Becker, George C. **Fishes of Wisconsin.**
Univ. of Wisconsin Pr. 1983. 1052p. illus., some color. maps. bibliog. index. LC 81-69813. ISBN 0-299-08790-5. $75. NAT HIST

Fishes of Wisconsin is clearly the best available regional or state fish book. Introductory chapters examine the heritage of Wisconsin's aquatic ecosystems and their fish and provide a glossary and detailed keys to identification. Individual species accounts dominate the volume; each includes a morphological description and details on systematics, distribution, status, habitat, biology, and importance and management. Black-and-white and/or color photographs illustrate each species. An expansive bibliography of over 1500 references attests to the comprehensiveness of the text. This expensive volume will be valuable to both professional biologists and laypersons interested in fish.—*James R. Karr, Ecology* ***Dept.****, Univ. of Illinois, Urbana-Champaign*

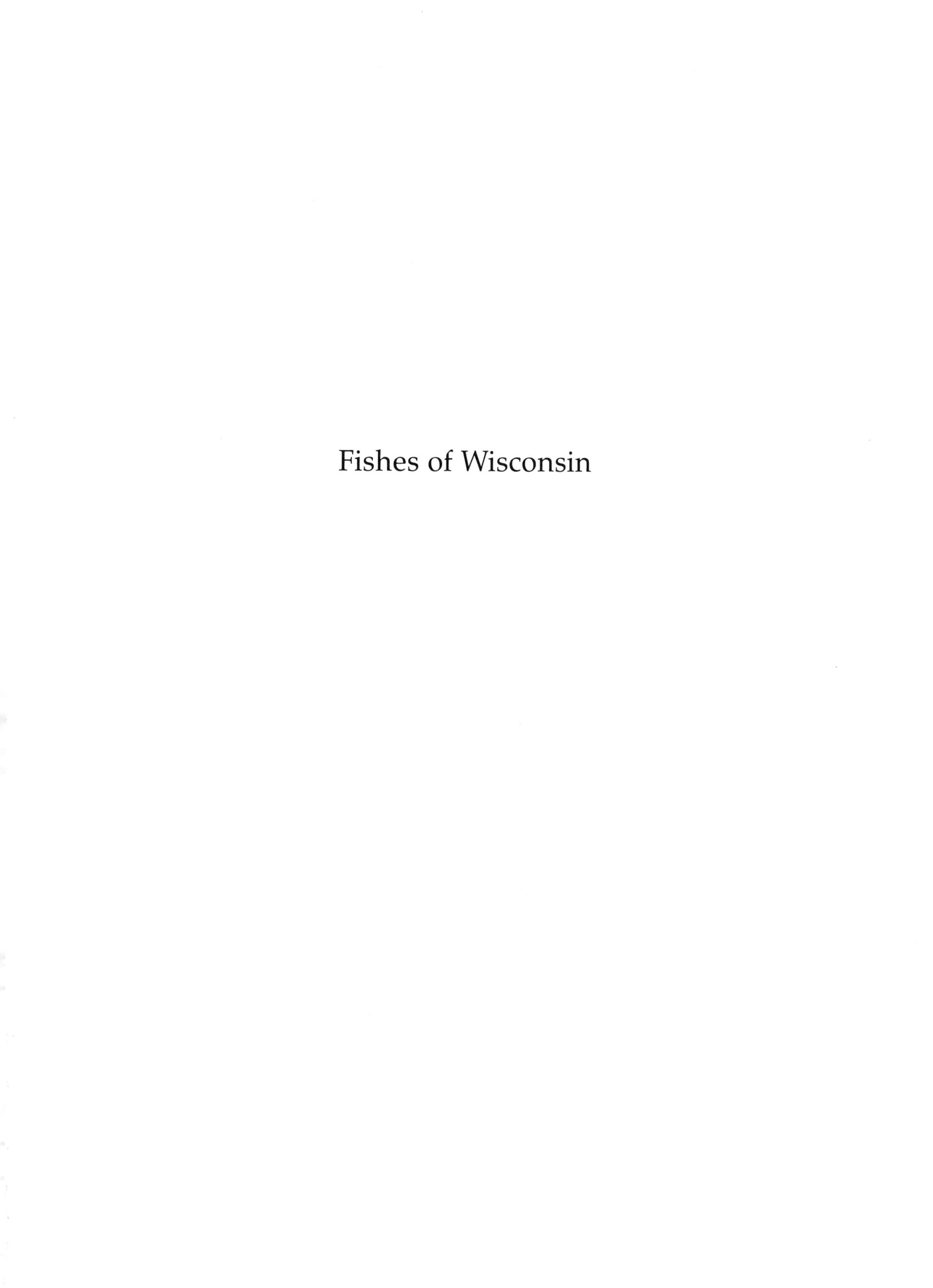

Fishes of Wisconsin

Publication of this volume
has been made possible in large part
through the generous support of the
University of Wisconsin Sea Grant Institute

FISHES OF WISCONSIN

GEORGE C. BECKER

The University of Wisconsin Press

Published 1983

The University of Wisconsin Press
114 North Murray Street
Madison, Wisconsin 53715

The University of Wisconsin Press, Ltd.
1 Gower Street
London WC1E 6HA, England

First printing

Printed in the United States of America

For LC CIP information see the colophon

ISBN 0-299-08790-5

Work on this book was funded in part by the University of Wisconsin Sea Grant College Program under a grant from the Office of Sea Grant, National Oceanic and Atmospheric Administration, U.S. Department of Commerce, and by the State of Wisconsin (Fed. grant #NA80AA-D-00086, Project #E/E-5). The U.S. government is authorized to produce and distribute reprints for government purposes notwithstanding any copyright notation that may appear hereon.

To four wonderful and long-suffering people

Sylvia Klenk Becker
Kenneth G. Becker
Dale R. Becker
David C. Becker

Contents

SPECIES ACCOUNTS

Preface

The idea of a fish book took root in the late 1940s when I became aware that there was no single up-to-date work available on the fishes of Wisconsin—a state renowned for its lakes, streams, and fishing. The need for a *Fishes of Wisconsin* became obvious when I began teaching ichthyology in the early 1960s and discovered that to properly identify the many species scattered in Wisconsin waters, I had to consult a number of reference books and texts, since there was no single work providing adequate keys and other identification information. Source books to which I had to make constant reference were *Fishes of the Great Lakes Region* by Hubbs and Lagler (1964), *Northern Fishes* by Eddy and Surber (1947), *Iowa Fish and Fishing* by Harlan and Speaker and keys by R. M. Bailey (1956), and *The Fishes of Illinois* by Forbes and Richardson (1920).

I began making fish collections in 1958, and in the early 1960s the program was greatly expanded with the help of teams of students. Each team, working in a designated area of the state, brought the collections of preserved fishes into the university laboratory at the University of Wisconsin–Stevens Point and with my help sorted, identified, and recorded them. The master sheets for these collections provided the bases of the distribution maps for the species. Many specimens from the collections contributed to the establishment of a division of fishes in the Museum of Natural History at the University of Wisconsin–Stevens Point. The thousands of specimens housed in the museum form the core of the present study.

After the completion of my *Inland Fishes of the Lake Michigan Drainage Basin* in early 1976, I began pulling together the species accounts for the *Fishes of Wisconsin*. A wealth of information was available in Wisconsin Department of Natural Resources research reports and technical bulletins, most of which dealt with sport species. I searched the literature to provide a basic life history for each species, including behavior and ecological requirements. I learned that for many nongame species very little is known. Unfortunately some of these are rare not only in Wisconsin but throughout their ranges. The accounts for these species are often fragmentary, and they point up the need for careful investigation to ensure the continued existence of such species.

As I prepared the distribution maps, it became evident that an irretrievable loss had occurred in the fish resource. Some species were extirpated. The species composition of Lake Michigan had changed radically within a few decades: in some basins several species had been completely eliminated, and exotic fishes had established successful populations, especially in waters undergoing extensive man-related changes. The fish complex was changing rapidly in parts of the state—much too rapidly to predict a secure future for some species.

My concern resulted in the preparation of introductory sections of text dealing with the water resource as it affects the fishes; past and present changes in water quality and anticipated effects if present demands for water continue; our early handling of the fishery resource, the manipulation of the fishery resource today, and the future values of fishes. I have suggested changes in management which may help to restore an ailing fish resource. Remedial action may be costly to implement, but this cost will be insignificant compared with the cost to our children who must mourn the missing pieces and who must struggle to reassemble the ecological disruptions we leave behind.

My taxonomic keys have been tested in a number of fish laboratories, and criticisms and suggestions have been honored in the latest revisions. But because fish did not evolve into species all fitting neatly into the slots provided within an artificial key, the key may break down unexpectedly. I would appreciate hearing from readers regarding problems with the keys.

I am also aware that in the life history accounts new knowledge will replace or modify old knowledge. It is difficult to keep abreast of all publications, bits of unpublished research, and isolated but important pieces of information. I therefore welcome such information and encourage you to write to me at the Department of Biology, University of Wisconsin–Stevens Point. Your suggestions will ensure a better future edition.

Acknowledgments

Throughout the preparation of *Fishes of Wisconsin* many individuals gave generously of time and funds. I am deeply indebted to my hundreds of ichthyology students at the University of Wisconsin–Stevens Point, who from 1960 to 1978 collected fishes from all sectors of Wisconsin on their own time and at their own expense. Many of them learned the joys of collecting and continued supplying the project with specimens long after their course obligations had been satisfied.

Fishes of Wisconsin was initiated in earnest in 1958 as a family collecting project. Until 1967, my sons, Kenneth, Dale, and David, assisted me in securing and preserving thousands of specimens in many hundreds of collections. During the writing period from 1976 to 1979, their help persisted in the field and extended into the laboratory and the darkroom. My wife, Sylvia, helped in the preparation of the manuscript while continuing to provide for her family's countless physical and spiritual needs. Through many of the early years, the devotion of my family to the fish project remained steadfast despite our hardships with the sampling gear, our struggles with the insect pests, and our endless struggle with my tyranny. This book, therefore, is a tribute to their selflessness and persistence.

I am grateful to the following persons who read, criticized, and offered suggestions for the portions of the manuscript sent to them: Merryll Bailey, Reeve Bailey, Paul Baumann, Dale Becker, Edward Brown, Jr., Clifford Brynildson, Lyle Christenson, Tom Claflin, Dan Coble, Fred Copes, Russ Daly, Billy Davis, Don Fago, Vernon Hacker, Arthur Hasler, John Held, Robert Hunt, Marlin Johnson, Lee Kernen, George King, Gary Lutterbie, John Magnuson, Patrick Manion, Harry Moore, James Moore, Susan Nehls, Joseph Nelson, Herbert Neuenschwander, Arthur Oehmcke, Gordon Priegel, Harold Purvis, Edward Schneberger, Paul Schultz, Howard Snow, Bruce Swanson, Stephen Taft, William Threinen, William Weiher, and LaRue Wells. For their careful attention to editorial matters, I give special thanks to Elizabeth Steinberg, Robin Whitaker, and Debra Bernardi.

The following people supplied me with specimens, information, or other materials: James Addis, Lloyd Andrews, Reeve Bailey, Paul Baumann, James Baumgart, Dale Becker, Brian Belonger, William Bodin, Henry Booke, Robert Braem, Ted Cavender, Don Dodge, Russell Dunst, Mark Ebbers, Don Fago, Arthur Fish, James Frostman, Harvey Hadland, Evald Heinonen, Russell Heizer, Ross Horrall, James Jaeger, Tom Johnson, Lee Kernen, Robert Kilcoyne, John Klingbiel, William LeGrande, Charles Long, Gary Lutterbie, Chris Madson, Edward Marks, Harold Mathiak, William McKee, Bernard Moes, Eileen Mullen, Carroll Norden, Weldon Paruch, Maryann Petesch, William Pflieger, Ronald Piening, Dennis Pratt, William Reeder, John Reynen, Harold Roberts, Don Samuelson, David Sanders, Randy Schumacher, Walter Scott, Philip Smith, Norbert Swaer, Ron Theis, Virgil Thiesfeld, William Thorn, William Threinen, Tom Thuemler, Donald Tills, Frederick Topel, Milton Trautman, John Truog, James Underhill, Walter Voight, Howard Weborg, Robert Welch, Matthew Wilgosz, and Steve Yeo.

The Wisconsin distribution maps were executed largely by Richard Duchrow, Joel Warnick, and Donna Yanda; the North American range maps by Kenneth Becker, William McKee, and Barbara Taylor. The Cartographic Laboratory at the University of Wisconsin–Madison prepared many of the other maps in this volume. The sketches of fishes in the keys were initially drafted by Tom Johnson, Stan Skutek, and Mike Tesmer. The final drawings are my own.

The black and white photographs were prepared by David Becker, Connie Frostman, Jack Lindberg, Nancy Ratner, and Randy Williams. Williams and I prepared the colored photographs of the fishes. I should also like to express my appreciation to the many people who made available color photographs and portraits; their names appear in the list of credits, p. 1023. Special thanks are due Virgil Beck, who executed the jacket illustration especially for this volume.

Early drafts of the manuscript were typed by Joey Humke, Marilyn Nelson, and Maryann Pietz; the final draft by Sylvia Becker.

This project was supported in part by the University of Wisconsin Sea Grant College Program under a grant from the National Oceanic and Atmospheric Administration, U.S. Department of Commerce, and the State of Wisconsin.

Fishes of Wisconsin

Wisconsin Waters

Glacial History

Available evidence indicates that the north central states were affected by at least four major glacial periods, which were separated by intervals during which the climate was warmer than at present. The last major glacial advance, known as the Wisconsin glaciation, moved south as far as mid-America. It is commonly accepted that fish in northern waters moved southward ahead of the lip of the advancing ice sheet, and northward as the ice sheet retreated. Students of fish distribution have noted that many Great Lakes fishes are related to species of the Mississippi River basin. An explanation for this relationship is found when the drainage patterns of the glacial Great Lakes are examined.

As the ice cap retreated, bodies of meltwater formed in the lake basins carved out by the glacier and drained in part into the Mississippi basin. Early in the Wisconsin glaciation, the first meltwater lake, known as Lake Chicago, appeared where southern Lake Michigan is located today; it drained by way of the Illinois River southwestward into the Mississippi River. Approximately 8 to 9 thousand years ago, when most of the Great Lakes were freed of glacial ice, an emerging Lake Superior, known as glacial Lake Duluth, drained southward by way of the St. Croix River into the Mississippi River system (see map, Main Algonquin stage). During the same period, Lake Ontario (glacial Lake Iroquois) drained eastward into the Hudson River system, providing an early entryway for Atlantic drainage fishes into the Great Lakes.

The present lakes and streams of northern and eastern Wisconsin have been largely shaped by past glaciations. The southwestern quarter of the state, however, lacks the features of erosion and deposition brought about by the continental glacier (see map of glacial lobes and the driftless area). This is the driftless area of Wisconsin, famous the world over because it is completely surrounded

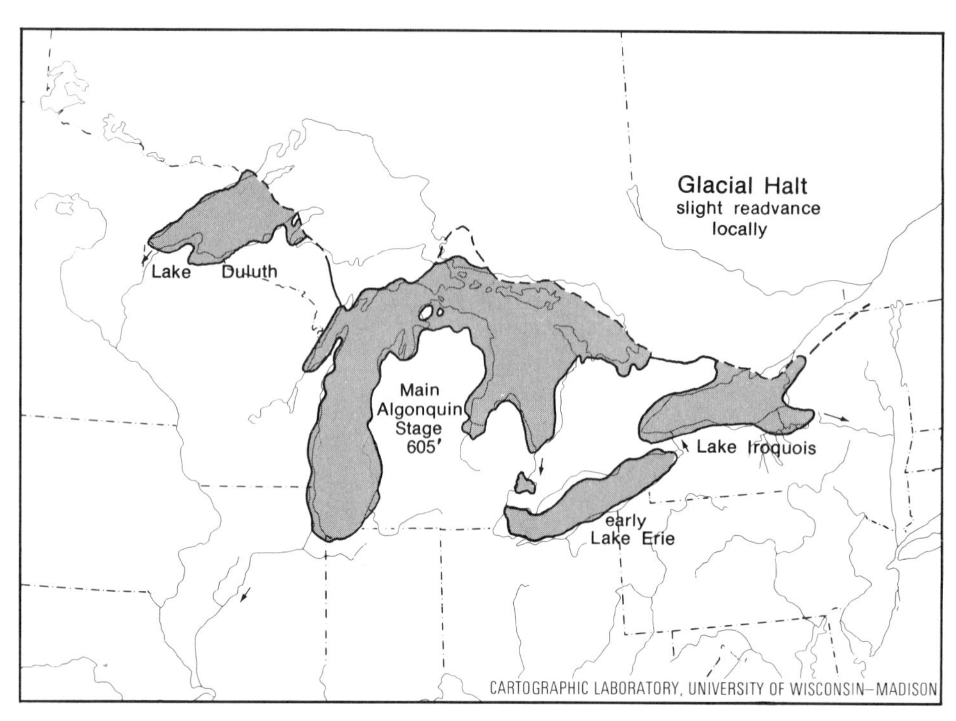

Main Algonquin stage (slightly modified from J. L. Hough *Geology of the Great Lakes*, p. 294. University of Illinois Press, Urbana. © 1958 by the Board of Trustees of the University of Illinois)

by glaciated regions: "It preserves a large sample of what the rest of Wisconsin, as well as northern and eastern United States, were like before the Glacial Period. Within the belts covered by the gigantic continental ice sheets of northeastern North America and northwestern Europe there is no similar region of substantial size which was left bare of glacial ice" (Martin 1932:82). Black (1959) suggested that early ice of the Wisconsin glaciation may have extended farther into the driftless area than is shown on most published maps.

The most sharply contrasting ecological conditions over wide areas of the state are between the driftless area and the area once covered by the glacier and glacial drift. Greene (1935:223–224) noted:

> Compared with the drift-covered area, the Driftless Area is rugged. Its central portion is floored principally by the Potsdam sandstone formation. In the northeast and extending in tongues down the valleys of the Black and Wisconsin rivers, the Archean granitic rock appears, while in the west and southwest the sandstone, overlain by a layer of limestone, is exposed only in the stream valleys. . . . The erosional system in the Driftless Area has been at work over a relatively long period of time and streams have carved for themselves a mature, efficient drainage system. Swampy conditions are localized in the lower relatively flat river valleys, and the only natural lakes are Pepin and St. Croix, formed in the courses of the Mississippi and St. Croix rivers respectively by delta dams.

The gradients of the streams in the driftless area are regular, with no natural swamps and no lake reservoirs. Such streams are subject to extreme fluctuation following wet and dry periods, and communities situated in their floodplains are subject to periodic flooding.

In the glaciated regions, streams are controlled by slopes which are not generally conducive to efficient runoff. In these regions, lakes, ponds, and marshes are the usual features. The phrase "imperfectly drained" is commonly used in

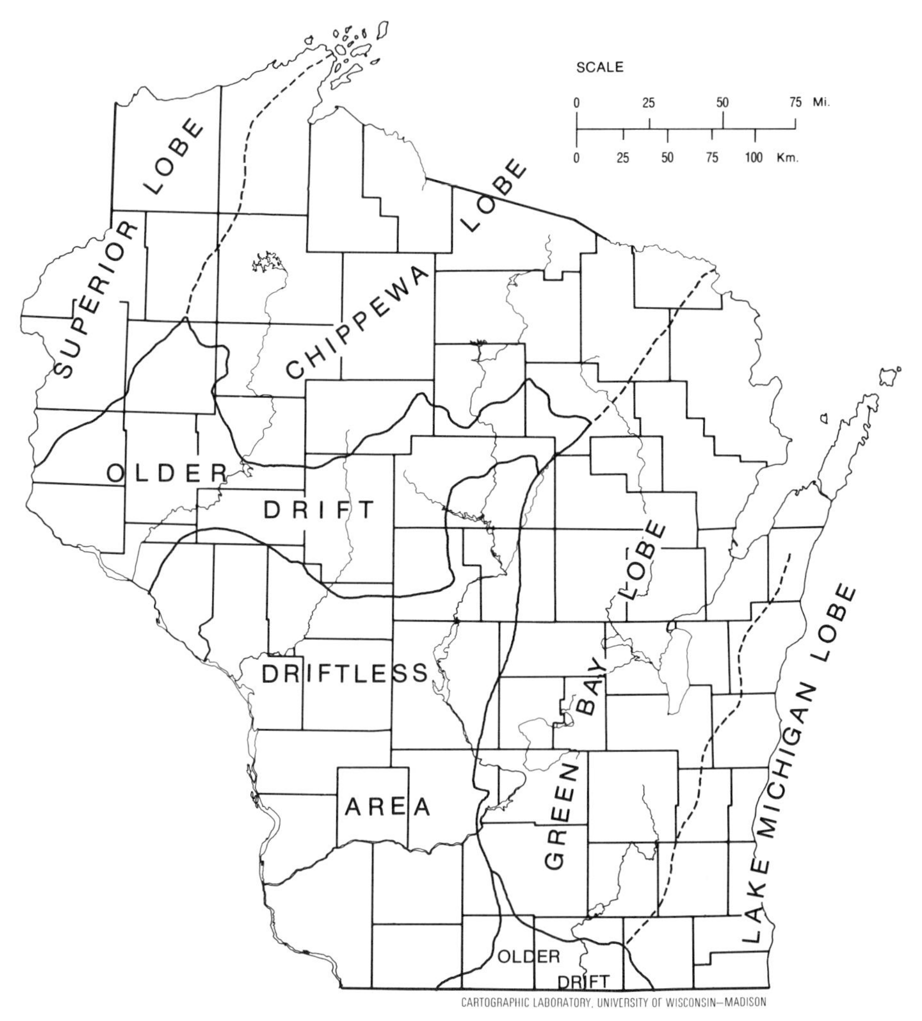

The glacial lobes at the Wisconsin stage of glaciation and their relation to the driftless area (after Martin 1932:87)

describing an area of youthful streams; such streams and their associated swamps and lakes are characterized by relatively constant volumes of water.

Because isolation is a known mechanism in the formation of new species of animal organisms, it has been suggested that new forms may have evolved within waters of the driftless area and may have been added to the varieties that moved in as the glacier retreated. The evolution of the largescale stoneroller (*Campostoma oligolepis*) has been ascribed to isolation within the driftless area of a stoneroller (*Campostoma* sp.) ancestor, and Greene (1935) argued that the driftless area was the center of distribution of the largescale stoneroller.

Water Resources

On the geological time scale, the Great Lakes are very young, their beginnings dating from only about 20 thousand years ago (Ragotzkie 1974). In area, Lake Superior, the largest and deepest of the Great Lakes, is the largest freshwater lake in the world. Superior is also the purest of the Great Lakes, its water containing only 52 ppm total dissolved solids. It lies in the path of outbreaks of polar air from central Canada, and is subject to long and cold winters. Lake Superior is close to being an arctic lake, and certainly can be classified as subarctic.

Lake Michigan, the world's sixth largest lake in both area and volume, is the only one of the Laurentian Great Lakes that lies entirely within the boundaries of the United States (Wells and McLain 1973). It resembles a long cul-de-sac and therefore flushes poorly, especially at its southern end. Its natural drainage is eastward through the Straits of Mackinac into Lake Huron, although 91 cms (3,200 cfs) is now being diverted from the Michigan basin through the Chicago Sanitary and Ship Canal. These waters flush the partly treated wastes from Chicago into the Illinois River. Elsewhere I have suggested that the Chicago Sanitary and Ship Canal between the Great Lakes and the Mississippi watershed serves as a potential passageway for fish between these major watersheds (Becker 1976).

Characteristics of Lakes Superior and Michigan

Lake	Lake area (km^2)	Drainage Basin Area (km^2)	Mean Depth (m)	Maximum Depth (m)	Elevation Above Sea Level (m)	Total Dissolved Solids, 1968 (ppm)	Mean Discharge (m^3/sec)
Superior	82,103	125,356	149	406	184	52	2,076
Michigan	57,757	118,104	89	281	177	150	1,558

Wisconsin has numerous inland lakes created by glacial action. The largest, Lake Winnebago, is 45.2 km long and 16.9 km wide, covers an area of 557 km^2, and has a maximum depth of 6.4 m. The deepest lake is Green Lake (Green Lake County), which covers 29.5 km^2 and has a maximum depth of 70.1 m (Wis. Dep. Nat. Resour. 1974). A total of 14,949 inland lakes have been documented; they cover almost 400,000 surface hectares (1 million surface acres). Named lakes number 5,695 and account for 95% of all lake surface (Les and Polkowski 1976).

Wisconsin has abundant water of good quality (U.S. Geol. Surv. 1976). The state is also crossed by 53,000 km (33,000 mi) of streams. Wisconsin has a northern climate typical of the continental landmass, characterized by average air temperatures of 18.9 to 21.7°C (66–71°F) in July and −5.6 to −12.2°C (22–10°F) in January (Threinen and Poff 1963). Moderate air temperatures coupled with large volumes of groundwater moving laterally into streams provide conditions favorable for trout. Wisconsin has over 1,500 trout streams with a combined length of 14,025 km (8,690 mi) (Kmiotek 1974).

Precipitation on land and water surfaces starts a pattern of circulation called the water cycle. Some of the water runs rapidly off the land surface into nearby streams and lakes to become surface runoff; some water evaporates immediately from the surface soil and plants; some returns to the air from plants through transpiration; and some seeps down through soils and rocks, reaching subsurface reservoirs (groundwater recharge) that eventually contribute base flow to streams and lakes.

More than two-thirds of the water that enters Wisconsin from precipitation leaves by evapotranspiration—the return of water to the atmosphere by a com-

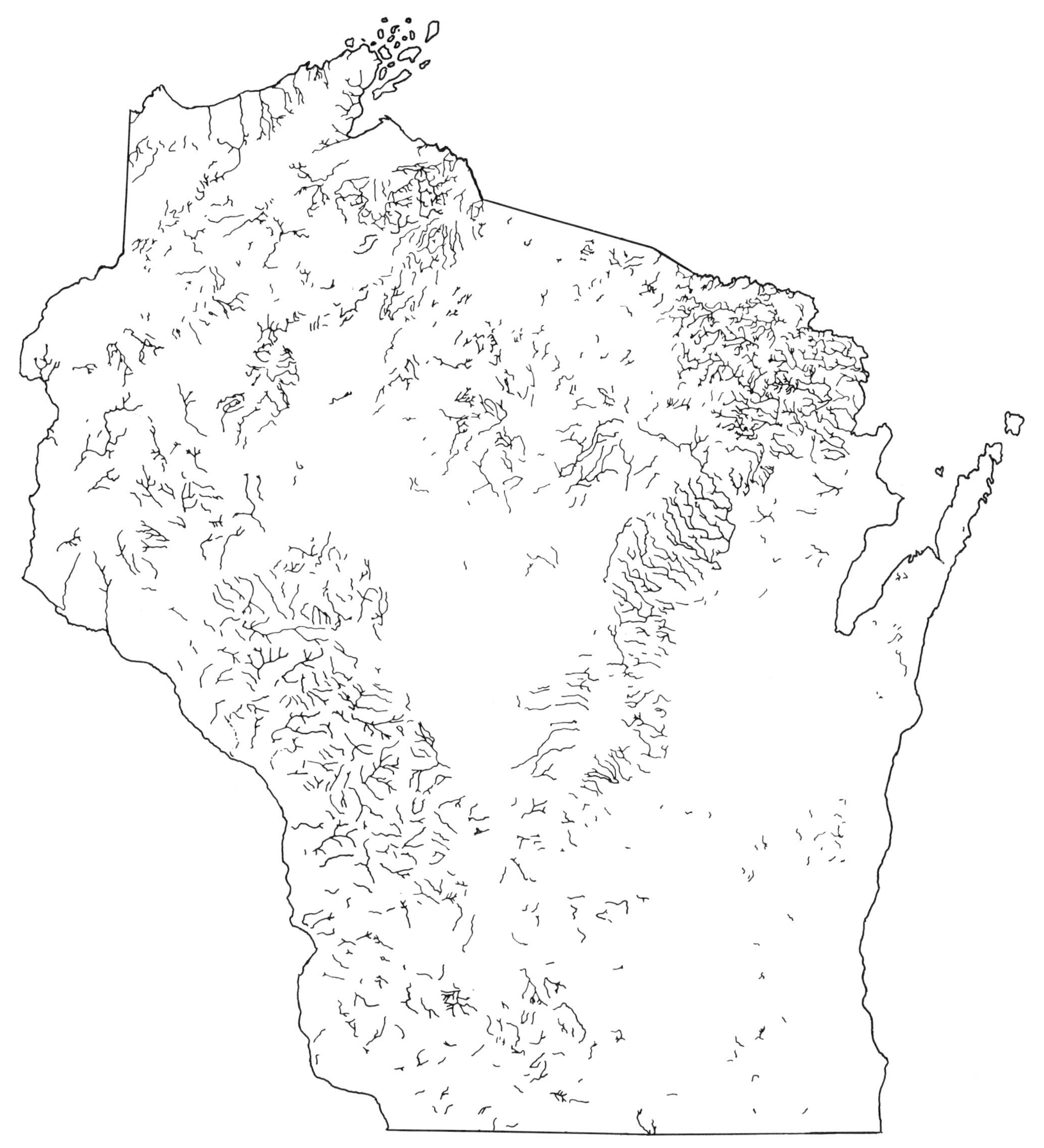

State hydrographic map with trout streams darkened (after Threinen and Poff 1963:58)

bination of evaporation from open water, foliage surfaces, the land surface, and transpiration from plants.

The average precipitation is 790 mm (31 in); the greatest amount falls in the southwestern and north central parts of Wisconsin. The average yearly streamflow or runoff leaving the state is equal to 25 cm (9.7 in)—which is 98 billion liters (26 billion gallons) per day, enough to fill Lake Winnebago 1,200 times in one year (U.S. Geol. Surv. 1976).

The exact amount of water in subsurface groundwater reservoirs changes from year to year, but increases and decreases balance out and the net change is zero. Not all of the groundwater discharged to lakes and streams is measured in streams leaving the state. Some is discharged directly to Lake Superior and to Lake Michigan, and some moves across the state line to Illinois.

Lakes and streams are replenished by precipitation on their surfaces, by overland flow, and by groundwater discharging into them. Nearly two-thirds of the streamflow in Wisconsin is contributed by groundwater bodies. The constancy of stream flow is controlled by many factors, including the number of lakes and wetlands, channel gradients, amount and type of vegetation, variations in geology and soil cover, size of the groundwater contribution, and man's regulation of surface reservoirs. Kettle lakes, occupying depressions in the land surface formed by glacial ice, are fed by groundwater discharging as seeps or springs.

The flow rates of selected streams from the Mississippi River, Lake Michigan, and Lake Superior drainage basins of Wisconsin follow. With few exceptions, the discharge rates of streams into Lakes Michigan and Superior are low.

Flow Rates of Selected Wisconsin Streams

	Drainage Area		Average Discharge	
Basin, River, and Station	km²	(mi²)	cms	(cfs)
Mississippi River Basin				
Mississippi, McGregor (Iowa)	174,870	(67,500)	936.4	(33,090)
Wisconsin, Muscoda	26,684	(10,300)	240.3	(8,491)
Chippewa, Durand	23,342	(9,010)	209.5	(7,404)
St. Croix, St. Croix Falls	15,363	(5,930)	117.3	(4,144)
Black, Galesville	5,492	(2,120)	46.5	(1,643)
Pecatonica, Martintown	2,679	(1,034)	19.1	(674)
Rock, Rockton (Ill.)	16,479	(6,361)	103.5	(3,658)
Lake Michigan basin				
Menominee, McAllister	10,415	(4,020)	96.0	(3,392)
Oconto, Gillett	1,756	(678)	16.2	(572)
Fox, Wrightstown	15,933	(6,150)	117.2	(4,140)
Milwaukee, Milwaukee	1,777	(686)	10.8	(382)
Root, Racine	484	(187)	3.9	(137)
Lake Superior basin				
Brule, Brule	311	(120)	4.8	(171)
Bad, Odanah	1,583	(611)	17.3	(611)
White, Ashland	723	(279)	8.2	(289)

Source: U.S. Geological Survey (1974).

Water Uses

A total of 12 billion liters (3.1 billion gallons) of water was withdrawn daily from lakes, streams, and the groundwater reservoir to meet the needs of Wisconsin homes, factories, and farms in the early 1970s. This did not include the water used each day for generating hydroelectric power. Most of the water withdrawn

Use of Water in Wisconsin (millions of liters per day)

Use	Source and Type of Supply				
	Groundwater			Surface Water	
	Public Supply				
	Municipal	Other	Private Supply	Public Supply (Municipal)	Private Supply
Domestic	235.0	15.5	266.1	271.4	0
Industrial and commercial[a]	344.4	4.9	350.1	471.2	821.7
Thermal-electric cooling	0	0	0	0	8,168.0
Irrigation	6.8	0	123.0	9.8	74.6
Stock	0	0	207.8	0	59.0
Other	158.2	10.6	42.4	210.8	4.9
Subtotal	744.4	31.0	989.4	963.2	9,128.2
Total		1,764.9		10,091.4	

Source: U.S. Geological Survey (1976).
[a]Excluding thermal-electric cooling.

for all uses was returned to streams and lakes for possible reuse, although often in somewhat modified form.

About 210 billion liters (55 billion gallons) per day of Wisconsin's river water passed through turbines to generate about 1.6 billion kilowatt hours of hydroelectric power. Most of this power was generated on the Wisconsin, Chippewa, Menominee, St. Croix, and Fox rivers (U.S. Geol. Surv. 1976). There were 1,600 dams from 1.8 to 21 m high in Wisconsin; of these, about 125 produced water power of more than 750 horsepower each.

Surface waters are still used as a water source by a number of Wisconsin municipalities. In 1970, 12 communities in Wisconsin were supplied by treated Lake Michigan water, and 3 communities were supplied from Lake Superior (Ruedisili 1972). Three communities were supplied by the Fox River, 1 community obtained water from Lake Winnebago, and 4 communities used surface waters from the Mississippi River basin. All other communities depended entirely upon groundwater.

Drilling approvals for irrigation purposes in Wisconsin jumped from about 14 per year in 1958 to 147 in the early 1970s (Calabresa 1977). In 1976, 330 approvals were issued. Most irrigation well development in the late 1950s occurred in the sand plains from the Whiting-Plover area south to Columbia and Adams counties; in parts of western Waushara and Waupaca counties; around Antigo; and in sand and gravel deposits of the Sarona, Rice Lake, and Chetek region. According to Calabresa, expansion of irrigation into new areas of the state will continue. Since the early 1960s, it has spread along the Wisconsin River between Sauk City and Gotham, as well as to Chippewa County, the Eau Claire area, St. Croix County, Green County, Walworth County, and other scattered places. In 1977, 240 permits were issued in Wisconsin for the diversion of surface water for irrigation, and an equal number of permit applications were pending.

Although irrigation is an intermittent activity that varies with normal precipitation and is carried on for only about 45 days a year, it is a highly consumptive use which reduces the amount of water reaching lakes and streams. In the central sand plains of Wisconsin, groundwater withdrawal has exceeded recharge and affected streamflow. It is estimated that during a severe drought depletion of summer streamflow could reach 60% of natural flow in Big Roche a Cri Creek and 90% in Tenmile Creek (Hine 1970, Weeks and Stangland 1971). Such severe reductions in stream stage could adversely affect trout by diminishing living space and food supply, and by allowing warming of the depleted waters above trout tolerance.

In Wisconsin, surface water may be taken directly from streams provided it can be demonstrated that it is surplus water. According to Wisconsin law, surplus water is any water of a stream which is not beneficially used. Beneficial users can be any private riparians on the stream: irrigators, owners of hydroelectric and nonhydroelectric dams, holders of discharge permits, industries connected to municipal systems, and suppliers of public water.

Provision is also made to protect public rights on a stream by assuring that an adequate flow remains to protect fish and the aquatic habitat. The public rights stage is defined as minimum water level to be sustained, as determined by an analysis of the components of the public rights in streams. These components include navigation, fish and wildlife, water-based recreation, esthetic enjoyment, and preservation of water quality. In large streams, if a stage cannot be determined but the investigator feels that there are fishery values or other public rights to be protected, the mean annual flow or the 7-day, 2-year low flow may be used to define the public rights requirement.

Special consideration is accorded to recognized trout streams, and no new permits may be issued for the diversion of water from any trout stream without the permission of the Wisconsin Department of Natural Resources. Consent must come from the district staff specialist for fish management, who grants "prior written approval." In the interest of conservation the department may also hold hearings to revoke permits for the diversion of water from trout streams.

More consideration must be given by public agencies to the definition of "surplus water." Normal water levels are extremely low during the months of July and August, when demands for the diversion of irrigation water are at their peak. This is also the critical period of the year for trout, since high air temperatures, coupled with low water levels, put severe physiological stress on trout and other fishes that require cool water temperatures for survival. A good argument can be made that in years of normal flow there is no surplus water for such coldwater species, and that removal of any water will allow high summer air temperatures to elevate the reduced water volume downstream from the site of water removal to critically high temperatures. When this occurs, one to several kilometers of trout water may be lost on the lower portion of the stream. According to Oehmcke and Truax (1964), in the Wolf River low flows and excessive irrigation on feeder streams have caused a warming of the water and destruction of the trout habitat.

Water policy evolution and a basic guide to water rights in Wisconsin have been summarized by Scott (1965) and Hine (1971), respectively. Zaporazec (1974) has compiled a bibliography and index of Wisconsin groundwater problems from 1851 to 1972.

The Pollution Problem

Wisconsin has a proud record of pollution regulation—from the first antipollution laws of the 1860s to the sweeping enactments of the 1960s. However, the last few decades of industrial and population expansion have so accelerated water pollution that it has become a major problem. In a report prepared for the Wisconsin Legislative Reference Bureau, S. Parker (1971:5) commented:

> A partial list, past and present, of what has found its way into Wisconsin waters shows the staggering extent of the pollution problem: nitrogen and phosphates from the new detergents; mercury, arsenic and cyanide from waste treatment facilities; numerous paper and pulp mill wastes such as wood fibers, sugars, sulfur, calcium, magnesium and ammonia; oil from leaking storage tanks, ruptured pipelines and outboard motors; manure and fertilizers from farmlands; pesticides, de-icers and eroded soil; daily tons of garbage and human wastes in the form of treated or raw sewage from inadequate septic tanks and drainage systems, overloaded municipal sewer facilities, pleasure boats and ships; the sandy wastes of taconite mining and the thermal pollution of power plants.
>
> This appalling outpour is aging the lakes prematurely by siltation and accelerated algae and weed growth, robbing the waters of oxygen, raising temperatures beyond levels suitable for aquatic life, spoiling recreational areas, and exposing humans and wildlife alike to noxious infections and potentially toxic substances. Municipalities, dependent on polluted lakes and rivers for the raw water they must treat to supply citizens with water pure enough for domestic use, are finding the process more difficult and costly.

Building and road construction, street runoff, litter, and all predominantly urban activities that potentially add pollutants to streams are also recognized as serious problems. The effects on water quality of urban management practices commonly used to alleviate such pollution have been reviewed by Oberts (1977).

According to S. Parker (1971), a great share of the pollution in this state comes from the paper and pulp mills clustered along the Wisconsin River and along the lower Fox River. Van Horn et al. (1949) demonstrated that waste waters from kraft paper mills were toxic to spotfin shiners and emerald shiners; they noted that when sufficient amounts of receiving water were available for dilution of such toxic wastes, the mixture became safe for fish and other organisms.

Municipal sewage plants rank second as major polluters. By the end of 1970 there were 475 municipal treatment plants in the state, nearly 20% of which offered only primary treatment—a system of screens and settling tanks which remove the heaviest one-third of the suspended solids and discharge the remainder into streams and lakes. The other treatment plants provided secondary treatment, 90% effective, in which bacteria, placed in contact with the sewage in trickling filters or oxygen-activated sludge, consume the organic portion of the wastes. S. Parker (1971:7) noted:

> There are a variety of reasons why municipal plants are such big polluters. Growing populations and new industries have overloaded many plants, lowering the normal efficiency of operation and decreasing the percentage of pollutants removed from the effluent.
>
> Many cities still have a combined sewer system carrying both sanitary sewage and storm water overflow. Heavy rains flood the system, discharging raw sewage into the lakes and streams. For example, when rains overflow Milwaukee's combined system, an extra 10,000 pounds of oxygen-demanding organic material per day pours into the waterways in addition to the normal daily runoff of 9,000 pounds.

The pollution of groundwater is a newly evolving problem. Pollution sources include industrial wastes, salt used for de-icing Wisconsin roads, spilled oil and gasoline, garbage dumps, barnyards and feedlots, septic tank effluents, and detergents, as well as such natural sources as sulfates, sulfides, and chlorides (Ruedisili 1972). Septic tank wastes, sinking into the ground, may contaminate the groundwater source used as a water supply. Crabtree (1972) found dangerous nitrate levels in 70% of the wells tested in Marathon County. Nitrate concentrations of more than 45 ppm can cause methemoglobinemia, an illness in which the blood is unable to carry oxygen to the cells of the body; the victim turns blue and eventually dies of oxygen starvation. The biggest threat is to babies who are given water from contaminated shallow groundwater aquifers.

Pollution From Heavy Metals

Ecological problems related to heavy metals arise when metal pollutants pass into ecosystems and end up in human food (Mount et al. 1970). Authorities have already indicated that the quantities of lead and cadmium in the diets of North Americans may be near the limit compatible with human health. Mercury contamination in fish has reached levels too high for fish to be safe for human consumption in many parts of the world.

In the Milwaukee, Racine, and Kenosha areas, metal wastes discharged into the air, water, and soil amount to more than 200,000 kg annually (Konrad and Kleinert 1974). These include arsenic, beryllium, cadmium, chromium, copper, lead, mercury, nickel, selenium, and zinc. An additional 70,000 kg of metal waste is discharged by lesser manufacturing centers over the state.

In Wisconsin, the highest mercury deposits have been found in waters below industrial discharges (chlorine–caustic soda plants and paper plants) (Konrad 1971). Significant amounts of mercury have also been found below several sewage treatment plants, along with other heavy metal contamination.

All Wisconsin fish analyzed in two studies contained some mercury (Kleinert and Degurse 1971, 1972). The mercury content varied in different species, and the larger fish often contained higher concentrations of mercury than smaller fish of the same species taken from the same water. Walleyes, suckers, redhorse, crappies, and bullheads frequently had high mercury concentrations; the panfishes, including bluegills, pumpkinseeds, and yellow perch, had low concentrations. Fish samples taken from the following areas had average mercury levels above the 0.5 ppm guideline established by the U.S. Food and Drug Administration: the 565-km sector of the Wisconsin River below Rhinelander, the 65-km sector of the Flambeau River between the Town of Cedar Rapids (Rusk Co.) and the junction of the Chippewa River, and the 81-km sector of the Chippewa River between the mouths of the Flambeau and Eau Claire rivers (Kleinert and Degurse 1972). Fishermen were warned to limit consumption of fish from these waters to one meal per week.

Levels of cadmium and chromium in all Wisconsin fish analyzed were less than 0.5 ppm (Kleinert et al. 1974). Arsenic, lead, zinc, cadmium, and chromium were not present in sufficient amounts to constitute a hazard to consumers.

Through the persistent application of copper sulfate for noxious plant control in lakes, large quantities of copper have been deposited on bottom substrates. In the waters of Lake Monona (Dane County), a buildup of 440 ppm was noted in the deeper layers of the mud bottom (15–17.5 cm), compared to 327 ppm in the top 2.5 cm (Antonie and Osness 1963). Hasler (1949), in reviewing the toxicity of copper treatments, found that even a single application of this substance may cause serious disturbances in the balance of aquatic environments.

Pesticides and PCBs

Among the toxicants causing great concern are the polychlorinated biphenyls (PCBs). Adult mink reproduction failures and mortality have been traced on many occasions to the eating of PCB-contaminated fish. PCBs have been implicated, along with chlorinated hydrocarbon pesticides, in the decline of raptors and fish-eating birds (Martin 1977). Insofar as is known, PCBs have not been implicated in observed fishkills in the wild, although laboratory investigations indicate the possibility that chronic low level ingestion of PCBs may adversely affect fish reproduction and/or growth rates. Ragotzkie (1974) reported that PCBs are known to affect the prenatal development of humans, and are carcinogenic to primates. PCBs have turned up in the milk of nursing mothers, and bird researchers have linked them with reproductive failures among aquatic birds of the Great Lakes.

In 1977, the Wisconsin Department of Health warned against eating more than one meal (one-half pound) of PCB-contaminated fish a week. The warning specifically included carp, trout, and salmon more than 51 cm (20 in) long from Green Bay and Lake Michigan; bullheads and catfish from southern Green Bay; catfish, carp, and white bass from the Mississippi River from Prescott through Lake Pepin; all fish except perch and northern pike from Little Lake Butte des Morts, and from the lower Fox River between Lake Winnebago and Green Bay; redhorse suckers and carp from the Milwaukee River between its mouth and Thiensville; carp from the Pike River (Kenosha County); and carp from the Root River between its mouth and the Horlick Dam. It was further recommended that nursing mothers, pregnant women, and any women who anticipated bearing children in the future, as well as children under six, not eat any of these fish. In early 1978, fish in three Sheboygan County streams were found to be contaminated with PCBs considerably above the allowable level of 5 ppm, and waters were posted against their consumption.

Of the 635 million kg of PCBs produced since 1929 (manufacture has now stopped in this country), an estimated 48 million kg were free in the environment in 1977. According to the U.S. Environmental Protection Agency, 345 million kg are still in use, mostly in transformers and in large and small high- and low-voltage capacitors (*Stevens Point Daily Journal* 7 June 1977).

Thermal Pollution

Our nation's economy is heavily dependent on electrical energy, and the demand for this energy is increasing rapidly. In the Great Lakes region, steam electric generating plants operate with open-cycle cooling systems, which generally eject waste heat directly into public waters. Unfortunately, open-cycle cooling damages or destroys large numbers of fish, as well as other aquatic organisms that serve as food for fish (Edsall 1976).

Edsall calculated the expected growth of the electricity-generating industry on Lake Michigan from 1968 to 2000 and estimated daily water consumption and the percentage of littoral zone waters that would be used (1976:456):

Year	Flow (cms)	Percentage of Littoral Zone Waters Used per Day
1968	188	0.082
2000	2,582	1.124

The above estimates were developed under the assumptions that stations would operate at 100% capacity and that the temperature of the cooling water would rise by 11°C (20°F). The littoral zone waters occupy the shoreline to the 9-meter depth contour.

Edsall (1976) and Tait (1973) noted that the littoral waters are used by almost all the fish in a large lake. The warmwater fishes of the Great Lakes are essentially permanent residents of the littoral waters. Species such as the lake trout and most whitefishes, generally inhabitants of the cold waters farther off shore, use the littoral waters during the cool portions of the year as feeding and spawning grounds, and also as nursery areas for their young. Several species of trout and salmon, and various other species which ascend tributary streams to spawn, must pass through the littoral waters on their way to and from the spawning grounds; and their offspring must pass through these waters when they migrate from the spawning streams to the open waters of the Great Lakes, where they grow to maturity and harvestable size. Studies clearly show that large numbers of fish are killed by impingement on intake screens of power plants and that fish eggs and fry are being entrained at power plants, with resulting high mortality.

During the years 1975–1976, an estimated 2,754,118 fish weighing a total of 49,630 kg were sucked into the cooling water intake of the Oak Creek power plant (Milwaukee County) (P. Hayes, *The Milwaukee Journal* 17 October 1976). Scientists estimated that more than 90% of these were alewives and smelt, but 635 trout and 190 salmon were also counted. At four power plants—Point Beach north of Manitowoc, Port Washington, Lakeside at St. Francis, and Oak Creek—almost 6 million fish weighing 149,053 kg were caught on the intake screens. Of these, 6,863 were trout or salmon weighing a total of 4,191 kg. At the same time, millions of newly hatched fish, fish eggs, and plankton were being sucked through the screens into the plant and then ejected, often with killing effect.

Investigators have noted that high concentrations of predator fish may gather in the plume from a thermal outfall; the fish are attracted by the abundance of food organisms (including other fish) which have passed through the cooling system, and which may be damaged or dead. Reports of mortalities caused by heat shock, cold shock, air embolisms, and chlorine treatment of cooling water are available in the literature.

According to Tait (1973), pesticides and heavy metals accumulate in the bodies of fishes much more rapidly in water of high temperatures. It has also been shown that some disease outbreaks in fish are much more severe at high environmental temperatures, and the concentration of fish in thermal plumes may facilitate the passage of disease organisms from one fish to another.

Acid Precipitation

Acid precipitation, resulting from wind-borne sulfur oxides from coal-burning industries and nitrous oxides from automobile exhausts, is a potential threat to fish life in approximately 80% of the lakes in the Northern Highland region of Wisconsin (Eilers et al. 1979, Staats 1979). Too much acidity in water can kill or deform fish; and, as has already occurred in 90 lakes in New York's Adirondack Mountains, a pH of about 4.5 renders waters fishless. Acid water releases toxic heavy metals such as mercury, copper, lead, manganese, nickel, zinc, and aluminum from the bottom sediments and permits them to get into the fatty tissues of fish. High levels of mercury in inland lake fish of the Lake Huron basin have already been linked with acid rain, and high levels of toxic metals in tributaries are known to deter Great Lakes fish from using those streams for spawning. The problem of acid precipitation in Wisconsin is currently (1980) being studied by state and federal agencies.

Eutrophication: Enrichment of Waters

In its infancy, a lake contains sterile waters which are clear, low in minerals, and low in algae and aquatic plants. The bottom water strata carry a good supply of oxygen all year round, along with low numbers of coldwater fishes. Such bodies of water are oligotrophic (low in nutrient levels). The Great Lakes up to the 1900s were good examples of oligotrophic waters, and Lake Superior is still classified as oligotrophic.

Over a period of time, however, as large quantities of nitrogen and phosphorus compounds wash into a lake (from natural sources, but also very largely from organic wastes produced by man and his activities), the water turns cloudy, and heavy algal blooms and thick mats of aquatic plants overrun the shallows. The bottom water strata in this now eutrophic (enriched) lake carry a poor supply of oxygen, and eventually will sustain only the most tolerant of warmwater fishes, such as bullheads and minnows. Materials are deposited rapidly upon the bottom of a eutrophic lake, the depth of the lake decreases, and eventually the lake fills in and disappears. This is the inevitable history of all lakes.

Fortunately, most Wisconsin lakes are only moderately eutrophic. Yet even Lake Michigan is becoming eutrophic in Green Bay and around the populated southern end of the lake. Numerous lakes in southern and central Wisconsin, and some in northern counties, are becoming choked with weeds and algae during the growing season. This process interferes with boating, swimming, fishing, and other recreational pursuits, and may lead to a sharp reduction in property values as desired lake values disappear. It is responsible for winterkills and summerkills of fishes.

Millions of state and federal dollars are being spent to slow down or reverse the eutrophication process. In Wisconsin a number of techniques have been used to control eutrophication. Lake flushing and dilutional pumping of Snake Lake (Vilas–Oneida counties boundary) have resulted in lowered phosphorus concentrations, the elimination of nuisance blooms of duckweed, and deepened littoral areas where compaction of the bottom followed drainage (Born et al. 1973a). The Marion Millpond (Waupaca County) generally exhibited less plant growth in areas where plastic sheeting and sand blankets were applied to the bottom than in untreated areas (Born et al. 1973b). In Horseshoe Lake (Manitowoc County), nuisance algal growth was curbed, transparency of the water improved, and dissolved oxygen increased by removing phosphorus from the water with the application of alum (Peterson et al. 1973).

A lake ringed with cottages, each equipped with its own septic tank system, soon becomes seriously eutrophic because of failure of the systems and seepage of enriched effluents into the lake. Relief for such a lake is immediate when it is surrounded by a sewer system that carries wastes to a treatment plant and diverts effluent waters out of the lake's basin.

Since the 1960s we have become increasingly aware that the marshes and swamps which surround a lake play an important role in its well-being. These wetlands are natural sponges which hold water and prevent floods; they are natural filters which remove organic nutrients from the waters flowing through them; and they are a vital refuge for fish and wildlife. Unfortunately, only about half (1 million hectares) of the wetlands natural to Wisconsin remain today (Harris and Sauey 1979). Of these, roughly 640,000 hectares are in private ownership and are particularly vulnerable to degradation and destruction.

Selected papers dealing with stream pollution, waste water, and water treatment are presented by Tarzwell (1960, 1965) and Keup et al. (1967). Nichols (1974) reviewed techniques for the control of nuisance aquatic plants, and Dunst et al. (1974) have prepared an extensive survey of techniques used in the rehabilitation of lakes.

Solving Pollution Problems

In recent years, advances in the treatment of waste water have progressed to the point where the product water is of high quality and purity. For example, the South Lake Tahoe sanitary district, using the physiochemical system for treatment of sewage wastes, created with its effluent water an artificial reservoir which supports a healthy population of rainbow trout and provides unrestricted recreation, including boating, water skiing, and swimming (Stevens 1971). The closed-cycle concept (the complete renovation of waste water and its immediate reuse) is not new. Culp and Culp (1971:2) noted:

> All municipal wastewater could be completely eliminated as a source of pollution in the United States and converted to a quality adequate to provide a valuable water resource for nearlyunrestricted reuse at a national cost of about 75 cents per person per month.

A system has been proposed which would eliminate, by planned stages, all discharge of industrial and municipal wastes into the Wisconsin River and its tributaries (Becker and Holland 1972). The plan calls for the most up-to-date treatment systems, and would eliminate discharge into public waters of raw, partly treated, and totally treated wastes. The clear, reusable water coming from centralized plants along the main stem of the river would be piped back for reuse to industries and municipalities. Any additional water needed would come from groundwater sources, but not from the basin's surface waters. The objective is to allow the natural systems of the rivers to reestablish themselves and to avoid the many problems resulting from the contamination of our lakes and streams.

Perhaps the most difficult obstacle to overcome in the implementation of such a plan is our own thinking regarding waste water disposal. For too long we have accepted the assumption that wastes must be released into the nearest river or lake. Hence we have many problems, some of which are becoming so serious that man's well-being is threatened. Enough studies have been made to demonstrate that water pollution catastrophes are very expensive and that the cheapest way to handle wastes is to treat them at or near the source, where they can be effectively converted into useful products or safely contained.

Continued pollution of our public waters will result in fishes becoming charged with higher levels of toxic wastes. Should this trend continue, ultimately man will be able to eat only those fish which are raised under carefully controlled conditions. Safe foods from public waters are already becoming increasingly rare; and just as problems have already arisen with mercury, DDT, Mirex, and PCBs, other problems—as yet not identified—are sure to surface. Today's most urgent problem is acid precipitation; it threatens the fishery resource in many northern Wisconsin lakes and may be uniquely difficult to control, since the airborne toxicants may be originating from locales thousands of kilometers away.

Our present efforts to control pollution problems are not succeeding. As population and industrial growth continue, we attempt to control increasingly complex wastes with antiquated and ineffectual treatment methods. Official pollution control agencies are still recommending for most municipal and industrial wastes primary and secondary (rarely tertiary) treatment systems—systems which are capable of coping neither with the present volume of waste water nor with the extraction of toxic substances. The sophisticated means available for waste control are dismissed as being too expensive. Frustrated, some observers have suggested that in the light of present trends man may be forced to adopt an enclosed environment, a sterilized test-tube culture, to ensure his own survival.

Wisconsin Fishes and Fishery Management

Early Limnological and Fishery Research

The University of Wisconsin has long been a leader in the science of limnology, which deals with the physical, chemical, meteorological, and biological conditions of ponds and lakes. Many basic limnological studies were conducted by the team of E. A. Birge and Chancey Juday, who contributed a legacy of more than 400 publications produced over more than four decades, beginning in the last quarter of the nineteenth century. Their enormous impact on the science of limnology is described at length by Frey (1963).

The Birge-Juday research attracted scientists from many foreign countries to Madison, Wisconsin. Basic research from 1940 to 1961 in such areas as plankton, odor detection by fish, homing migrations in fish, sun orientation in fish, and the chemical composition of bottom muds, has been summarized by A. D. Hasler (1963). The identification, investigation, and control of biologically associated problems in freshwater environments, based on Wisconsin experience, are discussed by Mackenthun et al. (1964) and Mackenthun and Ingram (1967).

The earliest list of fishes from Wisconsin was provided by Lapham (1846:71):

> Among the fish afforded by our lakes and rivers are whitefish, salmon, sturgeon, perch, bass, suckers, herring, pickerel or muskellunge, trout, catfish, sheep's head, lawyers, and many others, nearly all valuable as articles of food for man. They are caught in large quantities, and some are exported. The Indians at the north, where game is scarce and where agriculture has not yet been introduced, live almost exclusively upon fish, which are caught in vast quantities at the mouths of the rivers. The excellent qualities of these fish for the table are too well known to need description here.

Between 1872 and 1877, P. R. Hoy published a series of articles on Wisconsin fishes, culminating in 1877 (Hoy 1883) with a list of over 100 species, the longest list of Wisconsin fishes compiled to that time. Other early papers dealing with Wisconsin fishes were those by Marshall and Gilbert (1905), Wagner (1908, 1910a, 1910b, 1911), and A. S. Pearse (1918, 1921a, 1921b, 1924a, 1924b). In 1927, C. W. Greene reported 141 species of fish known from Wisconsin, and A. R. Cahn recorded 90 species from the Waukesha County area. W. Koelz's monumental work on the coregonid fishes of the Great Lakes appeared in 1929; Koelz drew heavily from fish collected from Wisconsin's inland lakes and from Lakes Michigan and Superior.

To date, the most significant contribution to our overall knowledge of Wisconsin fishes and their distribution is Greene's *The Distribution of Wisconsin Fishes*, which appeared in 1935. His work, a joint effort of the Wisconsin Geological and Natural History Survey and the Museum of Zoology of the University of Michigan, was based on more than 1,441 collections of fishes made between 1925 and 1928. Greene recognized 149 species, 14 of these having 2 or more recognized subspecies. *The Distribution of Wisconsin Fishes* was originally planned to be only a section of a larger report which was being prepared under the direction of Dr. C. L. Hubbs. Unfortunately, because of the large expense anticipated in its printing, the Hubbs work was never published.

Fish Culture and Stocking

The account of early fish management in Wisconsin that follows is derived mostly from Cox (1939) and from the annual and biennial reports of the Commissioners of Fisheries of Wisconsin (1876–1910).

The first Wisconsin fish commissioners were appointed in 1874 in response to a sagging Great Lakes fishery. The same year, the Wisconsin legislature was attempting to regulate the take in order to preserve the industry. Year by year the industry was shrinking because more gear was used for catching fish, but the loss of fish stocks was not fully comprehended.

The artificial propagation of fish was looked upon as a cure-all for preventing the exhaustion of the fish supply. In 1875 the first fish hatchery (the present Nevin hatchery) was established at Nine Springs, about 5 km southwest of Madison. In Milwaukee a temporary hatchery for whitefish and lake trout eggs was set up in the engine house of the water works, and attempts were also made to hatch these species at Pensaukee (Wis. Conserv. Dep. 1963).

In early days, milk cans were used as containers for fish to be stocked. The cans were transported aboard railroad express cars, from which they were transferred to any available conveyance for distribution to streams and lakes. Often this was a horse-drawn wagon, and the cooperator frequently had difficulty directing his load through deep mud and slumping snow banks to the stream or lake of destination.

Early in the propagation program exotic Atlantic and Pacific salmon eggs were obtained by purchase and donation from the U.S. Fish Commissioner. Much emphasis was placed on propagating the coldwater salmonid fishes, but these were stocked indiscriminately in warmwater lakes and streams where survival was impossible. For instance, in 1875 43,000 landlocked salmon eggs were hatched in Wisconsin's state or private hatcheries, and 10,000 fry were planted in Lake Mendota at Madison and a like number in Oconomowoc Lake (Waukesha County). From 25,000 Penobscot salmon eggs, 10,000 fry were planted in Devil's Lake (Sauk County).

In 1876 Lake Geneva (Walworth County) was planted with 250,000 lake trout, 100,000 whitefish, 50,000 brook trout, 10,000 landlocked salmon, 25,000 king salmon, and 1,000,000 walleyes. During 1877 lake trout were stocked in Browns Lake (Racine County); Delavan, Troy, Lauderdale, and Lake Pleasant (Walworth County); Oconomowoc, Pine, Pewaukee, North, Nagawicka, and Okauchee (Waukesha County); Lake Ripley (Jefferson County); Fox Lake (Dodge County); and Swan and Silver lakes (Columbia County).

In 1878, 20 graylings were held in Madison ponds; this was the first of a series of attempts to propagate the grayling in sufficient numbers to establish it in Wisconsin. In the same year plans were laid to take eggs from Lake Mendota ciscoes and to transport them to the Milwaukee hatchery for later stocking of inland lakes of Wisconsin.

Also in 1878, chinook salmon were stocked in Lakes Mendota and Monona (Dane County), in tributaries to the Mississippi River (Grant County), in Silver and Spring lakes (Columbia County), and in the Wisconsin River at Portage. In 1878, the Wisconsin hatchery superintendent wrote:

> I assert without any fear of contradiction, that the water selected by your commission for the planting of young fry [is] in every way suited for their welfare and growth, and that in a few years the people will enjoy the benefits accruing from our labors in pisciculture (5th Annu. Rep., Commnrs. Fish. Wis. 1878:28).

In 1879 the chinook salmon stocking program no longer seemed secure, and, although 1,100 salmon grew well at the Madison ponds, the Commissioners of Fisheries of Wisconsin (1879:16) noted that "it is still an unsolved problem whether they are adapted to our waters and can be successfully raised there or not." Extensive salmon culture ended in 1879 (except for the program of the late 1960s), though sporadic attempts were made to introduce exotic salmonids—e.g., the landlocked strain of the Atlantic salmon, which was stocked in Trout Lake (Vilas County) during the 1907–1908 period.

Millions of brook trout, whitefish, and lake trout were propagated from the beginning of the fish culture program. Successful yields from the stocking of lake trout were reported in 1901–1902 from Hammil Lake (Bayfield County), and Bass and St. Croix lakes (Douglas County). From 1901 to 1902, lake trout fry were distributed to Green Lake (Green Lake County), Lake Mendota (Dane County), Pine, Minocqua, and Tomahawk lakes (Vilas County), and others. As a result of the widespread stocking of lake trout, the distribution of native lake trout in the inland lakes of Wisconsin is not clear.

The exotic rainbow trout was secured from the U.S. Commissioner of Fisheries in 1880. The fish arrived in Wisconsin as eggs; about 2,000 young hatched from this initial shipment. In 1885, 600,000 rainbow trout were stocked in Wisconsin waters; in 1886, 620,000.

The first carp, 75 in number, were shipped to Wisconsin in 1880. They were bred upon arrival and produced 350 young the first year. Of these, 163 were distributed in 1881 to individuals in Rock, Columbia, Fond du Lac, Sauk, and Manitowoc counties. The commissioners, apparently little understanding the habits of the carp, reported (1884:15): "It is useless to undertake to grow carp where there are other fish. The carp must be cultivated in ponds expressly built for them and those of different ages must be kept by themselves." In 1891–1892, carp were distributed in Barron, Douglas, Eau Claire, Langlade, Marathon, St. Croix, Washburn, Bayfield, Chippewa, Marinette, Polk, Price, Sawyer, Shawano, and Taylor counties. In 1893, 8,050 carp were distributed in 37 counties; and in 1894, 8,125 in 36 counties. In all, between 1881 and 1895, over 131,000 carp fingerlings were distributed throughout Wisconsin. The last planting occurred in 1895, at which time this fish was well established in the state. By 1907 and 1908 it was the principal fish caught in the Mississippi River, and the superintendent of fisheries noted that fishermen were making more money catching and marketing "the despised carp" than they had made in past years from all other species.

Wisconsin initiated its walleye propagation program in 1883 and during that year produced 8 million fingerlings. Over a million Wisconsin muskellunge were propagated and planted in 1897. In 1887 Wisconsin imported 1,000 European brown trout eggs, which were hatched at the Bayfield Fish Hatchery at Bayfield (O. M. Brynildson et al. 1973). Exotic goldfish were received during the 1907–1908 period from the Nebraska Fish Commission in exchange for 100,000 eyed lake trout eggs; some goldfish were furnished to aquariums in Wisconsin, but the disposition of the remainder is unknown.

Lake sturgeon propagation plans were discussed in the Commissioners of Fisheries report for 1911–1912. At that time lake sturgeon were bringing the highest price of any freshwater fish, although in earlier days they had been caught in large numbers "and piled on the shores like so much cordwood." It was anticipated that lake sturgeon brood stock would be taken from the Wolf River; however, the plans never materialized. The problems associated with propagating the sturgeon have been discussed by Eddy and Surber (1947) and Eddy and Underhill (1974).

To improve the lake trout stocks in Lakes Michigan and Superior, the Wisconsin Commissioners allowed commercial fishermen, under permits, to catch lake trout during the closed season for the purpose of securing and fertilizing eggs (Bienn. Rep., Commnrs. Fish. Wis. 1909–1910). All expenses were incurred by the fishermen, who supplied as many eggs as were needed for the state hatcheries; those not needed were to be planted back on the lake trout reefs or spawning beds. During the 1909 season, 25 million eggs were sent to the hatcheries, and 15 million were planted back on the spawning beds.

In 1937, Wisconsin established a national record for state propagation and distribution of fish of all kinds, when over 1 billion fish were reared and planted in the state (Wis. Conserv. Dep. 1963).

Currently the Wisconsin Department of Natural Resources distributes fish from its own hatcheries, as well as from cooperative ponds, federal hatcheries, and private purchase. The program cultures mostly salmonids, largemouth bass, muskellunge, northern pike, and walleyes. In 1976, the department distributed over 436,000 brook trout, 1.1 million brown trout, 1.7 million rainbow trout, 1.1 million lake trout, 18,000 splake, 666,000 cohos, 1.1 million chinooks, 23,000 tiger trout, 609,000 largemouth bass, 12,000 smallmouth bass, 1.4 million muskellunge, 198,000 tiger muskellunge, 16 million northern pike, 54,000 perch, 62 million walleyes, 1.6 million whitefish, and lesser numbers of bluegills, catfish, crappies, sturgeon, sunfish, and rock bass (Wis. Dep. Nat. Resour. 1976a).

Fish Rescue and Transfer

From the late 1870s to the late 1930s, Iowa and Wisconsin Commissioners of Fisheries and the U.S. Fish Commission directed fish rescue and transfer programs to salvage Mississippi River fishes that were naturally imperiled.

In the June floodwaters on the Mississippi River, many fish that are ready to spawn seek the quiet backwaters to deposit their eggs. Conditions in the backwaters are favorable for the growth of the fish, and the young are often several centimeters long before the waters begin to subside. As the floods recede, the adult fish may return to the main channel, but many young fish are stranded in pools. Some pools become dry in a few days, others persist for weeks or months while the water slowly evaporates or seeps away, and a few remain until winter, when they freeze almost to the bottom. The landlocked fish die as the water diminishes or disappears, and as they are crowded, starved, and finally smothered when the pool freezes. A fish rescue and transfer program seeks to remove and distribute these fish before natural destruction occurs; the history and operational details of the program are given by Carlander (1954).

In 1898, the Wisconsin Commissioners of Fisheries reported that for several years they had collected small black bass from the sloughs and ponds along the Mississippi River for distribution to inland waters. In 1903–1904, over 117,000 bass rescued from Mississippi River sloughs were planted in inland waters. During the 1909–1910 period, of the almost 2 million fish taken from small Mississippi River ponds, approximately 600,000 were bass; over half of these were carried to the main river and the remainder were transported to inland lakes. In 1909, the Wisconsin legislature passed a law which directed that the license money paid by the commercial fishermen on the Mississippi River should create a separate fund to be used for the rescue of fish from the sloughs and bayous adjacent to the river (Carlander 1954).

In 1936, almost 10 million fish were transplanted in fish rescue operations conducted in the Mississippi, Wisconsin, Fox, and Wolf river bottoms, in flowages above power dams in some of the northern rivers, and in many lakes and streams where receding water or other conditions were detrimental to fish life (Wis. Conserv. *Bull.* 1937 2[1]:11). While the program was going on, private groups sent applications for rescued fish to be planted at their favorite fishing sites. When the fish cars made their trips inland, the applicants were notified where to meet the train to receive their quota of fish.

In the years for which it was possible to obtain records of the estimated numbers of fish caught, it appears that there were only 5 fish groups which in any year constituted more than 5% of the numbers of rescued fish:

> From 14 to 74 per cent of the fish were "catfish," including bullheads. "Sunfish" comprised 6 to 32 per cent of the annual catch and "crappies" varied from 3 to 37 per cent. Carp comprised from 0.6 to 39 per cent of the catch and "buffalo" from 0.6 to 16 per cent (Carlander 1954:38).

According to Carlander, the U.S. Fish Commission (Bureau of Fisheries) continued fish rescue operations on the Mississippi River until 1938 and retained crews for that purpose at Genoa and La Crosse. In the winter of 1939–1940, a crew of four men from the Wisconsin Conservation Department, working with local residents, seined Pool 10 near Cassville under the ice and rescued 100,000 fish. With this, the fish rescue and transfer program on the Mississippi River was nearing its end.

Although many regarded the fish rescue and transfer program as beneficial to fish stocks and to fishermen interested in exploiting these stocks, opposition to the program was growing for a number of reasons. Carlander (1954:35) noted:

> The sportsmen of the bordering states began to wonder if fish rightfully theirs were being sent to other parts of the country. . . . complaints that many game fish were being removed and the coarse fish returned to the river seem to have been somewhat justified since the records show that from twenty to ninety-three percent of the rescued "black bass" were transported to other waters.

The Wisconsin Conservation Commission (1949:89) noted that between 1920 and 1925 large numbers of rescued fish, mostly black crappies, were distributed to many northern Wisconsin lakes where they became extremely abundant. These "carp of the north" came into competition with and displaced sport fishes like walleyes and bass, and as a result of crowding often became stunted themselves. Thus the indiscriminate stocking of species outside their normal range may result in the reduction or loss of more desirable native fishes.

In retrospect, most fishery biologists now question the value of fish rescue for maintaining desired fish populations in Wisconsin waters. Stocking rescued fish in lakes, ponds, and rivers is also of doubtful value, since such stocking does not necessarily improve fishing. Most warmwater lakes and ponds are already overrun by large numbers of stunted fish, and any additional stocking merely aggravates this condition. Fish stocking is seldom needed except in new ponds and new artificial lakes.

The fish rescue and transfer program was undoubtedly responsible for the "discovery," years later, of isolated individuals far removed from the known distribution of their species. Attention is called to such perplexing cases in the species accounts.

Fishkills

Fishkills are by no means a recent phenomenon in Wisconsin, where they have occurred every year for as long as records have been kept. Today, many fishkills occur yearly, and in some waters, partial fishkills have become an anticipated yearly event. Some fishkills are traceable to fish diseases, but most are caused in late winter and late summer by oxygen depletion in heavily vegetated waters which are high in nutrients.

During July and August 1884, a die-off of an estimated 136 kilotons of fish occurred in Lake Mendota (Dane County). The cause was unknown, but an infestation of the protozoan *Myxobolus* was suspected. During the hot, dry summer of 1910, thousands of fish perished in the waters of Lake Winnebago and Green Bay, and from the latter part of July to the middle of August walleyes and perch were found floating over the surface of Green Bay. In 1925, a large number of fish were killed in the Flambeau River, probably as a result of industrial pollution.

In the early spring of 1967, over 50 large lake sturgeon perished in Lake Wisconsin (Columbia County); the suggested cause of death was industrial pollution. In 1968, there was a complete kill of brook trout along a 3.2-km stretch of the Little Wolf River (Marathon and Waupaca counties), which was traced to poison flushed from a potato-spray tank.

In 1974, heavy fishkills were reported from the lower Rock River (Rock County), Luxemburg Creek (Kewaunee County), Six Mile Creek (Dane County), and the Wisconsin River (Oneida and Wood counties); wastes from food and paper industries were partly responsible (U.S. Off. Water Plan. and Stand. 1975). In 1975, fishkills in Wisconsin were attributed to municipal operations (40%), industrial operations (20%), agricultural operations (20%), and other operations (20%) (U.S. Off. Water Plan. and Stand. 1977). Heavy kills were reported in 1975 from Manitowoc River (Manitowoc County), Cedar Creek (Washington County), Willow River (St. Croix County), and Oconto River (Oconto County).

A severe fishkill occurred in the Wisconsin River below DuBay Dam (Portage County) during the winter of 1976–1977. Most fish killed were black bullheads. The following July several hundred dead yellow perch, carp, and young-of-year walleyes were observed in the same area. In both instances the die-offs were caused by a shortage of dissolved oxygen.

In the mid-1970s, after treatment of the Rock River with toxicants for the elimination of carp, the sport fishes that had been stocked were winterkilled. The nutrient-rich waters produced heavy crops of aquatic vegetation, which decomposed and depleted the water below the ice of its oxygen. Repeated attempts over several years to reintroduce sport fishes to the system resulted in failure.

It is evident that the specific causes of fishkills are numerous. Some are natural, but municipal, agricultural, and industrial wastes introduced into our water systems are responsible for an increasing number of fishkills. Fishes stranded in overflow pools or in pools remaining after rapid drops in water level may die with the development of unfavorable conditions. Indeed, fishkills have become so commonplace that they seldom receive more than brief mention in local newspapers.

Fishing Demand and the Fish Resource

In Wisconsin sport fishing is the second most popular use of surface water resources. Only swimming attracts more water enthusiasts. Approximately 1 million anglers fished 18.5 million times and caught about 110 million fish in Wisconsin during the winter of 1970 and the summer of 1971 (Churchill 1971, 1972). Fishing, like other water-based activities, is concentrated most heavily on waters in the southeastern part of the state. Fortunately, these waters have the greatest capacity to produce fish pounds, although the population balance tilts toward nongame fish rather than sport fish.

It has been estimated that in 1960 only 9 Wisconsin counties could have exceeded 5,500 fishermen per summer Sunday; the estimate for 1980 was 14 counties. (In two of these counties, Oneida and Vilas, almost 40% of the projected 5,500+ fishermen per summer Sunday in 1980 were expected to be from Illinois.) (Wis. Dep. Resour. Dev. 1966.)

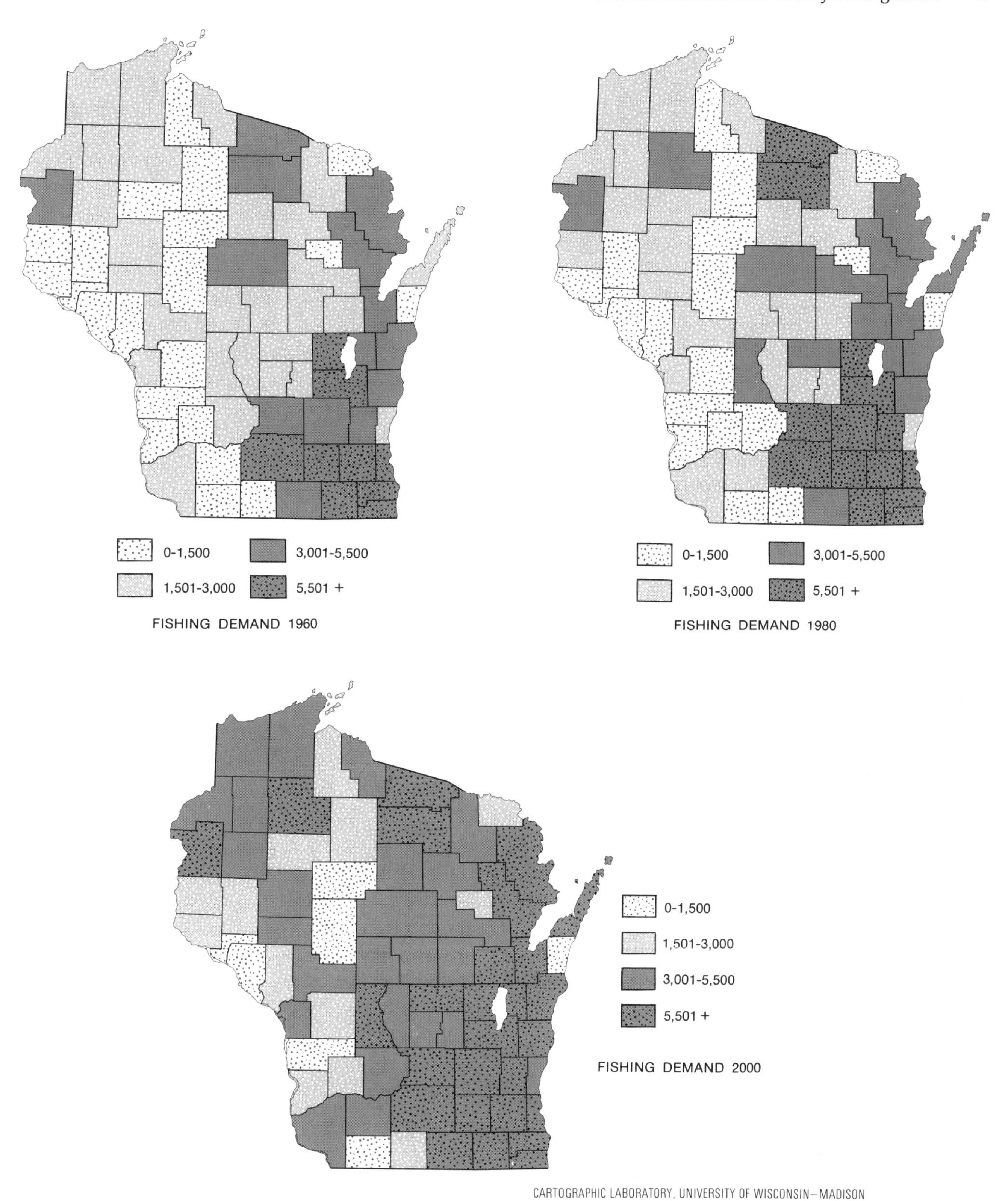

Numbers represent average number of fishermen per summer Sunday (after Wis. Dep. Resour. Dev. 1966:46–47).

In the year 2000, all but 20 counties should have over 3,000 fishermen on an average summer Sunday, and 27 of the counties, or more than one-third, may expect 5,500 fishermen; only 7 counties in Wisconsin might expect less than 1,500 fishing visits on the average summer Sunday. The increased fishing demand projected for the northwest sector is in part a reflection of increased demand by Twin Cities fishermen. The above data, however, do not reflect the increased fishing in those counties lying along the Great Lakes which resulted from the unanticipated salmon and trout bonanza that began in the late 1960s.

Statewide, Wisconsin fishing license sales continue to grow. Estimates indicate that about 25% of the public engages in fishing (Threinen 1964). Total sales of all Wisconsin fishing licenses were 1,374,531 in 1968, 1,386,208 in 1969, and 1,431,409 in 1970 (Kleinert and Degurse 1972). In 1970, the estimated fish taken included 4,579,000 trout, 204,000 salmon, 115,000 muskellunge, 3,282,000 northern pike, 4,651,000 walleyes, and 69,307,000 bass, perch, and other panfish (Wis. Legis. Ref. Bur. 1973).

Currently Lake Michigan sport fishing is an estimated $30-million-a-year business in Wisconsin. If state and federal agencies continue to stock trout and salmon in the lake, people will probably continue to fish for them.

Today there is a growing demand for food fish in the United States. Per capita fish consumption has increased from 4.8 kg in 1967 to 5.5 kg in 1975—a 14% increase over an 8-year period (Vilstrup 1975). The value of fish as a diet food and as a variety item in the menu has increased demand, and this trend is expected to continue.

The natural supply of fish has continued to decline as a result of increased commercial fishing pressure and environmental problems. Vilstrup (1975:46) stated:

> The yellow perch comes from Lake Erie with the bulk imported from Canada. Commercial catches from Lake Erie dwindled from a high of 15 million kg in 1969 to 6.8 million kg in 1974. It has been estimated that nearly 75% of the yellow perch are consumed in Wisconsin, and leading processors and distributors warn that prospects for an increased natural harvest appear limited.

In Lake Michigan's ecosystem the far-reaching effects of man's activities have included changes in water chemistry, benthos, plankton, and native fish populations. The changes in native fish stocks (mostly decreases in abundance) are primarily attributable to exploitation, the introduction of exotic fish species, and accelerated eutrophication and other effects of pollution (Wells and McLain 1973).

Although Lake Superior has not greatly changed from its pristine state, stocks of every fish species of commercial importance have been severely depleted (Lawrie and Rahrer 1973). The histories of all species suggest extensive overfishing long before the sea lamprey, known to have parasitized and reduced valuable fish populations, entered the lake. Recovery from these declines has been limited, but measures to control the sea lamprey, coupled with modern hatchery technology, clearly provide prospects for rejuvenating some existing stocks (e.g., lake trout) or developing entirely new ones (e.g., salmon spp.).

The fish resource is a matter of considerable complexity and is discussed in greater detail in the species accounts.

Fishery Management: Trends and New Developments

The goal of fishery management is to produce a sustainable yield of sport and commercial fishes. In Wisconsin, the Department of Natural Resources endeavors to sustain fish populations in waters where environmental deterioration has reduced the numbers of desirable fish species and where the fish have been overharvested. Managing water quality and fish populations is not an easy task. Early Wisconsin fish management activity is summarized in the "Fish Culture and Stocking" section, above. In the following paragraphs I bring together some recent management findings along with suggestions for the maintenance and rehabilitation of our waters.

Escanaba Lake in Vilas County has been an experimental lake since 1946, during which period fishing regulations have imposed no bag limits, no size limits, and no closed seasons for any sport fishes in its waters (Kempinger et al. 1975). Analysis of catch data from Escanaba Lake suggests that throughout Wisconsin the emphasis should be changed from managing the fish through fishing regulations to managing their habitat. Accordingly, for a number of species Wisconsin fishing regulations in recent years have been liberalized by reducing size limits and increasing bag limits. This trend is apt to continue.

The use of fish toxicants will undoubtedly be curtailed in the future (the negative effects of such treatment programs, discussed above, are also detailed in the species accounts). Dr. Willis King (Sport Fishing Inst. *Bull.* No. 262, March 1975, p. 7) commented that the pendulum has recently swung away from use of toxicants of all kinds in fresh waters, and has indicated that if new chemicals or new uses for old chemicals are wanted, the fish managers who want to use them are going to have to work for the money and personnel to do the basic environmental impact studies required. All new fish management projects should be highly coordinated by the Wisconsin Department of Natural Resources and should include the participation of all appropriate agencies (U.S. Soil Conservation Service, U.S. Environmental Protection Agency, U.S. Forest Service, state and local planning agencies, etc.) to promote the most comprehensive and effective effort for resolving fish management and water quality problems and managing aquatic systems.

One impediment to solving the fishery problems of the Great Lakes is conflict among approaches to fishery problems taken by the various management agencies having jurisdiction in different areas of the same lake (S. H. Smith 1973). Coordination of activities would contribute to attaining a common goal, once the goal has been defined.

Drastic measures must be taken to restore the Great Lakes (particularly Lake Michigan) to their original condition and to ensure that their native fish populations are not entirely extirpated. Ron Poff, Wisconsin DNR Great Lakes fisheries specialist, has suggested that PCBs be purged from the Great Lakes through the wholesale removal of alewives. Alewives contain up to 13 ppm of PCBs in their body tissues; and more than 100 million kg of alewives are available to bottom trawling in Lake Michigan.

Stanford Smith proposed making lake trout the primary planting fish for the Great Lakes, and converting all hatcheries to the rearing of trout instead of the salmon now propagated (R. C. Kienitz, *The Milwaukee Journal* 18 December 1977). Smith predicted that large concentrations of lake trout would depress and control the superabundance of alewives in the lakes, and that trout saturation would lead to natural reproduction of lake trout. In time, the hatcheries could be converted from lake trout reproduction to the propagation of whitefish, perch, chubs, and herring; stocking these native fishes would "drive the system further back to nature."

Our sport fishing culture in North America has been built around trophy rewards. Traditionally, the goal of a fishing vacation has been to bring home a large bass, muskellunge, or trout. However, times have changed, and there are now not enough large trophy-sized fish to go around. Recently nationwide sentiment has been supporting catch-and-release fishing as a management tool. Muskies, Inc., a Midwest-based organization interested in promoting conservation and fishing of the muskellunge, has strongly endorsed a catch-and-release program. In 1970, 19% of the total muskellunge caught by members were released back to the water; in 1976, 87%.

The spectacle represented by fishing tournaments has come under sharp criticism in recent years. Objections have been raised against promoters and others interested in financial gain through the abuse of the fish resource; fishing tournaments have also been viewed as putting a price on a fish's head or "killing fish for pay." Growing sentiment condemns the unnatural exploitation of fish and emphasizes the concept that fishing is a quiet, enjoyable, and private outdoor recreation.

More money and research will undoubtedly be directed toward solving the serious problems affecting some fish species. The stunting of panfishes has long been of concern to fish managers; however, remedies involving chemical treatments or predatory sport fishes have seldom been satisfactory. A new approach being explored is the introduction of native nongame predators, such as the burbot, bowfin, and gar, into waters with stunted panfish populations; these are the traditional top predators in many waters where stunting is seldom a problem.

A breakthrough in carp control is imminent. Recently it was discovered that carp move in tight schools under the ice. By outfitting a few "Judas" carp with transmitters, it may be possible to encircle and capture entire schools with nets, thus gaining valuable protein for man and effecting carp control at the same time. Such an example suggests that intensive research into fish behavior—an area in which we have little knowledge for many species—may pay dividends for future fish management.

Preserving Ecosystem Integrity: The Role of Nongame Fishes

In the "Report of Governor's Study Committee on the Use of Fish Toxicants for Fish Management," Cook et al. (1972) declared:

> The primary goal in the management of all our living resources must be to protect and enhance the integrity of ecosystems. A diversity of aquatic habitats and natural communities must be preserved to provide for education, research and esthetic enjoyment. It should be recognized that other generations will follow ours, and that we have a responsibility to maintain a suitable number of untampered ecosystems in representative habitats throughout the State and to place them "in trust" for the future.

Nongame fish (e.g., suckers, drums, gars, bowfins, minnows, and darters) constitute a large portion of our fishery resource, an important part that is often overlooked by sportsmen, resource managers, and research biologists. The management emphasis to date has been to establish sport fisheries, often for only a single species in a system. In Wisconsin, trout, muskellunge, northern pike, walleye, and bass have received most research emphasis. These species, at the tip of the food pyramid, constitute only a small part of the total fish volume in a given body of water; the nongame fishes outrank the sport species in total numbers of individuals, in combined weight, and in number of species present.

There are two arguments for the importance of every species of fish, regardless of how attractive or repulsive it may be. First, in terms of direct benefit to humans, there is no way to predict in advance which species may hold secrets useful in solving many kinds of problems. Koch (1975) quotes Joshua Lederberg:

> The variety of species is a great library of information literally encoded in the specific DNA molecules that characterize each type. It is paradoxical that, in this era of most rapid elimination of natural variety, we have begun to learn the keys to that code and to appreciate the subtleties of the evolutionary mechanism that it drives. Each different species is a unique adaptation to its own way of life, a lesson in 'how to live' that we never properly understand after we extinguish it.

It would be wrong to argue that every species has locked up inside its tissues a new food source or a cure for cancer. It is right to say, however, that every time we eliminate a species we eliminate the possibility of identifying its unique feature(s) and its possible value to humanity (Williams 1977). Second, all fish species are important as members of whole communities. It may seem, while you are fishing for walleyes or panfish, that gars, burbots, and bowfins are creatures with absolutely no redeeming virtues, but the quality of the walleyes and perch you catch may be directly dependent on the presence or absence of these predators. The lake fly (*Chironomus plumosus*) in the Lake Winnebago region may be a nuisance to the human population for a few days of the year, but to the lake sturgeon it is a prime food source throughout the year. Thus the strength of the lake sturgeon population is directly correlated with the "nuisance" level of the *Chironomus* larvae living in the lake muds.

Not enough effort has been made by fishery biologists to understand interspecific relationships, perhaps because the philosophy persists that nongame fishes are natural competitors with sport or other economically important fish species. According to Pister (1976), "management" has been manifested in nongame species destruction, often with virtually no biological justification.

Li (1975) has observed that (1) the evidence used to demonstrate interspecific competition is circumstantial in nature; (2) comparative dietary analysis of sport and nongame fish is inadequate; (3) sport fish territories, rather than food sources, may be limited in streams (sport fish are frequently the most aggressive fish in streams and unlikely to be displaced); and (4) predation (including fishing, a special form of predation) may be an important process governing community interactions. Li suggested that the concept of managing ecosystems should be promoted to replace single species management policies.

Probably the sucker is an example of a fish unfairly despised by many sportsmen, biologists, and fish managers. For decades it has been accused of depleting sport fish populations; yet a recent literature review (Holey et al. 1979) turned up no convincing evidence that sport fish populations were adversely affected by suckers. Although suckers eat the eggs and fry of some sport fishes, no evidence could be found that such predation was harmful. P. B. Moyle (1975) noted that trout and nongame fish can coexist in streams that support substantial trout populations.

Chemical treatment to control nongame fish in our streams is a management concept which must be reevaluated. In recent years the Wisconsin Department of Natural Resources has engaged in large-scale chemical treatment projects on lakes, reservoirs, and streams for the purpose of carp and "rough fish" control. According to Hasler (1973:214), although aquatic ecologists have decried the rising dangers of pollution,

> some are now supporting projects which may lead to the extermination of species or local populations of species under the justification of carp control. Entire drainage basins (e.g., Rock River, Wisconsin, 2,802 miles of streams and 100,400 acres of marshland) are poisoned with toxins, and such programs are labelled good conservation. I consider projects of this type contrary to the ecological ethic.

After treatment of the Rock River with antimycin A in 1970 and again in 1973, the major fishery consisted of bullheads, primarily black bullheads (Baumann 1975). The sport fish and panfish catch and the catch per unit effort fell dramatically between the second and third years after treatment on the upper section of the river, leaving in doubt the possibility of establishing a large natural population of predatory sport fish. Baumann noted no overall recreational improvement resulting from the reclamation. The sport fishery return has not noticeably increased, and continual restocking may be necessary to replace the sport fishes lost to winterkills and summerkills caused by the large increase in aquatic plants. Baumann concluded that a large, eutrophic river system cannot be effectively managed simply by treatment with toxicants and restocking with fishes.

Surveys of several chemically treated waters in Wisconsin have shown a sharp decrease in the total number of fish species following treatment (Becker 1975). A follow-up study of 1965 and 1967 antimycin field tests showed the persistence even as late as 1972 of an impoverished variety of fish species and for many species a reduction in numbers. Initial data in one study show that clams are particularly sensitive to fish toxicants, and that some species may have been eradicated in treated waters (H. Mathiak, pers. comm.).

The mass poisoning of waters appears to work contrary to those biological and ecological principles which support the concept that great species diversity leads to the stability of the environment. Hasler (1973:215) explained:

> To reduce the number of species in man's environment, then, is to invite instability, to reduce man's freedom to choose new species for exploitation and to impoverish the quality of his life. Driving a species to extinction is a process which cannot be reversed. Unlike a mineral which, though exploited until it is scarce, will always be somewhere on the earth—in a scrap heap or in the depths of the ocean—a biological species is unique, and, once lost, cannot be recreated. Over millions of years, evolution has experimented with countless biological types and has preserved those which are successful and well-adapted to their environment. They are the world's living museum and, as such, belong to humanity. No local group is justified in depriving future generations of species and their potential use by causing their extinction.

Pister (1976:13) said it this way:

> We still have a long way to go in the fish and wildlife professions before we reach an acceptable level of philosophical maturity. History alone will judge the value of what we do today. In the year 2076, society will be far less interested in the 1976 catch per angler in Crowley Lake or the degree of hunter success on a certain wildlife management area than in what happened to our native fauna if we fail to appreciate it enough to preserve, manage, and utilize it. We have inherited so much from our predecessors that we automatically assume an enormous debt to the future.

The approximately 25% of the Wisconsin populace who engage in fishing obviously have a stake in the state's fish resource, but we should not overlook the equally important and legitimate interest of the remaining 75%. Pister (1976) predicted a great expansion of nonconsumptive uses of fish and wildlife, with "a major increase in photography, species identification, behavioral studies, and similar 'research' pursuits. We should prepare for this inevitable demand and structure our management programs accordingly" (p. 12).

According to Pister, the only logical way to meet this demand is to manage and utilize the total fish and wildlife resource. This total resource, including both sport and nongame species, is vastly greater than the resource we have heretofore been concerned with. The management of nongame species is still embryonic in both practice and philosophy (Miller and Pister 1971, Pister 1974). During the late 1970s, Wisconsin's acting governor, addressing the Board of the Wisconsin Department of Natural Resources, recommended the establishment of an office within the department that would be concerned with nongame species. The move is especially commendable since it points up political recognition of a vast resource which in the past has had little attention.

In Wisconsin, official agencies continue to refer to many large nongame fish as "rough fish." This derogatory epithet engenders public animosity toward such species as buffaloes, burbot, redhorse suckers, freshwater drum, goldeye, carpsuckers, and quillback, all of which are excellent food fishes. Although the Governor's Study Committee on the Use of Fish Toxicants for Fish Management (Cook et al. 1972) recommended the deletion in writing and speech of "rough fish," the term persists in current fishing regulations (1980). The still common use of the terms "rough fish" and "trash fish" by fish managers is some indication of the extent to which management policies continue to be dictated by the public's rather narrow demands. In fact, sport fish are only important because of their present social and economic value. Li (1975) recommended that we broaden our management perspectives by trying to change the societal values which have resulted in the narrow policies of the past, and that we recognize the increasing need for fish protein to feed human populations. Carlander (1955) has shown that the total productivity of an aquatic system increases with the number of fish species which inhabit it. Butler (1976) predicted that we will soon protect and manage our freshwater sheepshead, suckers, carp, and other species for their value as sources of high quality protein.

In Wisconsin during the late 1970s, the commercial use of some white and longnose suckers was tested. These fish from Lakes Michigan and Superior were deboned, minced, frozen into 11.3-kg (25-lb) blocks, and shipped east. Some of the product, in the form of "fish crispies," sold in supermarkets at $1.96 per kilo (89¢ per pound). Consumers used the minced fish as a substitute for more expensive crabmeat in stuffing, in place of tuna in casseroles and salads, and in place of salmon in salmon loaf. Sucker meat is sweet tasting, low in calories and cholesterol, and highly nutritious.

Undoubtedly Bardach (1964) described the most pungent way of preserving nongame fish bounty—turning the fish into "cheese." The practice is of ancient origin and is widespread throughout the Orient. The recipe calls for certain thumb-long, short-lived fishes which are found in large numbers. After being cleaned and mixed with salt, the fish are allowed to rot in a vat. After 6 months—or, for the best results, even longer—the action of various bacteria will have turned the mixture into a white paste compounded of proteins and amino acids and laced with calcium from the softened bones. The odor is very strong, but approached without prejudice—and bearing in mind that Western cheese is of comparable origin—this "cheese" can be delicious.

Wisconsin fish processors and University of Wisconsin scientists have demonstrated that disagreeable fish processing wastes make a nutritious plant food and are trying to expand the market for it (*The Milwaukee Journal* 15 September 1977). The fertilizer is made by adding acids to organic material which break it down into nitrogen, phosphorus, and potassium while preventing bacterial fermentation.

Number of Species, Their Distribution, and Future Entries

This study recognizes 157 species of fish from Wisconsin waters. Of these species, 137 are present in the Mississippi River basin, 131 in the Lake Michigan basin, and 74 in the Lake Superior basin. By comparison, Greene (1935) reported 148 species from Wisconsin of which 132 were known from the Mississippi River basin, 111 from the Lake Michigan basin, and 58 from the Lake Superior basin. Since Greene (1935), the blue catfish (*Ictalurus furcatus*) has been removed from the state list of fishes (see p. 694), and the following species have been added: sea lamprey (*Petromyzon marinus*), alewife (*Alosa pseudoharengus*), pink salmon (*Oncorhynchus gorbuscha*), coho salmon (*Oncorhynchus kisutch*), chinook salmon (*Oncorhynchus tshawytscha*), pygmy whitefish (*Prosopium coulteri*), ironcolor shiner (*Notropis chalybaeus*), red shiner (*Notropis lutrensis*), river redhorse (*Moxostoma carinatum*), and bluntnose darter (*Etheostoma chlorosomum*). In addition to the species accounts for all Wisconsin fishes, I have treated separately the siscowet (*Salvelinus namaycush siscowet*), a subspecies of the lake trout. This form is now widely recognized and is receiving increased attention in Lake Superior waters from commercial fishermen and personnel of the Wisconsin Department of Natural Resources.

Since the late 1920s, a number of fish species have appeared in major Wisconsin drainage basins from which they had not been reported previously. In the Mississippi River basin, these are the red shiner, longnose sucker, river redhorse, bluntnose darter, and slimy sculpin; in the Lake Michigan basin, they are the northern brook lamprey, American brook lamprey, sea lamprey, shortnose gar, alewife, gizzard shad, pink salmon, coho salmon, chinook salmon, goldfish, ironcolor shiner, pugnose minnow, bigmouth buffalo, black redhorse, flathead catfish, pirate perch, yellow bass, warmouth, western sand darter, and river darter; and in the Lake Superior basin, the northern brook lamprey, sea lamprey, American eel, alewife, pink salmon, coho salmon, chinook salmon, pygmy whitefish, rainbow smelt, carp, blackchin shiner, yellow bullhead, channel catfish, stonecat, tadpole madtom, and spoonhead sculpin. The distribution of the species in the three watersheds is in conformity with the hypothesis that the Mississippi drainage is the center of origin of the Great Lakes fishes (Greene 1935).

The criterion used to add a fish species to the state list generally implies the successful establishment of that species, either through its own movement into state waters (e.g., the red shiner and the pink salmon) or through direct introduction by man (e.g., the coho salmon). There is little question about the successful establishment of the coho and chinook salmon as sport species; however, self-propagation of these species is not certain at this time, although limited reproduction is suspected in Lake Superior tributaries.

Wisconsin waters are expected to yield new species in the future. In Illinois, a number of species occur that may appear in Wisconsin by natural means or as introductions; these include the blue catfish (*Ictalurus furcatus*), the spotted gar (*Lepisosteus oculatus*), the silverjaw minnow (*Ericymba buccata*), the bigeye chub (*Hybopsis amblops*), the bigeye shiner (*Notropis boops*), the silverband shiner (*Notropis shumardi*), the freckled madtom (*Noturus nocturnus*), the redear sunfish (*Lepomis microlophus*), the spotted bass (*Micropterus punctulatus*), the greenside darter (*Etheostoma blennioides*), the orangethroat darter (*Etheostoma spectabile*), and the dusky darter (*Percina sciera*).

Crossover Connections

Crossover connections are frequently perched swamps or low, drained areas which, during high water or flooding, are covered with a sheet of water that connects drainage basins normally separated from one another. In the last 150 years there have been intermittent connections between the Mississippi River and Lake Michigan drainage basins, and possibly between the Mississippi and Lake Superior basins.

The best known Wisconsin crossover connection is the low divide between the Fox and Wisconsin rivers at Portage (Columbia County). Accounts persisted through the 1830s of floodwaters at this crossover deep enough to float canoes, and even government barges; undoubtedly unrestricted passage was available to fishes at such times. Commercial interests in the early 1800s agitated strongly for the establishment by the government of a canal. The first canal was completed about 1837 with a channel deep enough to float a canoe (Wis. Hist. Coll. 1895 13:345–347). In 1876 the federal government completed a canal 21 m wide, about 1.5 m deep, and 4 km long, with upper locks at the Wisconsin River and lower locks at the Fox River end. This canal remained in operation until July 1951. In the early 1960s, the upper locks were closed permanently, but still allowing a water flow of some 0.3 cms (10 cfs) from the Wisconsin River through the canal and into the Fox River. Since the late 1950s, a number of Mississippi River fishes have appeared in the Lake Michigan basin; these include the shortnose gar, bullhead minnow, pugnose minnow, blackstripe topminnow, western sand darter, and river darter. The Fox-Wisconsin connection at Portage is suspected to be the crossover point.

Greene (1935) called attention to the low divide between the headwaters of the Menomonee and Bark rivers (Washington County), and another low divide between the headwaters of the Root and Des Plaines rivers (Racine County). Until recently these may have been connections, at least intermittent ones, between the Mississippi and Lake Michigan basins.

After examining topographic maps, W. McKee (pers. comm.) suggested that crossover connections linking the Mississippi River and Lake Michigan basins may at one time have occurred between the Fox River and Menomonee River drainages at T7N R20E Secs 14 and 28, and the Bark River and Menomonee River drainages at T9N R19E Secs 35 and 36 (Waukesha County); between the Oconomowoc River and Cedar Creek drainages at T9N R19E Sec 3, the Pike Lake and Cedar Lake drainages at T10N R19E Secs 5, 6, 7, and 18, and the East Branch of the Rock River and Milwaukee River drainages at T12N R18E Secs 23, 24, 25, and 26 (Washington County); between the West Branch of the Rock River and East Branch of the Fond du Lac River drainages at T14N R15E Sec 12, and the West Branch of the Rock River and West Branch of the Fond du Lac River drainages at T15N R15E Sec 17 (Fond du Lac County); and between the Kimball Creek and Furbush Creek drainages at T39N R12E Secs 33 and 34, and the White Deer Lake and Butternut Lake drainages at T40N R12E Sec 34 (Forest County). Recent crossover connections linking the Mississippi River and Lake Superior drainage basins may have occurred between the Weber Creek and Pine Lake drainages at T43N R3E Sec 4 (Iron County); between the Upper St. Croix Lake and West Fork of the Brule River drainages at T45N R11W Secs 7 and 8; and between the Spruce River and Black River drainages at T45N R15W Secs 24 and 25 (Douglas County).

Present and past Illinois crossover connections between the Mississippi River and Lake Michigan basins include the low divide, about 2 km wide, between the Chicago and Des Plaines rivers, over which the early Jesuit missionaries paddled their boats during spring flood stages (Hubbs and Lagler 1964); and the Chicago Drainage Canal, which was completed in 1840 and further developed at the turn of this century into the Chicago Sanitary and Ship Canal. The recent entry of the gizzard shad into southern Lake Michigan is believed to have occurred via the Chicago Sanitary and Ship Canal.

For additional information on fish movements and dispersal routes, see Greene (1935) and Hubbs and Lagler (1964).

Exotic Fishes

As we have seen, non-native (exotic) fishes reach Wisconsin waters through direct introduction by man and through manmade waterways that facilitate passage around barriers. Early introductions apparently were made with little forethought: there was little understanding of the ecological requirements of the fish being introduced, little expertise to assure that the stocked fish had a reasonable chance of establishing itself, and little knowledge of or concern about the probable negative impact of the introduced exotic on the native fish population. During the nineteenth century, management philosophy permitted indiscriminate stocking of native and non-native fishes into as many new waters as possible (see the sections "Fish Culture and Stocking" and "Fish Rescue and Transfer," above).

Exotic fishes have also moved successfully through manmade waterways which were constructed in the interest of economic expediency. Economic interests were responsible for the construction of the Welland Canal (by-pass to Niagara Falls), which opened the upper Great Lakes not only to Atlantic shipping but to the anadromous Atlantic fishes, several species of which have already become scourges to the endemic fish community of the upper Great Lakes. Such open waterways continue to allow free passage for additional exotic species, and fish managers are wondering whether exotics of the future will be as damaging as those of the past. Several short accounts of Wisconsin's exotic species follow. For more detail, see species accounts in the literature cited.

In 1872, 25,000 American shad (*Alosa sapidissima*), native to the Atlantic Coast from Labrador to Florida, were introduced in the Mississippi River a few kilometers above St. Paul, Minnesota (Carlander 1954). In 1873, 70,000 young-of-year American shad were released into the Fox River at Appleton (Milner 1874b). The absence of progress reports following these records implies extirpation of the species in Wisconsin waters.

Rainbow trout (*Salmo gairdneri*) and brown trout (*Salmo trutta*) were introduced widely in Wisconsin waters during the late 1800s. Both are established and reproduce successfully; however, their numbers in lakes and rivers are augmented by an extensive stocking program.

Coho salmon (*Oncorhynchus kisutch*), chinook salmon (*Oncorhynchus tshawytscha*), and Atlantic salmon (*Salmo salar*) were widely stocked in Wisconsin waters during the 1870s. These introductions failed, and the program was discontinued except for occasional experimental plantings. With the use of new stocking techniques from the late 1960s to the present, coho and chinook introductions have provided a high rate of return to the angler. Atlantic salmon, stocked during the 1970s in Lake Michigan by the State of Michigan, have been caught along Wisconsin shores by Wisconsin anglers.

In 1959, the cutthroat trout (*Salmo clarki*) was introduced into a Washington County lake, and, in the 1970s, kokanee (*Oncorhynchus nerka*) were planted in a Langlade County lake. The success or failure of these plants has not been publicized; presumably self-propagation was nil. Hubbs and Lagler (1964) noted one record of the temporary establishment of the cutthroat trout in the State of Michigan.

The rainbow smelt (*Osmerus mordax*) appeared in the Wisconsin waters of Lake Michigan in the late 1920s and of Lake Superior in the 1930s. This strain was from a plant made in State of Michigan waters in 1912. The rainbow smelt reproduces successfully in the Great Lakes and in several inland lakes in Wisconsin where it has been introduced.

The alewife (*Alosa pseudoharengus*) and the sea lamprey (*Petromyzon marinus*) entered the upper Great Lakes via the Welland Canal and reached Wisconsin waters of Lakes Michigan and Superior in the 1930s and 1940s, respectively. Both species have reached pest numbers in Lake Michigan, and are undoubtedly responsible for the decline, if not the extirpation, of a number of endemic fish species in Wisconsin.

Four species of exotic minnows are known from Wisconsin. Best known is the carp (*Cyprinus carpio*), which was introduced successfully in 1881 and today is distributed in all but seven northern counties. The goldfish (*Carassius auratus*) has been introduced by man in a number of ponds, lakes, and streams of southeastern Wisconsin, where it has become successfully established, particularly in urban areas. The European rudd (*Scardinius erythrophthalmus*) was introduced into Oconomowoc Lake in 1917, and at least temporarily bred successfully. No recent records are known (Greene 1935). In the 1970s, Asiatic grass carp (*Ctenopharyngodon idella*) were illegally introduced into several private ponds in eastern and southern Wisconsin. The Wisconsin Department of Natural Resources has poisoned out these waters to prevent what may be another "carp problem."

Every year a number of tropical fishes from aquariums are illegally introduced into manmade warm water ponds. Occasionally these produce one or more broods during the summer of release. In the early 1960s I seined numerous guppies (*Poecilia reticulata*) and several unknown tropical fish from small ponds near Allenton (Washington County). Priegel (1967a) reported that a *Tilapia* species, a native of Africa, had been placed in Supple Marsh adjacent to Lake Winnebago, and that in August 1965 a 190-mm specimen was caught by an angler using worms as bait. Tropical fish are not known to survive Wisconsin's cold winters.

Although it is now unlawful to introduce exotic fishes into the waters of Wisconsin, the problem is a continuing one. More than 100 million fish were imported into the United States in 1972 alone, and some of these undoubtedly were released into public waters. The majority pose no danger to native fishes, but the probability exists that one or more species may become uncontrollable pests.

Extirpated and Endangered Fishes

Each species of fish has its evolutionary lifetime: infancy, when it is newly evolved from pre-existing forms; maturity, when it is expanding its range and becoming a part of the ecosystem; old age, when its numbers and range decrease; and ultimately death. Some species are like weeds. They are everywhere and successfully compete for space and food. Other species hang onto their identities by slim threads. They are vulnerable to fishing, to predators, and to slight changes in the environment.

The official Wisconsin Department of Natural Resources listings of fishes placed on endangered, threatened, and watch status are given in Wisconsin Department of Natural Resources Endangered Species Committee (1975) and Les (1979). I use these official listings for each troubled species in that part of the species account entitled "Distribution, Status, and Habitat." The following paragraphs give my personal listings of endangered species, which differ somewhat from those of the Wisconsin Department of Natural Resources, although they are based on the Department's definitions of endangered fish categories.

Extirpated Wisconsin species are the skipjack herring, blackfin cisco, deepwater cisco, longjaw cisco, shortnose cisco, ghost shiner, ironcolor shiner, creek chubsucker, and black redhorse. All were still present in Wisconsin waters in the late 1920s.

Endangered fishes are those in trouble. Their continued existence as a part of the state's wild fauna is in jeopardy, and without help they may become extirpated. They are officially protected by Wisconsin law (Chap. 29.415, Wis. Statutes). I consider the following species endangered: shortjaw cisco (Lake Michigan only; common in Lake Superior), kiyi (Lake Michigan only; abundant in Superior), gravel chub, striped shiner, and bluntnose darter.

Threatened fishes are those which appear likely to become endangered within the foreseeable future. Species I consider to be threatened are: paddlefish, blue sucker, river redhorse, goldeye, longear sunfish, pallid shiner, redfin shiner, Ozark minnow, pugnose shiner, starhead topminnow, crystal darter, western sand darter (Lake Michigan basin only; common in Mississippi River basin), mud darter, gilt darter, and slender madtom.

Fishes which may or may not be holding their own at the present time are given *watch* status. They are species suspected to have some problem which has not been identified or proved. They require special observation to identify conditions that might cause further decline, or factors that could help to ensure their survival in the state. I place the following under watch status: American eel, lake herring, bloater, pygmy whitefish, lake sturgeon, redside dace, speckled chub, pugnose minnow, red shiner, weed shiner, lake chubsucker, black buffalo, greater redhorse, pirate perch, and least darter.

The protection of fish species in trouble is a new concept in many states. How does one protect a lake or stream inhabited by an endangered species? What are the specific causes for its being endangered? How does one rally public support for preservation of endangered fishes? Fish species in trouble are mostly nongame fishes, often minnows and darters, which may be sensitive to the slightest alterations in their aquatic habitats. And man, the primary exploiter of and competitor for aquatic habitat with these species, is the only creature capable of restoring damaged habitat and its biotic treasures.

The Wisconsin Department of Natural Resources Endangered Species Committee (1975:1) observed that

> if wild creatures are disappearing, it is time to consider whether man too may be endangered. The survival of fish and wildlife and the survival of man are cut from the same fabric. Wild things are biological indicators of the health of our environment—barometers of the future of all life.
>
> What is really at stake is the well being of the total community of nature of which man is a part. We are concerned here with a remarkably interrelated whole, where each species has its place. If we eliminate one, we may lose another. Or we may cause the malfunctioning of the entire ecosystem. We don't know the complete role of many animals in the outdoor community. Until we do we cannot afford to lose any species.

Fish Parasites

Like other vertebrate animals, fishes have parasites. I have generally refrained from listing these in the species accounts; the material in this section is provided for the fisherman who is curious about parasites in fish he has just caught. I have simplified this section by listing only the most frequently encountered parasites. Further details dealing specifically with the parasites of Wisconsin fishes can be found in Marshall and Gilbert (1905), Pearse (1924a, 1924b), Cross (1938), Bangham (1944), Fischthal (1945, 1950, 1952, 1961), Degurse (1961), Anthony (1963), and Les (1975). Useful general works on the parasites of North American fishes are Davis (1956) and Hoffman (1970).

The YELLOW GRUB (*Clinostomum marginatum*) appears as a small (about 6 mm long) whitish or yellowish cyst deep in the flesh of the fish, or occasionally just beneath the skin. Yellow perch and bluegills are the prime targets, although northern pike, minnows, darters, and pumpkinseeds are commonly infected. The yellow grub has a complex life cycle. A fish parasitized by a yellow grub may be eaten by a great blue heron; the flesh of the fish is digested and the grub crawls to the throat and mouth of the bird, where it matures into an adult. The adult releases eggs, which are washed out of the heron's mouth into the water as the heron is feeding. The eggs hatch in the water into free-swimming larvae that penetrate certain species of snails. In the snail, each larva multiplies a thousandfold or more, and when a certain stage of development is reached the progeny leave the snail and become free-swimming again. These, upon contacting certain species of fish, burrow into the flesh and become yellow grubs. Light infections in the fish have no detrimental effect, but heavy infections cause the fish to swim more slowly, or may interfere with their growth. There is little danger of the yellow grub infecting man, and any parasites of this type are killed by thorough cooking.

The BLACK GRUB, or BLACK SPOT (*Neascus* spp.), is the most conspicuous parasite of fish. The parasite appears as a small black spot in the skin, about 1 mm

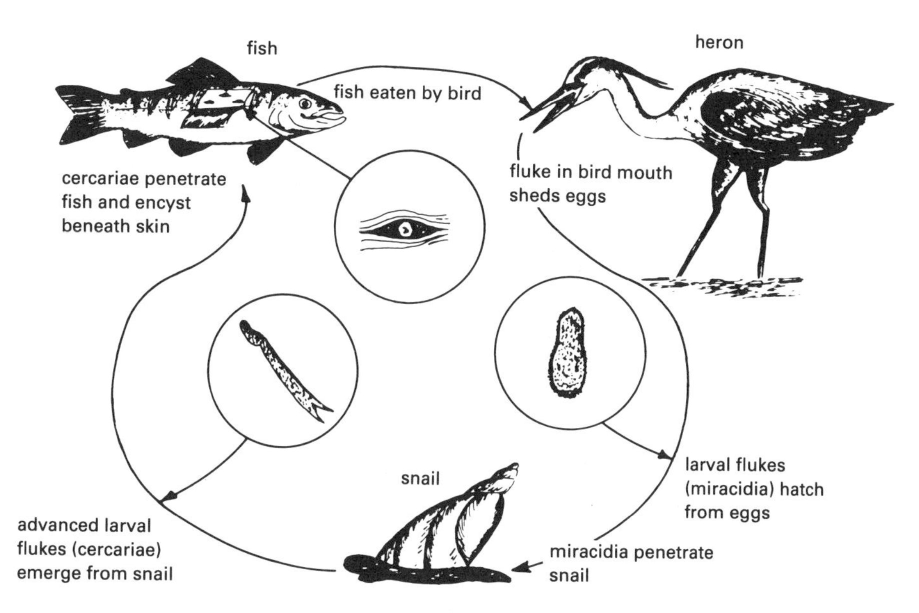

Yellow grub life cycle (Les 1975:3 after Northcote 1957)

diam. The encysted larva is surrounded by a thin inside wall laid down by the worm and a thicker wall on the outside deposited by the fish. The latter is black pigmented and is responsible for the black appearance of the cyst. Frequently the outer surface of a parasitized fish will have hundreds of cysts, some on top of one another, which give the fish a rough and distasteful appearance. Trout, bass, perch, northern pike, minnows, darters, and many other species may be infested.

The life cycle of the black grub is complex. A fish-eating bird, usually a kingfisher, eats the infected fish. The larva is digested out in the bird's intestine, where it transforms into an adult worm which lays eggs; these pass out into the water with the bird's droppings. The eggs hatch into larvae that swim about until they find and penetrate the right species of snail, where they multiply a thousandfold. Finally, free-swimming black grub larvae are released from the body of the snail; these larvae find a fish and penetrate beneath its scales or into the deeper layers of the fish's muscles. The cycle is then complete. It is suspected that heavy infections of black grub would have some unfavorable effect on the growth and vitality of fish. The black grub is not harmful to man, and it may be safely stated that infested fish are quite edible, even though they may not be pleasing to the eye. Skinning infested fish will remove most grubs, and normal cooking will destroy all grubs present.

The WHITE GRUB OF LIVER (*Posthodiplostomum minimum*) is a widespread and economically important larval fluke or trematode. It is most common in bluegills, pumpkinseeds, and rock bass; it occurs occasionally in black basses, minnows, and darters, but rarely in walleyes, perch, and bullheads. The grubs are present in thin-walled, transparent cysts in the liver, kidneys, spleen, reproductive organs, heart, and other body membranes. The complicated history of this grub begins when a parasitized fish is eaten, usually by the great blue heron. In the bird's intestine the grub matures into an adult, which produces eggs that are released into the water with the droppings of the bird. The eggs hatch into larvae and penetrate a particular species of snail, in which several generations of larvae develop and multiply. Eventually a free-swimming larva leaves the snail, finds a suitable fish, penetrates beneath the scales, and migrates to its destination in the liver and associated organs, where it encysts. If sufficient tissue is destroyed, the host fish will die; sometimes the liver is almost completely destroyed. The white grub of liver, even if swallowed alive, will not infect man. Moreover, since the parasite is not found in the fish's flesh, there is little danger of eating grubs, and normal cooking will destroy any grubs present should some accidentally cling to the body membranes in the dressed fish.

EYE GRUBS (*Diplostomulum* spp.) are small, flattened, and slightly elongated flukes found in the chambers or lenses of the eyes of nearly all species of fish. They have been taken from the eyes of suckers, perch, walleyes, sunfishes, northern pike, basses, crappies, rock bass, darters, trout, and burbot. A fish-eating bird, usually a gull, eats the infected fish and digests out the larvae, which then reach sexual maturity in the gut of the bird. The eggs of the eye flukes, evacuated with the droppings of the bird into the water, hatch into swimming larvae in 2 or 3 weeks. These penetrate a snail, where they develop further and multiply. Finally, a fork-tailed, free-swimming larva (cercaria) emerges and penetrates the fish host, where it becomes localized in the eye. A popeyed condition often results and sometimes develops rapidly. If the invasion is into the lens, the lens may become cloudy or opaque. If the infection results in blindness, the fish, no longer able to feed, gradually becomes emaciated and eventually dies.

The BASS TAPEWORM (*Proteocephalus ambloplitis*) occurs in both the adult and larval stages of fish. The adult and advanced larval stages (plerocercoid) of the bass tapeworm are very common in largemouth and smallmouth bass, and the bass tapeworm has also been found in trout, perch, pike, carp, and sturgeons. In the adult stage, mature segments of the tapeworm break off and pass into the water with the fish feces. These segments disintegrate and the eggs contained in them are eaten by microcrustaceans called copepods. Inside the copepods, the eggs develop into larvae. The copepods are eaten by young or adult fishes, which become infected with the tapeworm larvae; adult fishes are often infected by eating young fish. Although the adult stage of the bass tapeworm usually does little harm to the fish, a larval stage, the plerocercoid, may invade the fish's reproductive organs and cause infections; these often result in sterility. There is little chance of man being infected if the fish containing these larvae are thoroughly cooked.

The RIBBON TAPEWORM (*Ligula intestinalis*) is a yellowish white worm which may reach a length of over 0.6 m. It is most often found in minnows, but has been reported in perch, bass, suckers, and trout. The adult tapeworm is present in the intestines of fish-eating birds, and its eggs are shed into the water along with droppings from the bird host. The eggs develop into ciliated larvae, which are ingested by a copepod host; in the host they develop into small, wormlike procercoids. When the copepod is eaten by a fish, the procercoid larvae embed themselves in the intestine of the fish host, where they develop into the final larval stage, the plerocercoid. Fish infected with the ribbon tapeworm develop a swollen belly; heavy infestations may cause sterility in the fish (see picture of spottail shiner, p. 543). The ribbon tapeworm is eliminated when the fish is cleaned. Thorough cooking is recommended to ensure against infection.

Among other fish parasites are the SPINY-HEADED WORMS (Acanthocephala)

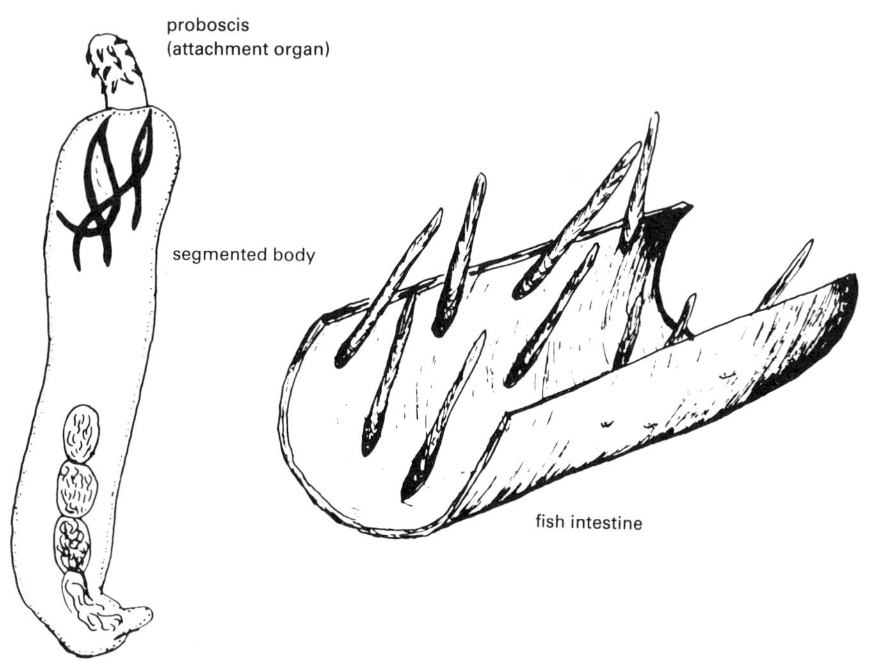

Spiny-headed worm and its position in fish intestine (Les 1975:10; drawing by D. Leveque)

and ROUNDWORMS (Nematoda), which occur in the intestine, although other internal organs may be invaded as well. Larval nematodes have been observed to cause considerable damage in the body cavity of fish. The kidney roundworm, which is found as a larva in the body cavity and viscera of bullheads and northern pike, may infect man. However, thorough cooking will destroy this parasite.

FISH LICE (*Argulus* spp.), GILL LICE (*Salmincola* spp.), ANCHOR WORMS (*Lernaea* spp.), and LEECHES (Hirudinea) are large, external parasites commonly encountered in Wisconsin fishes. Gill lice infect the gills of trout and salmon; in Wisconsin they are found primarily on brook trout. When the trout become crowded in a stream or a spring pond, the gill copepod also increases in number until the trout die or become so weak that they cannot avoid predators or disease. Anchor

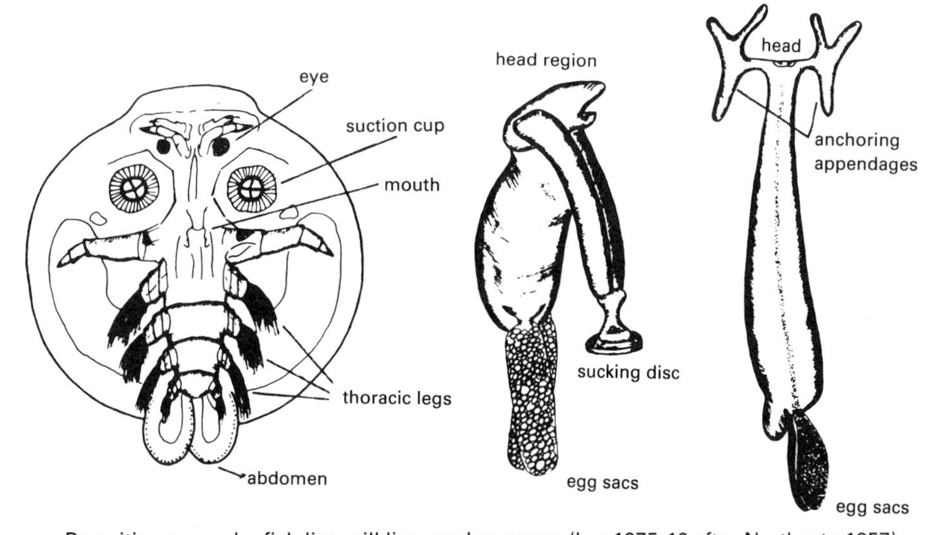

Parasitic copepods: fish lice, gill lice, anchor worm (Les 1975:13 after Northcote 1957)

worms, attached to the skin and bases of fins, have been reported from sunfish, trout, gars, bowfins, perch, drum, and minnows. Heavy infestations can slow the growth of a fish, cause it to lose weight, and even kill it. Leeches do not parasitize fish for prolonged periods, and damage from leeches to the fish population of a given lake or stream is usually slight.

Small white spots on the skin and fins of fish, and to a lesser degree on the gills, indicate the presence of the protozoan ICH (*Ichthyophthirius multifilis*). Although this is a disease parasite commonly associated with aquariums, it is a serious parasite in the wild, and heavy infestations can result in the death of fish. It is believed that all species of freshwater fish are vulnerable to ich.

A very destructive protozoan (Myxosporidea) causes the so-called whirling or tumbling disease, which affects fingerling trout. The organism, upon penetration of the cartilages of the trout's skull and its auditory organs, causes the fish to swim about with convulsive, rapid movements, at times turning on its back and even leaping from the water. A serious infection may be fatal. If the victim does recover, a deformity of the skeleton may affect the fish for life. Wherever the myxosporideans have penetrated cartilage, normal ossification is prevented, resulting in such deformities as shortened gill covers and fins, and fused cheeks which prevent the fish from shutting its mouth.

Fungi (*Saprolegnia* spp.), which appear as a white, cottony growth on the body of fish such as brown trout in Lake Michigan, can cause considerable damage and even death. Such infections of fish are of no danger to humans, but often result in fish having an unpalatable taste and unsightly appearance. Anglers frequently discard large fish, even of trophy size, that show signs of fungus.

The Species Accounts

Key to the Distribution Maps

From 1958 through 1978, 1,882 collections of fish specimens were made in Wisconsin waters by me, by student teams under my direction, by cooperating personnel from the Wisconsin Department of Natural Resources, and by cooperating commercial fishermen. The specimens from these collections were examined by me, and some were placed in the Museum of Natural History–Stevens Point (UWSP). The locations of these collections are indicated by *black dots* on the map of the fish collection stations and on the Wisconsin fish distribution maps accompanying each species account. Broadly overlapping symbols are omitted, and no attempt has been made to indicate the numerous repeat collections made at several collection sites.

The *black triangles* on the distribution maps accompanying the species accounts represent records from the Wisconsin Fish Distribution Study (1974–1979) of the Wisconsin Department of Natural Resources. They indicate spot locations given by computer printout data that were made available to me by the study—including the data for all species of fish from the Study's 1974 and 1975 collections, and data for rare and endangered species from the 1974 through 1978 collections. The fish from the Wisconsin Fish Distribution Study have been deposited in the Milwaukee Public Museum. I have examined and verified a number of specimens from these collections.

The *small open circles* on the species distribution maps represent reports given in the literature and unverifiable reports from many sources. The latter were mainly published and unpublished data from Marlin Johnson (UW–Waukesha) and from the Wisconsin Department of Natural Resources, including DNR district files, fish research reports, fish management reports, technical bulletins, and surface water resources reports. Surface water resources reports frequently

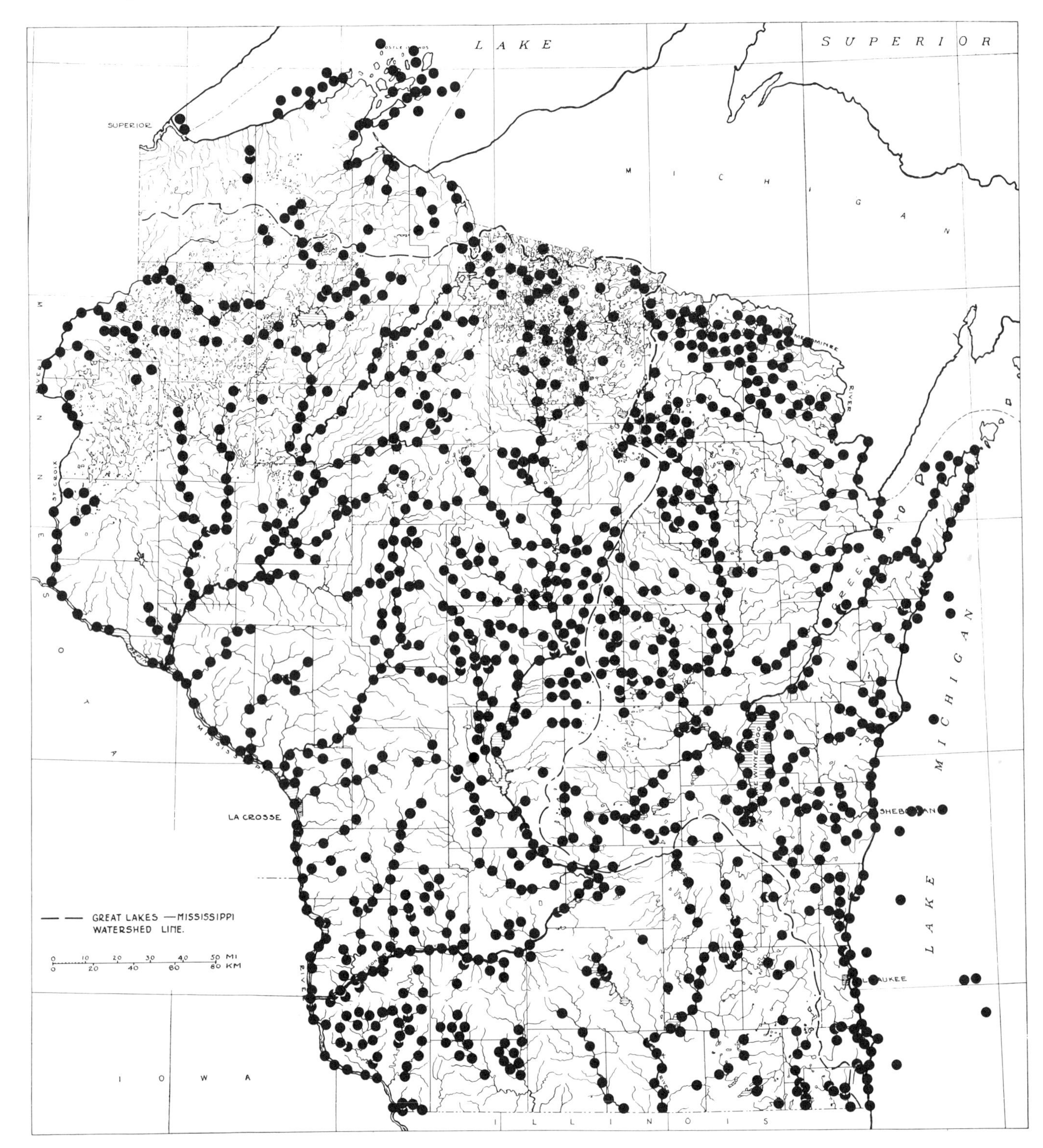

Fish collection stations (1958–1978)

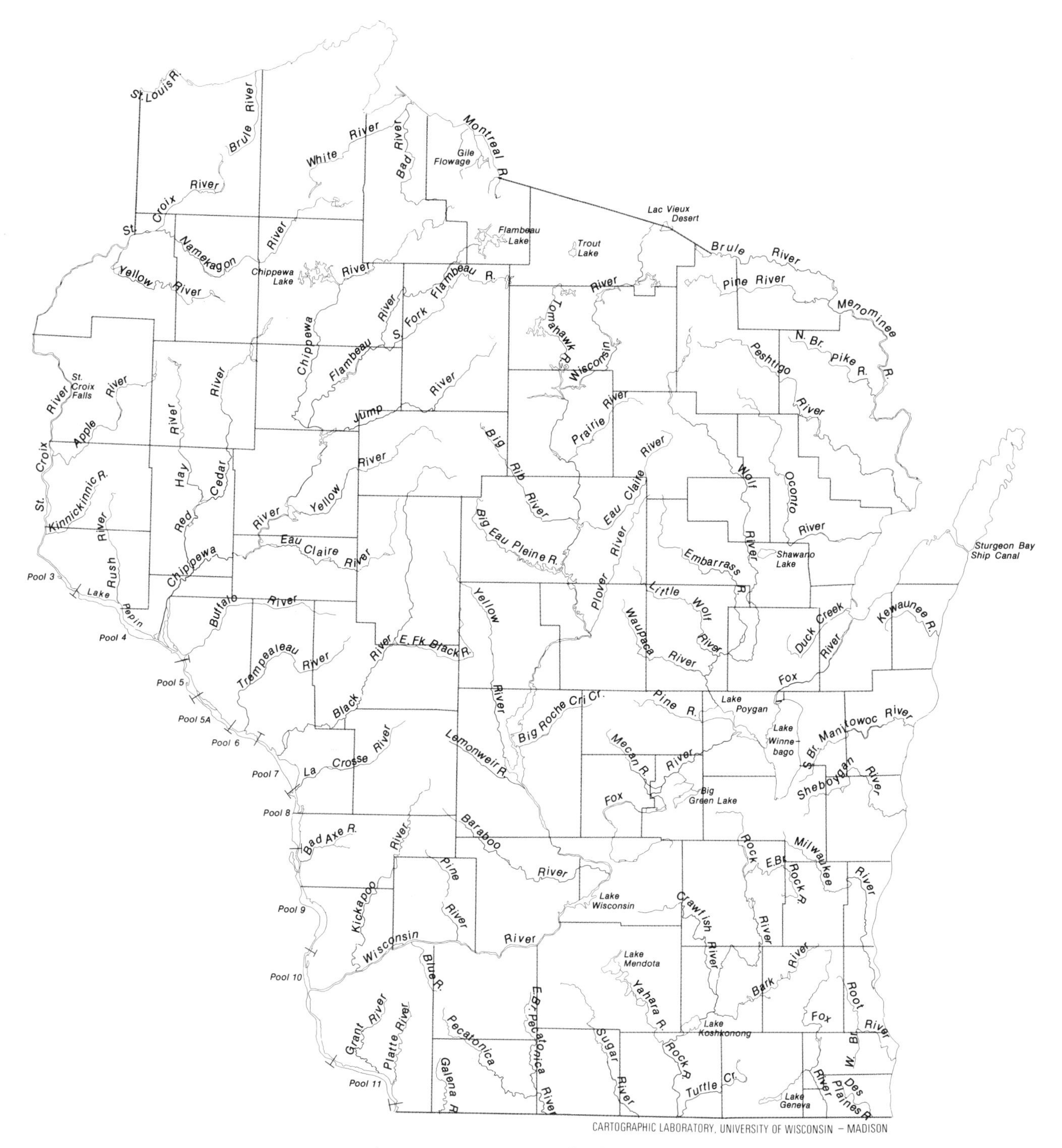

Important waterways of Wisconsin

Counties of Wisconsin

describe a species as being present in a river over a portion of, or along the length of, a county; in these cases I arbitrarily plotted a small open symbol at the midpoint of the designated county portion. For species found in lakes, the symbol was placed in the center of the lake.

The *large open circles* on the species distribution maps represent Greene's (1935) cumulative records from 1926 to 1928 and his early reports. They are useful for comparing the then-known distribution of a fish species with its present distribution.

Where several distribution sources tend to overlap broadly, the priorities given the different symbols follow the order of the explanations above: the *black dots* have first priority, and the *black triangles, small open circles,* and *large open circles* follow in that order. Thus a number of Greene (1935) records are not indicated on the species maps since those records have been superseded by more recent records or reports.

The small general range maps were prepared from materials appearing in recent published accounts. Where possible, attempts were made to pinpoint the range of a species to those waters in which it occurs—e.g., the range of the blue sucker appears on its map as a dendritic pattern along the major waterways where it is found, rather than as a solid black area.

Organization of the Species Accounts

In the text which follows, a family description precedes the accounts of the Wisconsin species found within that family. The family description gives the number of genera and species of that family found in Wisconsin as well as the number of genera and species found within the United States and Canada. When information on a fossil is available, the geologic age of the fossil is included.

Each family description also lists the anatomical or physiological features which distinguish that family from all others. In addition, features such as edibility, economic value, and habits common to the species of this family are discussed here. Also included is information pertaining to introduced species which have not yet become established in the state and deletions of species which have been incorrectly ascribed to Wisconsin waters.

The species accounts are designed to be useful to the fisherman and naturalist as well as to the fishery biologist. Highly technical language has been avoided wherever possible; where such terminology has been used, the Glossary (pp. 51–59) provides clarification. Species accounts include the following information about each Wisconsin fish species:

Species name and its derivation. The common and scientific names generally follow Robins et al. (1980).

Other common names. I have included the common names I encountered in the literature. Many are local names, while others are common names used over the entire range of the species; I have made no attempt to identify range of usage. Common names often result in much confusion, since the same name is often applied to a number of different species within a family (e.g., "sunfish") and even to species in different families (e.g., "stoneroller" for a minnow and for a sucker).

Description. The characters included are the family characters and the characters unique to the species. Thus, within a family the same characters are examined in all species for comparative purposes. Sexual dimorphism and hybridization are referred to when such information is available. The *systematic notes* are used to establish relationships between species, and to discuss subspecific differences and problems.

Color and markings are provided where they can aid identification of the species and differentiation of the sexes. Color and markings in breeding males and females (e.g., the fathead minnow) may be vastly different, so different that the nonexpert may take the two sexes for two different species.

Distribution, status, and habitat. The Wisconsin and general ranges are given for each species, followed by a discussion of the status of the species in Wisconsin. The scale used to define abundance follows Johnson and Becker (1970:265–266):

rare —one or two specimens taken at isolated intervals
uncommon —taken infrequently in very small numbers
common —taken frequently in moderate numbers
abundant —taken frequently in large numbers

In some accounts of species given endangered or threatened status in Wisconsin, it has been useful to review the status of such species in neighboring and other states. For such species I generally have given all known Wisconsin records and their sources in detail. Specimen collections alluded to will often bear a museum number. The key to museum abbreviations follows.

BMNH —Bell Museum of Natural History, University of Minnesota, Minneapolis
INHS —Illinois Natural History Survey, Urbana
MPM —Milwaukee Public Museum, Milwaukee
KU —University of Kansas Museum of Natural History, Lawrence
ROM —Royal Ontario Museum, Toronto
UF —Florida State Museum, Gainesville
UMMZ —University of Michigan Museum of Zoology, Ann Arbor
USNM —United States National Museum of Natural History, Washington
UWSP —Museum of Natural History, University of Wisconsin–Stevens Point
UWZM —University of Wisconsin Zoological Museum–Madison

The number of specimens in the collection is given in parentheses following the museum number. For example, "UWSP 3225 (11) Mississippi River, Pool 11 (Grant County) 1946" is interpreted as: "11 specimens under museum number 3225 in the Museum of Natural History, University of Wisconsin–Stevens Point, taken from Pool 11 of the Mississippi River opposite Grant County in 1946."

Generally a brief description is given of the habitat of the species. For some species, where considerable habitat information has been gathered, quantitative information (percent) may be given for turbidity, substrates, and river widths. The figures for substrates represent the bottom types (frequency percent) reported in the location of the collection, but may not necessarily represent the exact bottom over which the species was taken.

Biology. This section contains life history data, with special emphasis on fish behavior. Wherever possible, the following data are considered:

Spawning: dates, water temperature and velocity; nest site selection and construction; fighting, courtship and spawning behavior; factors influencing spawning success.

Fecundity, development, and growth: ratio of gonad to total body weight; egg size, color, and number; duration of incubation and development of embryo; hatching; yearly growth and maximum length and age attained; length and age at maturity for males and females.

Habits: food habits of young and adults, feeding behavior; daily and seasonal movements; relationships between individuals within the species and of species members to other species of fish; temperature tolerances.

Importance and management. The significance of the species to other fish species (including predators) and to other animals and birds, and its value to man as a bait fish, sport fish, and/or commercial fish are discussed briefly.

Research management for maximum production and yield per hectare are given where available. Selected experimental research programs and their probable impact on the fish population in a body of water are considered.

Glossary

abdominal—pertaining to the belly; the pelvic fins are abdominal when they are inserted far behind the bases of the pectoral fins.

acute—sharply pointed; an angle less than 90°.

adipose fin—the fleshy, rayless fin on the midline of the back between the dorsal and caudal fins, as in the trouts and bullhead catfishes.

age—age (growth) is determined by counting the annuli or growth rings deposited on scales, spines, or vertebrae. Age is expressed in arabic numerals (e.g., 1, 2, 3, etc.) or roman numerals (e.g., I, II, III, etc); 0 is young-of-year. The arabic numerals express the yearly lengths of each fish as determined by back calculating to each annulus (since the growth of the scales, spine, or vertebrae is essentially proportional to the linear growth of the fish). The roman numerals generally have been used to express the lengths of each age class as determined by the actual field lengths of the fish of that age class at the time of capture.

air bladder—see *swim bladder*.

alevin—the newly hatched, incompletely developed fish (usually salmonid) still in the nest or inactive on the bottom and living off stored yolk.

ammocoete—the burrowing, larval stage of the lamprey.

anal fin—the unpaired fin behind the vent.

anal fin height—the distance from the origin of the fin to the tip of its anterior lobe.

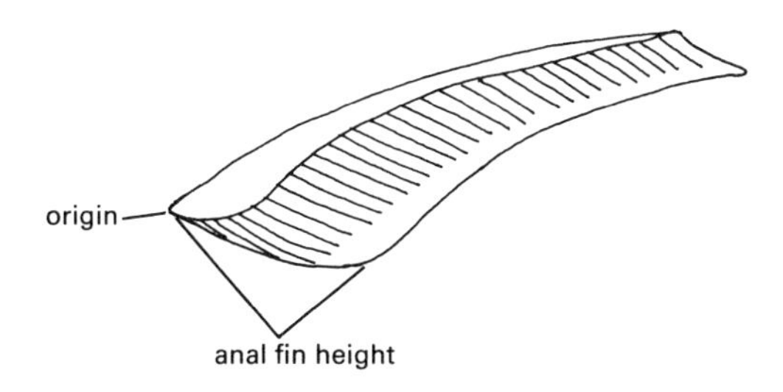

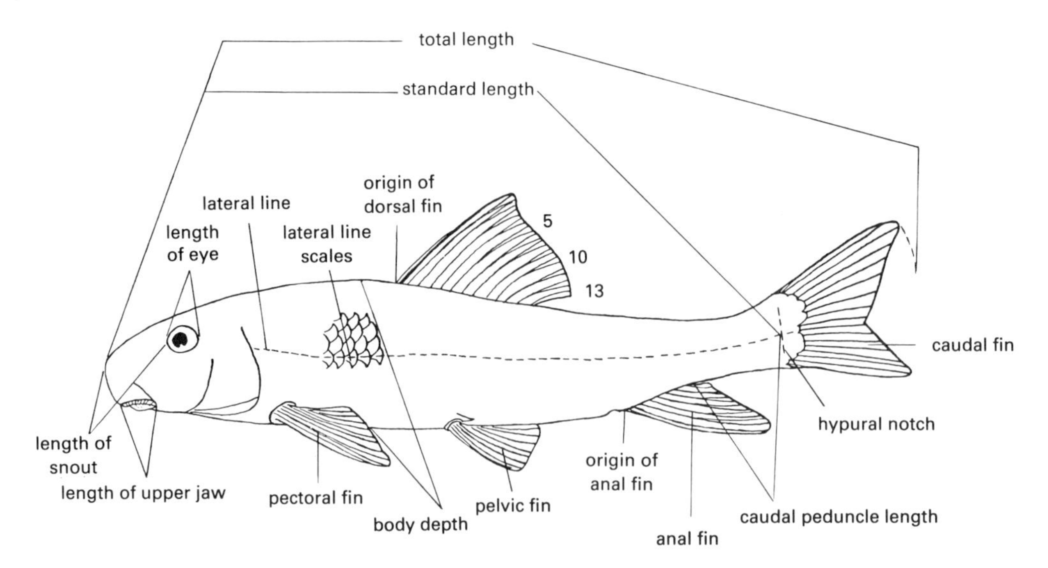

Topography of a sucker. The sucker pictured has 13 dorsal fin rays; note that the very small rays at the front end of this fin are not counted, and that the last fin ray (#13) is divided through its base.

annulus (pl. *annuli*)—the ringlike marking(s) on scales, spines, and vertebrae used to determine age.

axillary process (*pelvic axillary process*)—an enlarged, generally pointed scale projecting backward from the lateral insertion of the pelvic fin.

barbel—the slender, flexible process located near the mouth; functional in touch and taste. A small barbel is present in some minnow species (see illustration of creek chub, page 110).

basioccipital—the posteriormost bone on the underside of the skull. The pharyngeal pad against which the pharyngeal arches work is attached here.

benthos—fauna and flora of the bottoms of bodies of water.

bicuspid—having, or ending in, 2 points.

body depth—the greatest dorsoventral dimension of the body (excluding the fins and their bases).

body weight—the total weight of a fish.

bony plates, lateral—small to large platelike bones often arranged in a horizontal series on each side of the fish.

branchial diameter—the greatest lateral width of the branchial (gill-bearing) region (see illustration under *sucking disc*).

branchial groove—in lampreys, the longitudinal crease above the gill slit openings.

branchial myomere—in lampreys, the muscle segment in the region of the gill openings.

branchiostegals (*branchiostegal rays*)—the bones, ventral to the opercles, which support the gill membranes.

breeding tubercles—the hardened, often thornlike projections from the skin of the head, fins, and scales; present in the adult male (sometimes in the female) during the breeding season.

buccal cavity—the cavity of the cheeks or the mouth.

buccal epithelium—the lining of the cheeks or the mouth.

buccal funnel—the sucking disc of an adult lamprey; the expanded area, often armed with rasping teeth, about the mouth opening.

canine teeth—conical, pointed teeth which are larger than the other teeth.

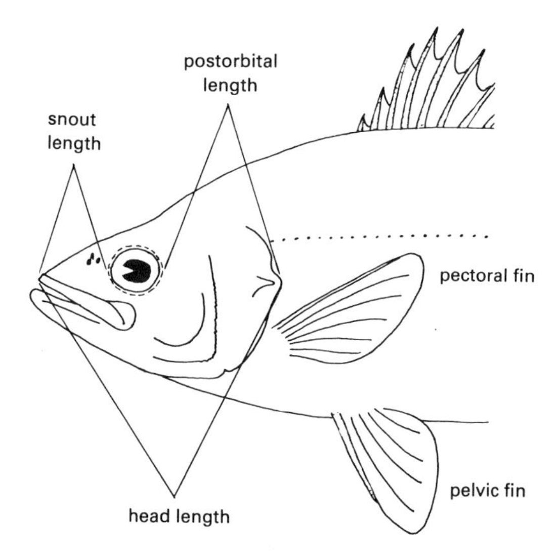

Anterior topography of a temperate bass

caudal (*caudal fin*)—the tail fin.
caudal fin, length of—distance from the hypural notch to the tip of the longest depressed lobe.
caudal peduncle—the narrow region of the body from the posterior end of the anal fin base to the base of the caudal fin.
caudal peduncle depth—the least depth of the caudal peduncle.
caudal peduncle length—the oblique distance from the end of the anal fin base to the midpoint of the hypural notch.
caudal peduncle scales—the least count of scales around the narrow part of the peduncle.
cheek—the area between the eye and the edge of the preopercle bone.
chromatophore—a pigment-bearing tissue element or cell.
circuli—concentric ridges on scales, generally surrounding the focus (inner circle).
circumferential scales—the (number of) scale rows crossing a line around the body immediately in the advance of the dorsal fin.
circumoral teeth—the large, often modified teeth, generally 3 or 4 in number, lying on either side of the mouth opening in adult lampreys.
cleithrum—the major bone of the pectoral girdle, extending upward from the pectoral fin base and forming the posterior margin of the gill chamber.
compressed—narrow from side to side; flattened laterally.
concave—curved inward (hollowed), as the free edge of the dorsal fin or the top of the head.
condition, coefficient of (*condition factor*; *K*)—The weight-length relationship of a fish, expressed as the solution to the equation:

$$K = \frac{W(10^5)}{L^3},$$

where K = coefficient of condition of fish in the metric system,
L = TL, SL, or FL in millimeters (the length used is indicated as a subscript to K: e.g., K_{SL}), and
W = WT of fish in grams.

convex—curved outward (arched) as the free edge of the dorsal fin or the top of the head.

ctenoid scale—a scale that bears a comblike row, or rows, of small teeth on its exposed (posterior) edge.
cycloid scale—a more-or-less rounded scale that bears no comblike teeth.
dentary—either of the pair of prominent bones of the anterior lower jaw, usually bearing teeth.
denticle—a small tooth or projection.
depressed dorsal fin length—the distance from the origin of the fin to the posteriormost point of the fin as the fin is held pressed to the back.
digestive tract length—the stretched-out length in situs of the digestive tract from the back of the pharynx to its endpoint (the anal opening).
disc length—the measurement in the adult lamprey along the midline of the sucking disc, including the external measurements of the papillary fringe.
dorsal—pertaining to the back; often used as an abbreviation for dorsal fin.
dorsal fin(s)—the median unpaired fin atop the back, as in the trouts and minnows; two dorsal fins—the first spinous and the second soft—as in the sunfishes, perches, and sculpins.
dorsal fin height—the distance from the origin of the fin to the tip of its anterior lobe.
dorsolateral scale count—the count of lateral scales (along any row from the third to the sixth above the lateral line) from a point below the origin of the dorsal fin and running anterior to the head.
epilimnion—the upper, warm stratum of water above the thermocline.
eye diameter—the greatest horizontal distance across the cornea.
falcate—curved like a sickle.
filament—an elongated, threadlike ray in a fin; a threadlike part of a gill.
fin ray—a bony or cartilaginous rod supporting the fin membrane.
fluke—a flattened, parasitic, trematode worm of the Order *Strigeatoidea.*
fontanelle—an aperture or opening in a bony surface, as in the upper skull of some suckers.
fork length (FL)—the distance from the anteriormost margin of the head to the posterior tip of the middle ray of the caudal fin.
gape, width of—the greatest transverse distance across the opening of the mouth.
gas bladder—see *swim bladder.*
genital papilla—the fleshy projection immediately behind the anus.
gill arch—one of the bony or cartilaginous arches or curved bars extending dorsoventrally and placed one behind the other on each side of the pharynx, and supporting the gills.
gill arch, ventral limb of—that portion of the gill arch ventral from the joint which is generally near the midpoint of the portion bearing gill rakers.
gill cover—the bones of the head that cover the gill chamber.
gill filaments—the threadlike respiratory structures projecting posteriorly from the gill arches.
gill membranes—the membranes below the bones of the head which close the gill cavity ventrolaterally, and which are supported by the branchiostegals.
gill rakers—anterior knobby or comblike projections from the gill arches.
gill slits (*gill openings*)—the openings between the opercle and the side of the head of the higher fishes. Lampreys have 7 gill slits on each side.
growth—see *age.*
gular membrane—the median soft tissue on the lower jaw or anterior throat, as in the mooneyes.
gular plate—the large, median, dermal bone on the lower jaw or anterior throat, as in the bowfin.

head length—the distance from the tip of the snout or upper lip to the most distant point of the opercular membrane.

hypolimnion—the lower, cold stratum of water below the thermocline.

hypural notch—the point between the end of the body vertebrae and the beginning of the caudal fin; the crease in the caudal peduncle made by bending the caudal fin to one side or the other.

included—a term referring to the partial fitting of the lower jaw into the upper jaw. "The lower jaw is *included*."

inferior—pertaining to the mouth when it is in a ventral or generally horizontal position.

infraorbital canal—the segment of the lateral line canal system that curves behind and beneath the eye and extends forward onto the snout (see illustration of mimic shiner, page 128).

insertion (of fin)—the anterior end of the bases of the paired fins.

interorbital distance—the least bony distance on the top of the head between the eye orbits.

interradial membrane—the membrane between the fin rays.

isthmus—the contracted part of the breast that projects forward between, and separates, the gill chambers.

jack—an early-maturing male salmon which returns to spawn a year or more before most males of its age group.

jaw, length of upper—the distance from the tip of the upper jaw to the posterior-most point of the maxillary.

jugular—pertaining to the throat; the pelvic fins are in jugular position when inserted in front of the bases of the pectoral fins.

K—see *condition, coefficient of.*

keel—a midventral ridgelike process, either fleshy, as in the golden shiners, or of strong spiny scales, as in the herrings.

lamina, transverse lingual—the anterior tongue plate, which can be straight (linear) from side to side, to strongly bilobed, or divided at the middle, as in the lampreys.

lateral length of mouth—the lateral (not diagonal) distance from the corner of the mouth to the tip of the lower jaw.

lateral line—the series of porelike openings along the sides of a fish.

lateral line canal system—in most fishes, an elaborate pressure- and sound-sensitive tubular system, identified by the presence of pored openings on the head and a lateral line.

lateral line scale count—the number of pored midlateral scales from the edge of the gill cover membrane to the hypural notch, including the scale (if half or more of scale) within the notch.

lateral scale count—the lateral scale count in the first row above the lateral line.

lateral series scale count—the number of unpored scales in the position which would otherwise be occupied by a lateral line, as well as any pored scales that may be present. Count begins from the edge of the gill cover membrane and terminates with the scale (if half or more of scale) within the hypural notch.

length (of fish)—same as *total length.* Where distances other than total length are used to measure a fish's length, they are so designated; see *fork length* and *standard length.*

length-frequency distribution—a method for indicating age based on the expectation that frequency analysis of the individuals of a species of any one age group collected on the same date will show variation around the mean length according to normal distribution (normal bell curve when graphed); it is based further on the expectation that when data for a sample of the entire population are plotted, there will be clumping of fish of successive ages around successive given lengths, making possible a separation by age groups.

lethal temperature, lower—the lowest temperature at which, after a 12-hour period of exposure and removal to a higher temperature, only 50% of the fish recover (Brett 1944).

lethal temperature, upper—the highest temperature at which 50% of the fish die if exposed for 12 hours (Brett 1944).

mandible—the lower jaw.

mandibular pores—small sensory openings on the undersurface of the lower jaw.

maxillary—the lateral bones of the upper jaw.

melanophore—a black pigment cell.

mouth, lateral length of—see *lateral length of mouth.*

muzzle—the projecting jaws and snout.

myomeres, trunk—the complete body segments from immediately behind the last respiratory pore up to, and including, the segment in front of the vent, as in the lampreys.

nape—the dorsal part of the body from the back of the head to the origin of the dorsal fin.

nonprotractile—not capable of being thrust out; pertaining to the upper jaw when the upper lip groove is not continuous over the snout.

notochord—the stiffening rod in the embryo which runs the length of the body from the head to the tail; the precursor to the backbone, persisting in primitive fishes such as the lampreys and sturgeons.

nuptial tubercles—see *breeding tubercles.*

oblique—having a slanting direction or position; inclined.

obtuse—broadly pointed; an angle greater than 90°.

opercle (*operculum*)—the large posterior bone of the gill cover.

opercular membrane—the thin membrane along the posterior edge of the gill cover.

oral valve—thin, transverse membranes, one near the front of each jaw, which function together in respiration.

origin (of fin)—the anterior end of a fin's base.

otolith—an ear stone or calcareous concretion appearing in the inner ear of a bony fish. Otoliths grow in size through the annual addition of a new concretion, which is interpreted as a growth (year) mark.

palatine teeth—the teeth borne by the palatine bones on the roof of the mouth.

palatines—the paired bones in the roof of the mouth, originating behind the anterior expanded tip of the vomer, and lying on either side of the roof between the shaft of the vomer and the upper jaw.

papilla (pl. *papillae*)—any small, blunt, soft, and rounded protuberance; a nipplelike structure.

papillary fringe—the membranous fringe surrounding the buccal funnel of the adult lamprey.

papillose—covered with papillae.

parr marks—the dark vertical marks or oval blotches on the sides of young salmonids.

pearl organs—see *breeding tubercles.*

pectoral fin length—the distance from the pectoral fin's insertion to its tip when the fin is depressed against the body.

pectoral fins—the paired fins directly behind the head, attached to the pectoral girdle at the side of the body or on the breast.

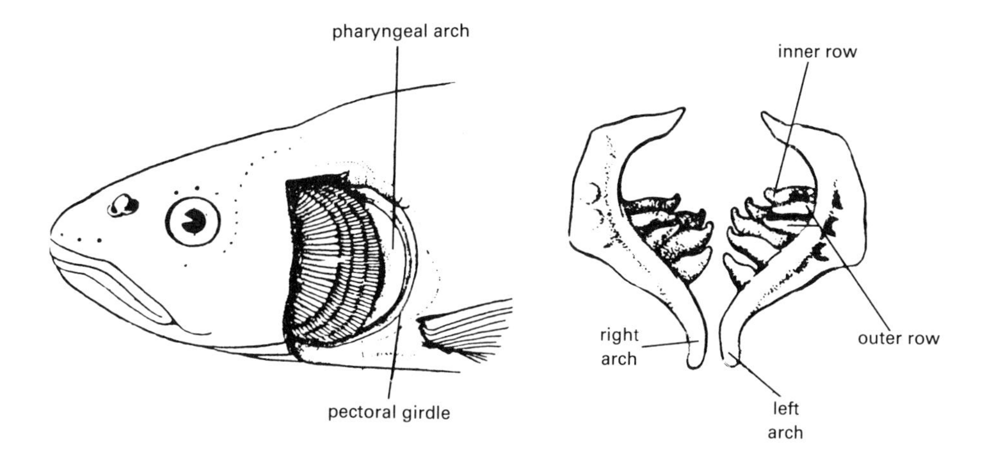

Anterior topography and pharyngeal teeth of a northern creek chub (Forbes and Richardson 1920:122)

pectoral girdle—the large bony or cartilaginous arches supporting the pectoral fins.

pelvic fin length—the distance from the pelvic fin's insertion to its tip when the fin is depressed against the body.

pelvic fins—the paired ventral fins, generally positioned between the pectoral fins and the anal fin.

pelvic girdle (*pelvic girdle complex*)—the bony plate supporting the pelvic (or ventral) fins.

peritoneum—the membranous lining of the body cavity.

pharyngeal arches—see *pharyngeal teeth.*

pharyngeal teeth—the bony toothlike projections from the modified fifth gill arches. (These arches are situated behind the gill-bearing arches and just medial to the large bones of the pectoral girdle.) Pharyngeal arches and teeth are useful in the identification of some minnows and suckers. In minnows, the teeth in each row are counted in order from the fish's left to its right: left arch outer row, inner row–right arch inner row, outer row. For the creek chub, illustrated above, the formula is 2,5–4,2. The common carp has teeth in 3 rows on each side (i.e., left arch outer row, middle row, inner row–right arch inner row, middle row, and outer row); the formula for the carp is 1,1,3–3,1,1.

pharynx—that part of the alimentary canal between the mouth cavity and the esophagus. The walls of the pharynx contain gills attached to gill (visceral) arches that are separated from one another by gill clefts.

physoclistous—having the swim bladder isolated from the esophagus.

physostomous—having the swim bladder connected to the esophagus by an open duct.

plicate—pertaining to pleatlike folds, or soft ridges alternating with grooves.

pored scale—a scale with an opening into the lateral line canal or a head canal (sensory canals).

postorbital length of head—the greatest distance between the posterior margin of the eye socket and the membranous margin of the opercle.

predorsal length—the distance from the tip of the snout or upper lip (whichever is more anterior) to the anterior base (origin) of the dorsal fin.

predorsal region—the portion of the fish anterior to the origin of the dorsal fin.

premaxillary—either of the paired bones at the front of the upper jaw.

preopercle—the sickle-shaped bone that lies behind and below the eye.
prickles—scales degenerated to points, as in the sculpins.
protractile—capable of being thrust out; pertaining to the upper jaw when the upper lip groove is continuous over the snout.
pyloric caeca—the fingerlike, blind sacs (pouches) attached in the area between the stomach and the intestine.
ramus—a projecting part or elongated process.
rays in paired fins, number of—all rays in the pectoral and pelvic fins are counted, including the smallest.
rays, soft—see *soft rays*.
rhombic scale—a type of heavy, bony, parallelogram-shaped, nonoverlapping scale, as in the gar.
rudimentaries (*rudiments*)—short, incomplete rays in fins, as in the bullhead catfishes.
sacculus—a cavity or sac of the inner ear.
scales around the body—see *circumferential scales*.
sensory pores—the openings of the lateral line canal system on the body and the head.
serrate—notched or toothed on the edge; sawlike.
sexual dimorphism—difference of form, color, or structure between sexes of the same species.
sieve apparatus—complexly branched papillae within the mouth of an ammocoete.
smolt—a young salmon which has undergone physiological changes (including enlargement of the thyroid gland, loss of parr marks, appearance of silvery scales, and development of the excretory salt cells) prior to downstream movement from the parental stream into the lake or sea.
snout—the part of the head anterior to the eye.
snout length—the distance from the anteriormost point on the snout or upper lip to the front margin of the eye socket.
soft ray—a segmented (cross-striated), flexible, and often branched support of the fin.
somite—a body segment.
spine—an unsegmented (not cross-striated), never branched, and usually stiff support of the fin. A pointed process on a bone, as the spines on the preopercle of a sculpin.
spinous (*spiny*) *dorsal fin*—the anterior of 2 dorsal fins in a number of fish families, such as the temperate basses, sunfishes, and perches.
spinous (spiny) ray—a spine of hardened soft rays, fused together, as in the dorsal and pectoral fins of the common carp and bullhead catfishes.
spiracle—the respiratory opening behind the eye which connects with the gill chamber, as in the lake sturgeon.
splint—the partial ray or half-ray at the front of the dorsal fin, as in the minnows.
standard length (SL)—the distance from the anteriormost projection of the head to the hypural notch.
subopercle—the bone lying immediately below the opercle and at the angle of the gill cover.
suborbital—below the eye.
subterminal—pertaining to a mouth which opens slightly ventrally (rather than opening at the anterior tip of the head), with the lower jaw sometimes closing within the upper jaw.

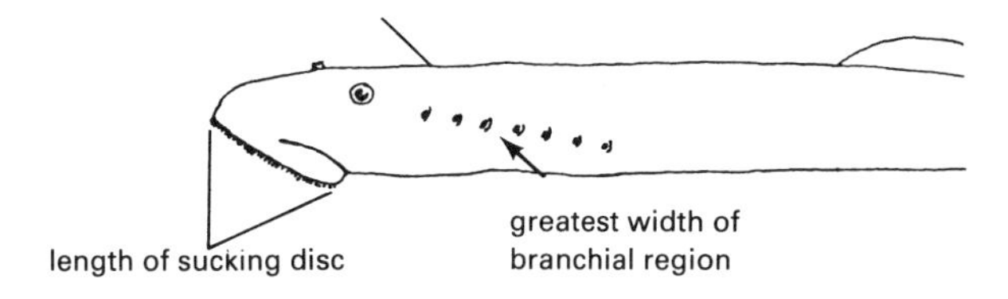

sucking disc—the buccal funnel; the expanded region (often armed with rasping teeth) about the mouth opening of an adult lamprey.

supraethmoid-ethmoid complex—the anteriormost structure in the upper skull which partially protects the brain. In the adult, the complex represents a fusion of 2 distinct bones and is used for differentiating the larger members of the bullhead catfish family.

supraoral cusps—the teeth of the tooth-bearing plate immediately above the mouth opening in the lamprey.

supraoral lamina—the tooth-bearing plate immediately above the mouth opening in the lamprey.

swim bladder—the membranous, gas-filled sac in the upper part of the body cavity which aids in creating buoyancy and in the respiration of some fishes.

symphyseal knob—the small knob or protuberance at the upper tip of the lower jaw.

symphysis—articulation of the 2 pharyngeal arches or the halves of the lower jaw in the median plane of the body (see illustration, page 608).

teeth—the hard, chewing, tearing, or holding structures usually on the bones of the mouth or throat; serrations.

teeth in lateral rows—those teeth originating with the circumoral tooth on each side of the supraoral lamina and radiating outward to the edge of the disc, but not including the deflected marginal teeth, as in the lampreys.

terminal—pertaining to a mouth in which the tips of the upper and lower jaws form the anteriormost part of the head.

thermal stratification—establishment of epilimnion, thermocline, and hypolimnion in a lake or pond.

thermocline—a layer of water marking a significant temperature change between the water above and the water below.

thoracic—pertaining to the thorax; pelvic fins are thoracic when they are inserted below or slightly behind the pectoral fins.

total length (TL)—the distance from the anteriormost projection of the head to the farthest tip of the caudal fin when the lobes of the fin are squeezed together.

transverse lingual lamina—see *lamina, transverse lingual.*

truncate—having the end even or square, as if cut off, as in the caudal fin.

tubercle—a soft or hardened lump or projection on the surface; see *breeding tubercles.*

unicuspid—pertaining to a tooth having, or ending, in one point.

vent—the external opening of the rectum or cloaca.

ventral—pertaining to the belly or to the lower surface.

vermiculate—wormlike; marked with irregular or wavy lines.

vertebral column—the spinal column running from the skull along the length of the fish, generally terminating at the base of the caudal fin, but occasionally extending into the dorsal lobe of the caudal fin, as in the sturgeons.

vomer—the bone lying in the roof of the mouth in the medial position, extending posteriorly from behind the jaw.

vomerine teeth—the teeth borne on the vomer bone in the roof of the mouth.

weight (WT)—the total weight.

Abbreviations, Signs, and Tables of Equivalents

avg	average(s)
C	centigrade
cfs	cubic feet per second
cm	centimeter(s)
cms	cubic meters per second
diam	diameter(s)
dm	decimeter(s)
F	Fahrenheit
FL	fork length(s) (see Glossary)
ft	foot (feet)
g	gram(s)
ha	hectare(s)
hr	hour(s)
in	inch(es)
K	condition, coefficient of (see Glossary)
kg	kilogram(s)
km	kilometer(s)
lb	pound(s)
m	meter(s)
mi	mile(s)
min	minute(s)
ml	milliliter(s)
mm	millimeter(s)
oz	ounce(s)
p. (pp.)	page(s)
(+)	(plus sign in parentheses) 1 or more
ppb	parts per billion
ppm	parts per million
ppt	parts per thousand
R	Range
sec	second(s)
Sec (Secs)	Section(s)
SL	standard length(s) (see Glossary)
sp. (spp.)	species singular (plural)
T	Township
TL	total length(s) (see Glossary)
wk	week(s)
wt, WT	weight(s)

Temperature—Fahrenheit to Centigrade

	0	1	2	3	4	5	6	7	8	9
30	−1.1	−0.6	0	0.6	1.1	1.7	2.2	2.8	3.3	3.9
40	4.4	5.0	5.6	6.1	6.7	7.2	7.8	8.3	8.9	9.4
50	10.0	10.6	11.1	11.7	12.2	12.8	13.3	13.9	14.4	15.0
60	15.6	16.1	16.7	17.2	17.8	18.3	18.9	19.4	20.0	20.6
70	21.1	21.7	22.2	22.8	23.3	23.9	24.4	25.0	25.6	26.1
80	26.7	27.2	27.8	28.3	28.9	29.4	30.0	30.6	31.1	31.7
90	32.2	32.8	33.3	33.9	34.4	35.0	35.6	36.1	36.7	37.2
100	37.8	38.3	38.9	39.4	40.0					

Weight—Pounds and Ounces to Nearest Gram

lb	0	1	2	3	4	5	6
oz	0	454	907	1361	1814	2268	2722
1	28	482	936	1389	1843	2296	2750
2	57	510	964	1418	1871	2325	2778
3	85	539	992	1446	1899	2353	2807
4	113	567	1021	1474	1928	2381	2835
5	142	595	1049	1503	1956	2410	2863
6	170	624	1077	1531	1985	2438	2892
7	198	652	1106	1559	2013	2466	2920
8	227	680	1134	1588	2041	2495	2948
9	255	709	1162	1616	2070	2523	2977
10	284	737	1191	1644	2098	2552	3005
11	312	765	1219	1673	2126	2580	3033
12	340	794	1247	1701	2155	2608	3062
13	369	822	1276	1729	2183	2637	3090
14	397	851	1304	1758	2211	2665	3119
15	425	879	1332	1786	2240	2693	3147

Note: 1 ounce = 28.35 grams

Lengths—Inches to Nearest Millimeter

in	mm	in	mm	in	mm	in	mm
0.5	13	8.0	203	15.5	394	23.0	584
1.0	25	8.5	216	16.0	406	23.5	597
1.5	38	9.0	229	16.5	419	24.0	610
2.0	51	9.5	241	17.0	432	24.5	622
2.5	64	10.0	254	17.5	445	25.0	635
3.0	76	10.5	267	18.0	457	25.5	648
3.5	89	11.0	279	18.5	470	26.0	660
4.0	102	11.5	292	19.0	483	26.5	673
4.5	114	12.0	305	19.5	495	27.0	686
5.0	127	12.5	318	20.0	508	27.5	698
5.5	140	13.0	330	20.5	521	28.0	711
6.0	152	13.5	343	21.0	533	28.5	724
6.5	165	14.0	356	21.5	546	29.0	737
7.0	178	14.5	368	22.0	559	29.5	749
7.5	190	15.0	381	22.5	572	30.0	762

Note: 1 inch = 25.4 millimeters

Keys to the Fishes of Wisconsin

Structure and Use of the Keys

Taxonomic keys are artificial devices. Species did not evolve from keys; rather, keys are man-made constructions designed to help in the identification of different species or forms.

The keys in this book are dichotomous; that is, the characteristics are grouped in pairs or couplets of contrasting statements. The user of the key chooses the statement which applies to the fish being identified, and then proceeds to the next couplet indicated. As inapplicable statements are progressively eliminated, it will eventually be possible to give the correct species label to the specimen.

The first of the keys that follow is the Key to the Families. Ten species in Wisconsin are the sole representatives of their families in the state. For these fishes, the family name is given, and a reference to the page in the book where the main species account is found. The families for which this occurs are the following: Paddlefishes, Bowfins, Freshwater Eels, Smelts, Mudminnows, Pirate Perches, Trout-perches, Codfishes, Silversides, and Drums. As an example, if the specimen keys out at 12a (PIRATE PERCHES, Aphredoderidae), the user of the key is referred directly to the pirate perch account on page 733 in the main text.

All other families of Wisconsin fishes are represented in the state by more than one species. For fishes in these 16 families, the family name is given, and a reference to a separate key to that family. These keys follow the Key to the Families. For instance, if the fish that is being keyed out is a minnow, the user of the key will be directed at 21a in the Key to the Families to a separate key—Key to the Minnows and Carps (page 107). In this key the 45 known species of Wisconsin minnows and carps are separated out and identified to species, and after careful searching it should be possible to arrive at the common and scientific names for the minnow specimen and the page number for that species account in the main text. Here additional data are given for shoring up the identification.

The keys which are given here have been profusely illustrated to provide visual clarification for the choices which must be made. These illustrations and the diagrams and definitions of technical terms in the Glossary should be consulted until the language of the keys becomes thoroughly familiar.

In addition, to aid in the identification of specimens, certain tools should be secured and be ready for use if needed. Gross structures can be seen easily, but small structures, particularly those in small minnows or young fish only a few centimeters long, may require the aid of a hand lens or a broadfield scope. Also, a dissecting needle and a sharp-tipped forceps may be helpful in making it possible to view hard-to-see fin rays, barbels, and other near-microscopic structures properly. For stepping off body distances, a divider is useful, and for the examination of internal characteristics, a small pair of scissors will be handy.

For many species of fish the keying process will not be simple. Indeed, the identification of some specimens may prove to be a lengthy, tedious, and frustrating pursuit. For some suckers and minnows, correct identification is akin to solving a difficult puzzle. Solution of the puzzle may lead to a sense of joy and a feeling of accomplishment. If the specimen does not key out properly, however, help can be obtained from the nearest university or from a nearby agency of the Wisconsin Department of Natural Resources. And, there is always the possibility of finding a "first" for the state.

Key to the Families

1a. Mouth a sucking disc or hoodlike and without jaws. Pectoral fins absent. One median nostril. Gill openings 7 on each side.
LAMPREYS
Petromyzontidae .... Page 77

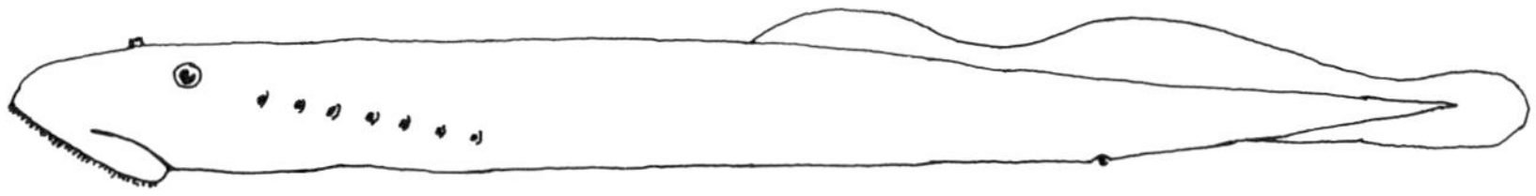

1b. Mouth with upper and lower jaws. Pectoral fins present. Two nostrils, 1 on each side. One gill chamber opening on each side of head 2

2a. Caudal fin forked with vertebral column turned upward and extending nearly to tip of upper lobe of fin 3

vertebral column turned upward,
extending nearly to tip
of upper lobe of fin

2b. Caudal fin unforked, or if forked, vertebral column not extending to upper lobe of fin 4

3a. Snout long and paddlelike. Scales absent, except for few on tail. Gill cover long and pointed posteriorly.
PADDLEFISHES
Polyodontidae .... Page 231

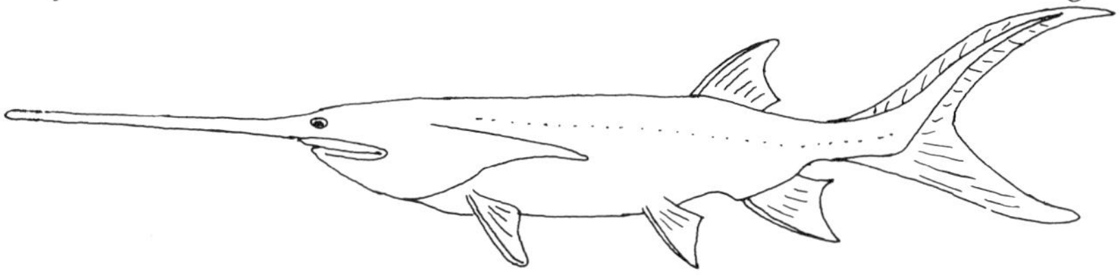

3b. Snout relatively short and rounded or shovel-shaped. Body with several rows of bony plates. Gill cover short and rounded.
STURGEONS
Acipenseridae .... Page 83

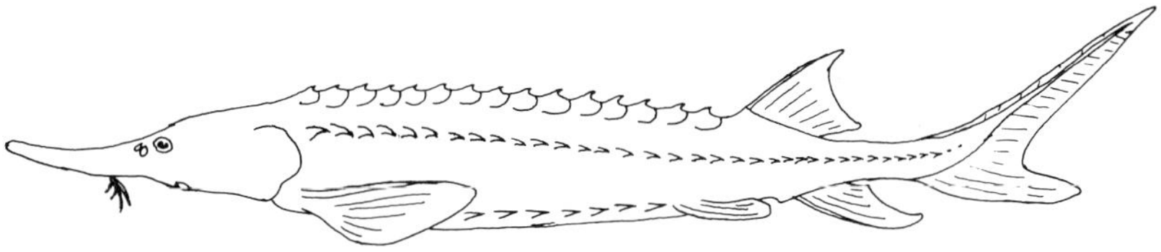

4a. Dorsal fin single, extending well over ½ of total length. Anterior nostrils at tips of tubelike extensions. 5

4b. Dorsal fin single or double but, if single, extending less than ½ of total length. Anterior nostrils not at tips of tubelike extensions 6

5a. Pelvic fins present. Gular plate present. Dorsal, caudal, and anal fins not continuous.
BOWFINS
Amiidae.. Page 249

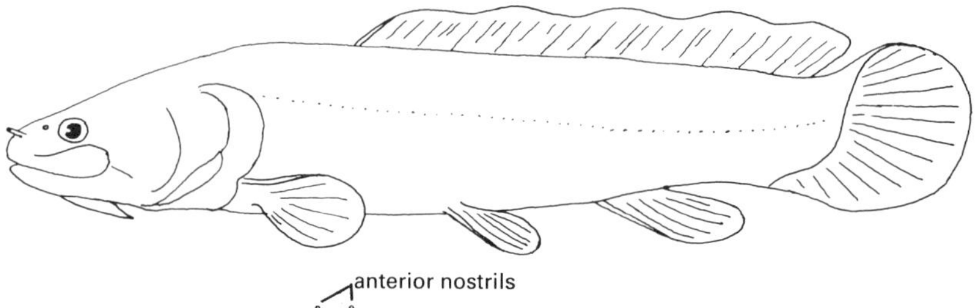

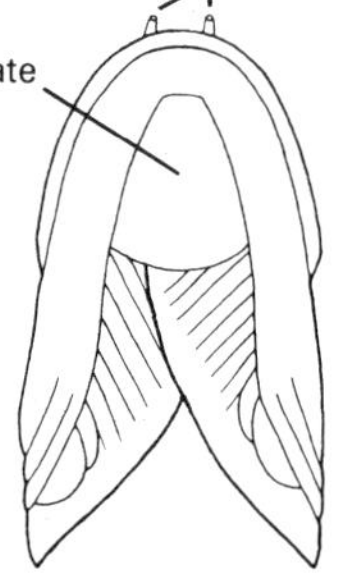

anterior nostrils

gular plate

5b. Pelvic fins absent. Gular plate absent. Dorsal, caudal, and anal fins continuous.
FRESHWATER EELS
Anguillidae.. Page 255

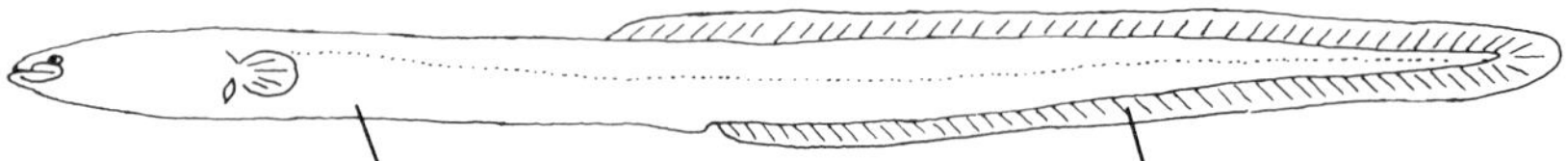

pelvic fins absent

dorsal, caudal, and anal fins continuous

6a. Jaws prolonged into narrow, strongly toothed beak. Scales rhombic.
GARS
Lepisosteidae... Page 85

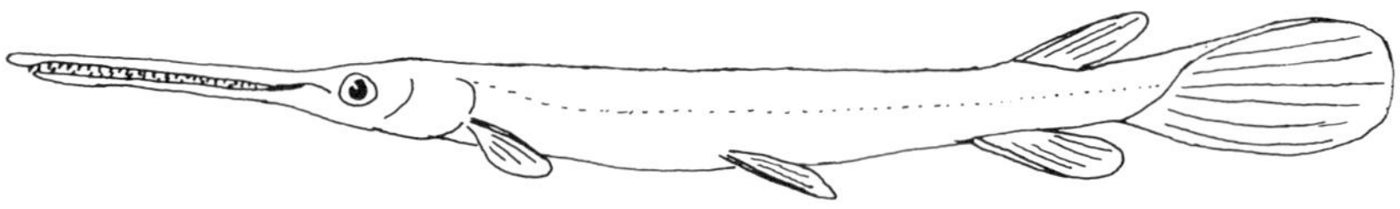

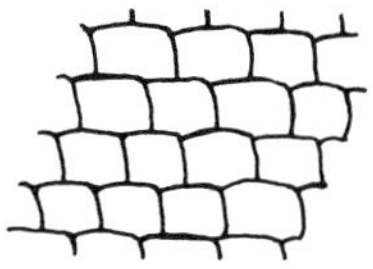

rhombic scales

6b. Jaws not prolonged into narrow, strongly toothed beak. Scales, if present, not rhombic.. 7

7a. Adipose fin present, sometimes as a low fleshy ridge joined to caudal fin 8

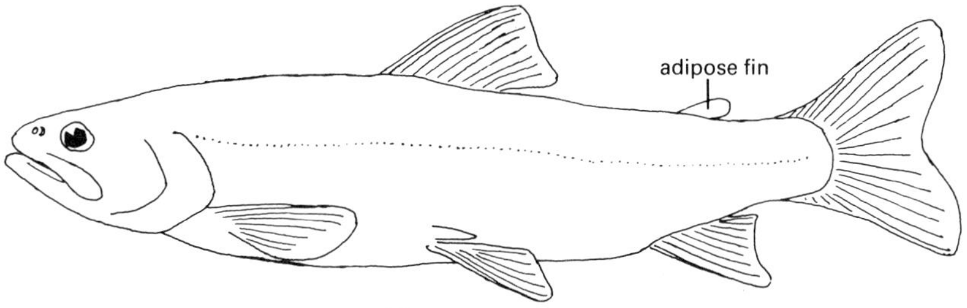

adipose fin

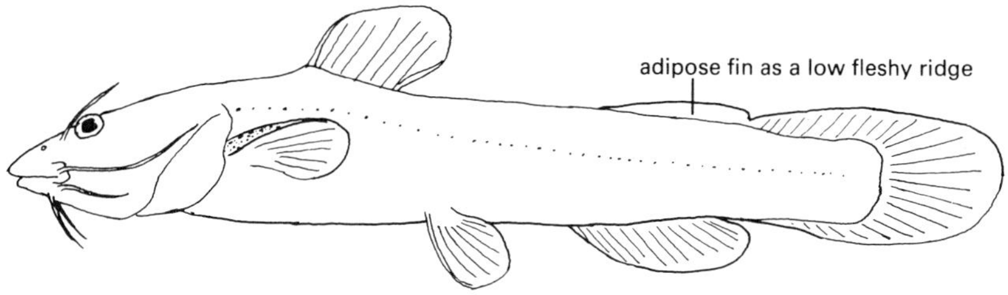

adipose fin as a low fleshy ridge

7b. Adipose fin absent. 11

8a. Barbels present, usually 8. Body naked. Each pectoral fin with a strong spinous ray.
BULLHEAD CATFISHES
Ictaluridae .... Page 143

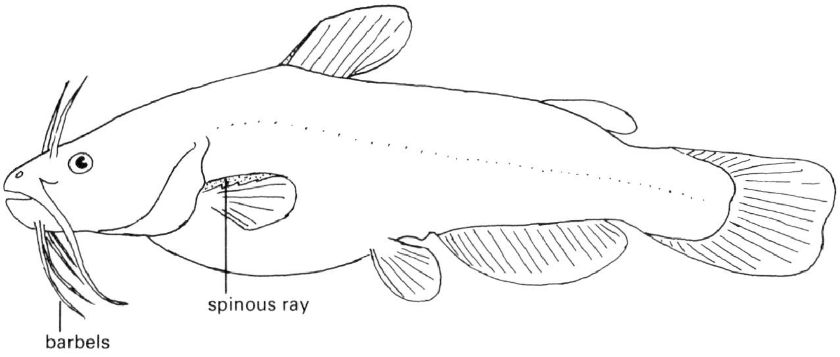

spinous ray

barbels

8b. Barbels absent. Body scaled. Pectoral fins entirely soft-rayed......... 9

9a. Scales with single row of teeth along posterior edge (ctenoid). Anterior base (origin) of pelvic fin below middle of pectoral fin.
TROUT-PERCHES
Percopsidae .... Page 739

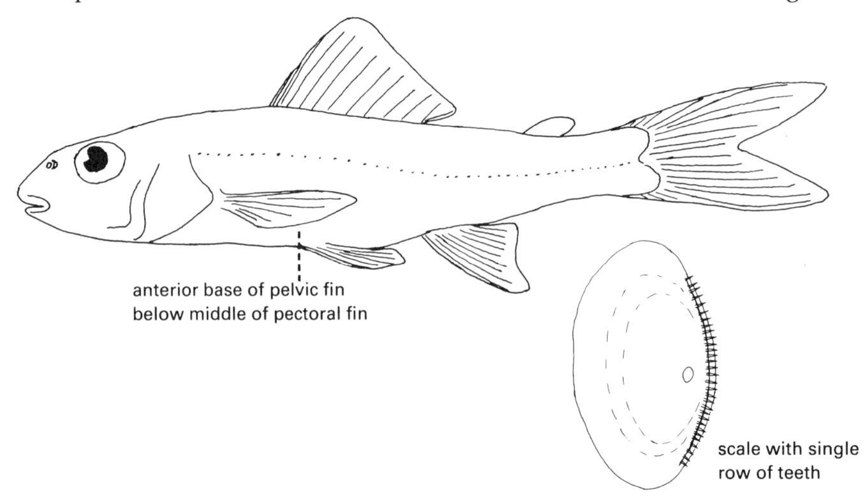

9b. Scales without teeth along posterior edge (cycloid). Anterior base (origin) of pelvic fin behind end of pectoral fin.............................. 10

10a. Pelvic axillary process present.
TROUTS
Salmonidae... Page 89

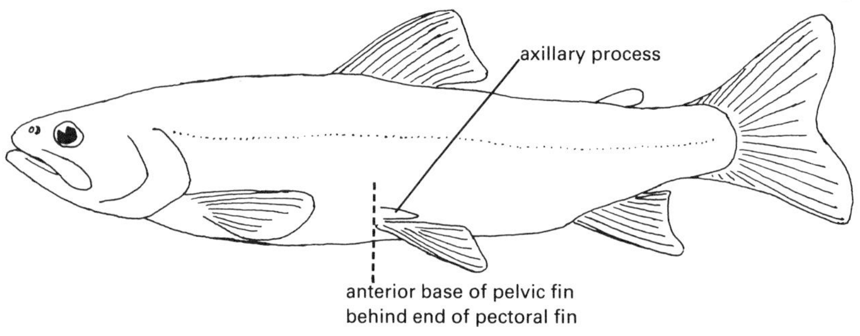

10b. Pelvic axillary process absent.
SMELTS
Osmeridae... Page 377

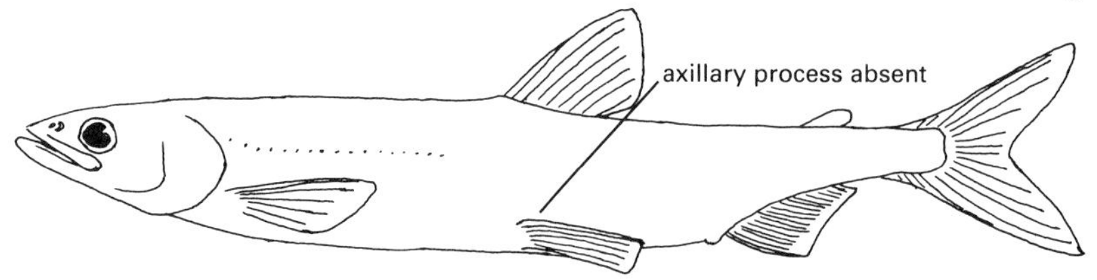

11a. One medial barbel under tip of chin.
CODFISHES
Gadidae .... Page 745

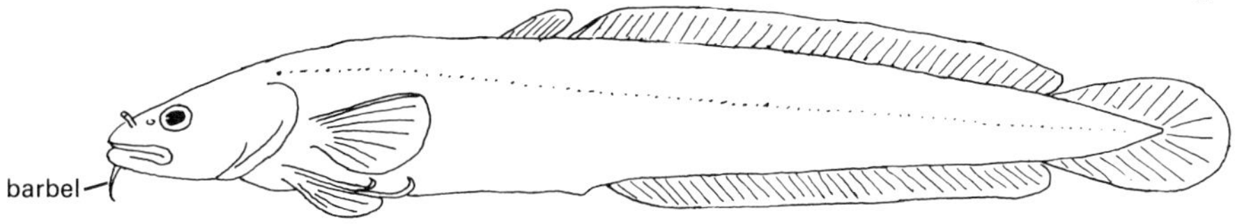

11b. Medial barbel on chin absent 12

12a. Anus far in front of anal fin, ahead of pelvic fins, except in young, where positioned at lesser distances in front of anal fin.
PIRATE PERCHES
Aphredoderidae .... Page 733

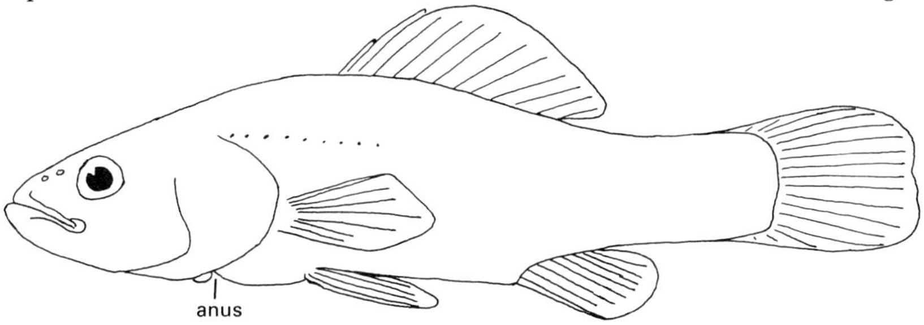

12b. Anus just in front of anal fin 13

13a. Four to 11 dorsal spines not connected to one another by membrane.
STICKLEBACKS
Gasterosteidae .... Page 149

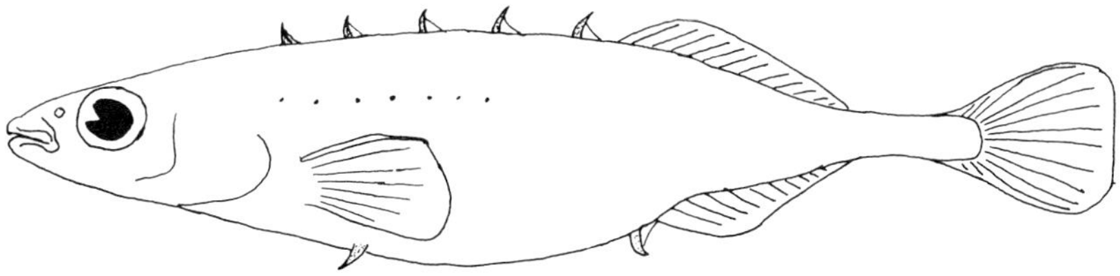

13b. Dorsal spines, when present, connected to one another by membrane. 14

14a. Dorsal fin single, without spines or with 1 stout sawtoothed spine ... 15

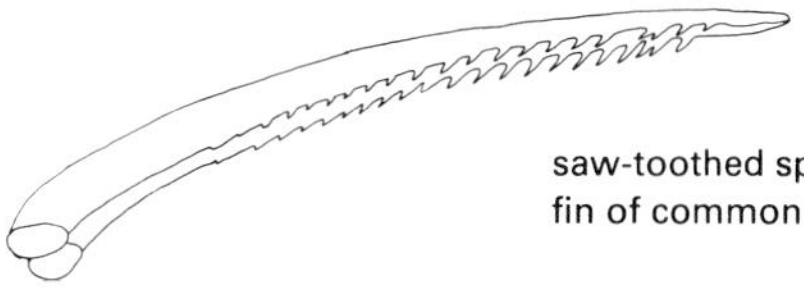

saw-toothed spine of dorsal fin of common carp

14b. Dorsal fin divided into 2 distinct parts, or single and with 4 or more spines 22

15a. Caudal fin rounded 16

15b. Caudal fin forked 17

16a. Most of length of pelvic fin behind anterior base (origin) of dorsal fin. Groove of upper lip not continuous over snout.
MUDMINNOWS
Umbridae .... Page 385

groove of upper lip not continuous over snout

most of pelvic fin behind anterior base of dorsal fin

16b. Most or all of length of pelvic fin lying in advance of anterior base (origin) of dorsal fin. Groove of upper lip continuous over snout.
KILLIFISHES
Cyprinodontidae .... Page 148

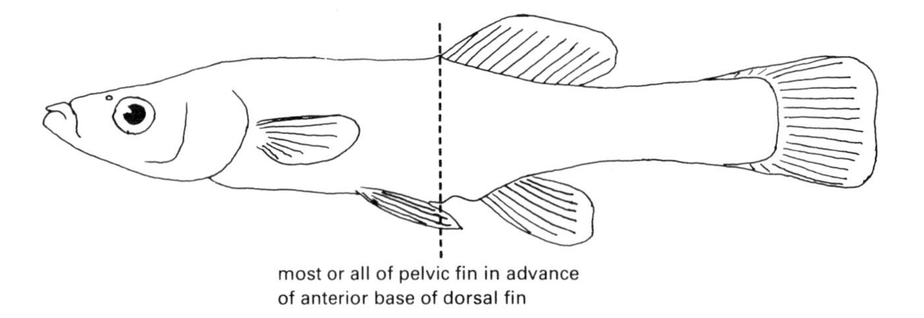

17a. Gill slits extended far forward below. Gill membranes free from throat with lower (anterior) margins overlapping on midline of throat 18

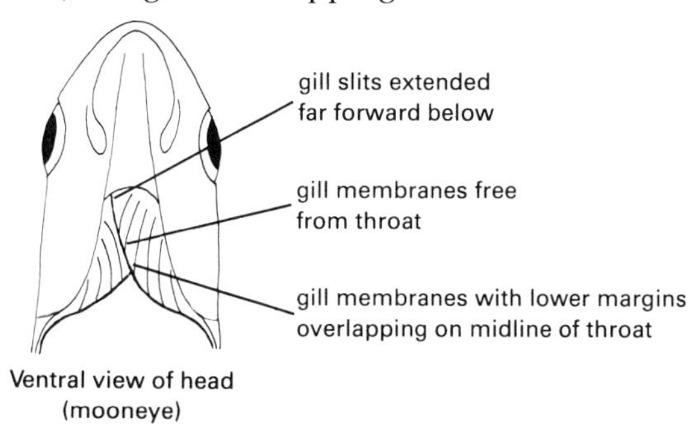

Ventral view of head
(mooneye)

17b. Gill slits not extended far forward below. Gill membranes united to throat either narrowly or broadly with lower (anterior) margins not overlapping on midline of throat 20

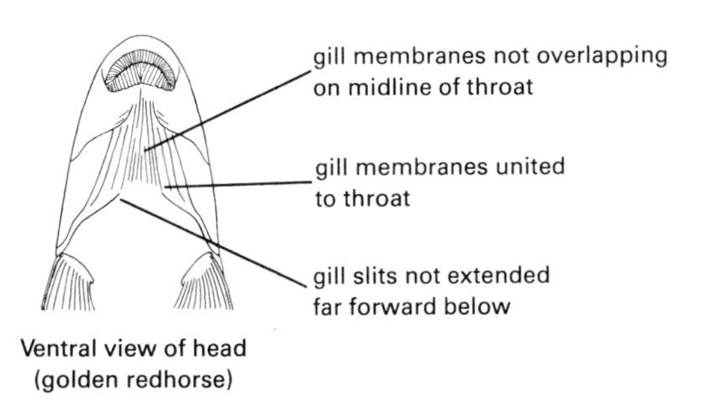

Ventral view of head
(golden redhorse)

18a. Snout strongly flattened dorsoventrally (shaped like a duck's bill). Scales present on side of head. Pelvic axillary process absent.
PIKES
Esocidae .... Page 105

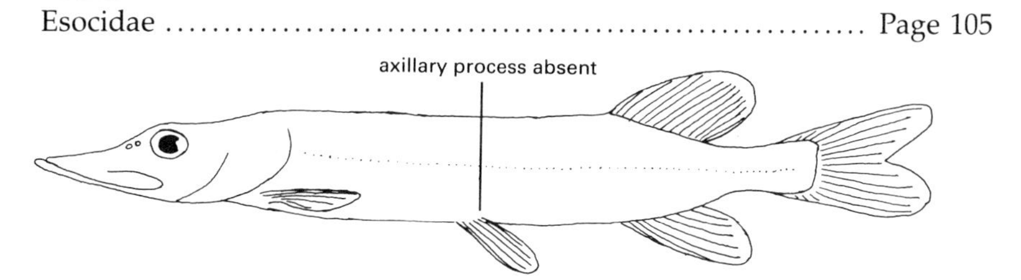

18b. Snout oval to rounded in cross section (not shaped like a duck's bill). Scales absent on side of head. Pelvic axillary process present.......... 19

19a. Midline of belly with strong spiny scales forming a sawlike keel. Lateral line absent. Gular membrane absent.
HERRINGS
Clupeidae.. Page 86

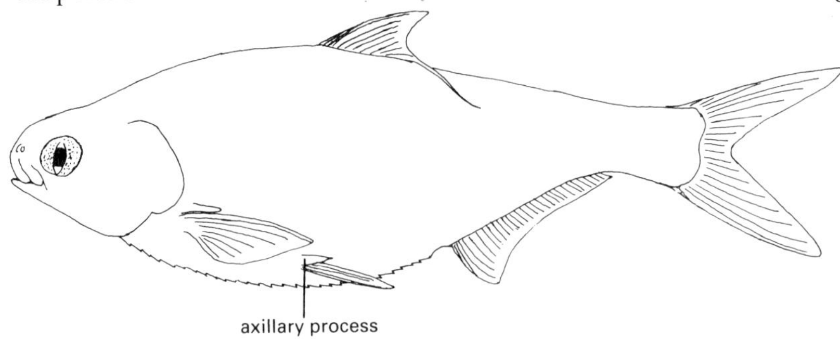

19b. Midline of belly without strong spiny scales. Lateral line present—at least in part. Gular membrane present.
MOONEYES
Hiodontidae.. Page 88

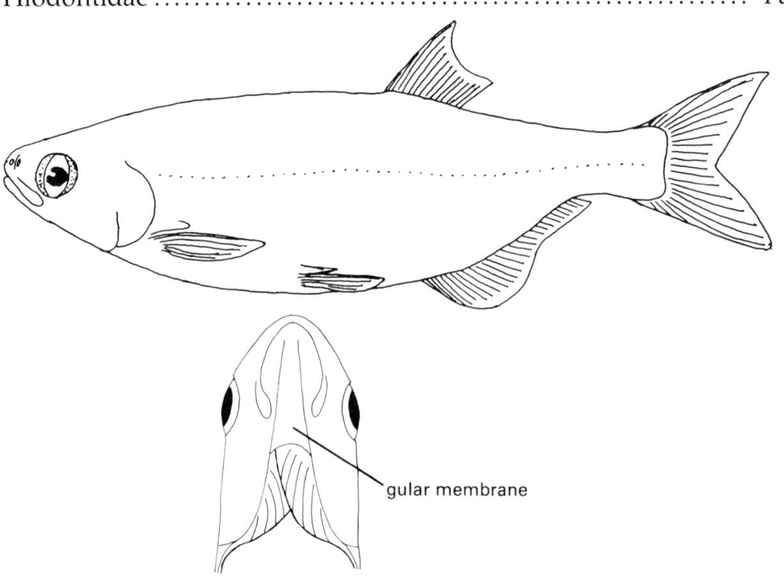

20a. Dorsal fin with 1 stout spine doubly saw-toothed posteriorly (see illustration under 14a).
COMMON CARP and GOLDFISH
Cyprinidae, in part .... Page 107

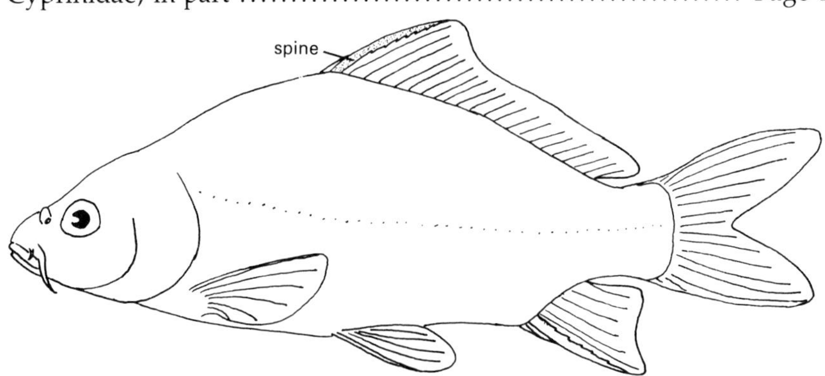

20b. One dorsal fin without spines 21

21a. Dorsal fin with 8 or 9 principal rays. Mouth not fitted for sucking. Anal fin placed forward; distance from front of anal fin to base of caudal fin (hypural notch) (B) contained less than 2.5 in distance from front of anal fin to tip of snout (A).
MINNOWS
Cyprinidae, in part .... Page 107

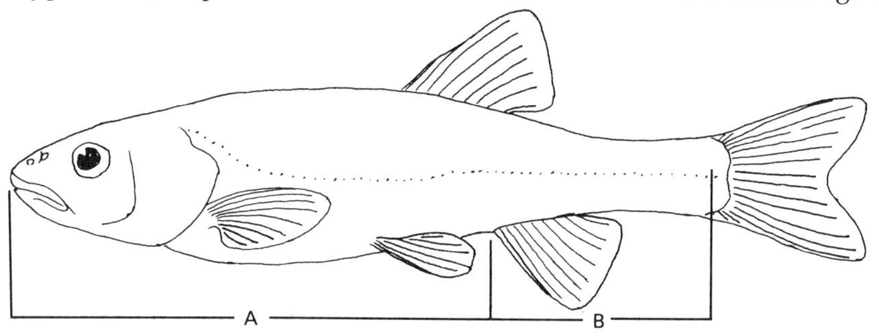

A/B equals less than 2.5

21b. Dorsal fin with 10 or more principal rays, or, if only 9, then lateral line absent or reduced to a few pores. Mouth generally inferior and fitted for sucking. Anal fin placed posteriorly; distance from front of anal fin to base of caudal fin (hypural notch) (B) contained more than 2.5 in distance from front of anal fin to tip of snout (A).
SUCKERS
Catostomidae.. Page 130

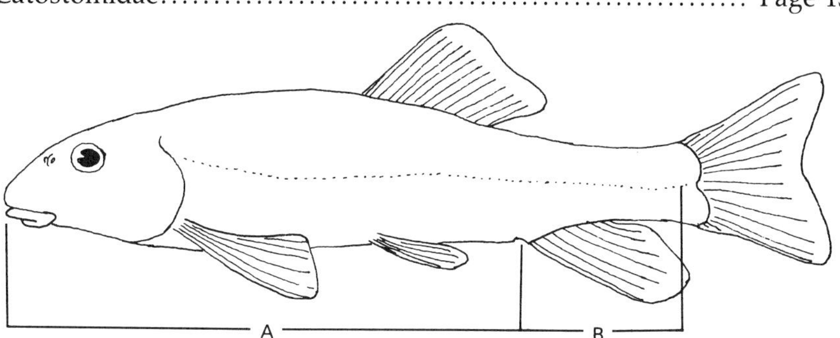

A/B equals more than 2.5

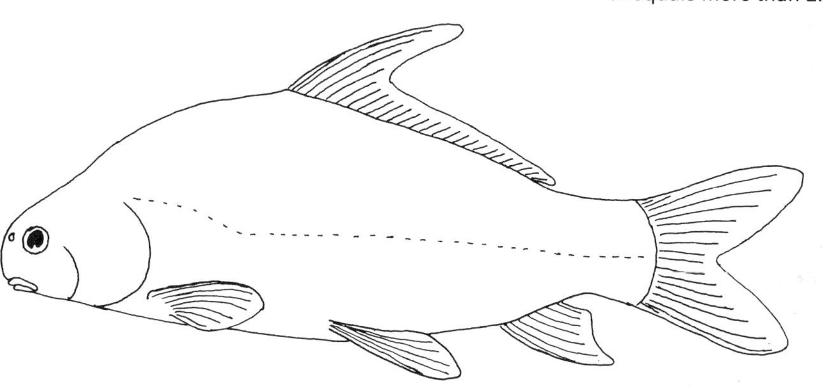

22a. Body scaleless, or with prickles only. Pelvic fin with 3 or 4 soft rays. Anal fin spines absent.
SCULPINS
Cottidae.. Page 168

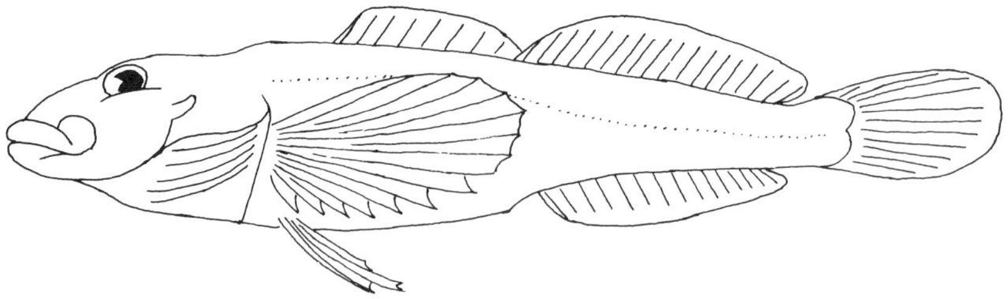

22b. Body scaled. Pelvic fin with 5 soft rays. Anal fin spines present, 1 or more.. 23

23a. Pelvic fin far back with anterior base below or behind end of pectoral fin. Mouthparts elevated and beaklike; mouth opening dorsally well above midline. Anal fin soft rays 20 or more.
SILVERSIDES
Atherinidae.. Page 767

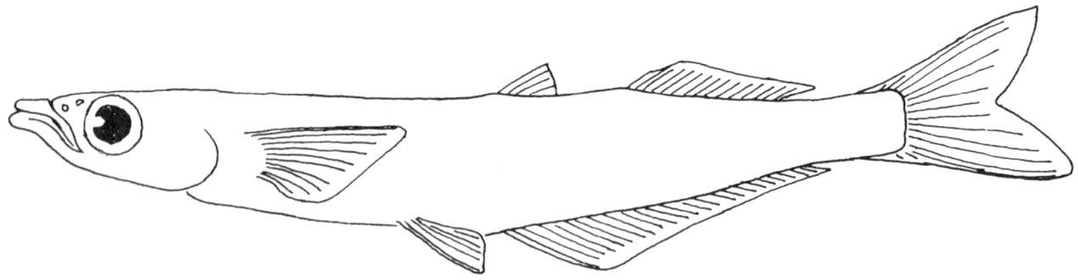

23b. Pelvic fin far forward with anterior base below middle or anterior half of pectoral fin. Mouthparts neither elevated nor beaklike; mouth opening at or below midline. Anal fin soft rays 18 or fewer........... 24

24a. Caudal fin bluntly pointed, central rays moderately elongated. Dorsal fin soft rays 24 or more. Lateral line extending to end of caudal fin.
DRUMS
Sciaenidae .... Page 955

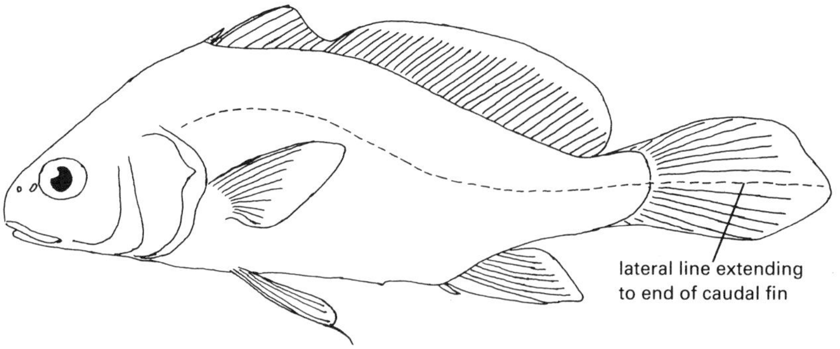

lateral line extending to end of caudal fin

24b. Caudal fin forked, square, or rounded. Dorsal fin soft rays 21 or fewer. Lateral line scarcely or not extending onto caudal fin.................. 25

25a. Anal fin spines 1 or 2.
PERCHES
Percidae.. Page 158

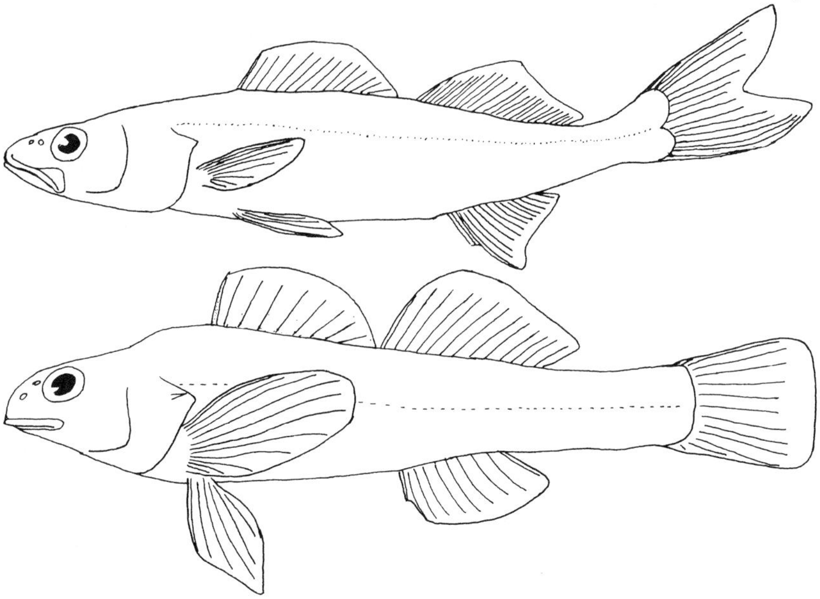

25b. Anal fin spines 3 or more.. 26

26a. Spinous dorsal fin and soft dorsal fin separate or only slightly connected. One sharp spine near back of gill cover. Margin of preopercle strongly saw-toothed.
TEMPERATE BASSES
Percichthyidae .... Page 150

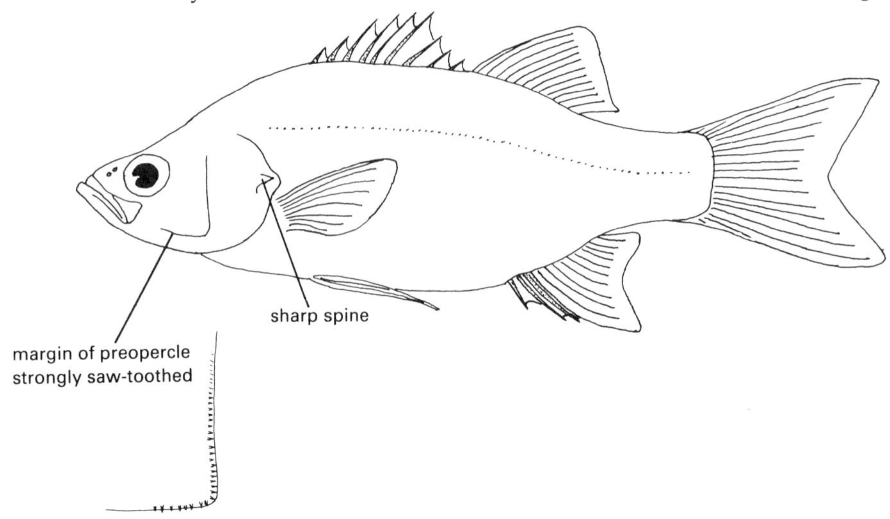

26b. Spinous dorsal fin and soft dorsal fin well connected with, at most, a deep notch between them. No sharp spine near back of gill cover. Margin of preopercle usually smooth; weakly saw-toothed in a few species.
SUNFISHES
Centrarchidae .... Page 151

Key to the Lampreys

1a. Two distinct dorsal fins either close together or well separated. Trunk myomeres 65 or more 2

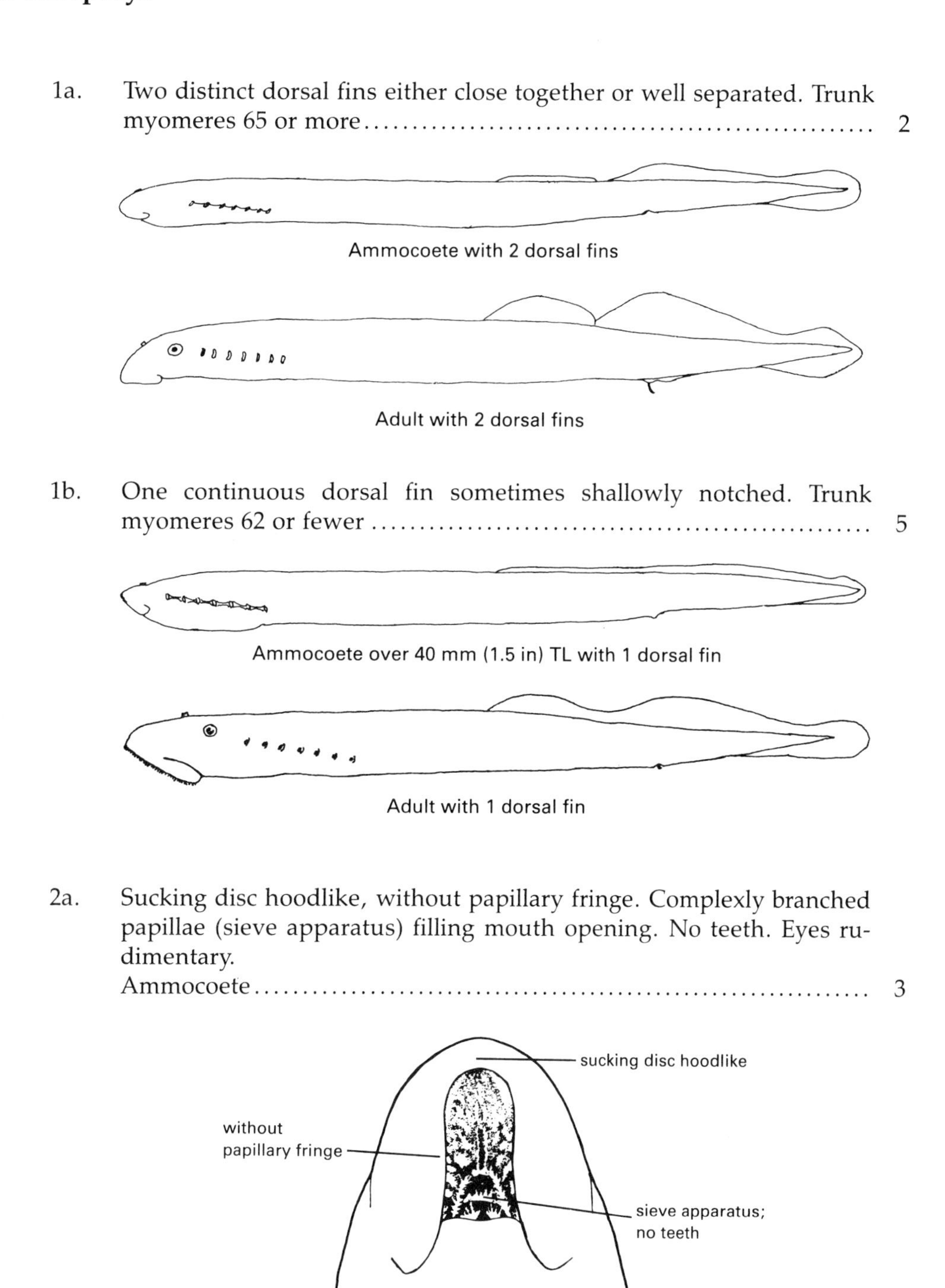

Ammocoete with 2 dorsal fins

Adult with 2 dorsal fins

1b. One continuous dorsal fin sometimes shallowly notched. Trunk myomeres 62 or fewer 5

Ammocoete over 40 mm (1.5 in) TL with 1 dorsal fin

Adult with 1 dorsal fin

2a. Sucking disc hoodlike, without papillary fringe. Complexly branched papillae (sieve apparatus) filling mouth opening. No teeth. Eyes rudimentary.
Ammocoete 3

American brook lamprey ammocoete
(P. W. Smith 1973:4)

2b. Sucking disc round or oval with papillary fringe. No sieve apparatus within mouth opening. Horny teeth present. Eyes functional. Adult 4

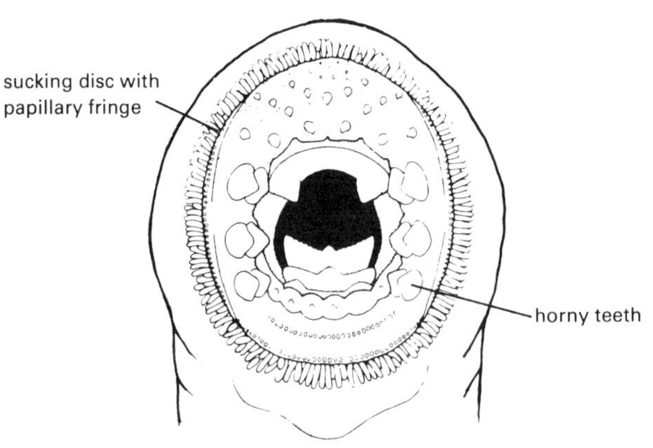

American brook lamprey adult
(P. W. Smith 1973:4)

3a. Caudal fin spade-shaped (bluntly pointed), with pigmentation concentrated on and near notochord only. Lower edge of caudal peduncle unpigmented. Lower half of upper lip unpigmented. Suborbital area completely unpigmented. Unpigmented band above branchial groove equal to about 2 widths of branchial myomere. Precursor of tongue darkly pigmented, swollen at base.
AMERICAN BROOK LAMPREY (ammocoete)
Lampetra appendix (DeKay).. Page 216

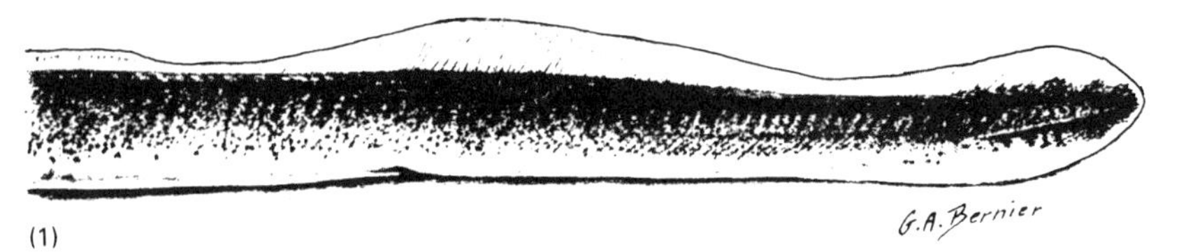

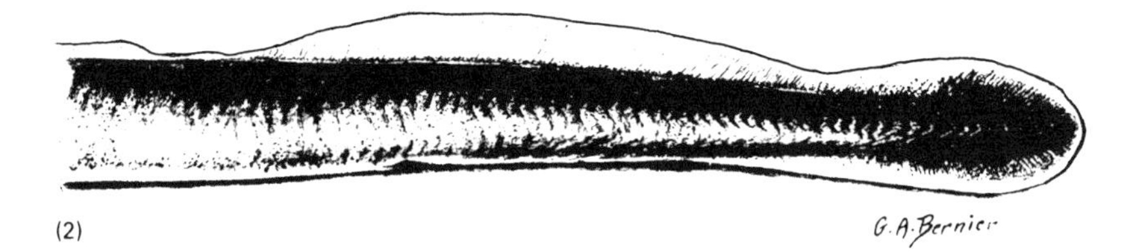

Tail region of (1) American brook lamprey ammocoete, and (2) sea lamprey ammocoete. Note in (2) beaver-tail shape of pigment on tail and well-pigmented lower edge of caudal peduncle. (Vladykov 1950:84)

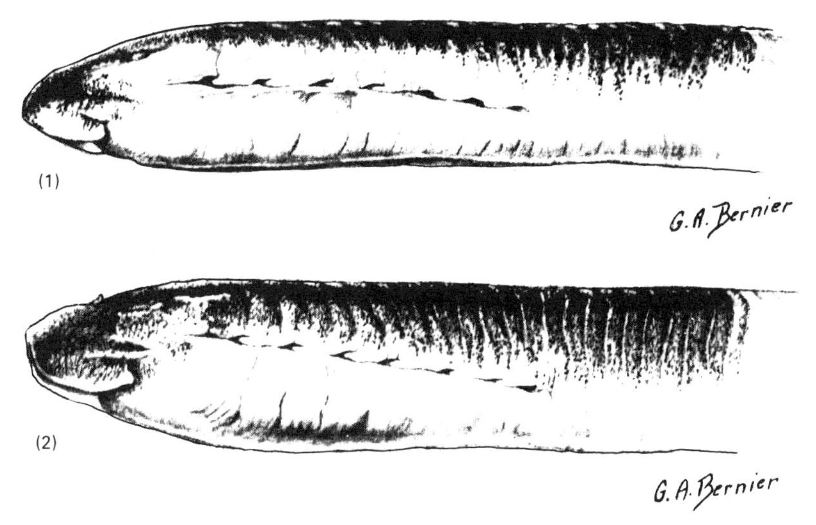

Head region of (1) American brook lamprey ammocoete, and (2) sea lamprey ammocoete. Note in (1) absence of pigment on upper lip and suborbital and branchial regions. (Vladykov 1950:82)

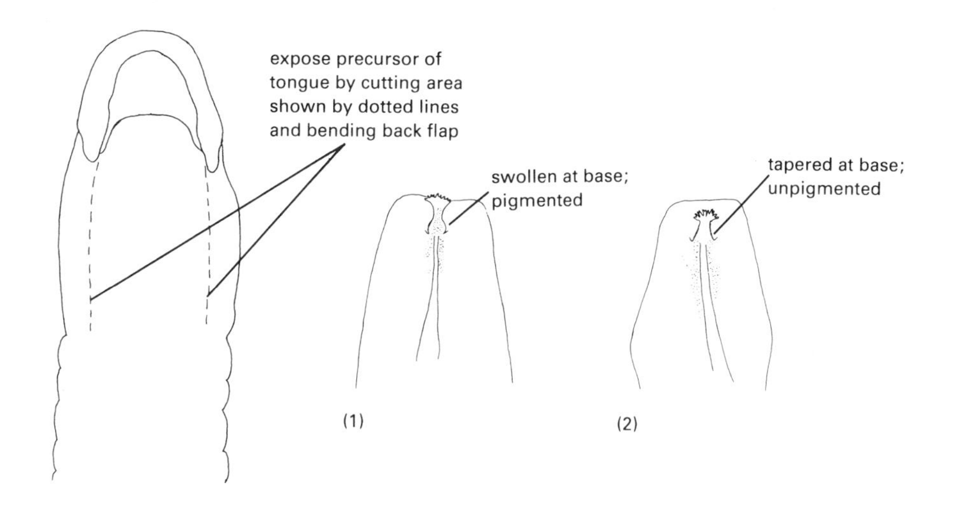

Precursor of tongue in (1) American brook lamprey ammocoete, and (2) sea lamprey ammocoete.

3b. Caudal fin typically rounded, with pigmentation from notochord toward extremity of caudal rays. Lower edge of caudal peduncle well pigmented. Lower half of upper lip pigmented nearly to lower edge. Suborbital area well pigmented. Unpigmented band above branchial groove less than width of single branchial myomere. Precursor of tongue unpigmented, tapered at base.
SEA LAMPREY (ammocoete)
Petromyzon marinus Linnaeus....................................... Page 211

4a. Supraoral lamina of sucking disc with 2 widely separated teeth; 3 pairs of bicuspid circumoral teeth, no lateral teeth beyond these.
AMERICAN BROOK LAMPREY (adult)
Lampetra appendix (DeKay) .... Page 216

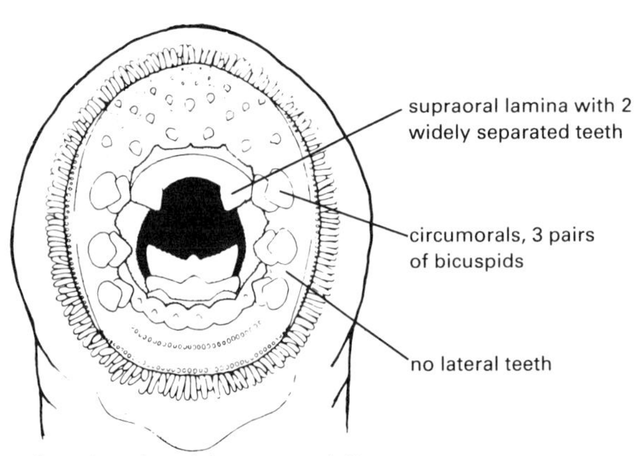

American brook lamprey adult
(P. W. Smith 1973:4)

4b. Supraoral lamina of sucking disc with 2 narrowly separated teeth; 4 pairs of bicuspid circumoral teeth, 5–7 lateral teeth per radiating row.
SEA LAMPREY (adult)
Petromyzon marinus Linnaeus .... Page 211

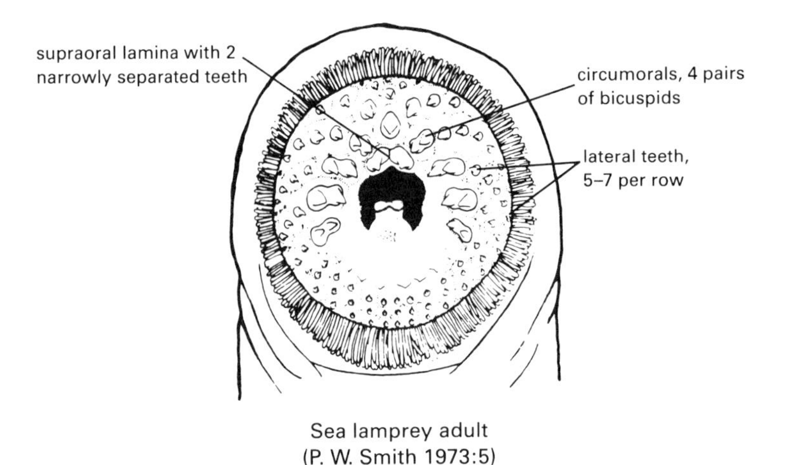

Sea lamprey adult
(P. W. Smith 1973:5)

5a. Sucking disc hoodlike, without papillary fringe. Complexly branched papillae (sieve apparatus) filling mouth opening. No teeth. Eyes rudimentary (see illustration under 2a).
Ichthyomyzon ammocoete. (Separation of the larval lampreys of this genus is not possible at this time.)

5b. Sucking disc round or oval with papillary fringe. No sieve apparatus within mouth opening. Horny teeth present. Eyes functional.
Ichthyomyzon adult 6

6a. Length of sucking disc into TL greater than 20. Disc small, greatest branchial diam into length of disc 0.4–0.9. Teeth degenerate—small, blunt.
NORTHERN BROOK LAMPREY
Ichthyomyzon fossor Reighard and Cummins .... Page 204

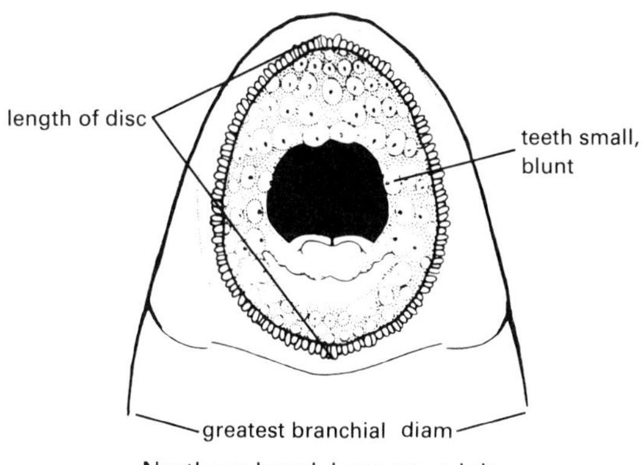

Northern brook lamprey adult
(P. W. Smith 1973:5)

6b. Length of sucking disc into TL less than 20. Disc large, greatest branchial diam into length of disc 1.0–1.8. Teeth functional—large, sharply pointed.. 7

7a. Circumoral teeth (with rare exceptions) all unicuspid; teeth in anterior row 3 (2–4); teeth in lateral rows 6 or 7 (4–8). Length of sucking disc into TL 11.1 (8.2–14.8). Trunk myomeres 51 (46–53).
SILVER LAMPREY
Ichthyomyzon unicuspis Hubbs and Trautman .... Page 201

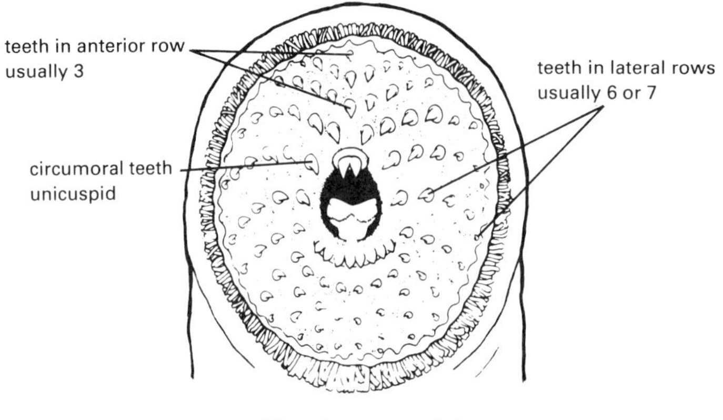

Silver lamprey adult
(P. W. Smith 1973:6)

7b. Circumoral bicuspid teeth 6 or 7 (3–8); teeth in anterior row 4 or 5 (3–6); teeth in lateral rows 7 or 8 (6–10). Length of sucking disc into TL 12.3 (10.3–16.2). Trunk myomeres 53 (51–56).
CHESTNUT LAMPREY
Ichthyomyzon castaneus Girard .... Page 208

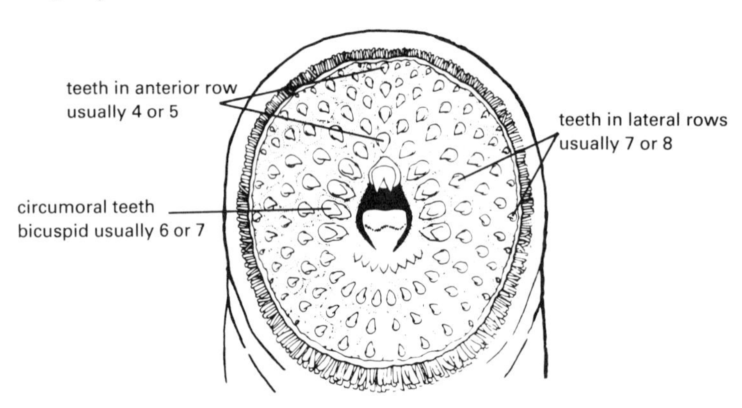

Chestnut lamprey adult
(P. W. Smith 1973:6)

Key to the Sturgeons

1a. Barbels smooth. Lower lip with 2 posterior lobes weakly to strongly papillose. Spiracle present at anterior end of the groove continuous with gill slit. Caudal peduncle partly naked; length of caudal peduncle (A) less than distance from origin of anal fin to insertion of pelvic fins (B). Dorsal lobe of caudal fin without a long filament.
LAKE STURGEON
Acipenser fulvescens Rafinesque .... Page 221

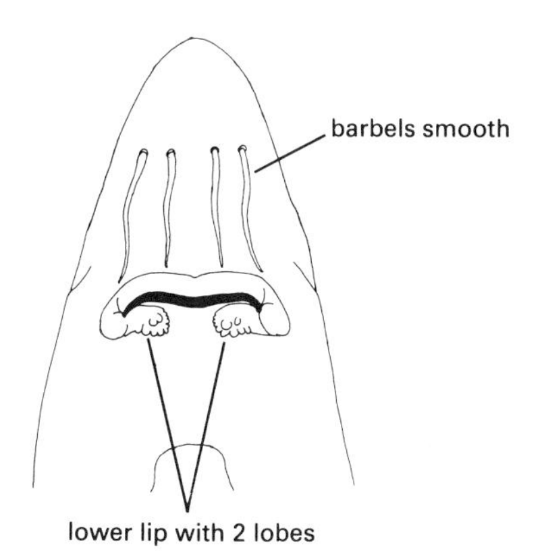

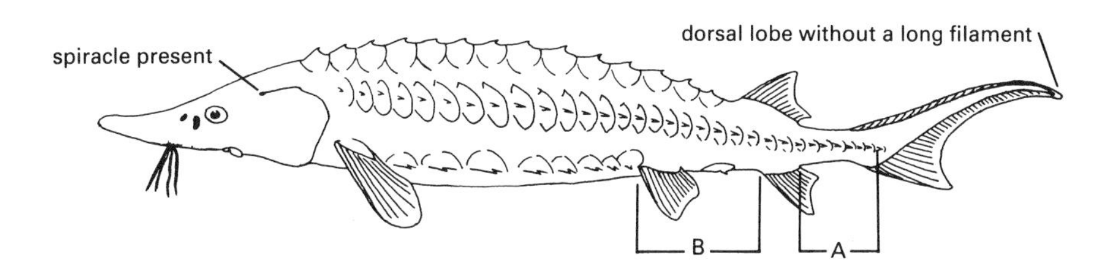

A is less than B

1b. Barbels fringed. Lower lip with 4 posterior lobes strongly papillose. Spiracle absent. Caudal peduncle covered with bony plates; length of caudal peduncle (A) greater than distance from origin of anal fin to insertion of pelvic fins (B). Dorsal lobe of caudal fin with a long filament (sometimes broken off).
SHOVELNOSE STURGEON
Scaphirhynchus platorynchus (Rafinesque) .... Page 227

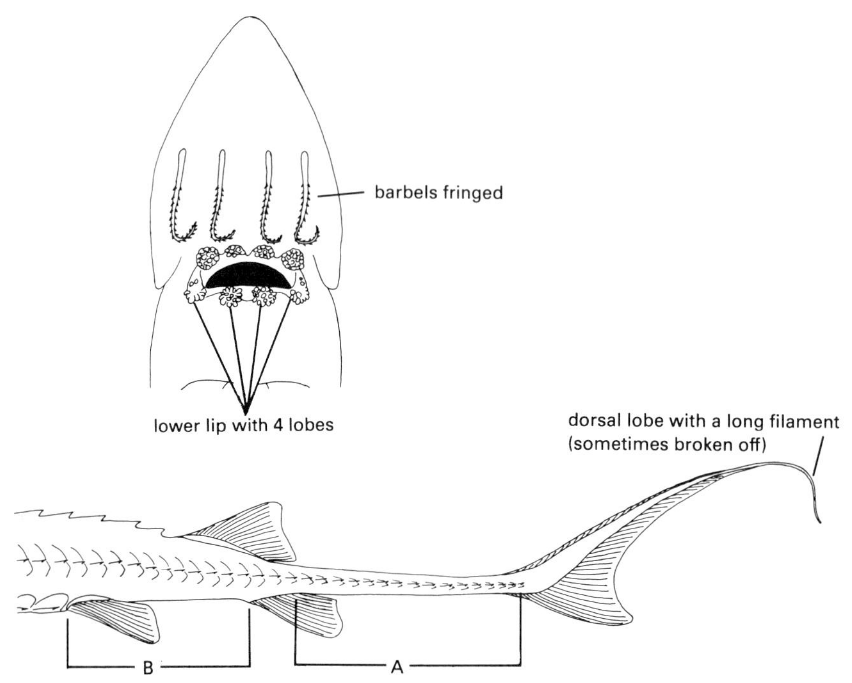

Key to the Gars

1a. Snout width at level of nostrils into snout length 15.6 (13.4–16.5); snout length into TL 4.7 (4.3–5.4). Head length into TL 3.3 (3.0–3.6).
LONGNOSE GAR
Lepisosteus osseus (Linnaeus).. Page 244

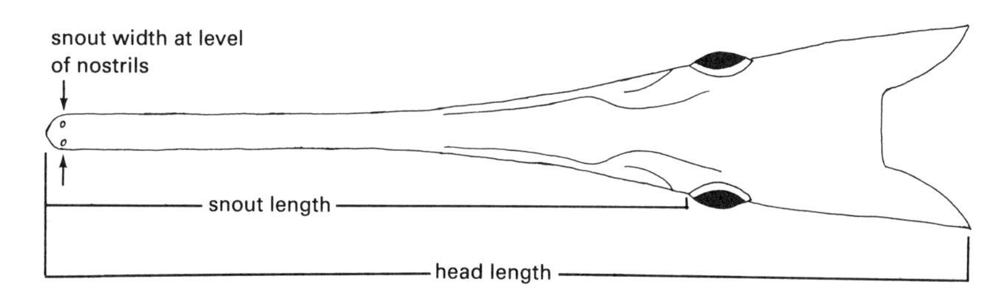

1b. Snout width at level of nostrils into snout length 6.8 (5.3–10.5); snout length into TL 7.1 (6.0–7.9). Head length into TL 4.1 (3.8–4.4).
SHORTNOSE GAR
Lepisosteus platostomus Rafinesque .... Page 241

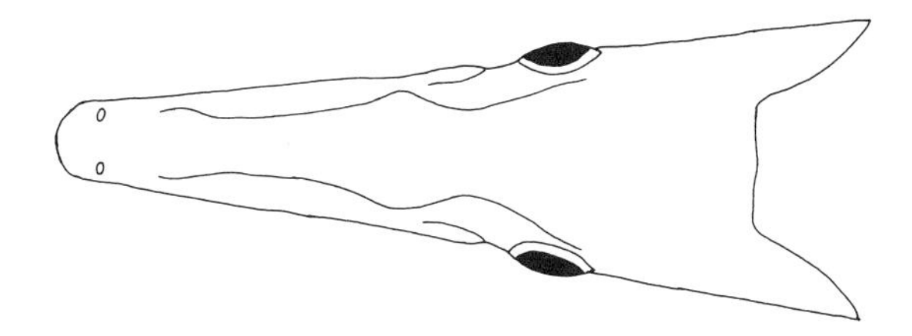

Key to the Herrings

1a. Snout blunt. Lower jaw included within upper jaw; mouth opening terminal or inferior. Last dorsal fin ray extending as a free filament, much longer than adjacent rays. Dorsal fin is behind origin of pelvic fin. Anal fin rays more than 20.
GIZZARD SHAD
Dorosoma cepedianum (Lesueur).................................... Page 273

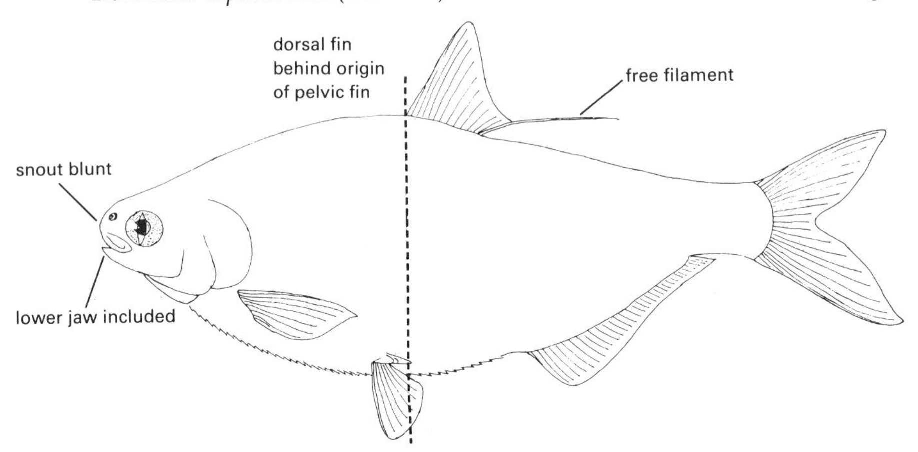

1b. Snout pointed. Lower jaw extends beyond upper jaw; mouth opening superior. Last dorsal fin ray about equal in length to adjacent rays. Dorsal fin is directly over or slightly in advance of pelvic fin. Anal fin rays fewer than 20 2

2a. Gill rakers on lower limb of first gill arch 41–44. Lateral series scales 42–50. Jaw teeth small, weak, and few; teeth on tongue absent. (Great Lakes drainage)
ALEWIFE
Alosa pseudoharengus (Wilson) .... Page 265

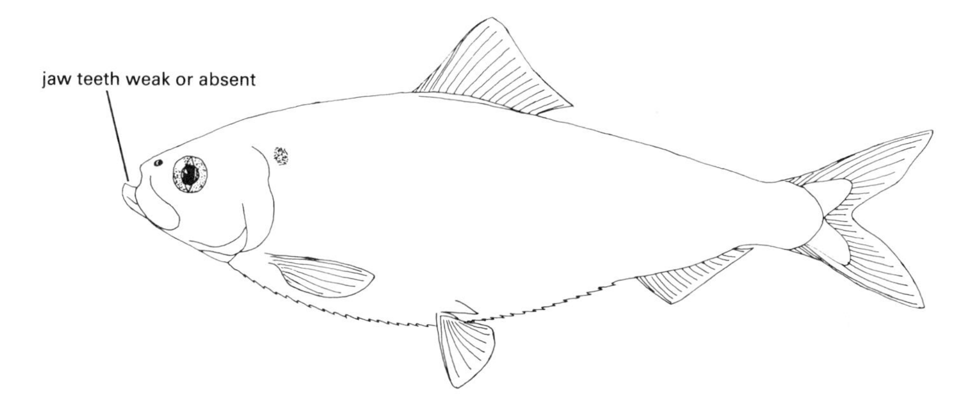

2b. Gill rakers on lower limb of first gill arch 20–30. Lateral series scales 53–60. Jaw teeth prominent; teeth on tongue in 2–4 rows. (Mississippi River drainage—extirpated in Wisconsin)
SKIPJACK HERRING
Alosa chrysochloris (Rafinesque).................................. Page 270

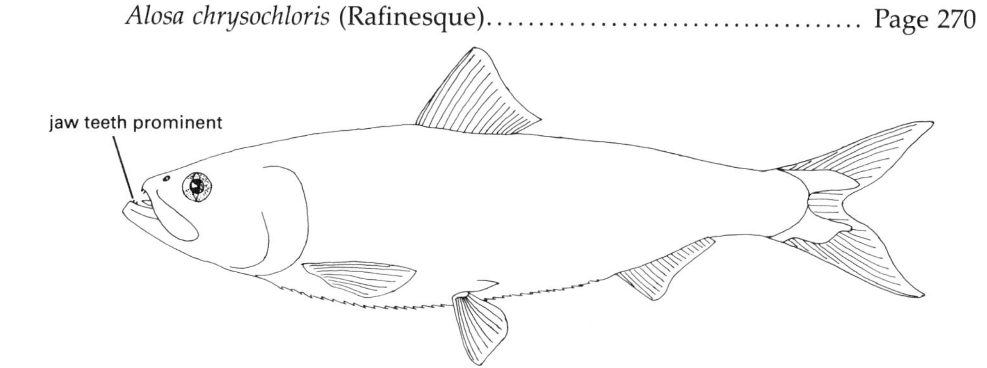

Key to the Mooneyes

1a. Anterior edge of dorsal fin in front of anal fin. Dorsal fin with 11 or 12 rays; its base about ½ anal fin base. Fleshy midventral keel from base of pelvic fin to vent. Maxillary short of, or just to, middle of pupil. Iris of eye silvery.
MOONEYE
Hiodon tergisus Lesueur .... Page 284

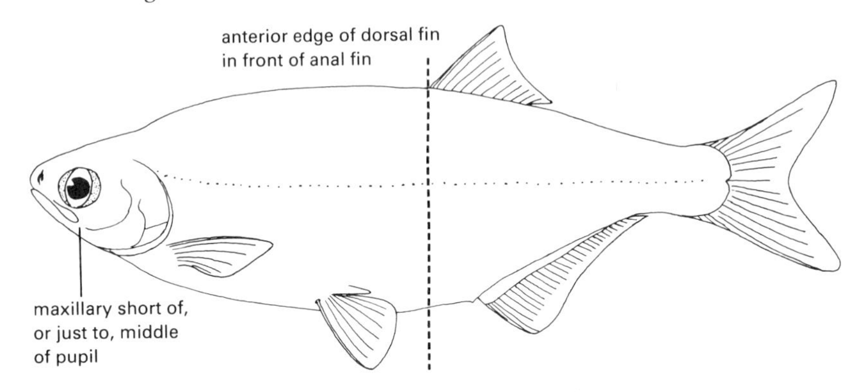

1b. Anterior edge of dorsal fin even with or slightly behind anterior edge of anal fin. Dorsal fin with 9 or 10 rays; its base about ⅓ anal fin base. Fleshy midventral keel from isthmus to vent. Maxillary extends beyond middle of pupil. Iris of eye yellow.
GOLDEYE
Hiodon alosoides (Rafinesque) .... Page 281

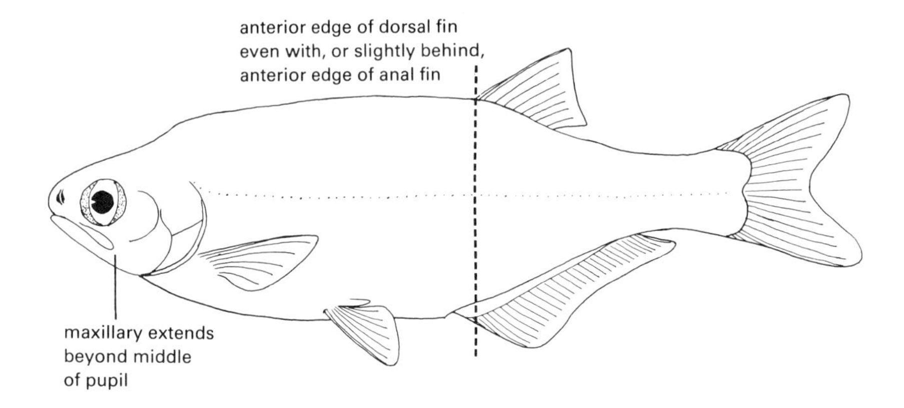

Key to the Subfamilies of the Trouts

1a. Mouth large; maxillary extends behind center of eye. Lower jaw (dentary) with a low dorsal lobe. Teeth on lateral parts of upper and on lower jaws. Scales in lateral line more than 100.
TROUTS and SALMONS
Salmoninae .... Page 90

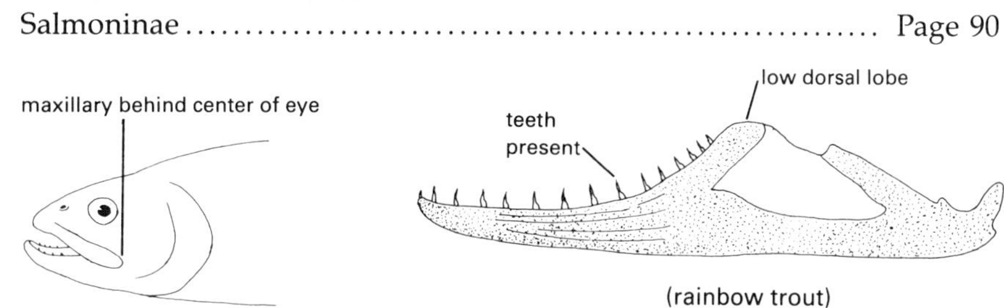

Head and dentary of Salmoninae

1b. Mouth small; maxillary does not extend beyond center of eye. Lower jaw (dentary) with a pronounced (often sail-like) dorsal lobe. Absence of teeth on lateral parts of upper and on lower jaws. Scales in lateral line fewer than 100.
WHITEFISH and CISCOES
Coregoninae .... Page 98

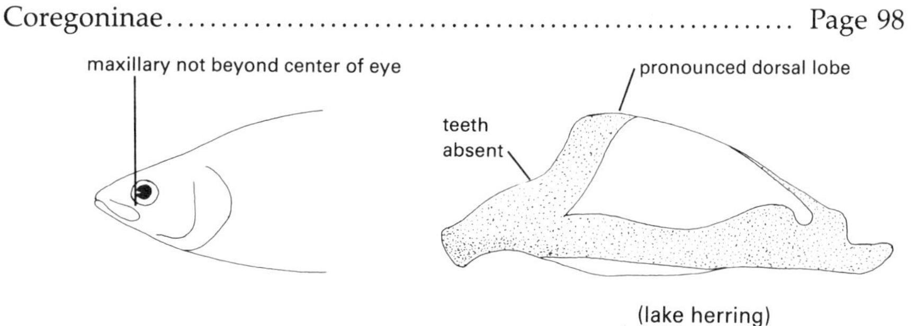

Head and dentary of Coregoninae

Key to the Trouts and Salmons (Salmoninae)

(See page 96 for young up to 125 mm)

1a. Mouth whitish in adults. Anal fin rays 8–12 (15). Branchiostegals usually 10–12 2

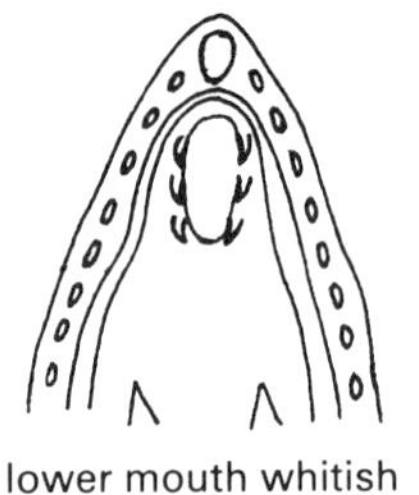

lower mouth whitish

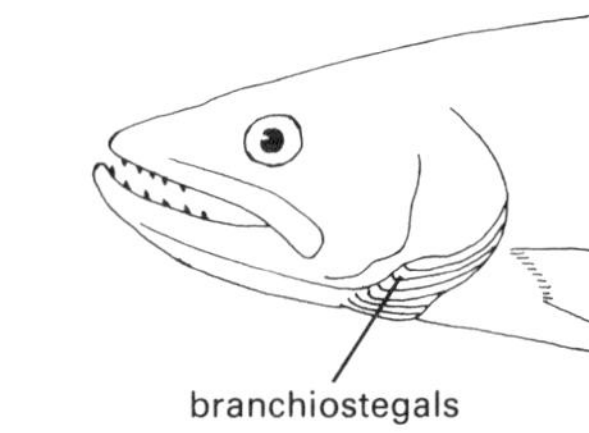

branchiostegals

1b. Mouth blackish in adults. Anal fin rays 13–19 (12). Branchiostegals usually 12–19.
Oncorhynchus spp. 7

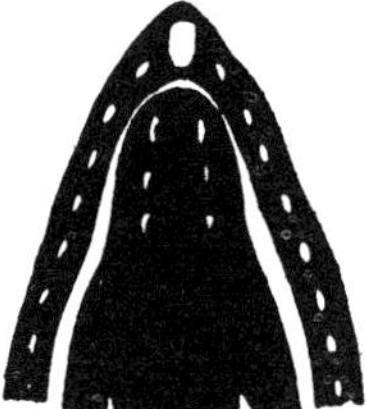

(chinook salmon)

(coho salmon)

lower mouth blackish

2a. Body with black or brown spots on light background (spots sparse in *Salmo salar*). Scales in lateral series fewer than 160. Teeth on head and shaft of vomer (often concealed by oral valve; see illustration under 2b).
Salmo spp. 3

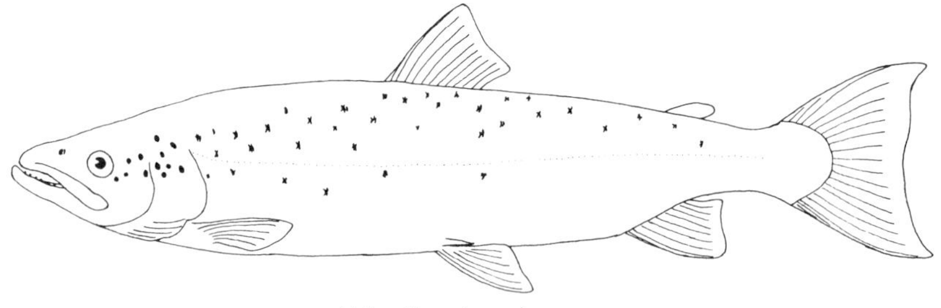

(Atlantic salmon)

2b. Body with light spots (occasionally red) on dark background. Scales in lateral series more than 160. Teeth on head of vomer only. *Salvelinus* spp. 5

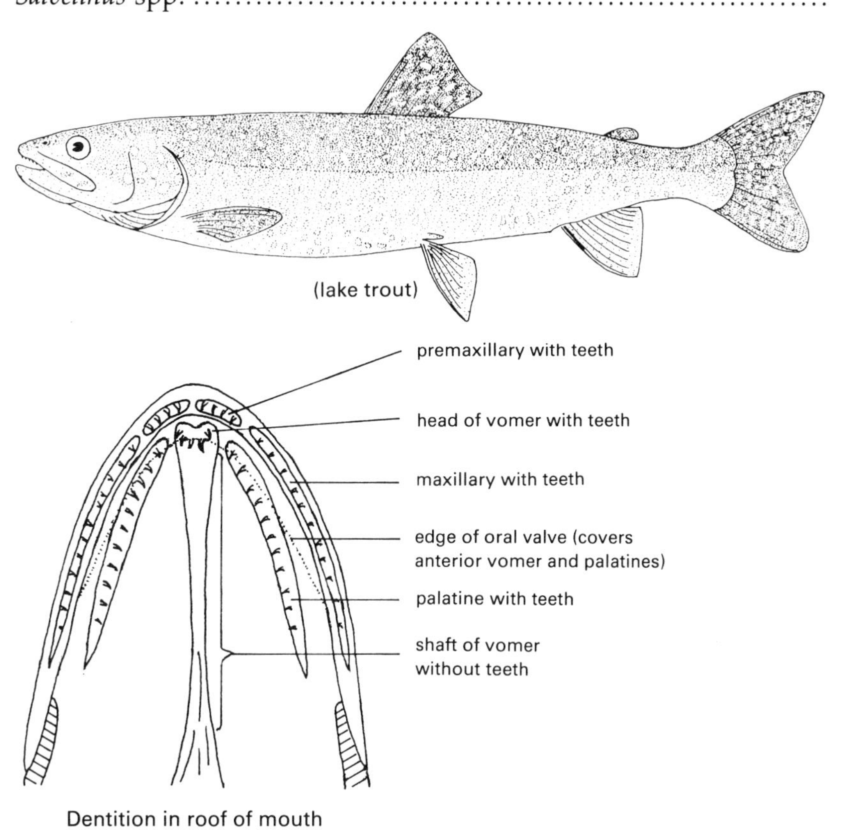

Dentition in roof of mouth
(brook trout)

3a. Vomerine teeth little developed, those on the shaft of the bone few and deciduous. Anal fin rays 9. Adults with X-shaped spots on side.
ATLANTIC SALMON*
Salmo salar Linnaeus .... Page 290

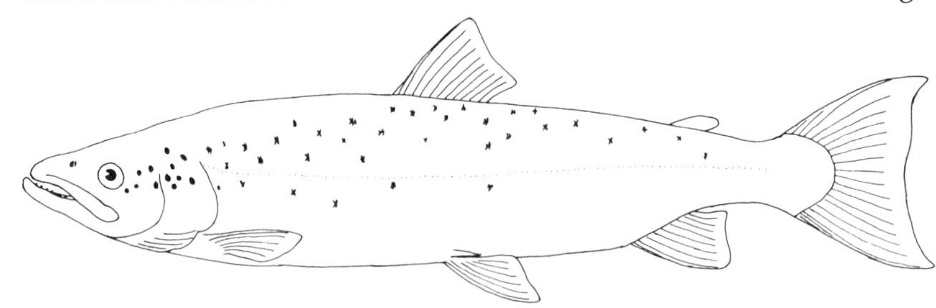

3b. Vomerine teeth well developed, those on the shaft of the bone numerous, persistent, and arranged in 1 zigzag or 2 alternating rows. Anal fin rays usually 10–13. Side usually with round spots. 4

4a. Black (or brown) spots large and diffuse, scarcely developed on caudal fin; reddish spots more or less strongly developed (often surrounded by a light border). Adipose fin orange or red-orange, without dark margin or spots. No pink to rose stripe along side of body.
BROWN TROUT
Salmo trutta Linnaeus .... Page 291

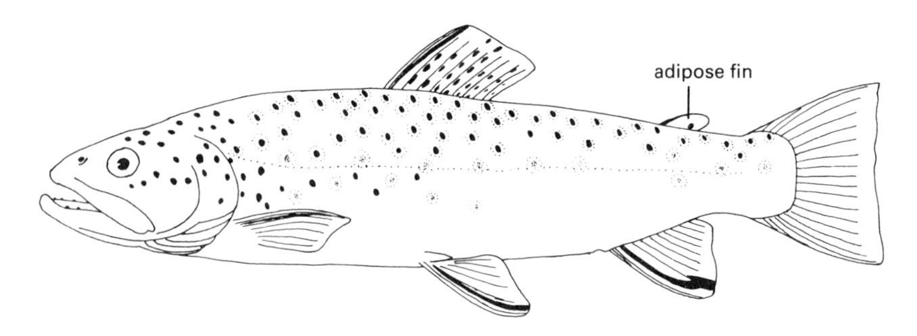

*The Atlantic salmon in spawning habit and the brown trout are confusing. Additional characters for separation are:

	Branchiostegal rays	*Dorsal fin rays*	*Red-orange on adipose fin*	*Lateral line scales*
Atlantic salmon	usually 11 or 12	11 or 12	none	109–121
Brown trout	usually 10	9–11	on margin	120–130

4b. Black (or brown) spots small and sharp, well developed on caudal fin; red spots totally absent. Adipose fin olive, with black margin or spots. Broad pink to rose stripe present along side of body.
RAINBOW TROUT
Salmo gairdneri Richardson .... Page 298

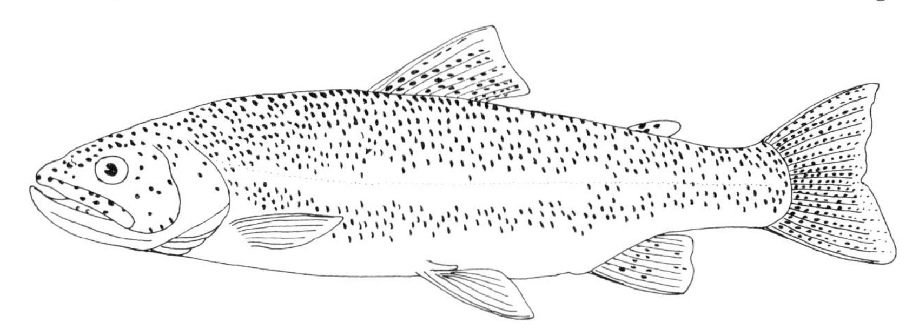

5a. Caudal fin little forked. Body red spotted in life. Lower fins each with black stripe near leading edge. Gill rakers 9–12. Mandibular pores usually 7 or 8 on each side.
BROOK TROUT
Salvelinus fontinalis (Mitchill) .... Page 316

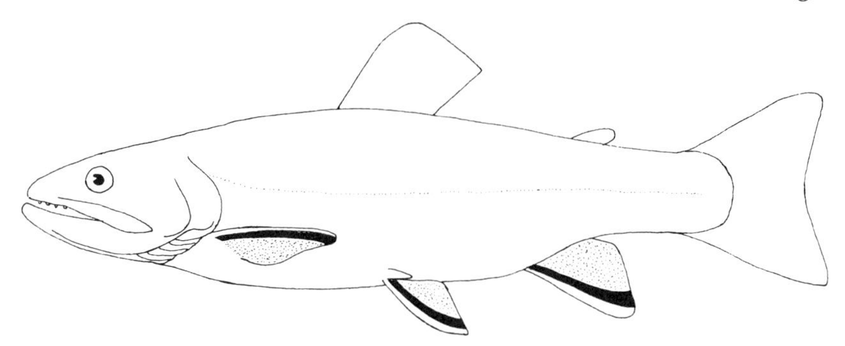

lower fins red with leading edge white followed by black stripe

5b. Caudal fin strongly forked. Body not red spotted in life. Lower fins without black stripe. Gill rakers 12–14. Mandibular pores usually 9 or 10 on each side 6

6a. Body depth into TL 3.8–5.5. Top of head describing a more-or-less straight line from back of head to tip of snout.
LAKE TROUT
Salvelinus n. namaycush (Walbaum) .... Page 323

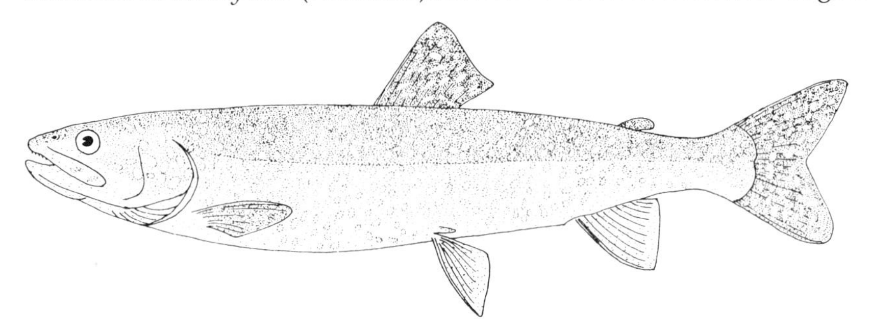

6b. Body depth into TL 3.1–3.8. Top of head a bent line above eye and a shortened snout.
SISCOWET
Salvelinus namaycush siscowet (Agassiz)* .... Page 330

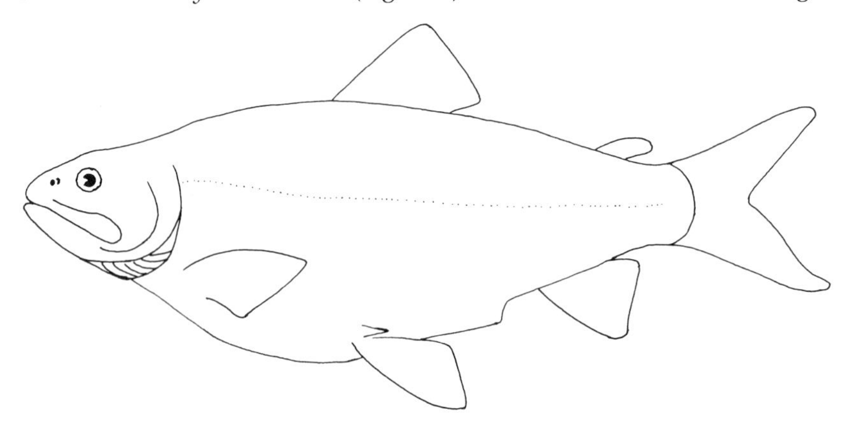

*Hubbs and Lagler (1964).

7a. Scales in lateral line 147–205. Large black spots on back and both lobes of caudal fin, largest as large as eye. Gill rakers on first arch 24–35. Breeding males with distinct humpback.
PINK SALMON
Oncorhynchus gorbuscha (Walbaum) .... Page 304

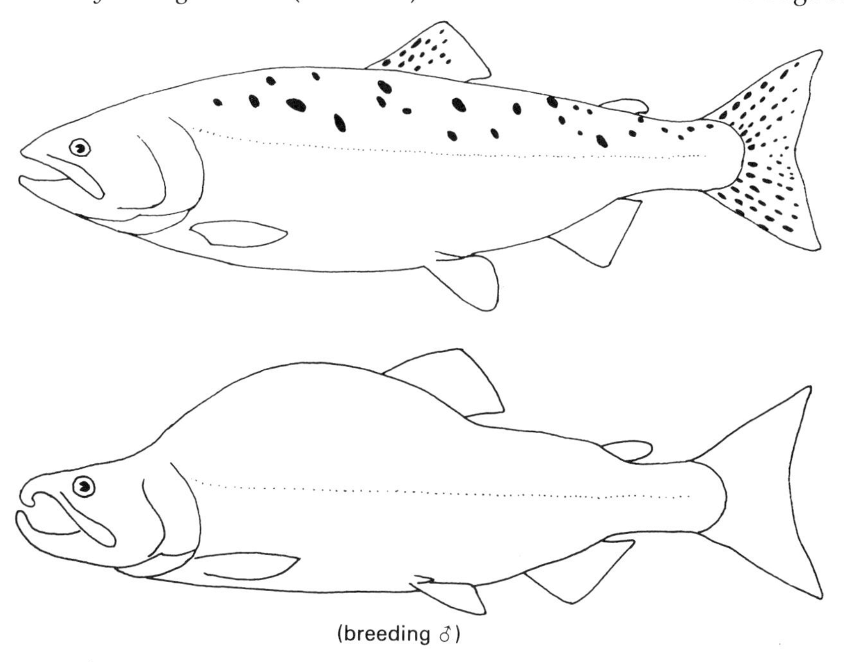

(breeding ♂)

7b. Scales in lateral line 112–165. Spots on back and caudal fin small, largest as large as pupil of eye. Gill rakers 16–26 on first arch. Breeding males without humpback... 8

8a. Entire mouth, including gums, black (see illustration under 1b). Anal fin rays 14–19. Pyloric caeca 140–185. Small black spots on both lobes of caudal fin.
CHINOOK SALMON
Oncorhynchus tshawytscha (Walbaum) .... Page 312

8b. Gums whitish (see illustration under 1b). Anal fin rays usually 11–15. Pyloric caeca 45–114. Small black spots, when present on caudal fin, on upper lobe only.
COHO SALMON
Oncorhynchus kisutch (Walbaum) .... Page 307

Key to Young Trouts and Salmons up to 125 mm*

1a. Rays in anal fin 8–12. Dark spots on dorsal fin present or absent...... 2

1b. Rays in anal fin 12–19. Dark spots on dorsal fin absent................ 6

2a. Dorsal fin without dark spots, and first dorsal ray not black.
LAKE TROUT
Salvelinus n. namaycush (Walbaum)................................ Page 323

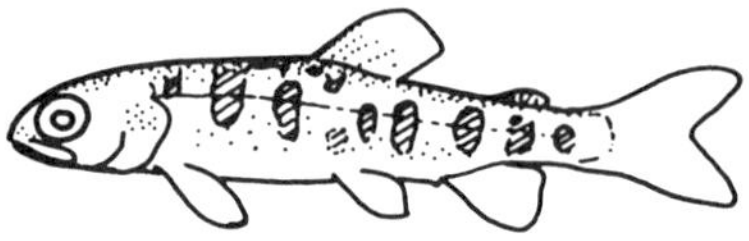

2b. Dorsal fin with distinct dark spots, or with first dorsal ray black 3

3a. Red or yellow spots on lateral line between or on parr marks (may be missing in hatchery-reared fish and in preserved specimens); combined width of dark areas along lateral line about equal to or greater than width of light areas 4

3b. Red or yellow spots absent; width of dark areas along lateral line less than width of light areas.
RAINBOW TROUT
Salmo gairdneri Richardson .... Page 298

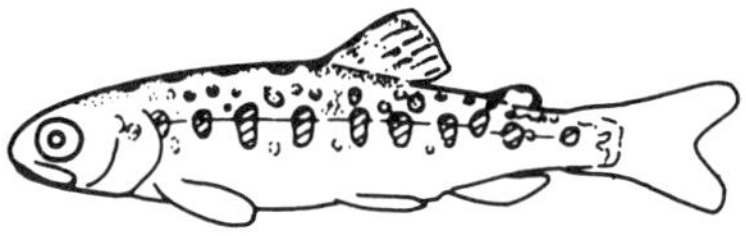

4a. Pectoral fins long, as long as depressed dorsal fin. Caudal fin deeply forked, center rays about ½ the length of longest.
ATLANTIC SALMON
Salmo salar Linnaeus .... Page 290

4b. Pectoral fins shorter than depressed dorsal fin. Caudal fin not deeply forked, center rays definitely more than ½ the length of longest...... 5

*After McPhail and Lindsey (1970:133–135) and Carl et al. (1967:56–58).

5a. No definite dark spots other than parr marks below lateral line; 8 or 9 wide parr marks, widest about equal to eye diam.
BROOK TROUT
Salvelinus fontinalis (Mitchill) .... Page 316

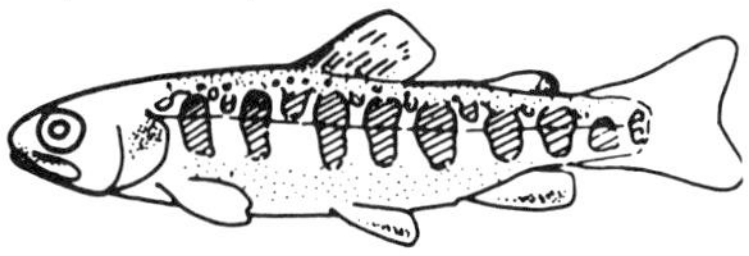

5b. Small black spots above and below lateral line in addition to parr marks; about 11 parr marks, none as wide as eye diam.
BROWN TROUT
Salmo trutta Linnaeus .... Page 291

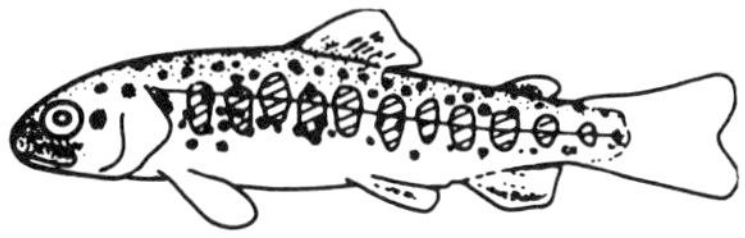

6a. Parr marks absent.
PINK SALMON
Oncorhynchus gorbuscha (Walbaum) .... Page 304

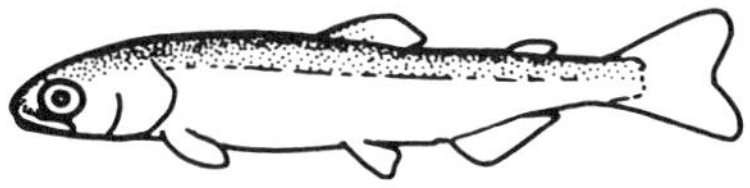

6b. Parr marks present as dark vertical bars or oval blotches 7

7a. First rays of anal fin elongated, producing concave outer margin to fin; leading edge of fin with white stripe followed by dark stripe (best seen when fish is immersed in water against dark background). Tail reddish.
COHO SALMON
Oncorhynchus kisutch (Walbaum) .... Page 307

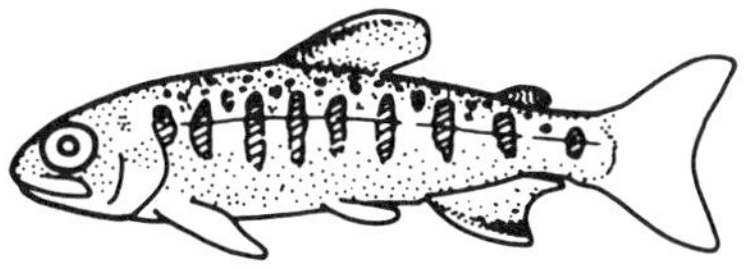

7b. First rays of anal fin not elongate; fins usually not colored.
CHINOOK SALMON
Oncorhynchus tshawytscha (Walbaum) .... Page 312

Key to the Whitefish and Ciscoes (Coregoninae)*

1a. Single flap between nostrils. Gill rakers fewer than 22.................. 2

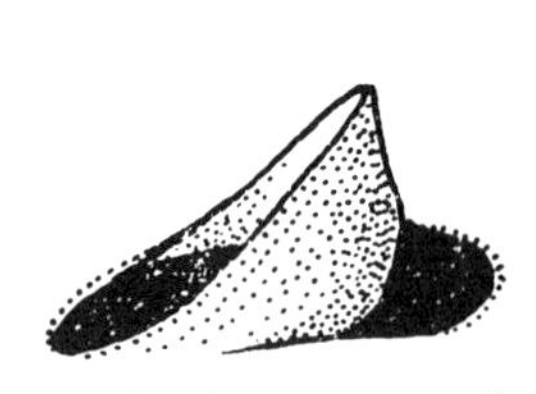

single flap between nostrils
(Koelz 1929:515)

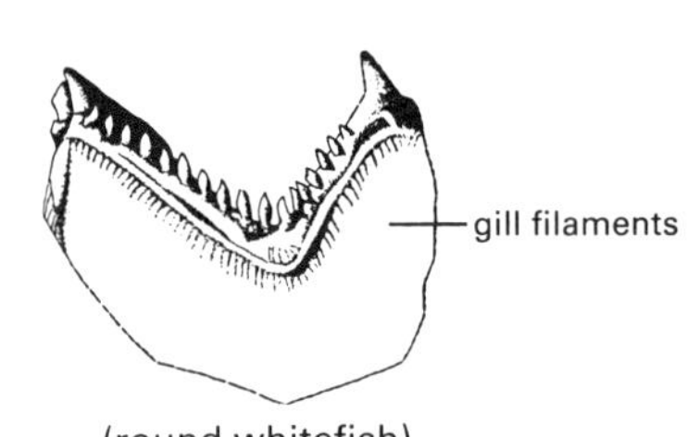

(round whitefish)
Anterior gill arches showing gill rakers
(Koelz 1929:327)

1b. Two flaps between nostrils. Gill rakers usually more than 22 3

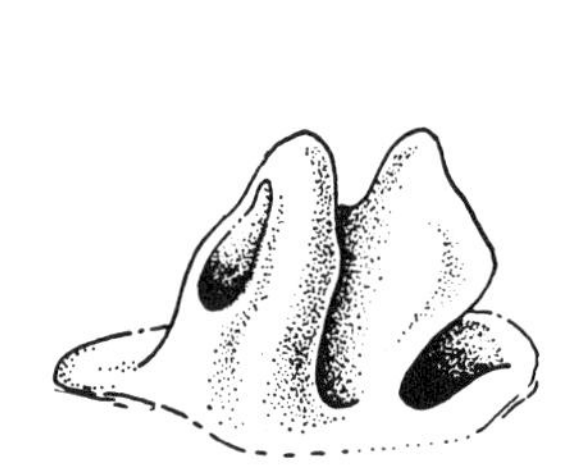

2 flaps between nostrils
(Hubbs and Lagler 1964:51)

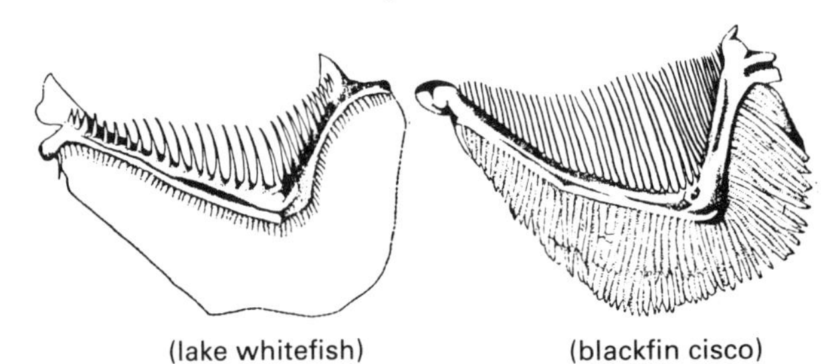

(lake whitefish) (blackfin cisco)
Anterior gill arches showing gill rakers
(Koelz 1929:327)

2a. Lateral line scales 55–70. Scale rows around body usually 33–37. Scales around caudal peduncle 18–20. Pyloric caeca 15–23.
PYGMY WHITEFISH
Prosopium coulteri (Eigenmann and Eigenmann).................. Page 369

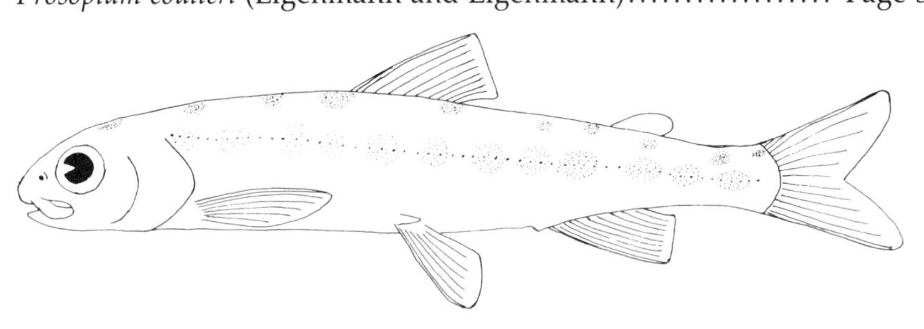

*Relative fin lengths for ciscoes are illustrated on page 104 below. For additional aid in identifying Great Lakes ciscoes, consult Parsons and Todd (1974).

2b. Lateral line scales 80–100. Scale rows around body usually 42–46. Scales around caudal peduncle 22–24. Pyloric caeca 87–117.
ROUND WHITEFISH
Prosopium cylindraceum (Pallas) .... Page 372

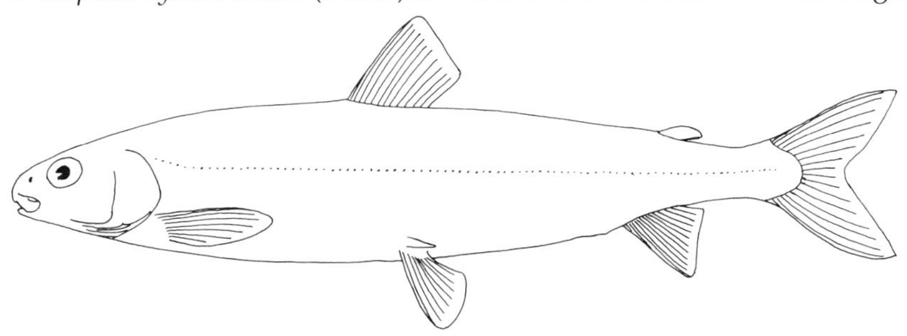

3a. Premaxillaries pointing backward, giving front of snout a rounded profile. Upper jaw usually contained 3 or more times in head. Gill rakers 19–33.
LAKE WHITEFISH
Coregonus clupeaformis (Mitchill) .... Page 335

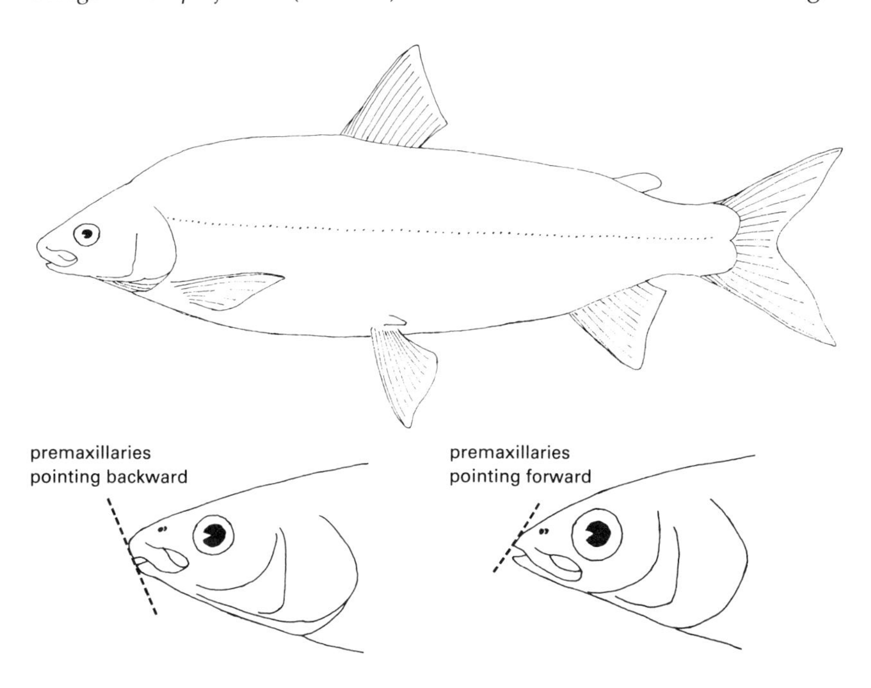

3b. Premaxillaries point forward, giving front of snout a pointed profile. Upper jaw seldom contained more than 3 times in head. Gill rakers usually more than 31* 4

*Some authors give the generic name *Leucichthys* to the 8 species of cisco which follow. For details substantiating a *Coregonus-Leucichthys* separation, see Vladykov (1970).

4a. Tip of lower jaw jutting beyond upper jaw. 5

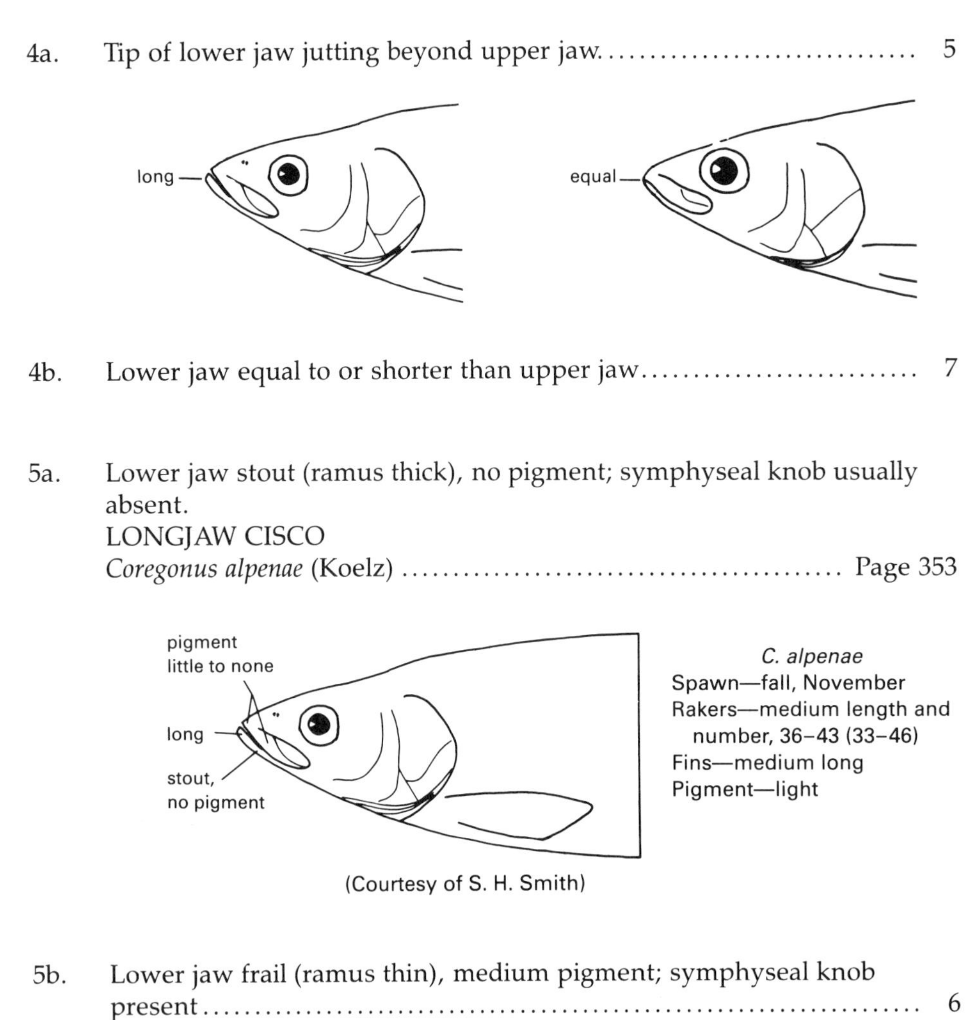

4b. Lower jaw equal to or shorter than upper jaw........................... 7

5a. Lower jaw stout (ramus thick), no pigment; symphyseal knob usually absent.
LONGJAW CISCO
Coregonus alpenae (Koelz) .... Page 353

(Courtesy of S. H. Smith)

5b. Lower jaw frail (ramus thin), medium pigment; symphyseal knob present 6

6a. Gill rakers medium long, about length of gill filaments, and usually 36–41. Paired fins very long, pelvics usually reaching to anus or beyond. Body deeper forward than medially. Eye very large, equal or nearly equal to snout.
KIYI
Coregonus kiyi (Koelz) .... Page 361

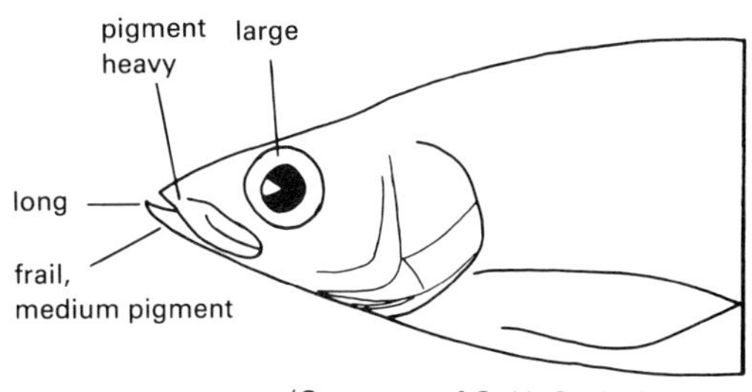

C. kiyi
Spawn—fall, October
Rakers—medium length and number, 36–41 (34–45)
Fins—very long
Pigment—medium
Thin body; large eye

(Courtesy of S. H. Smith)

6b. Gill rakers long, longer than longest gill filaments, and usually 41–44 (40–47 in some deepwater races). Paired fins long, but pelvic fins seldom reach anus. Body deepest medially. Eye large, but less than length of snout.
BLOATER
Coregonus hoyi (Gill) .... Page 356

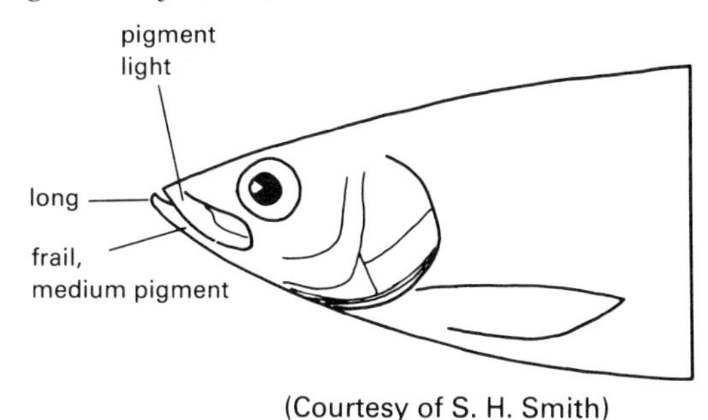

C. hoyi
Spawn—spring, (?) March (?)
Rakers—long and medium in number, 41–44 (37–48)
Fins—medium to long
Pigment—medium

(Courtesy of S. H. Smith)

7a. Lower jaw oblique and equal to upper jaw; posterior end of upper jaw usually reaching anterior edge of pupil 8

7b. Lower jaw underslung (ventral) and usually shorter than upper jaw; posterior end of upper jaw often reaching middle of pupil............ 10

8a. Gill rakers usually fewer than 33.
DEEPWATER CISCO
Coregonus johannae (Wagner).. Page 367

gill filaments

(deepwater cisco) (lake herring) (blackfin cisco)

(Koelz 1929:327)

8b. Gill rakers usually 46–50.. 9

9a. Body deepest medially. Lower jaw weak; symphyseal knob present. Body elongate and almost round in cross section.
CISCO or LAKE HERRING
Coregonus artedii Lesueur.. Page 341

pigment dark

equal

weak, medium pigment

C. artedii
Spawn—fall, Nov–Dec
Rakers—long and many, 46–50 (41–51)
Fins—medium
Pigment—dark

(Courtesy of S. H. Smith)

9b. Body deeper forward than medially. Lower jaw stout; symphyseal knob absent. Body broad and very deep.
BLACKFIN CISCO
Coregonus nigripinnis (Gill)... Page 364

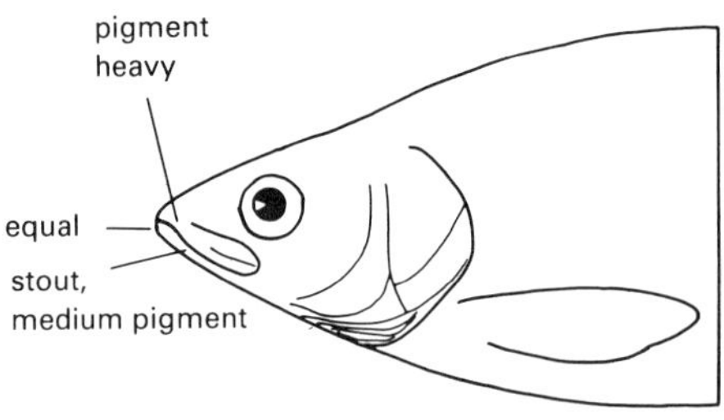

C. nigripinnis
Spawn—winter, Dec–Jan
Rakers—long and many 46–50 (41–52)
Fins—medium long
Pigment—very dark
Thick, deep body

(Courtesy of S. H. Smith)

10a. Snout long—snout into head length usually 3.3–3.6. Premaxillaries at angle of 60–70° with horizontal. Gill rakers usually 38–42 and approximately equal to length of gill filaments. Paired fins medium long.
SHORTJAW CISCO
Coregonus zenithicus (Jordan and Evermann) .... Page 350

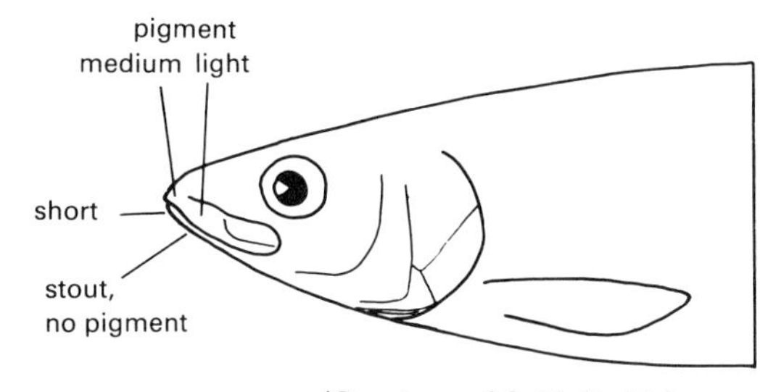

C. zenithicus
Spawn—fall, November
Rakers—medium length and number, 38–42 (35–44)
Fins—medium
Pigment—medium dark

(Courtesy of S. H. Smith)

10b. Snout short—snout into head length usually 3.4–4.0. Premaxillaries at large angle, often vertical (90°) with horizontal. Gill rakers usually 34–38 and shorter than gill filaments. Paired fins very short.
SHORTNOSE CISCO
Coregonus reighardi (Koelz) .... Page 347

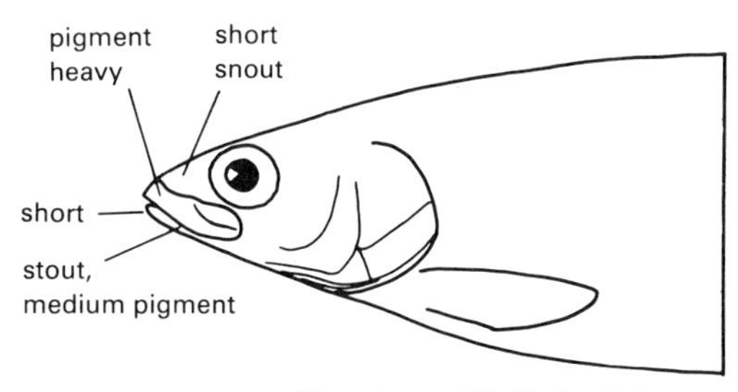

C. reighardi
Spawn—spring, April–May
Rakers—short and low in number, 34–38 (30–43)
Fins—very short
Pigment—dark
Short snout; adult small

(Courtesy of S. H. Smith)

Relative paired fin lengths of Great Lakes ciscoes*

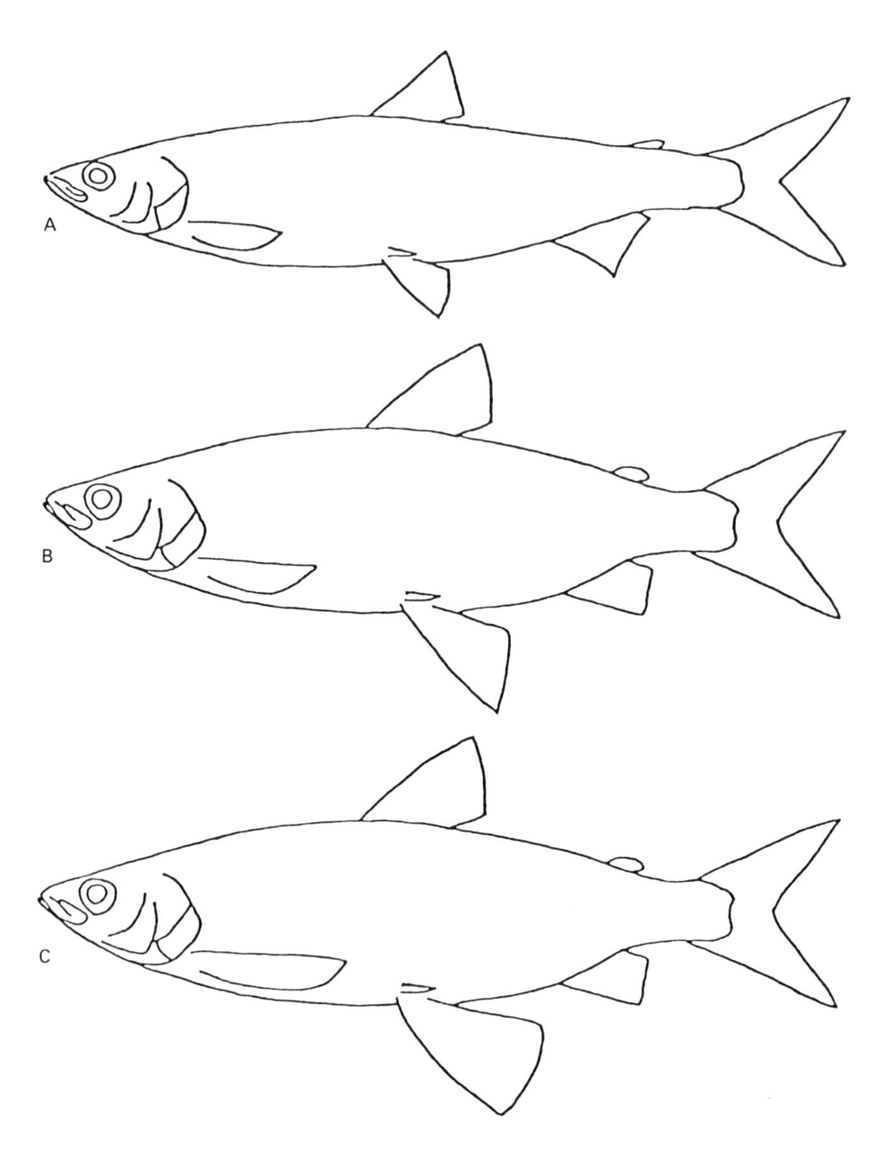

A. Short fins: typical of *C. reighardi* and large *C. artedii*.
B. Intermediate fins: typical of *C. artedii*, *C. hoyi*, *C. zenithicus*, and some *C. nigripinnis*.
C. Long fins: typical of *C. kiyi*, some *C. hoyi*, and some *C. nigripinnis*.

*After Parsons and Todd (1974).

Key to the Pikes

1a. Sensory pores on undersurface of jaw 4 on each side (rarely 3 or 5). Cheek and opercle fully scaled.
GRASS PICKEREL
Esox americanus vermiculatus Lesueur .... Page 393

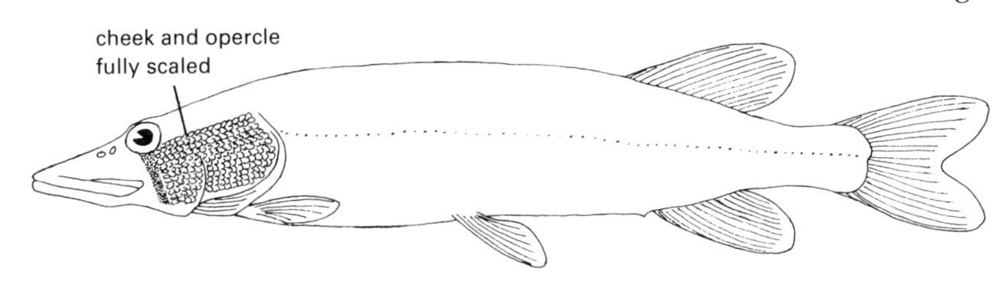

1b. Sensory pores on undersurface of jaw usually 5 or more on each side. Cheek and opercle not fully scaled 2

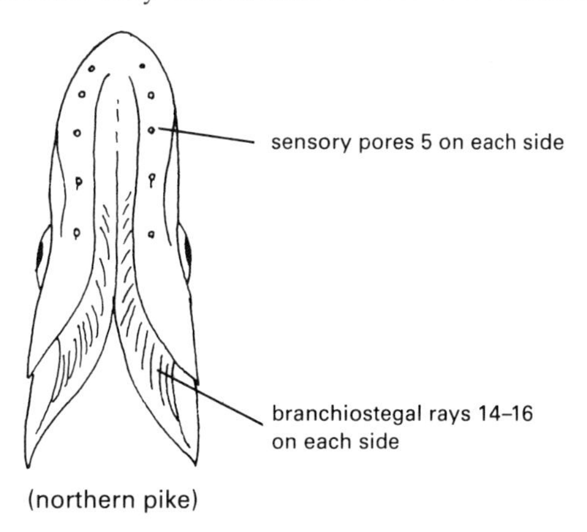

(northern pike)

2a. Sensory pores on undersurface of jaw 5 on each side (rarely 4 or 6). Cheek fully scaled; only upper portion of opercle scaled. Branchiostegal rays 14–16 on each side. Body a dark background color with horizontal rows of light-colored, bean-shaped spots in adults.
NORTHERN PIKE
Esox lucius Linnaeus .... Page 398

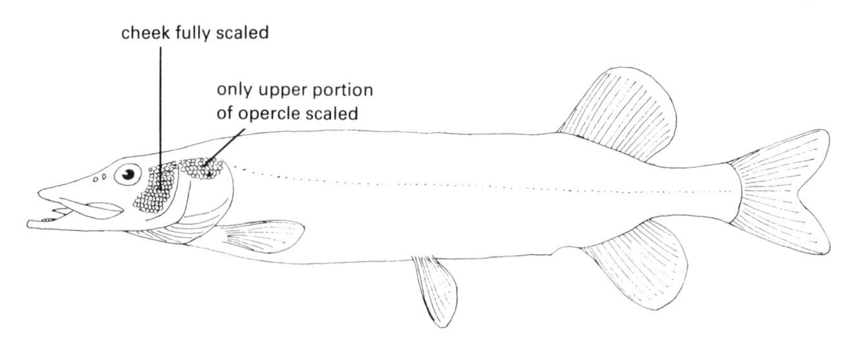

2b. Sensory pores on undersurface of jaw 6–9 on each side. Only upper portions of cheek and opercle scaled. Branchiostegal rays 16–19 on each side. Body a light background color with dark spots or narrow vertical bars.
MUSKELLUNGE
Esox masquinongy Mitchill.. Page 405

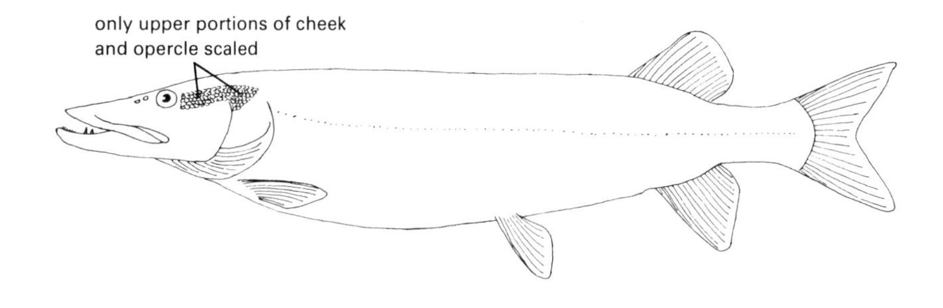

Key to the Minnows and Carps

1a. Dorsal fin with more than 11 soft rays. Dorsal and anal fins each with a strong, serrated, spinous ray.......... 2

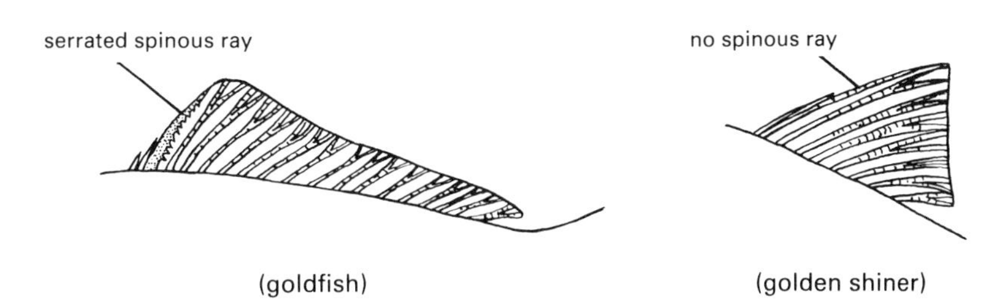

1b. Dorsal fin with fewer than 10 soft rays. No spinous ray in dorsal or anal fins.......... 3

2a. Upper jaw with 2 fleshy barbels on each side. Lateral line scales more than 32 (except in "leather" or "mirror" types). Gill rakers on first arch 21–27. Teeth 1,1,3–3,1,1.
COMMON CARP
Cyprinus carpio Linnaeus.......... Page 419

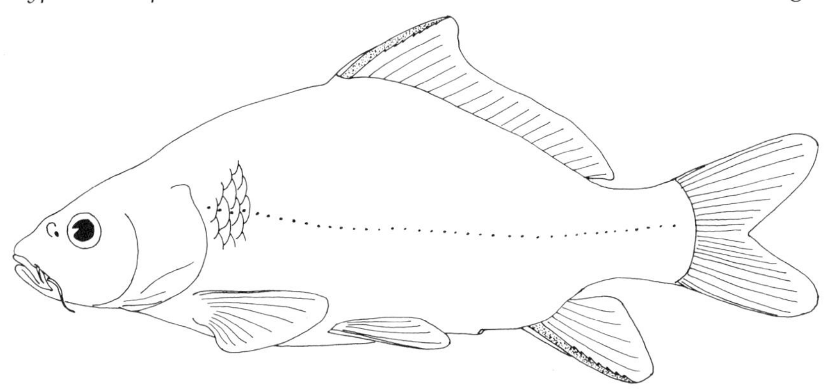

2b. No barbels on upper jaw. Lateral line scales fewer than 32. Gill rakers on first arch 37–43. Teeth 4–4.
GOLDFISH
Carassius auratus (Linnaeus).......... Page 428

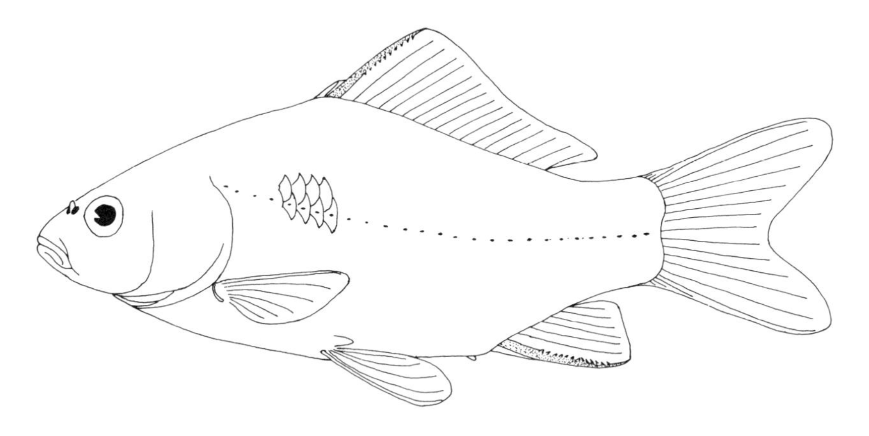

3a. Cartilaginous ridge ("chisel") of lower jaw prominent and separated from lower lip by definite groove. Intestine wrapped around swim bladder. Teeth 4–4 4

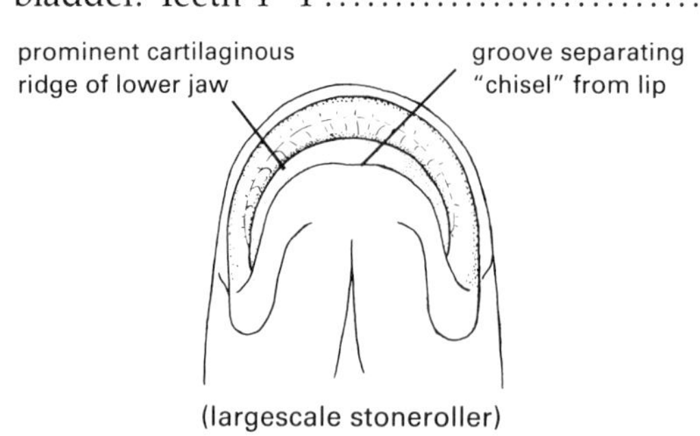

(largescale stoneroller)

3b. Cartilaginous ridge of lower jaw hardly evident and not separated by definite groove from lower lip. Intestine not wrapped around swim bladder. Teeth in 1 or 2 rows 5

4a. Scale rows around body just in front of dorsal fin usually 31–36. Lateral line scales usually 43–47.
LARGESCALE STONEROLLER
Campostoma oligolepis Hubbs and Greene .... Page 481

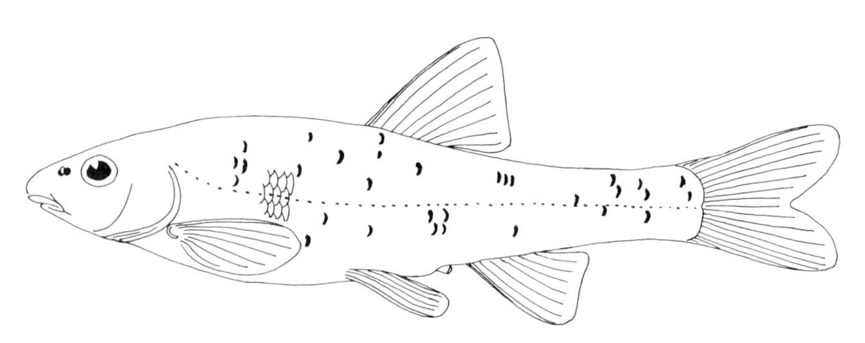

4b. Scale rows around body just in front of dorsal fin usually 39–46. Lateral line scales usually 49–55.
CENTRAL STONEROLLER
Campostoma anomalum (Rafinesque) .... Page 476

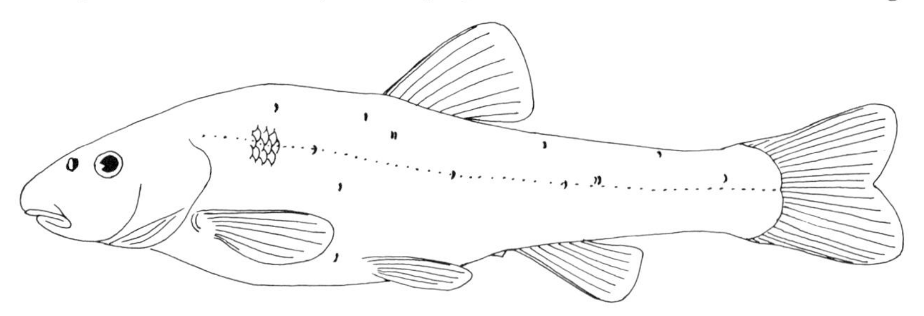

5a. Upper lip connected to snout by bridge of tissue (i.e., groove of upper lip is not continuous over snout) 6

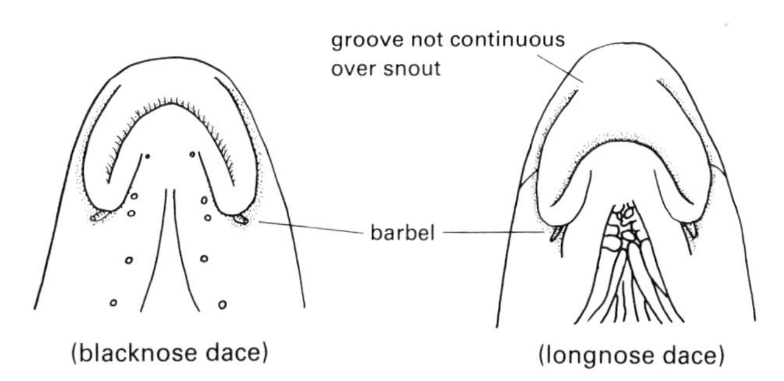

5b. Groove of upper lip continuous over snout (see illustration under 7a). . . 7

6a. Snout projecting beyond lower lip less than 1 mm. Mouth slightly oblique.
BLACKNOSE DACE
Rhinichthys atratulus (Hermann)................................... Page 467

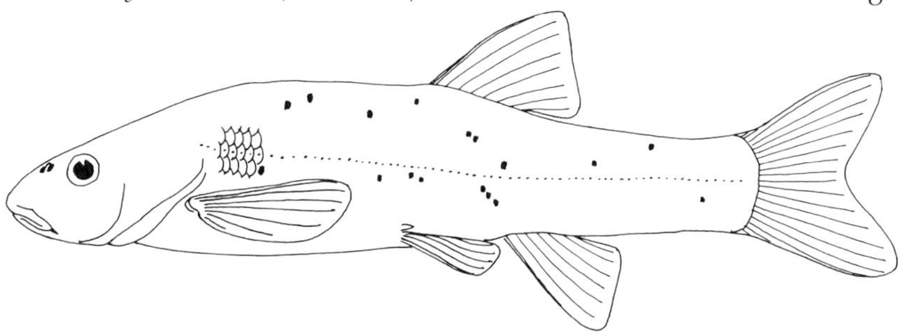

6b. Snout projecting beyond lower lip 1–3 mm or more. Mouth horizontal.
LONGNOSE DACE
Rhinichthys cataractae (Valenciennes) .... Page 472

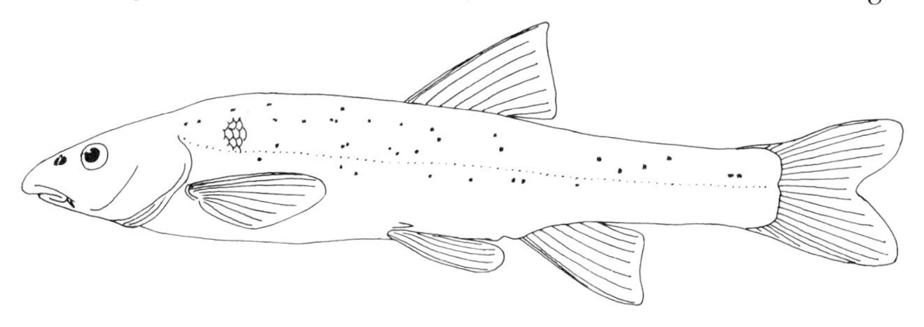

7a. Barbel flat or round, appearing in lip grooves at corners of lips or in groove of upper lip at a short distance anterior to corners 8

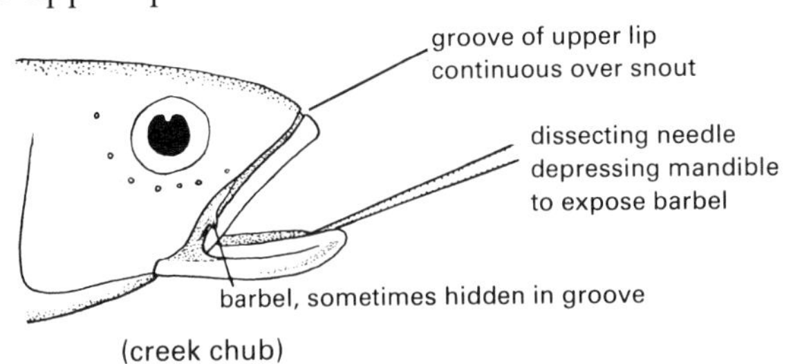

(creek chub)

7b. Barbel absent 16

8a. Barbel in lip grooves at corners of lips (as in blacknose dace; see illustration under 5a) 9

8b. Barbel in groove of upper lip at a short distance anterior to corners (as in creek chub; see illustration under 7a)................................ 14

9a. Dorsal fin membranes well pigmented, especially on midportion of membranes between first and fourth rays. Approximately 16 large tubercles in 3 rows on snout.
Breeding male of the
BLUNTNOSE MINNOW (See illustration under 32a.)
Pimephales notatus (Rafinesque) .... Page 595

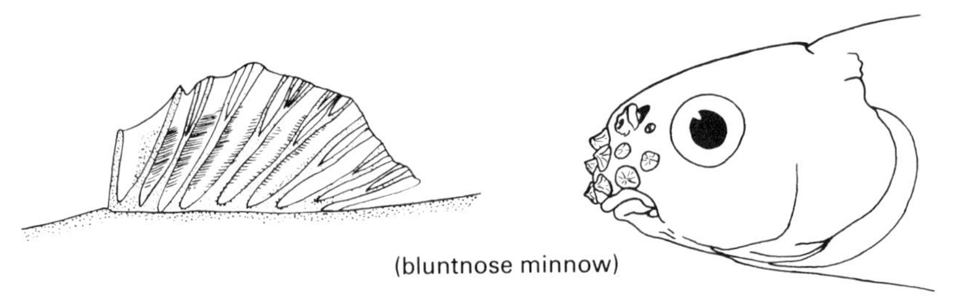
(bluntnose minnow)

9b. Dorsal fin membranes pigmented poorly or not at all. Tubercles, if present, scattered on other parts of head as well as snout............. 10

10a. Body with X-, V-, Y-, and variously shaped dark marks. Peritoneum black. Teeth 4–4.
GRAVEL CHUB
Hybopsis x-punctata Hubbs and Crowe............................ Page 489

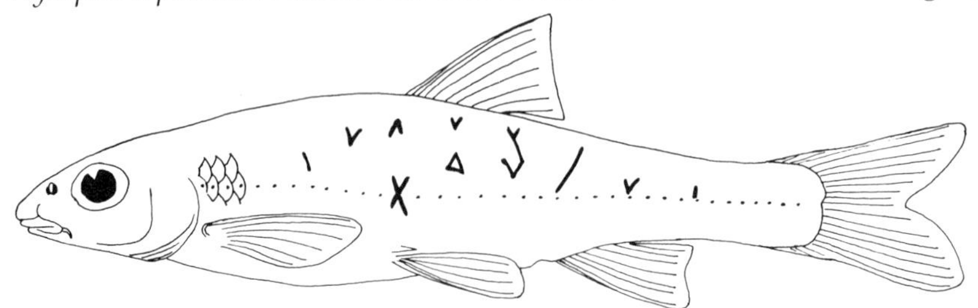

10b. Body not marked or with rounded spots on sides. Peritoneum silvery to dusky 11

11a. Length of protruding portion of barbel about equal to diam of pupil of eye. Prominent dark speckles on body. Teeth 4–4.
SPECKLED CHUB
Hybopsis aestivalis (Girard) .... Page 495

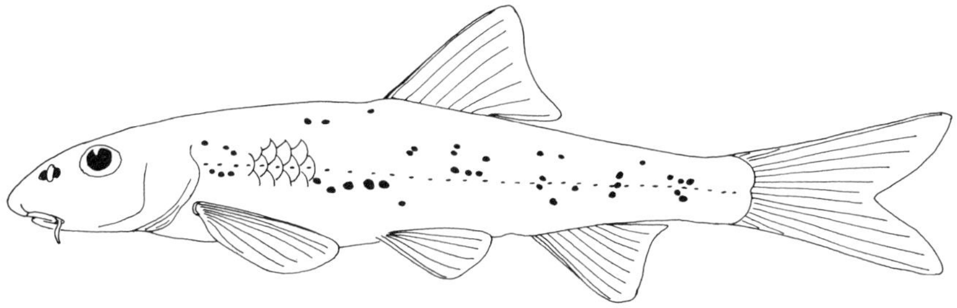

11b. Length of protruding portion of barbel considerably less than diam of pupil of eye. No dark speckles on body 12

12a. Lateral line scales more than 55. Teeth usually 2,4–4,2 but variable.
LAKE CHUB
Couesius plumbeus (Agassiz) .... Page 463

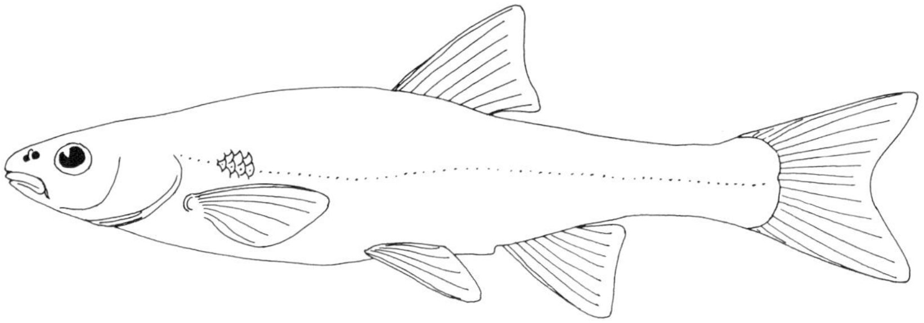

12b. Lateral line scales fewer than 45. 13

13a. Caudal fin length greater than head length. Caudal fin pigmented on rays and membranes except on last 2 ventral rays and membranes, hence showing a distinct white ventral edge. Teeth 1,4–4,1.
SILVER CHUB
Hybopsis storeriana (Kirtland) .... Page 492

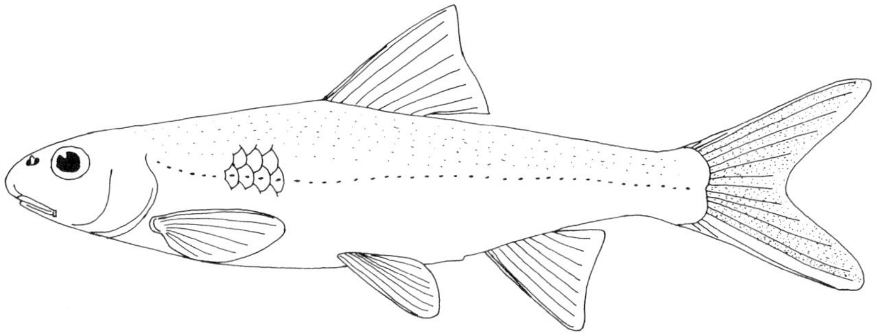

13b. Caudal fin length less than head length. Caudal fin, if pigmented, not showing a distinct white ventral edge. Teeth usually 1,4–4,1 (occasionally 4–4).
HORNYHEAD CHUB
Nocomis biguttatus (Kirtland).. Page 485

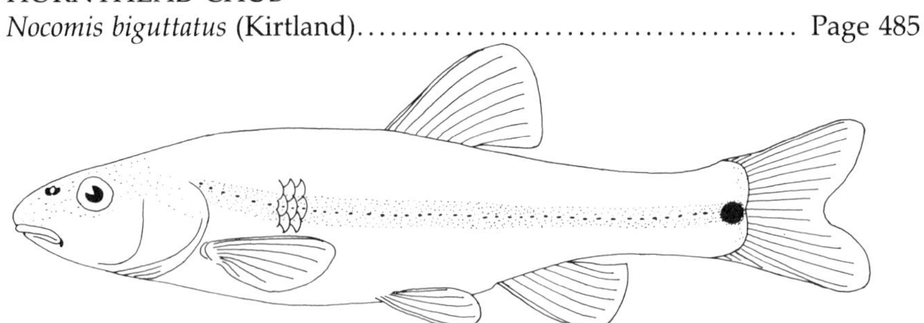

14a. Mouth large, upper jaw extending at least to below front of eye. Lateral line scales usually 50–60 (occasionally more). Black spot on dorsal fin near front of base (indistinct in young). Teeth 2,5–4,2.
CREEK CHUB
Semotilus atromaculatus (Mitchill).................................. Page 437

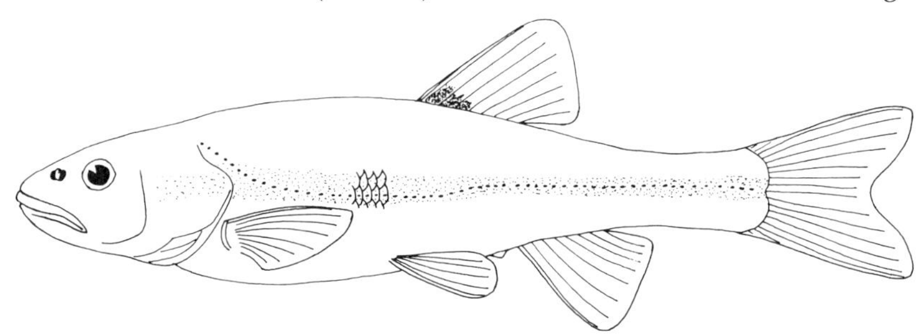

14b. Mouth small, upper jaw not extending to below front of eye. Lateral line scales usually 65 or more. Spot absent or indistinct on dorsal fin near base.. 15

15a. Lateral line scales usually 65–75. Sides frequently mottled by specialized dark scales. Teeth usually 2,5–4,2.
PEARL DACE
Semotilus margarita (Cope)... Page 442

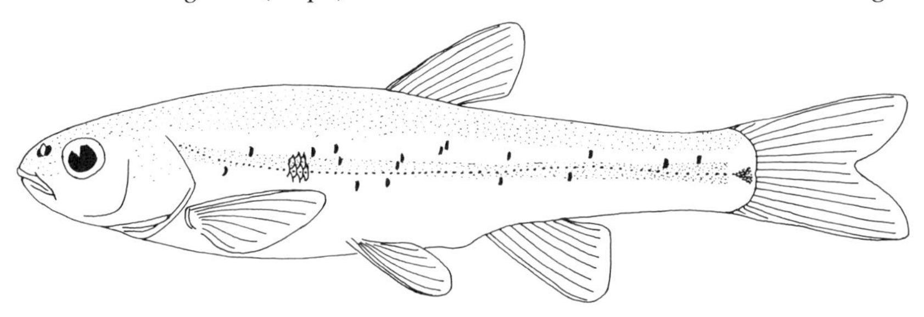

15b. Lateral series scales usually 80 or more (occasionally fewer). Sides not mottled by specialized dark scales. Teeth 5–5.
SOUTHERN REDBELLY DACE (See illustration under 20b.)
Phoxinus erythrogaster (Rafinesque)................................ Page 455

16a. Mouth very large; distance from anteriormost edge of lower lip (mandible) to corner groove almost ½ of head length. Teeth usually 2,5–4,2 (occasionally 1, 4–3,1).
REDSIDE DACE
Clinostomus elongatus (Kirtland) .... Page 446

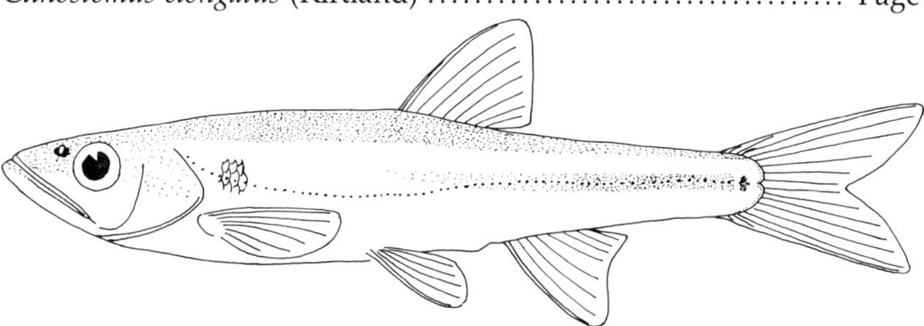

16b. Mouth smaller; distance from anteriormost edge of lower lip to corner groove about ⅓ of head length or less 17

17a. Principal rays of dorsal fin typically 9 (anterior half-rays are not included in the count). Interradial membranes of dorsal fin dusky to dark, except for membrane between rays 5 and 6 and parts of adjacent membranes which are clear and generally devoid of pigment. Teeth 5–5.
PUGNOSE MINNOW
Notropis emiliae (Hay) .... Page 575

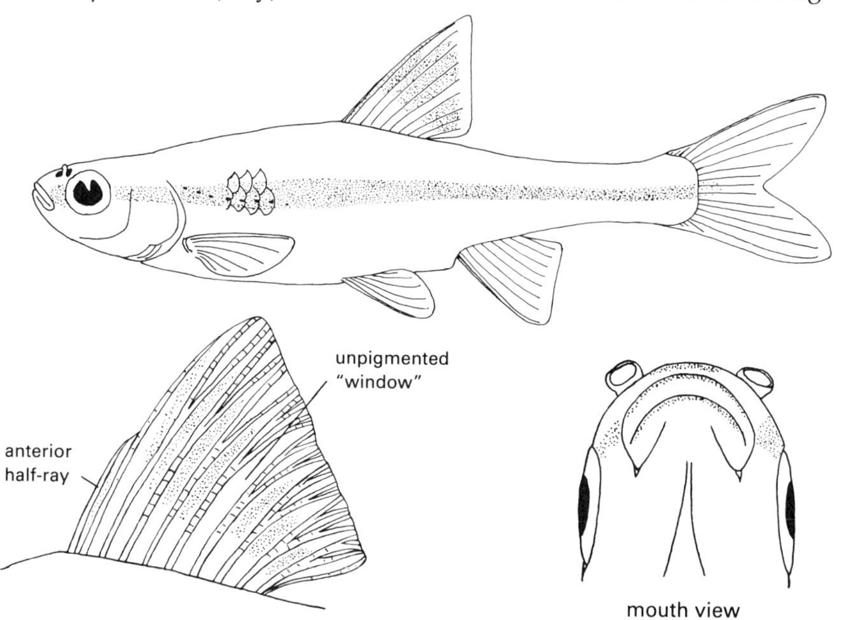

17b. Principal rays of dorsal fin typically 8 (anterior half-rays are not included in the count). Interradial membranes of dorsal fin clear or exhibiting different color pattern from above 18

18a. Lateral line scales (or lateral series scales) more than 65 19

18b. Lateral line scales (or lateral series scales) fewer than 60 21

19a. Body with single dusky lateral stripe; back with dark brown cape. Teeth 2,5–4,2.
FINESCALE DACE
Phoxinus neogaeus Cope .... Page 451

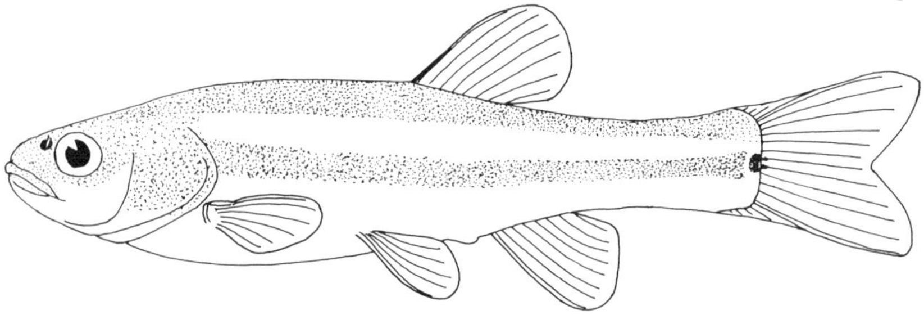

19b. Body with 2 dark lateral stripes; back without dark brown cape. Teeth 5–5 20

20a. Chin slightly anterior to upper lip. Mouth sharply oblique, usually more than 45° with horizontal, and more curved. Length of upper jaw less than, about, or a little more than ¼ length of head.
NORTHERN REDBELLY DACE
Phoxinus eos (Cope) .... Page 459

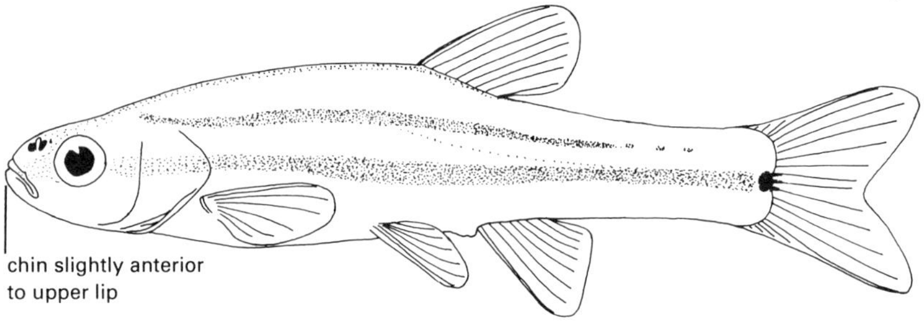

chin slightly anterior
to upper lip

20b. Upper lip anterior to lower lip and chin. Mouth slightly oblique, usually less than 45° with horizontal, and little curved. Length of upper jaw from about ¼ to considerably more than ¼ length of head.
SOUTHERN REDBELLY DACE
Phoxinus erythrogaster (Rafinesque) .... Page 455

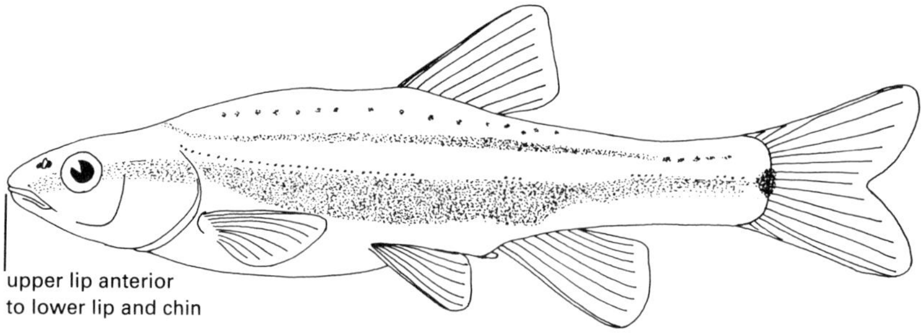

upper lip anterior
to lower lip and chin

21a. Lower lip with thickened lateral lobes which, with upper lip, gives scroll-like or fiddlehead appearance. Teeth 4–4.
SUCKERMOUTH MINNOW
Phenacobius mirabilis (Girard) .... Page 499

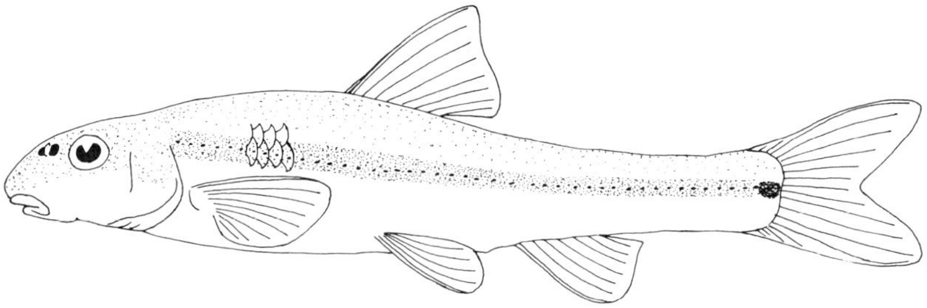

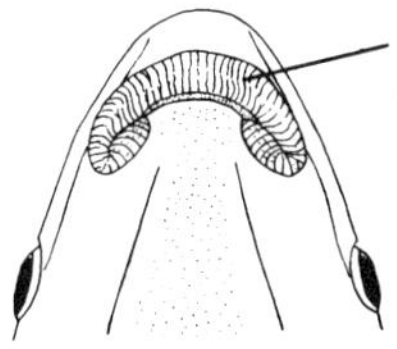

lips plicate
and papillose

(suckermouth minnow)

21b. Lower lip normal, without thickened lateral lobes 22

22a. Anal fin rays typically 9–13.. 23

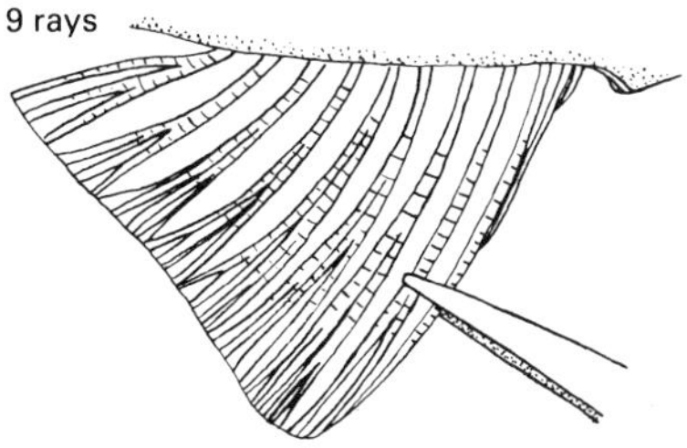

9 rays

(common shiner)

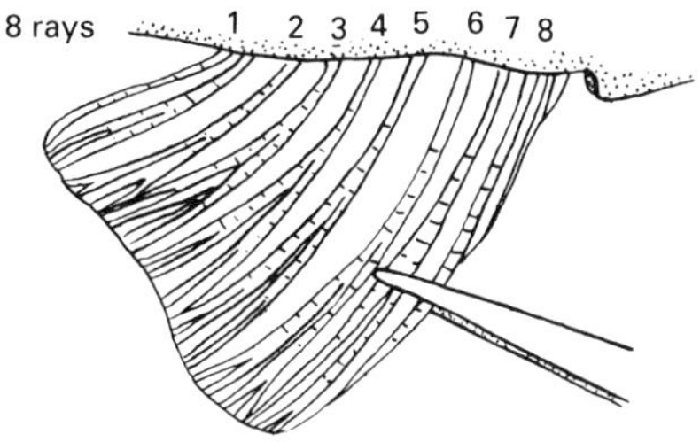

8 rays 1 2 3 4 5 6 7 8

(bigmouth shiner)

Note that the last ray of the fin, ray #1, is split to the base and appears as 2 closely spaced rays. It is identified as a single ray by the small space between the ray elements—a much smaller space than the spaces between the other fin rays

22b. Anal fin rays typically 7 or 8 29

23a. Origin of dorsal fin opposite origin of pelvic fin or slightly anterior. Anal fin rays typically 9 or 10 24

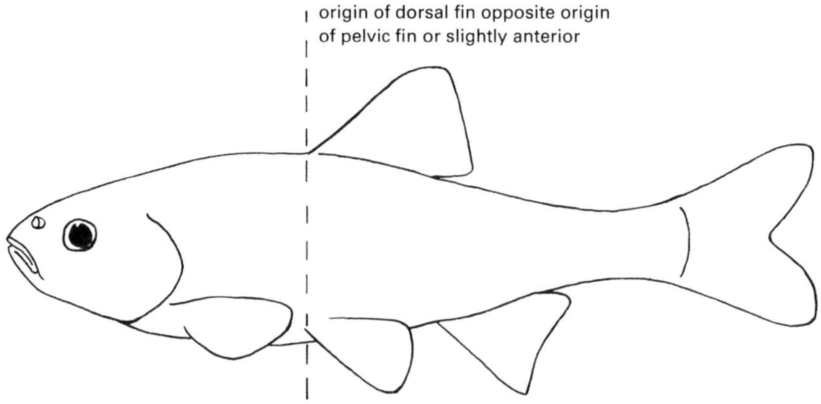

origin of dorsal fin opposite origin of pelvic fin or slightly anterior

(common shiner)

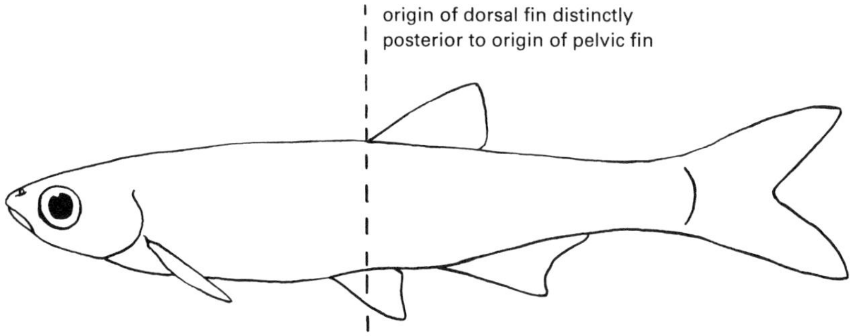

origin of dorsal fin distinctly posterior to origin of pelvic fin

(emerald shiner)

23b. Origin of dorsal fin distinctly posterior to origin of pelvic fin. Anal fin rays typically 11–13 (rarely 9, commonly 10) 26

24a. Dorsal fin membranes pigmented. Teeth 4–4 to 1,4–4,1.
RED SHINER
Notropis lutrensis (Baird and Girard) .... Page 554

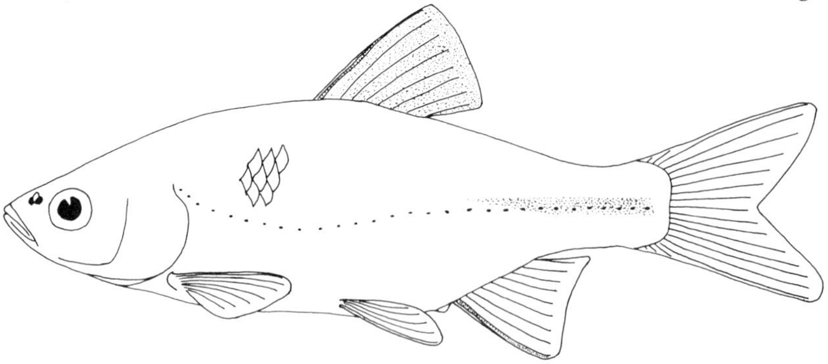

24b. Dorsal fin membranes unpigmented. Teeth 2,4–4,2 25

25a. Anterior dorsolateral scale count (from point below dorsal fin origin to head, along any row from third to sixth above lateral line) 18–24 (16–30). No dark stripes on back meeting in Vs posteriorly. Pigment on chin largely absent (a few chromatophores may be seen along edge of lower lip).
COMMON SHINER
Notropis cornutus (Mitchill) .... Page 518

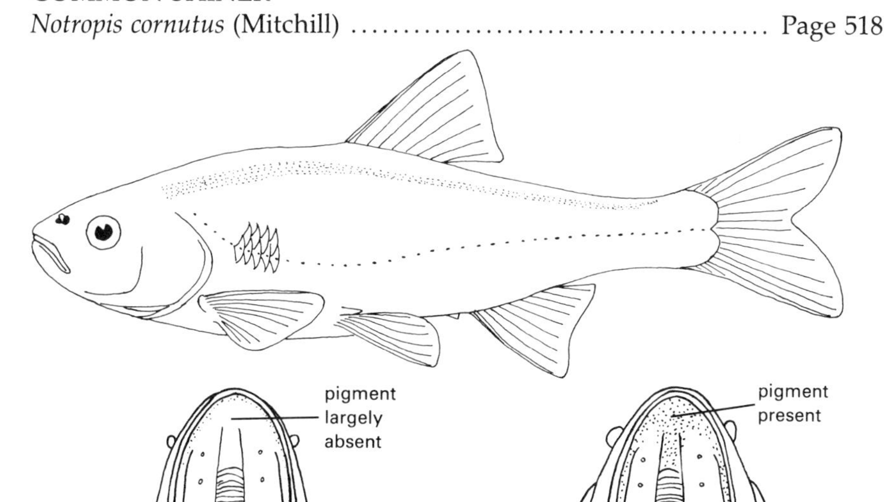

(common shiner) (striped shiner)

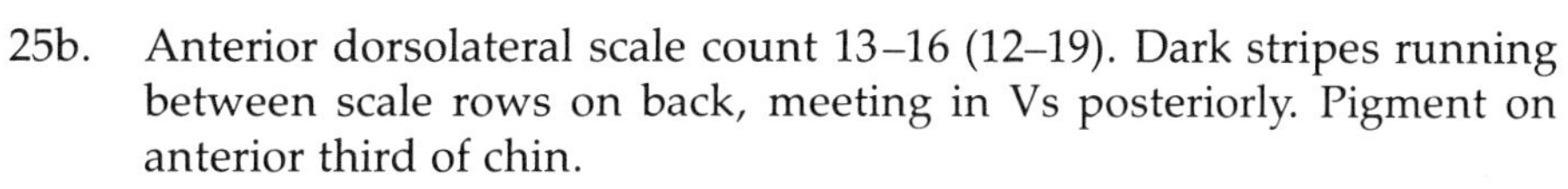

25b. Anterior dorsolateral scale count 13–16 (12–19). Dark stripes running between scale rows on back, meeting in Vs posteriorly. Pigment on anterior third of chin.
STRIPED SHINER
Notropis chrysocephalus (Rafinesque) .... Page 523

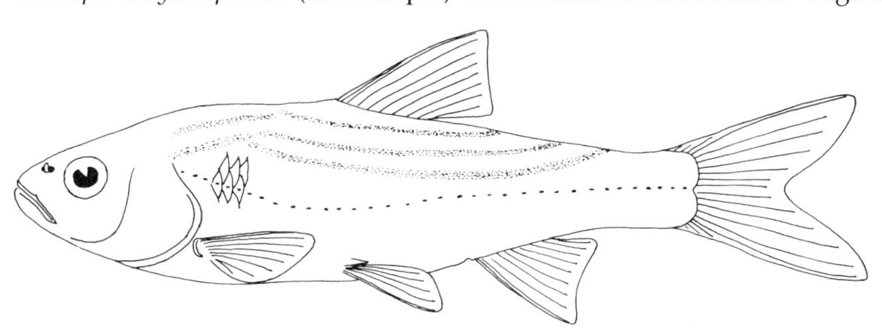

26a. Abdomen before vent with fleshy keel over which scales do not pass. Keel edged with half-scales. Teeth 5–5.
GOLDEN SHINER
Notemigonus crysoleucas (Mitchill) .... Page 432

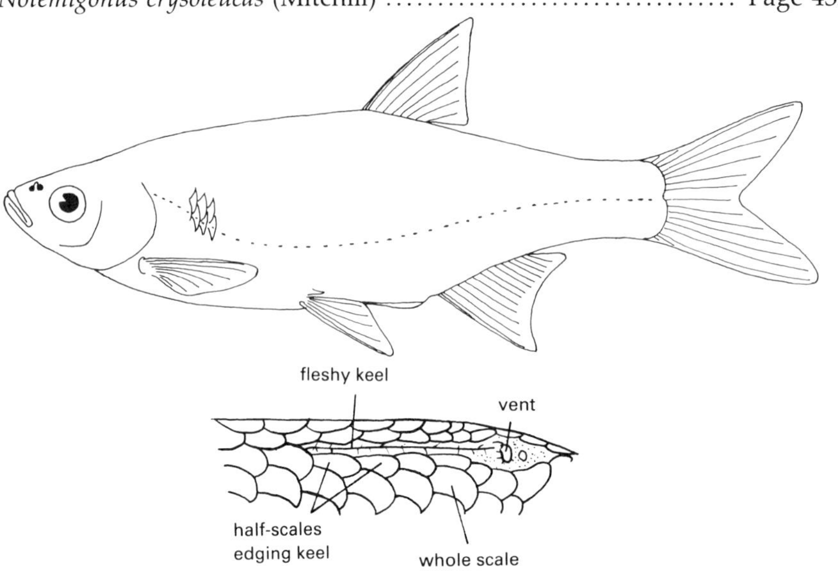

26b. Abdomen before vent rounded and scaled. Teeth 2,4–4,2 27

27a. Dorsal fin with black spot at its extreme base anteriorly. Lateral line scales 41–48.
REDFIN SHINER
Notropis umbratilis (Girard) .... Page 514

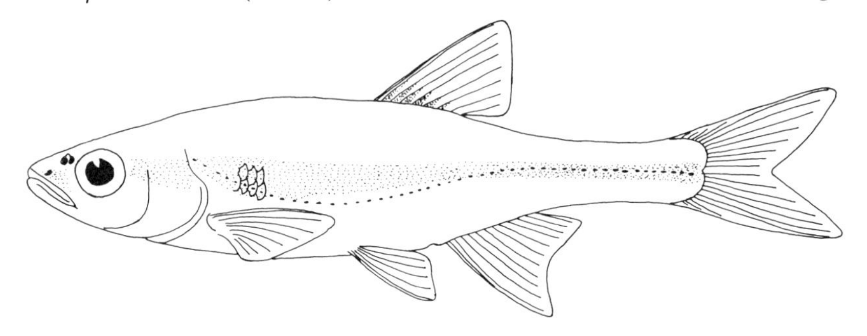

27b. Black spot at base of dorsal fin absent. Lateral line scales 36–41....... 28

28a. Head length in adult greater than ¼ SL. Snout elongated and sharp, its length greater than ⅔ distance from posterior margin of eye to posterior margin of head. Small chromatophores on chin usually confined to outside margin of chin.
ROSYFACE SHINER
Notropis rubellus (Agassiz) .... Page 510

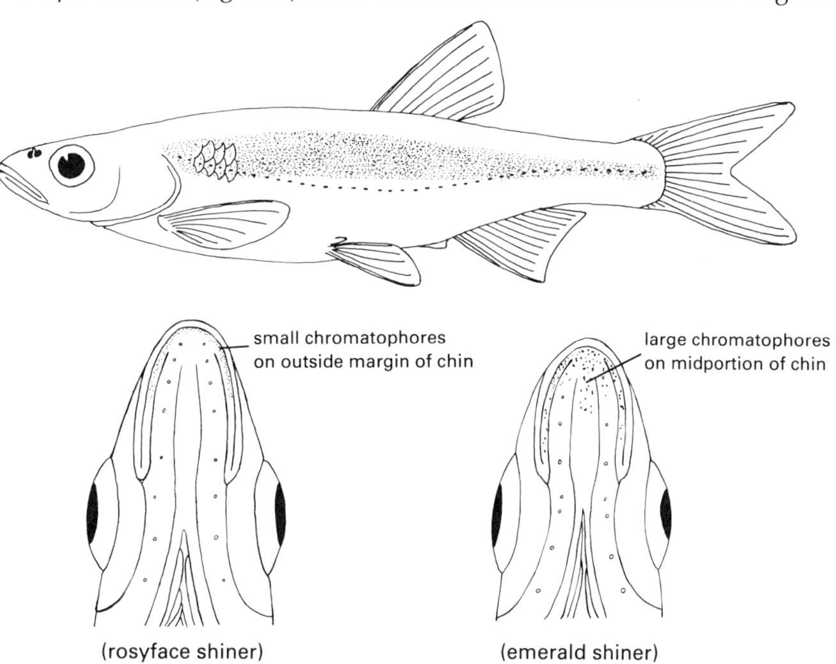

28b. Head length in adult less than ¼ SL. Snout short and blunt, its length less than ⅔ distance from posterior margin of eye to posterior margin of head. Large chromatophores on anterior half of chin, particularly on midportion.
EMERALD SHINER
Notropis atherinoides Rafinesque .... Page 505

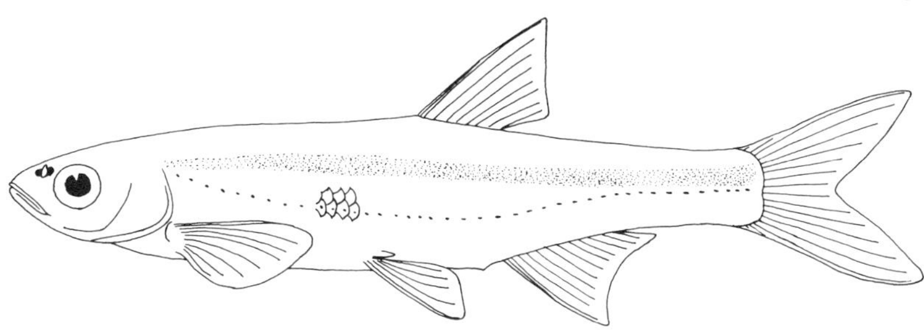

29a. Anal fin rays typically 7.. 30

29b. Anal fin rays typically 8.. 35

30a. Scales of back anterior to dorsal fin tightly crowded. Lateral scales 40 or more. Frequently a dark blotch on anterior membranes of dorsal fin near its base. First half-ray of dorsal fin separated from first full ray by membrane. Peritoneum silvery, blackish, or black. Teeth 4–4 .. 31

30b. Scales anterior to dorsal fin normal, not crowded. Lateral scales fewer than 40. Membranes of dorsal fin clear. First half-ray of dorsal fin closely attached to first full ray. Peritoneum silvery. Teeth in 1 or 2 rows...... 33

31a. Body deep, its depth into SL less than 4. Mouth almost vertical. Digestive tract long, 1.4–1.7 TL. Peritoneum black.
FATHEAD MINNOW
Pimephales promelas Rafinesque.................................... Page 600

31b. Body almost cylindrical, its depth into SL greater than 4. Mouth slightly oblique to almost horizontal. Digestive tract less than 1.3 TL. Peritoneum silvery or black... 32

32a. Snout protruding anterior to mouth. Mouth subterminal and almost horizontal. Body usually with distinct lateral stripe. Digestive tract moderately long, 1.0–1.2 TL. Peritoneum black.
BLUNTNOSE MINNOW
Pimephales notatus (Rafinesque) .... Page 595

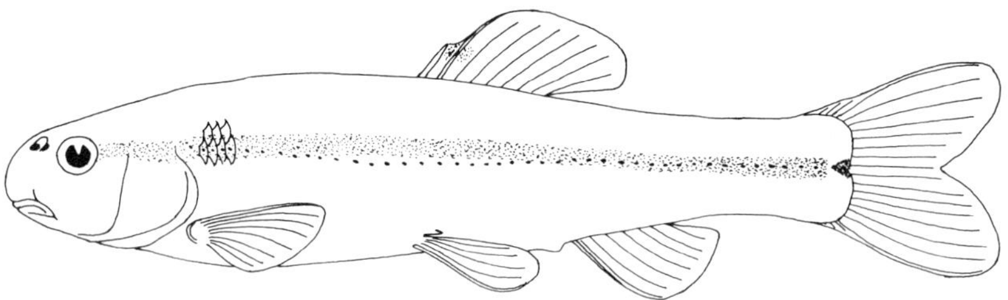

32b. Snout slightly protruding to even with upper lip. Mouth slightly subterminal to terminal and slightly oblique. Lateral stripe absent to faint. Digestive tract short, 0.6–0.7 TL. Peritoneum silvery.
BULLHEAD MINNOW
Pimephales vigilax (Baird and Girard) .... Page 591

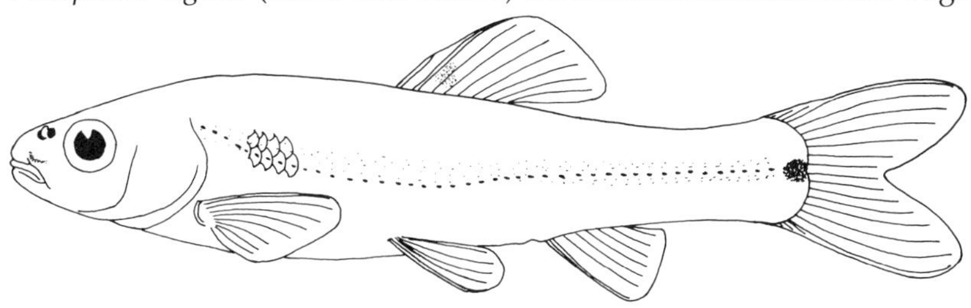

33a. Lateral stripe black, extending through eye and around upper and lower lips. Conspicuous black caudal spot. Breast naked. Teeth usually 2,4–4,2.
WEED SHINER
Notropis texanus (Girard)... Page 534

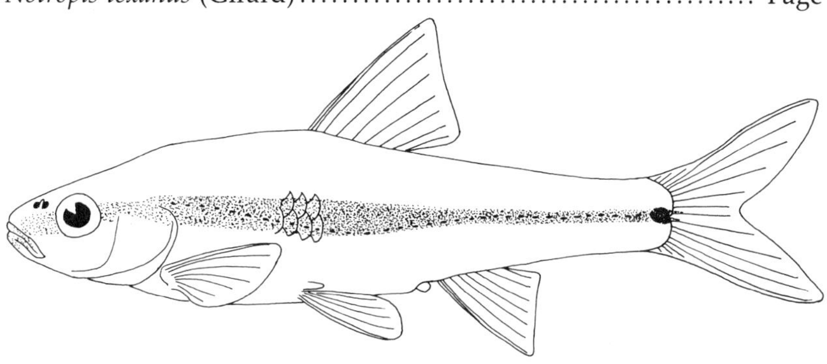

33b. Lateral stripe scarcely evident or absent. Caudal spot faint or absent. Breast scaled, at least in part 34

34a. Mid-dorsal stripe expanded in front of dorsal fin and interrupted at front of dorsal fin base. Pores of lateral line scales bounded above and below by paired dark chromatophores. Teeth 4–4.
SAND SHINER
Notropis stramineus (Cope) .... Page 562

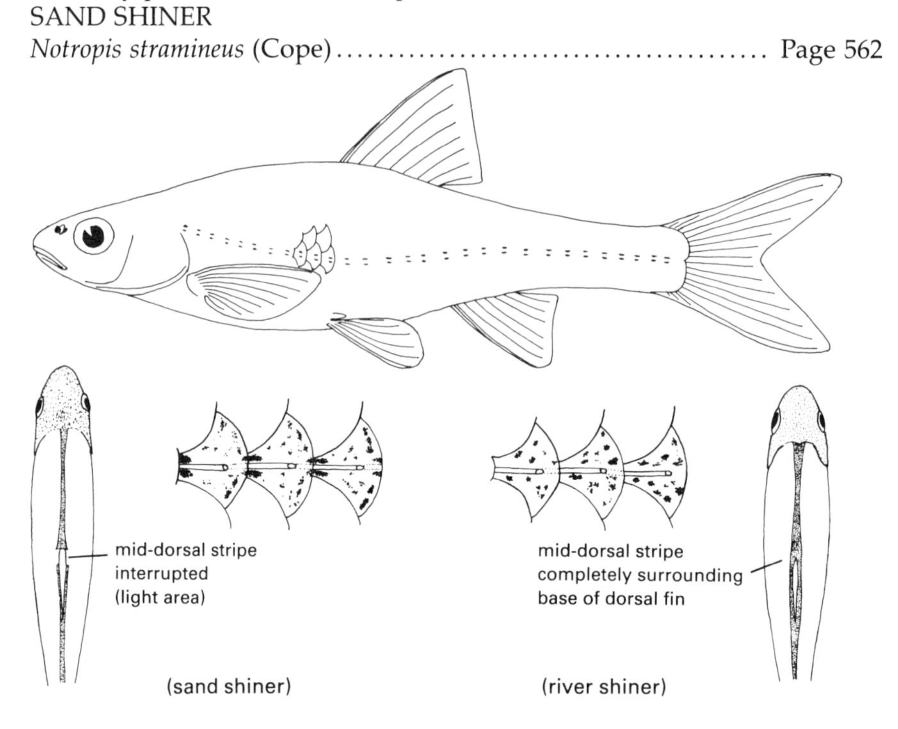

34b. Mid-dorsal stripe distinct and uniform in width, completely surrounding base of dorsal fin; stripe is not or is only slightly expanded immediately in front of dorsal fin origin. Pores of lateral line scales bounded irregularly by chromatophores or not at all. Teeth 2,4–4,2.
RIVER SHINER
Notropis blennius (Girard) .... Page 527

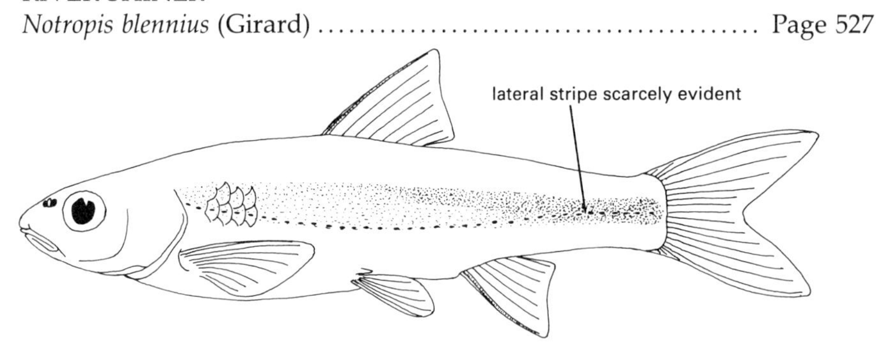

35a. Lateral scales 50 or more. (Either creek chub or pearl dace; see *Semotilus*, 14a and 15a.)

35b. Lateral scales fewer than 50 36

36a. Membranes of dorsal fin pigmented particularly between last 3 fin rays, or entirely pigmented 37

36b. Membranes of dorsal fin clear or otherwise pigmented................ 38

37a. Membranes of dorsal fin pigmented between last 3 fin rays; small young with at least a few chromatophores; in breeding males all membranes pigmented with last 3 especially black. Body depth into SL more than 3.5. Teeth 1,4–4,1.
SPOTFIN SHINER
Notropis spilopterus (Cope) .... Page 549

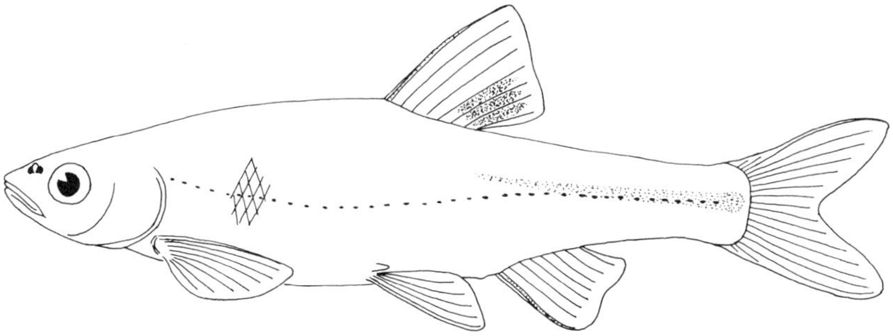

37b. Membranes of dorsal fin generally evenly pigmented. Body deep, its depth into SL usually 3.5 or less. Teeth 4–4 to 1,4–4,1.
RED SHINER
Notropis lutrensis (Baird and Girard) .... Page 554

38a. Prominent black spot (approximately diam of pupil of eye) at base of caudal fin (occasionally diffuse in Lake Michigan form). Teeth usually 2,4–4,2 (variable in outer row).
SPOTTAIL SHINER
Notropis hudsonius (Clinton) .... Page 540

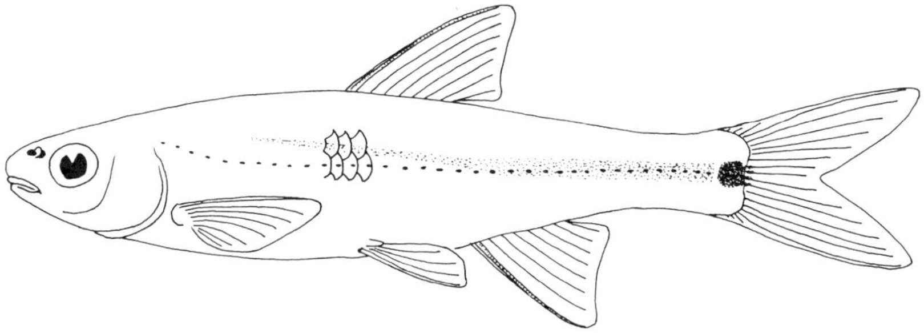

38b. Black spot at base of caudal fin absent or, if present, small............ 39

39a. Lateral stripe blackish (sometimes indistinct in life), continuing forward through eye and around muzzle 40

39b. Lateral stripe dusky or absent, usually not continuing forward through eye and around muzzle.. 44

40a. Black stripe continuing forward through eye primarily around tip of snout and to lesser degree upon upper lip, lower lip, and chin (as in blacknose shiner). Teeth 4–4... 41

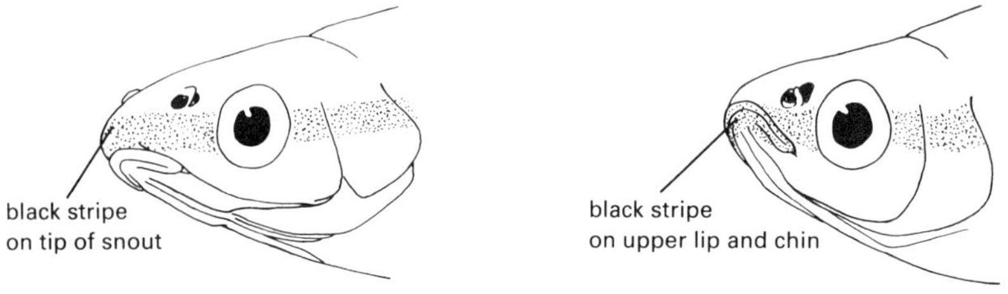

black stripe
on tip of snout

(blacknose shiner)

black stripe
on upper lip and chin

(blackchin shiner)

40b. Black stripe continuing forward through eye, onto upper lip, lower lip, and chin, scarcely if at all around tip of snout (as in blackchin shiner). Teeth in 1 or 2 rows... 42

41a. Lateral line scales with black crescent-shaped marks, the tips of which point backwards. Peritoneum silvery. Intestine S-shaped; when extended, reaching to caudal fin.
BLACKNOSE SHINER
Notropis heterolepis Eigenmann and Eigenmann .... Page 572

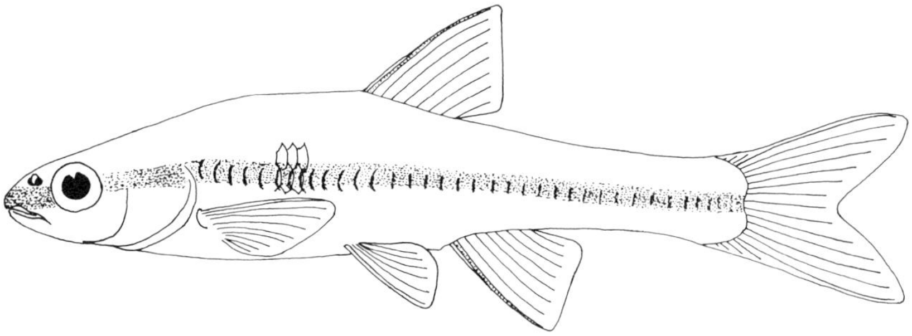

41b. Lateral line scales without crescent-shaped marks. Peritoneum black. Intestine much elongated and coiled; when extended, reaching to about twice TL.
OZARK MINNOW
Notropis nubilus (Forbes) .... Page 578

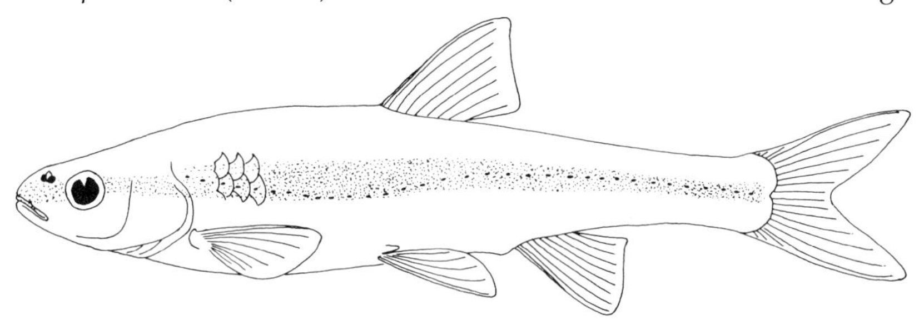

42a. Mouth vertical, about 80° with horizontal. Upper jaw extending only to below anterior nostril. Peritoneum dark brown to black. Teeth 4–4.
PUGNOSE SHINER
Notropis anogenus Forbes .... Page 558

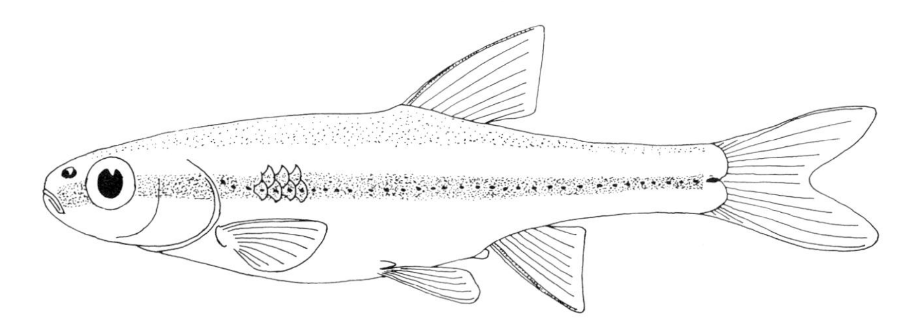

42b. Mouth oblique, about 45° with horizontal. Upper jaw extending at least to below posterior nostril. Peritoneum silvery (may have a few dark chromatophores) 43

43a. Breast scaled. Pigment absent on inner borders of jaws, on floor and roof of mouth, and on oral valve. Lateral stripe often producing a zigzag (scales of next row above lateral line with dark bars alternating with the black marks on lateral line scales). Teeth 1,4–4,1 or 4–4.
BLACKCHIN SHINER
Notropis heterodon (Cope) .... Page 537

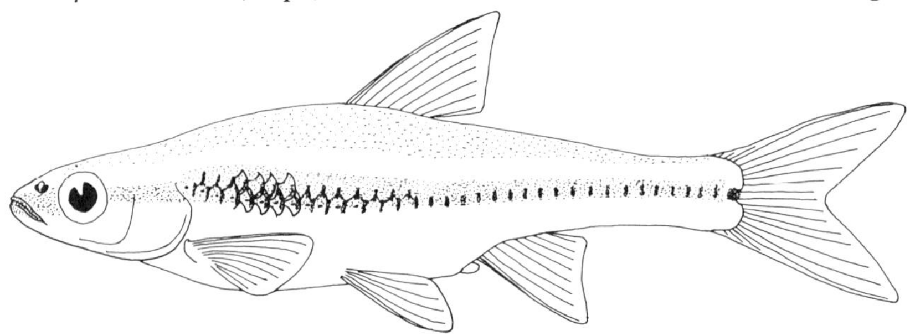

43b. Breast naked. Dark pigment conspicuous on inner borders of jaws, on floor and roof of mouth, and on oral valve. Solid dark lateral stripe 1 to 2 scales wide. Teeth 2,4–4,2.
IRONCOLOR SHINER
Notropis chalybaeus (Cope) .... Page 530

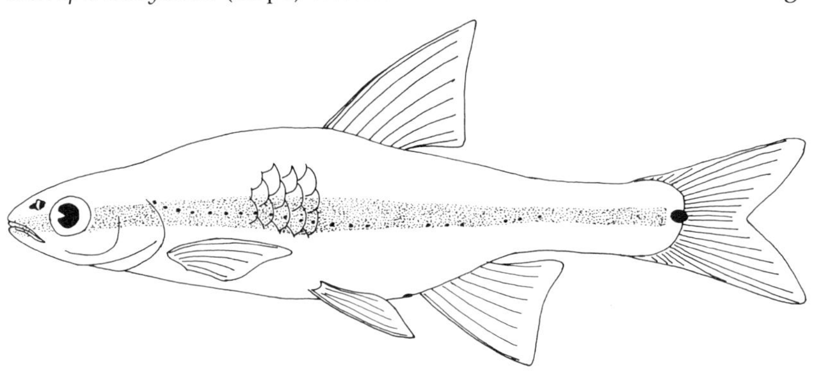

44a. Lateral length of upper jaw greater than eye diam. Teeth 1,4–4,1.
BIGMOUTH SHINER
Notropis dorsalis (Agassiz).. Page 545

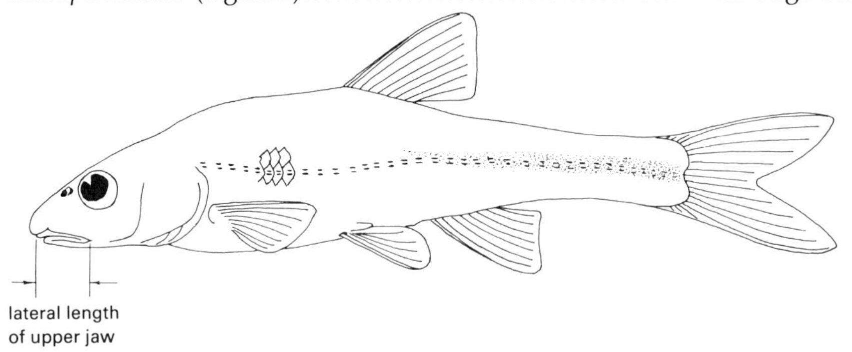

44b. Lateral length of upper jaw equal to or less than eye diam............ 45

45a. Belly blackish (i.e., dusky to black peritoneum visible through white belly tissue). Lateral line scales usually 36–39 46

45b. Belly white; peritoneum silvery (may contain some dark chromatophores). Lateral line scales usually 32–35 48

46a. Eye diam into head length 3.4–3.9. Teeth 4–4.
OZARK MINNOW (see illustration under 41b.)
Notropis nubilus (Forbes) .... Page 578

46b. Eye diam into head length 4.1–4.7 47

47a. In adult, eye diam equal to or greater than lateral distance from groove in corner of mouth (lip groove) to tip of snout. Relaxed dorsal fin rounded. Eye diam into head length 4.1–4.5. Lateral length of mouth into width of gape 2.3–2.7. Teeth 4–4 with oblique grinding surfaces.
BRASSY MINNOW
Hybognathus hankinsoni Hubbs .... Page 582

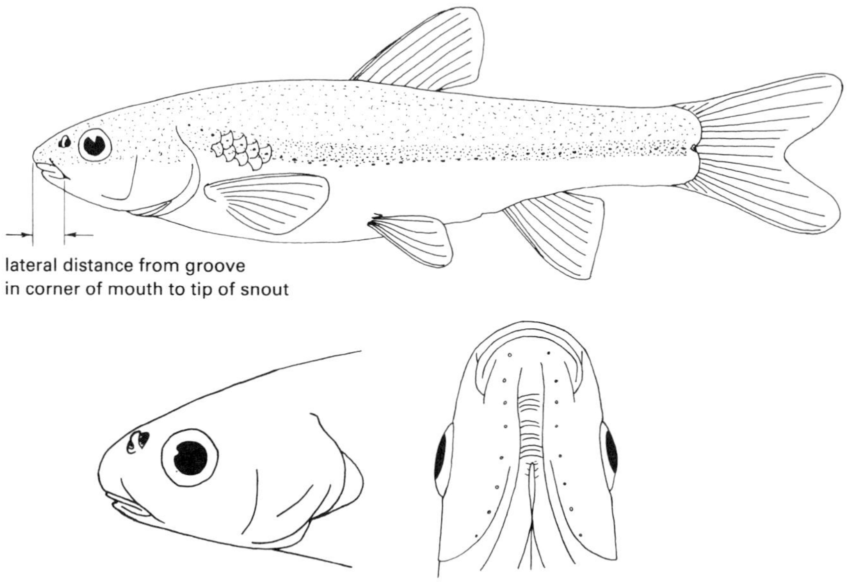

lateral distance from groove
in corner of mouth to tip of snout

47b. In adult, eye diam less than lateral distance from groove in corner of mouth (lip groove) to tip of snout. Relaxed dorsal fin pointed. Eye diam into head length 4.5–4.7. Lateral length of mouth into width of gape 2.0–2.3. Teeth 4–4 with oblique grinding surfaces.
MISSISSIPPI SILVERY MINNOW
Hybognathus nuchalis Agassiz .... Page 587

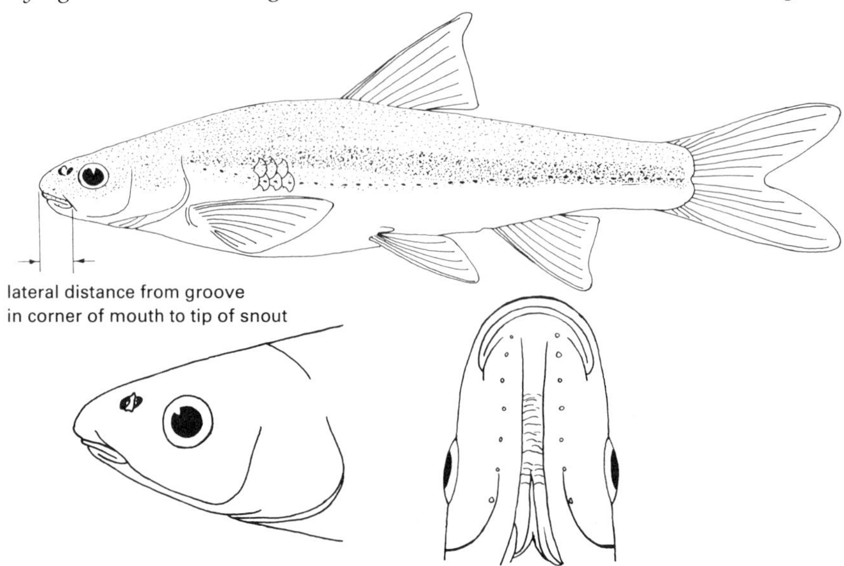

48a. Infraorbital canal short or undeveloped. Pigment absent on sides of body; chromatophores absent on lateral line scales. Teeth 4–4.
GHOST SHINER
Notropis buchanani Meek .... Page 570

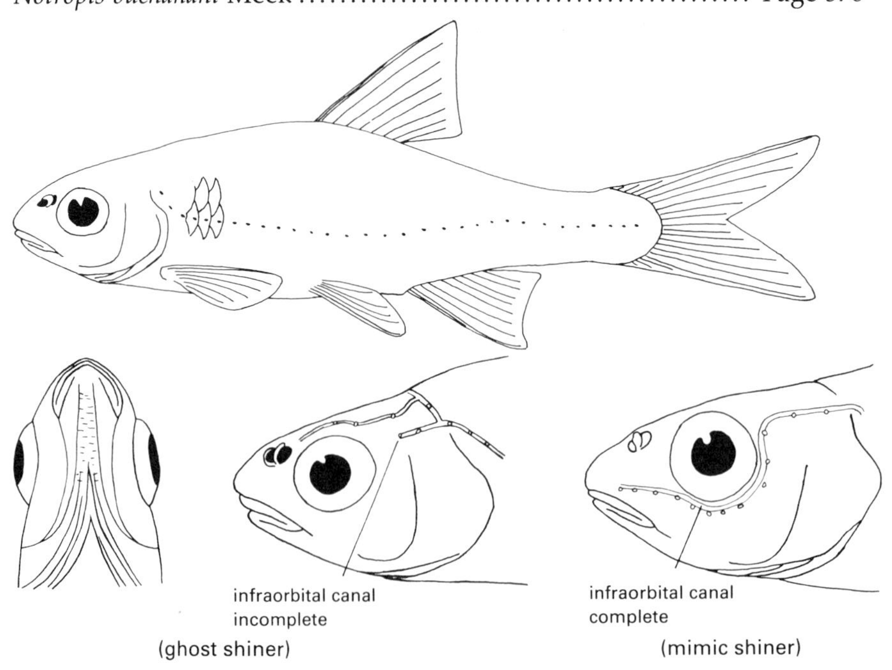

48b. Infraorbital canal entire, extending from lateral line canal along lower edge of eye toward nostril. Pigment present on side of body; chromatophores present on lateral line scales, and faint lateral stripe (often seen only under magnification in the pallid shiner).................... 49

49a. Mouth ventral, 25° or less with horizontal. Tip of snout in adult anterior to upper lip 0.4 mm or more. Teeth 1,4–4,1.
PALLID SHINER
Notropis amnis Hubbs and Greene .... Page 502

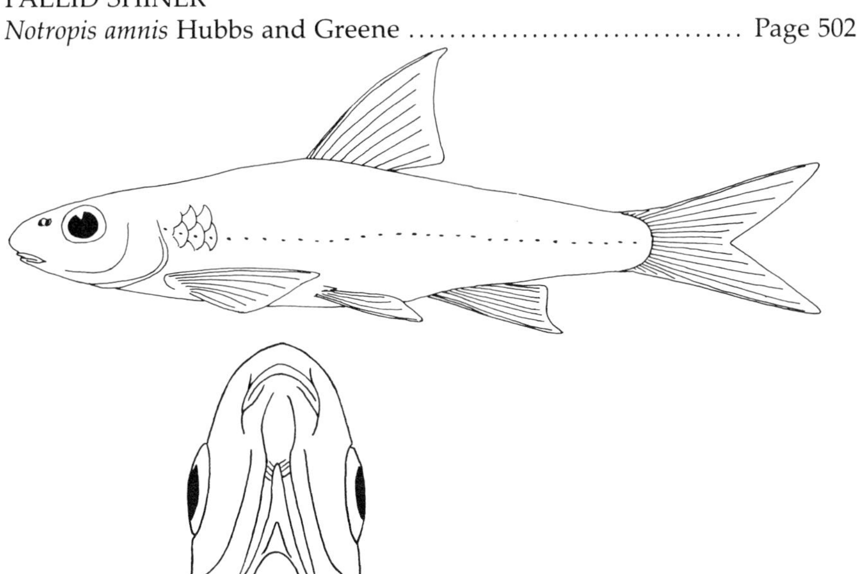

49b. Mouth oblique, 30° or more with horizontal. Tip of snout in adult scarcely anterior to upper lip. Teeth 4–4.
MIMIC SHINER
Notropis volucellus (Cope) .... Page 566

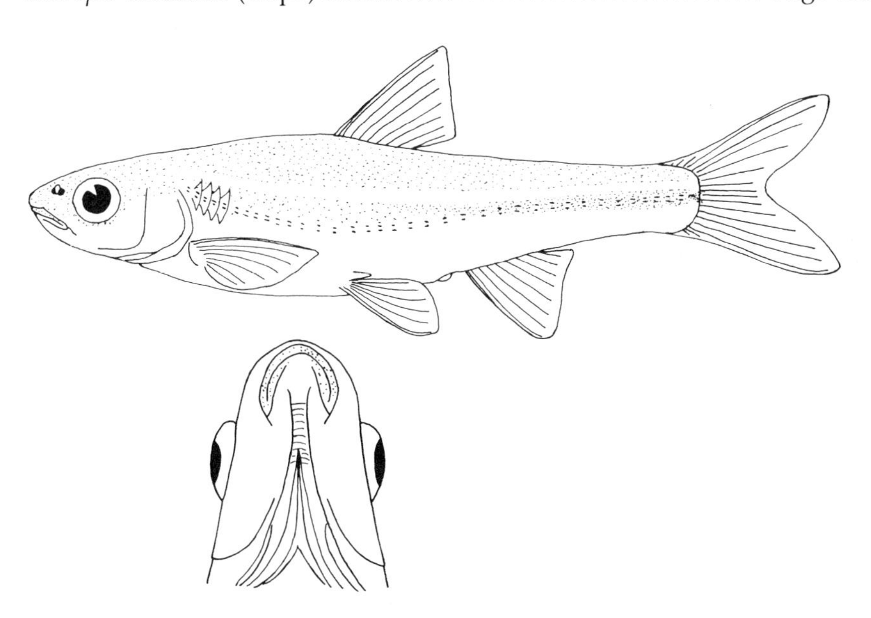

Key to the Suckers

1a. Dorsal fin with more than 20 rays; length of its base into SL less than 4.0 2

1b. Dorsal fin with 18 or fewer rays; length of its base into SL greater than 4.0 8

2a. Lateral line scales more than 50. Eye closer to posterior edge of opercular membrane than to tip of snout. Body depth into SL 4.0–4.4.
BLUE SUCKER
Cycleptus elongatus (Lesueur) .... Page 611

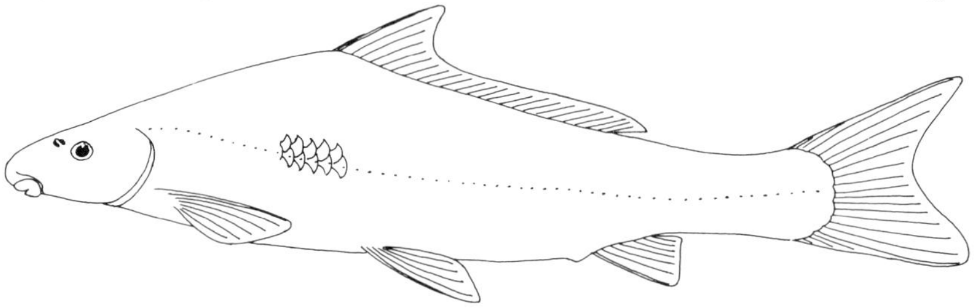

2b. Lateral line scales fewer than 50. Eye closer to tip of snout than to posterior edge of opercular membrane. Body depth into SL less than 4.0
Carpiodes spp. or *Ictiobus* spp. 3

3a. Subopercle broadest below middle. Distance A is about equal to B. Anterior fontanelle (locate by probing dorsal surface of head between nostrils) present. Lower fins cream-colored, colorless, or clear, almost lacking in pigment. Anterior lobe of dorsal fin essentially filamentous. Intestinal configuration of circular loops.
Carpiodes spp. (the carpsuckers) 4

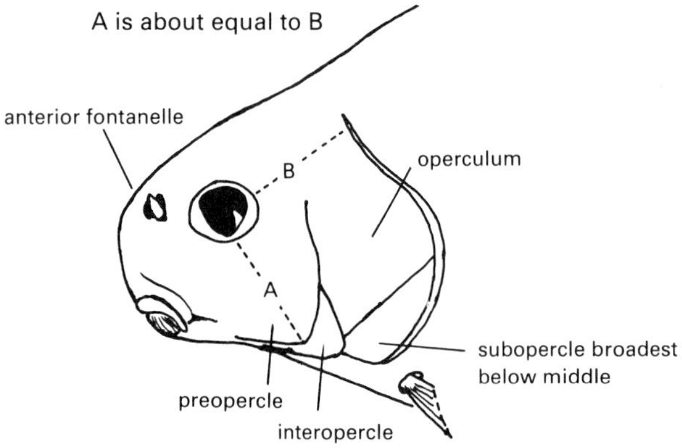

A is about equal to B
anterior fontanelle
B
operculum
A
subopercle broadest below middle
preopercle
interopercle

(river carpsucker)

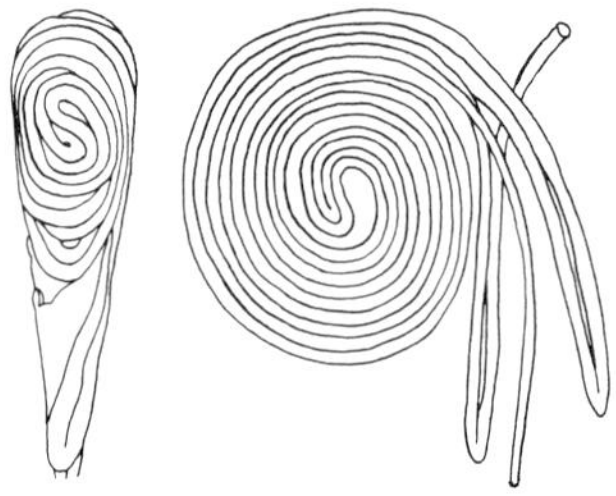

intestinal configuration (Berner 1948:141)

3b. Subopercle broadest at middle. Distance A is less than B. Anterior fontanelle much reduced or lacking. Lower fins darkly pigmented. Anterior lobe of dorsal fin rounded or pointed, but not filamentous. Intestinal configuration of elongated loops.
Ictiobus spp. (the buffaloes) 6

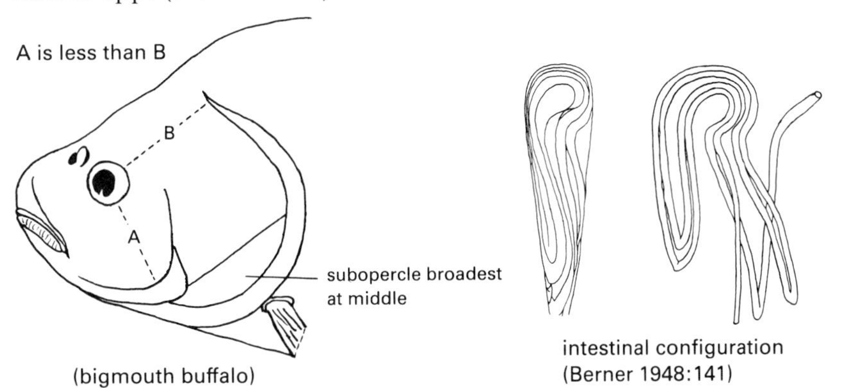

4a. No knob on tip of lower lip. Posterior edge of lower lip forming an acute angle. Tip of lower lip clearly in advance of anterior nostril. Snout in lateral view usually notched. Scales in lateral line usually 36–40. Body depth into SL 2.6–3.2. Head length into SL 3.2–3.8.
QUILLBACK
Carpiodes cyprinus (Lesueur)....................................... Page 630

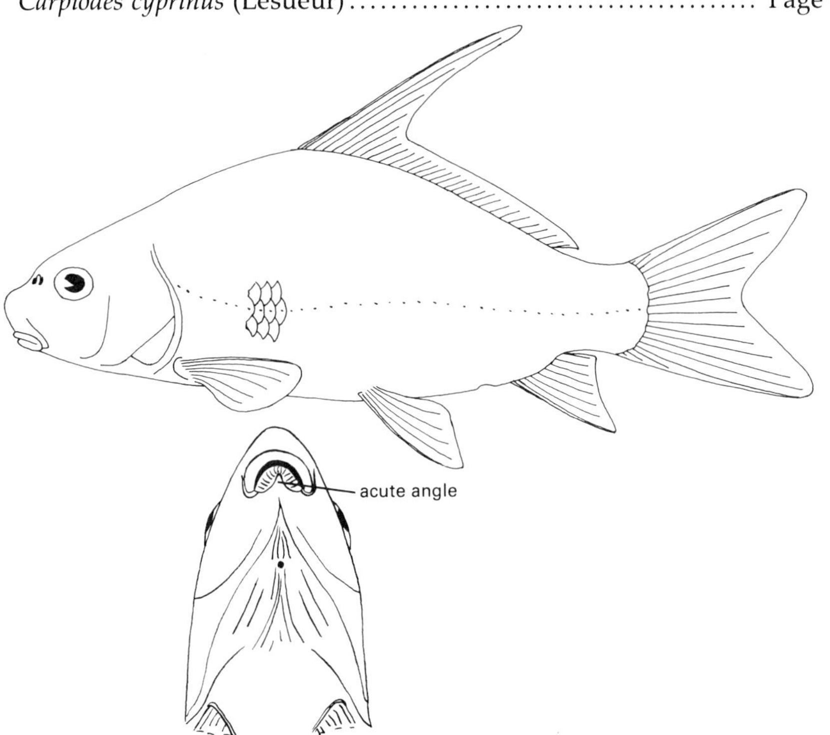

4b. Light knob on tip of lower lip. Posterior edge of lower lip usually forming an obtuse angle. Tip of lower lip scarcely or not at all in advance of anterior nostril. Snout in lateral view usually rounded and not notched. Scales in lateral line usually 33–37. Body depth into SL 2.2–3.1. Head length into SL 3.5–4.3.................................. 5

5a. Body depth into SL 2.5–3.1. Length of anterior rays of depressed dorsal fin usually less than ⅔ length of dorsal fin base.
RIVER CARPSUCKER
Carpiodes carpio (Rafinesque) .... Page 634

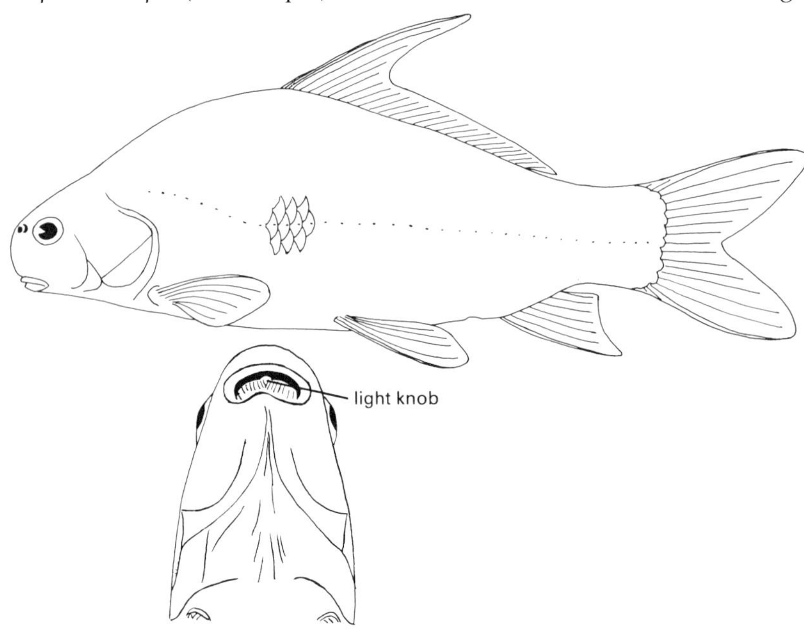

5b. Body depth into SL 2.2–2.6. Length of anterior rays of depressed dorsal fin usually greater than length of dorsal fin base.
HIGHFIN CARPSUCKER
Carpiodes velifer (Rafinesque) .... Page 638

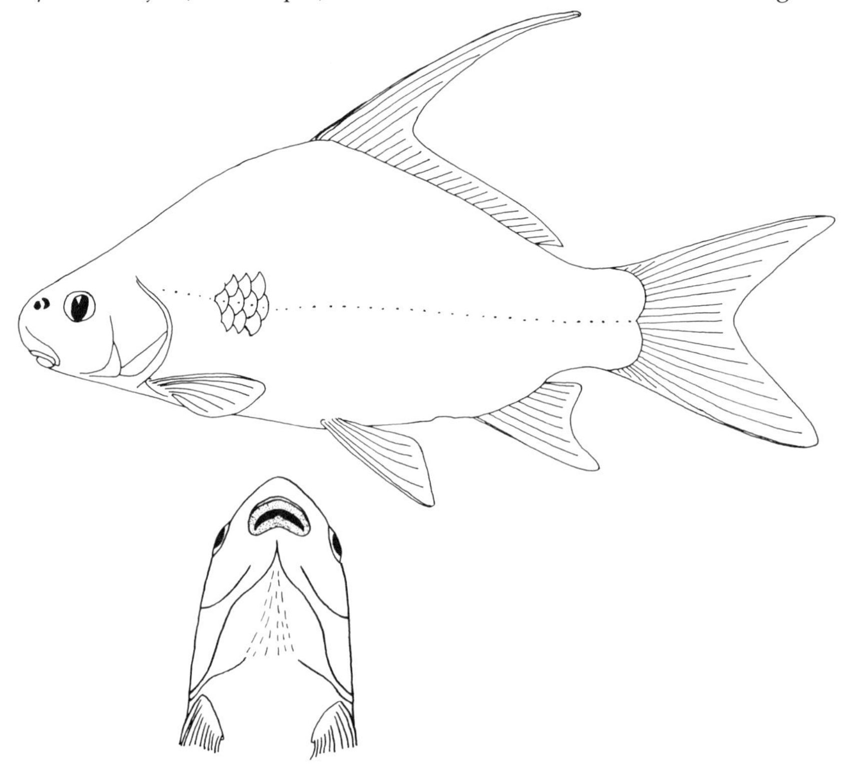

6a. Mouth large, terminal, and extremely oblique. Tip of upper lip about level with lower margin of eye. Lips thin and shallowly grooved. Length of upper jaw nearly equal to snout length.
BIGMOUTH BUFFALO
Ictiobus cyprinellus (Valenciennes) .... Page 615

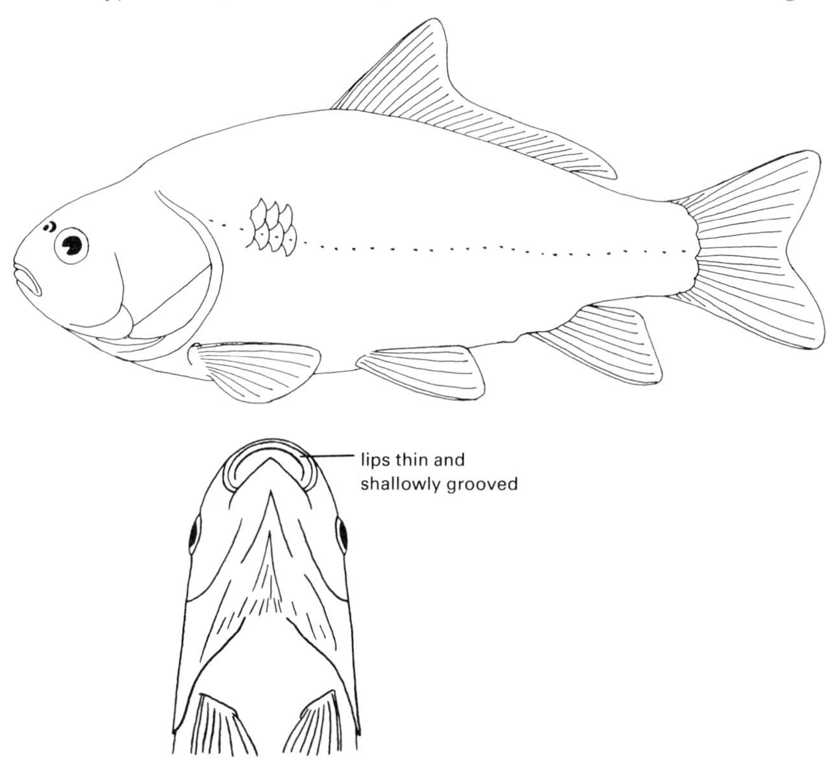

6b. Mouth smaller, subterminal, and almost horizontal. Tip of upper lip at a level far below lower margin of eye. Lips thick and deeply grooved. Length of upper jaw much less than snout length 7

7a. Body depth into SL 2.4–2.8. Back highly arched and compressed into mid-dorsal ridge (appearing humpbacked in combination with small head). Head small, its length into SL 3.4–4.1. Length of anterior rays of dorsal fin into dorsal fin base about 1.6. Length of upper jaw into snout length 1.5–2.0. Head thickness at opercular bulge into SL 5.2–6.1.
SMALLMOUTH BUFFALO
Ictiobus bubalus (Rafinesque) .... Page 625

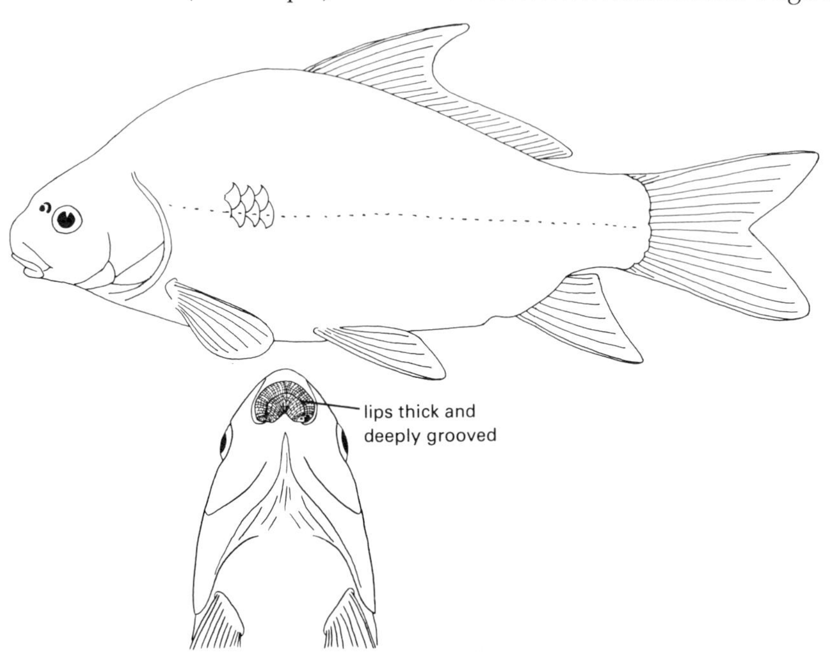

7b. Body depth into SL 2.9–3.5. Back not highly arched or ridged but rounded over top from side to side. Head large, its length into SL 2.9–3.8. Length of anterior rays of dorsal fin into dorsal fin base 2.2–2.5. Length of upper jaw into snout length 2.0–2.5. Head thickness at opercular bulge into SL 4.7–5.4.
BLACK BUFFALO
Ictiobus niger (Rafinesque) .... Page 621

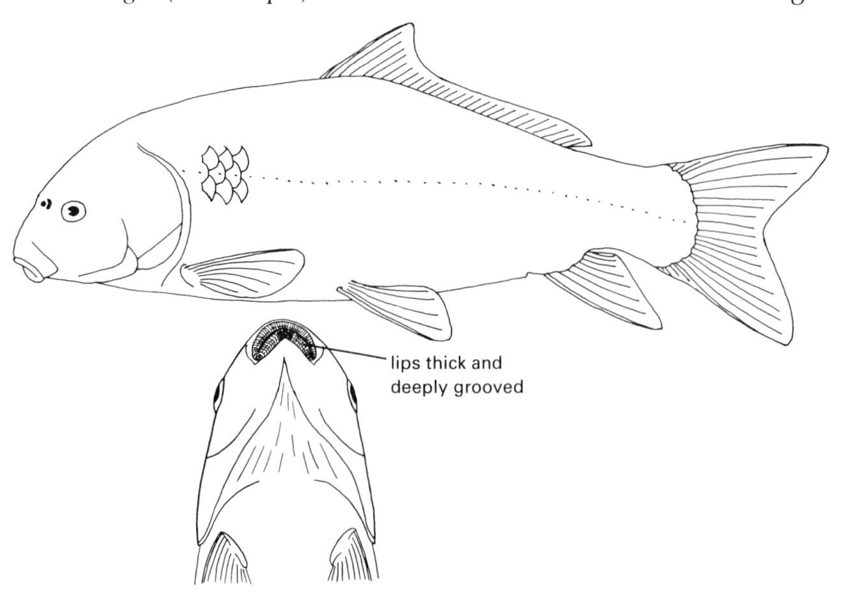

8a. Lateral line incomplete (developed anteriorly in adult spotted sucker) or absent 9

8b. Lateral line complete and well developed................................ 11

9a. Lateral series scales 42–46. Distinct blackish spot present on each scale base, resulting in series of longitudinal stripes which are most distinct (except in the smallest young where the faint spots and stripes may be restricted to region above anal fin base). Body depth into SL usually greater than 4.0. Lateral line somewhat developed anteriorly in adults.
SPOTTED SUCKER
Minytrema melanops (Rafinesque) .... Page 642

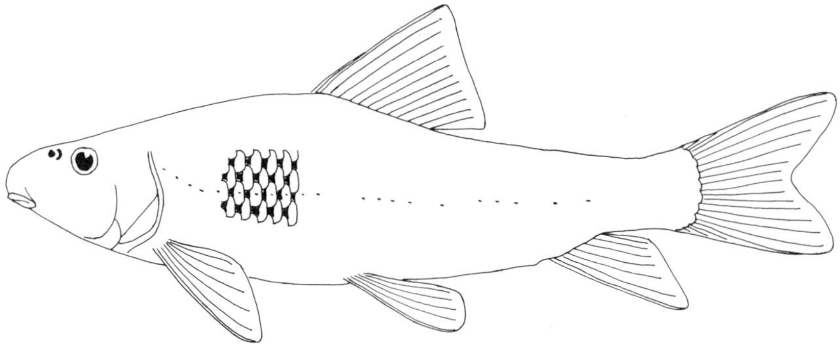

9b. Lateral series scales 35–41 (33–45). Blackish spot absent on each scale base. Body depth into SL usually less than 3.5. Lateral line lacking at all ages.
Erimyzon spp. (the chubsuckers).. 10

10a. Dorsal rays 11 or 12 (10–13). Lateral series scales 35–37 (33–40). Body depth into SL usually 3.3 or less. Unbroken, blackish lateral stripe very distinct in young, least distinct in large adults.
LAKE CHUBSUCKER
Erimyzon sucetta (Lacepède) .... Page 646

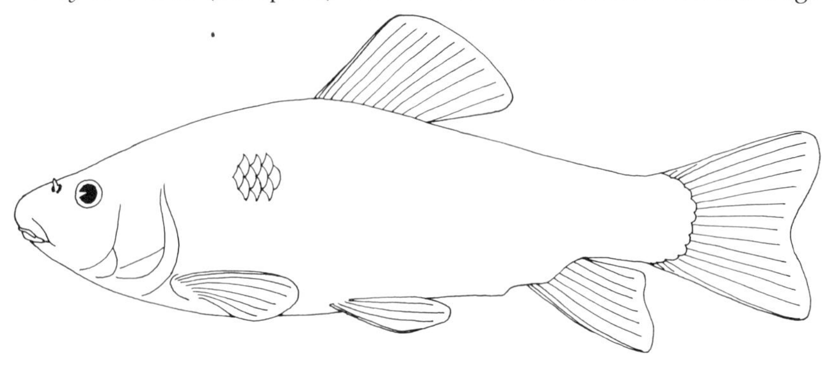

10b. Dorsal rays 9 or 10 (8–11). Lateral series scales 39–41 (37–45). Body depth into SL usually 3.3 or more. Dusky lateral stripe broken into series of more or less confluent blotches (these blotches sometimes very faint or absent in large adults).
CREEK CHUBSUCKER
Erimyzon oblongus (Mitchill) .... Page 650

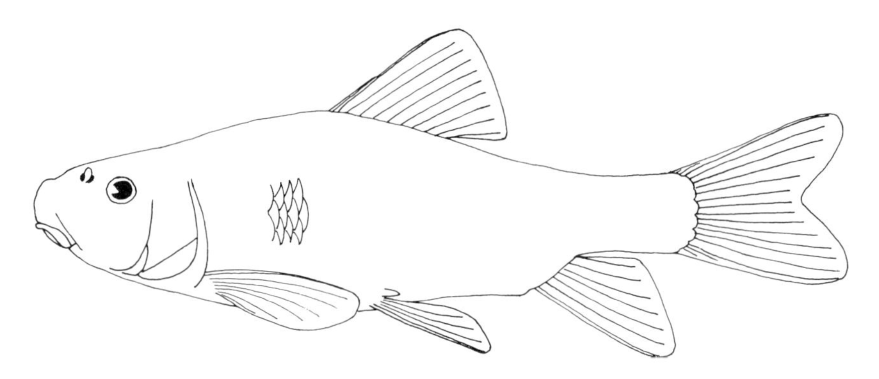

11a. Lateral line scales 55 or more.
Catostomus spp. 12

11b. Lateral line scales fewer than 54 13

12a. Lateral line scales 55–85. Snout short, scarcely protruding beyond upper lip.
WHITE SUCKER
Catostomus commersoni (Lacepède) .... Page 682

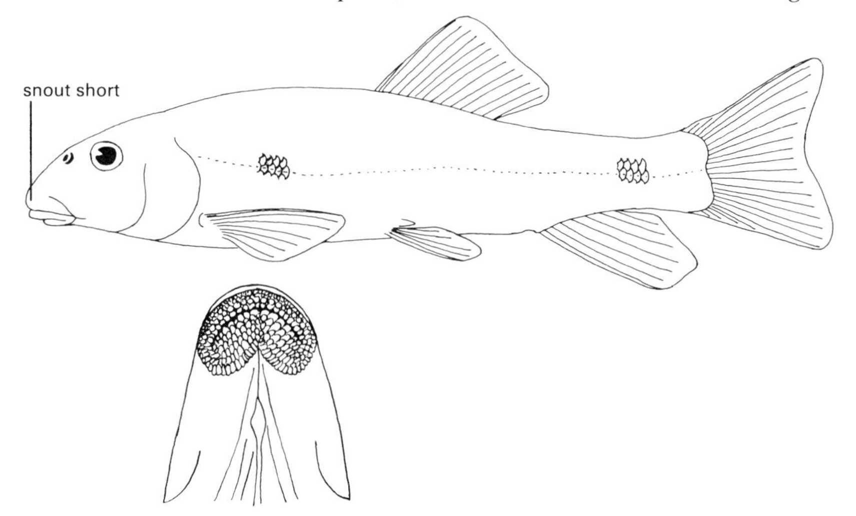

12b. Lateral line scales more than 90. Snout elongated, protruding well beyond upper lip.
LONGNOSE SUCKER
Catostomus catostomus (Forster) .... Page 688

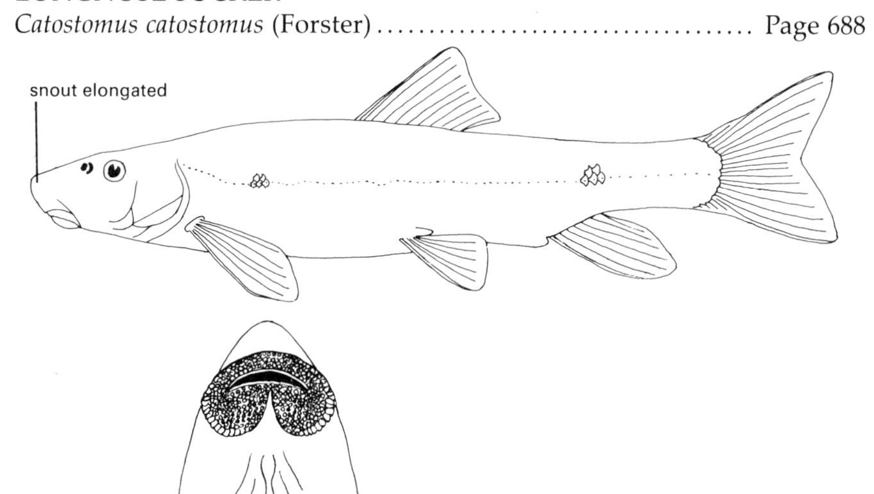

13a. Top of head between eyes concave. Body with 5 (4–6) dark, usually prominent oblique bars. Lips heavily papillose.
NORTHERN HOG SUCKER
Hypentelium nigricans (Lesueur) .... Page 678

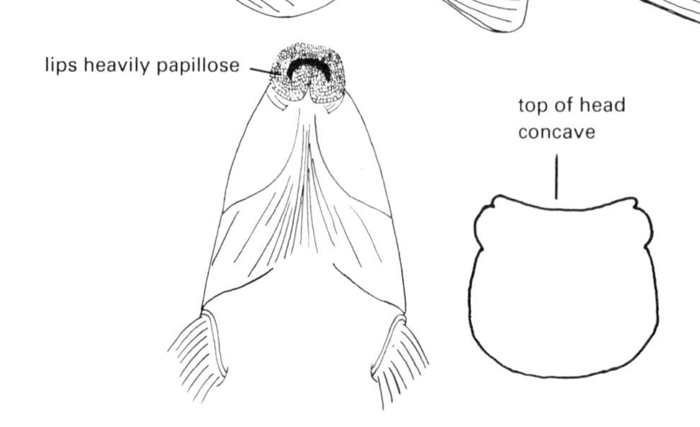

13b. Top of head between eyes usually convex. Body not marked with dark oblique bars. Lips primarily plicate, but may be papillose posteriorly and in corners.
Moxostoma spp (the redhorses)... 14

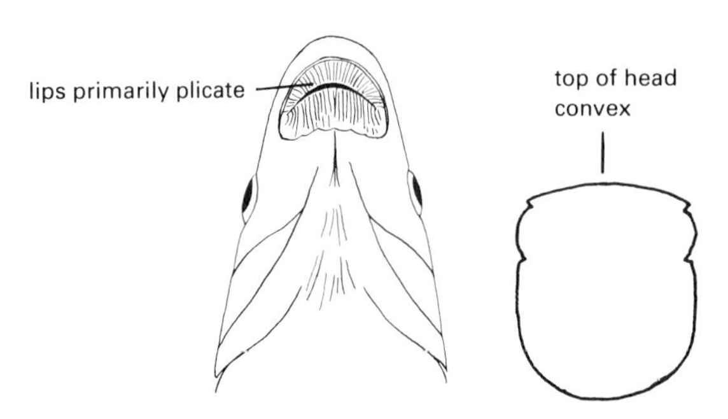

14a. Body scales, principally above lateral line, with distinct, dark spots at their bases. Tail always pink, red, or carmine in life; color soon fades in preserved specimens.. 15

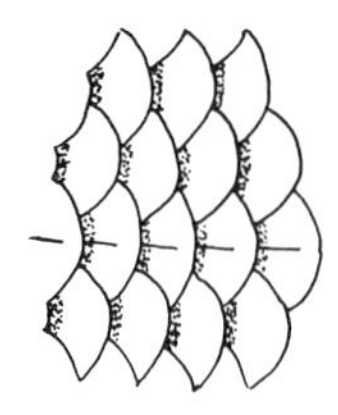

14b. Body scales without dark spots at their bases. Tail always slate-colored in life 17

15a. Scales around caudal peduncle 16 (7 above and 7 below the 2 lateral lines). Lower lip plicate with few papillae at corners. Dorsal fin slightly concave in young to convex in adults. Pharyngeal teeth heavy, comblike.
GREATER REDHORSE
Moxostoma valenciennesi Jordan .... Page 670

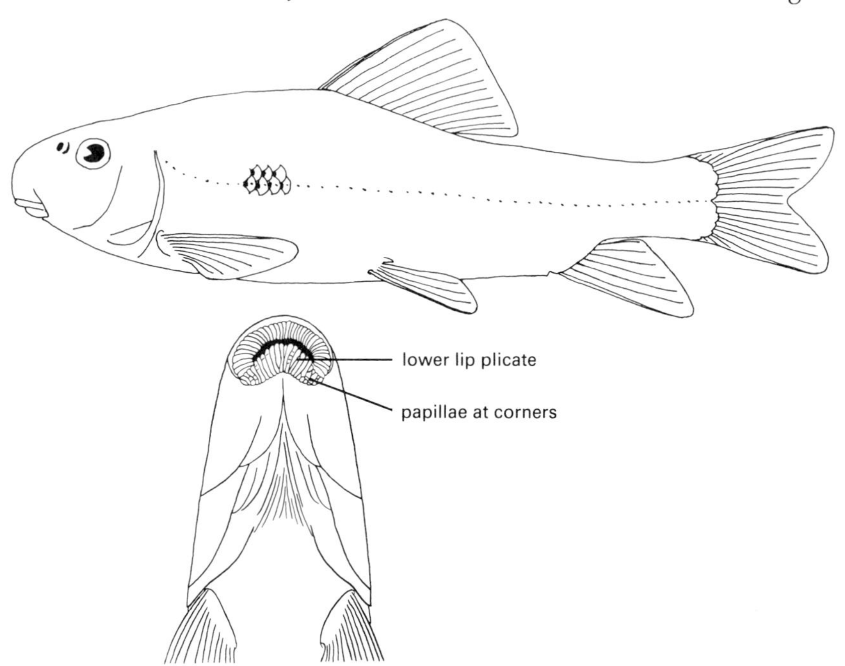

15b. Scales around caudal peduncle 12 (5 above and 5 below the 2 lateral lines). Lower lip either entirely plicate or partially papillose, especially along posterior half. Dorsal fin falcate to straight. Pharyngeal teeth thin, comblike, or thick, molarlike....................................... 16

16a. Head small and short, its length into SL usually 4.3–5.4 in yearlings and adults, 3.5–4.0 in young less than 76 mm (3 in) TL. Mouth small. Folds of lower lip transversely divided into large papillae; lower lip appearing swollen; posterior edge forming a straight line, rarely an obtuse angle. Pharyngeal teeth about 53 per arch, thin and comblike. Dorsal fin falcate.
SHORTHEAD REDHORSE
Moxostoma macrolepidotum (Lesueur) .... Page 665

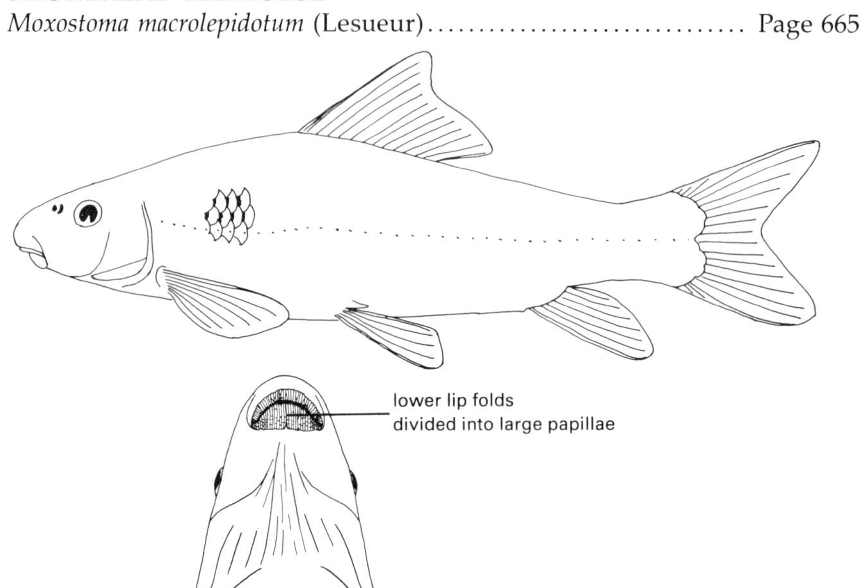

16b. Head bulky and long, its length into SL usually less than 4.3 in yearlings and adults, 3.0–3.8 in young less than 76 mm (3 in) TL. Mouth large. Folds of lower lip almost always smooth; papillae absent; lower halves nearly straight along posterior margin, which may be weakly scalloped. Pharyngeal teeth 33–45 per arch, large and molarlike. Dorsal fin straight or slightly concave in large young and adults.
RIVER REDHORSE
Moxostoma carinatum (Cope) .... Page 674

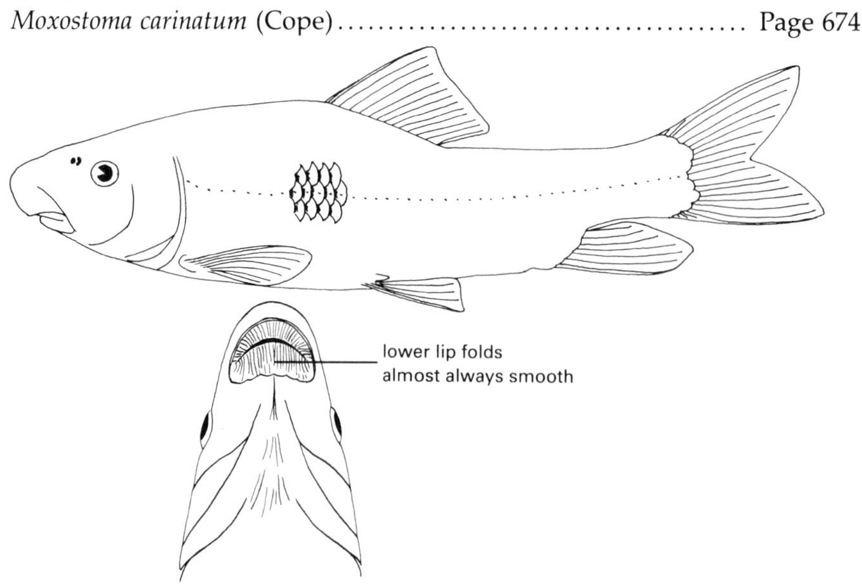

17a. Dorsal fin rays 15 (14–17). Length of dorsal fin base equal or almost equal to distance from back of head to dorsal fin origin. Lower lip folds partly or entirely dissected into fine, irregularly shaped papillae; lower lip halves forming an angle of about 90°. Dorsal fin slightly concave to convex.
SILVER REDHORSE
Moxostoma anisurum (Rafinesque) .... Page 661

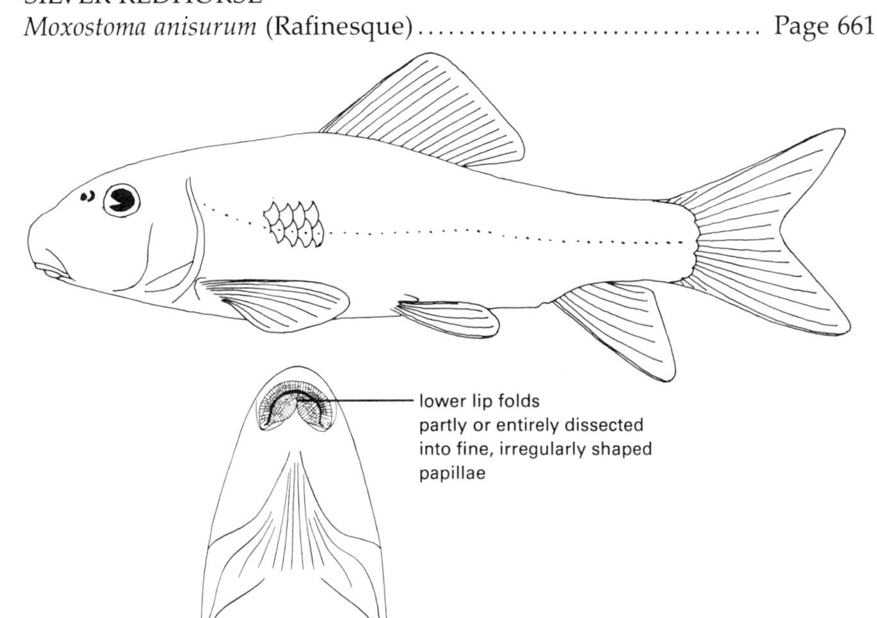

17b. Dorsal fin rays 12 or 13 (10–15). Length of dorsal fin base ⅔–¾ the distance from back of head to dorsal fin origin. Lower lip folds not dissected into papillae; lower lip halves in an almost straight line or broad obtuse angle, usually over 100°. Dorsal fin slightly falcate 18

18a. Lateral line scales 40–42 (37–45). Rays of pelvic fins usually 9, rarely 8 or 10. Least depth of caudal peduncle into its length usually less than 1.6. Snout blunt to rounded but not overhanging mouth. Head length into SL 3.9–4.3.
GOLDEN REDHORSE
Moxostoma erythrurum (Rafinesque) .... Page 657

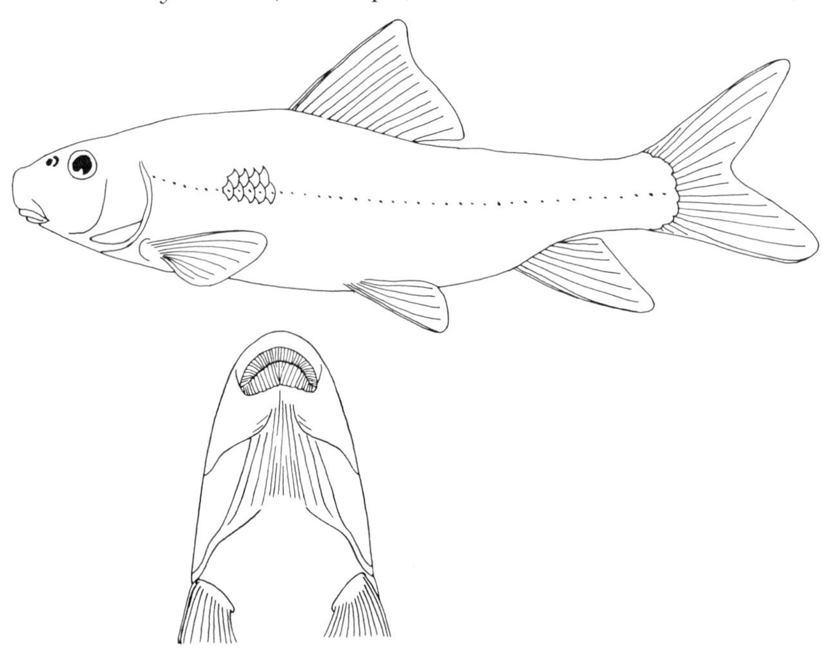

18b. Lateral line scales 44–47 (43–51). Rays of 1 or both pelvic fins usually 10 (8–11). Least depth of caudal peduncle into its length greater than 1.7. Snout rounded and swollen, slightly overhanging mouth ventrally. Head length into SL 4.1–4.8.
BLACK REDHORSE
Moxostoma duquesnei (Lesueur) .... Page 653

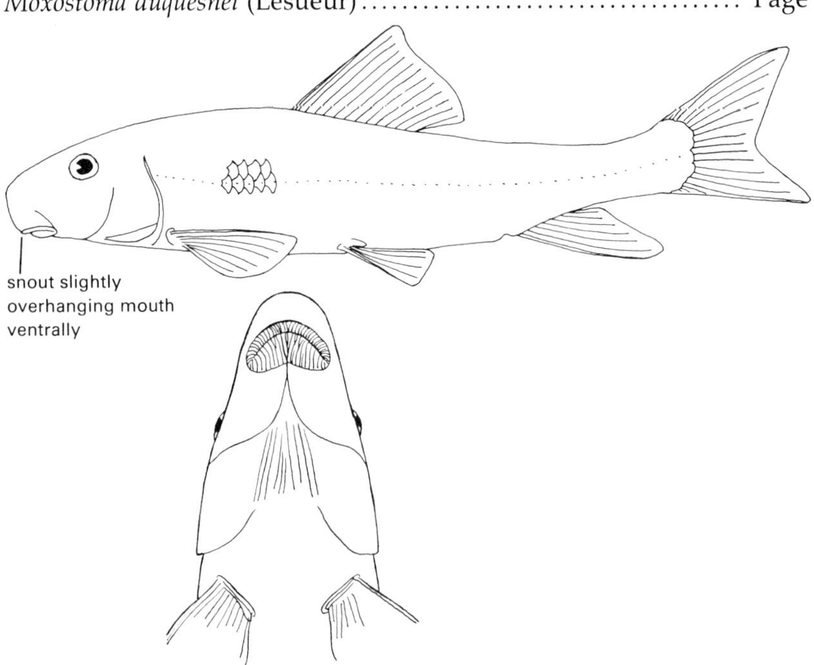

Key to the Bullhead Catfishes

1a. Adipose fin with its posterior margin flaplike and free, not fused to back or to caudal fin posteriorly 2

1b. Adipose fin with its posterior margin fused to back and to caudal fin, and separated from caudal fin by not more than an incomplete notch 7

2a. Caudal fin deeply forked 3

2b. Caudal fin not deeply forked, its rear margin rounded, straight, or with a slight notch 4

3a. Outer margin of anal fin rounded; anal fin rays 24–27 including rudimentaries. Body with dark spots except in large adults. Swim bladder of paired lateral chambers, no posterior chamber.
CHANNEL CATFISH
Ictalurus punctatus (Rafinesque) .... Page 712

3b. Outer margin of anal fin straight, anal fin rays 30–36 including rudimentaries. Body without dark spots. Swim bladder with paired lateral chambers and a posterior chamber.
BLUE CATFISH
Ictalurus furcatus (Lesueur) (Not in Wisconsin. See page 694.)

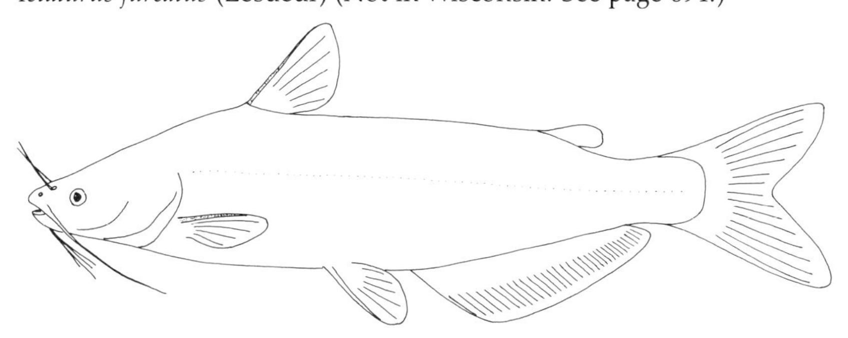

4a. Lower jaw protruding beyond upper jaw. Tooth patch on upper jaw with elongate lateral backward extensions. Length of anal fin base (A) less than distance from back of eye to rear margin of operculum (B). Pectoral fin spine strongly toothed along both anterior (teeth pointing toward base) and posterior (teeth pointing toward tip) edges.
FLATHEAD CATFISH
Pylodictis olivaris (Rafinesque) .... Page 728

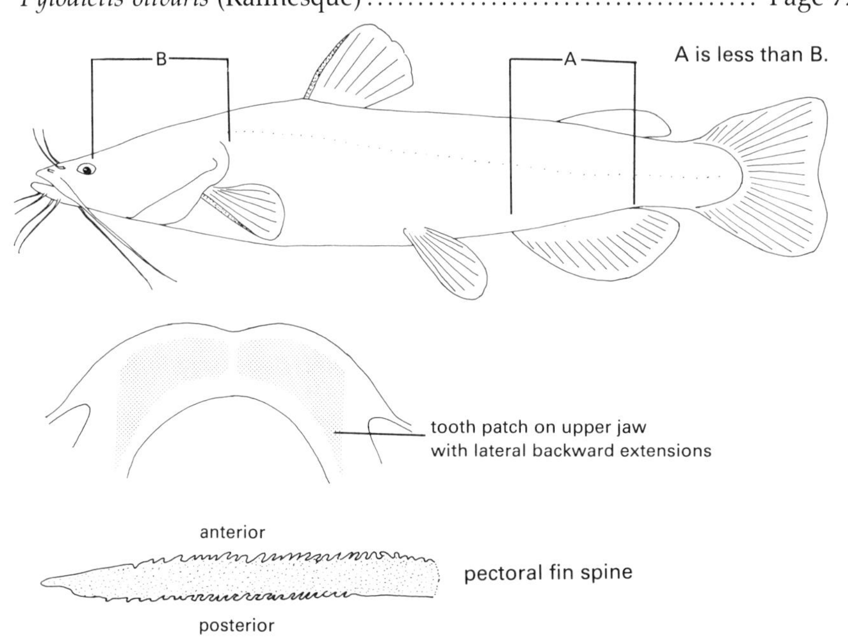

4b. Upper jaw extending beyond lower jaw. Tooth patch on upper jaw without lateral backward extensions. Length of anal fin base (A) greater than distance from back of eye to rear margin of operculum (B) (see illustration under 5a). Pectoral fin spine slightly rough to strongly toothed along posterior edge; along anterior edge weakly notched near tip 5

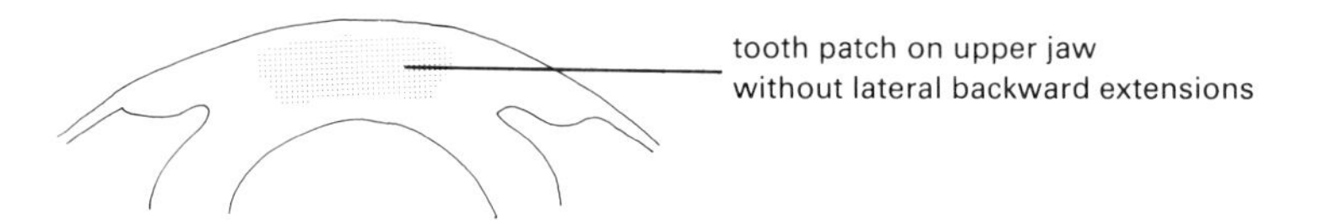

5a. Anal fin rays 24–27 including rudimentaries. Chin barbels whitish. Caudal fin rounded.
YELLOW BULLHEAD
Ictalurus natalis (Lesueur) .... Page 708

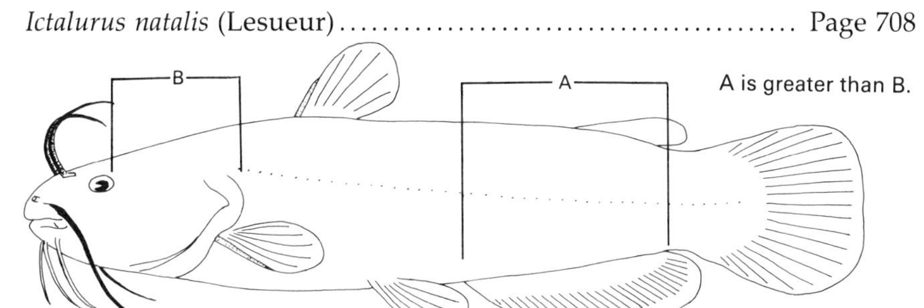

5b. Anal fin rays 15–24 including rudimentaries. Chin barbels gray to black. Caudal fin squarish and slightly notched 6

6a. Pectoral fin spine toothless along posterior edge or with irregular or poorly developed teeth. Side not mottled. Interradial membranes of fins jet-black. Adults with whitish bar at caudal fin base. Anal fin rays 15–21 including rudimentaries.
BLACK BULLHEAD
Ictalurus melas (Rafinesque) .... Page 697

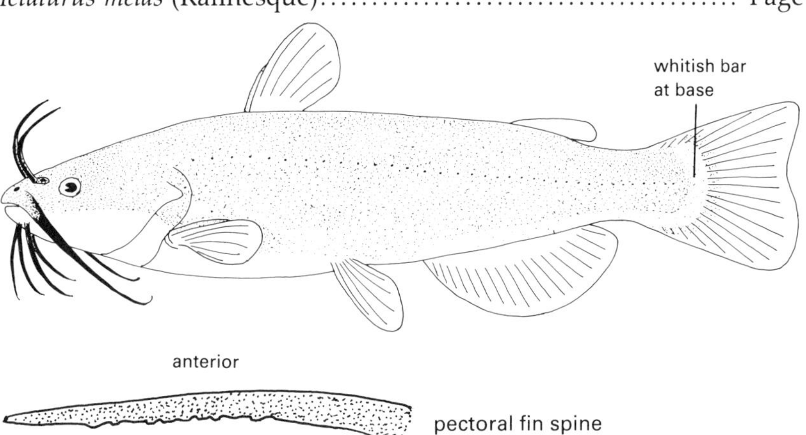

6b. Pectoral fin spine with strong, sawlike teeth along posterior edge. Side mottled. Interradial membranes of fins dark but not jet-black. Adults without whitish bar at caudal fin base. Anal fin rays 21–24 including rudimentaries.
BROWN BULLHEAD
Ictalurus nebulosus (Lesueur).. Page 702

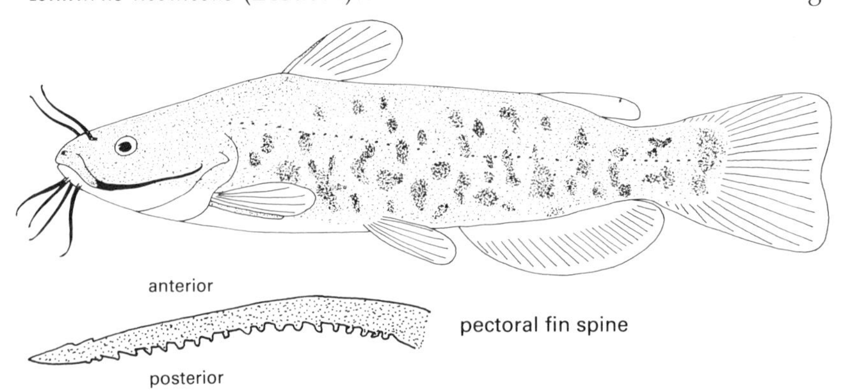

7a. Tooth patch of upper jaw with lateral backward extensions (see illustration under 4a). Tip of upper jaw projecting well beyond lower jaw. Caudal fin elongate, rectangular-appearing with more-or-less straight rear edge. Large, light, rectangular-shaped patch from back of head to near origin of dorsal fin; small, roundish, light patch immediately posterior to base of dorsal fin.
STONECAT
Noturus flavus Rafinesque .... Page 725

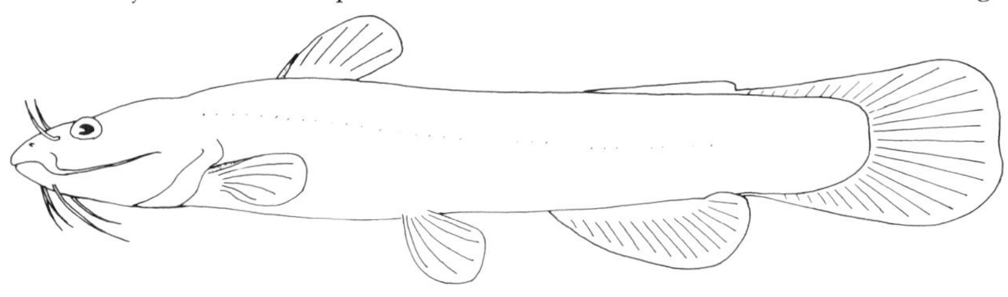

7b. Tooth patch of upper jaw without lateral backward extensions. Tips of jaws about equal. Caudal fin oval-appearing with rounded rear edge. Light patches behind head and dorsal fin absent or appearing as transverse bands 8

8a. Pectoral fin spine smooth on posterior edge. Distance from end of caudal fin to notch between adipose and caudal fins contained once or less in distance from notch to posterior base of dorsal fin. Usually 3 dark longitudinal streaks on each side and dark lines outlining the muscle segments. No transverse light bands behind head and dorsal fin. Anal, caudal, and dorsal fins not dark edged.
TADPOLE MADTOM
Noturus gyrinus (Mitchill) .... Page 719

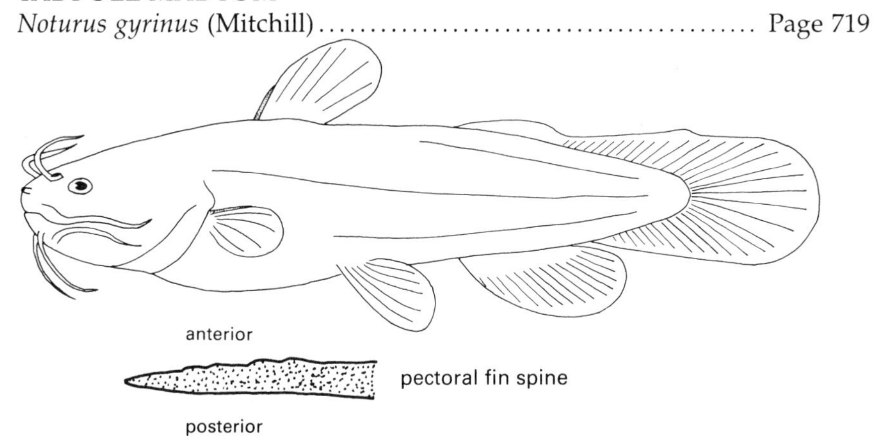

8b. Pectoral spine with well-developed teeth on posterior edge. Distance from end of caudal fin to notch between adipose and caudal fins contained decidedly more than once in distance from notch to posterior base of dorsal fin. Dark longitudinal streaks on sides absent; muscle segments not outlined with dark lines. Transverse light bands behind head and dorsal fin. Anal, caudal, and dorsal fins usually dark edged.
SLENDER MADTOM
Noturus exilis Nelson .... Page 722

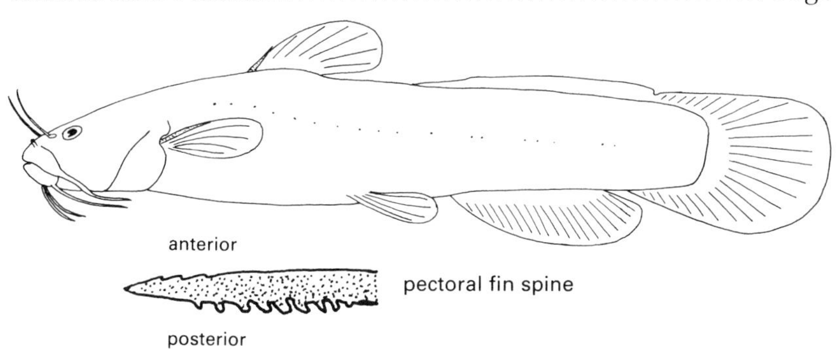

Key to the Killifishes

1a. Dorsal fin origin distinctly in advance of anal fin origin. Lateral series scales 39–43. No broad dark lateral stripe or dark blotch under eye.
BANDED KILLIFISH
Fundulus diaphanus (Lesueur).. Page 755

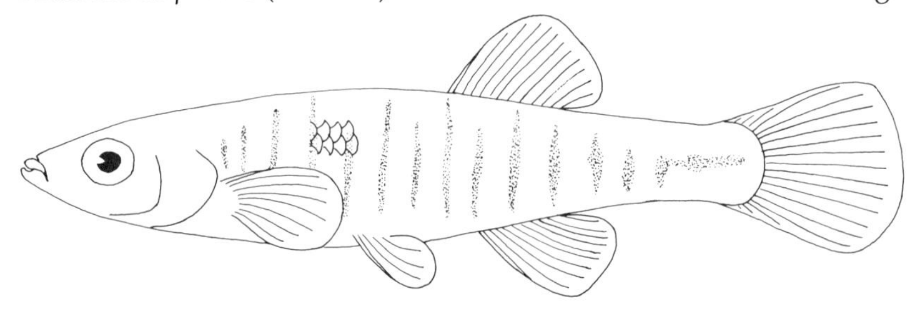

1b. Dorsal fin origin distinctly behind anal fin origin. Lateral series scales fewer than 38. Either broad dark lateral stripe or dark blotch under eye present 2

2a. Broad dark lateral stripe present; no thin, dotted horizontal stripes. No dark blotch ("teardrop") under eye. Body depth into SL generally greater than 4.
BLACKSTRIPE TOPMINNOW
Fundulus notatus (Rafinesque) .... Page 759

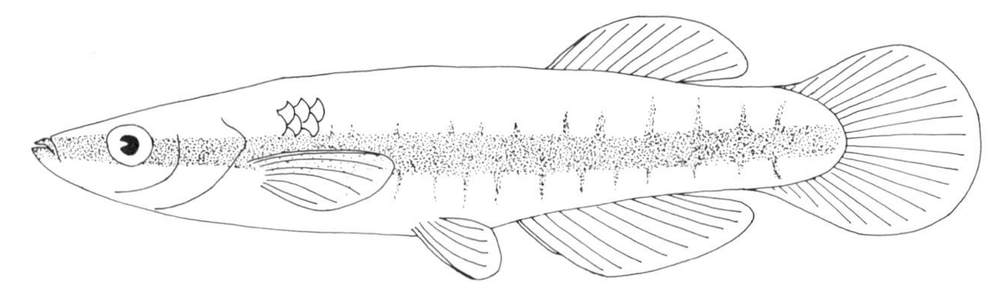

2b. Broad dark lateral stripe absent; instead, 7 or 8 thin, dotted horizontal stripes. Dark blotch ("teardrop") under eye. Body depth into SL usually 4 or less.
STARHEAD TOPMINNOW
Fundulus notti (Agassiz).. Page 763

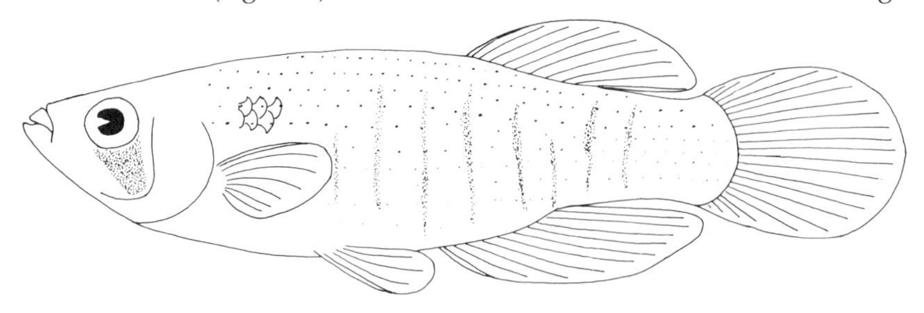

Key to the Sticklebacks

1a. Dorsal spines 4–6. Caudal peduncle deeper than wide, without trace of a lateral keel. Caudal fin rounded.
BROOK STICKLEBACK
Culaea inconstans (Kirtland) .... Page 777

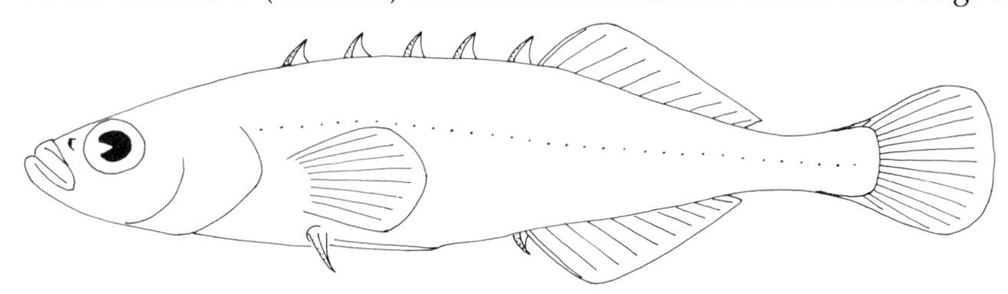

1b. Dorsal spines 8–11. Caudal peduncle wider than deep, with sharp lateral keels. Caudal fin truncate to slightly notched.
NINESPINE STICKLEBACK
Pungitius pungitius (Linnaeus)..................................... Page 782

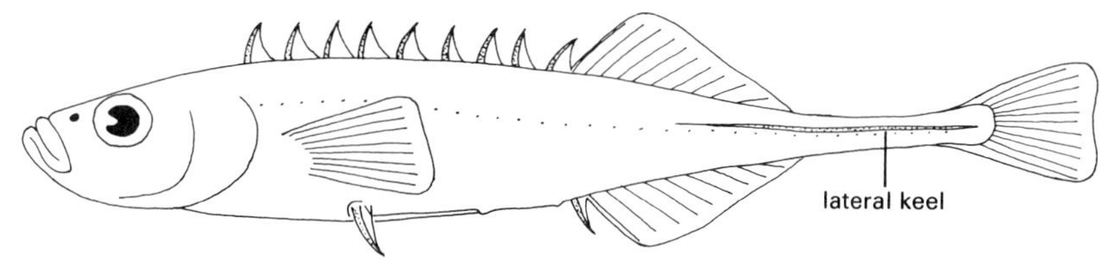

Key to the Temperate Basses

1a. Spinous dorsal fin and soft dorsal fin entirely separate. Anal spines graduated—first spine ⅓ or more length of second spine, third spine considerably longer than second; second and third spines about equally heavy. Soft anal fin rays 12 or 13. Color largely silvery; lateral stripes narrower and not usually broken or offset above origin of anal fin.
WHITE BASS
Morone chrysops (Rafinesque) .... Page 789

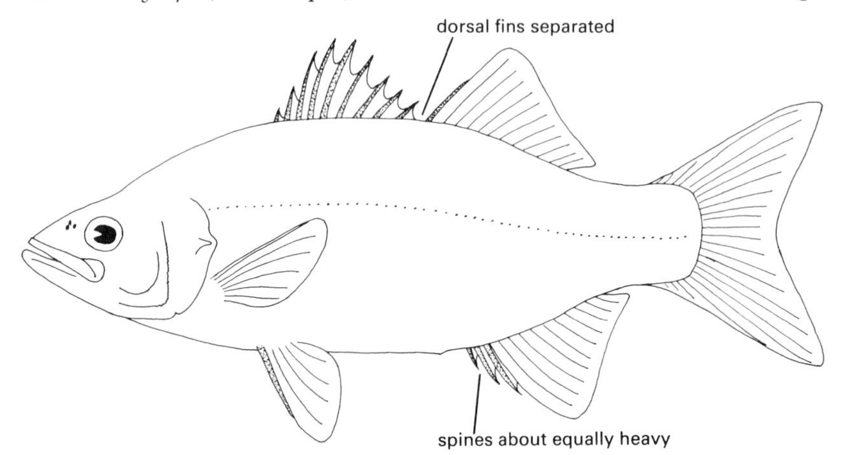

1b. Spinous dorsal fin and soft dorsal fin slightly connected by membrane. Anal spines not graduated—first spine less than ⅓ length of second spine, second spine almost equal to third; second spine much heavier than third. Soft anal fin rays 8–10. Color largely yellowish or olive; lower lateral stripes broader and usually sharply broken and offset above origin of anal fin.
YELLOW BASS
Morone mississippiensis Jordan and Eigenmann .... Page 794

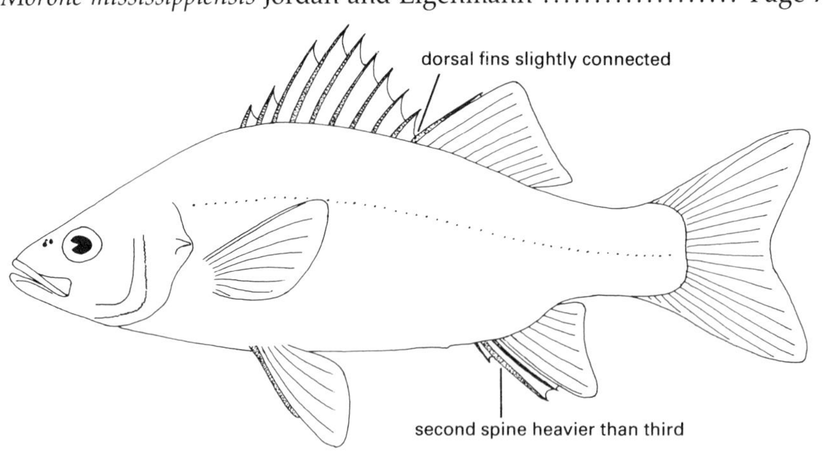

Key to the Sunfishes*

1a. Dorsal fin spines 6–8. Base of anal fin equal to or slightly longer than base of dorsal fin.
Pomoxis spp. (the crappies) 2

1b. Dorsal fin spines 10–12 (9–12). Base of anal fin much shorter than base of dorsal fin, anal fin base into dorsal fin base 1.5–3.0................. 3

2a. Dorsal fin spines 7 or 8 (6–9). Length of dorsal fin base about equal to distance from front of dorsal fin to eye. Irregular dark blotches and white spots on side; dorsal, caudal, and anal fins strongly vermiculate.
BLACK CRAPPIE
Pomoxis nigromaculatus (Lesueur) .... Page 863

2b. Dorsal fin spines 6 (4–7). Length of dorsal fin base much less than distance from front of dorsal fin to eye. Dark to faint vertical bars on side; dorsal and caudal fins strongly vermiculate, anal fin less so.
WHITE CRAPPIE
Pomoxis annularis Rafinesque...................................... Page 857

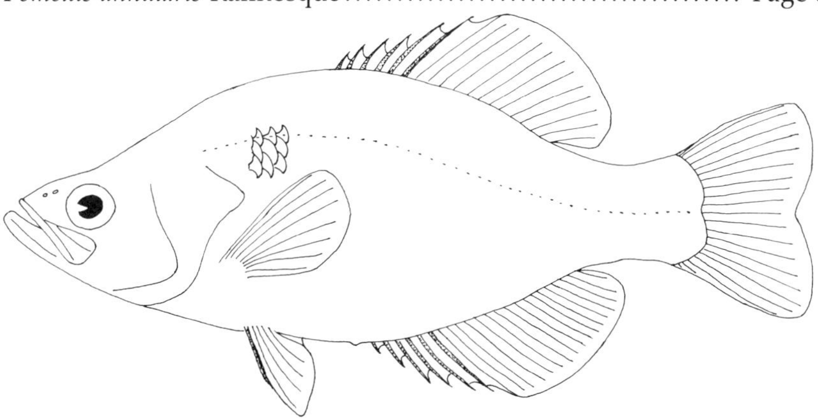

*Characteristics of common *Lepomis* hybrids are listed on page 157.

3a. Anal fin spines 5–7.
ROCK BASS
Ambloplites rupestris (Rafinesque) .... Page 852

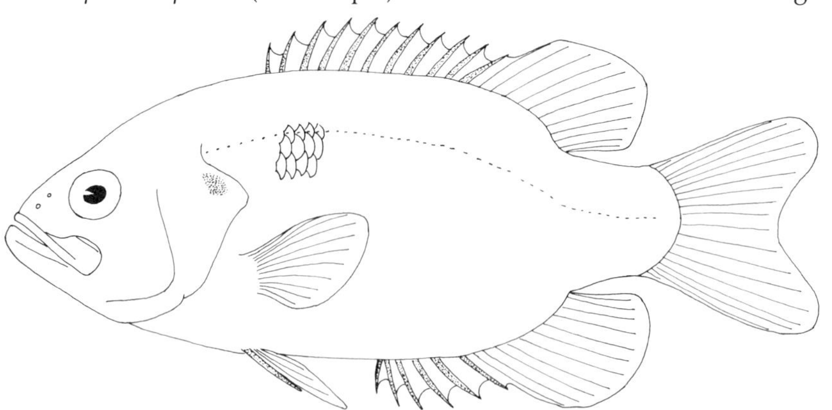

3b. Anal fin spines 3 4

4a. Scales small, more than 55 in lateral line
Micropterus spp. (the basses) 5

4b. Scales large, fewer than 55 in lateral line
Lepomis spp. (the sunfishes) 6

5a. Mouth large, upper jaw extending beyond posterior margin of eye in large fish. Lateral line scales 60–68. Dorsal fins almost divided, shortest posterior spine less than ½ the longest. Young with prominent lateral stripe and without colorful pigment on caudal fin.
LARGEMOUTH BASS
Micropterus salmoides (Lacepède) .... Page 809

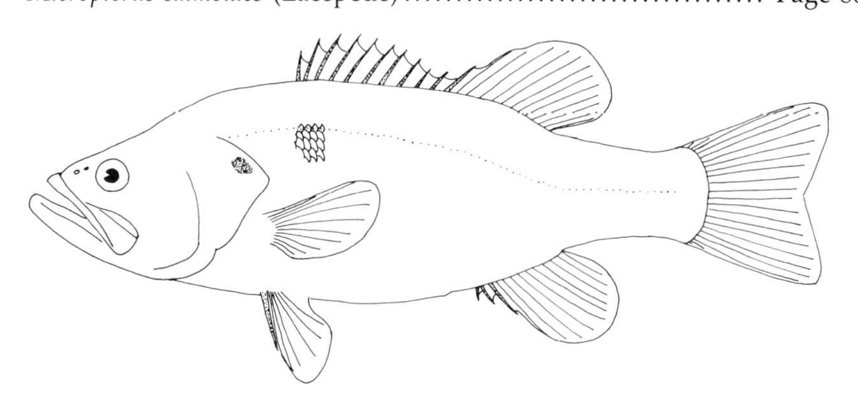

5b. Mouth moderate, upper jaw extending from middle to posterior margin of eye, never beyond. Lateral line scales 69–80. Dorsal fins moderately connected, shortest posterior spine greater than ½ the longest. Young without lateral stripe but having caudal fin with conspicuous yellow-orange base and dark crescent-shaped band through middle.
SMALLMOUTH BASS
Micropterus dolomieui Lacepède.................................... Page 801

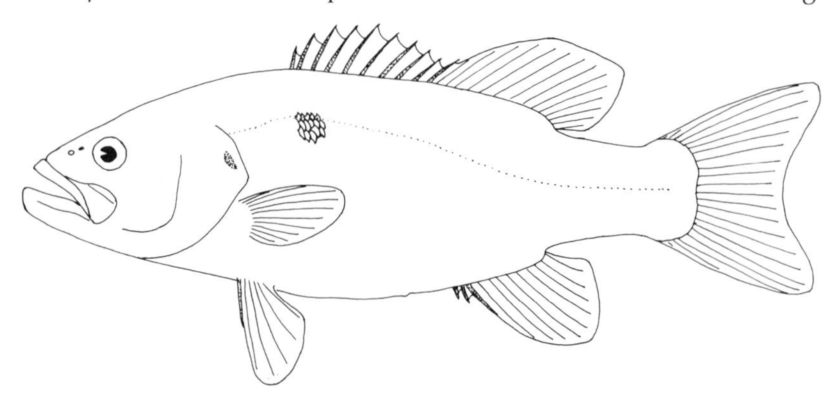

6a. Teeth present in midtongue. Supramaxillary well developed, its length greater than the greatest width of maxillary. Head with 3–5 distinct dark lines radiating posteriorly from eye; general body color pattern similar to that of rock bass.
WARMOUTH
Lepomis gulosus (Cuvier) .... Page 817

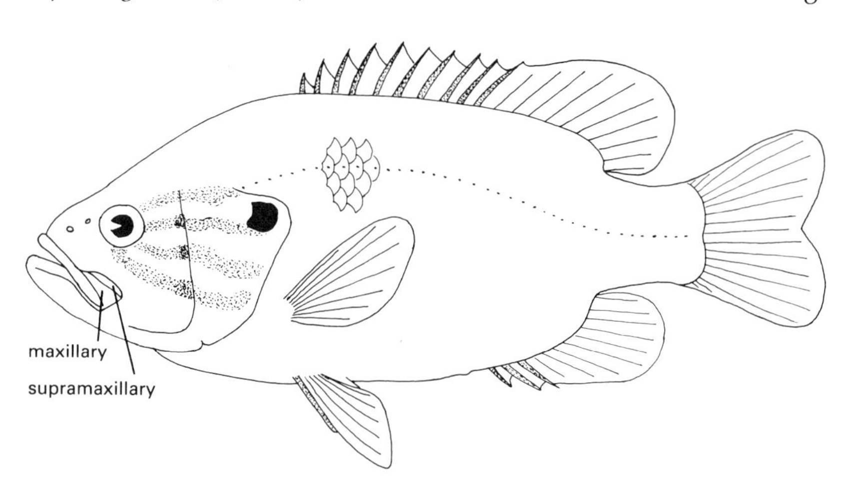

6b. No teeth on tongue (rarely a few in green sunfish). Supramaxillary reduced or absent, its length when present less than greatest width of maxillary. Head with no distinct dark lines radiating posteriorly from eye.. 7

7a. Pectoral fin when laid forward across cheek reaches anterior edge of eye or beyond; pectoral fin long and pointed, its length into SL about 3 8

7b. Pectoral fin when laid forward across cheek reaches only posterior edge of eye; pectoral fin short and rounded, its length into SL about 4 10

8a. "Earflap" has narrow, even, light-colored margin along entire edge. Sensory pores of head (just above lip groove) large and slitlike, width of largest opening greater than diam of anterior nostril. Anal fin soft rays 8 or 9. Largest seldom more than 100 mm (4 in) TL.
ORANGESPOTTED SUNFISH
Lepomis humilis (Girard)... Page 840

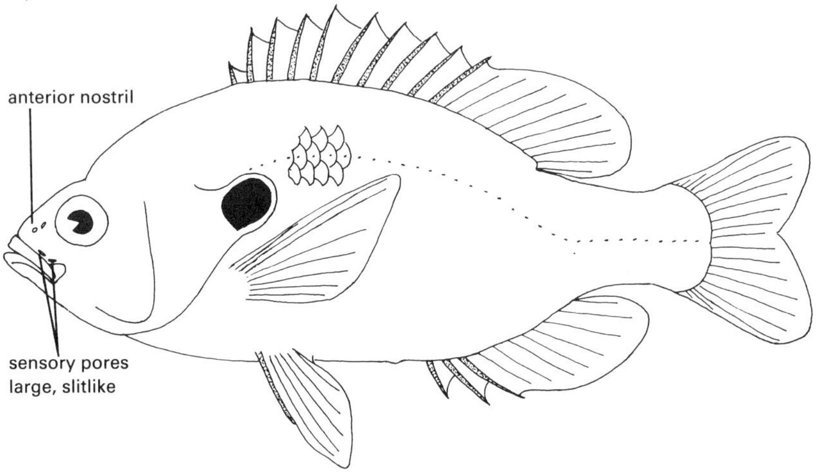

8b. "Earflap" is black or with margin becoming abruptly broader (light-colored spot, crimson in life) at posterior edge. Sensory pores of head small and round, width of largest openings less than diam of anterior nostril (see illustration under 9b). Anal fin soft rays 10–12. Often more than 125 mm (5 in) TL. 9

9a. "Earflap" black to edge without light-colored margin. Distinct black blotch present toward rear of dorsal fin. Gill rakers on first gill arch moderately long, straight, and pointed. (Young can be distinguished from pumpkinseed by long thin gill rakers and large, dark, well-defined oval to circular spots in last few interradial membranes of soft dorsal fin.)
BLUEGILL
Lepomis macrochirus Rafinesque .... Page 844

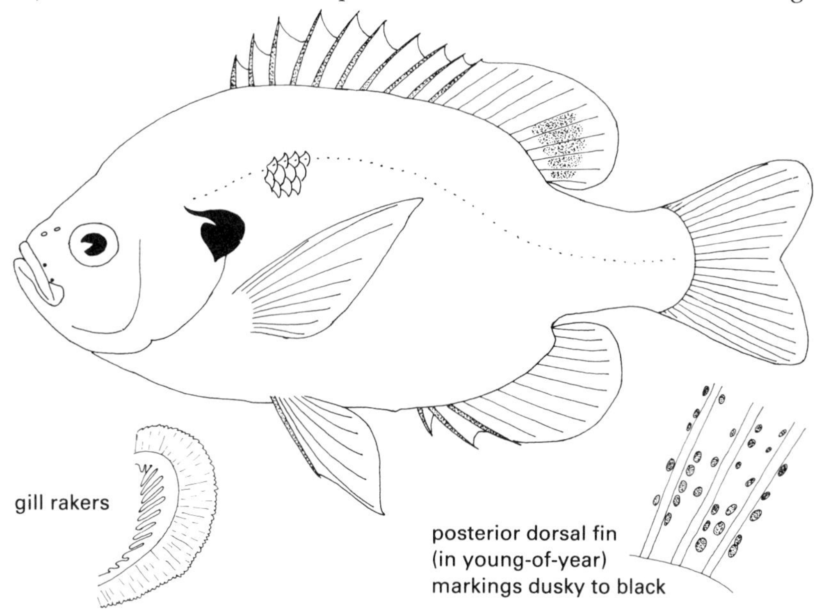

9b. "Earflap" with abruptly broader light-colored spot (crimson in life) at posterior edge. No distinct black blotch toward rear of dorsal fin. Gill rakers on first gill arch short, knobby, scarcely longer than wide. (Young can be distinguished from bluegill by short, bent gill rakers and diffuse irregular brown markings alongside last few dorsal fin rays.)
PUMPKINSEED
Lepomis gibbosus (Linnaeus).. Page 828

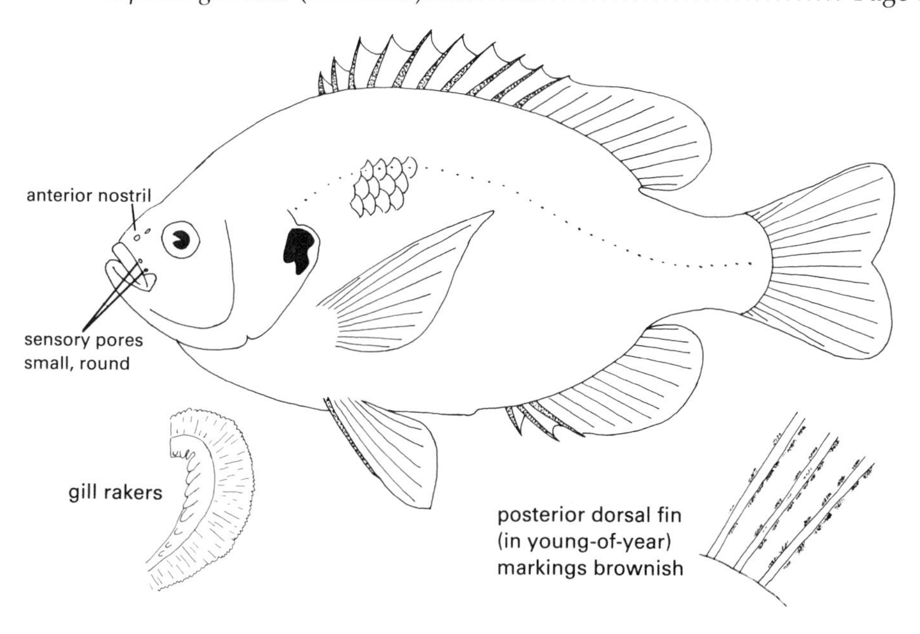

10a. Scales in lateral line 44–51. Gill rakers long, straight, pointed (see illustration under 9a). Posterior soft dorsal fin usually with dark blotch near base.
GREEN SUNFISH
Lepomis cyanellus Rafinesque .... Page 822

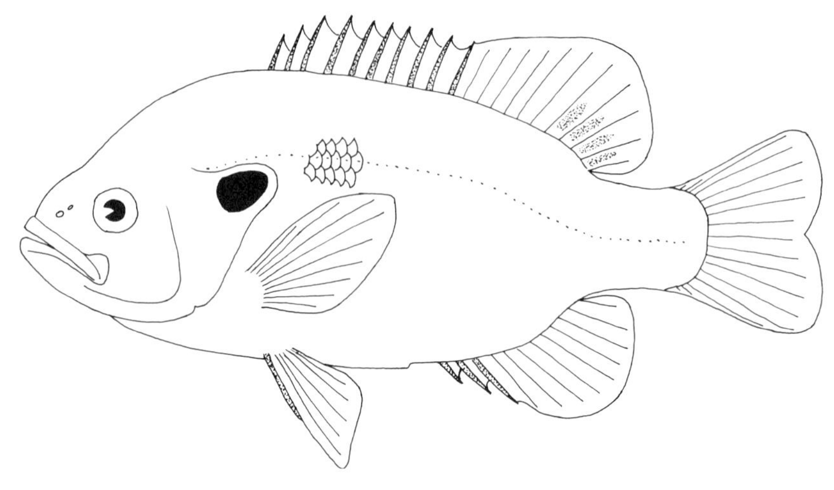

10b. Scales in lateral line 34–38. Gill rakers reduced to knobs. Posterior soft dorsal fin without dark blotch near base.
LONGEAR SUNFISH
Lepomis megalotis (Rafinesque)...................................... Page 834

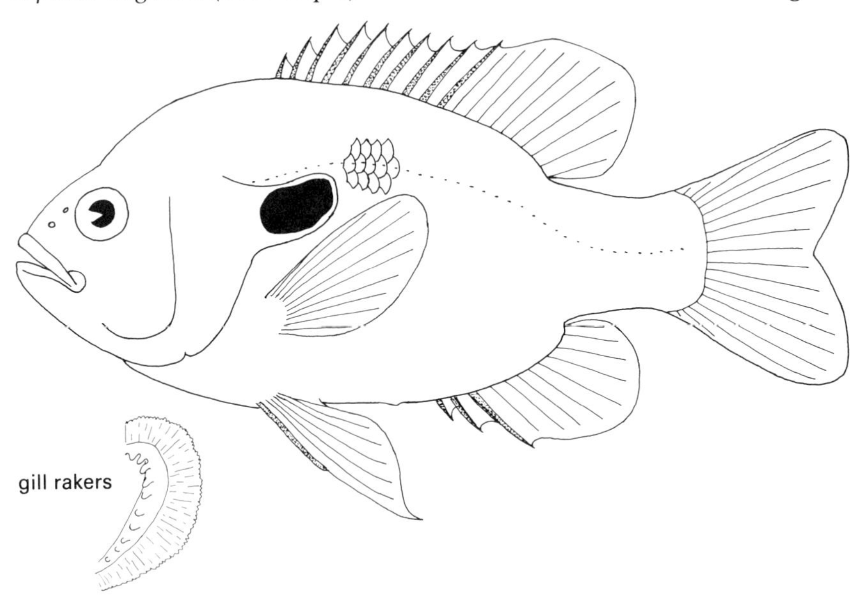

CHARACTERISTICS OF COMMON *LEPOMIS* HYBRIDS*

GREEN SUNFISH × PUMPKINSEED

Lepomis cyanellus × *Lepomis gibbosus*

Ear flap edged with wide, light-colored membrane and a red spot in life.

Pectoral fin laid forward, usually reaching between pupil and posterior edge of eye.

Gill rakers intermediate in length with some curvature—neither long and thin nor short, stubby, and bent.

Upper jaw reaching to below anterior edge of eye or beyond.

Posterior soft dorsal fin with diffuse dark spots between rays; anterior edge of pelvic fins and ventral edge of anal and caudal fins yellow or cream-colored.

Cheek and opercle with faint wavy lines radiating from eye to distal edge of opercle.

GREEN SUNFISH × BLUEGILL

Lepomis cyanellus × *Lepomis macrochirus*

Ear flap edged with a wide, uniformly gray-to-black membrane.

Pectoral fin laid forward, usually reaching between pupil and posterior edge of eye.

Gill rakers long and thin.

Upper jaw reaching to below anterior edge of eye or beyond.

Posterior soft dorsal fin with solid black pigmentation, not broken into diffuse spots; anterior edge of pelvic fins and ventral edge of anal and caudal fins yellow or cream-colored.

Cheek and opercle plain, without faint wavy lines radiating from eye to distal edge of opercle.

PUMPKINSEED × BLUEGILL

Lepomis gibbosus × *Lepomis macrochirus*

Ear flap black and edged with a narrow, light-colored membrane and a small red spot in life.

Pectoral fin laid forward, usually reaching anterior edge of eye.

Gill rakers intermediate in length with some curvature—neither long and thin nor short, stubby, and bent.

Upper jaw short, scarcely reaching to below anterior edge of eye.

Posterior soft dorsal fin with elongated dark markings, thinner and more irregular than in *L. macrochirus*, but not small circular spots as in adult *L. gibbosus*; anterior edge of pelvic fins light-colored, ventral edge of anal and caudal fins generally pigmented.

Cheek and opercle with faint wavy lines radiating from eye to distal edge of opercle.

*Prepared by Dale Becker

Key to the Perches

1a. Preopercle saw-edged. Upper jaw extending to middle of eye or beyond. Branchiostegal rays 7 or 8.
Perca sp. and *Stizostedion* spp. (yellow perch, walleye, sauger) 2

1b. Preopercle smooth-edged. Upper jaw usually not extending to middle of eye. Branchiostegal rays 5 or 6.
Ammocrypta spp., *Etheostoma* spp., and *Percina* spp. (the darters)...... 4

2a. No canine teeth in upper and lower jaws. Soft rays of anal fin 7 or 8. Body with distinct vertical bars. Body depth into SL 3.3–3.8.
YELLOW PERCH
Perca flavescens (Mitchill).. Page 886

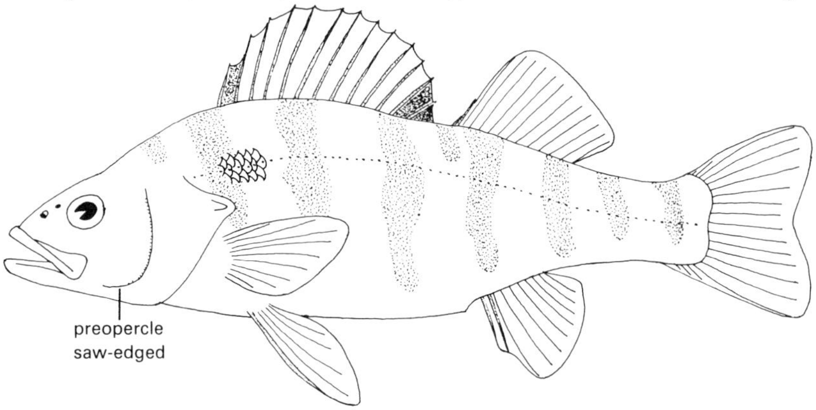

preopercle saw-edged

2b. Canine teeth in upper and lower jaws. Soft rays of anal fin 11–14. Body without distinct vertical bars. Body depth into SL 4.9–5.9. 3

3a. Spinous dorsal fin with large black blotch at posterior base. Pyloric caeca 3, each extending to posterior edge of stomach or beyond. Ventral lobe of caudal fin white-tipped. Soft dorsal fin rays 18–21. Cheeks sparsely scaled to naked.
WALLEYE
Stizostedion v. vitreum (Mitchill) .... Page 871

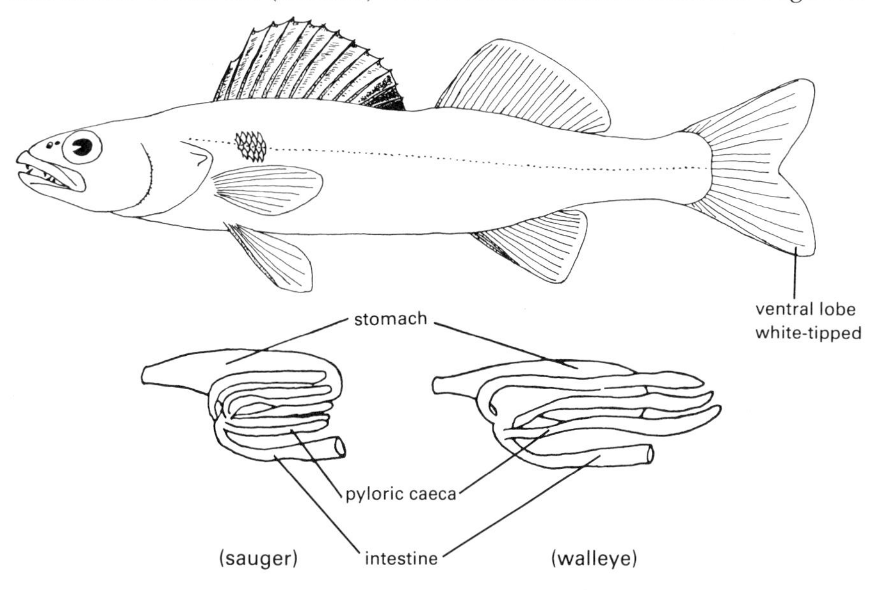

(Lutterbie 1975:22)

3b. Spinous dorsal fin with distinct dark spots; no large black blotch at posterior base. Pyloric caeca usually 4–6, each not extending to posterior edge of stomach. Ventral lobe of caudal fin usually without white tip. Soft dorsal fin rays 17–19. Cheeks well scaled.
SAUGER
Stizostedion canadense (Smith)...................................... Page 880

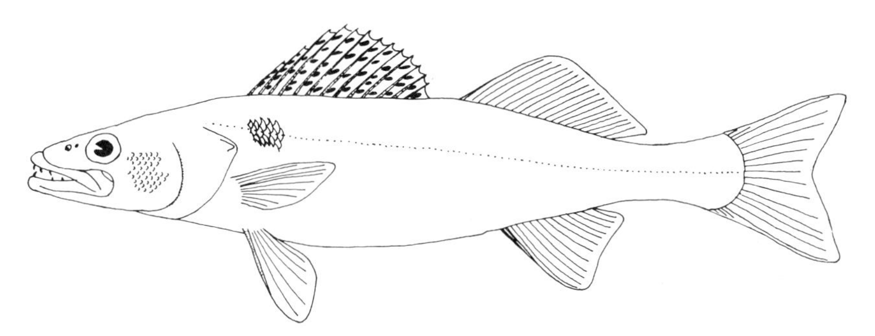

4a. Body depth into SL usually 7 or greater. Belly usually without scales. Anal fin with 1 spine.. 5

4b. Body depth into SL usually less than 7. Belly usually with at least a few scales. Anal fin usually with 2 spines (1 in johnny darter, bluntnose darter, and occasionally in the least darter)........................ 6

5a. Back with 12 or more small dark saddles along mid-dorsal line. Anal fin rays 7–10. Soft dorsal fin rays 9–12.
WESTERN SAND DARTER
Ammocrypta clara Jordan and Meek .... Page 918

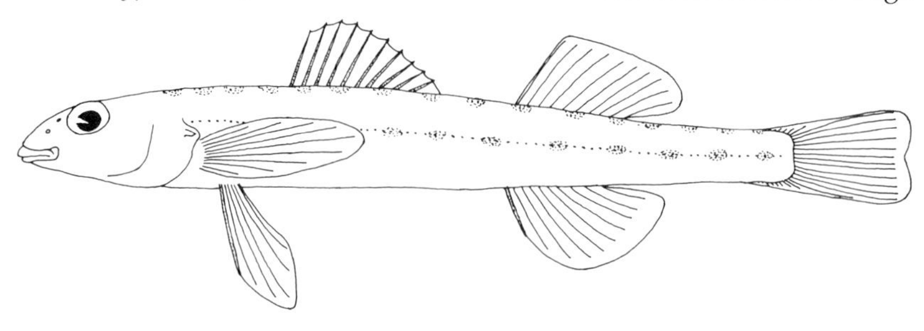

5b. Back with 3 or 4 broad saddle marks extending forward to lateral line. Anal fin rays 15 or 16. Soft dorsal fin rays 14–16.
CRYSTAL DARTER
Ammocrypta asprella (Jordan).. Page 915

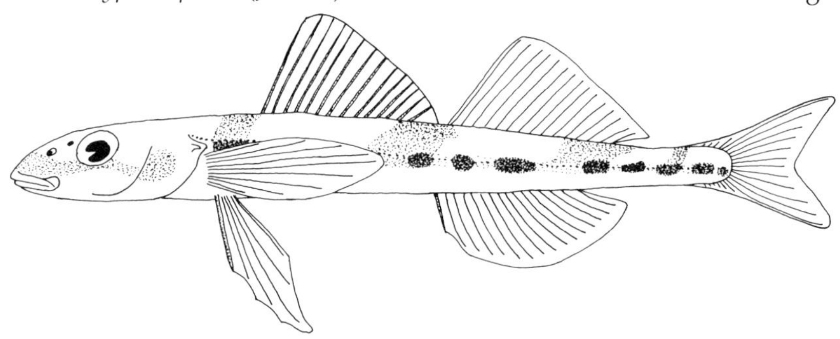

6a. No enlarged and modified scales between pelvic fins; midline of belly usually well scaled with scales of same type as those on sides. Anal fin usually smaller than soft dorsal fin. Lateral line complete or incomplete.
Etheostoma spp. 7

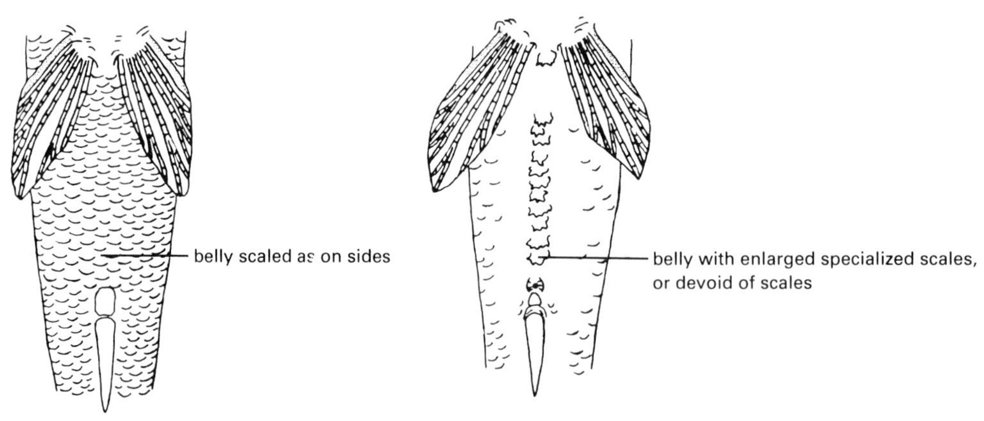

(Lutterbie 1975:23)

6b. One or more enlarged and modified scales between pelvic fins; midline of belly usually without scales or with a series of enlarged and modified scales, these bounded on each side by naked areas. Anal fin often nearly as large as or larger than soft dorsal fin. Lateral line always complete.
Percina spp. 14

7a. Spinous dorsal fin with 6 (5–7) spines. Lateral series scales 32–38, lateral line incomplete (0–7 pored scales). Pelvic fin extremely long, reaching to vent or beyond.
LEAST DARTER
Etheostoma microperca Jordan and Gilbert .... Page 950

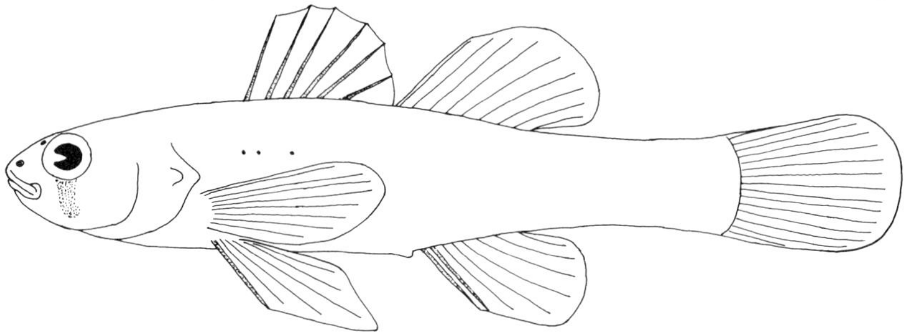

7b. Spinous dorsal fin with 7 or more spines. Lateral series scales 37 or more, lateral line complete or incomplete (more than 16 pored scales). Pelvic fin short, not reaching to vent 8

8a. Upper lip groove continuous over tip of snout. Anal fin spine 1....... 9

8b. Upper lip groove not continuous over tip of snout. Anal fin spines 2... 10

9a. Dark stripe extending from eye to snout interrupted medially on snout. Cheek usually naked. Soft dorsal fin rays usually 13. Dorsal fins only slightly separated, less than width of pupil. Lateral line complete.
JOHNNY DARTER
Etheostoma nigrum Rafinesque .... Page 921

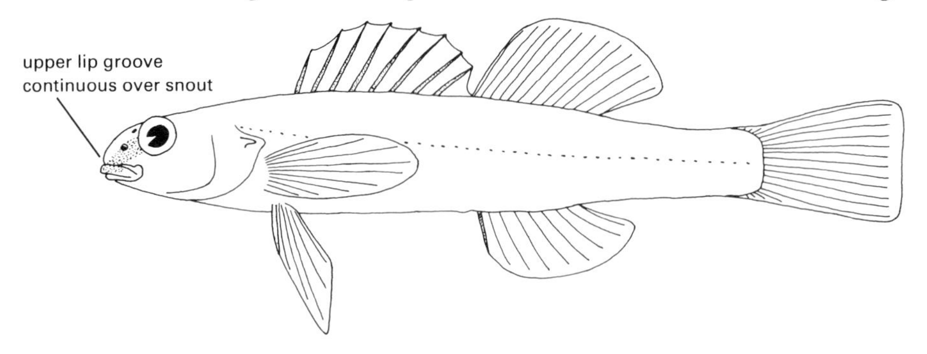

9b. Dark stripe extending from eye to snout continuous over tip of snout. Cheek scaled. Soft dorsal fin rays usually 9–11. Dorsal fins widely separated, about width of pupil or connected by thin membrane. Lateral line incomplete, with fewer than 25 pored scales.
BLUNTNOSE DARTER
Etheostoma chlorosomum (Hay) .... Page 926

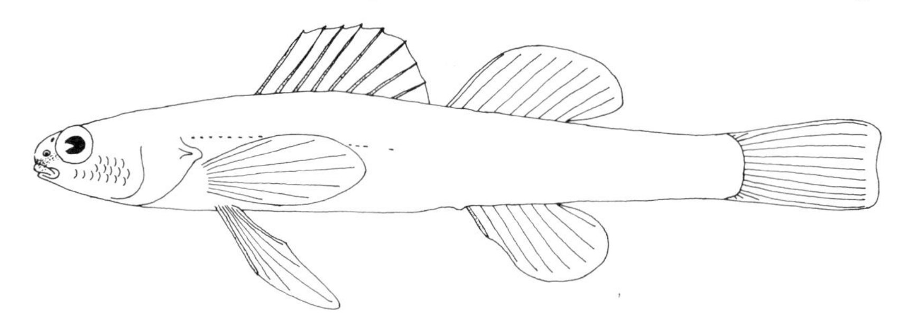

10a. Gill membranes broadly attached to one another 11

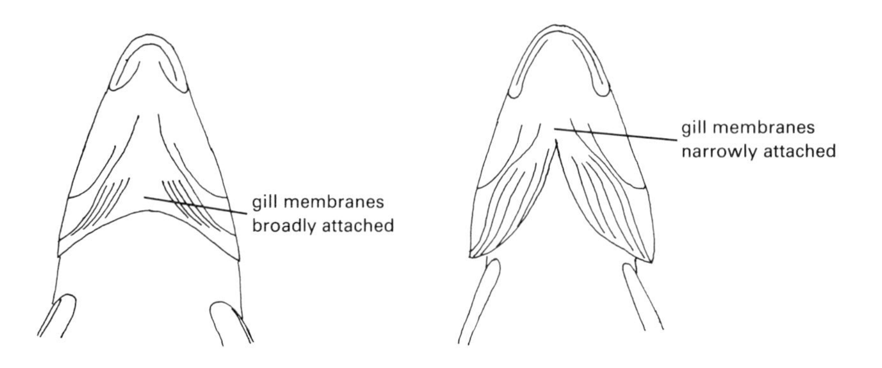

10b. Gill membranes narrowly or moderately attached to one another 12

11a. Cheek, opercle, and nape without scales. Spinous dorsal fin with 7 or 8 spines. Sides conspicuously marked with longitudinal rows of dots or dashes (central portion of each scale marked with dot or dash).
FANTAIL DARTER
Etheostoma flabellare Rafinesque .... Page 945

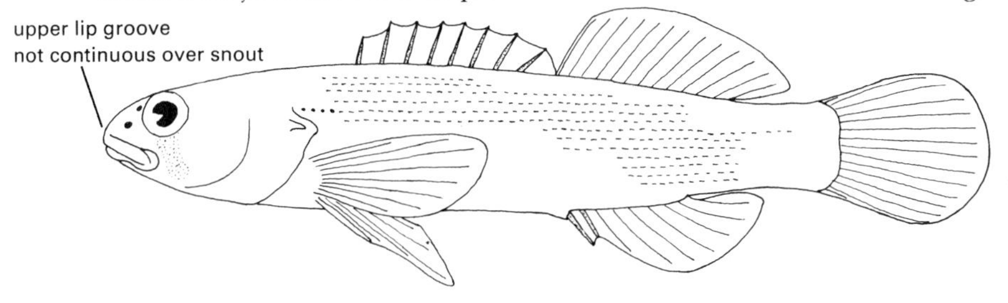

11b. Cheek, opercle, and nape scaled. Spinous dorsal fin with 10–12 spines. Sides not marked with longitudinal rows of dots or dashes.
BANDED DARTER
Etheostoma zonale (Cope) .... Page 929

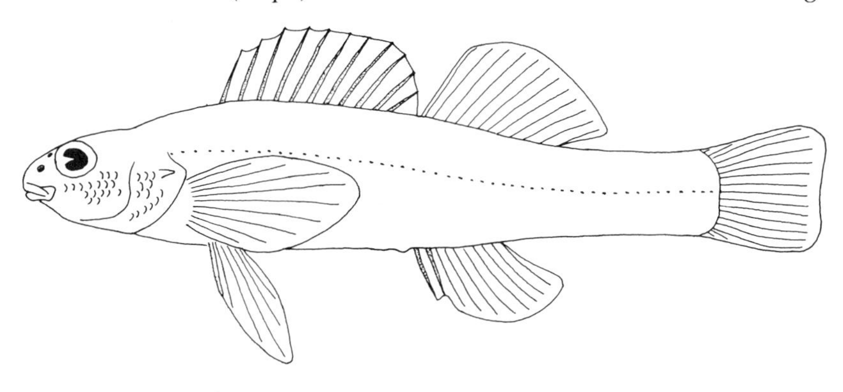

12a. Lateral series scales 55–65. Body depth into SL 4.8–5.5.
IOWA DARTER
Etheostoma exile (Girard) .... Page 940

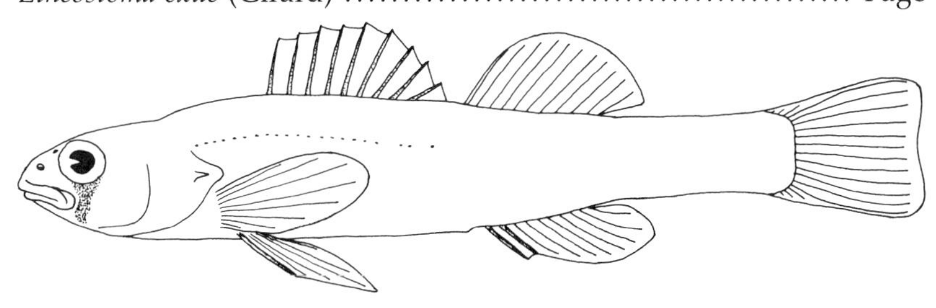

12b. Lateral series scales 50 or fewer. Body depth into SL 4.0–5.0 13

13a. Cheek naked or with row of scales along posterior border of eye. Anal fin soft rays usually 7. Without 3 dark spots at base of caudal fin. Males with a series of unbroken vertical bands on sides forming saddles over back.
RAINBOW DARTER
Etheostoma caeruleum Storer .... Page 932

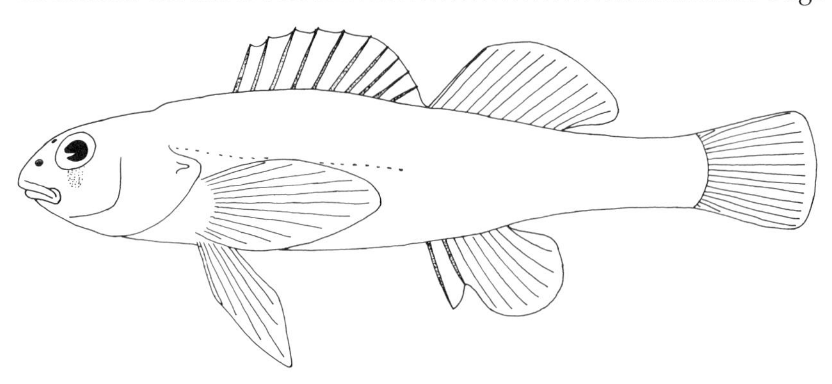

13b. Cheek scaled. Anal fin soft rays 8 or 9. Three small dark spots arranged vertically at base of caudal fin (occasionally interconnected). Males with a series of vertical bands on sides often confluent with one another and interrupted by lightly pigmented lateral scales.
MUD DARTER
Etheostoma asprigene (Forbes) .... Page 937

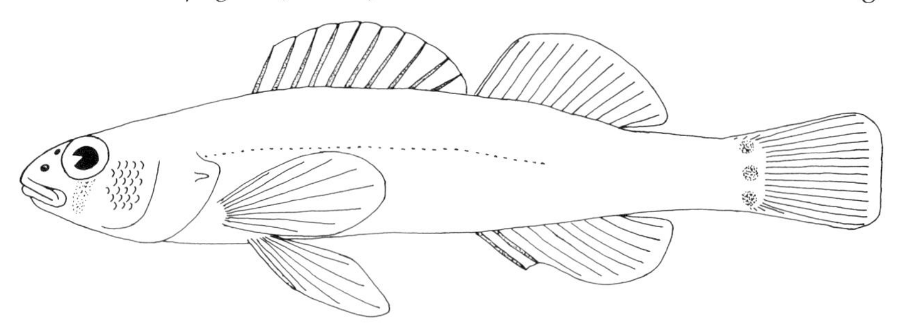

14a. Snout with conical protuberance. Lateral bands 15–25, narrow and zebralike, crossing over back and extending vertically down sides. Lateral line scales 71 or more.
LOGPERCH
Percina caprodes (Rafinesque) .... Page 907

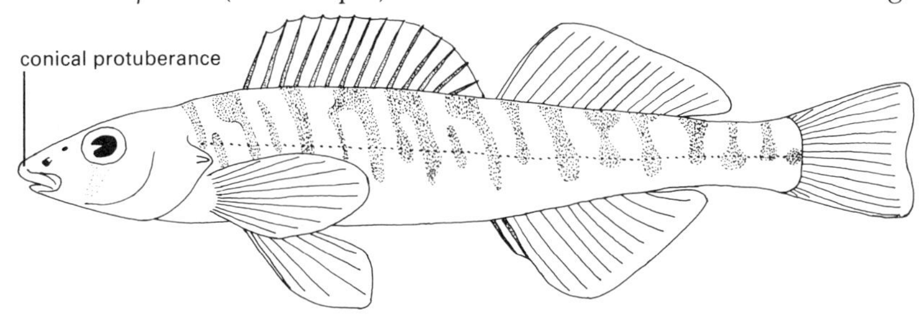

14b. Snout without conical protuberance. Lateral bands or blotches usually fewer than 15, irregular in width and often confluent. Lateral line scales usually fewer than 71 15

15a. Distance from tip of upper lip to junction of gill membranes (A) equal to or greater than distance from junction of gill membranes to back of pelvic fin base (B). Lateral blotches 10–16, dark and more-or-less confluent. Suborbital bar absent or faint.
SLENDERHEAD DARTER
Percina phoxocephala (Nelson) .... Page 894

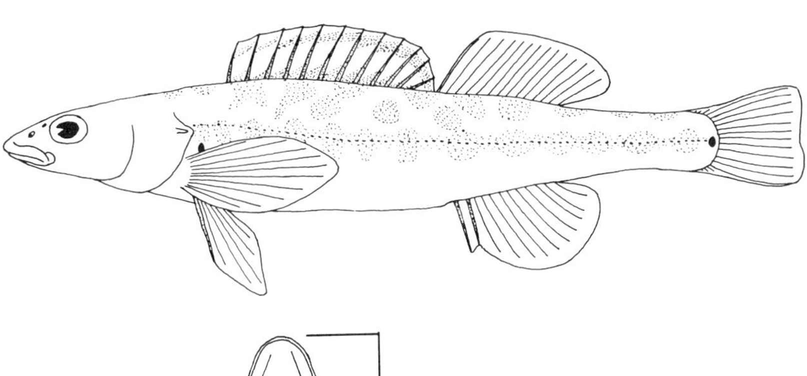

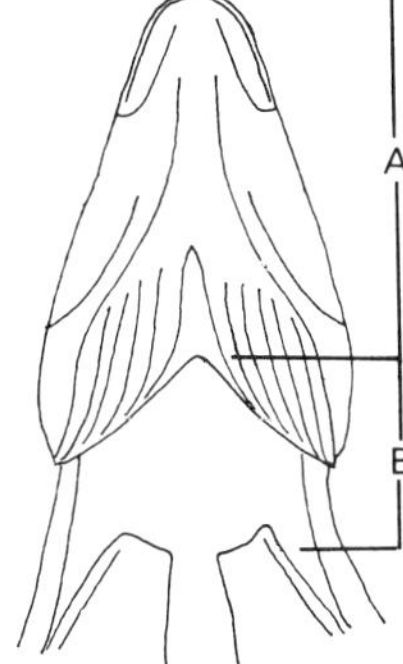

15b. Distance from tip of upper lip to junction of gill membranes (A) less than distance from junction of gill membranes to back of pelvic fin base (B). Lateral markings 5–11, blotches or becoming short vertical bars anteriorly. Suborbital bar distinct, black 16

16a. Spinous dorsal fin with black blotch on membrane behind first spine and larger black blotch on membranes between last 3 or 4 spines. Lateral blotches 8–11, becoming short vertical bars anteriorly. Lateral line scales 52–54 (48–60). Gill rakers on lower limb of first arch short, stout, bent, about 9.
RIVER DARTER
Percina shumardi (Girard) .... Page 912

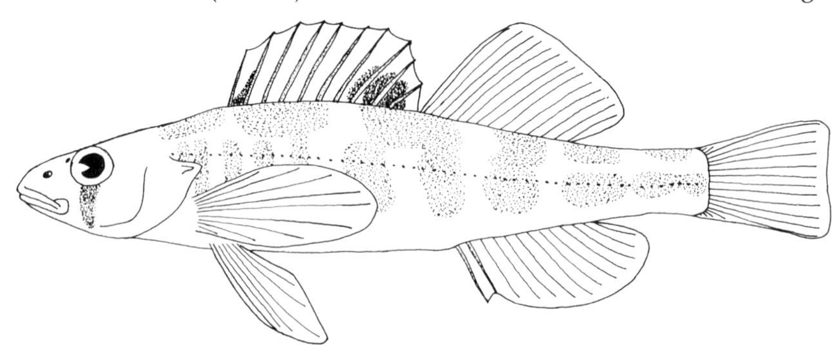

16b. Spinous dorsal fin almost totally pigmented or with heavy dark base, but not pigmented as in 16a. Lateral blotches 5–8. Lateral line scales 60–65 (56–71). Gill rakers on lower limb of first arch long, narrow, straight, 10 or 11 17

17a. Spinous dorsal fin with black pigment on lower half, becoming less intense posteriorly, extreme outer edge clear; spines 13 (12–15). Caudal peduncle scales 20–23. Back with 6–11 dark, saddle-type markings and dorsolateral vermiculations or checkerboard design. Lateral blotches usually connected, forming wide, irregular lateral stripe.
BLACKSIDE DARTER
Percina maculata (Girard) .... Page 898

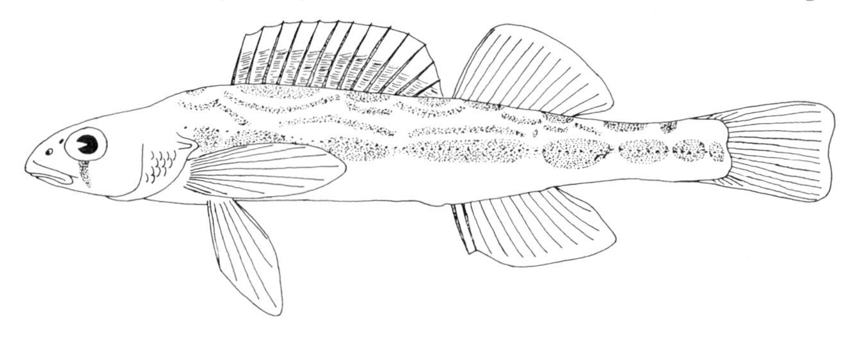

17b. Spinous dorsal fin more-or-less evenly pigmented, except extreme outer margin where whitish or clear; spines usually 12. Caudal peduncle scales 24–29. Back with 5–8 dark, squarish saddle bands; vermiculations or checkerboard markings absent. Lateral blotches separated, squarish, green-black, directly below saddle bands.
GILT DARTER
Percina evides (Jordan and Copeland) .... Page 903

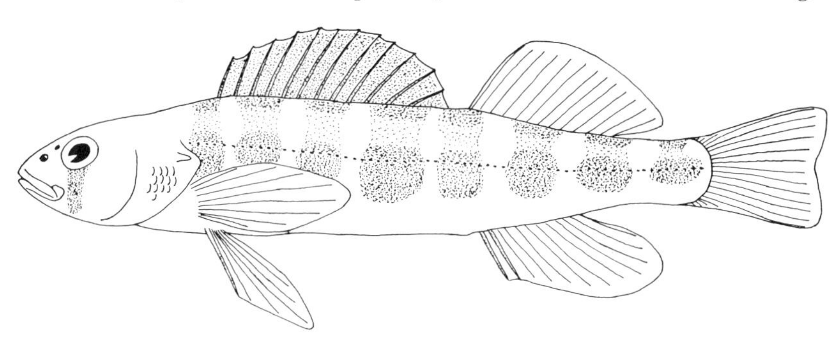

Key to the Sculpins

1a. Gill membranes meeting at acute angle, free from isthmus. Two to 4 conspicuous and partially naked preopercular spines on each side. Dorsal fins separated by space about equal to diam of eye.
DEEPWATER SCULPIN
Myoxocephalus thompsoni (Girard) .... Page 965

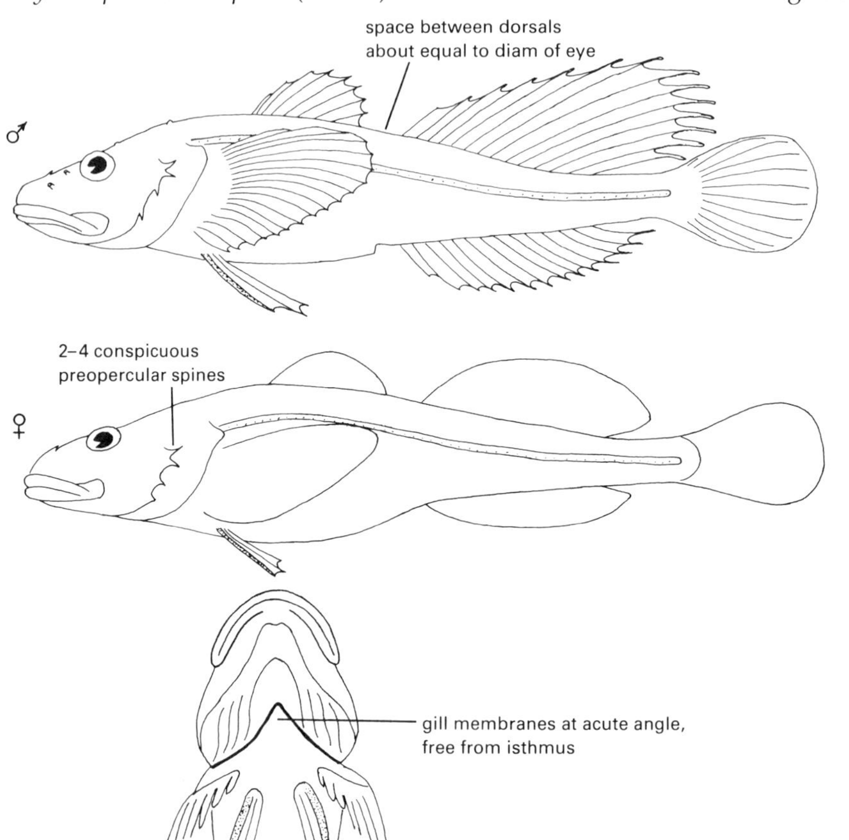

1b. Gill membranes broadly attached to isthmus. One conspicuous and partially naked preopercular spine on each side, other spines skin covered. Dorsal fins touching or narrowly joined.
Cottus spp. 2

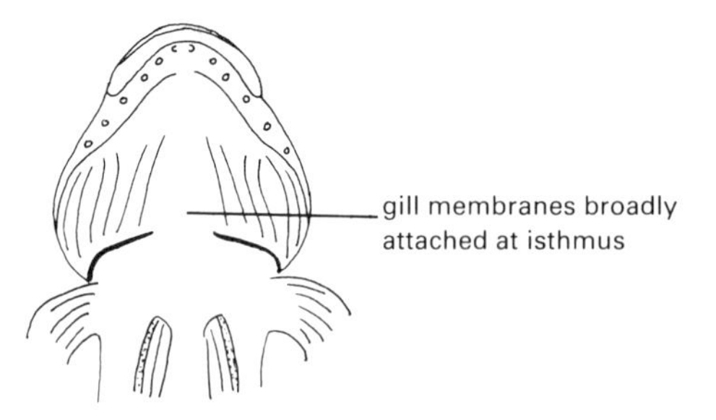

2a. Lateral line complete. One midline chin pore. Preopercular spine usually longer than ⅔ eye diam and curved strongly inward. Upper head and body covered with prickles. Pelvic fins with 1 spine and 4 soft rays appearing as 4 units (spine and first ray encased in single fleshy membrane). Chin membrane with brainlike convolutions and folds.
SPOONHEAD SCULPIN
Cottus ricei (Nelson) .... Page 979

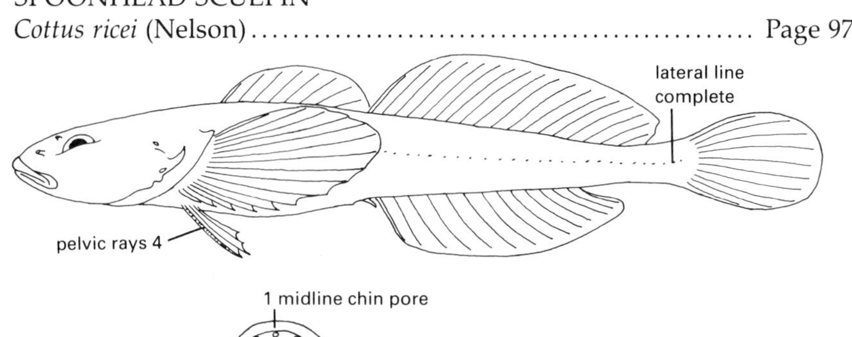

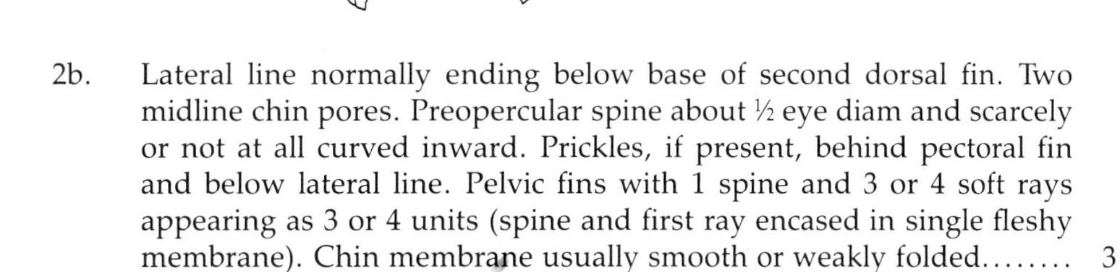

2b. Lateral line normally ending below base of second dorsal fin. Two midline chin pores. Preopercular spine about ½ eye diam and scarcely or not at all curved inward. Prickles, if present, behind pectoral fin and below lateral line. Pelvic fins with 1 spine and 3 or 4 soft rays appearing as 3 or 4 units (spine and first ray encased in single fleshy membrane). Chin membrane usually smooth or weakly folded........ 3

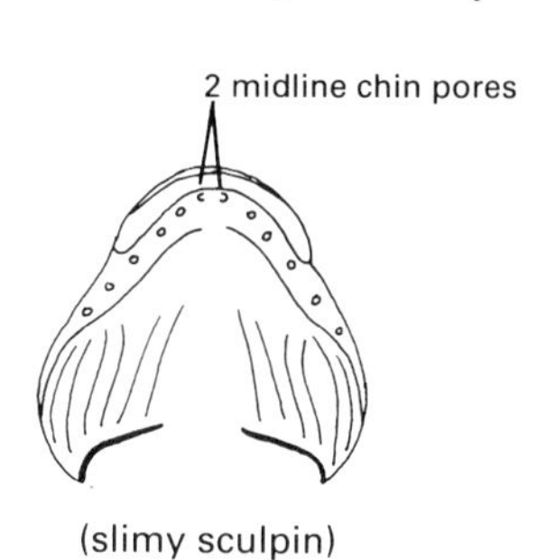

(slimy sculpin)

3a. Pelvic fin rays 4, last a little shorter than third. Caudal peduncle length less than postorbital distance. Last 2 rays of dorsal and anal fins arising from the same base. Palatine teeth usually present.
MOTTLED SCULPIN
Cottus bairdi Girard .... Page 969

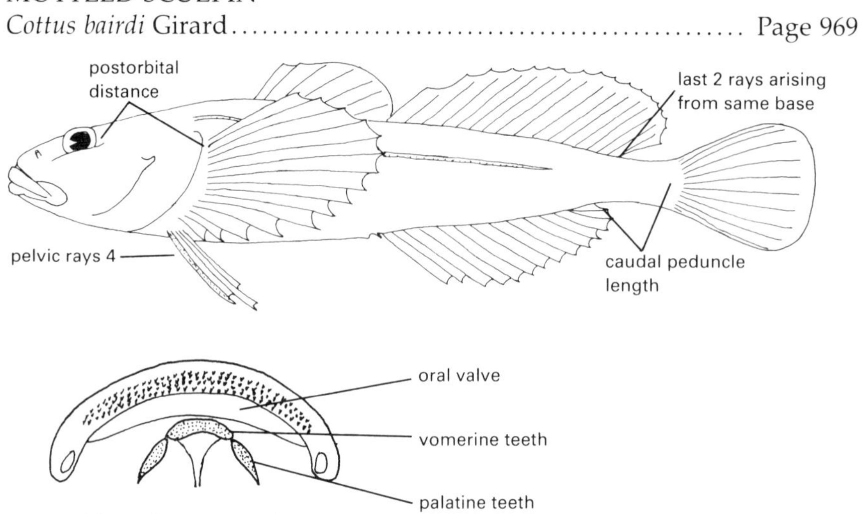

View of upper mouth

3b. Pelvic fin rays usually 3, if 4, last much shorter than third. Caudal peduncle length greater than postorbital distance. Last 2 rays of dorsal and anal fins separated, arising from separate bases. Palatine teeth usually absent.
SLIMY SCULPIN
Cottus cognatus Richardson .... Page 974

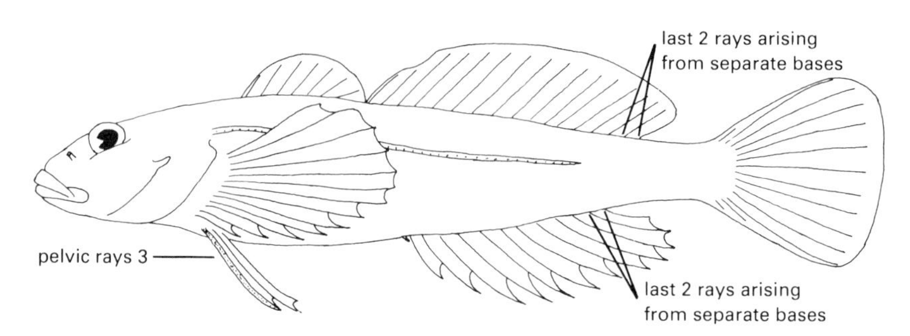

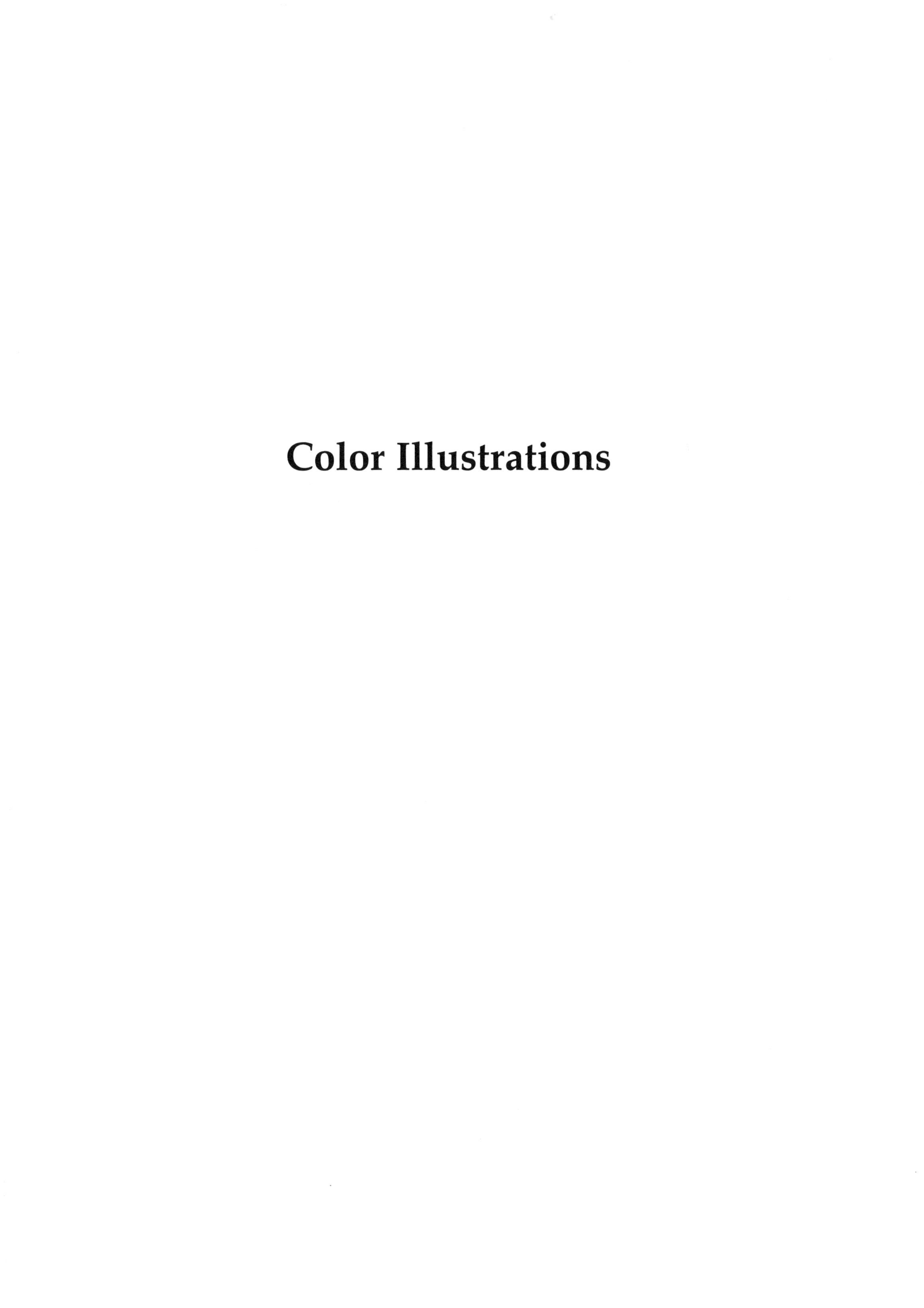

Color Illustrations

The photographs and portraits of fish in this section are arranged in the order in which the species are presented in the text. Color photographs of museum specimens, it should be pointed out, are not a reliable guide to the colors of living fish; among several species—for example, the suckers, minnows, and drums—the scales often lose the silvery luster of living individuals and photograph in varying shades of yellow and brown.

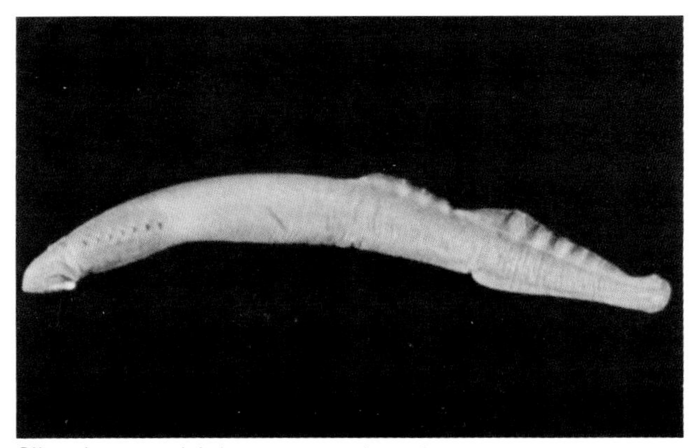
Silver lamprey *Ichthyomyzon unicuspis*

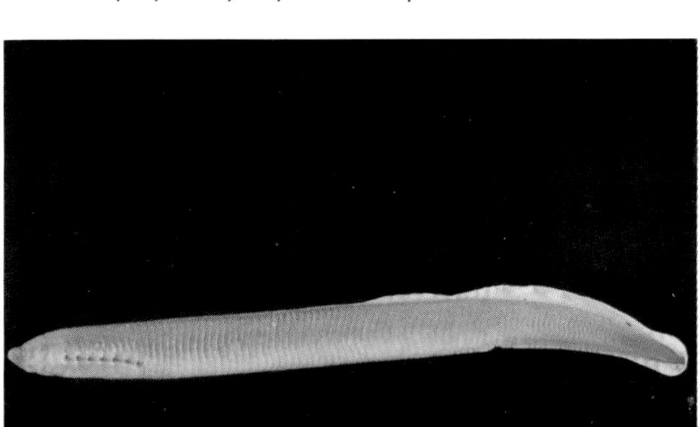
Northern brook lamprey *Ichthyomyzon fossor*

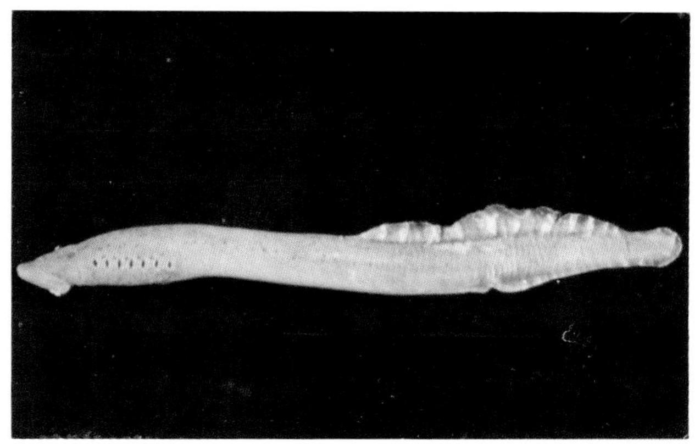
Chestnut lamprey *Ichthyomyzon castaneus*

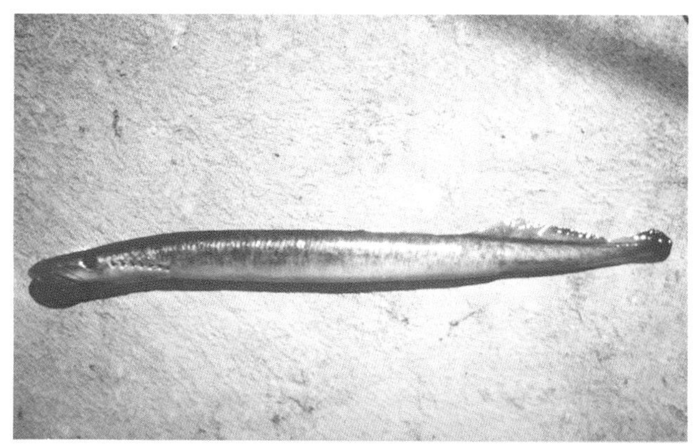
Sea lamprey *Petromyzon marinus*

Sea lamprey *Petromyzon marinus*, side view of head region

Sea lamprey *Petromyzon marinus*, view of buccal funnel

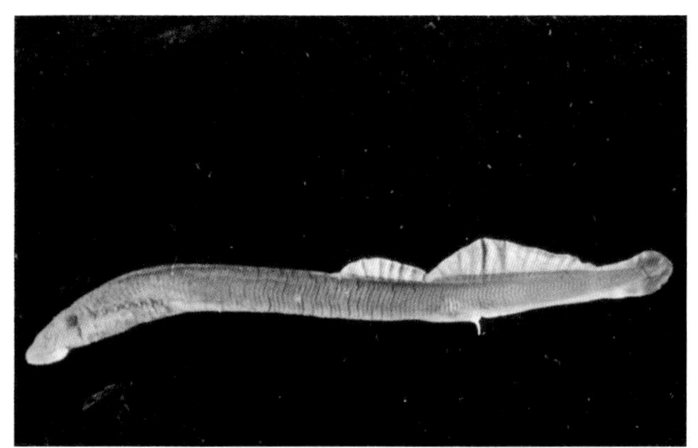

American brook lamprey *Lampetra appendix*, ♂

Lake sturgeon *Acipenser fulvescens*

Shovelnose sturgeon *Scaphirhynchus platorynchus*

Paddlefish *Polyodon spathula*

Shortnose gar *Lepisosteus platostomus*

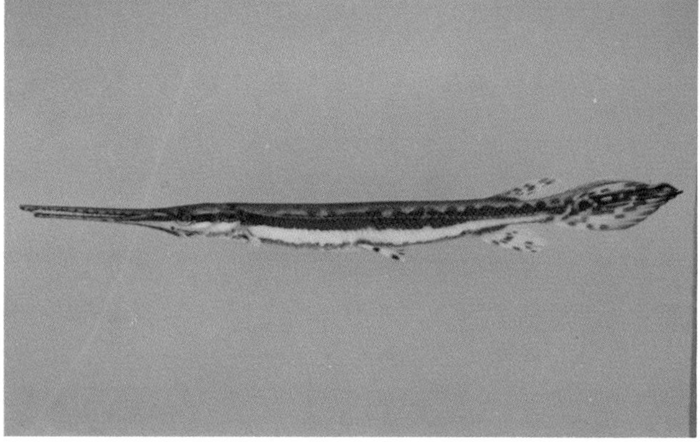

Longnose gar *Lepisosteus osseus*, immature

Longnose gar *Lepisosteus osseus*, adult

Bowfin *Amia calva*

Gizzard shad *Dorosoma cepedianum*

American eel *Anguilla rostrata*

Goldeye *Hiodon alosoides*

Alewife *Alosa pseudoharengus*

Mooneye *Hiodon tergisus*

Skipjack herring *Alosa chrysochloris*

Brown trout *Salmo trutta*

Rainbow trout *Salmo gairdneri*

Brook trout *Salvelinus fontinalis*, subadult

Pink salmon *Oncorhynchus gorbuscha*, ♂

Brook trout *Salvelinus fontinalis*, adult

Coho salmon *Oncorhynchus kisutch*

Tiger trout *Salvelinus fontinalis* × *Salmo trutta*, hybrid

Chinook salmon *Oncorhynchus tshawytscha*

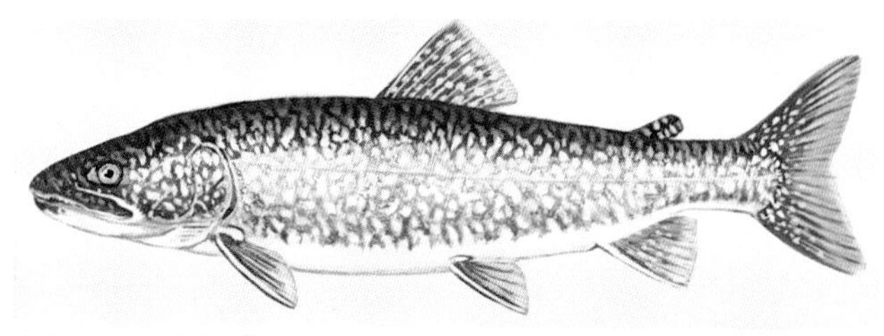

Lake trout *Salvelinus namaycush namaycush*

Lake whitefish *Coregonus clupeaformis*

Cisco or Lake herring *Coregonus artedii*

Shortjaw cisco *Coregonus zenithicus*

Shortjaw cisco *Coregonus zenithicus*, head view

Bloater *Coregonus hoyi*

Bloater *Coregonus hoyi*, head view

Kiyi *Coregonus kiyi*

Pygmy whitefish *Prosopium coulteri*

Round whitefish *Prosopium cylindraceum*

Northern pike *Esox lucius*

Rainbow smelt *Osmerus mordax*

Muskellunge *Esox masquinongy*

Central mudminnow *Umbra limi*

Grass carp *Ctenopharyngodon idella*

Grass pickerel *Esox americanus vermiculatus*

Common carp *Cyprinus carpio*

Goldfish *Carassius auratus*, gold phase

Goldfish *Carassius auratus*, gray phase

Golden shiner *Notemigonus crysoleucas*, immature

Golden shiner *Notemigonus crysoleucas*, adult

Creek chub *Semotilus atromaculatus*, ♂

Creek chub *Semotilus atromaculatus*, ♀

Pearl dace *Semotilus margarita*

Redside dace *Clinostomus elongatus*, ♀

Finescale dace *Phoxinus neogaeus*

Northern redbelly dace *Phoxinus eos*, ♂

Southern redbelly dace *Phoxinus erythrogaster*, ♂

Lake chub *Couesius plumbeus*

Southern redbelly dace *Phoxinus erythrogaster*, ♀

Blacknose dace *Rhinichthys atratulus*, ♀

Longnose dace *Rhinichthys cataractae*, ♂

Largescale stoneroller *Campostoma oligolepis*, ♂

Longnose dace *Rhinichthys cataractae*, ♀

Largescale stoneroller *Campostoma oligolepis*, ♀

Central stoneroller *Campostoma anomalum*, ♀

Hornyhead chub *Nocomis biguttatus*, ♂

Gravel chub *Hybopsis x-punctata*

Suckermouth minnow *Phenacobius mirabilis*, ♂

Silver chub *Hybopsis storeriana*

Pallid shiner *Notropis amnis*

Speckled chub *Hybopsis aestivalis*, ♀

Emerald shiner *Notropis atherinoides*

Rosyface shiner *Notropis rubellus*, ♀

Redfin shiner *Notropis umbratilis*, ♂

Redfin shiner *Notropis umbratilis*, ♀

Common shiner *Notropis cornutus*, ♂

Striped shiner *Notropis chrysocephalus*

River shiner *Notropis blennius*

Ironcolor shiner *Notropis chalybaeus*

Weed shiner *Notropis texanus*

Blackchin shiner *Notropis heterodon*

Spotfin shiner *Notropis spilopterus*, ♂ (top) ♀ (bottom)

Spottail shiner *Notropis hudsonius*

Red shiner *Notropis lutrensis*

Bigmouth shiner *Notropis dorsalis*, ♀

Pugnose shiner *Notropis anogenus*

Sand shiner *Notropis stramineus*

Blacknose shiner *Notropis heterolepis*

Mimic shiner *Notropis volucellus*

Pugnose minnow *Notropis emiliae*, ♂ (top) ♀ (bottom)

Ghost shiner *Notropis buchanani*

Ozark minnow *Notropis nubilus*

Brassy minnow *Hybognathus hankinsoni*

Bluntnose minnow *Pimephales notatus*, ♂ (top) ♀ (bottom)

Mississippi silvery minnow *Hybognathus nuchalis*

Fathead minnow *Pimephales promelas*, ♂ (top) ♀ (bottom)

Bullhead minnow *Pimephales vigilax*

Blue sucker *Cycleptus elongatus*

Bigmouth buffalo *Ictiobus cyprinellus*

River carpsucker *Carpiodes carpio*

Black buffalo *Ictiobus niger*

Highfin carpsucker *Carpiodes velifer*

Smallmouth buffalo *Ictiobus bubalus*

Spotted sucker *Minytrema melanops*

Quillback *Carpiodes cyprinus*

Lake chubsucker *Erimyzon sucetta*, immature

Golden redhorse *Moxostoma erythrurum*

Lake chubsucker *Erimyzon sucetta*, adult ♂

Silver redhorse *Moxostoma anisurum*

Creek chubsucker *Erimyzon oblongus*, ♂

Shorthead redhorse *Moxostoma macrolepidotum*

Black redhorse *Moxostoma duquesnei*

Greater redhorse *Moxostoma valenciennesi*

River redhorse *Moxostoma carinatum*, ♂

Black bullhead *Ictalurus melas*

Northern hog sucker *Hypentelium nigricans*

Brown bullhead *Ictalurus nebulosus*

White sucker *Catostomus commersoni*

Yellow bullhead *Ictalurus natalis*

Longnose sucker *Catostomus catostomus*, ♂

Channel catfish *Ictalurus punctatus*

Tadpole madtom *Noturus gyrinus*

Pirate perch *Aphredoderus sayanus*

Slender madtom *Noturus exilis*

Trout-perch *Percopsis omiscomaycus*

Stonecat *Noturus flavus*

Burbot *Lota lota*

Flathead catfish *Pylodictis olivaris*

Banded killifish *Fundulus diaphanus*

Blackstripe topminnow *Fundulus notatus*

Ninespine stickleback *Pungitius pungitius*

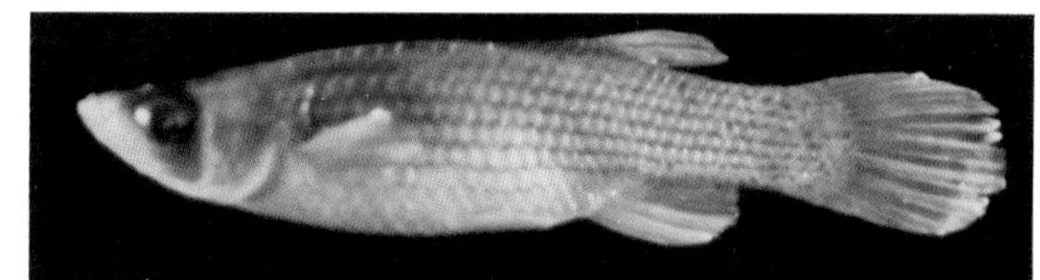

Starhead topminnow *Fundulus notti*, ♂ (top) ♀ (bottom)

White bass *Morone chrysops*

Brook silverside *Labidesthes sicculus*

Yellow bass *Morone mississippiensis*

Brook stickleback *Culaea inconstans*

Smallmouth bass *Micropterus dolomieui*

Pumpkinseed *Lepomis gibbosus*

Largemouth bass *Micropterus salmoides*

Longear sunfish *Lepomis megalotis*

Warmouth *Lepomis gulosus*

Orangespotted sunfish *Lepomis humilis*

Green sunfish *Lepomis cyanellus*, ♂

Bluegill *Lepomis macrochirus*

Rock bass *Ambloplites rupestris*, immature

Rock bass *Ambloplites rupestris*, adult

White crappie *Pomoxis annularis*

Black crappie *Pomoxis nigromaculatus*

Walleye *Stizostedion vitreum vitreum*

Sauger *Stizostedion canadense*

Yellow perch *Perca flavescens*

Slenderhead darter *Percina phoxocephala*

Blackside darter *Percina maculata*

River darter *Percina shumardi*

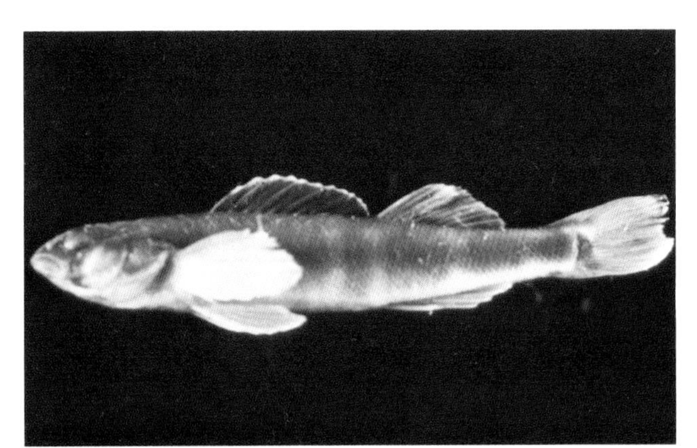

Gilt darter *Percina evides*

Crystal darter *Ammocrypta asprella*

Logperch *Percina caprodes*

Western sand darter *Ammocrypta clara*

Johnny darter *Etheostoma nigrum*

Bluntnose darter *Etheostoma chlorosomum*, ♂

Mud darter *Etheostoma asprigene*, ♂

Banded darter *Etheostoma zonale*

Iowa darter *Etheostoma exile*, ♂ (top) ♀ (bottom)

Rainbow darter *Etheostoma caeruleum*, ♂

Fantail darter *Etheostoma flabellare*, ♂ (top) ♀ (bottom)

Least darter *Etheostoma microperca*

Mottled sculpin *Cottus bairdi*

Freshwater drum *Aplodinotus grunniens*

Slimy sculpin *Cottus cognatus*

Deepwater sculpin *Myoxocephalus thompsoni*

Spoonhead sculpin *Cottus ricei*

The Species Accounts

Lamprey Family—Petromyzontidae

Five species of lampreys in three genera are known from Wisconsin. Of these, three are parasitic and two nonparasitic. In the United States and Canada, 17 species occur in 3 genera (Robins et al. 1980), and 13 of the species are strictly freshwater forms. A fossil specimen of *Mayomyzon piekoensis* was reported from the middle Pennsylvanian Francis Creek Shale of northeastern Illinois (Bardack and Zangerl 1968).

Lampreys are scaleless and cartilaginous with funnel-like mouths, often armed with horny teeth. A single, median nostril occurs anterior to the eyes. Seven pairs of gills open to the outside, each by an individual opening. A long single or double dorsal fin is continuous with the caudal fin; paired fins are absent.

All adult lampreys show the following traits: (1) In breeding females the anal fin fold is well developed and the tail turns upward, while in the males the anal fin fold is scarcely developed and the tail bends downward. (2) The lumen of the intestinal tract becomes nonfunctional and closes in fully mature individuals. (3) Between the time of peak physical development and spawning, the lengths and weights of adult lampreys of both sexes diminish. At spawning time sexually mature individuals are much smaller than they were a few months previously (Vladykov 1951).

Adults deposit their eggs in riffles of freshwater streams and then die. Upon hatching, the larval young burrow into silt and sand in quiet water where they filter-feed and grow. After 3 or more years, they metamorphose into adults during late summer and early fall. The nonparasitic forms spawn the following spring but the parasitic lampreys not until a year later. Nonparasitic lampreys spend their entire lives in streams; the parasitic forms may migrate downstream into widespreads of large rivers or into lakes where they prey on large fishes.

Lampreys are secretive. Except for the parasitic adults attached to large fishes, they are rarely taken. Even these may release themselves from the prey fish as they are being lifted from the water. In recent years, larger numbers of lampreys have been collected by electrofishing. The electric shock momentarily immobilizes the free-swimming adults. Lamprey ammocoetes are forced from their burrows in the stream bottom by the electric current and are collected in dip nets.

The role of the lampreys has not yet been defined. As a group, they are repulsive to the general public; some fishermen refuse to touch them. Erroneously, all lampreys are condemned as parasitic and harmful. The greatest populations of native parasitic lampreys occur in some of our best fishing waters, which suggests that generalizations regarding the harmful effects of lampreys on sport fish species may not be true and instead that some unknown salutary effect may be occurring. On the other hand, it must be recognized that the sea lamprey which invaded the Great Lakes basin has been responsible for considerable damage to our native fish stocks.

Silver Lamprey

Ichthyomyzon unicuspis Hubbs and Trautman. *Ichthyomyzon*—sucker of fish; *unicuspis*—unicuspid, characteristic of the circumoral teeth.

Other common names: northern lamprey, northern silver lamprey, river lamprey, brook lamprey, lamprey eel, lamper eel, blue lamprey, hitchhiker, bloodsucker.

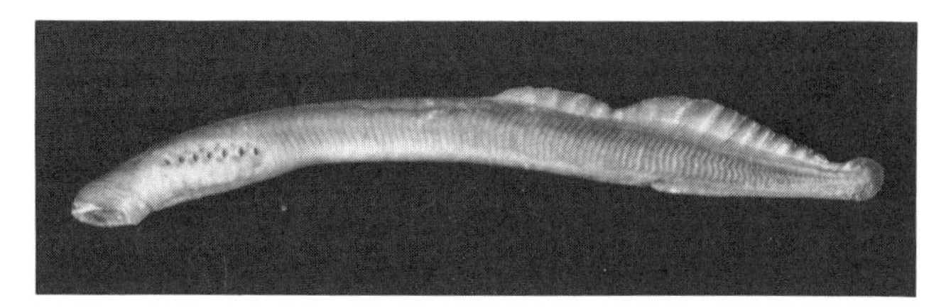

Adult 260 mm (specimen donated by Wisconsin DNR)

DESCRIPTION

Adult parasitic, cylindrical. Length 103–326 mm (4.1–12.8 in). Branchial diam into length of sucking disc 1.5 (1.0–1.8); length of sucking disc into TL 11.1 (8.2–14.8). Supraoral lamina with 2 (rarely 3) narrowly separated teeth. Circumoral teeth 4 on either side of the mouth opening, usually unicuspid (single point), the remainder bicuspid. Teeth in the anterior row of disc 2–4, usually 3. Teeth in lateral rows 4–8, usually 6 or 7. Transverse lingual lamina bilobed.

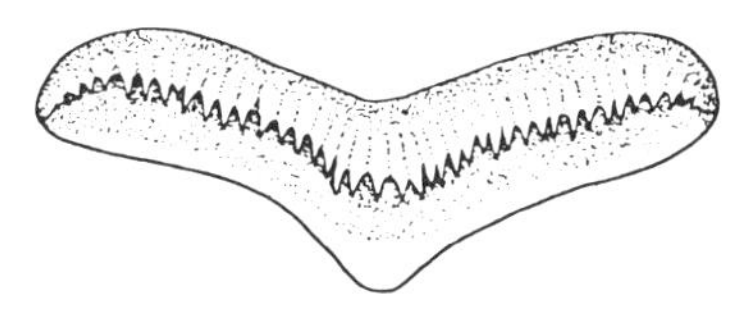

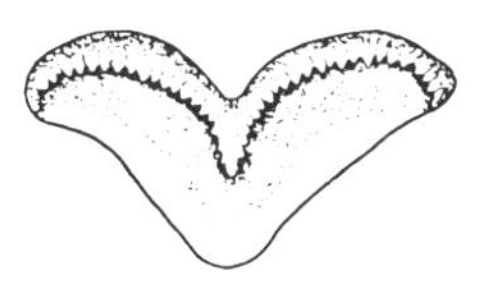

Transverse lingual lamina strongly curved to bilobed for silver lamprey (Hubbs and Trautman 1937:33)

Trunk myomeres 51 (46–53). Fins: 1 dorsal with a shallow notch, connected to a short round caudal fin.

Young adult usually light yellow-tan, lighter on belly and gradually darkening toward the back; sides sometimes mottled, occasionally slatey at any stage. Large mature specimen blue or blue-gray on the sides and black and grayish or bluish on the lower surface. Lateral line sense organs and those on the underside of the branchial region slightly darkened with increase over 150 mm TL but far less black pigment than in the chestnut lamprey.

Ammocoete indistinguishable from ammocoete of the northern brook lamprey (Purvis 1970).

Sexual dimorphism: Male with mid-dorsal ridge always present but not always prominent; urogenital papilla occasionally extending beyond ventral margin of body. Female with prominent post-anal fold, and body greatly distended from behind gill region to the cloaca.

Suspected hybrid: *I. unicuspis* × *I. castaneus* (Starrett et al. 1960). Experimental *I. unicuspis* × *I. castaneus*, *I. unicuspis* × *I. fossor* (Piavis et al. 1970).

DISTRIBUTION, STATUS, AND HABITAT

The silver lamprey occurs in all major drainages of Wisconsin, especially in the boundary waters, the lower Wisconsin River, and the tributaries and lower lakes of the Upper Fox and Wolf rivers.

The silver lamprey is endangered in Nebraska and South Dakota and rare in West Virginia (Miller 1972). In Wisconsin it is uncommon to common. It is widely distributed in the Lake Superior drainage but not taken in large numbers at any barrier (McLain et al. 1965).

This species is the common native parasitic lamprey of large rivers and large lakes. Its habitat coincides with waters bearing the greatest number of large host fishes, particularly the scaleless catfishes and the sturgeons. During spawning it is found in fairly clear medium- to large-sized rivers over gravel, and occasionally over sand. Feeding adults may be taken over a wide range of bottom types—heavy gravel to deep, soft mud, as in Lake Winnebago. In the Mississippi River it is occasionally taken with the chestnut lamprey. The ecological distribution of these two species is generally complementary. Hubbs and Trautman (1937) suggested that this mutual avoidance is due to competition and the resulting population pressure. They also suggested that the sea lamprey may partly or wholly replace *Ichthyomyzon* in Lakes Michigan and Superior.

BIOLOGY

Spawning in Wisconsin occurs in April, May, and possibly June. A sexually mature female (326 mm, 65.5 g), taken 8 April from the Waupaca River (Waupaca County), had ovarian weight of 9.71 g and an estimated 27,400 eggs 0.8–1.0 mm diam. In Canada a sexually mature female (201 mm, 13.5 g) had 15,474 eggs 0.8 mm diam (Vladykov 1951).

In the spring, after water temperature reaches 10°C (50°F) or more, the adults begin to migrate upstream to spawn in nests they build in the gravel and sand of riffles in medium-sized streams with moderate gradients (Trautman 1957). At a developmental temperature of 18.4°C (65°F), the burrowing larvae appear within 5 days (A. J. Smith et al. 1968). When the young leave the nest, they drift downstream and dig into bars and beds containing a combination of sand, dark muck, and organic debris which is free from

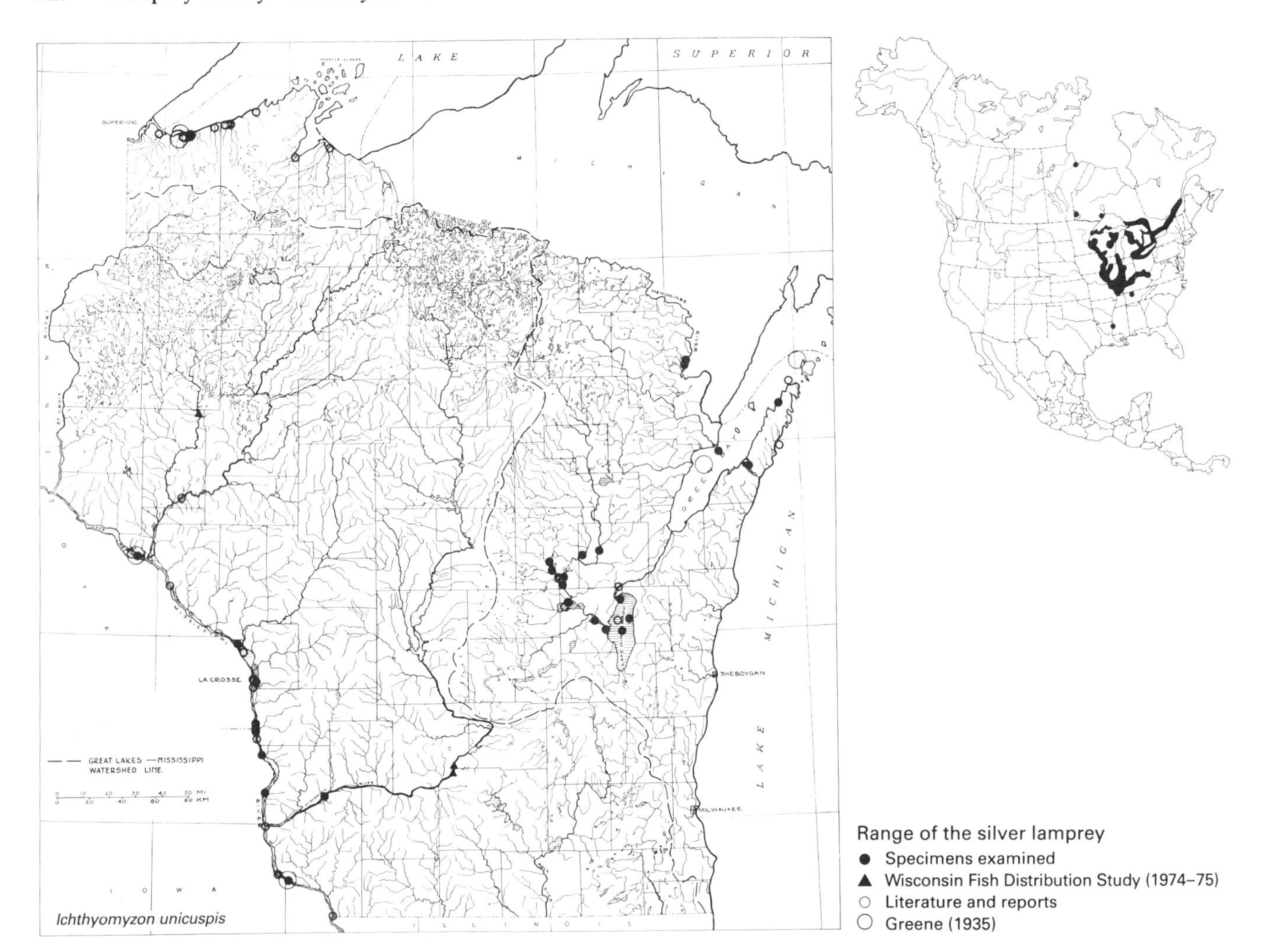

Ichthyomyzon unicuspis

clayey soil. There they remain for an indefinite period of time, possibly 4–7 years (Scott and Crossman 1973). They thrust their heads out from the upstream openings of their semicircular tunnels in order to feed upon the downstream-drifting microscopic food. The filter apparatus selects out algae, pollen, diatoms, and protozoans (Harlan and Speaker 1956). They are not parasitic as ammocoetes.

Metamorphosis or transformation begins in August while the ammocoetes are still in their burrows, and by the following spring they emerge from their burrows as small but transformed lampreys. In Wisconsin in May these are 103–139 mm (1.6–5.9 g); in Ohio, newly transformed silver lampreys (101–152 mm) enter Lake Erie in late April, May, and June (Trautman 1957); in Canada the ammocoetes (89–110 mm, 1–2 g) complete their transformation between 15 May and 15 July.

The adult is parasitic upon other fishes, attaching itself with its suction-cup mouth. The sharp teeth cut through the scales and the skin of the lamprey's prey, and the blood of the prey is extracted. Lampreys have been reported to parasitize northern pike, paddlefish, carp, lake sturgeon, suckers, white bass, and catfish.

In a laboratory experiment in which 23 species of fish were placed in tanks with silver lampreys, the silver lampreys chose brown bullhead, channel catfish, bowfin, white sucker, longnose sucker, American eel, carp, burbot, and black crappie as hosts (Roy 1973). Of these, the carp and black crappie were used as supports, not for feeding. According to Vladykov and Roy (1948), no vertebrates other than fishes are attacked by silver lampreys.

Observations in the laboratory show that this species is especially active at night; 81.5% of the attacks occurred during the night. The silver lamprey does not show any hesitation in its choice of a host, even if the fish in its tank are numerous. Sometimes an individual which appears indifferent toward several hosts will fix itself on a new fish, from among those recently introduced into the tank. An attack generally is made from the side, occasionally from the rear.

The period of greatest growth and most active

parasitic feeding occurs between June and September. The lengths and weights of adult silver lampreys from Wisconsin have been tabulated according to the month captured.

Lengths and Weights of Adult Silver Lamprey in Wisconsin (Preserved Museum Specimens)

	No. of Fish	TL (mm)		WT (g)	
		Avg	Range	Avg.	Range
May	6[a]	122	103–139	3.3	1.6–5.9
June	4	138	117–170	6.4	2.8–12.6
July	9	145	125–195	8.1	3.1–15.7
Aug.	1	181		13.1	
Sept.	3	228	190–263	34.4	18.2–57.8
Oct. to Dec.	—	—	—	—	—
Jan.	1	293		46.4	
Feb.	5	255	192–330	50.2	25.6–104.1
Mar.	4	262	242–275	45.1	37.2–51.2
Apr.	2[b]	276	225–326	48.9	32.4–65.5

[a]Newly transformed.
[b]Sexually mature.

Comparable mean-growth data for the period of active feeding and growth come from the St. Lawrence River of Canada (Vladykov and Roy 1948).

	Males		Females	
	TL (mm)	WT (g)	TL (mm)	WT (g)
May	107.9	2.1	113.0	2.7
Nov.	230.7	32.5	255.3	42.0

During the winter months following an active feeding period and until the time of spawning the next spring, lengths and weights of both sexes diminish. Roy (1973) found that some individuals in the laboratory continued feeding and did not reach maximum growth until mid-January and the end of February. Individuals placed in aquariums in November and kept alive from 2 to 6 months decrease 4–22% in length and 52–57% in weight (Vladykov and Roy 1948). Among the causes of shrinkage and weight loss are fasting up to 6 months, narrowing of the intestinal opening, and degeneration of the digestive tract until it becomes nonfunctional. Despite this, the gonads develop rapidly, with individuals ready to spawn in April and May. After spawning, the silver lamprey dies; the length of life for transformed individuals varies from 12 to 13 months.

In Wisconsin the largest silver lamprey reported (UWSP 2514) was 330 mm (13 in) long; in Quebec, 322 mm (Roy 1973); in Ohio, 328 mm (Hubbs and Trautman 1937); in Illinois, 395 mm (Starrett et al. 1960).

IMPORTANCE AND MANAGEMENT

The ammocoetes and small adults of the silver lamprey are doubtless preyed on by a variety of fishes, but its use as human food is probably minimal, although various reports concerning its edibility have been received. Occasionally small adults are used on the lower Wisconsin River and elsewhere as bait for sport fishes such as bass and catfish.

Although it is parasitic and feeds upon the body juices of host fishes to which it attaches, the silver lamprey is not considered especially destructive in Wisconsin (Brasch 1950).

Periodically, however, problems associated with this species do occur and the public clamors for remedial action. In late 1949 numerous "river lampreys" were reported parasitizing fish in Pool 11 of the Mississippi River (opposite Grant County). About 500 silver lampreys (153 mm TL) had done damage to various fish, mostly carp, but also catfish, paddlefish, and crappies. One commercial fisherman noted that "lampreyitis" was sweeping over the area. The state press carried a series of reports on the situation, and the comments of fish experts were quoted. A biologist assigned to the problem found that in all other sectors of the river silver lampreys were so scarce as to be no menace or not a serious drawback to the food and sport fish. The cause of the flare-up was unknown. The incident passed and no further outbreaks have occurred there.

In 1966 and 1967, there was concern over the possible effects of the native parasitic lampreys on the fishery of the Upper Fox and Wolf rivers and their lakes. R. Harris, former Department of Natural Resources area supervisor, stated:

> They've been here as long as the Indians have. We know they are capable of killing fish and have at times, but we also know they do not do the damage the sea lamprey does. . . . We've seen large carp carrying eight or 10 lampreys and counted sturgeon with 26 on them. . . . the fact that the silver and chestnut lampreys are native to the water and even in high cycles of population do not make much of an inroad on the fish leads us to say they cannot be classed as a menace such as the sea lamprey is (*Fond du Lac Commonwealth Reporter* 1 June 1967).

Among the best waters in Wisconsin for sport and commercial fishing are the Mississippi River and the lower portions of the Wolf and Fox rivers and their lakes, which coincide with the best silver lamprey waters in Wisconsin. Despite the occurrence of large numbers of lampreys from time to time, the overall fishing has seemed to be unaffected.

Northern Brook Lamprey

Ichthyomyzon fossor Reighard and Cummins. *Ichthyomyzon*—sucker of fish; *fossor*—a digger.

Other common names: Michigan brook lamprey, brook lamprey, Reighard's lamprey, bloodsucker.

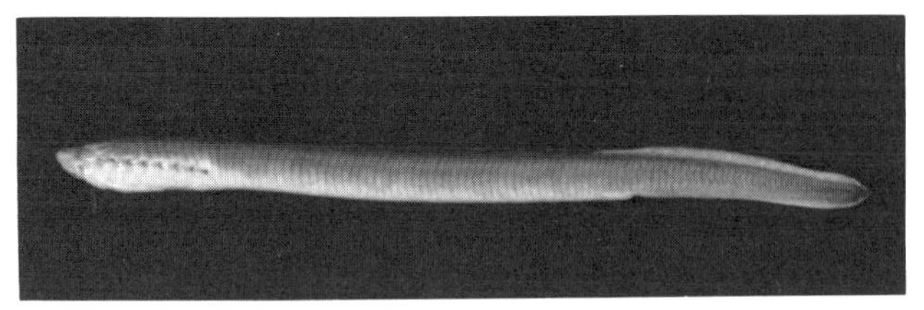

Ammocoete 143 mm, Tomorrow R. (Portage Co.), 17 Apr. 1962

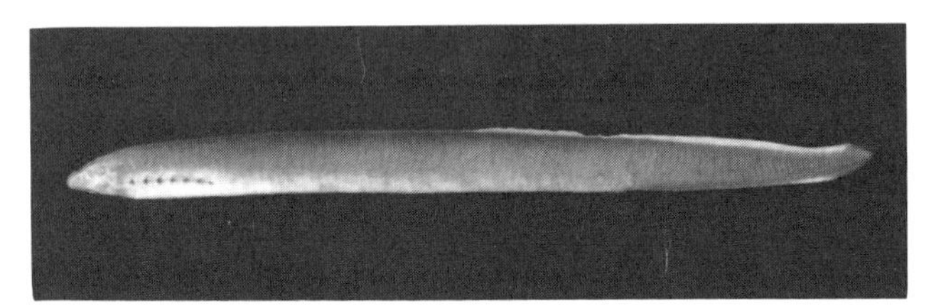

Adult 125 mm, Plover R., Jordan Park (Portage Co.), 10 Sept. 1969

DESCRIPTION

Adult nonparasitic, cylindrical. Length 105–162 mm (4.1–6.4 in). Branchial diam into length of sucking disc 0.65 (0.40–0.91); length of sucking disc into TL 31 (21–49). Supraoral lamina with 2 teeth, close together. Teeth of buccal funnel small and blunt. Transverse lingual lamina bilobed. Trunk myomeres 51 (46–56). Fins: 1 dorsal with or without a shallow notch, connected to a short round caudal fin. Chromosomes 2n = 164–166 (Robinson et al. 1974).

Adult color dark grayish brown on back and sides, pale gray or silvery white on belly. Pale median line against a dark back. Posterior part of tail about notochord dark gray, almost black. Sense organs of lateral line system generally of same color as trunk background. Following spawning until death, slate blue to black on back and sides, abrupt white or white-gray on belly.

Ammocoete back, sides, and caudal peduncle brown to gray-brown grading to tan on belly and a narrow strip at the base of the caudal peduncle. Anal fold unpigmented. Lateral line sense organs colored as background, occasionally posterior organs encircled with thin black line, visible under magnification. Pale median line along dark back. Suborbital area unpigmented or lightly pigmented, providing a whitish "window." Dorsal fin unpigmented or with scattered pigment, sometimes forming vertical columns. Precursor of tongue with swollen bulb at base pigmented black. Trunk myomeres 50 (45–55). Ammocoete indistinguishable from that of silver lamprey (Purvis 1970).

Sexual dimorphism: Breeding male with urogenital papilla 1–2 mm long protruding through swollen and inflamed cloaca. Breeding female with prominent, slightly convoluted post-anal fold, body greatly distended from behind gill region to cloaca and eggs visible through body wall.

Hybrids: Experimental *I. fossor* × *I. castaneus*, *I. fossor* × *I. unicuspis* (Piavis et al. 1970).

SYSTEMATIC NOTES

The northern brook lamprey was described by Reighard and Cummins (1916). Hubbs and Trautman (1937) consider this species a dwarf, degenerative, nonparasitic form derived from the larger, parasitic *Ichthyomyzon unicuspis*.

DISTRIBUTION, STATUS, AND HABITAT

The northern brook lamprey occurs in the Mississippi, Lake Michigan, and Lake Superior drainage basins. It is present in the Wisconsin, Red Cedar, and Rock river systems of the Mississippi drainage; in the Menominee, Peshtigo, and lower Wolf river systems of the Lake Michigan drainage; and in a number of tributaries to Lake Superior. It is probably more widely distributed than the records indicate.

This species is uncommon in the Wisconsin River system, and common in the Red Cedar and Wolf river systems.

Although the northern brook lamprey has been captured from small brooks (1–3 m wide) and large rivers (30–100 m wide), it is more common in streams of medium size, averaging 19 m wide and 0.7 m deep. Two large series of ammocoetes and adults were recovered over the following bottoms: mud 10%, sand 80%, gravel 10%; and hardpan 20%, sand and silt 80%. It usually occurs in moderately warm water, generally unsuitable for brook trout. The middle or lower portions of clear or muddy streams inhabited by this species often have water temperatures which fluctuate readily with changing air temperatures. In the Brule River (Douglas County) it is most numerous in fairly shallow pools having sand-silt bottoms and some rooted vegetation (Churchill 1945).

BIOLOGY

In central Wisconsin spawning occurs from late April to early June; in northern Wisconsin during June.

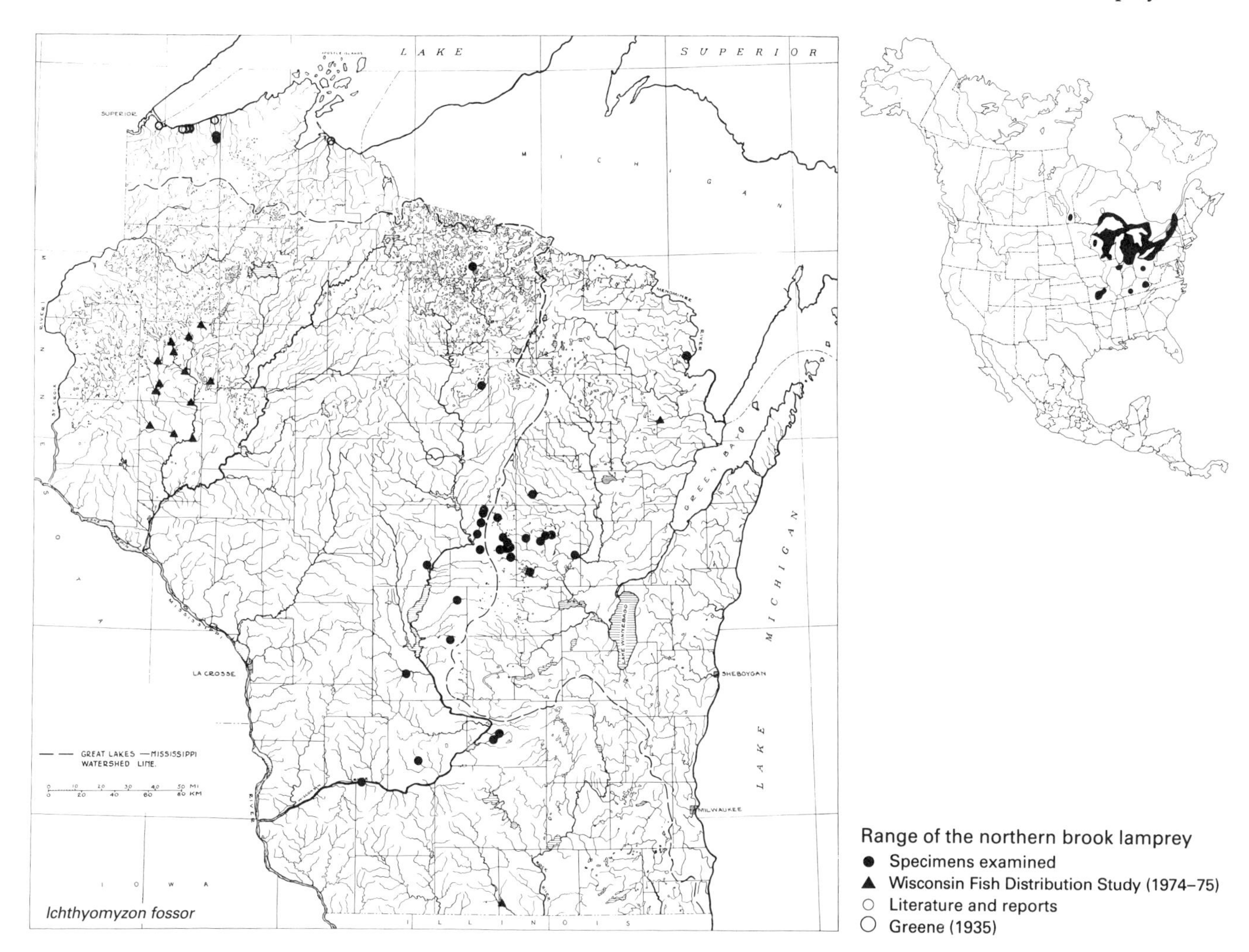

Tomorrow-Waupaca River (Portage County) specimens yield the following data: 17 April, a prespawning female (127 mm, 4.2 g) with 1,400 tight eggs (0.6–0.9 mm diam); 9 May, a visibly gravid female (147 mm, 6.4 g) with loose eggs (1.0–1.2 mm diam), a highly elevated dorsal fin, a caudal peduncle bent upward and in ready-to-spawn condition; 30 May, a spawned-out female (130 mm, 3.0 g) with only a single egg (0.9 mm diam) remaining in the ovary, emaciated with disc and anterior head degenerating.

Little Wolf River (Waupaca County) specimens: 18 April, two females with loose eggs (0.8–1.0 mm diam) and close to spawning; 26 May, five females completely spawned out (one with only four eggs left in ovary), one female with several hundred loose eggs (1.0–1.3 mm diam) still in abdominal cavity. Breeding was almost completed by this time. In nearby Blake Brook on 7 June, one female, gravid with eggs (0.8–1.0 mm diam), and four males were in ready-to-breed condition.

The differences in spawning times may be a function of water temperatures. The Little Wolf River provides brown trout water which warms up more readily in the spring than Blake Brook, a brook trout–brown trout stream. In the Tomorrow-Waupaca River, water temperatures fluctuate quickly in response to changes in air temperatures. During 1959, water temperatures from 9 to 30 May averaged 17 (7.4–23.9)°C. In Canada mature specimens were collected from 8 to 30 May at water temperatures ranging from 12.8 to 17.2°C, and spawning reached its peak at 13.3–15.6°C (Vladykov 1949). In Michigan spawning seldom takes place when the water is below 18°C; it is most vigorous at 20–22°C (Reighard and Cummins 1916).

Spawning was observed in Michigan from 23 to 27 May; the last adult was seen on 2 June (Reighard and Cummins 1916). The spawning site in Mill Creek was 9.14 m (30 ft) wide, from 0.2 to 0.5 m (8–20 in) deep over gravel 25–152 mm (1–6 in) diam. The current was strong. Adults attached themselves to pebbles, tossing them up and out from between the larger stones. Active lashing of the body at the same time served to stir up the sand, which was swept away by the current. Bright lights were avoided. Some spawning nests were ill-defined; some were 75–102 mm (3–4 in) diam and of about the same depth. As many as seven or eight individuals were involved in nest-building.

Because the spawning took place more or less hidden among stones, it was difficult to determine the exact details of the act. Apparently the male attaches himself by the buccal funnel either to a stone close to where the female is likewise attached or to the body of the female near her head. Then the bodies of both are thrown into spasmodic vibration and the eggs and milt are shed.

Hankinson (1932) determined that this species will also nest out in the open without any concealing stones or other large objects near the nests. He observed nests on 10, 11, and 13 May. All were depressions in bottom material of gravel shallows just above riffles; the water was about 0.3 m (1 ft) deep. From three to seven individuals were in the nests, coiling their bodies about one another. Spawning behavior was similar in every way to that of the American brook lamprey (*Lampetra appendix*).

In Missouri, Pflieger (1975) observed adults in the same nests as the chestnut lamprey, suggesting that nests excavated by the large parasitic species are sometimes utilized for spawning by this smaller species.

Optimum rearing temperature is 18.4°C (65°F) (A. J. Smith et al. 1968). The developmental period is about 12 days, after which the young wriggle free and for a time become free swimming (Leach 1940). About 14 days after fertilization many larvae attempt to burrow. They dig, head downward, tail vibrating, forming a burrow in the shape of a flattened U.

In the Brule River (Douglas County) ammocoete burrows are generally found among vegetation in a mixture of sand and silt in water 0.2–0.6 m (8–24 in) deep (Churchill 1945). Where conditions are optimum, the concentration is very high. At one station on a delta below a strong rapids, 153 lampreys were taken from an area of 15.6 m^2.

The food of the ammocoetes consists of microscopic organisms such as diatoms and unicellular algae (Churchill 1945).

Growth of the ammocoetes is rapid. A 19-mm young-of-year was taken on 16 October from the Tomorrow-Waupaca River. In the Sturgeon River, Michigan, Purvis (1970) determined annual increments of growth (based on October samples) as 37 mm (1.5 in) for the first year of life, 28 mm (1.1 in) for the second year, and 15 mm (0.6 in) for the third. For another year class the increments were 35, 39, and 27 mm (1.4, 1.5, and 1.1 in), respectively.

Sixty-nine ammocoetes from the Crystal River (Waupaca County) on 25 September 1971 appear to make the following age groupings based on lengths and weights: I: 27.5 mm, 0.065 g; II: 47–71 mm, 0.38–0.55 g; III: 75–102 mm, 0.61–1.66 g; IV: 104–123 mm, 2.10–3.22 g; V: 131–141 mm, 3.56–4.25 g; VI: 155 mm, 6.42 g. Many problems have been encountered in attempting to age ammocoetes through size, although it is generally conceded that of the nonparasitic lampreys this species is perhaps the longest lived (Okkelberg 1922, Hubbs 1925). The largest specimen collected came from the Tomorrow-Waupaca River (Portage County) and was 171 mm, 11.01 g (6.7 in, 0.4 oz).

Ammocoetes develop over 3 to 6 years prior to transformation (Purvis 1970, Okkelberg 1922, Hubbs 1925). Leach (1940) discusses the transformation process in detail. He found that after the transforming season there were always nontransforming ammocoetes which were longer than the largest transforming ammocoetes, and suggests that during the last year before transformation the ammocoete enters into a resting period during which there is cessation of feeding and a probable decrease in length.

In Wisconsin, transformation begins on the Brule River as early as 9 August (Churchill 1945). In central Wisconsin on 21 August I have seen transforming individuals which had well-formed eyes, transverse and horizontal lingual lamina defined, the sieve apparatus disappearing medially and retracting peripherally, and papillary fringe buds appearing. The disc length at this time is short (2–3 mm).

Although the transforming animals remain in their burrows during metamorphosis, they tend to leave the sand for longer intervals as the process advances (Leach 1940). Swimming does not become obvious, however, until late January and early February. It is assumed that the transformation process is complete only when the lampreys abandon their burrows. A period of about 3 or 4 months elapses between the completion of transformation and spawning. During the entire transformation and maturity period there is a reduction in the length of the animal. Leach estimates this as about 10% of the length at the onset of metamorphosis.

Early metamorphosis is described from an age-III population of this species in the Sturgeon River, Michigan. Thirty-two ammocoetes (6% of the lampreys 97–144 mm long) metamorphosed. The remaining ammocoetes of this year class would be expected to transform in succeeding years. Consequently a year class of this species contributes to two or more spawning populations. The length-frequency data demonstrate that this part of the year class metamorphosed at age III without an extended rest period (Purvis 1970).

Throughout the adult phase of life this species does not feed; the alimentary canal is nonfunctional and degenerates. Fifty adults from Wisconsin waters averaged 126 (105–162) mm long and 4.06 (1.9–7.0) g. Of 68 adults examined from the Brule River, 37 males averaged 110 (97–130) mm in length and 31 females, 123 (112–141) mm (Churchill 1945). The largest adult was 165 mm, 9.90 g (6.5 in, 0.3 oz); it was taken from Willow Creek (Rock County) on 5 November 1975 (Wis. Fish Distrib. Study 1974–75).

It is generally assumed that the adults die a few days after spawning. However, on 7 August 1958, 2 months following the spawning season, two fully mature adults, a male with spawned-out testis and a female with well-formed but undersized eggs (0.3–0.5 mm diam), were captured from the Tomorrow-Waupaca River.

In some streams of lower Michigan the northern brook lamprey inhabited waters of relatively low temperature (Morman 1979). In these the mean daily water temperatures during mid-June to August ranged from 14 to 20°C (57.2 to 68°F), with daily maximums up to 21.5°C (70.7°F).

Other lamprey species are seldom taken in the same water with the northern brook lamprey; however, in the Lake Superior drainage the northern brook lamprey occurs commonly in the same stream system with the silver lamprey and sea lamprey, but only occasionally with the American brook lamprey (H. Purvis, pers. comm.). It generally occurs in larger waters than the American brook lamprey and in smaller waters than the parasitic silver lamprey. Where ranges overlap, generally only one species is common.

IMPORTANCE AND MANAGEMENT

Since the northern brook lamprey is not parasitic, it has no harmful effect on other fishes. In the Brule River its activities are restricted to a single type of habitat, where its principal neighbors are burrowing mayfly nymphs and small mussels. All three of these forms feed directly on the microscopic organisms of the water and the mud-water interface and possibly compete with one another for food. The abundance of all three in the same area indicates that such competition does not have an adverse effect on their survival (Churchill 1945).

Occasionally this species is used as food by other fishes. The rock bass is a predator (Scott and Crossman 1973) and, in the Brule River, lampreys were taken from the stomachs of five rainbow trout (Churchill 1945).

We have no records of this species being used in Wisconsin as bait for catching sport fishes, as is the case in Canada (Vladykov 1949), nor are there published records that this small lamprey is used as food by man.

This species is sensitive to the lampricide 3-trifluoromethyl-4-nitrophenol (TFM), which has been used in control of the sea lamprey. Purvis (1970) estimated that, following two treatments with TFM, 65–95% of the northern brook lamprey were eliminated from the study area on the Sturgeon River, Michigan. In the 1971 Wisconsin fish control program for the Tomorrow-Waupaca River basin, approximately 81 km (50 mi) of mainstream and tributaries were treated with antimycin for a complete fishkill. The poisoning removed the lamprey population. Subsequent tests on various areas indicate that it has not reestablished itself. Care must be taken that this unusual species, which has a highly restricted range, is not jeopardized through the indiscriminate use of fish toxicants.

Chestnut Lamprey

Ichthyomyzon castaneus Girard. *Ichthyomyzon*—sucker of fish; *castaneus*—chestnut colored.

Other common names: western lamprey, northern lamprey, silver lamprey, brown lamprey, lamprey eel, river lamprey, lamper.

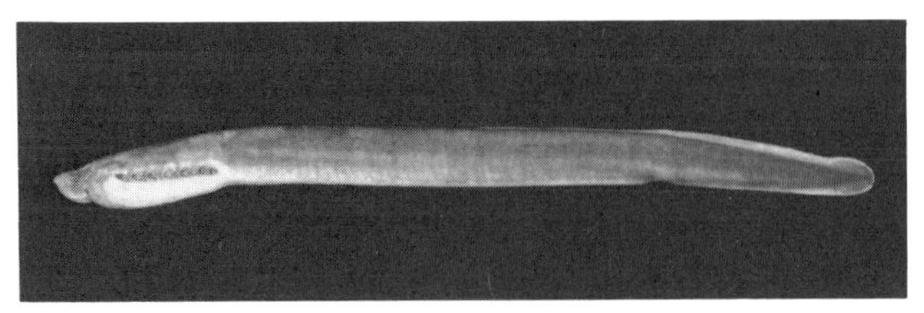

Ammocoete 140 mm, Prairie R. (Lincoln Co.), 3 Sept. 1976

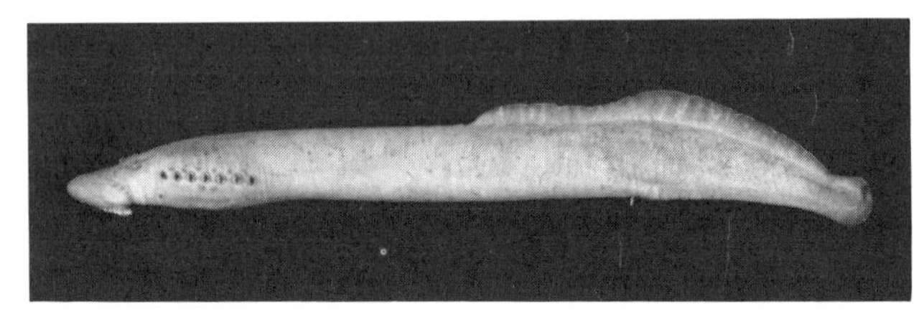

Adult male 255 mm (specimen donated by Wisconsin DNR)

DESCRIPTION

Adult parasitic, cylindrical. Length 125–271 mm (5–10.7 in). Branchial diam into length of sucking disc 1.4 (1.0–1.8); length of sucking disc into TL 12.3 (10.3–16.2). Supraoral lamina with 2 (3) narrowly separated teeth. Circumoral teeth 4 on either side of mouth opening, usually bicuspid 6.6 (3–8), the remainder (if any) unicuspid. Teeth in the anterior row of disc 3–6, usually 4 or 5. Teeth in lateral rows 6–10, usually 7 or 8. Transverse lingual lamina linear. Trunk

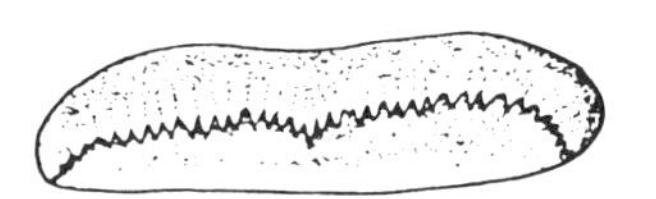

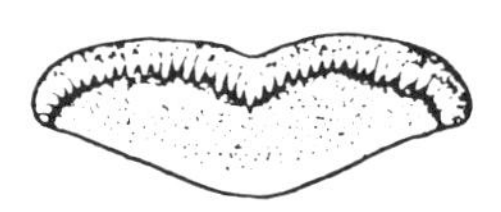

Transverse lingual lamina linear and weakly curved for chestnut lamprey (Hubbs and Trautman 1937:33)

myomeres 53 (51–56). Fins: 1 dorsal with a shallow notch, connected to a short round caudal fin.

Adult from light on belly to darker above with scarcely any bicolored effect; sides sometimes mottled. Occasionally slatey at any stage, becoming blue-black after spawning and prior to death (Hubbs and Trautman 1937). Lateral line sense organs and those of the underside of the branchial region with a concentration of black pigment.

Ammocoete back and sides gray (generally in the smallest individuals) to brown, grading to a cream-colored belly. Pale median line along back lacking. Base of caudal peduncle pigmented except for the anal fold and a narrow strip on either side. Lateral line sense organs with a concentration of black pigment. Suborbital area pigmented like the surrounding head region or slightly lighter. Dorsal fin with wide vertical bars (or portions thereof) consisting of pigment cells lying in horizontal layers one on top of the other. Precursor of tongue tapered and heavily pigmented.

Sexual dimorphism: Mature male with urogenital papilla occasionally extending beyond ventral margin of body. Female with prominent post-anal fold, and body greatly distended from behind gill region to the cloaca (A. J. Smith et al. 1968).

Suspected hybrid: *I. unicuspis* × *I. castaneus*, 242 mm (9.5 in) TL, from Pool 15 of Mississippi River (Starrett et al. 1960). Experimental crosses with *I. fossor* and *I. unicuspis* attained burrowing stage (Piavis et al. 1970).

DISTRIBUTION, STATUS, AND HABITAT

The chestnut lamprey occurs in the Mississippi and Lake Michigan drainage basins. It is not known from the Lake Superior basin.

In Iowa the chestnut lamprey is threatened (Roosa 1977); in Kansas it is rare; and in Nebraska, endangered (Miller 1972). In Wisconsin this species is uncommon to common in the Wisconsin, Mississippi, Chippewa–Red Cedar, St. Croix, and Namekagon river systems. In the Lake Michigan drainage it is rare; I have only one verifiable record, a specimen from the upper Fox River at Eureka (Winnebago County). The Greene (1935) record from Whitcomb Creek near Symco (Waupaca County) is based on an ammocoete unidentifiable as to species, which is now identified as *Ichthyomyzon* sp. (Hubbs and Trautman 1937). J. Kasper (pers. comm.) was unable to find the chestnut lamprey in Lake Winnebago; however, Priegel (1967a) reported it as rare in that lake. T. Wirth reported it from Lake Poygan (Becker 1964b).

In the Prairie (Lincoln County) and Namekagon (Sawyer County) rivers it is encountered at stream widths of 10–15 m (33–50 ft) at average depths of 25 cm (10 in), having bottoms that are typically gravel and rubble with shallows of sand and silt. Although occasionally found in impounded and other quiet water, this species generally inhabits flowing water. Unlike its close relative, the silver lamprey, it is more common in medium-sized streams than in large rivers. These species show a strong tendency toward mutual avoidance (Hubbs and Trautman 1937).

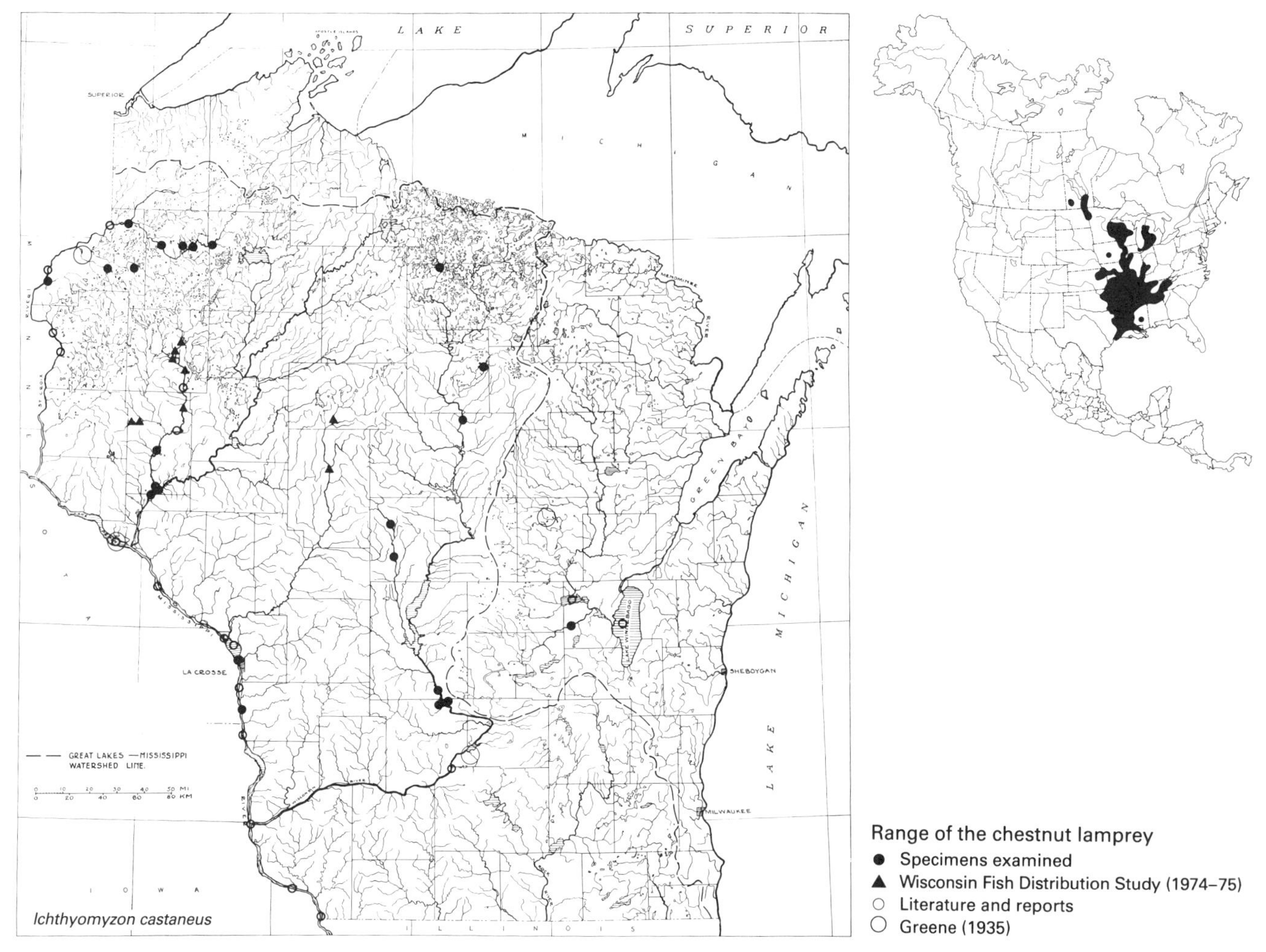

Range of the chestnut lamprey
● Specimens examined
▲ Wisconsin Fish Distribution Study (1974–75)
○ Literature and reports
◯ Greene (1935)

BIOLOGY

Spawning in Wisconsin occurs in April and May. A swarm of this species, consisting of hundreds of individuals, was seen attached to vegetation in the Yellow River (Wood County) in mid-April 1962 (D. Follen, pers. comm.). This was undoubtedly a spawning concentration of chestnut lamprey; one of them was captured (UWSP 1593).

In Michigan during a single night Hall (1963) saw 8–10 spawners on one nest under a log in 61 cm (2 ft) of moderately swift water. In the Rat River, Manitoba, about 50 individuals spawned over one nest (Case 1970).

Spawning behavior was described by Case (1970). Observations were made in mid-June in the Rat River, Manitoba. The river was 9.5 m (31 ft) wide, water temperature 16.5°C (61.7°F), and velocity approximately 1 m/sec. Approximately 50 chestnut lampreys moved stones with their discs and by 1700 hr a nest area 0.6 m × 1 m × 5 cm deep had been cleared. Then one individual, presumably a female, would attach itself to a large stone (3.5–5 cm diam) and begin rapid quivering movements of the body. A second individual, presumably a male, would then attach to the head of the first, and wrap its tail around the other's body. They quivered rapidly together. Sometimes a third individual would then attach to the head of the second. Up to five lampreys were observed attached to each other in this manner. (This phenomenon of up to five individuals attaching to each other in succession and undergoing rapid quivering has not been previously described.)

Those lampreys not engaged in mating were manipulating stones up to 5 cm diam from the upstream end of the nest back into the excavation. Thus eggs were probably covered as the nest was being expanded in an upstream direction. By 1030 hr next day the entire nest area, both excavated and filled in, extended 6.2 m upstream from the original nest-building site, indicating that spawning had continued throughout the night. The lamprey school was reduced in number to about 25. These were generally paired off; they scattered in the upstream end of the nest and spawned sporadically. Many small fishes, chiefly the common shiner, were present immediately downstream from the nest, probably feeding on lamprey eggs. Elliptical eggs (avg 0.635 mm × 0.560 mm), presumably from *I. castaneus*, were found in the stomachs of two adult male shiners. By 1430 hr only 10 lampreys remained in the spawning area, all at the head of the excavation. No further spawning activity was observed.

Ammocoetes of the chestnut lamprey select areas of moderate current, with stable bottoms of sand and silt with light growth of *Chara*. Larger ammocoetes have been found in quiet backwater areas of black muck and silt only in places where rooted vegetation was dense. The length of ammocoete life is unknown but is presumed to be 5 to 7 years (Scott and Crossman 1973).

The ammocoetes are filter feeders, extracting diatoms and desmids from the water and the bottom slurry. Twenty-one ammocoetes captured 22 June 1976 from the Prairie River (Lincoln County) averaged 128 (104–155) mm TL and 4.0 (1.9–7.34) g.

In the Manistee River, Michigan, metamorphosis begins in August or September of the final ammocoete year at 90–100 mm (3.6–4 in) TL and is completed in January (Hall 1963). The transforming adults may be briefly parasitic the first fall but are inactive over the winter and commence active predatory feeding the following spring. The adults feed from April to October, with the greatest feeding activity in July (when about 30% of the trout 178 mm [7 in] and longer observed in the study area had lampreys attached). The following winter the chestnut lampreys are inactive as they mature sexually.

Since the growth rate of the chestnut lamprey in the Manistee River study area did not keep pace with the very high rate of mortality of the adults, there was a steady decrease in the standing crop to about half of its initial value by the end of the season. Hall calculated the net production of the chestnut lamprey population in the study area at 1.48 kg/ha (1.32 lb/acre) from May through October 1961. Production was negligible during the rest of the year. In May 1961 there were approximately 2,000 adult lampreys in the marking area. The mortality rate was high; only 200 were present by October 1961. The average length of the lampreys increased from about 105 mm (4.1 in) in May to 175 mm (6.9 in) in October (avg wt increased from 1.8 to 9.1 g, respectively).

In Wisconsin, a newly transformed adult in April was 125 mm (4.9 in) TL and 2.5 g (0.1 oz). In June, seven adults averaged 166 (132–194) mm and ranged from 3.5 g to 16.7 g. By September and October chestnut lamprey adults averaged 194 and 236 mm (7.6 and 9.3 in) respectively (range 186–271 mm). In April of its second year as an adult in Yellow River (Wood County), a sexually mature female, 255 mm (10.0 in) TL and 37.7 g (1.3 oz), had an ovarian weight of 4.8 g and an estimated 13,400 eggs 0.6–0.7 mm diam. The foregoing are preserved lengths and weights.

The known maximum size of a chestnut lamprey in Wisconsin is 271 mm (10.7 in) TL.

IMPORTANCE AND MANAGEMENT

The effects of this parasitic lamprey on prey species is not known, at least not as clearly as those of a mammalian predator on its prey species (e.g., wolf-caribou). The terrestrial predator helps to bring about (1) population control, (2) selection against the weak and genetically inferior, and (3) establishment of a balance of nature. A similar role may be played by the lamprey in the aquatic ecosystem. Excellent trout populations exist in Wisconsin streams where the chestnut lamprey is found. Hence the possibility exists that the presence of the lamprey has some salutary effect, at this time not known and not understood.

In electrofishing runs on the Chippewa River between Eau Claire and Durand, chestnut and silver lampreys were seen clinging to numerous redhorse suckers and lesser numbers of paddlefish (1 individual with 12–15 lampreys attached to the belly), goldeye, and northern pike (D. Becker 1977, pers. comm.). On the St. Croix River (Wisconsin-Minnesota boundary) chestnut lamprey scars were seen on redhorse suckers, channel catfish, northern pike, carp, white sucker, and smallmouth bass (Kuehn et al. 1961). A scarring incidence of 25% was noted on redhorse in the St. Croix Falls reservoir. Kuehn et al. concluded that (1) lamprey scarring is closely governed by the abundance of lampreys, and (2) the abundance of redhorse suckers was not affected by lamprey predation. Chestnut lampreys have also been reported on brown trout in the Namekagon River.

In Michigan, data from lamprey studies suggest that the destructive potential (grams of fish killed per gram of growth) of the chestnut lamprey was directly related to the size of the lamprey and was similar to that of the sea lamprey of comparable size. Hall (1963) estimated the destruction of trout to be as much as 23.5 kg/ha (21 lb/acre), or about a third of the trout available to anglers during the 1961 trout season. Consequently, Michigan treated portions of the Manistee River to reduce predation on fish populations.

Sea Lamprey

Petromyzon marinus Linnaeus. *Petromyzon*—sucker of stone; *marinus*—of the sea.

Other common names: great sea lamprey, landlocked sea lamprey, lake lamprey, lamprey, lamprey eel, lamper eel, lamper.

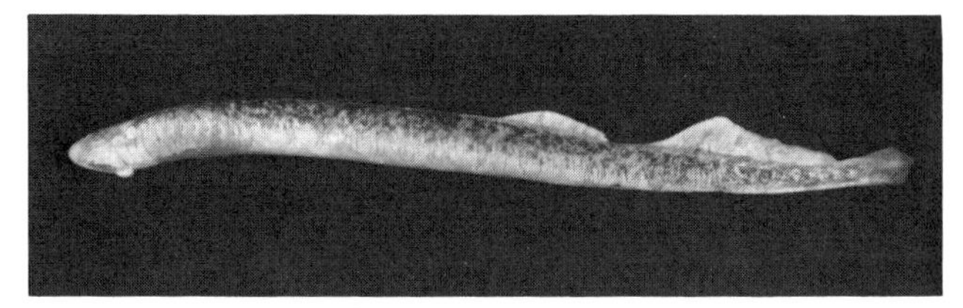

Adult 507 mm, L. Michigan, Algoma (Kewaunee Co.), 18 Apr. 1971

DESCRIPTION

Adult parasitic, cylindrical. Length 305–610 mm (12–24 in). Branchial diam into length of sucking disc 1.2 (1.0–1.4); length of sucking disc into TL 13.4 (11.7–16.6). Supraoral lamina with 2 narrowly separated teeth. Circumoral teeth 4 on either side of mouth opening, bicuspid. Teeth in lateral rows 5–7. Trunk myomeres 69 (63–73). Fins: 2 dorsal, generally well separated (occasionally close together in breeding males); separated by deep notch from a rounded, angular, or spade-shaped caudal fin. Chromosomes 2n = 168 (Potter and Rothwell 1970).

Newly transformed adults grayish blue above, grading to white on belly. Fully grown adults dark brown to black dorsally, light yellow to pale brown ventrally; dorsal half marbled in largest adults. Dark blotch of tail extending to margin of fin. Yellow variants possessing pigment pattern of dark forms noted by Manion (1972).

Ammocoete brown on upper sides and back, lighter on belly. Upper lip and suborbital region pigmented; branchial region above branchial groove pigmented except for light-colored band narrower than width of a branchial muscle segment; caudal peduncle entirely pigmented except for anal fold. In ammocoetes to 70 mm, body lining darkly pigmented and precursor of tongue generally unpigmented.

Sexual dimorphism: Breeding male with prominent ropelike ridge along back; urogenital papilla occasionally extending beyond ventral margin of body. Breeding female with prominent anal fold.

Experimental hybrids attempted with *Ichthyomyzon castaneus*, *I. unicuspis*, *I. fossor*, and *Lampetra appendix* (Piavis et al. 1970); best development with the last.

DISTRIBUTION, STATUS, AND HABITAT

The sea lamprey occurs in Lakes Michigan and Superior and in numerous tributaries to these lakes. An exotic, this species entered the upper Great Lakes via the Welland Canal. The first Wisconsin record, caught 23 March 1936, was a 406-mm (16-in) lamprey attached to a lake trout 24 km (15 mi) off Milwaukee in Lake Michigan (Hubbs and Pope 1937). In 1938 the sea lamprey was reported from Lake Superior. Today it is well established in Wisconsin waters and has become a dominant feature of the aquatic fauna.

Open dots on the map indicate known uppermost locales of tributary streams where the sea lamprey has been captured or observed. Its distribution in tributary streams is probably more extensive than is indicated by our records. In lower Michigan the sea lamprey demonstrated the greatest adaptability of all five species of lampreys, by occupying the widest range of streams and habitats (Morman 1979). Its habitat preferences are intermediate between the *Ichthyomyzon* spp. and the American brook lamprey.

In spring, mature lampreys require spawning habitat of gravel, sand, and rubble in tributary streams such as Hibbard's Creek and Peshtigo River in the Lake Michigan basin and the Bad, Middle, Amnicon, and Brule rivers of the Lake Superior basin. Nesting generally occurs close to the large lake, although in the Bad River drainage sea lampreys have been observed some 50 km (31 mi) upstream. After hatching, the larvae require eddies or pools of sandy silt, mud, and detritus. As a result of the drift, ammocoete larvae have been recovered from Lake Michigan itself within 0.4 km of the mouths of spawning streams (Wagner and Stauffer 1962). After metamorphosis, the young adults inhabit the deep waters of the lake, where they begin their parasitic phase, and, prior to breeding, they move into the shallows in the vicinity of stream mouths.

BIOLOGY

Migration up the tributaries of Lakes Superior and Michigan begins in early spring when stream temperatures rise above 4.5°C (40°F), and spawning occurs at water temperatures over 10°C (50°F). In southern Lake Superior streams, spawning runs usually peak by the end of May or during the first half of June (McLain et al. 1965) but in one Upper Michigan stream the spawning cycle occurred from 27 June to 20 July (Manion and McLain 1971). Sea lampreys seek out streams with gravel or sand bottoms and with moderately strong current.

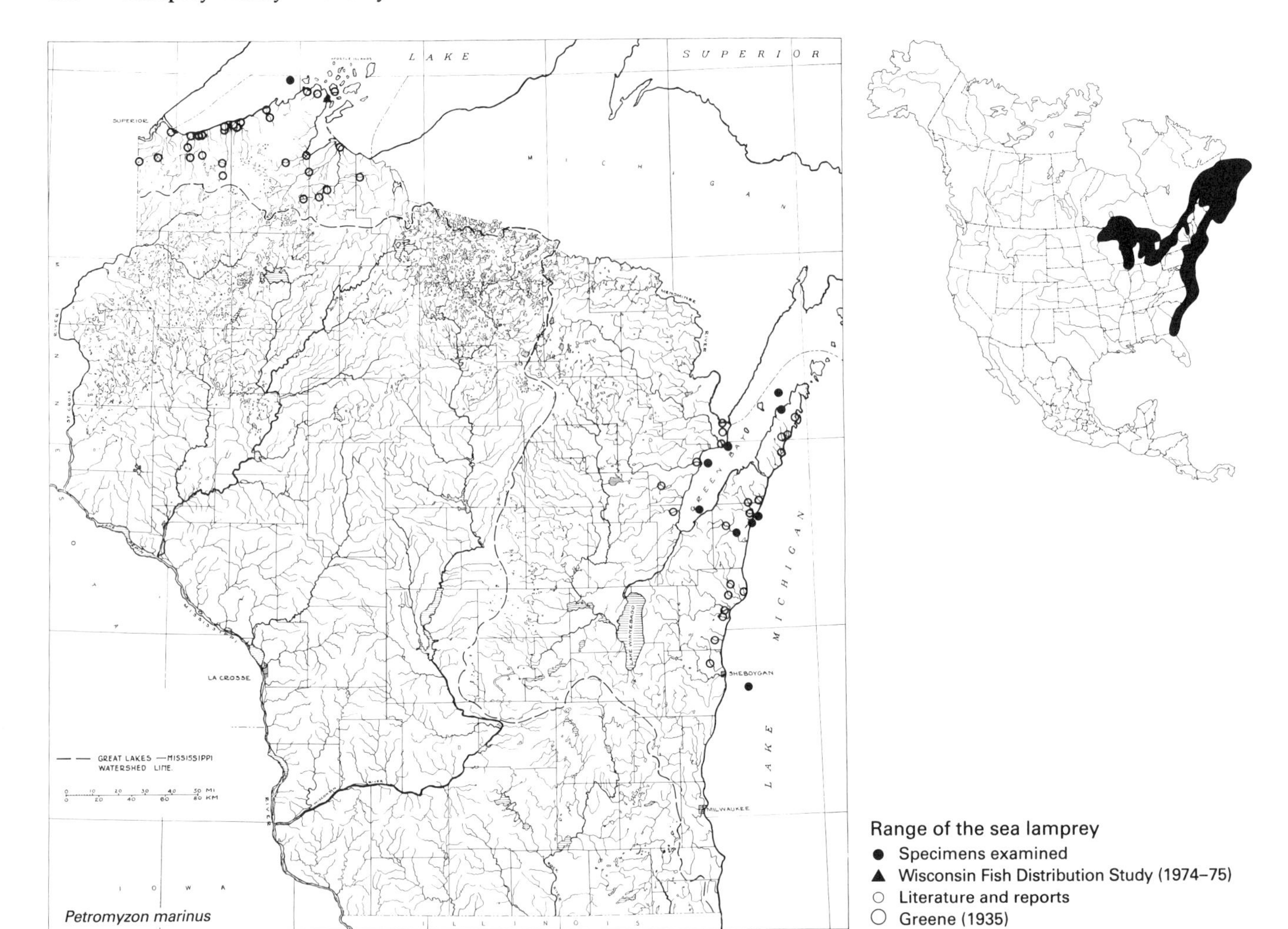

Petromyzon marinus

Range of the sea lamprey
● Specimens examined
▲ Wisconsin Fish Distribution Study (1974–75)
○ Literature and reports
◯ Greene (1935)

The following account is taken largely from Applegate (1950), Applegate and Moffett (1955), and Manion and McLain (1971). The male starts building a nest and is joined by a female who helps. They clear a small area about 0.6–0.9 m (2–3 ft) square, picking up stones with their mouths and piling them in a crescent-shaped mound (about 8 cm high) on the downstream side of the nest. Spawning begins during nest-building. While the female clings to a stone at the upper margin of the nest, the male seizes her at the back of the head with his mouth and presses his body against her side and loops his tail over her body. During copulation, which lasts 2 or 3 seconds, the female actively vibrates while the male holds his position, stirring up such a cloud of sand that the 20–40 sticky, fertilized eggs are at once concealed and covered, or are carried to the gravel rim of the nest, where they lodge in the spaces among the stones.

Such matings occur at intervals of from 1 to 5 min, persisting from 1 to 3 days, during which time 24,000–107,000 eggs are laid. Ten females (291–439 mm) from Hibbard's Creek (Door County) averaged 62,870 eggs (Vladykov 1951). Twenty-nine females (340–511 mm) from an Upper Michigan tributary to Lake Superior averaged 68,599 eggs (Manion 1973). Mature eggs are 0.8–1.3 mm diam (Parker and Lennon 1956). Following spawning, the adults die.

The eggs hatch in from 10 to 12 days. According to McCauley (1963), the range of temperatures necessary for successful hatching is 15–25°C (59–77°F); however, Manion and McLain (1971) noted successful hatches at 10–18.3°C (50–65°F) in the Big Garlic River, Michigan. About 6.3% of the eggs hatch (Manion 1968). The larvae remain buried in the sand and gravel until about the 20th day, when they (now 8.5 mm long) leave the nest and drift downstream until they reach quiet waters. Here they burrow into the sand or silt and undergo development over 3–5 or more years. Manion (pers. comm.) noted that ammocoetes in the Big Garlic River study area were over 17 years old. While they are developing, they filter-feed on diatoms and other materials which are carried in the water and come to rest on the bottom (Manion 1967).

The downstream drift of ammocoetes has been noted by Manion and McLain (1971). Most movement is in April and May at night, and during periods of activity an increase in water level commonly increases the extent of downstream drift. This drift may account for the presence of ammocoetes which are now being found in the estuaries and bays of the Great Lakes.

Transformation of ammocoetes into adults (100–180 mm long) begins in mid-July, and by October most are fully transformed (Manion and Stauffer 1970). Movement of recently metamorphosed sea lampreys begins in September and extends through May of the following year. Major movement occurs in October and November, with a lesser peak in April (Manion, pers. comm.). The new adults drift downstream and into the deep water of the Great Lakes, where they attach and feed on the blood and tissues of lake trout, large chubs, burbot, and other deepwater species. As the lampreys grow larger, they move shoreward, and in the fall they are found in relatively shallow water, where they now attack the lake whitefish, lake herring, walleye, yellow perch, round whitefish, sucker, and carp. As a sea lamprey feeds, an anticoagulant secreted by its buccal glands keeps the blood of the host fish from clotting, resulting in a free flow of food to the parasite (Schneberger 1947).

Toward the end of the winter, the sea lampreys now 300–600 mm (12–24 in) long, begin to mature sexually and gather with others off the mouths of streams. Beginning as early as January, prespawning adults cease feeding or feed at a greatly reduced rate (Anderson and Manion 1977). While the sex glands are developing rapidly, the digestive tract is degenerating, and further metabolism is dependent on the degeneration of the lamprey's muscles, skin, and even eyes. The adult phase lasts 12–20 months. The capture of tagged adults at least 2 months after the end of the normal spawning season, however, has indicated an extension of the parasitic phase of the life cycle beyond the usual 12–20-month period, possibly due to late-season maturation of the gonads, disease, or deleterious effects of tags (Moore et al. 1974).

The maximum length attained by the landlocked form of the Great Lakes sea lamprey is 76 cm (30 in) (MacKay and MacGillivray 1949). The saltwater (anadromous) form grows to 91.5 cm (36 in) and weighs 1.36 kg (3 lb) (De Sylva 1964).

Stauffer and Hansen (1958) reported that sea lamprey larvae in Michigan streams of the Lake Superior drainage were most numerous in streams with summer water temperatures of 10 to 26.1°C (50 to 79°F) and rarely occurred in cool spring-fed streams where brook trout and slimy sculpins were abundant.

The movement of adult sea lampreys is extensive. Recapture of tagged sea lampreys (Moore et al. 1974) has shown that many individuals have traveled long distances and that movement between lakes is common. Twenty-four lampreys tagged in Lake Huron were recaptured at widely scattered localities in northern Lake Michigan, and one was taken off Milwaukee, 426 km (264 mi) from the tagging site. The distance traveled by sea lampreys tagged in northern Lake Michigan was as great as 298 km (185 mi) to the south (off Manitowoc, Wisconsin) and 450 km (279 mi) to the southeast (Grand Bend, Ontario). But about half (268, or 56%) of the 477 sea lampreys recaptured had moved no more than 15 km from the point of release. The fastest movement recorded was 11.1 km (6.9 mi) per day.

Fish to which the sea lampreys are attached are probably responsible for some of their movement. Also, the sea lamprey has been known to fasten on to ships (B. R. Smith et al. 1974); divers who examined 125 ships passing through the Canadian locks at Sault Ste Marie found 18 sea lampreys attached to the hulls. The sea lamprey's habit of hitching onto ships has no doubt greatly increased the rate of infestation of Lakes Michigan and Superior.

In the laboratory, adult lampreys are more active during the daylight hours (Parker and Lennon 1956). Nonfeeding attachments on prey fish were observed to be common. A sea lamprey often attaches itself to a host for a considerable period of time and then shifts to one or more sites on the same fish before rasping a feeding hole. On the average, each sea lamprey made 87 attacks and spent 2,383 hours of feeding and 523 hours of nonfeeding attachment, and was responsible for 8.39 kilos (18.5 lb) of fish killed. Female lampreys made more attacks, fed more, killed more fish, and grew larger than males. The researchers estimate that the average fishkill by a wild sea lamprey exceeds and could be approximately double the number of fish killed by lampreys in the laboratory aquariums.

IMPORTANCE AND MANAGEMENT

The sea lamprey is a known host to glochidia of the mollusk *Anodontoides ferrussacianus* (Hart and Fuller 1974).

Sea lampreys are preyed on by several species of gulls, by herons, hawks, owls, bitterns, water snakes, raccoons, muskrats, mink, weasel, fox, and by northern pike, walleye, and brown trout (Scott and Crossman 1973). Minnows of genus *Notropis* and *Rhin-*

ichthys are known to feed on lamprey eggs as they are being laid.

Although only a small number of the eggs laid by the sea lamprey hatch into larvae, the success of this species has reduced a once-lucrative lake trout fishery to a fraction of its former wealth. A decade after its entrance into Lake Michigan the sea lamprey was firmly established; spawning runs had been reported in many streams and commercial fishermen had for several years been complaining of high incidences of sea lamprey wounds in their catches (Shetter 1949). Early reports indicated that the sea lamprey's primary victim was the lake trout, followed by whitefish, suckers, walleyes, yellow perch, and carp. Other species, particularly deepwater ciscoes and burbot, were also severely attacked.

In the Wisconsin waters of Lake Michigan the catch of lake trout by commercial fishermen declined from 1,124,140 kg (2,478,262 lb) in 1940, to 25 kg (56 lb) in 1954, and to none the following year (Wiegert 1958). In Lake Superior circumstantial evidence suggested that sea lamprey predation was a major factor in the high natural mortality of lake trout (Pycha and King 1975). Lakewide production dropped from 2.1 million kg (4.7 million lb) in 1949 to 168,300 kg (371,000 lb) in 1961—a 92% decline in little more than a decade.

In Lake Superior the prevalence of lamprey attacks in the late 1960s was apparent from the incidence of healed scars (Pycha and King 1975). In 1969, for example, 50% of 160 spawning trout 635–734 mm (25.0–28.9 in) long, 83% of 149 fish 737–836 mm (29.0–32.9 in) long, and 100% of 26 fish 838 mm (33 in) and longer bore healed scars. Fish in the smallest size group bore an average of 0.7 scar per fish and those of the largest-size group averaged 4.2 scars per fish. G. King (pers. comm.) estimated that the sea lamprey currently accounts for a 60–80% mortality among lake trout ages VII–IX and of spawning size.

In addition, the destruction of predators by the sea lamprey probably permitted the rapid expansion of the exotic alewife, which has unbalanced native stocks still further (S. H. Smith 1970).

In the Great Lakes the sea lamprey has been known to attach itself to long-distance swimmers, but it is quickly and easily dislodged. It does not attach itself to humans until long submersion has lowered their skin temperature; then it will attach and begin to rasp (Scott and Crossman 1973).

Historically, the adult sea lamprey has been an important food and a delicacy. In France, Germany, and the Baltic countries it is in great demand (Vladykov 1949), and through elaborate recipes is made into tasty dishes. In general, it is grilled, fried, marinated, steamed, served with different sauces, smoked, salted, and canned.

Sea lamprey control has progressed through three phases, with the use first of mechanical barriers, then electrical barriers, and subsequently chemical treatments. The first two were designed to entrap and destroy adult sea lampreys before they could spawn; the last, to remove generations of ammocoetes and so avoid the parasitic phase of the cycle. The program has been costly. In 1955 the International Great Lakes Fishery Commission was established, with membership from Canadian provinces and from the states bordering the Great Lakes, to enhance productivity of fish stocks of common concern and to eradicate or minimize sea lamprey populations in the Great Lakes. The chemical treatment of tributary streams to a single lake averages $1 million, and the program is repeated every several years.

In Lake Michigan sea lamprey control began in 1953 (Wells and McLain 1973). By 1958, barriers (mostly electrical, a few mechanical) had been placed across 65 streams to block upstream migration of sea lampreys. Barrier operations were discontinued in 1960 in favor of a more effective method of lamprey control—the treatment of streams with a toxicant selective for lamprey larvae. By 1966 all tributary streams known to harbor sea lamprey larvae had been treated, and many of the streams have since been treated a second time. The success of the treatment is shown by the sharp decline of spawning-run sea lampreys recorded at three barriers which had been left in operation to provide yearly indices of abundance: 12,886 lampreys were caught in 1961 and 1,168 in 1966. For financial reasons the "index" barriers were removed after the 1966 spawning season. Consequently, trends in lamprey abundance since that time are not easily ascertained.

In Lake Superior experimental control of the sea lamprey with electric barriers was begun in 1953 (McLain et al. 1965). Installed below spawning grounds in streams and rivers tributary to Lake Superior, these barriers were designed to prevent the sexually mature sea lampreys from reproducing. They were placed on the following rivers, among others: Bad, White, Cranberry, Brule, Poplar, Middle, Amnicon. Catches of sea lampreys on the Brule River for the years 1958, 1959, and 1960 were 22,842, 19,389, and 9,755, respectively. In the total operation along the south shore of Lake Superior, the catches dropped substantially, from 66,931 in 1958 to 52,173 in 1959 and to 39,783 in 1960. The development of a means of control by selective chemicals in 1958 superseded the barrier control system, which was given up at the end of the 1960 season. The barriers on the Brule and Amnicon rivers, however, are kept in operation, to assess the effectiveness of chemical control.

In Lake Superior the highest catch of sea lampreys was recorded in 1961 after 3 years of chemical operations, when 71,081 were taken at 37 barriers (B. R. Smith et al. 1974). In 1962, however, the numbers of adult sea lamprey fell suddenly and sharply. The 37 barriers captured only 9,992 individuals, a decline of 86% from the previous year. From 1962 through 1970 the numbers captured at 24 assessment barriers varied from 3,745 to 12,581.

The size and sex ratios of sea lampreys from Lake Superior changed as the control program progressed. The length and weight of adult lampreys decreased slowly from 1954 to 1961. In 1954, the average length was 455 mm (17.9 in) and the mean weight was 217 g (7.7 oz). By 1961 (the year of maximum lamprey population), mean length had decreased to 406 mm (16 in) and weight to 132 g (4.6 oz). In recent years, however, this trend has been reversed: the lampreys are becoming larger and heavier. Moreover, a greater ratio of females to males is appearing on the spawning beds.

At the present time, lampreys are controlled largely through use of the lampricide chemical 3-trifluoromethyl-4-nitrophenol (TFM) to kill the ammocoetes. Concentrations from 1 to 6 ppm for a period of 8 hours are lethal to sea lamprey larvae in most streams. In a few streams where the concentration of dissolved substances is high, 14 ppm TFM may be required (Baldwin 1968). Fish display varying degrees of resistance to the lampricide. Walleyes (*Stizostedion vitreum*) are almost as susceptible to it as lampreys, and particular care must be taken to maintain precise concentrations in rivers where these fish are present.

Although lamprey control is practised by chemically treating ammocoetes in streams, recruitment to parasitic populations of sea lampreys will presumably persist for some years, even if stream populations of larvae are exterminated (Wagner and Stauffer 1962), inasmuch as some streams have been found with ammocoete populations offshore. Control of these offshore populations is accomplished in several ways. When a combination of suitable offshore habitat and downstream drift is found, the streams are treated more frequently, to prevent recruitment to offshore areas. Bottom toxicants, which release chemicals on the bottom in habitats where ammocoetes are concentrated, have also been developed.

The Great Lakes Fishery Commission continues to search for new and effective means to control the sea lamprey. Among the other approaches to lamprey control that are being investigated are such biological methods as hormones directed toward the control of metamorphosis, and infection with viruses. Also, lamprey raised from eggs appear to be vulnerable in the embryo stage, suggesting the presence of yet another biological control. Currently being field-tested is the sterile-male technique, whereby a chemosterilant is injected into adult males, causing infertility without suppressing their spawning behavior. Their matings with normal females result in embryos which die during development.

Some fish experts challenge the methods now being used for lamprey control. Hasler (1973) has questioned the validity of a control program which destroys lampreys and other fish species rather than promoting their utilization by man. S. H. Smith (1973) has suggested that control agencies are establishing optimum conditions for the sea lamprey by thinning out lamprey stocks and thus providing the survivors with large numbers of lake trout.

Continued control of sea lamprey is basic, perhaps even crucial, to the maintenance of the valuable sport and commercial fishery in the Great Lakes. Finding a suitable control system will be a major challenge to man's ingenuity and to his interest in preserving what he can of the aquatic ecosystems so seriously undermined by the exotic lamprey.

American Brook Lamprey

Lampetra appendix (DeKay). *Lampetra*—sucker of stone.
Other common names: brook lamprey, lamprey eel, lamprey, rock-sucker, small black brook lamprey, small black lamprey.

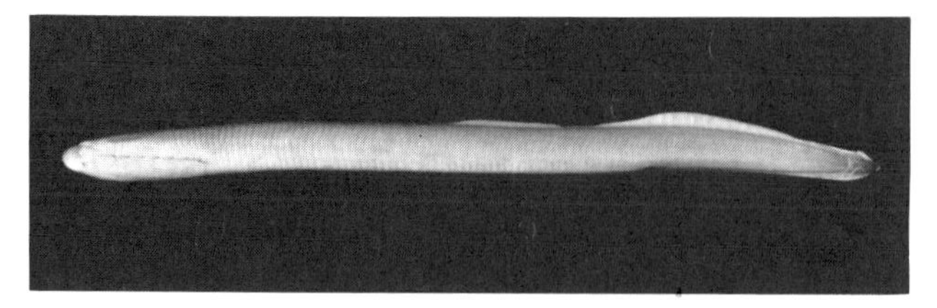

Ammocoete 187 mm, Pine R. (Richland Co.), 18 July 1962

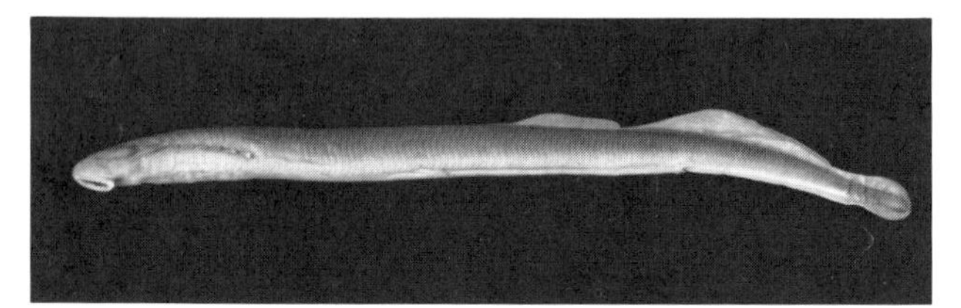

Adult male 173 mm, Little Plover R. (Portage Co.), 2 Apr. 1967

DESCRIPTION
Adult nonparasitic, cylindrical. Length 138–194 mm (5.4–7.6 in). Branchial diam into length of sucking disc 0.70 (0.35–1.00); length of sucking disc into TL 23.3 (16.6–37.4). Supraoral lamina with 2 widely separated teeth. Circumoral teeth 3 on either side of the mouth opening, bicuspid. Teeth in lateral rows none. Trunk myomeres 68 (64–75). Fins: 2 dorsal, narrowly to broadly separated, the second continuous with a triangular-shaped caudal fin. Chromosomes 2n = 164–166 (Robinson, Potter, and Webb 1974).

Adult brown, darker on back and paler ventrally. Fins with yellow tinge. Dark blotch at end of tail around the notochord not extending to the margin of the caudal membrane. Spawning adults slate gray to gray-brown, paler ventrally.

Ammocoete brown on upper sides and back, lighter on belly. Upper lip and suborbital region unpigmented; branchial region above branchial groove with broad unpigmented band equal to 2 widths of a branchial muscle segment; lower edge of caudal peduncle unpigmented. In ammocoetes to 70 mm (2.8 in), body lining unpigmented and precursor of tongue darkly pigmented (Vladykov 1950).

Sexual dimorphism: Breeding male with high dorsal fins separated by a sharp notch; long, threadlike genital papilla. Breeding female with low dorsal fins separated by broad notch; prominent anal fin fold.

Experimental hybrids with *Ichthyomyzon castaneus*, *I. unicuspis*, *I. fossor*, and *Petromyzon marinus* (Piavis et al. 1970); best development with *P. marinus*.

SYSTEMATIC NOTES
The long-used name *Lampetra appendix* was replaced by Hubbs and Trautman (1937) with *Entosphenus lamottenii* (Lesueur). Since then the species name, spelled *lamottenii* or *lamottei*, has been placed variably in *Entosphenus*, *Lampetra*, and *Lethenteron*. R. M. Bailey and F. C. Rohde (in prep.) recommend the suppression of *Lampetra lamottei* (Lesueur) (Bailey et al. 1970) as unidentifiable.

DISTRIBUTION, STATUS, AND HABITAT
The American brook lamprey occurs in the Mississippi and Lake Michigan drainage basins. It is known from the Upper Michigan drainage into Lake Superior but not from Wisconsin waters. Major centers of distribution are in the Red Cedar, Wisconsin, and Rock river systems, all in the Mississippi basin. In the Lake Michigan drainage, specimens were examined from Three Mile Creek (Kewaunee County), Wausaukee River (Marinette County), Tomorrow River (Portage County) and reported from East Twin River (Manitowoc County).

In Iowa this species is threatened (Roosa 1977); it is rare in Connecticut, Massachusetts, and Missouri (Miller 1972). In Wisconsin it is common in the Mississippi River drainage, but rare in the Great Lakes drainage.

This lamprey inhabits the headwaters of cool, clear streams over sand and small gravel, occasionally over silt, clay, large gravel, and rubble. It prefers small-sized streams, occasionally medium-sized rivers. In 15 different streams it occurred at average stream widths of 5.9 (2–15) m at depths of 0.7 (0.1–1.5) m. Common fish associates are sculpins, and brook and brown trout.

BIOLOGY
Spawning occurs in April and May. Males arrive at the spawning site first and spawning may begin at water temperatures of about 17.2°C (63°F). Prespawning activity was observed by Duane Steiner (pers. comm.) in Big Roche Cri (Adams County) on 29 April 1971. A male selected a site on one edge of a graveled area. Stones averaging 13 (6–50) mm diam were picked up with the buccal funnel and moved off to the side or on the upstream edge of the area being cleared. The nest, or redd, was an oval-shaped depression 150–180 mm (6–7 in) long, 100–125 mm (4–5 in) wide, and 25–50 mm (1–2 in) deep. The male

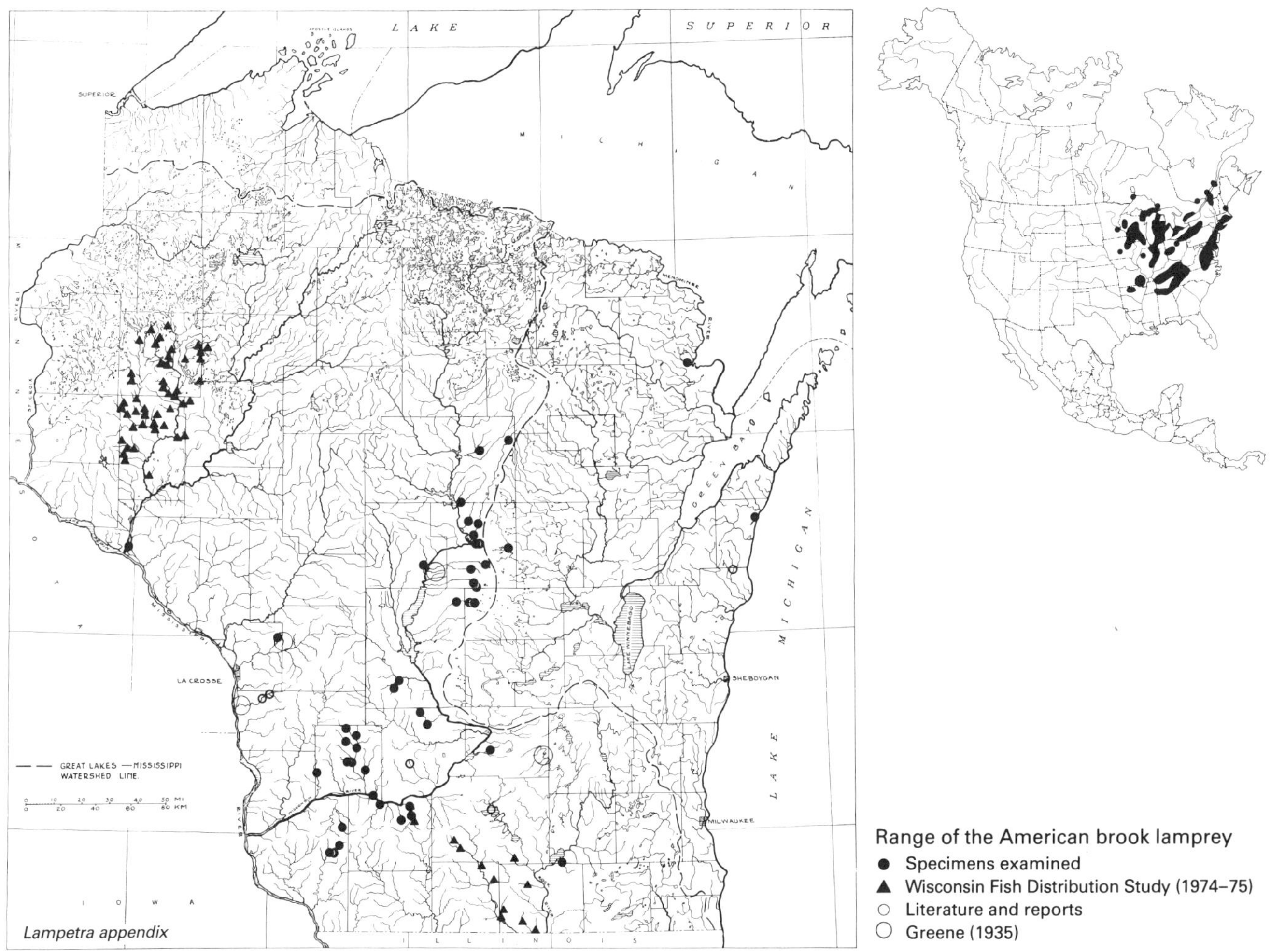

worked steadily but would pause now and then and attach to a rock. During one rest period another lamprey (undoubtedly a male) appeared and attached itself to the top of the first lamprey's head. The first lamprey released itself from the rock and both drifted downstream out of sight. In a few moments both reappeared, the first lamprey returning to its redd-building. The other selected a site nearby and initiated construction of another redd. P. Manion (pers. comm.) commented that the above episode was a typical example of fighting in males.

According to Breder and Rosen (1966), a nest may become a community affair for as many as 25–40 adults, although there is free movement among adjacent nests. A male attaches himself to the head of a female who is attached to a rock at the head end of the nest and twists his body partly around hers. Joint vibrations result in release of eggs and sperm. Adults die after spawning.

Embryological development is discussed by A. J. Smith et al. (1968). After hatching, the larvae are carried downstream to quieter water. There they burrow into sand and silt, often close to the slower currents at the water's edge. The length of time for ammocoete development is not known, although it may be as long as 5 years (Hubbs 1925). The ammocoetes feed mainly on diatoms and desmids (Creaser and Hann 1928).

Ten ammocoetes from the Pine River (Richland County), 18 July 1962, measured 196 (189–202) mm in length and weighed 13.58 (11.84–16.01) g. Manion and Purvis (1971) reported adult American brook lampreys, 260–299 mm (10.2–11.8 in) and 37–46 g (1.3–1.6 oz), from tributaries of Lake Michigan (Upper and Lower Michigan). Evidence suggests that these individuals may have fed parasitically.

In southern Wisconsin metamorphosis occurs in mid-August, when the eyes appear and the buccal hood consolidates into a disc or funnel. In the newly transforming adult the sieve apparatus is still visible, although much simplified, and the papillary fringe on the disc is rudimentary. By mid-September the bases of the disc teeth (still bearing traces of the sieve apparatus) are in place and the horny teeth appear, beginning in October. In a recently transformed (24 September) female (194 mm, 13.18 g) from the Platte River (Grant County) the ovary held well-formed eggs averaging 0.4 mm diam. The ratio of branchial diam into length of sucking disc increases from 0.35–0.50 at the time of transformation in August to 0.74–1.00 at spawning and death the following spring.

Maturity is completed in early April. On 11 April in Mt. Vernon Creek (Dane County), two males, 152 and 166 mm (6 and 6.5 in), weighed 6.95 and 10.33 g (0.2 and 0.4 oz); and six gravid females, 140–170 mm (5.5–6.7 in) in length, averaged 7.84 (5.47–10.70) g in weight. Eggs in the largest female were 1.0–1.2 mm diam. Spawning had not yet occurred in this population.

In the Little Plover River (central Wisconsin) two newly transformed (19 September) females (149 and 165 mm, 5.91 and 6.20 g) held well-formed eggs 0.3–0.5 mm diam. From the same stream a male with an elongated genital papilla was taken on 2 April, and two gravid females (148 and 172 mm, 7.31 and 12.42 g) were taken on 15 April. A 140-mm (5.73-g) female taken on 1 May contained 2,050 eggs 1 mm diam. These eggs were loose in the abdominal cavity. On 4 May, five males (139–159 mm, 4.60–6.32 g) were picked off the bottom of the stream where all had spawned and died. They were covered with a heavy mucus. In Wisconsin the adult stage lasts 8 or 9 months, during which time the adults do not feed.

IMPORTANCE AND MANAGEMENT

The American brook lamprey is a useful and inoffensive species. During its short existence after metamorphosing, it is food for sport fishes; moreover, according to Vladykov (1949:53), "Ammocoetes, due to their method of feeding by straining different materials from the oozy bottom and using them for body building, make a valuable link in the food chain of a brook."

This species is sensitive to pollution, including turbidity. The use of 3-trifluoromethyl-4-nitrophenol (TFM) as a sea lamprey larvicide has undoubtedly affected populations of the American brook lamprey in Lake Michigan tributaries. Fortunately, the American brook lamprey spawns upstream higher than the sea lamprey, and, according to P. Manion (pers. comm.), it always seems to be abundant throughout the river within a year after treatment.

Sturgeon Family—Acipenseridae

Two species of sturgeons in two genera are known from Wisconsin. In the United States and Canada, seven species in two genera are known (Robins et al. 1980). Of these, four (two on each coast) are marine species which spawn in fresh water.

Sturgeons are elongated fishes with an extended, hard snout and a ventral protrusible mouth preceded by four barbels. Prominent, bony scutes are arranged in five rows—one dorsal, two lateral, and two lateroventral. The tail is heterocercal (sharklike), with vertebrae extending into a much-elongated dorsal lobe.

In the same order is an extinct fossil family Chondrosteidae, known from the Lower Jurassic to the Lower Cretaceous. *Acipenser* is known from the Upper Cretaceous to Recent.

Sturgeons are among the important commercial fishes of the world. The meat is delicious and the eggs, converted into caviar, are in great demand. Unfortunately the worldwide stocks of sturgeons are dwindling because of dams, pollution, and exploitation. Many species are slow-growing and are easily exploited.

Priegel and Wirth (1971) reported that an occasional pallid sturgeon (*Scaphirhynchus albus*) occurs in the Wisconsin-Iowa boundary water of the Mississippi River. It has a lighter color, no scalelike plates on the belly, and the length of inner barbels into head length is more than 6. This species ranges in the Missouri and lower Mississippi rivers (P. W. Smith et al. 1971). An old report for Keokuk, Iowa (Coker 1930), is not accepted. I do not view this species as occurring in Wisconsin but acknowledge the possibility that it may, and it should be watched for.

Lake Sturgeon

Acipenser fulvescens Rafinesque. *Acipenser*—sturgeon; *fulvescens*—dull yellow color.

Other common names: freshwater sturgeon, Great Lakes sturgeon, rock sturgeon (usually the long-snouted, obviously plated young), stone sturgeon, red sturgeon, ruddy sturgeon, common sturgeon, shell back sturgeon, bony sturgeon, smoothback, rock fish, rubber nose, black sturgeon, dogface sturgeon.

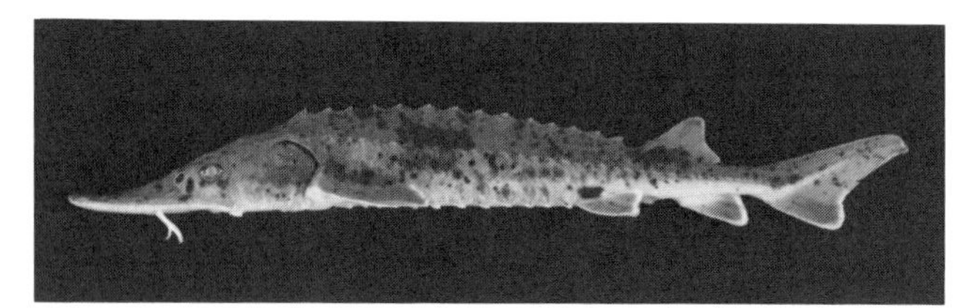

Immature 228 mm, Chippewa R. (Rusk Co.), 25 Sept. 1976

DESCRIPTION

Body heavy, torpedo-shaped, angular (5-sided) in young but round in adults. TL of adults 115 cm or more. Snout short, conical. Spiracle present. Caudal peduncle short, stout, partly naked. Lower lip with 2 lobes. Barbels on lower snout, smooth, 4. Upper lobe of tail fin pointed without threadlike (filamentous) extension.

Young gray or brown dorsally with dusky dorsal and lateral blotches. Adults gray to olivaceous dorsally, white ventrally.

DISTRIBUTION, STATUS, AND HABITAT

The lake sturgeon occurs in the Mississippi, Lake Michigan, and Lake Superior drainage basins. In the Mississippi River drainage it occurs in the Mississippi, St. Croix, Chippewa (and major tributaries), and Wisconsin rivers. In the Wisconsin River recent records place it upstream in the Castle Rock Flowage (Adams County). In Lake Superior it is found in the comparatively shallow waters of Keweenaw Bay, in the vicinity of the Apostle Islands, and it is known to spawn in the Bad River (Ashland County). It is occasionally taken in St. Louis Bay (Eddy and Underhill 1974). In the Lake Michigan basin it occurs in Green Bay, Lake Michigan, the Menominee River upstream to the White Rapids Dam, the Fox River upstream to Lake Puckaway, and the Wolf River upstream to Shawano. This system includes Lakes Winnebago, Butte des Morts, and Winneconne, and the Embarrass River (a tributary to the Wolf River). It has been introduced to lakes where natural reproduction did not occur: Big Cedar Lake (Washington County), Madison lakes (Dane County), Chain of Lakes (Waupaca County), Pear Lake (Washburn County), and others (Priegel and Wirth 1971).

The lake sturgeon is listed as a rare species in the United States (Committee on Rare and Endangered Wildlife Species 1966). Over most of its range in the United States it appears to be threatened (Miller 1972). It is depleted (possibly extirpated) in Alabama and Georgia; endangered or depleted in Missouri and West Virginia; rare and endangered in Iowa and Michigan; endangered in Nebraska, Ohio, Pennsylvania, South Dakota, and Vermont; and rare in Minnesota and New York.

In Wisconsin it is common in the Menominee River (Wisconsin-Michigan boundary), the lower Wolf River, Lakes Poygan and Winnebago, Lake Wisconsin (Wisconsin River), St. Croix River to Gordon Dam, Namekagon River below Trego Dam, and the Chippewa and Flambeau rivers. It is uncommon to rare in the lower Wisconsin River, Mississippi River, the Madison lakes, and Lakes Michigan and Superior. It is probably extirpated in the Wisconsin River in Wood, Portage, and Marathon counties and in the Baraboo River (Columbia and Sauk counties). The Wisconsin Department of Natural Resources has given this species watch status (Les 1979).

The lake sturgeon is a typical inhabitant of large rivers and lakes. It lives in shoal water in the Great Lakes. Inland it shows a preference for the deepest midriver areas and pools (Kuehn et al. 1961).

BIOLOGY

Spawning takes place during late April and early May in central Wisconsin. In northwestern Wisconsin in the St. Croix River, spawning migrations occur in May and early June (Eddy and Underhill 1974). The following account is taken from Priegel and Wirth (1971), unless otherwise indicated. In the Wolf River, during seasons when water flow is high and water temperatures rise slowly, spawning begins when the water temperatures reach 11.7°C (53°F). During seasons of low water flow and more rapid temperature rise, spawning does not begin until water temperatures reach 14.5–15.0°C (58–59°F). Males are observed at the spawning sites before females.

Often a dozen or more huge fish may be seen cruising the shallow shorelines or lying at the water's edge with their tails, backs, or snouts out of the water. Males cruise the spawning sites in groups often of eight or more fish, and are frequently so close to the bank that they can be readily captured.

Spawning begins as soon as a ripe female enters the group. Several males attend one female by swimming alongside her in the same direction, usually against the current. When actual spawning takes

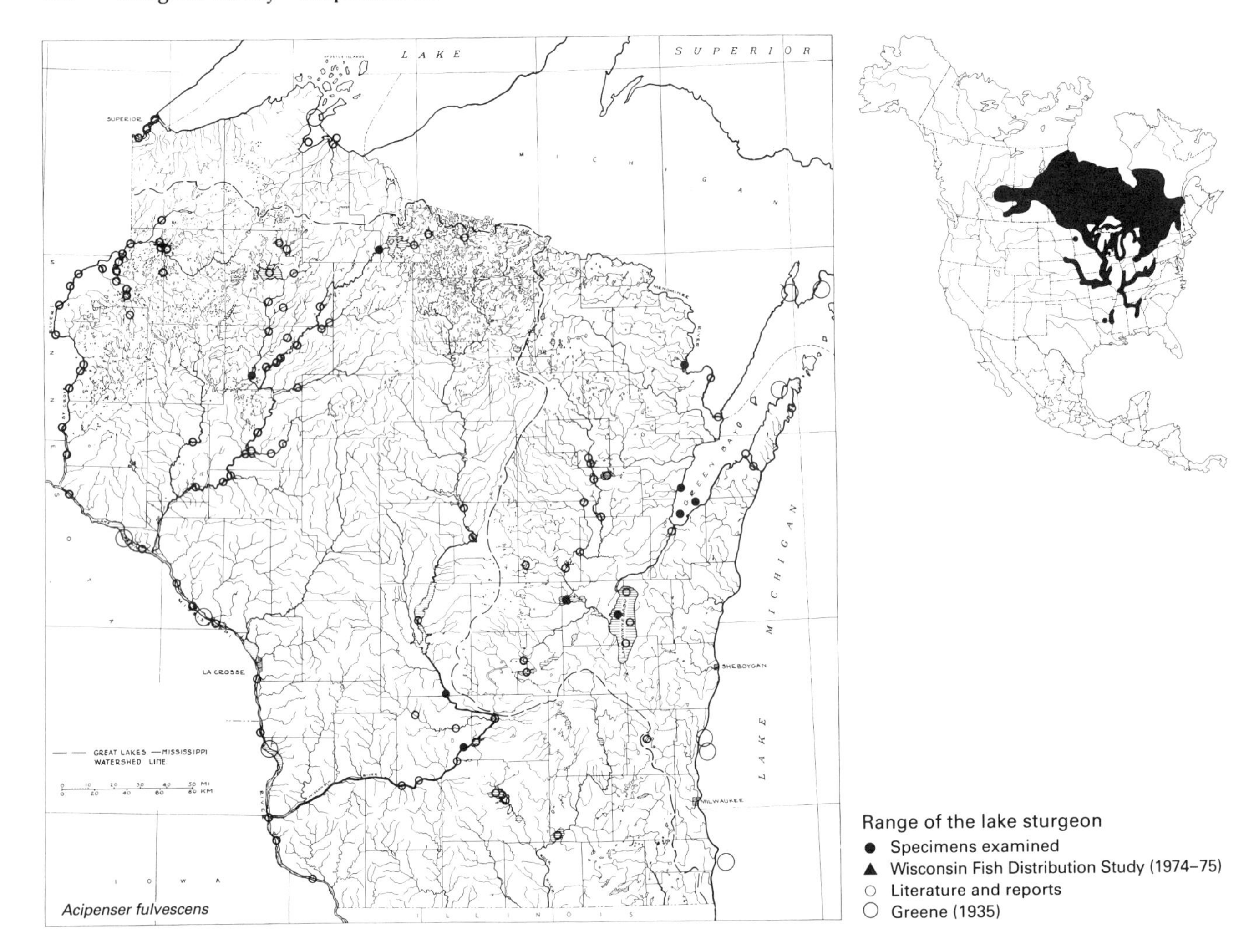

Range of the lake sturgeon
- ● Specimens examined
- ▲ Wisconsin Fish Distribution Study (1974–75)
- ○ Literature and reports
- ◯ Greene (1935)

place, one or more males vibrate simultaneously alongside a female. While milt is being released, the vibrating tail of the male may protrude from the water. "It produces a sound which could be compared to a ruffed grouse drumming or an old tractor starting up" (Priegel and Wirth 1971:7). The average spawning act lasts about 5 seconds; the spawning group drifts either downstream or out into deeper water, only to return, usually to the same site, to spawn again. The spawning activity for one female usually lasts from 5 to 8 or more hours but may extend over a period of a day or more, until she is spent.

Males release milt at the time the eggs are extruded, fertilizing the eggs. Spawning may occur in water only 0.3 m (1 ft) up to 4.6 m (15 ft) in depth. The eggs are black in color, very glutinous, about 3 mm diam. There is a considerable variation in the number of eggs produced by females of the same weight—anywhere from 50,000 to 700,000 eggs may be released.

On rare occasions, spawning occurs in Lake Winnebago along rocky west shore points. Spawning sites in the Wolf River are usually found on the outside bends of the river banks, especially where the current is upwelling or slowly boiling and where rocks, boulders, and broken slabs of concrete have been riprapped at a steep angle into the water. Spawning occurs at the Shawano Dam, Shiocton, and Northport. Some lake sturgeon move up into the Embarrass River. In the Berlin-Princeton area of the Fox River, spawning occurs during those years when the water is high enough for the sturgeon to get over the Eureka Dam.

Hatching time for the eggs is a function of water temperature. Priegel (1964a) followed egg development and recorded the initiation of hatching 8 days after the eggs were laid at water temperatures between 12.8 and 13.9°C (55–57°F), and in 5 days at or near 17°C (low 60s°F).

Harkness and Dymond (1961) illustrated the developmental stages and noted that the young are 8 mm long on hatching and nearly 21 mm at 16 days after hatching.

Since the lake sturgeon lacks scales, other methods have been sought for aging. Otoliths (inner ear bones) show growth rings through an elaborate method of preparation, but this method has its drawbacks (Schneberger and Woodbury 1944). A more reliable aging method involves the use of thin cross sections of the first pectoral fin ray (Probst 1954), and this is the method currently most often employed.

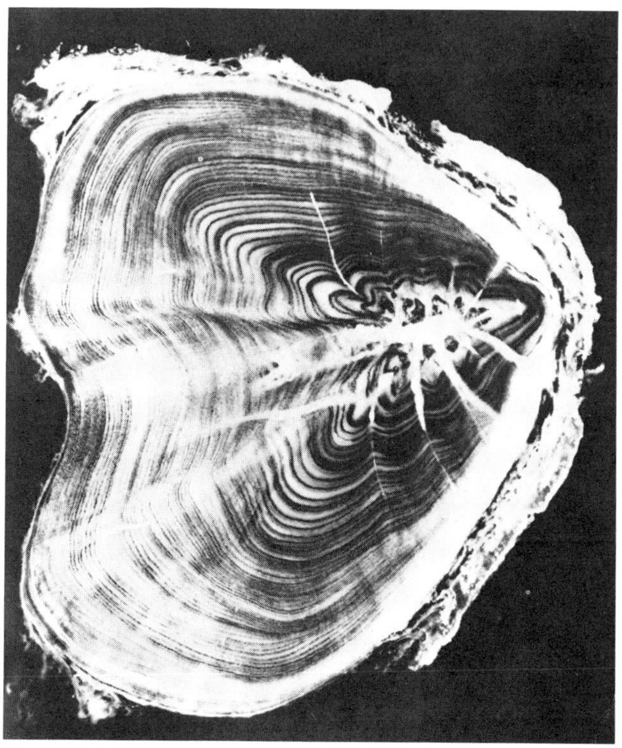

Cross section of a 2.01-m, 70.76-kg sturgeon 82 years old (Wisconsin DNR photo)

Ages, Lengths and Weights of Lake Sturgeon in Wisconsin

	L. Winnebago (Priegel 1973)		L. Poygan (Priegel 1964b)		Menominee R. (Priegel 1973)	
Age Group	TL (cm)	WT (kg)	TL (cm)	WT (kg)	TL (cm)	WT (kg)
1	27.9				15.2	0.045
3	58.4				30.5	0.136
6	83.8				53.3	0.680
9	111.8	8.62	86.4	3.63	73.7	2.13
11	116.8	9.98	94.0	4.54	86.4	3.10
14	124.5	13.15	111.8	7.26	99.1	5.31
17	132.1	15.42	119.4	9.53	116.8	11.11
20	144.8	19.05	127.0	11.79	124.5	11.48
25	149.9	24.04	137.2	15.88	134.7	17.69

Note: Growth varies considerably, as evidenced by the differences in L. Winnebago sturgeon, where, e.g., one 33-year-old fish weighed 49.90 kg (110 lb) and a 43-year-old fish weighed 19.50 kg (43 lb).

A female lake sturgeon reaches sexual maturity when she is 24–26 years old and about 140 cm (55 in) long. Thereafter, instead of spawning every spring, females spawn once every 4–6 years. Few males mature before they are 114 cm (45 in) long. Most males spawn every other year, but some do so every year.

In Wisconsin, male and female sturgeon grow at the same rate, but females live longer than males. Ninety-seven percent of the fish over 30 years of age are females (Priegel 1964b).

The largest lake sturgeon taken in recent years was an 81.65-kg (180-lb) fish (est. 82 years old) speared from Lake Winnebago in 1953 by E. Schroeder of Appleton. Oshkosh oldtimers, however, tell of an 85.05-kg (187.5-lb) fish caught 6 August 1913 on a set line by A. Haferman and Michael Goyke (*Milwaukee Journal*, March 1953). In the *Fond du Lac Journal* of 14 April 1881, I. Pollack is reported to have captured a sturgeon that weighed 134.72 kg (297 lb) and was 274.5 cm (9 ft) long. A lake sturgeon 229 cm, 140.62 kg (90 in, 310 lb), was caught from Batchawana Bay of Lake Superior in 1921 or 1922, at an estimated age of 100 years. In 1943 a fish of the same weight and 2.41 m (95 in) TL was reported from southern Lake Michigan, north of Benton Harbor, Michigan (Mich. Dep. Nat. Resour. 1975).

The lake sturgeon requires extensive areas of water less than 914 cm (30 ft) deep where abundant food is produced.

> Aquarium observations indicate that when the lake sturgeon searches for food, it swims close to the bottom with the ends of its sensitive barbels or feelers dragging lightly over the bottom. As soon as the feelers touch food, there is an instantaneous reaction: the tubular mouth is rapidly protruded and the food sucked in along with silt, gravel, and other bottom materials. The food items are rapidly strained as the soft bottom materials are puffed through the gills and the food items are retained. . . . Insect larvae found in the forward portion of their stomachs (i.e., the crop) are usually entire and still alive. Stomachs of larger fish have been found to contain a water-displaced volume of 66 ounces of midge lake larvae, estimated to number 60,000 individuals. Lake sturgeon in the Lake Winnebago area feed throughout the winter at water temperatures down to 34 F (Priegel and Wirth 1971:5).

At 19 mm, the young start feeding on minute crustaceans and continue on that diet until they are 178–203 mm long (Eddy and Underhill 1974). An examination of stomachs from 11 sturgeon in Lake Winnebago showed *Chironomus plumosus* exclusively in 10; the 11th contained, in addition to the *Chironomus*, leeches, numerous *Pisidium*, and small snails (Schneberger and Woodbury 1944). Chippewa River sturgeon feed largely on small snails. Lake sturgeon kept in confinement for long periods of time thrive on such grains as wheat and barley (Eddy and Surber 1947).

Lake sturgeon travel in loose aggregations, leaving them only at time of spawning. Lake Winnebago fish must pass through all of the upriver lakes to reach spawning grounds (as far as 200 km upstream) on the Wolf River, but yet "remember" to return to Lake Winnebago. Lake Poygan fish "remember" to drop off in Lake Poygan on their return trip from the spawning grounds, rather than continue on downstream to Lake Winnebago (Wirth and Schultz 1957). The lake sturgeon from Lake Winnebago and the upriver lakes will spawn together, but each returns to its home area.

Occasionally lake sturgeon will move downstream over a dam or a series of dams outside of the home basin. In the Menominee River, sturgeon have migrated downstream over the hydroelectric power dams (Priegel 1973). Three lake sturgeon tagged in Lake Winnebago were later captured by commercial fishermen who were fishing in the Little Bay de Noc and Escanaba areas of Lake Michigan (Priegel and Wirth 1971).

Local people along the Wolf River report sightings of large schools of small lake sturgeon over sand bars during the summer and early fall. During August 1969, large schools of 126–152-mm lake sturgeon were observed over gravel areas just below rapids in the Menominee River (Priegel and Wirth 1971). On 7 August 1971 in the Bad River 16.1 km upstream from Odanah, a 120-mm (4.7-in) fish was caught in shallow water over a sand bar by G. Ludwig (pers. comm. to Priegel). Such sightings are unusual. After their first year, young sturgeon are found in the same habitat as adults.

Lake sturgeon have the habit of leaping entirely out of the water until they appear to be standing on their tails. Sometimes just the head and upper third of the body slides up out of the water at a forward angle and falls back, creating a sliding splash. This leaping action may serve to get rid of parasitic lampreys attached to the sturgeon. Twenty-seven lampreys were removed from one 157-cm (62-in) sturgeon in Lake Winnebago. The lampreys probably do little damage, but they must be a nuisance.

IMPORTANCE AND MANAGEMENT

Fish are not known to prey on small lake sturgeon, but reliable sources have reported otter bringing small sturgeon onto the ice in the Lake Poygan area. The eggs of the lake sturgeon are preyed on by suckers, carp, catfish, and even other sturgeon. As previously noted, the adult sturgeon is an important host fish to the parasitic lampreys.

Until 1870 lake sturgeon were considered a nuisance by commercial fishermen, who destroyed them in great numbers by piling them on shore to rot (Milner 1874a). Today the sturgeon is a prized fish.

Lake sturgeon have been caught with angleworms, nightcrawlers, minnows, and snails. Occasionally they may be taken on small fish and cut pieces of fresh fish, but these are probably not as effective as natural food items. Hook and line angling for sturgeon is permitted in boundary and inland waters during a variable and limited open season, allowing one or two fish per season.

In Wisconsin, where spearing of lake sturgeon is still allowed, to spear a sturgeon falls in the same category of sport as bagging a deer or a bear. To the people in the four counties surrounding Lake Winnebago (accounting for 66–72% of the license sales annually), sturgeon-spearing is a festive occasion. Shacks are dragged out onto the ice and elaborate preparations are made. The spear fishermen often scatter a variety of perishable materials in the water, such as shelled corn, peeled potatoes, egg shells, or noodles. Through holes in the ice, they suspend decoys of various shapes, colors, and substances: ears of corn, wooden airplanes, beer cans, and even skillfully carved and painted replicas of fish. The decoys are thought to attract the curious lake sturgeon; they also help the spearers adjust their eyes to various depths. And if the length of the decoy is known, it can help the spearer decide if a sturgeon swimming beneath the hole is of minimum legal size. The spears have three to eight barbed tines, and are attached to wooden or metal handles 1.8–2.7 m (6–9 ft) long. The end of the handle is usually weighted with lead so that it can be propelled rapidly towards the target. The handle detaches when a fish is speared, making it possible to play the fish on a long line.

The largest catch on record was an estimated 2,828 lake sturgeon speared in Lake Winnebago and its upriver lakes in 1953; they weighed approximately

Lake sturgeon (Wisconsin DNR photo)

45,400 kg (100,000 lb) (Probst and Cooper 1955). From 1955 through 1970, an average yearly harvest of 15,000 kg (33,000 lb) of lake sturgeon has been taken from Lake Winnebago. Once abundant in Lake Michigan, the lake sturgeon is seldom taken there today. In 1880 the catch was 1,741,600 kg (3,839,600 lb); in 1966, only 907 kg (2,000 lb). In 1966 another 907 kg (2,000 lb) were caught from the combined United States and Canadian waters of Lake Superior.

In Wisconsin it is illegal to sell the flesh or roe of a Wisconsin-caught fish. Ontario, however, permits some commercial sturgeon-fishing. Its meat is delicious fresh or smoked and the eggs make a fine caviar. About one-fifth of the weight of a ripe female will be roe. Mature black eggs can be worked from the ovarian membrane through a sieve and then placed into a brine or similar preservative. Drained, washed, and packed in jars or kegs, this product is the famous caviar (Schlumpf 1941); until recently it sold for $36 per kilo. In the mid-1970s flesh of the fish on New York markets brought $7 per kilo.

In past years, various other products from lake sturgeon were marketed. The most widely known was isinglass, a form of gelatin obtained from the inner lining of the swim bladder of certain fish, chiefly lake sturgeon. Isinglass was used principally for clarifying wines, beers, and other liquids; it also had culinary and confectionery uses, in making jellies, stiffening jams, etc. Other lake sturgeon products included oil which was rendered from the fat, glue made from the gristly skeleton, and fine grades of ornamental leather made from the tanned skins (Priegel and Wirth 1971).

In Lake Winnebago there was no fishery for lake sturgeon from 1915 to January 1932, when a spearing season was established. Since then there has been an annual spearing season through the ice.

In order to curb overexploitation, the season bag limits have been changed from five fish (1932–1953), to three (1954–1955), to two (1956–1957), and then to one (1958–present). In 1955, the size limit was increased from 76.2 cm (30 in), which it had been since 1932, to 101.6 cm (40 in). In 1974 the minimum legal size was increased to 114.3 cm (45 in). Despite these restrictions, the exploitation rate on Lake Winnebago in the years from 1955 through 1969 was a legal kill of 599 sturgeon per year, according to Priegel and Wirth (1975). These researchers concluded that 540 fish is the maximum segment of the population of legal-size sturgeon (estimated at 11,500) that can safely be taken annually if the population present in 1969 is to be maintained.

With no more restrictions than length of season, size limits, and bag limits, there is no way to assure that overexploitation will not occur. For instance, there was a registered kill of 1,251 lake sturgeon in 1972, 936 in 1976, and 2,238 in 1982—harvests exceeding by a considerable margin the safe segment of 540. Even though such numbers are not cropped every year, large harvests may place the population in jeopardy. In addition to the registered kill are fish of sublegal size killed by spearing, fish carried off the ice improperly tagged and undeclared, and fish taken illegally by hook and line and by setlines during the closed season. All of these are unreported but may constitute an illegal kill as high as the legal kill.

The Menominee River (Wisconsin–Michigan boundary water) contains one of the last fishable lake sturgeon populations in Wisconsin and Michigan (Priegel 1973). Population estimates, in the best 42-km (26-mi) section (between the White Rapids and Grand Rapids dams), were 234 (1969) and 185 (1970) legal-size fish (106.7 cm [42 in] and larger). The calculated fishing pressure was 14,300 hours in 1969 and 11,400 hours in 1970. The estimated exploitation rate was 13% (58 fish) in 1969 and 17% (48 fish) in 1970, which is considered too high. To maintain a harvestable population, an exploitation rate of 5% would be desirable.

The 127-cm (50-in) size limit instituted on the Menominee River in 1975 would allow some male sturgeon there to reach sexual maturity, since 20-year-old males reach that size, and 20 years is the age at which males purportedly first attain maturity. Throughout the geographic range of the lake sturgeon, however, most females attain sexual maturity at age 25 (Harkness and Dymond 1961). Thus the 127-cm (50-in) size limit would offer little protection for females on the Menominee River (Priegel 1973).

In Lake Poygan the take of immature lake sturgeon has increased proportionately as a result of depletion of the sturgeon stock. The population data give an estimated percentage of immature females ranging from 70% in 1955 to 83.1% in 1957. The estimated population for Lakes Poygan and Winneconne is about 3,400 legal-size sturgeon. During the 1976 season, 85 sturgeon were registered; the largest fish taken was 168 cm (66 in) long and weighed 45.5 kg (100 lb). Average length was 129.5 cm (51 in) (Priegel and Wirth 1971). The population in Lakes Poygan and Winneconne is considered overexploited, and seasons have been drastically curtailed in recent years.

Closing the sturgeon fishery for a period of years was formerly considered a good management practice which would permit the population to return to something like its original abundance (Priegel and Wirth 1975). This beneficial effect has not occurred on the smaller upriver lakes (e.g., Poygan, Winneconne), which have had short, 2-day seasons every third year, although there might not yet have been enough time to determine whether those waters are recovering. In a review of the literature, Priegel and Wirth cited a number of instances in which overexploited sturgeon populations failed to recover after a closed period of many years. It is vital, they stated, that the lake sturgeon population and harvest in Lake Winnebago be sampled on a regular basis to watch for any signs of overexploitation and to initiate studies to determine causes of overharvest should evidence warrant it: "Once the population is over-exploited, it is almost a safe assumption that the population will never recover to former abundance, as has already been shown throughout the natural geographical range of the lake sturgeon" (p. 19).

In addition to the dangers of overexploitation there are other threats to the lake sturgeon population. Hydroelectric dams act as barriers to the traditional spawning grounds of the lake sturgeon. Because the sturgeon is a long-lived animal, populations isolated by dams may persist for many years, but eventually may die out from angling, spearing, or from natural or pollution-associated mortality. The disappearance of the lake sturgeon from the Wisconsin River upstream from Petenwell Dam (Adams County) may have occurred for those very reasons. In the Castle Rock Flowage a remnant population of lake sturgeon may still persist. There is no evidence, however, that it is sustaining itself, and after the last few fish are caught that segment of the population will be extirpated.

Not only are our best sturgeon-producing waters dammed, many are also lined with paper mills which alter the water quality by introducing highly organic effluents. Under certain conditions such wastes are capable of reducing the oxygen content in downstream waters, leading to serious fishkills. More than 50 large lake sturgeon from Lake Wisconsin (Columbia County) in the lower Wisconsin River were winterkilled during the spring of 1967. The problem was traced to pollution from paper mills.

Commercial sturgeon-poaching is also a serious and real problem, since the size and the value of these large fish apparently make the risk worthwhile.

To perpetuate the remaining lake sturgeon stocks, certain management procedures should be considered: (1) establish a quota system, applicable to all state waters, so that only a designated number of lake sturgeon may be harvested in any year by any method; (2) allow taking lake sturgeon only by hook and line, since it is a reasonable assumption that a number of sublegal fish are destroyed by spearing; (3) establish lake sturgeon refuges where the species is given full protection (year-round) and where, if necessary, all fishing is prohibited.

Shovelnose Sturgeon

Scaphirhynchus platorynchus (Rafinesque). *Scaphirhynchus*—spade snout; *platorynchus*—broad snout.
Other common names: hackleback, switchtail, sand sturgeon, flathead sturgeon.

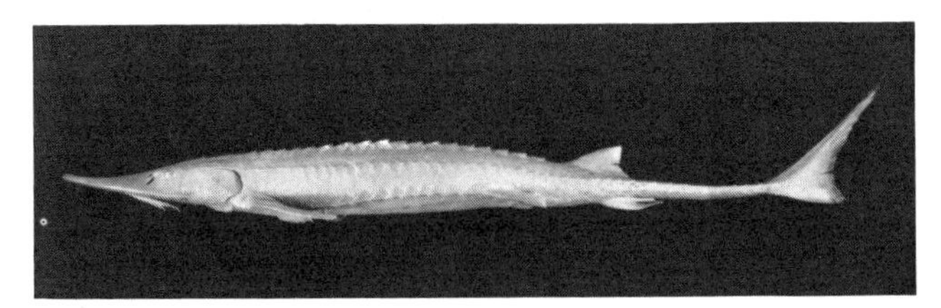

588 mm, Wisconsin R., Boscobel (Grant Co.), 19 June 1962

DESCRIPTION
Body much elongated, torpedo-shaped, angular (5-sided). Adult FL about 635 mm (25 in). Snout long, spade-shaped. Spiracle absent. Caudal peduncle slender, completely encased in bony plates. Lower lip with 4 lobes. Barbels strongly fringed. Upper lobe of tail fin elongated into a threadlike extension (often broken off). Chromosomes 2n = 112 (Ohno et al. 1969).

Adults tawny to gray or olivaceous dorsally, lighter ventrally.

DISTRIBUTION, STATUS, AND HABITAT
The shovelnose sturgeon occurs only in the Mississippi drainage basin, appearing in the Mississippi River, the Wisconsin River upstream to the Prairie du Sac Dam, the St. Croix River upstream to St. Croix Falls Dam, the Chippewa River up to the Eau Claire Dam, and the Red Cedar River upstream to the Menomonie Dam. Its presence in the Black River upstream to Black River Falls Dam is suspected but not documented (Christenson 1975).

The shovelnose sturgeon is depleted in Alabama, Mississippi, and South Dakota; endangered in Kentucky; rare and endangered in Oklahoma and Wyoming; rare to depleted in West Virginia; and rare in Minnesota (Miller 1972). In Wisconsin it is uncommon to common in the main channels of the Mississippi and lower Wisconsin rivers and in the lower Chippewa and Red Cedar rivers. Numbers in the Mississippi River have decreased sharply since the turn of the century.

This species inhabits deep channels of large rivers over sand or gravel in the presence of some current. On the Mississippi River it occurs in the tailwaters below wing dams and other structures which accelerate the water flow. In the Chippewa River (Dunn County) shovelnose sturgeon have been taken over sand and gravel; in the Red Cedar River (Dunn County) over bedrock (10%), rubble-gravel (40%), and sand (50%) (Christenson 1975). They tend to congregate wherever there are large quantities of small clams and snails (Trautman 1957). Rarely is the shovelnose sturgeon found in quiet water, although it has been reported in Lake Pepin (Wagner 1908). Coker (1930) noted that the capture of a specimen in a slough excited the interest of fishermen because the species is virtually never taken except in the river; it is a fish of the current.

BIOLOGY
Spawning in Wisconsin occurs during May and June. In the Red Cedar–Chippewa rivers during 1972, shovelnose sturgeon spawned the last week in May through the first week in June at water temperatures of 19.5–21.1°C (67–70°F) (Christenson 1975). According to Eddy and Underhill (1974), in the St. Croix River (Wisconsin-Minnesota boundary) large numbers migrate up from Lake St. Croix and gather under the dam at St. Croix Falls, where they probably are forced to spawn on the rocks in the swift water below the dam.

It is generally accepted that shovelnose sturgeon migrate upstream for spawning, and migrations into smaller streams have been reported (Forbes and Richardson 1920). Coker (1930) stated that runs of shovelnose sturgeon in the Mississippi River are variable: best when the river is low in spring and poor when it is high. Cross (1967) suggested that perhaps the species seeks an optimal volume of flow, departing from the largest rivers to enter tributaries for spawning in years when streams are high. During the run the shovelnose sturgeon swim near the surface, enabling fishermen to capture them by means of seines weighted to fish the top rather than the bottom (Jordan and Evermann 1923).

Helms (1974b) provided detailed anatomical data from Mississippi sturgeon. Gonads of immature males appeared as dark yellow longitudinal bands, 1–3 mm wide on the dorsal surface of the gonadal fat. They constituted 5% of the whole organ. Fully developed gonads exceeded 10 mm and were equal to or greater in volume than the attached fat. Mature testes were gray and appeared as a homogeneous mass.

In sturgeons from the Chippewa River, Christenson (1975) observed that the adhesive eggs appear to fall into three major groups: (1) yellow and/or white, (2) white and black, and (3) black (the mature eggs in the enlarged ovaries). Since at least three stages of

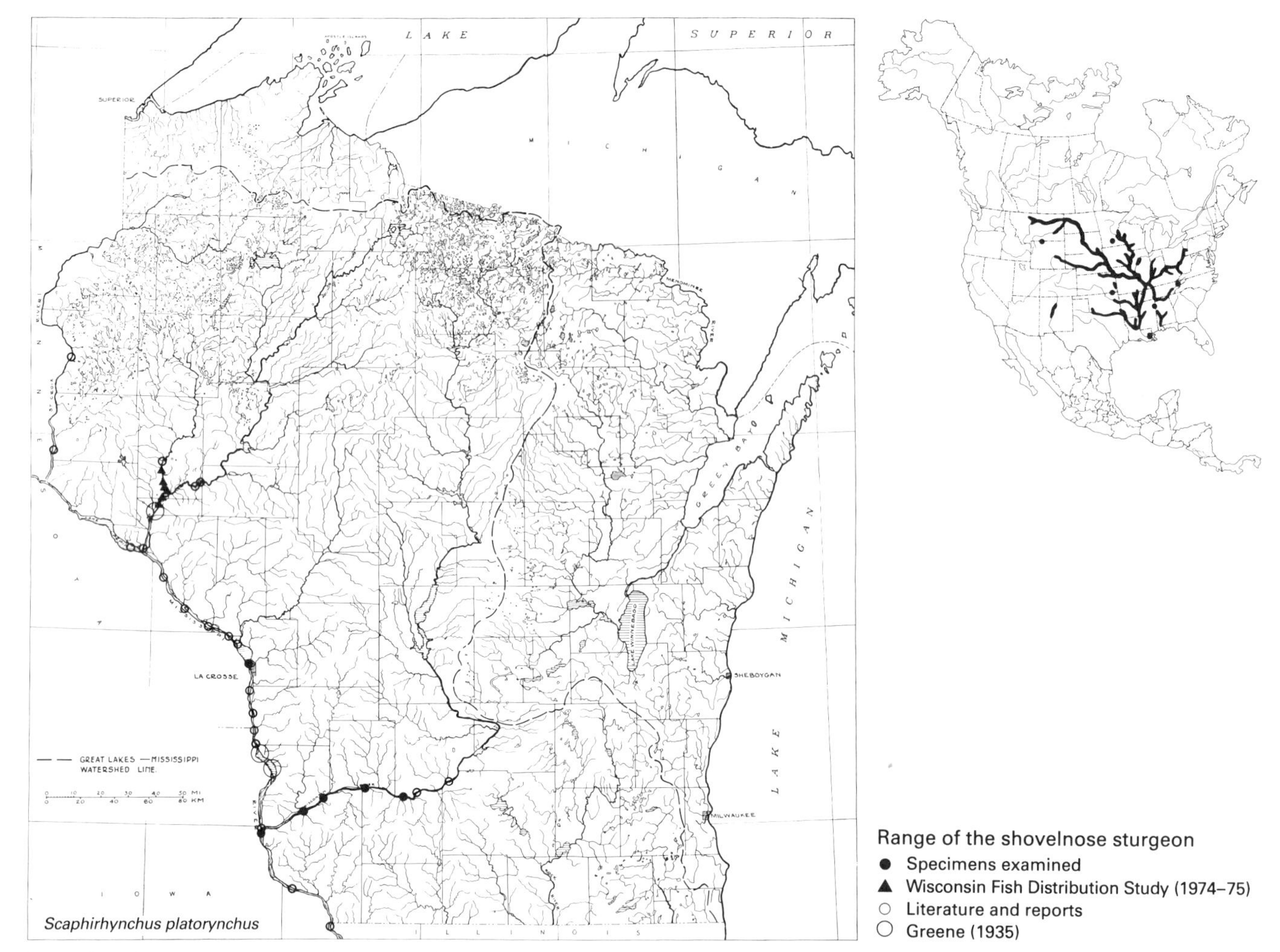

Range of the shovelnose sturgeon
● Specimens examined
▲ Wisconsin Fish Distribution Study (1974–75)
○ Literature and reports
◯ Greene (1935)

egg development occurred essentially without relation to the size of the female, it is apparent that females do not spawn every year; but the spawning chronology is not readily evident (Helms 1974b, Christenson 1975).

According to Helms (1974b), ovaries averaged 18.1% of the body weight in 24 gravid females from the Mississippi River ranging from 615 mm (24.2 in) to 853 mm (33.6 in) FL. Total counts of eggs averaged 27,592 (13,908–51,217). In the Red Cedar–Chippewa river system (Christenson 1975), estimated egg production ranged from 10,680 (in females 627 mm FL) to 50,971 (in females 805 mm FL), averaging 24,404. Mature egg diameter averaged 2.27 (2.05–2.43) mm.

A female taken 1 May 1972 from the Red Cedar River weighed 2.21 kg (4.88 lb), and was 805 mm FL (31.7 in). The ripening ovary constituted 18% of the body weight. A male of 2.58 kg (5.69 lb) body weight had testes which made up 6% of the body weight.

Little is known about early development of the shovelnose sturgeon. Young-of-year as small as 43 mm (1.7 in) FL were taken in the upper Mississippi River during late June by trawling (Helms 1974b). All successful trawl tows were rather far from shore; they were usually located in main channel or main channel border habitat. The most successful hauls were those associated with submerged rock wing dams. Coker (1930) noted that young taken on 11 July from the Mississippi River at Fairport measured 71 mm SL.

Shovelnose sturgeon are aged by length-frequency distribution and by determining the annuli appearing in a cross section of the pectoral fin ray taken close to the point of insertion (Zweiacker 1967, Helms 1974a, b). These methods did not prove feasible in the Red Cedar–Chippewa study, and Christenson (1975) calculated growth on empirical measurements of recaptured specimens.

Helms (1974a) placed 110 shovelnose sturgeon from Pool 13 (Mississippi River), collected from the end of October to the beginning of November, in a length-frequency distribution and aged them by examination of the pectoral rays. Young-of-year (age 0) averaged 226 mm (8.9 in) FL; age I—348 mm (13.7 in);

age II—480 mm (18.9 in); and age III—559 mm (22.0 in). In shovelnose sturgeon from Pool 9 (Helms 1974b), calculated FL as follows: I—213 mm (8.4 in), II—318 mm (12.5 in), III—409 mm (16.1 in), IV—478 mm (18.8 in), V—526 mm (20.7 in), VI—572 mm (22.5 in), VII—605 mm (23.8 in), VIII—635 mm (25.0 in), IX—658 mm (25.9 in), X—678 mm (26.7 in), XI—688 mm (27.1 in), XII—696 mm (27.4 in).

Helms (1974a) attributed the reduced rate of growth after the fourth year mostly to sexual maturity.

A Red Cedar River sample of 88 shovelnose sturgeon, taken by electrofishing, ranged from 559 to 747 mm FL (0.68–1.47 kg); a Chippewa sample, 509–810 mm (0.43–2.27 kg). Growth of tagged fish, most of which were sexually mature and at large for periods of up to 58 months, was virtually nil. Even allowing for the possibility that growth was retarded because of tagging, growth within the size range sampled must be characterized as extremely slow (Christenson 1975).

On the Mississippi River female shovelnose sturgeon mature at age VII, while most males spawn at age V. Only one age-V female was found with developing eggs (Helms 1974b). Monson and Greenbank (1947), in investigating the sexual maturity of 374 males and 503 females from fish markets at Lansing and Muscatine, Iowa, determined that, of fish under 635 mm (25 in) FL, 25% of the males and 7% of the females were mature; over 635 mm (25 in) FL, 62% and 58%, respectively.

Helms (1974b) reported a large female, 853 mm (33.6 in) FL and 2.81 kg (6.2 lb), from the upper Mississippi River. An 805-mm (31.7-in) FL, 3.18-kg (7.0-lb) fish, sex undetermined, was collected in the Chippewa River in July 1975 (L. Christenson, pers. comm.).

Christenson (1975) estimated that the shovelnose sturgeon population in the Chippewa River study area in 1973 approximated 2,300–2,700 (94–110 per km).

In aquariums, Cross (1967) observed that the sturgeon finds food by raking the bottom with the sensitive barbels that project downward from the snout. The highly protrusible lips are adapted for sucking.

At sampling stations in the Mississippi River near Keokuk, Iowa, this species was found to depend largely upon caddisfly larvae throughout the year (Hoopes 1960). In the 74 shovelnose sturgeon examined, the total stomach content consisted of 68% *Potamyia flava* larvae, 7% *Cheumatopsyche campyla* larvae, 17% *Hexagenia* naiads, and 8% other material, which included immature plecopterans, dipterans, and odonates.

In the upper Mississippi River, stomachs contained a preponderance of caddisflies, mayflies, and chironomids (Helms 1974b). Fish from a 3 May sampling were gorged with eggs. During May and early June there was moderately low food consumption. Increased volume of stomach contents was accompanied by an increase in condition on 6 September. Beginning 22 September, food intake was markedly reduced. Food consumption appeared to be unrelated to temperature.

In the Missouri River, aquatic insect larvae (Tendipedidae and Baetidae, primarily) were found in more than 97% of the stomachs, constituting 93% of the number and 88.1% of the volume of all organisms found (Held 1969). Crustaceans (*Daphnia* sp.) ranked second by number, volume (3.9%), and frequency of occurrence. Seven families of terrestrial insects constituted 3.1% of the total volume of all organisms.

Other items found in stomachs are dragonfly nymphs, snails, fingernail clams, algae, bits of higher aquatic plants, and organic detritus. Helms (1974b) and Modde and Schmulbach (1977) concluded that the shovelnose sturgeon is an opportunistic feeder whose food intake is controlled by availability.

Cholesterol concentrations in the shovelnose from the Chippewa River were considerably lower than those reported for other fishes, including the paddlefish (Hunn and Christenson 1977).

In the Mississippi River the movement of 122 shovelnose sturgeon recaptured by experimental netting showed mean upstream and downstream distances of 2.6 km (1.6 mi) and 0.8 km (0.5 mi) respectively. Movement of 155 sturgeon recovered by commercial fishermen showed 66% moving upstream, 25% downstream, and 9% taken at the tagging site; mean upstream and downstream distances were 15.3 and 1.9 km (9.5 and 1.2 mi), respectively, but the results may be biased by the high proportion of major commercial fishing units which were located a substantial distance upstream from the primary marking and releasing site (Helms 1974b). Interpool movement was always in an upstream direction. The greatest distance traveled, 194 km (120 mi), was covered by four fish which moved from Pool 13 to Pool 9 and which were recaptured 265–724 days after tagging. The sturgeon tended to congregate in the tailwaters of pools. During high-water years, the dam-control gates are out of operation much of the time and are not barriers to upstream movement.

In the Red Cedar River (Dunn County) over a period of 7–58 months, 57% (of 44 fish) moved upstream an average distance of 4.8 km (3 mi), while 39% moved downstream an average of 7.6 km (4.7

mi). Maximum upstream and downstream distances were 19.3 km (12 mi) and 16.9 km (10.5 mi), respectively. Two fish exhibited no movement (Christenson 1975).

IMPORTANCE AND MANAGEMENT

The shovelnose sturgeon is the host to the glochidia of the mollusks *Quadrula pustulosa*, *Obovaria olivaria*, and *Lampsilis teres* (Hart and Fuller 1974). It is the only known host for the hickory-nut clam (*Obovaria olivaria*), which inhabits water 1.2–1.8 m deep over sand or gravel in good current (Parmalee 1967). This coincides with the habitat of the shovelnose sturgeon.

Once this species was considered almost worthless, and, when taken in nets, was regarded by fishermen as a nuisance. It was the common practice to break the necks of the sturgeon or to throw them up high on the bank to die (Coker 1930). Today this species is considered a delicacy, and demand for it exceeds production.

Occasionally the shovelnose sturgeon is taken on hook and line in deep waters around snags, with worms and other live baits. During 1960 sport fishermen on the Wisconsin River between Prairie du Sac and Lone Rock creeled 11 shovelnose sturgeon in 3,243 fish caught; between Lone Rock and the mouth of the Wisconsin River, 60 sturgeon in 1,528 fish. These sturgeon averaged 580 (406–1,041) mm.

The largest numbers of shovelnose sturgeon are caught in trammel nets, drifted with the current (Cross 1967, Starrett and Barnickol 1955). The sturgeon are highly vulnerable to drift nets, regardless of mesh size, because the hooked scutes of the small sturgeon become entangled in the threads. In Wisconsin, they are taken in trammel nets, seines, setlines, buffalo nets, and bait nets. Setlines may be baited with cutbait, small fish, or worms.

Market values are among the highest for any commercial fish species in the upper Mississippi River basin. Processing by smoking adds considerable cost to the consumer product because it requires additional labor and is also apt to result in large loss in tissue weight. Loss in body weight by smoking for shovelnose sturgeon 568 g (1.25 lb) averaged 49.8%, while the weight loss for larger fish averaged 42.6% (Helms 1974b). Because of their small size, most shovelnose sturgeon are smoked, although a number are "hog dressed" (entrails removed but skin left intact).

In the mid 1970s, the average price paid to Iowa commercial fishermen ranged from $0.44 to $1.06 per kilo (2.2 lb), while the dressed price ranged from $0.99 to $1.87 per kilo. Smoked shovelnose sturgeon costs from $2.09 to $4.95 per kilo (Helms 1974b). In Wisconsin during 1975 the price paid to commercial fishermen was $0.64 per kilo and the catch of 2,980 kg had a value of $1,905.59 (Fernholz and Crawley 1976). Finished caviar from shovelnose sturgeon retails at about $33 per kilo (Helms 1974b). According to Eddy and Surber (1947), the roe has been made into excellent caviar and is often mixed with the roe of the paddlefish and even of suckers. The meat is delicious deep-fat fried, broiled, or smoked.

Harvest figures from the upper Mississippi River showed a steady decline until the last few decades (Helms 1974b):

Year	Kg
1894	192,000
1899	174,000
1922	54,000
1931	26,000
1947–1950	5,000–9,000
1950–1959	4,000–54,000
1960–1969	8,000–17,000
1970–1973	16,000–22,000

Since the construction of navigation dams, shovelnose sturgeon harvest has exceeded 45,000 kg (100,000 lb) only twice (in 1956 and 1958). Of the 11 pools bordering Iowa, Pools 9, 12, and 17 are generally the most productive.

According to Helms (1974b), populations of shovelnose sturgeon are undoubtedly much lower now than they were when the Mississippi River was a natural, unimpounded water course. The decline was undoubtedly a direct result of habitat destruction. Manipulation of the river to enhance navigation (including construction of 4-, 6-, and 9-ft channels) and establishment of impoundments have constricted shovelnose sturgeon habitat to small areas immediately downstream from navigation dams. At the present time in the upper Mississippi, shovelnose sturgeon populations have probably attained an equilibrium with the environment and seem capable of supporting a moderate commercial harvest. From the age structure, Helms estimated total annual mortality at about 60%; mortality from fishing ranged from 5 to 25% and did not affect total mortality.

A commercial fishing regulation adopted by both Wisconsin and Iowa establishes a nonfishing zone extending 274 m below navigation dams. The regulation undoubtedly affords the shovelnose sturgeon protection, since this is an area in which they congregate.

Paddlefish Family—Polyodontidae

In 1792 Walbaum described the American paddlefish as a new shark species, and in 1820 Rafinesque wrote an extensive description of it as an "entirely new shark genus." Sharks, however, are cartilaginous fishes (Chondrichthyes), while the paddlefish belongs to that group of fishes known as the bony fishes (Osteichthyes). The paddlefish, *Polyodon spathula*, is a smooth-skinned, bizarre-looking creature, with a long paddle-like snout and a tail with an elongated dorsal lobe.

Only one other species is known from this family: the Chinese sturgeon, *Psephurus gladius*, which inhabits the Yangtze-Kiang River in the Chinese lowlands and feeds on other fishes, whereas the American paddlefish feeds on plankton.

Paddlefish

Polyodon spathula (Walbaum). *Polyodon*—many toothed; *spathula*—spatula.
Other common names: spoonbill cat, duckbill cat, spadefish.

865 mm, Wisconsin R. (Sauk Co.), 25 May 1977. Lateral view above, dorsal view below.

DESCRIPTION
Opercular flap very long, pointed posteriorly and nearly reaching to pelvic fins, head plus opercular flap more than one-half total length. Adult length 102 cm. Scaleless except for a few rhomboid scales on tail. Long paddlelike snout, approximately one-third length of fish. Small teeth, fanglike, irregularly positioned and deciduous in single rows along upper and lower jaws and on the floor of the mouth on the basal portions of the gill arches. In a 63-cm (25-in) fish these teeth are less than 1 mm long. Gill rakers filamentous: in an 80-cm (30.5-in) fish the longest rakers on the first arch 32 mm long, 0.3 mm diam, and 423 total in a series (180 on the upper limb, and 243 on the lower); rakers arranged in 2 series per arch and separated by a thin cartilaginous plate which extends out from the gill arch almost to the tips of the longest rakers. Chromosomes 2n = 120 (Dingerkus and Howell 1976).

Gray to blue-black dorsally and laterally, whitish ventrally.

Sexual dimorphism. The urogenital papilla somewhat raised in males, more flattened and softer in females (Meyer and Stevenson 1962).

DISTRIBUTION, STATUS, AND HABITAT
The paddlefish is at present found in the Mississippi River, the St. Croix River upstream to St. Croix Falls Dam, the Chippewa River upstream to Eau Claire, the Red Cedar River upstream to Lake Menomin Dam, and in the Wisconsin River upstream to the Prairie du Sac Dam. A remnant population may exist in the Wisconsin River between Prairie du Sac and the Wisconsin Dells Dam and in the lower portion of the Baraboo River. A 132-cm (4-ft, 4-in) paddlefish with a 330-mm (13-in) bill was caught against the rack of the Island Woolen Mills Dam in West Baraboo on 6 June 1950 (*Baraboo News-Republic*, 7 June 1950).

This species has been recorded a very few times from the Great Lakes basin, and it is thought by some to have reached these waters via canals, but it is more likely that the species was encountered on the way to natural extirpation (Hubbs and Lagler 1964). All the Great Lakes reports date from before the turn of the century. Greene (1935) told of a paddlefish report from Lake Michigan, northeast of Port Washington, which seemed possible but highly improbable to him. If true, he suggested, the fish might have entered the lake through the Chicago canal.

A report of the general range of this species has been prepared by Carlson and Bonislawsky (unpublished manuscript); they found that the present distribution is somewhat reduced, with the northern subpopulations now extirpated. The paddlefish is rare, endangered, and depleted in West Virginia; endangered in Pennsylvania; and rare in Minnesota (Miller 1972). In Wisconsin it was given threatened status (Wis. Dep. Nat. Resour. Endangered Species Com. 1975), but more recently the paddlefish was placed on watch status (Les 1979).

Some researchers believe that the status of the paddlefish in the upper Mississippi River (Pool 9 area) has not changed in recent years and that presently it is holding its own. But although it was once abundant in Lake Pepin (when as many as 680 kg [1,500 lb] were taken in a single seine haul), today its numbers are greatly reduced. Spawning areas have been destroyed by the construction of dams and flood-prevention systems. Pollution in the Mississippi River has also undoubtedly had an adverse effect.

The paddlefish inhabits large rivers and their lake widespreads in waters of considerable depth (Coker 1930). From summer until early spring it occurs in lakes or impoundments where it moves in large schools over muddy bottoms (Wagner 1908). Numbers of paddlefish have been reported throughout the year from below the dam at Prairie du Sac on the Wisconsin River. The paddlefish is often associated with sturgeons, catfishes, carpsuckers, buffaloes, and the common carp.

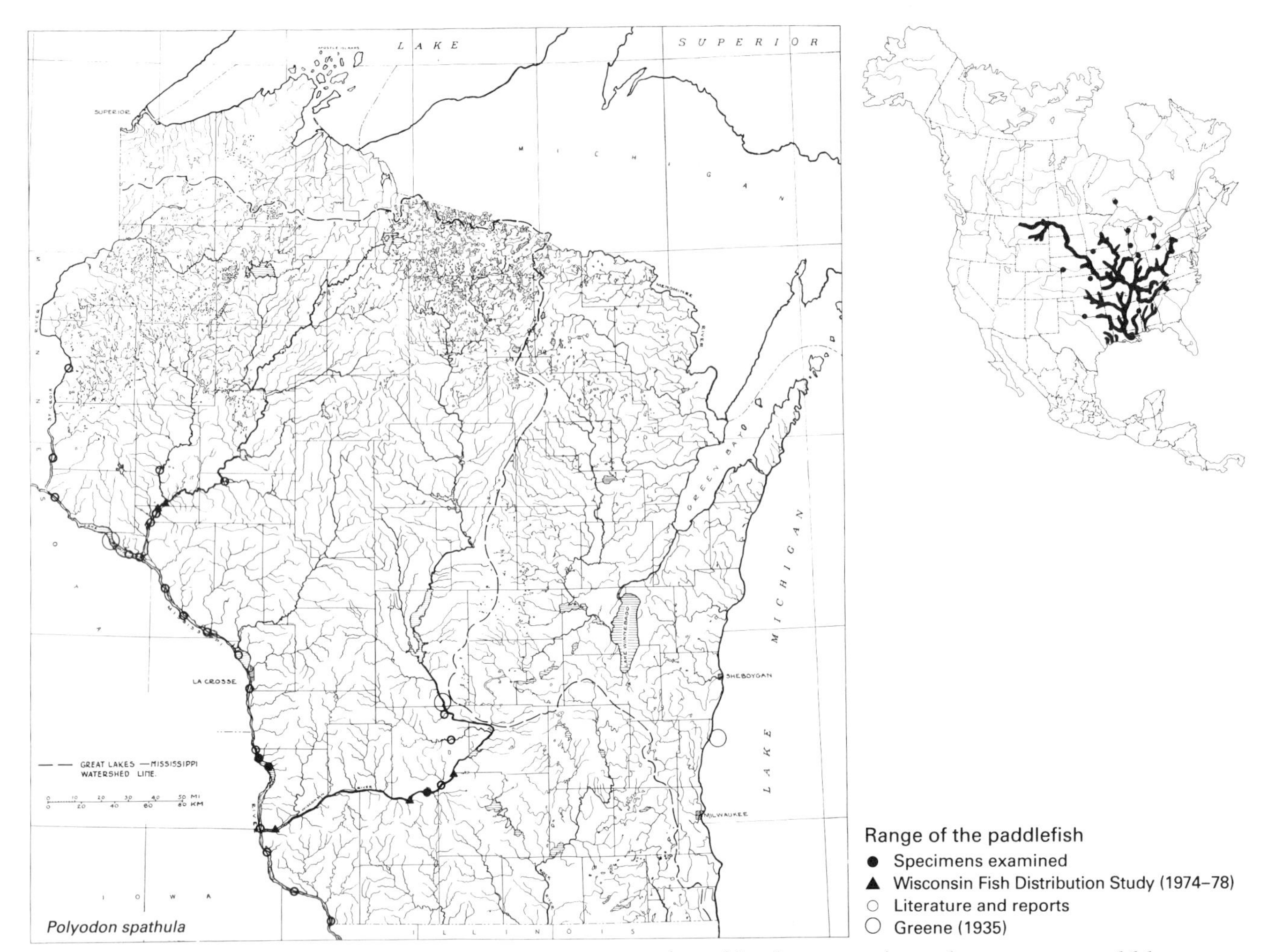

Range of the paddlefish
● Specimens examined
▲ Wisconsin Fish Distribution Study (1974–78)
○ Literature and reports
◯ Greene (1935)

BIOLOGY

Spawning occurs in early spring. No actual Wisconsin spawning has been recorded, but nearly ripe females have been taken from Lake Pepin (Pepin County) in late May.

Spawning details are described from the Osage River, Missouri, by Purkett (1961). Two conditions are necessary to initiate spawning: water must be warm enough, nearly 10°C (50°F), and water levels must rise. During spawning the paddlefish move in large schools near the surface. Spawning activity occurred over a large gravel bar in late afternoon and evening on 20 April, 7 days after a 2.7-m (9-ft) rise in water level at 16.1°C (61°F) water temperature. Several fish rose to the surface a number of times, with their caudal fins strongly agitating. This spawning rush probably signified the moment of egg release. Four days later, following a rapid fall in water level of about 2.1 m (7 ft), Purkett verified that spawning had occurred. Eggs and newly hatched larvae were found in the area where the current would have carried them from the spawning fish.

Upon fertilization, the eggs become adhesive and cling to the first objects they touch. The eggs hatch in 7 days or less at 18.3–21.1°C (65–70°F). Purkett (1961) discussed embryological and larval development. The larvae engage in a vertical (up-and-down) swimming motion while the current sweeps them into deep and quieter water (Purkett 1961, Needham 1965). Both eggs and larvae were found on the exposed drying gravel bars where spawning had taken place.

Spawning males in Missouri had an average length of 140 cm (55 in) and an average weight of 12.9 kg (28.5 lb). Females averaged 152 cm (60 in) in length and 18.8 kg (41.4 lb) in weight.

The ovaries weighed 2.7–3.6 kg (6–8 lb) in most ripe females from the Osage River (Purkett 1961), but Needham (1965) took 9.3 kg (20.5 lb) of eggs from a 33.1-kg (73-lb) female. A 18.1-kg (40-lb) fish from the

Osage River produced 371,480 eggs; and a 30.8-kg (68-lb) fish, 608,650 eggs. Ripe eggs are greenish black, nearly spherical, and 2 mm diam (Larimore 1950).

Early life history of the paddlefish is known largely from artificially propagated fish. Purkett (1963) stripped and fertilized eggs on 29 April. Hatching began on 10 May, 12 days after fertilization, and large numbers hatched through 14 May, with hatching dropping off to completion by 22 May. A number of the young were placed in a fertilized 0.2-ha (0.5 acre) pond. By 28 June these fish reached estimated lengths of 125–203 mm (5–8 in); by 8 August, 213–406 mm (8.4–16 in), weighing 37–256 g (1.3–9.0 oz). On 3 April, the two fish which survived a winterkill in the pond were 526 mm (20.7 in) and 551 mm (21.7 in) long, weighing 398 and 483 g (14 and 17 oz) respectively. At the age of 17 months they were 902 mm (35.5 in) and 864 mm (34 in) in length, and weighed 2.7 kg (6 lb) and 2.5 kg (5.5 lb).

Males attain sexual maturity when about 102 cm (40 in) long at about 7 years of age (Adams 1942). Mature females reach sexual maturity at 107 cm (42 in) at age 9 or 10. Mature adults probably do not spawn every year; however, the frequency of spawning is not known (Meyer and Stevenson 1962).

The otolith method of age determination is accurate only for fish under 10 years of age (Meyer 1960); over 10 years the annuli become crowded and difficult to read. The dentary bone gives best results (Meyer 1960, Adams 1942). In Illinois, the total length attained through 6 successive years of life was 297 mm (11.7 in), 714 mm (28.1), 902 mm (35.5), 991 mm (39.0), 111 cm (43.7), 114 cm (44.9) (Adams 1942). In the Fort Gibson Reservoir, Oklahoma, the estimated growth of a known-age population was 732 mm (28.8 in) at the end of the first year of life and 106 cm (41.7 in) at the end of the second year (Houser 1965). In Missouri, 26 fish averaging 148 cm (58.2 in) and 16.6 kg (36.6 lb) were 17 years old. Occasionally an individual will exceed 45.4 kg (100 lb); a 73.9-kg (163-lb) fish was taken from Lake Manitau, Indiana (Jordan and Evermann 1923). Ordinarily a large paddlefish weighs from 13.6 to 22.7 kg (30–50 lb). In 1974 a 165-cm (65-in) fish (UWSP 4714), weighing 26.3 kg (58 lb), was found dead in the Wisconsin River near Arena (Iowa County). Parts of the fish were missing, and the estimated live weight was 29.5 kg (65 lb).

The paddlefish—as one biologist put it—is a living plankton net. Its large mouth, extremely fine straining apparatus, and enlarged gill chamber and gill slits permit the rapid passage of enormous quantities of water. Thousands of small food organisms are filtered out by this system. The mouth is held wide open, and the snout weaves back and forth, giving the impression of a spiral-like movement. Since the paddlefish has weak jaws and only small teeth, it cannot catch other fish or crush mollusks.

1.65-m, 26.3-kg paddlefish, Wisconsin R., Arena (Iowa Co.) (specimen donated by H. Mathiak)

A study of 1,500 stomachs from Lake Pepin paddlefish disclosed the contents to be all plankton material, consisting of small crustaceans, algae, and ephemerid larvae (Wagner 1908). The latter were probably captured on their way to the surface of the water. In Illinois (Forbes and Richardson 1920) the paddlefish consumed mostly entomostracans, lesser quantities of larval mayflies, dragonflies, chironomids, and small amounts of adult aquatic insects, amphipod crustaceans, and leeches. Considerable quantities of algae and fragments of various aquatic plants were also found.

At sampling stations in the Mississippi River near Keokuk, Iowa, mayflies of the genus *Hexagenia* formed an important source of food for paddlefish during the winter, spring, and early summer months (Hoopes 1960). Naiads of *Hexagenia* constituted 46% of the total food content of the 64 paddlefish examined. Cladocerans, copepods, and algae were also significant food items, primarily in the late summer and fall months.

Although this species is primarily a plankton feeder, the food organisms found within the stomachs of the fish indicate that they occasionally feed at the bottom as well (Coker 1930). Contrary to popular opinion, the paddlefish does not use its bill to stir up or "dig up" the bottom. The bill is evidently a sensory organ which enables the fish to discern levels of plankton concentration. It also functions as a stabilizer, enabling the fish to swim at a horizontal level with least effort. Since the mouth is ventral in position, there would be a tendency for that large open cavity to draw the anterior end of the fish downward, which may be counteracted by the bill.

The paddlefish has the curious habit of leaping out of the water and landing, usually on its side, with great force. This phenomenon was reported in Lake Pepin (Wagner 1908) and also in numerous current reports for the Wisconsin River below the Prairie du Sac Dam. Such action may serve the purpose of dislodging the parasitic lampreys attached to the body.

Although the paddlefish normally inhabits deep water, during the summer it is found near the surface. Commercial fishermen report that it is frequently gilled in seines near the cork (floating) line. Paddlefish show a peculiar trait when surrounded by seines: upon striking the net, they become quiet and float to the surface of the water (Larimore 1950). Fishermen, taking advantage of this strange behavior, periodically collect the subdued fish in small rowboats.

IMPORTANCE AND MANAGEMENT

The paddlefish is heavily parasitized and used as a food source by lampreys of the genus *Ichthyomyzon*. Paddlefish with several lampreys attached to the gills have been reported from the Wisconsin River below the Prairie du Sac Dam (J. Diehl, pers. comm.). During May 1977 in the Chippewa River between Eau Claire and Durand almost all paddlefish had lamprey scars on sides and belly, and one had 12–15 silver lampreys and chestnut lampreys attached (D. Becker, pers. comm.).

The paddlefish seldom takes a baited hook and plays no role in sport fishery except in those states where a limited snagging season is permitted.

In the early 1900s, commercial fishermen in Wisconsin and Illinois used special rigging capable of hauling in 454–680 kg (1,000–1,500 lb) of paddlefish at a netting (Wagner 1908, Larimore 1950). Larimore reported seines 3.2 km (2 mi) long and 9 m (30 ft) deep, which were reeled in on a barge and herded the paddlefish in from open waters. Today, catches of paddlefish are mostly incidental while other species are being sought. The fish thus taken are shorter, on the average, than mature fish of this species, indicating that the majority of them have never spawned. Such information has led to recommendations for raising the size limits on paddlefish, but that protective measure may be of limited value, because the fish often die after being netted. Increasing length limits will not save sublegal fish that become trapped in commercial fishing gear.

The meat has high commercial value, for it is almost boneless and closely resembles that of the lake sturgeon in flavor and texture. It is a rare treat when smoked and in 1975 brought $2.20 per kilo at the Lansing, Iowa, fish market. The demand is greater than the supply. In addition, the eggs make an excellent caviar. Even in 1915 they were bringing $4.40 per kilo, while the flesh was worth only $0.22 per kilo (Larimore 1950). Occasionally the roe are mixed with that of the sturgeon and suckers.

The artificial propagation of this species has had limited success. Development and growth in an experimental 0.2-ha (.5-acre) pond was mentioned above (Purkett 1963). Fertilizer was added to maintain a plankton bloom, and 454 g (1 lb) of trout starter was scattered on the surface each day. It was not known whether this was consumed directly when the fish were small, but 229-mm (9-in) and larger fish were observed feeding on it regularly.

The growth rates of paddlefish receiving supplemental feeding in fertilized ponds are rapid (Swingle 1965). Seventeen paddlefish collected from the Tallapoosa River, Alabama, were stocked in two ponds which had varying fish populations and which were fertilized and supplied with fish food. When the ponds were drained, 114 and 144 days later, the 17 fish measured had increased in weight from 103 to 363%. Seven paddlefish from the pond drained after 114 days increased from a total weight of 15.4 kg (34 lb) to 37.1 kg (81.7 lb). In the other pond, 10 paddlefish which had totaled 21.5 kg (47.3 lb) weighed 56.2 kg (123.8 lb).

Commercial propagation of paddlefish is feasible provided a dependable supply of eggs is available. Relying on fishermen to secure sexually mature fish is impractical, and even seining will not produce fish that are ready to spawn. The use of chorionic gonadotropin to bring gonads to maturity was unsuccessful (Meyer and Stevenson 1962), but Needham (1965) succeeded in getting ovaries and testes to ripen under the injections of pituitaries from donor paddlefish. Needham found only limited response in the males to injection with donor carp pituitaries.

Recent attempts to secure live specimens for a zoo display through electrofishing have failed. More than 40 paddlefish were collected from the Wisconsin River below Prairie du Sac by personnel from the Wisconsin Department of Natural Resources. The fish were readily immobilized by the electrical current but none of them survived the jolt. Such sensitivity to electrical shock is unusual; most fish species recover within minutes.

Gar Family—Lepisosteidae

Two species of gars occur in Wisconsin. Five species, all in the genus *Lepisosteus*, are known in the United States and Canada (Robins et al. 1980). This family is almost exclusively North American, ranging southward to Costa Rica, Cuba, and Central America. Fossils are known from the Middle Eocene of North America.

The gars are long, cylindrical fish with a characteristic long, slender snout and jaws well armed with needlelike teeth. The gar's body is completely covered with rhomboidal scales which join to one another and provide an armorlike protection. It has a double skull in which inner parts of cartilage are overlaid by dermal bone. Kidney tubules open directly into the coelomic cavity in adults, a condition persisting only in the adult of primitive species.

A unique characteristic of these primitive fishes is the ability to breathe atmospheric air. The swim bladder is connected to the esophagus and operates as a primitive lung. The inner lining of the swim bladder is cellular and somewhat roughened, providing for additional gas-absorption area. Even in well-oxygenated aquariums they will surface briefly every few minutes. This is the act of "breaking," so familiar to many fishermen.

In breaking, the gar turns partly over on one side, emits a bubble of air, swallows, and then sinks below the surface. Supposedly this habit is discontinued in cold weather, and from October to April gars do not come to the surface to breathe (Forbes and Richardson 1920).

Eddy and Underhill (1974:132) noted:

> Their ability to breathe air enables them to live in polluted water unfit for any other fishes except the bowfins. We have seen cases of total oxygen depletion

where all the other species were killed, but the gars and the bowfins still swam about unconcernedly. We have known gars to drown when entangled in a net and unable to reach the surface for fresh air. Their air-breathing ability may be one of the characteristics which enabled these primitive fishes to survive.

All gars serve as hosts to the parasitic young (glochidia) of the most valuable of all freshwater mussels. The yellow sandshell (*Lampsilis anodontoides*) yields a shell with form, texture, and luster that compares most nearly, of all freshwater shells, to the marine "mother-of-pearl" (Coker 1930). At one time it was used not only for the manufacture of buttons of superior grade but also for the preparation of pearl handles for knives and for other novelties. Only gars function as hosts for this clam, and no other fish will answer. Without gars the mussel would disappear unless it could be maintained by artificial means. The shortnose gar is a known host to the glochidia of *Amblema plicata* and *Lampsilis teres* (Hart and Fuller 1974).

Gar skins have been used to a small extent for covering picture frames, purses, and fancy boxes, the plates being very hard and taking a fine polish (Forbes and Richardson 1920).

To anglers fishing with live bait, gars are sometimes a nuisance, since they steal the bait from hooks but are not themselves easily caught. They may, however, be taken by using a piano wire or copper wire snare on which a minnow is threaded; the snare is drawn tightly about the snout of the gar when it strikes the bait. Perhaps the most ingenious method for catching them is with a hookless lure which can be made at home. The only materials needed are a 75–100-mm (3–4-in) piece of nylon rope, 10 mm diam, and a short length of flexible wire. Stove pipe wire will do. The wire is attached to one end of the rope and fashioned into an eye to which a swivel leader can be attached. The other end of the rope is unraveled into its individual fibers until a fluffy "tail" results. The gar, which strikes a moving bait, will clamp down on the lure and its teeth will become snagged in the fibers (Sroka 1975).

Gars are of little commercial value. Some time ago, a crew operating in the Mississippi River near La Crosse made a haul of 1,134 kg (2,500 lb), which was sold to a rendering plant at $0.02 per kg (Wis. Conserv. *Bull.* 1948 13[2]:5). Both the longnose and the shortnose gar are taken from Wisconsin waters of the Mississippi River with setlines, gill nets, seines, buffalo nets, bait nets, and trammel nets. No distinction is made between the species in the commercial catch. For the 10-year-period 1956–1965, the average catch reported per year was 4,328 kg (9,542 lb); for the 1966–1975 period, 3,499 kg (7,713 lb). The record high for any year since 1953 was 13,218 kg (29,141 lb) in 1959, and the total value of the 1975 catch of 3,697 kg (8,151 lb) was $163.02 (Fernholz and Crawley 1976).

Shortnose Gar

Lepisosteus platostomus Rafinesque. *Lepisosteus*—scales of bone; *platostomus*—broad mouth.

Other common names: broadnosed gar, stubnose gar, shortbill gar, duckbill gar, billy gar.

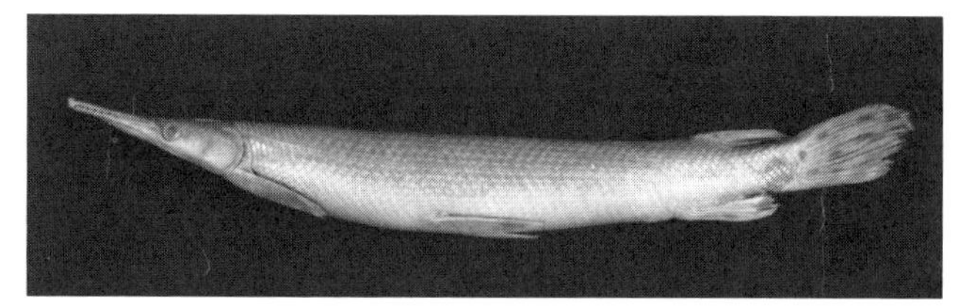

Adult 535 mm, L. Winnebago (Fond du Lac Co.), 28 Aug. 1961

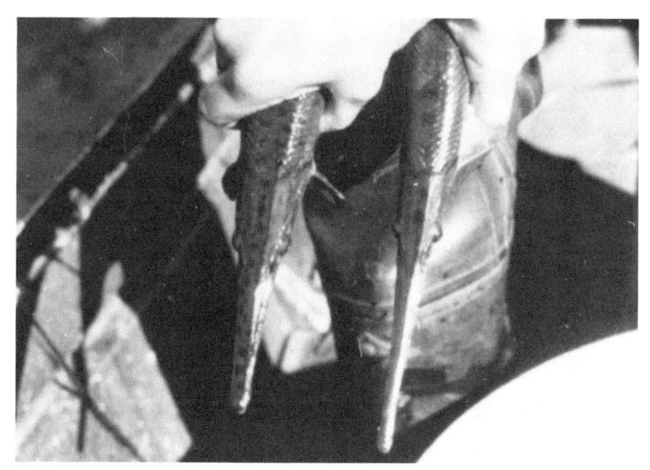

Dorsal view of heads of adult shortnose and longnose gars (photo by V. Hacker)

DESCRIPTION

Body long, cylindrical, depth into TL 10 (9–12). Adult length 460–480 mm. Head length into TL 4.1 (3.8–4.4). Snout length into head length 1.7 (1.6–1.8); snout length into TL 7.1 (6.0–7.9); least snout width into snout length 6.3 (5.2–9.3); snout width at level of nostrils into snout length 6.8 (5.3–10.5). Teeth numerous, villiform, sharp. Gill rakers rudimentary, irregularly arranged, 16–25. Scales ganoid (rhomboid); lateral line scales 61 (55–63). Tail abbreviate-heterocercal (vertebrae moving into dorsal portion of fin).

Adult brown, olive to slate dorsally; yellow or whitish below. Spots, when present, usually confined to the posterior third of the body. In fresh specimens from nonturbid water, large dark spots occasionally appear on bill and top of head; after death and with preservation, spots fade. Young less than 25 cm long similar to longnose gar of corresponding length (Trautman 1957).

DISTRIBUTION, STATUS, AND HABITAT

The shortnose gar occurs in the Mississippi River and its major tributaries (the St. Croix, Chippewa, Black and Wisconsin rivers) upstream generally to the first dam, and in the Rock River drainage (Greene 1935, Cahn 1927, McNaught 1963). I have not been able to verify Greene's report of this species from Pewaukee Lake (Waukesha County) in the Illinois-Fox drainage and have deleted it from the map.

The shortnose gar was recently reported for the first time in the Great Lakes drainage basin (Priegel 1963a, Becker 1964b); and it appears to be well established in the lower Wolf River, the lakes of the upper Fox River, the lower Fox River, and lower Green Bay. The presumed crossover point is the Fox-Wisconsin canal at Portage (Columbia County).

This species is uncommon to common in the lower Wisconsin and Mississippi rivers, the lower portions of their tributaries, in the lower Wolf River system, and in Green Bay. In some large rivers it may be more abundant than the longnose gar (Nord 1967). In the Rock River system it is rare, possibly extirpated. The shortnose gar prefers open, slow-moving, silty rivers. In large lakes it occurs over wave-washed shoals. Cross (1967) noted that it usually avoids the quiet backwaters, oxbows, and impoundments that often are inhabited by longnose gar.

BIOLOGY

The shortnose gar spawns in shallow, grassy sloughs from May to June. Spawning information was compiled by Carlander (1969). Shortnose gar spawned from May to June in 0.3–0.9 m (1–3 ft) of water in Illinois. In South Dakota during 1956, spawning occurred from 20 May to 15 June at water temperatures of 19–23.5°C (66–74°F); during 1957 and 1958 it occurred in late June and early July. The bright green eggs, about 2.5 mm diam, are deposited in small masses held together by a clear gelatinous substance and attached to grass, smartweed, etc. A 4.1-kg (9-lb) female produced 36,460 eggs (Potter 1926).

In Illinois the eggs hatched in 8 or 9 days (Richardson 1913). According to Echelle and Riggs (1972), spawning and hatching occur earlier in this species than in the longnose gar. The total length at hatching is 8 mm and in aquariums the average growth rate per day is 1.7 mm. The yolk-sac is absorbed 7 days after hatching (Richardson 1913). Young gar start feeding on entomostracans and mosquito larvae at 16 days after hatching. They are solitary in habit, floating near the surface, sometimes with their backs out of the water (Carlander 1969). Carlander has compiled the following growth data for young-of-year: 15–

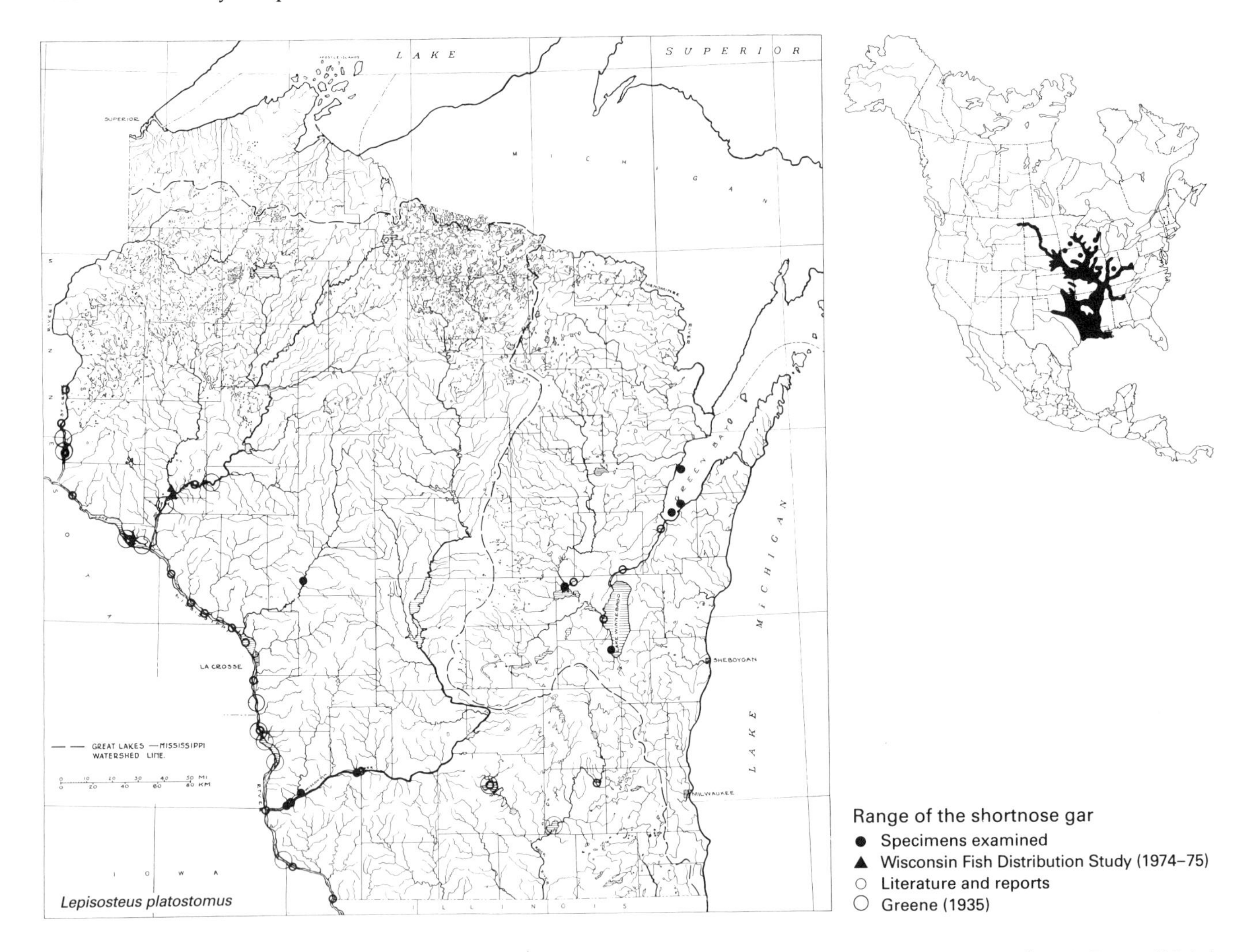

64 mm (0.6–2.5 in) in May (Illinois), 44 mm (1.7 in) in June (Illinois), 69 mm (2.7 in) in July (South Dakota), 64–127 mm (2.5–5 in) in August (Iowa), 102–152 mm (4–6 in) in October (Iowa), 178–254 mm (7–10 in) in October (Ohio).

In Lake Okoboji, Iowa, shortnose gar 483–584 mm (19–23 in) long fed mostly in the morning on crayfish, perch (165 mm), sunfish (114 mm), and bluegills (127 mm) (Potter 1923). On clear, warm days they lined up along the shore in 100–250 mm (4–10 in) of water, with their tails toward shore, waiting until prey were in easy reach. In Illinois (Richardson 1913) adult gars were observed coming to the surface to seize emerging gnats and mayflies. In South Dakota, Shields (1957) noted that shortnose gar fed heavily on carp until the latter were over 125 mm (5 in) long.

Growth of the shortnose gar is rapid. In South Dakota's Lewis and Clark Lake (Walburg 1964) mean total length at age I was 417 mm (16.4 in); II, 486 mm (19.1 in); III, 536 mm (21.1 in); IV, 587 mm (23.1 in); V, 605 mm (23.8 in); VI, 671 mm (26.4 in); VII, 734 mm (28.9 in). A few males matured at 457 mm (18 in) and females at 483 mm (19 in) (Carlander 1969). The largest shortnose gar reported by Carlander was 826 mm (32.5 in) TL and weighed 1.5 kg (3.4 lb). Trautman (1957) stated that adults are usually 406–762 mm (16–30 in) long and weigh 0.5–2.3 kg (1–5 lb). Potter (1926) reported a female from Iowa weighing 4.1 kg (9 lb). The shortnose gar is heavier for its length than the longnose gar but it attains far less length and weight and has a shorter life span.

Adult shortnose gars move in large schools both before and after the spawning season (Coker 1930). On 28 August I encountered a school of these gars alongside a concrete pier jutting into Lake Winnebago (Fond du Lac County) in open water devoid of aquatic vegetation. Five adults were quickly caught in a 6-m (20-ft) seine.

This species lies on the surface of the water in full sun, a habit which brings it into contact with water temperatures approximating high summer air temperatures. In Indiana, Gammon (1973) determined optimum temperatures for gars at 33–35°C (86–95°F), although Proffitt and Benda (1971) have taken them in the White River and Ilpaco Discharge Canal at 36.1°C (97°F). Adult shortnose gar are more abundant in shallow waters at night than during the daylight hours (Echelle and Riggs 1972).

IMPORTANCE AND MANAGEMENT

The eggs of this species are dangerous to vertebrate animals. Of two mice force-fed 0.2 ml of homogenized eggs, one died in less than 18 hr; the other became very sick but eventually recovered (Netsch and Witt 1962).

The shortnose gar is an excellent food fish when baked or smoked.

Durham (1955b) introduced the shortnose gar into small experimental ponds to test its effect on the populations of green sunfish, bluegill, largemouth bass, and black crappie. The results were inconclusive, but the shortnose gar tended to cause a reduction in the number of green sunfish and an increase in the number of bluegills. The maximum sizes of all the species of centrarchids increased.

The role of this species in maintaining a balanced fish population in some waters may be significant and warrants further study.

Longnose Gar

Lepisosteus osseus (Linnaeus). *Lepisosteus*—scales of bone; *osseus*—bony.

Other common names: northern longnose gar, gar, garpike, common garpike, billfish, billy gar, northern mailed fish.

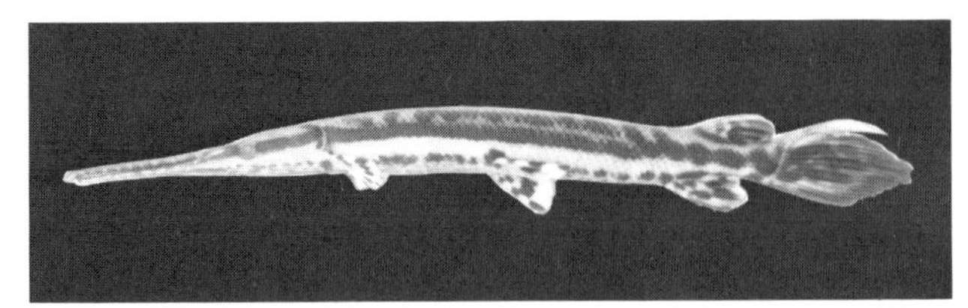

Immature 290 mm, Swan L. (Columbia Co.), 27 Sept. 1969

Adult 748 mm, Mississippi R., Pool 5a (Buffalo Co.), 28 July 1977. (See also photograph of heads of gars, p. 45)

DESCRIPTION

Body long, cylindrical, depth into TL 15 (12–18). Adult length 500 mm. Head length into TL 3.3 (3.0–3.6). Snout length into head length 1.5 (1.4–1.6); snout length into TL 4.7 (4.3–5.4); least snout width into snout length 16.1 (15.2–16.1), in young-of-year this measurement 11.6 (9.3–14.4); snout width at level of nostrils into snout length 15.6 (13.4–16.5), in young-of-year this measurement 10.6 (6.4–13.9). Teeth numerous, villiform, sharp. Gill rakers rudimentary, irregularly arranged 24–28. Scales ganoid (rhomboid); lateral line scales 62 (60–66). Tail abbreviate-heterocercal (vertebrae moving into dorsal portion of fin).

Adult olive to dark green above; whitish below with large round spots on dorsal, anal, and caudal fins. Young distinctly marked with a broad brown or blackish midlateral stripe from snout to base of caudal fin, with a striking white stripe immediately below, and a chocolate brown stripe on each side of belly. Fish (1932:305) noted: "The young are easily recognized by the greatly prolonged toothed jaws and elongate body, brilliant in seal, reddish brown, and bronze. . . . The most remarkable feature of this small and brilliant gar was the prolongation of the notochord into a fleshy filament, apart from the caudal fin, which kept up a rapid vibratory motion."

DISTRIBUTION, STATUS, AND HABITAT

The longnose gar occurs in the Mississippi, Lake Michigan, and Lake Superior drainage basins. The reports from Hacker (1975) do not designate the species of gar, but most reports undoubtedly pertain to the longnose gar, although occurrence of the shortnose gar is possible where the species are sympatric.

The longnose gar is common in the Mississippi and lower Wisconsin rivers. In the Lake Michigan drainage it is common in the Wolf and Fox rivers and their connecting systems. The 89-cm (35-in) gar reported in 1942 from Lake Michigan off Port Washington by commercial fishermen (*Milwaukee Journal* 27 September 1942) has not been verified as to species, but it was probably a longnose gar.

In northwestern Wisconsin the longnose gar is common in Big Sissabagama, Lac Court Oreilles, Grindstone, and Big Sand lakes (Sawyer County). It is common in the St. Croix River below St. Croix Falls Dam and abundant in the Island Lake Chain (Rusk County) and the Long Lake Chain (Chippewa County). This species is uncommon in northeastern Wisconsin.

I have seen a single report from the Lake Superior drainage: a 676-cm (26.6-in) male taken by a sport fisherman below the electric barrier on the Brule River (Douglas County) (Moore and Braem 1965).

The longnose gar is endangered (possibly extirpated) in Delaware and rare in South Dakota (Miller 1972). It appears secure in Wisconsin.

The longnose gar inhabits large, weedy lakes and reservoirs. In rivers (generally over 12 m wide) it occurs most frequently in backwaters or in quiet currents. In the lower Wisconsin River it was found in small numbers in the drop-offs between sand riffles and the shallow pools below. The frequencies of substrates associated with this species were gravel 29%, sand 25%, mud 17%, clay 13%, silt 8%, rubble 4%, and boulders 4%. It is an open-water fish, spending much time in the topmost stratum of a pelagic environment.

BIOLOGY

In Wisconsin spawning occurs from May to late June, and possibly early July. In southern Wisconsin the fish often ascend rivers to spawn over the weed beds of shallower waters (Cahn 1927). In lakes the longnose gar spawns in shoal water, usually in grass and

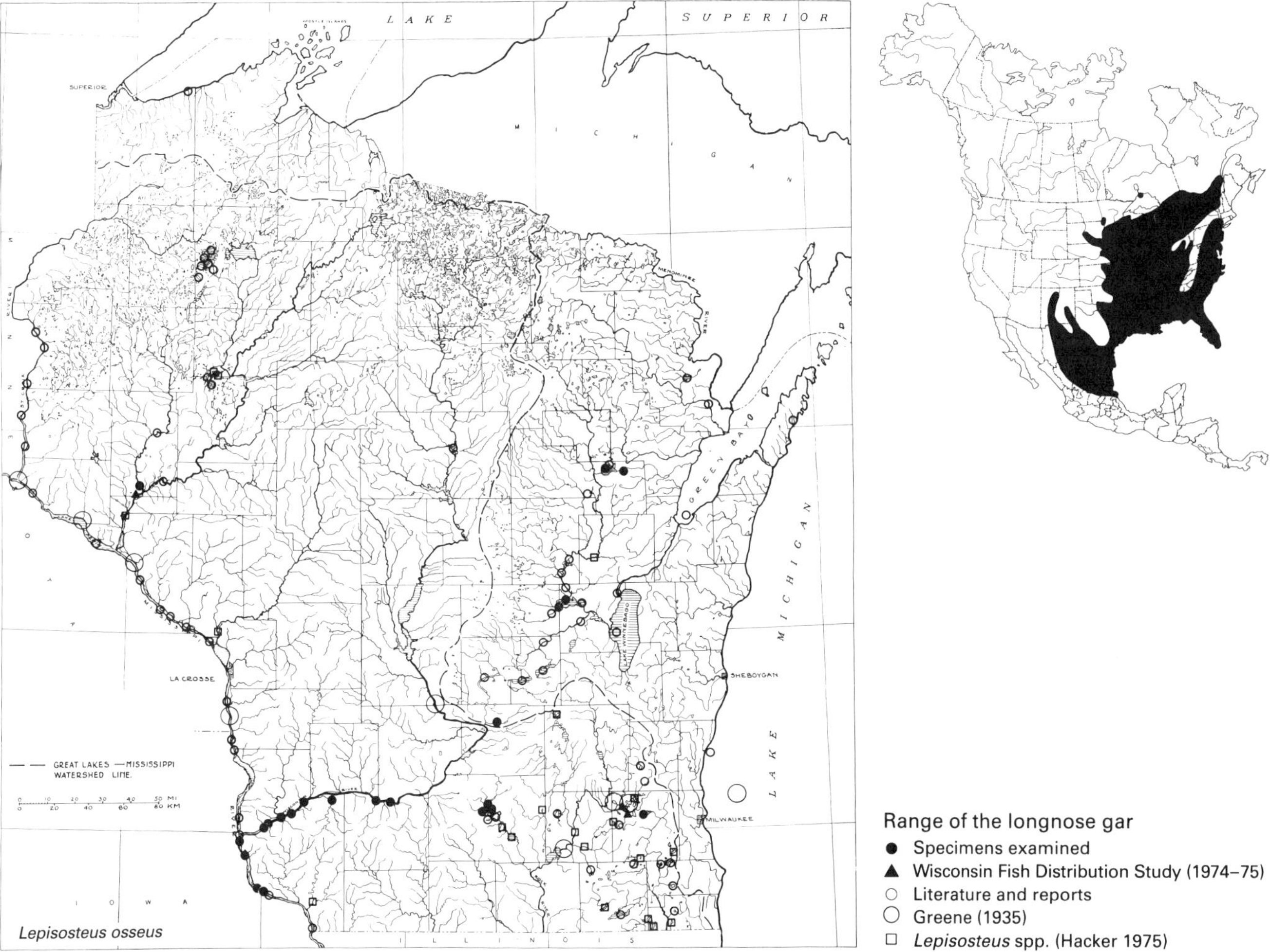

weeds, but it has been observed spawning about stone piles of railroad bridges (Forbes and Richardson 1920).

In Lake Mendota one spawning area was on a shallow gravel bar where the water was 0.3–0.9 m (1–3 ft) deep and bulrushes were present; the other was in 2 m (7 ft) of water over a substrate of boulders (Haase 1969). Spawning was associated with two ranges of temperature peaking at 19.5°C (67.1°F) and 21°C (69.8°F), and data suggest that spawning occurs with rising temperatures of the water—the immediate stimulus for the formation of the spawning groups. During each year there is usually more than one 3-day period of spawning, and these periods are concentrated within two ranges of temperature.

Detailed spawning behavior was reported by Haase (1969). As many as 15 males approach a female. If she is ready to spawn, she leads them in an elliptical path (apparently related to the shape of the spawning ground) for up to 15 minutes before spawning occurs. Over the spawning bed the males nudge the female with the ends of their snouts in the pectoral, lateral, and ventro-lateral areas. Frequent surfacing and gulping takes place during this phase. Then the spawning group positions itself at one place with heads down and snouts very close to or touching the bottom, and males continue to nudge the female. A rapid, violent quivering of the spawners follows as eggs and sperm are released. The quivering moves the spawning group forward and away from the spawning area. The eggs are green; those collected from Lake Mendota gars were 2.6–3.6 mm diam (Haase 1969).

H. Neuenschwander (pers. comm.) observed spawning at Picnic Point on Lake Mendota on 3 June 1948. Twenty-three gars swam an elliptical course about 3 × 8 m (10 × 26 ft) in 1–1.5 m (3–5 ft) of water over algal-covered boulders. Two to six males attended one female. The water temperature was 23.3°C (74°F).

Breder and Rosen (1966) reported that eggs may number more than 36,000 in a female of 101.6 cm (40 in) SL. Embryological development based largely on materials from Lac La Belle (Waukesha County) is described and depicted by Eycleshimer (1903). Hatching takes 3–9 days, depending on the temperature: 6 days at 20°C (68°F).

The emerging sac-fry, 9–10 mm long, while capable of swimming, are relatively inactive and, using an adhesive structure, hang vertically for long periods attached by their snouts to submerged objects such as vegetation and debris (Echelle and Riggs 1972). In aquariums they may attach to the surface film of the water. Shortly after absorption of the yolk-sac (about 9 days after hatching) and now 18–20 mm in length, the fry cease to hang vertically and are capable of resting motionless in a horizontal position at any depth in the water. At about this stage the gar takes its first aerial breath, becomes more active, and begins to feed. After absorption of the yolk-sac, the fry disperse. They do not exhibit a pronounced tendency to school.

Growth rate of the longnose gar during its first year of life is rapid. In aquariums Echelle and Riggs (1972) noted an average growth of 3.2 mm per day. In Portage Lake, Michigan, the estimated growth was 2.33 mm per day (Hubbs 1921); in Lake Mendota, Wisconsin, 1.5 mm per day (Haase 1969).

In Missouri 20 young-of-year raised experimentally for 52 days grew at the rate of 2.95 mm and 0.72 g per day (Netsch and Witt 1962). Their gross metabolic efficiency during this time was 43.1% and their food conversion factor was 2.34. Young-of-year longnose gars ate an average of 9.1% of their body weight per day, and digestion was completed at the end of 24 hours. Gar activity, or more appropriately inactivity, is probably the major factor contributing to the low food conversion factor. Throughout the experiments the gars were extremely inactive and made few unnecessary movements; even their method of feeding was one of apparent leisure. These factors contribute to their rapid growth, up to 6 times faster than that of other common large freshwater fishes.

Niemuth et al. (1959b) reported young-of-year 248–353 mm (9.8–13.9 in) long in early September in several Wisconsin lakes. Haase (1969) noted that young-of-year reach a maximum TL of 460 mm (18.1 in).

Age and growth of the longnose gar in central Missouri were determined from branchiostegal rays (Netsch and Witt 1962). Age-I males were 49.5 cm (19.5 in) long; females, 55.9 cm (22 in) long. Females continue to grow approximately 25 mm (1 in) a year for 13 or 14 years and outlive the males. Males mature between 3 and 4 years of age and females at about 6 years of age. At the end of the first year of life the females average 64 mm (2.5 in) longer than the males; this disparity in size increases with age to a point where the females are 178 mm (7 in) longer than the males at the end of the 11th year of life.

Compared to Missouri longnose gar, Wisconsin males (Lake Mendota) are 60–90 mm (2.4–3.5 in) smaller and females are 95–150 mm (3.7–5.9 in) smaller, with the maximum differences occurring at age I (Haase 1969). Lake Poygan males (age XVII) and females (age XVIII) are 309 and 380 mm (12.2 and 15 in) smaller than Missouri gars.

Haase (1969) noted that one-half of the maximum growth in length was attained during the first 2 or 3 years of life. The sexes are very similar in size at first,

Growth of the Longnose Gar in Wisconsin During First Year of Life (Preserved Museum Specimens)

Date	TL (mm)	WT (g)	Scalation	Location
19 June 1962	49	0.2	No scales	Wisconsin R. (Richland Co.)
7 July 1962	114	1.8	Side of caudal peduncle scaled	Blue R. (Grant Co.)
10 July 1962	140+	4.6	Lateral line, caudal peduncle, and sides posterior to pelvic fins scaled	Glass L., Mississippi R. (Grant Co.)
13 July 1962	62	0.4	No scales	Wisconsin R. (Grant Co.)
13 July 1962	71	0.5	No scales	Wisconsin R. (Grant Co.)
13 July 1962	133	3.6	Caudal peduncle & posterior half of lateral line scaled	Wisconsin R. (Grant Co.)
17 July 1962	119	2.5	Caudal peduncle & posterior half of lateral line scaled	Wisconsin R., Boscobel (Grant Co.)
3–5 Aug. 1960	74	1.0	No scales	Pewaukee L. (Waukesha Co.)
3–5 Aug. 1960	161	5.9	Lateral line scales complete	Pewaukee L. (Waukesha Co.)
3–5 Aug. 1960	168	7.8	Lateral line scales complete	Pewaukee L. (Waukesha Co.)
3–5 Aug. 1960	170	7.0	Lateral line scales complete	Pewaukee L. (Waukesha Co.)
8 Aug. 1962	141	4.7	Caudal peduncle and lateral lines scaled	Wisconsin R. (Iowa Co.)
10 Aug. 1974	138	4.8	Entirely scaled except ventrally from anus to isthmus	L. Mendota (Dane Co.)
10 Aug. 1974	147	5.3	Entirely scaled except ventrally from anus to isthmus	L. Mendota (Dane Co.)
10 Aug. 1974	167	9.2	Entirely scaled except ventrally from anus to isthmus	L. Mendota (Dane Co.)
10 Aug. 1974	204	16.1	Entirely scaled except ventrally from anus to isthmus	L. Mendota (Dane Co.)
19 Sept. 1971	366	72.9	Fully scaled	White Clay L. (Shawano Co.)
27 Sept. 1969	291	48.3	Fully scaled	Swan L. (Columbia Co.)
3 Dec. 1973	382	119.0	Fully scaled	Shawano L. (Shawano Co.)

but in Lake Mendota the females surpass the males at age III and in other lakes somewhat later. The oldest fish Haase recorded was a 32-year-old female from Lake Mendota, 123 cm (48.3 in) long. Males were up to 27 years old and under 99 cm (39 in) TL.

By age III all males more than 50 cm (19.7 in) long had sperm present (Haase 1969). The first maturity of females was noted at age IV, and most females had eggs in some stage of development by age IX.

A 142-cm (56-in) longnose gar was seined from Pewaukee Lake (Waukesha County) (Wis. Conserv. *Bull.* 1937 2[11]:39). In 1949 a 122-cm, 5-kg (48-in, 11-lb) gar was seined from Lake Wingra (Dane County) (Noland 1951). A 135-cm, 11.8-kg (53-in, 26-lb) fish was reported from Lake Beulah (Walworth County) in 1956 (H. Neuenschwander, pers. comm.). A female from the Oklawaha River, Florida, 142 cm and 14.5 kg (56 in and 32 lb), had an egg count of 77,156. The angler record is a 183-cm, 22.7-kg (6-ft ¼-in, 50-lb) fish from the Trinity River, Texas, 30 July 1954 (Walden 1964).

Fishes constitute the greatest bulk of stomach contents in all size-groups of longnose gars except those in the initial feeding stages (17–21 mm long) (Echelle and Riggs 1972), which select minute crustaceans, such as cladocerans and copepods. Very small fish appear early in the diet of the gar, however.

Haase (1969) noted a high percentage of fish in the diets of Wisconsin longnose gars reaching the swimming stage. Next to the fry of fishes, *Scapholeberis mucronata* (Cladocera) is the most important food item, but its importance diminishes rapidly as more fish is eaten. The fish portion of the diet of the young-of-year gar is mainly carp. The noncarp group includes silverside, bluegill, gar, largemouth bass, darters, spottail shiner, killifish, black crappie, and others. Gars 21–96 mm long are able to take prey up to one-third of their own length. Forbes and Richardson (1920) reported 16 larval minnows taken from the stomach of a 51-mm gar.

Adult longnose gars in southern Wisconsin are reported to have eaten brook silverside, blackstripe topminnow, sand shiner, largemouth and smallmouth bass, cisco, and white bass (Cahn 1927). Availability may be a major factor affecting the kinds of foods gars eat. Haase (1969) noted, however, that fishes important for sport fishing, like the largemouth bass, the yellow bass, the northern pike, and the walleye, were found infrequently in the stomachs of adult gars. Even though young-of-year largemouth bass were plentiful in Lake Mendota during 1967, gars fed on them sparingly.

A longnose gar feeds more actively at night than during daylight and much of the feeding is surface-oriented. It is adept at stalking a fish victim by swimming, not toward it, but off to one side, moving along in the water like a stick drifting with the surface current. Suddenly it flips its long beak to the side and catches its prey across the body in its jaws. The action is similar to the strike of a rattlesnake, occurring so quickly that the eye is unable to follow. Then, by a series of thrusts, the victim is turned so that it can be swallowed head first.

In the lower Wisconsin River a large longnose gar struck a seine so hard that it almost jerked the sticks out of the operators' hands, and it left behind in the torn mesh most of its upper jaw, which had broken off with the violence of its charge. Had it struck one of the seiners instead of the net, its pointed snout could easily have penetrated into the flesh several centimeters.

Young gars are commonly taken in the shallows, but as they grow larger they tend to go to deeper water and perhaps become more nocturnal (Haase 1969). During daylight they spend much time resting motionlessly close to submerged or overhanging objects near shore (Echelle and Riggs 1972). At night they are commonly found swimming actively in shallow, open waters. Certain individuals were found in identical spots day after day—one frequented the space beneath the same overhanging limb from mid-July until September. Saksena (1963) found that increased activity increased the rate of air-breathing.

Haase (1969) captured a number of longnose gars over spawning beds and transported them to the opposite side of Lake Mendota. A short time later 70% of them were recaptured spawning again in the same places.

The longnose gar prefers high water temperatures. In the Wabash River, Indiana, the longnose gar was attracted to the warmest zone available (Gammon 1973), and in the White River and Ipalco Discharge Canal the maximum temperature at which it was captured was 33.9°C (93°F) (Proffitt and Benda 1971).

Adult gars have the habit of basking near the surface on warm days or nights, and they may be seen floating like sticks of varying sizes. In Florida Holloway (1954) noted that gars are gregarious enough so that they are usually found in groups of two to five. I have seen such loose aggregations a number of times on the lower Wisconsin River, and Haase (1969) observed them on Lake Mendota.

IMPORTANCE AND MANAGEMENT

Haase (1969) showed that the main prey of the adult longnose gars were yellow perch, carp, bluegills, and pumpkinseeds. In addition, young-of-year gars fed heavily on young-of-year carp. He concluded that the gar probably doesn't harm fishing for sport fish and may in fact improve it.

Consideration has been given to gars as a possible aid in controlling overpopulation of sunfish and yellow perch. Niemuth et al. (1959b) noted that gars would be less vulnerable to overfishing than the sport fishes and suggested introducing gars into lakes with stunted populations of panfishes.

The longnose gar is classified as a nongame fish. Although it is seldom taken on hook and line, in recent years it has had its devotees among fishermen. Devices for catching gars have been discussed earlier. The meat is described as white, boneless, well-flavored, and wholesome. It is delicious baked on the "half shell" (Sroka 1975). It has been compared to roast pig and may be smoked with excellent success. When fried, it reportedly tastes like a combination of fish and pork chops. In Arkansas, gar meat recently sold on the market at $3.80 per kilo, and the demand was greater than the supply (V. Hacker, pers. comm.).

Although the flesh may be usable, gar eggs are highly poisonous to man as well as to chickens, cats, dogs, and mice. Vertebrate animals will normally avoid eating them. When 0.2 ml of egg homogenate from the longnose gar was force-fed to two mice they became quite sick, although both recovered within 2 days (Netsch and Witt 1962). On the other hand, gar eggs have been found in the stomach of a bluegill and in the intestine of a river carpsucker, and neither appeared to have suffered ill effects.

Because of its appearance and its known fish-eating habits, man has destroyed gars wherever possible. In 1900, the first fish contract granted by the state was one given to residents of Eau Claire and Chippewa Falls to remove "gar fish and other deleterious fish . . . " (V. Hacker, pers. comm.). A state rough-fish removal crew operating on Pewaukee Lake (Waukesha County) took 4,500 kg (10,000 lb) of gars in a single haul (Wis. Conserv. *Bull.* 1937 2[11]:39). The catch was converted into fertilizer.

Nowhere has the case against the longnose gar been stated more eloquently than by Forbes and Richardson (1920:32):

> This voracious, active and well-protected fish is a notable winner in the long struggle for existence which its species has maintained, but it is a wholly worthless and destructive nuisance in its relations to mankind. It is the enemy of practically all the other fishes in our waters, and so far as it eats anything but fishes, it subtracts from the food supply of the more valuable kinds. It has, in fact, all the vices and none of the virtues of a predaceous fish. On the other hand, it is preyed upon by nothing that swims, and is so well adapted to the varied features and vicissitudes of its habitat that it is proof against any but the most extraordinary occurrences.

Other fishery biologists are not sure that this species has earned such condemnation. Holloway (1954), while dealing with the management of gars, stated that it remains to be seen whether the reduction of gars will result in an increase or a decrease in the harvest of desirable species. Lagler et al. (1942) noted that gar populations are greatest (and perhaps most useful) where the largest populations of buffer, forage, and nonsport predators occur. Similarly Branson (1966:19) argued:

> . . . gars are especially important in waters where man's activities have upset the balance of nature in favor of the so-called "rough" fishes, i.e., carp, buffalofishes, and the like. It is here that gar populations often reach their greatest numbers and importance. In all of these environments, the gar exerts a profound controlling influence on the tendency of both rough and game species to overpopulate.

Bowfin Family—Amiidae

One species of bowfin is known from Wisconsin and North America.

By the late Palaeozoic period (200 million years ago) the first holostean fish, a form similar to the living *Amia*, had appeared, and from fishes such as these the teleosts evolved (Moy-Thomas and Miles 1971). Ancestral bowfins were especially well represented in middle Mesozoic strata, over 100 million years ago. Today there is only one living family, Amiidae, which is restricted to North America, and within this only one species, *Amia calva*, remains. This primitive fish is a phylogenetic relict, the lone survivor of a large family now found only as fossils in the rocks of Europe and the United States.

Amia has a rather primitive skeleton, partly bone and partly cartilage. It has a double skull: the outer bony, the inner cartilaginous but becoming bony around the openings through which the cranial nerves pass. The bony gular plate under the tip of the lower jaw is a skeletal oddity, as are the unicornlike clavicles in the pectoral girdle, peculiar serrated appendages believed to be remnants of organs which were larger and performed some function in more or less remote ancestors (Liem and Woods 1973).

Both bowfins and gars have kidney tubules opening directly into the coelomic cavity. This condition, common in the embryos of many fishes, persists in the adults of only primitive species; other adult freshwater rayfin fishes have their kidneys closed off from the body cavity.

On the other hand, *Amia* exhibits evolutionary advances: a gas bladder used as a primitive lung; an egg transport system similar to that of the shark and of terrestrial vertebrates; cellular elements in the headbones which produce all types of blood cells, thereby anticipating the blood-making function of the bone marrow of higher vertebrates; and a highly specialized reproductive habit in which parental care plays a conspicuous role. It is the only primitive ganoid showing such a highly specialized reproductive habit.

Bowfin

Amia calva Linnaeus. *Amia*—ancient name of a fish, probably the bonito, *Sarda sarda*; *calva*—bald.

Other common names: dogfish, mudfish, grindle, John A. Grindle, grinnel, lake lawyer, lawyer, cottonfish, blackfish, speckled cat, beaverfish, scaled ling, spot-tail.

Immature (Wisconsin DNR photo)

Adult female 632 mm, Crystal R. (Waupaca Co.), fall 1977

DESCRIPTION

Body moderately long, stout, oval in cross section. Adult length 500 mm. Head flattened above, head length into TL 3.8–4.9. Anterior nares or nasal tubes 2, prominent barbel-like structures on snout (9.5 mm long in 645-mm fish). Teeth numerous, caninelike; some short, peglike on upper and lower jaws. Gular plate heavy. Scales "polygono cycloid," large, 63–70 in lateral line. Dorsal fin long, soft-rayed, low, its length into TL 2.1–2.4. Caudal fin rounded, abbreviate-heterocercal (vertebrae moving into dorsal portion of fin). Chromosomes 2n = 46 (Ohno et al. 1969).

Back and sides olive-colored, often with dark, netlike mottling; belly cream-colored to white. Paired fins and anal fin bright green. Up to time of maturity both sexes with a round-to-oval black spot at the base of the upper caudal rays.

Sexual dimorphism: Mature male with black spot on upper caudal rays rimmed with orange-yellow. Mature female without black spot on peduncle; probably an inhibitory action of an ovarian hormone (Zahl and Davis 1932); female generally larger than male.

The caudal spot is an illustration of a deflective mark in a fish: a mark which deflects the attack of an enemy from a more or less vital part of the body to some other part (Lagler et al. 1962).

DISTRIBUTION, STATUS, AND HABITAT

The bowfin occurs in the Mississippi, Lake Michigan, and Lake Superior drainage basins. In the Mississippi River system it is distributed in the Mississippi and Wisconsin rivers, in their larger tributaries, and in the glacial lakes of the southeastern and northwestern sectors of the state. In the Lake Michigan watershed it occurs in the Fox and Wolf rivers, in their interconnecting lakes, and in lower Green Bay of Lake Michigan. Except for a single report from Milwaukee, Greene (1935) did not encounter this species in the Lake Michigan watershed. He had neither records nor reports from the Wolf-Fox system. This species may have been introduced into the Fox-Wolf system through fish rescue and transfer operations from the Mississippi River during the 1930s, or it may have made recent entry via the Fox-Wisconsin Canal at Portage. In the Lake Superior watershed it has been reported only from the St. Louis River (Sather and Johannes 1973) and Middle River (Moore and Braem 1965). In Wisconsin the bowfin is at the northern limit of its range.

In Wisconsin the bowfin is uncommon to common in large rivers and lakes. It is rare in Lake Winnebago (Priegel 1967a). This species is secure in Wisconsin.

The bowfin inhabits lakes and large sluggish rivers, generally in clear water with abundant vegetation. The smallest stream with a bowfin record is the Des Plaines River (Kenosha County), which, at the collection site, is a wide, sluggish stream, just above several miles of marsh (Greene 1935).

BIOLOGY

In southern Wisconsin spawning occurs from late April to early May (Cahn 1927); upstate it occurs as late as early June (Priegel 1963d). Optimum temperature for nest construction and spawning is 16–19°C (61–66°F) (Scott and Crossman 1973). The male builds a nest by biting off the vegetation in an area 46–76 cm (1.5–2.5 ft) diam in water from 61 to 152 cm (2–5 ft) deep. When he has cleared away the weeds, a bed of soft rootlets, sand, or gravel in a trough 10–20 cm (4–8 in) deep remains for the eggs. A female is attracted to the nest and spawning takes place, usually at night. The female lies on the bottom of the nest, the male circles about her for 10 or 15 minutes, sometimes nipping her snout or sides. The male then takes up a position beside the female, both fish violently agitate their fins, and eggs and milt are released over a period of less than 1 minute.

Richardson (1913) gave 2,000–5,000 eggs as the normal number per nest. Eddy and Underhill (1974) reported as many as 64,000 eggs in the ovaries of a

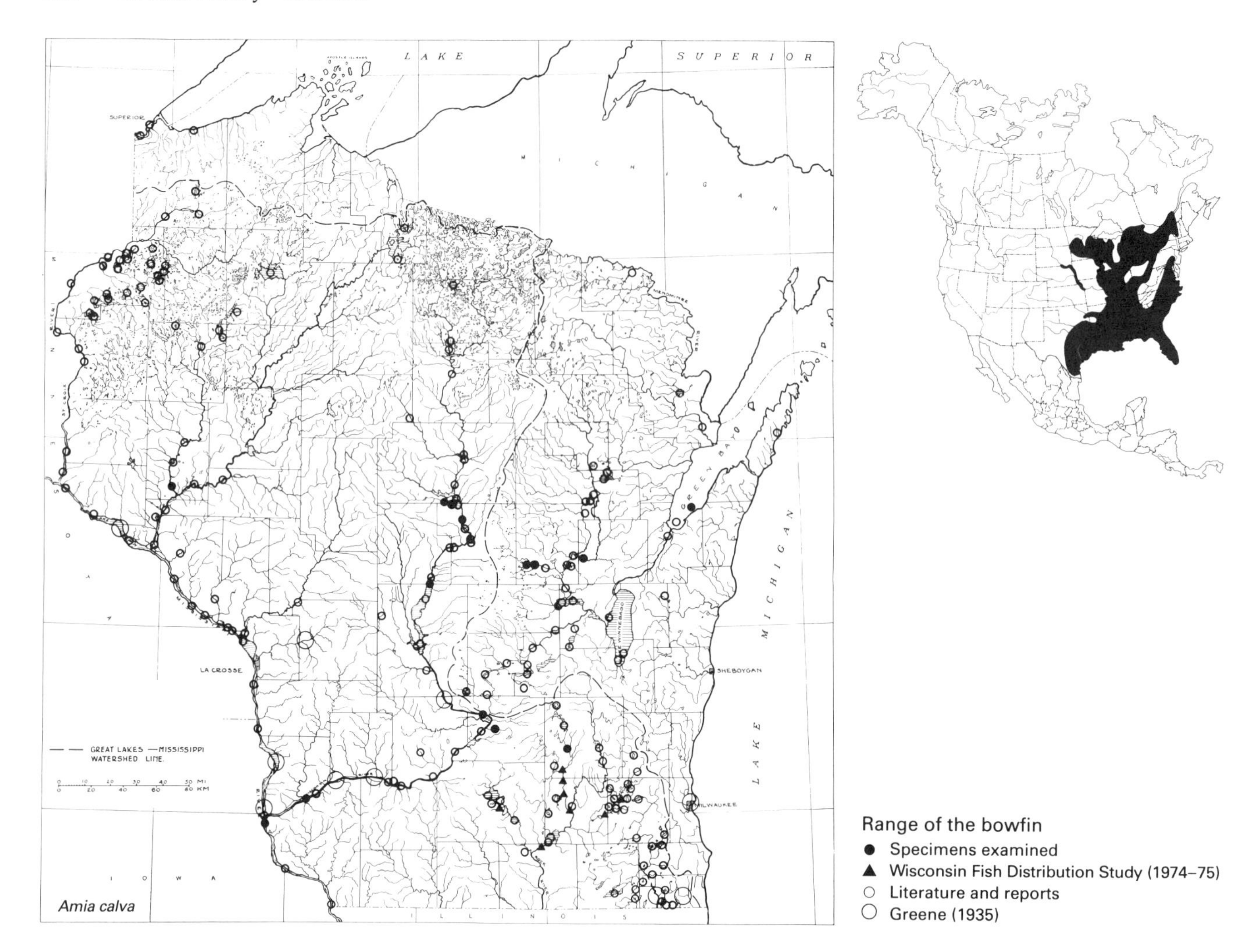

53-cm (21-in) fish. Bowfin eggs are slightly elliptical, 2.8 × 2.2 mm (Breder and Rosen 1966).

After one or more females have spawned in the nest, the male guards the eggs for the 8 to 10 days required for hatching (Purkett 1965). Upon hatching, the 8-mm-long larvae attach themselves to rootlets by an adhesive organ on their snouts or lie on their sides in the bottom of the nest until they are 9 days old and about 12 mm (0.5 in) long. The adhesive organ is no longer used, and the larvae will swim, begin feeding, and follow the male in a close school, often referred to as a ball of young. If one becomes separated from the parent, it swims in close circles until its protector reappears.

While in this vulnerable milling mass, the young are generally carefully guarded by the male. Some of the most unusual records of fish attacks are attributed to male bowfins protecting their young. Kelly (1924) reported that a 356-mm (14-in) fish, guarding 30–40 young, rushed him while he was standing on the bank. The attack carried the fish out of the water 203 mm (8 in) up a slightly sloping grassy bank and was repeated several times. When a pole was placed in the water, the fish attacked it and bit the end of it.

Cahn (1927:26) described the defense of the young by the male: "While guarding the young, the male dogfish will attack anything that threatens the precious mass of youngsters. I have had the parent attack nets, rakes, sticks—anything I thrust toward the ball of young; a vicious attack, a strike at the intruding object, a dash away to a distance of about six feet, a swift turn and another vicious attack. During this performance by the old fish, the school breaks up in every direction, the young going to the bottom and scurrying toward deeper water under the protection of the vegetation." Lagler et al. (1962) noted that the adult will create diversionary splashes in a direction away from the mass of young while the little school moves away.

Adults have also been known to take flight (Doan 1938). A vigorous sweep of a male's tail not only sent it out of sight but also threw the swarm of young fish to the bottom, where they were effectively screened from sight in the newly muddied water. After about

5 min the adult forced its way, unseen, through the bottom debris and became visible only when it raised its head up in the vicinity of the young. They immediately left their hiding places and collected again in a free-swimming school about the parent.

When the young fish reach a length of about 102 mm (4 in), some 2–2½ months after the males begin their nest-constructing activities, the juvenile school, having become progressively looser, breaks up. The fact that the young are rarely seen after the schools break up suggests they move to deeper water or to dense vegetation.

Growth is rapid; some young exceed 203 mm (8 in) during their first year of life. The ages and calculated growth at each annulus in the table below are tentative. The scale annuli were difficult to identify, and sample sizes were not large enough to check the validity of our determinations.

Noland (1951) reported a 737-mm (29-in) fish from Lake Wingra (Dane County) which weighed 3.9 kg (8 lb 10 oz); a 4.1-kg (9-lb) fish was caught from the Mississippi River at La Crosse in August 1978. Large bowfins may weigh in excess of 6.8–9.1 kg (15–20 lb) (Purkett 1965, Scott and Crossman 1973). A fish 109 cm (43 in) long was reported from New York (Rimsky-Korsakoff 1930). According to Carlander (1969), bowfins have been kept in captivity for periods of 20 years, 24 years, and 30 years.

Schneberger (1937b) encountered a school of 5,500 young which were 45–70 mm (1.75–2.75 in) long in a small bay off Lake Minocqua Thoroughfare near Woodruff. An analysis of 30 stomachs disclosed damselfly nymphs, *Hyallela*, chironomid larvae, and plankton crustaceans. Phytoplankton, especially filamentous algae, was found in each specimen. Ten bowfin young were placed in an aquarium and a dozen 19-mm (0.75-in) largemouth bass fry were put into the tank. The bass were viciously attacked by the small bowfins, and in a few seconds all were consumed. Schneberger concluded, however, that bowfins of this size in their native habitat have not yet become piscivorous.

In southeastern Wisconsin, Cahn (1927) reported that the bowfin's diet varies between fish and crayfish. He found many species of minnows, bluegills, pumpkinseed, largemouth and smallmouth bass, and perch—"in fact, small specimens of all of the game or food fishes." Pearse (1918) noted that 16 bowfins (383–465 mm long) from Lakes Mendota, Monona, and Wingra had 90.1% fish remains and 9.4% crayfish remains in their alimentary tracts. Other animals eaten are small rodents, snakes, turtles, frogs, large insects and their larvae, and leeches (Lagler et al. 1962, Harlan and Speaker 1956). The bowfin is an opportunist rather than a selective predator. It often feeds at night.

The bowfin's voracious feeding habits are commonly mentioned in the literature. Gluttony, the inclination to eat long after the normal capacity of the animal has been reached, has been described for the bowfin in aquariums (Lagler et al. 1962). Eddy and Underhill (1974) noted that one bowfin in their aquarium attacked another about half its size and carried the victim in its mouth for 24 hours before completely swallowing it.

The reputation of the bowfin's gluttony has grown to the point of exaggeration, and although it purportedly "has strong sharp teeth and is said to bite a 2-lb fish in two at a single snap," this is hardly likely. The bowfin is also capable of prolonged fasting; one was inadvertently left in an aquarium without food and was discovered a year later, still alive though quite gaunt (Eddy and Underhill 1974).

The air-breathing habit begins early in life, and when the ball of young fish is undisturbed, individuals will occasionally leave the school and surface for a gulp of air. Horn and Riggs (1973) noted that at temperatures of 4.4–10°C (40–50°F) air breathing is negligible. At 10°C and below, the bowfin is relatively inactive and is almost exclusively a water breather. Above 10°C the rate of air breathing consistently increases as the temperature increases. Air-breathing activity is greatest between 18.4 and 29.6°C (65 and 85°F) and during the 35.3°C (96°F) period—the critical

Date	No. of Fish	TL (mm)	Calculated TL at the Annulus (mm) 0	1	2	3	4	5	6	7	8	Location
2 July 1934[a]		45–70	45–70									Minocqua Thoroughfare (Oneida Co.)
13 July 1962	1	122	122									Wisconsin R. (Grant Co.)
13 July 1962	3	178–512		180	337	389	416	427				Wisconsin R. (Grant Co.)
23 Jan. 1968	8[b]	504–704		207	358	448	519	573	619	678	701	Wisconsin R. (Adams Co.)
28 Oct. 1967	1	251		153	190							Wolf R. (Outagamie Co.)
20 July 1975	1	320		177	253							Taylor L. (Waupaca Co.)
18 Sept. 1973	1	380		100	201	302						Beaver Dam R. (Dodge Co.)
9 June 1968	1	610		195	363	490	538	563	598			Green Bay (Brown Co.)

[a] Source: Schneberger 1937b.

[b] Includes four males, 585–690 mm (23.0–27.2 in) TL, all age VI; three females 604–704 mm (23.8–27.7 in) TL, ages VI–VIII; and one individual 504 mm (19.9 in), sex undetermined.

thermal maximum for this species. With increasing temperature and activity, the rate of oxygen depletion from the gas bladder increases progressively and the air-breathing rate increases. The bowfin has a higher breathing rate during darkness, correlated with an increase in the fish's activity.

That it is possible for the bowfin to survive prolonged air-breathing periods seems to be indicated by an incident reported from Alabama (Green 1966). A shallow pond that had been drained for half a year was filled with water and stocked during February and March with five sexually mature bowfins (two males, three females) taken from a nearby river slough. When the pond was drained on 22 April, 51-mm (2-in) young were seen, along with two bowl-shaped nests, suggesting that both male bowfins had incubated broods. Over a 21-day period, from 23 April to 11 May, this pond was dry. Seepage from other ponds made the bottom moist in many areas, but there was no accumulation of water. On 12 May the pond was refilled and stocked with about 150 goldfish. When it was drained again on 28 August, 24 bowfins were recovered with the goldfish. These bowfins averaged 406 mm (16 in) and 680 g (1.5 lb). Evidently some young had survived a prolonged air-breathing period.

Neill (1950) reported having unearthed an aestivating bowfin in a chamber 102 mm (4 in) below the ground surface and 203 mm (8 in) diam, 0.4 km (0.25 mi) from a river, the flood level of which had previously reached that location. Greenbank (1956) noted that, with a lowering of water level in the Mississippi River, bowfin, carp, northern pike, and crappies moved with the resultant current out of the backwaters. The fish appeared to be moving actively and were not merely swept along with the current. Some bluegills and largemouth bass, however, tended to remain in the backwaters, there to become trapped by the lowered water level.

Adult bowfins usually live in deep water, coming into shallows at night and during the breeding season. In winter they have been found closely huddled in gravelly pockets among water weeds (Coker 1930). Bowfins swim effortlessly, both forwards and backwards, by deliberate undulations of their elongated dorsal fins.

IMPORTANCE AND MANAGEMENT

The bowfin is host to the glochidia of the mollusk *Megalonaias gigantea* (Hart and Fuller 1974).

Most bowfins are caught while the angler is fishing for other species. Anglers discover that this fish is a rugged fighter that strikes hard and fights better than some highly rated sport fish; it is worth seeking for angling fun. When a large bowfin is hooked it will frequently sound and lie on the bottom like a water-soaked log. Spearing for bowfins may occur early in the year as the ice opens up and the bowfins congregate about the openings. I have seen more than 50 large bowfins 1.8–3.6 kg (4–8 lb) that had been speared and discarded on either side of a causeway on Petenwell Flowage (Adams County).

The bowfin is taken commercially by setlines, gill nets, seines, buffalo nets, and slat nets from the Mississippi River. During 1956–1965, a total of 30,770 kg (67,843 lb) were harvested from Wisconsin waters; during 1966–1975, 28,580 kg (63,006 lb). The largest catch was 5,626 kg (12,403 lb) in 1961. Its value to the commercial fisherman in 1975 was $0.04 per kilo.

Small bowfins make colorful, fascinating, and easily maintained aquarium subjects.

Reports as to the edibility of the bowfin are conflicting. Some describe its flesh as "soft, pasty, not especially palatable, unfit for use unless prepared in some special manner," while others say it is "very palatable, passably palatable, one of the best of all smoked fishes." V. Hacker (pers. comm.) noted that if bowfin flesh is frozen for 30–40 days before brining and smoking, it becomes hardened and makes very desirable eating. MacKay (1963) reported that it may be marinated in spices and vinegar before cooking, baked in highly seasoned dressing, or smoked. Scott and Crossman (1973) reported that the flesh is dry and has a mild flavor; when molded into patties, dipped in egg and bread crumbs or corn meal, it makes reasonably good eating.

Because the bowfin is not generally accepted as a food fish and because it feeds extensively on other fishes, it usually is considered undesirable. But since it inhabits waters likely to be populated by panfish or nongame fishes, the bowfin is often an asset. It may be quite effective in preventing stunting in sport fish populations (Purkett 1965, Scott and Crossman 1973, Berry 1955, Walden 1964).

The bowfin is frequently part of the fish fauna in many excellent sport and panfish waters in Wisconsin. In fact, the quality of such waters may be attributable in part to the presence of this species. Some fishery managers are considering the possibility of using this species, as well as the gar and the burbot, in lakes and ponds which are plagued with stunted panfish populations. On the basis of the scanty evidence we have today, it is possible that under certain circumstances the bowfin may be an essential part of a healthy aquatic ecosystem.

Freshwater Eel Family—Anguillidae

One species of freshwater eel is known from Wisconsin and North America. Its entire range lies east of the Rocky Mountains; there are no freshwater eels along the Pacific Coast of the United States. About 16 species, all in the single genus *Anguilla*, occur widely throughout the world, particularly in the region of southeast Asia and the southwestern Pacific Ocean, including Australia and New Zealand. The fossil record is from the Upper Cretaceous to Recent.

The body is excessively elongated and almost round in cross section. The gill openings are small, the pelvic fins absent, and the scales, when present, are small and embedded.

The Anguillidae or freshwater eels spawn in the sea, but early in life they move into fresh water, where they grow into adults. They are catadromous fishes: they run downstream to breed.

American Eel

Anguilla rostrata (Lesueur). *Anguilla*—eel; *rostrata*—beaked.
Other common names: common eel, freshwater eel, Boston eel, Atlantic eel, silver eel, elver.

850 mm, Zumbro R., Minnesota, 1977

DESCRIPTION
Body much elongated, snakelike. Lower jaw protruding beyond upper; mouth large, extending to below or beyond eye; jaws and vomer with numerous teeth somewhat unequal in length. Gill opening a small slit, about the length of base of pectoral fin. Fins: all soft-rayed; pelvic fins absent; dorsal fin beginning far behind head and in front of anal fin; dorsal, caudal, and anal fins continuous; caudal fin bluntly rounded. Scales minute and mosaic, separated from one another or meeting at their margins. Anterior nares at tips of short tubes close to upper lips near tip of snout. Chromosomes 2n = 38 (Roberts 1967).

Larval eel or leptocephalus ("thin-head") shaped like willow leaf and transparent. Transformed or "glass eels" with general shape of an eel, eyes pigmented but body transparent. In fresh water, immature eels yellowish, greenish or olive-brown; back darker, belly lighter. Mature adult at time of seaward migration with metallic sheen, back bronze or almost black and belly light or silvery (called "silver eel").

DISTRIBUTION, STATUS, AND HABITAT
The American eel occurs in the Mississippi, Lake Michigan, and Lake Superior drainage basins. In the Mississippi system, there are the following records and reports of eels outside the Mississippi River mainstem: Walworth County—Whitewater Lake (*Milwaukee Journal*, July 1950) 1950, Cravath Lake (*Janesville Gazette* 16 July 1974); Waukesha County—Lac La Belle (D. Mraz, pers. comm.) 1959, Lac La Belle and its outlet (Greene 1935), Upper Nemahbin Lake (L. Christenson, pers. comm.) 1951; Dodge County—Beaver (Dam ?) Lake (Greene 1935), Rock River between Hustisford and Watertown (H. Neuenschwander, pers. comm.) up to 1943; Jefferson County—Lake Koshkonong (*Janesville Gazette* 16 July 1974) 1954, Rock River at Watertown (D. Becker, pers. comm.) 1975; Dane County—Lake Monona (Neuenschwander 1946) 1880, Salmo Pond of Black Earth Creek (C. Brynildson, pers. comm.) 1976; Dane and Rock counties—Yahara River (Mackenthun et al. 1948) 1946; Rock County—Rock River below Monterey Dam at Janesville (*Janesville Gazette* 16 July 1974) 1965, lower Pecatonica River (C. Brynildson, pers. comm.) 1950s; Columbia County—Crawfish River T1ON R12E Sec 13 (*Columbus Journal Republican* 7 July 1976) 1976; Sauk County—Baraboo River (*History of Sauk County* 1880); La Crosse County—Neshonoc Lake (L. Christenson, pers. comm.) early 1950s; Dunn County—Lake Menomin (B. Apelgren, pers. comm.) about 1963; St. Croix County—Lake St. Croix (B. Apelgren, pers. comm.) 1964.

Lake Michigan records and reports: Ozaukee County—Lake Michigan off Port Washington (Greene 1935), Lake Michigan at Harrington State Park (UWSP 5666) 1977; Brown County—Green Bay at Red Banks (UWSP 2777) 1968, Fox River (Kernen 1974) 1974; Marinette County—Green Bay at Peshtigo Point (*Marinette Eagle-Star* 30 June 1974) 1974.

Lake Superior reports: Douglas County—Lake Nebagamon (W. Weiher, pers. comm.) 1966, 1970, 1973; Brule River at mouth (W. Weiher, pers. comm.) 1970; Superior harbor area (W. Weiher, pers. comm.) 1974. Additional Lake Superior basin areas outside Wisconsin: Minnesota shore Lake Superior (*Milwaukee Journal* 14 November 1971, Eddy and Underhill 1974) 1966–1971; Beaver Lake Creek in Upper Michigan (Moore and Braem 1965) 1957.

Wisconsin Fish Distribution Study (1974–1978) records and reports: Green County—Sugar River at Albany 1974; Dane County—Yahara River above Lake Mendota 1977; Sauk County—Wisconsin River T8N R4E Sec 3 1977; Grant County—Wisconsin River near Bridgeport 1977; Jackson County—Black River T22N R3W Sec 3 1975; La Crosse County—Black River T17N R8W Sec 4 1976; Dunn, Pepin, and Buffalo counties—three Red Cedar River collections 1963 and 1975, five Chippewa River collections 1977.

Eels reaching Wisconsin undoubtedly follow two routes: (1) the Mississippi River from the Gulf of Mexico and (2) the St. Lawrence Seaway. M. W. Smith and Saunders (1955) noted that eels avoid coolwater habitats. This may be responsible for their late

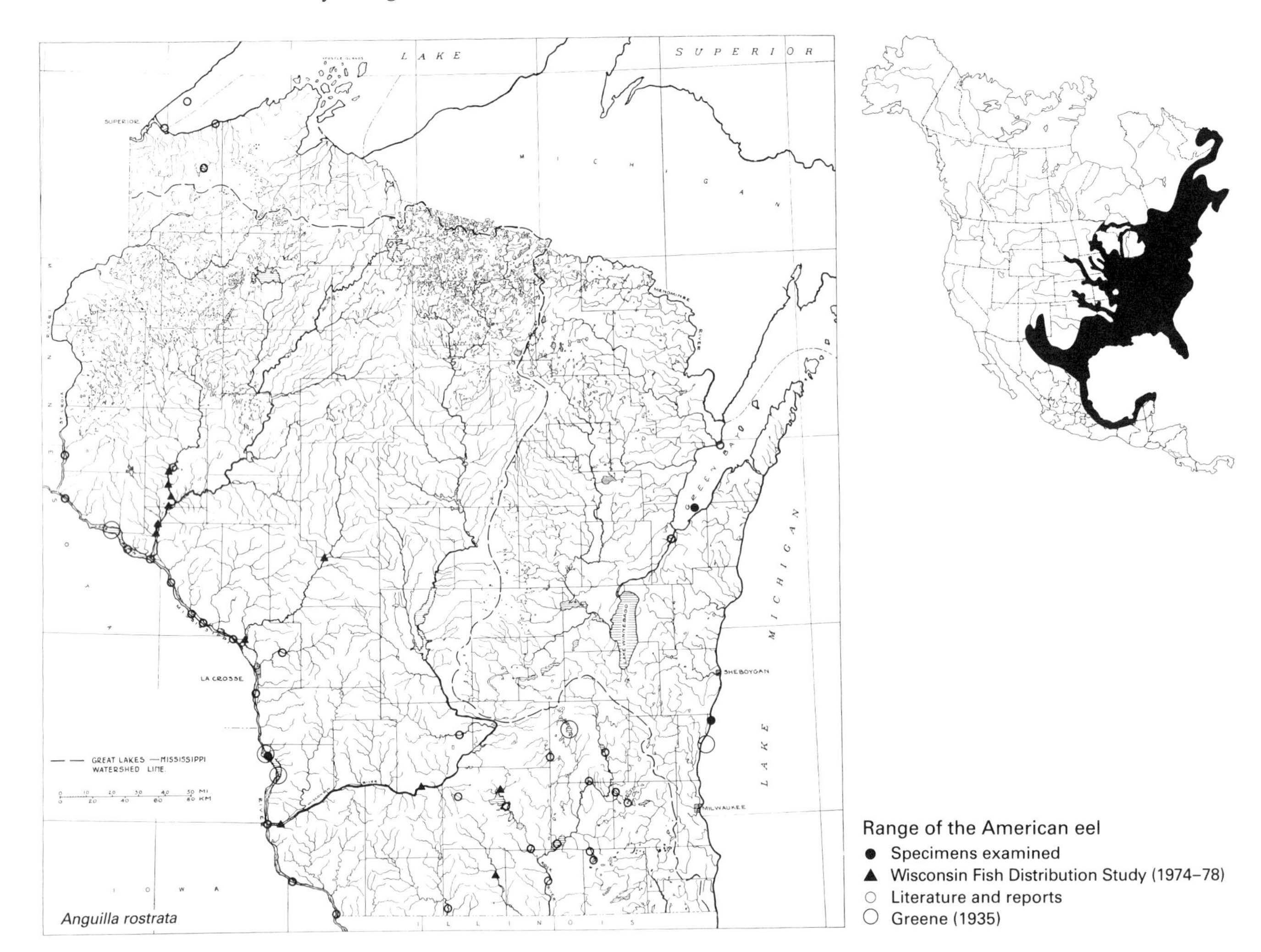

entry into the upper Great Lakes, especially Lake Superior.

The American eel is rare to uncommon in the Mississippi River and its tributaries. At one time it was common, but it has declined during the past half century. In recent years there has been little change in its status and its numbers do not appear to be diminishing. In the Lake Michigan and Superior basins this species is still an oddity. A capture off Peshtigo Point of Green Bay in 1974 was headlined "Fisherman Nets Strange Creature" (*Marinette Eagle-Star*). It is thought that the construction in 1974 of an eel ladder on the St. Lawrence River at Cornwall, Ontario, may increase the numbers of eels in the upper Great Lakes (Whitfield 1975). In Wisconsin this species has watch status (Wis. Dep. Nat. Resour. Endangered Species Com. 1975, Les 1979).

The eel inhabits large streams and lakes, seeking muddy bottoms and still waters. To reach these waters the eel has to traverse swift-flowing, medium-sized streams over a wide variety of bottoms. A prime requirement is sufficient food. The eel can tolerate habitats over a wide range of temperatures (Bigelow and Welsh 1925).

BIOLOGY

When she leaves fresh water to spawn, the female is very fat, with a very high oil content. This reserve of fat and oil undoubtedly sustains her on her journey to the breeding grounds thousands of miles away (Angel and Jones 1974). As the female eel leaves fresh water and enters the brackish estuaries, she is joined by the male eel. Presumably they leave North American shores and over a period of 2 or 3 months swim into the spawning area.

Schmidt (1922) says that breeding occurs in the Atlantic's Sargasso Sea between Bermuda and the Bahamas, but Vladykov (1964) makes a strong case for a breeding area much farther south than the Sargasso Sea. Assuming the Sargasso Sea center, it is difficult to explain the presence of adults of the American eel over their southern limits, i.e., Trinidad and Dutch Guiana, since the weak leptocephali would not be able to reach those sites against the strong North Equatorial Current.

The breeding season starts in late winter or early spring and extends into the summer (Breder and Rosen 1966). Spawning occurs in deep water and nothing is known of the mating activity. Presumably spawning occurs once, and is followed by the death of the adults. Males mature at 279–305 mm (11–12 in) and females at 457 mm (18 in) and at 5–20 years of age (Carlander 1969). The number of eggs has been reported at 5–20 million per female. It is presumed that the eggs and larvae require water of high temperature and high salinity for development.

The eel larvae (leptocephali) once considered distinct and separate fishes, are cigar-shaped in outline but very flat from side to side. They are usually as thick as an ordinary blotter and highly transparent, so much so that when laid on a printed page they offer practically no obstruction to reading.

The leptocephali arrive off our coastal waters in 1 year, at which time they assume the adult form and are 60–65 mm (2.4–2.6 in) long. As soon as they come under the influence of fresh water in our brackish bays, they become heavily pigmented and are nearly black. At this point they are 65–90 mm (2.5–3.5 in) long, and are called elvers (Scott and Crossman 1973).

Migration into fresh water occurs in spring. Most eels entering North American estuaries are females, although to the south of the American eel's range (from North Carolina to the Gulf of Mexico) a few males may be present (C. Huver, pers. comm.). The sex of this species is determined from a microscopic inspection of the gonads.

The males rarely move much above tidewater, and grow to maturity after spending years in brackish estuaries. The females, however, migrate into fresh water, some only a few kilometers and others hundreds or thousands of kilometers upstream. According to Dintaman (1975), elvers migrate upstream during the night, generally following the bank of the river or stream in very shallow water. When they approach a swift-running part of the stream, they move closer to the shoreline, often coming out of the water by clinging to wet grass or to the surface of wet rocks. They move overland until they have passed the swift section and can again enter the water to continue their upstream migration. They penetrate upstream by climbing, clinging, and crawling up the sides of rocks and, occasionally, of vertical fishways and dams. Walden (1964) noted that they surmount dams, negotiate tunnels, aqueducts, and underground streams, sometimes traveling over flooded or even dew-wet fields and turning up eventually in a pond or lake with no apparent access to any sea-connected river.

Scales do not form on young eels until they attain lengths of 16–20 cm (6.3–7.9 in) at about age III. In a length-frequency study, Hildebrand and Schroeder (1928) found lengths of 64 mm (2.5 in) at age I and 127 mm (5 in) at age II. By examining scales of eels in New Brunswick, M. W. Smith and Saunders (1955) determined age III at 241 mm (9.5 in); IV, 292 mm (11.5 in); V, 348 mm (13.7 in); VI, 368 mm (14.5 in); VII, 386 mm (15.2 in); VIII, 462 mm (18.2 in); IX, 500 mm (19.7 in); X, 549 mm (21.6 in); XI and older, 612–744 mm (24.1–29.3 in). Smith and Saunders read 10 scales for each fish but in the older fish many differences were noted in annulus counts, sometimes as much as 5 years in one individual. The highest reading was used as the age for that individual. Gunning and Shoop (1962) reported that in two Louisiana streams, eels were smaller in the stream with the higher population density. Of two eels tagged at lengths of 360 mm (14.2 in), one grew at least 138 mm (5.4 in) and the other, 325 mm (12.8 in) during 1 year of growth.

Female American eels 122 cm (48 in) TL and 7.26 kg (16 lb) have been recorded (Eales 1968). Male eels longer than 51 cm (20 in) are rare, but female eels up to 91 cm (3 ft) long are common, and they can reach a length of 152 cm (5 ft) (Angel and Jones 1974). In Wisconsin a number of eels of 91 cm (36 in) TL or longer and weighing 1.4–1.8 kg (3–4 lb) have been reported. On 30 April 1951 one was taken from Upper Nemahbin Lake (Waukesha County) 112 cm (44 in) TL, weighing 3.52 kg (7 lb 12 oz). Scott and Crossman (1973) reported the case of a European eel (*Anguilla anguilla*) kept in captivity from 1863, when 3 years old, to 1948, a life span of 88 years. No similar authentic records are known for North American eels.

Eels are voracious carnivores, feeding mainly at night and consuming a wide variety of fishes and invertebrate creatures. Contrary to earlier thinking, eels seek living rather than dead creatures and are not habitual eaters of carrion, although they do attack and partly consume fishes gilled in nets (Scott and Crossman 1973). They have also been known to feed on dead livestock that has washed into the stream (Harlan and Speaker 1956). Their snakelike movements permit them to move into extremely shallow waters and even overland for short distances in marshy or damp situations, and they have been observed in damp lowlands near streams, presumably in search of frogs, crayfish, and other foods. Ranthum (1969) reported an eel taken from Pool 19 of the Mississippi River that contained three small clams and a large number of *Hexagenia* naiads. A 676-mm (26.6-in) eel had eaten two crayfish; a 269-mm (10.6-in) eel had eaten a heptageniid mayfly naiad. In New York eels were found feeding mostly on fish, and also on chironomid larvae. It was observed that mayfly naiads and adults made up over half the food of 20 eels from the Delaware River in New York.

Freshwater eels can survive for more than a year without taking food (Lagler et al. 1962). The intestines of such starved fishes become nonfunctional and partly degenerate.

Eels, being nocturnal, usually spend the day hidden under rocks or logs or buried in the mud with only their snouts protruding. Adams and Hankinson (1926) noted that during the daytime they were caught in water from 9 to 18 m (30–60 ft) deep.

In winter, in cold regions like New England, the eel burrows in soft mud and hibernates. At Cape May eels burrow 152–203 mm (6–8 in), sometimes a little further, and often become more or less quiet or dormant (Adams and Hankinson 1926).

Eels make chirping or sucking noises, which Scott and Crossman (1973) report are frequently heard on warm August evenings in Canada. When highly excited, they produce high-pitched sounds by release of air from the bladder through the pneumatic duct (Lagler et al. 1962).

Eels have a remarkably acute sense of smell. The perceptual threshold for B-phenylethyl alcohol in the best-trained experimental eels (*Anguilla anguilla*) was a dilution of 1:2,857 trillion (Teichmann 1957). Teichmann estimated that 1–2 molecules of the scent in the nasal chambers could be detected by the eel. This sensitivity may operate as a homing device through which the mature adult seeks out ancestral spawning grounds.

Captive eels in the University of Minnesota aquariums lie quietly on the bottom while resting, sometimes upside down. They have occasionally escaped from their tanks and remained out of water for 24 hours without any apparent injury (Eddy and Underhill 1974).

The hardiness of the eel is almost proverbial, a view that has arisen largely because the eel can live out of water longer than most freshwater fish. Its gills are protected from dessication, and it appears to live at a low metabolic level.

IMPORTANCE AND MANAGEMENT

This species is host to the glochidia of the mollusks *Megalonaias gigantea*, *Arcidens confragosa*, *Actinonaias carinata*, and *Ligumia recta* (Hart and Fuller 1974).

The eel has been suggested as a biological control for lampreys. Perlmutter (1951) noted that the eel explores openings and crevices and roots through the mud for its prey. In an aquarium experiment, eels destroyed a considerable number of larval lampreys. The eel is too rare, however, in Lakes Michigan and Superior to have any effect on sea lamprey populations.

Adult eels appear to be well able to take care of themselves (Adams and Hankinson 1926), but young eels are eaten by walleye, great blue heron, American merganser, bald eagle, double-crested cormorant, black-crowned night heron, otter, mink, and water snake.

Catching an eel in Wisconsin by hook and line is generally a matter of chance, occurring usually while the angler is fishing for something else. Any bait will do to catch an eel. The eel is a fighter, pulling vigorously, tugging, and shaking. The simplest way to kill eels is to put them in a deep container, sprinkle them with salt, and add enough water to cover them. This method of killing eels helps to remove the slime layer (Berg et al. 1975).

The eel is an exceptionally good food fish. Whatever the season, and even in countries like the United States where most people are not accustomed to eating eel, it is considered a luxury food. In some countries, eel is traditionally served on certain days. In Italy, it is the traditional dish on Christmas Eve. In Japan, one day in July is set aside as "eel day," and great quantities are sold (Bardach et al. 1972).

The flesh is white and has a good flavor. It can be fried, baked, sauteed, jellied, made into chowder, smoked, and served with a variety of sauces. Smoked eel is by far the most popular mode of preparation. Berg et al. (1975) suggested that eels be skinned, rolled in crumbs, dipped in egg and deep-fried for 3–5 min.

At one time eels served to a limited extent as a source of oil, which was extracted and sold largely as a grease for harnesses and for medicinal purposes. Occasionally, eel skins were preserved and stretched over thin, narrow boards about a yard long to dry; the dried skins were used for lining buggy and riding whips. Skins also went into the production of fine bookbindings, and were shaped into suspenders and other items (Adams and Hankinson 1926).

In the Mississippi River adjacent to Wisconsin, eels are taken by setlines, bait nets, buffalo nets, and slat nets. During the 10-year period 1956–1965, a total of

435 kg (960 lb) was harvested from Wisconsin waters; during 1966–1975, 2,056 kg (4533 lb). The largest yearly catch was 343 kg (756 lb) in 1974 (Fernholz and Crawley 1976). Its value to the commercial fisherman of $0.51 per kilo in 1975 was exceeded only by the price for the catfish ($0.81) and the shovelnose sturgeon ($0.64).

During the 1970s, because of European demand, eels were bringing prices to commercial fishermen on the East Coast of $1.10 per kilo, and over 226,800 kg (500,000 lb) have been flown overseas in a single year. Most of them are shipped alive, and the demand is greater than the supply (Angel and Jones 1974).

Herring Family—Clupeidae

Three species of herrings in two genera are known from Wisconsin. In the United States and Canada 27 species in 9 genera are known (Robins et al. 1980).

The herring family contains many important marine species (e.g., herrings, shads, menhadens, and sardines), several of which are anadromous and enter fresh water to spawn. These fishes occur throughout the seas of the world, except for Antarctic waters. Among these are a few which have abandoned the marine phase of their existence. A few species live permanently in fresh water. Economically, the order Clupeiformes is an important group of fishes, and in terms of money value probably the most valuable in the world.

The herrings possess a row of modified scales, called scutes, along the midventral edge of the belly; these scales form a distinct sawtooth margin. All species have a transparent eye covering (adipose eyelid) with a vertical slit. All have the pelvic axillary process.

The herrings are spring spawners and the anadromous species crowd into streams in spectacular runs. Presumably, the eggs are deposited at random, and no care is given to them or to the newly hatched young.

Alewife

Alosa pseudoharengus (Wilson). *Alosa*—Saxon *Allis*, old name of the European shad, *Alosa alosa*; *pseudo*—false, *harengus*—herring.

Other common names: ellwife, sawbelly, sawbelly shad, shad, golden shad, branch herring, bigeyed herring, river herring, spring herring.

Adult 180 mm, L. Michigan (Door Co.), 3 July 1963

DESCRIPTION

Body oblong, strongly compressed laterally, depth into SL 3.0–3.7. Length 150–180 mm. Head length into SL 3.5–4.3. Mouth large, maxillary reaching below middle of eye; lower jaw projecting beyond upper jaw. Jaw teeth small, weak, and few. Gill rakers on lower limb of the first arch 41–44; upper limb of first gill arch about half the length of lower limb. Scales cycloid; lateral line absent; lateral series scales 42–50. Dorsal fin usually 13–14 rays, last ray not lengthened beyond the fin; dorsal fin insertion directly over or slightly in advance of pelvic fin insertion. Anal fin rays usually 17–18. Caudal fin deeply forked. Chromosomes 2n = 48 (Mayers and Roberts 1969).

Back gray-green or brownish green becoming silvery on sides and belly. Cheek silver. Single dark "shoulder" spot in most individuals. Adults with dark, longitudinal lines along scales above midline.

Larvae separable from gizzard shad larvae by ratio of snout to vent length/SL; values for alewife larvae 3.5–19.5 mm SL range from 0.82 to 0.74 (Lam and Roff 1977).

Possible hybrid *Alosa pseudoharengus* × *Alosa aestivalis* (Vincent 1960).

DISTRIBUTION, STATUS, AND HABITAT

The alewife reached the upper Great Lakes via the Welland Canal (bypass of Niagara Falls). It was first recorded from Lake Erie in 1931 and from Lake Huron in 1933. It appeared in Lake Michigan in 1949, had dispersed throughout most of the lake by 1953 (Miller 1957), and had become common throughout the lake by 1957. In the late 1950s and early 1960s the population increase was explosive. In Lake Superior it was first reported in 1953, and its numbers appear to be increasing there (McLain et al. 1965).

Movement of alewives into new areas occurred after high-water conditions, and the resultant increased current and high levels in the connecting canals and rivers may have served as a stimulus to the anadromous habits of this species (Graham 1954).

The alewife was observed running into Kangaroo Lake (Door County) and up the Pigeon River system in Sheboygan and Manitowoc counties, apparently establishing a permanent population in Pigeon Lake (L. Kernen, pers. comm.). It has been reported in East Twin River (Manitowoc County), Sheboygan River (Sheboygan County), Sauk Creek (Ozaukee County), and Milwaukee River (Milwaukee County). In Lake Superior it rarely occurs in tributary streams (McLain et al. 1965).

The alewife is abundant in Lake Michigan and common in Lake Superior. In Lake Michigan it constitutes 70–90% of the fish weight, and by sheer weight of numbers has dominated the fishery of the lake.

The present system in Lake Michigan—in which a single species, the alewife, makes up a major share of the forage fish of the lake—is not stable. According to S. H. Smith (1968a), the instability is accentuated because the alewife is highly sensitive and not well adapted to its life in fresh water. Its abundance has fluctuated widely in the other Great Lakes where it has already reached its peak. Causes of these fluctuations are not known and cannot be anticipated. Overfishing or overpredation during the low cycle of a fluctuation could cause the alewife population to collapse. It seems unlikely that the alewife can persist at its present level of abundance in Lake Michigan; a drop to a population level somewhat less than the present level may be expected.

In Lake Michigan the alewife inhabits all levels over all bottom types. It avoids cold water, and during the winter searches out the warmest areas—at the bottom in the deep portions of the lake. The cold water of Lake Superior may have deterred establishment of a substantial population there (S. H. Smith 1972).

BIOLOGY

Spawning occurs from June to August. In 1965 spawning in the harbor areas of Lake Michigan extended from the end of June to the first part of August, with the peak occurring during the first 2 weeks

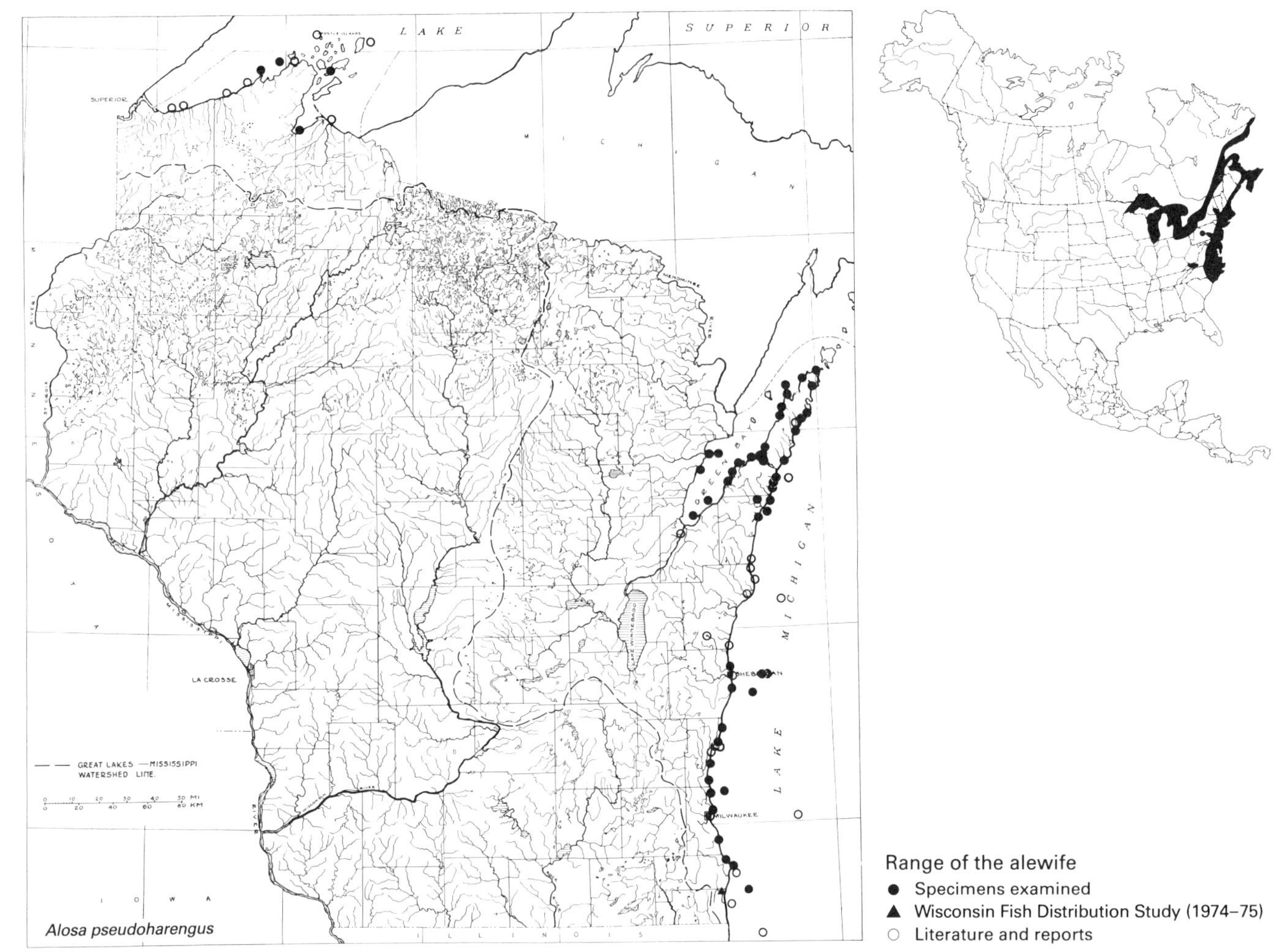

Range of the alewife
● Specimens examined
▲ Wisconsin Fish Distribution Study (1974–75)
○ Literature and reports

of July (Norden 1967a). The majority of spawning alewives were in age groups II and III (158–172 mm); the females produced from 11,000 to 22,000 eggs, compared to the 60,000–100,000 eggs in the larger marine alewife (Graham 1954). Norden noted some ripe individuals, mostly males, of age group I, but no age-0 fish were in spawning condition. In mature fish the testes made up about 5% of total body weight, the ovaries 10%.

In Lake Michigan, 5,000–6,000 spawning fish have been seen in schools 4.5–6 m (15–20 ft) diam (Threinen 1958). While on their inshore migration, they come into shallow water at night and remain offshore during the day.

In Lake Ontario spawning occurred at temperatures of 13–16°C (55–60°F). But temperatures during the spawning period may vary considerably, and L. Wells (pers. comm.) reported that, although during the same period of time alewives are found in water with temperatures ranging from 5°C (41°F) or less to 20°C (68°F) or more, most are found in water warmer than 8°C (46.4°F). Alewives tend to avoid temperatures greater than 22°C (71.6°F), but in some spawning streams they must occasionally endure temperatures of 25°C (77°F) or more. In the Milwaukee Harbor during July and August, Norden (1967b) collected developing eggs and larvae at surface water temperatures ranging from 17.5 to 21.1°C (63.5–70°F).

Spawning was observed by Edsall (1964) on the Kalamazoo River, Michigan, about 3.2 km (2 mi) upstream from Lake Michigan. Observations were made off a 24-m (80-ft) dock where the water depth was 3 m (10 ft). The spawning act involves two or more fish which swim rapidly with sides touching in a tight circle 20–30 cm (8–12 in) diam spiraling upward from the depths. The act terminates after one or two circles have been completed at the surface. The spawners then swim rapidly downward and out of sight. Spawning was first observed late in the afternoon (1700 hr) and reached a peak at 0200 hr, when spawning could be heard clearly. (The termination of the spawning act involves considerable splashing.) According to Odell (1934), there seems to be no preferred type of bottom.

Spawning itself has been thought to be a factor in alewife die-offs, but dead or dying alewives are seldom seen in areas where spawning is taking place (S. H. Smith 1968a). Norden (1967a) suggested that perhaps alewives spawn but once.

In Lake Michigan alewives, the eggs are pale yellow and about 1 mm diam (Norden 1967b). Newly hatched larvae average 3.8 mm TL; the yolk-sac is absorbed 3 days later when the larvae average 5.1 mm. Larvae 19.1 mm long begin to develop adult features, and at 35 mm (1.4 in) their body form closely resembles that of the adult. Instructions for distinguishing alewife larvae from those of trout, cisco, smelt, and gizzard shad are provided by Norden.

The smallest individual containing food (copepods) was 5.9 mm long (Norden 1968). Cladocerans first appeared in the digestive tracts of 9.5-mm larvae. Cladocerans and copepods generally constitute over 75% of the total number of organisms consumed, with *Cyclops* and *Bosmina* contributing a high percentage of the plankton eaten.

According to Threinen (1958), eggs kept in the laboratory at 13.3–15.6°C (56–60°F) in running water and at 15.6–23.3°C (60–74°F) in standing water hatch in 81–132 hours. Hatching begins in 2 days and is completed at the end of 6 days at 15.6°C (60°F).

Norden (1968) noted that attempts to rear larval alewives in the laboratory failed, death occurring after the absorption of the yolk-sac, about 3 days after hatching. Heinrich (1977) overcame this problem by presenting a mixture of wild zooplankton (mostly copepod nauplii, cyclopoid copepodites, and the cladoceran *Bosmina longirostris*, ranging in maximum dimension from 0.2 to 0.9 mm) twice each day, beginning the day of hatching. The fry are both phototropic and pelagic (Threinen 1958).

Morsell and Norden (1968) found that zooplankton predominate in the stomachs of fish taken from the shore zone (0–1.2 m depth) of Lake Michigan, Milwaukee Harbor, and Green Bay; whereas *Pontoporeia*, a deepwater amphipod, predominates in the littoral (9–30-m depths) and profundal zones (depths greater than 30 m). As the lengths of the alewives increase, a progressively greater proportion of *Pontoporeia* is found. *Limnocalanus macrurus* is the dominant zooplankton in the food of alewives caught in the winter, whereas *Cyclops bicuspidatus* and *Diaptomus* sp. dominate during the other seasons. *Mysis relicta* contribute a small portion of the profundal and littoral diet for those alewives longer than 139 mm (5.5 in). Tendipedid larvae and pupae are found in alewives from all zones but are important only in the shore zone, where they contribute 58.5% of the dry weight of the stomach contents of fish in the 60–119-mm (2.4–4.7-in) size group. Filamentous algae, mostly *Cladophora*, often constitute more than 50% of the volume of stomach contents from fish taken in the shore zone of Lake Michigan and Green Bay, probably ingested incidentally to feeding on zooplankton. A few gastropods are found in alewives in the littoral zone, indicating that alewives feed on the bottom to some extent.

Gannon (1976) suggested that positive selection of *Daphnia* by alewives probably takes place in southern Green Bay, although this was not indicated in electivity indices. Laboratory studies reveal the *Daphnia* are digested most rapidly by alewives and, therefore, are under-represented in stomach contents relative to other plankton species.

Fish eggs were found by Morsell and Norden (1968) in the stomachs of 46.2% of spawning alewives and were presumed to be alewife eggs. Larger eggs from another species of fish were also found in a few stomachs of alewives collected from the littoral zone. According to Edsall (1964), during intensive spawning activity, there is considerable egg predation from both nonspawning and spawning alewives as eggs are being released during the spawning act. In addition to the alewife eggs, stomachs of the larger alewives were tightly packed with scales (probably from spottail shiners). Edsall concluded that, although large alewives may feed only lightly on alewife eggs, small alewives appear to be very effective egg consumers.

From scales and otoliths, Norden (1967a) determined ages of more than 2,000 specimens from the Milwaukee area of Lake Michigan. During the first year of life 55.7% of the total length was reached; the second year, 24.5%; the third year, 11.2%; the fourth year, 8.6%. Growth by year was: 0, about 95 mm (3.7 in); I, 139 mm (5.5 in); II, 158 mm (6.2 in); III, 172 mm (6.8 in). After alewives attain their third annulus, additional annuli are crowded and difficult to read. Norden noted that errors in aging fish having more than three annuli are apt to be greatly magnified.

A 27 June die-off sample from Sturgeon Bay provided Brown (1968) with the following age and growth (mm) values:

	II	III	IV	V	All ages
Males	135	152	166	164	154
Females	132	154	166	180	163

Preliminary studies show that males mature earlier, are recruited at a younger age to the bottom stocks and to the spawning population, and die earlier than females. Most of the age-I fish taken on 1 June 1967 by trawl in Lake Michigan off Sturgeon Bay were between 70 and 99 mm (2.8 and 3.9 in) long.

Alewives from all four inland Great Lakes are considerably smaller than the anadromous form (occasionally 360 mm) along the Atlantic Coast. According to Norden (1967a), average length of the largest alewives from Lake Michigan was 193 mm (7.6 in), while in Massachusetts spawning alewives averaged 270 mm (10.6 in). Four individuals taken off Algoma in Lake Michigan (UWSP 035) averaged 230 mm (9.1 in); four individuals taken off northern Bayfield County in Lake Superior (UWSP 2260) averaged 246 mm (9.7 in).

Threinen (1958) noted that few alewives live beyond 5 or 6 years; Van Oosten (1932) reported that they will reach an age of 8 years.

In Lake Michigan the alewife has become the dominant fish species (S. H. Smith 1968a, 1968b). In the winter, adult alewives live in the deepest water, while in the spring and fall they pass through the nearshore mid-depths. In the summer, the alewives crowd the shore. All year the young alewives can be found in the central mid-depths of the lake, where they spend their first 2 years. At one time or another during the year all zones of the lake are dominated by vast swarms of alewives competing with and often eliminating the stocks of native fishes.

Norden observed the aggressive nature of the alewife in captivity with other species of fish. When feed is introduced into the aquarium, the alewives swarm into the food and consume it while the other species move off to one side and don't feed (*Milwaukee Journal* 12 March 1972).

One aspect of its behavior which distresses man is its dying, a biological endpoint over which the alewife has little control. Brown (1968:2) stated:

> The classic population explosion, which crested in the southern and central basins of the lake in 1966 . . . was accompanied by progressively heavier spring and summer dieoffs and was climaxed by a massive mortality in June and early July 1967. The 1967 dieoff was in progress by the first week of June and reached its greatest intensity by the third week, when huge windrows of fish were deposited by wind and waves on beaches in Michigan, Indiana, Illinois and Wisconsin.

In Wisconsin the mortality extended in Lake Michigan up to Sturgeon Bay and in Green Bay along the east shore. About 70% of the alewives in Lake Michigan died during the 1967 die-off (Wells and McLain 1972).

The alewife encounters sharp changes in water temperature between the deep, cold waters of the Great Lakes and the shallow, warmer waters inshore and in the tributaries. That the fish perhaps cannot adapt to severe temperature changes is one of the most plausible explanations suggested for the mortalities. Hoar (1952) suggested that fish may lose osmotic control in warm water because of an exhausted thyroid mechanism, possibly related to low levels of iodine in fresh water.

In some studies, alewives have been observed to die when subjected to temperatures below 3.4°C (38°F) and this lack of tolerance for cold is undoubtedly why in midwinter they must seek the deepest areas of lakes where the water is warmest—usually 3.9°C (39°F) (S. H. Smith 1968a). The fact that deep water in the Great Lakes can become colder than this during severe winters may explain why alewives sometimes start to die in the deepest waters in midwinter. Midwinter die-offs tend to go unnoticed because the fish remain on the bottom and do not wash ashore.

Adult alewives from Lake Michigan acclimated to 20°C (68°F) had an estimated upper incipient (beginning) lethal temperature of 24.5°C (76.1°F) (Otto et al. 1976). Young-of-year alewives acclimated to the same temperature were tolerant to temperatures 6°C higher than adults. The ultimate lower lethal temperature for this species is about 3°C (37°F).

IMPORTANCE AND MANAGEMENT

The prolific alewife has wrought profound changes in the fish population structure in the upper Great Lakes, particularly in Lake Michigan. The following detrimental effects are often mentioned: (1) It has reduced other species of fish in the lake, including the perch, herring, chubs, and minnows, by competing with the young of those species for plankton as food and actually preying on the young of other fishes (S. H. Smith 1972). (2) The die-offs litter the beaches. (3) The fish clog intakes of power plants and municipal water filtration plants. In addition, they have small commercial value, although they constitute over 80% of the fish biomass in Lake Michigan. As S. H. Smith (1968a:12) has stated:

> An upset of the entire fishery ecology of Lake Michigan was already well underway in 1949 when the sea lamprey was consuming the last vestiges of the lake trout (*Salvelinus namaycush*) and burbot (*Lota lota*)—the only abundant and widely distributed predators of the lake. Absence of large predators left the way wide open for a small and prolific species such as the alewife. Under this condition the alewife increased with almost unbelievable swiftness. In 1960 alewives represented about 8 per cent of the poundage of fish taken in experimental trawls in Lake Michigan; by 1966 they represented over 80 per cent. When undergoing its increase the alewives have reduced or replaced all of the previously very abundant species of the lake, and upset completely a very productive and stable multi-species balance that had existed since the glaciers retreated from the Great Lakes thousands of years ago.

However, the alewife also confers some benefits: (1) It is an excellent forage fish for high-value sport and commercial species such as salmon, steelhead, and lake trout. Biologists estimate that coho salmon are now consuming 36–45 million kg (80–100 million lb) of alewives each year, which amounts to less than 5% of the alewives in Lake Michigan (Downs 1974). (2) It is currently being harvested and converted into fish meal, which is primarily used to feed poultry. It does not find a market as mink feed, although Wisconsin leads the nation in mink production and 30% of the mink's diet is fish meal; because of the high levels of PCBs (polychlorinated biphenyls) in Great Lakes fish, mink ranchers use Canadian fish meal. (3) Its use as food for humans is being studied by University of Wisconsin food scientists, who are suggesting alewife hors d'oeuvres, alewife fish sticks, and "sardines." D. Stuiber (L. Berman, *Milwaukee Journal*, 7 October 1975) describes the alewife as tasting somewhat like a sardine (with the same nutritional content), but because it is a freshwater fish, it is softer. Larger alewives, though full of small bones, may be a valuable food fish for man and can be consumed fresh, as well as dry salted, pickled, and smoked.

Poff (1974:6) summarized the commercial importance of this species:

> Since 1970 the trend has been to stable production of alewives in these waters. Each year since 1966 the commercial harvest has been in excess of 18,000,000 pounds. This is phenomenal when one considers that production was negligible prior to 1956.
>
> A major harvest occurs in the areas bordering Pensaukee and Green Bay and off the ports of Manitowoc, Two Rivers and Milwaukee in Lake Michigan proper.

In 1974, the 18 million kg of alewives harvested were valued at $525,120. They amounted to 1,360 kilotons of fish meal, about 3% of the total United States production. Hardly 2% of the estimated 1 billion kg of alewives in Lake Michigan is being harvested and converted into fish meal.

The catch is split nearly equally between trawlers and pound netters. Much of it is carried to a firm at Oconto, where, every day during the height of the fishing season between May and December, an estimated 91,000–136,000 kg of alewives are processed into cat food and fertilizer (L. Berman, *Milwaukee Journal*, 7 October 1975).

The introduction of this species into East Coast water-supply reservoirs suffering from plankton blooms and other distasteful problems has resulted in a number of successes. The plankton blooms which were clogging pipes and filters disappeared, and the alewife exhibited remarkable growth. Such biological control of plankton blooms appears to be more effective than the conventional treatment with copper sulfate. Although the alewife introduction program is still in the experimental stages, it is dispelling certain erroneous impressions that the fish is nothing more than a pest (Worthington 1976).

Skipjack Herring

Alosa chrysochloris (Rafinesque). *Alosa*—Saxon *Allis*, old name of the European shad, *Alosa alosa*; *chrysochloris*—gold-green.

Other common names: skipjack, blue herring, golden shad, river shad, river herring, shad.

Immature 106 mm, Wabash R. (Posey Co.), Indiana, 7 Sept. 1966

DESCRIPTION

Body oblong, strongly compressed laterally, depth into SL 3.4–4.0. Length 300–400 mm. Head length into SL 3.6–4.0. Mouth large, reaching below eye; lower jaw projecting beyond upper jaw. Upper and lower jaw teeth present at all ages; tongue with small teeth in 2–4 rows. Gill rakers on lower limb of first arch 20–30. Scales cycloid; lateral line absent; lateral series scales 53–60. Dorsal fin usually 17 rays, last ray not lengthened beyond the fin; dorsal fin insertion directly over or slightly in advance of pelvic fin insertion; anal fin rays about 18. Caudal fin deeply forked.

Back bluish or greenish, sides silvery with golden reflections, belly silvery. Row of vague, dusky "shoulder" spots, absent in some individuals. Scales of back with dusky bases.

DISTRIBUTION, STATUS, AND HABITAT

All Wisconsin records are from the mainstem of the Mississippi River and the St. Croix River below St. Croix Falls where the skipjack herring reaches the northern limit of its distribution. Greene (1935) examined collections from the following places: St. Croix River above the railroad bridge at Hudson (St. Croix County) (UMMZ 78081, 20 August 1928); St. Croix River at Hudson (St. Croix County); Lake Pepin at Rest Island, Minnesota (opposite Pepin County); slough of Mississippi River 3.2 km (2 mi) north of Victory (Vernon County) (UMMZ 78194, 22 August 1928). Greene had reports from Lake Pepin at Lake City, Minnesota (opposite Pepin County); Lake Pepin at Maiden Rock (Pierce County); Mississippi River at Fountain City (Buffalo County); Mississippi River at Wyalusing (Grant County); Mississippi River at Genoa (Vernon County).

Additional records: UWZM 678 (2) Lake Pepin at Lake City (Wabasha County, Minnesota) August 1904; UWZM 706 (1) St. Croix River at Hudson (St. Croix County) 25 July 1908; UWZM 794 (12) Lake Pepin at Lake City (Wabasha County, Minnesota) August 1904; MPM 689 (2) Mississippi River at Wyalusing (Grant County) 23 July 1911; MPM 599 Lake Pepin at Maiden Rock (Pierce County) 2 August 1910.

The skipjack herring is rare in South Dakota (Miller 1972) and threatened in Iowa (Roosa 1977). No recent records are available from Wisconsin waters and this species, once abundant, is extirpated (Wis. Dep. Nat. Resour. Endangered Species Com. 1975, Les 1979).

A chronology of the status of skipjack herring in the upper Mississippi River follows:

1903–1904—Wagner (1908:34): "I was never able to hook one in Lake Pepin, but while fishing for black bass in the swift waters of the Mississippi several miles below the lake, I was forced to abandon minnows as bait, as the skipjack took all of them."

1911–1913—Eddy and Underhill (1974:145–146): "Between 1911 and 1913 many specimens from Lake Pepin were forwarded to the United States Bureau of Fisheries Laboratory at Fairport, Iowa. These included both adults and young, which indicated that they must have spawned somewhere in that vicinity."

1914–1916—Coker (1930:168): "There is no question that during the three years immediately following the construction of the dam there was a decided decline in numbers of fish appearing at Keokuk and in numbers taken in Lake Pepin. The records of collections in Lake Pepin by our seining crew for the years 1914, 1915, and 1916 were as follows: 4,189 in 1914, 2,288 in 1915, and 42 in 1916. These observations led us to suppose that the fish were rapidly decreasing in numbers in the upper part of the river."

1926—Coker (1930:168): "In August, 1926, the author witnessed several seine hauls in Lake Pepin, in each of which one or two river herring were taken. . . . It was the testimony of several commercial fishermen that 'the herring were coming back.'"

1950—Eddy and Underhill (1974:146): "In about 1950 a few specimens were reported from the Mississippi River on the Wisconsin side below Prairie du Chien, but no Minnesota specimens have been reported since those of Surber at Big Stone Lake (headwaters of the Minnesota River) in 1920."

1975—Moyle (1975:26) noted that the skipjack her-

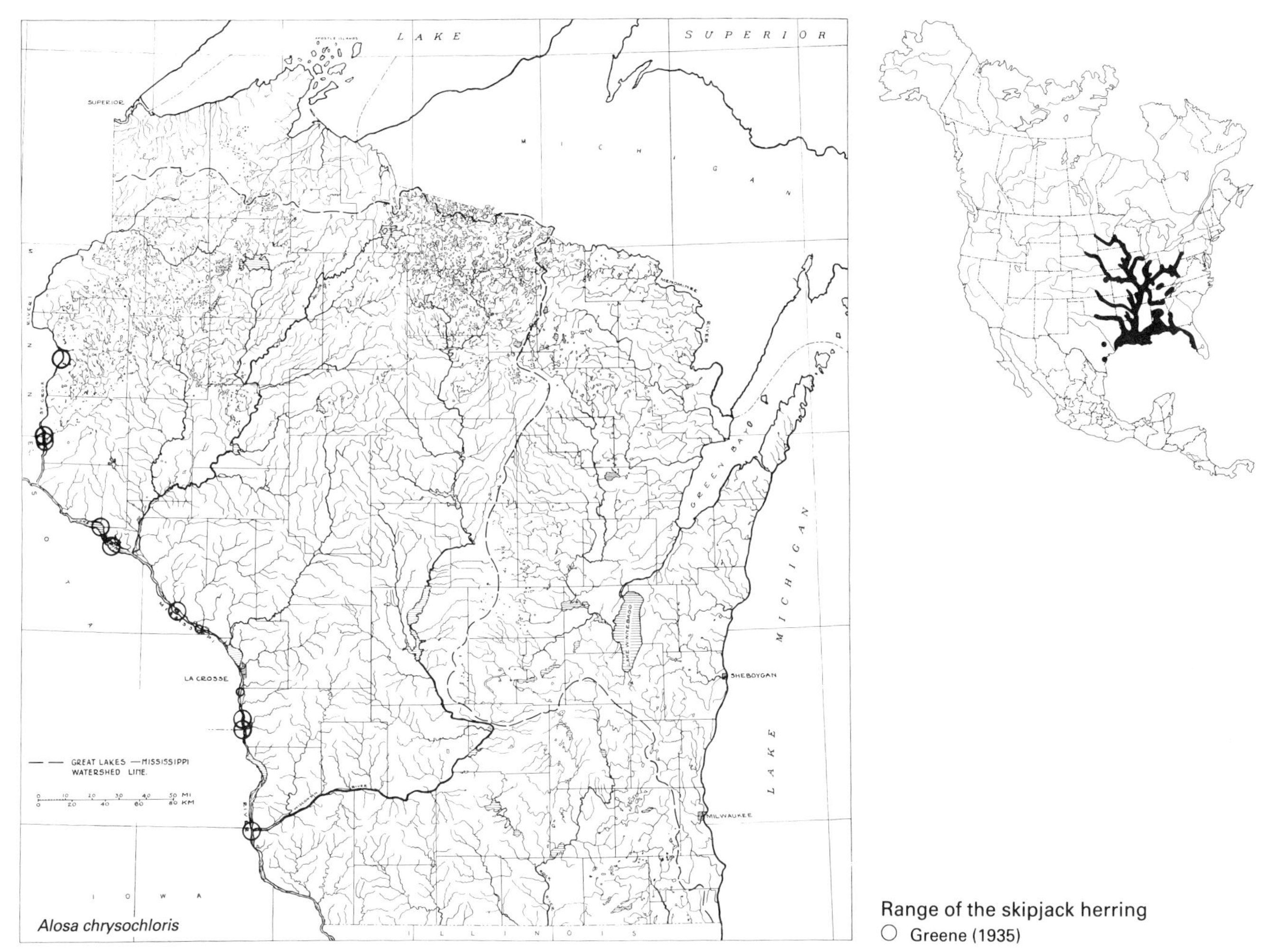

Range of the skipjack herring
○ Greene (1935)

ring is rare or extirpated in Minnesota: "It was once common in the Mississippi River as far upstream as Minneapolis, in the Lower St. Croix, and in the Minnesota River to its headwaters in Big Stone Lake. It has not been reported in recent years."

Today the skipjack herring is largely gone from the upper Mississippi River. P. W. Smith et al. (1971) noted that it is moderately common on the Mississippi River near the mouth of the Ohio River (southern tip of Illinois) and occasionally as far upstream as Pool 15 (environs of Muscatine, Iowa).

The skipjack herring inhabits the open waters of large rivers, and early in the year it often congregates in large numbers in the swift currents below dams and in the vicinity of wing dams. Occasionally it becomes an inhabitant of large river lakes. According to Trautman (1957) it appears to avoid turbid waters.

Undoubtedly one problem associated with the decline of the skipjack herring on the upper Mississippi River was its inability either to negotiate dams during the early spring migrations or to use canals bypassing the dams. Records show that great numbers of herring accumulated beneath the fastwater reaches below dams, but there is little evidence that many of the fish managed to get upstream either over or around the dams. Furthermore, nothing is known about how much unimpeded water is necessary to meet successful living and spawning requirements for this species, particularly near the northern limits of its range.

BIOLOGY

Little is known about the spawning habits of this species. At Keokuk, Iowa, fish in spawning condition were observed from the end of April through the beginning of July (Coker 1930). Although Coker was unsuccessful in determining the particular place and time of spawning, he concluded that the fish do not spawn in large aggregations, that during the spawning operations they are not readily captured by ordinary methods of fishing, and that spawning ends soon after the first of July. Fish full of roe were taken by Coker on 29 April 1914 at the very beginning of the run. Eggs and milt were exuded when pressure was applied. In 1915, eggs 0.8 mm diam were found on 24 May; 1.1 mm diam, 5 June. Milt issuing on pressure was first noted 23 June.

In Kentucky, young-of-year on 8 July were 21–30 mm SL and not completely covered with scales (Clay 1975). In Ohio, young-of-year during August were 25–102 mm (1–4 in) long and in October, 127–203 mm (5–8 in); adults, 305–406 mm (12–16 in) long, weighed 227–567 g (8–20 oz), and the largest specimen, 533 mm (21 in) long, weighed 1.59 kg (3 lb 8 oz) (Trautman 1957).

According to Harlan and Speaker (1956), the skipjack herring reaches a length of 254–305 mm (10–12 in) at maturity.

The skipjack feeds on plankton, small insect larvae, and small fishes (Eddy and Underhill 1975). In about 150 skipjack herring examined, approximately one-third were empty; a little more than one-third contained fish, chiefly minnows, with some mooneyes, gizzard shad, and others not determinable; and less than one-third contained insects and larvae, principally mayflies, some caddisflies, and others (Coker 1930).

Trautman (1957:179) described communal feeding:

> The species fed in large, swiftly swimming schools which forced the huge schools of emerald and mimic shiners to crowd together near the water's surface. Once the minnows were closely crowded together the skipjack dashed in among them, forcing the minnows to rise to the water's surface where they could be captured readily.

In pursuing its prey, the skipjack will itself frequently swim clear of the water. It is this phenomenon, recorded by many observers, that has given the fish the name "skipjack." In Lake Pepin Wagner (1908:34) noted: "Its peculiar habit of leaping out of the water while pursuing its prey is apparent here, especially at dusk, when the splashing of many specimens is almost continuous until long after dark."

The skipjack's movements are so swift that the eye can seldom follow them even in very clear water, as Eddy and Underhill (1974) noted, and its coloration also helps to obscure its movements.

In the Wabash River, Gammon (1973) noted that these fish actively avoided thermal inputs from an electrical power plant, all of which were warmer than 25.5°C (77.9°F).

IMPORTANCE AND MANAGEMENT

At one time the skipjack herring represented a very distinct economic asset because it helped perpetuate the ebony shell clam (*Fusconaia ebena*), which was regarded as the most valuable of all the pearly mussels of the Mississippi basin (Coker 1930). This clam was abundant in all the larger waters of strong current and yielded a shell of the best quality for buttons. The reproduction of the ebony shell clam, so far as all evidence goes, is accomplished largely through the parasitism of its young (glochidia) upon skipjack herring. Infection of the skipjack by larval mussels is heavy: one study showed 1,895 to 3,740 in a single fish, with a large number of fish infected (Baker 1928). By 1926, however, Coker found that the clam was a vanishing species in the upper river, and in 1929 not a living specimen of that species of clam could be found in Lake Pepin; there were only old shells (Eddy and Underhill 1974). Apparently only very old individuals are now to be found in the upper Mississippi River: a large, old specimen (103 mm) was obtained near Prairie du Chien in 1975 (Mathiak 1979).

The skipjack herring is also host to the glochidia of the mollusks *Megalonaias gigantea*, *Elliptio crassidens*, and *Anodonta grandis* (Hart and Fuller 1974).

The skipjack herring is criticized as being too bony to be of much value as a food fish and as lacking good flavor and food value. But no one faults it for its fighting qualities at the end of a line. Coker (1930:165–166) noted:

> . . . Its liveliness and vigor make it one of the gamiest fishes in the river, so that it affords real sport to the angler who fishes with live bait in swift water as about the ends of wing dams. An insight into its habits was had by the author and an aide as they fished for herring in the swift waters below the chute alongside the lock. The fish played about the boat in great numbers, darting through the water, leaping from the surface, taking the line and making the reels spin busily, only to release themselves when a strain was put upon the line. After a time it was found that the fish were taking the spindle-shaped lead in the mouth rather than the baited hook. The very swiftness of the fish prevented an earlier discovery of the trouble. With the leads removed from the lines and the bait kept close at the surface, the fish were caught in fair numbers.

The oil present in its flesh is said by fishermen to be very attractive to catfishes, and many skipjacks are caught specifically for use as jug or trotline bait (Pflieger 1975).

With the present state of knowledge, it is doubtful that any program geared to reestablishing this species will meet with success. Initially, research should be devoted to determining its life cycle and its special needs, if any, for successful propagation.

Gizzard Shad

Dorosoma cepedianum (Lesueur). *Dorosoma*—lance body; *cepedianum*—after Lacepède, naturalist and compiler of *Histoire Naturelle des Poissons* (*Natural History of the Fishes*).

Other common names: eastern gizzard shad, shad, hickory shad, mud shad, jack shad, sawbelly, hairy back, flatfish, skipjack, Norwegian herring.

Yearling 197 mm, Mississippi R. (Jackson Co.), Illinois, 1 July 1969

DESCRIPTION

Body oblong, deep, strongly compressed laterally, depth into SL 2.5–3.1. Length 270–350 mm. Head length into SL 3.2–4.0. Snout rounded, overhanging the ventral mouth; lower jaw short, fitting into upper jaw; maxillary reaching below anterior margin of eye. Jaw teeth and teeth on tongue absent (minute teeth on upper jaw in larval young, but soon lost). Gill rakers on lower limb of first arch about 190; upper and lower limbs of first gill arch subequal. Scales cycloid; lateral line absent; lateral series scales 52–70. Dorsal fin usually 10–12 rays, the last ray greatly prolonged beyond the fin (short or nonexistent in young); dorsal fin insertion slightly behind pelvic fin insertion; anal fin rays 27–34. Caudal fin deeply forked.

Back and upper sides silvery blue, grading into silvery and white on lower sides and belly. Shoulder spot prominent on young-of-year, becoming faint and disappearing early in second year of life.

Larvae separable from alewife larvae by ratio of snout to vent length/SL, values ranging 0.87–0.81 for gizzard shad larvae 3.5–19.5 mm SL (Lam and Roff 1977).

DISTRIBUTION, STATUS, AND HABITAT

The gizzard shad occurs in the Mississippi River and Lake Michigan drainage basins. It has not been reported from the Lake Superior drainage. In the Mississippi system, it is present in the St. Croix River upstream to St. Croix Falls Dam, the lower stretches of the Chippewa–Red Cedar rivers, and the Wisconsin River at least as far upstream as Portage (Columbia County). In the Lake Michigan drainage it is found in the upper and lower Fox River and in Lake Winnebago.

Although Miller (1957) presents a case for the gizzard shad's entry into Lake Michigan through the Chicago River canal, it is also probable that the Fox-Wisconsin canal at Portage (Columbia County) may have been another dispersal route. B. Moes (pers. comm.) noted that he had seen this species in Green Bay as early as 1953.

Priegel (1967a) reported it as abundant in the upper portions of the upper Fox River. It is uncommon to common in the lower third of Green Bay and rare in protected harbors along Lake Michigan. The numbers of the gizzard shad taken by the commercial fisheries in the Mississippi River have not warranted listing this species in the catch.

Although appearing in sizable numbers in some Wisconsin waters, this species has not reached pest levels. Populations appear to fluctuate greatly, undoubtedly because of the limiting effects of the low winter temperatures. Any trend, however, which warms the water (e.g., industrial hotwater effluent) may enable carryover of breeding stock through severe winters. The establishment and spread of this species in recent years in Lake Michigan may be supported by such artificial warm spots in harbors and industrial bays. At present the gizzard shad is secure in Wisconsin; it functions as a forage fish, and is an interesting part of Wisconsin's fish population.

It inhabits large rivers, reservoirs, lakes, swamps, bays, sloughs, and similar quiet open waters, from clear to very silty. Although it occurs in the relatively strong current of the upper Mississippi River, it prefers quieter waters and swarms in the sluggish lower parts of that river (Miller 1960). It is essentially an openwater species, usually living at or near the surface.

If the oxygen supply is adequate, the species may descend to depths of 33 m (108 ft), as in the Norris Reservoir in Tennessee (Miller 1960). In Green Bay during the summer and fall the gizzard shad is caught in pound, fyke, or gill nets set at 2–8 m (7–26 ft). In Lake Michigan, gizzard shad are generally caught within 1.6 km (1 mi) of shore and at depths of 6–13 m (20–43 ft) (L. Wells, pers. comm.).

BIOLOGY

In southern Wisconsin spawning occurs from late April and early May to early August. The adults may ascend smaller streams or ditches to spawn and the young are later abundant in such places if the gra-

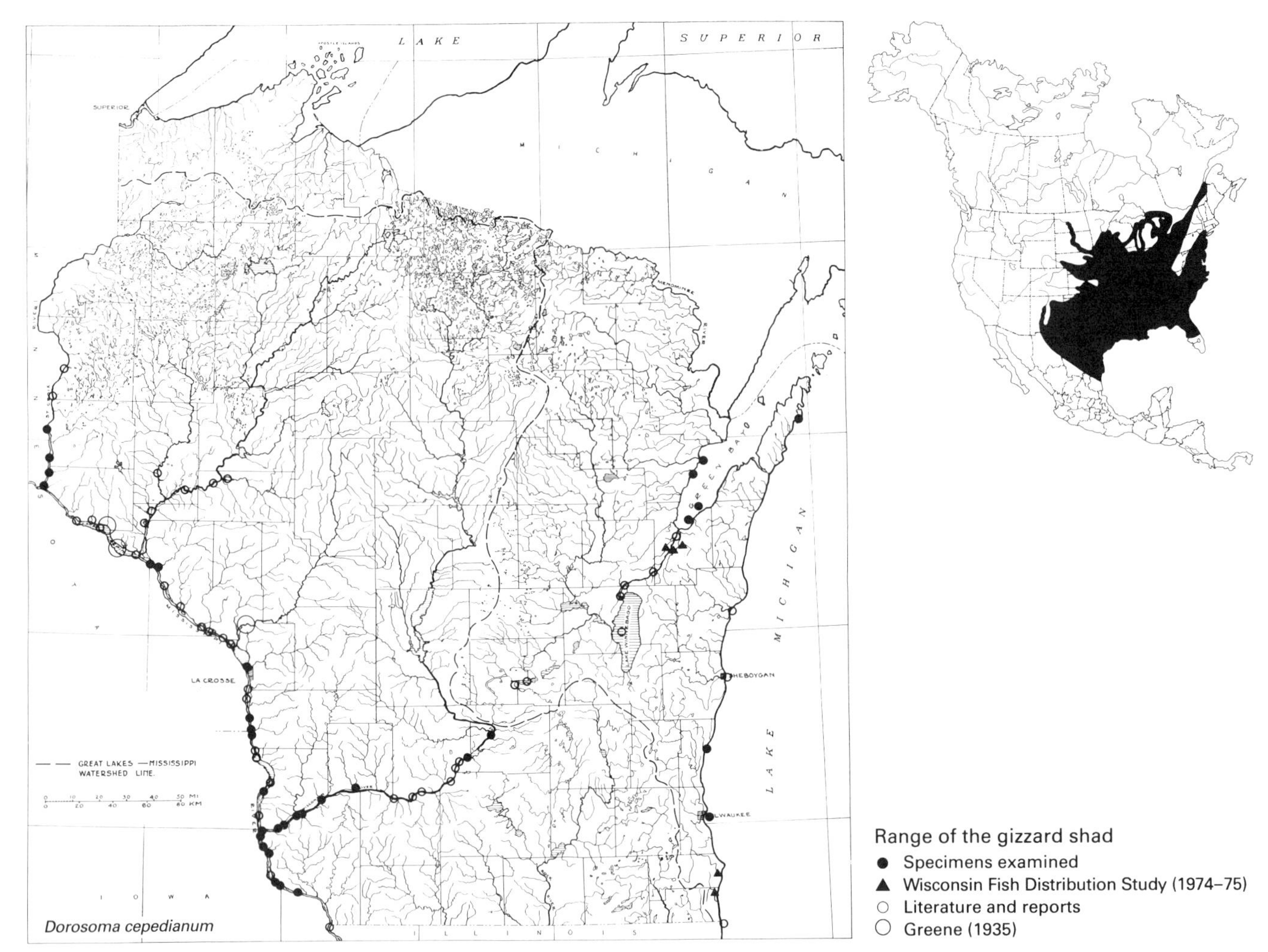

Range of the gizzard shad
● Specimens examined
▲ Wisconsin Fish Distribution Study (1974–75)
○ Literature and reports
◯ Greene (1935)

dient is sufficiently low (Miller 1960). Most populations inhabiting the warm-to-temperate waters of the United States spawn at 10–21°C (50–70°F).

According to Bodola (1966), only a few precocious male and female gizzard shad attain sexual maturity at age I. Almost all males and a good percentage of females mature at age II, and only rarely are age-III shad immature. Egg production is highest in the age-II fish, averaging 378,990 per individual.

During spawning the female is flanked on each side by males (Langlois 1954). Miller (1960:376) described the process:

> A group of males and females swimming near the surface begin to roll and tumble about each other in a mass, the eggs and sperm being ejected during this activity. The sticky eggs slowly sink to the bottom or drift with the current, readily becoming attached to any object they may contact.

The eggs, 0.75 mm diam, adhere to submerged aquatic plants and stones. Most spawning occurs at night.

Spawning sites for the gizzard shad from Green Bay or Lake Michigan are unknown, but it is likely that they may be similar to those described by Bodola (1966) for western Lake Erie. He observed shad spawning at 19.5°C (67°F) or more over a sandy, rocky bar in 0.6–1.2 m (2–4 ft) of water. After spawning, the fish returned to deeper water. That Green Bay shad probably spawn in rivers is indicated by capture of this species from the lower Fox River at De Pere (Brown County).

Not all mature eggs, according to observations of Bodola (1966), are expelled at the same time. Eggs which are not mature are held over for the next year, and those which develop to the spawning stage too late to be expelled are resorbed.

The eggs hatch into larvae 3.5 mm long after 95 hours at 16.1°C or 36 hours at 26.7°C. The movements of the newly hatched gizzard shad were an upward swimming and a downward settling—in each direction the head is foremost (Bodola 1966). This behavior continues for 3 or 4 days. On the fourth day the fry begin to swim horizontally as well as upward and downward. Their mode of swimming at this age, observed (in a petri dish) under a dissecting microscope, is largely by the pectoral fins which "vibrated seemingly with the rapidity of the wings of a bee in flight." Walburg (1976) noted that the larvae are weak swimmers for at least several weeks after hatching.

Young shad observed in an aquarium congregated on the lighted side. They began feeding about the fifth day and during the fifth or sixth day after hatching, green algae were recognized through the thin gut wall. By the 10th day they attained a length of slightly more than 6 mm (Bodola 1966).

A 22-mm young-of-year was seined from the Mississippi River (Crawford County) on 5 August 1976 (Wis. Fish Distrib. Study).

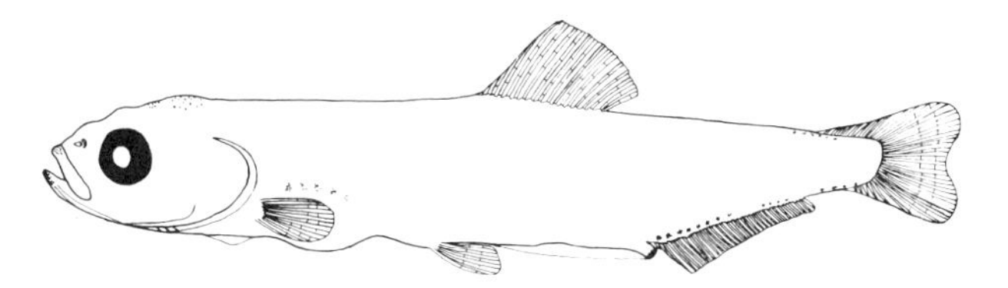

Gizzard shad 22 mm TL, Mississippi R. (Crawford Co.) 5 Aug. 1976 (drawing by D. Becker)

The annulus of the gizzard shad scale is a valid year mark and is laid down in May to July, a little later in the older fish than in the younger (Bodola 1966). Shad lengths remain practically constant from November until the time of annulus formation.

Christenson and Smith (1965) captured 716 gizzard shad from a backwater area of the Mississippi River near Fountain City (Buffalo County), ranging from 279 to 404 mm (11–15.9 in) TL. These fish were probably ages II–IV. A shad (UWSP 5427) from the Minnesota River (Hennepin County, Minnesota), 392 mm and 943 g (15.4 in and 2.1 lb), is clearly age IV. A 483-mm and 1.47-kg (19-in and 3.25-lb) gizzard shad was caught from Lake Michigan in February 1979. Shad in western Lake Erie (Bodola 1966) showed the following growth:

	SL at End of Year of Life (mm)				
	1	2	3	4	5
Males	141	273	313	343	349
Females	140	285	335	364	386

Bodola found three fish of age VI, the oldest taken. Patriarche (1953) reported an age-X fish from Lake Wappapello, Missouri.

Trautman (1957) reported an unusually large fish 521 mm and 1.6 kg (20.5 in and 3 lb 7oz). In Wisconsin a 483-mm, 1.5-kg (19-in, 3-lb 4-oz) fish was caught from Lake Michigan in February 1979.

The earliest food of the gizzard shad appears to be protozoans (Bodola 1966). At about 20 mm, shad feed almost wholly on the smaller zooplankton. After the fish grow to 30 mm, the digestive tract contains increasing percentages of phytoplankton. Bodola (p. 421) noted that the gizzard shad are filter feeders:

> . . . They filter the water of whatever particulate matter it contains. Shad captured in open waters contained mostly free-floating phytoplankton; those captured among the attached plants, such as *Cladophora*, *Myriophyllum*, and *Cera-*

Growth of the Gizzard Shad in Wisconsin

Date	Age Class	No. of Fish	TL (mm) Avg	TL (mm) Range	Calculated TL at Annulus	Location	UWSP No.
10 July	0	13	53	39–67		Mississippi R. (Grant Co.)	032
13 July	0	24	36	25–55		Green R. (Grant Co.)	027
13 July	0	39	40	28–73		Wisconsin R. (Grant Co.)	026
17 July	0	20	54	38–82		Wisconsin R. (Grant Co.)	028
13 Sept.	0	3	116	103–132		Buffalo R. (Buffalo Co.)	3214
19 Sept.	0	7	117	99–127		Mississippi R. (Grant Co.)	3216
20 Sept.	0	5	122	108–140		Wisconsin R. (Columbia Co.)	3125
21 Sept.	0	18	46	34–73[a]		Mississippi R. (Houston Co., Minn.)	3315
23 Sept.	0	4	122	116–129		St. Croix R. (Pierce Co.)	4410
24 Sept.	0	3	138	133–142		Mississippi R. (Grant Co.)	1465
24 Sept.	0	12	147	115–166		Wisconsin R. (Grant Co.)	1509
11 Oct.	0	10	140	120–160		Mississippi R. (Houston Co., Minn.)	3180
2 May	I	16	141	124–161	(Annulus not yet deposited)	Mississippi R. (LaCrosse Co.)	1836
May–Aug.	I	4	176	167–186	120	Green Bay (Oconto Co.)	2473
June–Sept.	I	1	174		121	Green Bay (Brown Co.)	2391
June–Sept.	II	1	281		I–118; II–272	Green Bay (Brown Co.)	2391
June–Sept.	II	1	296		I–110; II–283	Green Bay (Door Co.)	2479
6–13 June	II	1	276		I–104; II–235	Green Bay (Oconto Co.)	2403

[a]Late spawning—probably beginning Aug.

> *tophyllum*, ingested Cladocera, Copepoda, Rotifera, and small aquatic insect larvae; those captured in very turbid waters were filled largely with mud. That they do, however, add to their diet from the bottom debris is evidenced by the presence in the gizzard of sand particles of diameters in excess of 0.25 mm. This size of sand is not held in suspension even when the water is highly turbid. . . . The taking of sand when food is plentiful suggests its use as an aid in grinding by the gizzard—or that it may have been taken accidentally along with food.

Depending on their abundance in the water in which the fish are feeding, zooplankton or phytoplankton may predominate in the gut. Bodola noted that by the time the food reaches the intestine it has been macerated and partially digested so that it resembles mud. This fact may explain the frequently heard statement that shad eat mud.

The gizzard becomes evident in the 22.5-mm stage (Bodola 1966). In the adult it becomes a short, thick-walled muscular structure like the gizzard of a fowl; the intestine is long and much convoluted, with numerous folds on its inner surface and hundreds of pyloric caeca externally (Miller 1960). The presence of sand in the gut when ingested food is plentiful and its absence in winter when the gut is empty suggest that it may be taken as an aid in grinding the food in the gizzard. In the gizzard, algal and zooplankton items are always somewhat broken up.

Gizzard shad frequently travel in schools close to the surface. When they are surprised they will skip over the surface of the water, a habit that has caused fishermen in some places to give them the name "skipjack" (Eddy and Underhill 1974). Bodola (1966) noted that young gizzard shad are found in shallow water and the older fish in deeper water; the very oldest are captured only during the spawning season.

Severe winters limit the northern distribution of the gizzard shad. Gasaway (1970) observed large numbers of dead young-of-year shad frozen in the ice during the winters from 1954 to 1957; few survived the cold. Clark (1969) summarized temperature data for the gizzard shad as follows: preferred field temperature, 22.8–23.9°C (73–75°F); satisfactory growth, 33.9°C (93°F); upper lethal limit, 36.1°C (97°F). In White River and Ipalco Discharge, Indiana, the gizzard shad was captured at a temperature as high as 37.5°C (99.5°F) (Proffitt and Benda 1971). Clark noted that temperatures well below the lethal limit may be in the stress range. Miller (1960) stated that the species is particularly attracted by warm water flowing from industrial plants. In the Wabash River in Indiana, however, Gammon (1973) found that gizzard shad selected the coolest thermal region available, ranging from 22.2 to 28.9°C (72–84°F), and that they tended to avoid the warmer regions.

IMPORTANCE AND MANAGEMENT

The gizzard shad is host to the glochidia of the mollusks *Megalonaias gigantea*, *Elliptio dilatata*, *Anodonta grandis*, and *Arcidens confragosa* (Hart and Fuller 1974).

In the East, the gizzard shad has been taken on hooks baited with angleworm, small minnow, or even an artificial fly, but the few caught from Wisconsin waters are undoubtedly taken incidentally while fishing for other species.

Generally the gizzard shad is considered a poor bait fish, since the young are fragile and die quickly. But they have at times been gathered in large numbers for bait (*Milwaukee Journal*, January 1948):

> Durand, Wis.—Fishermen along the Chippewa River are interested in the appearance of large schools of gizzard shad. Gathering bait in unfrozen parts of the river, fishermen have been surprised at how quickly they can fill their bait cans. The shad have come up the river from Lake Pepin and the Mississippi, where they are reported to have increased by the millions.
>
> Along with the shad come flocks of seagulls to feed on them. For a time the taking of shad was prohibited but the ban has been lifted to permit bait fishermen to take them. They cannot, however, be used in any other waters than the Chippewa River.

The gizzard shad is not esteemed as food by man because of its soft, rather tasteless flesh and numerous fine bones. In the past, however, there has been a limited market for this species where a cheap fish was sought (Miller 1960). According to reports in the literature, it has also been used as hog, cattle, and trout food, and has been converted to fertilizer.

Young gizzard shad are important forage fish for sport and predator fishes. Hubbs (1934) spoke of them as "the most efficient biologically of all the forage fishes" because they are the short and efficient link in the food chain that directly connects basic plant life with sport fishes. Young-of-year about 51–127 mm (2–5 in) long form a major part of the diet of at least 17 important sport fishes (Miller 1960), and in some parts of the country the periodic mortality of the gizzard shad provides an important source of food for numerous species of waterfowl and wading birds.

Bodola (1966) reported that in Lake Erie the value of the gizzard shad as a forage fish is outweighed by the nuisance created when heavy mortality occurs and by the inconvenience caused to fishermen in whose nets they become entangled.

In some parts of its range, as in the East and the South, the gizzard shad has reached pest numbers; in some states reduction of the shad population is part of the fish management program. Under certain conditions in warm, shallow bodies of water that have a soft mud bottom, high turbidity, and relatively few predators, shad populations can explode and create problems (Hubbs 1934). Miller (1960) observed that under optimum conditions the gizzard shad is likely to get out of control, even if numbers of predator sport fishes are present, and this is particularly true if the species is not native to such waters.

The role of the gizzard shad in the ecology of fish populations is difficult to assess. Its value as a link in the food chain is not to be questioned. On the other hand, no use other than forage has been developed for shad, and their rapid growth soon makes them too large to be threatened by most predatory fish (Bodola 1966). Shad tend to overpopulate many waters to a degree that seems detrimental to other species.

In experimental gill nets fished in Lake Pepin during October 1965, when a total of 1,541 fish of 24 species were collected, the gizzard shad was the fourth most abundant species, constituting 8.2% of the catch.

Mooneye Family—Hiodontidae

The family Hiodontidae has one genus and only two species, both of which occur in Wisconsin. The mooneyes are North American in origin and distribution.

The mooneyes or "toothed herrings" superficially resemble the herrings in that they have adipose eyelids, a scaleless head, cycloid scales over the body, and a specialized scalelike projection, the axillary process, above the base of the pelvic fin. They differ in having a lateral line, prominent teeth, and the dorsal fin above the base of the anal fin rather than far forward. Also, the mooneyes lack the row of spiny scutes on the midventral ridge, so characteristic of the Clupeidae.

The mooneyes are exclusively soft-rayed, and have a large swim bladder and only a single pyloric caecum. The eggs are ovulated from the ovaries directly into the body cavity and are not conveyed through oviducts, structures present in most bony fishes. The lack of oviducts is a primitive feature.

Goldeye

Hiodon alosoides (Rafinesque). *Hiodon*—toothed hyoid; *alosoides*—shadlike, referring to the fish's general shape and similarity to shad (*Alosa*, Clupeidae). (*Amphiodon alosoides*—Greene 1935).

Other common names: Winnipeg goldeye, western goldeye, yellow herring, toothed herring, mooneye, shad mooneye, northern mooneye.

Adult male 372 mm, Wisconsin R. (Crawford Co.), 16 June 1977

DESCRIPTION

Body deep, depth into SL 2.8–3.3; greatest width into SL 8.3–12.5; midventral edge forming a fleshy keel (without serrate scales) from isthmus to vent. Length 200–300 mm. Head scaleless, length into SL 4.3–5.0; eye into SL 14–19. Snout bluntly rounded; mouth large and oblique with maxillary reaching beyond middle of pupil. Mouth well-toothed with small, sharp teeth on upper and lower jaws and roof of mouth; large, caninelike teeth on tongue. Gill rakers short, thick, 15–17. Branchiostegal rays 8–10. Dorsal fin insertion above or slightly behind anal fin insertion. Dorsal fin principal rays 9–10; anal fin principal rays 29–34, base covered by 1–3 rows of small scales. Pectoral fin 11–12 rays; pelvic fin 7 rays. Lateral line complete, almost straight; scales 57–62. Chromosomes 2n = 50 (Uyeno 1973).

Back dark blue to blue-green, upper sides and belly silvery to white. Iris of eye yellow.

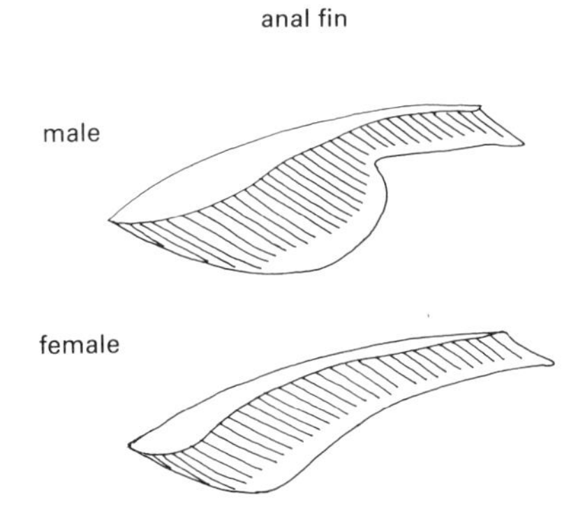

Sexual dimorphism: In mature male, anal fin with greatly expanded, round anterior lobe; in female, anal fin concave.

DISTRIBUTION, STATUS, AND HABITAT

The goldeye occurs only in the Mississippi River, the St. Croix River upstream to St. Croix Falls, and the lower Chippewa and Wisconsin rivers. The majority of records are from Nord (1967) and P. W. Smith et al. (1971). Two specimens (UWSP 4321) came from Pool 9 in 1975; two others (UWSP 2700) probably came from Pool 8. R. Sternberg (pers. comm.) reported 17 goldeyes from Lake Pepin (Pool 4) from 1967 to 1976 and 21 fish from Pool 5 from 1971 to 1974. Nord considers the goldeye uncommon in Pool 10.

The Wisconsin DNR Fish Distribution Study reported: (3) Mississippi River T4N R6W Sec 10 (Grant County) 1974; (1) Wisconsin River—South Channel T6N R6W Sec 15 (Grant County) 1977; (1) Wisconsin River T8N R2E Sec 6 (Iowa County) 1977; Wisconsin River T8N R2E Sec 11 (Iowa County) 1977; and Chippewa River T27N R10W Sec 35 (Eau Claire County) 1977.

The main distribution of the goldeye is in the western prairie provinces and states and, at our latitude, Wisconsin lies at the eastern edge of its distribution. In Wyoming it is listed as rare and endangered (Miller 1972). In the 1979 Wisconsin fishing regulations it is still classified as a rough fish, hence unprotected. On the other hand, the Wisconsin DNR Endangered Species Committee (1975) and Les (1979) accord it threatened status in Wisconsin waters.

This species frequents quiet, turbid waters of large rivers, the small lakes, ponds, and marshes connected to them, and the muddy shallows of larger lakes. According to Scott and Crossman (1973), it overwinters in deeper areas of lakes and rivers and moves toward the shallow, firm-bottomed spawning sites as the ice breaks up in the spring.

BIOLOGY

Scott and Crossman (1973:329) provided the following spawning summary:

> Spawning occurs in the spring from May to the first week in July, starting just after the ice breaks up and continuing over a period of 3–6 weeks. During this period temperature is 50°–55°F (10.0°–12.8°C). It takes place in pools in turbid rivers or in backwater lakes and ponds to these rivers. The spawning act has never been seen because of the turbidity of spawning sites, but it is assumed to take place at night. The small amount of sperm produced by the males suggests close approximation of single pairs during spawning. Females from 12 to 15 inches (305–381 mm) fork length con-

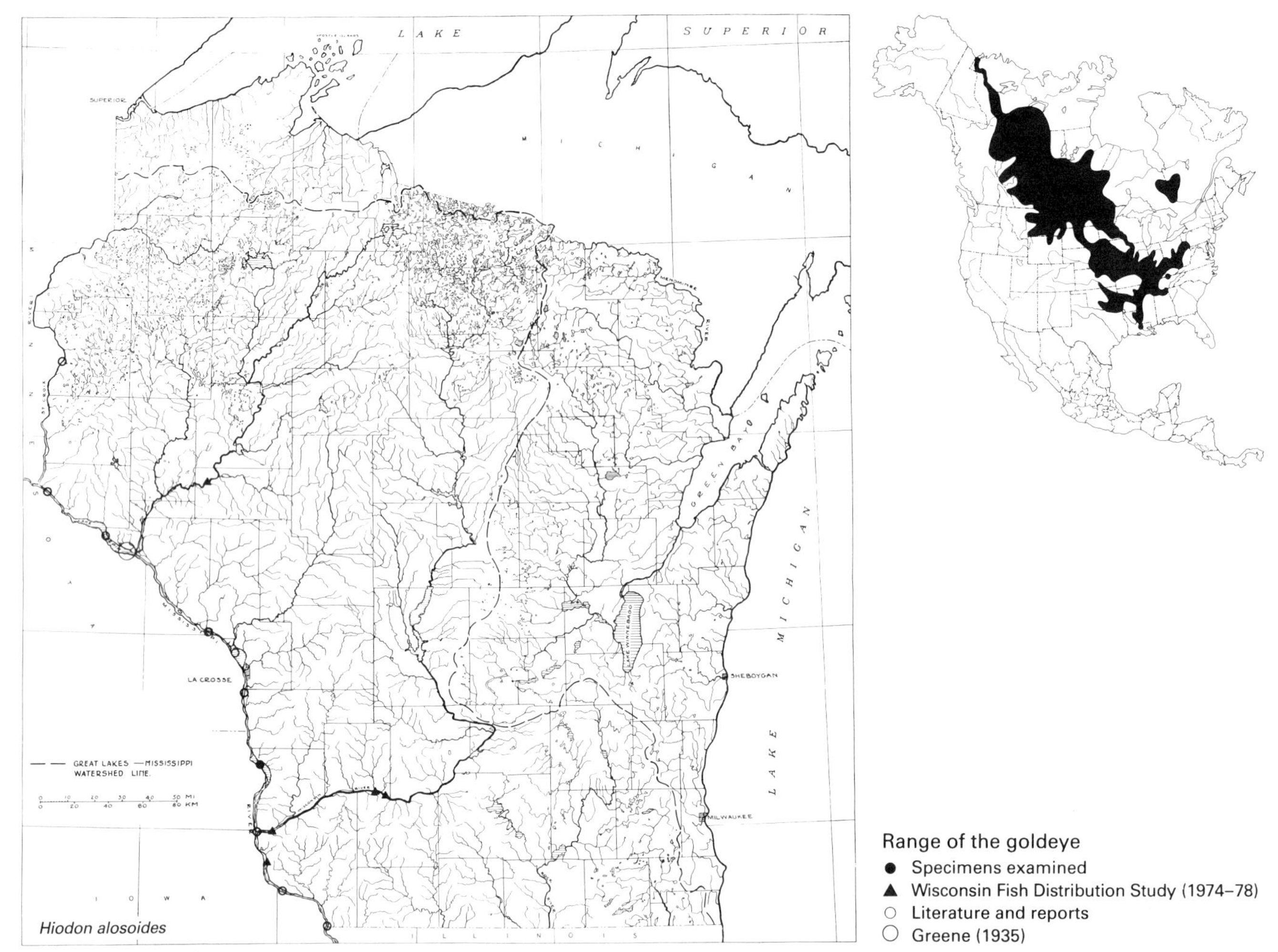

tain 5,761–25,238 eggs, which are approximately 4 mm in diameter after fertilization. Eggs contain a single, large oil globule, are steel-blue in colour when near maturity, translucent when shed and, unique among North American freshwater fishes, are semibuoyant. They hatch in about 2 weeks. Newly hatched larvae are just over 7 mm long and at first float vertically at the water surface.

Eggs spawned 7 June in Lake Mamawi, Alberta, hatched 19 June. Battle and Sprules (1960) described the early developmental stages of the goldeye and provided excellent drawings of postlarval young fish. The detailed caudal skeleton of a 19.5-mm fish was described by Cavender (1970).

Males reach maturity a year earlier than females, and the age at maturity tends to increase from south to north throughout the geographic range of the species. At our latitude some males may reach maturity at age II, but the majority of the males and females reach maturity at age III (Claflin 1963). According to Claflin, the testes of mature fish are very convoluted in the posterior region, and milt appears in isolated areas of the testes of ripe specimens. In the ripe females, the ovaries fill much of the body cavity and the eggs appear yellow because of their large fat content. Spent females have few or no eggs but possess an abundance of loose ovarian tissue in the body cavity. Claflin surmised that the relatively sharp decrease in growth in the third and fourth years of life is probably associated with the attainment of sexual maturity.

Location	No. of Fish	Calculated TL at the Annulus (mm)									Source
		1	2	3	4	5	6	7	8	9	
S. Dak., Missouri R.	266	115	200	266	302	326	343	351	358		Claflin (1963)
Minn., Red Lakes	1165	104	211	287	328	358	381	401	421	437	Grosslein and Smith (1959)
Mississippi R., Pool 9	2	117	197	229	288	317	340				UWSP 5321
Mississippi R., Pool 8(?)	2	135	225	281	333	356	381	451	462		UWSP 2700

In 17 goldeyes from Lake Pepin, the average weight was 799 g (1.76 lb), and the largest fish was 498 mm (19.6 in) TL and weighed 1.36 kg (3.0 lb). In Pool 5, 21 fish averaged 386 g (0.85 lb), and the largest fish was 406 mm (16.0 in) TL and weighed 635 g (1.4 lb) (R. Sternberg, pers. comm.). Maximum known size is a fish reported from Ohio, 508 mm (20 in) long weighing 1.42 kg (3 lb 2 oz) (Trautman 1957). Maximum age reported by Elrod and Hassler (1971) is XIV.

This species is essentially nocturnal; the eyes, having rods only, reflect light and are adapted to dim light conditions and to turbid habitat. There is a yearly upstream migration in the spring prior to spawning (Eddy and Underhill 1974, Scott and Crossman 1973); after spawning the adult fish continue upstream, apparently to feed (Scott and Crossman 1973). There is a downstream migration in the fall, and the fish are probably inactive in winter; in Canada, it has been observed that growth ceases during that period (Scott and Crossman 1973).

Results from one study showed that 75% of the oldest goldeyes were taken in midwater trawls within 5 m (16 ft) of the surface at night (Gasaway 1970). In marshes around the Saskatchewan River, movements of young fish were greatest near sundown and sunrise, and activity was generally greater at night than during the day (Grosslein and Smith 1959). Crepuscular movement was noted in the tailwater areas of Gavin's Point Dam (T. Claflin, pers. comm.).

The optimum temperature range for the goldeye, based upon selection and avoidance of thermal zones at the Wabash and Cayuga segments in Indiana, was 27–29°C (80.6–84.2°F) (Gammon 1973).

Food consists generally of almost any organism encountered, ranging from surface insects, crustaceans, and mollusks, to frogs, shrews, and mice. The goldeye has been known to eat northern pike, trout-perch, spottail shiner, yellow perch, log perch, other darters, and ninespine and brook sticklebacks. Young-of-year feed mainly on microcrustaceans, with minor amounts of insects and other invertebrates (Scott and Crossman 1973).

In Pool 19 of the Mississippi River (Hoopes 1960), *Hexagenia* naiads constituted 56% of the contents of the 44 goldeye stomachs collected; *Potamyia flava* larvae made up 19%. Immature Zygoptera and Odonata and fish formed the bulk of the remaining contents.

In the Red Lakes, Minnesota, study, the principal food organisms were aquatic insects, both larval and adult. The common occurrence of noctuid moths and fireflies in the contents of goldeye stomachs suggests that goldeyes are frequently surface feeders in shallow water (Grosslein and Smith 1959). In August 1939, Carlander (1969) found goldeyes feeding exclusively on grasshoppers in Upper Red Lake, Minnesota.

IMPORTANCE AND MANAGEMENT

Along the Mississippi River the goldeye and mooneye are generally classified as forage fish. They are eaten by northern pike, walleyes, birds, and mammals.

The angling value of the goldeye is slight, although the fish will occasionally rise to a fly or a small spinner. In Canada the usual method for catching goldeyes is to use a hook baited with insects or a small fish and held by a float about 30 cm below the surface. On light tackle goldeyes are said to provide good sport (Scott and Crossman 1973).

Reports concerning the palatability of the fresh goldeye vary. It has been described as soft, bony, and gray, but it has also been called an excellent food fish. There seems to be general agreement, however, that smoked goldeye is a gourmet delicacy. This product, whether it comes from Canada or the border states, is known as "Winnipeg goldeye," and since 1930 the demand has regularly exceeded the supply. Scott and Crossman (1973) quoted retail prices of from $3.28 to $4.40 per kilo for smoked goldeye and gave a lengthy discussion of its preparation.

The contribution of Wisconsin goldeyes as a food for human consumption is virtually nil, since the capture of goldeyes by commercial fishermen is rare. Wisconsin goldeyes and mooneyes from the Mississippi River are combined in the catch statistics, and the 498 kg (1,098 lb) reported for 1975 brought only $0.13 per kilo to the commercial fisherman (Fernholz and Crawley 1976).

In the Mississippi River between Dubuque and Burlington, Iowa, test nets in 1946 produced 84 goldeyes (0.67% of total number of fish) from 64% of the stations sampled, averaging 246 mm (122–450 mm) TL. Barnickol and Starrett (1951) noted that the goldeye was not collected in sufficient numbers to indicate potential importance as a commercial fish in that sector of the river.

It has been demonstrated that this species is vulnerable to heavy fishing. The decline in numbers of goldeyes in the Red Lakes, Minnesota, is attributable to overfishing, and it was suggested entrapment gear of some type be substituted for gill netting (Grosslein and Smith 1959).

Mooneye

Hiodon tergisus Lesueur. *Hiodon*—toothed hyoid; *tergisus*—polished, probably alluding to the fish's silvery coloring.

Other common names: toothed herring, cisco, river whitefish, notch-finned *Hiodon*, freshwater herring, white shad.

Adult male 266 mm, Wisconsin R., near Orion (Richland Co.), 28 July 1962

DESCRIPTION

Body deep, depth into SL 2.7–3.3; greatest width into SL 6.9–8.8; midventral edge forming a fleshy keel (without serrate scales) from pelvic fins to vent. Length 200–300 mm. Head scaleless, length into SL 4.2–4.8; eye into SL 14–15. Snout bluntly rounded; mouth slightly oblique with maxillary reaching, or just short of, middle of pupil. Mouth well-toothed with small, sharp teeth on upper and lower jaws, and roof of mouth; small, caninelike teeth on tongue. Gill rakers short, thick, 15–17. Branchiostegal rays 7–9, usually 8. Dorsal fin insertion in front of anal fin insertion. Dorsal fin principal rays 10–14, usually 12; anal fin principal rays 26–29, base usually covered by 2–3 rows of small scales. Pectoral fin rays 13–15; pelvic fin rays usually 7. Lateral line complete, almost straight; scales 52–57.

Back steel blue, sides silvery, belly white. Iris of eye silvery.

Sexual dimorphism: In mature male, anal fin with greatly expanded, round anterior lobe; in female, anal fin concave (p. 281).

DISTRIBUTION, STATUS AND HABITAT

The mooneye occurs in the Mississippi River and Lake Michigan drainage basins. It is not known from the Lake Superior system. It inhabits the Mississippi River, the St. Croix River upstream to the St. Croix Dam, the lower Chippewa River and its tributaries, the Eau Claire and Red Cedar rivers, the Wisconsin River upstream to the Prairie du Sac Dam, and the Kickapoo River. In the Lake Michigan drainage it occurs in the Wolf, Embarrass, and lower Fox rivers, Lakes Poygan and Winnebago, and Green Bay. The first specimen from Lake Michigan, an adult 214 mm (8.4 in) SL, was submitted for identification on 1 June 1922 by Smith Brothers, Port Washington (Van Oosten 1961).

The mooneye is endangered in Nebraska and South Dakota and rare in Michigan, Ohio, Vermont, and West Virginia (Miller 1972). In Wisconsin it is uncommon to common except in Green Bay and Lake Michigan, where it is rare.

The commercial statistics from the Mississippi River indicate that the numbers of mooneye are decreasing there. There is evidence that both the range and the density of this species is shrinking as a result of increased silting (Trautman 1957, Scott and Crossman 1973).

The mooneye is a large-water form, inhabiting the largest rivers and their interconnecting lakes. It prefers waters low in turbidity and is less tolerant of silted habitats than the goldeye.

BIOLOGY

Spawning occurs in April and May and probably later when adults migrate in large numbers up large, clear streams. On 17–19 May 1977 numbers of ripe males and females were taken from the swifter sectors of the Chippewa River between Eau Claire and Durand. The males were releasing milt and the females blue-gray eggs on handling (D. Becker, pers. comm.). A female produces 10,000–20,000 eggs.

Mooneyes hatch at about 7 mm TL as protolarvae (Snyder and Douglas 1978). In eastern Lake Erie, Fish (1932) found young at many places close inshore and at creek mouths. Larvae 12–15.5 mm long were taken on 7 June at the surface in water 5–6 m (15–19 ft) deep. The 6.5- and 14.2-mm stages were described and illustrated by Fish.

In western Lake Erie, mooneyes up to 39 mm long fed on entomostracans; those over 57 mm long, on insects and amphipods. The larger fish had taken their food largely from the surface of the water. Most of the insects had probably fallen into the water, but some were apparently caught in the act of emerging or preparing to emerge. While most of the food of fish 57–133 mm TL consisted of such insects, there were also some mayfly naiads (*Hexagenia*) and midge and caddisfly larvae (Boesel 1938).

The total stomach contents of 136 mooneyes from Pool 19 of the Mississippi River included 66% *Hexagenia* naiads and 17% *Potamyia flava* larvae (Hoopes

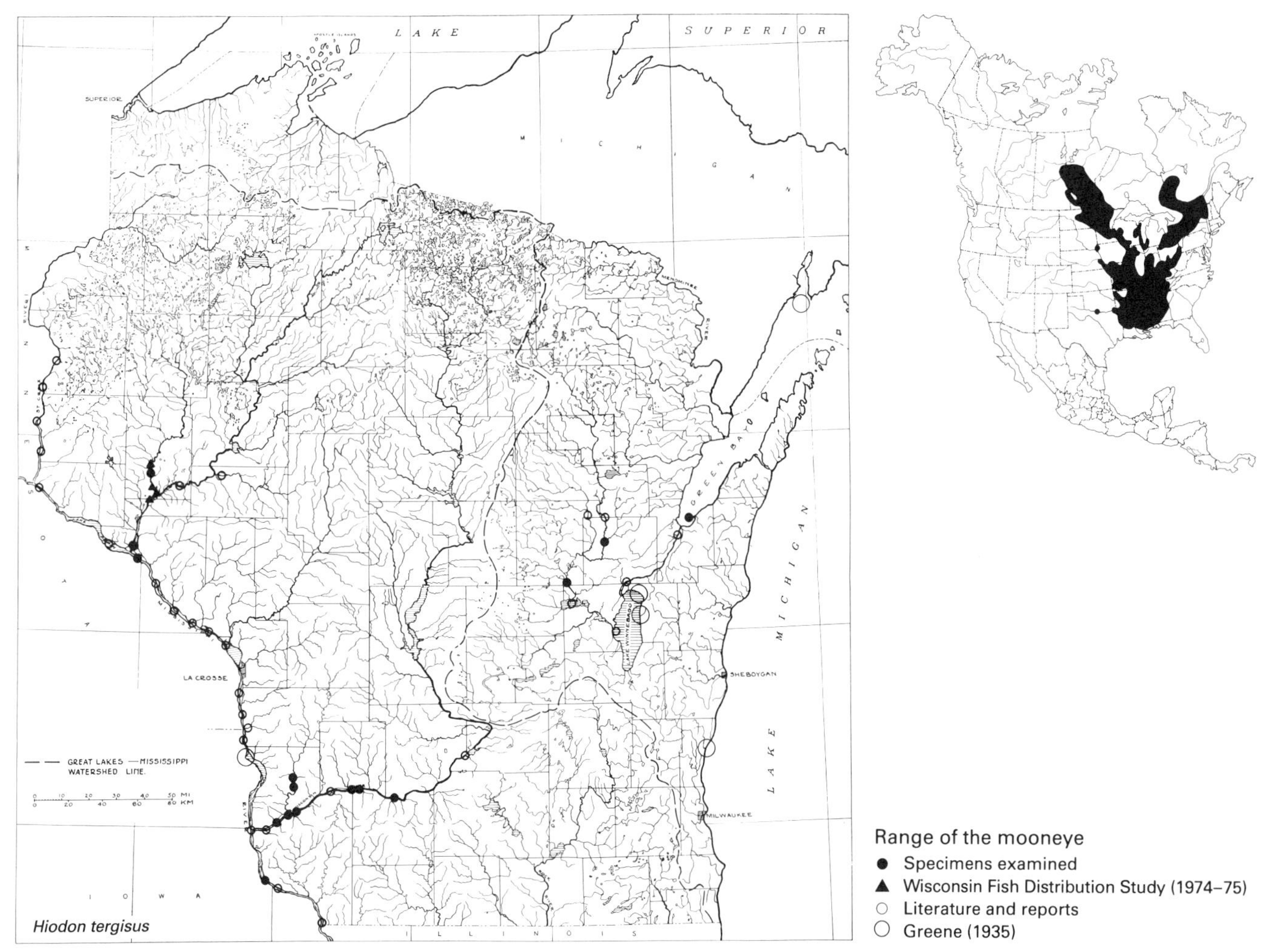

1960). Immature Plecoptera, Diptera, and Odonata made up the remainder.

In addition to terrestrial and aquatic insects, mooneyes consume mollusks, crayfish, small fishes, plankton, rotten wood, elm seeds, and other vegetable trash (Forbes 1878, Scott and Crossman 1973, Trautman 1957).

In five mooneyes (UWSP 1682) from the Wisconsin River (Richland County), the average TL calculated at each annulus was: 1—140 mm, 2—206 mm, 3—260 mm, 4—304 mm, 5—362 mm. A Wolf River female (UWSP 5575), 474 mm TL and 547 g preserved (18.7 in, 1 lb 3.3 oz) was in the 10th year of life.

A collection of 64 mooneyes from Pool 9 (Vernon and Crawford counties) of the Mississippi River, sampled from 12 to 15 June 1979, had total lengths ranging from 222 to 362 mm and weights from 116 to 546 g (P. Johnson, pers. comm.). The average lengths of the age classes taken were as follows: II—211 mm, III—255 mm, IV—300 mm, and V—350 mm.

Van Oosten (1961) gave the following calculated length and weight relationships for each age of Lake Erie mooneyes: 1—213mm (82 g), 2—244 mm (122 g), 3—295 mm (230 g), 4—310 mm (292 g), 5—320 mm (318 g), and 7— 333 mm (363 g). A 567-g (1-lb 4-oz) fish was taken from the Wisconsin River in 1977. A female from the Ohio drainage, 445 mm (17.5 in) TL, weighed 1.11 kg (2 lb 7 oz) (Trautman 1957).

Virtually all mooneyes are taken at depths less than 11 m (35 ft) (Trautman 1957). In Indiana the optimum temperature range for the mooneye, based upon selection and avoidance of thermal zones at the Wabash and Cayuga segments, is 27.5–29°C (81.5–84.2°F) (Gammon 1973). On Lake Winnebago numerous mooneyes are seen among the docks at Oshkosh on summer evenings.

IMPORTANCE AND MANAGEMENT

Occasionally a fisherman takes this species while angling for other species. The mooneye responds to artificial flies, lures, spinners, and minnows, and can provide much action, especially on light tackle. On the Wolf River, the mooneye may be called "cisco," and has been caught during the early walleye run in April.

Generally the mooneye is of minor importance as a food fish; its flesh is said to be dry, tasteless, and filled with small bones. In the Lake Pepin area it has been used locally for food—"only the dorsal part being retained in dressing" (Wagner 1908). The fish are smoked and marketed as smoked shiners; and when there are shortages of goldeye, the mooneye is often smoked and sold as goldeye (Langlois 1954).

In the Wisconsin commercial catch from the Mississippi River, mooneye and goldeye are combined in the statistics (Fernholz and Crawley 1976). Since the goldeye is rare to uncommon, it represents only a token portion of the total catch, and the figures which follow refer essentially to the mooneye. Statistics from 1953 to 1959 show catches in excess of 4,500 kg (10,000 lb) per year, with a high of 22,253 kg (49,058 lb) in 058 lb) in 1957. In the five-year period from 1971 to 1957. In the 5-year period from 1971 to 1975, the catch was 1,455, 1,295, 999, 1,754, and 498 kg, per year. The price to the commercial fisherman in 1975 was $0.13 per kilo. The mooneye is taken with seine, gill net, setlines, and buffalo and trammel nets.

Trout Family—Salmonidae

Nineteen species of trouts in five genera are known from Wisconsin. Of these, five species were established through the direct or indirect intervention of man. In the United States and Canada, 39 species in 7 genera are recognized (Robins et al. 1980).

The salmonids are medium- to large-sized fishes, and all bear an adipose fin. If the mouth is large, it is well toothed; if small, almost toothless. The scales are cycloid. The body is scaled, the head scaleless, the lateral line present, and the pelvic axillary processes present. Pyloric caeca are well developed and numerous.

Salmonids are freshwater fishes requiring low water temperatures. Some, like the Pacific salmon, are anadromous and move from large lakes up streams to spawn.

The salmonids are among the most important sport and commercial fishes in the state and provide a greater return in dollar value from Lakes Michigan and Superior than any other family of fishes. Many of Wisconsin's inland lakes and streams have important populations of native salmonids and, where conditions are suitable, additional waters have been converted into salmonid holdings through an extensive stocking program. The public views salmonids as elite fishes, surviving only in cold and clean water.

The family is composed of three subfamilies, two of which are known from Wisconsin: Salmoninae (p. 288) and Coregoninae (p. 333). A third, Thymallinae (p. 288), is represented by a single species which was native to Upper and Lower Michigan and in recent prehistory was probably present in Wisconsin waters.

Subfamily Thymallinae—Graylings

The Thymallinae have 17 or more dorsal fin rays, large scales whose embedded margins are indented, premaxillaries and maxillaries toothed, small eggs, young with parr marks, and parietals meeting at the midline (Norden 1961).

The arctic grayling, *Thymallus arcticus* (Pallas), once occupied the streams of the Lower Peninsula of Michigan from the Jordan River to the Muskegon River. The habitat of this fish in Michigan is essentially similar to that of the brook trout (Fukano et al. 1964). The eggs are laid in the shallows over sand and fine gravel. Aquatic insects and other invertebrates are its principal foods. Three reasons for the extermination of this beautiful fish in Michigan have been advanced: elimination by anglers and lumbermen using illegal methods of capture, destruction of eggs and fry by running logs in spring, and introduction of trout as predators or competitors (Hubbs and Lagler 1964, Fukano et al. 1964, Becker 1976).

Although the grayling is not native to Wisconsin, there have been numerous attempts to introduce it. Reports of the Commissioners of Fisheries of Wisconsin from 1878 to 1881 referred to grayling held in the Madison hatchery, but no stocking was recorded. In 1902, 180,000 fry were distributed from the Bayfield hatchery but no stocking locales were mentioned. In 1906, 30,000 eggs or fry were planted either in Lake Nebagamon or the Brule River by N. Clay Pierce, who had an estate on the Brule River (Douglas County). In 1908, 50,000 fry were planted in the Namekagon River at Cable (Bayfield County). The grayling was introduced into Mosquito Brook (Sawyer County) in 1937 and into Pine River (Waushara County) in 1938. No population was established anywhere.

The absence of grayling in Wisconsin may be due to the widespread distribution of brook trout in all waters which would be suitable for the grayling. It is probable that these species are not compatible and that the more aggressive brook trout persists at the expense of the grayling.

Subfamily Salmoninae—Salmon and Trout

The Salmoninae have 16 or fewer dorsal fin rays, small rounded scales, large-toothed premaxillaries and maxillaries, usually large eggs, young usually with parr marks, and parietals separate at the midline.

Wisconsin has only three native forms of this subfamily: brook trout, lake trout, and the fat lake trout (siscowet), all in the genus *Salvelinus*. Wisconsinites as well as residents of neighboring states have long been interested in coldwater fishes. Consequently, as early as the 1880s fish from Europe (brown trout), the East Coast (Atlantic salmon), and the West (rainbow trout, cutthroat trout, coho salmon, chinook salmon, pink salmon, kokanee) were being introduced into Wisconsin waters. Some of these (brown and rainbow trouts) took hold quickly and were soon reproducing naturally in their new habitats. Others have demonstrated at least partial adaptability (coho and pink salmon). In addition, a number of hatcheries and holding ponds in Wisconsin are producing millions of eggs, fingerlings, and yearlings of almost all species to meet the popular demand for bigger and better fishing.

The lake trout was for many years the mainstay of the commercial fishery of Lakes Michigan and Superior. With millions of kilograms being produced annually, the lake trout provided the state with an important food industry until the sea lamprey (in the 1940s and 1950s) destroyed it in Lake Michigan and seriously reduced it in Lake Superior. To this day the fishery is still depleted.

The brook trout is the favorite fish of thousands of Wisconsin anglers, and over 12,900 km (8,000 mi) of trout water are now listed for Wisconsin (Kmiotek 1974). All Wisconsin trout streams have recently been classified into three categories: Class 1—streams with conditions favorable for natural reproduction, with little or no stocking of hatchery fish needed to maintain good fishing; Class 2—streams with some native trout but fewer than can make use of the available food and space, with moderate to heavy stocking needed; Class 3—streams with marginal trout habitat, with stocking of legal-size trout necessary to provide trout fishing. Unfortunately, the maintenance of trout habitat does not correlate well with a growth in human population. Our native brook trout waters are deteriorating rapidly in some areas, especially in southern and eastern Wisconsin. In some headwaters, brook trout springs are guarded as irreplaceable treasures.

Opening weekend of the fishing season on many good trout streams consists of little more than elbow-to-elbow fishing and tangled lines. Even so, snagging for salmon and trout in those streams of Lake Michigan where they had been planted a few months earlier offers special rewards. The return in fish flesh for the investment in stocking is unusually high—about 7 kilos for every kilo stocked. The salmonids, especially in Lake Michigan, grow quickly on alewives and the other forage fishes available. During the early 1970s large cohos and chinooks were caught daily; several times during each season fish surpassed previous records.

It was not always so. After the sea lamprey destroyed the lake trout in Lake Michican (about 1955), the lake was nearly devoid of predators and was dominated by alewives. In 1965 the U.S. Fish and Wildlife Service began a massive reintroduction of lake trout, the traditional predator. Downs (1974:8) describes what followed:

> A year later, Michigan began to stock another predator fish that would patrol the upper and middle depths—the coho salmon. Within four years, 10.3 million coho "yearlings" had been released. Other Lake Michigan states joined enthusiastically in stocking these fish, bringing the total to 15.8 million fish by 1972. . . .
>
> In the fall of 1967, a virulent epidemic of "coho fever" struck in Michigan. Reports of three year old coho spawning off Frankfort and Manistee brought over 150,000 fishermen swarming to the water's edge. Despite storm warnings, nearly 6,000 vessels of all shapes and sizes headed out into the lake. A sudden

squall with nearly 15-foot waves capsized over 200 boats, and authorities considered it a minor miracle that only seven fishermen drowned.

Other imports, such as the chinook salmon and lake-run rainbow trout, have been stocked heavily in recent years and provide a bountiful harvest.

Meanwhile, the pink salmon, accidentally introduced into Lake Superior in 1956 at Thunder Bay, Ontario, had begun its long trek down the North Shore, infiltrating tributary streams of southern Lake Superior and northern Lakes Huron and Michigan. A species once considered unsuitable for introduction into the Great Lakes, it has become a successful exotic entirely on its own.

The stocking of kokanee (*Oncorhynchus nerka*) has met with little success in the Great Lakes basin (Becker 1976). A 283-mm, 207-g (11.2-in, 7.3-oz) male in breeding coloration was caught through the ice of a Langlade County lake in December 1976; apparently this individual was the product of private stocking. The status of this population is unknown.

Recent stocking of Atlantic salmon (*Salmo salar*) in the Lake Michigan basin has occurred primarily in streams of lower Michigan (Becker 1976). Smolts were stocked in the Boyne River each year from 1972 to 1974 and in the Platte River in 1974. Individuals from these plantings have appeared in Wisconsin waters, and several fish have been trolled in Lake Michigan off Manitowoc and Sheboygan shores. On 17 August 1976, a 88-cm, 6.15-kg (34.5-in, 13-lb 9-oz) Atlantic salmon was taken off Sheboygan (P. Schultz, pers. comm.). The state of Wisconsin attempted an Atlantic salmon release program in the Lake Superior basin. In 1972, the Department of Natural Resources imported 20,000 2- and 3-year-old Atlantic salmon from a private hatchery in Quebec to its Bayfield hatchery; and in 1973, 20,000 2-year-olds. These were released in Pike's Creek (Bayfield County). Through 1974, no Atlantic salmon were verified as having been caught in Wisconsin waters; however, one was taken off Marquette, Michigan, in the spring of 1974 (King and Swanson 1975). In 1978, 50,000 yearlings were released (J. Klingbiel, pers. comm.).

The revitalization of Lake Michigan with salmonine fish has been documented by Wells and McLain (1973) and Downs (1974); of Lake Superior, by Lawrie and Rahrer (1973) and Downs (1976).

The importation and restoration of these important fishes has brought many economic benefits. They have given new life to an ailing charter boat fishery and to the food and lodging industry along the lakes.

Unfortunately, fish and man are now threatened by man-made chemicals in the environment. DDT, dieldrin, PCBs, and other poisonous compounds reach the water and through biological magnification concentrate in the largest, oldest, and most valuable salmonid fishes.

Brown Trout

Salmo trutta Linnaeus. *Salmo*—Latin name for the salmon of the Atlantic; *trutta*—Latin for trout.

Other common names: German brown trout, German trout, Von Behr trout, English brown trout, Loch Leven trout, European brown trout, brownie, spotted trout.

Young-of-year 63 mm, Evergreen Cr. (Menominee Co.), 19 July 1966

Adult 225 mm, Crystal R. (Waupaca Co.), 24 Sept. 1971

DESCRIPTION

Body streamlined, laterally compressed. Adult stocky; caudal peduncle short and deep. Average size (age II) inland 310 mm and 317 g, Lake Michigan 546 mm and 2.5 kg, Lake Superior 498 mm and 1.55 kg. Head into TL about 4.3; mouth terminal, slightly oblique, large. Maxillary extending to below posterior edge of eye or beyond; teeth well developed on upper and lower jaws. Gill rakers 14–17. Branchiostegal rays usually 10. Dorsal fin rays 12–14; anal fin rays 10–12; pelvic fin rays 9–10. Lateral line scales 120–130. Pyloric caeca 30–60. Chromosomes 2n = 80 (Svardson 1945).

Inland brown trout brown to olive-brown shading to lighter brown on sides and creamy white below. Dorsal fin, back and sides above lateral line with large dark spots (each surrounded with light border). Few or no spots on caudal fin. Adipose fin orange to orange-red. Sides usually marked with prominent red spots with light borders. Migratory or lake-run brown trout with gray-silvery sheen, markings becoming an irregular pattern of dark crosses or checks on back and sides and gradually fading toward the belly. Young up to 125 mm with tip of chin pale or with a dusky patch or speckles much lighter than the pigment of eye; adipose fin orange; 7–10 distinct pale round spots along lateral line; dark speckling on abdomen.

Sexual dimorphism: Male lacking breeding tubercles, but developing hook on lower jaw at spawning. Female lacking breeding tubercles and hook on lower jaw.

Hybrids: Brown trout × rainbow trout, brown trout × brook trout.

The tiger trout, the brown trout × brook trout hybrid, is an extremely handsome fish, marked like a zebra, tiger, or giraffe, and apparently is less susceptible to fungus mortality, which is related to spawning stress. This hybrid is sterile. The tiger trout is a naturally occurring fish hybrid and has been taken from Little South Branch of the Pike River (Marinette County) (UWSP 3780 and 4482); Peterson Creek (Waupaca County); Tomorrow River (UWSP 1779 and 3572) and Emmons Creek (Portage County); Lunch Creek (UWSP 3543), Mecan River, West Branch White River, and Big Roche Cri Creek (Waushara County); Hatchery Creek (Sawyer County) (Sather and Threinen 1968); and Spring Creek (Chippewa County). Ten thousand hatchery-produced tiger trout were released in Door County waters of Lake Michigan in late September 1973. A 6.1-kg (13-lb 7-oz) tiger trout was caught in Lake Michigan off Kewaunee (Kewaunee County) on 25 July 1976; a 7.7-kg (17-lb) fish, off Sheboygan on 2 August 1977; and a 9.44-kg (20-lb 13-oz) fish, from the Sheboygan pier on 12 August 1978 (Sheboygan County).

DISTRIBUTION, STATUS, AND HABITAT

The brown trout occurs throughout Wisconsin and in all boundary waters except the Mississippi River. For detailed distribution see Kmiotek (1974).

This species was introduced into the United States from Central Europe in 1883. In 1887, Wisconsin imported 1,000 European brown trout eggs, which were hatched at the Bayfield Fish Hatchery. The Loch Leven or Scotch brown trout was first introduced into the United States from Scotland at approximately the same time. These two subspecies were crossbred and developed until the present strains known as the brown trout resulted (O. Brynildson et al. 1963).

The brown trout is common in coldwater streams of southern and central Wisconsin and in recent

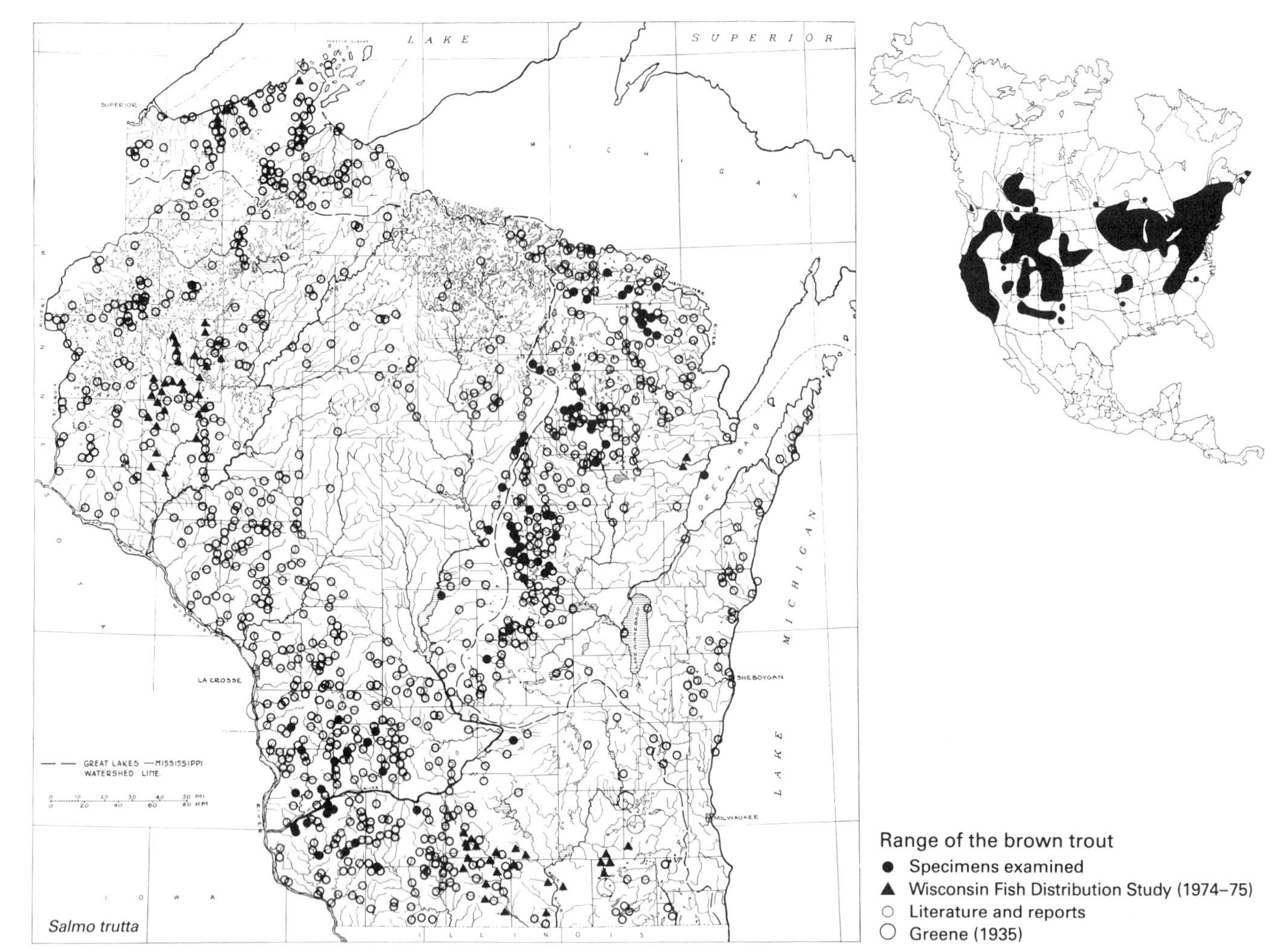

Range of the brown trout

years has assumed a larger role in stream fishing in northern Wisconsin. Although it has established self-perpetuating populations in most waters, in Lakes Michigan and Superior it is largely maintained by extensive stocking. Its future appears secure in Wisconsin.

The brown trout is best suited to waters rendered uninhabitable for brook trout because of increased summer temperatures and turbidity due to deforestation and agricultural activities. Streams containing both adult wild brook and brown trout may have mostly brook trout in the shallow headwaters and brown trout in the deeper, slower, and warmer water downstream. Frequencies of bottom types most commonly associated with this species were mud 10%, silt 15%, sand 21%, gravel 27%, rubble 14%, boulders 8%. The average width of streams where the brown trout has been found are: 1–3 m (25%), 3.1–6 m (28%), 6.1–12 m (25%), 12.1–24 m (19%), and 24.1–50 m (4%).

In the Great Lakes this species is found along the shore in relatively shallow water, seldom more than 15 m (50 ft) deep.

BIOLOGY

The brown trout spawns from October to December in waters ranging in size from large streams to small spring-fed tributaries, at depths of 15–61 cm (6–24 in).

O. Brynildson et al. (1963:5) noted:

> Seepage water is frequently present at or near the redd site. The redd is located in riffles or at the lips of pools to insure adequate circulation of water through the redd. The moving water brings oxygen to eggs and prevents deposit of silt which may suffocate them. Brown trout will spawn in areas where freezing winter water temperatures occur. But in areas where spring and seepage water is lacking, many eggs are killed.

The female excavates a saucer-shaped redd, or nest, in the gravel bottom of the stream. In streams where there is no gravel, spawning has occurred in areas of sand or hard clay particles.

The following account of spawning behavior of brown trout in the Brule River (Douglas County) was provided by A. Salli (pers. comm.). The female selects the site and builds the nest, and a single attending male defends the nest (probably only 1 in 100 males will help in nest construction). The nest is constructed through a process called "cutting," during which the pair of trout intermittently engage in courtship behavior. The male and female lie side by side or the male quivers (the male approaches the female from behind, turns his ventral side toward her, and quivers—"The sound produced is like that of a partridge taking off"). This spurs the female on with further nest construction. The female tests the nest, and when she is ready, she drops into the nest; then the male moves up, their mouths gape, and the gametes are shed in a 4-second orgasm. The female moves to the head of the nest and for half an hour cuts to cover the fertilized eggs. The male has to be present to stimulate the female to cut. During a 1-day observation period, at least 88 cuts (cutting periods) were engaged in by the female, and there were 102 courtship quivers (vibrations) by the male. Ten hours after the first spawning, a second spawning occurs. Salli observed no predation on eggs.

In the Brule River, the peak period for spawning occurs between mid-October and mid-November, with water temperatures ranging from about 12.8° to 1.7°C (55° to 35°F) (Niemuth 1967). Depth of water in which the nests are located ranges from 15 to 122 cm (6 to 48 in). The simple nest used by a pair of trout is usual, but Niemuth also reported construction of large "community" nests:

> . . . Through the individual efforts of a number of fish spawning closely together no distinct nest was formed, but a large, deep excavation and tailspill resulted. Laterally some of these community redds were several feet wide and the pit three or four feet deep. It was not uncommon to see from 6 to 12 large trout at a time in a community redd. These larger redds were built in areas where the water as well as the gravel was deeper (p. 40).

This species is considered intolerant of crowding with others of its kind, and spacing between individuals is normally observed. At certain times, however, there seem to be exceptions to this intolerance. Niemuth stated that after spawning it is not uncommon to see from 25 to 50 large brown trout in a single pool. He also observed brown trout moving upstream together in schools, spawning together, and moving downstream in collective groups. He observed some "spawning commotion," but generally speaking, the fish seemed tolerant of one another at that time.

Lake spawning has been reported from Lake Superior on rocky reefs along the shore (Eddy and Underhill 1974), and in Lake Michigan (Daly 1968b) along rocky and rubble-filled areas. Daly noted that the fish were so heavily concentrated in these areas that aggressive action and fighting occurred among the males.

In 1968, Daly observed that brown trout did not enter streams to spawn, largely because of low water flow. Unlike the salmon, the brown trout does not die after spawning, and an individual typically spawns more than once.

The number of eggs deposited by the female ranges from 400 to 2,000 or more, and is in proportion to her size. A migratory brown trout weighing 3.81 kg (8.4 lb) had a total egg production of 7,500 (Niemuth 1967). At 10.6°C (51°F) the young will hatch in 48–52 days. Needham (1969) noted that in water at 13.9°C (57°F) 30–33 days are required for hatching.

Growth of this species is rapid (O. Brynildson et al. 1963):

	Age Class			
	0 (6 mos.)	I (17 mos.)	II (29 mos.)	III (41 mos.)
Southern Wisconsin				
TL (mm)	124	259	345	421
WT (g)	17	176	434	811
Northern Wisconsin				
TL (mm)	107	193	274	330
WT (g)	11	68	201	352

Wild brown trout may mature after their second summer of life. In southern Wisconsin, some males are mature by October when they are 20 months old and 305 mm (12 in) long. In northern Wisconsin, brown trout generally do not mature until after their third summer of life unless they are growing as rapidly as their counterparts in southern Wisconsin.

Growth of the migratory brown trout in the Brule River (Niemuth 1967) is shown in the table below.

Migratory brown trout in the Brule River spend the first 2 years of life in the river, leaving the parent stream either late in the second year or early in the

	Age Class						
	III		IV		V		VI
	Males	Females	Males	Females	Males	Females	Females
TL (mm)	498	480	572	554	630	627	721
WT (kg)	1.55	1.36	2.22	2.04	2.99	2.99	4.45

third year of life. The most rapid growth occurs in early summer during their first year in the lake environment; little growth occurs during the winter. Most brown trout in the spawning population are 3 or 4 years old. There is no evidence of younger migratory brown trout entering the river on a prespawning run, as has been found in migratory rainbows.

Brown trout released into Lake Michigan in 1966 exhibited the same phenomenal growth as other salmonid species (Daly 1968b). Age-I, hatchery-raised fish were released in spring at 200 mm (8 in) and 113 g (4 oz); the following spring these trout (age II) measured 445 mm (17.5 in) and 1.59 kg (3.5 lb); 5 months later (after the second growing season in the lake), they averaged 546 mm (21.5 in) and 2.5 kg (5.5 lb).

Brown trout in Nebish Lake (Vilas County) averaged 373 mm and 524 kg (14.7 in, 1 lb 2.5 oz) at 28 months of age (O. Brynildson and Kempinger 1973).

The coefficient of condition (length–weight relationship) of brown trout usually declines during the winter months in northern Wisconsin streams, although in southern Wisconsin the average is generally high and uniform throughout the year.

A 762-mm, 6.58-kg (30-in, 14-lb 8-oz) brown trout was caught from the Rush River (Pierce County) on 5 May 1974. In Lake Michigan during 1971, a 787-mm, 8.9-kg (31-in, 19-lb 11-oz) fish was caught at Cave Point (Door County), and in August 1978 a 14.74-kg (32-lb 8-oz) fish was caught off Fox Point (Milwaukee County). In the Lake Superior basin, a 874-mm 10.43-kg (34.4-in, 23-lb) fish was captured from the Little Brule River by electrofishing in 1961; on 24 May 1971, a 13.41-kg (29-lb 9-oz) fish was captured from Lake Superior in Bayfield County. The record brown trout, weighing 17.92 kg (39.5 lb), came from Loch Awe, Scotland, more than a century ago. Longevity may be 18 or more years (Brown 1957, I:368).

In lakes, zooplankton is an important food for the smaller brown trout, although leeches, snails, pillclams, crayfish, freshwater shrimp, mayfly nymphs, and midge larvae are also eaten.

In Mt. Vernon and Black Earth creeks in southern Wisconsin, brown trout feed mainly on aquatic invertebrates during the cold months, whereas during the warm months a large part of their diet consists of terrestrial insects and worms. Results of one study indicated that brown trout up to 229 mm (9 in) in length appear to be insect feeders, but as they grow larger they turn to a crayfish and fish diet. Almost 70% of the diets of the largest brown trout are composed of young trout, sculpins, minnows, darters, and lampreys. The brown trout has a reputation for eating more fish than other trout species (O. Brynildson et al. 1963).

There are records of a brown trout having consumed a snapping turtle about the size of a silver dollar; of a 20-cm (8-in) mink in a 1.59-kg (3.5-lb) trout, and of a bluegill stuck in the throat of a helpless 3.8-kg (8-lb 5-oz) trout. Underhill caught a 35.6-cm (14-in) brown trout that contained seven medium-sized crayfish; the tail of the last victim still protruded from the trout's esophagus, "yet the glutton tried to take an imitation minnow" (Eddy and Underhill 1974). Peak feeding temperature for the brown trout is 15.6°C (60°F).

Newly stocked yearling brown trout in Lake Michigan initially inhabit water 3–15 m (10–50 ft) deep. As they grow and mature, they tend to move inshore into relatively shallow water (Daly 1968b).

The secretive habits of the brown trout make its presence almost unnoticed in many streams. These fish are generally inactive during the day, hiding in the depths of a pool or under some brush or an undercut bank. More active feeding occurs in the evening, night, and early morning. Brown trout will tolerate, without apparent difficulty, high turbidities for short periods of time, and therefore are permanent residents of many streams in southwestern Wisconsin which flood their banks (O. Brynildson et al. 1963).

Wild brown trout have been observed to disperse above and below the area where they were hatched. Fingerlings marked in such a spawning area were found scattered in limited numbers a year later up to 16 km (10 mi) below where they were marked and released. Hatchery-reared brown trout stocked as yearlings moved extensively downstream after being released in late March and early April when water levels and temperatures were unstable. During early summer or autumn, however, when water levels and temperatures were more stable in the same streams, the trout tended to move upstream from points of release (O. Brynildson et al. 1963). Stocked fingerlings moved mainly upstream.

Some migratory brown trout moved up the Brule River at a rate of 6.5 km (4 mi) per day despite electrical shock, handling, and tagging in the lower river (Niemuth 1967:18):

> The available information suggests that brown trout entering the Brule tend to move upstream through the lower one-third of the river rather quickly. Even though many trout continue their movement upstream, there is a definite tendency for many brown trout to "bunch up" and remain

in the slower, quieter water, and deeper pools found in the "meadows" area. This is particularly true in late summer and early fall prior to spawning.

Niemuth noted that brown trout movement is generally greatest when a rise in water level occurs, minimal during bright, sunny days, and increased on darker nights.

Brown trout (avg wt 1.04 kg) released in the Wisconsin waters of Lake Michigan (Daly 1968b) tended to remain within 24.2 km (15 mi) of point of release. After 1 year in the lake, however, some individuals had ranged as far as 323 km (200 mi) south to Waukegan, Illinois, and across the lake to Muskegon, Michigan.

The most active temperature range for this species is 10–18.3°C (50–65°F). The following temperatures were reported by Clark (1969): preferred temperature range in the laboratory generally for younger fish, 11.7–17.8°C (53–64°F), and recommendations by the Federal Water Pollution Control Administration for satisfactory growth 20°C (68°F) and for spawning 12.2°C (54°F). The upper lethal limit is 25.6°C (78°F), although the stress range may be well below that limit. Embody (1922) reported brown trout withstanding 28.5°C (83.3°F) briefly, and Needham (1969) noted that they will survive temperatures up to 27.2°C (81°F). Needham also cited Hewitt, who told of finding brown trout buried in gravel beds with only their dorsal fins showing, apparently in an effort to avoid uncomfortably high temperatures. The minimum dissolved oxygen tolerated at 20°C (68°F) is approximately 5 ppm; at lower temperatures lower oxygen concentrations can be tolerated.

Brown trout are frequently associated with the following species: blacknose dace, mottled sculpin, white sucker, creek chub, common shiner, bluntnose minnow, northern brook lamprey, and American brook lamprey. Other species occurring in brown trout water include the redside dace, fathead minnow, northern redbelly dace, johnny darter, and the longnose dace. Blacknose dace and mottled sculpin are considered "trout indicator" species.

IMPORTANCE AND MANAGEMENT

Although man is no doubt the adult brown trout's principal predator, otters, mergansers, and water snakes also take a toll. Dam-building by beavers results in impounding, and thus warming, waters in which the trout live, making them less suitable as habitat.

Heavy mortalities in lake-run brown trout have been caused by *Saprolegnia*, a parasitic fungus. In one spawning location, Daly (1968b) found 76% of the trout infected. He reported that the fungus invaded the lesions and scrapes produced by aggressive actions of the males, and that the females develop fungus on the head and tail regions as a result of nest-building activities.

The brown trout is highly esteemed as a food fish. The flesh is delicate and superior to the rainbow trout for eating. Its color ranges from white to pink, depending on age and diet of the fish. Generally, pinker meat is a characteristic of older and larger trout.

No other fish is considered as intelligent as a large brown trout or as difficult to catch. Larger browns are especially wary of the fisherman's hook. With skill, however, an angler may take them on either natural or artificial bait. Dry flies get good results, especially in early morning, late afternoon, and evening. Wet flies and nymphs, creepers, and sundry imitations of larval aquatic insects are used extensively. Small spinners ahead of wet flies and small metal spoons are often used, especially in the early spring or when the water is somewhat turbid. In midsummer and fall, when the water is low and clear, small flies attached to long, tapered leaders are very effective (Harlan and Speaker 1956).

Brown trout (Wisconsin DNR photo)

In lakes the brown trout is not as attracted to lantern fishing as is the rainbow trout (O. Brynildson and Kempinger 1973). Brown trout are taken by trolling, even during the day, and in Lake Michigan they are caught offshore in shallow water.

In Lake Superior from 1943 to 1955 a number of the large, migratory browns were harvested by commercial fishermen as "Sebago salmon" (Niemuth 1967); approximately 4,082 kg (9,000 lb) were harvested in 1950 and a similar amount in 1955. Since then this species has been legal only for the sport fisherman. In 1974 the average length of the trout that were taken was 467 mm (18.4 in); the total catch weighed 6,348 kg (13,994 lb) (King and Swanson 1975); in the same year 104,995 yearlings (14 per kg) were stocked in the Wisconsin waters of Lake Superior. In 1976, the sport fishery harvest in Lake Superior included 4,399 brown trout weighing 3,991 kg (8,800 lb) and in 1977, 1,943 fish weighing 1,763 kg (3,900 lb) (Sport Fish. Instit. *Bull.* No. 293, April 1978, p. 7).

In Lake Michigan the sport fishery catch of brown trout dropped from 25,000 fish in 1972 to 15,000 in 1973. Reasons for this decline are not clear, but one item which may be partly responsible is the noticeable decline of alewives—a food for the brown trout—along the beaches of Lake Michigan where in other years they had always been plentiful. (Daly et al. 1974). In 1973 most brown trout were taken by trolling (43%), followed by pier (24%), shore (18%), and stream (15%) fishing.

The habitat requirements of the brown trout are not as stringent as those of the native brook trout. As its habitat deteriorates and water temperatures become warmer, the brook trout may be seriously reduced in numbers or disappear. Habitat unsuitable for brook trout, however, may be favorable to supporting a good brown trout population, which may fill in the vacancy left by the native brook trout and continue to provide fishing. Moreover, the brown trout reaches a greater size than the brook trout and provides more trophy fishing.

Some investigators have found that under certain stream conditions habitat alteration can be an effective tool for increasing trout numbers and angler harvest (White and Brynildson 1967, Hunt 1969). Habitat alteration that is done on relatively undamaged streams, such as McKenzie Creek, and that mainly increases cover (such as installation of current deflectors and cover devices, bank revetment, brush felling, and removal of beaver dams) will probably not be rewarded by dramatic increases in the number of catchable-sized brown trout (Lowry 1971). But improving a sector of the Kinnickinnic River (St. Croix County) through fencing, planting vegetation, and installing of instream and bank stabilization devices resulted in a total trout population which quadrupled itself; in an unimproved section, the population remained static (Frankenberger 1968).

A dramatic recovery to former wild brown trout levels was demonstrated in Black Earth Creek, where high mortality occurred because of organic pollution (O. Brynildson and Mason 1975). Three years after a new sewage plant began operating in April 1968, the population had regained its original density, and after 4 years the wild brown trout had increased in numbers and weight to levels greater than those before the trout kill.

In coulee streams of southwestern Wisconsin, severe flooding prevented the trout population from reaching a high level of production; flash flooding and extended periods of turbidity were very detrimental to the trout population, especially yearling and young-of-year fish. (Frankenberger and Fassbender 1967). In Bohemian Valley habitat management techniques increased carrying capacity.

Considerable research has been devoted to the stocking and harvesting of the brown trout. In the Lower Willow River (St. Croix County), fall fingerling stocking at high densities indicated overwinter survival from 20 to 26% (Frankenberger 1969). Cost analysis on a per fish basis revealed that spring stocking of legal brown trout in numbers equal to the number of fall fingerling survivors would have been significantly cheaper and would have provided the angler with substantially larger fish.

Poisoning Nebish Lake (Vilas County) with rotenone for the removal of all fish and stocking with 4,500 fingerling brown trout and 4,500 fingerling rainbow resulted in a sport fishery harvest of trout flesh of 779 and 1,799 kg (1,717 and 3,965 lb), respectively (O. Brynildson and Kempinger 1973). For every kilogram of brown trout stocked there was a return of 5.2 kg to the creel. Six years after the initial stocking, an identical stocking was undertaken (Avery 1975), but the lake then contained adult smallmouth bass and an abundant, slow-growing yellow perch population. A month after the second stocking, large smallmouth bass captured in fyke nets regurgitated half-a-dozen fingerling trout during handling. Only one brown trout was captured during the next year, none appeared in the total angler harvest, and survival of fingerling trout in the lake was essentially nil after 5½ months.

Stocking both brown and rainbow trout in Nebish Lake had the advantage of offering the angler good fishing for large rainbow trout for 2 years and for large brown trout for 4 years after only one stocking. Where rapid production of fish flesh for the creel is not the goal and prolonged harvest of trout at lower fishing intensity is, brown trout should be stocked for future "quality" trout fishing.

Because female brown trout do not reach spawning size until their third autumn (age II), Hunt (1975) recommended establishing a size limit of at least 8 in (203 mm) statewide, or even a higher limit of perhaps 10 in (254 mm) for the southern half of the state.

Although in general introduction of the brown trout to our waters has been considered beneficial, there are nonetheless problems. W. C. Harris expressed some of these (cited by Eddy and Surber 1947:107):

> The brown trout has lost popularity among numbers of American fishing clubs and anglers because of its rapid growth, large size, and consequent ability and inclination to devastate waters in which our smaller trouts live. Being able to exist and thrive in waters of a higher temperature than is adapted to other trouts, they should never be placed in streams which the latter inhabit. True, most, if not all, of our native salmonoids are cannibals, in fresh or salt water; but owing to the size of the brown trouts and the practice of putting them in comparatively small and shallow trout streams, where they can ravage at will on fontinalis, planting of them should be discountenanced and discontinued.

Although Harris took an extreme view, he was correct in many particulars. The advantages of a brown trout stocking program have been reviewed above. It is a fact, however, that the presence of an exotic species, the brown trout, has contributed directly to the decline in range and numbers of the native brook trout, especially where habitat conditions are marginal for the brook trout.

Although the brown trout appears to have a place in our Wisconsin waters, its propagation and development should be thoughtfully limited. For instance, it seems unrealistic for fish management to destroy an entire native fish fauna in some of our waters to promote this species. This is precisely what has been done in many locales through mass poisoning procedures. The loss may not appear great now, but this may well be because of our lack of knowledge. We have not adequately determined the functions and interrelations of our native fishes, or their potential value in the aquatic ecosystem.

Rainbow Trout

Salmo gairdneri Richardson. *Salmo*—Latin name for the salmon of the Atlantic; *gairdneri*—after Dr. Meredith Gairdner, a naturalist in the employ of the Hudson's Bay Company.

Other common names: rainbow, steelhead trout, steelhead, Kamloops trout, coast rainbow trout, silver trout, Pacific trout, red-sided trout.

Adult (Wisconsin DNR photo)

DESCRIPTION

Body streamlined, laterally compressed. Average size in Lake Michigan 635–686 mm, 2.3–4.5 kg (25–27 in, 5–10 lb), in Lake Superior 533 mm, 1.68 kg (21 in, 3.7 lb). Head into TL about 5; mouth terminal, slightly oblique, large. Maxillary usually extending beyond eye; teeth well developed on upper and lower jaws. Gill rakers 16–22. Branchiostegal rays 9–13. Dorsal fin rays 10–12; anal fin rays 8–12; pelvic fin rays 9–10; pectoral fin rays 11–17. Lateral line scales 100–150. Pyloric caeca 27–80. Chromosomes 2n = 60 (Roberts 1967).

Adult blue to blue-green to brown on back, top of head, and upper sides; sides silvery to gray, sometimes with a broad, faint pink to rose stripe; many small dark or black spots mostly above lateral line, underparts whitish. Dorsal and caudal fins with rows of dark spots, adipose fin with black border and a few spots. Large, migratory adult (steelhead) of the Great Lakes and their tributaries, lustrous blue and silvery (often only faintly spotted). Young blue to green on back, whitish on sides and belly; 5–10 dark marks on back between head and dorsal fin, and 5–10 dark oval parr marks, the spaces between the marks wider than the parr marks: some small dark spots above but not below lateral line, black border of adipose fin with one or no breaks; dorsal fin with a white to orange tip and a dark leading edge.

Sexual dimorphism: Male lacking breeding tubercles, but developing hook on lower jaw at spawning. Female lacking breeding tubercles and hook on lower jaw.

Hybrids: Rainbow trout × brown trout, rainbow trout × brook trout, rainbow trout × lake trout (Schwartz 1972).

DISTRIBUTION, STATUS, AND HABITAT

The rainbow trout has been introduced statewide (Kmiotek 1974) into many streams and lakes.

In 1872 the first rainbow trout were propagated from imported spawn in private ponds, and 20,000 were reportedly liberated in Lake Geneva and the Madison lakes (Scott 1937). State hatcheries were soon established and by 1885–1886, 600,000 to 620,000 were planted at Mondovi, Juda, Mineral Point, Merrill, Milwaukee, Bloomer, Chippewa Falls, Crandon, Crivitz, Elkhart Lake, and Pine River.

The rainbow trout is common locally in streams and lakes over the state. Although it is continuously stocked in Lake Superior and its tributaries, self-perpetuating populations do occur in some large tributaries. In Lake Michigan its presence is dependent on continued stocking, and natural reproduction is insignificant. Of all our trout species, the rainbow trout is the most tolerant of high water temperatures.

This species prefers fast, whitewater sections of cool streams; however, it adapts readily to softwater, deep inland lakes. In Lakes Michigan and Superior it has a preference for shoal water 4.6–10.7 m (15–35 ft) deep (Daly 1968a) and is apt to be found in a stream influence area or near a peninsula. Although many of our streams carry stocked rainbow trout, conditions in them are not necessarily suitable for natural reproduction.

BIOLOGY

The general life cycle of this species requires a stream for spawning and early development, and a sea or large lake for maturation. Spawning occurs in the spring, and the rainbow parr generally spend the next 2 years of their lives in the parent stream, and then migrate to a large body of water. Here, 2 or more years are spent in maturation, followed by migration up the parent stream to spawn.

The following spawning information comes from Breder and Rosen (1966). The rainbow trout spawns on a rising temperature not later than 1030 hr or earlier than 1630 hr. After darkness there is little activity in either nest-building or spawning. The female alone engages in the construction of the nest, which is similar to that of the brook trout and may take as long as 2 days to excavate. The nest size is proportional to the size of the maker—larger than the female making it and deeper than her greatest body depth. Courtship consists of a vibratory performace in which the male touches the female with his snout

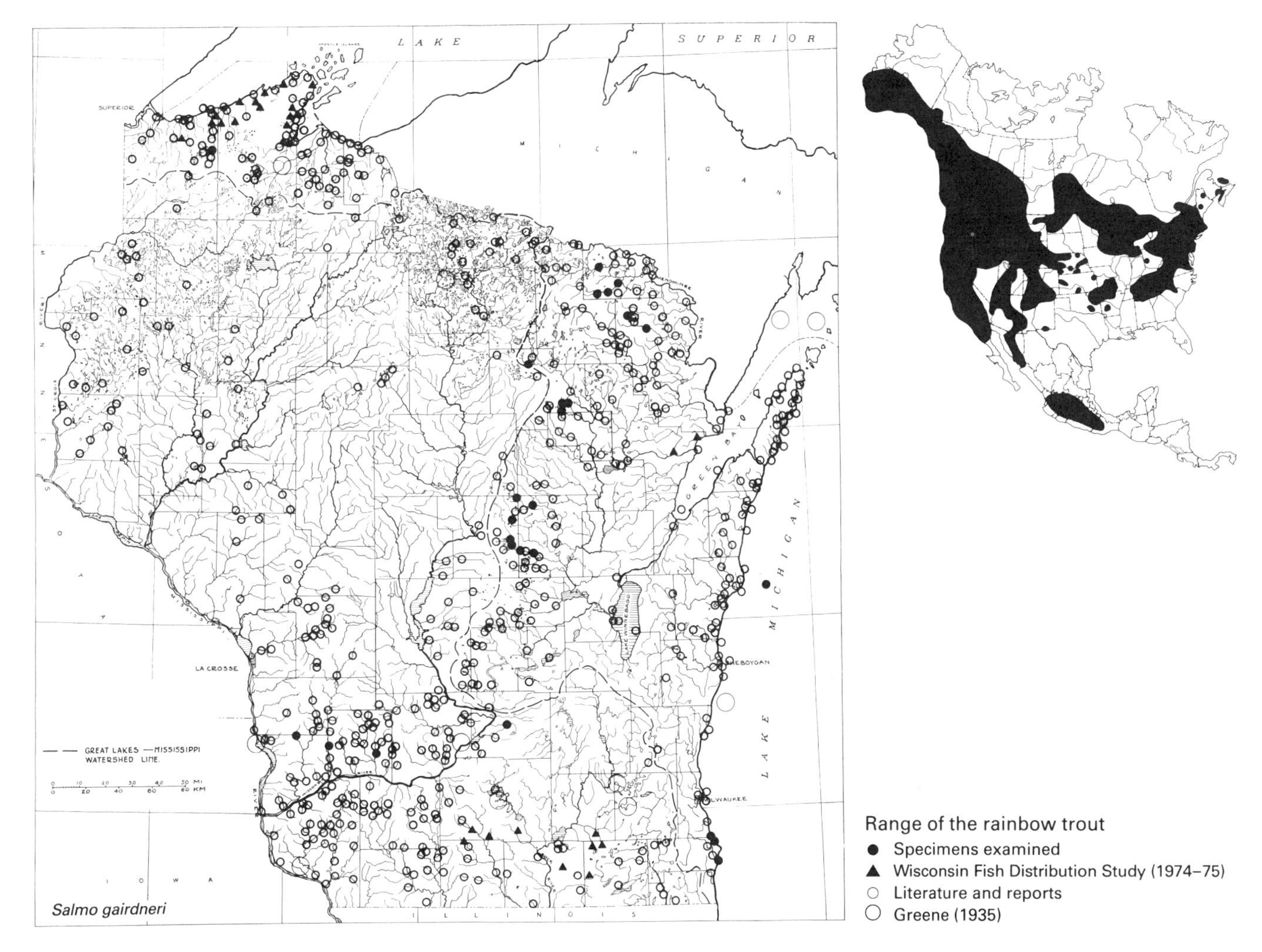

Range of the rainbow trout
- ● Specimens examined
- ▲ Wisconsin Fish Distribution Study (1974–75)
- ○ Literature and reports
- ◯ Greene (1935)

and stiffens and vibrates his body. The second phase is a simple nudging in the side of the female by the male. The third is a side-to-side swimming of the male over the female when she is resting at the bottom of the nest pit. Both male and female defend the nest against other fish; the male's vigorous defense is against intruders from downstream or the side; the female's, from upstream. In the spawning act, two males are typically present, one on either side of the female (p. 109):

> As they come into place, with fins spread against the bottom, they open their mouths. Both are seen to be tightly wedged against the female, the tails of the grouped fish in close contact. The force of the current, acting against the open mouth of each male, is transmitted into a strong pressure against the sides of the female as the three fish remain motionless for approximately five to eight seconds.

Spawning in the Brule River was documented by Niemuth (1970). The major spawning areas for migratory rainbows are located in areas almost identical to those used by the migratory brown trout. Brown trout spawning occurs in the fall; rainbow spawning starts toward the end of March and continues into May, peaking in mid-April, depending on weather conditions and the spring break-up. The primary spawning grounds in the Brule are located south of U.S. Highway 2. Four- and 5-year-olds make up the bulk of the actual spawners. During the period of greatest spawning activity, water temperatures range from 5 to 13°C (41 to 55°F). In prime areas, fish spawn in close proximity to one another with nests constructed close together. Niemuth reported that "some fighting and other spawning commotion takes place, but the fish seem to tolerate each other and the closeness of other neighboring fish does not seem to cause antagonism. It is not uncommon to see a hundred or more spawning rainbows in a relatively short stretch of the river. . . ." He also observed larger nests; it appeared as though a number of individuals used the same area and had constructed a community nest. R. Hunt (pers. comm.) refers to these as due to "superimposition": several females spawning successively at approximately the same ideal location.

In the Lake Michigan basin, spawning and nest-building was observed in Whitefish Bay Creek (Door County) and Little Scarboro and Stony creeks (Kewaunee County) (Daly 1968a, Avery 1974b).

Niemuth (1970) counted 2,200 eggs in a 432-mm (17-in) female and 3,800 in a 559-mm (22-in) female weighing 1.86 kg (4.1 lb). The incubation period varies with water temperature, averaging about 80 days at 4.4°C (40°F) and 19 days at 15.6°C (60°F) (Embody 1934). Embryonic and larval development is discussed by Knight (1963), who noted that eggs held at a constant 12.2°C (54°F) hatch in 23 days. The fry are about 18 mm long at hatching and 24 mm when they begin emerging from the gravel 2–3 weeks later (Wales 1941).

In migratory rainbow trout, growth in the stream during the first 2 years of life is slow. In Little Scarboro Creek, age-0 fish averaged 64 mm (2.5 in) in August and 86 mm (3.4 in) in October (Avery 1974b). In an April sample, age-I fish were 102 mm (4.0 in) TL; II, 163 mm (6.4 in); III, 226 mm (8.9 in). The average length of age-0 rainbow trout in Black River, Michigan, during the period from September through November was 74 mm (2.9 in) (Stauffer 1972).

Most rainbow trout observed in Avery's study migrated from Little Scarboro Creek at age I, sometime between early April and late August. A small segment of the population remained to migrate at age II, and a few individuals apparently never left the stream. In the Brule River, Niemuth (1970) found that most rainbow trout migrated at age II (range TL 157–274 mm), but peak downstream movement still occurred in May and June.

The lengths and weights of migratory adult rainbow in the Brule River for the period 1961–1965 (Niemuth 1970) are given in the table below.

In Lake Michigan the growth of stocked age-I rainbow trout has been phenomenal (Daly 1968a). The total lengths and weights for the known age groups are: I—203 mm, 0.11 kg; II—432 mm, 0.68 kg; III—635 mm, 2.27 kg; IV—686 mm, 4.54 kg; V—737 mm, 5.90 kg; VI—813 mm, 7.26 kg. Ages II through VI represent 1 through 5 years of growth in Lake Michigan. Rainbow trout weighing 2.27 kg (5 lb) in May increased to 3.2–3.6 kg (7–8 lb) by August, or a gain of 0.9–1.4 kg (2–3 lb) in 4 months.

In 1968, a 6.35-kg (14-lb) rainbow trout was caught below the North Avenue dam in the Milwaukee River. On 3 August 1973, a 9.3-kg (20.5-lb) rainbow trout was taken by trolling in Lake Michigan 15 km (9 mi) off Fox Point at a depth of approximately 14 m (45 ft). A few days later on 19 August 1973, an 11-kg (24-lb 4-oz) trout was taken off Sheboygan at a depth of 21 m (70 ft).

Excellent rainbow growth has been seen in inland lakes as well. Age-0 rainbow trout were stocked into Nebish Lake (Vilas County), a softwater lake which had been poisoned with rotenone to remove all resident fish (O. Brynildson and Kempinger 1973). Average total lengths and weights of trout captured by electrofishing, nets, and anglers (1967–1970) were: age 0 (June)—91 mm, 0.008 kg; age 0 (November)—284 mm, 0.24 kg; age I—396 mm, 0.67 kg; age II—480 mm, 1.36 kg; age III—493 mm, 1.38 kg. The fall-hatched rainbow trout, 28 months old, averaged 417 mm (16.4 in) TL in May. A similar rate of growth was recorded for winter-hatched rainbow trout released as May and June fingerlings in neighboring softwater Weber Lake (Burdick and Cooper 1956).

Rainbow trout stocked in Black Earth Creek in June at 76–127 mm TL averaged 241 mm (9.5 in) the following April (O. Brynildson et al. 1966).

Average growth of rainbow trout in Nebish Lake at all ages was better than the average growth of rainbow and brown trout in most other Wisconsin streams (O. Brynildson and Christenson 1961, O. Brynildson et al. 1966, Mason et al. 1966) and in inland lakes (O. Brynildson 1958, O. Brynildson and Christenson 1961, Mason et al. 1966).

Rainbow growth varies greatly among waters, the sizes ranging from those in small streams where adults rarely reach 203 mm (8 in), to those in Lakes Superior and Michigan, where individuals exceed 4.5–6.8 kg (10–15 lb). Rainbows can live as long as 7–11 years, depending on strain and locality, but few live more than 6.

This species eats a wide variety of foods, depending largely on availability. Immature and adult aquatic insects (principally caddisflies, mayflies, and dipterans), zooplankton, terrestrial insects, and fish are usually the most significant foods, although their relative importance varies greatly between waters

	Age Class							
	III	IV		V		VI		VII
	Both Sexes	Males	Females	Males	Females	Males	Females	Females
TL (mm)	361	483	486	579	574	630	650	734
WT (kg)	0.54	1.18	1.23	1.95	1.95	2.63	3.04	4.85
No. of Fish	203	72	107	97	130	17	31	2

and seasons (McAfee 1966). Other foods which are eaten less extensively, but which may be important locally at certain times, are oligochaetes, mollusks, fish eggs, amphipods, and algae. Unlike other North American trout, rainbows occasionally eat considerable quantities of vegetation, including algae and higher aquatic plants.

In Lake Michigan the alewife is the rainbow's primary food: one 3.63-kg (8-lb) rainbow contained the remains of 38 partially digested alewives (Daly 1968a).

O. Brynildson and Kempinger (1973) suggested that, for rapid growth, rainbow trout should be stocked in *Daphnia*-rich lakes; i.e., those lakes containing at least 10 1-mm-and-larger *Daphnia* per liter. Studies demonstrated that rainbow trout 178–432 mm (7–17 in) TL (O. Brynildson 1958, 1960, 1961, 1969) preyed mainly on crustaceans 1 mm and larger. In other Wisconsin lakes *Daphnia* was the major planktonic crustacean consumed by rainbow trout (W. E. Johnson and Hasler 1954).

Stocked rainbow trout in a northern Wisconsin spring pond fed upon immature chironomids, corixids, snails, and zooplankton (Carline et al. 1976). Whenever *Daphnia* were available, they were consumed in large numbers. Although forage fish were abundant in the pond, they did not constitute a significant part of the trout's diet.

This species has the reputation of being very mobile. Young fish have a strong tendency to move downstream, which has often resulted in the complete loss of rainbows shortly after they are stocked in a stream.

Migratory rainbows arrive in the Brule River from September to October and do not leave again until the following spring (April and May) (Niemuth 1970). After spawning they tend to move downstream out of the spawning areas and eventually out of the river. Although there is a spring run from Lake Superior for spawning, the fall-run rainbows constitute the backbone of the spawning population. Other smaller tributary streams, however, are known to have only spring rainbow spawning runs (e.g., Pikes Creek, Bayfield County).

Movement upstream in the fall migration is gradual from pool to pool and from one run to another (Niemuth 1970). The fish are usually most active during times of subdued light (cloudy days or towards dark) or at night, and when the water is relatively high and turbid.

According to Niemuth, downstream movement of smolts (age 1) was greatest at water temperatures of 13.3–20°C (56–68°F). Very limited activity was noted when water temperatures were below 8.9°C (48°F). Movement was greatest at times of declining water levels. Although the peak of the exodus for parr rainbows occurs in May, June, and early July, there seems to be a continuous trickle downstream throughout the summer and into the fall months. In the Black River, Michigan, Stauffer (1972) noted that most downstream migration occurred between 21 May and 30 June, at night, on subsiding water levels at water temperatures of 9–17°C (48.2–62.6°F).

A Brule River rainbow was caught in the Traverse River, Michigan, over 323 km (200 mi) on a straight-line measurement from the Brule River (Niemuth 1970). Another was taken over 161 km (100 mi) away, at the mouth of the Kodonce River of Minnesota's North Shore. Rainbows tagged in the Wisconsin waters of Lake Michigan (Daly 1968a) were recovered from streams in eastern Lake Michigan, as far south as the Indiana shore, and in Lake Huron (as far south as Saginaw Bay). Trout in spawning condition tagged in one stream have left that stream and ascended another stream where they were caught by anglers. Stream quality did not apparently have any bearing on such movement: trout tagged and released in Hibbard's Creek were captured in Stony Creek a month later, and the reverse occurred just as often.

Of all the trout, the rainbow is the most tolerant of a wide range of temperatures, from about 0.0 to 28.3°C (32–83°) (Embody 1934). When water temperatures are below 21.1°C (70°F), rainbow trout are usually near the surface, but as the upper layers become warmer, they move downward, tending to concentrate at levels between 15.6 and 21.1°C (60–70°F). Although they prefer well-oxygenated water, they can survive at very low oxygen levels, especially at lower temperatures and after longer periods of acclimation. For example, for wild New York rainbows averaging 97 mm (3¾ in), mean lethal oxygen concentrations ranged from 1.05 ppm at 11.1°C (52°F) to 1.51 ppm at 20°C (68°F) (Burdick et al. 1954). Rainbows do well in water of varying pH, ranging from at least 5.8 to 9.5.

IMPORTANCE AND MANAGEMENT

Numerous animals prey on the rainbow trout, including crayfish, insects, sculpins, black bass, trout, kingfisher, great blue heron, merganser, osprey, otter, raccoon, and bear (McAfee 1966b). Carline et al. (1976) suggested that kingfishers and—to a lesser degree—great blue herons are a major factor influencing trout survival in a northern Wisconsin spring pond. Since the lamprey eradication program has been in effect, the incidence of lamprey scarring on rainbows is very low. Niemuth (1970) noted that only

9 of more than 700 migratory rainbows handled bore lamprey scars or wounds, and these were confined primarily to larger fish (avg 540 mm).

There is no trout of comparable size that surpasses the rainbow in fighting qualities. Anglers like the rainbow because it is less wary than the brown trout, prefers faster water, and puts up a spectacular fight. It is a fine fish for eating—baked, fried, or smoked; however, many consider it the least delectable of the trout.

This species has been taken with a variety of baits. Stream fishermen catch rainbows on worms, insects, artificial flies, and minnows. Migratory trout are most often caught on salmon eggs or metal lures. In the big lakes they have been trolled for with boats or taken by spincasting from piers and breakwaters. In inland lakes a high percentage are caught at night by anglers stillfishing with corn, cheese, mayfly nymphs, and worms under the glare of gas lanterns.

A voluntary creel census conducted on the Brule River during 1962–1964 resulted in the registration of 938 rainbows weighing a total of 1,569 kg (3,458 lb). The average length registered was 528 mm (20.8 in), and the average weight was 1.68 kg (3.7 lb). The largest fish was 808 mm (31.8 in), and the heaviest was 6.12 kg (13.5 lb) (Niemuth 1970). In 1974, rainbow trout caught in the Lake Superior sport fishery (King and Swanson 1975) weighed 9,181 kg (20,240 lb) and constituted 29.4% of the harvest by weight. In 1976 the sport fishery harvest included 10,940 rainbow trout weighing a total of 12,406 kg (27,351 lb), and in 1977 the 7,647 harvested fish weighed a total of 8,671 kg (19,117 lb) (Sport Fish. Instit. *Bull.* No. 293, April 1978, p. 7).

In Lake Michigan the initial stocking of rainbow trout was made directly into selected streams to acclimate the fish before they entered the lake and to develop a tendency for homing to the stream of release (Daly 1968a). This procedure was discontinued after the first year because so many of the newly stocked fish were caught by fishermen before they got to Lake Michigan. Rainbows are now stocked directly into Lake Michigan at selected planting sites from Kenosha County northward. In Lake Michigan, rainbows finished a strong third in the creel in 1973, behind lake trout and coho salmon (Daly et al. 1974). Almost 33,000 were taken, mostly from the central and northern portions of the Wisconsin shoreline, about one-third of them by trolling.

Much experimental work in rainbow trout management has been carried on in Wisconsin. A number of strains of rainbow trout have been imported and stocked. In the late 1950s Crystal Lake in Vilas County was stocked with Kamloops trout. Nonmigratory strains of trout have been placed in streams in hopes of establishing permanent populations. In Wisconsin and other places, a strain of rainbow trout that spawns in the fall has been developed, primarily for hatchery production (Niemuth 1970). Spawning has been induced prematurely in trout with the aid of pituitary glands of carp (Hasler et al. 1939). Some male rainbows of hatchery origin may reach maturity in the fall, but most of the hatchery-stocked rainbows revert back to spring spawning characteristics when stocked in lakes and streams.

The rapid growth of trout in softwater Lake Nebish (Vilas County) demonstrates that such lakes can support fast-growing stocks if their production capacities are not taxed by large populations of stunted panfish (O. Brynildson and Kempinger 1973). In 1966 Lake Nebish was poisoned with rotenone to remove all resident fish and stocked the following year with 4,500 young-of-year rainbow trout. During the next 4½ years, 15 kg of rainbow trout were harvested by anglers for each kilogram stocked. In nearby Weber Lake (also a rotenone-treated lake), the stocking/harvest ratio was 4.4 kg harvested for each kilogram of rainbow stocked (Burdick and Cooper 1956). In 1973 Avery (1975) restocked Nebish Lake with 4,500 rainbow trout fingerlings, but by then there were smallmouth bass and numerous slow-growing yellow perch in the lake. Almost all of the trout died during the first 5½ months after they were put into the lake, and Avery suggested that stocking in a "two-story" lake with a competing fish population was inadvisable, partly, at least, because of fish predation.

Overstocking trout in some waters may lead to fewer returns. In a spring pond in Shawano County, Carline et al. (1976) determined that stocking with more than 100 kg/ha of trout resulted in a negative overwinter change in survival and biomass; when fall stocking was less than 100 kg/ha, overwinter growth rates and survival would be high and biomass would increase.

When domesticated brown and rainbow trout were released in Nebish Lake, Black Earth Creek, and Devil's Lake as June fingerlings or as April yearlings, production of the rainbow trout was greater, mainly because they survived better than the brown trout. When the trout were stocked in lakes, the growth of the rainbow trout was more rapid than the growth of the brown trout (O. Brynildson et al. 1966, C. Brynildson et al. 1970, O. Brynildson and Kempinger 1973). When both brown and rainbow trout were stocked in Nebish Lake at the same time, anglers were subsequently able to fish for large rainbow trout for 2 years and for large brown trout for 4 years.

Rainbow trout in inland streams are easily caught and, with the current size limit of 6 in (152 mm), they are often eliminated in many waters before reaching reproductive size. Female rainbow trout do not attain spawning size until their third autumn (age II), when they are approximately 254–305 mm (10–12 in) long. A size limit of at least 8 in (203 mm) statewide or, for the southern half of the state, a limit of perhaps 10 in (254 mm) has been proposed by Hunt (1975).

It has been demonstrated that remarkable salmonid growth can follow wholesale destruction by poisoning of the intrinsic fish population of a lake, and it has also been shown that such benefits are generally short-lived. For each apparent success there are a number of demonstrable failures. Since management plans are still experimental, care must be exercised to assure that the natural system will not be disturbed to the loss of native fishes and other organisms that may occur from the poisoning. The integrity of the natural system in every body of water is of top priority in any well-conceived management program.

Pink Salmon

Oncorhynchus gorbuscha (Walbaum). *Oncorhynchus*—hooked snout; *gorbuscha*—Russian name for this fish in Alaska.

Other common names: pink, humpback salmon, humpback.

Adult male 402 mm, Little Sioux R. (Bayfield Co.), 10 Sept. 1971

DESCRIPTION

Body streamlined, laterally compressed. Average size in Great Lakes 419 mm (16.5 in) TL. Head into TL 5 (less in breeding males). Eye small; snout greatly elongated; mouth terminal, slightly oblique, large. Maxillary extending beyond eye; teeth well developed on upper and lower jaws. Gill rakers 24–35. Branchiostegal rays 9–15. Dorsal fin rays 10–15; anal fin rays 13–19; pelvic fin rays 9–11; pectoral fin rays 14–17. Lateral line scales 147–205. Pyloric caeca 95–224. Chromosomes 2n = 52 (Roberts 1967).

Adult steel blue to blue-green on back, sides silvery, belly white; large dark spots (some as large as eye diameter) on back, upper sides, and on both lobes of caudal fin. Breeding males with head and back darker, sides pale red with brown to olive green blotches. Young blue-green on back, sides silvery, lacking parr marks, fins without black spots.

Sexual dimorphism: Breeding male lacking breeding tubercles but with prolonged hooked snout, mouth much deformed and gaping, and large hump before dorsal fin. Female lacking breeding tubercles, hooked snout, deformed mouth, or hump before dorsal fin.

Hybrids: Pink salmon × chinook salmon, pink salmon × coho salmon, pink salmon × sockeye salmon (Schwartz 1972).

DISTRIBUTION, STATUS, AND HABITAT

The successful, although accidental, introduction of this species into the Great Lakes is documented by Schumacher and Eddy (1960), Schumacher and Hale (1962), and Parsons (1973). In 1956 about 21,000 surplus fingerlings (1955 year-class) from the hatchery at Port Arthur, Ontario, were disposed of into the Current River, which flows into Lake Superior. By 1975 the pink salmon had distributed itself throughout Lake Superior and northern Lakes Huron and Michigan (Wagner 1976). It has spawned in 5 Wisconsin and 32 Michigan streams tributary to Lake Superior, 2 Michigan streams tributary to Lake Huron, and 6 Michigan streams tributary to Lake Michigan.

The first Wisconsin record (UWSP 5049) was a male collected with electrofishing gear 91 m (100 yards) upstream from the mouth of Little Sioux River (Bayfield County) on 10 September 1971.

In Wisconsin the pink salmon has been reported from the following streams (upstream distance in parentheses): Onion River (0.8 km), Sioux River (1.6 km) and its tributary, the Little Sioux River (0.8 km), and Fish Creek (8.1 km), all of Bayfield County; Montreal River (1.6 km) of Iron County (King et al. 1976). In the Lake Michigan basin it was reported in 1973 from the Ford River (Delta County, Michigan) less than 40 km from Door County, Wisconsin. In September 1977, a pink salmon, more than 483 mm long and weighing 964 g (more than 19 in, and weighing 2 lb 2 oz), was taken by angling below the Peshtigo Dam in the Peshtigo River (*Marinette Eagle-Star* 7 March 1978). This is the first Wisconsin record for the Lake Michigan basin.

During its maturation period the pink salmon of the Great Lakes is a pelagic species, occurring in open water near the surface, seldom at the bottom. Upon maturation it moves up tributary streams until it finds a gravel area suitable for spawning.

BIOLOGY

The pink salmon follows a 2-year cycle: each generation begins with the deposition of eggs and ends with the death of the spawning adult 2 years later. The strain in the Great Lakes is known as an "odd-year line," spawning every odd year, e.g., 1957, 1959, 1961, although an even-year spawning occurred in a Minnesota stream in 1976 (R. Daly, pers. comm.).

Spawning begins during the second week of September and is completed by the first week in October. Generally, spawning salmon are observed only in the first gravel area upstream from the mouth of the stream (Wagner and Stauffer 1975). In some Wisconsin streams tributary to Lake Superior, upstream migration may exceed 8 km (5 mi); in the Sturgeon River (Houghton County, Michigan) salmon runs of 65–81 km (40–50 mi) have been reported (Wagner 1976). In the Peshtigo River (Marinette County) upstream migration is more than 15 km (9 mi).

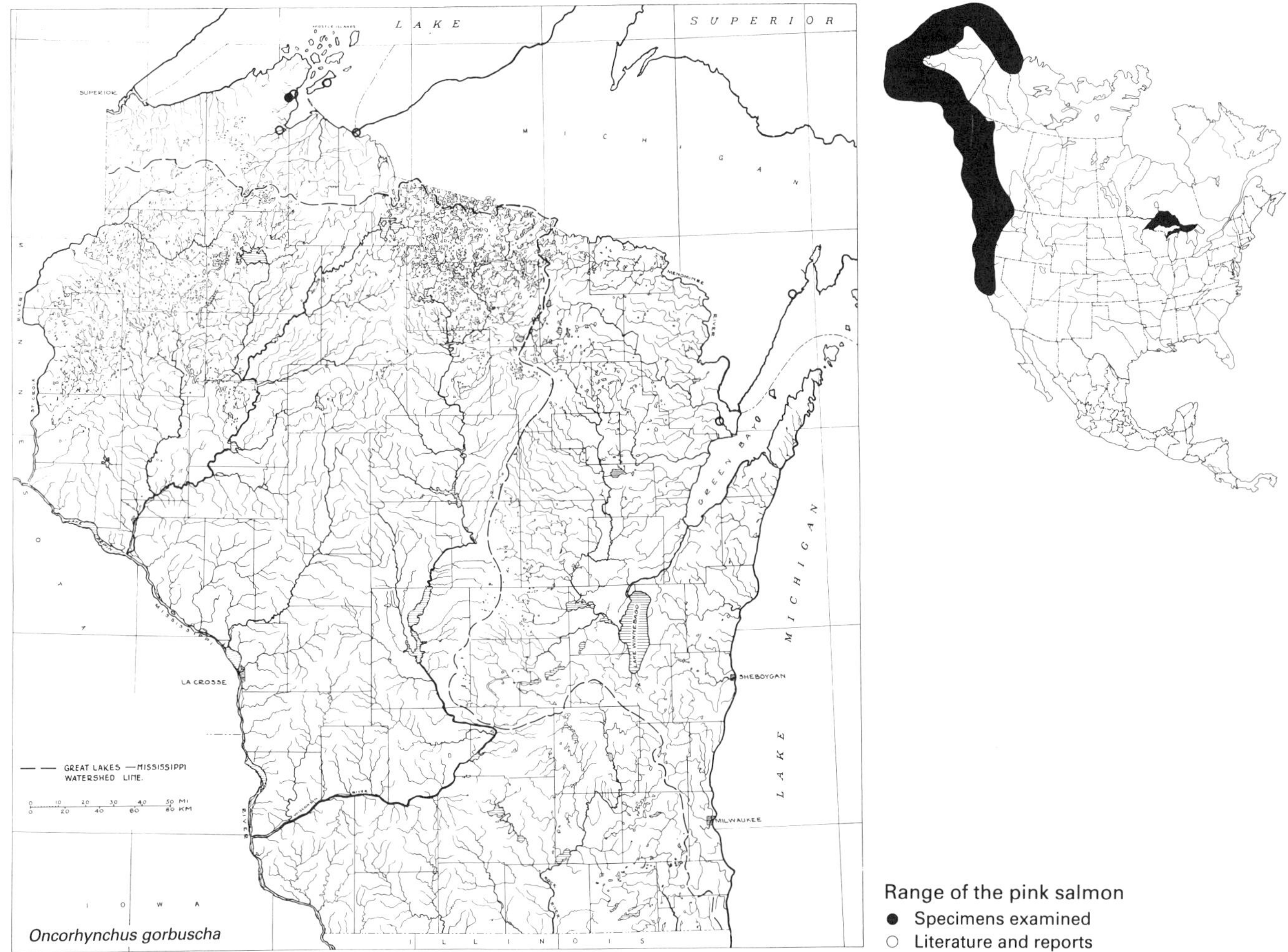

Range of the pink salmon
● Specimens examined
○ Literature and reports

The following generalized spawning information is taken from Scott and Crossman (1973). Spawning of early runs occurs at temperatures as high as 16°C (60.8°F) but spawnings of later runs peak at 10°C (50°F). The males are territorial and are aggressive toward other males; this trait is less highly developed in females. The female prepares the nest, an excavation in medium-sized gravel, 915 mm (3 ft) long and up to 457 mm (1.5 ft) deep, in about 305–610 mm (1–2 ft) of water. The female lies on her side and beats vigorously with her tail to remove silt and light gravel until she gets down to a firm gravel bed. Several males may spawn with a single female in one nest, a female may build more than one nest, and a single male may spawn with more than one female. Spawning usually occurs at night. The spawning fish settle near the center of the nest, their mouths gape widely, and eggs and sperm are released during vigorous vibration. After spawning, the female covers the eggs by digging (for 2–3 hr) at the upstream edge of the nest, which causes gravel to partly fill the nest.

About 1,900 eggs are laid (Helle 1970). The mean number of eggs in 12 females from Lakes Superior and Michigan was 1,161 (829–1,566) (Wagner 1976). The eggs are about 6 mm diam and orange-red in color. The spawning adults die within a few days or weeks. Depending on water temperature, hatching occurs from late December to late February. The hatchlings, called alevins, have large yolks, and remain in the gravel until the yolk is absorbed in April and early May; then they struggle up out of the nest and become free swimming. At that stage they are 33–38 mm long; they move downstream into the lake, either at night, when they are displaced by the current, or during the day when, as some reports suggest, they may school and move actively downstream.

After two growing seasons in the lake, they seek out a stream in which to spawn. On the West Coast the size of returning adults varies from 0.9 to 6.4 kg (2–14 lb), averaging 1.8 kg (4 lb). In the Great Lakes the adults are small at maturity. In a 1973 sample from Lake Superior, 53 fish averaged 411 mm (16.2 in) and 590 g (1.3 lb). The males were 386–480 mm

(15.2–18.9 in) long; the females, 361–460 mm (14.2–18.1 in). Ten mature salmon from Lake Huron tributaries averaged 432 mm (17.0 in) in length (Wagner and Stauffer 1975).

In a 1975 mixed sample from Lakes Superior, Michigan, and Huron, 98 males were 315–490 mm (12.4–19.3 in) long; 62 females, 363–445 mm (14.3–17.5 in). (Wagner 1976). In September 1975, a pink salmon 508 mm (20 in) long, weighing 1.11 kg (2 lb 7 oz), was caught near the mouth of the Silver River, near L'Anse, Michigan (Richey 1976).

In the ocean, during the first year of life the pink salmon feeds on small planktonic organisms; in the second year macrocrustaceans of pelagic habit make up much of the diet (Manzer 1968, 1969). If Great Lakes pink salmon have similar habits, they may be expected to prey upon *Mysis*, amphipods, and copepods, which are the mainstay of many resident fish, at least in Lake Superior (Anderson and Smith 1971b). On the Pacific Coast, adults do not normally feed after they begin the ascent of spawning rivers. In the Lake Superior population, however, fish showing early stages of transformation have been caught in the rivers by anglers using live bait.

The habits of this species once it migrates into the lake are not well known, but it appears to travel in schools and to inhabit the upper strata of the open lake. It is assumed that most of the adults return to the river in which they were hatched, but there is much wandering and some adopt a new stream for spawning. As a result, the pink salmon has spread from northern Lake Superior to streams in Lakes Huron and Michigan in less than 2 decades.

The minimal oxygen thresholds for the pink salmon are 1.99 ppm at 17°C, 3.36 ppm at 25°C (Privolnev 1963). The extremely low temperature of Hudson Bay may have been responsible for the failure of attempts to introduce the pink salmon there. It has also been observed that survival is low in some of the Lake Superior spawning streams, where spawning occurs in such shallow water that it is likely that a number of the spawning nests freeze out.

IMPORTANCE AND MANAGEMENT

On the West Coast, the young pink salmon are preyed upon by a variety of stream fishes, including trout, older salmon, sculpins, and probably even predacious birds like kingfishers and mergansers. The larvae of stoneflies may prey on eggs and alevins. In the Great Lakes, the sea lamprey undoubtedly takes its toll, although the adults are small and may be less attractive if larger associate species are present.

The presence of this new salmon in our waters has generated considerable excitement and enthusiasm. Both commercial fishermen and fishery biologists were amazed when in early September 1974 the lift of a trap net disclosed 29 pink salmon about 305 m (1,000 ft) off Madeline Island in Lake Superior.

On the West Coast the pink salmon makes up a substantial part of the commercial salmon catch and, although it is small, its abundance compensates for its lack of size. In the Lake Superior basin, the number of salmon observed in 1975 was frequently several times the number seen in the same streams in 1973 (Wagner 1976). The largest runs were in the Huron and Sturgeon rivers (Upper Michigan), which had an estimated 3,000 and 2,000 fish, respectively. It is expected that this salmon will thrive in the warmer waters of Lake Michigan and that before long it will become a target for both sport and commercial fishermen.

Currently there is a very limited sport fishery in the fall as these salmon come into the rivers to spawn. They provide the best sport when taken with small spinners, flies, spoons, or spawn bags. They can also be snagged with weighted hooks, since they are readily visible in shallow water, numerous in some streams, and not particularly wary.

There are differences of opinion about the eating qualities of the pink salmon during and just prior to spawning. Some people call them unpalatable, but others consider them palatable and just as good as the rainbow trout from the Great Lakes. Pink salmon caught out in the lake while they are still silvery and in prime condition are considered superb eating.

Concern has been expressed that this newcomer to our waters may displace our native endemic chubs, since it competes with them and with other native fishes for the kinds of foods eaten (Anderson and Smith 1971b, Lawrie and Rahrer 1973). According to Ron Poff, biologist for the Department of Natural Resources, the pink salmon may compete with the lake herring, just as the smelt is already doing.

The pink salmon of the Great Lakes is the only known self-perpetuating population of this species in fresh water. Its presence in the Great Lakes, which came about by chance, is an illustration of the ability of exotics to establish self-perpetuating populations in unexpected places.

Coho Salmon

Oncorhynchus kisutch (Walbaum). *Oncorhynchus*—hooked snout; *kisutch*—vernacular name for this species in Kamchatka.
Other common names: coho, silver salmon, sea trout, blueback.

Female 675 mm, Green Bay, L. Michigan (Oconto Co.), 5 Oct. 1980 (photo by S. Sommerfeldt)

DESCRIPTION
Body streamlined, laterally compressed. Average size in Lake Michigan 635 mm (25 in). Head into TL about 4.5 (less in breeding males). Eye small; snout greatly elongated; mouth terminal, slightly oblique, large. Maxillary extending beyond eye; teeth well developed on upper and lower jaws. Gill rakers 18–25. Branchiostegal rays 11–15. Dorsal fin rays 9–12; anal fin rays 12–17; pelvic fin rays 9–11; pectoral fin rays 12–16. Lateral line scales 112–148. Pyloric caeca 76 (45–114). Chromosomes 2n = 60 (Roberts 1967).

Adults steel blue to slightly green dorsally, sides silver, belly white; small dark spots on back, upper sides, base of dorsal fin and upper lobe of caudal fin. Breeding males with heads a dark blue-green, sides with a bright red stripe, gray to black on belly. Lower gums usually pale to gray. Young blue-green on the back, silvery sides, narrow parr marks 8–12, most bisected by the lateral line. Caudal fin and most of anal fin red-orange. Anal fin with first rays elongated, white on anterior edge with black stripe behind.

Sexual dimorphism: Breeding male lacking breeding tubercles but with prolonged hooked snout, mouth deformed, dorsal hump little developed to not developed. Female lacking breeding tubercles, hooked snout, deformed mouth, or hump before dorsal fin.

Hybrids: Coho salmon × pink salmon, coho salmon × chinook salmon (Schwartz 1972).

DISTRIBUTION, STATUS, AND HABITAT
The coho salmon inhabits Lakes Michigan and Superior and a number of their tributary streams. It has been stocked in Riley Lake (Chippewa County) and in Stormy and Pallette lakes (Vilas County).

A large-scale program for the introduction of coho salmon into Lake Michigan began in 1966 when 660,000 yearlings were released; a total of 10.3 million (mostly from the state of Michigan) were stocked through 1970 (Wells and McLain 1973). The state of Wisconsin contributed to this program by stocking approximately 500,000 coho salmon a year. Yearlings were stocked into rivers at or near South Milwaukee, Sheboygan, Manitowoc, Two Rivers, Algoma, Kewaunee, and Marinette, beginning with the Ahnapee River in 1968 and continuing to the present with most of the streams. Coho salmon were initially introduced into Lake Superior by the State of Michigan in 1966. Ontario and Minnesota joined the stocking program in 1969, but have since abandoned it. Coho salmon straying from these plants have appeared in Wisconsin streams in the vicinity of Chequamegon Bay since 1971, and in 1973 they were first seen in streams west of the Apostle Islands (Swanson 1976).

The presence of the coho salmon in Wisconsin is largely the result of intensive and continued stocking. Natural reproduction in the Lake Superior system is low, and it is generally insignificant in Lake Michigan.

In the Great Lakes the coho salmon occupies the upper strata, and is generally found within 16 km (10 mi) of shore. During the breeding season the coho migrate up a tributary stream (mostly into native trout water), where the first year of the young salmon's life is spent.

BIOLOGY
The coho salmon has a rather brief life cycle: 3 years elapse from the time eggs are laid until that generation dies following spawning. The eggs, laid in the fall of the year, hatch the following spring, and the juveniles live in the parent stream for an additional year. In the spring of their second year of life they migrate to the lake, live in the lake for 18 months, i.e., through two summer growing seasons, and then migrate back to the parent stream for spawning and certain death.

Coho salmon will ascend small tributary streams as far as they are physically able to do so, swimming up riffles with stream flows as low as 57 dm^3 (2 ft^3) per second and in water as shallow as 5 cm (2 in). Generally these are brook trout streams (Swanson 1976); however, in the Lake Michigan basin the cohos enter virtually all tributary streams.

The site for nest construction is typically near the head of a riffle composed of medium and small gravel

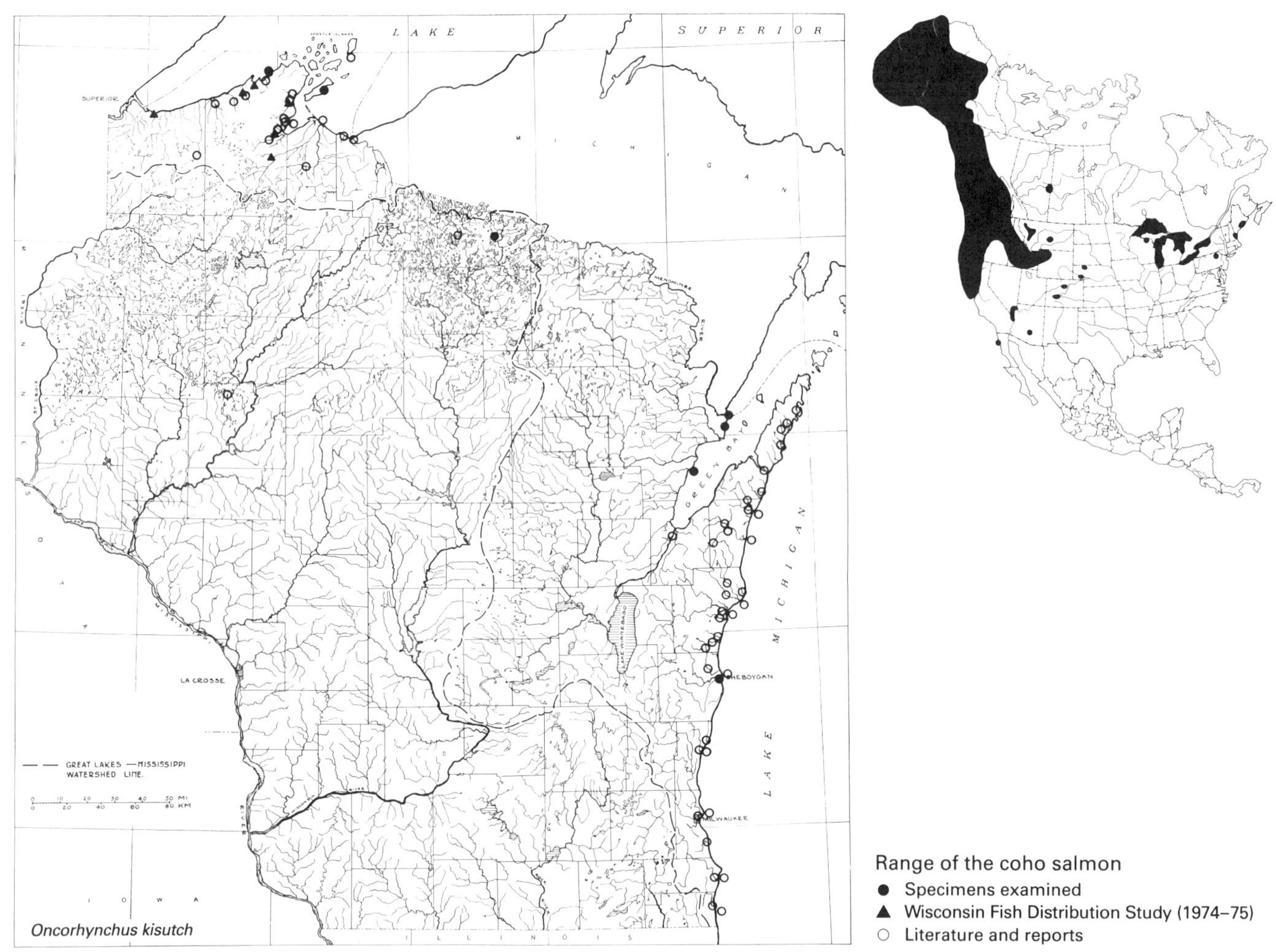

Range of the coho salmon
● Specimens examined
▲ Wisconsin Fish Distribution Study (1974–75)
○ Literature and reports

(Breder and Rosen 1966). The female constructs the nest. To dig it, she turns partly on her side and, with powerful and rapid movements of her tail, disturbs the bottom materials, which are then carried a short distance downstream by the current. The nest is an oval or roundish pit or depression at least as deep and long as the fish. While the nest is being built, several males in attendance may create a "great deal of commotion."

The early life history of the coho salmon has been determined for Little Scarboro Creek (Kewaunee County) in the Lake Michigan basin, and most of the following account comes from Avery (1974b). Mature coho salmon begin entering Little Scarboro Creek in late October and spawning activity peaks in November. The average number of eggs per adult was 3,807. Many false nests contained no eggs. A maximum of 250–300 eggs was found in the nests containing eggs, while most nests held fewer than 150. During the first week of March 10–15% of the eggs in an excavated nest that was examined were alive and in the eyed stage. In Little Scarboro Creek egg survival to hatching was 1.4%. The egg incubation period spanned 145–150 days, from late November to early April at water temperatures of 0.0–2.5°C (32–36.5°F). Avery found that intragravel dissolved oxygen in selected coho nests averaged 6.2 ppm, and stream discharge fluctuated two- to three-fold during the winter. He concluded that the general lack of suitable gravel substrates, cold winter water temperatures, and large variations in water level are responsible for the lack of significant natural reproduction in Lake Michigan tributaries. Another problem is associated with the spring spawning of rainbow trout, who superimpose their activities on the coho salmon nests. Trout excavations of coho nests increase coho mortality through premature excavation of young embryos.

Upon hatching, the alevins remain 2–3 weeks in the gravel until the yolk is absorbed and then emerge as free-swimming, actively feeding fry (Scott and Crossman 1973). During August 1971, a population of 1,634 age-0 cohos, along with lesser numbers of young-of-year rainbow trout and brook trout, were present in the lower 2.4 km (1.5 mi) of Little Scarboro

Creek. The average length and weight of the cohos were 91 mm (3.6 in) and 7 g. A population of 468 age-I cohos was present in the same sector in April 1972, and they averaged 112 mm TL and 13 g.

Approximately 1 year after they emerge from the gravel, the young smolts migrate rapidly downstream to the lake. This movement is usually completed before the end of May, although some do not leave the stream until mid-June. While in the lake they wander considerable distances from the parent stream, mixing with stocks from different streams. Apparently, however, this is of little significance in their later segregation and homing migration to the parent stream in the fall of the following year.

Streams tributary to Lake Superior appear to be more suitable for successful reproduction of coho salmon. In 1976 Department of Natural Resources biologists counted 814 cohos from North Fish Creek, 1,066 from Pine Creek, and 99 from Little Pine Creek. Most were young-of-year; six were smolts (age I), and two were jacks (D. Pratt, pers. comm.). In 1976, cohos composed 48% of the young-of-year and yearling salmonid community in Pine Creek, 41% in the Onion River, and 40% in Whittlesey Creek (Swanson 1976). In addition, coho young have been counted in Little Sioux River, Pikes Creek, Cranberry River, Flag River, and Bark River.

Age-0 cohos in North Fish Creek (Bayfield County) averaged 76 mm TL in June, 81 mm in July, and 84 mm (76–112 mm) in August. Smolts collected in June averaged 145 mm (114–179 mm) TL (D. Pratt, pers. comm.). Pine Creek (Bayfield County) during August–September 1976 yielded 659 age-0 cohos which averaged 81 mm (3.2 in) TL (another 406 were counted but not measured) and one age-I jack, 335 mm (13.2 in) TL. Another jack of the same length was captured in Little Pine Creek near the Lake Louise Dam. Coho jacks in the Big Huron River, Michigan, averaged 368 mm (14.5 in) TL and 499 g (1.1 lb) (Borgeson and Tody 1967). After two growing seasons in the lake, the returning spawners had an average weight of 1.3 kg (2.9 lb) (Lawrie and Rahrer 1973).

Reflecting Lake Michigan's higher productivity, the average total length and weight for first-year cohos is 381 mm (15 in) and 680 g (1.5 lb); for second-year fish, 635 mm (25 in) and 2.72 kg (6 lb) (Daly 1971).

First-year coho salmon frequently attain a weight of 1.81–2.74 kg (4–6 lb). One coho jack was 597 mm (23.5 in) TL and weighed over 3.18 kg (7 lb) (Borgeson and Tody 1967). A spawning Lake Michigan coho, taken at the Little Manistee, Michigan, weir, 27 October 1973, measured 108 cm (42.5 in) TL, and weighed 17.7 kg (39 lb 2 oz). In 1975 a coho 943 mm (37⅛ in) TL, weighing 11.06 kg (24 lb 6 oz), was taken off Shegoygan at a depth of about 20 m (65 ft).

Growth of the coho salmon in inland lakes is much less favorable. Avery (1973) noted that age-0 cohos stocked in Pallette Lake grew only 137 mm (5.4 in) in length and 116 g (4.1 oz) in weight during 3 years in the lake; age-I cohos, 107 mm (4.2 in) and 91 g (3.2 oz) in 2½ years. Few ever attained the minimum legal size of 254 mm (10 in). The food supply was not adequate for the fish to grow normally and eventually adopt a piscivorous diet. In Stormy Lake growth was better. From an average stocking size of 198 mm (7.8 in) and 82 g (2.9 oz), the cohos showed an average growth increment of 160–183 mm (6.3–7.2 in) and 197–362 g (6.9–12.7 oz) after 16–19 months in the lake. They grew to an apparent maximum of 457 mm (18 in) TL and 940 g (2 lb 1.2 oz) (McKnight and Serns 1977).

The coho salmon is a rapid-moving, wide-ranging species. A study of coho in Michigan streams showed yearlings moving 10.5 km (6.5 mi) downstream within 2 days after release; 32 km (20 mi), within a week (Borgeson and Tody 1967). Once out in the lake, the yearlings evidently dispersed widely, and from the beginning of August through September they were scattered over the northern half of Lake Michigan, including Green Bay and Two Rivers. In Lake Superior, cohos were captured 29 km (18 mi) west of the Big Huron River about 1 month after entering the lake. Six months after they had entered the lake, several cohos were caught 129 km (80 mi) east of the Big Huron River.

In Lake Michigan, overall movements of adult cohos indicate concentrations in the south end of the lake at the beginning of each year, with a gradual migration northward along the Wisconsin shore with the progress of the seasons. The cohos reach Kewaunee County in July and peak in September (Spigarelli and Thommes 1976).

The coho is active at temperatures between 6.7 and 14.4°C (44–58°F). Peak feeding temperature is 12.2°C (54°F). The schools are generally within 16 km (10 mi) of shore at depths up to 15 m (50 ft), although occasionally they are deeper.

In the Lake Michigan basin the transplanted cohos demonstrated at an exceptionally high level the ability to home back to the stream of their release in their new freshwater environment, although a few did stray to nearby streams. In the Lake Superior basin, because the initial plantings of yearlings in the Big Huron River moved out into the lake rapidly, it was surmised that the salmon did not imprint on their "home" stream, accounting for large numbers of spawning adults returning not to the "home" stream but to many other streams in the watershed.

Plantings in inland lakes which stratify thermally place rigid limits on movements of this coldwater species. In Pallette Lake, Engel and Magnuson (1971) noted that the coho was inshore in winter and spring, along with yellow perch and common shiner. In late summer it hovered with the cisco in the metalimnion in water 8–16°C (46–61°F). As a result, during the growing season the fish were in a zone which lacked an abundant population of young forage fishes, essential for good growth. Engel and Magnuson assumed that this separation of predator and prey interfered with the cohos' attaining maximum growth in small lakes in summer.

During April and June, yearling coho salmon in northern Lake Michigan feed largely on nymphs and larvae of aquatic insects (Peck 1974). More than 90% of the cohos examined in Peck's study had eaten insects, including mayflies, water boatmen, dipterans, stoneflies, and beetles. Crustraceans had been eaten by fewer than half of the cohos, and, fishes, including smelt, spottail shiner, and rock bass, had been taken by only a small percentage. As cohos grow, the incidence and the volume of the fish in the diet both increase. In Stormy Lake, the smallest coho examined with fish remains in its stomach was 216 mm (8.5 in) TL (McKnight and Serns 1974). Cohos in Lake Michigan subsist primarily on alewives, but they also eat smelt, ninespine sticklebacks, and insects. The diet of Lake Superior cohos includes insects, *Mysis relicta*, smelt, and ninespine stickleback.

In Pallette Lake, cohos consumed mostly terrestrial and aquatic insects. In November a few had eaten ciscoes and cisco eggs; however, the percentage of fishes eaten was only 1% by number (Engel and Magnuson 1971). In Stormy Lake during the winter, fishes constituted 93.3% of the volume of the coho stomachs, and among them were the northern pike, yellow perch, johnny darter, bluegill, and smallmouth bass (McKnight and Serns 1974).

IMPORTANCE AND MANAGEMENT

Kingfishers, herring gulls, loons, great blue herons, and brown trout prey on coho smolts (Borgeson and Tody 1967), but of 221 predatory fish examined in northern Lake Michigan, only one walleye and one northern pike had each eaten a smolt (Peck 1974). More than 90% of the fish eaten by fish predators were adult smelt, which apparently served as a buffer between yearling coho and the resident piscivorous fishes.

The coho salmon, in its turn, as well as all the other combined stocked salmonid species, preys on the alewife and is undoubtedly helping to curb alewife abundance in Lake Michigan. If the current level of stocking of salmon is continued, it may help prevent a repetition of the massive alewife die-off of 1967.

In the Lake Superior basin, it has been assumed that thus far the coho influx has had no detectable impact on established stream residents (Swanson 1976). In the Lake Michigan basin, coho competition with the native trout in the streams of Kewaunee County has been seen as potentially detrimental to the trout (Avery 1974b). Avery cited the problem of brook trout nests being disrupted by superimposed coho salmon nests.

The coho salmon is both a superb game fish and a superior food fish. It has been taken with "frost flies" in combination with flashing herring dodgers, multicolored spoons, and fresh and frozen baits, including alewives and smelt (Stephenson 1968). In spawning streams cohos are taken by conventional salmon baits or by snagging, which has recently been legalized. The coho, along with the chinook, has given the charter boat fishery and the supporting sporting goods, food, and lodging industries an economic boost. Lake Michigan has become the most popular salmon-fishing center in the world, attracting many out-of-state sportsmen. The catch, if properly prepared, can provide fine eating (Dudley et al. 1970; C. E. Johnson et al. 1974).

The coho's inherent capacity for very rapid growth provides an extremely high production potential. In the Wisconsin waters of Lake Michigan, the sport fishery reported 20,011 cohos in 1970, 33,984 in 1971, 60,621 in 1972, and 52,766 in 1973. Trolling was by far the most successful method, accounting for 46–78% of the total catch, followed by stream, pier, and shore fishing, in decreasing order of importance. In 1973, troll-caught cohos taken in the Kenosha (Illinois–Wisconsin state line) to Milwaukee sector constituted 62% of all cohos taken in Wisconsin waters. Many of these fish had started out in other states and were caught during their gradual northward movement along the Wisconsin shoreline from wintering areas in the south end of the lake (Daly et al. 1974).

In the Wisconsin waters of Lake Superior, the sport fishery for coho salmon reported 1,352 cohos in 1972, 3,316 in 1973, and 2,647 in 1974. Openwater fishing accounted for the greatest number, followed by stream fishing and ice fishing (King and Swanson 1975). In 1976 the sport fishery harvest included 2,598 coho salmon weighing 2,121 kg (4,675 lb), and in 1977, 2,273 fish weighing 1,856 kg (4,090 lb) (Sport Fish. Instit. *Bull.* No. 293, April 1978, p. 7).

The harvest of coho salmon in Stormy Lake, caught from May to September 1970 and after the following January, was estimated at well over 50% of the 1970 stocking (5,000 yearling cohos) (Serns and McKnight 1974).

The early experimental work done by Hasler and Wisby (1951) on odor discrimination in fishes was soon applied to the homing of salmon. The current coho stocking program makes certain that the salmon begin their migration in the Great Lakes with the chemistry of their "native" stream indelibly fixed in their "memory." When the salmon are smolting, less than 48 hours of exposure to spring water is sufficient for them to locate that water and identify it as "home" when they return to spawn (Jensen and Duncan 1971). Yearling cohos are transferred to holding ponds on tributary streams, and it is to these holding ponds that they are attracted some 18 months later; at that time they provide a bounty of lake-fattened fish for the fisherman.

An intriguing application of odor discrimination is the imprinting of juvenile salmon to morpholine or phenethyl alcohol, substances not known to occur in natural waters but which are detected by salmonids at low concentrations (about 1 drop morpholine to 473,000 liters of water) (Scholz et al. 1976). Yearling salmon exposed to the imprinting chemical for 1½ months and then released in Lake Michigan are attracted to the stream scented with the chemical to which they have been imprinted. As many as 98% of the fish recovered responded to the appropriate scent. Two advantages of the artificial imprinting technique over the use of holding ponds are immediately apparent (Daly et al. 1974). First, fish can be released in areas (for example, metropolitan areas such as South Milwaukee) which do not have adequate facilities for smolting ponds. Second, it may be that fish can be attracted or decoyed to fishing piers, fishing buoys, or breakwaters on shoreline parks if synthetic odor is dripped in at these sites. Increasing the number of places where the fish might be caught would lessen the sports fishing pressure and problems on some of the coho streams.

Coho salmon, as well as other salmonids, have become victims of chemical contaminants and pesticide residues in Lake Michigan. In 1969 federal agents seized coho from commercial warehouses when FDA analysis showed concentrations of dieldrin and DDT up to 19 ppm. In 1968, Dr. H. Johnson of Michigan State University noted a loss of up to 50% of alevins from Lake Michigan, which showed signs of DDT poisoning at the time they used the oils contained in the yolk-sac.

In early fall of 1971, PCB levels of 6–17 ppm (which exceeded the federal standard of 5 ppm) were discovered in several batches of coho salmon from Lake Michigan. Commercial sales of the fish were stopped and sports fishermen were advised to eat no more than one meal per week of the contaminated fish.

At the same time, eggs from Lake Michigan brood stock were showing much variability, with respect to fertilization, eye up stage, and hatching, and in state hatcheries a high mortality of fry was noted, due to an apparent fragility of the membrane about the yolk-sac, hemorrhages around the brain, and weakened membranes throughout the body system (Degurse et al. 1973). Testing showed that there was no correlation between the level of DDT or PCB and the mortality of the fry.

Chinook Salmon

Oncorhynchus tshawytscha (Walbaum). *Oncorhynchus*—hooked snout; *tshawytscha*—vernacular name of this species in Kamchatka.

Other common names: chinook, spring salmon, king salmon, king, tyee, quinnat, blackmouth.

Male 875 mm, Little R. (Marinette Co.), 10 Oct. 1980 (photo by S. Sommerfeldt)

DESCRIPTION

Body streamlined, laterally compressed. Average size in Lake Michigan 864 mm, 7.26 kg (34 in, 16 lb). Head into TL about 5 (less in breeding males). Snout elongate. Mouth terminal, slightly oblique, large. Maxillary extending beyond eye. Teeth large, sharp on upper and lower jaws. Gill rakers 16–26. Branchiostegal rays 13–19. Dorsal fin rays 10–14; anal fin rays 14–19; pectoral fin rays 14–17; pelvic fin rays 10–11. Lateral line scales 130–165. Pyloric caeca 140–185. Chromosomes 2n = 68 (Roberts 1967).

Adult iridescent green to blue-green on back, top of head, and upper sides; sides below lateral line silvery; belly silvery to white. At least a few black spots on back, top of head, upper sides, and all fins, including caudal fin. Lower gums black. Breeding fish olive-brown to purple, males darker than females. Young with parr marks 6–12 as wide as or wider than the spaces between, the lateral line passing through the center of most marks. Anal fin with first ray elongate, white, but usually no black stripe behind.

Sexual dimorphism: Breeding male lacking breeding tubercles, but with prolonged, hooked snout and a deformed mouth. Female lacking breeding tubercles; snout and mouth normal.

Hybrids: Chinook salmon × coho salmon, chinook salmon × pink salmon (Schwartz 1972).

DISTRIBUTION, STATUS, AND HABITAT

The chinook salmon, a Pacific Ocean salmon, was recently introduced into the Lake Michigan and Lake Superior drainage basins. From 1967 through 1970, 4.1 million fingerlings were released in Lake Michigan. The state of Michigan, which initiated the Pacific salmon program, released 93% of the chinook salmon planted through 1970, but all the other states bordering Lake Michigan have participated in the stocking effort (Wells and McLain 1973).

Wisconsin initiated its chinook salmon program in 1969 with the release of 65,000 fingerlings. In 1973 some 755,000 chinook fingerlings were released from 10 release sites—from the Pike River (Kenosha County) to Strawberry Creek (Door County) and the Little River (Marinette County) (Daly et al. 1974). All recent Wisconsin records in the Lake Superior basin are derived from state of Michigan plants. In the spring of 1967, 34,000 smolts were planted in the Big Huron River of the Upper Peninsula; from 1967 to 1970, 318,000 chinook young-of-year were planted in state of Michigan tributaries (Parsons 1973).

Attempts in the past century to stock the chinook salmon in Wisconsin resulted in failure (Introduction, p. 20). The success of the salmon program initiated in 1969 has resulted from the application of tested release techniques, and from annual stocking, which provides a constant return to the angler. The growth of the stocked salmon, especially in Lake Michigan, has been exceptional. In Wisconsin the salmon program is not dependent on natural reproduction; the emphasis is on artificial propagation, now largely dependent on brood stock from Lake Michigan. Limited natural propagation of this species is suspected to have occurred in some Lake Superior tributaries; however, even if propagation does occur, it is not sufficient to meet the demands of anglers.

The chinook salmon in Wisconsin provides an unusually successful fishery. It has become such an important feature among our Wisconsin fish fauna that its inclusion on the state list is expected. At the same time, it must be recognized that the chinook fails the criterion of self-perpetuation.

The preferred habitat of spawning chinooks is a large river with a clean gravel substrate. The young generally smolt soon after hatching, and migrate downstream to the sea, or large lake, where they grow quickly. Subadults and adults frequent mid-depth areas where food is abundant.

BIOLOGY

In its home on the West Coast there are many races of the chinook salmon, each moving inshore into its spawning river at a particular time of the year. Many rivers have more than one run (spring to winter chinooks), each made up of fish bound for different spawning grounds. The young of some races spend

Range of the chinook salmon
● Specimens examined
▲ Wisconsin Fish Distribution Study (1974–75)
○ Literature and reports

up to a year or two in the home stream and, although we generally think of the chinook as completing its life cycle in 4 years, some forms persist up to 9 years.

The chinook in Wisconsin is a salmon with a 4-year cycle. The fry are taken from hatcheries after 7 months. In the release ponds they are held for 3–4 weeks, and stocked directly into adjacent waterways. The next 3½ years are spent in the lake.

The following account of chinook spawning, based on data from West Coast streams, is taken largely from Scott and Crossman (1973). Chinook salmon generally spawn near riffles in large rivers or large tributaries. They tend to spawn in deeper water and on larger gravel than other Pacific salmon. Freshwater populations may spawn in rivers flowing into a lake, or on gravel shoals in the lake. The males and females are aggressive on the spawning grounds. The female digs the nest by lying on her side and thrashing the tail up and down. The nest, or redd, can be as much as 3.7 m (12 ft) long and 31 cm (1 ft) deep. Each female is attended by a larger, dominant male, and often by several smaller males. At spawning the female and the dominant male swim into the nest, the two fish lie side by side, their mouths gape, they vibrate, and eggs and sperm are released. Smaller males may dart into the nest and release sperm also. After spawning, the female digs at the head of the nest and covers the eggs with the displaced gravel; the eggs are generally buried about 1½ to 2 times the height of the body of the parent. The female may dig more than one nest and spawn with more than one male.

Several investigators have established that chinook salmon continue to build nests even after they have been stripped for fish-culture purposes; their work has shown that nest building is a function distinct from that of spawning, and unrelated to the presence of eggs in the ovary (Breder and Rosen 1966).

The number of eggs deposited varies with the stock and the size of the female. An average of about 8,500 eggs are deposited by Alaskan chinooks; in a New Hampshire freshwater population (Hoover 1936a), the average number was 2,500. The eggs are large, 6–7 mm diam, and orange-red in color. Optimum incubation temperatures are between 4 and 11°C (39 and 52°F). The female guards the nest, but usually dies within a few days to 2 weeks. Precocious males have been known to live 5 months after spawning.

The eggs hatch the following spring into alevins, which spend 2–3 weeks in the nest while the yolk is absorbed, after which the fry struggle up through the gravel to become free swimming. Some proceed almost directly to the sea or lake, but other stocks may remain in the home stream for a year or two.

The strain of chinook salmon brought to the Great Lakes matures in early fall. The first major spawning run of female chinook salmon in the Great Lakes occurred in the Little Manistee and Muskegon rivers (lower Michigan, in the Lake Michigan basin) in 1970. Nests were common on the shoals in some areas, and large numbers of eggs were deposited. In the spring of 1971 a few stream-hatched smolts were caught in these tributaries (Parsons 1973). In Wisconsin, successful spawning of chinook in some Lake Superior tributaries is suspected; however, no fry or smolts have been recovered.

Chinook smolts are 60 mm long and number more than 220 per kilogram. While still in the release stream, these young chinooks are most numerous in pools below riffles, or in low-velocity riffles where cover is available (Patten 1971). The optimum range of temperature in fresh water, which controls the rate of growth and survival of the young, is 13–17°C (55.4–62.6°F). Davidson and Hutchinson (1938) noted that constant temperatures above 17°C (62.6°F) retard growth and increase the mortality of the young; at 20°C (68°F) mortality is high. Constant temperatures below 13°C (55.4°F) also retard growth, and at 3°C (37.4°F) mortality is high. According to Brett (1952), the upper lethal temperature for fry is 25.1°C (77.2°F), and the preferred temperature is 12–14°C (53.6–57.2°F).

Smolts migrate downstream into a lake in May and June, and growth is rapid. In Lake Michigan the average total length and weight at the end of each year of life is: 1—254 mm, 227 g (10 in, 0.5 lb); 2—635 mm, 2.7 kg (25 in, 6 lb); 3—864 mm, 7.3 kg (34 in, 16 lb); and 4—1.02 m, 10.4 kg (40 in, 23 lb) (Daly 1971). In Lake Superior, age-II fish from the 1968 planting averaged 1.4 kg (3.1 lb), and age-III fish from the 1967 planting averaged 3.3 kg (7.2 lb) (Lawrie and Rahrer 1973). In chinook salmon sampled from Lake Superior during 1974–1975, the approximate calculated lengths at the annuli were: 1—325 mm, 2—500 mm, 3—625 mm, and 4—700 mm. Berg (1978) suggested that Lake Superior chinook salmon may not achieve a fifth year of life. The majority matured at either age II+ or III+ (Berg 1978). There was no significant difference in age between the sexes at the time of maturation.

A large number of 9–14-kg chinooks have been caught from Lake Michigan. An 18.3-kg (40-lb 4-oz) chinook was taken from the Menominee River on the upper Michigan–Wisconsin boundary in 1973.

The chinook is the largest member of the salmonid family, topping even the greatest recorded weights for lake trout. An Alaskan chinook 147 cm (58 in) long weighed 57.2 kg (126 lb).

In Lake Michigan, chinook salmon winter in the deeper areas off the Wisconsin shoreline, rather than moving en masse to the southern end of the lake, as coho salmon do (Daly et al. 1974). Chinooks live in mid-depth waters, and generally are not taken on the bottom in deeper water, although some chinooks have been taken on the bottom in gill nets.

Young chinook salmon in freshwater streams feed on terrestrial insects, crustaceans, chironomids, corixids, caddisflies, mites, spiders, aphids, phantom midge larvae, and ants. In a lake they undoubtedly consume insects and plankton until they reach sufficient size to eat fish. Smelt and alewives are important foods for the adult chinook in the Great Lakes. The chinook salmon's peak feeding temperature is 12.2°C (54°F), which during the summer lies within the thermocline.

IMPORTANCE AND MANAGEMENT

Predators on young chinooks include trout, salmon, sculpins, mergansers, kingfishers, and other diving birds. Field studies have indicated that a sculpin can digest a salmon 60 mm long in 24–28 hours (Patten 1971). Young chinooks compete with other salmon and trout for food, and the adult chinooks compete with other salmonids for spawning grounds.

When Captain Gray sailed his ship *Columbia* into the "Great River of the West" in 1792, he named the river after his vessel. He found there an Indian tribe called the Chinook living in aboriginal luxury on a species of large salmon that was abundant in the river. These fish later became known as chinook salmon. The Indians smoked and dried salmon, pounded the dried meat into powder, and used the surplus for trade. So abundant was this food supply, and so easy was its harvest, preservation, and storage, that the coastal Indians had time for the pursuit of leisure (Walden 1964).

In Lake Michigan, the chinook salmon is truly the king of all fish. It reaches the largest size of any fish in the lake, and is considered a prime food fish despite its contamination with industrial chemicals. It has been lured with shiny spoons, fluorescent-colored spoons, and baits. A preferred bait is the herring dodger, with a large hair fly trailed behind.

In Lake Michigan, the sport fishermen took 577 chinooks in 1970, 6,151 in 1971, 11,465 in 1972, and 27,660 in 1973. The increase in 1973 was influenced greatly by the catch of immature fish 330–432 mm (13–17 in) TL. These smaller chinooks were taken primarily along the southern part of the Wisconsin shoreline, both by trolling and by fishing from the pier or breakwater. The bulk of 3- and 4-year-old fish were taken in the Sturgeon Bay area during the spawning period (Daly et al. 1974). In Lake Superior, the sport fishery for chinook salmon produced 112 fish in 1973, and 66 in 1974 (King and Swanson 1975). In 1976, the sport fishery harvest included 254 chinook salmon with a total weight of 507 kg; in 1977, 415 chinooks were taken with a total weight of 828 kg (Sport Fish. Instit. *Bull.* No. 293, April 1978, p. 7).

Strawberry Creek near Sturgeon Bay was selected as the original chinook salmon release site in Wisconsin, since the large volume of water surging through the Ship Canal into Lake Michigan acts like a large river (Daly et al. 1974). This condition is especially attractive to chinooks as they come into spawning readiness. The Strawberry Creek site was also renovated into a spawn-taking and fish harvest facility. Some 1,500 chinooks were handled in 1972, and 600 in 1973. Eggs were taken for transport to hatcheries, where they were propagated artificially, and the surplus roe made available to the fish bait industry (Daly et al. 1974).

Chinook salmon management has some advantages over coho salmon management. Since chinooks require less rearing time and space in the hatchery, greater numbers of chinooks can be released for the same cost. Chinooks grow into larger fish, and so make better trophies than the cohos. Once a chinook release operation has been started, one release provides fishing for 3 years instead of the 2 years provided by one release of cohos (Daly 1971). Also, with each release chinooks consume more alewives, and ultimately convert these into larger quantities of salmon flesh.

Perhaps the greatest disadvantage of both chinook and coho salmon stocking programs is that, although the fishery is fast and hectic, it lasts only for a very limited period of time rather late in the year. Some chinook salmon may be caught all summer long, but large concentrations are not built up at stocking sites along the Lake Michigan shoreline (including the Sturgeon Bay Ship Canal) until late September. Peak abundance lasts only from late September to mid-November. According to Daly (1971), there is a need to develop strains of these salmon species which will be available earlier in the year to prolong the fishery.

Following the establishment of this fish-eating, but nonreproducing, species in the fresh waters of New Hampshire, it was suggested that the chinook salmon might be used in fresh water as a biological control of unwanted fish (Hoover 1936a). The chinooks exterminated smelt from a lake within 3 years, and then died out themselves, leaving the lake ready for the re-introduction of native trout.

Wholly freshwater and self-sustaining chinook populations now exist in only one fully documented transplant—in New Zealand. Several other attempts have "succeeded" temporarily, in that adult fish returned to the stream where eggs or fry had been released, but no permanent self-sustaining runs were established (Walden 1964).

Brook Trout

Salvelinus fontinalis (Mitchill). *Salvelinus*—an old name for char; *fontinalis*—living in springs.

Other common names: eastern brook trout, speckled trout, brookie, squaretail, squaretailed trout, speckled char, char or charr, common brook trout, mud trout, coaster (brook trout of Lakes Michigan and Superior), coaster brook trout, native trout, native, redspotted trout.

Immature 63 mm, Deerskin R. (Vilas Co.), 18 June 1977

Subadult 162 mm, West Branch of the Little Wolf R. (Menominee Co.), 19 July 1966

DESCRIPTION

Body streamlined, laterally compressed. Average size in inland streams 152–203 mm (6–8 in) TL. Head into TL 3.7–4.5. Snout somewhat rounded. Mouth terminal, slightly oblique, large. Maxillary extending beyond eye. Teeth on upper and lower jaws. Gill rakers 9–12. Branchiostegal rays 9–13. Dorsal fin rays 10–14; anal fin rays 9–13; pelvic fin rays 8–10; pectoral fin rays 11–14; caudal fin square, rarely slightly forked. Lateral line scales 210–244. Pyloric caeca 23–55. Chromosomes 2n = 100 (Roberts 1967).

Olive, blue-gray, or black on back, to white on the belly; wormlike overmarkings (vermiculations) on the back; red spots, sometimes surrounded by bluish halos, on sides. Black and white stripes along the front edges of the lower body fins; remainder of these fins reddish. Lower flanks and belly of breeding males becoming orange-red, with black pigmentation on either side of belly. Lake-run brook trout (coasters) more silvery over head and body, and less heavily pigmented. Young with 7–9 large, brown parr marks along lateral line. Sharp, dark brown line along tip of chin, almost as dark as pigment of eye. Young 45 mm (1.75 in) long, with a dark margin on adipose fin and a black stripe along front of dorsal fin, behind which diagonal rows of dark spots are added. Belly of very young with dark speckles.

One wild brook trout captured from Spring Creek (Chippewa County) had 2 anal fins (Hunt 1976).

Sexual dimorphism: Both sexes lacking breeding tubercles. Male developing a hook on lower jaw at spawning; absent in female.

Hybrids: Brook trout × rainbow trout, brook trout × brown trout, brook trout × lake trout (Schwartz 1972).

The brook trout has been crossbred with the brown trout to produce the infertile tiger trout, which possesses distinctive markings like that of a tiger, leopard, or giraffe. There are records of several such natural crosses from Wisconsin waters (see p. 291).

The splake is a hatchery-produced cross between the brook trout and the lake trout, *Salvelinus namaycush*. The fertile offspring appear to have a lower fecundity than either of the parent species (see pp. 323 and 329).

DISTRIBUTION, STATUS, AND HABITAT

The brook trout, the only stream-dwelling trout native to Wisconsin, occurs throughout the state, principally in central and northern Wisconsin, in Lake Superior, and in Lake Michigan (sustained through stocking in Lake Michigan). Many of the map locations have been plotted from the study done by Kmiotek (1974); he also classified each stream as to quality.

The brook trout is common in streams of central and northern Wisconsin, and rare to uncommon in southern Wisconsin, except in Richland, Columbia, Dane, and Sauk counties, where it is common in many streams. The Wisconsin Department of Natural Resources (Brasch et al. 1973) noted that the primary range of the brook trout in northern Wisconsin is probably fairly stable. In central and southern Wisconsin, the range seems to be decreasing; in some areas, it is all but gone.

The brook trout inhabits cool, clear, headwater spring ponds, springs, and spring-fed streams (see Threinen and Poff 1963). It has been successfully stocked in deep, softwater, stratified lakes (generally spring-fed) in which the lower stratum remains well oxygenated throughout the summer. It does best in water 20°C (68°F) or less. In my studies, the frequencies of bottom types most commonly associated with

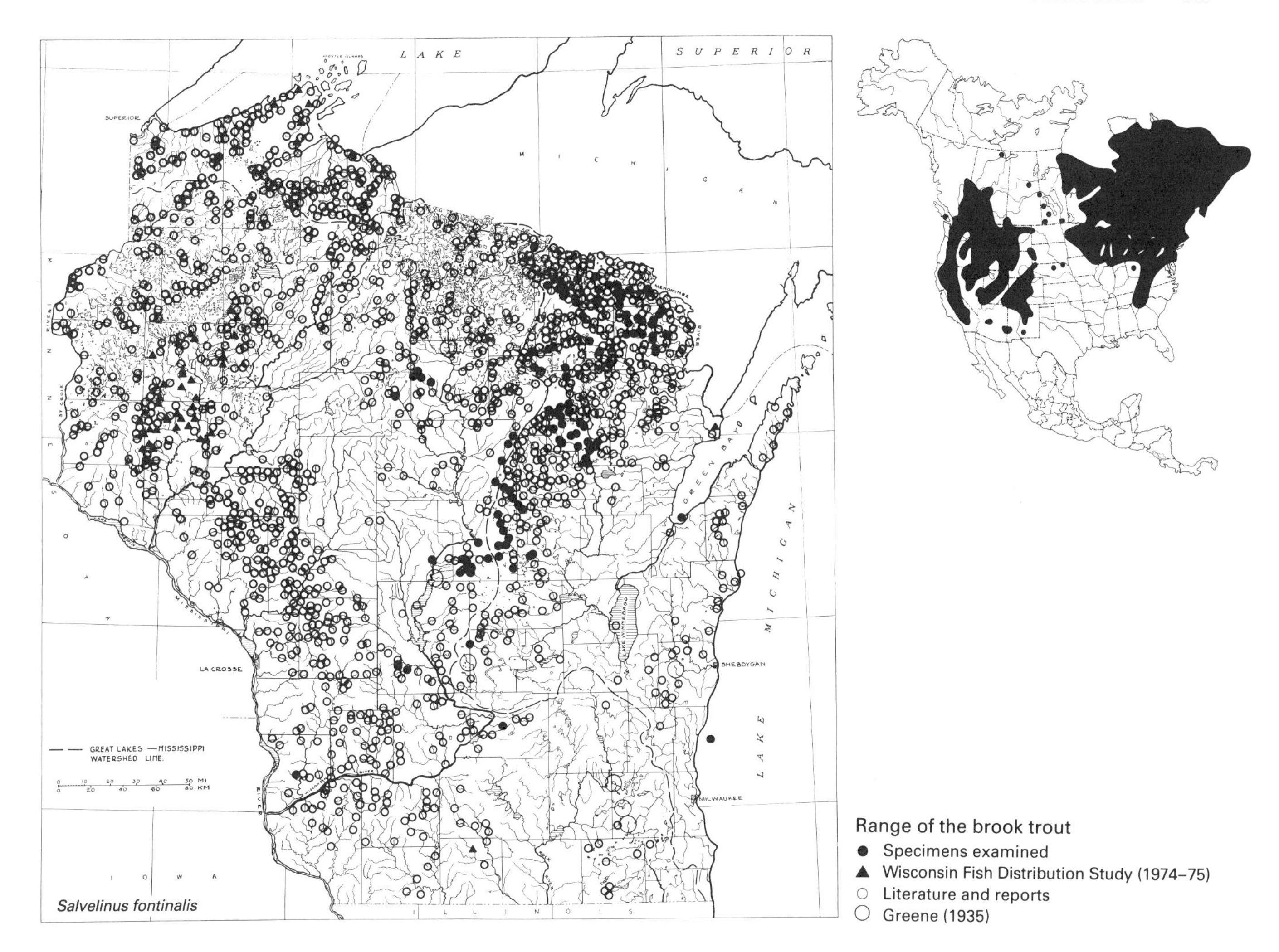

this species were: mud (10%), silt (17%), sand (26%), detritus (4%), gravel (23%), rubble (11%), and boulders (9%). The average widths of streams in which this species was encountered were: 1–3 m, 42%; 3.1–6.0 m, 25%; 6.1–12.0 m, 18%; 12.1–24 m, 13%; and 24.1–50 m, 1%.

BIOLOGY

Spawning in Wisconsin occurs late in the year, generally peaking in mid-November. As the spawning season approaches, mature brook trout seek gravel riffles in spring-fed tributaries, in a main stream, or in spring seepage areas in ponds (Brasch et al. 1973). Brook trout also spawn on the shores of lakes with moderately swift currents, and on lake bottoms where the updwelling water of spring seepage provides the oxygen necessary for the young to develop (Curtis 1949, MacKay 1963).

The female constructs the nest by darting upstream into the gravel, turning quickly on her side, and vibrating her body against the bottom; the nest-building act culminates with a sweep of the tail (Hazzard 1932). Construction of the nest may last as long as 2 days, with activity occurring at night as well as during the day. When completed, the nest is 0.3–0.6 m diam and several cm deep. A male in attendance fights off intruding males, but does not assist in nest construction.

Males display two types of courting activity. In one type, the male approaches the female as she lies in the nest, and pushes her gently from the center of the depression. In the other type, the male swims above the female, first in back and then in front of her dorsal fin, touching her with his body and fins (Hazzard 1932).

In spawning, the female takes a position at the bottom of the pit with pectoral and pelvic fins well spread against the stones (Greeley 1932). She remains motionless, with her vent close to the deepest part of the pit. The male, a larger fish than the female, darts to a position against one side of the female and curves his body toward hers in such a manner as to hold her against the bottom. For several seconds the male's body vibrates rapidly. Eggs and milt are extruded simultaneously.

After spawning, the female covers the nest by using her anal fin to sweep gravel over the pit from its edges (Curtis 1949). When the nest is finished, the eggs are beneath 4–20 cm of gravel.

A peculiar behavior on the part of small males was described by White (1930). While the nest-guarding male was chasing away another male, small males darted over the nest and seized the female by the ovipore. White assumed that this was a means of getting eggs to eat. Eddy and Surber (1947) noted that, although minnows and suckers took trout eggs from the nest, these were generally dead eggs lying at the surface of the nest.

The number of eggs produced during a spawning season varies with the size and age of the brook trout. The female probably produces 300–400 eggs. The number may vary from fewer than 100 in a 127-mm (5-in) female to about 1,200 in a 356-mm (14-in) fish. The eggs are large, 3–5 mm diam.

Fertilization of the eggs and survival to the fry stage is usually good (80–90%) under good habitat conditions (Brasch et al. 1973). Concentrations of spawning brook trout occur near springs, and the eggs are dependent upon the steady percolation of water through the gravel for aeration. The length of the egg incubation period depends upon water temperature. Development proceeds most rapidly and successfully with steady and moderate water temperatures. The mortality of eggs is high where water temperatures are low (near freezing). Groundwater springs are, therefore, essential for best development (Threinen and Poff 1963). At a constant 10°C (50°F), the development period is about 47 days, an optimum time for hatching. At 2.8°C (37°F) the development period is about 165 days.

When hatched, the larvae (sac-fry) remain in the gravel within the nest until the yolk is absorbed. They emerge from the gravel beds from January to April, depending on local conditions. The free-swimming fry are 20 mm (0.8 in) long. Hausle (1973) determined that low levels of dissolved oxygen (less than 6 ppm), and sand in excess of about 15% in the spawning gravel, reduced the number of fry emerging.

Survival from eggs to 9-month-old fingerlings in Lawrence Creek (Marquette County) is low, ranging from 1 to 2%. Overwinter survival of brook trout in Lawrence Creek is approximately 55% with little difference between age groups; large fingerlings have a higher overwinter survival than small fingerlings (Brasch et al. 1973).

Under normal conditions, the size attained for each year class of brook trout is: age 0—76–152 mm (3–6 in); age I—152–254 mm (6–10 in); and age II—203–330 mm (8–13 in) (Brasch et al. 1973). Slow-growing fish may not reach a length of 152 mm (6 in) until the third or fourth year of life. A September sample of brook trout in Lawrence Creek (Marquette County) averaged: age 0—94 mm (3.7 in); age I—170 mm (6.7 in); age II—208 mm (8.2 in); age III—292 mm (11.5 in); age IV—353 mm (13.9 in); and age V—366 mm (14.4 in). The male grows faster than the female. Because of high mortality, brook trout older than 3 years are rare. A few 4-, 5-, and 6-year-olds are probably caught each season. They range in size from 381 to 508 mm (15 to 20 in).

In fertile lakes, the growth rate of brook trout is often faster, with lengths of 457 mm (18 in) being attained in 2 or 3 years. Yearling trout 152 mm (6 in) TL, planted in Lake Michigan, reached an average of 345 mm (13.6 in) after 1 year in the lake (Daly 1968b). Such coasters usually weigh 907–1,361 g (2–3 lb), and may live to be 5 or 6 years old (Downs 1974). A 660-mm (26-in), 2.9-kg (6-lb 8-oz) coaster was taken at Bailey's Harbor (Door County) in 1971.

In Wisconsin, brook trout mature early in life. At Lawrence Creek, 5% of the males are mature at the end of the first summer of life; the smallest mature fish are about 89 mm (3.5 in) long. Most females (about 80%) mature as yearlings, at minimum lengths of about 127 mm (5 in).

The largest brook trout from Wisconsin was caught from the Prairie River (Lincoln County) on 2 September 1944; it weighed 4.5 kg (9 lb 15 oz). The maximum size for brook trout was a 6.6-kg (14.5-lb) specimen caught in Rabbit Rapids, Nipigon River, Ontario, in 1915 (Scott and Crossman 1973). From time to time, rumors of larger brook trout have been circulated, but none have been substantiated.

Brook trout are voracious feeders, consuming large amounts of animal matter, including aquatic insects (especially Trichoptera, Diptera, and Ephemeroptera), terrestrial insects, crustaceans, fish, and annelids. Availability often dictates what the trout will consume. Brook trout fry in Lawrence Creek consumed more chironomids, simuliids, and ephemeropterans than trichopterans or amphipods during their first 6 months of life (J. M. Miller 1974).

In the Little Plover River (Portage County), 68% of the brook trout had taken *Gammarus*, and in a 172-mm specimen there were more than 200 in the stomach. Caddisflies appeared in 40% of the stomachs. Other items included Coleoptera, Odonata, Hemiptera nymphs, annelids, unidentifiable plant seeds, and a 2-mm piece of brown glass which had lodged in a stomach wall (L. Lange, pers. comm.).

Brook trout in a spring pond (Shawano County) consumed gastropods, amphipods, chironomids, coleopterans, *Daphnia*, corixids, trichopterans, and other organisms (Carline et al. 1976). Whenever *Daphnia* were available (especially those 1 mm and larger), brook trout consumed them in large numbers. Forage fish were abundant in the pond, but were not heavily utilized by trout. Relatively small benthic invertebrates dominated the diet of all sizes of trout, although sticklebacks were important for the largest fish (Carline 1975). It is suspected that the absence of large brook trout in many spring ponds is due in part to the lack of large invertebrates and abundant forage fish.

Brook trout feed on insects mostly during early morning and evening periods of low light intensity, but feeding may occur at high noon on a bright day if a hatch of flies takes place. The optimum temperature for feeding is about 19°C (66°F).

Although commonly seen in groups, the brook trout is not a schooling species. It lies under cover, such as rocks, undercut banks, and logs, if available. In streams, the largest trout locate in deep holes or runs, only moving into unprotected waters and shallows when feeding.

The brook trout is largely stationary in habit. Wild brook trout in Lawrence Creek, during their first summer of life, move short distances from the nest, either upstream or downstream (usually the latter) (Hunt 1965b). The majority of tagged brook trout in the Au Sable River, Michigan, moved upstream an average of 0.8 km (0.5 mi), and about 20% remained in the locality where they were tagged (Shetter 1936). The bulk of the population moved downstream in the winter. Yearling brook trout stocked in Lake Michigan quickly enter tributary streams as far as 8 km (5 mi) from the point of release (Daly 1968b); there they remain until warm water temperatures drive them back into the lake.

According to data summarized by Clark (1969), the preferred temperatures of the brook trout, determined in the field, are 13.9–15.6°C (57–60°F). Temperatures recommended by the Federal Water Pollution Control Administration for satisfactory growth and for spawning are 20°C (68°F) and 12.8°C (55°F) respectively; the upper lethal limit is 25°C (77°F). Temperatures well below the lethal limit can be in the stress range (Clark 1969). The oxygen content of water must be at a minimum of 5 ppm throughout the year, and the water must be free of heavy silt, noxious gases, and other pollutants. The pH range of the water should be within 6.5 to 9, although trout may survive pH as low as 4.5 or as high as 10, if the change is not abrupt (Borell and Scheffer 1961).

The most consistent fish associate of the brook trout is the mottled sculpin; less common are the white sucker, creek chub, pearl dace, brook stickleback, and brown trout. Marginal brook trout waters are sometimes invaded by warmwater species such as northern pike, largemouth bass, yellow perch, and bluegills.

IMPORTANCE AND MANAGEMENT

The historical presence of the brook trout in all suitable waters in Wisconsin may well be the reason why the grayling (*Thymallus arcticus*) has not occurred in the state in recent times. In neighboring Michigan, sizable populations of graylings were present in coldwater streams of the upper and lower peninsulas, until man purposely introduced the more aggressive brook trout into those waters; by 1930, the grayling had been extirpated in Michigan. Where the brook trout has been introduced, in the mountain streams and lakes of the West it has generally succeeded at the expense of the native salmonid fishes.

Mergansers, loons, great blue herons, kingfishers, water snakes, otters, snapping turtles, bass, northern pike, and larger trout are all known to prey on brook trout. Under natural conditions, these depredations are generally harmless. In managed lakes, stocked with domestic trout, predators may be an important limiting factor (Brasch et al. 1973).

In the Bayfield, Wisconsin, hatchery many albino trout have appeared in the hatches. If the albino fry are not separated from the other fry, they are attacked by the normal fish, their pink eyes pecked out, and they die. This may account for the absence of albino fish in nature (Wahlquist 1939).

Perhaps no other trout is taken in greater numbers than the brook trout; anglers probably harvest at least one million wild brook trout from Wisconsin streams each year. It is readily caught on both live baits and artificial lures. Dry and wet flies catch more brook trout once the season is underway than any other lures. Large brook trout will take spinners and spoons; a small daredevil is particularly effective in lakes.

The brook trout is the most easily caught of all Wisconsin stream trout. Despite this, a few individuals reach 305–381 mm (12–15 in), even in streams which are heavily fished.

In addition to being easy to catch, the brook trout is tasty to eat. Its meat is firm and white, or lightly tinted with pink; its flavor sweet and delicate. To some connoisseurs, the brook trout is the supreme table fish, surpassing even the lake whitefish or the walleye.

In normally growing brook trout populations, most of the catch consists of yearling trout. Two-year-olds are also important in the angler's take; since they are heavier than yearlings, they are a higher quality fish. If a fisherman wants fish of a particular size limit, he should fish with artificial lures. Experiments have shown that 38% of stream trout taken on baited hooks die when returned to the water, whereas only 2.7% of the trout taken on flies die when returned.

Although they are rare, coaster brook trout (those spending part of their lives in the Great Lakes) have always supported a small, but exciting and unique, fishery. These fish have provided most of the brook trout over 900 g (2 lb) taken from Wisconsin waters. Coasters have an indefinable, perhaps sentimental, attraction all their own. Their value is out of all proportion to their numbers and size.

Brook trout were reestablished in Lake Michigan by a Wisconsin Department of Natural Resources Program, which began in 1967 with the release of 9,000 yearlings (Daly 1968b). The catch of brook trout from Lake Michigan has been encouraging, increasing from 4,952 fish in 1972 to 10,157 in 1973. In 1973, 40% of the fish were taken from shore; fish from streams accounted for 24%, trolling for 19%, and pier fishing for 19%. While brook trout do not attain the size of the other salmonids, they are highly prized by a select group of fishermen and are readily available in inshore waters.

Although native coaster brook trout persist in Lake Superior, in recent years Michigan has stocked this species. In 1974 the brook trout caught in the Wisconsin waters of Lake Superior averaged 282 mm (11.1 in) in length, weighed a total of 276 kg (608 lb), and constituted 0.9% of the sport fishing harvest by weight (King and Swanson 1975).

In 1976 the sport fishery harvest in Lake Superior included 1,369 brook trout weighing 621 kg (1,369 lb), and in 1977, 106 brook trout weighing 48 kg (106 lb) (Sport Fish. Instit. *Bull.* No. 293, April 1978, p. 7).

Yields of brook trout to anglers of 56 kg/ha of water have been reported from Wisconsin waters. This is several times the recorded, or the even expected, yields of sport fishes from moderately fertile warmwater lakes of the state (Brasch et al. 1973).

Electrofishing surveys conducted in 41 central and east central Wisconsin streams, all subject to fishing pressure, yielded from 48 to 8,750 brook trout per hectare (3–165 kg/ha) (Brasch et al. 1973). More intensive studies and comprehensive population estimates of fished portions of Lawrence Creek (Marquette County) gave spring standing crops of 34–101 kg/ha, and fall standing crops of 50–112 kg/ha. In an unfished refuge portion of Lawrence Creek, the standing crop built up to 277 kg/ha.

Lawrence Creek is one of the best researched trout streams anywhere. From a series of comprehensive reports, Hunt (1966, 1969, and 1971) provided estimates of annual fish production for 11 consecutive years—one of the longest and most reliable published records covering all age groups in a wild fish population. The series also spans lifetime production by eight generations of brook trout (the 1960–1967 year classes), and for five of these year classes it provides comparative data on total angler harvest.

In the upper section of Lawrence Creek, high production of brook trout resulted from a stream improvement program carried out in 1964 to increase pool area and streambank hiding cover for trout (Hunt 1974). Hunt observed:

> Despite the upward trend in production in developed Section A (the upstream study section) streamwide production remained quite stable because of concurrent downward trends in Sections C and D (two lowermost study sections). Comparison of annual production trends in improved Section A to annual production trends in the three unimproved sections revealed a high degree of intersectional dependence not previously realized from numerous analyses of standing stock data. . . .
>
> In this study, as in many ecological investigations, many "answers" are incomplete, many unresolved questions remain, many "pieces of the puzzle" are still missing. . . . The population demonstrated great adaptability and resiliency in attaining a level of approximately 500 kg of production each year. But why this level? Of all the associated unanswered questions that could be raised, this is perhaps the most intriguing. What environmental components limited this brook trout population to this level of production, despite substantial variations in population size, age structure and proportional distribution among the four study sections? (p. 14).

The effects of different angling regulations on a wild brook trout population and fishery were also studied at Lawrence Creek (Hunt 1962). Three sets of regulations were evaluated: a 6-in (152-mm) minimum size limit and bag limit of 10; no size limit and no bag limit; and a 9-in (229-mm) minimum size limit and bag limit of 5. The first two sets of regulations were much alike in their effect upon angler harvest. Few anglers were skillful enough to catch 10 or more wild brook trout, and few brook trout less than 6 in were kept when it was legal to do so. When the minimum size limit was raised to 9 in, the catch was dramatically reduced and fishing pressure declined. Simultaneously, the growth of trout declined, and instances of higher-than-normal summer and winter mortality due to natural causes reduced the possibility of stockpiling enough age-II brook trout to provide a yield (in terms of both number and kilograms) comparable to one that includes a significant percentage of age-I brook trout as well.

Much basic research on brook trout has been done in Wisconsin. White and Hunt (1969) noted that in two central Wisconsin brook trout streams age-0 brook trout followed a 2-year rhythm (cycle) of alternating upward and downward levels of abundance. This cycle persisted in both streams, despite somewhat different environmental characteristics and different general levels of trout populations in the two streams. The researchers concluded that it was unlikely that climate or predation gave rise to the cycle, and that competition between age-0 and age-I fish may have been responsible. They cited LeCren (1965), who found that the numerical density of trout fry was apparently a result of territorial behavior: fry not able to secure a territory drifted downstream and died of starvation.

Heding and Hacker (1960:22) reviewed the role of springs in brook trout reproduction and abundance:

> Detrimental land use practices, constructing dams on small streams, digging ponds, and creating small impoundments in spring-fed areas of our trout streams all have a disastrous effect on the natural reproduction of trout. . . . Springs are the "life blood" of our trout streams. Destroy that "life" in a trout stream and it's gone—forever.

The beaver has been cited as the cause for a serious decline of brook trout in some northern Wisconsin streams, where many small spring tributaries have been dammed by the animals (Christenson et al. 1961, Knudsen 1962).

Mason et al. (1967) suggested that wild strains of brook trout be introduced into potential brook trout streams, because wild strains survived longer in streams investigated than domestic and hybrid trout. O. Brynildson and Christenson (1961) concluded that the highest overwinter survival of fall-stocked, domestic brook, brown, and rainbow trout occurred in streams where ice cover was rare during winter, and where there was adequate instream cover and a low population of resident trout.

In a stream habitat development on the Kinnickinnic River (Saint Croix County), the population of brook trout more than 5.5 in long increased to 4 or 5 times its original size (Frankenberger 1968). Guidelines for the management of trout stream habitats in Wisconsin have been prepared by White and Brynildson (1967).

Brush removal from banks, as a technique for managing small trout streams, has been evaluated by Braatz (1974). Factors supporting the use of this technique, in areas where increases in water temperature would not be critical, included the availability of food for invertebrates, the abundance of invertebrates in the drift, and the greater amount of food found in trout stomachs.

Treating suitable lakes with fish poisons to eradicate the existing warmwater fish population, and the subsequent stocking of the lakes with brook trout, has introduced fishing for brook trout where it was not available prior to such management (Brasch et al. 1973). In these lakes, the growth of trout is usually good if proper stocking rates are used; prize fish are frequently taken.

Where hydraulic dredging of spring ponds has been used as a management tool, both the amount of fishing and the numbers of trout caught have increased (Carline and Brynildson 1977). Compared to other small lakes containing salmonids, standing crops and yields of trout from Wisconsin spring ponds have been among the highest reported.

In recent years the accelerated deterioration of Wisconsin's brook trout waters has been well documented. Habitat deterioration is a common result of grazing, the destruction of bank cover, the careless use of agricultural chemicals and irrigation, road construction, the dredging of ponds or spring feeders, and the damming of streams, to name only a few of the causes. Even such famous waters as the Brule River in Douglas County have shown a shrinkage of brook trout water. In the Brule at the turn of the century, brook trout were present in numbers throughout its 65-km length; today, wild brook trout inhabit only the upper third of the river. Introductions of competitive rainbow and brown trout may have had some part in this shrinkage.

Also, detrimental effects on native brook trout populations may occur with the introduction of exotic fishes such as the coho salmon. Avery (1974) gave evidence of brook trout nests in Kewaunee County which were being disrupted by superimposed coho salmon nests. Since only four small brook trout streams remain in that county, Avery recommended the placement of devices which would prevent any anadromous species, such as the coho salmon, from migrating into areas inhabited by the native trout.

Walden (1964:7) has penned an appropriate warning:

> In the northeastern United States millions of hatchery brook trout are stocked annually in the put-and-take game of modern fishing. But one is inclined to use the past tense in writing of the wild brook trout. Constitutionally incompatible with the advance of civilization, this exquisite fish is dying. Where man has dried up his springs by deforestation, polluted his waterways, straightened streams into ditches and denuded them of their natural cover, the wild brook trout has vanished. And with it has gone an essence of that early America which somehow it symbolized: rural peace, unmachined enterprise, and nature left to herself.

Lake Trout

Salvelinus namaycush namaycush (Walbaum). *Salvelinus*—an old name for char; *namaycush*—an American Indian name.

Other common names: Great Lakes trout, mackinaw trout, salmon trout, laker, lean trout, lean char, lean, gray trout, great gray trout, Great Lakes char, landlocked salmon, namaycush, forktail trout.

L. Superior (Wisconsin DNR photo, Lake Superior Work Unit, Bayfield)

DESCRIPTION

Body elongate, somewhat rounded. Average size 381–508 mm (15–20 in) TL. Depth into TL 3.8–5.5. Head into TL 3.6–4.8; in lateral view, top of head almost a straight line. Snout when mouth closed usually protruding slightly beyond upper jaw. Mouth terminal, slightly oblique, large. Maxillary extending beyond eye; teeth on upper and lower jaws. Gill rakers 12–24. Branchiostegal rays 10–14. Major dorsal fin rays 8–10; major anal fin rays 8–10; pectoral fin rays 12–17; pelvic fin rays 8–11; caudal fin deeply forked. Lateral scales 185–210 in diagonal rows. Pyloric caeca 120–180 (93–208). Chromosomes 2n = 84 (Roberts 1967).

Back, sides, head, and dorsal, adipose, and caudal fins light green, gray, or dark green with light spots; belly white. Pectoral, pelvic, anal, and caudal fins occasionally orange. Lower fins sometimes with narrow white border. Males display prominent black lateral stripe at spawning. Young with 7–12 parr marks, the spaces between parr marks equal to or greater than the marks themselves. Lake trout over 102 mm (4 in) with characteristic pale markings of char in young, hind edge of maxillary not reaching posterior edge of large eye.

Hybrids: Lake trout × brook trout, lake trout × rainbow trout (Schwartz 1972).

The splake (from *speckled* and *lake* trout) is a hybrid of the lake trout and the brook trout; in appearance and characteristics it resembles both parents. Usually it lacks the deeply forked tail of the lake trout; the dorsal and caudal fins are usually light spotted; and 65–85 pyloric caeca are present. For biology see p. 329.

DISTRIBUTION, STATUS, AND HABITAT

The lake trout is present in all three major drainage basins in Wisconsin. It occurs naturally in Lake Superior and in deep inland lakes, such as Trout Lake and Black Oak Lake (Vilas County). Until recently Lake Michigan sustained a native population, but this species no longer spawns in that lake (see Importance and Management). Because of extensive early distribution of lake trout fry into many northern Wisconsin lakes, its natural distribution is not known although it was reported from Keyes Lake (Florence County) in 1906, from upper St. Croix Lake (Douglas County) in 1908, and from Holly, Moon, and Hammil lakes (Bayfield County) in 1980 (D. Fago, pers. comm.). Greene (1935) examined specimens from Little Trout and Crystal lakes (Vilas County) and from Hammil Lake (Bayfield County). Fossil lake trout were taken from a Pleistocene clay bed at Menomonie (Dunn County) (Hussakof 1916).

The lake trout has been planted in a large number of Wisconsin's inland waters. In 1875 (Commnrs. Fish. of Wis. 1876) "250,000 salmon trout" were stocked in Lake Geneva, and "1 million" were stocked 2 years later. In 1877 such unlikely lakes as Browns (Racine County), Oconomowoc, Pine, Pewaukee, North, Nagawicka, and Okauchee (all in Waukesha County), and waters in Rock, Washington, Green Lake, Chippewa, and Saint Croix counties were stocked with this species.

In recent years the lake trout has been reported from the following inland lakes: Trout, Little Trout, and Crystal (all in Vilas County); Hammil, Lac Court Oreilles, and Little Court Oreilles (Sawyer County); Lucerne (Forest County); Big Green (Green Lake County); Keyes and Sea Lion (Florence County); Tomahawk and Big Carr (Oneida County); and Geneva (Walworth County). In most of these lakes fishing is maintained by continual stocking (Daly et al. 1962).

In Wisconsin the lake trout deserves close watching. It no longer spawns in Lake Michigan, where a population is currently sustained through extensive stocking. In Lake Superior, breeding lake trout populations have declined. The original status of this species in Wisconsin's inland lakes is virtually unknown since early records of the fish species present in these lakes were not kept. As noted above, the question of the original distribution of lake trout is confused further, because artificially propagated trout were stocked in many inland lakes early in the history of the Wis-

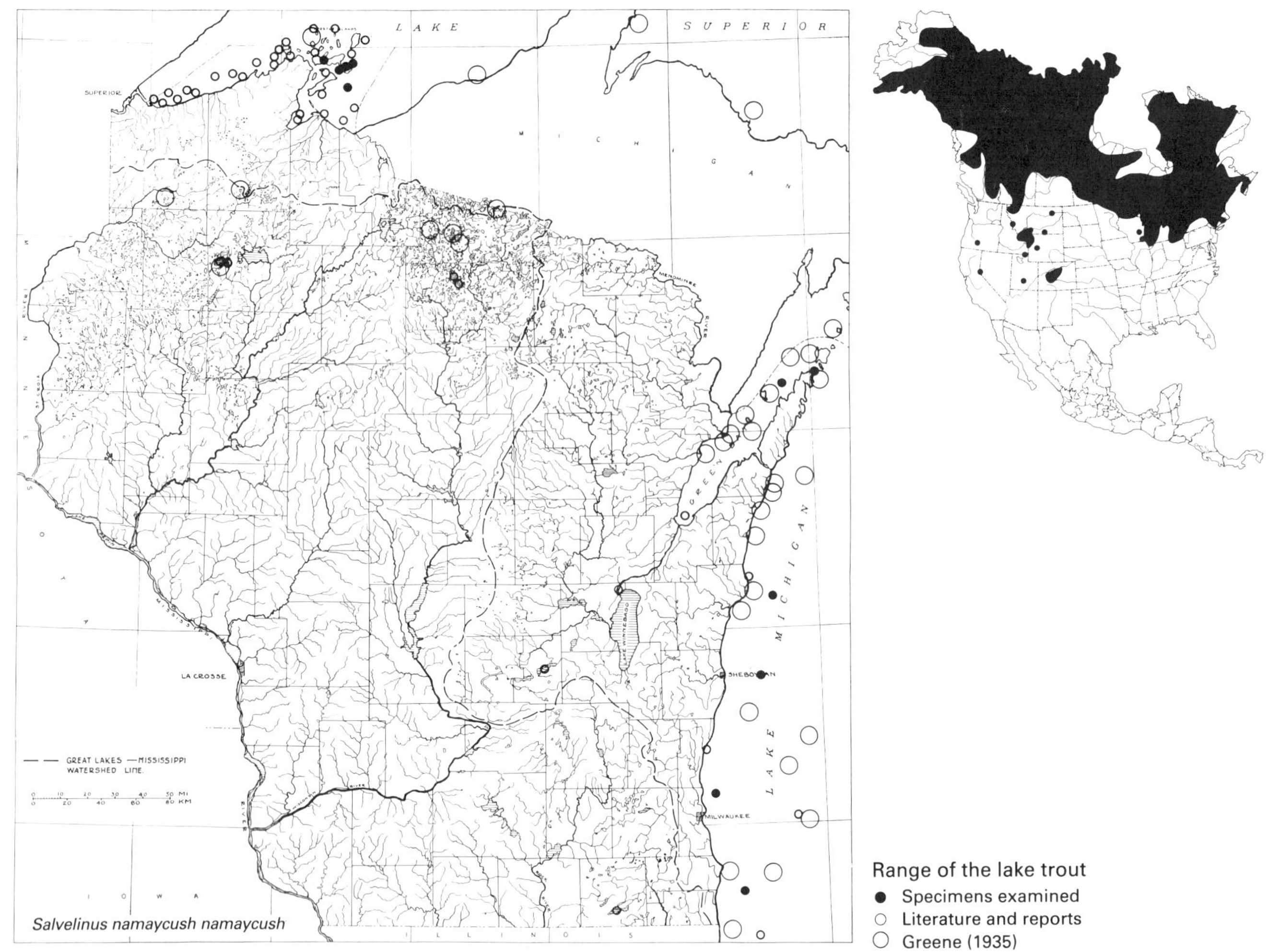

consin fisheries program. In summary, the lake trout appears to be decreasing in Wisconsin waters and its future will be increasingly dependent upon a vigorous propagation program.

Lake trout spend most of their lives in the deeper waters of cold lakes. They move about extensively, however, and may be found at any depth during certain seasons or at certain localities. In the Great Lakes, they are usually most abundant at depths between 30 and 90 m (100 and 300 ft). Generally, they live at or near the bottom, but some may also occur in the open water, far offshore, where they are caught commercially on setlines or in gill nets suspended below the surface. In smaller, inland lakes in the southerly part of their range, lake trout are restricted to deep water in summer by the warming of the surface water (Eschmeyer 1957).

BIOLOGY

Spawning occurs in fall, from mid-October to early December. The depth of the spawning grounds may be a few centimeters to 30 m or deeper (Daly et al. 1962). Most lake trout spawn on rocky bars which are kept free from silt by water currents. The Milwaukee and Sheboygan reefs in Lake Michigan and the Apostle Island reefs in Lake Superior were well-known spawning grounds. In southern Lake Michigan, before their extirpation, lake trout spawned on a clay bottom at depths as great as 60 m (200 ft) or more (Eschmeyer 1957). River-spawning populations of lake trout in eastern Lake Superior cast their eggs over large boulders intermixed with coarse gravel (Loftus 1958).

The spawning behavior of lake trout has been summarized by Eschmeyer (1957:3–4):

> No nest or redd is built by lake trout. The males, which outnumber the females on the spawning grounds, precede the females in congregating on the breeding area. They cruise over the bottom and clean it of debris, algal growth, and slime by fanning and rubbing the rocks. . . . Most activity occurs between dusk and midnight and reaches its peak shortly after dark, although a few males may be present at all times of the day during the height of the breeding season. Lake trout are polygamous and there is no vigor-

ous fighting or defense of territory. During courtship a marked, but transitory color change occurs among the males; the back becomes light and silvery while a dark, lustrous stripe appears along each side. Spawning may occur with only 1 or 2 males and 1 female taking part, or several males and several females may compose a compact spawning group. Typically, one or more males approach and nudge or nip at a female and then press against her side, with the vents in close proximity. The bodies of the fish quiver, their mouths open, and the dorsal fin of the male is held erect. Each act lasts for only a few seconds and undoubtedly must be repeated a number of times before spawning is completed. The fish breed at random over the cleaned area and no attempt is made to bury or otherwise care for the eggs, which sink into crevices among the rocks.

Individual male lake trout may remain on or near the spawning grounds for 3 weeks or more, but after the spawning season is over the adults disperse widely from the breeding area. Although lake trout may move to distant points between breeding seasons, most return to the same spawning grounds each year.

The principal spawning grounds of lake trout in southern Lake Superior are on rocky shoals at depths of less than 36 m. Spawning native lake trout on Gull Island Shoal were tagged, and subsequent returns of these fish indicated that nearly 100% homed back to Gull Island Shoal to spawn. Hatchery-reared lake trout spawning on Gull Island Shoal only achieved a 58.6% return. Such apparent wandering by hatchery-bred lake trout, in comparison to native lake trout, may greatly reduce their spawning potential (Swanson 1973). The largest runs of hatchery fish have been in inshore areas not known as major spawning grounds; most return to the areas where they were planted or to similar shore areas. Swanson noted that the Gull Island Shoal lake trout spawning population nearly doubled between 1963 and 1971.

In Lake Michigan and Green Bay, reef, shoal, or "honeycomb" rock in 2–36 m of water were chosen by lake trout as spawning grounds. No successful reproduction has occurred in Lake Michigan since the native trout population was extirpated in the mid-1950s.

The optimum water temperature for lake trout spawning in the Apostle Islands is 7.8–11.1°C (46–52°F). In small, inland lakes lake trout usually spawn just before the ice forms.

River spawning in streams of eastern Lake Superior (Loftus 1958) occurred in the second half of September and early October. The spawning bed at the Montreal River consisted of large boulders intermixed with coarse gravel, in an eddy near the lower end of a gorge some 200 m from Lake Superior. Eggs stripped from these lake trout, and incubated in a hatchery at the temperature of the lake water, hatched as early as late November.

The lake trout's eggs are 5–6 mm diam. The production of eggs by 70 lake trout 638–965 mm (25.1–38.0 in) TL and weighing 2.63–8.89 kg (5.8–19.6 lb), ranged from 2,476 to 17,119 (Eschmeyer 1955). The incubation period extends from 4 to 5 months, and hatching occurs from mid-February to the end of March. A newly hatched larva is 16 mm TL, with a large yolk-sac still attached. It spends another month among the rocks, resorbing the yolk-sac, and then moves into deeper waters. Fish (1932) illustrated a 21.5-mm sac-fry.

In southern Lake Superior, young-of-year lake trout increased from 30 mm (1.2 in) on 22–23 June to 79 mm (3.1 in) on 21–22 October.

Rahrer (1967) calculated total length and weight for Lake Superior lake trout as follows: I—102 mm, 9 g; II—160 mm, 27 g; III—216 mm, 73 g; IV—279 mm, 173 g; V—351 mm, 354 g; VI—427 mm, 658 g; VII—500 mm, 1.16 kg; VIII—579 mm, 1.90 kg; IX—668 mm, 2.95 kg; X—749 mm, 4.34 kg; XI—818 mm, 6.12 kg; and XII—876 mm, 8.29 kg.

In Lake Michigan (Van Oosten and Eschmeyer 1956), the growth of lake trout before the arrival of the lamprey was: I—86 mm; II—178 mm; III—257 mm; IV—320 mm; V—373 mm; VI—434 mm; VII—493 mm; VIII—536 mm; IX—587 mm; X—638 mm. Since 1966, yearling lake trout have been stocked from April to June in Lake Michigan. In May these yearlings average 132 mm and 18 g. In the lake, they attain the following total length and weight at the end of each year of life: 2—315 mm, 272 g; 3—414 mm, 635 g; 4—503 mm, 1.3 kg; 5—599 mm, 2.7 kg; 6—650 mm, 3.0 kg; 7—714 mm, 3.7 kg; 8—719 mm, 3.6 kg; 9—767 mm, 4.8 kg; 10—770 mm, 4.9 kg; and 11—785 mm, 5.2 kg (J. Moore, pers. comm.). In Green Lake stocked yearlings grew from 152 mm (6 in) to 406 mm (16 in) in 3 years (Daly et al. 1962).

In Lake Superior, male lake trout were first mature at age IV (520 mm TL), and females at age V (596 mm TL); however, the bulk of the fish in the spawning runs were ages VII and VIII (Dryer and King 1968). In most waters of Wisconsin, lake trout are mature when either 7 years old or about 610 mm (24 in) TL; the Green Lake population produced 610 mm males in 6 years (Daly et al. 1962). In general, males mature at an earlier age and are smaller than females. Varying numbers of mature lake trout in some lakes do not spawn each year, but may skip one or more seasons, during which they do not produce eggs or milt (Eschmeyer 1957).

Lake trout may live as long as 20 years (Van Oosten

1932). In 1971 and 1973, two age-XIII fish were caught in the sport fishery in Lake Superior (King and Swanson 1975).

The lake trout is the largest of all the trout; the average specimen generally weighs from 3.2 to 5.4 kg (7 to 12 lb). A 131-cm (51.5-in) fish, taken on hook and line in May 1952 from Lake Superior, weighed 28.6 kg (63 lb 2 oz) (Eschmeyer 1957); another, taken on 9 September 1946, weighed 21.3 kg (47 lb). A 16-kg (35-lb 4-oz) lake trout was taken in June 1957 from Big Green Lake (Green Lake County). A 79-cm, 7.2-kg (31-in, 15-lb 14.5-oz) fish was caught in 1971 at Cave Point (Door County) in Lake Michigan. A 46.3-kg (102-lb) lake trout was hauled out of Lake Athabaska, Saskatchewan, by a commercial fisherman in August 1961 (MacKay 1963).

In Lake Superior, the opossum shrimp *(Mysis)* was found to be by far the most important food of small lake trout. It was in 70% of the stomachs examined, and made up 84% of the food volume of young-of-year fish, 95% of the food of age-I fish, and 82% of the food of age-II fish. Other crustaceans, insects, and fish were less important in the diet (Eschmeyer 1956). As the lake trout grew larger, ciscoes, smelt, and cottids increased in the diet from 4.4% at 127–150 mm (5–5.9 in) to 93.9% at 406–429 mm (16–16.9 in) (Dryer et al. 1965).

Eschmeyer (1957) stated that lake trout eat whatever kind of fish happen to be available in the immediate environment. Small lake trout have been found only infrequently in the stomachs of lake trout, probably because of the greater relative abundance of other forage species rather than because of any scruples against cannibalism.

In Lake Michigan during the summer, lake trout consumed alewives (occurred in 53.7% of stomachs), unidentified fish remains (50.2%), sculpins (22.2%), smelt (20.7%), ninespine stickleback (0.5%), insects (1%), and fish eggs (0.5%); during the winter they consumed unidentified fish remains (46%), alewives (25.9%), sculpins (22.3%), smelt (16.5%), and invertebrates (mainly *Mysis relicta*) (15.1%) (Daly et al. 1974). Alewife remains have been found in lake trout as small as 208 mm (8.2 in) TL, and alewives become a more common food item in fish 254 mm (10 in) and larger. Cottid species are the preferred forage fish of newly stocked lake trout (Daly 1968b).

Adult lake trout in Big Green Lake feed on the cisco, sunfish, and lake emerald shiner (Hacker 1957). It is believed that in certain inland lakes predation by large lake trout may severely limit the density of their own population. In summer, when warming of the water prevents lake trout from reaching the upper levels occupied by their usual forage, they are driven to feed largely on zooplankton.

At certain times, lake trout become opportunistic and take advantage of other abundant foods. When large hatches of flies occur in late spring, the trout feed exclusively on the rafts of these insects on the water surface. On inland lakes, lake trout have been known to eat migrating shrews as they swam across the lake. Yellow warblers, apparently confused in flight by fog, have been found in the stomachs of surface-feeding lake trout (Daly et al. 1962).

The peak feeding temperature for the lake trout is 10.6°C (51°F).

Although lake trout are more abundant in some localities than in others in the lakes where they occur, they seldom form compact schools. Even the young are scattered and seem to have more or less solitary habits (Eschmeyer 1957). In Lake Superior during the summer months, young-of-year lake trout were found principally at depths of less than 36 m; in October, most were caught in water more than 36 m deep. All collections were made at water temperatures of 5.6–17.2°C (42–63°F). Most age-I and age-II trout were caught at depths of 36–62 m at temperatures of 3.9–11.7°C (39–53°F) (Eschmeyer 1956).

In the Apostle Islands region of Lake Superior, the lake trout was most common at depths of 18–53 m when data were combined for all seasons (Dryer 1966). In the spring an occasional lake trout was taken at depths to 143 m. In southern Lake Michigan, juvenile lake trout (mostly 305–381 mm) were concentrated at 73–90 m; in northern Lake Michigan, at 55–71 m.

The movement and migration of lake trout in Lake Superior is variable. Large-sized lake trout tagged near Keweenaw Point, Michigan, traveled west up to 307 km (190 mi), but if tagged over spawning grounds, there was a tendency for such trout to return to the same grounds, even though they may have wandered widely in the interim (Eschmeyer et al. 1953). Smaller lake trout (avg 462 mm), released in the Apostle Islands region, were recaptured during the first year, generally within an 81 km (50 mi) radius of the release site; however, some were taken from Grand Marais, Michigan, 412 km (255 mi) to the east. These tagging experiments supported the concept that the prevailing currents in Lake Superior were responsible, at least in part, for the long migrations recorded.

Pycha et al. (1965) noted that dispersal of yearling lake trout begins at planting and probably continues until the fish are mature. Most movement was eastward in southern Lake Superior, and followed the counterclockwise surface currents. Movement was most rapid in areas of strong currents, and slowest in areas of weak currents or eddies. In a recent tagging experiment, nearly one-third of all hatchery and native lake trout tagged on Wisconsin spawning grounds migrated into Michigan waters of Lake Superior in the summer (Swanson 1973). Natives returned to Wisconsin to spawn, whereas many of the hatchery fish did not return, at least not to the sampled spawning reefs. In summary, studies of the movement of native lake trout (including river-spawning lake trout) and hatchery-reared, planted lake trout indicate that most fish live within a radius of about 81 km (50 mi) of their points of hatching or planting. Some individuals, however, wander extensively (Lawrie and Rahrer 1973).

O. B. Smith and Van Oosten (1940) reported that it required 3 years for 1,416 tagged lake trout to become scattered through Lake Michigan. Most immature fish moved northward from the tagging site (near Port Washington) on the west-central shore and followed the shoreline. Mature fish were recaptured in all directions from the point of release, some having traveled more than 202 km (125 mi).

The lake trout seldom remains for extended periods in water of temperatures greater than 18.3°C (65°F); its preferred temperature is about 10°C (50°F) (Eschmeyer 1957). Lake trout can tolerate water temperatures up to 25°C (77°F); however, satisfactory growth of the young cannot take place in waters over 20°C (68°F). Higher water temperatures induce the rapid development and hatching of eggs; but beyond a certain point, the biochemistry goes awry and the eggs develop abnormally or not at all.

The principal associates of lake trout in the deeper water where it lives are sculpins, ciscoes, whitefish, and burbot.

IMPORTANCE AND MANAGEMENT

On the Great Lakes, lamprey predation is still a critical problem. Of the larger salmonid fishes, the lake trout is especially vulnerable to lampreys, since as young adults lampreys move into the deeper waters to parasitize the largest fish they can find. In northern Green Bay during 1973 there was an upward trend in the wounding of lake trout of all sizes, and an indication of increased lamprey activity. In Lake Michigan, from Algoma northward, 71% of the trout between 737 and 813 mm (29 and 32 in) long were scarred (Daly et al. 1974). In Lake Superior sea lamprey activity, after having increased in 1971 and 1972, declined in 1973 and held near that level in 1974. In 1974, over 10% of the trout 635 mm (25 in) TL and longer were wounded, but most bore old scars (King and Swanson 1975).

A known predator on lake trout eggs in Big Green Lake (Green Lake County) is the mudpuppy *(Necturus)*, which consumed the trout eggs as fast as they were laid (Weimer 1980). Up to 79 eggs were found in the stomach of one mudpuppy. Construction of an artificial spawning ground from large granite rock has resulted in modest lake trout spawning success.

The lake trout has always been a prized fish, whether taken by hook and line or secured through commercial fishing efforts. It has always commanded premium prices, either fresh or smoked. The flesh is firm, rich in flavor, and is white to red (often orange) in color. It is oily and has high energy value. One analysis found 73% water, 18% protein, 9.4% fat, and 1.0% minerals (Thurston 1962).

In the late 1940s, prior to the depredations by the sea lamprey, charter boat trolling for lake trout on Lakes Michigan and Superior was very popular. In Lake Superior (Belonger 1969) at the peak of the fishery in 1948, 33 charter trolling boats were in operation in Wisconsin waters. Lake trout in the 6.8-kg (15-lb) class, and catches of 23–45 or more kilograms were common.

In the late 1950s and early 1960s, lake trout sport fishing in Wisconsin waters reached its lowest point. Each year since 1962, however, sport fishermen have reported more lake trout taken per fisherman and more lake trout taken per trip. In 1967, 55.2% of the reporting fishermen caught lake trout up to 940 mm (37 in) TL.

The 1974 sport fishing catch of lake trout from Wisconsin waters of Lake Superior was 13,123 kg (28,931 lb), which represented 42% of the total sport harvest by weight, and made the lake trout the highest producer of all salmonid fishes (King and Swanson 1975). In 1976, the sport harvest of lake trout was 7,687 fish weighing 11,149 kg, and in 1977 the harvest was 9,184 fish weighing 11,086 kg (Sport Fish. Instit. *Bull.* No. 293, April 1978, p. 7). Despite the lake trout population levels suggested by these successes, inshore lake trout populations have become substantially depressed compared to the 1970 and 1971 population levels, and abundance levels have been further decreased by Indian fishing activity.

Lake trout bobbing in the Apostle Islands area has become a popular winter pastime. In 1972, 7,838 lake trout were landed. During February and March 1974, an estimated 6,177 bobbers harvested more than 2,937 lake trout (King and Swanson 1975). The average size of lake trout taken by bobbing increased from 505 mm (19.9 in) in 1972 to 549 mm (21.6) in 1974.

A successful program of stocking hatchery-reared lake trout in Lake Superior brought the lake trout population to a high level of abundance in the late 1960s and early 1970s (Wis. Dep. Nat. Resour. 1976). Releases of 16-month-old fish yielded returns to anglers of 5.7 to 37.3% (Pycha and King 1967). Returns from 9-month-old fish varied from only 2.1 to 6.4%.

Currently in Wisconsin there is a minimum commercial legal length for the lake trout of 17 in (432 mm). Since this species matures at a length of about 610 mm (24 in), it might be advisable to raise the limit to that level in bodies of water where natural reproduction is possible. This will not only provide future stock naturally, but it will also make available a quality fishery.

The history of the lake trout as a commercial species has been well documented for Lake Superior by Lawrie and Rahrer (1973), and for Lake Michigan by Wells and McLain (1973). In Lake Superior there appeared to be no significant long-term trend in yields until 1953, when a very steep decline set in; the decline continued at a rate of virtually 27% a year until 1962. This decline was attributable to depredations by the sea lamprey. The constant yields from 1962 to 1966, and the modest increase in yields in 1967 and 1968, occurred after the fisheries had been sharply restricted in 1962, and yields were controlled by the application of quotas on commercial fisheries.

Vying closely with the lake whitefish for first place as a table fish, usually produced in larger quantities, and cherished by the angler, the lake trout was the most important species in Lake Superior until its collapse. There is no doubt that throughout the history of the fisheries the lake trout was sought with the most diligence, persistence, and skill. In these circumstances, the long maintenance of high yields was possible because of the widespread distribution of a number of lake trout populations, each fished up individually. Hile et al. (1951b) documented an increase in effective fishing efforts over a large part of Lake Superior during the 1930s and 1940s, and thus provided convincing evidence that average stock densities were then falling despite the constant yields. Jensen (1978) noted that the fishing became overexploited at about the same time that the sea lamprey was first observed in the lake. Contributing to this excessive exploitation, at least in shallower waters, was the development of a lake trout sport fishery in the second quarter of this century, which averaged 39,000 kg (86,000 lb) from United States waters between 1944 and 1950.

In Lake Michigan the lake trout was the most valuable commercial species from 1890 until the mid-1940s. Production in Lake Michigan was usually the highest of any of the Great Lakes in that period (Wells and McLain 1973:26):

> In 1890–1911 the catch was rather consistently high, averaging 8.2 million pounds. The average annual yield then dropped to 7.0 million pounds in 1912–26, and declined further to 5.3 million pounds in 1927–39. The trend was reversed in 1940–44 when the catch was above 6 million pounds in every year, and the average was 6.6 million. The year 1945 marked the beginning of a precipitous decline that led to a catch of only 342,000 pounds in 1949 and a mere 34 pounds in 1954. Lake trout were extremely rare in 1955 (Eschmeyer 1957) and the species probably became extinct in the lake in 1956.

Even as early as the 1880s, declines in lake trout stocks were observed in certain areas of Lake Michigan. Since the declines were accompanied by appreciable decreases in average size, they probably were the result of exploitation. The gradual decrease in production from 1893 to 1938 was a result of excessive exploitation during a period of greatly increased fishing (Wells and McLain 1973). The sea lamprey had a powerful influence on the phenomenal decline of the lake trout in Lake Michigan after 1944 (Hile et al. 1951a, Eschmeyer 1957).

The lake trout rehabilitation program in Lake Michigan, coordinated by the Great Lakes Fishery Commission, began in 1965. Since then an average of nearly 2 million yearling lake trout (avg about 150 mm) have been stocked each year. The program has been highly successful in producing fish to spawning size, in spite of continued predation by the sea lamprey. The trout have grown rapidly, although no successful spawning is known to have occurred as yet in Lake Michigan. In the 1973 catch in Wisconsin waters of Lake Michigan, lake trout constituted 33⅓% of all salmonids creeled—an estimated 68,929 fish, and the greatest number of any salmonid species. Nearly all (99.44%) were taken trolling; the remainder were taken from pier, shore, and stream. These fish were caught primarily from Kewaunee north; recent plants from Kewaunee south should spread this fishery in future years. Wisconsin has also added some shore planting sites, which may make lake trout more available to a seasonal fishery from shallow, inshore areas (Daly et al. 1974).

When the natural populations of lake trout in Lake Michigan disappeared in the mid-1950s, the last known spawning lake trout disappeared with them. Despite the excellent growth shown by the stocked trout, there has been no indication that they are reproducing. To establish a reproducing population, 210,000 yearling trout were planted in 1976 on the

Milwaukee Reef, offshore from Sheboygan and Port Washington, and about one-third of the way across Lake Michigan. Another 70,000 yearlings were planted on Horseshoe Reef in Green Bay. These are known, historic spawning grounds, and the Milwaukee Reef was the chief breeding ground for the southern half of Lake Michigan before the lamprey problem. In 1978, lake trout fingerlings were lowered onto Horseshoe Reef in Green Bay in the hope that they would imprint to the area and return later to spawn.

A serious potential human health problem is associated with the lake trout, because this fish fixes considerable quantities of DDT, PCB, and other undesirable substances in its body tissues. It has been shown that after 152 days of exposure to dieldrin and DDT in water, yearling lake trout had accumulated an average of 478 ppb dieldrin or 352 ppb DDT (Reinert et al. 1974). In the early 1970s, high levels of toxic substances in Lake Michigan trout and salmon exceeded levels considered safe for human consumption by the FDA; the public and sport fishermen were warned not to eat more than one meal per week of such fishes. In May 1976, the Wisconsin Department of Natural Resources issued an order which banned all Lake Michigan lake trout sales for human consumption because of high PCB levels, and ordered that other means be found to dispose of trout caught in fishing boat nets.

SPLAKE, OR WENDIGO

The splake is a hybrid developed by fertilizing the eggs of a lake trout with the milt of a brook trout. This hybrid was mentioned in the 1884 Report of the Commissioners of Fisheries of Wisconsin, which noted that 2,000 splake had been raised to the age of 11 months. The fate of this experiment is not known.

The splake is produced in fish hatcheries and distributed in lakes. It grows rapidly and matures early (age III), but it is less fertile than either of the parent species. It is more littoral in habit than its parents, thus making it less susceptible to lamprey attacks.

This hybrid was first stocked in Little Bass Lake (8 km east of Woodruff) in 1958. Splake were reared in the Woodruff hatchery from fingerlings received from Michigan. Since then, the splake has been stocked in a number of Wisconsin lakes, including Crystal, Black Oak, Pallette (Vilas County); Left Foot (Marinette County); Ada (Langlade County); Lucerne (Forest County); Green Lake (Green Lake County); and Chain of Lakes (Waupaca County). It has also been stocked in Chequamegon Bay of Lake Superior.

A comprehensive study (O. Brynildson and Kempinger 1970) was made of yearling splake stocked in Pallette Lake in 1964. The average total length and weight of the fish at each year of life was: I—173 mm, 51 g; II—236 mm, 94 g; III—292 mm, 181 g; IV—351 mm, 346 g; V—388 mm, 481 g; VI—531 mm, 1.85 kg. In comparison, age-II splake from Green Lake (O. Brynildson 1966) averaged 76 mm (3 in) longer and weighed twice as much. In Pallette Lake, the largest splake taken was 648 mm (25.5 in) TL, and weighed 3.02 kg (8.85 lb). Splake were relatively easy to catch with minnows on hook and line in the thermocline (9–11 m) at 10–12.8°C (50–55°F).

A 6.46-kg (14-lb 4-oz) splake measuring 787 mm (31 in) long was caught on 7 June 1966 from Ada Lake; it was one of the fish originally stocked in that lake in 1959. It was 9 years old. According to Scott and Crossman (1973), in the Great Lakes individuals have been recaptured from 5 to 6 years after planting; some have weighed up to 7.26 kg (16 lb).

In Lake Huron (Budd 1957), the recapture pattern suggests that splake travel considerably. Two fish traveled a distance of about 161 km (100 mi) from the planting site. As the surface water warmed, the hybrids moved into deeper water. In general, however, they did not go as deep as the lake trout, and were taken in late October and early November on shoals where lake trout were known to have spawned in previous years.

Splake are omnivorous. In Pallette Lake they ate cisco and sucker eggs, plant materials (probably ingested incidentally while foraging for aquatic invertebrates), sand, and pebbles (O. Brynildson and Kempinger 1970). They selected the large (up to 18 mm long) cladoceran, *Leptodora kindtii*. Few fish appeared in the stomachs of yearling splake, but in age-V splake (381–584 mm), fish constituted nearly 100% of the food. The yellow perch was most common, followed by smallmouth bass, sculpins, and minnows. In Green Lake, splake 279–457 mm long consumed ciscoes. Splake food in South Bay, Lake Huron, was mainly sticklebacks and diptera larvae; other common items were young smelt, nymphs of Odonata, Trichoptera, Megaloptera, Ephemeroptera, and *Mysis* (Reckahn 1970).

In 1974, 17 splake caught in the Lake Superior sport fishery comprised 0.1% of the harvest of salmonid fishes (King and Swanson 1975). Preliminary results from stocking this hybrid have been encouraging, and the splake appear to have good growth rates. In 1976, the Lake Superior sport harvest included 106 splake weighing 72 kg, and in 1977 the harvest was 46 fish weighing 42 kg (Sport Fish. Instit. *Bull.* No. 293, April 1978, p. 7).

Siscowet

Salvelinus namaycush siscowet (Agassiz). *Salvelinus*—an old name for char; *namaycush*—an American Indian name for the lake trout; *siscowet*—an Indian name, probably from the same root as *cisco*.

Other common names: fat lake trout, fat trout, fats, fat char, half-breed.

Adult 860 mm, L. Superior (Ashland Co.), 29 Sept. 1977. Lateral view above and head view below.

DESCRIPTION

Body deep and stout. Length 43–84 cm (17–33 in). Depth into TL 3.1–3.8. Head length into TL 4.7–5.0; head very short and deep, its upper surface broad and short, covered by a skin so thick as to completely cover the bones; in lateral view, top of head rounded or angular above eye, with a shortened (pugnoselike) snout. Mouth terminal, slightly oblique; lower lip equal to upper or protruding slightly beyond snout. Maxillary extending beyond posterior edge of eye; teeth on upper and lower jaws. Branchiostegal rays 12–15. All dorsal fin rays 13–15; all anal fin rays 13–15; pectoral fin rays 14–15; caudal fin deeply forked. Lateral scales 163–183 (Eddy and Underhill 1974).

Back, sides, and head, and dorsal, adipose, and caudal fins light green or gray with light spots; distended belly white.

SYSTEMATIC NOTES

According to Lawrie and Rahrer (1973) commercial fishermen and buyers recognize and assign different monetary values to at least four variants: *lean trout* (lake trout), *fat trout* (siscowet), *half-breeds*, and *humpers* (bankers).

Two of the variants, the lean and the fat trout, are clearly distinct, at least at larger sizes, and have been accorded subspecific rank as *S. namaycush namaycush* and *S. n. siscowet* (Jordan and Gilbert 1883, Eddy and Surber 1947, Khan and Qadri 1970). Hubbs and Lagler (1964) provisionally retained the subspecific ranking of both variants; some authors (Agassiz 1850, Slastenenko 1958, Eddy and Underhill 1974) have raised the siscowet to specific rank. The siscowet and the lake trout differ in head length, postorbital distance, interorbital width, length of upper and lower jaws (all head characters), and in mean number of anal fin rays and ribs (Khan and Qadri 1970). The lake trout is salmonlike in appearance; the siscowet has a deep, stout body and a small head, which gives it a grotesque appearance. In the lake trout, the amount of fat in the tissues varies from 6.6 to 52.3%; in the siscowet, from 32.5 to 88.8%. The higher fat content in the fish has an adaptive significance in buoyancy regulation (Eschmeyer and Phillips 1965, Crawford 1966).

The lake trout and the siscowet clearly prefer different habitats—inshore shallow waters and offshore

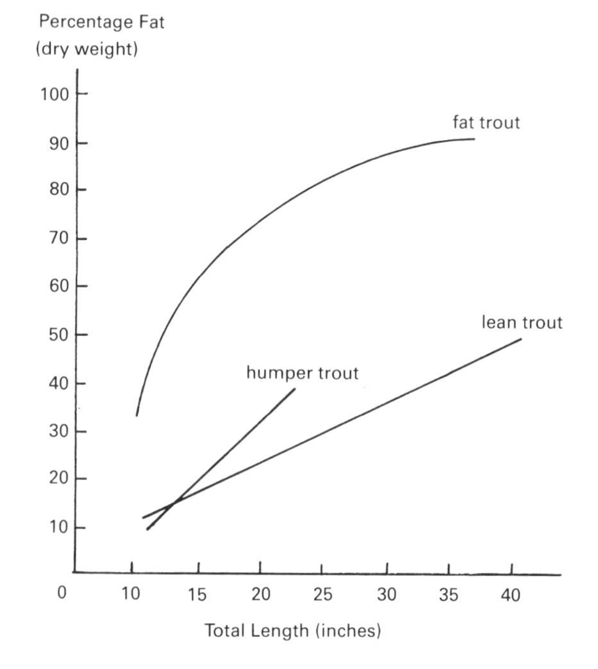

The percentage fat in the flesh of three variants of lake trout from Lake Superior (Lawrie and Rahrer 1973:35)

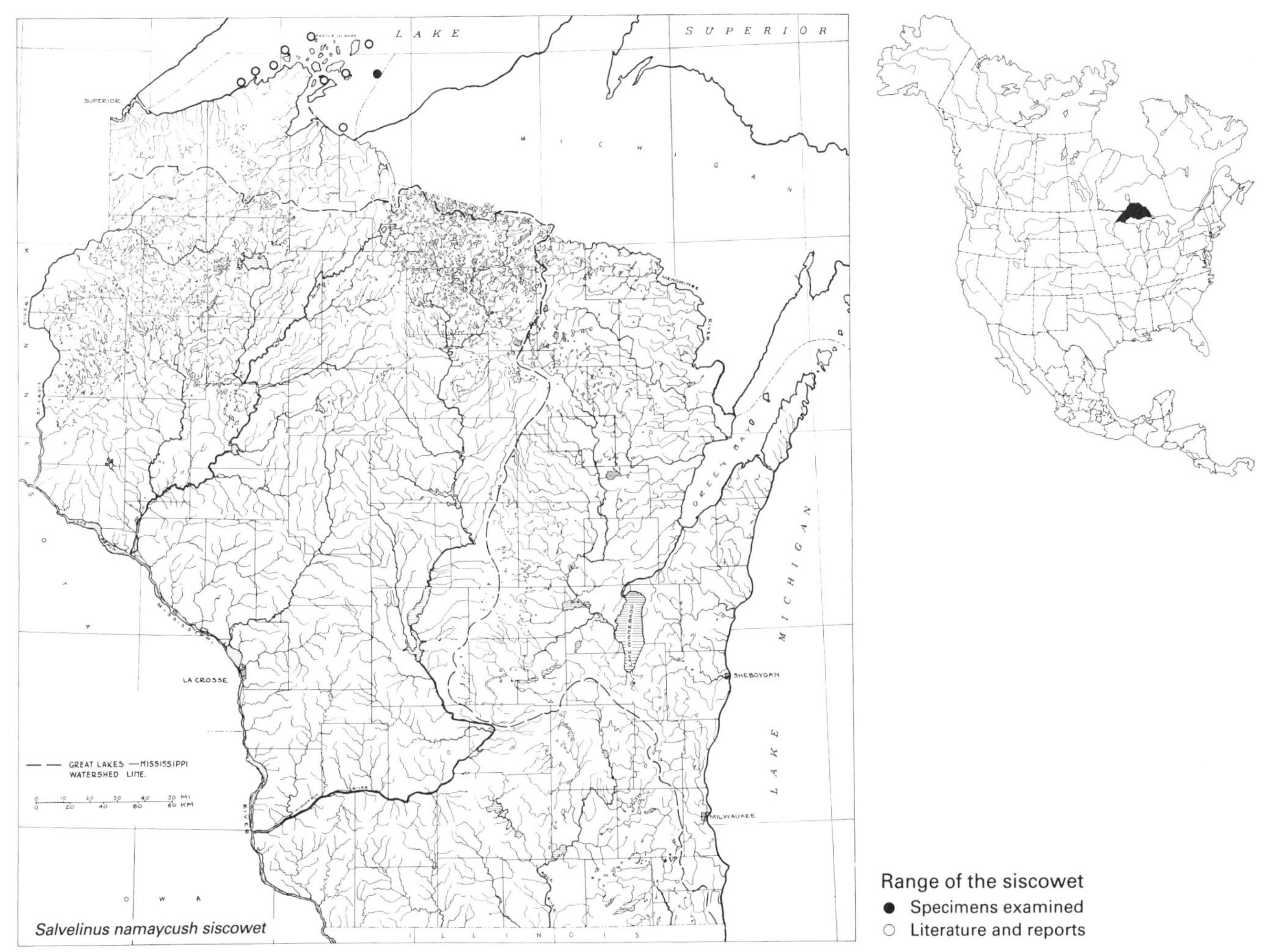

Salvelinus namaycush siscowet

Range of the siscowet
● Specimens examined
○ Literature and reports

deeper waters, respectively. Lake trout characteristically spawn between late September and early November on gravelly beaches and on rocky shoals in shallow waters; siscowets spawn from at least July to November (Eschmeyer 1955). Although the bathymetric segregation of these two forms is not total, they appear to be reproductively isolated. Eddy and Underhill (1974) suggested that the siscowet may represent a Pleistocene relict from the periglacial lakes which has survived to modern times only in Lake Superior.

The so-called half-breed is considered by fishermen to be the result of a cross between the lean lake trout and the fat siscowet. Khan and Qadri (1970) found no significant difference in the morphometry of half-breeds and siscowets or in their meristic counts, except for those of branchiostegal and anal fin rays. The fat content in relation to length of half-breeds is not significantly different from that for siscowets. Half-breeds are generally smaller than those fish unequivocally classified as siscowets by the industry (Lawrie and Rahrer 1973). Half-breeds are commonly taken at depths which lie within the deeper part of the lake trout range, close to the upper limit of siscowet bathymetric distribution. According to Lawrie and Rahrer, this suggests that half-breeds may reasonably be considered to be small siscowets, not yet large enough to be readily distinguished from lake trout. Such a conclusion is implicit in the discussions of Eschmeyer and Phillips (1965) and Khan and Qadri (1970).

The humper as described by Khan and Qadri (1970) on the basis of specimens used by Rahrer (1965) is more like the siscowet than the lake trout in many characters. Head length, postorbital distance, lengths of upper and lower jaws, predorsal length, and length of caudal peduncle are similar in the two variants, as are certain meristic characters, such as branchiostegals, anal fin rays, ribs, and vertebrae. Rahrer (1965) called attention to the external resemblance of the humper to the siscowet. However, he noted that the humper's thin ventral body wall ("paper-belly") and the limited amount of fat on its viscera would distinguish it from the siscowet. Kahn and Qadri (1970) regarded the humpers as constituting a distinct group, but offered no further comment. The taxonomic status of the humper trout is not yet clear.

DISTRIBUTION, STATUS, AND HABITAT

In Wisconsin, the siscowet occurs only in Lake Superior. It has been increasing in the commercial catch since the early 1970s, and its status appears secure.

The siscowet is normally taken below 91 m and is encountered most frequently at depths of 150–180 m. According to Eddy and Underhill (1974), it lives at depths of 550 m. Only rarely does it appear on the surface. It may spend its entire life at water temperatures that seldom exceed 4.5°C (40°F).

BIOLOGY

The siscowet spawns supposedly in deep water (91–146 m), probably from late July to late November, although two specimens—one nearly spent and another nearly ripe—were taken on 8 June (Eschmeyer 1955). The average egg production of the siscowet was 1,160/kg, 28% less than the average egg production (1,615/kg) of lake trout from southern Lake Superior. Siscowets 427–869 mm (16.8–34.2 in) TL produced 1,093–10,476 eggs; the egg diameter was 3.6–5.2 mm.

Siscowet females mature at smaller sizes than lake trout; a female measuring 427 mm (16.8 in) TL and weighing 862 g (1.9 lb) was 211 mm shorter than the shortest and 1.77 kg lighter than the lightest mature female lake trout taken in nine prespawning and spawning-run collections in southern Lake Superior in 1950. The catch also included a 399-mm, 590-g (15.7-in, 1.3-lb) ripe male siscowet (Eschmeyer 1955). Siscowets may exceed 23 kg (50 lb) in weight, and may reach 20 years of age.

The siscowet feeds primarily on deepwater fishes such as coregonids and sculpins, and occasionally on burbots and longnose suckers (Eddy and Underhill 1974). Of the stomachs of 42 siscowets taken at a depth of 183 m off Grand Marais, Minnesota, 18 contained small bloaters and kiyis; 2, large coregonids (probably shortjaw ciscoes); 25, 1 or more fourhorn sculpins; and 14, eggs of that sculpin. While some of the eggs may have been released from ingested sculpins, there was one stomach that contained nothing but eggs. A number of stomachs contained small pebbles. Occasionally siscowets are caught near the surface at night during June and July when the water temperature is about 4.5°C (40°F) (Thurston 1962). They apparently come up to feed on flies, bees, and millers that float on the surface, for the stomachs of specimens caught at the surface contain these insects as well as undigested bottom fish. A siscowet has very little room in its stomach for food. The amount present, Thurston (1962) noted, represents a small fraction of the food found in the stomach of a lake trout of the same size.

The siscowet is notable for its high fat content, which is among the highest of known fishes. The percentage of fat increased progressively with the increase in the length of the fish (see figure, p. 330). Eschmeyer and Phillips concluded that the wide difference in fat content between siscowets and lake trout is genetically determined. In an analysis of siscowet fillets, Thurston (1962) found 41.4% moisture, 9.6% protein, 48.5% oil, and 0.58% ash compared to 73.0%, 18.0%, 9.4%, and 1.02%, respectively, in lake trout fillets.

The siscowet does not blow up when taken from depths of 183 m whereas lake trout captured at only 73 m are ready to burst when brought to the surface (Thurston 1962).

IMPORTANCE AND MANAGEMENT

The siscowet is not generally available to the angler, and for that reason is not ranked highly as a sport fish.

Before the invasion of the sea lamprey (which almost depleted both the lake trout and the siscowet) some commercial fishermen specialized in siscowet fishing (Thurston 1962). In a single season two men in an 11-m (35-ft) boat, using gill nets, could take up to 18,000 kg (40,000 lb) of these fish, which sold for about the same price as lake trout. The catch was frozen and then smoked. The siscowets, according to Thurston, were usually not marketed in the Great Lakes area, but were shipped to the East Coast for sale to special customers.

In Wisconsin, the fishery for siscowets has been developing slowly since 1970, following the recovery of the siscowet population from the effects of sea lamprey predation. Recruitment to this population has been strong through several year classes. Market conditions have determined production levels in recent years: 1970—1,300 kg; 1971—9,400 kg; 1972—19,000 kg; 1973—20,000 kg; and 1974—42,000 kg (an additional 7,000 kg were taken in the Indian fisheries in 1974). The abundance of siscowets has increased as measured by catch per unit of effort data from commercial nets (King and Swanson 1975).

Subfamily Coregoninae—Whitefish and Chubs

The Coregoninae in Wisconsin consist of two species of *Prosopium* and nine species of *Coregonus* (the latter all valuable food fish). However, the genus *Coregonus* includes fishes which are among the most taxonomically difficult of any group of Wisconsin fishes. The lake whitefish (*Coregonus clupeaformis*) is easily identified but the other *Coregonus* species are not. Until about 1961, the others were called *Leucichthys* and comprised that large group of fishes called ciscoes and/or chubs. Five of these—*C. johannae* (deepwater cisco), *C. alpenae* (longjaw cisco), *C. reighardi* (shortnose cisco), *C. kiyi* (kiyi), and *C. hoyi* (bloater)—are restricted to the Great Lakes basin. They are known as endemic species and generally inhabit the deeper waters of the Great Lakes; they are not known to occur anywhere else. The other members of the genus, whose ranges extend into other drainage basins, are *C. artedii* (lake herring), *C. nigripinnis* (blackfin cisco) and *C. zenithicus* (shortjaw cisco).

The Coregoninae have no more than 15 dorsal fin rays, large rounded scales, no maxillary teeth, small eggs, young usually without parr marks, and parietal bones that meet at the midline.

The ciscoes and chubs have been a mainstay of a large and lucrative fishing industry in the Great Lakes, and, until the early 1960s, provided a healthy income for fishermen whose ancestors had learned the trade in the "old country" and taught it to them. Some coregonine fishes of Lake Michigan, however, could not tolerate heavy exploitation; and by the turn of the century the two largest species, the deepwater and the blackfin ciscoes, were already seriously depleted; even before the arrival of the sea lamprey in the 1940s, they were near extirpation. Meanwhile, the fishermen had turned to the medium-sized chubs using smaller gill-mesh sizes and intensifying their fishing efforts. The sea lamprey, after depleting Lake Michigan in the early 1950s of its favorite prey species, the lake trout, then began to prey on the larger remaining chubs. By early 1960 all cisco species in Lake Michigan were in serious trouble, and most of them were near extirpation. Only one small species, the bloater, managed to survive, increase in numbers, and sustain the smoked fish trade. Yet its success was short-lived, and by the early 1970s it also went into serious decline.

Another newcomer, the aggressive alewife, may have added to the chubs' problems by competing with them for food and for living space. The alewife also has been accused of eating unprotected chub eggs.

The trends in chub decline in Lake Superior have been similar to those in Lake Michigan, but the effects have been far less severe.

As a result of these population declines most boundary water cisco species have been extirpated or given endangered status. As of this writing, only two species, the lake herring and the bloater, remain in Wisconsin waters in any numbers, and even these forms have been greatly modified from their original descriptions, suggesting hybridization with each other and perhaps with other species. Details of this history have been supplied by Moffett (1957), S. H. Smith (1964, 1968b), and Woods (1970).

Elements of the taxonomy of cisco species have recently been scrutinized. Cisco identification has been primarily based on Koelz's monumental work, published in 1929, which for a long time went largely unchallenged. A recent review of Koelz's taxa by personnel from the Great Lakes Fishery Laboratory at Ann Arbor has indicated errors (Parsons et al. 1975, Parsons and Todd 1974, Todd 1977) and the need for a modern revision of the genus. Some proposed changes have been incorporated into my species accounts which follow.

In view of the above, my identification key to the species of ciscoes and the descriptions of the fish in my species accounts are perhaps more valuable from a historical perspective than of immediate use to the biologist with a fresh specimen in hand (especially if it is from Lake Michigan). Cisco identification has always been difficult, and even present-day experts are confused.

Lake Whitefish

Coregonus clupeaformis (Mitchill). *Coregonus*—angle-eye, coined by Artedi from the Greek meaning pupil of the eye and angle; *clupeaformis*—herring-shaped.

Other common names: whitefish, common whitefish, eastern whitefish, Great Lakes whitefish, inland lake whitefish, gizzard fish.

Adult 297 mm, Nipigon, Ontario, Canada, 29 Aug. 1969

DESCRIPTION

The following is based largely on Koelz's (1929) description of Lake Michigan specimens.

Body elongate, laterally compressed, its width equal to about 50% of its depth. Average length 457 mm (18 in). Depth into TL 3.9–4.3 (3.3–4.8). Head length into TL 4.4–4.8 (4.2–5.3). Snout into head length 3.4–3.7 (3.2–4.1). Premaxillaries with a backward slant (retrorse), making the mouth inferior and subterminal. Maxillary seldom reaching beyond the anterior edge of pupil; maxillary always pigmented; maxillary length into head length 3.2–3.4 (3–3.8). Lower jaw without pigment and symphyseal knob; lower jaw tip behind upper jaw; mandible into head length, 2.4–2.7. Eye into head length 3.8–5. Gill rakers short, the longest shorter than the longest gill filament; gill rakers 26–28 (19–33). Dorsal fin rays 11 (10–12); anal fin rays 11 (10–12); pectoral fin rays 15–16 (14–17); pelvic fin rays 11 (10–12); pectoral fin length into distance from pectoral origin to pelvic origin 1.7–2 (1.5–2.3); pelvic fin length into distance from pelvic origin to anal origin 1.5–1.8 (1.3–2). Scales in lateral line 81–88 (74–93); scales around body anterior to dorsal and pelvic fins 48–50 (46–52). Chromosomes 2n = 80 (Booke 1968).

Color in life silvery. Back pale pea green, palest behind the dorsal fin and fading toward the tail, obscured by wide bands of pigment around the free edges of the scales and fins. Sides bluish; belly whitish.

Breeding tubercles present on all males and majority of females; conspicuous on head and body, faint on fins. On first 4 rows above and below lateral line, 1 large tubercle in center of exposed portion of each scale and smaller tubercles possibly occurring on either or both sides. Head tubercles well developed and numerous, but small and irregularly distributed.

Hybrids: Lake whitefish × lake herring, lake whitefish × round whitefish (Schwartz 1972).

SYSTEMATIC NOTES

Koelz (1929) recognized three subspecies of *C. clupeaformis* in Wisconsin waters: *C. c. clupeaformis* in Lakes Michigan and Superior, *C. clupeaformis dustini* in Trout Lake (Vilas County), and *C. clupeaformis neohantoniensis* in Lake Lucerne (Forest County) and possibly in Keyes Lake (Florence County).

It is generally accepted that in large lakes like Superior and Michigan there are discrete populations with quite different growth characteristics within the same lake, even though these populations may be separated by relatively short distances (Lawrie and Rahrer 1973, Mraz 1964b). Through the electrophoretic analysis of muscle enzymes of lake whitefish from the Wisconsin and northern Michigan boundary of Lake Michigan, Imhof and Booke (1976) have assumed that this area contained two such distinct populations, and the results of a later study (Leary 1979) disclosed at least four populations of lake whitefish.

DISTRIBUTION, STATUS, AND HABITAT

In Wisconsin, the lake whitefish occurs in the Mississippi River, Lake Michigan, and Lake Superior drainage basins. It occurs in the littoral waters of Lakes Michigan and Superior. It has been reported inland from Trout and Allequash lakes (Vilas County)—the only records of this species from the Mississippi drainage basin. The Allequash Lake record consisted of one fish taken in Department of Natural Resources sets on 22 April 1949; this fish might have been a migrant from Trout Lake (T. McKnight, pers. comm.).

In the Lake Michigan basin, the lake whitefish is known from Lucerne Lake (Forest County); Keyes Lake, and the Brule River (Florence County); and the Menominee River (Marinette County) (McKnight et al. 1970). Lake whitefish were present in the Brule Flowage (Florence County) in a 1968 survey (L. Frankenberger, pers. comm.). A lake whitefish was taken by an eagle from the surface of Badwater Lake, a widespread of the Menominee River near Spread Eagle outlet (Florence County); the eagle was fright-

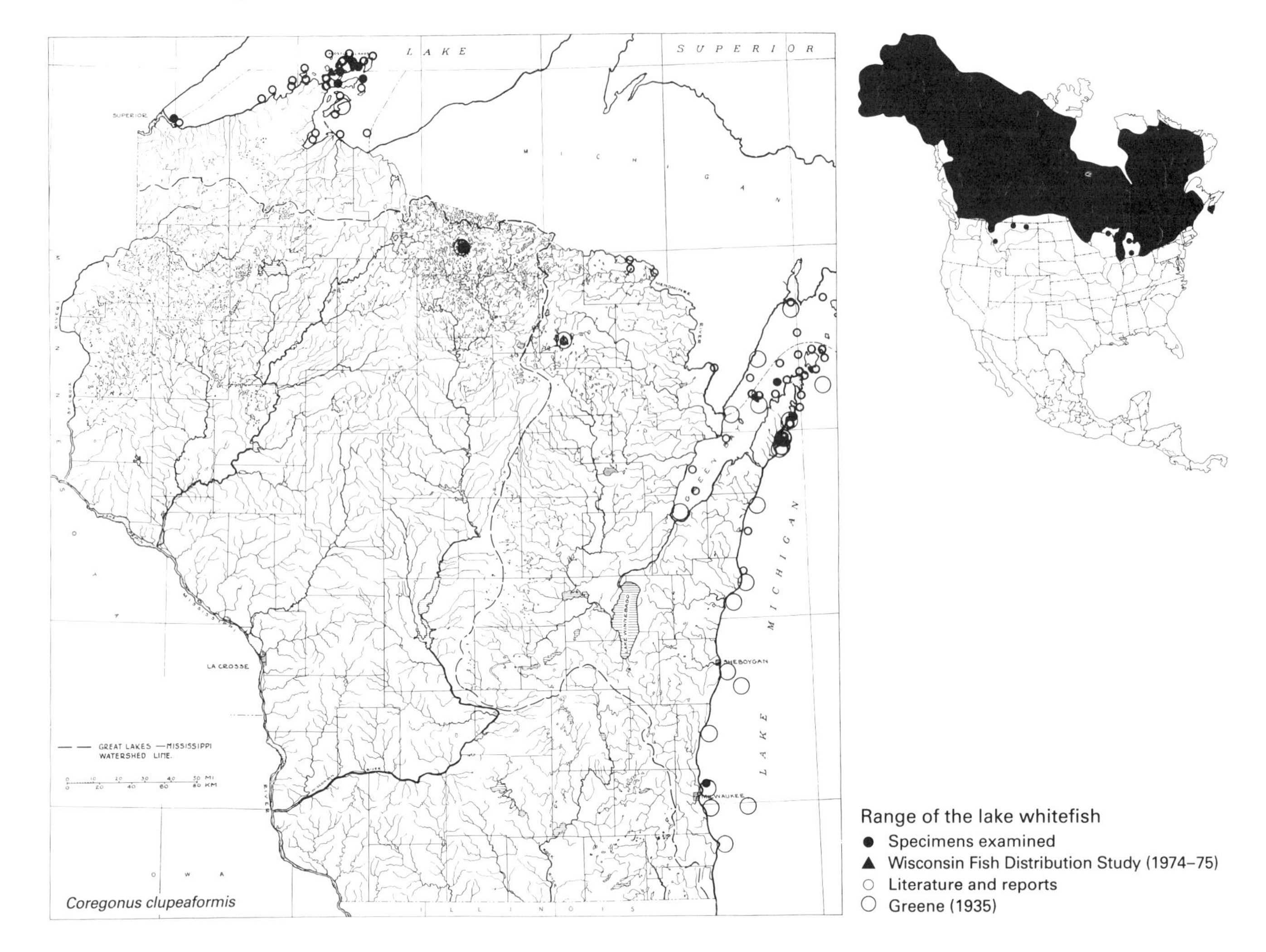

Range of the lake whitefish
● Specimens examined
▲ Wisconsin Fish Distribution Study (1974–75)
○ Literature and reports
◯ Greene (1935)

ened into dropping the fish (B. Jacob, pers. comm.). Jacob identified four lake whitefish from the Michigamme River (northern Michigan), which joins the Menominee River 5 km northeast of Florence (Florence County).

The lake whitefish is declining and possibly threatened in Lakes Erie and Ontario. It is common in Lake Huron, and abundant in Lake Superior and the northern half of Lake Michigan (Todd 1978). P. W. Smith (1979) has never seen specimens from the Illinois waters of southern Lake Michigan, but has received a 1972 report of its presence near Waukegan. In Wisconsin the lake whitefish is uncommon to common in Lakes Michigan and Superior; its status in inland lakes and rivers is not known.

The lake whitefish is essentially a shallow water coregonid. In the Apostle Islands region of Lake Superior, it generally inhabits depths of 18–37 m, and is not found below 71 m (Dryer 1966). In Green Bay during May, it occurs in less than 18 m; during September, it is found at 18–24 m (Van Oosten et al. 1946). As the ice leaves Lake Michigan, the lake whitefish is found in abundance at 37–55 m, and occasionally at 110 m or deeper; in July, as the water warms, it occurs at 5–37 m (Koelz 1929). In Trout Lake, it occurs at 15–33 m in July (Hile and Juday 1941).

BIOLOGY

In Lake Michigan, the time of spawning may vary from year to year, but it begins sometime between 25 October and 15 December, and continues for about 2–6 weeks. Historically, some Green Bay lake whitefish spawned in streams tributary to Green Bay (Wells and McLain 1973), but today spawning occurs over gravel, honeycomb rock, or small stones in 2–18 m of water along the shores of the lake and on the reefs around the islands.In late October and early November 1974, lake whitefish spawned over honeycomb rock in the Lake Michigan bays of northern Door County (L. Fredrich, pers. comm.).

In Trout Lake (Vilas County), lake whitefish spawn

from early through mid-November; at times they continue spawning through late November (McKnight et al. 1970). Shoal water temperatures recorded early in the season were 6.1–4.4°C (43–40°F).

Spawning occurs at night. It is accompanied by considerable jumping and playing. The fish rise to the surface, occasionally in pairs, and sometimes in trios composed of one female and two males; the female emits spawn on each rise, and the males, smaller-sized than the female, simultaneously discharge milt. The eggs are broadcast and settle to the bottom; they receive no parental care.

The production of eggs per female varies with size of fish. A 907 g (2 lb) female held 25,000 eggs, and a 5.90 kg (13 lb) fish held 130,000 eggs (Beard 1943). The eggs are orange-yellow in color, and have a diameter of 2.95 ± 0.01 mm (Booke 1970).

The eggs of the lake whitefish hatch during late March or early April; they require about 133 days of incubation at a water temperature of 1.7°C (35°F) (Beard 1943). A heavy mortality occurs among the developing eggs; probably not more than 13% survive to the eyed or fry stage. In the laboratory, the optimum temperature range for the incubation of eggs is 3.2–8.1°C (37.8–46.6°F), and the time from fertilization to median hatch is inversely related to water temperature; it ranges from 41.7 days at 10°C to 182 days at 0.5°C (Brooke 1975). At hatching, the lake whitefish larva is 13.25 mm long (Hinrichs 1977). The early development of the lake whitefish has been thoroughly described by Fish (1932), Price (1934, 1935), and Hinrichs (1979).

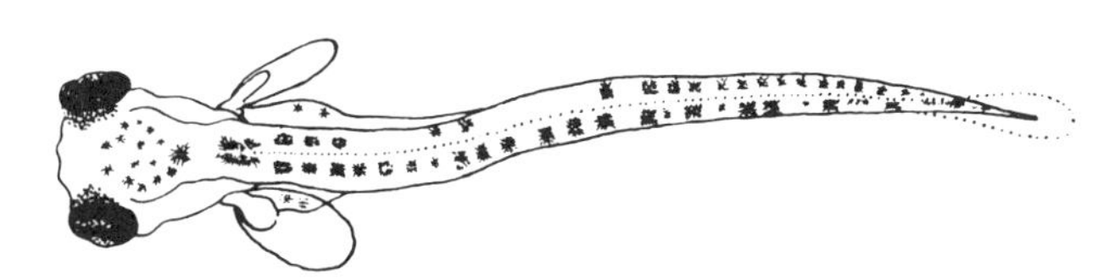

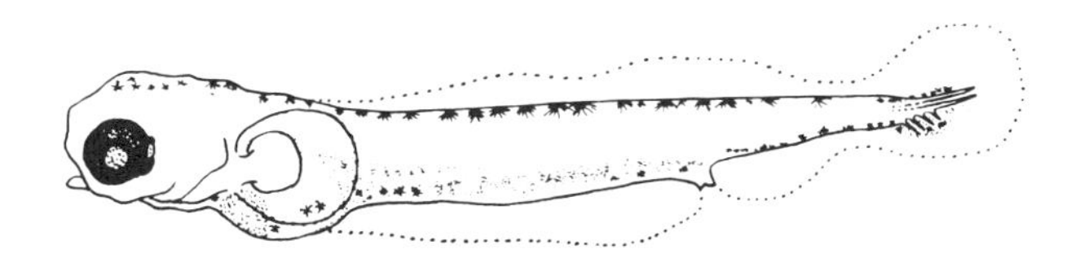

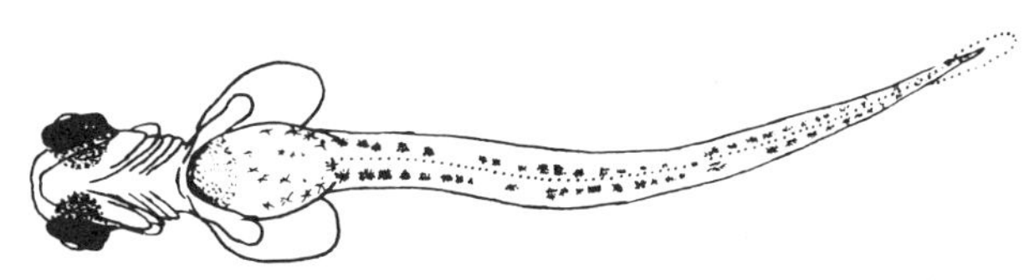

Preserved lake whitefish larva, South Bay, L. Huron. Dorsal view (top), lateral view (middle), ventral view (bottom). 13.6 mm TL; pre-anal myomeres, 39; post-anal myomeres, 13 (Faber 1970:494).

In South Bay of Lake Huron, larval whitefish were captured at depths of 10 m or less. Maximum numbers appeared to be closely associated with a water temperature of 4°C (39°F), which occurred at various times between the third week of April and the third week of May (Faber 1970). In late June and early July, postlarval lake whitefish (in South Bay) were sampled in shallow 17°C (63°F) water near emergent vegetation (Reckahn 1970). They were taken in association with spottail shiners. Their food consisted mostly of cladocerans, but bottom organisms, including alewife eggs, were also eaten. In early July, they left the shallows and migrated approximately 4 km toward deeper water, moving through a region inhabited by an abundant perch population. After this descent they were in 17°C (63°F) water, in company with large numbers of trout-perch. Near the end of August, they descended into deeper and colder waters (Reckahn 1970).

From 1974 to 1976, concentrations of larval lake whitefish appeared on inshore reefs in Moonlight Bay, North Bay, and the Rowleys Bay of Lake Michigan (Door County) shortly after ice-out in April (Fredrich 1977). They soon dispersed into a series of shallow, protected bays along the western shore of Lake Michigan. During April and May they fed on plankton, but by August, in deeper waters at the mouths of the bays, they had turned to *Pontoporeia*, the food mainstay of the adults. Growth was about 25 mm (1 in) per month during the first season.

Little is known about the life history of lake whitefish from the time the young are slightly more than 25 mm long until they appear in the fishermen's nets about 3 years later.

The Bayfield (Lake Superior) population was by far the slowest growing of the four lake whitefish populations from Lake Superior studied by Dryer (1963). Lake whitefish from Trout Lake (Vilas County) are especially slow growing, probably as a result of competition with a strong cisco population. A "dwarf" population was reported by Edsall (1960) from Munising Bay of Lake Superior, in which the average calculated total length at the end of the 9th year of life was 328 mm (12.9 in); at the end of the 16th year, it was only 411 mm (16.2 in). Calculated total lengths of lake whitefish at the end of each year of life are shown on the following page.

Annulus formation in Lake Superior lake whitefish occurred in mid-June. Records on the progress of the season's growth suggest that one-third or more of the total growth occurred after 15 August (Dryer 1963).

Lake whitefish from Bayfield, Lake Superior, shorter

Age and Growth (TL in mm) of the Lake Whitefish in Wisconsin

Location	1	2	3	4	5	6	7	8	9	14	Source
L. Superior, Bayfield	130	203	277	338	381	424	465	508	544		Dryer 1963
L. Michigan, Europe Bay	142	249	351	434	495	538	594	640	660[a]		Mraz 1964b
L. Michigan, Moonlight Bay	174	298	416	488	551	598	633	668[b]			UWSP 5548
Green Bay near Cedar R.	152	282	391	465	516	551	592	612	622[c]		Mraz 1964b
L. Michigan, Big Bay de Noc, Upper Michigan	142	239	351	455							Roelofs 1957
Trout L. (Vilas Co.)	81	117	151	181	207	230	251	275	303	366	Hile and Deason 1934

[a] 2.84 kg
[b] 5.16 kg
[c] 2.63 kg

than 368 mm (14.5 in), were immature, and those longer than 442 mm (17.4 in), mature. The youngest mature fish belonged to age-group V, and all fish older than age VII were mature (Dryer 1963). In Green Bay (Lake Michigan), the youngest mature male whitefish belonged to age-group II, and youngest mature females to age-group III. All age-IV fish were mature. The shortest mature males were 368–378 mm (14.5–14.9 in) long; the shortest mature females were 419–429 mm (16.5–16.9 in) long. All males longer than 505 mm (19.9 in) and all females longer than 467 mm (18.4 in) were mature (Mraz 1964b).

The lake whitefish is the largest of the coregonines. The largest specimens weigh 9 kg (20 lb) or more, but the average weight does not exceed 1.8 kg (4 lb). Individuals heavier than the average are termed "jumbos" by commercial fishermen. An 11.8-kg (26-lb) lake whitefish was taken from Drisco Shoals in Green Bay on 4 June 1938, and Van Oosten (1946) was informed of a 19.05-kg (42-lb) fish caught off Isle Royale, Lake Superior, in about 1918.

Adult lake whitefish generally consume *Pontoporeia*, pelecypods, gastropods, Diptera larvae, and pupae. Other common food items are *Mysis*, hydrachnids, isopods, ostracods, fish scales, and oligochaetes, and, occasionally, sticklebacks, and young alewives (Reckahn 1970).

In the stomachs of 160 lake whitefish collected off Alpena (Lake Huron), Carl Hubbs found primarily *Pontoporeia*, as well as *Sphaerium*, *Amnicola*, other small mollusks, sand, gravel, cinders, wood fragments, seed, Chironomidae larvae, and occasional bryozoan statoblasts, adult land insects, Trichoptera larvae, Corixidae, and sculpin sp. (cited by Koelz 1929). The stomachs of six whitefish (406–432 mm TL) from Torch Lake, Michigan, caught on hook and line were filled with nymphs of *Hexagenia* sp. (Colby and Washburn 1972).

In Torch Lake, Michigan, lake whitefish were observed feeding in an area chummed with bloater eggs. Upon arrival the school of whitefish dispersed and slowly swam about in random circular patterns at a list angle of 30 to 40° (Colby and Washburn 1972). Individual fish made abrupt, vertical turns, with their heads down and their tails toward the surface, while moving vigorously, as if to push their snouts as far as possible into the marl substrate. This behavior, and the cloud of suspended sediment it raised near the bottom, seemed to excite other lake whitefish and a few lake herring. Fish of both species darted about the suspended sediments as though feeding.

Cyclic movements characterize the behavior of the lake whitefish. Twice during the year, these fish move into shoal waters—in the spring, and again in the fall spawning period. In the Green Bay region of Lake Michigan, the best catches of legal and illegal whitefish in May were made in less than 18 m of water; in September, between 18 and 24 m (Van Oosten et al. 1946). In the mid-1970s, the best catches in Lake Michigan occurred during October (F. Copes, pers. comm.). As the water warms during the summer, lake whitefish migrate into deeper offshore areas; in eastern Lake Superior fishermen reported them at 110–128 m (Koelz 1929).

The total distance traveled by an individual lake whitefish is generally restricted. In one study, more than half of the tagged lake whitefish in the Apostle Islands area of Lake Superior were recovered within 8 km (5 mi) of the tagging site; the greatest distance traveled by an individual was 40 km (25 mi) (Dryer 1964). Of 101 tag returns in Lake Michigan lake whitefish, only 4 were recovered at distances greater than 40 km (25 mi) from the release site (O. B. Smith and Van Oosten 1940). Gunderson (1978) noted a substantial movement of lake whitefish which had been tagged in North and Moonlight bays (the open lake side of Door County), to the Peshtigo Reef and Chambers Island areas within Green Bay. This population also migrated back to North and Moonlight bays in the fall to spawn. In another study, one lake whitefish traveled 242 km (150 mi) from its tagging site in South Bay (Lake Huron), but tag returns suggest that the South Bay stock returns to South Bay during the winter or early spring (Budd 1957).

The lake whitefish is a strong schooling fish. All lake whitefish in one catch may be taken in one or two boxes of nets out of a gang of gill nets consisting of several boxes, and out of half a dozen pound nets in the same neighborhood, only one may take fish (Koelz 1929). It appears that schools of lake whitefish are local in their habits, and do not wander over wide stretches of a lake.

IMPORTANCE AND MANAGEMENT

The major predators of lake whitefish are the lake trout, northern pike, and burbot. Occasionally perch and ciscoes feed on whitefish larvae, and lake whitefish sometimes consume their own eggs (Scott and Crossman 1973).

In Wisconsin's inland lakes, fishermen angle for lake whitefish through the ice, jigging with various spoons, such as the "Swedish Pimple" and color-beaded hooks (McKnight et al. 1970). A number of 2.7–3.2-kg (6–7-lb) lake whitefish are taken from Lake Lucerne (Forest County) each winter. Trout Lake usually produces whitefish weighing between 0.3 and 1.4 kg (0.7 and 3 lb). During spawning, there is limited fishery with seines and dip nets.

The lake whitefish is considered to have the finest flavor—superior to lake trout—of any of Wisconsin's commercial fishes. It brings the highest price of any fish on the market, except for sturgeon, and its value as food is recognized throughout North America. Lake whitefish may be smoked, baked, pan-fried, or broiled with equal success. Whitefish eggs are a gourmet delicacy, and are marketed as caviar; in 1979, they sold for a price of $17 per kilo ($7.75/lb).

Historically, the lake whitefish played an important role in the Indian economy because of its ready availability. The Chippewas, who had a permanent village at Sault St. Marie on the Saint Mary's River connecting Lake Superior and Lake Huron, lived by fishing and making sugar on the maple islands. In the spring thousands of other Indians gathered there to trade furs at the warehouses and to gorge on lake whitefish from the river. Two men in a canoe could catch 2,270 kg (5,000 lb) of whitefish in half a day: they dipped whitefish weighing 2.7–6.8 kg (6–15 lb) out of the rapids with a scoop net on a pole. The Indians then feasted around campfires, and the wind carried the savory odor of roasting whitefish for many kilometers (Havighurst 1942).

With the opening of the upper Midwest to settlement, the lake whitefish was quickly exploited. Koelz (1929:522–523) wrote:

> In consequence of its food value, the whitefish, in the earlier days, was sought for the markets with the aid of every device that human ingenuity could invent. At no season was the pursuit relented, and no fish were too small to be taken. The smallest, together with the herring and the sturgeon, often were carried out onto the beach because they were so numerous that they interfered with the capture of the larger whitefish. Though originally whitefish were found in incredible abundance all along the shores of the lakes (in fact it is said that the species was the predominant one on the shoals), they could not endure long such drains on their numbers. Where for 1880 the Federal statistics show a production in Lake Michigan of over 12,000,000 pounds of whitefish, the catch for 1922 is given as a little over 1,500,000 pounds, despite the great increase in quantity and effectiveness of the fishing apparatus and increase in value of the fish taken. It is noteworthy, also, that the areas that produced the whitefish of 1880 are not those that yielded the bulk of the 1922 catch.

Lumbering and sawmill pollution also took their tolls of lake whitefish in Lakes Superior and Michigan. Commercial fishermen often complained that deep drifts of sawdust blanketed many whitefish spawning beds in the lakes, and they believed that these inhibited spawning and suffocated any eggs that had been deposited. Sawmill refuse in enormous quantities was thrown into streams to float out and sink in the lakes. Water-logged slabs tore and carried away fishermen's nets. Many of the lake whitefish spawning areas in streams (some streams were entered for spawning in early lumbering days) and in the lakes near river mouths must have been destroyed by lumbering operations (Lawrie and Rahrer 1973, Wells and McLain 1973).

The history of lake whitefish production is a study of highs and lows, but the reasons for this cyclic phenomenon are not clearly understood. In Lake Michigan, the highest production since 1940 occurred in 1947, when 819,281 kg (1,806,174 lb) were harvested. There was a drop to an all-time low of 4,182 kg (9,219 lb) in 1958. Production then gradually increased until 1974, when 532,620 kg (1,174,208 lb) were harvested; this was valued at $978,252. The bulk of the present commercial harvest occurs in the Door County area, with gill nets (114 mm stretch) and pound nets as the principal methods of harvesting (Wis. Dep. Nat. Resour. 1976c).

Wells and McLain have suggested that a contributing factor to the success of the 1943 year class in Lake Michigan (which was responsible for the excellent 1947 harvest) was the phenomenal decline of smelt in the winter of 1942–1943, which would have left the lake whitefish fry free of possible interference from smelt in 1943. Possibly substantial increase in the smelt population was a factor in the decline of lake whitefish numbers to the extremely low levels of the late 1950s.

After the lake trout's collapse in the early 1950s due to sea lamprey predation, the lake whitefish may also have been victimized extensively. Roelofs (1957) believed that a high mortality rate (94%) among lake whitefish between ages III and IV in Big Bay de Noc (northern Green Bay) in 1951–1954 may have been due to sea lamprey attacks; local commercial fishermen had reported that large numbers of dead, commercial-sized whitefish, showing a high incidence of lamprey scarring, had drifted into their nets. Wells and McLain (1973) and Poff (1974) attribute the increase of lake whitefish in Lake Michigan in the 1970s primarily to the decline of sea lamprey predation. Recent work in northern Lake Huron has shown that the scarring rate on lake whitefish is influenced not only by the abundance of the sea lamprey, but also by the abundance of other prey species such as the white sucker.

In Lake Superior, the highest production since 1940 occurred in 1949, when 347,000 kg (764,000 lb) of lake whitefish were harvested. In 1965 there was a drop to a low of 21,000 kg (46,000 lb); after that, production gradually increased to 102,000 kg (225,000 lb) in 1971. Production held at a fairly steady level in the 1970s. In 1974, 96,000 kg (212,000 lb) were netted by commercial fishermen and 23,000 kg (50,000 lb) were taken in the Indian fisheries (Wis. Dep. Nat. Resour. 1976c).

Lake Superior lake whitefish, which live in shallow waters, were protected from sea lamprey predation by the availability of preferred prey species, such as lake trout, large chubs, and burbot, which live in the deep waters with the sea lamprey. The sea lamprey did not prey heavily on lake whitefish in Lake Superior (S. H. Smith 1968b).

Jensen (1976) found that the whitefish populations in most areas of Lakes Superior and Michigan had been overexploited, and that yield in these areas was below the maximum sustainable yield before the sea lamprey took its toll.

In the Great Lakes region, the lake whitefish was once artificially propagated on a large scale to restore dwindling stocks, but this activity has been greatly curtailed because there is little evidence that the millions of fry planted at considerable expense have increased or even maintained the supply of fish.

Mid-1970s estimates of the North Bay and Moonlight Bay lake whitefish spawning stock (1.1 million) and of the Wisconsin Lake Michigan lake whitefish population (1.2–1.5 million) indicated that this spawning stock was a major component of the Wisconsin Lake Michigan lake whitefish population. Humphreys (1978) noted that the Wisconsin Lake Michigan fishery may be managed as a single stock. He suggested that more fish should be harvested at a smaller size to obtain a maximum yield, as 82% of the harvest was larger than the critical size of 489 mm. His data did not indicate that the 432-mm (17-in) size limit should be changed.

Cisco or Lake Herring[a]

Coregonus artedii Lesueur. *Coregonus*—angle-eye, coined by Artedi from the Greek meaning pupil of the eye and angle; *artedii*—of Artedi, after Petrus Artedi, the "Father of Ichthyology," and an associate of Linnaeus.

Other common names: shallowwater cisco, common cisco, Great Lakes cisco, freshwater herring, sand herring, the herring, chub, tullibee, grayback tullibee, blueback tullibee, blueback.

Adult 386 mm, Sunset L. (Portage Co.), 19 Sept. 1975

DESCRIPTION

The following is based largely on Koelz's (1929) description of Lake Michigan specimens.

Body elongate, almost round in cross section; side view decidedly elliptical. Average length 267 mm (10.5 in). Depth into TL 4–4.9 (3.6–5.3). Head length into TL 4.3–4.5 (4.1–5). Snout into head length 3.7–4 (3.3–4.3). Anterior maxillary darkly pigmented; maxillary length into head length 2.7–3 (2.5–3.3). Lower jaw weak, moderately pigmented; lower jaw with symphyseal knob; tips of upper and lower jaws equal. Eye into head length 4–4.2 (3.6–4.7). Gill rakers long, 46–50 (41–55). Dorsal fin rays 9–11 (8); anal fin rays 10–12 (13); pectoral fin rays 15–16 (14–18); pelvic fin rays 11 (10–12); pectoral fins medium long, pectoral fin length into distance from pectoral origin to pelvic origin 1.9–2.2 (1.6–2.6); pelvic fins medium long, pelvic fin length into distance from pelvic origin to anal origin 1.6–1.8 (1.4–2.3). Scales in lateral line 77–84 (68–94); scales around body anterior to dorsal and pelvic fins 40–42 (38–46). Chromosomes 2n = 80 (Booke 1968).

Color in life silvery with faint pink to purple iridescence on the sides. Back blue-green, pea green, or tan and gray; back usually darker than sides, thus accounting for the common names blueback and grayback.

[a]The name "lake herring" is commonly applied to the cisco of the Great Lakes, including Lakes Michigan and Superior.

Breeding tubercles present on all males; less well developed on females. A spent male specimen from Minocqua Lake (Oneida County) with small, scattered tubercles on head, and a single large tubercle (cornified pad) on the caudal edge of each body scale.

Hybrids: Cisco × lake whitefish, cisco × bloater, cisco × round whitefish (Schwartz 1972). According to S. H. Smith (1964), the "new" ciscoes resembling *artedii*, that have appeared in Lake Michigan, which are more robust and have broader, deeper bodies than typical *artedii*, are probably hybrids with the bloater.

SYSTEMATIC NOTES

C. artedii exhibits variations from one body of water to another. Koelz (1931) recognized 24 subspecies of *C. artedii*, 9 of which he assigned to ciscoes in inland lakes of Wisconsin. It is now accepted that these variations are primarily caused by environmental effects, since the cisco is sensitive to and responsive to changes in the environment. Some characters, however, are genetically fixed and do not readily change (e.g., gill raker numbers). The subspecific concept is being abandoned by current taxonomists. In some northern waters of Wisconsin, the deep-bodied form is commonly referred to as the tullibee.

DISTRIBUTION, STATUS, AND HABITAT

In Wisconsin, the cisco or lake herring occurs in the Mississippi River, Lake Michigan, and Lake Superior drainage basins. It inhabits relatively shallow waters of Lakes Michigan and Superior and more than 126 deep inland lakes of northern and southeastern Wisconsin (Hoy 1883, Koelz 1929, Frankenberger 1957, Wis. Dep. Nat. Resour. 1974, McKnight et al. 1970). A Lake Winnebago record is believed to have been a stray from Green Lake (Becker 1964b).

The cisco is endangered in Lakes Ontario and Erie, rare in Lake Huron, declining and possibly threatened in Lake Michigan, and declining in Lake Superior (Todd 1978, Parsons et al. 1975). In Wisconsin's northern inland lakes, the cisco is common to abundant. In the Madison area lakes, it is rare to extirpated; however, one individual was taken through the ice in Lake Monona in 1978. In Waukesha County, it is still known from Pine Lake, but is probably extirpated in Nagawicka, Fowler, Lac La Belle, Upper and Lower Nemahbin, Upper and Lower Nashota, Silver, and Dutchman lakes. In Wisconsin, the cisco (herring) has been given watch status (Wis. Dep. Nat. Resour. Endangered Species Com. 1975).

In southern Lake Michigan, the cisco has been collected at depths of 9–91 m, but most commonly at

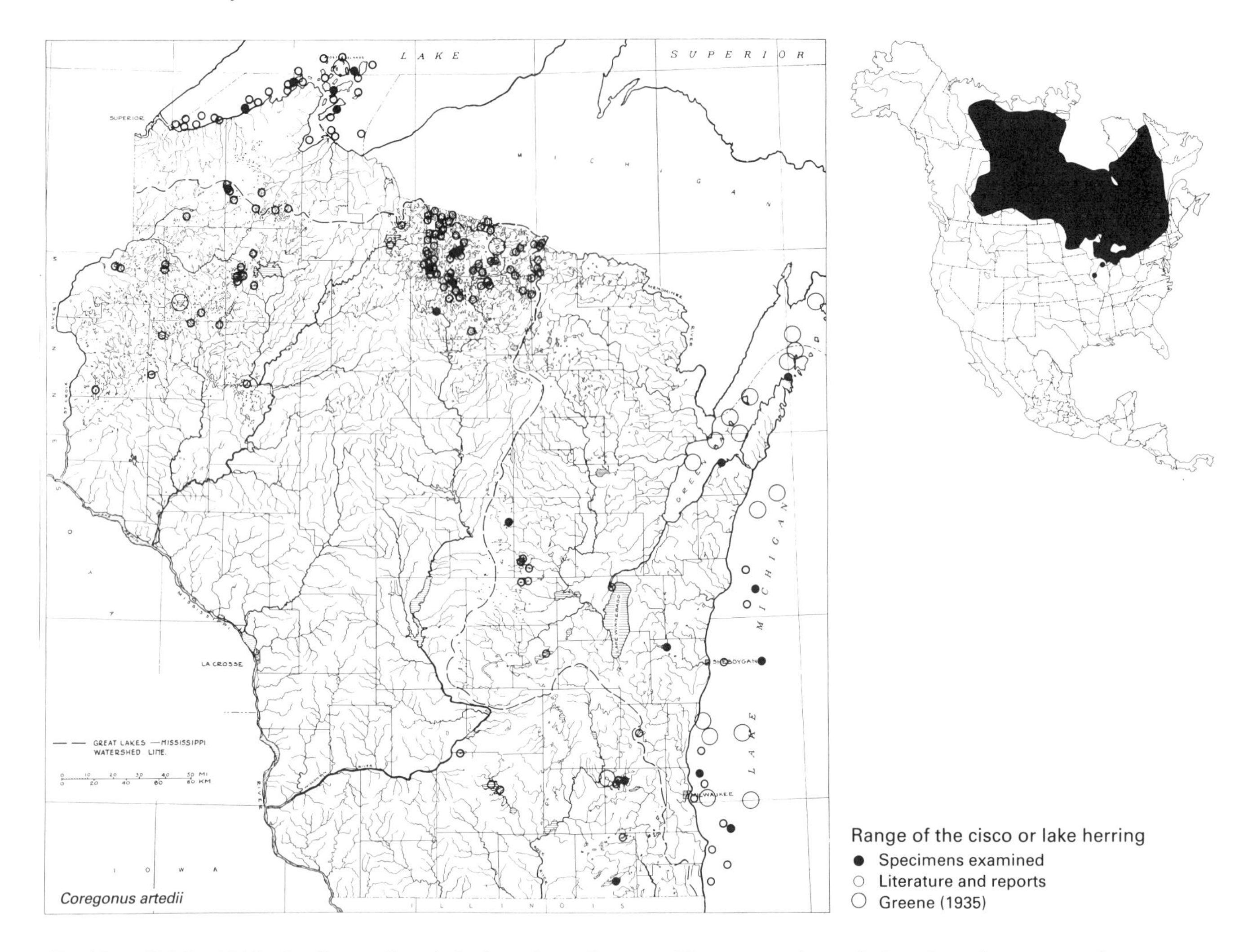

Range of the cisco or lake herring
- ● Specimens examined
- ○ Literature and reports
- ◯ Greene (1935)

27–46 m (Wells 1968). In Green Bay, it is found at all depths, but is never abundant below 46 m (S. H. Smith 1964). The all-season averages in the Apostle Islands region of Lake Superior indicate that it is most common at 18–53 m (Dryer 1966). Of all the cisco species, the lake herring or cisco is most frequently associated with inshore shoals and shallow water. It is found over a wide variety of bottom types.

The cisco requires deep inland lakes, generally more than 10 m deep and preferably with infertile waters. In northern Wisconsin, the cisco is rarely taken at water temperatures above 17–18°C (62.6–64.4°F), which mark the upper limit of its distribution, or at oxygen concentrations below 3 or 4 ppm, at the deeper limit of its distribution (Hile 1936).

BIOLOGY

The life history of the cisco or lake herring has been well researched in Wisconsin waters by Cahn (1927), Hile (1936), John (1954), S. H. Smith (1956, 1964, 1968b), Dryer and Beil (1964), and Dryer (1966).

The spawning of the cisco is apparently temperature-dependent, and occurs from early November to mid-December. In Lake Mendota (Dane County), ciscoes arrive on spawning grounds when the water temperature drops to 6–5°C (42.8–41°F), and spawning activities reach a peak when the temperature falls below 4°C (39.2°F) (John 1956). If the arrival of this temperature is delayed, spawning occurs anyway, but not until late in the season.

The spawning act of ciscoes from Oconomowoc Lake (Waukesha County) has been described by Cahn (1927). Spawning occurs in water 1–2 m deep over a bottom free of vegetation. Males arrive in the shallows from 2 to 5 days before the females, and breeding begins with the arrival of the females. At first as many as a dozen males follow a single female, but later on in the spawning season two males is more usual. The actions of the fish are deliberate, and there is no evidence of chasing or pugnacity. The female descends to within 15–20 cm of the bottom, leading the males, whose heads are about even with her anal opening. In a continuous swimming motion, the female extrudes eggs while the males release milt. The eggs are scattered over a considerable area and since they are slightly adhesive they become attached to rocks, vegetation, or debris on the bottom.

Spawning generally occurs at night. At night on Pallette Lake (Vilas County), I have heard considerable jumping and splashing by ciscoes, both out in the lake and within 5 m of the shore. This behavior has also been reported by fishermen of Green Bay to S. H. Smith (1956).

In Green Bay, most spawning lake herrings congregate in water 3–18 m (10–60 ft) deep, but catches of both ripe and spent fish have been made in nets fished at depths of at least 42 m. Spawning itself, however, occurs near the surface (pelagic spawning) over a wide variety of bottom types (S. H. Smith 1956).

Pelagic spawning by lake herring in Lake Superior has been substantiated by trawling at 18 m below the surface, where adult lake herring were captured, and in the same area at a depth of 37 m, where small numbers of lake herring eggs were taken. Dryer and Beil (1964) concluded that the eggs had drifted toward the bottom after they had been released from the fish. Off the north shore of Lake Superior, commercial gill nets floating 13 m below the surface in 146 m of water took large numbers of spawning lake herring. However, most of the commercial production comes from nets set on the bottom, and, as the fish move to the bottom some time during the night, it is possible that spawning may continue there.

Although at Wisconsin's latitude the cisco is a lake spawner, some river runs have been reported. One occurred in the Oconomowoc River (Waukesha County) from Fowler Lake up to the dam at the outlet of Oconomowoc Lake (Cahn 1927); others took place in the Brill River (Washburn County) up to the Long Lake Dam and the Red Cedar River (Barron County) below the Mikana Dam (Cooper 1956) and in the Tomahawk River (Oneida County) below the Willow Flowage Dam (UWSP 4915).

In a sample of Lake Superior females, 269–356 mm TL, the number of eggs ranged from 4,314 to 10,250 per fish. The average number of eggs per 28 g (1 oz) of fish for the entire sample was 842 (Dryer and Beil 1964). Comparable data from Green Bay (S. H. Smith 1956) showed more than 1,000 more eggs per fish, and nearly 100 additional eggs per 28 g of fish. The mean diameter of cisco eggs from Lake Superior and Lake Michigan was 1.88 mm.

Cisco eggs hatch in late April or early May. According to Colby and Brooke (1970), the optimum temperature range for normal development of the cisco is approximately 2–8°C (35.6–46.4°F); and at 5.6°C, development takes about 90 days. At 10°C (50°F), eggs hatched in the laboratory in 37–49 days (Hinrichs and Booke 1975). Early development from the egg to the 123-day juvenile stage has been illustrated and described by Hinrichs (1979). The cisco is completely scaled at 55 mm (Hogman 1970).

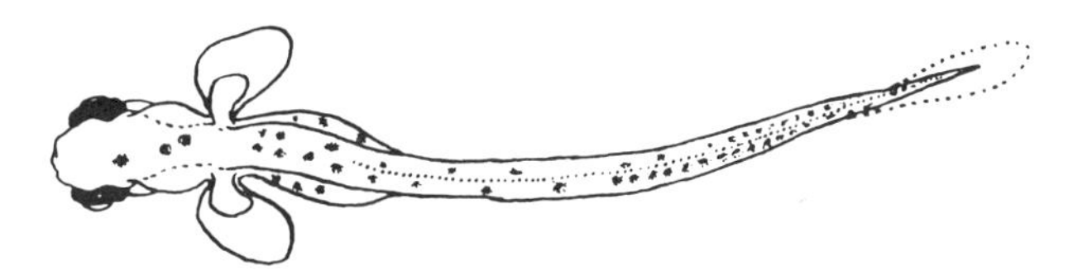

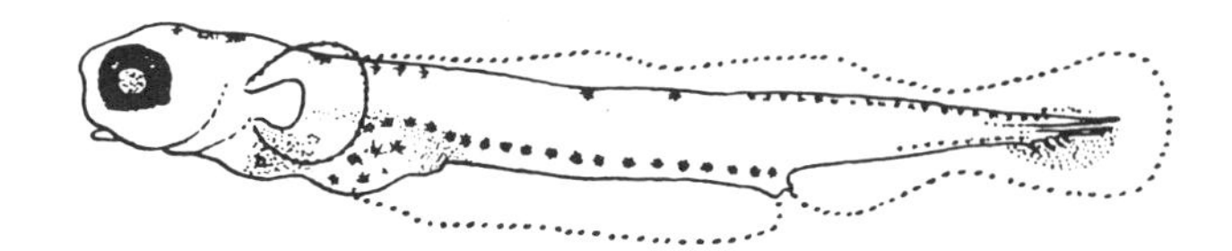

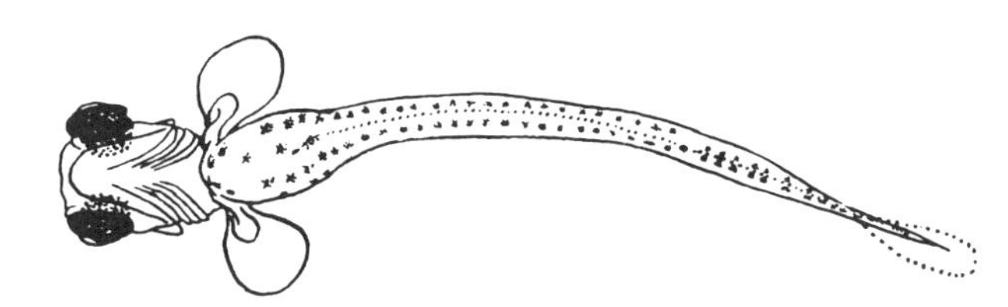

Preserved cisco (lake herring) larva, South Bay, L. Huron. Dorsal view (top), lateral view (middle), ventral view (bottom). 10.8 mm TL; pre-anal myomeres, 38; post-anal myomeres, 12 (Faber 1970:496).

In Canada (MacKay 1963), the fry range in the shallows of protected bays until they are a month old, when they disappear—probably into deeper water.

Calculated total lengths and weights of the lake herring in Wisconsin waters of the Great Lakes are as follows:

	L. Superior (Dryer and Beil 1964)				L. Michigan (S. H. Smith 1956)	
	Duluth		Bayfield		Green Bay	
Age	TL (mm)	WT (g)	TL (mm)	WT (g)	TL (mm)	WT (g)
1	109	11	119	14	127	
2	173	34	180	45	203	62
3	229	86	239	101	246	106
4	269	147	277	161	274	156
5	295	194	300	204	305	217
6	318	244	323	258	351	327
7	338	300	345	322	371	390
8	356	351	358	359		

In Lake Superior, age-groups III to V were best represented (Dryer and Beil 1964). The differences in the average lengths of the sexes were small.

Lake herring from Green Bay grow faster and weigh more than lake herring from Lake Superior. Annulus formation in Green Bay begins in May, is completed before mid-July, and occurs earlier in young fish and later in older fish (S. H. Smith 1956). The period for annulus formation in Lake Superior fish exceeds 8 weeks, and is completed by mid-August.

In northern Wisconsin, ciscoes in Clear Lake (Oneida County) showed the fastest growth of any population that Hile (1936) studied. Calculated total lengths of males (females) were: 1—110 mm (109 mm); 2—196 mm (199 mm); 3—255 (260); 4—287 (291); 5—308 (312); 6—323 (326); 7—335 (340); 8—345 (351); 9—354 (361); 10—(369); and 11—(376). The weight (g) of the females, which was consistently heavier than that of the males, was: I—80, II—306, III—530, IV—705, V—770, VI—841, VII—917, VIII—950, IX—1085, X—1062, and XI—1190. In southern Wisconsin (Oconomowoc Lake, Waukesha County) average total lengths and weights (sexes combined) were 5 months—62 mm, 22 g; II—135 mm, 105 g; III—174 mm, 166 g; IV—223 mm, 257 g; V—282 mm, 366 g; VI—315 mm, 445 g; VII—336 mm, 527 g; VIII—362 mm, 527 g; IX—374 mm, 623 g; and X—386 mm, 696 g (Cahn 1927).

In Green Bay, some lake herring reach maturity during their second year of life (age-group I), and most fish of both sexes mature during their third year of life (age-group II) (S. H. Smith 1956). In Lake Superior, the youngest mature lake herring belonged to age-group II, and all fish older than age III were mature; all lake herring shorter than 216 mm (8.5 in) were immature, and all fish longer than 302 mm (11.9 in) were mature (Dryer and Beil 1964). S. H. Smith (1957), summarizing published data on the maturity of ciscoes, showed that the age at which most fish mature in different populations varies from I to IV.

With the decline of lake herring stocks in recent years, there appears to have been an increase in the size of the remaining fish. During the early stages of the decline in the 1950–1962 period, the size and growth rate of the lake herring of Lake Superior increased, and the size continued to increase as abundance declined sharply after 1962 (Dryer and Beil 1964). Similar observations were made in Lake Michigan following the lake herring collapse in the late 1950s (S. H. Smith 1968b).

The cisco reaches large sizes in some waters. Cahn (1927) reported 13 fish, caught from Oconomowoc Lake in 1908, that weighed over 2 kg (4.5 lb) each. However, in 1924 the average weight of 244 ciscoes was only 116 g. A 2.1-kg (4-lb 10-oz) cisco was taken from Big Green Lake (Green Lake County) in 1969. A 3.63-kg (8-lb), 7-year-old female was caught from Lake Erie in 1949 (Scott and Crossman 1973).

The common food found in the lake herring stomachs during various seasons of the year gives strong support to the belief that this species is primarily pelagic. Its gill rakers are numerous and comblike—an efficient mechanism for straining out small plankton organisms. In one study of Lake Superior herring, 83% of the stomachs examined contained crustaceans (Dryer and Beil 1964). Copepods occurred in 71% of the stomachs sampled, and Cladocera *(Daphnia)* in 36%; Mysidacea (*Mysis relicta*) were important only in the December sample. Insects were found in the June–July and September–October collections, the Formicidae and Diptera being most common. Fish eggs (lake herring) were found in 62% of the stomachs in the December sample. Although the lake herring is known to prey on its own eggs, the question arises as to whether such eggs are a preferred food, or whether they are eaten incidentally with plankton. Since the major foods of the lake herring are pelagic, the eggs may simply be eaten as they drift toward the bottom after being released by pelagic spawners. Some eggs may be taken from the bottom; the lake herring's consumption of fingernail clams and water mites, though rare, gives evidence of occasional bottom feeding.

The food of immature ciscoes (up to 160 mm) in Oconomowoc Lake (Waukesha County) is 100% plankton organisms (*Cyclops, Daphnia, Diaptomus, Bosmina, Chydorus*, rotifers, and other animals of a similar nature) (Cahn 1927). Larger ciscoes are primarily plankton feeders, but they also eat mollusks, insect larvae, small fish (probably ciscoes), and vegetable matter. Insects eaten include the larvae of *Corethra*, Ephemerida, and Plecoptera, as well as adult insects picked off the surface in the summer, when the fish occasionally come up on quiet evenings. The vegetable matter consumed includes algae and plant debris from the bottom.

An examination of the stomachs of 35 ciscoes from Lake Geneva (Walworth County) revealed an average of 983 copepods in each of 27 stomachs; an average of 599 cladocerans were counted in 15 stomachs. Midge larvae also occurred in 15 stomachs, mayfly and stonefly naiads and insect fragments were found in 4, and the plant *Chara* in 1 (Nelson and Hasler 1942).

The cisco is a restless fish, constantly on the move, and was referred to by Cahn (1927) as "the most active of all our fishes." Cahn thought that this constant activity is related to its constant search for plankton food. However, it never wanders far—even in the Great Lakes the lake herring is not a distance traveler, and most individuals live out their lives within a few kilometers of their hatching sites. In Lake Michigan tagging operations, lake herring were not recovered at distances greater than 81 km (50 mi) from the point of tagging (O. B. Smith and Van Oosten 1940).

The lake herring engages in a seasonal migration cycle. For instance, in Green Bay during cool weather (September or October to May or June), they congregate in the shallow areas to depths of 10 m (S. H. Smith 1956). It is during this period that they are commonly taken in pound nets and are vulnerable to commercial fishing. Under the ice in midwinter, there may be some movement by lake herring into deeper waters. In June and July, they move laterally into pelagic waters, and are found anywhere between the surface and a depth of 10 m. With the warming of the surface waters, lake herring move into deeper water. During the warm summer months the lake herring hover some 2–3 m off the bottom in water deeper than 10–13 m; it is during this period that they have considerable protection from commercial exploitation. The cycle is completed with the coming of cool weather and the inshore movement of the fish.

Similar seasonal movements by ciscoes in Lake Superior have been described by Dryer and Beil (1964) and Koelz (1929). In Lake Superior, however, the inshore spawning areas in the fall are at all depths down to 165 m. In Lake Superior, as in Green Bay, the species congregates near the shores in the late fall, and it is at this time that the schools become the object of intensive fishing operations. About 90% of the annual lake herring catch is taken at this time, but in recent years aggressive fishing has occurred at other seasons as well (Wells and McLain 1973).

The seasonal cycle of the cisco in inland lakes follows a pattern similar to those of lake herring in Lakes Michigan and Superior, but on a smaller scale. From November to December the cisco is spawning inshore. With the coming of ice cover, there is often a movement into deeper water—a fact known by those who fish for this species through the ice. However, Cahn (1927) noted that in Oconomowoc Lake a vertical diurnal rhythm brings the cisco upward at night to feed on the minute crustaceans that move into the upper strata directly under the ice.

After the ice melts in Oconomowoc Lake and surface waters warm, the cisco seeks the lake's deepest level which provides cool, oxygen-abundant water. In spring, as thermal strata are established in the lake and oxygen is depleted from the hypolimnion, the cisco in Oconomowoc Lake are forced upward into the warmer temperatures of the thermocline (about 11 m from the surface). Late summer is the critical period of the year for the cisco in Oconomowoc Lake; a summerkill may occur, when, in order to get sufficient oxygen, the cisco is forced upward into a warm water layer higher than the cisco can tolerate. In the fall season, the waters cool and mix, again enabling the cisco to frequent surface and shallow waters prior to spawning.

IMPORTANCE AND MANAGEMENT

The lake herring has always been an important prey species for the lake trout (McKnight et al. 1970, Scott and Crossman 1973). Possibly the greatest mortality in the life cycle of the lake herring takes place immediately after the eggs are laid, as a result of predation by the lake herring itself. Predation on the eggs is apt to be heavy, since they lie unprotected on the bottom. The stomachs of 16 out of 19 feeding lake herring from Green Bay contained from 1 to 33 lake herring eggs each (S. H. Smith 1956). There is heavy predation on cisco eggs by brown bullheads and yellow perch, and occasional predation by lake whitefish and mudpuppies. Young ciscoes are preyed on by lake trout, and the larger adults by the sea lamprey.

The cisco seems to have only limited value as a sport fish in Wisconsin. Sport seining and dip-netting in 1966 produced an estimated statewide combined harvest of 26,400 ciscoes and lake whitefish that weighed 6,800 kg (Churchill 1967). In recent years, fishermen have found that when lake herring are feeding on mayflies they will also take artificial flies (S. H. Smith 1956); some large lake herring are taken with minnows. In some waters, bobbing for lake herring through holes in the ice with colored beads is a popular winter sport, and the spearing of ciscoes and whitefish in certain inland waters has become permissible under state regulations.

The flesh of ciscoes in some Wisconsin lakes is heavily infected with a tapeworm larva, rendering it obnoxious to human consumers. These worms are not harmful to man, and they die when the fish are cooked. Ciscoes from Lake Geneva (Walworth County) are often heavily infected, and have been rejected as food.

Historically, the lake herring has been the most productive commercial species in the Great Lakes. It is a fish of considerable value. Less fatty than the other chub species, it is in great demand when salted or smoked. In 1952, Green Bay produced 38.7% of the lake herring catch from all United States waters of the Great Lakes.

The unusual abundance of the lake herring in the past has led to carelessness in the handling and processing of the catch. Dryer and Beil (1964:499) noted that individual catches in Lake Superior, "often running as large as 10 tons, are piled in the gill net tugs and brought to shore where they are picked from the nets in warm sheds. Little care is taken in picking the fish from the nets. The rough treatment of this highly palatable but delicate fish often produces an inferior product. . . ." Apparently in the early fishery, man was not aware that this abundant and valuable species would some day decrease drastically in both Lakes Michigan and Superior, and that a seemingly inexhaustible resource would, within a few decades, dwindle to threatened status.

In Lake Michigan, the production of lake herring for 1899, 1903, and 1908 was 10.1, 7.0, and 11.0 million kg (22.2, 15.4, and 24.2 million lb), respectively (Wells and McLain 1973). The catch dropped drastically from almost 2.7 million kg (6 million lb) in 1952 to lows of 1,002 and 1,248 kg (2,209 and 2,752 lb) in 1972 and 1973. In 1974, when the catch of 2,772 kg (6,112 lb) was valued at $2,172, lake herring were taken incidentally to the lake whitefish in the Door County waters of Green Bay and Lake Michigan (83% of the harvest); the remainder of the catch (17% of the harvest) came from the Racine-Kenosha area, and was taken incidentally to the perch fishery (Wis. Dep. Nat. Resour. 1976c).

The early marked declines of lake herring in Lake Michigan were largely the result of heavy exploitation, although pollution must have contributed to the decline in southern Green Bay. It seems likely that the reduction of the lake herring to its present insignificance in Lake Michigan can be attributed to the resurgence of smelt populations by the early 1950s and the explosive increase of alewives which began in the mid-1950s (Wells and McLain 1973, Miller 1957). The ubiquitous and planktivorous alewife is not only a serious competitor for food, but is presumed to interfere with the successful spawning of the lake herring and to prey on herring eggs.

Wisconsin's lake herring production in Lake Superior has also dropped—from 2.1–2.9 million kg (4.6–6.5 million lb) in the 1940s to 1.0 million kg (2.2 million lb) in the late 1950s, and to less than 454,000 kg (1 million lb) after 1962. Production then dropped steadily to 63,000 kg (139,000 lb) in 1974, the lowest annual catch in recent years; an estimated additional 9,000 kg (20,000 lb) were taken in the Indian fisheries. Nearly half of the 1974 catch was taken incidentally in sets made for chubs. The lake herring population is not going to provide a major contribution to commercial production in the foreseeable future (Wis. Dep. Nat. Resour. 1976c).

Anderson and Smith (1971a) rejected overfishing as the primary cause of the post-1961 collapse of the lake herring in Lake Superior, and concluded that competition for food with the bloater and the smelt was the most probable cause of the decline. Lawrie and Rahrer (1973) presented evidence that the declines in lake herring abundance have followed intense commercial efforts which led to stock depletion. Selgeby et al. (1978) concluded that neither predation nor competition are the factors presently limiting the lake herring population in southwestern Lake Superior.

The stocking of ciscoes in deep, nonfertile lakes has been going on in Wisconsin since the early 1890s. In 1891, several million cisco eggs were taken from Lake Mendota and hatched in the Milwaukee hatchery; "some 12,000,000 of the fry were transported by baggage car to Ashland, and planted through three feet of ice into Chequamegon Bay" (Commnrs. Fish. of Wis. 1903). The venture was considered a success, although the fish did not reproduce.

Among the many inland lakes that have been planted with this species is Sunset Lake (Portage County), which was stocked with ciscoes from Pallette Lake (Vilas County). Sunset Lake has a reproducing population that has survived two poisonings of the lake. Crystal Lake (Sheboygan County) was also stocked, and has a reproducing population.

The greatest threat to cisco populations in inland lakes is the enrichment of the waters. During the summer this results in the depletion of oxygen in the lower stratum (hypolimnion), and forces the cisco into the upper strata, where temperatures are unfavorable for survival. Such lakes often exhibit serious cisco mortalities. In the past 100 years, summerkills of ciscoes in Lake Mendota have been commonly reported (Neuenschwander 1946). Summerkills of ciscoes were observed by Cahn (1927) from the following: Waukesha County lakes: Pine, Okauchee, Oconomowoc, Silver, and Lac La Belle; in Pine Lake (Waukesha County) kills have occurred in recent years (F. Ott, pers. comm.). Perhaps the greatest challenge to the management of cisco populations in inland lakes is stopping or reversing the eutrophication process.

Shortnose Cisco

Coregonus reighardi (Koelz). *Coregonus*—angle-eye, coined by Artedi from the Greek meaning pupil of the eye and angle; *reighardi*—of Reighard, after Jacob Reighard, ichthyologist, University of Michigan.

Other common names: Reighard's chub, Reighard cisco, shortnose chub, greaser (Lake Ontario).

Adult female 210 mm, L. Michigan, near Indiana City, Indiana, 1 Apr. 1921 (Koelz 1929:400)

DESCRIPTION

The following is based largely on Koelz's (1929) description of Lake Michigan specimens.

Body elongate, subterete in cross section, and only slightly compressed; body deepest anterior to dorsal fin. Average length 267 mm (10.5 in); TL = 1.18 SL. Depth into TL 3.9–4.5. Head length into TL 4.1–4.5 (3.9–4.8). Snout short; snout into head length 3.4–4.0. Premaxillaries heavily pigmented, and angled downward and forward at 60–90° with long axis of body; anterior maxillary pigmented; maxillary extending to about middle of pupil. Lower jaw stout, heavily tipped with black; lower jaw ventral and usually shorter than and included within upper jaw. Eye into head length 3.9–4.2 (3.6–4.6). Gill rakers short, longest shorter than longest gill filaments; gill rakers 34–38 (30–43). Dorsal fin rays 9–10 (8–11); anal fin rays 10–11 (9–12); pectoral fin rays 16 (15–17); pelvic fin rays 11 (10–12); pectoral fins very short, pectoral fin length into distance from pectoral origin to pelvic origin 2.0–2.5 (1.7–2.8); pelvic fins very short, pelvic fin length into distance from pelvic origin to anal origin 1.4–1.7 (1.2–1.9). Scales in lateral line 72–81 (66–96); scales around body anterior to dorsal and pelvic fins 40–43 (38–46). Details of skull and caudal skeleton provided by Cavender (1970). Chromosomes 2n = 80 (Booke 1968).

Color in life silvery, with underlying color of back usually pale pea green to blue-green with a pink iridescence.

Males and at least some females with tubercles during the breeding season. For a description of the breeding tubercles in males, see the deepwater cisco species account (p. 367).

Hybrids: Shortnose cisco × bloater (Parsons and Todd 1974).

SYSTEMATIC NOTES

The type specimen (Koelz 1924) is a female, 210 mm (8.3 in) SL, with large eggs, taken from Lake Michigan off Michigan City, Indiana, in 55–64 m of water on 1 April 1921.

Koelz (1929) recognized two subspecies from Wisconsin waters: *Coregonus* (subgenus *Leucichthys*) *reighardi reighardi* from Lakes Michigan and Ontario, and *Coregonus reighardi dymondi* from Lakes Superior and Nipigon.

C. r. reighardi is valid for Lake Michigan. However, Koelz's specimens of *reighardi* from Wisconsin waters of Lake Superior were reexamined, and all become *C. zenithicus* (Parsons et al. 1975, Todd 1977). Furthermore, *Coregonus r. dymondi*, known only from Canadian waters of Lake Superior, is regarded as a local population of *C. zenithicus* (Todd 1978).

DISTRIBUTION, STATUS, AND HABITAT

In Wisconsin, the shortnose cisco occurs in Lake Michigan and in Green Bay.

This species has been known from Lakes Ontario, Huron, and Michigan. It is endangered in Lake Huron, and extirpated in Lake Ontario. Its present status in Lake Michigan is endangered (Wis. Dep. Nat. Resour. Endangered Species Com. 1975). A single specimen (UWSP 2437) was taken 16–24 km (10–15 mi) east of Sheboygan in June 1968. The last known record from Lake Michigan came from Ludington, Michigan, on 18 May 1972 (Todd 1978). The extinction of this species seems inevitable.

The shortnose cisco ranges principally at depths of 37–110 m; the extremes at which it is found are 9 m and 165 m. It is most common in the upper zones of the deepwater areas, and it is distributed along the shores of Lake Michigan and probably on some of the reefs. It occurs at temperatures of 1.5–10.2°C (34.7–50.4°F).

BIOLOGY

The shortnose cisco spawns primarily from April to June at water temperatures of 3.8–4.7°C (38.8–40.5°F). The spawning season is quite variable, however, and may begin earlier or extend later in different years, according to Jobes (1943). In some years a few individuals do not spawn until September. S. H. Smith (1964) noted that, when large numbers of shortnose ciscoes are found in spawning condition in the fall in

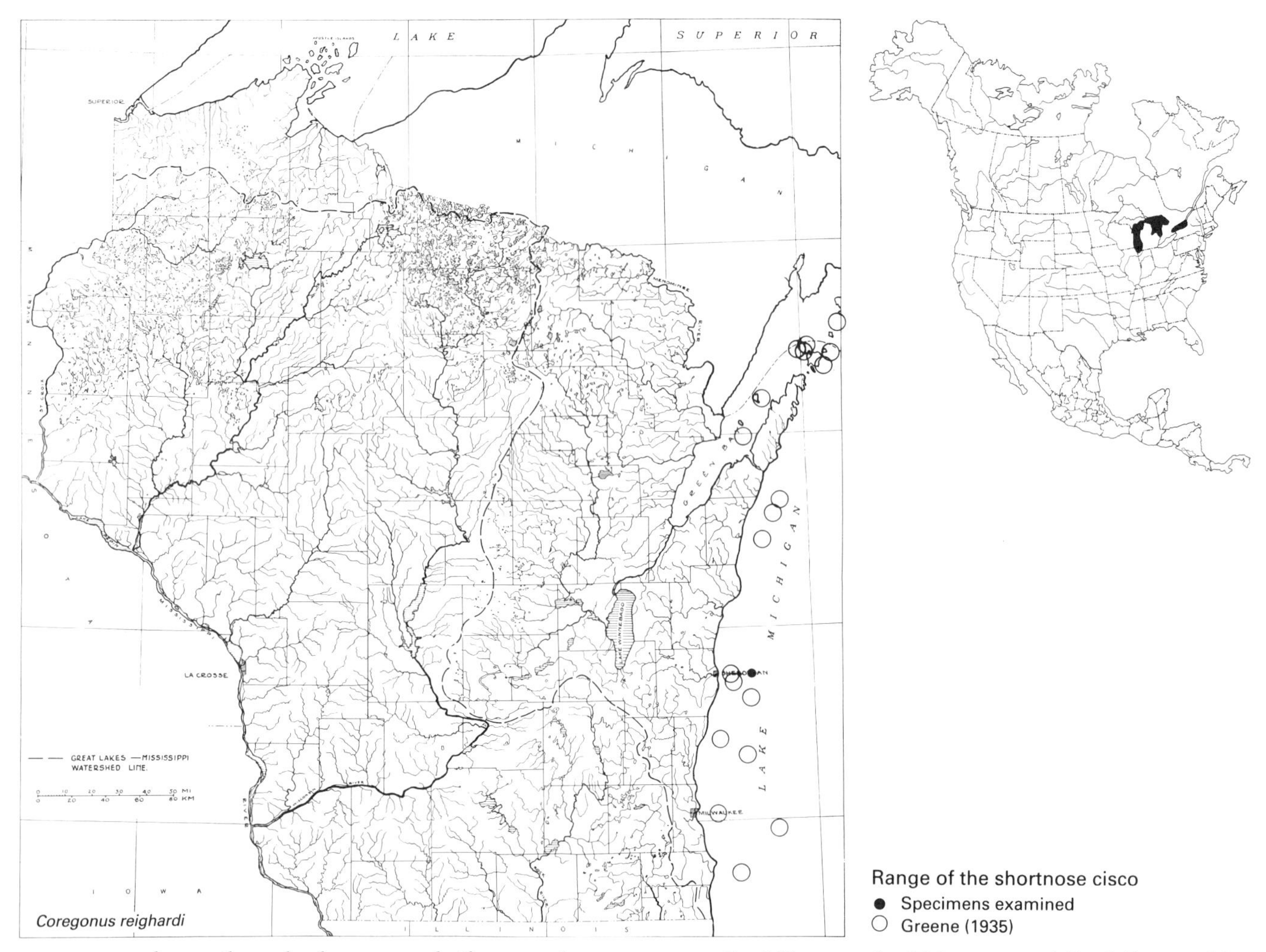

Range of the shortnose cisco
● Specimens examined
○ Greene (1935)

an area where they had spawned the previous spring, a biological change is indicated; such a change may increase the probability of hybridization with other fall-spawning cisco species.

In lower Lake Michigan, the shortnose cisco spawns at depths of 37–144 m; in the upper part of the lake, it spawns at 55–91 m; and in Green Bay, at 46 m (Jobes 1943). Spawning runs have been recorded off Sheboygan, Racine, Sturgeon Bay, Algoma, and Milwaukee, and a number of Michigan and Indiana ports, over bottoms of sand, silt, or clay (Koelz 1929, Jobes 1943).

The eggs of the shortnose cisco are yellow; they measure 2.0 mm diam (Booke 1970).

More than 7,570 shortnose ciscoes from upper Lake Michigan, 239–310 mm TL, were aged by Jobes (1943), who found that age-IV fish made up 50.2% of the total sample. Age, total length, and weight were: II—264 mm, 156 g; III—272 mm, 171 g; IV—277 mm, 171 g; V—284 mm, 185 g; and VI—290 mm, 199 g. The calculated total length at the end of each year of life was: 1—153 mm, 2—201 mm, 3—236 mm, 4—257 mm, 5—269 mm, 6—280 mm, and 7—269 mm (the last based on only one fish).

Shortnose ciscoes of both sexes taken by Jobes in November were relatively heavier than those taken in May, which suggests some loss of weight during the winter. Differences in growth between sexes was found to be unimportant. Jobes (1943) computed that 55% of the total growth in length (assuming 100% growth at age VI) was reached at the end of the first year of life. The coefficient of condition for all fish of ages II–VII, sexes combined, was 1.37.

In Jobes' study, females made up 85% of the total sample of shortnose ciscoes whose ages were determined, and they were dominant in all age-groups. Only females were found in age-groups VI and VII. In the sample taken, the sexes occurred in about equal numbers in May, after which the females dominated strongly in the catch all other months. Jobes assumed that the sexes of the shortnose cisco are segregated for the greater part of the year, and that they approach equality in numbers only during part of the spawning season, in May and June.

The largest shortnose cisco on record was a mature female, 371 mm TL and 445 g (14.6 in, 15.7 oz), taken off Escanaba, Michigan, on 13 May 1932. The longest male, 335 mm TL (13.2 in), was taken off Manistique, Michigan, on 6 July 1932; the heaviest known male, also caught off Escanaba, weighed 312 g (11 oz).

The stomach contents of 27 shortnose ciscoes from Lake Ontario were examined by Pritchard (1931). *Mysis relicta* and *Pontoporeia* were the major food items found, but small numbers of copepods, aquatic insect larvae, and fingernail clams had also been eaten.

The shortnose cisco seems to prefer the upper zones of deepwater areas. In lower Lake Michigan, Jobes (1943) found this species increasing in numbers with each 18-meter increase in depth down to 73 m; below that point the fish decreased in numbers as the depth increased. They were generally scarce or absent at depths of 128 m and more. In upper Lake Michigan, the greatest concentration of shortnose ciscoes occurred at 73–90 m, and in Green Bay, at 29–35 m.

IMPORTANCE AND MANAGEMENT

During the 1930s and 1940s, the shortnose cisco was a valuable commercial species in Wisconsin waters. Although only medium-sized, it was very fat and considered excellent when smoked. In 1930–1931, its numbers along the eastern shore of Lake Michigan were estimated to be more than seven times greater than along the western shore (Jobes 1943). This difference may have resulted from a more intensive fishery on the Wisconsin shore, where smaller-mesh nets were used. Jobes suggested that there was very little, if any, intermingling of the populations from the two sides of the lake.

In the comparison surveys of cisco species numbers, the U. S. Bureau of Commercial Fisheries used identical gangs of gill nets of various mesh sizes to sample the northern, central, and southern parts of Lake Michigan in different time periods (Smith 1964). In northern Lake Michigan the number of shortnose ciscoes caught (expressed as catch per 466-m gang net) were 12.0 in 1932, 6.5 in 1955, and 4.5 in 1961. In central Lake Michigan the number of shortnose ciscoes caught (expressed as catch per 777-m gang net) were 213.2 in 1930–1931, 20.4 in 1954–1955, and 6.8 in 1960–1961; and in southern Lake Michigan (expressed as catch per 777-m gang net), 60.5 in 1930–1931, 16.1 in 1954–1955, and 4.0 in 1960–1961. Each successive comparison survey showed a marked decrease from the previous one, and in the last series (1960–1961) less than 2% of the catch was composed of shortnose ciscoes.

The reasons for the near extirpation of the shortnose cisco in Lake Michigan are not known. Commercial exploitation and competition with alewives may have started or aided the decline. As reported earlier, there is evidence that shortnose ciscoes may have shifted their spawning time into the fall, when other cisco species are spawning, thus permitting the mixing of the gonadal products of several species at one time. With the explosion of the bloater population in Lake Michigan, the bloater became the dominant species of cisco in the lake; bloaters in spawning condition were found during every month of the year. This probably led to the contamination of the shortnose cisco gene pool as well as that of the bloater and other cisco species, and resulted in appearance of hybrid swarms of bloaterlike fish, along with a few "nonbloaters." Even these "nonbloaters," including the shortnose ciscolike specimens of the 1960s and early 1970s, were not as morphologically distinct as their ancestral species had been (S. H. Smith 1964, Wells and McLain 1973).

Shortjaw Cisco

Coregonus zenithicus (Jordan and Evermann). *Coregonus*—angle-eye, coined by Artedi from the Greek, meaning pupil of the eye and angle; *zenithicus*—named after Duluth, Minnesota, the Zenith City, where Jordan and Evermann (1909) saw hundreds of specimens of this species in the cold-storage plant of Booth and Company.

Other common names: shortjaw chub, longjaw, lightback tullibee, paleback tullibee, Lake Superior longjaw.

Keweenaw Bay, L. Superior, Michigan, 31 Aug. 1973 (U.S. Fish and Wildlife Service, Great Lakes Fishery Laboratory photo)

DESCRIPTION

Body elongate, subterete, with greatest depth at the front of the dorsal fin, depth into TL 4.2–4.8 (3.7–5.3). Average length 284 mm (11.2 in). Head into TL 3.8–4.1 (3.6–4.4). Snout into head length 3.3–3.6 (3.1–4). Premaxillaries medium pigmented, and angled downward and forward with long axis of body at 60–70°; anterior maxillary lightly pigmented, maxillary reaching to middle of eye. Lower jaw stout, without pigment and with no symphyseal knob; lower jaw ventral and usually shorter than upper jaw and included. Eye into head length 4.2–4.6 (3.9–5.1). Gill rakers medium long, with the longest equal in length to the longest gill filaments 38–42 (35–44). Scales in lateral line 74–84 (69–90); scales around body anterior to dorsal and pelvic fins 39–42 (37–45). Dorsal fin rays 10 (11); anal rays 11–12 (10–13); pectoral rays 16–17 (15–18); pelvic rays 12 (11). Pectoral fins medium long, length into distance from pectoral origin to pelvic origin 1.6–2.0 (1.3–2.4). Pelvic fins medium long, length into distance from pelvic origin to anal origin 1.3–1.6 (1.0–1.9).

Color in life, silvery with underlying color of back varying from dark blue-green to pale pea green. Dorsal fin margin and, often, distal half of pectoral and caudal rays, smoky to black. Black sometimes present on pelvics and anal fin, increasing in larger and older specimens.

Males, and sometimes females, with breeding tubercles during breeding season.

SYSTEMATIC NOTES

The type specimen (USNM 62517) is a male, 278 mm SL, taken off Isle Royale in Lake Superior in September 1908 (Jordan and Evermann 1909).

The bluefin cisco, *Coregonus nigripinnis cyanopterus*, formerly ascribed to Lake Superior waters, is synonymous with the shortjaw cisco (Todd and Smith 1980). Such bluefin ciscoes are merely large and old shortjaw ciscoes that were mistakenly considered to be a different species.

In central Canada the shortjaw cisco and *C. artedii* are the representative species from this genus (Clarke 1974).

DISTRIBUTION, STATUS, AND HABITAT

In the Great Lakes, the shortjaw cisco is known from Lakes Huron, Michigan, and Superior. In Lake Michigan it once occurred along all shores except in lower Green Bay. Where taken in recent years in Lake Michigan, this species inhabited the intermediate depths of the deepwater areas, formerly occupied by the longjaw cisco (*C. alpenae*) and the deepwater cisco (*C. johannae*) (S. H. Smith 1964). It is possible that the shortjaw cisco never was widely distributed in the northern part of Lake Michigan. But by 1960–1961 the species was seriously depleted in this lake (S. H. Smith 1964). An individual was captured in a trawl at 64 m off Benton Harbor, Michigan, on 19 April 1967 (T. Todd, pers. comm.); the last known occurrence in Lake Michigan was off Racine (Grid 2006:U.S. Fish Wildl. Serv. 1972) on 23 September 1975. Todd (1978) noted that the shortjaw cisco may have been extirpated in Lakes Michigan and Huron, but is still common in Lake Superior, although its numbers there are declining (Parsons et al. 1975). In Wisconsin this species has been given endangered status (Wis. Dep. Nat. Resour. Endangered Species Com. 1975).

In Lake Superior the shortjaw cisco is found along all shores, ranging between 18 m and 163 m, but most common at 55–126 m. In the Apostle Islands region it is most abundant in the spring at 110 – 126 m, in the summer at 55 – 71 m, and in the fall at 73–90 m (Dryer 1966).

BIOLOGY

T. Todd has reported populations of the shortjaw cisco spawning during the fall (December) and spring (May) in the Apostle Islands (Ashland County) and the Keweenaw, Michigan, areas of Lake Superior (pers. comm.). He also has data on August spawners

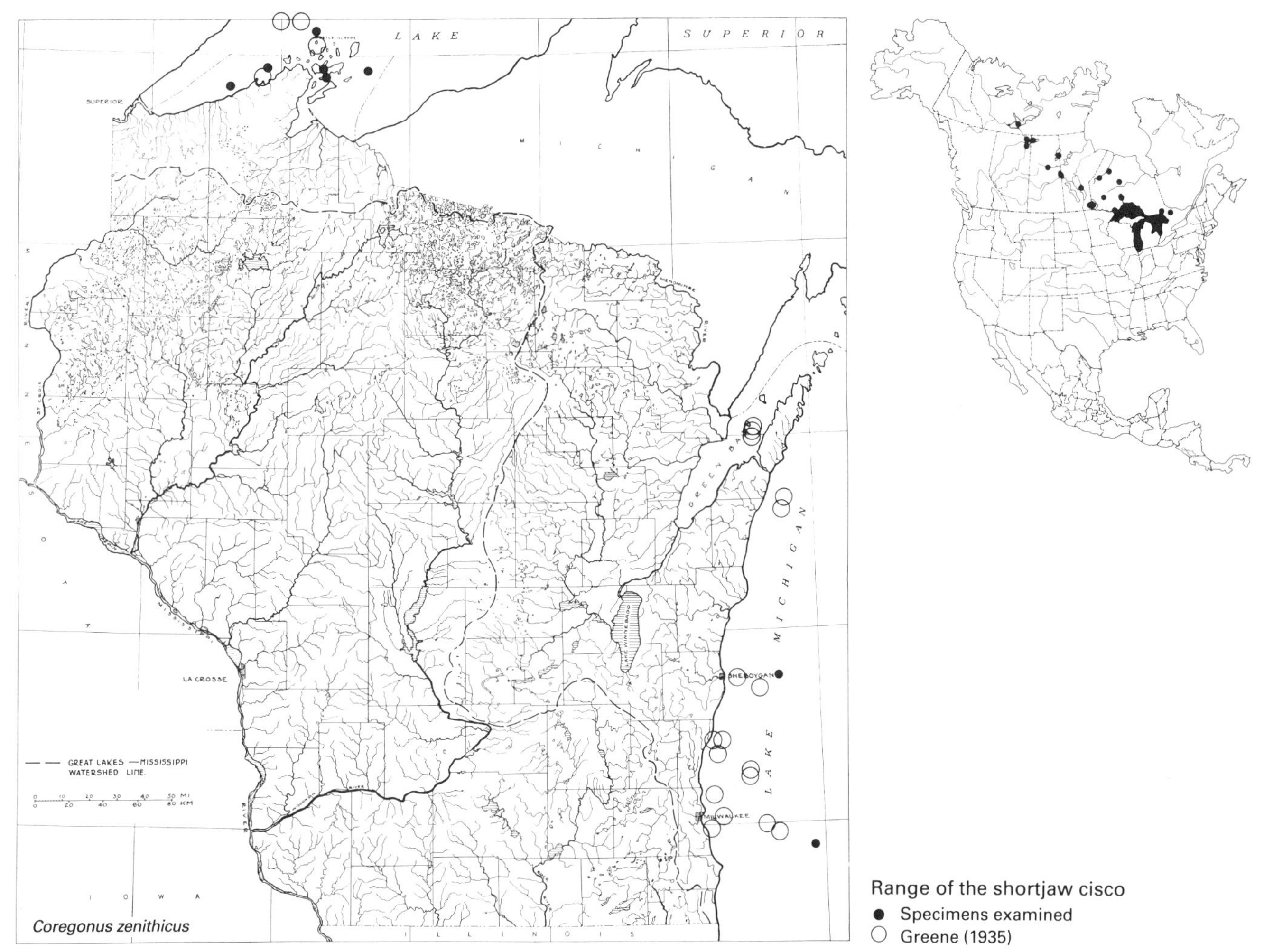

Range of the shortjaw cisco
● Specimens examined
○ Greene (1935)

from Isle Royale, Michigan, and from Grand Marais, Minnesota; he noted that spawning time for this species seems to be quite variable. Spawning probably occurs at depths of 37–73 m over clay bottom (Van Oosten 1937a). Individuals of 183 mm TL usually have maturing sex organs, and all fish of 243 mm TL or more (age IV) are sexually mature. The eggs are yellow, 2.14 ± 0.03 mm diam (Booke 1970).

In Lake Michigan, breeding grounds were reported off Milwaukee and possibly off Port Washington (Koelz 1929). Spawning took place over sand and clay at depths of 18–55 m. The fish congregated between the middle of October and the beginning of November and remained on the grounds about a month, the males arriving first.

Age and growth were determined by Van Oosten (1937a) from 589 shortjaw ciscoes collected from Lake Superior, near Duluth. Age group VII made up 41.3% of the catch; 93.2% of the sample ranged from 279 to 345 mm TL, with the mode at 305 mm. Van Oosten noted that length was a poor index of age, since fish of the same length could belong to as many as three or four different age groups. The average total length and weight for sexes combined were: IV—234 mm, 77 g; V—277 mm, 125 g; VI—297 mm, 150 g; VII—312 mm, 170 g; VIII—325 mm, 199 g; IX—351 mm, 249 g; and X—345 mm, 249 g. Calculated total length mm (TL = 1.2 SL) at the end of each year of life was: 1—97 mm, 2—130, 3—165, 4—200, 5—232, 6-261, 7-282, 8-300, 9—322. Compared to the increase in length, the increase in weight was small during the first years of life, but in later years it was relatively rapid.

As in many other ciscoes, growth compensation occurs in this species. Van Oosten observed that big yearlings were, on the average, the big fish in all succeeding years, but the maximum differences between the lengths of the size groups diminished each year, so that fish became more uniform in size during each successive year of age. The coefficient of condition, 0.99 in males and 1.04 in females, was low, indicating a species with a slender body form. The sexes were equally abundant in the population, although after the 8th year the males disappeared from the catch more rapidly than did the females; a few males survived to the 11th year of life.

The largest shortjaw cisco recorded was 404 mm (15.9 in) TL (Koelz 1929). The heaviest was an age-IX female, 368 mm (14.5 in) TL, weighing 312 g (11 oz) (Van Oosten 1937a).

In seven stomachs of shortjaw cisco collected off Cheboygan, Michigan, September 1917, *Mysis* and *Pontoporeia* constituted 95% of the food; *Pisidium*, pebbles, wood fragments, larval chironomids, and unidentifiable bottom material made up the rest (Koelz 1929).

IMPORTANCE AND MANAGEMENT

Early in the commercial fishery the old and large shortjaw ciscoes (erroneously called the bluefin) were the dominant deepwater chubs in Lake Superior. Eddy and Underhill (1974) noted that they often were found in the stomachs of lake trout and siscowets caught in very deep water; they also observed that when commercial fishing for lake trout was at its peak, the gill nets set at 122–183 m often caught a few shortjaw ciscoes.

The shortjaw cisco is delicious fresh or smoked. In 1922 (Koelz 1929) a lift in the Apostle Islands area of Lake Superior included 300 shortjaw ciscoes, but only one bloater, one blackfin cisco, and one shortnose cisco (the last two species are synonymous with the shortjaw cisco, but at that time were considered distinct species). By the mid-1930s, the shortjaw cisco was the only large chub common enough in Lake Superior to be taken in commercial quantities, and Van Oosten (1937a) noted that it ranked second to *artedii*, the lake herring, in abundance. He recommended that the shortjaw cisco be accorded protection through the sixth year of life, since there was an increase in weight from the fifth to the sixth year (about 53% for the males and 66% for the females) which would enhance the value of the commercial catch.

Marked changes occurred in the cisco population of Lake Superior between the mid-1930s and the late 1950s. During the 1958–1965 period, in the same area where Koelz had observed the lift of chub nets in 1922, and with gill nets of the same mesh sizes, Dryer and Beil (1968) obtained catches containing only 8% shortjaw ciscoes; 92% were bloaters. In 1965, an examination of 681 chubs from commercial landings at Bayfield, Wisconsin, revealed that shortjaw ciscoes made up 8% of the catch, kiyi 2%, and bloaters 90%. In 1974, the bulk of the deepwater cisco catch consisted of bloaters and insignificant numbers of shortjaw ciscoes and kiyi.

By 1961 the shortjaw cisco appeared close to extirpation in Lake Michigan (S. H. Smith 1964). In comparison surveys made during 1932, 1955, and 1961 the shortjaw cisco (compared to all other deepwater ciscoes) constituted 11%, 1.5%, and 0.5% respectively of the catch in northern Lake Michigan; 6.1%, 2.8%, and 0.7% of the catch taken off Grand Haven, Michigan; and 2.9%, 1.0%, and 0.9% of the catch taken off Ludington, Michigan.

Longjaw Cisco

Coregonus alpenae (Koelz). *Coregonus*—angle-eye, coined by Artedi from the Greek, meaning pupil of the eye and angle; *alpenae*—of Alpena, after Alpena, Michigan.

Other common names: the longjaw, longjaw chub.

Adult 269 mm, L. Michigan, near Charlevoix, Michigan, 15 June 1923 (Koelz 1929:364)

DESCRIPTION

The following is based largely on Koelz's (1929) description of Lake Michigan specimens.

Body elongate, with greatest depth medially, or nearly so; depth into TL 3.8–4.3. Average length 280 mm (11 in). Head into TL 4.1–4.4 (3.8–4.6). Snout into head length 3.4–3.6 (3.3–4.0). Premaxillaries usually slightly pigmented, and angled downward and forward with long axis of body at 45–60°; anterior maxillary little pigment to none, maxillary extending beyond anterior edge of pupil but seldom to center. Lower jaw without pigment and with no symphyseal knob; lower jaw stout and usually projecting beyond the upper jaw. Eye into head length 4.2–4.6 (3.8–5.2). Gill rakers medium long, with the longest about equal in length to the longest gill filaments 36–43 (33–46). Scales in lateral line 78–85 (71–96); scales around body anterior to dorsal and pelvic fins 41–43 (40–45). Dorsal fin rays 10–11 (9); anal rays 11–12 (9–13); pectoral rays 15–17 (12–18); pelvic rays 11 (10–12). Pectoral fins medium long; length into distance from pectoral origin to pelvic origin 1.9–2.2 (1.6–2.5). Pelvic fin medium long; length into distance from pelvic origin to anal origin 1.4–1.7 (1.2–1.9).

Color in life, silvery with a faint pink to purple iridescence which is strongest above the lateral line and absent on belly. Males with breeding tubercles similar to those described for the deepwater cisco (*C. johannae*).

SYSTEMATIC NOTES

The type specimen (USNM 87352) is a female, 269 mm SL, taken from Lake Michigan 36 km (22 mi) NNE Charlevoix, Michigan, on 15 June 1923 (Koelz 1929). The longjaw cisco, according to Koelz, resembles the deepwater cisco (*C. johannae*) more closely than it does any other cisco of the Great Lakes.

DISTRIBUTION, STATUS, AND HABITAT

The longjaw cisco is an endemic species occurring only in Lakes Michigan, Huron, and Erie. In Wisconsin it is known only from the waters of Lake Michigan and Green Bay. Its presence in Lake Erie has been documented by Scott and Smith (1962). It was last recorded in Lake Erie 13 November 1957; in Lake Huron, 12 June 1975; and in Grand Traverse Bay, Lake Michigan, in 1967. In the entire range, it currently is either extinct or so rare as to be beyond rehabilitation (Todd 1978).

The longjaw cisco is on the federal endangered species list (Office of Federal Register 1976). In Wisconsin it has been given endangered status (Wis. Dep. Nat. Resour. Endangered Species Com. 1975).

The longjaw cisco inhabits the open water of Lake Michigan and of Green Bay north of a line from the Sturgeon Bay Ship Canal to Marinette (Koelz 1929, Jobes 1949a). When not spawning it occurs at 51–128 m, with only stragglers found in shallower and deeper waters (extremes 9–165 m) (Koelz 1929). Jobes (1949a) took the maximum number at a depth of less than 73 m, within temperature extremes of 1.5–11.2°C (34.7–52.2°F). Because this species is seldom taken in water more than 128 m deep, Jobes reasoned that the longjaw ciscoes of the east and west shores of southern Lake Michigan are probably kept separate by the deep trough in the middle of the lake. He suggested that each side of the lake has its own population of longjaws, and that there is little if any intermingling of these populations.

BIOLOGY

The longjaw cisco is a fall spawner. Individuals taken 19 November 1920 off Michigan City, Indiana, would have spawned soon and probably nearby, although no fish with ripe eggs were found (Koelz 1929). Fishermen reported to Koelz that chubs (probably longjaws) came into shallow water (ca. 18 m) in the northern part of Lake Michigan to spawn in late October and November. A late spawning season agrees with the findings of Scott and Smith (1962), who noted that all of the longjaw ciscoes taken in Lake Erie on 11 November 1957 were ripe and had well-developed breeding tubercles.

Data indicate that spawning also may occur earlier in the season. Jobes (1949a) reported ripe females as follows: 5 August 1930, one fish off Ludington, Mich-

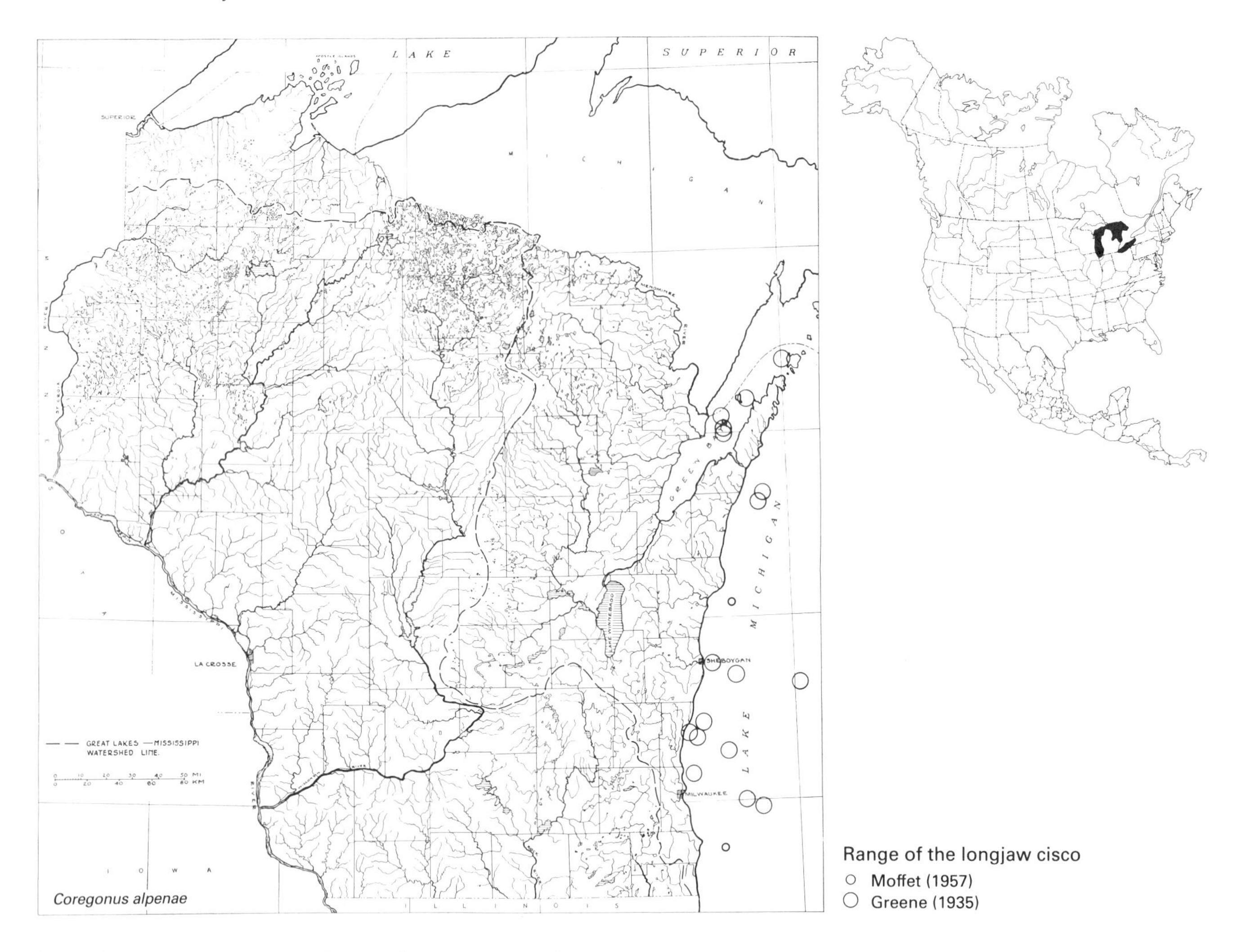

Range of the longjaw cisco
○ Moffet (1957)
◯ Greene (1935)

igan, from 48 to 49 m; 11 September 1931, one fish off Port Washington, Wisconsin, from 137 to 139 m; and 9 July 1932, one specimen off Manistique, Michigan, from 117 to 124 m. The earliest date on which a ripe male has been reported was 20 October 1931, off Milwaukee, Wisconsin, at 59–66 m. A "nearly ripe" male was taken 17 August 1932 off Charlevoix, Michigan, at 99–134 m. Spent females were taken off Sheboygan, Wisconsin, from 70 to 91 m on 16 October 1931, and off Racine, Wisconsin, in 77 m in November 1930. Spent males were taken on 12 November 1930 off Waukegan, Illinois, from 62 to 82 m.

The longjaw cisco reaches normal maturity in its third and fourth years of life (Moffett 1957).

Age and growth were investigated by Jobes (1949a). Longjaws from northeastern Lake Michigan (1923) and Grand Haven, Michigan (1929), were in age groups II–IX. In the 1923 sample, age group IV dominated (53.8%), followed by III (20.9%) and V (10.6%). Age group III (55.2%) dominated the 1928 collection, followed by age groups IV (31.0%) and II (12.1%).

In the 1923 sample, the average calculated total length and weight at the end of each year of life were: 1—123 mm, 20 g; 2—203 mm, 62 g; 3—251 mm, 122 g; 4—282 mm, 182 g; 5—312 mm, 244 g; 6—343 mm, 329 g; 7–371 mm, 414 g; 8—406 mm, 641 g. Most of the year's growth occurred before 15 June. In 1930, when all species of ciscoes were well represented in a sample studied, the average length of longjaw ciscoes was 274 mm (10.8 in) (S. H. Smith 1964).

The sexes grow at approximately the same rates (Jobes 1949a). The differences in relative heaviness between the sexes are so slight that the weighted average values of K for all males and all females are practically the same (1.30 for the males and 1.31, females). However, sex-ratio favored the females in 1930 (72.4% females) and in 1931 (67.5%). Jobes suggested a higher mortality in males as the cause of this difference.

By far the largest longjaw cisco reported was a female taken off Manistique, Michigan, on 1 September 1932, which was 546 mm (21.5 in) TL, and weighed

1,857 g (4 lb 1.5 oz). The largest male, captured off Ludington, Michigan, on 13 August 1930 was 439 mm (17.3 in) TL, and weighed 737 g (1 lb 10 oz) (Jobes 1949a).

Thirty stomachs examined by C. L. Hubbs from specimens taken off Alpena, Michigan (September 1917) at 110 m and deeper contained *Mysis* as the main food organism (Koelz 1929). About one-third of the fish examined had eaten a little sand and some plant remains of one kind or another; *Pisidium*, clay, fish scales, and cased invertebrate eggs were found in some stomachs. One specimen taken off Bay City, Michigan, 29 October 1921, had eaten larvae of the mayfly *Hexagenia* and some cased invertebrate eggs. A recent study of Lake Michigan longjaws (Bersamin 1958) disclosed that *Mysis* made up 95% of their food; the remaining 5% consisted of *Pontoporeia*. As many as 458 *Mysis* were counted in a single stomach.

IMPORTANCE AND MANAGEMENT

At one time the longjaw cisco constituted an important part of the commercial chub catch of Lake Michigan and of the smoked fish trade. Koelz (1929) reported that it occurred most abundantly in the northeastern end of Lake Michigan, between Frankfort and Manistique, Michigan, where it made up from 22 to 98% of the hauls. A second area of abundance lay off Michigan City, Indiana, at the southern end of the lake, where it made up from 10 to 33% of the chub lifts.

Surveys in which ciscoes were taken in identical gangs of gill nets in the same areas at different periods point up dramatically the decline of this species (S. H. Smith 1964). In northeastern Lake Michigan the longjaw catch was 35% of the sample in 1932, 1.6% in 1955, and 0.6% in 1961; in central and southern Lake Michigan at 46 m, it was 14.2% in 1930–1931, 4.3% in 1954–1955, and 0.7% in 1960–1961; in central and southern Lake Michigan, at 91–110 m; it was 15.4% in 1930–1931, 3.9% in 1954–1955, and 0.9% in 1960–1961. Apparently the decline of the longjaw cisco resulted primarily from intensive fishery, since its size made it vulnerable to reduced mesh sizes. It resulted secondly, and perhaps concurrently, from attacks by sea lamprey, which turned to the largest chubs when lake trout and burbot had been eliminated. It is likely that the longjaw cisco formed part of the food supply of the lake trout and burbot populations before these fishes were largely destroyed by the sea lamprey (Scott and Crossman 1973).

Bloater

Coregonus hoyi (Gill). *Coregonus*—angle-eye, coined by Artedi from the Greek, meaning pupil of the eye, and angle; *hoyi*—of Hoy, after P. R. Hoy, M.D., of Racine, Wisconsin, naturalist and ichthyologist.

Other common names: bloat, Hoy's cisco.

Whitefish Bay, near Whitefish Point, L. Superior, Michigan, 8 Aug. 1973 (U.S. Fish and Wildlife Service, Great Lakes Fishery Laboratory photo)

DESCRIPTION

Body elongate, with greatest depth medially; depth into TL 3.8–4.2. Average length 200–250 mm (8–10 in). Head into TL 4.0–4.2 (3.6–4.6). Snout usually a trifle longer than the large eye; snout into head length 3.7–4.0 (3.3–4.5). Premaxillaries pigmented, and angled downward and forward with long axis of body at about 40°; maxillary pigmented; maxillary into head length 2.5–2.6 (2.3–2.8), extending to pupil of eye. Lower jaw conspicuously pigmented (except in some Lake Michigan populations), and usually with prominent symphyseal knob; lower jaw longer than upper jaw, with mandibles frail, thin, and easily bent. Gill rakers long, longest usually longer than gill filaments 41–44 (37–48). Scales in lateral line 67–77 (60–84); scales around body anterior to dorsal and pelvic fins 40–42 (38–44). Dorsal fin rays 9–10 (7); anal fin rays 11 (10–13); pectoral fin rays 15–16 (14–17); pelvic rays 11 (10–12). Pectoral fins long; length into distance from pectoral origin to pelvic origin 1.7–2.0 (1.3–2.5). Pelvic fins long; length into distance from pelvic origin to anal origin 1.2–1.4 (1–1.7). Chromosomes 2n = 80 (Booke 1968).

Color in life silvery with some pink or purple iridescence and a greenish tinge above the lateral line; silvery white on belly. Fins usually weakly pigmented; dorsal and caudal fins dark edged.

Breeding tubercles develop on scales (1–3 per scale) on the sides of males and on some females.

When brought up from depths the air bladder expands, giving the fish a bloated appearance, hence its name. To its discoverer, Dr. Hoy, however, it was "the most beautiful of the white fish" (Hoy 1883).

Hybrids: Bloater × lake herring; bloater × shortnose cisco (Parsons and Todd 1974).

The problem of hybridization and introgression has been thoroughly discussed by S. H. Smith (1964), who made special note of a "new fish" which appeared to be a *hoyi* × *artedii* cross. The presence in Lake Superior of intergrades between these two species suggests that the same introgression is occurring there. Parsons and Todd (1974) noted: "The taxonomic variability among *C. hoyi* is so great that this form almost represents a potpourri of Lake Michigan ciscoes and suggests, whether true or not, the consequence of introgressive hybridization of the Lake Michigan species."

For Lake Michigan, Jobes (1949b) assumed the existence of at least two populations of bloaters—off the state of Michigan shore and off the Wisconsin shore—separated by the deep trough in the middle of the lake, which permitted little intermingling of the two populations, at least during most of the year.

DISTRIBUTION, STATUS, AND HABITAT

The bloater inhabits the underwater slopes of Lakes Superior and Michigan. In Lake Michigan in 1974 the major Wisconsin chub grounds ranged from Manitowoc to Kenosha counties.

In the Great Lakes the bloater has been known from Lakes Ontario, Huron, Michigan, and Superior. Currently it is rare to extirpated in Lake Ontario; the last specimen was taken on 4 May 1972 (Todd 1978). The Great Lakes Fishery Laboratory (Parsons et al. 1975) considers the bloater threatened in Lake Michigan and declining in Lake Superior. In Wisconsin the bloater has been given watch status (Wis. Dep. Nat. Resour. Endangered Species Com. 1975).

In Lake Michigan, bloaters are found at all depths from 22 to 178 m; in Lake Superior, from 18 to 165 m. It occurs within temperature extremes of 1.5–11.4°C (34.7–52.5°F).

BIOLOGY

In the Apostle Islands region of Lake Superior most spawning occurs from November to December (T. Todd, pers. comm.), although some ripe bloaters have been caught in all months and spent bloaters have been observed from September to February (Dryer and Beil 1968).

In Lake Superior spawning occurs at depths of 37–

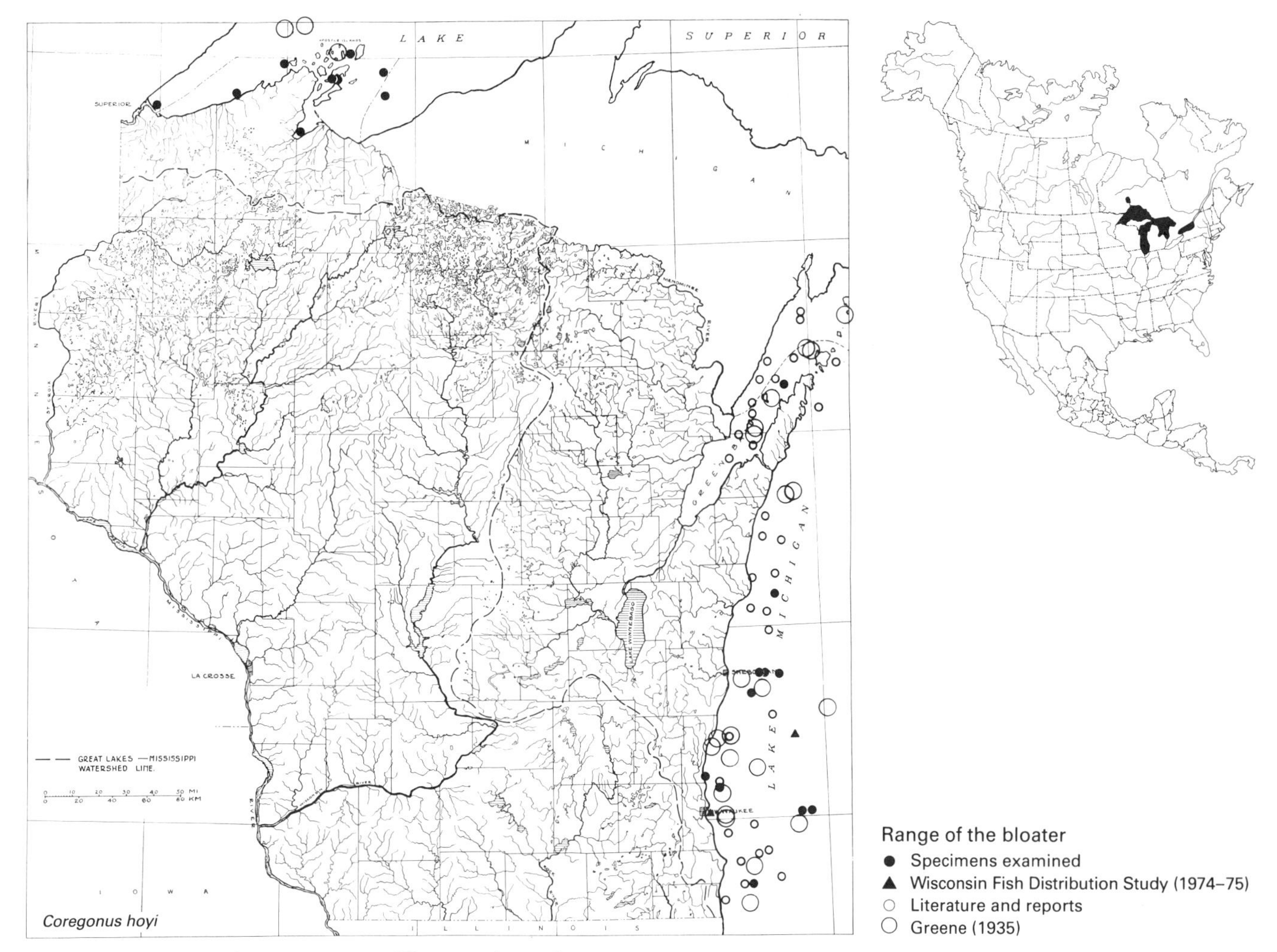

92 m over various bottom types. The number of eggs averages from 4,225 in a 213-mm (8.4-in) fish to 10,080 in a 297-mm (11.7-in) fish, or 1,241 eggs per 28 g (1 oz) of fish. The eggs constitute about 30% of the body weight (Dryer and Beil 1968). Egg color is yellow, 1.97 mm diam (Booke 1970).

In Lake Michigan (Emery and Brown 1978), spawning occurs mainly in January, February, and March. In addition a few bloaters may spawn during nearly all months of the year. Jobes (1949b) designated fish of both sexes as ripe, or nearly ripe, during the months of June through October, and five females taken in August were recorded as spent. In Lake Michigan, fecundity varies from 3,230 eggs (241-mm fish) to 18,768 (305-mm fish) (Emery and Brown 1978).

Spawning occurs in Lake Michigan at a depth of 51 m, but bloaters may spawn in shallower or deeper water (Koelz 1929); in southeastern Lake Michigan they spawn at 73–110 m in the midst of great alewife concentrations (Wells 1966). The character of the bottom selected is not known. Breeding grounds exist off Milwaukee and Port Washington, but considering the bloater's wide distribution there are undoubtedly numerous other spawning sites (Koelz 1929).

In eastern Lake Michigan hatching occurs from mid-May to mid-July, the average incubation period being about 4 months (Wells 1966). Hinrichs (1979) discussed in detail and illustrated development in the bloater from early cell division to the 145-day juvenile 45 mm TL.

Bloater larvae are 10.1 mm TL upon hatching (Hinrichs 1977). In Lake Michigan, Wells (1966) captured bloater larvae at all depths sampled, except 10 m; few were captured at 18, 27, and 37 m, but numbers increased steadily to 91 m (Wells 1966). The largest catches in deeper water tended to be near the bottom and clearly in very cold water. In late May, as surface warming continued and thermal stratification became more pronounced, the larvae concentrated even more at lower levels. Although all of these observations suggest a strong preference for cold water,

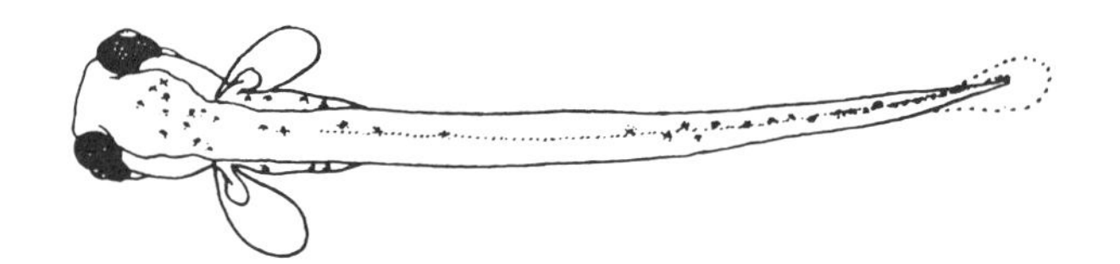
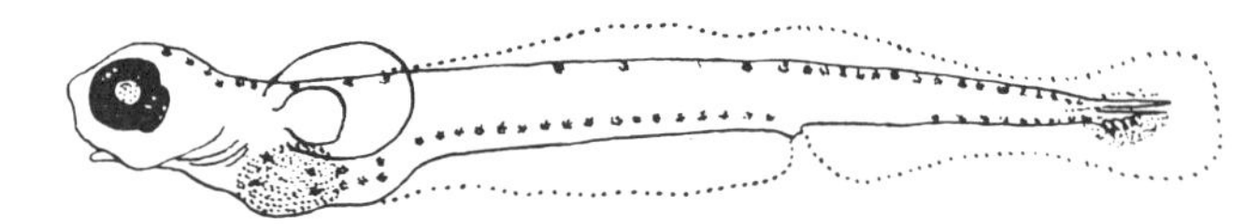
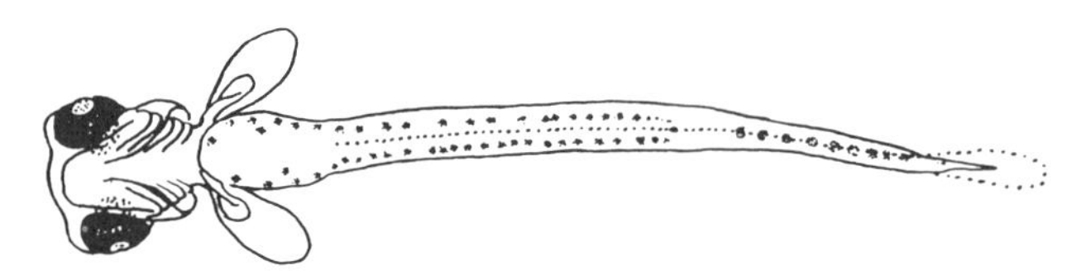

Preserved bloater larva, L. Michigan. Dorsal view (top), lateral view (middle), ventral view (bottom). 11.3 mm TL: pre-anal myomeres, 37; post-anal myomeres, 15 (Faber 1970:497).

the concentration near the bottom may also relate to the need for newly hatched larvae with rather large yolk sacs to rest occasionally on the bottom.

Historically, the bloater has been the smallest of all the chub species; however, in recent decades the average size has increased considerably. In the Apostle Islands region of Lake Superior catches in experimental gill nets showed that lengths increased from a mean of 226 mm (8.9 in) recorded between 1958 and 1961 to a mean of 254 mm (10 in) recorded between 1962 and 1965. The percentage of bloaters longer than 226 mm increased from 44.9 to 99.4 (Dryer and Beil 1968):

Calculated TL at the Annulus (mm)

	1	2	3	4	5	6	7	8	9	10
1958–1961	97	142	170	193	208	218	234	246	257	
1962–1965	99	150	183	208	226	239	254	269	284	297

The average size of the few age-I fish is nearly identical for the two periods, but during the 1962–1965 period bloaters at ages III–VII were 20–33 mm (0.8–1.3 in) longer and 31–37 g (1.1–1.3 oz) heavier than those taken from 1958 to 1961.

Growth in weight of Apostle Island bloaters, like growth in length, was faster in the 1962–1965 period than in the 1958–1961 period. Fish taken in the 1962–1965 period were 0.56 g (0.02 oz) heavier at the end of the first year of life, and 50 g (1.75 oz) heavier at the end of the ninth year, than fish of the same ages taken during the 1958–1962 period. Bloaters weighed 207 g (7.3 oz) at the end of 10 years of life.

Sex composition fluctuated irregularly and without trend from 1958 to 1965. In combined collections, the number of males exceeded females in age groups I–III, but the females outnumbered males in age groups IV–X. In combined samples 60.8% of all bloaters were females (Dryer and Beil 1968).

The youngest mature Apostle Island bloaters belong to age II, and all fish older than age III are mature. More males (91%) than females (89%) are mature at age II. All bloaters longer than 213 mm (8.4 in) are mature.

Similarly, in Lake Michigan the bloater appears to be increasing in size:

Calculated TL and WT for Bloaters (after Jobes 1946b)[a]

	1	2	3	4	5	6	7	8	9
1919									
TL (mm)	85	142	167	185	202	221	244	254	280
WT (g)	4	18	31	42	56	75	103	117	156
1928									
TL (mm)	93	149	178	201	225	242	260		
WT (g)	5	21	38	55	78	99	124		

[a]Bloaters taken off Grand Haven, Michigan; sexes combined and data converted from SL, using 1.21 SL = TL

Growth in length and weight for each age class was greater in 1928 than in 1919. In both years the females averaged about 6 mm (.25 in) longer than the males. The length of all fish in the samples taken in 1928 averaged about 25 mm (1 in) longer than those taken in 1919.

Fish size also increased in trawl hauls made between 1954 and 1966 at Grand Haven and Saugatuck, Michigan (S. H. Smith 1968b):

	1954	1960	1962	1963	1964	1965	1966
TL (mm)[a]	174	203	207	212	213	218	223
% greater than 229 mm (9 in)	4.2	12.1	12.7	18.1	18.9	28.8	38.2

[a]Includes all year classes.

The mean length in southern Lake Michigan increased 49 mm (about 2 in) during this period, and the percentage of bloaters large enough for the human food market (usually greater than 229 mm) increased from 4.2 to 38.2. In northern Lake Michigan the length increased about 25 mm (1 in) between 1955 and 1964, and the percentage of bloaters suited for human food rose from 25 to 67 (S. H. Smith 1968b).

A large female bloater taken in Green Bay on 21 May 1973 measured 366 mm (14.4 in) TL and weighed 332 g (11.7 oz).

The occurrence of fingernail clams and fish eggs in stomachs of Lake Superior bloaters suggests occasional bottom feeding, but bloaters are primarily pelagic feeders. A comparison of foods found in large (above 200 mm) and small (below 200 mm) bloaters revealed that copepods composed 98% of the total volume for small bloaters and 43% for the larger fish. *Pontoporeia* contributed 46% of the volume of food for the larger fish and only 1% for fish shorter than 200 mm. *Mysis* were found in the stomachs of 17% of the larger fish and 7% of the smaller fish (Dryer and Beil 1968).

Lake Michigan bloaters 33–145 mm TL, taken by midwater trawl at 42–73 m, contained 100% zooplankton (Wells and Beeton 1963). The predominant copepods were *Cyclops bicuspidatus* in summer and *Diaptomus* spp. in the fall. *Daphnia galeata mendotae* was by far the commonest cladoceran, especially in the fall. Other cladocerans were *Daphnia retrocurva* and *Bosmina longirostris*. In bloaters over 178 mm (7 in) long, *Pontoporeia* was the most important item in the diet, with some stomachs containing more than 200, although the usual number was fewer than 100. *Pontoporeia* is most commonly eaten in the shallower water, but it is important at all depths; as they grow larger, bloaters depend more on *Pontoporeia*. *Mysis relicta* is next in importance and is most commonly eaten in deeper water in the fall by fish 178–251 mm (7–9.9 in) long. Ordinarily individual stomachs held fewer than 50 *Mysis*, but one contained 181.

The ratio of *Pontoporeia* to *Mysis* decreases as depth increases from 27 to 73 m. *Mysis* is ordinarily found a meter or so above the bottom (Beeton 1960), whereas *Pontoporeia* is primarily a bottom dweller. The preponderance of *Pontoporeia* in the diet of bloaters more than 254 mm (10 in) long was probably due to the tendency of larger fish to feed directly on the bottom; this was borne out by the much higher percentage of bloaters longer than 254 mm (10 in) found to have mud in their stomachs.

According to Beeton, the clams *Pisidium* and *Sphaerium* spp. occurred in 33% of all bloaters combined; however, due to the small numbers present in individual stomachs, this item averaged only about 2% of the dry weight. The remaining food items made up a combined total of only 2% of the dry weight; they included fish eggs, midges, ephemeropteran nymphs, and fragments of other insect orders. Although found in 7.5% of the stomachs, ostracods constituted a negligible proportion of the dry weight.

Wells (1968) noted that bloaters live at midlevels in Lake Michigan until their third year. Few bloaters less than 178 mm (7 in) long are on the bottom. The larvae are in the hypolimnion in deep water, but the exact distribution of juveniles at mid-depths is unknown. The few that have been caught were taken in the thermocline or in upper levels when the water was cool. A few adult bloaters (age II or older) are taken at midlevels, almost invariably in or below the thermocline, but the largest catches of adults are made characteristically near the bottom (Wells 1968). Occasionally relatively good catches are made at 110–126 m, but at depths of 128 m and more the species ordinarily is scarce (Jobes 1949b). The temperature extremes of the water from which the bloater has been taken are 1.5–11.4°C (34.7–52.5°F), but the fish is encountered in greatest abundance at 3.8–7°C (38.8–44.6°F).

In the Apostle Islands region of Lake Superior some bloaters migrate into relatively shallow water 18–53 m during the summer and fall (Dryer 1966), although they are most abundant at 73–90 m at that time. In the spring they are evenly distributed at 55–108 m.

In Lake Michigan, Wells (1968) noted that this species engages in a shoreward movement in May, and that by July the greatest number are at depths shallower than 37 m. Bloaters avoid warm inshore water, but in a July trawl series, when the inshore water was cooled during an upwelling, the largest catches were at 9–22 m, and two bloaters were taken at 6 m. A single young-of-year was taken with a minnow seine at a depth of less than 1 m at Virmond Park beach (Ozaukee County) in September 1973.

IMPORTANCE AND MANAGEMENT

Historically the bloater was a small chub species and of little value to man. However, recent environmental advantages have resulted in increasing numbers and size, and the bloater has become the most important species of chub remaining in the fishery of Lakes Michigan and Superior. It is presently the mainstay of the chub fishery and provides the bulk of the smoked fish marketed for human consumption.

In Lake Michigan, as the lake trout declined in the late 1940s and early 1950s—a result of commercial fishing pressure and sea lamprey depredations—the bloater benefited by losing a key predator. At the same time the larger species of chubs were removed by the same pressures; by the early 1960s the largest deepwater ciscoes apparently had been exterminated, and the intermediate-sized species were uncommon. The smallest species, the bloater, exploded in numbers, beginning probably in the early or mid-1950s.

Apparently the bloaters' expansion was not only in numbers but also in territory; where previously bloaters had maintained breeding isolation, they now encroached upon the habitats and breeding cycles of other species of chubs. By 1969, a shortnose cisco or kiyi was only rarely caught in experimental nets, and even these few "nonbloaters" were not as distinct morphologically as formerly, their appearance suggesting hybridization with the bloater (Parsons and Todd 1974).

In Lake Superior the bloater expansion was made possible by the removal of the larger chub species through the use of progressively smaller mesh sizes in the commercial fisheries. All but the bloater had been fished to seriously reduced populations before the first sea lamprey was reported in 1946. Hence it is doubtful that either the sea lamprey or competition from the alewife played the role in Lake Superior that they apparently had in Lake Michigan (S. H. Smith 1968b). Moreover, the alewife in Lake Superior is not abundant enough to affect bloater populations (Lawrie and Rahrer 1973).

In recent years the bloater has become the mainstay of the chub fishery. Fishery surveys of Lake Michigan showed bloaters making up only 31% of the catch from 1930 to 1932, over 75% of the catch from 1950 to 1955 (Moffett 1957), and 93–95% of the catch in experimental gill nets from 1960 to 1961 (S. H. Smith 1964). They first entered the commercial fishery in the late 1950s with the introduction of trawl fishery, which provided an efficient means of catching them in large quantities at low cost for animal food and fish meal. During the same period even the gill net fishery became dependent on bloaters taken for human consumption when species of large chubs became scarce. The combined influence of the new trawl fishery and the increase in size of bloaters, which made them better suited for the gill net fishery, resulted in the largest chub catches of record: 5.0–5.4 million kg yearly during the 1960–1962 period. There was a sharp drop in production after deaths from botulism were attributed to improperly processed smoked chubs. Although the market and the fishery partially recovered, with catches of 2.3–2.7 million kg recorded during the 1968–1970 period, instability of the populations since has caused concern for the future of the industry and for the bloater stocks.

Fishery biologists in states adjoining Lake Michigan agree that the abundance of the bloater chub, the most common chub in the fishery, has been declining at the rate of 20% per year since 1969, and that the decline has been accompanied by increased growth rate, decreased reproduction, and a shift in the sex ratio (Poff 1973). The environmental factor or factors leading to poor year classes, which has been the main cause of this decline, are not clear. The alewife, however, is an obvious suspect. During its explosive increase in Lake Michigan from the 1950s to early 1967, the alewife must have become increasingly competitive with the bloater. The alewife altered the zooplankton population by greatly reducing the availability of large zooplankton species and the zooplankton biomass (Wells and Beeton 1963). Since young bloaters feed almost exclusively on zooplankton, the implications are obvious. Alewives may also feed on the eggs of bloaters (Morsell and Norden 1968).

As the number of bloaters has declined, their size has increased. Much of the increase up to the early 1960s was due to faster growth, but in recent years a greater proportion of older fish in the population has also been involved; the average age increased from 3.5 years in 1964 to 6 years in 1969 (Brown 1970). The proportion of females in the population rose from 75% in 1954 to 97% in 1961, then changed little through 1967 (Brown 1970). In the early 1970s, the sex ratio shifted back to a better representation of males, but the growth rate continued to increase. The sea lamprey's preying on larger bloaters was undoubtedly responsible for some bloater loss (S. H. Smith 1968b).

S. H. Smith (1968b) and Brown (1970) interpreted these changes as a response by the bloater to environmental stresses that probably will result in a disastrous decline in the stocks. Both Smith and Brown based their views on similar changes which preceded sharp declines in other coregonid populations, e.g., the lake herring in Birch Lake, Michigan (Clady 1967). Also, commercial fishermen have remarked that the average size of ciscoes was very large just before their drastic reduction in the middle and late 1960s in Lake Huron.

During the 1970s the Wisconsin Department of Natural Resources initiated an assessment fishery in Lake Michigan which was conducted out of ports from Two Rivers to Kenosha (Wis. Dep. Nat. Resour. 1976c). Commercial production of bloaters reached a low in the fall of 1975, but from 1976 to 1977 strong 1972 and 1973 year classes entered the fishery (P. Schultz, pers. comm.). From July 1981 to June 1982, 680,000 kg (1.5 million lb) were harvested from the Wisconsin waters of Lake Michigan.

Similar trends in the bloater economy have been documented for Lake Superior. In the 1930s the shortjaw cisco (*C. zenithicus*) dominated the chub fishery (Van Oosten 1937c), but by 1965 bloaters constituted about 90% of the commercial landings of chubs at Bayfield. In 1966 and 1967 the commercial catch exceeded 408,000 kg, but there has been a steady drop since (161,000 kg in 1974—Wis. Dep. Nat. Resour. [1976]) despite the high market value and excellent demand.

Kiyi

Coregonus kiyi (Koelz). *Coregonus*—angle-eye, coined by Artedi from the Greek meaning pupil of the eye and angle; *kiyi*—name used by commercial fishermen of Lake Michigan.

Other common names: bigeye, paperbelly, waterbelly, chub, mooneye.

Keweenaw Bay, L. Superior, Michigan, 5 Sept. 1973 (U.S. Fish and Wildlife Service, Great Lakes Fishery Laboratory photo)

DESCRIPTION

Body elongate, thin (strongly compressed laterally). Average length 259 mm (10.2 in). Greatest depth in front of dorsal fin, depth into TL 4.2. Head into TL 3.8–4.1 (3.7–4.3). Snout almost equal to eye diam. Premaxillaries heavily pigmented, and angled downward and forward with long axis of body at about 50°; maxillary heavily pigmented, extending beyond anterior edge of pupil but never to its center. Lower jaw conspicuously pigmented, usually with a prominent symphyseal knob; lower jaw frail (thin and easily bent) and projecting beyond the upper jaw. Eye into head length 3.8–4.2 (3.6–4.3). Gill rakers medium long, longest about as long as the longest gill filaments, 36–41 (34–45). Scales in lateral line 77–87 (71–91); scales around body anterior to dorsal and pelvic fins 41–44 (39–46). Dorsal fin rays 9–10 (11); anal rays 10–12 (9–16); pectoral rays 16–17 (15–18); pelvic rays 11 (12). Pectoral fins very long; length into distance from pectoral origin to pelvic origin 1.4–1.7 (1.1–2.1). Pelvic fins very long, length into distance from pelvic origin to anal origin 1–1.3 (0.96–1.4).

Color in life, silvery with faint pink to purple iridescence, strongest above the lateral line and absent on the lighter-colored belly. Pigment occurs on the sides above the lateral line, sparsely below. Dorsal and caudal fins widely margined with black; median rays of the caudal fin intensely pigmented with black.

Breeding tubercles appear in the males (Koelz 1929).

Hybrids: Kiyi × bloater (S. H. Smith 1964).

SYSTEMATIC NOTES

The type specimen (USNM 84100) is a female 191 mm (7.5 in) SL from Lake Michigan, taken 19 km east by south of the mouth of the Sturgeon Bay Ship Channel at 110–128 m on 23 August 1920 (Koelz 1921).

The kiyi is most easily confused with the bloater, since both have the protruding mandible with a pronounced symphyseal knob. The kiyi has a large eye, very long fins, and heavily pigmented mouth parts. Parsons and Todd (1974), noting the high degree of intergradation of taxonomic characteristics among most specimens of kiyis and bloaters in Lake Superior, have suggested that these two forms may be a single species. In using Koelz's (1929) data, only fish near the extremes of the range of characteristics could be readily identified either as kiyi or bloater.

DISTRIBUTION, STATUS, AND HABITAT

The kiyi occurs in Lakes Superior and Michigan. It has not been recorded from Green Bay. Recent verified records of kiyi occurrences from the Wisconsin waters of Lake Michigan are: 16–24 km east of Sheboygan, June 1968 (UWSP 2439); Milwaukee reef, 1974 (Fish and Wildlife Service, Ann Arbor); 23 km east of Algoma (Grid 1006) (U.S. Fish Wildl. Serv. 1972), April 1975 (Wis. Dep. Nat. Resour.).

This species is known from Lakes Ontario, Huron, Michigan, and Superior. The last known occurrence for Lake Ontario was 1964; for Lake Huron, 1973.

The kiyi is regarded as extirpated in Lakes Ontario and Huron, endangered in Lake Michigan, and declining in Lake Superior (Parsons et al. 1975, Mich. Dep. Nat. Resour. 1976, Wis. Dep. Nat. Resour. Endangered Species Com. 1975). Todd (1978) lists it as abundant in Lake Superior.

In Lake Michigan the kiyi's future is in jeopardy. S. H. Smith (1964) summarized its abundance as indicated at the most favorable sites in central and southern Lake Michigan. At 46 m the numbers of kiyi caught per 466-m gang net were 8.6 fish in 1930–1931, 9.6 in 1954–1955, and 1.5 in 1960–1961; at 91–110 m, the numbers caught were 73.7 fish in 1930–1931, 79.2 in 1954–1955, and 19.2 in 1960–1961.

The kiyi was abundant in Lake Michigan as recently as 1954–1955 (Moffett 1957), but had become greatly reduced by 1960–1961 (S. H. Smith 1964). It was nearly extirpated by 1964 (Wells 1966), although it was noted during trawling off the port of Saugatuck, Michigan. By 1969 (Wells and McLain 1973), ki-

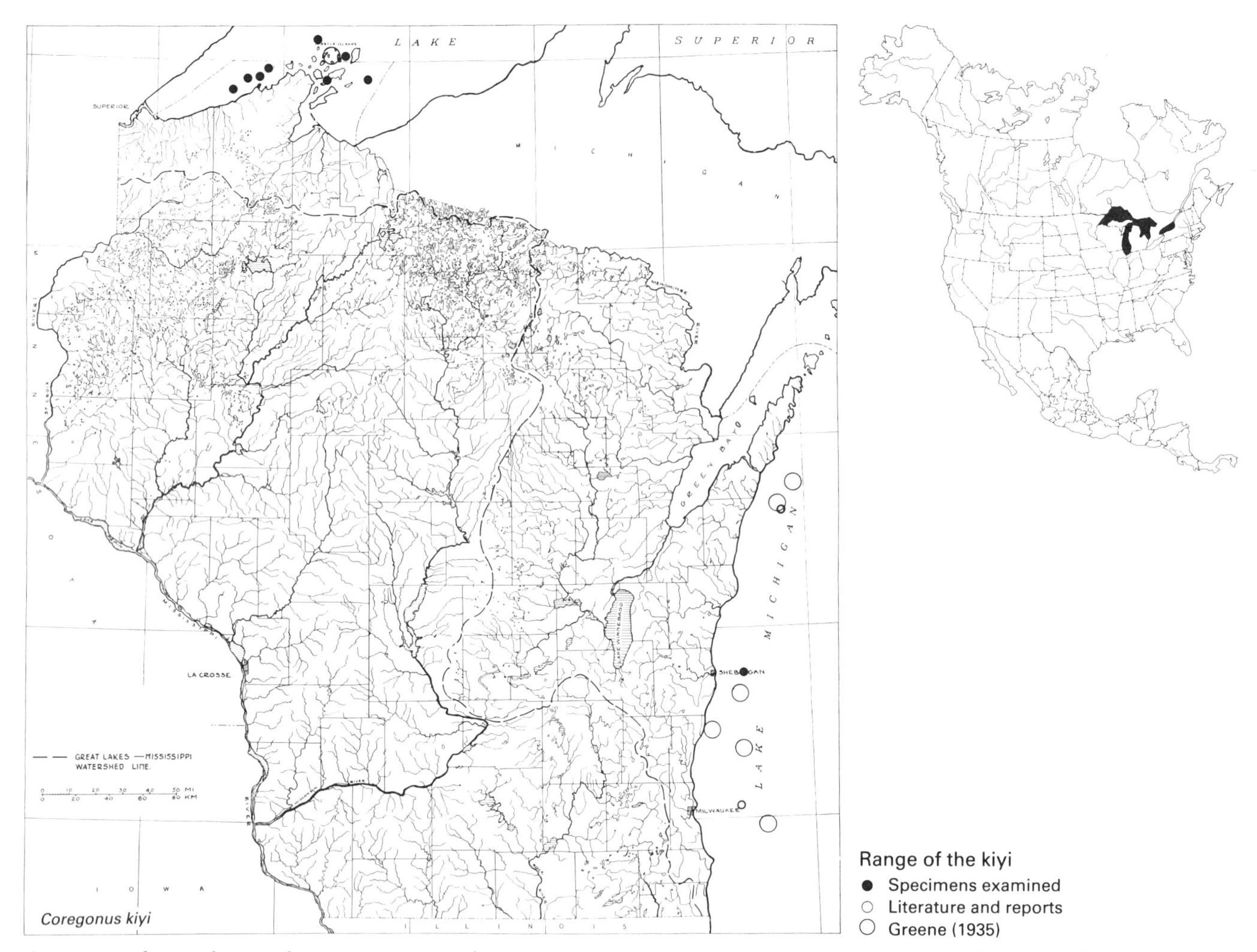

Coregonus kiyi

Range of the kiyi
● Specimens examined
○ Literature and reports
○ Greene (1935)

yis were only rarely caught in experimental nets; even these were not as distinct morphologically as formerly, their appearance suggesting hybridization with the bloater (S. H. Smith 1964).

The reasons for the decline of the Lake Michigan kiyi to an endangered status are not known, although the alewife is suspected. In midwinter, alewives are densely concentrated on the bottom in the deepest areas of the lake, in the identical areas occupied by the kiyi (S. H. Smith 1968b).

The kiyi has the deepest habitat of any of the chubs now present. In Lake Superior the kiyi is absent at depths of less than 37 m; it becomes increasingly abundant down to 183 m (Dryer 1966). In Lake Michigan it occurs throughout the central basins at depths of 73 m to at least 165 m, and occasionally in shallower waters.

BIOLOGY

The kiyi spawns in the fall. In southern Lake Michigan there is evidence that spawning begins as early as late September. A spent female was captured in shallow water off Racine on 24 September, and spent kiyis of both sexes occurred in collections made on 28 September (Hile and Deason 1947). Spawning activities proceed slowly during late September and early October and peak in mid-October. In northern Lake Michigan off Kewaunee on 15 October, 88% of the males and 69% of the females were ripe, although spent fish were scarce. By 30 October 47% of the males and 42% of the females were spent. Spawning may continue to mid-November. Hile and Deason (1947) assumed that the true length of the spawning season is 2 months or more. Known spawning areas in 1931 included Kewaunee, Sheboygan, and Racine in Wisconsin and Grand Haven in Michigan, at depths of 104–154 m. Koelz (1929) noted that in Lake Superior during the spawning season (late November to early December) the majority of kiyis were taken from 183 m.

The weight loss of male kiyis after spawning has been recorded as 1.6%; females, 11.8% (Deason and Hile 1947). Scale formation commenced between 27 and 32 mm TL and was completed at 51 mm TL (Hogman 1970).

Deason and Hile (1947) studied the age and growth of 1,649 kiyis captured at seven localities in Lake Michigan in 1931 and 1932. Only 10.4% of the total fish studied were males. Age IV was dominant (38.8%) in the combined collections. The average ages of the sexes were: males, 4.12; females, 4.56. The average total lengths and weights for all males were 257 mm and 136 g; females, 267 mm and 159 g:

Calculated TL at the Annulus (mm)

	1	2	3	4	5	6	7	8
Males	122	173	208	234	244	257	267	
Females	124	173	218	241	259	267	272	274

In northern Lake Michigan the growing season for the kiyi is 3–3½ months long, with 80% of the growth completed by 9 July and the remainder before 7 September. It is probable that the initiation of growth is a function of food or light rather than temperature (Deason and Hile 1947). The temperature of the central basin inhabited by the kiyi fluctuates between 2°C (35.6°F) in winter and about 4°C (39.2°F) in summer.

The K-factor of kiyis studied by Deason and Hile was greater than 1.35 for fish 221 mm (8.7 in) TL or longer. Ripe or nearly ripe females had an average K of 1.47; spent, 1.31. Corresponding figures for males were 1.37 and 1.36.

In Lake Michigan this coregonid matures at a small size: females at 173 mm (6.8 in) TL; males at 178 mm (7.0 in) (Hile and Deason 1947). In Lake Superior the smallest mature specimen examined was 161 mm TL (Koelz 1929).

The largest known kiyi was a spent male 351 mm (13.8 in) TL, weighing 332 g (11.7 oz), captured off Kewaunee in Lake Michigan on 5 November 1931. The largest female, a ripe fish taken off Racine on 30 October 1931, was 335 mm (13.2 in) TL weighing 329 g (11.6 oz) (Deason and Hile 1947).

Collections of kiyis from Lake Michigan were characterized at all times by a strong preponderance of females (Deason and Hile 1947). The dominance of females, however, was less pronounced in the spawning-run collections (75.2%) than in late spring, summer, and early autumn samples (90.2%). Deason and Hile conjectured that during the summer a greater proportion of the males were living at depths greater than those fished, or that they were somewhat above the bottom beyond the reach of the gill nets (which rested on the bottom and were only 1.5 m deep). A decline in the number of males as age increases may represent a higher natural death rate among the males, or a more rapid rate of destruction in the fishery.

In Lake Superior the bathymetric distribution of kiyis was at 0.2% for 37–53 m, 0.9% for 55–71 m, 0.9% for 73–90 m, 8.6% for 91–108 m, 27.0% for 110–126 m, 32.2% for 128–144 m, and 30.2% for 146–163 m (Dryer 1966).

Little is known of the kiyi's feeding habits. In Lake Huron, fish captured off Alpena had eaten *Mysis* almost exclusively (Koelz 1929). In Lake Ontario, *Mysis* were the principal food of 53 kiyis captured off Port Credit, whereas *Pontoporeia* ranked first in two fish from Main Duck Island (Pritchard 1931). *Mysis* also is considered an important food in Lake Michigan, but constituted only 30.3% of ingested food, compared with 69.7% *Pontoporeia* (Bersamin 1958).

IMPORTANCE AND MANAGEMENT

The kiyi is undoubtedly a food source for such predators as the lake trout and burbot, but it is inaccessible to the hook-and-line fisherman.

Its incidence in commercial fish hauls is minor. Examination of 681 chubs from Lake Superior commercial landings at Bayfield in 1965 revealed that kiyis composed 2% of the catch, shortjaw ciscoes 8%, and bloaters 90%.

Blackfin Cisco

Coregonus nigripinnis (Gill). *Coregonus*—angle-eye, coined by Artedi from the Greek meaning pupil of the eye and angle; *nigripinnis*: *niger*—black, *pinna*—fin.

Other common names: blackfin chub, blackfin tullibee, blackback tullibee, mooneye cisco.

Adult male 314 mm, L. Michigan, near Port Washington, 26 May 1922 (Koelz 1929:416)

Sketch of head and anterior gill arch of UMMZ 53119, L. Michigan, Racine, 3 July 1906

DESCRIPTION

The following is based on Koelz's (1929) description of specimens from Lake Michigan.

Body elongate, with greatest depth anteriorly. Average length 333 mm (13.1 in). Depth into TL 3.4–4.0. Head into TL 4.1–4.4 (3.8–4.7). Snout into head length 3.5–3.9 (4.1). Premaxillaries heavily pigmented, and angled downward and forward with long axis of body at 45–60°; anterior maxillary heavily pigmented, maxillary seldom extending much beyond the anterior edge of the pupil. Lower jaw conspicuously pigmented and no symphyseal knob; lower jaw stout and equal to the upper jaw. Eye into head length 4–4.4 (4.6). Gill rakers long, the longest greater in length than longest gill filaments, 46–50 (41–52). Scales in lateral line 80–87 (74–89); scales around body anterior to dorsal and pelvic fins 42–44 (41–45). Dorsal fin rays 10–11; anal rays 11–12 (10–13); pectoral rays 16–17 (15–18); pelvic rays 11–12. Pectoral fins medium long; length into distance from pectoral origin to pelvic origin 1.6–1.8 (1.5–2.2). Pelvic fin medium long, length into distance from pelvic origin to anal origin 1.2–1.5 (1.6).

Color in life, silvery, but the silvery cast is least conspicuous in this species because of the heavy pigmentation. Dorsal surface blue-black, almost obscuring the pea green to blue-green beneath. Below the lateral line pale blue-green is evident beneath the silvery layer. All fins, including the pelvics, usually blue-black. Males with breeding tubercles.

SYSTEMATIC NOTES

The blackfin cisco was named by Gill (see Hoy 1872a) from a specimen caught in Lake Michigan and sent to him by P. R. Hoy. "It has as yet been found only in the deepest water of Lake Michigan, where I had the pleasure of discovering it" (Hoy 1883). The type specimen is not extant according to Koelz (1929).

Koelz (1929), in his treatment of the coregonids of the Great Lakes, recognized two forms in Wisconsin waters: *Coregonus* (=*Leucichthys*) *nigripinnis nigripinnis*—the blackfin of Lake Michigan; and *Coregonus nigripinnis cyanopterus*—the bluefin of Lake Superior. Since Koelz, the literature of the fishes of the region has consistently reported the blackfin cisco from both lakes. However, recent work at the Great Lakes Fishery Laboratory in Ann Arbor, involving analysis of specimens upon which Koelz based his study, has shown that *nigripinnis* never existed in Lake Superior (Parsons et al. 1975, Todd 1977 and 1978, Todd and Smith 1980). Principal component analysis of Koelz's specimens indicate that all *C. n. cyanopterus* were merely large and old *C. zenithicus* and that *C. n. cyanopterus* is synonymous with *C. zenithicus*. The development of heavily pigmented fins in old and large *zenithicus* is probably responsible for occasional current reports of "bluefins" in Lake Superior. Early records of *C. nigripinnis prognathus* in Lake Ontario are also invalid; this species is not known to have occurred in that lake (Todd 1978).

Scott and Crossman (1973) noted that in inland waters of Canada it is often difficult to distinguish *nigripinnis* from *artedii*. Clarke (1974) determined that previous records of *nigripinnis* for Alberta and Saskatchewan are actually records of *C. artedii*.

DISTRIBUTION, STATUS, AND HABITAT

In the Great Lakes, the blackfin cisco is known only from Lakes Michigan and Huron. In Lake Huron the last known occurrence was at Wiarton, Ontario, on

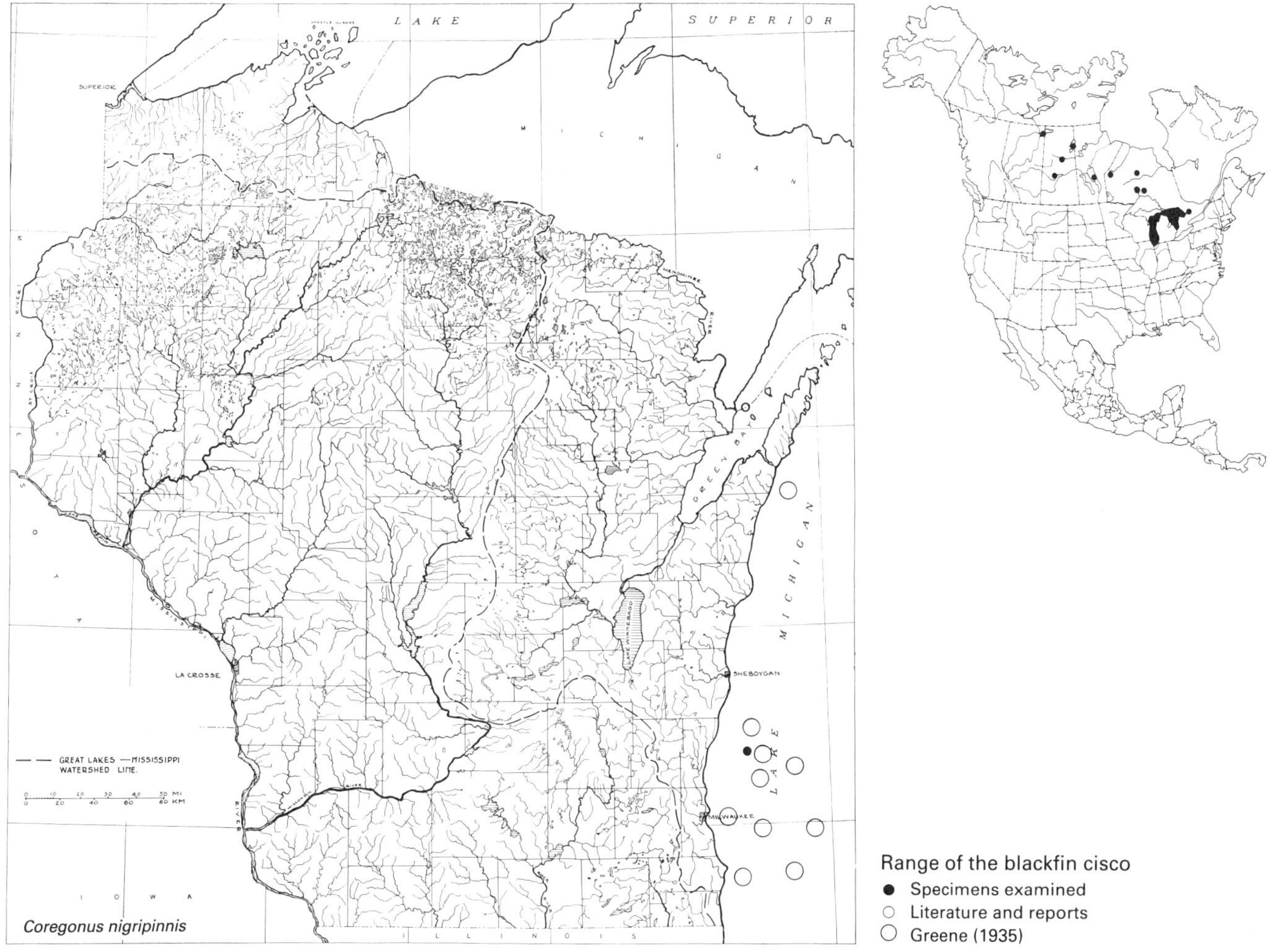

Range of the blackfin cisco
● Specimens examined
○ Literature and reports
◯ Greene (1935)

26 June 1923 (Koelz 1929). In Lake Michigan the last known blackfin cisco was taken in a trawl at 13 m off Marinette (Marinette County) on 26 May 1969. Two weeks earlier on 11 May two blackfin ciscoes were gill-netted from 146 m off Saugatuck, Michigan (T. Todd, pers. comm. and 1978). This species is probably extirpated in Lake Michigan (Parsons and Todd 1974, Lopinot and Smith 1973, Todd 1978, Wis. Dep. Nat. Resour. Endangered Species Com. 1975).

S. H. Smith (1964) suggested that the extirpation of the last few blackfin ciscoes may have occurred through introgressive hybridization due to a lack of their own species for spawning. The sheer numbers of bloaters present, also in spawning condition, could have overwhelmed the few blackfin eggs with bloater sperm.

The blackfin cisco occurred throughout Lake Michigan at depths of 55–165 m. It is probable that the blackfin seldom ranged above the 55 m contour. It was a characteristic cisco of the deepest waters, often in company with the deepwater cisco (*C. johannae*) and the kiyi (*C. kiyi*).

BIOLOGY

The Lake Michigan blackfin cisco spawns in December and January. Commercial fishermen reported spawning grounds 65 km ESE of Milwaukee in 110–165 m during late December and early January (Koelz 1929). During the same period spawning was reported 8–13 km west of Manistee in 73–146 m on clay.

The smallest specimen collected from Lake Michigan by Koelz (1929) measured 220 mm and was mature. Some much larger specimens have been immature.

This species is the largest of the endemic deepwater ciscoes in Lake Michigan, reaching an average length of 333 mm (13.1 in) in 1930 when all species of deepwater ciscoes were well represented (S. H. Smith 1964). The maximum size is not known, but Dymond (1926) gave a length of 388 mm (15.3 in) for Lake Nipigon specimens. The maximum age is probably 14 years (Van Oosten 1932).

Mysis appeared as the major food in 56 stomachs from fish collected off Alpena, Michigan, in September and October 1917, and in two fish taken in Georgian Bay on 6 October 1919. All fish came from depths of more than 110 m (Koelz 1929). In one or two stomachs a trace of plant fragments and of adult insects or a fish scale was found.

IMPORTANCE AND MANAGEMENT

The young of the blackfin cisco, along with other cisco species, were important foods of the lake trout in the deep waters of Lake Michigan. When the lake trout stocks were becoming exhausted in the early 1950s, the sea lamprey undoubtedly parasitized the last few surviving blackfins.

From the early days of the chub fishery to the time of its disappearance, the blackfin cisco was the prime target of the smoked fish industry (Hile and Buettner 1955). While on a fishing tug in 1951 off Port Washington, I saw a half dozen large blackfins which the fishermen had set aside from the remainder of the catch as the chubs which would bring the fanciest prices.

It seems almost certain that the large blackfin was simply overexploited in the early fishery, since it became scarce before a detrimental effect on this deepwater species would have been produced by any other factor (Wells and McLain 1973). Numbers were low in 1920 when Koelz collected specimens on Lake Michigan. In the comparison surveys of Lake Michigan, the blackfin cisco hardly became part of the record. Only 0.3 fish was caught per 466-m (1,530-ft) gang net set at 91 m in northern Lake Michigan in 1932. In 1930–1931 off Grand Haven, Michigan, 1.8 fish were caught per gang net set at 46 m and 91 m, and off Ludington, Michigan, 3.6 fish at depths up to 110 m. None of the comparison surveys of 1954–1955 and 1960–1961 caught blackfin ciscoes (S. H. Smith 1964).

Deepwater Cisco

Coregonus johannae (Wagner). *Coregonus*—angle-eye, coined by Artedi from the Greek meaning pupil of the eye and angle; *johannae*—of Johanna, "life companion" of George Wagner (Wagner 1910).
Other common names: the chub, deepwater chub.

Adult male 243 mm, L. Michigan, Michigan City, Indiana, 3 Sept. 1920 (Koelz 1929:364)

Sketch of head and first gill arch of UMMZ 54380

DESCRIPTION
Body elongate, moderately compressed. Average length 290 mm (11.4 in). Greatest depth forward, depth into TL 3.7–4.5. Head into TL 4–4.2 (3.8–4.4). Snout into head length 3.3–3.6 (3.2–4). Premaxillaries little or not at all pigmented, and angled downward and forward with the long axis of body at 50–60°; maxillary generally unpigmented, never extending to the center of the eye. Lower jaw unpigmented and moderately stout, about equal to upper jaw. Gill rakers short, longest generally shorter than the longest gill filaments, 27–32 (26–36). Scales in lateral line 80–90 (74–95); scales around body anterior to dorsal and pelvic fins 41–44 (38–46). Dorsal fin rays 9–10 (11); anal rays 11–13 (10–16); pectoral rays 16–17 (14–20); pelvic rays 11 (11–12). Pectoral fins medium long; pectoral fin length into distance from pectoral origin to pelvic origin 1.6–1.8 (1.5–2.1). Pelvic fins medium long; length into distance from pelvic origin to anal origin 1.2–1.5 (1.1–1.6).

Color in life, silvery with faint pink to purple iridescence above the lateral line; white on belly. This species closely resembles *C. alpenae*, the longjaw cisco (Koelz 1929, Scott and Smith 1962).

Males develop breeding tubercles in the breeding season. Tubercles 1 per body scale, except 2 on lateral line scales (1 on either side of the pore). Tubercles not present on scales along the back and the belly. Small tubercles of irregular shape and size, irregularly distributed on head; faint tubercles on some fins, especially the pelvics.

SYSTEMATIC NOTES
The type specimen (USNM 87353) is a ripe male 265 mm (10.5 in) long from Lake Michigan, taken about 29 km off Racine at a depth of about 46 m on 3 July 1906 (Koelz 1929).

DISTRIBUTION, STATUS, AND HABITAT
The deepwater cisco was formerly a widely distributed endemic species in the deeper waters of Lake Michigan (55–165 m) and Lake Huron (29–183 m). It was not known from lower Green Bay. In Lake Huron a specimen (ROM 19214) was last reported from Wolfsell, Ontario, on 4 August 1952 (Todd 1978). In Lake Michigan several specimens were identified from a commercial catch at 183 m in Grand Traverse Bay, Michigan, in June 1951 (Moffett 1957). S. H. Smith (1964) has suggested that the extinction of the last few *johannae* may have come about through introgressive hybridization due to a lack of their own species for spawning. Large numbers of spawning bloaters present during an attempted spawning of the few remaining deepwater ciscoes could—over a few generations—overwhelm the *johannae* gene pool to the point where it was no longer recognizable. It is presently considered extinct (Todd 1978, Wis. Dep. Nat. Resour. Endangered Species Com. 1975).

BIOLOGY
The deepwater chub spawned in late summer from mid-August to late September. Koelz (1929) noted that in Lake Michigan near Rock Island the few fish he had seen prior to August 1920 were not sexually mature. On 19 August he caught a number of males with freely flowing milt and with breeding tubercles; the females were not yet ripe but he assumed that they would spawn soon. In October he examined fish from a number of ports and noted spent females. He did not know at what depths nor over what bottoms the species spawned, and, upon examination of a number of fish, he assumed that a certain proportion spawned every other year.

This species was the second largest of the endemic

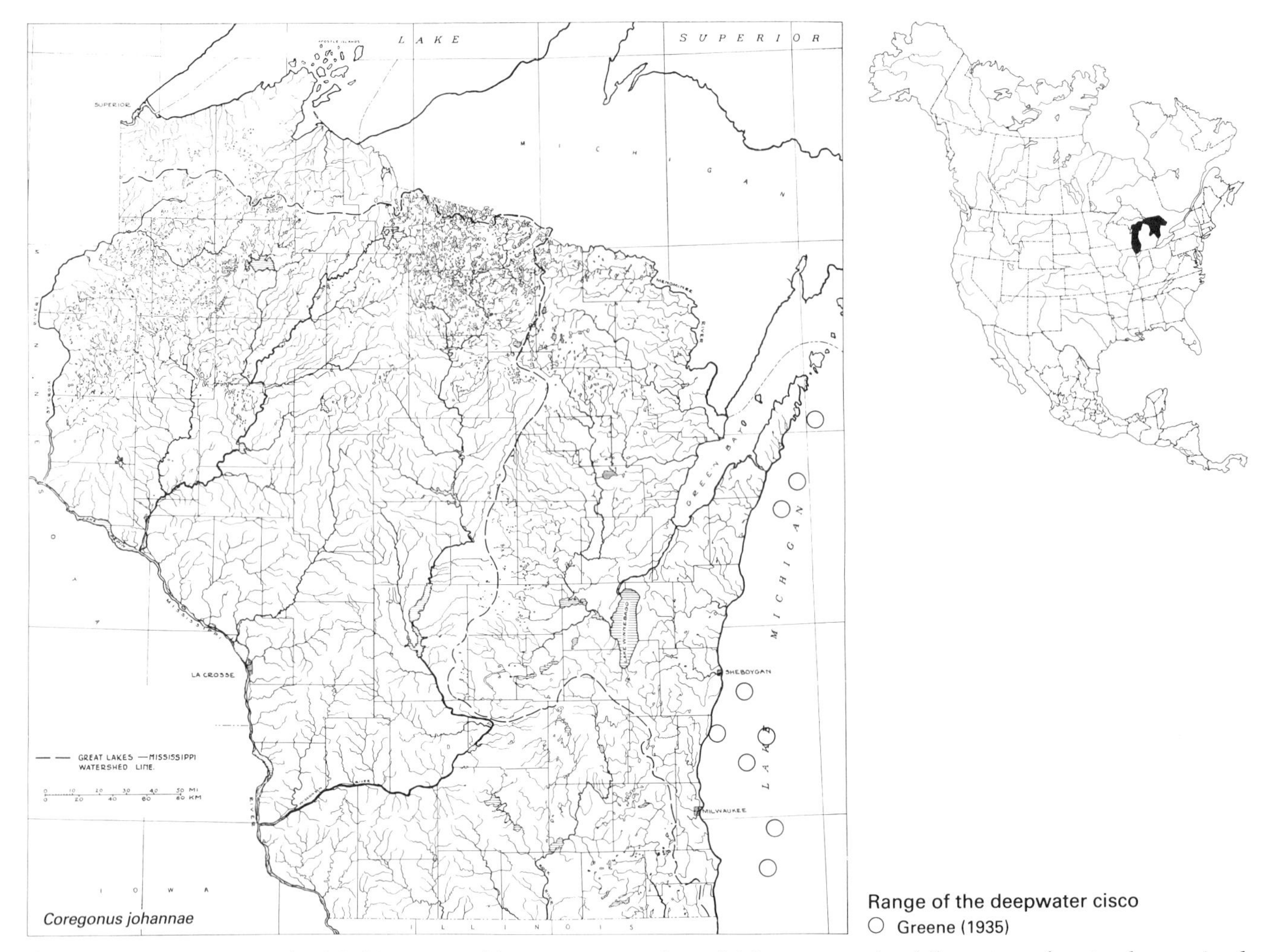

Range of the deepwater cisco
○ Greene (1935)

deepwater ciscoes in Lake Michigan, reaching an average length of 290 mm (11.4 in) and a weight of about 680 g (1.5 lb).

Hubbs examined 34 stomachs of *johannae* collected from Lake Huron off Alpena, Michigan, at 119–128 m during September and October 1917 (Koelz 1929). *Mysis* constituted 80–100% of the food in most of the stomachs. *Pisidium* and *Pontoporeia* were present in about one-third of the stomachs, usually only in small quantities. Half of all specimens had ingested sand, cinders, and wood fragments. Other objects included adult insects, larval and pupal Chironomidae, and fish scales.

IMPORTANCE AND MANAGEMENT

The deepwater cisco and the blackfin, our largest cisco species, were exploited heavily in a highly selective fishery from the mid-1800s to the early 1900s (Hile and Buettner 1955, S. H. Smith 1964). By 1920 the deepwater cisco apparently had been seriously depleted. During the summer and fall of that year Koelz (1929) examined lifts out of Milwaukee and Michigan City which contained between 5.7 and 51 kg of *johannae* to the kilometer of net when raised after 5 nights; he noted that they were uncommon. In only one lift, on 19 August 1920 near Rock Island, at 130–165 m, did he encounter a haul of *johannae* which he considered abundant: in a lift of 408 kg, about one-third were *johannae*—the remainder *kiyi*.

By 1930–1932, in experimental nets set in northeastern Lake Michigan, *johannae* constituted less than 1% of the chub catch; near Manitowoc and Racine, 1.5%; and near Ludington and Grand Haven, 3% (Moffett 1957). Identical sets made in the same or nearby locales in 1954–1955 and 1960–1961 produced no *johannae* (S. H. Smith 1964).

It seems certain that the large *johannae* were simply overexploited in the early fishery, since they became scarce before a detrimental effect on this deepwater species would have been produced by any other factors (Wells and McLain 1973). It was already scarce when the sea lamprey moved into Lake Michigan, and its moderately large size and deepwater habitat would have made it vulnerable to depredations by the sea lamprey during and particularly following destruction of the lake trout (Scott and Smith 1962).

Pygmy Whitefish

Prosopium coulteri (Eigenmann and Eigenmann). *Prosopium*—a mask, from the large bones in front of the eyes; *coulteri*—of Coulter, after Dr. J. M. Coulter, a distinguished botanist.

Other common names: Coulter's whitefish, brownback whitefish, pygmy.

100 mm, L. Superior, Cat Island (Ashland Co.), 7 Nov. 1979 (specimen donated by U.S. Fish and Wildlife Service, Ashland)

DESCRIPTION

Body elongate, rounded. Length 30–153 mm. Depth less than twice its width. Depth into TL 5.6–6.4. Head length into TL 4.9–5.5. Snout bluntly rounded and overhanging the ventral mouth. A single skin flap between the nostrils. Maxillary extends to anterior edge of eye or as far as center of eye; upper jaw length into head length 3.1–3.4. Lower jaw length into head length 2.3–2.6. Teeth absent except on tongue. Eye large, its diam greater than snout length. Gill rakers 16–20; raker length into head length 11–15. Scales in lateral line 56–66 (55–70); scales around body anterior to dorsal and pelvic fins 33–37 (31–40); scales around caudal peduncle 18–20 (16). Dorsal fin rays 11–13 (10–14); anal fin rays 13 (12–14); pelvic fin rays 9–10 (11). Pelvic fin length into distance from pelvic origin to anal origin 1.3–1.7. Pyloric caeca 15–23. Chromosomes 2n = 82 (Booke 1968).

Pale tan to brownish on back grading to whitish below. Along lateral line, 8–11 almost circular parr marks, becoming indistinct in large adults. Back with 12–14 dark spots.

Sexual dimorphism: Female deeper and broader; male with longer rayed fins. Breeding tubercles on top of head, on scales of back and sides, and on paired fins in both sexes, but more conspicuous in males.

Hybrid: Pygmy whitefish × round whitefish (Eschmeyer and Bailey 1955).

SYSTEMATIC NOTES

The pygmy whitefish is regarded as an early offshoot from the ancestral *Prosopium*, and has evolved characteristics represented by a reduction in the numbers of gill rakers, pyloric caeca, and lateral line scales (Norden 1970). It is the smallest species in the genus, and the one with the most disjunct distributional pattern.

McCart (1970) discussed the existence of sibling species of pygmy whitefish, suggesting that the Lake Superior population is sufficiently divergent from western populations to have had a Mississippi glacial refugium, while western populations may have redispersed from a Yukon-Bering Sea refugium (high gill raker form), or from a western refugium south of the ice sheet (low gill raker form).

DISTRIBUTION, STATUS, AND HABITAT

Bottom trawling by the United States Fish and Wildlife Service motor vessel *Cisco* in Lake Superior in 1952–1953 revealed a peculiarly isolated population of pygmy whitefish, which had previously been reported only from the Pacific drainage of northwestern North America. This disjunct Lake Superior population is over 1600 km (1000 mi) removed from its normal range (Eschmeyer and Bailey 1955).

The pygmy whitefish is widely distributed in Lake Superior, at least from the Apostle Islands east to Whitefish Bay (about 470 km) and north to Isle Royale. In the Great Lakes basin the pygmy whitefish is known only from Lake Superior, where it is rare (Todd 1978).

It seeks out the coldest of waters. In Lake Superior no seasonal changes appear in depth distribution (Dryer 1966). The all-season bathymetric range in southern Keweenaw Bay extends from 18 to 90 m, but the pygmy whitefish is most abundant at the 46–71 m interval.

BIOLOGY

Spawning in Lake Superior occurs during November or December. In the Apostle Islands from 17–20 November 1961, spawning and spent pygmy whitefish were trawled at depths of 31–46 m (M. Bailey, pers. comm.). Eschmeyer and Bailey (1955) captured young fish in the relatively shallow water (24–33 m) of Keweenaw Bay, Michigan.

All male pygmy whitefish of age-group II or older in collections from Keweenaw Bay and Siskiwit Bay (Isle Royale) were sexually mature. A few age-I males (7%) from Keweenaw Bay also were mature. The age at which 50% or more of the females were mature was 3 years (Eschmeyer and Bailey 1955).

Maturing eggs were counted in the ovaries of 63 pygmy whitefish collected in Lake Superior in 1953. Egg production averaged 362 (93–597) (Eschmeyer

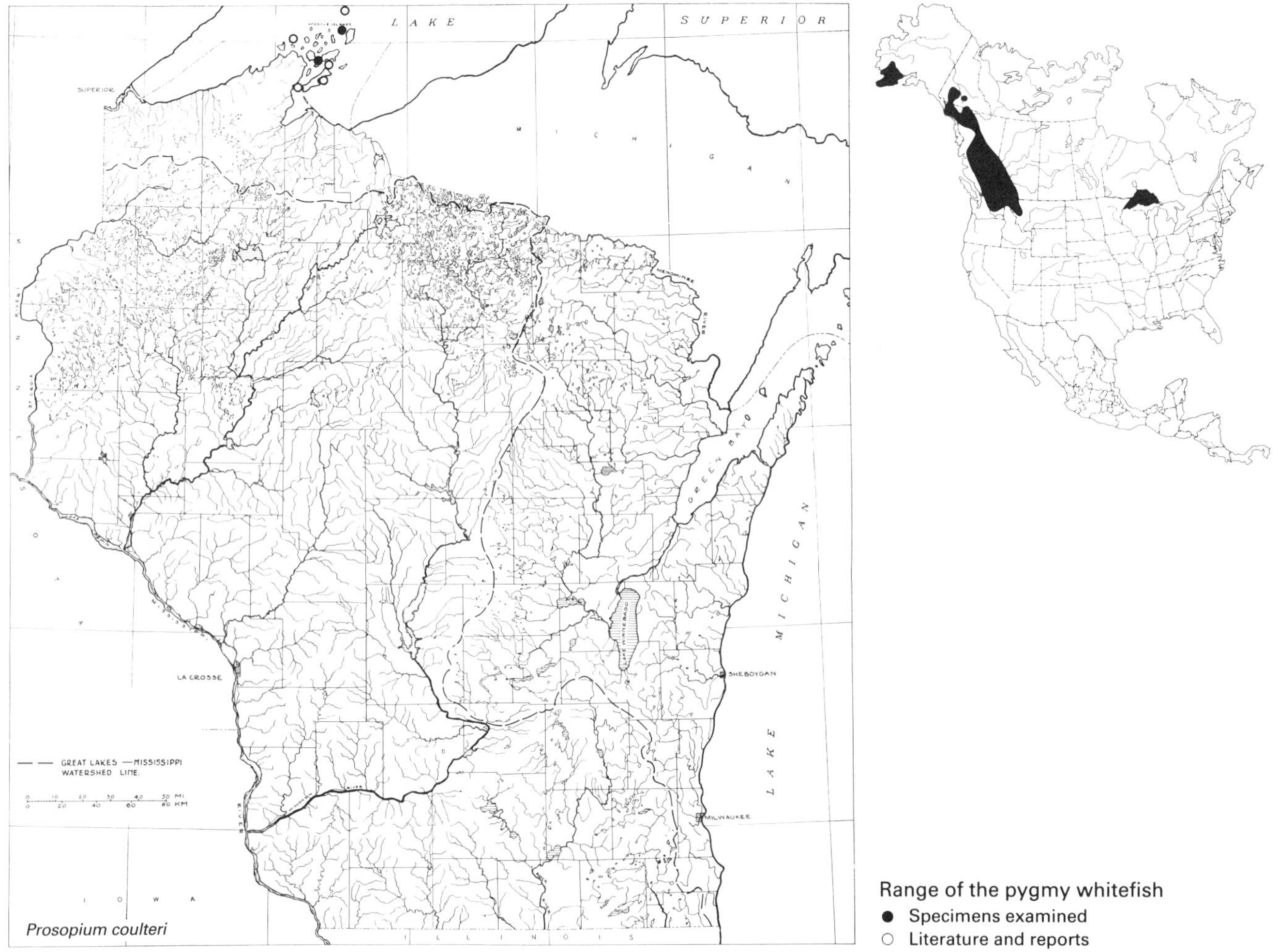

Range of the pygmy whitefish
● Specimens examined
○ Literature and reports

and Bailey 1955). The eggs are orange in color, 2.57 ± 0.03 mm diam (Booke 1970).

Female pygmy whitefish spawn in consecutive years. Mature ripe eggs are present in the abdominal cavity while smaller eggs, 1 mm diam, are developing in the ovaries (Weisel et al. 1973).

In the Northwest this lacustrine species moves from deep water to the mouths of inlet rivers, where spawning occurs. Spawning takes place generally in November and December, although Kendall (1921) found this species in a spawning run in Alaska in August. A late spawning was reported during the 26 December to 12 January period in Ross Creek, Montana (Weisel and Dillon 1954).

In Flathead Lake, Montana, pygmy whitefish males predominated during the early part of the spawning period at a ratio of 6.7:1. Of the age-I males, 74.5% were sexually mature and all males age II or older were mature. The percentage of maturity of the females was 27.8 at age I, 90.2 at age II, and 100 for older fish (Weisel et al. 1973). Four large spawners from Bull Lake had from 1,027 to 1,136 eggs.

Booke (1970) noted that large-egg coregonines spawn earlier than those with small eggs. From the information available, it appears that in Montana the large-egg mountain whitefish spawns about a month earlier than the small-egg pygmy whitefish (Weisel et al. 1973). Applying this to Wisconsin, we would anticipate that the spawning period for the round whitefish should occur before the known spawning period (November to December) of the pygmy whitefish.

Growth of young-of-year pygmy whitefish in Lake Superior is rapid. By 5 September average length is 31 mm; 30 September, 35–49 mm; 21 October, 47–51 mm (Eschmeyer and Bailey 1955). After this period, growth rates are slow: the two oldest fish from Keweenaw Bay, both nearing the end of their eighth growing season, were only 137 mm (5.4 in) long at the time of collection. Also, the average length of fish increased progressively with water depth, chiefly because the number of yearlings decreased from 100% at 18–26 m to none at 82–90 m.

According to Eschmeyer and Bailey, the average

calculated TL mm for females (males in parentheses) at the end of each year of life is: 1—46 (49); 2—69 (71); 3—88 (87); 4—107 (98); 5-117 (106); 6—123; 7—130. Females generally average longer and heavier at capture than do males of the same age. The percentage of males in the population decreases with age. In the populations studied males made up 51% of the fish in age groups I and II, 45% of those in age groups III and IV, and only 31% of those in age groups V-VII. Only females appear in age groups VI and VII. This trend is reflected in the average ages of the sexes: 2.4 years for males, and 2.9 years for females.

Pygmy whitefish from the Apostle Islands grow more rapidly than the Siskiwit or Keweenaw Bay populations. Calculated lengths (mm) of a gill net collection of females from the Apostle Islands at the end of each year of life were: 1—44; 2—68; 3—98; 4—117; 5—129; 6—139; 7—144. A large female 153 mm TL (UWSP 2718) was taken in the vicinity of Stockton Island (Ashland County) at 62 m on 29 May 1962. Scott and Crossman (1973) noted that in Maclure Lake, British Columbia, females of this species lived longer than in other waters; attaining an age of 9 years and a fork length of 271 mm (10.7 in), whereas males reached 6 years of age and a fork length of 225 mm (8.8 in).

In Lake Superior pygmy whitefish, crustacea occurred in 95% of the stomachs and composed 77% of the food volume (Eschmeyer and Bailey 1955); ostracods and amphipods (principally or entirely *Pontoporeia*) were the chief components. Copepods were in 26% of the stomachs, but were usually incidental in the diet of fish more than 89 mm (3.5 in) long. Cladocera (presumably *Daphnia*) and *Mysis* were unimportant items. Insects (principally larval and pupal chironomids) appeared in 62% of the stomachs and made up 9% of the food; adult insects were present in 20% of the stomachs, but represented only 1% of the volume. Larval clams (Sphaeriidae) occurred in 20% of the stomachs, making up 3% of volume. Fish eggs, presumably coregonine, were taken from May and January collections; when available, they may be important in the diet of this species. Small quantities of organic detritus and sand grains were present in a few of the fish examined.

A December collection of spawning pygmy whitefish from Ross Creek (Montana) demonstrated that these fish feed actively during their spawning period (Weisel et al. 1973). Fish eggs, laid by fellow spawners, were the most frequently ingested food and made up by far the greatest volume. Chironomids, however, were still taken in numbers, along with a few other insects.

In Lake Superior the most common associates of the pygmy whitefish are the cottid species, *Cottus cognatus* and *Myoxocephalus thompsoni*. The ninespine stickleback is next in importance, followed by the smelt, lake herring, deepwater ciscoes, lake trout, and trout-perch (Eschmeyer and Bailey 1955). M. Bailey (pers. comm.) also lists the spoonhead sculpin as a common associate of the pygmy whitefish.

IMPORTANCE AND MANAGEMENT

Wherever the pygmy whitefish comes to the surface during the spawning period it is vulnerable to predators. It has been caught by kingfishers in Washington and by terns in Alaska (Scott and Crossman 1973). Because of its small size and deepwater habitat in Lake Superior, it is most likely utilized by the lake trout, which were present in 57% of the hauls that took pygmy whitefish, and by burbot (18% of the hauls) (Eschmeyer and Bailey 1955).

Round Whitefish

Prosopium cylindraceum (Pallas). *Prosopium*—a mask, from the large bones in front of the eyes; *cylindraceum*—cylinderlike.

Other common names: the pilot, pilot fish, frost fish, Menominee, Menominee whitefish, cross whitefish, lake minnow.

Subadult 255 mm, North Bay, L. Michigan (Door Co.), 23 June 1977

DESCRIPTION

Body elongate, almost round in cross section. Average length 368 mm (14.5 in) in Lake Michigan. Depth into TL about 5. Head length into TL 4.9–5.6. Snout pointed and compressed laterally, rounded in lateral view and overhanging the ventral mouth. A single skin flap between the nostrils. Maxillary extends almost to anterior edge of eye in adults; upper jaw length into head length 3.9–4.8. Lower jaw length into head length 2.7–3.1. Teeth absent except on tongue. Eye moderate, its diam less than snout length. Gill rakers 16–18 (15–20); raker length into head length 20–27. Scales in lateral line 83–96 (80–100); scales around body anterior to dorsal and pelvic fins 42–46 (40–47); scales around caudal peduncle 22–24. Dorsal fin rays 14–15 (13); anal fin rays 9–11; pelvic fin rays 14–15 (13). Pelvic fin length into distance from pelvic origin to anal origin 1.7–2.5. Pyloric caeca 87–117. Chromosomes 2n = 78 (Booke 1968).

Color in life, silvery; dorsally dark brown to bronze, tinged with green. Scales of back margined with pigmented borders. Sides brownish. Basal half of the paired fins, and often the anal fin, orange. Young (under 200 mm) silvery, with 2 or more longitudinal rows of dark spots (2–4 mm diam) on sides, a row of 10 or more spots along the lateral line, and a series of 10 or more spots just below the midline of the back which may fuse with additional spots across the back.

Breeding tubercles well developed on males, less so on females, located 1 per scale on sides, none on head.

Hybrids: Round whitefish × pygmy whitefish. Artificial round whitefish × lake herring, and round whitefish × lake whitefish (Schwartz 1972).

SYSTEMATIC NOTES

The round whitefish has diverged somewhat more recently than the pygmy whitefish from an ancestral *Prosopium* (Norden 1970). Its evolution has been characterized by a shortening of head, snout, maxillary and gill rakers. It has evolved the greatest number of lateral line scales and a high number of pyloric caeca. The round whitefish has the widest geographical distribution of any species in the genus.

DISTRIBUTION, STATUS, AND HABITAT

The round whitefish ranges widely through northern North America and into northeastern Asia. It is known from all of the Great Lakes except Lake Erie. In Wisconsin waters it occurs in Lake Michigan, principally between Sheboygan and the tip of Door County, and in Lake Superior, where it is known to enter the lower reaches of the Brule, Amnicon, and Middle rivers of Douglas County.

The round whitefish is endangered in Lake Ontario and rare in Lake Huron (Todd 1978). Although it is considered common in Lakes Michigan and Superior, the stocks of this species appear to be declining in both lakes. In the Muskegon and Grand Haven areas of southeastern Lake Michigan, where the catch was 6,000 kg in 1929, the species has been seen only rarely since the late 1940s. The reasons for the apparent decrease are obscure (Wells and McLain 1973). Koelz (1929) gives only sporadic records of the round whitefish in southern Lake Michigan, although Hoy (1883) reported it spawning near Racine many years ago. In the Illinois waters of Lake Michigan it is probably extirpated (Lopinot and Smith 1973).

The round whitefish is essentially a shallow water form. In Lake Superior it is most abundant at less than 37 m, and none are taken at depths greater than 71 m (Dryer 1966). In northern Lake Michigan it is most common at 7–22 m, occasionally at depths to 59 m.

BIOLOGY

Spawning occurs in November and early December. During spawning there is a decided inshore movement of this species to shallower waters. In Lake Michigan the eggs are laid over honeycomb rock and gravel in 4–11 m of water. Hoy (1883) noted spawning about the first of December in 27 m of water "just outside the stony ridge north of Racine."

In Lake Superior spawning occurs in the mouths of rivers, on bottoms of boulders and gravel near shore, at depths of 4–11 m (Eddy and Underhill 1974). Concentrations have been noted in the Brule, Amnicon, and Middle rivers of Wisconsin's south

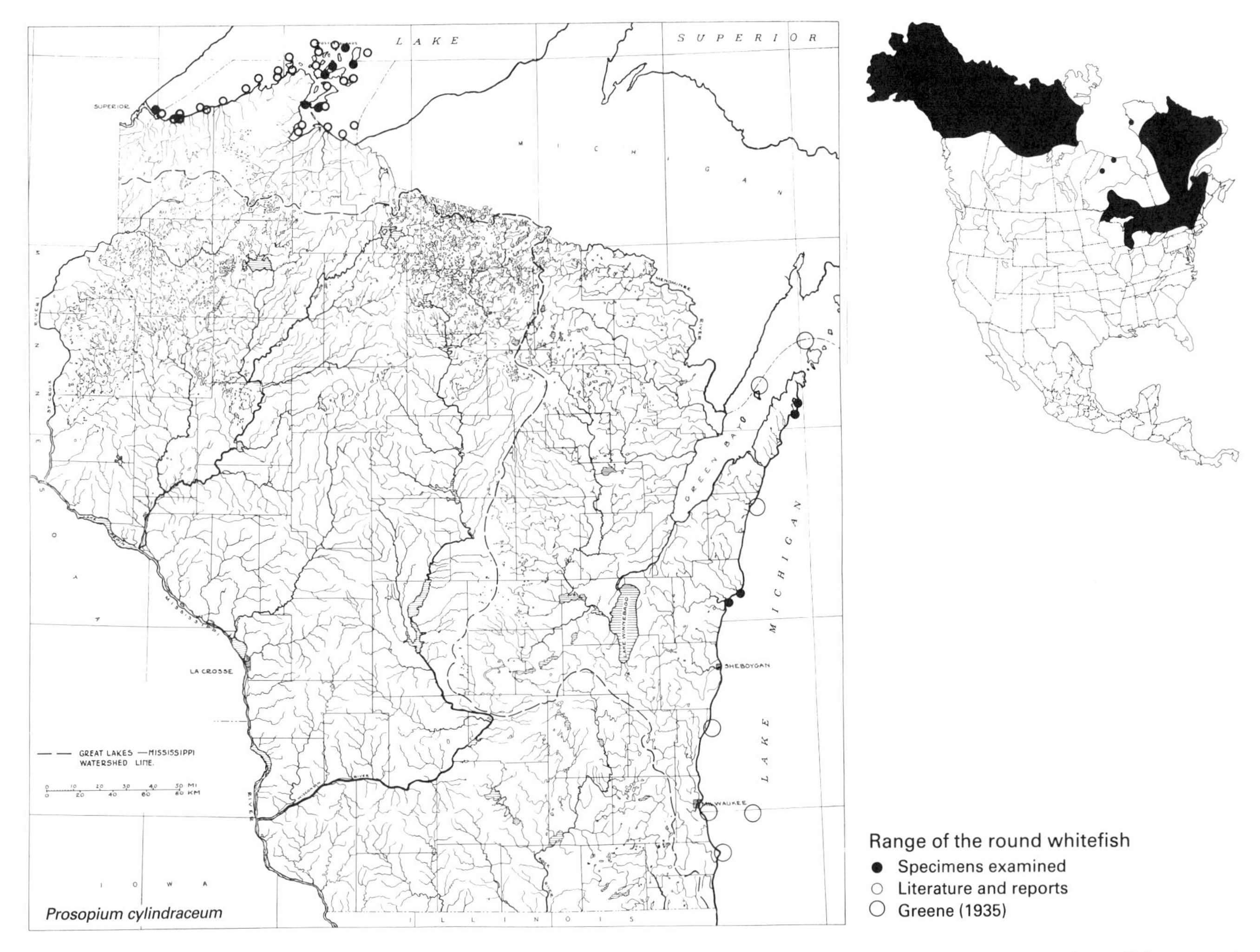

shore; in the Two Hearted River of Upper Michigan (McLain et al. 1965); in the Devil Track, Cascade, and French rivers of the north shore of Lake Superior (Eddy and Underhill 1974); and over the spawning beds of lake trout in the Montreal and Dog rivers of eastern Lake Superior (Loftus 1958). According to M. Bailey (pers. comm.), the last was probably not a spawning run since it occurred before the spawning period.

In Newfound Lake, New Hampshire, spawning occurred during the first three weeks of December over a large, shallow, rocky reef between 0.40 and 0.8 hectares (1–2 acres) in area (Normandeau 1969). Eggs were deposited at depths of just a few centimeters to 2 or more meters, at water temperatures of 4.4–2.8°C (40–37°F):

> Whitefish did not congregate into large groups, instead were observed swimming in pairs. Occasionally groups of 4 to 6 fish were seen in areas which apparently presented suitable spawning habitats. However, of the approximately 1,000 whitefish that were observed on this reef and along the nearby shore, no more than six to eight fish were seen in a single group at any one time. Even these fish seemed to be paired [p. 11].

Peak of hatching occurred during the last week of the following April, approximately 140 days from the time of fertilization, at a water temperature of 2.2°C (36°F). Upon hatching the fry remained on the bottom, but when disturbed could be seen swimming vigorously as they sought shelter in the rubble and beneath larger rocks. On 4 and 5 May, several round whitefish fry were collected from the spawning reef, and one was taken on 11 May, the last in a number of unsuccessful searches.

In Lake Superior average egg production in 36 round whitefish females was 5,330 (1,076–11,888) (Bailey 1963). Brice (1898) noted 12,000 eggs in a 795-g (28 oz) fish. The eggs are orange in color, 3.5 ± 0.03 mm diam (Booke 1970).

Round whitefish were 12.3 mm at hatching. Hinrichs (1977, 1979) noted that the oil droplets in the yolk-sac never unite during the developmental period; this is the only coregonid studied in which the droplets do not unite. A detailed description of the

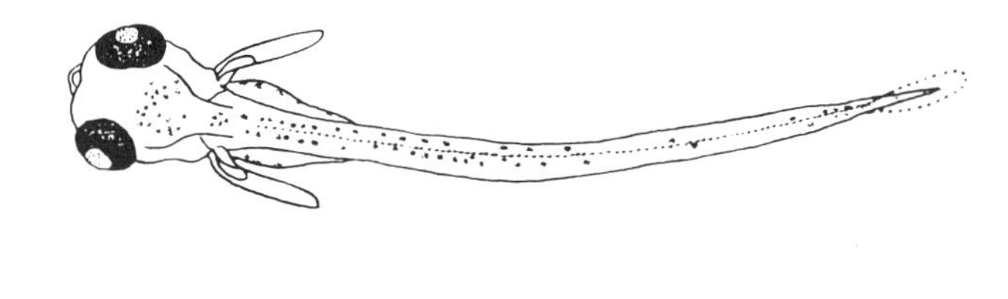

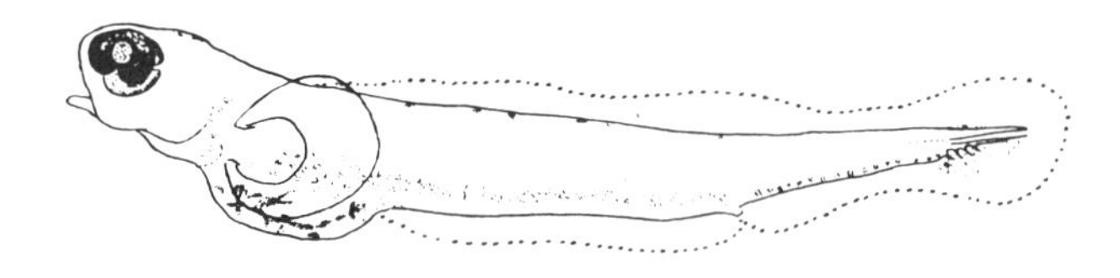

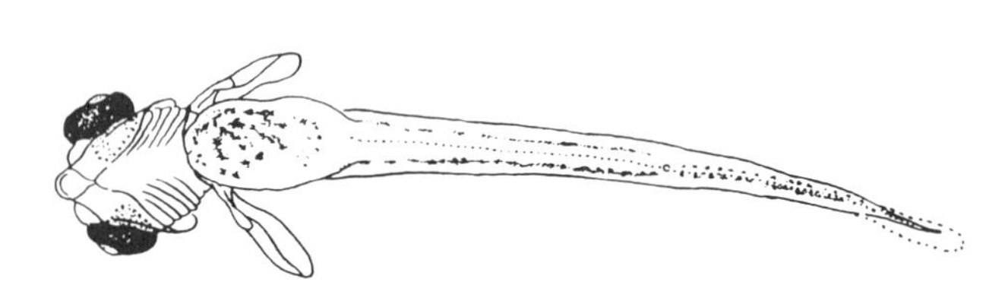

Preserved round whitefish larva, Newfound L., New Hampshire. Dorsal view (top), lateral view (middle), ventral view (bottom). 12.7 mm TL; pre-anal myomeres, 35; post-anal myomeres, 13 (Faber 1970:495).

early development of the round whitefish is provided by Hinrichs (1979).

Calculated total lengths and weights for year classes of round whitefish off the Sturgeon Bay Canal, Lake Michigan, were: 1—117 mm, 11 g; 2—229 mm, 74 g; 3—312 mm, 210 g; 4—363 mm, 341 g; 5—396 mm, 457 g; 6—427 mm, 582 g; 7—455 mm, 719 g; and 8—480 mm, 861 g. Mraz (1964a) noted that the females were heavier than the males by 2.8–22.7 g at all weight interval studies. In the Apostle Islands (Lake Superior), the calculated total lengths and weights were: 1—117 mm, 11g; 2—183 mm, 43 g; 3—231 mm, 88 g; 4—274 mm, 153 g; 5—307 mm, 224 g; 6—333 mm, 287 g; 7—356 mm, 358 g; 8—376 mm, 426 g; and 9—394 mm, 494 g (Bailey 1963). The data show that round whitefish from northwestern Lake Michigan had a decided advantage over the Lake Superior stock in both length and weight in every year of life beyond the first. The weights of Lake Michigan fish at the end of 7 and 8 years were twice the corresponding weights for the Apostle Islands stock.

Lake Michigan whitefish mature between 305 and 381 mm. The smallest mature males are 305–315 mm and the smallest mature females are 330–340 mm long. All males over 366 mm and all females over 378 mm are mature (Mraz 1964a). The majority of the males (95.2%) and females (85.7%) reach sexual maturity at age III.

Lake Superior round whitefish mature when they are as small as 178–188 mm, the youngest in age-group II. All fish larger than 328 mm are mature. All males older than age IV and females older than age V are mature.

An age-IX fish, 452 mm (17.8 in) TL, weighing 794 g (28 oz), came from Isle Royale (Bailey 1963). In Green Bay, Lake Michigan off Peninsula Point, Michigan, a 546-mm, 1.93-kg (21.5-in, 4-lb 4-oz) fish 8 years old was taken in a trap net on 1 August 1956 (Mich. Dep. Nat. Resour. 1975). The maximum age reported for this species is 14 years (Van Oosten 1932).

The round whitefish appears to be an opportunistic bottom feeder, ingesting small benthic invertebrates almost exclusively (Armstrong et al. 1977). In eastern Lake Michigan, snails (primarily *Physa* sp.) and midge larvae were found to be the organisms most frequently eaten by round whitefish in all seasons. Leeches and fish were seasonally important. During the summer, crayfish occurred in 14% of the stomachs, and one stomach taken in spring contained several rainbow smelt, the only incidence of fish predation observed.

According to Koelz (1929), the round whitefish is charged with the destruction of trout spawn by virtually every fisherman who is familiar with it. This accusation is supported by Loftus (1958) who noted that round whitefish were found in numbers over the spawning beds of lake trout in the Montreal and Dog rivers, where they empty into eastern Lake Superior. Stomachs of whitefish examined from the Montreal River contained as many as 150 lake trout eggs. However, M. Bailey (pers. comm.) noted contrary evidence in examination of many round whitefish and longnose suckers taken during the spawning run for lake trout on the reefs in Lake Superior: he found few, if any, trout eggs in their stomachs.

In Newfound Lake, New Hampshire, most of the stomachs of more than 200 round whitefish examined during spawning were empty. Prior to the onset of spawning, stomachs were usually filled with *Daphnia pulex* (Normandeau 1969).

It is generally believed that the round whitefish moves in schools along the shores, seldom into deep water. Unlike the lake whitefish, this species will not follow a lead readily and is rarely taken in pound or trap nets, but it is vulnerable to gill nets of 64–76 mm (2.5–3 in) mesh. Lake herring and perch are often taken with it (Koelz 1929).

The movement of the round whitefish follows a yearly cycle, which has been summarized for Lake Huron by Koelz (1929:552):

> . . . Thus all the records indicate that the pilot begin to move inshore in numbers on honeycomb rock and gravel about the middle of October, and that they remain there until the nets are pulled in (for the winter). Since few gill nets of a mesh suitable for pilot are set in the spring, not much is known about the offshore movement. The depth to which the fish migrate in summer is certainly not over 30 fathoms and probably not over 20.

Although normally a lake species, the round whitefish will move considerable distances against strong currents during the spawning run. Loftus (1958) noted that in eastern Lake Superior it had moved 3.2 km (2 mi) up the Dog River and had negotiated several steep rapids.

IMPORTANCE AND MANAGEMENT

The round whitefish is a source of food for other fishes. In Newfound Lake, New Hampshire, at the onset of the whitefish spawning run, there was a general increase in the activity of other fish species; among these were the white sucker, yellow perch, burbot, brown bullhead, and Atlantic salmon. Normandeau (1969) noted that the stomachs of white suckers were often full of whitefish eggs. Yellow perch, burbot, and brown bullheads also fed on the eggs, and on many occasions were seen swimming between the smaller rocks and crevices in search of food. Also, the stomachs of two Atlantic salmon were found to contain over 200 round whitefish fry. The stomach of one pickerel yielded the remains of a round whitefish 254 mm (10 in) long.

Generally, the flesh of the round whitefish is considered excellent and highly palatable. As a food fish for man it has never come into its own. It offers a limited fishery. Small catches are often sold as part of the shipments of other species, usually lake whitefish. This marketing procedure may contribute to a low estimate of round whitefish production, since "odd poundages" are not always listed by fishermen on their reports (Bailey 1963). Moreover, the 114-mm (4.5-in) mesh used for taking lake whitefish is too large for round whitefish.

Wells and McLain (1973:44) provided a summary of round whitefish production for Lake Michigan:

> Production of round whitefish was highest in the earliest years of record, 1893 and 1899—423,000 and 519,000 lb respectively. The annual catch averaged 106,000 lb in 1903–70.
>
> Although changes in production of round whitefish in Lake Michigan may not indicate abundance trends accurately, it is perhaps safe to speculate that the stocks have declined somewhat. Production in the late 1800s was considerably higher than that after 1900, and included (about 1885) catches of round whitefish "weighing 4 to 6 pounds each." . . . Few approach that size today.

In 1973, 5,839 kg (12,873 lb) were harvested in Lake Michigan; in 1974 the 4,280-kg (9,437-lb) harvest was worth $4,665. The round whitefish is not sought extensively by commercial fishermen because of its low market value. Lake Michigan waters along Door County, Wisconsin, account for 99% of the catch (Wis. Dep. Nat. Resour. 1976c).

In Lake Superior production generally has been small. The catch in United States waters of the lake averaged 12,065 kg in 1920–1959. The mean landings for the states were: Michigan, 6,670 kg; Wisconsin, 4,265 kg; Minnesota, 1,680 kg (Bailey 1963). The Wisconsin harvest in 1974 was 5,895 kg (12,995 lb) worth $3,575 (Wis. Dep. Nat. Resour. 1976c).

Smelt Family— Osmeridae

One species of smelt occurs in Wisconsin waters, introduced from Michigan when that state brought in smelt to provide food for salmon that were being stocked at the same time. The salmon perished, but the smelt prospered. The smelt family is essentially a marine family, and in the United States and Canada it includes nine species in six genera (Robins et al. 1980). All are Arctic or North Temperate.

The smelts are small, slender, silvery predacious fishes with thin, elongated bodies and large mouths. Teeth are either well developed or weakly developed on the jaws, the tongue, and the roof of the mouth. The scales are thin and cycloid. An adipose fin is present, but a pelvic axillary process is absent.

Rainbow Smelt

Osmerus mordax (Mitchill). *Osmerus*—Greek for odorous; *mordax*—biting.
Other common names: smelt, American smelt, freshwater smelt, frost fish, ice fish.

Adult male 155 mm, L. Superior, Ashland (Ashland Co.), 29 Apr. 1971

DESCRIPTION
Body slender, slightly compressed laterally. Average length 178 mm (7 in) TL. Depth into TL 7.2 (6.5–8.0). Head into TL 4.9 (4.6–5.4). Snout elongate and pointed. Mouth large, lower jaw protruding; maxillary extending to middle of eye or beyond. Teeth on upper and lower jaws, and on tongue and front of vomer where teeth are especially enlarged. Gill rakers long and slender 26–35. Branchiostegal rays 5–7. Scales cycloid; lateral scales 62–72, lateral line incomplete. Dorsal fin rays 8–11; anal fin rays 12–16; pectoral fin rays 11–14; pelvic fin rays 8. Pyloric caeca 4–8.

Breeding tubercles extensively developed on head, body, and fins of males; seldom on females.

Silvery; dorsal half of head and body steel blue, with sides lighter and belly white. A faint lateral stripe present in some large individuals. Fins generally clear.

DISTRIBUTION, STATUS, AND HABITAT
Although essentially a marine species with primary distribution along Canadian coastal waters, the rainbow smelt has intruded into fresh waters of the northeastern states and into the Great Lakes. It occurs in all major drainage systems in Wisconsin. In the Lake Superior basin it inhabits the lake proper and its tributaries; in the Lake Michigan basin, the lake proper, its tributaries, and Lake Lucerne (Forest County). In the Mississippi basin its presence has been established in Diamond, Sand Bar, and Tomahawk lakes (all within Bayfield County), and in Fence Lake and adjacent streams (Vilas County). The smelt was introduced "inadvertently" into the Fence Lake system in 1968 (M. Bailey, pers. comm.). The origin of the Lake Lucerne population is not known (A. Oehmcke, pers. comm.).

The rainbow smelt is an escape into Wisconsin waters. The seed stock, which came originally from Green Lake, Maine, contained a native freshwater race of the marine species common along the North Atlantic coast. Attempts to introduce this species in the upper Great Lakes go back to 1906, but it is generally accepted that the present strain spread from the 1912 stocking of 16.4 million smelt in Crystal Lake (Benzie County), Michigan. The rainbow smelt was first taken in Lake Michigan off the east shore near Frankfort, Michigan, in 1923 (Van Oosten 1936); by 1924 it had crossed the lake to Big Bay de Noc, an arm of Green Bay. It was first observed in Wisconsin waters in 1928 when a few were caught in gill nets near Little Sturgeon Bay (Door County). In 1929 a few smelt were taken in Lake Michigan off Gill's Rock and the Sturgeon Bay Canal. By 1930 it had reached Manitowoc, Port Washington, and Racine, and in 1931 it reached Kenosha, Wisconsin, and Michigan City, Indiana.

In Lake Superior the rainbow smelt appeared first at Whitefish Bay, at the eastern end of the lake, in 1930; it appeared in Keweenaw Bay in 1936, and probably reached the Wisconsin waters of Lake Superior in the late 1930s.

The rainbow smelt is common in lakes Superior and Michigan and is occasionally taken in large tributary streams.

In the Great Lakes, rainbow smelt inhabit waters 14–64 m deep and are most abundant in the 18–26 m zone. Occasionally they occur in small numbers to 91 m. The adults move inshore and congregate in dense schools in April, and, when spawning, some may move short distances up tributary streams.

BIOLOGY
The spawning season (late March through early May) normally lasts about 2 weeks, but climatic conditions such as cold rains and cold nights may extend it to a month (Daly and Wiegert 1958). Because of temperature differences between northern and southern Wisconsin waters the start of the spawning run may vary as much as 3 weeks between southern Lake Michigan and Lake Superior to the north. The run in southern Green Bay is normally a week to 10 days later than the run in northern Lake Michigan because the bay freezes over in winter and therefore warms up later.

Spawning is initiated when the water temperature reaches 4.4°C (40°F) or higher—shortly after the ice breaks up and moves out. At this time the bulk of

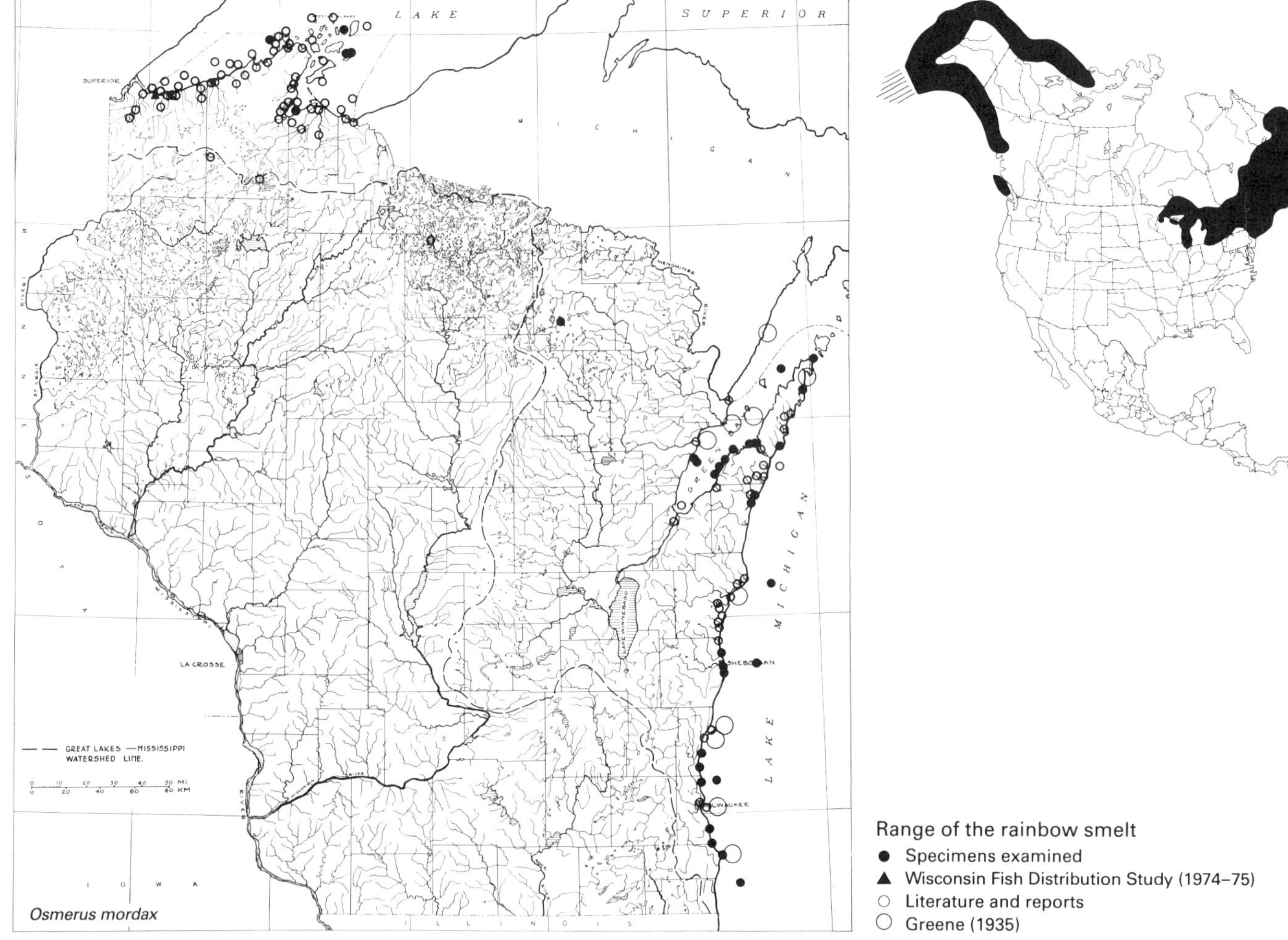

Range of the rainbow smelt
● Specimens examined
▲ Wisconsin Fish Distribution Study (1974–75)
○ Literature and reports
◯ Greene (1935)

the spawners migrate up streams to distances of 0.8–1.6 km (0.5–1.0 mi) above the stream mouths. In the Lake Superior basin, however, some migrations occur at greater distances: 13 km (8.0 mi) in the Brule River, 16 km (10 mi) in the Nemadji River, and 24 km (15 mi) in both the White and Bad rivers. The smelt also spawn on gravel deltas in lakes; such shore spawning generally occurs in less than 0.6 m (2 ft) of water (Rupp 1965).

The male assumes a position slightly anterior and slightly dorsal to the female in spawning and violently drives the female to the bottom or shoreward (Hoover 1936b). Spawning begins when males predominate over females 4 to 1, and increases later in the season when the sexes become more equal in numbers. The female never deposits more than 50 eggs at one time, no matter how violently she is thrown. Many females returning to the lake contain eggs, and it is probable that some enter the spawning runs several times. Spawning takes place principally during the night. Afterward many of the fish drift back to the lake with the current and seek out deep water. As a rule, relatively few of each night's spawners are found in the streams the following day. Those fish that remain are almost all males and, since the species is light sensitive, they seek darkness under banks and bridges.

In 1967, spawning occurred in late April in Lake Lucerne (Forest County) when rainbow smelt up to 183 mm (7.2 in) TL massed by the thousands in the shallows shortly after dark. The fish were so numerous that they bumped up against the legs of the seiners. The water temperature was 6.7°C (44°F).

Smelt eggs sink to the bottom immediately after they are released, and become attached to the substrate by a short pedicel (stalk) formed from the outer shell membrane (Rupp 1965). In rainbow smelt from western Lake Superior the eggs averaged 0.86 mm diam (Bailey 1964), and the average number of eggs for smelt 185–224 mm (7.3–8.8 in) long was 31,338 (21,534–40,894). When the eggs absorb water after fertilization, egg size increases to 0.9–1.3 mm diam (Van Oosten 1940).

Development takes about 20–30 days at normal water temperatures and 10 days at 15.6°C (60°F) (Webster 1942). Schneberger (1937a) found developing embryos in 74% of the eggs examined from spawning grounds in Green Bay. Mortality may be great, however, and Rupp (1965) noted mean survival-to-hatching of 0.03–2.10% for shore-spawning smelt.

The newly hatched fry are 5.5–6.0 mm long, very delicate, and transparent. Soon after hatching the fry are carried downstream by the current, and no doubt many die within a short time (Van Oosten 1940). Fry from St. Louis Bay, Lake Superior, absorbed their yolk-sacs before they reached a length of 7 mm (Siefert 1972). *Cyclops bicuspidatus*, copepod nauplii, diatoms, and nonmotile green algae were found in digestive tracts of first-feeding smelt.

Rainbow smelt can be aged by reading characteristic annuli on scales. The calculated growth of a small sample (UWSP 1844) from Lake Michigan at Sheboygan was: 1—82 mm; 2—127 mm; 3—180 mm. Excellent growth occurred in Green Bay (Van Oosten 1940): III—254 mm; IV—305 mm; V—356 mm (approx. 227 g). In comparing the growth of rainbow smelt from Green Bay with those taken from Crystal Lake, Michigan (Creaser 1925), Schneberger (1937a) found that the Green Bay smelt grew at a faster rate, averaging 356 mm (14 in) at age V, compared to 274–305 mm (10.8–12 in) at age V in Crystal Lake.

The calculated total lengths and weights at the end of each year of life for smelt from western Lake Superior (Bailey 1964) were:

	1	2	3	4	5	6	7
Males							
TL (mm)	66	150	183	203	218		
WT (g)	1.7	20.4	41.5	55.7	64.2		
Females							
TL (mm)	66	150	193	221	239	257	310
WT (g)	1.7	20.4	44.6	64.2	80.7	93.7	108.5

In spite of certain variations with age and possible annual differences, it appears that annulus formation begins near mid-June and is completed about the middle of August. Younger smelt form annuli earlier than do the older fish (Bailey 1964).

In Lake Superior all rainbow smelt shorter than 127 mm (5.0 in) are immature; all fish longer than 170 mm (6.7 in) are mature. All smelt are immature after only one growing season, but they are all mature after three or more growing seasons. Among age-II fish, 40.7% of the males and 17.7% of the females had reached maturity. Bailey determined the sex of mature smelt by gross inspection of the gonads, but immature fish of age-group II required microscopic examination. Sex could not be determined with confidence for smelt of age-group 0 or of age-group I until near the end of the second growing season.

The peak feeding temperature of this species is 10°C (50°F). Full-grown rainbow smelt in the Great Lakes continue to subsist principally on the larger crustaceans. In the inshore waters they may consume large numbers of fishes. During the spawning season smelt, especially the females, virtually stop feeding.

When 198 smelt from northern Lake Michigan and northern Lake Huron were examined, many of their stomachs were gorged with opossum shrimp (*Mysis relicta*). Thirty-nine (20%) had eaten young-of-year alewives. The only other fish found in smelt stomachs were a 68-mm young-of-year smelt and a 60-mm ninespine stickleback. O'Gorman (1974) noted that large smelt commonly prey on young alewives during the fall when the two species occupy the same depth zones. He surmised that the quantity of young alewives consumed by smelt may represent an important part of the alewife's total mortality during its first year of life.

Rainbow smelt in Lake Superior (King and Swanson 1975) showed the following food preferences (occurrence percent): *Mysis relicta* (70.1%), *Pontoporeia affinis* (21.2%), copepods (3.5%), fish (3.3%). Of the identifiable fish there were six sculpins, five ninespine sticklebacks, and one young-of-year smelt, all ranging in size from 12 to 84 mm (0.5 to 3.3 in). Additional contents were midgefly adults and larvae, ephemeropterans, unknown terrestrial insects, corixids, plecopterans, cladocerans, and an unknown invertebrate larva.

Van Oosten (1940) noted that this species is highly cannibalistic, and that after attaining a length of 152 mm (6 in) it may turn to eating fishes, mostly its own kind. The following varieties of fish have been found and identified in smelt stomachs: smelt (most common), emerald shiner, yellow perch (not common), sculpin (*Cottus*—in Green Bay smelt), burbot (from 5 Green Bay smelt), rock bass (not common), coregonid (lake herring?—one specimen from Lake Michigan), and stickleback. Smelt eggs were also found. In Crystal Lake, Michigan, 147 rainbow smelt fed almost entirely (98%) on emerald shiners; the remaining food consisted of chironomid and mayfly larvae and pupae (Creaser 1925).

In Lake Michigan the rainbow smelt move in increasing numbers from pelagic to a bottom existence as they grow older (Wells 1968). Age-0 fish live in the upper levels until the fall or very late summer, when at least some move to the bottom. Age-I fish may be either at midlevels (commonly in the thermocline) or on the bottom. Age-II fish and older are mostly on the bottom.

Adult smelt on the bottom occupy shallow and intermediate depths in southeastern Lake Michigan. They have been observed widely scattered from 13 to 64 m on 13 February, but by 11 March had abandoned the deeper water (Wells 1968). Most older smelt move into shallow spawning areas by 15 April, and on 5 May they appear at depths of 5–18 m. By 26 May they extend their range to 36 m. At this time they avoid the warm water near shore.

In northern Lake Michigan, where the smelt are far more abundant than in the southeastern portion of the lake, adult smelt extend their summer range to 46–64 m, and occasionally in small numbers to 91 m, although the greatest numbers are at 27 m (usually the shallowest water fished).

In Lake Superior, most of the ago-0 and age-I smelt are taken at less than 18 m, and only an occasional fish is taken below 35 m (Dryer 1966). The age-II and older smelt from trawls are nearly evenly distributed between 18 and 71 m; they are rarely captured above 18 m, and none are found below 71 m. During the winter smelt occur at depths of 14–18 m in Lake Lucerne (Forest County).

Optimum temperatures for the smelt are 6.1–13.3°C (43–56°F).

Because of the timing of spawning and of the outward migration of the young, smelt have been able to utilize relatively polluted areas which other anadromous species cannot use (Dow 1972). Since the adults spawn during a period when there is generally heavy runoff, polluted waters are greatly diluted and unfavorable water conditions are less apt to develop. Also, the developmental period in the egg is very short, enabling the young to emigrate from spawning areas which may become seriously polluted later when the water volume drops.

IMPORTANCE AND MANAGEMENT

The rainbow smelt has clearly supplanted the chubs (Coregonus spp.) as the principal food of Lake Superior's lake trout population (Dryer et al. 1965). Published records indicate that the following fish have fed in various degrees on smelt: brook trout, lake trout (extensively in Great Lakes), whitefish, lake herring, eel, walleye (extensively in Great Lakes), yellow perch (commonly in Great Lakes), northern pike (occasionally), gar, and burbot (commonly in Great Lakes). On Lake Lucerne, walleyes caught in late August 1974 contained smelt 50–150 mm (2–6 in) long; a 406-mm (16-in) walleye had seven smelt; a 356-mm (14-in) walleye had five (F. Koshere, pers. comm.).

To many people the smelt is known as a tasty food fish. Smelt are most palatable when rolled in flour, corn meal, or cracker meal and fried in plenty of oil, until golden brown. Baked smelt is also a treat for those with fastidious tastes. Van Oosten (1940) included a recipe for pickled smelt which purportedly makes a very palatable appetizer. In the spring smelt can be bought fresh; during the remainder of the year an excellent frozen product is available.

Dipping and seining for the small, silvery fishes during their spawning migration has become a way of life for men, women, and children (*Stevens Point Daily Journal* 28 April 1977):

> Kings and queens were once crowned in their honor, complete with speeches, fireworks and parades.
>
> People came hundreds of miles to celebrate their arrival, and grown men, fully clothed, jumped into the water to catch them with their bare hands.
>
> Back in the '40s, they called this phenomenon "smelt-mania." We may not use that term today but the mania for smelt is still with us.
>
> Smelt fishing is a spring ritual along the shores of the Great Lakes. Beginning about the first week in April in

Smelt dipping (Wisconsin DNR photo)

Smelt harvest (Wisconsin DNR photo)

southern Lake Michigan, sportsmen line the shores, armed with everything from "bedsprings to bird cages." With these weapons, fishermen scoop up the small silvery smelt, making their annual spawning run to shore.

By early May, hundreds of bonfires glow against the night sky along Lake Superior as smelt fishermen patiently await their quarry. Because smelt are sensitive to light and warm temperatures, they run primarily at night.

Some old-timers say that on a quiet night you can actually hear them coming in with a soft wooshing sound.

And when they come, they come by the thousands. . . .

That carnival called smelting reached its zenith in the 1930s when Oconto and Marinette, Wisconsin, attracted 20–30 thousand visitors to dances, banquets, and parades that stretched for 3 miles. There was the "smestling" match which was held in a ring covered with 2 tons of smelt; the wrestlers fought to see who could stuff the most smelt in his opponent's trunks. The event got newsreel coverage from all of the news services of the day; newspapers all over the United States carried stories on Wisconsin's phenomenal smelt run; radio stations told their listeners about the run; and part of the fun for thousands of people was lining up elbow to elbow, vying with one another for a share of the silvery fish.

The impact of the event, triggered by this small, exotic fish that arrived on the Wisconsin scene at a time when the country was fighting its way out of the depression, was summed up by Van Oosten (1940):

> The smelt, therefore, has not only added a new source of food for the residents and fish of the Great Lakes area and a new source of revenue for the commercial fisherman and unemployed during the winter, and stimulated all types of business generally during a normally slack period of the year, but has provided additional recreation for the citizens during the fall and winter with hook and line, during the spring with dip nets and other paraphernalia, and even during the summer with fly fishing when the smelt school near the surface.

According to E. Schneberger (pers. comm.), in about 1934 a family of very limited means living in a shacklike home at the mouth of the Peshtigo River discovered a bonanza. The mother asked her sons to fill a couple of wash boilers with water from the river so she could get an early start on Monday's laundry. When the boilers were filled, the boys discovered that many smelt had been dipped up. They got busy catching smelt and filled every available container with fish. The next day they made several trips to the fish market to sell the smelt, and with the money they paid off debts and bought food and clothing.

Schneberger (1937a) reported that commercial fishermen operating set hooks for lake trout in northern Green Bay preferred smelt over the native chubs as bait. In Lake Michigan commercial smelt production in 1940 was 800,000 kg, but by 1944 production had dropped to zero. The almost total mortality of smelt in Lakes Huron and Michigan during the fall and winter of 1942–1943 was referred to as "the smelt disaster," and its cause is still a mystery. After considering many possible explanations, scientists concluded that this disaster had probably been caused by a communicable disease, either bacterial or viral (Van Oosten 1947). The smelt population rebounded to a high of almost 1.4 million kg in the 1957–1958 period, and dropped to several hundred thousand kilograms yearly from the early 1960s to the present. Smelt production in 1974 was reported at 152,630 kg and valued at $15,301—the largest catch since 1969. The harvest was primarily from Green Bay and off Manitowoc and Kewaunee counties. Pound nets were used during spring spawning runs and they accounted for 86% of the 1974 catch. Smelt production in recent years has been related more to market conditions than to relative abundance (Wis. Dep. Nat. Resour. 1976c).

In Lake Superior no significant commercial landings of smelt were reported until 1952, when 20,400 kg were taken in United States waters. Commercial production of smelt in Wisconsin waters of Lake Superior was 281,000 kg in 1963 and 217,000 kg in 1974 (King and Swanson 1975).

In spite of its many positive attributes, the smelt has had its antagonists. Commercial fishermen claim that the smelt have driven out the lake herring, the lake whitefish, and the lake trout. There is no evidence, however, that these species constitute a significant item in the diet of the smelt. Schneberger (1937b) reported that stomach analyses had been made on 200 smelt taken within 0.4 to 0.8 km of the reefs where approximately 500,000 lake trout fry had been planted 2 days previously. The smelt had eaten *Mysis* and smelt; no lake trout fry were found in the smelt stomachs.

Berst and Spangler (1973) noted that when smelt populations of Lake Huron underwent an explosion in the late 1930s and early 1940s, the production of lake trout, whitefish, ciscoes, and chubs began a major decline. In the winter of 1942–1943 the smelt population of Lake Huron collapsed. The following spring saw the emergence of the greatest year class of whitefish ever recorded for Lake Huron. "It is obvious that the larger smelt populations prior to 1942 were utilizing vast quantities of food organisms near the base of the production pyramid. We suspect that in the virtual absence of the smelt population following the die-off of 1942–43, populations of whitefish and ciscoes may have capitalized on this large reservoir of available energy" (Berst and Spangler 1973:32). Similarly, Anderson and Smith (1971a) rejected overfishing as the primary cause of the post-1961 collapse of the lake herring in Lake Superior, and concluded that competition for food with the smelt was the probable cause of the decline.

An earlier summary relative to this controversy was expressed by Hubbs and Lagler (1964:57): "Relationships of smelt to other species of commercial importance, such as the lake trout, are as yet little understood. The smelt is known to be a predator, it is also eaten by large fish. Whether it does more good than harm in the economy of a lake is not known."

Mudminnow Family—Umbridae

One species of mudminnow occurs in Wisconsin, but four species in three genera are known from the United States and Canada (Robins et al. 1980). Although best represented by the North American species, they are considered of European ancestry. They are known from the Lower Eocene in Europe and Oligocene in North America.

The mudminnows are characteristic inhabitants of small bog lakes, shallow muddy ponds, and slow-moving, vegetated streams. They are small fishes with rounded caudal fins, short snouts, and somewhat flattened heads. The pectoral fins are small to large and fanlike; the pelvic fins, small and abdominal. Mudminnows have a functional duct from the pharynx to the swim bladder and are capable of breathing atmospheric oxygen.

Central Mudminnow

Umbra limi (Kirtland). *Umbra*—a shade, or dark, possibly referring to its habitat (they were once thought to inhabit caves); *limi*—mud.

Other common names: western mudminnow, mud minnow, Mississippi mudminnow, mudfish, dogfish.

Male 98 mm (top), female 99 mm (bottom), Hemlock Cr. (Wood Co.), 6 Apr. 1974

DESCRIPTION

Body robust, almost round in cross section anteriorly. Average length 60 mm (2.4 in). Depth into TL 4.9–7.0. Head into TL 3.8–4.9; top of head, cheeks and opercles scaled. Snout short and blunt. Maxillary extending to anterior edge of pupil. Lower jaw protrudes slightly. Mouth medium; groove of upper lip interrupted, not extending over tip of snout. Small villiform teeth on premaxillary, lower jaws and roof of mouth. Gill rakers 13–15, short and stout. Branchiostegal rays 4–5. Scales large, cycloid; lateral series 34–37, lateral line absent. Lateral line canals present on head (Schwartz and Hasler 1966b). Dorsal fin rays 13–15; anal fin rays 7–9; pectoral fin rays 14–16; pelvic fin rays 6–7; all fins rounded on free edge. Osteology discussed by Dineen and Stokely (1954). Chromosomes 2n = 22 (Roberts 1967).

Back and sides dark olive green to brown-black, mottled with up to 14 distinct to vague dark brown vertical bars; belly yellow to white. A prominent vertical black bar at base of tail; fins brownish.

Sexual dimorphism: Male with long anal fin, almost reaching base of caudal fin; female with short anal fin, not reaching base of caudal fin. Anal fin of male developing a bluish green coloration, especially intense during the breeding season.

DISTRIBUTION, STATUS, AND HABITAT

The central mudminnow occurs throughout Wisconsin, although it is less commonly distributed in the southwestern quarter of the state than elsewhere. It is common to abundant in many marshes, ditches, and streams.

This species is associated with moderately to densely vegetated waters. Plant types recorded are cattail, waterweed, eel grass, bullrush, pondweed, yellow water lily, water buttercup, and filamentous algae. In a number of Wisconsin collections it occurred in some bog lakes, but was more commonly distributed in streams as follows: streams 1–3 m wide, 46%; 3.1–6.0 m, 19%; 6.1–12.0 m, 13%; 12.1–24.0 m, 13%; 24.1–50.0 m, 10%. Bottom materials most commonly associated with it were gravel (24%), sand (22%), silt (18%), mud (15%), rubble (8%), boulders (6%), and detritus (5%). The central mudminnow prefers pools or areas lacking water flow, tolerates slow or moderately flowing water, and avoids fast water. It has been most commonly encountered in water up to 0.5 m deep; it is less common in deeper water. In Wisconsin it prefers clear water, light to dark brown in color, and is less frequent where turbidity is high.

BIOLOGY

Numerous literature references indicate upstream migrations of the mudminnow prior to spawning, many of these lateral into overflow ponds. In Dodge County waters, migrations occur during March and April, but spent females do not appear until after 20 April (H. Neuenschwander, pers. comm.).

Spawning occurs at a water temperature of 12.8°C (55°F), and possibly at temperatures up to 15.6°C (60°F). The breeding season is correlated with the flooding of adjacent areas. The rise in water temperature and forming of suitable breeding habitats act as stimuli for spawning (Peckham and Dineen 1957). Areas of overflow provide excellent breeding grounds for adults and protected habitats for the young. The eggs, adhesive and demersal, are deposited singly on leaves of plants and no nest building occurs. In Indiana, spawning is completed by 29 April (Peckham and Dineen 1957), but in southeastern Wisconsin Cahn (1927) noted no spawning after 12 April.

Egg production is from 425 to 450 eggs per female

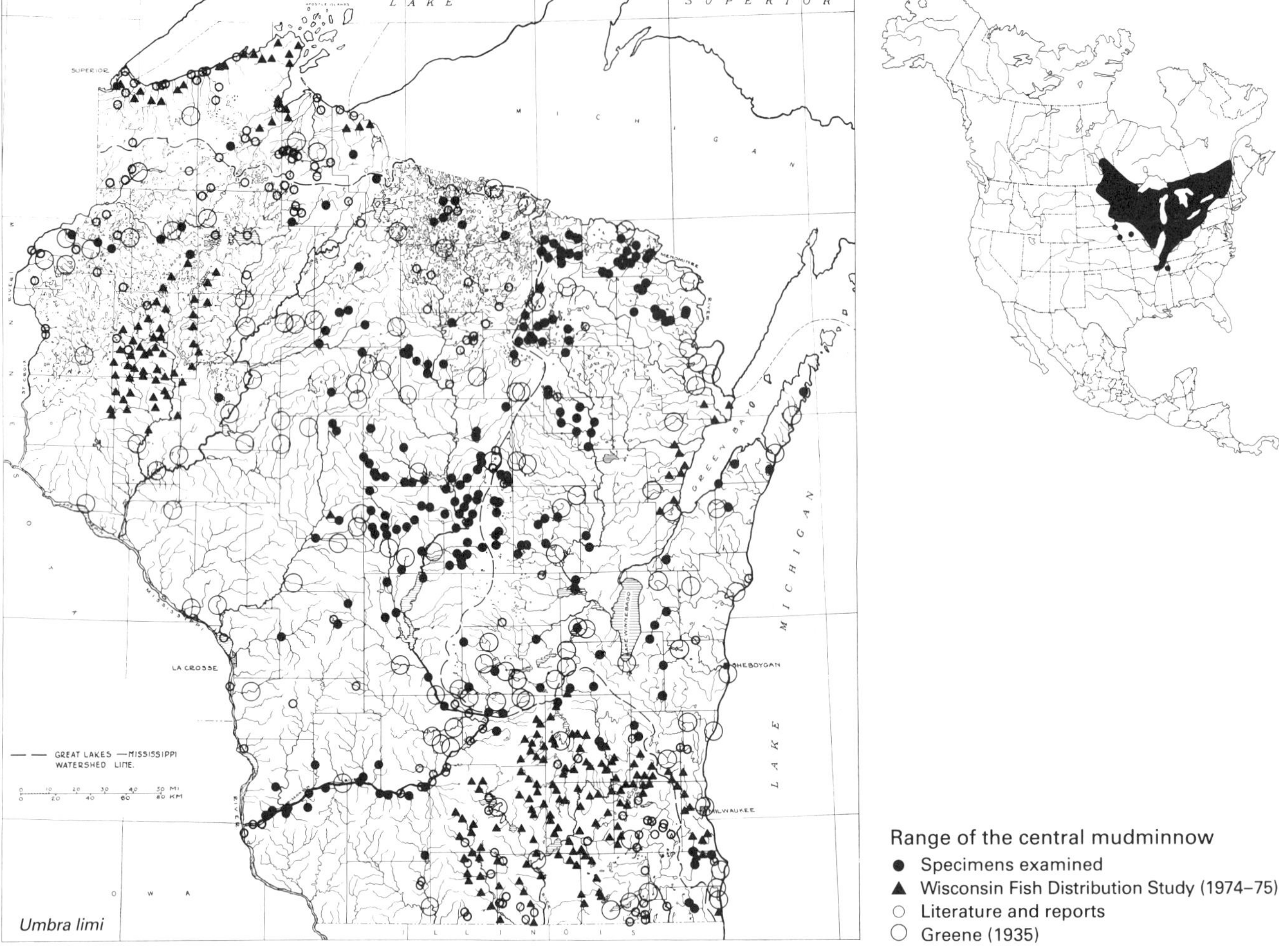

Range of the central mudminnow
● Specimens examined
▲ Wisconsin Fish Distribution Study (1974–75)
○ Literature and reports
◯ Greene (1935)

(Evermann and Clark 1920). Westman (1938) noted that in the central mudminnow the guarding female will pick out and devour undeveloped eggs. Eggs are yellow or orange colored, about 1.6 mm diam. The transparent fry is 5 mm long when it emerges on the sixth day (Langlois 1941). By the 16th day the fry becomes pigmented and dark. Fish (1932) described the 24.75 mm stage; the embryonic development of the related eastern mudminnow (*Umbra pygmaea*) was pictured by Mansueti and Hardy (1967).

Up to the time they are 25 mm (1 in) long the young have a notochordal lobe above the developing caudal fin, similar to that in gars. This may help orient the fish before feeble movement is possible with the poorly developed fins. The young move from the breeding areas back to the main stream when they are about 30 mm (1.2 in) long (Scott and Crossman 1973).

In southern Wisconsin young-of-year are 28 mm long in late June, 35 mm by 15 July, 39 mm by 29 July, 43 mm by 12 August, and 55 mm by October; in northern Wisconsin they are 23 mm by mid-July and 41 mm by the beginning of September.

The scales of the central mudminnow are not adapted to age determination, since the circuli are roughly longitudinal in relation to the antero-posterior axis and characteristic annuli are absent. The opercula and otoliths are useful in the aging process. A sample of mudminnows (UWSP 531) collected 11 July 1966 from an unnamed creek in Langlade County was aged from otoliths (F. Hagstrom, pers. comm.):

Age Class	No. of Fish	TL (mm)		Calculated TL at Annulus (mm)			
		Avg	Range	1	2	3	4
0	1	23					
I	4	42.8	31.3–64.5	37.0			
II	39	54.5	41.1–71.5	39.3	51.3		
III	17	66.7	49.3–83.5	49.4	59.9	65.5	
IV	3	79	71.9–89.2	57.9	65.1	73.8	79.0
Avg (weighted)				42.8	54.5	66.7	79.0

A Wisconsin specimen in the UWSP Museum is 120 mm (4.7 in) long. Trautman (1957) reported this species up to 132 mm (5.2 in). In ponds near Okauchee Lake (Waukesha County), Cahn (1927) reported mudminnows up to 140 mm (5.5 in).

In Wisconsin the growth rate of central mudminnows is similar to the growth exhibited in Indiana (Peckham and Dineen 1957), New York (Westman 1941), and Michigan (Applegate 1943). Scott and Crossman (1973) suggested that mudminnows live at least to 7 or 9 years of age, basing this calculation on known-age fish and expected yearly increments.

The mudminnow is primarily a bottom feeder. In Indiana (Peckham and Dineen 1957), young mudminnows (19 mm long) had eaten newly hatched snails; *Physa* was the predominant molluscan in the diet. Chironomids, copepods, ostracods, and cladocerans were the principal food items of the young-of-year. Adults selected chironomids, mayflies, caddisflies, and mollusks as their chief foods. A few fish were eaten by the mudminnows, but plant material appeared to be incidental in their diet. One blacknose dace (30 mm) was found in the stomach of an 80 mm mudminnow, and two unidentified fish were found in the stomach of an 85 mm mudminnow. Mudminnow scales were common in the mudminnow stomachs.

Stomach analyses by various researchers have shown that the digestive tracts of mudminnows contained the following average percentages of food and other items: insects, 45.6; amphipods, 11.1; entomostracans, 16.3; mollusks, 12.3; arachnids, 0.16; plants, 7.1; surface drift, 4.6; algae, 1.4; miscellaneous, 1.24; and silt, 0.2 (Dobie et al. 1948). Stasiak (1972) found the pharyngeal teeth of minnows in the digestive tracts of several large mudminnows. Cahn (1927) found particles of *Hydra* in the intestine.

The mudminnow is a very slow swimmer and lies concealed in mud or vegetation much of the time. The prey is attacked with a sudden rush (Keast and Webb 1966). In an Indiana study a higher percent of the stomachs contained food in winter than in any other season, and, as in other species, many were empty during the breeding season (Peckham and Dineen 1957).

The central mudminnow is sensitive to disturbances of the water that affect deeper water layers and produce a water displacement surface. A single drop of water, falling from a height of 5 cm, produced surface waves strong enough to release a response in a fish 69–74 cm away (Schwartz and Hasler 1966a). The fish swam toward the stimulus initially at a maximum speed of 10.2–13 cm/sec decreasing to about 3 cm/sec; the reaction ended after moving about 4.5 cm. Fright reactions are sometimes carried out much faster and over longer distances, often 40–50 cm. Schwartz and Hasler assumed that the ability to perceive ripples on the water aided in detecting prey. The mudminnow responds to water currents as small as 1.6 mm/sec.

On the mudminnow's habits, Eddy and Underhill (1974:197) wrote:

> . . . The mudminnow is rarely seen by the average fisherman because it lives in waters rarely frequented by panfish and game fish, and it is difficult to seine. . . . Students at the Lake Itasca Forestry and Biological Station carried out mark-and-recapture studies on the mudminnows in some roadside ditches which provided optimum conditions for seining and which did not give the fish an opportunity to migrate. They observed mudminnows diving into the mud and detritus near the margins of the ditches but could not capture them with either seine or dip nets. However, once the water had become stirred up and turbid, the fish could be taken in the seines. After five weeks of daily sampling the students were still capturing unmarked mudminnows.

Mudminnows have usually been described in early reports as burrowing quickly into the mud, tail first, to escape predation or to survive drought conditions, and as hibernating in the mud in winter. Later observations show that they do flee into the thick detritus and flocculent ooze, but do not burrow into the mud (Scott and Crossman 1973). During the winter the fish remain active in the vegetation under the ice. According to Schneberger (pers. comm.) they are usually able to escape the effect of fish toxicants used to eradicate fish populations.

In Wisconsin the mudminnow is one of the hardiest fishes and has been found in ponds where the oxygen concentration is very low. Eddy and Underhill (1974) reported that it has been found in ponds where the oxygen concentration was less than 1 ppm. The mudminnow has both alveoli and gas absorbing and secreting organs in the swim bladder, and when oxygen levels in the water are insufficient to meet its needs, it gulps air at the surface (Lagler et al. 1977). It is often the only species to survive a severe winter kill and is capable of utilizing air bubbles under the ice. Reportedly it can be superficially frozen in ice and will revive upon thawing (Hubbs and Lagler 1964).

The mudminnow is also able to survive high water temperatures in pools which become isolated, stagnant, and as warm as 28.9°C (84°F) in August (Scott and Crossman 1973). However, a water temperature of 38°C (100.4°F) in a shallow Michigan pond caused appreciable mortality in this species (Bailey 1955). Some of these characteristics help to explain why the mudminnow is often the only species of fish inhabiting swamps, shallow ponds, and bog pools.

In central Wisconsin's Buena Vista Marsh, where considerable channelization has occurred, this species is common, particularly in old ditches and in newly ditched areas. The greatest numbers (more than 3,000 in a 200-m sector) occurred in an old downstream ditch where the mudminnow was the most common species (Headrick 1976). There it was taken from beneath undercut banks—cover which was absent from new downstream ditches and natural streams. Data for upstream study areas (whether natural or ditched) showed no consistent preference.

Central mudminnows and associate species in a collection from Pedro Creek (Menominee County) were: central mudminnow (23), northern redbelly dace (135), pearl dace (43), brook stickleback (43), white sucker (30), brassy minnow (23), golden shiner (12), common shiner (11), fathead minnow (5), black bullhead (2), johnny darter (1), and creek chub (1). In Drew Creek (Langlade County), 74 central mudminnows were taken along with blacknose dace (158), mottled sculpin (51), white sucker (32), creek chub (20), longnose dace (16), northern redbelly dace (14), brook stickleback (3), common shiner (5), and finescale dace (1). In the outlet of Williams Lake (Marquette County), 46 central mudminnows were taken with Iowa darter (8), largemouth bass (3), fathead minnow (2), and black bullhead (numerous fry in several schools).

IMPORTANCE AND MANAGEMENT

Mudminnows are preyed on by a variety of larger stream forms, including grass pickerel, chain pickerel, northern pike, sunfishes, and catfishes; many are devoured by birds, muskrats, and foxes. In one study (Peckham and Dineen 1957) the chief predator was the mottled sculpin: the stomach of a 111-mm male contained a 72-mm female mudminnow with eggs; a 102-mm sculpin had eaten a 65-mm female. Hence some potential young are lost to predation by sculpins.

The central mudminnow is used extensively as a bait minnow in Wisconsin and other states where it is plentiful, because it is able to live for a long time in the bait bucket as well as on the hook. In southern Wisconsin it is a preferred bait for walleyes. There is considerable disagreement as to its value as a bait fish because of its drab appearance compared to a shiner minnow. Good fishermen, however, maintain its excellence. It is used for taking bass and northern pike, and is a good bait to have in one's minnow pail. Its dark color, which is thought by some to render it unsuitable as bait, may be brightened somewhat by keeping the fish over a light background in bright light (Hubbs and Lagler 1964).

The mudminnow is a fish of considerable beauty and makes an attractive, interesting aquarium fish. It is easily taught to take small pieces of meat, earthworm, or cereal.

Although dredging, draining, and increased turbidity may have eliminated suitable habitats in much of its range (Trautman 1957), in Wisconsin this species is among the first to enter such newly created habitats, provided that the turbidity is only temporary. In many areas, man's activities have resulted in the expansion of its range.

Pike Family—Esocidae

Three species of pike occur in Wisconsin. The family includes five species in one genus. One species, the northern pike, occurs in North America, Europe, and northern Asia; one species is endemic to Siberia; and three are endemic to eastern North America. Although best represented by four species in North America, this family is of Eurasian ancestry. In the Old World it is known from the Middle Eocene; in North America it is known from the Pliocene.

The body is elongate and the head is much depressed anteriorly; it is often said to be duckbilled. The jaws and mouth are well armed with teeth. Intermuscular bones are forked or Y-shaped. A single dorsal soft-rayed fin is positioned far back on the body.

All pike are fish eaters and highly predacious; the stomachs are long and the intestines short. Two species, the northern pike and the muskellunge, are among the largest carnivorous fish in Wisconsin and are much sought after by sport fishermen.

Grass Pickerel

Esox americanus vermiculatus Lesueur. *Esox*—an old European name for the pike; *americanus*—from America; *vermiculatus*—vermiculated, alluding to the wavy bars of the color pattern.

Other common names: western grass pickerel, mud pickerel, little pickerel, pickerel, central redfin pickerel, grass pike, mud pike, slough pickerel.

Adult 190 mm, Richland Cr. (Crawford Co.), 11 July 1962

DESCRIPTION

Body elongate, cylindrical, almost round in cross section. Average length 203 mm (8 in). Depth into TL 5.7–8.3. Head into TL 3.2–3.8; top of head unscaled, cheeks and opercles fully scaled. Snout short, into head length 2.4–2.7; snout flattened dorso-ventrally and concave on top. Mouth large, maxillary usually not reaching beyond middle of pupil. Large canine teeth in lower jaws, flattened to rear. Sensory pores on undersurface of lower jaw 4 (3–5 on each side). Gill rakers reduced to sharp, toothlike structures. Branchiostegal rays 12 (10–14). Scales cycloid, lateral line scales 97–118, usually fewer than 110; lateral line complete. Principal dorsal fin rays 12–13; principal anal fin rays 11–12; pectoral fin rays 14–15; pelvic fin rays 9–10; all of these fins rounded on edge; caudal fin forked. Chromosomes 2n = 50 (Beamish et al. 1971).

Olive- or yellow-brown dorsally; sides barred or mottled with darker browns, barred pattern more regular above lateral line, irregular mottling below. A distinct dark brown to black teardrop below eye. Fins clear to lightly pigmented. In young-of-year (20–75 mm), a distinctive pigment-free line below the lateral line extending from snout to tail. In older young, body pattern consists of dark, reticulated markings against a light background. [See Kleinert and Mraz (1966) for the distinction between immature grass pickerel and northern pike.]

Hybrids: Four natural hybrids of grass pickerel and northern pike were taken from Rice Creek, T42N R6E Secs 7 and 8 (Vilas County), 19–23 April 1971 (UWSP 3983-6). These specimens are 464–585 mm TL (690–1670 g) and in age-groups IV or V. Their coloration is similar to that of the grass pike: 33–39 narrow, oblique, light-colored body bands (some beaded) alternating with broader, dark brown bars. Below the lateral line, markings are more mottled and less regular. The lower half of the opercle is scaled anteriorly, the scaled portion often describing a diagonal from the midposterior edge of the opercle to the base of its anterior edge. The mandibular sensory pores are 4 (seldom 5). The subocular (teardrop) bars are faint to absent. The descriptions follow Schwartz (1962) and McCarraher (1960). For additional details, see Serns and McKnight (1977).

A similar hybrid has been reported from the East Fork Raccoon Creek, T1N R12E Sec 31 (Rock County) (Wis. Fish Distrib. Study 1974). The grass pickerel × northern pike hybrid is infertile. Artificial grass pickerel × muskellunge have been produced in Ohio (Tennant and Billy 1963).

DISTRIBUTION, STATUS, AND HABITAT

The grass pickerel occurs in the lower Wisconsin, Rock, Fox, and Des Plaines river systems of the Mississippi drainage. In the Mississippi River it has been reported from southern Vernon County downstream (P. W. Smith et al. 1971). The records from the Menomonee and Root river systems of the Lake Michigan basin are all old (Greene 1935), and it is doubtful that this species persists there any longer. The recent northern occurrences in Vilas County (Partridge, High, and Fishtrap lakes) and Oneida County (Minocqua Thoroughfare, connecting Minocqua and Tomahawk Lakes) are isolated and may be accidental introductions from the fish transfer operations of the early 1940s. [See Kleinert and Mraz (1966) for additional distribution details.]

Two possible entry routes of the grass pickerel into Wisconsin are indicated: from the Mississippi River, through the Des Plaines, Fox, and Rock rivers; or from southern Lake Michigan (Becker 1976). Greene (1935) noted that its habit of spawning in shallow flood waters favors its chances of crossing low divides such as those between the Root and Des Plaines rivers and between the Menomonee and lower Fox rivers.

The grass pickerel is common in lakes and sluggish waters of extreme southeastern Wisconsin, except in the streams of the Lake Michigan basin, from which it has been extirpated. It is common in the lower Wisconsin River and uncommon in the Mississippi River. It appears to have extended its range in recent years.

This species prefers quiet water (lakes and sloughs), but it has occasionally been taken from fast currents in small streams. I have found it in streams of the

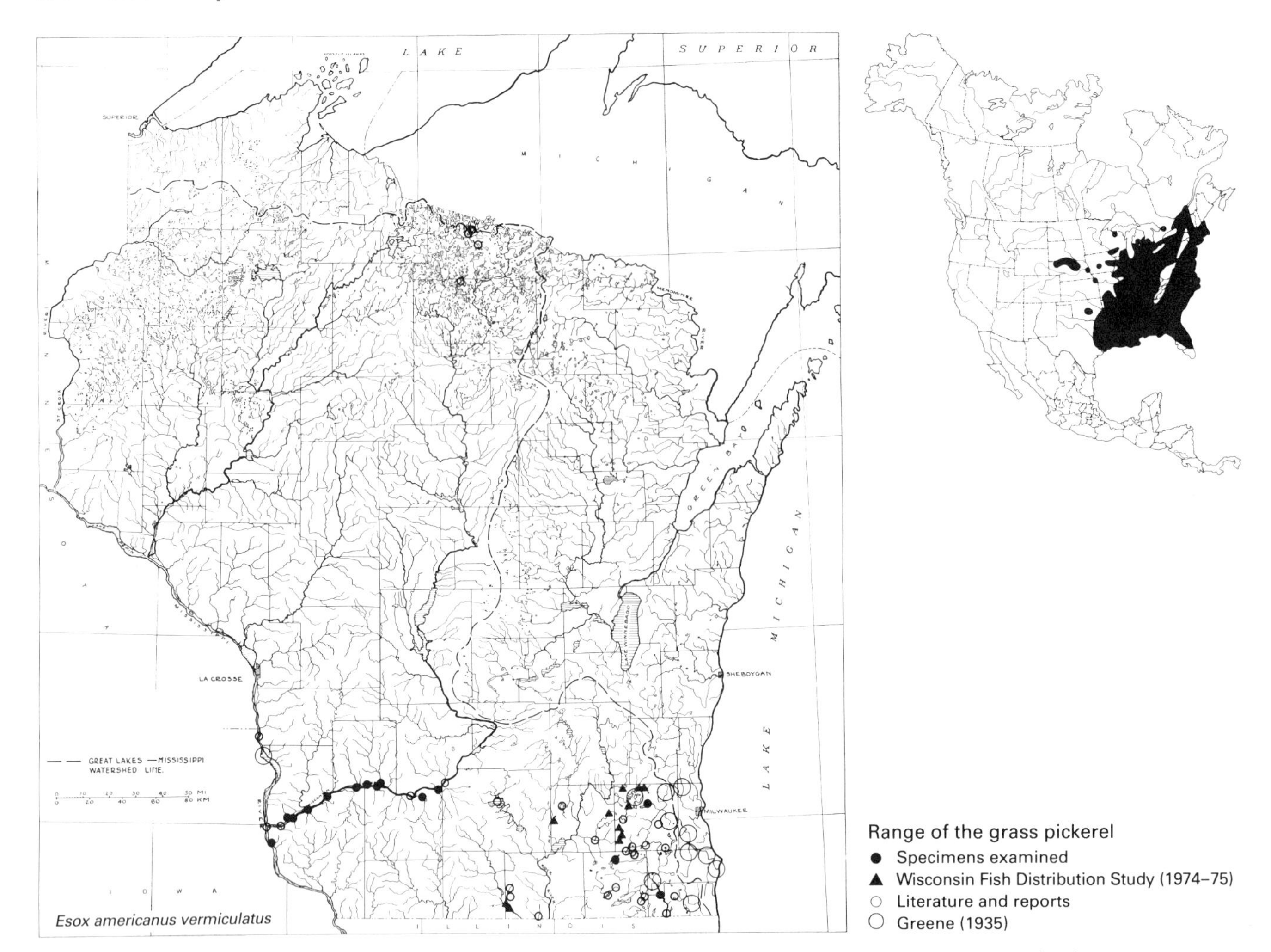

Esox americanus vermiculatus

following widths: 1.0–3.0 m (11%), 3.1–6.0 m (44%), 6.1–12.0 m (22%), and 12.1–24.0 m (22%). The frequency of substrates encountered were sand (21%), gravel (21%), mud (17%), clay (13%), rubble (13%), silt (8%), and boulders (8%). The grass pickerel has appeared in clear to turbid water; highest population densities occur in shallow, weedy locations (Kleinert and Mraz 1966), containing such plants as leafy liverworts, water lilies, pondweeds, filamentous algae, and broadleaf cattails. I have encountered small populations of this species in sand-bottomed backwaters, sloughs, and landlocked pools of the lower Wisconsin River which were virtually devoid of all types of vegetation. In southeastern Wisconsin Cahn (1927) noted that the grass pickerel is present where the water has been muddied by carp activity, is normally 0.6 m deep, and is slow and sluggish but not stagnant, with a bottom mixture of sand and mud.

BIOLOGY

Spawning occurs mainly in the spring (March–April) immediately after the ice goes out at temperatures of 4.4–11.7°C (40–53°F). No nest is built; the eggs are broadcast and abandoned, settling and adhering to vegetation. The spawning in Pleasant Lake (Walworth County) was described by Kleinert and Mraz (1966:18):

> Water in the East Bay slough warms before the lake in early spring, and pickerel aggregate as soon as the ice begins to recede. Spawning takes place almost immediately and continues for approximately two weeks, as evidenced by the presence of ripe pickerel in the area and the presence of eggs on the bottom. Although pickerel are most numerous in the slough at spawning time, a few can be seen scattered about the other shorelines and bays, suggesting that spawning occurs in many locations. However, eggs and fry are abundant only in the slough and are difficult to find elsewhere in the lake.
>
> During the spawning period pickerel were most often seen in groups of two to six or more fish in the few inches of water bordering the margin of the slough. Females could often be identified at sight by their bulging abdomens. Pickerel were wary at this time, darting into deeper water when approached by an observer. Numerous attempts were made to observe the spawning behavior during the three springs of the study; however, cloudy weather, wind

and the wariness of the fish prevented observation of the spawning act.

Evidence of a second, low intensity spawning period, occurring in summer or fall, was reported by Lagler and Hubbs (1943), who collected young in Michigan in November of 1941 comparable in size to young collected in June. Scott and Crossman (1973) postulated that changing water temperatures (upward in spring, downward in fall), not just the increase in temperature, are the stimuli for spawning. The capture in May of large fingerlings (31.5 and 37 mm) from Pleasant Lake, along with small fingerlings (6.5–17 mm) which had hatched a few days previously, made Kleinert and Mraz (1966) suspect that the former were fall-hatched fingerlings.

A combined sample of nine females was caught in Pleasant (Walworth County) and Rock (Jefferson County) lakes on 30 March 1963, just prior to spawning. Counts of the mature eggs in the ovaries ranged from 843 for a 160-mm (6.3-in) fish to 4,584 for a 325-mm (12.8-in) fish. Mature eggs were clear, yellow amber in color, and from 1.5 to 2.4 mm diam in contrast to the smaller, white opaque immature eggs also contained in the ovary. In September and October clear, yellow amber eggs similar to mature eggs were seen in less than 28% of the females from a number of southeastern Wisconsin lakes. These females averaged 254 mm (10 in) TL; females with only white, immature eggs averaged 196 mm (7.7 in) long (Kleinert and Mraz 1966).

Eggs hatch in 11–15 days at water temperatures of 7.8–8.9°C (46–48°F). The young, at this time 6.2 mm long, are inactive. They remain near the bottom, possibly attached to vegetation, and live from 10 to 14 days on the yolk (Scott and Crossman 1973). In Wisconsin, early growth in different years appears to be similar and it is rapid; 6.5–11.5 mm on 24 April, 10–17 mm on 9 May, 25–29 mm on 25 May, and 31–49 mm on 3 June (Kleinert and Mraz 1966). [In Illinois young had grown to a length of 51–64 mm by 25 May (Richardson 1913).] The average length of fingerlings caught in three September surveys was 127 mm (5 in).

Scale analysis of a combined sample of 280 pickerel from Pleasant, Upper Phantom, Beulah, Pickerel, Ripley, and Eagle Spring lakes indicates average lengths at different ages as: 0—145 mm (5.7 in); I—208 mm (8.2 in); II—251 mm (9.9 in); III—287 mm (11.3 in); and IV—356 mm (14.0 in). Females are longer than males at ages 0, I, and II; no males of age III or older were encountered, providing further evidence that females exceed males in growth and longevity (Kleinert and Mraz 1966).

Both yearling males and females can be sexed in the spring. The males showed milt and the females ripe eggs at spawning time, indicating that both sexes mature at age I (Kleinert and Mraz 1966).

The species is small in size; fish exceeding 305 mm (12 in) are rare. Among pickerel measured at Pleasant Lake, only 10% exceeded 254 mm (10 in) and less than 1% exceeded 305 mm (12 in) (Kleinert and Mraz 1966). The largest known grass pickerel from Wisconsin is a 5-year-old, 376-mm, 352-g (14.8-in, 12.4-oz) female (ROM 32061) taken from Rice Creek (Vilas County) (Serns and McKnight 1977). Trautman (1957) recorded the maximum size as 381 mm (15 in) and 397 g (14 oz).

In a Wisconsin study, food of pickerel 9.5–15 mm long consisted principally of cladocerans, copepods, and occasionally ostracods; food of pickerel 15–40 mm long included cladocerans and copepods with tendipedid larvae, Odonata nymphs, and fish (Kleinert and Mraz 1966). Zooplankters were rarely found in fish 40–80 mm long; their diet was almost entirely tendipedid larvae, Odonata and ephemerid nymphs, small fish, and scuds (*Hyalella* spp.). Three species of fish were found in fingerling pickerel stomachs: blackchin shiners, lake chubsuckers, and smaller pickerel. Of 104 grass pickerel 152–343 mm (6–13.5 in) TL from Pleasant Lake, Lower Phantom Lake, Pickerel Lake, and Beulah Lake, 93 contained fish, 7 contained dragonfly nymphs, and 2 contained crayfish. Small bluegills and pumpkinseeds were the predominant fish eaten, followed by bluntnose minnows and blackchin shiners. Certain grass pickerel showed a capacity to ingest very large food fish: a 102-mm (4-in) bluegill was found in the stomach of a 244-mm (9.6-in) pickerel, and a 76-mm (3-in) perch was found in a 198-mm (7.8-in) pickerel. The fish-eating inclination begins early for some individuals—a large fingerling 37 mm (1.5 in) long held 13 young-of-year 6.5–11.5 mm long in its stomach.

In an Ontario creek (Crossman 1962), 22 species of fishes were present, but grass pickerel fed on only 9 species in this descending order of importance: central mudminnow, golden shiner, grass pickerel, white sucker, pumpkinseed, common shiner, creek chub, yellow perch, and johnny darter.

The grass pickerel feeds mostly in the late afternoon or early evening; little feeding occurs at night.

Scott and Crossman (1973) reported the grass pickerel's lower tolerance level for oxygen concentration as 0.3–0.4 ppm in Michigan. The range of pH in Canadian habitats is 6.26–8.32. The final preferred temperature has been experimentally determined as 25.6°C (78°F); maximum temperatures of some habitats are as high as 28.9°C (84°F), and cruising speed has been demonstrated experimentally to increase with increased acclimation temperature. The grass pickerel is adapted to high temperatures, enabling it to be successful during drastic decreases in the water level and the minimum flow typical of its habitat. Young-of-year live in the shallows along the shore, but older fish are found in the deeper portions of the streams and ponds.

Failure of year classes has been traced to declining water levels which strand many fingerlings and adults in slough nursery areas (Kleinert and Mraz 1966). Further, in winter the remaining water in the slough is depleted of oxygen, eliminating any surviving pickerel. However, it can become abundant in a lake environment; there was an estimated maximum fall population level in Pleasant Lake (Walworth County) of 3.92 kg/ha (3.5 lb/acre).

In Glass Lake slough (near Bagley, Grant County) of the Mississippi River fish species associated with 4 grass pickerel were: longnose gar (1), gizzard shad (32), bigmouth buffalo (2), spotted sucker (4), white sucker (1), golden shiner (76), pugnose minnow (4), spotfin shiner (2), spottail shiner (32), weed shiner (1), tadpole madtom (4), northern pike (5), white bass (3), yellow bass (3), yellow perch (36), walleye (8), logperch (6), johnny darter (1), mud darter (1), largemouth bass (112), bluegill (2), black crappie (509), white crappie (6), and brook silverside (28). In Indian Creek (Richland County) the following association of fish appeared: grass pickerel (3), lake chubsucker (1), white sucker (13), central stoneroller (368), blacknose dace (13), creek chub (244), southern redbelly dace (21), bluntnose minnow (35), suckermouth minnow (1), bigmouth shiner (23), brassy minnow (1), Mississippi silvery minnow (3), northern pike (2), johnny darter (173), and rainbow darter (1).

The relationship of the grass pickerel to northern pike has intrigued fishery biologists and managers. These species were stocked prior to spawning in three Delafield ponds at the ratio of approximately three pickerel to one northern pike (Kleinert and Mraz 1966). When the ponds were drained in September a greater number of pickerel fingerlings were in one pond, a greater number and poundage of northern pike fingerlings were in the second pond, and northern pike fingerlings and adults remained in the third pond, with no surviving pickerel. Northern pike brood fish showed a higher April-to-September survival in two ponds; both species showed similar survival percentages in one pond. Also, evidence supported Crossman's (1962) observations that grass pickerel apparently move infrequently and for only short distances to hunt for food or shelter.

Since grass pickerel are sometimes abundant in lakes where northern pike populations are low, it has been theorized that competition between northern pike and grass pickerel may deplete the northern pike population. Kleinert and Mraz (1966) could not document such competition, however. Observations of the grass pickerel and northern pike association at Pleasant Lake showed that these species shared similar spawning times and locations and that the time required for hatching and development to the feeding stage was similar for both species when hatched and held at the Delafield station.

Trautman (1957) noted, however, that there seems to be a marked interspecific competition between the grass pickerel and other species of pikes, for the grass pickerel was rare or absent in any locality where another species of pike was abundant.

IMPORTANCE AND MANAGEMENT

Grass pickerel are eaten by catfishes, sunfishes, yellow perch, and by grass pickerel themselves. Large fingerlings and adult grass pickerel cannibalize pickerel smaller than themselves.

The fisherman's interest in this species is small because the overall size of the fish is insufficient for the pan. It is usually mistaken for the young of the northern pike and returned to the water to "grow up." It will take baited hooks, however, and can provide enjoyable sport on very light tackle.

Among those fishermen recognizing the species, the prevalent notion is that grass pickerel are "verminous" and a nuisance fish which should be discarded. It is of no importance in the commercial and sport fishery of the Mississippi River (Barnickol and Starrett 1951).

The grass pickerel makes a handsome aquarium fish and is easily maintained, but it usually requires live fishes or crayfishes as food.

The grass pickerel may be valuable as a predator since its diet consists almost entirely of fish. Richardson (1913) suggested that grass pickerel fry 51–64 mm TL fed on carp fry, which were less than 16 mm long by 1 June in Illinois. The larval and swim-up fry stages of muskellunge are also highly vulnerable to grass pickerel predation in waters where the two species occur together (A. Oehmcke, pers. comm.).

In samples taken from many Wisconsin locales, the grass pickerel was represented by only a single individual, indicating that its density level may be extremely low. There have been no complaints that this species has reached pest levels. Its role in the aquatic ecosystem appears to be part of the balance of nature, a delicate relationship between predator and prey in which neither harms the other but in which each performs some salutary environmental function.

The assumption prevails that grass pickerel may be detrimental to the northern pike, and Kleinert and Mraz (1966) have suggested that present management efforts should be directed toward preventing the spread of the species.

Grass pickerel and northern pike have been crossed artificially (Schwartz 1962). Muskellunge and grass pickerel have also been artificially hybridized, the resulting hybrids being heavier bodied than the parents. But the desirability of pickerel–northern pike and pickerel-muskellunge hybrids as potential sport fishes has yet to be determined.

Northern Pike

Esox lucius Linnaeus. *Esox*—an old name for the pike in Europe; *lucius*—the supposed Latin name for this species.

Other common names: great northern pike, jack, jackfish, pickerel, great northern pickerel, common pike, snake, snake pickerel.

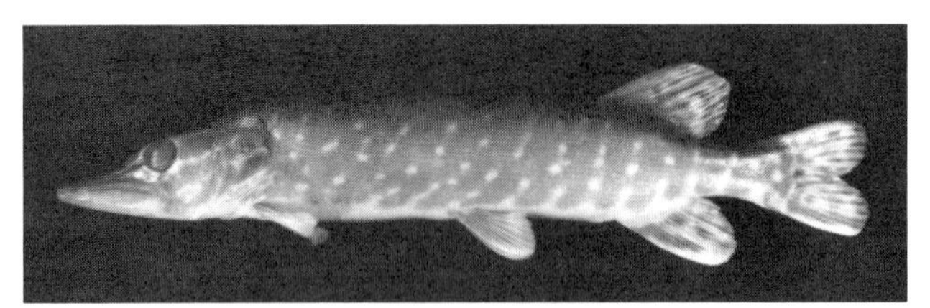

Immature 195 mm, Tomorrow R. (Portage Co.), 7 Aug. 1963

Adult (Wisconsin DNR photo)

DESCRIPTION

Body elongate, cylindrical, almost round in cross section. Average length approximately 508 mm (20 in). Body depth into TL 6.0–9.0. Head length into TL 3.3–4.0; top of head unscaled, cheeks usually fully scaled, opercles usually scaled on top half only. Snout long, into head length 2.1–2.4, but longer than postorbital head length; snout flattened dorso-ventrally, duckbill-like. Mouth large, maxillary usually reaching at least to midpupil. Lower jaw with large, strong canines (peglike posteriorly) and short, sharp, recurved brushlike teeth on roof of mouth and tongue. Sensory pores on undersurface of lower jaw (mandibular pores), usually 5 on each side. Gill rakers reduced to sharp, toothlike structures. Branchiostegal rays 14–16. Scales cycloid, lateral series usually more than 120 (105–148); lateral line complete. Principal dorsal fin rays 15–19; principal anal fin rays 12–15; pectoral fin rays 14–17; pelvic fin rays 10–11; all of these fins rounded on edge; caudal fin moderately forked, tips more rounded than the muskellunge. Chromosomes 2n = 50 (Nygren et al. 1968).

Light to dark olive dorsally, becoming white ventrally; light bean-shaped horizontal markings dispersed in oblique rows on sides; vertical fins commonly orange-yellow. Young northern pike (under 279 mm) with oblique dark bars; fingerlings lack pigment-free line below lateral line which is characteristic of grass pickerel, *E. americanus* (see Kleinert and Mraz 1966). Young solid black-green on back, contrasted with cream-colored stripe on back of muskellunge fingerling.

Sexual dimorphism: In female, many longitudinal folds (convoluted tissue) between urogenital protuberance and anus; in male, urogenital opening associated with slitlike concave, transverse depression, the rim of which is usually level with surrounding tissue and does not show prominently uplifted folds between slit and anus (Casselman 1974).

Hybrids: Northern pike × grass pickerel from Rice Creek (Vilas County) in 1971 and East Fork, Raccoon Creek (Rock County) 1974 (p. 393). Northern pike × muskellunge (tiger muskellunge) (pp. 405, 412).

Mutant: The silver pike is a mutation or "sport" of the northern pike. It is a solid silver or gray color, sometimes flecked with gold, and not marked like the typical northern pike, although the number of scales, fin rays, pores under the jaws, and other features are the same as for the northern pike. In Wisconsin, populations of silver pike have been reported from Bear and Munger lakes (Oconto County) by M. Burdick and T. Thuemler (Biologists, Wis. DNR). (See UWSP 5047.) This variant is also reported from northern Minnesota (Eddy and Surber 1947, Eddy and Underhill 1974), and according to Scott and Crossman (1973) it is now known to occur sporadically throughout the world distribution of the northern pike. It breeds true, and when crossed with muskellunge produces a hybrid similar to that of the muskellunge–northern pike cross, which is speckled like a crappie. It has also been named silver muskellunge, but properly the common name should be silver pike.

DISTRIBUTION, STATUS, AND HABITAT

In Wisconsin the northern pike occurs in the Mississippi River, Lake Michigan, and Lake Superior drainage basins. It is widely distributed throughout the state except in the unglaciated area, where it is sparsely dispersed except in large river systems and impounded areas. It occurs in the shallow waters of Lakes Superior and Michigan, particularly Green Bay.

The northern pike is generally common except in the southeastern quarter of the state, where populations are seriously depressed. It is reportedly absent from the Chippewa River and its lakes above Radisson (Sawyer County). Historically the lakes and rivers of the highlands of northern Wisconsin have been devoid of northern pike, but man-connected activities in recent years have promoted the expansion of the northern pike into most of these lakes.

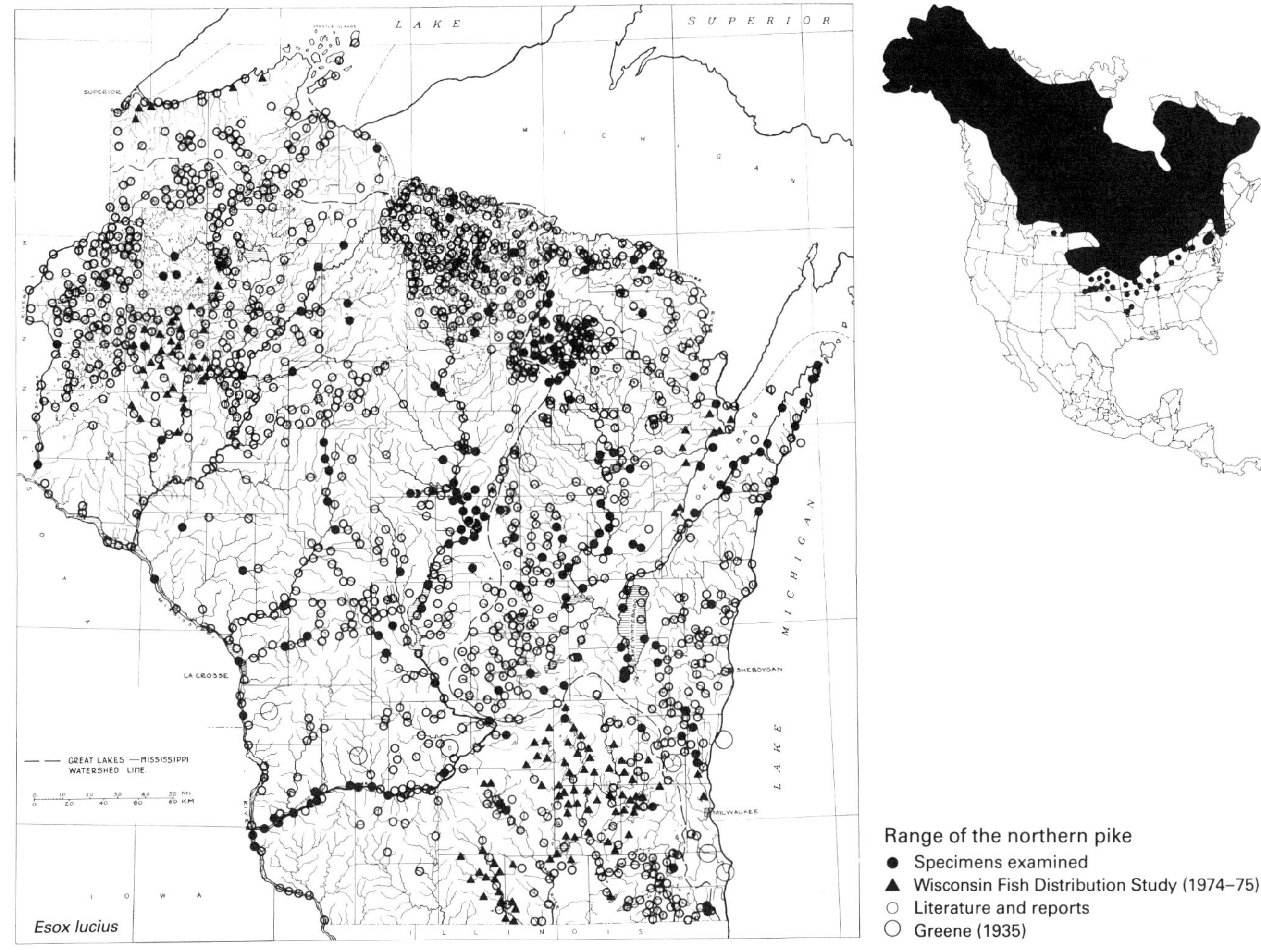

The northern pike inhabits cool to moderately warm weedy lakes, ponds, and sluggish rivers. In a number of Wisconsin collections it is a common resident of most medium- to large-sized lakes with inlet streams. Its frequency in streams of various widths was: 1.0–3.0 m wide, 13%; 3.1–6.0 m, 9%; 6.1–12 m, 14%; 12.1–24.0 m, 30%; 24.0–50.0 m, 27%; and more than 50 m, 7%. In streams it was present in quiet pools to fast currents. Frequencies of substrates reported for this species were sand (27%), mud (21%), gravel (18%), rubble (11%), silt (10%), boulders (9%), detritus (4%), and clay (1%). It is present in areas of light to dense aquatic vegetation, and has been captured over a wide range of turbidity, although it is much more common in clear and only slightly turbid water.

BIOLOGY

Spawning may occur from late March to early April, as soon as the ice begins to break up in the spring. Migrations into the spawning areas take place during the night; the peak of the run is between 2100 and 2400 hr (Franklin and Smith 1963, Carbine 1942). Spawning sites are located in shallow, flooded marshes associated with lakes or with inlet streams to those lakes. Spawning runs into a slough in Minnesota occurred at water temperatures between 1.1 and 4.4°C (34 and 40°F), but 2.2–2.8°C (36–37°F) was the preferred temperature range (Franklin and Smith 1963).

There is general agreement that northern pike congregate in spawning areas a few days before spawning actually occurs. Apparently temperatures, daily light intensity, and the presence of suitable vegetation work together to stimulate spawning. The spawning habitat is basically a flooded area with emergent vegetation. Grasses, sedges, or rushes with fine leaves appear to make the best substrate for egg deposition.

Certain characteristics of the spawning population from Gilbert and Big Cedar lakes (Washington County) were noted by Priegel and Krohn (1975): (1) Males tended to move into and out of the spawning area faster than females. The average sex ratio ranged from 1 female to 2.0–2.3 males. (2) As the run progressed, the average size of males increased; after the peak, their size decreased. The size of female northern pike showed no such trend. (3) Fecundity was roughly proportional to the weight of the female northern pikes sampled. There was an average of 10,300 eggs per pound of fish. (4) Immigration into the spawning areas began in mid-March, with major spawning activity occurring from late March through early April. Peak emigration took place in early April, but continued through early May. In Minnesota, Franklin and Smith (1963) observed spawning only between 1400 and 1800 hr, at surface water temperatures of 11.1–17.2°C (52–63°F).

The spawning act involves a female and from one to three attendant males. Clark (1950) described the spawning act: A spawning group moves slowly; the female is generally slightly in front of the males, but often the males are adjacent to her. Just prior to spawning the group slackens its speed and each male moves into position with its urogenital opening on about the same line as that of the female. Each male curves the caudal portion of its body outward and brings it against the female with a slap. All then dart forward from the spawning site.

Each spawning act is accompanied by the shedding of 5–60 eggs. The actual spawning act takes from 3 to 10 seconds, and is repeated about once a minute for as long as an hour (Breder and Rosen 1966). Priegel and Krohn (1975) noted that after spawning many of the fish had gashes on their bodies and their fins were badly frayed. Some died after spawning.

In the Murphy Flowage (northwestern Wisconsin), Snow (1958) estimated that 600 northern pike will dispense about 9 million eggs. The smallest female contributes about 8,000 and the largest about 100,000 eggs. Due to predation on eggs and the young by insects and other fish, including the northern pike itself, their number is reduced by well over 99% within a few months; only about 18,000 young remain alive by the end of the summer.

Eggs may be deposited in water only 152–254 mm (6–10 in) deep (Threinen and Herman 1958), on vegetation to which they adhere. At deposition the eggs are 2.3–3.2 mm diam, amber, and have no visible oil globules (Kleinert and Mraz 1966). Eggs hatch in 12–14 days, depending upon water temperatures; from 210 to 270 degree-days above 32°F (0°C) are required to bring the embryos to hatching. Water temperatures in nature during egg development usually vary from 7.2 to 15.6°C (45 to 60°F).

Newly hatched northern pike vary from 6.5 to 8 mm. These prolarvae do not have a developed mouth and remain in this stage from 4 to 15 days, quiescent on vegetation or near the bottom (Franklin and Smith 1963). They adhere to vegetation by using a sucker-type membrane on the top of the head. With absorption of the yolk-sac the survival of the young becomes dependent upon the availability of plankton food.

Feeding begins about 10 days after hatching when the fish reach a length of 11–12 mm. As with all species, northern pike young are highly dependent upon plankton pulses when they first hatch; early developing plankton species such as *Polyphemus* are important to their welfare (Threinen et al. 1966). In Minnesota the principal food items taken include cladocerans, copepods, and insects (especially Tendipedidae larvae and Ephemeroptera and Zygoptera nymphs) (Franklin and Smith 1963). Insects become more important in the diet after fish reach a length of 20 mm. Cyclops are replaced by scuds (*Hyalella* spp.) at a fish length of about 45 mm. Small fish soon become part of the northern pike's diet and, after migrating back to the lake, become the preferred food. Among these are darters (most common), bass juveniles, small perch, killifish, silversides, and minnows (*Notropis* spp.).

In Minnesota, the average increment in total length of pike expressed in mm/day was: 0.5 mm—0–20 days; 2.0 mm—20–50 days; 1.0 mm—50–90 days (Franklin and Smith 1963). In Michigan the average daily increase in the length of young pike was 1.8 mm per day during the first 82 days after hatching in 1939 (Carbine 1942). In Gilbert Lake (Washington County, Wisconsin), young northern pike attained an average total length of only 44 mm 54 days after hatching (Priegel and Krohn 1975).

When fingerlings average 20 mm (18–24 days after hatching), they emigrate from the spawning marsh into the lake or river. Spawning marshes function successfully as nurseries only with proper water levels. Water is required in spawning marshes for at least 3 months after egg deposition for the best survival rate.

Growth of the northern pike is especially rapid during the first and second years of life.

In Murphy Flowage of northwestern Wisconsin, northern pike during the second year of life attain lengths of 330–610 mm (13–24 in) (Snow 1958). Average age-III fish are 635 mm (25 in) long, with some as long as 762 mm (30 in). An age-VII fish is about 1.02 m (40 in) long and weighs 8.17–9.07 kg (18–20 lb).

At a length of 457 mm (18 in) a northern pike weighs 600 g (1.32 lb); at 762 mm (30 in), 3,000 g (6.6 lb). The female grows faster and larger than the male.

A male may mature in 1 year, always in 2, and the female matures in 2 years, always in 3. The size at maturity varies. In most lakes, males mature at 406–457 mm (16–18 in), and females at 508–559 mm (20–

Age and Growth (TL in mm) of the Northern Pike in Wisconsin

Age	Northern Wisconsin (Snow 1969)	Sturgeon Bay L. Michigan (Van Engel 1940)	L. Mendota (Dane Co.) (Van Engel 1940)	Plover R. (Portage Co.) (Paragamian 1976)
1	216	190	290	250
2	351	429	541	438
3	442	584	683	586
4	503	676	770	681
5	561	752	856	
6	612	795	922	
7	668	828	963	
8	668		993	
9			988	

22 in) (Threinen et al. 1966). In the Black River near the Onalaska Spillway, ripe males ranged in length from 279 to 864 mm (11 to 34 in), with the majority falling in the 483–711 mm (19–28 in) range; females ranged from 508 to 914 mm (20 to 36 in), with the majority 508–711 mm (20–28 in) (Finke 1966a). In Pool 8 of the Mississippi River, ripe males averaged 617 mm (24.3 in), while ripe females averaged 630 mm (24.8 in) (Wright 1973).

The data indicate that the growth rate of northern pike is decreased by any reduction in oxygen concentration. Below about 3 ppm there is decreased food consumption and decreased food conversion efficiency (Adelman and Smith 1970).

Northern pike usually live about 7 years, although some have approached the age of 25 in nature. In captivity, they have lived to 75 years (Lagler et al. 1977).

The northern pike is one of our larger fishes, and every year fish in the 4.5–9.1-kg (10–20-lb) class are caught. A 17.2-kg (38-lb) fish was taken from Lake Puckaway (Green Lake County) on 6 August 1952, and a 20.4-kg (45-lb) pike was taken from Fox Lake (Dodge County) on 15 July 1907. A 20.9-kg (46-lb 2-oz) northern pike was reported from Sacandaga Reservoir in New York State on 15 September 1940.

Early in its life the northern pike becomes a voracious feeder on fish and other vertebrate animals. In Lake Geneva, Wisconsin, of 14 pike weighing from 1.4 to 4.5 kg (3 to 10 lb), 13 contained cisco exclusively and 1 contained mimic shiners exclusively. The stomach contents of 13 smaller pike weighing 0.6–1.4 kg (1.25–3 lb) contained cisco, mimic shiners, yellow perch, a smallmouth bass, a rock bass, an unidentified centrarchid, and a crayfish (Nelson and Hasler 1942).

In the Murphy Flowage northern pike fed on bluegills, perch, minnows, and crappies, in that order (L. D. Johnson 1969). Although bluegills were the predominant prey species, the pike appeared to select the perch, a more cylindrical species. Johnson noted that the body depth of a forage fish is its critical measurement, and that 84% of the items found in all northern pike stomachs were between 13 and 38 mm (0.5 and 1.5 in) in depth. The length of the forage fish does not seem to be a critical factor in the predator's ability to swallow it. But occasionally large northern pike are found to have choked on prey too large to swallow.

The food of northern pike 381–660 mm (15–26 in) long in a central Wisconsin trout stream was 54% trout (rainbow and brown trout, avg 168 mm [6.6 in] long). Other items in decreasing order of importance were mottled sculpin, white sucker, blacknose dace, crayfish, and muskrat (Hunt 1965a).

Some fishes eaten by northern pike are brown bullhead, pumpkinseed, yellow perch, golden shiner, fathead minnow, northern redbelly dace, white sucker, blacknose shiner, central mudminnow, Iowa darter, and brook stickleback (Lagler 1956). In one report, an 813-mm (32-in) northern pike had swallowed another pike 457 mm (18 in) long. Other vertebrates known to have been eaten by northern pike include ducks, red squirrels, sandpipers, moles, shrews, mink, fully grown muskrats, frogs, and a blackbird. An unusual insect-feeding northern pike has been reported from Lac Brochet, Quebec (L. D. Johnson 1969).

The gastric glands in the northern pike's stomach secrete hydrochloric acid and pepsinogen, effective in combination to split large protein molecules. In typically carnivorous fishes such as the northern pike, gastric acidities of pH 2.4–3.6 have been measured (Lagler et al. 1977).

Northern pike feed almost entirely during the daytime. This species is known as a sight feeder with a peak feeding temperature of 18.9°C (66°F). Feeding methods are described by Threinen (1969:2):

> . . . Observations indicate northern pike usually locate in some type of concealment from which they dash out after unsuspecting prey. No doubt they also make feeding forays, slowly moving about looking for unsuspecting schools of fish when they are hungry. Such behavior is not specifically detailed in available literature, but has been inferred from extensive angling observations and skin diving sightings.

The species is not known to be a wary fish. The small size of the brain (1/1305 of weight of the body), as compared with animals higher on the evolutionary scale, supports this observation (Threinen et al. 1966).

Many anglers believe that northern pike shed their teeth in the summer because they bite less frequently then, but this is not true. Investigation has shown that the teeth are not shed entirely at any one time. Worn-out or broken-off teeth are replaced as they are lost by new ones, which grow alongside the larger ones. In August the northern pike does not bite well because food production is then at its peak for the year and they are consequently well fed; at this time they are also likely to seek the cooler and deeper waters (Eddy and Underhill 1974).

The depth distribution of this species is variable from one time of the year to another. During the winter period they were taken at all depths in Lake Mendota, and in the spring they were taken between 1.5 and 5.8 m (5 and 19 ft) (Tibbles 1956). During the summer they occur just off the sand bars at 5.5–7.6 m (18–25 ft) in the lakes of southeastern Wisconsin. In Lake Geneva, Nelson and Hasler (1942) noted differential distribution with respect to size: small northern pike were found at 3.1–6.1 m (10–20 ft), medium-sized fish at 6.1–12.2 m (20–40 ft), and large fish (1.4 kg or over) at greater depths.

Through contraction of the gill chambers, water is jetted toward the tail and jet propulsion seems to constitute an important part of the thrust for speed in the northern pike's take-off from rest (Lagler et al. 1977). This species has been recorded moving at 4.7 km/hr (2.92 mi/hr). The northern pike travels extensively; planted fish have appeared in the lower Fox River 36–57 km (22–35 mi) below the upriver lakes where they were released (Priegel 1968a). Snow (1974a) noted that 25–30% of the northern pike stocked in Murphy Flowage went over the flowage dam to downstream areas. Further analysis indicates that such movement may be a density adjustment to avoid overpopulation.

In a tagging experiment with northern pike on the Black River (LaCrosse County), 92% of the returned tags were taken in the Black River within 8 km (5 mi) of the tagging site (Finke 1966a). The longest recorded movement was 34 km (21 mi) downstream to the vicinity of Stoddard. Another fish traveled 32 km (20 mi) up the La Crosse River to West Salem. Results of the study indicate that northern pike congregate below the Onalaska Spillway prior to spawning, spawn in the marshes near the spillway, and remain mostly in the Black River until late summer. Krohn (1969) noted that northern pike disperse rapidly soon after stocking.

For sustained growth and survival in northern pike, the mean water temperature should not exceed the optimum temperature. This increases from 21° C (69.8° F) upon hatching to 26° C (78.8° F) for juvenile pike (Hokanson et al. 1973). As lake waters warm in midsummer, northern pike seek cooler waters near spring inlets or seeps. They are most active when temperatures range between 12.8 and 23.3° C (55 and 74° F). When northern pike acclimated at 25.0, 27.5, and 30.0° C (77, 81.5, and 86° F) were exposed to lethal trials between 32.0 and 35.3° C (89.6 and 95.5° F), they would not feed, and most of the longterm deaths at the lower test temperatures seemed to be due to starvation, as indicated by their emaciated appearance at death (Scott 1964).

Privolnev (1963) has noted that the northern pike has an increased oxygen threshold in warmwater: 0.72 ppm at 15°C (59°F), and 1.4 ppm at 29°C (84.2°F). In winter, northern pike are quite tolerant of low oxygen conditions and will withstand levels as low as 0.3 and 0.4 ppm (Cooper and Washburn 1949). However, they succumb to winterkill when the oxygen is depleted (Hanson 1958).

Supersaturation of oxygen is equally fatal. In 1940 a sudden mortality of fishes, among them northern pike, occurred in Lake Waubesa (Dane County). Large, mature adults had damaged gills, with most filaments containing gas emboli large enough to block the capillaries and to obstruct blood flow. Death was due to respiratory failure (Woodbury 1941). Northern pike have also been known to succumb to summerkill, and perhaps to algae-produced toxins. Mackenthun et al. (1948) noted a mass fish mortality, which included northern pike, on the Yahara River (southcentral Wisconsin) as a result of the decomposition of algae in early fall.

Fish associates of northern pike include the many fishes found in Wisconsin marshes, lakes, and streams. The list includes virtually all of the warmwater fishes and most of the coldwater fishes, except those in the Great Lakes which dwell in the deepest and darkest waters.

IMPORTANCE AND MANAGEMENT

Both perch and small minnows prey on recently hatched northern pike (Hunt and Carbine 1950, Carbine 1942), and bluegills have preyed on northern pike fingerlings in a slough outlet (Franklin and Smith 1963). Silver lamprey attach themselves to the northern pike, particularly in river situations, and sea lamprey attacks have been noted in the Great Lakes. The northern pike is a host to the glochidial stage of the mollusk *Amblema plicata* (Hart and Fuller 1974). Hatchery populations, and presumably wild fish, are susceptible to the bacterial disease furunculosis (*Aeromonas salmonicida*).

Northern pike are popular with Wisconsin and out-of-state anglers, closely following the popularity of walleyes and largemouth bass. Northern pike bite readily and are a highly prized catch. Catch data from Wisconsin lakes and adjoining states indicate that sport fishermen catch up to 50% of the population present at the beginning of a season (Threinen and Herman 1958). In fact, the pike's biggest predator is man, who will even poach the spawning fish by spearing them in shallow water (Threinen et al. 1966).

Northern pike feed continuously during the daylight hours, so fishermen would likely find one time of day as good as any other for catching them. Small minnows and midwater lures are the most successful baits. In a 9-year study, spoons and spinners were the most successful artificial lures (L. D. Johnson 1969). Ice fishing produces excellent northern pike yields. The best seasons for pike fishing are late spring and early summer, late summer and fall, and early in the winter soon after ice forms.

Northern pike are tasty and have flaky, white flesh. Except for the Y-shaped bones—which mar even the fillets—they present a high-quality meat. When chunks of a freshly caught fish are dipped in pancake batter and deep-fat fried, even the bones cannot detract from the flavor treat. Unfortunately, in evaluating cooked northern pike from water affected by paper mill wastes, a taste test panel found them to have undesirable flavors and aromas in three of four seasons (Baldwin et al. 1961). In central Wisconsin, the Wisconsin River carries large amounts of paper mill wastes which have contaminated the flesh of all fish, including northern pike. However, recent efforts to treat the paper mill wastes before they are released to the stream have resulted in some improvement in the edibility of the fishes from those waters.

Commercial fishing for northern pike occurs in Green Bay, primarily off the western shoreline. In 1973 the commercial harvest was 14,180 kg (31,262 lb), valued at $5,962 (Poff 1974). In 1974 the harvest decreased to 10,299 kg (22,705 lb), valued at $5,694 (Wis. Dep. Nat. Resour. 1976). Fyke nets account for two-thirds of the reported catches. Northerns are also taken in large-mesh gill nets.

The northern pike is no longer a commercial species in the Mississippi River fishery, but it is a considerable factor in the sport fishery there. In 1967–1968 the projected sport fishery catch in Pools 4, 5, 7, and 11 was 22,208 fish weighing 42,663 kg (94,054 lb) (Wright 1970). The average weight per fish was an estimated 1.92 kg (4.24 lb). The northern pike diminishes rapidly in numbers in the lower pools; the estimated catch for Pool 11 near the southern state line was a mere 308 fish weighing 419 kg (924 lb).

A key management problem with northern pike has been expressed by C. Brynildson (1958:9):

> Probably no other Wisconsin game fish has been more adversely affected by increased shoreline "improvements" on many of our lakes than the northern pike. Gone are many of the large northern pike spawning runs that occurred every spring into the adjacent marshes and flooded lowlands in southern Wisconsin.
>
> Why? Because spawning grounds have been destroyed. Northern pike waters today are confined mainly to the north and isolated lakes in the southern part of the state which still have good spawning marshes. The greatest loss of pike spawning grounds has taken place in the southeastern tier of counties, where the demand for lake frontage is greatest.

Concern has been shown over the destruction of northern pike spawning grounds through environmental alterations, including dredging and filling operations (Borgeson and Tody 1967, Threinen et al. 1966, Threinen and Herman 1958, Threinen 1969, Fago 1973).

In areas where the habitat has already been lost, the construction of northern pike spawning marshes may be effective in restoring the population. Attempts to manage Perrys Marsh, adjacent to Lake Ripley (Jefferson County), for northern pike production resulted in small numbers (218/ha/yr) of pike (Kleinert 1970); low zooplankton food levels may have been responsible for this low production. In the Pleasant Lake marsh (Walworth County), annual production varied from 131 to 1,312 fingerlings per hectare (324 to 3,243/acre) (Fago 1977). Production and growth were better in this marsh than in some natural marshes; the survival rate of 2.6% (12,000 fingerlings) from the estimated deposition of 446,000 eggs was nine times higher than the .03% reported from some completely natural marshes in Michigan.

A northern pike habitat is created when a small stream is converted into a lake. Since impoundments always have extensive shallows and marshy spawning habitat, they are invariably good northern pike habitats (Threinen 1969).

The development of a strain of northern pike which does not require flooded marshes for spawning may relieve the spawning problem where flooded marshes have been depleted.

Normally the northern pike is present in natural environments in low densities. The population of northern pike was estimated to be between 1,400 and 2,500 mature fish (20–35/ha, or 8–14/acre) in different years at the Murphy Flowage, a 73-ha (180-acre) shallow impoundment in Rusk County. The standing crop ranged between 17 and 28 kg/ha (15 and 25 lb/

acre). At Cox Hollow Lake, a newly flooded impoundment in Iowa County which had not been opened to fishing, a population of 3,896 (101.5/ha, or 40.6/acre) and a standing crop of 56.4 kg/ha (50.3 lb/acre) were reported (Threinen et al. 1966). The Plover River (central Wisconsin) held an average population density of 54 fish (28.9 kg) per hectare (Paragamian 1976a).

Wherever present, the northern pike is a key predator of anything of size which moves in or on the water. It has been estimated that, in good waterfowl marshes, predation by pike may destroy 4.3 young waterfowl per hectare (1.7 per acre). In prime Canadian delta areas (Saskatchewan River and Athabaska River) the destruction of young waterfowl by pike may amount to 1.5 million individuals per year, or 9.7% of the average annual production of these areas (Solman 1945).

Attempts to use northern pike to control fish populations, particulary panfish like the bluegill and yellow perch, have intrigued the fish manager. The results were reviewed by Beard (1971). Control of bluegills by the introduction of northern pike has had limited effect in some instances and moderate success in others. In many instances the presence of the northern pike was not sufficient to keep the panfish population in balance, and panfish stunting persisted. Snow (1974a) noted that the northern pike should not be stocked to control stunted bluegills. Such control is unlikely to occur, because once bluegills are so abundant that their growth is stunted, the number of predator fish needed to control them is apt to be higher than the carrying capacity of the waters involved.

Stocking of northern pike in waters which already have sizable populations will have a number of adverse effects (Snow 1974a:18):

1. Competition between stocked and native pike may force the stocked pike to move out of an impoundment or drainage lake. Unintentional movement into downstream areas where pike are not needed or wanted may do more harm than good.
2. Overstocking or high densities of pike may increase the susceptibility of these fish to parasitic infection or exceptionally high mortality from other causes.
3. Heavy stocking of pike into waters where native pike are already present may have an unfavorable effect on angling success.

Snow suggested that after stocking, the total density of large fingerlings (254–457 mm, or 10–18 in) should not exceed 20/ha (8/acre). Krohn (1969) suggested the food and space available to support northern pike is limited in most waters. When this capacity is exceeded by stocking or other factors, competition develops and is manifested through events such as increased natural mortality or poor growth that tend to restore a more suitable density of northern pike. In waters containing an excellent natural northern pike population, stocking is not necessary and if stocked, the return to the angler is low. Priegel (1968a) reported that anglers recaptured only 8.7% of the fish released in Lake Poygan, and 4.3% of those released in Lake Butte des Morts, over periods of 3 and 2 years respectively.

At the present time the northern pike is the biggest threat to the future of Wisconsin's muskellunge. Historically the lakes and rivers of the highlands of northern Wisconsin have been muskellunge domain. Threinen and Oehmcke (1950) explained:

> Waters like the Island Lake chain in Rusk county are now dominated by the northern pike, whereas 15 years ago a northern could not be caught there. Lac Court Oreilles now has northern pike. In the north-central part of the state the tremendous Flambeau flowage, Manitowish chain and the Pike Lake chain in the Flambeau drainage have northerns. . . .

It is suspected that competition between these species occurs soon after hatching. Northern pikes hatch out about 2 weeks earlier and grow faster than the muskellunge. It has been suggested that the larger northern pike fry turn on the smaller muskellunge for food. In a pond stocked with 25,000 northern pike fry and 25,000 muskellunge fry, 402 northern pike and only 4 muskellunge remained about a month later.

Concern with the probable adverse effect of northern pike populations on muskellunge has resulted in the establishment of liberal bag limits for the pike. In the early 1950s a year-round northern pike fishing season, with a bag limit of 25 fish a day, was opened on 18 choice muskellunge lakes in Price, Sawyer, Rusk, and Oneida counties. In recent years the tendency has been to observe liberal bag and size limits on northern pike, except in those counties of the southeastern quarter of the state where populations are seriously depleted. Study of the 18-in (46-cm) size limit on northern pike has indicated that in some waters this limit did not accomplish its intended purpose, and that it is not generally an effective management technique (Snow and Beard 1972). After the size limit was established in Bucks Lake (Rusk County), the total catch of northern pike (including sublegals) declined by 29%, and the catch of northern pike over 46 cm (18 in) long decreased by an estimated 55%.

Muskellunge

Esox masquinongy Mitchill. *Esox*—an old name for the pike in Europe; *masquinongy*—in Cree "mashk" means deformed and "kinonge" is a pike.

Other common names: Great Lakes muskellunge, Ohio muskellunge, Wisconsin muskellunge, muskie (musky), lunge, northern muskellunge, leopard muskellunge, maskinonge, tiger muskellunge (generally reserved for the muskellunge × northern pike hybrid).

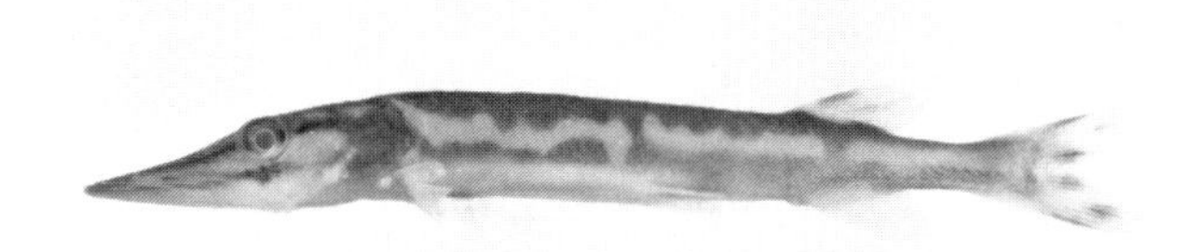

Immature 80 mm, North Twin L. (Vilas Co.), 18 June 1977

Wisconsin muskellunge (top), northern pike (middle), and muskellunge–northern pike hybrid (bottom) (Wisconsin DNR photo)

DESCRIPTION

Body elongate, moderately compressed laterally, somewhat flattened dorsally. Average length approximately 813 mm (32 in). Greatest body depth into TL 6.1–9.7. Head length into TL 4–4.3; top of head unscaled, cheeks and opercles usually scaled on top half only. Snout long into head length 2.1–2.3; snout flattened dorso-ventrally, duckbill-like. Mouth large, maxillary extending to midpoint or posterior edge of pupil. Lower jaw with large, strong canines (peglike posteriorly) and short, sharp, recurved brushlike teeth on roof of mouth and tongue. Sensory pores on undersurface of lower jaw (mandibular pores), usually 6–9 on each side. Gill rakers reduced to sharp, toothlike structures. Branchiostegal rays 16–19 on each side. Scales small cycloid, lateral series 147–155 (130–157); lateral line complete. Principal dorsal rays 15–19; principal anal rays 14–16; pectoral fin rays 14–19; pelvic fin rays 11–12; all of these more or less rounded on edge; caudal fin moderately forked, tips pointed, at least more so than in northern pike. Chromosomes 2n = 50 (McGregor 1970).

Silvery background with dark, variable markings, often as oblique stripes, spots, or blotches, or even with scarcely any markings. Belly white with small spots. Fins green to red-brown with dark blotches. Young (less than 150 mm) with broad scalloped bars of olive green along sides and gold mid-dorsal stripe on back; belly white.

Hybrids: Tiger muskellunge, the muskellunge × northern pike hybrid, is a naturally occurring form in several large lakes (Lac Vieux Desert, Big St. Germaine, and Plum lakes of Vilas County; Tomahawk and Minocqua lakes of Oneida County) where the northern pike has entered the native fishery. An estimated 40–50% of the "muskellunge" caught annually from Lac Vieux Desert on the Wisconsin-Michigan boundary are natural hybrids (Oehmcke 1969). The males are always sterile, but females are often fertile. A description of the young and adult tiger muskellunge, along with illustrations of hybrids, parent species, and backcrosses between hybrid females and northern pike are provided by Black and Williamson (1946).

Natural hybridization between the muskellunge and the northern pike is rising in muskellunge waters where northern pike are now present. This crossbreeding of native species is of definite management concern and needs research attention (Oehmcke 1969).

An artificial muskellunge × grass pickerel hybrid has been produced in Ohio (Tennant and Billy 1963).

SYSTEMATIC NOTES

Three subspecies of muskellunge have been recognized: *E. m. masquinongy* (spotted)—St. Lawrence River, the Great Lakes and tributaries; *E. m. immaculatus* (no pattern or barred)—Wisconsin, Minnesota, northwestern Ontario, and southeastern Manitoba; and *E. m. ohioensis* (barred or diffuse spots and blotches)—Ohio River and tributaries. Of these, the first two have been ascribed to Wisconsin by Greene

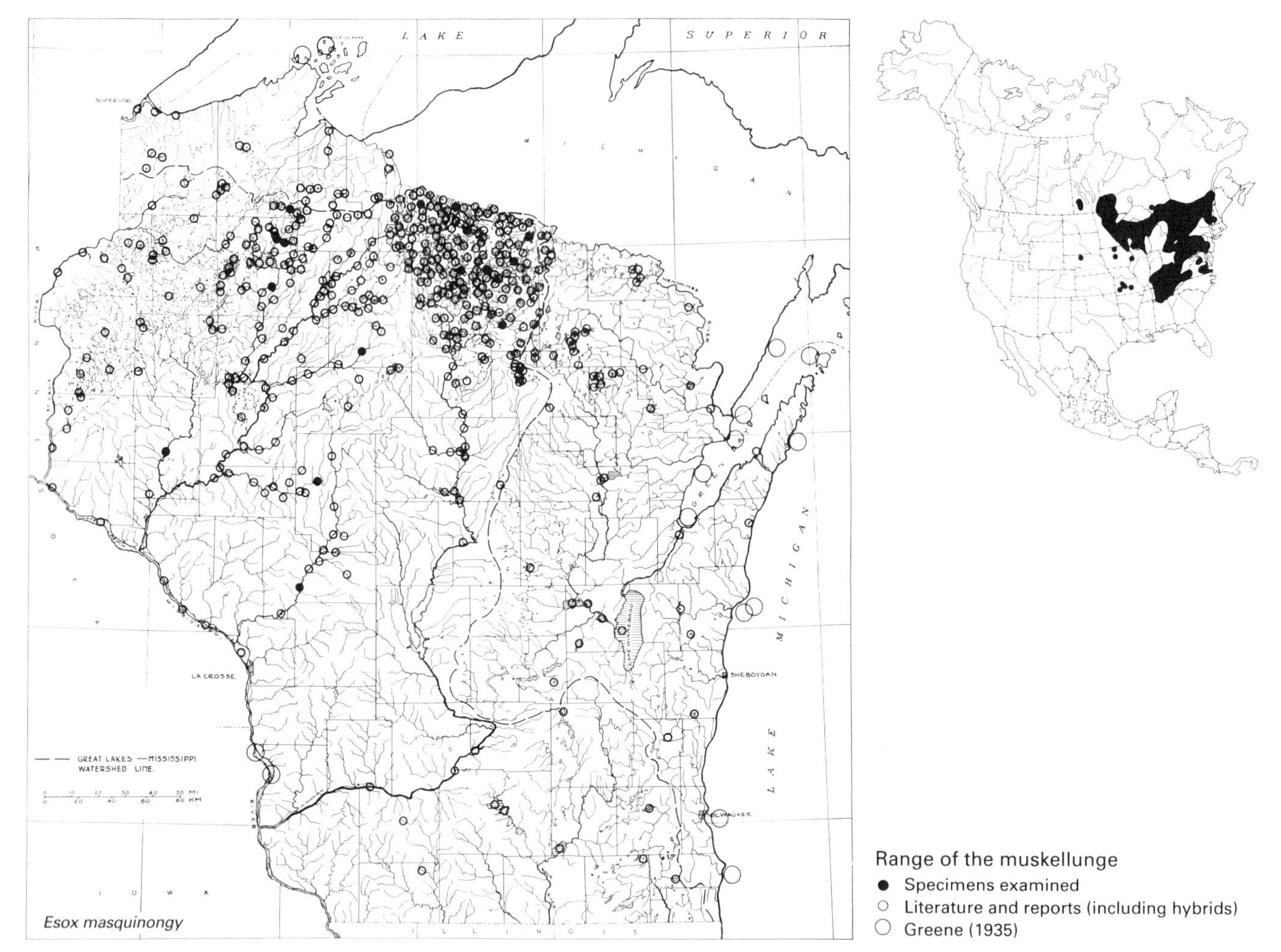

Range of the muskellunge
● Specimens examined
○ Literature and reports (including hybrids)
◯ Greene (1935)

(1935). Greene applied the name "tiger muskellunge" to *E. m. immaculatus*, but in recent years this name has been assigned to the natural and artificial hybrid with the northern pike.

There is such variation in the markings and patterns of the muskellunge in Wisconsin inland and outlying waters that the tendency has been to treat the complex as a single variable species. Taxonomic difficulties have been compounded as a result of fish cultural activities and extensive plantings, and hybridization has added to the confusion.

DISTRIBUTION, STATUS, AND HABITAT

The muskellunge occurs in all three drainage basins in Wisconsin, but is most widely distributed in the Chippewa, Flambeau, St. Croix (upstream to Trego Dam), Black, and Wisconsin rivers of the Mississippi basin. Its original inland range is given by Oehmcke et al. (1965, updated 1977). In recent years no records exist of this species from the Mississippi River below Lake Pepin. A total of over 700 lakes and flowages and 43 muskellunge streams, comprising over 126,284 ha (312,048 acres), hold this species (Wis. Dep. Nat. Resour. 1968a). About 25% of all muskellunge populations in Wisconsin have been created through stocking (Oehmcke 1969).

Its presence in central and southern Wisconsin is the result of widespread stocking of fry and fingerlings; stocked waters include Pewaukee Lake (Waukesha County), Little Green Lake (Green Lake County), Lake Wisconsin (Columbia County), and Chain O' Lakes (Waupaca County). Hybrid muskellunge × northern pike have been stocked principally in nonmuskellunge waters of southern and central Wisconsin.

The muskellunge is common in the lakes and rivers in the headwater regions of the Chippewa, Flambeau, and Wisconsin rivers, and in the St. Croix River upstream to Trego Dam. It is rare to common in the lakes and rivers of central and southern Wisconsin, and rare in Lakes Michigan and Superior.

Muskellunge typically occur in lakes with numerous submerged weed beds, but sometimes are found in clear, sterile lakes with virtually no weeds. Large

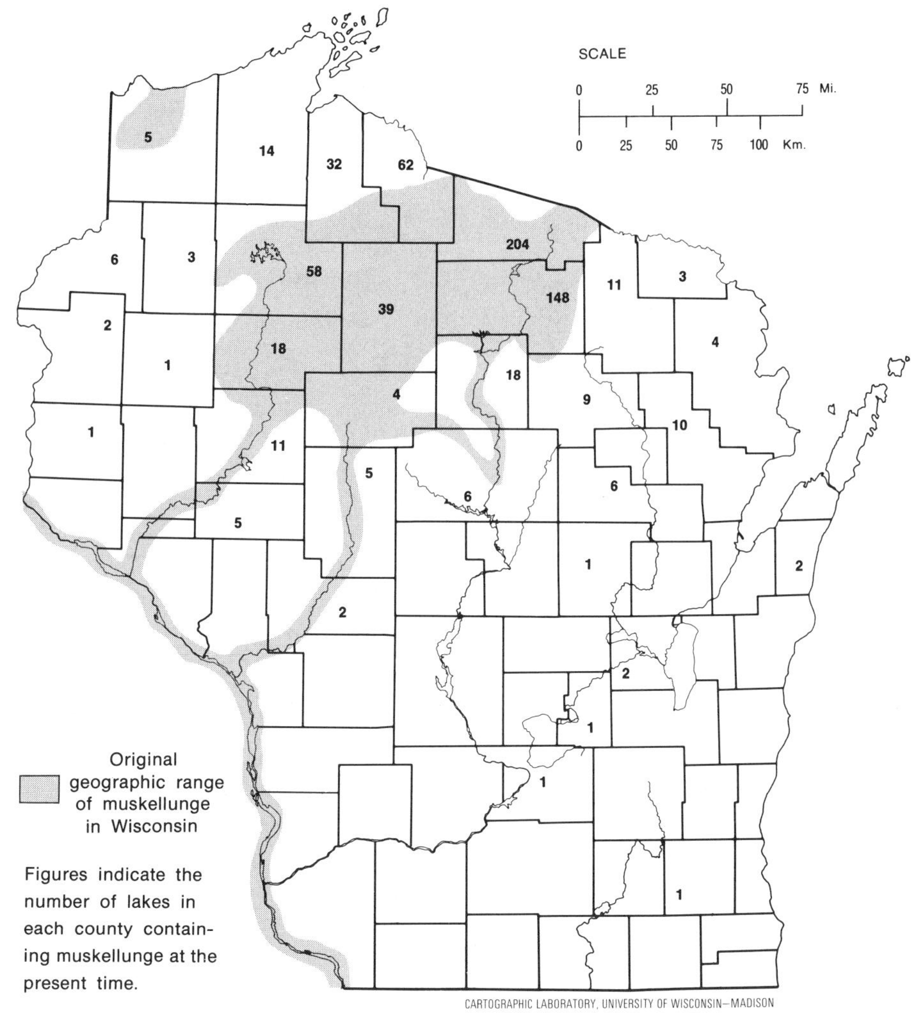

Past and present distribution of Wisconsin muskellunge (after Oehmcke et al. 1965; updated 1977)

lakes which have both extensive deep and shallow basins and tributary streams are preferred waters and provide necessary forage and cover requirements. In medium to large rivers, muskellunge inhabit pools and slower water. They are a shallow water form, usually found in less than 5 m (15 ft) of water, but occasionally they are found at depths of 12–15 m (40–50 ft). Cool water temperatures are preferred, ranging from 0.6 to 25.6°C (33 to 78°F), but muskellunge can withstand temperatures up to 32.2°C (90°F) for short periods. This species is more tolerant of low levels of oxygen than many other game fish species found in the same habitat (Oehmcke et al. 1965).

BIOLOGY

The following account is derived largely from Oehmcke et al. (1965) and Oehmcke (1969). Within the north and south limits of the Wisconsin muskellunge range, spawning occurs from mid-April to mid-May, with the peak occurring early in the season. Spawning usually takes place in shallow bays over a muck bottom covered with dead vegetation and other detritus. Water depth is 15–76 cm (6–30 in), and the optimum temperature is about 12.8°C (55°F), but may range from 9.4 to 15.6°C (49 to 60°F). In Sawyer County lakes, Dombeck (1979) noted that the movement of muskellunge greatly increased in early spring before water temperatures began to rise. This suggests that factors other than temperature influence the onset of spawning. It is likely that a combination of environmental factors such as temperature, increasing photoperiod, and increasing oxygen levels may initiate movement to spawning areas. Spawning activity was observed between 1900 and 0300 hr.

Oehmcke et al. (1965:5) provide the following details:

> Eggs are deposited indiscriminately over several hundred yards of shoreline . . . The male swims side by side with the female and eggs and milt are deposited simultaneously at intervals over the bottom. There is no parental care. Adult spawners return to the same spawning ground in consecutive years.

Muskellunge from 64 to 135 cm (25 to 53 in) produce 22,000–180,000 eggs about 3.2 mm diam (Galat 1973). The number of eggs correlates with fish length and weight—larger females produce greater numbers of larger-sized eggs. An 18-kg (40-lb) female produced 225,000 eggs.

Females can be induced to spawn by administering pituitary extract (Hasler et al. 1940). Eleven female muskellunge captured below the dam on the Chippewa River near Winter (Sawyer County) were injected with 50 mg of acetone-dried carp pituitary glands. Nine of the injected females spawned 3–4 days after a single injection of carp pituitary, while two were given two injections each and spawned 6 days after the first injection. The number of eggs recovered from these 11 individuals ranged from 22,092 to 119,928.

Egg development varies with water temperatures during incubation. The young muskellunge hatches within 8–14 days after fertilization in rising water temperatures ranging from 12.2 to 16.7°C (54 to 62°F). Galat (1973) noted that at a constant incubation temperature of 13°C (55.4°F) most hatching occurs on the 14th day and some on the 15th. A detailed development of the muskellunge from fertilization to hatching (sac-fry stage) is described and illustrated by Galat.

Only 6 days of incubation may be required at 20°C (68°F). Incubation at 3.9°C (39°F) results in 100% mortality by the end of 35 days (L. D. Johnson 1958). In the hatchery, muskellunge sac-fry are held in hatching jars for an additional 10–14 days until the yolk-sac is almost gone and the swim-up fry have reached about 13 mm total length. At this point the fry are transferred from hatchery jars to ponds which have been fertilized and inoculated for zooplankton, such as *Daphnia* spp. Swim-up muskellunge begin to feed immediately on live forage zooplankton. After 4 days they prefer to eat live fish, if available. In hatchery ponds, sucker fry are introduced 8–10 days after the muskellunge to ensure a desirable food source. Once the fish-eating habit of the muskellunge begins, it persists throughout life.

A number of factors limit reproduction in this species: cold water temperatures (below 10°C) and fluctuating water levels at spawning time, predation by other fish and invertebrates (e.g., bluegills, perch, rock bass, northern pike, several species of minnows, diving beetle larvae, dragonfly nymphs, and back swimmers) on both eggs and fry, quantity and size of live zooplankton and fish forage available for the muskellunge fry, and hybridization with the northern pike.

> A lack of optimum conditions determined by these limiting factors appears to have a direct bearing on the survival of muskellunge from fry to maturity. Natural events occurring in the early life of the muskellunge account for the greatest mortality. Northern lakes are subject to severe climatic variations during the spring months because of the latitude. Since muskellunge eggs and fry are extremely sensitive to water-temperature fluctuations, they are affected adversely (Oehmcke et al. 1965:5).

The muskellunge grows most rapidly during the first 3 years of life, after which time its rate of growth gradually decreases (Schloemer 1936). Since it is difficult to determine the age of muskellunge as they get older and larger, it is advantageous to use a number of different aging methods for arriving at the best estimate. Three methods in common use are the scales, fin bones, and vertebrae; all three show characteristic year marks (L. D. Johnson 1960). Discussing the problems entailed in aging this fish, L. D. Johnson (1971) noted that by the time the fish attain an age of XII, the outside edges of the fin sections are so trans-

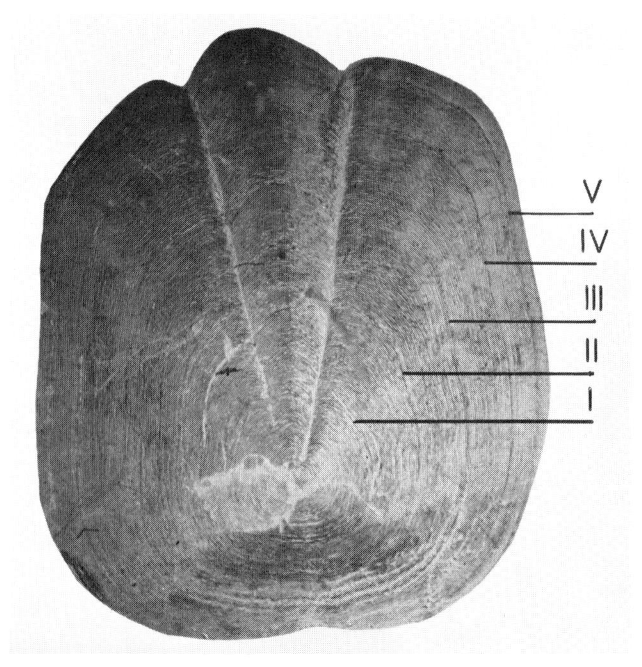

Muskellunge scale, age V (Wisconsin DNR photo)

lucent and scale edges so eroded that outer annuli cannot be distinguished, making both methods of aging inaccurate. At age X, less than 30% accuracy is obtained from fish of known age. To provide a more accurate estimate of the true length at the time of annulus formation, an adjustment of 76 mm (3 in), which signifies the length of the muskellunge at the time of scale formation, is added to the back calculated lengths.

Muskellunge growth in length is quite rapid for the first 5 years. Thereafter, growth in weight is greater (Oehmcke 1965:8).

Age	TL (mm)	WT (g)
Hatched fry	13–18	
1 month	43–76	
2 months	104–178	8
5 months	147–312	136–227
1 year	178–457	136–454
3 years	406–762	318–5,443
5 years	457–1,041	907–7,711
10 years	813–1,321	3,629–14,969
15 years	1,143–1,448	6,350–23,587
19 years	1,329–	

Average calculated SL for northern Wisconsin muskellunge at end of each year of life (Schloemer 1936) is: 1—178 mm (7.0 in), 2—366 mm (14.4 in), 3—503 mm (19.8 in), 4—620 (24.4), 5—716 (28.2), 6—792 (31.2), 7—859 (33.8), 8—925 (36.4), 9—965 (38.0), 10—1008 (39.7), 11—1046 (41.2), 12—1095 (43.1), 13—1128 (44.4), 14—1158 (45.6), 15—1201 (47.3), 16—1194 (47.0), 17—1258 (49.5), 18—1262 (49.7), 19—1298 (51.1).

Muskellunge growth is different in different lakes; the variability is so great that we may speak of poor, average, and excellent lakes (L. D. Johnson 1965). In some of the poor lakes, mature spawning muskellunge may live to a maximum age of 8 years without ever attaining the 30-inch (76-cm) legal size limit. Poor lakes are those with cold waters, low fertility, and, as a result, low forage fish production. In Big Spider Lake (Sawyer County) no muskellunge reached 76 cm (30 in) until age VIII (L. D. Johnson 1971).

In average muskellunge lakes the 76-cm (30-in) growth is attained within 5 years, and muskellunge live to a great age; there are many 8- to 15-year-old fish. World record muskellunge have been taken from some of the average waters. Lac Court Oreilles (Sawyer County) muskellunge are 76 cm (30 in) long at age V, and reach 104 cm (40.8 in) at age X.

There are only a few excellent muskellunge lakes, where a muskellunge may attain 76 cm (30 in) within 4 years. These fish are stocky and heavy as a result of abundant food. The excellent lakes are not usually native muskellunge waters, but lakes where muskellunge have been introduced from hatcheries. Growth rates are rapid, but the muskellunge do not usually live to old age; 12 years is about the maximum age for the excellent lakes, and we have no world records listed from them. In Little Green Lake (Green Lake County) stocked muskellunge reach 79.5 cm (31.3 in) at age III, and 117.9 cm (46.4 in) at age XII (Hacker 1973). The heaviest fish weighed 12.5 kg (27.5 lb).

Female muskellunge are usually longer and heavier than males of the same age. Age-V females will be 76–152 mm (3–6 in) longer than males at that age.

Sexual maturity is usually attained at ages III–V. L. D. Johnson (1971) reported that some males in Bone (Polk County), Lac Court Oreilles, and Big Spider lakes are mature spawners at age III and some females are mature at age IV. All male muskellunge are mature at age IV and all females at age V. The smallest mature male was 495 mm (19.5 in) long and the smallest mature female was 559 mm (22 in); both were from Big Spider Lake.

Greatest growth occurs in early summer (June) and early fall (September) when available forage is at a maximum and water temperatures are favorable (about 20°C). For young muskellunge, it takes 5–7 kg of live fish forage to produce 1 kg of muskellunge.

The average age of most creeled muskellunge is 3–6 years. One known-age fish had reached the age of 26 years (L. D. Johnson 1975), while record fish have been 30 years old or older. The largest record Wisconsin fish was 31.6 kg (69 lb 11 oz), taken on 20 October 1949 from the Chippewa Flowage (Sawyer County). The accepted world rod-and-reel record is a muskellunge just 113 g (4 oz) heavier (31.7 kg or 69 lb 15 oz) taken from the St. Lawrence River on 22 September 1957. An unofficial record, 133 cm and 31.9 kg (52.5 in, 70 lb 4 oz), was reported from Middle Eau Claire Lake (Bayfield County) (L. D. Johnson 1954).

In northern Wisconsin, Couey (1935) reported the use of perch, darters, and chubs as food. Hacker (1966) reported bluegills, minnows, and largemouth bass from the stomachs of Little Green Lake muskellunge; one 881-mm (34.7-in) muskellunge had a 318-mm (12.5-in) largemouth bass in its stomach. Generally the literature calls attention to perch, suckers, and small minnows as preferred fish food of muskellunge. Cannibalism is common to muskellunge of all sizes, and Parsons (1958) found a 406-mm (16-in) muskellunge in the stomach of a 711-mm (28-in) fish.

Occasionally muskellunge consume small muskrats, ducks and shorebirds, shrews, chipmunks, gophers, frogs, salamanders, crayfish, and large water insects.

The feeding behavior of young-of-year muskellunge has been observed in Parsons (1958:10–11):

> . . . The young muskellunge showed considerable patience, skill and efficiency in capturing their prey. Usually the young fish remained motionless along the shore's edge, in patches of aquatic vegetation, aside submerged branches, or in patches of shade only to dart out and capture a fish passing a few inches away. Almost all forage fish were grabbed in the middle, thoroughly 'munched' as evidenced by spewing scales, and swallowed end first.
> . . . When feeding, small muskellunge would often remain 15 minutes in one position whenever forage fish were near. Had the patience of the observer equalled that of the muskellunge, probably longer interims would have been observed. A young muskellunge often concentrated so intently on potential prey that it could be approached and touched with a stick before showing alarm. It is probably under these conditions when young muskellunge are most subject to predation or cannibalism.

Peak feeding temperature is 17.2°C (63°F), and feeding drops off in water temperatures above 29.4°C (85°F). Feeding is hampered by turbid waters because muskellunge depend primarily upon sight for the capture of their prey. Muskellunge habitat in some large rivers has been destroyed by increasing water turbidity (Oehmcke et al. 1965). Adult muskellunge are unpredictable in their feeding habits, sometimes biting readily and at other times remaining inactive. As in the case of many other fish, they seem to be most active in the early morning or late afternoon and evening hours (Wis. Dep. Nat. Resour. 1968a).

In a controlled feeding experiment, fingerling muskellunge (102–127 mm) were placed in aquaria and fed minnows. Their daily intake of prey averaged approximately 6.4% of their initial body weight. The average gross conversion ratio of 2.73 approached that of northern pike, and was much lower than that of either smallmouth or largemouth bass (Gammon 1963).

Fish forage supplied in Wisconsin's muskellunge propagation program generally consists of white sucker fry, naturally spawned bluegill fry, and naturally spawned fathead minnow fry (L. D. Johnson 1958). Other fish that have proven satisfactory as forage are brook stickleback and lake emerald shiners, whereas black crappie and northern pike fingerlings are undesirable because they grow too large to be swallowed by the muskellunge, and because they are predacious.

The behavior of the muskellunge has been summarized by Oehmcke et al. (1965:4–5):

> The muskellunge are lone, sedentary fish that usually lurk concealed among vegetation, near channels, bars or near rocky ledges and shoals, ready to dart after prey. A specific home range appears to be occupied by individual muskellunge because of desirable food and cover. There is no roaming tendency unless food is in short supply. Migration is limited usually to shallow marshy spawning areas in April and May, and to deeper waters after spawning. Muskellunge are again found in shallow water from September through October. If the muskellunge makes his home in rivers, downstream migration occurs in the fall and upstream migration in the spring. Factors that influence behavior include water temperatures, water-level fluctuations, food supply and movements of food supply.

Planted fingerlings 178–305 mm (7–12 in) will travel 11.3 km (7 mi) from the point where they were introduced in 1 week (L. D. Johnson 1963), generally along shorelines. The fingerlings stop off at favorable habitats along the way, in the same places where native muskellunge fingerlings of similar size are found. Within 2 weeks, even in lakes as large as 2,000 ha (5,000 acres), all the suitable shoreline will have muskellunge fingerlings.

Mature muskellunge, captured on their spawning grounds and tagged, will spread out; they are caught at distances up to 16 km (10 mi) from the tagging site (L. D. Johnson 1963). One record indicated a minimum straight-line travel distance of at least 40 km (25 mi), passing from one lake through a channel into another lake, within 1 week. The actual travel distance would probably have been far greater.

In northwestern Wisconsin, muskellunge whose movements were being followed by means of radio transmitters attached to them showed peak movement in the fall, followed by minimum movement during the winter months (Dombeck 1979). Greater activity was noted again in the spring, followed by intermediate movement during the summer. One fish traversed half the length of Moose Lake (Sawyer County) four times in less than 1 month during the fall; the same fish remained within a radius of 0.4 km (¼ mi) during the winter. Activity was related to water temperature, with peak activity occurring at 8–10°C (46.4–50°F) and minimum activity at 0.2°C (32.4°F). During the summer tagged muskellunge were never observed in water less than 21°C (69.8°F) and showed low activity in water temperatures above 27°C (80.6°F).

Johnson observed legal-size muskellunge swimming in such unlikely places as among bathers at a beach. Movements have been tracked by following a bobber attached by a 3-m (10-ft) line to the back of the muskellunge. Muskellunge seldom submerged more than 1.5 m (5 ft) during normal travel, even though the bottom may have been 27 m (90 ft) below. By means of bobbers, muskellunge speed has been paced at 1.6 km (1 mi) per hour, including two or three resting periods of 5–10 min during each hour.

In George and Corrine lakes (Vilas County), young and yearling largemouth bass congregated in the same brush piles and beds of vegetation frequented by the muskellunge (Gammon and Hasler 1965). Largemouth bass populations subsequently decreased, with virtually no bass surviving to the third summer of life, but the number of smallmouth bass increased. Shortly after hatching, the smallmouth schools scattered, with individuals or small groups moving into shallow water near shore, often in rocky or sandy areas, the smallmouth thus reduced contact between themselves and the muskellunge.

Species associated with the muskellunge are numerous; generally, they are the coldwater to warmwater fishes in northern Wisconsin lakes and streams where the muskellunge is found. In North Twin Lake (Vilas County) the yellow perch, common shiner, logperch, pumpkinseed, and white sucker have been taken with young-of-year muskellunge.

IMPORTANCE AND MANAGEMENT

Young muskellunge are preyed on by northern pike, walleye, yellow perch, smallmouth bass, largemouth bass, rock bass, and sunfishes, as well as other muskellunge. Scott and Crossman (1973) note that in hatchery situations, and possibly in nature as well, diving beetles, electric light bugs, and the large larvae of some aquatic insects are significant predators on newly hatched muskellunge. Large muskellunge are nearly free of predation except from poaching.

During the 1961 season about 170 resorts and other businesses in northwestern Wisconsin were asked to keep records of the muskellunge caught by their guests or patrons. In all, 2,022 legal fish were reported (Klingbiel 1962). A statewide survey of muskellunge fishermen gave an estimated harvest of one fish for every 5.6 acres—a possible total harvest of 47,700 from the state's muskellunge water (Oehmcke et al. 1965). The "Musky Marathon," sponsored by the Vilas County Chamber of Commerce from 1966 to 1968, recorded a total of 4,510 fish weighing 24,500 kg (53,966 lb), or an average of 5.43 kg (11.96 lb) per fish (Oehmcke 1969).

The muskellunge harvest has been estimated by Churchill (1968) as follows: 1964—110,000, 1965—110,000, 1966—94,000, 1967—92,000. For that time period, the estimated yearly catch was 101,000 legal muskellunge. I consider these estimates to be high. Based on the available muskellunge water, the muskellunge life table, and estimated mortality, I estimate the yearly take of legal muskellunge at 30,000 to 32,000. From 20 to 30% of the total estimated harvest may be due to the stocking effort (Oehmcke 1969, Snow 1969, Hacker 1966).

The economic value of muskellunge fishing to resort, sporting goods, and associated businesses is high. A study of Fine and Werner (1960) showed that resident and nonresident fishermen spent an estimated $188.5 million in 1960. If the conservative estimate of 10% of this figure represented spending by licensed fishermen who fished for muskellunge, the economic impact of the muskellunge fishery is quite obvious (Oehmcke 1969).

The muskellunge is Wisconsin's most famous fish, and more has been written about fishing for the muskellunge than for most other game fishes. Any legal muskellunge becomes a trophy fish; there are thousands of fishermen who spend hundreds of hours in search of such a prize. When it is caught, it is frequently honored by being mounted at considerable expense.

> In typical waters, the muskellunge lurk near the drop-offs from rock or sand bars in the middle of the lake, along weed beds, in small weed-covered bays and in shady waters close to shores that are fringed with overhanging trees. Casting or trolling over these areas is most rewarding (Oehmcke et al. 1965).

The muskellunge is a spectacular fighter, violently twisting underwater, leaping out of the water to shake the hook, or bulldogging the bottom like an unyielding snag. Favorite lures are bucktails, spoons, and wobbling underwater baits. But in heavy weeds, surface lures retrieved with noisy and erratic action often entice an otherwise uninterested muskellunge. The most effective live bait is a sucker 23–36 cm (9–14 in) long which is fitted to a harness.

In 1955 the Wisconsin legislature recognized the muskellunge's quality by designating it as the official state fish. Like television, movie, or baseball stars, the muskellunge has its avid fans. There are loner muskellunge fishermen who fish only for this species and who do it in solitude—the more solitude the better. There are also those more gregarious in nature who band together to fish for "Mr. Big" in competitive fever. Muskies, Inc., has been formed to promote and to perpetuate the sport of muskellunge fishing. A small group of muskie-struck fishermen from northern Wisconsin calls itself KMK (Killer Musky Klub) and publishes a newsletter biannually.

Private fishing clubs exist in Wisconsin on private lakes which hold natural or planted muskellunge. Under some membership rules, muskellunge may be caught, but they also must be returned to ensure action for other members.

The muskellunge on a platter is the gourmet's delight. Although the meat—like that of the northern pike—has rows of Y-shaped bones, these generally are large, easily extracted, and hardly detract from the white, flaky, and firm meat.

The artificial propagation of muskellunge in Wisconsin was initiated in 1899 at Woodruff. For more than 25 years little effort was directed toward rearing muskellunge beyond the sac-fry stage. Today the program is geared to producing large fingerlings, ranging from 203 to 381 mm (8 to 15 in), for all high-priority muskellunge plantings. Present stocking procedures call for scatter planting whenever possible to eliminate concentrations of small fish (Oehmcke 1969). Oehmcke noted that biologists and fish managers base their recommendations for the stocking rates for individual bodies of water on such factors as available forage, exploitation rates, and general conditions of the fishery. When the actual catch from a given lake is known, fingerling stock of twice the annual harvest is recommended; otherwise, a standard rate of five fingerlings per hectare (2/acre) is used.

The loss of stocked fish is rapid. The life expectancy table in the next column shows how many muskellunge remain alive after each year of life from an initial stocking of 1,000 fingerlings about 20–25 cm (8–10 in) long (L. D. Johnson 1975:20). The large number of fish dying between years 5 and 10 reflects the take in the fishery. At age V the fish reach the legal length of 76 cm (30 in), and at that time there are only 9.4% of the original number remaining.

Tiger muskellunge have been artificially hybridized in Wisconsin hatcheries since 1940. During 1976, 164,926 fry and 33,341 fingerlings (the latter weighing 2,700 kg) were distributed in Wisconsin waters. Many hybrids have been stocked in nonmuskellunge lakes in central and southern Wisconsin. This hybrid is a hardy fish, shows greater thermal resistance than either parent (Scott 1964), and exhibits phenomenal growth. In Little Green Lake (Green Lake County), hybrids 2.5 years old may be 838 mm (33 in) long (Hacker 1973). A tiger muskellunge weighing 22.79 kg (50 lb 4 oz) was taken on 28 June 1951 from Lac Vieux Desert (Vilas County).

Muskellunge Life Table

Age Interval	No. Alive at Beginning of Year	No. Dying During Year of Age	No. Dying per 1000 Alive at Beginning of Year	Avg Number of Years of Life Remaining at Beginning of Year of Life
0.5–1	1000	886	886	1.4
1–2	114	5	44	7.1
2–3	109	5	46	6.4
3–4	104	5	48	5.7
4–5	99	5	51	5.0
5–6	94	29	308	3.2
6–7	65	13	200	3.4
7–8	52	16	307	3.2
8–9	36	10	277	3.3
9–10	26	7	269	3.2
10–11	19	5	263	3.2
11–12	14	1	71	3.2
12–13	13	4	307	2.5
13–14	9	2	222	2.3
14–15	7	2	285	1.8
15–16	5	3	600	1.3
16–17	2	0	0	1.5
17–18	2	0	0	0.5

While hybrids supply a rapid return to the fishery, there are several disadvantages that must be considered. Hybrid muskellunge bite on live baits during the winter months, when the season is closed, and hooked fish are invariably killed. They also bite well during the summer and are particularly vulnerable under legal size (Hacker 1973). As a result, many tiger muskellunge are destroyed and do not become part of the legal catch.

A number of problems persist in the muskellunge-rearing program. Supplying the demand for forage minnows to feed young muskellunge is still the primary key to successful fingerling production. A basic requirement is the feeding of proper-sized forage fish at each critical stage in fingerling development. The fourth and fifth week of rearing have been identified as one weak point in the muskellunge pond program (Oehmcke 1969).

Rearing costs rose from $14.65/kg ($6.66/lb) in 1964 to an estimated $22/kg ($10/lb) in 1977, and probably will continue to rise. The Wisconsin Department of Natural Resources has successfully used sewage treatment plant ponds for raising muskellunge fingerlings from 76 mm (3 in) to about 305 mm (12 in). Such ponds can also be used to raise food for muskellunge fingerlings. From 45 kg (100 lb) of fathead minnows stocked in a sewage treatment pond in Whitehall (Trempealeau County) over 3,270 kg (7,200 lb) of fatheads were harvested in 3.5 months (A. Oehmcke, pers. comm.). The use of sewage treatment ponds, and the help of outside groups supplying minnows for muskellunge food, could trim expenses from rearing costs.

Since muskellunge are among the largest of the fish predator species, they are important in maintaining fish population balance. Studies by Gammon and Hasler (1965) and by Schmitz and Hetfeld (1965) showed that increasing growth rates of perch were accompanied by decreases in their numbers after muskellunge were introduced into two bass-perch bog lakes in northern Wisconsin. In the same experiment largemouth bass populations decreased markedly, due undoubtedly to predation from the muskellunge. In another experiment, involving a stunted bluegill population (Clear Lake, Sawyer County), the stocking of muskellunge fingerlings resulted in good muskellunge growth but had no apparent affect on the growth rate of the bluegills, although these were undoubtedly used by the muskellunge as forage (Snow 1968). Snow suggested that when the density of a bluegill population is above a certain unknown level, predator stocking can exert little, if any, control on the population. In High Lake (Vilas County), Helm (1960) noted that after stocking yearling muskellunge there was improvement in the native muskellunge population, in walleye fishing, and in the quality of perch taken.

A major problem associated with the muskellunge stocking program is the 20–80% mortality which occurs within 3 weeks of stocking (Snow 1968). There is evidence that muskellunge stocked in High Lake were preyed on by other species of fish: the tag from a muskellunge, 251 mm (9.9 in) long when stocked, was taken from the stomach of a 1.13-kg (2.5-lb) walleye (Helm 1960). Although Island Lake (near Winter, Sawyer County) in 1972 had the highest predator index (northern pike, walleye, bass) of any lake studied, it also had the highest survival (96%) of stocked fingerlings (L. D. Johnson 1974). Very heavy aquatic vegetation cover in Island Lake appeared to lower fingerling mortalities due to predation.

Enough circumstantial evidence exists to suggest that a serious competitor of the muskellunge is its close relative, the northern pike. Natural hybridization between the species produces progeny with curtailed reproductive potential. Also, the probable competition between the fry of the northern pike and the muskellunge, at the expense of the latter, has been mentioned previously (p. 404).

Lakes that formerly contained muskellunge exclusively are now dominated by the northern pike—waters like the Island Lake chain (Rusk County). Almost all of the best remaining muskellunge waters also have northern pike. The two species appear to be incompatible, and the northern pike is gradually replacing the native muskellunge in many waters. To counteract this competition, management measures have been imposed (Oehmcke et al. 1965): northern pike removal programs, heavy stocking of fingerling or yearling muskellunge to support muskellunge populations, and increased bag limits on northern pike in counties having numerous muskellunge waters.

In Escanaba Lake (Vilas County), which was opened to fishing under experimental regulations stipulating no size and bag limits and no closed seasons on any species of fish, the muskellunge population remained more stable throughout the study period (1946–1969) than populations of the other fish species (Kempinger et al. 1975). Anglers harvested 550 muskellunge that weighed a total of 1,181 kg (2,604 lb). Muskellunge constituted 0.1% of the total catch and 1.9% of the total weight harvested. From 1954 to 1969, the average annual muskellunge size varied from 546 to 742 mm (21.5 to 29.2 in), and 27% of those caught were 762 mm (30 in) or larger. The muskellunge population was supported by substantial plantings of fingerling and yearling fish.

The current inland and boundary waters limits for muskellunge—76-cm (30-in) size, and one fish bag per day—have been in effect for more than 30 years. The open season for muskellunge begins near the end of the spawning season in May, and extends until mid-November. The average muskellunge fisherman is far less successful than the average deer hunter. Since the muskellunge never occurs in dense populations and is intensively fished, Oehmcke et al. (1965) suggested that season bag limits be established for individual waters. Also, compulsory registration of harvested muskellunge would provide needed management information.

I have suggested that muskellunge fishing be continued on a catch-and-release basis (Becker 1976). Large muskellunge which would be continually returned to the water might serve as checks on the competitive northern pike, and would provide a continual source of fishing for other fishermen. A single trophy fish, rather than ending up on one person's table or wall, might instead be commemorated by successful fishermen either through the "thrill of the moment" or through a snapshot taken prior to releasing the fish to the water. As an added protection to the fish, only artificial baits with single hooks should be allowed. Catch-and-release programs work by offering more fishing fun, and by providing the moral satisfaction that comes with leaving something for the next fisherman rather than contributing to the exhaustion of an already strained resource. In waters where there may be an overpopulation of this species, and where cropping is necessary to preserve a healthy population, a controlled permit season may be instituted.

Our current problems with muskellunge fishing will undoubtedly accelerate with the anticipated growth of the human population, with increased leisure time, and with the steady decline of the muskellunge range and reserves. As noted by Threinen and Oehmcke (1950:12), the future of this species appears doubtful:

> Looking at the problem in retrospect and taking into account the present limited distribution of the muskellunge, we could conclude that the muskellunge is a relict species apparently doomed by time. This process has been accelerated by man's breaking down the natural barriers.
>
> But where man has in his power to tear down, perhaps he can also build up. We hope that sound fish management activities can adequately cope with the situation.

Minnow and Carp Family—Cyprinidae

Forty-five species of minnows in 15 genera are known from Wisconsin; of these, 43 species are native. In the United States and Canada more than 200 species are recognized (Robins et al. 1980), and every year additional species are accepted. The Cyprinidae include some 275 genera and more than 1,500 species. Of Eurasian origin, it is the largest of all fish families. It is known from the Paleocene of Europe, the Eocene of Asia, and the Miocene of North America.

Minnows are small to large, soft-rayed fishes with toothless jaws, pharyngeal teeth in the back of the mouth cavity which grind food against a plate fastened to the skull beneath the hind brain, and well-developed fins and scales.

The pharyngeal teeth, usually ascribed to the fifth branchial (gill) arch, have been studied in Wisconsin minnows by Peterman (1969), and in depth in Minnesota minnows and suckers by Eastman (1970). Eastman provided a key to the minnow species based solely on these teeth and their arches. Evans and Deubler (1955) noted that the number and arrangement of teeth on the arch is rather constant for the species. In our native North American species the teeth are arranged in one or two rows, and tooth replacement is continuous throughout life.

What appear to be spines in the dorsal and anal fins of such forms as the carp and the goldfish are actually hardened bundles of soft-ray elements which have fused embryonically to give rise to spinous rays. These are not true spines, such as are encountered in the basses and the sunfishes.

In most insectivorous minnows, the digestive tract is a simple S-shaped structure which, when extended, is generally less than the minnow's total length. The lining of the body cavity is silvery, and it may be lightly speckled with dark pigments. Vegetable-feeders, however, have elongated digestive tracts in which additional loops develop from the original S-shaped structure. As the intestine lengthens, the lining of the body cavity darkens to dusky or black.

During the breeding season, the males of many minnow species sport bright, attractive colors and breeding tubercles in various shapes and numbers. These features have made our North American minnows attractive to European fish fanciers. Breeding tubercles have three functions: they aid in the construction of the nest, they are weapons of combat between fighting males, and they enable males to hold females during spawning (Reighard 1903).

Between the swim bladder and the inner ear is the Weberian ossicle device, a chain of three bones derived from the anteriormost vertebrae. These increase the minnow's hearing sensitivity, and Winn and Stout (1960) suggested that perhaps this has been a reason for its success in the fresh waters of the world.

Another successful feature in many minnow species is continuous spawning over a long season, commonly called fractional spawning. Nikolsky (1963) noted that fractional spawning decreases the chance that one or more entire generations will be lost to unfavorable environmental conditions, such as high water or flood stages.

Many intra- and occasionally inter-generic hybrids occur. Minnow hybridization may result from drought conditions on small, spring-fed streams that support large populations of fishes (Cross and Minckley 1960). Unusual crowding of spawning fishes would increase the opportunity for fertilization of the eggs of one species by sperm from another species, and, as noted by Hubbs (1955), hybridization of fishes seems most common in areas that have been subject to radical climatic change within the past 20,000 years, and in streams that have been altered recently by the activities of man.

The use of and demand for bait minnows has led to the development of an important business in and around resort or fishing areas. In 1957, the Wisconsin Department of Natural Resources issued 853 bait dealer licenses. The dealers sold almost 23.5 million minnows with an estimated value of $783,000. The total volume of all minnows used was estimated at 36 million, with a market value of about $1.2 million (Niemuth 1959).

Great demand and uncertain supply have caused many minnow dealers and people who handle live bait to propagate and rear minnows in natural or artificial ponds. Today some people supplement their incomes by raising minnows, while others live entirely off the profits derived from raising and selling minnows. Procedures and methods for raising minnows are discussed by Hasler et al. (1946), Dobie et al. (1956), and Hubbs and Cooper (1936). In recent years tank trucks have transported thousands of golden shiners from Arkansas to Wisconsin to help meet the demand.

The minnow is one of the most important commercial food fishes in the state. In 1976 over 1.25 million kg (2.75 million lb) of carp worth

$179,142 were harvested from the Wisconsin waters of the Mississippi River (Fernholz and Crawley 1977). They weighed over 64% of the total commercial catch, and were surpassed in value only by the catfish catch.

Fish management and research biologists who have conducted surveys with shocking units in southern Wisconsin trout and bass streams have shown that an immense number of minnows are present in most streams having reasonably good habitat (C. L. Brynildson 1959). A minnow dealer who was given a contract to remove forage fish from Milner Branch, Little Grant River (Grant County) seined 174 kg/ha in 1955 and 140 kg/ha in 1956, a high harvest. Subsequent shocking showed that the number of suckers remained essentially constant, and that the number of creek chubs and common shiners increased through natural reproduction and movement. Investigations strongly indicate that forage fish production continues to be high regardless of the intensity of the harvest.

High-density populations of forage fish undoubtedly compete with trout and bass for space and food, but the degree of competition is difficult to measure. Minnows have additional value in that they serve as a "buffer" food for predators that would otherwise deplete trout and bass more extensively.

In addition to the carp and the goldfish, which are well established in Wisconsin waters, other introductions have occurred. According to Baughman (1947), 90 European tench, *Tinca tinca* Linnaeus, were stocked in Wisconsin during 1895–1896. This minnow, which reaches 25–30 cm and about 250 g in 3 to 4 years, has 95–120 small scales along the lateral line, and the skin is thick and slimy (Muus and Dahlstrom 1971). It feeds on the larvae of insects, mostly midges, and on small clams, and snails. The fate of this stocking in Wisconsin is unknown.

In 1916, B. O. Webster, superintendent of hatcheries with the Wisconsin Department of Natural Resources, secured "several pails" of European rudd, *Scardinius erythrophthalmus* (Linnaeus), from the New York Aquarium and stocked them in Oconomowoc Lake (Waukesha County) (Cahn 1927). Cahn reported two successful spawnings; however, no subsequent records are available. This minnow, similar in body form to the golden shiner, has 40–43 scales, and pelvic, anal, and caudal fins which are bright red on the extremities. The eyes are yellow to orange. It averages 20–30 cm and 200–400 g in about 10 years, and feeds on aquatic vegetation, insects, snails, and occasionally fish eggs (Muus and Dahlstrom 1971).

A more recent introduction to Wisconsin has been the grass carp, *Ctenopharyngodon idella* (Valenciennes). It was imported into the United

Grass carp 189 mm, Arkansas State Hatchery, 21 May 1976

States in 1963 by the Bureau of Sport Fisheries and Wildlife to the Fish Farming Experimental Station in Stuttgart, Arkansas, and was soon introduced in waters of Arkansas, Alabama, and Oregon (Greenfield 1973). Illegal importations and stockings of this species into Wisconsin ponds occurred in 1974. In November 1975, 44 grass carp were removed from Maloney Pond near Brodhead (Green County), 1 of which was 490 mm (19.3 in) and weighed 1.56 kg (3 lb 7 oz). Of the 12 grass carp originally stocked in a dairy pond near Manitowoc (Manitowoc County), 1 was killed in April 1975 during rotenone treatment; another was found dead on the shore prior to treatment. V. Hacker (pers. comm.) noted that fingerlings 20–23 cm in May sometimes reach 55 cm (21.5 in) and 1.8 kg (4 lb) by November.

The grass carp has 36–40 lateral line scales and pharyngeal teeth (2,4–4,2). It is reported to reach a length of over 1.2 m and a weight of 45 kg (4 ft and 100 lb) in its native range.

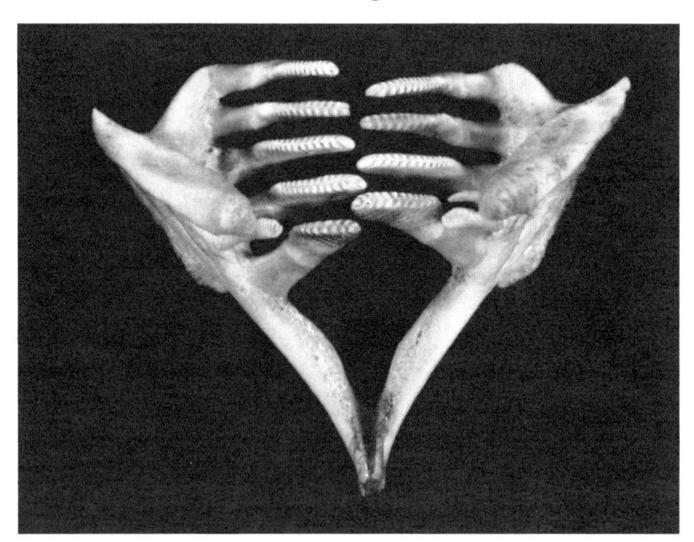

Grass carp pharyngeal teeth

The grass carp was imported into this country as a biological control for aquatic vegetation. If it becomes established in natural waters, it may, like the carp, become a serious pest. It is feared that the grass carp may destroy fish and waterfowl habitat by eliminating all aquatic vegetation in waters where some vegetation is desirable.

Potentially the biggest threat from the grass carp may come from the central Mississippi River, where a number of specimens have been reported by commercial fishermen. A 9.53-kg (21-lb) specimen was caught in 1971 in the Mississippi River near Chester, Illinois (Pflieger 1975). Stroud (1976:4) noted:

> It is indisputable that grass carp are now resident in the Mississippi and Missouri rivers. Since they have already reproduced in two Mexican rivers, there is every reason to expect grass carp to do so in the Mississippi River system and its tributaries. The presence of this fish portends both good and bad for American fishery resources.

Common Carp

Cyprinus carpio Linnaeus. *Cyprinus*—Greek name of the carp; *carpio*—Latinized form of carp.

Other common names: carp, German carp, European carp, mirror carp, leather carp, leatherback, German bass, buglemouth.

Immature 120 mm, Mississinewa Reservoir (Wabash Co.), Indiana, 2 Mar. 1968

Immature 90 mm, (mirror variety), Mississinewa Reservoir (Wabash Co.), Indiana, 2 Mar. 1968

Adult 476 mm, Wisconsin R., Stevens Point (Portage Co.), 22 Sept. 1977

DESCRIPTION

Body robust, compressed laterally. Average size 406–457 mm (16–18 in); TL = 1.24 SL (200 mm); TL = 1.23 SL (400 mm). Depth into TL 3.0–3.9. Head length into TL 3.7–4.3. Snout long; mouth of moderate size reaching to below nostril, 2 fleshy barbels on each side of upper jaw, the smaller hanging from edge of snout, the larger from near corner of mouth. Pharyngeal teeth molarlike, larger teeth often with blackened ridges 1,1,3–3,1,1. Gill rakers 21–27. Dorsal fin originating slightly anterior to or directly below pelvic fin; dorsal fin long, of 1 spinous soft-ray serrated posteriorly, and 15–23 rays; anal fin of 1 spinous soft-ray serrated posteriorly and 4–6 rays; pectoral fin rays 14–17; pelvic fin rays 8–9. Lateral line 32–41; lateral line complete. Digestive tract about 1.6 TL. Chromosomes 2n = 104 (Ohno, Wolf and Atkin 1968).

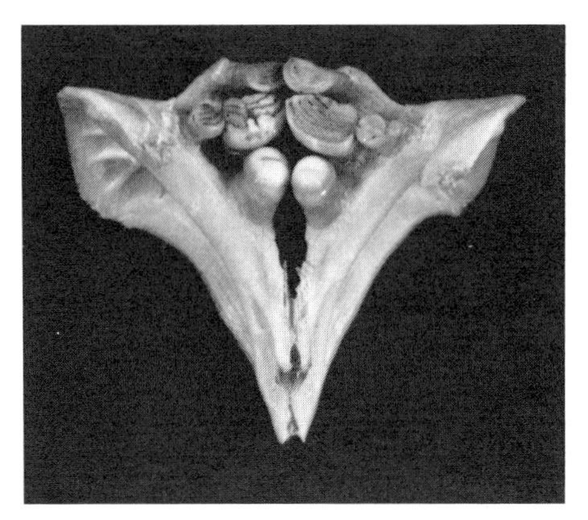

Carp pharyngeal teeth

Brassy olive above, lower sides golden yellow; belly yellow-white. Basal half of caudal and anal fins often reddish; stronger coloration in adults. Each scale on back and sides with dark basal spot. Peritoneum dusky.

Fine breeding tubercles on head and pectoral fins in male, rarely in female. Male obviously darker during the spawning season.

Hybrids: Common carp × goldfish (UWSP 3263), from the Milwaukee River at Estabrook Park (Milwaukee County); from the Crawford River (Dodge County) and the Milwaukee River (Milwaukee County) (Wis. Fish Distrib. Study 1975).

SYSTEMATIC NOTES

The scaled carp with its large, thick cycloid scale, the mirror carp with its occasionally enlarged and scattered scales, and the leather carp in which the scales are absent, are varieties of the same species. The progeny of the mirror and the leather carp are mostly fully scaled. Of the 345 fish imported to the United States as brood stock, 227 were mirror and leather carp and 118 were scaled carp, but nearly all offspring were fully scaled. Mirror and leather carp are quite rare today, constituting less than 2% of all wild carp (Walden 1964). The genetic basis for these varieties is discussed by Wohlfarth and Lahman (1963).

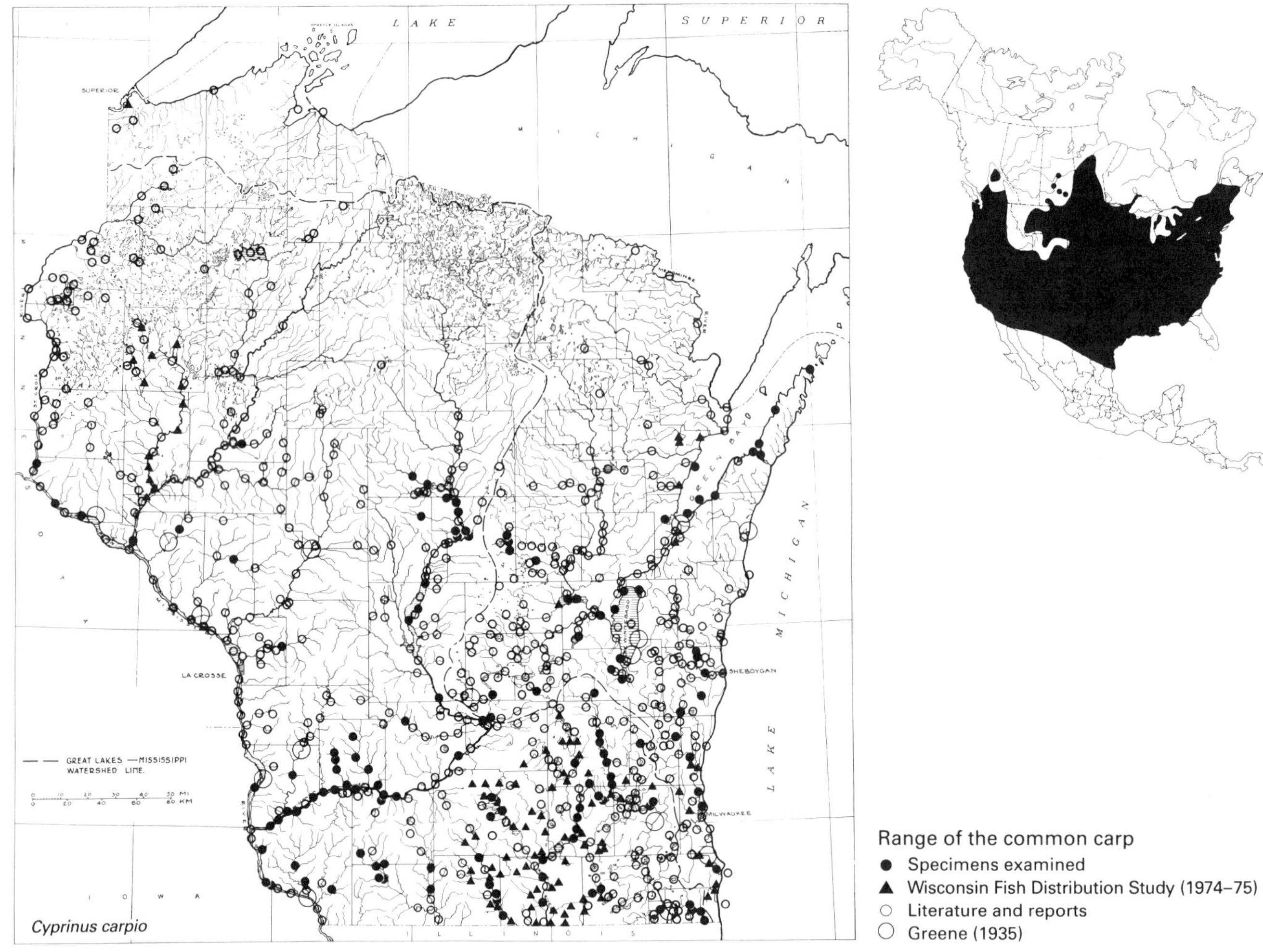

Range of the common carp
● Specimens examined
▲ Wisconsin Fish Distribution Study (1974–75)
○ Literature and reports
◯ Greene (1935)

DISTRIBUTION, STATUS, AND HABITAT

The common carp occurs in all three drainage basins in Wisconsin, and has been steadily extending its range in the state. It is rare in the Lake Superior basin, and on the south shore of Lake Superior the yearly catch is six or fewer individuals; it has been recorded from several streams throughout the area (McLain et al. 1965). In 1958 (Druschba 1959), it had not been reported from Bayfield, Ashland, Iron, Vilas, Florence, Langlade, Lincoln, Oneida, Price, Rusk, and Sawyer counties. In 1975, Hacker (1975) noted this species from all counties except Bayfield, Florence, Iron, Vilas, Oneida, Langlade, Menominee, and Price.

The carp, native to Asia, was mentioned in the 1876 report of the Commissioners of Fisheries of Wisconsin as "a species eminently calculated for the warmer waters of the country." The 1879 report carried a reprint of "A Distinguished Immigrant—Prof. Baird's European Carp." In 1880, 75 carp were obtained from Prof. Baird of the U.S. Commission and forwarded from the carp ponds at Washington, D.C., to the Nevin Hatchery in Madison, Wisconsin. The first year's hatch produced 350 young. In 1881, 163 carp fingerlings in lots of 20–22 were distributed to individuals in Rock, Columbia, Fond du Lac, Sauk, and Manitowoc counties. As many as 35,000 were placed into Wisconsin waters in 1890; distribution continued until 1895, when the program was discontinued. By that time plantings had been made throughout the state, including the northern and central counties of Barron, Douglas, Eau Claire, Langlade, Marathon, St. Croix, Ashland, Marinette, Polk, Price, Sawyer, Shawano, Taylor, and Washburn.

The exotic carp is a characteristic and abundant species in large, shallow lakes and streams in southern and central Wisconsin. In recent years it has become common in some northern Wisconsin waters.

Although the carp is known to survive under a wide range of conditions, it prefers warm streams, lakes, and shallows containing an abundance of aquatic vegetation. The carp is tolerant of all bottom types and of clear or turbid waters, but is not normally found in clear, cold waters or streams of high gradient. The carp is not found in chara-type lakes (Threinen 1952). In Wisconsin it was encountered most frequently in turbid water at depths of 0.6–1.5 m over substrates of sand (frequency 29%), mud (19%), clay (10%), gravel (23%), silt (9%), rubble (6%), boulders (3%), and detritus (1%). It occurred in rivers of the following widths: 1.0–3.0 m (8%), 3.1–6.0 m (13%), 6.1–12.0 m (22%), 12.1–24.0 m (42%), 24.0–50.0 (15%).

BIOLOGY

In Wisconsin the spawning period for carp extends from April to August (Miller 1942). The greatest activity occurs in late May or early June when water temperatures range from 18.3–23.9°C (65–75°F) (Cahn 1927, Mraz and Cooper 1957b). Spawning occurs in shallow, weedy areas of lakes, ponds, tributary streams, swamps, temporary flood plains, and marshes at depths of 8 cm to about 183 cm (3 in to 6 ft) (Mansueti and Hardy 1967). Intermittent spawning may last several days to several weeks, possibly with two spawning peaks in some areas.

Carp segregate into small groups typically consisting of one pair, or of a female and two to four males, or of one female with six to seven males. Swee and McCrimmon (1966) described spawning behavior (p. 377):

> In the prespawning phase, each group of fish swam locally in a compact school within the relatively open areas of the marsh with their dorsal fins and backs exposed above the water. The males initiated the spawning act by repeatedly pushing their heads against the body of the female. Each prospective spawning group gathered in a shallow area, usually in less than 12 inches of water where there was an abundance of vegetation on which the adhesive eggs could be broadcast. On stimulation by the males, the female responded by raising her caudal peduncle and tail. Her tail lashed violently and, as she propelled herself forward, the eggs were scattered over the vegetation. Simultaneously, the males came along the side of the female with their tail region proximate to the female genital opening and, by violent movements of their tail region, discharged their milt.

Spawning was observed on 28 May in the early afternoon (W. McKee, pers. comm.) at the mouth of the Mink River (Door County): "The spawning was very intense, as I only had to stand still for a minute or two and the spawning activity resumed around me. Several times I had carp bump against my ankles. And on several occasions I witnessed 'picture perfect' mating units of one large female flanked on either side by two smaller males. If I caused a commotion by running through the water a very literal acre of water around me came alive with startled carp!"

In Lake St. Lawrence, Ontario, spawning did not occur at water temperatures below 16°C (60.8°F), activity was comparatively low at 16–18°C (60.8–64.4°F), reached an optimum between 19 and 23°C (66.2 and 73.4°F), and ceased at temperatures above 28°C (82.4°F). Temperature is the primary environmental stimulus to spawning (Swee and McCrimmon 1966).

Carp in holding ponds apparently do not spawn successfully (Black 1948). Even if spawning is attempted in the pond, the thorough working the carp give the bottom daily would almost certainly prevent any of the eggs from surviving long enough to hatch.

The individual female deposits her eggs in groups of from 500 to 600 in an area roughly 2 m diam (Jester 1974). These eggs are 0.9–2.0 mm diam and of a grayish white to yellowish color. The adhesive eggs either stick to debris or plants or sink to the bottom, where they lie disregarded by both parents.

Despite the fact that no males were present, females which were temporarily held in a large tank at a Wisconsin hatchery spawned by bumping against the side of the concrete tank while swimming alongside it (Mraz and Cooper 1957b). Soon the entire tank, which was more than 6 m long, had a layer of eggs sticking to the bottom.

Fecundity is variable, depending on the size of the female. In an age-IV female about 391 mm (15.4 in) TL, 56,400 eggs are produced; in an age-XVI female 851 mm TL, more than 2.2 million eggs are produced (Swee and McCrimmon 1966). In the Madison region females weighing 4.5–6.8 kg (10–15 lb) produce more than 1 million eggs each (Miller 1952). The number of eggs discharged at the primary spawning is from 50,000 to 620,000 (Mansueti and Hardy 1967).

The incubation period extends from 3 to 16 days, depending on the temperature: 3–5 days at 20°C (68°F); 5 days at 15°C (59°F) (Mansueti and Hardy 1967). At hatching the yolk-sac larvae are 3.0–6.4 mm TL. Mansueti and Hardy describe and illustrate stages between 4 mm and 30 mm TL. Scales become evident anteriorly on sides at 22.5 mm, and scalation is complete at 30 mm.

The artificial breeding of carp has been difficult because of the sticky layer which develops on the surface of the eggs, causing them to clump together when they come in contact with water. A solution of 0.6% sodium chloride (salt) temporarily inhibits the stickiness of the eggs and permits them to be poured uniformly into hatching trays (Blaylock and Griffith 1971).

For the first 2 days of life, the young carp are attached to vegetation or lie near it. After 4–5 days, the yolk-sac is gone and the young move to the bottom. At 18 days, young carp may be nearly 25 mm (1 in) long and will tend to move into slightly deeper water. The young fish remain in this habitat for much of the summer, a trait which makes them relatively unavailable to many of the predacious fish which might eat them while they are small. By the time the young carp leave the shallow, weedy habitat, they are often 76–102 mm (3–4 in) long and are relatively safe from predation (Sigler 1958). Small crustaceans (Entomostraca) are a major food of young carp (Moen 1953).

The growth of young-of-year has been recorded as follows:

Date	No. of Fish	TL (mm) Avg	TL (mm) Range	Location
18 June	1	46		Wisconsin R. (Grant Co.)
27 July	7	22	20.5–24	Wisconsin R. (Portage Co.)
7 Aug.	5	52	32–69	Mill Cr. (Richland Co.)
14 Aug.	8	99	80–117	Sugar R. (Green Co.)
17 Sept.	18	93	70–107	Wisconsin R. (Portage Co.)

Carp are generally aged by analyzing scale annuli, although this method is not always reliable. Opercular bones were used by Sigler (1958). A method of sectioning carp spines for growth studies was described by English (1952).

In Lake Monona (Dane County) age-II males on 21 June were 360 mm TL; age-II females were 366 mm TL (Frey 1942). Similar growth was found in Lake Kegonsa. In Lake Waubesa age-III males were 388 mm TL and females, 424 mm TL. The first annulus formed in late May; the second and third annuli formed from middle of June into second half of July. Miller (1952) determined that Lake Waubesa carp less than 3 years old were 419 mm (16.5 in) TL and weighed 1.09 kg (2.4 lb).

In four large carp from the Wisconsin River (Juneau County) collected 21 July 1976, the calculated total length at the annuli was: 2—304 mm, 3—404 mm, 4—490 mm, 5—543 mm, 6—584 mm, 7—622 mm, 8—643 mm, 9—667 mm, 10—695 mm, 11—746 mm, and 12—761 mm (W. McKee, pers. comm.). The first annulus was not readable on the scales. Three of the fish were age X, and one was age XII. Carp from the Mississippi River near Fountain City had the following calculated total lengths at time of annulus formation (sexes combined): 1—196 mm, 2—376 mm, 3—486 mm, 4—561 mm, and 5—655 mm (Christenson and Smith 1965).

Selective breeding has developed some fast-growing races of carp in other parts of the world. In Israel, carp from selected stock weighed over 907 g (2 lb) in October in the first year of life (Carlander 1969).

In Wisconsin, male carp may mature at age II and females at age III (a few at age II) (Miller 1952, Frey 1940).

A 25.91-kg (57-lb 2-oz) carp was caught from Lake Wisconsin (Columbia County) on 28 August 1966. A 27.9-kg (61-lb 8-oz) carp was taken from Big Wolf Lake (Jackson County, Michigan), in 1974. A carp weighing 37.88 kg (83.5 lb) was taken at Pretoria, South Africa (Walden 1964).

The usual longevity of the carp is 9–15 years; maximum observed longevity is 47 years (Brown 1957).

Carp are omnivorous. In 42 carp up to 460 mm TL from the Madison, Wisconsin, area, 49% of the contents of the digestive tracts consisted of immature and adult individuals from the following insect orders: Diptera, Ephemeroptera, Trichoptera, Hemiptera, and Coleoptera (Pearse 1918). In addition Pearse found entomostracans (20.9%), amphipods (6.9%), snails (6.9%), and lesser quantities of oligochaetes, mites, rotifers, plants, silt, and debris. In Lake Mendota (Pearse 1921a) carp averaging 383 mm TL had taken fish (35%), snails (32.8%), plants (2.8%), and bottom ooze (27.9%). Although the literature occasionally reports fish in the carp's diet, the percentage of fish in this report is exceptionally high.

In Iowa (Moen 1953), the diet of carp of all sizes is predominantly animal material from three principal groups: insect larvae, crustaceans, and mollusks. In addition, Moen noted oligochaete worms, freeliving flatworms, leeches, and water mites. His data indicated that carp will take walleye (*Stizostedion vitreum*) eggs during the spawning period, but the predation is not extensive. One stomach from an April collection of 37 Spirit Lake carp contained 3 walleye eggs. In carp from the Des Moines River (Harrison 1950), insects made up 53% of stomach contents and included mayflies, dipterans, caddisflies, aquatic beetles, and hemipterans. Terrestrial insects were consumed by many individuals, but made up only a small part of the volume. The plant material (32%) consisted of green leaves from lowland trees, grasses, twigs, rootlets, and green algae. Bryozoans, crayfish, earthworms, fish scales, and fry of the spotfin and the bullhead minnows were also identified. During winter months animal organisms (crustaceans and dipterous larvae) made up 100% of the diet, with only traces of plant material (Moen 1953). Fish taken during low oxygen conditions (less than 1.0 ppm) were all empty.

In Elephant Butte Lake (New Mexico), the algae

Chlorophyta and Chrysophyta were the most important food items in the carp diet (Jester 1974). Plant materials made up 43.5% and animal materials, mostly Copepoda and Cladocera, 10.2%. Jester concluded that carp are versatile omnivores, eating whatever food is available.

Cannibalism by large carp larvae of smaller larvae, even in the presence of abundant plankton, was reported by Kudrynska (1962). Sigler (1958) cited a report of young carp (25–51 mm) taken from the stomachs of 5- to 9-kg (10–20-lb) carp.

Carp appear to utilize a sequence of tactile and gustatory cues in the prey selection process (Stein et al. 1975). They have taste sensations similar to mammals and can sense salty, sweet, bitter, and acid stimuli (Lagler et al. 1962).

In general, carp do little feeding in water below 10°C (50°F), and none at 1.7–4.5°C (35.1–40.1°F) (Carlander 1969).

The carp adapts to a wider variety of conditions than almost any native North American fish. Habitat requirements permit carp to range the state's extensive warm waters with little concern for low oxygen content, pollution, or sudden temperature changes. Carp are able to withstand turbidities far in excess of those found in most natural waters, but 165,000 ppm (silicon dioxide equivalents) are fatal to 3-inch carp (Sigler 1958). Fatal turbidities are considerably lower for largemouth bass, pumpkinseed, channel catfish, and rock bass, but higher for the black bullhead and golden shiner. The carp has the capacity to adjust to higher than normal salinity—up to 17 ppt, which is a concentration of salts considerably higher than that in their own bodies (Lagler et al. 1962).

The carp's ability to tolerate low oxygen levels is well known and often it is one of the last survivors in oxygen-depleted waters. This relates to its ability to use atmospheric oxygen (MacKay 1963).

In a widespread fish-kill due to supersaturation of oxygen from an algal bloom, only a few carp suffered mortality. The fish looked normal except for small gas bubbles, under the skin and in the fin rays, which obstructed the flow of blood (Mackenthun et al. 1948).

Aquarium-held carp (Sigler 1958) in water 1.7°C (35.1°F) are quite inactive, with no apparent inclination to move about. At 2.2°C (36°F) these carp move away when approached, but show no inclination to feed. When the temperature is raised to 26.7°C (80.1°F), they dash frantically around the aquarium, frequently hitting the sides when an observer approaches. Wild carp have been observed to begin activity at a water temperature of 3.3°C (37.9°F).

Sigler speculated that an average optimum water temperature for carp is 20°C (68°F). This is the maximum temperature at which carp will spawn. Growth would be slow at this temperature, but the fish would be long-lived. In a Canadian study dealing with temperature preference (Pitt et al. 1956), carp selected water at 32°C (89.6°F). In Wisconsin the preferred water temperature was 31.8°C (89.2°F); in the field (Lake Monona power plant outfall), this temperature was 30.6° (87.1°F) (Neill and Magnuson 1974). This is obviously above the temperature at which carp can either reproduce or survive for a long period of time on short rations; however, they can probably live at this temperature for long periods if sufficient food is available. The upper lethal temperatures are between 31 and 34°C (87.8 and 93.2°F) when carp are acclimated at 20°C (68°F), and 35.7°C (96.3°F) when they are acclimated at 26°C (78.8°F) (Black 1953). The lower lethal temperature is a body temperature of −0.7°C (30.7°F) (Bardach et al. 1966).

Sigler (1958) reported that with rising temperatures activity among carp increases and some leaping may be seen. No one knows exactly why carp leap and splash, although it has been called "playing." The larger fish move into shallow waters in the afternoon or evening, often in enormous concentrations (Nord 1967).

Carp normally seek quiet waters and dark holes, avoiding swift water except during the spring spawning runs. They are rarely reported below depths of 30 m (100 feet), even in deep lakes. This reluctance to inhabit deep water may be due to avoidance of the low water temperatures found at greater depths.

Except in the spring, carp are usually wary and dash for cover or deep water at the slightest disturbance. At other times they swim about in a leisurely and almost lazy fashion. A change in the weather can cause them to alter their habitual movements; even a slight change in the water level affects them. For example, in Illinois, Sigler watched carp moving freely into flooded corn fields as long as the water level was rising; however, a drop in the water level as slight as a few inches sent them scurrying back to the protection of the river.

Carp seining operations are intensified in the spring and in the fall during those seasons when the carp form schools, making it possible to catch them in large numbers (Miller 1952). A seine haul in November 1973 by a Wisconsin Department of Natural Resources crew on Lake Koshkonong produced a record 340,000 kg (750,000 lb) (V. Hacker, pers. comm.). Schooling is also characteristic under the ice.

Carp may range extensively. One fish tagged in Missouri was recaptured 28 months later in South

Dakota, after traveling at least 1,088 km (674 mi) (Sigler 1958). Recently the Nebraska Game and Parks Commission reported a carp which covered 1,629 km (1,009 mi) on the Missouri, Mississippi, and White rivers. One carp tagged in Lake Winnebago, at Supple's Marsh near Fond du Lac, was recaptured in the Embarrass River, approximately 148 km (92 river miles) away (Priegel and Morrissette 1971). In Lake Winnebago and connecting waters most carp have been recaptured within a few kilometers of tagging sites.

Almost all warmwater fish are associated at one time or another with carp. In the Baraboo River (Sauk County), the carp is associated with the bluegill, black bullhead, largemouth bass, white crappie, and northern pike. In a collection from the Blue River (Grant County), the following species (number) were found together: common carp (26), quillback (1), bigmouth buffalo (1), shorthead redhorse (21), white sucker (3), central stoneroller (2), creek chub (6), golden shiner (1), bullhead minnow (22), bluntnose minnow (9), suckermouth minnow (1), common shiner (12), emerald shiner (13), spotfin shiner (102), sand shiner (3), bigmouth shiner (11), Mississippi silvery minnow (230), stonecat (1), johnny darter (23), and banded darter (1).

IMPORTANCE AND MANAGEMENT

Predators of carp, particularly the young, are bass, crappies, northern pike, bowfin, turtles, snakes, loons, mergansers, grebes, and goshawks. Predacious water insects destroy small carp, as do frogs and toads. The eggs are eaten by minnows, catfish, and sunfish. The adults are parasitized by lampreys. In a feeding preference test (Coble 1973), northern pike always selected carp and fathead minnows over green sunfish and bluegills. A great blue heron was killed by a 31-cm (12-in) carp which it tried to swallow (Ryder 1950); apparently the carp was too large for the heron to swallow, but the bird was unable to regurgitate the fish because the dorsal spine pierced the gullet and held the fish fast.

Carp are an important source of gonadotropins for many game fishes. Both mature eggs and sperm were obtained from rainbow trout in advance of the normal spawning period in Wisconsin by intraperitoneal injections of fresh or acetone-dried pituitary glands of the carp (Hasler et al. 1939).

Carp have been proposed as a source of forage for game fish (Sorenson 1971). A major problem in muskellunge culture is the establishment of a reliable source of fry, and carp may provide a solution. Injection of carp females with carp pituitary induces spawning within 12 hours.

Carp have been used as weed control agents; many shallow fishing lakes would soon become choked with aquatic vegetation if it were not for their activities (Moyle and Kuehn 1964). The eradication of carp in many southern Wisconsin river impoundments has resulted in weed-choked waters.

Carp in some localities are important as eradicators of fluke diseases that attack sheep (Adams and Hankinson 1926). In grass bottomlands during annual overflows, carp eat the snails (*Limnaea*) that harbor stages in the life history of the flukes. Lastly, the carp makes an excellent bioassay animal, because it is hardy, seldom subject to diseases, and highly productive.

Problems associated with the carp were recognized as early as 1891–1892 when the Wisconsin superintendent of fisheries, noting carp habits in California, called them "a great nuisance to the sportsman who uses a gun . . . " because they destroy wild river beds "by their ground hog proclivities." At the 1901 meetings of the American Fisheries Society in Milwaukee, a special roundtable discussion was held on the carp. General E. E. Bryant, a member of the Wisconsin Conservation Commission, noted that within a radius of 8 km of Madison there were "billions of carp," and that every fisherman saw them, cursed them, and refused to catch them. George Peabody of Appleton reported that the introduction of carp in Lake Koshkonong had destroyed the fishing for black bass and pike, roiled the waters, and ruined duck hunting through the destruction of wild rice and celery (Black 1944).

There are many illustrations of the loss of aquatic vegetation where carp are abundant (Threinen and Helm 1954). At Madison, Wisconsin, during 1944–1945 carp were stocked at an equivalent of 532 kg/ha (475 lb/acre) in a pond with a dense growth of waterweed (*Anacharis canadensis*), sago pondweed (*Potamogeton foliosus*), and lesser amounts of pickerel weed (*Potamogeton richardsonii*), coontail (*Ceratophyllum demersum*), and wild rice (*Zizania aquatica*) (Black 1946). Fifty-one days later the aquatic vegetation was reduced to a very critical stage: the wild rice had been uprooted within a few days of stocking, the sago pondweed was torn out quickly, and the coontail soon after; only the waterweed, heavily grazed, and the pickerel weed remained. When the pickerel weed was attacked, however, it was destroyed completely in less than 2 weeks.

Competition exists between young largemouth bass and carp of all ages for the available food, and in areas of spawning the largemouth is at a definite disadvantage (Sigler 1958, Mraz and Cooper 1957b). Competition between the carp and the green sunfish for available habitat takes place because both fish frequent shallow water and occasionally compete for the same spawning area (Sigler 1958). Competition between the carp and the black bullhead is for habitat, food, and spawning areas: "The more aggressive carp move into available spawning areas at the expense of bullheads, and the excessive activity of spawning carp is probably disturbing to them" (Sigler 1958).

The contention that the presence of carp even in small numbers is detrimental to game fish is strongly disputed by the fact that nearly every lake in southern Wisconsin has carp present, yet game fish thrive except in those lakes where a dense carp population exists (Mraz and Cooper 1957a). Nonetheless, there is constant pressure by the public to remove carp, even from waters where their numbers are known to be small.

Dymond (1955) believes that the success of carp and the disappearance of other species in some waters are probably attributable to changed ecological conditions incident to the clearing of land. Two such conditions that favor carp more than most other fish are the high temperatures of the streams and the silting of lakes and streams. High water temperatures result from the removal of bank and land cover. Silting results from the erosion of agricultural and other lands. Ellis (1973) noted that the carp is a symptom, not a cause. Its abundance is due to ecological changes in the habitat that represent improved conditions for carp and deteriorating conditions for game species.

Highly polluted waters, such as the Illinois River (Mills et al. 1966), have noticeable effects on carp. First, the length-to-depth ratio of individuals increases as pollution increases. By dividing the depth into the standard length, an index is obtained; if the fish's length is 3 or more times greater than its depth, it is too thin for commercial uses. Any index under 3 would indicate a satisfactory commercial fish. Second, carp exhibit a rachitic bone malformation, known as "knothead" condition, which becomes more conspicuous with increased pollution.

Sigler (1958) summarized the basic carp problem in the following statement:

> Granted that carp may be more able competitors than many game fish, or that carp may be able to replace game fish only after the habitat has sufficiently deteriorated, it still remains that carp can and do alter a habitat in such a way that it is less suitable for game fish—and even for carp themselves. However, in general, it is expected that game fish will be handicapped more by these habitat changes than will carp, and that carp will therefore become dominant.

Once a carp population has established itself in an area, other factors may operate along with selective harvesting to account for population balance in favor of carp (Sigler 1958). One factor is the comparatively few fatal diseases that plague carp; another is the wild carp's comparative freedom from harassment by effective enemies.

Izaak Walton (1653) early extolled the virtues of this species:

> The carp is the Queen of Rivers, a stately, a good, and a very subtil fish. . . .

There are many devotees to fishing for this species, in Wisconsin and elsewhere, and carpophiles from over the world come to the United States—the center of the finest carp fishing in the world (Gapen 1973).

Dr. Increase Lapham wrote in 1882: "The day will come when the people of the state (Wisconsin) will thank the men who have introduced and planted this extra fine species of fish (carp)." In 1882 the city council of Ripon passed an ordinance "prohibiting fishing in all waters within the city limits, for the protection of the trout and carp, for two years." To make certain that the carp would succeed, the 1884 report of the Commissioners of Fisheries of Wisconsin noted: "It is useless to undertake to grow carp where there are other fish. The fish must be cultivated in ponds expressly built for them and those of different ages must be kept by themselves."

In many lakes and rivers in southern Wisconsin, the carp today is first in numbers and fish biomass. To many it is a sport fish; and it is sought with hook and line, using doughballs and other soft baits; it has also been speared, hunted with bow and arrow, netted, and snagged. In Pools 4, 5, 7, and 11 of the Mississippi River in 1967–1968, the estimated sport fishery catch of carp was 4,367 fish weighing a total of 8,375 kg (18,463 lb) (Wright 1970).

The carp has become an important commercial species in Wisconsin. Before 1903 it was not taken in Lake Pepin in any large quantities; by 1907 this wide spread of the Upper Mississippi River was producing more carp than any other species of fish: " . . . (fishermen) of Bay City caught, in December 1907 with one haul of a seine . . . 55,000 pounds of carp for which they received four and one-half cents per pound" (Commissioners of Fisheries of Wisconsin, 1907–1908).

In the Wisconsin portion of the Mississippi River during the 1960–1964 period, the carp harvest rose from 1.144 million to more than 1.862 million kg (2.522 million to 4.105 million lb). The average price per kilo varied between 7 and 9¢. Seines and gill nets accounted for 96% of the carp caught. Lake Pepin was by far the greatest carp-producing area in the Wisconsin boundary waters, and Pools 8 and 9 were next in carp production. In 1974, carp amounted to 63% (1.26 million kg or 2.78 million lb) of the total commercial catch in the Mississippi River. In 1975, the value per kilogram was 12¢ or $93,345.72 for 769,848 kg (1.70 million lb) (Fernholz and Crawley 1976).

The time of the carp's first appearance in Lake Michigan is not known. Commercial production records started in 1893, with an entry of 900 kg (2,000 lb), and by 1899 the catch had increased to 11,300 kg (25,000 lb). Production passed 454,000 kg (1 million lb) in 1934. The annual average was 680,000 kg (1.5 million lb) from 1934 to 1965 and 1.04 million kg (2.3 million lb) from 1966 to 1970 (Wells and McLain 1973). The 1975 catch was 1.47 million kg (3.24 million lb)—1.16 million kg (2.56 million lb) from haul seines and 261,923 kg (577,431 lb) from 18-cm stretch (7-in stretch) gill nets. The value of the carp fishery was $142,850 in 1974 (Wis. Dep. Nat. Resour. 1976c). A large percentage of the catch has been from southern Green Bay, although some carp are taken in nearly all shallow areas of the lake, particularly in the southeastern portion.

In 1976 Wisconsin Department of Natural Resources fish removal crews took 5,000 kg (11,020 lb) of carp from Lake Winnebago (Wis. Dep. Nat. Resour. 1976b).

From 1949 to 1976, 80.7 million kg (178 million lb) of underutilized fish, of which 62% were carp, were removed from Wisconsin waters. Most of the carp are used as human food (Hacker 1975). Large carp are sent to markets in New York, Philadelphia, Chicago, Memphis, and other cities in the southern states. In 1978 prices paid to the commercial fisherman for fresh fish in the round are only 11–22¢/kg, but the consumer paid $2.20/kilo or more for carp fillets and smoked chunks. Smoked carp is becoming increasingly popular, and carp meat products are finding a growing market.

Wisconsin carp are in demand for fee-fishing ponds in southern states, where fishermen are turning to carp for sport fishing. During 1951 over 91,000 kg (200,000 lb) of carp removed from Wisconsin waters were transported alive to other states to stock fishing ponds, where fishermen may catch Wisconsin carp with hook and line after paying an admission fee (Miller 1952). In 1967, nearly 454,000 kg, at a price of $0.12/kg, were shipped from Wisconsin to southern states for fee-fishing ponds (DeLoughery 1975).

When properly prepared the meat of carp is excellent. Carp may be skinned, and the dark streak running along each side cut out and discarded. After the meat has been soaked in salt water from 2 to 6 hours, it may be cooked by any of the usual methods. There are many folders, bulletins, and cookbooks containing recipes in which carp is the basic protein ingredient. Carp delicacies may be prepared by consulting Mattingly (1976). Hacker (1976) provides recipes for carp chowder, pickled fish, carp sandwich, and hors d'oeuvre of smoked carp. In *The Art of Viennese Cooking* (Morton 1970) recipes are provided for boiled carp, fish stock, Polish carp, and fish goulash; Gapen (1973) provides recipes for steaks, steamed carp, French fried carp, carp rolls, and carp cakes.

In recent years the use of carp as human food has taken a dramatic setback. Polychlorinated biphenyls (PCBs), toxic industrial chemicals, have accumulated in the fats of carp in some Wisconsin waters and fish consumers are therefore warned against eating more than one meal of carp per week. Wisconsin fishing regulations should be consulted for information as to the waters affected.

In Wisconsin a number of years ago canned carp were sold for human consumption under the title "Lake Fish," and the sales went well (E. Schneberger, pers. comm.). When the company was required to place "carp" on the label, sales dropped and the business halted. In Minnesota, however, an entrepreneur is currently making carp into baloney, dips, country-style fish sausage, fish breakfast links, wieners, and even a mock tunafish sandwich spread.

The so-called "muddy" taste in carp was researched by Lewis (1939), who reported that microorganisms of the group *Actinomyces* were responsible. Sigler (1958) noted that carp lose objectionable tastes if they are taken alive and placed in clear, running water for 5–10 days or more.

The following measures for controlling carp have been instituted or suggested:

1. Seining is often the most practical method of removing carp, but it may be expensive (Miller 1952, Peterson 1956). In Lake Wingra, during a 2-year period in which the population was reduced by about 90% by the seine fishery, as well as by natural mortality, carp reproduction remained negligible (Neess et al. 1957, Churchill 1976).
2. Barriers can be erected to prevent carp from entering new waters or from reinvading waters from which they have been removed. Movement of carp may be restricted through the use of wood traps (Miller 1952), screens, and dams, each peculiarly suited to certain conditions.

3. Water level fluctuations may be used effectively against eggs and sac-fry. Lowering the water in an impoundment just a few inches may be sufficient to destroy eggs and larvae by exposing them to air.
4. Parasites and diseases specific to carp may be introduced as a means of control. To date these measures have not proved themselves; they may be dangerous (Sigler 1958).
5. Electricity may be used to direct fish movements, capture fish, and kill fish.
6. Chemicals may be used in shallow impoundments and ponds where the level of lakes or reservoirs can be sufficiently lowered. Several kinds of toxicants, such as rotenone, toxaphene, and antimycin have been used in fish control programs in the past; rotenone and antimycin are still in use. With chemical programs care must be taken that the native fish species are not destroyed.
7. Sonar and radio-telemetry tracking of carp during the winter can be used to locate and capture large schools of these fish when they are under ice (Johnsen and Heitz 1975).
8. Prohibiting the use of carp as bait will prevent the contamination of new waters and the reentry of carp into cleared waters. Wisconsin regulations forbid the use of carp as bait fish.

It is generally conceded that the exploitation of the commercial and sport possibilities of carp is the solution that offers the most promise for carp control (Sigler 1958, Nord 1967). According to Sigler, the use of carp as a high protein supplement offers promise, but further technological advances are needed before carp meal can compete with marine fish products. In order to increase human consumption of carp, it would be necessary to advertise carp as a product to the general public. Sigler (p. 58) continues:

> The problem is important because, heretofore, little has been done to bring to light the undeveloped potential of an abundant and seemingly inexhaustible natural resource. It is important because at the present time a low-cost, high-protein food supply and animal feed supplement is available to the people of the state. It is important because the recreational, commercial, and industrial values of our carp populations should be exploited as part of the tremendous social and economic expansion. . . . Finally, it is important because in times of possible national emergency, we have within our borders a readily obtainable food supply.

Although Sigler wrote this in behalf of Utah, the concepts are applicable to Wisconsin. There is no other species of fish in our state that equals the carp in the production of protein pounds. Although the Wisconsin Department of Natural Resources has attempted in many ways to promote utilization of this species as a worthwhile food product for man and animal, segments of the public refuse to accept such a useful perspective.

Unless we are willing to spend millions of dollars to pull out dams and restore the watersheds of our streams in Wisconsin, we will have carp in abundance. The best way to handle the carp is to utilize it as a sport fish, as a food fish, and as a "desirable" species.

Goldfish

Carassius auratus (Linnaeus). *Carassius*—Latinization of the vernacular names Karass or Karausche (German for Crucian carp); *auratus*—gilded.

Other common names: golden carp; Indiana, Baltimore, and Missouri minnow.

110 mm, L. Michigan, Port Washington (Ozaukee Co.), 15 Sept. 1973

DESCRIPTION

Body deep and stout, moderately compressed. Average length 152–203 mm (6–8 in). Depth into TL 2.9–3.6. Head length into TL 3.8–4.1. Snout pointed. Maxillary short, reaching to below nostril. Mouth terminal, oblique; barbels absent. Pharyngeal teeth 4–4 on heavy arch, 1 tooth conical and 3 with crowns expanded laterally, compressed dorso-ventrally, and sheared off at an angle. Gill rakers 37–43. Fins heavy, rounded on edge; dorsal originating over or slightly ahead of pelvic fin; dorsal fin long, of 1 spinous soft-ray serrated posteriorly and 15–19 rays; anal fin of 1 spinous soft-ray serrated posteriorly and 5 (6) soft rays; pectoral fin rays 15–16; pelvic fin rays 9 (8). Lateral line scales 27–30; lateral line complete. Digestive tract, of several loops, about 1.5 TL. Chromosomes 2n = 100 (Kobayasi et al. 1970).

Color variable from olive green to red, orange or gold, commonly orange variegated with black. General dull gray-olive in some populations. Scott and Crossman (1973) suggested that the highly colored fish became more rare, partly as a result of selective predation by fish-eating birds, such as herons. Peritoneum dusky to black. Young variable from green, bronze to black.

Sexual dimorphism: In males, fine breeding tubercles on opercles, back, and on pectoral fins. Male with longer pectoral and pelvic fins than female.

Hybrids: Goldfish × common carp (UWSP 3263), from the Milwaukee River at Estabrook Park (Milwaukee County); from the Crawford River (Dodge County) and the Milwaukee River (Milwaukee County) (Wis. Fish Distrib. Study 1975).

DISTRIBUTION, STATUS, AND HABITAT

The goldfish occurs in the southeastern quarter of Wisconsin. Since it has been reported from southeastern Minnesota, it may also occur in the Mississippi River. In Waukesha County goldfish have been liberated in Oconomowoc Lake and Lac La Belle, where, according to Cahn (1927), schools of large goldfish (up to 0.9 kg) "have established themselves, reproducing in considerable numbers." Wisconsin Department of Natural Resources biologist D. Mraz (pers. comm.) stated that Peters Lake (Walworth County) has had a common goldfish population for years: "They run about 12 in. long and are a real sight to see." In 1974, Department of Natural Resources biologist D. Dodge (pers. comm.) observed goldfish up to 305 mm (12 in) long, weighing 0.45–0.91 kg (1–2 lb), in the lower 0.8 km (0.5 mi) of Sauk Creek (Ozaukee County).

The goldfish, a native of Asia, has been introduced into many American waters. The direct importation of oriental goldfish into the United States began at a comparatively recent date. The first specimens seem to have been brought over by Rear Admiral Daniel Ammen, USN, in 1878, and fish of that lot were presented to the United States Fish Commissioner and extensively bred at the government nurseries in Washington. Subsequently, large numbers of Japanese goldfish were brought into the United States by private fanciers and by regular dealers; other importations were made from Europe.

At the World's Columbian Exposition in Chicago in 1893, goldfish were kept in pools and lagoons as exhibits, and afterward were released or escaped into Lake Michigan (Woods 1970). Large goldfish can still be seen in the weed beds of the yacht harbors in the area.

In Wisconsin, the earliest stocking of the goldfish was in Lake Mendota in 1855 by Governor Farwell (McNaught 1963). Today the most frequent reports of goldfish in Wisconsin come from Milwaukee County. They have been observed in the Milwaukee River from near the Ozaukee county line to the downtown area. Small schools of goldfish are often seen near the surface of the water below the State Street and Wells Street bridges. Many Milwaukee ponds and lagoons are ideally suited to this species, which has been reported from Saveland Park Pond (Poff and Threinen 1964), Jackson Park, and Mitchell Park. Richard Howmiller (pers. comm.) noted: "Many years ago I caught hordes of goldfish, all colors, to about 14 inches in Mitchell Park—could be a sizeable population there."

Some of the goldfish that have been reported in Wisconsin may have been unwanted pets that were released into public waters. In a Department of Natu-

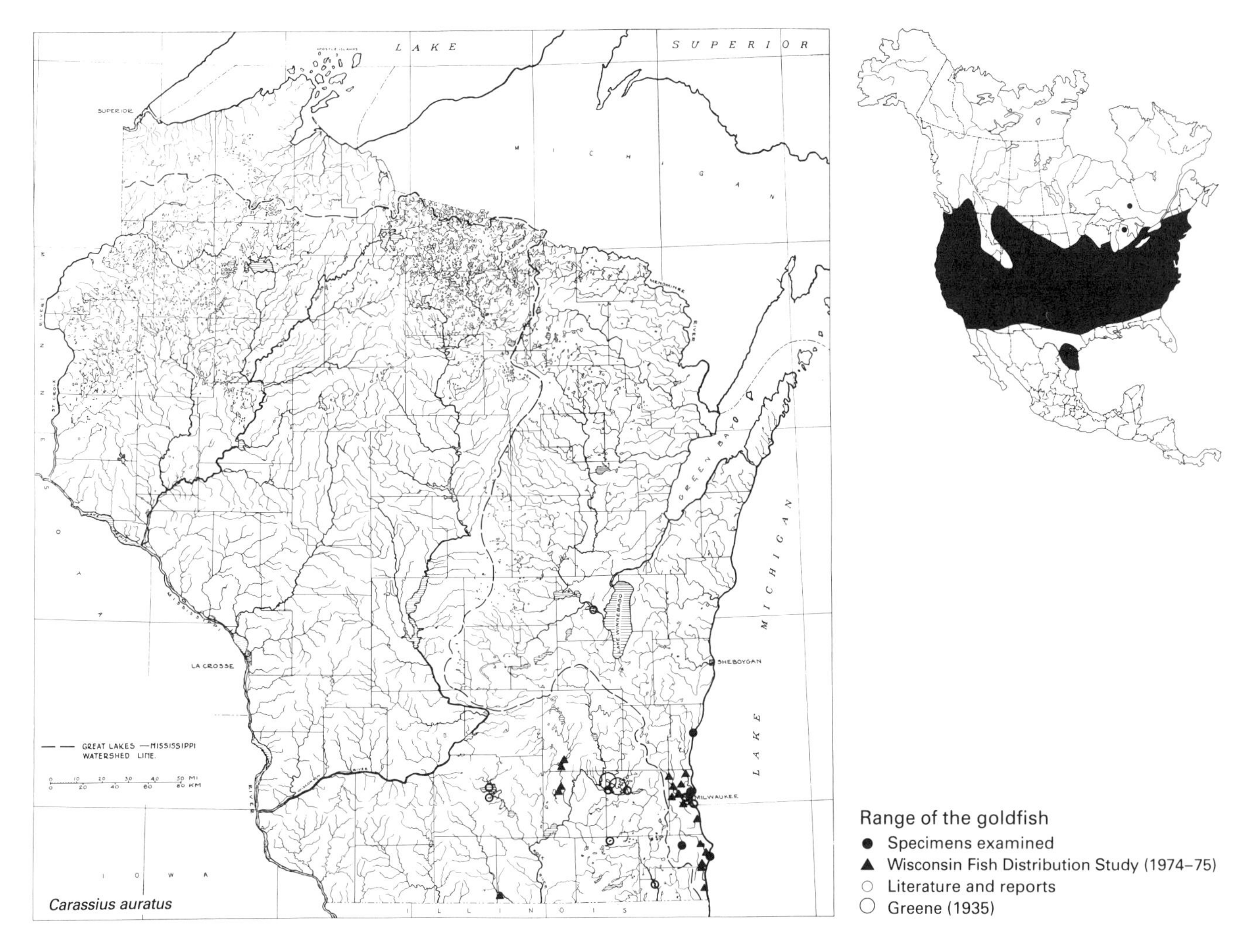

ral Resources survey in 1942 (Noland 1951) only a single specimen (weight 0.5 kg) was taken from Lake Wingra. Wisconsin's northernmost goldfish record is of an isolated individual taken from Lake Butte des Morts (Winnebago County)—"a goldfish the size of a large white bass . . . caught by Elmer Sauer, Neenah" (Wis. Conserv. *Bull.* 1943 8[8]:27).

In Wisconsin, the goldfish is common in some sluggish streams and in the lakes and lagoons of urban centers. It is found occasionally in protected areas of Lake Michigan.

The goldfish inhabits shallow water with dense vegetation in warm lakes, reservoirs, rivers, and quiet streams. The adults generally are near the bottom, but sometimes appear in schools at the surface.

BIOLOGY

Spawning occurs when the water temperature reaches 15.6°C (60°F), and spawning continues throughout the summer if the temperature remains above 15.6°C and the fish are not overcrowded. In Wisconsin the season may run from April to August. After the population reaches a high density, an excretion from the goldfish represses further spawning (Swingle 1956).

The spawning behavior of the goldfish is not generally accompanied by as much splashing as that of the carp, in part because goldfish are smaller. The female may be accompanied by two or more males, and the eggs are released at depths of 15 cm over submerged aquatic plants or willow roots. According to Webster (1942), several males "wildly chase the female" as she scatters the eggs. Spawning starts at about daybreak and lasts into the afternoon.

The first spawn of the season is generally the largest, with individual fish spawning 3–10 lots of eggs at intervals of 8–10 days. A female may lay 2,000–4,000 eggs at one time. Her ovaries hold 160,000–380,000 eggs (Muus and Dahlstrom 1971). The eggs are usually attached singly, rarely in twos and threes, to aquatic plants and other fixed objects, at intervals of 12–25 mm (Mansueti and Hardy 1967); the eggs are adhesive and stick to any object they touch. The male fertilizes the eggs immediately.

The eggs are about 1.6 mm diam, smaller if from small fish. They are clear when laid and turn brown as they develop. Dead eggs are cloudy and opaque. The incubation period is from 46 hours to 14 days, depending on temperature: 8–10 days at 15°C (59°F), 5 days at 20°C (68°F), 46–54 hours at 29°C (84.2°F) (Mansueti and Hardy 1967). At hatching the yolk-sac larvae are 3.0–5.0 mm long, possibly as long as 8.0 mm. The elaborate developmental process is described and illustrated up to the 30 mm stage by Mansueti and Hardy (1967). When first hatched the larvae cling to plants or remain quietly on the bottom, but after 1–2 days they become free-swimming.

In many parts of Europe, male goldfish are not found and the whole population consists of females. The mode of reproduction in a goldfish population without males is discussed by Muus and Dahlstrom (1971:134):

> . . . These females reproduce by pairing with males of related species such as carp, crucian carp, etc. During spawning true fertilization does not take place, for the spermatozoa penetrate the outer membranes of the eggs but perish before their nuclei combine with those of the eggs. However, the mere presence of the sperm stimulates the egg nuclei to start dividing and thus produce new individuals. The offspring produced in this way will have received only the hereditable genes of the female, and therefore can only become females. This form of reproduction is known as gynogenesis, and is extremely rare among animals.

Goldfish from the Milwaukee River (Milwaukee County) collected in September 1966 showed the following growth during the first 4 years of life:

Age Class	No. of Fish	TL (mm)		Calculated TL at Annulus (mm)		
		Avg	Range	1	2	3
0	5	84.4	81–87			
I	9	120.2	106–140	67.3		
II	6	151.3	132–168	66.6	125.8	
III	3	188.0	170–200	81.7	134.7	168.3
Avg (weighted)				69.5	128.8	168.3

In New York (Carlander 1969, citing G. C. Embody) growth of the goldfish was: 0—64 mm FL, I—89 mm TL, II—127–152 TL. In Ontario, the fork length-weight relationship from wild specimens taken from Silver Lake, Port Dover, was: 222 mm—340 g, 229 mm—397 g, 260 mm—510 g, and 267 mm—680 g (Scott and Crossman 1973).

In Iowa the condition factor (K_{SL}) for 197 fish, 79–228 mm SL, averaged 3.54 (Carlander 1969).

Experiments with goldfish grown in water previously inhabited by other goldfish have shown that such experimental fish grew better than the controls did in "unconditioned" water. The improved growth may have been due to the uptake of regurgitated food from the conditioned water. More likely, however, it was due to the presence of a growth-promoting substance that could be isolated from the slime in the tanks with conditioned water. This substance was found to be effective in stimulating growth at dilutions as low as 1.2 ppm (Lagler et al. 1977).

In the Milwaukee River some goldfish purportedly grow to 457 mm (18 in) (*Milwaukee Journal* 30 July 1972). In Ohio, adults are usually 254–406 mm long and weigh 340–1,588 g (12 oz–3.5 lb) (Trautman 1957). Trautman noted that specimens more than 457 mm TL almost invariably show some hybrid characters.

Sexual maturity varies depending on the strain. Some fantail varieties may mature in 9 months, while other varieties may not do so for 3 or 4 years (Breder and Rosen 1966). Trautman (1957) noted that individuals from small ponds spawn at a length of 127 mm (5 in). Normally maturation occurs at an age of 3–4 years, at lengths of 150–200 mm (Muus and Dahlstrom 1971).

The usual longevity of goldfish is 6–7 years. The maximum observed longevity is 30 years (Brown 1957).

Goldfish have developed an organ in the roof of the mouth (palatal organ) where food is tested by taste and touch (Lagler et al. 1977). They are omnivorous feeders, consuming a variety of larvae and adult aquatic insects, mollusks (such as small clams and snails), crustaceans, aquatic worms, and aquatic vegetation (Scott and Crossman 1973).

Goldfish frequent the deep water off of bars during most of the year, but in spring they move into the shallows (Cahn 1927). According to Trautman (1957), the goldfish has about the same ecological requirements as the carp; however, it seems to be less tolerant than the carp of moderate or high gradients, cool water, great turbidity, and domestic and industrial pollutants. It often reaches greater numbers than the carp in shallow water and in dense aquatic vegetation.

The preferred temperature for younger goldfish in the laboratory is 27.8–28.6°C (82–83.5°F); the upper lethal limit, according to the Federal Water Pollution Control Administration, is 41.4°C (106.5°F) (Clark 1969). Goldfish in a warm environment were trained to cause a small drop in their environmental temperature by pressing a lever; temperatures between 33.5 and 36.5°C (92.3 and 97.7°F) were subsequently selected by the fish most of the time (Rozin and Mayer

1961). Riege and Cherkin (1971) noted that memory retention in goldfish increased when the temperature increased from 10 to 30°C (50 to 86°F).

The speed of travel of the goldfish is 3.6 km/hr (2.23 mi/hr) (Lagler et al. 1977). Removal of the forebrain leaves the goldfish with less initiative and spontaneity in exploring its environment.

Endocrinal studies have shown that ACTH (adrenocorticotropic hormone) of the pituitary has a stimulating effect on melanin (black pigment) production in the xanthic goldfish. Also, small doses of thyroxine cause thickening of the epidermis and a paling of the goldfish (Lagler et al. 1977).

The goldfish, although a freshwater fish, has the capacity to adjust to higher than normal salinity and can tolerate salinities up to 17 ppt (Lagler et al. 1977).

IMPORTANCE AND MANAGEMENT

Predation on goldfish by other animals is minimal, especially since the highly colored fish are eliminated from the population. The effect of this species on the aquatic ecosystem is not clearly understood. Greeley (1936) considered it "a worthless although apparently not seriously destructive addition to the fish population." Dobie et al. (1956) noted that many states prohibit the use of goldfish for bait because of the danger of introducing them into valuable game-fish waters: "Experience in some of these States has shown the goldfish to be as vigorous as carp in destroying game-fish habitats." Cross (1967) noted that thoughtless release of goldfish endangers native fishes through competition: "The goldfish has no advantages as a bait-minnow over various native species. Therefore, the production and use of goldfish as bait involves unnecessary risk that anglers ought not be willing to accept." In Wisconsin it is unlawful to use goldfish for bait.

The center for the commercial production of goldfish in the United States is Lake Erie, where in 1936 commercial fishermen took 30,800 kg (67,800 lb) (Wis. Conserv. *Bull.* 1938 3[9]:53). In 1966, 61,200 kg (135,000 lb) of goldfish valued at $4,050 were removed from Lake Erie by haul seines (Lyles 1968). These fish had lost their bright color and resembled carp. Fishermen have taken enormous quantities of goldfish in seines from the lower Hudson River (New York). They have usually been used as fertilizer, or sold in winter at a small price for food, "but they are rarely purchased twice by the same person, they are so bony" (Greeley 1936).

The goldfish is the best known of our domesticated fishes. Available in novelty stores, along with all sorts of fishbowls and aquariums to accommodate them, goldfish often become the showy centerpiece of our living rooms. They are hardy and easily kept, often surviving long periods of neglect.

All goldfish have scales, but in the course of cultivation varieties have been developed whose scales are so thin and transparent as to be inconspicuous, or, under certain conditions, almost invisible. Fanciers call them "scaleless," but "transparent-scaled" would be more correct. Many varieties have become popular: the Telescopes (popeyed fish with defective sight), the Comets, Fringetails and the Veiltails, the Nymphs, the Fantail, the Veiltail Telescopes, the Veiltail Moor Telescope, the Lionhead, the Oranda, and the Shubunkin. Goldfish have been called the "peacocks" of the fish world. They have been produced by Chinese, Japanese, and American breeders after long-term, careful development of the breeding stock. Much is known about the genetics of the goldfish, which has been treated chiefly in the Japanese literature.

Farming of the showy goldfish varieties in the United States started about 1889 in Maryland. Large-scale production now occurs in Indiana, Iowa, Kansas, and elsewhere. The goldfish is a good bait fish in the southeastern states, where it is legal, because it is hardy, can live in crowded pails even during hot weather, reproduces in large numbers, and grows rapidly. Goldfish farming for bait has been well described by Dobie et al. (1956) and Prather et al. (1953). In hatcheries where a heavily stocked brood pond provides fry for eight or ten growing ponds, the production will reach 200,000–300,000 bait fish to the acre (500,000–750,000/ha).

Goldfish production can be increased in most ponds by supplementing the natural food with artificial food. Soybean meal, peanut meal, poultry mash, and cottonseed meal are good supplementary foods for goldfish (Dobie et al. 1956).

Because it is easily produced and is hardy, the goldfish has become a favorite experimental animal. Many fish biologists use the goldfish as an assay animal; subjects pursued deal with the toxicity of new chemicals, temperature sensitivity, respiration rates, biochemical changes in fish tissues, energy extraction efficiency, thermal shock, photoperiodism, and endocrines. The goldfish is the aquatic counterpart of the guinea pig and the rabbit in experimental research.

Golden Shiner

Notemigonus crysoleucas (Mitchill). *Notemigonus*—back, half, angle; the back being almost keeled; *crysoleucas*—gold, white.

Other common names: bream, American bream, roach, American roach, butterfish, eastern golden shiner, sunfish, dace, bitterhead, chub, gudgeon, young shad, windfish, goldfish.

Immature 52 mm, L. Poygan (Winnebago Co.), 8 Aug. 1971

Adult 110 mm, Mill Cr. (Dodge Co.), 8 Sept. 1973

DESCRIPTION

Body deep, strongly compressed laterally. Average length 102 mm (4 in) TL. Depth into TL 3.8–5.8. Head triangular, length into TL 5–5.8. Snout pointed. Mouth small, almost vertical (strongly oblique), the maxillary not reaching front of eye; barbel absent. Pharyngeal teeth 5–5, slender, strongly hooked at tip with well-developed (often serrated) cutting edges below; arch slender. Eye into head length 3–4.2. Gill rakers long, slender, about 16. Dorsal fin origin distinctly posterior to pelvic fin origin; dorsal fin straight to slightly falcate, rays usually 8; anal fin rays usually 11–13; pectoral fin rays 15–17. Pelvic fin rays 9(8), pelvic process in some populations. Lateral line scales 42–54; lateral line strongly decurved, complete. A pronounced fleshy keel between pelvic fins and anal origin over which the scales do not pass. Digestive tract (end of pharynx to anus) is a single S-shaped loop 0.6–0.7 TL. Chromosomes 2n = 50 (Gold and Avise 1977).

Back golden underlaid with olive green; sides more golden with silvery reflections; belly yellowish or yellow-silvery; fins light olive or yellow. Young and immature with a definitive lateral stripe about the width of pupil from eye or snout to caudal base. Peritoneum dusky or silvery with large dark speckles.

Sexual dimorphism: Breeding male with red-orange pelvic fins and orange, black-margined anal fin; back swollen at nape. According to Forbes and Richardson (1920), the lateral body scales are rough with minute tubercles.

DISTRIBUTION, STATUS, AND HABITAT

The golden shiner occurs in all three drainage basins in Wisconsin, although it is less extensively distributed in the unglaciated southwestern quarter of the state. In Wisconsin the golden shiner is common to abundant.

It inhabits lakes, ponds, reservoirs, and river areas with limited current, where it is generally found in sloughs and pools, seldom in riffles. In Wisconsin it occurred in rivers of the following widths: 1.0–3.0 m (10% frequency), 3.1–6.0 m (15%), 6.1–12.0 m (15%), 12.1–24.0 m (36%), 24.1–50 m (18%), and more than 50 m (7%). It was encountered most frequently in clear water over substrates of sand (33% frequency), mud (20%), gravel (19%), silt (11%), rubble (5%), detritus (4%), boulders (3%), clay (3%), bedrock (1%), and marl (1%) at depths of 0.6–1.0 m. Specifically a fish of weedy waters, the golden shiner prefers shoals where aquatic vegetation is moderate to very dense, and is seldom found on the wave-washed, sand-bottomed shoals of lakes where vegetation is absent.

BIOLOGY

At Wisconsin's latitude, the golden shiner has a long spawning season, extending from the time the water reaches 20°C (68°F) through the rest of the summer (Dobie et al. 1956). In Michigan spawning has been observed from June to August, with some evidence that the season begins in May (Hubbs and Cooper 1936); in New York spawning usually begins in May and continues into August (Forney 1957); in Connecticut, it occurs from mid-June to mid-August (Webster 1942).

During the spawning period there are sometimes four or five distinct spawning peaks (Mansueti and Hardy 1967). Spawning occurs at temperatures between 20 and 27°C (68 and 80.6°F); when the water temperature exceeds 27°C, spawning activity ceases unless a cool rain reduces the water temperature sufficiently to shock the fish into further spawning activity. The time of spawning is usually early morning to noon.

Spawning occurs over beds of submerged vegetation. One or two males pursue a female, nosing her cheeks, opercles, and the sides of her abdomen; she drops her eggs as she swims (Webster 1942). Greeley and Greene (1931) observed fish swimming back and

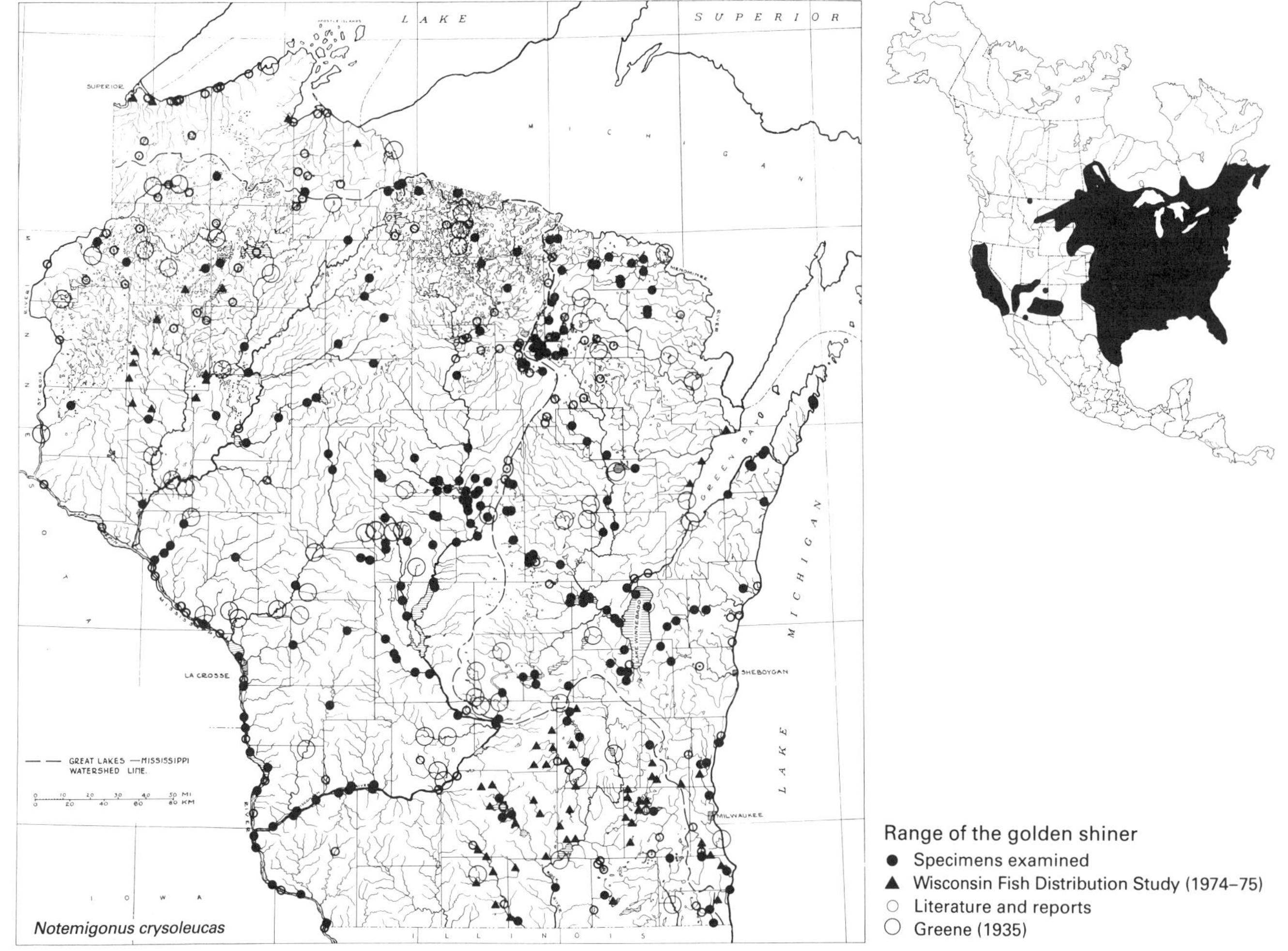

Range of the golden shiner
● Specimens examined
▲ Wisconsin Fish Distribution Study (1974–75)
○ Literature and reports
◯ Greene (1935)

forth over beds of vegetation with rapid circling movements; later considerable quantities of golden shiner eggs were found clinging to the vegetation and to stones.

Golden shiners have occasionally failed to spawn successfully in ponds lacking aquatic vegetation (Forney 1957). Mats of straw submerged along the shore provide a suitable spawning site in ponds where dense plankton blooms prevent the growth of filamentous algae.

In Minnesota, golden shiners were observed spawning in largemouth bass nests (Kramer and Smith 1960b). In a 3-year period, 4–75% of the active bass nests in a lake, and 40–94% of them in an adjoining slough, were used by golden shiners. Schools of 25–100 shiners deposited eggs in bass nests 1–2 days after the bass had spawned, and the male bass guarding the nest did not interfere with the spawning activity of the shiners, except during 1 year of the 3-year study. Eggs were deposited on mats of needle rush (*Eleocharis acicularis*), humps of fibrous organic debris, and bare sand.

Kramer and Smith noted that golden shiner eggs which had been laid in unused largemouth bass nests disappeared before hatching, while those laid in occupied nests hatched at about the same time as the bass eggs. The abundance of young-of-year in the summer was directly proportional to the percentage of bass nests used for spawning in the spring.

On 14 June 1965 in Long Lake (Florence County), a female (133 mm TL), with ripe ovaries constituting 10% of total body weight, contained an estimated 2,290 yellow mature eggs 1.1 mm diam, and 390 white immature eggs 0.7 mm diam. A second female (141 mm TL) had ovaries constituting 7.2% of the body weight with a total of 4,670 eggs. The mature eggs were 1.0 mm diam, and the immature eggs were 0.4 mm diam, in a ratio of 1:1. Mansueti and Hardy (1967) report fecundity up to 200,000. The eggs are adhesive and lack oil globules. Incubation is 4 days at 23.9–26.7°C (75–80°F) (Dobie et al. 1956).

M. Fish (1932) described and illustrated the 18.0-mm stage of the golden shiner, and noted that although a 24-mm specimen was fully scaled, it possessed a fleshy keel on the belly behind the pelvic fins over which the scales did not pass. The juveniles are found in schools near the periphery of ponds, or in the open water of shallows not far from vegetation. In lakes with rock shores, the young remain in deeper water where vegetation may be found.

In Minnesota ponds, total length has been calculated for age in terms of days (Dobie et al. 1956): 8 mm—10 days, 15 mm—20 days, 23 mm—30 days, 30 mm—40 days, 38 mm—50 days, 46 mm—60 days, and 53 mm—70 days.

In Wisconsin, the growth of young-of-year follows:

Date	No. of Fish	TL (mm) Avg	TL (mm) Range	Location
10 July	26	43.5	33–52	Mississippi R. (Grant Co.)
18 July	5	30.6	26–36	L. Poygan (Waushara Co.)
18 July	2	50.0	49–51	Mississippi R. (Crawford Co.)
3 Aug.	10	43.5	35–50	Pewaukee L. (Waukesha Co.)
8 Aug.	18	47.3	36–57	L. Poygan (Winnebago Co.)
9 Aug.	28	48.4	39–55	L. Poygan (Winnebago Co.)
10 Aug.	29	43.0	30–58	Collins L. (Portage Co.)
14 Aug.	43	45.1	34–55	Sugar R. (Rock Co.)
14 Sept.	84	55.4	39–67	Lemonweir R. (Monroe Co.)
18 Sept.	36	53.2	46–65	White Clay L. (Shawano Co.)
18 Sept.	5	64.6	61–68	Moonlight Bay, L. Michigan (Door Co.)

Age is determined by reading scales. In this species the annuli are very clear. Golden shiners from Pool 10 of the Mississippi River (Grant County), collected 10 July 1962, showed the following growth:

Age Class	No. of Fish	TL (mm) Avg	TL (mm) Range	Calculated TL at Annulus (mm) 1	2	3
0	26	43.5	33–52			
I	43	97.0	85–110	44.1		
II	6	122.5	107–132	35.8	86.0	
III	1	153		32.2	83.6	123.0
Avg (weighted)				42.9	85.6	123.0

Shiners from Pool 7 of the Mississippi River (LaCrosse County), collected 2 May 1968, showed the following growth:

Age Class	No. of Fish	TL (mm) Avg	TL (mm) Range	Calculated TL at Annulus (mm) 1	2	3	4	5
II	3	112.3	102–130	51.5	112.3			
III	3	140.7	136–146	30.9	88.6	140.7		
IV								
V	1	200		28.0	91.9	137.3	188.3	200
Avg (weighted)				39.3	99.2	139.9	188.1	200

An 8-year-old, 195-mm-long golden shiner (UWSP 4539) from Arbor Vitae Lake (Vilas County) had the following growth at the annuli: 1—28 mm, 2—59 mm, 3—83 mm, 4—127 mm, 5—154 mm, 6—172 mm, and 7—185 mm. However, this species lived for 10 years in a New York aquarium (Nigrelli 1959). It purportedly reaches 305 mm (12 in) TL and a weight of 680 g (1.5 lb) (Adams and Hankinson 1926).

There is considerable variation in rate of growth. The golden shiner grows more rapidly in the warmer waters in southern Wisconsin than in the cooler waters in northern parts. Females grow faster, attain a larger size, and live longer than males (Hubbs and Cooper 1936). This species may mature in 1 year in warm regions at a length of 64 mm (2.5 in), but in most of the lake states it probably does not mature before age II (Dobie et al. 1956).

From lakes near Madison (Dane County) golden shiners 25–152 mm (1–6 in) TL had eaten large quantities of cladocerans (57.6%), copepods (16.5%) and insects (9.7%, largely Diptera), and lesser amounts of amphipods, ostracods, mites, mollusks, plant remains, silt, and debris (Pearse 1918). In golden shiners from Waukesha County (Cahn 1927), the food consisted largely of entomostracans, *Hyallela*, young waterboatmen and backswimmers, and occasionally young leeches. Aquatic vegetation comprised about 20% of the food.

In Missouri, Divine (1968) noted that a wide variety of food organisms was consumed by shiners, and that the dominant organism was never the same from one month to the next in the same pond. Each size group appeared to concentrate on consuming foods of a particular type; for instance, the 13- to 37-mm group ate protozoans, copepods, cladocerans, and plant fragments, and the 38- to 59-mm group consumed *Hexagenia*, bushy pondweed (*Najas*), and bur marigold (*Bidens*). Although they consumed a wide variety of foods, three or fewer items usually made up more than 90% of the diet. In some ponds, filamentous algae made up the bulk of the diet during certain months. The 60- to 89-mm group relied on insects in July, August, and September, but in June *Closterium* was important, and plant materials replaced insects in September. Bur reed (*Sparganium*) was the most extensively used of the higher plants, and *Spirogyra* and *Oedogonium* made up the bulk of the filamentous algae. The 90- to 129-mm group consumed the greatest variety of forage organisms, from protozoans, rotifers, cladocerans, copepods, and *Hexagenia* to filamentous algae, colonial algae, and higher plant material.

The food habit studies made by many researchers reveal that the golden shiner feeds more on animal plankton (chiefly water fleas) than on any other main group of food organisms. Insects, both aquatic and terrestrial, and diatoms and other algae, are of considerable importance, especially in certain localities, but they are of less significance than the minute crustaceans. Other food items recorded include small clams, snails, protozoans, water mites, and small fishes (Hubbs and Cooper 1936).

Golden shiners are classified as sight feeders. Their mouths are uptilted, and they feed mostly at or near the surface. The bacteria *Escherichia*, *Aerobacter*, *Pseudomonas*, and *Flavobacterium* are believed to be regular inhabitants of the intestines of golden shiners in southern Illinois (Franklin 1964).

The golden shiner is easily damaged by handling, and it is very excitable; consequently it is not recommended as a bioassay animal (Ward and Irwin 1961). It will jump out of the water at a sharp noise from a boat or from the shore. Although generally associated with shallow water, many shiners 203 mm or larger have been noted in water 1.5–3.7 m (5–12 ft) deep where plants were not especially numerous (Adams and Hankinson 1926).

The golden shiner is the only fish that survives in some ponds and sloughs where the oxygen is completely exhausted in winter. In field studies, the lowest observed oxygen tension at which all fish survived for 48 hours was 1.4 ppm, and the highest observed oxygen tension, which killed all fish within 48 hours, was 0.0 ppm (Moore 1942). At oxygen levels of 0.2–0.0 ppm in Michigan lakes, there was some survival of golden shiners, but there was a heavy kill of game and panfish (Cooper and Washburn 1949). Moore noted that small individuals are less tolerant of low oxygen levels than are larger individuals of the same species, at both summer and winter temperatures.

In a Canadian study the shiner was an associate of the rock and smallmouth bass at water temperatures of 20.7–21.4°C (69.3–70.6°F), but was never taken with the mottled sculpin and the brook trout, which frequented waters at temperatures of 15.7–16.6°C (60.3–61.9°F) (Hallam 1959). The upper tolerance limit of golden shiners is about 34°C (93.2°F). In a shallow Michigan pond at water temperatures as high as 38°C (100.4°F), high mortality occurred in the umbrid, castostomid, cyprinid, ictalurid, and percid groups (Bailey 1955); among the species undergoing appreciable mortality was the golden shiner. Carlander (1969) reported freely swimming golden shiners in water at 30°C (86°F); when frightened in waters of 27–35°C (80.6–95°F), some shiners died but others regrouped.

In water salinities of 2, 4, 6, and 8 ppt, the eggs of both golden shiners and goldfish were only slightly affected. Immediately after hatching, however, a marked reduction in salinity tolerance was observed. Total mortality of fry of both species occurred in the 8 ppt salinity tanks. Salinities as low as 2 ppt reduced survival in both species. Only 7% survival of the golden shiner fry occurred at the end of 3 weeks at salinities of 6 ppt (Murai and Andrews 1977).

Fish associates observed in the Wisconsin River (Grant County) were: golden shiner (205), paddlefish (1), gizzard shad (156), quillback (8), river and/or highfin carpsuckers (5), bigmouth buffalo (2), white sucker (6), bullhead minnow (35), bluntnose minnow (3), pugnose minnow (72), emerald shiner (10), spotfin shiner (493), spottail shiner (7), river shiner (5), Mississippi silvery minnow (3), black bullhead (48), northern pike (3), white bass (25), yellow perch (4), western sand darter (3), johnny darter (4), logperch (2), smallmouth bass (11), largemouth bass (8), pumpkinseed (1), bluegill (8), black crappie (42), white crappie (2), brook silverside (11), and freshwater drum (4).

IMPORTANCE AND MANAGEMENT

The golden shiner is used extensively as a food minnow by many game fishes, including crappies, bass, and muskellunge. It is eaten by pied-billed grebes, mergansers, bitterns, green herons, night herons, greater yellowlegs, fish hawks, kingfishers, and crows (Adams and Hankinson 1926). It is a tribute to the reproductive capacities of the golden shiner that it can remain abundant while living in a habitat with so many animals which use it for food.

The golden shiner is a known host to the glochidial stage of the clam known as the floater, *Anodonta grandis*, hence contributing to the success of that mollusk species.

The golden shiner has a reputation as an excellent bait minnow for game and panfishes, and it is a good bait for walleyes. The greatest demand for it comes in those seasons when the water is cold. A very delicate minnow, it is hard to keep alive in a bait pail in the summer.

Large golden shiners will take artificial flies, and may provide some sport on light tackle. There is a diversity of opinion as to the palatability of golden shiners, and perhaps this is a matter of regional tastes. In the East, large individuals have been used for home consumption, and constitute a potential supply of nourishing human food (Hildebrand and Schroeder 1928, Adams and Hankinson 1926). Forbes and Richardson (1920) mention it as an excellent panfish.

Natural reproduction of golden shiners does not meet the needs of the bait industry in Wisconsin, and many tankloads of this minnow are raised in Arkansas and trucked into the state for distribution to bait stations. In its first season, the golden shiner makes excellent bait for crappie fishing by September, when it is 51 mm (2 in) long; during its second season it is good bass bait.

The golden shiner is an interesting and attractive aquarium fish.

The golden shiner may be a valuable mosquito destroyer in stagnant water (Adams and Hankinson 1926). When a shiner specimen was introduced into a barrel swarming with mosquito wrigglers, it devoured practically all of them in a few days. The mouth opening on the upper surface of the shiner's head, and its feeding habits at the surface and in midwater ideally suit this species for mosquito control, although its impact on natural populations of mosquitoes is not known.

In 1973, the estimated adult population of golden shiners in Lake Wingra (Dane County) was 7,300 or 54/ha (Churchill 1976). In Flora Lake (Vilas County), the population was estimated at different times to be 25–287 fish, or 0.9–11.2 kg/ha (Parker 1958).

Methods of propagation of the golden shiner have been outlined in Dobie et al. (1948), Dobie et al. (1956), Langlois (1941), Prather (1957a), and Forney (1957). It spawns readily in ponds, and reaches bass size in 6–12 months. Golden shiners 70 mm (2.75 in) long can be seined, transported, and sold even in warm weather if treated with care (Forney 1957). However, to raise golden shiners, ponds must be free of fathead minnows to ensure spawning success (Dobie et al. 1956).

In New York, fertilized ponds consistently produce greater weights and numbers of golden shiners than unfertilized ponds. In a 2-year period, the wholesale value of golden shiners produced in ten fertilized ponds was $1,620/ha, while the value of shiners produced in three unfertilized ponds was only $433/ha. The cost of the fertilizer applied was approximately $150/ha, a small expense for such an increase in production (Forney 1957). Fertilizers increase the production of microscopic plants, which, as food, increase the production of animals used by minnows as food.

The production of eight Minnesota golden shiner ponds averaged 163 kg/ha (145 lb/acre), and the maximum was 437 kg/ha (390 lb/acre). When production was above 336 kg/ha (300 lb/acre), about 5% of the fish were large enough to be used as pike bait; when production was around 168 kg/ha (150 lb/acre), 70% of the fish were large enough for pike bait.

Evidence is presented by Hubbs (1934) that in ponds in which adult golden shiner are kept there is practically no bass reproduction, since the large minnows consume the bass fry. On the other hand, Regier (1963) noted a reduction of golden shiners in management ponds stocked with largemouth bass and golden shiners. In these the bass preyed on the shiners to the point of eliminating them entirely.

Creek Chub

Semotilus atromaculatus (Mitchill). *Semotilus*—banner (i.e., dorsal fin), spotted; *atromaculatus*—black, spot.

Other common names: horned dace, northern horned dace, common chub, northern creek chub, tommycod, brook chub, silvery chub, mud chub, blackspot chub.

Adult male 125 mm, Wakefield Cr. (Florence Co.), 22 June 1965

Adult female 105 mm, Wakefield Cr. (Florence Co.), 22 June 1965

DESCRIPTION

Body robust, almost cylindrical, slightly compressed posteriorly. Average length 102 mm (4 in) TL. TL = 1.21 SL. Depth into TL 3.8–5.9. Head length into TL 4.0–4.7. Snout bluntly pointed. Mouth terminal, slightly oblique, large and extending to below anterior part of eye; upper and lower lips thick, upper lip groove continuous over tip of snout; a flaplike barbel in upper lip groove slightly in advance of the corner. Pharyngeal teeth usually 2,5–4,2 (occasionally 2,4–4,2 or 2,4–5,2), strong, hooked; sturdy arch. Eye into head length 3.8–6.6. Gill rakers short, conical, widely spaced on lower limb, about 8. Dorsal fin origin slightly behind origin of pelvic fin; dorsal fin rays 8 (a distinct dark spot at base of first 3 rays); anal fin rays 8; pectoral fin rays 16–17; pelvic fin rays 8. Lateral line scales 49–66 (average, Lafayette County 55.1, Portage County 58.03, Florence County 58.43, with number apparently increasing from south to north); lateral line usually complete, sometimes interrupted. Digestive tract simply S-shaped 0.6–0.7 TL. Chromosomes 2n = 50 (W. LeGrande, pers. comm.).

Back dark olive, sides lighter to silvery (often with violet and purple iridescence in large males); belly silvery white. Young with a distinct narrow lateral stripe which begins behind the eye and ends in a small, black basicaudal spot. Lateral stripe becoming faint and diffuse in adults, disappearing in the oldest and largest fish. All fins with rays edged in pigment, the dorsal and caudal fin membranes darkly pigmented. Peritoneum silvery to light gray.

Breeding males with 6 to 10 or 12, large sharp tubercles on each side of head, smaller tubercles on opercle, on first 6–8 rays of pectoral fin, and on upper scales of caudal peduncle. Body, sides of head, and fins usually with a rosy tint; occasionally yellow, blue, and purple on sides of head and body.

Sexual dimorphism: In male, pectoral fin length in SL 5.4–6.6, generally 6 or less; in female 6.2–6.7.

Hybrids: Creek chub × redside dace (Greene 1935), creek chub × common shiner (Raney 1940a, Greeley 1938), creek chub × southern redbelly dace and creek chub × stoneroller (Cross and Minckley 1960, Cross 1967), creek chub × longnose dace (Slastenenko 1957).

SYSTEMATIC NOTES

Two subspecies, *Semotilus a. atromaculatus* (Mitchill) and *S.a. thoreauianus* Jordan, are recognized (Hubbs and Lagler 1964). The former is wide-ranging, and is found in Wisconsin; the latter is found in the eastern parts of the Gulf of Mexico drainage (extreme southeastern United States). The major distinguishing feature between the two subspecies is difference in scale size, which is clinal in nature; subspecific distinctions may be unwarranted (Bailey et al. 1954).

DISTRIBUTION, STATUS, AND HABITAT

The creek chub is widely distributed in all three drainage basins in Wisconsin. Although it has been reported in the Great Lakes to 13 m (Hubbs and Lagler 1964), no recent reports are known from Lakes Michigan and Superior. It is frequently recorded at the mouths of streams entering these lakes, and it has been taken in the shallows of lower Green Bay.

The creek chub is abundant in small- and medium-sized streams and rivers over the entire state. It is rare in large rivers and in lakes. It is a common Wisconsin minnow, and although its populations are easily exploited, they restore quickly. This species is tolerant of considerable pollution: a native fish with the tenacity of a weed. Its status appears secure.

The creek chub was encountered over substrates of gravel (23% frequency), sand (22%), silt (15%), rubble (11%), mud (11%), boulders (6%), clay (5%), bedrock (4%), and detritus (3%). It occurred in clear to dark brown waters, preferring silt-free to slightly turbid waters, although it was also taken from a number of locales with turbid water. It occurred in streams of the following widths: 1.0–3.0 m (28%), 3.1–

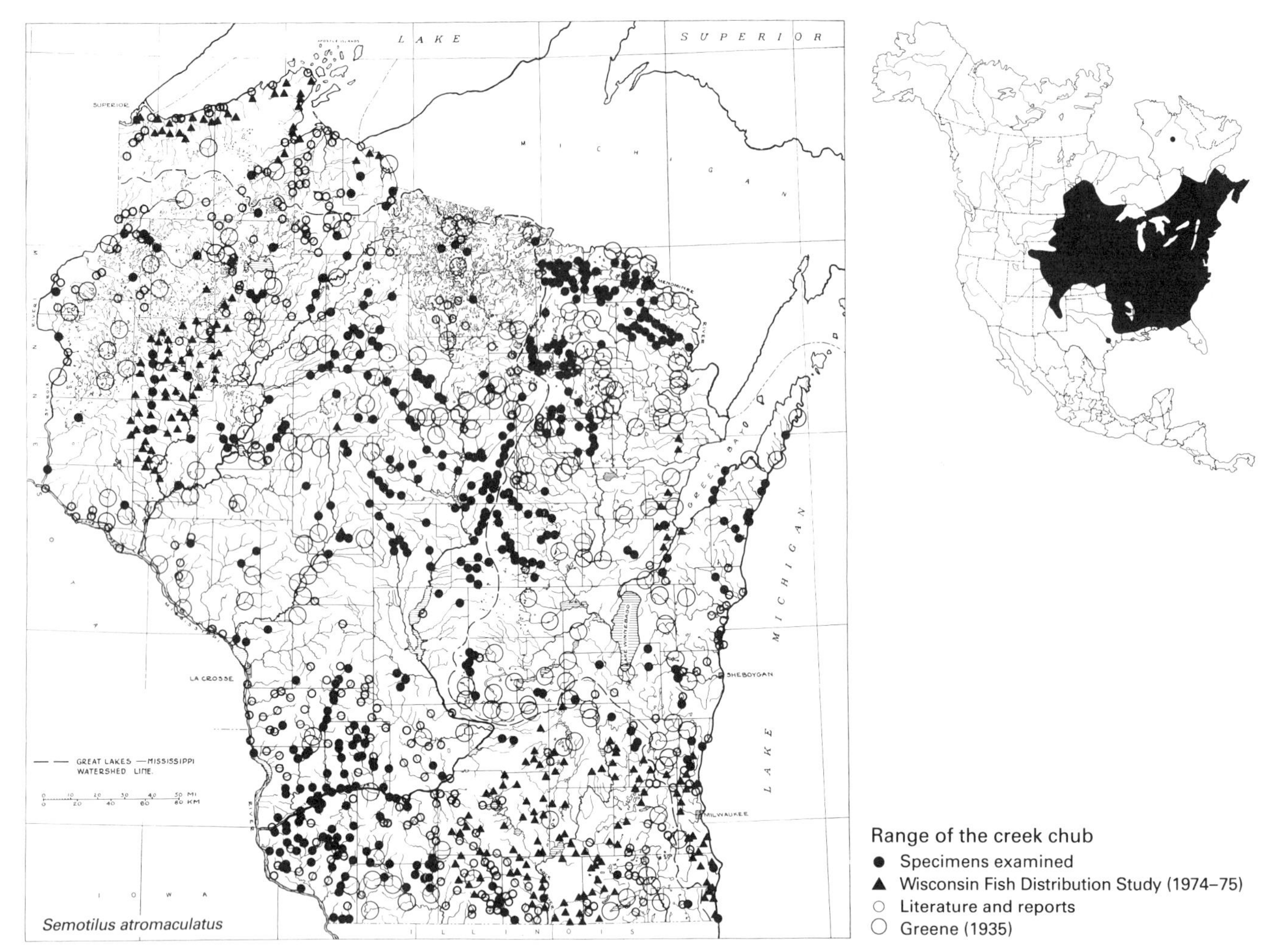

6.0 m (26%), 6.1–12.0 m (20%), 12.1–24.0 m (15%), 24.1–50.0 m (7%), and more than 50 m (4%).

The creek chub occurs infrequently in lakes. Of the 441 localities from which Greene (1935) collected this minnow, only 9 were lakes. In 256 lake collections, I found it in only 6. In 18 of 20 Wisconsin lakes, creek chubs are believed to have been introduced by bait fishermen (Copes 1978).

BIOLOGY

Spawning occurs from May to July, with most spawning completed early in the season. Spawning usually begins at a water temperature of 12.8°C (55°F); the upper limit is near 17°C (62.6°F). It occurs over coarse gravel runs in currents of 0.3–0.7 m/sec (1–2.4 ft/sec), and over littoral areas of gravel in lakes.

In some streams creek chubs migrate into suitable spawning areas. In Iowa (Paloumpis 1958), the early run consisted of males, but about 2 weeks later, it was predominantly females. In a small headwater stream in Illinois (T. Storck, pers. comm.), nearly all mature males, 80% of the mature females, and large numbers of immatures undertook at least short upstream migrations. Larval chubs drifted downstream in early summer, but there is evidence that no other age-groups made substantial downstream migrations.

The nest-building and spawning behavior of the creek chub was originally described by Reighard (1910), whose observations were summarized by Miller (1964:326):

> In brief, he found that spawning occurs in a shallow pit excavated by the male. By picking up stones in the mouth and depositing them on the upstream edge of the pit, the male creates a small pile. As digging and stone carrying continue, the male gradually fills in the anterior portions of the pit and extends the excavation farther downstream. Prolonged activity forms a ridge of gravel one to several feet long and about a foot wide covering a previously excavated trench and a shallow pit (newest section of the trench) just downstream to the ridge. The male defends the pit and sometimes parts of the ridge against other male predators. Spawning occurs when a female enters the nest and approaches the male, which clasps her between pectoral fin and body. When the clasp of less than a second,

egg release, and fertilization are over, the female floats upward for a few seconds apparently stunned, then swims away. Since spawnings are interspersed with nest-building the eggs become imbedded in a shallow gravel pile that probably deters predators after the male deserts the spawning site and protects the eggs from sediment.

The spawning embrace of the creek chub. The male is curved about the body of the female, which he has flipped into an upright position (Reighard 1910:1130).

Probably not more than 25–50 eggs are released at one time. The female drifts downstream, but may return shortly for another spawning in the same or another nest.

Ross (1976) observed three types of nest-entry behavior of female creek chubs: moving passively downstream into the nest tail first, swimming in circles as the nest was being approached, and assuming a prespawning position in the nest before being detected by the nesting male; otherwise, a direct entry into the nest produced male aggression, and the female was driven away.

Communal nesting sites (Ross 1977) are attended by several males: the nesting male who is the dominant male that controls the nesting territory, and the nest-watching male(s) who, when the nesting male is chasing an intruder away or parallel-swimming, enters the nest and initiates nest building. Upon return, the nesting male chases the nest-watchers from the nest. These remain near the periphery of the nest, watching for another opportunity to enter. Occasionally a nest-watcher will have the opportunity to spawn with a female when the dominant nesting male is absent.

Combat between chubs seldom involves bodily contact, despite the following account from Reighard (p. 1128):

> . . . If the male dace that approaches the nest is of the same size as the nest occupant a battle frequently ensues. The two strike at each other with their heads in apparent efforts to inflict wounds with the sharp pearl organs. They often struggle together fiercely in these encounters, but neither fish appears to suffer any injury.

Recent studies (Ross 1977, Miller 1964) have shown that fighting is rare. Nesting male chubs seldom swing their heads with enlarged tubercles against other fishes while around the nest, and overt aggression rarely occurs during creek chub interactions. Ritualized, rather than overt, aggression is common in vertebrate social systems, and appears characteristic of creek chubs.

The parallel swim is a ritual combat between a resident male and an intruding male. During the parallel swim, which carries the antagonists one or more meters upstream from the nesting site, the dorsal, anal, and pectoral fins are spread wide, and forward movement by the strong, undulating caudal beats is relatively slow (Miller 1964). Several clearly observed fish had their mouths open during parallel-swimming, but this may not always occur. Progression seems to be slow because the caudal beats not only propel the fish, but intimidate the opponent. Thus they resemble the tail-beating movements common in many species inhabiting still waters. The tail-beating effect is probably of primary importance because it often is begun when the fish are still side by side, and is prominent especially when one fish is somewhat ahead of the other. When this happens, the forward fish stops, but continues to make caudal undulations, directing the tail blows at the head and forebody of the other.

The creek chub occasionally appropriates spawning pits from stoneroller minnows, which are driven away. The creek chubs may also move into a nest containing one or more common shiners, and dig or carry stones without opposition (Miller 1964). At times, shiners are so active that they bump and jostle a chub working in the same nest; when this hinders the chub, he turns and swings his head toward the nearest shiners, driving them back a few centimeters. After a minute or two, the shiners usually crowd into their original positions, and the chub threatens again. Often many male common shiners are actively engaged in digging, courting, spawning, and fighting in a milling swarm around a pit-digging chub.

Copes (1978) observed spawning in the Tomorrow River (central Wisconsin) in nests which were never over 36 cm (14 in) wide, 15 cm (6 in) deep, and 76 cm (30 in) long. After one to three females had entered the nest, the male came alongside, wrapped his caudal peduncle around a female, pressed her to the bottom, and quickly straightened his body, or else the male pressed the female against the side of the nesting depression, and eggs were released. The spawning act lasted less than 2 seconds. One large female entered two nests in less than 10 minutes.

Gravid females were collected from the Tomorrow River on 4 May 1959. A 96-mm fish with ovaries 20.1% of body weight held an estimated 1,115 mature eggs, 1.4–1.5 mm diam; a smaller number of immature eggs 0.7–0.8 mm diam were present. A 120-mm fish with ovaries 23.5% of body weight had 2,255 mature eggs 1.6–1.7 mm diam, and fewer immature eggs 0.7–0.9 mm diam.

Eggs are covered with gravel by the males after each spawning act, protecting them from potential predators. Raney (1969) noted that the spawning activities and the nest of the creek chub are attractive to the common shiner and the blacknose dace, which usually occupy the nest without being attacked. Dobie et al. (1956) observed that at least 30% of the males and 15% of the females die each year after spawning.

The eggs hatch within the nest, and the young make their way out through the chinks between the stones. Copes (1978) collected fry 10–12 mm on 20 July 1974 from the Tomorrow River, and on 11 July from the Plover River (Portage County). M. Fish (1932) illustrated and described the 14-mm stage. According to Copes, scales begin to appear when the fish reach 26 mm, and scales of 30-mm individuals had two to three circuli. Growth of young-of-year is rapid, sometimes attaining 89 mm (3.5 in) or more before the end of the first year.

Creek chubs from Big Rib River (Taylor County), collected 12 October 1974, showed the following growth:

Age Class	No. of Fish	TL (mm)		Calculated TL at Annulus (mm)		
		Avg	Range	1	2	3
0	8	39.9	36–47			
I	13	70.2	65–82	43.4		
II	4	104.5	98–111	46.4	76.4	
III	8	141.9	127–160	45.6	81.6	117.9
Avg (weighted)				44.6	79.9	117.9

In Iowa (Dinsmore 1962), mean total lengths at the first 3 annuli were 58.2, 94.6, and 127.6 mm. In southern Illinois the calculated TL (mm) at the end of each year was 58, 94, 132, and 160 (Gunning and Lewis 1956). In Sand Creek (Wyoming) during September growth was: 0—38.6 (26–52) mm; I—74.2 (50–94) mm; II—108.3 (80–135) mm; III—141 (120–161) mm; IV—163 (147–184) mm; V—184.5 (175–203) mm (Copes 1978). New annulus formation appeared 1 July, and most growth ceased by early September.

Males grow more rapidly than females, and Copes noted that maturity occurs at age III in males, and in some age-I females. Few creek chubs live longer than age VI. One 292-mm, age-VIII chub was collected from the Tomorrow River in August 1965. The largest known creek chub, 330 mm TL, was caught by hook and line from the Pembina River in North Dakota in 1964 (Copes 1978).

The creek chub is best described as an opportunist and a carnivore, feeding on whatever organisms are available, from surface drift to benthos. Digestive tracts of adult creek chubs from Castle Creek (Bayfield County) contained: fish (62%), insect remains and vegetation (17.5%), amphipods (6.4%), adult Coleoptera (4.4%), Ephemeroptera nymphs (4.1%), Odonata larvae (2.3%), and Diptera adults (2.1%) and larvae (1.2%). Copes did not find fish in creek chubs smaller than 95 mm TL. Fish made up 90% of the volume of food in creek chubs 175 mm or larger.

Observations on the feeding habits of the creek chub are provided by Copes. Schools of young-of-year feed actively throughout the day on drift and benthic organisms, and search in vegetation for food organisms. Age-I and smaller age-II fish feed extensively in vegetated areas of streams. In April and early May larger creek chubs were not observed feeding before 1100 hr. Copes noted that schools of creek chubs usually do not leave the sheltered areas where they spend the night until water temperatures have increased a few degrees from the daily minimum. Schools of larger chubs are seen foraging on the bottom and in vegetation for a 1- to 2-hr period; they then return to a pool or to a deep run, and appear to lie in wait for drift items. Copes noted that as a drift organism neared the creek chub aggregation, from 2 to 50 chubs rushed to consume it. During July and August drift items consumed by chubs included leaves, small sticks, willow buds, insects, and other matter; they also pursued invertebrates, smaller fish, and tadpoles.

In Iowa, fish identified in the stomachs of creek chub included the spotfin shiner, common shiner, and bigmouth shiner, the bullhead minnow and fathead minnow, and johnny darter (Harrison 1950). Adams and Hankinson (1926) noted that the creek chub is very fond of the eggs and fry of the brook trout. Even young bullheads have been found in creek chub stomachs (Hubbs and Cooper 1936).

The creek chub is classified as a sight feeder by Evans (1952) because the taste lobes of the brain are not enlarged.

The creek chub is primarily a schooling species. Copes observed schools of age-0 creek chubs active in shallow runs throughout the day during August. Age-I and small age-II creek chubs usually are found in schools which occupy the edges of pools and deeper runs. Creek chubs larger than 180 mm generally do not school; they occupy a sheltered spot in a deep pool or run at the edge of the current.

Creek chubs winter in deeper pools and runs. They can be seen lying on the bottom of streams, and many have been collected from under stream shelters in November. When alarmed, a school of creek chubs breaks up, and individuals swim rapidly toward vegetation and other shelter. In a tagging experiment, Copes noted that recaptured fish had moved no more than 30 m from where they had been tagged.

The upper temperature at which the water becomes lethal to the creek chub during mid-summer in Algonquin Park (Ontario) is 32.5°C (90.7°F); the lower lethal temperature is 1.7°C (35.1°F) (Brett 1944).

This species is able to tolerate a wide range of species associates under widely varying environmental conditions. In Gran Grae Creek (Crawford County) 285 creek chubs were collected with the northern hog sucker (1), white sucker (51), central stoneroller (530), longnose dace (3), blacknose dace (1), bluntnose minnow (117), common shiner (50), spotfin shiner (10), weed shiner (56), bigmouth shiner (146), brassy minnow (5), Mississippi silvery minnow (26), central mudminnow (1), grass pickerel (2), northern pike (1), walleye (3), johnny darter (10), mud darter (1), fantail darter (1), and warmouth (1).

IMPORTANCE AND MANAGEMENT

Creek chubs are eaten by a variety of natural predators such as loons, kingfishers, mergansers, walleyes, brown trout, northern pike, and smallmouth bass; large creek chubs eat smaller fish of their own species.

The creek chub is the host to the glochidia of the clams *Anodonta imbecilis* and *Strophitus undulatus*; hence it is partially responsible for the success of those mollusks (Hart and Fuller 1974).

In Wisconsin the creek chub is a popular bait minnow for pan and gamefish. Where spearing pike through the ice is allowed, the creek chub makes an ideal decoy. It is a hardy minnow, and holds up well in the bucket or on the hook. It can tolerate considerable exposure to sudden changes in water temperature. Some anglers prefer to "sour" their chubs by placing them in a capped fruit jar in the sun for a few hours before using them (Harlan and Speaker 1956).

This minnow readily takes a hook baited with worm or a piece of fish, and frequently will take an artificial fly. It furnishes thrills to thousands of boys and girls of all ages who fish along smaller streams. Its flesh has a fine flavor and is said to taste like smelt.

Creek chubs have been accused of competing with game fishes for food and of being trout predators, since large chubs are known to feed to some extent on small trout fingerlings. Hubbs and Cooper (1936:60) analyzed the problem:

> . . . Under natural conditions in a stream, a population of large trout would probably keep the abundance of this and other minnows in check by eating them, but under existing conditions, the survival of these large, competing minnows is favored since the intensive fishing on almost all of our . . . trout streams continually removes most of the larger fish-eating trout. Thus fishermen by removing the large trout cause an increase in abundance of chubs, which by competing for food with the remaining smaller trout decrease the growth and the numbers of trout. On the other hand, an increase in the abundance of the chubs in a trout stream augments the food supply for the larger trout that are not taken by the angler. In this way the harm done by the minnows may be compensated for. The whole problem is extremely complicated, and has not been thoroughly studied by fisheries investigators. It is probable that a large population of creek chubs is desirable in some trout streams, but undesirable in others.

The propagation of creek chubs is outlined by Dobie et al. (1956), Washburn (1948), and Langlois (1941). It is well suited for production in large numbers in artificial ponds. Creek chubs can be ripened by injections of carp pituitary (Ball and Bacon 1954). When held in tanks at 7.8–17.8°C (46–64°F), they can be stripped of eggs in 48 hours.

Stocking of creek chub fry in growing ponds is especially successful if there is an incoming flow of spring water; however, even without such a water supply, 125,000 fry can be stocked to a hectare of water. At the end of 6 weeks at water temperatures of 21.1–23.9°C (70–75°F) when fry have reached 38 mm (1.5 in) TL, larger items of food, such as fathead minnow fry, are recommended.

Pearl Dace

Semotilus margarita (Cope). *Semotilus*—banner (i.e., dorsal fin), spotted; *margarita*—a pearl.

Other common names: northern pearl dace, northern dace, northern minnow, nachtrieb dace.

Adult male 97 mm, Big Roche a Cri Cr. (Waushara Co.), Sept. 1958

Adult female 122 mm, Walczak Cr. (Oneida Co.), 5 July 1966

DESCRIPTION

Body elongate, almost cylindrical, slightly compressed posteriorly. Average length 89 mm (3.5 in). TL = 1.24 SL. Depth into TL 4.8–6.3. Head into TL 4.2–5.3. Snout bluntly pointed to rounded. Mouth terminal, slightly oblique, moderate-sized, extending to below nostril; upper lip groove continuous over tip of snout; a small flaplike barbel in upper lip groove slightly in advance of the corner, occasionally lacking on one side, less frequently on both. Pharyngeal teeth usually 2,5–4,2 (occasionally 1 less tooth on inner or outer row), slender, hooked, with a short cutting surface. Eye into head length 3.3–4.6. Gill rakers short, conical, to knoblike on lower limb, 6–8. Dorsal fin origin behind origin of pelvic fin; dorsal fin rays 8; anal fin rays 8; pectoral fin rays 15–16; pelvic fin rays 8. Lateral line scales 62–75; lateral line complete (occasionally interrupted). Digestive tract simple S-shaped loop 0.7–0.9 TL. Chromosomes 2n = 50 (W. LeGrande, pers. comm.).

Back dark olive, sides light olive to lateral stripe; belly below stripe white to silvery white. Patches of darkened scales on sides, few on young. Dusky lateral stripe distinct in young and ending in distinct basicaudal spot; lateral stripe less distinct in large specimens, especially anteriorly. Fin rays edged in dark pigment; dorsal, caudal and anal fin membranes with scattered dark chromatophores. Peritoneum silvery with dark speckles.

Breeding males with a few minute tubercles on head and opercles, densely tuberculate on edges of branchiostegal rays; lateral body scales and breast scales with tubercles on posterior edges; close-set and pointed tubercles on rays 2–6 of pectoral fins. Large breeding female occasionally with fine tubercles on rays 2–6 of pectoral fins. Adult male with orange to bright red stripe along flank below lateral stripe; females yellow to orange, occasionally red. Vivid colors often present in the fall and persisting through spawning.

Sexual dimorphism: In male, length of pectoral fin into SL 4.8–5.7; in female, 6.1–7.0 (R. Theis, pers. comm.).

Hybrids: Pearl dace × northern redbelly dace and possibly a tri-hybrid with the northern redbelly and finescale daces (Legendre 1970). Pearl dace × central stoneroller from the South Fork of the Hay River (Barron County) (Wis. Fish Distrib. Study, pers. comm.).

SYSTEMATIC NOTES

The systematic position of this species is not clear. It has recently been placed in the genus *Semotilus* (Bailey and Allum 1962). Also, there is evidence for placing it in the genus *Phoxinus*, and Legendre (1970) suggested that the pearl dace is more closely related to the finescale dace (*Phoxinus neogaeus*) than to other members of the genus *Semotilus*. Three subspecies are recognized (Hubbs and Lagler 1964), of which only the northern pearl dace *Semotilus margarita nachtriebi* occurs in Wisconsin.

DISTRIBUTION, STATUS, AND HABITAT

The pearl dace occurs in all three Wisconsin drainage basins. It is widely distributed except in the Lake Superior watershed, in the unglaciated southwestern quarter of the state, and in the southern tier of counties.

The pearl dace is listed as rare in Connecticut and Nebraska, rare and depleted in Maryland and West Virginia, rare and endangered in Wyoming, and endangered in South Dakota and Iowa (Miller 1972, Roosa 1977). In Wisconsin the pearl dace is common in small streams of central and northern Wisconsin, except in streams of the Lake Superior drainage, where it is rare. It is uncommon in medium and large rivers.

In Wisconsin its typical habitat is cool, clear headwater streams and bog drainage streams; only rarely is it found in lakes. It was encountered in clear to slightly turbid water most frequently at depths less than 0.5 m (seldom more than 1.5 m), over substrates of sand (26% frequency), gravel (22%), silt (18%),

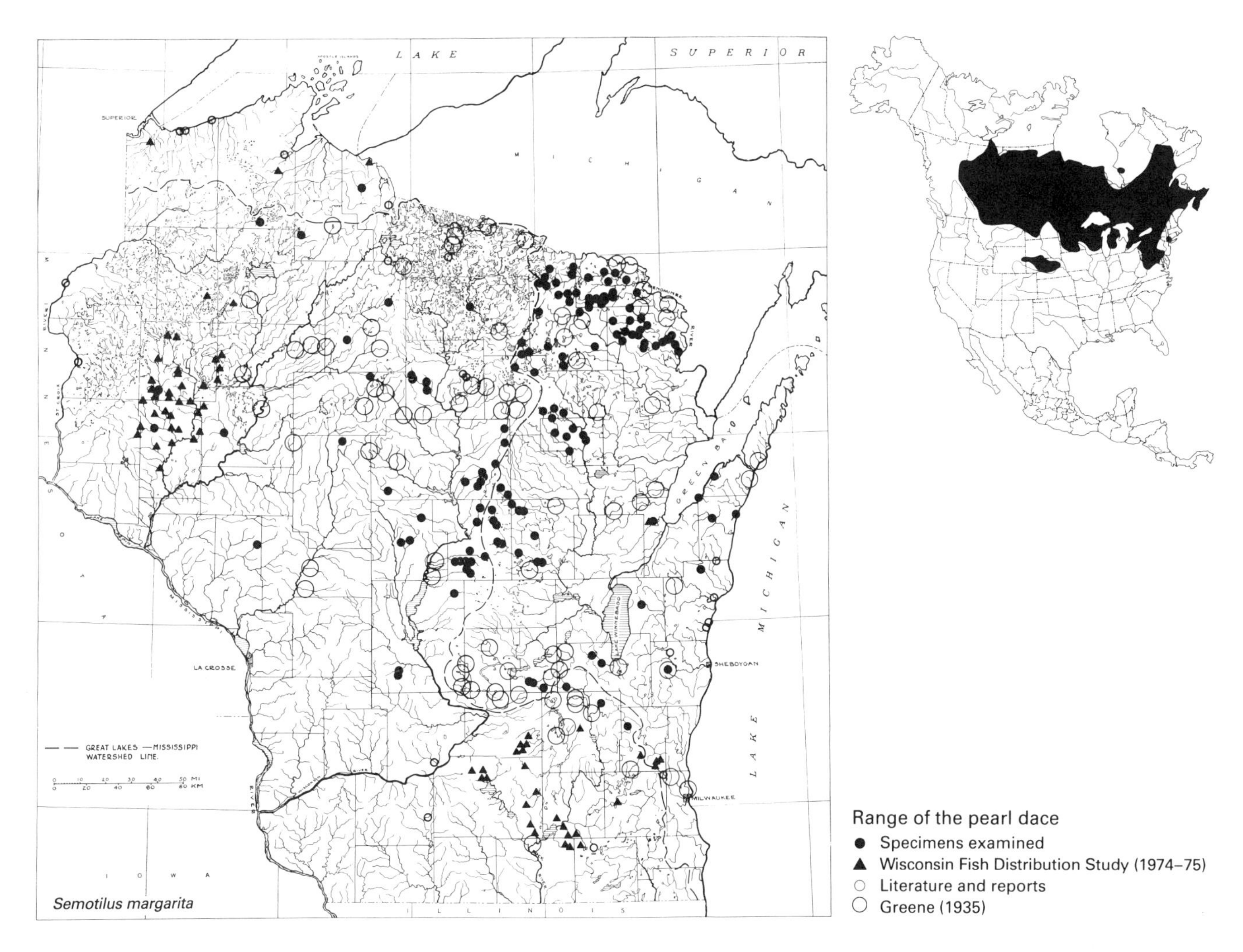

Range of the pearl dace
● Specimens examined
▲ Wisconsin Fish Distribution Study (1974–75)
○ Literature and reports
◯ Greene (1935)

mud (10%), rubble (9%), detritus (6%), boulders (6%), bedrock (2%), and clay (1%). It occurred in streams of the following widths: 1.0–3.0 m (44%), 3.1–6.0 m (19%), 6.1–12.0 m (16%), 12.1–24.0 m (13%), 24.1–50.0 m (7%), and more than 50 m (1%). It was generally taken from light brown to dark brown water in areas of sparse vegetation.

BIOLOGY

In Wisconsin, spawning occurs from late March to the end of April or later. Spawning was observed in two streams in lower Michigan on 12–13 June at water temperatures of 17.2–18.3°C (63–65°F) (Langlois 1929). Activity occurred in a strong current, in a moderate current, and in a pocket where the water was nearly quiet; dace were seen pairing only over coarse gravel, fine gravel, and sand, though there were other substrate materials accessible. The streams were about 5 m (15 ft) wide and 0.5–0.6 m (1.5–2 ft) deep where the fish were breeding.

Large males, smaller males, and breeding females were present. According to Langlois (1929), each adult male maintained a small area of the stream bottom about 20 cm (8 in) across as his private spawning ground, guarding it against intrusion by other males, and apparently restricting his own spawning to this area most of the time. A male's holding was without definite outline, and was defined only by the behavior of its proprietor. No transporting of material was seen, and there were no signs of either mounding or excavating. The two closest holdings in the areas observed were 2 m (6 ft) apart. The smaller males maintained no holdings, and frequently invaded the holdings of other males, only to be driven out when their owners returned. The smaller males also pursued females and occasionally succeeded in pairing with them. Adult females were constantly pursued by males.

Langlois described parallel-swimming, a type of behavior also referred to as deferred combat (Reighard 1910). An interesting facet of this behavior was seen by Langlois (p. 162): "Sometimes, at the moment when the intruder apparently refuses to be led farther away, the two males pose for an instant with their heads abreast as if they had started to pass each other and then stopped suddenly. From this position the stranger almost invariably makes another dash for the holding."

Langlois detailed the pearl dace's spawning behavior (p. 162):

If the stranger should be a female, and if she permits the male to drive her into his holding instead of fleeing, and if, once there, she stays and permits the male to pair with her, the process occurs in this manner. The two fish come to a position side by side, close at bottom, and, if there is a current, heading upstream. The oversized tubercle-roughened pectoral fin of the male is slipped beneath the anterior part of the body of the female, and his tail is crossed over her back, just behind her dorsal fin. Then as his tail presses her vent and tail tightly to the bottom, her pectoral fin raises the forepart of her body to an angle of about 30 degrees from the bottom, in this way stretching tight her belly wall and probably assisting oviposition. When this position has been reached both fishes vibrate the posterior parts of their bodies rapidly, the tail of the female stirring up the bottom behind them, while the male's tail fans the bottom alongside and about mid-way between the female's pectoral and pelvic fins. If the male is considerably shorter than the female his tail may not reach the bottom, and in this case it vibrates in the water at whatever angle it attains. The eggs and milt are without doubt extruded while the fish are vibrating, but they were not seen. When the spawning vibrations have ceased, the female resumes a horizontal position at once, swimming forward out of the holding without the momentary relaxation and floating belly-upward that occurs in the case of the horned dace immediately following the spawning act.

The spawning act lasts about two seconds, and since each female repeats the act many times during the breeding season she must extrude but a few eggs each time.

The pearl dace exhibits an interesting stage in the development of nesting in fishes—the establishment of a territory. A further stage in nesting development is illustrated by the creek chub, which digs a nest pit and places gravel in an upstream ridge (Raney 1969).

Egg development occurs early in this species. For five females 89–112 mm TL, collected 8 November from Tenmile Creek (Portage County), the weight of the gonads was 15–19% of the total weight; for eight males 54–88 mm TL it was 2.6–3.3%. These are high levels of gonadal development in view of the fact that spawning was some 5 months away (E. Curtis and D. Korth, pers. comm.).

At the onset of spawning on 27 March in Big Roche a Cri Creek (Adams County), gravid females 102–123 mm TL had ovaries 18–21% of body weight (R. Theis, pers. comm.). A 119-mm fish held an estimated 4,240 mature eggs, 1.3 mm diam; a 122-mm fish, 4,005 eggs, 1.4 mm diam. The ovaries contained eggs in only one stage of development; partially ripe eggs were not observed.

Pearl dace from Big Roche a Cri Creek (Adams County), collected 14 September 1960, showed the following growth:

Age Class	No. of Fish	TL (mm) Avg	TL (mm) Range	Calculated TL at Annulus (mm) 1	2	3
0	39	41.5	34–48			
I	36	77.6	53–99	53.4		
II	10	113.3	107–117	64.0	99.4	
III	4	121.0	119–123	56.5	88.0	109.6
Avg (weighted)				55.8	96.0	109.6

Age-I males, 65–99 mm TL, had orange to bright red stripes on the flanks. Age-I females over 80 mm had yellow stripes on the flanks; all age-II and age-III females, orange to red. In this collection no males were over age I, and both males and females at this age were becoming sexually mature and would have bred the following spring.

In southern Ontario (Chadwick 1976), lengths of females at the first 3 annuli were 55.0, 89.2, and 114.5 mm; lengths of males at the first 2 annuli were 58.5 and 85.6 mm. Only two age-II males were recovered; no males were age III.

Sexual maturity is attained in both sexes at age II, and it is possible that males die off shortly after spawning. A few females may reach age IV.

The largest pearl dace reported is 158 mm (6.25 in) TL from Charlie Lake, Peace River (western Canada) (Lindsey 1956).

The studies available have shown that insects are preferred food of the pearl dace, but this species has been known to feed on phytoplankton, mollusks, surface drift, and water mites (Dobie et al. 1956). In New York, the diet of 13 individuals was entirely plant material of algae and diatoms (Rimsky-Korsakoff 1930). In Canada (McPhail and Lindsey 1970), stomachs contained insects (primarily beetles), filamentous algae, *Chara*, and vegetable debris. The pearl dace has taken flies from the surface after the manner of trout, and they have been said to eat animal plankton and various aquatic organisms, including small fish.

In 200-m study areas of a natural headwater stream in central Wisconsin, M. Headrick (pers. comm.), using a mark-recapture technique estimated populations of 1,999 ± 663 pearl dace in August, and 1,375 ± 233 in September. In an area which had been ditched, the populations were 1,820 ± 819 and 3,888

± 836 respectively. The populations dropped off drastically in larger downstream waters which had been ditched.

In Canada, Hallam (1959) noted that this species is commonly associated with the brook trout and mottled sculpin at average water temperatures of 15.8–16.6°C (60.3–61.9°F), and seldom with the smallmouth bass and rock bass at 20.8–21.5°C (69.3–70.6°F). The upper lethal temperature for pearl dace in August is 31.1°C (88°F), and for dace immersed in cold tanks, the lower lethal temperature in August is −0.2°C (31.6°F) (Brett 1944).

In Tenmile Creek (Portage County), 37 pearl dace were taken with brook trout (2), white sucker (160), creek chub (51), bigmouth shiner (2), fathead minnow (12), blacknose dace (28), northern redbelly dace (8), johnny darter (11), central mudminnow (1), mottled sculpin (7), and brook stickleback (3).

IMPORTANCE AND MANAGEMENT

The value of the pearl dace as a forage species in Wisconsin is not known. It has been noted in the diet of kingfishers in eastern Canada (Scott and Crossman 1973).

The importance of the pearl dace is difficult to assess. It undoubtedly has only limited use as a bait minnow in Wisconsin, since it is seldom taken in large numbers.

Dobie et al. (1956) suggested that the pearl dace might be reared successfully in artificial ponds, and that bait large enough to catch panfish could be raised in one season: "Because it makes a fine growth in northern boggy waters, this fish could be raised in northern areas in places where land is cheap. For dealers with little working capital, this species seems to offer excellent opportunities" (p. 103).

Redside Dace

Clinostomus elongatus (Kirtland). *Clinostomus*—inclined mouth; *elongatus*—elongated.
Other common name: red-sided shiner.

Adult male 67 mm, tributary to Little Sandy Cr. (Marathon Co.), 29 May 1961

Adult female 82 mm, Melancthon Cr. (Richland Co.), 19 July 1962

DESCRIPTION

Body elongate, thin, strongly compressed laterally. Average length 65 mm (2.5 in). TL = 1.22 SL. Depth into TL 5.0–5.8. Head length into TL 4.3–4.6. Snout sharply pointed and long. Lower jaw projecting beyond upper; barbels absent; maxillary long, reaching to below eye (almost half of head length—largest in minnow family). Mouth very large and terminal, oblique. Pharyngeal teeth slightly hooked, usually 2,5–4,2 (occasionally 1,4–3,1). Gill rakers rudimentary, but variable in size. Dorsal fin originating slightly behind pelvic fin; dorsal fin rays 8; anal fin rays 9 (8–10); pectoral fin rays 14–16; pelvic fin rays 8. Lateral line scales 69 (62–75); lateral line complete. Digestive tract short with only a single loop. Chromosomes 2n = 50 (W. LeGrande, pers. comm.).

Back usually green or blue-green; below this on each side a narrow light stripe followed by a dark lateral stripe, vague in its beginnings but becoming clearer below dorsal fin and continuing posteriorly to caudal peduncle; laterally below the stripe a broad orange or red streak extending from opercle to at least below dorsal fin; white ventrally. Sides speckled with darkened scales. Peritoneum silvery.

Sexual dimorphism: Pectoral fins of male longer (and thicker during breeding season) than in female; male pectoral length into head length 1.15–1.19 (ages I and older); in female, 1.36–1.41 (Schwartz and Norvell 1958).

Hybrids: Redside dace × common shiner, redside dace × creek chub: common, and rate of hybridization in Wisconsin at 2% (Greene 1935). Redside dace × southern redbelly dace (Trautman 1957).

SYSTEMATIC NOTES

The striking feature in the disposition of the breeding tubercles on the breast of the redside dace is the similarity to those encountered in the genus *Phoxinus* (formerly *Pfrille* and *Chrosomus*) (Koster 1939). In each of these genera there develops a series of "very regular comb-like rows of nuptial organs" on the breast just anterior to the pectoral fin. Hubbs and Brown (1929), who first called attention to this feature, considered it evidence of a direct relationship between these genera, and were unable to find anything even suggestive of this arrangement in other genera.

According to Koster, the color pattern of a ripe male pearl dace is strikingly similar to that of the redside dace, and offers further evidence of the close relationships between these genera. Morphologically, the redside dace appears to have more in common with the pearl dace than with the redbelly daces (*Phoxinus*). The tendency of males to maintain territories resembles the behavior of the pearl dace, while the male habit of pursuing females resembles the behavior of the redbelly daces (*Phoxinus*).

DISTRIBUTION, STATUS, AND HABITAT

The redside dace occurs in the Mississippi River and Lake Michigan drainage basins. Populations are isolated in a disjunct distribution pattern, confined primarily to small headwater streams.

The overall range of this species is constricted, disjunct, and decreasing. In Minnesota it is largely confined to the extreme southeast. In lower Michigan, where it has threatened status, the only recent record (1970) comes from a tributary to Lake Erie. It has disappeared from Iowa (Harlan and Speaker 1956, Roosa 1977), and there is only a single record from northeastern Kentucky (Clay 1975). In Ohio, it has decreased drastically in abundance, and in some sections disappeared entirely (Trautman 1957). In Canada (Scott and Crossman 1973), it is restricted to tributaries into western Lake Ontario, and its "sensitivity to turbidity suggests that this dace will become increasingly rare."

In Wisconsin, the redside dace populations which once were found in Milwaukee and Racine counties

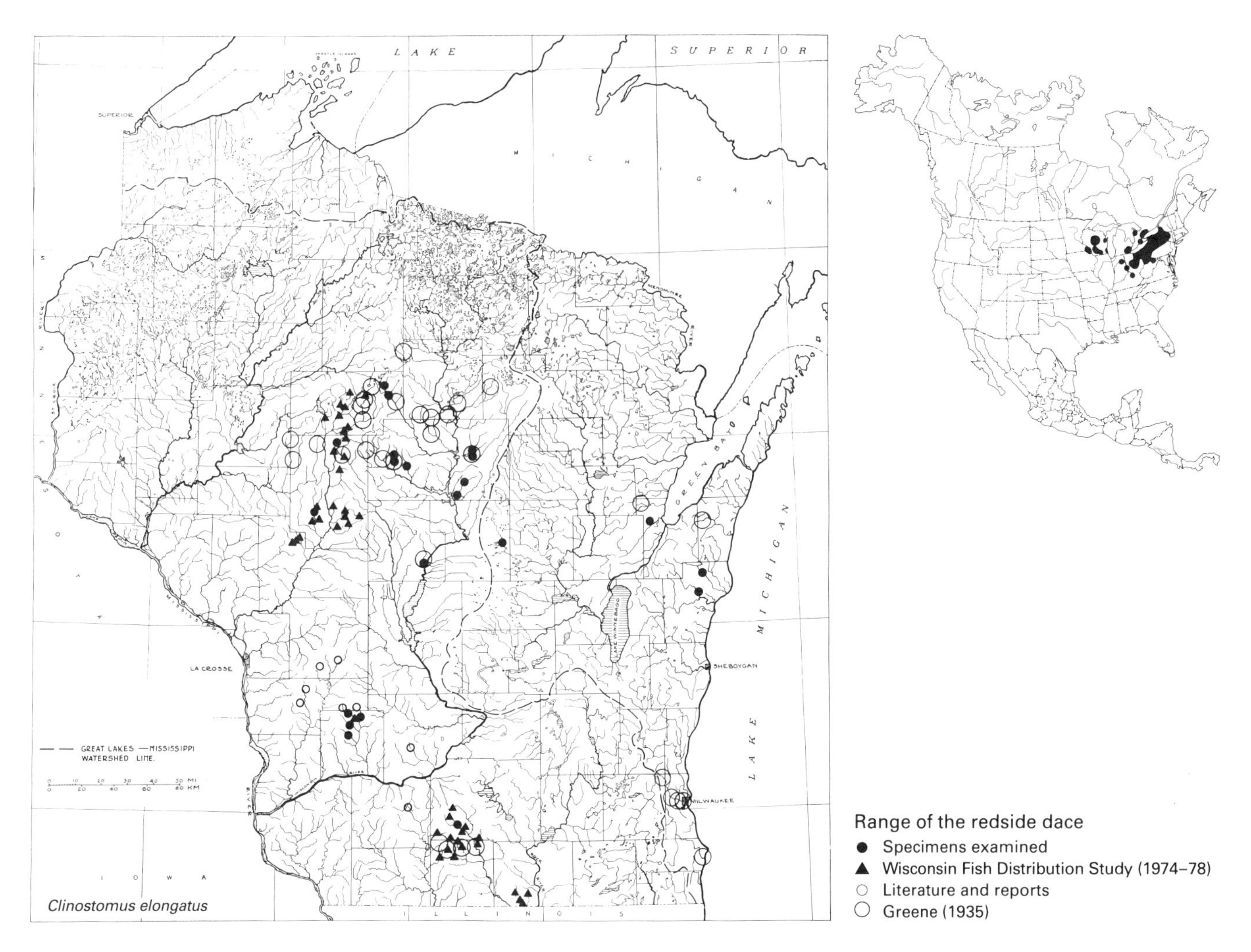

Clinostomus elongatus

Range of the redside dace
- ● Specimens examined
- ▲ Wisconsin Fish Distribution Study (1974–78)
- ○ Literature and reports
- ◯ Greene (1935)

have disappeared, and other populations in central and southern Wisconsin have been severely decimated. The stream habitat in which this species is found frequently coincides with intensive human use. These streams are in low-gradient areas given to farming, golf courses, and homes, and such uses invariably lead to modification of the stream in a number of ways unfavorable to the redside dace.

Difficult decisions face the Wisconsin Department of Natural Resources. Although that regulatory agency is alert to the problem of the redside dace, it is doubtful that it will be able to provide the constant vigilance needed to prevent deterioration of the water resource specifically required by that species. In the 1970s, federal and state agencies planned and instituted watershed changes to promote flood control. Among the redside dace streams which underwent modification were Brick Creek (Clark County), Hamann Creek (Marathon County), and Pine River (Richland County).

Greene (1935) suggested that the redside dace is moving toward extirpation. He called attention to its spotty distribution then, and noted that following glaciation it had probably had a more continuous distribution. He was concerned with the high degree of hybridization which this species had with the common shiner and the creek chub. Koster (1939) observed that if the redside dace has been largely or entirely restricted to spawning in creek chub or common shiner nests, it may have become over specialized in its spawning habits. He also noted that the spottiness of its distribution may be evidence that it is not fully synchronized with the host species as regards season of spawning.

The problems associated with spawning and hybridization do not appear as serious today as Greene and Koster indicated. Large populations of this minnow are frequently encountered along with other minnow species. Nevertheless, its habitat requirements are very narrow, and these most likely limit its distribution.

The redside dace has been placed on watch status

by the Wisconsin Department of Natural Resources Endangered Species Committee (1975) and Les (1979), but it will take more than "watching" to reverse the loss of habitat which threatens this species. Until we understand better what its specific needs are, one or more scientific areas should be established for this species.

In Wisconsin the redside dace has been taken from pools and quiet riffles of small streams with moderate gradients and cool waters. This species avoids both warm and very cold water. The substrates over which it has been taken were: gravel (50% frequency), sand (14%), clay (14.%), silt (7%), rubble (7%), and bedrock (7%). It occurred in pools and riffles at depths of 0.1–0.5 m, rarely deeper, in streams 1.0–3.0 m (25%) and 3.1–6.0 m (75%) wide. In almost all instances the area adjacent to the stream was meadow or pasture, and the water clear to slightly turbid.

Pools containing this species usually have a moderate current flowing through them, and many have overhanging grasses, brush, or trees along the banks for emergency cover.

BIOLOGY

In Wisconsin, spawning occurs in May. The following account of spawning is taken from observations by Koster (1939) on redside dace populations in northern New York.

With the approach of the spawning season, the adult males left the pools and approached the spawning beds. Three days before actual spawning was observed, males began courtship pursuit. If a female ventured near a male or a group of males, she was pursued with great vigor back to the upper pool. A second sign of the approaching season was the defense of small territories by the males. These were usually located behind a creek chub nest, and were small territories, generally no larger than the fish defending them. Deferred combat (never actual fights) between males was in the form of side-by-side swims—intimidation swims some 2–3 m upstream (see Reighard 1920).

The territorial instinct became weaker as the actual spawning period approached. During spawning the adult redside dace congregated in dense schools closely behind the pits of the nests. Males formed the body of the group; females were restricted to the sides and downstream margins of the school. When a female left her position and swam toward the pit of the nest, males joined her and spawning occurred in the depression of the nest. The spawning group commonly consisted of four to six or more males which gathered about the back and sides of the female. A simpler combination consisted of two single males, one on each side of the female, and each with his body as close as possible to hers while they were in the pit. Milt and eggs were apparently emitted at this time. At the anterior edge of the depression, following spawning, the group broke apart and individuals drifted downstream to rejoin the main school. The spawning act might be repeated four to six times per minute, or several minutes might elapse between successive matings. Spawning was observed at 18°C (65°F) or higher.

According to Koster (1939):

> The reaction of the male horned dace (creek chub) and shiners (common shiners) to the redside dace was one of tolerance. At one time a spawning group of *Clinostomus* actually pushed a fairly large male *Semotilus* aside without provoking an attack. The redside dace were often driven away from the tail of the redd during the battles for the possession of the redds by the horned dace and shiners but were not made the object of special persecution.

Most of the body of the male redside dace bears scattered, small, breeding tubercles. These are obviously of value in enabling males to maintain position against a female in a current during spawning. A highly tuberculate male (86 mm TL) was taken 29 April 1962 from the West Twin River (Manitowoc County) (UWSP 2338). A gravid female (89 mm TL, 5.23 g) from the same collection had ovaries which were 9.6% of the body weight, and which held an estimated 1,160 eggs. The eggs were white-yellow in color and 0.8 mm diam; they appeared to be well developed and loose in the ovaries. One yellow-colored egg was 1.6 mm diam.

Artificially fertilized and water-hardened eggs are somewhat ovoid in shape, 1.2–2.4 mm diam (Koster 1939), and are not adhesive at any time. Koster counted 409–1,526 eggs in 15 females. The 23.25-mm larval stage has been described and figured by Fish (1932).

Growth of young-of-year in Wisconsin has been recorded as follows:

Date	No. of Fish	TL (mm) Avg	TL (mm) Range	Location
15 Aug. (1976)	5	45	43–48	Brick Cr. (Clark Co.)
21 Aug. (1959)	4	38	34–40	Moccasin Cr. (Wood Co.)
17 Sept. (1974)	1	42		Wedges Cr. (Clark Co.)
8 Sept. (1974)	47	41	31–47	Fenwood Cr. (Marathon Co.)

The redside dace can be aged from its scales, although there is a considerable variation of circuli and annuli patterns, even on the same fish. Redside dace from the West Branch Pine River (Richland County), collected on 18 July 1962, showed the following growth:

Age Class	No. of Fish	TL (mm)		Calculated TL at Annulus (mm)	
		Avg	Range	1	2
I	12	60.7	53–70	49.1	
II	11	89.0	84–94	56.0	84.0
Avg (weighted)				52.4	84.0

A small sample from Little Sandy Creek (Marathon County), collected on 29 May 1961, contained 10 age-I fish 54.5 mm TL (41–67 mm) whose calculated TL at the end of the first year of growth was 45.2 mm.

As the redside dace gets older, the growth rate of the female is greater than that of the male. Koster (1939) presented the following SL (mm) for specimens caught in New York in May:

Age Class	SL (mm)	
	Males	Females
I	38.0 ± 2.5	37.3 ± 2.8
II	55.6 ± 2.9	57.0 ± 2.7
III	61.7 ± 3.4	69.1 ± 3.2

In Linesville Creek, Pennsylvania, the standard lengths (sexes combined) of redside dace for each year group were 0—39.57 mm, I—55.18 mm, II—67.72 mm, and III—74.54 mm (Schwartz and Norvell 1958).

The redside dace matures at age II, occasionally at age III. The largest Ohio specimen was 114 mm (4.5 in) long (Trautman 1957). An age-III, 117.5-mm (4.6 in) female (UWSP 5441) was collected from Hamann Creek (Marathon County) on 27 August 1976.

The redside dace occurs in schools, and spends its daylight hours searching for food. In both its natural habitat and in aquariums it will jump several inches into the air to catch a hovering insect.

Observations by Schwartz and Norvell (1958) have shown that this species is a midwater or surface feeder. Insects comprised 95.0% of the total food by volume in the specimens studied. Terrestrial insects made up 76.9% of this total, while 17% consisted of bottom forms such as Diptera pupae (11.2%), Ephemeroptera (3.9%), and Odonata (1.7%), with traces of other bottom insects. The remaining 5% of the food eaten was composed largely of spiders and related forms (3.0%); water mites, roundworms, plants, and debris contributed a little more than 1% to the redside diet. Plankton was not found in any of the stomachs; however, one stomach contained a quantity of debris (mud and wood particles).

According to Schwartz and Norvell, the size of food is an important factor in determining whether it will be eaten. There is a general increase in the size of food organisms consumed as the size of the fish increases. Year group 0 fed mostly on small Diptera and a few Coleoptera and Hemiptera. Specimens of year group I consumed Coleoptera and Hymenoptera in preference to Diptera. Specimens in year group II also preferred adult Coleoptera and Hemiptera to Diptera.

The pharyngeal teeth of the redside dace are effective instruments for reducing the ingested food to digestible size (Evans and Deubler 1955). These are replaced in a definite order of succession with equal frequency, and tend to be replaced before they show wear.

The preference of the redside dace for cooler waters has been illustrated in a southern Ontario study (Hallam 1959). The frequency occurrence of the redside dace was greater with the brook trout (2%) and the mottled sculpin (11%) than with the rock bass (1%) and the smallmouth bass (0%). Hallam noted that the brook trout and mottled sculpin were taken from waters which averaged more than 4.5°C (8°F) colder than those from which the rock bass and smallmouth bass were taken.

In southern Wisconsin's Pine River (Richland County), the following associate fish species were taken with 50 redside dace: American brook lamprey (2), northern hog sucker (4), white sucker (72), central stoneroller (181), blacknose dace (176), creek chub (95), bluntnose minnow (95), common shiner (190), bigmouth shiner (114), johnny darter (179), fantail darter (82), and redside dace × common shiner (1). In central Wisconsin's Little Sandy Creek (Marathon County), the following species were taken with 18 redside dace: white sucker (34), blacknose dace (21), creek chub (24), northern redbelly dace (55), bluntnose minnow (6), fathead minnow (1), common shiner (3), bigmouth shiner (19), brassy minnow (25), central mudminnow (1), blackside darter (6), johnny darter (42), fantail darter (3), and brook stickleback (10).

IMPORTANCE AND MANAGEMENT

The redside dace competes with trout for food (Raney 1969, Greeley 1936), a fact inferred from the following account. In Story Creek in southern Wisconsin, Mason et al. (1967) noted that the stocked section contained only 32 kg of wild and carry-over stocked brown trout per hectare; however, a high density of the redside dace was observed. Population levels of other minnows and white suckers were relatively low. It is not known whether the redside dace is a competitor of significance, but it is extremely quick in striking at surface food and often hits artificial flies intended for trout.

The redside dace has been reported from the tanks of minnow dealers in central Wisconsin, undoubtedly the harvest of minnows from area streams. Since it inhabits quiet pools in open, readily accessible areas, it is easily taken by seine.

With its high color and active nature, this species would make a fine aquarium pet if high water temperatures could be avoided. Diminishing numbers, however, suggest that demands from the pet fish trade might endanger an already threatened species.

Finescale Dace

Phoxinus neogaeus Cope. *Phoxinus*—tapering, the old name of the European minnow; *neogaeus*—new, world.

Other common names: bronze minnow, New World minnow, rainbow chub, chub, leatherback.

Adult male 68 mm, tributary to Grand R. (Green Lake Co.), Sept. 1972

Adult female 71 mm, tributary to Grand R. (Green Lake Co.), Sept. 1972

DESCRIPTION

Body stout, almost cylindrical anteriorly, compressed posteriorly. Average length 61 mm (2.4 in). TL = 1.23 SL. Depth into TL 4.5–6.5. Head length into TL 3.8–5.0. Snout blunt. Mouth terminal, moderately oblique and straight, and extending to below anterior margin of pupil of eye; barbel absent. Pharyngeal teeth 2,5–4,2 (variable, with 1 less in a row on one or both sides, but always 2 rows); teeth strong, hooked, arch sturdy. Eye into head length 2.9–4.8. Gill rakers short, conical, widely spaced on lower limb, up to 9 per side. Dorsal fin distinctly posterior to pelvic fin origin; dorsal fin rays 8; anal fin rays 8; pectoral fin rays 15; pelvic fin rays 8. Lateral scale series 72–89; lateral line very short, incomplete. Digestive tract short, simple S-shaped 0.6–0.8 TL. Chromosomes 2n = 50 (W. LeGrande, pers. comm.).

Back dark brown, extending halfway between the mid-dorsal line to the lateral stripe. Between the back and the lateral stripe, a light olive stripe. A distinct, dark lateral stripe commencing on the snout (pigmented lips), proceeding through eye, opercle, along the length of the body, and terminating in a distinct basicaudal spot. Lower half of body lightly pigmented above to silvery white on midventral surface. Sides in mature male below lateral stripe often with a yellow, orange, or reddish wash; female with a light yellow stripe. Fin rays edged in dark pigment; interradial membranes mostly yellow but colorless at tip. Peritoneum black, occasionally dusky.

Sexual dimorphism: In breeding male, tubercles in several rows of weltlike structures between the pectoral origin and the nearest opercular edge, and on the scales of the lower half of the caudal peduncle to the anterior base of the anal fin. The first 5 or 6 rays of the pectoral fins thickened and stiffened, and with a swelling on each ray about one-fourth the length of the ray from the tip, causing the outer part of the fin to curve upward. In female, pectoral fin short and narrow. In male, pectoral fin length/SL 0.2098; in female, 0.1709 (Stasiak 1972). Lengths of dorsal, anal, pelvic, and caudal fins significantly larger in the male.

Hybrids: Finescale dace × northern redbelly dace hybrids are common and have been reported from New York, Michigan, Ontario, Quebec, South Dakota, Minnesota, and Wisconsin. In New York, hybrid individuals are frequently more numerous than either of the parent species (Greeley and Greene 1931, Greeley and Bishop 1933). An intensive study of hybrids (New 1962) disclosed only females, but Legendre (1970) reported both sexes and demonstrated interfertility. The ratio snout length divided by upper jaw length is 0.8817 (always less than 1) for the finescale dace, 0.989 (near 1.0) for the hybrids, and 1.102 (greater than 1) for the northern redbelly dace (Hubbs and Brown 1929). New illustrated the parent species, the hybrid, and their intestinal tracts, and suggested the possibility of introgressive hybridization with a shift toward the redbelly dace.

SYSTEMATIC NOTES

In the past there has been considerable shifting of the generic placement of this species. Originally *Phoxinus* (Cope 1869), it was placed in *Pfrille* (Hubbs 1926), where it is retained by some workers (see Stasiak 1972), and in *Chrosomus* (Hubbs and Lagler 1964). Recently, however, it was merged with the northern and southern redbelly dace in *Phoxinus* (Bailey et al. 1970). Although there are considerable internal differences between the finescale and the redbelly daces, the external characters of these three species are very similar, and the large incidence of hybridization strongly supports an intrageneric relationship.

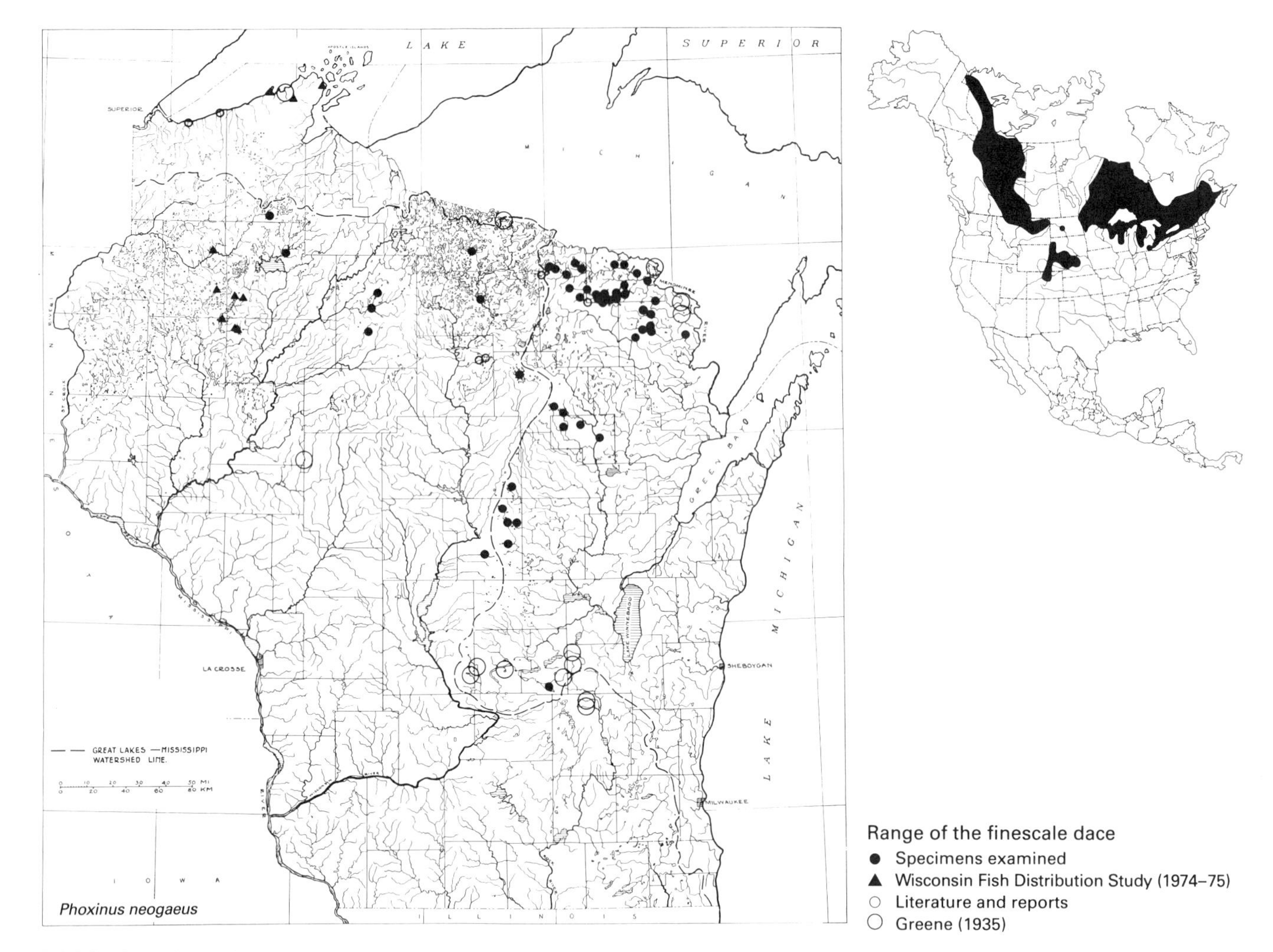

Range of the finescale dace
- ● Specimens examined
- ▲ Wisconsin Fish Distribution Study (1974–75)
- ○ Literature and reports
- ◯ Greene (1935)

McPhail and Lindsey (1970) suggested that this species may form an unusual link between New World and Old World minnows.

DISTRIBUTION, STATUS, AND HABITAT

The finescale dace occurs in all three drainage basins in Wisconsin and its distribution generally coincides with the Wisconsin Drift. Distribution is spotty, with occurrence in small drainages which may be many kilometers apart from one another.

The finescale dace is uncommon to common in small streams and ponds in northern Wisconsin. In central Wisconsin, at the southern limit of its range, it has been eliminated from a number of locales in recent years (see Greene 1935), but it still occurs in the smallest of headwater streams, where it is rare.

This species is found in cool, boggy waters of lakes, ponds, and sluggish creeks. It was encountered most frequently in light brown to dark brown waters at depths of 0.1–0.5 m over substrates of sand (25% frequency), gravel (22%), silt (19%), mud (11%), detritus (8%), bounders (7%), rubble (5%), and clay (2%). It occurred in streams of the following widths: 1.0–3.0 m (56%), 3.1–6.0 m (15%), 6.1–12.0 m (10%), 12.1–24.0 m (15%), and 24.1–50.0 m (3%).

BIOLOGY

In Wisconsin, spawning occurs from April to June. Tuberculate males and females with ripe eggs have been taken as early as 19 April in northern Wisconsin, and females with a few ripe eggs have been taken in mid-June.

The most extensive study of this species was made in the French Creek beaver ponds at Lake Itasca, Minnesota, by Stasiak (1972). The following data are from Stasiak, except where other sources are cited.

In Itasca Park, spawning fish were observed in late April when the air temperature ranged from −5 to 13°C (23 to 55.4°F), and the water temperature reached as low as 11°C (51.8°F); many of the larger lakes in the park region were still partly covered with ice. The shallow water in the beaver ponds was subject to wide fluctuations in temperature. Spawning on 6–8 May occurred in waters from 13 to 18°C (55.4 to 64.4°F).

Stasiak suggested that spawning is triggered by the sudden rise and fluctuation in water temperature which takes place following the disappearance of the ice. Fish collected from French Creek Bog in water 15°C (59°F), and released the following day in water 24°C (75.2°F) in a large aquarium at the University of Minnesota, spawned vigorously almost immediately. Stasiak described their behavior:

. . . The fish (5 males, 4 females) had been placed in a well-established 20 gallon aquarium containing rocks and live vegetation. Almost immediately, two males began chasing the largest female (in the field, the females initiated the chase). The males would nip at the caudal and anal region of the female as they chased from behind; whenever the female was close to a rock, vegetation or the side of the aquarium, the male would swim alongside the female, placing his large pectoral fin directly behind the pectoral fins of the female. The large, scoop-shaped pectoral fin of the male perfectly fit the body contour of the female and allowed the male to somewhat control the swimming of the pair. With the pectoral fins thus located, the male tried to force the female against some object such as a rock or the side of the aquarium; whenever the male was successful in doing this, it would curl its tail over the tail of the female. In this position, the tubercles above the anal fin of the male were usually adjacent to the vent of the female. The two fish vibrated in this position for several seconds, and then the male released the female.

In the field, spawning occurred where depressions in the pond were covered by fallen logs or a group of branches. The water was usually 0.5–0.9 m (1.5–3 ft) deep. Large schools of finescale dace were seen swimming near the surface; fish of all sizes were clearly present, including large ripe females, immature fish born the previous spring, and males in bright breeding colors. The large males did not defend any territory, did not build any nests, nor did they fight among themselves.

Although males were often seen following females closely, females invariably induced chasing. This occurred when one to three females suddenly left the school in the direction of some cover, usually a fallen log. They swam with a definite zigzag motion, and one to three males almost immediately began to chase the zigzagging females. The spawning group swam into a depression under logs or branches where the substrate was either mud or fine gravel. Stasiak assumed that spawning occurred at this time, although he was unable to observe the act.

In Wisconsin, mature females were collected on 13 June 1966 from a feeder to the Pike River (Marinette County). A 76-mm fish with ovaries 16% of total weight held an estimated 820 ripe eggs 1.0–1.1 mm diam; an 87-mm female with ovaries 17.2% of total weight held an estimated 1,600 eggs. A 68-mm male had testes 5.7% of total weight. Spawning was in progress and some females had few eggs remaining in their ovaries. On 21 June in Slough Creek (Marinette County), a 69-mm female with ovaries 4% of total weight held 250 eggs 1.0–1.2 mm diam.

In Minnesota, a female with ovaries 18.8% of total weight (the highest value found in females) was collected 10 May 1969; the highest testes to total weight value for males was 1.68% on 8 May 1970 (Stasiak 1972). The largest number of ripe eggs (1.1 mm diam) found in a single specimen was 3,060. A prespawning female (82 mm SL) had 5,850 eggs. Stasiak noted two distinct size classes of eggs: the yellow-orange mature eggs, and numbers of smaller (0.3–0.5 mm) recruitment eggs.

Artificially fertilized eggs hatched into larvae 4.2 mm TL exactly 4 days after fertilization. The larval fish began to swim for very short periods 3 days after hatching, first fed actively 7 days after hatching, and at 10 days ate small particles of dry prepared food from the surface of the water. At 19 days the minnows had very obvious dorsal, anal, and caudal fins. Eggs spawned naturally developed at a rate similar to those developing in the laboratory. In nature, the diet of finescale dace during the first 2 months consisted of Diptera (larvae and adults), Cladocera, Ostracoda, and Copepoda. Aquatic Hemiptera formed an increasing percentage of the food after June, as did Coleoptera larvae and adults. Finescale dace less than 35 mm SL did not consume mollusks.

In Minnesota, young-of-year attained the following growth (SL): 23 June—17.8 mm, 20 July—25.6 mm, 10 August—30.0 mm, and 23 November—35.3 mm.

Analysis of the scales of finescale dace collected 13 June 1966 from a feeder stream to the North Branch of the Pike River (Marinette County) showed the following growth:

Age Class	No. of Fish	TL (mm) Avg	TL (mm) Range	Calculated TL at Annulus (mm) 1	2	3	4
I	13	36.0	33–41	21.4			
II	14	56.7	51–61	30.4	54.6		
III	4	71.5	69–75	25.6	63.7	71.5	
IV	1	88		24.3	66.8	77.4	85.0
Avg (weighted)				26.0	57.2	72.7	85.0

In Minnesota, age-I females were 38 mm, males 41 mm; age-II females 49.5 mm, males 50 mm; age-III females 56.5 mm, males 56 mm; age-IV females 66 mm, males 60 mm; age-V females 76.5 mm, males 67 mm; age-VI females 83 mm. Complete sexual maturity was attained by age II in both sexes. Stasiak obtained the best results for calculating age from scales removed from the caudal peduncle; he also used the right opercular bone.

A 107-mm female was collected from a beaver flowage in Weasel Creek (Sawyer County).

The diet of finescale dace from a feeder stream in Marinette County consisted of dipterans, crawling water beetles (Haliplidae), moth remains, back swimmers (Corixidae), unidentifiable insect remains, filamentous algae, detritus, and sand (V. Starostka, pers. comm.). A number of tracts were empty; others contained large amounts of plant debris.

In Minnesota, mollusks are the major food organisms of adult fish. Fingernail clams, or snails, or both are always found in at least 30% of the stomachs examined. The sharp, heavy pharyngeal teeth of finescale dace allow them to exploit this food source. Trichoptera larvae, Diptera larvae, and aquatic Hemiptera (mostly Corixidae) are consistently found in the diet. Animals occurring less frequently include Diptera adults, Coleoptera larvae and adults, Ephemeroptera larvae, and Hydracarina. Plant material, which contributes about 22% of the intestinal contents in some collections, is in the form of undigested filamentous Chlorophyta. This material is probably ingested incidentally to other food items, and probably does not contribute much food value. Sand and mud are also found in stomachs. Miscellaneous food items include spiders, ants, small Odonata, and fish eggs. These eggs are taken at the time of year when the northern redbelly dace is spawning in the ponds.

Many small fish of suitable eating size were present in the Minnesota ponds, but Stasiak found none in the specimens examined. In an aquarium, however, I have seen finescale dace avidly feeding on small guppies, and in all probability larval fish are consumed occasionally.

The finescale dace is capable of withstanding a wide temperature range. In Canada (Brett 1944), the lower lethal temperature for midsummer was 1.3°C (34.3°F), and the upper lethal temperature was 32.3°C (90.1°F).

The finescale dace is largely a schooling fish and frequents those waters in which competition with other fish species is low. Hubbs and Cooper (1936) noted that boglike lakes, beaver ponds, and small weedy, muskeg streams frequently contain an association of minnows which includes pearl dace, finescale dace, northern redbelly dace, brassy minnows, and fathead minnows. In Morgan Creek (Florence County), 35 finescale dace were associated with: brook trout (4), white sucker (1), blacknose dace (8), hornyhead chub (20), pearl dace (1), northern redbelly dace (358), fathead minnow (1), common shiner (80), blacknose shiner (5), brassy minnow (8), johnny darter (3), mottled sculpin (2), and brook stickleback (22).

IMPORTANCE AND MANAGEMENT

According to Stasiak, the chief predators of this species in French Creek Bog in Minnesota are insects such as large, predacious diving beetles and the giant water bug. He suspected that backswimmers (Notonectidae) consume considerable numbers of the young minnows, and on two occasions he found pharyngeal teeth in the stomachs of mudminnows. Stasiak also suspected that herons, kingfishers, grebes, and loons, as well as northern pike and brook trout, constitute potential vertebrate predators of the finescale dace.

Finescale dace make interesting aquarium pets and are not sensitive to wide variations in water temperature.

In northern Wisconsin there is limited use of this species as a bait minnow. It is hardy, survives well in crowded containers, and makes satisfactory pike bait.

Southern Redbelly Dace

Phoxinus erythrogaster (Rafinesque). *Phoxinus*—tapering, the old name of the European minnow; *erythrogaster*—red belly.
Other common name: red-bellied dace.

Adult male 65 mm, tributary to Pecatonica R. (Lafayette Co.), 28 June 1960

Adult female 67 mm, tributary to Pecatonica R. (Lafayette Co.), 28 June 1960

DESCRIPTION

Body elongate, almost cylindrical. Average length 64 mm (2.5 in). TL = 1.24 SL. Depth into TL 4.1–5.8. Head length into TL 4.5–5.2. Snout blunt. Mouth terminal, with tip of upper lip protruding beyond lower lip; mouth moderately oblique (about 36° with horizontal axis) and straight, extending to below posterior nostril; barbel generally absent (present in groove in upper lip anterior to angle of mouth in some individuals from the Blue River, Grant County). Pharyngeal teeth 5–5, slender, slightly hooked. Eye into head length 3.8–4.9. Gill rakers short, conical, 7–9. Dorsal fin origin distinctly posterior to origin of pelvic fin; dorsal fin rays 8; anal fin rays 8; pectoral fin rays 14–15; pelvic fin rays 8. Lateral scale series 67–90; lateral line very short or incomplete. Digestive tract 1.6–1.7 TL, increasing in length with size and age of fish. Chromosomes 2n = 50 (W. LeGrande, pers. comm.).

Back above lateral stripe light olive, below lateral stripe silvery white with red, yellow, or pink wash. Lateral stripe beginning on side of snout and terminating in a distinct wedge-shaped basicaudal spot. A thin, dorsolateral stripe on upper back between lateral stripe and mid-dorsal stripe appears as a solid line from operculum to behind dorsal base, after which it becomes a series of dots. Irregular spots on upper back on either side of the mid-dorsal stripe, approximately 12 or more per side. Peritoneum black or dark brown.

Breeding male southern redbelly dace are among the most strikingly beautiful of all Wisconsin fishes. Intense reds cover the lower sides, breast, abdomen, chin, lower head, and the base of the dorsal fin. All fins are a vivid yellow edged in white. The 2 black lateral stripes enclose a broad yellow band. Breeding females occasionally have red pigment about the base of the pectorals, and a reddish wash from above the pelvic fins to the base of the anal fin. Specimens which have been in the UWSP collection for 15 years continue to retain these colors, an unusual occurrence since in formalin and alcohol most pigments fade within a short time.

Breeding male finely but densely tuberculate on head, on body scales, on rays of all fins except the caudal fin; about 8 rows of closely apposed tubercles in a unique patch anterior to the pectoral base and parallel to the opercular margin. Breeding female with scattered tubercles on top of head.

Sexual dimorphism: In male, the distance from the end of the pectoral to the pelvic origin is usually less than one-fourth the length of the pectoral fin; in female, the distance is usually greater than four-tenths the length of the pectoral fin. In male, pelvic fin into SL 5.1–5.9; in female, 6.6–8.8.

Hybrids: Reported with the common shiner, creek chub, redside dace, finescale dace, and central stoneroller minnow (Greenfield et al. 1973, Cross and Minckley 1960, Hubbs and Bailey 1952, Slastenenko 1957, Trautman 1957).

SYSTEMATIC NOTES

A thorough study in Minnesota (Phillips 1969a) showed that the southern and northern redbelly dace are morphologically distinct and do not interbreed where sympatric.

Koster (1939), on the basis of the similarity of triangular patches of tubercles near the pectoral fins, concluded that the groups *Chrosomus* (= *Phoxinus*)—*Pfrille* and *Margariscus*—*Clinostomus*—*Couesius* form a closely related series. The discovery in Wisconsin of a population of southern redbelly dace, with barbels typical of *Semotilus* (subgenus *Margariscus*), further supports this relationship.

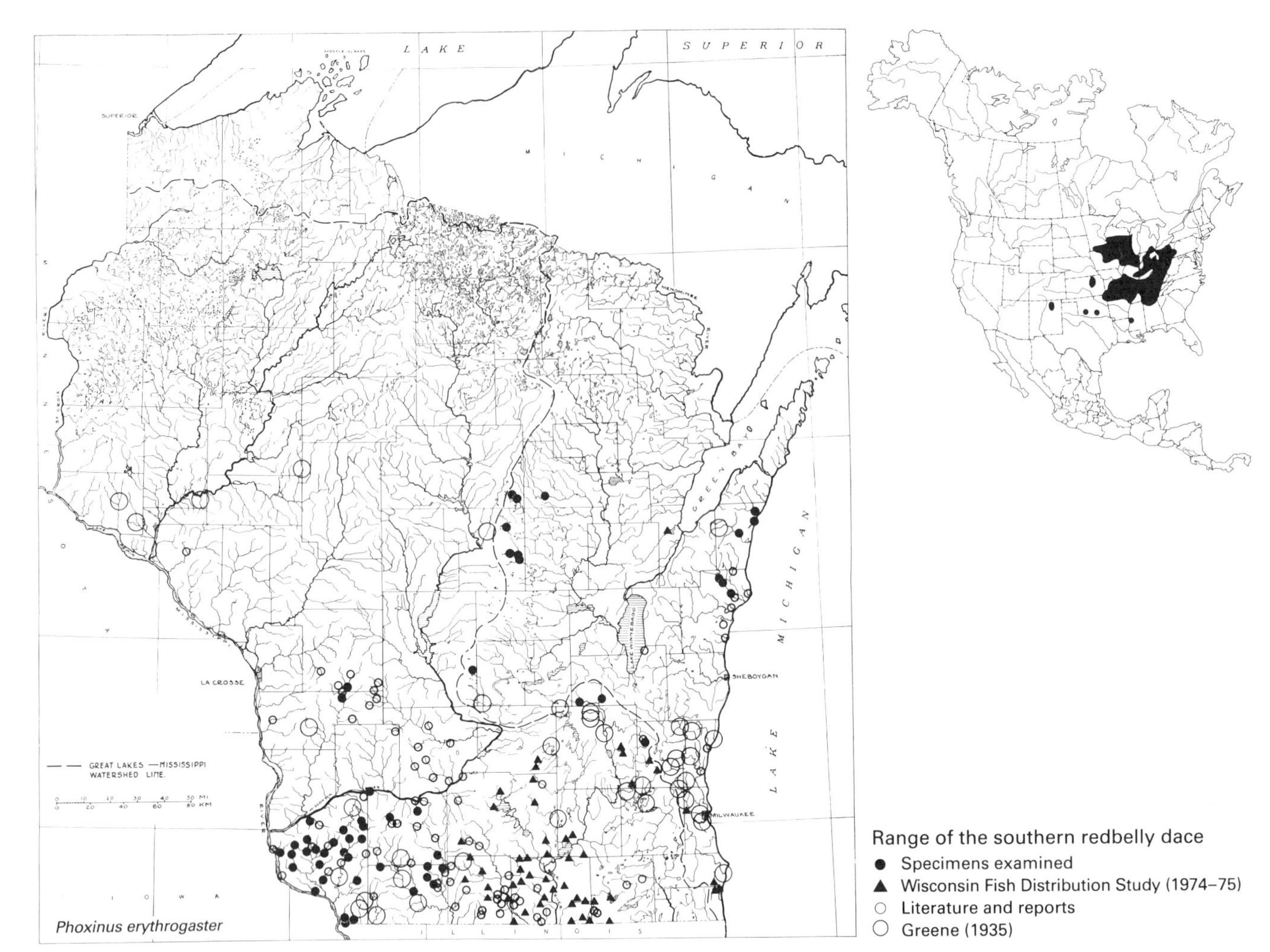

DISTRIBUTION, STATUS, AND HABITAT

In Wisconsin, the southern redbelly dace occurs in the Mississippi River and Lake Michigan drainage basins, and ranges northward through the center of the state. The overall range appears to be similar to that of the species in the 1920s (Greene 1935); however, many additional sites within that range have been recorded since then.

In southern Wisconsin the southern redbelly dace is abundant in small- to medium-sized streams, although it is absent in many likely looking streams of Crawford and Richland counties. It appears to have moved into a number of new localities in central Wisconsin; throughout this region it is rare to uncommon. Its status in the lower Lake Michigan drainage of Wisconsin is insecure, and it appears to have disappeared from a number of locales in the Milwaukee, Menomonee and Root river drainages.

In Wisconsin the southern redbelly dace was encountered only in streams, generally in clear water, and less commonly in slightly turbid and turbid waters. It was found at depths of 0.1–1.5 m over substrates of gravel (27% frequency), rubble (21%), silt (19%), sand (10%), mud (6%), boulders (6%), clay (5%), and bedrock (5%). It occurred in rivers of the following widths: 1.0–3.0 m (54%), 3.1–6.0 m (24%), 6.1–12.0 m (14%), and 12.1–24.0 m (8%). Vegetation is sparse to absent in its habitat.

BIOLOGY

In Wisconsin, spawning begins in early May and extends into late July, although males may retain their brilliant colors into August. Gravid females with ripe eggs were collected from a feeder stream to the Grant River (Grant County) on 24 July, but all females examined in August were spent.

Extensive observations of spawning behavior were made near Lake Forest, Illinois, a few miles south of the Wisconsin-Illinois line (B. G. Smith 1908). No aggression between males was observed. Competition was limited to the struggle to get a position next to the female:

> . . . Several males pursue one female; as the foremost males gain a position alongside the female, the flight and

pursuit attain almost lightning-like rapidity. At length two males spawn with the single female as follows: One on each side presses the side of his head against that of the female, all three facing up stream. The two males then crowd laterally against the female, held between them; their entire flanks are thus pressed against the sides of the female. While the males are in this position, a rapid vibration of their bodies occurs. The wave of pressure begins at the anterior end of the body and passes backward as a sidewise undulating movement. Other males may attempt to crowd in. So far as observed, the female remains passive (p. 13).

Smith noted that immediately after spawning other fishes poked their noses into crevices between pebbles, just downstream from where the spawning occurred, evidently in an attempt to get at the scattered eggs to eat them.

Smith observed that an entire school, in a compact body, may spawn on the pebbly margin of a stream in a "writhing mass of several hundred fishes . . . rasping over the pebbles and wriggling into water so shallow that their dorsal surfaces are exposed." He noted that in shallows where the participants were wedged among large pebbles and were in close contact with the bottom, their positions might be held indefinitely, and that they might lie for many minutes without motion, except for the frequent rapid vibration of their bodies. In one instance a male crowded the female laterally against some pebbles and curved his tail up over her body, thus holding her firmly against the bottom; his body vibrated rapidly and the water became cloudy with milt.

The southern redbelly dace also uses abandoned nests of *Nocomis* (Hankinson 1932) and probably creek chub (Smith 1908). In an abandoned nest, Smith noted a school of a dozen or more males crowded together to await the arrival of one or more females; spawning occurred in the hollow of the nest. Sometimes males left the nest in a body and returned to it repeatedly; their movements appeared to be excited, and suggested that they were attempting to entice or drive a female into the nest.

In Wisconsin, mature ripe females were collected on 28 June 1960 from a feeder to the Pecatonica River (Lafayette County). A 67-mm fish with ovaries 26% of total weight held 862 ripe orange-yellow eggs 1.2–1.3 mm diam; immature yellow-white eggs about 0.7 mm were less numerous than mature eggs. A 68-mm fish with ovaries 24% of body weight held 1,020 ripe eggs. On 20 July 1962 in Bacon Branch (Grant County), a 59-mm female with ovaries 14% of body weight held 230 eggs 1.25 mm diam, and a 76-mm fish with ovaries 5% of body weight held 550 maturing eggs 0.75–1.0 mm diam. In the latter fish, immature eggs were about 0.5 mm diam.

Phillips (1969c) estimated the total number of eggs (including undeveloped eggs) per female (58.7–81.5 mm TL) as 7,748–20,966. This potential fecundity level probably is not realized in the production of mature eggs during the 1–3 years that a female may breed.

By scale analysis, southern redbelly dace, collected 24 July 1962 from a tributary of Rogers Branch (Grant County) showed the following growth:

Age Class	No. of Fish	TL (mm)		Calculated TL at Annulus (mm)		
		Avg	Range	1	2	3
I	38	53.5	40–64	34.2		
II	9	69.2	65–73	33.5	61.1	
III	7	73.7	71–76	31.4	56.2	68.1
Avg (weighted)				33.7	59.0	68.1

Age-I southern redbelly dace under 50 mm TL are immature; those over 50 mm TL are mostly mature. All age-II and age-III fish are mature. Females average slightly smaller than males. The largest Wisconsin dace seen was a male, 76 mm (3.0 in) TL.

The diet of southern redbelly dace taken from Blue River (Grant County) consisted of large amounts of plant matter and sand with only a single, unidentifiable trace of animal matter (V. Starostka, pers. comm.). In southeastern Wisconsin, Cahn (1927) found Entomostraca, algae, and particles of aquatic vegetation, and an occasional *Hyalella* or *Gammarus*.

In general, this species feeds chiefly on microscopic plants (Forbes 1883, Raney 1969, Rimsky-Korsakoff 1930). Zooplankton may be present in stomachs in trace amounts. Mud, sand, silt, and detritus constituting up to 90% of the volume of ingested materials are freely consumed. In Minnesota, Phillips (1969b) noted that food items generally correspond to what is available in the stream, and that feeding activity is higher in the daytime than at night. Food is obtained by nibbling or sucking slime from the stones and other objects on the bottom. The elongated intestine is designed to handle plant digestion; Phillips observed that it increases in length with age at a rate faster than body growth.

Clear and shaded waters are the prime habitat of the southern redbelly dace. If undercut banks are absent, this species when frightened forms closely packed schools in midwater, instead of scattering to hide under objects as many other brook species do.

The schooling behavior of this species is strong, even after the spawning season is over.

In Bacon Branch (Grant County), 199 southern redbelly dace were associated with the following species: white sucker (22), central stoneroller (185), longnose dace (3), hornyhead chub (10), creek chub (22), bluntnose minnow (9), suckermouth minnow (2), common shiner (53), bigmouth shiner (5), johnny darter (11), fantail darter (43), and largemouth bass (3).

IMPORTANCE AND MANAGEMENT

The southern redbelly dace has been used as bait for crappies in southern Minnesota, although it is not as hardy as the northern species (Dobie et al. 1956). The southern redbelly dace is highly vulnerable to capture. Trautman (1957) observed that in a few hours two commercial bait seiners could capture 75% of the dace population in a half-mile of stream. In frequently seined streams, the dace populations are very low, even in those brooks containing a large amount of suitable habitat.

The southern redbelly dace is a good bioassay animal and aquarium species if handled with reasonable care (Ward and Irwin 1961). Eddy and Underhill (1974) note that, if the day length is controlled, these fish retain their brilliant red pigmentation for a long period of time. In caring for this species, a large tank, well-oxygenated water, and plenty of swimming space is required. Sterba (1973) recommended summer temperatures of 15–23°C (59–73.4°F), and winter temperatures of 12–15°C (53.6–59°F); spawning will occur in spring at temperatures of 20–24°C (68–75.2°F). This native fish is not as sensitive to temperature as many of the tropical species.

Although accounts of the southern redbelly dace as a forage species are not known, its strong schooling habit in exposed shallows, especially during spawning, suggests vulnerability to fish-eating birds and mammals.

Northern Redbelly Dace

Phoxinus eos (Cope). *Phoxinus*—tapering, the old name of the European minnow; *eos*—sunrise.
Other common names: redbelly dace, red-bellied dace, leatherback, yellowbelly dace.

Adult male 53 mm, tributary to Little Sandy Cr. (Marathon Co.), 29 May 1961

Adult female 59 mm, tributary to Little Sandy Cr. (Marathon Co.), 29 May 1961

DESCRIPTION

Body elongate, almost cylindrical. Average length 51 mm (2 in). TL = 1.24 SL. Depth into TL 4.4–6.3. Head length into TL 4.4–5.1. Snout bluntly pointed. Mouth terminal, with chin generally protruding beyond upper lip; mouth strongly oblique (about 50°, with horizontal axis) and curved, extending to below midnostril; barbel absent. Pharyngeal teeth 5-5 (occasionally 1 or 2 missing on one side), slender, hooked. Eye large, into head length 2.7–4.3. Gill rakers short, conical, about 10. Dorsal fin origin distinctly posterior to origin of pelvic fin; dorsal fin rays 8 (7); anal fin rays 8; pectoral fin rays 13–15; pelvic fin rays 8. Lateral scale series 77–81 (70–90); lateral line incomplete, decurved. Digestive tract elongate with 2 crosswise coils 1.1–1.6 TL. Chromosomes 2n = 50 (Legendre and Steven 1969).

Back above lateral stripe dark olive; below lateral stripe silvery white, yellow or red, the colors usually a condition of spawning. Lateral stripe beginning on snout and terminating in a basicaudal spot. A thin, dorsolateral stripe on upper back between lateral stripe and mid-dorsal stripe appears as a solid line from operculum to behind the dorsal base, after which it becomes a series of dots. Irregular spots in a line on upper back on either side of the mid-dorsal stripe generally unclear, diffuse, or absent, 10 or less per side. Peritoneum black or dark brown.

Breeding male with about 6 rows of minute tubercles on breast below opercular margin. Tubercles on pectoral fin rays, and on scales of lower half of caudal peduncle. Intense red on abdomen of male; occasionally bright yellow on abdomen throughout breeding season.

Sexual dimorphism: The length of pectoral, pelvic depressed dorsal and anal fins is significantly greater in males than in females (Phillips 1969a). Sexual variation is not apparent until a total length of 30–40 mm is attained.

Hybrids: Northern redbelly dace × common shiner (Gilbert 1964), northern redbelly dace × finescale dace (New 1962, Legendre 1970). Legendre reported northern redbelly dace × pearl dace and suspected tri-hybrid northern redbelly dace × finescale dace × pearl dace.

SYSTEMATIC NOTES

The northern redbelly dace and southern redbelly dace are generally regarded as two species, although

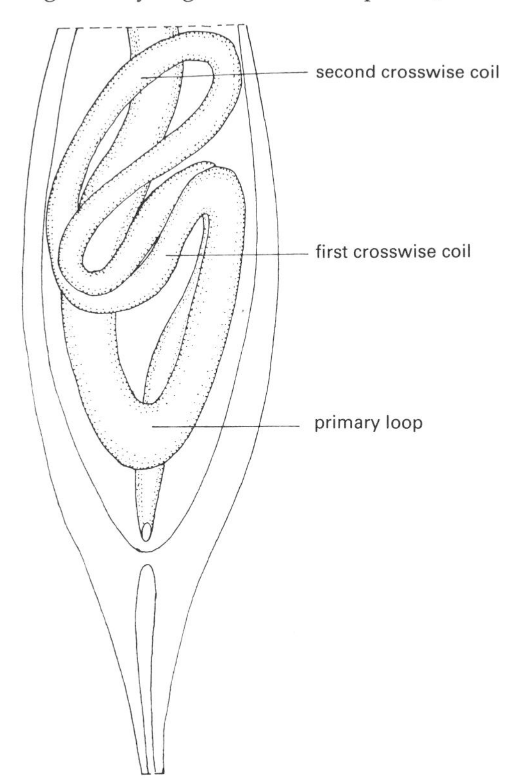

Ventral view of the alimentary tract of the northern redbelly dace with ventral body wall and viscera removed

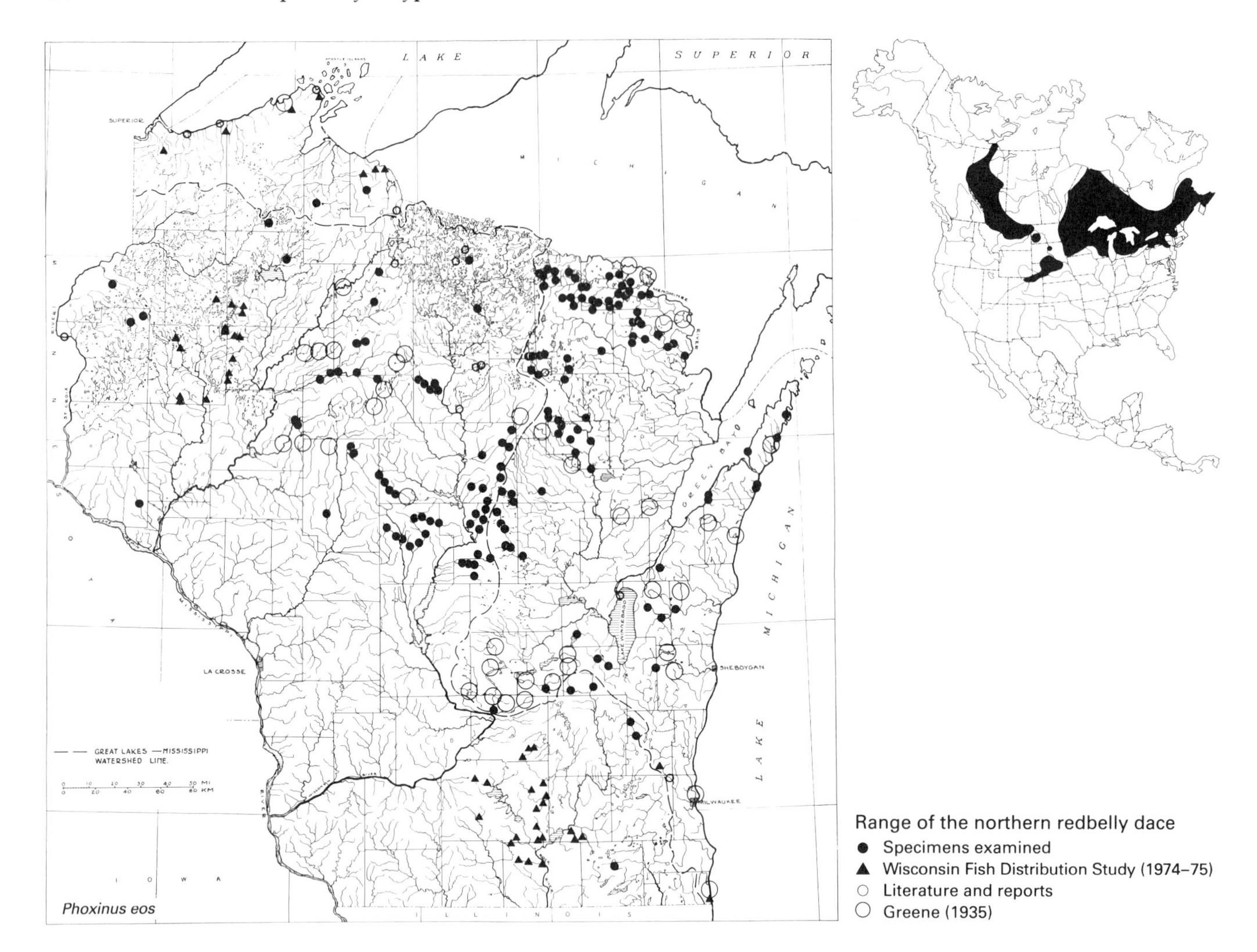

the northern redbelly dace has also been considered a subspecies of the southern redbelly dace (Jordan and Evermann 1896). A thorough study in Minnesota (Phillips 1969a) showed that these forms are morphologically distinct, do not interbreed where sympatric, and hence are distinct species.

DISTRIBUTION, STATUS, AND HABITAT

In Wisconsin, the northern redbelly dace occurs in all three drainage basins. In the Mississippi River basin it generally avoids the unglaciated southwestern quarter of the state, and, although it almost reaches the Illinois line, this species has never been collected in that state. It occurs rarely in the shallows of Lake Superior and northern Lake Michigan.

The northern redbelly dace is abundant in small streams and in bog lakes of central and northern Wisconsin. In the lower half of the Lake Michigan basin it is gone from a number of locales where it was found in the late 1920s, but over the remainder of its range it appears secure.

This dace prefers the quiet waters of beaver ponds, bog ponds, and small lakes, as well as quiet, pool-like expansions of headwater streams, often over bottoms of finely divided brown detritus or silt. In such locations the water is often stained the color of tea and may be slightly acid. In Wisconsin this species was encountered most frequently in clear to slightly turbid water at depths of 0.1–0.5 m (less frequently at 0.6–1.5 m) over substrates of sand (27% frequency), gravel (23%), silt (17%), mud (10%), boulders (9%), rubble (7%) detritus (5%), and clay (1%). It was taken once over bedrock; it has seldom been taken over marl. It occurred in streams of the following widths: 1.0–3.0 m (44%), 3.1–6.0 m (17%), 6.1–12.0 m (18%), 12.1–24.0 m (11%), 24.1–50.0 m (7%), and more than 50 m (3%). The northern redbelly dace is often associated with vegetated areas.

In central Wisconsin, the analysis of six habitat types—upstream and downstream sectors of new ditch, old ditch, and natural stream—showed that the northern redbelly dace was most abundant in the upstream natural stream and in the downstream ditches, and scarce or absent in downstream natural stream and in the upstream ditches (Headrick 1976).

The northern redbelly dace and its closely related form, the southern redbelly dace, live in very different types of habitats. In some waters, however, as in the lower Tomorrow River (Portage and Waupaca counties), they occur together. In this river the northern redbelly dace was the only form taken years ago, but the southern redbelly dace has appeared in increasing numbers in recent years.

BIOLOGY

At the latitude of Wisconsin the spawning season extends from the latter part of May into August. The condition of museum specimens suggests that most spawning in Wisconsin occurs in June and July.

The spawning behavior of the northern Redbelly dace has been studied in Michigan by Hubbs and Cooper (1936:65):

> . . . Spawning occurs in pairs or in a group of one female and several males. The breeding males can be easily recognized by their more brilliant colors, the breeding females by the swollen abdomen, due to the presence of large eggs. The great activity of the female, when ready to spawn, immediately attracts the ripe males, which then pursue her, in what appears to be a type of spawning courtship. The female followed closely by 1 to as many as 8 males, darts through the water for several feet as if attempting to escape. The first male to be attracted to the female, sometimes the only one, takes up a position a few inches behind and just below the female; other males joining the pursuit take up positions behind for several feet, the female darts headlong into a mass of filamentous algae, almost immediately followed by 1 or more males. The entire spawning group appears to struggle against the obstruction offered by the entangling algal filaments. The male, when only one is involved, takes a position directly alongside the female; several males, when present, form a dense cluster about the female, each approximately parallel to the female. It is not evident whether more than one male spawns with one female at the same time. The spawning act, lasting 2 to 4 seconds, is accompanied by a vigorous vibration of the bodies of the spawning fish. After the first spawning act the pair or group, in courtship pursuit, darts from one algal mass to another, performing a similar spawning act in each. By careful examination, it is seen that these masses of algae contain a few (5 to 30) non-adhesive eggs, scattered through and entangled among the filaments.

In Wisconsin, mature females were collected on 18 June 1960 from Hemlock Creek (Wood County). A 60-mm fish with ovaries 20% of total weight held 435 ripe orange-yellow eggs 0.9 mm diam; immature yellow-white eggs were 0.3–0.6 mm diam. A 58-mm fish with ovaries 15% of total weight held 410 ripe eggs 1.0 mm diam; immature eggs were in several stages of development up to 0.6 mm diam. Such differences in the egg generations within a single female suggest that a female has two or more distinct spawning periods during one season. The eggs hatch in approximately 8–10 days at water temperatures of 21.1–26.7°C (70–80°F) (Hubbs and Cooper 1936). In Michigan young-of-year grew 0.23–0.28 mm per day (Chapoton 1955).

Scales of the northern redbelly dace are difficult to read; however, when used in conjunction with a length-frequency analysis of 401 fish collected 30 June 1966 from Simpson Creek (Forest County), I was able to make the following estimate of growth: age 0—25–31 mm, age I—33–56 mm, age II—58–60 mm. A collection taken 19 July 1966 from the outlet creek to McCall Lake (Menominee County) was interpreted to consist of the following year classes: I—44–49 mm, II—52–69 mm, and III—70–77 mm.

According to Hubbs and Cooper, the rate of growth and the age of maturity of northern redbelly dace vary considerably according to the time at which the young hatch. Those hatching early in the season will spawn the following year at age I; those individuals hatching late probably do not spawn until age II. At the latitude of Wisconsin some fish live at least 3 years. In Canada, Scott and Crossman (1973), citing Legendre, reported this species reaching 5 years, and a maximum age of 8 years.

The largest Wisconsin fish observed was a 77-mm female from the outlet to McCall Lake (Menominee County). M. Johnson (pers. comm.) reported an 80-mm fish from the Menomonee River (Waukesha County) in 1967.

The food of the northern redbelly dace consists mainly of algae such as diatoms and filamentous algae, but it also includes zooplankton and aquatic insects. In aquariums, redbelly dace will eat smallmouth bass fry 8–9 mm long (Scott and Crossman 1973).

The northern redbelly dace frequently occurs in waters which are too warm for trout. With proper acclimation this dace tolerates midsummer temperatures ranging from 4 to 32°C (39.2 to 89.6°F) (Brett 1944).

In a tributary to Little Sandy Creek (Marathon County), 245 northern redbelly dace were associated with the following species: white sucker (27), blacknose dace (42), creek chub (23), redside dace (8), fathead minnow (1), common shiner (102), brassy minnow (2), central mudminnow (7), johnny darter (3), and brook stickleback (14).

IMPORTANCE AND MANAGEMENT

The northern redbelly dace probably has a host of predators, such as other fishes, kingfishers, and mergansers. In New York (Greeley and Greene 1931), it has been exterminated in most ponds where perch or bass have entered. Elsewhere there have been reports of predation by brook trout; to what extent brook trout prey on this dace in Wisconsin is not known. Hubbs and Cooper noted that since this dace is almost exclusively a plant eater, and therefore competes very little with trout for food, it appears to be a more desirable forage minnow for trout streams than some other minnows, such as the creek chub and the blacknose dace.

The northern redbelly dace is occasionally sold as a bait fish in Wisconsin. In spite of its small size, it is a good bait for perch, crappies, rock bass, and bluegills. It is extremely hardy and lives well under crowded conditions in a minnow pail (Hubbs and Cooper 1936).

When taken with its brilliant breeding colors, the northern redbelly dace surpasses in splendor many tropical fishes. It makes an attractive aquarium fish, and can be spawned successfully by using a synthetic fiber mat as a site for egg deposition (Eddy and Underhill 1974). Fry bred in aquariums have been raised to maturity. The northern redbelly dace thrives on dried aquarium foods.

The experimental propagation of this minnow in a small pond in Grand Rapids (Michigan), at the rate of 320,000 fish/ha (128,000/acre), has shown that it can be reared for bait. Since it feeds to a considerable extent on bottom ooze and plant matter, it uses the foods most readily available in the food chain.

Lake Chub

Couesius plumbeus (Agassiz). *Couesius*—after Dr. Elliot Coues, American ornithologist, collector of type specimens; *plumbeus*—lead colored.

Other common names: northern chub, lake northern chub, chub minnow, plumbers minnow, Moose Lake minnow, bottlefish.

Adult male 151 mm, L. Michigan, Kroeff Cr. (Sheboygan Co.), 19 Apr. 1974

Adult female 197 mm, L. Michigan, Kroeff Cr. (Sheboygan Co.), 19 Apr. 1974

DESCRIPTION

Body elongate, almost round in cross section. Average length 127 mm (5 in). TL = 1.22 SL. Depth into TL 4.8–6.9. Head length into TL 4.5–5.3. Snout bluntly rounded and slightly overhanging the mouth. Mouth large, almost reaching to anterior margin of eye; long, prominent barbel present in corner of mouth. Pharyngeal teeth hooked, usually 2,4–4,2 (variable 2,4–4,1; 1,3–4,2, etc.). Gill rakers short, 4–9. Dorsal fin originating over pelvic fin; dorsal fin rays 8; anal fin rays 8; pectoral fin rays 15–16 (13–18); pelvic fin rays 8. Lateral line scales 63 (60–67); lateral line complete. Digestive tract with only a single loop, length less than TL. Chromosomes 2n = 50 (Legendre and Steven 1969).

Back and upper sides lead gray, silver to silver-white below lateral line. An occasional darkened scale on the sides. During breeding season rosy colors appear in both sexes. In male, faint rosy wash at corner of mouth, on upper lip and above lip groove; faint rosy color at upper angle of opercle extending into opercular cavity; intense rosy spot on body surrounding base of pectoral fin, and rosy spot above base of pelvic fin; faint rosy stripe (3–6 mm wide) along side of body just above paired and anal fins; during courtship a distinct black lateral stripe. In female, rosy color on body about base of pectoral fin. Peritoneum silvery.

Breeding tubercles appear in both sexes. In male, fine tubercles on top of head, opercles and cheeks, on edges of scales of back, on scales of sides to lateral line, on breast, caudal peduncle, and on rays of pectoral and pelvic fins. In female, same as in male except less heavily tuberculate, with only the anteriormost rays of the paired fins tuberculate.

Sexual dimorphism. In male, pectoral fins long and subcircular; gap between end of pectoral fin and origin of pelvic fin about half the length of pectoral fin. In female, pectoral fins short and ovate; gap between end of pectoral fin and origin of pelvic fin about three-fourths the length of the pectoral fin.

Hybrids: Lake chub × longnose dace uncommon, but reported from Isle Royale (Hubbs and Lagler 1949) and Upper Michigan (Taylor 1954). Although a pearl dace × lake chub hybrid has been reported, it has not been proved (Hubbs 1942). *Couesius* is relatively resistant to hybridization.

SYSTEMATIC NOTES

Bailey (1951) submerged *Couesius* in *Hybopsis* Agassiz. However, recent studies indicate that *Hybopsis* is an unnatural assemblage, and Jenkins and Lachner (1971) recognized *Couesius* as a genus rather than a subgenus of *Hybopsis*. The *Couesius* group shows affinity with *Semotilus*, particularly with *Semotilus margarita*, in barbel position, scale pattern, tuberculation, breeding color, scale morphology, vertebral numbers and other features.

Earlier, Koster (1939) noted the similarity of tuberculate scale patches in *Phoxinus*, *Semotilus margarita*, and *Clinostomus*, and suggested that these species form a closely related series.

DISTRIBUTION, STATUS, AND HABITAT

In Wisconsin, the lake chub is found in the shore waters of Lakes Superior and Michigan, more commonly about the mouths of streams at depths of 1 m or less. Along shores it occurs over sand bottom interspersed with large-sized boulders. Tributary streams to Lake Michigan appear to be used only for spawning during the spring; tributaries to Lake Superior, including those which have intermittent flows, appear to hold permanent populations.

Although not reported from the Mississippi drainage basin in Wisconsin, in 1954 the lake chub was taken from Twin Springs Creek, northwest of Dubuque, Iowa, and across the Mississippi River from Grant County, Wisconsin. Like *Cottus cognatus*, which lives in the area, the lake chub's occurrence in northeastern Iowa far south of the main range of the spe-

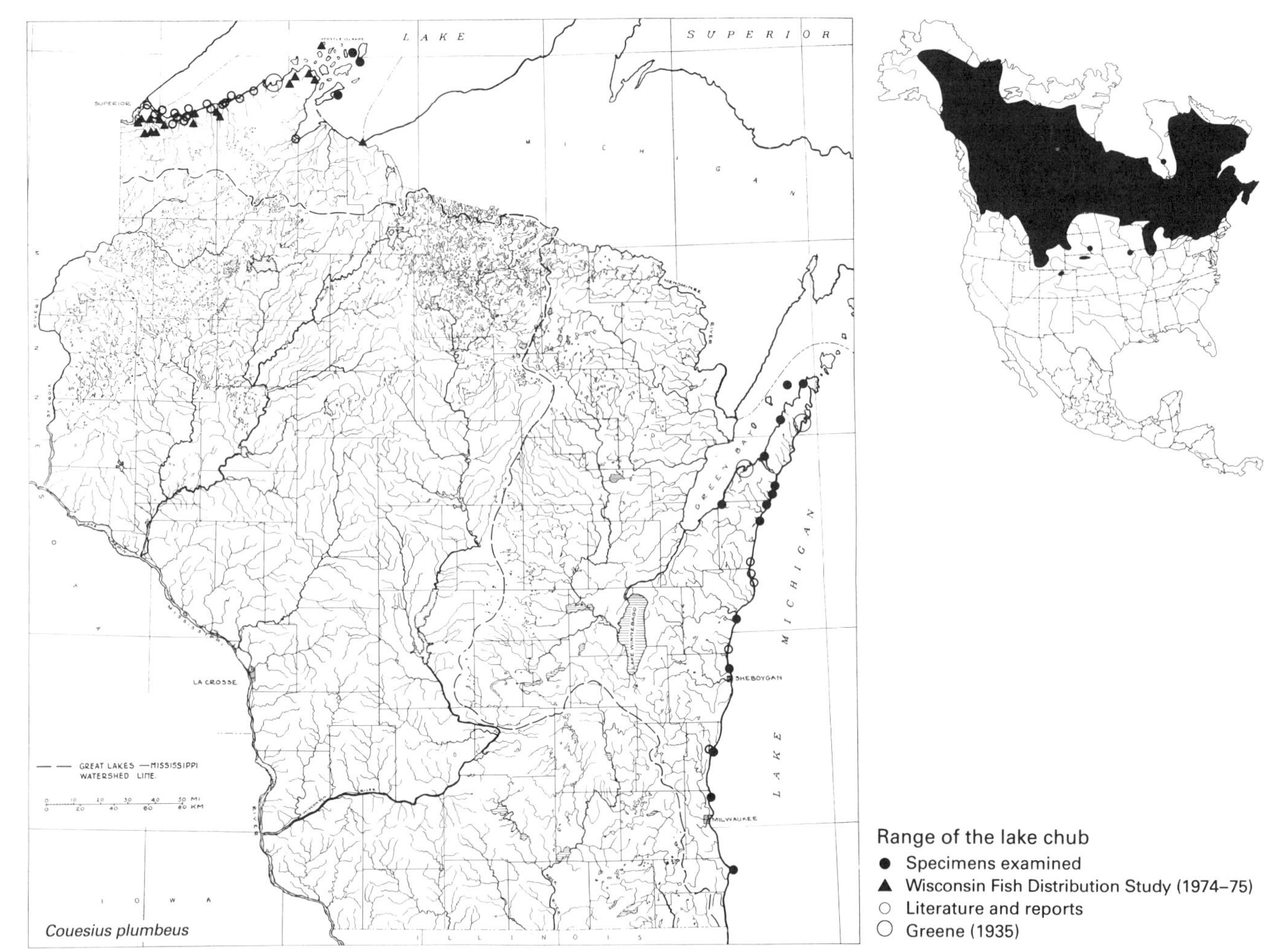

Range of the lake chub
● Specimens examined
▲ Wisconsin Fish Distribution Study (1974–75)
○ Literature and reports
◯ Greene (1935)

cies is explainable as a glacial relict (Bailey 1956). Streams with *Cottus cognatus* populations have been found in southwestern Wisconsin, and the possibility exists that the lake chub may occur as a relict species in one or more of those streams. It is also likely that this species may inhabit deep lakes containing ciscoes or lake trout, since it is a common associate of these species in the inland lakes of Canada, the Upper Peninsula of Michigan, and northern New York (Greene 1935).

Streams in the Lake Superior drainage with lake chub populations which occur many kilometers upstream are: Bluff Creek (to 22 km upstream), Nemadji River (9 km), Bardon Creek (12 km), and Poplar River (10 km) (all in Douglas County); Reefer Creek (16 km) and Sand River (14 km), (both in Bayfield County). Streams in Lake Michigan basin from which this species has been reported are Sauk Creek (Ozaukee County), Kroeff Creek and Sevenmile Creek (Sheboygan County), and Red River into Green Bay (Kewaunee County).

The lake chub is common in shoal waters of stream mouths in Green Bay and Lake Michigan, and in the Bayfield and Douglas county tributaries to Lake Superior. The future of this species appears secure if water conditions along the shores of the Great Lakes remain unchanged.

The lake chub tolerates a wide variety of environments, and has the most widespread northern distribution of any North American minnow. It frequents lakes and streams, including both clear and turbid waters, and even the outlets of hot springs (McPhail and Lindsey 1970).

Little is known about this species and its habits. In the southern parts of its range it is more common in lakes, but northward it is more common in rivers. The lake chub sometimes occurs in large schools, and is essentially a shallow water species. In large lakes, it can be taken by seining shoals.

In collecting the lake chub from Lake Michigan, I noted that the greatest inshore density was at depths of 15 cm to 1 m just out of the mouth of a tributary stream. Hauls of 7–10 individuals were taken here. As we moved along the shore from this center, the number of fish captured dwindled. At 100 m from the mouth of the creek, the lake chub was no longer captured. Catches were especially common along large boulders.

The lake chub's presence in deeper water appears to be sporadic. Several extensive fish surveys of deep waters have failed to report this species. No lake chubs were reported by Wells (1968), who trawled at depths between 5.5 and 91.5 m in southeastern Lake Michigan; nor were they reported by Dryer (1966), who trawled at 4–109 m and set gill nets at 4–160 m in the Apostle Islands region of Lake Superior. Hubbs and Lagler (1949) reported 178-mm (7-in) adults taken in experimental gill nets set in 6–11 m of water in Middle Islands Passage (Isle Royale in Lake Superior), and the Museum of Natural History (UWSP) has received specimens which were gill netted from both Lake Superior and Lake Michigan by commercial fishermen at depths of 5 m or more.

The lake chub prefers cool waters, and is considered a trout indicator (Greeley and Greene 1931, Hubbs and Cooper 1936).

BIOLOGY

In the Great Lakes region, spawning occurs in the spring, usually in late April and May. In British Columbia, spawning occurs from late June to early August, and in Montana it occurs throughout the summer (Brown et al. 1970).

The ability of the lake chub to breed successfully in a diversity of habitats (i.e., in river shallows, along rocky shores, and in shoals of lakes) and over a variety of substrates (silt, leaves, gravel, and rocks) may be an important factor in its abundance and distribution (Brown et al. 1970).

In Saskatchewan, spawning occurred at the margins of the Montreal River in about 5 cm of water. Chubs began moving into shallow spawning areas in the morning; most spawning occurred in the afternoon, although some took place until at least midnight (Brown et al. 1970). Courtship and spawning behavior were observed in an aquarium. Males showed aggression by holding their positions before an introduced object, twitching their bodies and fins, and giving chase. When a female was introduced, the males pursued her from beneath with persistent nosing in her vent region. This forced the female upward, often causing her to break surface. Males sometimes swam beside a female with their snouts just behind her operculum; if several males were present they swam side by side, apparently competing for position beside the female. The lateral body stripe of males became darker and more distinct during courtship, and the mouth was rapidly opened and closed.

Courtship pursuit continued until the female swam alongside or beneath a rock. A male then forced himself against her, and, as he vibrated vigorously and she appeared to struggle, the nonadhesive eggs freely dispersed. On one occasion when no rocks were available, a spawning act was observed over a gravel substrate. Spawning was generally consummated several times per minute, with each act lasting about 1 second. Only a small number of eggs were released during each act. Spawning was at times interspersed with feeding, and both sexes were observed to devour eggs. There was no evidence of parental guarding, nor was there any nest construction.

In the Lake Michigan basin, spawning migrations of up to 1.6 km (1 mi) have been reported from Sauk Creek in Ozaukee County, but migration distances are generally less than 0.8 km (0.5 mi). In a tributary stream to Lake Saugay, Quebec, temperatures at spawning have been reported as 14°C (57°F); in the lake as 19°C (66.2°F) (Scott and Crossman 1973). In Saskatchewan, Brown et al. (1970) noted spawning in the Montreal River in late May, but there was no spawning in Lac La Ronge until mid-June when surface temperatures reached 10°C (50°F). Although a preponderance of afternoon spawning was indicated, spawning also took place at night and continued until at least midnight.

On 19 April 1974, two prespawning lake chub males from Lake Michigan (Sheboygan County), 164 and 169 mm TL and weighing 51 and 49 g, had testes 2.9 and 3.1% of total weight. On 26 April 1975, two prespawning Lake Michigan males, 159 and 164 mm TL, had testes 3.3 and 3.1% of total weight. Ahsan (1966b) determined that temperature is the major environmental factor controlling the development of sperm. Low temperatures of 5–12°C (41–53.6°F) during the winter preceding spawning are essential for normal gonadal proliferation and formation of the primary spermatocytes. Higher temperatures, 16–21°C (60.8–69.8°F), hasten or terminate sperm production in prespawning fish.

Ahsan (1966a) also noted that there is continual sperm production in the testes during spawning, making repeated sperm discharges possible. When the ratio of males to females is low, repeated sperm discharges may be an advantage that ensures fertilization of eggs. Photoperiod does not appear to dominate sperm development at any stage.

On 26 April 1975, three prespawning Lake Michigan females of 168, 175, and 181 mm TL had ovarian weights which were 22.4%, 22.7% and 22.9% of total weight. The ovaries contained 5,290, 5,820, and 6,630 eggs respectively; they averaged 1.6 mm diam. A female of 194 mm and 104 g collected 19 April 1974, had ovaries 25.2% of total weight containing an estimated 11,440 eggs, 1.65 mm diam.

In Saskatchewan, egg production in a 100-mm female was about 800, and in a 130-mm fish it was as high as 2,400 (Brown et al. 1970). Of 919 eggs collected from among silt, leaves, and wood fragments, 519 (56%) were viable. Silt apparently had no adverse effect on early egg development. Eggs incubated at temperatures between 8 and 19°C (46.4 and 66.2°F) hatched after 10 days (Brown et al. 1970).

Growth of lake chubs is rapid, and by mid-September the young-of-year in Lake Michigan are 44–70 mm TL. Lake chubs from Lake Michigan (Door County) collected 3 July 1963 (UWSP 2254) showed the following growth:

Age Class	No. of Fish	TL (mm)		Calculated TL at Annulus (mm)			
		Avg	Range	1	2	3	4
I	1	71					
II	8	109.6	101–124	67.3	101.1		
III	5	130.6	127–136	78.3	102.4	130.6	
IV	2	165.5	165–166	72.5	104.5	134.5	165.5
Avg (weighted)				71.7	102.0	131.7	165.5

A sample collected at the mouth of Kroeff Creek (Sheboygan County) on 19 April 1974 (UWSP 4656) showed growth as follows:

Age Class	No. of Fish	TL (mm)		Calculated TL at Annulus[a] (mm)				
		Avg	Range	1	2	3	4	5
III	11	155.1	150–164	80.2	120.8	155.1		
IV	5	168.6	159–175	72.0	106.6	142.0	168.6	
V	5	177.8	170–183	75.4	109.4	139.2	160.6	177.8
Avg (weighted)				77.1	114.7	148.2	164.6	177.8

[a]The annulus for the year of capture had not yet been deposited; length at time of capture is given. The annulus is deposited from June to the beginning of July.

The 19 April sample was a prespawning population; all males and females were ready to spawn. The males (151–169 mm TL) were the smallest fish in the collection and were all age III, except the 169-mm male, which was age IV. The females ranged from 150 to 197 mm TL, and all were age IV or older. The scales in age IV and older fish were difficult to read. In four large females, 192–197 mm TL, scales could not be read at all; consequently these, which were estimated to be 6 or 7 years old, were not included in the above table.

In Lake Michigan the lake chub matures at age III, and few fish live beyond age V.

The largest known individual came from Lake Mattagami, Quebec. It was 227 mm (over 8.9 in) TL (Scott and Crossman 1973).

The food of young lake chubs consists of cladocerans and copepods; that of older fish is essentially insects. Stomachs of 15 chubs taken from Lake Michigan off Door County showed that 7 had ingested ephemeropteran larvae, 6 had ingested dipteran larvae, and 1 an Odonata larva; 4 stomachs were empty. Anderson and Smith (1971b) noted that lake chubs from western Lake Superior had eaten small amounts of crustaceans, including *Mysis*, copepods and cladocerans, and large quantities of chironomids and dipterans. In a July collection, one lake chub held unidentifiable fish remains, and an October collection yielded stomachs containing snails and fish eggs. The lake chub's almost total lack of external taste buds suggests that the fish is almost an obligatory sight feeder (Davis and Miller 1967).

Species associated with 1 lake chub in Lake Michigan off Wind Point (Racine County) were: longnose dace (5), emerald shiner (1), and mottled sculpin (1). Associated species taken off Kroeff Creek (Sheboygan County) included: lake chub (c. 25), longnose dace (13), white sucker (1), slimy sculpin (2), and ninespine stickleback (1); taken off Bear Creek (Door County) were: lake chub (43), longnose dace (112), alewife (117), white sucker (7), fathead minnow (1), creek chub (3), bluntnose minnow (6), common shiner (2), spottail shiner (27), sand shiner (1), mottled sculpin (1), and brook stickleback (1).

IMPORTANCE AND MANAGEMENT

The literature points to the lake chub as an important forage fish for such predators as lake trout, burbot, and walleyes. Scott and Crossman (1973) cite records of predation by northern pike, mergansers, and kingfishers. Unfortunately, there is no documentation of such predator-prey relationships in Wisconsin waters.

In Canada (Scott 1967) this species is sometimes sold by bait dealers for early spring fishing for lake trout, and walleyes, and other species. The lake chub has been observed to interfere with brook trout angling (Scott and Crossman 1973), for "it is almost impossible to make a cast without catching one of these minnows."

In the spring of the year the larger lake chubs are taken by smelt fishermen and mistakenly eaten as smelt. Larger lake chubs have been smoked. They are reportedly very good, and taste a great deal like ciscoes.

Blacknose Dace

Rhinichthys atratulus (Hermann). *Rhinichthys*—snout, fish; *atratulus*—probably from *atratus*, meaning clothed in black as for mourning.

Other common names: western blacknose dace, dace, striped or redfin dace, brook minnow, slicker, "potbelly" or "pottlebelly" because it is frequently distended with parasitic worms.

Adult male 75 mm, tributary to Little Sandy Cr. (Marathon Co.), 29 May 1961

Adult female 101 mm, Tomorrow R. (Portage Co.), 5 Sept. 1960

DESCRIPTION

Body stout, spindle-shaped, slightly compressed laterally. Average length 64 mm (2.5 in). TL = 1.19 SL. Depth into TL 4.4–6.6. Head length into TL 4.3–5.1. Snout overhanging mouth by less than 1 mm. Mouth slightly inferior, upper lip groove not continuous over snout; mouth slightly oblique and extending to below nostril; pointed barbel in groove at angle of mouth. Pharyngeal teeth 2,4–4,2, slender, hooked without grinding surface. Eye into head length 3.5–6.0. Gill rakers short, conical, widely spaced, 6–7. Dorsal fin origin slightly posterior to origin of pelvic fin; dorsal fin rays 8; anal fin rays 7; pectoral fin rays 13–16; pelvic fin rays 8. Lateral line scales 60–75; lateral line complete. Digestive tract 0.8–0.9 TL. Chromosomes 2n = 50 (Howell and Villa 1976).

Upper part of body brownish black and spotted with black blotches; lower part of body silvery and speckled with black spots; belly white. Faint, diffuse lateral stripe in some fish; young-of-year with a distinct broad stripe of black chromatophores extending from tip of snout to end of body, terminating in a black spot at base of caudal fin and extending out on to fin. Fin rays lightly etched in dark pigment. Peritoneum silvery to dusky.

Breeding males with minute tubercles on head, over body scales, and on pelvic fins; a reddish lateral stripe retained until fall, when it fades to a rust brown retained during winter. Membranes between pectoral rays 2–5, swollen near fin tip into breeding pad, occasionally light orange in color. Colored lateral stripe absent in female.

Sexual dimorphism: In male, end of pelvic fin reaches base of anal fin; in female, end of pelvic fin does not reach base of anal fin. In male, free end of anal fin describes a right or near right angle with body axis; in female, free end of anal fin describes an elongated loop.

Hybrids: Artifical blacknose dace × longnose dace (Howell and Villa 1976). The combination of one-to-one pairing, spawning in slow waters, and burying eggs would successfully prevent the blacknose dace from forming natural hybrids with either the longnose dace or other cyprinid species.

SYSTEMATIC NOTES

Several subspecies are recognized (Hubbs and Lagler 1964), of which the western blacknose dace, *R. atratulus meleagris* Agassiz, ranges in Wisconsin. This subspecies is distributed through the entire Great Lakes basin (except about the east end of Lake Ontario) to northeastern Nebraska and Manitoba.

DISTRIBUTION, STATUS, AND HABITAT

In Wisconsin the blacknose dace is widely distributed in all three drainage basins. It is rarely taken in the shoals of Lake Superior and northern Lake Michigan.

In Wisconsin this species is common to abundant in small, cool headwater streams; it is uncommon to common in clear medium-sized streams. Its status appears secure.

This species prefers small headwater creeks with moderate to rapid water. With the exception of the related longnose dace, the blacknose dace shows a greater preference for swift water than any other Wisconsin minnow. It was encountered most frequently in clear or slightly turbid water at depths of 0.1–0.5 m over substrates of gravel (24% frequency), sand (24%), rubble (14%) silt (13%), boulders (9%), mud (8%), clay (3%), detritus (3%), and bedrock (3%). It was rarely taken in lakes or reservoirs. It occurred

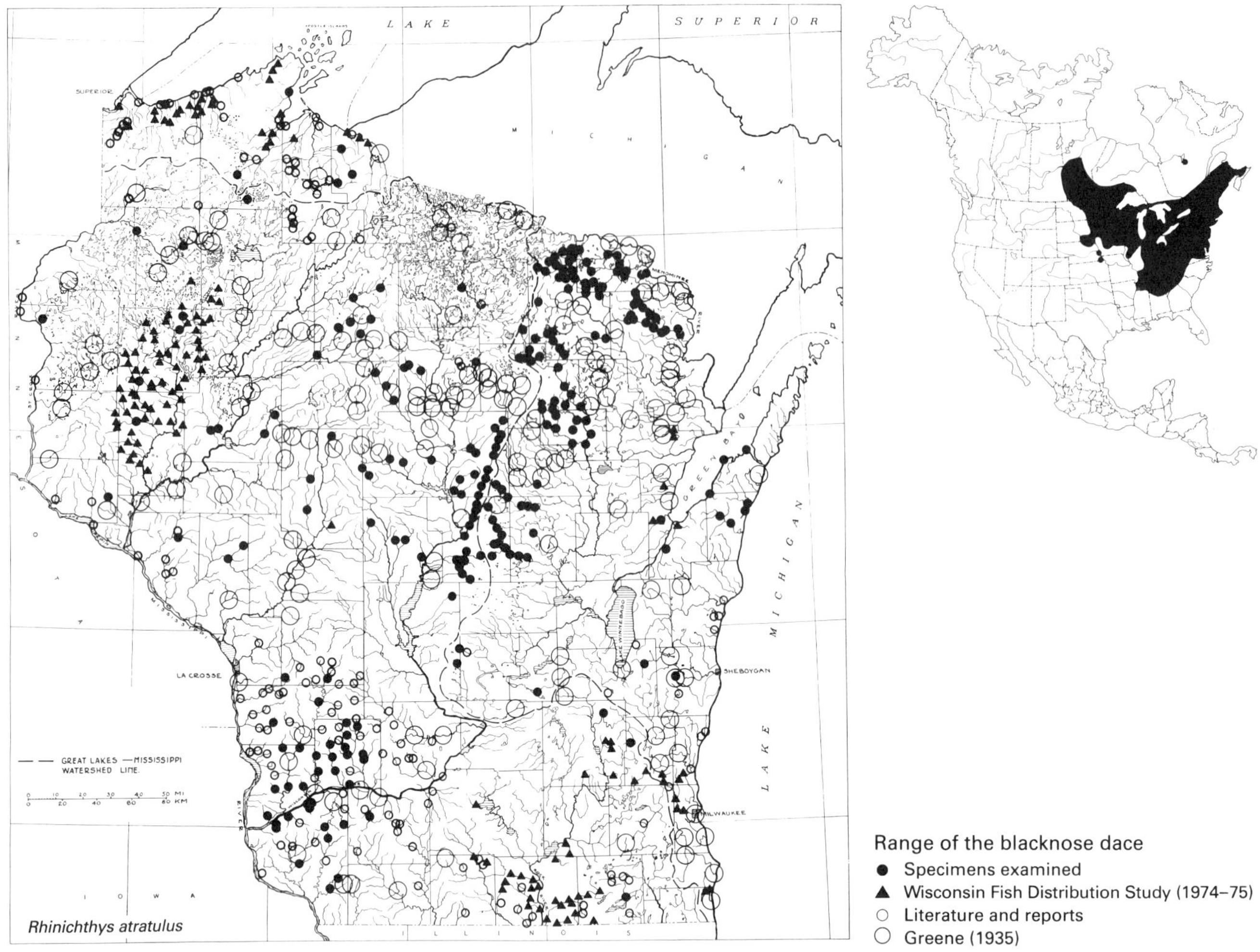

Range of the blacknose dace
● Specimens examined
▲ Wisconsin Fish Distribution Study (1974–75)
○ Literature and reports
◯ Greene (1935)

in streams of the following widths: 1.0–3.0 m (42%), 3.1–6.0 m (20%), 6.1–12.0 m (16%), 12.1–24.0 m (15%), 24.1–50.0 m (7%), and more than 50 m, none.

BIOLOGY

In Wisconsin, spawning occurs in May and June, and may extend into early July. In Iowa, spawning is reported from early May through July over gravel (Noble 1965). Spawning temperature for the blacknose dace is 21°C (69.8°F) in Pennsylvania (Raney 1940a). In central Wisconsin, water temperatures during the spawning period average 20.6°C (69°F), but fluctuate widely from 12.0 to 27.4°C (53.5 to 81.3°F) (Becker 1962). Tarter (1969) suspected that photoperiod plays an important role in the gonadal maturation and spawning of western blacknose dace in Kentucky, as a result of the somewhat thermal constancy of the stream.

The breeding behavior of the western blacknose dace has been observed in Minnesota (Phillips 1967) and Pennsylvania (Raney 1940a). The following account is primarily drawn from these sources.

During spawning, prolonged displays of combat are observed in blacknose dace. A pair of males swims rapidly in tight circles, with the head of one fish at the other's tail. While thus occupied, they are moved some 3–5 m downstream by the current, where they break off circling maneuvers; they then return to the area from which they started, swimming parallel to one another and bumping sides.

Territorial behavior was not observed in Minnesota, but in Pennsylvania large adult males guarded and spawned in the same territories for 3 consecutive days. These holdings were over areas of sand and fine gravel, and stood out clearly from the rest of the bottom. The territory varied somewhat in size, but was usually an area 0.6 m (2 ft) or less in diameter. A male occasionally attacked another male beyond this limit. Near the center of each holding there was a small depression 10–13 cm diam and up to 5 cm deep. These depressions, Raney observed, were not dug out by the male, but were the result of a large number of spawnings at the same spot. Considerable sand was stirred up during each successful breeding act, and some of it drifted a few inches downstream.

Raney described the spawning act as follows (p. 401):

> The females were more retiring and remained in the deeper parts of the pools until ready to spawn. When a female came into or near a territory she was immediately greeted by a cluster of males who undoubtedly recognized her by sight. The guarding male attempted to keep her for himself and dashed at his rivals who temporarily consisted of males from adjoining territories as well as small males with no holdings. He was usually successful in driving them away but the female would often retire to the pool only to return to the same or another holding very shortly. Finally when the female had taken a position in the center depression of the territory the male took his place along side with his caudal peduncle thrown over hers. In the spawning act both vibrated violently and at the same time the end of the anal papilla was forced downward into the sand. The vibration lasted two seconds at times although occasionally shorter periods were sufficient. Considerable silt was raised at the moment the eggs were laid and some at least were buried.
>
> After spawning the female usually hurriedly retreated to the deeper area in the pool. However, on one occasion a female was seen to remain at one spot for 10 seconds after spawning. A female would return and spawn with the same male at the same territory many times. She would also spawn with other males in their territories and much less often with a small male on the edge of a holding of a large male. On several occasions a territory holding male was seen to go into another territory and guide a female back into his own holding by placing his body so as to block her when she attempted to move in a contrary direction.

Spawning is at its height in late morning, although at times it may continue into early afternoon.

According to Phillips, other fishes frequently interfered with spawning pairs. Smaller blacknose dace harassed spawning couples by diving in on them, obviously seeking eggs to eat. Interlopers frequently knocked spawning partners off balance before spawning could occur. On one occasion after spawning had occurred, approximately 10 small blacknose dace and common shiners converged on the pair, the male drove them away with one dash and then lingered a moment, apparently moving grains of sand with his snout. Raney listed the creek chub, striped shiner and rainbow darter as the three most frequent egg-eating fish, other than blacknose dace, to intrude into blacknose dace spawning sites.

In the East, Traver (1929) described courtship behavior in which the male swam back and forth six or seven times beneath the body of the female, occasionally passing over or in front of her. If the water was too shallow for this, the male darted back and forth in front of the female several times. Traver also reported the peculiar behavior of two males who could find no females (p. 119):

> . . . One, a large male, was swimming restlessly about, and the other, a smaller less brightly-colored male, was resting near a tuft of grass, head upstream. Frequently the two approached each other, the smaller beneath the larger, his head pressing upward against the underside of the body of the larger in the region of the pectoral fins, the caudal fins of the two fishes approaching one another and moving with a peculiar fan-like vibration.

In Wisconsin, mature females were collected from a tributary to Little Sandy Creek (Marathon County) on 29 May 1961. An 85-mm fish with ovaries 10.6% of total weight held an estimated 1,360 ripening eggs 1.0 mm diam; a lesser number of immature eggs 0.6–0.8 mm diam were present. A 90-mm fish with ovaries 19.1% of total weight had an estimated 920 eggs 1.4 mm diam, and fewer immature eggs 0.6–0.9 mm diam. A 72-mm female with a gonad/WT index of 17.9% had an exact count of 373 ripe and loose eggs 1.4 mm diam. A late-spawning, 10.4-g female, collected from the Pine River (Florence County) 25 June 1965, had a gonad/WT index of 17.4% and ovaries with ripe eggs.

Traver (1929) noted that fry were 5 mm long upon hatching. Early in free life fry begin to feed on chironomid larvae with mayfly nymphs second in importance. Total insect material taken by this age-group amounts to 67% of the food consumed; plant material forms 23% of the food, of which 18% is diatoms. Crustacea are taken sparingly during the first summer and autumn. Very young blacknose dace feed largely from the surface.

M. Fish (1932) described and illustrated the 17.25-mm stage of the blacknose dace. Noble (1965) noted that scale formation proceeded forward from the caudal peduncle at 16–20 mm SL, that annuli formed each year between March and May, and that fish which lacked scales until spring of the second year also lacked the first annulus.

Individuals 31 and 34 mm TL were captured from Bear Creek (Portage County) on 16 September 1965.

The growth of blacknose dace from Lily River (Forest County), collected 5 July 1966, is shown in the table on the following page. Annulus 3 was just being deposited. The calculated lengths at age I of some of the larger fishes (75 mm or greater) were unusually high, suggesting perhaps that the first

Age Class	No. of Fish	TL (mm)		Calculated TL at Annulus (mm)		
		Avg	Range	1	2	3
I	23	57.2	46–69	33.1		
II	29	79.6	73–90	40.6	67.3	
III	1	95.0	—	48.2	73.8	95.0
Avg (weighted)				37.5	67.5	95.0

annulus was missing. If this is the case, then the ages for some of these fish may have been underestimated.

In a sample collected 13 July 1960 from a tributary to Bear Creek (Portage County), the dace showed the following lengths: I—59.3 (49–67) mm; II—73.2 (66–83) mm (R. Bruch, pers. comm.).

In two Massachusetts streams (Reed and Moulton 1973), mean TL for each age group at capture was: I—54.3 and 55.1 mm; II—61.0 and 66.5 mm; and III—74.0 and 73.7 mm. The back calculated TL values to the annuli were: 1—42 and 44.4 mm; 2—52.4 and 56.4 mm; and 3—66.8 and 66.6 mm.

The blacknose dace begins to mature late in its second year of life, and is mature at age II (Noble 1965, Hubbs and Cooper 1936).

Insects are the major foods of the blacknose dace, but diatoms and other algae may contribute about 25% of the diet (Breder and Crawford 1922, Carlander 1969). Fish collected from Millville Creek (Grant County) 23 June 1962 had eaten insects from the trichopteran, ephemeropteran, and chironomid groups. Some stomachs contained dytiscids, *Gammarus*, filamentous algae, and debris (J. Dine, pers. comm.). In Iowa (Noble 1965), Diptera larvae, primarily chironomids, appeared in 58% of the stomachs and in every collection. The high utilization of chironomids during June and July may be related to the high growth rate of dace during that period. In late November and in March desmids and diatoms were important food items. Some authors believe that the various plant materials are not digested to any great extent, and are consequently of little value as food (Hubbs and Cooper 1936). Numerous reports have indicated that the blacknose dace eats its own eggs, as well as those of other species such as white suckers (Reighard 1920).

The blacknose dace is very active, darting from one resting place on the bottom to another. It finds protection from the current by resting beneath and behind stones and pebbles. Its agility is best appreciated by anyone who attempts to collect specimens with a seine from the rocky bottom of a swift stream: a few of the dace jump over the top of the seine, while many dart beneath boulders to escape the lead line. The inexperienced collector is surprised at the small number which he actually captures.

In summer the larger blacknose dace are found in the deeper pools, while the very young are found over shoals. In winter all are found close up under the banks in the deepest water available. They move upstream early in spring.

Kuehne (1958) studied the schooling behavior of this minnow in detail. The blacknose dace forms a loosely knit school which often includes creek chubs and other minnow species. Groups of fish less than 50 mm long remain apart from schools of larger, older specimens. Aggregations are active during the summer and fall, but not in the winter. Spring spawning tends to disrupt schooling.

In schools, the lead fish tend to swim more erratic paths, and thus greater distances, than the following fish. Leadership alternates among fish in the group. All fish prefer large rather than small numbers of their own species, and prefer fish of nearly the same size. They are also more attracted to active than to sluggish individuals. The response to movement is a key mechanism involved in schooling. There is no evidence that any sense other than sight is involved in the schooling reaction. Blinded fish do not school, and they swim more slowly and steadily than normal fish. Kuehne suggested that the schooling habit might aid in orientation, in feeding, and in predator avoidance.

The blacknose dace is frequently taken with the longnose dace, trout, darters, sculpins, stickleback, white sucker, creek chub, and common shiner. In the Little Green River (Grant County), 198 blacknose dace were associated with brown trout (+), white sucker (54), central stoneroller (2), longnose dace (21), creek chub (32), southern redbelly dace (2), fathead minnow (2), bigmouth shiner (8), and fantail darter (29).

In Wisconsin on the Tomorrow-Waupaca River (Portage County), significant differences in counts and measurements of blacknose dace were found in two populations separated by a dam and its reservoir, but few differences were found in populations from the Tomorrow-Waupaca River and the Little Wolf River (Becker 1962). Schontz (1963) noted significant variations in a number of characteristics in blacknose dace populations, and suggested that these differences are a result of genetic isolation, rather than mere phenotypic responses to environmental differences.

IMPORTANCE AND MANAGEMENT

There is little evidence that the blacknose dace is an important forage fish. It has been reported as food for trout (Hubbs and Cooper 1936, Scott and Crossman 1973), and has been found in the stomach of a creek chub (Noble 1965).

Because the blacknose dace is a common inhabitant of trout streams, it has been called a trout indicator. Wherever blacknose dace are found trout may also be expected, although in some instances the dace appears to tolerate higher temperatures than the trout. The blacknose dace probably does good service by devouring the mosquitoes and blackfly larvae that thrive along trout streams (Adams and Hankinson 1926).

The blacknose dace is an attractive aquarium pet, and does well when the aquarium water is circulated. Propagation of the blacknose dace is possible. The milt and eggs may be stripped from ripe males and females, and artificial fertilization is practical (Dobie et al. 1956).

Longnose Dace

Rhinichthys cataractae (Valenciennes). *Rhinichthys*—snout, fish; *cataractae*—of the Cataract, the original type being from Niagara Falls.

Other common names: longnosed dace, Great Lakes longnose dace, stream shooter.

Adult female 90 mm, Namekagon R. (Washburn Co.), 17 Sept. 1976

DESCRIPTION

Body elongate, almost cylindrical, slightly compressed posteriorly. Average length 76 mm (3 in). TL = 1.21 SL. Depth into TL 5.2–6.8. Head length into TL 4.0–5.2; head flattened ventrally. Snout elongate, overhanging mouth, extending beyond lower lip 1–3 mm or more. Mouth inferior, upper lip groove not continuous over snout; mouth extending to below posterior nostril; pointed barbel in groove at angle of mouth. Pharyngeal teeth 2,4–4,2 slender, hooked, cutting edge short. Eye into head length 4.2–6.0. Gill rakers short, conical, widely spaced on lower limb, 6–8. Dorsal fin origin slightly to distinctly posterior to origin of pelvic fin; dorsal fin rays 8; anal fin rays 7; pectoral fin rays 13–15; pelvic fin rays 8. Lateral line scales 61–75; lateral line complete, almost straight. Digestive tract simple S-shaped 0.6–0.8 TL. Chromosomes 2n = 50 (Howell and Villa 1976).

Back olive green to brown, but grayish in large lakes; sides lighter, belly silvery white. Back and sides mottled by scattered, darkened scales. Adults with a dark stripe ahead of eye; young with stripe continuing posteriorly to a broadening blotch in front of caudal fin. Lateral stripe fades away in adults as pigmentation of the dorsal half of body increases. In the field this minnow can be identified as a species with 2 white spots on a dark field: the origin of the dorsal fin and dorsal origin of the caudal fin are white to cream-colored.

Breeding males with minute tubercles over top of head, on posterior edges of most of the dark-colored body scales above the lateral line, but fewer on scales below lateral line; strongly pointed tubercles in paired rows on first 4–5 rays of pectoral fin. In males, the premaxillary, cheek, axis of pectoral fin, process of pelvic fin, base of anal fin, and the base of the caudal fin, are orange to salmon; in females, yellow to orange (Becker 1962). These colors may persist beyond the spawning season with a secondary surge of color during October.

Sexual dimorphism: In male, distance from end of pectoral fin to pelvic origin less than diam of eye; in female, greater than diam of eye.

Hybrids: Longnose dace × river chub (Raney 1940b), longnose dace × creek chub (Slastenenko 1957), longnose dace × lake chub (Hubbs and Lagler 1949), longnose dace × central stoneroller (Greeley 1938), and longnose dace × common shiner (Ross and Cavender 1977). Experimental longnose dace × blacknose dace (Howell and Villa 1976).

DISTRIBUTION, STATUS, AND HABITAT

The longnose dace occurs in all three Wisconsin drainage basins. Since the 1920s, it has extended its range southward into the southwestern counties which drain into the Mississippi River and the lower Wisconsin River; also, numerous records now appear from the shores of Green Bay and Lake Michigan.

The longnose dace is abundant in fast water in medium-sized streams of the northern half of Wisconsin. It is common in small, fastwater streams of southwestern Wisconsin, and common to abundant in wave-swept shallows of Lakes Michigan and Superior. This species appears secure.

The longnose dace in Wisconsin occurs in riffles or torrential water over a bottom of boulders and gravel; it generally avoids pools and quiet runs. It was encountered most frequently in clear, warm water at depths of 0.1–0.5 m. Substrates over which it was found include gravel (23% frequency), rubble (22%), sand (20%), boulders (14%), silt (10%), mud (7%), clay (2%), bedrock (2%), and detritus (1%). It occurred in streams of the following widths: 1.0–3.0 m (26%), 3.1–6.0 m (19%), 6.1–12.0 m (19%), 12.1–24.0 m (23%), 24.1–50.0 m (12%), and more than 50 m, none.

In central Wisconsin, the longnose dace is the species of fish frequently found in torrential parts of streams over bottoms of small rubble and coarse gravel, at water depths of 0.3–0.6 m (1–2 ft). The most favorable habitat, however, is a long, fast slick over a bottom of fine gravel which is interspersed with beds of aquatic vegetation—a habitat type less frequently encountered in this region of the state.

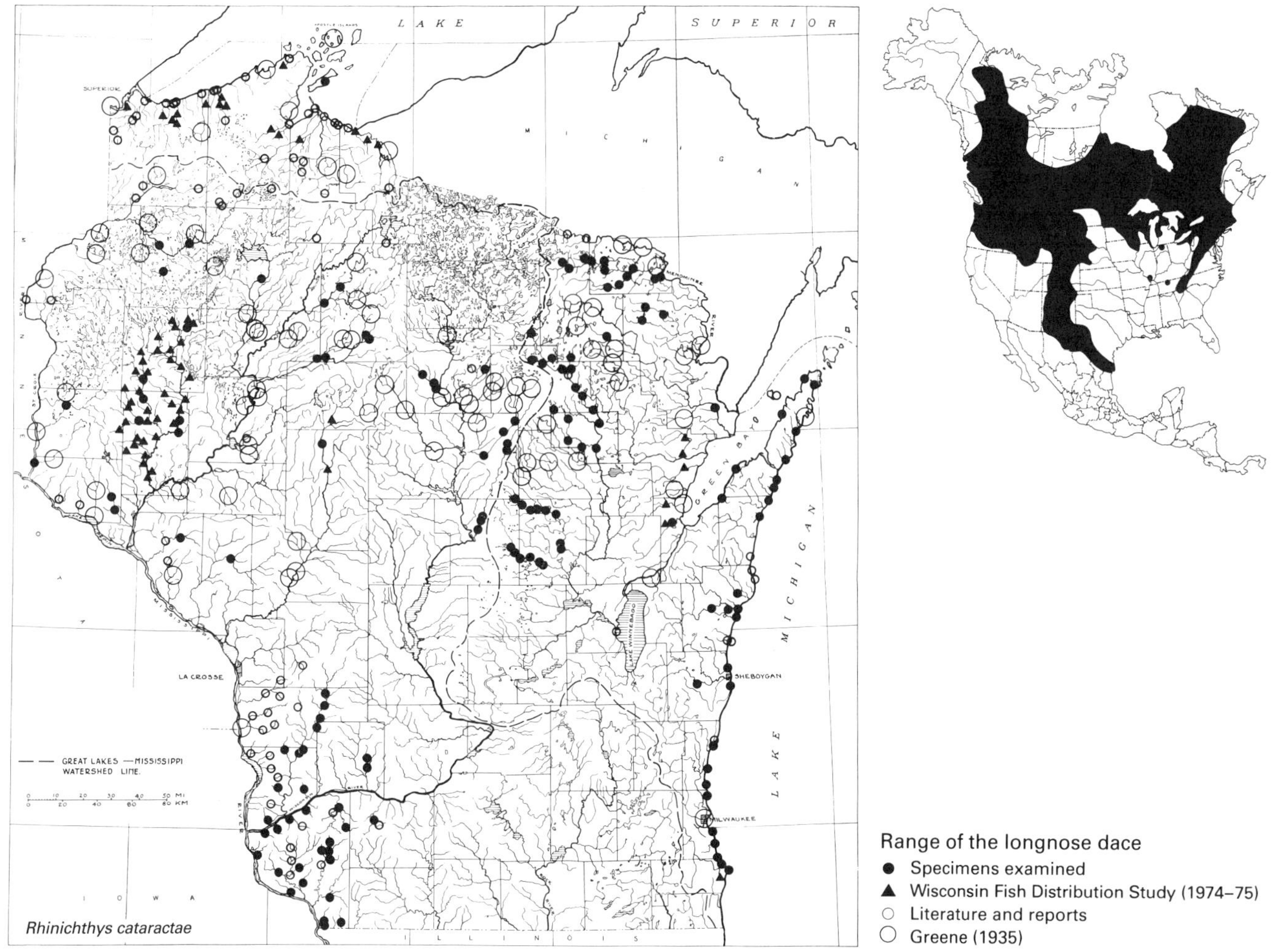

BIOLOGY

The longnose dace spawns early, from late April to mid-June (Becker 1962). The height of spawning in a central Wisconsin stream occurred from 5 to 8 May at an average water temperature of 17.2°C (63°F); water temperatures ranged between 11.1 and 23.3°C (52 and 74°F).

Greeley and Bishop (1933) observed spawning in New York state on 16 July. A school of at least 25 fish, mostly males, swam over an area of fine gravel in a strong current in water 5–10 cm deep. A single spawning act was seen. A female stopped on the bottom, and a dense group of at least six males, individuals which had been following her closely, hid the female from view for a brief second or two as they crowded against her sides and dorsal area. Following this, several males were seen to thrust their noses downward in an evident search for eggs. A search of the gravel disclosed a number of eggs.

Gravid females were collected 4 May from the Tomorrow-Waupaca River (Portage County) (Becker 1962). A 103-mm fish held 181 ripe eggs 1.5 mm diam, constituting 15% of the ovarian weight; the ovary also contained immature eggs in various stages of development. An 85-mm fish had eggs which were 1.7 mm diam, the largest eggs seen. A 99-mm fish, taken 23 May, had 655 ripe eggs, the greatest number encountered. The average total number of eggs per ovary in all stages of development was 2,440 (1,400–2,870). For several females taken on 9 May the ovaries were 25–27.2% of the total weight.

Early development of the longnose dace has been described by McPhail and Lindsey (1970:249):

> Eggs are laid in a group down amongst stones, and are probably guarded by one parent. In Manitoba, females lay from 200 to 1200 eggs, which are adhesive, transparent, and so colourless as to be almost invisible under water. These hatch in 7–10 days at 16 C (60 F). The yolk sac is absorbed about 7 days later; the young then rise to the surface and inflate the posterior lobe of the gas bladder with air. They then become pelagic, living in still shallow water at the river margin. After about 4 months they begin selecting faster current, and gradually move into deeper water (J.H. Gee, personal communication).

M. Fish (1932) illustrated and described the 13.7-mm stage.

Longnose dace from Lake Michigan near Algoma (Kewaunee County), collected 19 September 1965, showed the following growth:

Age Class	No. of Fish	TL (mm) Avg	Range	Calculated TL at Annulus (mm) 1	2	3	4
0	10	43.1	35–53				
I	14	74.9	65–80	53.8			
II	16	88.3	80–96	51.8	75.8		
III	5	109.0	102–115	54.3	79.1	99.4	
IV	1	122.0		49.1	68.4	92.7	109.9
Avg (weighted)				52.8	76.2	98.3	109.9

Growth in Lake Superior is similar to that of Lake Michigan. The calculated lengths at the annuli of longnose dace from Madeline Island (Ashland County) were: 1—54.3 mm, 2—73.7 mm, 3—86.5 mm, and 4—100 mm (S. Gutreuter, pers. comm.). These fish, taken 4–8 June 1968, showed the following growth: II—82 (77–89) mm, III—98 (95–100) mm, and IV—113 (105–118) mm.

The calculated total lengths at the annuli for a Tomorrow-Waupaca River (Portage County) collection were: 1—50.6 mm, 2—71.9 mm, and 3—86.7 mm (S. Gutreuter, pers. comm.). These fish, taken 17 April 1962, showed the following growth: I—52 (45–57) mm, II— 77 (68–90) mm, and III—87 (83–95) mm.

In Minnesota, Kuehn (1949b) encountered longnose dace that were 5 years old with a calculated total length of 98–99 mm. In Massachusetts (Reed and Moulton 1973), the calculated lengths in several collections at age 4 ranged from 97 to 106 mm, and at age 5, from 118 to 119 mm. Only females reach age V.

Maturity is reached at age II. In central Wisconsin, the condition (K_{TL}) of males and females on 25 April was 1.07. The highest value for females, 1.15, was recorded 9 May 1959 (Becker 1962).

The largest longnose dace that have been reported were "seven-inch adults" (178 mm) taken off Isle Royale in Lake Superior (Hubbs and Lagler 1949).

In central Wisconsin, the longnose dace is primarily a dipteran feeder (Becker 1962). Diptera constituted 81% of all animal organisms counted. Most common were Tendipedidae, less common were Simulidae; and Tipulidae, Rhagionidae, Tabanidae, Psychodidae, and Anthomyiidae appeared infrequently. Nymphs of Ephemeroptera constituted almost 10% of the total number of organisms taken, and caddisfly larvae (Trichoptera) made up almost 9%. A few water mites appeared entangled in masses of algae found in the stomachs. Small amounts of algae, fine roots, and other plant materials, as well as fine sand and gravel, were found in over 62% of all stomachs examined. These materials had been ingested for the most part along with the animal organisms which formed the bulk of the minnow's diet; caddisfly cases, midgefly tubes, and old *Physa* shells constituted additional by-products.

The literature notes that annelid worms, crustaceans, mollusks, and fish eggs are taken occasionally by the longnose dace (Copes 1975, Dobie et al. 1956, Dymond 1926).

In central Wisconsin, I found that the longnose dace feeds lightly from December to March, and feeds heavily in April and May. The degree of feeding drops off slightly in June and continues at moderate levels during the summer and early fall, with the heaviest intake occurring in November. I was able to induce feeding in this species (Becker 1962:167–168):

> As I walked across the stream in water six to eight inches deep my boot would strip bare portions of the stones on the bottom. Within a few seconds dozens or a hundred fish would cluster about these disturbed areas. A rock that had been stripped would be approached by numbers of fish, such that the bared area on the top surface was a milling mass. As the fish touched their noses to the cleaned surface they suddently set their tails into intense vibration with nose and mouth in lateral vibration against the rock as if shaking loose minute organisms which were still clinging . . .
>
> The swarms of minnows on the cleaned surfaces lost interest within a minute or two, and the fish would then scatter, some returning downstream. . . .Some . . . would linger and investigate the cleaned areas, but without the aforementioned vibrations.
>
> Infrequently . . . one or two . . . would strip the algae from the upstream edge of the cleaned surface, removing it in small sheets by pushing with the nose, using the nose in the manner of a chisel between the sheet of algae and the rock.

In nature the longnose dace was never seen feeding at the surface; however, in the laboratory it will take food from the surface, and during feeding periods it will break the surface of the water with violent thrusts.

Greene (1935) noted that, in the rugged country of higher altitudes where biological competition is not very keen, the longnose dace is commonly found in moderate current and even in lakes. It occurs in the Great Lakes where the currents along windswept shoals resemble surging, strong undercurrents of rivers. This species is usually found in water currents of over 0.5 m per second (Gee and Northcote 1963).

Although young longnose dace, which have well-developed swim bladders, are pelagic during the day, at night they move offshore to depths greater than 0.3 m. (Gee and Northcote 1963). Adults at depths of less than 0.3 m usually do not show such nocturnal movement. In adults, the swim bladder is poorly developed and occupies less than 7% of the dace's total volume, enabling the fish to adapt to a bottom existence.

The longnose dace is able to withstand rapid changes in environmental conditions. Water temperatures which fluctuate widely in a matter of minutes appear to have no harmful effects on a large central Wisconsin population, nor do summer temperatures up to 27.8°C (82°F) for short periods of time. During the heat of summer, the longnose dace is absent from the shores of Lake Erie and apparently moves into offshore waters (Trautman 1957). For short periods of time this species can endure both heavy turbidity, in which visibility is less than 15 cm (6 in), and low oxygen levels. In laboratory experiments, given only 0.3 ppm oxygen, the longnose dace rose to the surface, and, in vertical position (as if walking on its tail), gulped air.

During the winter, the longnose dace becomes sedentary and inactive in relatively quiet and shallow pools, or in shallow, flat, sand- and gravel-bottomed slicks adjacent to the typical summer habitat. These areas are several meters wide and 15–30 cm deep, and may be covered with ice. Often the longnose dace is the only species of fish captured from such habitat.

In southern Canada, Hallam (1959) observed that the longnose dace was more commonly associated with the smallmouth bass and the mottled sculpin than with the rock bass and brook trout. In central Wisconsin, the longnose dace shared its typical habitat with the hornyhead chub, common shiner (absent in winter), creek chub (absent in winter), northern hog sucker, mottled sculpin, largescale stoneroller, johnny darter, fantail darter, and banded darter.

IMPORTANCE AND MANAGEMENT

Smallmouth bass, brown trout, and brook trout have preyed on the longose dace. I captured a mottled sculpin, 59 mm TL, which had swallowed and partially digested a 51-mm longnose dace; a few millimeters of the victim's tail were still protruding from the sculpin's mouth. There may be a numerical correlation between these species: stream segments with large numbers of longnose dace have few mottled sculpins, and where sculpins are abundant, longnose dace are present in reduced numbers.

In Michigan (Lagler and Ostenson 1942), the longnose dace is the early spring food of the otter.

Because of its abundance and presence in specialized habitat, the longnose dace has been the subject of several experiments. In Pennsylvania (Reed 1959), an estimated 1,137 adults occurred over a 472-m (1,550-ft) experimental area. The density of this species was about 0.9 adult dace per square meter of riffle habitat. In Minnesota, the longnose dace has been propagated at least once. It seems to do well in long, narrow ponds supplied with a small amount of running water (Dobie et al. 1956).

I have attempted to establish a population of longnose dace in a sector of the Tomorrow River containing large numbers of mottled sculpin and brook trout. Forty-four dace, taken from a population 21 km (13 mi) downstream, were transplanted into a typical dace riffle (Becker 1962). Failure may have been due to predation, the limited numbers of dace stocked, or prolonged cool water temperature. Further investigation should determine the dace's environmental needs and its relationships with associate fish species.

The longnose dace has been suggested as a possible biological control against nettlesome black flies (*Simulium*) (Adams and Hankinson 1926).

The longnose dace can be kept alive for 2 years or more in laboratory tanks where the water is kept cool. It is not highly excitable and is easily handled.

Central Stoneroller

Campostoma anomalum (Rafinesque). *Campostoma*—curved mouth; *anomalum*—extraordinary.

Other common names: stoneroller, Mississippi stoneroller minnow, stone lugger, racehorse chub, steel-backed chub, rotgut minnow, doughbelly, mammy, tallow-mouth minnow, common stoneroller.

Adult male (tuberculate) 145 mm, Zumbro R. (Dodge Co.), Minnesota, 18 Mar. 1974

Adult female 117 mm, Zumbro R. (Dodge Co.), Minnesota, 18 Mar. 1974

DESCRIPTION

Body generally slender, nearly round. Average length 102 mm (4 in). Head length into SL 3.6–4.3. Snout rounded, protruding slightly beyond mouth. Mouth ventral, lower jaw having a distinctive cartilaginous "cutting" edge not covered by skin (insert dissecting needle into mouth and depress lower lip to see this); barbels absent; maxillary short, reaching to below nostril. Pharyngeal teeth 4–4, hooked slightly or not at all. Eye into head length 3.5–5.8. Fins small, rounded; dorsal fin originating over pelvic fin; dorsal fin rays 8; anal fin rays 7; pectoral fin rays usually 15; pelvic fin rays usually 8. Lateral line scales 49–55; lateral line complete. Scales around body (circumferential scales) 39–46; sum of two preceding counts 87–102. Intestine long, in transverse loops completely surrounding swim bladder. Chromosomes 2n = 50 (W. LeGrande, pers. comm.).

Back and sides brown, dark olive, or gray, abruptly white ventrally. Scattered dark scales on sides. Fins clear, except dark crescents in dorsal and anal fins of adults. Peritoneum black.

Breeding males dark slate with white belly; dorsal fin with orange wash basally and a prominent black stripe medially; caudal and anal fins with basals of orange; pelvic and pectoral fins dark pigmented and suffused with yellow; lips a bright white. Breeding tubercles on head, between nostrils and on most scales of body. It is the most ornately tubercled of all Wisconsin fishes.

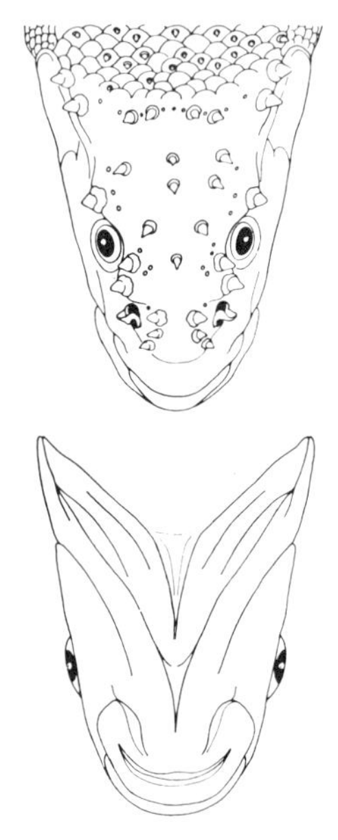

Dorsal and ventral views of head tubercle pattern in a full nuptial male (Burr and Smith 1976:526)

Sexual dimorphism: Adult male with large pectoral fins almost circular in shape; female with small pectoral fins somewhat elongate and narrow.

Hybrids: Between the central stoneroller and the common shiner (Trautman 1957), the southern redbelly dace (Hubbs and Bailey 1952), the creek chub (Cross and Minckley 1960), the hornyhead chub, and the pearl dace (Wis. Fish Distrib. Study).

SYSTEMATIC NOTES

During the survey of the Wisconsin fish fauna in the late 1920s, it became apparent that two distinctive *Campostoma* forms occur in the state (Hubbs and Greene 1935). Hubbs and Greene determined that the central stoneroller (*Campostoma anomalum pullum*), a small-scale form, is the typical form known from southern Wisconsin, and they recognized as a new subspecies the Wisconsin stoneroller minnow (*Campostoma anomalum oligolepis*), a large-scale form which

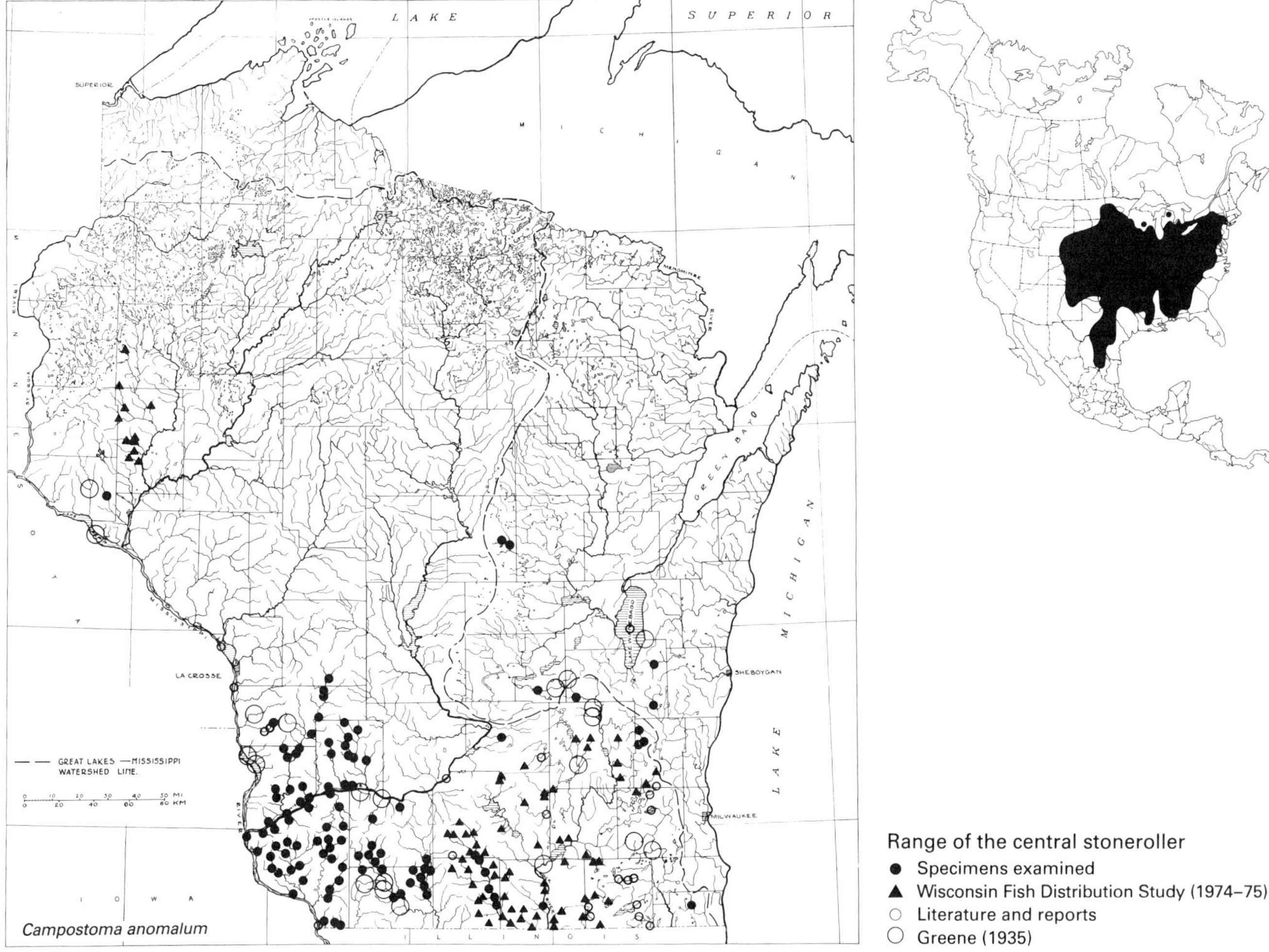

Range of the central stoneroller
● Specimens examined
▲ Wisconsin Fish Distribution Study (1974–75)
○ Literature and reports
◯ Greene (1935)

is commonly distributed through the central and northern parts of the state. Soon the common name of largescale stoneroller was applied to the new form (Hubbs and Lagler 1947 and 1964). In 1968 and in 1971, Pflieger presented evidence that these subspecies are in fact distinct species, thereby elevating the largescale stoneroller, *Campostoma oligolepis*, to the rank of a full species.

Difficulties exist in the identification of the central stoneroller and the closely related largescale stoneroller, *Campostoma oligolepis*, both of which occur in Wisconsin. The comparison shown in the table on the following page provides characters for their separation.

DISTRIBUTION, STATUS, AND HABITAT

In Wisconsin, the central stoneroller occurs in the Mississippi River and Lake Michigan drainage basins. In the former, it is found primarily in the lower Mississippi and Wisconsin rivers and in the upper Rock River drainages. Disjunct distribution centers exist in the lower Chippewa and Red Cedar watershed of northwestern Wisconsin, and in the Tomorrow River drainage of the Lake Michigan basin. It is absent from the Lake Superior basin.

The central stoneroller is abundant in small, swift-flowing streams of southern Wisconsin and is occasionally taken in quiet pools. It was the most abundant species in smaller streams during a 1960–1963 survey in southwestern Wisconsin (Becker 1966); several hundred individuals were captured at each of a number of stations.

The central stoneroller inhabits swift-flowing headwater streams, and it appears occasionally in medium- to large-sized rivers. It is rarely found in lakes, but it has been reported from Lake Winnebago (Greene 1935, Priegel 1967a) and Pewaukee Lake (McCutchin 1946). It was generally taken from riffle and pool sections of streams over the following bottom types: gravel (33% frequency), sand (17%), rubble (15%), clay (10%), silt (10%), mud (8%), boulders (6%) and bedrock (1%). It occurred in waters that were clear to turbid at the following stream widths: 1.0–3.0 m (26% frequency), 3.1–6.0 m (34%), 6.1–12.0 m

Characters for Separation of the Central Stoneroller and Largescale Stoneroller (After Burr and Smith 1976:522)

Characters	Central Stoneroller	Largescale Stoneroller
Circumferential scales	39–46 (38–50)	31–36 (29–38)
Lateral line scales	49–55 (47–58)	43–47 (41–48)
Circumferential plus lateral line scales	Usually 87–102	Usually 74–83
Gill rakers	26–35	19–26
Interorbital distance[a] into distance from back of eye to upper end of gill opening	Usually less	Equal to or greater
Snout (from side or above)	More pointed (does not extend beyond upper lip, or extends only slightly)	More globose, blunt (extends beyond upper lip)
Ventral view of mouth	Circular, slightly wider than long (mouth almost as wide as head)	Oval, decidedly wider than long (mouth less wide than head)
Head width	Narrow and strongly tapering	Wide, weakly tapering
Form of body	Generally slender	Generally robust
1–3 tubercles along inner margin of nostrils in breeding males	Present	Generally absent (occasionally 1–2 present on one side)
Black crescent in anal fin of breeding males	Present	Absent (sometimes incomplete faint marks)

[a] Least width of skull between eyes.

(20%), 12.1–24.0 m (14%), 24.1–50.0 m (5%), and more than 50 m (2%). The stoneroller is best adapted to warm waters, but sometimes inhabits borderline trout waters.

During the winter, stonerollers may congregate under stones, leaves, or other bottom debris (Miller 1964).

BIOLOGY

Spawning occurs in southern Wisconsin from the end of May to June and possibly into July. During the first warm weather of spring, when water temperatures reach 14.4–23.9°C (58–75°F), schools of stonerollers begin ascending streams, jumping small dams when necessary to reach the smallest headwaters. Miller (1964:323–324) provided a summary of nest building and reproductive behavior:

> . . . First the males leave pools and deeper areas and begin to dig small pits in shallow areas. Digging may occur in slow water or in riffles, but usually results in well-defined pits only in the former situation. Males deepen the pits by picking up stones in the mouth and ejecting them at the edge of the pit, by pushing the head down into the gravel and writhing, thereby loosening smaller particles, some of which are carried downstream by the current, and by occasionally pushing or lifting a stone with the head or body until it is partially out of the pit. While nest building, large dominant males vigorously drive away smaller males trying to enter their diggings. Dominant males, however, rarely spend more than a few minutes at any one nest pit. They move constantly from pit to pit. Territorial defense is most conspicuous when males defend a digging, though smaller, peripheral males show some aggression when companions approach too closely. When many males are crowded into a small area territorial defense breaks down occasionally, and several fishes work in a nest for a few minutes. Females, which generally school in deeper water near the spawning beds, move out over the nests and dip down into a pit from time to time. As soon as a female enters a pit, all nearby males dart in beside her and attempt to press against her. Since the spawning act is extremely brief, some males crowding into the nest probably do not fertilize eggs. When a male presses her side, the female deposits some eggs and darts away. The female is in the pit for a fraction of a second to several seconds. The flurry of activity during spawning and subsequent digging cover the eggs with sand and fine gravel.

O. R. Smith (1935) described nest building as a community affair, with 2–5 males working at a small pit in a clean area about 1 m (3 ft) long and 0.6 m (2 ft) wide at water depths of 15–20 cm (6–8 in). Fighting between two males of equal size started with the two fish side by side over a pit; one gave the other a quick "body check" in the ribs with his "shoulder" above the pectoral fins, then the attacked fish, without giving any ground, returned the blow. These body checks were sometimes exchanged several times before one of the contestants gave up. Males often chased each other with such abandon as to throw themselves out on the shore.

Stonerollers prefer a nest with a deep pool or a bank overhang nearby as shelter in times of disturbance (Miller 1964), but they can modify their behavior enough to spawn successfully in various stream conditions and over a wide temperature range. These characteristics account in part for the stoneroller's wide distribution and its success in ecologically diverse systems.

While most spawning occurs in pits dug by male stonerollers, occasionally stonerollers parasitize the nests of the river chub, hornyhead chub, and the creek chub (Miller 1964). Sometimes common shiners and creek chubs take over stoneroller nests. As soon as an intruder enters a stoneroller nest, the resident stoneroller leaves without opposing the intruder and moves elsewhere to dig, or swims into a deeper pool and ceases activity. When stonerollers occasionally return to such nests, the shiners drive them away with frontal attacks. In most instances, stonerollers lose the competition for preferred spawning sites to males of the common shiner, creek chub, and river chub.

In Wisconsin, breeding central stonerollers are age II or III. Specimens examined from Crooked Creek (Grant County) on 26 June had not yet spawned. An age-II female (103 mm TL) had ovaries 11.2% of total weight with 563 ripening amber-colored eggs 1.28 mm diam; a second generation of small, yellow-white eggs averaged 0.62 mm diam. Another female (92 mm TL) had ovaries 13.2% of body weight with 623 near-ripe eggs 1.3–1.5 mm diam. In the same collection some large females examined had no maturing eggs, and in other individuals the ovaries were undeveloped. It appears that spawning in this small stream (which is trout water in its upper reaches) may be delayed until the end of June or the beginning of July. In a collection taken from nearby Millville Creek on 23 June, males were tuberculate, but the females were not yet ripe.

Males develop incipient tubercles in September or October, and by early the following spring they are well armed.

Reed (1958) noted that the mature egg is 2.0 mm diam. When an egg is placed in water, the chorion is released from the yolk and slowly fills with water to 2.4 mm diam. The unfertilized egg is dull gray in appearance, while the fertilized egg turns bright yellow and is adhesive. At 21.1°C (70°F), stoneroller larvae hatch out in 69–71 hr after fertilization; they are 5.7 mm long at hatching. The 9.75-mm stage has been described by Fish (1932).

The growth of young-of-year in southern Wisconsin has been observed as shown in the table at the top of the next column.

Central stonerollers from the Platte River (Grant County) collected on 24 September 1966 showed the growth which follows in the second table, next column.

The condition value (K_{TL}) of yearling and age-II central stonerollers taken 4 October 1975 from the Milwaukee River (Fond du Lac County) was 1.11.

In Roaring Springs Creek (southern Illinois) the calculated total lengths (mm) at the annuli were: 1—51 mm, 2—79 mm, and 3—99 mm (Gunning and Lewis 1956). Age-group II was the most abundant, making up 65% of the stoneroller sample. In Big Creek

Date	No. of Fish	TL (mm)	
		Avg	Range
11 July	5	34	31-36
15 July	14	37	28-42
13 Aug.	10	46	40-53
26 Aug.	6	46	39-51
16 Sept.	5	54	21-65

Age Class	No. of Fish	TL (mm)		Calculated TL at Annulus (mm)		
		Avg	Range	1	2	3
0	6	55.8	45-66			
I	16	96.6	83-113	62.3		
II	24	122.3	110-138	60.2	96.6	
III	2	154.5	148-161	51.0	88.5	121.0
Avg (weighted)				60.5	96.0	121.0

(Great Smoky Mountains National Park) the length range of each age-group was: 0—56 mm, I—79–104 mm, II—117–132 mm, III—127–206 mm, IV—165–239 mm, and V—173–226 mm (Lennon and Parker 1960). In the West Prong Little River (Great Smoky Mountains National Park), none of the age-II stonerollers were mature, and, of the age-III fish, most males were immature and most females were mature (Lennon and Parker 1960). All age-V fish of both sexes were mature.

The largest fish in Wisconsin collections are tuberculate males; in the Platte River (Grant County) 135–161-mm males were age II and III. Priegel (1967a) noted that this species reaches a length of 203 mm (8 in). Eddy and Underhill (1974) reported maximum sizes of 203–254 mm (8–10 in). In Great Smoky Mountains National Park (Lennon and Parker 1960), the largest female was 188 mm (7.4 in), and the largest male was 287 mm (11.3 in).

The stoneroller is adapted for removing attached growths (the microscopic algae known to most people as brown slime or scum) from the rocks of stream bottoms. It has a special device on the lower jaw: a hardened, gristly, leading edge that is used to scrape surfaces for food. The minute particles of food are directed into the pharynx by numerous elongated gill rakers. Algae, diatoms, desmids, small amounts of zooplankton, a few aquatic insects (tendipedids), and plant tissue are eaten, along with the sand and clay which are probably taken along with the foods (Hubbs and Cooper 1936, Cahn 1927, Kraatz 1923). A study of 20 specimens from the Oswego River system (New York) showed food composition as follows:

midge larvae (10%), diatoms (50%), algae (10%), and sand and silt (30%) (Dobie et al. 1956).

In the Yellowstone River (Lafayette County), the following associate species were taken with 266 central stonerollers: white sucker (45), hornyhead chub (1), creek chub (37), southern redbelly dace (8), bluntnose minnow (67), common shiner (42), johnny darter (9), fantail darter (1), and bluegill (9).

IMPORTANCE AND MANAGEMENT

Many stonerollers are eaten by herons and bitterns (Cahn 1927). At sites where smallmouth bass and rockbass are common, stonerollers are relatively scarce; smallmouth bass appear to control the number of stonerollers (Lennon and Parker 1960).

In streams in the Great Smokies (Lennon and Parker 1960), stoneroller populations ranged up to 23,800 fish and 585 kg/ha. They constituted 21–62% of the weight of fish in six streams studied. Where stonerollers were removed, other fish increased in average length and weight. These results indicate that abundant populations can be reduced substantially by exploitation. There was little movement of stonerollers into the harvested sections from adjacent upstream and downstream areas.

Lennon and Parker (1960) noted that the nest building activities of stoneroller minnows soon obliterated all traces of rainbow trout nests that had been built 2 months earlier. They concluded that the stoneroller competes with the rainbow trout for spawning beds before the trout eggs hatch, although the stoneroller spawns later than the trout. The limiting factor in rainbow trout spawning success appears to be severe competition between rainbow trout and stonerollers for spawning grounds. It also appears that trout populations in stoneroller areas can be improved only by stocking more trout, or by reducing the number of stonerollers.

The stoneroller has been rated as an excellent bait for bass, walleyes, and catfish. There are many references in the literature to its hardiness and to its good qualities as a bait minnow, but I have found that, compared to other minnows from the same water, it is delicate and will quickly succumb to crowding and high water temperatures in a holding can.

In Wisconsin, where the stoneroller is small, it is seldom eaten. In parts of the East, particularly the Great Smokies region, it is a prized food fish, and the Tennessee Game and Fish Commission has reported that there are fishermen who throw back trout and keep stonerollers.

The stoneroller has been propagated in shallow ponds supplied with a slow-moving current. The first attempts were moderately successful (Dobie et al. 1956). Langlois (1941) reported that stoneroller eggs can be artificially fertilized.

Largescale Stoneroller

Campostoma oligolepis Hubbs and Greene. *Campostoma*—curved mouth; *oligolepis*—few scales.
Other common name: Wisconsin stoneroller minnow.

Adult male (tuberculate) 151 mm, Eau Claire R. (Marathon Co.), 29 May 1961

Adult female 122 mm, Eau Claire R. (Marathon Co.), 29 May 1961

DESCRIPTION
Body elongate, robust, nearly round. Average length 102 mm (4 in). Head length into SL 3.9–4.2 (3.5–4.2). Snout globose, extending beyond upper lip. Mouth ventral, lower jaw having a distinctive cartilaginous "cutting" edge (0.3 mm wide or wider) not covered by skin (insert dissecting needle into mouth and depress lower lip); barbels absent; maxillary short, reaching to below nostril. Pharyngeal teeth 4–4, most slightly hooked. Fins small, rounded; dorsal fin originating over pelvic fin; dorsal fin rays 8; anal fin rays 7 (8); pectoral fin rays 16 (13–17); pelvic fin rays 8 (9). Lateral line scales 43–47 (41–48); lateral line complete. Scales around body 31–36 (29–38); sum of two preceding counts 74–83 (70–86). Intestine long, 3.3–5.2 times TL, in transverse loops completely surrounding swim bladder.

Back and sides dark olive or gray, abruptly whitish ventrally. Scattered dark scales on sides. Fins clear, except dark crescent in the dorsal fin of adults (occasionally some pigmentation in middle of anal fin).

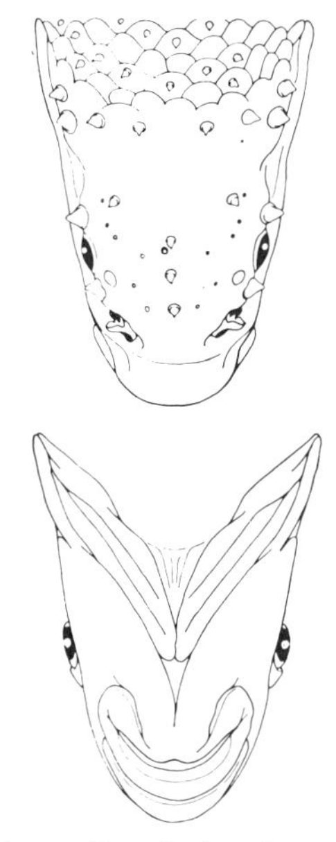

Dorsal and ventral views of head tubercle pattern in a full nuptial male (Burr and Smith 1976:526)

Prominent dark spot on membranes of caudal fin immediately behind lateral line. Peritoneum black. Young, lighter pigmented; a pronounced lateral stripe about the width of pupil to width of eye.

Breeding males with head brownish dorsally and laterally, light ventrally; pink spot on either side of snout immediately above lateral edge of upper lip; iris reddish. Back almost black, lighter on sides and belly. Dorsal fin with heavy dark crescent; anal fin without such a mark, or with a similar mark disappearing toward the anterior edge. Pelvic fins, anal fins, and ventral body scales with a reddish wash. Breeding tubercles as in central stoneroller, except tubercles along inner margin of nostrils generally absent in largescale stoneroller (occasionally 1–2 present on one side).

Difficulties exist in the identification of the largescale stoneroller and the closely related central stoneroller, *Campostoma anomalum*. See p. 478 for additional characteristics by which the two species may be separated.

SYSTEMATIC NOTES
During the survey of Wisconsin fish fauna in the late 1920s, it became apparent that two forms of stoneroller (*Campostoma*) were appearing in the collections (Hubbs and Greene 1935). One form, the central stoneroller (*C. a. pullum*), was the typical form of the Great Lakes region, and was taken largely in southern Wisconsin; the other, the largescale stoneroller, was recognized as a new subspecies, *Campostoma an-*

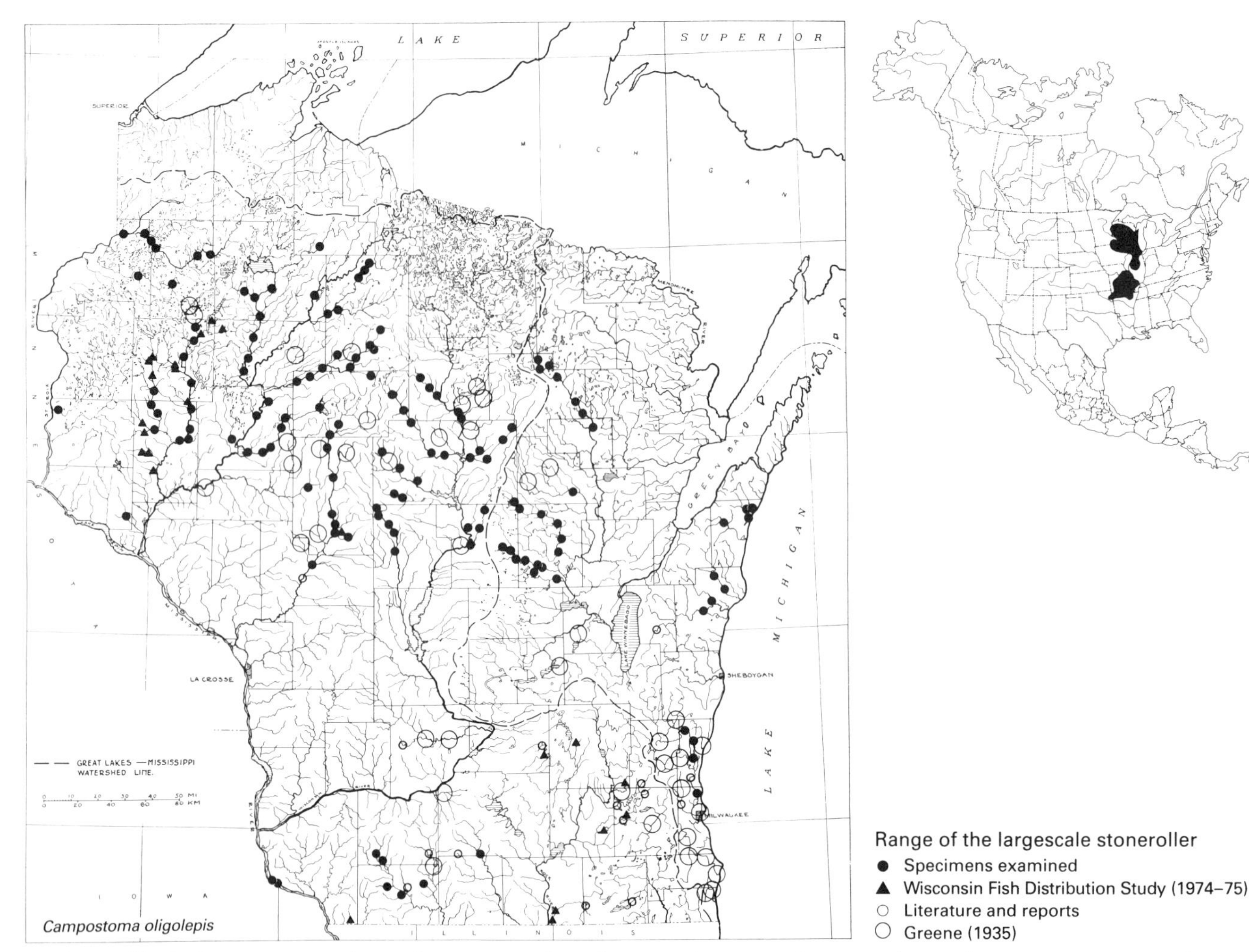

Range of the largescale stoneroller
● Specimens examined
▲ Wisconsin Fish Distribution Study (1974–75)
○ Literature and reports
◯ Greene (1935)

omalum oligolepis, common throughout central and northern Wisconsin, although absent from the Lake Superior drainage. At that time the largescale stoneroller was known only from Wisconsin, which accounts for the common name "Wisconsin stoneroller minnow" (Greene 1935).

The type specimen of the largescale stoneroller (UMMZ 75582), a breeding male 92 mm SL, was collected by Greene and Stuart in Little Rib River 4 km (2.5 mi) east of Hamburg (Marathon County), Wisconsin, on 19 June 1927 (Hubbs and Greene 1935). Numerous paratypes were deposited in the University of Michigan Museum and at the University of Wisconsin—Madison.

Hubbs and Greene commented that where the two *Campostoma* occurred together there were no intergrades, although Nybakken (1961) reported a few intergrades in a later study. Bailey (1956) suggested that, although the two may be different species, it was also possible that *oligolepis* was an environmentally produced variant found in regions where springs of relatively uniform temperature affected early developmental stages in such a way as to produce a structurally different fish.

Hubbs and Lagler (1964) noted that *oligolepis* was probably a distinct species. Pflieger (1968) elevated *oligolepis* to specific rank, and presented a detailed rationale for this action (Pflieger 1971). According to Burr and Smith (1976), no intermediates of *oligolepis* and *anomalum* have been found where they are sympatric.

In Wisconsin, sympatric populations are known from the following locales: Ebert Lake Creek T23N R10E Sec 20, and Tomorrow River T23N R10E Secs 27 and 28 (Portage County); Middle Branch of the Pecatonica River T5N R2E Sec 29, Mineral Point Branch T4N R2E Sec 10, and T5N R2E Sec 36; Dodge Branch T5N R5E Sec 30; Ames Branch T2N R3E Sec 11 (Lafayette County); Sinsinawa River T1N R1W Sec 27 (Grant County); and Sugar River T5N R8E Sec 33 (Dane County).

Greene (1935) suggested that the largescale stoneroller originated in the driftless area of southwestern Wisconsin. Burr and Smith (1976) did not accept

Greene's hypothesis, and assumed that the largescale stoneroller became differentiated from the central stoneroller in the Ozark region during a glacial maximum, most likely the Illinoian. Following the retreat of the last (Wisconsin) glaciation, both the central stoneroller and largescale stoneroller dispersed northward, and occupied streams in the recently glaciated landscape. Human modification has since resulted in a deterioration of optimal habitat for the largescale stoneroller, and enabled the central stoneroller, which is less rigid in its ecological requirements, to supplant the largescale stoneroller in many areas. This has resulted in a disjunct range for the largescale stoneroller.

DISTRIBUTION, STATUS, AND HABITAT

In Wisconsin, the largescale stoneroller occurs in the Mississippi River and the Lake Michigan drainage basins. It is not known from the Lake Superior basin. Its distribution is principally in the northern half of the state and in the southeastern corner.

The largescale stoneroller is abundant in medium-sized, swift-flowing streams of central and northern Wisconsin. Frequently it was the most abundant fish encountered at a collection site. It is absent from a number of streams in the Lake Michigan drainage from Washington to Kenosha counties where it was commonly distributed 50 years ago (Greene 1935), which suggests that it has been unable to cope with alterations of the stream bed and/or water quality brought about by man's activities.

The largescale stoneroller occurs primarily in pools associated with riffles in medium- to large-sized streams; it is seldom found in small streams. It has been taken over the following bottom types: boulders (23% frequency), sand (23%), gravel (20%), silt (12%), rubble (12%), mud (9%), and clay (2%). It is essentially a fish of clear water, and occurred in streams of the following widths: 1.0–3.0 m (5%), 3.1–6.0 m (8%), 6.1–12.0 m (13%), 12.1–24.0 m (34%), 24.1–50.0 m (29%), and more than 50 m (11%).

BIOLOGY

In central and northern Wisconsin spawning occurs in June. Pflieger (1975), who observed spawning in Missouri, noted that the breeding habits resembled those of the central stoneroller. Perhaps where the two species occur together in southern Wisconsin, ecological isolation is maintained throughout the breeding season, allowing the largescale stoneroller to utilize the fast, deep, rocky riffles, and the central stoneroller to utilize the quieter, shallow, headwater situations (Burr and Smith 1976).

In five female largescale stonerollers collected 29 May (Marathon County), the ovarian weight was 8.2–14.7% of the total weight. In only one female were a few eggs almost ripe; in all others the eggs were undeveloped. Egg color is yellow-amber. An age-II female, 111 mm and 14.74 g, held 1,510 eggs 1.4 mm diam in ovaries 2.31 g in weight.

Eggs of the largescale stoneroller have been stripped, artificially fertilized, and hatched in the laboratory; the offspring have been reared in ponds (Pflieger 1971).

In Wisconsin growth of the young is rapid:

Date	No. of Fish	TL (mm)		Location
		Avg	Range	
11 July	7	30	25–41	Wolf R. (Langlade Co.)
14 July	11	39	31–44	Wolf R. (Menominee Co.)
18 July	5	38	34–39	Wolf R. (Langlade Co.)
7 Sept.	32	47	41–58	New Wood R. (Lincoln Co.)
9 Sept.	11	50	44–54	Embarrass R. (Shawano Co.)
27 Sept.	86	59	40–85	Eau Claire R. (Marathon Co.)
13 Sept.	9	52	47–56	Black R. (Clark Co.)
1 Oct.	19	62	54–69	South Fork Flambeau R. (Price Co.)
4 Oct.	41	58	43–63	Hay R. (Dunn Co.)

In Missouri, fry of the largescale stoneroller placed by themselves in a small, unfertilized pond in mid-May averaged 114 mm (4.5 in) by October (Pflieger 1975). Pflieger noted that this is far more rapid growth than is normally achieved in streams.

Largescale stonerollers from the Eau Claire River (Marathon County) collected on 29 May 1961 showed the following growth:

Age Class	No. of Fish	TL (mm)		Calculated TL at Annulus[a] (mm)		
		Avg	Range	1	2	3
I	5	55.6	50–60	55.6		
II	35	90.3	66–122	58.5	90.3	
III	4	126.3	104–154	57.8	97.8	126.3
Avg (weighted)				58.1	91.1	126.3

[a]The annulus for the year of capture had not been deposited; length at time of capture is given. The annulus is deposited from the end of May to the beginning of June.

From the same river another sample had a calculated growth at the annulus as follows: 1—62 mm, 2—106 mm (W. McKee, pers. comm.). The average condition (K_{TL}) on 27 September 1975 for 56 individuals 76–155 mm long was 1.04.

The largescale stoneroller lives in large schools near the bottom at depths of 0.3–1.0 m, and feeds primarily on algae scraped from submerged objects. Digestive tracts of largescale stonerollers from the Eau Claire

River (Marathon County) contained large quantities of algae and diatoms, some fine gravel and debris, and small tendipedid larvae (the last undoubtedly dwelling within the algae and taken with the plant material).

An anchor-worm (*Lernaea* sp.) parasite was attached to a 55-mm largescale stoneroller taken from the Embarrass River (Shawano County). Serious infestations of black grub (*Neascus* sp.) occur in some populations and numerous white grubs (*Posthodiplostomum* sp.) have been noted on the gut in some individuals.

The following associate species were collected with 27 largescale stonerollers in the New Wood River (Lincoln County): white sucker (4), rainbow darter (2), pumpkinseed (11), smallmouth bass (1), hornyhead chub (1), common shiner (85), logperch (2), fathead minnow (2), longnose dace (1), creek chub (35), and northern hog sucker (2).

IMPORTANCE AND MANAGEMENT

The largescale stoneroller is particularly valuable because it is a primary consumer which feeds on basic plant foods and converts them into animal protein. Undoubtedly, the largescale stoneroller is used by other fishes, by birds, and by mammals as a ready source of protein food.

Hornyhead Chub

Nocomis biguttatus (Kirtland). *Nocomis*—an Indian name, applied by Girard to a group of fishes; *biguttatus*—two-spotted.

Other common names: hornyhead, horned chub, river chub, jerker, Indian chub, redtail chub, chub.

Adult male (tuberculate) 139 mm, Wolf R. (Forest Co.), 4 July 1966

Adult female 143 mm, Wolf R. (Forest Co.), 4 July 1966

DESCRIPTION

Body robust, almost round. Average length 89 mm (3.5 in). TL = 1.20 SL. Depth into TL 4.1–5.1. Head length into TL 4.1–4.6. Snout bluntly rounded. Mouth large and slightly oblique, reaching to below front of eye; barbel present in corner of mouth groove. Pharyngeal teeth usually 1,4–4,1 (occasionally 4–4), broad at base and strongly hooked at tip; arch stout. Eye into head length 3–5. Gill rakers short and conical, about 9. Dorsal fin usually originating over pelvic fin origin, sometimes slightly behind; dorsal fin rays 8; anal fin rays 7; pectoral fin rays 14–17; pelvic fin rays 8. Lateral line scales 38–48; lateral line complete. Digestive tract (from end of pharynx to anus) a single S-shaped duct about 0.9 TL. Chromosomes 2n = 50 (W. LeGrande, pers. comm.).

Back olive brown, sides silvery, belly white. Lateral stripes inconspicuous on living specimens, distinct on most preserved fish. A large, diffuse caudal spot, most prevalent on young. Young with a reddish caudal fin. Peritoneum brownish to dusky.

Breeding males with approximately 60–100 conspicuous tubercles on upper part of head, some tubercles with heavy "spines" pointing anteriorly. First 4 pectoral rays with peglike tubercles in single row at base of fin ray, doubling toward the tip. A prominent reddish "ear spot," and orange on dorsal and anal fins. Lachner (1952) described an intense black horizontal stripe on midside of body, and a light middorsal stripe about as wide as a scale prominent during breeding period only. Faint "tubercle spots" may appear on the heads of breeding females.

Sexual dimorphism: In mature male, pectoral fin large; the distance from the end of the pectoral fin to the origin of the pelvic fin about 0.5 the pectoral fin length. In female, pectoral fin short; the distance from the end of the pectoral fin to the origin of the pelvic fin 0.7–1.0 the pectoral fin length. In male, pectoral fin almost circular in ventral view; in female, narrow and elliptical in ventral view.

Hybrids: Hornyhead chub × striped shiner, hornyhead chub × common shiner, hornyhead chub × Ozark minnow (Schwartz 1972); hornyhead chub × common shiner from Walworth, Waukesha, Columbia, and Washington counties (Wis. Fish Distrib. Study 1974–1975).

SYSTEMATIC NOTES

Formerly known as *Hybopsis kentuckiensis* (Forbes and Richardson 1920) and *Hybopsis biguttatus* (Bailey 1951, Johnson and Becker 1970). Until recently *Nocomis* (Girard) has been included as a subgenus in the polymorphic genus *Hybopsis* Agassiz. *Nocomis* is diagnosed and recognized as a genus primarily on the basis of sexual dimorphic features, its mound-nest building behavior, general coloration, physiognomy, scale radii, and vertebral numbers (Jenkins and Lachner 1971). *Nocomis* and *Couesius* are more closely related to the genus *Semotilus* Rafinesque than to any group remaining in *Hybopsis*.

DISTRIBUTION, STATUS, AND HABITAT

The hornyhead chub occurs in all three drainage basins in Wisconsin, and is generally distributed in all parts of the state except the unglaciated southwest quarter. Since Greene (1935) made his studies in the late 1920s, this minnow appears to have spread into waters of the lower Wisconsin River and its tributaries.

The hornyhead chub appears to be decreasing over its general range. Intensive land cultivation with attendant increases in the siltation and intermittent flow of streams may be important factors in its de-

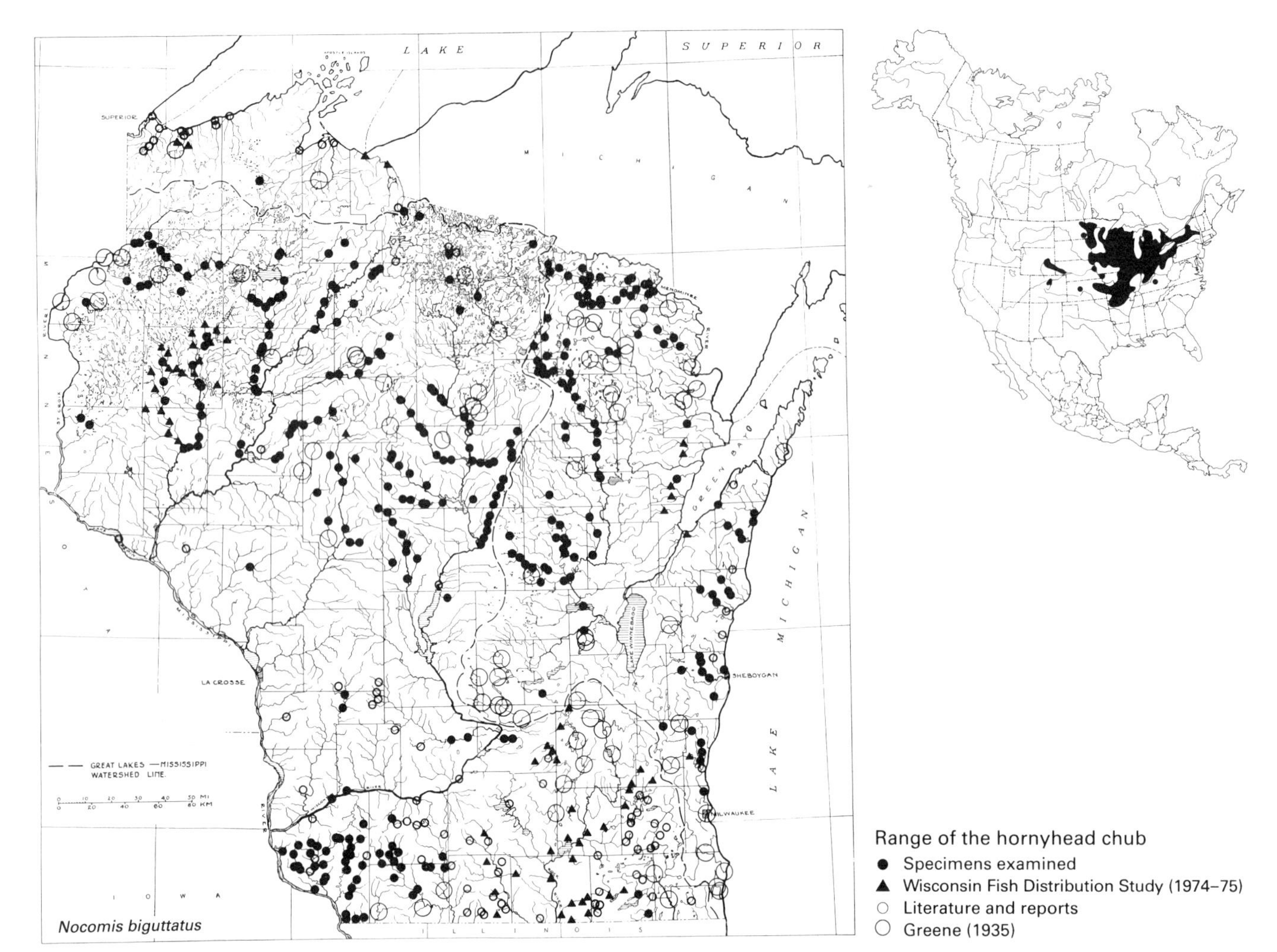

Range of the hornyhead chub
● Specimens examined
▲ Wisconsin Fish Distribution Study (1974–75)
○ Literature and reports
◯ Greene (1935)

clining abundance in parts of Missouri (Pflieger 1975). Although at one time it was widespread in Ohio and was widely used there for food and bait, by 1950 it existed there only in widely scattered relict populations (Trautman 1957). In Canada, it is probably much less common now than formerly (Scott and Crossman 1973).

The hornyhead chub is common in clearwater, medium-sized streams of northern and central Wisconsin. In a central Wisconsin study, it constituted 6.6% of the total number of minnows collected (Becker 1959). It is uncommon in the southwestern quarter of the state, except in the southern tier of counties, where it is common. Cahn (1927) noted that it was formerly abundant in the Oconomowoc River, but that its numbers there have become greatly reduced.

In Wisconsin, the hornyhead chub was encountered most frequently in clear water; its numbers decrease as turbidity increases. It was essentially a shallow water fish, most common at depths of 0.6–1.5 m, and less common at depths of 0.1–0.5 m; it was found over substrates of gravel (27% frequency), sand (20%), rubble (12%), boulders (13%), silt (12%), mud (9%), clay (2%), detritus (2%), bedrock (2%), and marl (1%). It occurred in streams of varying widths: 1.0–3.0 m (17% frequency), 3.1–6.0 m (24%), 6.1–12.0 m (18%), 12.1–24.0 m (26%), 24.1–50.0 m (11%), and more than 50 m (5%). It was rarely encountered in softwater lakes of central and northern Wisconsin.

The hornyhead chub inhabits riffles and the pools between riffles. Larger chubs will often seek shelter under slab rocks. In northeastern Wisconsin, the water color of streams where it has been captured was generally light brown; fewer fish were taken from dark brown streams. In its habitat the vegetation is sparse to dense.

BIOLOGY

In Wisconsin, the hornyhead chub spawns from May through July. Several nests were seen on 22 July 1958 in the Little Wolf River (Waupaca County), from which both males and females in breeding condition were collected. Nests of this species were also seen on 23 June 1966 at the Pine River outlet of Butternut Lake (Forest County); one nest was in a narrows of the lake itself where a current was established. The Pine River nests were at water depths of 0.3 and 1.0 m (1 and 3 ft), and were 457 mm (18 in) diam and 76 mm (3 in) high. They were constructed of cleaned gravel 13–25 mm diam. Two females (25.2 and 23.9 g), collected from the Pine River sites, had ovaries 11.9 and 8.8% of total body weight.

In two prespawning females (130 and 124 mm TL), taken 17 June 1966 from the Pike River (Marinette County), the ovaries were 10.3 and 11.6% of the body weight, and contained 995 and 952 maturing eggs respectively. These eggs were 1.3–2.0 mm diam; a small number of white, immature eggs 0.3–1.0 mm diam were also present.

Spawning occurs at water temperatures of 18.3°C (65°F) or warmer (Hankinson 1932). Hubbs and Cooper (1936:44–45) provided the following description of nest building and spawning:

. . . A slight concavity in the stream bottom is either selected for the site of the nest or such a cavity is constructed either by sweeping or carrying material away from the area by the breeding fish. Carrying of pebbles onto the nest is done entirely by the male. Short periods of carrying pebbles are alternated with short breeding acts. In the final nest, consequently, the eggs are thoroughly scattered through the pile of pebbles. In this way the eggs are not only shielded from most egg predators, but are also kept in a slight current and free from silt. Each nest is occupied by a single male Horny-head, who probably spawns with several females. The pile of gravel comprising the nest varies considerably in size, from approximately 1 ft. × 2 ft. in diameter × 2 in. deep to 3 ft. × 3 ft. × 6 in.

In nest building the male carries the stones in his mouth, or rolls or pushes them with lips and snout. The nest increases in size with successive spawnings. A.H. Carter (see Scott and Crossman 1973) believed that as many as 10 females spawned in one nest under observation. The total egg complement is not deposited in one nest at one time, since at each spawning an individual female deposits only eggs which are ripe. The eggs attach to gravel or to plant roots.

The nest piles of the hornyhead chub are used as spawning sites by other stream fishes, including the blacknose dace, stoneroller minnow, common shiner, rosyface shiner, southern redbelly dace, and the blackside darter. The relationship of the hornyhead chub to the common shiner on the chub's nest is most unique; it has been described by Hubbs and Cooper (1936:45):

. . . One male of each species often occupies the nest simultaneously (Hankinson 1920), neither paying any attention to the presence of the other. However, any other fish approaching the nest is driven away. In this commensalistic association, the function of the male Common Shiner is restricted to the protection of the nest, while the male Hornyhead functions both as a transporter of pebbles and as a guardian of the nest. The Common Shiner is most active in driving off small intruders such as shiners, while the Chub brings his sharp horns into use in driving off larger egg-marauders, such as the Hog Molly (northern hog sucker). Each species is benefitted by the part played by the male of the other species in protecting or constructing the nest.

Other species associated with the common shiner over hornyhead chub nests, either to spawn or to search for eggs as food, are the bluntnose minnow, rainbow darter, and johnny darter.

Hankinson (1932) described an instance when a hog sucker about 381 mm (15 in) long crept slowly up on a chub nest; its protective markings seemed to conceal it from the guarding fish for a time, but suddenly it was noticed by the male hornyhead, which was carrying stones. The hornyhead immediately gave the sucker a blow on the side of the head with his tubercle-roughened snout of sufficient force to send the sucker several centimeters over to one side. A few more blows started the sucker on an upstream retreat, with the hornyhead following for four or more meters. The encounter showed the effectiveness of the nuptial tubercles as organs of offense. The hornyhead was probably not a quarter of the size of the sucker.

Female hornyheads generally produce fewer than 1,000 eggs each. Lachner (1952) found from 460 to 725 eggs in four females 80–89 mm SL. The development of the embryo has not been studied. In Wisconsin, young-of-year have not been collected before September. On 4 October, seven were taken from the Milwaukee River (Fond du Lac County) which were 48.9 mm (40–61 mm) TL. In Ohio, young-of-year were 25–76 mm (1–3 in) long in October (Trautman 1957). According to Pflieger (1975), the young frequent areas without current, and are often found in association with higher aquatic plants.

Hornyhead chubs from the Plover River (Portage County), collected 2 October 1968, showed the following growth:

Age Class	No. of Fish	TL (mm)		Calculated TL at Annulus (mm)		
		Avg	Range	1	2	3
0	5	35.6	29–47			
I	4	65.5	48–90	43.2		
II	20	97.9	75–114	42.4	65.6	
III	3	125.7	120–130	40.0	63.9	95.2
Avg (weighted)				42.3	65.4	95.2

In central Wisconsin, this species grows slowly during the first year. An individual collected on 27 January 1959 from the Tomorrow River (Portage County) was only 39 mm TL, and age-II hornyheads taken 2 March 1959 were 66 and 85 mm TL. In Ontario waters (Scott and Crossman 1973), the size range (SL) from young-of-year to age-IV chubs was age 0—24–36 mm, age I—44–58 mm, age II—64–83 mm, age III—86–100 mm, and age IV—131 mm.

The annulus is generally deposited in May, but appears earlier in younger fish. Males grow to a larger size than females of the same age-group. In a collection from the Pike River (Marinette County), mature males were 129–167 mm TL, and gravid females were 94–130 mm TL. According to Lachner (1952), the growth increment is somewhat greater during June and July than in August and September. Maturity is reached at age II in fast-growing fish, and at age III in others. This species rarely exceeds 4 years of age.

The largest known Wisconsin hornyhead chub (UWSP 5155) is an age-IV male 225 mm TL and 140.9 g, collected from Sunset Lake (Portage County) on 11 July 1975. Its estimated lengths at annuli are 1—71 mm, 2—128 mm, 3—189 mm, and 4—209 mm. Trautman (1957) reported a hornyhead chub 236 mm (9.3 in) long which weighed 170 g (6 oz). The largest hornyheads are almost invariably males, as is common in all species of minnows in which males build nests and guard eggs.

The hornyhead chub feeds mostly by sight. The barbels have few tastebuds (Davis and Miller 1967). The food of young-of-year taken in July from Sandy Creek, New York, was Ostracoda (36.1% of volume), Cladocera (8.6%), Gastropoda (13.8%), Ephemeroptera (8.6%), Trichoptera (5.9%), *Chironomus* larvae (10.7%), insect remains (6.2%), and filamentous algae (9.8%) (Lachner 1950). The food of adults consisted of vascular plant remains (44.5%), filamentous algae (11.1%), crayfish (32.2%), Coleoptera larvae (8.9%), and Trichoptera (3.3%).

In summary, the food of hornyhead chubs includes both plant and animal tissues. In Canada, the young eat cladocerans and aquatic insect larvae; older fish eat crayfish, snails, annelids, aquatic insect larvae, and fish (Scott and Crossman 1973). Snails become quite important in the diet of age-I and older fish. Although filamentous algae, seeds of grasses, and the remains of other plants have been recorded in hornyhead chub stomachs, these are probably of little value as food (Hubbs and Cooper 1936). The rather short digestive tract of this chub makes proper digestion and absorption of vegetative matter highly unlikely.

Species collected with 140 hornyhead chubs from the Platte River (Grant County) included white sucker (47), central stoneroller (17), longnose dace (8), creek chub (1), bluntnose minnow (61), suckermouth minnow (3), common shiner (88), rosyface shiner (25), sand shiner (1), Ozark minnow (20), stonecat (3), johnny darter (7), fantail darter (21), smallmouth bass (11), green sunfish (2), and bluegill (6). Species collected from the Eau Claire River (Marathon County) with 67 hornyhead chub included shorthead redhorse (16), northern hog sucker (4), white sucker (38), largescale stoneroller (397), longnose dace (5), creek chub (30), bluntnose minnow (3), common shiner (244), rosyface shiner (39), mimic shiner (22), bigmouth shiner (50), blackside darter (1), logperch (2), and fantail darter (1).

IMPORTANCE AND MANAGEMENT

Little is known about predators of the hornyhead chub, although Scott and Crossman (1973) assumed that they fall prey to rock bass and smallmouth bass. In a laboratory experiment in which common shiners, white suckers, and hornyhead chubs were exposed to predation of smallmouth bass, 21% of the hornyhead chubs were eaten during the time of exposure (Paragamian 1976b). Paragamian found neither white suckers nor hornyhead chubs in the stomachs of smallmouth bass electrofished from the Plover River (Portage County), a natural stream, although common shiners, white suckers, and hornyhead chubs were present in equal numbers.

The hornyhead chub is an excellent bait fish, hardy on the hook or in storage tanks. In Iowa, it is one of the most sought after baits for bass and catfish, and is used extensively for walleye fishing (Harlan and Speaker 1956). Because of its large size, it is said to make an excellent bait fish for northern pike. In southeastern Wisconsin (Cahn 1927), thousands of hornyhead chub have been captured yearly for use as casting minnows, and "two guides . . . have taken not less than 600 of these chubs a week for five months a year for more than forty years, from the Ashippun river, and still the fish are abundant."

Hornyhead chubs bite readily on hook and line—the method by which they formerly were captured for bait. I have caught them on dry flies and eaten them fried. They are tasty, although the flesh of hornyheads caught in late summer tends to be on the soft side. I have spoken with others who have eaten them a number of times, and who find them quite acceptable. Because they are easily taken on worms and dry flies, they provide fishing action when game fishing is slow.

Gravel Chub

Hybopsis x-punctata Hubbs and Crowe, *Hybopsis*—gibbous face; *x-punctata*—x-dotted.
Other common name: spotted chub.

Male 71 mm, Rock R., Beloit (Rock Co.), 27 Sept. 1970

DESCRIPTION

Body slender, almost round—only slightly compressed. Average length 76 mm (3 in). TL = 1.25 SL. Depth into TL 5.9–6.8. Head length into TL 4.7–5.0. Snout rounded and long, overhanging mouth. Mouth horizontal, ventral, small, reaching below posterior nostril; a slender, small but conspicuous barbel near the end of the maxillary. Pharyngeal teeth 4–4, slender (upper teeth sometimes bent posteriorly), and strongly hooked at tip. Eye large, into head length 3.0–3.3. Gill rakers short, conical, about 9. Dorsal fin slightly falcate, distinctly in advance of pelvic fin origin; dorsal fin rays 8; anal fin rays 7; pectoral fin rays 13–16; pelvic fin rays 8. Lateral line scales 40–43; lateral line complete. Digestive tract with several loops, longer than TL.

Olive green dorsally, silvery on sides, and silvery white on belly. Scale margins randomly outlined in black on sides, resulting in X- or Y-shaped marks. A small, black spot often present at base of tail fin. Peritoneum black.

Breeding male with tubercles very small, even minute, on head and branchiostegals, and sometimes on most scales on anterior part of body. Pectoral fins bearing conical tubercles, larger than those on body, in single file on basal part and distal branches of rays 2–9; other fins lacking tubercles (Cross 1967).

Hybrids: Gravel chub × streamline chub (Trautman 1957).

SYSTEMATIC NOTES

This species was long treated with *Erimystax dissimilis* (Kirtland), and was so reported from southern Wisconsin by Greene (1935), and from southeastern

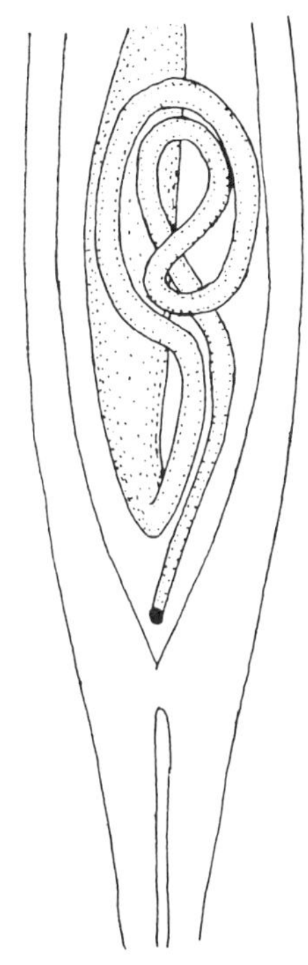

Ventral view of the alimentary tract of the gravel chub with ventral body wall and viscera removed

Minnesota by Eddy and Surber (1947). It was reported as *Hybopsis dissimilis* (Kirtland) from Illinois by Forbes and Richardson (1920). Hubbs and Crowe (1956) described a new species, *Hybopsis x-punctata*, and assigned it to the populations in these states. Two subspecies are recognized: *H. x-punctata x-punctata* from the Mississippi River and its northern tributaries, and *H. x-punctata trautmani* from the Ohio River basin of Illinois.

DISTRIBUTION, STATUS, AND HABITAT

In Wisconsin, the gravel chub is known only from the lower Rock River drainage of the Mississippi River drainage basin, including the lower Pecatonica River, the lower Sugar River, the main channel of the Rock River, and lower Turtle Creek. Greene (1935) collected it only once from the Sugar River at Brodhead (Green County).

Specimens recorded in the 1970s include (number): UWSP 3688 (2) Rock River T1N R12E Sec 35 (Rock County) 1970; UWSP 4712 (2) Sugar River T1N R10E Sec 17 (Rock County) 1974. The Wisconsin Fish Distribution Study reported: seven collections (1–42) from Turtle Creek T1N R12E Sec 36 to T1N R13E Sec 3 (Rock County) 1975–1977; two collections (3–14) from Rock River T1N R12E Sec 35 (Rock County) 1976; nine collections (1–26) from Sugar River T1N R10E Sec 17 to T2N R9E Sec 23 (Rock and Green counties) 1974; three

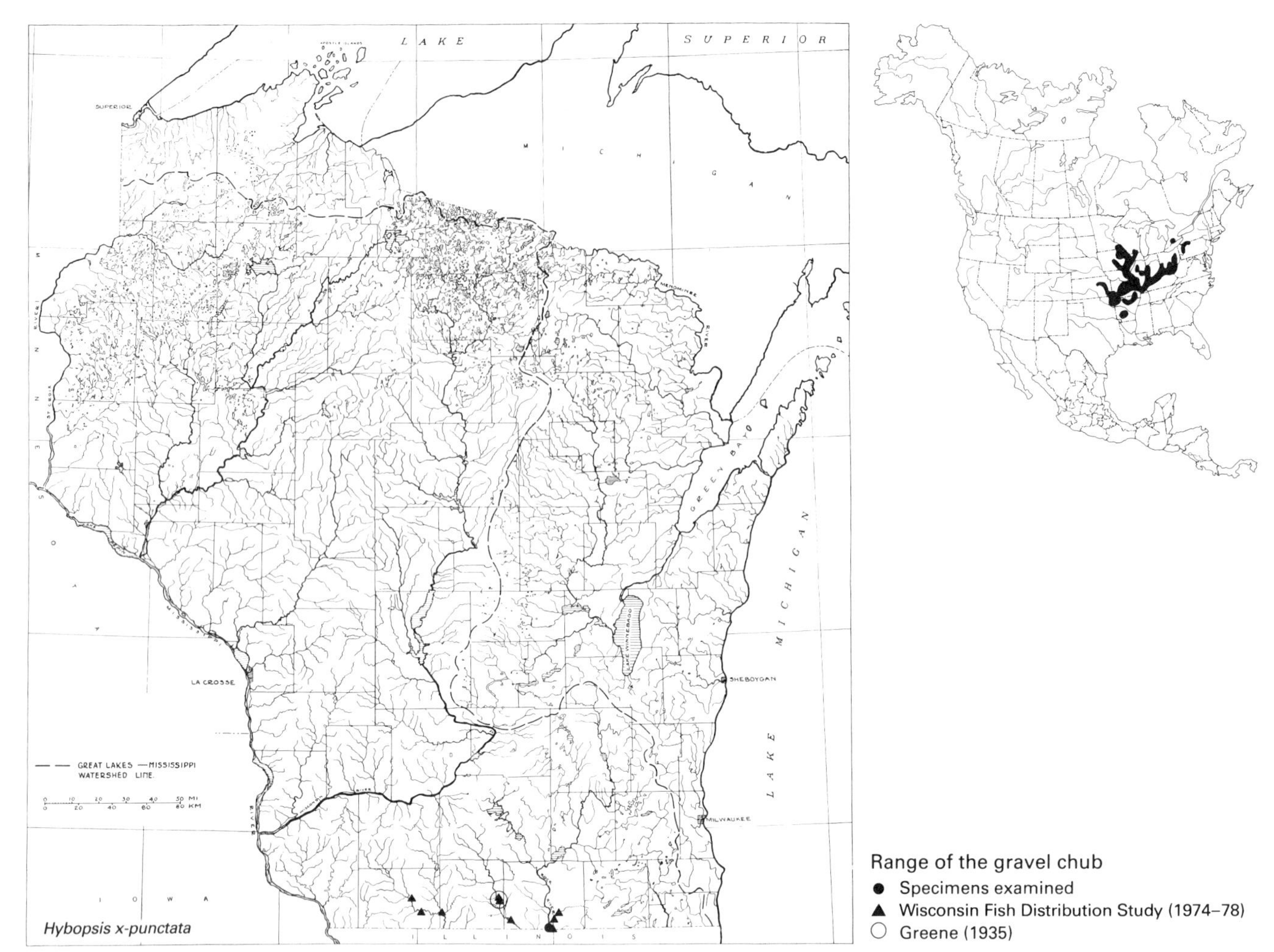

collections (1–2) from Pecatonica River T1N R6E Sec 6 to T2N R4E Sec 17 (Green and Lafayette counties) 1976.

Over its general range, there is some pessimism for the gravel chub's future. In Ohio, it disappeared from many riffles and bars immediately after the sand and gravel of stream bottoms became heavily covered with silt (Trautman 1957). In Minnesota, Phillips and Underhill (1967) noted its presence in the Root and Iowa rivers, but stated also that it is rare and may be dwindling. In Iowa (Roosa 1977), it is threatened. P.W. Smith (1965) stated that in Illinois it is occasional in the Rock River and its tributaries, and sporadic in the Wabash and lower Mississippi rivers.

In Wisconsin, the gravel chub has endangered status (Les 1979). It seems especially susceptible to turbidity and siltation which are increasing in its remaining Wisconsin range as agricultural use of the land increases. In addition, there is the ever-present threat of impoundment of the few remaining riffle areas which are essential to its survival. Turtle Creek (Rock County), which has perhaps the best remaining population of this minnow in the state, has been proposed as the site of a reservoir for flood control by the U.S. Army Corps of Engineers.

This species is usually found in medium- to large-sized rivers in deep, swift water over a pea-gravel bottom. The following description of the Sugar River site (T2N R9E Sec 23, Green County) was provided by D. Becker (pers. comm.):

> West channel above Hwy F west of Brodhead, 100 yds above bridge, a swift-flowing gravel riffle 1–3 ft deep, gravel 1–2.5 inches in diameter, bottom clear of vegetation, water turbid. The entire area suitable for gravel chub approx. 150–200 ft long—30 to 40 ft wide. 3 specimens collected with boom shocker on Aug 1, 1974—Fago and Priegel. 11 specimens collected with seine on Aug 5, 1974, from same area—5 returned. —Fago, Siegler, Becker.

The habitat requirements of the gravel chub are so strict that populations are isolated and confined to special riffle areas with special bottom types. In northern Illinois, the gravel chub has been taken chiefly in swift water flowing over sand (Forbes and Richardson 1920). In the Ozarks (Pflieger 1971), it tends to be most abundant in the downstream sections of the larger streams, where the gradient is less, and where the water is warmer and less clear than in the headwaters. Trautman (1957) noted that in Ohio the gravel chub was present in the largest numbers in the slower flowing, deeper waters where silt was lacking. In northeastern Oklahoma, it resides among or under rubble in relatively deep riffles in fast-moving water (B. Davis, pers. comm.).

BIOLOGY

The spawning time of the gravel chub in Wisconsin is not known. In Missouri (Pflieger 1975), it spawns on swift, gravelly riffles in the early spring. In Kansas (Cross 1967), spawning gravel chubs were taken on 9 April when the water temperature was 15.6°C (60°F); adults that freely extruded eggs or milt were concentrated in water 0.6–0.9 m (2–3 ft) deep adjacent to a gravel bar where the current was swiftest. It is presumed that spawning is limited to a brief period in early spring. In Illinois, males with well-developed gonads, but without tubercles, were taken in the middle of June (Forbes and Richardson 1920).

The growth of gravel chubs (UWSP 1598) taken 10–13 October 1948 from Missouri (Louis County) was recorded as follows:

Age Class	No. of Fish	TL (mm)		Calculated TL at Annulus (mm)	
		Avg	Range	1	2
I	5	80.3	75.5–86	56.3	
II	4	90.8	88–95.5	52.6	81.4
Avg (weighted)				54.7	81.4

Little information is available on the growth of this species in Wisconsin. Two age-I gravel chubs (UWSP 3688) taken from the Rock River (Rock County) on 27 September were 69 and 70.5 mm TL, and were an estimated 46.3 mm long at the first annulus. One age-I fish (UWSP 4712) taken from the Sugar River (Rock County) on 5 August was 53 mm TL, and was an estimated 34.7 mm long at the first annulus. A young-of-year from the same collection (UWSP 4712) was 40 mm TL.

In Ohio, young-of-year in October are 28–61 mm (1.1–2.4 in) long; at 1 year, 43–71 mm (1.7–2.8 in) long (Trautman 1957). Breeding adults are usually 64–97 mm (2.5–3.8 in); the largest specimen recorded was 99 mm (3.9 in) long.

The digestive tract of a Meramec River, Missouri, gravel chub contained an abundance of desmids and diatoms of many species, as well as plant debris and sand grains. No animal matter was present.

The gravel chub probably feeds by probing under rocks and in crevices with its sensitive snout (Davis and Miller 1967). The taste buds on the barbels are usually large, sometimes attaining a length of 100 microns; they project downward at oblique angles to give a branched appearance.

The curved dorsal surface and the pectoral fin serve to keep the gravel chub on or near the bottom of fast water whenever it leaves sheltered areas. Moore and Paden (1950) suggested that the specific microhabitat of the gravel chub may be beneath rocks in the riffle areas, where the effects of swift water would be reduced. When disturbed, the chub has been observed to dart swiftly away to hide under rocks; the retreat chosen was often too small to accommodate the entire body, but as soon as the head was hidden the fish became motionless.

Fish species associated with two gravel chubs in the Rock River at Beloit (Rock County) were: black crappie (5), white crappie (3), smallmouth bass (3), orange-spotted sunfish (15), bluegill (150), northern pike (2), black bullhead (1), brook silverside (4), logperch (1), johnny darter (1), spotfin shiner (462), spottail shiner (6), and sand shiner (108).

IMPORTANCE AND MANAGEMENT

There are no records of the gravel chub as a prey for fish-eating predators; nor are there records of man's use of this species as a bait minnow.

Silver Chub

Hybopsis storeriana (Kirtland). *Hybopsis*—gibbous face; *storeriana*—after David H. Storer, early American ichthyologist.
Other common name: Storer's chub.

Male 148 mm, Sneed Cr. (Iowa Co.), 3 Aug. 1962

DESCRIPTION

Body stout and almost round. Average length 140 mm (5.5 in). TL = 1.29 SL. Depth into TL 4.1–5.9. Head length into TL 4.8–6.1. Snout relatively long, abruptly decurved and protruding slightly beyond mouth. Mouth reaching between nostril and anterior eye; a well-developed barbel at posterior end of lip groove in corner of mouth. Pharyngeal teeth 1,4–4,1, hooked at tip. Eye large, into head length 3.0–4.3. Gill rakers, slight protruberances or short fleshy lobes, 10. Dorsal fin originating slightly anterior to pelvic fin; dorsal fin rays 8; anal fin rays 8 (7); pectoral fin rays 17; pelvic fin rays 8. Lateral line scales 37–41; lateral line complete. Digestive tract short with a single S-shaped loop 0.6–0.7 TL. Chromosomes 2n = 50 (W. LeGrande, pers. comm.).

Pale gray-green dorsally, becoming silvery on sides and silvery white on belly. Iris of eye white-yellow. Faint dusky lateral stripe usually present. Caudal fin lightly pigmented, except the lower 3 or 4 rays, which are completely unpigmented. Peritoneum silvery.

Breeding males with tubercles confined to rays 2–8 on pectoral fins. Head bears minute sensory buds, but not breeding tubercles (Cross 1967).

DISTRIBUTION, STATUS, AND HABITAT

The silver chub occurs in the Mississippi River drainage basin, largely from Lake Pepin (Wagner 1908) downstream in the Mississippi River, and in the lower Wisconsin River. Occasionally it occurs in the lower extremities of small to large tributaries. In 1974 (Wis. Fish Distrib. Study) it was taken from the Sugar River (Green County), which is part of the Rock River drainage system.

The silver chub is rare in Michigan and in South Dakota (Miller 1972). It is ironic that the best study of this species was done by Kinney (1954) in Lake Erie, where the silver chub is believed extirpated. Its disappearance was probably related to the loss of its prime food, the large mayfly (*Hexagenia*) (Britt 1955). According to Scott and Crossman (1973), this fish's disappearance is regrettable, "since it suggests an ever-narrowing faunal base in that woefully abused body of water."

In Wisconsin, the silver chub is uncommon. Barring catastrophic deterioration in water quality, it probably will survive as part of our fish fauna in limited numbers.

In Wisconsin, the silver chub was encountered most frequently at depths of 0.6 m or more over substrates of sand (47% frequency), mud (24%), clay (19%), and gravel (10%). It occurs in streams 3.1 m wide or wider—most frequently in large, low-gradient rivers more than 50 m wide. It is taken in water of slow to fast current, from riffles, deep, quiet pools, and sloughs with moderate amounts of vegetation or no vegetation at all. The silver chub seems to have the least specific habitat requirements of the three *Hybopsis* species in the state.

BIOLOGY

Spawning occurs in June and July in Wisconsin. Most spawning information comes from Lake Erie (Kinney 1954). There is a shoreward migration in the spring, which is probably a positive thermotropic response. Spawning begins with the water temperature at 18.9°C (66°F), and reaches its peak with the water temperature at 22.8°C (73°F). Spawning is thought to occur in open water. Trautman (1957) noted large numbers of spawned adults lying dead along Lake Erie beaches during the June and July spawning season; this suggests that some adults died after spawning.

On the Mississippi River (Crawford County) on 27 June, two mature gravid females with ovaries about 9% of total weight held ripe eggs 1.5 mm diam. On 28 July in the Wisconsin River (Richland County), the ovaries of a female were 5% of the body weight, with eggs 1.3 mm diam (E. Peters, pers. comm.).

In Lake Erie, ovary weights varied from about 10% of the body weights of small specimens (20–30 g) to 20% of the body weights of large specimens (70–80 g) (Kinney 1954). The formula for the number of mature eggs produced is: Number of eggs = 365 + 746.64 × ovary weight (g). Time to hatching is not known, but Fish (1932) described and illustrated four larval stages from 5 to 21 mm, and Taber (1969) illustrated stages from 6.5 to 17.7 mm. In Lake Erie, larval

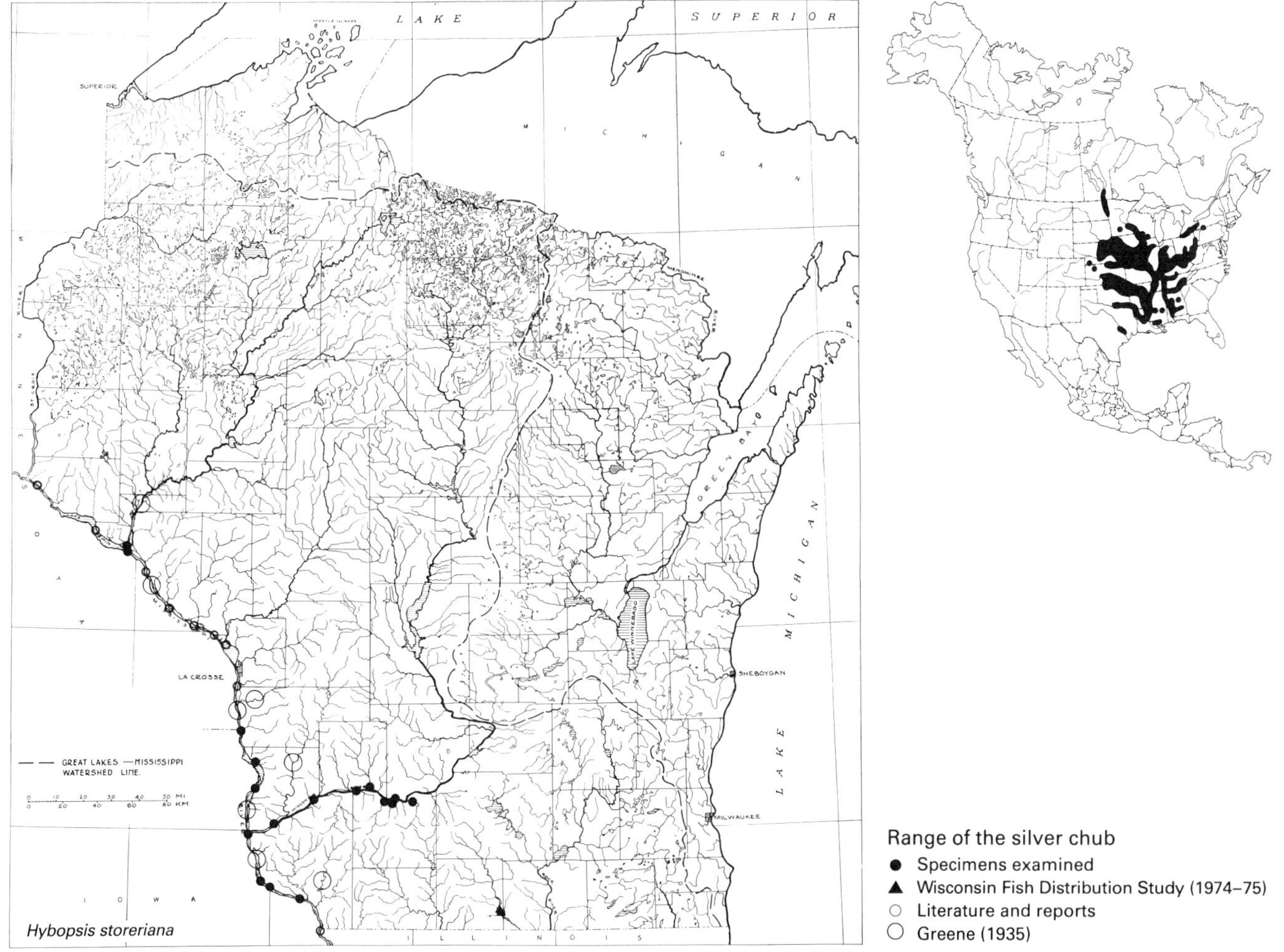

stages up to 7.5 mm were taken during the latter half of June and the first week of July, usually in bottom hauls at depths of 18–20 m. Greeley (1929) secured young-of-year at stream mouths to Lake Erie.

The growth (mm) of young-of-year in Wisconsin follows:

Date	No. of Fish	TL (mm) Avg	TL (mm) Range	Location
16 July	13	33.2	32–42	Mississippi R. (Grant Co.)
11 Aug.	3	44.5	43.5–45	Mississippi R. (Grant Co.)
13 Aug.	1	35.0	—	Mississippi R. (Grant Co.)
19 Sept.	11	46.6	34–56.5	Mississippi R. (Grant Co.)
24 Sept.	3	62.8	53–68	Mississippi R. (Grant Co.)

The young are fast-growing. The largest collections were made in shallow, flowing waters over an expansive gravel and clay beach near Cassville (Grant County).

The scale method of age determination is valid for silver chubs. Annulus formation occurs after 23 May, and by 27 June it is completed in age-I fish and almost completed in age-II fish.

Growth of silver chubs from the lower Wisconsin River (July samples):

Age Class	No. of Fish	TL (mm) Avg	TL (mm) Range	Calculated TL at Annulus (mm) 1	2	3
I	4	131	124–136	79.5		
II	10	147.1	132–154	77.8	128	
III	1	165		92.9	116.1	145.1
Avg (weighted)				79.3	126.9	145.9

Age-I silver chubs taken on 28 September 1974 from the confluence of the Chippewa and Mississippi rivers (UWSP 4938) were 133 (108–146) mm TL, age-II fish, 158 and 160 mm TL; in Pool 9 of the Mississippi River, calculated lengths to the first annulus averaged 46.6 mm; in Pool 11, 54.4 mm; and above Pool 5, 60.3 mm. In silver chubs from the lower Wisconsin River the calculated lengths to the first annulus averaged 79.3 mm.

The oldest specimen in Wisconsin collections is 3-

plus years. In western Lake Erie, male silver chubs seldom lived more than 3 years, while females attained an age of almost 4 years. The maximum total length of Lake Erie chubs was slightly over 200 mm, and the weight about 90 g.

The silver chub is one of our largest native minnows. A Wisconsin silver chub female 165 mm (6.5 in) long (UWSP 2245) was collected from the Wisconsin River at Boscobel (Grant County). From Ohio, Trautman (1957) reported a silver chub 231 mm (9.1 in), 170 g (6 oz).

The diet of silver chubs taken from the Mississippi River (Crawford County) consisted of Trichoptera (most abundant), *Gammarus*, *Pisidium*, Coleoptera, Ephemeroptera, and Diptera (E. Peters, pers. comm.). Food items consumed by silver chubs from the Wisconsin River (Richland County) included Hemiptera (Corixidae), which were found in almost all stomachs, as well as Trichoptera (Limnephilidae and Brachycentridae), *Pisidium*, Diptera, Ephemeroptera, and Coleoptera.

Young-of-year in Lake Erie fed on Copepoda (39.5%), Tendipedidae (34.7%), *Daphnia* (10.9%), Trichoptera larvae (4.6%), Sphaeriidae (4.1%), Ostracods (2.9%), Oligochaeta (1.3%), and *Gammarus*, Baetidae, and Coleoptera (1.8%) (Kinney 1954). During the first part of Kinney's study, adults fed principally on *Hexagenia* nymphs (66.7%), small Mollusca (17.3%), *Daphnia* (5.2%), and *Gammarus* (3.1%). During September 1953, Britt (1955) found that, because of low oxygen conditions, the *Hexagenia* population had suffered a drastic decline. Food habit studies conducted after the *Hexagenia* decline showed that Tendipedidae, *Daphnia*, and *Gammarus* made up the bulk of the food eaten by adult silver chubs. Kinney estimated that the silver chub ate 10% of its weight in *Hexagenia* per day.

In aquarium studies, feeding by silver chubs occurred only at or near the bottom of the tank (Davis and Miller 1967). When not feeding, the fish rested quietly near a bottom corner of the aquarium. The selection of food items appeared to be under both sight and taste control. Capture of live or dry food seldom involved movement of more than 2–4 cm. When a fish was touched by either type of food an apparent feeding response was elicited, but if the initial movement was unsuccessful, there were no subsequent attempts to obtain that food item. If given a choice between live and dry food, the fish showed a slight preference for live food. Often when there was dry food on the bottom, fish picked up material, appeared to chew on it momentarily then ejected large quantities of sand. In captivity, this chub is easily excited by vibration or movement near the aquarium (Davis and Miller 1967).

According to Davis and Miller, the silver chub relies more on taste to secure food than do other species of the subgenus. External taste buds are slightly more numerous than in other species, and well-developed compound taste buds occur in the interradial membranes of the pectoral fins.

The silver chub is a southern species which seems to require 6–7 months with water temperatures above 7.2–10°C (45–50°F); 3 of these must be above 21.1°C (70°F). Water temperature is the main factor in determining the northern edge of its range, while salinity is the limiting factor at the southern edge. It is essentially a bottom fish, and before its disappearance from Lake Erie it was commonly taken in bottom hauls at depths of 18–20 m (60–66 ft). In shallows where this species is not collected during the day, it is often collected in large numbers at night (B. Davis, pers. comm.).

Trautman (1957) noted that, when pools in large rivers became excessively silted, the silver chub moved into gravelly streams with clearer water. During the winter on the Mississippi River, the silver chub frequents deep holes. Individuals were collected during March in the vicinity of Alma (Buffalo County) from holes 9–12 m deep (M. Ebbers, pers. comm.).

In the lower Wisconsin River, 10 silver chubs were associated with the following species: shovelnose sturgeon (1), mooneye (4), quillback (1), river carpsucker (5), highfin carpsucker (2), shorthead redhorse (97), golden redhorse (47), northern hog sucker (65), common carp (12), speckled chub (1), bluntnose minnow (1), emerald shiner (15), spotfin shiner (23), river shiner (1), sand shiner (36), sauger (6), walleye (1), crystal darter (6), river darter (3), slenderhead darter (11), logperch (31), smallmouth bass (21), black crappie (1), and freshwater drum (2).

IMPORTANCE AND MANAGEMENT

The silver chub is a forage fish; it is known to be eaten by burbot, *Stizostedion* sp., and other large fish-eating species (Kinney 1954). A 108-mm silver chub was taken from the stomach of a flathead catfish (Coker 1930).

The silver chub is an excellent bait minnow in Iowa, when available (Harlan and Speaker 1956). It does not live long either in the bait bucket or on the hook, but because of its size it is highly prized for large-fish angling, and it is taken occasionally on worms. Apparently it is of little direct food value to man because of its numerous bones.

Speckled Chub

Hybopsis aestivalis (Girard). *Hybopsis*—gibbous face; *aestivalis*—pertaining to summer.

Other common names: long minnow, northern longnose chub.

Adult 65 mm, Wisconsin R., Arena (Iowa Co.), 3 Aug. 1962

DESCRIPTION

Body elongate and slender, round in cross section. Average length 45–55 mm (1.8–2.2 in). TL (males) = 1.24 SL; TL (females) = 1.29 SL. Depth into TL 6.2–8.3. Head length into TL 4.5–5.2. Snout fleshy, protruding far forward of horizontal mouth. Mouth reaching to below anterior edge of eye; a fleshy barbel from the corner of mouth groove in length about equal to diam of pupil. Gill rakers, short, pointed, and fleshy, 8. Pharyngeal teeth 4–4, slender with a short cutting edge and strongly hooked at tip; pharyngeal arch slender and weak. Dorsal fin usually originating slightly anterior to pelvic fin; dorsal fin falcate, rays 8; anal fin rays 8; pectoral fin rays 12–15; pelvic fin rays 8. Lateral line scales 36–40; lateral line complete. Digestive tract a simple S-shaped duct 0.5–0.7 TL. Chromosomes 2n = 50 (J. Gold, pers. comm.).

In life, pale and translucent; belly white. Sides with a silvery longitudinal stripe; dark speckles on sides. Dark blotch near base of each lobe of caudal fin. Peritoneum silvery.

Fine tubercles in both male and female over the entire head and branchiostegal region, along the rays of the pectoral fins, the anterior rays of the pelvic fins, and in some individuals on the dorsal body scales and the breast scales. The breast scales may have tubercles as thick as sandpaper. Tuberculation appears in the larger young-of-year in October, and is retained throughout life.

Sexual dimorphism: In mature male, the space between the end of the pectoral fin and the origin of the pelvic fin is usually 1 mm or less; in female, 2 mm or more. In the male, the long pelvic fins usually extend posterior to the tip of the anal papilla; in females, the pelvic fins are anterior to or barely reach the tip of the anal papilla.

SYSTEMATIC NOTES

Hybopsis aestivalis is the only species in the subgenus *Extrarius*. This species is composed of six nominal subspecies: *Hybopsis aestivalis aestivalis* (Girard) of clear Rio Grande River tributaries, *H. a. hyostomus* (Gilbert) of streams east of the Mississippi River, *H. a. marconis* (Gilbert) of the San Marcos River, *H. a. sterletus* (Cope) of the Rio Grande River proper, *H. a. tetranemus* (Gilbert) of the Arkansas River, and *H. a. australis* (Hubbs and Ortenburger) of the Red River of Oklahoma–Texas (Davis and Miller 1967).

Ascribed to Wisconsin is the large-eyed form *H. a. hyostomus*, which inhabits relatively clear waters and possesses a single pair of relatively short barbels.

Small-eyed forms, *H. a. tetranemus* and *H. a. australis*, inhabit turbid waters and may have one or two pairs of barbels. *H. a. australis* in the upper Red River always has two pairs of long barbels. Specimens are sometimes found with three barbels on one side (B. Davis, pers. comm.), although as many as seven have been reported. It has been suggested that barbel development was a recent compensatory adaptation for reduced vision in turbid habitats.

DISTRIBUTION, STATUS, AND HABITAT

The speckled chub occurs in the Mississippi River upstream to its junction with the Chippewa River, and in the Wisconsin River upstream to near Wisconsin Dells. It is an inhabitant of large rivers, but is occasionally taken in medium-sized tributaries to these rivers.

Greene (1935) collected this species from the Mississippi River, and once from the Wisconsin River basin, where he found it only in Otter Creek, about 1 mi north of Clyde in Iowa County. Since then it appears to have expanded its range upstream in the Wisconsin River. The possibility exists that it may cross into the Lake Michigan drainage basin via the Fox-Wisconsin canal at Portage.

In Wisconsin, the speckled chub is at the northern limits of its range. It varies in abundance from year to year. Starrett (1951) suggested that this variation is related to the success or failure of the yearly breeding cycle. He noted that a change in the time of floods from spring and early summer to midsummer, when spawning occurs, might have a drastic effect on this species. Starrett also gave evidence that a very limited population of speckled chubs can produce a large population the following year. Other factors influencing speckled chub numbers are the population densities of other fishes and the amount of space available.

In Wisconsin, the speckled chub is generally un-

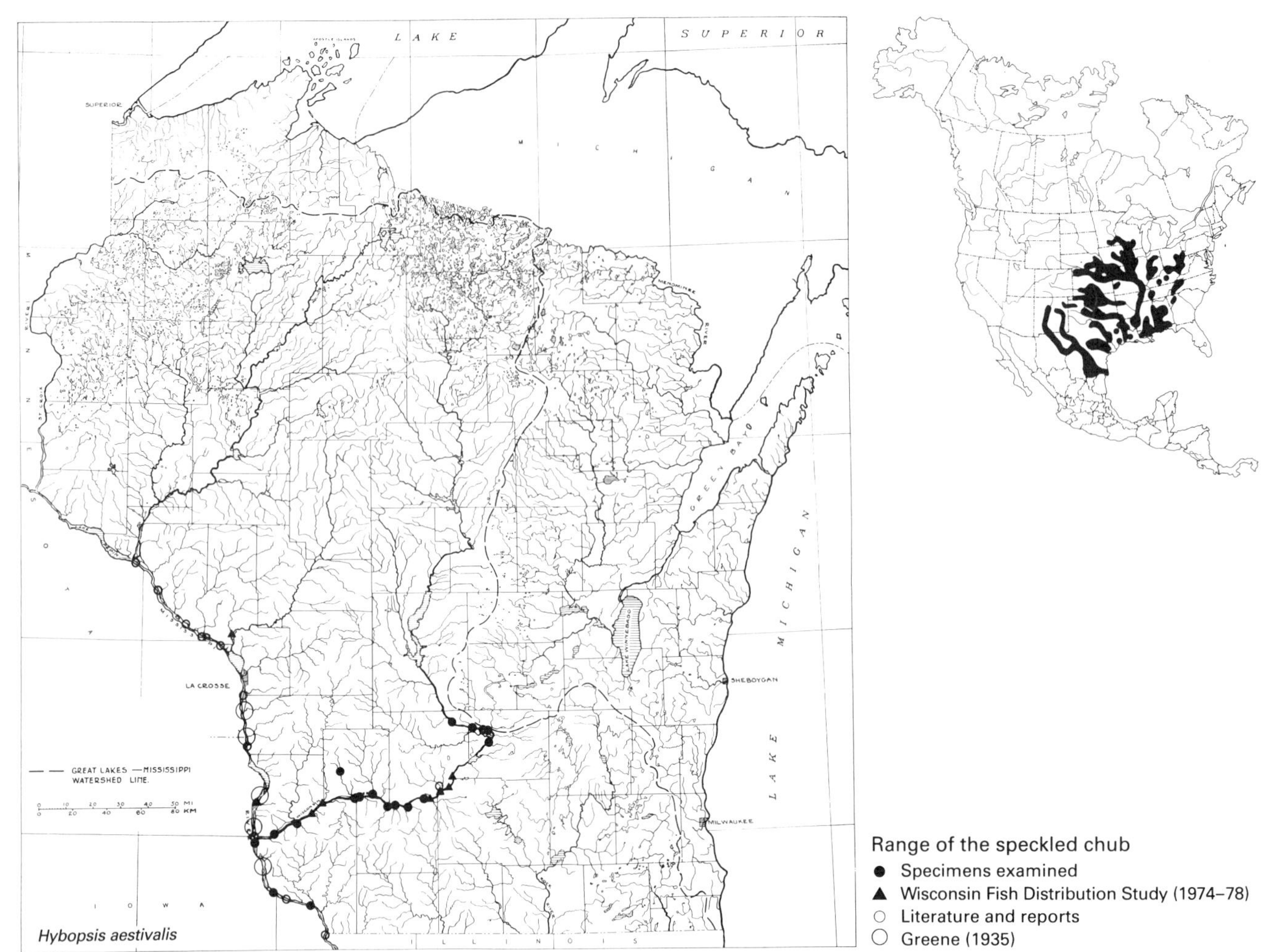

Range of the speckled chub
● Specimens examined
▲ Wisconsin Fish Distribution Study (1974–78)
○ Literature and reports
◯ Greene (1935)

common in the lower Wisconsin and Mississippi rivers and in the lower portions of their larger tributaries. It has been given threatened status (Les 1979).

In Wisconsin, the speckled chub was encountered most frequently in broad, shallow riffles over substrates of sand (62% frequency), mud (23%), clay (8%), and gravel (8%). Once it was taken from a hard, sand-bottomed slough. It occurs in rivers generally over 50 m wide; it has been found twice in streams 12–24 m wide. At collection sites, aquatic vegetation is generally lacking, and the water is slightly turbid to turbid.

BIOLOGY

Spawning begins in May or June and continues sporadically into August. In Kansas, Cross (1967) noted that the reproductive period seems long, inasmuch as tuberculate males and egg-laden females have been taken from late May through August, always when water temperatures exceeded 21.1°C (70°F).

In the Wisconsin River (Iowa County) on 3 August, a speckled chub 61 mm TL, 1.73 g, had ovaries 12.2% of the total weight which contained 796 mature yellow eggs 0.9 (0.7–1.0) mm diam, and white, immature eggs 0.2 (0.1–0.3) mm diam. On 8 August, a female 55 mm TL, 1.38 g, had ovaries 9.4% of the body weight which contained 559 eggs, about half of which were mature, and which were 0.7 (0.65–0.8) mm diam. On the latter date a number of females had soft abdomens, suggesting that they may have spawned recently; some females still bore a number of mature eggs 0.8 mm diam. In September, females were without ripe eggs.

Spawning occurs around noon, and the eggs are broadcast by the females in the deeper part of the stream current (Bottrell et al.1964). The fertilized eggs are only slightly heavier than water; they develop as they drift in the currents. Hatching time is about 23 hr after blastula formation. The larvae are completely transparent, with no visible pigmentation. In the laboratory, newly hatched larvae swam upward in a spiral fashion, sank to a depth of several centimeters, or to the bottom of the tank then repeated the process. They began to feed 2–3 days after hatching.

Juvenile speckled chubs do not form schools. They feed aggressively, and grow rapidly—19 mm (0.75 in) in three weeks. Most of the food is taken from the bottom, or as it falls through the water; no food is taken from the surface.

The growth of young-of-year speckled chubs follows:

Date	No. of Fish	TL (mm) Avg	Range	Location
16 July	5	27.8	27.0–29.3	Mississippi R. (Grant Co.)
20 Sept.	18	35.0	30.0–37.5	Wisconsin R. (Columbia Co.)
21 Sept.	21	34.3	30.5–37.0	Wisconsin R. (Sauk Co.)
24 Sept.	12	34.4	29.0–38.0	Wisconsin R. (Grant Co.)
21 Oct.	12	38.0	35.0–41.0	Wisconsin R. (Grant Co.)

The speckled chub is short-lived, seldom surviving more than 1.5 years. Reproduction is accomplished by year-old fish. Of 195 age-I speckled chubs collected 8 August 1962 from the Wisconsin River (Iowa County), the 109 males were 47.3 (43–54) mm TL; the 86 females were 52.2 (45–61.5) mm TL. In Iowa, age-I fish in May were 18–53 mm SL; in July, 24–49 mm SL; and in October, 34–51 mm SL (Starrett 1951). In Ohio, Trautman (1957) reported 46–76 mm TL for breeding adults. The maximum size reported for this species in Ohio (Trautman 1957) has been 76 mm (3 in) TL. B. Davis (pers. comm.) reported a 73.1-mm SL specimen from the Rio Grande at Albuquerque, "which would make the New Mexico specimen something over 80 mm TL."

Adult speckled chubs have seldom been captured in Wisconsin collections at the end of September, which implies a decrease through mortality. On the other hand, the young-of-year begin to appear in numbers at that time.

The diet of the speckled chub consists mostly of immature aquatic insects. In 22 speckled chubs collected 8 August from the Wisconsin River (Iowa County), the following food items were identified: Trichoptera, Hemiptera, Odonata, Coleoptera, cycloid fish scales, and debris. Ten digestive tracts were empty (F. Camenzind, pers. comm.).

In Iowa, this species has been classified as a Diptera feeder (Starrett 1950b). During the summer it consumed Diptera larvae and adults, Ephemeroptera nymphs, Trichoptera larvae, Corixidae, larvae and adults of terrestrial insects and small amounts of plant material. In addition, Entomostraca appeared in several stomachs during the winter.

Aquarium feeding behavior was reported by Davis and Miller (1967):

> Occasionally, they would stop and turn to pick up materials from the bottom. Cutaneous taste buds on the barbels, fins, and body probably had detected the food. After a short interval, small quantities of sand were ejected from the mouth. Introduction of live *Daphnia* sp. elicited no response until the *Daphnia* touched or swam close to the fish. When dry food was introduced, no response occurred until it had sunk almost to the bottom. Usually at this point, the nearest fish would initiate a rapid searching movement with pectorals spread widely and barbels in contact with the sand. Almost immediately, other fish began the same behavior. Whether this resulted from activity of the first fish or independent detection of food is not known. When live and dry food were introduced simultaneously, fish began feeding on the dry food first, perhaps because of the rapid diffusion of strong sapid materials from the dry food. Feeding behavior in [this species] is primarily taste oriented, although vision may play an important role in securing food close to the head. Fish were kept in aquaria for over three months with no apparent change from taste to sight feeding, even though the water was clear at all times.

Davis and Miller described and illustrated the brain morphology for most subspecies of *H. aestivalis*. They noted many taste buds on barbels, and compound taste buds in the first interradial membrane of the pectoral fins. In a bottom-dwelling fish, chemoreceptors on the pectoral fins would greatly increase the sensory area, and thus increase the efficiency of energy expenditure during food searching behavior. The speckled chub has numerous taste buds in the pharyngeal region, undoubtedly for efficient food sorting. Behavioral observations by Davis and Miller (1967) revealed a sustained "chewing motion" by this chub, after which expulsion of material was noted. No behavioral differences were detected among the observed subspecies.

The speckled chub is adapted for bottom dwelling by possession of a depressed body, elongate snout, subterminal mouth, well-developed barbels, and large pectoral fins. It exhibits more morphological plasticity than any other species in the genus *Hybopsis*, probably because of its highly variable habitat preferences. It is found in both clear and turbid waters.

The speckled chub is sedentary, resting quietly on the stream bottom when not moving about in search of food (Pflieger 1975). Trautman (1957) noted that it usually remains in waters more than 1.2 m (4 ft) deep during the day, especially if the waters are clear, and ventures into the shallows only on dark nights. On three nights specimens were collected in shallow water until the bright moon began to shine, after which none could be taken.

This minnow uses the channel of a river more than other minnows do (Starrett 1950a). During the winter of 1946–1947 it continued to use the river channel of the Des Moines River at Fraser (Iowa) even though it was not covered with ice; other species of minnows at this station in winter were seldom collected from the ice-free channel.

The speckled chub frequently inhabits fast water over shifting sand bottoms, where it is easily overlooked because such a barren habitat is seldom productive to the seiner. It is here, however, that one may expect to encounter the speckled chub, as well as the western sand darter, a common fish associate. Eddy and Underhill (1974), noting the difficulty in getting speckled chub specimens, observed that "the shifting sand is so loose that it is difficult to seine, and the little chub apparently dives into the sand when disturbed."

In the Wisconsin River (Iowa County) 270 speckled chubs were associated with the following species: quillback (4), shorthead redhorse (2), bullhead minnow (62), emerald shiner (16), spotfin shiner (320), river shiner (7), bigmouth shiner (4), brassy minnow (1), western sand darter (9), johnny darter (4), bluegill (1), and brook silverside (8).

IMPORTANCE AND MANAGEMENT

Game fish in deeper waters may prey upon speckled chubs to meet their energy requirements.

In Wisconsin the speckled chub is little known. It frequents waters which are not normally sampled by fishermen. Minnow seiners avoid the sand riffles of large rivers, since minnow species seldom occur there in any numbers. The speckled chub is small and lacks the showiness of minnows desirable for fishing, although it is of some value as bait and forage in New Mexico (Koster 1957).

Suckermouth Minnow

Phenacobius mirabilis (Girard). *Phenacobius*—deceptive, life (its appearance suggests an herbivorous species with long intestines, which it really is not); *mirabilis*—wonderful.

Other common names: sucker-mouthed minnow, plains suckermouth minnow, sucker-mouth dace.

Adult male (tuberculate) 76 mm, Trout Cr. (Crawford Co.), 11 July 1962

Adult female 69 mm, Trout Cr. (Crawford Co.), 11 July 1962

DESCRIPTION

Body slender, almost cylindrical. Average length 76 mm (3 in). TL = 1.22 SL. Depth into TL 5.1–5.9. Head length into TL 4.9–5.3. Snout bluntly rounded and extending beyond ventral mouth. Upper lip thick and lower lip with prominent lateral lobes ("fiddlehead"). Mouth extending to below nostril; barbel absent. Pharyngeal teeth 4–4, slender, slightly hooked to not hooked at all. Eye small, into head length 4.2–5.0. Gill rakers short, conical to irregular, knoblike; about 9. Dorsal fin origin anterior to origin of pelvic fin; dorsal fin rays 8; anal fin rays 7(6); pectoral fin rays 14; pelvic fin rays 8. Lateral line scales 43–51; lateral line complete, slightly decurved. Digestive tract short, S-shaped, 0.6–0.7 TL. Chromosomes 2n = 50 (W. LeGrande, pers. comm.).

Back dark olive with dark edges to scale pockets; dusky lateral stripe ending in a prominent black, elongated, basicaudal spot; lower sides and belly silvery white. Pectoral, dorsal, and caudal fins darkly pigmented, especially in adult males; other fins whitish. Breeding males brightly covered with an iridescent blue and silver pigmentation (Eddy and Underhill 1974). Peritoneum silvery with scattered dark speckles.

Breeding male with minute tubercles over top of head and opercles, dorsolateral scales, and on rays of pectoral, pelvic, dorsal and anal fins. Breeding female occasionally lightly tuberculate on top of head.

Sexual dimorphism: In male, pelvic fins reaching or almost reaching anus; in female, a considerable gap between end of pelvic fin and anus. Pectoral fins in male, large, broad, and fan-shaped; in female, small, narrow, and elongate.

DISTRIBUTION, STATUS, AND HABITAT

In Wisconsin, the suckermouth minnow occurs only in the Mississippi River drainage basin, primarily in the nonglaciated southwestern quarter of the state. Since 1930, using the Mississippi River as a connective, it appears to have expanded northward into Buffalo County. In the Rock River basin it has expanded through the southern tier of counties. Greene (1935) noted that the distribution of this species in Wisconsin is typical of stream fishes with a southern center of distribution which have entered Wisconsin through the Mississippi River and its tributaries, and have found the streams of the driftless area favorable habitats.

The suckermouth minnow is uncommon to common in tributaries to the lower Wisconsin and Mississippi rivers. With the modification of streams as a result of farming, this species has been spreading its range and multiplying. The extension of its range has been documented for Indiana and Ohio (Trautman 1957), and is occurring in Wisconsin. After first invading a locality, the suckermouth minnow often becomes unusually abundant; as it becomes a permanent part of the fish population its numbers decrease noticeably. This phenomenon is illustrated in the streams of the lower Rock River basin, where 20 to 80 specimens of suckermouth minnows per collection are common.

The suckermouth minnow is primarily a riffle fish which prefers warm streams with moderate or low gradients. In Wisconsin, it was encountered most frequently at depths of 0.6–1.5 m over substrates of gravel (38% frequency), rubble (17%), sand (13%), silt (13%), clay (10%), mud (9%), and boulders (1%). It occurred in streams of the following widths: 1.0–3.0 m (22%), 3.1–6.0 m (44%), 6.1–12.0 m (24%), and 12.1–24.0 m (10%). The suckermouth is present in clear waters, but occurs in the greatest numbers in

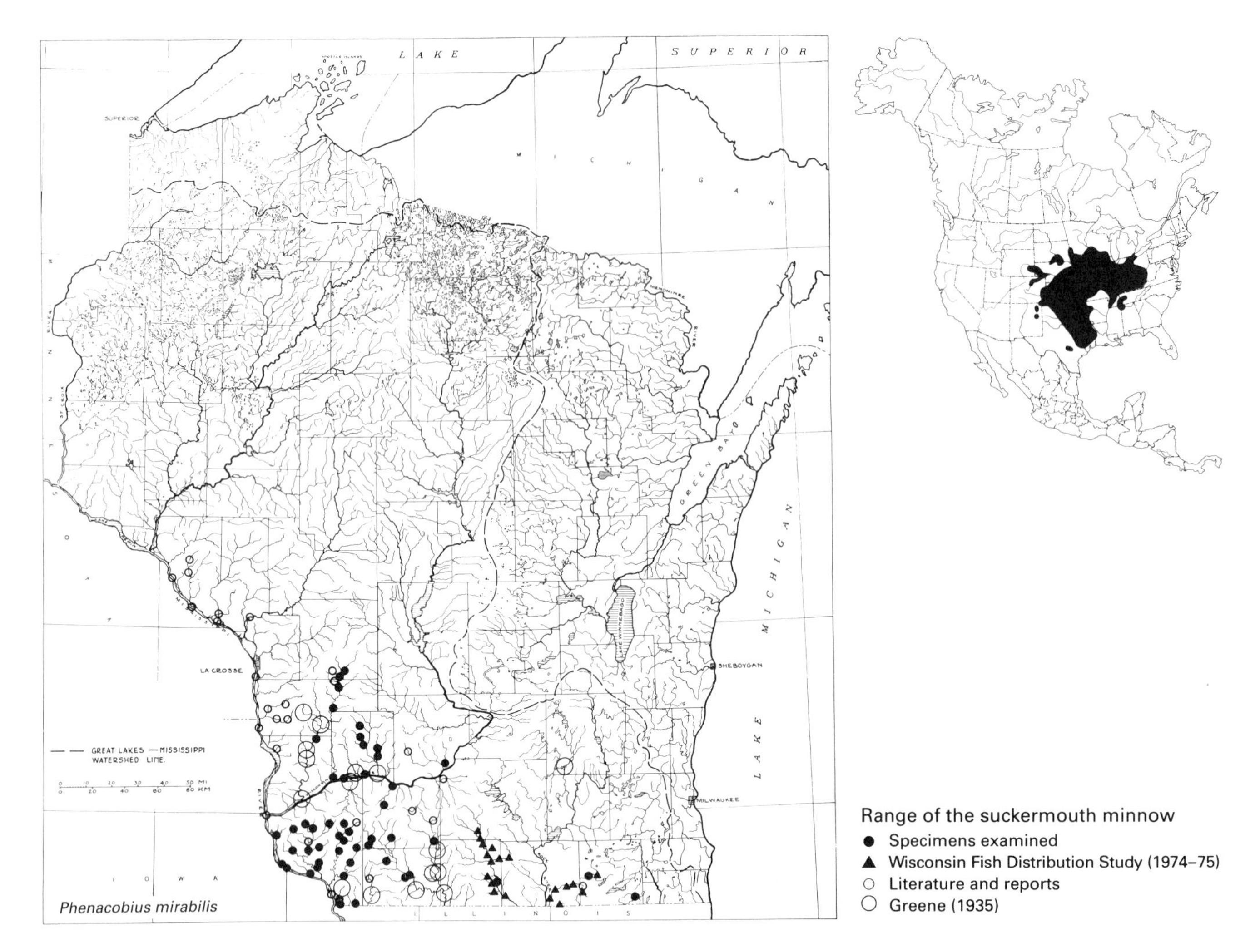

highly turbid waters, and is seldom associated with instream vegetation.

In Ohio (Trautman 1957), this species selects riffles of streams whose waters are usually turbid and rich in organic material, and whose gradients are sufficiently high so that the gravel on the riffles remains comparatively free from silt. It usually reaches large population densities in large streams and rivers, especially when competitive pressure from other riffle species is low. Populations are low or absent in the clearest streams, in streams of high gradients, and in normally turbid streams whose gradients are too low to prevent silt accumulations from covering the stones on the riffles.

BIOLOGY

In Wisconsin, spawning extends at least from early July to the end of August, although males with breeding tubercles have been taken from June into mid-September. The wide range in size of young-of-year implies a long spawning season. In Kansas (Cross 1967), the suckermouth minnow has a longer reproductive period than any other riffle fish; specimens bearing tubercles and having enlarged gonads have been taken in all months from April through August. Cross has suggested that during this 5-month period males remain reproductively active, and that females spawn two or more times.

In Oklahoma (Cross 1950), suckermouth minnows in spawning condition were taken at water temperatures of 14–25°C (57.2–77°F). Nothing is known about the spawning site of this species, or about its reproductive behavior; it is surmised to spawn on gravelly riffles.

In Wisconsin, gravid females were collected from a branch of the Platte River (Grant County) on 20 July 1962. A 90-mm fish with ovaries 24% of total weight held an estimated 1,640 orange-yellow, ripe eggs 1.3 mm diam. A second generation of yellow, immature eggs 0.8 mm diam numbered less than one-fourth the number of mature eggs. A 91-mm fish with ovaries 12% of total weight held 830 mature eggs 1.25

mm diam; immature eggs were 0.7 mm diam, and numbered approximately one-third the number of mature eggs.

The growth of young-of-year in Wisconsin has been reported as follows:

Date	No. of Fish	TL (mm) Avg	Range	Location
10 Aug.	7	43	37–47	McCartney Br. (Grant Co.)
14 Aug.	34	41.2	27–47	Little Platte R. (Grant Co.)
14 Sept.	2	43	36–50	Kickapoo R. (Monroe Co.)
15 Sept.	1	54		Kickapoo R. (Vernon Co.)
21 Sept.	2	41.5	41–42	Otter Cr. (Sauk Co.)

The fish in this sample probably represent the largest young-of-year present at the time the collection was made, since the gear used (6 mm-mesh seine) selected larger fish over smaller individuals.

Suckermouth minnows from Kuenster Creek (Grant County), collected 9 August 1962, showed the following growth:

Age Class	No. of Fish	TL (mm) Avg	Range	Calculated TL at Annulus (mm) 1	2	3
I	4	46.8	42–50	34.8		
II	20	78.5	73–87	35.9	61.0	
III	9	90.0	79–104	37.4	62.0	85.2
Avg (weighted)				36.2	61.3	85.2

Suckermouth minnows mature at age II. The largest specimen, 122 mm (4.8 in), was reported by Trautman (1957).

The food of suckermouth minnows is composed largely of aquatic dipteran larvae and caddisfly larvae; at times bottom ooze, detritus, and plant material make up a small part of stomach contents (Eddy and Underhill 1974, Stegman 1969, Starrett 1950b, Forbes and Richardson 1920). The suckermouth minnow, which lives on the bottom, obtains its food by rooting in gravel and rocks with its sensitive snout and lips (Pflieger 1975). In the aquarium the suckermouth minnow rests on the sand like a darter, supported by its pectoral fins; the head moves gently up and down with the opening and closing of the gills (Forbes and Richardson 1920).

In the Little Platte River (Grant County), 39 suckermouth minnows were associated with the following species: shorthead redhorse (1), white sucker (57), common carp (1), central stoneroller (73), blacknose dace (1), hornyhead chub (64), creek chub (1), bluntnose minnow (11), common shiner (21), sand shiner (8), bigmouth shiner (2), logperch (10), johnny darter (4), fantail darter (1), and smallmouth bass (9).

IMPORTANCE AND MANAGEMENT

In Iowa, the suckermouth minnow is used extensively as bait by anglers (Harlan and Speaker 1956). In Wisconsin, it is far too uncommon to be of any consequence as a bait or forage fish.

Pallid Shiner

Notropis amnis Hubbs and Greene. *Notropis*—back, keel; *amnis*—of the river.

Adult 57 mm, Mississippi R., Wyalusing (Grant Co.), 15 July 1962

Adult (note well-defined lateral stripe) about 64 mm, Mississippi R. (Grant Co.), 10 Aug. 1976

DESCRIPTION

Body slender and fragile, moderately compressed laterally. Average length 51 mm (2 in). TL = 1.31 SL. Depth into TL 5.7–6.3. Head length into TL 4.8–5.4. Snout blunt, extending beyond upper lip. Mouth almost horizontal, small, reaching below posterior nostril; the upper jaw extending posteriorly beyond the corner of mouth, usually fleshless and completely concealed beneath the suborbital; barbels absent. Eye into head length 2.7–3.4. Pharyngeal teeth 1,4–4,1, short, hooked at tip, cutting edge short. Gill rakers about 5 small knobs near union of upper and lower limbs of first gill arch. Dorsal fin origin below or slightly in advance of pelvic fin origin. Dorsal fin high and pointed with anterior rays much elongated, almost as long as or longer than predorsal distance; dorsal fin rays 8; anal fin rays 8 (9); pectoral fin rays 12 (11–14); pelvic fin rays 8 (7). Scales highly deciduous; lateral line scales 34–37; lateral line complete.

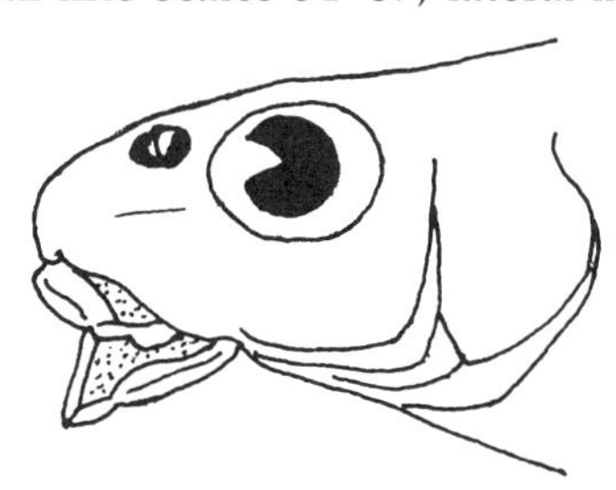

Mouth arrangement of the pallid shiner (after Douglas 1974:119)

Digestive tract short with a single S-shaped loop about 0.5 TL.

Back pale olive yellow, the scale pockets faintly dark at the edges; sides silvery, belly silvery white, fins unpigmented. A faint lateral stripe of stipplelike dots around tip of snout and behind eye, ending at the base of caudal fin. Mid-dorsal stripe of faint striations, sometimes absent. Peritoneum silvery, occasionally with a few dark speckles.

Breeding male with tubercles on cheek, branchiostegal rays, and along pectoral fin rays.

SYSTEMATIC NOTES

Notropis amnis is accredited to Hubbs and Greene (Greene 1935). A thorough review of this species' status appeared in Hubbs (1951b). The holotype (UMMZ 75435), an adult 43 mm SL, was seined by L.P. Schultz and C.M. Tarzwell on 27 August 1928 in a channel of the Mississippi River, 1 mile north of Prairie du Chien (Crawford County). Hubbs recognized two subspecies: northern pallid shiner, *Notropis amnis amnis*, and southwestern pallid shiner, *Notropis amnis pinnosa*. The former occurs in the Wisconsin, Minnesota, Iowa, northern Illinois, and northern Missouri sectors of the Mississippi River and its tributaries.

Hubbs noted that *Notropis amnis* most closely resembles *Hybopsis amblops*, but called attention to the absence of barbels in the pallid shiner, and a mouth structure quite unlike that in *H. amblops*. The immediate relationships of the pallid shiner within the genus are not apparent, and it may be made the type of a distinct subgenus when *Notropis* receives a much needed general revision.

DISTRIBUTION, STATUS, AND HABITAT

In Wisconsin the pallid shiner occurs in the Mississippi River and the lower parts of its major tributaries. It reaches its northern limit of distribution in Wisconsin.

Specimens examined: UWSP 1476 (1) Mississippi River at Wyalusing (Grant County) 1966; UWSP 1555 (5) Mississippi River above Fountain City (Buffalo County) 1946; UWSP 2671 (1) Mississippi River at Wyalusing (Grant County) 1962; UWSP 2672 (1) Wisconsin River T6N R5W Sec 6 (Grant County) 1962; UWSP 3150 (1) Mississippi River above Red Wing dike, Minnesota, 1947; UWSP 3223 (17) Mississippi River above Potosi (Grant County) 1946; UWSP 4884 (1) Mississippi River at Wyalusing (Grant County) 1963; UWSP 3273 (1) Mississippi River 2.4 km north of the Iowa-Minnesota line, Minnesota, 1969; and UWSP 5673 (8) Mississippi River at Cassville Slough (Grant County) 1976.

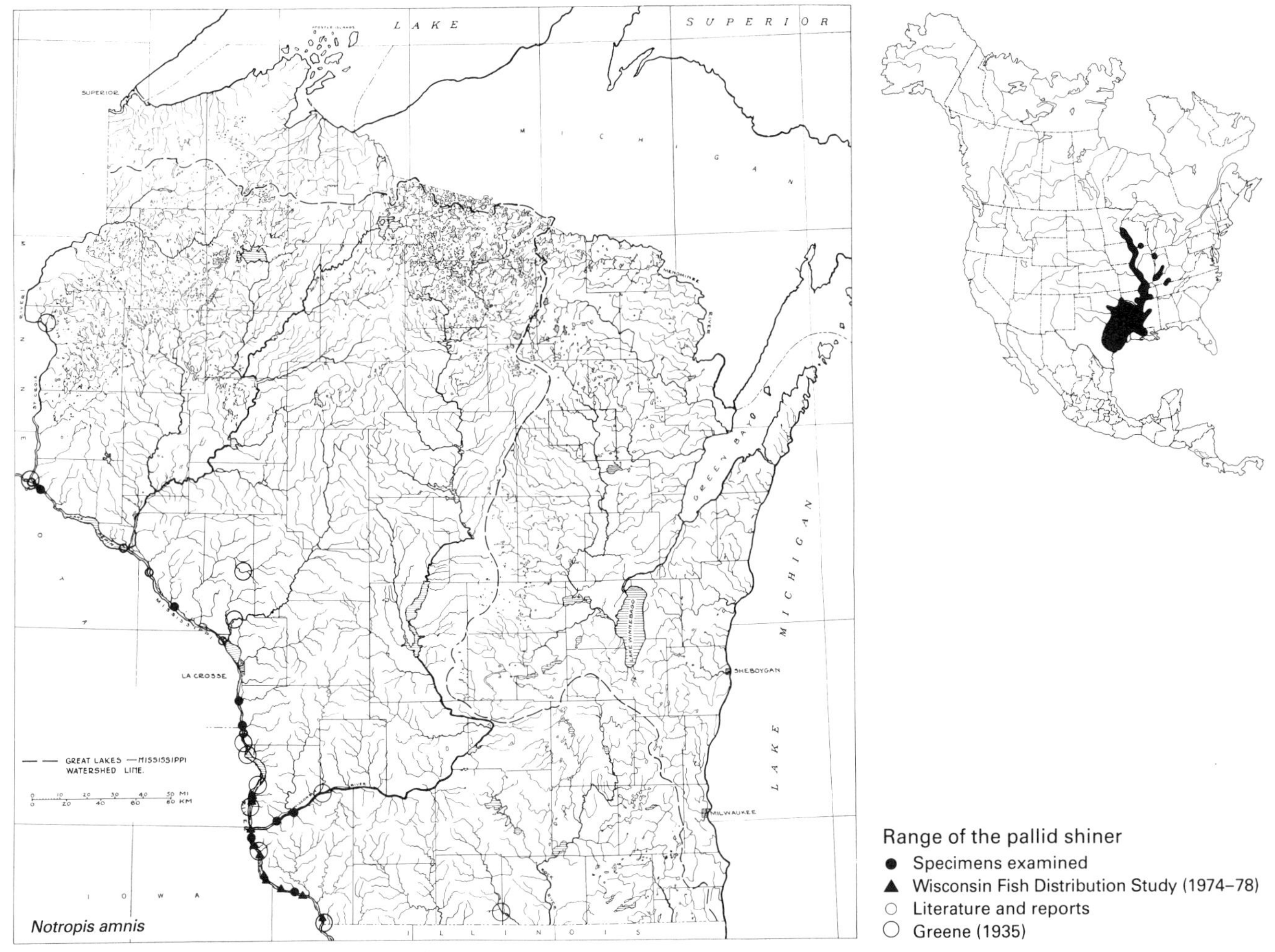

Range of the pallid shiner
● Specimens examined
▲ Wisconsin Fish Distribution Study (1974–78)
○ Literature and reports
◯ Greene (1935)

In 1976, the Wisconsin Fish Distribution Study reported 23 collections of pallid shiners from the Mississippi River between T1N R2W Sec 29 (southern Grant County) and T8N R7W Sec 36 (southern Crawford County). The Upper Mississippi River Conservation Committee reported supplemental records from Pools 3, 4, 5, 9, and 11 (P. W. Smith et al. 1971). Four specimens were seined from the Mississippi River near Brownsville (Houston County), Minnesota, in 1965 (Phillips and Underhill 1967).

The status of the northern populations of this species is a matter of concern. According to Hubbs (1951b), the pallid shiner appears to be a rare species, except for isolated local populations; it may be headed toward extirpation. In the upper Mississippi River it constitutes less than 1% of the minnow population. It is rare in Minnesota, where it has been collected on only a few occasions (Eddy and Underhill 1974). In Illinois, this species has endangered status (Lopinot and Smith 1973). In Missouri it was widespread in the eastern part of the state as recently as the early 1940s, but no specimens have been taken since 1956 in spite of collectors' efforts (Pflieger 1975). No other Missouri fish has shown such a marked decline in abundance and according to Pflieger it probably is on the verge of being eliminated from the state, if it has not already gone.

In Wisconsin, the range of the pallid shiner appears to have shrunk since 1930. Greene (1935) recorded it not only from the Mississippi River and the lower Wisconsin River, but also from their tributaries—i.e., the Black and Trempealeau rivers (Trempealeau County), and the Sugar River (Green County). In spite of intensive collecting in these and adjacent waters from 1958 through 1978, the pallid shiner has been captured only in the mainstem of the Mississippi River and the lower Wisconsin River; this suggests a loss of range.

The number of recent records (1958–1978) of the pallid shiner in the Mississippi River from Vernon to Grant counties implies a stable, but low-level, population in that sector of the river. In Wisconsin, the pallid shiner is accorded threatened status (Wis. Dep. Nat. Resour. Endangered Species Com. 1975, Les 1979).

In Wisconsin, the pallid shiner has been taken over sand and mud in sloughs, over sandbars with slow-moving water, and from impoundments without current. In Iowa, it is reported in flowing water over sandbars (Harlan and Speaker 1956).

In its northern distribution through the central United States, the pallid shiner is confined mainly to the larger lowland rivers; in the south, it more commonly inhabits small- to medium-sized streams (Hubbs 1951b). Avoidance of the excessive turbidity of the main streams in the south may be the chief factor in this differential habitat selection, but temperature is perhaps also involved. In the north, this essentially southwestern species avoids the smaller streams, which are generally cooler, and may find only the larger waters sufficiently warm.

BIOLOGY

Nothing is known about the spawning or feeding habits of the pallid shiner.

I have attempted to age pallid shiners by reading scales. In a number of specimens, no scales were available which could be used for aging, since the scales are deciduous; in other specimens, the scales still intact were often replacement scales, which are useless for aging purposes. Therefore the following data on age and growth in the pallid shiner are tentative.

Young-of-year attained a growth of 30–32.5 mm TL by 4 November in Pool 5A of the Mississippi River (Buffalo County). In seven pallid shiners 56–59.5 mm TL from the Mississippi River (Grant to Vernon counties), estimated lengths at the annuli were: 1—34 mm and 2—49 mm. The annulus appears to be deposited in July.

The condition (K_{TL}) of 10 pallid shiners from the Mississippi River during early August 1976 was 0.79 (range 0.74–0.85).

The largest Wisconsin specimen observed was 64.5 mm (2.5 in) TL. The largest specimens from Louisiana (Douglas 1974) were slightly over 70 mm (2.75 in).

Ecological information on this species is quite variable. In the pallid shiner's habitat aquatic vegetation is absent about as often as it is present, but it is occasionally recorded as dense (Hubbs 1951b). The habitat bottom varies from very soft mud to sand, gravel, or rock. The summer temperatures recorded for the pallid shiner grade from "cold" (presumably meaning cool) to "warm," with two records of nearly 23°C (73.4°F) for the northern pallid shiner, and five or more averaging 33°C (91.4°F) for the southwestern pallid shiner. Reports on water currents favored by this species are about equally divided between "none" or "almost none" and "slow" to "rapid," with slow flows recorded most often. The delicate fins and skin and the moderately streamlined build of the pallid shiner indicate that it is adapted best for slow currents.

Records also indicate that the pallid shiner is tolerant of a wide range of turbidity (Hubbs 1951b). In waters where this fish is found reports are about equally divided between "clear" or "almost clear" and "moderately turbid" or "muddy," with a few locales noted as "murky" or "very muddy."

In the lower Wisconsin River 1 pallid shiner was associated with the following species: shortnose gar (1), longnose gar (1), gizzard shad (35), bigmouth buffalo (4), shorthead redhorse (1), common carp (5), bullhead minnow (83), bluntnose minnow (18), pugnose minnow (22), emerald shiner (4), spotfin shiner (519), spottail shiner (3), weed shiner (3), river shiner (9), sand shiner (4), Mississippi silvery minnow (30), trout-perch (1), white bass (34), yellow perch (2), western sand darter (4), logperch (2), johnny darter (53), smallmouth bass (3), largemouth bass (10), black crappie (273), white crappie (13), brook silverside (2), and freshwater drum (6).

IMPORTANCE AND MANAGEMENT

Nothing is known about the use made of the pallid shiner by man, game fish, or predatory birds.

Emerald Shiner

Notropis atherinoides Rafinesque. *Notropis*—back, keel; *atherinoides*—from *atherina*, silversidelike.

Other common names: lake shiner, Milwaukee shiner, lake emerald shiner, common emerald shiner, river emerald shiner, shiner, lake silverside, buckeye shiner, Lake Michigan shiner.

Adult 120 mm, L. Michigan (Kenosha Co.), 20 Mar. 1959

DESCRIPTION

Body slender, often fragile, strongly compressed laterally. Average length 51–76 mm (2–3 in). TL = 1.27 SL. Depth into TL 5.0–7.0. Head length into TL 4.7–5.8. Snout bluntly pointed. Mouth oblique, terminal, large, extending to below nostrils; barbel absent. Pharyngeal teeth usually 2,4–4,2, occasionally 1 tooth fewer in inner or outer row on one side; hooked, sturdy; strong arch. Gill rakers short, conical, 9–11. Eye into head length 2.9–3.8. Dorsal fin origin posterior to pelvic fin origin; dorsal fin rays 8; anal fin rays 11 (10–12); pectoral fin rays 13–17; pelvic fin rays 8 (axillary process sometimes present). Scales deciduous; lateral line scales 36–41; lateral line complete. Digestive tract short with a single S-shaped loop, 0.5–0.6 TL. Chromosomes 2n = 50 (J. Gold, pers. comm.).

Body silvery with blue-green to green on back, iridescent in living fish; sides silvery, belly silvery white. Young fragile and translucent. Fins clear. Peritoneum silvery with brown speckles. In preserved specimens, a dark lateral stripe posteriorly, vague anteriorly.

Breeding male with minute tubercles on pectoral fin rays 2–10. No brilliant colors during spawning; faint rosy pigment or none.

SYSTEMATIC NOTES

Hubbs and Lagler (1964) recognized two subspecies: the river emerald shiner, *Notropis a. atherinoides*, and the lake emerald shiner, *Notropis a. acutus*. The former is the typical form of large rivers and lakes; the latter is the typical form in Lake Michigan, intergrading in Lake Superior (at least about Isle Royale) with *N. a. atherinoides*. The lake emerald shiner is considered the small-headed, terete form.

A comparison of small collections from Lake Michigan, Lake Winnebago, and Pewaukee Lake failed to show significant differences. This species is quite plastic, and the recognition of subspecies at this state of our knowledge is unwarranted.

DISTRIBUTION, STATUS, AND HABITAT

The emerald shiner occurs in all three drainage basins in Wisconsin, and in Lakes Michigan and Superior. It is widely distributed in the larger waterways and lakes of central and southern Wisconsin, but it is absent from the northern sectors of the Lake Michigan and Mississippi River drainages, except for a few widely disjunct lakes in the latter.

The emerald shiner is common to abundant in the inland waters of Wisconsin. It is rare in Lake Michigan, and declining in Lake Superior (Parsons et al. 1975). See "Importance and Management" for historical details.

In the West, this species has become more common because of the establishment of reservoirs. The creation of the navigational pool system on the Mississippi River undoubtedly benefited the species.

The emerald shiner inhabits large lakes and rivers, and the lower reaches of streams tributary to such rivers. In Wisconsin, it was encountered most frequently in clear water at depths of 0.6–1.5 m, over substrates of sand (43% frequency), gravel (17%), mud (16%), silt (9%), rubble (6%), clay (5%), and boulders (4%). It occurred more frequently in stagnant and slow-moving water than in riffles, in streams of the following widths: 3.1–6.0 m (5%), 6.1–12.0 m (17%), 12.1–24.0 m (54%), 24.1–50.0 m (22%), and more than 50 m (2%). The low numbers of this species recovered from the largest rivers is not an indication of low populations as much as of its unavailability. In large waters this species is at middepths or at the surface, where it is less vulnerable to the seine—hence the low frequency of recovery from main stem rivers. The emerald shiner frequents open waters. Vegetation does not appear to be an important requirement—many collections have been taken from areas totally devoid of vegetation.

BIOLOGY

The emerald shiner is a summer spawner. Spawning may occur in Wisconsin as early as late May, and extends to the beginning of August, although the major spawning period is in June and July. Gravid females appear in the lower Wisconsin River in June, and by August most females are spent.

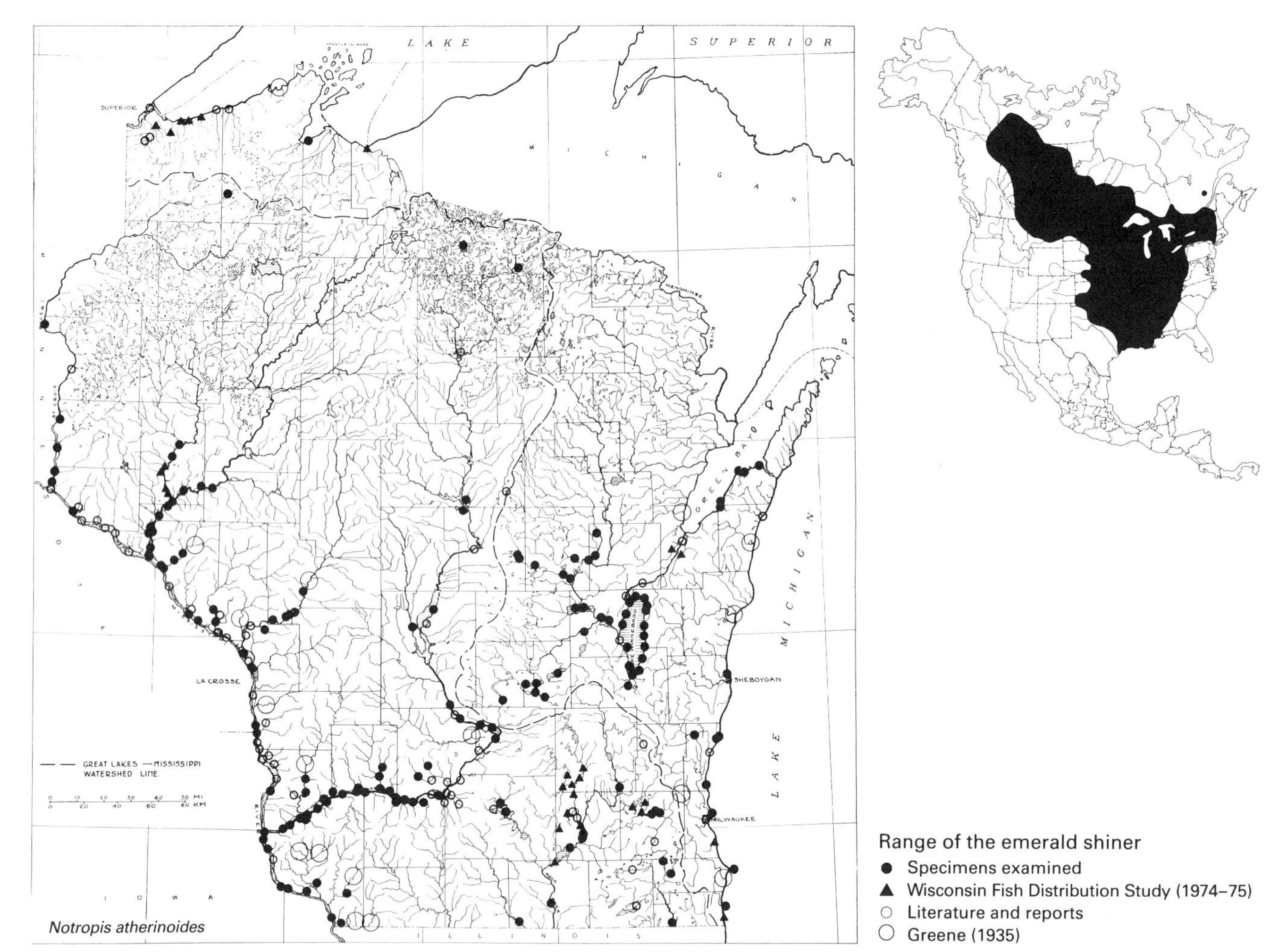

Notropis atherinoides

Range of the emerald shiner
● Specimens examined
▲ Wisconsin Fish Distribution Study (1974–75)
○ Literature and reports
◯ Greene (1935)

Spawning is temperature dependent. It begins not long after the 22.2°C (72°F) threshold temperature is exceeded (Flittner 1964). In southern Canada, gravid females were taken from water temperatures ranging from 20.1 to 23.2°C (68.2 to 73.8°F) (Campbell and MacCrimmon 1970). The spawning substrate is normally gravel shoals (Dobie et al. 1956), although rounded boulders, coarse rubble and sand (Campbell and MacCrimmon 1970), and hard sand or mud swept clean of detritus (Flittner 1964) are also used. Spawning occurs offshore at night at depths of 2–6 m (7–20 ft), in spawning schools that may number millions of fish in a given area. Flittner (1964:73–74) noted:

> The shiners first appear about 1 to 2 feet below the surface, milling and darting rapidly and erratically in a circular path. The smaller males appear to pursue the larger females for a few seconds at a time. As these pairs swim about in a 10- to 20-foot circle, the male overtakes the female and presses closely on either the right or left side, in what appears to be an interlocking of pectoral fins. The pair gyrates a second or two, and then slows down as the female arches her side upward producing the "flash" visible to the observer. As the pair arches together, it stops for an instant, rolling over further, after which either the female or both sound, diving out of view. Several males were observed to dart from one female at the instant of rolling and assume a similar mating position near another female; thus they may repeat the process several times.
>
> Emission of sex products appears to take place at the instant of rolling. However, the turbidity of the water, the darkness, and the lack of a diagnostic milky color in the male spermatic fluid made verification impossible.

Since the spawning of the emerald shiner in any body of water lasts for several weeks, each fish may spawn more than once. Mature females contain eggs in two stages of development (Fuchs 1967). Fuchs and Flittner concluded that post spawning mortality of the emerald shiner is severe in Lewis and Clark Lake (South Dakota) and in Lake Erie.

In the Wisconsin River (Richland County) on 27 June 1962, an age-I female 69 mm TL, with ripe ovaries constituting 33% of total weight, contained an estimated 2,990 mature yellow eggs 0.9 mm diam. Immature white eggs were also present—about one-fourth the number of mature eggs. A female (probably age II) 75 mm TL, taken 17 July 1962 from the Wisconsin River (Crawford County), held an estimated 2,040 mature eggs averaging 0.8 mm diam.

The fertilized nonadhesive eggs sink to the bottom, where they hatch in 24–32 hr. Flittner (1964) discussed embryonic development in detail. At hatching the young fish is about 4 mm; at 4.9 mm the estimated age is 30 hr; at 6.1 mm, 90–96 hr; and at 8.9 mm, about 11 days. Prolarvae remain near the bottom for 72–96 hr; during this period their swimming movements are directionless. At about 96 hr they become free-swimming postlarvae. Most are planktonic in the upper 2 m of water, and are therefore subject to drifting with downstream water movement or wind-induced currents. The fry gather in enormous schools, and may often be seen on the surface in the center of a lake, where they move about and feed.

M. Fish (1932) noted that in Lake Erie net tows from 2 July to 20 August contained from 1 to 500 young emerald shiners. She described and illustrated the 4.9–13.5-mm stages. On the lower Wisconsin River (Grant County), young-of-year 30–37 mm TL appeared in collections taken in the middle of July. By the middle of August they were 30–49 mm long; in mid-October, 38–60 mm long. In Lake Winnebago, young-of-year were 19–46 mm in mid-July; Priegel (1960) recorded 16–41-mm lengths in August, 26–51-mm lengths in September, and 28–53 (avg 40.1)-mm lengths in October.

A sample of emerald shiners from the Wisconsin River (Crawford County), collected 18 August 1966, was aged by scales:

Age Class	No. of Fish	TL (mm)		Calculated TL at Annulus (mm)		
		Avg	Range	1	2	3
0	4	42.8	38–45			
I	16	50.4	45–61	37.4		
II	17	80.2	73–95	44.6	67.9	
III	6	91.8	89–97	41.1	67.8	89.2
Avg (weighted)				41.1	67.9	89.2

In this mid-August collection, the first annulus was in place, the second annulus had been deposited in some of the age-II fish, and the third annulus was just being placed.

In Lake Erie (Flittner 1964), very rapid growth has been observed; it averaged 63 mm in the first year, 91 mm in the second, 104 mm in the third, and none in the fourth year among the few surviving females collected. Females were of larger average sizes at each age than males. Also, females were longer lived than males; no males with 3 annuli on their scales were collected, but females with 3 annuli were relatively common. A small percentage of females lived to spawn in the fifth summer (age IV), but none survived beyond midseason. Flittner found that nearly all of the seasonal growth occurred in 90 days from June to September.

A large emerald shiner 124 mm (4.9 in) long (UWSP 2909) was collected from Lake Michigan at Kenosha in 1961.

Emerald shiners captured in St. Louis Bay, Lake Superior, began to feed when 5 mm long, and had absorbed the yolk-sac by the time they were 6 mm long (Siefert 1972). The rotifer *Trichocera* is the dominant food of first-feeding fish, and, along with other rotifers, it remains an important food of emerald shiners of all sizes. Other foods selected by young up to 12 mm long are: copepod nauplii, cladocerans, nonmotile green algae, blue-green algae, diatoms, and protozoans.

The food of older emerald shiners consists largely of insects, most of which are terrestrial (Dobie et al. 1956). Their diet includes entomostracans, algae, small fish, fish eggs, terrestrial insects, aquatic insects, and oligochaete worms. Studies by several workers show that, in general, the percentages of different foods consumed are as follows: water fleas 26.8%, algae 7.9%, water boatman 1.0%, mayflies 1.3%, caddisflies 2.1%, chironomids 9.7%, terrestrial insects 7.9%, miscellaneous insects 26.3%, fish eggs 2.9%, crustacean debris 10.7%, and miscellaneous 3.2%. The stomach contents of six emerald shiners from western Lake Superior were entirely mayfly larvae (Anderson and Smith 1971b). Alewife eggs and shiner scales were taken from the stomach of one emerald shiner, according to Edsall (1964).

In aquarium feeding experiments, this species fed on the food floating on the surface (Mendelson 1972). In spite of decreasing concentrations of food at the water surface, it continued to remain at the surface for some time before moving toward the bottom to feed on descending food particles and on bottom food.

The emerald shiner tends to remain in the midsection of deep water or on the bottom during the daytime whenever the water is clear, or when there are waves. It seldom, if ever, penetrates below the late-summer thermocline (normally from 11 to 15 m). It is typically a fish of the open waters, and most often is decidedly pelagic. In summer it comes to the surface at dark to feed upon the small midges and other flying insects that hover just above the water's surface (Trautman 1957, Raney 1969). Studies in Lake Winnebago bear out these movements; daylight bottom trawling captured numbers of emerald shiners, but night trawling seldom captured this species (Priegel 1960).

Differences in water temperature seem to strongly influence the seasonal distribution pattern of the emerald shiner. The preferred temperature of the species, as determined in a vertical temperature gradient tank, was 25°C (77°F) (Campbell and MacCrimmon 1970). The maximum temperature at which it was captured in the White River and the Ipalco Discharge Canal, Indiana, was 31.1°C (88°F) (Proffitt and Benda 1971).

In the spring, peak populations of emerald shiners move up Roxbury Creek (Dane County), a small tributary (less than 3 m wide, and rarely deeper than 1 m in the deepest pools) of the Wisconsin River (Mendelson 1972). The emerald shiner, the spotfin shiner, and the sand shiner constitute the bulk of the population. By mid-June, most of the fish have left Roxbury Creek and returned to the river, and the emerald shiner and the sand shiner have disappeared completely from the stream; neither species has ever been collected in Roxbury Creek during the summer months.

Similar migrations occur in the fall in the Wisconsin River region. Day-to-day observations indicate that, once emerald shiners have entered a stream in numbers, they tend to remain there for several and sometimes for many weeks. Very little movement to or from the Wisconsin River seems to occur. Mendelson (1972) made the following observations:

> One interesting exception to this, however, occurred during the days 26 to 28 September, 1971, in Prentice Creek. On each of these days large schools of *atherinoides* entered the stream in mid-afternoon, the upstream movement of fishes continuing for several hours until early evening. Fish remained in the creek through the night. In early morning a downstream movement began and by 9 A.M. most of the fish had returned to the river. On the afternoon of September 26, fish moving upstream were observed to pass a given point at the rate of twenty fish per second. During two hours of observation, an estimated 140,000 fish passed this point. Fish were still moving upstream at 1730 hours when observations were discontinued.

In McCartney Branch (Grant County) the associate species of 18 emerald shiner were shorthead redhorse (8), golden redhorse (1), white sucker (20), central stoneroller (223), longnose dace (1), hornyhead chub (2), creek chub (27), southern redbelly dace (58), bluntnose minnow (30), fathead minnow (4), suckermouth minnow (11), common shiner (16), sand shiner (2), yellow bullhead (2), johnny darter (18), largemouth bass (4), and green sunfish (1).

IMPORTANCE AND MANAGEMENT

The emerald shiner is an important food source for game and panfishes. It has been found in the stomachs of perch, smelt, burbot, lake trout, rainbow trout, rock bass, pumpkinseed, northern pike, sauger, and white bass. Predation on emerald shiner eggs can be substantial on heavily used spawning shoals. Many fish-eating birds, such as gulls, terns, mergansers, and cormorants, feed heavily upon emerald shiners, whose surface-swimming habit makes them particularly susceptible to this kind of predator (Scott and Crossman 1973).

Emerald shiners have been seined and introduced into hatcheries as forage for game fishes. They live well in fish ponds and in lakes where they have been introduced, but there is no evidence that such fish will reproduce successfully in the hatchery or in inland lakes. At one hatchery it was noted that larger adult shiners ate bass fry quite readily.

Emerald shiners are an excellent aquarium fish. Their glistening sides, unique form, and graceful movements make them attractive.

The emerald shiner is often used for bait despite the fact that it dies quickly and loses its scales easily. It is good bait for bass, perch, and walleye. Because it is hardy in cold weather, it is a favorite bait for winter fishing. In Wisconsin it is sold as the "Milwaukee shiner," because large numbers of them were once taken from southern Lake Michigan.

Until the early 1950s an important bait fish in Wisconsin was the emerald shiner, commonly called the lake shiner. It occurred in tremendous abundance in the waters of the Great Lakes. In the spring and fall, emerald shiners came inshore in such enormous schools that they darkened the water. Sometimes these concentrations appeared for only one day and then were gone. From 1958 to 1962 concentrations were reported in Lake Michigan at Kenosha, Milwaukee, Port Washington, Sheboygan, Algoma, and Manitowoc (R. Simpson, pers. comm.)

The emerald shiner almost disappeared from Lake Michigan in the early 1960s, at a time when the alewife population increased dramatically. It is thought that the shiner was unable to compete for food with the alewife. Young shiners were particularly vulnerable since they remained inshore until midsummer, by which time their habitat was shared with huge numbers of young alewives and many adult alewives. Wells and McLain (1973:46) noted:

> The emerald shiner has undergone perhaps the most extraordinary change in abundance of any species in Lake Michigan. Until about 1960, it was so abundant that it was regarded as a nuisance when it congregated in harbors in spring and fall. It occasionally clogged cooling water intake screens of power plants and vessel engines. Statements by residents around Lake Michigan indicate that the emerald shiner once provided a substantial commercial fishery for the fish-bait market; no production records were kept however.

Rosyface Shiner

Notropis rubellus (Agassiz). *Notropis*—back, keel; *rubellus*—reddish.

Other common names: rosy-faced minnow, skipjack.

Adult male (tuberculate) 66 mm, Ames Branch (Lafayette Co.), 27 June 1960

Adult female (gravid) 64 mm, Ames Branch (Lafayette Co.), 27 June 1960

DESCRIPTION

Body slender, moderately compressed. Average length 61 mm (2.4 in). TL = 1.26 SL. Depth into TL 5.6–7.1. Head length into TL 4.3–5.4. Snout pointed. Mouth terminal, slightly oblique, tip of upper lip almost at top of pupil; mouth extending to below anterior margin of eye; barbel absent. Pharyngeal teeth 2,4–4,2 (but variable, with 1 or more teeth missing in outer or inner rows on one side or both), slender, slightly hooked; arch moderately sturdy. Eye large, into head length 2.8–4.0. Gill rakers knoblike to short, conical; up to 8. Dorsal fin slightly posterior to pelvic fin origin; dorsal fin rays 8; anal fin rays 10 (9–11); pectoral fin rays 12–13; pelvic fin rays 8. Lateral line scales 37–40; lateral line complete, slightly decurved. Digestive tract short with a single S-shaped loop 0.5–0.6 TL. The gut configuration and brain pattern are illustrated and described by R. J. Miller (1963).

Preserved specimens silvery; olive yellow cast above lateral stripe, whitish below. Lateral stripe narrow on caudal peduncle, but broadens to width of eye anteriorly. Mid-dorsal stripe well defined and ending at anterior base of dorsal fin. Dorsal scales with dark edges. Fins clear. Peritoneum silvery, thickly sprinkled with dark speckles. In living fish, a beadlike, iridescent emerald line running length of body above the lateral line.

Breeding male orange to orange-red on head, proximal part of pectoral fin and insertions of anal, dorsal, and caudal fins, and on body behind opercular flaps. Light orange to orange-yellow on rest of body. Breeding female less highly colored; light orange on head and insertions of pectoral, dorsal and caudal fins, but color sometimes absent.

Breeding male with 100 or more minute tubercles on upper half of head from snout to occiput; mandible with single file of about 12 tubercles; body scales above lateral line generally edged with 1–5 or more tubercles; anterior 3 rays on pectoral fins tuberculate. Breeding female with minute and weakly scattered tubercles on top of head, sides of snout, and posterior edges of body scales above the lateral line.

Sexual dimorphism: Pectoral fin length and width greater in male than in female; male pectoral length into TL 6.9; female, 8.0.

Hybrids: Rosyface shiner × common shiner, rosyface shiner × striped shiner, rosyface shiner × spotfin shiner, rosyface shiner × mimic shiner (Schwartz 1972, R. J. Miller 1963 and 1964, Bailey and Gilbert 1960). Hermaphroditism reported several times (Reed 1954).

DISTRIBUTION, STATUS, AND HABITAT

In Wisconsin, the rosyface shiner occurs in the Mississippi River and Lake Michigan drainage basins, but is absent from much of the central and upper regions of the driftless area, the St. Croix River system, and the northern portion of the Lake Michigan system. It has not been reported from the Lake Superior drainage basin, except in the extreme eastern sector (Michigan and Ontario).

This species is common in southwestern Wisconsin, common to abundant in central Wisconsin, and uncommon to common in northeastern Wisconsin. Since the 1920s it has disappeared from Cedar Creek and from the Menomonee River of the Lake Michigan drainage in southern Wisconsin.

The rosyface shiner generally inhabits medium-sized, clear, swift streams; it rarely occurs in lakes. In Wisconsin, it was encountered most frequently in clear water at depths of 0.6–1.5 m over substrates of gravel (29% frequency), rubble (21%), sand (15%), mud (13%), silt (10%), clay (5%), boulders (4%), and bedrock (2%). In lakes it generally occurred in the vicinity of connecting streams. In streams it inhabited moderate to swift riffles and pools. It occurred in rivers of the following widths: 1.0–3.0 m (11%), 3.1–6.0 m (23%), 6.1–12.0 m (23%), 12.1–24.0 m (29%), 24.1–50.0 m (9%), and more than 50 m (6%).

Although known as a clear-water form, with turbidity as a limiting factor in its distribution, strains of rosyface shiner have developed in the Pecatonica and

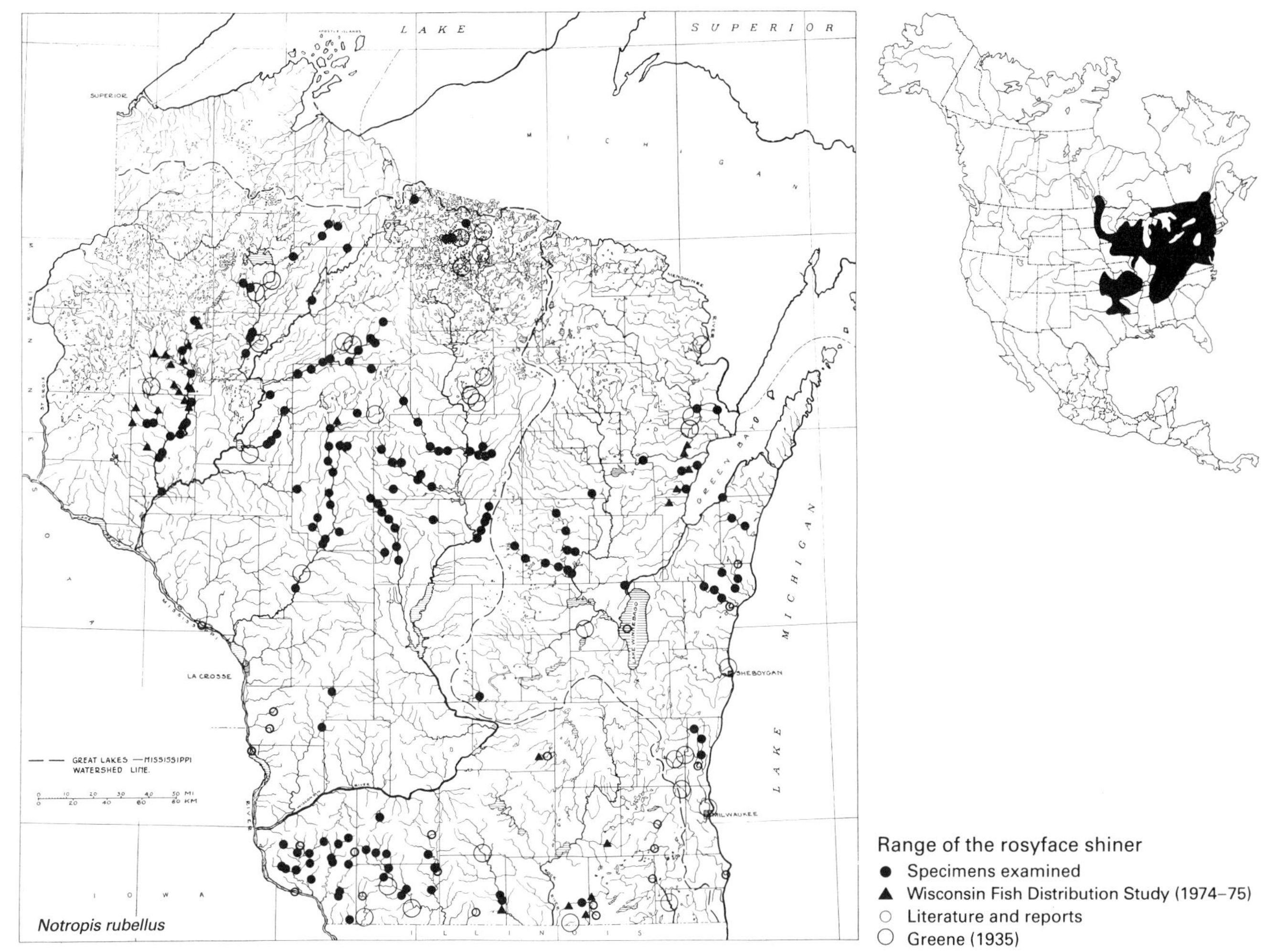

Range of the rosyface shiner
● Specimens examined
▲ Wisconsin Fish Distribution Study (1974–75)
○ Literature and reports
◯ Greene (1935)

Sugar river basins in southwestern Wisconsin which are capable of withstanding considerable turbidity. A number of references in the literature, however, indicate that highly silted water has adverse effects on this species, probably because it interferes with the sight stimuli necessary for its existence.

BIOLOGY

In Wisconsin, the rosyface shiner spawns principally from May to June, although there is evidence that some spawning occurs later. Spawning occurs at temperatures of 21.1°C (70°F) or higher (Miller 1964), often above nesting common shiners and hornyhead chubs in nests constructed by the latter.

Prespawning activities of the rosyface shiner were observed in a stream in New York on 10 June 1941 (Pfeiffer 1955). A school of approximately 100 fish swam a circular course through two pools and its connecting riffle. At times a small group of about 15 or 20 fish broke away from the main body and circled by themselves. The speed at which the schools moved was at all times uniformly swift. Three days before spawning was observed, the coursing movement of the schools ceased, and they maintained a stationary position immediately below the upper riffle.

Actual spawning began on 23 June, and continued from 25 to 28 June. The number of spawning individuals was reduced daily, until only 10 fish were spawning on the last day. The water temperature on the first day was 24.4°C (76°F). During the remainder of the spawning period, the average water temperature was 26.9°C (80.3°F).

Spawning occurred during bright, sunny days in a shallow area containing nests of minnows. A school of rosyface shiners suddenly dashed into the spawning area, and separated into 4 or 5 groups of 8–12 minnows each; each group came to rest in a nest depression. Males and females then vibrated their bodies in unison, causing the water to break at the surface as if it were boiling. Both sexes crowded one another; the sides of their bodies were in contact, but they scarcely held one position during the brief spawning act. This thrashing and lashing about in the depression lasted 5 or 6 seconds, and was followed by relative quiet for about 30 seconds; some minnows remained quiet in the depressions, while a few moved to other nests. Vibration and body shaking was then repeated, followed again by a short period of quiet. These spawning and resting periods lasted for a total of about 5 minutes. The school then dashed back to its former position in the pool. After 10 minutes, the whole procedure began again with a sudden dash from the pool into the shallow waters of the spawning site. Pfeiffer (1955) noted that two male striped shiners vibrated in unison with the spawning rosyface shiners.

The spawning site of the rosyface shiner has been described as in midstream or several inches above the gravel (Hubbs and Cooper 1936, Hankinson 1932), generally above the other fish of the aggregation. According to Miller (1964), rosyface shiners in spawning schools frequently jockey for position and make attack and parallel-swimming movements, but males never defend a fixed territory over the gravel as do common shiner males. Typically, males swim back and forth, with no fixed position, over the nest or in the school. Often two fish brush or butt each other about the head and anterior parts of the body. These encounters are usually momentary, after which the fish return to their hovering activities. The parallel-swim involves two fish (usually males, but possibly a male and a female), which generally move upstream a few centimeters or as far as 2 m. Parallel-swimming males seldom move farther than 2–5 cm apart, and usually appear to be almost touching much of the time. The number of head butts during parallel-swimming behavior is high in this species.

Prespawning, circular swimming behavior, similar to that described above, was observed on 25 May 1967 in the Yellow River (Wood County). A number of rosyface shiners were captured from the school; milt was flowing freely from the vents of the males, and the females were gravid. Seven highly colored males (62–71 mm TL, 2.24–3.00 g) had testes that represented 3–5.7% of their total weight. Eight females (66–78 mm TL, 2.53–3.92 g) had ovaries 14.1–19.2% of their total weight, and ripe eggs 1.0–1.2 mm diam. At least one female was partially spent, and in two the eggs had not yet ovulated.

In Ames Branch (Lafayette County) on 27 June 1960, a 65-mm female with ovaries 16% of total weight held 610 ripe eggs 1.1 mm diam; an equal number of white, immature eggs 0.5 mm diam were also present. A 69-mm female with ovaries 19% of total weight held 900 mature eggs. Both females were 2 years old.

The eggs are demersal and sticky; they attach to the first object with which they come in contact. When an egg is placed in water, the chorion is released from the yolk and slowly fills with water; the egg attains a size of 1.5 mm diam (Reed 1958). The larvae hatch out 57–59 hr following fertilization, and are 5.1 mm SL at hatching. M. Fish (1932) described and illustrated the 15-mm stage.

A 20-mm young-of-year was taken 15 September 1974 from the Jump River (Rusk County). The small size at this date suggests a late spawning, probably in August. Age-I rosyface shiners from Turtle Creek (Rock County) on 21 May 1975 were only 34–42 mm TL.

Rosyface shiners from the Jump River (Price County), collected 18 October 1969, showed the following growth:

Age Class	No. of Fish	TL (mm)		Calculated TL at Annulus (mm)		
		Avg	Range	1	2	3
0	1	35				
I	25	56.6	52–60	38.9		
II	25	63.2	58–75	37.0	56.9	
III	4	71.3	69–76	28.6	53.5	66.2
Avg (weighted)				37.2	56.4	66.2

In New York, Pfeiffer (1955) found that age-I males were larger than females, but that females were slightly larger at ages II and III. The largest female was 75 mm SL (about 94.5 mm TL); the largest male was 71 mm SL (about 89.5 mm TL).

Reed (1957a) considered this species omnivorous. Young-of-year 22–30 mm long preferred algae and diatoms (65.5%) to insects (28.2%)—nearly a complete reversal of adult preferences, which were algae and diatoms 22.4% and insects 68.4%. Reed also found that in Pennsylvania, the rosyface shiner ceased feeding from 19 November 1953 until 19 March 1954. During this period, the minnow had left its riffle habitat for the deeper pools and eddies. It fed only to a limited extent at the time of spawning; only 5.5% of the fish examined had some food in their stomachs.

In a spawning population from Ames Branch (Lafayette County) on 27 June 1950, 9 of 30 stomachs examined were empty, and in another 8 stomachs the contents could not be identified. The remaining rosyface shiners had eaten Diptera (culicids and chironomids), Ephemeroptera, Hemiptera, and Trichoptera. No vegetation was evident in stomach contents (J. Palmisano, pers. comm.).

Among rosyface shiners examined in New York, aquatic insects made up 72% of the total volume of food, and terrestrial insects made up 25%. Vegetation was found in a few stomachs, and 15 stomachs contained fish eggs which were not identified. Pfeiffer (1955) observed rosyface shiners feeding off the bottom, and also at the surface of the water. Feeding was not restricted to any particular time of the day. According to R. J. Miller (1963), the rosyface shiner has an overall brain pattern typical of the predominantly sight-feeding fish.

Rosyface shiner males and hybrid males differ in behavior from male common shiners mainly in that the rosyface shiners fight less for position and do not drive away predators even slightly larger than themselves. In fact, rosyface shiners exhibit a well-defined attraction to other species during early prespawning periods when three or four individuals swim close together behind breeding common shiners or creek chubs (Miller 1964). Miller noted that the rosyface shiner is highly attracted by members of its own species, but that it is stimulated to aggression at certain times when companions of its own species venture too close. Thus males are both attracted by other males and stimulated to attack them.

The rosyface shiner was a dominant species in a collection from the Milwaukee River (Ozaukee County). Species associated with 64 rosyface shiners were: white sucker (1), largescale stoneroller (17), hornyhead chub (5), common shiner (69+), striped shiner (34+), spotfin shiner (4), redfin shiner (1), and rock bass (12). A Waupaca River (Waupaca County) collection produced rosyface shiner (48), shorthead redhorse (1), hornyhead chub (5), bluntnose minnow (76), fathead minnow (3), common shiner (56), spotfin shiner (33), sand shiner (7), mimic shiner (9), northern pike (2), yellow perch (94), western sand darter (48), river darter (3), logperch (1), Iowa darter (1), and black crappie (4).

IMPORTANCE AND MANAGEMENT

The rosyface shiner is often eaten by largemouth bass and northern pike (Cahn 1927). During the spawning season its eggs are vulnerable to the rainbow darter, the northern hog sucker, and the stoneroller minnow which have been observed feeding on the eggs being deposited on the nest (Reed 1957b). Apparently the rosyface shiner ignores these marauders.

In areas where the rosyface shiner is abundant it is commonly used as a bait minnow. Hundreds of rosyface shiners were seen in one bait dealer's tanks, but a number of the fish were dead. Rosyface shiners do not keep well in crowded tanks, although they are considered excellent bait for yellow perch, crappies, and black bass.

The rosyface shiner is an excellent fish for the home aquarium, especially when taken in breeding colors. It often retains its colors for a number of weeks.

Redfin Shiner

Notropis umbratilis (Girard). *Notropis*—back, keel; *umbratilis*—remaining in the shade.

Other common names: northern redfin shiner, redfin, compressed redfin.

Adult male (tuberculate) 74 mm, Hutchins Cr. (Union Co.), Illinois, 29 May 1969

Adult female 68 mm, Hutchins Cr. (Union Co.), Illinois, 29 May 1969

DESCRIPTION

Body slender to moderately deep, strongly compressed. Average length 56 mm (2.2 in). TL = 1.25 SL. Depth into TL 4.1–5.5. Head length into TL 5–5.2. Snout bluntly pointed. Mouth terminal, slightly oblique, tip of upper lip at level of upper pupil; mouth extending to below posterior nostril; barbel absent. Pharyngeal teeth 2,4–4,2, slender, slightly hooked; arch slender. Eye large, into head length 2.9–4.0. Gill rakers knoblike to short, conical; about 8. Dorsal fin origin slightly posterior to origin of pelvic fin; dorsal fin rays 8; anal fin rays usually 11 (10–12); pectoral fin rays 12–13; pelvic fin rays 8. Lateral line scales 41–48; lateral line complete, strongly decurved. Digestive tract short with a single S-shaped loop 0.5–0.6 TL. Chromosomes 2n = 50 (Gold et al. 1980).

Back bluish gray, sides and belly silvery, upper sides often with fine V-shaped markings. Dusky lateral stripe in preserved specimens. Anterior base of dorsal fin with a diffuse dark spot disappearing posteriorly on base; fins dusky or unpigmented.

Breeding males dark with bluish iridescence; all fins flushed with pink or red. Breeding tubercles, small and sharp, on head, branchiostegals, and most scales of body; only occasionally found on belly and caudal peduncle, on pectoral fin rays, and anterior edges of dorsal, anal, and pelvic fins. The pattern of head tuberculation was figured by Snelson (1972) and Snelson and Pflieger (1975).

Sexual dimorphism: Male significantly greater in head length, snout length, caudal peduncle length and depth, and length of all fins (Snelson and Pflieger 1975). Urogenital papilla of adult female enlarged and protruding during warmer portion of year; papilla in male absent.

Hybrid: Redfin shiner × red shiner (Pflieger 1975).

SYSTEMATIC NOTES

Snelson and Pflieger (1975) clarified the nomenclature of *Notropis umbratilis* and presented an updated synonymy. Two subspecies are recognized: *N. u. umbratilis*, which is distributed in the Salt River drainage, the Missouri River drainage, and the central Arkansas River drainage; and *N. u. cyanocephalus*, which has a complementary distribution in the central Mississippi River basin and in the Great Lakes basin, including Wisconsin. The two subspecies are recognized primarily on details of pigmentation and tuberculation.

DISTRIBUTION, STATUS, AND HABITAT

In Wisconsin, the redfin shiner occurs in the Mississippi River and Lake Michigan drainage basins, where it is at the northern limit of its range. It is absent from the Lake Superior basin. This species is disjunctly distributed in the lower half of Wisconsin. It is well established in one of the Gardner ponds in the University of Wisconsin Arboretum at Madison, and has access via Murphy Creek to Lakes Mendota, Monona, Wingra, Waubesa, and Kegonsa when the pond overflows during times of high water (McNaught 1963).

The redfin shiner is locally rare to common in slow-moving, turbid waters of southeastern Wisconsin. Old records (Greene 1935) indicate that it was once present in widely isolated streams throughout the southern half of the state. It has since disappeared from a number of locales. During the early 1970s it was eliminated from a number of sites in the upper Rock River system (Washington and Fond du Lac counties) through the widespread use of toxicants in a carp control program. Unfortunately, no attempts were made to save any of the redfin shiner populations prior to treatment. The redfin shiner has watch status in Wisconsin (Les 1979).

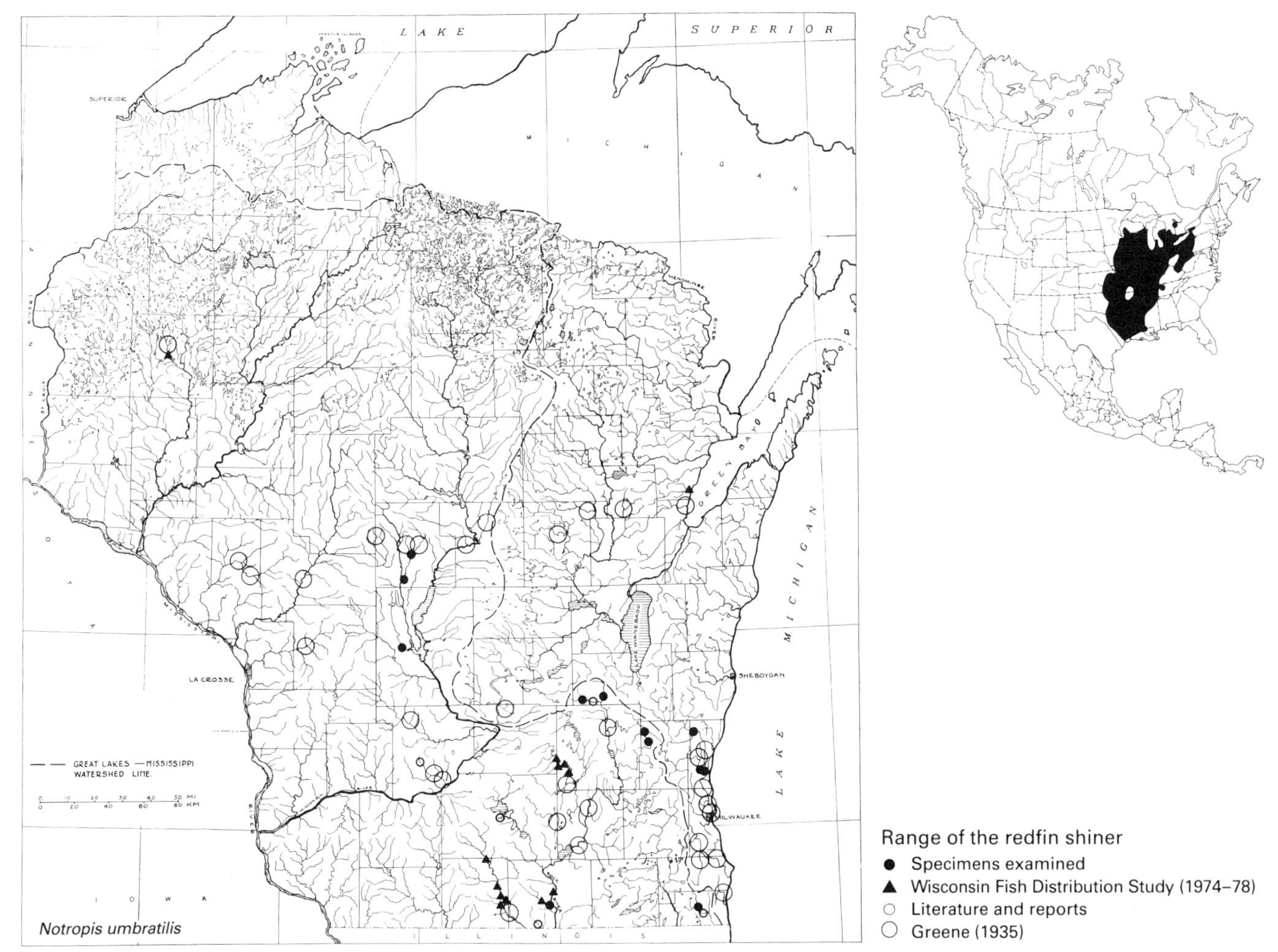

In Wisconsin, the redfin shiner was encountered occasionally in clear water, but it was more frequently found in turbid water at depths of 0.1–1.5 m over substrates of silt (29%), gravel (24%), rubble (24%), boulders (12%), sand (6%), and detritus (6%). It occurred in the pool areas of low-gradient streams of the following widths: 3.1–6.0 m (9%), 6.1–12.0 m (18%), 12.1–24.0 m (36%), 24.1–50.0 m (18%), and more than 50 m (18%).

Basically, the redfin shiner is a pool-dwelling species, and schools may often be seen near the surface. In high-gradient streams with a strong base flow, such as those of the Ozark uplands (Pflieger 1975), this species is found most often in protected inlets and in overflow pools away from the main channel. Streams kept cool by inflowing water from springs are usually avoided.

BIOLOGY

In Wisconsin, spawning extends from early June to mid-August. Highly tuberculate males were captured on 15 June from Allenton Creek (Washington County). On 19 August 1963 spent females, and others with small numbers of ripe eggs, were taken from the same stream; although no fully tuberculate males were seen, one male still had a few tubercles and scars. Cross (1967) noted that in Kansas spawning occurs at water temperatures of 21.1°C (70°F) or higher.

Hunter and Wisby (1961) and Hunter and Hasler (1965) studied the spawning behavior of the redfin shiner extensively after it was introduced in 1954 into ponds at the University of Wisconsin Arboretum, Madison. The following account is largely from those sources.

It is apparent there is an intimate and widespread reproductive association between the redfin shiner and species of *Lepomis*. Hunter and Hasler have found that the release of milt and eggs by spawning green sunfish attracts redfin shiners to the sunfish nests and stimulates the shiners to spawn above the nests. On subsequent days, some of the male shiners return to the sunfish nests, reestablish their territories, and continue spawning. The role of the sunfish cannot be discounted, since the number of shiners decreases when sunfish are removed. Hunter and Hasler have only rarely observed male redfin shiners holding territories over nests unoccupied by an adult sunfish. Apparently the presence of the male sunfish plays a role in the recognition of a spawning site by redfin shiners; more shiners were attracted by milt and a moving latex model than by milt alone.

The number of redfin shiners over a particular green sunfish nest varies from 1 to more than 100. When only one shiner has a territory over an isolated sunfish nest, the territory extends 1–1.5 m beyond the nest. However, the formation of very dense spawning aggregations is a distinct feature of the redfin shiner's reproductive behavior. Aggregations consist of a nucleus of 30–100 male redfin shiners, which is surrounded by a more diffuse ring of male and female shiners. The central cluster of males extends from the water surface downward to within 2 or 3 cm of the bottom. Males of all sizes are found at all depths in the cluster, but usually there are more large males near the bottom. Many of the male redfin shiners within the aggregation defend small territories, some only slightly larger in diameter than the length of the fish itself. Males that possess no territory move through the mass, fighting and being chased by other male shiners. Males within the mass are constantly whirling, pursuing each other, striking other males with their snouts, and spawning with females that swim rapidly through the aggregation.

The spawning act has been described as follows (Hunter and Hasler 1965:269–270):

> Female shiners remained outside the cluster of males which were holding territories over a green sunfish nest. As a female swam toward the group of males, one of the males approached the female, aligned, and the 2 fish swam parallel to each other, the female often located slightly below the male. Spawning nearly always took place high above the nest of the green sunfish. The 2 minnows closed ranks as they swam over the nest and it appeared that spawning was accomplished when the male executed unusually wide undulations of his body against the body of the female. Other males holding territories over the nest frequently pursued and crowded about the spawning pair.

Redfin shiners do not remain on the spawning grounds overnight, but move on and off the site each day. The number of redfin shiners on the spawning grounds increases during the morning hours, reaches a maximum between 1030 and 1430 hr, and gradually decreases thereafter.

The male green sunfish only rarely chase or snap at redfin shiners that hold territories over their nests. If species other than the redfin shiner approach the nest, however, they are immediately chased or threatened. The advantage to a minnow species using a centrarchid nest is that nearly all centrarchids continue to defend and fan their nests long after spawning. If the minnows spawn while the sunfish is constructing its nest or is spawning, the minnow eggs may be protected from predators and from silting until the young are free-swimming.

Snelson and Pflieger (1975) have observed reproductive activities of the redfin shiner over the nests of the green sunfish, orangespotted sunfish, and longear sunfish in Arkansas, Ohio, Oklahoma, and Missouri.

Hunter and Hasler (1965) never saw young or adult redfin shiners eating the eggs they or the sunfish had deposited in the nest. Juvenile sunfish, on the other hand, were seen feeding on both redfin shiner and sunfish eggs when the nests were not occupied by male sunfish. Apparently sunfish moved in to feed on redfin eggs during spawning observed on the South Branch of the Rock River (Fond du Lac County) in early June 1960 (V. Hacker, pers. comm.).

A gravid female redfin shiner (55 mm TL) from the East Branch of the Rock River (Washington County) on 15 July 1971 held 525 mature yellow eggs 0.75 mm diam; the ovarian weight was 13% of total body weight. Also present were immature white eggs 0.25–0.5 mm diam. A 53-mm female with an ovarian weight 9% of total weight held an estimated 645 ripening eggs 0.6–0.7 mm diam.

Hunter and Wisby (1961) noted that the average mortality of redfin shiner egg samples collected from green sunfish nests is 54%. In both the redfin shiner and the green sunfish, the postlarval stage is attained in the laboratory 7–10 days after the eggs are deposited.

The growth of young-of-year redfin shiners in southern Wisconsin has been reported as follows:

Date	No. of Fish	TL (mm) Avg	TL (mm) Range	Location
1 Aug.	3	33	31–35	Cedar Cr. (Ozaukee Co.)
10 Sept.	23	29	22–39	Milwaukee R. (Ozaukee Co.)

Redfin shiners from Allenton Creek (Washington County), collected 19 July 1963, showed the following growth:

Age Class	No. of Fish	TL (mm)		Calculated TL at Annulus (mm)		
		Avg	Range	1	2	3
0	1	23				
I	13	48.2	44–51	30.6		
II	27	57.7	50–62	31.8	51.8	
III	1	68		36.8	52.4	68
Avg (weighted)				31.5	51.8	68

The annulus of the year had not yet been placed in some of the older and larger fish.

Six age-I redfin shiners collected 6 April from Hemlock Creek (Wood County) averaged 41.7 (36–45) mm. In central Missouri (Pflieger 1975), the redfin shiner attains a length of about 28 mm (1.1 in) by the end of its first summer of life, and averages about 43 mm (1.7 in) by the end of its second summer. Most sexually mature adults are in their second or third summer (ages I and II), and the life-span seldom exceeds 3 summers.

Male redfin shiners are significantly larger than females. The largest male recorded was 67.4 mm SL (estimated 84 mm TL); the largest female was 62.0 mm SL (78 mm TL) (Snelson and Pflieger 1975).

The redfin shiner feeds on aquatic and terrestrial insects, and on other small animal life that may be available. At times it seems to feed extensively on filamentous algae and bits of higher plants (Eddy and Underhill 1974).

In Allenton Creek (Washington County), 172 redfin shiners were associated with the following species: white sucker, central stoneroller, creek chub, golden shiner, bluntnose minnow, fathead minnow, common shiner, central mudminnow, blackstripe topminnow, and johnny darter.

IMPORTANCE AND MANAGEMENT

In Wisconsin, the redfin shiner is too uncommon to be a useful bait or forage species.

Specimens taken during the breeding season make striking aquarium pets. In view of what is known about stimuli for spawning, redfin shiners should challenge the aquarist who prides himself on raising his own fish.

Common Shiner

Notropis cornutus (Mitchill). *Notropis*—back, keel; *cornutus*—horned.

Other common names: eastern shiner, redfin shiner, silver shiner, dace, silverside, rough-head, hornyhead, creek shiner, skipjack, shiner.

Adult male (tuberculate) 99 mm, tributary to Little Sandy Cr. (Marathon Co.), 29 May 1961

Adult female 160 mm, North Twin L. (Vilas Co.), 18 June 1977

DESCRIPTION

Body moderately deep, laterally compressed. Average length 64–102 mm (2.5–4.0 in). TL = 1.25 SL. Depth into TL 4.3–6.3. Head length into TL 4.3–5.3. Snout bluntly pointed. Mouth large, terminal, extending to between nostril and anterior margin of eye; barbel absent. Pharyngeal teeth 2,4–4,2 (occasionally a tooth absent in outer row on one or both sides); most teeth strongly hooked; arch sturdy. Eye into head length 2.8–4.3. Gill rakers short, conical to flat-topped; about 9. Dorsal fin origin over pelvic fin origin; dorsal fin rays 8; anal fin rays 9 (8); pectoral fin rays 15–17; pelvic fin rays 8. Lateral line scales 34–40; lateral line complete, decurved. Digestive tract S-shaped, about 0.8 TL; sections long and extending length of visceral cavity (see R. J. Miller 1963). Chromosomes 2n = 50 (W. LeGrande, pers. comm.).

Light olive dorsally with a broad mid-dorsal stripe, sides silvery with scattered dark scales, belly white-silver. Dark stripes on upper sides do not meet on back behind dorsal fin. Fins clear. Peritoneum dark brown overlying a silvery background.

Breeding males with lead blue on head and back; sides of body and fins pink to rose. Large tubercles on top of head and on snout; a single row along edge of lower jaw. Scales of back from nape to dorsal fin with small tubercles. Anterior ray of dorsal fin and anterior rays of pectoral fins with well-developed tubercles. Color and tubercles lacking in females.

Difficulties exist in the identification of the common shiner and the striped shiner. For aids in separation consult p. 523.

Sexual dimorphism: Adult male, pectoral fin width into pectoral fin length 1.4–1.9; female, 2.1–2.2.

Hybrids: Hybrids of the common shiner have been reported with the stoneroller, northern redbelly dace, southern redbelly dace, redside dace, hornyhead chub, rosyface shiner, striped shiner, lake chub, creek chub, and longnose dace (Gilbert 1964, Greenfield et al, 1973, Cross and Minckley 1960, Trautman 1957, Miller 1962 and 1963, Ross and Cavender 1977). In Wisconsin hybrids have been reported between the common shiner and the hornyhead chub, rosyface shiner, emerald shiner, and striped shiner (Wis. Fish Distrib. Study 1974–1975). Hermaphroditism in a common shiner × rosyface shiner hybrid is described by R. J. Miller (1962).

SYSTEMATIC NOTES

Gilbert (1964) revised *N. cornutus* and closely related species, retaining the present form *Notropis cornutus frontalis* and elevating *Notropis cornutus chrysocephalus* to *Notropis chrysocephalus*.

DISTRIBUTION, STATUS, AND HABITAT

The common shiner is widespread in the Mississippi River, Lake Michigan, and Lake Superior drainage basins.

This species is abundant, and is one of the most common stream and river minnows. It is occasionally found in clearwater lakes over silt-free bottoms. Although the population of common shiners may not be seriously threatened, Hubbs and Cooper (1936) suggested that some thought should be given, at least by bait dealers, to conservation of the species.

In Wisconsin, the common shiner was encountered in clear waters (47%), slightly turbid waters (33%), and turbid waters (20%) at average depths of 0.1–0.5 m (53%), 0.6–1.5 m (41%), and more than 1.5 m (6%). It occurred over the following substrates: gravel (24% frequency), sand (23%), mud (12%), silt (11%), rubble (11%), boulders (11%), clay (4%), detritus (2%), hardpan (1%), and bedrock (1%). It has

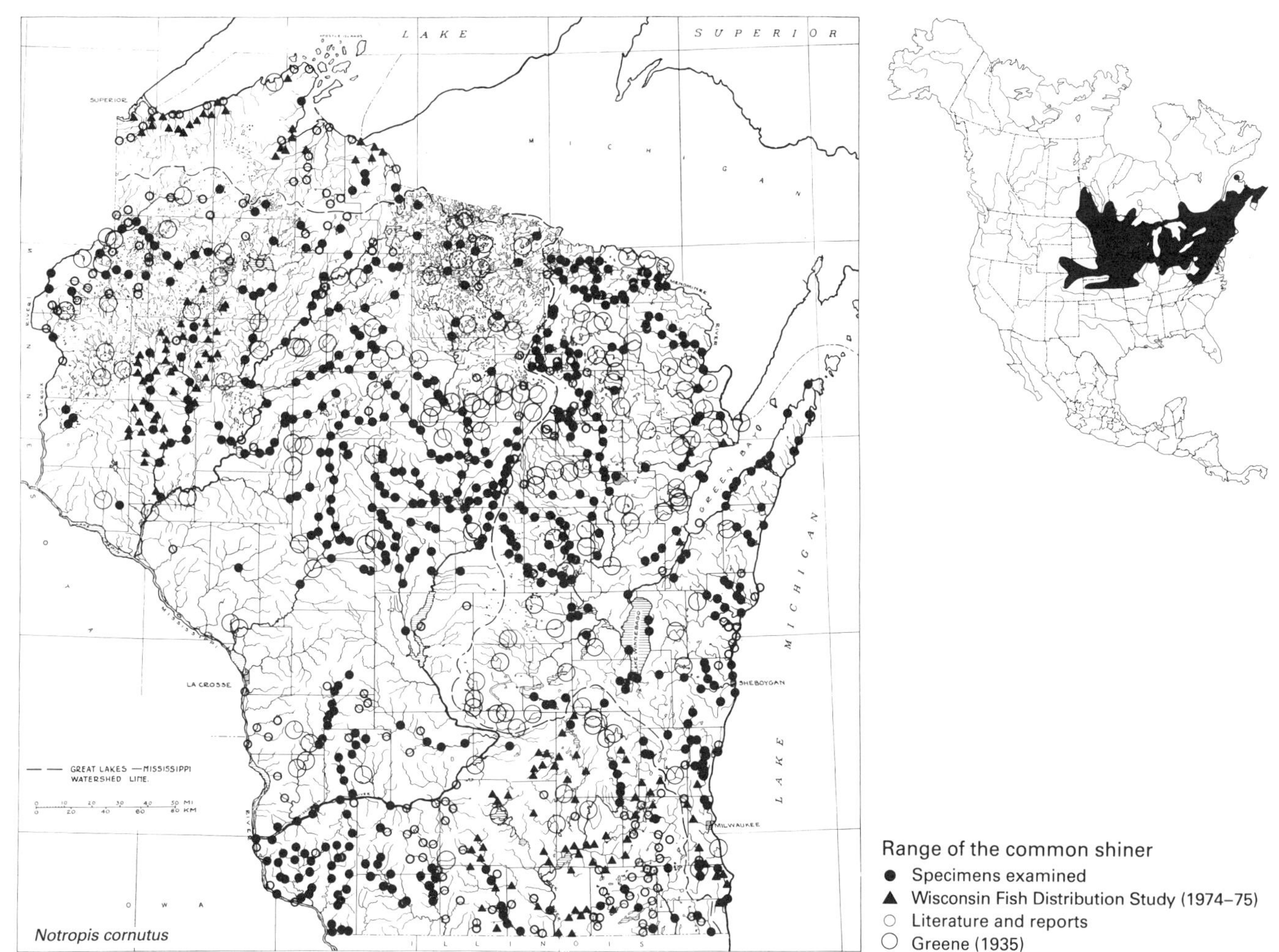

been reported from a number of lakes and reservoirs, and in rivers of the following widths: 1.0–3.0 m (21%), 3.1–6.0 m (19%), 6.1–12.0 m (18%), 12.1–24.0 m (25%), 24.1–50.0 m (12%), and more than 50 m (5%). It occurs at sites without cover as well as sites with moderate vegetative cover.

BIOLOGY

In Wisconsin, spawning occurs from late May to the end of July in stream riffles over gravelly bottoms. The common shiner's abundance in some inland lakes suggests that it may also spawn successfully over the gravel shoals of these lakes. Spawning activity occurs early in the season in southern Wisconsin, and later in the northern part of the state.

According to Breder and Rosen (1966), spawning usually begins when the water has reached a temperature of 15.6–18.3°C (60–65°F). At any one locality spawning lasts about 10 days, and is limited to the daylight hours. The common shiner may (1) spawn over gravel beds in running water, (2) excavate a small depression in gravel or in running water, or (3) use nests built by other species, such as the hornyhead chub, creek chub, and stoneroller minnows, whether these are built in running water or the still waters of shallow pools. Hunter and Wisby (1961) cited the use of smallmouth bass nests as well. The common shiner prefers to spawn over the nests of other species when these are available.

When the common shiner uses the active nest of another species, there is a commensal relationship between the two species. Hankinson (1932) described an instance where the male hornyhead carried stones and the large shiner chased away intruders; they were mutually helpful, but never interfered with each other.

Miller (1964) provided a thorough discussion of the spawning activities of the common shiner. The following description is largely derived from his account. In the establishment of territories, fighting occurs among the shiner males. When attacking, a male turns toward the intruder and rushes at him; at times the attacker tilts his head tubercles and dorsum toward the intruder and butts him. Frequently, a defending fish erects his fins and tenses his body before turning to attack; these movements are sometimes sufficient to cause the other fish to flee. Mature males often can be found with large portions of their heads and bodies injured and covered by fungus at the end of the season.

Another form of aggressive behavior seen in territorial males is the parallel swim. This occurs when an intruder swims into a nest guarded by a resident male. Two males of approximately the same size swim upstream into the current 25–200 mm (1–8 in) apart, parallel to each other, for a distance of several centimeters to 2 m (6 ft) or more. The body is always taut, with the caudal peduncle and tail often slightly raised. The rigid movements resulting from these muscular contractions give the impression that their behavior is formalized or ritualized. The males may turn and butt each other singly or in unison. After the terminal butt, they usually return to their original positions, although occasionally the intruder takes over the territory.

The prespawning behavior known as "tilting" precedes all successful common shiner spawnings, and is one of the most prominent activities of all spawning males. Raney (cited by R. J. Miller 1964:333) observed:

> With the female above the male and the male alternately inclining himself to a semi-recumbent position first to one side then the other, conditions are set for the spawning act. The female dips down beside that side of the male which is inclined toward the bottom or making the more acute angle.

Males were sometimes seen swimming in circles while tilting at females that were swimming away from the center of the territory.

In the spawning act itself, the female swims down behind the male, and remains there long enough for him to swing his caudal peduncle over her back while he places his pectoral fin under her breast, thereby forming a sigmoid flexure about her body. The two anal openings are close together for a fraction of a second; during this time the eggs are ejected and fertilized. After the spawning clasp has been completed, the female immediately darts upward, frequently breaking the surface. The lunge toward the surface is almost always present, and has the appearance of a reflexlike movement, perhaps a mechanical reaction to the sudden violent contractions of spawning.

Spawning common shiners are found in two seemingly different types of social groups, which Miller (1964) called the massed aggregates and the dominant male associations. The massed aggregate occurs at the beginning of the spawning period, when 40–100 males mass in areas about 0.6 m (2 ft) square over cleared gravel just above a riffle, or in a gravel depression, cleaned and deepened by the males, in less than 25 cm (10 in) of water at the side of the stream where the current is slight. In such aggregates all males are visibly aggressive, constantly swinging their heads toward one another, sometimes butting, biting, and chasing each other for a few centimeters. In spite of the constant activity, little more than 2–4 cm is cleared around each fish. Some digging is done by most common shiner spawning groups, but it is done most frequently by the large aggregates, and in creek chub and stoneroller nest pits. Miller noted that spawning does not occur until the fourth day the aggregate has been active.

In addition to this focal spawning aggregate, other spawning groups appear in outlying clearings which are used for only a day or two at a time and then deserted. Miller referred to these as dominant male associations. In such a group a dominant male located in the anterior nest pit. In a typical case observed by Miller, the dominant male spawned eight times during a 5-min period, and gave 36 courting tilt displays.

Current speed over spawning nests can vary from swift to very slow, but spawning has never been observed in backwaters without current. Large common shiner spawning aggregates occur only in weak currents. Females tend to prefer spawning in nests over slow rather than fast water. Territorial defense and spawning by the common shiner have only been observed in nature over gravel.

Miller (1964) stated that water temperature appears to affect social behavior of common shiners in at least two ways. In early spring, it seems to influence the development of breeding colors and tubercles and the beginning of spawning activities in males, and ovulation and associated behavior in females. In very cold springs, these developments are delayed. Thus temperature may augment the developmental processes controlled and coordinated by photoperiodic stimuli. Secondly, sharp drops in water temperature often seem to inhibit social behavior to an unexpected extent. A drop in temperature from 24.4 to 16.7°C (76–62°F) halted appreciable activity among shiners for three days. Miller noted that fish just reaching peak activity continued to spawn for some time after the advent of unfavorable weather, while fish which had already spawned for several days ceased spawning; they resumed spawning only after a long time had passed.

In North Twin Lake (Vilas County) on 18 June 1977, a gravid female 98 mm TL and 11.91 g, with ovaries about 22% of total weight, held 3,630 eggs 1.2 mm diam. A 114-mm, 17.9 g female, also with ovaries 22% of body weight, held 3,940 eggs 1.3 mm diam.

The demersal eggs become adhesive after water-hardening in about 2 min after being laid and dropped between pebbles on the bottom of the nest to which they adhere. When first laid they are orange and average 1.5 mm diam (Breder and Rosen 1966).

Laboratory experiments (Miller 1964) indicate that common shiner eggs stripped into small jars containing stream water can be fertilized by common shiner milt as much as 2 min later, and still result in 100% fertilization and hatching, and normal development of the young. Such delayed fertilization enables sperm from other breeding species to fertilize the common shiner eggs, resulting in hybrids.

Considering its abundance and its wide distribution, little is known about the common shiner's early development and growth. This is undoubtedly similar to that of *Notropis chrysocephalus*, for which M. Fish (1932) has described and figured a number of stages from 6.9 to 13.2 mm.

Common shiners from the Wolf River (Menominee County), collected 21 July 1966, showed the following growth (M. Miller, pers. comm.):

Age Class	No. of Fish	TL (mm)		Calculated TL at Annulus (mm)			
		Avg	Range	1	2	3	4
0	7	32.7	29–35				
I	3	73.3	65–83	41.2			
II	19	80.3	71–92	34.4	66.6		
III	21	103.5	82–127	29.3	58.7	89.0	
IV	5	121.2	92–138	33.6	59.6	83.0	105.0
Avg (weighted)				32.5	62.1	87.8	105.0

A 182-mm male, collected 18 June 1977, from North Twin Lake (Vilas County) had the following calculated lengths at the annuli: 1—46.3 mm, 2—108.3 mm, 3—156.6 mm, and 4—168.9 mm.

In southern Illinois, the average calculated TL at each annulus was: 1—36 mm, 2—74 mm, 3—102 mm, 4—122 mm, and 5—165 mm (Lewis 1957). In Iowa (Fee 1965), the estimated SL at each annulus for the male common shiner was: 1—46.34 mm, 2—66.95 mm, 3—78.25 mm, 4—97 mm, and 5—116 mm; the annulus was deposited in May and early June. Male common shiners grow faster than females. This species requires 2 or 3 years to reach maturity.

Hubbs and Cooper (1936) stated that breeding males often attain a length of 203 mm (8 in) or more, and Trautman (1957) reported a maximum length of 208 mm (8.2 in). Although common shiners seldom reach age VI, the estimated greatest age recorded is 9 years (Van Oosten 1932).

The common shiner is omnivorous in its feeding habits; and it is also opportunistic. Its diet is divided nearly equally between plant and animal matter. In the Platte River (Grant County), stomachs contained the filamentous alga *Ulothrix*, mayfly, cranefly, and caddisfly larvae, and higher plant materials (C. Hasler, pers. comm.)

In Iowa, Fee (1965) noted plant matter, including such algae as diatoms, *Cladophora*, *Spirogyra*, as well as higher plant matter, and nearly equal amounts of such animal matter as *Plumatella repens*, *Lumbricus* sp., Plecoptera, Ephemeroptera, Hemiptera, Trichoptera, Diptera, Coleoptera, and other adult and larval insects. In an earlier study from the Des Moines River, the diet was 71% plants, 18% insects, 8% fish, and 2% organic debris (Harrison 1950). The fish materials identified included the Topeka shiner, an undetermined minnow, and several scales.

Breder and Crawford (1922) found that young common shiners eat the same types of food as the older fish. In both groups animal food constituted 59% of the diet, and vegetable plus debris, 41%. These authors found no correlation between the length of the fish and type of food eaten. Observed in captivity, common shiners were noted to rise to the surface of the water with both the force and the grace of a trout, although they also seemed quite adept at securing food from the bottom. The percentage of empty stomachs in winter indicated a cessation of active metabolism during the cold season.

Common shiners migrate upstream from the deeper pools where they had wintered. Miller (1964) found that in general common shiners marked in one area were found in the same or a nearby area for several weeks after marking; in some areas (usually backwaters) fish marked in November were recaptured in the same areas as late as the following April, despite early spring rains which had several times flooded the entire area.

In Long Lake (Minnesota), common shiners occurred primarily in two areas: (1) shiners under 100 mm were usually found in shallow water, either mixed in with mimic shiner schools, or in small schools on the outside edges of mimic shiner schools; (2) large shiners swam about in schools of 5–15 fish 0.5–1.0 m above aquatic plants, at depths of 1–4 m. (Moyle 1969).

In a compilation of temperature tolerances of the common shiner, Carlander (1969) listed lethal highs up to 33.5°C (92.3°F). The common shiner in nature adjusts to a wide range of average temperatures.

Hallam (1959) noted that the common shiner associated with both coldwater fish (brook trout and northern muddler) and warmwater fish (rock bass and smallmouth bass). In the Wisconsin River (Grant County), 255 common shiners were associated with the following species: quillback (17), river carpsucker (1), spotted sucker (1), white sucker (1), central stoneroller (1), creek chub (4), bullhead minnow (11), bluntnose minnow (246), fathead minnow (2), pugnose minnow (7), emerald shiner (12), spotfin shiner (1002), spottail shiner (1), weed shiner (1), river shiner (1), sand shiner (8), bigmouth shiner (1), Mississippi silvery minnow (5), central mudminnow (1), grass pickerel (7), northern pike (13), blackstripe topminnow (3), pirate perch (1), yellow perch (8), walleye (18), western sand darter (3), johnny darter (32), smallmouth bass (1), largemouth bass (8), bluegill (2), orangespotted sunfish (5), black crappie (14), and white crappie (1).

IMPORTANCE AND MANAGEMENT

A laboratory experiment (Paragamian 1976b) indicated that the common shiner is vulnerable to predation by smallmouth bass. Forty-eight percent of the common shiners were eaten by the bass, compared to 21% of the hornyhead chubs and 4% of the white suckers. These results were consistent with field observations from the Plover River (Portage County), in which 40% of the fish contained in the stomachs of smallmouth bass were identifiable as *Notropis*, including the common shiner. In addition to its use by game fish, the common shiner has been eaten by the pied-billed grebe, green heron, kingfisher, and bald eagle.

The common shiner is an important forage fish in Wisconsin, and one of the principal fishes available at bait dealers. It is an attractive bait minnow for northern pike (especially in winter), black bass, and walleyes, but it does not persist well on the hook.

The common shiner is readily available to the fisherman who goes after his own bait. I have seen glass minnow traps, baited with pieces of bread, fill with hundreds of common shiners a few minutes after setting. At times, glass traps become so filled with minnows that movement within the trap is scarcely possible. This method is successfully used by commercial minnow dealers.

While fishing for trout, I have taken the common shiner a number of times rising to my dry flies; it often provides fishing activity when trout fishing is slow. Larger specimens of shiners are acceptable food fish.

The common shiner makes an interesting and easily acquired aquarium fish. Males in breeding colors are strikingly attractive with their dark blue heads, bodies washed in pink, and paired orange fins. This fish is active, but it is not a very durable aquarium pet, since its mortality rate in captivity is high.

To raise this species commercially, rearing ponds must be arranged to allow adult fish to swim upstream from the ponds to lay their eggs. The young will then drift downstream and grow in the ponds. (Dobie et al. 1956).

Striped Shiner

Notropis chrysocephalus (Rafinesque). *Notropis*—back, keel; *chrysocephalus*—golden head (Greek).
Other common names: central common shiner, common shiner, shiner, redfin shiner.

Adult 116 mm, Milwaukee R. (Ozaukee Co.), 10 Sept. 1972

DESCRIPTION

Body moderately deep, laterally compressed. Average length 58–102 mm (2.3–4.0 in). TL = 1.27 SL. Depth into TL 4.4–4.9. Head length into TL 4.4–5.0. Snout bluntly pointed. Mouth large, terminal, extending to below anterior margin of eye; barbel absent. Pharyngeal teeth 2,4–4,2, sturdy and strongly hooked; arch stout. Eye into head length about 4.3. Gill rakers short, pointed, some flat-topped or dentate; about 9. Dorsal fin origin over pelvic fin origin; dorsal fin rays 8; anal fin rays 9 (8–10); pectoral fin rays 14–16; pelvic fin rays 8. Lateral line scales 36–40; lateral line complete, decurved. Digestive tract S-shaped, 0.7–0.8 TL. Chromosomes 2n = 50 (W. Legrande, pers. comm.).

Green- or blue-olive dorsally; sides blue-silver in adults; belly white-silver. Mid-dorsal stripe prominent, broad, and slate colored. Dark, wavy lines between scale rows of back, meeting on back posterior to dorsal fin. Sides with scattered dark scales. Fins generally clear, or tinged with white. Peritoneum dark brown overlying a silvery background.

Breeding male with lead blue on head and back; sides pink, distal third of dorsal, caudal and anal fins pink. Large tubercles on top of head, snout, and lower jaw. Scales of back, leading edge of dorsal fin with small tubercles. Anterior rays of pectoral fins with well-developed tubercles. Color and tubercles lacking in female.

Hybrids: Striped shiner × central stoneroller, striped shiner × Mississippi silvery minnow, striped shiner × hornyhead chub, striped shiner × common shiner, striped shiner × rosyface shiner (Gilbert 1964), striped shiner × common shiner from Pigeon Creek (Ozaukee County) (reported by Wis. Fish Distrib. Study).

SYSTEMATIC NOTES

Until recently, *Notropis chrysocephalus* was accorded subspecific rank as *Notropis cornutus chrysocephalus*. In 1964, Gilbert elevated this form from a subspecies of *Notropis cornutus* to specific rank, *Notropis chrysocephalus*, and it is so recognized by the Committee on Names of Fishes (Bailey et al. 1970). Several authors disagree with the change, noting that the distinctions are not clear-cut; these authors continue to recognize it as a subspecies of *Notropis cornutus* (Scott and Crossman 1973, Menzel 1976, R. J. Miller 1968, Miller and Robison 1973).

In the middle and lower Milwaukee River (Ozaukee to Milwaukee counties) the two species are taken side by side in the same collections. They are so distinctive in their markings that they can readily be separated in the field. Aids for their identification follow:

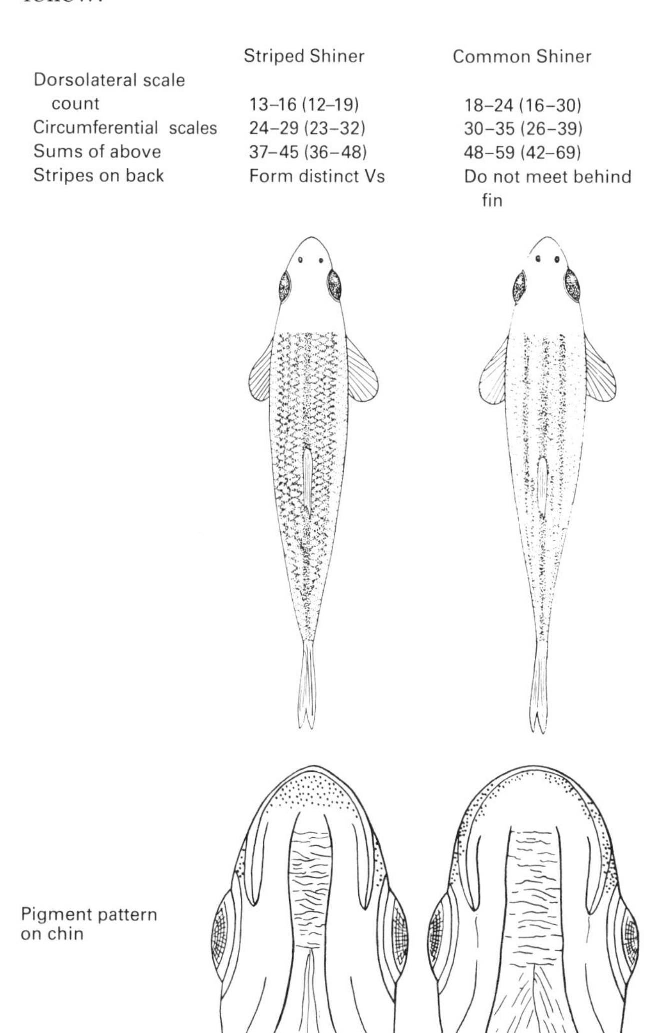

	Striped Shiner	Common Shiner
Dorsolateral scale count	13–16 (12–19)	18–24 (16–30)
Circumferential scales	24–29 (23–32)	30–35 (26–39)
Sums of above	37–45 (36–48)	48–59 (42–69)
Stripes on back	Form distinct Vs	Do not meet behind fin

Characters for the separation of the striped shiner and the common shiner (Gilbert 1964:144, 170)

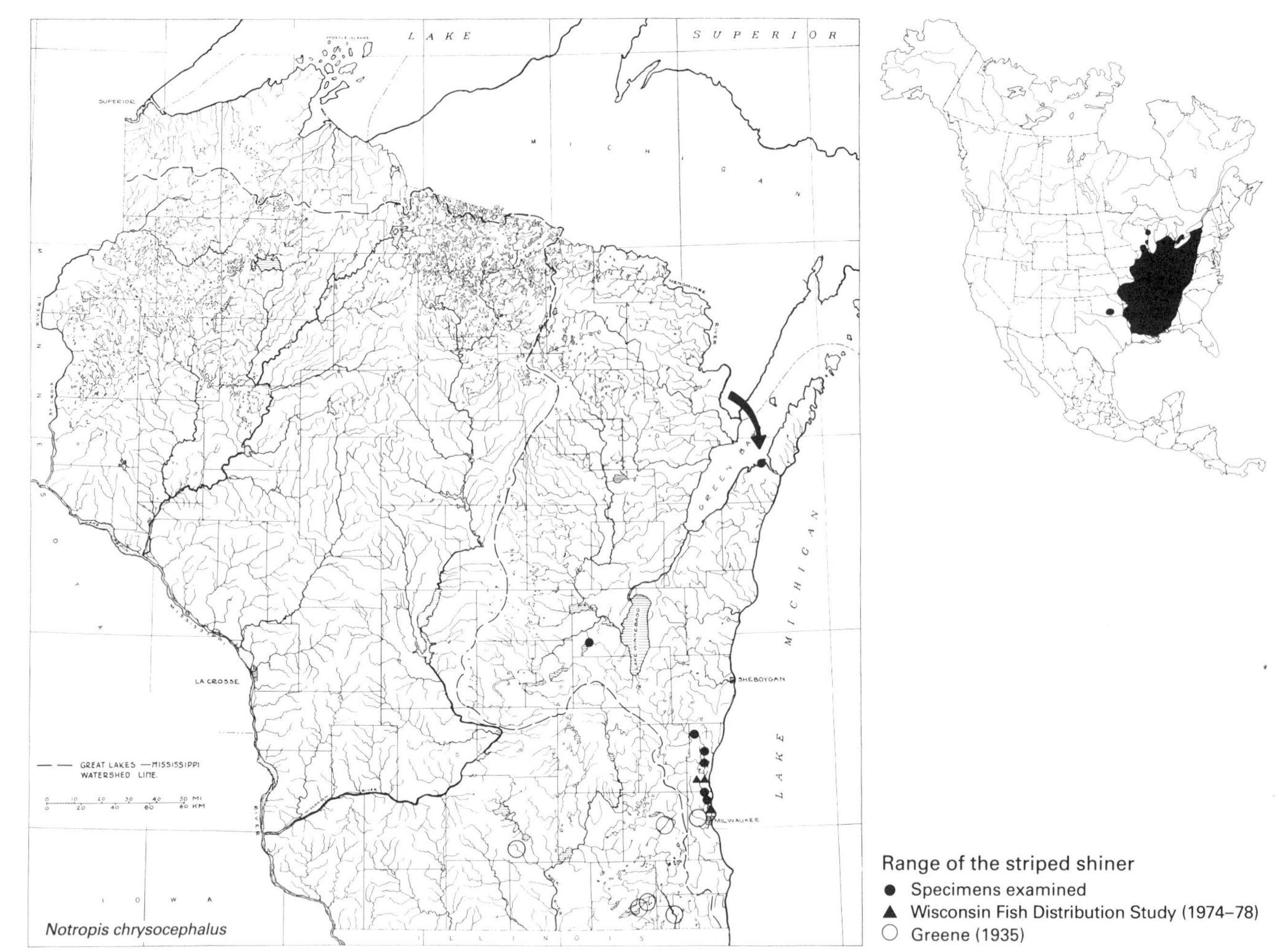

DISTRIBUTION, STATUS, AND HABITAT

The striped shiner occurs in the Rock River and Illinois and Fox river watersheds of the Mississippi River basin and in the Lake Michigan basin.

Specimens examined: UWSP 211 (34) Milwaukee River 0.8 km north of Grafton (Ozaukee County) 1963; UWSP 2089 (71) Milwaukee River 1.2 km north of Saukville (Ozaukee County) 1963; UWSP 2864 (1) Green Bay at mouth of tributary stream T28N R25E Sec 28 (Door County) 1962; UWSP 3207 (11) Milwaukee River at Kletzsch Park (Milwaukee County) 1969; UWSP 3264 (26) Milwaukee River 0.8 km north of Grafton (Ozaukee County) 1963; UWSP 3707 (11) Milwaukee River north of Good Hope Road (Milwaukee County) 1970; UWSP 3762 (4) Milwaukee River 100 m below Range Line Road (Milwaukee County) 1970; UWSP 4173 (108) Milwaukee River at County A (Ozaukee County) 1972; UWSP 4174 (14) Milwaukee River at Highway 57 (Ozaukee County) 1972; UWSP 4176 (23) Milwaukee River at County T (Ozaukee County) 1972; UWSP 5738 (1) Rush Creek T17NR14E S13 (Winnebago County) 1978.

The Wisconsin Fish Distribution Study, in addition to reporting numerous Milwaukee River records duplicating the above locales, has reported this species from these tributaries of the Milwaukee River: (16) Pigeon Creek T9N R21E Sec 22 (Ozaukee County) 1975, and Cedar Creek T10N R21E Sec 26 (Ozaukee County) 1967.

Compared to the common shiner, the range of the striped shiner is very constricted. In Missouri (Pflieger 1971), the striped shiner is not uniformly abundant over its range, and in some streams it seems to have declined since the 1890s. The reasons for its decline are not apparent. In Ohio, Trautman (1957) predicted that, as the waters of the state warmed up and became more turbid, the range of the striped shiner, finding such changes favorable, would expand.

In Wisconsin, the distribution of the striped shiner has decreased since Greene (1935) surveyed the state in the late 1920s. In recent years it has not been reported from Dane, Waukesha, Walworth, and Kenosha counties. Except for records from Green Bay and Rush Creek (Winnebago County), the striped shiner has been collected and reported only from the Milwaukee River and the lower portions of two tributaries, Cedar Creek and Pigeon Creek. The striped shiner occurs only in the central and lower sectors of the Milwaukee River, from Waubeka (Ozaukee County) downstream to Glendale (Milwaukee County). The closely related common shiner is found throughout the Milwaukee River system, where it is more abundant than the striped shiner.

The state of Wisconsin has given the striped shiner endangered status (Les 1979). To ensure its continuation in Wisconsin, it is imperative that the Milwaukee River be watched; perhaps a section of the river should be set aside for the protection of the striped shiner, since it is the only known reservoir of this species in the state.

In the Milwaukee River, the striped shiner occurs most frequently in clear to slightly turbid water at depths of 0.1–1.5 m over substrates of gravel (22% frequency), rubble (17%), boulders (17%), silt (17%), sand (17%), mud (6%), and bedrock (6%). It is often associated with dense aquatic vegetation.

Pflieger (1975) noted that in Missouri the striped shiner frequently occurs just below riffles in a slight to moderate current, but is more often found in nearby backwaters or short, rocky pools with little or no current.

BIOLOGY

Since the striped shiner was long considered conspecific with the common shiner, *Notropis cornutus*, few attempts were made in the past to differentiate its biology from that of the common shiner. Hankinson (1932), who was acquainted with the striped shiner and the closely related common shiner, reported that they appear to have identical spawning habitats and behavior. He observed the two species spawning in territorial holdings adjacent to each other in the same shallows.

The spawning season for the striped shiner in Wisconsin is not known. In southern Michigan, this season extends from the latter part of May into June (Hubbs and Cooper 1936); in Missouri, from late April to mid-June.

Hankinson (1932) provided most of the following spawning information. Water temperature must be at 18°C (64.4°F) for the initiation of spawning activities. A spawning group of striped shiners seen at a *Hybopsis* (*Nocomis*?) nest in southern Michigan was dominated by a large, breeding male who kept away intruding fish, while many shiners, mostly mature females, schooled closely around the male. Larger males would dispossess the smaller males. Where two fish seemed equally formidable, they swam side by side in a zigzag manner upstream, often for several meters, after which they separated. Such ceremonial behavior determines which male will be dominant in the spawning process that follows.

Spawning was accomplished in a fraction of a second. Preliminary to the act, the dominant male corralled the females toward the middle of the nest, and then threw his body into a curve on the inside of which the selected female was held always with her head pointed upward. The spawning act is like that of the creek chub, as it was observed by Reighard (1910). The male is often accompanied on the nest by a group of females, and undoubtedly spawns with several of them.

Hankinson noted that late in the spawning season only small males were found with holdings, perhaps because the spawning beds had been occupied by the larger and more formidable males earlier in the season, or possibly because the small males matured later than the large ones. The first explanation seems more likely, for Hankinson saw very small males spawning elsewhere early in the season.

The development of the striped shiner was described by Fish (1932). Eggs and larvae were found in a tributary creek to Lake Erie on 14 June. The eggs were 1.6 (1.45–1.9) mm diam. Upon hatching the larva was 6.9 mm TL. Fish described and figured stages through 13.2 mm.

Striped shiners from the Milwaukee River (Ozaukee County) collected 2 August 1963, showed the following growth:

Age Class	No. of Fish	TL (mm)		Calculated TL at Annulus (mm)			
		Avg	Range	1	2	3	4
0	4	33.8	29–45				
I	46	70.1	57–84	42.4			
II	20	92.1	86–101	47.8	86.6		
III	2	103.3	103–104	57.0	86.1	103.3	
IV	1	119.0		48.0	87.7	105.7	119.0
Avg (weighted)				44.5	86.6	104.1	119.0

Both the first annulus and, in most fish, the second annulus, were deposited by early August; the third and fourth annuli were in the process of formation. In central Ohio, the annulus is placed in May (Marshall 1939).

In Ohio (Trautman 1957) growth, is similar to that in the Milwaukee River. Young-of-year in October are 25–64 mm; at about 1 year, 38–89 mm; adults are 76–178 mm. Specimens more than 203 mm (8.0 in) long are uncommon. The largest striped shiner reported was 236 mm (9.3 in) long.

Stomachs of striped shiners from the Milwaukee River (Ozaukee County) contained Hymenoptera, Corixidae, Coleoptera, Diptera, unidentifiable insect remains, filamentous algae, and other vegetative material.

Marshall (1939) cited a study by R.C. Ball, presumably of this species, which indicated that it is an omnivorous feeder, and that food is found in the stomachs at all seasons, although the amount of food taken in the winter months is relatively small. A large portion of the diet consisted of insects, though plant material was taken freely at certain times; the kind of food depended on its seasonal abundance.

In Ohio (Trautman 1957), the largest populations of striped shiners are present in brooks and smaller streams where the gradients are moderate or high, the waters normally clear, the bottoms primarily of gravel, boulders, bedrock, and sand, and where brush or other escape cover is present in the pools.

According to Trautman (1957), many adults and young move downstream after the spawning season to winter in the larger, deeper waters of lower gradients; during the winter or in drought periods many are present in the Ohio River. Trautman noted that the striped shiner differs ecologically from the common shiner, in that the former seems to prefer warmer waters, moving downstream in larger numbers after spawning and occupying deeper and larger downstream waters in winter. Also, in Ohio the striped shiner seems to be more tolerant of turbid waters, silt on the stream bottom, and lower stream gradients. The reverse relationship seems to exist in Missouri (Pflieger 1971), where the common shiner occupies the warmer, more turbid prairie streams, and the striped shiner inhabits the cooler and clearer streams of the Ozark uplands.

In the Milwaukee River near Saukville (Ozaukee County), 77 striped shiners were associated with the following species: common shiner (151+), golden redhorse (3), bluntnose minnow (3), largescale stoneroller (16), hornyhead chub (5), creek chub (2), spotfin shiner (5), rosyface shiner (24), redfin shiner (4), sand shiner (32), black bullhead (1), smallmouth bass (1), pumpkinseed (3), longear sunfish (29), rock bass (5), logperch (1), blackside dace (1), and johnny darter (1).

IMPORTANCE AND MANAGEMENT

Smaller striped shiners undoubtedly serve as forage for game fishes. In the South, this minnow is used extensively as bait (Cook 1959), but in Wisconsin such use is practically nonexistent.

River Shiner

Notropis blennius (Girard). *Notropis*—back, keel; *blennius*—blenny, from the convex bluntnose profile.

Other common name: shiner.

Adult 100 mm, L. Winnebago (Calumet Co.), 18 Aug. 1960

DESCRIPTION

Body stout, slightly compressed laterally. Average length 61–89 mm (2.4–3.5 in). TL = 1.27 SL. Depth into TL 5.2–6.3. Head length into TL 4.4–5.2. Snout rounded and slightly overhanging the mouth. Mouth slightly oblique, reaching below anterior edge of eye to anterior edge of pupil; barbel absent. Pharyngeal teeth 2,4–4,2 (a tooth is commonly absent on one or both sides in outer row), stout, strongly hooked. Eye large, into head length 3.0–3.9. Gill rakers short, knoblike to conical, 6–9. Dorsal fin origin over pelvic fin origin; dorsal rays 8; anal fin rays 7 (rarely 8); pectoral fin rays 13–15; pelvic fin rays 8. Lateral line scales 32–36; lateral line complete, only slightly decurved. Digestive tract short with a single S-shaped loop 0.6–0.7 TL.

Silvery, but light yellow-brown dorsally; silvery midlateral stripe, silvery white on belly. Mid-dorsal stripe well defined, surrounding base of dorsal fin. Lateral line not marked by paired melanophores. No bright breeding colors. Peritoneum silvery.

Breeding male with minute tubercles on snout, top of head, on rays of pectoral fins and on front edges of dorsal and anal fins.

Sexual dimorphism: Pectoral fins in male longer and broader than in female.

SYSTEMATIC NOTES

In the past some confusion has existed in the terminology referring to this species. *Notropis jejunus* by Jordan and Evermann (1896–1900) and by Forbes and Richardson (1920) becomes *Notropis blennius*, and their *Notropis blennius* becomes the sand shiner, *Notropis stramineus*.

Hubbs and Lagler (1964) recognized two subspecies: *Notropis blennius jejunus* (Forbes), and *Notropis blennius blennius* (Girard). These authors assigned the Wisconsin populations to *Notropis blennius jejunus*.

DISTRIBUTION, STATUS, AND HABITAT

The river shiner occurs in the Mississippi River drainage basin in the Mississippi and lower Wisconsin rivers, in the lower reaches of larger tributaries, and in the Rock River system. In the Lake Michigan drainage basin it has become firmly established only in Lake Winnebago, but has been recorded nowhere else in the basin. It is absent from the Lake Superior basin.

Greene (1935) published records of the river shiner based on the literature and on reports from Lake Mendota (Dane County) and from several lakes in northwestern Waukesha County. The origin of the Lake Mendota report is unknown, and probably is in error. The Waukesha County reports undoubtedly originated with Cahn (1927), whose *Notropis blennius* is obviously the sand shiner, *Notropis stramineus* (see "Systematic Notes" above). These locales have been deleted from the range map.

Next to the spotfin shiner, *Notropis spilopterus*, the river shiner was the species most commonly captured from the Mississippi River; at a number of my collection sites on the Mississippi, more than 400 river shiners were taken. In Lake Winnebago it was next to the emerald shiner in abundance (Becker 1964b). It is common on the lower Wisconsin River, and rare in the Rock River system.

Greene (1935) collected this species well upstream on a number of tributaries to the Mississippi River and lower Wisconsin River. Its current absence in these locales implies a loss of range in recent years which cannot readily be accounted for.

The river shiner is typically an inhabitant of large rivers and river lakes. In Wisconsin, it was encountered most frequently at depths up to 1.5 m over substrates of sand (46% frequency), rubble (18%), mud (16%), gravel (16%), and clay (5%). It has been taken from a tributary stream 9 m wide, but most collections have come from sloughs, eddies, and sandbars of the lower Wisconsin and the Mississippi rivers. Several collections have been made over moderate to swift riffles. It is taken from clear to turbid water, and it is tolerant of continuous turbidity. Vegetation is completely lacking to dense in its habitat.

BIOLOGY

The river shiner is classified as a late spawner (Starrett 1951). In Wisconsin, spawning occurs from June

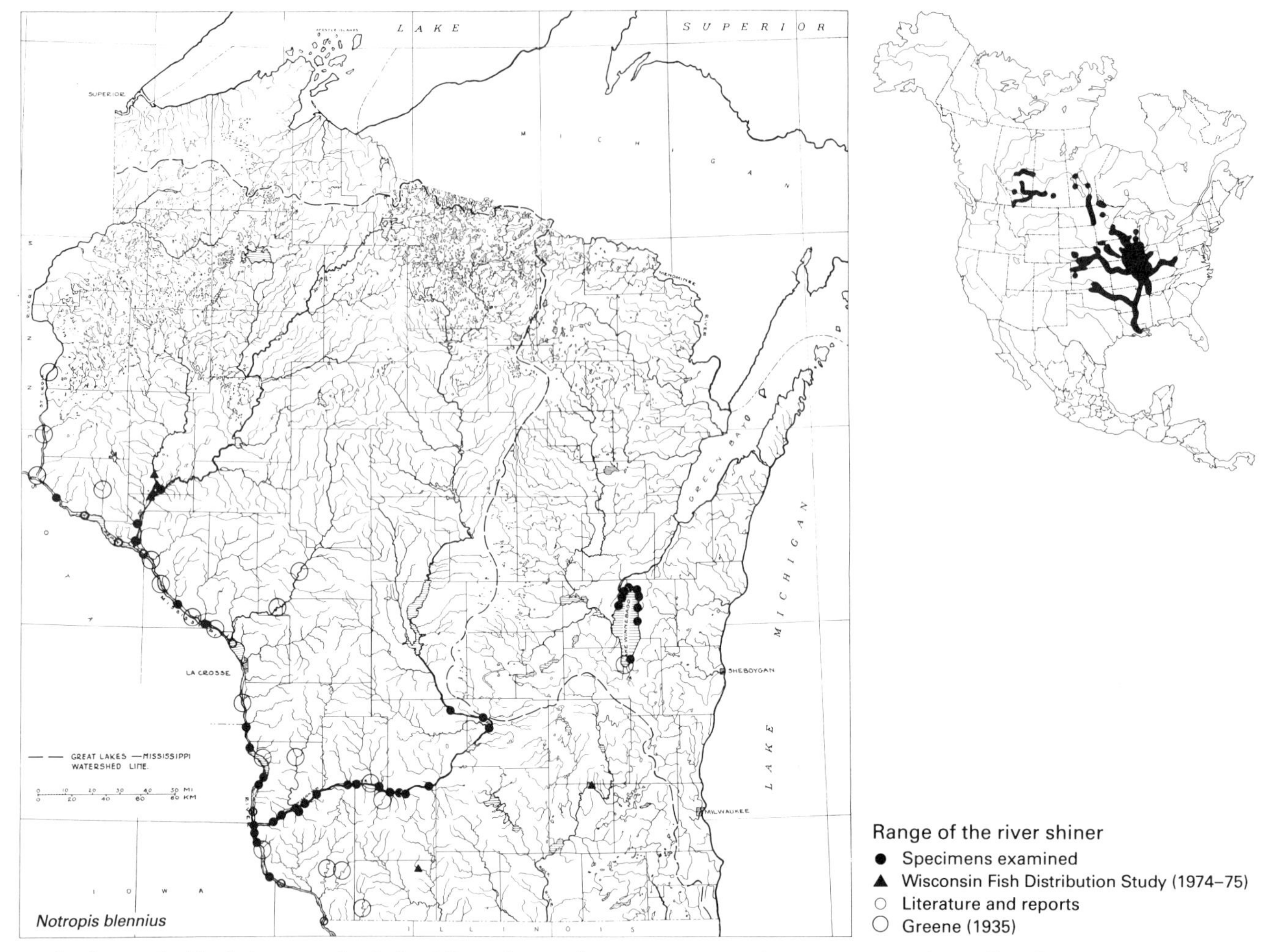

Range of the river shiner
● Specimens examined
▲ Wisconsin Fish Distribution Study (1974–75)
○ Literature and reports
◯ Greene (1935)

to the latter half of August. In Lake Winnebago, females were still gravid on 18 August but all were spent by 29 August. In Illinois, gravid females were reported from the last of June to 27 August (Forbes and Richardson 1920). In Ohio, spawning occurs over gravel and sand bars (Trautman 1957).

Nothing is known about its spawning behavior.

The fecundity of select females taken during the spawning season (some may have been partially spent) was reported as follows:

Date	TL (mm)	Ovarian WT as % of Total WT	No. of Mature Eggs	Egg Size (mm)	Location	UWSP No.
18 June	91	19.8%	2,840	0.94	Wisconsin R. (Crawford Co.)	2630
13 July	89	11.5	3,005	0.76	Wisconsin R. (Grant Co.)	3024
15 July	71	10.4	2,270	0.81	Mississippi R. (Grant Co.)	3039
15 July	82	16.8	1,895	0.83	Mississippi R. (Grant Co.)	3039

A second generation of small, white immature eggs was also seen; they were generally more numerous than the mature eggs.

In Lake Winnebago, young-of-year were 19–33 mm long by 18 August.

River shiners from the Mississippi River (Grant County), collected 24 September 1966, showed the following growth:

Age Class	No. of Fish	TL (mm)		Calculated TL at Annulus (mm)			
		Avg	Range	1	2	3	4
0	18	37.1	28–46				
I	20	58.4	46–64	38.4			
II	19	76.5	70–84	33.9	68.5		
III	9	87.3	82–92	28.1	58.4	80.2	
IV	6	97.3	89–108	28.5	62.4	83.3	93.3
Avg (weighted)				34.0	64.8	81.4	93.3

Age-I males in August are tuberculate and mature. Gravid females are generally age II and older.

In Ohio, Trautman (1957) found age-0 river shiners

in October 20–56 mm TL; age-I fish were 25–64 mm; adults were 52–132 mm. The largest river shiner was 132 mm (5.2 in) long.

The river shiner is primarily an insect feeder. In mid-July, stomachs of shiners from the Mississippi River at Wyalusing contained *Daphnia*, Corixidae, Trichoptera, Ephemeroptera, and tendipedid larvae. Algae and other plant matter as well as insects, have been noted from river shiners taken in the Wisconsin River.

Several adult river shiners in the Mississippi River collection had the acanthocephalan parasite *Pomphorhynchus bulbocolli* in the intestine, with the proboscis and bulblike neck extending through the intestinal wall into the body cavity.

Trautman (1957) reported that in Ohio the river shiner usually remains in water deeper than 1 m (3 ft) throughout the day, whenever these waters are clear; it ventures into shallower waters only at night when the waters are clear, or in the daytime only when they are turbid.

In the Mississippi River at Wyalusing (Grant County), 428 river shiners were associated with the following species: longnose gar (10), bowfin (1), gizzard shad (89), quillback (187), smallmouth buffalo (1), shorthead redhorse (3), golden redhorse (7), common carp (2), central stoneroller (1), silver chub (1), golden shiner (110), bullhead minnow (145), pugnose minnow (8), emerald shiner (340), spotfin shiner (245), spottail shiner (589), sand shiner (6), mimic shiner (2), bigmouth shiner (1), brown bullhead (2), tadpole madtom (1), northern pike (1), white bass (119), yellow bass (4), yellow perch (5), sauger (2), walleye (2), western sand darter (5), river darter (1), logperch (11), johnny darter (36), smallmouth bass (1), largemouth bass (31), pumpkinseed (1), bluegill (173), orangespotted sunfish (8), rock bass (1), black crappie (178), white crappie (14), brook silverside (118), and freshwater drum (17).

IMPORTANCE AND MANAGEMENT

The river shiner undoubtedly serves as forage for predator fish.

Little is known about the river shiner. Considering its abundance, excellent opportunities exist to learn about the basic life requirements of this fascinating minnow.

Ironcolor Shiner

Notropis chalybaeus (Cope). *Notropis*—back, keel; *chalybaeus*—iron-colored.

Adult 51 mm, canal, 2 km west of Grant City (Scott Co.), Missouri, 9 June 1964

Adult 48 mm, Fox R. opposite Lock 25 (Columbia Co.), 26 Aug. 1925

DESCRIPTION

Body moderately robust; slightly compressed. Average length 47 mm (1.8 in). TL = 1.27 SL (Swift 1970). Depth into TL 4.7–5.8. Head length into TL 4.5–4.8. Snout blunt. Mouth terminal, oblique (about 45° to body axis), tip of upper lip extending to level of mid-pupil; mouth extending below posterior nostril to anterior margin of eye; barbel absent. Pharyngeal teeth 2,4–4,2, slender, hooked with long cutting edge; arch slender. Eye large, into head length about 3.0. Gill rakers short, conical to knoblike, and widely separated on lower limb, 6–7. Dorsal fin origin over or slightly posterior to origin of pelvic fin; dorsal fin rays 8; anal fin rays 8; pectoral fin rays 12–14; pelvic fin rays 8. Lateral series scales 33–34 (31–36); lateral line incomplete, with 10 or more unpored scales posteriorly; infraorbital canal interrupted above and behind eye. Digestive tract with a single S-shaped loop about 0.6 TL.

Back olive green, belly whitish. Dark pigment conspicuous on inner borders of jaws, floor, and roof of mouth and on oral valve. Lateral stripe, almost diam of eye at its widest, extending onto head and around snout on upper lip and tip of chin; a small rounded or elongated basicaudal spot, subequal to lateral stripe and slightly, but distinctly, separated from it, extending well out onto the caudal rays. Distinct mid-dorsal stripe in advance of dorsal origin. Dorsal scale pockets pigmented so as to form a diamond-shaped scale pattern. In 1–1.5 scale rows above the lateral stripe the scale pockets are only lightly pigmented, resulting in a distinctive light streak between scales of the back and the lateral stripe; melanophores lightly lining in part the first scale pockets below the lateral stripe. Breast anterior to pectoral bases naked. Fins clear, rays occasionally lightly pigmented. Peritoneum silvery with numerous dark speckles.

Breeding males with sharp, saw-edged tubercles ringing lower jaw, which merge into a well-developed group of 8–12 tubercles at tip of slightly swollen symphysis. Tubercles of varying size on anterior end of snout, and small patches of tubercles arranged in bands on the rays of the pectoral fins. A slight growth of tubercles similar to male pattern sometimes seen on larger, probably older, females (Marshall 1947). Males with orange to rose tint over the entire body, but most intense on the dorsal and caudal fins and on the ventral surface of the caudal peduncle; in females tints on dorsal and caudal fins faint or absent.

SYSTEMATIC NOTES

Variations in the meristic and morphometric characters of the ironcolor shiner in different parts of its ranges are treated by Swift (1970). In appearance this species is easily confused with *Notropis texanus* and *Notropis heterodon*.

DISTRIBUTION, STATUS, AND HABITAT

In Wisconsin, the ironcolor shiner has been taken only twice—both times in headwater sectors within the Lake Michigan watershed, where it is at the extreme northern limits of its range. In the Midwest, it occurs in widely disjunct populations, generally at low population levels. In lower Michigan, it is found only in the St. Joseph River drainage (Becker 1976).

The two collections which Greene (1935) originally catalogued as *Notropis texanus* contained specimens of this species (Swift 1970). There were 7 ironcolor shiners among 41 fish collected from the Fox River opposite Lock 25 (Columbia County), 26 August 1925, and 2 ironcolors among 75 from Blake Creek (Waupaca County), 9 July 1926. These are on deposit at the Museum of Zoology in Ann Arbor, Michigan (nos. 188734 and 188735).

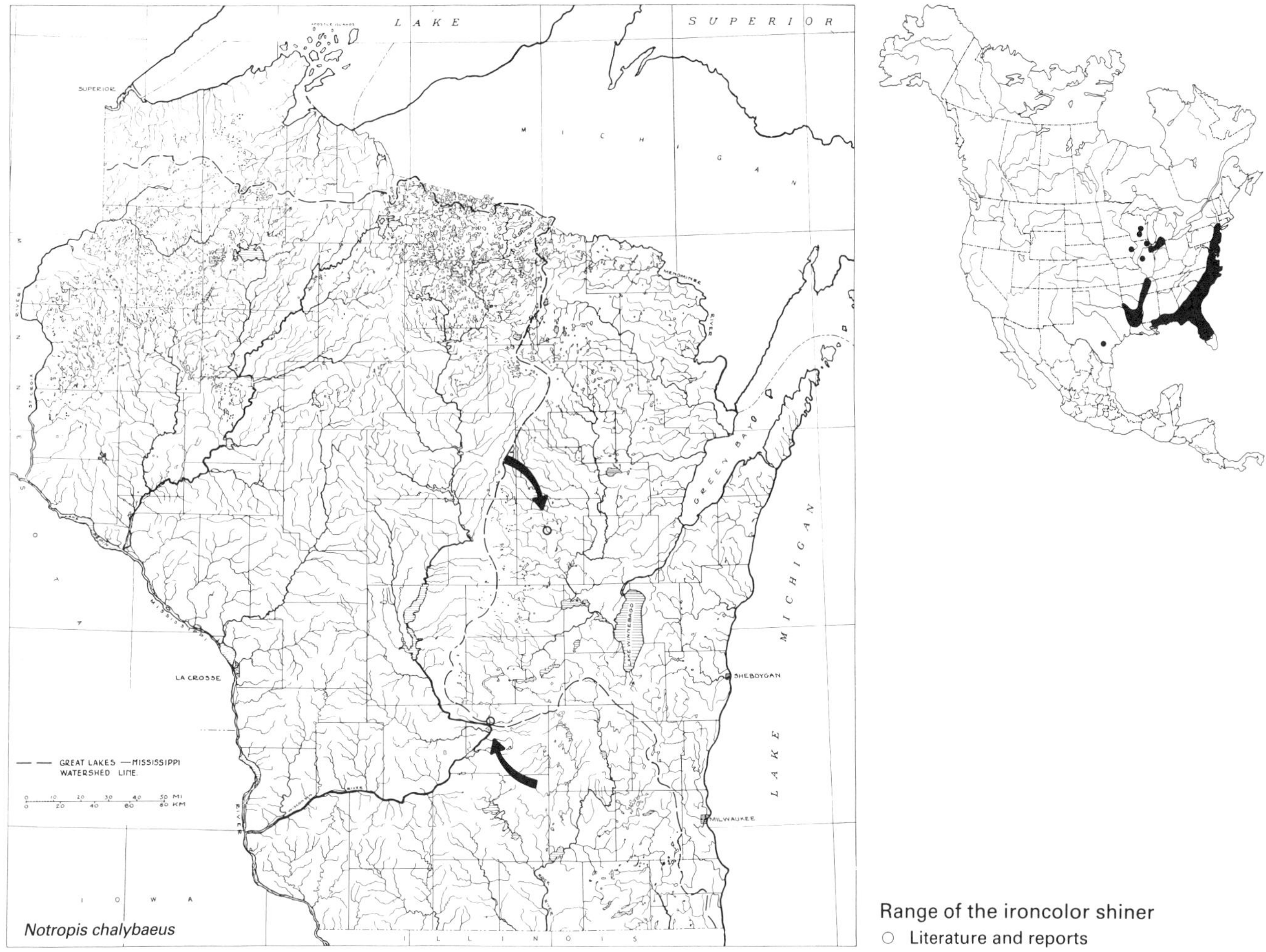

Range of the ironcolor shiner
○ Literature and reports

In Iowa (Harlan and Speaker 1956, Roosa 1977), the ironcolor shiner has not been taken since around the turn of the century, and may be extirpated. It is rare in Michigan (Miller 1972). In Wisconsin, its presence is based entirely on the nine specimens from the two collections previously mentioned; no other known collections have been made since the mid-1920s. It is probable that this species is extirpated in Wisconsin.

Although the ironcolor shiner occurs in shallow waters and in swift currents, it is primarily an inhabitant of sluggish, acid streams in small, quiet, sand-bottomed pools with an abundance of aquatic vegetation. These pools are its preferred habitat, and are important in its breeding.

The ironcolor shiner occurs in waters with temperatures close to the air temperature; the water is usually a few degrees cooler. Marshall (1947) noted that in such waters, temperatures may fluctuate rapidly.

The movements of this species are associated with changes in the stream contours and the water level. It exhibits a general tendency to move into quiet water whenever possible.

BIOLOGY

The extent of the ironcolor shiner's spawning season in Wisconsin is unknown. A tuberculate male was taken from Blake Creek (Waupaca County) on 9 July. Other records from its northern range show that highly tuberculate males and females with large eggs were observed as early as 30 May in Bucks County, Pennsylvania, and 7 June in Orange County, New York (Swift 1970).

In Florida, where the biology of this species is best understood (Marshall 1947), spawning occurs from early or mid-April through the end of September. No distinctive migratory movements are correlated with spawning, which occurs in sand-bottomed pools. No nest is built.

Marshall described the ironcolor shiner's spawning behavior (p. 172):

> . . . Throughout the daylight hours of the breeding season the males chase the females about the area . . . an individual will chase first one female and then another, apparently selecting any ripe female that ventures nearby. . . . Whereas sexual chasing may be observed during times of

high water and rapid currents, the culmination of courtship behavior has been observed only when there was little current in the populated areas. Just prior to spawning the sexual chasing described becomes more intense. Eventually the females discontinue their retreat from pursuing males and the actual union of individuals soon follows . . . a male and female swim side by side with their silvery, ventral surfaces pressed close together and their dorsal surfaces apart. In such close proximity they dash quickly across the pool and then separate. . . . Such a spawning behavior tends to distribute the eggs in a broadcast manner about the pools.

The ironcolor shiner seems to have little affiliation to a particular spawning area. When disturbed and driven out of one spawning area to an adjacent site, these shiners resume spawning almost immediately.

A gravid female, collected 9 June from Scott County, Missouri, held 246 mature, orange-yellow eggs 0.7–0.8 mm diam, and an equal number of immature, yellow-white eggs 0.4–0.5 mm diam. The ovaries were 12% of the body weight.

The fertilized eggs sink and adhere to sand grains and similar particles on the stream bottom. In the laboratory females in breeding condition were stripped of eggs by the application of slight pressure to the abdomen, a treatment often fatal to the fish. At mean water temperatures of 16.7°C (62°F), the eggs hatched in about 52–56 hr. According to Marshall (1947), the newly hatched prolarvae are 2.3 mm TL. At 6 mm SL (at the age of 30 days in aquarium-reared fish), the larvae—several of which have been illustrated by Marshall—undergo a gradual metamorphosis into the juvenile form. When they have attained 14.8 mm TL, at age 69 days, fin development is complete or nearly so, and in gross external appearance they resemble the adult except for their size, lack of scales, and lack of adult pigmentation. Swift (1970) suggested that this growth rate is probably slower than the growth rate in the wild. In Wisconsin, young-of-year are 29 mm TL by the end of August.

In nature, larvae of the ironcolor shiner were collected from the surface in or near the spawning areas, where they swam in aggregations, completely independent of and unattended by adults. Although it is possible that a single aggregation might be composed of the young of one parent, it is probable, as indicated by the heterogeneous sizes within an aggregation, that the young of several different parents and different hatching dates are intermixed. The larvae showed a tendency to swim into the current, but they had practically no ability to maintain a position in the current. Larvae occur generally in protected, miniature embayments and harbors of various sorts.

Sometime after development, juvenile ironcolor shiners become an integral part of the adult schools, which are composed of fish of many sizes, with both sexes represented in about equal numbers. The composition of schools is definitely unstable: groups sometimes split and sometimes unite, and there is a considerable exchange of members among groups. Sometimes individuals remain isolated, or form small groups of two to five minnows. Schooling is retained by visual stimuli, and at night there is a partial dispersal.

The Wisconsin specimens of the ironcolor shiner were aged by scale analysis. In the Fox River collection (Columbia County) of 26 August 1925, three young-of-year were 27.2 (24–29) mm TL, and four age-I fish were 43.6 (33–48) mm TL. The calculated length at the first annulus was 29.0 mm. The two shiners collected 9 July 1926 from Blake Creek (Waupaca County), were age I and 40.5 and 43 mm TL; they were an estimated 28.5 mm at the first annulus. One of these was a well-tuberculated male; hence maturity in males may occur at age I. A 52-mm ripe female, collected 9 June 1964 from a canal near Grant City, Missouri, was 2 years old.

Marshall (1947) noted that females, on the average, are larger than males. The known maximum size is 51 mm SL, or approximately 64 mm (2.5 in) TL (Bailey et al. 1954).

According to Marshall, the ironcolor shiner feeds by sight on a variety of aquatic insects, insect fragments, and any other animal material small enough to be ingested. Although the digestive tract of examined specimens showed a high percentage of algae and plant detritus, with very few recognizable animal remains, this species has the anatomy of a decidedly carnivorous minnow. There is no indication that the plant materials are digested, since those found at the anal end of the intestinal tract are in the same condition as those at the anterior end. Marshall suggested that the plant content was a mass of the more resistant plant tissues from within animals eaten by the shiner. In feeding experiments in which the shiner was given a variety of microcrustacea, on which it fed voraciously, it was observed on dissection that the long, hooked pharyngeal teeth had torn the crustaceans into shreds and fragments, leaving the visible plant material behind.

The ironcolor shiner's normal feeding activities continue during the breeding season. Throughout the daylight hours these minnows may be seen approaching particles that drift by in the current; in sluggish pools, they may be seen ranging about in quest of food. Not all particles approached are taken into the mouth, and, of those that are, not all are acceptable; many are soon ejected. No feeding has been noted at night.

Since 1960, collections at the sites in Wisconsin where this species was once known to occur produced the following species: from the Fox River (Columbia County)—white sucker (1), central mudminnow (3), common carp (13), northern redbelly dace (1), bluntnose minnow (79), fathead minnow (18), golden shiner (37), spotfin shiner (17), blacknose shiner (1), sand shiner (9), brassy minnow (1), black bullhead (4), tadpole madtom (20), banded killifish (2), blackstripe topminnow (7), johnny darter (10), banded darter (2), rock bass (1), pumpkinseed (1), and brook stickleback; from Blake Creek (Waupaca County)—rainbow trout (1), northern hog sucker (5), white sucker (9), hornyhead chub (52), creek chub (4), bluntnose minnow (16), common shiner (72), spotfin shiner (4), stonecat (2), blackside darter (5), johnny darter (12), banded darter (4), fantail darter (3), pumpkinseed (1), bluegill (9), and rock bass (5).

IMPORTANCE AND MANAGEMENT

In Wisconsin, the ironcolor shiner has no value as a bait or forage fish. It has been recovered in the south from the stomachs of the grass pickerel, *Esox americanus* (Marshall 1947). The eggs and young are probably subject to predation by almost any carnivorous fish, including the adults of their own species. Other possible predators are such birds as the kingfisher and the heron.

Weed Shiner

Notropis texanus (Girard). *Notropis*—back, keel; *texanus*—of Texas.

Other common names: northern weed shiner, Richardson shiner (the northern subspecies); Evermann shiner (the southern subspecies).

Adult 51 mm, Buffalo R. (Buffalo Co.), 13 Sept. 1969

DESCRIPTION

Body moderately robust, slightly compressed. Average size 51 mm (2 in). TL = 1.25 SL. Depth into TL 5.5–6.1. Head length into TL 4.8–5.3. Snout blunt. Mouth terminal, oblique (less than 45° to body axis), tip of upper lip extending to level of midpupil; mouth extending below posterior nostril to anterior margin of eye; barbel absent. Pharyngeal teeth 2,4–4,2 (occasionally 1 or 2 teeth of outer row missing on one side); slender, slightly to strongly hooked; arch moderately sturdy. Eye large, into head length 2.8–3.3. Gill rakers on lower limb, 3, knoblike; in joint and on upper limb 4, short, conical. Dorsal fin origin slightly anterior to origin of pelvic fin; dorsal fin rays 8; anal fin rays 7; pectoral fin rays 12–14; pelvic fin rays 8. Lateral line scales 34–37; lateral line complete, slightly decurved. Digestive tract with a single S-shaped loop 0.6–0.7 TL. Chromosomes 2n = 50 (Campos and Hubbs 1973).

Back olive green with brassy tinge; silvery on sides, belly whitish. Dark pigment essentially absent from inside of mouth except for a few melanophores on oral valve. Lateral stripe, about half diam of eye at its widest, extending onto head and around snout on upper lip and tip of chin; a small square or rounded basicaudal spot subequal to lateral stripe and slightly, but distinctly, separated from it. Mid-dorsal stripe distinct and expanded to a dark spot in advance of dorsal origin. Dorsal scale pockets pigmented so as to form a diamond-shaped scale pattern. In 1–1.5 scale rows above the lateral stripe the scale pockets are only slightly pigmented, resulting in a distinctive light streak between scales of the back and the lateral stripe. Melanophores lightly lining the scale pockets below the lateral stripe in a distinct diamond-shaped pattern for as many as 2 scale rows. Breast anterior to pectoral bases unscaled. Fins clear, rays occasionally lightly pigmented. Peritoneum silvery, with a few dark speckles, to dusky.

Breeding males with tubercles well developed on top of head and snout, lower jaw, and on most pectoral rays; few tubercles on scales of nape to origin of dorsal fin. Breeding colors of males collected 13 May in Kalamazoo River (Michigan) "with strong amber wash, dorsal and caudal with strong wash of orange, females not so bright" (Carl Hubbs cited by Swift 1970).

Hybrid: Weed shiner × mimic shiner (reported by Wis. Fish Distrib. Study).

SYSTEMATIC NOTES

Notropis roseus (Jordan) and *Notropis nux* Evermann become *Notropis texanus* (Girard) *fide* Suttkus (1958). If a northern subspecies is recognized, *N. roseus richardsoni* Hubbs and Greene becomes *N. texanus richardsoni* (Hubbs and Greene). In Wisconsin, Greene (1935) recognized the southern subspecies from the Platte River (Grant County), and the northern subspecies from the remainder of its Wisconsin range.

DISTRIBUTION, STATUS, AND HABITAT

In Wisconsin, the weed shiner occurs in the Mississippi River and Lake Michigan drainage basins; it is not known from the Lake Superior basin. The distribution records indicated by Greene (1935) have been revised according to Swift (1970).

Greene (1935) suggested that the weed shiner crossed into the Lake Michigan drainage basin at Portage.

This southern minnow is at the northern limits of its range in Wisconsin and Minnesota. It is regarded as threatened in Iowa (Roosa 1977). In Wisconsin, the weed shiner is uncommon in the lower Wisconsin River, in the Mississippi River, and in the lower portions of their tributaries. Populations are widely disjunct. Although it was quite common at one time above St. Croix Falls, the Museum of Natural History at Stevens Point has had only a single, unverifiable report since the 1960s; according to Eddy and Underhill (1974), no specimens have been taken by them in that area since the 1950s. Since 1958 I have collected at sites in the upper Fox River watershed (Marquette, Green Lake, and Columbia counties) where Greene (1935) collected weed shiners in the late 1920s, but I have been unable to find any there. Most records from the Lake Michigan basin are old, and the few recent records are distributed northward (Outagamie and Marinette counties). The only recent records

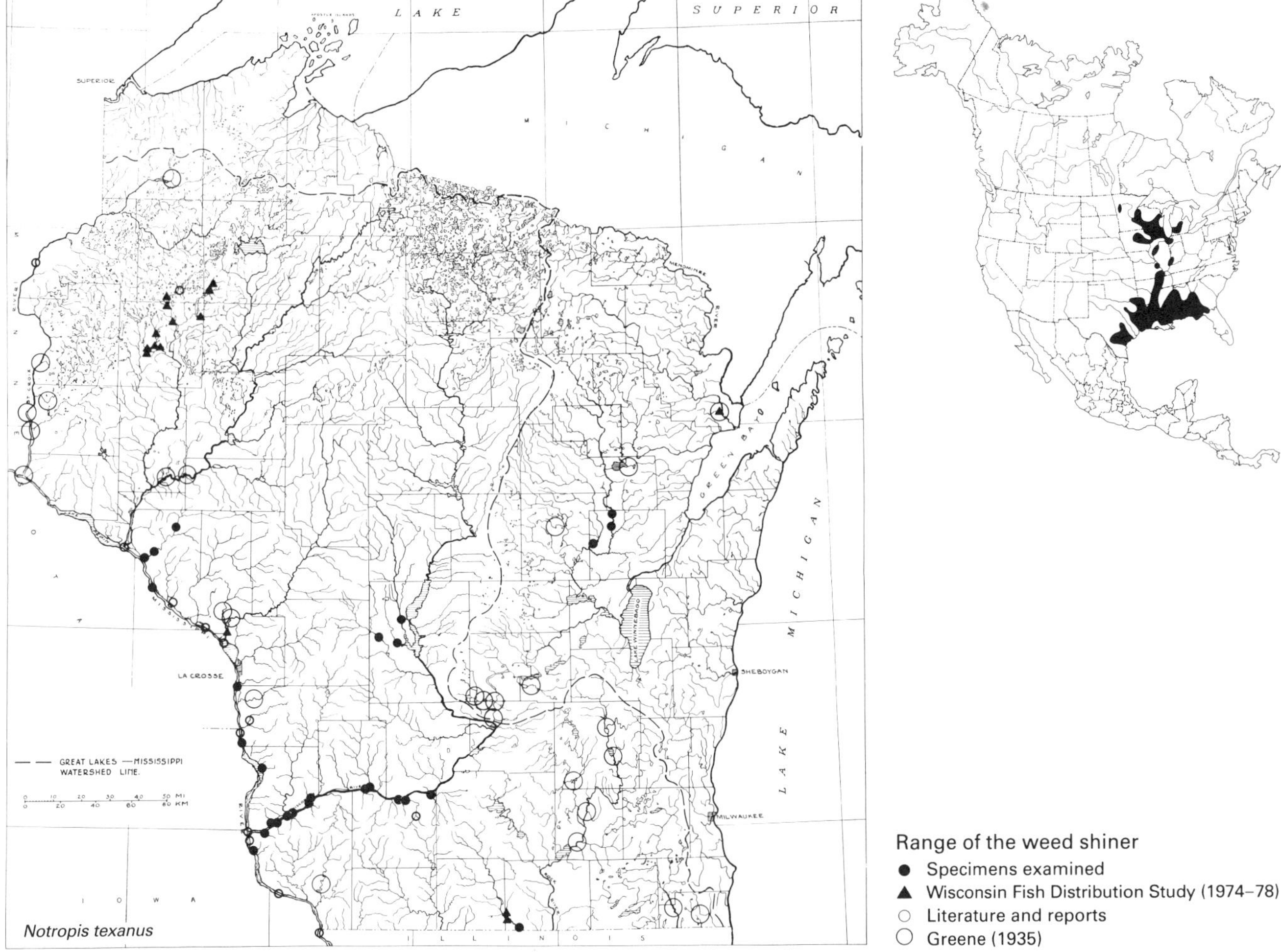

from southeastern Wisconsin come from the Sugar River.

The weed shiner must be extremely sensitive to environmental deterioration or changes, although the factors operating are not understood. It should be monitored closely in those areas where known populations exist. In Wisconsin it has been given watch status (Les 1979).

The weed shiner is an inhabitant of sloughs, lakes, and the quiet or sluggish sections of medium-sized streams and larger rivers. Occasionally it is taken from the lower reaches of small tributary streams; in one instance the tributary was only 1–1.5 m wide, but the weed shiner occurs more commonly in tributaries 12.1–24.0 m wide. In Wisconsin, it was encountered most frequently in water 0.1–1.5 m deep over substrates of sand (37% frequency), mud (32%), clay (11%), silt (5%) detritus (5%), gravel (5%), and boulders (5%). It occurs in waters of slow current, or without current. Despite the implication of its common name, "weed shiner," it is not always associated with weedy habitats.

BIOLOGY

In Wisconsin, spawning occurs in late June and July. Inspection of museum specimens indicates that most spawning is completed by mid-July. In the state of Mississippi (Cook 1959), spawning may occur from February to May.

A pre-spawning age-II, 52-mm female, collected from the Wisconsin River on 18 June 1962, and with ovaries 14% of total weight, held 420 mature yellow eggs 0.8 mm diam; an almost equal number of immature white eggs were 0.5 mm diam. A second age-II female, 50 mm TL, with ovaries 15% of body weight held 307 mature yellow eggs, and an equal number of immature white eggs.

Weed shiners from Buffalo River (Buffalo County), collected 13 September 1969, showed the growth presented in the table on the following page. The estimated length of the weed shiner at the time of scale deposition is 13 mm (R. Schmal, pers. comm.).

Age-I fish taken from Barron Flowage (Barron County) on 29 July 1976 were 32, 33, and 34.5 mm TL (UWSP 5567). Swift (1970) noted that the weed

Age Class	No. of Fish	TL (mm) Avg	Range	Calculated TL at Annulus (mm) 1	2
I	17	42.0	36–46	28.9	
II	33	52.4	47–57	32.5	47.1
Avg (weighted)				31.3	47.1

shiner reaches a maximum of 70 mm SL (87.5 mm TL) (UMMZ 163518).

Analysis of stomach samples of weed shiners from a slough in the Wisconsin River disclosed mostly plant debris, including filamentous algae. Animal material was present, but unidentifiable.

The weed shiner lives in midwater and is a schooling fish. Species associated in the Buffalo River (Buffalo County) with 141 weed shiners were: emerald shiner (41), spotfin shiner (45), golden shiner (6), bluntnose minnow (7), fathead minnow (39), white sucker (1), spotted sucker (1), largemouth bass (2), black crappie (1), green sunfish (2), and johnny darter (1). In Gran Grae Creek (Crawford County), species associated with 56 weed shiners were: northern hog sucker (1), white sucker (51), central stoneroller (530), longnose dace (3), blacknose dace (1), creek chub (285), bluntnose minnow (117), common shiner (50), spotfin shiner (10), bigmouth shiner (146), brassy minnow (5), Mississippi silvery minnow (26), central mudminnow (1), grass pickerel (2), northern pike (1), walleye (3), johnny darter (10), mud darter (1), fantail darter (1), and warmouth (1).

IMPORTANCE AND MANAGEMENT

The weed shiner's use as a forage fish is probably low, even in those areas where numbers have been taken. It has no significance as a bait minnow. The capture of a few specimens is a collecting event.

Blackchin Shiner

Notropis heterodon (Cope). *Notropis*—back, keel; *heterodon*—varying teeth (in reference to tooth number).

Other common names: black-striped minnow, black-chinned minnow, shiner.

Adult male 65 mm, Lac Vieux Desert (Vilas Co.), 18 June 1977

Adult female 67 mm, Lac Vieux Desert (Vilas Co.), 18 June 1977

DESCRIPTION

Body robust, only slightly deeper than wide. Average length 56 mm (2.2 in). TL = 1.26 SL. Depth into TL 4.1–6.7. Head length into TL 4.2–5.0. Snout bluntly pointed. Mouth small, terminal, oblique (about 45° to body axis) and extending below anterior margin of eye; barbel absent. Pharyngeal teeth variable, 1,4–4,1 or 4–4, strongly hooked, with well-developed cutting edge; arch stout. Eye large, into head length 2.5–4.0. Gill rakers short, conical, up to 8. Dorsal fin origin generally directly over origin of pelvic fin; dorsal rays 8; anal fin rays 8; pectoral fin rays 12–14; pelvic fin rays 8. Lateral scales 31–38; lateral line incomplete to complete or interrupted, slightly decurved; breast scaled at least in part. Digestive tract S-shaped, 0.7–0.8 TL; all three segments running the full length of body cavity.

Silvery over a background yellow dorsally, and whitish ventrally. Scales immediately above the dark lateral stripe lack dark edges, producing a marked light streak, but all scales above this are edged in pigment. Lateral stripe dark and distinctive, extending from the caudal fin onto the head, through the eye, around the snout, and slightly onto the chin; lateral stripe often forming a zigzag pattern (scales of next row above lateral line with dark bars alternating with the black marks on the lateral line scales). Basicaudal spot small. During breeding season adults develop a marked yellow tinge ventrally. Fins generally clear, except for rays edged in dark pigment. Peritoneum silvery, with brown speckles, to dusky.

Breeding male with fine tubercles on top of head and upper surface of pectoral fins.

Sexual dimorphism: In male pectoral fin length into SL 5.7; in female 6.8.

DISTRIBUTION, STATUS, AND HABITAT

The blackchin shiner occurs in the Mississippi River, Lake Michigan, and Lake Superior drainage basins in Wisconsin. In the Mississippi basin it is generally absent from the unglaciated region. Its range is closely associated with glacial lakes and streams. In the preparation of the range map, I have followed the revisions noted by Swift (1970) for the upper Fox River materials deposited by Greene (1935) in the University of Michigan Museum of Zoology.

The blackchin shiner is rare in North Dakota, and endangered in Pennsylvania and South Dakota (Miller 1972). In Minnesota, the species has vanished in many places, probably as a result of increased siltation and accompanying turbidity (Eddy and Underhill 1974). In Iowa, it is probably extirpated, since it has not been collected for many years (Harlan and Speaker 1956). It quickly disappeared from Ohio when waters became turbid and the bottom silty, or when vegetation vanished (Trautman 1957). In Illinois it is rare (Lopinot and Smith 1973).

In early Wisconsin the blackchin shiner was abundant. Cahn (1927) reported schools numbering 200 individuals from Waukesha County lakes like Oconomowoc, La Belle, Golden, Keesus, Pewaukee, and Pine. Although still present in several of these lakes, it is greatly diminished in numbers. It was reported as one of the most common species during 1913–1914 in Lake Wingra (Dane County) (Noland 1951); today it is extirpated there. In Wisconsin, the blackchin shiner still appears secure in the northern counties, where it is common in lakes and bog ponds; elsewhere it has been reduced or eliminated. This glacial relict bears close watching.

The blackchin shiner inhabits glacial potholes and lakes, and streams which are usually lake outlets or inlets. In Wisconsin, it was encountered most frequently in clear to slightly turbid water at depths of 0.1–0.5 m, and less commonly in deeper waters. It

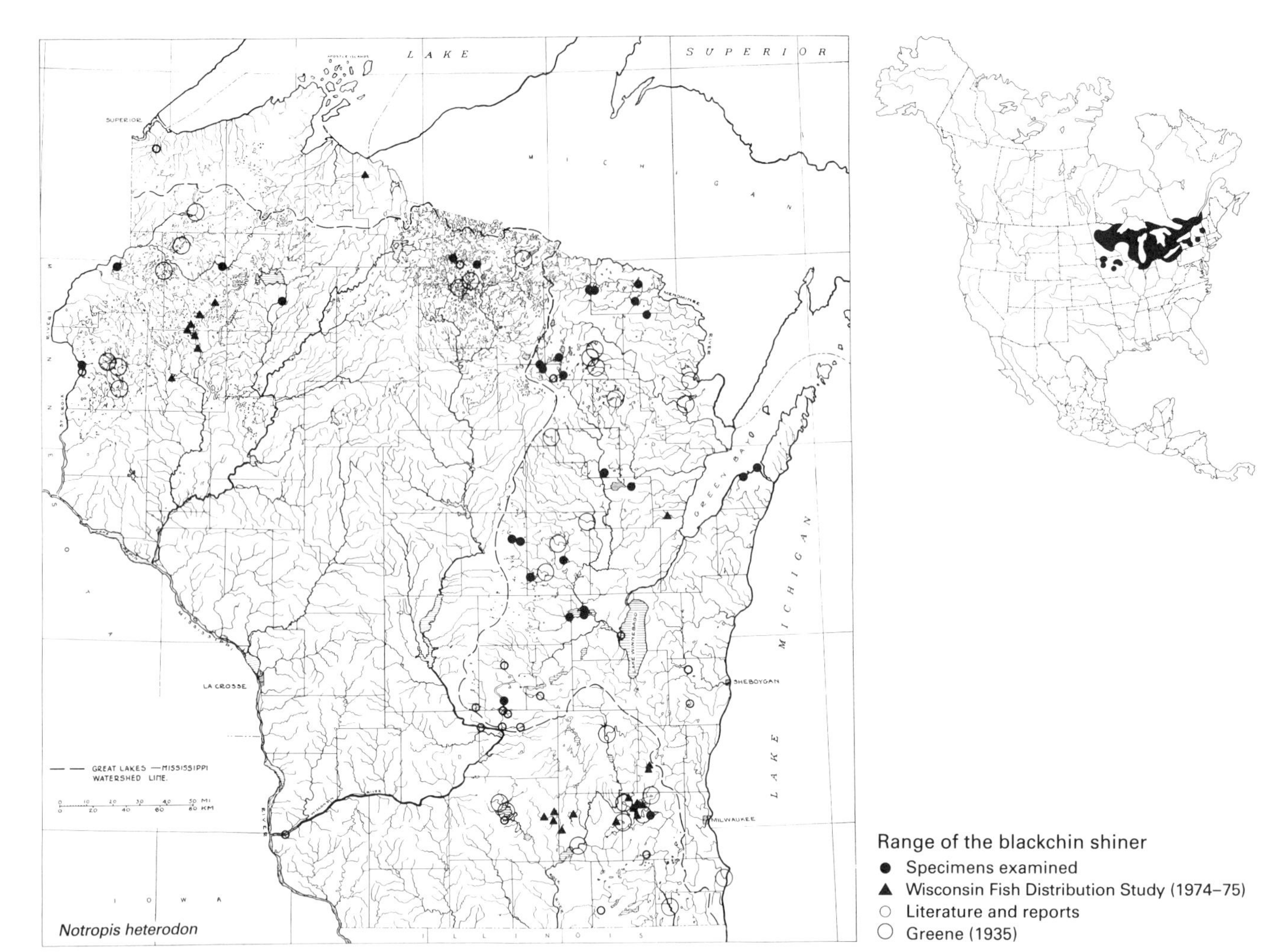

Range of the blackchin shiner
● Specimens examined
▲ Wisconsin Fish Distribution Study (1974–75)
○ Literature and reports
◯ Greene (1935)

was found over substrates of sand (30% frequency), gravel (21%), mud (18%), silt (14%), boulders (7%), detritus (4%), clay (2%), rubble (2%), and marl (2%). Lakes were preferred, although it occurred in quiet streams of the following widths: 1.0–3.0 m (33%), 3.1–6.0 m (17%), 6.1–12.0 m (25%), and 12.1–24.0 m (25%). It is associated with sparse to dense vegetation.

BIOLOGY

In Wisconsin, spawning occurs from June to August. Gravid females were collected in many samples taken through 9 August, and inspection of ovaries indicated a wide range in egg development. This suggests that, for one individual, spawning probably extends over a period of several weeks.

On 15 June in Spider Lake (Marinette County), a female 61.5 mm, 2.46 g, with ovaries 17% of body weight, held 675 mature or maturing eggs 0.8–1.2 mm diam; the immature white eggs, which were not counted, were 0.3–0.7 mm diam. A 54-mm, 1.66-g female, collected from Lake Poygan (Winnebago County) on 8 August, held 705 mature or maturing eggs 0.5–1.0 mm diam; the ovaries were 16% of body weight, and contained 2.5 times as many immature white eggs, 0.2–0.4 mm diam as mature or maturing eggs. A 55-mm, 1.47-g female, collected from Pewaukee Lake (Waukesha County) on 5 August, held 1,070 mature eggs 0.8–1.1 mm diam in ovaries 20% of the body weight; the number of mature eggs was greater than the immature eggs, which were 0.3–0.5 mm diam.

Nothing is known about the spawning habits and the early development of the blackchin shiner. Young-of-year in the Chippewa River (Sawyer County) were 33–33.5 mm on 1 October.

Blackchin shiners from Spider Lake (Marinette County), collected 15 June 1963, were aged by analysis of the scales, and showed the growth presented in the table on the following page (K. Oliver, pers. comm.).

A collection of blackchin shiners taken from Lake Poygan (Winnebago County) 8 August 1963 contained 34 age-II fish, 45–54 mm TL, with these esti-

Age Class	No. of Fish	TL (mm) Avg	Range	Calculated TL at Annulus (mm) 1	2	3
I	11	47.6	37–53	39.2		
II	79	55.1	48–62	32.8	46.5	
III	8	63.5	61–67	30.0	46.6	57.8
Avg (weighted)				33.3	46.5	57.8

mated lengths at the annuli: 1—28.0 mm, 2—42.9 mm (B. Bacon, pers. comm.). Condition (K_{SL}) for 10 individuals was 1.99 (1.56–2.31).

In Ohio (Trautman 1957), young-of-year in October were 18–36 mm; age-I fish were 25–51 mm; and adults were 41–71 mm. The largest specimen taken was 71 mm (2.8 in) long. Lopinot and Smith (1973) noted that the blackchin shiner is sexually mature at one year, and spawns annually.

The intestinal contents of 16 blackchin shiners from Lake Poygan in July contained hydrachnids, Diptera larvae and adults, a Hymenoptera adult, Trichoptera, Ephemeroptera, a tubificid, leeches, a glochidium, unidentifiable vegetable matter, small feathers, and debris (D. Jaeger, pers. comm.). In southeastern Wisconsin, Cahn (1927) noted that blackchin shiners fed most frequently upon Entomostraca, followed by insect larvae, *Hyalella*, *Physa* (snails), and leech cases (*Placobdella parasitica*).

Similarly, the intestinal tracts of blackchins taken from the Madison lakes (Pearse 1918) contained cladocerans (33.4%), copepods (11%), insect larvae pupae and adults (26%), oligochaetes (2.1%), rotifers (2.2%), plant remains (3.9%), algae (11.7%), debris (4.1%), and sand (2.4%). Pearse implied that the scarcity of ostracods and oligochaetes in the diet indicated that the blackchin does not feed on the bottom, and that its food is found on aquatic vegetation. In two New York samples (Rimsky-Korsakoff 1930), plants, including the algae *Oedogonium* and *Spirogyra*, constituted 90 and 70% of the intestinal contents.

According to Keast (1965), in Ontario the blackchin shiner is a very specialized feeder; the overwhelming bulk of the food found in stomachs was Cladocera and flying insects (mostly small Diptera) taken at the surface. Among the Cladocera, *Chydorus*, and *Bosmina* were the main genera consumed—400–700 occurring per 10 stomachs in June and July. Some of the larger *Daphnia* were taken in August. Some filamentous algae and diatoms were present in mid and late summer.

Little is known about the ecological requirements of the blackchin shiner. It has been observed that blackchin shiners are abundant in Lake Itasca (Minnesota) for several years, and then become rare for several years, before becoming abundant again (Eddy and Underhill 1974). These fluctuations seem to correlate with rising and falling water levels caused by differences in annual rainfall. High and stable water levels are followed by population increases.

This shiner is able to withstand severe depletion of dissolved oxygen under the ice. Some blackchins survived in a Michigan lake in which the approximate oxygen concentration in the upper 0.3–1.2 m (1–4 ft) of water was 0.2–0.0 ppm (Cooper and Washburn 1949).

As a result of high (38°C or 100.4°F) water temperatures in a shallow Michigan pond, a large number of fish perished. The greatest mortality occurred in the umbrid, catostomid, cyprinid, ictalurid, and percid groups, and the blackfin shiner was among the species killed in large numbers (Bailey 1955).

Twenty-four blackchin shiners were collected from Halls Creek (Florence County) along with the white sucker (2), blacknose dace (3), bluntnose minnow (88), common shiner (96), blacknose shiner (2), brassy minnow (3), black bullhead (2), central mudminnow (7), largemouth bass (1), and mottled sculpin (1).

IMPORTANCE AND MANAGEMENT

The blackchin shiner undoubtedly is a desirable forage minnow for many game fishes, although its importance may be minimal due to its low numbers. Occasionally this minnow is sold as a bait minnow, in a bag mixed with other minnows. Cahn (1927) noted it as a hardy bait minnow that was much used for "silver bass" fishing.

Spottail Shiner

Notropis hudsonius (Clinton). *Notropis*—back, keel; *hudsonius*—named from the Hudson River.

Other common names: spawneater, spottail minnow, spottail, sucking carp, shiner.

Adult female 93 mm, mouth of tributary to L. Michigan (Door Co.), 3 July 1963

DESCRIPTION

Body moderately robust, laterally compressed. Length 51–76 mm (2–3 in). TL = 1.28 SL. Depth into TL 4.3–6.4. Head length into TL 4.7–5.7. Snout bluntly rounded and projecting slightly beyond upper lip. Mouth small, nearly horizontal, extending to below anterior margin of eye; barbel absent. Pharyngeal teeth 2,4–4,2, but highly variable in outer row (from 0 to 2); teeth broad at base, flat, hooked; arch heavy. Eye large, into head length 2.5–4. Gill rakers short, conical, up to 9. Dorsal fin origin directly over origin of pelvic fin; dorsal fin rays 8; anal fin rays 8 (7); pectoral fin rays 13–15; pelvic fin rays 8. Lateral line scales 36–41; lateral line complete. Digestive tract short, S-shaped, 0.6–0.7 TL.

Silvery over pale olive dorsally, sides silvery, belly silvery white. Fins clear, except for black spot at base of caudal fin which is most conspicuous on small fish, but in larger fish becomes somewhat hidden by the silvery pigment of the scales; size of caudal spot about the size of the pupil of the eye. No bright colors during breeding season. Peritoneum silvery with scattered dark chromatophores.

Breeding male with small tubercles on top and sides of head, on scales of back (up to 10 tubercles on posterior edge), on first 7–10 rays of pectoral fins, and occasionally on branchiostegal rays. Female minutely tuberculate on top of head, with tubercles continuing on back to dorsal fin.

Sexual dimorphism: In male the distance from the end of the pectoral fin to the pelvic fin origin is usually less than half the pectoral fin length; in female, the distance is usually more than half the pectoral fin length.

SYSTEMATIC NOTES

Hubbs and Lagler (1964) recognized two subspecies from Wisconsin: the northern spottail shiner, *Notropis hudsonius hudsonius*, from the Mississippi River and Lake Superior drainage basins, and the Great Lakes spottail shiner, *Notropis hudsonius* subspecies, from Lake Michigan and its tributary waters. The two are separated in the northern spottail shiner by the larger, more intense caudal spot and the full complement of teeth (2,4–4,2), and in the Great Lakes spottail shiner by the smaller, more diffuse caudal spot and the absence of one inner row tooth on one or both sides.

DISTRIBUTION, STATUS, AND HABITAT

The spottail shiner occurs in the Mississippi River, Lake Michigan, and Lake Superior drainage basins in Wisconsin. It is well distributed in the shallow water of the Great Lakes and the boundary rivers, and has its greatest inland distribution in the Wisconsin River, the Rock River, and the Fox and Wolf river systems.

In Iowa, the spottail shiner was once the most numerous minnow in the larger natural lakes, but its numbers seem to have become depleted from commercial exploitation (Harlan and Speaker 1956). In Wisconsin, it is locally common in very large inland lakes, in Lakes Michigan and Superior, and in large, slow-moving rivers such as the lower Wisconsin, the Mississippi, and the St. Croix.

The spottail shiner is a big river, big lake minnow that is found in the quiet water of river sloughs and in water with moderate currents. In Wisconsin, it was encountered in inland water of varying clarity at depths of 0.1–1.5 m over substrates of sand (39% frequency), gravel (20%), mud (13%), silt (13%), rubble (6%), hardpan (3%), bedrock (3%), boulders (1%), clay (1%), and detritus (1%). It occurred in streams of the following widths: 1.0–3.0 m (5%), 3.1–6.0 m (5%), 6.1–12.0 (5%), 12.1–24.0 m (45%), 24.1–50.0 m (22%), and more than 50 m (18%). It is found in or near areas with sparse to moderate amounts of vegetation. In Lakes Michigan and Superior it occurs in shoal waters (reported to depths of about 46 m in Lake Michigan).

BIOLOGY

In inland waters, spawning generally occurs in late May and early June. Spawning migrations up the tributary streams of Green Bay (Sugar Creek, Door County; Red River, Kewaunee County; and Little Suamico River, Oconto County) have been noted from early June, although in some years these migra-

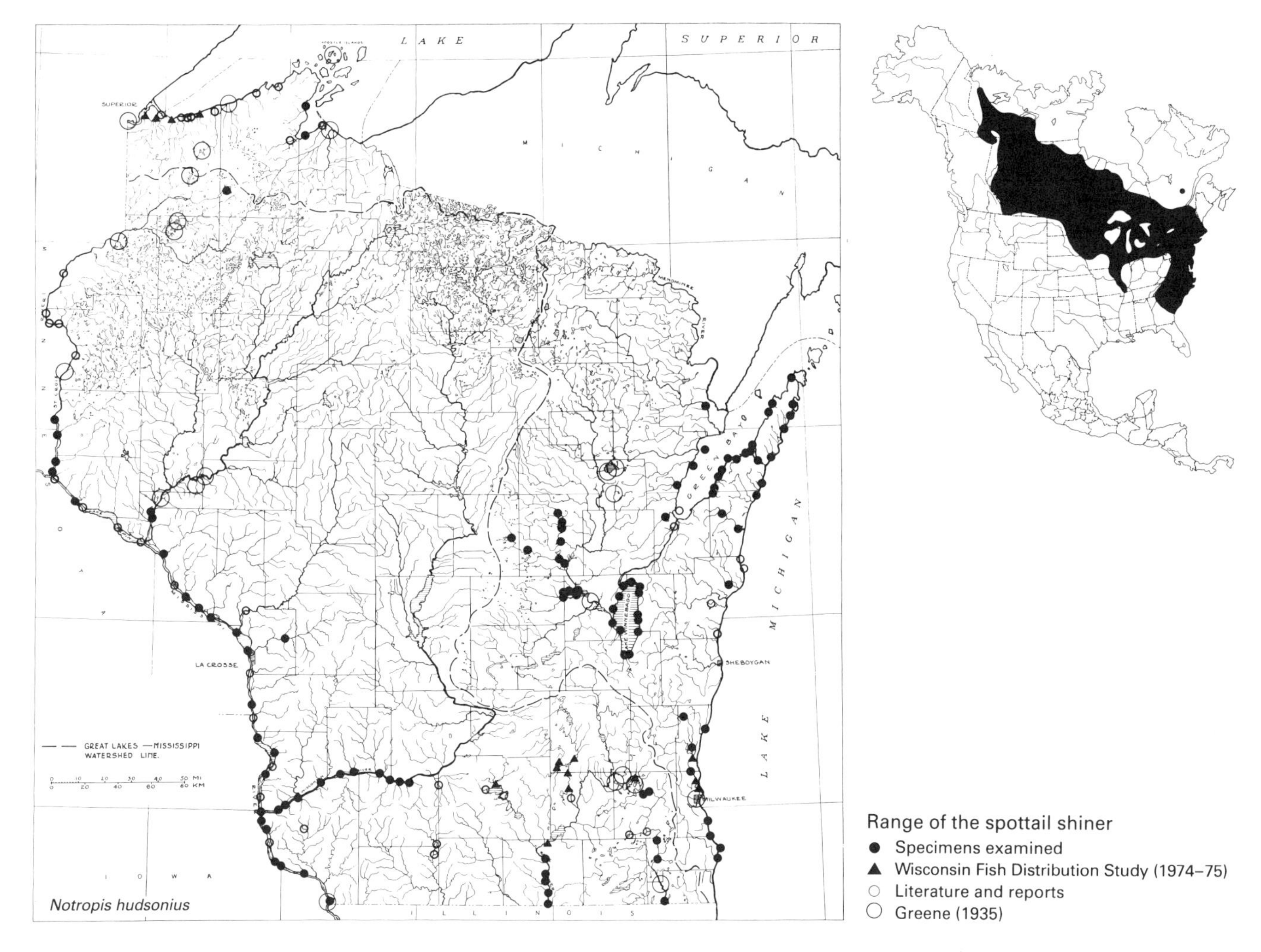

tions may begin in late April (R. Simpson, pers. comm.). In southeastern Lake Michigan, spawning normally occurs from late June to late July, but following a cold spring it is delayed and occurs from mid-July to late August or early September (Wells and House 1974). Data indicate that spawning is either prolonged, or that the time of spawning varies greatly from year to year in a given body of water, depending on the seasonal weather.

In Iowa, Griswold (1963) noted that although most spawning occurs in late May and early June, a few spottails apparently spawn in August. The water temperature at spawning is unknown, but ripe individuals were observed in probable spawning areas when the temperature was 18.3°C (64.9°F) (Mansueti and Hardy 1967).

Spawning occurs in closely packed groups or massed aggregations over areas of gravelly riffles near the mouths of brooks, or along the sandy shoals of lakeshores. There is no evidence of nesting. Thousands of spottail shiners were observed milling about in Sugar Creek (Door County) on 6 June 1962 in what appeared to be a spawning run. The stream, 1.2–3.1 m (4–10 ft) wide and up to 0.45 m (1.5 ft) deep, had a moderate current and a gravel bottom. Both males and females were in ripe condition.

Details of spawning behavior are not clear. Greeley and Greene (1931) observed a large number of individuals milling around in a close group in a small brook tributary to the St. Lawrence River. The fish were actively spawning, and eggs were later found to be numerous in the sand. With one scoop of a 2-m seine, Greeley and Greene collected 3 liters of spottail shiners.

In Lake Michigan, spawning was observed at a depth of 4.6 m, above a water intake crib which was located where the bottom depth was 9.1 m (Wells and House 1974). Several females were seen depositing eggs in patches of *Cladophora*, about 4 cm high, growing on the crib. An estimated 500–1,000 males and females, most apparently ripe, were above and in the *Cladophora*.

From the aforementioned Sugar Creek collection, a mature, partially spawned age-V female, 124 mm

TL and 18.26 g, with ovaries 8% of body weight, held 1,090 ripe eggs, uniform in size at 1.0 mm diam. Immature eggs (many more than the number of ripe eggs), averaging 0.6 mm diam, appeared in a cluster in the dorso-anterior portions of the ovary.

A 127-mm, 22.66-g female, collected from Little Suamico River (Oconto County) on 9 June 1962, held 4,640 ripe eggs, 1.1 mm diam, in ovaries comprising 15% of the body weight. There were approximately as many ripe eggs as immature eggs, the latter 0.7 mm diam. This female was estimated to be 3 years old.

Ten mature females from Lake Michigan, 97–131 mm long and ranging in age from II to V, contained 915–3,709 mature eggs (Wells and House 1974). The number of eggs generally increased with the length of the fish. The largest number of eggs, 8,898, was reported from a female taken from Lake Erie.

M. Fish (1932) described and figured the 5-mm and 14.25-mm stages, and described the 19.0-mm stage. Mansueti and Hardy (1967) illustrated the 27.5-mm stage. There is a correlation between the water temperature during embryonic development and the number of vertebrae appearing in the embryo. Hubbs (1923) concluded that in Douglas Lake, Michigan, the largest young in the coldest temperatures had the highest average number of caudal vertebrae, whereas the intermediate and smallest young which were hatched during a much warmer period had a lower average number of vertebrae. Scott and Crossman (1973) submitted limited data which suggest that western populations in Canada have a higher number of vertebrae than eastern populations.

After hatching, the growth of the spottail shiner is dependent on temperatures. In Iowa during 1957, the daily increment in the size of the young from 24 July to 28 August was 0.68 mm, at a mean air temperature of 26.8°C (80.3°F); in 1961, growth was only 0.55 mm, at a mean air temperature of 21.7°C (71°F) (McCann 1959). In Lake Michigan, the growing season begins as early as mid-May, and continues as late as September or early October (Wells and House 1974).

Scale platelets begin forming when the young are 14 mm long, but no circuli appear until the young reach 20 mm TL (McCann 1959).

In Wisconsin, the growth of young-of-year has been observed as shown in the table at the top of the next column.

Spottail shiners from Sugar Creek (Door County), collected 6 June 1962, showed the growth presented in the second table in the next column.

In Lake Michigan (Wells and House 1974), the calculated total lengths (mm) of spottail shiners at the end of each year of life were: 1—males 62, females 63; 2—males 95, females 97; 3—males 108, females 114; 4—males 117, females 123; and 5—males 129, females 131.

Date	No. of Fish	TL (mm)		Location
		Avg	Range	
13 July 1962	8	33.6	29–41	Wisconsin R. (Grant Co.)
17 July 1962	42	44.4	29–48	Wisconsin R. (Crawford Co.)
19 July 1960	34	30.3	20–35	L. Poygan (Waushara Co.)
23 July 1960	46	35.7	28–39	L. Poygan (Waushara Co.)
8 Aug. 1961	39	47.2	42–52	L. Poygan (Waushara Co.)

Age Class	No. of Fish	TL (mm)		Calculated TL at Annulus[a] (mm)				
		Avg	Range	1	2	3	4	5
I	5	84.2	82–88	78.6				
II	9	99.3	89–105	66.4	98.3			
III	41	109.2	88–116	60.6	94.9	109.1		
IV	1	124		68.6	112.9	119.6	124	
V	1	124		58.3	101.9	111.1	116	124
Avg (weighted)				63.2	96.0	109.4	120	124

[a]In most individuals the annulus for the year of capture had not been placed. This sample was part of a spawning population; predominantly male. Five individuals, 110–124 mm, were female.

Annulus formation is generally late. In Iowa, yearling spottails did not develop an annulus until mid-July (Griswold 1963). In Minnesota, the first annulus forms in late June, but later annuli form in the second week of July after spawning (L. L. Smith and Kramer 1964). Female shiners tend to have higher condition factors than males, but the difference is not significant.

Apparently spottail shiners do not mature until they are over 66 mm at the spawning season. In Clear Lake (Iowa), they may mature at age I (McCann 1959). In Lake Michigan, 53% of the males and 40% of the females at age I, and all fish at age II, were mature (Wells and House 1974).

A Wisconsin specimen 137 mm (5.4 in) long was captured from Lake Monona (Dane County) in 1977 (C. Brynildson, pers. comm.).

Stomach contents of spottail shiners from Sugar Creek (Door County) consisted of Diptera larvae, mayfly larvae, spiders, ants, algae and other plant materials, debris, and sand (M. Kosmerchock, pers. comm.). Cahn (1927) reported that 80% of the food in stomachs of fish from southeastern Wisconsin was animal matter—mostly entomostracans, and occasionally young mollusks. In Clear Lake (Iowa), McCann (1959) noted that spottails fed on a wide variety of materials, which included water mites, Diptera larvae and adults, Trichoptera larvae, Cladocera, grass seeds, and plant fiber.

McCann also noted that in several cases spottails from a single seine haul showed considerable variation in their feeding. In one sample, some of the spottails had fed almost entirely on surface organisms, others had fed almost entirely on plankton organisms, and a third group had fed almost entirely on bottom organisms. Further study in the same lake (Griswold 1963) showed that spottails tended to be selective in their choice of food; all food in the stomach and the intestine of the same fish was similar. Griswold reported a distinct feeding period just before sundown.

In an intensive study of the food habits of the spottail shiner in Red Lakes (Minnesota), L. L. Smith and Kramer (1964) found that food selection definitely changed when the size of the fish increased. This change became evident at about 70 mm TL. Cladocera, Copepoda, and Ostracoda were the most important foods in the smaller fish, but in fish larger than 70 mm, insects predominated. Rotifers and algae were eaten by a significant number of fish only in the size group below 10 mm. Fish larger than 49 mm TL ate spottail shiner eggs; 33.3% of the largest fish (110–117 mm) ate spottail eggs. Smith and Kramer reported algae in stomachs of the very young; otherwise plant materials were not noted in the diet. The spottail shiner consumed only certain groups of bottom organisms; although oligochaetes and clams larger than 4 mm were present in substantial numbers, they were not eaten.

In Lake Michigan (at the mouth of the Kalamazoo River), a number of spottail shiners had eaten alewife eggs, and one 76-mm (3.0-in) shiner held 125 alewife eggs (Edsall 1964). Many of these shiners had also eaten shiner scales. It has also been reported that larger spottails eat both their own eggs and their young; it is this habit that has led to the name "spawneater" for this fish.

In Lake Poygan (Waushara County), a broad and shallow lake, the spottail shiner was not encountered in the breakwater or shallows areas, but in the open water well out in the lake near patches of *Scirpus* sp. Most spottails were taken from the open lake beyond the last emergent vegetation, in water 0.6–0.9 m (2–3 ft) deep, where they were captured along with white bass, yellow bass, redhorse suckers, and yellow perch.

The spottail shiner is more susceptible to capture by night seining, since it has a tendency to move into shallower water at night (McCann 1959, Scott and Crossman 1973), although Hubbs (1921) noted movement into deeper water at night. In winter it was caught through the ice on Lake Mendota in 15 m (50 ft) of water; the angler was fishing off the bottom with gall wasp larvae (Black 1945b).

In Lake Michigan, considerable yearly movement has been noted for this species. Wells (1968) presented evidence that the spottail shiner seeks out water from 13°C (55.4°F) to the warmest available, and that there is a tendency for the fish to move with the warmest layer of water wherever it lodged. Considerable yearly movement has been noted in this species. From February to April, it is irregularly distributed to depths up to about 46 m, with greatest numbers at 5.5–31 m. By early May a definite shoreward movement is evident, and from the end of May to the end of August this species is seldom caught at depths greater than 12.8 m. By mid-October spottail shiners scatter into water as deep as 31 m.

Spottail shiners in Lake Michigan off Grand Haven, Michigan, were concentrated in the warmest water available during mid-September trawls (Brandt 1978). More were captured in water of 15–20°C (59–68°F) than at any other temperature.

Some spottail shiners have been observed in water at 35°C (95°F) (Trembley 1960), although juveniles suffered 100% mortality when they passed into the lower end of a discharge canal from a nuclear power plant where water temperatures were greater than 30°C (86°F).

In Green Bay, extensive bottom trawl explorations caught spottail shiners in nearly a quarter of all trawl drags. They were most abundant at the 9-m interval, and 97% were taken in 22 m or less (Reigle 1969a). The largest catch was 59 kg (130 lb) in a 20-min drag at a depth of 13 m south of Oconto.

Heavy infestations of the plerocercoid of *Ligula* (tapeworm parasite) have occurred in the body cavities of large adults from the Red River outlet (Kewaunee County) and Green Bay. Infected specimens are usually collected near colonies of terns, which have been reported as definitive hosts to the parasites.

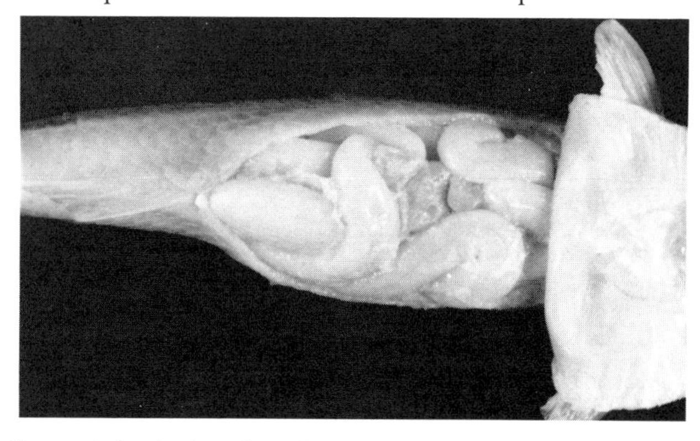

Open abdominal cavity of a spottail shiner showing *Ligula* parasites *in situ*

Two hundred six large spawning spottail shiners were collected from Sugar Creek (Door County) near its mouth into Green Bay on 6 June 1962. Species associated with it were: white sucker (5), creek chub (6), pearl dace (1), longnose dace (43), blacknose dace (32), common shiner (6), blacknose shiner (1), sand shiner (1), bluntnose minnow (32), fathead minnow (8), hornyhead chub (3), northern pike (1), black bullhead (2), central mudminnow (1), brook stickleback (3), and barred fantail (1).

IMPORTANCE AND MANAGEMENT

The spottail shiner is an important prey species for white bass, smallmouth bass, northern pike, and muskellunge, and it has been taken by the loon, common tern, American merganser, and kingfisher. The spottail is a competitor with young-of-year northern pike and yellow perch for food (Hunt and Carbine 1950).

The spottail shiner is considered a bait minnow of high rank. It has been used in different parts of the country as bait for yellow perch, bass, northern pike, and walleye; in New York it is also a popular muskellunge bait. The spottail's bright, silvery color makes it attractive; it is active and vigorous on the hook, and swims clear of the vegetation. Its reputation for hardiness varies.

The spottail shiner has been found to be a useful biological indicator of organochlorine contaminants in nearshore habitats (Suns and Rees 1977). The limited home range of young-of-year spottails and their relatively short exposure to contaminants enabled researchers to determine residue levels from recent contaminant discharges.

Bigmouth Shiner

Notropis dorsalis (Agassiz). *Notropis*—back, keel; *dorsalis*—pertaining to the back.
Other common names: Gilbert's minnow, big-mouthed shiner, central bigmouth shiner.

Adult 59 mm, Rocky Cr. (Wood Co.), 18 June 1960

DESCRIPTION
Body slender, back arched; body slightly compressed laterally, flattened ventrally (especially anteriorly). Average length 64 mm (2.5 in). TL = 1.26 SL. Depth into TL 5.0–6.0. Head length into TL 4.0–4.9. Snout bluntly pointed, projecting slightly beyond ventral mouth. Mouth large, lateral length of upper jaw greater than eye width, extending to below pupil; barbel absent. Pharyngeal teeth 1,4–4,1, some strongly hooked; arch slender. Eye large, into head length 3.3–4.1; pupil of eye skewed dorsally and "looking upward." Gill rakers knoblike to short, conical, up to 8. Dorsal fin origin over or slightly behind pelvic fin origin; dorsal rays 8; anal fin rays 8 (7–9); pectoral fin rays 14–15; pelvic fin rays 8. Lateral line scales 32–37; lateral line complete, almost straight. Digestive tract short, S-shaped, 0.4–0.5 TL.

Pale brown dorsally, and silver or white laterally and ventrally. Dorsolateral scales weakly outlined. Mid-dorsal stripe dark, conspicuous, and divided at dorsal base. Lateral line marked by fine paired "mouse tracks." Fins unpigmented. No bright breeding colors. Peritoneum silvery.

Breeding male with minute tubercles on top and sides of head, best developed below eye. Scattered tubercles on nape and on rays 2–10 of pectoral fins.

Distinguishing the bigmouth shiner, the sand shiner, and the mimic shiner from each other is difficult. Characters useful in separation of these species are shown in the table below.

SYSTEMATIC NOTES
Synonym: *Notropis gilberti* Jordan and Meek. Three subspecies are recognized by Hubbs and Lagler (1964): our form, named central bigmouth shiner, *Notropis dorsalis dorsalis* (Agassiz), which occurs throughout the central portion of the range for this species; the western bigmouth shiner, *N.d. piptolepis* (Cope), which occurs in Colorado and Wyoming in the Platte River system of the Great Plains; and the eastern bigmouth shiner, *N.d. keimi* Fowler, which occurs in the Allegheny River system of Pennsylvania and New York, and in the Genesee River and Oneida Lake in the Lake Ontario drainage of New York.

Underhill and Merrell (1959), who investigated the morphological differences in the populations of this shiner from different areas in Minnesota, concluded that there were micro-geographic races. It was impossible to decide from the available evidence whether meristic characters in fishes are primarily determined by the environmental complex or by the genotype.

DISTRIBUTION, STATUS, AND HABITAT
In Wisconsin, the bigmouth shiner occurs in the Mississippi River drainage basin and in the Lake Michigan drainage basin, where it was recently estab-

Characters for Separation of the Bigmouth Shiner, Sand Shiner, and Mimic Shiner
(after Eddy and Underhill 1974:256)

Characters	Bigmouth Shiner	Sand Shiner	Mimic Shiner
Anal fin rays	8	7	8
Pharyngeal teeth	1,4–4,1	4–4	4–4
Eyes	Pupils skewed upward	Pupils medial	Pupils medial
Predorsal scales	Irregular size and pattern	Regular in pattern and uniform in size	Regular in pattern and uniform in size
Lateral length of mouth	Greater than eye diameter	Less than eye diameter	Less than eye diameter
Mouth position	Horizontal, ventral	Slightly oblique, subterminal	Slightly oblique, subterminal
Snout shape, dorsal view	V-shaped	V-shaped	U-shaped
Pigment about vent and at base of anal fin	Absent or faint	Absent or faint	Darkly pigmented
Mid-dorsal stripe (before dorsal fin)	Prominent and continuing on either side of dorsal fin	Prominent, broadening before dorsal fin and interrupted at anterior base of dorsal fin	Absent; or poorly defined as several faint striations or a line of crosshatch marks

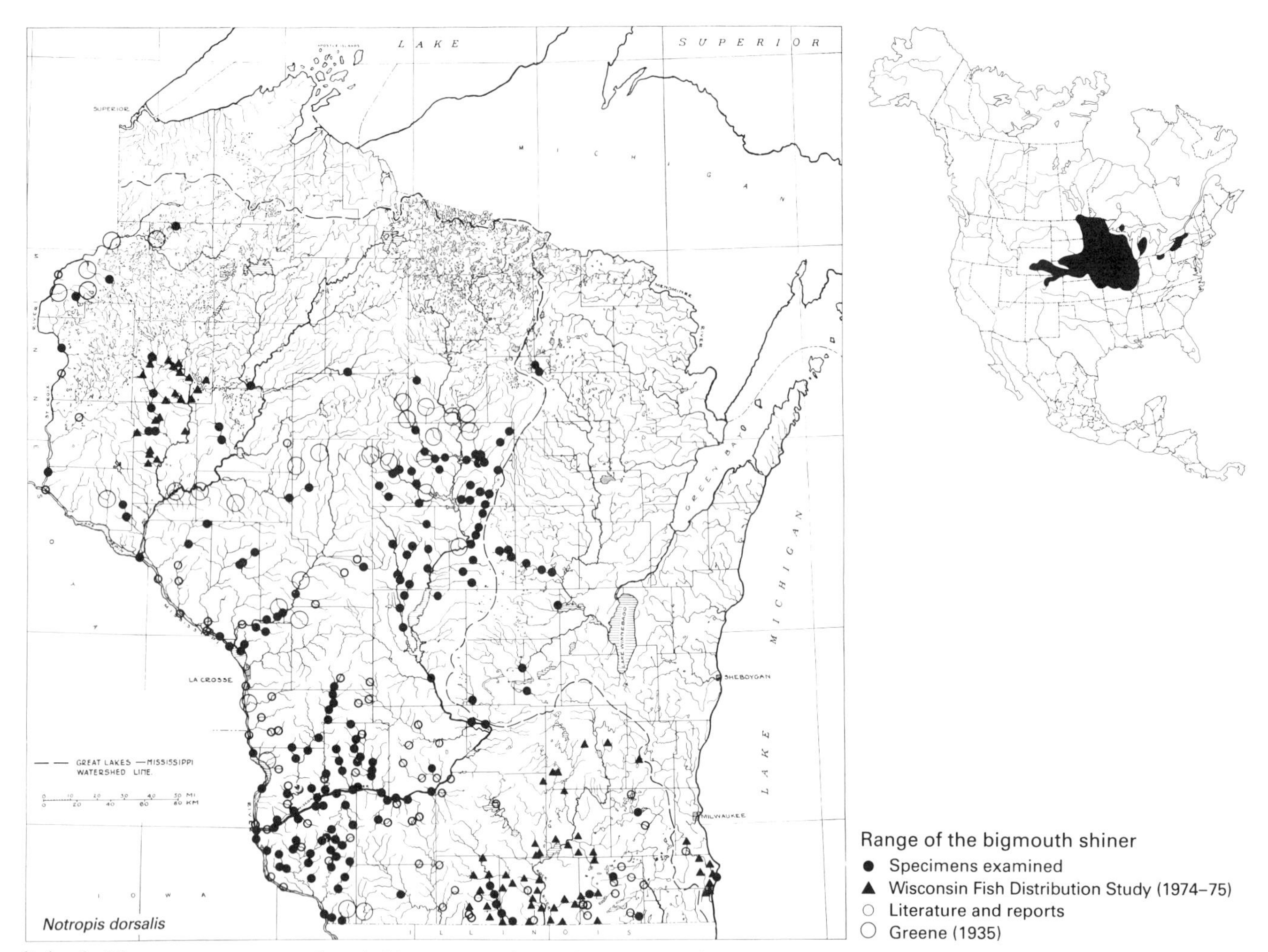

Range of the bigmouth shiner
● Specimens examined
▲ Wisconsin Fish Distribution Study (1974–75)
○ Literature and reports
◯ Greene (1935)

lished. There are no records of this species from the Lake Superior basin.

Greene (1935) noted the bigmouth shiner's strong distribution in the unglaciated portion of Wisconsin. He explained his single record from the Fox River (Green Lake County) of the Lake Michigan drainage basin as the result of a crossover at Portage, through either glacial or modern connections. This species has appeared at a number of sites in the Fox and Wolf river watershed, all of which can be explained through the connection at Portage, except collections from the upper Wolf River in Langlade County. Since it is unlikely that this minnow could move over the dam at Shawano, I would ascribe its presence in the upper Wolf River to minnow pail introduction. Similarly, recent collections in the Root and Pike river systems of Racine and Kenosha counties are more likely to have resulted from minnow pail introductions than by the minnow's overcoming the low divide between the headwaters of the Root and Des Plaines rivers.

The status of the bigmouth shiner is changing in parts of its range. In Ohio (Trautman 1957), it is being replaced by the silverjaw minnow, and Trautman predicts that, if this process continues, extirpation of the bigmouth in that state is inevitable. In northern Missouri, extensive channelization of prairie streams over several decades has increased conditions favorable to the bigmouth shiner, accounting for its increase in abundance.

In Wisconsin, the bigmouth shiner is common. Since the 1920s it has extended its range markedly, especially into the Pecatonica, Sugar, Rock, and Fox river systems of the Mississippi River drainage basin, as well as into the Lake Michigan drainage basin. Increasing siltation and turbidity appear to favor this species; the bigmouth shiner will be secure if present trends continue.

In Wisconsin, the bigmouth shiner was encountered most frequently in clear water at depths of 0.1–1.5 m over substrates of gravel (29% frequency), sand (24%), rubble (15%), silt (11%), clay (10%), mud

(9%), and boulders (3%). Although it has been collected occasionally from pools, sloughs, and lakes, it occurred generally in the flowing waters of rivers of the following widths: 1.0–3.0 m (18%), 3.1–6.0 m (33%), 6.1–12.0 m (33%), 12.1–24.0 m (13%), 24.1–50.0 m (4%), and more than 50 m (1%). It inhabits open water free of vegetation.

The literature calls attention to the bigmouth shiner's preference for sterile sand flats, and for sandy stretches in streams, rivers, and lakes (Harlan and Speaker 1956, Taylor 1954, Hubbs and Cooper 1936, Eddy and Surber 1947, and Eddy and Underhill 1974).

BIOLOGY

In Wisconsin, spawning begins in late May and in some areas probably extends into August. Gravid females have been taken in Marquette County on 29 July. Starrett (1951) classified this minnow as a late spawner in the Des Moines River (Iowa), where it spawned from late July through August. Keeton (1963) noted that high water levels in June may delay the spawning of the bigmouth shiner.

Nothing is known about the spawning habits of the bigmouth shiner. Moore (1944) suggested that its spawning habits may be similar to those of the Arkansas river shiner, *Notropis girardi*. The Arkansas river shiner spawns in midstream over a bottom of fine sand. The eggs are fertilized, and then swept by the current downstream; they develop as they travel. Hatching occurs in 1–2 days, and is followed by a peculiar "vertical swim" by the larvae with their yolk-sacs: whenever they touch the substrate, they swim vigorously upward to the surface; as the process is repeated over a period of about 2 days the yolk-sacs become greatly diminished in size, and horizontal swimming begins.

In Little Sandy Creek (Marathon County) on 29 May 1961, an age-II female, 61 mm TL and 2.30 g, with ovaries 19% of body weight, held 1,000 eggs 0.9–1.0 mm diam. On 15 June 1965 in the Plover River (Portage County), an age-II female, 66 mm TL and 2.81 g, held an estimated 1,275 ripe yellow eggs 0.9 mm diam; also present were a slightly greater number of immature white eggs 0.5 mm diam.

The growth of young-of-year bigmouth shiners in central and northern Wisconsin has been observed as shown in the table at the top of the next column. The wide range in length on a particular date implies a long spawning season, especially in moderate-sized streams. In small creeks, the low mean lengths of some populations late in the season imply delayed spawning. This suggests a temperature-related condition—smaller streams generally reach the required spawning temperature level later than larger streams.

Date	No. of Fish	TL (mm)		Location
		Avg	Range	
9 Sept.	63	30.5	20–44	Big Sandy Cr. (Marathon Co.)
19 Sept.	37	32.9	21–54	Eau Claire R. (Eau Claire Co.)
19 Sept.	75	33.5	25–48	Eau Claire R. (Eau Claire Co.)
23 Sept.	45	41.8	34–52	Plover R. (Portage Co.)
27 Sept.	14	31.6	28–39	Little Eau Claire R. (Marathon Co.)
27 Sept.	19	46.0	35–53	Eau Claire R. (Marathon Co.)
28 Sept.	13	33.1	22–45	Johnson Cr. (Marathon Co.)
4 Oct.	11	48.0	43–54	Hay R. (Dunn Co.)

Bigmouth shiners from Gran Grae Creek (Crawford County), collected 24 September 1966, showed the following growth:

Age Class	No. of Fish	TL (mm)		Calculated TL at Annulus (mm)	
		Avg	Range	1	2
0	22	44.8	38–51		
I	39	60.9	54–66	45.3	
II	16	67.2	66–70	44.4	63.6
Avg (weighted)				45.0	63.6

An 80-mm (3.2-in) male from Hay River (Dunn County), collected 4 October 1977, had the following estimated growth at the annuli: 1—45 mm, 2—58 mm, and 3—70 mm.

Maturity is attained at age II. Pflieger (1975) suggested that in central Missouri the bigmouth shiner probably reaches maturity during its second summer (age I).

In a Pine River (Richland County) collection, the digestive tracts of bigmouth shiners contained filamentous algae, dipterans, and hydrachnids (W. Gelwicks, pers. comm.). In Roxbury Creek (Dane County) in June, bigmouth shiners fed largely upon *Calopsectra* (60%), the tipulid *Dicranota* (8.3%), chironomid larvae of the tribe Chironomini (7.2%), and chironomid pupae. A classification of items in the diet into habitat categories suggested that over 70% of the food consumed by bigmouth shiners from Roxbury Creek was of benthic origin; only 10.3% was from the drift (Mendelson 1972).

In Iowa bigmouth shiners fed primarily on Ephemeroptera and Diptera, and on some green and blue-green algae (Griswold 1963, Starrett 1950b).

Aquarium experiments demonstrate that the bigmouth shiner will take food from the surface, but once a particle of food is seized the minnow retreats quickly to midwater or to the bottom (Mendelson

1972). Waterlogged food particles drifting from the surface toward the bottom at first attract little attention from the fishes still feeding on the surface. After a lag of several minutes, two species, the bigmouth shiner and the sand shiner, begin to drop out of the surface assemblage. This phase is often initiated among bigmouths by a single fish picking a particle of food from the substrate of the aquarium. In a short time, all bigmouth shiners are engaged in this way, moving over the bottom, their bodies more or less parallel to the sand bottom.

According to Pflieger (1975), sight is apparently less important to the bigmouth shiners than taste in locating food. When food was introduced in aquariums, the minnows swam about rapidly over the bottom, taking in mouthfuls of sand from which they sorted out the food. The sand was forcefully rejected from the mouth or gill openings.

C. Hubbs (1941) suggested that dorsoventral flattening and ventral mouths are associated with bottom-dwelling and bottom-feeding habits. The bigmouth shiner is a pioneer species in the smaller streams, and is capable of adapting to the changing habitat conditions in unstable streams. Starrett (1950a) noted that it is sometimes collected over newly covered sandbars in the Des Moines River (Iowa), suggesting an ability to use newly formed habitats.

Movement by this species apparently is more frequent at night than during the day. Mendelson (1972) observed bigmouth shiners moving unhurriedly from pool to pool after dark. Trapping at night showed that after dark this species had a tendency to locate in shallow water, or near the surface in deeper water; apparently, under cover of darkness, it ventured into the potentially more dangerous regions of the stream.

In Trout Creek (Crawford County), 95 bigmouth shiners were associated with these species: shorthead redhorse (3), golden redhorse (1), northern hog sucker (20), white sucker (182), central stoneroller (173), longnose dace (12), blacknose dace (192), creek chub (86), bluntnose minnow (61), suckermouth minnow (31), spotfin shiner (5), brassy minnow (21), blackside darter (1), johnny darter (21), fantail darter (4), and brook stickleback (11).

IMPORTANCE AND MANAGEMENT

The bigmouth shiner is undoubtedly an important forage fish in Wisconsin streams, and in some areas it is an important bait minnow. In Iowa, it is widely used as bait for panfishes, especially crappies and perch (Harlan and Speaker 1956).

It makes an interesting aquarium minnow if the water is kept clean and well aerated.

The bigmouth shiner has been rated a poor test species because it is difficult to sort from other species without excessive handling, is susceptible to disease, and is excitable in test containers (Bunting and Irwin 1965).

In view of the bigmouth shiner's abundance and wide distribution in Wisconsin, opportunities are excellent for learning the life history of this species.

Spotfin Shiner

Notropis spilopterus (Cope). *Notropis*—back, keel; *spilopterus*—spotted fin.

Other common names: silverfin minnow, satinfin minnow, blue minnow, steelcolored shiner, lemonfin minnow.

Adult male (tuberculate) 73 mm, L. Poygan (Waushara Co.), 23 July 1960

Adult female 69 mm, L. Poygan (Waushara Co.), 23 July 1960

DESCRIPTION

Body moderately deep, compressed laterally. Average length 64 mm (2.5 in). TL = 1.26 SL. Depth into TL 4.7–5.6. Head length into TL 4.3–5.3. Snout long and sharply pointed. Mouth strongly oblique (about 45° to body axis), tip of upper lip at end of upper pupil; mouth extending to below posterior nostril; barbel absent. Pharyngeal teeth 1,4–4,1, slender, strongly hooked; cutting edge serrate; arch sturdy. Eye into head length 3.0–4.5. Gill rakers short, conical, about 9. Dorsal fin origin slightly behind origin of pelvic fin; dorsal fin rays 8; anal fin rays 8; pectoral fin rays 13–15; pelvic fin rays 8. Lateral line scales 36–37 (35–39); lateral line complete, slightly decurved. Digestive tract short with a single S-shaped loop, 0.6 TL. Chromosomes 2n = 50 (W. LeGrande, pers. comm.).

Living fish silvery, underlaid with a bluish cast on back and sides. Small young with at least a few chromatophores on last 2 or 3 membranes of dorsal fin; large young and adults with dusky or black blotch on these membranes. Lateral stripe in preserved fish mainly on caudal peduncle. Color in preserved fish, dorsal half olive yellow, sides bluish silver, belly whitish. Mid-dorsal stripe well defined and surrounding dorsal fin. Dorsal scale pockets with dark pigment, resulting in a distinctive and regular diamond-shaped design visible through the scales. Peritoneum silvery, with numerous dark speckles, to dusky.

Breeding males steely blue with broad, dusky stripe posteriorly; lower fins yellow, whitish near tips; all membranes of the dorsal fin dusted with dark speckles with the last 3–4 more darkly pigmented. Breeding tubercles in male in a dense patch across snout; numerous large tubercles on head with tips directly forward; a few tubercles on lower jaw, on anterior edge of pectoral fin, on anal rays, and on posterior edge of scales on sides above and anterior to anal fin. Dorsal 3 scale rows on each side of midline may have an additional large tubercle in center of exposed portion of each scale. In females, tubercles occasional on top of head and on mid-dorsal scales before dorsal fin.

Hybrids: Spotfin shiner × rosyface shiner, spotfin shiner × red shiner (Schwartz 1972). Artificial spotfin shiner × steelcolor shiner (Pflieger 1965); the hybrid (F_1) females exhibit no reduction in fertility when backcrossed with male spotfin shiners, and both males and females of the backcross seem to be fertile.

SYSTEMATIC NOTES

Notropis spilopterus is closely related to *Notropis lutrensis*, the red shiner, and both undoubtedly were derived from a common stock (Gibbs 1957a).

Gibbs (1957b) recognized two subspecies: the eastern spotfin shiner, *Notropis spilopterus spilopterus* (Cope), and the western spotfin shiner, *Notropis spilopterus hypsisomatus* (Gibbs). The Wisconsin form is assigned to the latter, and differs chiefly by usually having 36 or 37 lateral line scales, instead of 37–39; by its deeper body, modally 26% of SL, rather than 24%; and by the greater development of the tubercles on the lower part of the caudal peduncle in the breeding male. Intergrades are understood from the western drainage into Lake Michigan, including parts of the Fox and Wolf rivers and Green Bay.

DISTRIBUTION, STATUS, AND HABITAT

The spotfin shiner occurs in the Mississippi River and Lake Michigan drainage basins. It generally avoids the northern tier of counties, and does not occur in the Lake Superior basin.

The spotfin shiner is abundant in medium- to large-sized rivers, and common in large lakes. This

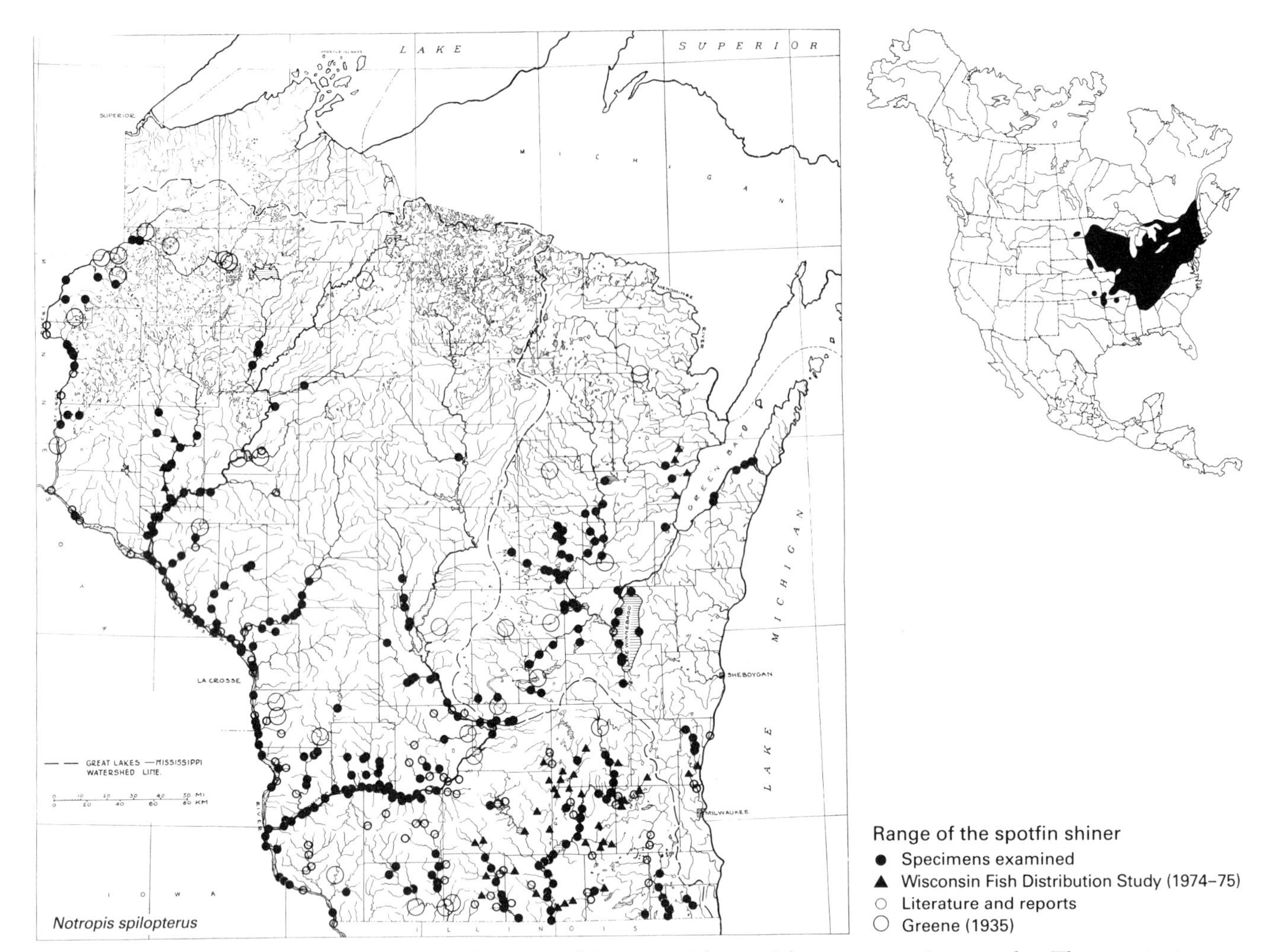

Range of the spotfin shiner
● Specimens examined
▲ Wisconsin Fish Distribution Study (1974–75)
○ Literature and reports
◯ Greene (1935)

species is tolerant of a wide variety of habitats, and is usually the most numerous shiner where waters are turbid. It can tolerate considerable siltation, and domestic and industrial pollution. Modern land use programs favor this species, and the spotfin shiner appears to have expanded its distribution since the late 1920s (see Greene 1935).

A potential threat to the spotfin shiner is the red shiner (*Notropis lutrensis*), with which the spotfin is not compatible. The red shiner appears to be extending its range northward into Wisconsin; where it has done so in Illinois, it has displaced the spotfin shiner (Page and Smith 1970).

In Wisconsin, the spotfin shiner was encountered most frequently at shallow depths (0.1–0.5 m) over substrates of sand (31% frequency), mud (21%), gravel (19%), clay (11%), silt (9%), rubble (7%), and boulders (3%). It occurred in rivers of the following widths: 1.0–3.0 m (1%), 3.1–6.0 m (18%), 6.1–12.0 m (24%), 12.1–24.0 m (35%), 24.1–50.0 m (18%), and more than 50 m (4%). It occurs in riffles, pools, or sloughs, and is found in clear to highly turbid water with or without vegetation nearby. The greatest numbers of spotfin shiners are taken from a moderate current in shallow water over a sand bottom; they are less common in the quiet waters of sloughs.

BIOLOGY

In Wisconsin, spawning begins toward the end of May and may extend into early September. Favorable spawning temperatures are 21.1–23.9°C (70–75°F). Gale and Gale (1977) found that spotfins are fractional spawners. A pair in an outdoor wading pool spawned 12 times between 16 June and 10 August, releasing from 169 to 945 eggs (total 7,474) at intervals of 1–7 days; 5-day intervals were the most common. Spawning usually occurred before 1000 hr, but sometimes afternoon spawning occurred.

This species seems to be exacting in its choice of a spawning substrate. It has been known to spawn in selected rock crevices, on logs having loose bark or crevices, and on the top of a minnow pail.

Among spotfin shiners territoriality is strong, and defense of a spawning site is vigorous. Pflieger (1965) noted that males held small territories over a log, which they defended against other males, but the position and boundaries of the territories changed frequently. When two males came into close proximity, they often engaged in threatening displays in which they erected their dorsal fins and swam along stiffly side by side. Usually there was no bodily contact, but occasionally they struck at each other repeatedly with their snouts.

Gale and Gale (1977) observed that a territorial spotfin shiner sometimes grabs the pelvic or anal fin of its opponent with its mouth and drags its adversary from the spawning area. They saw one fish drag another about 30 cm (12 in) across a spawning boulder. When two males grasp each other by the pelvic fins simultaneously, they swim in a circle, slowly at first, then with increasing speed, until only a blur is seen.

A male spotfin shiner often makes several prespawning display passes along a crevice before swimming out to seek a female. Gale and Gale suggested that touching the crevice is an integral part of the male's prespawning behavior, and that tactile stimulation provides positive reinforcement. In the laboratory, male spotfins sometimes made 30 or more prespawning passes before the actual spawning.

If a female does not approach the crevice to spawn when the male has completed his prespawning passes, the male swims to a group of females (generally in the current just downstream) and tries to crowd or drive one of them to the crevice. As they approach the crevice, the male usually orbits the female.

The spawning act has been described by Pflieger (1965:4):

> When a female was about to spawn, she swam up over the spawning site and was approached by 1 or more males. Usually, 1 male succeeded in driving the others off, and he then took a position above the female with his head approximately even with her pectoral fins and his ventral surface touching her back. When spawning, he appeared to press her against the log and both vibrated rapidly. They often proceeded farther up the log with the male maintaining his position above the female and performed the spawning act 2 or 3 more times.

When spawning on the undersurface of bark, the female and male spotfins were upside down. They maintained the same position relative to each other and to the spawning substrate as they did when spawning in an upright position (Pflieger 1965).

Crevice spawning affords protection from depredation, the spawning activities of other fish, abrasion by water-borne materials, dislodgement by strong currents, smothering in silty or muddy bottoms, settling silt, and direct sunlight (Gale and Gale 1977). The chances of eggs being fertilized are enhanced in a crevice. These authors suggested that, when the breeding habits of more of our fishes are known, fractional spawning may not be uncommon. The cyprinids in general have long breeding seasons, and many of them may be fractional spawners.

Gale and Gale (1977) observed the egg-laying process of the spotfin shiner (p. 174):

> . . . The eggs "sprayed" out, somewhat like shot from a gun; some traveled several centimeters before adhering to the bottom of the crevice. Eggs may not have become adhesive for a second or two after release for they sometimes seemed to "roll" across the plate before adhering. The numbers of eggs in groups ranged from 10 to 97. In some instances, the number of eggs per group declined progressively during a spawning session but more often groups of eggs were almost as large at the end of a session as at the start.

Between spawnings, the male was observed eating eggs which had missed the spawning site. Since these exposed eggs were usually eaten by the spawning male, Pflieger suggested that egg eating is part of the spawning ritual, rather than a simple feeding reaction. Gale and Gale, however, found that egg feeding slowed after about an hour, and that several females shared in egg consumption. They concluded that such feeding was not ritualistic, or at least not entirely so.

Highly gravid spotfin females with many ripe eggs up to 1.2 mm diam were collected on 6 June 1962 from Green Bay (Door County). Four beautifully colored and tuberculate males, 70–84 mm TL (UWSP 3810) were collected from the Wisconsin River (Sauk County) in early September 1970, suggesting that spawning occurs at this late date in southern Wisconsin.

The eggs in the ovary are of several size classes. Water-hardened eggs found sticking to a log were 1.5 mm diam (Hubbs and Cooper 1936).

Hatching begins in 5 days at 22°C (71.6°F) (Gale and Gale 1977). Scales first form at 15–16 mm on the caudal peduncle (Stone 1940).

Spotfin shiners from the Black River (Jackson County), collected 27 September 1975, showed the growth presented in the table on the following page.

A 97-mm, 10.81-g male in breeding habit, collected from the Red Cedar River (Dunn County) 8 July 1975, was estimated to be 4 years old, and had the following calculated lengths at the first 3 annuli: 1—23.3 mm, 2—49.1 mm, and 3—69.1 mm.

The smallest sexually mature spotfin shiners of

Age Class	No. of Fish	TL (mm) Avg	Range	Calculated TL at Annulus[a] (mm) 1	2	3
0	3	27.3	25–30			
I	19	53.3	45–59	32.2		
II	15	62.1	55–67	27.1	52.1	
III	13	75.2	70–86	26.0	55.2	74.1
Avg (weighted)				28.9	53.6	74.1

[a]The annulus for the year of capture had not been placed in the larger and older fish. The males were larger than the females in each age group; but the females apparently lived to a greater age.

each sex to be reported were 38 mm SL (est. 47.9 TL) (Pflieger 1965). Both sexes mature at age I, though some individuals may not spawn until age II (Stone 1940).

The largest known male was 108 mm (4.2 in), and the largest known female was 93 mm (3.7 in) (Stone 1940).

The food of the spotfin shiner consists mostly of insects (Dobie et al. 1956). It ingests both aquatic and terrestrial insects, small fishes, vegetable matter, small crustaceans, plankton, and carp eggs. Food studies by several workers show that, in general, the food preferences of the spotfin are as follows: midge larvae (17.5%), mayfly nymphs (6.2%), insects (64.7%), and miscellaneous (11.5%). As noted above, between spawnings males and females are observed eating exposed eggs of their own species.

In Roxbury Creek (Dane County) spotfin shiners selected food from 92.5% of the aquatic fauna available, and from 90.0% of the terrestrial fauna (Mendelson 1972). In one sample, they fed on *Gammarus* (51.8%), chironomid pupae (18.2%), terrestrial insects (7.6%), copepods (6%), *Calopsectra* (5.3%), orthoclads (5%), and a variety of other items, including the trichopterans *Pycnopsyche* and *Hydropsyche*, the hydrophilid beetle *Anacaena*, and *Simulium*. A large terrestrial oligochaete (23 mm in length) was ingested by one spotfin shiner.

In aquarium feeding experiments, spotfins fed on food floating on the surface (Mendelson 1972). In spite of decreasing concentrations of food at the water surface, the emerald shiner and the spotfin shiner remained in this region long after the bigmouth and sand shiners had left. Then they, too, moved toward the bottom and began feeding on descending food particles and on bottom food. Spotfin shiners seized each food particle individually, with their bodies held at a relatively steep angle to the bottom.

According to Mendelson, in pools the spotfin shiner was usually captured in mid water during the day, but at night there was a tendency for it to locate near the surface. An analagous movement into shallow water at night was noted by Starrett (1951) in the Des Moines River.

It has been suggested that the spotfin shiner produces sounds similar to those produced by *Notropis analostanus* (Winn and Stout 1960, Gale and Gale 1977). These sounds are produced when males fight, and when males and females court. A purring sound occurs when a male actively courts a female, but isolated females also produce fainter, less frequent knocking sounds, so that it was impossible to know which sex made the sound during courtship. It is possible that these sounds may be species specific, acting as an isolation mechanism when closely related species are spawning nearby.

The spotfin shiner is capable of withstanding high temperatures. When juvenile spotfin shiners, collected from water 27–31°C (80.6–87.8°F), were exposed to temperatures of 15–35°C (59–95°F) for 14–20 hours, there was a decrease in swimming performance when the temperature changes were rapid (Hocutt 1973); swimming performance peaked between 25 and 30°C (77 and 86°F). The maximum temperature at which this species was captured in the White River and the Ipalco Discharge Canal, Indiana, was 31.1°C (88°F) (Proffitt and Benda 1971).

In the Wisconsin River (Grant County), 4,686 spotfin shiners were associated with the following species: quillback (5), river and/or highfin carpsucker (30), blue sucker (1), white sucker (1), creek chub (+), bullhead minnow (237), bluntnose minnow (1), emerald shiner (44), sand shiner (389), bigmouth shiner (1), Mississippi silvery minnow (1), yellow perch (6), walleye (19), western sand darter (14), johnny darter (3), smallmouth bass (64), and largemouth bass (1). In Neenah Creek (Marquette County), 467 spotfin shiners were taken with the northern hog sucker (1), white sucker (4), creek chub (7), bluntnose minnow (48), rosyface shiner (5), sand shiner (221), bigmouth shiner (32), central mudminnow (1), blackstripe topminnow (3), johnny darter (9), banded darter (1), and black crappie (1).

IMPORTANCE AND MANAGEMENT

Little is known about the spotfin shiner's use by other fishes as forage, although where the spotfin shiner is abundant it is undoubtedly eaten frequently. Spotfin shiner eggs are lifted from crevices by crayfish; one crayfish ate more than 100 eggs at a single feeding (Gale and Gale 1977). There is also a record of the spotfin shiner eating the eggs of carp, but this habit probably has little economic significance because the two species do not commonly occur in the same habitat (Hubbs and Cooper 1936).

This brilliantly colored minnow is reported to be a good bait species for crappies and pike. There is disagreement as to its hardiness on the hook and in the live box; hence it is seldom used by anglers in the lake states, despite its abundance in certain areas.

This species has been suggested as very desirable for bait culture (Gale and Gale 1977). Large numbers of eggs could be collected in a short time; all larvae in the transfer pond would be the same age, uniform in size, with a minimum of grading. Later spawnings could be placed in separate ponds, permitting minnows to be harvested at regular intervals, rather than all at one time. The spotfin's long spawning period might make it possible for some ponds to be used for rearing two groups of fish in the same year. If fractional spawning increases fecundity, it would follow that the number of females needed as broodstock would be reduced. Gale and Gale observed that few males are needed to fertilize the eggs, and that a ratio of 1:10 or 1:20 might be sufficient for bait culture.

Few of our native minnow species can be spawned successfully in the home aquarium; the spotfin shiner, however, is an exception. Pflieger (1965) kept adult spotfins in an aquarium over the winter and induced them to spawn in March. He kept water temperatures at 21.1–23.9°C (70–75°F), supplied living and high-protein food, and provided a piece of slab wood as a spawning surface.

The spotfin shiner is rated as a poor bioassay animal (Bunting and Irwin 1965).

Red Shiner

Notropis lutrensis (Baird and Girard). *Notropis*—back keel; *lutrensis*—of the otter; the species was first known from Otter Creek, Arkansas.

Other common names: redfin shiner, redhorse shiner.

Adult male 67 mm, Menominee Cr. (Grant Co.), 14 Sept. 1969

Adult female 63 mm, Menominee Cr. (Grant Co.), 14 Sept. 1969

DESCRIPTION

Body deep and greatly compressed. Average length 51 mm (2 in). TL = 1.26 SL. Depth into TL 3.6–4.3. Head length into TL 4.7–5.0. Snout bluntly pointed. Mouth oblique (about 45° to body axis), reaching to below posterior nostril; barbel absent. Pharyngeal teeth 4–4 (0,4–4,1 and 1,4–4,1 have also been reported), moderately slender, hooked; arch sturdy. Eye small, into head length 4.0 or more. Gill rakers short, narrow, round tipped. Dorsal fin origin over or slightly behind origin of pelvic fin; dorsal fin rays 8; anal fin rays 9 (8–10); pectoral fin rays usually 14; pelvic fin rays 8. Lateral line scales 32–36; lateral line complete, decurved. Digestive tract S-shaped (all 3 segments run the length of the body cavity), 0.7–0.8 TL. Chromosomes 2n = 50 (Gold et al. 1980).

Olive green dorsally, sides silvery, belly white. Dorsal and lateral scales edged in pigment, resulting in a symmetrical, diamond-shaped design. Dorsal and caudal fins uniformly pigmented (anterior membranes as dark as posterior membranes). Peritoneum silvery, with numerous large, dark chromatophores.

Breeding male pale blue on sides, with prominent purplish crescent behind head; top of head red, its sides rosy; dorsal fin entirely dark; caudal and paired fins red or orange. Breeding male with dense patch of tubercles on snout and on top of head. Large scattered tubercles with tips directed forward on chin; 0–4 tubercles on lower jaws, occasionally a file of 3–4 on each side of nape. Tubercles along margins of body scales and on rays of all fins, a single, heavy tubercle per scale in the vicinity of the anal fin. Breeding female finely tuberculate on head, and on midline of back before dorsal fin.

Hybrids: The red shiner hybridizes readily with the spotfin shiner, *Notropis spilopterus*, occasionally forming hybrid swarms where their ranges come together (Page and Smith 1970). Where mass hybridization between the two species has occurred, turbidity has apparently been a factor leading to both the invasion of a stream by the red shiner, and to the breakdown of reproductive isolating mechanisms, which are probably manifestations of species recognition. According to Page and Smith (p. 269):

> . . . The bright yellow fins of breeding male spotfin shiners and bright red fins of breeding male red shiners suggest that species recognition in both species is visual. In addition, sounds emitted by several species . . . including *N. lutrensis* during courtship . . . suggest audio recognition as an isolating mechanism. A high concentration of silt particles in suspension in the breeding habitat could disrupt the transmission of both light and sound and result in the improper identification of spawning partners.

Page and Smith suggested that the hybrids were partially fertile, since a wide range of variation, probably representing backcrosses, was noted in their collections.

DISTRIBUTION, STATUS, AND HABITAT

In Wisconsin, the red shiner occurs only in the Mississippi River drainage basin. It was added to the ichthyofauna of Wisconsin when two students, M. Hudson and H. Pearson, collected a male (67 mm TL) and a female (63 mm TL) (UWSP 3200) from Menominee Creek (Grant County), SE ¼ Sec 34 T1N R2W, on 14 September 1969. The site, almost on the Wisconsin-Illinois line, was described as follows: a high, wooded ridge on the western side of the stream; a cattle pasture on the east bank, the cattle having direct access to the stream at most points; water turbid; average width of stream at most points 3 m (10 ft); depth variable.

Although Hubbs and Lagler (1964) reported that the red shiner had become recently established in lagoons of Lake Michigan at Chicago, there is no evi-

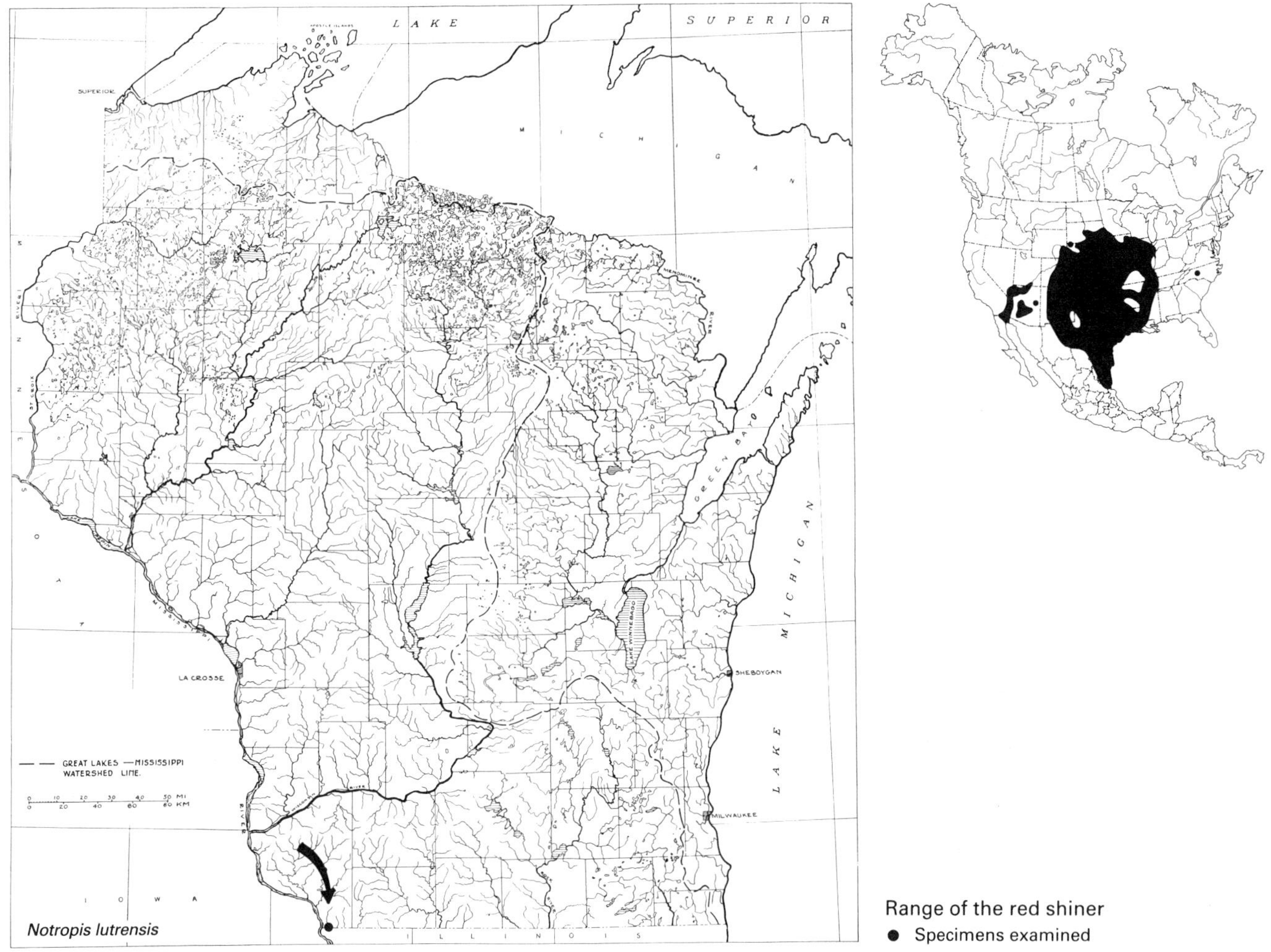

dence to substantiate its presence there (Becker 1976).

Although the number of red shiners in Wisconsin may be low, many waters in southern Wisconsin suit its requirements, and it is likely that in the future the red shiner will appear in a number of streams and become a secure member of our Wisconsin fish fauna.

The red shiner adapts well to new habitats, and consequently is easily introduced into new areas via the minnow pail or the aquarium. Also, the red shiner appears to be expanding naturally to the north. Wisconsin has placed the red shiner on watch status (Wis. Dep. Nat. Resour. Endangered Species Com. 1975, Les 1979).

The red shiner is tolerant of high turbidity and siltation, and avoids waters that are continuously clear or cool. Its habitats are quite variable, ranging from small, intermittent streams to medium and large rivers and lakes; the largest populations occur in small- to medium-sized streams. It is taken over a variety of bottom types, which vary from clean sand or gravel to almost pure silt. Its tolerance for silt is undoubtedly a major factor in its abundance in the agricultural areas of Illinois (Page and Smith 1970).

BIOLOGY

At the latitude of Wisconsin, spawning probably occurs from June to August. In Iowa, all red shiner males longer than 40 mm clearly indicated breeding maturity (Laser and Carlander 1971). In Kansas, spawning was reported over nests of the green sunfish and the orangespotted sunfish in an open-water area measuring 5 × 5 m. No interspecific activity was noted between the sunfish and the red shiners. The water temperature was 23°C (73.4°F), and the bottom was gravel, sand, and mud. Minckley (1959:421–422) described red shiner spawning in Kansas:

> The red shiners moved rapidly at the surface of the water, with one male (rarely two or more) following one female. The male followed closely, passing the female and causing her to change direction. At the moment of the female's hesitation, prior to her turn, the male would erect his fins in display, at the side and a little in front of the

female. After brief display, usually less than two seconds, the male resumed the chase, swimming behind and around the female in a spiral fashion. After a chase of two to three feet, the female would sometimes allow the male to approach closely on her left side. The male nudged the female on the caudal peduncle and in the anal region, moving alongside with his head near the lower edge of the left operculum of the female, thus placing his genital pore about a head-length behind and below that of the female. At this time spawning must have occurred; however, possibly because of the speed of the chase, I observed no vibration of the fish as described for other species of *Notropis* at the culmination of spawning. . . . While the spawning act presumably occurred the pair was in forward motion in a straight course for three to five feet, at the end of which the male moved rapidly away, gyrating to the side and down. The female then swam away at a slower rate. In instances when the female failed to allow the male to move alongside, the male sometimes increased his speed, striking the female, and often causing her to jump from the water.

Some conflict between males was observed, usually when two or more followed one female. The males would leave the female, swerve to one side, and stop, facing each other or side by side. At this moment the fins were greatly elevated in display. There was usually a rush on the part of one male, resulting in the flight of the other, and the aggressive male would pursue for about two feet. Many times the pursued male jumped from the water.

According to Cross (1967), in Kansas spawning occurs in both lakes and streams at water temperatures of 15.6–29.4°C (60–85°F) from May to October, but most spawning probably takes place in June and July. Cross observed males apparently patrolling individual territories adjacent to small patches of vegetation or to fine tree roots; he also observed groups of more than 50 nuptial males surrounding the end of a large stump, which had been polished by the cleaning activity of the fish. Pflieger (1975) noted that in Missouri male red shiners occupy small territories around the margins of sunfish nests, and guard these territories vigorously against the intrusion of other males. The Topeka shiner, the redfin shiner, and the red shiner have similar spawning habits, and all three minnow species commonly spawn simultaneously on the same sunfish nest. The redfin shiner normally spawns in midwater over the nest, while the red shiner and the Topeka shiner spawn near the bottom, around the edges of the nest.

Life history studies of the red shiner are available from central Iowa (Laser and Carlander 1971). In 50 gravid females examined at various times through the summer, there were 485–684 eggs per female; there was no correlation between the number of eggs and the length or weight of the female. At least three egg sizes were recognized in most females; two sizes were predominant in the larger gravid females. The variation in egg size suggests intermittent spawning through the summer. Spent females were recorded in mid-July, but others were gravid in August. Taber (1969) illustrated the developmental stages from 3.3 mm to 9.5 mm for the red shiner.

Young-of-year at 30–35 mm were collected in the greatest numbers on 1–3 July, indicating that the peak of spawning was probably in late May or early June (Laser and Carlander 1971). Sizes (mm) of red shiners by age groups, as indicated by scales in June and early July 1968, were: 0—29 (17–35), I—50 (37–65), and II—72 (69–75). The condition factor (K_{TL}) of these age groups was 1.16, 1.18, and 1.06 respectively.

In central Missouri (Pflieger 1975), the red shiner averages 23 mm long by the end of its first summer of life, and 46 mm by the end of its second summer. Most adults mature in their second or third summer; few live beyond 3 summers (age II). Growth in new impoundments is much more rapid than in streams.

Laser and Carlander (1971) analyzed the digestive tract contents of red shiners taken from 1 July to 5 August. The percentage of plant material (mostly algal, with little evidence of higher-plant tissue) consumed during this time was 67.8; the percentage of insect material was 32.2. During the high-water period, the percentage of plant material consumed increased, and the percentage of insect larvae consumed dropped.

In Missouri ponds, during August (Divine 1968), red shiners less than 34 mm long consumed Collembola in the greatest volume. In September, higher plant materials and *Closterium* made up 75% of the diet; however, in one pond the fish consumed approximately 75% copepods, rotifers, and protozoans, with the remaining volume consisting of plant materials. In red shiners of the 35–50 mm group, insects constituted more than 50% of the volume. In fish greater than 51 mm, stomachs held insects almost exclusively in June, July, and August, although in June, Cladocera and higher plant materials were also important components.

In Oklahoma (Hale 1963), filamentous algae composes as much as a third of the total volume of the red shiner's food, but its food value is in doubt because of its apparently low digestibility. Hale reported that the relatively large variety of terrestrial insects in the red shiner's diet indicates that this species is inclined to feed at the surface. Others report that the red shiner is an extremely active fish, which commonly breaks the surface of the water while feeding. It feeds primarily by sight, and takes its food at all water levels.

The red shiner probably tolerates the highest temperature reported for cyprinids—it was taken in a warm spring in New Mexico at 39.5°C (103.1°F) (Brues 1928).

Metabolic activity was lowered when red shiner males were exposed to their mirrored image, or to red shiner or blacktail shiner females. Delco and Beyers (1963) speculated that since red shiners are weakly schooling fish, metabolic depression may be related to the schooling habit. We may assume that the individual fish lowers his metabolism when in a group, because he need not be very alert to the dangers of predation or to the opportunities for obtaining food; such dangers and opportunities are shared by members of the group. The energy thus saved may be used for tissue repair, growth, gamete production, sound production, pigment production, courtship activities, and other activities.

Delco (1960) found that female red shiners produced sounds which attracted males of the same species. He concluded that the sounds produced by females might serve as a signal to males that the females are ready for courtship. Since male red shiners do demonstrate positive discrimination, female sounds would appear to act as a species recognition device.

The red shiner seems to thrive under conditions of intermittent flow, frequent high turbidity, and other environmental variations that characterize many plains streams. Cross (1967) noted that during droughts the red shiner predominates in streams having steep gradients, while many other species decline in abundance. In the first year or two of a wet cycle, the red shiner continues to abound, occupying nearly all available habitats from swift riffles to quiet pools, regardless of the depth and the nature of the stream bottom. If the wet cycle continues, the red shiner population declines, disappearing first from riffles, then diminishing on gravel shoals, until only residual populations remain in shallow pools with silted bottoms.

Where stream environments are relatively stable, the red shiner is at a competitive disadvantage in the presence of species that concentrate their reproductive effort in brief intervals at precise locations.

The range of the redfin shiner is complementary to that of the spotfin shiner. Ecological incompatibility apparently exists between these species, since the range of the red shiner expands as the spotfin shiner's is reduced. With changes in habitat favoring the red shiner, the spotfin shiner's range has become significantly reduced since the 1920s. Page and Smith (1970) provided a detailed discussion of this problem as it occurred in Illinois.

Pflieger (1975) found that the red shiner lives in schools in midwater or near the surface, and is most often found in association with the sand, redfin, bigmouth, Topeka, and ghost shiners. In collections from Menominee Creek (Grant County), 2 red shiners were associated with the following species: white sucker (1), common shiner (191), emerald shiner (12), bigmouth shiner (3), bluntnose minnow (2), central stoneroller (1), longnose dace (50), southern redbelly dace (1), suckermouth minnow (1), hornyhead chub (5), smallmouth bass (1), and fantail darter (8).

IMPORTANCE AND MANAGEMENT

In parts of its range the red shiner is undoubtedly an important forage minnow for game fishes and fish-eating birds.

Because it is hardy, the red shiner makes a desirable aquarium pet. This minnow has been marketed in a pet shop under the name "rainbow dace" (Moore et al. 1976).

The red shiner can be used with reasonable care as a bioassay animal, although it has nervous habits (Ward and Irwin 1961).

Pugnose Shiner

Notropis anogenus Forbes. *Notropis*—back, keel; *anogenus*—without chin.
Other common names: pug-nosed shiner, shiner.

Adult female 53 mm, L. Poygan, Boom Bay (Winnebago Co.), 8 Aug. 1963

DESCRIPTION
Body slender, fragile, moderately compressed laterally. Average length 46 mm (1.8 in). TL = 1.23 (1.19–1.28) SL. Depth into TL 4.6–5.6. Head length into TL 4.5–5.4. Snout blunt, shorter than eye. Mouth very small, almost vertical to body axis; posterior edge of mouth below anterior nostril; barbel absent. Pharyngeal teeth 4–4, strongly hooked, truncated portion below sometimes weakly serrated; arch slender. Eye large, into head length 2.9–3.8. Gill rakers knoblike to short, conical, up to 8. Dorsal fin origin slightly behind origin of pelvic fin; dorsal rays 8 (9); anal fin rays 8 (7–10); pectoral fin rays 12–14; pelvic fin rays 8. Scales deciduous; lateral line scales 34–37; lateral line complete. Digestive tract basically S-shaped, 0.6–0.7 TL; terminal ascending and descending segments forming a semi-loop where they join anteriorly.

Silvery, with yellow cast dorsally; sides and belly silvery. A lead-colored lateral stripe, extending from a small, wedge-shaped dark spot on base of caudal fin along sides and through eye, abruptly terminating close to side of mouth. Fins unpigmented to faintly dusky, especially pectoral fins along anterior edge. No bright breeding colors. Peritoneum dark brown overlying a silvery background.

Breeding male with minute tubercles on top of head; dorsal surfaces of pectoral rays, and sometimes pelvic rays, thickened and roughened.

Sexual dimorphism: In male the pelvic fin extends to or beyond the anal opening; in female, the pelvic fin does not reach the anal opening.

The pugnose shiner is superficially similar to the pugnose minnow (*Notropis emiliae*), and can easily be confused with it. Bailey (1959) has provided an excellent comparison based on 10 characters.

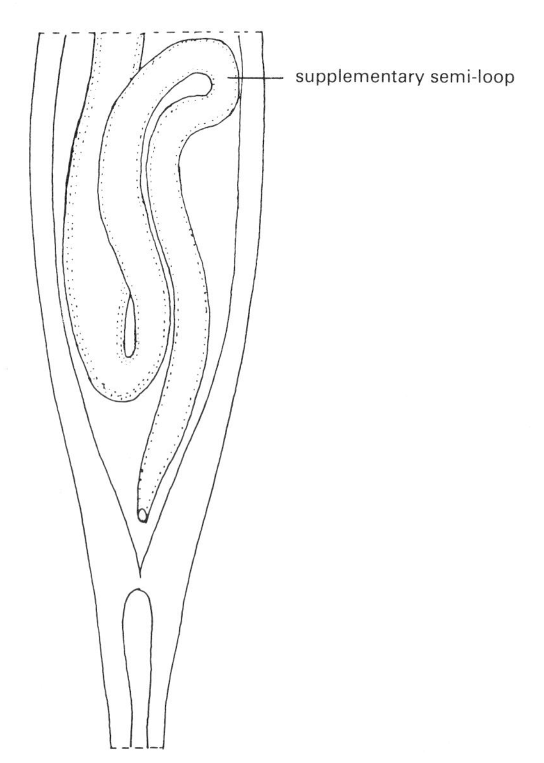

Ventral view of the alimentary tract of the pugnose shiner, with ventral body wall and viscera removed

SYSTEMATIC NOTES
Notropis anogenus was described by Forbes (1885) from 24 specimens collected in the Fox River at McHenry (McHenry County) in northern Illinois, a few miles south of the Wisconsin state line. According to Bailey (1959), no holotype was designated. Of the eight specimens still in the collection of the Illinois State Natural History Survey, Bailey found six *Notropis anogenus* and two *Notropis heterodon*, which emphasized the close similarity of these two species. From the syntypes, he selected an adult 43 mm SL as lectotype.

Bailey suggested that among the many species of *Notropis* the pugnose shiner, *N. anogenus*, may be most intimately related to the Topeka shiner, *Notropis topeka* Gilbert, with which it shares many structural characters, and to which it bears a strong resemblance.

DISTRIBUTION, STATUS, AND HABITAT
The pugnose shiner occurs in the Mississippi River and Lake Michigan drainage basins in Wisconsin. Two widely separated centers of distribution are apparent: eastern Wisconsin (especially the southeast),

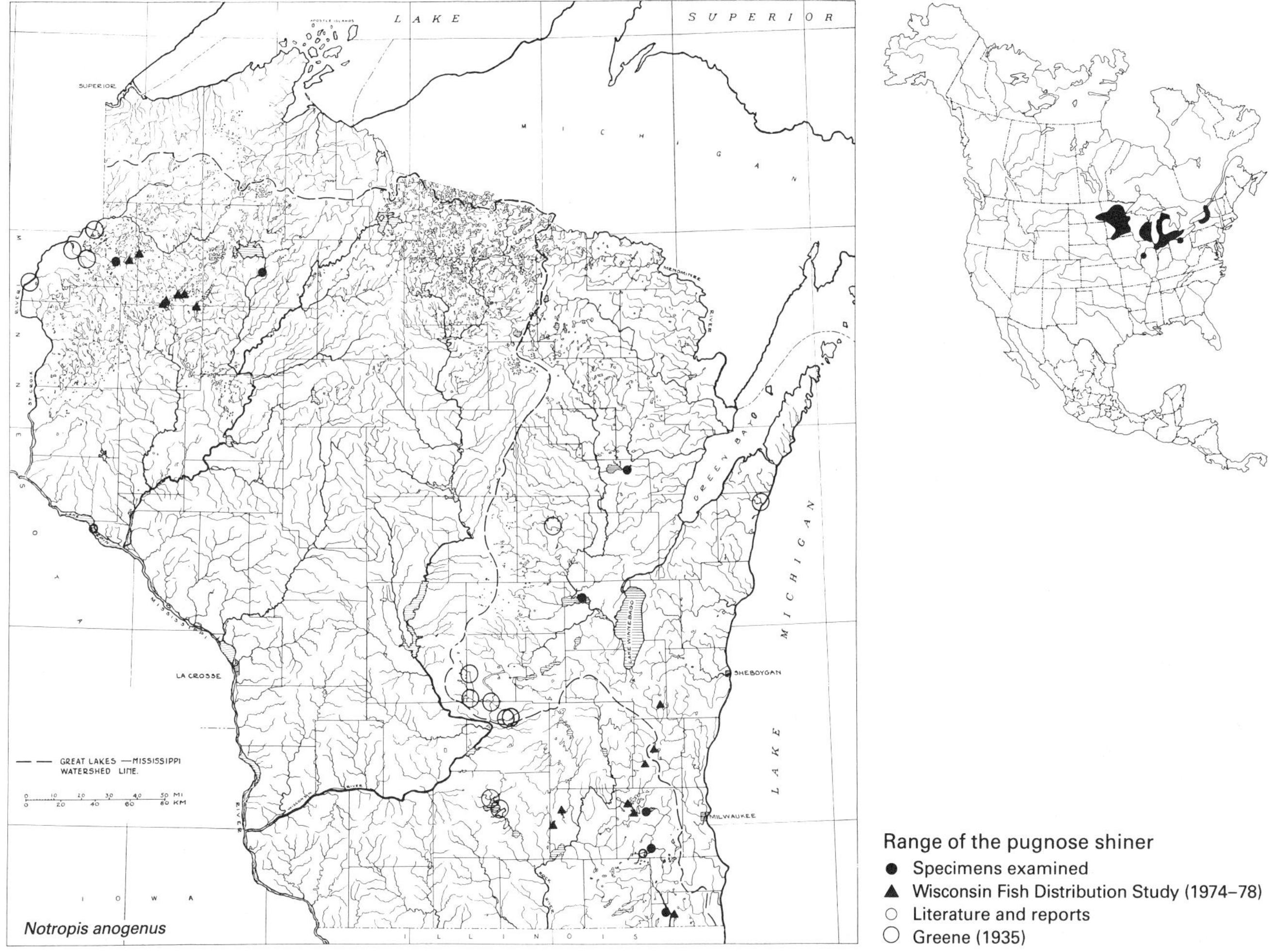

Range of the pugnose shiner
● Specimens examined
▲ Wisconsin Fish Distribution Study (1974–78)
○ Literature and reports
◯ Greene (1935)

and northwestern Wisconsin. The general distribution of this species was thoroughly reviewed by Bailey (1959). He suggested that the species apparently had a glacial refugium in the upper Mississippi basin, from which it dispersed over its present known range.

Specimens examined: UWSP 2829 (2) Pewaukee Lake T7N R18E Sec 24 (Waukesha County) 1960; UWSP 2830 (2) and 2831 (27) Lake Poygan, east shore of Boom Bay (Winnebago County) 1961 and 1963; UWSP 3168 (1) and 3967 (2) White Clay Lake (Shawano County) 1967 and 1971; UWSP 4591 (1) Yellow River T39N R15W Sec 23 (Burnett County) 1974; UWSP 4615 (2) Pike Lake (Waukesha County) 1974; UWSP 4974 (3) Lake Ripley (Jefferson County) 1974; and UWSP 5444 (1) Chippewa River overflow pond T38N R6W Sec 3 (Sawyer County) 1976. M. Johnson submitted for verification a specimen from Bassett Creek T1N R19E Sec 12 (Kenosha County), and reported another from the Fox River T5N R19E Sec 19 (Waukesha County).

Since 1974 the Wisconsin Fish Distribution Study has reported this species from Lake Ripley and Rock Lake (Jefferson County); Lower Nemahbin Lake, Lake Nagawicka, Oconomowoc Lake, and Okauchee Lake (Waukesha County); Pike Lake and Big Cedar Lake (Washington County); Bear Lake, Long Lake, and Kekegama Lake (Washburn County). Rasmussen (1979) noted this species from Pool 4 of the Mississippi River; if this is a valid record, it is undoubtedly a stray from a tributary stream.

The pugnose shiner appears to be in serious trouble over its range. Scott and Crossman (1973) concluded that it has a diminishing range in Canada, and that at one time it probably occurred along the northern shores of Lakes Ontario and Erie, between the two widely separated areas where it is now found. In Ohio (Trautman 1957), the pugnose appeared to be extremely intolerant of turbid water—presumably a primary factor in its extirpation from Ohio waters. In Illinois (Smith 1965), it is known only from Channel Lake in northwestern Lake County; its status is that of an endangered species (Lopinot and Smith 1973). In Minnesota, it is not presently endangered or threatened, but it is rare and has become a "species of special interest" (Moyle 1975). Eddy and Underhill (1974) suggested that removal of aquatic plants from the shallow margins of many lakes to create swimming beaches will probably eliminate the pugnose shiner from such waters in the near future. The pugnose shiner is threatened in Iowa (Roosa 1977).

In Wisconsin, the pugnose shiner has been found in a number of new locales since the 1960s. However, earlier known populations in Dane, Marquette, and Columbia counties may have disappeared, since repeated efforts to capture specimens have failed (Becker 1961, 1971). Most site records of this species are based on the capture of one or two individuals, suggesting low population levels, but it may be locally abundant. The pugnose shiner has been accorded the status of a threatened species by Wisconsin (Les 1979).

The pugnose shiner has been collected from clear, weedy shoals of glacial lakes, and from streams of low gradient over bottoms of sand, mud, gravel, or marl. Characteristic vegetation in its habitat includes pondweed species, water milfoil, *Elodea*, eel grass, coontail, bullrush, *Chara*, and filamentous algae (especially *Spirogyra*). The pugnose shiner is taken mostly from shallows during the warm months of the year, and undoubtedly spends the remainder of the year in deep water.

BIOLOGY

Life history information on the pugnose shiner is lacking. D. Becker, who has studied this species in depth, has graciously allowed me to use his raw data to prepare this account. Unless indicated otherwise, the following data are from him.

Gravid females appear from mid-May into July. Pugnose shiners in breeding condition were collected from Lower Nemahbin Lake (Waukesha County) on 27 and 29 May. On those dates, water temperatures were 21.1°C (70°F) and 22.8–23.9°C (73–75°F) respectively. On 20 June, at a water temperature of 28.9°C (84°F), some females were still gravid while others were partially or entirely spent. In northern Wisconsin lakes (Washburn County), gravid females appeared in a 28 May collection. A partially spent female with a few ripe eggs was taken 11 July.

In Lake Poygan, I noted that female pugnose shiners taken 8 August had ovaries which still contained a few mature eggs; some were undergoing atresia. Apparently, this species does not always lay a full complement of eggs.

In Lower Nemahbin Lake on 15 May, eight gravid females with ovarian weights constituting 7–14% of body weight held 530–958 eggs each. The eggs were in two stages: yellow, mature to maturing eggs 0.5–0.7 mm diam, and white, immature eggs. Most females in this collection were not in breeding readiness.

In a collection taken 29 May, a gravid female 54.5 mm TL and 1.905 g had ovaries 12.6% of body weight, with approximately 30% of the eggs mature or almost mature. A second female, 55.5 mm TL and 2.141 g with ovaries 16.8% of body weight, held 1,275 eggs, of which 21% were mature (0.7–1.3 mm diam), and the remainder immature (0.2–0.6 mm diam).

I estimated the growth of pugnose shiners through analysis of the scales from a Lake Poygan (Winnebago County) population, collected 8 August 1963:

Age Class	No. of Fish	TL (mm)		Calculated TL at Annulus[a] (mm)		
		Avg	Range	1	2	3
I	7	42.0	38–44	31.9		
II	18	46.3	45–49	24.3	38.3	
III	2	52.5	52–53	21.5	29.5	46.5
Avg (weighted)				26.0	37.4	46.5

[a]The annulus is placed in May or June.

A young-of-year pugnose shiner taken from Lower Nemahbin Lake on 10 September 1977 was 20.5 mm long.

D. Becker reported a female 60 mm TL and 2.446 g from Lower Lake Nemahbin, collected 29 May, with the following estimated lengths at the annuli: 1—29 mm, 2—43 mm and 3—57 mm. The largest male in this collection was 50 mm TL, but a number of females were larger. The condition factor (K_{TL}) for 10 females was 1.17 (1.02–1.26); for 8 males it was 1.01 (0.94–1.13).

The pugnose shiner grazes on plants, and its elongated intestine is indicative of this habit (Snelson 1971). Analysis of the digestive tract of a large female disclosed filamentous green algae and an equal amount of cladocerans (*Daphnia* sp., *Chydorus* sp.).

In aquariums, the pugnose shiner selected plant foods, such as *Chara* and *Spirogyra*, in preference to high-protein animal foods. Heavy plant growth was soon grazed to the bottom. Animal food, including high-protein flake food, was accepted mostly after the plant food supply had become nearly exhausted.

I observed an aquarium, holding eight pugnose shiners and eight blackchin shiners, in which almost all of the pugnose shiners hid in a dense stand of *Elodea* rooted at one end of the aquarium. When food was introduced on the surface, two to four pugnose shiners left cover and joined the blackchin shiners in feeding. Occasionally, one pugnose shiner swam quickly to the surface, took food, and returned to midwater to rejoin the others; the approach to the surface was delicate, and, except for the tip of the snout, no part of the body left the water.

The pugnose shiners fed mostly in midwater. Often a food particle dropped between individuals of the two species, and each would hurry to get the morsel for itself. Each species shared in the success. I could detect no avoidance reaction by the pugnose shiners, although they were smaller than the blackchin shiners. Occasionally the pugnose shiners sucked in food as if voracious, only to eject it in a puff. The same fish did this a number of times. In spite of their minute mouths, the pugnose shiners ingested food particles up to 2 mm diam as effectively as the blackchin shiners did. Particles twice the length of the mouth were dispatched quickly; hence the small size of the mouth is no criterion for predicting the size of the food which can be swallowed.

D. Becker, in studying the pugnose shiner of Lake Ripley (Jefferson County) and Lower Lake Nemahbin (Waukesha County), found that it did not move into the shallows until beds of submergent vegetation appeared at or near the time of spawning. In Lake Ripley, one individual was captured on 18 May, one individual at each of two stations on 26 May, and one individual on 27 June. In Lower Lake Nemahbin during 1975, this species began appearing in numbers on 15 May (44 fish) and 22 May (26 fish); it was associated particularly with large stands of the green alga *Chara*, as well as with higher aquatic weeds.

What may have been a record catch of pugnose shiners occurred on 14 May 1977 from Lower Nemahbin Lake, when, in a single 8-m haul with a bag seine, more than 1,000 fish were caught, 610 of which were pugnose shiners. Also present were at least 200 blacknose shiners, 25 blackchin shiners, and 50 bluntnose minnows, as well as numerous bluegills, pumpkinseeds, rock bass, largemouth bass, and black crappies. Five hundred sixty pugnose shiners were returned to the water, and 50 were retained for aquarium and laboratory study. Becker suggested that this was a prespawning school; a number of the females, both large and small, were gravid.

From repeated observations, the normal pugnose shiner school size appears to number 15–35 individuals. After the breeding season school size is reduced to 6–12 individuals; these fish cruise over heavy beds of *Chara* 15–20 cm (6–8 in) apart from one another, in the company of other fishes such as blacknose shiners and lake chubsuckers.

The pugnose shiner is timid and secretive. When a school is threatened, the fish immediately drop to the bottom and conceal themselves in the densest vegetation available. This reaction to danger makes the species less susceptible to conventional entrapment devices; hence it may appear to be less common than it actually is. In the aquarium, the pugnose shiner is never far from cover, and any motion or disturbance from outside the aquarium sends it into hiding. By contrast, the blackchin shiner is far more open and active, swimming in a loose school on the periphery of the water weed within which the pugnose shiner hides.

Although the pugnose shiner appears to avoid the surface, and has never been seen jumping out of the water, evidence suggests that this does occur. While cleaning around an aquarium, I came upon two pugnose shiners (41 and 44 mm TL) which had leaped a minimum height of 51 mm to the edge of the aquarium, with enough forward thrust to carry them 15 mm across the lip of the aquarium. When the water was lowered to 71 mm below the aquarium rim, there were no further losses.

IMPORTANCE AND MANAGEMENT

The value of the pugnose shiner as a forage fish is unknown. This species is so rare as to be unknown to most fishery biologists, even in those areas where it is still found.

Sand Shiner

Notropis stramineus (Cope). *Notropis*—back, keel; *stramineus*—made of straw.

Other common names: straw-colored minnow, shore minnow.

Adult 53 mm, Waupaca R. (Waupaca Co.), 13 June 1960

DESCRIPTION

Body slender, slightly compressed. Average length 62 mm (2.4 in). TL = 1.26 SL. Depth into TL 5.6–7.7. Head length into TL 4.6–5.3. Snout blunt, viewed dorsally V-shaped. Mouth terminal, slightly oblique, extending to below anterior margin of eye; barbel absent. Pharyngeal teeth 4–4, hooked; arch moderate. Eye large, into head length 3.0–3.3. Gill rakers short, conical, widely spaced, about 8. Dorsal fin origin over origin of pelvic fin; dorsal fin rays 8; anal fin rays 7 (6); pectoral fin rays 13–14; pelvic fin rays 8. Lateral line scales 33–36; lateral line complete, slightly decurved. Digestive tract with a single S-shaped loop, 0.7–0.9 TL. Chromosomes 2n = 50 (J. Gold, pers. comm.).

Back olive yellow, the scales edged in pigment; sides silvery, with lateral line pores bounded by "mouse tracks" (paired spots); belly silvery white. Mid-dorsal stripe well defined and expanding at front of dorsal fin, where it becomes interrupted. Basicaudal spot small, generally narrower than the short lateral stripe on caudal peduncle. Fins unpigmented. Peritoneum silvery with a few dark speckles. Bright breeding colors absent.

Breeding male with minute tubercles on top and sides of head and along rays of pectoral fins. Breeding female occasionally finely tuberculate on top of head.

Separation of the sand shiner, the bigmouth shiner, and the mimic shiner is difficult. Characters useful in separation of these species are tabulated on p. 545.

SYSTEMATIC NOTES

Until 1928, the sand shiner was confused with several other species of shiners (Hubbs and Greene 1928); literature references previous to 1928 are of little value. Suttkus (1958), in reviewing the extant type materials under *N. deliciosus*, found there was no referable specimen and adopted *stramineus*, the next available name. Hubbs and Lagler (1964) recognized two subspecies: the northeastern sand shiner, *Notropis stramineus stramineus* (Cope), pertaining to the Wisconsin form, and the southern sand shiner, *N. stramineus* subsp. The subspecific question was reviewed by Bailey and Allum (1962), who applied the name *Notropis stramineus missuriensis* (Cope) to the form which lives in all major drainages of western South Dakota.

DISTRIBUTION, STATUS, AND HABITAT

The sand shiner occurs in the Mississippi River, Lake Michigan, and Lake Superior drainage basins. It is widely distributed in southern Wisconsin, and sporadically distributed northward.

In Ohio, which historically has had a wide distribution of this species, the sand shiner has decreased markedly in some areas, probably because of its inability to adjust to increased erosion and siltation (Trautman 1957). Trautman noted that it seems tolerant of some inorganic pollutants, such as mine wastes, as long as the sand and gravel of the bottom are not covered.

In Wisconsin, the sand shiner is rare in small streams, and common to abundant in medium- to large-sized streams and rivers of central and southwestern Wisconsin. Elsewhere, it is uncommon to common. It is taken infrequently, and generally in small numbers, in lakes.

In Wisconsin, the sand shiner occurs in lakes, sloughs, and streams of moderate current, in water of varying clarity and depth. It was most common at 0.1–1.5 m, over substrates of gravel (27% frequency), sand (24%), mud (12%), silt (11%), clay (8%), rubble (8%), boulders (8%), detritus (1%), and bedrock (1%). In our collections it occurred in rivers of the following widths: 1.0–3.0 m (7%), 3.1–6.0 m (12%), 6.1–12.0 m (21%), 12.1–24.0 (39%), 24.1–50.0 m (17%), and more than 50 m (4%). It was frequently taken where vegetation was scanty or absent, and even where the water was highly contaminated with organic wastes.

BIOLOGY

In Wisconsin, the spawning season extends from late May to at least mid-August. Females with ripe eggs were taken from Green Bay (Door County) from 6 June through the summer; they were taken as late as 15 August from Cottage Inn Branch (Iowa County). In late May and early June, Cahn (1927) noted

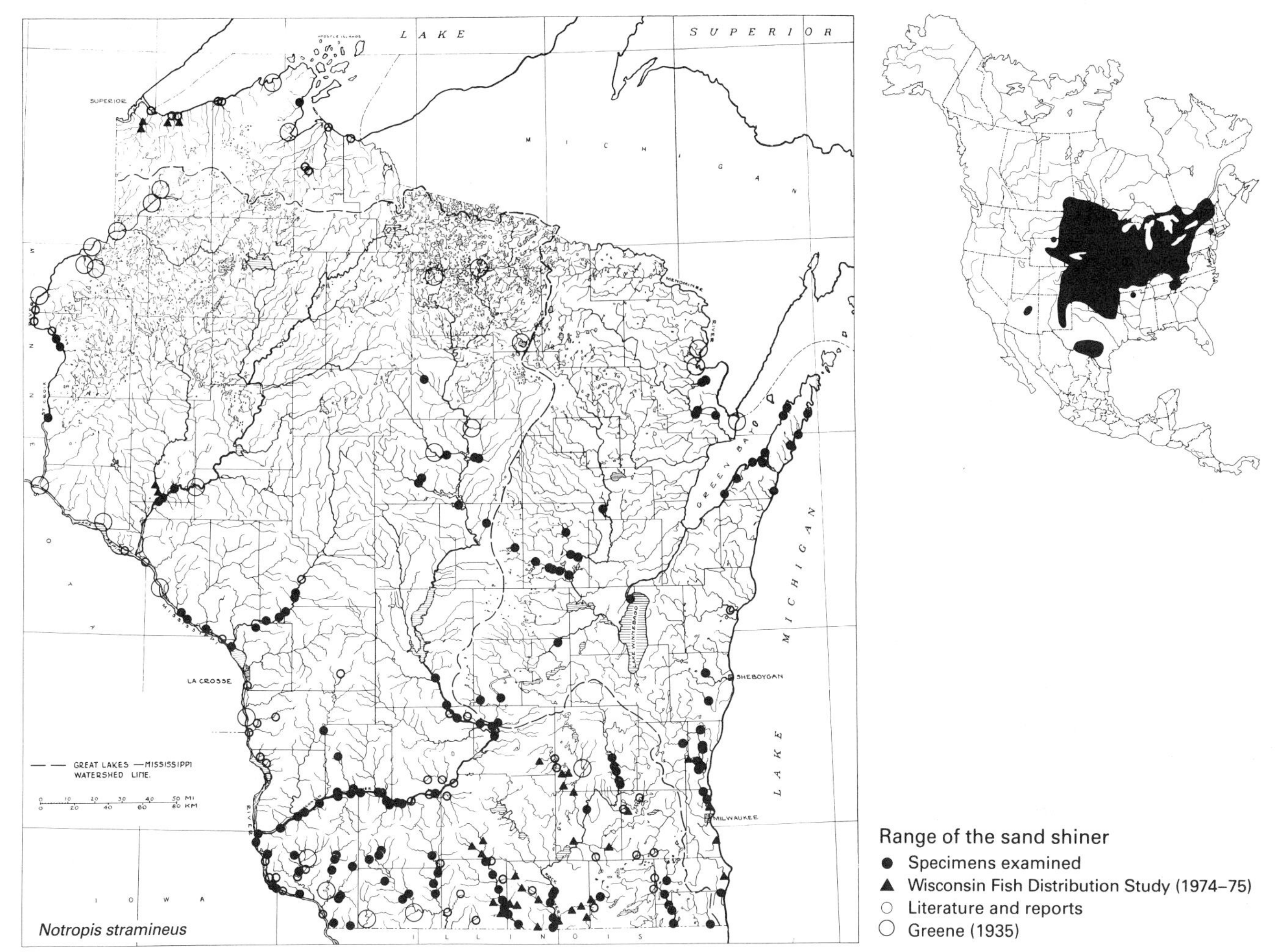

Range of the sand shiner
● Specimens examined
▲ Wisconsin Fish Distribution Study (1974–75)
○ Literature and reports
◯ Greene (1935)

spawning along southeastern Wisconsin lakeshores in shallows 31–46 cm (12–18 in) deep, usually under the protection of submerged vegetation.

In Kansas (Summerfelt and Minckley 1969), peak spawning in late July and August coincided with the highest temperatures (31°C in 1965, and 27–37°C in 1966), which was also a time of minimal rain and runoff during the hot, dry portion of the summer. The authors suggested that summer spawning at high temperatures might be an adaptation to enhance survival of sand shiner fry in Great Plains rivers, where spring is characterized by drastic water level fluctuations and flood conditions.

A mature female sand shiner 55 mm TL, collected from the Wisconsin River (Crawford County) on 18 June 1962, with ovaries 11% of body weight, held 270 ripe eggs 0.8 mm diam. The ovaries also contained several generations of colorless to white immature eggs 0.1–0.4 mm diam. Another female, 60 mm TL, with an identical gonosomatic index held 1,060 eggs 0.8 mm diam.

In Iowa, Starrett (1951) reported that during July age-I females contained about 250 eggs, age-II females about 1,100 eggs, and age-III females about 1,800 eggs.

Little is known about sand shiner spawning behavior and the early development of the embryo. Fish (1932) reported 4.7–11.5-mm stages in Lake Erie on 28 July 1928, and a 16.3-mm fish on 22 August. She described the 5.0-, 6.5-, 7.5-, 12.0-, and 28.6-mm stages, and illustrated the 5.0-, 7.5-, and 12.0-mm stages.

Summerfelt and Minckley reported a length of 10.5 mm for the size of the sand shiner at the time of scale formation. Young-of-year 20–24 mm TL appeared in Kansas collections in May and June, and probably represented the progeny of very early spawners; larger numbers of young-of-year, 25–34 mm, first appeared in the September and December collections.

Twenty-two young-of-year sand shiners, collected from Big Sandy Creek (Marathon County) on 9 September 1975, averaged 23.5 (18–32) mm TL. The condition (K_{TL}) of 12 young-of-year, 37–44 mm TL, from the Eau Claire River (Eau Claire County) on 19 September 1975, was 0.85 (0.78–1.02).

Sand shiners from Neenah Creek (Marquette County), collected 29 July 1960, showed the following growth:

Age Class	No. of Fish	TL (mm)		Calculated TL at Annulus[a] (mm)		
		Avg	Range	1	2	3
I	24	53.3	48–57	35.2		
II	10	61.5	59–64	38.4	57.2	
III	5	66.4	64–68	33.2	57.1	65.7
Avg (weighted)				35.8	57.2	65.7

[a]The annulus for the year of capture had not yet been deposited in some age-II and age-III fish.

A sample from a breeding population of sand shiners, collected from Cedar Creek (Ozaukee County) on 1 August 1963, consisted of five males and five females in age-group III; they were 66–72 mm TL, and had the following calculated lengths at the annuli: 1—38.7 mm; 2—56.0 mm; and 3—68.7 mm. The third annulus was in the process of being placed.

Sand shiners spawn at age I, and generally there is a sharp decline in the abundance of age-II fish following their second spawning (Summerfelt and Minckley 1969). Starrett (1951) attributed the collapse of the age-II group to senility.

The largest sand shiner observed, 80 mm TL and 4.74 g, was a breeding male collected from Green Bay (Door County) on 6 June 1962.

Mendelson (1972) found that the food habits of the sand shiner in Roxbury Creek (Dane County) were influenced by the large quantity of algae present in the water column. Algae constituted 29% of the volume of food in stomachs examined, accounting for the very high presence (45.6%) of copepods, since harpacticoids were particularly prominent in algal mats. In addition, the sand shiner consumed *Calopsectra*, *Paratendipes*, chironomid pupae, and some *Gammarus*. Terrestrials were absent from gut contents. In southern Illinois (Stegman 1969), stomachs contained bottom ooze, aquatic insects, and dipterous larvae.

Starrett (1950b) classified the sand shiner as an omnivorous feeder, and noted that in the Des Moines River (Iowa) its summer diet was bottom ooze (68% of volume), aquatic nymphs and larvae, Ephemeroptera nymphs, Trichoptera larvae, adult terrestrial insects, adult and emerging Ephemeroptera, dipterans, corixids, and a small amount of plant material. Young sand shiners fed mostly on bottom ooze diatoms.

Aquarium feeding experiments (Mendelson 1972) showed that the sand shiner approaches the surface rapidly at a steep angle. Once a particle of food has been seized, the fish retreats quickly to midwater or to the bottom. When waterlogged food particles drift down from the surface, the sand shiner begins to feed on particles of food in the water column from a position close to, but not on, the bottom. Very infrequently the fish removes food from the substrate itself, seizing food particles individually, with its body held at a relatively steep angle to the bottom.

The movements of the sand shiner have been followed by Mendelson (1972) in Roxbury Creek, a stream less than 3 m (10 ft) wide, and 1 m (3 ft) deep in the deepest pools. Peak spring populations occur in Roxbury Creek from mid-April until early June. By mid-June, most sand shiners have left the creek and have returned to the Wisconsin River. During the summer months, this species is absent from the creek. In the fall, large numbers return to the stream, beginning in mid-September and continuing until mid-October; peak populations occur again from this time through the end of November. A gradual reduction in numbers follows over the winter months. Mendelson suggested that this attrition is due in part to the death of fishes, and in part to movement back to the river. In the spring, the remaining winter residents in the creek are supplemented by new populations from the river.

In Lake Erie (Fish 1932), the sand shiner is found at the surface, as well as on the bottom at depths of 11–34 m (36–106 ft). During the winter in the Des Moines River (Starrett 1951), the sand shiner remains mostly under the ice cover along shore.

Daily movements of the sand shiner have also been described. Mendelson noted a movement at night from deep water into the shallows and to the surface; during the day sand shiners were found on the bottom or in midwater.

The sand shiner is a schooling fish. An early report from Oconomowoc Lake noted schools containing at least 5,000 individuals (Cahn 1927).

In reviewing the success and failure of sand shiner production in the Des Moines River, Starrett equated poor recruitment with higher population density and the lower amount of available space. Implied is a built-in control, which keeps the population within the carrying capacity of the environment. Harlan and Speaker (1956) noted that in Iowa there was a trend toward a decline in the sand shiner population and an upsurge in the bigmouth shiner population.

Ten sand shiners lived in, and showed no distress in, test solutions to which no oxygen was applied. An oxygen level of 1.4 ppm produced no fatalities. Test solutions had a pH range of 8.4–7.4 (Gould and Irwin 1962).

In the Waupaca River (Waupaca County) 430 sand shiners were associated with these species: golden redhorse (20), northern hog sucker (9), white sucker (24), largescale stoneroller (38), hornyhead chub (2), creek chub (2), pearl dace (18), bluntnose minnow (94), common shiner (176), rosyface shiner (12), spotfin shiner (33), blacknose shiner (4), mimic shiner (72), bigmouth shiner (95), logperch (4), johnny darter (47), bluegill (1), rock bass (2), and brook stickleback (2). From the Wisconsin River (Richland County), 550 sand shiners were collected with quillback (13), river and/or highfin carpsucker (69), shorthead redhorse (3), silver redhorse (2), bullhead minnow (281), bluntnose minnow (19), emerald shiner (80), spotfin shiner (2,450), river shiner (7), Mississippi silvery minnow (1), white bass (6), yellow perch (16), walleye (3), western sand darter (2), logperch (1), johnny darter (2), smallmouth bass (4), largemouth bass (4), and black crappie (5).

IMPORTANCE AND MANAGEMENT

The sand shiner probably serves as an important forage fish because of abundance in certain areas.

Historically, the sand shiner was the standard bait minnow of southeastern Wisconsin (Cahn 1927). In more recent years it has been included occasionally in a mixed bag of minnows.

Gould and Irwin (1962) noted that sand shiners are good bioassay animals because they are easy to transport, withstand low oxygen conditions, and will take dry food readily.

In Kansas, the life history of the sand shiner has been studied intensively to aid in monitoring the effects of pesticides on the ichthyofauna of the Smoky Hill River basin. The larger study involves a comprehensive evaluation of possible pesticidal contamination of soils, water, and wildlife, resulting from the intensification of agriculture and the increased use of pesticides associated with irrigation (Summerfelt and Minckley 1969).

Mimic Shiner

Notropis volucellus (Cope). *Notropis*—back, keel; *volucellus*—a diminutive of swift.

Other common names: channel mimic shiner, shiner.

Adult 67 mm, Eau Claire R. (Marathon Co.), 29 May 1961

DESCRIPTION

Body slender, somewhat compressed. Average length 51 mm (2 in). TL = 1.27 SL. Depth into TL 6.1–7.4. Head length into TL 4.6–5.3. Snout blunt, protruding slightly beyond mouth. Mouth subterminal, slightly oblique, tip of upper lip at level of lower eye margin; mouth extending to below anterior margin of eye; ventral view of mouth, small and U-shaped; barbel absent. Pharyngeal teeth 4–4 slender, slightly to strongly hooked; slender arch (see Gilbert and Bailey 1972). Eye into head length 2.6–3.5. Gill rakers short, conical to knoblike, about 5. Dorsal fin origin over or slightly behind origin of pelvic fin; dorsal fin rays 8; anal fin rays 8; pectoral fin rays 12–15; pelvic fin rays 9. Lateral line scales 33–38; lateral line complete, slightly decurved. Digestive tract short with a single S-shaped loop, 0.6–0.7 TL. Chromosomes 2n = 50 (Gold et al. 1980).

Back olive yellow to lateral line; below, whitish. In preserved specimens, lateral stripe on caudal peduncle, faint to absent anteriorly. Dorsal scales dark edged, pore of lateral line scale with spot above and below ("mouse tracks"). Mid-dorsal stripe, appearing as several faint parallel striations, or mid-dorsal scales pigmented posteriorly, resulting in a series of transverse bars ending in some diffuse pigment just before the dorsal fin. Fins generally clear; caudal rays at times heavily edged with pigment. Black pigment about anus and along the base of anal fin. Peritoneum silvery, with numerous speckles, to dusky.

Breeding male with minute tubercles over head, branchiostegals, and along rays of pectoral fin. No special breeding colors. Breeding female occasionally with minute, sharp tubercles on snout.

Hybrids: Mimic shiner × rosyface shiner (Bailey and Gilbert 1960), mimic shiner × weed shiner (Wis. Fish Distrib. Study).

Separation of the mimic shiner from the bigmouth shiner and the sand shiner is difficult. Characters useful for separating these species are given on p. 545.

SYSTEMATIC NOTES

Several subspecies have been recognized: *Notropis volucellus volucellus*, the northern mimic shiner; *Notropis volucellus wickliffi*, the channel mimic shiner, a form which inhabits the larger rivers in the upper parts of the Mississippi River system; and *Notropis volucellus buchanani*, the ghost shiner, which has been elevated to specific level, *Notropis buchanani* Meek (Bailey 1951).

The following account does not distinguish between the northern mimic shiner and the channel mimic shiner. Although Jenkins (1976) elevates the channel mimic shiner to specific status, *Notropis wickliffi*, I have no real confidence in the systematic separation of *wickliffi* from *volucellus*.

DISTRIBUTION, STATUS, AND HABITAT

In Wisconsin the mimic shiner occurs in the Mississippi River, Lake Michigan, and Lake Superior drainage basins. It is less generally distributed in the unglaciated southwestern quarter of the state. In the Great Lakes, it appears sporadically in the shallows of protected bays.

This species is locally uncommon to common in medium-sized streams and large rivers, and in lakes in central and northern Wisconsin; it is rare in the southwestern quarter of the state. It has disappeared from a number of locales in southern Wisconsin since the late 1920s.

The mimic shiner prefers clear, moderately weedy lakes; in central and southern Wisconsin, it is generally found in the pools and backwaters of creeks. In Wisconsin, the mimic shiner was encountered most frequently at depths of 0.1–1.5 m over substrates of sand (18% frequency), silt (18%), gravel (18%), mud (14%), detritus (9%), rubble (9%), boulders (9%), and marl (5%). It occurred in streams of the following widths: 6.1–12.0 m (14%), 12.1–24.0 m (57%), 24.1–50.0 m (14%), and more than 50 m (14%).

BIOLOGY

In Wisconsin, spawning extends from May through July, and possibly into August. Females with ripe eggs have been taken through 24 July.

The breeding site and spawning habits of mimic shiners are unknown. It has been suggested that they broadcast their eggs over the weeds in the deeper, weedy littoral areas, and that spawning oc-

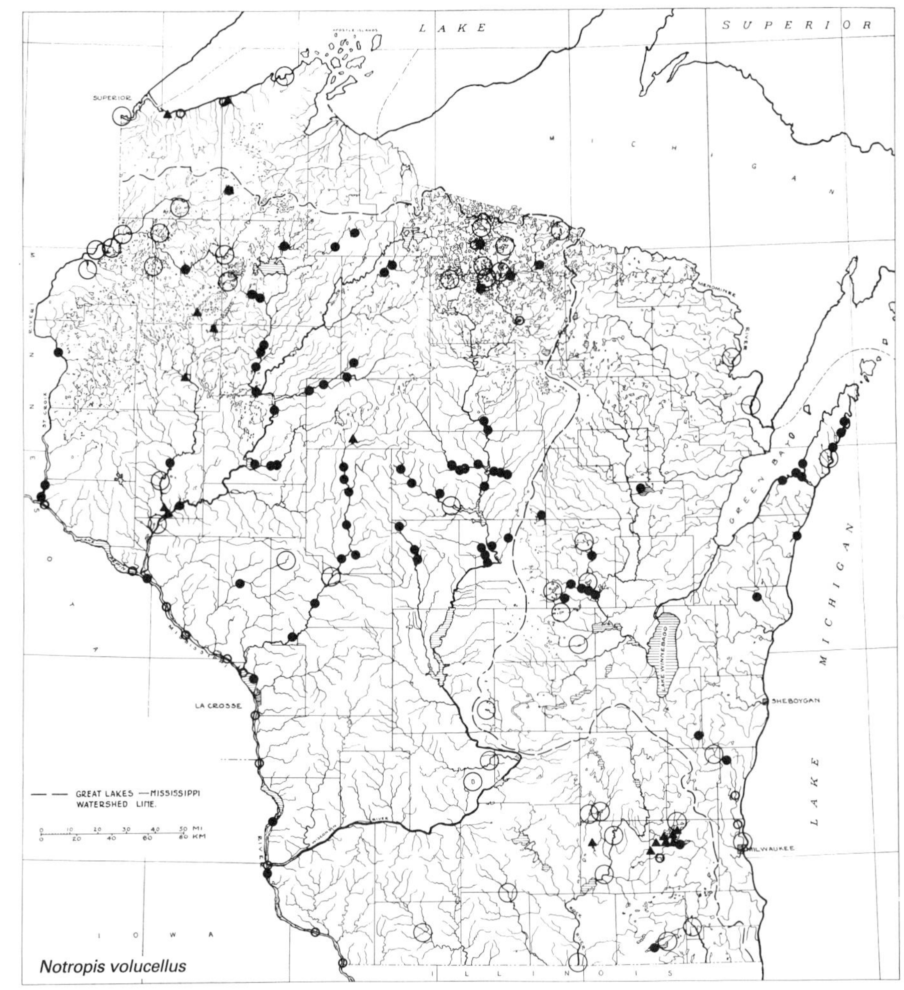

Range of the mimic shiner
● Specimens examined
▲ Wisconsin Fish Distribution Study (1974–75)
○ Literature and reports
◯ Greene (1935)

curs at night (Black 1945a). In Minnesota, Moyle (1969) reported formation of large, midsummer schools for spawning. The females outnumbered the males about 2 to 1. Spawning occurred in 1966 between 26 July and 10 August, and in 1967 it began on 11 August; in 1968 there was no spawning at all, possibly because the cold and rainy summer limited the availability of surface insects for food.

In Wisconsin, a 67-mm, age-III female, taken May 1974 from the Rock River (Jefferson County), held eggs up to 1 mm diam. Gravid females were collected from the Waupaca River (Waupaca County) on 13 June 1960. A 62-mm female with ovaries 22% of body weight held 635 orange, ripe eggs 0.75 mm diam. A 65-mm female with ovaries 17% of body weight held 960 ripe eggs. A generation of smaller eggs, 0.50 mm diam, was found in fewer numbers. Black (1945a) found that in Shriner Lake, Indiana, the average number of eggs produced was 367 per fish.

The growth of young-of-year mimic shiners has been recorded as follows:

Date	No. of Fish	TL (mm) Avg	TL (mm) Range	Location
1 Aug.	2	28.5	28–29	Milwaukee R. (Ozaukee Co.)
9 Sept.	53	26.5	18–32	Big Sandy Cr. (Marathon Co.)
13 Sept.	2	26	16–35	Black R. (Clark Co.)
10 Oct.	4	24	19–26	Black R. (Clark Co.)

The small fish present in mid-October suggest that there was late spawning.

Mimic shiners from Black River (Clark County), collected 13 September 1968, showed the following growth:

Age Class	No. of Fish	TL (mm)		Calculated TL at Annulus (mm)	
		Avg	Range	1	2
I	8	47.8	43–52	29.5	
II	22	58.3	52–65	29.9	50.2
Avg (weighted)				29.8	50.2

In Indiana (Black 1945a), age-I mimic shiners were 48 mm long, and age-II fish were 55 mm. The breeding population was made up almost entirely of 1-year-old fish. Black noted a period of extremely rapid growth during the month of July, for 3 or 4 weeks just after spawning, followed by a slowing of the growth rate. The maximum life span was 2 years.

In Minnesota, sexually mature mimic shiners were those over 42 mm long (Moyle 1973).

The males are smaller than the females. The largest mimic shiner reported from Wisconsin was a 73-mm female with ripe eggs, collected from the Yellow River (Chippewa County) on 24 July 1970.

The food of the mimic shiner has been studied intensively in Long Lake, Minnesota (Moyle 1969). In the early morning, mimic shiners feed heavily (84%) on midwater organisms, especially *Daphnia pulex*. During the day, midwater organisms are a small part of the diet (7–11%); they are replaced by emerging Diptera and terrestrial insects, especially leafhoppers, ants, and beetles (61–62%), and by invertebrates, algae, and detritus browsed from the bottom (28–32%). In the evening mimic shiners feed more extensively on dipteran pupae, ephemeropteran adults, and *Hyallella azteca* than they do during the day. The only food items positively correlated with daytime feeding are cicadellids and algae. Copepods, abundant in evening plankton samples, are almost completely ignored by the mimic shiners.

There is a correlation between Moyle's study of the mimic shiner's food habits in Minnesota and Black's study of its food habits in Shriner Lake, Indiana. Black (1945a) considered the mimic shiner omnivorous. He found these foods in a more or less decreasing order of use: Entomostraca, green algae, blue-green algae, fish scales, insects (mostly adult or immature Chironomidae), plant debris, diatoms, and desmids. He noted that mimic shiners have an opportunity to feed on the zooplankton only in the morning, when the ascending minnow schools cross the path of the descending plankton, and in the evening, when this movement is reversed. Limited data suggest that the mimic shiner feeds at night also.

The mimic shiner is a schooling fish. Moyle (1973) noted that during most of the day schools swim back and forth along the shore. Toward evening large, shallow-water schools break up into groups of 10–15 fish, most of which swim out into deeper water, following the surface of the aquatic plant growth. Scuba diving observations at night showed that mimic shiners and bluntnose minnows spend the dark hours lying on the bottom, scattered about on bare areas at depths from 0.1 to 8 m. In the early morning small groups of minnows are again evident; these groups soon join to form the large daytime schools. As the summer progresses the daytime schools become larger; 25 schools containing a total of 3,000 fish were observed on 25 July, and on 2 September a single school containing 15–20 thousand fish was noted. This phenomenon was also observed by Black (1945a) in Indiana:

> In late July and August of 1935 these minnows sometimes congregated several layers deep and as closely packed as they could swim in the shallow water along the south shore of the lake—forming a solid school that extended well over 150 yards along shore and averaging not less than five yards in width.

The population level of mimic shiners fluctuates from year to year. Black recorded a large drop in numbers between the years 1935 and 1936 in Shriner Lake. Dr. C. L. Hubbs suggested to Black that cannibalism might be the explanation for this decrease. Superabundant adults might have been so pressed for food that they consumed most of the fry. Black noted that mimic shiners of the same age attained a greater size when the total population of the species in the lake had been reduced.

In southern Ontario streams, Hallam (1959) found that the mimic shiner was associated with rock bass and smallmouth bass, which occurred at downstream and warm water collection sites. The mimic shiner was not taken with the coldwater brook trout and mottled sculpin.

In the East Fork of the Chippewa River (Ashland County), 147 mimic shiners were associated with these species: white sucker (4), golden redhorse (93), rock bass (2), hornyhead chub (21), common shiner (125), rosyface shiner (6), bluntnose minnow (13), creek chub (4), brook stickleback (1), fantail darter (1), johnny darter (12), blackside darter (13), and central mudminnow (1).

IMPORTANCE AND MANAGEMENT

The mimic shiner has seldom been taken in quantities at any of the Wisconsin collection sites. Its use as a forage or bait minnow is probably low.

The principal check on the mimic shiner's numbers appears to be the various predatory fishes, especially the largemouth and smallmouth bass, black crappie, yellow perch, and northern pike. Black (1945a) reported the kingfisher, green heron, and probably the great blue heron as birds which prey on the mimic shiner. He also observed a water snake (*Natrix*) swallowing a mimic shiner, and turtles eating dead fish of various species, including the mimic shiner.

Black reported that the large population of mimic shiners in Shriner Lake provided the principal food for all species of predatory birds and fish at the site, and also served as the food supply for fishes at the Tri-Lakes hatchery. Mimic shiners from Shriner Lake were also used in huge quantities as bait, and were caught for use as fertilizer by the people living along the lakeshore.

Ghost Shiner

Notropis buchanani Meek. *Notropis*—back, keel; *buchanani*—named for Dr. John L. Buchanan, president of Arkansas Industrial University.
Other common name: shiner.

Adult 44 mm, Mississippi R. (Vernon Co.), 25 July 1944

DESCRIPTION

Body delicate, moderately deep, strongly compressed laterally. Average length 41 mm (1.6 in). TL = 1.30 SL. Depth into TL 5.0–6.2. Head length into TL 4.4–5.8. Snout short, rounded, protruding slightly beyond mouth. Mouth subterminal, slightly oblique, tip of upper lip at level of mideye; mouth extending to below anterior margin of eye; ventral view of mouth U-shaped; barbel absent. Pharyngeal teeth 4–4. Eye large, into head length 2.8–3.9. Sensory canal (infraorbital) behind and beneath eye absent. Gill rakers short, conical to knoblike, about 6. Dorsal fin origin slightly behind origin of pelvic fin; dorsal fin pointed and falcate, depressed fin longer than head; dorsal fin rays 8; anal fin rays 8; pectoral fin rays 13 (12–14); pelvic fin rays 8 (9). Lateral line scales 30–35. Digestive tract short with a single, S-shaped loop, about 0.6 TL.

Back, sides, and belly pale yellowish white, usually with a few scattered dark melanophores edging the top 3 rows of scales along the back, and a concentrated patch of melanophores on posterior head. Fins clear. General lack of pigmentation accounting for common name. Peritoneum silvery.

Breeding male with small tubercles over most of head, forward part of body, and along rays of pectoral fins; tubercles largest on snout and top of head (Pflieger 1975).

SYSTEMATIC NOTES

The widespread southwestern distribution of the ghost shiner suggests an origin in Gulf of Mexico coastal drainages west of the Mississippi River. Formerly *Notropis volucellus buchanani*, it has been elevated to specific level, *Notropis buchanani* Meek (Bailey 1951).

DISTRIBUTION, STATUS, AND HABITAT

In Wisconsin, the ghost shiner occurs only in the Mississippi River where it is at the northern limit of its range. Specimens examined: UWSP 3225 (11) Mississippi River, Pool 11 (Grant County) 1946; UWSP 5024 (3) Mississippi River, Pool 7, vic. Dakota, Minnesota, 1946; UWSP 5025 (5) Mississippi River, Pool 9, 1.6 km above De Soto (Vernon County) 1944; UWZM 2911 Mississippi River, Pool 9 (Allamakee County) Iowa, 1944; UMMZ 100915 (1) Mississippi River between Lansing and upper Iowa River (Allamakee County), Iowa, 1932; UMMZ 147196 (10) Mississippi River, Pool 9 (Allamakee County) Iowa, 1945. The ghost shiner has been reported from Iowa in UMRCC (1953): Mississippi River vic. New Albin and vic. Lansing (Allamakee County); Mississippi River vic. Marquette and vic. Millville (Clayton County). P. W. Smith et al. (1971) and the Upper Mississippi River Conservation Committee (1953) noted its distribution in upper Mississippi River opposite Pierce, Pepin and Buffalo counties, Wisconsin, in Pools 3, 4 and 5A. Underhill (1957) cited a Minnesota report from the junction of the Root and Mississippi rivers.

P. W. Smith et al. (1971) stated that the ghost shiner has become quite rare, and may be extirpated, above Pool 14 of the Mississippi River. This species has not appeared in recent Mississippi River surveys opposite Wisconsin, and no collections are known to have been made since the 1940s. In Wisconsin, the ghost shiner is regarded as extirpated (Wis. Dep. Nat. Resour. Endangered Species Com. 1975, Les 1979).

In Wisconsin portions of the Mississippi River, the ghost shiner has been taken from the main channel over sand and some mud up to 10 m from shore, at depths up to 0.5 m. In other parts of its range it has been collected from slow current where there were rushes and sedges in medium abundance, and from the mouths of bayous. It has not been taken in Wisconsin from tributary streams or from small streams, as is the case in the South. This species usually occupies gentle eddies adjacent to strong currents in the main channels of rivers. Cross (1967) noted its presence at the confluence of small, intermittent creeks and large rivers, where the current sweeps past backwaters in the creek mouths; he also found it along the lower edges of gravel bars in the mainstream, where the direction of flow is reversed.

The ghost shiner is generally associated with warm, sluggish, and turbid water (Knapp 1953, Cross 1967, Metcalf 1959). It has also been reported from moderately clear to clear water (Pflieger 1971, Trautman 1957).

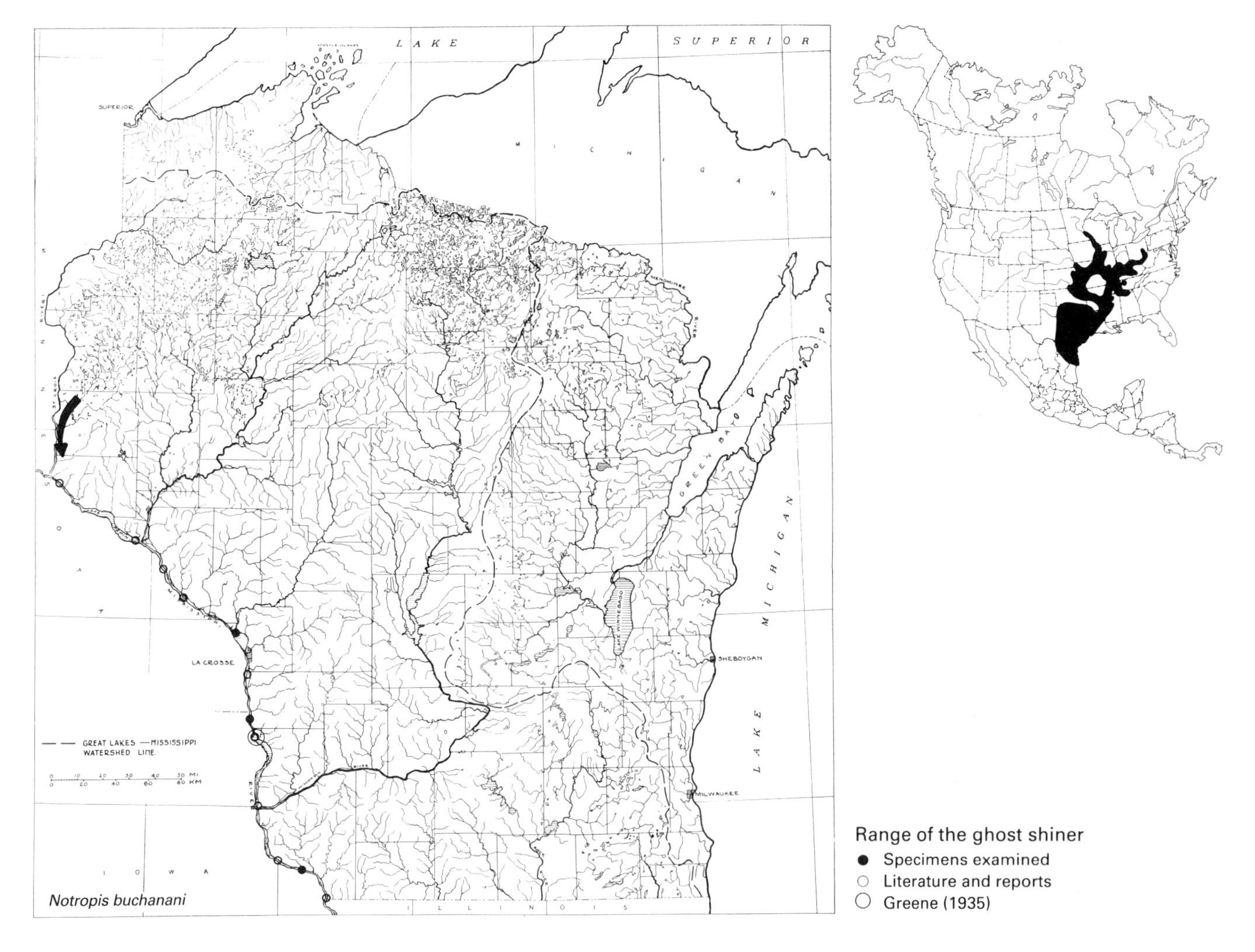

BIOLOGY

In Wisconsin, the spawning of the ghost shiner probably occurred from June to August. In Kansas, this species reproduces between early May and mid-August (Cross 1967). A female, with well-developed eggs, and a tuberculated male were captured near a sandbar in the main channel of the Blue River, Kansas, on 14 August (Minckley 1959).

On 1 June a 42-mm female from the Mississippi River at Jackson County, Illinois, held immature eggs 0.2–0.3 mm diam. She was in the third year of life, although the second annulus had not yet been deposited. Spawning probably occurs at age II.

The ghost shiner is aged by the examination of scales. Unfortunately, its scales are deciduous, and Wisconsin specimens available for aging have lost all scales, or retain only a few anterior lateral line scales. In the largest Wisconsin specimens examined (44–48 mm TL), no scales could be read, although these individuals were estimated to be 2 years old. The calculated total length at the first annulus for 16 smaller Wisconsin specimens was 24 mm. The largest individual seen was 51 mm TL (UWZM 2911).

In Ohio, young-of-year ghost shiners were 20–38 mm long, age-I fish were 28–58 mm, and adults were 33–64 mm (Trautman 1957). The largest specimen reported was 64 mm (2.5 in).

Ghost shiners have been observed resting behind large stones that littered the bedrock, then darting out for bits of food borne downstream by the current (Cross 1967). They are usually found in the company of the mimic shiner (Harlan and Speaker 1956).

IMPORTANCE AND MANAGEMENT

The ghost shiner must have assumed an insignificant role as a forage species. This delicate minnow offers an opportunity to the fish biologist whose desire to make a contribution to knowledge is limited by time and expense. Through a study of southern populations much can be learned, since so little is known.

Blacknose Shiner

Notropis heterolepis Eigenmann and Eigenmann. *Notropis*—back, keel; *heterolepis*—various scale (in reference to the variation in the shape of the scales).

Other common names: northern blacknose shiner, black-nosed minnow, blacknose dace, black-sided minnow, blunt-nosed minnow, Cayuga minnow.

Adult 53 mm, Eske L. T24N R10W Sec. 19 (Portage Co.), summer 1959

DESCRIPTION

Body slender, only slightly deeper than wide. Average length 51 mm (2 in). TL = 1.25 SL. Depth into TL 4.7–7.5. Head length into TL 4.3–5.1. Snout bluntly pointed and projecting slightly beyond lower jaw. Mouth slightly oblique, extending to below nostril or anterior margin of eye; barbel absent. Pharyngeal teeth 4–4, slender, slightly to strongly hooked; arch moderately sturdy. Eye large, into head length 2.7–4.0. Gill rakers knoblike to small, conical protuberances, up to 7. Dorsal fin origin more or less directly over origin of pelvic fin; dorsal rays 8; anal fin rays 8 (7); pectoral fin rays 12–14; pelvic fin rays 8. Lateral series scales 33–37; lateral line incomplete; breast scaled. Digestive tract short, S-shaped, 0.4–0.6 TL.

Silvery over pale, olive yellow back; the scales immediately above the dark lateral stripe lack dark edges, thereby contrasting sharply with the dark-edged scales of the back. Sides silvery, and belly silvery white. Lateral stripe extends around snout (thus the name blacknose shiner), but not onto the lower lip and chin, which are white. Pockets of lateral scales with vertical black, crescent-shaped "new moon" marks, whose tips point backward; basicaudal spot absent. No bright colors during breeding season. Fins essentially unpigmented. Peritoneum silvery with a scattering of dark chromatophores.

Breeding male with fine tubercles on top of head.

Hybrids: Blacknose shiner × brassy minnow (Hubbs 1951a); it is presumed that the scarcity of the blacknose shiner in Kansas during the 1880s was conducive to its hybridization with other forms, including the brassy minnow.

SYSTEMATIC NOTES

This species was formerly named *Notropis cayuga* Meek (Jordan and Evermann 1896–1900, Forbes and Richardson 1920). Two subspecies are recognized in the Great Lakes basin: *Notropis heterolepis heterolepis*, which includes the Wisconsin form, and *Notropis heterolepis regalis* Hubbs and Lagler, the typical form confined to Harvey Lake on Isle Royale, Lake Superior (Hubbs and Lagler 1949, and 1964). A third subspecies, which is characterized by a complete lateral line, and which has gradually been approaching extinction, is represented southward in the central Mississippi Valley, both east and west of the Mississippi River.

DISTRIBUTION, STATUS, AND HABITAT

In Wisconsin, the blacknose shiner occurs in the Mississippi River, Lake Michigan, and Lake Superior drainage basins. It inhabits the area once covered by the glacial drift, and has also been recorded from the driftless area formerly occupied by glacial Lake Wisconsin. Greene (1935) suggested that these records represent a holdover from the glacial period when waters in the driftless area served as a refuge for some fish species.

Although the distribution of this species on the general range map appears to be extensive, populations are actually widely scattered within this range. The blacknose shiner appears to be most secure in Minnesota, Wisconsin, Michigan, and Canada.

In Missouri, the blacknose shiner is decreasing in range and abundance, and if this trend continues it may soon be eliminated (Pflieger 1975). In Iowa, the blacknose shiner is endangered (Roosa 1977); other than one lake record (Harlan and Speaker 1956) and four stream records (Dowell 1962) in the northwestern corner of Iowa, no other recent records are known, even though at one time the blacknose was widespread in the state. It was once one of the common cyprinids of eastern South Dakota, but has not been collected recently (Bailey and Allum 1962), and in all probability has been extirpated. In Ohio, the blacknose shiner may be gone in the near future, if it has not already disappeared (Trautman 1957). In Pennsylvania, it is endangered (Miller 1972). In Illinois, it remains in only a few locations in the northern part of the state, and is listed as rare (Lopinot and Smith 1973).

The blacknose shiner requires clear and vegetated waters. The species has disappeared rapidly when

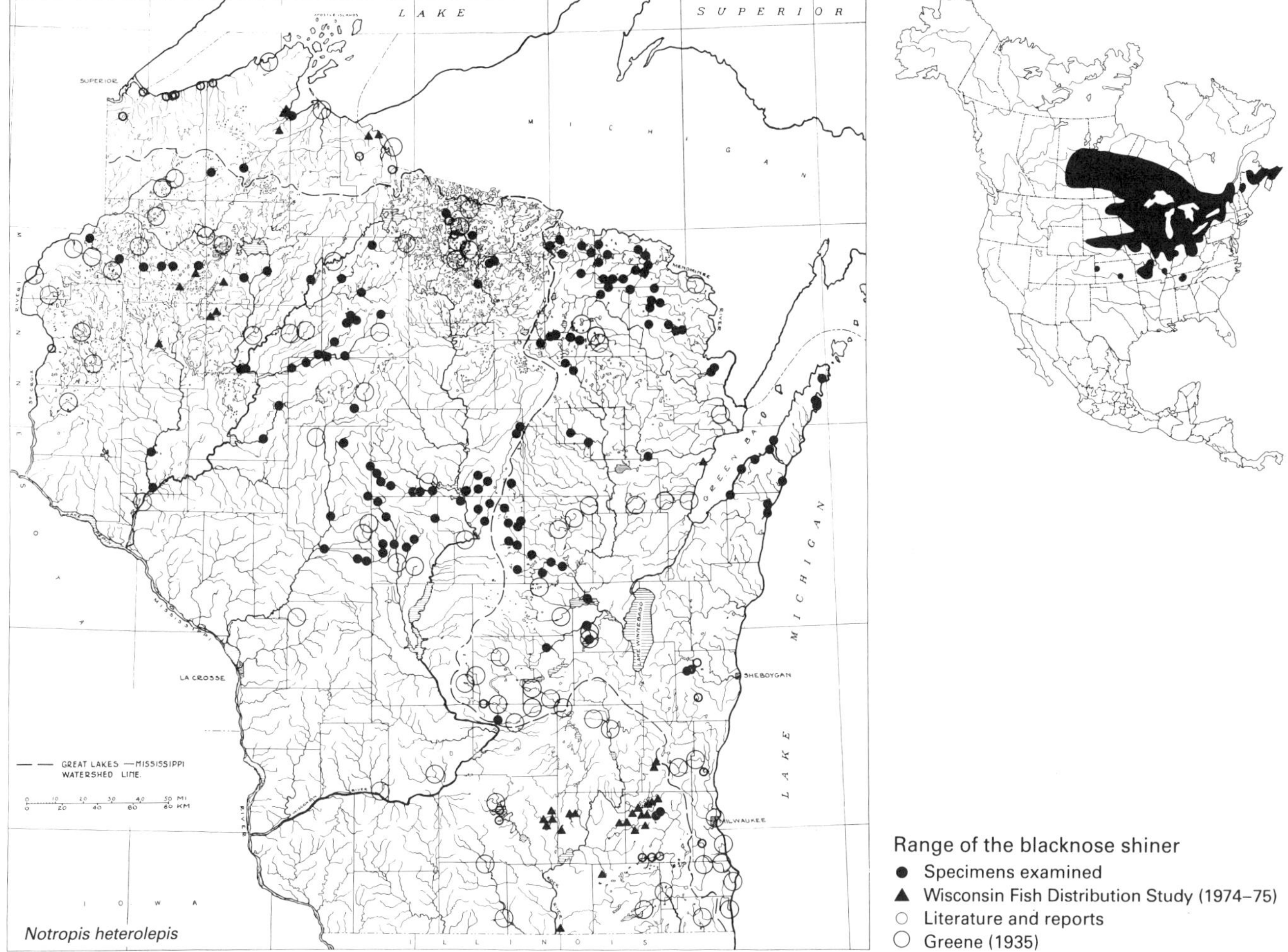

these waters have become turbid, the bottoms have silted over with clay, and the aquatic vegetation has been reduced in amount or eliminated entirely. As a result of drought and intensive land use, the habitat has been greatly restricted during recent years throughout the plains and prairie regions from South Dakota to Ohio. Problems exist even in those states where healthy populations of blacknose shiners remain. Eddy and Underhill (1974) expressed concern that the elimination of higher aquatic plants from bathing beaches and from private lake fronts might result in the scarcity or disappearance of the species.

In the southeastern quarter of Wisconsin, where the blacknose shiner was reported by Greene (1935), it apparently has disappeared from a number of locales. During 1913–1914 it was reported from Lake Wingra (Cahn 1915), but there are no recent records from that lake (Noland 1951). The blacknose shiner is rare in the southwestern quarter of the state. Elsewhere, it is common in lakes and in slow-moving streams.

In Wisconsin, the blacknose shiner occurred at depths of 0.1–1.5 m in the weedy shoals of glacial lakes and reservoirs, and in the quiet waters of connecting streams between lakelike widespreads. It was found in streams of the following widths: 1.0–3.0 m (24% frequency), 3.1–6.0 m (16%), 6.1–12.0 m (12%), 12.1–24.0 m (28%), 24.1–50.0 m (16%), and more than 50 m (4%). It is taken in sparse to dense vegetation; including filamentous algae, bulrush, wild rice, waterweed, pondweed, and arrowhead. The blacknose was found in water which is clear to slightly turbid, and rarely in turbid water, and then probably only where the turbidity is temporary.

BIOLOGY

In Wisconsin, I have seen gravid female blacknose shiners in June, although Cahn (1927) indicated that gravid females have usually been taken in July, and several as late as 10 August. The spawning behavior and habits of this species are unknown: however, it is suspected that the blacknose shiner spawns over sandy places.

In Halsey Lake (Florence County) on 15 June, a

gravid, age-I female, 59 mm and 1.85 g, with ovaries 14% of body weight, held 850 yellow mature eggs 0.8 mm diam. White immature eggs were 0.4 mm diam, and more than twice the number of mature eggs. In a nearby impoundment of the South Branch of the Popple River on 18 June, a gravid, age-II female, 72 mm and 3.18 g, with ovaries 15% of body weight, held 1,420 yellow mature eggs 0.9 mm diam. White immature eggs were 0.5 mm diam, and approximately twice the number of mature eggs. According to Lopinot and Smith (1973), the blacknose shiner is sexually mature in 1 year, and reproduces annually.

M. Fish (1932) described and illustrated the 20-mm stage. The blacknose shiner's ventral mouth, parallel to the body axis, and its white chin, are diagnostic at this stage and throughout life.

In central Missouri, the blacknose shiner reaches a length of 20–38 mm (0.8–1.5 in) by the end of its first summer of life.

Blacknose shiners from Severson Lake (Portage County), collected 4 August 1970, showed the following growth:

Age Class	No. of Fish	TL (mm) Avg	TL (mm) Range	Calculated TL at Annulus (mm) 1
0	7	30.6	27–35	
I	8	48.8	45–55	43.3

The smallest young-of-year blacknose shiners possessed scales only along the bases of the dorsal and the pectoral fins. A number of year-old fish had not had an annulus placed at this late date.

Twenty-five age-I blacknose shiners, collected 14 September 1974 from Rocky Run Creek (Wood County), were 53–63 mm long, and had calculated lengths at the first annulus of 43.9 mm. The smallest age-I fish taken anywhere was collected 21 April 1974 from the Fox River (Green Lake County); it was 32.5 mm TL.

Thirty-nine age-I blacknose shiners, collected 15 June 1965 from Halsey Lake (Florence County), were 36–60 mm TL, and had an average calculated length at the first annulus of 43.6 mm. One age-II fish, 81 mm long, had the following calculated lengths at the annuli: 1—53 mm, and 2—73 mm (J. Cox, pers. comm.).

The maximum known length of a blacknose shiner, 81 mm SL (est. TL 101 mm), was reported from Harvey Lake on Isle Royale in Lake Superior (Hubbs and Lagler 1949).

The diet of 20 blacknose shiners from Eske Lake (Portage County) included zooplankton, small mollusks and crustaceans, dipterans, plant materials, arachnids, and eggs (possibly fish eggs) (F. Van Hulle, pers. comm.). Cahn (1927) reported a diet largely composed of Entomostraca, although insect larvae and a little algae were often found in the stomachs he examined. In Minnesota (Nurnberger 1928), foods included algae, sponges, insects, and their larvae.

The ventral position of the mouth and short digestive tract of the blacknose shiner suggest that this species feeds primarily on the bottom on animal foods.

Apparently the blacknose shiner is able to tolerate severe oxygen depletion in winterkill lakes. In a southeastern Michigan lake, in which the approximate amount of dissolved oxygen in the upper 0.3–1.2 m (1–4 ft) of water was 0.2–0.0 ppm, some survival of this minnow was noted, although no bass and bluegills survived.

My observations of the blacknose shiner indicate that its numbers fluctuate greatly from year to year in a given body of water (Becker 1964a). In Eske Lake (Portage County) during 1959, this minnow was seen by the thousands along the southeastern shore of the lake, and hundreds were easily captured with a square-yard dip net. The following year none were seen in the same area, but a few were captured in the small creek draining the lake. In larger lakes, the blacknose is taken in protected bays, generally on the north side of the lake.

In Moen Lake (Marathon County), 30 blacknose shiners were associated with the following species: creek chub (19), northern redbelly dace (40+), golden shiner (14+), fathead minnow (18+), common shiner (1), black bullhead (4+), central mudminnow (2), yellow perch (1), Iowa darter (16+), and green sunfish (8+).

IMPORTANCE AND MANAGEMENT

The blacknose shiner undoubtedly forms a significant part of the diet of predacious fishes that live in the same habitat. This species makes a good bait minnow.

Pugnose Minnow

Notropis emiliae (Hay). *Notropis*—back, keel; *emiliae*—named for Mrs. Emily Hay.

Other common names: pug-nosed minnow, small-mouthed minnow.

Adult male 51 mm, south shore of L. Poygan (Winnebago Co.), 19 July 1960

Adult female 53 mm, south shore of L. Poygan (Winnebago Co.), 19 July 1960

DESCRIPTION

Body slender, moderately compressed laterally, with slim, elongated caudal peduncle. Average length 50 mm (2 in). TL = 1.25 (1.19–1.29) SL. Depth into TL 4.7–6.5. Head length into TL 5.0–5.8. Snout blunt and rounded, its length less than eye diam. Mouth very small, almost vertical to body axis, extending below anterior nostril; barbel absent (but occasionally present on one or both sides). Pharyngeal teeth 5–5 (occasionally 4 on one side), slender, strongly hooked, and serrated; arch slender (see Gilbert and Bailey 1972). Eye moderate, into head length 3.0–3.3. Gill rakers short, irregular, knoblike, up to 8. Dorsal fin origin over or slightly behind origin of pelvic fins; dorsal fin rays usually 9; anal fin rays 8 (7); pectoral fin rays about 15; pelvic fin rays 8. Lateral line scales 35–41; lateral line usually complete. Digestive tract short with a single, S-shaped loop, 0.5 TL. Chromosomes 2n = 48 (Campos and Hubbs 1973).

Silvery with yellow to green cast dorsally; silvery laterally and ventrally. Dorsal and lateral scales edged in pigment, appearing diamond shaped. Mid-dorsal stripe obscure or absent; a narrow midlateral stripe commencing at margin of upper lip (not encircling snout) and extending posteriorly to base of caudal fin. Base of central caudal rays pigmented. Fins generally unpigmented, except for dorsal fin in adults (especially well marked in breeding male), in which the interradial membranes are dusky to dark, and only the membrane between rays 5 and 6 is clear and generally devoid of pigment. No bright breeding colors. Peritoneum silvery with scattered dark speckles.

Breeding males with compact patch of tubercles above upper lip and a compact cluster on lower jaw (Gilbert and Bailey 1972), minute tubercles covering rest of head, and small tubercles on anterior 5–7 branched pectoral rays.

Sexual dimorphism: Adult male usually with pectoral fin length 6.4–7.5 into TL; adult female, 8.3–9.7 into TL.

The pugnose minnow is superficially similar to the pugnose shiner (*Notropis anogenus*), and can easily be confused with it. Bailey (1959) provided an excellent comparison based on 10 characters.

SYSTEMATIC NOTES

The pugnose minnow, long known as *Opsopoeodus emiliae* (Hay), has recently been interpreted as a specialized derivative of *Notropis*, and, on the evidence adduced, Gilbert and Bailey (1972) downgraded *Opsopoeodus* to subgeneric status in *Notropis*. According to these authors, the pugnose minnow agrees closely with *Notropis* in the aggregate of its characters. Two of the most distinctive features of *emiliae*, the pharyngeal tooth count (5–5) and the conspicuous marking of the dorsal fin in breeding males, lose force as "generic" characteristics in that they vary geographically: in peninsular Florida, the teeth number 5–4, and the "flag fin" is undeveloped. Two subspecies are recognized: *N. emiliae emiliae* (Hay), which occurs in the Upper and Lower Mississippi–Gulf Coast drainage, and along the Atlantic coast; and *N.e. peninsularis*, which occurs in the Florida peninsula, and intergrades in northern Florida and southern Georgia.

DISTRIBUTION, STATUS, AND HABITAT

In Wisconsin, the pugnose minnow occurs in the low- or base-gradient streams of the Mississippi River drainage basin, where it reaches the northernmost limits of its distribution. It appears to be well

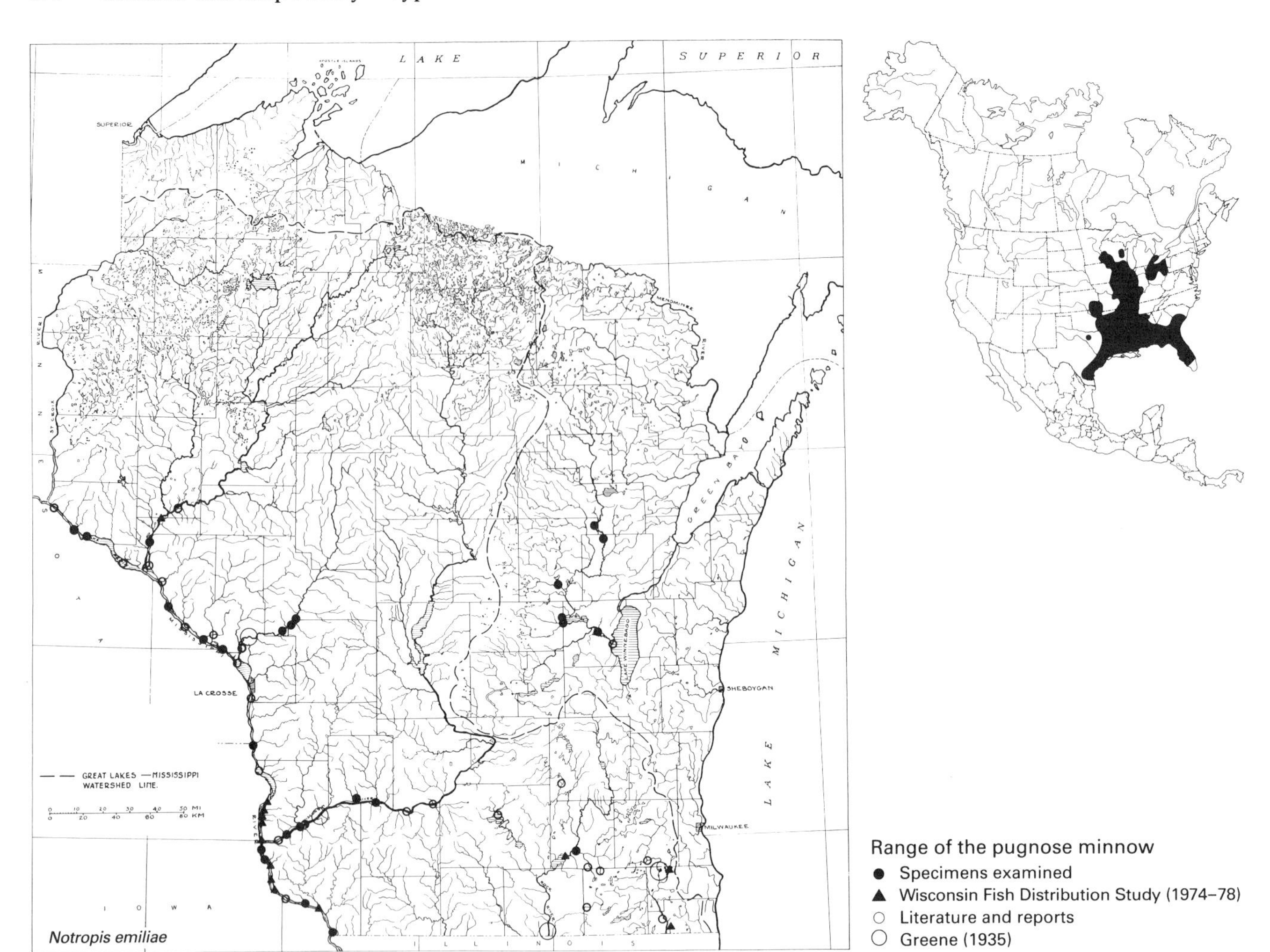

Range of the pugnose minnow
● Specimens examined
▲ Wisconsin Fish Distribution Study (1974–78)
○ Literature and reports
◯ Greene (1935)

distributed in the Rock River watershed. Cahn (1927) recorded two reports from the Oconomowoc and Ashippun rivers, but no locales were specified.

In the Lake Michigan drainage, the pugnose minnow is known only in the Fox and Wolf river watershed, where it appears to have become recently established, probably through the Fox-Wisconsin canal at Portage. The only other record from the Lake Michigan drainage is from Wolf Lake, Indiana (Meek and Hildebrand 1910), where the pugnose probably has been extirpated (Becker 1976). It is not known from the Lake Superior drainage.

At the northern part of its general range the pugnose minnow appears to be declining in numbers. In Ohio, since 1930 it has drastically decreased numerically or disappeared from most localities where it was formerly taken; at present it appears to be threatened with extirpation (Trautman 1957). In Missouri, it may be disappearing (Pflieger 1975).

In Minnesota, recent pugnose minnow collections have been made from the Mississippi River south of Red Wing, and from the Zumbro and Root rivers. Eddy and Underhill (1974) suspected that this minnow is more common in southeastern Minnesota than was previously thought.

In Wisconsin, the pugnose minnow is uncommon to rare at most collection sites, although it may be more common than it is believed to be. The records suggest that adults frequent deeper waters than are normally reached by minnow seines. Most of our collections consist of young fish, which apparently frequent the shallows. The pugnose minnow has been given watch status (Wis. Dep. Nat. Res. Endangered Species Com. 1975, Les 1979).

The pugnose minnow was encountered at variable depths over substrates of mud (41% frequency), sand (41%), rubble (7%), silt (4%), clay (4%), and gravel (4%). It occurred in quiet, weedy waters of lakes, reservoirs, and sloughs, and in rivers of low gradient, 12.1 m or more wide.

BIOLOGY

Spawning in southern Wisconsin extends at least from mid-June to mid-July. Little is known about the spawning habits and behavior of the pugnose minnow.

Pugnose minnows with greatly distended abdomens were taken from the Wisconsin River (Grant County) on 21 June 1962. Three gravid females, 50, 48, and 48 mm, held 312, 320, and 340 eggs respectively; the eggs were 0.9–1.1 mm diam. On 27 June, a few kilometers upstream in the Wisconsin River four females were captured with 200–240 eggs each, and on 10 July in the Mississippi River (Glass Lake near Bagley) an individual with 200 eggs was taken. These egg counts are unusually low for a minnow (V. Starostka, pers. comm.).

In Illinois, gravid female pugnose minnows and tuberculate males were reported between 10 and 20 June (Forbes and Richardson 1920). In Florida, breeding males were collected from March to September, and gravid females were collected from January to September, suggesting that this species has a protracted breeding season (Gilbert and Bailey 1972).

Growth of young-of-year pugnose minnows is rapid, but variable. The appearance of small individuals late in the season suggests an extended spawning season (possibly into early August) in some Wisconsin waters. The following growth has been recorded in Wisconsin:

Date	No. of Fish	TL Range (mm)	Location
13 July	72	24–30	Wisconsin R. (Grant Co.)
26 July	2	21–27	Mississippi R., Pool 6
23 Aug.	1	33	Black R. (Jackson Co.)
7 Sept.	4	34–38	L. Poygan (Waushara Co.)
14 Sept.	1	24	Lemonweir R. (Monroe Co.)
15 Sept.	21	28–40	L. Butte des Morts (Winnebago Co.)
24 Sept.	1	33	Chippewa R. (Pepin Co.)

On 24 September 1966, pugnose minnows collected from the Mississippi River (Grant County) showed the following growth: 12 young-of-year—37.1 (33–40) mm TL; 40 age-I fish—42.2 (38–47) mm TL; the estimated length at the first annulus was 34.8 mm. Eight age-II adults, collected at the end of June and the beginning of July 1962 from the lower Wisconsin River and a nearby locale on the Mississippi River, were 52.3 (49–54) mm TL; the estimated lengths at annuli were: 1—39.7 mm; and 2—53.3 mm.

In Ohio, young-of-year in October were 25–43 mm TL; age-I fish were 33–51 mm; and adults were 38–58 mm (Trautman 1957). The largest pugnose minnow reported was 64 mm (2.5 in).

The condition factor (K_{TL}) of adult pugnose minnows from southern Wisconsin in late June and early July was 0.80 (0.69–0.90) for six males, and 0.90 (0.82–0.97) for eight females.

Little is known about the diet of the pugnose minnow. Pugnose minnows from the Wisconsin and Mississippi rivers had ingested filamentous algae, unidentifiable debris, plant fibers, eggs (of parasites?), crustacean parts, and sand (V. Starostka, pers. comm.). In pugnose minnows from southeastern Wisconsin, Cahn (1927) reported Entomostraca and small crustacea (*Hyalella*). Gilbert and Bailey (1972) cited studies by W. McLane, who found the following foods in stomachs from pugnose minnows in Florida (in descending order of frequency): chironomid larvae, filamentous algae, unidentifiable animal matter, copepods, cladocerans, and hydrachnids, with minute amounts of fish eggs, sand, and, possibly, larval fish.

The pugnose minnow's almost vertical mouth suggests that this species feeds on items from midwater or near the surface. The serrations on its pharyngeal teeth are apparently adapted to its feeding habits, and particularly to its consumption of microcrustaceans (Gilbert and Bailey 1972).

In the lower Wisconsin River (Grant County), 72 pugnose minnows were associated with the following species: paddlefish (1), gizzard shad (156), quillback (8), river and/or highfin carpsucker (5), bigmouth buffalo (2), white sucker (6), golden shiner (205), bullhead minnow (35), bluntnose minnow (3), emerald shiner (10), spotfin shiner (493), spottail shiner (7), river shiner (5), Mississippi silvery minnow (3), black bullhead (48), northern pike (3), white bass (25), yellow perch (4), western sand darter (3), logperch (2), johnny darter (4) smallmouth bass (11), largemouth bass (8), pumpkinseed (1), bluegill (8), black crappie (42), white crappie (2), brook silverside (11), and freshwater drum (4).

IMPORTANCE AND MANAGEMENT

The pugnose minnow is too rare and too restricted in its distribution to be of any importance as a forage or bait fish. It undoubtedly is taken by predatory fish and birds, although, considering its limited numbers, consumption is probably at low levels.

In the state of Mississippi, where the pugnose minnow is locally common, it is used as a bait minnow (Cook 1959).

Ozark Minnow

Notropis nubilus (Forbes). *Notropis*—back, keel; *nubilus*—Latin, meaning dusky, in reference to the body color.

Other common name: Forbes minnow.

Adult male (tuberculate) 65 mm, Apple R. (Lafayette Co.), 19 May 1976

Adult female 71 mm, Apple R. (Lafayette Co.), 19 May 1976

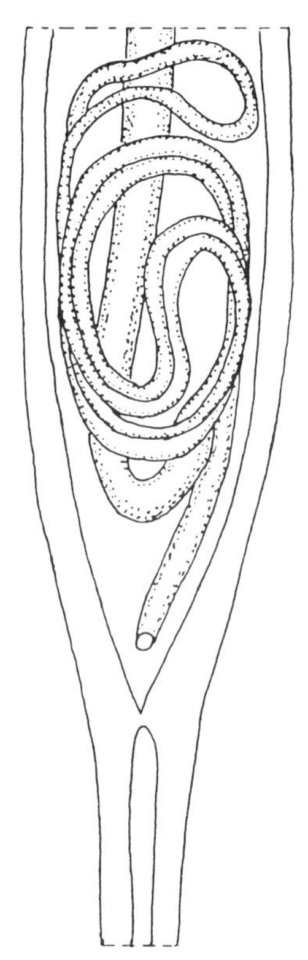

Ventral view of the alimentary tract of the Ozark minnow, with ventral body wall and viscera removed

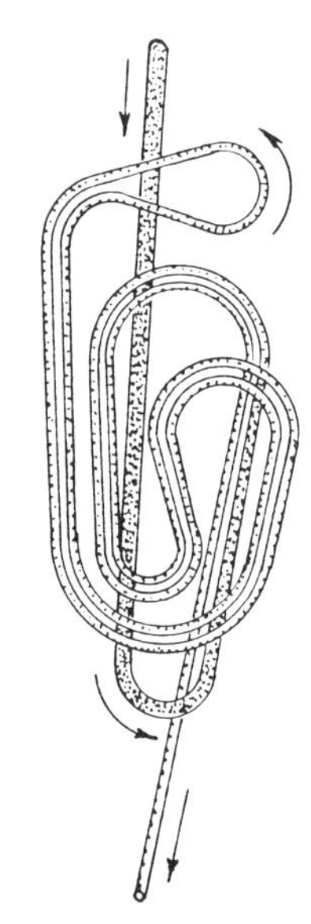

Alimentary tract of Ozark minnow, diagrammatic

DESCRIPTION

Body slim, almost round, weakly compressed laterally. Average length 56–75 mm (2.2–3.0 in). TL = 1.22 SL. Depth into TL 4.9–5.8. Head length into TL 5.0–5.5. Snout blunt, extending beyond mouth. Maxillary reaching below nostril. Mouth subterminal, slightly oblique, with corner of upper lip slightly swollen; barbels absent. Pharyngeal teeth 4–4 (upper 3 teeth often with elongate cutting edges); teeth short, slender, and hooked. Eye large, into head length 3.7 (3.4–3.9). Gill rakers short and fleshy, 8. Dorsal fin originating over origin of pelvic fin; dorsal, anal, and pelvic fin rays 8; pectoral fin rays 13–15. Lateral line scales 36–38; lateral line complete and nearly straight. Digestive tract elongate, with regular coils, 1.9–2.4 TL.

Back and upper sides dark olive yellow. Midline of back with a prominent dusky stripe overlaid with a series of golden spots in live fish. Sides silvery, with a prominent dusky stripe (almost width of eye) extending anteriorly onto head and around tip of snout above upper lip. Belly silvery white. Caudal fin generally with a small, black spot at base. Fins transparent. Peritoneum black.

Breeding male with lower half of body and fins tinged with yellowish orange; underside of head orange. Breeding tubercles scattered over top of head, and over sides of head behind and below eyes; body scales (except on belly) edged with 6–9 tubercles,

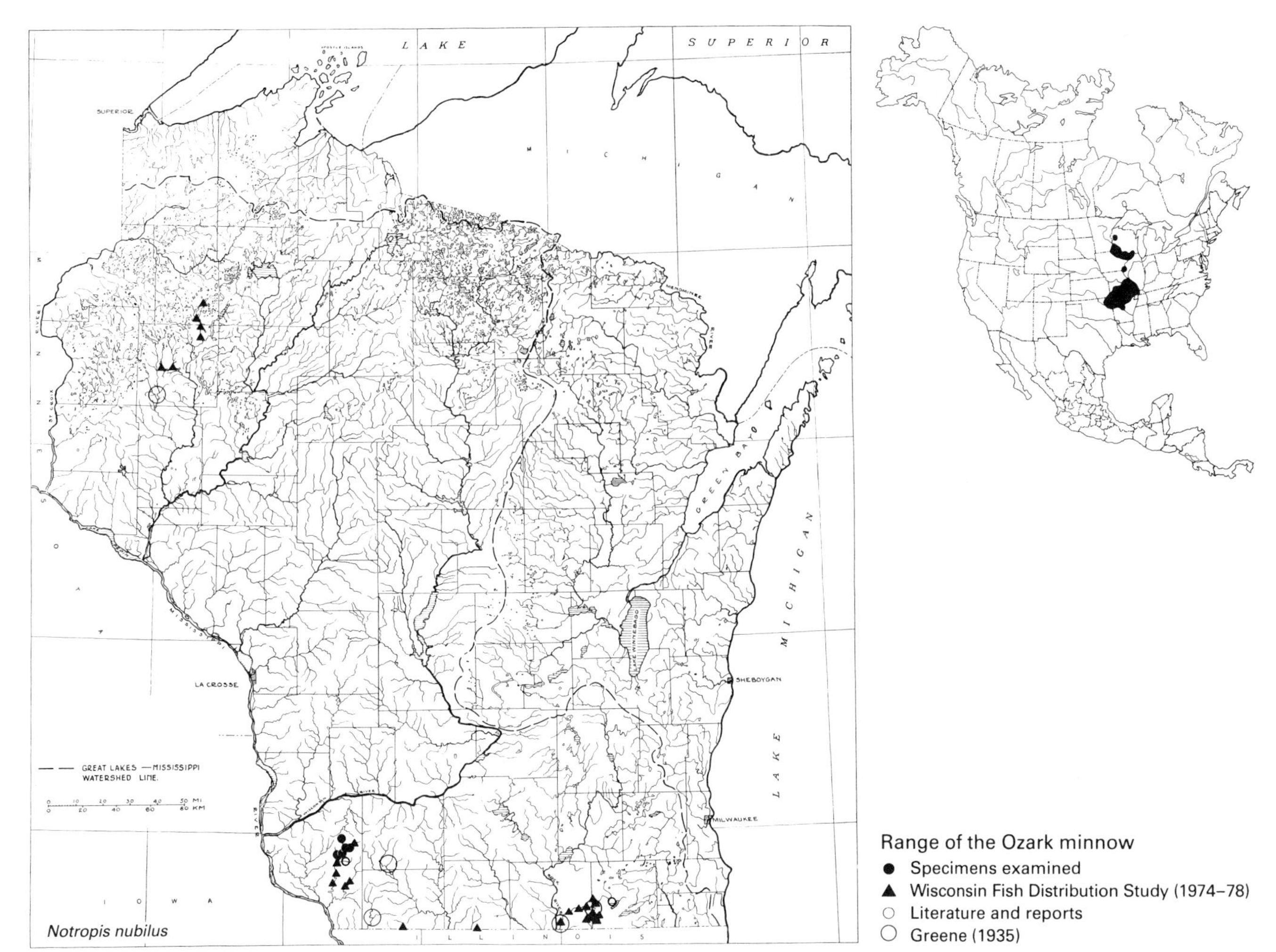

and a vertical row of 3–4 tubercles in center of each scale; anterior half of pectoral rays with large tubercles. Breeding females yellowish; lightly to moderately tuberculate on head.

Hybrids: Ozark minnow × hornyhead chub (Schwartz 1972), Ozark minnow × bleeding shiner, and Ozark minnow × duskystripe shiner (Pflieger 1975).

Sexual dimorphism: In males the pectoral fin is almost as broad as it is long; in females it is more elongate. In males the distance between the end of the pectoral fin and the origin of the pelvic fin is less than half the pectoral fin length; in females this distance is more than half the pectoral fin length.

SYSTEMATIC NOTES

The Ozark minnow was formerly in the genus *Dionda*, primarily because of its elongate intestine and black peritoneum, although some *Notropis* species show these characters. Swift (1970) allied *Dionda nubila* (Forbes) with *Notropis chrosomus* (Jordan) and *N. leuciodus* (Cope) under the subgenus *Hydrophlox* of *Notropis*, by transferring the species *nubila* from *Dionda* to *Notropis*. Members of the subgenus *Hydrophlox* share uniserial tubercles on the upper surface of most pectoral fin rays in breeding males, fine tubercles over most of the body and head in both sexes, and bright red, orange, or yellow colors in both sexes in the breeding season. The hybridization between *nubilus* and *Notropis* spp. indicates the close relationship of these groups.

DISTRIBUTION, STATUS, AND HABITAT

In Wisconsin the Ozark minnow occurs only in the Mississippi River drainage basin. It is found in isolated areas of the southern tier of counties (Grant, Iowa, Lafayette, Green, Rock and Walworth), and in a widely removed population in the upper Red Cedar system (Dunn and Washburn counties), where it is at the northernmost limit of its range.

According to Pflieger (1971), the Ozark minnow has probably long occupied the Ozark uplands. The disjunct populations in Wisconsin's driftless area may have been established by a postglacial dispersal from an Ozark refugium, although it is equally plausible that the species was present in or near the driftless area throughout the Wisconsin glacial period. The Ozark minnow was undoubtedly more widely distributed following the glacial retreat than it is today. G. R. Smith (1963) reported it in a late-Illinoian fauna in southwestern Kansas, thus providing evidence of a more western distribution during glaciation. The general distribution pattern of the Ozark minnow is very similar to that of the largescale stoneroller, although the ecological requirements of the latter are less fixed.

Wisconsin collections I have examined: UWSP 187 (1) and 2632 (7) Crow Branch T5N R1W Sec 19 (Grant County) 1962; UWSP 1472 (4) Platte River T5N R2W Sec 24 (Grant County) 1966; UWSP 2631 (7) Branch to Platte River T5N R2W Sec 33 (Grant County) 1962; UWSP 2633 (19) Platte River T5N R2W Sec 26 (Grant County) 1962; UWSP 5440 (6) Apple River T1N R3E Sec 33 (Lafayette County) 1976.

From 1974 to 1978, the Wisconsin Fish Distribution Study collected the Ozark minnow from a total of 25 locales from the Turtle River system (Rock and Walworth counties); East Branch Richland Creek (Green County); Apple River (Lafayette County); Little Platte River, and Platte River system (Grant County); Vermillion, Brill, and Red Cedar river systems (Barron County); and Long Lake (Washburn County).

Greene (1935) examined collections of Ozark minnows from the Hay River at Prairie Farms (Barron County); Galena River 3 km south of Benton (Lafayette County); Mineral Brook Branch of the West Pecatonica River at West Mineral Point (Iowa County); South Branch of Turtle Creek at Allen Grove (Walworth County); and Turtle Creek at Beloit and "near Beloit" (Rock County). Cahn (1927) reported it from Scuppernong Creek, but since the specific locale and county were not recorded, I have been unable to map this report.

The Ozark minnow is absent from a number of Wisconsin locales from which it had been previously reported. It appears to be intolerant of excessive turbidity and siltation. Unfortunately, most of the streams in which this species is still found are in regions of heavy agricultural land use, and it appears that the needs of the Ozark minnow are incompatible with man's demands on the same waters. This species is considered threatened in Wisconsin (Les 1979).

The Ozark minnow occurs in clear, small- to medium-sized streams of low gradient, with gravel to rubble bottoms. In the Platte River it was taken from clear water at depths of 0.3–0.5 m, over a substrate of clean gravel; in the nearby Crow Branch it was taken from a pool 3.0–4.5 m wide and up to 0.6 m deep, over a gravel bottom covered with fine silt. Both areas were devoid of submergent and emergent vegetation, and both had a gentle current. Only a single lake record is known from Wisconsin.

In its Ozark range, the Ozark minnow inhabits streams with a predominance of gravelly or rocky bottoms, and a permanent, strong flow. It is most often found in protected backwaters near riffles, or in pools immediately below riffles where the current slackens (Pflieger 1975, Miller and Robison 1973).

BIOLOGY

The Ozark minnow has a long spawning period. In southern Wisconsin, spawning begins in May and continues through July, and possibly into August. In Missouri, spawning occurs from late April to early July, but peaks in May and June; it takes place over nests of the hornyhead chub (Pflieger 1975).

In the Apple River (Lafayette County), a prespawning, heavily tuberculated male had testes 1% of total body weight on 19 May. On the same date, a female, 69 mm TL and 3.43 g, had ovaries 8% of body weight, and a total egg count of 1,021. The eggs were in two size classes: 0.6–0.8 mm diam and yellow, and 0.3–0.4 mm diam and whitish; the numerical ratio was 2:1, respectively. A larger female, 71 mm TL and 4.00 g, had ovaries 12.8% of body weight, and 557 yellow mature eggs 1.0–1.2 mm diam. A smaller egg size class, 0.4–0.8 mm diam, appeared whitish, and made up about one-fourth of the egg complement of the ovary.

On 20 July, 282 mature eggs were counted in the ovaries (13.3% of body weight) of a female 64 mm TL and 2.10 g from Crow Branch of the Platte River (Grant County). On 26 July, 443 mature eggs were in the ovaries (18% of body weight) of a female 63 mm TL and 2.55 g taken from the Platte River (Grant County).

The calculated lengths at the annuli for combined collections from the Platte River and tributaries (Grant County), taken 20–26 July 1962, were:

Age Class	No. of Fish	TL (mm)		Calculated TL at Annulus (mm)		
		Avg	Range	1	2	3
I	8	48.2	41–52	33.4		
II	26	62.5	56–75	34.9	58.6	
III	1	80		38.9	60.6	75.7
Avg (weighted)				34.7	58.7	75.7

The oldest known Ozark minnow from Wisconsin is a 3-year-old female. Females of this species attain a larger size than males. Both sexes reach maturity and spawn at age II.

A large female Ozark minnow (UWSP 4589) was taken from Goose Creek (Washington County) Arkansas on 9 September 1973. She was 93 mm (3.7 in) TL, and 4 years old.

The digestive tracts of Ozark minnows from southwestern Wisconsin contained microscopic green algae, blue-green algae, and diatoms, and large quantities of unidentifiable vegetative material and sand. Diatoms of a number of species were particularly abundant, probably indicating the permanency of the frustules. Bottom detritus, diatoms, and other periphytes were undoubtedly derived from the gravel and rubble substrate. Cahn (1927) reported that the digestive tract contents of Ozark minnows from Waukesha County consisted almost entirely of algae (*Spirogyra, Zygnema, Closterium*, with occasional Entomostraca and small insect larvae.

In the laboratory, Ozark minnows were fed dry meal, *Daphnia*, and chironomid larvae, but were never observed to eat actively. They became progressively thinner, and lost their color completely (Bunting and Irwin 1965). One or two fish died each day during the last week of the holding period.

The Ozark minnow is a schooling fish which lives near the bottom in rather shallow water. D. Becker (pers. comm.) provided ecological data for a collection site. In the Apple River (Lafayette County), the water was moderately turbid, and the bottom was not visible beyond 0.6 m (2 ft). The substrate consisted of gravel (40%), sand (30%), and muck (30%). The stream was 4.6–6.1 m (15–20 ft) wide, and 0.3–0.6 m (1–2 ft) deep. Emergent vegetation was absent, and submergent vegetation and algae were scarce. The current was moderate, and water temperature was 21.1°C (70°F) in mid-May. The surrounding area was entirely upland pasture.

Cahn (1927) noted that the water of Scuppernong Creek was dark grayish brown because of a large amount of suspended fine silt and muck. The bottom was soft; the water was 46 cm (18 in) deep, and had little current. The conditions described by Cahn are marginal for the Ozark minnow and perhaps explain its absence from the Scuppernong system today.

Twenty Ozark minnows from the Platte River were associated with the following species: white sucker (47), central stoneroller (17), longnose dace (8), hornyhead chub (140), creek chub (1), bluntnose minnow (61), suckermouth minnow (3), common shiner (88), rosyface shiner (25), sand shiner (1), stonecat (3), johnny darter (7), fantail darter (21), smallmouth bass (11), green sunfish (2), and bluegill (6).

IMPORTANCE AND MANAGEMENT

Considering the rarity of the Ozark minnow, it must be of small consequence as forage for game species. It is probably not used much as bait by Wisconsin anglers because of its limited distribution in the state.

Brassy Minnow

Hybognathus hankinsoni Hubbs. *Hybognathus*—protruding jaw, probably in reference to upper jaw or snout; *hankinsoni*—after ichthyologist T. L. Hankinson of Michigan.

Other common names: grass minnow, Hankinson's minnow.

Adult 72 mm, tributary to Little Sandy Cr. (Marathon Co.), 29 May 1961

DESCRIPTION

Body elongate, slightly compressed laterally. Average length 58–71 mm (2.3–2.8 in). TL = 1.25 SL. Depth into TL 4.0–6.2. Head length into TL 4.4–5.2. Snout long, blunt, and rounded, slightly overhanging upper jaw. Maxillary short, scarcely reaching to below nostrils; barbels absent. Pharyngeal teeth 4–4 with oblique grinding surfaces, not hooked. Eye into head length 4.1–4.5. Gill rakers short, slender, and pointed,

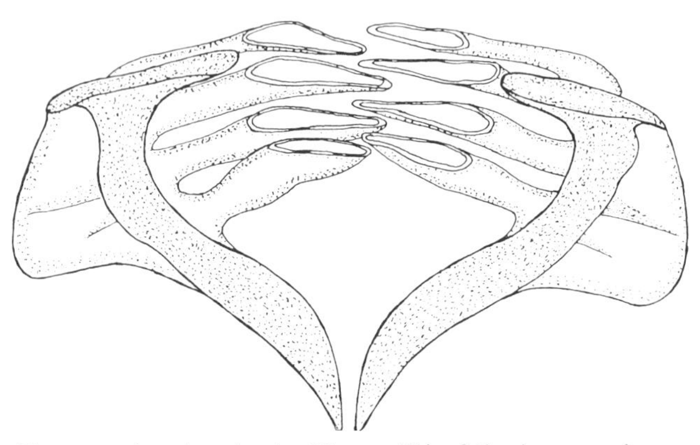

Pharyngeal arches (male, 80 mm TL) of the brassy minnow. Note the long, flat cutting edges of the teeth and the absence of hooks.

8. Dorsal fin slightly in advance of pelvic fin origin; dorsal fin rounded, rays 8; anal fin rays usually 8, sometimes 7; pectoral fin rays 13 (14–15); pelvic fin rays 8. Scales with about 20 radii of varying lengths. Lateral line scales 35–38; lateral line complete. Digestive track "coiled like a watch spring," with elongated stomach almost the length of peritoneal cavity; ventral to the stomach are a series of alternating loops and coils, first counterclockwise (ventral view), then clockwise—the last loop clockwise into the anus; tract about 3.8–4.1 TL.

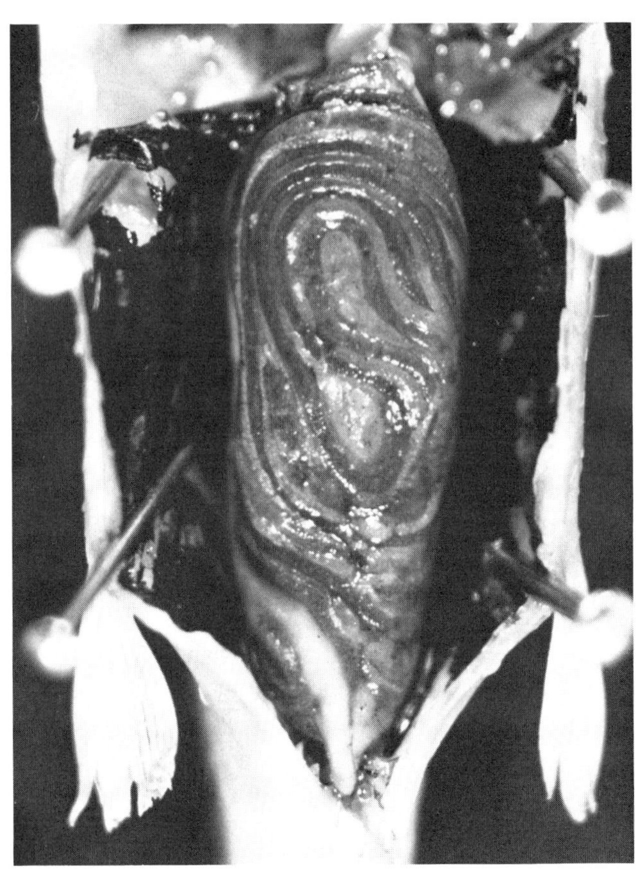

Ventral view of multi-coiled intestine of the brassy minnow (Tomorrow R., Portage Co., specimen). Note black peritoneum (photo by D. Damitz).

Dark silvery cast dorsally and laterally, grading to creamy white below. Peritoneum black.

Breeding male usually changes in color from the silvery cast to a brassy or golden hue. Fins also with a brassy tinge. Breeding tubercles appear in the middle rays of the pectoral fins of some males.

Sexual dimorphism: In males the distance from the end of the pectoral fin to pelvic fin origin is less than half the pectoral fin length; in females, more than half the pectoral fin length. In males the width of the pectoral fin is about three-fourths its length; in females, about half its length.

Hybrids: Brassy minnow × blacknose shiner (Hubbs 1951a).

SYSTEMATIC NOTES

Bailey (1954) reviewed the range, classification, and description of the brassy minnow. The lectotype

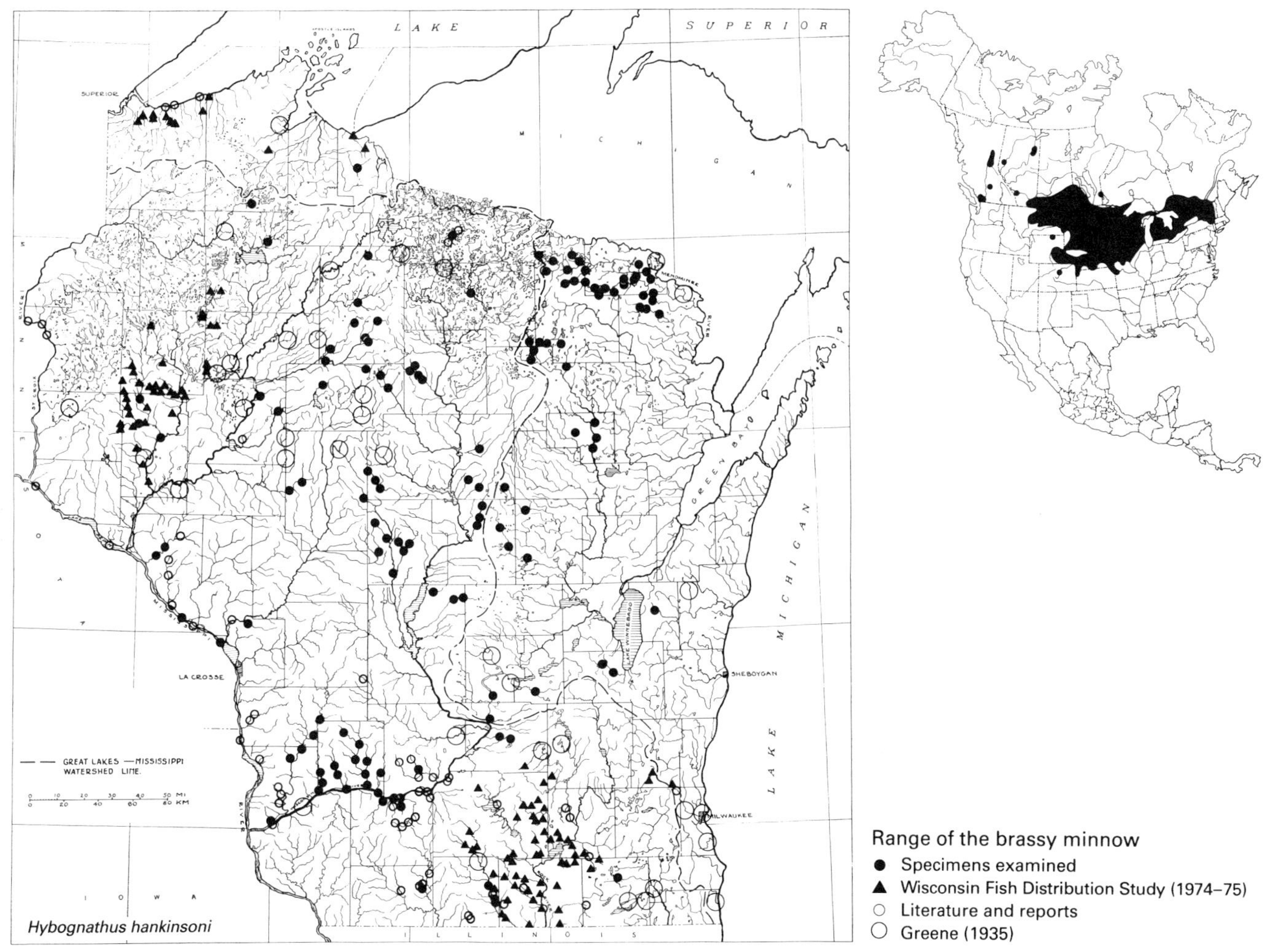

(UMMZ 84266) was collected in the Dead River, T48N R26W Sec 8, in the Lake Superior watershed (Marquette County), Michigan, on 20 July 1927 by C. A. Montague.

DISTRIBUTION, STATUS, AND HABITAT

In Wisconsin, the brassy minnow occurs in the Mississippi River, Lake Michigan, and Lake Superior drainage basins, with principal distribution in the Mississippi watershed. Since the 1920s, this species has moved into streams within the unglaciated area, and expanded its distribution in both the Lake Michigan and Lake Superior drainages. It appears to have been eliminated from waters in the extreme southeastern corner of the state.

The brassy minnow is common in slow-moving streams, except in northwestern Wisconsin, where it is uncommon. It is rare in large rivers and lakes. The brassy minnow appears secure in its Wisconsin range.

In Wisconsin the brassy minnow occurs in small- to medium-sized streams of moderate to slow current; in large rivers it is supplanted by the Mississippi silvery minnow (*Hybognathus nuchalis*). It appeared most frequently in clear to slightly turbid waters at depths of 0.1–1.5 m over substrates of sand (26% frequency), gravel (23%), silt (15%), mud (10%), rubble (8%), hardpan (7%), clay (5%), detritus (4%), boulders (1%), and bedrock (1%). It occurred in streams of the following widths: 1.0–3.0 m (19%), 3.1–6.0 m (28%), 6.1–12.0 m (23%), 12.1–24.0 m (22%), 24.1–50.0 m (7%), and more than 50 m (1%). Copes (1975) noted that in Wyoming the brassy minnow prefers a habitat with little or no current (generally less than 0.6 m/sec), a mud or silt bottom, and some vegetation. It is common in overflow ponds adjacent to moderate-sized streams or small rivers (Harlan and Speaker 1956).

BIOLOGY

Spawning in Wisconsin occurs in May and June. Copes (1975) provided the following spawning data, based largely on populations observed in Sand Creek, Wyoming. The length of the spawning seasons appears to be 7–10 days at water temperatures of

16–27°C (60.8–80.6°F). Spawning occurs from 1100 to 1700 hr, peaking at about 1400 hr, in and over vegetation.

Sexually mature brassy minnow males leave schools during the spawning season and scatter among aquatic vegetation and in flooded marshes. The males exhibit no territorial behavior. When schools of 100–200 brassy minnows swim in the flooded lateral depressions, from 1 to about 15 males approach a female near the periphery of the school and swim either above, below, or beside her. The female swims quickly in either a spiral or a straight path, pursued by the males, toward a bed of vegetation, where spawning occurs. About half of the time the pursued female spirals upward and jumps several centimeters out of the water; males then discontinue their pursuit. Copes (1975:61) described spawning behavior as follows:

> Spawning appeared to take place in the vegetation with one or more males vibrating rapidly from one to three seconds while pressing against the female. The vibrating stirred up bottom sediments, making the water turbid and observation of the details of the spawning act impossible. By 2 PM on May 27 and 28, 1969, the water of the entire spawning area became very turbid from feeding and spawning activities of fish in a lateral pond of Sand Creek, and fish could be seen flashing everywhere. It was estimated there were 4 to 6 thousand fish in a single lateral depression. Eggs were collected from the vegetation and mud bottom. The eggs were slightly adhesive to the vegetation.

When the water temperature dropped suddenly from 16.7 to 10.0°C (62.1 to 50°F), spawning ceased; it resumed 5 days later when the water temperature returned to 16.7°C.

Dobie et al. (1956) reported spawning by the brassy minnow early in the spring, when the water temperatures reached 10–12.8°C (50–55°F). In Iowa, spawning occurs in June (Starrett 1951).

A prespawning female, 55 mm TL, and 2.15 g, collected 29 May from Little Sandy Creek (Marathon County), had ovaries 14% of body weight which contained 1,151 yellow mature eggs 0.5–0.7 mm diam; a second generation of smaller, white eggs was 0.1–0.3 mm diam. In a collection from Marinette County on 25 June, the females looked gravid, but all were soft-bellied and had recently spawned out. A probable late spawning for nothern Wisconsin was suggested by a 79-mm female, collected 24 June from Jones Creek (Forest County), that carried a total of 2,500 eggs of two sizes: yellow eggs 0.7–0.8 mm diam, and white eggs 0.2–0.3 mm diam.

Fry, 5–9 mm TL, were collected on 19 July from the lower end of Sand Creek (Wyoming) (Copes 1975). Scales were evident at 20–26 mm TL, and all fish above 30 mm were scaled.

Aging of the brassy minnow is accomplished through analysis of scales. Copes (1975) noted that most growth ceases by early September, and does not resume until the following May.

The average growth and weight of a September sample of brassy minnows in Sand Creek, Wyoming, were: 0—32.4 (22–44) mm (0.25 g); I—57.1 (44–68) mm (1.9 g); II—70.8 (68–80) mm (3.6 g); and III—83.0 (82–84) mm (4.7 g). In the Tomorrow and Plover rivers in Wisconsin the growth and weight of October samples was: 0—37.1 (28–49) mm (0.26 g); I—56.4 (49–69) mm (2.0 g); II—71.2 (62–78) mm (3.5 g); and III—82.5 (76–85) mm (4.9 g). Few fish in Wyoming and in Wisconsin had reached age III (Copes 1975). Females were not significantly larger than males. The condition factor (K_{TL}) averaged 0.93 for the four age-classes. Copes computed a population turnover about every 4 years.

Sexual maturity is reached at age II (Dobie et al. 1956), although a few Wisconsin and Wyoming age-I females were sexually mature (Copes 1975).

A large female (UWSP 518), 95 mm TL, was collected from Pedro Creek (Oneida County) in July 1966.

The digestive tracts of brassy minnows in Wyoming (Copes 1975) contained the following items: algae (94% of volume), organic debris (remains of higher plants, 5%), and animal matter (less than 0.5%). Diatoms and desmids made up at least 50% of the algae in the stomachs. The animal matter consisted of diptera larvae, copepods, and cladocerans. No change in the diet was evident with increased age.

Dobie et al. (1956) found the following items in brassy minnow stomachs: zooplankton (25.9% of volume), phytoplankton (31.6%), aquatic insects (21.3%), plants (3.4%), surface drift (16.1%), and silt (1.7%). The digestive tracts of 20 brassy minnows from the Tomorrow River (Portage County) contained diatoms and desmids (95% frequency), filamentous algae (80%), higher plant material (40%), and animal remains (10%) (D. Damitz, pers. comm.).

In aquarium studies, Copes (1975) fed brassy minnows dry meal (trout food), midgefly and mosquito larvae, small amphipods, early instars of mayflies, copepods, cladocerans, damselflies, nematodes, and nematomorphs. The fish appeared to be opportunists, feeding on any live food item that could be swallowed.

Copes also recorded the feeding behavior among brassy minnows in Wyoming. In April and early May no feeding was noted until early afternoon, and then only for a 1–2 hr period. Feeding activity in the summer months usually occurred after the water temperature increased 2–4°C (3.6–7.2°F) from the daily minimum, and the most intensive feeding occurred from 1300 to 1500 hr. Schools of brassy minnows moved slowly upstream, feeding on drift and on organisms in the aquatic vegetation. In the early spring and late fall, schools were seen feeding on detritus and ooze. The food value of ooze was not determined, but decomposing organic material, protozoans, and bacteria in the ooze are believed to be an important source of energy.

In Wyoming brassy minnows fed extensively during high water in flooded areas. Mosquito larvae were abundant in isolated lateral depressions in June and early July. A school of minnows appeared to follow the mosquito larvae into water less than 25 mm deep; after 2 days of intensive feeding no mosquito larvae remained. On two occasions, schools were observed feeding on cow manure. In late September and October the brassy minnow engaged in communal feeding, in which individual fish stirred up bottom sediments that were fed upon by several members of the school. At times, communal feeding activity was so intense that it made the water turbid. Copes (1975) noted only two instances in which surface drift was eaten. Feeding continues during the spawning season in this species.

In field studies (Copes 1975), the brassy minnow survived a maximum water temperature of 28.9°C (84°F), prolonged periods of minimum temperatures near 0°C (32°F), and daily variations in water temperature of as much as 17.8°C (32°F). In Ontario, this species tolerates a wide temperature range, and appears to be equally distributed from the coldwater habitat of the brook trout (3% frequency) and mottled sculpin (10%) to the warmer water habitats frequented by the rock bass (5%) and smallmouth bass (6%) (Hallam 1959).

Brassy minnows remained fairly quiet and stayed close together in a test container (Gould and Irwin 1962). They survived an oxygen level of 1.5 ppm. Test solutions had a pH range of 8.7–7.4.

The brassy minnow is a schooling species. In Wyoming, the schools have no apparent leader, move slowly at a uniform speed, and generally remain in areas of little or no current with a mud bottom. In August and September, schools of immature brassy minnows were observed in lateral depressions and shallow vegetated areas, but never appeared in large pools or deep runs (Copes 1975). The schools of immature brassy minnows were mainly monospecific, except for occasional small fathead minnows, creek chubs, or white suckers. Adult schools were found in pools with many creek chubs and white suckers. Large schools (200–500 brassy minnows) frequented shallow flooded areas when these became 2–4°C (3.6–7.2°F) warmer than the stream itself. They left the flooded areas at dusk, or when water temperatures dropped below that of the stream. They then ceased feeding, broke up into smaller schools, and moved into quiet areas, where they became inactive.

During the summer, schools of small brassy minnows spent the night in muskrat channels and other openings in the aquatic vegetation of runs. In early spring and in the late fall, schools spent the night in pods (masses of fish in physical contact with each other), or scattered over the bottom. Copes (1975) observed fish stacked up six deep. The brassy minnows wintered in pools and deep runs that contained shelter. In November, pods were found in masses of willow roots and under shelter; other brassy minnows were found buried in debris on the bottom. Four fathead minnows were collected with brassy minnows in one such pod. The brassy minnow is generally inactive from November through March.

Copes notes no intra- or interspecific aggressive behavior among brassy minnows. When alarmed, large schools broke up into smaller schools, which swam erratically up and down the stream. Individual fish buried themselves in the silt bottom, others moved into beds of vegetation, while some formed fright schools (each fish tried to reach the middle of the group, or tried to hide behind others in the school).

Fish species associated with 57 brassy minnows taken in Rocky Creek (Wood County) were: white sucker (2), blacknose dace (11), creek chub (15), northern redbelly dace (31), bluntnose minnow (10), fathead minnow (35), common shiner (20), central mudminnow (1), johnny darter (1), and brook stickleback (29). In the Kickapoo River (Crawford County), 74 brassy minnows were captured with longnose gar (1), shorthead redhorse (1), silver redhorse (17), northern hog sucker (5), white sucker (29), central stoneroller (69), longnose dace (1), creek chub (23), bluntnose minnow (605), fathead minnow (22), spotfin shiner (134), bigmouth shiner (61), slenderhead darter (1), johnny darter (5), green sunfish (4), and white crappie (1).

IMPORTANCE AND MANAGEMENT

The brassy minnow is most abundant in habitats having only a few or no predacious fish. It is very vulnerable to fish predation.

The brassy minnow has been found in the stomachs of creek chubs, walleyes, black crappies, brook and brown trout, northern pike, and rock bass. Snowy egrets, great blue herons, and belted kingfishers have been seen feeding on brassy minnow schools (Copes 1975). One minnow was taken from the stomach of a leopard frog.

In Wisconsin, the brassy minnow is a valuable forage and bait minnow. It is extensively sold as walleye, crappie, and perch bait. In a study of more than 150 samples (Copes 1975), brassy minnows made up 2–40% of the minnows sold as local mixed bait, 2–15% of the minnows sold as fathead minnows, and 5–20% of the minnows sold as Milwaukee (lake emerald) shiners.

Gould and Irwin (1962) classified the brassy minnow as a poor bioassay animal.

Mississippi Silvery Minnow

Hybognathus nuchalis Agassiz. *Hybognathus*—protruding jaw, probably in reference to upper jaw or snout; *nuchalis*—pertaining to the nape.

Other common names: silvery minnow, blunt-jawed minnow.

Adult male 95 mm, Black R. (Jackson Co.), 27 Sept. 1975

Adult female 88 mm, Black R. (Jackson Co.), 27 Sept. 1975

DESCRIPTION

Body elongate, slightly compressed laterally. Average length 76–102 mm (3–4 in). TL = 1.26 SL. Depth into TL 4.9–5.8. Head length into TL 4.8–5.5. Snout slightly rounded (more pointed than in *Hybognathus hankinsoni*), overhanging mouth. Maxillary short, reaching to below nostrils; barbels absent. Pharyngeal teeth 4–4, with oblique grinding surfaces; some barely hooked at tip (see p. 582). Eye into head length 4.5–4.7. Gill rakers short, pointed, 8–10. Dorsal fin slightly in advance of pelvic fin origin; dorsal fin pointed (posterior margin somewhat falcate); dorsal fin rays 8; anal fin rays usually 8, occasionally 9; pectoral fin rays 15–16; pelvic fin rays 8 (7). Scales with 8–11 long radii; lateral line scales 38–40; lateral line complete. Digestive tract (see p. 582)"coiled like a watch spring," with elongated stomach almost the length of peritoneal cavity; ventral to the stomach are a series of alternating loops and coils, about 5.4–5.8 TL. Chromosomes 2n = 50 (W. LeGrande, pers. comm.).

Silvery in life. Preserved specimens brown dorsally and on upper side; a faint lead-colored lateral stripe posteriorly; light brown-yellow ventrally. Peritoneum black.

Breeding male with light yellow along the sides and the lower fins, and small tubercles on the body and fins. According to Forbes and Richardson (1920), in spring male the nuchal region is somewhat swollen. Breeding female occasionally with a few tubercles (Eddy and Underhill 1974).

Sexual dimorphism: In males the distance from the end of the pectoral fin to the pelvic origin is less than half the pectoral fin length; in females, usually more than half the pectoral fin length.

SYSTEMATIC NOTES

Recently the Committee on Names of Fishes (Robins et al. 1980) recommended the addition of Mississippi to the common name, a modifier indicative of its geographic range, and supported the proposal by Pflieger (1971) of elevating the eastern silvery minnow *Hybognathus nuchalis regius*, previously treated most often as a subspecies, to a specific rank *Hybognathus regius*.

DISTRIBUTION, STATUS, AND HABITAT

In Wisconsin the silvery minnow occurs in the Mississippi River and in the lower portions of its tributaries, including the Rock River system. Cahn (1927) reported this species from the Menomonee River of the Lake Michigan drainage basin, although the three specimens are no longer extant, and the possibility exists that he may have confused this species with the closely related brassy minnow. The silvery minnow was reported once from the mouth of the Chicago River at the head of the Chicago Drainage Canal (Forbes and Richardson 1920); however, Hubbs and Lagler (1964) were unable to verify this report, and believed that it may have been based on *H. hankinsoni*. Trautman (1957) supposed that the silvery minnow's early disappearance from southern Ohio was caused by increased turbidity of the waters and the killing of aquatic vegetation by silt.

In Wisconsin, the silvery minnow is uncommon to rare. In the upper Rock River, where it was taken in the 1920s, it seems to have disappeared from some localities. Extensive state fish poisoning programs may have removed this species from some waters in the Rock River basin.

The Mississippi silvery minnow inhabits medium to large rivers, and the lower extremities of small streams opening into such waters. Occasionally it has been taken from pools, backwaters, and oxbows adjacent to large streams. In Wisconsin, it was encoun-

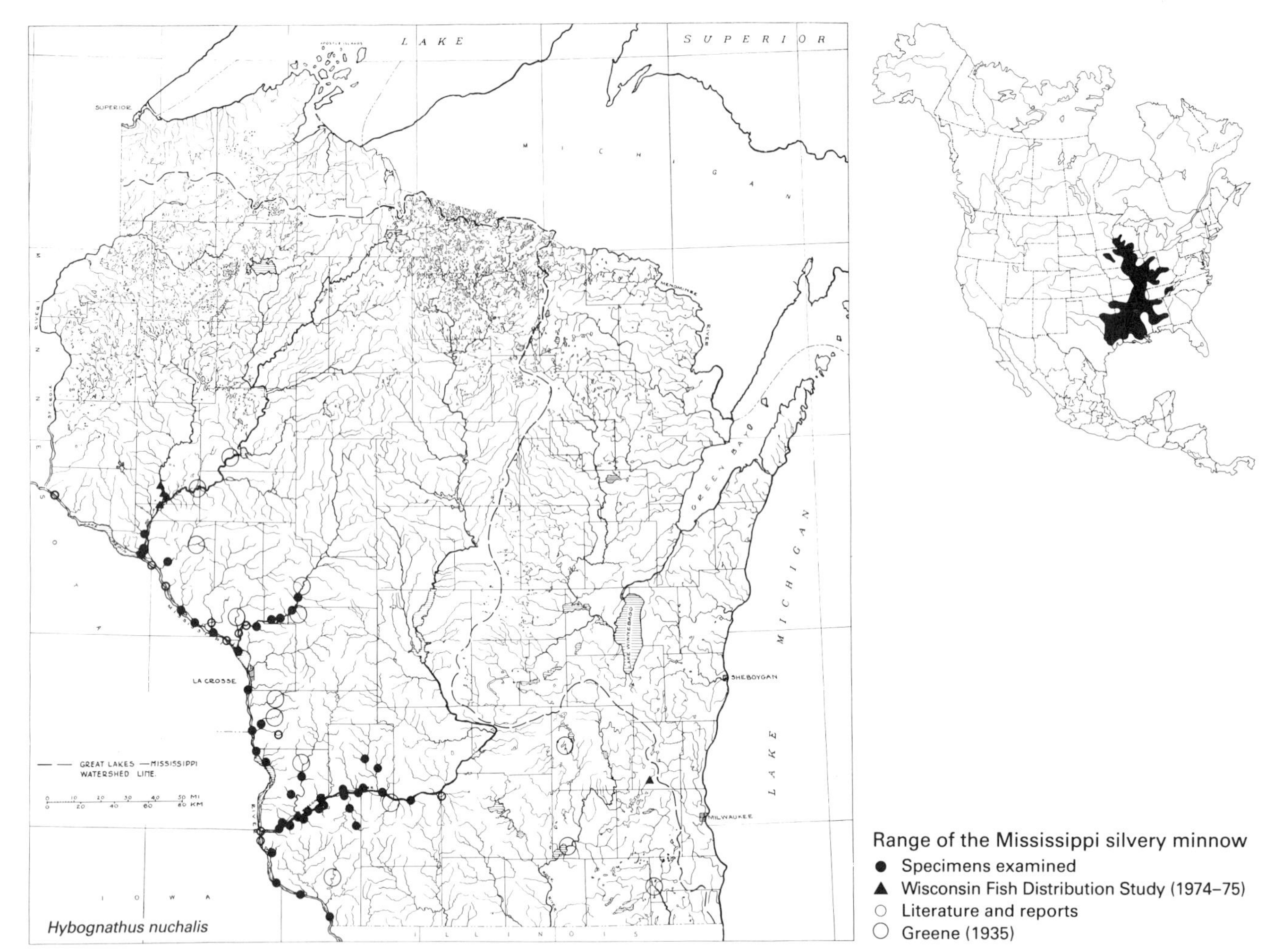

Range of the Mississippi silvery minnow
● Specimens examined
▲ Wisconsin Fish Distribution Study (1974–75)
○ Literature and reports
◯ Greene (1935)

tered most frequently in clear water at depths up to 1.5 m, over substrates of sand (49% frequency), mud (11%), gravel (20%), rubble (9%), silt (7%), and clay (4%). The sites were generally sparsely vegetated. It occurred in tributary streams of the following widths: 1.0–3.0 (7%), 3.1–6.0 (57%), and 6.1–12.0 (36%). Most collections of this species have been made in the lower mouths of tributary streams close to large rivers. It is possible that the silvery minnow is far more common in large rivers than our collections indicate, since collection bias may have occurred. Cross (1967) reported this minnow from relatively deep water in the Missouri River, where the flow is sluggish and the bottoms silted.

The eastern silvery minnow, *Hybognathus regius*, has been reported from lakes. No lake records for the Mississippi form are known for Wisconsin.

BIOLOGY

In southern Wisconsin, the silvery minnow spawns from the end of April or early May until at least the end of July. Females with mature eggs 0.8 mm diam were taken from Saunders and Gran Grae creeks, tributaries to the lower Wisconsin River, on 17 and 30 July. No gravid females were found in any collections made in August and September. The silvery minnow breeds principally in creeks and rivers in shallow water, in or near riffles (Adams and Hankinson 1926).

The spawning habits of the closely related eastern silvery minnow from Cayuga Lake in New York State were described by Raney (1939). The details are included here for information and are not to be construed as the typical spawning habits of the Mississippi silvery minnow. Spawning occurred in late April and early May at temperatures of 13–20.5°C (55.4–68.9°F). Spawning activities started in the morning about 1000 hr, and continued until about 1600 hr; spawning peaked between 1200 and 1400 hr. The nonadhesive eggs were laid on the bottom ooze in the quiet waters of coves. No territory was held, and no fighting was observed among the males. Individuals of both sexes were occasionally seen coming to the surface to gulp air. Raney described spawning as follows (pp. 677–678):

> When ready to spawn a female will move slowly toward the shallow water at the side of the cove. From one to ten males will move at once toward her. The first two to get to her swim slightly underneath on opposite sides and nose her slightly in the region in front of and above the anus. The other males will attempt to squeeze out the two males which first reached her. If they fail to replace the lower males they swim along close to the female's back and sides. The female followed by her retinue of males may at times move quickly in a curved path which usually ends in the center of the cove among the rest of the nonactive females. When pursued in this manner a female would often jump out of the water a few inches and travel as much as three feet while in the air. Usually, however, she continues toward a grassy area and spawning occurs.
>
> Breeding is usually accomplished with a male close to either side of a female, near the base of newly sprouted grass in from 2 to 6 inches of water. The eggs are apparently laid as the three vibrate rapidly for a second or two. The breeding vibration although momentary is violent enough to disturb the bottom ooze making the water slightly turbid. When spawning occurs quite close to shore the grass could be seen waving considerably. At times one male appeared to spawn by crowding a female against a clump of vegetation. On other occasions a single female would be accompanied by from 4 to 10 males when spawning took place. However, it appears that only the two males close alongside the female are effective. Because of the ooze stirred up it was impossible to see details at the moment of spawning.
>
> After spawning the female returns to the deeper waters in the center of the cove. The males again take up their movements near the shore looking for other females. . . . It was not determined how soon a female would spawn again nor how many eggs were laid at one spawning although the number is likely quite small.

Sometimes eggs of the eastern silvery minnow are buried to a depth of a few millimeters (Mansueti and Hardy 1967). They are essentially nonadhesive, although occasionally they become attached to bits of bottom debris. Incubation time is 6–7 days when daytime temperatures vary from 13.3 to 20.5°C (55.9 to 68.9°F).

The yolk-sac larvae are 6.0 mm TL at hatching. They remain near the bottom, and, following yolk absorption, they concentrate in small schools near shore, usually among emergent vegetation. Juvenile silvery minnows leave tributary nursery grounds and enter lakes by 15 July in New York.

Mansueti and Hardy (1967) described and illustrated stages from 5.7 to 17.3 mm TL.

In the Wisconsin River on 19 June, a silvery minnow, 102 mm TL and 8.84 g, had ovaries 9.3% of the body weight, which contained 2,054 yellow mature eggs 0.8–0.9 mm diam. A second female, 107 mm TL and 10.75 g, held 3,105 mature eggs 0.7–0.9 mm diam; the ovaries were 9.3% of the body weight. No smaller, white, immature eggs were observed.

The growth of the young-of-year silvery minnows is rapid. Observations in Wisconsin showed the following.

Date	No. of Fish	TL (mm)		Location
		Avg	Range	
19 June	7	33.57	31–38	Wisconsin R. (Richland Co.)
20 June	4	44.75	43–45	Indian Cr. (Richland Co.)
20 June	111	34.66	24–42	Blue R. (Grant Co.)
23 June	21	30.48	27–32	Wisconsin R. (Grant Co.)
25 June	18	34.33	28–39	Blue R. (Grant Co.)
27 June	4	38.25	34–40	Mississippi R. (Vernon Co.)
18 Aug.	1	66.00		Wisconsin R. (Crawford Co.)
7 Sept.	2	69.00	64–74	Mississippi R. (Crawford Co.)
28 Sept.	3	52.33	44–59	Chippewa R. (Buffalo Co.)

Aging was done by reading scale annuli. The annulus was recognized by following the circuli onto the lateral fields, where they become irregular and showed cutting over. Adults in southern Wisconsin collections, 18–25 June 1962, showed the following growth:

Age Class	No. of Fish	TL (mm)		Calculated TL at Annulus[a] (mm)	
		Avg	Range	1	2
I	9	75.2	59–83	61.2	
II	17	100.3	90–110	77.7	100.1
Avg (weighted)				72.0	100.1

[a]Annulus deposition begins in May for age-I fish, and in middle to late-June for age-II fish.

Growth in New York of pond-raised eastern silvery minnows (Raney 1942) was similar to that of southern Wisconsin fish. By 20 June the young-of-year averaged 31 mm TL; by 15 July, 45 mm; and by late September, 61 (41–72) mm. Age-I fish averaged 80 (65–89) mm; age-II males, 82 (76–87) mm, and age-II females, 88 (78–96) mm. The original progeny spawned for the second time (at age III) the following year.

Maturity occurs at age II in both sexes, although Mansueti and Hardy (1967) noted that some females reach maturity at age I. Only one Wisconsin fish, a 107-mm female, had reached age III; her calculated lengths at the annuli were: 1—65.7 mm, 2—86.6 mm.

The largest specimen from Wisconsin waters in the UWSP museum collection is 110 mm (4.3 in) TL.

The silvery minnow has the long intestine, the simple pharyngeal teeth with well-developed grinding surfaces, and the few, short gill rakers characteristic of the "mud-eating minnows," and its food corresponds to these structural pecularities (Forbes and Richardson 1920). The digestive tracts of silvery minnows from the lower Wisconsin River contained green algae, blue-green algae, and diatoms. Numerous diatom species, *Oscillatoria* spp., and filamentous algal fragments were found in quantity, along with sand grains and much unidentifiable organic debris, all microscopic in size.

The Mississippi silvery minnow is a schooling fish which moves along the bottom and feeds predominantly on the bottom. Schools of 50–100 fish have been seen in deep and quiet water (Forbes and Richardson 1920). Because of the silvery minnow's reluctance to break formation, dealers who seine for bait are able to collect large numbers of them. During early fall I have seen adults in small schools frequenting the sandy bottoms of streams of various sizes, from small tributaries to large rivers.

In the lower Wisconsin River, 68 Mississippi silvery minnows were taken with the following species: gizzard shad (1), quillback (67), bigmouth buffalo (2), common carp (1), golden shiner (1), bullhead minnow (102), bluntnose minnow (5), emerald shiner (4), spotfin shiner (1,004), spottail shiner (9), river shiner (33), bigmouth shiner (1), channel catfish (1), northern pike (1), white bass (18), walleye (1), western sand darter (9), logperch (1), johnny darter (53), smallmouth bass (7), largemouth bass (5), bluegill (2), black crappie (3), white crappie (1), and freshwater drum (6). A collection from the Blue River (Grant County) contained these species: Mississippi silvery minnow (230), quillback (1), bigmouth buffalo (1), shorthead redhorse (21), white sucker (3), common carp (26), central stoneroller (2), creek chub (6), golden shiner (1), bullhead minnow (22), bluntnose minnow (9), suckermouth minnow (1), common shiner (12), emerald shiner (13), spotfin shiner (102), sand shiner (3), bigmouth shiner (11), stonecat (1), johnny darter (23), and banded darter (1).

IMPORTANCE AND MANAGEMENT

The use of the silvery minnow as a forage species, except by the largemouth bass, loon, and common tern, is unknown, but its schooling habit in shallows undoubtedly makes it vulnerable to other predators as well.

The silvery minnow is considered a good bait minnow in parts of the United States. In the East it has been used extensively for food; there it takes the hook freely during the spawning season, and is a desirable bait for black bass, perch, and northern pike (Adams and Hankinson 1926).

In Wisconsin, the silvery minnow is not hardy, and is consequently an undesirable live bait. Moreover, its numbers are not sufficient to ensure a continual bait source. Since this minnow is small in Wisconsin, its use as a food source to man is probably nil.

The eastern silvery minnow has been suggested as a possible forage minnow in the propagation of muskellunge, which requires an early breeding minnow to provide food for the newly hatched young (Raney 1942).

Raney noted a mortality rate of 5% among eastern silvery minnows in pond culture, which he attributed, in part, to depredations by kingfishers, largemouth bass, and the disease fungus *Saprolegnia*. He successfully propagated this species (110 thousand young per hectare) in a shallow, earthen pond, 0.06 ha in area. The pond was fertilized several times, but only natural food was available to the minnows.

Bullhead Minnow

Pimephales vigilax (Baird and Girard). *Pimephales*—fat, head; *vigilax*—watchful.

Male 70 mm, Wisconsin R. (Columbia Co.), 20 Sept. 1969

Female 53 mm, Wisconsin R. (Columbia Co.), 20 Sept. 1969

DESCRIPTION

Body stout, slightly compressed laterally. Average size 64 mm (2.5 in). TL = 1.24 SL. Depth into TL 4.9–5.8. Head length into TL 4.9–5.3; top of head and back behind head slightly flattened. Snout blunt, even with or scarcely protruding beyond upper lip. Mouth small, terminal to almost terminal, and slightly oblique; mouth extending to below region between posterior nostril and anterior margin of eye; barbel absent. Pharyngeal teeth 4–4, slender, hooked, with elongate cutting edges; sometimes serrated. Eye into head length 3.2–4.0. Gill rakers knoblike to short, conical, 6–8. Dorsal fin origin over or slightly behind origin of pelvic fin; dorsal fin rays 8 (short ray at front of dorsal fin not tightly bound to first principal ray, as is the case in most minnows); anal fin rays 7; pectoral fin rays 15–16; pelvic fin rays 8. Lateral line scales 40–45; lateral line complete, slightly decurved. Scales on back before dorsal fin small and crowded. Digestive tract a simple S shape, 0.6–0.7 TL. Chromosomes 2n = 50 (W. LeGrande, pers. comm.).

Back light olive, sides and belly silvery. In preserved fish, a faint lateral stripe about width of pupil of eye, ending in a conspicuous basicaudal spot. Dorsolateral scale pockets faintly edged in pigment; pores of lateral line scales often distinctly marked with melanophores ("mouse tracks"). Dark blotch on dorsal fin near anterior base. Fins near base yellowish or clear. Peritoneum silvery, with scattered dark speckles, to dusky.

Breeding male dark on head and body; intense dark blotch on dorsal fin; outer half of dorsal and caudal fins darkened; anterior 2 rays of pectoral fin dark pigmented; a golden orange band as wide as dorsal fin base extending from dorsal fin to belly (Parker 1964). Large pointed tubercles in 2 rows on snout, usually 4 in upper row, 5 in lower; fleshy gray rugose pad of "skin" extending from nape to dorsal fin. In breeding female, minute tubercles in pits on snout.

Tuberculate male 77 mm, with fleshy pad on nape and back, Wisconsin R. (Grant County), 23 June 1962

Hybrids: Bullhead minnow × bluntnose minnow (Trautman 1957).

SYSTEMATIC NOTES

The bullhead minnow has formerly appeared under the generic names *Ceratichthys, Cliola* and *Hypargyrus*; it has had a thorough taxonomic review by Hubbs and Black (1947). Two subspecies are recognized: *Pimephales vigilax perspicuus* (Girard), the northern form, whose range extends from Wisconsin to the Alabama River system in Alabama and the Trinity River system in Texas (avoiding the upper part of the Red River system in Oklahoma and Texas) (Hubbs and Lagler 1964); and *P.v. vigilax* (Baird and Girard), the southwestern form, whose range extends from the upper Red River system to south of the Trinity River as far as the Rio Grande basin in Texas and Mexico.

DISTRIBUTION, STATUS, AND HABITAT

In Wisconsin the bullhead minnow occurs in the Mississippi River and Lake Michigan drainage basins. It is found in the Mississippi River and in the lower ex-

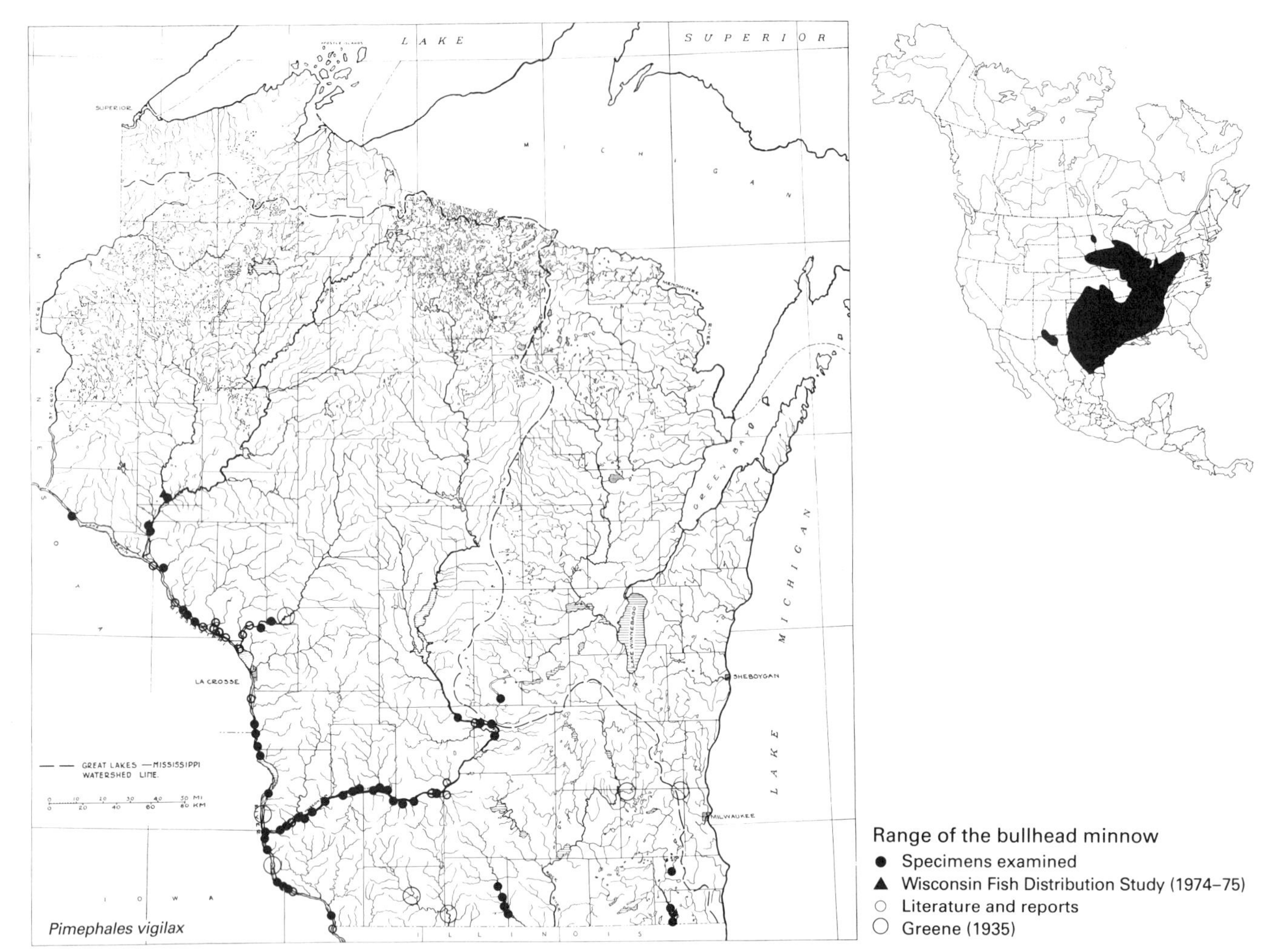

tremities of its tributaries, including the Rock River system and the Fox River.

Early in this century the bullhead minnow was reported in the Lake Michigan drainage from the Menomonee River (tributary of the Milwaukee River) by Cahn (1927); Greene (1935) suggested that this fish may have been a bait bucket release, or a recent immigrant via highwater connections between the Rock and Milwaukee river systems. No specimens are known to substantiate this report. On 29 July 1960, however, nine specimens (UWSP 2318) were collected from the upper Fox River (Marquette County). The site (T14N R9E Sec 23) is near the Wisconsin-Fox canal at Portage, the likely crossover point from the Mississippi River watershed. More collecting on the upper Fox River is needed to determine the extent of the bullhead minnow population in those waters. The continued poisoning of portions of the Fox River and adjacent waters with antimycin or other fish toxicants, for the purpose of carp removal, may jeopardize or wipe out the only known Great Lakes population of the bullhead minnow.

In the lower Wisconsin River, the bullhead minnow is common to abundant. In the Mississippi River it is among the most abundant species in the river.

The bullhead minnow inhabits sluggish waters of large inland streams, connected backwaters, and silty streams. In Wisconsin, it was encountered most frequently over substrates of sand (44% frequency), mud (24%), clay (11%), gravel (11%), rubble (5%), and silt (5%). It occurred in waters of varying clarity, at different depths; it was found in large rivers and in the lower portions of tributaries 3.1–6.0 m wide. It was seldom taken in riffles. Vegetation may or may not be present.

BIOLOGY

In Wisconsin, spawning extends from June to August. Gravid females have been taken from southern Wisconsin waters from late June to the beginning of August. In Illinois, gravid females have been taken as early as 21 May (Forbes and Richardson 1920).

The spawning of the bullhead minnow takes place beneath flat stones or debris in shallow pools or slowly flowing water. Its reproductive habits are similar to those of the bluntnose minnow. The following account comes from Parker (1964), who witnessed bullhead minnows spawning in aquariums.

Spawning occurs at water temperatures of 25.6°C (78°F) or higher. The nest is constructed by the male under boards, rocks, stones, tree trunks, limbs, concrete, metal pipes, or tile. As spawning time approaches the males are aggressive, attacking intruding males "with great speed and vigor." At times, females go in and out of the nest while the male is there. At other times, a female remains outside the nest opening for hours without moving away. Parker (1964:233) provided this description:

> . . . One male selected a nest site on 22 July, 26 days before a female located herself in front of it. Here she remained most of the day and night, moving away from the opening only during the feeding periods and returned soon after feeding. Several days later, the female was observed entering the nest where she remained for a short period before returning to her former position. Occasionally the male would come out and the female would enter. When she came out, he re-entered. The exchange of positions occurred several times and finally the male took his former position in the nest and began to move from side to side. Both fish swam in a circular manner when entering or leaving the nest and while moving about the aquarium during the spawning activities.

A spawning session lasted about 10 minutes. Parker did not see the actual release of eggs and sperm, but he recorded that the male protects the eggs, driving away fish twice his size. Constant movement of the male beneath the eggs keeps the water agitated, and, in brushing the eggs with the skin pad of his back, he keeps them free of sediment.

Parker noted that eggs hatch in 4.5–6 days at water temperatures of 26.1–28.3°C (79–83°F). Taber (1969) illustrated the developmental stages from 5.7 to 12.7 mm. According to Parker, in nature young bullhead minnows feed primarily on bottom ooze diatoms.

In Wisconsin, gravid fish were collected 19 June from the Wisconsin River (Richland County). A 65-mm fish, with ovaries 16.1% of body weight, held 390 orange, mature eggs 1.2 mm diam; yellow, immature eggs of about equal number were 0.1–0.7 diam. A 55-mm fish, with ovaries 19.9% of body weight, had 320 ripe eggs 1.0 mm diam; and a 56-mm fish, with ovaries 17.2% of body weight, held an estimated 335 ripe eggs 1.1 mm diam.

In the Wisconsin River (Iowa County), on 8 August young-of-year were 20–36 mm TL. On 21 October in a downstream site (Grant County), the smaller young-of-year were 26–32 mm TL, implying a late spawning.

Bullhead minnows from the Wisconsin River (Richland County), collected 19 June 1962, showed the following growth:

Age Class	No. of Fish	TL (mm)		Calculated TL at Annulus[a] (mm)	
		Avg	Range	1	2
I	28	49.4	33–62	34.4	
II	12	68.6	61–79	39.0	63.9
Avg (weighted)				35.8	63.9

[a]The annulus for the year of capture had not yet been deposited in the largest and oldest fish.

The eight largest fish in this sample, 65–79 mm TL, were males of a breeding population. Females are generally smaller than males. Maturity is reached at age I in fish over 50 mm long. The condition (K_{TL}) of bullhead minnows collected from the Black River (Jackson County) on 24 September 1975 averaged 0.98 (0.84–1.09)(C. Piantino, pers. comm.).

A large bullhead minnow, 94 mm (3.7 in) long, was reported from Ohio (Trautman 1957).

The bullhead minnow is omnivorous. In Minnesota, it feeds extensively on algae and other vegetation, but it may also feed on small snails, on *Hyallela*, and on other small, bottom-dwelling animals (Eddy and Underhill 1974). In Oklahoma (Parker 1964), insects were found in all bullhead minnow stomachs examined; they consisted of many small aquatic larvae and adults, among which chironomids and psychodids were the most common. Small crustaceans constituted the greatest volume and cladocerans were the most abundant. The total volume of plant food was relatively small. In a few stomachs, filamentous green and blue-green algae constituted a large proportion of the food. Diatoms, which were numerous in many stomachs, were usually associated with mud and debris; their total volume was never more than 5% of the content of any one stomach.

Parker observed that the bullhead minnow took food 15–20 min after being brought to the laboratory (pp. 230–231):

> If they did not catch the food while it was falling, they secured it from the bottom by tilting the body slightly so that the long axis of the body formed a 35–40° angle with the tank bottom. Ground shrimp, apparently preferred to other foods, was usually caught as it fell through the water. The fish captured *Daphnia* by rapid pursuit. Prepared dry foods or other nonmotile foods were readily taken if no live foods were in the aquaria, but were refused sometimes when live foods were available.

The bullhead minnow is a schooling fish during the daytime, and disperses at night while resting (Parker 1964). Vision plays an important role in the formation and maintenance of schools. The minnows in schools are at a small, nearly uniform distance from one another. Individuals in the school engage in circular movements ("milling") while the rest of the school remains relatively stationary; milling begins when the school makes a sharp turn of 180° or more. When undisturbed, the school tends to break up, becoming "diffuse and amorphous," but, when the aquarium is approached or is vibrated by sound, the fish hasten to reschool. Parker suggested that schooling is part of a "fear" reaction, which has been reported in many other species of fish. Parker noted that schools do not form during spawning, but reform after spawning activities have occurred.

In the Wisconsin River (Iowa County) 1,206 bullhead minnows were associated with the following species: river and/or highfin carpsucker fry (21), shorthead redhorse (1), speckled chub (3), bluntnose minnow (5), fathead minnow (1), emerald shiner (31), spotfin shiner (1,704), river shiner (1), sand shiner (1), bigmouth shiner (6), brassy minnow (5), yellow bass (1), yellow perch (4), walleye (1), logperch (3), johnny darter (14), smallmouth bass (1), largemouth bass (10), bluegill (3), and brook silverside (4).

IMPORTANCE AND MANAGEMENT

In Iowa, the bullhead minnow is an excellent forage fish, and is used extensively by anglers as bait for panfish and bass (Harlan and Speaker 1956). It is not known to what extent this minnow ends up in the bait buckets of Wisconsin fishermen, but the large numbers available suggest at least limited use.

Bullhead minnows transport and hold well in tanks, and eat dry food readily, but are too nervous to be good bioassay animals (Gould and Irwin 1962).

Bluntnose Minnow

Pimephales notatus (Rafinesque). *Pimephales*—fat, head; *notatus*—spotted.

Other common names: blunt-nosed minnow, blue-nosed chub, bullhead minnow, fat-head chub.

Male (tuberculate) 82 mm, Mud Branch Cr. (Lafayette Co.), 29 June 1960

Female 77 mm, Pewaukee L. (Waukesha Co.), 9 Sept. 1961

DESCRIPTION

Body elongate, cylindrical, and weakly compressed laterally. Average length 64 mm (2.5 in). TL = 1.21 SL. Depth into TL 4.9–6.9. Head length into TL 4.7–5.5; top of head and back before dorsal fin broad and flattened. Snout blunt and rounded, slightly protruding anterior to the upper lip. Mouth inferior, slightly oblique to horizontal, extending to below posterior nostril; barbel absent (breeding male with a blisterlike swelling of skin at corner of mouth). Pharyngeal teeth 4–4, broad and flattened; teeth slightly hooked, with long, often serrated, cutting edges. Eye into head length 2.7–4.0. Gill rakers short, pointed, flattened (like tip of leaf), 8–10. Dorsal fin origin slightly behind origin of pelvic fin; dorsal fin rays 8 (short ray at front of dorsal fin thickened and separated from first principal ray, rather than splintlike and tightly bound to first major ray, as is the case in most minnows); anal fin rays 7; pectoral fin rays 15–16; pelvic fin rays 8. Lateral line scales 40–44; lateral line complete, slightly decurved. Scales on back before dorsal fin small and crowded. Digestive tract 1.0–1.2 TL. Chromosomes 2n = 50 (W. LeGrande, pers. comm.).

Back light olive green, sides silvery, belly silvery white. Fins with yellow to olive tint; dorsal fin often with a dusky blotch near front about one-third of way up from base. Scale pockets, especially above

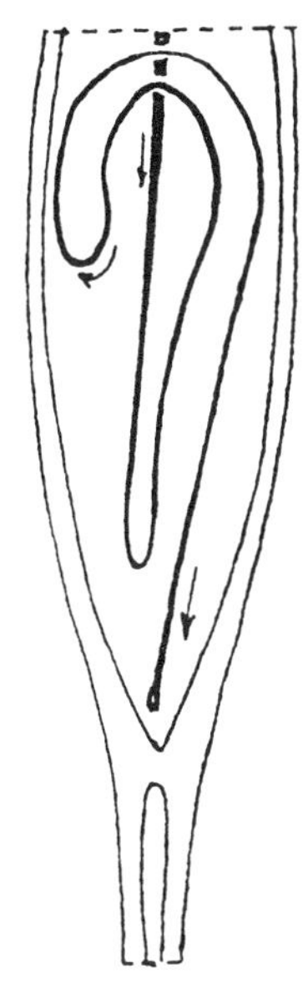

Alimentary tract of the bluntnose minnow, diagrammatic

lateral stripe, edged in pigment. Faint lateral stripe about width of pupil of eye extends from behind eye to caudal peduncle, terminating in a distinct, wedge-shaped basicaudal spot. Caudal spot and lateral stripe sometimes absent from living fish, and best seen in preserved specimens. Peritoneum black.

Breeding male almost black, with whitish pad on forward part of back; often lower fins have an orange hue. Tubercles (about 14–17) large, sharp, in 3 rows across the snout, not extending above the nostrils; small tubercles may occur on anterior pectoral rays. A thickened, barbel-like swelling at corner of mouth.

Hybrids: Bluntnose minnow × fathead minnow, bluntnose minnow × bullhead minnow (Trautman 1957).

DISTRIBUTION, STATUS, AND HABITAT

In Wisconsin the bluntnose minnow occurs in the Mississippi River, Lake Michigan, and Lake Superior drainage basins. It is widely distributed, except in the Lake Superior basin, where distribution is spotty.

From the standpoint of distribution and numbers, the bluntnose minnow is the most successful fish species in Wisconsin. It appears to be doing well even in the heavily populated sectors of the state. It probably benefits from the increased spawning sites made available to it by man—rocks, concrete, metals, wood, and trash which are thrown into our waterways. Its status appears to be secure.

The bluntnose minnow occurs in lakes, ponds, rivers, and creeks in a wide variety of habitats. In Wisconsin, it was encountered most frequently in clear water, and commonly in slightly turbid to turbid

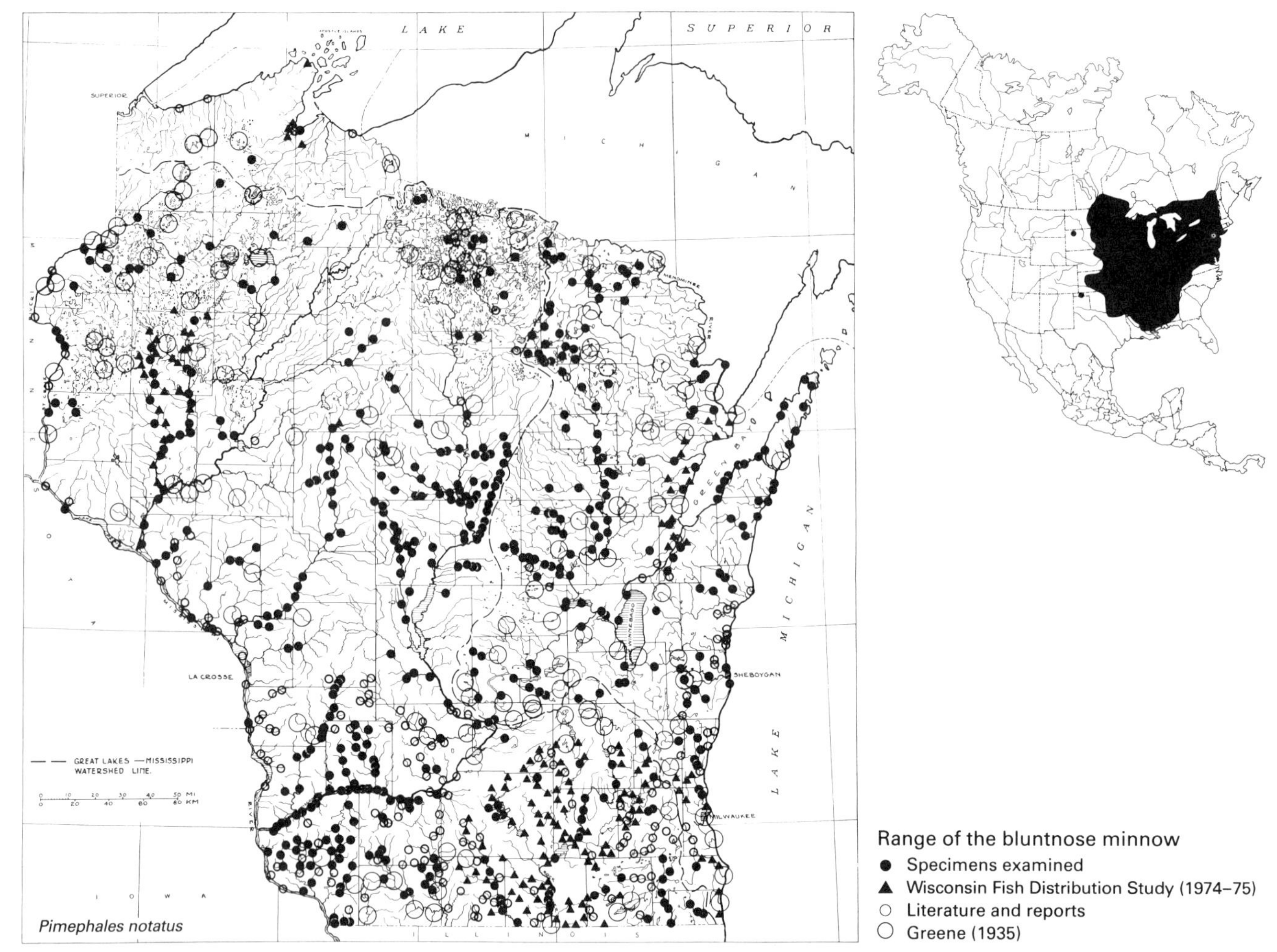

Range of the bluntnose minnow
● Specimens examined
▲ Wisconsin Fish Distribution Study (1974–75)
○ Literature and reports
◯ Greene (1935)

water. It was found at varying depths over substrates of gravel (24% frequency), sand (23%), mud (13%), silt (13%), rubble (11%), clay (7%), boulders (6%), detritus (2%), and bedrock (1%). It is seldom taken over marl. It occurred in streams of the following widths: 1.0–3.0 m (19%), 3.1–6.0 m (24%), 6.1–12.0 (23%), 12.1–24.0 (25%), 24.1–50.0 m (7%), and more than 50 m (3%). It was often associated with submerged vegetation.

BIOLOGY

In Wisconsin, spawning probably extends from May to August. In central Wisconsin, gravid females and tuberculate males were taken as early as 25 May, and a male in full breeding habit was taken as late as 19 August. Water temperatures at spawning are 21.1–26.1°C (70–79°F).

The spawning and nesting behavior of the bluntnose minnow have been thoroughly discussed by Hubbs and Cooper (1936), and most of the following account has been taken from that source.

Nests are constructed over sand or gravel shoals, at water depths of a few centimeters to 2.5 m. The adhesive eggs are stuck to the underside of any convenient flat object, such as a log, piece of bark, hardpan clay, rock, or mussel shell. If natural objects are absent, the bluntnose minnow male constructs the nest under a tin can, board, tile, piece of tar paper, barrel, metal wash basin, milk can top, etc.

Hubbs and Cooper have described nest construction by the male (p. 69):

> . . . After the site was definitely selected, he began constructing the nest—a long task which consisted chiefly of making a shallow cavity in the bottom underneath the object, and cleaning off the under surface of the object where the eggs were to be laid. In excavating the cavity, the male cleaned out the silt, sand and small pebbles by violent sweeps of the tail, and pushed out stones, sticks and other larger objects with his horny snout. In cleaning that part of the under surface of the chosen object which forms the roof over the cavity, the male used his mouth and his spongy back. The entire process of selecting the nesting site and building the nest required an hour or two.

Each nest is constantly protected by a single male, who guards it against the intrusion of all fishes other than his own mates. He is able to drive away fishes twice his size. Often he constructs a narrow slit between the spawning object and the bottom so that no fish much larger than himself could reach the nest, even if he failed to guard it. The bluntnose minnow's ability to guard its nest against larger intruders has been described by Hubbs and Cooper (1936:71):

> . . . A school of a dozen or more of these sunfish (green sunfish) kept constant vigil about each nest, all facing the nest in an almost perfect two-foot circle. They were obviously waiting their chance to dash into the nest for the eggs, or to eat the newly-hatched fry as soon as the latter left the nest. Occasionally one of the sunfish became bold enough to approach within a few inches of the nest, when suddenly a black streak was seen to dart at the intruder, who immediately retreated as the male Blunt-nosed Minnow returned to his post. Rarely, if ever, was the intruding sunfish so bold as to stay and "fight it out" with the male minnow.

Occasionally a nesting object, such as a long board, has under it closely associated groups of nest-guarding males; there may be one nest per linear foot of board. When such nesting objects are disturbed and the males driven off, a riot ensues (p. 71):

> . . . they (the males) usually do not return until after a lapse of several minutes. Each male then spends several minutes thoroughly examining the entire area about and beneath the spawning object before he becomes sufficiently oriented to again assume the guardianship of his nest. When the males are thus seeking out their own nests, the general region about the nesting object becomes a tumult of confusion. They swim about from one nest to another, fighting every male encountered; like tiny bulls, they lunge into one another with their horns. The general confusion is often further complicated by the presence of supernumerary males or of small fishes that have entered the nest to feed on the eggs. The battle royal, which usually lasts several minutes, ends when each male again becomes resigned to the guardianship of his own nest.

Spawning frequently occurs at night (Westman 1938), but Hubbs and Cooper (1936) found that spawning also occurs in the daytime. Westman concluded that not only will several females spawn with a single male, but also that more than one female will spawn with the same male during a single night.

A female bluntnose minnow may spawn a batch of 40–408 eggs (Westman 1938) per spawning. Spawning may occur two or more times a year. The eggs are usually placed close together in one layer in a roughly circular or oblong patch 8–10 cm or larger; another layer may be added if space is limited. Observation of nests indicates that not all spawning takes place at one time; nests normally contain both freshly laid eggs and eggs in an advanced state of development. Hubbs and Cooper observed that individual females entered nests, laid 25–100 eggs, and left within 10–30 min. More than 5,000 eggs were laid in a single nest within 48 hr, presumably by several females.

The presence of the parent bluntnose male is necessary to ensure a continuous movement of water over the eggs, and to keep the nest free from sediment. Westman (1938) observed that eggs which had not reached the eyed stage in development would die within 12 hr after the parent male was removed. Hankinson (1908) noted that the male stood guard even after the minute young had hatched and swum away; he also observed a male bluntnose minnow guarding an empty nest for more than a day after the eggs had all been hatched.

Gravid females were collected from Mill Creek (Richland County) on 29 June 1962. A 64-mm fish, with ovaries 12.6% of body weight, held 390 yellow-white, ripe eggs 1.2 mm diam. A 65-mm fish, with ovaries 10.5% of body weight, held 485 maturing eggs 1.0–1.1 mm diam. A third female, 68-mm TL, with a gonad/body weight index of 7.3%, had evidently just spawned; she contained only about a dozen ripe eggs, and 320 immature eggs 0.3–1.0 mm diam, suggesting a second spawning later in the season.

In New York ponds (Westman 1938), all eggs observed became eyed after a period of 3–5 days on the spawning tile, and hatched after 6–10 days. Dead eggs were never found in the nests, and Westman suggested that such eggs either drop from the tile and remain undeveloped, or that they are removed from the tile by the male.

The newly hatched larva is 4.6 mm, and at 3 days, 5.5–5.7 mm (Fish 1932). Fish has illustrated the stages through 12 mm, and described the stages through the 17.8-mm young adult. The young appear in groups near the surface of the water 8 days after hatching.

In ponds near Madison (Dane County), bluntnose minnows were 23 mm on 10 July, and averaged 42 mm TL on 17 October (Neess 1947). This retarded growth rate was thought to be due to the late spring in 1947, since in previous years about one-half of the population was 45 mm long or longer at the end of the first year.

In Michigan, Hubbs (1921) estimated growth early in the bluntnose minnow's first summer as 0.48 mm per day during a 30-day period. In Minnesota (Lux 1960), young-of-year showed the following growth: 15 mm on 28 June, 18 mm on 15 July, 26 mm on 27 July, 32 mm on 14 August, and 38 mm on 28 August. The young bluntnose minnows live on or near the shallow-water breeding grounds of their parents.

The bluntnose minnow in Pewaukee Lake (Waukesha County) grows rapidly, attaining a calculated total length of 51.3 mm at the first annulus. The age composition of a 9 September collection was: 0—43.5 (38–49) mm; I—61.3 (54–67) mm; and II—82.2 (77–85) mm. In a 27 September collection from the western end of Lake Mendota (Dane County) (D. Schmitt, pers. comm.), the calculated total length at the first annulus was 43.3 mm, and the age composition was: 0—43.1 (24–57) mm; I—60.9 (55–66) mm; and II—75.1 (71–80) mm. In a 16 September collection from the Plover River (Portage County), the calculated total lengths at the first and second annuli were 39.5 and 60.9 mm respectively, and the age composition was: I—52.5 (50–55) mm; II—64.0 (58–70) mm; and III—86.7 (81–92) mm. The annulus for the year was just being deposited for the largest and oldest fish in these collections.

Females reach maturity at age I, and males at age II (Westman 1938). Females may pass through at least two spawning seasons, and possibly a third.

Males reach a length of 102 mm (4 in), and females, 76 mm (3 in) (Dobie et al. 1956). The maximum known total length reported is 108 mm (4.3 in) (Trautman 1957).

The bluntnose minnow is primarily a bottom feeder, supplementing its diet with surface insects and plankton (Moyle 1973). Keast (1965) classified this species as a specialized feeder, since the bulk of the diet is made up of three items. Food consists chiefly of small organisms taken from the bottom, from water plants, and from the water. The literature includes a number of reports in which diatoms and filamentous algae constitute a substantial part of its diet. In Minnesota during the winter, Moyle found the gut of this minnow packed with 90% large diatoms and 10% filamentous algae; he suggested that algae probably make up most of the winter diet of this species.

In August and September, the bluntnose minnow in Green Lake (Green Lake County) consumed insect larvae (50%) and insect pupae (50%); in Lake Mendota (Dane County), it consumed adult insects (25.6%), cladocerans (31.4%), copepods (14.1%), plants (14.3%), algae (10%), and bottom ooze (4.3%) (Pearse 1921a). It is also known to eat fish eggs, fish fry, oligochaetes, debris, silt, and even its own young (Dobie et al. 1956). Hankinson (1908) saw individuals feeding on the eggs of black bass, johnny darters, sculpins, and sunfish of three species.

In Long Lake (Minnesota), Moyle (1973) observed that in the early morning bluntnose minnows feed heavily on emerging chironomids. Apparently these fish move out of their normal habitat among the aquatic plants and into shallow areas at each end of the lake, where there are swarms of chironomids. Scuba observations indicate that bluntnose minnows are not active at night, but rest quietly on the bottom in open areas.

In Lake Mendota (Dane County) during the winter the bluntnose minnow is found on the bottom at depths of 11–18 m (35–60 ft) (Black 1945b). When the ice cover has gone, the bluntnose enters the shoal areas. It occasionally leaves the shore regions if temperatures, wind, or other factors, such as the presence of enemies, produce unfavorable conditions. Hankinson (1908) noted that the bluntnose is much less common in shallow water during the summer than in the spring. He also noted that in Walnut Lake (Michigan) it is most common over gravel bottoms and near submerged plants, rather than where the bottom is marly.

In Long Lake (Minnesota), Moyle (1973) noted two seemingly contradictory tendencies in the bluntnose minnow's habitat preference: (1) a tendency to associate with larger schools of mimic shiners in water less than 1 m deep, and (2) a tendency to stay in small schools in water 2–4 m deep, among aquatic plants. Moyle observed an interesting relationship with the mimic shiners, in which the bluntnose minnows in independent schools of 10–15 fish swam immediately behind and slightly beneath the large schools of mimic shiners. He presumed that the bluntnose were attracted by the protection and feeding advantages that a large school of fish could afford. Among aquatic plants, bluntnose minnows were usually found in independent schools of 10–20 fish, which sought out the silty-bottomed openings that were scattered among the beds of aquatic plants.

That the bluntnose minnow has a keen sense of smell, and can discriminate between the odors of aquatic plants, suggests that in nature it can separate odors as it swims about, much as a dog follows a trail amid a distracting host of odors (Walker and Hasler 1949). These authors imply that odor discrimination may guide fish to feeding grounds, and may prevent immature fish from straying from cover. The original work done by Hasler and others with the bluntnose minnow suggested that other natural odors may be responsible for directing migratory fishes (such as salmon) to locate their own homing areas.

At an acclimation temperature of 25°C (77°F), the bluntnose minnow has an upper tolerance limit of 33°C (91.4°F); at an acclimation temperature of 15°C (59°F), it has a lower tolerance limit of 1°C (33.8°F)

(Bardach et al. 1966). Numbers of bluntnose minnows died in a shallow Michigan pond as a result of a 38°C (100.4°F) water temperature (Bailey 1955).

With its wide distribution in most aquatic habitats, the bluntnose minnow comes into contact with most species of Wisconsin fishes. In Spencer Lake (Waupaca County), 922 bluntnose minnows were associated with these species: hornyhead chub (1), creek chub (3), fathead minnow (25), common shiner (118), blacknose shiner (1), mimic shiner (83), yellow perch (2), johnny darter (3), green sunfish (3), and bluegill (8).

IMPORTANCE AND MANAGEMENT

The bluntnose minnow undoubtedly serves as an important forage fish, and is probably taken by black bass, walleyes, northern pike, burbot, and other piscivores. Its eggs are probably eaten by crayfish, minnows (including nonspawning bluntnose males), leeches, and sunfish, especially when the nests have been disturbed by large animals such as man, and wading cattle; the eggs may also be eaten by turtles and snails (Hubbs and Cooper 1936).

In Wisconsin, this minnow is used extensively as bait for bass, perch, crappies, white bass, and other panfishes. It is considered a good bait minnow, for it lives well on the hook, although it succumbs when crowded in small containers, especially during warm weather.

Since the diet of the bluntnose minnow is partly herbivorous, and since its animal food consists chiefly of the smaller organisms, it lends itself to pond culture. In a small pond in Michigan, it has been propagated at the rate of 262,000 fish and 280 kg/ha (104,800 fish and 250 lb/acre). In Ohio, 1,183,000 bluntnose minnows have been raised to a hectare of water (Dobie et al. 1956). Neess (1947) noted that there was an average of about 50 young produced per pair of adults planted in newly dug ponds near Madison (Dane County).

Fathead Minnow

Pimephales promelas Rafinesque. *Pimephales*—fat, head; *promelas*—in front, black.

Other common names: northern fathead minnow, blackhead minnow, Tuffy minnow, fathead.

Male (tuberculate) 85 mm, Tomorrow R. (Portage Co.), 2 July 1958

Female 65 mm, Tomorrow R. (Portage Co.), 2 July 1958

DESCRIPTION

Body short, stout, slightly compressed laterally, often with a fat belly. Average length 51 mm (2 in). TL = 1.22 SL. Depth into TL 3.6–5.0. Head length into TL 4.0–4.9; top of head and back behind head slightly flattened. Snout blunt, extending slightly beyond upper lip. Mouth small, almost terminal, strongly oblique to almost vertical; mouth extending to below anterior nostril; barbel absent. Pharyngeal teeth 4–4; teeth slender, scarcely hooked, with elongate cutting surfaces. Eye into head length 3.3–5.4. Gill rakers short, pointed, flattened (like tip of leaf), 12–14. Dorsal fin origin over, to slightly in advance of, origin of pelvic fin; dorsal fin rays 8 (short ray at front of dorsal fin not tightly bound to first principal ray, as is the case in most minnows); anal fin rays 7; pectoral fin rays 15–16; pelvic fin rays 8. Lateral series scales 43–49; lateral line short, incomplete. Scales on back before dorsal fin, small and crowded. Digestive tract long, 1.4–1.7 TL. Chromosomes 2n = 50 (Gravell and Malsberger 1965).

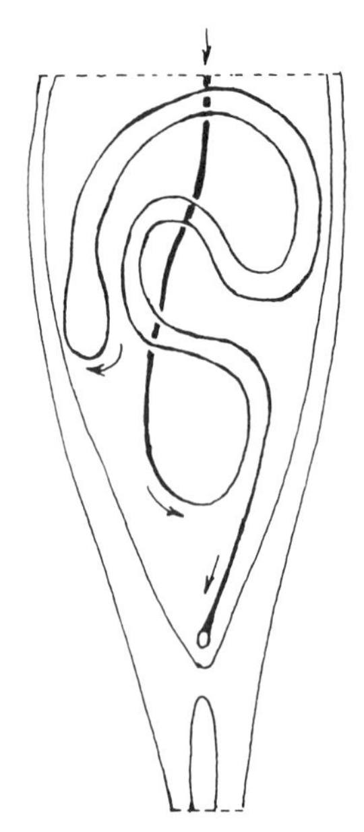

Alimentary tract of the fathead minnow, diagrammatic

Back and sides to lateral stripe dark olive; below lateral stripe, whitish with black peritoneum showing through belly. Lateral stripe, extending from caudal peduncle to head, faint to distinct in young, in nonbreeding adults, and in breeding females; in breeding males stripe is absent, or, if present, diffuse anteriorly. Basicaudal spot small to absent. Males with a black blotch on lower third of first 2 or 3 rays. Scale pockets above lateral stripe distinctly edged in pigment; scale pockets below stripe, only faintly pigmented. Peritoneum black.

Breeding male black on head; rest of body, including fins, dark. Breeding tubercles in 3 main rows on snout, several tubercles on lower jaw, scattered minute tubercles on top of head. Fleshy gray pad of "skin" extending from nape to dorsal fin. Breeding female with distended belly.

Sexual dimorphism: A protruding urogenital structure (ovipositor) evident in female at least 1 month prior to spawning; absent in male (Flickinger 1969).

Hybrids: Fathead minnow × bluntnose minnow (Trautman 1957).

SYSTEMATIC NOTES

The subspecies ascribed to Wisconsin is the northern fathead minnow, *Pimephales promelas promelas* Rafinesque (Hubbs and Lagler 1964). The apparent subspecific differences between the northern (north central United States) and southern (Texas and Oklahoma) forms were examined by Taylor (1954), who found that the characters used for separating the forms are highly variable and not conclusive.

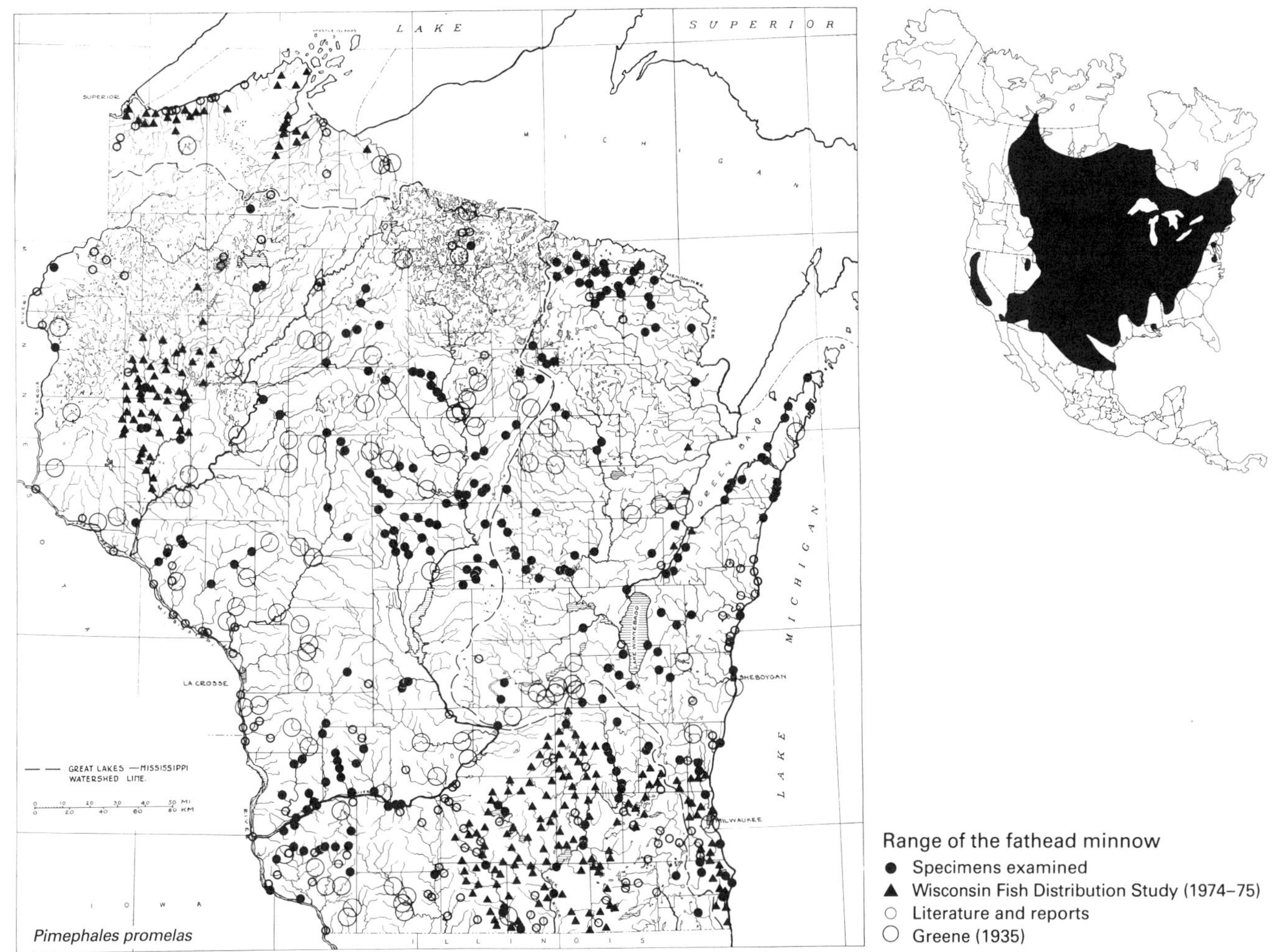

Pimephales promelas

DISTRIBUTION, STATUS, AND HABITAT

In Wisconsin, the fathead minnow occurs in all three drainage basins, where it is widely distributed. In the late 1920s (Greene 1935), its distribution center was clearly in the unglaciated region of the state. Greene attributed this to the fathead's preference for waters which are subject to heavy silting.

In Wisconsin, the fathead minnow is common to abundant, and the status of this species appears secure. Since the 1920s, its incidence has increased, particularly in the southeastern quarter of Wisconsin; the frequency occurrence of no other Wisconsin species has risen as abruptly. Although the fathead minnow is the dominant fish in some isolated sloughs, small shallow ponds, and ditches, it seldom is taken in large numbers.

In northern Wisconsin, the fathead minnow frequents boggy lakes, ponds, and streams; in southern Wisconsin, it frequents small ponds and low-gradient, silty streams and ditches. It was encountered in waters of varying clarity at depths up to 1.5 m over substrates of sand (20% frequency), rubble (19%), gravel (18%), silt (13%), mud (11%), boulders (9%), clay (5%), detritus (3%), bedrock (1%), and marl (1%). It occurred in streams of the following widths: 1.0–3.0 m (28%), 3.1–6.0 m (21%), 6.1–12.0 m (23%), 12.1–24.0 m (19%), 24.1–50.0 m (9%), and more than 50 m (1%). Rooted aquatic plants may or may not be present, but where fathead minnows are abundant much floating and submerged algae is present.

BIOLOGY

In Wisconsin, spawning begins in late May and early June and lasts until the middle of August (Thomsen and Hasler 1944). In the Madison area, the peak occurs in early July. At the Woodruff hatchery, spawning occurred from 28 May to 30 June, and little activity in northern Wisconsin was noted beyond that date (Williamson 1939). According to Markus (1934), the breeding dress of the males appears approximately 30 days before the first eggs are deposited, and these secondary sex characters fade immediately after the close of the spawning period.

It is not clear whether temperature, photoperiod,

or both trigger spawning in fathead minnows (Andrews and Flickinger 1974). Although some minimum temperature requirement is indicated, the large number of first spawnings in May strongly support day length as the major influence initiating spawning activity. Temperature may be more important than photoperiod, however, once the reproductive cycle has started. Spawning begins in the spring when water temperatures reach 15.6°C (60°F), and continues until they drop in the fall to 15.6–18.4°C (60–65.1°F) (Prather 1957b).

In southern Wisconsin ponds, the fathead prefers a spawning substrate of sand to marl or gravel; the last is chosen only when all other spawning areas have been taken over (Thomsen and Hasler 1944). The eggs are generally deposited on the underside of hard surfaces; in Thomsen and Hasler's study, eggs were deposited on boards with one end elevated, and on stones, tiles, and strips of sheet metal. From the 320 nests Thomsen and Hasler observed, about 80% were at a depth of 0.75 m (2.5 ft). Some of the nests were excavated under the board itself, and others were placed approximately 76 mm (3 in) above the bottom of the underside of the board. The majority of nests were at the point of contact between the board and the bottom. Even lily pads and old tires may become nesting sites (McMillan 1972).

The male chooses the nesting site, and if the object selected lies flat on the bottom he digs a cavity under it; depending on the composition of the bottom, he works from 1 to 10 hr. This process has been described by Andrews and Flickinger (1974:763):

> . . . Males cleaned the underside of the object selected for the nest site, using the head tubercles in a scraping action and pulling pieces of algae and associated debris off the nest surface with the mouth. Clearance beneath objects located on the substrate was achieved by creating a depression beneath the object by a sweeping action of the caudal fin.

Investigations by R. J. Smith and Murphy (1974) indicate that the spongy dorsal pad of the fathead male may play an important role in the preparation of the spawning site. Histological examination shows that the pad contains many mucus cells. Mucus secreted by these cells is deposited on the spawning surface during contact movements; it has been suggested that this layer may improve conditions for egg attachment, may serve as a chemical signal marking the breeding site, and may improve egg survival, since mucus is known to increase resistance to disease and parasites in fish. In addition, taste buds in the dorsal pad allow chemosensory sampling of the spawning surface, eggs, and hatching young.

The nest undergoing construction is defended against all fish. Males with prepared nest sites allow some gravid females to approach the site, but drive off males that approach within 50 cm of the nest. A defending male may engage in tail-beating, a process whereby an intruding male is side-swiped with a thrust of the defender's tail. Tail-beating probably serves an intimidatory function, operating through the pressure-sensitive lateral line system of the threatened fish. According to McMillan (1972), males may also engage in snout-butting contests. In every observation, the incumbent male won out regardless of size. One worker noted that males also drove ripe-looking females from the nest, and a great amount of persistence was required by the female before the male accepted her in the vicinity of the nest.

Burrage (1961) described the courting behavior of a captive male and female. Three different activities were noted: sometimes the male simply admitted the female into the nest; at other times the male vigorously chased the female and coerced her into the nest area; or, he entreated the female to enter the nest. In the last type of activity, the male swam from the nest in search of the female and, upon finding her, maneuvered in front of the female, while directly facing her. The male would then cease maneuvering and return to the nest. This he did several times, the female approaching closer to the nest each time, before she finally entered the nest.

McMillan (1972) noted a number of prespawning sessions in which the male and female, generally moving in a circular course, made close lateral contact with each other and vibrated rapidly while portions of their dorsal surfaces touched the roof of the nest. McMillan described the spawning act (p. 75):

> Finally, when a sufficient degree of vibratory stimulation has been reached, the male lifts and presses the female's ventral surface against the object's underside. In doing so, he turns so that he is beneath the female and can use the posterior part of his body to manipulate her upward. The tubercles on his large pectoral fins also help him to grip the female tightly. As the fishes' bodies are taut and strained in this position, the female emits one or perhaps several eggs, and the male probably releases sperm at this instant. Then they abruptly separate, although a new bout of vibrating may begin only seconds later.

The buoyant, adhesive eggs stick to each other and to the undersurface of the nesting object. The eggs are usually deposited at night (Andrews and Flickinger 1974), and after egg deposition has been completed, the male drives the female from the nest.

One female fathead lays from 80 to 370 eggs at a

time, and undoubtedly spawns several times during the summer (Thomsen and Hasler 1944). Markus (1934) observed 36–12,000 eggs per nest. If it is early in the spawning season, the male usually accepts more than one ripe female; and more than one female deposits eggs in the nest cared for by a single male; eggs are sometimes two layers deep over one part of the nest. Consequently, eggs of several different ages may be found in a single egg mass. When the breeding season draws to a close, males abandon nest sites and move to deeper water, seldom rejoining the large schools of mature females (Andrews and Flickinger 1974). Whether one male remains at a nest site for the duration of the spawning season, or whether there is a succession of males at that site, is unknown.

Each nest is guarded by one fathead male, who constantly swims back and forth beneath the eggs, stroking them with his back. His function is threefold: to protect eggs from predators (even females eat the eggs if given the chance), to provide fresh water and remove wastes by agitating the water about eggs, and to keep the eggs free from sediments (Markus 1934). McMillan (1972) observed that while caring for the eggs the male nibbles at the egg mass to remove fungus-infected or otherwise "bad" eggs, which he eats; the rest of the batch is then protected from infection.

According to Dobie et al. (1956), males die 30 days, and females 60 days, after the onset of spawning. In rearing ponds, Markus (1934) found that most age-I fish die after spawning, and that only 15–20% of the population reaches age II.

In Wisconsin, gravid female fathead minnows were collected from Sawyer Bay (Door County) on 5 June 1962. A 65-mm fish with ovaries 16.4% of body weight had 695 orange, mature eggs 1.0 mm diam, and a greater number of immature, yellow eggs 0.3–0.7 mm diam. A 62-mm fish with ovaries 13% of body weight held 1,325 ripening eggs 0.8 mm diam, and an equal number of immature eggs 0.2–0.6 mm diam. In Iowa (Carlson 1967), total egg counts of females from the Skunk River on 5 July 1966 were 802–2,622, of which about one third were ripe. At Fairport (Iowa), Markus (1934) recorded one female depositing eggs on the same male's nest 12 times between 16 May and 23 July; a total of 4,144 offspring were recovered from this pair.

The eggs hatch in 4.5–6 days at 25°C (77°F) (Hasler et al. 1946). Manner et al. (1977) have investigated the ultrastructure of the chorion of the fathead minnow and Niazi (1964) discussed the development of the Weberian system and early embryology. The length of the newly hatched fry is 4.75 mm (Markus 1934). Fish (1932) illustrated and described the 11.6-mm stage. The average length at scale formation is 16.3 mm (Andrews 1970).

After hatching, young fathead minnows remain near the nest until the yolk-sac has been absorbed. Their growth rate is rapid. They may reach adult size during their first summer of life, depending on the amount of food available. At Fairport (Iowa), Marcus reported that male fish hatched on 28 May showed secondary sex characters by 18 July, and females held mature eggs by 24 July. They spawned immediately and their young attained a length of 55 mm before winter, and were sexually mature for the early spawning period the following spring. Young only 25–30 mm at the time winter set in did not spawn early the following spring, but began later in the season. Early-hatched fish may spawn later the same year, even as far north as Iowa and Minnesota (Isaak 1961, Lord 1927).

The rate of growth of the young fathead under normal conditions follows: 20 days—10 mm, 40 days—19 mm, 60 days—29 mm, 80 days—39 mm, 100 days—50 mm, and 120 days—58 mm. In Elk Creek (Buffalo County), young-of-year collected 27 September 1975 were 26–48 mm TL.

In a collection from Meadowbrook Creek (Forest County) taken 28 June, the calculated total lengths at the first and second annuli were 29.5 and 56.3 mm respectively (M. Ebener, pers. comm.). The age-length composition of this collection was: I—50.6 (47–55) mm, and II—64.7 (57–72) mm. In a 5 June collection from Sawyer Bay (Door County), Ebener calculated lengths of 32.6 and 54.4 mm at the annuli; age-length composition was: I—53.8 (45–60) mm, and II—61.4 (52–70) mm. In a 28 September collection from Pigeon Creek (Trempealeau County), all individuals were age I; they were 52–71 mm TL (M. Fero, pers. comm.), and had a calculated total length of 36.8 mm at the first annulus. In all populations male fathead minnows grow more rapidly, and to a larger size, than females. This is characteristic of species of minnows in which the males guard the nest, whereas the female is usually larger where no nest-guarding occurs.

As indicated above, some populations of fathead minnows may mature in the same year they are hatched (age 0). Other instances of such rapid development to maturity are unknown or rare among fishes in the northern part of the United States. In Wisconsin, where the water temperatures are lower than the Fairport (Iowa) Hatchery ponds, most individuals will not mature until at least their second summer of life (age I), and some individuals probably do not mature until their third summer (age II). Age-III fish rarely appear in collections (Carlson 1967, Held and Peterka 1974, Chadwick 1976).

The largest fatheads observed, 90–101 mm TL, were reported from Smithys Lake (Nebraska) (McCarraher and Thomas 1968).

The fathead minnow is an opportunistic feeder. In northern Wisconsin ponds, the stomach contents of fatheads consisted of algae, fragments of higher plants, and mud (Williamson 1939). In southeastern Wisconsin (Cahn 1927), the fathead was observed to be a bottom feeder, grubbing in the soft bottom for insect larvae, which formed over 90% of its diet.

In a Missouri pond (Divine 1968), fathead minnows less than 35 mm long ate a variety of foods, including higher plant materials, filamentous algae, and colonial algae. In another pond, the dominant food item changed each month: filamentous algae (*Spirogyra*, *Mougeotia*) in June, copepods in July, Cladocera in August, and insects in September. All larger fish consumed a greater variety of organisms, including—in addition to those mentioned above—protozoans, rotifers, and insects; insects constituted more than 85% of the diet in August.

The upper limit of the fathead minnow's temperature tolerance (permitting 50% survival) is 33°C (91.4°F); the lower limit is 2°C (35.6°F) (Bardach et al. 1966). Temperature preference, determined experimentally, was 22.6°C (72.7°F) (Jones and Irwin 1962). Brungs (1971) evaluated the chronic effects of constant elevated temperatures on this species: the number of eggs produced per female, the number of eggs per spawning, and the number of spawnings per female were gradually reduced at successively increased temperatures above 23.5°C (74.3°F). No spawning or mortality occurred at 32°C (89.6°F).

The fathead minnow probably exhibits the greatest ecological diversity of all cyprinids occurring in North America. Cross (1967) referred to it as a "pioneer" (p. 151):

> . . . It is one of the first species to invade intermittent drainage channels after rains, and it commonly progresses upstream into farm ponds via their spillways. It is one of the last species to disappear from small, muddy, isolated pools that remain in stream channels during droughts. This species has other attributes of hardiness that enable it to flourish where few other fish survive. It seems unusually tolerant of pollution, in streams having little oxygen as a consequence of sewage influx or barnlot drainage, and in other streams that are saline owing to effluents discharged by the petroleum industry.

The fathead is often found in lakes where most other species succumb to winterkill; it may survive in muskrat burrows at such times (Carlander 1969). It is tolerant of both clear and turbid waters, and of a wide range of pH.

In Little Hemlock Creek (Wood County), 190 fathead minnows were collected with these species: white sucker (75), blacknose dace (28), creek chub (75), pearl dace (6), northern redbelly dace (32), bluntnose minnow (13), common shiner (178), blacknose shiner (12), bigmouth shiner (6), brassy minnow (3), black bullhead (1), central mudminnow (13), blackside darter (1), johnny darter (13), pumpkinseed (3), and brook stickleback (6).

IMPORTANCE AND MANAGEMENT

The fathead minnow is an ideal forage fish, since it is widely distributed, small, and highly prolific, and has a prolonged spawning period, assuring the availability of recently hatched or small fatheads to predators throughout the summer months. All fish-eating birds and fishes associated with it must at one time or another use this minnow as food. Isaak (1961) noted that large leeches and painted turtles prey on the eggs of fathead minnows and destroy many fathead nests. The male's attempts to ward off these predators are futile.

The fathead minnow is unable to maintain itself in streams or lakes which have a heavy population of predacious fish. In Wisconsin, the fathead is least common in streams which support numerous other kinds of fish; where the fathead does occur in such waters, it is generally found to be at depressed population levels. It becomes abundant in streams "peculiar in having emergent vegetation in pools, and a scarcity of other minnows" (Starrett 1950a).

In Wisconsin, the fathead minnow is a major bait fish, available at most bait stations. It is ideal bait for crappies, perch, white and yellow bass, and rock bass; the largest adults are suitable for walleyes, bass, and larger game fish. The fathead is one of the hardiest of fishes, and, if hooked through the lips or the tail, or under the dorsal fin, it will stay alive for a number of hours.

The fathead minnow has been used extensively as a testing animal, and culture units of fathead minnows for this purpose are maintained at research laboratories (Benoit and Carlson 1977). Numerous studies of the effects of toxic substances on the fathead minnow's body tissues, eggs, and fry are reported in the literature.

When St. Louis encephalitis, in epidemic proportions, precipitated serious concern throughout most of Illinois in the summer and fall of 1975, the fathead minnow, the blackstripe topminnow, and the golden shiner were recommended as possible natural controls against its vector, the mosquito (P. W. Smith 1975).

In recent years, the fathead minnow has been used in Minnesota for mosquito control. Eddy and Underhill (1974:249), writing of the program in the St. Paul-Minneapolis area, observed:

> . . . The Metropolitan Mosquito Control District has abandoned insecticides and has stocked these minnows in the sloughs, ponds, and ditches where mosquitoes breed. The minnows have been successful in reducing the populations of larval mosquitoes in these areas to a satisfactory abatement level. Because the shallow depth of many ponds results in frequent winterkills, those ponds will require continued stocking, but the cost will probably be less than that for chemical controls and will eliminate any possible side effects from insecticides. The program provides us with a good example of biological pest control.

In Iowa, Konefes and Bachmann (1970) suggested introducing fathead minnow fry into one or more tertiary holding ponds whose water source is the effluent of a sewage treatment plant. Such effluent waters, after having received primary and secondary treatment (trickling filters), still contain high concentrations of plant nutrients, such as nitrates, ammonia, and phosphorus. Huggins (1969) found that when the effluent water passes through several ponds arranged in a series, the water quality progressively improved; the final pond released into the receiving stream or downstream reservoir a discharge water from which significant amounts of nutrients had been removed and unwanted algal blooms diminished.

Since the chemical elements in the holding ponds are the same as the fertilizers purchased by fish culturists and dispersed by them in their ponds to increase minnow productivity, tertiary ponds inherently save the cost of the fertilizer. If fathead minnows are stocked to holding ponds where they will be able to feed on the algae produced in the nutrient-rich waters, and where they can reproduce and grow to adult size, they will be converting effluent nutrients into minnow flesh. As the fathead minnows are harvested, the organic load within the tertiary ponds will be reduced. Also, the moneys earned from the minnow sale might be used to help offset the costs of construction and maintenance of the tertiary ponds. Konefes and Bachmann observed that the use of such ponds for fathead minnow production seems to be a viable approach toward both environmental preservation and conservation of natural resources.

In Wisconsin, from 45 kg (100 lb) of fathead minnows stocked in a sewage treatment pond in Whitehall (Trempealeau County) over 3,270 kg (7,200 lb) of fatheads were harvested in 3.5 months (A. Oehmcke, pers. comm.). Sewage ponds are currently being used as holding ponds for feeding-out muskellunge fry prior to stocking (see p. 412).

The propagation of the fathead minnow has a rich literature. Details of propagation have been outlined in Hasler et al. (1946), Markus (1934), Dobie et al. (1956), Hedges and Ball (1953), Forney (1957), and Prather (1957b and 1958). In one study (Lord 1927), the production of fatheads was recorded as 505,000 fish at approximately 133 kg/ha (202,000 fish and 119 lb/acre).

Sucker Family—Catostomidae

Nineteen species of suckers in 8 genera are known from Wisconsin. The suckers are a compact group of 12 living genera and about 60 species, essentially North American. In the United States and Canada, 59 species are listed in 11 genera (Robins et al. 1980). Only two representatives are found in eastern Asia—an ancient monotypic genus in China (*Myxocyprinus*), and *Catostomus catostomus*; the latter represents a recent invasion of a species widespread in northern North America.

Fossil remains of suckers have been taken from deposits in British Columbia, Nevada, and Colorado. The earliest reliably dated remains of the family in North America are from the Eocene, and are some 55 million years old (Miller 1959). It is believed that suckers arose in southeastern Asia and soon crossed a Bering land bridge to America, leaving a relict in China.

It is generally held that the suckers are ancestral to (or at least more primitive than) the minnows; however, Eaton (1935), while studying the upper jaw mechanism in the bony fishes, concluded that suckers descended from minnows. The fact is that suckers are closely related to minnows, and frequently appear confusingly minnowlike.

The sucker family is readily distinguished from native minnows by a difference in the distance from the front of the anal fin to the base of the caudal fin. In suckers, this distance is contained more than 2.5 times in the distance from the front of the anal fin to the tip of the snout; in minnows, the anal-caudal distance is contained fewer than 2.5 times in the distance from the anal fin to the snout tip. Old World minnows, such as the carp and the goldfish, resemble suckers in this respect, but may be distinguished from suckers by their hardened spinelike rays at the front of the dorsal and anal fins. In suckers, the pharyngeal teeth are numerous, often comblike, and in a single row on each arch; in minnows, there are fewer than nine teeth per arch, and these may be arranged in one to three rows.

In suckers, barbels are absent. The scales are cycloid. The mouth, usually on the lower portion of the head, is suckerlike; it is protrusible in many species. The lips are fleshy, with many folds or papillae, or both. Parts of the first four vertebrae are highly modified into a device known as the Weberian apparatus—a characteristic shared with minnows and many other freshwater fishes. The flesh of most sucker species is filled with numerous Y-shaped (intermuscular) bones.

The pharyngeal teeth in the suckers are diagnostic in a number of species. Most have thin, comblike teeth; a few have strong, flat-topped, and molarlike teeth. Branson (1962) discusses in detail the structure and function of the pharyngeal teeth. The sucker's food is ground and swallowed by means of elaborate spindloid muscles, which move the pharyngeal arches against a massive dorsal pad.

The pharyngeal pad in many suckers is swollen and thickened ventrally, and it almost fills in the pharyngeal and mouth cavities, leaving only a narrow slit between the gill arches and the pad. In *Carpiodes* and *Ictiobus* only small animal and plant foods are ingestible. Their pharyngeal teeth are small and weak, and the arches accordingly may be paper thin and extremely fragile. Large food organisms with hard parts cannot easily be accommodated by such a system.

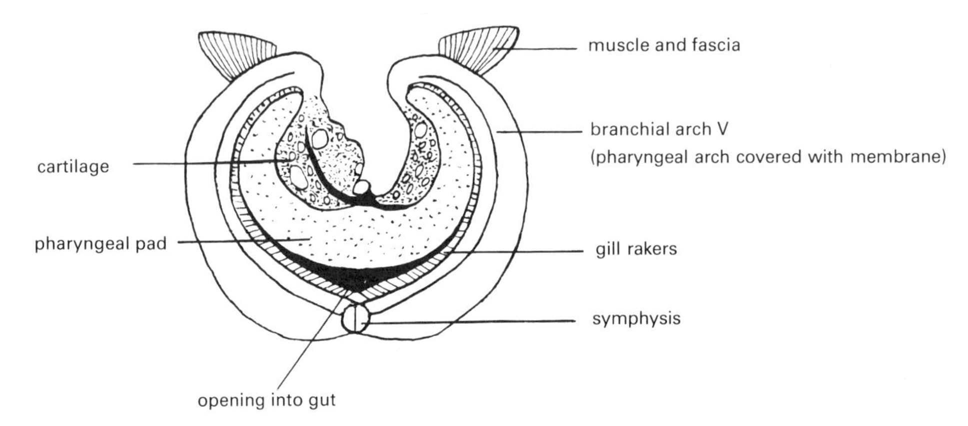

Cross section just anterior to the arches bearing the pharyngeal teeth in the smallmouth buffalo

Suckers play an important role in the early stages of the food chain. They feed largely on aquatic insects and their larvae, and on small mollusks, algae, and minute crustaceans. They are effective vacuum cleaners, taking their food from the bottom muds, rocks, plants, and logs, and from the water itself. They are able to find their food by touch and taste as well as by sight. Such versatility may be responsible for their large numbers. In many Wisconsin waters, the total weight of the suckers surpasses the total weight of all the other fishes combined. Their value as a forage fish is well known, and suckers have been stocked in some waters as a food source for large sport fish.

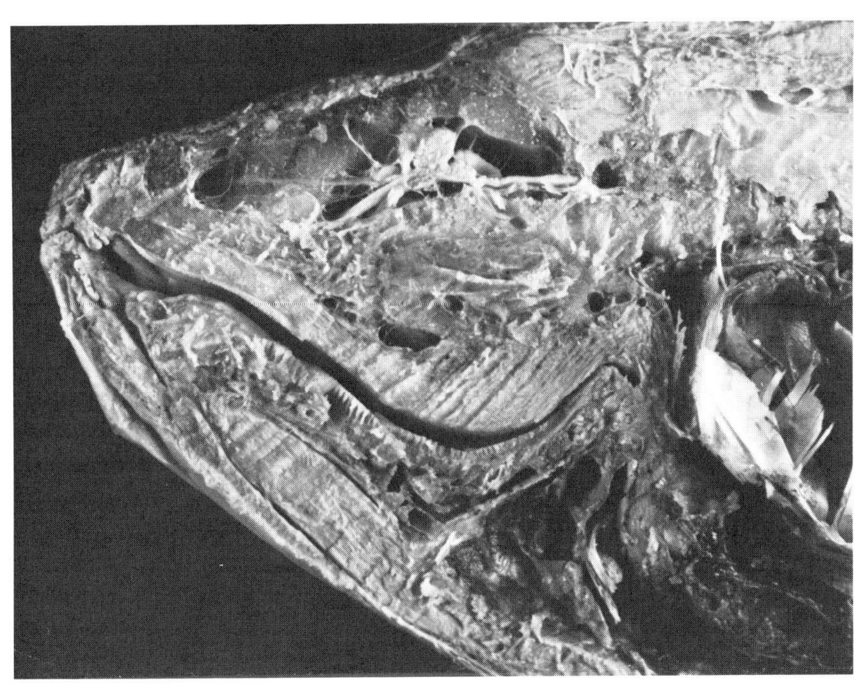

Midsagittal section through the head of the bigmouth buffalo, showing the small mouth and pharyngeal cavities

Although suckers have been harvested by commercial fishermen in all Wisconsin drainages for many years, the small amounts they receive in price hardly pay the cost of handling. In the Wisconsin waters of Lake Michigan, sucker production in 1974 was 141,400 kg, which was valued at $8,787 (Wis. Dep. Nat. Resour. 1976c); the waters of Green Bay with 85% of the harvest are the principal areas of production, and most suckers are taken incidentally to perch, whitefish, and alewives. In Lake Superior, the commercial catch for 1974 was 24,000 kg, and in the Mississippi River it was 21,300 kg.

The catches noted above reflect the poor market conditions for suckers. Potentially, suckers could provide substantially more commercial production than the figures reported, since sucker populations are at high levels, with strong spawning runs and consistent year class strength. It has been estimated that 1.4–1.8 million kilograms of suckers could be taken annually from the American side of the Great Lakes. In Wisconsin, thousands of kilograms could be harvested yearly from many of our inland lakes and streams without harming the seed stock.

In Wisconsin consideration should be given to elevating the suckers to the level of sport fishes. Large suckers are spectacular fighters when hooked, and on the table they pose excellent fare. They are a notable resource which has been unjustly overshadowed by sport fish, some of which are inferior in fighting and eating qualities.

Unfortunately, the sucker's image as a "trash fish" and "rough fish" has not been corrected by our public agencies, and the public persists in the view that suckers are valueless, tasteless, nuisance fish. The fact is that, as fish flesh goes, suckers are among the largest and tastiest of fishes. They have other desirable qualities: they are low in cholesterol, high in protein, and can be refrigerated for long periods without much deterioration in quality. Suckers, in fact, represent a valuable food resource whose day in the sun is yet to be seen. Recipes for cooking suckers are given in *A Fine Kettle of Fish* (Hacker 1977).

Sucker distribution in Wisconsin is generally healthy, but the story in neighboring states is not as favorable. The growth of industrialization in the Great Lakes states, the increase in atomic energy and fossil fuel plants, the proliferation of irrigation projects and high-intensity farming, and the expansion of towns and cities, with their increasing amounts of sewage effluents and automotive wastes, have all contributed to a shrinkage of the sucker's range. Some suckers are delicately balanced in ecosystems which are being seriously altered, and accounts of massive fishkills frequently list "suckers and redhorse" as victims. Ultimately, the result may be the decimation, extirpation, and extinction of sucker species.

Two sucker species, the black redhorse and the creek chubsucker, were eliminated early in this century from their known ranges in southern Wisconsin. Efforts should be made to ensure the continued health of the remaining 17 species.

Blue Sucker

Cycleptus elongatus (Lesueur). *Cycleptus*—circle, slender (meaning "small round mouth," according to Rafinesque); *elongatus*—elongate.

Other common names: Missouri sucker, razorback, slenderheaded sucker, gourdseed sucker, blackhorse, bluefish, sweet sucker, suckerel, "muskellunge" in the lower Wabash River in Indiana.

Adult female 601 mm, Wisconsin R. (Sauk Co.), 25 May 1977

DESCRIPTION

Body elongate, oval in cross section. Average length 610 mm (24 in). TL = 1.24 SL. Depth into SL 4.0–4.4. Head into SL 5.0–5.4. Snout pointed, slightly bulbous at tip, projecting far anterior to upper lip. Mouth small, lips heavily papillose. Pharyngeal teeth 34–40 per arch, large medial teeth widely spaced; arch moderately stout, symphysis short. For comparative osteology of the skull and appendages, see Branson (1962). Dorsal fin long, sickle-shaped, with 28–33 rays; dorsal fin base into SL 2.5–3.0. Anal fin rays 7 (8); pelvic fin rays 9. Lateral line scales 53–58; lateral line complete. Chromosomes 2n = 96–100 (Uyeno and Smith 1972).

Back and sides blue to blue-black; belly whitish. Fins dusky to black.

Breeding males almost black; minute tubercles over most of the head, on scales, and on rays of all fins, persisting long after spawning. Breeding female tan to light blue.

Tuberculate male 591 mm, Chippewa R. (Dunn Co.), 17 May 1977

SYSTEMATIC NOTES

The genus *Cycleptus* contains only one species, which is restricted in its range to the Mississippi Valley and the Southwest into Mexico. It is in the subfamily Cycleptinae, along with the Asiatic genus *Myxocyprinus* (also with only one species).

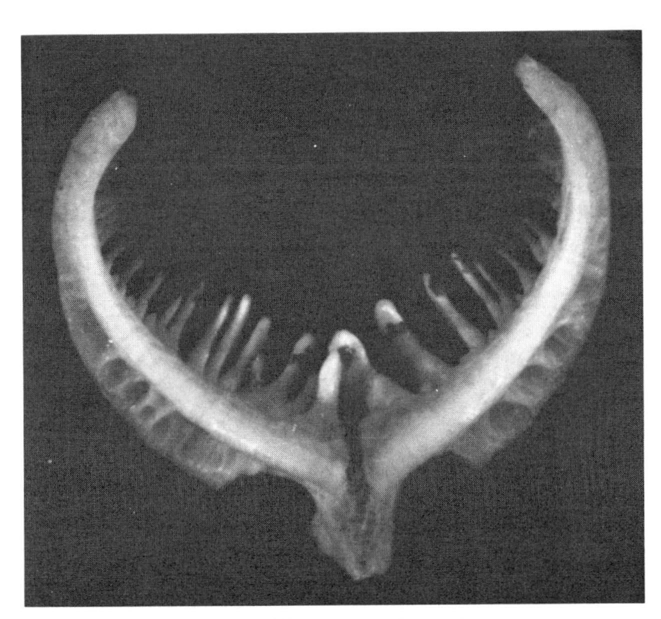

Pharyngeal arches of the blue sucker, front view

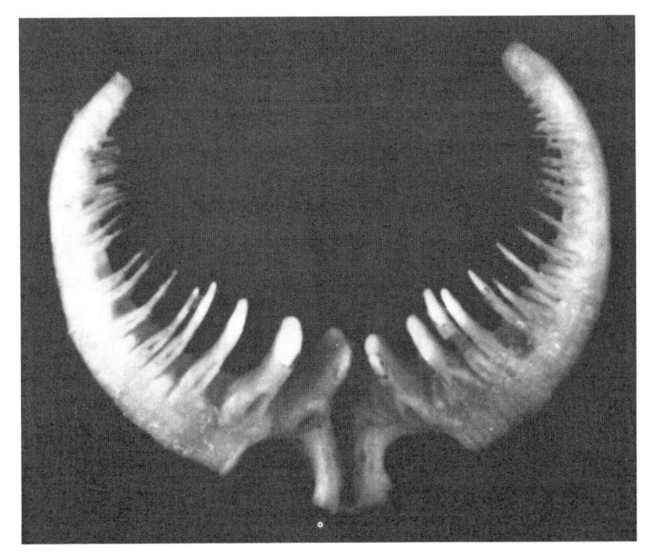

Pharyngeal arches of the blue sucker, back view

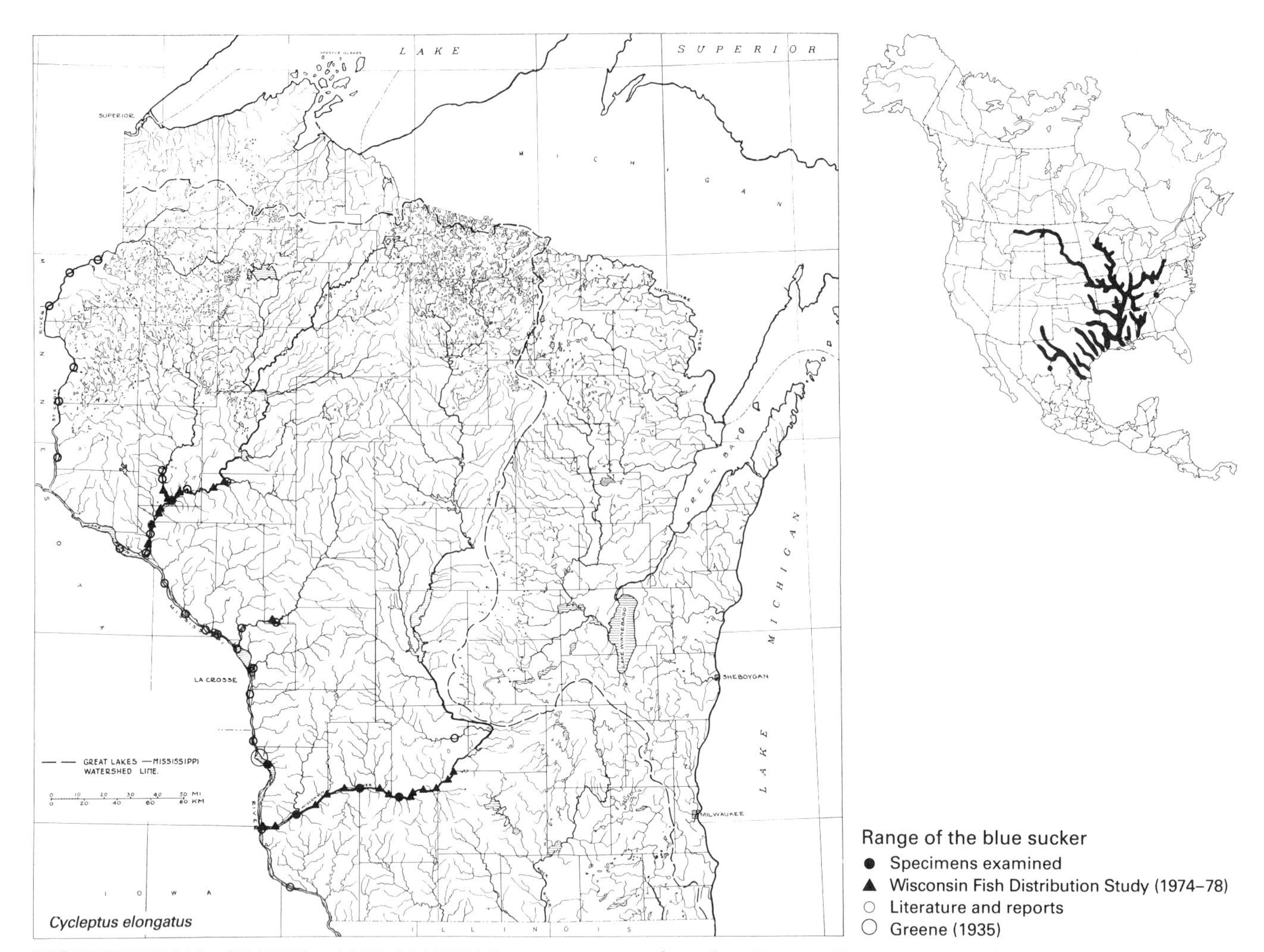

DISTRIBUTION, STATUS, AND HABITAT

In Wisconsin the blue sucker occurs only in the Mississippi drainage basin, frequenting the Mississippi River and the lower portions of the St. Croix, Red Cedar, Chippewa, Black, La Crosse, and Wisconsin rivers. Its distribution in these tributaries is generally to the first barrier dams, except in the St. Croix, where it appears in small numbers above the St. Croix Falls Dam (Kuehn et al. 1961). The Baraboo River (Sauk County) record (Hoy 1883) was listed without a specific location; it is doubtful that this species exists above the Prairie du Sac Dam today. For detailed distribution notes, see Christenson (1974).

Specimens examined: UWSP 107 (1) Wisconsin River 1.2 km east of Muscoda (Iowa County), 1962; UWSP 794 and 815 (3) Wisconsin River between Spring Green and Lone Rock (Sauk and Richland counties), 1962; UWSP 3982 (1) Mississippi River off Ferryville (Crawford County), 1971; UWSP 5585 (1) Chippewa River T25N R13W Sec 9 (Pepin County), 1977; UWSP 5615 (2) Wisconsin River T8N R4E Sec 30 (Sauk County), 1977; and CD Rice Div. of NUS Ohio Corp., Pittsburgh, Pa., collection (1) Chippewa River T26N R12W Secs 29 and 30 (Dunn County), 1973.

Specimens reported by Marlin Johnson from the Wisconsin River below Prairie du Sac Dam (Sauk County), 1970; 36 collections reported by the Wisconsin Fish Distribution Study, from the Wisconsin, Black, Red Cedar, and Chippewa rivers, 1975–1977; reported by P. W. Smith et al. (1971) and Rasmussen (1979) from the Mississippi River, Pools 4–11, mostly 1964 or earlier.

The blue sucker appears to be rare over much of the northern and central parts of its general range. Recent surveys on the upper Mississippi River demonstrate this (Barnickol & Starrett 1951, Kuehn et al. 1961, P. W. Smith 1965, P. W. Smith et al. 1971). Its status is rare in Kansas (Platt et al. 1973), Minnesota (Phillips and Underhill 1971, J. B. Moyle 1975), Iowa (Harlan and Speaker 1956), and Missouri (Pflieger 1975). It is sporadic in Illinois (P. W. Smith 1965). The state of Wisconsin has given the blue sucker threatened status (Wis. Dep. Nat. Resour. Endangered Species Com. 1975, Les 1979).

At the turn of the century the blue sucker was a common inhabitant of the Mississippi River and its major tributaries. Coker (1930), in reference to the blue suckers in the upper Mississippi River, wrote (pp. 182–183):

> . . . we have . . . the oral reports of fisherman [*sic*] at many points on the Mississippi, as far north as Wisconsin, that until 10 or 15 years ago there were important spring runs and lesser fall runs of blue suckers . . . it was the habit of the blue sucker to assemble in considerable numbers only for brief seasons and in the swiftest waters of the river, where, in the absence of effective protective legislation, it was comparatively easy to take them; while in other seasons they had retired to places unknown, probably the deeper parts of the river, from which they were taken only occasionally. The fish could, therefore, be known to commercial fishermen as abundant while regarded by scientific collectors as rare, unless by chance the collections happened to be made at the right season and in the right place.

Reasons for the blue sucker's decimation include the construction of dams. Coker has presented evidence that the reduction of blue sucker numbers in the upper Mississippi River followed the construction of the dam at Keokuk, Iowa. The dam probably interfered with the spawning migrations of these fish, and possibly inundated former important spawning areas. The dams on the middle and upper Mississippi River have virtually eliminated riffle areas which may have been blue sucker spawning sites.

Christenson (1974) noted during the early 1970s that the level of abundance of blue suckers in the lower Chippewa and Red Cedar rivers (Dunn and Pepin counties) was well above that reported for other waters throughout its range:

> . . . Those areas may well represent the northernmost bastion of this species if not the last outpost throughout much of its range. If so, Wisconsin has a custodial responsibility for this species which extends well beyond its borders (p. 4).

Blue suckers characteristically inhabit large, deep rivers, and the deeper zones of reservoirs. In rivers, they occupy narrow chutes where the channel has been constricted, and where the current is moderate to swift. Juveniles occupy the broader, less turbulent riffles. The preferred bottom is gravel or rubble.

BIOLOGY

Little is known of the breeding habits of the blue sucker. The literature indicates that an upstream spawning migration into riffle areas takes place; some of these areas have a heavy current. Spawning occurs from late April to early May, at temperatures of 10–15.6°C (50–60°F) (Harlan and Speaker 1956, Cross 1967). In the Mississippi River, eggs are deposited in May and June (Coker 1930).

Blue suckers in postspawning condition were reported on 17–19 May 1977 from the Chippewa River between the Eau Claire Dam and Durand (D. Becker, pers. comm.). Some 50–60 individuals were taken while boom shocking or seining over hard gravel and rubble in water 0.9–1.5 m (3–5 ft) deep with a swift current of 0.3–0.6 m (1–2 ft)/sec. Some males were still tuberculate, but none produced milt. One female extruded eggs when handled.

Two young-of-year blue suckers, 25 and 26 mm TL, were collected from the Wisconsin River near the Iowa-Dane county line on 24 May 1977. A single young-of-year, 34 mm TL, was seined from the Wisconsin River near Muscoda (Iowa County) on 20 June 1962 (UWSP 107). The site was a broad sheet of slow-moving water less than 0.3 m (1 ft) deep over a large sand flat.

Blue suckers 545, 555, and 737 mm TL from the lower Wisconsin River, collected 4 August 1966, showed the following growth at the annuli: 1—73 mm, 2—193 mm, 3—370 mm, 4—519 mm, 5—572 mm, 6—691 mm, and 7—722 mm. The two smaller suckers were 5 years old, and the largest was 7.

Twelve blue suckers, collected from the Red Cedar River (Dunn County) on 8–9 July 1975, were 4–11 years old and ranged in size from 582 to 750 mm (TL). The calculated lengths at the annuli were: 1—89 mm, 2—226 mm, 3—377 mm, 4—487 mm, 5—537 mm, 6—575 mm, 7—611 mm, 8—641 mm, 9—666 mm, 10—689 mm, and 11—727 mm.

The differences in the growth rates between blue sucker populations in southern and northern Wisconsin are considerable. Initial growth appears to be much more rapid in the Red Cedar River population, but between ages III and IV the Wisconsin River fish exhibit a faster growth rate.

The condition (K_{TL}) values of 15 blue suckers collected 8–9 July 1975 from the Red Cedar River averaged 0.92 (0.57–1.29). Using the length-weight relationships given in Table 3 (Christenson 1974), the condition values for the Chippewa River suckers averaged 0.78; for the Red Cedar River suckers, 0.88.

Christenson noted that Red Cedar River specimens are appreciably heavier than those from the Chippewa River. This difference is best illustrated in the 635–658-mm (25.0–25.9 in) size interval, in which nine Chippewa River specimens and six Red Cedar

River fish averaged 2.09 and 2.50 kg (4.6 and 5.5 lb) respectively. According to Christenson (1974:3):

> . . . This weight differential suggests that the habitat in the Red Cedar River may be more favorable. In that regard, it should be noted that a shifting sand bottom with, by implication, limited bottom fauna production, is characteristic of the lower Chippewa River but not of the lower Red Cedar River.

In the combined collections of 181 specimens for which Christenson recorded lengths, total lengths ranged from 457 to 759 mm (18.0 to 29.9 in).

According to commercial fishermen, blue suckers weighing up to 9.07 kg (20 lb) were common at one time in the Missouri River (Pflieger 1975). In Ohio (Trautman 1957), rivermen have reported maximum lengths of 914–1,016 mm (36–40 in), and weights of 5.44–6.80 kg (12–15 lb). A 750-mm (29.5-in) blue sucker from the Red Cedar River (Dunn County) weighed 4.6 kg (10 lb 2 oz).

The food of the blue sucker consists largely of insects and their larvae, crustaceans, and plant materials, including algae (Harlan and Speaker 1956, Koster 1957).

The blue sucker is a gregarious fish which lives in the deeper water of river channels, except during the spawning migration. In the lower Wisconsin River between Spring Green (Sauk County) and Lone Rock, I boom-shocked nine fish from deepwater channels with strong currents, which were adjacent to islands with badly eroded banks.

One young adult (age IV) was seined in October 1971 from an atypical habitat—a mud-bottomed slough (Crawford County) of the Mississippi River. Lotus and arrowhead were present.

In the lower Wisconsin River, 9 blue suckers were associated with these species: shovelnose sturgeon (1), mooneye (1), quillback (1), river carpsucker (20), highfin carpsucker (3), smallmouth buffalo (1), black buffalo (1), shorthead redhorse (20), golden redhorse (4), northern hog sucker (2), common carp (15), silver chub (6), speckled chub (2), bluntnose minnow (2), bullhead minnow (17), emerald shiner (199), spotfin shiner (92), spottail shiner (1), Mississippi silvery minnow (1), channel catfish (1), white bass (1), yellow perch (1), sauger (14), walleye (10), river darter (1), slenderhead darter (1), logperch (8), smallmouth bass (7), black crappie (1), and freshwater drum (3).

IMPORTANCE AND MANAGEMENT

Predators on the blue sucker are not known. It is likely, however, that fish-eating birds may prey to a limited extent on newly hatched young which occasionally frequent shallow water.

According to Coker (1930), blue suckers may be caught in the Mississippi River on set lines, in fyke nets, in seines, or in floating trammel nets drifted over the rapids at night. Catches of 363–408 kg (800–900 lb) in a single night have been reported in the past, but blue suckers are now rarely taken.

The flesh of the blue sucker is firm, flaky, and well flavored. The blue sucker is well known, highly valued as a food fish, and preferred to any other sucker as a food source.

Bigmouth Buffalo

Ictiobus cyprinellus (Valenciennes). *Ictiobus*—fish, bull; *cyprinellus*—little carp.

Other common names: redmouth buffalo, common buffalofish, gourdseed buffalo, roundhead buffalo, bullhead buffalo, stubnose buffalo, brown buffalo, bullmouth buffalo, bullnose buffalo, slough buffalo, trumpet buffalo, chubnose buffalo, mud buffalo, white buffalo, lake buffalo, blue buffalo, gourdhead buffalo, pugnose buffalo.

Immature 294 mm, Wisconsin R., near Portage (Columbia Co.), 13 Feb. 1976

DESCRIPTION

Body robust, somewhat compressed, back not prominently arched or ridgelike (as in the smallmouth buffalo); ventral line curved up anteriorly. Average length 394 mm (15.5 in). TL = 1.26 SL. Depth into SL 2.4–2.9 (3.3). Head into SL 2.6–3.6. Snout bluntly rounded, often with a slight depression before the eyes, giving it a turned-up appearance. Mouth terminal, large, wide, and oblique; tip of upper lip on a level with lower margin of eye; lips thin and nearly smooth, lower lip finely striated. Pharyngeal teeth short and fragile, about 165 per arch; crown of tooth with a small, pointed cusp at anterior edge; arch paper-thin and ribbonlike; symphysis much elongated. Subopercle broadest at middle. Dorsal fin sickle shaped; longest anterior rays into length of base 1.5–2.0; dorsal fin rays 24–32, dorsal fin base into SL 2.5–2.9. Anal fin rays 8–10, pelvic fin rays 10–11. Lateral line scales 34–39; lateral line complete. Digestive tract much elongated, with loops running parallel to body axis.

Back olive brown to bronze; sides and belly lighter. Fins with light brown to dusky pigment; caudal fin almost black at spawning.

Hybrids: Bigmouth buffalo × smallmouth buffalo (Trautman 1957). Artificial bigmouth buffalo × smallmouth buffalo, and bigmouth buffalo × black buffalo (Stevenson 1964).

DISTRIBUTION, STATUS, AND HABITAT

In Wisconsin, the bigmouth buffalo occurs in the Mississippi River drainage basin, and probably in the Lake Michigan basin. It is widely distributed in the Mississippi River and its large tributaries, and is most widely distributed in the Rock River system of southern Wisconsin.

A bigmouth buffalo, caught in the mid-1960s from Big Lake (Vilas County) and mounted and on display in a service station in Boulder Junction, weighed 27.2 kg (60 lb). It represents an individual from a disjunct population far removed from any other natural Wis-

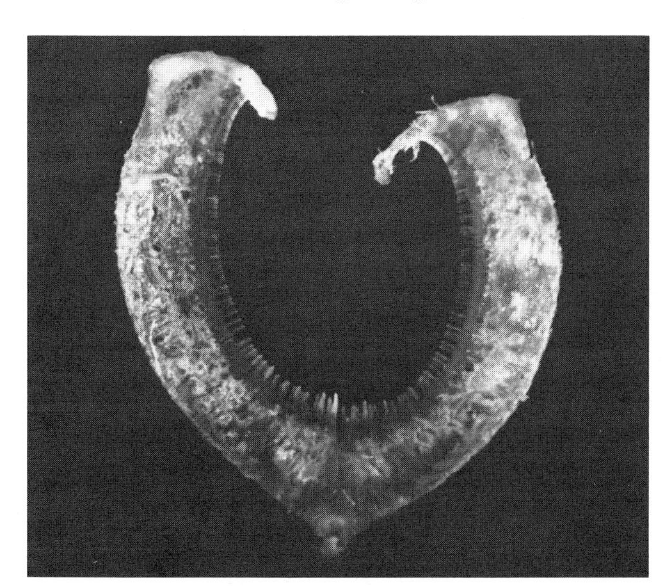

Pharyngeal arches of the bigmouth buffalo, front view

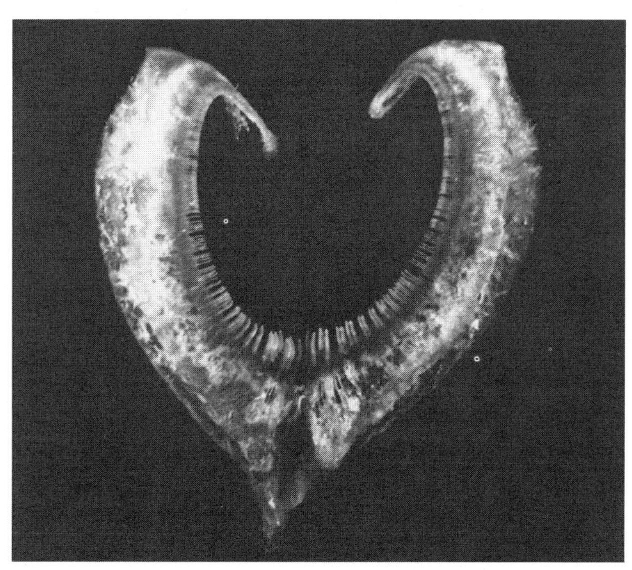

Pharyngeal arches of the bigmouth buffalo, back view

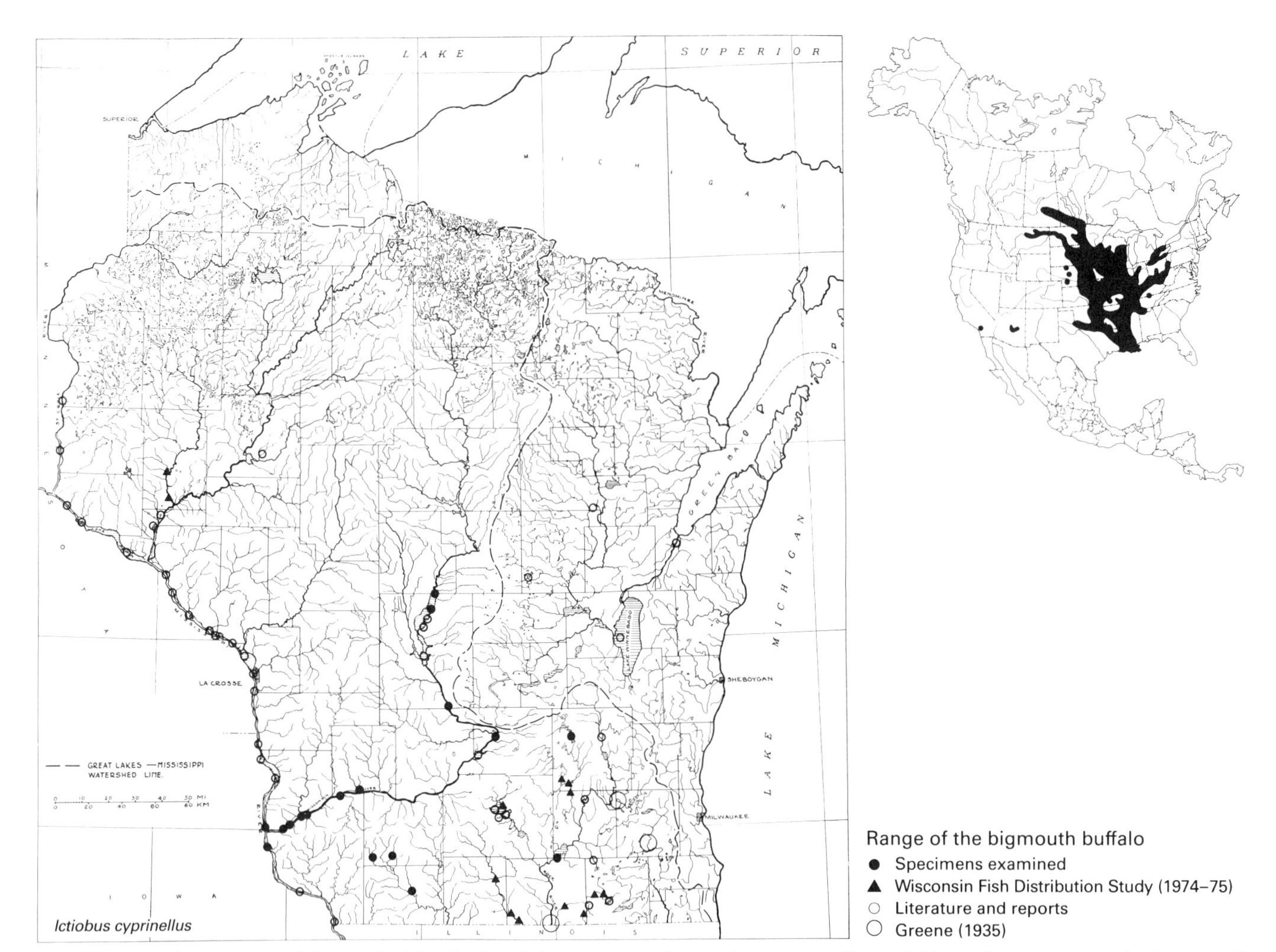

Range of the bigmouth buffalo
● Specimens examined
▲ Wisconsin Fish Distribution Study (1974–75)
○ Literature and reports
◯ Greene (1935)

consin populations, and is probably derived from a fish rescue and transfer operation.

Despite a number of reports from the Lake Michigan drainage basin, no specimen of the bigmouth buffalo from those waters is available for verification. These reports are from Lake Winnebago (Winnebago, Calumet, and Fond du Lac counties) (Priegel 1967a, Becker 1964b, and Miller 1971), the lower Fox River (Brown County) (Kernen 1974), Round and Pine lakes (Shawano County) (Andrews and Threinen 1968), and Long Lake (Waupaca County). The Long Lake record is based on photographs supplied by V. Hacker of a 1.09-m, 21.8-kg (42.8-in, 48-lb) fish; experts agree that it is *Ictiobus*, but the identification to species is not conclusive.

The bigmouth buffalo is uncommon to common in medium-sized to large rivers in slow, sluggish, or still water; it frequents oxbow and flood plain lakes, sloughs, bayous, and shallow lakes. It is essentially a big-water fish, although in the southern third of the state it occurs occasionally in streams only 6–12 m (20–40 ft) wide. It was encountered most frequently in water more than 1.5 m deep over substrates of mud (27% frequency), silt (18%), sand (18%), gravel (18%), clay (9%), and rubble (9%).

BIOLOGY

In Wisconsin, spawning occurs in late April and May. The following account of bigmouth buffalo spawning requirements and behavior is taken largely from the notes of H. E. Neuenschwander, who for 40 years has observed the spawning of this species in the Rock River (Dodge County) marshes.

No nest site is prepared by the parent fish. Clear, clean water, free of heavy sedge, cattail growth, matted bluejoint, and canary grass, is preferred by the bigmouth. Favored are flooded marshes which were cut for hay or burned over during the previous year, leaving a mat of green grass 15–20 cm (6–8 in) high in water 0.3–0.9 m (1–3 ft) deep.

The first bigmouth buffaloes enter marshes or flooded river bottoms as stragglers when water temperatures rise suddenly during an early "heat wave," which may occur as early as 10 April. Spawning may follow a succession of warm, calm nights, during which the marsh temperature seldom drops below 12.8°C (55°F), and daytime water temperatures of 15.6–23.9°C (60–75°F) prevail. Spawning occurs at 12.2–25°C (54–77°F), but most often at 15.6–18.3°C (60–65°F).

From 3 to 30 spawning units of three to five fish per unit may spawn in a single suitable area at one time. A spawning unit consists of a female and two to four males; together they engage in a series of continuous rushes, in which each rush may be 4.6–6.0 m (15–20 ft) or more long. The dark tails of the large females frequently break water during spawning. Females also create big, rushing wakes or swirls at the surface of the water, make loud, splashing turns, and often throw water into the air with their large tails. This activity can be heard 0.4 km (¼ mi.) or more away.

Coker (1930), in describing spawning on the Mississippi River, reported that the female is at the center of the spawning unit. When she sinks to the bottom to deposit her eggs, the males crowd around and under her, pushing her to the top of the water until their tails and fins are out. They then make a tremendous rush, causing the water to foam. The natives called this activity "tumbling."

Neuenschwander noted that in the Rock River marshes spawning occurs at all hours of the day and night, and will even occur on very windy days and during light rain. It may be interrupted for a few hours when clouds darken the sky and water temperatures drop, but it resumes again when warm sunshine returns. The spawning period is relatively short, and the stay on the flooded marsh may be for only 1 day, rarely for 3. Within a few hours after spawning, the spent fish leave the marshes and return 0.8–1.6 km (0.5–1.0 mi) to the main stream channel from which they had come. If spring flood waters are of short duration and the weather is cold, spawning may occur over a sand and gravel bottom in the main river.

In Beaver Dam Lake (Dodge County), before its eradication by toxicants, the bigmouth buffalo spawned over sand and gravel bars. In South Dakota, Walburg (1976) noted that in some years, when suitable spawning habitats are not available, the bigmouth buffalo does not spawn at all.

Egg production is a function of female size: a 4.54-kg (10-lb) female bigmouth buffalo holds 400,000 eggs (Harlan and Speaker 1956); a 6.53-kg (14.4-lb) fish holds an estimated 750,000 eggs (R. P. Johnson 1963). The eggs average 1.5 (1.2–1.8) mm diam. They are released into the water, and adhere to any object they contact. Hatching is adversely affected by turbidities in excess of 100 ppm, or by marked fluctuations in the water level (Walburg and Nelson 1966).

The eggs are left unattended until they hatch. From 8 to 14 days are required for incubation, depending upon the temperature of the water (Harlan and Speaker 1956). At about 17°C (62°F), hatching occurs in 9–10 days (Eddy and Surber 1947).

Young bigmouth buffaloes tend to gather in shallow bays. In South Dakota, they fed primarily on benthic organisms, including tendipedid pupae and larvae (63% volume), benthic cladocerans (12%), copepods (22%); and *Daphnia* (3%) (Starostka and Applegate 1970). Food habits of the young were similar in Saskatchewan, with the addition of diatoms (R. P. Johnson 1963).

In Wisconsin, growth of young-of-year bigmouth buffaloes has been reported as follows:

Date	No. of Fish	TL (mm)		Location
		Avg	Range	
20 June	1	20		Blue R. (Grant Co.)
26 June	52	54	41–66	Wisconsin R. (Juneau Co.)
10 July	2	59	53–65	Mississippi R. (Grant Co.)
13 July	4	51	44–59	Wisconsin R. (Grant Co.)
13 July	2	78	71–84	Wisconsin R. (Grant Co.)

Scales had not yet formed in the specimen taken on 20 June, but all other young were fully scaled.

The growth of the bigmouth buffalo in Wisconsin is rapid. Eleven specimens from Pool 8 of the Mississippi River (in the vicinity of La Crosse County) were: age 0—63 (49–125) mm; IV—427 (404–449) mm; V—526 mm; and VI—556 (549–567) mm (Bur 1976). The condition values (K_{TL}) of the adults averaged 1.74.

Bigmouth buffaloes 305–415 mm TL, taken from Lake Koshkonong (Rock County) on 8 September 1968, were all age III, and averaged the following lengths at the annuli: 1—124 mm, 2—247 mm, and 3—301 mm (S. Lybeck, pers. comm.).

The calculated total lengths at the end of each year of growth for 1,130 buffaloes, mostly from the Rock River drainage basin, were: 1—146 mm, 2—297 mm, 3—393 mm, 4—474 mm, 5—537 mm, 6—591 mm, and 7—593 mm (Frey and Pedracine 1938). These data pertain essentially to the bigmouth buffalo, but since the fish analyzed included 141 specimens from the Wisconsin River, it is possible that some smallmouth and black buffaloes were included in these figures. The authors noted that the growth rates of buffaloes from the Wisconsin River were similar to those of buffaloes from Lake Koshkonong, the Crawfish River, and the Rock River.

Age and Growth of the Bigmouth Buffalo Taken 21 July 1976 from the Wisconsin R. (Juneau Co.)[a]

Age Class	No. of Fish	TL (mm)		Calculated TL at Annulus (mm)											
		Avg	Range	1	2	3	4	5	6	7	8	9	10	11	12
IX	1	600		105	190	300	360	415	475	520	555	585			
X	6	676	641–696	124	240	311	360	422	481	529	583	632	666		
XI	5	779	723–825	129	241	312	372	441	501	561	622	672	722	763	
XII	4	862	842–898	151	311	406	463	523	566	617	664	712	756	805	845
Avg (weighted)				131	255	335	393	453	508	561	614	662	709	782	845

[a]R. Jackson (pers. comm.)

The age of the bigmouth buffalo at maturity varies from age I in southern U.S. latitudes (Swingle 1957b) to age X and older in southern Canada (R. P. Johnson 1963). At the Fort Randall Reservoir in South Dakota, 90% of the males and 95% of the females were mature at age III (Walburg and Nelson 1966); these fish averaged 375 mm TL and 815 g. In Saskatchewan, growth of the bigmouth is slow, and fish reach 20 years of age (R. P. Johnson 1963).

Ordinarily, the bigmouth buffalo is the largest fish of the genus—the giants of the species attain a weight of 34.02 kg (75 lb) (Carson 1943). The maximum size known is a fish of over 36.3 kg (80 lb) from Spirit Lake, Iowa (Harlan and Speaker 1956).

The bigmouth buffalo has a short food chain and it is in direct competition with the carp, river carpsucker, and smallmouth buffalo for available plankton and bottom fauna (Walburg and Nelson 1966). The most important food organisms for the bigmouth are copepods and cladocerans (McComish 1967, Cross 1967). Phytoplankton is of minor importance and is probably eaten only incidentally, although in one study (Starostka and Applegate 1970), blue-green algae were seasonally important. In Canada, R. P. Johnson (1963) reported aquatic beetles, aquatic bugs, mollusks, and amphipods in the bigmouth buffalo's diet, plant material, mainly diatoms, was present in negligible quantities. Harlan and Speaker (1956) noted such unusual items of food in stomachs as small fish and fish eggs, seeds from both aquatic and terrestrial plants, and, in the spring, the "cotton" from cottonwood trees.

Johnson described feeding behavior which he called "skipping." The fish were observed swimming, both forward and backward; at an angle of about 55° to the bottom. When they touched the bottom, swirls of muddy water were raised as they searched for food through the mud and debris.

A midsagittal section through the head of the bigmouth buffalo shows the very small mouth and pharyngeal cavities required for handling minute particles of food (see the illustration on p. 609).

The bigmouth buffalo is able to endure low oxygen tensions and high water temperatures. No deaths occurred among bigmouths subjected to a test concentration in which oxygen was reduced to 0.9 ppm (Gould and Irwin 1962). The maximum temperature at which this species was captured in the White River and the Ipalco Discharge Canal, Indiana, was 31.7°C (89°F) (Proffitt and Benda 1971).

The bigmouth buffalo has a pronounced tendency to school—a behavior pattern which occurs throughout the summer (R. P. Johnson 1963). It is partly pelagic in habit, differing in this respect from other deep-bodied suckers (*Ictiobus* and *Carpiodes*), all of which are essentially bottom dwellers (Cross 1967). R. P. Johnson (1963:1425) observed:

> On warm still days buffaloes spread out over the entire surface of the lakes where they rest quietly, often in the midst of a dense algal bloom. The upper 2 ft of water is preferred for this "loafing." Often the dorsal fin projects above the water. Representative dates and surface water temperatures in Echo Lake in 1955 when this occurred were: July 26, 22.0°C; August 22, 20.4°C; September 2, 20.0°C. This behavior was never observed on windy days, for when the water was choppy the buffaloes congregated in protected bays in somewhat deeper water.

The bigmouth buffalo prefers shallow waters. In South Dakota, Walburg and Nelson (1966) collected 65% of their fish from water less than 1.2 m (4 ft) deep; the rest were taken at depths of 2.4–3.1 m (8–10 ft).

Bigmouth buffaloes may make upstream runs to dams in the spring, and also in September or October if high flood waters are present (H. E. Neuenschwander, pers. comm.). In South Dakota's Lake Oahe, the movement of marked fish was extensive (Moen 1974): 44% were recaptured downstream from the point of release, and 38% were retaken upstream. Females showed a stronger tendency to move downstream than males. The maximum distance traveled was 379 km (235 mi), and the maximum rate of travel was 6.5 km (4 mi) per day.

During late January 1976, 38 bigmouth buffalo were netted from Lake Wisconsin (Columbia County) along with black buffalo (5), smallmouth buffalo (60), common carp (100), white bass (2), freshwater drum (24), lake sturgeon (70), and silver redhorse (1).

IMPORTANCE AND MANAGEMENT

Predation on the bigmouth buffalo is probably slight; growth of the young is so rapid that they soon become too large for most predators.

The buffaloes have enthusiastic followers among sport fishermen. The bigmouth buffalo has been referred to as "the musky of the southern Wisconsin streams, the sportiest, wariest, most mysterious and most sought-after native fish that swims, and, when smoked, a supreme gourmet's delight" (H. E. Neuenschwander, pers. comm.).

The bigmouth buffalo seldom takes a hook, and is only rarely caught with other fishes. In the lower Mississippi Valley, it is frequently taken on set lines baited with balls of dough (Jordan and Evermann 1923).

In Wisconsin each spring, fishermen seek the bigmouth buffalo with square dipnets from river banks and bridges, or, armed with sturdy 3.7-m (12-ft) spears, they pursue it on flooded marshes from rowboats and skiffs. Such modern pursuit of the buffalo is tame compared to the historical account given by Jordan and Evermann (1923:39):

> In certain lakes in the Mississippi Valley . . . extraordinary runs of very large buffalo fish occur occasionally. These runs take place in the spring at the spawning time of the fish, and usually at the time of a heavy rain when the tributary streams are full and the connecting marshes are flooded. Then these fish come up from the lake, in great numbers, crowding the inlets and spreading over the flooded marshes. They remain only a few days, and soon disappear as suddenly and mysteriously as they came; but their brief stay has been long enough to permit great slaughter by the farmers of the surrounding country, who kill great numbers with pitchforks, clubs and other primitive weapons, and haul them away in wagon loads.

The bigmouth buffalo is becoming increasingly popular as a table fish. The meat is nutritious, and in taste it is considered inferior to catfish but superior to carp. It is unexcelled when smoked.

The bigmouth buffalo was rated as a poor test species by Gould and Irwin (1962). Frequent changes of the water in holding tanks was required because of fouling; the fish appeared to be susceptible to parasites, were easily disturbed by stimuli throughout the holding period, and were available in a size suitable for testing only during a part of the first growing season.

At the turn of the century, the bigmouth buffalo was abundant in Lake Pepin and was caught and shipped in larger quantities than any other fish (Wagner 1908).

In the Wisconsin portion of the Mississippi River, during the 5-year period 1960–1964, there was a 66% increase in kilograms of buffaloes (combined species) caught (Finke 1967). During this period the total buffalo harvest was 1,257,000 kg (2,771,000 lb); the price per kilogram ranged from 18 to 22¢ (8 to 10¢/lb). The gill net was the most effective gear for taking buffaloes, accounting for 680,000 kg (1,500,000 lb) over the 5-year period. Pool 9 yielded the most buffaloes—254,000 kg (560,000 lb)—followed by Pools 7 and 8, each of which produced slightly less than 227,000 kg (500,000 lb). The best months for catching buffaloes were March and April, which accounted for 215,000 kg (474,000 lb) and 186,000 kg (410,000 lb) respectively.

Recent production in Wisconsin waters of the Mississippi River for the combined species of buffaloes was: 1965—286,820 kg (632,319 lb); 1970—372,105 kg (820,337 lb); 1975—195,286 kg (430,525 lb); and 1976—243,962 kg (537,834 lb). At slightly more than 47¢/kilo (21.5¢/lb), the 1976 catch was valued at $115,634, ranking third in value to the $188,437 realized from the catfish catch, and the $179,142 for the carp catch that year (Fernholz and Crawley 1977). The bigmouth buffalo constituted the greatest portion of the above figures for buffalo species.

Inland catches of buffaloes in Wisconsin are also significant. In 1947, 11,300 kg (25,000 lb) [probably bigmouth buffalo—author] were taken from Beaver Dam Lake (Dodge County) (*The Milwaukee Journal*, 2 November 1947). During one week in July 1976, commercial fishermen removed 2,700 kg (6,000 lb) of bigmouth buffaloes from Castle Rock Reservoir (Juneau County) (J. Diehl, pers. comm.). In 1970, under the rough and detrimental fish removal program supported by the Wisconsin Department of Natural Resources, 117,259 kg (258,508 lb) of buffaloes [combined species but mainly bigmouth buffalo—author] were removed by state and contract fishing crews (Miller 1971). Most were harvested from Delavan Lake (Walworth County), Lake Koshkonong (Jefferson County), and the Rock River (Rock County). The 95,804 kg (211,208 lb) harvested by the state crews brought $33,520.98, and were mostly sold for human consumption. In 1975–1976, contract crews removed about 230,000 kg (500,000 lb) of bigmouth buffaloes from Delavan Lake (R. Schumacher, pers. comm.).

In listing the standing crops of fishes in North American lakes and reservoirs, Carlander (1955) reported bigmouth buffaloes at the top, with production even greater than carp. Bigmouth buffaloes averaged about 195 kg/ha (174 lb/acre), with a maximum of over 1,100 kg/ha (1000 lb/acre).

The buffaloes, probably more than any other group of Wisconsin fishes, have a great potential for producing fish flesh and high-level protein. A single trial of bigmouth buffalo in a 1/25-ha (1/10-acre) pond at the University of Kansas in 1961 resulted in a yield of 287 kg/ha (256 lb/acre), without fertilization of the pond or feeding of the fish (Cross 1967). This is about twice the production obtained using channel catfish under similar conditions.

Consideration should be given to the use of ponds receiving treated effluent water from sewage plants, and cooling ponds at power generation sites, for the prolonged and accelerated growth of the bigmouth buffalo. Additional potential for producing fish flesh may come from the hybridization of buffalo species (Stevenson 1964). In one study, bigmouth and black buffalo hybrids were approximately twice the length of the nonhybrids, and 4 times their weight, after 216 days.

The bigmouth buffalo is classified in the Wisconsin fishing regulations as a rough fish, and state and commercial fishermen have been removing it from state waters for many years. It seems strange that this native species, which is not harmful to other fishes, which is avidly sought after by a special group of dipnet sportsmen, and which is an excellent food fish, should be indiscriminately eliminated from Wisconsin's public waters. In its war against the carp on the upper Rock River, the Wisconsin Department of Natural Resources has used toxicants which eliminated not only the carp but all species of fish. The Department has given little consideration to the potential loss of the bigmouth buffalo as a fish protein resource. As a result, the bigmouth buffalo has been eliminated from many areas of the upper Rock River drainage above Watertown, where, until the 1960s, it was a common and valuable resource.

The bigmouth buffalo appears to be secure over most of its range in Wisconsin, but the loss anywhere of this valuable fish is an inexcusable tragedy. Serious consideration should be given to accord the bigmouth buffalo sport fish status.

Black Buffalo

Ictiobus niger (Rafinesque). *Ictiobus*—fish, bull; *niger*—black.

Other common names: mongrel buffalo, round buffalo, current buffalo, chopper, buglemouth buffalo, bugler, router, blue router, reefer, prairie buffalo, kicker, blue buffalo, blue rooter, chucklehead buffalo, bastard buffalo, pumpkinseed buffalo, deepwater buffalo, buoy tender.

Adult 980 mm, L. Wisconsin (Columbia Co.), 26 Jan. 1976

DESCRIPTION

Body slightly compressed, almost round, and more slender than other species of buffalo; back not prominently arched; ventral line straight. Average length 406 mm (16 in). TL = 1.24 SL. Depth into SL 2.6–3.5. Head into SL 2.9–3.8. Snout blunt and broadly rounded. Mouth small, ventral, and almost horizontal; tip of upper lip is far below the lower margin of eye; lips moderately full and striated. Pharyngeal teeth short, narrow, and fragile, about 195 per arch; well-developed crown of tooth with cusp at anterior edge; arch moderately strong, with large, honeycomb spaces on anterior edge; the symphysis short, on moderately long stems of the arch. Subopercle broadest at middle. Dorsal fin sickle shaped; longest anterior rays into fin base 2.2–2.5; dorsal fin rays 27–31; dorsal fin base into SL 2.6–2.7; anal fin rays 8–9; pelvic fin rays 9–11. Lateral line scales 36–39; lateral line complete. Digestive tract much elongated, with loops running parallel to body axis. Specimens less than 305 mm (12 in) difficult to separate from smallmouth buffalo (Trautman 1957).

Back slate to bronze, with a greenish overcast; sides bronze, belly lighter. Fins dark olive to slate.

Breeding male with minute tubercles on sides of head, on scales (10–15), and on anterior rays of pelvic fins. Breeding males often blackish and without tubercles.

Hybrids: Black buffalo × smallmouth buffalo (Moore 1968). Experimental black buffalo × bigmouth buffalo (Stevenson 1964, Hollander and Avault 1975).

DISTRIBUTION, STATUS, AND HABITAT

In Wisconsin the black buffalo occurs only in the Mississippi River drainage basin. It inhabits the Mississippi River upstream to Lake Pepin, the Wisconsin River upstream to and including the Wisconsin Dells Flowage, and the lower Pecatonica River. It is doubtful that this species occurs in Lac La Belle (Waukesha County), although it was formerly reported there by Cahn (1927). No Lac La Belle specimen is extant, and if Cahn actually found this species there, it undoubtedly was the product of a fish rescue and transfer

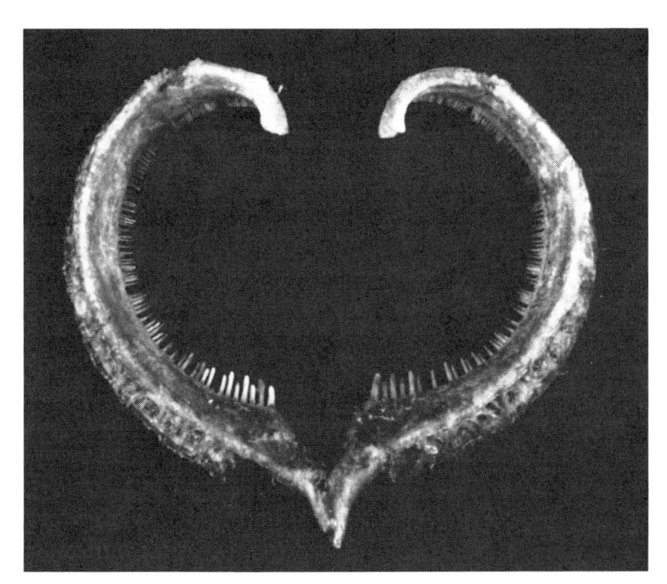

Pharyngeal arches of the black buffalo, front view

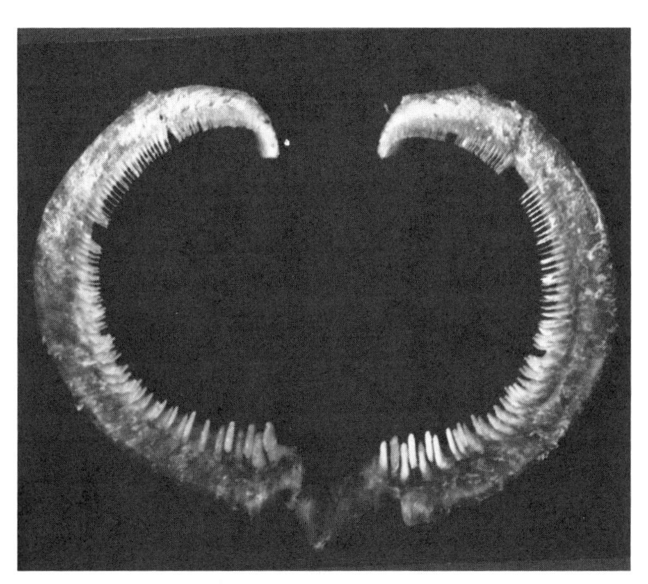

Pharyngeal arches of the black buffalo, back view

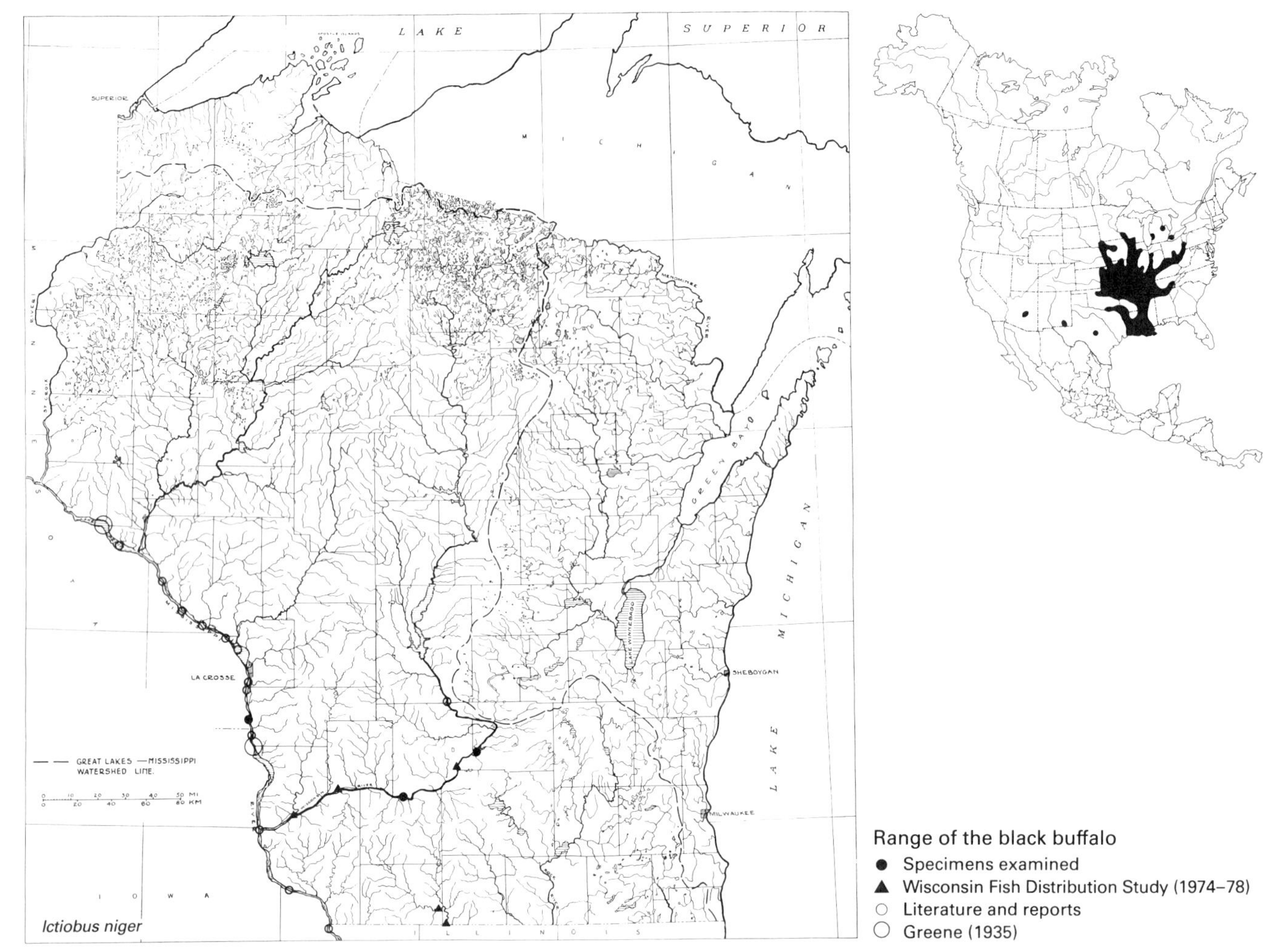

operation from the Mississippi River. I have deleted this report from the map.

Specimens examined: UWSP 813 (1) Wisconsin River between Spring Green and Lone Rock (Sauk and Richland counties), 1962; UWSP 1647 (1) Mississippi River in Pool 9 below Genoa (Vernon County), 1967; UWSP 5272 (1) and 5405 (1) Lake Wisconsin Flowage of Wisconsin River (Columbia County), 1975 and 1976 respectively; UWSP 5641 (1) Wisconsin River between the Wisconsin 18 and 35 bridge and Millville (Grant County), 1977; MPM 8901 (1) Lake Wisconsin Flowage of the Wisconsin River (Columbia County), 1975.

The Wisconsin Fish Distribution Study reported the following black buffalo specimens: (2) Pecatonica River T1N R6E Sec 33 (Green County), 1976; (1) Pecatonica River T1N R5E Sec 11 (Lafayette County), 1976; (1) Wisconsin River T7N R6W Sec 14 (Grant County), 1977; (1) Wisconsin River T9N R2W Sec 36 (Richland County), 1977; (1) Wisconsin River T10N R6E Sec 25 (Columbia County), 1977; (5) Wisconsin River at Lake Wisconsin T10N R8E Sec 6 (Columbia County), 1976; (1) Wisconsin River at Lake Wisconsin T11N R8E Sec 33 (Columbia County), 1975. Other reports include: Lake Pepin (Pepin County) (Greene 1935); Mississippi River at Pool 7, 1970–1972 (R. Ranthum, pers. comm.); Mississippi River at Pools 4 through 12 (P. W. Smith et al. 1971); Wisconsin River in Wisconsin Dells Flowage, 10 km upstream from Wisconsin Dells, 1976 (J. Diehl, pers. comm., with confirming photograph).

The black buffalo is rare to uncommon in Wisconsin waters, where it is at the northern limit of its distribution. Ranthum (pers. comm.) noted that in Pool 7 of the Mississippi River it appeared more frequently than such species as the paddlefish, lake sturgeon and blue sucker. He also observed that at certain locations and times black buffaloes made up a large part of the catch and a high proportion of the exceptionally large fish taken. During the winter of 1975–1976, when the Lake Wisconsin Flowage (Columbia County) was opened to commercial fishing, 5 black buffaloes appeared in a catch of 100 buffaloes of all species. Wisconsin has placed the black buffalo on threatened status (Les 1979).

Although the black buffalo, a large river form, occurs in sloughs, silty backwaters, and impoundments, it appears to prefer stronger currents than either the smallmouth or bigmouth buffaloes, and it is occasionally taken in the main channel. Cross (1967) captured the black buffalo in deep, fast riffles where the channel narrowed. The black buffalo is taken from the main channel of the Mississippi River, hence its name "buoy tender." It occurs in water of varying turbidity over a wide variety of bottoms.

BIOLOGY

Spawning probably occurs in April and May, although a tuberculate male was captured from the lower Wisconsin River in mid-June.

A possible spawning of the black buffalo, observed by L. E. Yeager in the state of Mississippi, was reported by Breder and Rosen (1966:236):

> . . . the fish aggregated in large numbers from 10 a.m. to 5 p.m. in overflowed land adjacent to a swamp. They were in such a state of milling and excitement that they could be approached without caution. They broke water continually although seldom cleared the surface. . . He [Yeager] suggested, without definitely saying so, that pairs separated themselves from the group for mating. Three days later the water had receded, and the shores were found strewed with rotting egg masses. Yeager implied that this observation covered a very unusual spawning mode because of the great loss of eggs and the fact that local people knew nothing of such procedures at other times.

Experimental hybrid black buffaloes (male) × bigmouth buffaloes (female) were hatched out in about 72 hours at 21°C (69.8°F) (Hollander and Avault 1975). The eggs tolerated salinities as high as 15 ppt, which was the upper salinity limit of the test. The fry had the best survival at 9 ppt.

In Louisiana, young-of-year black buffaloes, from ponds which had been stocked with adults 197 days before, were 19 mm long on 15 October (Perry 1976). In Ohio, young-of-year were 38–102 mm (1.5–4.0 in) long in September (Trautman 1957).

Four black buffaloes of ages V–VIII, from the Mississippi and Wisconsin rivers, had the following calculated lengths at the annuli: 1—52 mm, 2—148 mm, 3—333 mm, 4—409 mm, 5—462 mm, 6—518 mm, 7—532 mm, and 8—566 mm. An especially fast-growing black buffalo, 625 mm TL and 4.54 kg, was taken under the ice from Lake Wisconsin with an entanglement net; its estimated age was 6 years, and it had a condition value (K_{TL}) of 1.86. A 101-cm, 21.8-kg (39.8-in, 48-lb) fish taken from the same locale on 26 January 1976 was estimated to be 20 years old.

In the south, black buffaloes reach maturity at age II (Perry 1976). In Illinois, so few specimens of black buffaloes have been examined that the maturity size for this species has not been determined. The smallest ripe female noted in Illinois was 470 mm (18.5 in) long (Barnickol and Starrett 1951). A 15.42-kg (34-lb) fish from Illinois was 24 years old (Carlander 1969).

In Pool 7 of the Mississippi River, the black buffalo ranged from 4.5 to 6.8 (possibly 9.1) kg (10 to 15, possibly 20 lb) in weight (R. Ranthum, pers. comm.). According to Carson (1943), it usually weighs less than 9.1 kg (20 lb), but may weigh as much as 31.8 kg (70 lb).

The food of the black buffalo is similar to that of the bigmouth buffalo (Forbes and Richardson 1920). Sixty-seven percent of its diet is animal matter, largely mollusks and insects. An occasional young crayfish is taken, but more than half of the animal food is made up of insects. The vegetable food eaten includes water plants, such as duckweed and algae. Cross (1967) noted that the black buffalo and the smallmouth buffalo are sometimes found together on shallow riffles, where their fins and backs break the surface as they forage for insects and epiphytes on stones.

In Arizona (Minckley et al. 1970), the introduced clam (*Corbicula manilensis*) made up most of the volume of the black buffalo diet. Diatoms, blue-green algae, and crustaceans were relatively high in frequency of occurrence, but in numbers and volume made up only a minor part of the diet. The clams consumed were juveniles to small adults, with measurements from less than 1.0 to more than 15.0 mm across the valves. Organic detritus constituted 30% of the digestive tract contents, and sand, 10.3%. When feeding, black buffaloes were observed diligently searching the bottom, stirring the softer sediments, and delving beneath twigs, stones, and other debris.

Hybrid adult and fingerling buffaloes (black buffalo × bigmouth buffalo) in experimental ponds used less supplemental feed than channel catfish, tilapia, and Israeli carp (Williamson and Smitherman 1975). The hybrids ate mostly supplemental feed and Entomostraca (mainly ostracods), followed by debris and traces of unicellular algae and filamentous algae. The hybrid buffalo is primarily a benthic feeding omnivore.

In the Wabash River of Indiana, buffaloes (species

not indicated) preferred 29.0–31.0°C (84.2–87.8°F) temperatures, which are probably within the optimum temperature range for the black buffalo (Gammon 1973). Waters of low salinity (up to 9 ppt) are beneficial for black buffalo production, whereas waters in excess of 12 ppt salinity are not suitable for buffalo fish culture.

In Lake Wisconsin during late January 1976, 5 black buffaloes were netted along with bigmouth buffalo (35), smallmouth buffalo (60), common carp (100), white bass (2), freshwater drum (24), lake sturgeon (70), and silver redhorse (1).

IMPORTANCE AND MANAGEMENT

To what extent the black buffalo is preyed on by fish predators is unknown. The black buffalo is seldom caught on natural or artificial lures. In Kansas, however, it is taken on worms or doughballs (Cross 1967).

Smallmouth Buffalo

Ictiobus bubalus (Rafinesque). *Ictiobus*—fish, bull; *bubalus*—buffalo.

Other common names: razorback buffalo, suckermouth buffalo, round buffalo, quillback buffalo, router, roachback buffalo, humpback buffalo, channel buffalo, baitnet buffalo, thicklipped buffalo, white carp, liner buffalo, brown buffalo.

Adult 435 mm, Mississippi R., Bellevue, Iowa, 21 Oct. 1978

DESCRIPTION

Body deep, especially in large fishes, and highly compressed; back highly arched and ridgelike; ventral line nearly straight. Average length 30–40 cm (11.8–15.8 in). TL = 1.28 SL. Depth into SL 2.4–2.8 (2.2–3.0). Head into SL 3.4–4.1. Snout blunt. Mouth small, ventral, almost horizontal; tip of upper lip far below lower margin of eye; lips moderately full and striated. Pharyngeal teeth small and fragile, about 180–190 per arch; well-developed crown of tooth with cusp at anterior edge, arch moderately strong; large honeycomb spaces along anterior edge of each arch; the symphysis short. A large pharyngeal pad virtually fills the pharyngeal cavity, leaving only a narrow slit between the pad and the pharyngeal arch. Subopercle broadest at middle. Dorsal fin sickle shaped, longest anterior rays into length of base about 1.6, dorsal fin rays 26–31; dorsal fin base into SL 2.4–2.6. Anal fin rays usually 9; pelvic fin rays 9–11. Lateral line scales 36–38; lateral line complete. Digestive tract much elongated, with loops running parallel to body axis.

Back bronze or slate olive; sides bronze, lighter on belly. Fins slate brown. With age, colors lighten; old individuals from turbid waters pale yellow-gray.

Breeding male with fine tubercles on head (Branson 1961).

Sexual dimorphism: Longest dorsal ray significantly longer in female than in male (Phillips and Underhill 1971).

Hybrids: Smallmouth buffalo × bigmouth buffalo (Trautman 1957). Experimental smallmouth buffalo × bigmouth buffalo, and smallmouth buffalo × black buffalo (Stevenson 1964).

DISTRIBUTION, STATUS, AND HABITAT

In Wisconsin the smallmouth buffalo occurs only in the Mississippi River drainage basin. It has been reported from the lower portions of the St. Croix, Red Cedar, Chippewa, and Wisconsin rivers, and from the mouths of small tributaries to these rivers.

Isolated reports of buffaloes from the Big Lake and Island Lake region in Vilas County are substantiated by a 17.2-kg (38-lb) smallmouth buffalo caught from

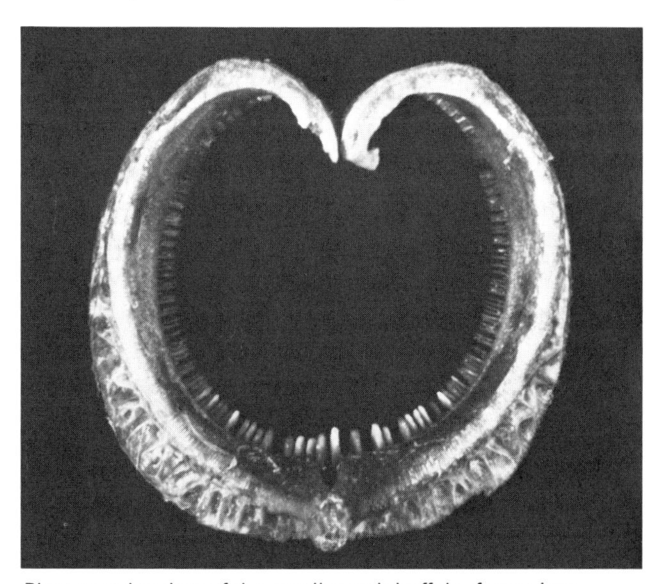

Pharyngeal arches of the smallmouth buffalo, front view

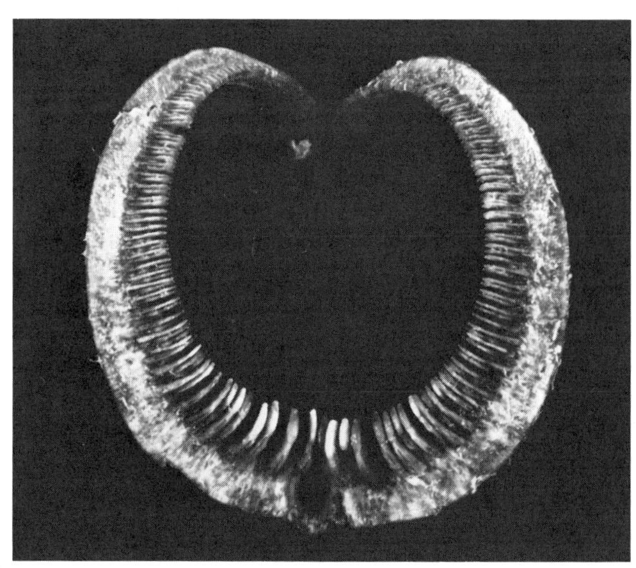

Pharyngeal arches of the smallmouth buffalo, back view

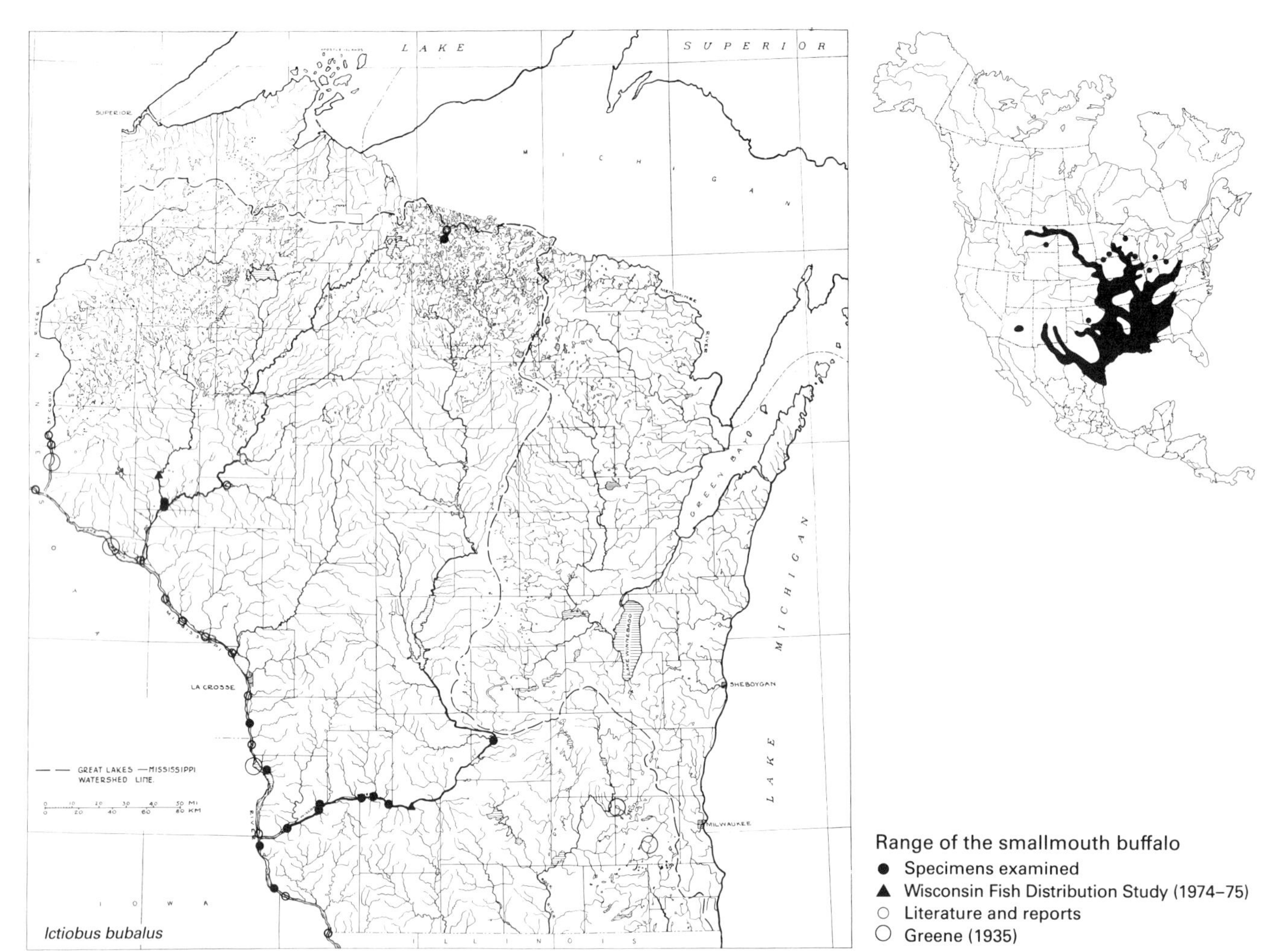

Island Lake in the 1960s. It was mounted by Neal Long of Sayner and displayed at the Sportsmans Bar in Arcadia (Trempealeau County) in the 1970s. This fish probably derived from fish-rescue plantings from the Mississippi River, which were made during the 1930s. Cahn (1927) observed the smallmouth buffalo from Lac La Belle (Waukesha County), and noted that it was more common in the Rock River. He also observed one specimen from the Fox River near Waukesha that weighed 5.9 kg (13 lb). The Waukesha County reports probably represent the last remnants of a disjunct population; specimens for verification of these reports are not available. H. E. Neuenschwander (pers. comm.) reported that the smallmouth buffalo was taken from the Rock River between Hustisford and Watertown as late as 1965.

The smallmouth buffalo is uncommon to common in Wisconsin; in some large waters it is the dominant buffalo species.

The smallmouth buffalo is found in pools, oxbow lakes, and deeper waters of large rivers. It prefers clear, clean water. Occasionally young are taken from the mouths of small streams tributary to large rivers.

BIOLOGY

At the latitude of Wisconsin spawning occurs from April to early June at temperatures of 15.6–18.3°C (60–65°F). The presence of smallmouth buffalo in spawning condition in a small creek suggests that they sometimes ascend small streams to spawn (Coker 1930). Attempts to propagate buffaloes at the fisheries biological station of Fairport, Iowa, have been described by Coker (p. 192):

> . . . natural propagation . . . met with no success until the spring of 1917, when the conditions were varied by keeping the pond about half full of water in the early part of the season and allowing it to fill gradually early in May. A few days after the production of this artificial flood stage the splashing of buffalo fish was observed (May 11 and again May 17, 18 and 19) in overflow regions along the margins of the pond, and propagation was found to have been successful. . . . The rise should begin when the temperature

of the water is 56°F. and should be so controlled that it is completed in 10 to 15 days, with the water at 62 to 64°F. Spawning begins at 56 to 58° but is more active at 60 to 62°, so that the fish have spawned out when the rise is concluded. The largemouthed buffalo fish (*cyprinella*) may be bred without the artificial rise, but the smallmouth (*bubalus*) does not do well without it. The rise is found desirable for both species, as the weathered grounds seem to offer a more favorable environment for the eggs during incubation.

In South Dakota (Gasaway 1970, Walburg 1976), spawning of the smallmouth buffalo is most successful in years when water levels rise in the spring to flood marshes or low-lying meadows. The eggs are deposited at random over the bottom, or in vegetation; they adhere to any object they touch.

Jester (1973) has provided much spawning information for the smallmouth buffalo in Elephant Butte Lake, New Mexico. The following account is derived from Jester unless otherwise noted.

Spawning for the smallmouth buffalo occurs from early May to September, and water temperatures during spawning ranged from 19.1 to 27.5°C (66.4 to 81.5°F), with peaks of activity occurring between 22 and 26.5°C (71.6 and 79.7°F) (Jester 1973). The latest observed spawning by female smallmouth buffaloes occurred in September at a water temperature of 26.4°C (79.5°F), and apparently was terminated by the exhaustion of eggs rather than by the occurrence of a threshold temperature. Free-flowing milt was observed in males during every month of the year, indicating that the spawning season of the smallmouth buffalo is controlled entirely by the incidence of ripe females.

Male smallmouth buffaloes begin to concentrate on shoals 1.2–3.1 m (4–10 ft) deep in March and April, just prior to the spawning season. Additional males apparently join the concentration as they ripen, and leave when they are spent. Individual females also join the concentration as they ripen and leave when they are spent, so that large numbers are present just prior to and at the peak of spawning activity.

According to Jester, smallmouth buffaloes spawn at depths of 1.2–2.4 m (4–8 ft) among recently inundated terrestrial vegetation. Eggs are broadcast at random over shoals, and are abandoned to sink into whatever bottom conditions may exist at the spawning site.

Fecundity varies from 18,200 eggs in an age-II female to 525,500 in an age-XV female (Jester 1973). Incubation requires from 8 to 14 days, depending on the water temperature (Nord 1967). Young smallmouths have been taken in relatively shallow water over mud bottoms; they tend to school, although this is not a pronounced habit.

A young-of-year smallmouth taken 11 July from Richland Creek (Crawford County) was 44 mm TL; 12 young taken on 15 July from the Wisconsin River (Grant County) averaged 60 mm (42–72 mm); 2 young taken on 17 July from the Wisconsin River (Crawford County) were 48 mm and 61 mm long; and 1 young fish taken on 25 August from the Red Cedar River (Dunn County) was 47 mm TL.

Eight smallmouth buffaloes, 239–358 mm TL (9.4–14.1 in), taken from the Mississippi River at Fountain City (Buffalo County), were 1 year old and 147 mm (5.8 in) long at the formation of the first annulus (Christenson and Smith 1965). Twenty-six specimens from Pool 8 of the Mississippi River (in the vicinity of La Crosse County) were: age 0—84 (71–105) mm; III—324 mm; IV—427 (423–431) mm; V—468 mm; and VI—487 mm (Bur 1976).

Specimens from the Wisconsin River and from the contiguous portion of the Mississippi River at its mouth were: age I—270–275 mm; V—401–450 mm; and VI—462 mm. The calculated lengths at the annuli were: 1—112 mm; 2—245 mm; 3—346 mm; 4—391 mm; 5—428 mm; and 6—462 mm. A 183-mm specimen, taken on 13 September from the cooling lake at the Columbia (County) Power Plant on the Wisconsin River, exhibited no annulus. The yearly growths of smallmouth buffaloes from the Wisconsin River and from the Salt River, Missouri (Purkett 1958a), were almost identical. The condition values (K_{TL}) for smallmouth buffaloes in one study in New Mexico (Jester 1973) averaged 1.44 (1.22–1.67).

The age of smallmouth buffaloes at maturity is variable. In the middle Mississippi River, Barnickol and Starrett (1951) determined sexual maturity for this species at 381 mm (15 in). Age at maturity is usually 3 years (Nord 1967, Harlan and Speaker 1956). In some South Dakota waters, maturity is as late as 7–9 years for males and 10–11 years for females (Walburg and Nelson 1966). In New Mexico (Jester 1973), males may mature at 1 year and females at 2 years. According to Jester, at formation of annuli 9 through 13 females are heavier than males of approximately the same length.

This species has reached age XV in New Mexico, and it is estimated that only 2 smallmouth buffaloes out of 1 million hatched reach this age (Jester 1973). Occasionally this species reaches a weight over 15.9 kg (35 lb).

In one study of young-of-year smallmouth buffaloes (McComish 1967), copepods and cladocerans made up 99% of the food volume in the stomachs; sand constituted the remaining portion. Earlier observations revealed that the food of young smallmouth buffaloes consists of algae, duckweed, protozoans, rotifers, insect larvae, and insect eggs (Forbes and Richardson 1920, Gowanloch and Gresham 1965).

The smallmouth buffalo is an opportunist and feeds on organisms that are abundant (McComish 1967). In South Dakota's Lewis and Clark Reservoir, and in the Missouri River, zooplankton and attached algae were the primary foods. There was a general decrease in the volume of zooplankton consumed, and an increase in the volume of attached algae consumed, from late spring to early fall. The high frequency of insect larvae, attached algae, detritus, and sand in the diet indicated that the smallmouth buffalo fed on the bottom, primarily in shallow shoreline areas. Chironomidae, Baetidae, and Trichoptera were all found in smallmouth buffalo stomachs, although Chironomidae were most important.

In central Arizona (Minckley et al. 1970), the diet of smallmouth buffaloes varied radically from one season of the year to another. In January and February the diet was largely composed of diatoms, but in March and April a combination of Cladocera, Copepoda, and green algae constituted more of the food than diatoms. In May and June, a large component of the diet was clams; from July through October, the largest component was blue-green algae; and in November and December, diatoms and blue-greens prevailed.

Buffaloes (species not identified) selected water temperatures of 31.0–34.0°C (87.8–93.2°F) in the Wabash River, Indiana, and appeared to be as thermophilic as carp (Gammon 1973). The maximum temperature at which the smallmouth buffalo was captured in the White River and Ipalco Discharge Canal, Indiana, was 33.6°C (92.5°F) (Proffitt and Benda 1971).

In Elephant Butte Lake, New Mexico, the movements of the smallmouth buffalo are not clearly understood. Evidence exists of shifts upstream during the spring and summer and downstream during fall and winter; corresponding changes in population densities appear to be small, however, apparently because buffaloes continuously move into upstream areas where local commercial harvesting has reduced smallmouth buffalo numbers (Jester 1973). Although considerable movement was noted, bona fide migrations and heavy seasonal concentrations of smallmouth buffaloes do not occur except into spawning areas in spring. About two-thirds of the fishes marked in Elephant Butte Lake were recaptured less than 12.8 km (8 mi) from the sites where they had been marked, and about one-half were recaptured less than 9.6 km (6 mi) from marking sites. The longest distance moved was 23.2 km (14.5 mi).

According to Minckley (1969), competition was not severe among the three species of buffalo in Apache Lake, Arizona. Bigmouth buffaloes were the most widespread, occurring in open water and sometimes concentrating in shallow bays. Smallmouth and black buffaloes remained near the bottom in deeper bays and inlets, with the smallmouth associated with mud and sand bottoms and the black buffalo associated with cliffs, other cover, and gravelly bottoms. Jester (1973) noted that interaction between buffaloes, river carpsuckers, and carp (to a lesser extent) were quite strong. When the buffaloes were harvested from shoals in carpsucker and carp habitat, the carpsuckers increased in numbers and weight. Jester concluded that there is interspecific competition where these species occupy the same habitat.

In the Mississippi River near Cassville (Grant County), 12 smallmouth buffaloes were associated with the following species: longnose gar (1), mooneye (1), gizzard shad (25+), quillback (10), highfin carpsucker (1), common carp (7), largescale stoneroller (1), silver chub (7), speckled chub (2), golden shiner (3), bullhead minnow (7), fathead minnow (1), suckermouth minnow (1), emerald shiner (52+), spotfin shiner (4), spottail shiner (300+), river shiner (300+), sand shiner (6), tadpole madtom (1), white bass (150+), yellow bass (7+), western sand darter (14), river darter (2), logperch (12), johnny darter (4), largemouth bass (20+), bluegill (50+), black crappie (6), brook silverside (9), and freshwater drum (25).

IMPORTANCE AND MANAGEMENT

Although the smallmouth buffalo is an important component of the fish community in several waters, the extent to which it is used as food by carnivorous fishes is not known. In New Mexico, Jester (1973) noted that it had not been found in the stomach of any other fish.

The smallmouth buffalo is caught commercially with gill net and seine; it is seldom taken by sport fishermen on hook-and-line. It is a valuable food fish, and is said to have a finer flavor than the other buffaloes; purportedly there is less waste in cleaning a smallmouth buffalo because it has a smaller body cavity. Recipes for the preparation of buffaloes are given by Hacker (1977); especially tasty is his recipe for baked fish with stuffing.

The acceptability of the flavors and the aromas of the smallmouth buffalo, river carpsucker, carp, and channel catfish was tested in New Mexico (Wisdom 1972). The catfish was ranked first, smallmouth buffalo second, river carpsucker third, and carp last. Jester (1973) concluded that since the identity of the fishes was unknown to members of the taste panel, these results imply that differences in market acceptability and prices are determined more by the prejudices of consumers than by the flavor and the aroma of the fish.

Over much of its range the smallmouth buffalo is a valuable commercial fish. In the Wisconsin waters of the Mississippi River from 1965 to 1976, the catch for the combined species of buffaloes averaged 269 thousand kg (592 thousand lb) yearly (see p. 619). Just what proportion of the buffalo catch was made up of smallmouth buffaloes is not known, although this species is second in abundance to the bigmouth buffalo in upper Mississippi waters. Medium-sized smallmouth buffaloes generally bring premium prices, hence they are proportionately a more valuable part of the catch; in 1975, I recall seeing a light-colored smallmouth buffalo, about 3.6 kg (8 lb) which the fish wholesaler had set aside because "it brings a much better price."

Commercial production of buffaloes has apparently been stable since the early 1950s. Two factors appear to have reduced buffalo production from the large numbers which were known at the turn of the century: competition from the exotic carp, and the construction of flood-control dams and levees, which destroyed potential breeding grounds by inhibiting flooding.

A standing crop biomass of 780 kg/ha (700 lb/acre) has been reported for smallmouth buffaloes (Jester 1973). It appears that continued heavy fishing pressure would cause a rapid decline of buffaloes, to the point where a profitable commercial fishery could not be maintained.

Quillback

Carpiodes cyprinus (Lesueur). *Carpiodes*—carplike; *cyprinus*—after the island of Cyprus, from which the carp was supposedly introduced into Europe.

Other common names: quillback carpsucker, lake quillback, silver carp, carpsucker, eastern carpsucker, coldwater carp, quillback sucker, white sucker, broad mullet, mullet, carp, lake carp, white carp, long-finned sucker, breme, drum.

Immature 141 mm, Wisconsin R., Boscobel (Grant Co.), 18 June 1962

DESCRIPTION

Body stout, compressed; back may be much arched; ventral line nearly straight anteriorly. Average length 356 mm (14 in). TL = 1.32 SL. Depth into SL 2.6–3.2. Head into SL 3.2–3.8. Snout long, bluntly pointed, its upper surface between nostrils and tip typically notched (clearcut crosswise depression) in lateral view. Mouth ventral, tip of lower lip well in advance of anterior nostril; no knob at tip of lower lip; the halves of the lower lip meeting in an acute angle; lips thin and flesh-colored in life. Pharyngeal teeth small, about 210 per arch, each tooth bearing an enamel-like cap on cutting edge with a small cusp anteriorly; arch medium stout, the anterior edge with large honeycomb openings; the symphysis short. Subopercle broadest below middle. Dorsal fin long, falcate; anterior dorsal ray filamentous, its depressed length falling between middle and end of fin base and sometimes beyond; dorsal fin base into SL 2.4–2.6; dorsal fin rays 22–30; anal fin rays 7–8; pelvic fin rays 9–10. Lateral line scales usually 36–40; lateral line complete. Digestive tract much coiled.

Back silvery gray to light olive; sides silvery; belly whitish. Fins colorless, almost lacking in pigment.

Breeding male with small tubercles on the sides and ventral surface of the head (see Huntsman 1967), on the first dorsal ray, and on at least the first 8 or 9 pectoral rays and the first 2 pelvic rays. Large breeding female occasionally with a few tubercles on the side of the head.

Hybrid: Quillback × highfin carpsucker (Wis. Fish Distrib. Study #1385).

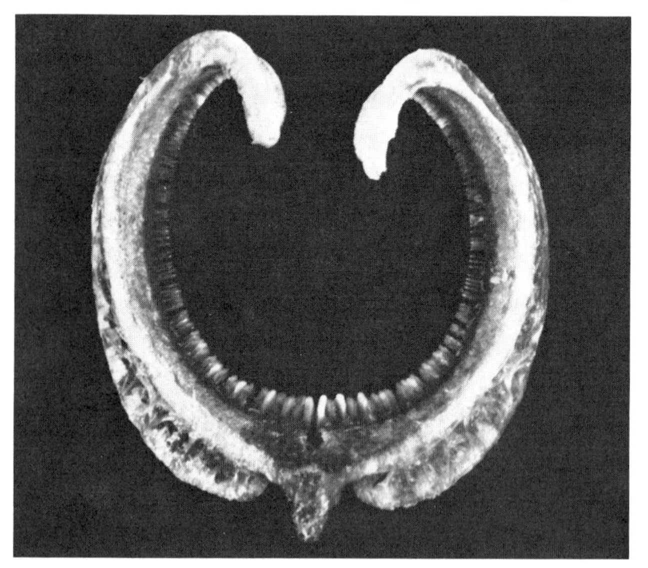

Pharyngeal arches of the quillback, front view

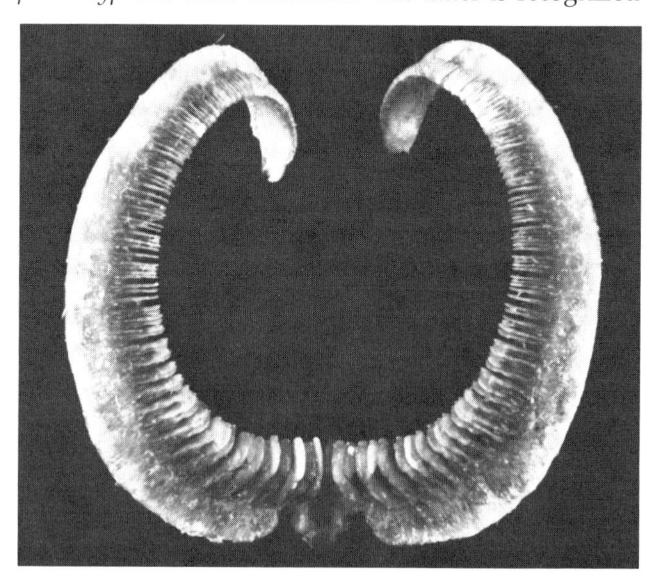

Pharyngeal arches of the quillback, back view

SYSTEMATIC NOTES

Carpiodes forbesi, formerly distinguished from *C. cyprinus* by its more slender form, large head and mouth, and the lower and more posterior dorsal fin, is now recognized as an environmental variant of *C. cyprinus* (Bailey and Allum 1962).

Two subspecies are recognized: the northern quillback carpsucker, *Carpiodes cyprinus cyprinus* (Lesueur), and the central quillback carpsucker, *Carpiodes cyprinus hinei* Trautman. The latter is recognized

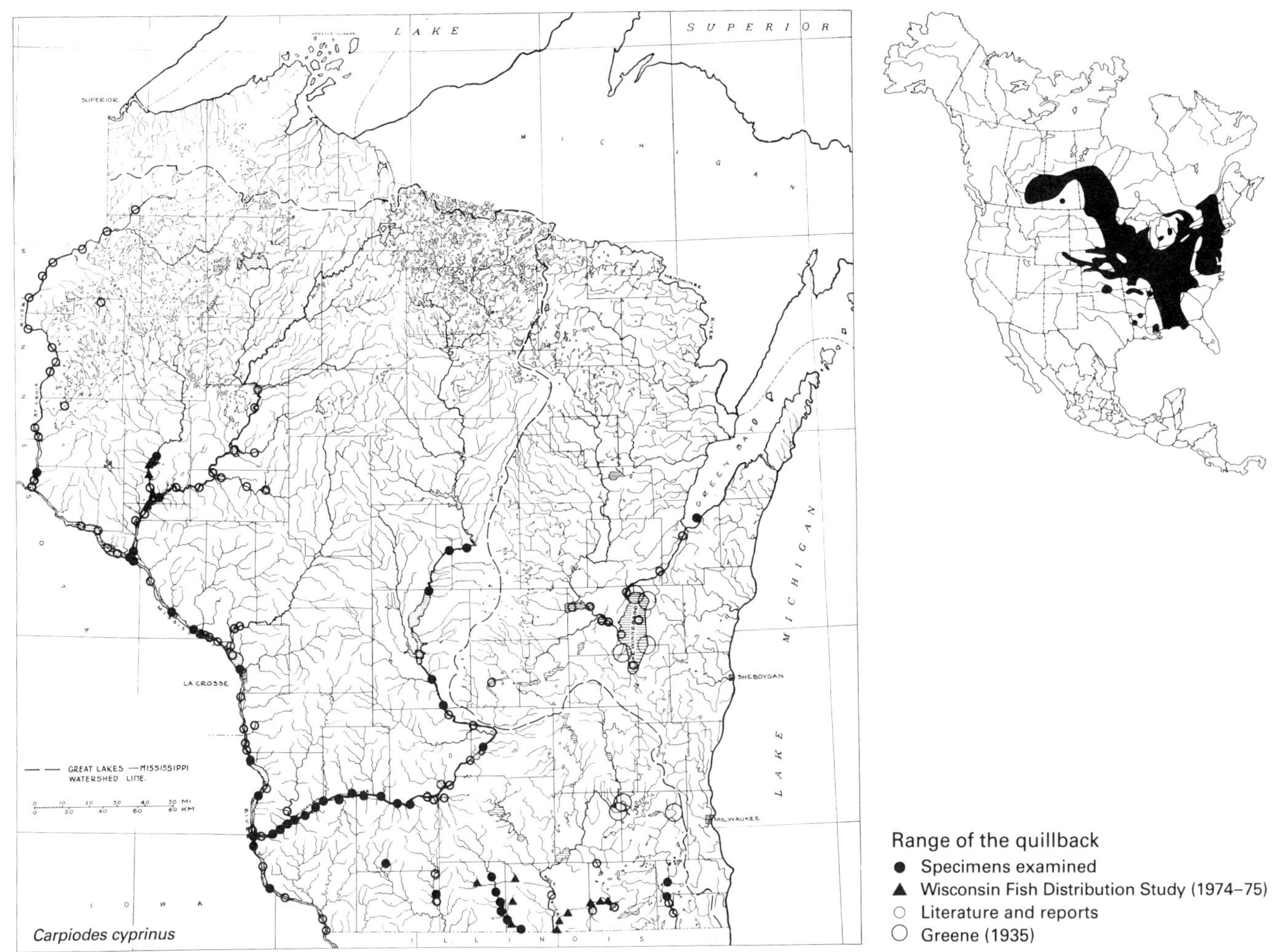

by its larger size, deeper body, and smaller eyes. Some specimens from the southern parts of Minnesota and Wisconsin and from northern Iowa are thought to be intergrades (Hubbs and Lagler 1964, Trautman 1957).

DISTRIBUTION, STATUS, AND HABITAT

In Wisconsin the quillback occurs in the Mississippi River and Lake Michigan drainage basins. It is present in the entire Mississippi boundary water, the St. Croix upstream to Douglas County, the lower Chippewa and Red Cedar rivers, the Wisconsin River upstream to Portage County, and in the Rock and Illinois-Fox river systems. It was listed erroneously by Cahn (1927) as *C. velifer* from the Rock and Fox rivers in Waukesha County. In the Lake Michigan basin it occurs in the upper and lower Fox River and its connecting lakes, in Lake Poygan, and in Green Bay.

In Wisconsin, the quillback is abundant in the lower Wisconsin River, the Mississippi River, and in Lake Winnebago. Over most of the remainder of its Wisconsin range it is considered common. Its status appears to be secure.

The quillback was encountered in clear to turbid waters at depths of 0.1 to more than 1.5 m, over substrates of sand (44% frequency), gravel (20%), silt (12%), mud (12%), clay (8%), and rubble (4%). It occurs in medium- to low-gradient rivers and in their lakes and sloughs, and in streams down to 6.1 m wide.

BIOLOGY

The extent of the spawning season in Wisconsin is not known, although tuberculate males have been reported from the Chippewa River as early as 17–19 May. A tuberculate male was taken from the Red Cedar River (Dunn County) on 15 June, and others from the junction of the Chippewa and Mississippi rivers as late as 28 September.

In Ohio the quillback appears to have a lengthy spawning period, and ripe males and females have been taken from late June through September. Water temperatures usually range from 19.0 to 28.0°C (66.2 to 82.4°F) during the spawning period (Woodward and Wissing 1976). According to Trautman (1957), spawning adults ascend small creeks in the spring, and have been found in base and low gradient, dredged ditches of less than 3 m (10 ft) in average width. In Iowa, spawning probably occurs from May through July (Buchholz 1957, Vanicek 1961). According to Harlan and Speaker (1956), the eggs are deposited in a random fashion over sand and mud bottoms in quiet waters of streams. No nest is built, and no care is given the young.

Eggs in a 601-mm female quillback from the Red Cedar River (Dunn County) were 1.6–1.8 mm diam. Fecundity in this species ranges from 15,235 eggs for an age-VI fish to 63,779 for an age-X fish (Woodward and Wissing 1976).

M. Fish (1932) illustrated and described the 21-mm stage.

The growth of young-of-year quillbacks in southern Wisconsin has been recorded as follows:

Date	No. of Fish	TL (mm) Avg	TL (mm) Range	Location
18 June	10	24	23–28	Wisconsin R. (Grant Co.)
27 June	9	32	27–38	Wisconsin R. (Richland Co.)
13 July	13	41	34–48	Wisconsin R. (Grant Co.)
8 Aug.	8	61	54–72	Wisconsin R. (Iowa Co.)
15 Aug.	8	66	56–80	Sugar R. (Green Co.)
16 Sept.	2	110	96–123	Mill Cr. (Richland Co.)
24 Sept.	9	100	70–123	Mississippi R. (Grant Co.)

Considering the size of these young-of-year, and the natural growth sequence as the season progresses, we may surmise a May to June spawning period in Wisconsin.

Frequently large numbers of young quillbacks are taken from quiet, broad flats no more than 15 cm (6 in) deep. Such quiet areas are often overlaid with silt.

In the lower Wisconsin River, age-I quillbacks are 144 (134–155) mm TL by mid-July; age-II fish average 202 mm. The ages and growth of select quillbacks were:

Date	Age Class	TL (mm)	Location
25 Aug. 1972	IV	374	Wisconsin R. (Wood Co.)
18 Aug. 1962	V	422	Wisconsin R. (Crawford Co.)
26 June 1962	VI	428	Wisconsin R. (Grant Co.)
28 July 1962	IX	457	Wisconsin R. (Richland Co.)
27 Sept. 1974	XI	601	Red Cedar R. (Dunn Co.)
15 July 1974	XII	552	L. Menomin (Dunn Co.)

In Ohio (Woodward and Wissing 1976), total lengths (mm) of 194 quillback carpsuckers (sexes combined) calculated back to the annuli were: 1—84; 2—156; 3—206; 4—242; 5—280; 6—312; 7—342; 8—368; 9—398; 10—428; and 11—448. This rate of growth was similar to that of the quillback in Iowa (Vanicek 1961). The males are generally larger than the females at each annulus. The condition (K_{TL}) was highest (1.38) in age-I fish; the lowest values occurred in the age-X (1.08) and age-XI (1.13) fish.

The largest Wisconsin quillback observed was 601 mm (23.7 in) TL, and weighed 3.67 kg (8.1 lb). Trautman (1957) noted a maximum length of 660 mm (26 in) and a maximum weight of 4.08 kg (9 lb).

The quillback feeds freely on debris in the bottom ooze, on plant materials, and on insect larvae. According to Harrison (1950), only small amounts of identifiable material are found in the visceral contents: 86% undeterminable debris, 12% algae, and 2% insect remains, with a trace of other invertebrates. Very small tendipedids, sometimes occurring by the thousands, were the only insects found intact in the digestive systems examined. Other insects were represented by larvae cases, detached legs, and wings. In southeastern Wisconsin (Cahn 1927), the quillback's food consisted of fragments of aquatic vegetation and algae, occasional *Chironomus* larvae, and a variety of snails (*Planorbis, Physa*), and small clams.

The quillback inhabits quiet water except when spawning. In Indiana, it prefers 29.0–31.0°C (84.2–87.8°F) water temperatures, which are probably within the optimum for that species (Gammon 1973). Gerking (1945) noted that it is seldom found among aquatic vegetation.

The quillback overwinters in large, turbid waters of low gradient over clayey silt bottoms, although it is known from clear waters and clean bottoms as well. A downstream migration of both young and adults occurs in the late summer and early fall in Ohio (Trautman 1957).

In the Mississippi River at Wyalusing (Grant County), 187 quillbacks were associated with these species: longnose gar (10), bowfin (1), gizzard shad (89), smallmouth buffalo (1), shorthead redhorse (3), golden redhorse (7), common carp (2), silver chub (1), golden shiner (110), bullhead minnow (145), pugnose minnow (8), emerald shiner (340), spotfin shiner (245), spottail shiner (589), river shiner (428), sand shiner (6), bigmouth shiner (1), brown bullhead (2), tadpole madtom (1), northern pike (1), white bass (119), yellow bass (4), yellow perch (5), sauger (2), walleye (2), western sand darter (5), river darter (1), logperch (11), johnny darter (36), smallmouth bass (1), largemouth bass (31), pumpkinseed (1), bluegill (173), orangespotted sunfish (8), rock bass (1), black crappie (178), white crappie (14), brook silverside (118), and freshwater drum (17).

IMPORTANCE AND MANAGEMENT

The quillback is undoubtedly available as a forage species, especially during the first year of life when the young commonly frequent shallows. After that, most quillbacks are too large to serve as forage fish.

Although quillbacks are not of any particular importance to the angler, more of them are taken by anglers than any other carpsuckers. Because of their abundance in most streams, considerable numbers are taken incidentally to other catches (Harlan and Speaker 1956). Doughballs, bread, small worms, and grubs are generally used by the few fishermen who attempt to catch them. Illegal snagging devices are also used, especially in the fast waters below dams. This method is wasteful, however, since not only the quillback, but other species as well, are injured in the unsuccessful attempts when the hook pulls out of the flesh.

The quillback flesh is white, flaky, sweet, and very tasty, particularly in the spring. Its suitability as a food fish is marred by the large number of bones, which make it hard to process (by machines or by hand) and to eat. Better methods of processing the carpsucker are sorely needed. Its potential as a future food resource is excellent.

In the Lake Michigan basin, limited commercial fishing and fish removal programs account for the few hundred kilograms of quillbacks taken yearly from Lake Poygan (Becker 1964b). In Lake Winnebago, 0.5 to 16 thousand kg of quillbacks are removed annually (Priegel 1967a); state fishermen removed 848 kg in 1976 (Wis. Dep. Nat. Resour. 1976b).

In reports of the commercial catch for the Mississippi River, the quillback is not distinguished from the other carpsucker species; the term "quillback" in such reports represents mostly the quillback, but also includes the river carpsucker and the highfin carpsucker. Quillbacks constituted the bulk of the following catches from Wisconsin waters of the Mississippi River: 1965—6,461 kg (14,245 lb), $285 total value; 1970—10,362 kg (22,845 lb), $571 value; 1971—11,257 kg (24,816 lb), $496 value; 1975—9,652 kg (21,278 lb), $851 value; and 1976—8,529 kg (18,802 lb), $752 value (Fernholz 1966, 1971, 1972; Fernholz and Crawley 1976, 1977).

River Carpsucker

Carpiodes carpio (Rafinesque). *Carpiodes*—carplike; *carpio*—carp.
Other common names: carpsucker, white carp, quillback, silvery carp, northern carpsucker.

Immature 90 mm, Kansas R., Topeka (Shawnee Co.), Kansas, 13 Aug. 1972

Adult 415 mm, Wisconsin R., Prairie du Sac Dam (Sauk Co.), 10 May 1977

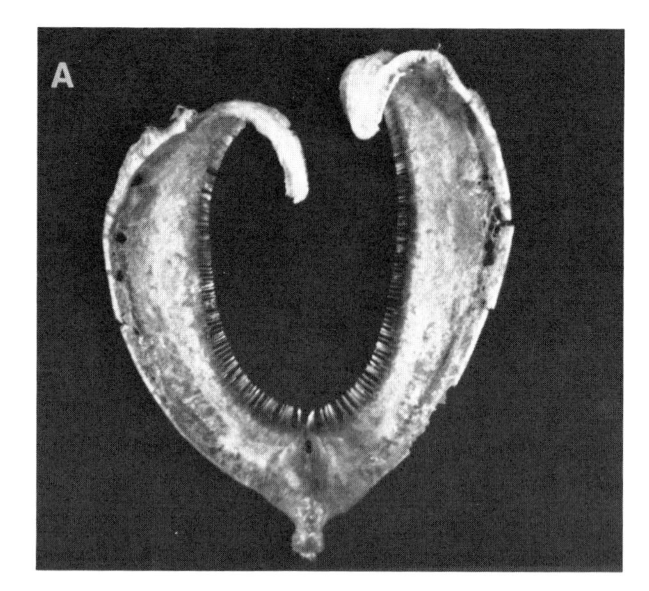

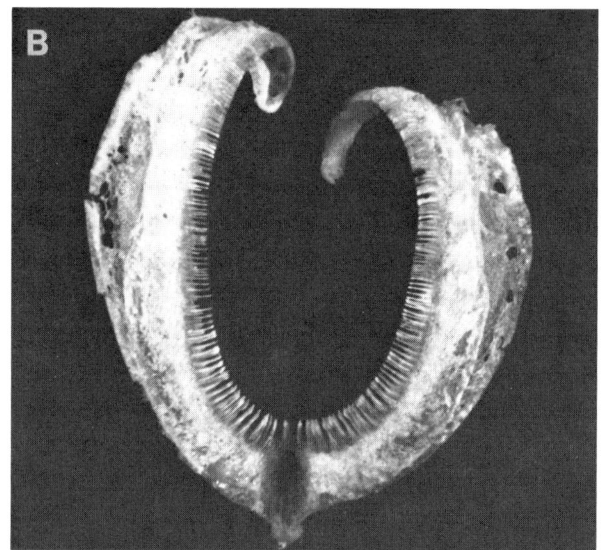

Pharyngeal arches of the river carpsucker. A. Front view. B. Back view.

DESCRIPTION

Body stout, back moderately compressed and slightly arched; ventral line nearly straight. Average length 320 mm (12.6 in). TL = 1.31 SL. Depth into SL 2.3–3.1. Head length into SL 3.5–4.1. Snout bluntly rounded, its upper surface between nostrils and tip seldom notched. Mouth ventral; a small, median knob on lower jaw, tip of knob scarcely or not at all in advance of anterior nostril; lips thin and white in life, the halves of the lower lip meeting in a wide angle. Pharyngeal teeth minute, narrow, and fragile, about 255 per arch; arch broad, paper thin. Subopercle broadest below middle. Dorsal fin long, falcate; anterior dorsal ray never filamentous, usually less than two-thirds length of dorsal fin base; dorsal fin base into SL 2.4–2.7; dorsal fin rays 23–27; anal fin rays 7–8; pelvic fin rays 9 (8–10). Lateral line scales 34–36; lateral line complete. Digestive tract much coiled. Chromosomes 2n = 96–100 (Uyeno and Smith 1972). *C. carpio* and *C. velifer* less than 75–100 mm TL are difficult to separate since distinctive characteristics do not appear until later.

Back brown-olive; sides silvery; belly whitish. Fins generally clear; in large, old fish the fins are pigmented.

Breeding male with minute tubercles on top and sides of head (see Huntsman 1967), scales of nape, and upper surfaces of pectoral and pelvic fin rays.

Hybrids: According to Trautman (1957), hybridization is possible with the highfin and quillback carpsuckers, but such hybrids are difficult to detect since these species already resemble one another in their morphological characters.

DISTRIBUTION, STATUS, AND HABITAT

In Wisconsin the river carpsucker occurs in the Mississippi River drainage basin, principally in the Mis-

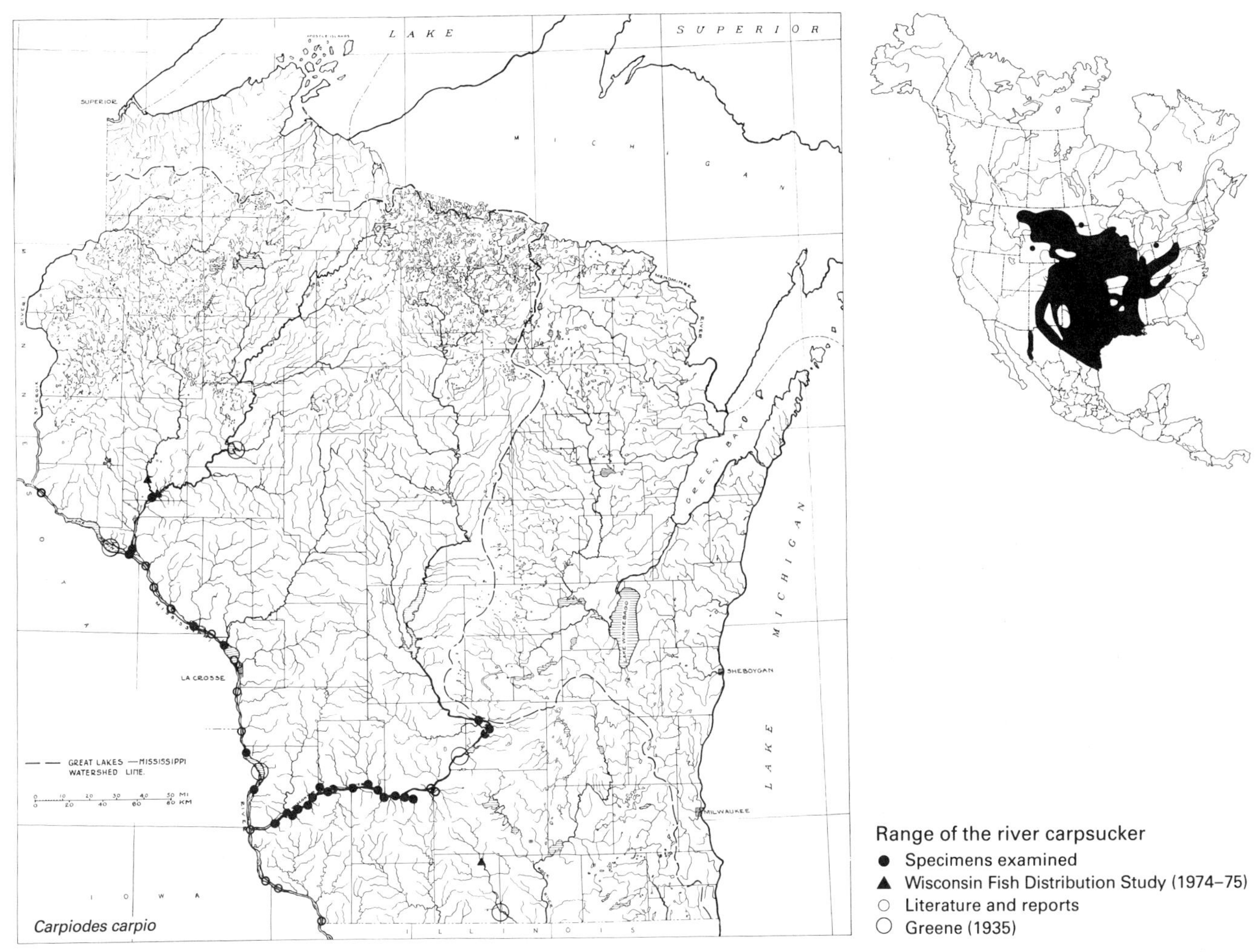

Range of the river carpsucker
● Specimens examined
▲ Wisconsin Fish Distribution Study (1974–75)
○ Literature and reports
◯ Greene (1935)

sissippi, Chippewa, Wisconsin, and Sugar rivers, and occasionally in the mouths of their tributaries.

The river carpsucker is limited in both numbers and range. In the Chippewa and Wisconsin river systems it is uncommon to common.

In Wisconsin, this species occurs in large, silty rivers over sand and silt. It prefers slow-moving water, sloughs, and pools.

BIOLOGY

In Wisconsin, spawning occurs in May and probably later. In Iowa, spawning begins in late April or early May (Harlan and Speaker 1956); the greatest spawning activity in the Des Moines River occurs in mid-June to early July (Behmer 1965). The eggs are deposited at random, and left unattended until they hatch. In New Mexico, spawning may occur from early April through early August at water temperatures of 18.3–24.0°C (64.9–75.2°F) (Jester 1972).

Spawning was observed in Oklahoma by R. M. Jenkins (Walburg and Nelson 1966:14):

> Spawning occurred after dark between 8:30 and 10:30 p.m. over firm sand bottom on the leeward side of a large island in water 1 to 3 feet deep. Spawning was a noisy performance with much slapping at the water surface. Eggs were apparently broadcast loose in the water since a number were found adhering to the float of a gill net nearby. Surface water temperature was 75°F (23.9°C).

According to Behmer (1965), ripe females were collected in Iowa in mid-August. There was no clearly defined spawning peak, and female carpsuckers did not ripen synchronously. Some carpsuckers probably spawn more than once a year. In South Dakota (Walburg 1976), spawning is most successful in years when water levels rise in the spring to flood marshes or low-lying meadows. Cross (1967) noted spawning in a narrow zone along a bank that was eroded by the current. He reported that the roots and some fallen stems of rushes, exposed by undercutting, provided substrates for the deposition of the eggs.

A gravid age-V female, taken from the lower Wisconsin River on 24 May, held ripe eggs 1.4–1.5 mm diam, and a 487-mm female, taken from the Chippewa River (Dunn County) on 18 May, held mature eggs 1.2–1.5 mm diam.

Behmer (1969a) found fecundity ranging from

4,430 eggs in a 183-g female to 154,000 eggs in a 737-g fish. The ovaries in the latter were more than 20% of the body weight. He reported eggs in three size groups; the smallest group was the most numerous, and contained very small, yolkless, transparent eggs (Behmer 1965).

The eggs hatch in 8–15 days. The 12- and 14-mm stages have been illustrated by May and Gasaway (1967). Growth is rapid. Ten young from the Sugar River (Rock County) were 44 (38–51) mm TL on 14 August, and 51 young from the Wisconsin River (Columbia County) averaged 60 mm on 20 September.

Age-I river carpsuckers from the Mississippi River (Buffalo County) were 183–216 mm TL (Christenson and Smith 1965). In Pool 8 of the Mississippi River (Vernon and La Crosse counties), carpsuckers 385 mm TL were age IV; 466 mm, age V; and 511 mm, age VI (Bur 1976). The condition (K_{TL}) for each age group was 1.47, 1.52, and 1.25, respectively.

In the Wisconsin River (Dane County), adults 397–410 mm TL had the following estimated lengths at the annuli: 1—173 mm; 2—280 mm; and 3—365 mm. River carpsuckers 446–493 mm TL from the Chippewa River (Dunn County) showed the corresponding lengths: 1—120 mm; 2—265 mm; 3—366 mm; 4—404 mm; 5—439 mm; and 6—460 mm.

Growth is more rapid in cutoff lakes and sloughs than in the mainstream Missouri River (Morris 1965). There is some evidence that high water levels contributed to the reduced growth of carpsuckers in the Des Moines River (Keeton 1963), and there is some correlation between high water temperatures and more rapid growth.

Maturity usually occurs at age III for males, and at ages III or IV for females; however, maturity has been reported for both sexes at age II (Carlander 1969). In most populations, numbers drop off abruptly after age V or VI, although specimens up to age XI have been reported.

The largest river carpsucker from Wisconsin waters was 528 mm TL (Christenson and Smith 1965). A 526-mm, 2.04-kg male from the Red Cedar River (UWSP 5323) was estimated to be 8 years old. A 635-mm, 4.65-kg (25 in, 10 lb 4 oz) specimen was reported from Ohio (Trautman 1957).

In the Des Moines River (Iowa), the most common foods of young-of-year river carpsuckers are phytoplankton, followed by *Difflugia*, diptera larvae, and rotifers (Buchholz 1957).

The river carpsucker is essentially a bottom feeder, which browses on the periphyton associated with submerged rocks and debris; sand and silt found in stomachs confirms its bottom-feeding habits. There is little variation in diet by age or season. River carpsuckers ingest a wide variety of the small planktonic plants and animals which are found in quiet pools and backwaters of most rivers and streams. They have fine gill rakers, and a highly efficient taste system in the buccal epithelium (Miller and Robison 1973).

In the Des Moines River, river carpsuckers 15–25 cm (6–10 in) long contained 60% unidentifiable organic material and 40% plants; fish 25 cm (10 in) and longer contained 64% plants, 26% insects, and 10% invertebrates other than insects (Harrison 1950). The insects were largely bloodworms and larval caddisflies.

In Indiana, Gammon (1973) determined the optimum temperature range for the river carpsucker at 31.5–34.5°C (88.7–94.1°F). The maximum temperature at which the river carpsucker was captured in the White River and Ipalco Discharge Canal, Indiana, was 37.5°C (99.5°F) (Proffitt and Benda 1971).

Tagging and recapture experiments on the Des Moines River (Iowa) suggest that the river carpsucker has a sedentary nature (Behmer 1969b), and that individual carpsuckers may remain together in preferred habitats. In one instance, a carpsucker was recaptured 10 km (6 mi) downstream the year following tagging.

Behmer estimated a population of 6,932 fish longer than 150 mm for his 4 km study area, and a weight of approximately 500 kg per river kilometer.

In the Wisconsin River (Sauk County), 20 river carpsuckers were associated with the following species: shovelnose sturgeon (1), mooneye (1), quillback (1), highfin carpsucker (3), smallmouth buffalo (1), black buffalo (1), blue sucker (9), shorthead redhorse (20), golden redhorse (4), northern hog sucker (2), common carp (15), silver chub (6), speckled chub (2), bullhead minnow (17), bluntnose minnow (2), emerald shiner (199), spotfin shiner (92), spottail shiner (1), Mississippi silvery minnow (1), channel catfish (1), white bass (1), yellow perch (1), sauger (14), walleye (10), river darter (1), slenderhead darter (1), logperch (8), smallmouth bass (7), black crappie (1), and freshwater drum (3).

IMPORTANCE AND MANAGEMENT

The river carpsucker is undoubtedly available as a forage species, especially during the first year of life when the young commonly frequent shallows. After that most of them are too large to serve as forage fish.

In Wisconsin, angling for the river carpsucker is incidental to angling for other species. In Iowa (Harlan and Speaker 1956), a few fishermen are adept at catching river carpsuckers and find considerable pleasure in the sport. Usually very small hooks, numbers 8 to 10, are baited with tiny doughballs or small pieces of moistened bread rolled into balls the size of a pea. The best fishing places are around large drift or brush piles in the stream, or immediately below dams.

The river carpsucker has an excellent taste when smoked (Brown 1971), and the meat is white and sweet. However, the numerous bones prevent its wide use as a table delicacy.

Commercial fishing reports for the Wisconsin waters of the Mississippi River include river carpsuckers in the catch with the quillback and the highfin carpsucker under the heading "quillback." River carpsuckers constitute only a small part of the yearly catch of carpsuckers (see p. 633).

Highfin Carpsucker

Carpiodes velifer (Rafinesque). *Carpiodes*—carplike; *velifer*—sailbearer.

Other common names: highfin, humpbacked carp, white carp, quillback carp, highfin sucker, silver carp, river carp, carpsucker, bluntnose river carp, spearfish, sailfish, skimback, skimfish.

Adult 222 mm, Wisconsin R. (Grant Co.), 24 Sept. 1966

DESCRIPTION

Body deep, much compressed laterally, with back highly arched; ventral line straight anteriorly, curved posteriorly. Average length 216 mm (8.5 in). TL = 1.34 SL. Depth into SL 2.2–2.6. Head into SL 3.7–4.1. Snout bluntly rounded, its upper surface between nostrils and tip seldom notched. Mouth ventral; a small, median knob on lower jaw, tip of knob directly below or slightly in advance of anterior nostril; lips weakly plicate, the halves of lower lip meeting at a 70–90° (sometimes greater) angle. Pharyngeal teeth minute, narrow and fragile, about 270 per arch; arch broad, paper thin, with symphysis much elongated. Subopercle broadest below middle. Dorsal fin long, falcate; anterior dorsal ray filamentous, its depressed length (if unbroken) longer than length of fin base; dorsal fin base into SL 2.6; dorsal fin rays 23–27; anal fin rays 8–9; pelvic fin rays 9–10. Lateral line scales usually 33–35; lateral line complete. Digestive tract much coiled. *C. velifer* and *C. carpio* less than 75–100 mm TL are difficult to separate since distinctive characteristics do not appear until later.

Back brown-olive; sides silvery; belly whitish. Fins generally colorless, almost lacking in pigment.

Breeding male with small tubercles on top and bottom of head, on snout (see Huntsman 1967), on most scales, and on the rays of the fins.

Hybrids: According to Trautman (1957), hybrids

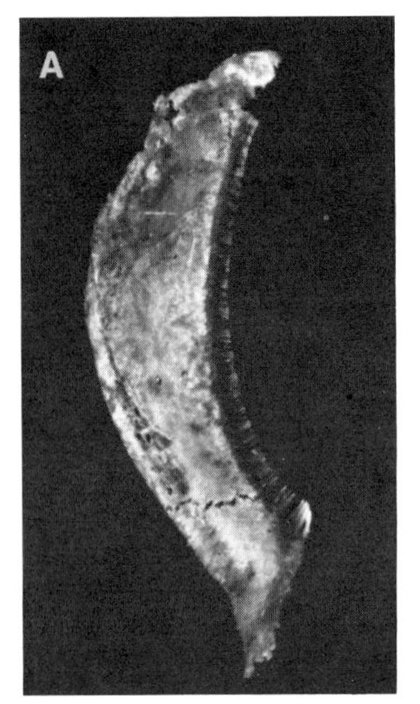

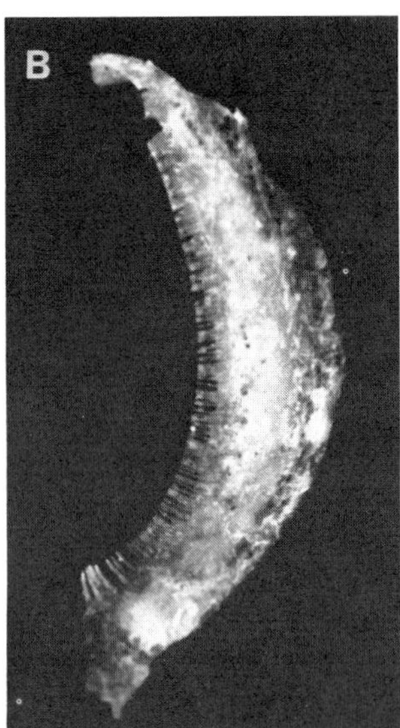

Right pharyngeal arch of the highfin carpsucker. A. Front view. B. Back view.

are possible with the quillback and river carpsucker. A highfin carpsucker × quillback was taken from the Cassville slough of the Mississippi River (Grant County) on August 1976 (Wis. Fish Distrib. Study, #1385).

SYSTEMATIC NOTES

C. velifer of Cahn (1927) is erroneous, and refers to *C. cyprinus*. *C. difformis* Cope of Forbes and Richardson (1920) refers to the present species, *C. velifer*.

DISTRIBUTION, STATUS, AND HABITAT

In Wisconsin the highfin carpsucker occurs presently only in the Mississippi River drainage basin, where it reaches the northern limit of its range. It has been reported from the Mississippi, lower St. Croix, lower Chippewa, and lower Wisconsin rivers.

Its presence in the Lake Michigan basin is based on two old records—one from the Calumet River in Illinois, and the other, which is questionable, from the Lake Michigan drainage basin. The latter was reported from "Root River, Michigan"; however, Hubbs (1926) concluded that it was more likely the Root River of Wisconsin. It is doubtful that the highfin carpsucker now exists in the Lake Michigan basin (Becker 1976).

Of all carpsuckers, the highfin has the most restricted range, and a number of reports indicate diminishing numbers in many parts of its range. In Iowa, it is found primarily in the large inland rivers, and only rarely in the Mississippi and Missouri rivers (Harlan and Speaker 1956). In Missouri, it is rare and appears to be confined to reservoirs in the Ozarks

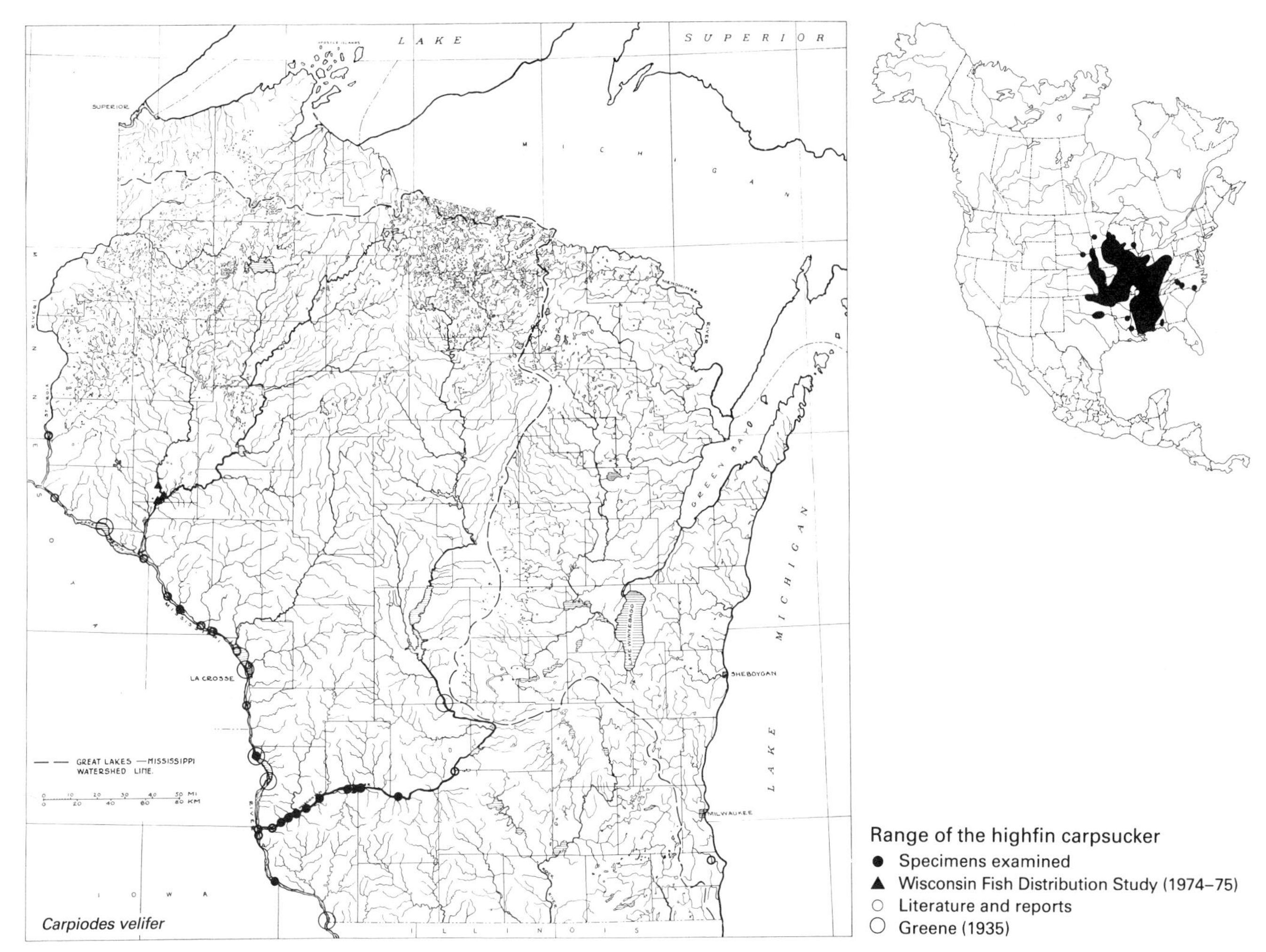

Range of the highfin carpsucker
● Specimens examined
▲ Wisconsin Fish Distribution Study (1974–75)
○ Literature and reports
◯ Greene (1935)

(Pflieger 1975); it has disappeared "from streams where it occurred 30 years ago." In Kansas, it is an endangered species (Platt et al. 1973), and in Nebraska it is endangered and possibly extirpated (Miller 1972).

On the upper Mississippi River, the highfin is rarely taken where it was once common (P. W. Smith et al. 1971). In the Minnesota-Wisconsin boundary waters of the Mississippi and St. Croix rivers, Eddy and Underhill (1974) noted a decline in the highfin population; only a single specimen was taken in Lake St. Croix in a 4-year period.

In Wisconsin, the highfin carpsucker appears to be common in two areas: the lower Wisconsin River, as attested by a number of collections made in 1962; and the lower Chippewa River between Eau Claire and Durand, where in 1977 a number of individuals (75+), 23–31 cm long and up to 450 g in weight, were collected by boom shocking and seining (D. Becker, pers. comm.).

In Wisconsin, the highfin carpsucker is found in large rivers where the current is moderate to swift, or in the quiet waters immediately adjacent to the river channels. It occurs over substrates of sand and gravel in areas which are essentially free of vegetation.

In contrast to its habitat in Wisconsin, in the southern portions of its range the highfin carpsucker often occurs in small streams or rivers. This phenomenon has been observed in other species, such as the smallmouth bass, the southern redbelly dace, and the central stoneroller minnow, which tend to frequent "big water" in the northern portions of their ranges and "little water" in the southern portions.

BIOLOGY

In Wisconsin, highfin carpsuckers in breeding condition have been reported from the Red Cedar and Chippewa rivers from mid-May to July, and from the Wisconsin River toward the end of July. In Iowa (Harlan and Speaker 1956), breeding fish migrate in large numbers to the shallow areas and the overflow ponds of streams.

In Ohio, the fecundity of four females (ages V–VII) ranged from 41,644 to 62,355 eggs per individual

(Woodward and Wissing 1976). The average diameter of the eggs in a Red Cedar River (Dunn County) female was 1.2 mm. Young-of-year from the Wisconsin River (Grant County) were 58 (49–72) mm on 24 September, and 56 (43–78) mm on 21 October. The lack of growth between the dates these collections were made suggests that growth for the year ceases in the early fall.

In the lower Wisconsin River (Sauk to Grant counties), the highfin carpsucker showed the following growth:

Age Class	Month Captured	No. of Fish	TL (mm) Avg	TL (mm) Range
I	June	3	77	72–82
I	July	29	101	81–120
II	Sept.	1	221	
III	Sept.	1	249	
IV	July	1	308	
V	July	3	322	307–333
VI	July–Aug.	2	325	312–337

Back-calculated values at the annuli were: 1—51 mm; 2—121 mm; 3—192 mm; 4—257 mm; 5—303 mm; and 6—312 mm.

In the Red Cedar River (Dunn County), two highfins captured in early July were age IV and had the following estimated lengths at the annuli: 1—42 mm; 2—142 mm; 3—218 mm; and 4—290 mm. Apparently these fish were the product of a late spawning; they showed little growth during the first year of life. The condition (K_{TL}) for the male (340 mm TL) was 1.65; for the female (322 mm TL), it was 1.38. In Pool 8 of the Mississippi River, Bur (1976) determined the ages and weights for four fish: I—153 mm (58 g); V—460 mm (1,455 g) and 472 mm (1,630 g); and VI—496 mm (1,720 g). Their condition (K_{TL}) values were 1.62, 1.49, 1.55, and 1.41 respectively.

According to Woodward and Wissing (1976), male highfins are generally larger than females at each annulus, although the actual differences in length and weight vary greatly. Sexual maturity is attained during the third year of life (Harlan and Speaker 1956). Trautman (1957) noted that in Ohio many females are mature at 229 mm (9 in).

The maximum size reported for the highfin carpsucker is the 496-mm, 1.72-kg (19.5-in, 3.8-lb) specimen from Pool 8 of the Mississippi River (Bur 1976), noted above.

The digestive tract of a single adult highfin carpsucker from Pool 8 of the Mississippi River contained 25 copepods and 2 tendipedids. Another fish was empty (Bur 1976). The stomach contents of highfins 15–25 cm (6–10 in) long from the Des Moines River, Iowa, consisted of 93% bottom ooze and algae, and 7% insects (Harrison 1950); in fish over 25 cm (10 in) long, these ratios were 78% and 22%. The insects were very small bloodworms "sometimes occurring by the thousands. . . . Other insects were represented by partial remains such as larvae cases, detached legs, wings. . . ."

D. Becker (pers. comm.) has suggested that the highfin carpsucker is a schooling fish, since on several occasions large numbers were turned up at one time with the boom shocker. This species prefers a habitat with moderately deep to deep water, differing thus from the quillback. In Iowa in July, when water levels were low, the highfin was generally found in riffle areas. Pflieger (1971) noted that the highfin is generally found in clearer waters and over firmer bottoms than other carpsuckers, and that the highfin is less tolerant of high turbidity and siltation.

The maximum temperature at which the highfin carpsucker was captured in the White River and Ipalco Discharge Canal, Indiana, was 33.9°C (93°F) (Proffitt and Benda 1971).

An upstream migration of highfin carpsuckers occurs in a number of Ohio rivers during May; a downstream movement occurs in late August and September (Trautman 1957).

Trautman (1957) observed that C. S. Rafinesque called this species the "sailor fish, flying fish and skimback" because of its curious habit of skimming along the surface with part of its back and its dorsal fin exposed, and because it frequently jumps above the water's surface. Trautman noted that skimming and jumping occur most often on quiet evenings in the late spring and early summer. The habit is indulged in by all species of carpsucker, but the highfin appears to skim and jump more frequently than do the others, including the river carpsucker.

In the Wisconsin River near Boscobel (Grant County), 49 highfin carpsuckers were associated with these species: longnose gar (1), gizzard shad (23), quillback (31), river carpsucker (1), smallmouth buffalo (2), shorthead redhorse (2), silver redhorse (1), golden redhorse (1), white sucker (1), golden shiner (10), bullhead minnow (195), fathead minnow (1), emerald shiner (24), spotfin shiner (666), spottail shiner (95), weed shiner (5), river shiner (29), Mississippi silvery minnow (47), grass pickerel (5), northern pike (9), pirate perch (1), white bass (49), yellow perch (93), walleye (22), western sand darter (8), blackside darter (1), logperch (10), johnny darter (85), smallmouth bass (18), largemouth bass (150), pumpkinseed (1), bluegill (16), orangespotted sunfish (4), black crappie (47), white crappie (6), brook silverside (10), and freshwater drum (5).

IMPORTANCE AND MANAGEMENT

The use of the highfin carpsucker as a forage fish by predator animals is unknown. Although the highfin carpsucker has been accused of competing with the small channel catfish for food, and with all fish for space in the rivers it inhabits (Harlan and Speaker 1956), it is doubtful that the small highfin population is of much consequence to the fish community.

The highfin carpsucker is host to the glochidial stage of the mollusks *Amblema plicata* and *Megalonaias gigantea*, and assists in the perpetuation of those clam species.

The highfin carpsucker is not important to the angler. A few are caught incidentally with other fish, or by the methods used to catch quillbacks and river carpsuckers.

Only a small part of the commercial catch from the Mississippi River includes the highfin, which is categorized under "quillback," along with the quillback and river carpsucker, in Mississippi River catch reports (see p. 633). Because of smaller size, the highfin would be less vulnerable to capture with the commercial gear commonly used.

Spotted Sucker

Minytrema melanops (Rafinesque). *Minytrema*—reduced aperture (an allusion to the imperfections of the lateral line); *melanops*—black appearance.

Other common names: spotted redhorse, corncob sucker, striped sucker, speckled sucker, black sucker, winter sucker.

Immature 142 mm, L. Poygan (Waushara Co.), 19 July 1960

Adult 411 mm, Mississippi R. (Pool 6), near Winona, Minnesota, 3 Aug. 1972

Breeding male 385 mm, Black R. (Jackson Co.), 2 May 1978

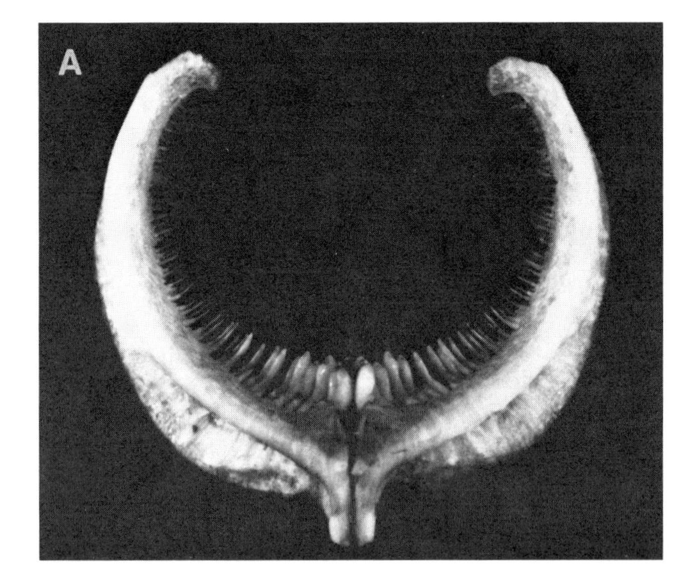

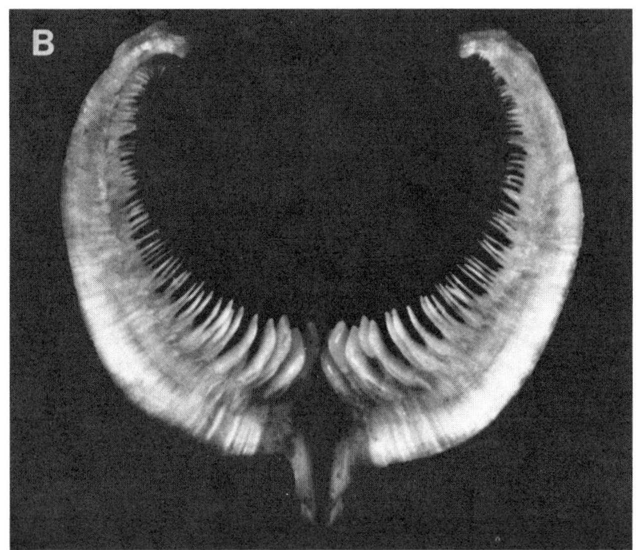

Pharyngeal arches of the spotted sucker. A. Front view. B. Back view.

DESCRIPTION

Body elongate, almost round in cross section; ventral line curved. Average length 279 mm (11 in). TL = 1.29 SL. Depth into SL 3.9–4.5. Head into SL 3.9–4.6. Snout bluntly pointed. Mouth ventral or slightly oblique, lips thin; upper lip with faint plicae; lower lip plicate and forming a sharp angle posteriorly. Pharyngeal teeth about 83 per arch; crown of each tooth with prominent cusp on anterior edge; arch moderately strong with large, honeycomb openings; the symphysis much elongated. Dorsal fin short, slightly sickle shaped in adults, straight in young; dorsal fin base into SL 5.0–6.0; dorsal fin rays 11–12; anal fin rays 7; pelvic fin rays 9–10. Lateral series scales 42–46; lateral line absent or incomplete (as few as 4 unpored scales).

Back dark green or brown-olive; sides coppery green; belly gray to silvery. Fins dusky, paired fins dusky to white; black pigment on outer quarter to third of dorsal fin. Anterior exposed edges of scales with pronounced squarish spots, lined up in regular horizontal rows.

Breeding male with tubercles on snout, over eye,

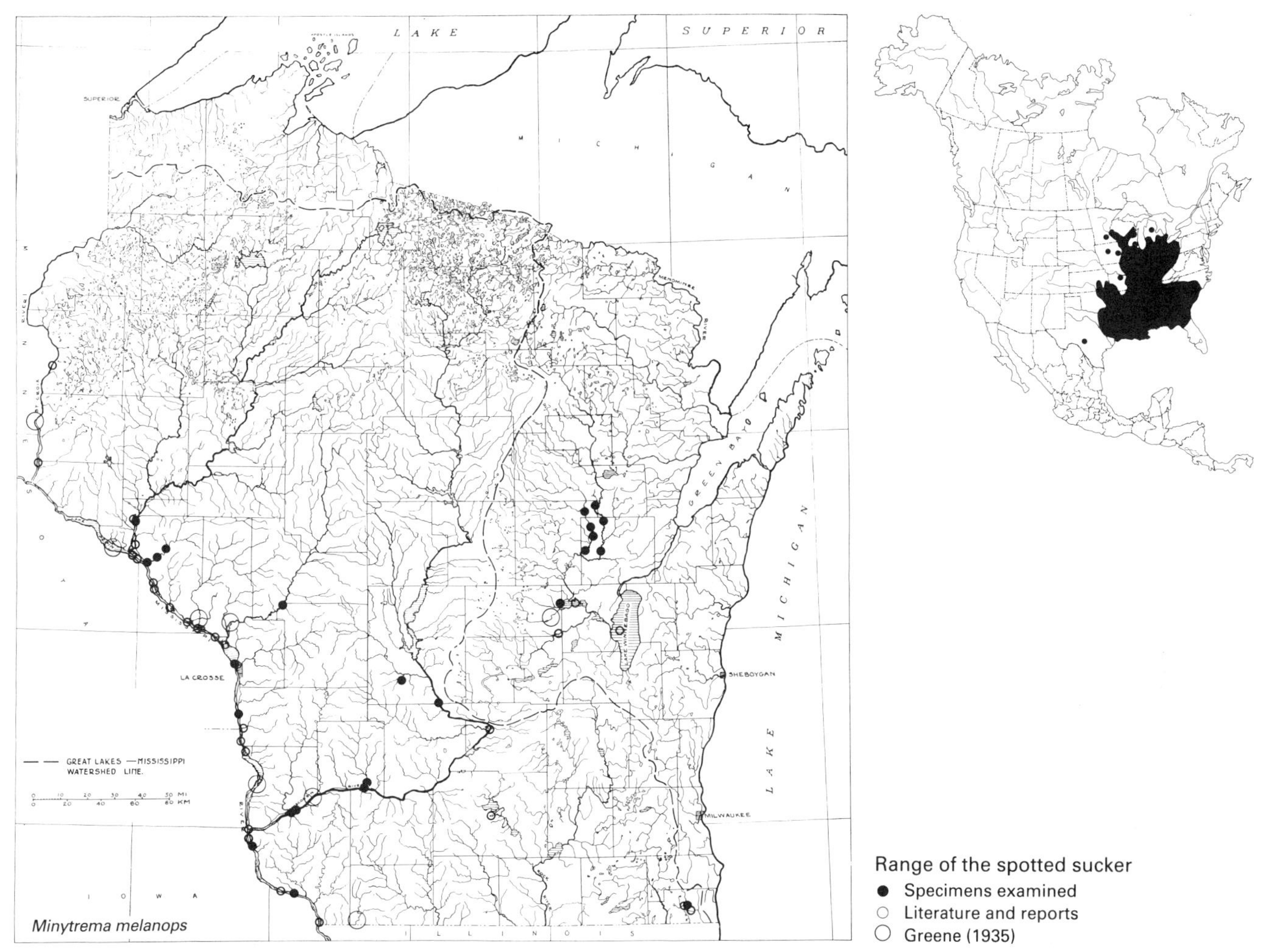

Range of the spotted sucker
● Specimens examined
○ Literature and reports
◯ Greene (1935)

on cheeks, along ventral edges of head; and a strongly tuberculated anal fin. In some males, small tubercles on other fins and on scales of the back. Males with 2 dark, nearly black, midlateral stripes separated by a pinkish red stripe (McSwain and Gennings 1972). In some breeding females, small tubercles on anal fin and a faint, pink midlateral stripe.

SYSTEMATIC NOTES

Only one species is recognized in the genus *Minytrema*. *Minytrema* is closely related to the chubsuckers in the genus *Erimyzon*.

DISTRIBUTION, STATUS, AND HABITAT

In Wisconsin the spotted sucker occurs in the Mississippi River and Lake Michigan drainage basins. Primarily a species of large rivers and their sloughs and reservoirs, it occurs in the Mississippi, St. Croix, Chippewa, Black, Des Plaines, and Wolf rivers, and in the lower parts of their tributaries. It has been reported from the upper Fox River and Lake Winnebago (Priegel 1967a, Fassbender et al. 1970). On the St. Croix River, it is reported upstream to St. Croix Falls (Polk County) (Phillips and Underhill 1971). In Lake Wingra (Dane County), a single specimen was taken in 1944 (Noland 1951); it was probably introduced from the Mississippi River in fish rescue and transfer operations.

In most areas at the northern limit of its range the spotted sucker appears to be declining in numbers. In Illinois, it has declined sharply since the beginning of the century (P. W. Smith 1965, Larimore and Smith 1963). In Iowa, it is doubtful whether the spotted sucker now exists anywhere but in the Mississippi River (Harlan and Speaker 1956). In Ohio, it was widely distributed throughout the state before 1900, but since 1920 it has been rather locally distributed (Trautman 1957). Its decrease in Ohio was caused primarily by destruction of the habitat. Trautman noted that this small-mouthed sucker with closely bound gill covers "seemed to be particularly intolerant to turbid waters, various industrial pollutants, and to lake and stream bottoms covered with flocculent clay silts." Cross (1967) suggested that the reduction in spotted sucker numbers in Kansas since early in the century may be traced to unfavorable environmental changes (mainly siltation) resulting from the intensive cultivation of watersheds along the low gradient streams that are preferred by this species.

In Wisconsin, the spotted sucker is common locally in the lower Wisconsin and in the Mississippi rivers and in their larger tributaries. It has apparently expanded its range in the Wolf-Fox and Des Plaines river drainages since Greene (1935) collected in the late 1920s. In Wisconsin this species seems to be secure.

In Wisconsin the spotted sucker occurs most frequently over a soft bottom of muck or sand where there is plant detritus. It is generally found in slightly turbid water, which is either quiet or has a sluggish current; it is frequently found in areas with heavy aquatic vegetation. Atypical habitats are known for this species. In Kansas it occurs in some intermittent streams which become turbid after rains, and in streams with bottoms that vary from bedrock to muck, but are always firm (Cross 1967).

BIOLOGY

In Wisconsin the spotted sucker spawns in May. On 9 May 1968, specimens from the St. Croix River at Taylor's Falls (Chisago County), Minnesota, were stripped of eggs or milt and returned to the river (Phillips and Underhill 1971).

In Georgia, spawning occurred from 11 March to 4 May at water temperatures of 12.2–19.4°C (54–66.9°F) (McSwain and Gennings 1972). The jumping activity of spotted suckers, which drew attention to the spawning site, was most obvious in pool-like areas near the riffle on which spawning was observed. Spawning occurred from the late morning into the afternoon over limestone rubble, in a riffle area 0.3–0.5 m deep. The flow rate of the riffle area was estimated at 1.4 m^3/sec, and the surface velocity at 0.24 m/sec. McSwain and Gennings described prespawning activity (1972:738):

> . . . From three to seven males, positioned with head upstream, established loosely defined territories over a 6 m by 3 m area. Active defense of territories was observed in which the defender swam directly toward the intruder, chasing him several meters before returning to his territory. Confrontations resulted when a cruising male swam too close to an already positioned male. These confrontations rarely involved actual physical contact. The males did not defend their territories against the intrusion of minnows that were present on the riffle. Established territories became temporarily indistinct with the appearance of a female. When a female swam into the riffle, the nearest males immediately darted toward her and began bumping and prodding her about the abdomen, back, and head with their snouts. Males often swam back and forth over the female during this prespawning activity.

McSwain and Gennings noted that spawning usually involved two males and a female. During spawning, the female settled on the bottom with a male on each side of her; all three fish were positioned with their heads upstream. The males clasped the posterior half of the female's body between their posterior halves, and vibrated their caudal portions vigorously for 2–6 sec. During the vibratory period, the trio rose toward the surface in a tails-down angle. Eggs were shed near the end of this period; they drifted downstream directly below the spawning site. At completion of the spawning act, the spawners often broke the surface of the water as they separated. The female immediately moved away, leaving the males to resume their territorial positions. Rarely, a single male would pin a female between his body and a prominent rock, but eggs were not observed during these unions. When spawning was in progress, whether involving one male or two, the intrusion of an additional male broke up the union.

Spotted sucker eggs hatch in 7–12 days (Carlander 1969). Just prior to hatching, the eggs are 3.1 mm diam; at hatching the larvae are 8.0–9.2 mm TL (White 1977). White illustrated the larval stages from 8.5 to 23.5 mm long. He noted that scale formation begins at 24–26 mm, and is completed by 32–33 mm.

In Wisconsin, the growth of young-of-year spotted suckers has been recorded as follows:

Date	No. of Fish	TL (mm) Avg	TL (mm) Range	Location
2 Aug.	10	44	38–49	Pine R. (Richland Co.)
5 Aug.	4	54	53–55	Snake Hollow Cr. (Jackson Co.)
23 Aug.	1	64		Black R. (Jackson Co.)
28 Aug.	2	53	51–55	Des Plaines R. (Kenosha Co.)
8 Sept.	2	65	59–70	Embarrass R. (Outagamie Co.)
13 Sept.	9	46	37–58	Buffalo R. (Buffalo Co.)
16 Sept.	2	58	52–63	Wolf R. (Outagamie Co.)
16 Sept.	1	78		Wolf R. (Waupaca Co.)

Three age-I fish taken from the Mississippi River (Grant County) on 10 July 1962 averaged 145 (130–150) mm TL. Seven spotted suckers taken 2 May 1968 from Pool 8 of the Mississippi River were 145–460 mm TL; they were 2–8 years old, and calculated lengths at the annuli were: 1—61 mm; 2—131 mm; 3—197 mm; 4—327 mm; 5—387 mm; 6—425 mm; 7—

442 mm; and 8—457 mm (W. Resheske, pers. comm.). At the time of capture, the annulus for the year had been placed in age-II fish, but had not yet appeared in fish age III or older.

One hundred twenty-two spotted suckers taken during the summer of 1975 from Pool 8 of the Mississippi River ranged from 130 to 495 mm TL; they were 1–6 years old (Bur 1976). The calculated lengths at the annuli were: 1—63 mm; 2—169 mm; 3—270 mm; 4—348 mm; 5—391 mm; and 6—450 mm. Weights ranged from 1.8 g for young-of-year to 1.73 kg (3 lb 13 oz) for a six-year-old.

The calculated lengths at the annuli for 85 spotted suckers from the Mississippi River at Fountain City (Buffalo County) were: 1—61 mm; 2—203 mm; 3—284 mm; 4—351 mm; 5—396 mm; and 6—414 mm (Christenson and Smith 1965).

A 150-mm female spotted sucker, taken from the Mississippi River at Bagley (Grant County), had eaten mostly ostracods and tendipedid larvae, and lesser amounts of ephemeropteran larvae, amphipods, copepods, filamentous algae, and higher plant material. Most of the food organisms were less than 3 mm TL.

In Pool 8 of the Mississippi River, copepods and ostracods constituted 19.4%, and cladocerans 77.2%, of the volume in spotted sucker digestive tracts (Bur 1976). Bur noted that many of the digestive tracts of the fish examined were empty; he concluded that the spotted sucker did not feed during periods of changing light intensities. White and Haag (1977) found, however, that the young feed in schools during the day, while the adults feed mainly at dawn and dusk. This species feeds actively during the breeding season (McSwain and Gennings 1972).

Ten spotted suckers were collected from the Pine River (Richland County) along with river carpsucker (1), shorthead redhorse (2), white sucker (4), silver chub (2), speckled chub (1), golden shiner (7), bullhead minnow (31), bluntnose minnow (2), fathead minnow (3), suckermouth minnow (4), emerald shiner (7), spotfin shiner (118), weed shiner (1), brassy minnow (1), channel catfish (1), black bullhead (80), central mudminnow (3), grass pickerel (1), walleye (1), johnny darter (19), largemouth bass (9), green sunfish (26), pumpkinseed (5), bluegill (4), and black crappie (4).

IMPORTANCE AND MANAGEMENT

Young spotted suckers are probably preyed on by other fishes and by birds (Scott and Crossman 1973).

The spotted sucker is occasionally taken by anglers. On the Wolf River it bites on worms or grubs, and is referred to by fishermen as a "corncob sucker." It is an excellent food fish.

In the Mississippi River, the spotted sucker constitutes only a small part of the commercial catch referred to in statistics as "suckers and redhorse," although occasionally it may be a prominent part of a catch.

From Alabama to Wisconsin, standing crops of the spotted sucker averaged 8.7 kg/ha (7.8 lb/acre), and ranged from 2.9 to 20.0 kg/ha (2.6 to 17.8 lb/acre) (Carlander 1955).

Lake Chubsucker

Erimyzon sucetta (Lacepède). *Erimyzon*—sucker; *sucetta*—from sucet, French for a sucker or sucking fish.

Other common names: chubsucker, pin sucker, pin minnow, sweet sucker.

Adult male 219 mm, Pleasant L. (Walworth Co.), 26 Mar. 1974

DESCRIPTION

Body moderately deep, slightly compressed; tapered at both ends. Average length 188 mm (7.4 in). TL = 1.22 SL. Depth into SL less than 3.3, usually 2.9–3.1. Head into SL 3.5–4.1. Snout tapered to a blunt point. Mouth subterminal, slightly oblique; lips plicate, halves of lower lip forming an acute angle. Pharyngeal teeth short and fragile, 80 or more per arch, with a sharp cusp on anterior edge of crown; arch weak, symphysis moderately long. Dorsal fin convex, dorsal fin base into SL 5.2; dorsal fin rays 11–12 (10–13); anal fin rays usually 7; pelvic fin rays usually 9. Lateral series scales 35–37 (33–40); lateral line absent. Scales square in appearance, with both dorsal and ventral edges straight and parallel to one another; similar scale structure in *Erimyzon oblongus*. Chromosomes 2n = 96–100 (Uyeno and Smith 1972).

Back olive brown; sides lighter and more yellow; belly olive yellow. The scales prominently dark edged. Fins olive to slate colored. Young with a clear black stripe from tip of snout to base of caudal fin; caudal fin reddish; dorsal fin with dark chromatophores on interradial membrane between first and second ray, thinly scattered chromatophores on distal portions of second and third membranes, chromatophores absent from the rest of the membranes.

Breeding male with 3 large tubercles on each side of snout; anal fin sickle shaped.

SYSTEMATIC NOTES

Literature records for *Erimyzon* prior to 1930 are unreliable because the species were not properly distinguished until then (see Hubbs 1930b). Two forms are recognized: the eastern lake chubsucker, *Erimyzon sucetta sucetta* (Lacepède), which occurs east of the Allegheny Mountains from New York to Florida; and the western lake chubsucker, *Erimyzon sucetta kennerlii* (Girard), which occurs west of the Allegheny Mountains from the lower Great Lakes above Niagara Falls to Texas, including Wisconsin. The western form usually has 11 dorsal rays and 36–38 lateral series scales; the eastern form usually has 12 dorsal rays and 35–36 lateral series scales.

DISTRIBUTION, STATUS, AND HABITAT

In Wisconsin, the lake chubsucker occurs in the Mississippi River and Lake Michigan drainage basins. In the former, it is confined mainly to the lower Wiscon-

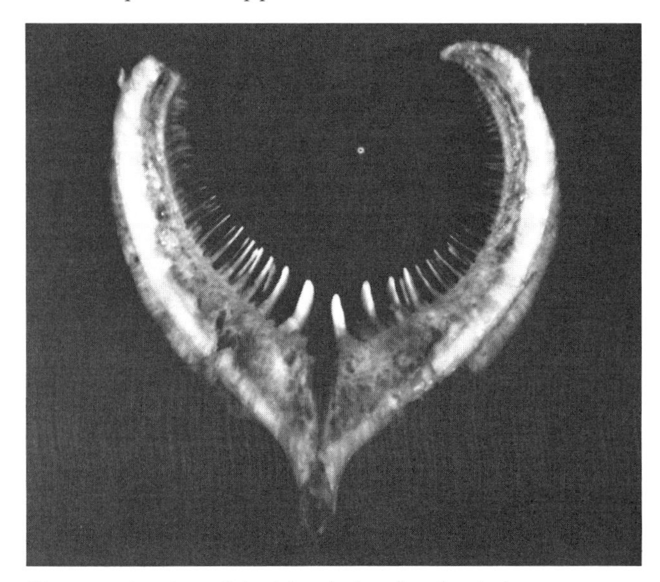

Pharyngeal arches of the lake chubsucker, front view

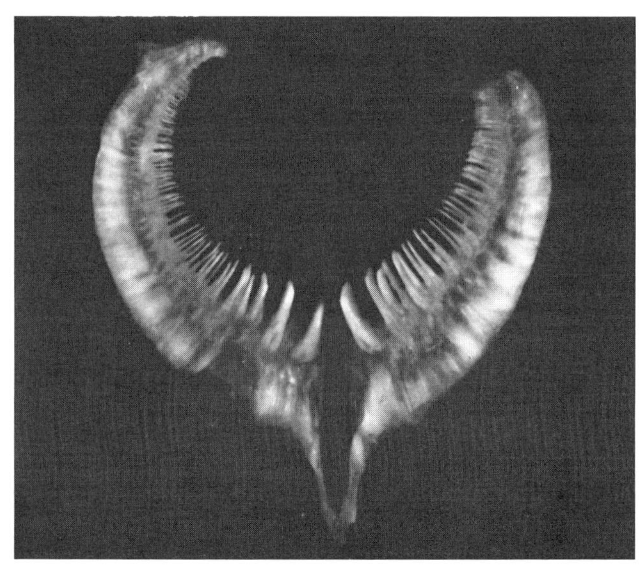

Pharyngeal arches of the lake chubsucker, back view

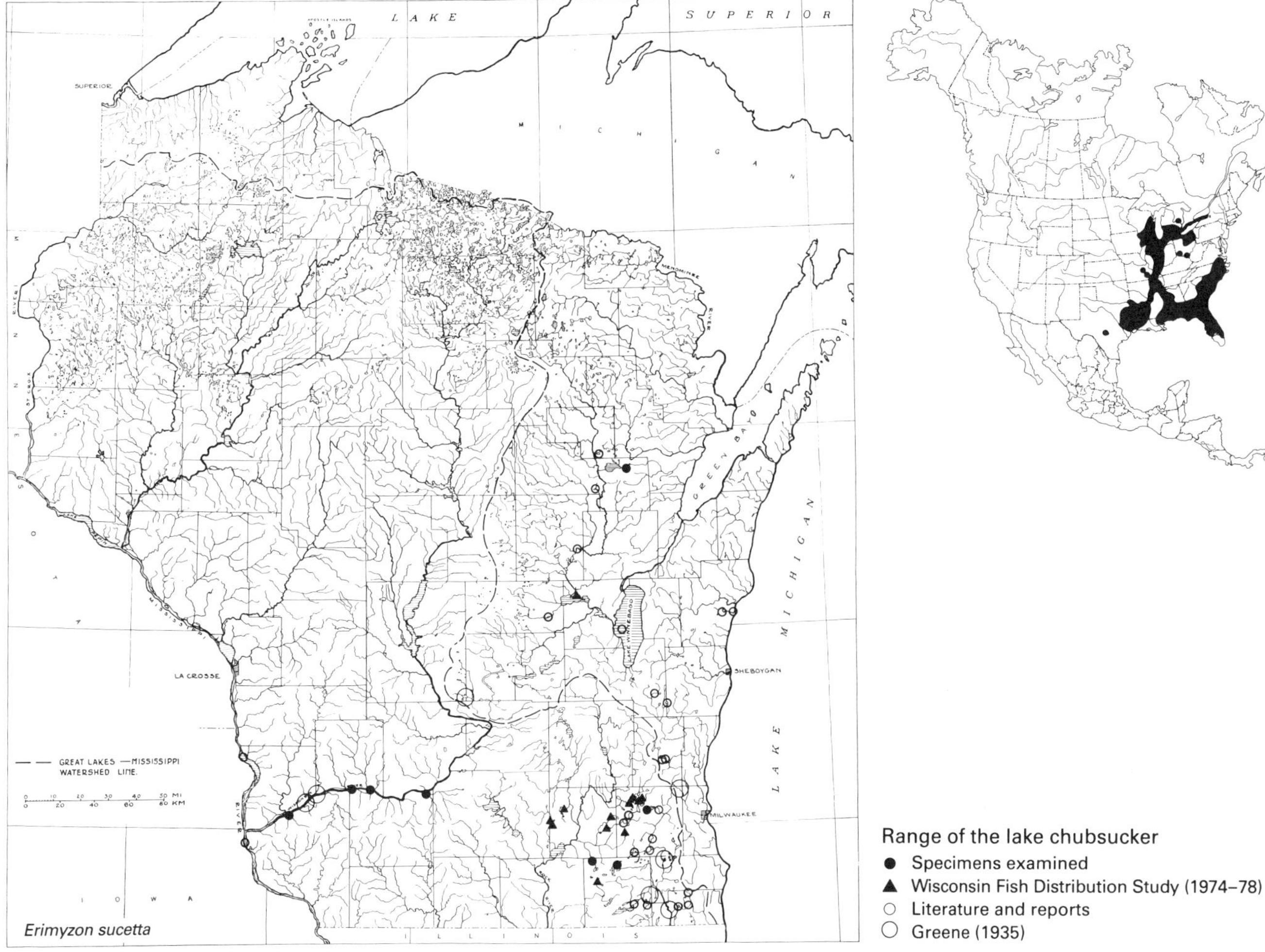

Range of the lake chubsucker
● Specimens examined
▲ Wisconsin Fish Distribution Study (1974–78)
○ Literature and reports
◯ Greene (1935)

sin River and its tributaries and the upper Rock River and Illinois-Fox River watersheds. This species reaches its northern limit of distribution in the Wolf River system of the Lake Michigan basin.

In Wisconsin, the lake chubsucker appears to have spread northward, particularly in the Lake Michigan drainage basin, since Greene (1935) made his survey in the late 1920s.

Specimens examined: UWSP 109 (1) Indian Creek at Hwy 60 (Richland County), 1962; UWSP 110 (1) Wisconsin River slough east of Big Green River (Grant County), 1962; UWSP 126 (1) Pewaukee Lake (Waukesha County), 1960; UWSP 2824 (1) Tripp Lake (Walworth County), 1968; UWSP 4020 (1) Wisconsin River T8N R5E Sec 9 (Iowa County), 1969; UWSP 4605 (4) Pleasant Lake (Walworth County), 1974; UWSP 5484 (4) Oconomowoc River T8N R17E Sec 34 (Waukesha County), 1976; and UWSP 5656 (1) White Clay Lake (Shawano County), 1967.

The Wisconsin Fish Distribution Study made 25 collections of lake chubsucker from 1974 to 1978 in Waukesha, Walworth, Jefferson, and Fond du Lac counties. On file with the same study are a number of state and private reports from the Rock, Illinois-Fox, and Fox-Wolf river systems. Other reports of lake chubsuckers include: Moshawquit Lake (Menominee County) and Pine Lake (Shawano County) (T. McKnight, pers. comm.); Auroraville Pond (Waushara County) (V. Hacker, pers. comm.); Lake Winnebago (Priegel 1967a); and Silver Creek (Manitowoc County) (M. Johnson, pers. comm.).

The lake chubsucker has disappeared or decreased over much of its range. It is extirpated in Iowa (Harlan and Speaker 1956, Roosa 1977), and has decreased in Illinois (P. W. Smith 1979), Missouri (Pflieger 1975), and Ohio (Trautman 1957). It is seldom abundant, and it is often disjunct in its distribution.

In Wisconsin seldom are more than one or two lake chubsuckers collected at a site, even in those areas where known populations exist. In the lower half of Wisconsin, the lake chubsucker is rare to uncommon locally in the larger rivers and the lower portions of their tributaries. It is occasional in lakes from the Wolf River watershed, and has been reported as abundant in the Auroraville Pond (Waushara County) (V. Hacker, pers. comm.). It appears to be most secure in the lakes and streams of the extreme southeastern corner of Wisconsin. In Waukesha County, this species was captured in 7 of 40 lakes sampled (Poff and Threinen 1963). The lake chubsucker has recently been given watch status (Wis. Dep. Nat. Resour. Endangered Species Com. 1975, Les 1979).

The lake chubsucker characteristically occurs in lakes, oxbow lakes, and sloughs of large rivers and quiet streams. In Wisconsin, it was encountered most frequently in clear water at depths of 0.1–0.5 m, over substrates of gravel (30% frequency), rubble (20%), sand (20%), boulders (10%), mud (10%), and silt (10%). It occurred in streams 3.0–24.0 m wide. It is frequently associated with dense vegetation over bottoms composed of sand or silt mixed with organic debris.

BIOLOGY

In Wisconsin, lake chubsucker spawning begins in late March and probably occurs in some waters until early July.

During spawning the eggs are scattered at random with no apparent prior preparation of the spawning site. In Michigan forage fish ponds, lake chubsuckers scattered their eggs abundantly over both large and small beds of *Amblystegium riparium*, among masses of filamentous algae, and in dead grass stubble on submerged pieces of sod (Cooper 1936). The spawning season, somewhat modified by the method of handling the breeders, lasted about 2 weeks in each pond. Underhill (1941) noted movement of lake chubsuckers along the shores of a pond before and during spawning.

A prespawning female, 273 mm long and weighing 337 g, collected 26 March from Pleasant Lake (Walworth County), had ovaries 3.6% of body weight, and held an estimated 15,055 maturing eggs 0.75–1.0 mm diam; an egg size class of 0.3–0.7 mm diam was more numerous. Both egg size classes were yellow-white, with a few of the largest eggs yellow-orange in color.

In Michigan, the number of eggs deposited by lake chubsuckers varied from 3,000 to 20,000 (Cooper 1936). At water temperatures of 22.5–29.5°C (72.5–85.1°F), eggs hatched into 5–6 mm fry in 6–7 days. Detailed chemical analyses which were made of developing lake chubsucker embryos (Shaklee et al. 1974) were correlated with the structural stages described for the white sucker by Long and Ballard (1976).

Young lake chubsuckers have an estimated growth of 0.50 mm per day during a 30-day period early in the first summer of life (Hubbs 1921). In the lower Wisconsin River, young-of-year were 32 mm on 13 July, and 63 mm on 2 November. They are frequently found in weedy areas. Small chubsuckers, 30–42 mm, fed on copepods, cladocerans, and chironomids (Ewers and Boesel 1935).

In Pleasant Lake (Walworth County), lake chubsuckers showed the following growth at the annuli: 1—64 mm; 2—147 mm; 3—208 mm; 4—221 mm; 5—247 mm; and 6—269 mm. The largest fish, a 273-mm, 337-g female, was 6 years old. A 223-mm, age-III lake chubsucker from Pewaukee Lake (Waukesha County) exhibited a growth rate similar to the chubsuckers from Pleasant Lake. Three age-II chubsuckers, 99–120 mm TL, from Scuppernong Creek (Washington County) averaged 46 and 105 mm at the first and second annuli.

The maximum known size of a lake chubsucker is a 387-mm, 907-g (15.2-in, 2.0-lb) fish taken in Silver Springs, Florida (Carlander 1969).

Lake chubsuckers generally grow rapidly during the first 3 or 4 summers of life, after which the growth rate drops quickly. Both sexes reach maturity at age III (Cooper 1936).

The lake chubsucker is a bottom feeder which ingests diatoms, algae, mollusks (*Sphaerium*, *Physa* and *Planorbis*), insect larvae, and occasionally adult insects. Vegetable matter may make up about 70% of the diet (Cahn 1927). In Florida (Shireman et al. 1978), lake chubsuckers 83–103 mm long fed primarily on filamentous algae (100% occurrence), cladocerans (25% occurrence), and chironomid larvae (25% occurrence); copepods were of lesser importance (13% occurrence). Chubsuckers, 127–152 mm long, fed primarily on copepods (50% occurrence) and algae (25% occurrence); cladocera, ostracods, and chironomid larvae (13% occurrence) were eaten with equal frequency.

Lake chubsuckers are tolerant of environmental stresses. Gerking (1945) noted that, in the Kankakee River region of Indiana, this species was present in Beaver Lake before the area was ditched and the lake eliminated; the lake chubsucker persists, however, in Beaver Lake Ditch.

The lake chubsucker can tolerate low oxygen thresholds in winterkill lakes (Cooper and Washburn 1949). In Michigan lakes, its toleration level of approximately 0.4–0.3 ppm was similar to that of the yellow perch, grass pickerel, pumpkinseed, and northern pike; this was lower than the level of about 0.6 ppm tolerated by largemouth bass and bluegills.

The lake chubsucker has been collected from White

Clay Lake (Shawano County) along with the pugnose shiner, brown bullhead, largemouth bass, rock bass, yellow perch, Iowa darter, and johnny darter.

IMPORTANCE AND MANAGEMENT

The lake chubsucker is a valuable forage fish for predators, and largemouth bass feed readily upon the fry. Bennett and Childers (1966) observed (p. 89):

> . . . It apparently fills a niche not occupied by any of the predatory or semipredatory sport fishes, and its presence broadens the food web for basses (Centrarchidae) where these are dependent on crayfish, aquatic insects, and their own young for food. Moreover, the lake chubsucker is so retiring and unobtrusive that it is seldom seen except during the height of the spring spawning season. This is a clear-water species, and its feeding does not roil the bottom and thereby increase the turbidity of the water.

The lake chubsucker is of little or no importance to the angler because of its scarcity in most waters and its small size. It can be taken on a small hook. However, its flesh is bony and without flavor. In Alabama, it is occasionally taken in large numbers by commercial fishermen (Smith-Vaniz 1967).

Fingerling lake chubsuckers seem ideally suited for use as bait minnows, since they have round cylindrical bodies, soft fins, and a golden color; they are also hardy and can withstand the stress of handling. The production of lake chubsuckers for bait is possible in heated ponds at Wisconsin's latitude.

Bennett and Childers (1966) have proposed that the lake chubsucker be stocked as forage fish in artificial ponds, quarry pits, and small lakes, if the owners are interested in bass fishing.

The lake chubsucker is capable of maintaining a sizeable population, but seldom produces an overpopulation. In Ridge Lake, Illinois, there were an estimated 468 chubsuckers per hectare (187/acre). From Florida to Wisconsin, standing crops of the lake chubsucker averaged 24.3 kg/ha (21.7 lb/acre), and ranged from 0.7 to 80.7 kg/ha (0.6 to 72.0 lb/acre) (Carlander 1955). A recent study in Florida produced a mean biomass estimate of 514 kg/ha (458 lb/acre) (Shireman et al. 1978).

Creek Chubsucker

Erimyzon oblongus (Mitchill). *Erimyzon*—sucker; *oblongus*—oblong.
Other common names: chubsucker, sweet sucker.

Immature 84 mm, Little Cr. (Grant Parish), Louisiana, 14 Sept. 1969

DESCRIPTION
Body elongate, slightly compressed. Length 114–178 mm (4.5–7.0 in). TL = 1.24 SL. Depth into SL 3.2–4.2, usually more than 3.4. Head into SL 3.4–3.7. Snout well rounded, in ventral view barely extending beyond tip of upper lip. Mouth subterminal, slightly oblique; lips plicate but papillose at corners, halves of lower lip forming an acute angle. Pharyngeal teeth narrow, fragile, about 68 per arch, with an elongate, sharp cusp on anterior edge of crown of each tooth; arch weak, symphysis short. Dorsal fin base into SL 5.3–5.8; dorsal fin convex, with 9–10 (8–11) rays; anal fin rays usually 7; pelvic fin rays usually 9. Lateral series scales 39–41 (37–45); lateral line absent. Scales square in appearance, with both dorsal and ventral edges straight and parallel to one another; similar scale structure in *Erimyzon sucetta*.

Back olive brown; sides lighter and more yellow; belly yellow to white. The scales prominently dark edged. Dorsal and caudal fins olive or slate colored; lower fins yellowish white. In young, a series of 5–8 blotches along sides, with a saddle band directly above each; adults with lateral stripe or lateral blotches more or less confluent. Young with amber caudal fin; dorsal fin with brown chromatophores in interradial membranes between first and third rays, thinly scattered chromatophores on distal portions of remaining membranes. Breeding males with 3 large tubercles on each side of snout.

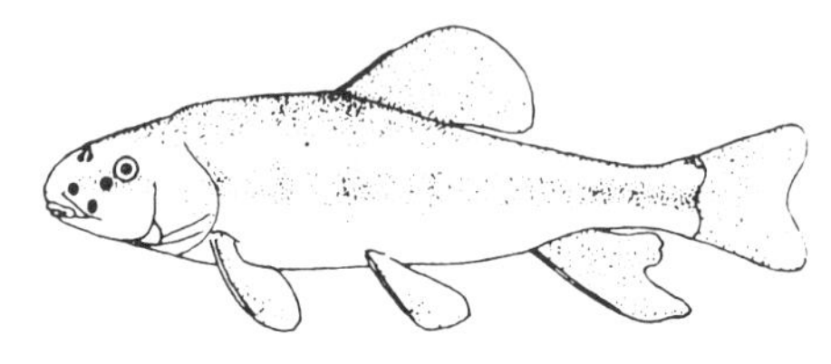

Breeding male with three tubercles on side of snout; anal fin sickle shaped (from *The Fishes of Ohio*, by Milton B. Trautman [Columbus, Ohio: Ohio State University Press, 1957, 280])

Sexual dimorphism: Male with anal fin sickle shaped; female with anal fin lobed or shallowly indented on free edge.

SYSTEMATIC NOTES
Literature records for *Erimyzon* prior to 1930 are unreliable because the species were not properly distinguished until then (see Hubbs 1930b). Three subspe-

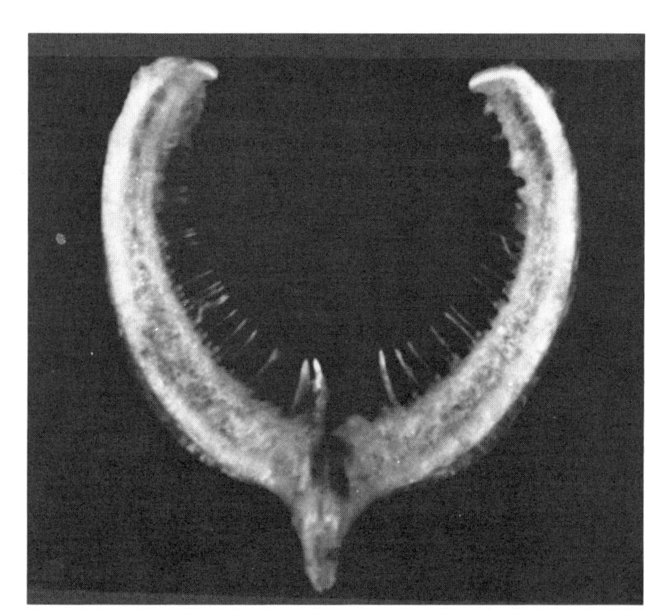

Pharyngeal arches of the creek chubsucker, front view

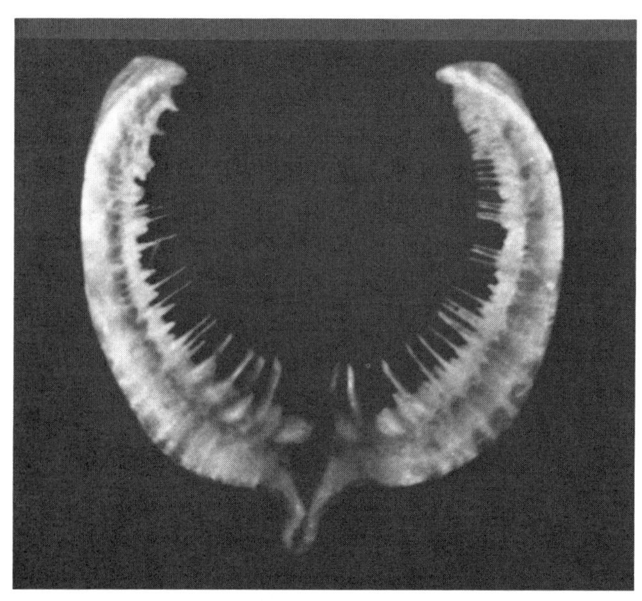

Pharyngeal arches of the creek chubsucker, back view

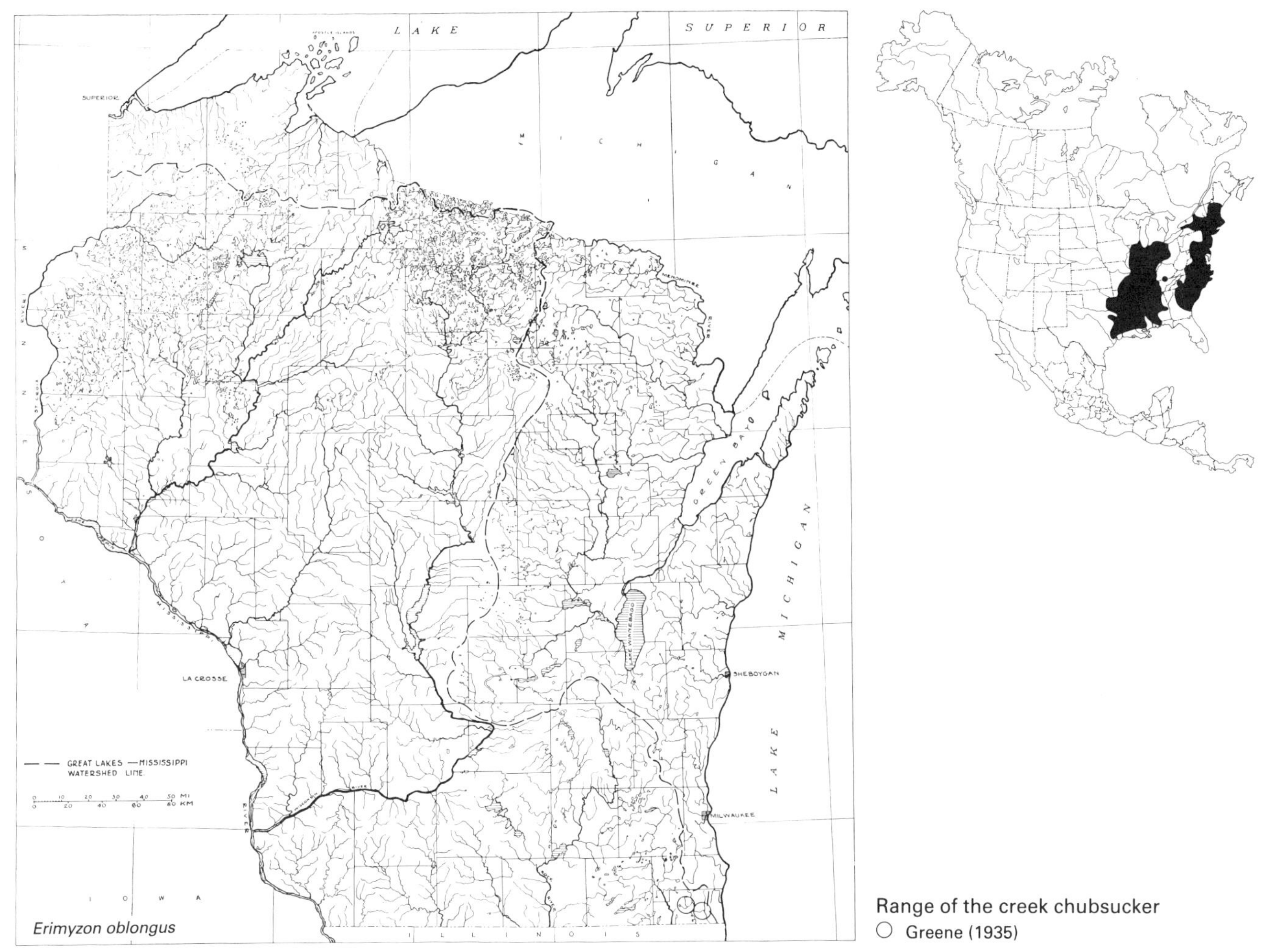

Range of the creek chubsucker
○ Greene (1935)

cies for *Erimyzon oblongus* are recognized: the eastern creek chubsucker, *E. o. oblongus*, which occurs in the Atlantic drainage from New England at least to Virginia, including the Lake Ontario basin; *E. o. connectens*, which occurs in the Altamaha River system, Georgia; and the western creek chubsucker, *E. o. claviformis*, which occurs west of the Allegheny Mountains from the lower Great Lakes above Niagara Falls to Oklahoma and Alabama, including Wisconsin. The last subspecies is characterized by a small dorsal fin, usually with only 10 rays, and a very small size—usually less than 25 cm (10 in).

DISTRIBUTION, STATUS, AND HABITAT

In Wisconsin, the creek chubsucker occurred in the extreme southeastern corner of the Lake Michigan drainage basin, in Kenosha County. Two records are provided by Greene (1935)—one from the Des Plaines River, and another from a tributary. I have examined the former (UMMZ 78465), which consists of eight specimens taken by Schultz and Tarzwell on 28 August 1928 from the Des Plaines River 3.2 km (2 mi) east of Bristol (Kenosha County). Another collection of two specimens (UWMZ 623), collected 27 June 1906 by George Wagner, is from a creek 3.2 km (2 mi) northeast of Salem (Kenosha County).

Environmental effects adverse to the creek chubsucker have been reported. In Illinois, P. W. Smith (1971) noted that the dessication of stream systems during droughts has been particularly devastating to headwater and creek species like the creek chubsucker. In Ohio, Trautman (1957) found many dead chubsuckers in a stream choked with clayey silt; the silt had been washed into the stream from recently cultivated cornfields during a brief summer shower and packed about the gills of the chubsuckers, suffocating them.

In Wisconsin, the creek chubsucker is considered extirpated (Wis. Dep. Nat. Resour. Endangered Species Com. 1975, Les 1979). It probably reached the northern limit of its range in the Des Plaines River, and the deterioration of the watershed there may have eliminated the remnant population by the mid-20th century.

Where the creek chubsucker was captured, the Des Plaines River is 5–8 m (15–25 ft) wide. According to Pflieger (1975), this species is an inhabitant of clear, quiet waters with thick growths of submergent vegetation, and bottoms composed of sand or silt mixed with organic debris. It commonly occurs in the deeper and more sluggish pools of small creeks, but it is more often found in protected inlets and overflow pools. The creek chubsucker is more characteristic of small creeks than of rivers. The eastern subspecies also occurs in sizeable impoundments and in lakes.

BIOLOGY

Spawning occurs from early spring to early June. In the East, where spawning has been observed, creek chubsuckers move upstream in large numbers, and spawn throughout the day and night in riffles or at the outlets of lakes (Whitworth et al. 1968, Everhart 1958). Although the eggs are generally scattered at random with no apparent prior preparation of the spawning site, spawning may occur over a prepared substrate. In Illinois, Hankinson (1920) observed two tuberculate males pulling at the stones of a gravelly shoal; later these two individuals were seen flanking one of the several smaller associate chubsuckers which Hankinson considered females. The behavior he witnessed was very similar to the spawning act of the white sucker (see p. 684).

In Black Moshannon Lake, Pennsylvania (Wagner and Cooper 1963), egg production for the population as a whole averaged about 9,000 eggs per adult fish; for the largest females (381 mm) it averaged 29,000. In North Carolina, the number of eggs per female ranged from 8,694 to 72,360 in females 111–970 g (Carnes 1958).

The ripe eggs are spherical, 1.84 mm diam. Incubation at about 20°C (68°F) requires 96 hours (Mansueti and Hardy 1967), and the early embryonic stages, yolk-sac larvae, larvae, and juveniles are illustrated and detailed by Mansueti and Hardy. Upon hatching, the young are 4.8 mm TL. Young creek chubsuckers remain in small schools over vegetation along lake shores, or in quiet pools of small streams.

Seven young-of-year creek chubsuckers from the Des Plaines River (Kenosha County), taken 28 August, averaged 45 (39–53) mm TL. An age-II fish from the same collection was 100 mm TL.

The average standard lengths (weights) of western creek chubsuckers collected in August from southern Illinois (Lewis and Elder 1953) were: I—85 mm (14 g); and II—122 mm (40 g). Their calculated standard lengths at the annuli were: 1—40 mm, and 2—86 mm. In Missouri, adults are commonly 114–178 mm long, and may attain a maximum of about 236 mm (9.3 in) (Pflieger 1975). In Ohio (Trautman 1957), the smallest breeding males with tubercles and bifurcate anal fins were only 61 mm (2.4 in) long.

By comparison, the growth of the eastern creek chubsucker is substantially greater. In Black Moshannon Lake, Pennsylvania, age-I fish were 71–132 mm TL. Males age II were 244 mm TL (212 g); III—305 mm (410 g); IV—323 mm (487 g); and V—353 mm (600 g); females age II were 246 mm (219 g); III—277 mm (309 g); IV—320 mm (465 g); V—330 mm (511 g); VI—358 mm (675 g); and VII—376 mm (750 g). No males were found older than age V. In most age groups in which sample sizes were moderately large, males appeared to grow faster than females.

In Virginia, the food of creek chubsuckers consisted of Entomostraca, rotifers, small insects, and algae (Flemer and Woolcott 1966). Pflieger (1975) suggested that the terminal mouth of this species may indicate that it feeds less on the bottom than many suckers.

After spawning, or in the early summer, adult creek chubsuckers migrate downstream into the larger creeks, where they remain throughout the fall and winter.

IMPORTANCE AND MANAGEMENT

In New York, the creek chubsucker is, next to the golden shiner, probably the most important forage fish of the smaller lakes; it is also a frequent associate of pickerel, perch, and largemouth bass (Greeley 1936). In New Hampshire, it is used as a forage fish by such game species as large and smallmouth bass and chain pickerel (Scarola 1973).

In the south, where the creek chubsucker bites readily on small hooks, it gives children and other pole fishermen considerable sport (Cook 1959). The creek chubsucker may be used as bait in lieu of large minnows (Luce 1933). The flesh, however, is bony and considered flavorless.

The creek chubsucker occurs for the most part at low population levels. Black Moshannon Lake in central Pennsylvania held an estimated population of about 20 breeding adults per hectare (8/acre) (Wagner and Cooper 1963). Although a high annual mortality rate was observed in the population, Wagner and Cooper considered such a mortality rate to be an advantage to the management of lakes producing predatory game fishes, since a small population of adult chubsuckers is sufficient to produce a large number of small forage fish without using a major part of the fish food production of the lake to maintain the adult suckers.

Black Redhorse

Moxostoma duquesnei (Lesueur). *Moxostoma*—sucking mouth; *duquesnei*—after Fort Duquesne (now Pittsburgh), Pennsylvania, the type locality.

Other common names: blackhorse, black mullet, finescale mullet, finescale redhorse, white sucker, blue sucker.

230 mm, Spring R. (Sharp Co.), Arkansas, 1 June 1977

DESCRIPTION

Body slender and elongate, almost round in cross section; ventral aspect straight, slightly curved caudally. Adult length about 250 mm (10 in). TL = 1.27 SL. Depth into SL 3.9–4.8. Head into SL 4.1–4.8. Snout rounded and swollen, overhanging mouth ventrally (almost concealing upper lip). Mouth ventral and horizontal; lips plicate, occasionally slightly wrinkled, papillae absent; lower lip much broader than upper, with posterior edge in straight line or at a broad angle (100–170°). Pharyngeal teeth narrow, fragile, about 65 per arch; crown of tooth with single, definitive cusp at anterior edge; arch moderately strong, symphysis short. Dorsal fin slightly sickle-shaped or moderately concave, rarely straight; dorsal fin base into SL 4.4–5.4, length of base about three-fourths the distance from back of head to dorsal fin base; dorsal fin rays 12–14; anal fin rays 7; pelvic fin rays usually 10 (8–11), but almost invariably 1 or both pelvic fins have 10 rays. Postweberian vertebral numbers 40–41 (39–43). Lateral line scales 44–47 (43–51); lateral line complete. Scales around caudal peduncle 12. Chromosomes 2n = 96–100 (Uyeno and Smith 1972).

Back dark olive green; sides golden to brassy; belly whitish. Caudal and dorsal fins slate colored, although pale red in larger juveniles and adults in some drainages; lower fins typically orange hued or reddish orange, most intense in anterior rays. Scales without dark spots at their anterior exposed bases.

Breeding male with minute tubercles over all surfaces of head; tubercles on most body scales and on all caudal fin rays, with largest tubercles on lower lobe. Anal fin rays tuberculate except on outer third to fifth of rays; minute tubercles generally present on anterior rays of paired fins and dorsal fin. Breeding males with light pinkish midlateral stripe from operculum to base of caudal fin. Genital papilla swollen, opaque white in male; translucent, with small reddish tip, in female. Breeding female with minute tubercles on head and most of body; tubercles absent on fins. Breeding female shows no change in color.

Sexual dimorphism: In male, the lengths of the depressed dorsal fin, the dorsal fin base, the pelvic fin, and the anal fin are significantly longer than in female (Phillips and Underhill 1971).

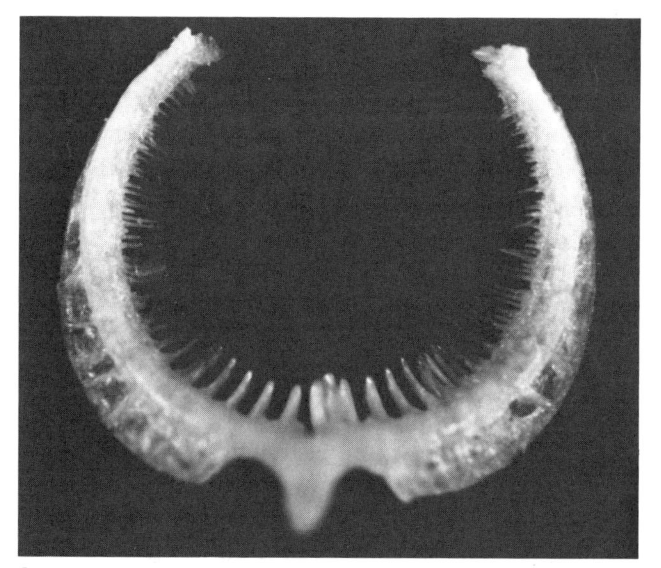

Pharyngeal arches of the black redhorse, front view

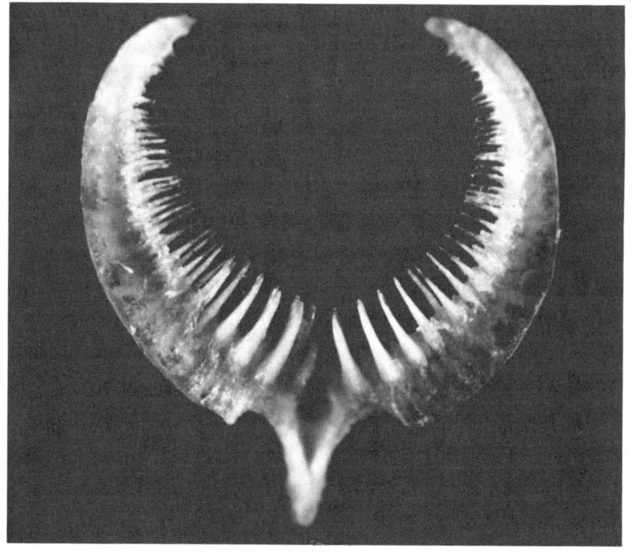

Pharyngeal arches of the black redhorse, back view

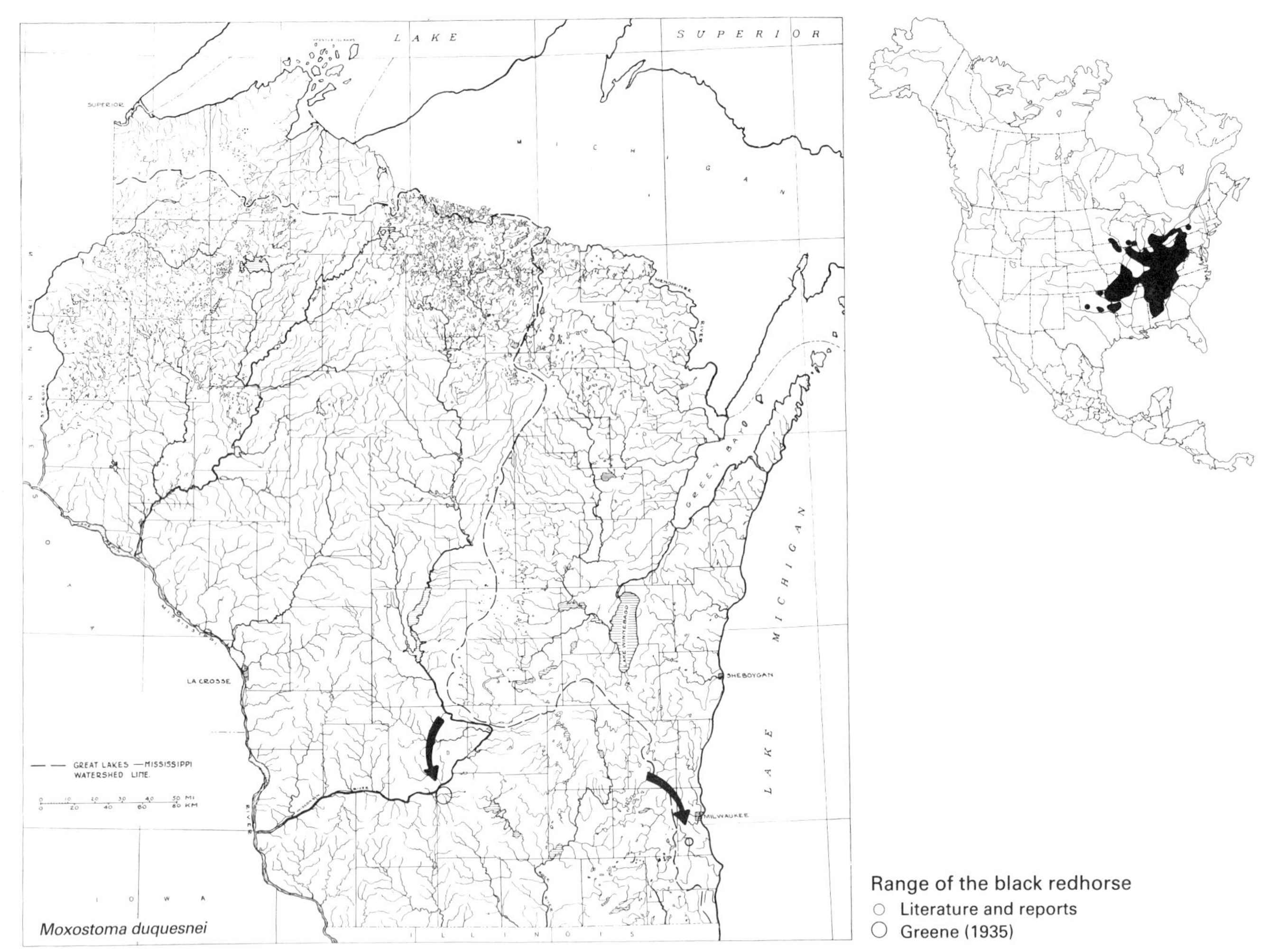

Range of the black redhorse
○ Literature and reports
○ Greene (1935)

DISTRIBUTION, STATUS, AND HABITAT

The inclusion of the black redhorse in the fish fauna of Wisconsin is based on two specimens: UMMZ 47641, from Black Earth Creek, 1.6 km southeast of Mazomanie (Dane County), collected by Scholz and Tarzwell 7 August 1928; and USNM 20272, from the Root River, probably near Milwaukee or Racine in the Lake Michigan drainage basin, collected by S. F. Baird during the mid-1800s.

In Minnesota, the black redhorse has been given changing or uncertain status (J. B. Moyle 1975). It is endangered in Iowa (Roosa 1977), and possibly extirpated in Canada (Scott and Crossman 1973).

The black redhorse was probably eliminated early from the Root River in southeastern Wisconsin. In Black Earth Creek, the placement of the impoundment at Mazomanie was probably responsible for its disappearance there. Today it is considered extirpated in Wisconsin (Wis. Dep. Nat. Resour. Endangered Species Com. 1975, Les 1979), although a faint possibility exists that it may still occur in some restricted sector of suitable water in southern Wisconsin which has been overlooked.

The narrow spawning requirements of the black redhorse, which include a proper substrate, water flow, and stream size, may have contributed to its disappearance in Wisconsin.

The black redhorse inhabits the swiftly flowing sections of small- to medium-sized streams. It is found in clear water over gravel, bedrock, and sand where siltation is at a minimum. According to Jenkins (1970), it is generally absent from small headwater tributaries averaging less than 3 m (10 ft) in width, and it is the redhorse most restricted to higher gradients and smaller streams. The Black Earth Creek specimen was collected where the stream was about 18 m (60 ft) wide, and ran swiftly over gravel and rubble (Greene 1935).

In Missouri, streams with average annual discharges of 14–17 m^3/sec (500–600 cfs) yielded larger proportions of black redhorse than streams having greater volumes of flow (Bowman 1970); at lesser flow volumes, limited observation has shown that there is a decrease in black redhorse densities.

BIOLOGY

Unless otherwise designated, the following information on the black redhorse is derived from Bowman (1970), whose studies were based on research in the Niangua and Big Piney rivers in Missouri.

Adult black redhorses begin moving to spawning areas in March or early April from the deeper holes of rivers; they move both upstream and downstream to reach spawning riffles. At least 30 tagged individuals were observed to have moved upstream a distance of 9.7 km (6 mi) to a spawning riffle, passing approximately 20 shoal areas to reach a spawning shoal. Adults do not "home" to any particular spawning shoal.

Spawning occurs during the latter part of April, at water temperatures of 13.3–22.2°C (56–72°F). During spawning the black redhorse is highly select about the water depth and the bottom substrate of the spawning site; few of the many shoals observed were used intensively for spawning. The chief requirements are a water depth of 0.2–0.6 m (0.5–2.0 ft), and a substrate composed of approximately 70% fine rubble, 10% coarse rubble, and 20% sand and gravel.

Well-developed tubercles on mature males appear at least 17 days before spawning, and regress completely within 2 weeks after spawning. Spawning activities occur over a 4-day period, and are continuous from dawn to dark; they may also occur throughout the night.

To defend a territory, which averages 0.5 m (1.5 ft) in diameter, the male black redhorse swims toward intruding males of the same species with extended dorsal, pectoral, and pelvic fins; the intruder immediately moves away. No body contact has been observed between males in territorial defense. Infrequent jumping, consisting of a roll to the surface followed by a return to their territories, has been noted among territorial males.

Females remain in a pool immediately upstream from the spawning shoal. Prior to spawning they drift with the current, tail first, into the spawning area. At that time two territorial males position themselves on each side of the female. In the spawning act, the males clasp the posterior half of the female's body between the posterior halves of theirs and vibrate their caudal halves rapidly. During this period, which averages 3.4 seconds, the eggs are shed and fertilized. At the completion of spawning, the trio is in a tails-down position. After spawning, the female returns to the deeper water of the upstream pool, and the males return to the center of their respective territories.

Young-of-year black redhorses are most commonly observed among beds of water willow (*Justicia americana*) in relatively quiet pools. The young occur in schools, and feed near emergent aquatic vegetation. The food of the young, 65 mm or less, is principally phytoplankton. In the population studied, fry were not observed leaving spawning areas, but they were subsequently found immediately upstream from spawning shoals. In Ohio (Trautman 1957), young-of-year in October were 51–89 mm (2.0–3.5 in) long.

The Wisconsin black redhorse specimen from Black Earth Creek (Dane County) is 291 mm SL, an estimated 370 mm TL; and 7 years old. Its lengths calculated to the annuli were: 1—42 mm; 2—145 mm; 3—230 mm; 4—273 mm; 5—299 mm; 6—336 mm; and 7—360 mm. Two individuals from the North Fork of the Apple River (Jo Daviess County), Illinois, which is a few kilometers south of the Wisconsin line, were 3 years old and an estimated 54 mm, 128 mm, and 207 mm at the annuli. The growth of the black redhorse during the first year of life in northern streams is extremely slow; however, in subsequent years growth is more rapid and similar to that reported by Purkett (1958b) for Missouri populations of this species: 1—89 mm; 2—165 mm; 3—236 mm; 4—279 mm; 5—307 mm; and 6—325 mm.

The age at which black redhorses reach maturity is variable. In Missouri, Bowman (1970) found no sexually mature fish younger than age II, and found some fish in age groups IV and V which were still not sexually mature. Males tend to mature at smaller sizes than females.

Adult black redhorses 254–406 mm (10–16 in) long usually weigh 170–696 g (6.0–24.5 oz). Although this species is the smallest of the redhorses, an unusually large individual, 658 mm and 3.18 kg (25.9 in and 7 lb), was taken from the Eleven Point River in Missouri (Pflieger 1975).

Black redhorses longer than 65 mm consume mostly aquatic insects—primarily Diptera, some Ephemeroptera, and smaller amounts of Cladocera, Copepoda, and Nemathelminthes (Bowman 1970). Dipterans were the most important single food item taken by adult black redhorses collected from March through October in Missouri. Analysis of 775 stomachs disclosed no fish eggs.

Black redhorses feed in the early evening. Mature fish generally feed in schools of 15–20 fish immediately above or below a riffle. They have been observed moving slowly over the substrate of streams, sucking in bottom material, and expelling silt and waste, which leaves behind a trail of "drift." Not all bottom materials are separated from food items; most of the stomachs examined contained numerous fine grains of sand.

In the summer, the black redhorse prefers pools, where it remains in loose aggregations. In October and November it moves into deeper wintering holes. Even heavy spear fishing pressure does not drive the fish from these holes.

IMPORTANCE AND MANAGEMENT

The use of the black redhorse as forage by animal predators is not known. A comparison of food of the black redhorse with that of the smallmouth bass showed that the black redhorse did not compete directly with smallmouth bass fingerlings. The bass consumed principally *Hemiptera*, mollusks, and small fishes (Bowman 1970).

In Missouri, black redhorses may be caught on small worms and other live bait, but most are taken by gigging (spearing), snagging, or snaring. In the clear streams of the Ozarks, most redhorses are taken by spearing (Pflieger 1975). Snagging and snaring are most successful during the spring spawning season, when large numbers of fish concentrate in shallow water.

The flesh of the black redhorse has a sweet, delicate flavor which ranks with that of the finest food fishes. When scored and fried in deep fat, the numerous small bones disappear.

Golden Redhorse

Moxostoma erythrurum (Rafinesque). *Moxostoma*—sucking mouth; *erythrurum*—red tailed (a misnomer, since the tail of adult is slate colored).

Other common names: golden mullet, smallheaded mullet, golden sucker, white sucker.

Male (tuberculate) 323 mm, Yellow R. (Wood Co.), 25 May 1967

Female 323 mm, Yellow R. (Wood Co.), 25 May 1967

DESCRIPTION

Body slender to stout, moderately compressed; ventral aspect curved. Adult length about 280 mm (11 in). TL = 1.27 SL. Depth into SL 3.4–4.4. Head into SL 3.9–4.3. Snout bluntly pointed to rounded, but not overhanging mouth. Mouth large, ventral, and horizontal; lips coarsely plicate, papillae absent; lower lip slightly broader than upper lip, posterior edge forming a broad angle (90–130°). Pharyngeal teeth narrow, fragile, 53–63 per arch; crown of each tooth with a single definitive cusp at anterior edge; arch moderately strong, symphysis short. Dorsal fin slightly falcate or moderately concave, infrequently straight in adult; dorsal fin base into SL 5.3–5.6, length of base about two-thirds the distance from back of head to dorsal fin base; dorsal fin rays 13 (10–15); anal fin rays 7; pelvic fin rays 9. Postweberian vertebral numbers 37–38 (35–39). Lateral line scales 40–42 (37–45); lateral line complete. Scales around caudal peduncle 12 (11–14). Chromosomes 2n = 96–100 (Uyeno and Smith 1972).

Back brassy to bright gold; sides bronze to yellowish; belly whitish. Three diffuse, dusky saddle bands in young-of-year and age-I fish. Caudal and dorsal fins slate colored in life (caudal fin pale reddish in small specimens); lower fins yellowish orange to reddish in adults, with free edges whitish. Scales without dark spots at their anterior exposed bases. Scales in anterior dorsolateral area with distinctly dark margins, except in breeding males.

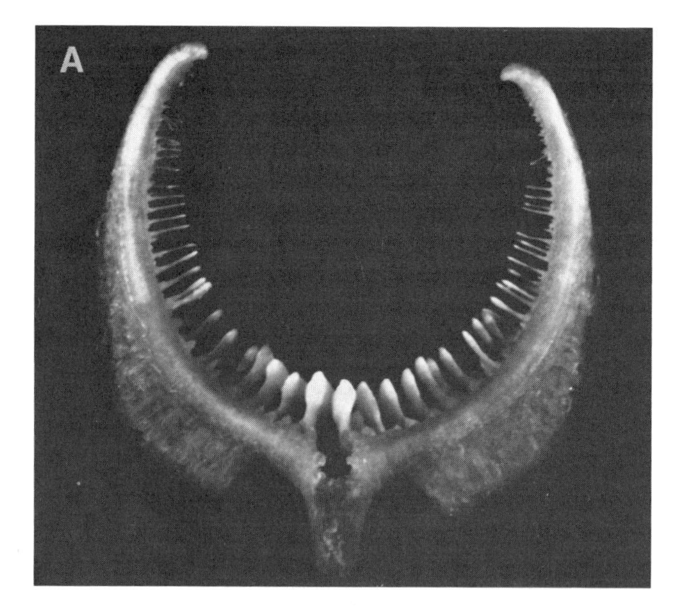

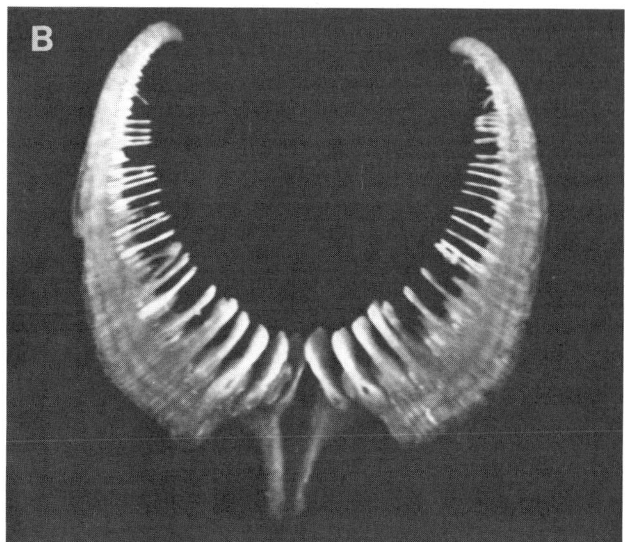

Pharyngeal arches of the golden redhorse. A. Front view. B. Back view.

Breeding male with large, sharp tubercles (1–2 mm at base) on snout to anterior eye and anterior cheek; minute tubercles on upper surface of head. Scales of breast and sides scattered or margined with minute tubercles. Anal and caudal fin rays strongly tuberculate; occasionally distal portions of pectoral fin rays with minute tubercles on both upper and lower sur-

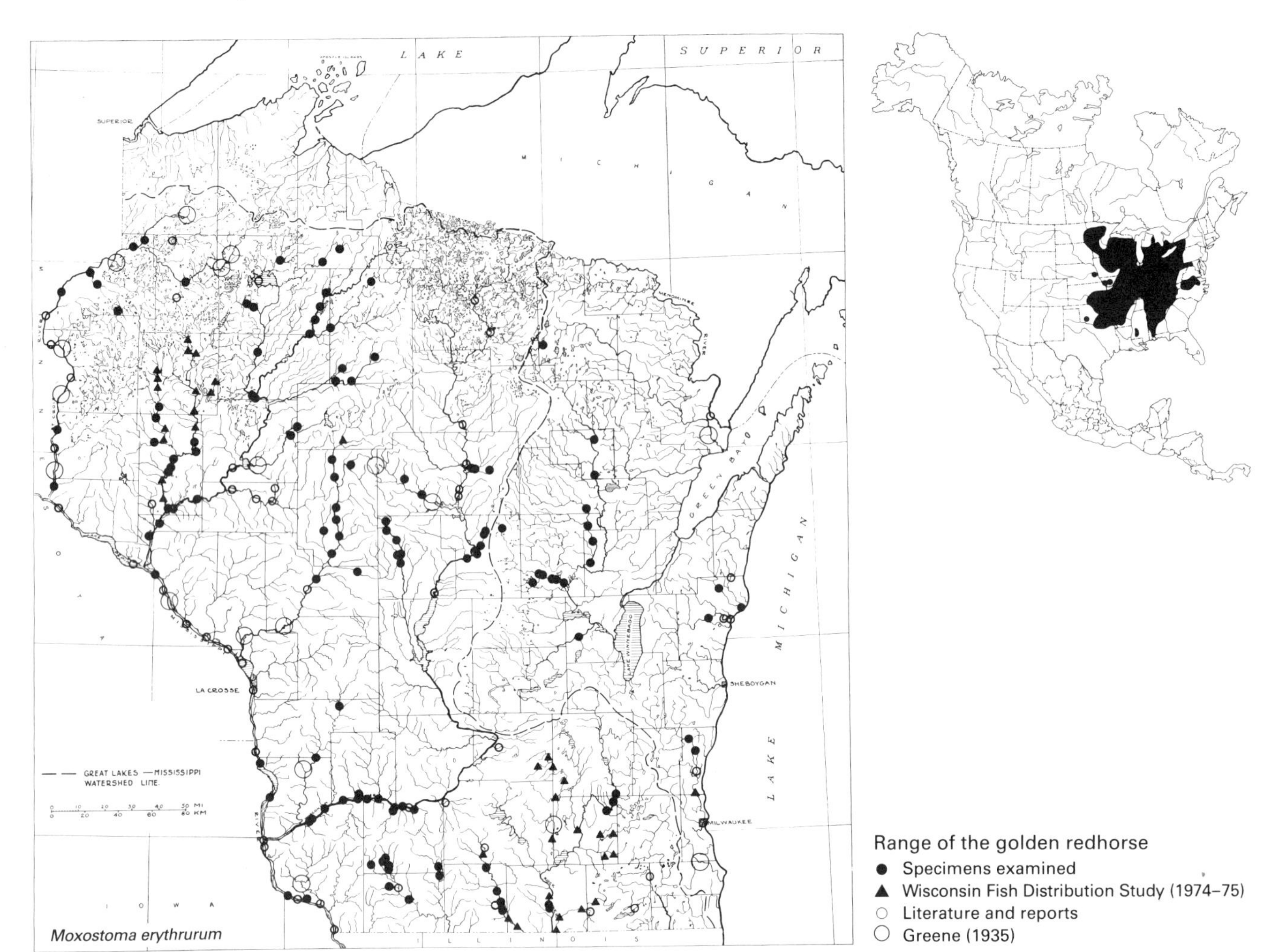

faces. Breeding female with slightly thickened anal rays, and thickened epidermis over lower portion of caudal peduncle.

Sexual dimorphism: The pelvic fin shape differs in males and females, as it does in the white sucker (see p. 684); the medial edge of the fin in females is not quite as rounded.

DISTRIBUTION, STATUS, AND HABITAT

In Wisconsin the golden redhorse occurs in the Mississippi River and Lake Michigan drainage basins. It has not been reported from the Lake Superior watershed.

The golden redhorse is a common sucker in Wisconsin. Care must be exercised in fish toxification programs that this valuable resource is not eliminated. It is sensitive to most toxicants, and can be extirpated from a river system if precautions are not taken.

The golden redhorse inhabits streams and river reservoirs, but seldom occurs in lakes. It prefers pools in river bends with undercut banks and fallen trees, where aquatic vegetation is almost nonexistent. In Wisconsin, it was encountered most frequently in clear water at depths of 0.6–1.5 m, over substrates of sand (24% frequency), gravel (20%), mud (14%), rubble (13%), boulders (12%), silt (9%), and clay (8%). It occurred in medium- to large-sized rivers of the following widths: 1.0–3.0 m (4%), 3.1–6.0 m (8%), 6.1–12.0 m (6%), 12.1–24.0 m (38%), 24.1–50.0 m (26%), and more than 50 m (18%).

BIOLOGY

In Wisconsin the golden redhorse spawns in May. Males in breeding habit, 320 and 323 mm TL, were collected from the Yellow River (Wood County) on 25 May. Active spawning occurred on 22 and 23 May on the lower Plover River (Portage County), when numbers of fish were seen breaking the water in fast runs (smooth ripples). These runs were in water 0.3–1.0 m deep, over large gravel, on either side of an island. Jumping and rolling activity was observed similar to that described for the black redhorse. The spawning site was located immediately downstream from the pool below McDill Dam. The river width at this point was about 45 m (150 ft). The golden redhorse normally spawns on riffles in the main stream; in Indiana, according to Gerking (1953), it ascends small streams to spawn only if such streams are near its home territory. No nest construction has been observed.

In Michigan, spawning occurred when the water temperature was 22.2°C (72°F) (Hankinson 1932). However, Meyer (1962) suggested that, based on gonadal development, spawning may occur when water temperatures are slightly above 15.6°C (60°F).

Male golden redhorses apparently congregate on spawning grounds to defend home territories before and during the spawning periods (Meyer 1962, Jenkins 1970). Jenkins noted that, when territories are invaded, the large head tubercles are frequently used in frontal attacks, which commonly result in body contact.

Spawning males tend to be as large as or larger than females. During the spawning act two males are present—one on each side of the female (Jenkins, pers. comm.). Females remain nearby in pools, or in deep water along the shore; they enter the shallows occupied by males only briefly to spawn.

A partially spent golden redhorse female, 453 mm and 1.15 kg, collected 22 May from the Plover River (Portage County), had ovaries 15% of the body weight, which held 21,000 eggs 2.2–2.5 mm diam. From the same collection, a male, 346 mm and 397 g, had testes 6.5% of its body weight.

In early August, young-of-year golden redhorses from several sites in southern Wisconsin were 25–45 mm long. By mid-September, in central and northern Wisconsin, they were 22–79 mm long. Nine taken from the Waupaca River (Waupaca County) on 9 September averaged 73 mm TL; seven young taken from the South Fork of the Jump River (Price County) on 20 September averaged 37 mm TL. In Ohio, young-of-year were 64–114 mm long during October (Trautman 1957).

Six golden redhorses in age groups IV–VII, from Cary Pond in the Crystal River (Waupaca County), were 339–424 mm TL; they had the following estimated lengths at the annuli: 1—52 mm; 2—111 mm; 3—186 mm; 4—259 mm; 5—316 mm; 6—363 mm; and 7—392 mm. The annulus is placed by 18 June in age-I fish in the lower Wisconsin River and in the Plover and Waupaca rivers of central Wisconsin. In older fish, the annulus is placed later.

Thirty-seven golden redhorses in age groups I–VII, from Pool 8 of the Mississippi River were 128–483 mm TL; they had the following calculated lengths at the annuli: 1—57.2 mm; 2—155.7 mm; 3—264.8 mm; 4—339.1 mm; 5—396.0 mm; 6—454.0 mm; and 7—492.0 mm (Bur 1976). Their weights ranged from 28 g for age-I fish to 1,750 g for age-VII fish.

In Wisconsin, the golden redhorse occasionally exceeds 457 mm (18 in) TL and 1.1 kg (2 lb 8 oz). In Oklahoma it has been reported up to 625 mm (24.6 in) TL and 2.22 kg (4.9 lb) (Carlander 1969).

The age at which the golden redhorse reaches maturity is variable. In Iowa (Meyer 1962), males begin to mature at age III, and females at age IV.

The food of 20 golden redhorses from Pool 8 of the Mississippi River consisted of Trichoptera (46.5% volume), Tendipedidae (27.1%), Ephemeroptera (13.6%), Sphaeriidae (3.4%), Copepoda (2.1%), and other items (7.4%) (Bur 1976). In the Plover River (Portage County), 12 fish had eaten Diptera (75% occurrence), Ephemeroptera (58%), Trichoptera (58%), Mollusca (67%), Coleoptera (17%), Hemiptera (8%), and algae (84%) (D. Gamble, pers. comm.).

Algae constitutes at least a portion of the golden redhorse's diet in some areas. In the Des Moines River, filamentous algae made up 25% of the volume of the diet, and was the only plant material found in stomachs examined (Harrison 1950).

The golden redhorse is intolerant of both cold and warm waters; it seeks out an intermediate temperature range. In the Wabash River of Indiana, its optimum temperature range was 26–27.5°C (78.8–81.5°F) (Gammon 1973). Gammon concluded that it will probably be permanently reduced in areas warmed by thermal waters from electric generating plants. The golden redhorse actively avoided hot and mixed temperature zones below one power plant on the Wabash, and showed a tendency to concentrate in the cooler water above the plant. The golden redhorse and some other species with low temperature preferences apparently endure periods of thermal stress for short periods during the summer in the natural, unheated portions of the Wabash River.

According to Greene (1935), the golden redhorse has a greater tolerance for silt and sand bottom streams than do the other species of redhorse.

The golden redhorse occurs in small, compact schools. In Ohio (Trautman 1957), it ascends smaller streams in the spring, moves downstream during the summer and fall, and winters in the larger streams. In Iowa, golden redhorses showed significant downstream movement during a low-water period (Meyer 1962). In Iowa the redhorse population tended to be sedentary, rather than mobile, during the summer.

Twenty-two golden redhorses were collected from the Middle Branch of the Pecatonica River (Iowa County) along with the shorthead redhorse (10), silver redhorse (2), northern hog sucker (5), white sucker (16), largescale stoneroller (1), central stoneroller (5), hornyhead chub (2), bluntnose minnow (3), common shiner (4), rosyface shiner (4), sand shiner (1), stonecat (1), blackside darter (9), johnny darter (4), fantail darter (2), smallmouth bass (5), and rock bass (2).

IMPORTANCE AND MANAGEMENT

According to Scott and Crossman (1973), young and adult golden redhorses probably do not compete as significantly as was once thought for food or space with species more valued by man.

The golden redhorse is occasionally used as bait for large game fish, which may explain why strays are found in lakes where this species does not normally occur (e.g., Collins Lake, Portage County). The release of bait fish from minnow buckets into natural waters is illegal, but it is commonly practiced.

The golden redhorse is not especially important to anglers, but occasionally it is taken on worms and other live baits. In the Ozark region, redhorses have long been the object of a substantial spear fishery (Cross 1967). Practiced at night from boats, the spearing of these fish is an exciting sport demanding alertness and skill.

The flesh of the golden redhorse is sweet and tasty, although bony. It is the general consensus among those who have sampled them that redhorses are excellent food fishes, and superior to many game fish in the flavor and the texture of the meat. The troublesome bones can be avoided by scoring the meat, or by grinding it up to make fish patties.

A small number of the larger adult golden redhorses are taken in the commercial fishery from the Mississippi River. The golden redhorse contributes to the "sucker and redhorse" catch, which in 1976 totalled 18,100 kg (39,903 lb), and was valued at $1,795.63 (Fernholz and Crawley 1977).

The potential of the golden redhorse as a food resource for man should be explored. It undoubtedly can withstand greater exploitation than it is currently sustaining.

Silver Redhorse

Moxostoma anisurum (Rafinesque). *Moxostoma*—sucking mouth; *anisurum*—unequal tail, in reference to the differences in the upper and lower lobes of the caudal fin.

Other common names: silver mullet, whitenose redhorse, white sucker, bay mullet, redfin mullet, longtailed sucker.

Immature 178 mm, South Branch of the Manitowoc R. (Manitowoc Co.), 14 Apr. 1974

Adult male 505 mm, junction of the Chippewa and Mississippi rivers (Buffalo Co.), 28 Sept. 1974

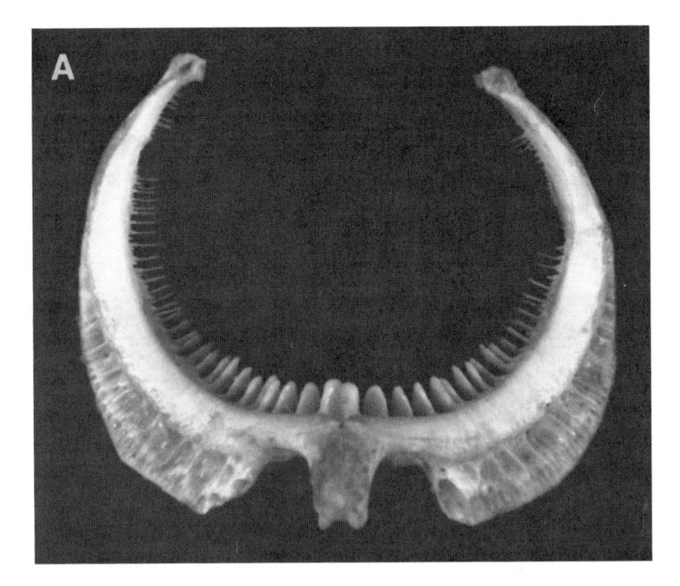

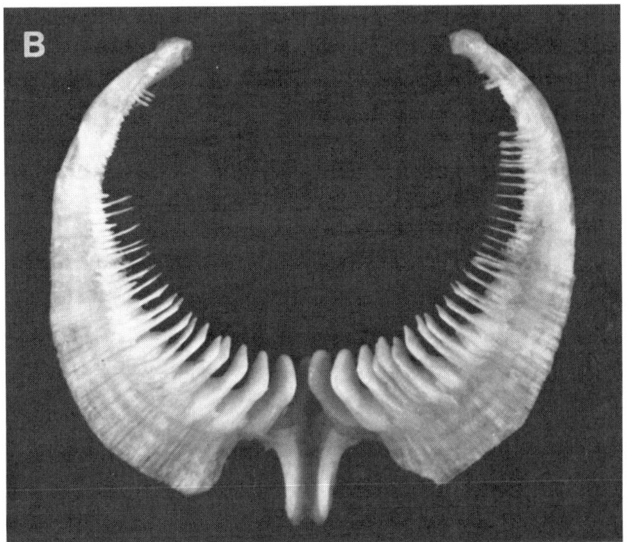

Pharyngeal arches of the silver redhorse. A. Front view. B. Back view.

DESCRIPTION

Body stout, deep, and compressed, heavy forward; the back elevated, rather humped in old specimens; ventral line curved. Adult length about 300 mm (12 in). TL = 1.27 SL. Depth into SL 3.1–4.1. Head into SL 3.5–4.3. Snout blunt, slightly rounded to square (truncate); snout does not overhang mouth. Mouth ventral and horizontal; lips plicate, folds on lower lip surface partly or entirely dissected into fine, irregularly shaped papillae; lower lip halves forming an angle of about 90°. Pharyngeal teeth about 80 per arch, with teeth larger on lower portion of arch; most crowns of teeth with prominent cusp anteriorly; arch strong with large, honeycomb openings, the symphysis much elongated. Dorsal fin slightly concave to slightly convex, occasionally straight in young; dorsal fin base into SL 4.2–5.2, length of base slightly shorter than to about equal the distance from back of head to dorsal fin base; dorsal fin rays 15 (14–17); anal fin rays 7; pelvic fin rays 9. Lateral line scales 41–42 (38–46); lateral line complete. Scales around caudal peduncle 12.

Silvery, with back darker and sides sometimes with faint yellow reflections; belly silvery white. Caudal and dorsal fins slate colored in life; lower fins white or light reddish, red in spawning season. Scale bases generally not darkened, but occasionally darkened in large, old fish.

Breeding male with minute tubercles moderately to densely concentrated on upper head, more sparse on ventral surface of head. Body with minute tuber-

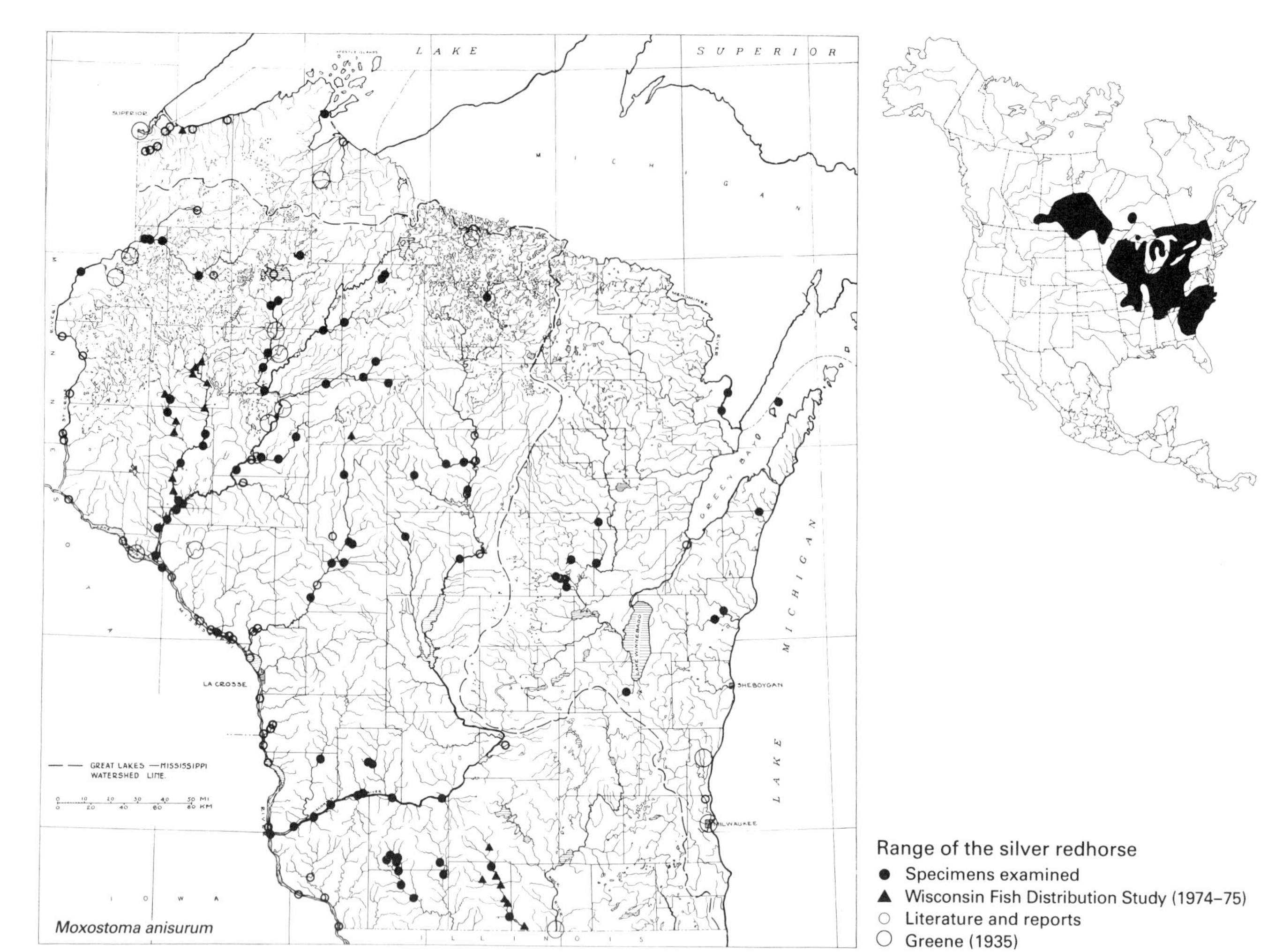

Range of the silver redhorse
● Specimens examined
▲ Wisconsin Fish Distribution Study (1974–75)
○ Literature and reports
◯ Greene (1935)

cules on all scales, averaging slightly larger on lower portion of caudal peduncle. Anal fin well tuberculated on all rays; other fins with minute tubercles on anterior rays, occasionally on all rays. Breeding female lightly tuberculate on head, lower caudal fin and anal fin; lower caudal peduncle and anal area with moderately to rather thickened skin.

DISTRIBUTION, STATUS, AND HABITAT

In Wisconsin, the silver redhorse occurs in the Mississippi River, Lake Michigan, and Lake Superior drainage basins. It is most widely distributed in the larger river systems of the western half of the state. It is also present in the shoal waters of Lakes Michigan and Superior.

The silver redhorse is uncommon to common in most of the Wisconsin waters where it is found. It has been considered rare at the barriers in the larger deep and sluggish river tributaries to Lake Superior (McLain et al. 1965). Its distribution may be more general than is indicated by the collection records, because its habits make it difficult to capture unless deepwater sampling equipment, such as a gill net or a boom shocker, is used.

The silver redhorse is extremely sensitive to fish toxicants, and, where they are used, populations are quickly eliminated. This occurred in 1971 in the Waupaca River (Waupaca County) when antimycin was applied during a stream rehabilitation program instigated by the Wisconsin Department of Natural Resources. Prior to treatment, this species had been abundant in the reservoir at Weyauwega (Waupaca County) and in the Waupaca River between Weyauwega and its mouth (Becker 1976).

In Wisconsin, the silver redhorse was encountered most frequently at depths of 0.6 m or more over substrates of gravel (24% frequency), sand (18%), mud (14%), clay (14%), rubble (14%), boulders (10%), and silt (7%). It occurred in large-river reservoirs and in streams of the following widths: 1.0–3.0 m (3%); 3.1–6.0 m (16%); 6.1–12.0 m (9%); 12.1–24.0 m (31%); 24.1–50.0 m (34%); and more than 50 m (6%). It avoids streams with high gradients and with excessive turbidity.

BIOLOGY

The spawning of the silver redhorse occurs in April and May, often as soon as the ice goes out. In Iowa, spawning reaches its peak during the first week of May, when the water temperature is 13.3°C (56°F) (Jenkins 1970); this is slightly later than the spawning peak of the shorthead redhorse.

According to Meyer (1962), in Iowa, the male silver redhorses precede the females in reaching spawning readiness. Males congregate on the spawning grounds, apparently to defend home territories, before and during the spawning periods. The sex ratio on the spawning grounds was 75 males to 37 females, indicating the brevity of the female's stay. At a spawning site in the main channel of the Des Moines River, Iowa, the water was 0.3–0.9 m (1–3 ft) deep and flowed over a bottom of gravel and rubble. A pair of large, adult silver redhorses was observed spawning in the Chippewa River (Ontario) on 9 June 1954 at a depth of about 1.5 m (5 ft) (Scott 1967).

Egg development proceeds rapidly in the fall prior to spawning. Well-developed eggs, 1.1–1.3 mm diam, were found in a female (416 mm TL) from the East Twin River (Manitowoc County) on 3 September. An 8-year-old female (571 mm, 2.21 kg), collected 24 April from the Biron Flowage (Wood County) of the Wisconsin River, held 34,800 eggs averaging 2.2 mm diam; the ovaries were 10.3% of the body weight. In Iowa (Meyer 1962), egg production by three females ranged from 14,910 in a 340-mm, 5-year-old fish to 36,340 in a 490-mm fish of unknown age.

M. Fish (1932) illustrated and described the 19.5-mm stage.

In Iowa, young silver redhorses remain in smaller streams throughout their first year of life (Harlan and Speaker 1956).

The growth of young-of-year silver redhorses in Wisconsin has been recorded as follows:

Date	No. of Fish	TL (mm) Avg	TL (mm) Range	Location
2 July	4	35	33–39	Wolf R. (Menominee Co.)
14 July	7	72	63–78	Sugar R. (Green Co.)
16 July	10	30	23–34	Kickapoo R. Crawford Co.)
21 July	2	42	42–43	Little Wolf R. (Waupaca Co.)
5 Aug.	8	69	60–81	Sugar R. (Green Co.)
15 Aug.	2	68	67–68	Sugar R. (Green Co.)
9 Sept.	3	93	90–94	Waupaca R. (Waupaca Co.)
20 Sept.	15	50	44–60	South Fork Jump R. (Price Co.)

Nine silver redhorses taken from the Pecatonica River (Iowa County) on 30 June 1960 were of the following age-groups and average lengths: I—89 mm; II—203 mm; III—238 mm; and V—261 mm.

Eighteen silver redhorses taken from the Waupaca River at Weyauwega (Waupaca County) on 10 September 1971 were in age-groups IV to XII, and were 358–492 mm TL (K. Sroka, pers. comm.). The calculated lengths at the annuli were: 1—98 mm; 2—173 mm; 3—235 mm; 4—287 mm; 5—323 mm; 6—347 mm; 7—369 mm; 8—390 mm; 9—416 mm; 10—430 mm; 11—449 mm; and 12—470 mm.

One hundred thirty-four silver redhorses taken from Pool 8 of the Mississippi River during the summer of 1975 were in age-groups I to IX, and were 145–636 mm TL (Bur 1976). The calculated lengths at the annuli were: 1—66 mm; 2—198 mm; 3—312 mm; 4—396 mm; 5—450 mm; 6—492 mm; 7—527 mm; 8—554 mm; and 9—580 mm. The growth of the silver redhorse in the Mississippi River appears to be more rapid than in inland waters.

Among silver redhorses, most growth for the year occurs in late July, August, and early September (Jenkins 1970). Annulus formation in southern Wisconsin occurs early in June in age-I fish, but not until late in June in age-III fish. In Iowa, older and larger silver redhorses complete annulus formation as late as August (Meyer 1962). Meyer noted that maturity begins at age V.

Occasionally the silver redhorse attains a large size. A 570-mm, 3.40-kg (22.4-in, 7.5-lb) fish was taken from the Red Cedar River (Dunn County) on 27 September 1974; it was 10 years old. A 635-mm, 3.52-kg (25.0-in, 7.75 lb) silver redhorse, taken on 12 August 1974 from Lake Superior off Pikes Creek (Bayfield County), was an estimated 14 years old. According to Trautman (1957), Ohio River commercial fishermen have reported maximum weights up to 4.54 kg (10 lb) for silver redhorses. Trautman reported a 635-mm (25-in) specimen weighing 3.74 kg (8 lb 4 oz).

In Iowa, silver redhorses consume the same food items throughout the summer and fall as do the golden and shorthead redhorses, and all three species consumed the same foods in approximately equal amounts (Meyer 1962); the principal foods for redhorses longer than 102 mm (4 in) were, in the order of their frequency of occurrence: immature Chironomidae (91%), immature Ephemeroptera (62%), and immature Trichoptera (18%). In an earlier study from the Des Moines River, Iowa (Harrison 1950), the food of 11 silver redhorses consisted of 64% insects, 21% plants, 8% organic material, 4% fish, and 3% crustaceans. The insects were basically bottom forms, including mayflies, stoneflies, caddisflies, dipterous flies, backswimmers, water boatmen, beetles, and a few terrestrial insects. The plant material was filamentous algae. Two individuals had preyed upon spotfin shiner fry, another contained a scale of a large fish, and one specimen had eaten part of a crayfish.

In the Des Moines River, Iowa, young silver redhorses inhabit slow-moving waters over soft-bottom areas near overhanging banks, presumably for protection from predators (Meyer 1962). During the summer the silver redhorse population tends to be sedentary rather than mobile.

In the Kickapoo River (Crawford County), 17 silver redhorses were associated with longnose gar (1), common carp (2), and sauger (2).

IMPORTANCE AND MANAGEMENT

The extent of predation on the silver redhorse is not known. Scott and Crossman (1973) suggested that the young may be vulnerable to a wide range of warmwater predators in rivers, but that adults are probably relatively safe from predation.

The silver redhorse is taken by anglers on worms, on grubs, and occasionally on dough bait. A redhorse 610 mm (24 in) long from an Ontario lake, believed to be of this species, was battled for 2 hours, according to Scott and Crossman (1973); these authors noted that where this species is locally abundant it "may constitute a potential sport fish of some significance."

The silver redhorse, although bony, is an excellent food fish, and can be prepared in a variety of ways. It is superb when canned in a tomato and vegetable oil sauce.

The silver redhorse is taken more frequently by commercial seine than by angling. Wisconsin production of "suckers and redhorse" (including the silver redhorse) in the commercial fishery of the Mississippi River has been fairly constant since the 1950s: 1955—30,507 kg (67,257 lb); 1960—13,509 kg (29,781 lb); 1965—12,325 kg (27,172 lb); 1970—18,957 kg (41,792 lb); 1974—21,310 kg (46,979 lb); and 1976—18,100 kg (39,903 lb). To the commercial fisherman, the value of the 1976 catch was $1,795.63. The silver redhorse constituted only a small part of this catch, although in some areas it represented a significant percentage of the catch. Bur (1976) noted that, in Pool 8 of the Mississippi River, the silver redhorse was the second largest group of catostomids sampled in his study; they constituted 26.4% of those taken during the summer of 1975.

In Lakes Michigan and Superior, the silver redhorse appears only rarely in the commercial catch. There is no documentation for the claim by Forbes and Richardson (1920) that, at some points in Lake Michigan, the silver redhorse contributes a considerable percentage to the catch of suckers.

Shorthead Redhorse

Moxostoma macrolepidotum (Lesueur). *Moxostoma*—sucking mouth; *macrolepidotum*—large scaled.

Other common names: redfin, redfin sucker, red sucker, redhorse mullet, common mullet, shorthead mullet, mullet, bigscale sucker, common redhorse, northern redhorse, Des Moines plunger.

Adult female 470 mm, Mississippi R. (Buffalo Co.), 28 Sept. 1974

DESCRIPTION

Body elongate, slender, moderately compressed; ventral aspect slightly curved. Adult length about 280 mm (11 in). TL = 1.25 SL. Depth into SL 3.5–4.3. Head into SL 4.3–5.4. Snout pointed to slightly blunt, but not overhanging mouth. Mouth small, ventral, and horizontal to slightly oblique; lips deeply plicate, the folds of lower lip transversely divided into large papillae; lower lip much broader than upper lip, lower lip appearing swollen, with posterior edge forming a straight line, rarely a very obtuse angle. Pharyngeal teeth narrow, fragile, about 53 per arch; crown of each tooth with a pronounced cusp on anterior edge; arch moderately strong, the symphysis short. Dorsal fin moderately falcate, rarely straight; dorsal fin base into SL 5.3–5.6, length of base about two-thirds the distance from back of head to dorsal fin base; dorsal fin rays 12–14 (11–15); anal fin rays 7 (8); pelvic fin rays 9 (8–10). Lateral line scales 42–44 (39–46); lateral line complete. Scales around caudal peduncle 12–13. Chromosomes 2n = 96–100 (Uyeno and Smith 1972).

Back dark olive to tan olive; sides olive yellow; belly whitish. Caudal and dorsal fins pale to bright red in life (fades to gray in formalin or alcohol); paired fins salmon to reddish orange; anal fin orange or red with whitish edge. Scales with dark spots at their anterior exposed bases.

Breeding male with minute tubercles on head, body scales (larger tubercles on caudal peduncle), rays of caudal and anal fins, and at least on anterior rays of paired and dorsal fins. Breeding female with minute tubercles concentrated on dorsal surface of head, occasionally on rays of anal and lower half of caudal fins; a thickened epidermis over lower portion of caudal peduncle.

Sexual dimorphism: In adult males, the posterior rays of the dorsal fin are longer in relation to the anterior rays than in females (Jenkins 1970). The depressed dorsal fin, dorsal fin base, and anal fin are longer in males than in females (Phillips and Underhill 1971). The pelvic fin shape differs in shorthead redhorse males and females as in white sucker (see p. 684); the medial edge of the fin in females is not quite as rounded.

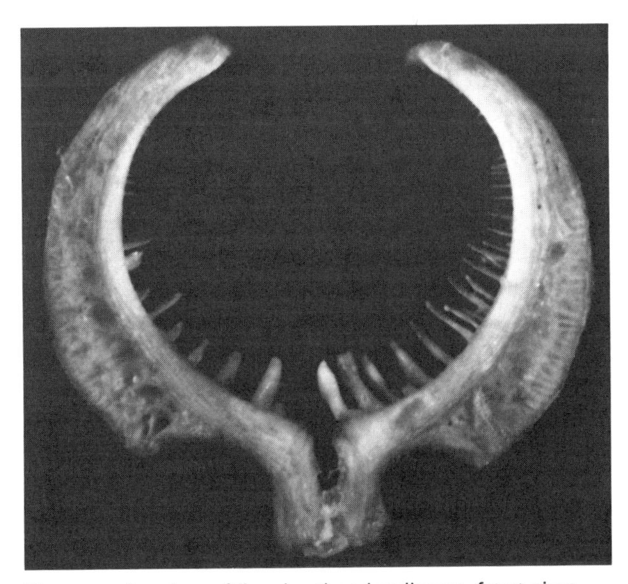

Pharyngeal arches of the shorthead redhorse, front view

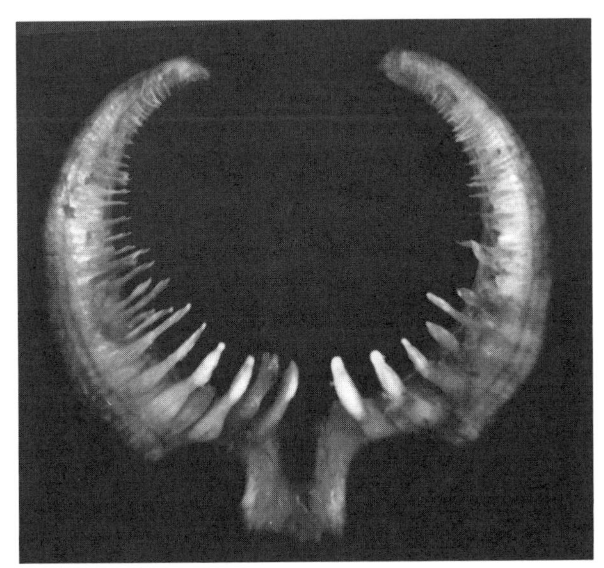

Pharyngeal arches of the shorthead redhorse, back view

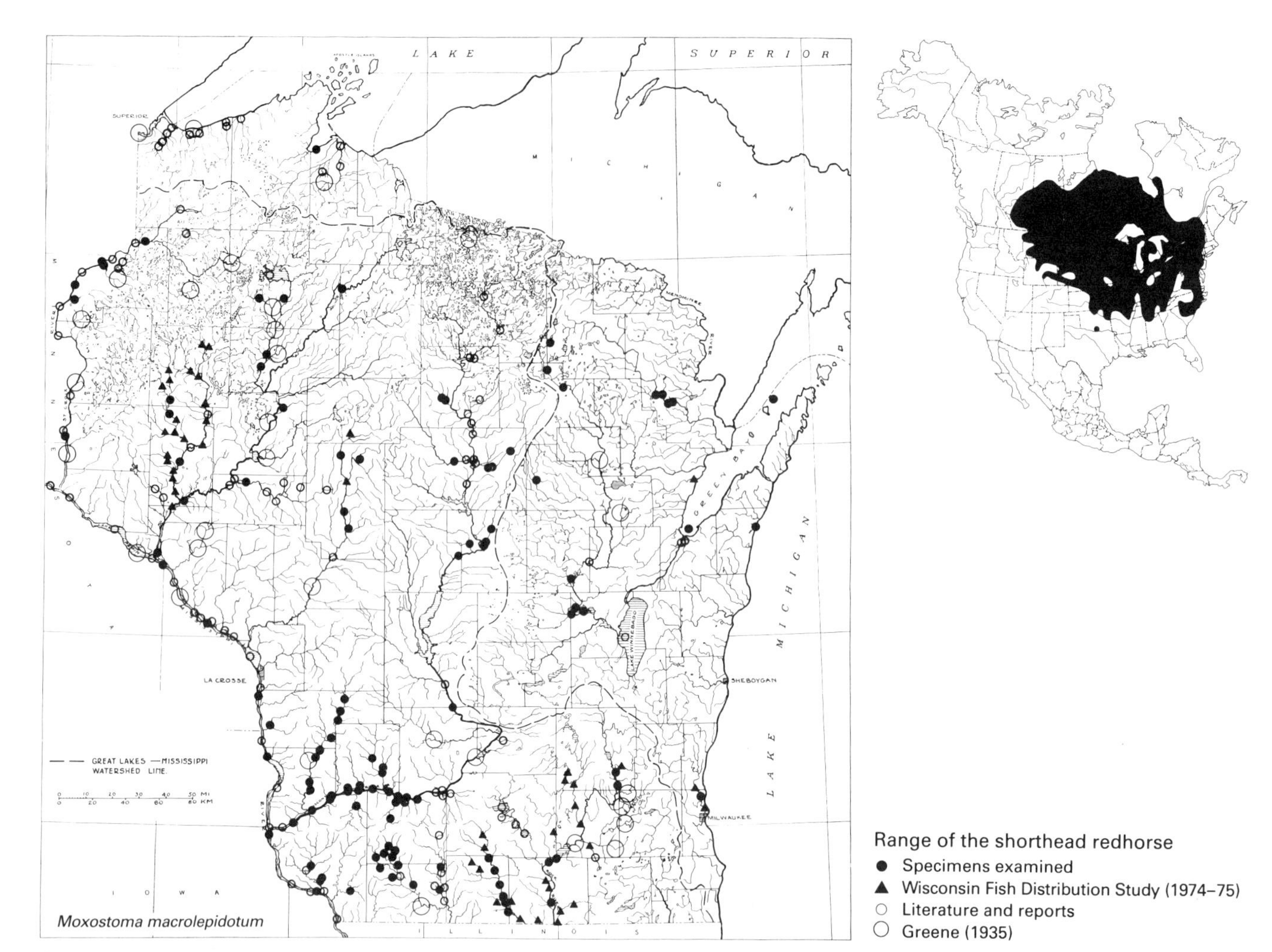

Range of the shorthead redhorse
● Specimens examined
▲ Wisconsin Fish Distribution Study (1974–75)
○ Literature and reports
○ Greene (1935)

SYSTEMATIC NOTES

Three subspecies are recognized: *Moxostoma m. macrolepidotum*, described above and including Wisconsin in its wide range; *Moxostoma m. pisolabrum* Trautman and Martin, the pealip redhorse, which differs from other forms by having the medial upper lip much enlarged and smoothly cornified, and which is mainly Ozarkian in its distribution; and *Moxostoma m. breviceps* (Cope), the Ohio redhorse, which usually has a 10-ray count, rather than 9, in one or both pelvics, and a dorsal fin which is more falcate, and which appears in the Ohio River basin (Jenkins 1970).

DISTRIBUTION, STATUS, AND HABITAT

In Wisconsin the shorthead redhorse occurs in all three drainage basins. It is distributed in medium- to large-sized rivers, in large, inland lakes of central and northern Wisconsin, and in Green Bay.

The shorthead redhorse is common statewide, and is perhaps the most successful redhorse in distribution, if not in numbers. It is more common in many river collections than the golden redhorse, and is also more common than the silver redhorse, which is similarly dispersed. Despite its apparent ability to adapt to a wide variety of habitat conditions, the creation of artificial reservoirs in good shorthead redhorse streams has led to a reduction in its numbers within impounded areas (Coker 1930, Trautman 1957, Jenkins 1970).

The shorthead redhorse is a common species in lakes, in stream reservoirs, and in the largest rivers of Wisconsin. There are no records from Lake Superior or from Lake Michigan (other than Green Bay). It was encountered most frequently in clear to slightly turbid waters at depths of 0.6 m or greater, over substrates of sand (28% frequency), gravel (22%), mud (19%), clay (11%), rubble (10%), silt (5%), boulders (3%), and bedrock (2%). It occurred in streams of the following widths: 1.0–3.0 m (4%); 3.1–6.0 m (22%); 6.1–12.0 m (22%); 12.1–24.0 m (31%); 24.1–50.0 m (16%); and more than 50 m (4%). The apparent drop in frequency in the larger rivers resulted from the lack of adequate deepwater sampling equipment. In lakes, it prefers the clear shallows; however, it has

Gravid female from the Wisconsin R., Wisconsin. Ovarian covering removed to expose eggs. Weight of roe over 225g. (Photo by S. Taft)

been taken in some lakes at depths of 3–12 m and occasionally deeper. This species of redhorse is more plastic in its habitat requirements than any other redhorse.

BIOLOGY

The shorthead redhorse spawns in April and May at water temperatures of 8.3–16°C (47–60.8°F). According to H. Neuenschwander (pers. comm.) redhorse suckers have appeared in numbers below the Hustisford Dam (Dodge County) toward the end of April. In northeastern Wisconsin's Peshtigo River, spawning was observed in early May (M. Hawley, pers. comm.). Males reach spawning readiness before females, and congregate on the spawning grounds apparently to defend home territories, before and during spawning periods (Meyer 1962).

In northeastern Illinois (Burr and Morris 1977), spawning occurred on 18 May at 16°C (60.8°F), from 1100 to 1300 hr and from 1400 to 1600 hr. The fish were active near the edge of a sandbar, on a shallow riffle (15–21 cm deep), in troughs and circular "nests" containing coarse stones and rubble. The "nests" and troughs may have been depressions resulting from bottom disturbances during the spawning activity.

Spawning occurs when a female moves onto the riffle where the males have congregated. The spawning act has been described by Reighard (1920:19):

> . . . When she had come to rest on the bottom one of the males approached and placed himself by her side. After half a second the other male took his place on her opposite side and spawning occurred very much as in the white sucker. The backs of the two males were strongly arched so that their dorsal fins were carried well above that of the female and fully spread. Their caudal and anal fins were close pressed against those of the female and against each other as in the white sucker. . . . The spawning and vibrations lasted two or three seconds. The fish then separated and the female went up stream.

In southern Michigan, the breeding grounds of the shorthead redhorse are the quieter, upper parts of rapids in streams not less than 9–12 m (30–40 ft) wide and in shallow water with gravel bottom.

Six female shorthead redhorses, 460–537 mm TL and 1.31–1.93 kg, collected 24 April from the Wisconsin River (Wood County), held 22,000–44,000 eggs averaging 1.9 (1.6–2.1) mm diam. The largest female had ovaries 13.2% of body weight.

M. Fish (1932) described and illustrated the 7.5 mm stage. Young-of-year shorthead redhorses on the Wisconsin River are scaled, except on the breast, by 8 August.

Young-of-year in some waters of northern Wisconsin are 36–39 mm in early July, and 43–45 mm by the end of September. In southern Wisconsin, they are 37–52 mm TL in early August, and 76–87 mm by mid-September. Young shorthead redhorses show rapid growth in Lake Poygan: 58–70 mm on 9 July, and 96–103 mm by 9 September.

Five shorthead redhorses, from the Middle Branch of the Embarrass River (Shawano County), in age-groups VI–IX, and 338–391 mm TL, had the following estimated lengths at the annuli: 1—32 mm; 2—96 mm; 3—170 mm; 4—223 mm; 5—266 mm; 6—303 mm; 7—329 mm; 8—351 mm; and 9—370 mm. Six fish, ages VI–XI and 460–537 mm TL, from Biron Reservoir of the Wisconsin River (Wood County) had the following calculated lengths at the annuli: 1—48 mm; 2—111 mm; 3—248 mm; 4—348 mm; 5—408 mm; 6—445 mm; 7—476 mm; 8—491 mm; 9—504 mm; 10—513 mm; and 11—531 mm.

The average calculated lengths for 220 shorthead redhorses, 125–528 mm TL and in age-groups I–VII, collected from Pool 8 of the Mississippi River were: 1—103 mm; 2—209 mm; 3—295 mm; 4—365 mm; 5—420 mm; 6—470 mm; and 7—527 mm (Bur 1976).

In Iowa, young redhorses (shorthead, golden, and silver) generally form annuli in June; older and larger redhorses complete annulus formation as late as August (Meyer 1962). A comparison of growth beyond the last annulus indicated that most of the growth occurred in late July, August, and early September. There were no pronounced differences in the growth rates between sexes. In South Dakota (Gasaway 1970), growth in this species increased after impoundment.

Maturity in the shorthead redhorse occurs generally at age III (Carlander 1969).

The maximum length reported for shorthead redhorses is 620 mm (24.4 in) (Trautman 1957); the maximum weights reported are 3.63–4.54 kg (8–10 lb) (Eddy and Surber 1947). A 2.72-kg (6-lb) fish was reported from a central Wisconsin reservoir of the Wisconsin River (R. White, pers. comm.).

The food of 22 young-of-year shorthead redhorses, 51–78 mm TL, from Pool 8 of the Mississippi River, included Tendipedidae (86.4% occurrence), Amphipoda (77.3%), Ostracoda (72.7%), Copepoda (59.1%), Cladocera (40.9%), and Trichoptera (4.5%) (Bur 1976).

The food of 100 shorthead redhorses, 150–500 mm TL, from Pool 8 of the Mississippi River, consisted of Tendipedidae (41.2% volume), Trichoptera (39.3%), Simuliidae (12.5%), Sphaeriidae (1.7%), and other (5.2%) (Bur 1976). In 21 shorthead redhorses from the Plover River (Portage County), the diet included Diptera larvae, Ephemeroptera larvae, Trichoptera larvae, mollusks, and some green algae (M. Hawley, pers. comm.). Similar food items were taken from Peshtigo River shorthead redhorses, which had also consumed one Odonata larva and three mature Diptera.

In Iowa, Harrison (1950) noted that shorthead redhorses had consumed mostly insects, and considerable plant materials (algae and traces of green leaves), crayfish, earthworms, bryozoa, a spotfin shiner fry, and a single fish egg.

While feeding, Ohio redhorses (*Moxostoma m. breviceps*) flicked their fins rapidly, and pushed between small stones and gravel with their snouts. Fin flicking may be a means of finding food by stirring up small or softer bottom materials (Jenkins 1970).

The shorthead redhorse descends freshwater streams to brackish water in Hudson Bay (Scott and Crossman 1973). It has a salinity tolerance of 3.0 ppt (Mansueti and Hardy 1967).

Eighteen shorthead redhorses were collected from Mineral Point Branch (Iowa County) along with the silver redhorse (2), golden redhorse (10), northern hog sucker (31), white sucker (10), largescale stoneroller (9), central stoneroller (6), hornyhead chub (19), bluntnose minnow (1), stonecat (1), blackside darter (5), johnny darter (3), fantail darter (4), smallmouth bass (5), and rock bass (1).

IMPORTANCE AND MANAGEMENT

The young shorthead redhorse is probably preyed on by a number of fish-eating predators. Cahn (1927) reported that young redhorses are occasionally found in the stomachs of walleyes, northern pike, and, less frequently, black bass. The shorthead redhorse is host to the glochidial stage of the mollusk *Alasmidonta marginata*; hence it assists in the distribution and perpetuation of that clam.

Young shorthead redhorses have been used as bait for large bass, northern pike, walleyes, and muskellunge. They are hardy and live well on the hook.

In the early spring shorthead redhorses are readily taken on worms, grubs, hoppers, crickets, small pieces of meat and stream flies. Its virtues as a sport fish have been extolled by Eddy and Underhill (1974:287):

> The northern redhorse is the only Minnesota redhorse that bites readily on the baited hook and may on occasion take a wet fly or plug. Northern redhorses are good sport when taken on a fly rod, particularly in fast water. . . . A 2-pound redhorse in fast water will provide even the trout purist with an exciting battle. Another virtue of redhorse fishing is that there is no wait between bites. Fishing in rapids below dams is particularly productive when the fish are on their spawning run.

H. Neuenschwander (pers. comm.) caught 84 redhorses in one vertical lift of a 1.98-m (6.5-ft) square dipnet during the spring run below the Hustisford Dam (Dodge County).

Historically the shorthead redhorse has been the most important food fish of the genus. According to Jordan and Evermann (1932), in the upper Mississippi Valley states, it had always been held in considerable esteem by farmers, who were in the habit of snaring, seining, or trapping them in great numbers in the spring, and salting them for winter use.

Many people regard the shorthead as the best food fish of the suckers, for the flesh is white and flaky and is excellent, particularly when baked. The biggest objection many people have to the suckers—and to smaller suckers especially—is the presence of needlelike, Y-shaped bones which make eating bothersome. This problem can be avoided by scoring the meat, or by running the fillets through a food chopper and fashioning the finely ground meat and bones into patties. With the proper seasoning and chopped onions, such fillets can be delicious. Commercial and home canning of the shorthead redhorse has great potential, but past attempts to increase such use have met with little success (Scott and Crossman 1973).

In Wisconsin, the shorthead is the most common redhorse in the large rivers. In Pool 8 of the Mississippi River during the summer of 1975, Bur (1976) collected 607 shorthead redhorses, compared to 324 silver redhorses, 48 golden redhorses, 168 spotted suckers, and 19 white suckers. If this collection is a guide to relative abundance, it is likely that, in the commercial fishery statistics which list these species mentioned together as "suckers and redhorse," the shorthead represents about 50% of the listed catch. In 1976, the total catch for the Wisconsin waters of the Mississippi River was 18,100 kg (39,903 lb), which was valued at $1,795.63 (Fernholz and Crawley 1977). For additional commercial catch statistics, see p. 664.

Considering all of its attributes, it seems inconceivable that the shorthead redhorse persists in the minds of many fishermen and regulatory agencies as a "rough fish." Serious consideration should be given to elevating this species to "sport fish" status.

Greater Redhorse

Moxostoma valenciennesi Jordan. *Moxostoma*—sucking mouth; *valenciennesi*—after M. A. Valenciennes, the famous French naturalist who first described this species on the basis of a specimen from Lake Ontario.

Other common names: common redhorse, redhorse.

Female 261 mm, St. Croix R. (Polk Co.), 28 Sept. 1978

DESCRIPTION

Body elongate to moderately stout, almost round in cross section; ventral aspect slightly curved. Adult length about 460 mm (18 in). TL = 1.23 SL. Depth into SL 3.6–4.2. Head into SL 3.7–4.4 (3.3–3.7 in young up to 76 mm). Snout slightly to moderately rounded, but not overhanging mouth ventrally. Mouth large, ventral and horizontal; lips deeply plicate, folds smooth surfaced except occasionally "wrinkled" on lateral portion of lower lip; lower lip broader than upper lip; lower lip often appearing swollen; lower halves forming an obtuse angle (100–160°). Pharyngeal teeth heavy, about 55 per arch (80 according to Jenkins 1970); crown of each tooth with pronounced cusp on anterior edge; arch moderately strong, symphysis short. Dorsal fin slightly concave (in young) to slightly convex (in adults); dorsal fin base into SL 4.9–5.3, length of base about ¾ the distance from back of head to dorsal fin base; dorsal fin rays 13–14 (11–15); anal fin rays 7; pelvic fin rays 9 (8–10). Lateral line scales 42–45 (41–45); lateral line complete. Scales around caudal peduncle 16 (14–17).

Back brown olive with bronze overcast; sides more golden; belly whitish. Dorsal, caudal, and anal fins red in life (fade to gray in formalin and alcohol); anterior rays of pelvic and pectoral fins whitish, remainder reddish. Scales with dark spots at their anterior exposed bases.

Breeding male with minute tubercles on entire dorsal and lateral surfaces of head and on body scales. Large tubercles on rays of lower lobe of caudal fin, fewer on rays of upper lobe. Breeding female with small and bluntly tipped tubercles on all fins except dorsal, but less widely distributed and generally smaller than in male; tubercles absent from female body, except on lower caudal peduncle.

SYSTEMATIC NOTES

The confusion associated with the identification and nomenclature of this species is discussed by Jenkins (1970) and by Scott and Crossman (1973). Synonym: *Moxostoma rubreques* Hubbs (1930b).

DISTRIBUTION, STATUS, AND HABITAT

In Wisconsin, the greater redhorse occurs in widely scattered localities within the Mississippi River and

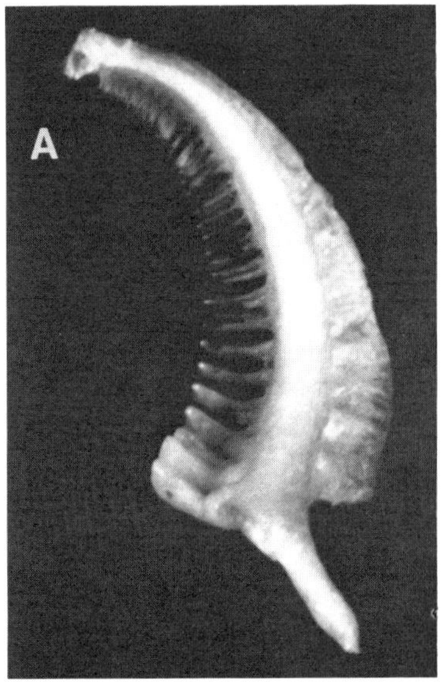

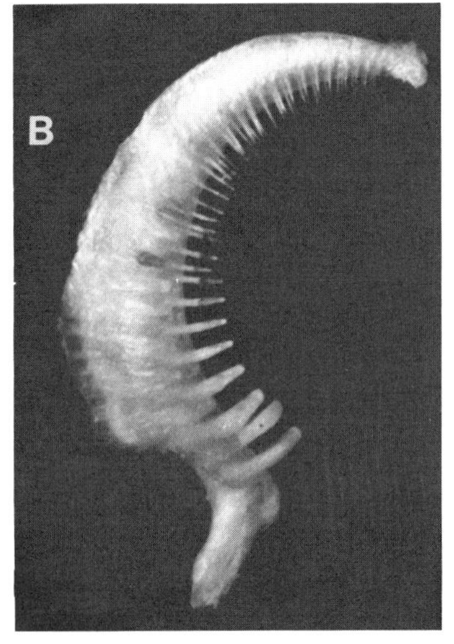

Left pharyngeal arch of the greater redhorse. A. Front view. B. Back view.

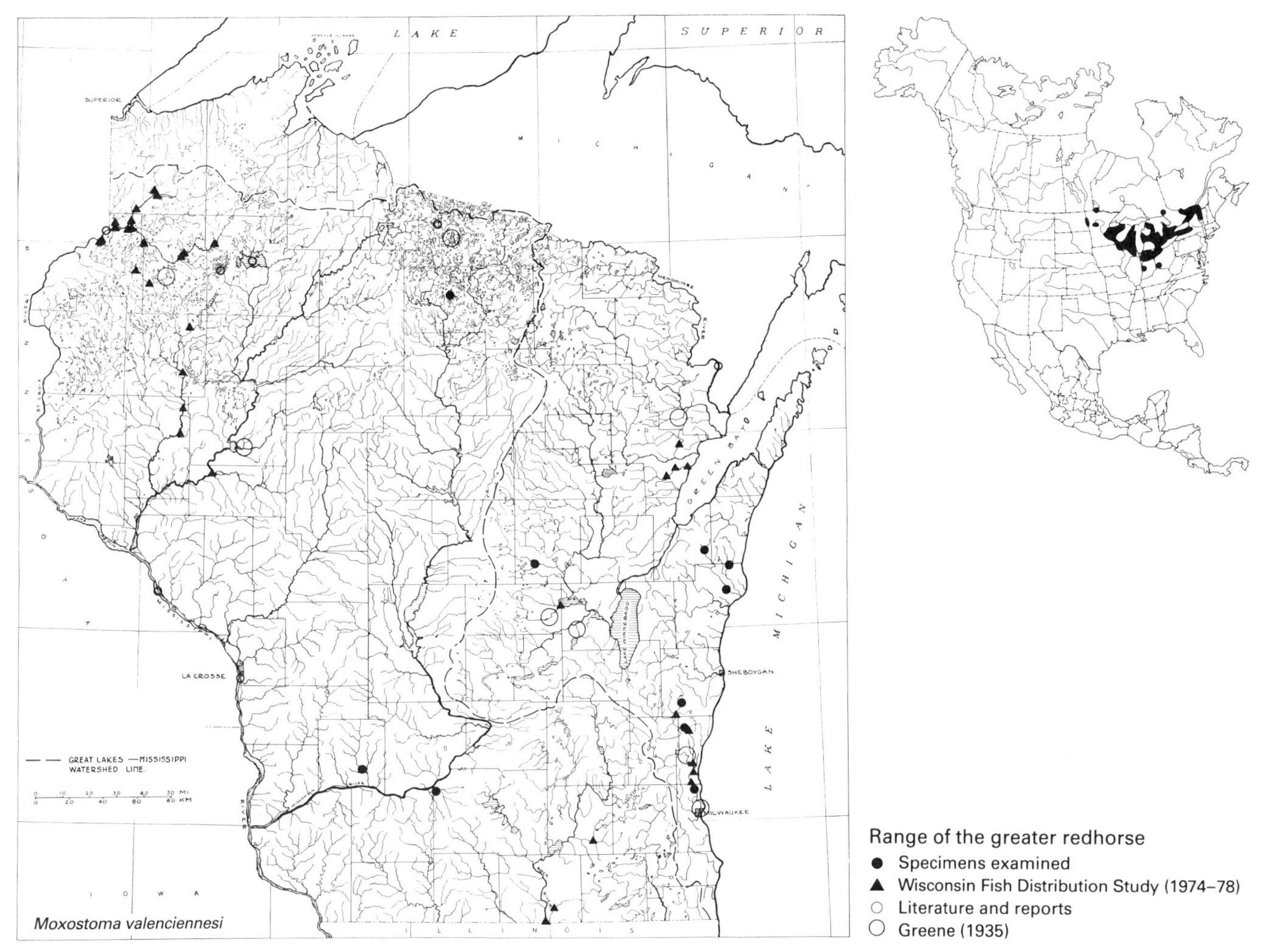

Range of the greater redhorse
● Specimens examined
▲ Wisconsin Fish Distribution Study (1974–78)
○ Literature and reports
◯ Greene (1935)

Lake Michigan drainage basins. It has not been reported from the Lake Superior basin.

Specimens examined: UWSP 3163 (1) Bearskin Lake (Oneida County), 1967; UWSP 3802 (1) Cary Pond of Crystal River (Waupaca County), 1971; UWSP 4323 (1) Neshota River T22N R22E Sec 10 (Brown County), 1973; UWSP 4763 (1) East Twin River T21N R24E Sec 6 (Manitowoc County), 1974; UWSP 5082 (1) Turtle Creek T1N R13E Sec 9 (Rock County), 1975; UWSP 5426 (1) West Twin River T20N R24E Sec 29 (Manitowoc County), 1976; MPM 12799 (1) Yellow River T39N R14W Sec 15 (Burnett County), 1976; UWSP 5725 (1) St. Croix River T34N R18W Sec 19 (Polk County), 1978; UWZM 4355 (1) Black Earth Creek (Dane County), 1957; UWSP 5577 (1) Pensaukee River T27N R21E Sec 12 (Oconto County), 1977; UWSP 5719 (1) Pensaukee River T27N R21E Sec 13 (Oconto County), 1978; UWSP 5655 (1) Yellow River T41N R16W Sec 28 (Burnett County), 1977; and MPM 6222 (9) Pine River T9N R1E Sec 2 (Richland County), 1972. From the Milwaukee River; UWSP 4358 (1) at Brown Deer Road (Milwaukee County), 1969; UWSP 5328 (1) T10N R22E Sec 30 (Ozaukee County), 1975; UWZM 4378 (1) at Waubeka (Ozaukee County), 1959; and MPM 6994 (1) T13N R21E Sec 8 (Sheboygan County), 1973.

The Wisconsin Fish Distribution Study from 1974 to 1978 reported these specimens: (3) Brill River T36N R10W Sec 30 (Barron County), 1975; (1) Chippewa River T27N R9W Sec 18 (Eau Claire County), 1977; (4) Turtle Creek T1N R13E Sec 9 (Rock County), 1975; (1) Rock River T1N R12E Sec 35 (Rock County), 1976; (1) Bark River T5N R15E Sec 11 (Jefferson County), 1976; (1) Lake Poygan T19N R13E Sec 13 (Waushara County), 1974; (1) Little River T28N R21E Sec 5 (Oconto County), 1975; and (1) Whitefish Lake T39N R9W Sec 14 (Sawyer County), 1974. From the Red Cedar River: (2) T29N R11W Sec 8 (Dunn County); (1) T31N R11W Sec 26 (Dunn County), 1975; and (4) T33N R11W Sec 14 (Barron County), 1975. From the Milwaukee River: (3) T9N R21E Sec 36 (Ozaukee County), 1975; (2) T9N R22E Sec 18 (Ozaukee County), 1975; and (17) T10N R22E Sec 30 (Ozaukee County), 1975. From Pensaukee River: (1) T27N R21E Sec 18 (Oconto County),

1975; (3) T27N R20E Sec 32 (Oconto County), 1975; and T27N R21E Sec 12 (Oconto County), 1975. The Wisconsin Fish Distribution Study also received specimens in 1976 and 1977 from Department of Natural Resources fish research (T. Beard) taken from Brill River (Barron County); St. Croix River, Yellow River, Loon Creek, Chases Brook, Dogtown Creek, and Namekagon River (Burnett County); Yellow River, McKenzie Creek, Namekagon River, and Spring Creek (Washburn County); Namekagon River (Sawyer County); and Saint Croix River and Moose Creek (Douglas County).

Jenkins (1970) reported: UMMZ 96086 (1), UF 14567 (1), and USNM 117557 (1) Spooner Lake Outlet (Washburn County), 1928; UMMZ 156836 (1) Mississippi River at La Crosse (La Crosse County), 1948; KU 4879 (1) St. Croix River at the Burnett-Pine county line, 1959; UMMZ 73885 (1) Willow Creek (Waushara County), 1926. Jenkins noted that 4 of the upper Mississippi River and Lake Michigan basin records for Wisconsin by Greene (1935) were either not specifically located, or were misidentified. The report from the Wisconsin River in Becker (1966) is incorrect. Additional reports: Mississippi River, Pools 5 and 8 near Buffalo and La Crosse respectively (P. W. Smith et al. 1971); Chippewa Flowage (Sawyer County) (Dunst and Wirth 1972); Island Lake (Vilas County), 1977 (K. Linquist, pers. comm.); and Menominee River on the Wisconsin-Michigan boundary (Marinette County) (Taylor 1954).

The greater redhorse's status has been reviewed by Jenkins (1970), who noted that it is uncommon or rare over most of its range. In parts of its range, the greater redhorse probably has been extirpated, or has had its populations reduced to low levels as a result of siltation and other forms of pollution. It may also be inherently rare in certain portions of its range.

The greater redhorse in the states immediately surrounding Wisconsin is nonexistent, or in precarious condition. Its presence in the Red River of the north Minnesota–North Dakota boundary, where the three existing records date from the 1890s, is doubtful. In Minnesota it has been reported from the Mississippi River at La Crosse (1948) and at Minneapolis (1926) (Phillips and Underhill 1971). In Michigan, it has been reported from the Menominee River on the Wisconsin-Michigan boundary and from Kelly Creek (Menominee County) (Taylor 1954). In Illinois, the greater redhorse is extirpated (P. W. Smith 1973). In Iowa, there are no records of this species. The general range map I have provided indicates the historical range of the greater redhorse; it does not define the constrictions of its present range or its sporadic distribution within that range.

The status of the greater redhorse in Wisconsin is probably brighter than anywhere else in its range; however, our recent records are often substantiated by only one or a few specimens. Since the greater redhorse is sensitive to chemical pollutants and turbidity, small populations are vulnerable and may be reduced or extirpated. It is possible that the population from Cary Pond (Waupaca County) may have been eliminated by a Department of Natural Resources carp control project in 1971. Other populations are threatened with domestic sewage and particulate runoff.

In Wisconsin, the greater redhorse has watch status (Les 1979). The establishment of a sanctuary containing a healthy population of the greater redhorse should be instituted, and the biological needs of the species studied carefully. Such a reservoir must be set aside if the greater redhorse is to continue as part of Wisconsin's fish fauna.

The greater redhorse inhabits mainly medium-sized to large rivers, river reservoirs, and large lakes. Scott and Crossman (1973) suspected that it occurs in limited numbers in the Great Lakes themselves, near the mouths of tributary streams. Adults may occur throughout the year in streams as narrow as 5–9 m (18–30 ft) with an average depth of less than 1 m (3 ft). The greater redhorse prefers clear water over sand, gravel, or boulders.

BIOLOGY

The greater redhorse is said to spawn in May or June in the moderately rapid water of streams (Scott 1967). The following information about spawning is from Jenkins (1970, and pers. comm.).

Spawning occurred in the Thousand Island area of the St. Lawrence River from 28 June to 8 July 1967, and from 25 June to 7 July 1968, at water temperatures of 16.7–18.9°C (62–66°F). Although these dates are late for catostomid spawning, St. Lawrence River water in the Thousand Islands area warms relatively late, and the greater redhorse run closely follows that of the white sucker, *Catostomus commersoni*.

An Oneida Lake (New York) male showed developing tubercles on 19 April, and in the Ausable River (Michigan), three tuberculate males apparently were spawned out by 23 June. Spawning beds generally consist of gravel with admixtures of sand and small rubble, in moderate to swift currents. Following the movement or migration to these areas, male greater redhorses hold positions or territories, and are periodically visited by females for spawning. No nest construction has been observed. Spawning is accomplished, in typical redhorse fashion, by a trio of two males and a female. Jenkins noted a functional reproductive dimorphism, whereby males tend to spawn with females larger than themselves.

In the Pine River (Richland County) on 23 August, nine young-of-year greater redhorses were 37–50 mm TL. In the Milwaukee River (Ozaukee County) on 10 September, 14 young-of-year were 53–75 mm TL and 1.7–4.8 g. In the Pensaukee River (Oconto County) on 28 October, three young were 57–74 mm and 1.99–2.85 g.

The growth of the greater redhorse varies in different parts of the state. In the Pensaukee River (Oconto County), three greater redhorses, in age-groups III, V, and VI, were 173 mm. 321 mm, and 395 mm TL respectively; they had the following average calculated lengths at the annuli: 1—28 mm; 2—128 mm; 3—232 mm; 4—295 mm; 5—335 mm; and 6—378 mm. Four fish collected from Red Cedar River (Barron County) on 24 June, were in age-groups IX and X, and were 584–616 mm TL and up to 3.25 kg in weight (23–24.2 in, 7 lb 2.8 oz); they had the following calculated lengths at the annuli: 1—34 mm; 2—131 mm; 3—231 mm; 4—351 mm; 5—424 mm; 6—478 mm; 7—519 mm; 8—549 mm; 9—572 mm; and 10—559 mm. The annulus for the year was just being placed in the largest and oldest fish.

In view of known growth rate of young-of-year greater redhorses, the calculated growths at the first annulus in the above assessments are unusually low. No correction has been made for this bias.

Two 8-year-olds from Turtle Creek (Rock County), were 547 and 666 mm TL; the latter weighed 2.32 kg (5 lb 1.8 oz). They had the following lengths at the annuli: 1—53 mm; 2—186 mm; 3—279 mm; 4—373 mm; 5—451 mm; 6—519 mm; 7—560 mm; and 8—607 mm.

The largest greater redhorse, 673 mm TL and 4.85 kg (26.5 in, 10 lb 11 oz), was taken from Whitefish Lake (Sawyer County) on 25 or 26 June 1974. Back-calculated lengths at the annuli were: 1—80 mm; 2—157 mm; 3—275 mm; 4—382 mm; 5—462 mm; 6—511 mm; 7—540 mm; 8—563 mm; 9—588 mm; 10—613 mm; 11—635 mm; and 12—652 mm. An age-X fish from Lake Poygan (Waushara County), 618 mm and 3.06 kg (24.3 in, 6 lb 12 oz), showed a yearly growth rate identical to that of the specimen from Whitefish Lake.

The greater redhorse is the largest of the redhorses; adults frequently exceed 2 kg (4.4 lb). In the Lake Ontario drainage, it has been reported at 5.90 kg (13 lb) (Dymond et al. 1929). According to Jenkins (1970), maturity, which is based on tuberculation, occurs in males between 380 and 540 mm SL (about 467 to 664 mm TL). Males probably mature at ages V and VI.

The food of the greater redhorse consists principally of aquatic insects and mollusks. The stomach of a 24-cm (9.4-in) fish from Lake Champlain (New York) contained the following food: midge larvae (5% volume), mollusks (25%), crustaceans (60%), and plants (10%) (Rimsky-Korsakoff 1929).

In Bearskin Lake (Oneida County), species associated with the greater redhorse included the hornyhead chub, largemouth bass, bluegill, pumpkinseed, yellow perch, johnny darter, muskellunge, northern pike, and walleye.

IMPORTANCE AND MANAGEMENT

The value of the greater redhorse as a prey species is not known. The greater redhorse is seldom taken by angling. It is probably only rarely a small part of the commercial "suckers and redhorse" catch reported from the Mississippi River and Lake Michigan.

River Redhorse

Moxostoma carinatum (Cope). *Moxostoma*—sucking mouth; *carinatum*—keeled.

Other common names: greater redhorse, redfin redhorse, pavement-toothed redhorse, big-jawed sucker, river mullet.

Adult female 638 mm, Chippewa R. between Eau Claire and Durand (Dunn Co.?), 17–19 May 1977

DESCRIPTION

Body moderately stout, usually round, often quite compressed in adult males; ventral line curved. Adult length about 300 mm (12 in). TL = 1.26 SL. Depth into SL 3.3–4.0. Head into SL 3.6–4.2. Snout squared at tip or slightly rounded. Mouth ventral and horizontal; lips deeply plicate, folds almost always smooth, papillae absent; lower lip much broader than upper lip, with lower halves nearly straight along posterior margin, which may be weakly scalloped. Pharyngeal teeth 33–45 per arch; teeth of lower half very large and molarlike, with a somewhat flattened grinding surface; arch heavy and strong. Dorsal fin straight to slightly concave; dorsal fin base into SL 4.5–5.0, length of base about three-fourths the distance from back of head to dorsal fin base; dorsal fin rays 13–15; anal fin rays 7; pelvic fin rays 9 (8–10). Lateral line scales 42–44 (41–46); lateral line complete. Scales around caudal peduncle 12–13.

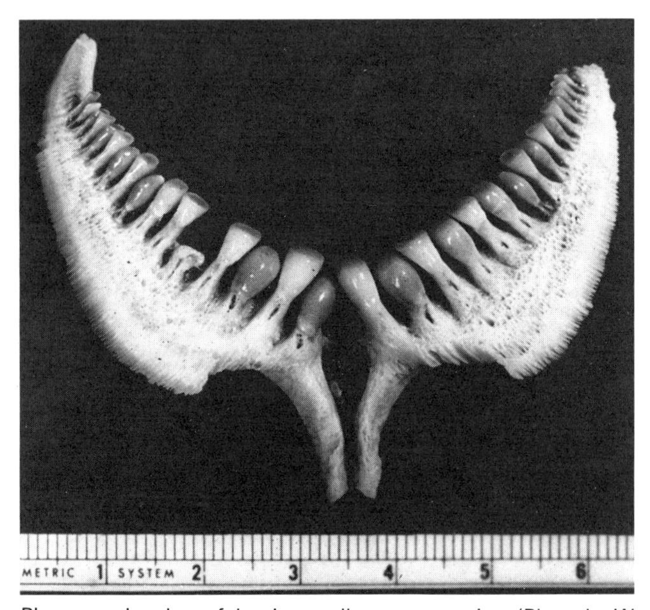

Pharyngeal arches of the river redhorse—rear view (Photo by W. Schmid and J. Underhill, University of Minnesota)

Back bronze olive; sides and belly yellowish, brassy, or bronzed. Caudal and dorsal fins red in life, lower fins orange to reddish orange. Scales usually with dark spots at their anterior exposed bases.

Breeding male with moderate to large tubercles on snout to cheek, on throat, on back of head, and occasionally a few on opercle and nape; minute tubercles occasionally on margins of scales on upper half of body, on all caudal and anal fin rays, and, in larger male, on anterior rays of paired fins. Breeding male with a midlateral, dark stripe extending from snout to above anal region. Breeding female with thickened epidermis of lower caudal peduncle.

Sexual dimorphism: Males in Lake St. Croix (Wisconsin-Minnesota boundary) with a significantly lesser head depth, slimmer caudal peduncle, and longer anal fin than females (Phillips and Underhill 1971).

Hybrid: A possible hybrid between this species and either the shorthead or the golden redhorse has been reported from the South Fabius River system, Missouri (Jenkins 1970).

DISTRIBUTION, STATUS, AND HABITAT

In Wisconsin, the river redhorse occurs only in the Mississippi River basin.

Specimens examined: UWSP 3557 (2) Lake St. Croix near Stillwater, Minnesota, 1968; UWSP 5576 (1) and MPM 12800 (1) Rock River T8N R15E Sec 4 (Jefferson County), 1976; UWSP 5584 Chippewa River T27N R9W Sec 19 (Eau Claire County), 1977.

The Wisconsin Fish Distribution Study reported: 6 collections (1–61) Rock River T8N R15E Sec 4 (Jefferson County), 1976 and 1977; (7) Rock River T9N R15E Sec 33 (Jefferson County), 1977; (1) Sugar River T2N R9E Sec 25 (Green County), 1974; (1) Sugar River T2N R9E Sec 23 (Green County), 1974; (1) Wisconsin River T6N R7W Sec 13 (Grant County), 1977; (3) Black River T19N R6W Sec 27 (Jackson County), 1978; (1) Black River T19N R5W Sec 1 (Monroe County), 1977; 4 collections (1–2) Chippewa River T24N R14W Sec 23, T26N R12W Sec 3, T27N R10W Sec 35, T27N R9W Sec 19 (Pepin, Dunn, and Eau Claire counties), 1977; (1) Yellow River T41N R16W Sec 28 (Burnett County), 1977; St. Croix River T42N R15W Sec 33 (Burnett

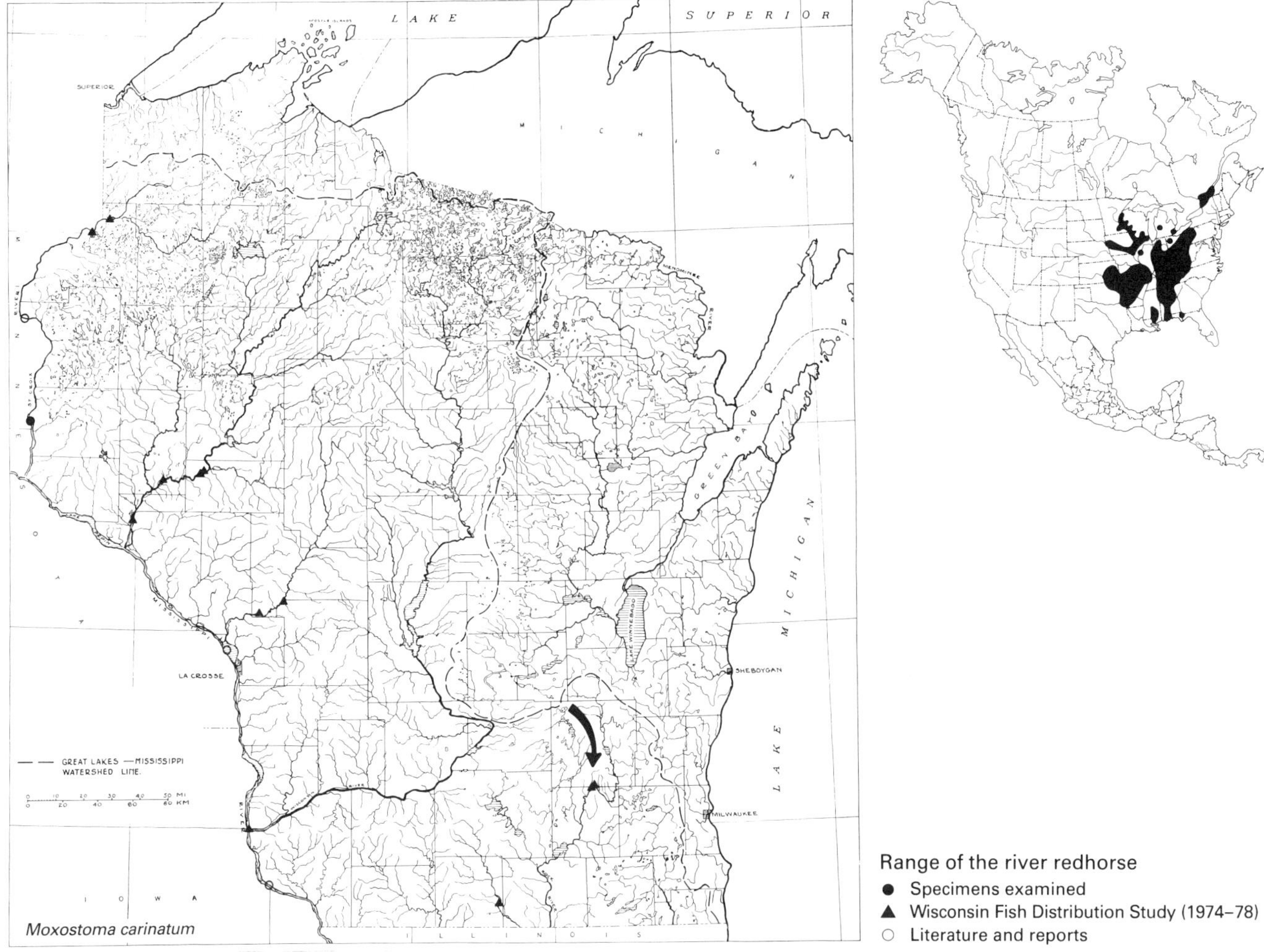

Range of the river redhorse
● Specimens examined
▲ Wisconsin Fish Distribution Study (1974–78)
○ Literature and reports

County), 1977. Other reports: Mississippi River at Cassville (Grant County) (Jenkins 1970); Mississippi River near Dresbach, Minnesota (W. Thorn, Minn. Dep. Nat. Resour., pers. comm.).

Over much of its range, the river redhorse is in serious trouble and has declined markedly within the past century. It is probably extirpated in Michigan (Becker 1976), Iowa (Roosa 1977), and Indiana (Gerking 1945). It has been placed on the rare and endangered species lists for Illinois (Lopinot and Smith 1973) and Kansas (Platt et al. 1973). Turbidity and other forms of pollution in such areas as eastern Kansas, Iowa, Illinois, western Pennsylvania, and northern Missouri may have been major factors in the decline and extirpation of river redhorse populations (Jenkins 1970).

In Ohio, the river redhorse declined after 1940 (Trautman 1957). In Alabama, it once constituted as high as 24.3% of the total weight of fish collected in rotenone samples (Hackney et al. 1968), but has not been recorded in similar studies of the same areas since the impoundment and inundation of the river habitat. Apparently the river redhorse population has been severely reduced and possibly extirpated over much of its former range within Alabama.

In Wisconsin, the river redhorse is a threatened species (Wis. Dep. Nat. Resour. Endangered Species Com. 1975, Les 1979). It appears only in those rare areas on large rivers where the channel is constricted sufficiently to cause water to flow rapidly over a hard, silt-free bottom. I have suggested the establishment of refuges in such areas to ensure the perpetuation of the river redhorse and other species that require similar conditions.

Jenkins (1970) called attention to the fact that species of suckers which are essentially molluscan feeders, such as the river redhorse, have all apparently suffered a great loss of range within historical times, or have become extremely localized in their distribution compared to related species. Mollusks are particularly sensitive to toxicants, and are among the first organisms killed where toxicants are applied.

The river redhorse prefers large rivers and the lower portions of their main tributaries. It inhabits reservoirs, pools, and moderate to swift water over clean gravel and rubble, and is seldom encountered in deeper waters with mud, silt, or sand bottoms.

BIOLOGY

The river redhorse is a late spawner. In the southern part of its range, spawning occurred from 10 to 17 April at water temperatures of 22.2–24.4°C (72–76°F) (Hackney et al. 1968). In Quebec, tuberculate males were taken on 1–3 June; males with scars were taken only from 1–7 July (Jenkins 1970).

The following spawning data were supplied by D. Becker (pers. comm.). While electrofishing the Chippewa River between the Eau Claire Dam (Eau Claire County) and Durand (Pepin County) on 17–19 May 1977, between 12 and 17 river redhorses were taken in 0.6–1.2 m (2–4 ft) of water, over gravel and rubble, in a current 0.6–1.0 m/sec. Water temperatures varied from 20°C (68°F) in the morning to 23.3°C (74°F), in the afternoon. The sides of the males were dark olive, and the caudal and anal fins showed signs of wear. The females were a "rich gold" on the sides. The males emitted milt and the females emitted eggs as they were handled for measurements. The largest specimen weighed more than 4.99 kg (11 lb). In the downstream portion of the sampling area, specimens had tubercle scars only, and spawning apparently had been completed. During the same time period, the golden redhorse (*Moxostoma erythrurum*) was spawning in shallower areas, where the river was 0.3–0.6 m (1–2 ft) deep.

The spawning behavior of the river redhorse was observed in Alabama and reported by Hackney et al. (1968:327):

> River redhorse in the Cahaba River spawn on gravel shoals. The males precede the females onto the shoals. . . . The redds were excavated by using the caudal fin in a sweeping motion, the mouth in a sucking motion, and the head in a pushing motion. Redds were observed in water from 6 inches to 3.5 feet deep. The size of the redds varied from 4 to 8 feet across and were excavated to a depth of 8 to 12 inches into the gravel. Frequently there were overlaps from one redd to another. A minimum of eight redds were found on all spawning sites. After the redds were constructed the male took a position on the redd facing upstream. This practically motionless position was maintained until a female neared the redd. At this point the male darted back and forth across the redd in somewhat of a nuptial dance. In all spawning instances observed a second male came onto the redd, and in perfect harmonic motions, joined the first male in the nuptial dance. After the two males remained for a few seconds in this rhythmic movement the female took a position between the two males . . . (who) then pressed tightly against the female and all three began a series of tetanic vibrations. During these vibrations the eggs were released, fertilized and buried in the gravel. On several occasions one of the males left the formation after the tetanic vibrations had started, subsequently leaving one male and one female in the spawning act. In no instances did a female come onto a redd to spawn when only one male was present.

A gravid female river redhorse, 645 mm and 3.69 kg, collected from the Chippewa River (Eau Claire County) on 17 May 1977, held eggs averaging 3.0 (2.7–3.1) mm diam. In Alabama, females 455–561 mm (17.9–22.1 in) held from 6,078 to 23,085 eggs, 3–4 mm diam (Hackney et al. 1968).

Eggs which were incubated in the laboratory at 22.2°C (72°F) hatched in 3–4 days. Somites developed approximately 48 hours following fertilization (Hackney et al. 1968). These laboratory-held fish were 13 mm long on 21 April, and 104 mm long on 9 August. They were extremely wary and skittish, even with daily feeding; such behavior may explain in part why juveniles are difficult to capture.

Five river redhorses taken from Wisconsin waters were in age-groups IV–XII, and were 347–645 mm TL. The calculated lengths at the annuli were: 1—40 mm; 2—128 mm; 3—221 mm; 4—310 mm; 5—394 mm; 6—446 mm; 7—490 mm; 8—527 mm; 9—580 mm; 10—615 mm; 11—629 mm; and 12—645 mm. In Missouri, Purkett (1958b) determined the following length-weight relationships: 152 mm—40 g; 254 mm—184 g; 381 mm—607 g; 508 mm—1.42 kg; 635 mm—2.74 kg; and 711 mm—3.83 kg.

The standard lengths of mature males, whose maturity was determined by tuberculation, ranged between 300 and 459 mm (Jenkins 1970). In Alabama (Hackney et al. 1968), adult females had an average length shorter than that of adult males.

The river redhorse reaches 76 cm (29.9 in) TL in the St. Croix River (Phillips and Underhill 1967). In the Chippewa River, individuals have been reported to exceed 4.99 kg (11 lb).

The chewing structures of river redhorses furnish an effective mill for crushing mollusks, which apparently are this species' primary food. The river redhorse's molarized teeth and enlarged pharyngeal arches and associated structures are apparently adapted for masticating a greater percentage of mollusks than those of most other suckers (Jenkins 1970). In the Cahaba River, Alabama, the river redhorse feeds largely on the Asiatic clam *Corbicula* sp; other food items which are present in stomachs, but in insignificant quantities, include larval Ephemeroptera, Chironominae, and Trichoptera (Hackney et al. 1968). One-third of the food consumed by two Illinois specimens was mollusks; the remainder was composed of insect larvae, mainly mayflies and hydrophilid beetles (Forbes and Richardson 1920).

The river redhorse may make upriver spawning migrations. This possibility is supported by the tendency of the young and of small juveniles to occur more frequently than adults in moderate- and small-sized streams (Trautman 1957).

Of 286 tagged river redhorse adults from the Cahaba River, Alabama, 4 were recovered; 1 had shown no movement over a 12-day period, and another had moved 24 km (15 mi) upstream during the same period; 2 had each moved 16 km (10 mi) upstream during a 22-day period (Hackney et al. 1968).

The river redhorse is quickly restored to waters from which it has been eliminated if there is a reservoir population nearby (Jenkins 1970). An apparently complete fishkill in the Clinch River, Virginia, during mid-June 1967 was followed in late summer by the restoration of a population of young river redhorses, probably from the mouth of a nearby tributary. Residents reported that the river redhorse was again common in the Clinch River in 1969.

IMPORTANCE AND MANAGEMENT

The river redhorse is rarely taken on a baited hook, but it may be caught incidentally while angling for other fish. In Alabama, where a small number of anglers bait areas to attract this species (Hackney et al. 1968), two principal methods are used by sport fishermen to catch shoaling redhorse: snaring, in which a wire loop attached to a stout pole is passed over the fish's head and drawn tight; and snagging, with unbaited treble hooks. There is also some interest in spear and bow fishing, both of which are legal methods for taking nongame fish in Alabama.

The flesh of the river redhorse, like the flesh of all redhorses, is edible and tasty, although bony. The presence of river redhorse bones in Indian middens suggests it was eaten by Indians (Scott and Crossman 1973).

Difficulty in identifying the river redhorse makes it impossible to assess the numbers which are actually caught. In the commercial catch of the Mississippi River, the river redhorse is categorized with "suckers and redhorse." In Canada's St. Lawrence River near Montreal, commercial fishermen rank the river redhorse as a species of minor importance. During fall and winter fishing in Canada, it constituted about 2% of the catch of suckers (Scott and Crossman 1973). In 28 days one fisherman caught 90 river redhorses which weighed a total of 163 kg (360 lb).

One Wisconsin population of the river redhorse, discovered in 1976 by the Wisconsin Fish Distribution Study between the two dams on the Rock River at Watertown (Dodge and Jefferson counties), became the central figure in a controversial carp control program. The fish toxification program called for the destruction of all fish from Hustisford (Dodge County) to the lower dam at Watertown. Fortunately, a pretreatment survey with a boom shocker disclosed a unique population of river redhorses in the sector between the dams—a distance of approximately 1.6 km (1 mi). None was found either above or below the dams. Forty-one river redhorses were removed and placed in holding ponds at Delafield, and treatment plans were revised to allow toxicants only in the waters above the upper dam, leaving the critical area between the two dams untreated. After treatment, the redhorses were returned to the area from which they had been removed.

It remains to be seen whether the area between the dams continues to offer a suitable habitat to this species. It was impossible to prevent some of the antimycin from spilling over into the control area, since the upper dam leaked. The possibility exists that some undesirable effects may have occurred, such as the reduction or the destruction of the molluscan food supply of the river redhorse.

The river redhorse is a unique fish resource and is worthy of special attention. Steps should be taken to ensure that adequate reservoirs of this species are quickly set aside in Wisconsin waters and that life history research is instigated toward determining its critical environmental demands.

Northern Hog Sucker

Hypentelium nigricans (Lesueur). *Hypentelium*—below, 5 lobes, supposedly in reference to 5-lobed lower lip; *nigricans*—blackish.

Other common names: hogmolly, hognose sucker, black sucker, stoneroller, spotted sucker, riffle sucker, bigheaded sucker, hammerhead sucker, hog mullet, crawl-a-bottom, stone lugger, stone toter, pugamoo.

Male 232 mm, Elk R. (Price Co.), 2 Oct. 1976

DESCRIPTION

Body elongate, cylindrical; heavy forward, much tapered posteriorly. Average length 203 mm (8 in). TL = 1.20 SL. Depth into SL 4.5–5.2. Head into SL 3.6–4.5; top of head between eyes concave; eyes looking upward. Snout long and strongly decurved. Mouth ventral, horizontal or oblique, often protruding anteriorly into a "vacuum cleaner"; lips very thick and strongly papillose, the upper lip almost as thick as the lower, with 8–10 series of papillae. Pharyngeal teeth 44–50 per arch; medial teeth enlarged, with expanded heads bearing a distinctive cusp anteriorly; arch moderately stout, symphysis short. Dorsal fin falcate, dorsal fin base into SL 5.1–6.5; dorsal fin rays 11–12 (9–12); anal fin rays 7(8); pelvic fin rays usually 9; pectoral fins very long, into SL 4.5–4.9. Lateral line scales 47–51 (46–54); lateral line complete. Reduced swim bladder volume compared to most other catostomids. Chromosomes 2n = 96–100 (Uyeno and Smith 1972).

Back olive to brown; sides variable, lighter olive, brown or yellow; belly whitish. The back and upper sides of young marked with 5 dark, oblique saddles. Scales of sides greatly mottled. Lips orange or reddish orange in life. All fins red, orange, or yellow; caudal and anal fins usually red. Lower fins reddish with some dusky mottling on pectorals and pelvics.

Breeding male with minute tubercles densely covering head dorsally and laterally; anal, pelvic, and caudal fins tuberculate; tubercles occasionally persisting long after spawning. In old males, some body scales with minute tubercles. Breeding female with small tubercles on fins, occasionally persisting on anal fin into September.

Sexual dimorphism: Males with third and seventh pelvic rays of about equal length, giving fin a square appearance when spread (when relaxed, medial edge appears longest). Females with third and fourth pelvic rays longest, giving fin a rounded appearance when spread (when relaxed, lateral edge much longer than medial edge).

SYSTEMATIC NOTES

Originally the hog sucker was listed in genus *Catostomus*, subgenus *Hypentelium*, but the subgeneric status has been raised to generic level. Further investi-

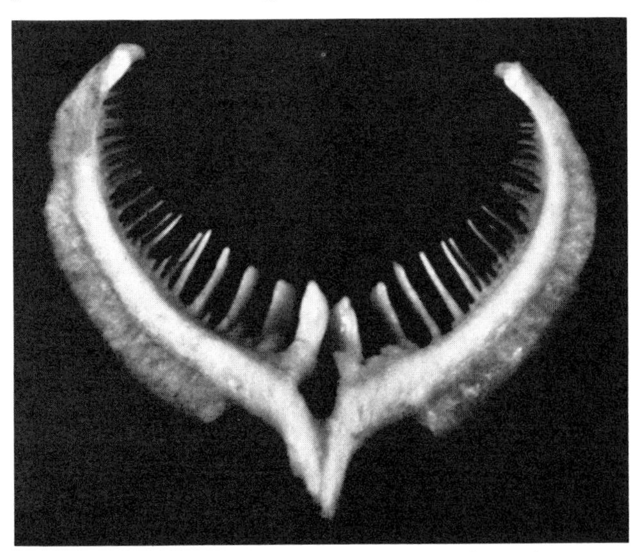

Pharyngeal arches of the northern hog sucker, front view

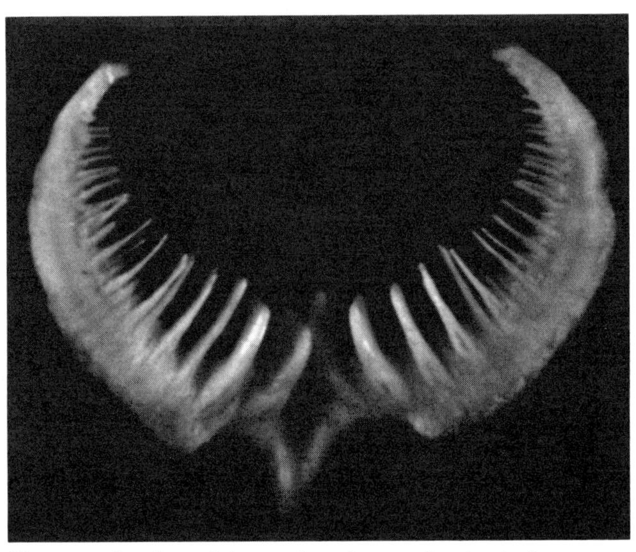

Pharyngeal arches of the northern hog sucker, back view

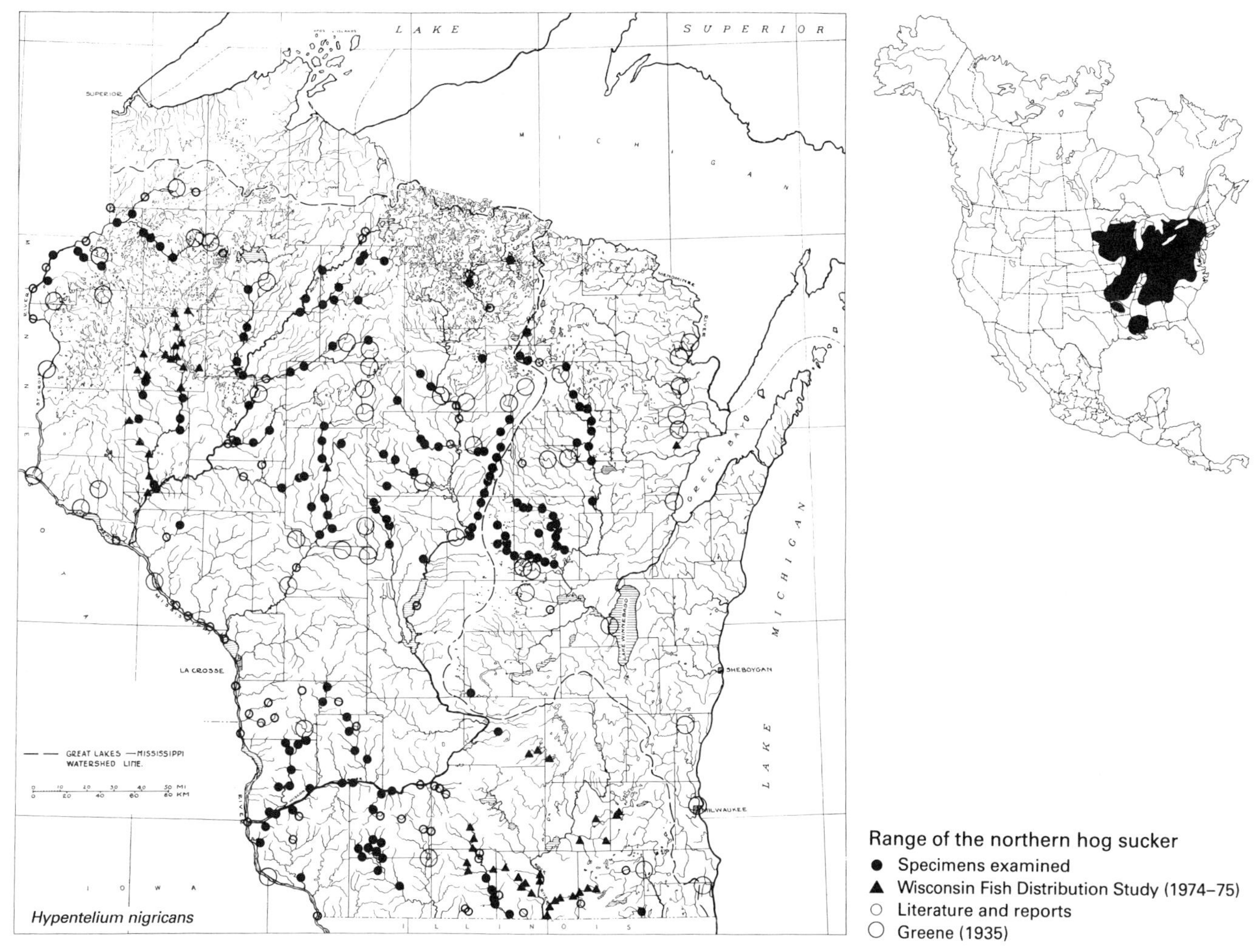

gation has placed this genus closer to the redhorses than to the finescaled suckers (Jenkins 1970). Three species are recognized, but only one is known from Wisconsin.

DISTRIBUTION, STATUS, AND HABITAT

In Wisconsin, the northern hog sucker occurs in the Mississippi River and Lake Michigan drainage basins. It is not known from the Lake Superior basin. All of our records come from streams, but a single report has been ascribed to Grindstone Lake (Sawyer County) (Sather and Threinen 1968).

In Wisconsin, the northern hog sucker avoids lakes, and is present only sparingly in the larger streams. It is uncommon in the Mississippi River, perhaps as a result of man's conversion of the riffle or fastwater sectors to a series of impounded pools. In the driftless area, it is locally abundant, and in a survey in southwestern Wisconsin more than 200 individuals were taken in 32 of 153 collections (Becker 1966). The northern hog sucker appears to have disappeared from the Milwaukee and Pike river systems of the lower Lake Michigan basin, perhaps as a result of acute environmental changes which have occurred in that part of the state. The northern hog sucker appears to be secure in Wisconsin.

The northern hog sucker frequents the clear parts of streams or rivers, especially riffle areas where the current is sufficiently rapid to keep the bottom scoured of silt. It was encountered most frequently in clear to slightly turbid water at depths of 0.1–1.5 mm, over substrates of gravel (26% frequency), sand (26%), boulders (15%), rubble (12%), mud (8%), silt (6%), clay (5%), and bedrock (1%). It occurred in streams of the following widths: 1.0–3.0 m (5%); 3.1–6.0 m (20%); 6.1–12.0 m (23%); 12.1–24.0 m (24%); 24.1–50.0 m (23%); and more than 50 m (6%).

BIOLOGY

Spawning occurs in April and May in riffles, or in the downstream ends of pools. No nest is built, but during prespawning activities the aggressive males clean an area of gravel. In New York, ripe males have been collected as early as 19 April, when the water temperature was 15.6°C (60°F) (Raney and Lachner 1946). Females are usually found in the riffles only when they are ready to shed eggs; at other times they frequent nearby pools.

The spawning of the northern hog sucker, observed in shallow water near the downstream end of a pool, has been described by Raney and Lachner (1946:77):

> . . . The pool, just below an impassable falls, harbored some 35 to 40 hog suckers which varied in length from 6 to 12 inches. They tended to gather in groups of 3, 5, 7 and 12 fishes, each group with a single female, and swam about the pool, the males attempting to crowd about the female. The female when ready to spawn would take a position over the bottom in a restricted area of sand and gravel about three feet in diameter where the water was about 3 to 5 inches deep. The males, usually two or three in numbers, followed immediately and caused a great commotion as they attempted to pack in about the female, their tails and caudal peduncles crowded against her sides. As she extruded the eggs the males became greatly excited and often stood on their heads with the threshing tails protruding from the surface and beating the water into foam. The breeding act lasted approximately two seconds and is repeated after a short period of rest of 4 to 7 minutes during which the female retires to the deeper water but is still followed by her retinue of males. It was noted that a small 6 inch male was one of the most successful of all those present and did not once leave the side of a female during a period of several hours.

The demersal, nonadhesive eggs are broadcast and abandoned; the eggs and young receive no parental attention. As the eggs were laid, many minnows, eastern blacknose dace (*Rhinichthys a. atratulus*), and northern creek chub (*Semotilus a. atromaculatus*) rushed in to feast upon them. The northern hog suckers showed no interest in food at this time, even though an earthworm was dangled in front of their mouths. They showed little concern over the presence of an observer standing only a few feet away.

Eggs hatch in 10 days at a mean water temperature of 17.4°C (63.3°F). Newly hatched larvae measure 9.1–10.6 mm TL. Buynak and Mohr (1978) have illustrated and described the stages from protolarvae 10.2 mm long to juveniles 27.8 mm TL.

In Wisconsin, the growth of young-of-year northern hog suckers follows:

Date	No. of Fish	TL (mm) Avg	TL (mm) Range	Location
18 July	18	34	29–44	Wolf R. (Langlade Co.)
25 July	14	54	43–60	Red Cedar R. (Dunn Co.)
16 Sept.	3	62	57–68	Plover R. (Portage Co.)

Eight northern hog suckers collected 12 July 1970 from the Plover River (Portage County) showed the following growth at the annuli: 1—38 mm; 2—101 mm; 3—175 mm; and 4—241 mm. The specimens were of the following age classes and lengths: II—146–154 mm; III—203–206 mm; and IV—266–283 mm. The condition (K_{TL}) of the above collection averaged 1.05 (0.98–1.29).

Female northern hog suckers grow faster than males, but males mature sooner than females. In New York (Raney and Lachner 1946), some of the larger males mature and breed when they are only 2 years old and are about 135 mm (5.3 in) long; practically all males are mature when they are 3 years old and 180 mm (7.1 in) long. On the other hand, most females mature at 3 years, when they average 170 mm (6.7 in) TL. The slower growing females do not spawn until they are 4 years old and are 213 mm (8.4 in) long.

The largest museum specimen (UWSP 5428) of a northern hog sucker, collected 11 September 1976 from the Hay River (Barron County), is 378 mm (14.9 in) TL and 8 years old. Females up to 508 mm (20 in) have been reported in Minnesota (Eddy and Underhill 1974).

A young northern hog sucker nearly 25 mm long was reported to have eaten 95% small crustaceans (Chydorinae) and 5% midge larvae, along with a trace of rotifers and diatoms (Greeley 1927).

In southern Wisconsin, the northern hog sucker feeds almost entirely on animal matter, largely insects and larvae, with only a small proportion of the diet consisting of mollusks (6%), and vegetable matter (12%) (Cahn 1927). In central Wisconsin, it consumed Coleoptera (40% volume), small clams (30%), small amounts of dragonflies, damselflies, and freshwater shrimp, and traces of sand and gravel (L. Meyer, pers. comm.).

The northern hog sucker's feeding behavior has been described by Forbes and Richardson (1920:87):

> . . . It seeks its food in the more rapid parts of streams, pushing about the stones upon the bottoms and sucking up the ooze and slime thus exposed, together with the insect larvae upon which it mainly depends for food.

Along with its food the northern hog sucker sucks up sand and small rocks which it quickly ejects. This species feeds ravenously, and is not easily disturbed by intruders (Harlan and Speaker 1956).

The seasonal movements of the northern hog sucker in Ohio have been described by Trautman (1957). During the spawning season, this species congregates in high-gradient streams over stony riffles. After spawning, many adults and some young begin to drift downstream into larger waters with lower gradients. The downstream movement continues throughout the late summer and fall until the fish reach the larger, deeper waters where they winter. There they remain until the water temperatures rise to above 4.4°C (40°F), after which they begin their spring migrations upstream. In New York, Raney and Lachner (1946) noted that these fish are sluggish and generally inactive in water below 10°C (50°F), and that in water as cold as 4.4°C (40°F) they are extremely sluggish and have been seen lying beside a log or a stone in a riffle without moving for long periods.

Individual northern hog suckers are often found in the swiftest flowing portions of riffles, where their streamlined bodies and widely spread pectoral fins, and the downward push of the current on their depressed heads, hold them in position; even recently killed specimens, if properly placed, will remain on the bottom without being swept downstream (Trautman 1957). The northern hog sucker avoids profuse amounts of aquatic vegetation. Eddy and Surber (1947) noted that it "loves to bask in the sun, lying atop some large rock or in a shallow riffle."

In Moccasin Creek (Wood County), 13 northern hog suckers were associated with these species: American brook lamprey (5), brook trout (2), white sucker (153), largescale stoneroller (3), blacknose dace (53), creek chub (49), redside dace (9), bluntnose minnow (8), common shiner (27), bigmouth shiner (22), yellow bullhead (1), black bullhead (1), central mudminnow (2), blackside darter (13), johnny darter (29), and fantail darter (6).

IMPORTANCE AND MANAGEMENT

The northern hog sucker is beneficial to minnow species present in its habitat by making available to them food to which they normally would have little access. While overturning stones during the feeding process, the northern hog sucker dislodges many food items which float downstream to foraging minnows. Hence the minnows are commensal species, dining at the table prepared by the sucker.

The northern hog sucker is host to the glochidial stage of the mollusk *Alasmidonta marginata*; it is one of a number of fish species responsible for the distribution and perpetuation of that clam species.

The northern hog sucker is sometimes used as a bait in still-fishing. However, it is generally considered too dull in color and too prone to seek the bottom to be an effective bait fish, even though it lives well on the hook and is active. In the East, large northern hog suckers are sometimes used as bait for muskellunge, northern pike, and other large game fishes (Raney and Lachner 1946).

The northern hog sucker is rarely taken on a small worm or a wet fly by anglers. Although the flesh of this species has been described as coarse and not very desirable, I have found the opposite to be true. A small northern hog sucker, filleted, salted, dusted with flour, and deep-fat fried, is tasty and sweet; the meat may be soft in consistency, but the flavor is superior to that of some panfish I have tried.

White Sucker

Catostomus commersoni (Lacepède). *Catostomus*—inferior mouth; *commersoni*—after P. Commerson, an early French naturalist.

Other common names: common sucker, common white sucker, coarse-scaled sucker, fine-scaled sucker, eastern sucker, brook sucker, gray sucker, black sucker, common mud sucker, sucker, mullet, black mullet, slender sucker, June sucker, whitehorse, carp.

Female 217 mm, Hay R. (Dunn Co.), 4 Oct. 1976

DESCRIPTION

Body elongate, round in cross section. Average length 241 mm (9.5 in). TL = 1.23 SL. Depth into SL 4.2–5.0. Head into SL 3.8–4.5. Snout rounded and slightly pointed, but sometimes square; in ventral view snout barely extends beyond tip of upper lip. Lips heavily papillose. Pharyngeal teeth about 56 per arch, with a pronounced cusp on anterior edge of crown of each tooth; lower 5 teeth on each side with moderately expanded crowns; arch moderately strong, widely flared into wings beginning at the level of third tooth; symphyseal stem short. Dorsal fin slightly convex to straight to slightly concave; dorsal fin base into SL 5.7–7.0; dorsal fin rays 10–13; anal fin rays 7; pelvic fin rays 10–11. Lateral line scales 60–70 (55–85); lateral line complete. Digestive tract long, undifferentiated, with 4–5 coils. Chromosomes 2n = 100 (*Chromosome Atlas* 1973).

Back olive to brownish; belly lighter to whitish. Dorsal and caudal fins light slate, remaining fins whiter or tinged with orange. Scales generally dark margined. Usually 3 prominent dark blotches (diam of eye or larger) along sides in young-of-year and age-I fish, which disappear in older fish.

Breeding male with tubercles on rays of anal fin, lower lobe of caudal fin, on some caudal peduncle scales, on head, and along caudal edge of each body scale. Breeding male usually with a well marked, dark, lateral stripe or a crimson lateral stripe. Breeding females occasionally with poorly defined tubercles on anal and caudal fins.

Sexual dimorphism: In adult males, the tip of the anal fin reaches or is less than 4 mm of the lowermost full ventral ray of the caudal fin; in females, there is a gap of 4–13 mm. In males, the seventh pelvic ray exceeds the third in length by 0.5–3.5 mm; in females, the seventh ray is from 1 to 5 mm shorter than the third. (See figure on p. 684.)

Hybrids: White sucker × longnose sucker, and with other closely related catostomids (Brown 1971, Hubbs et al. 1943, Nelson 1973).

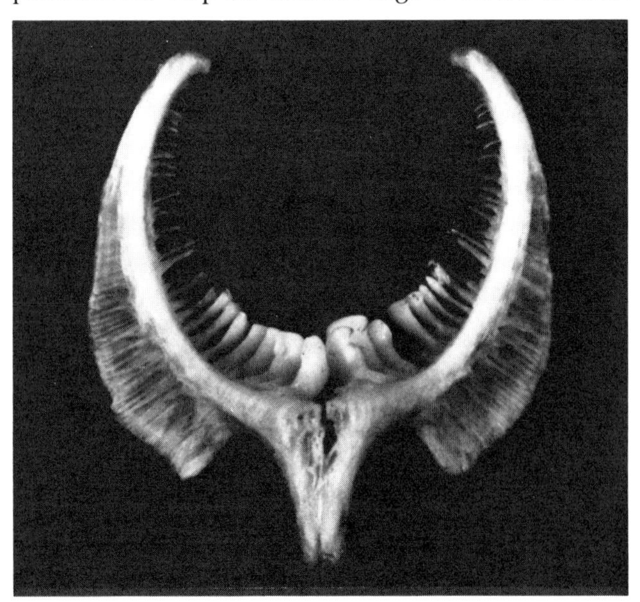

Pharyngeal arches of the white sucker, front view

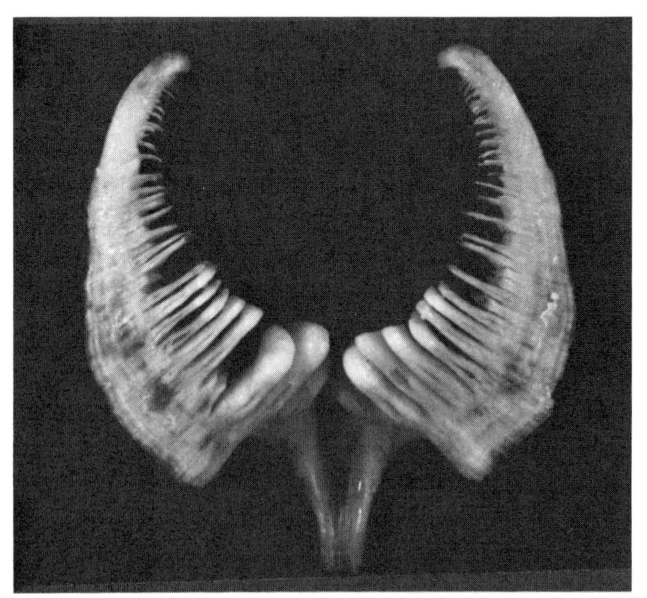

Pharyngeal arches of the white sucker, back view

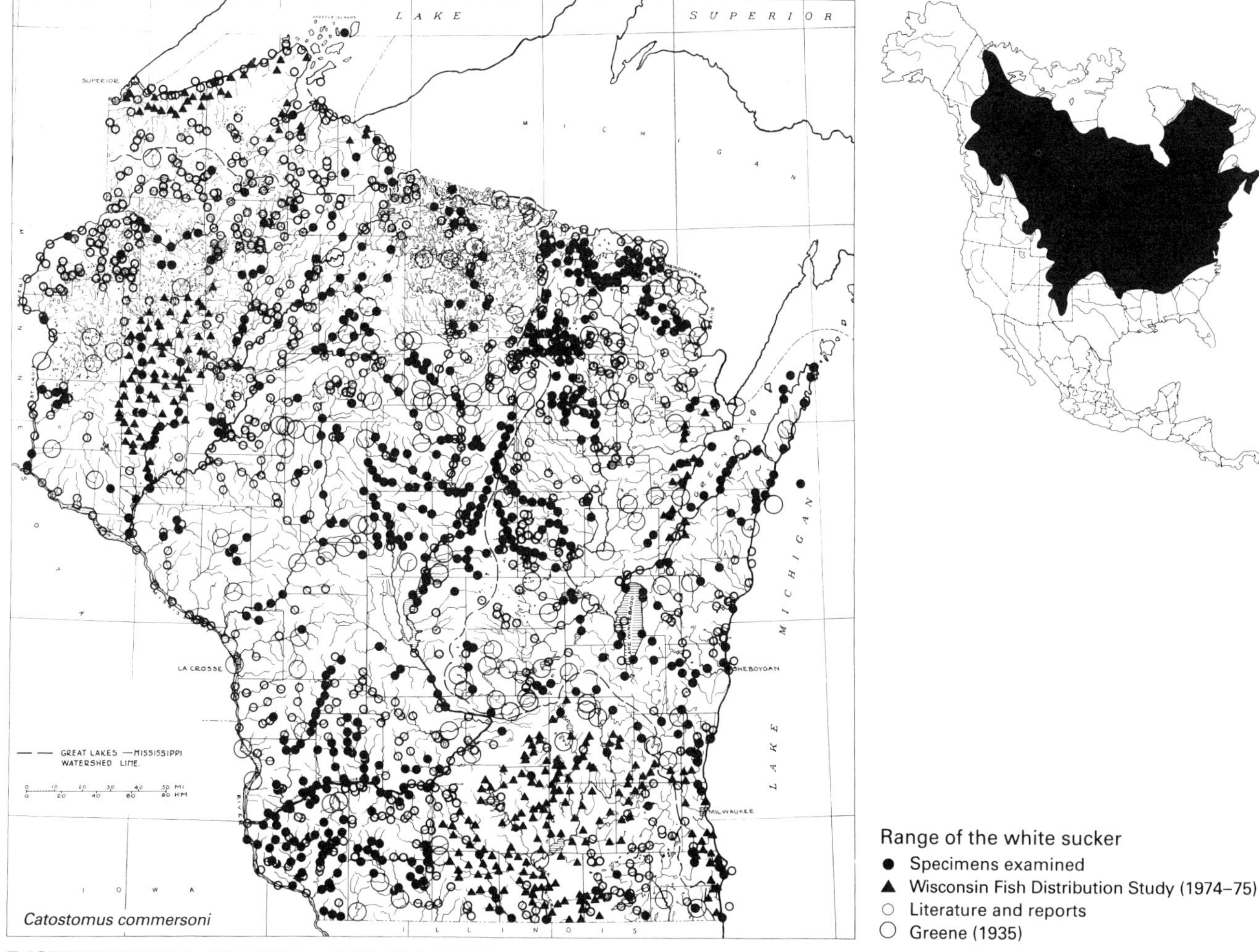

DISTRIBUTION, STATUS, AND HABITAT

In Wisconsin, the white sucker occurs in all three drainage basins, and is widely distributed in lakes and streams throughout the state.

The white sucker is probably the most widespread of all fishes in Wisconsin, where it is common to abundant in most streams and in large lakes. In the Mississippi River it is rare to uncommon. In a central Wisconsin study, this species appeared in 56 of 59 collections, and the total combined weight of the white suckers exceeded the total weight of all other species taken (Becker 1959).

The white sucker is a common inhabitant of the most highly polluted waters of southeastern Wisconsin, and of the most turbid waters of southwestern Wisconsin. It is generally more tolerant of a wide range of environmental conditions than any other species of fish in Wisconsin.

In Wisconsin, the white sucker tolerates all stream gradients from the lowest to the highest. It was encountered most frequently in clear to slightly turbid water at depths up to 1.5 m, over substrates of gravel (23% frequency), sand (22%), silt (14%), rubble (13%), mud (12%), boulders (9%), clay (5%), detritus (2%), and bedrock (1%). It was taken once over marl. The white sucker occurred commonly in lakes or reservoirs in areas with sparse vegetation. It was found in streams of the following widths: 1.0–3.0 m (24%); 3.1–6.0 m (27%); 6.1–12.0 m (17%); 12.1–24.0 m (17%); 24.1–50.0 m (10%); and more than 50 m (4%).

BIOLOGY

In Wisconsin, the white sucker generally spawns from April to early May. In northern Wisconsin, spawning has been observed in late May and early June (Spoor 1935), and it may possibly occur in late June (Faber 1967). Spawning occurs shortly after ice-out, when the water temperature reaches about 7.2°C (45°F). Spawning is associated with migratory runs which, according to Magnuson and Horrall (1977), may be initiated by water runoff from early melting snow. Water temperature may be an important factor in determining the peak of the spawning migration and the duration of the run. The major migration

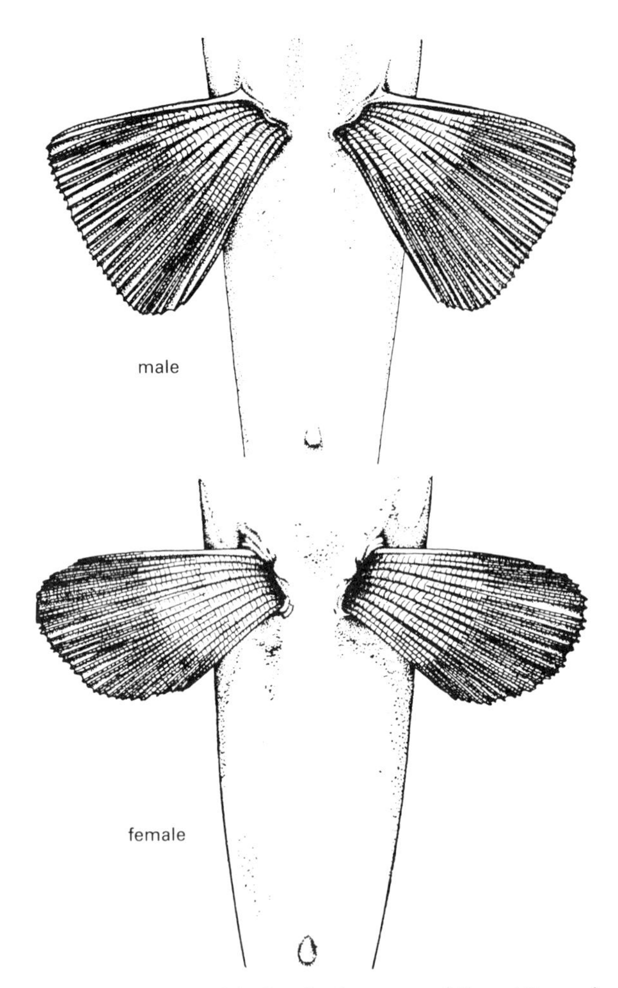

Comparison of the pelvic fins in the sexes of the white sucker (Spoor 1935)

usually takes place at night, starting at dusk; its greatest intensity is reached between 2200 and 2300 hr (Schneberger 1972c).

Male white suckers are more numerous than females on the spawning areas, and they arrive 2–3 days before the females. No nests are prepared, and no territories are defended. Spawning occurs in swift water or rapids, over a bottom of gravel; however, the white sucker occasionally spawns in lakes, if conditions are suitable (Breder and Rosen 1966).

The spawning behavior of the white sucker has been described by Reighard (1920). While the males are numerous on the rapids, the females locate in deeper water above or below the rapids. When a female moves into the rapids and comes to rest quietly on the bottom, she is approached by from one to ten males. A male coming within a few centimeters of the waiting female may stop, spread his pectorals, erect his dorsal fin, protrude his jaw, and for a second vibrate his head rapidly from side to side. "Head trembling" also occurs when one male approaches another on the spawning grounds.

The spawning act frequently occurs between a single female and two males with one male on each side of her. The males spread their adjacent pectorals beneath the female, and press their caudal fins against hers. The backs of the males are arched, and their dorsal fin rays spread like the ribs of an extended fan. When the fish have come into position, all three fish vibrate rapidly. If they are in shallow water their backs may be exposed. The powerful movement of their tails stirs up the gravel, releasing a cloud of sand, which is washed downstream. The spawning act lasts about 1.5 seconds.

Although additional white sucker males may be present during the spawning act and may attempt to interfere, they take no part in the normal spawning. There is no combat between the males that crowd about the female to gain a place at her side; when not at the side of the female, males seem to pay no attention to one another.

After spawning, the female white sucker moves on, usually upstream, where she soon pairs with other males on another part of the spawning grounds. The eggs from one female are scattered in small lots over a considerable area—probably over more than one rapids.

In a Canadian study (Geen et al. 1966), the estimated spawning mortalities of adults for two successive years were 16% and 20%, although the percentages are probably high.

In northern Wisconsin, female white suckers 406–533 mm (16–21 in) TL produced 20–50 thousand eggs (Spoor 1935). An age-VI, 406-mm female from Pleasant Lake (Walworth County), with ovaries 16% of the body weight, held more than 35,600 eggs (K. Landauer, pers. comm.). In Minnesota (Vessel and Eddy 1941), 483–508-mm (19–20-in) white suckers contained 93–139 thousand eggs.

The eggs are demersal and adhesive when laid. They stick to, and are partially covered by, bottom materials. Fertilized eggs are 2.0–3.0 mm diam. No care is given to the eggs.

According to Dobie et al. (1956), water temperatures from 13.9 to 20°C (57 to 68°F) are best for hatching white sucker eggs. In this temperature range, the incubation period is 5–7 days. A thorough description of the development from fertilization to the exhaustion of the yolk supply has been prepared by Long and Ballard (1976). Information on the development of later stages has been supplied by Mansueti and Hardy (1967), who have reported that scale formation is first evident at about 22.0 mm and is completed by 25.0 mm, when the young are about 40 days old.

Approximately 1 month elapses between the first appearance of white sucker spawners and the downstream migration of the fry (Geen et al. 1966). The young remain in the gravel at the spawning grounds for 1–2 weeks after hatching, before they emerge to move downstream. These fry, 12–14 mm TL, move downstream almost entirely at night. According to Clifford (1972), as the fry become larger, many more move downstream near the surface of the water than near the stream's substrate.

In Erickson and John lakes (Vilas County) white sucker larvae were first collected in late May and in June (Faber 1967). Large numbers of larval white suckers were observed schooling in very shallow water (2–5 cm) near shore, and were regularly caught in the limnetic region after dark.

Larval white suckers (12–25 mm long) have oblique mouths and short intestines (Cross 1967). They feed near the surface on protozoans, diatoms, small crustaceans, and bloodworms brought by currents into areas occupied by the schools of fry. As the young grow, the mouth becomes ventral, the intestine elongates, and the fish seek food mainly on the bottoms of streams or lakes.

Young white suckers are typically gregarious, and, during the first year of life, may form schools of a few fish to several hundred fish. They usually spread out side by side, facing the shore (Schneberger 1972c); when alarmed they hide in deep water, but usually return to shallow water in a few minutes. In lakes, white suckers under 51 mm (2 in) long usually feed in water 15–20 cm (6–8 in) deep along the shore.

The growth of young-of-year white suckers in northern Wisconsin reached 29 (24–33) mm on 4 July in the Wolf River (Forest County), and 44 mm by 20 September in the Jump River (Price County). In central Wisconsin, they reached 33 (28–38) mm on 25 June in the Little Eau Claire River (Portage County), and 66 (60–78) mm on 16 September in the Plover River (Portage County). In southern Wisconsin, young-of-year attained 30 (23–34) mm on 30 June in the Pecatonica River (Iowa County).

White suckers for age-groups I through VIII appear in the table below. No 6- or 7-year-old males were taken from Lake Winnebago. Priegel determined that the average age at maturity was 2 for both males and females. All fish were mature at 3 years or older.

From sections of the pectoral fins, Vondracek back calculated total lengths (mm) at the annuli for white suckers from the Pensaukee River, a tributary to Green Bay: 1—males 175 (females 180); 2—292 (301); 3—357 (374); 4—389 (415); 5—406 (438); 6—403 (445); 7—414 (460); 8—421 (463); 9—429 (461); and 10—438 (471). In white suckers from Green Bay and Lake Michigan, a small number of males mature at age II, and some females mature at age III. Most white suckers are mature at age IV. Data presented by Vondracek indicate that white suckers in Green Bay grow at a faster rate than they do in Lake Michigan.

In Spauldings Pond (Rock County), white suckers 384–398 mm (15.1–15.7 in) TL were 3 years old (Threinen and Helm 1952). A 525-mm fish, collected from Roberts Lake (Forest County) on 8 July 1966, was estimated to be 11 years old; age was calculated by analysis of pectoral fin-ray sections (R. Puckett, pers. comm.). Beamish and Harvey (1969) found that, for some populations of white suckers, the scale method for calculating age is inaccurate after the fish have reached 5 years of age.

The largest known Wisconsin white sucker, which weighed 2.50 kg (5.5 lb), was taken from Lake Mendota (Dane County) on 11 March 1976.

The condition (K_{TL}) of white suckers, collected from the Biron Flowage of the Wisconsin River (Wood County) on 24 April, averaged 1.14 (0.85–1.36). All fish were in postspawning condition.

Both adult and juvenile white suckers feed throughout the day and night, but they feed more actively at night than in broad daylight. Observations at night have indicated that after dark adults move into shallower water to feed (Moyle 1969). This species has diversified feeding habits, taking any food

Age and Growth (TL in mm) of the White Sucker in Wisconsin

Location	I	II	III	IV	V	VI	VII	VIII	Source
Muskellunge L. (Vilas Co.)[a]	71	117	163	203	231	262	290	310	Spoor (1938)
L. Winnebago									
Males	163	320	401	427	442				Priegel (1976)
Females	163	330	411	452	448	498	523		
L. Michigan, Green Bay									
Males		324	355	388	410	417	427	424	Vondracek (1977)
Females		311	369	414	439	442	466	472	

[a]Data converted by Vondracek (1977) from SL or FL, using conversion factors presented in Carlander (1969).

that may appear, including fish and fish eggs (Dobie et al. 1948). It has eaten mud, plants, mollusks, insects, entomostracans, diatoms, desmids, rotifers, crustaceans, and protozoans. Stomach analyses have shown 100% insects in some collections, 100% higher plants in others, 95% mollusks in one collection, and 50% drift in other stomachs. The average percentages of food items in stomachs examined by several workers were: insects 39.0, crustaceans 3.3, mollusks 10.3, surface drift 2.1, plankton 26.3, higher plants 9.7, miscellaneous 8.8, and bryozoans 0.5.

The white sucker is essentially a bottom fish. In deep lakes, few if any are captured more than 46 cm (18 in) off the bottom (Spoor and Schloemer 1939). They move inshore in the evening and offshore in the morning. In Green Bay (Lake Michigan), they were most numerous at the 9-m interval, although a few were captured at 37 m (Reigle 1969a). According to Hile and Juday (1941), the maximum depths of occurrence of white suckers varied from 5 to 10 m in Lake Mendota (Dane County) to 10 to 15 m in Lake Geneva (Walworth County) and Green Lake (Green Lake County).

In streams, the largest white suckers occur in the deep holes; they are easily stunned with electrofishing equipment, although such treatment is seldom fatal. White suckers keep poorly in holding tanks on hot days. They may survive low oxygen levels if the water temperature is low.

White suckers move about extensively (Olson and Scidmore 1963), dispersing widely after spawning. In South Bay of Lake Huron, white suckers traveled 0.6–12.9 km (0.4–8 mi) from the tagging site; one was reported 56 km (35 mi) away, 5 years after it was tagged (Coble 1967b).

In northern Wisconsin lakes, the white sucker prefers water temperatures of 11.8–20.6°C (53.2–69.1°F) (Ferguson 1958), generally at the lower part of the epilimnion and the upper part of the thermocline. On 1 August, the upper lethal temperature was 31.2°C (88.2°F) (Brett 1944).

Beamish (1972) determined that the low to lethal pH for the white sucker is 3.0–3.8. In Lake Waubesa, and in the Yahara River below the lake, a sudden mortality of fishes occurred when the water became super-saturated with oxygen (Woodbury 1941); among the fish most affected were large, mature white suckers.

IMPORTANCE AND MANAGEMENT

In Wisconsin the sucker is an important forage fish. Muskellunge are known to feed on the white sucker and, in some areas, they are preyed upon by walleyes, basses, burbots, brook trout and sea lampreys. Small white suckers are also prey to such fish-eating birds as the bald eagle, heron, loon, and osprey. Spawning suckers in streams fall prey to bears and other animals.

The white sucker is a host to the glochidial stage of the mollusks *Alasmidonta marginata* and *Anadonta implicata*; it is one of several fish species responsible for the distribution and perpetuation of those clam species (Hart and Fuller 1974).

The chief economic value of the white sucker lies in its use as food for sport fishes. From the time they emerge from the egg until they reach a length of 203 mm (8 in), white suckers are the natural food of walleyes and northern pike (Eddy and Surber 1947). In Maine, the white sucker is one of the principal foods of lake trout over 2.27 kg (5 lb) (Everhart 1958). The vulnerability of white suckers to predation by smallmouth bass was almost nil. (Paragamian 1976b).

In the past, the white sucker has been criticized for eating the eggs of walleyes and muskellunge. Schneberger (1972c), who examined several hundred white sucker and redhorse stomachs collected during spawn-taking operations, found that fish eggs were only occasionally ingested: "Apparently the sucker does not make a special effort to seek out fish eggs for food but merely sucks them up incidentally with its regular food." In Ontario, it has been shown that predation by suckers on brook trout eggs is insignificant compared with predation by the trout themselves (MacKay 1963). In summation, the evidence for white sucker predation on spawning grounds of more desired species is variable and nonconclusive (Scott and Crossman 1972).

In Wisconsin, the white sucker is an important bait fish. White suckers from 76–356 mm (3–14 in) are used as live bait for walleyes, northern pike and muskellunge. In 1968, Wisconsin licensed bait dealers reported a total of 194,264 kg (428,272 lb) of suckers sold during the year. Schneberger (1972c) estimated the value of the sucker bait industry that year as approximately $300,000.

The white sucker is generally fished for by sportsmen early in spring, with worms used as bait. They are also speared or dip netted; and occasionally they will hit wet flies or spinning lures fished near the bottom (Reece 1963). Sucker hordes during spring runs are especially vulnerable to spearing or netting.

The flesh of the white sucker is white, sweet, and good tasting, although not quite as firm as that of most sport species. White sucker meat is a delicacy when smoked. Sucker recipes, bearing such exotic names as "Hunters Creek Home Fried," "Tasty Frontier Fritters," "Macatawa Bake," "Waterfront Casserole," and "Calumet Combo," do justice to its edibility (Mattingly 1976). Detracting from the pleasure of eating white suckers are the large Y-shaped bones between the muscle segments. These may be avoided by filleting or by grinding the meat and bones fine and fashioning them into fish patties. White suckers may also be canned; the canning process softens the bones, as it does in canned salmon.

Commercial fishermen take white suckers by seines, fyke or drop nets, pound nets, gill nets, and trawls. The catch is used for both human and animal food, much of it for cat and dog food. The white sucker, when cooked, can be used as a food supplement with the freshwater drum for the domesticated mink (Priegel 1976). Several years ago, the canning of suckers was attempted by a Michigan producer; and although the canned suckers were delectable, they could not compete with the more desirable canned salmon (Schneberger 1972c).

In Green Bay from 1963 through 1965, suckers (primarily white suckers) were the third most abundant species in the total trawl catch; they occurred in 36% of the drags (Reigle 1969a). In the Pensaukee River (Oconto County), suckers are exploited heavily by a contract fishery. A yearly mean of 158,858 kg (350,217 lb) was removed from 1967 to 1976 (Magnuson and Horrall 1977). (For further information on suckers in the commercial fishery of Lake Michigan waters, see p. 691). In Lake Superior, white suckers are of little commercial importance. During 1970, contract fishermen removed 241,918 kg (533,328 lb) of suckers from the inland waters of Wisconsin, while state crews removed 4,158 kg (9,167 lb), for a combined total of 246,076 kg (542,495 lb) (Miller 1971). The catch consisted mostly of white suckers.

The population dynamics of white suckers are not always understood. In a northern Wisconsin lake, white suckers were numerous over a period of years when the panfish populations were abundant. Although the white sucker population was not exploited, it declined just prior to the panfish population decline, and remained low (Kempinger et al. 1975). In another Wisconsin lake, with a relatively fast-growing population of white suckers, the numbers of fish of other species were lowered by removal. The suckers in the lake grew faster, despite a continued rise in their own numbers (Parker 1958).

Studies have been made of the removal of white suckers from trout streams in southern Wisconsin. In a 3-year study in Milner Creek (Grant County), 5,050 white suckers were removed during the first year, and 7,700 fish were removed 2 years later; a total of more than 499 kg (1,100 lb) of fish were removed. In October of the last year, C. Brynildson and Truog (1958) estimated that 7,411, 13- to 38-cm white suckers still remained in the stream.

The production of white suckers has been described at length by Dobie et al. (1956), Forney (1957), and Schneberger (1972c). Ponds of moderate fertility usually produce the most suckers. Where chironomid larvae are present in the bottom muds, good sucker crops may be produced consistently year after year. On the other hand, where filamentous algae grow over the bottom, sucker production is poor and may be reduced to almost zero.

The white sucker from Oklahoma to Michigan has standing crops averaging 12.2 kg/ha (10.9 lb/acre), and ranging from 0.1 to 35.3 kg/ha (0.1 to 31.5 lb/acre) (Carlander 1955).

Considering its wide distribution, its high numbers, and its delectability, the white sucker is potentially the most valuable food and sport fish in Wisconsin. It is an important and unusually persistent resource. All efforts should be directed toward its utilization, and toward improving its image before sportsmen and the general public. The white sucker represents a pool of millions of kilograms of valuable protein, which can be harvested yearly without depleting the seed stock.

Longnose Sucker

Catostomus catostomus (Forster). *Catostomus*—inferior mouth.

Other common names: sturgeon sucker, red sucker, redside sucker, mullet, northern sucker, finescale sucker, black sucker.

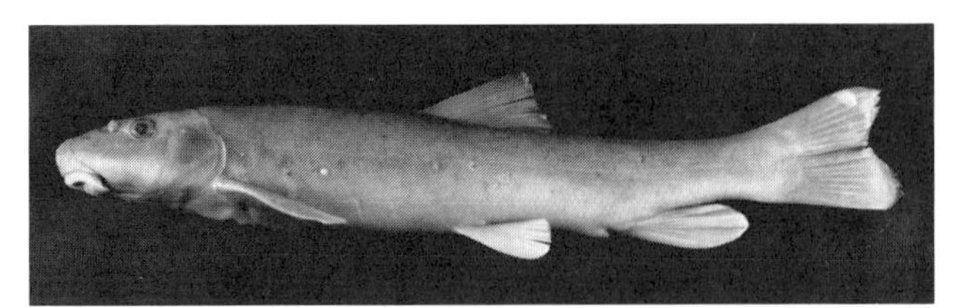

227 mm, Poudre R. (Larimer Co.), Colorado, 14 Apr. 1970

DESCRIPTION

Body elongate, rounded in cross section. Average length 406 mm (16 in). TL = 1.21 SL. Depth into SL 4.2–4.6. Head into SL 3.6–4.2. Snout strongly pointed and tapered sharply backward and ventrally to mouth; in ventral view, snout extends far anterior to upper lip. Lips heavily papillose. Pharyngeal teeth with sharp cusps on anterior cutting edges of crowns, about 52 per arch; arch medium stout, with pronounced, winglike flange arising at level of fourth tooth from center; symphysis short, but with strong ventral plates. Dorsal fin straight in young to slightly concave in adults; dorsal fin base into SL 6.6–8.0; dorsal fin rays 10 (9–11); anal fin rays 7; pelvic fin rays usually 9. Lateral line scales crowded anteriorly, usually more than 95 (91–115); lateral line complete. Digestive tract long, undifferentiated, with 2 or 3 coils. Chromosomes 2n = 98 (Beamish and Tsuyuki 1971).

Back dark slate; sides lighter; belly whitish; generally an abrupt change in color from sides to belly. Dorsal and caudal fins light slate, remaining fins milky white or transparent. Young with 3 large, diffuse, black lateral blotches (present in Lake Superior fish up to 175 mm).

Breeding male with tubercles on head, anal fin, and ventral lobe of caudal fin; the upper surface of the body almost black; a bright red midlateral stripe running length of body.

Hybrids: Longnose sucker × white sucker, and other closely related catostomids (Nelson 1973, Paetz and Nelson 1970, Brown 1971, and Hubbs et al. 1943).

DISTRIBUTION, STATUS, AND HABITAT

In Wisconsin the longnose sucker occurs in the Lake Superior and Lake Michigan drainage basins; its probable occurrence in the Mississippi River drainage basin is based on the single report (Wis. Dep. Nat. Resour.) from North Twin Lake (Vilas County). The site of this report is a few kilometers northwest of the site of the Kentuck Lake (Vilas County) record (UWSP 3709), which is in the Lake Michigan watershed. Two old records from the upper Peshtigo River (Forest County) suggested to Greene (1935) that some of the deeper lakes tributary to this river may be inhabited by this species.

The longnose sucker is the only species of North American suckers which has invaded another continent. It is known from the Yana, Kolyma, and Anadyr rivers of eastern Siberia, which it apparently in-

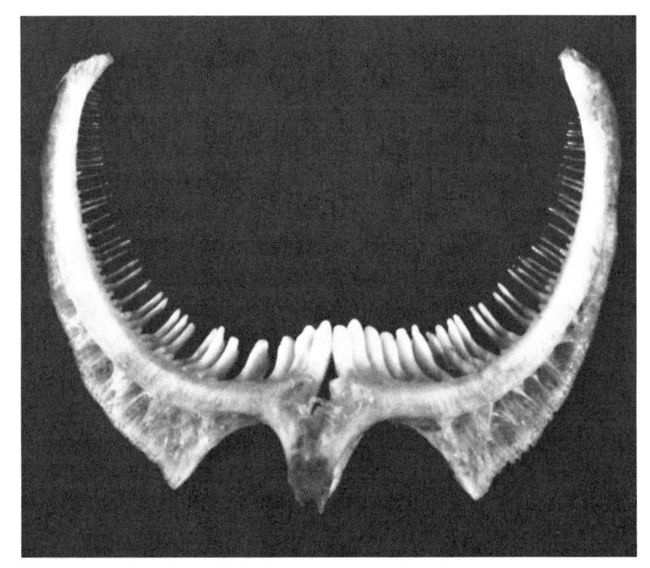

Pharyngeal arches of the longnose sucker, front view

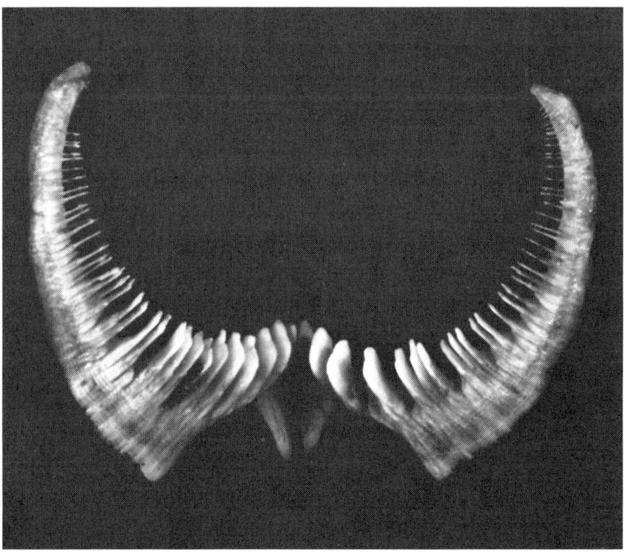

Pharyngeal arches of the longnose sucker, back view

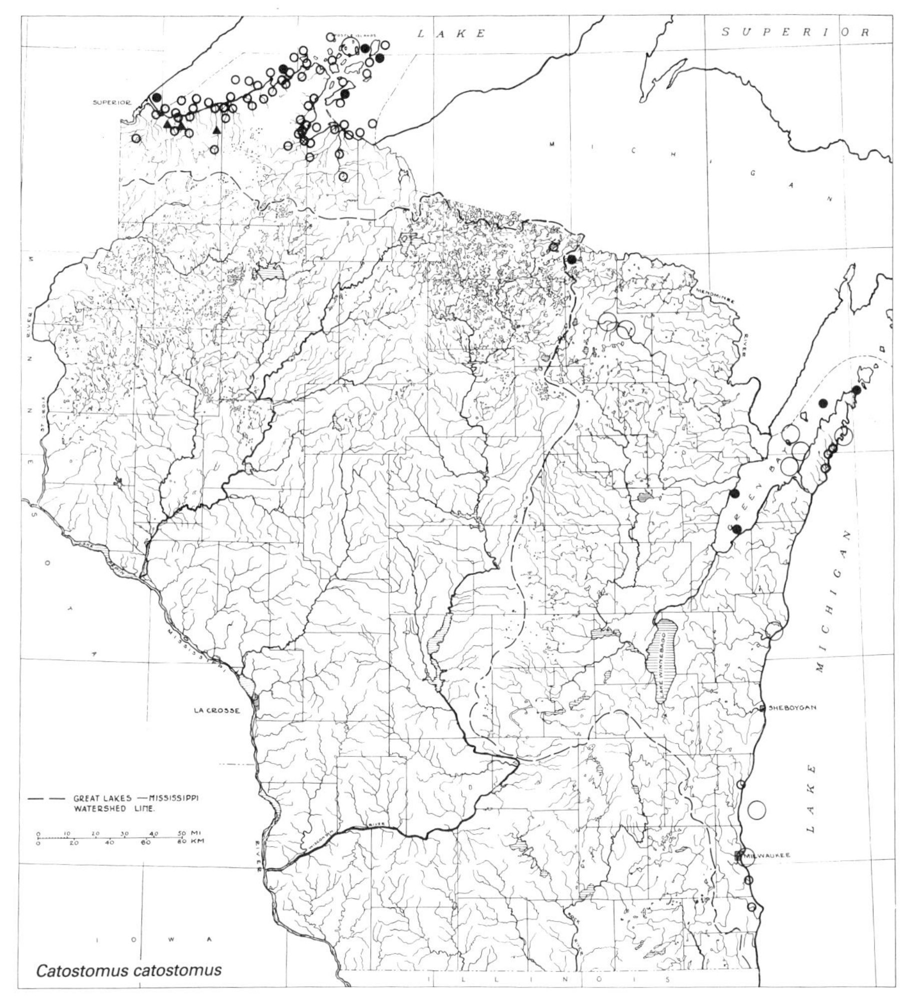

Range of the longnose sucker
● Specimens examined
▲ Wisconsin Fish Distribution Study (1974–75)
○ Literature and reports
◯ Greene (1935)

vaded recently via the Bering Straits. This species occurs in brackish water about the mouths of Arctic streams (Scott and Crossman 1973).

The longnose sucker is abundant in Lake Superior and its tributaries during spawning. In that basin it appears to be secure. In northern Lake Michigan, it is common, but it is rarer to the south, and has probably been extirpated at the southern tip of the lake. The longnose sucker rarely appears in Lake Michigan tributaries.

In Lake Michigan, the longnose sucker occurs in shallow waters, but it is occasionally found in deeper water. During bottom trawl explorations of northern Lake Michigan (Reigle 1969b), the largest catch was made at 24 m. In Lake Superior, the longnose sucker is most abundant at less than 37 m; it is seldom found deeper than 55 m (Dryer 1966).

BIOLOGY

In Wisconsin, the longnose sucker spawns in April and May. Longnose suckers were observed spawning in the company of white suckers at Fond du Lac (St. Louis River near Duluth, Minnesota) on 15 May (Eddy and Surber 1947). A male in breeding condition was collected from Kentuck Lake (Vilas County) in May. In the Brule River (Douglas County), the dates of peak spawning migration varied from 19 April to 25 May (Bailey 1969). The spawning migration intensified as the river water temperature approached 12.8°C (55°F), but fell off sharply when water temperatures exceeded 15.6°C (60°F). Spawning takes place over the gravelly bottoms of streams; it may also occur in shoal waters as is probably the case in some areas of Lake Michigan.

In the spawning run of the Brule River (Bailey 1969), male longnose suckers outnumbered females 91 to 79. The mean length of the males was 386 mm (15.2 in); that of the females was 421 mm (16.6 in). In age, the males averaged 7.2 years; the females averaged 8.0 years.

The spawning behavior of longnose suckers was observed in a British Columbia stream about 3 m wide and 15–30 cm deep (Geen et al. 1966); the current varied from 30 to 45 cm/sec over gravel 0.5–10 cm diam. The spawning act was described as follows (p. 1771):

. . . During spawning, individual females left the still water and moved into the midst of the males. Two to four males usually escorted the female a short distance and crowded beside her. During egg deposition the group of three to five fish thrashed about for 3 or 4 sec, the males apparently either clasping the female with their pelvic fins or vibrating against her with the anal fin. The dorsal fins appeared to be held stiffly erect during spawning. Following the spawning act the female returned to still water or to the cover of the bank and the males returned to previously occupied positions.

Spawning occurred during daylight hours. After dark no splashing was heard, indicating the egg deposition had ceased. No nest was built; the pale yellow eggs, adhesive and demersal, were laid a few at a time, and adhered to the gravel and other substrate material.

Although some male longnose suckers held specific positions through 1 or 2 days, no aggressive behavior or area defense was noted. Males occasionally drifted backward downstream, however, and brushed their tails against the heads of other males (Geen et al. 1966).

In Brule River (Douglas County) longnose suckers, the average number of eggs was 26,000, and ranged from nearly 14,000 for the shortest fish (353 mm) to more than 35,000 for a 450-mm female; the eggs from one female averaged 2.2 mm diam. Under laboratory conditions (Scott and Crossman 1973), eggs hatch in 8 days at a water temperature of 15°C (59°F), and in 11 days at 10°C (50°F).

Young longnose suckers remain in the gravel of the bottom for 1–2 weeks before emerging. When the fry are between 10 and 12 mm TL, they begin to migrate downstream during nighttime hours (Geen et al. 1966).

Attempts by Bailey (1969) to locate young-of-year longnose suckers in the Brule River and adjacent streams were unsuccessful. The only age-0 longnose suckers taken in his study were captured in trawls fished about 0.8 km (0.5 mi) off Duluth, Minnesota. Bailey concluded that larval suckers spend little time in the Brule River and adjacent streams, and that they drift to Lake Superior soon after hatching.

Bailey determined the following growth at the annuli of longnose suckers from western Lake Superior: 1—102 mm; 2—152 mm; 3—188 mm; 4—229 mm; 5—274 mm; 6—340 mm; 7—368 mm; 8—396 mm; 9—424 mm; 10—437 mm; and 11—462 mm. The period of annulus formation extended from mid-May to late September. More than 6 years were required for suckers to reach 454 g (1 lb), and nearly 10 years were needed to reach 907 g (2 lb). The youngest mature males were 4 years old, and all males were mature at age VIII. Females first matured at age V, and all were mature at age IX.

The back-calculated lengths at the annuli of nine longnose suckers from the Chambers Island area of Green Bay in Lake Michigan (UWSP 2399) were: 1—67 mm; 2—123 mm; 3—168 mm; 4—216 mm; 5—252 mm; 6—278 mm; 7—309 mm; and 8—344 mm (D. Breitzman, pers. comm.). The yearly growth of a 330-mm, age-VI male from Kentuck Lake (Vilas County) (UWSP 3709) was: 1—74 mm; 2—128 mm; 3—179 mm; 4—230 mm; and 5—280 mm. This fish was collected in May, and the annulus for its last year of life had not yet been placed.

A large longnose sucker, 642 mm (25.3 in) FL and weighing 3.31 kg (7.3 lb) was gillnetted from Great Slave Lake, Canada (Harris 1962). It was estimated to be 19 years old (Keleher 1961).

In one study, the food of young, 11–18 mm longnose suckers was plankton; 20–90-mm young grazed on weeds and solid surfaces, taking no mud (Hayes 1956). Weisel (1957) noted that adults frequent deep water during the heat of summer days, but in the evening and at night they approach the shores to feed. In western Lake Superior, the food habits of 231 longnose suckers and 24 white suckers in the Duluth-Superior and Apostle Islands areas were studied together (Anderson and Smith 1971b). Amphipods were the most important crustaceans, followed by lesser quantities of cladocerans, isopods, copepods, ostracods, and *Mysis*. Chironomids were the most commonly eaten insect, along with Ephemeroptera, Trichoptera, Coleoptera, and Hemiptera. Also present were fingernail clams, snails, coregonid eggs, Araneae, oligochaetes, Hydracarina, plant material, and a substantial amount of unidentified material.

Stenton (1951) reported longnose suckers 356–406 mm (14–16 in) long which had 0–98 brook trout eggs in their digestive tracts. It was known that these eggs had been exposed to predation by the superimposition of nests on limited spawning grounds, and may have been dead when eaten.

Although it is considered to be a shallow-water fish, the longnose sucker has been found as deep as 183 m (600 ft) in Lake Superior (Scott and Crossman 1973). Evidence indicates that it moves offshore in the fall (Dryer 1966). The upper lethal temperature for the longnose sucker has been calculated as 26.5°C (79.8°F) when the fish is acclimated at 14°C (57.2°F) (Black 1953).

In Green Bay near Oconto (Oconto County), the

longnose sucker is associated with these species: brown trout, coho salmon, alewife, rainbow smelt, shortnose gar, lake sturgeon, white sucker, burbot, gizzard shad, northern pike, common carp, common shiner, spottail shiner, black bullhead, white bass, smallmouth bass, rock bass, trout-perch, walleye, sauger, and yellow perch.

IMPORTANCE AND MANAGEMENT

Young longnose suckers probably fall prey to a wide variety of predacious fishes and fish-eating birds (Scott and Crossman 1973). Even large longnose suckers are taken by northern pike. Adult longnose suckers in spawning streams are probably taken by bear, by other mammals, and by ospreys and eagles.

The longnose sucker has been criticized in the past as a competitor with sport fish for space and food (Everhart and Seaman 1971, Scott 1967). Some researchers, however, feel that its value as a forage fish may outweigh its negative values as a competitor for food (Baxter and Simon 1970). Brown (1971), recognizing the problem, stated that the "true ecological relationship of suckers and game fishes is poorly understood but it may be that suckers are important to, or compatible with, good game fish populations at least in some instances."

The longnose sucker has contributed to commercial fish production in Lakes Superior and Michigan. Unfortunately, longnose suckers, white suckers, and redhorses (*Moxostoma* spp.) are categorized together in the statistics on yearly catches. In the Lake Superior catch, the longnose sucker is the most abundant sucker, followed by the white sucker and the redhorses. In Lake Michigan, the white sucker is most abundant, followed by the longnose sucker and the redhorses.

Sucker production in the Wisconsin waters of Lake Michigan in 1974 was 141,390 kg (311,700 lb), which was valued at $8,787; this was a decrease of 62,500 kg (137,803 lb) from the 1973 harvest. The waters of Green Bay, which are the principal areas of sucker production, account for 85% of the harvest. Most suckers are taken incidentally to the perch, whitefish, and alewife fishery (Wis. Dep. Nat. Resour. 1976c).

The production of suckers in the Great Lakes has been so strongly dependent on market demand that the catch figures are generally not useful as indices of abundance. It appears likely, however, that the severe drop in production which began in 1950 in Lake Michigan was at least partly a result of decreased sucker abundance caused by sea lamprey predation (Wells and McLain 1973). After the lamprey had decimated the lake trout populations, it turned to other species, including the suckers. The increase in sucker production in 1969–1970 might have been related to decreased sea lamprey predation following the implementation of a lamprey control program, and to an increase in the lake trout population. The same authors have suggested that the abundance of suckers may have declined to some extent over the years, particularly in Green Bay, as a result of the degradation of spawning streams.

In Lake Superior, longnose sucker populations are at high levels, with strong spawning runs and consistent year class strengths. Still, commercial production is limited because of poor market conditions. The sucker species could provide substantially more commercial production in Lake Superior than the 24,000 kg (53,000 lb) reported in 1974, which was valued at $2,291 (Wis. Dep. Nat. Resour. 1976c).

In the Great Lakes region, the longnose sucker seldom bites on a baited hook. It is usually taken by sportsmen by spearing or snagging during the spawning migration.

The flesh of the longnose sucker is firm, white, flaky, and sweet, and is superior to that of the white sucker. It is delicious when smoked; according to Eddy and Underhill (1974), "even the most discriminating gourmet would have difficulty distinguishing it from more exotic smoked fish."

Bullhead Catfish Family—Ictaluridae

Eight species of bullhead catfish in three genera are known from Wisconsin. The ictalurid catfishes are representatives of exclusively soft-rayed families of North American origin. In the United States and Canada, there are 5 genera and 39 species of catfish (Robins et al. 1980). Fossils occur in Miocene and Recent deposits.

The head of the catfish is often large and flattened. The teeth of the upper and lower jaws are minute and sharp, and are arranged in broad pads. The swim bladder is connected with the Weberian ossicles, and is involved in the reception and production of sound. An often elongate, adipose fin is a distinctive character. All members possess eight prominent, whiskerlike barbels, sensitive to touch and to chemical stimuli; in addition, many taste buds are distributed over the scaleless bodies of a number of species, enabling them to locate food at night when most members of the family are active.

A well-known feature of the bullhead catfishes is the spinous ray in the dorsal fin and in each pectoral fin. These spines are morphologically hardened bundles of soft-ray elements which have fused embryonically. The madtoms have poison glands associated with these spines, which are capable of inflicting a painful, but not dangerous, wound. According to Walden (1964:195), it is probable that all catfishes are so equipped: "The poison glands do not affect the flesh for eating purposes and do not seem to bother the predator fish whose powerful digestive juices dissolve any madtom or small stonecat in short order."

The spines of the different species of bullhead catfish can be used to distinguish one species from another, although, even within the same species, there may be considerable variation of the spine pattern in populations from different parts of its range. A useful key to the identification of Illinois bullhead catfishes through spines was prepared by Paloumpis (1963). The supraethmoid-ethmoid complex is also used for separating the larger members of the family (Calovich and Branson 1964, Paloumpis 1964).

Wisconsin catfishes can be divided into two groups: the small, secretive madtoms, and the large species which include the bullheads and the trophy-sized fishes. The bullheads and large catfishes provide considerable quantities of food for man. The most valuable commercial species in the Mississippi River is the channel catfish, which brings the highest price per kilogram and generally has the total highest value year after year.

All of the larger catfishes and bullheads provide excellent food, and in many restaurants along the Mississippi River catfish dinners are a specialty. The meat is white or beef colored. It is not necessary to skin the smaller catfishes before cooking them; skinning is a difficult task, which has discouraged many people from preparing these abundant fish for the table.

Bullheads are typical inhabitants of glacial lakes in central North America which are nearing extinction. They are adapted to lakes of low oxygen content, high carbon dioxide content, abundant vegetation, abundant food, low transparency, and increasing acidity. As the lakes of Wisconsin age, conditions generally will favor the warmwater fishes, and the bullheads in particular.

As a lake becomes silted in and weed-choked, bullheads explode numerically and dominate the waters, whereas the former sport and panfish disappear. This trend is inevitable, and the public should be aware that in such lakes the fishing has not "deteriorated," but shifted to another group of fishes, just as tasty as, if not more tasty than, the former inhabitants. Lakes reaching this stage are winterkill lakes. Bullheads are hardy, and among the last survivors before the lake is filled in and becomes extinct.

Bullheads often withstand domestic pollutants better than most fish. Also, along with the bowfins and the gars, they are best able to endure high concentrations of poisons, including 20 ppb of antimycin—a concentration at which other species are killed.

Because bullhead catfish require a minimum of attention and will eat any kind of food presented to them, including dog food, members of this family make interesting aquarium pets. Since they are hardy, they are able to survive aquarium conditions that would eliminate most other fishes.

The blue catfish, *Ictalurus furcatus*, was formerly included with the fishes of Wisconsin, based on two collections reported by Greene (1935) for lower Lake Pepin (Pepin County) and the Mississippi River near Lansing, Iowa (opposite Crawford County). Unfortunately, the specimens for these reports were not saved. R. Bailey suggested to me and to Dr. Greene that these probably were misidentified channel catfish, *Ictalurus punctatus*, which, during the spawning season, lose their characteristic spots and could easily be confused with the blue catfish. Dr. Greene concurred, and the blue catfish is herewith removed from the Wisconsin list.

Imm. blue catfish 95 mm, Tensaw R. (Baldwin Co.), Alabama (specimen donated by H. A. Swingle)

The blue catfish is known from the Mississippi River, but rarely from above its juncture with the Missouri River. However, a specimen (INHS 2148), 23 cm SL, was taken in 1972 from the Mississippi River 2 km northeast of Bellevue, Iowa; this site is approximately 32 km (20 mi) from the Wisconsin-Illinois line, and its presence there supports the possibility that at some time the blue catfish may appear in Wisconsin waters. The blue catfish should be watched for, and I have included it in the taxonomic keys. Suspected specimens should be carried to the nearest Department of Natural Resources agency or museum for verification.

Black Bullhead

Ictalurus melas (Rafinesque). *Ictalurus*—fish cat; *melas*—black.

Other common names: bullhead, common bullhead, black catfish, black cat, yellow belly bullhead, horned pout, brown catfish, stinger, river snapper.

Adult 182 mm, tributary to Green Bay (Door Co.), 5 June 1962

DESCRIPTION

Body robust, rounded anteriorly, compressed posteriorly. Length 165–229 mm (6.5–9.0 in). TL = 1.19 SL. Depth into TL 4.0–5.1. Head length into TL 3.8–4.2. Snout bluntly pointed in lateral view, broadly rounded in dorsal view; elongated barbels of snout just anterior to posterior nostrils. Mouth short but wide, terminal and horizontal; very long barbel sweeping posteriorly from the upper jaw at each corner of the mouth; 4 shorter barbels attached in a transverse line on the lower chin. Numerous minute needlelike teeth in broad bands on upper and lower jaws. Dorsal fin origin about midway between pectoral and pelvic fins; dorsal fin with a stout spine and 5–6 rays; dorsal adipose fin free at posterior end. Anal fin rays including rudimentaries 15–21; pelvic fin rays 8; pectoral fin with a stout spine, slightly rough to irregularly toothed on posterior edge; caudal fin somewhat square and slightly notched at midpoint. Scaleless. Lateral line complete. Digestive tract 0.8–1.5 TL. Chromosomes 2n = 60 (LeGrande 1978).

Dorsal region of head, back, and upper sides olive to black; sides lighter; belly whitish to yellowish, with color usually extending up to base of caudal fin as a pale bar. Barbels black or gray. All fins dusky, with dark edges and black interradial membranes.

Breeding male black with bright yellow or white belly.

Sexual dimorphism. Male with distinctive urogenital papilla extending posteriorly; absent in female. One opening behind the vent in male, 2 openings behind the vent in female (Moen 1959).

Hybrids: Black bullhead × brown bullhead from Lost Lake and Crawfish River (Dodge County) (Wis. Fish Distrib. Study 1974–1975). Experimental black bullhead × channel catfish, black bullhead × yellow bullhead, black bullhead × white catfish, black bullhead × blue catfish (Dupree et al. 1966).

DISTRIBUTION, STATUS, AND HABITAT

In Wisconsin, the black bullhead is widely distributed in the Mississippi River, Lake Michigan, and Lake Superior drainage basins.

The black bullhead is the most abundant of Wisconsin's bullhead species. It is also the most tolerant of agricultural siltation, industrial and domestic pollutants, and warm water. In the Lake Superior basin, the black bullhead is classified as widespread and common in the streams of western Lake Superior (McLain et al. 1965). Its distribution, especially in northern Wisconsin, is much more extensive today than it was in the mid-1920s.

Quiet backwaters, oxbows, impoundments, ponds, lakes, and low-gradient streams are typical habitats of the black bullhead. In Wisconsin, it was encountered in water of varying turbidity, most frequently at depths of less than 1.5 m, over substrates of sand (24% frequency), gravel (20%), mud (16%), silt (15%), rubble (9%), boulders (9%), detritus (4%), clay (1%), hardpan (1%), and bedrock (1%). It was taken in streams of the following widths: 1.0–3.0 m (13% frequency), 3.1–6.0 m (15%), 6.1–12.0 m (12%), 12.1–24.0 m (31%), 24.1–50.0 m (18%), and more than 50 m (11%).

BIOLOGY

The spawning of the black bullhead usually occurs from April through June, but ripe females have been taken at Wisconsin's latitude as late as early August (Forney 1955). When the water temperature reaches 21°C (69.8°F), saucer-shaped nests 15–36 cm (6–14 in) diam are constructed in the mud or sand in water 0.6–1.2 m (2–4 ft) deep. The nests are built beneath matted vegetation, woody debris, or overhanging banks, or in muskrat burrows. The female constructs the nest (Wallace 1967:853):

> . . . The excavation was carried out by downward fanning of the pelvic fins, side-to-side fanning of the anal fin, and pushing of small pebbles toward the periphery of the depression with the snout. The male was nearby, but did not assist in the excavation. When the male swam over the nest the female butted him in the abdominal area as if to push him from the nest.

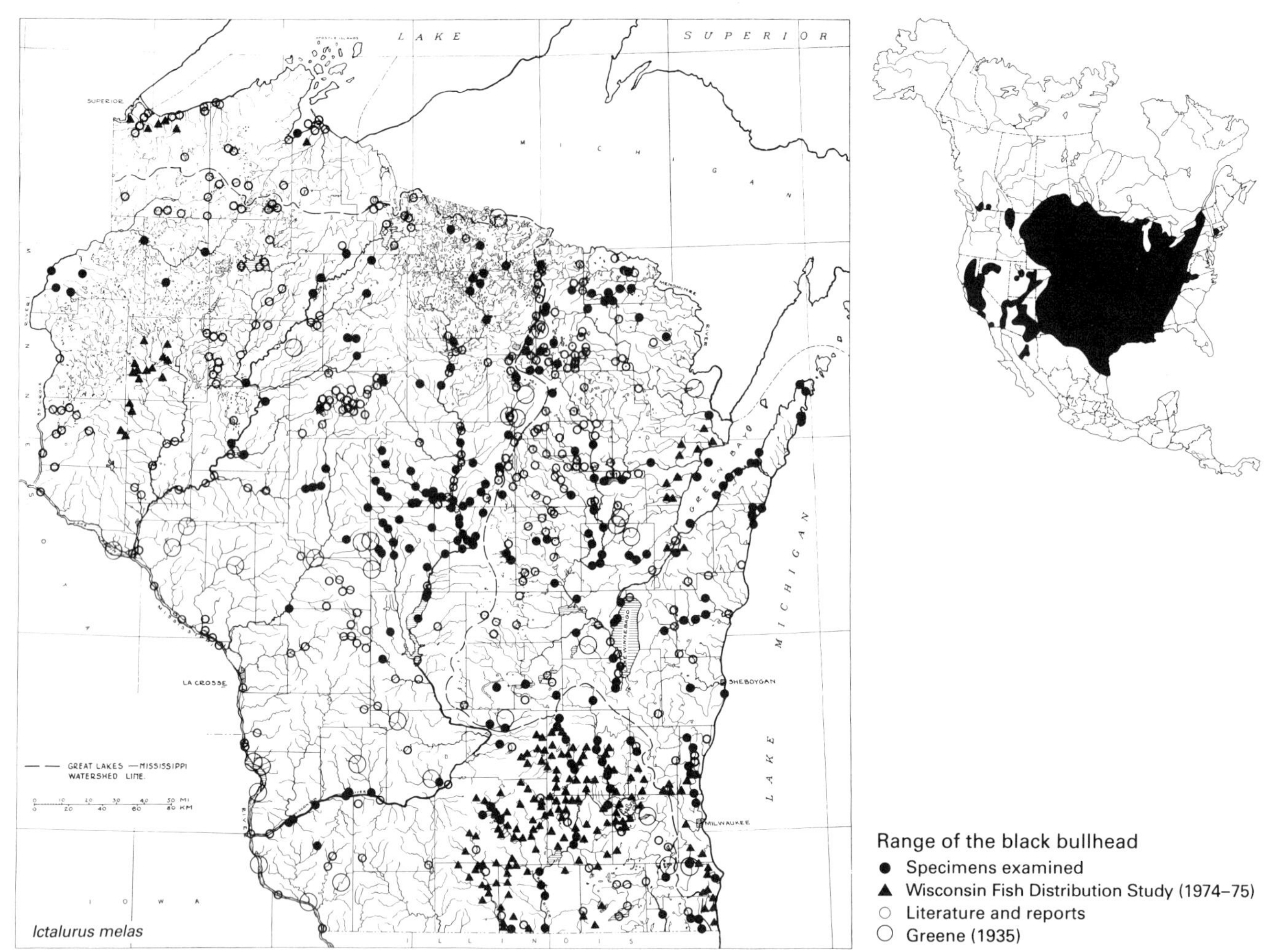

Ictalurus melas

Wallace also described the black bullhead's spawning behavior (p. 853):

> . . . While the male and female were oriented in opposite directions, the male twisted his caudal fin to one side toward the female so that it was over her head and eyes. . . . The male held the female in this way for a period of several seconds. The male's caudal fin was more tightly twisted over the female's head, and the ventral part of his body anterior to the twisted portion was arched almost in a 45° angle toward the abdomen of the female. The female's body was not arched, but her caudal fin was bent slightly toward and almost over the male's head. The male's mouth was widely opened as if "yawning," and his head was bent slightly downward. . . . During the fourth embrace, the female quivered for about one sec and the eggs were deposited. The male remained perfectly still with its mouth wide open. . . . After the female stopped quivering both fish moved apart and lay still for about one min on the bottom of the aquarium.

After a spawning session, both fish began to swim as before; the female passed back and forth over the center of the nest, fanning the eggs with her pelvic and anal fins, and butting the male's abdomen when he swam near the eggs. Spawning occurred five times within 1 hour. The female fanned and guarded the eggs during the first day, but on the second and third days after spawning the male guarded the nest.

The eggs are laid in gelatinous masses with a gelatinous coat. Eggs examined 21 hours after spawning had developed to the late gastrula stage (Wallace 1967). Incubation takes 5–10 days, depending on the water temperature.

A prespawning female black bullhead, 145 mm and 48 g, collected from the Yellow River (Wood County) on 25 May, had ovaries 3% of the body weight; she held yellow, maturing eggs 0.8–1.3 mm diam. A gravid female, 196 mm and 129 g, taken from Green Bay (Door County) on 6 June had ovaries 6.3% of the body weight; she held 4,005 yellow, almost mature eggs, 1.2–1.6 mm diam.

The care of eggs by adult black bullheads is undoubtedly similar to that of the brown bullhead (see p. 704), in which the pelvic fins slap up and down against the egg mass, or the anal fin swirls the mass about or even breaks it up. The process undoubtedly provides the developing eggs with needed aeration and water circulation.

After the eggs hatch, the activity of paddling with the pelvic fins stops and the parent fish become more gentle in their movements, swimming about over the young that huddle in a compact mass encumbered by large yolk-sacs. By the time the young are able to rise off the bottom, they have attained most of their coal black coloration. The young fish rise in a cloud-like mass, and the parents try to keep them in a compact school by swimming about them, more or less in circles; the involuntary orientation of the young themselves, which is almost entirely visual, also tends to keep them together.

Young black bullheads remain in compact, swirling schools for 2 weeks or longer; the conspicuous "balls" of black young move slowly near the surface in moderately deep water. When the young are about 25 mm long, the adults cease tending them, and the fry move into shallower water (Forney 1955). Their first food consists of cladocerans, other small crustaceans, and very small midge larvae.

The growth of young-of-year black bullheads in Wisconsin has been recorded as follows (Paruch 1979):

Date	No. of Fish	TL (mm) Avg	TL (mm) Range	Location
18 July	5	24	23–25	St. Croix R. (Burnette Co.)
29 July	45	29	22–39	Williams L. (Marquette Co.)
14 Sept.	4	29	26–31	Little Yellow R. (Juneau Co.)
19 Sept.	1	41		Little Sturgeon Bay (Door Co.)

Analysis of the annuli on the pectoral spines of 330 black bullheads, taken from the Wisconsin River below the Du Bay Dam (Portage County), showed the following growth: 1—67 mm; 2—148 mm; 3—181 mm; 4—209 mm; and 5—233 mm (Paruch 1979). These fish, collected 21 January 1977, showed the following length-weight relationship: $\text{Log } W = -10.811311 + 2.924228 \text{ Log } L$, where W is total weight (g) and L is total length (mm).

In Little Lake Butte des Morts (Winnebago County), black bullheads averaged 206 (147–295) mm TL. The length-weight relationship of the mid-October sample is expressed by $\text{Log } W = -0.60180 + 2.92398 \text{ Log } L$, where W is total weight (g) and L is total length (in). According to Priegel (1966a), no stunting existed in this population and the sample fell into three age-classes: II—198 (157–216) mm; III—211 (150–267) mm; and IV—267 (239–295) mm. The condition value (K_{TL}) calculated from Priegel's figures was 1.30.

The age of the black bullhead at maturity is variable. According to Cross (1967), maturity is reached in the second, third, or fourth summer, depending on the population density and the available food supply.

Most large black bullheads seldom exceed 318 g (0.7 lb). The largest known Wisconsin fish, caught in 1978 from Black Oak Creek (Vilas County), weighed 1.30 kg (2 lb 14 oz). The official record for a black bullhead caught on sporting tackle is a 610-mm, 3.63-kg (24-in, 8-lb) fish taken from Lake Waccabuc, New York, in 1951 (Walden 1964).

Black bullheads are opportunistic feeders that eat whatever food is available, including carrion. In the Wisconsin River below the Du Bay Dam (Portage County), the diet of this species consisted of *Daphnia*, cladocerans, *Cyclops* and other copepods, plant matter, and unidentifiable insect parts and eggs (K. McQuin, pers. comm.).

Black bullheads 40–60 mm SL from Cedar Creek (Ozaukee County) had eaten: *Hyallela azteca* (54.1% of volume), insect larvae (19.2%), organic detritus (15.1%), insect adults (4.5%), fungi and algae (3.4%), small crayfish (2.8%), and miscellaneous (0.9%) (Darnell and Meierotto 1962). In the Madison area (Pearse 1918), they had eaten, in addition to the above foods, snails, leeches, oligochaetes, silt, and debris. Midge larvae make up a considerable part of the black bullhead's insect food.

In Iowa (Harrison 1950), about 5% of the black bullhead's diet consisted of fish—scales and chunks of larger fish found dead on the stream bottom. Welker (1962) found that as many as 18% of the stomachs examined in August in Clear Lake, Iowa, contained small fish (common shiners and perch?). Larger bullheads also take frogs (Carlander 1969).

Young black bullheads exhibit two distinct feeding periods—one just before dawn, and another shortly after dark (Darnell and Meierotto 1962). Little food of any kind is taken during the middle of the day or around midnight. Nocturnal fishes, such as bullheads, rely largely on smell, taste, and touch and probably also use their lateral-line sense organs to locate and catch their prey (Lagler et al. 1977).

Bullheads are highly sensitive to touch on the head and on the barbels. Taste buds are densely concentrated on the barbels, but they also occur in the pharynx and the gill cavity, and cover the head and the body (Bardach et al. 1967); there are an estimated 100,000 taste buds on the body of a bullhead (Lagler et al. 1977). Taste alone can guide the black bullhead to sources of chemical stimuli many fish lengths away. Bullheads are also able to perceive both the intensity of, and the range of, vibrations from 16 to 13,000 cycles per sec (Lagler et al. 1977).

Subadult black bullheads avoided the effluent-outfall area of a power plant on Lake Monona (Dane County), where the maximum temperatures approached 35°C in summer and 14°C in winter (Neill and Magnuson 1974). When acclimated at 23°C (73.4°F), the upper lethal temperature for the black bullhead was 35°C (95°F) (Black 1953). At summer temperatures of 22–23°C (71.6–73.4°F), black bullheads survived for 24 hr at oxygen thresholds as low as 3.4 ppm (Moore 1942). In Michigan, this species was reported to survive winterkill oxygen concentrations of less than 0.2–0.3 ppm (Cooper and Washburn 1949).

Black bullheads are gregarious and travel in large schools. Adults apparently remain inactive in weed beds during the daylight hours, but they move around extensively at night. Trapping evidence suggests that the adults tend to forsake pools during the early hours of darkness, and return shortly before dawn (Darnell and Meierotto 1965). Carlander and Cleary (1949) noted that black bullheads came into shallow water more frequently between 0200 and 0600 hr than at other times. According to Darnell and Meierotto, feeding behavior is associated with periods of dim light, whereas schooling takes place during periods of bright light.

During late April and early May following a heavy rain, more than 2,500 sexually mature black bullheads engaged in a nocturnal movement from an Illinois reservoir, over the spillway, and into the stream below (Lewis et al. 1968).

In Cedar Creek (Ozaukee County), 50 black bullheads were associated with the following species: white sucker (4), central stoneroller (15), creek chub (10+), bluntnose minnow (1), fathead minnow (6), common shiner (20), sand shiner (1), tadpole madtom (15+), and green sunfish (1).

IMPORTANCE AND MANAGEMENT

Black bullheads are eaten by white bass (MacKay 1963), but predation by other fishes, even on young black bullheads, is apparently very low (Scott and Crossman 1973). This may be a result, in part, of the protection afforded by the bullhead's spines and its nocturnal habits. Turtles have purportedly preyed on bullheads, and there is a report of a 150-mm (6-in) bullhead being caught by a 0.6-m (2-ft) snake.

The black bullhead is a host to the glochidial stage of the mollusks *Megalonaias gigantea* and *Quadrula pustulosa*; it is one of several fish species responsible for the distribution and perpetuation of those clam species.

In Wisconsin, the black bullhead is used as setline bait for taking large catfishes, such as the flathead catfish. Fishing for the black bullhead is a sport valued by many fishermen; it bites readily on worms, liver, or almost any kind of meat. G. W. Peck, a former governor of Wisconsin and a noted humorist of his day, immortalized the bullhead (Peck 1943:17)

> . . . There is a species of fish that never looks at the clothes of man who throws in the bait, a fish that takes whatever is thrown to it; and when once it has hold of the hook never tries to shake a friend, but submits to the inevitable. . . . It is a fish that is a friend of the poor and one that will sacrifice itself in the interest of humanity. That is the fish that the state should adopt as its trade-mark and cultivate friendly relations with and stand by.

According to Wisconsin Fishing Regulations (1980), all bullheads are by definition game or sport fish. At present there are no restrictions on bullhead fishing—no closed season, no daily bag limit, and no minimum length.

The flesh of the black bullhead is firm, reddish or pink, and well flavored when taken from clean water. Connoisseurs compare the flavor to that of chicken. The flavor of bullheads from muddy waters can be improved by keeping them alive in clean water for a week or more.

Man has used the black bullhead extensively as a test fish. It adjusts readily to laboratory conditions, and does not jump from containers, although it does foul the water in holding tanks (Ward and Irwin 1961). Its desirability as a test animal for toxic chemicals stems from its ability to resist larger doses of toxins than most fishes (McCoy 1972, Ferguson and Goodyear 1967). As a test fish, the black bullhead has contributed to our knowledge of the function of the pituitary gland (Chidambaram et al. 1972).

In the Wisconsin waters of the Mississippi River, commercial fishermen take bullheads (all species) most effectively by setlines, which account for 64% of the total catch (Finke 1967). Next in effectiveness are bait nets and slat nets. During 1960–1965, a total of 123,000 kg (272,000 lb) of bullheads was taken; the best catches occurred in Pools 8 and 9 of the Mississippi River. During 1976 (Fernholz and Crawley 1977), 13,989 kg (30,841 lb) were taken; this catch was valued at $4,626, and the black bullhead probably constituted a large part of the catch.

During 1970, contract fishermen removed 30,800 kg (67,900 lb) of bullheads (all species) from inland waters of Wisconsin (N. J. Miller 1971). In 1974, the commercial harvest from fyke nets in southern Green Bay produced 15,085 kg (33,257 lb) of bullheads, which was valued at $4,165 (Wis. Dep. Nat. Resour.

1976c). An improved market could definitely lead to an increase in the total catch of bullhead species, as there are many other areas of Lake Michigan and Green Bay where bullheads could be harvested. In 1979 "bullheads" were bringing $2.20/kilo ($1/lb) on the retail market in Wisconsin food stores.

The black bullhead is a good farm pond species, and, in waters where winterkill is prevalent, it is frequently the only survivor. When bullheads are planted in a pond, only they should be planted, as they will probably overtake any other species present (Sharp 1950). When the black bullhead becomes overabundant, as it usually does, stunting occurs; the result is a fish which is too small to be desirable. Carlander (1969) noted that growth tended to be faster in clear water than in turbid water, and in uncrowded rather than crowded conditions. In Iowa, bullheads transferred from crowded to uncrowded conditions at age V grew from an average of 100 g (3.6 oz) to an average of 254 g (9 oz) in 3.5 months. In Kansas (Cross 1967), ponds in which fish were given a daily supplemental feeding of food pellets produced black bullheads 152 mm (6 in) or more in the year that they hatched; these fish weighed 450 g (1 lb) or more as yearlings. Allbaugh and Manz (1964) noted that when large amounts of food were artificially fed to bullheads there was greater growth in males than in females.

In the 1960s, Beaver Dam Lake (Dodge County) was treated with the toxicant rotenone to control carp. The result was an explosion of black bullheads by the mid-1970s, and in 1978 there was still a large, fishable bullhead population. According to Carlander (1969), after treatment of a reservoir in Iowa with rotenone, bullheads became very abundant; yet a few years later they were almost nonexistent in the area.

Brown Bullhead

Ictalurus nebulosus (Lesueur). *Ictalurus*—fish cat; *nebulosus*—clouded, in reference to mottled coloring.

Other common names: northern brown bullhead, marbled bullhead, marble cat, speckled bullhead, speckled cat, common bullhead, bullhead, brown catfish, common catfish, small catfish, catfish, mudcat, red cat, horned pout, bullpout.

Adult 275 mm, Half Moon L. (Eau Claire Co.), mid-Apr. 1978

DESCRIPTION

Body robust, rounded anteriorly, compressed posteriorly. Length 152–254 mm (6–10 in). TL = 1.20 SL. Depth into TL 3.8–5.7. Head length into TL 3.8–4.4. Snout bluntly pointed in lateral view, broadly rounded in dorsal view; elongated barbels of snout just anterior to posterior nostrils. Mouth short but wide, terminal and horizontal; upper jaw slightly longer than lower jaw, with very long barbel sweeping posteriorly from the upper jaw at each corner of the mouth; 4 barbels (outer 2 much elongated, inner 2 thinner and shorter) attached in a transverse line on the lower chin; numerous small, sharp teeth arranged in several irregular rows on upper and lower jaws. Dorsal fin origin at about midpoint between pectoral and pelvic fins; dorsal fin with a stout spine and 6–7 soft rays; dorsal adipose fin free at posterior edge. Anal fin rays, including rudimentaries, 21–24; pelvic fin rays 8. Pectoral fin with an elongated spine barbed on posterior edge, near tip with barbs inclined toward the base of spine, barbs becoming erect near middle, and barbs inclined toward the tip near base (see Key, p. 146). Caudal fin edge straight, occasionally slightly indented at middle. Scaleless. Lateral line complete. Digestive tract coiled, 1.1–1.4 TL. Chromosomes 2n = 60 (LeGrande 1978).

Dorsal region of head, back, and upper sides yellowish brown to almost black; lower sides mottled with lighter yellowish brown to gray; ventral region of head and belly pale yellow to white. Barbels dark brown to nearly black, except sometimes barbels on chin yellow to white. All fins dark colored, similar to body; interradial membranes slightly darker, but not black.

Hybrids: Brown bullhead × black bullhead from Lost Lake and Crawfish River (Dodge County) (Wis. Fish Distrib. Study 1974–75). Experimental brown bullhead × yellow bullhead, brown bullhead × blue catfish, brown bullhead × white catfish, brown bullhead × channel catfish (Dupree et al. 1966).

SYSTEMATIC NOTES

Two subspecies are recognized; *Ictalurus n. nebulosus* (Lesueur) is found in Canada, the Dakotas, Wisconsin, and the northern part of the Ohio Valley to Virginia; this form has been extensively introduced into western North America. *Ictalurus n. marmoratus* ranges from southern Illinois and northeastern Oklahoma to the Carolinas and Florida.

DISTRIBUTION, STATUS, AND HABITAT

In Wisconsin,the brown bullhead occurs in the Mississippi River, Lake Michigan, and Lake Superior drainage basins. Its major distribution is in the Rock and Fox-Wolf River systems of eastern Wisconsin, and the Chippewa River system of northwestern Wisconsin. It is present in the shallows of Lake Superior, Lake Michigan, and Green Bay, and in the lower courses of tributary streams. Although the brown bullhead has been reported frequently from a number of sources, some of these reports may be in error since this species is easily confused with other species of bullheads. I have plotted these reports on the distribution map when there was no opportunity to check them. As an example, I have not personally seen a specimen of the brown bullhead from the Wisconsin River basin, although it is commonly reported from that system.

According to McLain et al. (1965), the brown bullhead is widespread in the mouths of tributaries to Lake Superior; in these waters its numbers fluctuate widely from year to year, but the trend is toward increasing numbers. Priegel (1967) described the brown bullhead as abundant in Lake Winnebago. In general, its distribution over Wisconsin is sporadic and its numbers are low. It is the least common of the state's three species of bullheads, and its status has probably changed little since the 1920s.

The brown bullhead inhabits the weedy waters of warmwater lakes and sluggish streams. In the Mississippi River it occurs in sloughs and backwaters. It

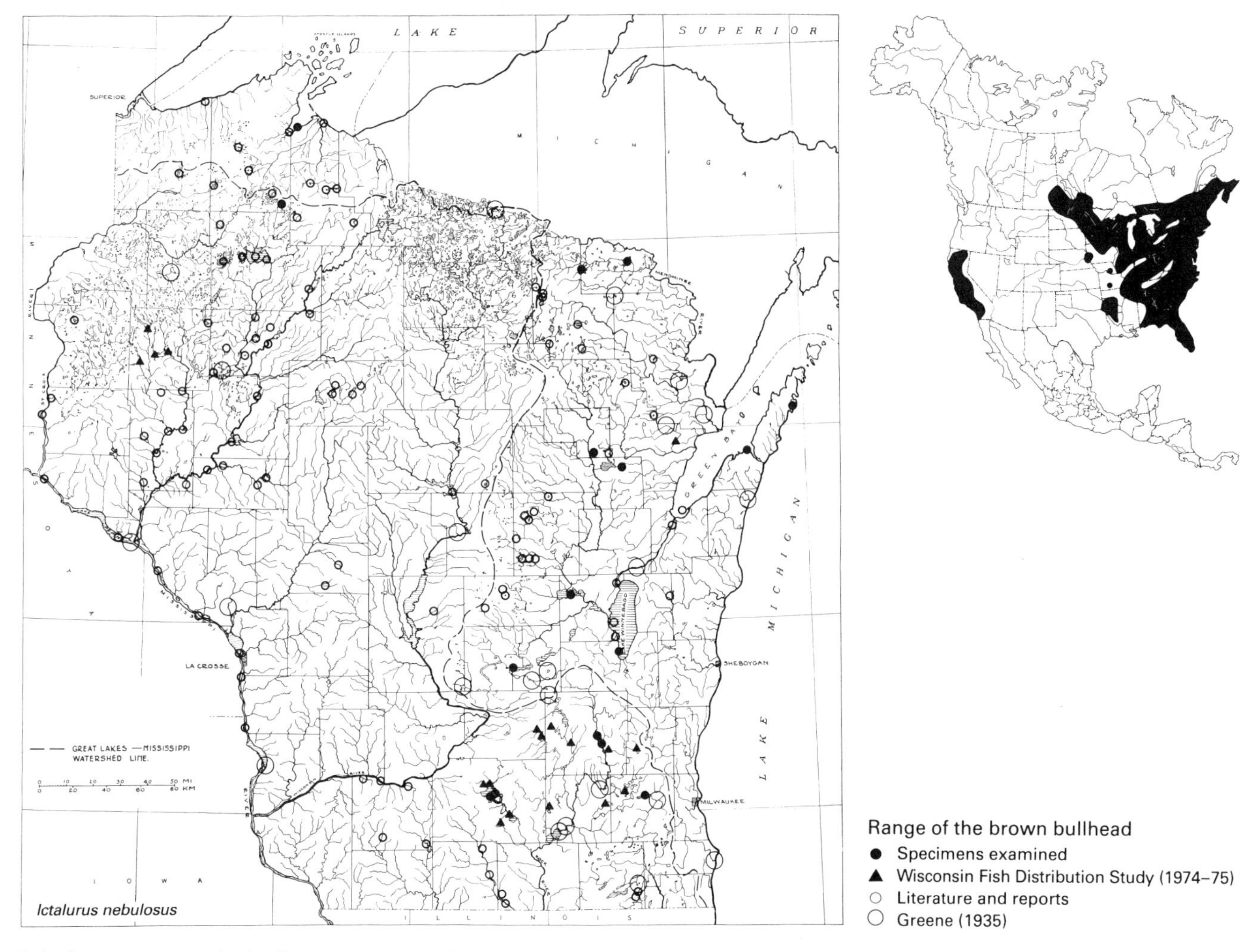

Range of the brown bullhead
- ● Specimens examined
- ▲ Wisconsin Fish Distribution Study (1974–75)
- ○ Literature and reports
- ◯ Greene (1935)

inhabits vegetated shallows over sand, rock, mud, and silt, in lakes and low-gradient streams of varying size. It is tolerant of high turbidity and of waters modified by domestic and industrial effluents.

BIOLOGY

Spawning occurs in June and July in central and northern Wisconsin, and probably in May in the southern part of the state. Throughout the brown bullhead's range spawning occurs from late spring to August or later; it takes place from early morning to 1400 hr, at water temperatures of 21–25°C (69.8–77°F) (Mansueti and Hardy 1967).

The brown bullhead's nest is constructed by the female, occasionally by both parents. They suck pebbles up to 25 mm (1 in) diam into their mouths and transport them away from the nesting site (H. M. Smith and Harron 1903). Nests consist of open excavations in sand, gravel, or (rarely) mud, often in the shelter of logs, rocks, or vegetation. Occasionally these fish excavate holes in a bank, or make burrows up to 1 m long under roots of aquatic plants. Cavities of old stumps, stovepipes, old pails, and terra-cotta pots are occasionally used as nesting sites (Mansueti and Hardy 1967).

It is not clear how a male and female, instead of two fish of the same sex, come to occupy a single cavity (Breder 1935). That the brown bullhead is capable of sound production is well known, but there is no evidence that sounds have any significance in sex recognition. While the nest is being constructed, the male drives other bullheads away from the nesting area. Breder and Rosen (1966) described spawning behavior (pp. 252–253):

> After the nest has finally been completed the prospective spawners spend much time lying side by side with their tails to the opening of the nest. At such times they are usually in contact. This quietude is interrupted by swimming in a nearly circular path, the one fish following close to the other. Not infrequently at such times the tail of one fish, apparently accidentally, slips into the mouth of the other. If the latter closes down on the intruded tail, and it usually does, the bitten fish leaves the nest as though shot from a gun. After swimming about for a while it returns to resume the activities.

Finally they flatten so as to merge into a simple quiescent side to side position, with the fish facing in opposite directions and with their bodies in close contact. In this position spawning takes place. A large number of 'spawning acts' occur until the female is emptied of her eggs. . . . They are of a pale cream color, and average about 3 mm in diameter. . . . Between every spawning effort the fishes rest, the male in a seemingly exhausted state. The fishes separated slightly at this time, sometimes the male half falling to one side.

From 50 to 10,000 or more eggs are deposited per nest. The eggs are adhesive, and are deposited in clusters, similar to masses of frogs' eggs. One or both parents usually guard the clusters (Mansueti and Hardy 1967). According to Adams and Hankinson (1926), the guard fish, generally a male, suffers sores on his head when he locks jaws with another male while fighting for possession of the female brooding the eggs. However, this behavior has not been supported by more recent observations.

A partially spawned, 193-mm brown bullhead female, collected 15 July from Chippewa Lake (Bayfield County), had ovaries 9.6% of body weight (98 g); she held an estimated 2,190 yellow-white eggs, 2.2–2.7 mm diam. In Minnesota (Vessel and Eddy 1941), fecundity for females 267–330 mm (10.5–13 in) long was 6,180–13,000 eggs.

The brooding of the eggs, an elaborate procedure, has been described by Breder and Rosen (1966:253):

While it is difficult to be certain about the identity of the sexes of these fish, it appears that the female does most of the actual incubating and the male most of the guarding. . . . Both fishes were seen to defend their nest against other fishes. . . . Both parents were seen to incubate the eggs. . . . Most commonly the parent fish would settle down on the eggs with the ventral fins widespread so as to cover the mass as well as possible. Then these fins would be paddled up and down alternately, actually striking the eggs with considerable force. In a few days, generally, this action was sufficient to loosen the mass entirely from its place of attachment, so that subsequent fanning caused the entire mass to slap up and down against the floor of the tank in rhythm with the fins. Sometimes this kind of motion was alternated with a swimming movement in which the long anal fin served to swirl the mass about, or even break it up. At other times the mass of eggs, or part of it, would be taken into the mouth and 'chewed' in such a fashion as to roll them over and over, after which they would be ejected with considerable violence. Rarely at such times would the cluster be swallowed.

After the eggs hatch, the adults stop brooding acactivities but continue swimming over the young which are encumbered by large yolk-sacs. The time required for brown bullhead eggs to hatch is 6–9 days, at water temperatures of 20.6–23.3°C (69–74°F). The young remain on the nest for 7–10 days before they begin to swim. When the young rise off the bottom, the parents swim about them in circles to keep them in a compact school; strays are caught in their parents' mouths and returned to the school. In nature, it is probably at this point that the parents leave the young to fend for themselves. H. M. Smith and Harron (1903) observed young brown bullheads being sucked into the parents' mouths, but the parents did not always blow them out, ". . . the feeding instinct becoming paramount to the parental instinct."

The details of the brown bullhead's embryonic development from cleavage (1.2 hr) through hatching (8 days) to the 17-day stage are given by Armstrong (1962). The length at hatching is 4–8 mm (Mansueti and Hardy 1967). Fish (1932) illustrated and described the 22-mm stage.

Juvenile brown bullheads sometimes occur in schools throughout their first summer. Such schools are found among vegetation, or near other suitable cover over more or less muddy bottoms.

In Wisconsin, the growth of young-of-year brown bullheads has been recorded as follows (Paruch 1979):

Date	No. of Fish	TL (mm) Avg	TL (mm) Range	Location
14 July	16	36	25–39	La Motte L. (Menominee Co.)
2 Aug.	1	39		White Clay L. (Shawano Co.)
19 Aug.	1	51		L. Poygan (Winnebago Co.)
28 Aug.	1	57		L. Winnebago (Fond du Lac Co.)
12 Sept.	2	65	53–76	Rock R. (Dodge Co.)
26 Sept.	18	68	56–84	L. Mendota (Dane Co.)
15 Oct.	1	89		Rock R. (Dodge Co.)

In brown bullheads from Little Lake Butte des Morts (Winnebago County), Priegel (1966a) determined the following age-length relationships: II—152 mm; III—193 (157–246) mm; IV—241 (203–290) mm; and V—267 (257–290) mm. The condition value (K_{TL}) averaged 1.25. A 243-mm fish from Green Bay (Door County) showed the following growth at the annuli of the pectoral spine: 1—66 mm; 2—135 mm; 3—162 mm; and 4—216 mm (Paruch 1979). The age of the brown bullhead at maturity is 3 years (Mansueti and Hardy 1967).

In Wisconsin, the brown bullhead seldom attains a length of more than 356 mm (14 in). A 1.70-kg (3-lb 12-oz) brown bullhead was taken from Nelson Lake (Sawyer County) in 1972. The maximum length reported for this species from Florida lies between 508 and 532 mm (20 and 21 in) (Carlander 1969). A 2.50-kg (5-lb 8-oz) brown bullhead was reported from Veal Pond, Sandersville, Georgia, in 1975.

Fry and fingerlings up to 75 mm long eat zooplankton and chironomids; adult brown bullheads feed on insects, fish, fish eggs, mollusks, and plants (Carlander 1969). In lakes near Madison, Wisconsin, brown bullheads consumed dipteran larvae, amphipods, cladocerans, oligochaetes, a wide variety of aquatic insects in lesser amounts, and traces of plants and algae (Pearse 1918). In Green Lake (Green Lake County), they consumed these foods (in order of decreasing amounts): snails, crayfish, plants, oligochaetes, insect larvae, amphipods, algae, clams, mites, and cladocerans. In Lake Mendota brown bullheads ate insect larvae, algae, amphipods, plants, leeches, cladocerans, crayfish, ostracods, bottom ooze, insect pupae, snails, and sand (Pearse 1921a).

Availability frequently determines what kind of food is ingested. In Illinois (Forbes and Richardson 1920), the brown bullhead's diet consisted chiefly of "small bivalve mollusks, larvae of insects taken upon the bottom, distillery slops, and accidental rubbish. One of the specimens had eaten 18 leeches." In West Virginia (Klarberg and Benson 1975), the brown bullhead met its nutritional requirements with detritus, sewage, and acid-tolerant invertebrates. Small fishes are eaten occasionally. The brown bullhead has consumed the eggs of the cisco in Lake Ontario, of herring in the Potomac River, and of lake trout in Maine, Ontario, and Quebec (Emig 1966a).

Brown bullheads are able to find food by an elaborate sense of taste. Brown bullheads (19–27 mm) from Michigan lakes could find distant chemical clues by means of taste alone and moved in the direction of the chemical in the absence of a current (Bardach et al. 1967). Even inactivation of their sense of smell did not impair their searching ability. Typically, a bullhead showed that it had perceived a chemical by what is best described as a startled response: the barbels stiffened, the body became rigid for a moment, the head began a slow to-and-fro movement, and the fish almost immediately began swimming. Keast and Welsh (1968) noted that brown bullheads were exclusively nocturnal in their feeding habits in Canadian lakes. In Iowa, they are reported to feed at all times of the day and night (Harlan and Speaker 1956).

The brown bullhead prefers warm water. In Ontario (Hallam 1959), it is associated with rock bass and smallmouth bass in waters at temperatures of 20.8–21.4°C (69.3–70.6°F). At an acclimation temperature of 36°C (96.8°F), the upper lethal temperature for brown bullheads was 37.5°C (99.5°F)(Brett 1944); at an acclimation temperature of 21°C (69.8°F), the lower lethal temperature was −1.0°C (30.2°F).

The brown bullhead has been observed swimming in 37–38°C (98.6–100.4°F) water, and entering 40°C (104°F) water for worms (Trembley 1960). In a shallow Michigan pond (Bailey 1955), many brown bullheads died as a result of a 38°C (100.4°F) water temperature. In a thermal gradient trough, this species selected 27.3°C (81.1°F) (Richards and Ibara 1978).

The brown bullhead's metabolic rate is positively correlated with temperature, and inversely correlated with carbon dioxide concentrations. It tolerates relatively high carbon dioxide levels and low oxygen levels (Emig 1966a). In the Monongahela River of West Virginia, it is the most abundant species and is distributed over the widest pH range (3.4–7.7) of any species present (Klarberg and Benson 1975). It endures a maximum salinity of 7.6 ppt (Mansueti and Hardy 1967). In a southeastern Michigan winterkill lake, many brown bullheads survived with a minimum concentration of dissolved oxygen of 0.5–0.05 ppm, and some survived in another lake at 0.2–0.0 ppm (Cooper and Washburn 1949). In Minnesota (Moyle and Clothier 1959), the brown bullhead survived well when oxygen levels fell to near 1 ppm. This species, as well as the other bullheads, is known to gulp air at the surface when the oxygen level in the water becomes critically low.

In one study (Loeb 1964), the respiratory movements of the brown bullhead were more or less continuous at all temperatures, but were so weak at water temperatures below 2.8°C (37°F) that the pulsations could not be counted. At any temperature above 6.1°C (43°F), steady pulsations occurred, increasing as the temperature rose (e.g., 73 per min at 16.7°C).

In the late fall, brown bullheads become sluggish and cease feeding, often "mudding up," or burying themselves in soft, leafy ooze along the shore. This occurs at temperatures ranging from 0.0 to 18.3°C (32 to 65°F) (Loeb 1964). At water temperatures of 7.8°C (46°F) and above, the mouth could always be seen above the mud or in a funnel just below the surface, and breathing was more or less continuous. At 6.1°C (43°F) and below, sediment often covered the mouth for hours and some fish remained buried for up to 24 hours.

Loeb (1964) recorded the brown bullhead's method of entry into bottom sediments consisting of organic ooze, silt, and dead leaf material (pp. 120–121):

> . . . Bullheads buried themselves by thrusting with the head in a strong swimming motion. The fish, which may have been meandering leisurely over the surface of the mud, quickly tilted the body to an almost vertical position and drove its entire body into the sediment with a few vigorous movements. . . . After burial the body was covered with from a fraction of an inch to 2 inches of sediment, the long axis of the body was horizontal or tilted slightly up toward the mouth, and the lateral axis was canted at an angle so that one gill more or less pointed up and the other down. . . . The mouth was brought into direct contact with the free water above the surface of the mud . . . [or] the buried fish often made contact with the free water by sucking in the inch or 2 of sediment covering its mouth and expelling the material in geyser fashion from the uppermost gill. In this way a small funnel was formed over the mouth and the material from the funnel was deposited over the gill in a volcano-like mound so that an open passage of water extended from the gill to the top of the mound.

Loeb noted that two bullheads were found buried for several hours beneath 5 cm of sediment without the presence of a funnel over the mouth, or of a passage over the gill. It was assumed that they were breathing through the 5 cm of organic botton ooze. Older literature references indicate that bullheads can survive several weeks in cocoonlike clods of nearly dried mud; however, this has not been substantiated.

In Folsom Lake, California, tagged brown bullheads released at the point of capture traveled an average of 2.7 km (1.7 mi) before they were recaptured by anglers. The longest distance traveled was 26.1 km (16.2 mi) (Emig 1966a).

The brown bullhead is chiefly nocturnal in its habits, and its activity increases with the approach of darkness. Normally, this species is not accused of stirring up bottom sediments and creating turbidity; however, when brown and yellow bullheads were removed from an Alabama pond which had been very muddy for years, the water clarified, and a dense growth of algae followed (Tarzwell 1941). Tarzwell concluded that the bullheads limited vegetation and food production by stirring the bottom and by keeping the water continually roiled.

In 1969, 35 brown bullheads were collected from Rebholz Creek (Door County) along with bluntnose minnow (35), fathead minnow (4), golden shiner (18), northern redbelly dace (24), common shiner (64), spottail shiner (3), blacknose shiner (50), sand shiner (6), mimic shiner (12), black bullhead (25), white sucker (3), smallmouth bass (1), rock bass (10), pumpkinseed (7), northern pike (2), central mudminnow (5), and banded killifish (10).

IMPORTANCE AND MANAGEMENT

The brown bullhead has been preyed on by lampreys, northern pike, snapping turtles, water snakes, and green herons. In Lake Winnebago during the fall of 1960, it was the third most important fish item consumed by the walleye; only perch and white bass were consumed more often (Priegel 1963b).

The brown bullhead is a host to the glochidial stage of the mollusks *Megalonaias gigantea* and *Quadrula pustulosa*; it is one of several fish species responsible for the distribution and perpetuation of those clam species (Hart and Fuller 1974).

Man catches the brown bullhead over soft bottoms where there is considerable aquatic vegetation. The hook is baited with raw beef, worms, or minnows. Hankinson has caught the brown and yellow bullheads with just a chunk of beef tied on a line and no hook (Adams and Hankinson 1926); often two fish were pulled in at one time, persistently clinging to the meat.

The name "red cat" for the brown bullhead comes from the red color of its flesh, and is used in areas where the dressed fish are sold commercially. The meat is very tasty, especially when the bullheads are taken from clean water in the spring and fall.

Man has used the brown bullhead extensively as a laboratory animal in assessing physiological changes involving factors such as temperature, taste, oxygen consumption, blood group agglutinins, and osmoregulation. It has also been subjected to toxicity bioassays, in which petroleum refinery effluents were used as toxicants (Bunting and Irwin 1965).

In the commercial harvest of bullheads in Wisconsin (see Black Bullhead, p. 700), the brown bullhead is categorized with the black and yellow bullheads, and probably constitutes only a small portion of the bullhead catch; it is probably of the least importance. Restaurants prefer to buy brown bullheads (called "red cats") which weigh 91–318 g (0.2–0.7 lb) alive, so that one or more fish can be included in one serving (Swingle 1957a).

In Connecticut (Marcy and Galvin 1973), brown bullheads constituted 12% of the estimated number of fish caught in the heated discharge canal of a nuclear power plant. The winter catch (January through March) at the canal was dominated by carp, followed by the brown bullhead. During this period the temperature of the canal water was about 14°C (57.2°F). There appeared to be a relationship between water temperature and the catch rate: on and immediately after days when the plant reduced its power level enough to lower the water temperatures considerably, the catch rate declined.

In Alabama (Swingle 1957), production of brown bullheads of marketable size, and up to 835 kg/ha (745 lb/acre), was obtained with supplemental feeding. The most successful method of commercial production was to stock fry or fingerlings in the spring, fertilize the pond until fall, feed the fish during fall and spring months, and drain the pond before reproduction could occur. Such fish were 151–227 g (0.3–0.5 lb)—the most desirable size for sale. Swingle (1957a) provided a summary of management procedures for the commercial production of brown bullheads; these methods should yield approximately 1,110 kg/ha (990 lb/acre).

In Wisconsin, the potential exists for raising brown bullheads in the heated waters of power plants and in the tertiary pools of sewage plants.

Brown bullhead populations are subject to very limited management in most states. They are classified as sport fish in Wisconsin, California, Michigan, and Washington; as panfish in Massachusetts; and as rough or coarse fish in Minnesota, North Carolina, Alabama, and Florida.

Yellow Bullhead

Ictalurus natalis (Lesueur). *Ictalurus*—fish cat; *natalis*—having large nates, or buttocks.

Other common names: northern yellow bullhead, yellow catfish, yellow cat, yellowbellied cat, brown catfish, brown bullhead, white-whiskered bullhead, Mississippi bullhead, greaser.

145 mm, Plover R., Stevens Point (Portage Co.), 2 Oct. 1968

DESCRIPTION

Body robust, rounded anteriorly, compressed posteriorly. Length 165–235 mm (6.5–9.3 in). TL = 1.19 SL. Depth into TL 4–5.2. Head length into TL 3.7–4.5. Snout bluntly pointed in lateral view, broadly rounded in dorsal view; elongated barbels of snout just anterior to posterior nostrils. Mouth short but wide, terminal and horizontal; upper jaw slightly longer than lower jaw, with very long barbel sweeping posteriorly from the upper jaw at each corner of the mouth; 4 shorter barbels attached in a transverse line on the lower chin; numerous minute, needlelike teeth in broad bands on upper and lower jaws. Dorsal fin origin slightly anterior to midpoint between pectoral and pelvic fins; dorsal fin with a stout spine and 6 soft rays; dorsal adipose fin free at posterior end. Anal fin rays, including rudimentaries, 24–27; pelvic fin rays 8; pectoral fin with a stout spine, regularly barbed on posterior edge with barbs near tip inclined toward the base of spine; caudal fin rounded. Scaleless. Lateral line complete. Digestive tract about 1.3 TL. Chromosomes 2n = 62 (LeGrande 1978).

Dorsal region of head, back, and upper sides yellow, olive, or black; sides lighter; ventral region of head and belly yellow to white. Snout and upper jaw barbels dark pigmented, chin barbels whitish, occasionally grayish in large individuals. All fins dusky, with pencil-line black margins; the interradial membranes dark but not black; anal fin usually with dark horizontal median band.

Hybrids: Experimental yellow bullhead × channel catfish, yellow bullhead × blue catfish, yellow bullhead × white catfish, yellow bullhead × brown bullhead, yellow bullhead × black bullhead, yellow bullhead × flathead catfish (Dupree et al. 1966).

DISTRIBUTION, STATUS, AND HABITAT

In Wisconsin, the yellow bullhead occurs in the Mississippi River, Lake Superior, and Lake Michigan drainage basins. It does not generally occur in Lakes Superior and Michigan, except in Green Bay. It is widespread in inland waters, except in the southwest quarter of the state, where it is sporadic.

The yellow bullhead is generally uncommon in the Mississippi River, and common in the Wisconsin River and in Lakes Winnebago and Poygan. It is the typical bullhead in clear, medium-sized streams and clear lakes. Its status in Wisconsin appears to be secure.

In Wisconsin, the yellow bullhead was encountered most frequently in clear water at depths of 0.6–1.5 m, over substrates of sand (26% frequency), mud (21%), gravel (18%), silt (13%), boulders (13%), rubble (5%), detritus (3%), and bedrock (1%). It was occasionally found in slightly turbid to turbid waters. It occurred in quiet, weedy sectors of lakes and reservoirs, and in streams of the following widths: 1.0–3.0 m (13% frequency); 3.1–6.0 m (17%); 6.1–12.0 m (17%); 12.1–24.0 m (29%); 24.1–50.0 m (8%); and more than 50 m (17%). It has occasionally been taken from streams with gentle to fast currents.

BIOLOGY

The spawning of the yellow bullhead may begin in May, and in northern Wisconsin it extends into July. The nests are usually saucer-shaped excavations at depths of 0.5–1.2 m (1.5–4 ft), located beside or beneath a bank, a log, or a tree root. Nests also have been reported in burrows 0.6 m (2 ft) deep, under boards, in cans, under crockery, and in the entrances of deserted muskrat burrows (Adams and Hankinson 1926). In lakes, nests occur in heavy banks of weeds (Cahn 1927). The burrow may be excavated by both sexes. Often small roots from the surrounding vegetation are left in the burrow; these frequently serve as anchorage for the yellowish white, adhesive eggs. Usually 300–700 eggs are deposited in a nest.

A partially spawned, 172-mm yellow bullhead, collected 23 June from Sevenmile Creek (Florence County), had ovaries 13.6% of body weight (84 g); she held an estimated 1,190 yellow-orange, mature eggs 2.2–3.0 mm diam. A 171-mm, 77-g female, with ovaries 10.7% of body weight, held 860 eggs 2.5–3.0 mm diam.

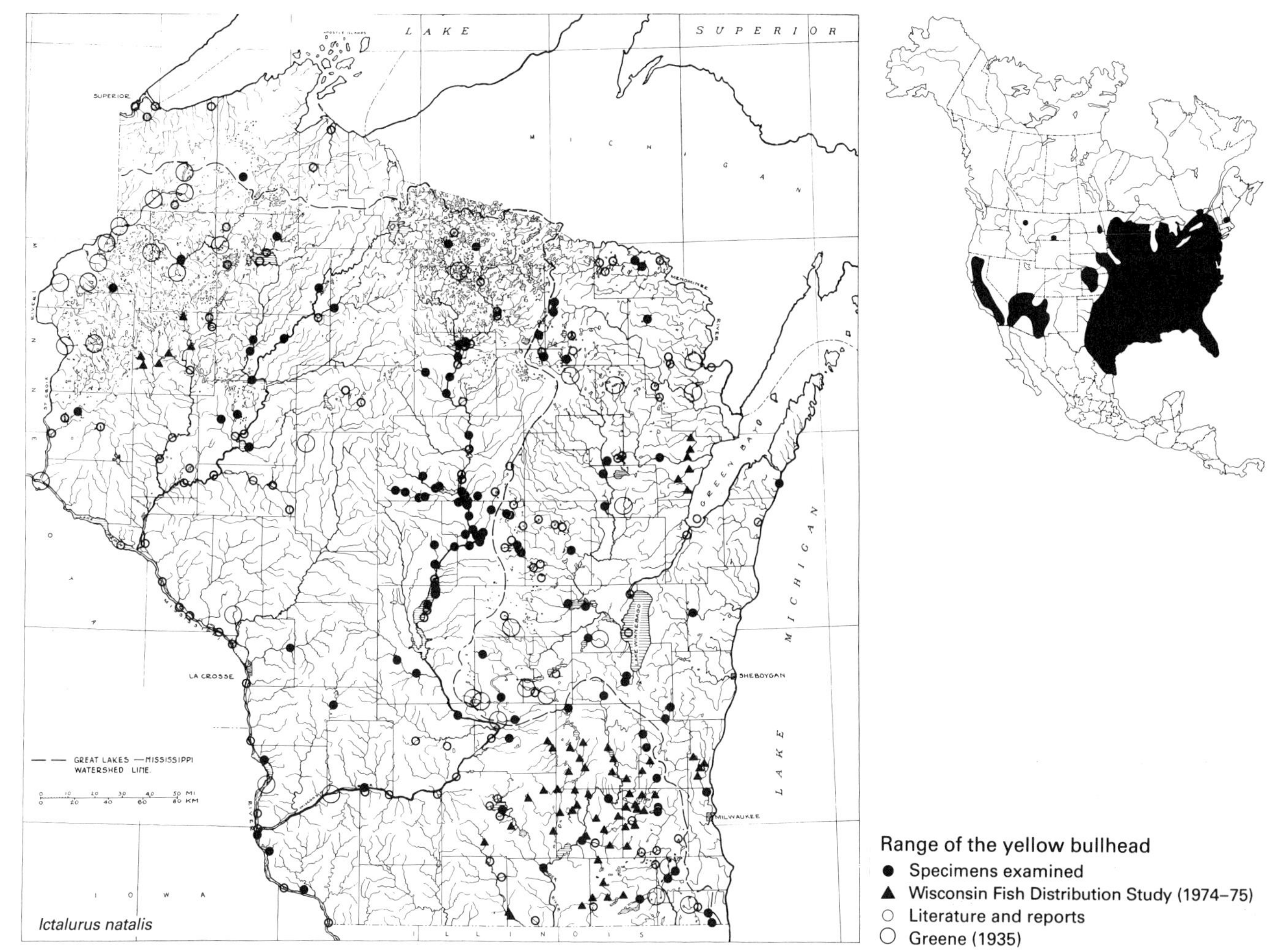

Ictalurus natalis

According to Mansueti and Hardy (1967), the fecundity rate per female is 1,650–7,000 eggs. In Minnesota, during the first week of July, three fish, 254–279 mm TL, had egg counts of 3,950–4,270 (Vessel and Eddy 1941).

The eggs hatch in 5–10 days. Fish (1932) described and illustrated the 17-mm stage, and Mansueti and Hardy (1967) provided a drawing of a 21-mm juvenile. The larvae and juveniles are guarded by parent fish until late July or August, or until the young are about 50 mm long (Mansueti and Hardy 1967). The estimated growth within a 30-day period early in the first summer's existence is 0.60 mm per day (Hubbs 1921).

In quiet water, schools of several hundred young yellow bullheads feed and move in compact groups near the surface; the guardian parent remains 0.3–0.6 m away, warding off all intruders (Harlan and Speaker 1956). In the autumn, the young hide under logs and stones in shallow water (Adams and Hankinson 1926).

The growth of young-of-year yellow bullheads in Wisconsin has been reported as follows (Paruch 1979):

Date	No. of Fish	TL (mm) Avg	Range	Location
12 July	9	19	15–20	Wolf R. (Langlade Co.)
14 July	4	26	22–29	La Motte L. (Menominee Co.)
10 Aug.	2	41	32–50	Collins L. (Portage Co.)
10 Aug.	2	57	53–60	McCartney Cr. (Grant Co.)
27 Sept.	4	46	35–63	Little Eau Pleine R. (Marathon Co.)
14 Dec.	1	76		Wisconsin R. (Portage Co.)

The age and growth of 102 yellow bullheads from Wisconsin (UWSP specimens) are summarized in the table on the following page (Paruch 1979).

In yellow bullheads from Little Butte des Morts (Winnebago County), Priegel (1966a) has determined the following age-length relationships: II—206 (180–244) mm; III—226 (193–274) mm; and IV—272 (226–295) mm. The condition value (K_{TL}) averaged 1.38. Maturity in yellow bullheads is reached during the third year of life (Harlan and Speaker 1956).

A 337-mm yellow bullhead weighing 508 g (1 lb 1.8

Age Class	No. of Fish	TL (mm) Avg	Range	Calculated TL at Annulus (mm) 1	2	3	4	5	6	7
0	28	35	16–76							
I	14	129	69–177	54						
II	34	167	122–244	43	109					
III	19	207	165–252	49	111	159				
IV	4	263	242–291	86	152	193	223			
V	2	263	226–300	69	135	197	214	235		
VII	1	345		145	200	218	236	272	290	309
Avg (weighted)				51	115	169	222	247	290	309

oz), was taken from Lake Wingra (Dane County) in 1945 (Noland 1951). A 1.4-kg (3-lb 3-oz) yellow bullhead was caught from Nelson Lake (Sawyer County) in 1972. The maximum known length reported is 465 mm (18.3 in) (Mansueti and Hardy 1967).

Young yellow bullheads feed principally on entomostracans and insect larvae; adults eat a wide variety of living and dead material in the water. In Lake Mendota (Dane County), yellow bullheads ate crayfish, amphipods, cladocerans, insect larvae, copepods, snails, and algae (Pearse 1921a). In Green Lake (Green Lake County), this species ate fish, insect larvae and adults, amphipods, cladocerans, and plant matter. In Sinissippi Lake (Dodge County), it consumed fathead minnows (H. Neuenschwander, pers. comm.).

In a northern Alabama pond (Tarzwell 1941), yellow bullheads ate largely chironomids, corixids, and golden shiners, and lesser amounts of many aquatic and terrestrial insects and oligochaetes.

According to Harlan and Speaker (1956), the yellow bullhead appears to be more selective and more nocturnal in its feeding habits than the other two species of bullheads. Like the other species, the yellow bullhead responds to odors in the water; when a food pellet is dropped into water frequented by a yellow bullhead, the bullhead's fins spread and its barbels stiffen; the timing of this response is roughly proportional to the fish's distance from the place where the food was dropped. The fish then swims to the pellet and picks it up.

In a Michigan lake, no homing or territorial tendency was noted in marked yellow bullheads (Fetterolf 1952). In Wisconsin, Greenbank (1956) observed movement of this species into and out of a shallow Mississippi River backwater lake. During January and February about twice as many yellow bullheads entered the lake as left it, most activity occurring when heavy snow covered the ice.

In winterkill lakes of southeastern Michigan, the yellow bullhead survived where the minimum oxygen concentrations were 0.3–0.1 ppm, and some individuals survived at 0.2–0.0 ppm (Cooper and Washburn 1949). In the laboratory, yellow bullheads were held to an average oxygen level of 2.7 ppm for 8 hr a day, for 9 days; they showed no significant stress patterns in serum protein fractions (Bouck and Ball 1965).

Although the yellow bullhead can endure severe environmental stresses, its taste buds erode and its swimming and feeding behavior are modified when it is exposed to concentrations of commercial detergents at 0.5 ppm (Bardach et al. 1965). In laboratory experiments, such fish found food pellets only when they accidentally swam over them or touched them with their lower jaws or their lips. The researchers concluded that fishes such as bullheads, that rely mainly on their chemical senses for finding food, feed less efficiently in waters which persistently contain 0.5 ppm of detergents.

Four yellow bullheads were collected from Sevenmile Creek (Florence County) along with white sucker (6), blacknose dace (1), creek chub (2), pearl dace (6), finescale dace (4), northern redbelly dace (54), blacknose shiner (16), black bullhead (2), central mudminnow (20), Iowa darter (6), pumpkinseed (2), mottled sculpin (1), and brook stickleback (1).

IMPORTANCE AND MANAGEMENT

No records have been found of the yellow bullhead being taken by other predators, although this doubtless happens.

The yellow bullhead is known as a host to the larval stage of the clam *Anodonta grandis* (Hart and Fuller 1974); it probably acts as an important link to future generations of clams.

The yellow bullhead is frequently taken on worms, liver, and meat scraps. It bites as dusk approaches, and continues biting well into the night. It is an excellent food fish; the flesh is fine in texture, firm, and delicious, and it has few bones. It is probably more difficult to skin than other bullheads because its skin is thin.

In experimental trawls in Green Bay, the yellow bullhead and 11 other species of fish composed only 0.7% of the total catch. Reigle (1969a) concluded that it has no potential commercial importance for bottom trawling. In that stretch of the Mississippi River from the Wisconsin line to Caruthersville, Missouri, yellow bullheads and brown bullheads are too scarce to be of any commercial importance (Barnickol and Starrett 1951).

In the commercial harvest in Wisconsin (see Black Bullhead, p. 700), the yellow bullhead is categorized with the black and brown bullheads, and probably constitutes only a small portion of the bullhead catch; it is perhaps second in importance to the black bullhead.

Little is known about management of yellow bullheads. In a shallow pond in northern Alabama, bullheads comprised 197 kg/ha (176 lb/acre) (Tarzwell 1941). Of the 521 bullheads from this pond that were measured, 127 were yellow and 394 were brown; the yellow bullheads attained a larger size than the brown bullheads. After the bullheads and golden shiners were removed from the pond, the muddy water cleared up and a dense algal growth formed in a few days. Tarzwell concluded that the usual turbidity of this pond was due to the bullheads stirring up the bottom and keeping the waters roiled.

Artificial habitats for the yellow bullhead were inadvertently produced along the banks of the Plover River (Portage County), which flows through a public park in Stevens Point, when the banks were riprapped with flat stones placed loosely together. The yellow bullheads frequented the cavities between the stone slabs, and were readily brought out of their hiding places with shocking gear.

Channel Catfish

Ictalurus punctatus (Rafinesque). *Ictalurus*—fish cat; *punctatus*—spotted.

Other common names: channel cat, spotted catfish, spotted cat, Great Lakes catfish, lake catfish, northern catfish, fiddler, white cat, blue cat, lady cat, chucklehead cat, willow cat, cat.

256 mm, Sugar R., near Brodhead (Green Co.), 15 Aug. 1963

DESCRIPTION

Body slender, somewhat compressed, especially posteriorly; not humpbacked before dorsal fin; the profile of the back from the dorsal fin forward gently sloping and curved. Length 305–508 mm (12–20 in). TL = 1.27 SL. Depth into SL 3.8–4.7 (6.6). Head small, length into SL 3.6–4.3. Snout profile bluntly pointed, broadly rounded in dorsal view; barbels of snout short, threadlike, and just anterior to posterior nostril. Mouth short but wide, subterminal and horizontal. Lower jaw much shorter than and included in upper jaw; long barbel (decidedly exceeding head length) sweeping posteriorly from the upper jaw at each corner of the mouth; 4 short barbels attached in a transverse line on the lower chin, with the median pair shorter. Numerous small, sharp teeth in broad bands on upper and lower jaws. Dorsal fin origin far anterior to midpoint between pectoral and pelvic fins; dorsal fin with a dorsal spine less than, to slightly greater than, distance from tip of snout to back of eye; dorsal fin soft rays 6–7; dorsal adipose fin free at posterior edge. Anal fin with free edge generally rounded and with 24–27 rays, including rudimentaries; pelvic fin rays 8; pectoral fin with a narrow spine about same length as dorsal spine, regularly barbed on posterior edge with barbs all inclined (and becoming smaller) toward the base of spine; caudal fin deeply forked. Scaleless. Lateral line complete. Chromosomes 2n = 58 (LeGrande 1978).

Dorsal half of head and body pale blue to pale olive with silvery overcast; ventral surface whitish; sides with spots of varying size and number. Old males become dark in color and lose their spots (these are commonly referred to as "blue catfish" and mistaken by some observers for *Ictalurus furcatus*, the bona fide blue catfish). Fins lightly pigmented. Maxillary barbels darkly pigmented; snout and chin barbels lightly pigmented, except bases of chin barbels generally unpigmented.

Sexual dimorphism: Males with a distinctive urogenital papilla extending posteriorly, which is absent in females; hence one opening behind the vent in males, and two openings behind the vent in females (Moen 1959). In males the head is wider than the body; in females the head is scarcely as wide as the body (Davis 1959). Breeding males are often a brighter blue or deep blue-black on the back and sides than females; the region above and behind the eye is swollen in breeding males.

Hybrids: Channel catfish × flathead catfish (Slastenenko 1957). Experimental channel catfish × blue catfish, channel catfish × white catfish, channel catfish × flathead catfish, channel catfish × brown bullhead, channel catfish × yellow bullhead, channel catfish × black bullhead (Sneed 1964, Dupree et al. 1966).

SYSTEMATIC NOTES

The northern catfish *Villarius lacustris* (Walbaum) of Green Bay and Lake Michigan (Greene 1935) is now recognized as a synonym of *Ictalurus punctatus*. Hubbs and Lagler (1964) noted that the former does not now appear to be sufficiently set off to be recognized, but the whole problem is in need of critical analysis.

DISTRIBUTION, STATUS, AND HABITAT

The channel catfish occurs in all three drainage basins in Wisconsin. In the Lake Superior basin, it is known only from the St. Louis River (Moore and Braem 1965, Eddy and Surber 1947, Eddy and Underhill 1974). In the lower two-thirds of the state it is widely distributed in the larger rivers, their lake systems, and the lower courses of their tributaries. In the Wisconsin River, it occurs regularly as far upstream as the Castle Rock Dam (Adams and Juneau counties), but rarely beyond this point. Greene (1935) noted a report from the mouth of the Plover River (Portage County), and S. Becker (1972) reported that a "28-pound catfish" (probably this species) was taken from the Wisconsin River near Stevens Point early in the century.

The channel catfish is not known from the Rock River above Hustisford (Dodge County); it was introduced between Hustisford and Watertown in 1954, although it is native in the Crawfish and Beaverdam

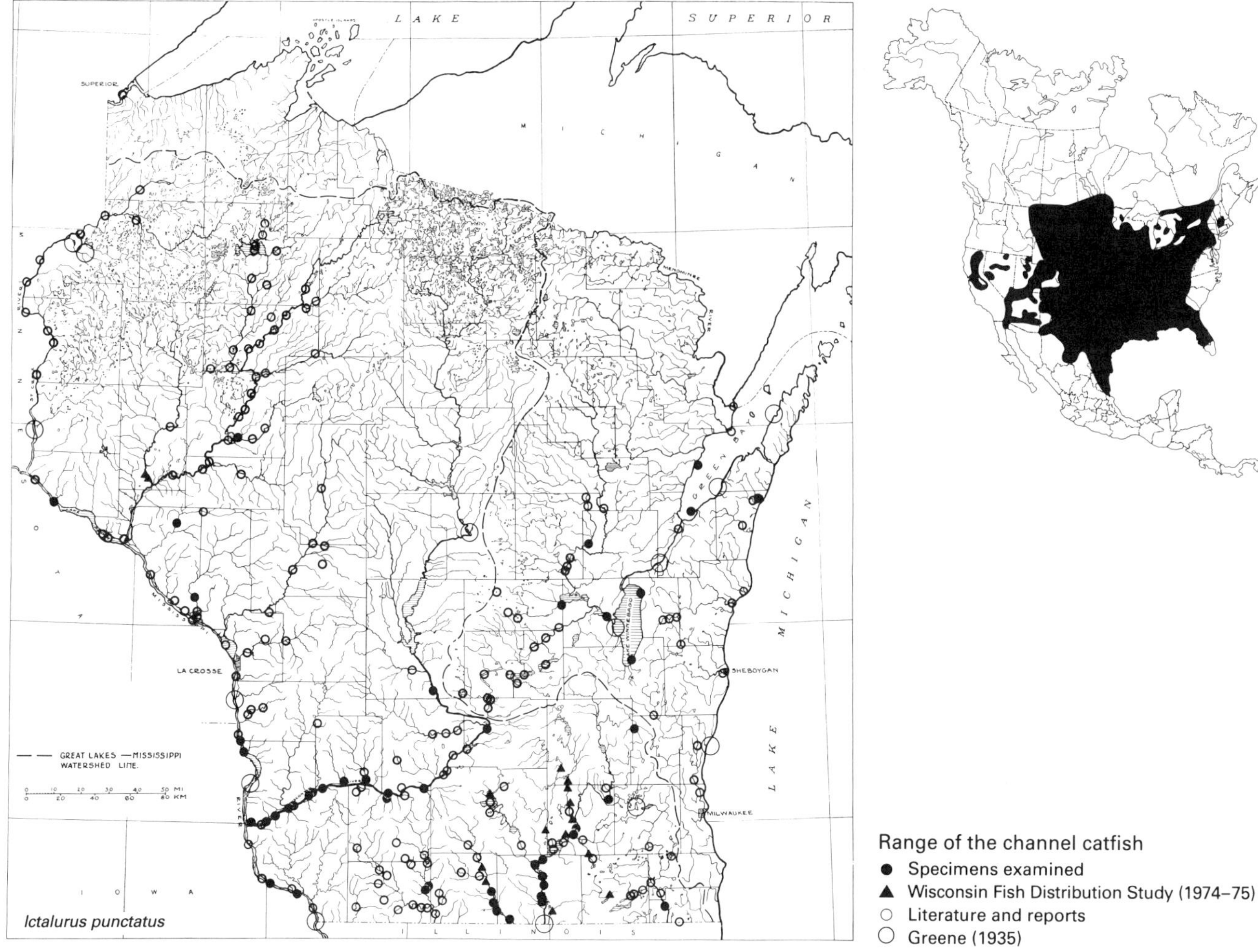

rivers (Dodge County) (H. Neuenschwander, pers. comm.). It was introduced into Waukesha County lakes (Cahn 1927); in 1955 it was introduced into Lake Helen (Portage County), where it winterkilled by the following spring (Becker 1969).

The channel catfish was introduced into the West Twin River (Manitowoc County) in 1957, followed by plants in the Manitowoc, Sheboygan, Onion, and Mullet rivers (Manitowoc and Sheboygan counties) (Schultz 1969). Sustaining populations now occur in the East and West Twin rivers and in the Manitowoc and Sheboygan rivers. Apparently it was not found in these streams prior to introduction, although a small population has always existed in Lake Michigan and in Green Bay.

The channel catfish is uncommon to common in the larger waterways and their connecting lakes in the southern half of Wisconsin. It is less common northward, and rare to uncommon in Lake Michigan and Green Bay.

The channel catfish is found in a wide variety of habitats. It occurs in clear, rocky, well-oxygenated streams, as well as in slow-moving, silty streams; it is often found downstream from power dams where the water is fairly rapid. In streams, young channel catfish inhabit shallow riffles and turbulent areas near sand bars; adults spend the day under big rocks, in deep pools, or under log jams, and enter shallow water at night. Channel catfish may also be found in sluggish streams, lakes, and large reservoirs. They prefer warm water averaging 21.1°C (70°F). Not much is known about the habitat of young channel catfish in lakes.

In Wisconsin, the channel catfish was encountered in turbid water over substrates (decreasing order of frequency) of mud, sand, clay, gravel, silt, rubble, and boulders. It has been taken a number of times from large rivers and streams 12.1–24.0 m wide, in quiet water and in moderate currents.

BIOLOGY

Spawning occurs from May to July, when the water temperature reaches about 23.9°C (75°F); the optimum temperature for spawning is about 26.7°C

(80°F). Adult channel catfish may make extensive excursions upriver in the spring. The male locates a suitable dark cavity or crevice in the stream, under a ledge where rock strata outcrop in the channel, or beneath the roots of a tree undercut by the current. Under highly turbid conditions in a lake or a reservoir, nests may be made directly on the bottom in the mud. Neither a current nor a rocky substrate is necessary for spawning, or for normal development of the young channel catfish. In ponds and hatcheries, nail kegs, earthenware crocks, or milk cans are provided for the fish to spawn in. In clearwater ponds, it is necessary to produce a "hollow log" by telescoping two to three nail kegs together after the bottoms have been knocked out; the spawn is usually deposited in the middle keg (Marzolf 1957).

Prior to spawning, the male cleans the nest site by vigorous fanning with his fins and body, and waits for a female that is ready to deposit eggs (Davis 1959). Pairing may occur before the female is actually ripe, and she may stay nearby while the male cleans the nest. The female usually takes no part in preparing the nest, or in guarding the nest and the young. According to reports, the largest or oldest fish spawn first; the smallest fish are usually the last to spawn.

The following spawning behavior by channel catfish was observed in aquariums (Clemens and Sneed 1957); the female had been injected with fish pituitaries (p. 3):

> Any biting on the part of the female, directed towards other females or towards males, was accepted as a sign of readiness to spawn, since paired catfish (both male and female) usually drove other fish away. . . . In pairing acts in which aggressiveness occurred, it was observed that if the fish were going to pair, the bites of the male became progressively less severe until they were more like a nudge in the region of the vent.
>
> A few hours before the event, there were some rather positive signs that spawning was to take place. The female occasionally would make what we called "runs" along the bottom. In this type of behavior the female moved over the spot where the eggs were to be deposited in a wiggling motion, the pelvic and pectoral fins alternately beating against the bottom. These runs were short, about 4 to 6 inches. This same behavior was later a part of the spawning act and was repeated many times.

When a male attempted to spawn with a female, they were headed in opposite directions to one another (p. 5):

> . . . Then he wrapped his tail around her head so that his caudal fin covered her eyes. . . . Then the male's body quivered, during which time his pectoral fins beat, but his pelvics remained rather motionless and pointed backwards, and in some cases slightly to the side. . . . If the female responded, she usually did so within 5 seconds. When she participated she wrapped her tail around the head of the male and quivered in unison with him. Both her pelvic and pectoral fins were motionless during this act. With each reflex a contraction of the abdominal muscles of the female moved the eggs posteriorly and progressively produced a flattened area behind the pectoral fins. She then lunged forward about 3 to 5 inches as the eggs spurted out. A current of water, produced by the lunge, caused the eggs to swirl up before they settled to the bottom. . . .
>
> It was believed that the male released milt at the end of the reflex at the same moment that the female released eggs.

Clemens and Sneed noted that a spawning period lasted from 4–6 hr, and that about 150 eggs were laid about nine times each hour, for a total of 8,000 eggs. Generally, females weighing 0.45–1.81 kg (1–4 lb) produced about 8,800 eggs per kilogram of body weight. According to Clemens and Sneed, when female catfish spawn, they usually void all of their eggs.

The eggs of channel catfish average 3.2 mm diam with the chorion removed. They are light yellow, demersal, and adhesive; they adhere to each other.

The incubation period of the eggs is from 5 to 10 days, at water temperatures between 21.1 and 29.4°C (70 and 85°F). At mean water temperatures of about 26.7°C (80°F), the time from the first deposition of eggs to the time when the first egg hatches ranges from 6 to 7 days. Eggs that are laid first are the last to hatch; the gradient of the oxygen tension between the top and the bottom eggs probably accounts for the differences in hatching time. Clemens and Sneed (1957) noted that during the deposition period both parents provided aeration for the eggs (pp. 6, 8):

> . . . At the end of the spawning period the male for the first time began paddling on the top of the eggs, while the female rested quietly to one side. From then on the female was permitted less and less to be near the eggs. The male drove her away as he did any other intruder.
>
> The most striking activity was exhibited by the male when he vigorously wiggled his body and pressed and packed the eggs with the flat side of his pelvic fins in a manner that shook the entire egg mass. He moved forward from one end of the egg pile to the other, which gave the impression that he was walking on his fins. This action was similar to the "run" of the female during the spawning act.
>
> . . . Vigorous males worked the eggs every 5–10 min the first day or 2, but late in the incubation period the workings were less frequent. . . . The eggs were loosened more when the male pulled at the eggs with his mouth. . . . No channel catfish were observed taking the eggs completely

in their mouths. One male was seen trying to move a loose egg mass that had shifted from the center of the aquarium by placing his snout under the edge of the mass and carrying it a little forward as he swam.

Upon hatching, the channel catfish fry accumulated in a mass on the bottom of the aquarium, usually in a corner, where they remained for about 2 days; then they began to come to the surface. By the third day, they had started to feed and to move about the aquarium.

Marzolf (1957) noted that channel catfish fry in ponds normally remain in the nest about 7 days, and are defended by the male fish. When the nest no longer needs to be defended, the male fish is ready for the second spawn. The minimum size of the fry at hatching is about 6.4 mm. The early development of young channel catfish through the pectoral fin-bud stage at 34 hr was examined by Saksena et al. (1961). Yolk-sac larvae, larvae, and juveniles were described by Mansueti and Hardy (1967). Fish (1932) illustrated the 32.6 mm juvenile, which has the true channel catfish appearance, including the spots.

Channel catfish larvae which are guarded by the male initially mass on the bottom and later make excursions to the surface. They may travel in schools for several days or for weeks (Mansueti and Hardy 1967). After dispersal, the juveniles feed singly in quiet, shallow water over sand bars, around drift piles, and among rocks; some juveniles winter under boulders in rather swiftly flowing water.

In Lewis and Clark Lake, South Dakota, channel catfish yolk-sac larvae shorter than 15 mm were collected from the old river channel at depths of 10–12 m in early July (Walburg 1976). The young remained in schools for the first several weeks after hatching, but apparently dispersed when they were about 25 mm (1 in) long.

In Wisconsin, the growth of young-of-year channel catfish has been reported as follows:

Date	No. of Fish	TL (mm)		Location
		Avg	Range	
13 July	1	35		Wisconsin R. (Crawford Co.)
14 Aug.	8	49	30–63	Sugar R. (Green Co.)
16 Aug.	2	54	50–57	Wisconsin R. (Richland Co.)
7 Sept.	9	67	64–73	Mississippi R. (Crawford Co.)
11 Sept.	5	68	61–73	Rock R. (Rock Co.)
16 Sept.	3	67	55–82	Yellow R. (Chippewa Co.)
26 Sept.	2	87	82–91	Mississippi R. (Pierce Co.)

For channel catfish taken from Pool 9 (Lansing, Iowa) of the Mississippi River, lengths calculated from the vertebrae at the end of each year of life were: 1—75 mm; 2—161 mm; 3—231 mm; 4—299 mm; 5—361 mm; 6—423 mm; 7—488 mm; 8—536 mm; 9—610 mm; 10—676 mm; 11—658 mm; and 12—709 mm (Appleget and Smith 1951). From the same collection the relationship of length to weight at selected size intervals was: 196 mm—54 g; 264 mm—136 g; 391 mm—526 g; 521 mm—1,510 g; 643 mm—3,588 g; and 721 mm—4,314 g.

A 506-mm channel catfish from Lake Poygan (Waushara County) had the following estimated growth at the annuli of the pectoral fins: 1—90.4 mm; 2—198.8 mm; 3—325.3 mm; 4—397.5 mm; and 5—469.8 mm (Paruch 1979).

In Virginia (Stauffer et al. 1976), channel catfish in the heated discharge (34.4°C) from a power plant had significantly lower condition than fish from an upstream reference area, where the temperature was 26.7°C. The condition factor (K_{FL}) for fish from the heated area was 1.18; for fish from the reference area it was 1.23.

The age of channel catfish at maturity varies greatly from one body of water to another. In Pool 9 of the Mississippi River, Appleget and Smith (1951) noted that no fish in their first 4 years of life were mature, but that in the fifth year both sexes (17.6%) showed some degree of sexual development. In the beginning of the ninth year of life, 100% of the males and 90% of the females were mature. Neither sex reaches maturity at less than 305 mm (12 in), but many fish in the 330-mm (13-in) group are mature. In the south, Davis (1959) noted that some channel catfish become sexually mature in their second year, and that most of them spawn for the first time when they are 3 years old.

Few channel catfish live more than 8 years, although occasionally large catfish over 15 years old are taken in Wisconsin waters (Finke 1964). Such fish may exceed 762 mm (30 in) in length and weigh 6.80 kg (15 lb) or more. A 19.96-kg (44-lb) channel catfish was taken from the Wisconsin River in 1962. The maximum size known, a 26.31-kg (58-lb) fish, was caught in the Santee Cooper Reservoir, South Carolina, in 1964.

Young channel catfish tend to feed primarily on aquatic insects or on bottom arthropods; after they reach 100 mm they are usually omnivorous or piscivorous (Carlander 1969). In Lake Oahe, South Dakota (Starostka and Nelson 1974), the diet changed from zooplankton to fish as the channel catfish increased in length.

In the Wisconsin River (Adams County) during September, adult channel catfish had eaten insects (including Diptera, Coleoptera, Hymenoptera, Trichoptera, Orthoptera, and Hemiptera), and annelids, seeds, plant materials, and detritus (K. Primmer, pers. comm.). There were no fish in the stomachs of the 22 catfish examined.

In Pool 19 of the Mississippi River, channel catfish stomachs contained 68% *Hexagenia* naiads and subimagos, but only 3% *Potamyia flava* larvae. Mayfly subimagos appeared only in channel catfish stomachs collected between 24 June and 16 July, and their presence always coincided with periods of peak mayfly emergence. The remainder of the contents included immature Plecoptera and Diptera, clams, snails, and algae (Hoopes 1960).

According to Finke (1964), items taken from channel catfish stomachs include insects, frogs, crayfish, snails, fish, clams, worms, algae, pondweeds, elm seeds, wild grapes, "cotton" from cottonwood trees, pieces of dressed rabbit, chicken necks, canned corn, shrimp, beef bones, and much more. Carlander (1969) listed such unusual items from catfish stomachs as a snake skin, an adult bobwhite, and hydroids.

In food preference studies (Lewis et al. 1965), channel catfish showed a pronounced preference for crayfish of the right size over fathead minnows, and a preference for fathead minnows over fingerling bluegills, green sunfish, and golden shiners. Fingerling carp and bullheads were poorly utilized, and tadpoles were killed but not eaten.

Dead fish and other animals are sometimes included in the channel catfish diet (Davis 1959). The occurrence of grasshoppers and other terrestrial insects in stomachs indicates that channel catfish take some food from the surface of the water, although they usually feed near the bottom. They have been known to eat refuse discarded by people, and to congregate near places where garbage is dumped into streams and lakes.

Adult channel catfish usually feed on the bottom in a random manner, detecting food by touch and smell. The eyes of the channel catfish, which are proportionately larger than those of other species of catfish, seem to be adapted to sight feeding to some degree (Davis 1959). This is consistent with its use of minnows as food when the water is the clearest (Bailey and Harrison 1948).

The channel catfish feeds most actively from sundown until about midnight, at water temperatures between 10 and 34.4°C (50 and 94°F) (Bailey and Harrison 1948). In the winter this species rarely feeds, and the available evidence indicates that adults do not feed during the breeding season.

Channel catfish are most active when water levels are rising—following a rain, for example, or the opening of a power dam. With rising water, these fish are on the move, searching for food washed into the stream. They often feed in submerged grassy areas, which act as strainers that catch and hold all kinds of food.

At temperatures of 25, 30, and 35°C (77, 86, and 95°F), the lethal oxygen levels for channel catfish are at 0.95, 1.03, and 1.08 ppm respectively (Moss and Scott 1961). At 25°C channel catfish embryos and the resulting larvae developed properly when the dissolved oxygen concentrations and control concentrations were near air saturation, but survival at 25°C was statistically less at 2.4 and 4.2 ppm oxygen (Carlson et al. 1974). No embryos hatched at 1.7 ppm oxygen. At all reduced oxygen concentrations at 25 and 28°C (77 and 82.4°F) embryo pigmentation was lighter, the hatch period was extended, feeding was delayed, and growth was reduced.

Channel catfish 6 days old and 11 months old, acclimated at 26, 30, and 34°C (79, 86, and 93°F), had upper lethal temperatures at 36.6, 37.3, and 37.8°C (97.9, 99.1, and 100°F), respectively (Allen and Strawn 1967). Kilambi et al. (1970) determined that the optimum conditions for raising channel catfish included a water temperature of 32°C (89.6°F) and a 14-hr photoperiod; they based their findings on an evaluation of growth, food consumption, food conversion efficiency, and mortality. In the Wabash River, Indiana, the optimum temperature range for this species was 30 to 32°C (86–89.6°F) (Gammon 1973). In the White River and Ipalco Discharge Canal, Indiana, the maximum temperature at which the channel catfish was captured was 37.8°C (100°F) (Proffitt and Benda 1971). Juvenile channel catfish exposed to rapid temperature changes have shown decreased swimming performance (Hocutt 1973).

A preliminary tagging study in the lower Wisconsin River indicated a general downstream movement of channel catfish into the Mississippi River during late summer and autumn (C. Brynildson et al. 1961). An upstream spawning run into the Wisconsin River was anticipated during the latter part of May and early June. One channel catfish tagged in the lower Wisconsin River moved 78 km (48 mi) to Avoca Lake (Iowa County); this was the greatest upstream movement recorded (C. Brynildson 1960). The greatest downstream movement was made by an individual tagged at Prairie du Sac (Sauk County) and captured in the Mississippi River near De Soto (Crawford County), a distance of about 190 stream km (118 stream mi). C. Brynildson (1964) noted that, in the lower Wisconsin River, the average downstream movement was 22 km (13.8 mi), and the average upstream movement was 12 km (7.3 mi).

In Kansas (Cross 1950), extensive upstream migrations of channel catfish were observed during high-water periods in June and July. In Lake Sharpe, South Dakota, channel catfish moved upstream from April through June, and a second peak of upstream movement occurred in September and October (Elrod 1974); most fish appeared to move downstream in November or early December.

There is no evidence to indicate that channel catfish will travel a great distance to return to home territory (Hubley 1963a). Channel catfish tagged in the upper Mississippi River between Lansing, Iowa, and upper Lake Pepin moved essentially downstream prior to capture. The greatest downstream movement was recorded for two fish released at Reads Landing, Minnesota, which were recaptured at Potosi, Wisconsin, 275 km (171 mi) downstream, 14 to 16 months after their release. The greatest upstream movement was recorded for a fish released at Lake City, Minnesota. It was recaptured 33 months later, 345 km (214 mi) upstream in the Minnesota River at New Ulm, Minnesota. The fastest movement was recorded for an individual that moved 179 km (111 mi) downstream in 36 days, at an average rate of 5 km (3.1 mi) per day. Three fish passed through eight dams before recapture.

Eighty-nine percent of the channel catfish tagged in Trempealeau Bay (Trempealeau County) were recaptured within 21 km (13 mi) of their release point. The remaining 11% were caught at distances of 32–185 km from the release sites (Ranthum 1971). One fish had traveled up the Trempealeau River a distance of 61 km (38 mi) from the point of release; another had gone up the Chippewa River within Eau Claire County a distance of 136 km (84 mi); and a third fish reached Pool 11 of the Mississippi River, 186 km (115 mi) from the point of release.

IMPORTANCE AND MANAGEMENT

Because of their long spines, larger channel catfish suffer little from predation. Young catfish, however, are vulnerable to predacious insects and other fish. In ponds, the young are especially preyed upon by bluegills and bass (Marzolf 1957). Bailey and Harrison (1948) found some cannibalism on young channel catfish by catfish 306 mm (12 in) or over which was directly proportional to the density of the young fish present.

The channel catfish is a known glochidial host to the following mollusks: *Amblema plicata*, *Megalonaias gigantea*, *Quadrula nodulata*, and *Quadrula pustulosa*. It is one of several fish species responsible for the distribution and perpetuation of those clam species (Hart and Fuller 1974).

The channel catfish ranks high as a sport fish in Wisconsin. In the upper Mississippi River, it was rated ninth in numbers taken in 1957, and third in 1962–1963 (Nord 1967). In 1967–1968, the estimated sport fishery catch of the channel catfish in Pools 4, 5, 7, and 11 of the Mississippi River was 39,494 individuals, with an average weight per fish of 586 g (1.29 lb) (Wright 1970). In the lower Wisconsin River, channel catfish make up almost 50% of the catch. On the Minnesota side of Lake Pepin, where snagging for channel catfish under the ice is allowed, 14,277 fish weighing 8,549 kg (18,847 lb) were harvested during 1962–1963 and the following 2 winters (Skrypek 1965).

The channel catfish takes a hook most readily on moonlit nights from about twilight on into the night. Baits used to catch channel catfish include minnows, worms, grasshoppers, crayfish, and uniquely odiferous concoctions calling for such ingredients as cheese trimmings, rolled oats, spoiled clams, liver strips, and fish and/or chicken entrails along with a volatile additive, such as anise or chicken blood. The flesh of the channel catfish is white, crisp, juicy, tender, and of excellent flavor.

In Wisconsin, fishing regulations pertaining to the channel catfish are liberal. In 1980 in inland waters and in Wisconsin-Minnesota boundary waters the daily bag limit was 10–25 fish; and there was no limit in Wisconsin-Iowa boundary waters.

According to Scott and Crossman (1973), the spines of the channel catfish and other species of catfish have always been found among Indian artifacts. The bases of the spines were rounded off, the barbs removed, and the spines used as awls for leather work; if the holes in the bases were intact, the spines were used as needles. One such artifact, from the shores of Lake Huron in Ontario, was carbon dated at 1,000 years B.C.

The channel catfish has become a basic test animal for determining chemical transfers, immune responses, and antibody formation. Channel catfish embryos can be obtained, even in the fall of the year, by injecting a female with pituitary materials.

The channel catfish is probably the most valuable commercial fish in the upper Mississippi River; it is the most sought-after fish in the river, and brings the best overall price. The channel catfish is harvested mainly for human consumption. Since 1960, the commercial catch has averaged 181–227 thousand kg

(400–500 thousand lb) yearly. The highest catch was made in 1964, when 277,659 kg (612,125 lb) were boated (Fernholz and Crawley 1977). In 1976, 194,261 kg (428,266 lb) of channel catfish, at 97¢/kg (44¢/lb), had an exvessel value of $188,437—the most valuable fishery on the river. In that year, the channel catfish were taken by the following gear: set lines, 130,597 kg; bait nets, 22,340 kg; slat nets, 14,371 kg; gill nets, 12,816 kg; buffalo nets, 10,092 kg; seines, 4,433 kg; and trammel nets, 66 kg.

Set lines are stationary lines stretched across a likely area, to which hooks are attached at intervals (Finke 1964). Regulations limit each commercial fisherman to a certain number of hooks; these are baited with various substances, including cut fish, cottonseed cake, dough balls with cheese, and other homemade products. One fisherman reported great success with pieces of white soap. Slat nets, or basket traps as they are frequently called, consist basically of wooden boxes of slats with flexible throats; this type of gear is very selective, and will usually catch only catfish. Set in a current during the spawning season, slat nets apparently attract the fish as they seek dark places in which to build their nests. Often the trap is baited with a live, gravid female, who attracts males searching for a mate.

In 1953 on Lake Poygan, 3,530 catfish made up 62.9% of the total catch in 64-mm (2½-in) trap nets. On the same lake, Wisconsin Department of Natural Resources research crews captured 4,100 catfish in the period between December 1958 and December 1959 (Becker 1964b).

In 1966, the gill net catch of channel catfish from the Wisconsin waters of Lake Michigan was 91 kg (200 lb); the catch was valued at $43. In 1974, catfish had a reported harvest of 791 kg (1,743 lb) and a value of $461 (Wis. Dep. Nat. Resour. 1976c).

Attempts to raise channel catfish usually resulted in failure until workers at the U.S. Bureau of Fisheries in Fairport, Iowa, discovered in 1916 that the species could be raised in ponds by providing proper nesting conditions (Davis 1959). Two methods of raising channel catfish have proved satisfactory (Davis 1959). In the pen method, a pair of fish is placed in an enclosure containing a nail keg or some other nest structure. After spawning has been completed, the female is removed so that she cannot eat the eggs, and the male is left to care for the eggs until they hatch. The young are then placed in troughs for the first stage of rearing. In the pond method of rearing, brood fish are allowed to pair of their own accord, in a pond that is supplied with nest structures. Eggs are removed from the nests as soon as possible after they are deposited; they are hatched in jars or in wire baskets through which water flows continuously.

In the South, channel catfish, grown at 7,500/ha (3,000/acre) in 0.04-ha (0.1-acre) ponds for a growth period of 220 days, produced 3,656 kg/ha (3,262 lb/acre). In Illinois, 113-g (4-oz) fingerlings, placed into warmwater ponds and fed a prepared fish food, averaged 340 g (12 oz) in 4 months; some fish weighed more than 450 g (1 lb) (L. H. Osman, *Milwaukee Journal*, 26 July 1964).

An objectionable, "earth-musty" flavor is frequently found in intensively cultured catfish which renders the fish unmarketable. Lovell and Sackey (1973) determined that blue-green algae could impart this undesirable flavor in the fish. When fish which had been in the algae tanks for 14 days were transferred to flowing, charcoal-filtered water, the unpleasant flavor disappeared after 10 days.

Roughly 40% of the weight of catfish which enter a processing plant turns up as waste at the end of the processing line. Conversion of this offal into a dry and/or moist swine and catfish food holds considerable promise (Lovell 1973).

Impoundments with moderately turbid waters are less likely to require special management for channel catfish production than impoundments with clear waters. In clear waters, predatory fish and insects probably limit the survival of catfish by preying on the young. The survival of young catfish was not nearly as high in ponds containing adult largemouth bass and either bluegill or redear sunfish as it was in ponds containing only channel catfish (Marzolf 1957). In one instance, 15 25-mm (1-in) catfish were found in the stomach of a 178-mm bluegill taken from the nest of a channel catfish. Marzolf noted that the survival of fingerling catfish is directly correlated to the amount of turbidity in the water. It is assumed that turbid water furnishes cover for the fry and fingerlings. Heavy vegetation in clear ponds often conceals enormous numbers of predacious insects and insect nymphs, which may feed upon the fry.

The culture, stocking, and management of catfish in Arkansas and other southern states has led to a considerable amount of research in the private, state, and federal sectors. The outpouring of technical writing and bulletins has been extensive. Unfortunately, in Wisconsin the application of these techniques is made difficult by our long winters and short growing season; to realize a crop, an enterprising fish farmer must extend the growing season by heating the water. Heated discharge ponds at power plants hold some promise for catfish farming, although this idea needs a closer look.

Tadpole Madtom

Noturus gyrinus (Mitchill). *Noturus*—back tail, in reference to the connection between the adipose and the caudal fins; *gyrinus*—tadpole.

Other common names: madtom, tadpole stonecat, tadpole cat, bullhead.

Adult 109 mm, Pine R. (Florence Co.), 25 June 1965

DESCRIPTION

Body heavy, round, and potbellied anteriorly (rarely elongate); strongly compressed posteriorly. Length 64–89 mm (2.5–3.5 in). TL = 1.23 SL. Depth into TL 4.4–6.0. Head length into TL 3.8–4.4. Snout blunt, with a barbel arising from collar surrounding each posterior nostril; barbels long and reaching almost to back of head. Mouth short but wide, horizontal; lips fleshy. Lower jaw slightly shorter than upper jaw; barbel attached to upper jaw at each corner of mouth almost reaching to opercular opening; 4 barbels (outer 2 about length of maxillary barbels, inner 2 slightly shorter) attached in a transverse line on the lower chin. Numerous small, sharp, or peglike teeth in broad bands on upper and lower jaws; tooth patch on upper jaw without elongate, lateral backward extensions. Dorsal fin origin decidedly in advance of midpoint between pectoral and pelvic fins; dorsal fin swollen at base with a short spine (about one-third fin height), and usually 6 rays; dorsal adipose fin long, low, continuous with caudal fin and delimited from it by a shallow notch. Anal fin rays 14–16; pelvic fin rays usually 8. Pectoral fin spine about two-thirds fin length; notches on anterior edge delicate or absent; posterior edge of spine barbless; poison glands associated with dorsal and pectoral fins. Caudal fin broadly rounded posteriorly. Scaleless. Lateral line incomplete. Digestive tract 1.0–1.4 TL. Chromosomes 2n = 42 (LeGrande 1978).

Dorsal and lateral regions of head, back, and upper caudal peduncle dark slate brown; lighter brown on sides of caudal peduncle; ventral region of head and belly tan to yellow-brown. Fins generally darkly pigmented; paired fins usually less pigmented. Barbels darkly to lightly pigmented. Generally 3 dark, longitudinal streaks per side; the prominent middle streak follows the position of the vertebral column, and from this streak dark lines outline the muscle segments dorsally and ventrally.

Hybrids: Tadpole madtom × brindled madtom (the latter not found in Wisconsin) (Trautman 1957, Menzel and Raney 1973).

SYSTEMATIC NOTES

Synonyms: *Schilbeodes gyrinus* (Greene 1935), *Schilbeodes mollis* (Hubbs and Lagler 1947), *Schilbeodes gyrinus* (Hubbs and Lagler 1958), and *Noturus gyrinus* (Hubbs and Lagler 1964, Taylor 1969, Bailey et al. 1960 and 1970, Robins et al. 1980).

DISTRIBUTION, STATUS, AND HABITAT

The tadpole madtom occurs in all three drainage basins in Wisconsin. It is present in sheltered bays of western Lake Superior, and it is distributed throughout Wisconsin except in the driftless area, where it is seldom taken.

In Wisconsin, the tadpole madtom is common in medium to large rivers. It is considered rare at the barriers in tributaries of Lake Superior (McLain et al. 1965). In large lakes it is rare to common. This species appears to be secure in Wisconsin.

In Wisconsin, the tadpole madtom was encountered most frequently at depths of 0.1–1.5 m in clear to slightly turbid water; it was also found in darkly colored water. This species occurred over substrates of sand (27% frequency), gravel (20%), mud (18%), boulders (16%), silt (10%), rubble (8%), clay (1%), and detritus (1%). It prefers thick growths of submergent plants, or accumulations of organic debris, including dense branches, leaves, trash, and empty mussel shells. It occurred in lakes, reservoirs, and sloughs, and in slow to moderate current in pools and riffles in streams of the following widths: 1.0–3.0 m (3%); 3.1–6.0 m (6%); 6.1–12.0 m (15%); 12.1–24.0 m (53%); and 24.1–50.0 m (24%). The tadpole madtom is more commonly found in natural and artificial lakes than either of the other two members of this genus in Wisconsin. In Canada, it has been taken as deep as 25 m (81 ft).

BIOLOGY

The tadpole madtom spawns in June and July. Spawning is known only for single pairs under objects or in cavities in the bottom. There is apparently little formal nest preparation. The eggs are deposited

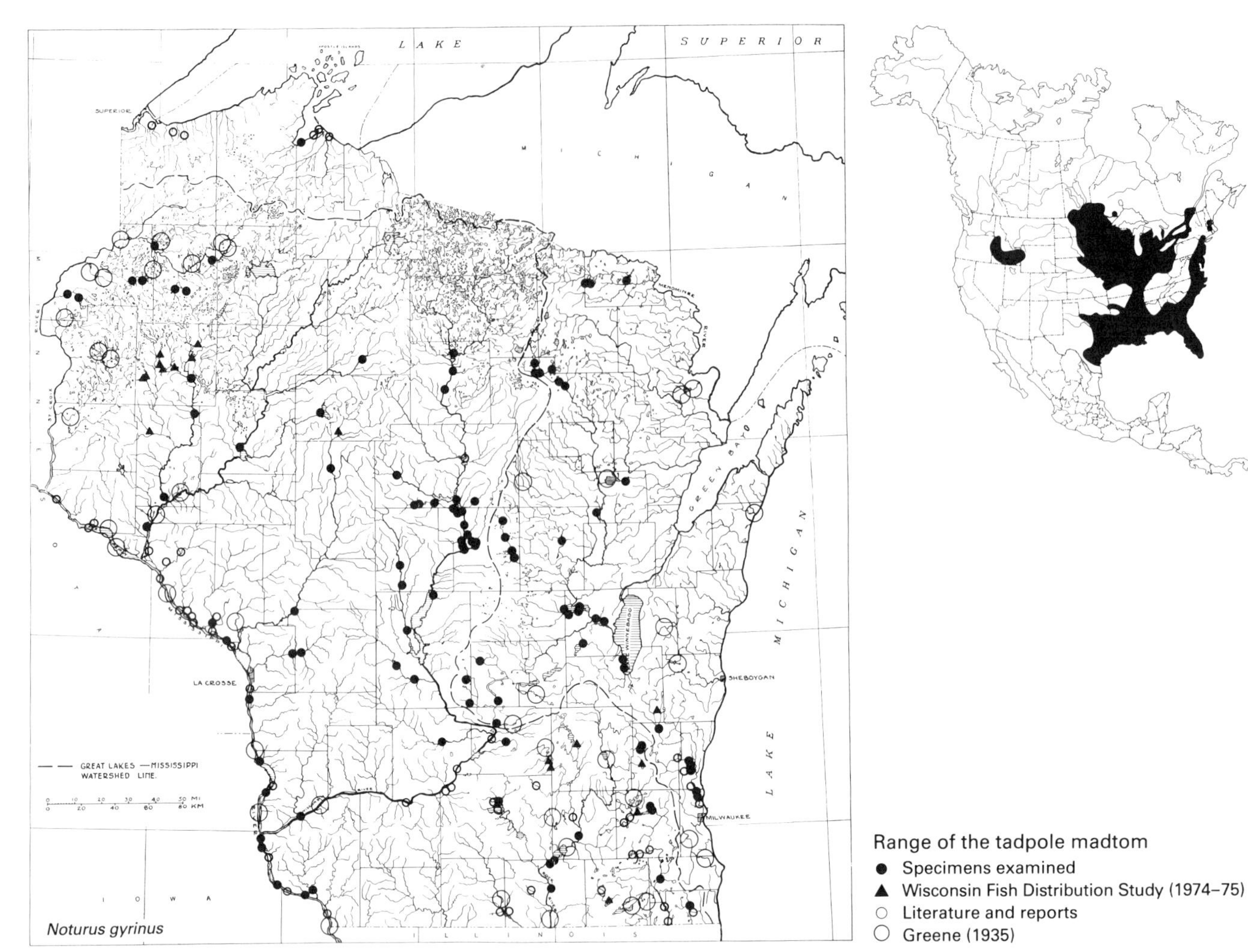

in clusters beneath boards or logs, in crayfish burrows, in holes in mud, under roots, and in old tin cans (Mansueti and Hardy 1967). The number of eggs varies; it has been reported to average 50 per fish, or as high as 117 per fish (Scott and Crossman 1973, Bailey 1938). Egg-guarding individuals are in most cases males (Taylor 1969). There is no evidence that parent tadpole madtoms care for their broods after hatching.

Unlike female bullheads and catfishes, which typically liberate all of their eggs in a single spawning, female madtoms normally mate several times during the breeding period (Menzel and Raney 1973). Evidence for this is indirect, and is based in part on published accounts which indicate that the number of eggs in a clutch may be considerably less than the number of eggs in the ovary in several species of madtoms. The available evidence also indicates that the mating pair bond is less enduring among madtoms than among other catfishes.

A maturing tadpole madtom female, 90 mm and 14.02 g, collected 25 June from the Pine River (Florence County), had ovaries 9.2% of the body weight, and held 159 orange eggs 2.0–2.5 mm diam. A mature female, 87 mm and 10.72 g, collected 12 July from the Hunting River (Langlade County) had ovaries 14.9% of the body weight, and held eggs 2.4–2.6 mm diam. In New York state, Menzel and Raney found 82–179 eggs in the ovaries of four females. Upon deposition, the eggs adhere to each other and to the substrate, and the whole egg mass is surrounded by another gelatinous envelope.

Young tadpole madtoms are essentially like adults when they have attained about 25 mm TL.

In Wisconsin, the growth of young-of-year tadpole madtoms has been reported as follows (Paruch 1979):

Date	No. of Fish	TL (mm) Avg	TL (mm) Range	Location
19 Aug.	2	22	21–23	L. Poygan (Winnebago Co.)
28 Aug.	4	43	35–50	L. Winnebago (Fond du Lac Co.)
9 Sept.	1	53		Pewaukee L. (Waukesha Co.)
18 Sept.	3	30	29–30	White Clay L. (Shawano Co.)
24 Sept.	27	38	30–46	Trempealeau L. (Trempealeau Co.)
4 Oct.	23	35	29–63	Milwaukee R. (Fond du Lac Co.)

In Iowa, young-of-year ranged from 18 to 56 mm at the end of August and the beginning of September (Griswold 1963).

The ages and growth of 145 tadpole madtoms from Wisconsin (UWSP specimens), aged by analysis of the pectoral spines, are summarized below (Paruch 1979):

Age Class	No. of Fish	TL (mm)		Calculated TL at Annulus (mm)		
		Avg	Range	1	2	3
0	82	35.3	21–52			
I	34	45.0	35–89	45.2		
II	20	76.0	51–117	42.7	64.6	
III	9	86.9	80–95	35.6	66.5	86.9
Avg (weighted)				43.0	65.2	86.9

On 15 August, tadpole madtoms from a Minnesota lake (Hooper 1949), aged by analysis of vertebrae, were: 0—26.4 (15–38) mm SL; I—61.6 (43–85) mm SL; and II—89.1 (78–104) mm SL. Average weights were 0.32, 4.16, and 16.32 g respectively. Of more than 4,000 fish examined, only 270 were age II.

An age-II tadpole madtom 117 mm long (UWSP 5207) was collected from Mason Lake (Adams County) in 1975.

In Trempealeau Lake (Trempealeau County), the tadpole madtom consumed ostracods, cladocerans, Trichoptera, Coleoptera, unidentifiable insect and animal remains, algae, and eggs (K. Ball, pers. comm.). In the Madison area, it fed on insects (44% volume), oligochaetes (18.3%), small crustaceans (including amphipods, ostracods, and copepods) (28.3%), plants (5.9%), mites (+), snails (0.1%), algae (0.1%), and silt and debris (3%) (Pearse 1918). The tadpole madtom is also known to have consumed small fishes, a planarian worm, and dragonflies (Forbes and Richardson 1920, Scott and Crossman 1973). It feeds mainly at night. The items in the tadpole madtom's diet show that it gets its food on the bottom and from among aquatic plants. The smaller individuals apparently depend on crustaceans and oligochaetes; larger fishes rely more on insects.

At a high water temperature of 38°C (100.4°F), the tadpole madtom suffered an appreciable mortality in a shallow southern Michigan pond (Bailey 1955). In a winterkill lake of southeastern Michigan, with 0.2–0.0 ppm of dissolved oxygen in the upper 0.3–1.2 m of water, some tadpole madtoms survived but no largemouth bass or bluegills survived (Cooper and Washburn 1949).

The tadpole madtom tolerates at least a moderate amount of salinity; it has been reported from the tidal portions of Virginia rivers (Mansueti and Hardy 1967). It has also been taken from dark, stained water with a pH of 4.5 (Holder and Ramsey 1972).

Like all madtoms, the tadpole madtom is secretive, spending the daylight hours lurking in the protection of cavities, cutbanks, debris, or vegetation (Scott and Crossman 1973, Pflieger 1975). At night it leaves its cover and feeds actively in shallows.

In a rotenone kill project of a 5-ha (12.5-acre) lake in northern Minnesota, 40 kg (88 lb) of tadpole madtoms were recovered out of a total of 114 kg (251 lb) of fish of all species (Hooper 1949). Other species present were northern pike, pumpkinseeds, yellow perch, and black bullheads. Approximately 16,770 madtoms were present in the lake at the time of the rotenone poisoning, based on the counts of fish removed from the lake and on the counts of fish remaining in the lake that could not be efficiently recovered.

In Cedar Creek (Ozaukee County), 15 tadpole madtoms were associated with these species: white sucker (4), central stoneroller (15), creek chub (10+), bluntnose minnow (1), fathead minnow (6), common shiner (20), sand shiner (1), black bullhead (50), and green sunfish (1).

IMPORTANCE AND MANAGEMENT

Where they are abundant, tadpole madtoms probably contribute significantly to the food supply of sport fishes. The tadpole madtom is also known to have been eaten by a garter snake (Scott and Crossman 1973).

This madtom is a host to the glochidia for the mussels *Actinonaias carinata* and *Lampsilis radiata luteola* (Hart and Fuller 1974).

Tadpole madtoms are excellent bait for black bass, and a preferred bait for walleyes, along the Mississippi River. When hooked through the lips, madtoms survive for a long time, and several walleyes can be taken on a single madtom. In the late 1970s, madtoms sold for bait cost the fisherman about $1.50 per dozen. They are collected by digging into detritus with a hand scoop—a long handle affixed to a metal frame, which is covered with 3/8-in (9.5-mm) hardware cloth. Bait dealers use tin cans to extract the madtoms from holding tanks: the can is lowered into the tank, and the fish, seeking cover, voluntarily swim into the can. Often a piece of burlap is thrown into the holding tank to provide them with cover.

Its fondness for still water and its small size make the tadpole madtom an interesting aquarium resident (Walden 1964, Sterba 1973, Scott and Crossman 1973).

Slender Madtom

Noturus exilis Nelson. *Noturus*—back tail, in reference to the connection between the adipose and the caudal fins; *exilis*—slender.
Other common name: slender stonecat.

Adult male 123 mm, Oconomowoc R. (Waukesha Co.), 14 May 1977

Adult female 111 mm, Oconomowoc R. (Waukesha Co.), 14 May 1977

DESCRIPTION
Body elongate, cylindrical anteriorly, compressed posteriorly. Length 76–102 mm (3–4 in). TL = 1.17 SL. Depth into TL 5.2–6.8 (4.4). Head length into TL 3.9–4.7. Snout blunt, short barbels of snout arising from collar surrounding posterior nostrils. Mouth short but wide, horizontal lips thick. Upper jaw slightly longer than lower jaw, longest barbel (decidedly less than head length) attached to upper jaw at each corner of the mouth; 4 barbels (outer 2 almost as long as the upper jaw barbels, inner 2 slightly shorter) attached in a transverse line on the lower chin. Numerous small, sharp, or peglike teeth in broad bands on upper and lower jaws; tooth patch on upper jaw without elongate lateral backward extensions. Dorsal fin origin decidedly in advance of midpoint between pectoral and pelvic fins; dorsal fin generally swollen at base with a short spine (less than half of fin height), and 6–7 soft rays; dorsal adipose fin continuous with caudal fin and delimited posteriorly by a shallow notch. Anal fin rays 18–21; pelvic fin rays 8–9. Pectoral fin spine short, strongly notched on its anterior edge from tip of spine to at least its midpoint; well-developed barbs (generally inclined toward base) on posterior edge of spine. Caudal fin rounded to slightly squarish. Scaleless. Lateral line incomplete. Digestive tract coiled, 1.1–1.3 TL. Chromosomes 2n = 54 (LeGrande 1978).

Dorsal region of head, back, and caudal peduncle yellowish brown, dark olive, or slate gray; lower sides and belly cream white. Transverse light bands behind head and across back behind dorsal fin. Dorsal, caudal, and anal fins generally dark edged; other fins light edged. Paired fins often with dark pigment near base. Upper barbels dark pigmented; chin barbels white to light pigmented.

DISTRIBUTION, STATUS, AND HABITAT
In Wisconsin, the slender madtom occurs in the Rock and Pecatonica river systems, where it is at the northern limit of its distribution.

An early Wisconsin record of the slender madtom (USNM 1420) from the Root River in the Lake Michigan basin is doubted (Taylor 1969). Some confusion seems to have been associated with this report, and the specimens are not available.

Specimens examined: UWSP 5150 (4) Oconomowoc River T8N R18E Sec 19 (Waukesha County), 1975; UWSP 5151 (5) and 5344 (5) Bark River T8N R18E Sec 26 (Waukesha County), 1975; UWSP 5578 (30) Oconomowoc River T8N R18E Sec 19 (Waukesha County), 1977.

Taylor (1969) reported USNM 1412 Oconomowoc River, Lac La Belle; INHS (Cahn coll.) Honey Creek, tributary to Rock River, Watertown. The Wisconsin Fish Distribution Study during 1974–1977 made 19 collections of this species from Darien Creek, Little Turtle Creek, Bark River, Rock River, Oconomowoc River, and Mason Creek in the Rock River system; and 12 collections in East Branch Richland Creek (Illinois site), Dodge Branch, Unnamed Creek, Otter Creek, Wood Branch, Bonner Branch, Cottage Inn Branch, Pedler Creek, Mineral Point Branch, Livingston Branch, and the Pecatonica River in the Pecatonica River system.

Additional reports: Oconomowoc River at Stonebank (Waukesha County), and twice from Mukwonago River (Waukesha County) (Cahn 1927); (3) Bark River T5N R15E Sec 11 (Jefferson County) (T. Engel, pers. comm.); Oconomowoc River T8N R18E Sec 19 SE ¼ (Waukesha County), 1973 (M. Johnson, pers. comm.).

The slender madtom is rare in the upper Pecatonica basin, and rare to uncommon in the Bark and

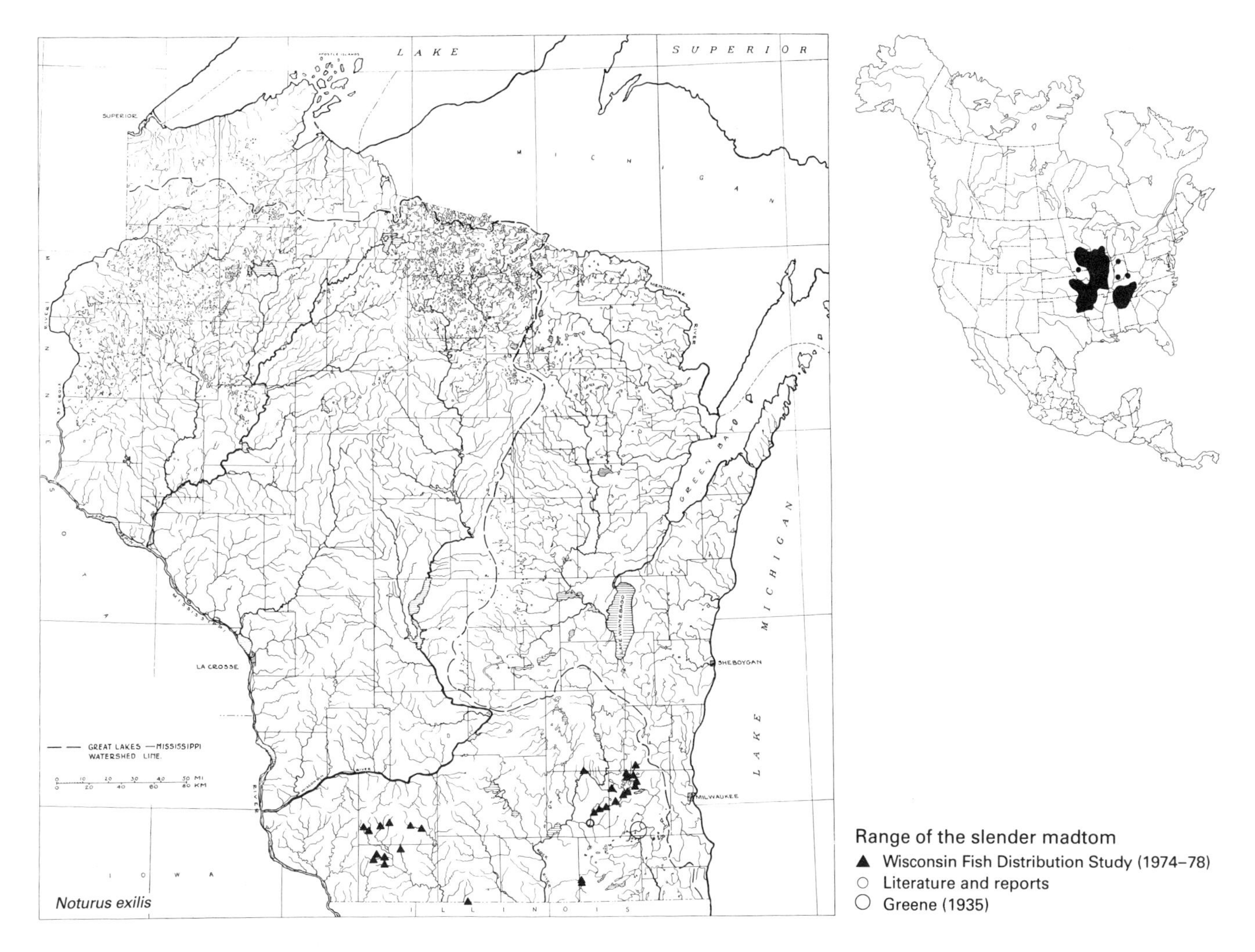

Range of the slender madtom
▲ Wisconsin Fish Distribution Study (1974–78)
○ Literature and reports
◯ Greene (1935)

Oconomowoc rivers of the Rock River system. It has been accorded endangered status in Wisconsin (Les 1979).

In Wisconsin, the slender madtom is generally encountered in clear, moderate to swift water, at depths of 1–3 dm (4–12 in) over substrates of gravel and boulders interspersed with fine sand. It occurs in streams 9–12 m wide; however, a few records from large rivers support the concept that it may occur in large rivers where the current and the substrate are suitable. In Missouri, Pflieger (1971) noted that the slender madtom occurs in rocky pools where there is sufficient current to keep the bottom free of silt; and in Kansas (Cross 1967) it is sometimes found in deep leaf-litter of calm pools, if their waters remain clear and cool.

BIOLOGY

In Wisconsin, spawning occurs in late May and in June. The spawning habits of the slender madtom are not known, but are probably like those of the closely related margined madtom, *Noturus insignis* (Richardson). The margined madtom deposits a compact mass (up to 55 mm diam) of large, adhesive eggs in a nesting cavity which has been excavated beneath a flat rock 0.3 m diam or larger (Fowler 1917). The nest is positioned in such a manner that a current of water can percolate through the egg mass. The eggs apparently are cared for by the male. Newly hatched young crowd together in a constantly moving compact mass.

A prespawning slender madtom female, 106 mm and 16.99 g, taken 14 May from the Oconomowoc River (Waukesha County), had ovaries 5.5% of the body weight, and held 160 light yellow immature eggs, 1.7–2.5 mm diam. A 114-mm, 19.2-g fish had 181 eggs, 2.0 mm diam. A 106-mm, 16.55-g female in spawning readiness, taken on 28 May from the Bark River (Waukesha County), had ovaries 18.6% of the body weight, and held 169 mature eggs, 3.5 mm diam and yellow-orange in color.

Slender madtoms, collected on 14 May 1977 from

the Oconomowoc River (Waukesha County), showed the following growth (Paruch 1979):

Age Class	No. of Fish	TL (mm) Avg	Range	Calculated TL at Annulus (mm) 1	2	3
I	6	76.3	74–81	69.6		
II	6	99.7	88–113	42.4	99.7	
III	18	111.7	96–126	37.9	71.9	111.7
Avg (weighted)				45.2	78.9	111.7

Age-I and age-II fish each had condition (K_{TL}) means of 1.31, and age-III fish had a condition mean of 1.22 (1.04–1.62).

The largest Wisconsin specimen seen was a 126-mm (5-in) slender madtom from the Oconomowoc River sample. The largest slender madtom known was a specimen retained in an aquarium at the Museum of Zoology, University of Michigan, for 1½ years; it had attained 113 mm SL (estimated 132 mm TL) (Taylor 1969).

The slender madtom is insectivorous. In late May, the stomach contents of a fish from the Bark River contained mostly caddisflies, a trace of midgeflies, unidentifiable insects parts, filamentous algae, and debris. In aquariums this species will take a variety of foods, including earthworms, insect larvae, and dry rations. According to Miller and Robison (1973), it hides under stones and in weeds during the day, venturing forth after dark to feed on insect larvae and other small animals.

Several slender madtoms were studied in a large aquarium in the Museum of Natural History at Stevens Point, Wisconsin. In one end of the aquarium, a number of large stones was heaped up. Each of the six madtoms selected a niche for itself among the stones, and seldom ventured from this except when food was introduced into the aquarium. When one slender madtom followed food into another's occupied den, there was a struggle for at least a piece of the worm (W. Paruch, pers. comm.). The fish chased and nipped one another when territorial rights were violated.

With the lights on in the room and the aquarium bathed in light, there was little activity among the fish. Normally, each individual rested quietly in its crevice, and only at long intervals shifted its position. Sometimes a fish assumed a rigid headstand or tailstand position for 15–30 min or more, using a vertical side of a rock as a prop. An individual fish in physiological distress would swim frantically up and down the side of the aquarium opposite the mound of rocks, and, within hours, or up to a few days later, such fish died.

With the lights extinguished in the museum and the aquarium in darkness, the slender madtoms swam from their holes and soon cleaned up food from the floor of the aquarium just as they entered open shallows to feed during the night in their native waters. Bunting and Irwin (1965) noted that daylight seining for madtoms proved ineffective because the fish were located on the bottom among rocks and debris at that time; but at night, when madtoms moved into open water, more than 600 specimens were taken.

When the aquarium lights were turned on late at night, there was a frantic flurry of activity. Some individuals headed directly for the mound of stones, but others swam violently from one side of the aquarium to the other, their unscaled bodies undulating from side to side like oversized tadpoles. An occasional individual, totally disoriented, swam the entire length of the 50-gallon aquarium, and at full speed struck the glass with such a thud that it could be heard the length of the museum. On several occasions, an individual knocked itself senseless for a few seconds.

According to Bunting and Irwin (1965), during a holding period of 20 days, a number of slender madtoms died when the aeration pump stopped for 24 hours during a power failure. When aeration was reestablished, surviving specimens were in poor condition but recovered within a few hours.

When subjected to toxicity bioassay, using petroleum refinery effluent as a toxicant, the slender madtom exhibited little reaction to the test solutions. Only when the toxic concentrations were high was there an initial and brief distress.

IMPORTANCE AND MANAGEMENT

Predation on the slender madtom by fish or wading birds is probably low because of its secretive daytime habits. It may be more vulnerable at night when it leaves cover. However, the slender madtom can maneuver and swim quickly for short distances, and probably elude most pursuers. For their size, these madtoms are fast swimmers and quite energetic.

The slender madtom is much too small to be used as a food fish for people, although it is occasionally taken with worms on small hooks.

Several authors agree that the slender madtom is an interesting, adaptable aquarium fish. "Its loach-like form, serpentine swimming-motions, and odd poses when at rest add to its interest as a novelty in aquaria" (Cross 1967).

Stonecat

Noturus flavus Rafinesque. *Noturus*—back tail, in reference to the connection between the adipose and the caudal fins; *flavus*—yellow.

Other common names: yellow stonecat, stone catfish, stonecat madtom, catfish, white cat, doogler, beetle-eye, mongrel bullhead, deepwater bullhead.

Adult 162 mm, mouth of Plover R. (Portage Co.), 9 July 1958

DESCRIPTION

Body elongate, cylindrical anteriorly, slightly compressed posteriorly. Length 127–152 mm (5–6 in). TL = 1.18 SL. Depth into TL 4.6–7.8. Head length into TL 4.1–4.7. Snout pointed, fleshy; barbels arising from collar surrounding posterior nostrils, with tips reaching beyond middle of eyes. Mouth short but wide, horizontal; lips thick and fleshy. Lower jaw shorter than upper jaw; longest barbel (less than half of head length) attached to upper jaw at each corner of mouth; 4 barbels (outer 2 almost as long as the upper jaw barbels, inner 2 about ⅔ length of outer barbels) attached in a transverse line on the lower chin. Numerous small, sharp, or peglike teeth in broad bands on upper and lower jaws; tooth patch on upper jaw with elongate lateral backward extensions. Dorsal fin origin decidedly in advance of midpoint between pectoral and pelvic fins; dorsal fin swollen at base, dorsal fin with a short spine (¼–⅓ fin height) and 6–7 rays; dorsal adipose fin long, low, continuous with caudal fin and delimited from it by a shallow notch. Anal fin rays 15–18; pelvic fin rays 8–10. Pectoral fin spine short (¼–⅔ fin length), strongly notched on its anterior edge from tip of spine to more than half of its length; posterior edge of spine smooth and barbless; poison gland opening by pore above base of pectoral fin (Scott and Crossman 1973, Reed 1907). Caudal fin roughly rectangular in shape. Scaleless. Lateral line incomplete. Digestive tract coiled, about 1.3 TL. Chromosomes 2n = 48–50 (LeGrande 1978).

Dorsal region of head, back, and upper caudal peduncle brown to slate gray; sides yellow-brown; belly yellowish to whitish. Light rectangular patch between back of head and origin of dorsal fin; small light patch immediately posterior to base of dorsal fin. Pelvic fins generally unpigmented; all other fins lightly to heavily pigmented and light edged. Upper barbels lightly pigmented to mottled; chin barbels whitish.

DISTRIBUTION, STATUS, AND HABITAT

In Wisconsin, the stonecat occurs in all three drainage basins. It is well distributed in streams within the southern one-third of the Mississippi River drainage in Wisconsin, and northward it appears in widely separated streams within the drainage systems of the Wisconsin, Black, and Chippewa rivers. In the Lake Superior basin, it appears mostly in the mouths of tributaries to the lake. In the Lake Michigan basin, disjunct populations occur in the Wolf, upper Fox, Milwaukee, and Root river systems. There are no records of the stonecat from Lakes Superior and Michigan. Because of its rubble-type habitat, this species is seldom captured by seine; the usual method is by electrofishing.

The stonecat is common in tributaries to Lake Superior (Moore and Braem 1965, McLain et al. 1965). In the southern two-thirds of Wisconsin, it is uncommon to common in medium-sized streams of moderate current. Its status is secure.

In Wisconsin, the stonecat was encountered most frequently in clear water at depths of 0.6–1.5 m, over substrates of gravel (34% frequency), rubble (24%), sand (12%), boulders (10%), mud (8%), silt (6%), clay (4%), and bedrock (2%). It occurs in moderate to fast current in riffles, in pools, and around the rock pilings of bridge abutments. It is found in streams of the following widths: 1.0–3.0 m (4%), 3.1–6.0 m (44%), 6.1–12.0 m (20%), 12.1–24.0 m (16%) 24.1–50.1 m (16%), and over 50 m (occasional). The crevices among rock slabs which have been loosely placed together to form a bank riprap, serve as habitat niches for this species. Its typical habitat is a stream with many large, loose rocks.

This species has been reported from Saginaw Bay in Lake Huron and from Lake Erie, where it occurs from shallows along the shore to depths of 9 m or more (Fish 1932, Scott and Crossman 1973), in areas where there is a minimum of current but much wave action (Taylor 1969).

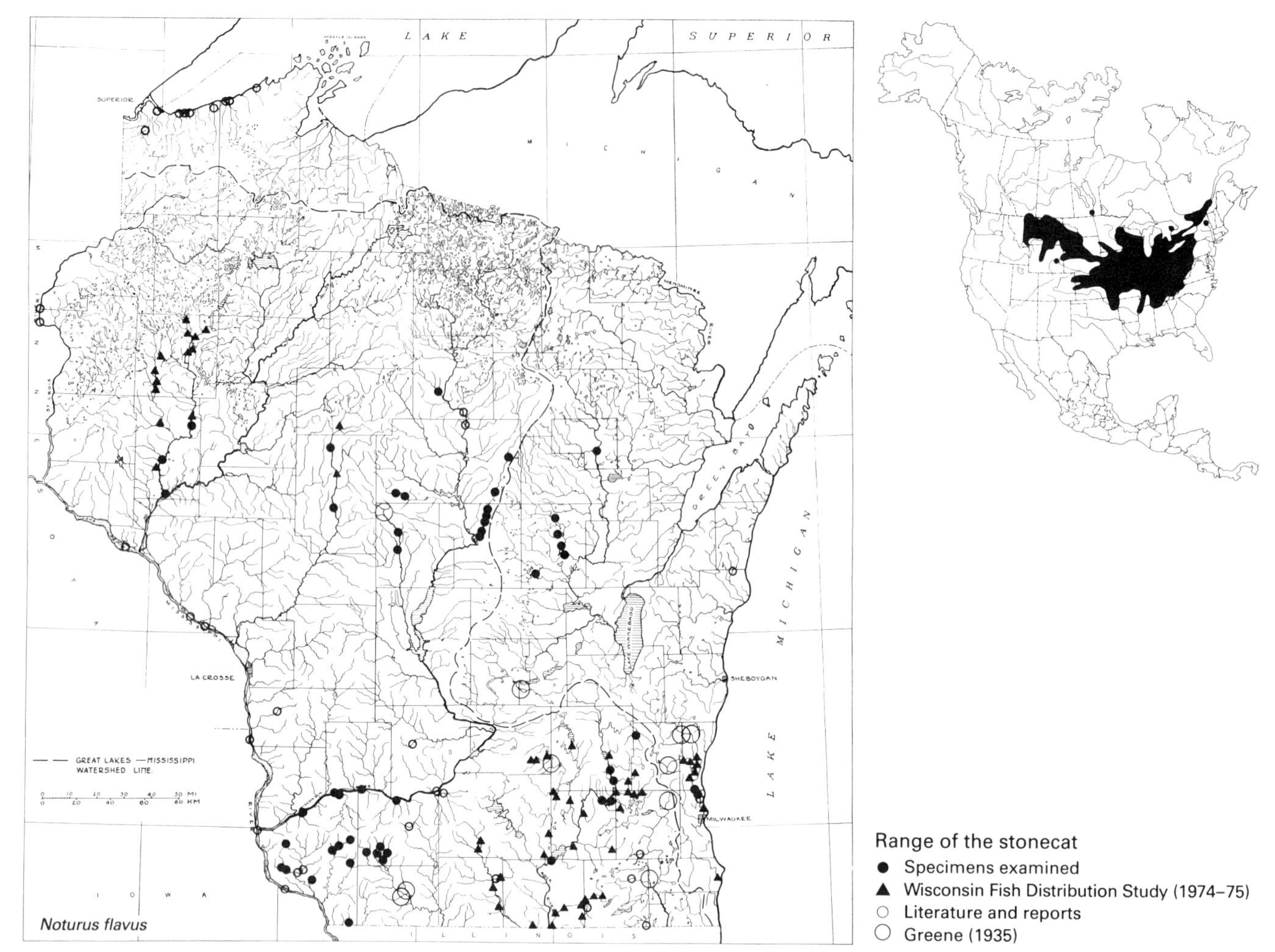

BIOLOGY

In Wisconsin, the stonecat probably spawns in June or July, and possibly continues to spawn as late as August. Spawning begins when the water temperature reaches 27.8°C (82°F). The eggs are placed under stones, and are guarded by one or both parents.

In New York state, Greeley (1929) found two egg masses under flat stones on 13 July at a water temperature of 27.8°C. Two fishes, probably the parents, guarded one mass, and a male was hidden beneath the other. About 500 yellow, opaque eggs, 3.5–4.0 mm diam, were held together in a round mass by an adhesive jelly. In western Lake Erie, stonecats spawn in early June on bouldery shoals, or in the lowermost riffles of tributary rivers (Langlois 1954). The females had well-developed eggs on 27 June; each female held from 767 to 1,205 eggs.

M. Fish (1932) described and illustrated the 20-mm stage. In the Wisconsin River (Richland County), 14 young-of-year averaged 47 (21–61) mm TL in mid-August, and on the Platte River (Grant County), a single young fish was 32 mm TL on 24 September.

The age and growth of 74 stonecats from Wisconsin (UWSP specimens), aged by analysis of the pectoral spines, are summarized below (Paruch 1979):

Age Class	No. of Fish	TL (mm) Avg	TL (mm) Range	Calculated TL at Annulus (mm) 1	2	3	4	5
0	27	46	29–83					
I	20	102	49–142	55				
II	19	148	88–173	48	100			
III	5	159	146–169	42	88	124		
IV	1	199		54	90	145	163	
V	2	187	185–188	51	72	114	147	162
Avg (weighted)				51	95	124	152	162

In 10 stonecats, collected 9 August from Kuenster Creek (Grant County, the total lengths calculated, to the annuli were: 1—52.9 mm; 2—96.4 mm; and 3—102.9 mm (Paruch 1979).

In the Vermillion River, South Dakota (Carlson 1966), the stonecat averages 79 mm TL at the end of its first year of life, and attains lengths of 99, 114, and 137 mm by the ends of succeeding years. The largest specimen examined was 196 mm, and was in its seventh year of life.

In Ohio streams (Gilbert 1953), the calculated standard lengths of stonecats according to an analysis of the vertebrae were: 1—54mm; 2—73 mm; 3—89 mm; 4—104 mm; 5—116 mm; and 6—129 mm. In Lake Erie, the yearly growth was somewhat greater: 1—68 mm; 2—121 mm; 3—162 mm; 4—181 mm; 5—195 mm; 6—203 mm; 7—208 mm; 8—224 mm; and 9—237 mm. The more rapid growth in Lake Erie was believed to be due to the abundance of mayfly naiads as food. No difference in the growth of the sexes was noted.

The maximum known size for a stonecat is 312 mm (12.3 in) and 482 g (1 lb 1 oz) (Trautman 1957).

The food of the stonecat consists of aquatic insects, mollusks, minnows, crayfishes, and plant materials. In Iowa (Harrison 1950) the stonecat ate the following items: aquatic riffle insects (64% of volume); fish, including spotfin shiners, common shiners, and a bullhead minnow (14%); crayfish and earthworms (9%); filamentous algae and weed seeds of terrestrial origin (7%); and undetermined organic matter (5%). In Missouri, Pflieger (1975) found that stonecats consumed the immature stages of various riffle-dwelling insects, supplemented with an occasional darter or other small fish.

Stonecats seek food by their sense of smell or taste, and they use their barbels as they cruise along close to the bottom. They probably feed at night. During feeding, they may work their way into quiet water (Taylor 1969).

Compared to most other members of the family, the stonecat is a solitary catfish. During the warmer months stonecats may become common on riffles or shoals. As colder weather approaches, however, most stream stonecats leave the riffles and migrate to water as deep as 2.4 m (8 ft) (Gilbert 1953); only a few scattered individuals remain behind. As warm weather approaches, they again return to the riffles.

The stonecat tolerates pollution and oxygen depletion which few other fish can survive. Although a relatively northern species of *Noturus*, the stonecat is seldom found in water cold enough to maintain salmonids. In southern Ontario, a single stonecat was taken in association with the brook trout at an average water temperature of 15.7°C (60.3°F), but it occured more commonly with the rock bass and smallmouth bass at water temperatures of 20.7–21.5°C (69.3–70.6°F) (Hallam 1959).

In warmwater streams of southern Ontario with typical water temperatures of 23.9–26.7°C (75–80°F) during the summer months, the stonecat was an important member of a white sucker–blacknose dace–creek chub–common shiner association (M. G. Johnson 1965). In three stream sections studied, there were 58–410 stonecats per hectare, representing standing crops of 0.34–3.70 kg/ha (0.3–3.3 lb/acre).

In Kuenster Creek (Grant County), 10 stonecats were associated with these species: white sucker (+), central stoneroller (26+), hornyhead chub (26+), creek chub (1), bluntnose minnow (2), suckermouth minnow (19), common shiner (23), rosyface shiner (1), bigmouth shiner (1), johnny darter (1), fantail darter (18), and smallmouth bass (4).

IMPORTANCE AND MANAGEMENT

Although the stonecat is not subject to much predation, it has been eaten by smallmouth bass and a by a watersnake (Scott and Crossman 1973). In some areas, the stonecat is said to be of considerable importance as food for the smallmouth bass, and its level of abundance becomes an excellent index of smallmouth bass abundance (Trautman 1957). There exists a report of a healthy brown trout, 381 mm (15 in) long, that had disgorged a 100-mm (4-in), partially digested stonecat (Walden 1964).

The stonecat is used as channel and flathead catfish bait by anglers fishing the lower Wisconsin River. Adams and Hankinson (1926) noted its value as a bass bait. On the Ohio River prior to 1925, commercial fishermen caught it in numbers to be used as trotline bait.

Jones (1964) has written of the stonecat, "Often mistaken for the black bullhead, the stonecat is a fair food fish and is taken in numbers by youthful fishermen who consider the sting of its poisonous spine inconsequential." Because of its secretive, nocturnal habits, the stonecat is not often seen, but like many fish it will go after a tempting bait that comes along during the day. Although it is of little value as a commercial fish or a sport fish, the flesh of the stonecat is excellent (Greeley 1929).

Flathead Catfish

Pylodictis olivaris (Rafinesque). *Pylodictis*—mud fish; *olivaris*—olive colored.

Other common names: flathead, Mississippi bullhead, Mississippi cat, Hoosier, goujon, shovelnose cat, shovelhead cat, mudcat, yellow cat, Johnny cat, Morgan cat, flatbelly, Appaluchion, pied cat, Opelousas cat, granny cat.

(Forbes and Richardson 1920:180)

DESCRIPTION

Body elongate, head and body depressed dorsoventrally. Length 508–762 mm (20–30 in). TL = 1.15 SL in adults; 1.21 SL in young-of-year. Depth into TL 5.3–7.6. Head broadly flattened; head length into TL 3.4–3.8. Snout pointed in lateral view; barbels arising from collar surrounding posterior nostrils and tips of barbels scarcely reaching back of eye. Mouth short but wide, horizontal. Lower jaw protruding beyond upper jaw; long barbel (almost reaching edge of opercular flap) attached to upper jaw at each corner of mouth; 4 barbels (outer 2 about ½ length of maxillary barbels, inner 2 decidedly shorter) attached on chin. Numerous small, sharp teeth in broad bands on upper and lower jaws; tooth patch on upper jaw with elongate lateral backward extensions. Dorsal fin origin barely in advance of midpoint between pectoral and pelvic fins; dorsal fin spine about ½ fin height; dorsal fin rays usually 6; dorsal adipose fin long (almost as long as depressed dorsal fin), separated from caudal fin and forming a free, flaplike lobe. Anal fin rays 14–16; pelvic fin rays 9; pectoral fin spine ½ to ⅔ fin length, saw-edged both anteriorly and posteriorly; caudal fin straight and slightly notched posteriorly, not forked. Scaleless. Lateral line complete. Digestive tract about 1.0 into TL. Chromosomes 2n = 56 (LeGrande 1978).

Color variable with size and habitat. Dorsal region of head, back, and sides light brown to yellow, mottled with dark brown or black (mottling tending to disappear in adults from turbid water); ventral region of head and belly yellowish to cream colored. Caudal fin darkly pigmented, except upper lobe, which has a distinct white patch along dorsal border (white patch disappears with age); other fins pigmented like adjacent parts of body. All barbels slightly to darkly pigmented. Young more contrastingly colored than adults.

Sexual dimorphism: In males, a single urogenital opening behind anus; in females, two openings urinary and genital; these openings more pronounced in adults than in young, especially during spawning season (Moen 1959).

Hybrids: Experimental flathead catfish × channel catfish, flathead catfish × yellow bullhead, flathead catfish × blue catfish, flathead catfish × white catfish (Sneed 1964, Dupree et al. 1966).

DISTRIBUTION, STATUS, AND HABITAT

In Wisconsin, the flathead catfish occurs in the Mississippi River and Lake Michigan drainage basins. In the Mississippi basin, it is known from the St. Croix, Red Cedar, Chippewa, La Crosse, Wisconsin, Pecatonica, and Sugar river systems. It reaches the northern limit of its distribution in the St. Croix River. According to Cahn (1927), the flathead catfish was taken from the Mississippi River overflows and introduced into Oconomowoc and Nagawicka lakes. The introduced fish did not spawn and are undoubtedly extirpated. In the Lake Michigan basin, this species occurs in the lower Wolf and upper Fox rivers and in their lakes. Greene (1935) did not report this species from the Lake Michigan drainage, and the possibility exists that he overlooked it in his survey. It probably entered the Lake Michigan drainage via the Fox-Wisconsin crossover connection or the canal at Portage.

In Wisconsin, the flathead catfish is rare to common in the Mississippi River and in the lower portions of its major tributaries. Priegel (1967a) listed it as common in Lake Winnebago. It is uncommon to common in sectors of the lower Wolf River and the upper Fox River.

In comparing his results on the Mississippi River with the earlier findings of Barnickol and Starrett (1951), Schoumacher (1968) concluded that flathead catfish are being exploited quite heavily by commercial fishermen. Many fishermen feel that fewer fish, especially large fish, are being taken now as compared with past years.

Little is known about the biology and the population structure of the flathead catfish in Wisconsin. To ensure sustained fishing and a viable population, a long-term, active research program is advised.

Young flathead catfish are often found among rocks on riffles, occupying the same habitat as the riffle-dwelling madtoms. Adults occur in deep pools cre-

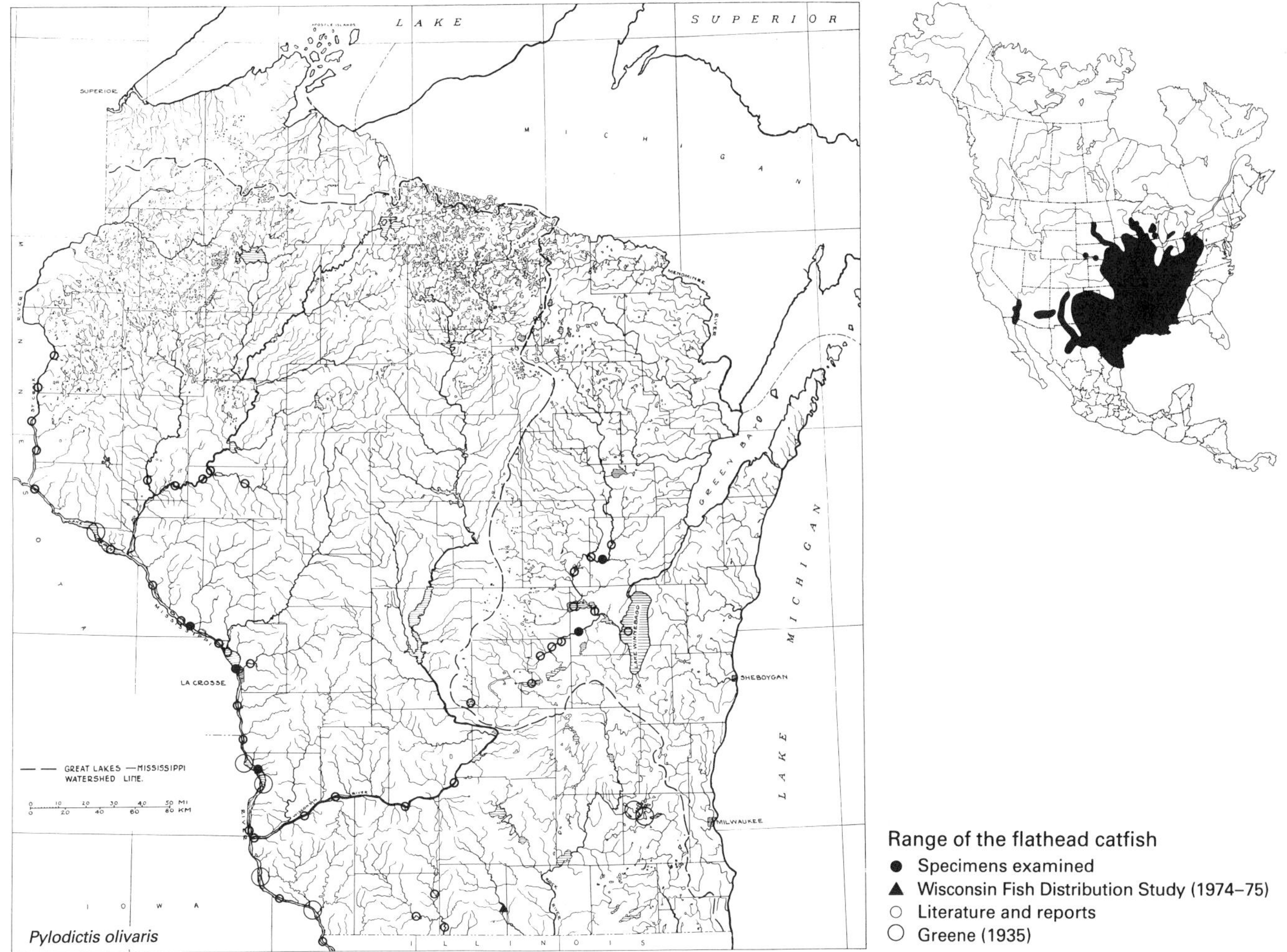

ated by swirling currents. Cross (1967) found: "Many such pools now exist below concrete aprons of low dams, and adjacent to bridge-supports that trap driftwood. Such obstructions in the channel disrupt the streaming flow of the current, leaving deep pockets in the otherwise shallow beds. . . ." The flathead catfish prefers tangled timber, piles of drift, or other cover.

BIOLOGY

The spawning of the flathead catfish takes place in June and July in secluded shelters and dark places. Spawning occurs at water temperatures of 22.2–23.9°C (72–75°F). A large nest is built. Cross (1967) reported finding a bank nest that had been dug into a steep clay bank with an entrance about 355 mm (14 in) diam, which widened to 813 mm (32 in) inside the nest chamber. The bottom of the nest was silt free, and there was a ridge of clean gravel at the entrance.

Nest construction was observed at the Shedd Aquarium, Chicago (W. Chute in Breder and Rosen 1966). Both male and female (about 1.2 m long) used their tails and mouths to make a hollow in the sand down to the bare gravel and rock in one corner of the tank; the completed nest was approximately 1.5 m diam.

Spawning was witnessed in the Dallas Aquarium (Fontaine 1944:50–51):

> As breeding approached the male was often seen with the female, swimming over and beside her, gently rubbing his belly on her back and sides. His barbels apparently had some effect as they were brought into play almost constantly as he rubbed her. There was no apparent change in color during spawning, such as has been observed in many other species of fish. Presently the male came to rest on the bottom with his caudal peduncle and caudal fin encircling the head of the female. There was then a strong quivering movement on the part of the male. This was repeated from time to time and was observed at irregular intervals for almost two weeks. When the female was ready to spawn she began to deposit her eggs in a depression in the gravel that she and the male had prepared, behind an old tree stump on the ledge to the rear of the tank. The female expelled the eggs in masses of 30 to 50 which were

then fertilized by the male. At this time the two fish lay side by side, with heads in the same direction, turning their bellies together. At times the female quit the nest for a few minutes while the male fluffed and arranged the eggs. During this observation the egg-laying was carried out in about four and one-half hours. Within an hour after the female had quit spawning she was removed from the tank, as past experience had shown that she would crush or eat the eggs. The male took up guard over the nest at once.

Observers of flathead catfish spawning noted that when the male settled over the mass of eggs after spawning, he ventilated them strongly with his ventral fins, created a current of water with his anal fin, and fluffed the eggs by lifting the egg mass with his ventral fins; he also turned the eggs in a half-arc by using his mouth or ventral fins to move the egg mass, and by slipping his caudal fin under the egg mass he gave it a good shaking in a movement much more violent than one would expect to see. The male continued to drive away the female or any other fish coming near the nest: he fought fishes of his own size or smaller and gently eased the larger fishes away.

In Texas hatchery pens, the males were vicious while guarding eggs, and would "tear the female to pieces" if she attempted to enter the spawning jar containing the eggs (Henderson 1965). Henderson also noted that a number of females that had spawned had been killed by the male, even though laboratory workers tried to remove the female as soon as possible.

The egg mass of the flathead catfish in the Shedd Aquarium contained an estimated 100,000 eggs. The size of the flathead catfish spawn varies, depending on the size of the female. Snow (1959) reported an egg mass which weighed slightly less than 1,089 g (2.4 lb), and contained about 15,000 eggs. In small hatchery-reared brood fish, the spawns numbered from 3,000 to 5,000 eggs (Henderson 1965). In Kansas, three females, 305–610 mm TL, held 6,900–11,300 eggs, averaging 2.8–3.2 mm diam (Minckley and Deacon 1959).

In Oklahoma, estimates of the fecundity of flathead catfish ranged from 4,076 to 31,579 eggs for fish 1.05–11.66 kg (Summerfelt and Turner 1971). Ripe eggs averaged 3.7 mm diam. Forty-five percent of the sexually mature females probably did not spawn, and mature eggs of the unspawned females were resorbed.

Giudice (1965) reported that the hatching of flathead catfish eggs occurred in 6–7 days at 23.9–27.8°C (75–82°F); Snow (1959), reported hatching in 9 days at 24–25.9°C (75–78.6°F), into fry which were about 11 mm long.

The male flathead continues to guard the young after hatching. The young remain tightly schooled for several days while the large yolk-sac is being absorbed. Cross (1967) noted that by mid-June the young leave the nest, and are afterward found mostly on shallow riffles, beneath stones or other cover. Young-of-year flathead catfish feed mainly on aquatic insect larvae, including Chironomidae, Ephemeroptera, and Trichoptera.

The age and growth of flathead catfish are determined in most studies by analyzing the rings on sections of the pectoral spines. From one to three early annuli are missing on some of the spines from larger fish (Muncy 1957).

In the Mississippi River bordering Iowa (Schoumacher 1968), flathead catfish, ages II to XVI, demonstrated the following growth: II—356 mm; III—406 mm; IV—462 mm; V—533 mm; VI—556 mm; VII—686 mm; VIII—663 mm; IX—655 mm; X—620 mm; XI—734 mm; and XVI—864 mm. In an earlier study (Barnickol and Starrett 1951) of catfish from the Iowa-Illinois sections of the Mississippi River, the growth in older flatheads appeared to be substantially greater: I—193 mm; II—297 mm; III—373 mm; IV—429 mm; V—490 mm; VI—561 mm; VII—608 mm; VIII—795 mm; IX—895 mm; X—838 mm; XI—902 mm; XIII—940 mm; and XIV—978 mm.

A 1.12-m, 24.95-kg (44.1-in, 55-lb) flathead catfish, caught 23 August 1974 from the Fox River at Eureka (Winnebago County), had the following calculated lengths for each year of growth: 1—109 mm; 2—234 mm; 3—404 mm; 4—497 mm; 5—528 mm; 6—559 mm; 7—606 mm; 8—652 mm; 9—683 mm; 10—698 mm; 11—745 mm; 12—776 mm; 13—833 mm; 14—884 mm; 15—962 mm; 16—976 mm; 17—1,008 mm; 18—1,024 mm; 19—1,040 mm; 20—1,048 mm; 21—1,063 mm; 22—1,071 mm; 23—1,087 mm; and 24—1,100 mm (Paruch 1979).

In Oklahoma (Turner and Summerfelt 1971), the average K_{TL} for 124 females and 90 males was 1.30 and 1.25 respectively.

Carlander (1969) noted that the growth of flathead catfish was more rapid on shallow mud flats than in clear rocky areas. Minckley and Deacon (1959) suggested that in Kansas the flathead catfish grew faster in the Big Blue River than in the Neosho River, because it fed on fish at an early age.

In the Mississippi River, flathead catfish mature at ages IV or V (Barnickol and Starrett 1951). The size at maturity varies considerably: a few are mature at 381 mm (15 in), but most are not mature until they reach 457 mm (18 in). According to Minckley and Deacon (1959), the loss of the light patch at the tip of the upper lobe of the caudal fin may indicate sexual maturity.

Large flathead catfish are reported yearly from Wisconsin. In the Lake Michigan basin, individuals weighing 9.1–18.1 kg (20–40 lb) are common. A 27.7-kg (61-lb) fish was caught from the Fox River at Eureka (Winnebago County) in 1966. In the Mississippi River, commercial fishermen have reported specimens as large as 1.5 m (5 ft) and 45.4 kg (100 lb) (Harlan and Speaker 1956). In 1911, two flathead catfish weighing 53.5 and 56.7 kg (118 and 125 lb) were reported caught on setlines (Bachay 1944).

In Wisconsin, a 419-mm (16.5-in) channel catfish was taken from the stomach of an 18.1-kg (40-lb) flathead from the Pecatonica River, and a 457-mm (18-in) northern pike was taken from the stomach of a 7.26-kg (16-lb) flathead from Lake Puckaway. Unlike the channel catfish, the flathead is not a scavenger; it rarely eats dead or decaying matter. Stomachs usually contain small quantities of debris consisting of mud, sand, gravel, pieces of wood, and leaves. Bullhead and channel catfish spines have been found imbedded in the stomach wall or mesenteries of flathead catfish.

In flathead catfish measuring more than 250 mm (10 in) from the Big Blue River, Kansas (Minckley and Deacon 1959), fishes occurred in 90% of the stomachs that contained food and comprised 79% volume. The ingested fishes identified from Kansas collections were suckers, minnows, channel catfish, madtoms, darters, sunfish, and freshwater drums. In the Neosho River, crayfish constituted a large part of the diet of larger flatheads.

Flathead catfish feed most actively in May and early June, and from July to September; they feed less during the winter months and in late June and early July, when spawning occurs. The flathead is often a passive predator that lies in wait for its victim (Minckley and Deacon 1959:347):

> We twice observed the feeding behavior of a 14-inch specimen in an aquarium. The fish lay motionless, except for slight movements of the eyes and opercles, and allowed the food-fish (*Notropis lutrensis*) to draw near, on one occasion touching the barbels. Then, with a short lunge by the catfish, the minnow was eaten.

Trautman (1957) has observed flathead catfish feeding at night on riffles so shallow that their dorsal fins stuck out of the water; he has also seen them lying on the bottom, usually beside a log or other object, with their mouths wide open. Ohio River fishermen have reported that they have seen frightened fish dart into the open mouths of flatheads, to be swallowed immediately. The large numbers of such hiding species as rock bass, spotted black bass, and small catfishes found in the stomachs of large flatheads lend credence to these statements.

In the Wabash River, Indiana, the optimum temperature range for the flathead catfish was 31.5–33.5°C (89–92°F) (Gammon 1973). Gammon noted that the flathead catfish is sedentary, and that tagging studies suggest that it does not move about enough to encounter the other thermal possibilities. In 1971, electrofishing catches of flathead catfish were uniformly low among nearly all of the zones studied. In the same year the Cayuga power plant began releasing heated effluents into the river which, according to Gammon, was responsible for a "dramatic . . . increase . . . in the density of flathead catfish in the heated zones alone." He reported that in 1972 "the major increase came from large numbers of 100 to 200 mm long fish, presumably the result of a highly successful 1971 year class, the first year class to follow the introduction of heated effluents into the river."

According to Minckley and Deacon (1959), young-of-year flatheads move or are carried from the place of hatching to swift, rubble-bottomed riffles where they remain until they are 51–102 mm (2–4 in) TL. At that size, the young fish become more evenly distributed in the stream; some remain on the original riffles, but more move into pools, deeper riffles, and into almost all other habitats. This random distribution seems to be the rule among fish ranging from 102 mm (4 in) to approximately 305 mm (12 in) long. Large individuals, more than 406 mm (16 in) long, are found near the more massive logs and drift piles, and usually in or near deep holes in the stream bed. A drift pile usually yields only one, or at most two or three adults. Each individual has a favorite resting place where it can be counted on to be each day unless disturbed (Pflieger 1975). In the Mississippi River during the winter, the flatheads go into a "pseudo-hibernation state, embedding themselves in muddy holes in forty to sixty feet of water" (Bachay 1944).

Two out of three flathead catfish, implanted with ultrasonic transmitters and displaced a distance of 1.3–2.7 km (0.8–1.7 mi) from their site of capture, showed a strong tendency to return to the point of release (Hart 1974). Funk (1957) classified the flathead catfish as a semimobile species. He reported that 48.9% of tagged flathead catfish which were recaptured were found less than 1.6 km (1 mi) from the point of tagging; 72.1% were found less than 8.1 km (5 mi) from the point of tagging. No fish was recovered more than 80.7 km (50 mi) from the point of release.

Fighting between members of this species appears to be common. When a female flathead was returned to the tank with a male with which she had spawned previously, the two were soon fighting; after they were separated each returned to its respective place in the tank. However, fighting erupted once more (Fontaine 1944:51):

> . . . It was not until late in the afternoon that day that they started fighting again. After sparring for a few minutes the female backed away from the male a distance of about 18 inches, made one rush and struck him in the side. He rolled over and floated to the surface, belly up. He was removed to a reserve tank and lived for two days then died. An autopsy revealed that the blow had injured his intestine, stomach and several other organs.

IMPORTANCE AND MANAGEMENT

The flathead catfish is not particularly vulnerable to predators because of its rapid growth and secretive habits; however, the survival of 38–51-mm fingerling flatheads stocked in ponds containing adult sunfishes and fathead minnows (*Pimephales promelas*) was low—from 0 to 1.5% (Hackney 1966). In ponds where there were large numbers of crayfish present, the flathead fingerling mortality rate was very high (Henderson 1965).

The flathead catfish is host to the glochidia of a number of freshwater mussels, including *Amblema plicata*, *Megalonaias gigantea*, *Quadrula nodulata*, *Quadrula pustulosa*, *Quadrula quadrina*, and *Elliptio dilatata* (Hart and Fuller 1974).

Along the lower Wisconsin River, the flathead catfish is sometimes called the "candy bar," attesting to the superb flavor and texture of its flesh. It is a much sought-after prize, and some fishermen specialize in catching it by setline or bank pole. The methods used for catching flatheads are similar to those used for taking channel catfish, except that only live or freshly killed baits are effective with the flathead. J. Kincannon (pers. comm.), who kept a record of the flathead catfish he took from the lower Wisconsin River near Blue River (Grant County) from 22 May to 15 June 1963, caught 12 flatheads totalling 79.4 kg (175 lb); they ranged in size from 2.27 to 15.88 kg (5 to 35 lb), and were taken on bullheads and channel catfish up to 330 mm (13 in) long. They were caught along steep, grassy banks where old tree roots and logs were in evidence.

During 1960, on the Wisconsin River between Prairie du Sac and Lone Rock, sport fishermen creeled 11 flathead catfish (averaging 660 mm) out of 3,243 fish caught. Between Lone Rock and the mouth of the Wisconsin River, 16 flatheads (averaging 648 mm) were caught out of a total of 1,528 fish (C. Brynildson 1960). During 1967–1968, in Pools 4, 5, 7, and 11 of the Mississippi River, the estimated sport fishery catch was 1,909 flathead catfish weighing 1,280 kg (2,821 lb) (Wright 1970). Bachay (1944) reported that in a hole below a wing dam near Dresbach (Pool 7), Minnesota, the Kramer brothers took a yearly average of 3.2–4.5 thousand kg (7–10 thousand lb) of flathead catfish on setlines; their largest catch was taken from December through February. During the winter of 1942, the Kramer brothers took more than 5.4 thousand kg (12 thousand lb) of flathead catfish in gill nets.

In the upper Fox River, fishermen fish for flatheads with setlines and bank poles using large white suckers, redhorse suckers, carp, sheepshead, and yellow bullheads on 5/0 and 7/0 hooks. Fishing is done at night from 2000 to 0630 hr. B. Curless (pers. comm.) and another fisherman caught 28 flathead catfish ranging from 4.54 to 19.05 kg (10 to 42 lb) in the vicinity of Berlin (Green Lake County) and Eureka (Winnebago County) between 1 July and 14 September 1973.

In the commercial fishery statistics for the Mississippi River, the flathead catfish is included with the channel catfish under the caption "catfish." The ratio of flathead catfish to channel catfish is very low; in the Iowa waters of the Mississippi River (Schoumacher 1968), it is 1:49.

Some success in the propagation of the flathead catfish has been achieved since the 1950s (Giudice 1965, Henderson 1965, Sneed et al. 1961, and Snow 1959). Snow, citing Swingle, reported that in rearing ponds the flathead catfish grew at a rate of 905 g (2 lb) per year, had an excellent flavor, and appeared promising as a commercial species. Yearling flathead catfish stocked in May at 178 mm (7 in) and 45 g (0.1 lb), averaged 384 mm (15.1 in) and 635 g (1.4 lb) 6 months later (Stevenson 1964). From Oklahoma to Wisconsin, the standing crop of flathead catfish averaged 24.9 kg/ha (22.2 lb/acre); it ranged from 1.6 to 103.6 kg/ha (1.4 to 92.4 lb/acre) (Carlander 1955).

The flathead catfish has for some time been used as a fish-control species. Swingle (1964) noted that large flathead catfish are predatory and in several cases eliminated larger bluegills. Small flatheads (51–127 mm) eliminated almost all fathead minnows, while larger flatheads apparently preferred bluegills to fathead minnows; they eliminated all the large bluegills they could swallow, except for a few in the 178-mm (7-in) group, and left very few bluegills in the 102–152-mm (4–6-in) group. Hackney (1966) noted that 125 large flathead catfish per hectare (50/acre) did not completely correct the balance in a population of stunted bluegills in 320 days.

Pirate Perch Family—Aphredoderidae

A single living species is known for this family, which is of North American origin, and is confined to the fresh waters of the eastern United States. The pirate perch is in the last surviving genus of the family Aphredoderidae. Another genus lived during the Oligocene or Miocene but is now extinct.

The trout-perch and cavefishes (Amblyopsidae) are distant cousins of the pirate perch. Like cavefishes, the pirate perch has its anus and urogenital apertures in the throat region; however, it lacks the adipose fin of the trout-perch.

The pirate perch is a spiny-rayed fish with ctenoid scales bearing a single row of teeth along the exposed edges of the scales. The swim bladder is simple, and the pneumatic duct to the pharynx is lost (physoclist). There are 12 pyloric caeca.

Pirate Perch

Aphredoderus sayanus (Gilliams). *Aphredoderus*—more correctly "Aphododerus," meaning excrement throat (from the position of the vent); *sayanus*—for Thomas Say, the distinguished entomologist.

Common name: Forbes and Richardson (1920) attributed the common name, "pirate perch," to Charles C. Abbott, a pioneer ichthyologist, who observed that a specimen he had in an aquarium ate only other fish.

Adult 67 mm, Wisconsin R. (Sauk Co.), 21 Sept. 1969

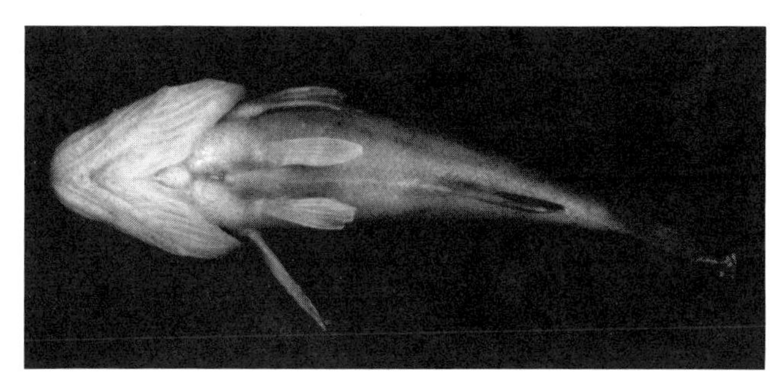

Ventral view. Vent is directly behind throat knob.

DESCRIPTION

Body stout, slightly compressed laterally, elevated at base of dorsal fin; caudal peduncle thick. Length 83–100 mm (3.3–3.9 in). TL = 1.26 SL. Depth into SL 2.8–3.4. Head into SL 2.6–3.0; head broad below, preopercle edge strongly toothed and rough to the touch; strong spine near upper edge of opercle. Snout pointed. Mouth large, oblique, with lower jaw projecting; numerous minute, villiform teeth in wide bands on upper and lower jaws; back of upper jaw reaching to anterior edge of eye. Dorsal fin convex, nearer snout than base of caudal fin, and behind pelvic fins; dorsal fin with 2–3 short spines, 10–11 rays; anal fin 2–3 spines, 6–7 rays; pelvic fins 1 spine, 6 rays. Scales strongly adherent, ctenoid, with a single row of teeth on exposed edges; cheeks and opercles fully scaled. Lateral series scales 48–59; lateral line incomplete, developed anteriorly. The sensory canal system on head is well developed, and consists of relatively large sensory canals and numerous sense organ clusters (see Moore and Burris 1956). Digestive tract 1.2–1.6 SL; in adults, anal opening immediately behind the throat knob.

Back dark olive to black; sides lighter; belly yellowish. In life, specks of iridescent blue (occasionally copper, green, or silver) on back and sides. Two narrow, vertical bars separated by a pale interspace at base of caudal fin. Dorsal and caudal fins slate colored, other fins more lightly pigmented.

Breeding males blackish on head and dorsal half of body, and tinged with violet.

DISTRIBUTION, STATUS, AND HABITAT

In Wisconsin, the pirate perch occurs in the Mississippi River and Lake Michigan drainage basins, where it reaches the northern limit of its distribution. The principal population centers of the species are the lower Mississippi River, the lower Wisconsin River and its tributaries, and the Des Plaines River watershed.

Specimens examined: UWSP 1181 (2) Bear Creek T18N R2E Sec 3 (Richland County), 1962; UWSP (1) Wisconsin River T7N R4W Sec 15 (Grant County), 1962; UWSP 1183 (1) Wisconsin River opposite Boscobel (Crawford County), 1962; UWSP (1) Wisconsin River T8N R3W Secs 23 and 24 (Grant County), 1962; UWSP 1495 (1) Wisconsin River T7N R4W Sec 21 (Grant County), 1966; UWSP 1910 (2) Des Plaines River T1N R21E Sec 4 (Kenosha County), 1968; UWSP 2035 (22) Wisconsin River T11N R9E Sec 6 (Columbia County), 1968; UWSP 3127 (1) Wisconsin River T13N R6E Sec 25 (Sauk County), 1969; UWSP 3772 (1) South Branch, Embarrass River T28N R10E Sec 25 (Marathon County), 1970; UWSP 4345 (1) ditch into Lemonweir River T17N R2E Sec 16 (Juneau County), 1973; UWSP 4393 (1) Yellow River T18N R4E Sec 19 (Juneau County) 1973; UWSP 4401 (1) Lemonweir River T14N R2E Sec 11 and 12 (Juneau County), 1973; UWSP 4441 (1) Lemonweir River T17N R3W Sec 32 (Juneau County), 1973; and UWSP 5617 (1) Lyndon Creek T14N R5E Sec 1 (Juneau County), 1977.

Wisconsin Fish Distribution Study (1974–1978) collections: (1) Kilbourn Road ditch T1N R22E Sec 6 (Kenosha County), 1976; (19) unnamed channel, Black River T17N R8W Sec 17 (La Crosse County), 1978. M. Johnson (pers. comm.) reported this species from the Root River, the Des Plaines River, and Brighton Creek, (Kenosha County), 1965–1968. L. Andrews (pers. comm.) reported it from Swamp Creek below Swamp Lake, and lower Rocky Run Creek near its

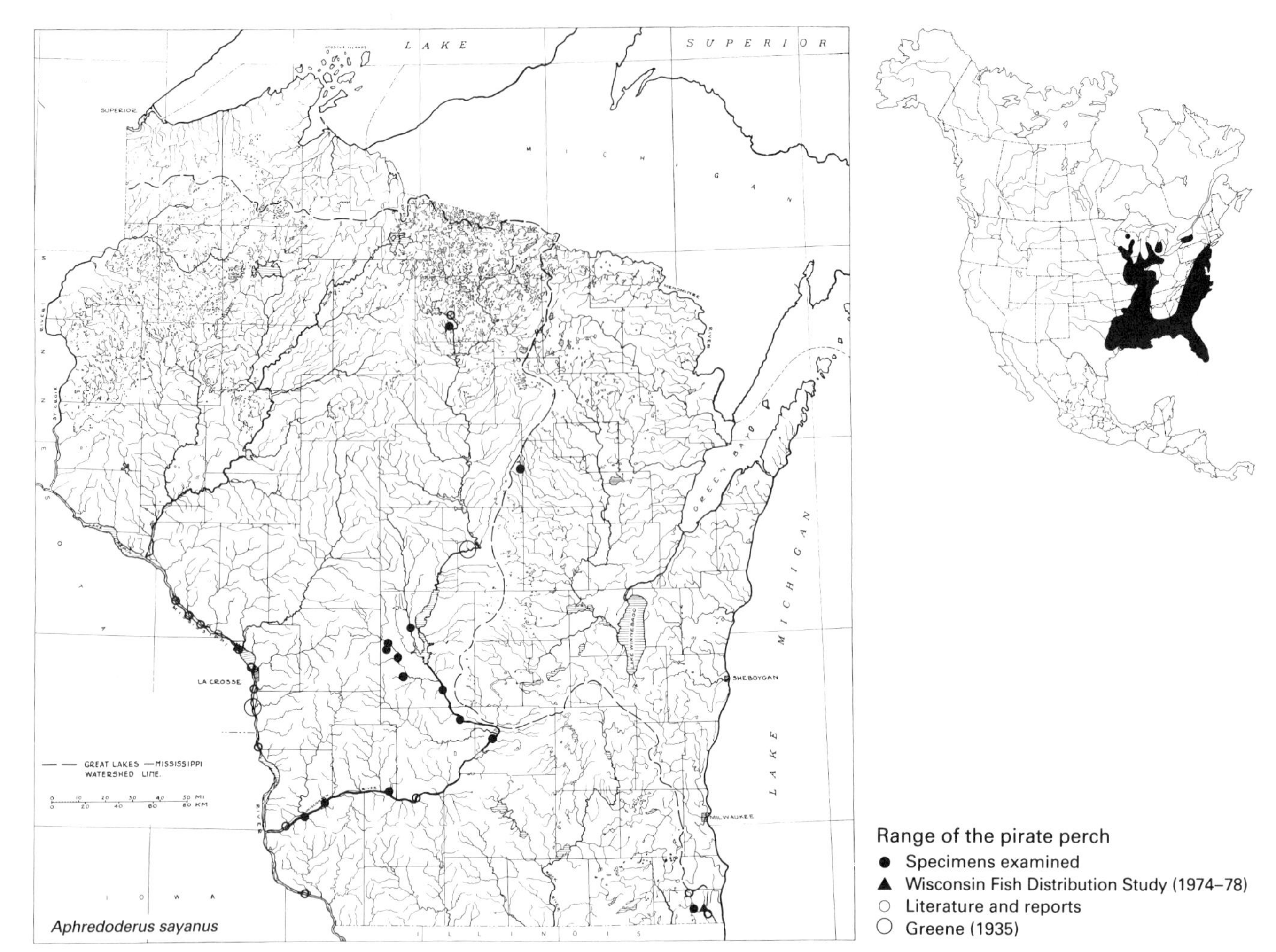

outlet into the Tomahawk River (Oneida County), 1977.

In Wisconsin, the pirate perch is rare to uncommon in sloughs of the Mississippi River, the Wisconsin River and the lower portions of its tributaries, and the Des Plaines River system. Populations are widely separated. It seems probable that the records from the Embarrass River (Marathon County) in the Lake Michigan basin, and from the upper Wisconsin River system (Oneida County), resulted from introductions. This species has been given watch status in Wisconsin. (Wis. Dep. Nat. Resour. Endangered Species Com. 1975, Les 1979).

The pirate perch occurs in oxbows, overflow ponds, sloughs, marshes, ditches, and the pools of low-gradient (0.57 m/km, 3 ft/mi) streams. It is found over sand, or over soft, muck bottoms covered with organic debris. Frequently it is associated with brush piles or dense aquatic vegetation. The streams generally are medium- to large-sized rivers, but occasionally may be creeks less than 3 m wide. This species occurs mostly in quiet water, seldom in a sluggish or stronger current.

The best collection of pirate perch was made with a minnow seine from backwater of the Wisconsin River, which had been flooded less than a week previously. The bottom was a gray, organic muck overlaid with leaves and sticks at depths of 0.6–1.0 m (2–3 ft). No current was discernible.

BIOLOGY

The spawning of the pirate perch occurs in the spring, probably in May. It has been suggested in the literature that the pirate perch builds a nest which is guarded by both parents. However, Pflieger (1975) reasoned that since the urogenital pore is situated on the throat, the eggs are more likely to be incubated in the gill cavities, as they are in some cavefishes whose urogenital pore is similarly located. This concept is supported by the work of Martin and Hubbs (1973), who observed that, as the eggs were expressed from a female pirate perch, they tended to move along a groove into the gill chamber; these authors suggested the possibility of buccal incubation.

At water temperatures of 19–20°C (66.2–68°F), the hatching of pirate perch eggs occurs over 5–6 days (Martin and Hubbs 1973). These authors give developmental details from the time of fertilization to the 10-day larval stage. Forbes and Richardson (1920) observed that the young are protected by the parents until they are about 8 mm (5/16 in) long.

In pirate perch, the anterior shift of the vent is accompanied by a similar shift of the urogenital duct (Mansueti 1963). The shift begins at the preanal fin region in the 9-mm fish, and proceeds progressively forward to the jugular area as the fish grows larger. In Wisconsin, this movement occurs throughout the first growing season, and is completed during the second year of life. On 21 June, the vent is directly posterior to the insertions of the pelvic fins; by 22 September, the vent is anterior to the pelvic fins, about one-fourth the distance from the pelvics to the knob of the throat; by 24 October, the vent is about one-half this distance.

In Wisconsin, young-of-year pirate perch were 21.5 mm by 18 June, 31 mm by 17 July, 44 mm by 28 August, and 49 mm by 24 September.

Twenty-two pirate perch, 51–108 mm TL, collected 1 October 1968 from a Wisconsin River slough (Columbia County), had the following calculated lengths at the annuli: 1—52 mm; 2—85 mm; and 3—103 mm. The K_{TL} averaged 1.73 (1.38–2.28). The largest fish was a female which weighed 19.32 g.

In Oklahoma (Hall and Jenkins 1954), the calculated total lengths of pirate perch at the end of each year of life were: 1—55.8 mm; 2—84.5 mm; 3—101.6 mm; and 4—116.4 mm. The rate of growth was most rapid during the first 2 years of life. In North Carolina (Shepherd and Huish 1978), females were more numerous than males, and grew faster in their second and third years than males.

The largest pirate perch reported, 126 mm (5 in) TL, came from Sub-Prison Lake, Oklahoma (Hall and Jenkins 1954).

The intestinal tracts of two small pirate perch from the Wisconsin River (Columbia County) contained quantities of green algae. The stomachs of larger fish contained ostracods, *Hyallela*, ants, and fish scales (J. Small, pers. comm.).

In a Virginia study (Flemer and Woolcott 1966), the pirate perch had consumed (in decreasing frequency of occurrence): Diptera larvae, Ephemeroptera nymphs, Hemiptera, Amphipoda, Megaloptera larvae, Copepoda, Trichoptera larvae, Decapoda, plant matter, Plecoptera nymphs, Diptera pupae and adults, Odonata nymphs, fishes, Ostracoda, and unidentifiable plant and animal materials.

In nature, the pirate perch is largely insectivorous. Its feeding activity has been described by Parker and Simco (1975: 573–574):

> . . . A high correlation exists between the activity of the food item offered and the willingness of the fish to feed. Very small fish would feed at the surface but only rarely would larger fish do so. The larger fish would readily take earthworms from the bottom and did so by forming a negative pressure in the oral cavity and quickly opening the mouth to pull in the prey. When feeding in this manner fish did not approach the prey directly, but swam along side and then turned the head abruptly as the vacuum pressure was released. Smaller fish did not feed in this manner but instead picked at the food item repeatedly with the mouth.

Richard Howmiller (pers. comm.), who kept pirate perch in an aquarium, suggested that this species probably was rare because it would only take food which was moving and was within 6 mm of its snout.

The pirate perch has the reputation of being a sluggish fish that swims infrequently during the day. Its activity patterns are circadian, and demonstrate the nocturnal nature of this species (Parker and Simco 1975). Its nocturnal activities may be related to its feeding patterns: it becomes active just before dark when many insects and other invertebrates also become active, and its activity peaks at dawn, coinciding with the activity of a large number of possible prey organisms. The activity of the pirate perch is largely restricted to the bottom. Quinn (1976) observed that the pirate perch is "a creature of the night in search of prey."

During the day pirate perch have been observed to pass a considerable time at rest, with their heads upstream, their large dorsal fins expanded, their caudal fins partly closed, and their pectorals moving slowly (Becker 1923). Parker and Simco (1975) noted that pirate perch always sought cover, such as rocks, limbs, or plants, when available; using their pectoral fins, they assumed odd positions on plants, either head up or head down at 30–90° from the horizontal. The fish could maintain these positions for hours. All such actions may be an attempt to avoid light, an example of fright behavior or perhaps a camouflaging technique.

In an aquarium, the larger, more active, pirate perch always fed before the smaller ones; however, the larger fish was subordinate to the smaller fish in the one area of the aquarium to which the smaller fish confined its activities and which it defended. Parker and Simco noted that, when a large fish entered this area, the two fish took up a side-by-side position only briefly before the large fish was driven out. To drive out the larger fish, the smaller fish occasionally nipped, but primarily it used the dorsal portion of its head as a battering ram.

When confined, the pirate perch's aggression is turned to other species as well as members of its own. Five pirate perch in an aquarium attacked and killed three black bullheads, three emerald shiners, and four central mudminnows (J. Small, pers. comm.). Quinn (1976) noted a general thinning out of tank tenants, as well as nipped tails on the larger fish, in aquariums containing pirate perch.

Fish species associated with the pirate perch in a slough of the Wisconsin River (Columbia County) were: central mudminnow, black bullhead, tadpole madtom, grass pickerel, northern pike, largemouth bass, bluegill, black crappie, golden shiner, emerald shiner, pugnose minnow, and fathead minnow.

IMPORTANCE AND MANAGEMENT

The ecological importance of the pirate perch is not known. In the north, where it is rare, its presence in the natural community is probably inconsequential.

The pirate perch makes an attractive aquarium fish if kept by itself in a planted, well-aerated, and well-matured tank at a room temperature no higher than 22°C (71.6°F) (Sterba 1973). It must be provided with suitable hiding places among stones or under pieces of broken flowerpot. It will accept live foods only: minnows, earthworms, *Daphnia*, and mosquito larvae.

Trout-Perch Family— Percopsidae

A single genus and only two species are recognized in this family, which is placed in the same suborder with the Aphredoderidae (pirate perch) and Amblyopsidae (cavefishes). Regarded as of North American origin, the trout-perch is thought to have repopulated North America in post-glacial times from a refugium in the Mississippi Valley.

The trout-perch is a surviving remnant of a fauna which marked the transition from soft-rayed, herringlike forms to the later appearing groups of spiny-rayed fishes. It resembles both a trout and a perch: its adipose fin and naked head are features of the Salmonidae, its ctenoid scales and fin spines, and the form of its mouth, make it appear to be related to the Percidae.

The trout-perches possess large heads, and nonprotractile premaxillaries which form the border of the upper jaw. Their dorsal, pelvic and anal fins are each preceded by one to two weak spines. The scales are small, and have only a single row of weak ctenii on their exposed edges.

Trout-Perch

Percopsis omiscomaycus (Walbaum). *Percopsis*—perch-like; *omiscomaycus*—probably an Algonkian Indian name that includes the root "trout" (McPhail and Lindsey 1970).

Other common names: grounder minnow, sand roller, silver chub.

Adult 111 mm, Green Bay (Door Co.), 6 June 1962

DESCRIPTION

Body elongate, cylindrical, but slightly compressed laterally; caudal peduncle long and tapered. Average length 76–102 mm (3–4 in). TL = 1.24 SL. Depth into SL 3.9–4.5. Head into SL 3.3–3.6. Snout long, pointed; upper lip groove not continuous over tip of snout. Mouth large, horizontal to slightly oblique; corner of mouth below nostril and far short of anterior edge of eye; numerous minute, villiform teeth in wide bands on upper and lower jaws. Dorsal fin slightly falcate, nearer tip of snout than base of caudal fin, its origin over the origin of pelvic fins; dorsal fin with 2 spines, 10–11 rays; small dorsal adipose fin; anal fin 1 spine, 6–7 rays; pelvic fin 1 spine, 8–9 rays. Scales ctenoid, with a single row of teeth on exposed edges. Lateral line scales 47–52; lateral line complete. Digestive tract 0.5 TL; 10–14 pyloric caeca.

Translucent appearance in life. Back and sides pale olive; belly whitish. A silvery stripe along lateral line; 5 distinct rows of dark spots—2 rows along either side, and 1 mid-dorsal row; the lateral line row consisting of 10–12 conspicuous spots. Fins lightly pigmented along rays; membranes occasionally lightly pigmented in dorsal, caudal, and anal fins.

Sexual dimorphism: According to Kinney (1950), in males, the urogenital opening is small, and cannot accept a 0.5 mm diam probe; in females, the opening accepts a 1 mm probe. Scott and Crossman (1973) were unable to employ this test for sexing trout-perch successfully, particularly with ripe or spawning fish.

SYSTEMATIC NOTES

The species treated here—the trout-perch, *Percopsis omiscomaycus* (Walbaum)—is the common widespread form within this genus. The sand roller or western trout-perch, *Percopsis transmontana* (Eigenmann and Eigenmann), is found in the lower Columbia River system of Washington, Oregon, and Idaho; this species has two stout spines in both the dorsal and anal fins.

DISTRIBUTION, STATUS, AND HABITAT

In Wisconsin, the trout-perch occurs in all three drainage basins. It is a characteristic species in large rivers and widely scattered lakes of the Mississippi River and Lake Michigan basins; in the Lake Superior watershed, it occurs in almost all of the tributary streams.

In Wisconsin, the trout-perch is uncommon to common in the Mississippi and Wisconsin rivers. It is common in the Chippewa River and its connecting lakes in Sawyer County, and in Lake Superior and its tributaries. It is common to abundant in Lakes Poygan, Winnebago, and Michigan.

This species prefers the shallow and intermediate depths of Lakes Superior and Michigan and large inland lakes; it avoids shallow, mud-filled bays. It is present in tributary streams, particularly during spawning. I encountered it most frequently in clear to slightly turbid water. It was found over substrates of sand (39% frequency), mud (23%), gravel (23%), and boulders (15%).

BIOLOGY

In Wisconsin, the spawning of the trout-perch occurs from late April to June, and probably longer. In Lake Winnebago (Priegel 1962a), spawning was observed from late May to mid-June, at water temperatures of 15.6–20°C (60–68°F), over rocks. Sand bars in lakes are usually selected for spawning, but trout-perch in Lake Winnebago were observed spawning among rocks. Two or three males accompany each female during the spawning act. Priegel observed the following unusual spawning phenomenon (p. 113):

> . . . In some cases, wave action forces the fish onto the rocks and as the water recedes, the fish are left on the moist rocks where the eggs and milt are released. Upon return of the next wave, the fish are swept back into the water and the eggs scattered about. The eggs do not adhere to the rocks but fall between them.

Since the trout-perch are random spawners, no care is given to the eggs or fry by either parent.

Details of trout-perch spawning behavior in streams

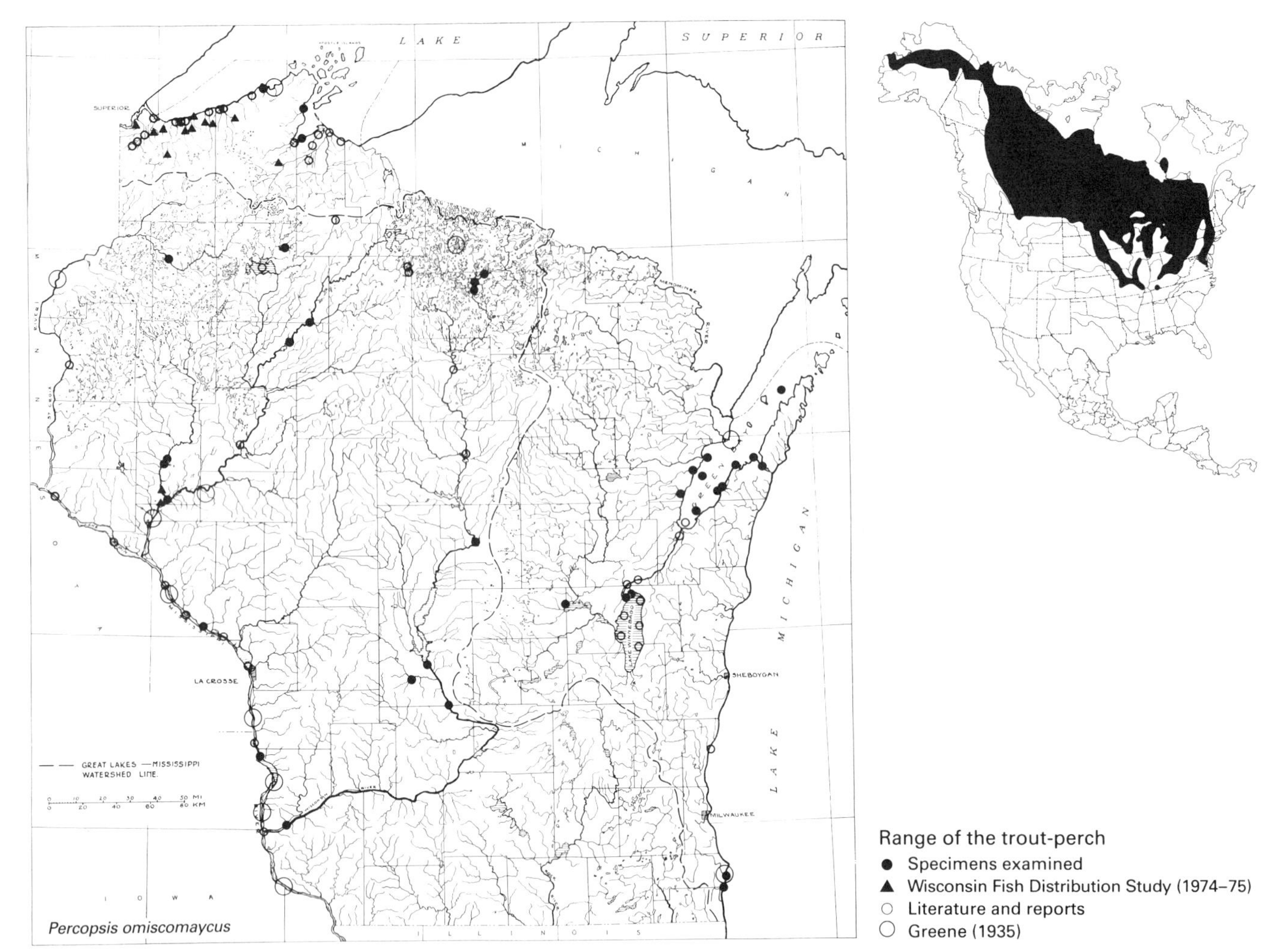

Range of the trout-perch
● Specimens examined
▲ Wisconsin Fish Distribution Study (1974–75)
○ Literature and reports
◯ Greene (1935)

have been provided by Magnuson and Smith (1963). Trout-perch congregated off the mouth of Mud Creek (tributary to Lower Red Lake, Minnesota) before sunset and moved into the creek after dark; as the fish swam into the creek, they moved from warm lake water into relatively cooler creek water. Most of the trout-perch moved out of the creek again by sunrise. However, during the first half of July spawning was observed regularly in Mud Creek at midday (p. 93):

> . . . Spawning in Mud Creek took place within 4 or 5 inches of the surface and was concentrated near the edges of the stream. Two or more males clustered around a single female and just before the eggs were extruded the males pressed close to the sides of the female and all 3 fish occasionally broke the surface of the water as the eggs and milt were simultaneously released. The eggs, which are more dense than water and have a sticky surface, sank as they drifted with the current until they touched the bottom to which they adhered.

Based on the size of the young-of-year sampled, Magnuson and Smith concluded that in Minnesota the trout-perch has a spawning season of approximately 2½ months (from May until August), with two or more periods of increased spawning, or greater egg and fry survival. In Lower Red Lake, spawning occurred along the beaches in water less than 1.1 m (3.5 ft) deep.

Magnuson and Smith noted that the age composition of the spawning population was: 31%—age I; 61%—age II; 8%—age III; and 1%—age IV. Males generally mature and spawn at a younger age than females, have a higher mortality rate, and consequently disappear from the population at a younger age. Age I spawning males are subject to high mortality, which seems to be coincident with the period of the highest water temperature and the peak of trout-perch spawning. In 1957, this peak occurred in mid-July. Priegel (1962a) noted that in Lake Winnebago, adult trout-perch which have just spawned are washed ashore in great numbers; these are erroneously reported by local residents as a large die-off of small walleyes. In western Lake Erie, most trout-perch spawn at age I and few males or females live to spawn at age II (Kinney 1950).

A number of gravid female trout-perch were taken over sand and rock in the Red Cedar River (Dunn County) on 19 April 1974. As these fish were handled, eggs poured from the genital opening. One female, 126 mm TL and 20.56 g, with ovaries 19.4% of the body weight held 1,825 yellow, ripe eggs, 1.3–1.5 mm diam; and an approximately equal number of white, immature eggs, 0.7–1.0 mm diam. Magnuson (1958) believed that the immature eggs do not ripen during the same spawning season, and that each female therefore spawns once each season. He determined the relationship between the number of mature eggs held by a female and the total length of the ripe female by the formula $\log y = -3.247 + 3.029 \log x$, where x = total length of ripe female trout-perch and y = number of mature eggs in both ovaries.

Artificially fertilized trout-perch eggs were 1.87 mm diam, and hatched out in 6.5 days at water temperatures of 20–23°C (68–73.4°F) into larvae approximately 5.3 mm long (Magnuson and Smith 1963). The yolk-sac was absorbed 4–5 days later at a length of approximately 6.2 mm. Fish (1932) illustrated and described the 6-, 7-, 9.5-, and 35.5-mm stages. At 39.5 mm the trout-perch is fully scaled and has assumed the adult appearance.

In northern Wisconsin, young-of-year trout-perch are 27 mm long by 27 June, and by late September they range from 43 to 57 mm. In Lake Winnebago (Priegel 1962a), they were 25–30 mm in June, and at the end of the first growing season (mid-October) they were 71–81 mm long. By comparison, in western Lake Erie (*Commercial Fisheries Review* 1961) growth is terminated by 15–30 October at an average length of 84 mm (3.3 in).

In Green Bay, 50 trout-perch, 63–146 mm TL, showed the following growth at the annuli: 1—70 mm; 2—90 mm; 3—109 mm; and 4—135 mm (P. Kanehl, pers. comm.). Trout-perch in Lake Winnebago (Priegel 1962a) were 81–91 mm (3.2–3.6 in) in the fall of their second year of life. In Minnesota, the average calculated growth of male trout-perch from Lower Red Lake was: 1—50.8 mm; 2—88.2 mm; 3—103.5 mm; growth of females was: 1—51.4 mm; 2—92.2 mm; 3—108.3 mm; and 4—114.7 mm. Fish lengths were calculated with an intercept of 8.32 mm (Magnuson and Smith 1963). These authors noted spawning checks (false annuli resulting from growth interruption during spawning) located just outside the first annulus. In older fish such false annuli were not seen, since growth for the year did not occur until after spawning took place. The annulus for the year was deposited in age-I fish in June, and in age-II fish in late July or early August.

A large Wisconsin specimen 152.5 mm long (UWSP 2467) was taken from Green Bay near Pensaukee Harbor (Oconto County) during the summer of 1968.

Young trout-perch consume greater numbers of zooplankton than larger fish of the same species (Tomlinson and Jude 1977). In Lake Winnebago, the young feed primarily on cladocerans, copepods, and rotifers (Priegel 1962a).

In the Duluth-Superior and Apostle Islands areas of Lake Superior, crustaceans (principally amphipods and *Mysis*) were the predominant food of trout-perch, followed closely by insects (primarily chironomids) (Anderson and Smith 1971b); mollusks (Sphaeriidae), plant material, oligochaetes, and Hirudinea also were consumed. In southeastern Lake Michigan (Tomlinson and Jude 1977), chironomid larvae appeared most frequently in stomachs (80% occurrence), followed by amphipods (48%), cladocerans (39%), and copepods (29%). *Pontoporeia affinis* was the primary amphipod, and *Chironomus* the most frequently consumed chironomid; *Cyclops* was the most common copepod, and the benthic *Eurycercus* was the most common cladoceran in trout-perch stomachs. Fish eggs were observed in only two stomachs. In Lake Winnebago (Priegel 1962a), trout-perch feed on lake fly larvae (*Chironomus plumosus*), other insect larvae, and leeches. Occasionally small minnows and darters are eaten (Kinney 1950).

Even in waters where the trout-perch is abundant, it is seldom seen, for it appears to stay in deep water during the day and to move into shallow shore waters after dark. It is seldom caught during lake surveys, except by night seining, although it can be caught by otter trawls in the daytime. During the 1960–1961 survey of Lake Winnebago (Becker 1964b), in 23 daytime seinings along all shores of the lake only a single individual appeared, although it is one of the most common fishes in the lake.

In the Apostle Islands region of Lake Superior, no seasonal trends in the distribution of trout-perch were noted (Dryer 1966). The all-season averages indicated that trout-perch were widely distributed down to 90 m, and most abundant at 18–35 m and at 55–71 m. In southeastern Lake Michigan, this species is restricted to shallow and intermediate depths (Wells 1968), and it is mainly found in water of 10–16°C (50–60.8°F). Wells observed that in 1964, most trout-perch in the small catches of February–April were taken at 22–31 m. In May, they were concentrated nearer shore at 9–13 m, and during the summer this continued to be the depth at which they were found in greatest abundance. By 14 October, they were back in deeper water at 18–37 m, the largest numbers at 22 m. In a

4-day period in mid-August, Wells noted a pronounced shift of the population into deeper water following a sudden increase in water temperature.

During early September 1977, trout-perch in Lake Michigan off Grand Haven, Michigan, were captured more frequently at night than during the day (Brandt 1978). Data suggest that either the trout-perch were avoiding the bottom trawl during the day, or that extensive onshore-offshore migrations were occurring. During the day, trout-perch concentrated where water temperatures were greater than 15°C (59°F); the thermal distribution of trout-perch expanded at night to 7–18°C (44.6–64.4°F).

Fish species associated in Green Bay (Door County) with 98 trout-perch were: white sucker (1), alewife (3), creek chub (1), bluntnose minnow (5), fathead minnow (2), common shiner (3), blacknose shiner (1), spottail shiner (68), rainbow smelt (1), black bullhead (4), yellow perch (10), and fantail darter (1).

IMPORTANCE AND MANAGEMENT

Trout-perch are eaten by walleyes, northern pike, burbot, lake trout, brook trout, sauger, yellow perch, and freshwater drum. In Canada (Lawler 1954), 63 trout-perch were found in the stomach of 1 northern pike. In Minnesota, sheepshead which moved into the trout-perch spawning streams contained as many as 19 trout-perch per fish (Magnuson and Smith 1963). In Lake Winnebago, fry of trout-perch were eaten by 10- to 50-mm walleyes to a limited extent, and, along with the freshwater drum, were the most important forage consumed by 51- to 75-mm walleye fingerlings (Priegel 1970b).

The trout-perch makes its greatest contribution as major link in the food cycle of many waters. Although trout-perch are competitive with larger fish in that they occupy the same habitat and feed upon the same foods as the young of all the important game and food fishes, they have become a major source of food to many game fishes.

The trout-perch is readily taken on a hook baited with angleworms. It has sometimes been used as a panfish.

The fact that the trout-perch has large eggs, and that lake populations have a prolonged spawning period, suggests that this species may be useful in laboratory studies in which eggs are required—and, indeed, it has been used in a limited way for such studies (Scott and Crossman 1973).

In many waters, the trout-perch is a common part of the fish fauna. In Green Bay, where it is abundant, this species occurred in 32% of the drags, and its overall catch rate was 0.91 kg (2 lb) per drag. One large catch of 45 kg (100 lb) was made at 15 m off Sturgeon Bay (Reigle 1969a). In Lake Poygan the trout-perch constituted 53.4% of the catch; in Lake Winnebago, 62.4% (Becker 1964b). In the Mississippi River, R. C. Nord (pers. comm., 1964) noted that fairly large numbers of trout-perch have been trawled in the vicinity of La Crosse and in Lake Pepin. However, in many waters populations fluctuate strongly from year to year. In Lake Winnebago (Priegel 1965), during July and August 1960, 208 and 155 fishes were captured per haul during the day, and 113 and 74 fish at night. During July and August 1961, the catch per haul of trout-perch decreased to 29 and 11 fish during the day and 9 fish at night. In Lake Superior streams the trout-perch is widespread, but its numbers fluctuate widely.

Cod Family—Gadidae

Only one species, the burbot, appears in Wisconsin. It is a truly freshwater form and is circumpolar in distribution. The family Gadidae is represented by 25 species in the United States and Canada, 23 of which inhabit the Atlantic and Pacific oceans. This is the well-known marine family which contains the cod, the haddock, and many other important food species.

The cods have large heads and wide gill openings. Their jaws are terminal or nearly so, and both jaws and vomer are equipped with numerous small teeth in wide bands; there is a small barbel at the tip of the chin. The scales are small and cycloid. All the fins are soft rayed, and the pelvic fins are set far forward. In the burbot, the pelvic fins are in the throat region and are anterior to the pectoral fins; this is the only Wisconsin species with the pelvic fins positioned in front of the pectorals. In the cods, the caudal vertebrae become smaller posteriorly, and the pneumatic duct from the swimbladder to the pharynx is lost (physoclist).

Burbot

Lota lota (Linnaeus). *Lota*—the ancient name used by Guillaume Rondelet, a French zoologist; in French, la Lotte.

Other common names: lawyer, lake lawyer, ling, ling cod, eelpout, freshwater cod, cusk, spineless catfish, gudgeon, mud blower, mother eel (Kansas), maria (Saskatchewan, Manitoba, northern Ontario), methy (northern Canada), lush (Alaska), dogfish (Minnesota).

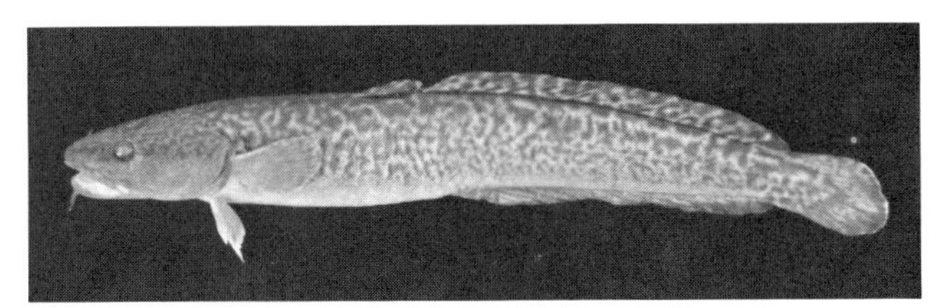

258 mm, Beaver Cr. (Trempealeau Co.), 28 June 1977

DESCRIPTION

Body elongate, cylindrical anterior to anus; laterally compressed posterior to anus. Length 305–483 mm (12–19 in). TL = 1.08 SL. Depth into SL 6.2–7.7. Head into SL 4.4–4.8; head flattened dorsoventrally. Snout pointed; upper lip groove continuous over tip of snout. Mouth large, almost horizontal; posterior edge of upper jaw behind pupil of eye; numerous minute teeth in wide bands on upper and lower jaws. One median chin barbel, and barbel-like, tubular extensions for each nostril opening. Dorsal fins 2; first dorsal low, short with 8–16 rays; second dorsal low, long with 61–81 rays. Anal fin rays 52–76; pelvic fin rays 5–8, the second ray prolonged into a tapering filament. Scales cycloid, embedded in cheeks, opercles, and body, so small as to be almost invisible except in large adults; under microscope the scales have heavy circuli which appear like growth rings in a gymnosperm twig; lateral line complete. Pyloric caeca 31–150. Large liver without gall bladder.

Adults uniformly yellow, or light brown to black, or mottled with dark brown or black on back and sides; belly whitish. Young fish conspicuously speckled, or with dark vermiculations. Dorsal, caudal, and anal fins mottled and more or less dark edged; pectoral fins mottled; pelvic fins white to slightly pigmented.

DISTRIBUTION, STATUS, AND HABITAT

In Wisconsin, the burbot occurs in all three drainage basins and in all boundary waters. Its distribution is mainly associated with the St. Croix, Chippewa–Red Cedar, Wisconsin, Rock, and Wolf-Fox river systems. Its distribution in the unglaciated portion of the state is sporadic.

The chronology of the changes in abundance of burbot in Lake Michigan suggests that the sea lamprey was responsible for the burbot's decline in the mid-1940s, and that sea lamprey control led to an upswing in burbot numbers in the late 1960s. (Wells and McLain 1972). The burbot is uncommon in the Mississippi River, although at one time it was reported as common in Lake Pepin (Wagner 1908). It is common in the Flambeau watershed and in the tributaries to Lake Superior; it is abundant in Lakes Poygan and Winnebago. Its status in Wisconsin appears to be secure.

The burbot frequents cool waters of large rivers, and the lower reaches of their tributaries, and lakes—particularly in northern Wisconsin. It is encountered most frequently at depths over 1.5 m (immatures at lesser depths) over substrates of mud, sand, rubble, boulders, silt, and gravel. It was found in streams of the following widths: 1–3 m (13%), 3.1–6.0 m (25%), 12.1–24.0 m (25%), and more than 50 m (38%). It prefers patches of plants and trash when young, stony-bottomed riffles when half-grown, and undercut banks when adult (Hubbs and Lagler 1964).

BIOLOGY

The burbot is the earliest spawner of all Wisconsin fishes. Spawning occurs in mid-winter, or in the early spring before the ice has melted. In the Lake Michigan basin, adults spawn from January to March. In Lake Winnebago, burbot spawn on rock and gravel reefs from late January to early February (Weber 1971). In the Bayfield area of Lake Superior, most burbot collected had spawned by late February and early March; spawning in the Apostle Islands region may continue into late March (Bailey 1972).

Burbot spawn in deep water in some areas, but the spawning site is usually in shallow bays in 0.3–1.2 m (1–4 ft) of water over sand or gravel, or on gravel shoals 1.5–4.6 m (5–15 ft) deep. Spawning usually takes place at night, and the spawning grounds are deserted in the daytime. The surface water temperature is close to freezing; no nest is built, and no care is given the young.

The spawning act of the burbot has been observed a number of times. E. Fabricius noted (Breder and Rosen 1966:376):

> The female slowly swam about on a sand bottom in a tilted posture, with lifted tail and her head pointed downwards, dragging the chin barbel and the prolonged second rays of the pelvics along the ground. The male approached her from

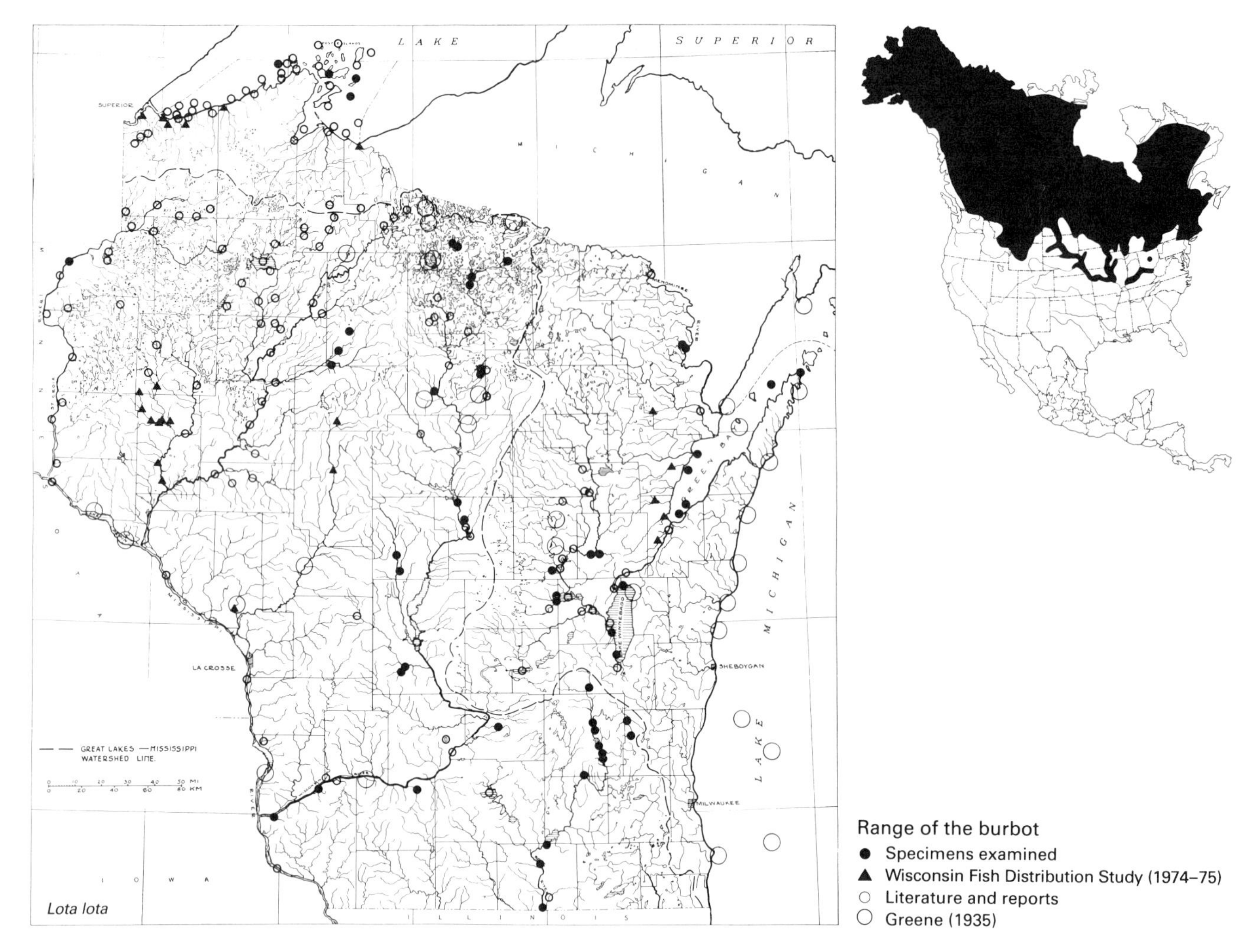

behind, swam in under her belly and placed his head under hers, so that her chin rested on his crown. In this position the couple swam about at the bottom for some minutes. The male suddenly rotated his body half a turn, pushing his belly against the vent of the female. In this mating act a cloud of eggs and sperm was released. After mating the male and female separated for a moment, the female performed a series of powerful tail beats which stirred up the sexual products and scattered the eggs. The eggs were carried about by the water movements caused by this activity, but they finally sank down to the bottom.

This activity was repeated until the female was spent.

Cahn (1936) observed probable spawning by the burbot in Minnesota (p. 164):

On the night of February 12 the interesting phenomenon of breeding was observed. . . . At first a dark shadow was noted at the edge of the ice, something which appeared to be a large ball. Eventually this moved out into view and it was seen to be indeed a ball—a tangled, nearly globular mass of moving, writhing lawyers. The fish were all intertwined, slithering over one another constantly, slowly, weaving in and out of the living ball. About a dozen fish were involved. . . .

The mass of fish, about 76 cm (30 in) diam, was in water about 1.2 m (4 ft) deep.

In Lake Superior burbot (Bailey 1972), the estimated number of eggs in the ovaries of eight females, 373–541 mm (14.7–21.3 in) long, ranged from 268,832 to 1,154,014. In New York (Robins and Deubler 1955), a 643-mm, 2.8-kg (25.3-in, 6.1-lb) female held 1,362,000 eggs. The average diameter for the semipelagic eggs varies with the region, but generally ranges from 1.25 to 1.9 mm.

The incubation period of burbot eggs is from 4 to 5 weeks, at a water temperature of 4°C (39.2°F) (Breder and Rosen (1966). Fish (1932) provided sketches from the 3.5- to 19-mm stages, along with descriptions of these and the 30.5-mm stage. The median barbel is recognizable in the 10.9-mm stage.

Many newly hatched young burbot are found on the shallow, sandy bottoms of lakes (Eddy and Surber 1947) and in trout streams which may act as nursery streams (Harlan and Speaker 1956). In Lake Huron, burbot production occurs in the large bays, but, like smelt, the young disperse throughout the surface waters over deep water and display a limnetic pattern of distribution (Faber 1970). In Lake Erie, Fish (1932) noted larval and postlarval stages 3–15 mm long at 5–60 m from mid-June to mid-August.

Age is determined by counting the annular rings of the otoliths. Burbot from western Lake Superior (Bailey 1972) showed a considerable overlap in lengths from year to year, but the average estimated lengths were: 0—145 mm; I—254 mm; II—300 mm; III—340 mm; IV—376 mm; V—409 mm; VI—439 mm; VII—478 mm; VIII—513 mm; IX—551 mm; X—594 mm; XI—645 mm, and XII—711 mm. The estimated annual weight increments ranged from 27 g to 118 g through age VI, and from 163 g to 586 g from age VII through age XII.

About 59% of the Lake Superior males, but only 5% of the females, were mature at age I; all burbot of both sexes were mature at age V. The shortest mature male was 246 mm (9.7 in) long; all males more than 417 mm (16.4 in) long were mature. The shortest mature female was 272 mm (10.7 in) long, and all females longer than 404 mm (15.9 in) were mature.

Burbot specimens up to 1 m (39.4 in) long, with weights of 25–30 kg (55–66 lb) and ages of 15–20 years, have been reported, mainly from Siberia (Muus and Dahlstrom 1971). Large burbot from Lake Winnebago reach a length of nearly 76 cm (30 in) and weigh 3.6–4.1 kg (8–9 lb) (Lewis 1970).

In Lake Superior (Bailey 1972), burbot of all ages had eaten fish and crustaceans. The fish consumed in order of frequency were sculpins (slimy and spoonheads), smelt, bloater, ninespine sticklebacks, trout-perch, and lake trout. Fish eggs, probably the eggs of lake herring (*Coregonus artedii*), occurred in 21.4% of the burbot stomachs during the fall. The crustaceans *Mysis relicta* and *Pontoporeia affinis* appeared in over half of the stomachs examined, and fingernail clams occurred in 26% of the stomachs. Insects were relatively unimportant. The presence in burbot stomachs of rocks, wood chips, clinkers, plastic, and other inert materials suggests that their feeding had been rather indiscriminate.

In Lake Michigan and Green Bay (Van Oosten and Deason 1938), food consisted of fish (74% volume) and invertebrates (26%). The dominant items in southern Lake Michigan were sculpins (76%); in northern Lake Michigan, coregonid chubs (51%) and *Pontoporeia* (37%); and in Green Bay, trout-perch (34%) and *Mysis* (26%). The consumption of invertebrates decreased with increases in the size of the burbot. Fishes were eaten after burbots reached 330 mm (13 in) or more in size. One must keep in mind, however, that this study of food habits was made before the advent of the alewife brought about dramatic changes in the fish populations of these waters. The diet of the burbot today may be quite different than it was in the 1930s, and it now probably includes the abundant alewife.

According to Scott and Crossman (1973), in streams small burbot 51–305 mm (2–12 in) long feed on *Gammarus*, mayfly nymphs, and crayfish. Adult burbot become voracious, feeding on most available fishes and crayfishes, dead or alive. Perch up to 254 mm (10 in) long have been reported from Wisconsin burbot stomachs. A 559-mm (22-in) burbot, seined from Lake Winnebago, had swallowed all but the tail of a 406-mm walleye (Colburn 1946). One 483-mm (19-in) burbot contained five 76-mm perch, six 51-mm crayfish, six large burrowing mayfly nymphs, and one dragonfly nymph (Wis. Conserv. *Bull.* 1948 13[4]:31). Adams and Hankinson (1926) remarked about the burbot's capacity for food (p. 518):

> If he can procure food he will not desist from eating so long as there is room for another particle in his capacious abdomen. He is frequently taken with his abdomen so much distended with food as to give him the appearance of the globe or toad-fish.

Adult burbot do not feed during the spawning period, but begin to prey heavily on forage fish immediately after spawning. They supposedly come into shallow water to feed at night.

Optimum temperatures (Scott and Crossman 1973) for the burbot are 15.6–18.3°C (60–65°F); 23.3°C (74°F) appears to be its upper limit. The preferred temperature of young burbot as determined by laboratory experiments is 21.2°C (70.2°F) (Ferguson 1958).

During the warm summer months, and in the fall when the water temperature has declined, the larger burbot is usually found in the deepest part of a lake or stream. In the Apostle Islands region of Lake Superior the burbot shows a wide distribution from the shallowest water to 126 m, with the largest catches taken at 18–35 m. Koelz (1929) noted that the burbot was taken in numbers near Stannard Rock at a depth of 210 m. In northeastern Lake Michigan, there was a characteristic monthly inshore concentration of burbot at 13–18 m or at 19–21 m, and a second concentration at 31–34 m, or at more than 34 m (Van Oosten et al. 1946).

IMPORTANCE AND MANAGEMENT

Burbots are eaten by other fishes. At Two Rivers (Lake Michigan), a lake trout 597 mm (23.5 in) long had 76 mm (3 in) of a burbot tail projecting from its mouth;

the head had been digested, but the body was 356 mm (14 in) long without it. Young burbot are eaten by smelt, yellow perch, and other fishes.

The burbot is readily caught through the ice in late winter, with minnows used as bait at the end of hand lines, tip-ups, and conventional rods and reels. Since the goal of Wisconsin ice fishermen is generally walleyes, however, the burbots caught are unwelcome and are frequently left on the ice. In the East, burbots are said to attract large numbers of herring gulls which come down to within a few feet of fishermen; there are reports of substantial windbreaks being made of the carcasses of these fish.

The burbot is classified a rough fish by the state of Wisconsin. Liberal regulations permit fishermen to spear and to net it, and there are no restrictions on fish size or on bag size. Spearing for burbot is allowed in tributaries to Lake Superior when the spearing season for other species has been closed.

In Siberia, the skin of the burbot has been used instead of glass (Adams and Hankinson 1926). In recent years, Lake Winnebago burbot have been trucked alive to Indiana and Ohio for stocking fee fishing ponds.

In Wisconsin, the burbot has never been of great commercial importance because of its low market demand. Even in the very early commercial fishery most burbot were discarded, except for the few sent to local markets (Milner 1874a). In Lake Michigan, burbot production reached an all-time high in 1974 with a total harvest of 93,363 kg (205,826 lb) (Wis. Dep. Nat. Resour. 1976c:1):

> . . . This was 91,859 pounds greater than the 1973 harvest and 68,826 pounds higher than the previous high produced from Wisconsin waters of Lake Michigan and Green Bay in 1917. The increase may not indicate as drastic an increase in relative abundance as production figures indicate, although burbot numbers have increased tremendously in the last ten years, especially in Green Bay. The increase is definitely related to fishermen being allowed the sale of 10% lake trout as an incidental catch of their legal catch—burbot being used to increase their legal catch. The value of the burbot fishery was reported at $7,693 or less than four cents a pound.

In Lake Superior, the burbot population is at a high level of abundance, and commercial catches are considerably higher than the 455 kg (1,000 lb) reported by the fishery: "This high quality food species is capable of sustaining a fairly large annual catch but no markets are available to the Lake Superior fishermen" (Wis. Dep. Nat. Resour. 1976c). Bailey (1972) commented that, although the burbot ranks among the most nutritious of the freshwater fishes, catches by commercial fishermen have often been discarded because of the lack of a profitable market.

In the Wisconsin waters of the Mississippi River in 1973, burbot landings totaled 9,500 kg (21,000 lb) and were valued at $3,000 (Pileggi and Thompson 1976). In 1970, 10,991 kg (24,230 lb) were removed by state crews from Lake Winnebago, and 1,678 kg (3,700 lb), from Lake Poygan (Miller 1971); some were sold for domestic mink food.

The flesh of the burbot resembles that of the cod and haddock, and in flavor it is the equal of many game fishes. For best results, the fish must be skinned and used fresh since the meat gets tough when frozen and has a rubbery texture when it is thawed.

In the mid-1920s fishery biologists predicted that, as a source of human food, the burbot appeared to be a fish of the future. That prediction is still awaiting fulfillment. Canada initiated a program to promote burbot as a food fish (MacKay 1963). Burbot, cleaned and skinned, were supplied to various hotels and restaurants in Toronto, and their chefs were asked to cook the fish and to give their opinions on the burbot's quality. The results were positive—"excellent"; and, "compare very favourably with any fish which I have obtained from the wholesalers." Nevertheless, attempts to encourage public acceptance of the burbot in Canada as a quality food fish, or as a processed fish for industrial use, have not been encouraging (Scott and Crossman 1973).

In the early decades of this century, the former United States Bureau of Fisheries urged the use of burbots for food through an extensive distribution of economic circulars and display cards. Excellent recipes for preparing this fish were provided. Mattingly (1976) provided burbot recipes with such intriguing names as White Pine Pan Fried, Crispy Kinde, Goodells Golden Puffs, Jiffy Jasper Jamboree, and Lakeland Cocktail. From Montana comes a recipe for Barbecued Ling (B. Miller 1974). In Wisconsin, Poor Man's Lobster is simplicity itself (Weber 1971:23):

> Fillets are cut into small 1- to 2-inch pieces, boiled in salt water for 3 minutes and drained. With melted butter poured over them, and appropriate seasoning, the taste will delight the most delicate palate . . . similar in taste to the more expensive lobster imported to the supermarket.

Burbot roe is a delicacy and, when seasoned and served on hot buttered toast, is as attractive as any roe (MacKay 1963).

The vitamin D potency of burbot liver oil is as high as that obtained from cod liver (Scott and Crossman 1973). In many European (especially Scandinavian) countries burbot livers are eagerly sought, and are a valuable commodity when smoked and canned. The Fisheries Research Board of Canada has experimentally canned Canadian burbot livers; the product is considered to be of high quality, especially for such uses as the making of canapes. Despite all these accolades, over much of its range this species still bears the tag of a rough fish, and, in Wisconsin, except for a small market that has developed in some eastern counties, it is a despised fish species.

Perhaps the most valuable contribution of the burbot to the ecology of lakes is its predatory nature. It is at the top of the food chain, and consumes all species of fish, large and small. In a managed ecosystem, this contribution to population control may help to prevent stunting in some fish species—a major problem in many lakes and streams. After burbot from Lake Winnebago were introduced into Shannon Lake (Vilas County), which has a large stunted perch population, the burbot were observed to be feeding heavily on the perch. Some Wisconsin fish managers look on the burbot, along with the gars and the bowfin, as possible natural biological controls; the purposeful stocking of such predators may provide a balance of fish species and a yield that could be arrived at in no other way.

Killifish Family—Cyprinodontidae

Three species of killifish in one genus occur in Wisconsin. Only one species has a wide north-south distribution in the state; the other two appear in southern Wisconsin as the northernmost populations of southern forms.

The family Cyprinodontidae is represented by 48 species in 10 genera in the United States and Canada, a number of which are both marine and freshwater in habit (Robins et al. 1980). The family includes the Devils Hole pupfish, Owens River pupfish, Comanche Springs pupfish, and Pahrump killifish of the southwest, all of which are endangered and have been the subjects of congressional conservation measures.

The killifish are small fishes which inhabit shallows and are adapted to surface feeding. Their jaws have well-developed teeth, their heads are flattened above, and they have small, more or less dorsal mouths. The gill membranes are free from the isthmus, and the scales are cycloid. Killifish possess soft-rayed fins; a single dorsal fin is located posteriorly. In adult killifish, the duct between the swim bladder and the pharynx is lost (physoclist).

Banded Killifish

Fundulus diaphanus (Lesueur). *Fundulus*—fundus, meaning bottom, the abode of the "Fundulus mudfish"; *diaphanus*—transparent.

Other common names: eastern banded killifish, western banded killifish, freshwater mummichog, freshwater killy, grayback minnow, freshwater killifish, killifish, topminnow, menona killifish, menona topminnow, barred minnow, hardhead.

Adult 62 mm, Rinehart L. (Portage Co.), 13 June 1977

DESCRIPTION

Body elongate, laterally compressed, somewhat flattened at back of head and nape. Length 51–64 mm (2.0–2.5 in). TL = 1.23 SL. Depth into SL 4.8–5.6. Head into SL 3.3–3.7. Snout bluntly pointed. Mouth small, oblique, and opening dorsally; lower jaw projecting; minute, needlelike teeth in bands on upper and lower jaws. Dorsal fin far posterior on back, but distinctly in advance of anal fin origin; dorsal fin rays 10–13; anal fin rays 9–11; pelvic fin rays 6; caudal fin rounded to truncate. Scales cycloid; lateral series 39–43; lateral line absent, top of head scaled. Intestine, with single loop, about one-half length of body. Chromosomes 2n = 48 (Chen and Ruddle 1970).

Body light olive on back and sides, yellow-white on lower half, including belly. Usually 12–20 narrow, vertical bars on sides (more apparent in preserved specimens). Dorsal and caudal fins lightly pigmented; ventral fins lightly pigmented or clear.

Breeding males with vertical bars, and dorsal and anal fins enhanced during spawning; dorsal fin may exhibit green-gold iridescence and a suggestion of a band or two of black pigment (Scott and Crossman 1973).

Sexual dimorphism: Dorsal and anal fins usually larger in male than in female; vertical bars on sides more numerous in male.

Hybrids: Banded killifish × mummichog (Chen and Ruddle 1970).

SYSTEMATIC NOTES

Two subspecies are recognized (Hubbs and Lagler 1964): the eastern banded killifish, *Fundulus diaphanus diaphanus* (Lesueur), which is found from South Carolina north to the Maritime provinces and Newfoundland, including the eastern parts of Pennsylvania; and the western banded killifish, *Fundulus diaphanus menona*[a] Jordan and Copeland, which is found from western New York to the eastern parts of the Dakotas, including Wisconsin. The western form usually has less scales in the lateral series, and has less rays in the dorsal, anal, and pectoral fins. Also, in the western form the bars on caudal peduncle generally are fused into a median lengthwise stripe, whereas in the eastern form they are often short but not fused.

DISTRIBUTION, STATUS, AND HABITAT

In Wisconsin, the banded killifish occurs in the Lake Michigan and Mississippi River drainage basins. There are no records from the Lake Superior basin. In the Mississippi basin it has been recorded from each of the two northern lake areas (Burnett and Vilas counties) and is probably more common than the record indicates. Its main centers of distribution in the Mississippi basin are the Rock River and the Des Plaines watershed of southeastern Wisconsin. The only record known from the driftless area is from the upper Sugar River (Dane County) (Greene 1935).

The banded killifish is common to abundant in many lakes of southeastern Wisconsin, and in the Green Bay and Lake Michigan shallows of Door and Kewaunee counties. Elsewhere in the eastern half of Wisconsin, it is rare to uncommon and occasionally common. Its status in Wisconsin appears to be secure.

The banded killifish inhabits the shoal waters and estuaries of large lakes, and the quiet backwaters and sections of slow current in medium- to large-sized streams. It has a strong preference for broad, sandy shallows during the warm season of the year, in the open or in the vicinity of sparse aquatic vegetation. It avoids the swift, cold water of trout streams. It was encountered most frequently in clear water at depths to 0.6 m, over subtrates of gravel, sand, silt, marl, mud, clay, detritus, and rubble.

[a]Type specimen collected by P. R. Hoy from the outlet of Lake Monona near Madison.

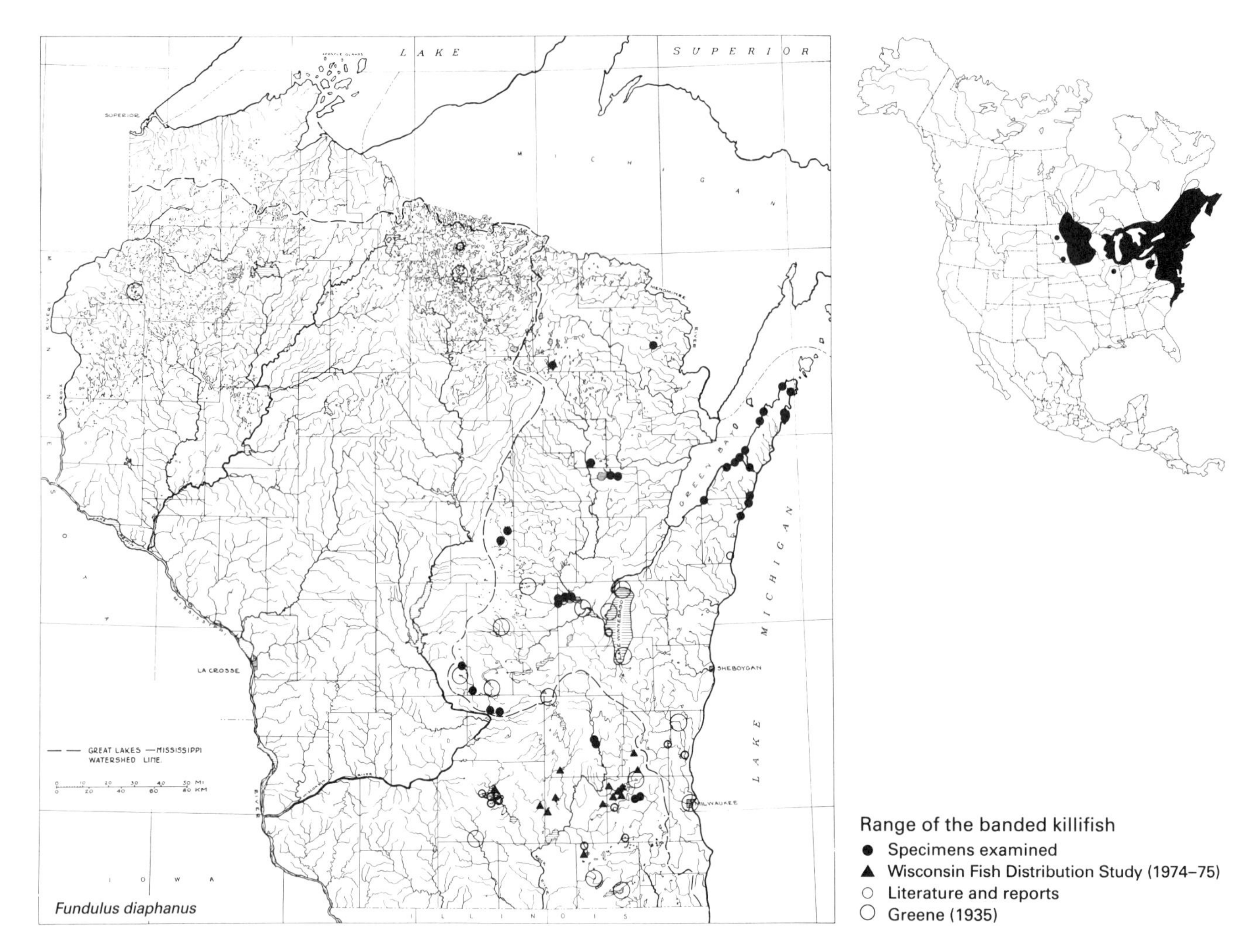

BIOLOGY

In Wisconsin, spawning occurs from June to at least mid-August. Partially spawned banded killifish appeared in collections from mid-June to early August.

Details of spawning by this species have been described by Richardson (1939). The banded killifish began spawning after water temperatures were held at 21.0°C (69.8°F). Combat between males was common, but it was not especially vicious, and it did not result in evident damage to the fighters. When placed in aquariums at water temperatures of 23°C (73.4°F), mating began almost immediately. Combat occurred between males, followed by pairing and the male's pursuit of the female. The male drove the female towards a mass of floating weeds, then pressed her body into the weeds with his body and fins. Vibration followed, causing the female to release a cluster of 5–10 eggs; fertilization occurred simultaneously. Adhesive threads which became entangled in the weeds were attached to the eggs (p. 166):

> On several occasions the cluster failed to break up, and the female, having been released by the male, moved away with the eggs still suspended below her until the thread caught on a weed, when the thread would break away from the papilla.

The spawning act was repeated every 15–30 seconds over a period of 5 minutes, during which time about 50 eggs were deposited.

Spawning over an unprepared bottom, in 20 cm (8 in) of water at 32.2°C (90°F), was described by Webster (1942). The spawning pair sank to the sandy bottom while turning on their sides, the male assuming the uppermost position. This was followed by a rapid vibration which lasted 2–4 seconds.

A gravid banded killifish female, 62 mm TL and 2.77 g, collected in Green Bay (Door County) on 5 June, had ovaries 19.9% of body weight. She held 163 maturing (yellow-orange) to mature (orange) eggs, 1.1–2.0 mm diam, and a number of immature, white eggs, 0.4–0.6 mm diam. A second female, 63 mm and 2.52 g, with ovaries 15.5% of body weight, held 182 maturing to mature eggs, 0.9–2.0 mm diam, and an undetermined number of immature eggs, 0.4–0.6 mm diam. These females, both with highly distended abdomens, were in prespawning condition.

Early development of the banded killifish was studied by Cooper (1936). He took eggs 2 mm diam, from masses of filamentous algae in a small Michigan pond and placed them in aerated jars at water temperatures of 22.2–26.7°C (72–80°F). The 6–7-mm fry hatched in 11–12 days. M. Fish (1932) sketched and described the 7.1- and 12.3-mm stages. Scales form quickly in this species and 22-mm young from Lake Emily (Portage County) are completely scaled except for nape and top of head.

In eastcentral Wisconsin, young-of-year banded killifish from Lake Emily (Portage County) averaged 32.7 (23–40) mm on 10 August; young from Bear Lake (Waupaca County), 37.5 (36–39) mm on 12 September; and young from Green Bay (Door County), 41.9 (36–48) mm on 18 September. In a southeastern Minnesota lake (Lux 1960), banded killifish were 15 mm on 9 July, 39 mm on 14 August, and 50 mm on 24 September.

Banded killifish from Lake Emily (Portage County), collected 10 August 1960, showed the following growth:

Age Class	No. of Fish	TL (mm)		Calculated TL at Annulus (mm)		
		Avg	Range	1	2	3
I	10	56.6	48–65	39.8		
II	9	64.9	60–69	35.3	58.9	
III	1	70.0		28.0	58.0	66.0
Avg (weighted)				37.2	58.8	66.0

The annulus in larger and older killifish is deposited in late July and early August.

According to Cooper (1936b), in some localities both sexes of banded killifish mature at age II; the females reach a larger size than the males. A large age-II female banded killifish 80 mm (3.2 in) long was collected from Pewaukee Lake (Waukesha County) in September 1961. A 114-mm (4.5-in) banded killifish was taken from Oneida Lake (New York) Adams and Hankinson 1926).

The principal foods of banded killifish from Lake Emily (Portage County) were small crustaceans, including copepods, amphipods, and cladocerans (P. La Mere, pers. comm.). A large number of mayfly nymphs were eaten, as well as plant seeds, but the seeds passed through the digestive tracts intact. Beetle larvae, snails, and protozoans were eaten less often.

In Green Lake (Green Lake County), the diet of banded killifish consisted of insect larvae and pupae, amphipods, cladocerans, ostracods, nematodes, and sand (Pearse 1921a). In Lake Mendota, its diet contained insect larvae, pupae and adults, amphipods, cladocerans, copepods, ostracods, plant material, and sand. In Illinois, Forbes (1883) noted that about four-fifths of the food consisted of animal substances; the remaining fifth included algal filaments and seeds in a quantity too large to have been taken accidentally.

Young banded killifish feed almost entirely on planktonic crustacea and chironomid larvae (Keast 1965).

Keast (1965) referred to the banded killifish as a generalized feeder, since so many different food items are ingested at any one time. Still, its heavy use of ostracods throughout life is largely a banded killifish characteristic not shared by other species in Lake Opinicon, Ontario, and Keast suggested that this trait could have survival value if other resources should fail. In Ontario, this versatile feeder ingests chironomid larvae, cladocerans, ostracods, copepods, amphipods, turbellarians, small flying insects, trichopterans, newly hatched Odonata nymphs, and small mollusks. Fleshy plant seeds appear in the diet in midsummer, along with some algal material.

The banded killifish is a schooling fish, and it feeds as a member of a school. It feeds effectively at all water depths, despite the dorsal position of the mouth, and it is largely diurnal in its feeding habits. Keast and Welsh (1968) found that it obtained most of its food between 1300 and 1750 hr; thereafter, the stomachs emptied until about 0100 hr, when 70% of the fish contained no food. A second, shorter period of feeding commenced before dawn; by 1000 hr, 65% of the stomachs were empty.

The preferred position of the banded killifish is near the surface of the water, although, of the three species of killifish in Wisconsin, this is the least "topwater" of the group. It appears less commonly in the upper 2.5 cm of the water column, and it prefers the depths beneath this zone (Schwartz and Hasler 1966a). It frequently seeks out vegetation; its protective coloration and quiet habits make it difficult to see.

In a laboratory experiment, after being brought to an acclimation of 14 ppt salinity (the approximate isosmotic level for blood), the banded killifish endured temperatures up to 33.5°C (92.3°F), which was the lethal temperature (50% mortality level) (Garside and Jordan 1968). The upper lethal temperature for the banded killifish in distilled water (0 ppt) and sea water (32 ppt) was 27.5°C (81.5°F). Many banded killifish died as a result of 38°C (100.4°F) water temperature in a shallow Michigan pond (Bailey 1955); however, the greatest mortality in the pond occurred among the mudminnow, sucker, minnow, bullhead catfish, and perch groups.

IMPORTANCE AND MANAGEMENT

Reports regarding the banded killifish's value as a forage fish are conflicting, although it has been preyed upon by black bass, northern pike, trout, and the salamander *Necturus*. It is also known to have been consumed by many fish-eating birds, including belted kingfishers, mergansers, grebes, bitterns, night herons, and herons (Adams and Hankinson 1926).

There are conflicting reports as to the value of the banded killifish as a bait minnow. Several authors note that it is a poor bait fish, for it will not stand handling and confinement in a minnow pail. But Scott and Crossman (1973) noted that it is hardy and lives well in a minnow pail: "It is also said to live for many hours packed in leaves in a tin can . . . it could live this way, without water for several days. It must indeed be a hardy species!"

The banded killifish lives well in an aquarium and makes an interesting, although not very conspicuous, aquarium fish. In many respects it challenges the observer "to locate the killifish," since its quiet behavior and camouflage make it a "ghost" fish rather than an aggressive inhabitant. Under certain conditions, however, it becomes aggressive and purportedly injures the fins of other fishes.

The banded killifish has been propagated in a small pond in Michigan at the rate of approximately 200,000/ha (80,000/acre) (Cooper 1936). It is a promising species for propagation as a forage fish for bass-rearing ponds.

Blackstripe Topminnow

Fundulus notatus (Rafinesque). *Fundulus*—fundus, meaning bottom, the abode of the "Fundulus mudfish"; *notatus*—spotted.

Other common names: topminnow, blackband topminnow.

Male 54 mm, Neenah Cr. (Marquette Co.), 29 July 1960

Female 54 mm, Neenah Cr. (Marquette Co.), 29 July 1960

DESCRIPTION

Body elongate, almost cylindrical, top of head and nape flattened. Length 43–60 mm (1.7–2.4 in). TL = 1.25 SL. Depth into SL 4.0–5.5. Head length into SL 3.2–3.7. Snout pointed in lateral view. Mouth small, oblique, and opening dorsally; lower jaw slightly projecting; minute, needlelike teeth in bands on upper and lower jaws. Dorsal fin far posterior on back, distinctly behind origin of anal fin; dorsal fin rays 9 (8–10); anal fin rays 12; pelvic fin rays 6; caudal fin rounded. Scales large, cycloid; lateral series 31–36, top of head and parts of cheeks and opercles scaled. Cephalic lateral line system detailed by Schwartz and Hasler (1966a); body lateral line system with few pored scales, incomplete. Intestine short and straight, or with a single forward loop. Chromosomes 2n = 40 (Black and Howell 1978).

Back and upper sides olive; lower half of body white or yellowish. Sides with a prominent dark stripe, nearly straight edged in females, with crossbars in males. Dorsal, anal, and pelvic fins bright yellow in males; little or no yellow in the fins of females; dorsal, caudal, and anal fins with dark spots, more intense and sharp in males; pectoral and pelvic fins in both sexes generally without spots, but occasionally with a small pigmented area at base of pectorals. Chin of males blue. Branchiostegals yellow in males, white in females.

Sexual dimorphism: Anterior base of anal fin clasped in distinct fleshy sheath in females; anal and dorsal fins longer and larger in males than in females.

SYSTEMATIC NOTES

The synonymic assignments ascribed to this species are listed by Braasch and Smith (1965).

DISTRIBUTION, STATUS, AND HABITAT

The blackstripe topminnow occurs in the Mississippi River and Lake Michigan drainage basins in southern Wisconsin, where it is at the northern limit of its distribution. The upper Fox River population (Columbia and Marquette counties) probably represents a recent crossover from the Wisconsin River at the Portage Canal. Since the 1920s this species has expanded westward into streams of the unglaciated area.

In southeastern Wisconsin, the blackstripe topminnow is found in many waters but never in large numbers. Frequently it can be seen moving ahead of a seine near the surface of the water. Its status appears to be secure, even in waters which have been heavily disturbed by man. It has a wider distribution in Wisconsin today than it had 50 years ago.

The blackstripe topminnow inhabits a variety of habitats such as pasture creeks, sloughs, bottomland lakes, drainage ditches, and the quiet margins and highwater pools of rivers. Generally, it inhabits low-gradient streams where the current is moderate or lacking; it is rarely found in lakes. In my studies it was encountered in water of varying turbidity and depth over substrates of gravel (31% frequency), silt (19%), mud (15%), sand (15%), rubble (12%), clay (4%), and boulders (4%). It occurred in streams of the following widths: 1.0–3.0 m (7%); 3.1–6.0 m (7%); 6.1–12.0 m (43%); 12.1–24.0 m (36%); and 24.1–50.0 m (7%).

BIOLOGY

In Wisconsin, the spawning of the blackstripe topminnow occurs in June and July. At the same latitude in Michigan, reproductive activity begins at least by early May, and females retaining eggs have been taken as late as the third week of August (Carranza and Winn 1954).

Carranza and Winn provided most of the following observations on blackstripe topminnow spawning behavior. Territoriality occurs within an area 6–12 m long, parallel with and no more than 4 m from shore. Within this area, pair activity takes place, and somewhere in the middle of this territory is a small cover or protected pocket to which the female re-

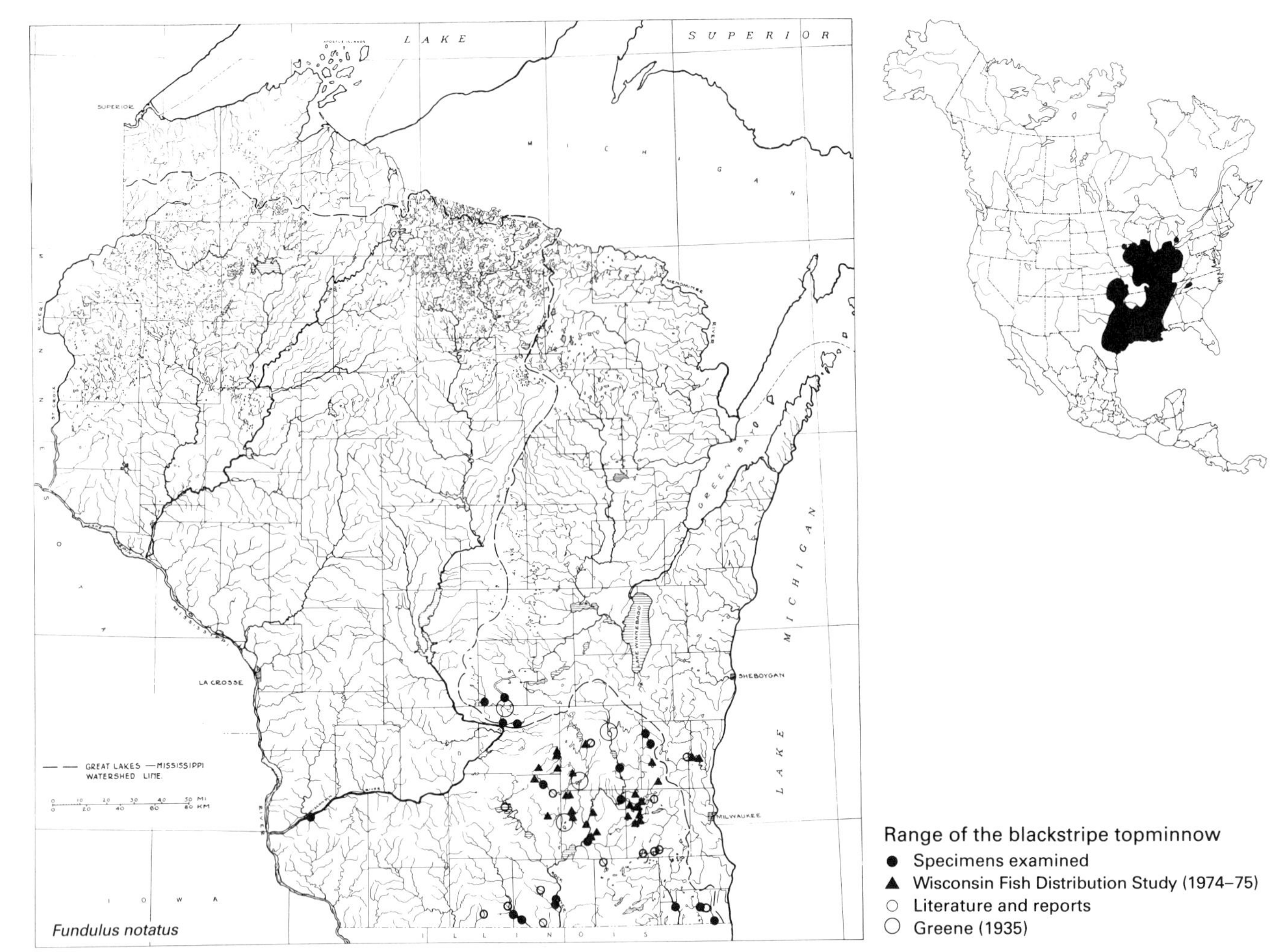

Range of the blackstripe topminnow
● Specimens examined
▲ Wisconsin Fish Distribution Study (1974–75)
○ Literature and reports
◯ Greene (1935)

turns, usually accompanied by the male. Observers have noted four instances when a female left a side pocket near shore to intercept groups of cruising males. Each time she returned with a male who followed her for a short time and then swam away. Other pairs may appear in this territory unmolested, but when the intruding pairs approach closely, the resident male vigorously chases the other male away. The attacked male retreats rapidly, often breaking the surface in what seems to be a series of skips. Females alone in a territory will drive an intruding female away. The female apparently can lead the male almost anywhere in her area. He usually follows slightly below and behind the female.

Among blackstripe topminnows kept in aquariums, aggressive behavior between males results in prolonged fights (Carranza and Winn p. 276):

> . . . The males take positions parallel to each other, facing in opposite directions, with all the fins except the pectorals stiffly spread and with the throat area expanded. Then each makes abrupt dashes and nips at the caudal region of his opponent. The abrupt dashes start with the caudal bent about 90 degrees, which is similar to the position of this fin during the spawning act. In so doing, the antagonists turn in a circle, and the larger male always was the winner.

There is little that can be called courtship in the blackstripe topminnow's behavior. When the female swims slowly or stops, the male often moves forward or upward beneath her, with his head slowly moving up and down. The significance of this characteristic head "dipping" is unknown; it has been observed only when the fish are paired, and usually when the male is out of view of the female.

When the female is ready to spawn, she swims to some algae or other plants (Carranza and Winn p. 276):

> . . . The behavior that stimulates the male's spawning reaction seems to be the close presence of a female beside or on top of some vegetation well below the surface of the water. Frequently males would try to spawn with females feeding in the algae on the bottom of the tank, but the females always swam away. It is obvious from this that the female determines the time and place to spawn. . . .

In the spawning position, the dorsal and anal fins of the

male are folded over the corresponding fins of the female . . . [his] body assumes an S-shape with the caudal fin at a right angle to the body. . . . Both sexes rapidly vibrate for one or two seconds. The throats are expanded. The vibration is ended with a flip of the caudal fin, usually by the male, which throws the single egg into the algae. The egg is frequently released from the female by the vibrations, but it often remains attached to her by a mucous thread until the final flip that throws it into the vegetation.

When the female has finished spawning, she swims rapidly to the surface. One female was observed to spawn 30 times in 20 minutes with three different males. Carranza and Winn suggested that a female may lay 20–30 eggs over a short period, and then wait, perhaps several days, until she produces more ripe eggs.

Abnormal spawning situations were observed in aquariums. Once a female was seen spawning by herself, although a male was courting her all the time. In at least four observed instances, two males tried to spawn with one female at the same time, with one male on each side of the female or both males on the same side.

Under natural conditions, the blackstripe topminnow is not likely to eat its eggs, since this fish feeds almost exclusively at the surface. However, in the laboratory (Carranza and Winn 1954) eggs were readily eaten by the females and by nondominant males. The dominant male slowed this process somewhat by chasing other males and by trying to spawn with the females when they went down to the algae to eat the eggs.

A partially spawned blackstripe topminnow female, taken from the Wisconsin River (Grant County) on 21 June, had ovaries 12.8% of body weight. She held 170 maturing (yellow) to mature (yellow-orange) eggs, 0.7–1.8 mm diam, and a small number of white, immature eggs, 0.3–0.6 mm diam. These eggs were difficult to count, because they appeared to be connected to one another by fine transparent threads.

An age-I female, taken from the East Branch of the Rock River (Washington County) on 15 July, had ovaries 9% of body weight, and held a few mature eggs, 0.9–1.6 mm diam. An age-II female, 65 mm TL, with ovaries 5.2% of body weight, had only a few eggs remaining; they were 1.6 mm diam.

The growth of young-of-year blackstripe topminnows in Wisconsin is presented in the table at the top of the next column.

Age-I blackstripe topminnows, taken 21 March from the Fox River (Columbia County), averaged 38.1 (36–41) mm TL.

Blackstripe topminnows from the East Branch of

Date	No. of Fish	TL (mm) Avg	TL (mm) Range	Location
29 July	3	26.7	26–27	Fox R. (Marquette Co.)
14 Aug.	16	36.4	33–40	Sugar R. (Rock Co.)
28 Aug.[a]	4	36.8	35–39	Illinois-Fox R. (Kenosha Co.)
28 Aug.[a]	23	33.4	29–37	Des Plaines R. (Kenosha Co.)
25 Sept.	41	34.5	26–43	Waterloo Cr. (Dane Co.)

[a]Two young, 33 and 35 mm long, were parasitized with anchorworms (*Lernaea* sp.).

the Rock River (Washington County), collected 15 July 1971, showed the following growth (sexes combined):

Age Class	No. of Fish	TL (mm)		Calculated TL at Annulus (mm)	
		Avg	Range	1	2
I	38	48.1	41–54	32.6	
II	4	62.8	60–65	27.3	49.8
Avg (weighted)				32.1	49.8

Growth is slightly greater in females than in males during the first year of life.

The blackstripe topminnow reaches a length of 76 mm (3 in) (Trautman 1957, Braasch and Smith 1965).

In an Illinois study of the blackstripe topminnow's food habits (Forbes 1883), insects (largely terrestrial) amounted to 73% of the food consumed. Additional animal items included mollusks (*Physa*), spiders, and small quantities of cladocerans, ostracods, and copepods. Vegetation, almost wholly filamentous algae, was taken in such quantities by various individuals as to suggest that its presence was not accidental. In southeastern Wisconsin, Cahn (1927) noted that about 75% of the blackstripe's food was filamentous algae, with *Spirogyra* and *Zygnema* predominating, and that the remainder of its diet was insects picked from the surface.

Schwartz and Hasler (1966a) observed that the blackstripe topminnow takes food which drops on the surface, even when the food is relatively far away and perhaps out of sight. Not only the eye, but other sense organs such as the cephalic line system, enable these fish to detect their food.

In a southeastern Michigan lake where there was a severe winterkill of bluegills (Cooper and Washburn 1949), there was good survival of blackstripe topminnows, although the approximate minimum concentration of dissolved oxygen in the upper 0.3–1.2 m of the water was only 0.8–0.5 ppm.

In the winter, the blackstripe topminnow stays in the deeper water, apparently in bottom vegetation

(Carranza and Winn 1954). It migrates from deep water in late March or early April to the shallow shore zone, where it assumes a surface swimming habit. Schwartz and Hasler (1966a) noted that in aquariums it hovers in the top 2.5 cm of water 63% of the time, and that in three out of four observations, it is found in direct contact with the surface film. This distribution changes radically if the water surface is disturbed by aeration or stirring; the fish then remain in the deeper water. The blackstripe topminnow achieves closer and more frequent contact with the water surface at night than during the day, and, if artificial lights are turned on at night, they drop to the bottom, where they remain for at least 2 minutes.

While in contact with the surface film, this species responds to surface waves approaching from all directions. The response is composed of a quick orientation of the head in the direction of the wave source, and an immediate movement toward that source. Schwartz and Hasler noted that up to a distance of 40 cm the blackstripe topminnow achieved an almost 100% positive reaction, and that a distinct response might frequently be elicited at distances beyond 90 cm.

In the Fox River (Marquette County), 8 blackstripe topminnows were associated with these species: common carp (1), bullhead minnow (9), bluntnose minnow (22), emerald shiner (43), spotfin shiner (25), sand shiner (7), yellow bullhead (1), tadpole madtom (4), northern pike (3), yellow perch (5), johnny darter (20), largemouth bass (3), bluegill (10), black crappie (5), and brook silverside (1).

IMPORTANCE AND MANAGEMENT

The blackstripe topminnow is one of the staple foods of the smallmouth bass (Cahn 1927), and undoubtedly serves as forage for other predators, including wading birds.

It has been suggested that the blackstripe topminnow might be used as a biological control against mosquito larvae which wriggle on the surface of quiet waters. Unfortunately, the isolated microhabitats of mosquitoes and topminnows are not always the same.

The blackstripe topminnow makes a conspicuous and interesting aquarium pet in its preferred habitat, just under the surface. Cross (1967) suggested that it can be propagated by placing a string-type mop on the aquarium floor upon which the eggs are deposited.

Starhead Topminnow

Fundulus notti (Agassiz). *Fundulus*—fundus, meaning bottom, the abode of the "Fundulus mudfish"; *notti*—named for Dr. Nott, its discoverer.

Other common names: topminnow, striped minnow, striped topminnow, blackeyed topminnow.

Male 47 mm, Wisconsin R. (Iowa Co.), 31 July 1965

Female 50 mm, Wisconsin R. (Iowa Co.), 31 July 1965

DESCRIPTION

Body deep, moderately compressed, top of head and nape flattened. Length 47–55 mm (1.9–2.2 in). TL = 1.30 SL. Depth into SL 3.5–4.0. Head length into SL 3.3–3.7. Snout pointed in lateral view, broadly rounded in dorsal view. Mouth small, oblique, and opening dorsally; lower jaw slightly projecting; minute, needlelike teeth in bands on upper and lower jaws. Dorsal fin far posterior on back, distinctly behind origin of anal fin; dorsal fin rays 8–9; anal fin rays 11; pelvic fin rays 6; caudal fin rounded. Scales large, cycloid; lateral series 30–34; lateral line absent. Digestive tract short, about three-fourths SL. Chromosomes 2n = 46 (Chen 1971).

Back and upper sides light olive to tan; lower sides and belly lighter to yellowish. Series of red to brown dots forming 7–8 horizontal lines along sides. Prominent dark blotch ("teardrop") beneath eye, slanting slightly posteriorly. In male the dorsal, caudal, and anal fins with dark spots (reddish in life), sometimes arranged in bands; in female, fins not so marked. Pectoral and pelvic fins lightly pigmented or clear.

Sexual dimorphism: Male with 11–12 narrow, upright bars along side; bars diffuse or absent in female. In male, dorsal and anal fins large and long, reaching or almost reaching rayed base of caudal fin; in female, distance from the ends of the dorsal and anal fins to the rayed base of caudal fin about half the length of each fin.

SYSTEMATIC NOTES

Although Wiley and Hall (1975) and Wiley (1977) treated the *notti* complex as a series of five species, the Committee on Names of Fishes (Robins et al. 1980) retained all (excepting *F. lineolatus*) in species *notti*. Geographic populations can be recognized as subspecies. The Wisconsin form is *Fundulus notti dispar*.

DISTRIBUTION, STATUS, AND HABITAT

In Wisconsin, the starhead topminnow occurs in the Mississippi River drainage in four specific, disjunct centers: in the Spring Green to Sauk City sector of the Wisconsin River; in the lower Sugar River and Coon Creek of the Rock River drainage; in the Mukwonago River watershed of the Fox River basin; and in the Black River near La Crosse.

Specimens examined: UWSP 1192 (5) Wisconsin River slough T8N R5E Sec 1 (Iowa County), 1965; UWSP 5185 (1) Wisconsin River slough T9N R6E Sec 20 (Dane County), 1973. The Wisconsin Fish Distribution Study (1974–1978) reported: (2) unnamed drainage ditch T1N R1OE Sec 19 (Rock County), 1974; (1) unnamed channel Black River T17N R8W Sec 17 (La Crosse County), 1978. Other reports: Taylor Creek T1N R1OE Sec 6 (Rock County), 1965 (M. Johnson); Coon Creek T1N R11E Sec 27 (Rock County) (L. Lovshin); Lake Beulah (Walworth County) (Greene 1935); Mukwonago Millpond = Phantom Lake (Waukesha County) (Cahn 1927); Mukwonago River below Phantom Lake Dam (Waukesha County), 1968 (M. Johnson) and 1974 (Seeburger 1975); Mukwonago River at Hwy 83 (Waukesha County), 1975 (T. Krischan); three sites (specifics lacking, not plotted on map) in sloughs along the Wisconsin River between Hwy 14 at Spring Green and Sauk City (Sauk County), 1968 (M. Johnson).

Although Greene (1935) recorded the starhead topminnow from Lake Beulah (Walworth County), it has not been taken there since the 1920s (Seeburger 1975). In the fall of 1974, it was reported as common in the Mukwonago River below the Phantom Lake Dam (Waukesha County); 18 specimens were taken from a slough of the Wisconsin River (Iowa County) in 1965.

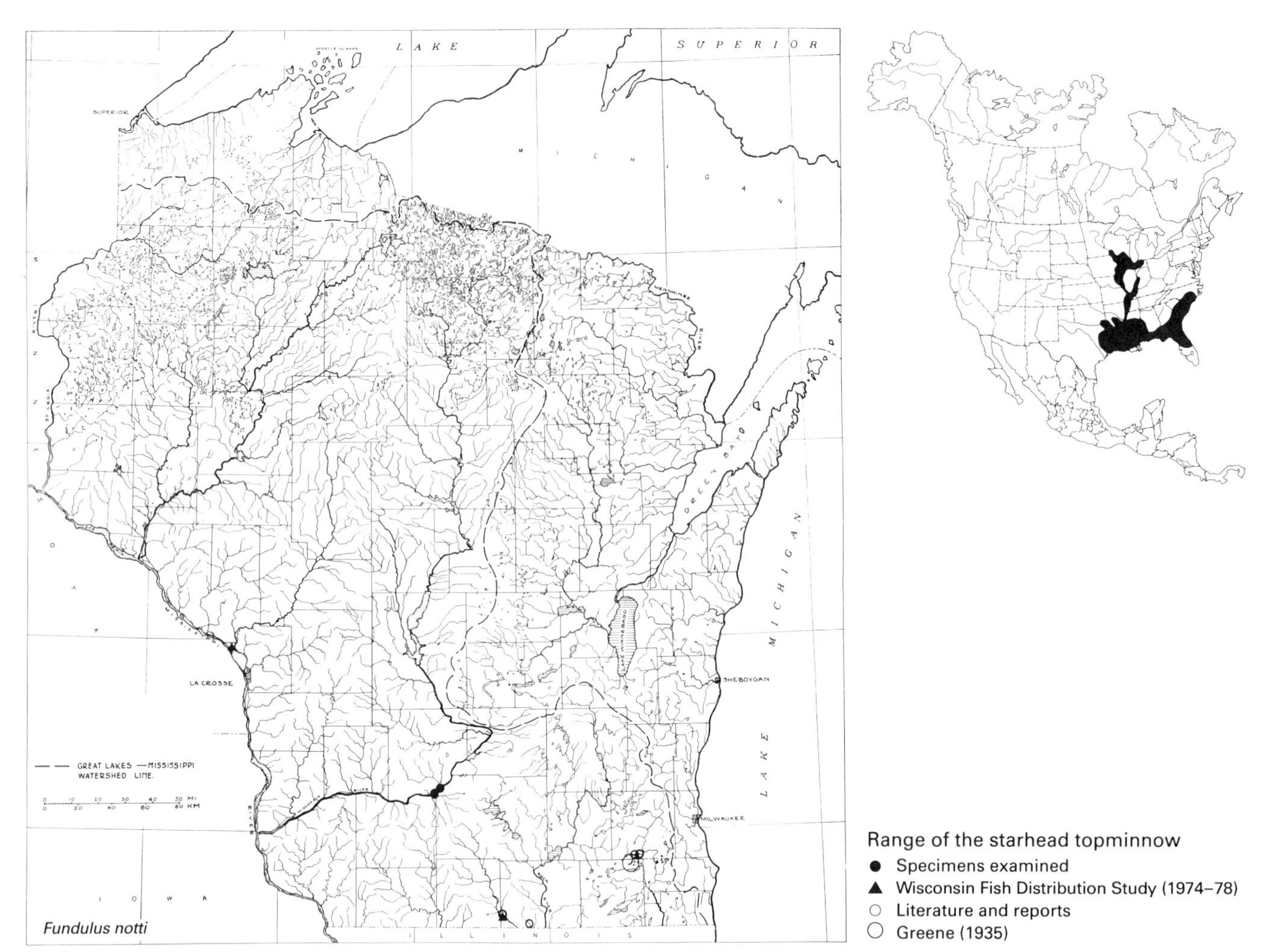

Wisconsin has given the starhead topminnow endangered status (Les 1979). Care must be taken that it is not lost from our waters, where it is at the northern limit of its distribution. The establishment of a topminnow sanctuary is recommended; it would be unique in the Midwest. The related pupfish of the arid Southwest have received special protection from the federal government.

The characteristic habitat of the starhead topminnow is a quiet, shallow backwater having clear to slightly turbid waters and an abundance of submerged aquatic plants. Cahn (1927) noted that in the Mukwonago millpond habitat the water was dark, the banks mucky, and the shores reedy. Below the dam, where the river was 15–18 m wide, this species occurred over gravel and rock in shallows with dense vegetation.

BIOLOGY

Spawning occurs from June to July. In Illinois, ripe male and female starhead topminnows were taken at the end of May (Forbes and Richardson 1920).

A gravid starhead topminnow female, 50 mm TL, taken from the Wisconsin River (Iowa County) at the end of June, had ovaries 16% of body weight; she held 136 yellow, maturing or mature eggs, 0.7–1.8 mm diam, and a small number of white, immature eggs, 0.3–0.6 mm diam. Five specimens from this Wisconsin River collection, age II and 47–55 mm long, had the following estimated lengths at the annuli: 1—30 mm, and 2—49 mm. Maturity is reached at age II. The mortality of a year class is almost complete by the end of the third year of life; few starhead topminnows reach age III.

A 60-mm male starhead topminnow, collected 30 May from a swamp (Union County, Illinois), was 3 years old. According to Pflieger (1975), adults reach a maximum of about 81 mm (3.2 in).

In Illinois (Forbes and Richardson 1920), about half of the food ingested by starhead topminnows consisted of insects, half of which were terrestrial insects that had fallen into the water. Mollusks, crustaceans, and delicate aquatic vegetation constituted the remainder of the starhead's diet.

The starhead topminnow normally occurs singly or in pairs. It skims along just beneath the surface of the water, with a bright silvery spot showing on the top of the head; it will not dive even when pursued. Cahn (1927) noted that it sometimes swims slowly with its dorsal fin out of water, and that when it is disturbed it zigzags rapidly, usually to return very shortly to the spot it left.

In South Carolina, starhead topminnows from various shores of a small woodland pond were placed in unfamiliar surroundings. These fish had the ability to orient themselves with respect to the sun for moving in a direction which would return them to the land-water interface from which they had been captured. Even when placed on land surfaces, the fish were able to move toward the water by using the position of the sun to align their bodies for a series of overland jumps. On heavily overcast days, however, many fish were unable to orient their bodies in a consistent direction from jump to jump. Goodyear (1970) noted an unusual escape maneuver by the starhead topminnow (p. 604):

> In five instances *F. notti* which were being chased by bass, were seen to jump onto the bank and remain there for several minutes before jumping back into the pond. The bass remained only a few seconds after the *F. notti* left the water and were gone when the starhead topminnow returned.

IMPORTANCE AND MANAGEMENT

Considering its scarcity in Wisconsin, the starhead topminnow must have limited value as a forage species.

Silverside Family — Atherinidae

Only one species of silversides is known from Wisconsin. It is a strictly freshwater form with an extensive range over the eastern United States. Hubbs (1921) suggested that its "habitat reactions" were inherited from its marine ancestors and hence were developed in the sea.

Twelve species of silversides in eight genera are listed from the United States and Canada (Robins et al. 1980). Of these, 10 occupy typical saltwater coastal or estuarine habitats. Most silversides are small fishes. They include the well-known California grunion, a spectacular fish which during high tide is thrown up onto the beach sands to spawn. Rosen (1964) demonstrated that the silversides, halfbeaks, and killifishes were closely aligned families, probably with a common Eocene ancestry in the fresh and brackish waters of Australia, from which they spread around the world.

The members of this family have scaled heads, two dorsal fins (the first small and spiny), pectoral fins high on the body, and both pelvic and anal fins each with a small spine. The swim bladder is present, but loses its pneumatic duct connection with the pharynx (physoclist).

Brook Silverside

Labidesthes sicculus (Cope). *Labidesthes*—a pair of pincers, for eating; *sicculus*—dried, found in half-dry pools.

Other common names: silverside, northern silverside, skipjack, friar, topwater.

Adult 95 mm, Rinehart L. (Portage Co.), 13 June 1977

DESCRIPTION

Body slender and elongate, translucent, slightly compressed; top profile of head straight, and head flattened. Length 51–76 mm (2–3 in.). TL = 1.18 SL. Depth into SL 7–10. Head length into SL 4.6–5.2. Snout beaklike, with lower jaw slightly projecting. Mouth long, almost horizontal near tip, and strongly oblique posteriorly; minute, needlelike teeth on upper and lower jaws. Two dorsal fins on posterior half of back, first dorsal with 4 spines, second with 1 spine and 9–11 rays. Anal fin with 1 spine and 20–26 rays; pelvic fin with 1 spine and 5 rays; caudal fin forked. Scales small, cycloid; lateral series scales 75–84; lateral line incomplete. Digestive tract short, S-shaped, about 0.5 TL. Pyloric caeca absent.

General color pale green; body translucent in life. Dorsal scales outlined with pigment; prominent lateral silvery stripe. Preserved fish light colored (but opaque), lower jaw and top of head pigmented; scales of back outlined with pigmented dots; prominent dark midlateral stripe fading out anteriorly. Fins clear to lightly pigmented along edges of rays; spinous dorsal fin pigmented near tip.

Breeding male with short, conical urogenital papilla behind anus; female with a broad, round, fleshy-lipped genital papilla with large opening. Male with prominently black-tipped first dorsal fin; first dorsal fin in female only lightly pigmented (J. Yrios, pers. comm.).

DISTRIBUTION, STATUS, AND HABITAT

The brook silverside occurs in the Mississippi River and Lake Michigan drainage basins in Wisconsin. The northernmost report is from the St. Croix Flowage in Douglas County (Sather and Johannes 1973). Although we have no Wisconsin record from the Lake Superior drainage basin, it has recently been collected from the Dead River at Marquette, Michigan (Berg et al. 1975).

The brook silverside is common in many lakes and rivers in Wisconsin. Because of its visible habits, large numbers are documented for many waters. Its status appears to be secure.

In Wisconsin the brook silverside was encountered most frequently at the surface in clear water, 0.1–1.5 m deep, over substrates of sand (39% frequency), gravel (22%), mud (15%), silt (9%), clay (6%), rubble (6%), and boulders (3%). It occurred in lakes and in lake-like habitats such as sloughs, reservoirs, and pools of large rivers. Occasionally it was taken in moderate currents of medium-sized rivers 12–50 m wide. It is frequently associated with sparse vegetation, seldom with dense vegetation.

BIOLOGY

The brook silverside spawns only one season, at age I, and dies shortly thereafter. In Wisconsin, spawning begins as early as May (Cahn 1927), reaches its height in June and July, and probably extends into early August. The pairing of fish begins when water temperatures reach 18°C (64.4°F); spawning occurs at 20°C (68°F), and the peak of spawning is reached at 22.7°C (72.9°F).

In Michigan (Hubbs 1921), each male brook silverside appeared to command a rather ill-defined area of surface water, 2–4 m long by 1–2 m wide, in moderate current. From this area each guardian male vigorously drove off invading males, then usually returned to his original position. Hubbs noted, however, that during the height of the breeding activities, territorial restrictions were lost as both males and females "were engaged in their wild spawning."

Cahn (1927), who made extensive observations on this species in Oconomowoc Lake and adjacent lakes in Waukesha County, did not observe the establishment of territories. The following account, unless otherwise specified, is taken from Cahn. All of the spawning activities described took place in shallow water near shores.

The prespawning activity of the brook silverside is in the form of vertical pairing, during which the male swims on the surface of the water, and the female swims in perfect alignment with the male, approximately 25–30 cm below him. The female determines the direction of movement. Frequently two or more males may be present, but generally one male drives the others away. Early in the season the progress of the fish is leisurely—30 cm is traveled in 3–4 seconds. As the water warms up, the fish travel in

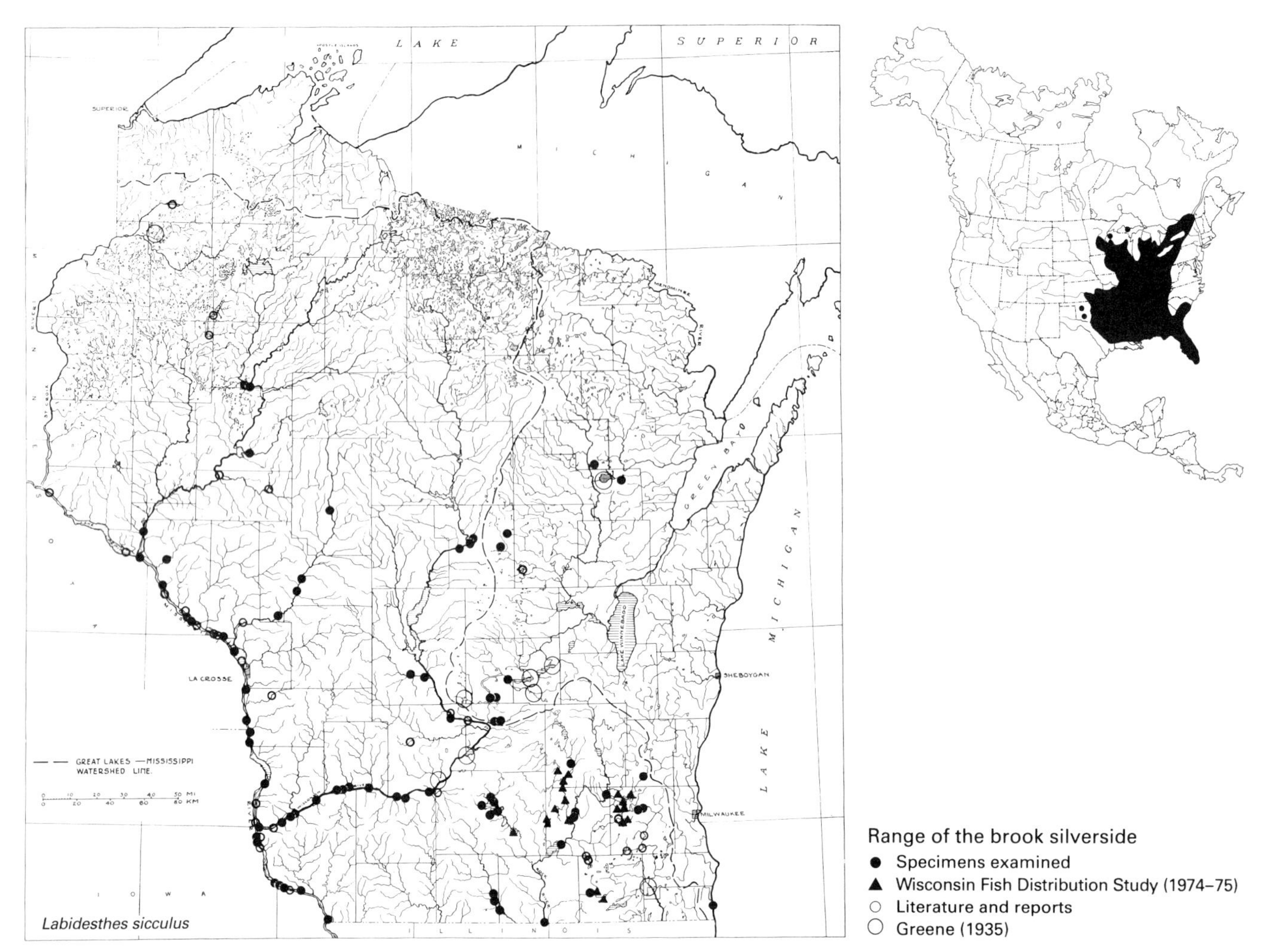

Range of the brook silverside
● Specimens examined
▲ Wisconsin Fish Distribution Study (1974–75)
○ Literature and reports
◯ Greene (1935)

spurts, and the interval of alignment decreases to about 5 cm. When the breeding season reaches its peak, the position of the fish shifts to a horizontal alignment with the male following the female as she "travels at a furious pace."

When the spawning activities are in full sway, a school of silversides presents a wild sight (Cahn p. 65):

> . . . In and out dart the females, pursued by one or more males, darting this way and that, shooting an inch or more out of the water and landing again three or four inches from the spot of their emergence amid a spatter of spray, followed immediately by the attending male retinue. Suddenly the female slows down her pace and comes to what amounts to *comparative* rest. The first male to reach her approaches from the rear and draws up along side. This apparently is the signal for the departure of any males that may be pursuing that particular female. . . . Other males simply disperse and join in the chase of other females. The paired fish now begin a downward glide, approaching the bottom at an angle of approximately 30°. During the descent, the fish bring the edges of their abdomens into repeated momentary contacts—from eight to twenty-one times being the extreme numbers observed, with fourteen as an average of forty-six observations. During the descent the eggs are extruded from the body of the female and may be seen slowly settling toward the bottom in the wake of the descending pair. Fertilization takes place in the water immediately after the eggs leave the female, the spermatozoa being extruded by the male coincident with the momentary contact with the abdomen of the female. . . .

Cahn observed that, after completion of the descent, 26 females showed empty ovaries, and that only a few females had retained some half-dozen eggs. The males ascend at once to the surface where they take off in pursuit of other females.

In the brook silverside populations I have looked at, it is obvious that all eggs do not ripen at once, nor is the entire complement of eggs released at one time. On the lower Wisconsin River, spawning was well under way by 19 June. An 81-mm, 2.77-g female, with ovaries 15.5% of body weight, held 785 maturing to mature (orange) eggs, 0.6–1.0 mm diam;

an immature, white-yellow generation of eggs was 0.3–0.5 mm diam. From a nearby area on the same date, a 75-mm, 2.08-g female in prespawning condition, with ovaries 10% of body weight, held 450 maturing eggs, 0.5–0.8 mm diam, and a small number of immature eggs, 0.2–0.5 mm diam.

On 17 July in the Wisconsin River at Boscobel (Grant County), an 80-mm 2.46-g fish, with ovaries 14% of body weight, held 700 maturing to mature eggs, 0.8–1.1 mm diam, and a few immature eggs, 0.4–0.6 mm diam. Females examined from Pewaukee Lake (Waukesha County) on 3 August and from Lake Monona (Dane County) on 10 August still had well-developed ovaries containing a number of ripe eggs. It is likely that spawning may continue over a period of days or weeks. In Indiana, Nelson (1968b) noted similar ranges in egg sizes and differences in egg generations.

The brook silverside's egg is well supplied with a number of oil globules and with a flotation-adhesive organ in the form of a gelatinous filament, which is about 6 times as long as the diameter of the egg. In a water current, this filament may act as a flotation body transporting the egg for some distance. The sticky filament becomes attached to the first thing with which it comes into contact, either vegetation or bottom material such as bulrushes or gravel. The egg itself is not sticky.

In Oconomowoc Lake, the eggs hatched out in 8–9 days at depths of 41–94 cm in 22.8–24°C (73–75°F) water. In Indiana (Nelson 1968b), eyed eggs from Crooked Lake hatched in the laboratory into young 4 mm TL. Fish (1932) described and iillustrated the 27-mm stage.

After hatching, young brook silversides wiggle to the surface, and assemble in schools of 30–200 individuals. They confine themselves to the upper 3 cm below the surface, are constantly active, and move as a school from the shallow water outward to assume a pelagic habitat over deep water. This habitat may be over water 3–5 m deep, but it is generally over water 10–20 m deep.

In their offshore habitat, the young eat largely zooplankton and grow rapidly. The small size of young brook silversides, together with their inconspicuous coloring and nearly transparent bodies, gives them protection from enemies. Despite their camouflage, they have been seen scattering wildly with the approach of a tern or a large fish. Hubbs (1921) and Cahn (1927) emphasized the constant activity of the young. The brook silverside is among the most active of our freshwater fishes, and, according to Cahn, young fish 22-mm long swam an average distance of 211 cm in 2 minutes, or an estimated 886 m in the course of a day.

With the coming of darkness at night, young brook silversides become inactive and float motionless just under the surface. Members of the school point in all directions, and there is no marked orientation. From mid-July on the young engage in increasingly frequent nocturnal migrations to the shallows, from which they return to their pelagic habit over deep water during the day. Cahn has suggested that this movement is triggered by differences in water temperature: at night the young seek out the warmer surface temperature of the shallow water (1 m deep) rather than the colder surface temperature of the deep water (16 m). This shoreward journey is accomplished rapidly (Cahn 1927:78–79):

> . . . they swim at top speed straight for the shore. . . . The minnows arrive together, which fact is significant. In from ten to twenty-five minutes the entire silversides population of the lake is inshore.

Upon completing their inshore movement, the young have joined the adult silversides that typically inhabit inshore surfaces through the 24-hour day. Following hatching, young brook silversides grow 1 mm per day for 2 weeks, after which growth is slower. In Oconomowoc Lake, the average growth during the first year of life was: 22 June, 11.2 mm; 6 July, 28.6 mm; 17 August, 46.2 mm; 28 September, 63.9 mm; and 26 October, 65.6 mm. Growth ceases in mid-October and resumes the following May: 18 May, 68.6 mm; 1 June, 72.2 mm; 22 June, 75.2 mm, and 1 August to 1 September, 76.2 mm. Most growth (approximately 80–90%) occurs during the first year of life. The total life-span of the brook silverside is 15–17 months. The single annulus is deposited in June and July. In Indiana, Nelson observed brook silversides about 100 mm FL, which must have been between 21 and 23 months old; none lived into a second breeding season.

The largest known Wisconsin specimens of brook silversides were 96 and 98 mm TL; they were captured 3 August from Pewaukee Lake (Waukesha County). In Indiana (Nelson 1968b), one brook silverside was 109 mm (4.3 in) FL.

In Oconomowoc Lake, young brook silversides prior to their inshore migrations at night, ate *Cyclops*, *Daphnia*, *Bosmina*, rotifers, diatoms, and other algae. While inshore in mid-August they consumed mostly insects, including Diptera, Coleoptera, and unspecified larvae; they also ate copepods, cladocerans, ostracods, *Mysis relicta*, plant remains, and arachnids. Accompanying the change in environment, there was a change from the micro-organism diet to a predominantly insectivorous diet.

In Lake Mendota (Pearse 1921a), brook silversides had eaten insect pupae and adults and cladocerans. In an earlier study (Pearse 1918), brook silversides in the Madison area had eaten insect eggs, larvae, pupae and adults, as well as spiders, mites, ostracods, copepods, cladocerans, rotifers, protozoans, and algae.

In Illinois (Forbes 1883), spiders and terrestrial insects, accidentally washed or fallen into the water, amounted to 12% of the brook silverside's food. Mullan et al. (1968) reported that terrestrial organisms were of major seasonal importance to this species. In an Indiana stream, dance flies (Empedidae), which frequently hover above waters in large swarms, constituted 21% of the food items consumed by these fish (Zimmerman 1970). Fish remains have been reported from several brook silverside stomachs, and *Labidesthes* fry and centrarchid fry were taken from the stomachs of silversides collected from an Indiana lake (Nelson 1968b).

Keast (1965) noted that the brook silverside is specialized for catching flying insects in the air. Its long, closely set gill rakers with their numerous denticles suit it admirably for straining micro-organisms from the water. In Ohio, this species often stopped feeding in the daytime when the water became turbid, and lay listlessly at the surface as it does at night (Trautman 1957).

In a southeastern Michigan winterkill lake, with oxygen levels of 0.8–0.5 ppm in the upper 0.3–1.2 m of water, there was good survival of brook silversides. Cahn (1927) determined that it tolerates pH levels of 7.5–8.3, with the optimum pH tolerance at 7.65–7.7.

The brook silverside is positively phototropic. At night Cahn was able to lead a small school of these fish 1.4 km across Oconomowoc Lake with the beam of his flashlight. In Lake Mendota, Tibbles (1956: 185) reported that, when spotlights and Coleman lanterns were directed onto the water, brook silversides began to appear and remained in the areas of highest illumination, whereas yellow perch, which were also attracted, stayed on the periphery of the illuminated arc, or in the shadow of the boat:

> When a spotlight was moved to change the field of light intensity—the skipjacks "en masse" would rapidly follow to keep within the illuminated area. Any unfortunate skipjack that was unable to adjust rapidly enough and follow the beam of light was immediately taken by the perch which remained in the darker zones.

Moonlight can also precipitate activity among brook silversides. If the night is dark and calm, with no moon or only part of a moon, the fish lie suspended and motionless in the water. When the moon is almost full or full, the shallows become the scene of one of the most startling scenes in the fish world (Cahn 1927:81):

> . . . The silversides seem to go crazy, as if they were moonstruck. They dart about at a most startling speed, dashing here and there, leaping out of the water again and again, bumping into each other, splashing, circling, behaving in a most exaggerated manner . . . and the gentle splashing of the "breaks" is the characteristic night sound of the lake. Such activity goes on during the entire night if the light holds. . . .

The brook silverside's habit of leaping out of the water and through the air in a low, graceful arch, at times for distances at least 10 times its own length, is a source of wonder, even to the casual observer. Hubbs (1921) observed that occasionally such a leap was repeated from one to four times before the fish finally dove out of sight. He noted that the fishes seemed to be at play, although they could have been avoiding a predator, securing insect food, or skipping prior to spawning.

The brook silverside is the most characteristic of our surface fishes—more than any other Wisconsin fish, it locates at the surface of the water. Immature individuals can scarcely be driven more than a few centimeters below the surface, and even the adults spend most of their time within 10–12 cm of the surface and seldom venture below the upper meter of water.

During the winter the brook silverside generally remains inshore over water up to 2 m deep. Its movements are slow and sluggish. Its food habits revert back to those of the immature fish, but it apparently lives on a maintenance ration only since there is no visible growth during the winter.

IMPORTANCE AND MANAGEMENT

When young brook silversides are over deep water, they are preyed upon by the black tern, common tern, longnose gar, cisco, smallmouth bass, and largemouth bass. In shallow water they have been taken from smallmouth bass, largemouth bass, bowfin, northern pike, rock bass, green sunfish, bluegill, pumpkinseed, white bass, yellow perch, grass pickerel, cisco, American bittern, least bittern, belted kingfisher, red-breasted merganser, mudpuppy, snapping turtle, water snake, crayfish spp., and mink (Adams and Hankinson 1926).

The brook silverside is almost never used as a bait fish, since it keeps poorly in a minnow bucket. In Canada, larger specimens are occasionally used for bait. Adams and Hankinson (1926) stated that two or three dead silversides on a hook will catch perch, bluegills, and black crappies. Cahn (1927) noted that in southeastern Wisconsin brook silversides are usually replaced carefully by fishermen "who uniformly believe them to be young ciscos."

The brook silverside makes an interesting and unique addition to the aquarium, but it is difficult to keep alive.

It has been suggested that the brook silverside may be of value in destroying mosquitoes. However, its fragility would make it of little use for stocking bodies of water where mosquitoes breed.

Stickleback Family—Gasterosteidae

Two species of sticklebacks in two genera are known from Wisconsin. Members of this family occur in North America, northern and central Asia, and Europe. Six species in five genera are found in the United States and Canada (Robins et al. 1980). Of these, two species are strictly coastal saltwater forms, three occupy shallow, inshore areas of marine waters and fresh waters, and only one is a strictly freshwater form.

The sticklebacks are a family of small, scaleless fishes with well-developed pelvic spines and isolated dorsal spines. Lateral bony plates are often developed. The pelvic girdles are generally large, and the pectoral fins are fanlike, set high on the sides, and have their bases in a vertical line.

The behavioral patterns of our Wisconsin species, the brook stickleback and the ninespine stickleback, are quite elaborate. Their behavior is similar to that of the threespine stickleback, whose behavior has been studied intensively for many years and is perhaps better understood than the behavior of most animals known to man. Pertinent references dealing with the biology of sticklebacks are provided by Reisman and Cade (1967) and Wootton (1976).

Brook Stickleback

Culaea inconstans (Kirtland). *Culaea*—coined from the former generic name *Eucalia*; *inconstans*—changeable, variable.

Other common names: fivespined stickleback, variable stickleback, freshwater stickleback, common stickleback, pinfish, sixspined stickleback, black stickleback.

Adult 68 mm, Slough Cr. (Marinette Co.), 21 June 1966

DESCRIPTION

Body deep, compressed laterally. Length 38–61 mm (1.5–2.4 in). TL = 1.15 SL. Depth into TL 4.7–5.4. Head length into TL 3.4–4.3. Mouth small, oblique, and dorsal, with lips swollen. Lower jaw projecting beyond upper jaw; minute, needlelike teeth in several irregular rows on upper and lower jaws. Dorsal spines 4–6, separate, and each with its own membrane, followed by dorsal fin with 9–11 rays. Anal fin with 1 spine and 9–10 rays; pelvic fin with 1 heavy spine and 1 ray (pelvic skeleton absent in some populations—see J. S. Nelson 1969 and 1977). Pectoral fin 9–11 soft rays; caudal fin rounded to truncate. Body scaleless, but with 30–36 small, bony plates along the lateral line (see J. S. Nelson 1969); lateral line complete. Digestive tract about 0.5 TL. Chromosomes 2n = 46 (Chen and Reisman 1970).

General color olive green on back and sides, with white spots of varying sizes and shapes, or with light vertical, wavy lines; belly and ventral region of head of lighter greenish color to whitish. All fins lightly to darkly pigmented.

Breeding male with body and fins jet black, sometimes tinged with copper.

SYSTEMATIC NOTES

The brook stickleback was known for many years by the generic name *Eucalia*. It was shown by Whitley (1950) that *Eucalia* Jordan, 1878, in the Gasterosteidae is preoccupied by *Eucalia* C. Felder, 1861, in Lepidoptera (Nymphalidae). Bailey and Allum (1962) saw no alternative to the adoption of *Culaea* Whitley, 1950, as the generic name for the brook stickleback.

In examining populations of the brook stickleback throughout its range, J. S. Nelson (1969) found a clinal variation in dorsal and pelvic spine lengths, with the longest spines occurring in the Wisconsin to Ohio area. He suggested that the long spines of the Midwest forms act as protection against predators in an area where predators have a large selection of prey species. In the West, however, where the prey-predator ratio is less, natural selection favors short-spined individuals with streamlined bodies and light pelvic skeletons which are better able to escape into dense vegetation. In southern Manitoba, Moodie (1977) noted the small body size of a population of brook sticklebacks which are exposed to predatory fishes.

DISTRIBUTION, STATUS, AND HABITAT

The brook stickleback occurs in all three drainage basins in Wisconsin. It is widely distributed in most small river basins, particularly in headwater reaches; it occurs in shoal waters of Lakes Superior and Michigan, and in inland lakes, especially northward.

Where the brook stickleback is found, it is often a common species. It is rare in Lake Winnebago (Priegel 1967a) and occasional in Lakes Superior and Michigan. Its position in state waters appears to be secure.

In Wisconsin, the brook stickleback was encountered most frequently in clear to slightly turbid water at depths up to 1.5 m, over substrates of sand (24% frequency), gravel (21%), silt (16%), mud (11%), rubble (9%), boulders (9%), clay (5%), detritus (4%), and bedrock (2%). It occurred in spring holes, boggy lakes, and occasionally in well-protected bays of large lakes. This species preferred moderate currents in streams of the following widths: 1.0–3.0 m (36%), 3.1–6.0 m (36%), 6.1–12.0 m (11%), 12.1–24.0 m (8%), 24.1–50.0 m (7%), and more than 50 m (2%). It occurs in the Great Lakes in shallows down to 31 m (Hubbs and Lagler 1964), and in Lake Huron at all depths to 55 m (Scott and Crossman 1973). It is usually found in the colder waters, and invariably is associated with a moderate to dense vegetation cover. In southwestern Wisconsin, it is frequently encountered in highly turbid waters, suggesting the development of silt-tolerant populations.

BIOLOGY

In Wisconsin, spawning may begin as early as April, and is known to occur from May to mid-June. Jacobs (1948) stated that the water must attain a minimum temperature of 8°C (46°F) before the brook stickleback begins to spawn. However, nests have been found normally at 15–19°C (59°–66°F) (Winn 1960);

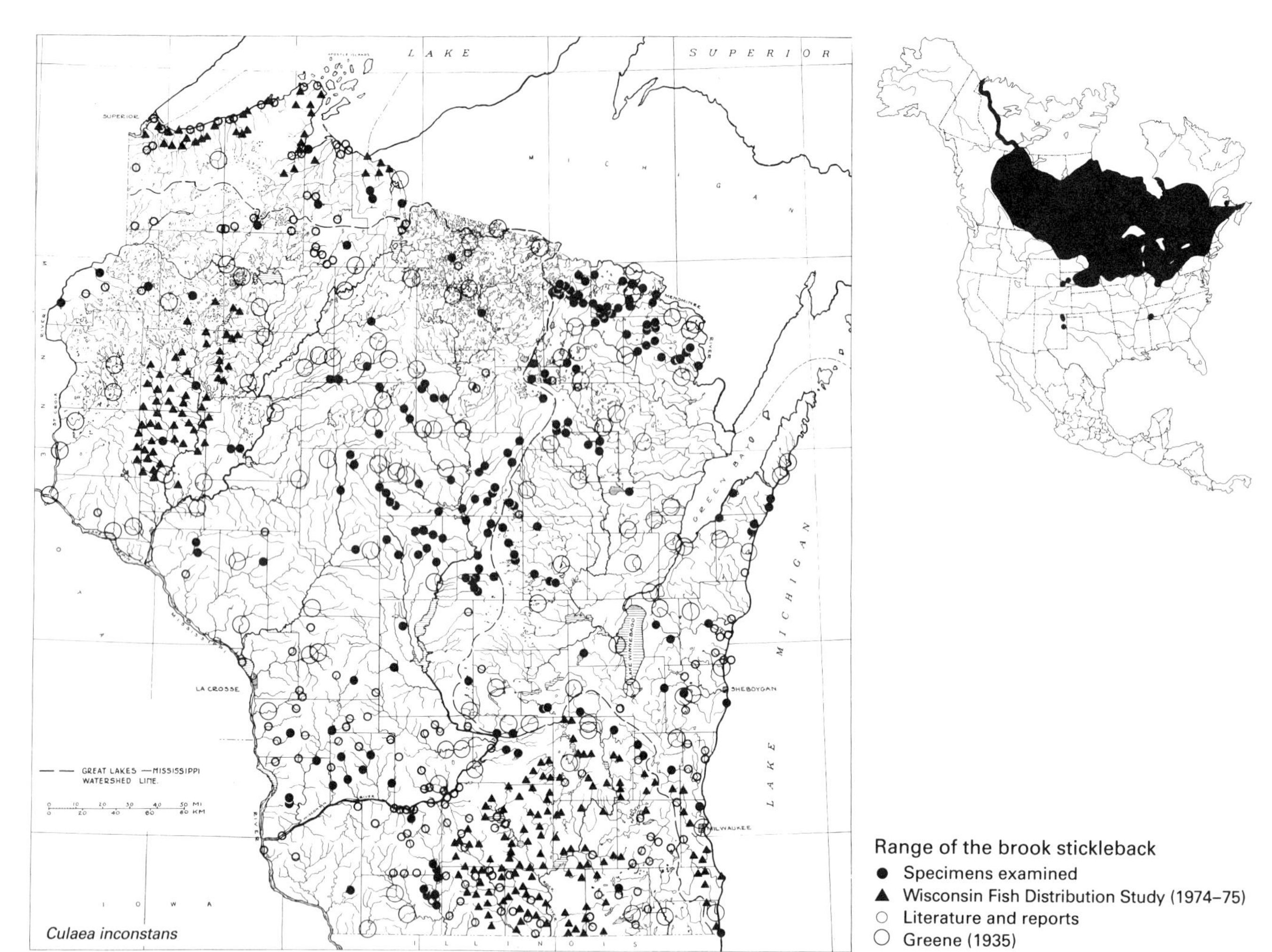

outside of this temperature range, nest building and courtship are seriously impaired. In addition to a suitable water temperature, the environmental requirements for successful spawning include vegetation for nest construction and clear water for courtship displays (Winn 1960, MacLean and Gee 1971).

During the spring, adult brook sticklebacks move from deep, cold water into shallow, warm water, where they establish territories and start to build nests. According to Winn (1960), the territories are defended against individuals of a reasonable size and of most species, including darters and trout. Rather narrow boundaries exist between the territories, which the male sticklebacks are able to recognize. A male, chasing another male, often crosses his boundary and thus in turn is chased. Ritualized fighting, called "lateral display," has been identified and described by Reisman and Cade (1967:267):

> . . . [It] consisted of a parallel head-to-head or head-to-tail orientation with simultaneous fluttering of the bodies and with the dorsal and ventral spines maximally erect. It was usually followed by a very quick attack by one of the fish and an equally rapid counterattack by the other. Such attacks were sometimes followed immediately by a reorientation of the fish into the lateral display . . . this display occurred only between territorial males, which always darkened in color during the display and attack and showed conspicuous black vertical bands through their eyes.

In general, the brook sticklebacks' nests are roughly globular in shape, 1.5–5.0 cm diam, and are constructed by the males of organic debris, filamentous algae, and other materials (Winn 1960). The nests are usually attached to a stem somewhere between the bottom and more than 0.3 m above the bottom. They increase in size over the season as eggs are added and as the male adds material to the nest. The bottom where nests are located varies from organic debris to sand and various mixtures of both. Some nests observed in Lake Michigan were attached to *Scirpus* stalks and to blades of grass bound together. A preferred building site is *Chara*. The nesting materials are attached to their support and to each other by a whitish cement which is produced by the kidneys and associated structures, including the muciparous tubules, urinary ducts, bladder, and common urinary duct. All of these become modified to produce the secretion (Breder and Rosen 1966). All nests, according to Winn (1960), have one opening prior to the deposition of eggs by a female. She creates a second hole upon leaving the nest through the side opposite the entrance maintained by the male.

While the nest is under construction, even a ripe female may be attacked vigorously. Winn observed a male hitting the body of a female with his snout several times until she left. Generally, however, females swim in aggregations or individually outside of the male's area. When a female is ready to spawn, her color changes from a uniform pale green to a variegated dark and light pattern. She then enters the male's territory where she is attacked. She responds in one of four ways to the male's nips and butts: she moves toward the nest, she remains motionless, she goes to the bottom, or she moves on to another territory. If she remains still or goes to the bottom, the male frequently goes to the opening of the nest (Winn 1960:433):

> . . . If she did not come to the nest, he would go back to her and the process was repeated. Several times nudges by the male appeared to direct the female towards the nest. Eventually the female entered a nest. In this position, with her head and tail sticking out each side of the nest, the male prodded her ventral region and her caudal peduncle. This resulted in her vibrating vigorously at which time presumably she laid eggs. After the female had vibrated, usually several to many times, she swam out of the nest where she was attacked frequently by the male. . . . She fled immediately to an area outside of the males' territories.

After the departure of the female, the male enters the nest momentarily and fertilizes the eggs.

According to Hubbs and Lagler (1964), fewer than 100 eggs are usually produced, and these are zealously guarded by the male. After the eggs have been laid in the nest, the male pushes them to the side and down. The male brook stickleback may repair the second hole in the nest created by the exit of the female; such repairs were observed much less often near the end of the spawning season. According to numerous observers (Winn 1960, McKenzie 1974), the male positions himself in front of the nest entrance and fans a current of water through the nest by a vigorous, alternate beating of his pectoral fins; while fanning, his position is maintained by a strong compensatory beating of his tail.

During the parental phase, the male may also build another nest at a different site, and transfer the eggs to a new nest. McKenzie noted that males used pieces of the old nest to build the new. Before the old nest is completely demolished, the male transfers the eggs by grasping them in his mouth and swimming to the new nest. If a clutch of eggs falls out of the nest, the male retrieves the clutch by grasping it in his mouth; he then swims to the nest entrance and relodges the eggs.

In the Waupaca River (Waupaca County) on 13 June 1960, a 52-mm, 1.63-g female brook stickleback in prespawning condition with ovaries 8.9% of body weight, held 182 maturing (orange) eggs, 0.9–1.1 mm diam; she also held a few immature (white) eggs, 0.3–0.6 mm diam. In the Popple River (Florence County) on 16 June 1965, when spawning was under way, a partly spawned, 52-mm, 1.40-g female, with ovaries 10.7% of body weight, held 90 mature eggs, 1.2–1.3 mm diam; she also held a few immature eggs, 0.3–0.5 mm diam. A 53-mm, 1.37-g female, taken from the Pecatonica River (Lafayette County) on 28 June 1960, had ovaries 11.7% of body weight, and held 94 mature eggs, 1.2–1.3 mm diam; in these eggs, the egg membrane had lifted from the yolk and exhibited a clear (perivitelline) space.

The brook stickleback's eggs are demersal and adhesive. Winn (1960) observed hatching in 8–10 days at water temperatures of 16–17°C (61–63°F), and in 9–11 days at 17–18°C (63–64°F). McKenzie (1974) reported hatching in 7 days at 17.5–18°C. The larvae are 5 mm long. Although some observers have reported that the larvae remain attached by their heads to various materials for several days, Winn suggested that this apparent attachment may be explained by movement of the pectoral and caudal fins rather than by any viscid spot.

According to McKenzie, on the day of hatching the male constructs a nursery by pulling apart the upper portion of the nest until it is a loose network of material. Such a nursery may aid in the aeration of the embryos, and may also prevent the newly hatched fry from escaping before they can swim freely and fend for themselves. As the embryos hatch they rise upwards, and most of them become enmeshed in the nursery. A few escape and rise to the surface of the water, but these are quickly retrieved by the male, who catches them in his mouth one at a time and spits them into the nursery. He then fans the fry briefly. In a day or two, the young escape so fast from the nursery that the male is unable to retrieve them all, and he either abandons them or eats them.

M. Fish (1932) illustrated and described the 19.6-mm stage.

The growth of young-of-year brook sticklebacks in Wisconsin follows:

Date	No. of Fish	TL (mm) Avg	Range	Location
18 June	14	25.1	20–33	Rocky Run Cr. (Wood Co.)
20 June	4	24.8	22–26	K C Cr. (Marinette Co.)
30 June	10	33.9	27–40	Pecatonica R. (Lafayette Co.)
30 June	23	32.3	22–38	Pecatonica R. (Iowa Co.)
4 July	14	26.7	22–31	Pedro Cr. (Oneida Co.)
16 July	9	33.4	30–35	Duffy Cr. (Crawford Co.)
22 July	25	33.7	26–38	Tributary to Waupaca R. (Waupaca Co.)
19 Sept.	8	30.9	25–35	L. Michigan (Door Co.)
20 Sept.	8	42.1	40–45	Mill Cr. (Wood Co.)
24 Sept.	86	39.6	31–47	Citron Cr. (Crawford Co.)
29 Sept.	21	46.0	39–49	Wolf R. (Langlade Co.)

Based on their length-frequency distribution, brook sticklebacks captured 22 July from a tributary to the Waupaca River (Waupaca County) were: age 0—26–38 mm; age I—40–58 mm; and age II—60–63 mm. On 24 June in Popple Creek (Forest County), the estimated length-frequency distribution was: age 0—29–32 mm; age I—35–54 mm; age II—56–59 mm; and age III—68 mm. The last age group was represented by a single individual, and age group II was weakly represented.

Sexual maturity is attained in 1 year.

A large, 76-mm, 4.65-g brook stickleback was taken from Rock Creek (Barron County) (Wis. Fish Dist. Study 1975). The maximum size reported for this species is 87 mm (3.5 in) (Scott and Crossman 1973).

The brook stickleback is carnivorous. A wide variety of aquatic insects, especially larvae and crustacans are the principal food items. In the Madison area (Dane County), more than 47% of the volume of food eaten consisted of insects, and 38% consisted of entomostracans (Pearse 1918). Winn (1960) noted that fish eggs, its own and those of other species, are a minor item in the brook stickleback's diet.

In Illinois (Forbes 1883), half of the stomach contents of four brook sticklebacks consisted of filamentous algae and the other half of insects (nearly all aquatic larvae of *Chironomus*) and Entomostraca (with Cladocera the most abundant). In Minnesota (Nurnberger 1928), brook sticklebacks had eaten algae, sponges, Entomostraca, and insects and their larvae.

Individual brook sticklebacks show some aggressive behavior of a nonreproductive type called food-fighting (Reisman and Cade 1967). Food-fighting appears to involve the establishment of a hierarchy, especially under crowded conditions. Large food objects are shaken vigorously while held in the mouth; this action serves not only to kill and to break up the prey into smaller pieces, but also to signal communal feeding, during which the large pieces of food are grabbed from mouth to mouth by five to seven participating individuals, attempting to steal the food away. Degraeve (1970) noted two instances in which brook sticklebacks burrowed their heads into the silt of the bottom in search of food.

When acclimated to water temperatures of 25–26°C (77–79°F), the brook stickleback's upper tolerance limit (permitting 50% survival) is 30.6°C (87.1°F) (Brett 1944). Preliminary tests have shown that this species can be acclimated to survive for months at lower tolerance temperatures of 0.0 to −2.0°C (Reisman and Cade 1967).

Nitrite toxicity of 5 ppm killed brook sticklebacks (McCoy 1972) in 3–5 hours; they were less sensitive to this toxicity level than the yellow perch, but far more sensitive than carp, black bullheads, common suckers, and quillbacks. Salinity tolerance experiments have indicated that brook sticklebacks have a considerable tolerance to salt water, at least for short periods; they continued to feed in salinities of 50% sea water (17.5 ppt), but ceased all activity at salinities of 70% (Nelson 1968c). Natural populations of brook sticklebacks are found in salt or brackish water, but such populations are unusual (Scott and Crossman 1973).

The marked spring and early summer natural breeding season of the brook stickleback suggests the stimulating effect of a long photoperiod, i.e., about 14–15.5 hours per day (Reisman and Cade 1967). In the nonreproductive state, these fish are relatively passive and congregate in schools.

Three types of burrowing behavior have been ascribed to the brook stickleback (Degraeve 1970). In one type, the fish burrow into silt by diving into it head first, and then rapidly lash their tails to propel their bodies beneath the silt; they may remain buried for periods exceeding 30 minutes. In another burrowing action, the fish "tunnel" through the silty substrate at about 15 cm per second for distances as great as 0.6 m, before they emerge again. Burrowing into silt in search of food, which has been described above, is the third type of behavior.

Spectacular downstream movements of the brook stickleback have been recorded. Large numbers were trapped moving down Silver Creek, Ontario, into Georgian Bay in Lake Huron, during a week in mid-June; similar numbers were trapped during a week from the end of June to early July of the following year (Lamsa 1963). In an upper Michigan tributary to Lake Superior, brook sticklebacks moved downstream chiefly in winter (Manion 1977); movement increased in October, peaked in January, then gradually tapered off through May. Most migration thus took place when stream temperatures reached their annual lows, and when water levels were nearly constant.

Headrick (1976) reported that, in central Wisconsin streams and ditches, the brook stickleback was abundant where bank vegetation trailed in the water in the presence of submergent *Ranunculus*, and where there was also a maximum density in watercress cover. Reed canary grass in upstream ditches was not good stickleback habitat because it sheltered brook trout which preyed on sticklebacks.

Sixty-four brook sticklebacks were collected from the South Branch of the Popple River (Florence County) along with white sucker (14), blacknose dace (28), creek chub (20), pearl dace (20), finescale dace (24), northern redbelly dace (69), bluntnose minnow (22), common shiner (46), brassy minnow (1), central mudminnow (5), johnny darter (3), and mottled sculpin (1).

IMPORTANCE AND MANAGEMENT

The brook stickleback is preyed upon by brook trout, smallmouth bass, northern pike, bowfin, yellow perch, largemouth bass, and walleye. It undoubtedly falls prey also to fish-eating birds, such as kingfishers, herons, terns, and mergansers.

The brook stickleback is a host species for the glochidial stage of the floater mussel, *Anodonta grandis*, hence helping to perpetuate that mussel.

In Wisconsin, the brook stickleback is not a preferred bait species, and it has little direct economic significance. However, in many waters it is effective in the control of mosquitoes, for it feeds on the "wrigglers" and often lives in habitats that other fishes can not tolerate (Hubbs and Lagler 1964).

Brook sticklebacks make interesting aquarium fish, and as such could be used in behavior studies if a supply of live brine shrimp could be maintained to feed them. Reproductive behavior can be induced in the aquarium by following basic procedures (Reisman 1961). However, because of its aggressive nature, the brook stickleback will kill other small fishes kept with it.

Ninespine Stickleback

Pungitius pungitius (Linnaeus). *Pungitius*—pricking.
Other common names: stickleback, tenspine stickleback, many-spined stickleback, pinfish, tiny burnstickle.

Adult 67 mm, L. Michigan, near Sheboygan (Sheboygan Co.), 23 Apr. 1967

Dorsolateral view. Note arrangement of spines and expanded caudal peduncle.

DESCRIPTION

Body slender, compressed laterally, tapering to an elongate, slender caudal peduncle broader than deep. Average length 57 mm (2.3 in). TL = 1.12 SL (1.14 in Lake Superior [Griswold and Smith 1973]). Depth into TL 6.0–7.2. Head length into TL 3.8–4.5. Mouth small, oblique and dorsal, with lips swollen. Lower jaw projecting beyond upper jaw; minute, needlelike teeth in several irregular rows on upper and lower jaws. Dorsal spines 9 (8–11), separate, and each with its own membrane, followed by dorsal fin with 9–11 rays. Anal fin with 1 spine and 8–10 rays; pelvic fin with 1 heavy spine and 1 ray; pectoral fin with 10 rays; caudal fin truncate to slightly notched. Scaleless, but with small, bony plates usually along anterior portion of lateral line, at bases of dorsal and anal fins, and on lateral keels of caudal peduncle; lateral line complete. Digestive tract short, about 0.4 TL. Chromosomes 2n = 42 (Chen and Reisman 1970).

Dark green to yellow-green above, with irregular dark bars or mottling; lower head and belly silvery. Fins unpigmented. Male with dark gray iris, ventral spines a conspicuous bluish white, and a midventral gray patch extending from vent anteriorly to area between opercula; female with pale gray iris, ventral spines an inconspicuous light gray, and no dark patch on ventral surface.

Breeding male often with jet black belly and white pelvic fin membranes. In both sexes, reddish tints about head.

SYSTEMATIC NOTES

For North America two morphological forms have been suggested (McPhail 1963): the Bering form, which occurs in coastal areas from Alaska across the top of the continent to New Jersey on the Atlantic coast; and the Mississippi form, which occurs from the lower Great Lakes north and westward to the MacKenzie River, and includes the Wisconsin populations. The latter form has a higher gill raker count than the Bering form, and a low to intermediate dorsal spine count. McPhail suggested that *Pungitius* survived glaciation in two ice-free refugia, and assumed that the southern refugium was in the upper Mississippi Valley. The evidence suggests that the differences between these forms are genotypic.

DISTRIBUTION, STATUS, AND HABITAT

In Wisconsin the ninespine stickleback occurs in the shoal waters of Lakes Superior and Michigan, and occasionally in the mouths of tributaries to these lakes. Records and reports appear for Lake Superior in Anderson and Smith (1971b), Dryer (1966), Moore and Braem (1965), McLain et al. (1965), and Anderson (1969); for Lake Michigan, they appear in Wells (1968), Wells and McLain (1973), Smith (1968b), and Reigle (1969a, b, c).

No records exist of this species from the inland lakes in Wisconsin, although there is a possibility that it may be present in one or more deep, coldwater lakes. It is known from four interior lakes in the state of Michigan (Hubbs and Lagler 1964), and from one interior lake in Indiana (Nelson 1968a, c).

The ninespine stickleback is common to abundant in shoal areas of Lake Superior, and uncommon in streams of its drainage basin. It is rare to uncommon in shoal areas of Lake Michigan. An increase in ninespine stickleback abundance in southern and east-central Lake Michigan is indicated since the late 1960s; this increase may be related to a decrease in the abundance of alewives (Wells and McLain 1973).

The ninespine stickleback is a fish of cool, quiet waters, and in Wisconsin it is almost wholly confined to the marginal waters of Lakes Superior and Michigan at depths up to 110 m.

BIOLOGY

An extensive life history of the ninespine stickleback in the Apostle Islands (Ashland County) of Lake Superior was prepared by Griswold and Smith (1972 and

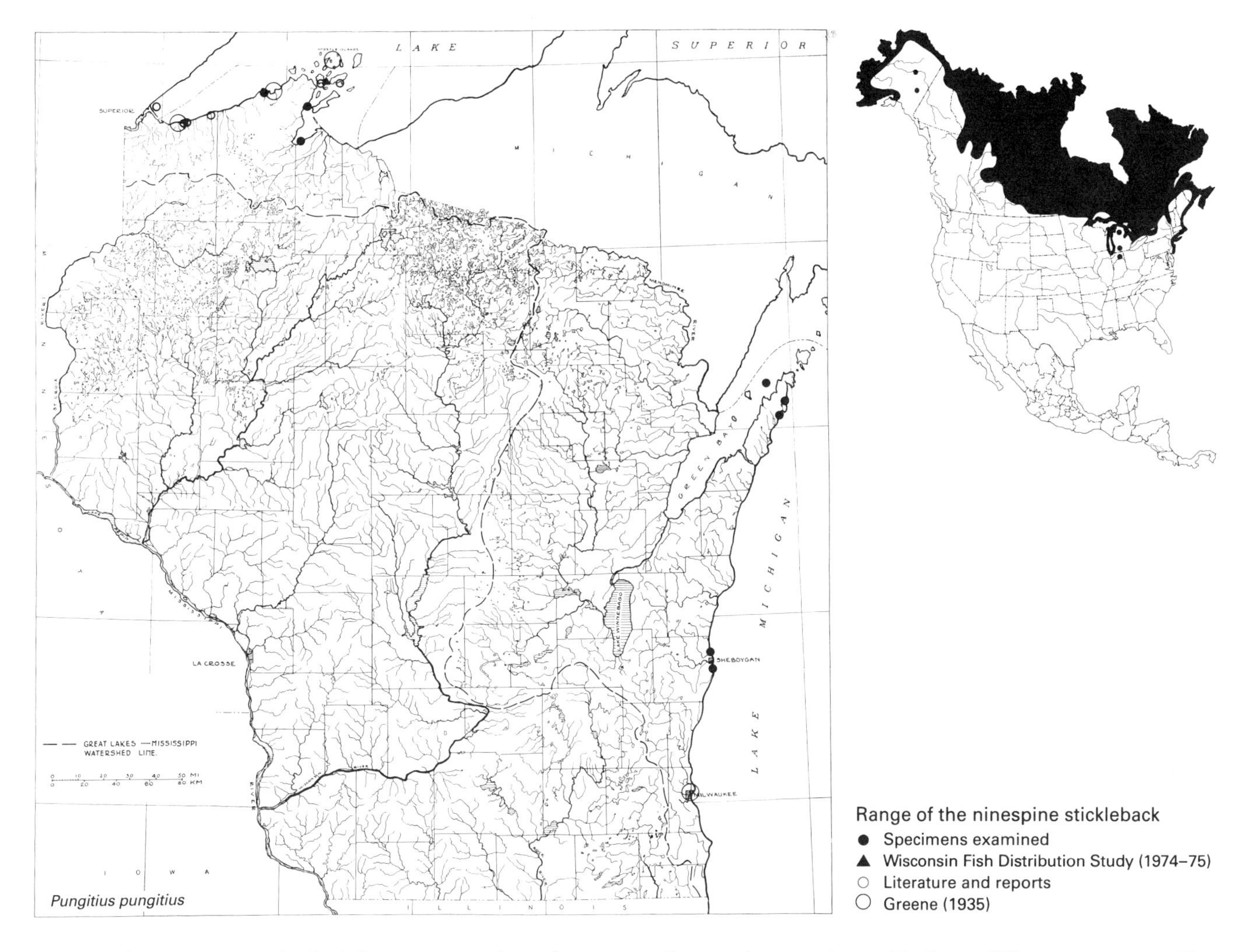

Range of the ninespine stickleback
- ● Specimens examined
- ▲ Wisconsin Fish Distribution Study (1974–75)
- ○ Literature and reports
- ◯ Greene (1935)

1973). The account which follows was taken from these sources, unless otherwise indicated.

The ninespine stickleback begins spawning in early June in Lake Superior. The first spent females were observed on 6 June. By the end of July, all but 1 of 38 fish were spent, and that 1 was partly spent. In aquariums, spawning activity was most frenzied when the water temperature was 11–12°C (51.8–53.6°F).

In the Apostle Islands, the only substratum in which territories were established and successful nesting took place was in highly organic bottom muds. It was over these muds, at depths of 16–40 m, that gravid females and males in breeding condition were collected by trawl in the lake. Nests built in this substratum were simple burrows about 1 cm diam and 3–4 cm long. The nests had one opening; fish entering the nest for spawning went in head first, turned around, and deposited their sex products. Males entered the nests to fertilize the eggs immediately after the female had vacated it. Males commonly spawned twice, usually with different females; one male was observed spawning with three different partners. Females always spawned twice within a period of 6–48 hours; and two female acts were with different males.

In Lake Huron (McKenzie and Keenleyside 1970), most ninespine stickleback nests are built under or between rocks, and are distributed from 25 to 150 cm from shore at depths of 25–80 cm. A few nests are built in relatively exposed locations, such as in surface pits of large rocks or very close to shore; most of these are eventually destroyed by wave action. Successful nests are well hidden among rocks and are not exposed to turbulence. Nests consisting entirely of algae fragments are found under rocks and in crevices between rocks; the algae is loosely packed together with leaf fragments and rootlets. The male, who constructs the nest alone, bores into this mass, probably gluing it from the inside with secretions from his kidneys. He pushes and mends the outside of the nest, but no external gluing has been observed. Sand digging in which the male picks up substrate material from the floor of the nest in his mouth and spits it out away from the nest has been seen in aquariums in which rocks were placed on the sand.

Territories are established by the male ninespine sticklebacks (McKenzie and Keenleyside 1970:57):

> Resident males responded to territorial intrusion by another male either by rapid charging, or nipping, biting and chasing, or by a slower approach followed by mutual circling by the 2 fish, slight head-down posture, with ventral spines erect. This was followed by the intruding fish swimming away, or by the circling developing into rapid roundabout fighting, with each fish biting at the other's tail. Mouth fighting was occasionally seen at the height of these vigorous encounters.

The raising of the dorsal and ventral spines is common fighting behavior in this species. The head-down posture indicates a high level of aggression, and a head-up posture indicates submission.

McKenzie and Keenleyside did not see male ninespine sticklebacks dragging other males away from their nests, as described by Morris (1958), although they noted that occasionally the males grasped small, intruding sculpins and suckers by the dorsal or the caudal fin and dragged them away from the nest site. These authors describe a fighting posture called "shivering" (p. 57):

> Occasionally, as two males slowly circled around each other, the resident fish oriented towards its opponent, settled onto the bottom, and then vigorously shivered, or vibrated the whole body, including the tail, for one or two seconds. Intruding fish either stopped advancing or retreated when the resident shivered, suggesting that it has signal value as a threat display.

In the "stationary charge," the ninespine stickleback points itself directly at its opponent, with the tail and posterior part of the body beating rapidly in intense lateral movements while the fish remains stationary (Morris 1958). This display, as in the lateral display of the brook stickleback, usually develops into a charge and a bite.

The female ninespine stickleback is invited into the male's nest with an elaborate ritual (McKenzie and Keenleyside 1970:58–59):

> A South Bay male courted by swimming straight at a ripe female, stopping near her, briefly twisting his body into a slight S-bend, erecting both ventral spines, then turning and swimming straight back to the nest. The female either followed the male to his nest and entered it, or followed part way and stopped. The male usually responded to such a hesitant female by quickly approaching her and dancing, in which he tilted head-down and jumped around the female in a series of short jerky movements, turning slightly laterally between jumps. After a bout of dancing he swam directly to the nest again. If the female did not follow, he either ignored her or repeated the approach, dance and lead sequence, but dancing was not done while leading. When following a leading male, a female swam slightly head-up and with her snout close to the male's black patch.

The female deposits a cluster of 20–30 eggs in the nest and departs. The male then enters the tunnel-shaped nest and fertilizes the eggs, swimming through the tunnel without stopping (Scott and Crossman 1973). As many as seven females may be encouraged to deposit eggs in one nest. While caring for the incubating young, the male may build a second nest.

The fecundity of females collected from Lake Superior on 27 June ranged from 65 to 114 eggs. "Green" fish before spawning held 82–158 eggs. Griswold and Smith (1972) suggested that atresia of some eggs occurs in maturing ninespine sticklebacks just prior to spawning, and that this may be a physical reaction to the pressure caused by the growing ovary. In maturing females, several developmental groups of eggs can be distinguished. Water-hardened eggs 15 min after release are 1.76 (1.53–1.98) mm diam. The mean weights of ovaries in terms of body weight were 10.2% and 9.8% at two different stations in the Lake Superior study.

In Lake Superior, no ninespine stickleback eggs were found in more than 150 ninespine stickleback stomachs studied during the spawning period.

The fertilized eggs are guarded and fanned by the male ninespine stickleback. During incubation the time spent fanning peaks shortly before hatching, and then falls off sharply until the young are free-swimming. Lake Huron males do not build a nursery (a loose collection of plant fragments, into which European male ninespine stickleback spit young fish which have strayed from the nest [Morris 1958]); rather, when the young are free-swimming, the male catches them in his mouth and spits them back into the nest. Those that escape the male scatter on the bottom and hide among the rocks. A male parent has never been seen eating his own fry.

After hatching, young ninespine sticklebacks congregate in shallow, sandy areas where they are unavailable to predatory lake trout and to most other species. By the time they leave the shallow water in late fall, they have grown to 45 mm or more. Ninespines of this length are found in trout stomachs the following spring.

In aquarium studies (Griswold and Smith 1972), the average length of ninespine sticklebacks at hatching was 5.65 mm. After 1 day they measured 5.95 mm; 6 days—6.75 mm; 11 days—7.56 mm; 13 days—8.64 mm; 18 days—10.77 mm; and 22 days—12.91 mm.

Copepods, rotifers, and brine shrimp were provided as food. Cannibalism was observed among fry, and usually resulted in the death of both the cannibal fish and its victim.

Ninespine sticklebacks of Lake Superior were aged by reading annuli on otoliths. The annuli are deposited in late June and early July. According to Griswold and Smith, the growth rates of females and males from the Apostle Islands varied. The average empirical lengths of females in spring prior to annulus formation were: 1—47 mm; 2—62 mm; 3—69 mm; 4—74 mm; and 5—80 mm. Males averaged: 1—47 mm; 2—60 mm; and 3—66 mm. Ninety percent of the males were mature at age I, but only 40% of the females were mature at that age. All individuals of both sexes are mature at age III.

Females predominated in the Apostle Island samples. In age-group 0, the male-female ratio was 0.930 to 1; by age III it was 0.125 to 1; and at age IV all specimens were female. High mortality occurred among males during the spawning season. In the laboratory, seven out of eight males that raised broods to the point where the fry swam actively about, died within a month after spawning. In the St. Lawrence River system (Quebec), Coad and Power (1973) noted that the longevity of the river form of the ninespine stickleback was 1 year and some months, whereas the lake form lived for more than 2 years.

The largest ninespine sticklebacks taken from Lake Superior were two females, 80–81 mm long (Griswold and Smith 1973). A large specimen 77 mm long (UWSP 1575) was collected from the mouth of a tributary to Lake Michigan in Sheboygan County.

In western Lake Superior, crustaceans (amphipods, mysids, and copepods) made up 50% of the ninespine's diet in April, and 97–100% of its diet in May through November (Anderson and Smith 1971b). In the Apostle Islands (Griswold and Smith 1973), ninespines less than 50 mm long fed primarily on *Pontoporeia* and copepods, which made up 70 and 13% of the total food volume respectively; of minor importance were cladocerans, mysids, chironomids, diptera larvae, and a filamentous green alga. In fish 50 mm and longer, *Pontoporeia* constituted 61% of the volume of food, *Mysis* 21%, copepods 8%, and miscellaneous other items 10%. Late fall and early spring stomach samples suggest that coregonid eggs may be an important food item in the winter. In Lake Huron (Reckahn 1970), ostracods were the major food item, and other common items included cladocerans, diptera larvae, amphipods, and isopods.

In the Apostle Islands, ninespine sticklebacks were found in the warmer, deep water in early spring, but were evenly distributed at all depths during spring turnover (when the waters mix and the water temperatures are the same at all depths) (Griswold and Smith 1973). In midsummer they congregated on warm, shallow shoals where water temperatures reached as high as 20°C (68°F). On a sandy beach they were found in 1–4 m of water, and on a steep slope covered with a dense growth of *Nitella* sp. they were found in 15–20 m of water. When the fall turnover occurred in September, they were again fairly evenly distributed at all depths. By November, the fish began to congregate in the deeper water, and were found there in great numbers during December. It is assumed that a deepwater habitat is used in midwinter, since the fish are abundant there the following spring. In northern Lake Superior, a large number of ninespine sticklebacks were taken at 69–77 m (Scott and Crossman 1973).

In southern Lake Michigan, Wells (1968) collected only three ninespine sticklebacks at depths of 37–91 m. In northern Lake Michigan, the fish were found at depths of 18–90 m, but were most frequently caught at the 18 and 27 m intervals; in northern Green Bay, they were most often taken at 9–31 m (Reigle 1969a, b). In Crooked Lake, Indiana, the ninespine stickleback was found between 5 and 30 m (Nelson 1968a).

The ninespine stickleback, introduced into a lake with adverse oxygen conditions in the winter and spring, survived low oxygen levels of 0.8–1.46 ppm (Zhiteneva 1971). At the beginning of winter, red blood cells stored in the spleen are released into the blood. An anemic state began after 4.5–5 months. There was an increase in the percentage of immature red blood cells and of the phagocytic cells. It was determined that if the ninespine stickleback lives for more than 5 months under adverse oxygen conditions, the blood-forming organs become overstrained; polymorphism is noted among the red blood cells.

In the Canadian parts of its range the ninespine stickleback exhibits modifications of the pelvic complex (= girdle). This complex may be abnormal in some areas, absent in others (Coad 1973), and commonly absent in some areas (Nelson 1971). The function of the pelvic complex appears to be twofold: it serves as a support for the pelvic spines which are used in defense against predators; and, in male fish during the breeding season, it serves as a signaling device for leading females to the nest. The loss of this structure would seem to place an individual at a selective disadvantage.

The ninespine sticklebacks differ from many other

fish in that their pectoral fins are more important as swimming organs than their tails. During slow and medium speed propulsion, the tail is not employed at all, but is held still and straight (Morris 1958).

Ninespine sticklebacks were seined from a public beach of Lake Superior (Ashland County) along with trout-perch and spottail shiners.

IMPORTANCE AND MANAGEMENT

The ninespine stickleback is an important forage fish. In Lake Superior, lake trout, brown trout, rainbow trout, burbot, and various sculpins feed on ninespine sticklebacks. In Lake Nipigon (Ontario, Canada), ninespines are eaten by walleyes, brook trout, lake trout, yellow perch, and burbot (Dymond 1926).

In the Apostle Islands region, Griswold and Smith (1973) found ninespine sticklebacks in 7.5% of the lake trout less than 28 cm long; and, in 42% of the lake trout 28–38 cm long, ninespine sticklebacks constituted 39% of the volume in the diet. In lake trout longer than 38 cm, smelt are the major food, although ninespine sticklebacks are still found in a few stomachs. In the best lake trout nursery area in the Apostle Islands, ninespine sticklebacks are the predominant food item, even though juvenile smelt are more abundant. The availability of ninespine sticklebacks at the various stations is probably important in the lake trout's selection of these areas as nursery sites; no good trout nursery areas are known where ninespine sticklebacks are not abundant.

In northern Lake Michigan, the ninespine stickleback was found in 18.1% of the lake trout stomachs examined and constituted 10% of the volume of food in those stomachs. In Green Bay, the ninespine was found in 0.3% of the stomachs examined; it was not found in stomachs from southern Lake Michigan (Van Oosten and Deason 1938).

Studies reported by Griswold and Smith (1973) have shown that young northern pike rejected ninespine sticklebacks as food, first exhibiting a negative reaction upon coming into contact with the spines, and then a visual avoidance. Upon reaching a certain size, however, northern pike prefer ninespine sticklebacks as food.

Temperate Bass Family—Percichthyidae

Two species of temperate basses in one genus are known from Wisconsin; both are strictly freshwater species. In the United States and Canada the temperate basses consist of seven species in four genera (Robins et al. 1980). Five species are essentially marine; two, the white perch and striped bass, run up coastal streams to spawn. Gosline (1966) has separated the temperate basses from the sea basses (Serranidae).

The percichthyids are deep-bodied, percoid fishes with well-developed jaws armed with numerous teeth. Their upper jaws are bordered by the premaxillaries, with the maxillaries expanded posteriorly. They have seven branchiostegal rays, and the pelvic fins are in a thoracic position without an axillary process.

Although superficially resembling the black basses and sunfishes, the temperate basses are not closely related to them, and differ from them in a number of characteristics: temperate basses are random spawners and they do not build nests or care for their eggs and young, as do most members of the sunfish family.

White Bass

Morone chrysops (Rafinesque). *Morone*—derivation unknown; *chrysops*—golden eye.

Other common names: silver bass, white lake-bass, striped bass, silver fish, streaker.

Adult 241 mm, L. Poygan (Winnebago Co.), 9 Aug. 1961

DESCRIPTION

Body robust and deep, strongly compressed laterally. Length 203–254 mm (8–10 in). TL = 1.27 SL. Depth into TL 3.5–3.8. Head length into TL 3.4–3.9. Mouth moderate, slightly oblique. Lower jaw projecting beyond upper jaw; minute, needlelike teeth in several irregular rows on upper and lower jaws. A sharp spine near back of gill cover; margin of preopercle (bone just ahead of gill cover) strongly saw toothed. Dorsal fins 2; first dorsal fin 9 spines and separated from second dorsal fin of 1 spine and 13–15 rays. Anal fin of three spines and 12–13 rays; anal spines graduated from short to long in distinct steps, with the first spine one-third or more the length of the second spine; the second anal spine not notably heavier than the third. Pelvic fin far forward (almost below pectoral fin), with 1 spine and 5 rays; caudal fin forked. Scales ctenoid, 52–60 in lateral line; lateral line complete. Scales on gill covers, cheeks, and top of head to between eyes. Digestive tract into TL about 1.3.

Overall silvery in life; in preserved fish, back and upper sides olive gray, shading to white on lower head and belly. Sides with 6–7 horizontal, dark stripes. Vertical fins pigmented; little or no pigment on paired fins.

Sexual dimorphism: In male, a single urogenital opening behind the anus; in female, 2 openings (genital and urinary) behind the anus (Moen 1959).

Hybrids: White bass × yellow bass from Lake Mendota (Dane County), 16 June 1975 (Wis. Fish Distrib. Study 1975).

SYSTEMATIC NOTES

Morone chrysops is a synonym of *Lepibema chrysops* (Hubbs 1929) and *Roccus chrysops* (Bailey 1956). See Bailey et al. (1970) for clarification of the current name *Morone*.

DISTRIBUTION, STATUS, AND HABITAT

In Wisconsin the white bass occurs in the Mississippi River and Lake Michigan drainage basins. It is found in the bays of Lake Michigan, and particularly in southern Green Bay. Earlier reports by Greene (1935) from Lake Superior have been deleted from the map; there are no known records of its occurrence in the Lake Superior drainage. The white bass has been introduced in Long Lake (Manitowoc County), Pelican Lake (Oneida County), and in the following lakes of Waukesha County: Lac La Belle, Pewaukee, Oconomowoc, and Nagawicka (Cahn 1927, McCutchin 1946). Undoubtedly the fish rescue operations of the early 1900s, or panfish stocking by the former Wisconsin Conservation Department were responsible for a number of existing populations in these and other locations. In 1978 the white bass was reported from Lake Alice (Lincoln County) (L. Andrews and S. Serns, pers. comm.).

The white bass is common in large lakes and rivers of the southern half of Wisconsin, and in the St. Croix River upstream to the St. Croix Falls Dam. It is abundant in Lake Winnebago. In Wisconsin, its status appears to be secure, although in some waters it is being displaced by the yellow bass.

The white bass occurs in open, clear to turbid waters of lakes and reservoirs, and in large (occasionally medium-sized) rivers with moderate currents. It was encountered most frequently in water less than 6 m deep, over substrates—in decreasing frequency—of sand, mud, rubble, gravel, silt, clay, hardpan, and boulders.

BIOLOGY

Spawning occurs from late April to June, and is temperature dependent. In Lake Mendota, the spawning runs of the white bass occurred from late May through June, at water temperatures of 12.5–26.1°C (54.5–79°F); peak spawning occurred at 16.9–22.6°C (62.4–72.7°F) (Horrall 1962). High temperatures early in the season were associated with an early run, and a rapid rise in temperatures was correlated with an increase in the intensity of spawning and with a shorter spawning period.

White bass apparently prefer the running water of tributary streams for spawning, but when such wa-

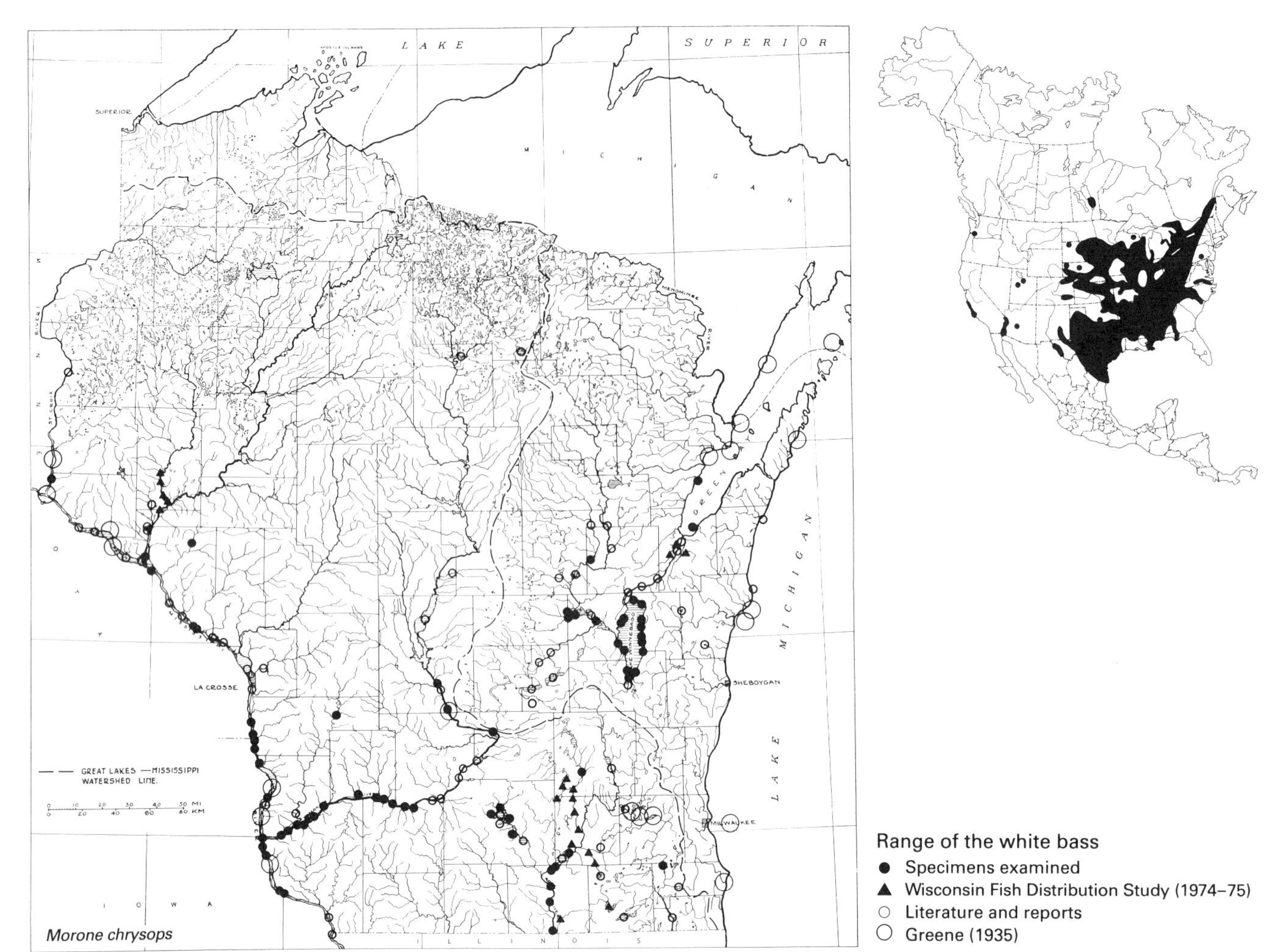

Range of the white bass
● Specimens examined
▲ Wisconsin Fish Distribution Study (1974–75)
○ Literature and reports
◯ Greene (1935)

ters are lacking they spawn along windswept lake shores in water 0.6–2.1 m deep. A firm bottom of sand, gravel, rubble, or rock is required for successful spawning (Riggs 1955), although spawning has been observed on rooted aquatic plants, filamentous algae, and logs (Chadwick et al. 1966).

During spawning (Riggs 1955), several males surround a female and the group swims "rapidly and erratically around scattering the demersal eggs at or near the surface." Riggs noted that the eggs are fertilized as they sink, and since the eggs are adhesive, they attach to gravel, vegetation, and other materials standing in the water.

Active spawning occurs both day and night (Chadwick et al. 1966). The length of the spawning period is from 3 to 4 days (Cahn 1927) to several weeks. In Lake Mendota (Dane County), Horrall (1962) noted that spawning by white bass at Maple Bluff and Governor's Island began in late May and continued through June in some years.

Horrall observed that, on the spawning shoals early in the season, either the female white bass outnumber the males, or there is about a 1:1 ratio. Following this period, there is a rapid build-up of a strongly male-dominated spawning population (about nine males to one female), which persists over the greater portion of the run and characterizes the active spawning period. During the run a ripe female moves from deeper water onto the spawning shoals just long enough to expel her eggs, after which she returns to deeper or open water. The end of the run is typified once more by a 1:1 sex ratio, or by a slight female dominance. Such bisexual feeding schools are composed of spawned-out fish and of late female spawners.

Horrall has demonstrated that there is a decrease in the average size of white bass on the spawning grounds from the beginning to the end of the spawning period—the result of a decrease in the number of older fish and an increase in the number of younger fish. The recruit spawners, in age groups II and III, reach a maximum number during the last portions of the spawning period. Horrall concluded that the majority of the white bass continue to spawn on the same spawning ground each year.

The number of white bass eggs produced per female varies from 241 to 933 thousand, and averages 565 thousand (Riggs 1955). The number of eggs presumably is related directly to the size of the female. In Lewis and Clark Lake, South Dakota, females spawned only about 50% of their eggs; the large eggs were shed during spawning, and the smaller eggs were retained and resorbed by late July or early August (Ruelle 1977). White bass eggs are 0.7–1.0 mm diam immediately before spawning and with water-hardening they are 0.7–1.2 mm diam. In South Dakota white bass ovaries in April were 9.8% of body weight, and averaged 10–15% of body weight in May.

Eggs from Lake Mendota white bass hatched at 20.2°C (68.4°F) in 45 hours and another group of eggs at a temperature of 21.5°C (70.7°F) hatched in 41 hr (Horrall 1962). The yolk-sac is absorbed in about 8 days. No parental care is given to the eggs or to the young. Newly hatched larvae are about 2 mm long (Yellayi and Kilambi 1970). Sac larvae of the white bass exhibit unique swimming behavior (Siefert et al. 1974:188):

> . . . They swam vertically to near the surface, where they became inactive and dropped, head down, to the bottom of the chamber. Upon touching, they swam actively to the surface again. This behavior was noted at all oxygen concentrations at 16 C soon after hatching, and it continued for 3 days at oxygen concentrations of 35% saturation and above. On the 4th day the larvae at these concentrations maintained a horizontal swimming position.

M. Fish (1932) illustrated and described the 5.0-, 5.1-, 10.5-, and 12.6-mm stages. Taber (1969) pictured developmental stages from 2.4 to 19.0 mm.

Young white bass, when hatched, remain in shallow water for a while, then migrate to the deeper waters. In Lewis and Clark Lake, South Dakota, most larvae 4–10 mm long were planktonic (1–2 m below the surface) and were collected near shore (Walburg 1976). Fish longer than 10 mm were found near the bottom in water 2–4 m deep.

In Lake Winnebago (Priegel 1970a), the growth of young-of-year white bass was: June—18–25 mm; July—29–73 mm; August—51–110 mm; September—59–114 mm; and October—87–141 mm. Although young-of-year continued to grow through mid-October, 50% of their growth was completed by 1 August (Priegel 1971a). The average total length by mid-October 1966 was 104 mm.

White bass are generally aged by scales, which usually show well-marked annuli that are easy to read. In Lake Mendota (Dane County), Horrall (1962) noted that annulus formation did not occur in fish age-III or older until after the spawning period. He determined the following age and mean total length for males (females): III—263 (271) mm; IV—278 (290) mm; V—287 (303) mm; VI—297 (310) mm; VII—313 (321) mm; and VIII—326 mm.

In Lake Winnebago (Priegel 1971a), the calculated lengths at the end of each year of life were: 1—97 mm; 2—190 mm; 3—254 mm; 4—274 mm; 5—287 mm; 6—302 mm; 7—307 mm; and 8—320 mm. The length-weight relation of Lake Winnebago white bass is expressed by the regression $\text{Log } W = -5.63167 + 3.29933 \text{ Log } L$, where W is weight in grams and L is TL in millimeters. No significant difference in growth between the sexes was found, so the data were combined. The three largest fish seen from Lake Winnebago were 358, 363, and 386 mm TL. In Lake Geneva (Walworth County), white bass 6 years old were 305 mm SL (Nelson and Hasler 1942).

More rapid growth was exhibited by white bass from the Mississippi River. White bass from Pools 3–6 had the following calculated growth to the annuli: 1—130 mm; 2—246 mm; 3—313 mm; 4—353 mm; and 5—351 mm (Kittel 1955). A small sample taken in October from Lake Pepin (Upper Miss. R. Conserv. Com. 1967) was: 0—132 mm; I—241 mm; II—297 mm; III—351 mm; and IV—376 mm. From a backwater area near Fountain City (Buffalo County), white bass were: 0—99 mm; I—236 mm; II—328 mm; and III—363 mm (Christenson and Smith 1965).

White bass are generally sexually mature at age III, although some precocious males mature at age II (Horrall 1962). In Lake Winnebago (Priegel 1971a), 8% of the males were mature at age II, and all were mature at age III; 42% of the females were mature at age III, and all were mature at age IV.

A 1.7-kg (3-lb 12-oz) white bass was caught from Pelican Lake (Oneida County) in 1963, and in 1977 a 1.99-kg (4-lb 6-oz) specimen from Okauchee Lake (Waukesha County). A 2.41-kg (5-lb 5-oz) white bass was taken in 1972 from Ferguson Lake, California.

White bass are carnivorous. They feed on microscopic crustaceans, insect larvae, and fish. In Lake Mendota (Voigtlander and Wissing 1974), young white bass consumed largely cladocerans and chironomids, some copepods, *Hyalella azteca*, ephemeropteran nymphs (*Caenis* sp.), and fish (brook silversides) which appeared only twice in the samples, and were probably incidental captures. Yearling white bass in Lake Mendota consumed *Daphnia*, *Leptodora*, *Hyalella*, chironomids, Odonata, ephemeropterans, and fish. The frequency of occurrence of fish in the diet of these yearlings was 14–50% in seven samples taken; they included crappies spp., sunfish spp., spottail shiner, *Notropis* sp., bluntnose minnow, carp, bullhead sp., temperate bass sp., brook silverside, yellow perch, and logperch. A 203-mm yearling white bass had a food volume of 7.20 ml, which consisted of seven crappies sp. (30–40 mm), one sunfish sp. (25 mm), and one *Notropis* sp. (25 mm). In an earlier study McNaught and Hasler (1961) determined that zooplankters of the genus *Daphnia* comprised the bulk of the food of the white bass in Lake Mendota. These white bass were able to locate high concentrations of *Daphnia*, and the pattern of their feeding activity was shown to correspond with the morning and evening concentrations of *Daphnia* in the surface waters.

In 56 white bass collected from Pool 19 of the Mississippi River (Hoopes 1960), *Hexagenia* naiads constituted 54% of the total stomach contents. The larvae of *Potamyia flava* formed 9% of the contents, and immature Odonata and Zygoptera, Hemiptera, amphipods, crayfish, and fish were also present.

In Lake Winnebago, young-of-year white bass consumed 100% invertebrates, including *Daphnia*, *Leptodora*, *Cyclops* and *Diaptomus*, *Hyalella*, ostracods, oligochaetes, chironomids, and *Limnephilus* (Priegel 1970a). Yearling and older white bass relied especially on *Daphnia* and *Leptodora*, and consumed young fish shortly after they hatched; among these were yellow perch, sauger, white bass, freshwater drum, and trout-perch. The freshwater drum and trout-perch occurred most frequently in white bass stomachs.

McNaught and Hasler (1961) determined that yearling white bass pick up individual *Daphnia* when feeding. Older white bass make a subsurface sweep some 20–40 cm in length, at a depth of 10–20 cm, with mouths agape and opercles spread. They then break through the surface film, causing the disturbance by which their schools are readily sighted. There is a progressive shift by white bass to larger food items as light levels decrease. Preliminary studies indicate that white bass feed more by sight than by scent (Greene 1962).

In the laboratory, Wissing (1974) determined that the daily food energy consumed by white bass represented about 6% of the caloric value of the whole fish. Of this, roughly 27% was egested, while the remainder was assimilated and then apportioned to growth and maintenance.

Heated zones in the Wabash River, Indiana (Gammon 1973), seemed to attract small white bass. Analysis of their selection and avoidance of thermal zones, suggested that the probable optimum temperature for the species lay between 28.0 and 29.5°C (82.4 and 85.1°F). At the Colbert Power Plant on the Tennessee River, the white bass was captured from the 34.4°C (93.9°F) discharge (Churchill and Wojtalik 1969).

Chadwick et al. (1966) noted that white bass thrive over a wide range of limnological conditions. In Oklahoma they do well in shallow impoundments with small annual fluctuations, and with moderate alkalinities of 80–110 ppm.

Studies of the movements and depth distribution of white bass were made in Lake Mendota (Tibbles 1956). From early spring to the fall, usually in the early morning and late afternoon, white bass were seen singly, in schools, or in schools in such large numbers that an entire surface area seemed alive with their commotion. Such activity ceased shortly after sunrise, and began again a few hours before sunset. Throughout the summer, over 90% of the catch of white bass was within the top 6 m of water. The white bass were not observed quiescent on the bottom with the yellow perch, but they were observed under floating aquatic vegetation or in the shadow of buoys. They apparently moved little at night. Limited data suggest that white bass prefer a habitat in the surface waters during the summer, but move into deeper waters for the rest of the year. Horrall (1962) observed that the littoral zone is frequented by the white bass only in the early stages of life, in old age, and during the spawning season. Young bass avoid dense vegetation and shallow areas with organic bottoms; they prefer shallow water over sandy beaches. Wissing and Hasler (1971) noted that young-of-year white bass demonstrated a high degree of excitability when an individual fish was isolated from other members of a school.

In a tagging study in the Mississippi River, white bass were rather mobile and were capable of undertaking extended journeys (Finke 1966b). After the spring migration into the tailwaters of Lock and Dam No. 3, the white bass ranged widely: A small portion of the population continued upstream and entered tributaries such as the St. Croix 24–50 km (15–31 mi) upstream from the tagging site; the majority of the fish moved downstream 18 km (11 mi) to Lake Pepin, where they remained; others made long downstream movements of up to 211 km (131 mi). The 394-mm white bass which journeyed 211 km was at large for 131 days before it was recaptured. The average distance traveled by 57 white bass before recapture was 34 km (21 mi).

The white bass has a strong homing tendency which is directed toward a specific spawning ground (Hasler et al. 1958, Horrall 1962). In Lake Mendota, most recaptured fish had homed correctly, and even those fish which had been removed to a different spawning area returned to the spawning area where they had first been captured. Hasler et al. (1969) demonstrated that spawning and nonspawning white bass which were displaced from their capture sites, and which were provided with ultrasonic transmitters in the stomachs, showed a distinct directional preference for the eastern half of the lake where the spawning grounds were located. Water currents, wind-generated surface waves, and the sun were considered as possible directional cues used by the fish.

In Lake Mendota, the common schooling associates of adult white bass are the yellow perch and the crappie (*Pomoxis*). The spottail shiner is common in schools of yearling white bass (McNaught and Hasler 1961).

IMPORTANCE AND MANAGEMENT

The white bass is a host to the glochidial stage of the following mollusks: *Megalonaias gigantea*, *Lampsilis radiata luteola*, *Amblema plicata*, *Anodonta grandis*, *Actinonaias carinata*, *Anodonta implicata*, and *Fusconaia ebena* (Hart and Fuller 1974, Surber 1973).

The white bass is one of the most handsome of freshwater fishes, and ranks fairly high as a food fish. The flesh is firm, white, and palatable when either fresh or smoked. When the spectacular yearly runs occur in the Wolf River, hundreds of anglers gather in the vicinity of Fremont, Gills Landing, and Winneconne. Both anglers and white bass also concentrate on the Fox River at Omro and Eureka, and below the dams on the Mississippi River and its larger tributaries. The white bass responds to live minnows, grubs, angleworms, artificial flies, and flashy spinning lures. Stringers of large numbers of white bass are not unusual. Even lake fishing will produce large catches, and John (1954) reported that two fishermen in 1911 caught 611 white bass from Lake Mendota during 1 day of fishing.

On the Mississippi River in 1957, the white bass ranked fifth in the sport catch, and in 1962–1963 it ranked fourth (Upper Miss. R. Conserv. Com. 1967). The estimated sport fishery catch of white bass in Pools 4, 5, 7, and 11 during 1967–1968 was 55,484 fish weighing 22,130 kg (48,787 lb) (Wright 1970).

The commercial harvest of white bass from the lower Green Bay waters of Lake Michigan in 1974 was reported at 1,730 kg (3,815 lb) (Wis. Dep. Nat. Resour. 1976c).

In 1955 (Kittel 1955), test netting from Pool 3 to the head of Pool 6 in the Mississippi River showed that, next to black crappies (17.5 fish per lift), white and yellow bass (3.6 fish per lift) were the most common. Other experimental nets may show greater numbers of channel catfish, saugers, yellow perch, and gizzard shad, but the white bass is frequently among the leaders. Finke (1966b) noted that in the upper Mississippi River white bass are lightly harvested, even in areas like Lake Pepin where they congregate after the spring migration. In Lake Winnebago, the white bass is the most abundant panfish species; however, according to Priegel (1971a) it is cyclic, and even when numerous it is only harvested in appreciable numbers during its spring spawning migration up the Fox and Wolf rivers.

White bass may dominate an impoundment within a few years after introduction (Chadwick et al. 1966); however, white bass populations do not seriously affect other game fish. The standing crop of white bass from Oklahoma to Wisconsin averaged 3.6 kg/ha (3.2 lb/acre), and ranged from 0.1 to 25.9 kg/ha (0.1 to 23.1 lb/acre) (Carlander 1955).

Yellow Bass

Morone mississippiensis Jordan and Eigenmann. *Morone*—derivation unknown; *mississippiensis*—of the Mississippi River.

Other common names: brassy bass, gold bass, streaker, barfish, striper, striped bass, black-striped bass.

Adult 210 mm, L. Winnebago (Fond du Lac Co.), 28 Aug. 1961

DESCRIPTION

Body robust and deep, strongly compressed laterally. Length 152–203 mm (6–8 in). TL = 1.25 SL. Depth into TL 3.3–3.6. Head length into TL 3.6–3.8. Mouth moderate, scarcely oblique. Lower jaw scarcely projecting beyond upper jaw; minute, needlelike teeth in several irregular rows on upper and lower jaws. A sharp spine near back of gill cover; margin of preopercle (bone just ahead of gill cover) strongly saw toothed. Dorsal fins 2; first dorsal fin has 9 spines, slightly connected by membrane to second dorsal, which has 1 spine and 11–13 rays. Anal fin of 3 spines and 8–10 rays; anal spines not graduated from short to long in distinct steps: the first spine is less than one-third length of the second, and the second and third spines are almost of equal length; second spine notably heavier than the third. Pelvic fin far forward (almost below pectoral fin), with 1 spine and 5 rays; caudal fin forked. Scales ctenoid, 49–51 in lateral line; lateral line complete. Scales on gill covers, cheeks, and top of head to between eyes. Digestive tract into TL about 1.5.

Overall, golden yellow in life; in preserved fish, back and upper sides yellow-olive, shading to yellow or yellow-white on lower head and belly. Sides with 6–7 horizontal, dark stripes. Vertical fins pigmented; little or no pigment on paired fins.

Sexual dimorphism: In male, a single urogenital opening behind the anus; in female, 2 openings (genital and urinary) behind the anus (Moen 1959).

Hybrid: White bass × yellow bass from Lake Mendota (Dane County), 16 June 1975 (Wis. Fish Distrib. Study 1974–75).

SYSTEMATIC NOTES

Synonyms: *Morone interrupta* (Carlander and Cleary 1949), *Roccus interruptus* (Cook 1959), and *Roccus mississippiensis* (Bailey 1956). See Bailey et al. (1970) for clarification of the current name.

DISTRIBUTION, STATUS, AND HABITAT

The yellow bass, a southern species, is a recent addition to the fish fauna of Wisconsin, where it reaches the northern limit of its distribution. The first records came from the Mississippi River in the vicinity of Prairie du Chien and Lynxville (Crawford County) (Greene 1935). Since the late 1920s it has been reported upstream in the Mississippi as far as Lake Pepin, in the lower Chippewa River basin, and in the lower Wisconsin River upstream to the Prairie du Sac Dam. This species also occurs in the Lake Michigan drainage basin and in the Rock River basin, where it undoubtedly was introduced.

Helm (1964) summarized the expansion of the yellow bass in Wisconsin (p. 124):

> . . . By 1958 specimens had been collected or reliably reported from 22 lakes or ponds in six river systems within the State, in addition to the Mississippi River. Most of the expansion within the State appears to be the result of transferring fish from the Mississippi River, while the remainder is due to the stocking of children's fishing ponds. As a result of these stocking activities, the range of the yellow bass has been extended from the Mississippi drainage into the Great Lakes drainage.

Helm suggested that the appearance of this species in the Madison lakes occurred as a result of salvage fish transfers into Lake Wingra during the 1930s. Wright (1968) determined its recent dispersal in the Madison lakes region.

The yellow bass is uncommon to common in the Mississippi and lower Wisconsin rivers. It is common and increasing in Lakes Poygan and Winnebago, and in the Madison lakes. Its status appears to be secure.

The yellow bass is primarily an inhabitant of lakes and connecting lakes, sloughs, and reservoirs on large rivers. It prefers wide expanses of open water free of weeds, over substrates of sand, gravel, rubble, and silt, and over firm substrates overlaid with a thick layer of mud. It is found in clear to turbid water, up to at least 7 m deep.

BIOLOGY

In Wisconsin, the yellow bass spawns in May or June. It commonly moves into tributary streams to spawn, or it may spawn in a lake over gravel or rock reefs in water 0.6–1.0 m deep. Spawning begins when water

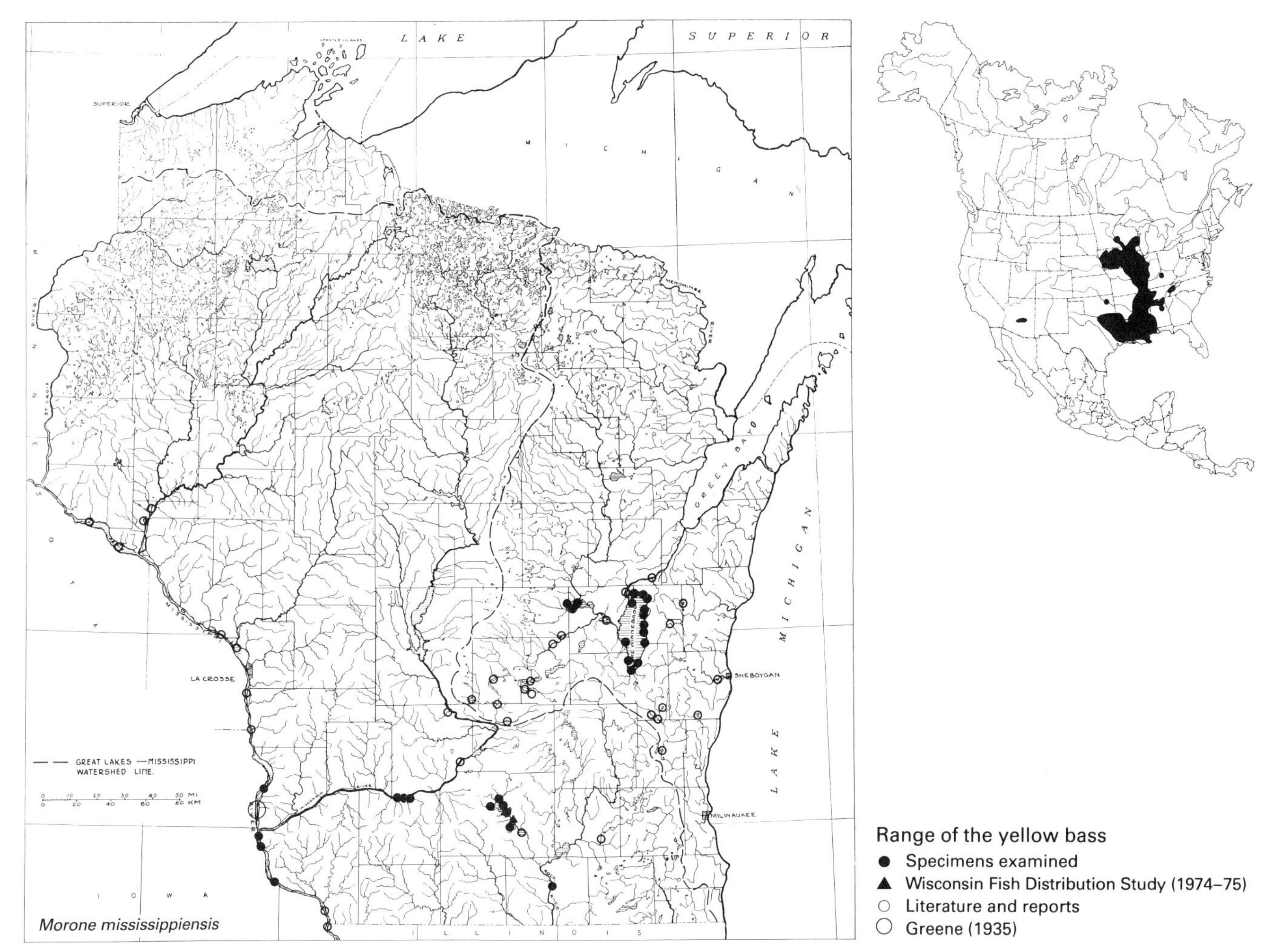

Morone mississippiensis

temperatures approach 15°C (59°F) (Bulkley 1970), after a rapid temperature rise of 3.5–4.5°C over several days; however, spawning is probably more intense at 20–22°C (68–71.6°F) (Burnham 1909, Shields 1965).

The time of breeding corresponds with that of the white bass. In 1960 in Lake Mendota (Horrall 1962), a number of ripe male and female yellow bass were captured from the white bass spawning grounds at Maple Bluff. Previously large numbers of yellow bass had been known to spawn in the Yahara River below the dam at the outlet of Lake Mendota.

Preliminary to spawning, yellow bass pair off and swim swiftly along side by side; the male swims about 8 cm away from the female, and both appear to be excited (Burnham 1909). When spawning occurs, the fish swim very slowly or stop for a few seconds while the eggs and milt are emitted (p. 104):

> In the act of spawning the female lies partly on her right side with vent toward the male, ejecting the eggs with a tremulous or wavy motion of her entire body. The male does not lie sideways but remains upright beside the female, so that his vent is directly over the eggs as they come from the female. He ejects the milt on the eggs without any perceptible movement of his body except as necessary to maintain his position beside the female. The eggs are not all voided at once, and the fish swim around together during the interval between spawnings, which continue for an hour or more. After spawning the fish usually remain still near the bottom for some time as if resting.

No care is given to the eggs or to the young.

In Lake Wingra, the average egg production of yellow bass 148–168 mm TL was 19,300 (14,300–39,400) (Churchill 1976). Bulkley (1970) noted that in Iowa there was a wide variation in the effective fecundity of yellow bass females, not only among females of similar lengths, but from year to year. Atresia of developing eggs was estimated at 20% during the period from December to May, and was attributed to poor nutrition.

In Iowa at spawning time, the ovaries of adult yellow bass constituted up to 16% of body weight, and testes constituted up to 8% of body weight. Freshly ovulated eggs averaged 0.8 ± 0.1 mm diam. Not all of the eggs were laid; Bulkley reported retention of approximately 34% of the total egg production.

The eggs of the yellow bass are semibuoyant and sink slowly. Many are eaten or smothered, and many are unfertilized when they reach the bottom (Burnham 1909). Shields (1965) noted that the percentage of eggs which hatch is usually low. The strength of year classes may be very erratic, and an abundance of yellow bass usually occurs in only 1 year out of 3. At a water temperature of 21.1°C (70°F) the eggs hatch in 4–6 days into colorless, transparent larvae approximately 3.2 mm long. The yolk-sac is absorbed in about 4 days, after which the fry begin swim-up movements (Burnham 1909:105):

> [the fry] rise straight toward the surface head first by vigorous movements of the tail, and when their exertions cease turn quickly and sink head first to the bottom without moving the body or fins while descending. Touching bottom they immediately turn and swim upward again, occasionally stopping before reaching the surface.

Swim-up fry may be seen near the surface in water about 0.6 m deep, and in 2–3 days they drift toward the shores and can be found in water 3–25 cm deep. The minute fry swarm in schools once they have absorbed their yolk-sacs and can swim freely. These schools remain in the shallows, where they feed on minute zooplankton. At this stage they are vulnerable to predation. After they begin to feed, yellow bass fry grow rapidly, reaching a length of 25 mm in about 3 weeks. Their natural food is terrestrial and aquatic insects.

In Lake Wingra, young-of-year yellow bass were 45–51 mm (1.8–2.0 in) long in early August, and were 74–93 mm (2.9–3.7 in) long by late October (Helm 1964). In Lake Winnebago in mid-August, young yellow bass averaged 50 (35–57) mm (J. Gunderson, pers. comm.).

The use of scales for determining the age of yellow bass is not always reliable. During certain years, especially when yellow bass are slow-growing, the annuli fail to form (Helm 1964, Frey and Vike 1941, Buchholz and Carlander 1963).

In Lake Wingra (Churchill 1976), the average calculated total lengths at the annuli were: 1—97 mm, 2—136 mm, 3—153 mm, and 4—159 mm. Yellow bass 105–130 mm long, captured from Lake Monona on 10 August, were 90 mm long at the time of first annulus deposition (J. Gunderson, pers. comm.). A 210 mm fish from lake Mendota, captured 10 August, had the following calculated values at the annuli: 1—68 mm, 2—125 mm, 3—148 mm, 4—168 mm, and 5—185 mm.

More rapid growth was exhibited by yellow bass from the Wolf-Fox basin. The calculated lengths of 202 yellow bass from Lake Poygan were: 1—76 mm; 2—162 mm; 3—234 mm; 4—253 mm; 5—274 mm; and 6—300 mm (Priegel 1975). The length-weight relation is $\text{Log } W = -4.0289 + 2{,}700 \text{ Log } L$, where W is WT in grams, and L is TL in millimeters. Priegel found that the growth of Lake Poygan yellow bass was greater than that reported from most areas of the United States.

In this species, maturity is reached at age III (Priegel 1975, Shields 1965).

Few yellow bass live more than 3 or 4 years. The annual survival rate after the first year of life is about 20–40%. Buchholz and Carlander (1963) reported a life span of 9 years for few individuals of this species.

A 964-g (2-lb 2-oz) yellow bass was caught 18 January 1972 from Lake Monona (Dane County). A large 6-year-old yellow bass, 411 mm (16.2 in) long and weighing 1.42 kg (3 lb 2 oz), was caught from Lake Poygan in state fish management nets in January 1964 (Stevens Point *Daily Journal*, 20 March 1964).

The yellow bass is carnivorous. In Lake Wingra, the foods of major importance were Cladocera (92% occurrence), Copepoda (92%), Chironomidae larvae (68%), Chironomidae pupae (52%), Chaoborinae (16%), fish remains (20%) and Ostracoda (28%). Ephemeroptera, Hydracarina, and Corixidae occurred less frequently (Helm 1964). Plankton was the most important food consumed during the day, and chironomids were most important at night. Helm noted no significant differences in the foods consumed by small, medium, and large fish.

In Iowa, young yellow bass ate primarily entomostracans, but started taking significant numbers of immature insects when the bass reached 50 mm (Welker 1962). Forage fish were found in only 2% of the adult yellow bass examined in 1960, compared with 24% in 1952 and 86% in 1943, when the yellow bass population consisted of larger fish. In 1953–1954 Collier (1959) found adult yellow bass consuming large numbers of young-of-year yellow bass, gizzard shad, and insects; but during the summers of 1956 to 1958, forage fish were of minor importance in their diet, and the yellow bass fed mainly on immature insects and minute crustaceans. Bulkley (1970) and Kraus (1963) also reported that adult yellow bass ate young-of-year of their own species as a major food item during the late summer and autumn.

In Lake Wingra during July, yellow bass exhibited a definite feeding pattern (Helm 1964)—feeding shortly after dark and again at daylight. Unlike white bass, they do not regularly feed on the surface, but usually feed at mid-depths or near the bottom (Helm 1958, Shields 1965).

In Lake Monona, during the summer months, large yellow bass were concentrated during the day in a power plant outfall area with water temperatures approaching 35°C (95°F) (Neill and Magnuson 1974). Small- and medium-sized yellow bass were more abundant, day and night, in the unheated areas, and appeared to avoid the outfall areas. Burnham (1909) reported that this species is tolerant of water temperatures higher than 32.2°C (90°F).

In Lake Wingra during the spring, yellow bass did not move into the shallows until the water had warmed up to nearly 15°C (59°F). In the fall, they occurred in the shallows in reduced numbers when the water temperature dropped below 10°C (50°F), but none remained in the shallows when it dropped to 4°C (39.2°F) (Helm 1964). Young-of-year were captured in Lake Wingra with seines in shallow water at night, but very few were ever captured in the same areas during daylight. The lake bottom was the preferred habitat during daylight hours when light intensities were high. Some individuals tended to move up into the middle depths, and even to the surface, when light intensities were low.

Kraus (1963) found that yellow bass were most active between 2000 and 0400 hr. Carlander and Cleary (1949) reported that the two main periods of activity for yellow bass in water over 3 m were from 2000 to 0200 hr and from 0800 to 1600 hr. It is generally agreed that the yellow bass is far less active in the daytime than it is at night.

In the Wisconsin River at Spring Green (Sauk County), 22 yellow bass were associated with these species: quillback (1), river carpsucker (8), shorthead redhorse (6), golden redhorse (13), speckled chub (5), bullhead minnow (330), bluntnose minnow (137), emerald shiner (32), spotfin shiner (995), spottail shiner (1), weed shiner (1), river shiner (23), bigmouth shiner (3), brassy minnow (48), Mississippi silvery minnow (2), white bass (7), western sand darter (14), blackside darter (1), logperch (5), johnny darter (16), smallmouth bass (1), bluegill (1), and brook silverside (10).

IMPORTANCE AND MANAGEMENT

According to Shields (1965), small yellow bass provide excellent forage for many species of fish, including larger yellow bass.

In Lake Wingra (Dane County), yellow bass contributed 11% to the estimated total spring biomass in 1973, and 30% in 1974; in 1972, the estimated biomass of yellow bass was about 35–40 kg/ha (31–36 lb/acre) (Churchill 1976).

In Lakes Waubesa, Monona, and Kegonsa in the Madison area, most anglers do not actively fish for yellow bass, but it is becoming common in catches in these lakes, whereas white bass are rarely taken; it has multiplied to the point where it now makes up 90% or more of the total white bass–yellow bass catch (Wright 1968). Whether the decline in white bass numbers is due to habitat deterioration, the introduction of the yellow bass, or a combination of these and other factors cannot be stated. Wright has suggested that the Madison lakes may be changing in such a manner as to confer a selective advantage upon the yellow bass. From a number of stations in Lake Winnebago during August 1960, I seined 707 yellow bass (mostly young-of-year) and only 76 white bass.

The yellow bass is small, but quite gamy on light tackle. It will take almost any small lure or bait, including worms, minnows, cut-bait, flies, spinners, spoons, small plugs, and sometimes even flyrod poppers. In Wisconsin, the angling regulations for 1980 allow continuous fishing for yellow bass with no size or bag limit.

The flesh of the yellow bass is white, firm, flaky, and delicious. It is often compared to that of the yellow perch, and it is usually considered superior to the flesh of the white bass.

Sunfish Family—Centrarchidae

Eleven species of centrarchids in four genera are known from Wisconsin. In the United States and Canada, 32 species in 9 genera are known. According to Miller (1959), the Centrarchidae probably arose from some specialized serranid progenitor which invaded fresh water during or before the Eocene period. The hypothetical primitive centrarchid probably was a free-swimming inhabitant of lowland waters, with a shape and size comparable to that of *Ambloplites*. From the distribution of present species and of species and genera known only as fossils, it would appear that the centrarchid center of origin was located in the Mississippi Valley (Branson and Moore 1962). By the beginning of the Pleistocene many of the extant genera, and some that disappeared before the close of that period, were in existence.

The sunfishes are typically spiny-rayed fishes, with 6–13 spines in the anterior dorsal fin, and 3–9 spines in the anterior part of the anal fin. The spinous and soft-rayed dorsal fins are generally joined as one fin. The fish are for the most part deep bodied and strongly compressed laterally. Fine teeth appear in brushlike bands on both the upper and lower jaws, and the lower pharyngeal arches broaden into pads bearing conical or molarlike teeth ("throat-teeth"). The swim bladder is isolated from the esophagus (physoclistous condition). The pectoral fins are moderately high on the body, and the pelvic fins are located almost directly below them and slightly posteriorly. The caudal fin is notched or slightly forked.

All sunfish species tend to be nest builders, although occasionally some species use the nests of other fishes that have already spawned.

The male generally builds the nest, cares for the eggs and young, and often is quite vicious in his protective role.

Hybridization, especially within the genus *Lepomis*, is common in many of our waters, especially in the southern sector of Wisconsin. This occurs when spawning fish of several species are unduly crowded, or when there is a great scarcity of one species coupled with the abundance of another, or when the individuals of the sparse species seem to have difficulty in finding their proper mates (Hubbs 1955). Hybrids have also been produced by placing male individuals of one species into a pond with females of another (Childers 1967). There seems to be a general agreement among ichthyologists who study centrarchids that behavioral isolation is probably the most important type of isolating mechanism in this group (Gerald 1971). That is, behavioral patterns which are specific to only one species are used to keep the different sunfishes separated from one another, especially during the critical spawning period. This conclusion has come about largely through the process of elimination, however, and the actual cues used by sunfish are still largely unknown. Auditory communication is only one of several types of cues used by fish.

The sunfishes are among the most colorful and attractive of our fishes and the bass species of the family are important game fish, avidly sought after by a large body of fishermen. The total production of the members of the sunfish family is astounding. In Wisconsin, they are among the most common of our fishes, and they furnish the bulk of the fish coming to creel. They are standby fishes for a shore lunch, or for that easy meal when the larger game fishes are not biting. Because of their popularity, the sunfishes have been widely stocked in Wisconsin.

Unfortunately, because they are prolific and hardy, sunfishes also present a serious and difficult fish management problem. Many waters produce millions of stunted sunfish, to the dismay of fishermen and biologists. Consequently, size and bag limits have largely been removed in Wisconsin, and fishermen are encouraged to increase their harvest.

"Panfish cannot be accumulated or stockpiled for future use. What man does not utilize, nature will eliminate" (Snow 1960:14).

Smallmouth Bass

Micropterus dolomieui Lacepède. *Micropterus*—small fin; *dolomieui*—after M. Dolomieu, a French mineralogist and friend of Lacepède, for whom dolomite was named.

Other common names: northern smallmouth bass, smallmouth black bass, smallmouth, bronzeback, Oswego bass, black bass, yellow bass, brown bass, green bass, redeyed bass, redeye, white or mountain trout.

Immature 45 mm, Wisconsin R. (Juneau Co.), 26 June 1977

Subadult 166 mm, L. Winnebago (Winnebago Co.?), 18–21 Aug. 1960

Adult (living) (Wisconsin DNR photo)

DESCRIPTION

Body slender to robust, slightly compressed laterally, oval in cross section. Length 233–349 mm (9.1–13.7 in). TL = 1.23 SL. Depth into TL 3.7–4.8. Head length into TL 3.2–3.9. Mouth moderately large, slightly oblique. Upper jaw reaching from middle to posterior edge of eye but never beyond; lower jaw slightly longer than upper jaw; conical, pointed teeth in brushlike pads on upper and lower jaws; lower pharyngeal arches narrow, with numerous fine teeth. Gill rakers on first gill arch long, straight, pointed. Dorsal fins 2, but joined and appear as 1; first dorsal fin with 10 spines, second with 13–15 soft rays. Anal fin with 3 spines, 10–11 soft rays; pelvic fin thoracic, with 1 spine and 5 rays; pectoral fin short and rounded, when laid forward across cheek not reaching eye; caudal fin moderately forked. Scales ctenoid, in lateral line 69–80; lateral line complete. Chromosomes 2n = 46 (W. LeGrande, pers. comm.).

Back and head brown, or yellow-brown, or olive to green; sides lighter; belly light yellow to white. Most scales on sides with bronze reflections. Vertical bars faint, 9–16 (generally more numerous and prominent in young), not fused into a lateral band. Usually 3 dark streaks on each side of head, radiating backward from snout and eye; dark opercle spot about size of pupil of eye. Eye usually red or orange. Fins lightly pigmented, caudal fin in adults with darker edge; in young, caudal fin strikingly marked with yellow at base, pronounced dark crescent band through middle, and a whitish edge.

Breeding male darkens to blackish on back and sides; breeding female has intensified colors.

Hybrids: Smallmouth bass × spotted bass (Scott and Crossman 1973). Artificial smallmouth bass × largemouth bass (Schwartz 1972, *Sports Afield* June 1977:147–148).

DISTRIBUTION, STATUS, AND HABITAT

In Wisconsin, the smallmouth bass occurs in all drainage basins. It seems probable that it was quite generally dispersed in early postglacial time, and was distributed over the state approximately as it is at present before any introductions were made (Greene 1935). Over 5,650 km (3,500 mi) of smallmouth bass streams are listed for Wisconsin (Wis. Dep. Nat. Resour. 1968b).

Originally the smallmouth bass ranged from northern Minnesota to Lake Nipissing (Ontario) and Quebec, with a relict population from the Nipigon River (Ontario) south to the Tennessee River drainage of Alabama and to eastern Oklahoma (Hubbs and Lagler 1964). A range map was prepared by Hubbs and Bailey (1938). The smallmouth bass has been extensively introduced in American waters, in the waters of most European countries, and in the waters of Guam, Hawaii, Hong Kong, Japan, and Vietnam (Robbins and MacCrimmon 1974).

The smallmouth bass is common in medium to

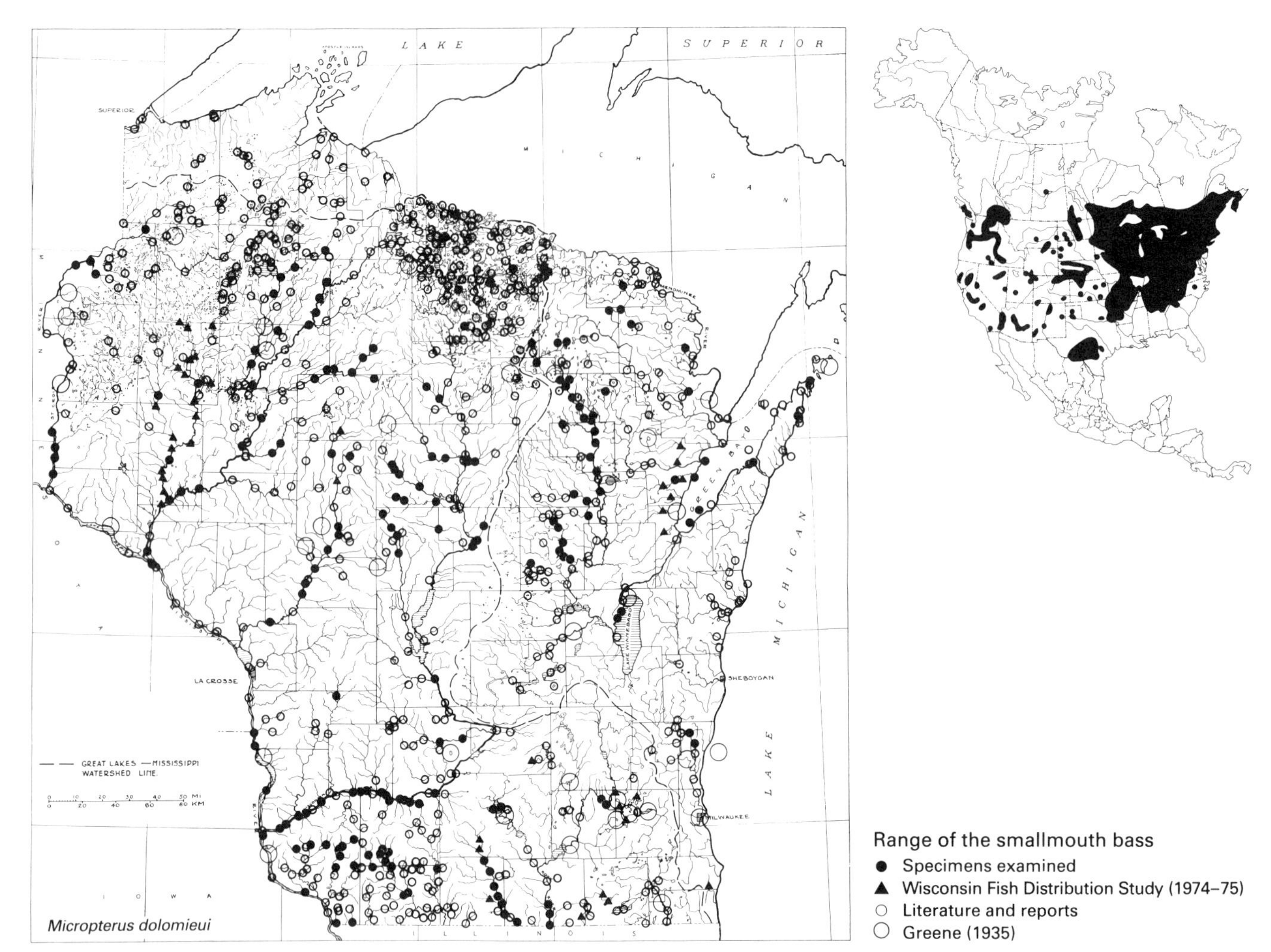

large streams and in large, clearwater lakes throughout Wisconsin. In Lake Winnebago, it is abundant along the north and east shores (Priegel 1967a). In Waukesha County, it was reported from 10 of 40 lakes sampled (Poff and Threinen 1963). It is common in upper Green Bay of Lake Michigan and in Chequamegon Bay of Lake Superior. Fair numbers are present in moderate to swift currents along the rocky banks of the lower Wisconsin River, and numerous young-of-year have been captured from eddies along Wisconsin River sand banks (Becker 1966). The streams draining into the Wisconsin River north of the east-west highland ridge traversing Grant and Iowa counties contain few or no smallmouth bass; south of the ridge the streams, including those less than 3 m wide, contain substantial populations of smallmouth bass. The smallmouth bass is uncommon on the Mississippi River, where "much of the favored habitat . . . has been altered or destroyed since the inception of the 9-foot navigational channel. The species now appears to be quite spotty" (R. Nord, pers. comm.). This species is uncommon at barriers in the mouths of tributaries of Lake Superior (McLain et al. 1965).

Smallmouth bass are less abundant in Wisconsin today than they were formerly. In the Fox River (Green Lake County), they were once so abundant that local farmers near Princeton netted them for hog food (Fassbender et al. 1970). In Lake Wingra (Dane County), during the 1936 carp seining, smallmouth bass were present in fair abundance (Noland 1951); however, none were reported in the 1944 carp seining, and the species is no longer listed from that lake (Churchill 1976). The smallmouth bass was common in the Rock River between Hustisford and Watertown (Dodge County) until about 1940, but it has become rare in that River since then (H. Neuenschwander, pers. comm.). Smallmouth bass fishing at most points along the Great Lakes shoreline is no longer of the excellent quality described for earlier years (Borgeson and Tody 1967).

The distribution of smallmouth bass in Wisconsin is typical of the distribution of a glacial lake species. In the northern part of the state it is found in both lakes and streams, but southward it is more common in swift, clear streams and rivers than in lakes. It prefers cool, flowing streams, and large, clear lakes over rocky and sandy bottoms. Lakes over 6.1 m (20 ft) deep, with rooted aquatic vegetation and clean, gravel shores provide the optimum habitat. In Lake Michigan, the smallmouth bass is confined to shoal waters of protected bays. It commonly avoids sluggish or muddy water.

In Wisconsin, the smallmouth bass was encountered most frequently in clear to slightly turbid, shallow water, over substrates of sand (27% frequency), gravel (23%), rubble (15%), boulders (14%), mud (11%), silt (7%), clay (3%), bedrock (1%), and detritus (1%). It was taken from lakes and streams with various currents: riffles 42%, pools 46%, and sloughs 13%, and with varying widths: 1.0–3.0 m (2%), 3.1–6.0 m (16%), 6.1–12.0 m (13%), 12.1–24.0 m (29%), 24.1–50.0 m (23%), and more than 50 m (16%). In lakes, the smallmouth bass seeks out rock ledges and rocky bottoms, but may also be found along weedy shorelines. It often occurs in streams containing trout, but typically inhabits the warmer water sections below trout water. Many streams hold trout in the headwaters and grade into smallmouth bass near the mouth.

BIOLOGY

Excellent summaries of the life history of the smallmouth bass are provided by Coble (1975) and Hubbs and Bailey (1938).

In reviewing water temperatures related to smallmouth bass spawning and nest building, Cleary (1956) noted that temperature thresholds are variable. Although commonly reported as spawning at water temperatures of 16.7–17.8°C (62–64°F), smallmouths have been found spawning at 11.7°C (53°F). In southern Wisconsin, the smallmouth bass spawns from the middle of May through June, when the water temperature ranges between 12.8 and 23.9°C (55 and 75°F). In Lake Geneva, Mraz (1960) noted nest construction at minimum water temperatures of 15–16.1°C (59–61°F), but females did not appear. In the Door County area of Lake Michigan (Wiegert 1966), some smallmouths spawned in sheltered shallow bays as early as 20 May when the water temperature rose above 15.6°C (60°F); other smallmouths caught on exposed reefs and shorelines had not yet spawned in late July. In the St. Croix River, spawning occurred as early as 11 May and as late as 7 June (Kuehn et al. 1961).

In Clear Lake (Oneida County), nesting activity was observed at 18°C (64.4°F), and spawning occurred at 19°C (66.2°F) (Marinac 1976); however, activity ceased when the water temperature fell to 16°C (60.8°F) in early June, and resumed when the temperature rose to 18°C (64.4°F) in the third week of June.

In the Red Cedar River (Dunn County), there was some evidence of upstream movement by smallmouth bass in the spawning period (Paragamian 1973). C. Brynildson (1957) stated that two factors adversely affected the success of smallmouth spawning in streams: a sudden drop in the water temperature, and the siltation of nests during floods. Mraz (1964d) reported that when the water temperature dropped from 18.3°C (64.9°F) to 7.2°C (45°F), the males deserted the nests, but first apparently fanned silt over the eggs. A few days later, after the water temperature again rose to 18.3°C (64.9°F), the males reappeared and cleared the nests of silt, and fresh egg deposits were found. None of these nestings were successful, however, as both old and new eggs were lost to a fungus infection.

In lakes, smallmouth bass nests are more common and are built earlier on the west and north shorelines, where the water temperatures are usually higher and the shores are best protected from prevailing winds (Mraz 1964d). Nests are constructed on gravel, preferably beside a natural or an artificial obstruction such as a stone crib, log, oil drum, large boulder, or stump. Concrete blocks placed in Lake Geneva (Walworth County) were accepted as nesting locations, and frequently two nests were found on either side of one block.

In Lake Michigan, most smallmouth nests were observed at water depths of 0.4–1.5 m on gravel and rubble; fewer nests were built on sand and bedrock with overlying gravel (Wiegert 1966). In Lake Geneva (Mraz 1960, 1964d), most of the smallmouth nests were located in 2.4–3.7 m of water, although some were more than 6 m below the surface.

Most nest building takes place in the early morning. A male apparently builds several "practice nests" until he finally settles on one as suitable (Mraz 1964d, Cleary 1956). Nest construction requires from 4 to 48 hr or more (Hubbs and Bailey 1938). After selecting a satisfactory nest site, the male begins construction by assuming a nearly vertical position in the water, head up, and sweeping vigorously with his tail. Silt, sand, and small stones settle at the periphery of the nest, which in diameter is about twice the length of the male. With his mouth he may remove large objects, and he roots and overturns the bottom material, especially in the center of the nest. Mraz (1964d) noted that he has never found a smallmouth nest that could be described as other than a perfect nest: a large, perfectly circular, clean gravel structure.

When the nest has been constructed, the smallmouth bass male awaits a female. When a female appears, the male makes short rushes at her. The female may be driven into the nest repeatedly, and may remain in the nest a little longer each time (Breder and Rosen 1966). As the female moves into the nest, the male on the periphery turns on his side with the fully distended dorsal spines pointing toward her. This may be a threat signal, and is similar to behavior exhibited by the threespine stickleback as the female enters a stickleback nest.

When the female is ready to spawn, there is a marked change in her appearance. The dark mottlings on her body become prominent as the background color pales. Breder and Rosen, quoting J. Reighard, described behavior in the nest (1966:408):

> . . . The two fish lie side by side on the bottom. The female is turned partly on her side so that her median plane forms an angle of about 45° with the plane of the horizon. The male remains upright with his head just back of the pectoral of the female or opposite it! The male is quiet during the process while the female exhibits certain peculiar fin movements. The eggs are emitted at periods when the female is with the male in the nest.

Reighard noted four such periods of 4–6 seconds each, which were separated by periods of about 30 seconds. The female that he observed remained in the nest with the male for 2 hours and 20 minutes. When she departed the male pursued her, but he returned to care for the eggs, which had adhered to the bottom stones of the nest.

A female smallmouth bass may spawn in more than one nest. Ordinarily, a male spawns with only one female at a time, but one male is known to have spawned with two females in the same nest at the same time; the females alternated egg-laying periods, and both females left the nest at about the same time after their eggs had been laid (Breder and Rosen 1966).

The male smallmouth bass protects the nest against intruders of his own and other species; however, Latta (1963) reported that the common shiner had spawned in smallmouth nests in eastern Lake Michigan. Mraz (1964d) observed the total loss of many smallmouth bass nests due to predation by minnows, bluegills, pumpkinseeds, and green sunfish. Their method of operation was simple (p. 8):

> . . . One lead fish approaches the nest or school and the male leaves to chase the fish away. At once, the remainder dart in and feed, then dart away at the male's return. This is repeated until the nest or school is cleaned up or the group of predators decide to leave.

The number of smallmouth bass eggs per nest varies from 2,000 to 10,000 (Wis. Dep. Nat. Resour. 1968b). The eggs and newly hatched fry are vulnerable to floods. If the nest is destroyed, renesting may occur—a habit which is a distinct advantage when earlier nesting has not been successful (Nord 1967). Kuehn et al. (1961) observed one nest which survived a 2-m rise in the water level.

The fecundity of three smallmouth bass females, ages IV and V, from Lake Geneva, which were 335, 406, and 414 mm TL was 4,896, 5,402, and 5,364 eggs respectively (Mraz 1960). The eggs of smallmouth bass average 2.2 (1.8–2.5) mm diam (Fish 1932, Latta 1963, Meyer 1970), and are deposited in the center of the nest (Mraz 1964d).

Hatching time for this species ranges from 9.5 days at a water temperature of 12.8°C (55°F) to 2.25 days at 23.9°C (75°F) (Emig 1966b). According to Mraz (1964d), if spawning occurs during a rapid water temperature rise which levels off at about 23–25°C (73–77°F), the eggs may hatch in 48 hr or less. Developing smallmouth bass embryos were subjected to a temperature rise from 11.7 to 25°C (53 to 77°F) with zero mortality (Webster 1945).

Fish (1932) described and illustrated the 8.8-, 9.5-, 10-, and 19-mm stages of the smallmouth bass. Meyer (1970) illustrated the 10.2-mm (12-day), 15.6-mm (49-day), and 24.0-mm (66-day) stages. A series of early developmental stages through 24 days is depicted by Hubbs and Bailey (1938). The approximate length of smallmouths when all fin rays are formed is 10.7–11.0 mm, and larvae about 24 mm long develop distinctive, dark, vertical patches along the lateral line. After the smallmouth fry have taken on a dark pigmentation, they are readily visible. Smallmouth nests then look as if tar has been poured into them, hence the term "black fry." The young bass remain in this stage for 2–4 days, after which the dark pigmentation disappears, the yolk-sac is absorbed, and the school is ready to move away from the nest (Mraz 1964d). Young smallmouth bass may remain in the nest for 6–15 days, after which they rise in a school above the nest. The male herds them together as they weave about, in the fashion of cichlid fishes (Breder and Rosen 1966).

The young are usually protected by the male from 2 to 9 days, but at times he guards them for as long as 28 days, even after they have become widely dispersed in the shallow water near shore (Hubbs and Bailey 1938). The smallmouth bass thus cares for its young for a longer time than other sunfishes do, with the exception of the largemouth bass.

Pflieger (1966) stated that there seemed to be a marked reduction in the abundance of smallmouth fry within the first few days after they left the nests, suggesting that mortality was high at that time. Wiegert (1966) observed predation on smallmouth bass fry by minnows and small perch in the Sawyer Harbor area (Door County) during the 1964 season. In Missouri (Pflieger 1966), a marauding bluegill consumed 39 smallmouth bass fry after the male smallmouth bass was frightened away. On one occasion Pflieger saw smallmouth fry produced during the first nesting period feeding on fry from the second nesting.

In southern Wisconsin (Grant, Richland and Lafayette counties), young-of-year smallmouth bass averaged 26 mm long in June, 55 mm in July, and 69 mm in August and September (S. Krause, pers. comm.).

Annulus formation occurs in late June and early July, and there is no difference in the growth rates of the sexes. Coble (1967a) determined that the total yearly growth of age-III to age-V smallmouth bass in South Bay, Lake Huron, was directly related to the mean surface water temperature for the period July through September. However, bass from Lake Opeongo, Ontario, and older bass from Lake Opeongo and South Bay showed no relationship between growth and surface water temperatures.

The weights at the annuli of the Red Cedar River population shown in the table below were: 0.01, 0.09, 0.29, 0.52, 0.84, 1.02, 1.17, and 1.35 kg (Paragamian and Coble 1975). Smallmouth bass from Lake Geneva weighed 0.45 kg at 318 mm long; they weighed 0.91 kg at 406 mm, and 1.36 kg at 470 mm (Mraz 1960). In eastern Lake Michigan, the K_{SL} of smallmouth bass ranged from 2.53 to 3.35 for fish 165–470 mm long; the condition generally increased with the size of the fish (Latta 1963). Smallmouth bass, 100–259 mm SL, from Muskellunge Lake (Vilas County) had K_{SL} values of 2.04–2.56 (Bennett 1938).

The age at maturity for smallmouth bass is 3–4 years (Nord 1967). Some Lake Geneva smallmouth bass mature at 3 years of age, or at about 279 mm (11 in) (Mraz 1960). In Lake Michigan, the fastest growing male smallmouth bass reached sexual maturity at 3 years (259 mm), and the fastest growing female reached maturity at 4 years (325 mm); all males were mature at 5 years (avg TL 277 mm), and all females, at 7 years (avg TL 361 mm) (Latta 1963).

A 4.1-kg (9-lb 1-oz) smallmouth bass was taken 21 June 1950 from Indian Lake (Oneida County).

Young smallmouth bass begin their carnivorous existence as they rise from the nest. Before the yolk-sac is fully absorbed, they feed actively on minute midge larvae, *Daphnia*, or other small crustacea (Moore 1922). Unlike adult bass, which do most of their feeding during the early morning and early evening, the young bass feed throughout the day, and perhaps also at night (Hubbs and Bailey 1938). By the time the smallmouth bass are 38 mm (1.5 in) long, insects and small fishes make up the bulk of their food, and at about 76 mm (3 in) they begin to feed on small crayfishes. Fishes of suitable size and of almost any species living in the same waters—including perch, sunfishes, minnows, darters, sculpins, suckers, catfishes, sticklebacks, and young bass—are eaten by smallmouth bass, and form a large part of the diet of all juvenile and adult smallmouths. Usually dead food is rejected, but when the food supply is insufficient dead animals are eaten. The smallmouth has needlelike teeth which grab and hold the prey so that it may be swallowed whole.

In the Red Cedar River (Dunn County), young-of-year smallmouths and one yearling had eaten primarily aquatic insects, including larval and adult *Hydropsyche* and larval mayflies (Paragamian 1973). In smallmouth bass more than 162 mm long, crayfish, fish, and aquatic insects had been eaten, in that order of importance; the fish food included the smallmouth bass, white bass, bluegill, and logperch. In smallmouth bass 135–329 mm long from the Plover River (Portage County), fish was the most important food item (48% occurrence), followed by crayfish

Age and Growth (TL in mm) of the Smallmouth Bass in Wisconsin

Location	1	2	3	4	5	6	7	8	9	10	11	12	13	Source
L. Michigan and Green Bay (Door Co.)	79	160	234	264	302	333	381	404	414	445	432	470	505	Wiegert (1966)
19 lakes & 1 stream, Northern Wisconsin	61	135	208	269	318	358	388	424	447	465	480			Bennett (1938)
Clear L. (Oneida Co.)	92	142	185	240	297	354	394	427	453	473	487			Marinac (1976)
Red Cedar R. (Dunn Co.)	100	190	274	329	383	407	424	444						Paragamian and Coble (1975)
Plover R. (Portage Co.)	91	158	220	297	366	410	440	455	476					Paragamian (1973)
L. Geneva (Walworth Co.)	71	173	277	356	409	452	478							Mraz (1960)

(24%), and aquatic insects (4%); the fish eaten included the common shiner, shorthead redhorse, fantail darter, smallmouth bass, black bullhead, and stonecat. In the laboratory (Paragamian 1976b), the common shiner was most vulnerable to predation by the smallmouth bass, and the hornyhead chub ranked second; the white sucker was the least vulnerable. In angler-caught smallmouths 147–350 mm long from Clear Lake (Oneida County), crayfish made up 65% of the volume of the stomachs, fishes (cyprinids and percids) 22%, and insects 13% (Marinac 1976). In Lake Mendota (Dane County), smallmouth bass averaging 356 mm consumed adult insects (82.5% volume), plant matter (5%), bottom ooze (9.5%), amphipods (2.5%), and insect larvae (0.5%) (Pearse 1921a). In Green Lake (Green Lake County) 114-mm smallmouths consumed cladocerans (37.6% volume), insect larvae (31.9%), fish (13.6%), insect pupae (7.8%), insect adults (5%), amphipods (4.1%), plants (0.2%), and sand (0.2%).

Cahn (1927) reported catching a smallmouth bass which had consumed eight honey bees; this fish had undoubtedly been feeding at the surface. Lachner (1950) reported a 68-mm smallmouth bass which had eaten a 46-mm darter.

W. E. Williams (1959) reported that the smallmouth bass demonstrated a conversion factor of 4.50; i.e., it converted to flesh 1 part of 4.50 parts of food consumed.

In northern Wisconsin lakes during the summer (Hile and Juday 1941) the smallmouth bass inhabited waters at temperatures of 20.3–21.3°C (68.5–70.3°F). According to Emig (1966b), it prefers water temperatures of 21.1–26.7°C (70–80°F), and becomes lethargic at 10°C (50°F). A water temperature of about 10°C (50°F) marks the beginning and ending of the period of nonactivity and of reduced or suspended growth (Hubbs and Bailey 1938). In the laboratory (Larimore and Duever 1968), smallmouth fry acclimated to 30 and 35°C (86 and 95°F) failed to swim in waters which were warmer than their acclimation temperatures. Emig (1966b) noted that, at 21.1°C (70°F), concentrations of dissolved oxygen of 0.96 ppm in Deer River and 0.87 ppm in Beebe Lake (both in New York) were lethal to smallmouth bass.

Smallmouth bass occur most consistently in shallow water, and appear to be almost exclusively inhabitants of the epilimnion. In Nebish Lake (Vilas County), they were captured in water shallower than 7 m, and in Muskellunge Lake they were captured in the epilimnion at about 3 m (Hile and Juday 1941). In Green Lake (Green Lake County), Pearse (1921a) netted smallmouth bass at depths above 20 m, and in Lake Geneva Nelson and Hasler (1942) captured most smallmouths at 6–9 m, although they ranged freely between 3 and 12 m.

During the day adult smallmouths retire to pools, undercut banks, or lairs in fairly deep water. Hubbs and Bailey have described their activity between dusk and dawn (1938:33):

> . . . At dusk they move about more freely, and in lakes are then frequently seen splashing at the surface far from shore. They may remain active on moonlight nights, but ordinarily lie on the bottom in their open-eyed sleep until awakened by the first rays of dawn, hardly perceptible to man. Hunger then seems to impel them to search vigorously for food, which they often find on the very shallow marginal waters into which the forage fish have gone to catch a little rest. They may move so far inshore that their backs are exposed, and splash noisily as they lunge about after fishy morsels.

In winter, smallmouth bass go to deep waters and lie about rocks, ledges, or roots in a semidormant manner; they evidently do not take food at this time.

There appears to be a niche separation between the smallmouth bass and the largemouth bass in waters where these two species occur together. During their first year of life, smallmouths definitely seem to avoid the thick weedbeds of shallow water in which largemouths commonly congregate (Hubbs and Bailey 1938). Smallmouth young seek shelter in the lee of a stone or a brick, or in the cavity under a flat object. In lakes, smallmouths prefer to rest in the proximity of a rock ledge, a submerged log, or a boulder. In flowing water, smallmouths commonly lie in the protective backwater of a large boulder, a stump, or a rock ledge, where a minimum of physical exertion is required to retain their positions. Adult smallmouths are rarely taken near beds of submerged or floating plants, which are the favored retreats of largemouth bass.

In laboratory experiments designed to clarify aspects of the niche separation between the largemouth and the smallmouth bass, both species exhibited crepuscular activity, but the largemouth also showed a midday activity peak. The smallmouth bass avoided bright light, and its peak activity periods occurred at the beginning and at the end of the dark periods. The activity of the largemouth bass was much more depressed during dark periods, and rose sharply at the onset of light periods.

The smallmouth bass apparently has much less inclination to school than the largemouth bass (Mraz 1964d). Schooling is common among smallmouth fry in the nest, but they soon disperse.

Emery (1973) noted two kinds of daytime activity

among smallmouth bass. In one of these, loosely aggregated pods of smallmouths moved slowly over an area, describing a path which led them back to a position of rest; often this was done in association with rock bass schools. In the other activity, smallmouths traveled from one area or range to another, moving in shallow water for as much as several kilometers a day.

Larimore (1952) found that smallmouth bass which had been transferred overland and released in other parts of a stream were capable of returning to their home pools from either upstream or downstream. Latta (1963) concluded from a 3-year study that this species was essentially nonmigratory; although 1 out of 3,141 tagged smallmouths had traveled 149 km (92 mi), only 11 individuals moved more than 32 km (20 mi). Smallmouth bass which were tagged and recaptured in Green Bay and in the Lake Michigan side of the Door County peninsula tended to remain in a given area (Wiegert 1966); only a few larger fish moved any great distances—a 33-cm fish tagged in Little Sturgeon Bay was recovered in the Ahnapee River (Kewaunee County) after traveling approximately 73 km (45 mi). In Missouri streams, 63% of the smallmouth bass had moved less than 1.6 km (1 mi) from their place of release, and over 97% were taken within 40 km (Funk 1957).

In the Black River (Clark County), 10 smallmouth bass were associated with the following species: blackside darter (18), northern hog sucker (17), shorthead redhorse (10), rock bass (4), slenderhead darter (1), rainbow darter (17), banded darter (18), golden redhorse (7), hornyhead chub (8), blacknose shiner (74), common shiner (33), largescale stoneroller (10), brook silverside (1), white sucker (1), johnny darter (6), and stonecat (1) (R. Urban, pers. comm.).

IMPORTANCE AND MANAGEMENT

Young smallmouth bass are preyed upon by older generations of bass, sunfish, perch, and large fish predators, as well as by crayfish, birds, frogs, and snakes.

The smallmouth bass is a known host to the glochidial or larval stage of the mucket clam (*Lampsilis siliquoidea*) (Hart and Fuller 1974).

Wisconsin anglers use a wide variety of tackle when fishing for smallmouth bass; sophisticated spinning and flyrods are used alongside the old-time cane pole. All of these, fished with minnows, angleworms, hellgramites, crayfish, and adult mayflies, attract the smallmouth. Dry flies, wet flies, and casting and spinning baits complete the smallmouth arsenal. Harlan and Speaker (1956) concluded that it "is almost impossible to tell the angler what kind of bait to use" when fishing for the smallmouth.

Jordan and Evermann (1923) quoted a Dr. J. A. Henshall, who wrote of the smallmouth bass (p. 356):

> . . . He is plucky, game, brave and unyielding to the last when hooked. He has the arrowy rush of the trout and bold leap of the salmon, while he has a system of fighting tactics peculiarly his own. . . . I consider him, inch for inch and pound for pound, the gamest fish that swims.

The smallmouth bass is distinctly a sport fish, and commercial harvesting is not permitted in Wisconsin. Fishing regulations for this species are liberal; since 1955 they have included an early opening for both the smallmouth and largemouth bass seasons in the 12 southern counties, and no size limit. The open season allows a daily bag limit of 5 to 10 smallmouths, and a size limit is imposed only in some northwestern counties where the minimum length must be 10 in. Liberal regulations in southern Wisconsin have been justified on the grounds that natural mortality and predation eliminate many smallmouth bass before they reach 10 in (254 mm); thus the removal of the minimum size limit provides more fishing without depleting future stocks (C. Brynildson 1957). For details pertaining to specific waters, current state fishing regulations should be consulted.

The best-known smallmouth bass fishing waters are those of Green Bay and Lake Michigan, which surround the tip of Door County. In one study, about 81% of the smallmouth bass caught there were taken after 1 July, and only 19% were taken during June (Wiegert 1966). In Lake Michigan south of Door County, the numbers of smallmouth bass taken drop off quickly. Only seven were reported caught from the Point Beach Nuclear Plant fishing pier (Manitowoc County) during 1972 and 1973 (Spigarelli and Thommes 1976).

According to Nord (1967), there are few bona fide smallmouth bass fishermen on the Mississippi River, and most smallmouths are taken incidentally with other species. In 1957, the smallmouth bass ranked sixteenth in the Mississippi River sport fishery, and the majority of the fish were taken above Pool 8; in 1962–1963, it ranked fifteenth. The projected sport fishery catch of smallmouth bass in Pools 4, 5, 7, and 11 in 1967–1968 was 5,351 fish weighing 2,233 kg (4,918 lb) (Wright 1970).

The flesh of the smallmouth is white, firm, and flaky, with a fine savor and a juicy, succulent quality. It is considered by gourmets to be superior to any fish except the lake whitefish of the Great Lakes. Its flesh is nutritious, and it has a low fat content which permits the successful angler to freeze his catch for later enjoyment (Schneberger 1972d).

Before the establishment of its walleye population, Escanaba Lake (Vilas County) was highly regarded for its smallmouth bass fishing (Kempinger et al. 1975). In the early years, smallmouth bass accounted for 1–11% of the annual total weight harvested by anglers, but in recent years it has amounted to less than 1%. From 1946 to 1969, 4,397 smallmouth bass were caught from Escanaba Lake, weighing a total of 993 kg (2,189 lb). In the Red Cedar River (Dunn County) the estimated harvest of smallmouth bass during 1973 was 5.1 kg/ha (Paragamian 1973). In Clear Lake (Oneida County), during 1974 and 1975, the smallmouth harvest ranged from 2.1 to 3.8 bass/ha (Marinac 1976).

In Livingston Branch (Iowa County), the standing stock of smallmouth bass was 51.6–82.9 kg/ha (C. Brynildson and Truog 1965). In the Red Cedar River (Dunn County) Paragamian (1973) estimated 132 smallmouth bass/ha and a standing crop of 15.1 kg/ha; in the Plover River (Portage County), he estimated 118 smallmouth bass/ha and 17.5 kg/ha. In Clear Lake (Oneida County), Marinac (1976) estimated 8.7 bass/ha and 1.1 kg/ha.

Smallmouth bass management is beset with many unanswered questions. In northern Illinois, when stocked in 12 ponds representing most kinds of warmwater pond habitats, the smallmouth bass reproduced successfully in 6 ponds and failed to reproduce in the other 6. This failure may have resulted from an absence of sexually mature fish, or from the inability of the smallmouths to compete successfully with largemouth bass and green sunfish (Bennett and Childers 1957). These researchers concluded that smallmouth bass are most successful in ponds by themselves, and that if they have to compete with such species as largemouth bass, green sunfish, bluegills, and bullheads, their growth and survival rates are reduced. Larimore (1954) noted that when smallmouth bass were introduced into a stream already containing native smallmouth bass, there was a decline in the number of native smallmouths in several pools which contained a concentration of stocked fish. This decline may have been caused by the movement of native smallmouths to other parts of the stream, or by a lack of native fish to replace those removed by anglers.

In Canada, the introduction of ciscoes in Lake Opeongo as food for lake trout proved to be detrimental to the smallmouth bass, and resulted in a drastic decline in the smallmouth bass resource (Emery 1975).

A smallmouth bass, unlike a salmonid fish, cannot be safely stripped of its eggs; however, it will perform normal spawning activities in artificial ponds if satisfactory conditions are provided (Hubbs and Bailey 1938). To create such conditions, a large pond may be stocked with forage minnows, crayfishes, and microcrustaceans; and aquatic vegetation allowed to grow up; gravel spawning beds should be prepared. Bass introduced in such ponds spawn and remain throughout the season in the ponds with the young fish. No subsequent food or care is needed, except for the fertilization of the water to increase the growth of natural foods. The costs of labor are slight, and little or no expense is involved in feeding the fish, but production is inefficient for the area utilized because of losses through cannibalism, insufficient food, and predation. Pond management techniques, and techniques for trapping and transporting smallmouth bass are given by Mraz (1964d). The details of feeding and caring for the young are discussed by Hubbs and Bailey (1938), and by Langlois (1936).

Largemouth Bass

Micropterus salmoides (Lacepède). *Micropterus*—small fin; *salmoides*—troutlike, in gameness and in quality as food, and often called "trout" in the South, where the original was captured.

Other common names: northern largemouth bass, largemouth, bigmouth bass, black bass, largemouth black bass, green bass, line side, green trout, Oswego bass, bayou bass, slough bass, lake bass.

Immature 52 mm, outlet of Williams L. (Marquette Co.), 29 July 1960

Subadult 184 mm, L. Poygan (Winnebago Co.), 23 July 1960

DESCRIPTION

Body slender to robust, slightly compressed laterally, oval in cross section. Length 229–305 mm (9–12 in). TL = 1.24 SL. Depth into TL 3.5–4.2. Head length into TL 3.2–3.5. Mouth large, slightly oblique. Upper jaw reaching at least to posterior edge of eye in adults, and from middle to posterior edge in young-of-year; lower jaw heavy, blunt, decidedly longer than upper jaw; conical, pointed teeth in brushlike pads on upper and lower jaws; lower pharyngeal arches narrow, with numerous fine teeth. Gill rakers on first gill arch stout, long, straight, and pointed. Dorsal fins 2, scarcely joined; first dorsal fin with 10 spines and second with 12–14 soft rays. Anal fin with 3 spines, 11 (10–12) soft rays; pelvic fin thoracic, with 1 spine and 5 rays; pectoral fin short and rounded, when laid forward across cheek not reaching eye; caudal fin moderately forked. Scales ctenoid, in lateral line 60–68; lateral line complete. Chromosomes 2n = 46 (W. LeGrande, pers. comm.).

Back and head dark green to light green; sides lighter; belly and ventral region of head whitish. A prominent lateral stripe from snout through eye to base of tail, interrupted anteriorly as a series of blotches of varying diameters, and becoming a solid, even stripe on caudal peduncle (in young-of-year, stripe appearing as a series of vertical blotches). Streaks on each side of head, radiating backward from snout or eye either faint or absent; dark opercle spot about size of pupil of eye. Eye golden brown. Vertical fins lightly pigmented, paired fins generally clear; caudal fin alike in young and adult, without the bright colors of the smallmouth young. Adults from mud-bottom lakes are dark olive brown to black, with markings hardly discernible.

In breeding male, colors darken.

Sexual dimorphism: Males over 350 mm with circular, scaleless area around urogenital opening; females with pear-shaped, scaleless area (W. D. Parker 1971).

Hybrids: Artificial largemouth bass × smallmouth bass (see p. 816), largemouth bass × rock bass, largemouth bass × bluegill, largemouth bass × warmouth, largemouth bass × black crappie (West and Hester 1966, Schwartz 1972, *Sports Afield* June 1977:147–148).

DISTRIBUTION, STATUS, AND HABITAT

In Wisconsin, the largemouth bass occurs in all three drainage basins; it is least widespread in the driftless area of southwestern Wisconsin. Wisconsin is near the northern limit of distribution, and it has been suggested that its presence in the state, especially in the northern counties, resulted from introductions. In the neighboring Upper Peninsula of Michigan, its absence in early reports and records prompted Taylor (1954) to suggest that the largemouth bass may not have been native to the Upper Peninsula, although it is widely distributed there today. Unfortunately, early records of its status in northern Wisconsin are not available. In northwestern Wisconsin it was present in at least 61 of 65 lakes sampled from 1975 to 1977 (H. Snow, pers. comm.). In Waukesha County, it was found in 29 of 40 lakes sampled (Poff and Threinen 1963).

The largemouth bass originally ranged east of the Rocky Mountains from southern Quebec and Ontario through the Great Lakes and the Mississippi Valley to the Gulf of Mexico, and from northeastern Mexico to Florida and the Carolinas (Hubbs and Lagler 1964). Details of its original range and of its present range (a result of extensive introductions) are given by Rob-

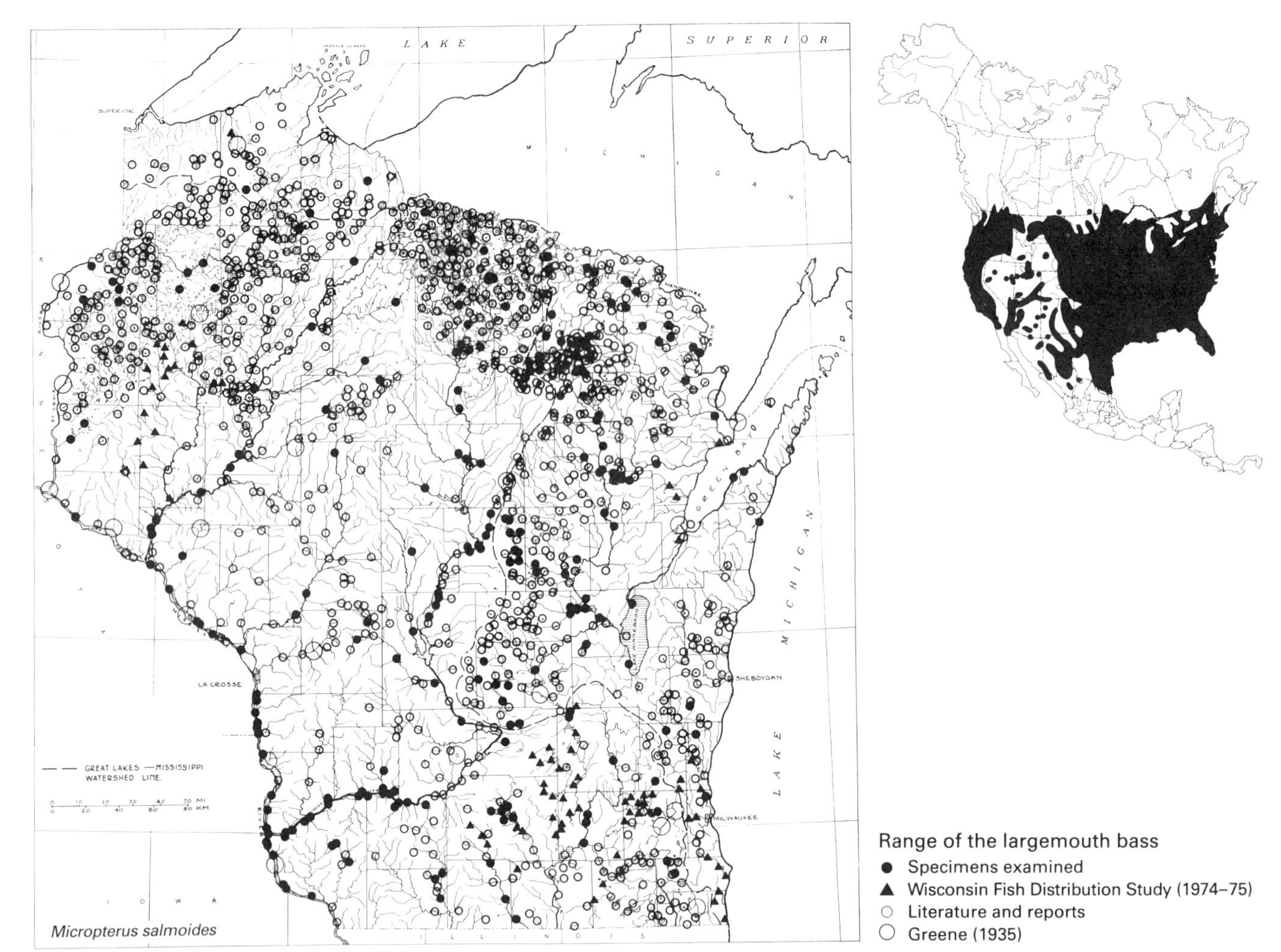

Range of the largemouth bass
● Specimens examined
▲ Wisconsin Fish Distribution Study (1974–75)
○ Literature and reports
◯ Greene (1935)

bins and MacCrimmon (1974). Its present world distribution includes North America, Central America, South America, Africa, Europe, Guam, Hawaii, Japan, Lebanon, New Zealand, and the Philippines.

The largemouth bass is abundant in medium to large rivers, and occasional in the lower extremities of small streams opening into them. It is common in lakes, ponds, sloughs, and backwaters, and in some landlocked pools of the Wisconsin and Mississippi rivers. Priegel (1967a) considered it common in the weedy bays along the western shore of Lake Winnebago. It occurs in a number of Milwaukee County lagoons. It is rare at the barriers of the tributaries to Lake Superior (McLain et al. 1965). Impoundments in streams without native largemouth bass populations are soon stocked with this species; hence it is quickly expanding its range into new areas.

In Wisconsin, the largemouth bass was encountered most frequently in clear to slightly turbid water at depths up to 1.5 m, over substrates of sand (31% frequency), gravel (20%), mud (20%), silt (9%), rubble (7%), boulders (6%), clay (4%), and detritus (3%). It occurred in rivers of the following widths: 1.0–3.0 m (19%), 3.1–6.0 m (13%), 6.1–12.0 m (17%), 12.1–24.0 m (28%), 24.1–50.0 m (19%), and more than 50 m (4%). The largemouth bass occurs mostly in shallow areas with sparse to dense vegetation—the same type of habitat that produces bluegills.

BIOLOGY

An excellent single reference for basses is Stroud and Clepper (1975). The following account is largely derived from Mraz et al. (1961) and Mraz (1964d).

The spawning of the largemouth bass in Wisconsin occurs from late April to early July. Nests were observed in Browns Lake (Racine County) as early as 3 May and as late as 25 May. The average spawning date was 9 May at the former Burlington Hatchery (Racine County), and 15 May at the Delafield Research Station (Waukesha County). Largemouth bass spawn about 2 weeks later in the northern part of the state than in the south. In Vilas County lakes, largemouth bass had finished spawning by the third week of June, according to Parker and Hasler (1959).

The selection of nest sites begins when water temperatures reach 15.6°C (60°F), and eggs are laid when the water temperatures are at 16.7–18.3°C (62–65°F). It is generally assumed that the largemouth bass does not spawn at temperatures much below 17.8°C (64°F) (Breder and Rosen 1966). The species is self-sustaining in Puerto Rican reservoirs where water temperatures average 25.5°C (78°F) throughout the year (Robbins and MacCrimmon 1974). In Minnesota near the Twin Cities, the first spawning of largemouth bass occurred 2–5 days after the daily mean water temperature had reached and remained above 15.6°C (60°F). Such temperatures occur first in shallow bays, which are generally warmer than the main body of water.

In water containing both largemouth and smallmouth basses, the largemouth spawns a little sooner than the smallmouth. The shallower, protected spawning sites among emergent vegetation in quiet bays, which are preferred by the largemouth, warm to the optimum temperatures sooner than do the deeper, rockier sites used by the smallmouth (Scott and Crossman 1973). In a Delafield (Waukesha County) pond with carp present, three largemouth bass nests originally constructed along a gravel shore were deserted before the eggs were laid, and the bass renested within a very heavy bed of coontails and water buttercups (Mraz and Cooper 1957b); inside the dense vegetation, the nests were constructed on a bottom of mud and plant fibers. Successful hatches of bass fry were produced from these nests.

The male largemouth bass usually selects a sand or gravel bottom upon which to build a nest; however, largemouths will also nest on soft bottoms, where they are able to expose such hard objects as roots, twigs, and snail shells on which to deposit the eggs (Hubbs and Bailey 1938). The largemouth bass nest is placed in about 0.2–1.8 m of water; the average depth is about 0.6 m (Breder and Rosen 1966). The male largemouth constructs a nest by using his fins to sweep out a huge basin, which may be 1 m diam and 0.3 m into the bottom. Mraz noted that deep depressions may be dug to get down to sand, or gravel, or even to a firm layer of sticks. Largemouth bass usually nest about 9 m apart from each other, and never nest in colonies as do most sunfishes.

Territorial defense against intruders is practiced by the largemouth bass as it is by other sunfishes. Eddy and Surber (1947) found that the guarding largemouth male strikes almost anything within at least a 7-m radius of the nest; he does not feed on food objects, but chews on them and then ejects them some distance away.

According to Reighard (1906), the spawning of the largemouth bass takes place at dusk (p. 15):

> . . . The male was in the nest or near it and repeatedly the female approached. The male circled to her outer side and bit her flank and she then went away. Three or four other bass, probably males, were seen ten or 15 feet outside the nest. I returned at 7 P.M. and found the same conditions. The female was seen to approach the nest and to turn on her side with her head pointed obliquely downward and to float thus, as though half dead. In this position she entered the nest and the male followed and took up a similar position. What happened in the nest could not be clearly seen. The tails of the two fish lay side by side on the bottom with their tails together and parallel. It could also be seen that sometimes one and sometimes apparently the other fish lay turned partly on its side. At this time no doubt the eggs were emitted. After being in the nest for a short time the fish came out, and the female was seen to be still floating, head downward. They then returned to the nest and continued thus for half an hour, alternately lying on the bottom within the nest and floating on its border. It was then too dark to make further observations.

The male largemouth bass receives more than one female in his nest. The eggs may be deposited in the center of the nest, along the rim, or even outside of the nest. According to Mraz et al. (1961), adult females carry 2,000–20,000 eggs in their ovaries; the number of eggs per female is largely a function of size. Not all the eggs will be emitted at once, and one female may lay eggs in several nests. Each nest usually contains about 5,000 eggs. The eggs are demersal and adhesive, and amber to pale yellow in color; when fertilized they are 1.5–1.7 mm diam (Scott and Crossman 1973, Merriner 1971a).

Hatching time in stable, warmwater temperatures is from 3 to 7 days. At the Burlington Hatchery, the average hatching time was 7 days, according to 20 years of records. A sudden drop in water temperature delays hatching time and may even kill eggs, but eggs carried in the nest for as long as 2 weeks have hatched successfully. It is generally believed that the welfare of the eggs is dependent upon the nest cleaning and water circulation provided by the male when he fans the nest. The eggs in many well-guarded nests have developed fungus infections and have been lost, however. Bass eggs left unattended have sometimes been hatched in porcelain trays. Kelly (1968) showed that temperature is not the main cause of largemouth bass egg mortality in the 12.8–23.9°C (55–75°F) range.

On hatching, young largemouth bass are transparent and 3 mm long. Counts made in Punch Lake (Vilas County) showed as many as 6,000 largemouth bass fry were produced in one nest, with an average of 3,000 fry per nest and a total production, in a good year, of about 37,500/ha (15,000/acre). After hatching, the fry remain in the bottom of the nest until the yolk is absorbed, usually a period of 6 or 7 days. They then rise from the nest, and begin feeding and schooling (Scott and Crossman 1973, Kramer and Smith 1960a). At this time, the fry are 5.9–6.3 mm long. They may remain in a brood as long as 31 days, and are guarded over part or all of this time by the male. At this stage young largemouths are a pale green, rather than black like the smallmouth bass.

Meyer (1970) illustrated the largemouth fry at the 5.4-mm, 10.2-mm (19-day), and 15.5-mm (31-day) stages. Fish (1932) illustrated and described the 75-mm stage.

Largemouth bass begin life as a swarm of fingerlings. The swarm is generally composed of young from a single nest, although the joining of 2–5 schools is common; in such cases, the respective males accompany the group. As feeding begins and the fish start to grow, the swarm spreads out until it covers several square meters. During this period, the male remains with the group and valiantly defends his brood of young against all comers. Nevertheless some young are lost to predation, and others may starve to death if plankton supplies are insufficient when feeding begins after yolk-sac absorption. Some predation is in the form of cannibalism by larger young on newly hatched broods. The bass which feed on fish grow more rapidly than the others during the first year, and retain that advantage in later years.

In early July, young-of-year largemouth bass in northern Wisconsin lakes averaged 32 mm TL; in Lake Poygan (Waushara County) during mid-July, they averaged 42 (28–51) mm TL; and in the Mississippi River (Grant County) on 24 September, they averaged 67 (55–86) mm TL. In Pewaukee Lake (Waukesha County), young largemouths averaged 40 mm in early August, and 68 mm on 10 September.

The growth of largemouth bass in Wisconsin is more moderate than the growth of this species in some southern states. Stroud (1949) noted that it reaches 190-, 343-, and 371-mm (7.5-, 13.5-, and 14.6-in) TL in Douglas Lake, Tennessee, during the first 3 years of life. Northern largemouth bass are longer lived than southern fish, which seldom live beyond 5 years.

Largemouth bass register great increases in length during the first 2 years of life; thereafter, weight gains are greater.

Padfield (1951) determined that females tended to be longer and heavier than males for each age group studied, but the differences between the sexes were slight. Differential mortality occurs, however; females reach a maximum of 9 years of age, and males reach a maximum of only 6 years. Females appear to be better fitted for survival under adverse conditions than males.

The growth of largemouths ceases at temperatures below 10°C (50°F). Stunted populations occur mostly in small, infertile lakes, many of which are found in northern Wisconsin; a lake with a stunted population may contain no fish over 254 mm (10 in) long (Mraz et al. 1961).

Young largemouth bass up to 76 mm (3 in) long are abundant in many waters, and frequently make up a large percentage of the fish taken in research nets; however, only a small number of the young reach maturity. Mature fish are generally 3–4 years old and 254–305 mm (10–12 in) long; they continue to reproduce year after year. There seems to be no mortality associated with the stresses of reproduction. The old-

Age and Growth (TL in mm) of the Largemouth Bass in Wisconsin

Location	1	2	3	4	5	6	7	8	9	10	11	12	13	Source
Northern Wisconsin lakes	71	165	246	297	335	353	386	424	450	470	490	486	490	Bennett (1937)
Birch L.[a] (Washburn Co.)	81	193	257	325	363	391	432							Snow (1969)
Clear L.[a] (Sawyer Co.)	56	165	224	262	333	386	419							Snow (1969)
Flora L. (Vilas Co.)	107	173	231	284	315	345	381	404	437	470				Parker (1956)
Punch L. (Vilas Co.)	56	137	193	236	254									Mraz et al. (1961)
Mississippi R. (Buffalo Co.)	102	244	325											Christenson and Smith (1965)
Cox Hollow L.[a] (Iowa Co.)		155	183	211	318	381	465	513						Dunst (1969)
L. Wingra (Dane Co.)	96	166	208	251	293									Churchill (1976)
L. Mendota (Dane Co.)	114	246	320	366	396	437	460	478	480	503	518			Bennett (1937)
Browns L. (Racine Co.)	91	170	229	272	305	345	411	452	467	478	498	521	511	Mraz and Threinen (1957)

[a]Lengths at capture.

est largemouth bass reported was age XVI, and was 541 mm (21.3 in) TL (Carlander 1977).

Most largemouth bass do not exceed 0.9–1.4 kg (2–3 lb) in weight, but occasionally a 2.7-kg (6-lb) fish is taken. The heaviest largemouth bass known from Wisconsin was 5.07 kg (11 lb 3 oz) taken on 12 October 1940 from Lake Ripley (Jefferson County). A record 819-mm, 10.09-kg (32¼-in, 22-lb 4-oz) fish was caught in Montgomery Lake, Georgia, in 1932. The giants of this species occur in Florida and Georgia.

The foods of fingerling largemouth bass are principally microcrustaceans—copepods, cladocerans, and ostracods. As largemouths reach a size of 51–76 mm, insects, insect larvae, and fish begin to appear in their diets. Larger largemouth bass eat fish, crayfish, frogs, and larger insects (Mraz et al. 1961, Keast 1965).

In Lake Mendota (Dane County), seven largemouths averaging 135 mm (5.3 in) TL contained the following amounts of food: fish 45%, algae 14.2%, amphipods 13.4%, crayfish 12.1%, insect adults 10.7%, and plants 3.6% (Pearse 1921a). In Murphy Flowage (Rusk County), crayfish comprised 54.6%, fish 38.8%, and insects 1.5% of the total weight of all items consumed (Snow 1971). The fish eaten, in decreasing order of importance, were bluegills, tadpole madtoms, brown bullheads, yellow perch, black crappies, minnows, and largemouth bass. Dragonfly nymphs were the predominant insects consumed; other items eaten were frogs, inorganic materials (stones up to 19.5 g), plant materials, mammals, tadpoles, annelids, and pelecypods. Shorttail shrews were found in two largemouth stomachs.

Snow (1971) noted that, after a drawdown of water in a northern Wisconsin flowage, which was accompanied by a known decline in the abundance of aquatic vegetation and an apparent decline in the abundance of crayfish, largemouth bass increased their consumption of bluegills. He suggested that a drawdown might be used to alter the feeding habits of bass to make them prey more selectively on bluegills.

Largemouth bass which had eaten golden shiners were found to have eaten more food than largemouths that had eaten insects. Largemouths also grew more rapidly on a diet of fish than on a diet of insects, regardless of whether they ate the same amount or not (MacKay 1963). In the largemouth, foods are converted to fish flesh in a ratio of 4:1—4 kg of food produces 1 kg of flesh (Mraz et al. 1961). Small largemouth bass fed in colder waters than big largemouths, but no large bass took food voluntarily in water below 10°C (Markus 1932).

Aquarium tests have shown that bass will readily swallow forage fishes whose maximum depth of body is equal to the mouth width of the bass (MacKay 1963). Largemouths are sight feeders that hunt for food; a small school of 5–10 largemouth bass roaming the shallows is a common sight. Apparently they feed at all hours, but feeding is most often observed in early morning or late in the day. The actual prey-capture behavior was discussed by Nyberg (1971), who indicated that the attack velocity was greater for moving prey, such as minnows, than for crayfish and worms. In some cases, the prey was not completely swallowed up initially; it was caught and held in the jaws until the forward motion of the bass stopped—then it was sucked in. McKnight (1968) demonstrated that largemouth fingerlings that were fed minnows grew better and weighed more than bass which were fed a commercially prepared, pellet-type feed. He suggested that the bass prefer live, swimming foods.

Barkalow (1950) reported that a largemouth bass which swam slowly beneath and behind a feeding duck in the shallows may have been feeding as well. He postulated that largemouth bass follow other animals and feed on the prey that are flushed from hiding by these animals.

The largemouth bass is truly a warmwater fish that prefers shallow water; it is seldom found in water more than 6 m deep. It prefers temperatures of 27.2–30°C (81–86°F) and its upper lethal limit is 35.6°C (96°F) (Clark 1969). Immature largemouth bass, however, have been collected from water with temperatures as high as 37°C (98.6°F) (Siler and Clugston 1975), and largemouths were known to survive a 38°C (100.4°F) water temperature in a shallow Michigan pond (Bailey 1955).

In Lake Monona (Dane County), largemouth bass tended to concentrate in the heated outfall of a power plant (Neill and Magnuson 1974). They preferred water temperatures of 29.1°C (84.4°F) in the laboratory and 29.7°C (85.5°F) in the field. Sonic tracking studies (Clugston 1973) have suggested that largemouth bass regularly migrate in and out of thermal plumes. During the winter (Gibbons and Bennett 1971), largemouth bass sought out heated areas in a reservoir receiving heated effluent from a reactor.

Water temperature plays an important role in determining the swimming performance of largemouth bass. Hocutt (1973) found that at 5°C (41°F) the largemouth bass swam sluggishly, but at temperatures of 15–35°C (59–95°F), it swam at speeds above 13.7 m/min.

Water temperature is an important limiting factor in the adaptation of largemouth bass to new waters within and beyond the native range (Robbins and MacCrimmon 1974). High lethal temperatures limit the success of largemouths in tropical lowlands, and the need for warm waters for successful spawning limits the northward dispersal of the species in North America and Europe.

In Minnesota field studies performed by suspending largemouth bass in live boxes at varying depths, Moore (1942) observed largemouth bass mortality within 24 hr at a water temperature of 15°C (59°F) and at an oxygen level of 3.1 ppm. At winter water temperatures, all bass died within 48 hr at an oxygen level of 2.3 ppm. In winterkill lakes of southeastern Michigan, largemouth bass and bluegills had a toleration threshold for dissolved oxygen of about 0.6 ppm (Cooper and Washburn 1949).

Carlander (1977) cited references which classifed largemouth bass as suitable for slightly alkaline waters, and for brackish waters of up to 24.4 ppt salinity.

Given a modestly abundant food supply, largemouth bass seem to be capable of feeding and maintaining themselves even in permanently turbid water (Miller 1975). Miller postulated that turbidity inhibits mating and adversely affects the survival of eggs and the young rather than the survival of juvenile or adult bass.

Numerous authors have noted the strong schooling tendency of largemouth bass fry, and the schoollike behavior of small groups of immature and mature bass that range the edges of shallow waters in lakes and ponds. Similar behavior has seldom or never been observed among other bass species, and the cause and function of such movements by the largemouth can only be speculated upon at present (Miller 1975).

During the day, largemouth bass cruise above aquatic plants at depths of 1–3 m, or lie under lily pads or in the shade of overhanging trees, piers, or brush. In the evening, largemouths tend to move into shallow water, apparently to feed. After dark they return to deeper water, where they rest on the bottom under logs or trees (Moyle 1969). They rest with the throat region touching the substrate, with the pelvic and median fins erect, and with the tail slightly elevated (Miller 1975). They are seldom found at depths greater than the deepest water in which rooted vegetation grows.

Largemouth bass generally move into deeper waters in winter (Lewis and Flickinger 1967), but usually remain more active than smallmouth bass during the winter months. In the spring, largemouths migrate into bays that have warmed up sooner than the main body of water.

Largemouth bass that were displaced during the spawning season tended to return to the site where they had originally been captured (Parker and Hasler 1959). They returned in an indirect way—by following the shoreline rather than swimming directly to the site from the center of the lake, where they had been released. Hasler and Wisby (1958) noted that displaced largemouth bass did not return to their capture area with the same precision as did green sunfish. A strong tendency by largemouths to remain in a home area within 91 m of their point of capture was reported by Lewis and Flickinger (1967). However, one largemouth bass which had been fitted with a transmitter, traveled a minimum distance of 3.1 km (2 mi) in 33 min after its release, or 3.6 times its total length per second, at a water temperature of 25°C (77°F) (Larimore and Dufford 1976). MacKay (1963) cited a study of largemouths in which the distance from the point of tagging to the point of recapture averaged 4.3 km (2.7 mi).

In areas of the world where the largemouth bass has become naturalized, there is little evidence that introductions into larger bodies of open water have resulted in appreciable declines in the population levels of native species. In smaller lakes, ponds, and reservoirs, however, introduced largemouths may result in a population explosion of the bass, the decimation of all forage species, and the stunted growth of the bass (Robbins and MacCrimmon 1974).

In Wisconsin, almost all species of fish are associated with the largemouth bass, except for the coldwater fishes. The largemouth lives principally with bluegills, pumpkinseeds, golden shiners, and bullheads. Competing predator species have been thought to cause a decline in largemouth bass populations; the introduction of walleyes into landlocked lakes in northeastern Wisconsin inhabited only by bass and panfish, for example, had this effect (Mraz et al. 1961).

For details on the niche separation between the largemouth bass and the closely related smallmouth bass, consult the smallmouth bass species account.

IMPORTANCE AND MANAGEMENT

Young largemouth bass are eaten by other centrarchids, by esocids, and by the larger percid fishes. Since adult bass are rapid swimmers, it is unlikely that they often become the prey of birds and other fish. Adams and Hankinson (1926) reported on one largemouth bass from Oneida Lake, New York, which had a lamprey scar from a wound that may have been responsible for its death. Perhaps a more important enemy of the largemouth bass is the bass tapeworm, which attacks the reproductive organs and renders the bass sterile.

The largemouth bass is host to the glochidial stage of a large number of important clams, including *Amblema plicata, Fusconaia ebena, Megalonaias gigantea, Quadrula nodulata, Andonta grandis, Lasmigona complanata, Strophitus undulatus, Actinonaias carinata, Lampsilis ovata, Lampsilis siliquoidea, Lampsilis teres, Ligumia recta,* and *Ligumia subrostrata* (Hart and Fuller 1974).

The largemouth bass is eagerly sought by anglers in Wisconsin. In a survey of vacationers, 28% preferred bass over other species and the bass had a higher popularity rating as a sport fish than all other species.

The largemouth bass bites on almost any type of bait as long as it moves. Live baits such as worms, minnows, frogs, insect larvae, and crayfish have all been successful. Surface plugs or underwater plugs work well, and fly fishermen usually use a large popper. Laboratory experiments have shown that the largemouth bass is able to distinguish colors quite readily. It prefers red, which it is able to distinguish easily from all other colors except violet (Mraz et al. 1961). Colors have been worked into a wide assortment of bass plugs and artificial flies. Evening and early morning hours are usually the best fishing times. Snow (1971) analyzed baits and methods of capture for largemouth bass in Murphy Flowage (Rusk County).

In the Mississippi River, the largemouth bass ranked 12th in the sport fishery in 1957, and 10th in 1962–1963 (Nord 1967). For 1967–1968, the estimated sport fishery catch in Pools 4, 5, 7, and 11 was 30,545 fish weighing 19,960 kg (44,010 lb) (Wright 1970).

In Murphy Flowage (Rusk County) from 1955 through 1969, anglers caught 7,176 largemouth bass weighing 3,370 kg (7,426 lb); the annual harvest averaged 6.8 fish and 3.1 kg/ha (Snow 1978). In Escanaba Lake (Vilas County) from 1946 through 1969, anglers caught 2,271 largemouth bass weighing 1,184 kg (2,611 lb). This species never provided more than 2% of the total annual catch from Escanaba Lake, and never more than 8% of the total annual weight harvested (Kempinger et al. 1975). At Browns Lake (Racine County) in 1953, anglers caught 2,671 largemouths, or about 4.5 kg/ha (4 lb/acre). Early in the history of the impounded Yellowstone Lake (Lafayette County), a partial and incomplete creel census placed the yearly harvest of largemouths at 65–183 fish and 10.1–31.4 kg/ha (9–28 lb/acre) (Mraz et al. 1961).

Largemouth bass young are useful as bioassay animals. They adjust readily to captivity and are not sensitive to handling (Ward and Irwin 1961).

According to Bennett (1951), legal length limits have no value in largemouth bass conservation, and there appears to be no advantage in closed seasons and in bag limits. There has been no correlation established between the number of largemouth bass of spawning size in a population and the number of young bass produced. In Browns Lake (Racine County), Mraz (1964c) found that, with liberal angling regulations (including no size limit and an earlier opening of the season), there were slightly better growth rates among largemouths toward the end of a 6-year study. He concluded that, during the study period, liberalization of bass-fishing regulations afforded an increased opportunity for anglers to pursue their sport without harm to the largemouth population.

Largemouth bass meat is moderately firm and has a mild flavor. It is also nutritious; analyses show that an edible portion contains 76.7% water, 20.6% protein, 1.8% fat, and 1.2% ash. The low fat content allows largemouths to be kept frozen for a long time. In the early part of the fishing season, largemouths from weedy waters with mud bottoms have been known to retain a muddy flavor acquired from the lake bottom during their partial hibernation (Eddy and Underhill 1974).

The management of largemouth bass has challenged fishery researchers for many years. Population estimates on three separate occasions at Browns Lake, a 158-ha bass-bluegill lake in Racine County, placed the largemouth population at between 88 and 138 individuals more than 152 mm long, and the standing crop weight at 30.3–37 kg/ha (27–33 lb/acre) (Mraz et al. 1961); about 34 kg/ha (30 lb/acre) were regarded as normal for this glacial lake.

Like a bluegill population, a largemouth bass population may become overcrowded and stunted. Punch Lake (Vilas County) contained only one species of fish—a slow-growing population of large mouth bass which reached 254 mm (10 in) in the fourth or fifth year (Churchill 1949a). After a removal program was instituted, the size of the fish at the end of the third summer's growth had increased from 178 mm (7 in) in 1939 to 203 mm (8 in) in 1942. The introduction of hybrid muskellunge × northern pike to further control the population resulted in a greater increase in largemouth growth; the average size of the bass in 1948—at the end of the third summer following the introduction—was 241 mm (9.5 in). Following a thinning operation in Flora Lake (Vilas County), in which bluegills, pumpkinseeds, rock bass, yellow perch, white suckers, and golden shiners were removed in large numbers yearly, no change in the linear growth of largemouth bass was observed, but there was an increase in weight (Parker 1956).

Though variable from year to year, the natural reproduction of largemouth bass is generally adequate to sustain satisfactory fishable populations. Formerly bass hatcheries were an important fish management activity in Wisconsin, but in recent years they have been reduced or eliminated. Stocking is confined to winterkill lakes, or to new or rehabilitated waters. The introduction of a few pairs of adult largemouths is sufficient to achieve repopulation; natural nurseries, such as small ponds with large numbers of stunted bass, can be tapped for such seed stock.

An analysis of the production of young largemouths in ponds in southern Wisconsin suggests that high populations of carp may depress the production of largemouth bass (Mraz and Cooper 1957b). This is not true in all cases, however, for two ponds containing carp and largemouth bass yielded 2,540 and 14,125 young bass per hectare. Compared with the stocking rates of fingerling largemouth bass commonly employed in fish management work, this rate of production would appear to be entirely adequate to maintain bass populations, if other conditions were suitable.

Where excessive carp populations have caused turbidity and destroyed vegetation, the usual management approach has been either to eliminate the carp by fish toxicants or to reduce them by seining. A substantial carp reduction results in clearer water, which is necessary for sight feeders like the largemouth bass, and in restored weed beds, with the food resources they harbor (Mraz et al. 1961).

Where the primary interest of a pond owner is sport fishing and large fish are preferred, a combined population of largemouth bass and golden shiners is superior to a bass-bluegill combination, in that bass reach a catchable size in a shorter time. In Wisconsin, largemouth bass can be raised alone, or with golden shiners or fathead minnows as a food source (Klingbiel et al. 1969). In most cases, the minnows disappear in about 4 years, but the bass may do almost as well without them. Golden shiners are generally favored over fathead minnows because the adult shiners become larger and, therefore, are less apt to be eaten. Although largemouth bass and bluegills are a recommended combination in many states, this combination is not recommended in Wisconsin (Klingbiel et al. 1969:14–15):

> . . . Generally bluegills become overpopulated and stunted. These fish are of no value because they are too large for largemouth bass to eat, and too small for angling. Bluegills will also compete for food with the smaller bass and will eventually stop bass reproduction by eating the young. Bass-bluegill management has been successful in very few ponds in Wisconsin.

The recommended stocking rate for largemouth bass is 250 25–51-mm fingerlings per hectare; such fingerlings are available in July. Golden shiners or fathead minnows may be stocked with the bass at the rate of 1,000 adults per hectare. Fishing should begin when the bass are 3 years old; harvesting is extremely important because overpopulation occurs easily, particularly in the northern part of Wisconsin, where growing seasons are short and waters are relatively infertile. The angler should keep no fish larger than about 300 mm (12 in), since large bass help to control the numbers of small fish. For example, a 450-mm (18-in) bass can eat a 200-mm (8-in) bass.

Largemouth females and smallmouth males have been artificially crossed to produce the "meanmouth" hybrid, which as a yearling is 203–305 mm (8–12 in) long and weighs up to 454 g (1 lb). This hybrid is fertile, can reproduce at age I, and has the ability to backcross with the parent species. It is very aggressive. There is concern that, if released into the natural environment, the genetic swamping of either the smallmouths or largemouths might result. Consequently, the hybrids have not been considered for use in fisheries management (*Sports Afield*, June 1977: 147–148).

Warmouth

Lepomis gulosus (Cuvier). *Lepomis*—scaled operculum; *gulosus*—gluttonous.

Other common names: warmouth bass, goggle-eye, black sunfish, wide-mouthed sunfish, stump-knocker, mud bass, wood bass, weed bass.

Adult 142 mm, Rinehart L. (Portage Co.), 13 June 1977

DESCRIPTION

Body deep, compressed laterally. Length 89–127 mm (3.5–5.0 in). TL = 1.24 SL. Depth into TL 2.6–3.0. Head length into TL 2.8–3.1. Mouth large, oblique. Upper jaw reaching to middle of eye or beyond, with supramaxillary well developed; lower jaw decidedly longer than upper jaw; conical, pointed teeth in brushlike pads on upper and lower jaws; well-developed teeth on pad in midtongue; lower pharyngeal arches narrow with bluntly conical teeth. Gill rakers on first gill arch long, thin and straight. Opercular flap inflexible. Dorsal fins 2, but broadly joined and appear as 1; base of dorsal fins about 2.3 times length of anal fin base; first dorsal fin with 10 spines, second with 9–10 soft rays. Anal fin with 3 spines, and 8–10 soft rays; pelvic fin thoracic (almost directly beneath the pectoral fin), with 1 spine and 5 rays; pectoral fin rounded, moderately long, and when laid forward across cheek reaching posterior edge of eye; caudal fin scarcely forked. Scales ctenoid, gill covers and cheeks scaled. Scales in lateral line 36–40; lateral line complete. Chromosomes 2n = 48 (W. LeGrande, pers. comm.).

Body brown, with obscure vertical bars or with lines of dark dots along scale rows; ventral region of head and belly light brown. Sides of head with 3–5 distinct dark lines, radiating outward from eye. Iris red or reddish brown. Vertical fins darkly pigmented and mottled with spots in irregular parallel lines; dorsal fin lacking a distinct basal blotch; paired fins lightly pigmented.

Breeding male bright yellow and eye bright red.

Hybrids: Warmouth × pumpkinseed, warmouth × green sunfish, warmouth × bluegill, warmouth × redbreast sunfish, warmouth × redear sunfish (Childers 1967). Artificial warmouth × largemouth bass (Merriner 1971b).

SYSTEMATIC NOTES

Until recently the warmouth was the sole species within the genus *Chaenobryttus*. Bailey et al. (1970) noted that it is closely related to the typical sunfishes of the genus *Lepomis*, and that it does not differ structurally from the closest of these (*cyanellus*) any more than *cyanellus* does from the more divergent forms. *Gulosus* is now regarded as a species of *Lepomis*, and *Chaenobryttus* is downgraded to subgeneric rank.

DISTRIBUTION, STATUS, AND HABITAT

In Wisconsin the warmouth occurs in the Mississippi River and Lake Michigan drainage basins. In the Mississippi basin this southern species reaches the northern limit of its distribution. It is not known from the Lake Superior basin.

Greene (1935) had no records of the warmouth from the Lake Michigan basin. Recent records place it in the headwaters of the Wolf and Fox river systems, which suggests a migration into that system via the Fox-Wisconsin canal at Portage. It is also likely that the warmouth was introduced through fish rescue transfers from the Mississippi River into eastern Wisconsin. Extensions of the warmouth's range in northwestern Wisconsin are based on the following reports: Moose Ear Creek (Barron County) (Wis. Fish Distrib. Study 1974–1975); Chain Lake (Chippewa County) (Sather and Threinen 1963); Long Lake and Upper Ox Lake (Douglas County) (Sather and Johannes 1973); and Town Line Lake (Chippewa County) (H. Snow, pers. comm.).

Few specimens of this species have been taken in Wisconsin. Since 1962, collections placed in UWSP are (number of individuals in parentheses): #1505 (1) Gran Grae Creek (Crawford County); #908 (1) and #4183 (1) Mills Creek (Richland County); #3576 (2) Severson Lake (Portage County); #4160 (3) Petenwell Flowage (Adams County); #4164 (1) Fox River (Columbia County); #4614 (3) Pleasant Lake (Walworth County); #5580 (3) Rinehart Lake (Portage County); and #5722 (1) Lake Alice (Lincoln County).

The warmouth has been reported from 9 of 40 Waukesha County lakes sampled (Poff and Threinen 1963), and it has also been reported as present among

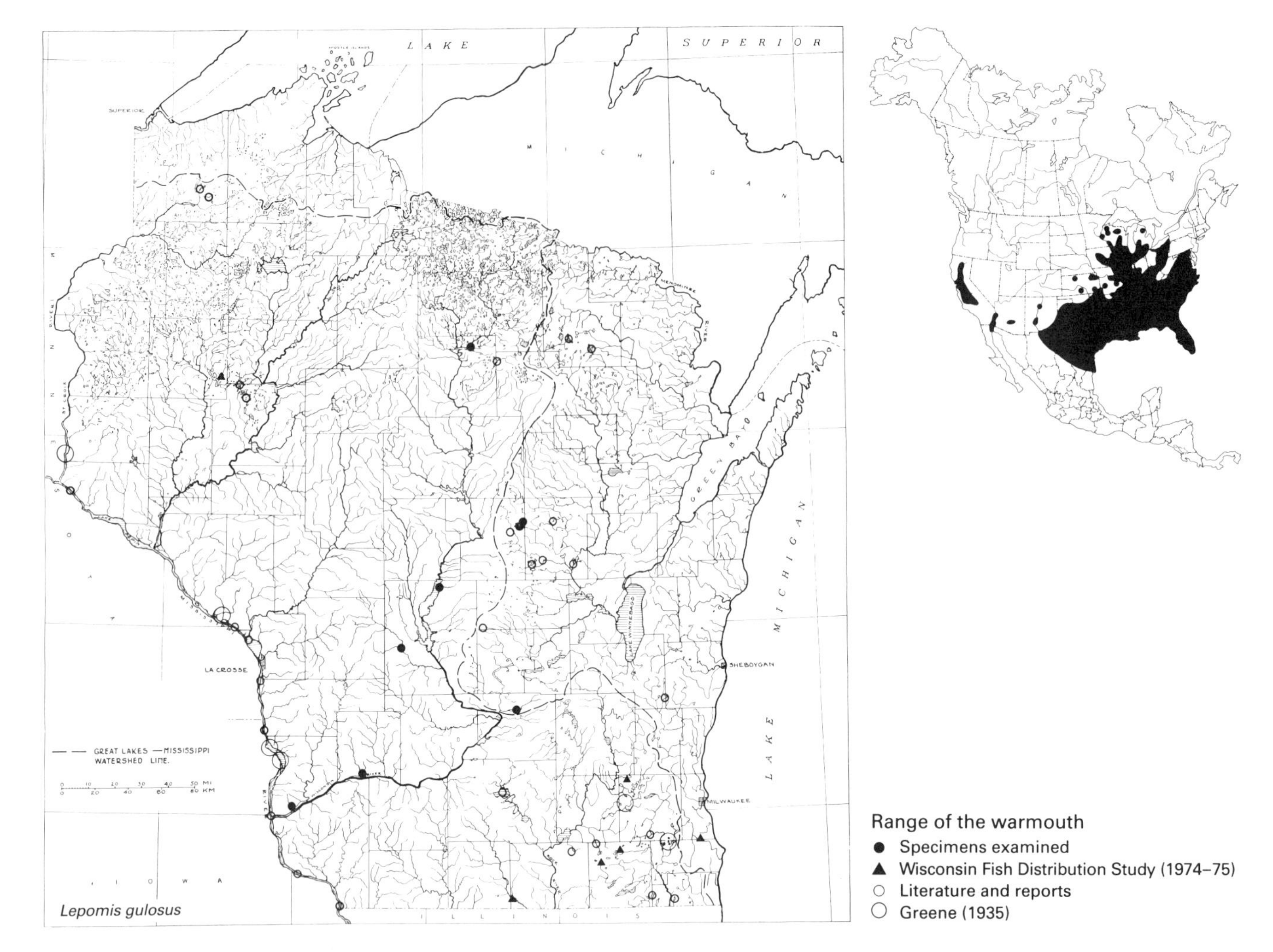

the fish in smaller lakes (Laura and Skidmore ponds, Genesee) in the same county (Cahn 1927). Mackenthun (1946) reported it from Turtle Lake (Walworth County), Silver and Powers lakes (Kenosha County), Storrs Lake (Rock County), and Forest Lake (Fond du Lac County).

Throughout Wisconsin the warmouth is rare to uncommon. Except for the southeastern corner of the state, populations appear to be widely scattered. Apparently its range in Wisconsin is expanding as a result of the establishment of reservoirs, the increasing siltation of our waters, and inadvertent transport and stocking. The warmouth is probably more commonly distributed in southern and central Wisconsin than the record indicates, since it can easily be overlooked. Even when the warmouth is known to exist in small numbers in a given body of water, its secretive habits in dense vegetation obscure its presence.

In Wisconsin, the warmouth occurs in lakes, ponds, low-gradient streams, and drainage ditches. It is associated with muddy or turbid waters, dense growths of aquatic weeds, and bottoms of soft mud, sand, or gravel. According to Seeburger (1975), in Walworth County the warmouth prefers lakes, ponds, and smaller rivers with mud bottoms. In the Mississippi River it is associated with quiet backwater lakes.

BIOLOGY

The life history of the warmouth has been extensively studied in central Illinois by Larimore (1957). Unless otherwise designated, the following account is derived from his work.

In Illinois, the nesting season of the warmouth begins during the second week of May, reaches its peak early in June, and starts to decline after the first of July; however, it often extends well into August. The length of the nesting season differs among populations in different lakes, and probably varies considerably from year to year. Evidence indicates that a warmouth may spawn several times during a summer. It spawns at water temperatures approaching 21.5°C (70.7°F).

The warmouth's nesting sites are on bottoms of loose silt, sand with loose silt, silt containing sticks and leaves, rubble, or rubble covered with a thin layer of silt. Warmouths show some preference for rubble lightly covered with silt and detritus, and are careful to select a spot near a stump, root, rock, clump of vegetation, or some similar object. Nests are not found in an area that is completely exposed, or in an area of clear sand, such as the bluegill selects. Nests are usually built at depths of 0.6–0.8 m (0.2–1.5 m).

The warmouth is not a colonial nester; the nests are usually widely separated unless the nesting areas are restricted, in which case nests are sometimes found close to one another. Richardson (1913) reported that a dozen nests of this species had been found at Havana, Illinois, in a circle 6 m diam, in water 15–25 cm deep. The nests were 10–15 cm across and of irregular shape; they evidently had been quickly and carelessly made, compared to bluegill and bass nests.

As in other sunfish species, the male warmouth excavates the nest. Violent sweeping motions of his tail clear loose debris away from the selected spot and produce a shallow irregular concavity. As he enters the nest site, he turns abruptly upward, giving three or four violent sweeps with his tail while balancing in an almost vertical position and checking his forward motion with his pectoral fins.

The nesting site is guarded from intruders by the male warmouth. According to Larimore (1957:66):

> . . . He assumes a belligerent attitude by swimming toward the intruder with his mouth open and his opercles spread; at the same time, his eyes become red and his body becomes light yellow in color. As the nesting male nears the intruder, he usually turns abruptly to one side or upward and, with vigorous movements of his tail fin, forces small pulses of water toward the intruder. He may also nip. . . .

When a female warmouth that is not yet ready to spawn is placed in a tank with a nesting male, she is charged, nipped, and driven to the surface. Unable to escape the male in an aquarium, she may eventually be killed by his continued aggression.

In getting a female to his nest, the male warmouth assumes an aggressive attitude. He approaches her with opercles widely spread and his mouth open; his body changes colors in courtship as it does when he fights off an intruder—an adjustment requiring only 5–10 sec. If the female is ready to spawn, she is easily directed toward the nest, and spawning soon follows. Spawning behavior has been described by Larimore (1957:44):

> On entering the nest site, both male and female begin to circle, the female being nearer the center of the nest, slightly on her side and somewhat beneath the male. . . . As they circle inside the nest, the female works her jaws three or four times and suddenly jerks her body violently, giving the male a sharp thump on the side. Each time the female jerks, she extrudes about 20 eggs. The thump she gives the male probably stimulates a discharge of sperm, although no milt was ever seen coming from the genital pore. After circling the nest several times, the female interrupts the activities and leaves the nest site. The male usually follows her a short distance but returns quickly to the nest to assume guardianship. At this point in the spawning activity, males often have been observed to fan the nest with sweeping motions of the tail in a manner similar to that exhibited when nest building.

Male warmouths ripen slightly earlier in the season than females, and they remain sexually active somewhat longer than females. Larimore determined that warmouths over 137 mm (5.4 in) long attained spawning condition sooner and spawned over a longer period of time than did 89- to 137-mm (3.5- to 5.4-in) fish. The male protects and fans the eggs.

Larimore noted that hybrids can be produced in the laboratory between the warmouth and a number of species of *Lepomis*, yet such hybrids seldom occur in large numbers in natural populations. In the laboratory, male warmouths have courted green sunfish and bluegill females, but have not succeeded in spawning with them and have seldom been able to guide them to the nest depressions. Such reproductive isolation may be explained by the characteristic sounds produced by males of some *Lepomis* species (see Gerald 1971), which enable females of different species to recognize males of their own species.

Fecundity is a function of the size of the female warmouth. From April to June in Park Pond, Illinois, females 89–180 mm (3.5–7.1 in) long held 4,500–37,500 eggs. In Venard Lake in May, females 94–137 mm (3.7–5.4 in) long held an estimated 17,200–63,200 eggs. The diameter of fertilized warmouth eggs is 0.95–1.03 mm. At water temperatures of 25–26.4°C (77–79.5°F), the eggs hatch in 34.5 hr.

Immediately upon hatching, the warmouth prolarvae drop down onto the sand and silt between the coarse gravel particles of the nest. After 36–48 hours they begin to make feeble jumps 2 cm or so above the bottom of the nest. The yolk-sac is exhausted by the fourth day. The young begin active swimming at the end of the fifth day, and swim about the nest in rather compact groups. In outdoor tanks, they begin to feed by at least the seventh day after hatching. The schools gradually dissolve as individuals begin independent searches for food. No juvenile warmouths have been observed in large groups.

Larimore (1957) described development to the 15.7-mm juvenile stage, and photographed stages from hatching (3.4 mm) to the 12.0-mm postlarva. The 15.7-mm young is essentially like an adult in body form.

In ponds and lakes, warmouth fry scatter into dense weed masses, making it impossible for the male parent to keep the young together for close care. After the fry leave the nest area, they receive no parental care. In several Illinois lakes, minnows and sunfishes were observed destroying warmouth eggs and larvae in unprotected warmouth nests. Postlarval and juvenile warmouths which had left the nest were eaten in great numbers by larger fish. Largemouth bass 44 mm (1.75 in) long fed voraciously on warmouths 19 mm (0.75 in) long, which in turn had been eating large numbers of postlarval warmouths. In the laboratory, a 19-mm warmouth ate 11 postlarvae (4 days old) in 5 min; another ate 12 in the same length of time. The survival of late warmouth broods is frequently higher than that of early broods because as the season advances the aquatic vegetation becomes more dense and there is less danger of drops in water temperature.

In Severson Lake (Portage County), young-of-year warmouths were 35 mm long on 4 August. In southern Wisconsin streams in the second half of September, young warmouths were 44 mm TL.

For combined Wisconsin collections of warmouths, the calculated length at each annulus was: 1—37 mm; 2—74 mm; 3—90 mm; 4—126 mm; and 5—147 mm. The best growth was demonstrated by warmouths from Pleasant Lake (Walworth County), which had values of 40, 79, 108, 143, and 160 mm at the annuli.

In Iowa, the calculated total lengths at the annuli (estimated weights in parentheses) were: 1—41 mm (1 g); 2—91 mm (15 g); 3—147 mm (68 g); 4—178 mm (129 g); 5—190 mm (175 g); 6—203 mm (214 g); and 7—221 mm (242 g) (Lewis and English 1949). In Illinois (Larimore 1957), these values were: 1—42 mm (2 g); 2—86 mm (12 g); 3—125 mm (40 g); 4—163 mm (91 g); 5—189 mm (153 g); 6—204 mm (196 g); 7—215 mm (232 g); and 8—217 mm (239 g). In Enright Pond, Illinois, fish of the first brood produced in the lake attained a length of 152 mm (6 in) during their first 13 months. The less turbid the water, the greater is the growth of warmouths.

In Illinois, annuli usually form about the first week in May. The condition value (K_{TL}) for warmouths 81–208 mm (3.2–8.2 in) TL ranged from 2.01 to 2.29. Larimore noted that there was a decline in condition for the larger warmouth in the early fall and again in winter. No consistent differences in condition were evident between males and females.

In Venard Lake, Illinois, both sexes matured at age I, when they had reached lengths between 79 and 86 mm (3.1–3.4 in); in Park Pond they did not mature until they had reached age II and a minimum length of 89 mm (3.5 in).

Larimore found that the majority of large warmouths were males. A 244-mm, 454-g (9.6-in, 1-lb) male (age VI) was collected from Park Pond, Illinois. Trautman (1957) reported a specimen 284 mm (11.2 in) long, with a weight of 454 g (1 lb), from Ohio. A warmouth in Georgia in 1974 weighed 907 g (2 lb 0 oz).

In Illinois, young warmouths feed on plankton, insects, and small crustaceans. Those over 127 mm (5 in) long, feed largely on small fishes. In Park Pond, Illinois, warmouths consumed crayfish (29.7% volume), fish (20.5%), damselflies (15.7%), dragonflies (5.2%), diptera larvae (4.6%), mayflies (2.9%), Entomostraca (0.7%), Hemiptera (0.3%), miscellaneous insects (12.2%), and miscellaneous items (8.2%). In Lake Venard in central Illinois, fish constituted only 5.9% of the volume of the warmouth's diet, but dragonflies made up 23.8%. In Park Pond, where many species of minnows were present, small sunfish were more commonly taken by warmouths. Warmouths may feed upon any items that are readily available, including snails.

When a food item is sighted, the warmouth turns toward it, judges its acceptability as food, and then may move in quickly to snap it up. A motionless object is seldom picked up by a warmouth. The large size of its mouth is better suited to a fish-eating diet than that of most sunfishes. During the summer months, the warmouth's feeding activity reaches a peak early in the morning and practically ceases in the afternoon.

The critical oxygen level for warmouths is 3.6 ppm at a water temperature of 20°C (68°F) (Larimore 1957). The warmouth's ability to survive at low oxygen concentrations allows it to range into habitats that would be unfavorable to other fish species. It is among the last species of fish to die when collections of live fish are concentrated in tanks, tubs, or buckets containing water. However, there was a heavy kill of warmouths in a Michigan lake during the winter when the oxygen level dropped to 0.0–0.2 ppm in the upper 0.3–1.2 m of water (Cooper and Washburn 1949). Gould and Irwin (1962) stated that the warmouth had withstood concentrations of 1.0 ppm oxygen without fatality; it also endured test concentrations of pH ranging from 8.5 to 7.4.

Although essentially a freshwater species, warmouths have been reported in waters with 4.1 ppt salinity in Louisiana (Carlander 1977).

The warmouth's association with turbid water, organic silt deposits, and dense vegetation indicates a greater tolerance of these conditions than most other sunfish have. This may be a factor in lessening its competition with other species.

In learning experiments (Witt 1949), isolated warmouth individuals learned about as quickly as bluegills and more quickly than largemouth bass, but in groups the warmouths made more errors than either largemouths or bluegills. Warmouths could learn to distinguish a worm on a hook from a free worm. After being penalized for making an error, the warmouth was not as cautious as the bluegill in approaching a hooked worm.

According to Larimore (1957), an order of dominance in a natural warmouth population has not been observed. However, in a restricted group, such as that in an aquarium, a hierarchy is quickly established. The aggressiveness of a fish in its pursuit of food or space, and the dominance of the fish relative to other members of the group, determine its position in the hierarchy. The smaller the group, the more stable and definite the order of dominance appears. In groups of more than three or four fish, the order may change frequently.

Warmouths of less than 127 mm (5 in) TL remain in protective cover in shallow water the year around; larger individuals spend more time in deep water than in shallow water. There is no school formation even during the winter, when many fishes form groups. The warmouth has a quiet disposition. It moves around relatively little, displays no show activity except during the spawning season, seeks the cover of weeds and other hiding places, and avoids intense light.

Warmouths were collected from Silver Lake (Kenosha County) along with the common carp, bluegill, black crappie, walleye, bullhead (sp.?), largemouth bass, pumpkinseed, rock bass, bowfin, and other species (Mackenthun 1946).

IMPORTANCE AND MANAGEMENT

The warmouth plays a role in the ecology of the mussels *Amblema plicata*, *Alasmidonta marginata*, *Carunculina parva*, and *Lampsilis teres*, since it is host to the glochidial stage of those species (Hart and Fuller 1974).

Known as an excellent small sport fish, the warmouth will take earthworms, minnows, grasshoppers, crickets, grubs, and artificial baits. In Walworth County, warmouths up to 15 cm have been taken with flyrod and popper late in the spring (Seeburger 1975). In five southern Wisconsin lakes, warmouths composed an average of 2.6% (0.7–7.5%) of the catch (Mackenthun 1946). Other fish species commonly taken from the same lakes were bluegills and green sunfish, and, to a lesser extent, rock bass, largemouth bass, and black crappies.

Exploitation rates are usually lower for the warmouth than for other sunfishes inhabiting the same waters primarily because of the difficulty of fishing in the dense cover that warmouths prefer. Most warmouths are taken incidentally while fishing for other sunfishes. In Wisconsin, the regulations for taking panfish, including warmouths, from inland waters are liberal; an aggregate of 50 panfish may be caught in 1 day. In the boundary waters there is no bag limit on panfish, except in Wisconsin-Minnesota waters where there is a limit of 25 per day.

The warmouth is a desirable laboratory fish. Its prolonged spawning season makes suitably sized specimens available for much of the year. It transports well, withstands crowding and low oxygen tensions, and is large enough to be easily handled and yet small enough to be accommodated in most aquariums. It is a good animal for bioassay, but it needs live food and is difficult to collect because it remains in weedy areas (Gould and Irwin 1962).

Unlike other *Lepomis* species, warmouths have no tendency to become dominant at the expense of other species. This has been indicated by the relatively low proportions of warmouths reported in fish populations of Illinois and other states. Larimore (1957) found that, in 17 ponds in central Illinois stocked with 11 different fish combinations (including largemouth bass, smallmouth bass, and several panfish), warmouths tended to establish small broods each year without seriously restricting the reproduction or growth of companion species. However, Larimore also pointed out that small numbers of warmouths which had been introduced into a pond overcrowded with other sunfish seemed unable to establish a population. In ponds in which other populations of fishes had been thinned, an increase in the growth rate of warmouths was noticed.

Green Sunfish

Lepomis cyanellus Rafinesque. *Lepomis*—scaled operculum; *cyanellus*—blue.

Other common names: green perch, black perch, logfish, blue-spotted sunfish, sunfish, little redeye, blue bass, creek sunfish, rubbertail, sand bass.

Adult 130 mm, Pine R. (Richland Co.), 7 Aug. 1962

DESCRIPTION

Body robust, strongly compressed laterally. Length 102–127 mm (4–5 in). TL = 1.25 SL. Depth into TL 2.4–2.9. Head length into TL 2.8–3.1. Mouth large, terminal, slightly oblique; lips large. Upper jaw extending to about middle of eye; small, blunt teeth in brushlike pads on upper and lower jaws; rarely, a few teeth on tongue; lower pharyngeal arches narrow and strong with conical, blunt teeth. Gill rakers on first gill arch long, straight and thin. Opercular flap inflexible. Dorsal fins 2, but broadly joined and appear as 1; base of dorsal fins about 2.5 times length of anal fin base; first dorsal fin with 9–11 spines, second with 10–12 soft rays. Anal fin with 3 spines and 9–10 soft rays; pelvic fin thoracic, with 1 spine and 5 rays; pectoral fin rounded, moderately long, and when laid forward across the cheek barely reaching eye; caudal fin scarcely forked. Scales ctenoid, gill covers and cheeks scaled. Scales in lateral line 44–51; lateral line complete. Chromosomes 2n = 46 (Roberts 1967).

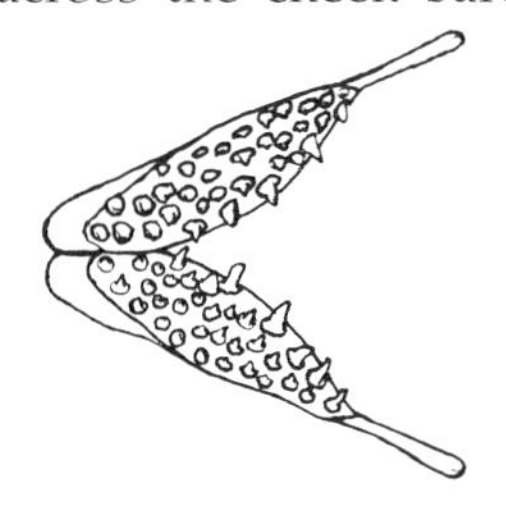

Dorsal view of the lower pharyngeal arches of the green sunfish, showing their narrow width and bluntly conical teeth (from *The Fishes of Ohio*, by Milton B. Trautman [Columbus, Ohio: Ohio State University Press, 1957, 499])

Dorsal region brown to olive, with many emerald reflections; sides lighter, with 7–12 faint dark, vertical bars; belly yellow to white. Head with emerald spots, and at times with backward radiating emerald lines; opercular flap with black center and with a broad, light-colored margin. Fins generally pigmented; bases of rear dorsal and anal fins usually with a vague, dark blotch. Young similar to adults, but lacking bands on sides and spots on cheeks and fins.

Breeding male with prominent, yellowish white line along margin of the dorsal, caudal, and anal fins, and with dark, vertical bars along sides (Hunter 1963).

Hybrids: Green sunfish × bluegill, green sunfish × pumpkinseed (Wis. Fish Distrib. Study 1974–1979); green sunfish × longear sunfish, green sunfish × orangespotted sunfish, green sunfish × redbreast sunfish, green sunfish × redear sunfish (Childers 1967).

DISTRIBUTION, STATUS, AND HABITAT

In Wisconsin, the green sunfish occurs in the Mississippi River and Lake Michigan drainage basins. It is well distributed in streams and lakes in the southern one-third of the state, and it is widely dispersed northward. It has not been reported from the Lake Superior basin with the exception of two records from Houghton County, Michigan, where it was probably introduced (Taylor 1954).

The green sunfish was present in over 30% of the Waukesha County lakes sampled (Poff and Threinen 1963); it was rare in Pewaukee Lake (Becker 1964a). It is rare to uncommon in the Wisconsin and Mississippi rivers, and it is generally common in moderate-sized streams and lakes of southern Wisconsin.

The green sunfish usually inhabits quiet pools in warm, shallow waters of ponds, lakes, small brooks, and rivers of low gradient. In Wisconsin, it was encountered in clear to turbid water at depths generally less than 1.5 m over substrates of gravel (23% frequency), sand (17%), silt (17%), rubble (12%), mud (12%), clay (8%), boulders (8%), detritus (1%), and marl (1%). It occurred in low-gradient streams of the following widths: 1.0–3.0 m (18%), 3.1–6.0 m (22%), 6.1–12.0 m (22%), 12.1–24.0 m (28%), 24.1–50.0 m (8%), and more than 50 m (2%).

BIOLOGY

In southern Wisconsin, spawning commences in late May or early June, continues through June and July,

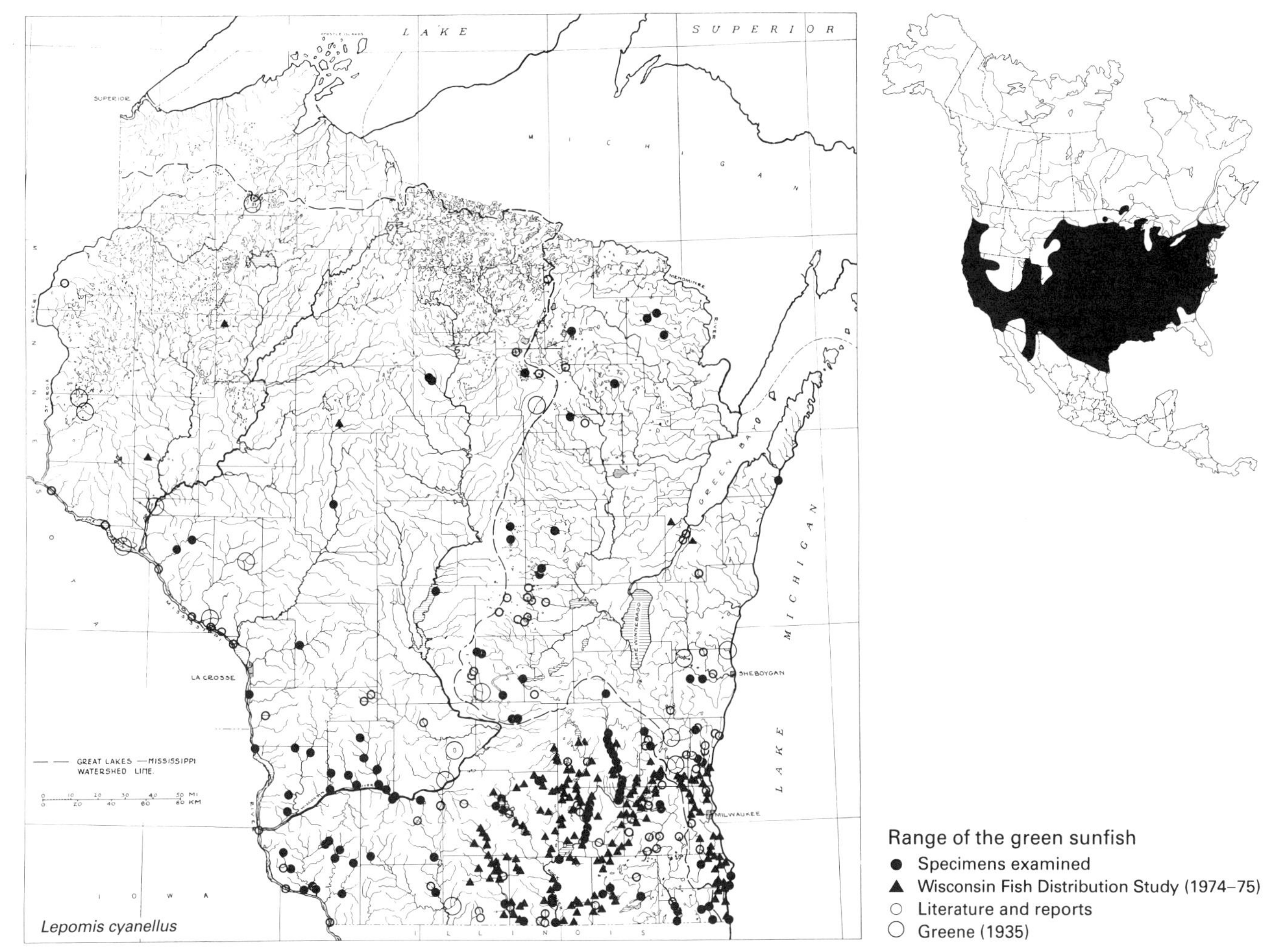

Lepomis cyanellus

and terminates in early August (Hunter 1963). The green sunfish builds and spawns at water temperatures of 15–28°C (59–82.4°F). Breeding activities take place every 8–9 days during the season, and the peak of nest establishment nearly always coincides with a rise in the mean water temperature.

Hunter (1963) discussed in detail the reproductive behavior of the green sunfish in Madison (Wisconsin) ponds. The following account is from this source, unless otherwise indicated.

Green sunfish nests are seldom located in water deeper than 35 cm, and small males may construct nests in water as shallow as 4 cm. The nests are built in the shelter of rocks, logs, and clumps of grass, if these are available; occasionally the abandoned nests of other sunfishes are used.

The nest is constructed by the male, who rises vertically above the nest site and delivers a burst of vigorous outward thrusts with his tail; each thrust displaces some sand and gravel, and gradually a shallow depression is formed. Carlander (1977) indicated that males may remove larger pebbles with their mouths. Each nest is between 15 and 38 cm diam (Carlander 1977), and as many as 25 nests have been observed within a 15 square meter area (Sigler and Miller 1963). Large males occasionally dig several trial nests prior to spawning, generally within a meter of their previous nests. Small landmarks in the vicinity of a nest appear to play a major role in nest recognition.

Hunter observed that aggregations of female and male green sunfish of all sizes gathered around the periphery of the nests of the first males that spawned; he counted 114 fish assembled near the nest of one spawning male. As other nests were constructed and colonization began, the number of fish around individual nests decreased.

Fighting occurs only when the male green sunfish are engaged in constructing nests and spawning. Nesting territories are defended against intruders. The resident male responds aggressively by spreading the opercles wide and by vigorously driving the trespassing fish from the nest. Two male combatants may press their open mouths to their opponent's opercle and rotate in this position. Sigler and Miller

Fighting posture of two male green sunfish (Hunter 1963:15)

(1963) noted that attacking male green sunfish meet their opponents head on, and sometimes even grasp them by the jaw during the engagement.

Witt and Marzolf (1954) reported that male longear sunfish defended larger territories when their nests were isolated than when the nests were a part of a colony. Hunter drew similar conclusions about the green sunfish and observed that where nests of this species were 30 m apart the males defended an area of 1–1.5 m diam, but that where nests were close together the males defended only the area encompassed by the nest.

Gerald (1971) noted that male green sunfish make a grunting sound while courting a female. A nesting male, upon sighting a female, repeatedly rushed toward her and then backed toward his nest, while producing a series of gruntlike sounds. Gerald had the impression that the female produced a single grunt as she first approached the male. The mechanism of sound production is unknown.

The spawning behavior of the green sunfish has been described by Hunter (1963:15):

> . . . Spawning was accomplished in the manner typical of all centrarchids: the male and female circled in the nest side by side, paused momentarily and released sperm and eggs. The consummatory act took place when the female reclined on her side and vibrated while the male remained in an upright position. An isolated pair might circle and spawn in a nest for considerable periods of time but in crowded colonies the male frequently interrupted spawning to chase intruding fish. After spawning, the male expelled the female from the nest with a nip. Both sexes usually spawned with more than one individual. Occasionally a male spawned simultaneously with more than one female. While a pair of sunfish were circling in the nest another female entered the nest, aligned itself with the male, and when the first female rotated on her side the intruding female also slid beneath the male and vibrated.

The presence of a male in a nest appeared to be sufficient stimulus to cause a female to enter the nest. Hunter (1963:15–16) saw females during the latter part of the nesting period move from nest to nest in old sunfish colonies, often being expelled from every nest:

> . . . Females sometimes darted beneath a male, immediately rotated on their sides and vibrated. Sometimes mating was accomplished in this fashion but often the male remained sexually passive, in which case the female was eventually driven from the nest.

During spawning periods, male green sunfish are more active than at any other time during their reproductive cycle. Within a 10-min period, Hunter observed one male execute five spawning acts, make ten trips in and out of the nest, threaten his neighbor once, and gyrate in the nest 39 times.

Gonadal growth is stimulated in both sexes of green sunfish by the simultaneous influence of high water temperature [greater than 15°C (59°F)] and long photoperiods (15 hr or more) (Kaya and Hasler 1972). However, long photoperiods and elevated temperatures [24°C (75.2°F)] will not prevent gonadal regression from occurring during the postspawning period (Kaya and Hasler 1972).

The eggs of the green sunfish are numerous, demersal, and adhesive. Varying egg sizes have been reported: 0.8–1.0 mm diam (Kaya and Hasler 1972), 1.2–1.3 mm (Taubert 1977), and 1.0–1.4 mm (Meyer 1970). In nests over mud and marl, the eggs become attached to the roots of sedges and bulrushes (Hankinson 1908). Eggs held at water temperatures of 24–27°C (75.2–80.6°F) hatch into prolarvae 3.5–3.7 mm long in 35–55 hr (Taubert 1977). Swim-up, following absorption of the yolk-sac, occurs in the 6-mm stage by 145 hours. Taubert illustrated the 3.6-, 5.8-, 8.3-, and 9.3-mm stages, and described the stages up through the 22-day-old metalarva. Meyer (1970) figured the 5.4-mm (9-day), 10.2-mm (30-day), 15.1-mm (37-day), and 23.7-mm (57-day) stages.

Green sunfish were induced to spawn in aquariums at 25°C (77°F) with a daily, 16-hr period of light (W. E. Smith 1975). Within several days a male had established territorial rights, and spawning occurred within 14 days. The eggs hatched 2 days later at 25°C. Larval swim-up and the beginning of feeding took place 5 days after hatching, and the fry fed successfully on newly hatched brine shrimp nauplii. At 30 days after hatching, the mean total length of the fry was 3 cm, and at this time frozen adult brine shrimp were introduced as food. At the age of 16 weeks, green sunfish males were about 10 cm long, and females about 6 cm long. Spawning occurred at 16 weeks and continued at intervals of 6–10 days to the end of the study period, 2 months later. All of these individuals had been brought to maturity together, and there was little aggression exhibited. With the use of the proper cultural techniques, the green sunfish will spawn at less than 6 months of age.

In Wisconsin waters, young-of-year green sunfish were about 29 mm long in mid-July, and 27–37 mm at the end of September. In Madison (Dane County) ponds, young-of-year were 4–9 mm in June, 11–28 mm in July, 19–35 mm in August, and 21–40+ mm in September (Siewert 1973).

The green sunfish is aged by reading scales. Hubbs and Cooper (1935) called attention to a spawning mark on scales, which indicates an abrupt, though temporary, slackening or cessation of growth during the breeding season.

Green sunfish taken from the Pine River (Richland County) on 7 August 1962 had the following calculated growth at the annuli: 1—24 mm; 2—54 mm; 3—91 mm; and 4—117 mm (J. Morzinski, pers. comm.). In Michigan (Hubbs and Cooper 1935), green sunfish exhibited the following growth: 0—8–44 mm; I—24–90 mm; II—54–142 mm; III—68–142 mm; IV—84–168 mm; V—114–188 mm; VI—130–188 mm; and VII—168–196 mm. In Minnesota (Kuehn 1949a), the calculated total length at each annulus was: 1—43 mm; 2—74 mm; 3—99 mm; 4—127 mm; 5—150 mm; 6—168 mm; and 7—183 mm. In the upper Saint Francis River, Missouri (Purkett 1958b), the green sunfish reached a calculated length of 196 mm at the 10th annulus. Males grow faster than females, and tend to live longer.

In Madison ponds, some age-I male green sunfish started to spawn in late July or early August (Hunter 1963). In Michigan (Hubbs and Cooper 1935), few age-I fish were mature, but all age-III fish were mature. The overall size at maturity for both sexes of green sunfish averaged slightly more than 76 mm in southern Michigan, and slightly under that figure in the northern part of the state.

Siewert (1973) demonstrated that a 5°C (9°F) increase in the water temperature above the ambient temperature, with the heat released from the bottom of a body of water, can improve conditions for green sunfish growth in northern latitudes, and that the growth of young green sunfish was better in a heated pond than in the unheated reference pond. Gerking (1952) noted that a 10-g green sunfish used about 33% of the absorbed protein for growth, compared to 20% for a 55-g fish. Carlander (1977) reported that growth among green sunfish was more rapid after poisoning and restocking, and after an almost complete winterkill.

Although the green sunfish is normally small, occasionally a large individual is caught. A 709-g (1-lb 9-oz) green sunfish was taken from Wind Lake (Racine County) on 23 August 1967. A 964-g (2-lb 2-oz) fish came from Stockton Lake, Missouri, on 18 June 1971. Carlander (1977) cited a report of a green sunfish from a Utah reservoir which was 279 mm (11 in) long.

Siewert (1973) observed that young green sunfish consumed zooplankton, and that adults consumed zooplankton, insects, snails, and young-of-year green sunfish. Stomachs examined also contained *Chara* and *Spirogyra*, but Siewert concluded that not much nutritional value was gained from such plant material. In Michigan (Sadzikowski and Wallace 1976), plant materials and odonates were important food sources for the green sunfish and the bluegill, and both of these species consumed more plant materials than the pumpkinseed. The green sunfish has a larger mouth than the bluegill, and its diet contained food items of a larger average size than those in the bluegill's diet, despite the similarities of the food items. Thus, even though these two species eat similar foods, they may actually be exploiting quite different food sources.

Other foods taken by green sunfish include crayfish, terrestrial insects, and fish. In one population, green sunfish ate more largemouth bass eggs and fry than other sunfish, but the number taken was not significant after mid-May (Mullan and Applegate 1968), when the green sunfish turned to gizzard shad and sunfish young for food. Green sunfish 51–99 mm long contained a volume of about 33% fish larvae in late June. Forbes and Richardson (1920) reported that more than one-third of the diet of green sunfish in Illinois was made up of fish, the remainder of insects and crayfishes. In California, green sunfish eliminated mosquitofish and threespine sticklebacks from a pool in a stream as water levels decreased (Greenfield and Deckert 1973).

According to Sigler and Miller (1963), green sunfish prefer to eat animal materials, but are able to shift to plant materials when animals are unavailable. Unusual animal items reported eaten include a short-tailed shrew (Sigler and Miller 1963) and a bat (Carlander 1977).

Green sunfish survive water temperatures as high as 33–34°C (91–93°F) (Sigler and Miller 1963) and even 36°C (97°F) (Proffitt and Benda 1971). In the laboratory, they actively avoided temperatures of more than 30.3°C (86.5°F) and less than 26.5°C (79.7°F), and preferred a median temperature of 28.2°C (82.8°F) (Beitinger et al. 1975). Jones and Irwin (1962) determined a temperature preference of 26.8°C (80.2°F) for this species. The green sunfish was able to withstand sudden changes of temperature as great as 11°C (20°F) without immediate mortality, provided the upper lethal limit was not exceeded; some delayed mortalities were noted, however (Nickum 1967).

Green sunfish tolerated pH changes from 7.2 to 9.6, and from 8.1 to 6.0, at water temperatures of 17–19.5°C (63–67°F), with 4–9 ppm of oxygen (Wiebe 1931). At winter temperatures, they survived at an oxygen level of 3.6 ppm, but died when the oxygen level was at 1.5 ppm over a 48-hour period (Moore 1942). Green sunfish showed an initial decline in feeding and growth when exposed to concentrations of ammonia greater than 2 ppm (Jude 1973). When exposed to 3, 7, and 15 ppm of cadmium, green sunfish exhibited reduced food intake and growth. Cadmium elimination after exposure to high concentrations for short periods was complete within 60 days. Siewert (1973) reported a complete kill of green sunfish in a pond in which hydrogen sulfide had developed during June.

The green sunfish can stand more turbidity and silt than any other sunfish species except the orangespotted sunfish. In several green sunfish studies high levels of silt turbidity did not seem to affect feeding or attack behavior but did affect the social hierarchy and resulted in increased scrubbing movements against the bottom or side of the aquariums (Heimstra et al. 1969). In clear water, one fish in a group typically made almost all attacks, with attacks generally ending in a chase, and it appeared as though a definite social hierarchy was established. Under the turbid conditions, attacks were less frequent, activity was reduced among the fish, and there was not as much indication of a social hierarchy. Horkel and Pearson (1976) found that an increase in the amount of clay suspended in water resulted in increased ventilation rates among the fish, and an overall reduction in their activity. In high turbidity, green sunfish engaged in "coughing,"—a quick, short expulsion of water from the oral cavity, which, according to Lagler, Bardach, and Miller (1962), is a violent sweeping of water over the gill lamellae to free them of accumulated detritus.

The green sunfish seeks the warm, shallow waters of smaller lakes and reservoirs, and spends much of its time in the vicinity of weed beds. Its aggression appears to be directed against members of its own species, rather than against other species. Hunter and Wisby (1961) noted that when swarms of redfin shiners appeared above the nests of spawning green sunfish the male sunfish only rarely responded aggressively toward them. The green sunfish enters small streams when moving upstream in the spring. According to Walden (1964), there is a legend in Missouri that the green sunfish forsakes the streams for the meadows after a heavy fall of dew.

The green sunfish is quite sedentary. In one tagging experiment, 77.8% were recaptured less than 1.6 km (1 mi) from the point of release, and 95.6% were recaptured within 16 km (10 mi) (Funk 1957). This species is most active while illumination levels are changing at dawn and dusk (Beitinger et al. 1975). Green sunfish 7.1–9.7 cm long, stimulated by water draining into a pond from a discharge pipe, jumped to heights 10 times their body lengths and leaped a horizontal distance of 0.6 m (Ellis 1974).

When displaced, green sunfish appeared to return to the home area more than did bluegills, pumpkinseeds (Kudrna 1965), and largemouth bass (Hasler and Wisby 1958). Green sunfish took less time to home than the other centrarchids studied; they started directly toward the site of capture rather than swimming in circles in a searching fashion. Hasler and Wisby noted that individual green sunfish in shallow ponds appeared to return in the spring to the same area occupied the previous summer.

Fifty-nine green sunfish were collected in 1971 from the Rock River (Dodge County) along with the common carp (66), spotfin shiner (79), fathead minnow (4), shorthead redhorse (1), black bullhead (48), stonecat (1), orangespotted sunfish (1), and black crappie (1).

IMPORTANCE AND MANAGEMENT

In a desert impoundment, green sunfish were the major food for the largemouth bass (Biggins 1968). In food preference studies (Lewis et al. 1965), channel catfish selected green sunfish after crayfish and fathead minnows.

The green sunfish acts as a host to the glochidial stages of a number of mussels (Hart and Fuller 1974): *Amblema plicata*, *Fusconaia ebena*, *Quadrula metanevra*,

Anodonta grandis, *Anodonta imbecilis*, *Lasmigona complanata*, *Strophitus undulatus*, *Actinonaias carinata*, *Lampsilis teres*, *Leptodea subrostrata*, and *Ellipsaria lineolata*.

The green sunfish bites readily on worms, grasshoppers, crickets, and artificial flies, and puts up a fight about equal to that of a rock bass. Because of its small size, the green sunfish is most often caught incidentally by anglers fishing for bluegills. Fishermen regard green sunfish as bait stealers. The occasional large green sunfish which is taken makes an excellent panfish. Wisconsin's fishing regulations for panfish from inland waters, including green sunfish, are liberal; an aggregate of 50 panfish may be caught in one day. In most boundary waters there is no bag limit on panfish, except in Wisconsin-Minnesota waters where there is a limit of 25 panfish.

The green sunfish has been used as an experimental animal, since it is easily handled and makes a good bioassay animal (Ward and Irwin 1961).

Because of its small size and frequent abundance, the green sunfish is often regarded as a nuisance (Eddy and Underhill 1974, McKechnie and Tharratt 1966). Many overcrowded populations show evidence of stunting. The largest populations of green sunfish occur in habitats where there is little competition from other sunfish species, and since the green sunfish is more tolerant to turbidity and siltation than other sunfishes, it tends to be favored in such waters. Trautman (1957) noted an increase in green sunfish numbers in several streams where a decrease in longear sunfish numbers was most marked. Although the green sunfish is stunted in Utah and competes for both food and space with some sport fish, Sigler and Miller (1963) concluded that it is probably not detrimental enough to warrant expensive steps to curtail it.

The natural hybridization of green sunfish with other sunfish species is quite common, and is thought to result from the rarity of one of the parental species and the abundance of the other in a body of water. A scarcity of nesting sites may also lead to hybridization (Cross 1967). Hybrids exhibit hybrid vigor in that they are larger than the parents and are more aggressive in taking anglers' lures. According to Cross, such hybrids can be produced in a pond by stocking the pond with a few male bluegills and a few female green sunfish. The young hybrids can then be seined and transferred to other ponds in limited numbers to ensure their growth to a large size.

Hubbs (1955) described green sunfish × pumpkinseed hybrids in a Michigan stream, in which the hybrids constituted about 95% of the sunfish population. The hybrids had migrated upstream about 8 km (5 mi) from a pond which held the parent species.

A golden color mutation in the green sunfish has been found and developed in Texas (White 1971). Called the "Texas golden green," it is highly prolific and reaches sexual maturity in less than 6 months. Its golden color makes it extremely vulnerable to predation. Studies are being conducted on its use as a forage fish.

Pumpkinseed

Lepomis gibbosus (Linnaeus). *Lepomis*—scaled operculum; *gibbosus*—formed like the nearly full moon, referring to the body shape.

Other common names: pumpkinseed sunfish, yellow sunfish, common sunfish, sunfish, round sunfish, punky, sunny, sun bass, pond perch, bream.

Adult 135 mm, Hilbert L. (Marinette Co.), 21 June 1966

DESCRIPTION

Body very deep, strongly compressed laterally. Length 127–190 mm (5.0–7.5 in). TL = 1.26 SL. Depth into TL 2.4–3.1. Head length into TL 3.3–4.0. Mouth short, terminal, slightly oblique. Upper jaw scarcely reaching front of eye, or not reaching eye; lower jaw slightly longer than upper jaw; small blunt teeth in brushlike pads on upper and lower jaws, no teeth on tongue; lower pharyngeal arches with pads almost as broad as long, and with a few large, low, molarlike teeth. Gill rakers on first gill arch short and knobby, scarcely longer than wide. Opercular flap flexible only at tip. Dorsal fins 2, but broadly joined and appear as 1; base of dorsal fins about 2.3 times length of anal fin base; first dorsal fin with 10–11 spines, second with 10–12 soft rays. Anal fin with 3 spines, and 10–11 soft rays; pelvic fin thoracic with 1 spine and 5 rays; pectoral fin pointed, long, and when laid forward across cheek reaching front of eye; caudal fin scarcely forked. Scales ctenoid, gill covers and cheeks scaled. Scales in lateral line 38–43; lateral line complete. Chromosomes 2n = 48 (W. LeGrande, pers. comm.).

Dorsal view of the pumpkinseed's broad and heavy lower pharyngeal arches with large, molarlike teeth (from *The Fishes of Ohio*, by Milton B. Trautman [Columbus, Ohio: Ohio State University Press, 1957, 519])

Back brown to olive; sides lighter; breast and belly orange to red-orange. Back and sides speckled with orange, yellow, blue, and emerald spots. Sides of body with 7–10 faint vertical bands (especially prominent in female). Several narrow, wavy, emerald or blue lines alternating with orange-brown lines radiate backward from snout and eye. Opercular flap with black center and with a thin, light-colored margin which enlarges posteriorly into a halfmoon crimson spot (fading to white in preserved specimens). Membranes of soft dorsal, caudal, and anal fins with brown pigmented spots (diffuse brown chromatophores in young-of-year) but no pronounced large, black blotch; small faint orange to olive spots on soft dorsal and caudal fins; pectoral and pelvic fins with slight dark pigmentation. Young similar to adult female, but lacking the bright colors.

Breeding male more brilliantly colored than female; breeding female exhibiting more prominent dark, vertical bands.

Hybrids: Pumpkinseed × warmouth, pumpkinseed × green sunfish, pumpkinseed × bluegill, pumpkinseed × orangespotted sunfish, pumpkinseed × redbreast sunfish, pumpkinseed × longear sunfish (Childers 1967). Pumpkinseed × green sunfish, and pumpkinseed × bluegill. (Wis. Fish Distrib. Study 1974–1979).

DISTRIBUTION, STATUS, AND HABITAT

The pumpkinseed occurs in all three drainage basins in Wisconsin and in the shallow, protected bays of Lakes Michigan and Superior. It is widely distributed throughout the state except in the unglaciated region, where its populations are disjunct.

The pumpkinseed is taken occasionally in protected bays in Lakes Superior and Michigan, and in Green Bay. It has been reported generally in small numbers from the mouths of tributary streams to Lake Superior (Moore and Braem 1965, McLain et al. 1965). The pumpkinseed was reported from 23 of 40 Waukesha County lakes sampled (Poff and Threinen 1963). It is a common inhabitant of many ponds, lakes, and streams. The establishment of impoundments on many creeks and rivers has created favorable habitats for this species. It is easily established in new waters.

In Wisconsin, the pumpkinseed was encountered most frequently in cool to moderately warm waters

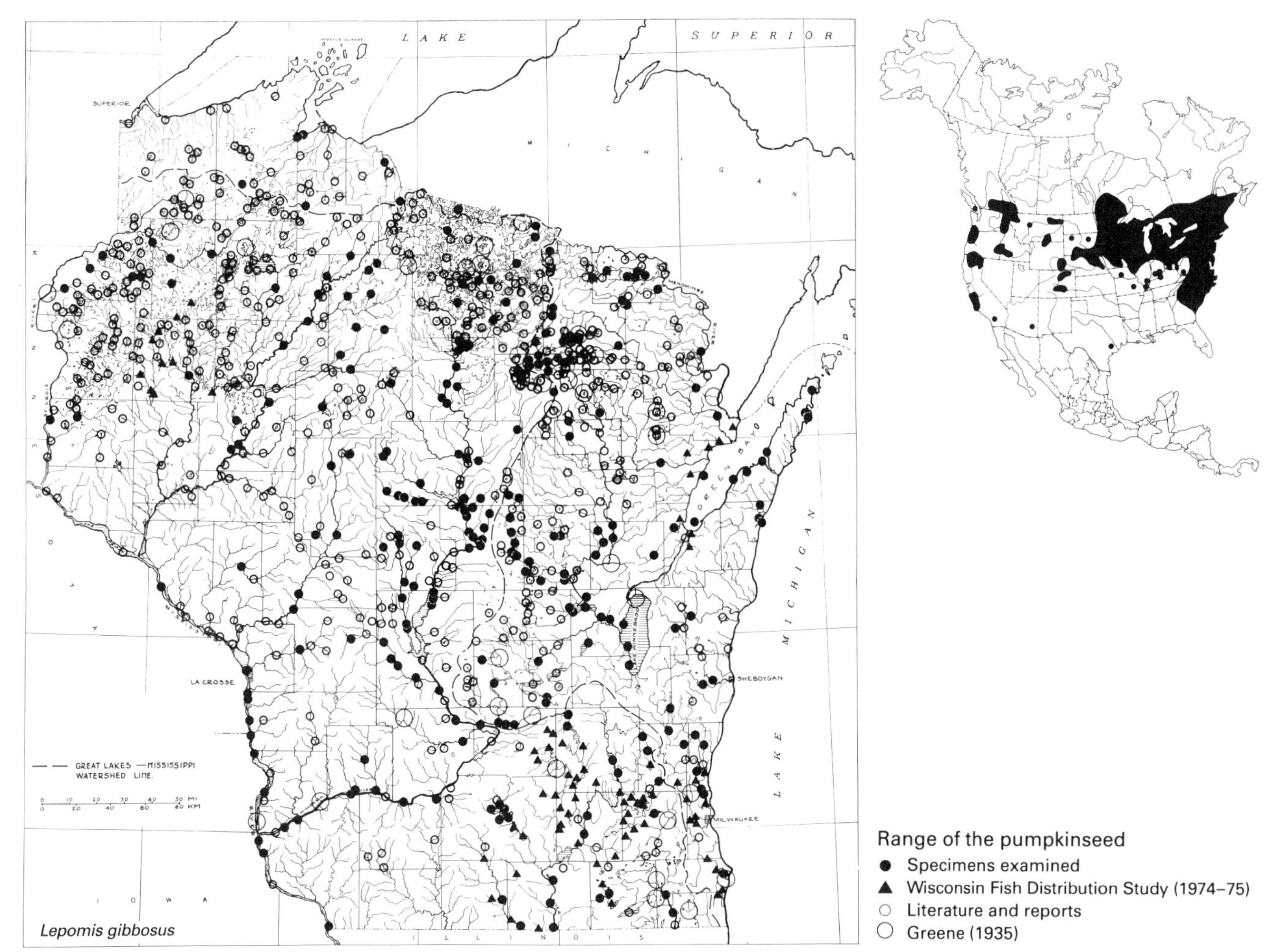

which are clear to slightly turbid; it was found at depths of less than 1.5 m, over substrates of sand (28% frequency), gravel (19%), mud (18%), silt (13%), boulders (8%), rubble (7%), detritus (4%), clay (2%), hardpan (1%), and bedrock (1%). It occurred in weedy ponds, lakes and reservoirs, and in low-gradient streams of the following widths: 1.0–3.0 m (13% frequency); 3.1–6.0 m (12%); 6.1–12.0 m (9%); 12.1–24.0 m (36%); 24.1–50.0 m (20%); and more than 50.0 m (11%).

BIOLOGY

Pumpkinseeds spawn sometime between early May and August. C. E. Johnson (1971) noted that in Wisconsin pumpkinseeds prefer to spawn from late May to July at water temperatures of 19.4°C (67°F), on sand or gravel in shallow, warm bays. Nest building starts when water temperatures reach 13–17°C (55–63°F). Nests are usually found in 0.3–0.8 m of water, and are about 31–38 cm diam (Wis. Conserv. Com. 1958). As many as 10–15 nests may be seen together in a small area, although Clark and Keenleyside (1967) found that pumpkinseed nests in two ponds were an average of 60 and 54 cm apart, and were more scattered than the nests of bluegills, which were 50 and 32 cm apart. In Michigan, Carbine (1939) noted that pumpkinseed nests occurred singly or in groups of two or three and that occasionally pumpkinseed nests were found within a bluegill colony.

The nest is constructed by the male pumpkinseed. It is a more or less circular depression in the bottom, made by a fanning movement of the tail. Objects too large or heavy to be removed by this method are pulled away with the mouth (Adams and Hankinson 1926). Males defend territories around their nests with typical sunfish aggressive behavior—spreading of the opercula, charging, biting, chasing, and, rarely, mouth-fighting. Pumpkinseeds maintain larger territories than bluegills; approaching fish of either species were often attacked by nesting pumpkinseeds when they were about 1 m from the nest (Clark and Keenleyside 1967). R. J. F. Smith (1970) noted that prespawning aggression among male pumpkinseeds failed to occur when water temperatures had dropped to 11–13°C (52–55°F).

While nest building is going on, female pumpkinseeds spend most of their time in the deeper water. Breder (1936) noted that if a female cruised out in the vicinity of the nests she was pursued by one or more males; and that such attention usually drove the female back to the inactive group of females which remained somewhat removed from the nests. Eventually, after considerable play of this kind, the female settled closer to the bottom and withstood the male's attack; in this case, the male usually began to court her—i.e., to drive her into his nest. Breder has described this behavior (1936:30):

> . . . The direction of 'driving' appears to be determined entirely by the direction the pursued elects to follow. This view would give the role of spawning determination to the female. That is to say, the males having established themselves on a nest pursue practically anything, giving up the chase only when it leads far away from the nest. This view fuses the 'fighting' and 'courting' behavior into one, with the behavior of the female as the determining element.

When a gravid female enters a nest, the male and female swim side by side in a circle, making approximately 11 circuits per minute, while touching bellies. During a rotation, the female inclines to one side at about 45°, and emits some eggs, and the male simultaneously releases sperm. According to Breder, spawning may last an hour. In an aquarium in which three females and one male were present, a spawning pair was joined by a second female, and the three fish attempted perhaps with success to spawn together. The male was upright between the two females, which inclined on either side of him; all were facing in the same direction.

Breder and Rosen (1966) reported that a male pumpkinseed sometimes actually operated over two nests intermittently. Males may spawn at least twice in a season in the same nest, with the same or with other females.

The male pumpkinseed guards the eggs against other fishes, and he will go so far as to bite hands and fingers held near the nest. The spreading of his gill covers and the display of his colors appear to be instrumental in driving away intruders, as well as in attracting the female.

It has been generally assumed that the pumpkinseed and other sunfish relatives guard only the eggs and not the young. In this connection, Breder and Rosen (1966) cited a report of a male pumpkinseed which was found tending the young in the bottom of a nest. The young were rather active, and now and then one of them left the nest and swam up to the surface. When the parent fish snapped up the stray, he appeared at first to be devouring his young; it was soon discovered that each time the parent took a young fish in his mouth he immediately returned to the bottom of the nest, head downward, and spat the young into the nest near the ground. Breder (1936) noted that a few students have seen sunfishes transporting their young by oral or other means, but that he has never seen such behavior himself.

The production of Lake Wingra (Dane County) pumpkinseeds, which were 112–141 mm TL on 31 May 1972, was 5,800 (4,100–7,000) eggs; the production of 119–135-mm fish on 29 June was 4,500 (2,400–6,700) eggs (Churchill 1976). Two females from northern Wisconsin, 122 and 126 mm TL, held 5,460 and 5,850 eggs in late June (G. Lutterbie, pers. comm.). In Deep Lake, Michigan, Carbine (1939) collected 1,509 fry from one nest and 14,639 from another.

Pumpkinseed eggs, which are about 1 mm diam, are demersal and adhere to bottom objects such as soil particles, small stones, roots, and sticks. Hatching occurred in 47 hr at temperatures of 19.0–24.7°C (66–76.5°F) (Balon 1959); and in about 3 days at 27.8°C (82°F) (Breder 1936). Balon provided extensive details and illustrations of the embryonic development of the pumpkinseed from fertilization to the 5.2-mm prolarva at 157 hr. Fish (1932) described and illustrated the 18.5-mm stage.

Young pumpkinseeds live on or near the shallow water breeding areas. According to Cahn (1927), they leave the nest almost at once, after which no further parental care is displayed. Young-of-year in central

Age and Growth (TL in mm) of the Pumpkinseed in Wisconsin

Location	1	2	3	4	5	6	7	Source
Bucks L. (Rusk Co.)	46	81	137	170	188	190		Snow (1969)
Murphy Flowage (Rusk Co.)	43	69	94	119	137	155		Snow (1969)
Lowland L. (Chippewa Co.)		51	64	79	94	97		Snow (1969)
Flora L. (Vilas Co.)	54	79	106	128	151	171		Parker (1958)
Flora L. (Vilas Co.)[a]	53	76	99	122	144	154	173	Parker (1958)
L. Wingra (Dane Co.)	48	87	120	134	137			Churchill (1976)

[a]Pumpkinseed × bluegill hybrids.

Wisconsin lakes were 38 (28–46) mm TL in August, and 46 (39–57) mm in September.

Snow (1969) suggested that there may be a higher growth rate among pumpkinseeds found in drainage lakes, where alkalinity is high, than among those found in seepage lakes, where alkalinity is low.

In nature pumpkinseeds reportedly reach age X, although most do not exceed ages VI–VIII. They have lived up to 12 years in captivity (Carlander 1977). Fast-growing males may mature at age I; others mature at ages II and III.

A 454-g (1-lb) pumpkinseed was caught 15 January 1976 from Bishop Lake (Forest County). Mackenthun (1948) reported one pumpkinseed from southern Wisconsin in the 241–251-mm (9.5–9.9-in) group.

The stomachs of 24 Wisconsin pumpkinseeds, 50–169 mm long, contained crustaceans, rotifers, snails, clams, flatworms, aquatic insect larvae, and terrestrial insects (D. Bendlin, pers. comm.). In Green Lake (Green Lake County) during late summer, pumpkinseeds which were 146 mm long had eaten insect larvae (59.5% volume), clams (6.1%), snails (26.5%), and leeches (7.5%). In Lake Mendota (Dane County), pumpkinseeds which were 118 mm long, had consumed insect larvae (29.3% volume), insect pupae (0.5%), insect adults (4.2%), amphipods (3%), ostracods (29.5%), snails (11%), leeches (5.9%), plant material (5.5%), and sand (11.1%).

In Illinois (Forbes 1880), the food of nine adult pumpkinseeds consisted of mollusks (46%), (including *Planorbis*, *Amnicola*, and *Valvata*), insects (20%), crustaceans (22%), and vegetation (12%); the plants were *Chara*, *Myriophyllum* and algae. In southern Canada (Keast 1965), fish fry and mollusks were important in the pumpkinseed's midsummer diet. Scott and Crossman (1973) reported that larval salamanders have been eaten by pumpkinseeds. Except for specimens less than 70 mm long, pumpkinseeds of all sizes consume more gastropods than the other sunfish species (Sadzikowski and Wallace 1976). This is made possible by the pumpkinseed's wide pharyngeal arches and round, molarlike teeth, and probably helps to minimize competition for food with other cohabiting sunfish.

Evidence in one study showed that the pumpkinseed fed daily from 0500 to 0730 hr, that steady feeding began about 0930 hours, and was followed by a marked acceleration in feeding between 1500 and 1730 hours (Keast and Welsh 1968). A brief period of feeding occurred after midnight. Keast noted that the pumpkinseed is a diverse feeder—8–10 different food items were present in significant volumes in its diet. In laboratory experiments, at a water temperature of 22.7°C (73°F), the pumpkinseed digested all digestible organic matter it had eaten within 22 hr (Kitchell and Windell 1968).

The water temperature preference of small pumpkinseeds tested in the laboratory, was 31.5°C (88.7°F) (Coutant 1975). Reynolds and Casterlin (1977) noted that published preferred temperatures for this species ranged from 24.2°C (75.6°F) to 32°C (89.5°F). Young pumpkinseeds that were found in the thermal outfall of a power plant on Lake Monona (Dane County) in August had body temperatures higher than 29°C (84°F) (Neill and Magnuson 1974). In a shallow Michigan pond, a 38°C (100.4°F) water temperature resulted in a large fish mortality among umbrid, catostomid, cyprinid, ictalurid, and percid species; among the more resistant species was the pumpkinseed. In southern Canada (Hallam 1959), the pumpkinseed associated with rock bass and smallmouth bass at an average summer water temperature of 21°C (70°F).

O'Hara (1968) determined that the bluegill is better adapted to higher temperatures than the pumpkinseed. In general, the pumpkinseed lives in cooler waters than other members of the genus. However, O'Hara (1968) also determined that small pumpkinseeds are better adapted to warmer temperatures than larger fish, because temperature has less effect on the respiratory metabolism of small fish.

Power and Todd (1976) studied the effects of increasing temperatures on the social behavior of pumpkinseeds in territorial groups. When subjected to a 1°C temperature increase every other day until they succumbed, their social behavior remained remarkably unchanged by thermal stress until the temperature reached nearly lethal levels. As the temperature rose, ritualized behavior increased in frequency and then fell off; behavioral and physiological signs of stress appeared at temperatures of 31–38°C (88–100.4°F).

The pumpkinseed has been used as a test animal to predict the ecological impact of cold shock during the winter when thermal discharges from power stations were terminated. Becker et al. (1977), determining the pumpkinseed's resistance to abrupt and to gradual cold shock, found that the lower 50% mortality temperature limit was 12.3°C (54.1°F) among fish acclimated to a 30°C (86°F) temperature, 9.6°C (49.3°F) among fish acclimated to 25°C, and 4.5°C (40.1°F) among fish acclimated to 20°C (68°F). Prior to death, the fish suffered from a loss of equilibrium at temperatures slightly higher than the lower mortality limit. Such fish are in a helpless state and will eventually succumb.

At a summer temperature of 26°C (79°F), the lowest observed oxygen tension at which pumpkinseeds survived for 24 hours was 4.3 ppm; at a temperature of 15°C (59°F), 3.1 ppm (Moore 1942). In southeastern Michigan lakes (Cooper and Washburn 1949), the pumpkinseed showed a relatively high tolerance of oxygen deficiency; it survived in waters in which the oxygen level dropped to 0.2–0.3 ppm during winter stagnation.

In one study, reproductive isolation appeared to be complete between pumpkinseeds and longear sunfish (Steele and Keenleyside 1971). Female pumpkinseeds showed a preference for pumpkinseed males even in the absence of visual cues, but pumpkinseed males did not discriminate between females of the two species in either the presence or absence of visual cues. The female's choice of a spawning partner of the same species may be an important ethological isolating mechanism between these two species. It is probable that auditory recognition, as described by Gerald (1971), plays some role in species isolation. When equal numbers (1:1 sex ratio) of pumpkinseeds and bluegills were stocked in ponds in southern Ontario (Clark and Keenleyside 1967), no spawning between the two species was attempted, nor were any hybrids found in the large numbers of yearling and 2-year-old offspring. The biologists determined that behavioral isolation through the visual recognition of mates of the same species was probably the major barrier to hybridization.

Observations by scuba divers have disclosed that juvenile pumpkinseeds travel in abundant and loose schools in shallow water (0.5–0.1 m) in areas of emergent water plants (Emery 1973). The young swim near the surface. Adults, however, are found in deeper water over rocky or plant-covered substrates, and only rarely school. Adults are often observed in pairs or in small aggregations of three or four individuals.

Pumpkinseeds are active by day. At dusk they move toward the bottom, where they rest. Resting areas are usually in interstices of rocky cliff areas or near fallen logs. Emery noted that pumpkinseeds become pale and barred at night.

There is evidence that the pumpkinseed is a homing fish. In an Iowa study, 64% of the displaced pumpkinseeds had homed (Kudrna 1965). A greater percentage of large fish homed than small fish. According to Kudrna, pumpkinseeds, when displaced in a new territory, initially spent time moving in circles as if searching for familiar landmarks. Reed (1971) noted that many displaced pumpkinseeds returned to their original home range within 24 hr, and that most fish tagged and released in the general area of capture showed little, if any, tendency to stray.

Forty-five pumpkinseeds were collected from a pond on the south branch of the Popple River (Florence County) along with white sucker (1), pearl dace (2), finescale dace (25), northern redbelly dace (58), golden shiner (319), fathead minnow (3), common shiner (4), blacknose shiner (695), brassy minnow (2), black bullhead (2), yellow perch (6), and Iowa darter (3).

IMPORTANCE AND MANAGEMENT

Small pumpkinseeds form part of the food of almost all predatory fishes such as basses, walleyes, yellow perch, northern pike, and muskellunge. Even larger pumpkinseeds and other sunfish may eat the young. Because the pumpkinseed spends much time in shallow water, it is exposed to many enemies. It is known to have been eaten by cormorants, mergansers, and herons (Adams and Hankinson 1926).

The pumpkinseed is host to the glochidial stage of the mollusks *Amblema plicata* and *Anodonta implicata* (Hart and Fuller 1974).

Adams and Hankinson have suggested, with "abundant confirmation," that the pumpkinseed destroys mosquito larvae.

Although the pumpkinseed has been termed the "small boy's fish," it is sought by adult anglers as well. It can be caught by still-fishing methods with worms, grasshoppers, and other small, live baits, but it also responds to small dry flies, to poppers, or to standard wet fly trout patterns. It is caught during the day, and especially in late afternoon. Its flesh is white, flaky, sweet, and delicious.

In Escanaba Lake (Vilas County), the total sport fishery harvest of pumpkinseeds from 1946–1969 was 138,338 fish weighing 11,140 kg (24,559 lb) (Kempinger et al. 1975). Pumpkinseeds ranked second in the number of fish caught; they constituted 36.3% of the total numerical catch, and a third (17.8%) of the total weight. The pumpkinseed population in Escanaba Lake, based on fish 114 mm long and larger, was estimated at 52,000 in 1959; too few were taken, however, to provide estimates from 1966 through 1969. Pumpkinseeds comprised 1.5%, 8.0%, and 3.4% of the total catches from Black, Oak, and Laura lakes (Vilas County) from June through August 1970 (Serns and McKnight 1974). In Murphy Flowage (Rusk County), the total harvest of pumpkinseeds from 1955 to 1970 constituted 1.9% of the total fish catch by number and 1.4% by weight (Snow 1978).

In Wisconsin, the regulations for taking panfish,

including the pumpkinseed, from inland waters are liberal. An aggregate of 50 panfish may be caught in one day. In most boundary waters there is no bag limit on panfish, except in Wisconsin-Minnesota waters, which have a limit of 25.

The pumpkinseed is undoubtedly among the most strikingly colorful and beautiful of Wisconsin fishes. Jordan and Evermann (1923) called it "a very beautiful and compact fish, perfect in all its parts, looking like a brilliant coin fresh from the mint." It makes an interesting and attractive aquarium fish.

In Lake Wingra (Dane County), the estimated biomass (kg/ha) of pumpkinseeds during 1972–1974 ranged from 3 to 4 for juveniles and from 4 to 11 for adults (Churchill 1976). The total biomass of Lake Wingra in 1973 was 668 kg/ha; it consisted of pumpkinseeds (14 kg/ha), bluegills (503 kg/ha), white crappies (56 kg/ha), black crappies (20 kg/ha), and yellow bass (75 kg/ha).

In waters which are overpopulated with pumpkinseeds, stunting is a problem. The thinning of such populations either by mechanical means or by partial poisoning may help, although biological controls in the form of fish predators may provide a more satisfactory solution. When the numbers of bluegills, pumpkinseeds, and their hybrids were reduced in Flora Lake (Vilas County) by netting operations, all responded favorably with an increase in the linear rate of growth, and the pumpkinseeds showed an increase in weight at all lengths (Parker 1958).

Longear Sunfish

Lepomis megalotis (Rafinesque). *Lepomis*—scaled operculum; *megalotis*—great ear, in reference to the prominent opercular flap.

Other common names: northern longear, Great Lakes longear, longear, blue and orange sunfish, pumpkinseed.

Adult male 94 mm, Milwaukee R. (Ozaukee Co.), 2 Aug. 1963

Adult female 80 mm, Milwaukee R. (Ozaukee Co.), 2 Aug. 1963

DESCRIPTION

Body deep, strongly compressed laterally. Length 71–94 mm (2.8–3.7 in). TL = 1.26 SL. Depth into TL 2.4–3.0. Head length into TL 2.7–3.4. Mouth moderately large, oblique, with jaws of equal length. Upper jaw reaching pupil of eye; conical, pointed teeth in brushlike pads on upper and lower jaws, no teeth on tongue; lower pharyngeal arches narrow, with pointed teeth. Gill rakers on first gill arch short, thick, knoblike (about as long as wide), and crooked. Opercular "ear flap" flexible and often much elongated in adults. Dorsal fins 2, but broadly joined and appear as 1; base of dorsal fins about twice the length of anal fin base; first dorsal fin with 10 spines, second with 10–11 soft rays. Anal fin with 3 spines, and 9–11 soft rays; pelvic fin thoracic with 1 spine and 5 rays; pectoral fin short, bluntly pointed to rounded, and when laid forward across cheek barely reaching posterior edge of eye; caudal fin slightly forked. Scales ctenoid, in lateral line 34–38; lateral line complete. Chromosomes 2n = 48 (W. LeGrande, pers. comm.).

Back olive to rusty brown; sides lighter; breast and belly yellow to orange-red. Back and sides with specks of yellow, orange, emerald, and blue; 8–10 vertical bars conspicuous to absent. Cheeks orange with wavy blue streaks radiating back from mouth and eye. Ear flap black, narrowly edged with pale red to yellow (white in immature and all preserved specimens). Dorsal and anal fins olive, often with rusty orange wash; in preserved specimens, soft dorsal fin with parallel rows of light dots. Pectoral fins clear to lightly pigmented.

Breeding male iridescent green above and bright orange below; the vertical fins a deep rusty orange, and the pelvic fins blue-black. Scale pockets with dark-pigmented crescents pointing anteriorly. Breeding females less brilliantly colored.

Hybrids: Longear sunfish × orangespotted sunfish, longear sunfish × green sunfish, longear sunfish × bluegill, and longear sunfish × pumpkinseed (Childers 1967).

SYSTEMATIC NOTES

The Wisconsin form is *Lepomis megalotis peltastes* (Cope), the northern longear sunfish. *L. m. megalotis* (Rafinesque), the central longear sunfish, is distributed south of the Lake Erie—Ohio River divide to Louisiana (Trautman 1957). The northern longear sunfish differs from the central longear sunfish by having an ear flap which usually extends upward at a 45° angle, rather than almost horizontal to the body axis; by having a single large, reddish spot in the white border of the ear flap, rather than several small reddish spots; and by reaching a length of about 100 mm, compared to 230 mm.

DISTRIBUTION, STATUS, AND HABITAT

The longear sunfish occurs in three widely separated distribution centers in southeastern, eastcentral, and northwestern Wisconsin within the Mississippi River and Lake Michigan drainage basins. It has not been reported from the Lake Superior basin. In Wisconsin, the longear sunfish is near the northern limit of its distribution.

Specimens examined (numbers of individuals in parentheses): UWSP 862 (32) Milwaukee River at Saukville and Waubeka (Ozaukee County), 1963;

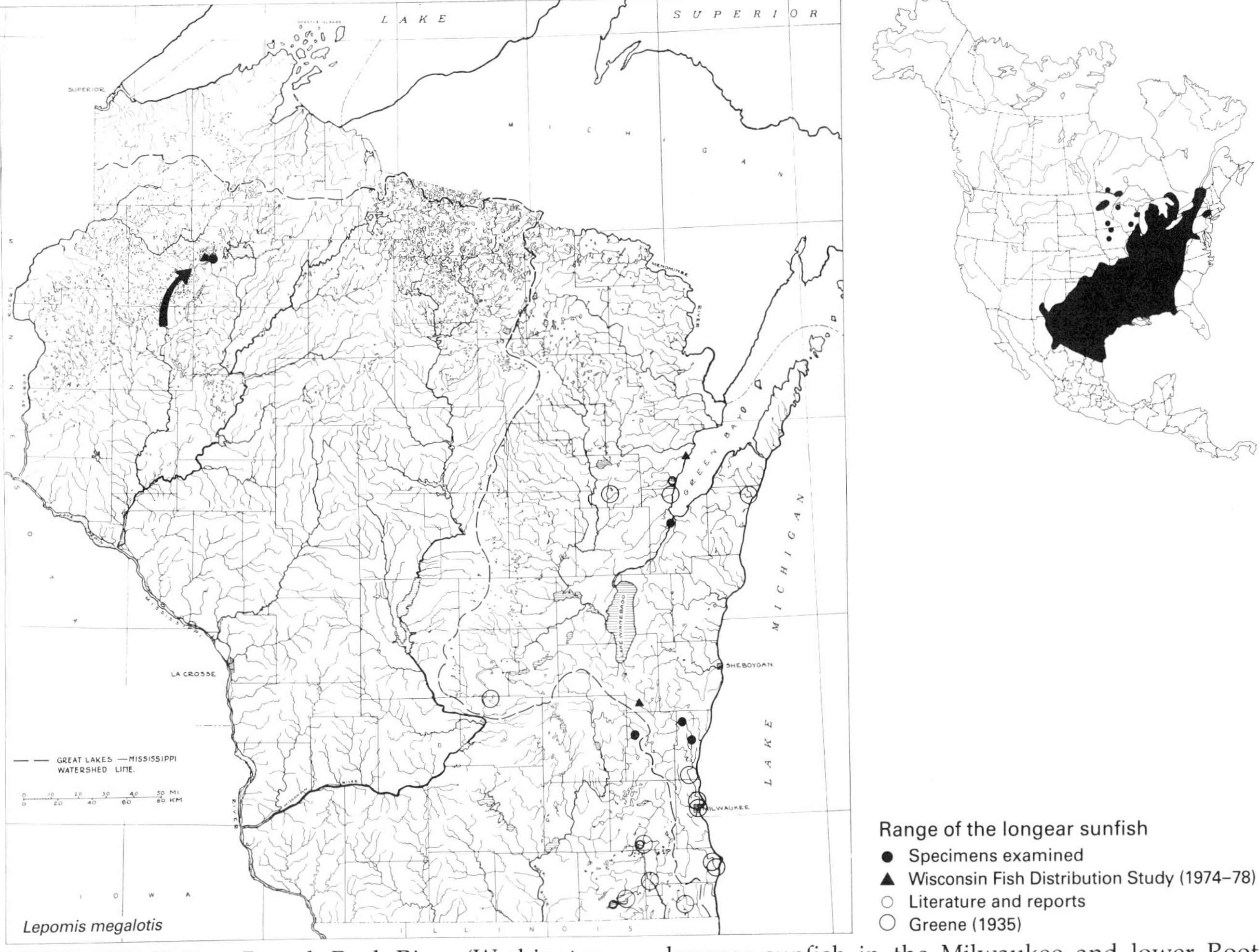

UWSP 4607 (2) East Branch Rock River (Washington County), 1971; UWSP 5009 (1) Fox River (Brown County), 1973; UWSP 5561 (1) Little Lac Court Oreilles (Sawyer County), 1976; and UWMZ 4373 Pensaukee River (Oconto County), 1957.

The Wisconsin Fish Distribution Study (1974–1978) reported: (4) Lac Court Oreilles (Sawyer County), 1968; (6) Pensaukee River (Oconto County) 1975; and (7) West Branch Milwaukee River (Fond du Lac County) 1978. Greene's (1935) mapped records are all indicated by large open circles on my map. Seeburger (1975) reported the longear sunfish from Mukwonago River below Phantom Lake (Waukesha County) 1972. Other reports: M. Johnson and J. Weckmiller (pers. comm.), Mukwonago River below the dam in Mukwonago (Waukesha County), 1968; C. Norden (pers. comm.) (6) Milwaukee River at Saukville (Ozaukee County), 1966; R. Heizer (pers. comm.) (12) Little Suamico River (Oconto County), 1974; Mraz (1960) (6) Lake Geneva (Walworth County), 1958.

Greene (1935) suggested that the presence of the longear sunfish in the Milwaukee and lower Root rivers may have resulted from crossovers from the Des Plaines and Illinois-Fox rivers at high water, or by means of stream capture, probably the former. Its presence in the headwaters of the upper Fox, in the Wolf River system, and in the Suamico River near its mouth indicates its probable dispersal into these waters by means of the glacial Fox connectives. Its occurrence in the mouth of the Ahnapee River (upper Kewaunee County) indicates its possible derivation from glacial Lake Oshkosh during a later stage, when that lake drained into Lake Chicago.

According to Gerking (1953), the longear sunfish is a very abundant, if not the most abundant, centrarchid fish in smaller midwestern streams. However, its numbers have decreased in large Ohio streams as a result of its intolerance of turbid conditions (Trautman 1957). In recent years it has been eliminated from the Root River (Racine County), the lower Milwaukee River (Ozaukee and Milwaukee counties), the East Branch of the Rock River (Washington County), and at least some sectors of the Illinois-Fox and Des Plaines rivers (Walworth, Racine, and Kenosha counties). The population from the East Branch of the Rock River (Washington County) was lost through the use of antimycin in a massive carp control project; unfortunately, no attempts were made to salvage this longear sunfish population. The population losses in other locales were undoubtedly caused by the effects of serious soil erosion and turbidity.

Wisconsin accords the longear sunfish threatened status (Wis. Dep. Nat. Resour. Endangered Species Com. 1975, Les 1979). Many sports fishermen confuse this species with the common pumpkinseed, and there appears to be little protection afforded to the longear by the fishing regulations. Perhaps the best way to ensure its protection is to establish a suitable refuge in a sector of a stream already containing sizeable populations (e.g., the Saukville to Waubeka sector of the Milwaukee River). Since the longear sunfish is a sedentary species that seldom moves beyond a home range of 30–60 m, a refuge of a few kilometers of stream would appear to be adequate.

The longear sunfish usually inhabits streams of clear, shallow, nearly still, and moderately warm water, in or near areas of aquatic vegetation. In its habitat in the Milwaukee River 1 km above Saukville, the stream is 18–24 m wide, has an average depth of 0.3 m (greatest depth 0.5 m), and a bottom composed of rubble, gravel, and some sand. The water is clear, and moderate amounts of aquatic vegetation are present. At Waubeka, where the river forms a pondlike widespread, the rocks, boulders, and rubble are overlaid with a thin layer of silt. Occasionally the longear sunfish occurs in lakes.

BIOLOGY

In Wisconsin, the longear sunfish probably begins to spawn in June and is known to spawn in early August. At the same latitude in Michigan, spawning occurs from late June to August when water temperatures are 23.3–25°C (74–77°F) (Hubbs and Cooper 1935). Spawning has been reported in late July in Kansas, when temperatures were as high as 30.5°C (87°F) (Cross 1967).

The male longear sunfish builds the nest in gravel, if it is available; otherwise the nest is built in sand or hard mud. Males construct their nests by a sweeping action of the tail similar to that of nest-building bluegills (H. C. Miller 1963).

Nests may be built in water 0.2–3.4 m deep, although they are most frequently reported at 0.25–0.36 m (Boyer and Vogele 1971, Adams and Hankinson 1926, Witt and Marzolf 1954). The longear generally appears to nest in small colonies of 5–13 nests which are from a few cm to about 0.3 m apart (Hankinson 1920, H. C. Miller 1963), although colonies of several hundred nests are known (Keenleyside 1972). Often the nests within the colony are so close together that their rims nearly touch. Nests are approximately 0.5 m diam, and more or less circular, but some nests are irregular in shape and difficult to discern except for the attending fish (Hankinson 1920).

The male longear is highly territorial, and although a guarding male aften chases intruders through the territories of other males, the territory itself appears to include only the immediate nest area and the space above the nest to approximately 1 m (Boyer and Vogele 1971). A territorial male defends a nest from individuals of his own and of other nonpredatory species of fish, but does not defend it from such surface-feeding fishes as the blackstripe topminnow. When a largemouth bass 46 cm long approached one longear nest for an instant, the sunfish turned toward the intruder as if to challenge him, but then abruptly turned and fled, seeking the meager cover offered by a small, dead branch (Witt and Marzolf 1954). Within seconds after the bass had left the vicinity, the longear was back in its own nest.

Boyer and Vogele have called attention to lateral threat displays which occur between male longear sunfish near spawning colonies and between males guarding adjacent nests. A weak lateral display was seen when a spawning female quickly spread and folded the dorsal spines upon reentry of a male who had chased excess females from the nest. According to Boyer and Vogele, the frontal threat, in its various forms, is the most frequent type of aggressive behavior among longears, and particularly common and vigorous during reproductive activities (p. 22):

> . . . The longest displays were by males on adjacent nests. Each male spread his fins except the spiny dorsal fin and made alternate short thrusts forward followed by backing into a lateral position. While the male was in the lateral position, the rayed portion of his dorsal fin often was quivered repeatedly; this appeared to be an intention movement for the thrust which soon followed.

Aggressive encounters with contact, especially in the early nest building phase, probably account for superficial injuries observed on guarding males. In one Boyer and Vogele study, the rayed portion of the dorsal fin of nearly every guarding male had been split, and many other males had portions of their fleshy opercle lobes torn away. Among even-aged longear sunfish raised in the laboratory, there was less extreme aggression, and no injuries to either males or females (W. E. Smith 1975). On the other hand, Miller (1963) reported that longear females were killed by continued male attacks, especially when the fish were confined in small aquariums.

When single male longear sunfish in aquariums were presented simultaneously with two female sunfish (one a longear female, and either a pumpkinseed or a bluegill female) the nesting male longears courted females of their own species more vigorously than they did those of the other species (Keenleyside 1972). The longear males were generally more aggressive toward longear females than toward bluegill females but were equally aggressive toward their own and pumpkinseed females. Gerald (1971), in preliminary experiments on the courtship sounds produced by nesting males, noted that both male and female longear sunfish responded by swimming toward such calls, at least during spawning. Male longear sunfish were induced to court and call to dead females that were manipulated on a string.

When female longear sunfish were seen entering a nesting colony, the males began leading. Leading involved spreading the fins (except the spined portion of the dorsal fin, which was only sometimes spread briefly), swimming straight toward a female, and then returning directly to the nest (Boyer and Vogele 1971). If a female followed a male into his nest area, the male swam in a descending spiral toward the bottom, with one side tilted inward toward the side of the female.

A spawning or prespawning female sometimes made peculiar movements upon entering a nest, before she began to circle with a male: she bit the substrate, then turned on one side and darted away. When turned on her side, the female's back was directed either toward or away from the pursuing male. At other times, a female entered a nest, bit the substrate, and immediately began to circle with the male (Boyer and Vogele 1971).

Spawning in a longear sunfish colony typically increases in frequency during the day, and peak activity occurs in the afternoon when water temperatures are at their peak. Spawning details have been given by Witt and Marzolf (1954:189):

> . . . The male circled within the 8-inch center of the nest, always keeping the female between him and the center of the nest. They circled within the nest both clockwise and counter-clockwise, the direction dependent upon how the male reentered the nest after chasing an intruder. The male always remained in an upright position, while every 10 to 15 seconds the female would roll on her side, to within 20 degrees of the horizon, and bring her vent in close proximity to his. This posture lasted only 2 seconds, during which time both fish shuddered, the female more violently than the male.

Interruptions known as intrusions sometimes occur at the height of spawning. Keenleyside (1972) determined that the main function of nest intrusion by females is to eat eggs; males apparently intrude to fertilize the eggs in another male's nest.

Spawning sessions reported by Boyer and Vogele (1971) usually ended immediately following a spawning movement, with the female darting from the nest and the male chasing her. A female leaving one nest after only a few spawning movements often went immediately to another nest to spawn. Two or more females were often present in one nest at the same time, and two females were frequently observed circling on the inside of a single male. The male usually forced out one of the females (usually the female farthest on the inside), and thus limited the occupancy of the nest to only one female at a time. From 7 to 20 eggs are emitted in one spawning movement.

Immediately after the female leaves, the male begins to fan the nest. At first he maintains a normal attitude over the center of the nest while he moves his paired fins and his caudal peduncle rapidly. He then assumes a vertical posture over the nest, standing on his tail; in this position he fans the nest vigorously enough to dislodge small pebbles. Witt and Marzolf (1954) assumed that the first method of fanning insures a complete mixing of sperm and eggs, and possibly cleans the eggs of excess sperm, and that the second method of fanning drives the eggs deep into the interstices between the large pebbles, where they are probably more protected from predators.

Hankinson (1920) observed a longear nest from which the sunfish had been driven away and which had been entered by bluntnose minnows, redfin shiners, and stoneroller minnows. The stonerollers were seen consuming sunfish eggs. Longear sunfish eggs are also eaten by hog suckers, white suckers, and redhorse suckers (Keenleyside 1972). Boyer and Vogele (1971) observed defending male longear sunfish feeding in or adjacent to their nests, and even consuming eggs from their own nests.

Longear sunfish eggs are demersal and adhesive, and may become attached to the roots of plants after the plants have been cleaned of bottom mud (Breder 1936). In the Milwaukee River on 1 August 1963, an age-II, gravid female (75 mm, 9.5 g) with ovaries 12% of body weight, held an estimated 745 eggs, 1.3 mm diam. An age-III female (93 mm, 18.99 g) had ovaries 13.4% of body weight, and held an estimated 1,620 ripe eggs; a few immature, white eggs were present in various sizes up to 0.7 mm diam.

The number of longear sunfish eggs found in 12 nests varied from 137 to 2,836; the number of larvae varied from 52 to 1,132 (Boyer and Vogele 1971). Taber (1969) illustrated developmental stages from 6.0 to 19.0 mm. Hatching occurs in 3–5 days, although in the laboratory, at 25°C (77°F), embryos hatched in 2 days, and swim-up and feeding began 7 days later (W. E. Smith 1975). In nature, larvae left the nest as each clutch developed, rather than all at one time. Boyer and Vogele (1971) noted that the lengths of 70 advanced larvae collected from one nest were 5.8–7.5 mm; the average length was 6.9 mm. Males often continued to guard the nest even after the last larvae had emerged (Huck and Gunning 1967). In October, the young are 20–56 mm TL (Trautman 1957).

Longear sunfish from the Milwaukee River (Ozaukee County), collected 1 August 1963, showed the following growth:

Age Class	No. of Fish	TL (mm)		Calculated TL at Annulus (mm)			
		Avg	Range	1	2	3	4
I	14	65.5	52–73	30.1			
II	7	76.9	71–83	26.4	55.7		
III	9	90.3	84–94	27.2	60.9	76.0	
IV	2	99.0	96–102	32.0	55.0	75.0	92.0
Avg (weighted)				28.6	58.2	75.8	92.0

In southern Michigan (Hubbs and Cooper 1935), the calculated lengths at the annuli (sexes combined) were: 1—44 mm; 2—57 mm; 3—73 mm; 4—78 mm; 5—111 mm; and 6—105 mm. Growth in males was slightly greater than in females. Hubbs and Cooper have discussed the validity of the spawning mark in this species. Aging of the longear is by scale analysis. Relatively few longear sunfish live to be older than 4 years; but in Michigan one fish was found to be approximately 9 years old.

At Wisconsin's latitude, maturity begins at age II. According to Hubbs and Cooper, however, occasional large yearling longears in scattered localities may mature soon enough to spawn in their second summer.

Of 1,129 longear sunfish collected in Michigan, the majority were from 53 to 89 mm long; the largest was about 140 mm (5.5 in). A 115-mm fish (UWSP 4607), collected from the East Branch of the Rock River (Washington County), is the largest Wisconsin specimen known. Trautman (1957) reported a maximum size of 236 mm (9.3 in) and 284 g (10 oz).

In northern Arkansas (Mullan and Applegate 1968), longear sunfish up to 48 mm long consumed aquatic insects (49.5% volume, mostly midgeflies), microcrustaceans (41.2%), fish eggs (9.1%), and terrestrial foods (0.1%). Longears 51–99 mm long consumed aquatic insects (64.7% volume and mostly midgeflies), fish eggs (15.4%), terrestrial foods (7.7%), detritus (4.9%), microcrustacea (4.2%), mollusks (0.8%), bryozoans (0.7%), filamentous algae (0.7%), fish (0.7%), and mites (0.2%). Fish 102–201 mm long ate aquatic insects (42.1% volume, and mostly midgeflies), terrestrial foods (18.6%), fish (12.0%), detritus (12.0%), fish eggs (10.8%), malacostracans (3.1%), microcrustacea (1.0%), bryozoans (0.3%), and mollusks (0.1%). Large longear sunfish also ingested moderate to heavy quantities of young bass in May, and newly hatched sunfish in June. In a Kentucky study (Lotrich 1973), fish were the principal food of longear sunfish.

Longear sunfish apparently feed more extensively at the surface of the water than some other sunfishes. Mature insects constitute a large percentage of their food. On two occasions longears were observed following hog suckers and feeding on organisms that the suckers stirred up (Huck and Gunning 1967). Gerking (1952) determined that young longear sunfish used about 33% of the protein that they consumed for growth, but that the oldest longear sunfish (105 g) used only 5% of the available protein for growth.

A number of behavioral characteristics of the longear sunfish have been observed by researchers. H. C. Miller (1963) referred to the longear sunfish species as "quite timid" though not as timid as the orangespotted sunfish. The comfort movement most frequently observed among longear sunfish was chafing, during which the fish brushed their sides or bellies along the substrate or a protruding stick (Boyer and Vogele 1971). Convulsive coughing occurred occasionally in individuals that were rapidly eating eggs from a nest; such coughing resulted in the ejection of gravel from the mouth. Observers have reported that longear sunfish become inactive at night, although surface feeding has been observed under bright moonlight in late summer. In intense darkness the fish rested on the bottom with their pelvic fins and the forward parts of their bodies, (from the midventral line to the chin) touching the substrate; the pectoral fins were spread at right angles to their bodies.

The typical home range of the longear has been estimated to be from 30 m to no more than 60 m of stream (Gunning 1965, Gerking 1953). In one study, the majority of longear sunfish that were displaced to a new location migrated back to their original home. Gunning (1959) presented evidence to show that blinded longears are able to return to their home range as quickly and accurately as fish not visually impaired; he concluded that blind fish apparently recognize the home area by a characteristic odor or a combination of odors. Olfaction is probably more important than vision in the homing ability of the longear sunfish.

During the winter in Louisiana, at least some longear sunfish desert their home ranges. Only about one-third of the fish marked in the summer range were taken in the same section during the winter (Berra and Gunning 1972). In Arkansas during March, longear sunfish were seen hiding singly or in small groups under rocks or stumps on the bottom, but as the water warmed they became more active; aggregations of fish dispersed when the water temperature reached 17.8°C (64°F) (Boyer and Vogele 1971). The longear has been found at water temperatures up to 37.8°C (100°F) (Proffitt and Benda 1971).

In a Missouri movement study, 70% of the recaptured longear sunfish had made no movement, 20% had moved downstream, and 10% had moved upstream (Funk 1957).

Hallam (1959) found that longear sunfish in southern Ontario commonly associated with rock bass and smallmouth bass at an average water temperature of 21°C (70°F). The longear avoids association with coldwater mottled sculpins and brook trout, having been taken only once with the latter.

In Illinois, the longear sunfish is a frequent companion of the green sunfish (Forbes and Richardson 1920). In the Milwaukee River at Saukville (Ozaukee County), 29 longear sunfish were taken with these species: golden redhorse (3), largescale stoneroller (16), hornyhead chub (5), creek chub (2), bluntnose minnow (3), common shiner (151+), striped shiner (77), rosyface shiner (25), spotfin shiner (5), sand shiner (32), redfin shiner (5), black bullhead (1), blackside darter (1), logperch (1), johnny darter (1), smallmouth bass (1), pumpkinseed (3+), and rock bass (5).

IMPORTANCE AND MANAGEMENT

In Wisconsin, the longear sunfish is too small to be considered a food fish for man, and its populations are too sparse to be of much importance as food for other fishes and animals; nor is it abundant enough anywhere in the state to be a serious competitor of other fishes. Worms, grasshoppers, and small minnows are good natural baits.

The longear sunfish adjusts well to captivity. It is not susceptible to injury from handling, is not unduly aggressive, and appears to be a promising species for use as a laboratory test fish (Ward and Irwin 1961, W. E. Smith 1975). In the laboratory, W. E. Smith was able to get this species to spawn, to raise the young to maturity in 22 weeks (males 10–12 cm, females 7–9 cm), and to produce successive generations under conditions of long photoperiod and a water temperature of 25°C (77°F). The adults continued to spawn with regularity every 6–10 days for 14 months.

In Bull Shoals, Arkansas, where the longer sunfish has become the predominant sunfish, it is a highly successful competitor, and production in 1968 was at 45.8 kg/ha (41 lb/acre) (Boyer and Vogele 1971). In Jordan Creek, Illinois, 2,015 longear sunfish weighed 38.6 kg, compared to 32.8 kg for 369 smallmouth bass and 108.2 kg for 32,361 minnows collected from the study areas (Durham 1955a).

Orangespotted Sunfish

Lepomis humilis (Girard). *Lepomis*—scaled operculum; *humilis*—humble, insignificant.

Other common names: orangespot, redspotted sunfish, dwarf sunfish, pigmy sunfish, pumpkinseed.

Adult 107 mm, Pecatonica R., above Mifflin (Iowa Co.), 15 Aug. 1962

DESCRIPTION

Body moderately deep, compressed laterally. Average length 51–76 mm (2–3 in). TL = 1.25 SL. Depth into TL 2.8–3.5. Head length into TL 2.8–3.3. Mouth small, oblique. Upper jaw reaching to front of eye; lower jaw slightly longer than upper jaw; conical, pointed teeth in brushlike pads on upper and lower jaws, no teeth on tongue; lower pharyngeal arches narrow, with short, pointed teeth. Sensory head pores greatly enlarged, especially those above the upper lip groove—more so than in any other species of *Lepomis*. Sensory pits (2 depressions in skull between eyes) larger than in any other sunfish, the width of each pit about equal to distance between the pits. Gill rakers on first gill arch blunt and straight, the longest 3–4 times longer than wide. Opercular ear flap prominent, often elongate, flexible. Dorsal fins 2, but broadly joined and appear as 1; base of dorsal fins about 2 times length of anal fin base; first dorsal fin with 10–11 spines, second with 10 soft rays. Anal fin with 3 spines, and 8–9 soft rays; pelvic fin thoracic with 1 spine and 5 rays; pectoral fin rounded to bluntly pointed, and when laid forward across cheek reaching to about anterior edge of eye; caudal fin scarcely forked. Scales ctenoid, gill covers and cheeks scaled. Scales in lateral line 36–41; lateral line complete. Chromosomes 2n = 44–46 (W. LeGrande, pers. comm.).

Male: back olive, sides lighter, and ventral region of head and belly yellow to white. Back and sides with up to 7 broad, dark bands; orange spots on sides of head and body; black spot on ear flap, margined with white. Vertical fins usually not mottled, but broadly margined with red-orange in life. Female: head and body brown, no orange. Soft dorsal fin and caudal fin base mottled with brown spots; paired fins largely unpigmented. This species provides an excellent example of sexual dichromatism in central North American fish; the males are more brilliantly colored than the females.

Breeding male brilliantly colored, with conspicuous orange-red spots, orange fins; and orange-red eye; anterior pelvic fin and entire anal fin margined with black.

Hybrids: Orangespotted sunfish × green sunfish, orangespotted sunfish × bluegill, orangespotted sunfish × longear sunfish, and orangespotted sunfish × pumpkinseed (Childers 1967).

DISTRIBUTION, STATUS, AND HABITAT

In Wisconsin, the orangespotted sunfish is known only from the Mississippi River drainage basin. Greene (1935), who collected in the late 1920s, recorded it at several locales from the Mississippi River upstream to the Victory-Genoa sector (Vernon County); his only other collection came from the Galena River (Lafayette County), almost on the Illinois line. The literature report from the headwaters of the Fox River at Lannon (northeastern Waukesha County) was supplied by Cahn (1927). Since the late 1920s, the orangespotted sunfish has infiltrated the lower Wisconsin River basin, the Sugar and Rock river basins, and the Mississippi River upstream to its junction with the St. Croix River.

The orangespotted sunfish, probably more than most species, has extended its range in recent years, and, considering its habitat needs, will probably continue to extend its range northward. The orangespotted sunfish is found in soft-bottomed pools, and it is tolerant of silt and some pollution. The extension of its range is promoted by the tilling and clearing of land.

The orangespotted sunfish is uncommon to common in Wisconsin. Its status appears to be secure, although in Illinois, where the habitat seems to be increasing, there has been evidence of a decline in its numbers in some areas (P. W. Smith 1968).

In Wisconsin, the orangespotted sunfish was encountered most frequently in turbid water, over substrates of mud (31% frequency), gravel (22%), clay (16%), sand (13%), silt (6%), rubble (6%), and boulders (6%). It was found in sloughs, in backwater

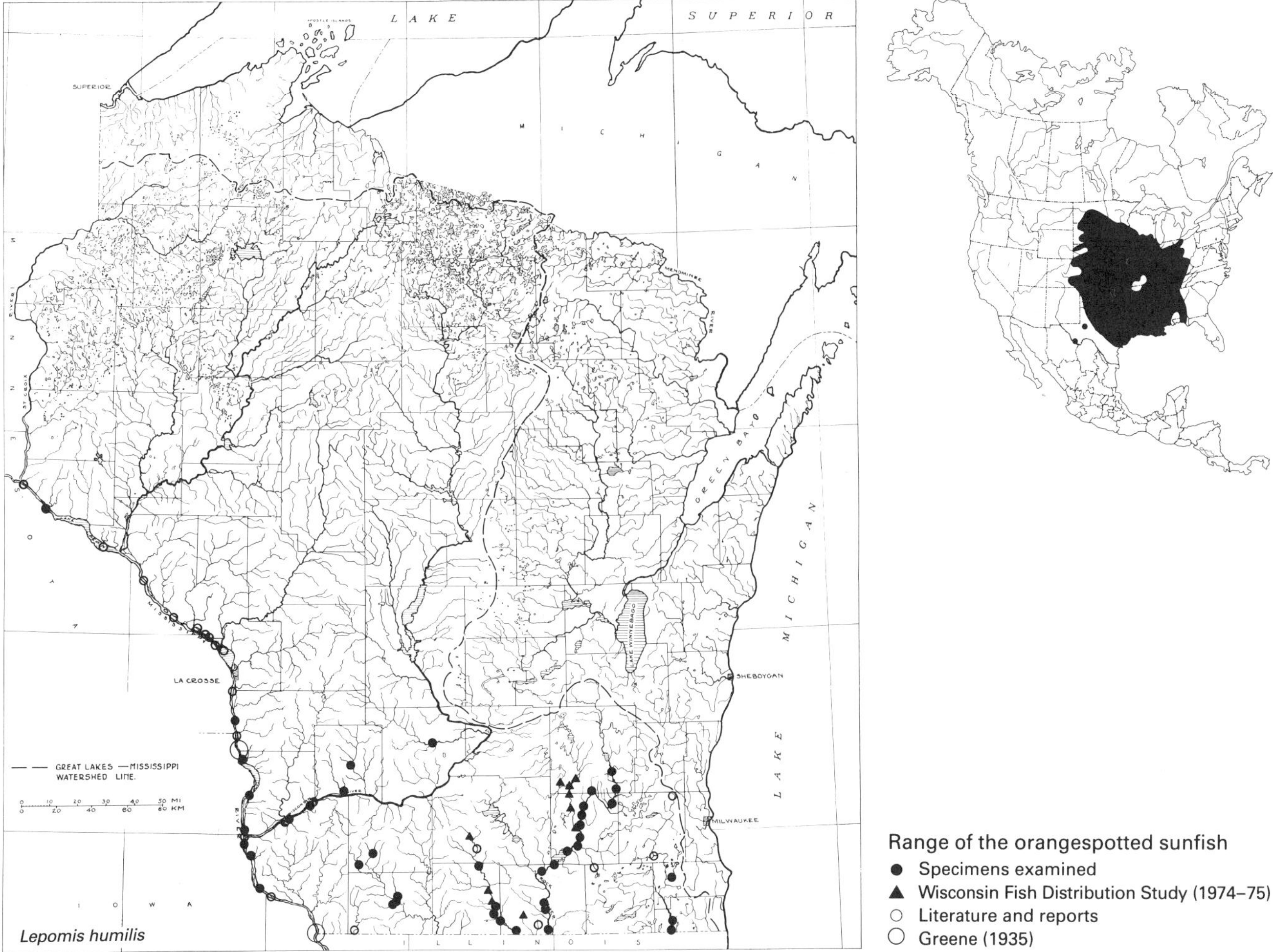

Range of the orangespotted sunfish
● Specimens examined
▲ Wisconsin Fish Distribution Study (1974–75)
○ Literature and reports
◯ Greene (1935)

lakes, and in sluggish streams down to 5 m in width, in waters supporting a scanty to moderate amount of vegetation.

BIOLOGY

Spawning at Wisconsin's latitude occurs from late May to August. It begins when water temperatures reach about 18.3°C (65°F), and continues at temperatures of 23.9–31.7°C (75–89°F) in water depths of 10–61 cm. The nest of the orangespotted sunfish is similar to the nests of other sunfishes, but somewhat smaller—15–18 cm diam, and 3–4 cm deep. According to Barney and Anson (1923), the nest is constructed by the male, which, by powerful pushes with his head, and "by flirts of the tail, combined with active trembling of the fins, removes the smaller pebbles and lighter sand from a bowl-shaped pocket." The nest is circular, or nearly so. The following account of nesting and spawning behavior is derived from Barney and Anson (1923) unless indicated otherwise.

The nests of the orangespotted sunfish are often built in colonies. In a freshly drained Iowa pond, some 960 nests were counted along a bank that was 111 m long; the nests had been excavated through an 8–10 cm deposit of mud until a solid bottom of gravel had been exposed. In Kansas, Cross (1967) reported that males of this species defended individual territories of 30–60 cm diam. When frightened from their nests, several males may move together into deep water before returning, seconds later, to their respective breeding territories.

Breeding behavior has been described by Barney and Anson: "The two fish after much maneuvering and occasional splashing come to a position with the bellies touching each other, whereupon the eggs and sperm are delivered." The females leave the nest after spawning, while the male remains on the nest until the eggs have hatched.

In central Missouri (Pflieger 1975), the red shiner and redfin shiner have been observed spawning over nests of the orangespotted sunfish.

The number of eggs produced by orangespotted sunfish is a function of the size of the female. A 105-

mm female held 4,700 eggs (Barney and Anson 1923). In southern Wisconsin (G. Lutterbie, pers. comm.), on 27 June, a 57-mm female held about 795 eggs; and in mid-July, fish 64- and 69-mm long held an estimated 718 and 1,159 eggs respectively. The transparent, amber eggs are about 0.5 mm diam. They are slightly adhesive, and cling to stones, pebbles, and sand grains on the floor of the nest, where they are continually fanned by the quivering fins of the male. Occasionally the male leaves the nest to fight off intruding males intent on feeding on the eggs; at such times the eggs are vulnerable to predation by minnows (e.g., red shiners), which will instantly swarm into an unguarded nest (Cross 1967). Barney and Anson also observed darters and spottail shiners raiding nests when the orangespotted sunfish males were engaged in fighting off their own kind.

Orangespotted sunfish eggs hatch in 5 days at water temperatures of 18.3–21.1°C (65–70°F). In Wisconsin, the growth of young-of-year has been reported as follows (G. Lutterbie, pers. comm.):

Date	No. of Fish	TL (mm)		Location
		Avg	Range	
11 Sept 1971	67	30	19–41	Rock R. (Jefferson Co.)
19 Sept. 1971	16	34	26–40	Rock R. (Jefferson Co.)
27 Sept. 1970	20	37	31–45	Rock R. (Rock Co.)

On the Mississippi River near Fountain City (Buffalo County), the average calculated lengths at the annuli were: 1—28 mm, and 2—66 mm (Christenson and Smith 1965).

In Iowa ponds, Barney and Anson (1923) determined the lengths for each year class of orangespotted sunfish: 0—10–24 mm (July to September); I—25–45 mm; II—40–55 mm; III—49–74 mm; and IV—56–93 mm. In Oklahoma (Jenkins et al. 1955), orangespotted sunfish had the following calculated growth at the annuli: 1—53 mm; 2—81 mm; and 3—99 mm; in Illinois (Lopinot 1958), these values were: 1—71 mm, 2—89 mm, 3—94 mm, and 4—137 mm.

Orangespotted sunfish that hatch early attain sexual maturity by August of the following year (i.e., at age I). The great majority, however, lay their first eggs in May of the third year of life (i.e., at age II). Barney and Anson noted that there is a normal retardation of growth as the sunfish reaches sexual maturity.

The largest Wisconsin orangespotted sunfish seen was 112 mm (4.4 in) long. In a Louisiana collection (Carver 1967), the maximum total length of this species was 147 mm (5.8 in).

In the stomachs of 11 Wisconsin orangespotted sunfish, D. Gaudet (pers. comm.) reported insect larvae (Trichoptera, Ephemeroptera, Plecoptera, Odonata, unidentifiable parts), crustaceans (*Daphnia*, copepods, *Gammarus*), mites, and ctenoid fish scales. In Illinois (Stegman 1969), 28 orangespotted sunfish had eaten crustaceans, aquatic insects, and dipterous larvae as primary foods. In 41 stomachs from Iowa fish, Kutkuhn (1955) found that insects (Trichoptera, Ephemeroptera, Diptera, Homoptera, Hemiptera) constituted 87% of the volume of food, crustaceans (Eucopepoda, Cladocera) 8% and Hydracarina 4%; he also found traces of algae and debris. In another Iowa study (Harrison 1950), stomach contents were almost 100% aquatic insect remains, but part of a butterfly and a terrestrial beetle were also observed. Barney and Anson agreed that the orangespotted sunfish feeds primarily on crustaceans and insect larvae, but they reported that it occasionally eats small fish; a 75-mm orangespotted sunfish had eaten two small individuals of its own species.

The orangespotted sunfish is able to tolerate low levels of dissolved oxygen. Gould and Irwin (1962) reported that this species had the ability to withstand oxygen concentrates of 1.7 ppm without sustaining casualties. The majority of the orangespotted sunfish tested in another study tolerated rapid changes of pH, from 7.9 to 9.2, and from 8.1 to 6.0, when the dissolved oxygen was 8 ppm (Wiebe 1931). Wiebe observed this species spawning in water at pH 9.3. Carver (1967) noted that this species was not collected in salinities exceeding 0.74 ppt.

According to Gerald (1971), male orangespotted sunfish produce courtship sounds which are species specific. Males were induced to court and to call to dead females that were manipulated on a string. Also, 11 orangespotted sunfish responded to playback of orangespotted male courtship sounds, and 3 orangespotted sunfish responded to the courtship calls of the longear sunfish.

In the Illinois-Fox river system (Waukesha County), Cahn (1927) reported that the associates of the orangespotted sunfish were the grass pickerel and the central mudminnow. In the Sugar River (Rock County), I found this species associated with: the quillback, river carpsucker, northern hog sucker, white sucker, creek chub, golden shiner, bluntnose minnow, fathead minnow, common shiner, emerald shiner, spotfin shiner, weed shiner, sand shiner, bigmouth shiner, channel catfish, black bullhead, blackstripe topminnow, johnny darter, smallmouth bass, green sunfish, pumpkinseed, and black crappie.

IMPORTANCE AND MANAGEMENT

In an Iowa pond which was stocked with adult largemouth bass and adult yearling orangespotted sunfish, the latter were apparently used extensively as forage fish by the bass. Although the bass reproduced successfully, there were no signs of orangespotted sunfish reproduction; Barney and Anson (1923) suggested that the small adult and young orangespotted sunfish served as food for the bass. Cross (1967) noted that, where it is abundant, the orangespotted is a significant forage item for larger centrarchids. On the other hand, the orangespotted sunfish may also compete for food with young bass, bluegills, and crappies (Cross 1967, Clark 1960).

Barney and Anson also noted that it may play a role in the natural history of freshwater mussels. It may be the host of glochidial stages of *Anodonta corpulenta* (Coker et al. 1921), and perhaps of other noncommercial mollusks. A natural infection of the orangespotted sunfish with the glochidia of the valuable yellow sand shell mussel (*Lampsilis anodontoides*) has been reported, but this is of doubtful significance, as the yellow sand shell has never been carried through its transformation into adult form experimentally other than on the gars.

The orangespotted sunfish has little or no value as a sport or a food fish, although it takes the hook readily when it reaches 75–100 mm (3–4 in).

It is used occasionally as an aquarium fish because of its brilliant colors, and it appears to live well in captivity as long as it has sufficient *Daphnia* and other live foods (Harlan and Speaker 1956).

This species makes a good bioassay animal because it transports and holds well, and it is not particularly excitable (Gould and Irwin 1962).

Barney and Anson (1923) suggested that in some locales, the orangespotted sunfish may be a valuable fish for mosquito control.

The standing crop of orangespotted sunfish in an Oklahoma pond was 2.9 kg/ha, with a net annual production of 1.6 kg/ha (Whiteside and Carter 1973).

Trautman (1957) noted that, as the orangespotted sunfish moved eastward in Ohio, the first specimens collected on the eastern frontier were hybrids between the orangespotted sunfish and some other sunfish species. When he collected in the same locality a few years later, after the eastern frontier had moved beyond this locality, pure orangespotted sunfishes were taken, usually in far greater numbers than the hybrids.

Bluegill

Lepomis macrochirus Rafinesque. *Lepomis*—scaled operculum; *macrochirus*—large hand, possibly in reference to the size of the pectoral fin.

Other common names: bluegill sunfish, northern bluegill sunfish, common bluegill, blue sunfish, bluemouth sunfish, sunfish, pale sunfish, chain-sided sunfish, bream, blue bream, bluegill bream, coppernosed bream, blackear bream, roach, dollardee, sun perch, strawberry bass.

Adult 143 mm, Waupaca R. (Waupaca Co.), 13 June 1960

DESCRIPTION

Body deep, strongly compressed laterally. Length 127–178 mm (5–7 in). TL = 1.25 SL. Depth into TL 2.2–2.6. Head length into TL 3.5–3.9. Mouth small, strongly oblique. Upper jaw almost reaching to anterior edge of eye; lower jaw decidedly longer than upper jaw; conical, pointed teeth in brushlike pads on upper and lower jaws, no teeth on tongue; lower pharyngeal arches moderately wide, with thin, pointed teeth. Gill rakers on first gill arch long, straight, and pointed. Opercular "ear flap" flexible. Dorsal fins 2, but broadly joined and appear as 1; base of dorsal fins less than twice length of anal fin base; first dorsal fin with 10 spines, second with 10–12 soft rays. Anal fin with 3 spines, and 10–12 soft rays; pelvic fin thoracic with 1 spine and 5 rays; pectoral fin long, pointed, and when laid forward across cheek reaching to and generally beyond anterior edge of eye; caudal fin slightly forked. Scales ctenoid, gill covers and cheeks scaled. Scales in lateral line 39–45; lateral line complete. Chromosomes 2n = 48 (W. LeGrande, pers. comm.).

Back olive brown; sides vary from brown to green, with 5–9 vertical, double chainlike bars (more prominent in young); side at times with blue or purple reflections; throat and belly white, yellow or orange-red. Ear flap black to edge. Pale blue lines extending backward from mouth and chin. Fins brown pigmented; a prominent dark blotch toward rear of soft dorsal fin, occasionally present toward rear of anal fin (in young-of-year, dorsal spot appears as a series of microscopic round, distinct chromatophores in the last few interradial membranes). Colors vary according to habitat: fish from dark waters are dark olive or almost black dorsally, and somewhat lighter ventrally; fish from clear waters are light blue-green dorsally, and almost white ventrally.

Breeding male with bright orange to rusty breast and a bluish sheen over body; pelvic and anal fins dusky.

Sexual dimorphism: In mature bluegills, the urogenital opening in the male usually terminates in a small, funnel-shaped pore; in the female, the opening resembles a small, swollen, doughnutlike ring—probably the result of a slight eversion of the urogenital tract (McComish 1968).

Hybrids: Bluegill × pumpkinseed, bluegill × green sunfish (UWSP specimens, Wis. Fish Distrib. Study 1974–1975). Other natural hybrids: bluegill × warmouth, bluegill × orangespotted sunfish, bluegill × redear sunfish, bluegill × redbreast sunfish, bluegill × longear sunfish, bluegill × spotted sunfish (Childers 1967). Artificial hybrids: bluegill × white crappie, bluegill × black crappie (Carlander 1977).

SYSTEMATIC NOTES

Synonyms are *Lepomis pallidus* (Mitchill), *Helioperca incisor* (Cuvier and Valenciennes), and *Helioperca macrochira* (Rafinesque). The Wisconsin subspecies is the northern bluegill, *Lepomis m. macrochirus* Rafinesque. The form *Lepomis machrochirus purpurascens* (Cope), which is distributed in Atlantic Coast streams from the Carolinas to Florida, may be a distinct species, according to Hubbs and Lagler (1964).

DISTRIBUTION, STATUS, AND HABITAT

The bluegill occurs in all three drainage basins in Wisconsin. Originally it was not found in the Lake Superior basin (Greene 1935), but as a result of widespread stocking it is now present and reproducing in many lakes and rivers. It is considered rare at the barriers of tributary streams to Lake Superior (McLain et al. 1965). In Waukesha County, bluegills occurred in 32 of 40 lakes sampled, and, along with the black crappie, it had the highest frequency occurrence of any species (Poff and Threinen 1963). It is present in most medium-sized streams to large rivers, and in nearly all lakes throughout the state. The bluegill is

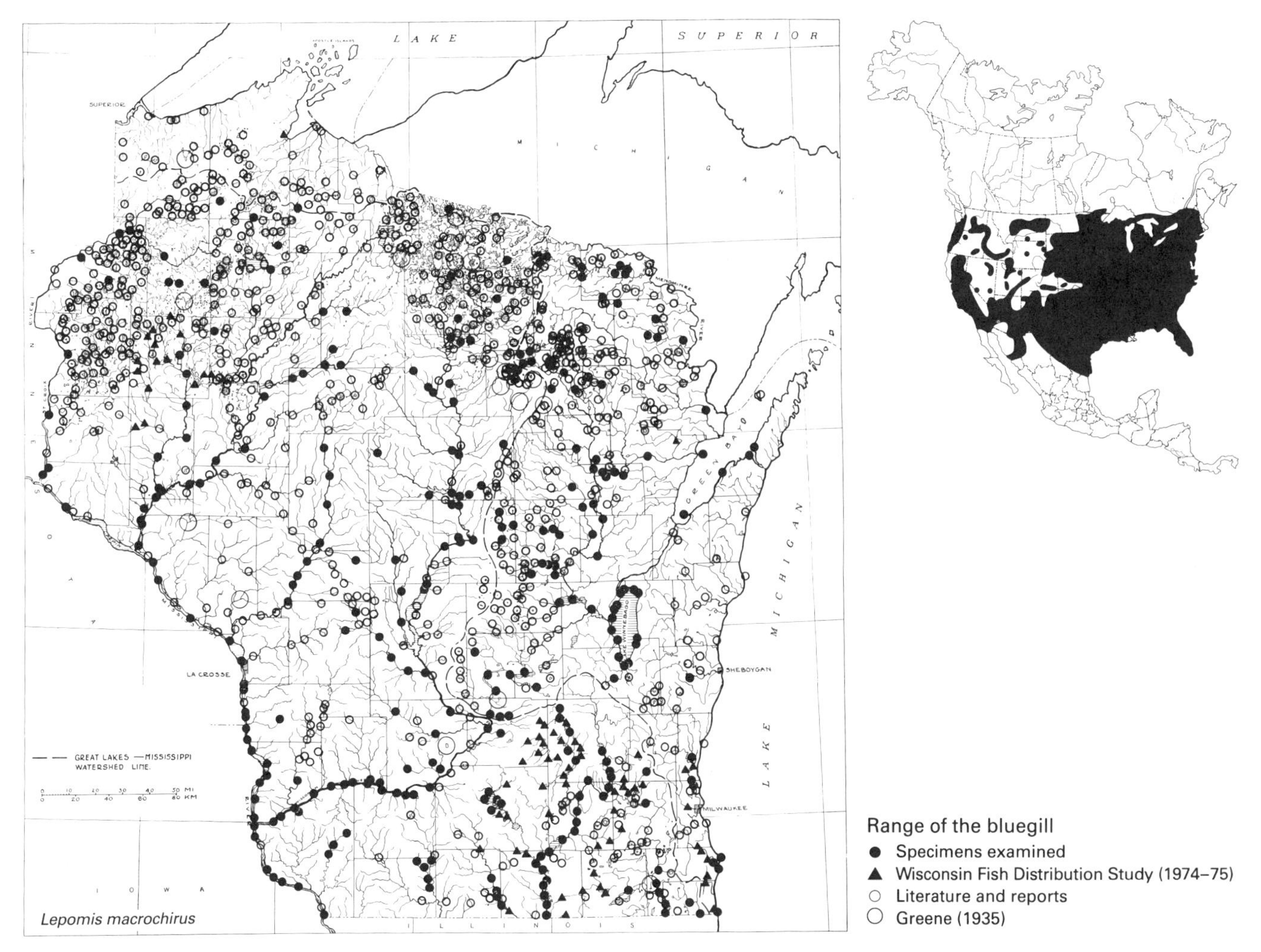

the most abundant sunfish and centrarchid in Wisconsin.

In Wisconsin, the bluegill was encountered most frequently in clear water (occasionally in slightly turbid and turbid water) at varying depths, over substrates of sand (29% frequency), gravel (20%), mud (17%), silt (11%), rubble (8%), boulders (7%), clay (4%), detritus (2%), hardpan (1%), marl (1%) and bedrock (trace). It is an inhabitant of lakes, ponds, reservoirs, and backwater sloughs, and it was found in quiet to moderately swift waters in streams of the following widths: 1.0–3.0 m (12%); 3.1–6.0 m (7%); 6.1–12.0 m (20%); 12.1–24.0 m (32%); 24.1–50.0 m (22%); and more than 50.0 m (6%). It prefers warmwater habitats with a moderate amount of rooted vegetation.

BIOLOGY

In Wisconsin, bluegill spawning occurs at water temperatures of 19.4–26.7°C (67–80°F) from late May to early August; spawning peaks in June. Clugston (1973) noted that water temperatures which exceed 20°C (68°F) for long periods may extend bluegill spawning, and that ripe female bluegills were collected all year from a primary cooling pond.

Winter aggregations of bluegills break up when the water temperature reaches 10°C (50°F) (Scott and Crossman 1973). The males appear first in the shallow water of spawning areas; they generally select a sand or gravel bar which can be hollowed out for a nest. A shallow depression, 5–15 cm deep and about 30 cm diam, is swept out by the male in water 0.8 (0.3–1.5) m deep. H. C. Miller (1963:111) has described this process:

> Nest sweeping begins with side to side undulations of the caudal peduncle while the male is horizontal and stationary. The undulations become strong, and the body bends at the base of the caudal peduncle first to one side then to the other. . . . Pectoral fins are held at right angles to the body, spread, and flat. They move alternately pushing forward and up to counter the tendency for forward or upward locomotion. Dorsal, anal, and pelvic fins are depressed. These movements bring . . . males to a nearly vertical position, slightly ahead of their starting point.

The effect of this vigorous sweeping is to stir the loose substrate material with the caudal fin, much as a broom would. Repeated sweepings create a depression, with the loosest and finest bottom materials forming a rim around the edge. The nest resembles a miniature volcanic crater that has been weathered away close to the ground (Harlan and Speaker 1956).

Occasionally a bluegill builds an isolated nest, but usually bluegills construct colonies of 40–50 nests within a radius of 18–21 m (Harlan and Speaker 1956); in some colonies, the nests almost touch one another (Snow et al. 1962). Occasionally bluegills use the nests of the pumpkinseed and the rock bass; bluegills may also use their own nests several times during the season (Carbine 1939).

The male bluegill defends the nest, before and after spawning, against all species, but most vigorously against other male sunfishes. Lateral displays, with maximum fin erection and caudal fin elevation, occur commonly among nesting male bluegills (H. C. Miller 1963). The most aggressive and frequent behavior observed in most species of *Lepomis* is the frontal threat display. In this behavior, the dorsal, anal, and pelvic fins are displayed, and the fish moves forward toward the opponent; the caudal fin has a locomotive function and is not involved in the display posture. The attack consists of a butt or a bite, usually directed at the side of the other fish, but more frequently the display ends short of attack and is better described as a thrust, rush, chase, or swipe. Miller reported bluegill attacks in which highly aggressive males rushed each other and hit mouth to mouth.

H. C. Miller (1963:122) called attention to behavior exhibited by males which she called rim circling:

> . . . Males over their nests repeatedly circle the rim of the nest with fins in Lateral Display position. As they circle, their fins and the vertical bars on the sides become darker. Color fades when the circling stops. . . . The sight of spawning fish was a stimulus which made males without partners circle their rims faster and more persistently.

The approach of females or other fish caused males to rim circle more frequently and rapidly. Since this behavior makes the performing male conspicuous, it may serve to attract females to the nest.

The factors involved in the male bluegill's recognition of the female bluegill when females of other species of sunfish are present are not clearly understood. When male bluegills were presented simultaneously with a female bluegill and a female pumpkinseed, they responded more strongly to the former (Keenleyside 1967). Male bluegills produce courtship calls which may be characterized as a series of grunts (Gerald 1971). In preliminary experiments, the response of bluegills to play back of their recorded calls indicated that bluegills may be attracted by their conspecific calls, at least during spawning.

After a female bluegill enters the nest, the male and female swim about the nest in a circular path; they eventually come to rest with the male upright and the female at an angle, with their bellies touching. A few eggs and some milt are released, and the spawning behavior is repeated. A female does not necessarily deposit all of her eggs in one nest, nor is one nest necessarily used by only one female.

The egg production of Lake Wingra (Dane County) bluegills (122–144 mm) on 25 May was estimated at 4,800 (2,900–8,000); on 29 June it was estimated at 2,900 (1,900–4,600). Churchill (1976) suggested that the earlier figure may provide a better estimate of the total production, but even that figure is probably low, since most of the fish were completely ripe at capture and may have already deposited some of their eggs. In Minnesota, Vessel and Eddy (1941) estimated fecundity for age-IV to age-VIII fish at 25–46 thousand eggs; they noted a tendency for egg production to increase with increases in the weight, age, and length of the fish.

The bluegill's eggs are small, demersal, and adhesive. Egg diameter varies from 1.09 mm after water hardening (Merriner 1971a) to 1.2–1.4 mm (Meyer 1970). Hatching occurs in 71 hr at a water temperature of 22.6°C (72.7°F), in 34 hr at 26.9°C (80.4°F), and in 32.5 hr at 27.3°C (81.1°F) (Carlander 1977). During incubation the male aerates the eggs and keeps them clean of debris with gentle fanning, and drives all intruders from the nest.

Newly hatched bluegill fry are 2–3 mm long. According to Meyer (1970), larvae are free-swimming at 5.0–5.5 mm, 3 days after hatching. At 8.9–9.4 mm all fin rays are formed. Meyer illustrated the 5.5-mm and 10.3-mm stages, and Taber (1969) illustrated the stages from 5.2–21.5 mm.

In Michigan, 4,670–61,815 bluegill fry were reported per nest—the average for 17 nests was 17,914 fry (Carbine 1939). In northern Wisconsin, Churchill (1949b) reported 22 thousand fry per nest. Shortly after hatching, the male abandons the young, which in northern Wisconsin appear in the limnetic zones from late June through July (Faber 1967).

The growth of bluegills is rapid. In Murphy Flowage (Rusk County), bluegills average about 19 mm long in August, and about 38 mm long in September (Snow et al. 1962).

Bluegills are typically aged by analysis of their

Age and Growth (TL in mm) of the Bluegill in Wisconsin

Location	1	2	3	4	5	6	7	8	9	10	11	Source
Murphy Flowage (Rusk Co).	38	74	104	135	155	170	180	203	229			Snow (1969)[a]
Clear L. (Sawyer Co.)	36	56	66	81	97	104	127	137	147			Snow (1969)[a]
Muskellunge L. (Vilas Co.) (1935–1938)												
Males	44	75	96	120	140	154	165	174	169	180	184	Schloemer
Females	44	74	98	119	135	144	158	163	166			(1939)
Flora L. (Vilas Co.)	53	72	88	110	124	138	149	163	165	176		Parker (1965)
L. Wazeecha (Wood Co.)	44	76	109	138	175	195	219					Wolff (1974)
L. Sherwood (Adams Co.)	62	91	119	133								Wolff (1974)
Upper Mississippi R., Pools 3–6	56	104	147	160	185	198						Kittel (1955)
Mississippi R. (Buffalo Co.)	51	112	163	213								Christenson and Smith (1965)
L. Mendota (Dane Co.)	43	95	135	163	181							El-Shamy (1976)
L. Wingra (Dane Co.)	50	88	122	139	152							Churchill (1976)

[a]Average empirical length for year.

scales. The annuli are generally clearly depicted, although care must be taken to identify false annuli. Coble (1970) determined that false annuli may form as a result of handling the fish, or of interrupted feeding during the growing season. Southern Wisconsin bluegills average better growth than bluegills from northern Wisconsin, although they are not as long lived. More than 500 southern Wisconsin bluegills had condition values (K_{TL}) averaging 1.83 (1.63–2.18, with the largest bluegills exhibiting the best condition).

Male bluegills grew more rapidly than females in some populations that were studied, but the differences were usually small; in a few populations, females grew larger than males (Carlander 1977). In other studies, no differences in the growth of the sexes were detected. Swingle (1956) reported a repressive factor, probably a hormone in the water, which increases with population density and retards reproduction, but does not retard it sufficiently to prevent crowding and slow growth. The growth and condition of bluegills is better in waters with strong predator populations than in waters with few predators.

In the South, a few bluegills may reproduce during their first summer of life. At Wisconsin's latitude, some individuals mature at age I, and most mature at age II or III.

In most Wisconsin lakes, an age-IV bluegill is about 15 cm long and weighs 71 g. A 227-g (8-oz) bluegill is about 7 years old. A 305-mm, 1,588-g (12-in, 3.5-lb) bluegill was taken in a fyke net from Sand Lake (Washburn County) in 1945 by Wisconsin Department of Natural Resources personnel (Fischthal 1948), and a 1,701-g (3-lb 12-oz) fish was caught in Little Clam Lake (Ashland County) in 1953 (Snow et al. 1962). A 381-mm , 2.16-kg (15-in, 4-lb 12-oz) bluegill was taken from Ketona Lake, Alabama, in 1950 (*World Almanac* 1976).

When bluegills 5.0–5.9 mm long first start to feed, their food consists of rotifers and copepod nauplii (Siefert 1972). At 7 mm other rotifers and *Cyclops* spp. appear in the digestive tracts. In 8-mm fish, cladocerans become dominant in the diet; they include *Bosmina, Ceriodaphnia, Chydorus, Daphnia,* and *Polyphemus.*

Adult bluegills feed mainly on aquatic insects, small crayfish, and small fish (Carlander 1977). In six fish (avg 147 mm) examined from Lake Geneva (Walworth County), aquatic vegetation (*Chara*) occurred in five stomachs, insects (midge larvae, mayfly and stonefly naiads, insect fragments) in three, and snails in one (Nelson and Hasler 1942). In Lake Mendota (Pearse 1921a), four bluegills had eaten insect larvae (0.5% volume), insect adults (11.2%), snails (0.8%), oligochaetes (0.8%), plants (75.6%), and algae (10%). In Green Lake (Green Lake County), 165 bluegill digestive tracts held insect larvae (33% volume), insect pupae (1.7%), insect adults (12.9%), mites +, crayfish (9.2%), amphipods (14.8%), cladocerans +, snails (0.5%), sponges (0.5%), plants (21.3%), algae (1.7%), bottom ooze (2.2%), and sand (2.2%).

In three northern Wisconsin lakes, 65% of the diet of bluegills consisted of insects, including Diptera larvae, mayfly nymphs, caddisfly larvae, dragonfly nymphs, ants, and miscellaneous insects (Couey 1935). Plants constituted 10% of the total food consumed, but made up 30% of the food from one lake; in the other two lakes no plant food had been eaten. The plants consisted mostly of fragments of leaves and terminal buds of large aquatic plants, and a small amount of filamentous algae. The mollusks present were snails from the genera *Physa, Planorbis,* and *Amnicola.*

Kitchell and Windell (1970) noted that plant material makes up about 20% of the volume of the annual diet of natural bluegill populations. In controlled feeding experiments in the laboratory, those bluegills that were fed algae (*Chara*) in addition to a maintenance level of animal food showed a slightly greater percentage increase in weight than comparable fish fed on a maintenance diet of animal food alone. It was also evident that bluegills do gain some nutritional value from algae; however, bluegills neither will nor can consume enough *Chara* to meet metabolic requirements.

Leeches and fish eggs are also eaten by bluegills. When food is scarce, bluegills commonly eat their own eggs; male bluegills, especially, eat early spawns (Swingle and Smith 1943).

The optimum temperature for feeding by bluegills has been given as 27°C (81°F), and the maximum temperature at which bluegills feed has been given as 31°C (88°F) (Kitchell et al. 1974, Stuntz 1976). Feeding decreases at temperatures below 10–12.8°C (50–55°F). Baumann and Kitchell (1974) found that bluegills tended to be limnetic during the daytime, feeding largely on plankton, but that they moved to littoral areas about sundown to feed on benthic organisms and organisms attached to or living on aquatic plants. The bluegill is a grazing fish, taking this and that, and often hunting individual dipteran midge larvae or plankters. It is also a sight feeder that readily takes insects which fall on the surface of the water; these are eaten with a sucking, popping sound. Bluegills feed almost continuously during the growing season, although feeding peaks occur at 1500 hours in the afternoon and again in the evening after 2030 hours (Keast and Welch 1968). Intermittent feeding occurs at night; in one population that was examined, only 20% of the fish had empty stomachs by 0730 hours.

The kind of food eaten by bluegills may be dictated in part by the kinds of associate fishes that are present. Werner and Hall (1976) demonstrated that, when the bluegill is stocked alone, prey from the vegetation made up 61% of its diet; when bluegills were stocked with pumpkinseeds and green sunfish, however, the bluegills concentrated on prey from the open water column, such as *Bosmina* and *Cyclops*. The bluegill's long, fine gill rakers retain small prey, making such a niche shift possible. Similarities in the food eaten by bluegills and green sunfish may not be what they seem (Sadzikowski and Wallace 1976). The green sunfish has a larger mouth, and ingests food items of a larger average size; thus, even though these two species consume similar kinds of food, they may actually exploit quite different food sources.

In winter, the bluegill feeds sparingly, usually on planktonic cladocerans and copepods (Moyle 1969). In summer, at a mean water temperature of 20°C, bluegills may consume average weekly rations of up to 35% of the body weight (about 5% per day); during the winter, when the water averages between 2 and 3°C, bluegills may consume less than 1% of body weight per week (about 0.14% per day) (Lagler et al. 1977).

The temperature preferred by young bluegills in the laboratory was 31.2°C (88.2°F) (Beitinger 1974). When suddenly exposed to water at 36.1°C (97°F), 35% of the fish died, and, among those fish that survived, thermoregulatory performance was slightly impaired. Nickum (1967) found that bluegills were able to withstand sudden changes in temperature as great as 11.1°C (20°F), if the upper lethal temperature limit was not exceeded; delayed mortalities sometimes occurred, however. Young bluegills in a Lake Monona (Dane County) thermal outfall area had estimated acclimation temperatures between 29.4 and 31.3°C (84.9 and 88.3°F) (Neill and Magnuson 1974); the highest body temperatures among 31 bluegill specimens was 31.8°C (89.2°F). Clugston (1973) found bluegills at 35–41°C (95–105.8°F) in heated effluent waters from a power plant.

When juvenile bluegills in aquariums were given a choice between an environment at their preferred temperature (31.0°C) with a large, socially dominant bluegill present, or an environment at a higher or a lower temperature without the presence of the dominant fish, they selected the latter (Beitinger and Magnuson 1975).

In winterkill lakes, the toleration threshold of bluegills for dissolved oxygen was about 0.6 ppm (Cooper and Washburn 1949). Moore (1942) determined an oxygen threshold of 0.8 ppm for the bluegill. Bluegills will not tolerate low oxygen nearly as well as northern pike, perch, and bullheads (Snow et al. 1962). Bluegills and largemouth bass are among the first fish to die off in winterkill lakes.

Woodbury (1941) presented evidence of a sudden mortality of adult bluegills when oxygen in Lake Waubesa (Dane County) reached a super-saturation level during late April. In death all of the fish looked normal, except for small gas bubbles under the skin and in the fin rays. The gills were damaged extensively, and most filaments contained gas emboli large enough to block the capillaries and to obstruct blood flow. Analysis of the water showed very high amounts of dissolved oxygen caused by algal bloom.

Trama (1954) found that bluegills tolerated a pH ranging from 4.00 ± 0.15 to 10.35 ± 0.15. Although there was 100% survival at these ranges, adverse physiological reactions occurred. Bluegills have been taken in water with 4.5 ppt salinity (Bailey et al. 1954).

Bluegills travel in loose schools, and 10–20 fish can often be seen swimming together. Activity and feeding are greatest at dawn and dusk, although feeding occurs at low levels during other times of the daily cycle. Bluegills on the Mississippi River were most active from 0800 to 1000 hr and from 1600 to 2200 hr (Ranthum 1969). During the day, large bluegills remain in or near cover (Stuntz 1976), while at night they disperse into all areas of a shallow lake. In early spring, when vegetation has not yet emerged to provide cover, bluegills select habitats in areas of shade, or in areas where cover is permanent, such as in the shelter of a beaver lodge or a fallen tree. According to Stuntz, the substrate is important in habitat selection only during the spawning season; temperature does not appear to influence habitat selection in the field. In a deep, northern Wisconsin lake (Hile and Juday 1941), bluegills, rock bass, and smallmouth and largemouth basses inhabit the warmwater of the epilimnion, most commonly at depths of 3 m. The young occupy the shallows continuously.

In Lake Wingra (Dane County) during September, bluegills moved onshore after sunset and offshore after sunrise. All size classes sampled appeared to participate in these movements (Baumann and Kitchell 1974). In winter, bluegills remain near the bottom of a shallow lake, or they may collect below the discharges of power plant condensers (Snow et al. 1962). In the spring, they migrate up sluggish streams or into channels which have warmed up before the main body of water.

The bluegill has a home range particularly during the spawning period. In an Iowa study (Kudrna 1965), 60% of the larger bluegills that were displaced had homed. When bluegills were released in a displaced area, however, they swam about as if searching before they began to home.

In the Platte River (Grant County), fish associated with 6 bluegills were: the white sucker (47), central stoneroller (17), longnose dace (8), hornyhead chub (140), creek chub (1), bluntnose minnow (61), suckermouth minnow (3), common shiner (88), rosyface shiner (25), sand shiner (1), Ozark minnow (20), stonecat (3), johnny darter (7), fantail darter (21), smallmouth bass (11), and green sunfish (2).

IMPORTANCE AND MANAGEMENT

Bluegill fingerlings are preyed upon by largemouth bass, northern pike, yellow perch, black crappies, pumpkinseeds, bullheads, and by bluegills themselves. Herons and otters take smaller bluegills. Two- to three-year-old bluegills are eaten by adult largemouth bass and by northern pike; however, the bodies of larger bluegills are too deep to be swallowed by predators.

The bluegill is a host to the glochidial stage of the following mussels: *Amblema plicata*, *Fusconaia flava*, *Megalonaias gigantea*, *Anodonta grandis*, *Quadrula metanevra*, *Quadrula nodulata*, *Pleurobema cordatum*, *Actinonaias carinata*, *Carunculina parva*, *Lampsilis ovata*, *Lampsilis radiata luteola*, *Ligumia recta*, and *Ligumia subrostrata* (Hart and Fuller 1974).

The bluegill in Wisconsin is perhaps the best known and the most sought-after sunfish. It is easily caught. Small terrestrial or aquatic baits, including worms, grasshoppers, crickets, and grubs, are all acceptable to the bluegill. Artificial popping bugs and flies are particularly effective when bluegills are concentrated in the shallows during nesting. Wintertime jigging in weed beds, with a fly grub for bait, also produces excellent results. The bluegill is a game fighter, carries the lure in tight circles, and uses the flat of its side against the pull of the line.

In Pools 4 to 6 on the Mississippi River (Kittel 1955), the bluegill, carp, black crappie, and white bass yielded the greatest numbers taken per trap net lift. High yields persisted between the years 1957 and 1977 (Ebbers and Hawkinson 1978). The estimated sport fishery catch of bluegills in Pools 4, 5, 7, and 11 for 1967–1968 was 311,008 fish weighing 48,140 kg, or about 154 g (⅓ lb) per fish (Wright 1970). In 1970, the bluegill provided catch rates of 0.31 and 0.34 fish per man hour—the highest for any species in two Vilas County lakes (Serns and McKnight 1974). From 1955 through 1970, a total of 373,520 fish of various species were caught by 53,637 anglers from Murphy Flowage (Rusk County); of these, 312,342 (84%) were bluegills (Snow 1978).

In Wisconsin, bluegills are not permitted in the commercial catch, but liberal sport fishing regulations exist. In inland waters, an aggregate of 50 panfish, including bluegills, may be caught in 1 day. In most boundary waters there is no bag limit, except in Wisconsin-Minnesota waters, where there is a limit of 25 per day (Wis. Dep. Nat. Resour. 1979).

As a food fish, the bluegill is highly respected, and it is often referred to as the "bread and butter fish." Its flesh is firm, white and flaky. Since the flesh has little fat, bluegills may be kept frozen in storage for long periods.

The bluegill is an easily cared-for aquarium fish, and, because it is readily available, it is perhaps our most common native fish kept in home aquariums.

Dense populations of bluegills are possible because they are largely primary consumers, producing fish flesh directly from the most basic foods. In many of Wisconsin's lakes, the bluegill is the most common sport fish present. Lake Wingra (Dane County), for instance, is a very productive lake, with an average standing crop of about 494 kg/ha of fish over 75 mm long (Churchill 1976). Most of the crop consists of panfishes, and about 75% of the biomass consists of bluegills. During one period of study, the biomass of bluegills over 75 mm long varied from 140 to 500 kg/ha, while the number of bluegills over 2 years old varied from 7,000 to 25,000 per hectare. In October 1972, Churchill estimated a population of 3.4 million bluegills in Lake Wingra that were age I or older.

From Stewart Lake (Dane County), C. Brynildson (1955) recovered 440 kg/ha of fish, which were mostly bluegills, and he felt that the recovery was incomplete. On the other hand, in Escanaba Lake (Vilas County) from 1956 through 1969, bluegills made up 3% or less of the available standing crop of sport fishes (Kempinger et al. 1975). In some lakes managed for walleyes, coho salmon, and other sport species, bluegill numbers may be low, with correspondingly low returns to the angler (Serns and McKnight 1974).

The stunting of bluegills and yellow perch occurs in many waters throughout Wisconsin, and has often been called the number one fish management problem in the state. Wisconsin and other states have attempted to correct the problem by reducing or eliminating these populations through seining, trapping, angling, and the use of poisons (e.g., rotenone and antimycin). Predators have been introduced in some waters to curb bluegill numbers. Where it has been possible to do so, levels have been lowered in lakes or impoundments to concentrate fish for removal, or to facilitate predation.

In Flora Lake (Vilas County), bluegills, pumpkinseeds, and hybrids of these two species responded favorably in linear rate of growth after their numbers had been reduced by trapping, but only the pumpkinseeds were heavier at the overall mean length (Parker 1958). In Cox Hollow Lake (Iowa County), a new impoundment, stocked bluegills, largemouth bass, and northern pike showed an initial rapid population expansion and superior growth, followed by a tremendous decline in both population size and growth (Dunst 1969). The majority of Cox Hollow Lake anglers during the 1970s caught many small, thin bluegills that were less than 15 cm (6 in) long.

When stunted bluegills are transferred to a lake that has no existing sport and panfish populations, phenomenal growth may occur. Bluegills 97–152 mm long and weighing 11–71 g were placed in Sand Lake (Washburn County), where previous populations had been winterkilled; within 1 year the bluegills were 188–226 mm long and weighed 153–338 g. In that year they had increased their average lengths approximately 1.7–1.9 times, and their average weights 9–17 times (Fischthal 1948). Two years after the fish population of Stewart Lake (Dane County) had been removed and the lake restocked with 722 largemouth bass fingerlings and 2 pairs of adult bluegill breeders, the lake was opened to fishing. An estimated 300 bass (330–406 mm long) and 2,000 bluegills (127–203 mm long) were creeled during the opening day of fishing (McCutchin 1949).

Attempts have been made to control extremely slow-growing bluegill populations by introducing predators. In Clear Lake (Sawyer County), where the bluegills appeared to be suffering from intense intraspecific competition, muskellunge were stocked at several times the normal level, and walleyes were heavily stocked (Snow 1968). There was no appreciable change in the growth of the bluegills, and no drastic change in their abundance—they continued to make up 85–95% of the total population. The walleyes showed poor survival, which raised the issue of their importance as a predatory species. Snow suggested that, when the density of a bluegill population is above a certain unknown level, predator stocking can exert little, if any, control on the bluegill population. The stocking of northern pike in Murphy Flowage (Rusk County) also failed to reduce the numbers of bluegills; in fact, the numbers of bluegills, particularly small ones, continued to increase, while their growth continued to decline. The impact of the stocked pike on the native pike population and on angler harvest was unfavorable (Snow 1974a).

The failure of predators to control stunted bluegill populations is mentioned in the literature (Beyerle 1971, Carlander 1977). An evaluation of the effects of thinning on panfish populations was provided by Buchanan et al. (1974). Carlander suggested that bluegill growth stops when the carrying capacity of a given body of water is reached, i.e., when any factor becomes limiting. For example, growth slowed after thermal stratification occurred and oxygen depletion concentrated bluegills near the surface.

In addition to the limiting factors that affect their growth bluegills over age III to IV sustain an annual mortality rate of 57–99% (Carlander 1977). In Murphy Flowage (Rusk County), Snow (1978) determined that bluegills sustained a total average mortality rate of 61% annually, and an estimated annual natural mortality rate of 53% in the absence of fishing.

Even where management techniques succeed in

reducing bluegill populations, success is usually temporary, and overcrowding and stunting recur within a few years. It is difficult to achieve a balance in the ecosystem which keeps populations at an optimum level.

The bluegill is commonly stocked in new farm impoundments and in newly dug farm ponds. At Delafield (Waukesha County), Mraz and Cooper (1957b) demonstrated that bluegill reproduction in ponds was more consistent than that of carp, largemouth bass, and black crappies. Bluegills spawned successfully in all ponds; they averaged nearly 10,000 fish per hectare in six trials, and ranged from 1,235 to 33,900 young fish per hectare. Such a reproductive capacity soon leads to overcrowding unless a relatively large population of predator fish has been established before the bluegills are introduced.

Although largemouth bass and bluegills are a recommended combination of species for farm ponds in many states, this combination is not recommended in Wisconsin. Klingbiel et al. have summarized the problem in Wisconsin (1969:14–15):

> . . . Generally bluegills become overpopulated and stunted. These fish are of no value because they are too large for largemouth bass to eat, and too small for angling. Bluegills will also compete for food with the smaller bass and will eventually stop bass reproduction by eating the young. Bass-bluegill management has been successful in very few ponds in Wisconsin.

Rock Bass

Ambloplites rupestris (Rafinesque). *Ambloplites*—blunt armature; *rupestris*—living among rocks.

Other common names: northern rock bass, redeye, redeye bass, goggle eye, rock sunfish.

Adult 129 mm, Blake Cr. (Waupaca Co.), 7 June 1960

DESCRIPTION

Body robust, compressed laterally. Length 152–203 mm (6–8 in). TL = 1.25 SL. Depth into TL 2.7–3.3. Head length into TL 2.9–3.4. Mouth large, slightly oblique. Upper jaw extending to beyond middle of eye, and lower jaw projecting beyond upper jaw; small, blunt teeth in broad bands on upper and lower jaws; pharyngeal pads with teeth at back of throat. Dorsal fins 2, but broadly joined and appear as 1; base of dorsal fins twice as long as anal fin base; first dorsal fin with 10–12 spines, second with 10–12 rays. Anal fin with 5–7 spines and 9–11 soft rays; pelvic fin thoracic with 1 spine and 5 rays; pectoral fin rounded, short, and when laid forward across the cheek does not reach eye; caudal fin scarcely forked. Scales ctenoid, gill covers, cheeks, and back of head scaled. Scales 39–43 in lateral line; lateral line complete. Chromosomes 2n = 48 (W. LeGrande, pers. comm.).

Dorsal region of head, back, and upper sides brown to olive; ventral region lighter. Eyes bright red to orange. All fins pigmented; vertical fins with distinct white spots posteriorly. Each scale pocket below lateral line with a prominent black spot, forming 8–10 horizontal rows of spots. In young up to 51 mm, sides variably marbled in black and white. Breeding males blackish, with eye color intensified.

Sexual dimorphism: In male, a single urogenital opening behind the anus; in female, 2 openings (genital and urinary) behind the anus (Moen 1959).

Hybrids: Artificial rock bass × black crappie, rock bass × bluegill, rock bass × banded sunfish, rock bass × warmouth, and rock bass × largemouth bass (Hester 1970, Tyus 1973).

DISTRIBUTION, STATUS, AND HABITAT

In Wisconsin, the rock bass occurs in the Mississippi River, Lake Michigan, and Lake Superior drainage basins. It is present in the shallow waters of the Great Lakes, and in many of the softwater lakes in northern Wisconsin, but it is less common in lakes southward.

The rock bass is common in medium to large streams and in lakes throughout Wisconsin, except in the southwestern quarter, where it is rare. According to McLain et al. (1965), it is common in the mouths of tributaries to Lake Superior. In some lakes where the waters are becoming enriched, the rock bass population has declined. This species was common in the Rock River between Hustisford and Watertown up to 1920, but has since become rare in that area (H. Neuenschwander, pers. comm.).

Although the rock bass is found in many kinds of water, it shows a distinct preference for clear, cool to warming waters over a gravel or rocky bottom, with some vegetation present. It was encountered in clear water (60% frequency), slightly turbid water (27%), and turbid water (13%) of varying depths, over substrates of sand (26% frequency), gravel (20%), mud (13%), rubble (12%), boulders (12%), silt (9%), bedrock (4%), clay (2%), detritus (1%), hardpan (1%), and marl (1%). It was found in lakes and reservoirs, and in streams of the following widths: 1.0–3.0 m (6% frequency), 3.1–6.0 m (15%), 6.1–12.0 m (9%), 12.1–24.0 m (31%), 24.1–50.0 m (24%), more than 50 m (16%).

BIOLOGY

In Wisconsin, the rock bass moves into areas of very shallow water during late May and early June when water temperatures reach 15.6–21.1°C (60–70°F). Spawning is initiated when water warms to 20.5–21°C (69–70°F) and may continue to 26°C (79°F) (Carlander 1977). Spawning takes place in water from a few centimeters deep to more than 1.0 m deep, in circular, dish-shaped nests. The male builds the nest by fanning out sand and debris over a bottom of coarse sand or gravel to create a depression of 20–25 cm (8–10 in) diam.

Details of the spawning behavior of rock bass are provided by Trautman (1957), Breder (1936), and Breder and Rosen (1966). Immediately preceding and during the spawning season, adult females congregate in pools. A female approaches a nest only when

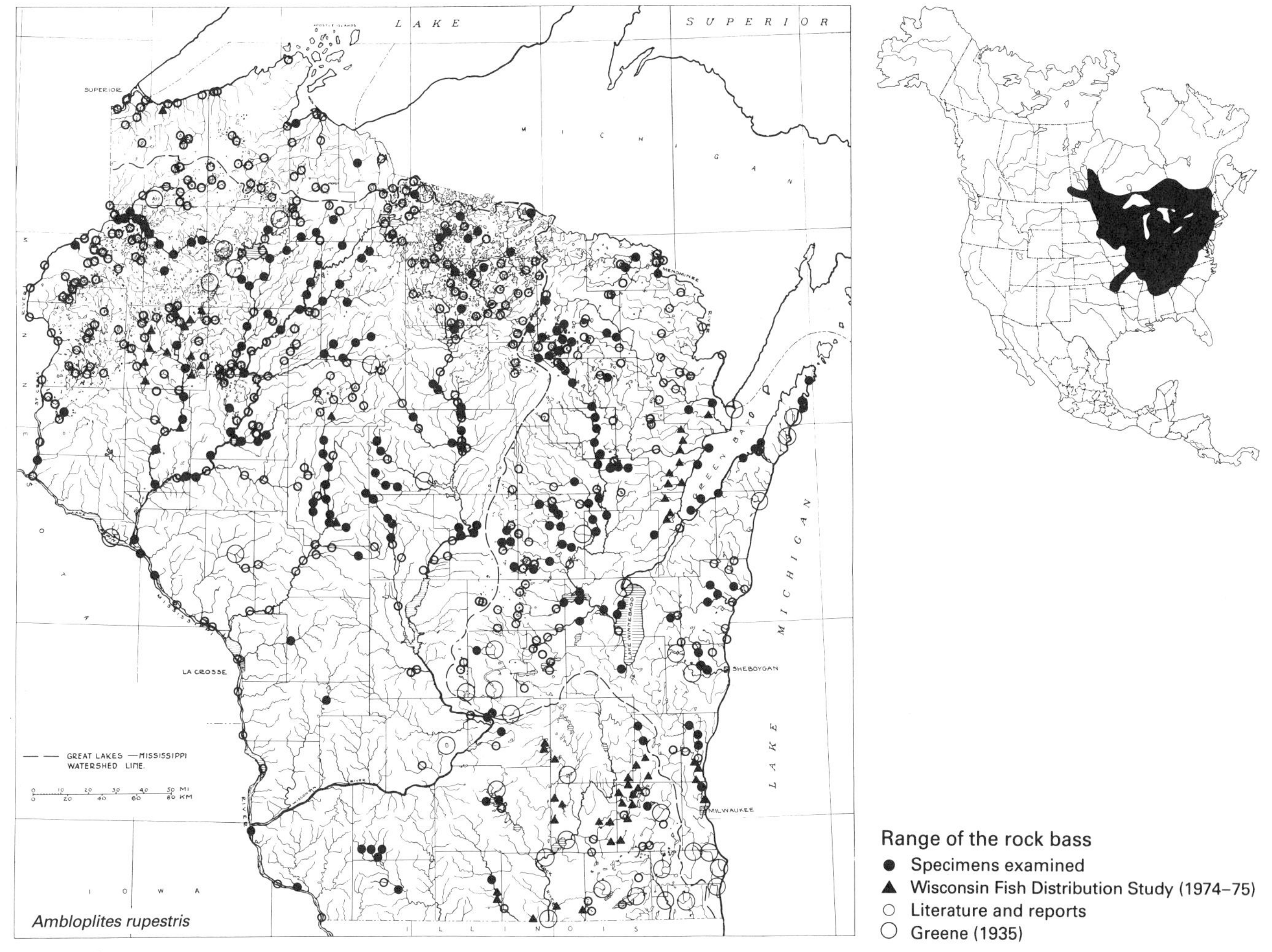

she is ready to deposit her eggs. She is driven into the nest by the male, who guards her carefully until the eggs have been deposited. During spawning and fertilization, the female reclines on her side and the male remains upright. The two fish engage in a peculiar rocking motion in a head-to-tail position. Only a few eggs at a time are extruded, and at each deposition milt is extruded by the male. This behavior may continue for an hour or more, after which the female leaves the nest and does not return. The eggs are carefully looked after by the male, who takes up a position above the nest, and every now and then fans the eggs with his fins. A few days after the eggs have hatched, the fry gradually rise out of the nest; the male soon leaves them to shift for themselves.

Observations of rock bass in aquariums disclosed a female with a distinctly blunt and red ovipositor who attempted to mate with a male that was fanning a batch of eggs. She quivered considerably, and the two fish performed the peculiar rocking motion in a head-to-tail position. This male continued with little interruption to fan the eggs he was guarding. During the fanning period, males in the aquarium drove off large crayfish (*Cambarus*), which were kept as scavengers, whenever the crayfish got within a few centimeters of the eggs. Such struggles continued for an hour until the crayfish eventually withdrew.

A 173-mm, 136-g female rock bass captured 7 June from Blake Creek (Waupaca County), had ovaries 14.2% of her body weight. She held an estimated 6,300 mature (orange) eggs, 1.7–1.9 mm diam, and a small number of immature (white-yellow) eggs, 0.7–1.3 mm diam. In Minnesota (Vessel and Eddy 1941) the fecundity of rock bass varied from 2,000 to 11,000 eggs, depending on the size of the fish. Females 18–20 cm long and weighing 227–340 g produced 2,000–7,000 eggs. The average female lays about 5,000 eggs.

Rock bass eggs are adhesive, and hatch in 3–4 days at water temperatures of 20.5–21.0°C (69–69.8°F) (Eddy and Surber 1947). In Michigan (Carbine 1939), the number of rock bass fry per nest varied from 344 to 1,756; there was an average of 796 fry for each of the nine nests counted.

Fish (1932) illustrated and described the 10.5-mm stage. The young rock bass remain for several months in shallows near or within vegetation.

In Wisconsin, the growth of young rock bass varies with the latitude and with the characteristics of the water:

Date	No. of Fish	TL (mm) Avg	TL (mm) Range	Location
11 June	2	20	19–21	Wolf R. (Langlade Co.)
9 Aug.	3	27	25–29	L. Poygan, south shore (Winnebago Co.)
8 Aug.	2	39	39–40	L. Poygan, north shore (Winnebago Co.)
10 Aug.	11	35	29–39	L. Mendota (Dane Co.)
19 Aug.	13	28	19–37	L. Winnebago (Winnebago Co.)
18 Sept.	48	36	29–55	Namekagon R. (Washburn Co.)
20 Sept.	33	39	25–50	Butternut L. (Price Co.)
1 Oct.	15	43	37–61	Flambeau R., south fork (Price Co.)

The paper on Wisconsin rock bass by Hile (1941) is a classic in the treatment of growth data and in the comparison of growth increments from different years.

The calculated weights for the Muskellunge Lake rock bass, years 1 through 11, were: 1, 4, 10, 20, 36, 56, 82, 108, 141, 165, and 187g (Hile 1942).

The general growth curves for the Lake Nebish population show that male rock bass grow more rapidly than females, and that the differential growth of the sexes is not distinctly apparent before the fourth year. Hile noted that most of the season's growth had been completed by the time of capture in late July and early August. Good growth was correlated positively with high temperatures, especially in June and September. Good growth and heavy precipitation in June also were correlated positively. Hile suggested that the correlation between rainfall, fluctuations in growth, and the strength of year classes may depend on the enrichment of Lake Nebish by materials washed in during periods of heavy downpour. Temperatures may have a direct effect on the physiological processes of the fish, and may also affect the abundance of fish food in the lake.

In Nebish Lake, most rock bass reach maturity at ages II and III. The slower-growing fish do not reach maturity until age IV (Hile 1941). Most rock bass survive for 6–8 years, although individuals of this species have lived at least 18 years in captivity (Breder 1936).

Normally rock bass do not exceed 227 g (.5 lb) in weight, but a 794-g (1-lb 12-oz) individual was caught from Green Lake (Green Lake County) on 14 February 1971. A 1.5-kg (3-lb 5-oz) rock bass was taken in Lake Cadillac, Michigan, in 1946. Scott and Crossman (1973) reported an individual 340 mm long which weighed 1.64 kg (3 lb 10 oz). Adams and Hankinson (1926) reported rock bass weighing up to 1.70 kg (3.75 lb).

In Illinois, young-of-year rock bass fed on cladocerans, *Cyclops*, corixid, chironomid and neuropteran larvae, and some land insects (Forbes 1880). In northern Wisconsin lakes, insects (including dipteran, ephemerid, and caddisfly larvae, dragonfly nymphs, and ants) were the most important foods consumed by rock bass, followed by crayfish and fish (Couey 1935). In Green Lake (Green Lake County), rock bass had ingested crayfish (64% volume), cladocerans (12%), insect larvae (11.8%), mites (4.2%), amphipods (2.9%), insect pupae (0.6%), ostracods (0.2%), and sand (4.2%) (Pearse 1921a). In Lake Mendota (Dane County) rock bass, Pearse found crayfish (50%), cladocerans (14%), plant materials (10%), amphipods (5.8%), insect adults (5%), algae (3%), insect larvae (2%), and sand (11.2%). Of 24

Age and Growth (TL in mm) of the Rock Bass in Wisconsin

Location	No. of Fish	1	2	3	4	5	6	7	8	9	10	11	12	13	Source
Birch L. (Washburn Co.)	117	46	71	112	150	175	208								Snow (1969)[a]
Bucks L. (Rusk Co.)	27	56	130	183	229	249	292								Snow (1969)[a]
Clear L. (Sawyer Co.)	33	46	58	99	124	157	178								Snow (1969)[a]
Nebish L. (Vilas Co.)															
Males	395	43	77	112	145	170	187	199	209	216	224	233			Hile (1941)
Females	586	41	76	110	138	159	173	183	190	198	205	212	218	227	
Allequash L. (Vilas Co.)		44	67	88	111	139	163	179	190						Hile (1942)
Muskellunge L. (Vilas Co.)		40	62	83	106	128	149	168	185	203	214	222			Hile (1942)
Trout L. (Vilas Co.)		39	62	87	113	148	181	198	216	227					Hile (1942)
Wolf R. (Oneida Co.)	26	27	66	113											B. Mauch (pers. comm.)
Pecatonica R. (Iowa Co.)	5	41	73	148											B. Mauch (pers. comm.)

[a]Empirical means, not measured to annulus.

stomachs examined from Lake Geneva (Walworth County), 4 held *Micropterus* sp., 8 held mimic shiners, and 14 held crayfish (Nelson and Hasler 1942).

Keast (1965) noted that the rock bass was a fairly diverse feeder, and that the larger fish avoided small food items because of the high energy outlay necessary to obtain a sufficient quantity of them. He found that there were two periods of feeding: in the evening from 1700 to 2100 hr, and in the morning from 0730 to 1200 hr.

During the summer in lakes of northern Wisconsin, the rock bass was found at 14.7–21.3°C (58.5–70.3°F) (Hile and Juday 1941); in streams of southern Ontario (Hallam 1959) it occurred at 20.7°C (69.3°F). The preferred temperatures of rock bass from Lake Monona (Dane County) were 27.3°C (81.1°F) in the laboratory and 27.5°C (81.5°F) in the field (Neill and Magnuson 1974). In a shallow Michigan pond (Bailey 1955), a water temperature of 38°C (100.4°F) resulted in the deaths of large numbers of fish, including rock bass.

In winter, rock bass inhabit deeper water, where they remain in a condition of semihibernation. After spawning they are usually found in 2–5 m of water in the region of submerged vegetation (Schneberger 1973). In lakes of the northeastern highlands during July and August, rock bass were taken down to the following depths (depths at which the greatest number were taken given in parentheses): Nebish Lake 10.9 m (6 m); Muskellunge Lake 12.9 m (4 m); and Trout Lake 6.9 m (5 m). Fish of all sizes showed a preference for the warmer epilimnion, except in Nebish Lake, where larger rock bass were found in the upper thermocline, 2–4 m below the smaller fish. Penetrations by rock bass into deeper regions of the water are rare. In Lake Geneva (Walworth County), Nelson and Hasler (1942) captured most rock bass at 9 m, although small numbers occurred down to 12 m.

Moore (1942) determined that rock bass were unable to tolerate oxygen tensions of 2.3 ppm at winter temperatures. In the laboratory at 22.8°C (73°F), Bouck (1972) noted that rock bass hyperventilated and stopped feeding during the low-oxygen periods, and showed impaired growth when the oxygen level of the water was lowered from near saturation to 3 ppm for an 8 hr period per day over 9 consecutive days.

Mercury-contaminated yellow perch and rock bass from Lake St. Clair, which were stocked in two earthen ponds and held for a 26-month period, increased 88% and 183% respectively in mean weight during that period (Laarman et al. 1976). Although the concentrations of total mercury in the fillets had declined 53% in the yellow perch and 59% in the rock bass, all of the reduction in mercury concentrations was attributable to dilution by growth. The data suggested an initial redistribution of residues from other tissues to the muscle and a continued incorporation of background amounts of mercury during growth.

A trapping study (Spoor and Schloemer 1939) revealed that rock bass were captured in far greater numbers at night than during the day. The highest rate of capture was between 1900 and 2100 hr, and a slight increase occurred between 0300 and 0400 hr. The study offered little evidence of daily inshore and offshore movements.

In an extensive tagging effort in Missouri streams, Funk (1957) classified the rock bass as sedentary; 64% of the rock bass were captured within 1.6 km (1 mi) of the point of release and 98% within 40 km (25 mi). In Indiana (Scott 1949), rock bass showed a strong tendency to remain in a very limited area, ranging within a 1.6 km section of stream during the 2-year study; however, a few fish wandered widely—as much as 30 km (19 mi) upstream and 13 km (8 mi) downstream from the point of tagging. MacLean and Teleki (1977) determined that rock bass along the north shore of Long Point Bay in Lake Erie inhabit a restricted home range during the nonreproductive season, but undertake a 36–40 km (22–25 mi) spawning migration to the Inner Bay in the spring.

In northern waters, the rock bass is often associated with the smallmouth bass, perch, bluntnose minnow, hornyhead chub, rosyface shiner, northern hog sucker, johnny darter, rainbow darter, and fantail darter.

The rock bass can change color with great rapidity—from silver to almost solid black, or to silver with black splotches (Eddy and Surber 1947). Pflieger (1975) called it "the chameleon of the sunfish family."

IMPORTANCE AND MANAGEMENT

It is not known to what extent rock bass are preyed upon by other species. The rock bass does serve as a host to the glochidial stage of a number of important mussels, including *Amblema plicata*, *Amblema marginata*, *Arcidens confragosa*, *Actinonaias carinata* and *Lampsilis radiata luteola* (Hart and Fuller 1974).

The rock bass is not considered an important sport fish in Wisconsin, and is usually caught only incidentally while fishing for other species. It will take worms, white grubs, minnows, spoons, spinners, bucktails, cut-bait, crayfish, and grasshoppers, and occasionally it will rise to a fly. It usually hits the angler's lure with much vigor and begins a strenuous fight, but it tires easily.

In the Mississippi River, the estimated sport fishery catch of rock bass in Pools 4, 5, 7, and 11 during 1967–1968 was 2,888 fish weighing 340 kg (747 lb) (Wright 1970). The numbers of rock bass in the catch diminish rapidly as one moves downstream. In three Vilas County lakes during 1970 (Serns and McKnight 1974), the estimated catch of rock bass was 1,015 from Stormy Lake, 1,001 from Black Oak Lake, and 605 from Laura Lake. The fish averaged 15–18 cm long.

In Escanaba Lake (Vilas County), from 1946 to 1969, 13,171 rock bass weighing 1,657 kg (3,652 lb) were caught by anglers (Kempinger et al. 1975). The estimated population, based on rock bass 10 cm and larger, varied annually from 1,000 to 5,600 from 1956 through 1963. In Murphy Flowage (Rusk County), from 1955 to 1969, 8,084 rock bass weighing, 1,059 kg (2,335 lb) were caught by angling (Snow 1978).

At one time, Wisconsin imposed a size limit on this species. Currently all minimum size limits, bag limits, and closed seasons have been eliminated (Wis. Dep. Nat. Resour. 1979). The rock bass is classified as a sport fish in Wisconsin.

There are conflicting reports concerning the palatability of the rock bass, but most reports indicate that the flesh of fish from clear, cool water is firm and white and has an excellent flavor.

The propagation and stocking of rock bass are not commonly practiced in Wisconsin or in neighboring states. It is a prolific fish in nature. When the fish population was thinned by trapping in Flora Lake (Vilas County), rock bass exhibited a marked increase in their linear growth rate, even though the total number of rock bass present also increased (Parker 1958). In a Michigan lake, partial poisoning with rotenone resulted in an increased growth rate in rock bass of all ages (Beckman 1941).

White Crappie

Pomoxis annularis Rafinesque. *Pomoxis*—sharp opercle; *annularis*—having rings, the vague vertical bars of the sides.

Other common names: silver crappie, pale crappie, ringed crappie, crappie, crawpie, silver bass, white bass, newlight, bachelor, campbellite, white perch, strawberry bass, calico bass, tinmouth, papermouth, bridge perch, goggle-eye, speckled perch, shad, John Demon.

Adult 166 mm, L. Winnebago (Calumet Co.), 17 Aug. 1960

DESCRIPTION

Body deep, strongly compressed laterally (slab-sided). Length 165–229 mm (6.5–9.0 in). TL = 1.29 SL. Depth into TL 2.7–3.9. Head length into TL 3.2–4.0. Mouth large, moderately oblique. Upper jaw reaching at least to middle of eye; lower jaw heavy, tip jutting beyond tip of upper jaw; minute conical, pointed teeth in brushlike pads on upper and lower jaws; lower pharyngeal arches long and narrow, with numerous fine teeth. Gill rakers on first arch close-set, long, slender, and straight; about 28. Dorsal fins 2, but completely joined and appear as 1; 6 (4–7) spines, 12–16 rays, base length of dorsal much shorter than distance from dorsal origin to eye; base length of dorsal fin equal to or slightly shorter than base length of anal fin. Anal fin with 6 spines and 17–18 rays; pelvic fin thoracic, with 1 spine and 5 rays; pectoral fin elongate, and when laid forward across cheek reaching eye; caudal fin slightly forked. Scales ctenoid, in lateral line 39–46; lateral line complete. Chromosomes 2n = 48 (W. LeGrande, pers. comm.).

Back and upper head dark green with many blue, green, and silvery reflections; sides lighter, with 5–10 vague, vertical bands composed of dark blotches which become indistinct on lower sides of body; ventral region of head and belly whitish. Eyes yellow to green. Irregular dark opercle spot scarcely larger than diam of pupil of eye. Dorsal, caudal, and anal fins heavily vermiculated, contrasting with round to oblong light-colored spots (which are less evident in the anal fin); paired fins unpigmented to lightly pigmented. Spots almost absent in large adults (especially the females) from turbid waters.

Breeding male usually darker and more distinctly marked than female; males may be as heavily spotted as male black crappie (Trautman 1957).

Hybrids: White crappie × black crappie (Hubbs 1955, Trautman 1957), white crappie × flier (Burr 1974). Hybrids are predominantly males (Schneberger 1972b).

DISTRIBUTION, STATUS, AND HABITAT

In Wisconsin, the white crappie occurs in the Mississippi River and Lake Michigan drainage basins, where it is near the northern limit of its distribution. It has not been taken from the Lake Superior watershed. In the past 50 years this species has extended its distribution to the lower Chippewa–Red Cedar basin, the midreaches of the Wisconsin River, the Madison lakes region, the Beaver Dam and Crawfish rivers, and the Fox-Wolf river system of the Lake Michigan basin. Earlier records from the Lake Michigan drainage were only from the Root River in extreme southeastern Wisconsin (Greene 1935).

Although some range extension was undoubtedly a result of this species' natural expansion into suitable habitats, some also resulted from the intended or the inadvertent stocking of white crappies with other species. Stocking has been suggested as the source of the Smith Lake record of the upper St. Croix drainage (Sawyer County) (Greene 1935, Schneberger 1972b). The white crappie's continued presence in the St. Croix River above the St. Croix Falls Dam (Polk County) has been verified by two specimens (UWSP 4819) taken in June 1974. In the Madison Lakes, white crappies were first reported in the 1944 carp seining of Lake Wingra, where, according to Noland (1951), the crappies appeared in large numbers and were the most abundant panfish in the lake. Noland concluded that the white crappie had probably been introduced as a result of fish rescue and transfer operations.

The establishment of the white crappie in the Fox-Wolf river system of the Lake Michigan drainage is of recent occurrence, although it could have been overlooked by Greene in his survey during the 1920s. Its means of entry is uncertain, but three possibilities exist: (1) via the Fox-Wisconsin canal at Portage, (2)

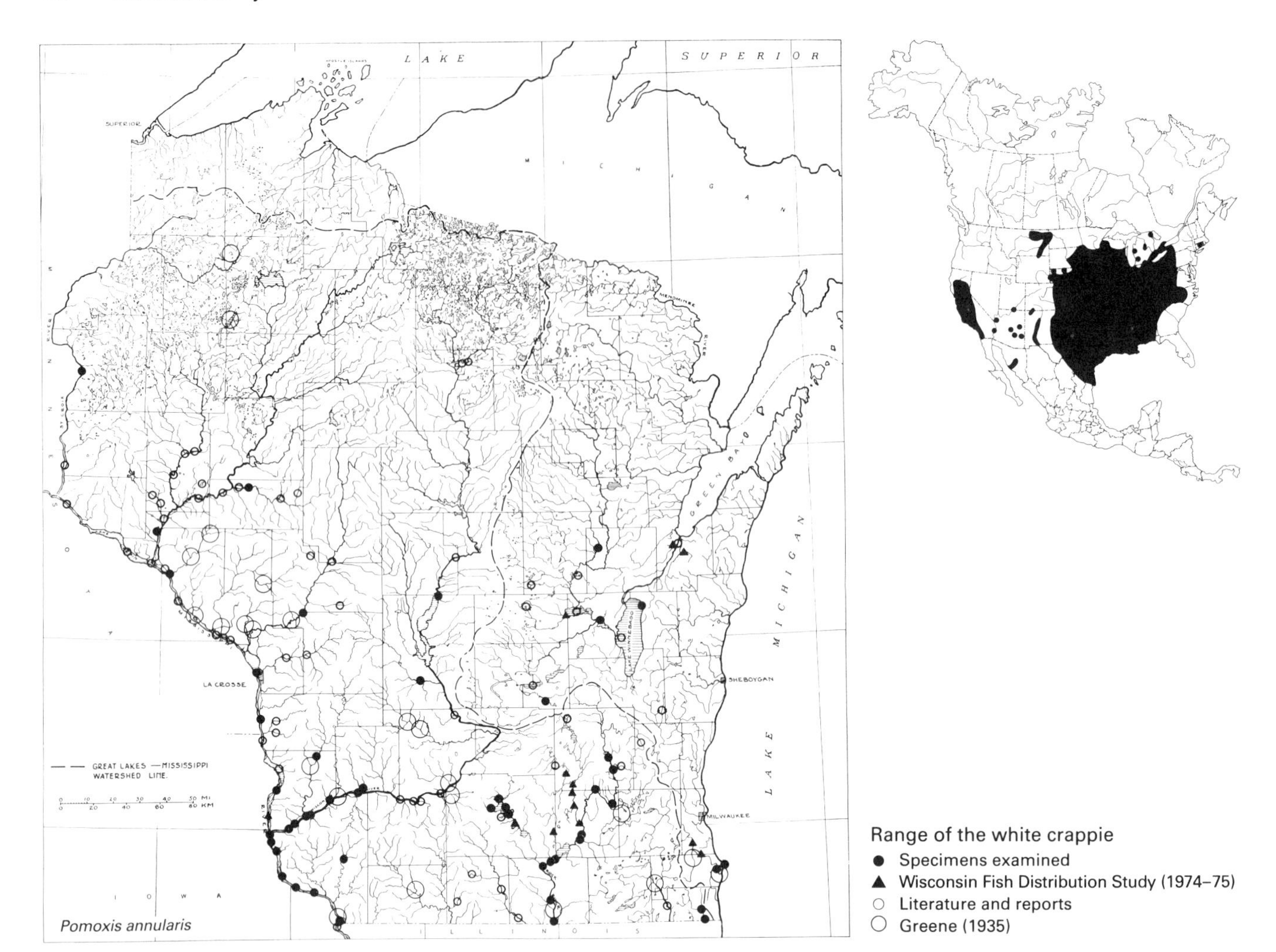

Range of the white crappie

via fish rescue and transfer operations from the Mississippi River, and (3) via southern Lake Michigan into Green Bay. The first two means of entry seem most likely, because if the species had entered from Lake Michigan it would have left some seed stock in tributary streams along western Lake Michigan, and this is not the case. Earlier Greene (1935) suggested that the white crappie's means of entry into the Root River watershed (Milwaukee and Racine counties) may have been through the drainage ditch connecting the Illinois-Fox river and the Root River watersheds during high water.

Although Cahn (1927) reported that the white crappie was found in nearly all of the larger lakes and in some of the smaller lakes in Waukesha County, it was more recently reported (Poff and Threinen 1963) in only 2 of 40 lakes sampled in Waukesha County. Priegel (1967a) considered the white crappie rare in Lake Winnebago, and V. Hacker (pers. comm.) reported it as common in Kingston Pond of the Grand River (Green Lake County). The white crappie is common to uncommon in the Rock, the lower Wisconsin, and the Mississippi rivers. In addition to extending its range in Wisconsin, the white crappie appears to be increasing in numbers.

In Wisconsin, the white crappie occurs in sloughs, backwaters, landlocked pools and lakes, and in the pools and moderate currents of moderate-sized to large streams. It inhabits areas of sparse vegetation. It prefers slightly turbid to turbid water, and occurs at varying depths within the warm, shallow-water upper layer, over substrates of sand, mud, gravel, rubble, clay, and silt.

BIOLOGY

Rutledge (1971) has prepared a bibliography of literature containing specific life history references to white and black crappies. The spawning of the white crappie has been dealt with at length by Hansen (1951, 1965), Morgan (1954), and Siefert (1968, 1969a); unless otherwise indicated, the following account is based on these sources.

Spawning occurs in May and June at water temperatures of 14–23°C (57–73°F) with most spawning occurring at 16–20°C (61–68°F). Contrary to what has been observed in other centrarchid species, the white crappie does not desert the nest when the water temperature drops. The white crappie may nest at depths of 5 cm to 1.5 m, generally within 10 m of the shore, on hard clay or gravel, or on the roots of aquatic or terrestrial plants. Hansen reported white crappie nests in water 10–20 cm deep along an undercut sod bank of red clay. In one nest, the eggs were attached to blades of lawn grass and to grass roots which were dangling in the water only 5 cm below the surface; the fish guarded this nest from a position below the eggs.

The white crappie nests in colonies, and as many as 35 nests have been reported in one colony; solitary nests are rare. Nests in circular colonies were spaced 0.5–0.6 m apart; those in linear colonies were found to be 0.6–1.2 m apart. White crappies nest in or near plant growth if it is available. Well-defined nest depressions are generally absent, and a nest may consist of a circular area 12–15 cm across, from which a thin layer of silt has been swept. In some habitats, the nest may be 30 cm across. Siefert has described nest construction (1968:254):

> Nest preparation consisted of short vigorous periods (3 to 5 sec) of body movement as the abdomen touched, or nearly touched, the substrate. During this time the fish remained in an upright position. Sediment was swept out of the nest with fin and body movements, but only the loose silt layer was removed and a well-defined nest depression was not constructed. Occasionally the female exhibited the same nest sweeping movements as the male immediately before and during the spawning run.

Territorial behavior was observed among white crappies places in breeding pens. The territorial crappies were aggressive, and vigorously chased all intruders from the defended area, usually by snapping or butting at intruders, and by flaring their opercles. Territories averaged 1 m^2, and generally were established near a submerged tree branch or a corner of the pen; they did not always correspond to a later nesting site.

Spawning acts by white crappies in breeding pens were observed between 0850 and 1600 hr, and most spawning began before 1200 hours. Siefert described spawning behavior (1968:255):

> . . . The female, after being repulsed from the territory a number of times, would finally stop retreating from the territory when chased, and would be accepted by the male. After circling the nest several times the female would position herself beside the male and face the same direction as the male. They would remain motionless for a few seconds, and then the sides of their bodies would touch. Both fish then would slowly move forward and upward with their bodies quivering. The female would slide under the male in the process, pushing him up and to the side, causing the pair to move in a curve as the sex products presumably were emitted. The male exerted a steady pressure on the female's abdomen. Each spawning act lasted from 2 to 5 sec with most lasting 4. Intervals between acts ranged from one half to 20 min. Maximum number of acts in one spawning run was 50, and the longest duration of any run observed was 145 min.

In two instances, Siefert watched an intruding male quickly position himself on the unoccupied side of the female and participate in the spawning act; however, immediately following spawning, he was chased from the area by the defending male. On another occasion, a female mated with a second male guarding a nest site which was about 1 m away from the territory of her first mate. The male of the primary spawning vigorously chased the female away from the second male's nest; the second male, in turn, chased the invading first male back to his own territory.

Following egg laying, the male white crappie guards the eggs (Breder and Rosen 1966:424):

> . . . The male fish jealously guarded the eggs and kept the water about them in constant motion with his pectoral fins. Other fish were kept away and objects that came near the eggs were savagely bitten. If a person placed his hand within six inches of the surface of the water, the male fish would leap clear of the water and strike the hand viciously.

The white crappie's eggs average 0.89 mm diam, and are demersal and adhesive. They are usually scattered over an area larger than the actual nest (Siefert 1968). Nests surrounded by *Chara* contain more eggs on the periphery than in the middle. The eggs sampled from two white crappie nests showed evidence of multiple spawning over a period of less than 2 days; the eggs were in two distinct stages of development.

Lake Wingra (Dane County) females, 159–187 mm TL, held an average of 12,000 (6,200–24,000) eggs on 25 May. On 29 June, females 163–176 mm TL averaged 3,300 (300–5,100) eggs (Churchill 1976). These egg counts appear to be low, and probably represent females which had already partly spawned. In Ohio (Morgan 1954), the total number of eggs produced by white crappies varied from 1,908 in a 149-mm fish to 325,677 in a 330-mm fish.

The hatching time of white crappie eggs kept at water temperatures of 21.1–23.3°C (70–74°F) varied between 24 and 27.5 hr (Morgan 1954). The embryos hardly encircled the yolk at hatching, and the movements of the larvae were quite feeble. The larvae were 1.215–1.98 mm long, and so poorly developed that Morgan did not expect them to live. Siefert (1969b) found that the minimum total length of white crappie upon hatching was 2.56 mm, and that the yolk material was absorbed before the fish reached 5 mm.

Morgan (1954) illustrated and described the white crappie's embryonic development from fertilization through the 6-mm stage (14.5 days after hatching). There has been no evidence of scale formation on fish less than 16 mm TL, and the first fully scaled fish observed was 27 mm long (Siefert 1965). Larval white and black crappies (5–16 mm long) in Missouri River reservoirs can be separated by the number of post-anal myomeres and the number of total myomeres: for the white crappie, these are 19 or less and 30–31 respectively; for the black crappie, they are 21 or more and 32 respectively (Siefert 1969b). In larvae greater than 16 mm, there are 5–6 dorsal spiny rays in the white crappie, and 7 in the black crappie.

In western reservoirs, the white crappie larvae are initially collected in nursery areas near coves and boat basins, but during the summer they move out of protected areas into the open reservoir (Siefert 1969a). In Lewis and Clark Lake, South Dakota, the young are in the pelagic zone during July and August, but in September larger numbers of fish are taken with bottom trawls in water less than 6 m deep (Gasaway 1970).

The average yearly growth of male and female white crappies is about the same; however, late in life females grow faster than males (Morgan 1954).

Determining the age of white crappies by counting the number of annuli present is difficult, because the annulus may be formed over a period of several months, or not at all during some years (Morgan 1954, Hansen 1951).

In Iowa, the condition (K_{TL}) of white crappies 102–260 mm long averaged 1.29 (1.11–1.42) (Neal 1961). In Illinois, the highest coefficient of condition (K_{SL}) for a 279-mm fish was 3.38 (Hansen 1951).

Maturity occurs at age II in some individuals, but most white crappies are mature at ages III and IV (Nelson 1974, Siefert 1969a, Morgan 1954).

As a rule, the white crappie is short-lived; few survive more than 5 years. In an Illinois study (Starrett and Fritz 1957), a natural death rate of over 50% occurred in large broods during their third year of life. An exceptionally old fish—age XIII, with a weight of 1.62 kg (3 lb 9 oz)—was reported by Harlan and Speaker (1956) from Corydon Reservoir, Iowa.

The largest white crappie reported by Christenson and Smith (1965) from the Mississippi River (Buffalo County) was 325 mm (12.8 in) long. A 1.59-kg (3-lb 8-oz) fish was taken by Cahn (1927) from the Neosho Mill Pond (Dodge County). A record white crappie, 533 mm long and weighing 2.35 kg (21 in and 5 lb 3 oz), came from Enid Dam, Mississippi, in 1957 (*World Almanac* 1976).

The first foods eaten by white crappies are rotifers and copepod nauplii, followed, as the fish increase in size, by *Daphnia, Diaptomus,* and *Leptodora*. Zooplankton are almost the only food eaten during the first year, but a few amphipods and chironomids are taken in late fall and spring (Carlander 1977).

Entomostraca continue to be a significant food throughout the life of white crappies in most waters, but insects and forage fish are usually the major foods of large crappies. In Pool 19 of the Mississippi River, the food of 83 white crappies included *Hexagenia* naiads (42%) and *Potamyia flava* larvae (11%); the remainder of the food was composed chiefly of immature Diptera, Odonata, Zygoptera, Hemiptera, and fish (Hoopes 1960). In a later study (Ranthum 1969), fish were the most important food item in the white crappie diet, followed closely by chironomids, and *Hexagenia* mayfly naiads and adults; other insects contributed little to the food volume. Five of the crappies in this study contained two or three gizzard shad each; another contained a bluegill or a crappie; in another specimen four minnows were found. Schneberger (1972b) has suggested that the white crappie eats its own young.

In an Iowa study (Neal 1961), plant materials and insect adults never accounted for more than 5% of the stomach contents of white crappies. Food items found in the stomachs included ostracods, fish eggs, plant seeds, algae, Hydracarina, nematodes, unidentified Crustacea, and insect eggs.

In a Pennsylvania reservoir, during most months young white crappies fed exclusively on zooplankton, mostly in the morning and early afternoon; an

Age and Growth (TL in mm) of the White Crappie in Wisconsin and Other Northern Waters

Location	1	2	3	4	5	6	7	8	9	Source
L. Wingra (Dane Co.) 1972–1973	92	140	165	175	179					Churchill (1976)
Mississippi R. backwater (Buffalo Co.)	66	152	231	277	297					Christenson and Smith (1965)
Clear L. (Iowa)	72	144	184	208	231	272	272			Neal (1961)
Avg for northern waters	66	138	193	238	268	286	313	318	363	Carlander (1977)

estimated 14–17 hr period elapsed for the food to pass through the stomach (Mathur and Robbins 1971). These researchers suggested that plankton feeding by adult white crappies of all sizes is related to their long gill rakers.

Gammon (1973) determined that the optimum water temperature range for the white crappie, based on its selection and avoidance of thermal zones, was 27.0–28.5°C (80.6–83.3°F). Triplett (1976) noted that the initiation of power plant operations resulted in a nearly continuous congregation of fish in the outfall area. The maximum temperature at which the white crappie has been captured was 31.1°C (88°F) (Proffitt and Benda 1971). The white crappie is active at summer water temperatures as high as 30.6°C (Morgan 1954). During the winter months when warm-acclimated fish in a warmwater outfall (28–30°C) were forced into a cold lake water (0–2°C), they manifested apparent oxygen hunger, and continued exposure to the cold water was fatal (Agersborg 1930). From June to August, no white crappies were found in water with less than 3.3 ppm oxygen (Grinstead 1969). This species tolerates pH ranging from 6.2 to 9.6 (Schneberger 1972b).

The white crappie is a schooling species. White crappies in the Mississippi River are more nocturnal than diurnal; their activity peaks between 2000 and 2200 hr and between 0400 and 0600 hours. There is a rapid decline in movement between the evening and morning peaks and a more gradual decline between the morning and evening peaks. In Ohio, test net catches have shown that white crappies are most active between 1700 hours and 0500 hours (Morgan 1954). Sport fishermen are most successful in the late afternoon or early evening, at which time the crappies come into the shallow waters near shore to feed on minnows and small fishes, or on insects that appear on the water (Harlan and Speaker 1956).

In a Missouri study, Funk (1957) determined that 30% of the tagged white crappies moved less than 1.6 km (1 mi) from the point of release; 40% moved less than 16 km (10 mi); and 70% moved less than 40 km (25 mi). The movements of white crappies appear to be random or haphazard. In Illinois, four white crappies were recaptured 5.6, 12.9, 25.8, and 29.1 km upstream, from tagging points; others were retaken 1.8 and 3.2 km downstream (Thompson 1933). White crappies have a strong, positive reaction to water currents, and this may be a factor in their migration (Schneberger 1972b). Siefert (1969a) determined that a substantial portion of tagged white crappies emigrated from Lewis and Clark Lake (South Dakota) into the tailwaters below Gavins Point Dam; these fish passed unharmed through the turbines, since no other water releases occurred, and contributed to the tailwater white crappie fishery.

In the Mississippi River at Wyalusing (Grant County), 14 white crappies were associated with the following species: longnose gar (10), bowfin (1), gizzard shad (89), quillback (187), smallmouth buffalo (1), shorthead redhorse (3), golden redhorse (7), common carp (2), central stoneroller (1), silver chub (1), golden shiner (110), bullhead minnow (145), pugnose minnow (8), emerald shiner (340), spotfin shiner (245), spottail shiner (589), river shiner (428), sand shiner (6), bigmouth shiner (1), tadpole madtom (1), northern pike (1), white bass (119), yellow bass (4), yellow perch (5), walleye (2), western sand darter (5), river darter (1), logperch (11), johnny darter (28), smallmouth bass (1), largemouth bass (31), pumpkinseed (1), bluegill (173), orangespotted sunfish (8), rock bass (1), black crappie (178), brook silverside (118), and freshwater drum (17).

IMPORTANCE AND MANAGEMENT

The white crappie is preyed upon by large game fishes, including largemouth bass, smallmouth bass, northern pike, and muskellunge (Schneberger 1972b).

The white crappie is host to the glochidial stages of the following mollusks: *Amblema plicata, Fusconaia ebena, Fusconaia flava, Megalonaias gigantea, Quadrula pustulosa, Elliptio dilatata, Anodonta grandis, Lasmigona complanata, Actinonaias carinata, Carunculina parva, Lampsilis ovata, Lampsilis radiata luteola, Lampsilis teres, Ligumia recta,* and *Proptera laevissima* (Hart and Fuller 1974).

The white crappie is taken with small minnows and a variety of artificial baits. Hansen (1951) noted that in the morning more black crappies were caught than white, and that in the evening the reverse was true. Extreme care must be taken in landing this fish, since its mouth is very tender, and the hook is easily pulled out. The white crappie is considered an excellent panfish.

Compared to the black crappie, which is much more abundant in Wisconsin and has a statewide distribution, the white crappie is of limited angling and economic importance. Commercial fishing for either crappie species is not allowed in Wisconsin. However, liberal angling regulations for inland waters permit a daily bag limit of 50 panfish, including crappies and there is no bag limit in boundary waters, except in Wisconsin-Minnesota waters, where the daily bag limit is 25 panfish (Wis. Dep. Nat. Resour. 1979). Up-to-date fishing regulations should be consulted for current regulations, since these are subject to change.

In suitable waters, the production of white crappies may be considerable. In Lake Wingra (Dane County), the estimated population and biomass (kg/ha) during May 1972 were 31,000 and 12 kg/ha respectively; during May 1973, they were 120,000 and 56 kg/ha; and during May 1974, they were 43,000 and 13 kg/ha (Churchill 1976). In Alabama (Swingle and Smith 1939), 10 white crappies weighing 1.87 kg (4 lb 2 oz) were stocked in February in a 0.72-ha, unfertilized pond; on draining the pond the following November, 3,780 white crappies weighing 16.38 kg (36 lb 2 oz) were recovered.

The white crappie is an easy fish to propagate. It thrives in fairly warm water in shallow ponds, lakes, and reservoirs where the bottom may be muddy. Vegetation is not essential to its existence. When fish of this species are needed for stocking in newly created or rehabilitated waters, sufficient numbers can be obtained by netting in waters where an abundant population exists. Consideration should be given, however, to the desirability of introducing this species in areas where limited growth may occur.

Fluctuations in the numbers of white and black crappies have been reported from a number of waters (Ball and Kilambi 1973, Starrett and Fritz 1957). In Beaver Reservoir, Arkansas, Ball and Kilambi noted that black crappies were dominant in the early impoundment period, whereas white crappies became dominant during the late impoundment period. They ascribed this pattern of dominance to the feeding habits of the two species: white crappie adults consumed fishes all year round, whereas black crappie adults consumed benthic insects in the spring and fishes in other seasons; the apparent reduction in the number of insects and earthworms during the late impoundment gave the advantage to the white crappie.

As is the case in other species of the centrarchids, stunting occurs among white crappies where the fish population level is too high for the available food. It has been shown that the growth of white crappies improved after population was thinned (Carlander 1977), but there was no clear-cut improvement in growth following the removal of carp from fish populations (Scidmore and Woods 1960). After an extensive review of the factors affecting crappie growth and dominant year classes, Rutledge and Barron (1972) suggested a number of methods to correct stunting. These included increasing the food supply; stocking predators like largemouth bass and northern pike (there has been little evidence of success with the longnose gar); the introduction of sterilized fish to control year class abundance; encouraging crappie harvest; and thinning populations by the use of toxicants, by trapping and seining, and by fluctuating the water level.

Black Crappie

Pomoxis nigromaculatus (Lesueur). *Pomoxis*—sharp opercle; *nigromaculatus*—black spotted.

Other common names: crappie, crawpie, calico bass, strawberry bass, speckled crappie, specked perch, speckled bass, speck, grass bass, Oswego bass, shiner, moonfish, barfish, silver bass, lake crappie, butter bass, bitterhead, banklick bass, lamplighter.

Subadult 116 mm, L. Winnebago (Fond du Lac Co.), 19 Aug. 1960

Adult (living) (Wisconsin DNR photo).

DESCRIPTION

Body deep, strongly compressed laterally (slab-sided). Average length 178–254 mm (7–10 in). TL = 1.30 SL. Depth into TL 2.9–3.5. Head length into TL 3.3–3.8. Mouth large, moderately oblique. Upper jaw reaching at least to middle of eye; lower jaw heavy, tip jutting beyond tip of upper jaw; minute conical, pointed teeth in brushlike pads on upper and lower jaws; lower pharyngeal arches long and narrow, with numerous fine teeth. Gill rakers on first arch close-set, long, slender and straight; about 29. Dorsal fins 2, but completely joined and appear as 1; 7–8(6–9) spines, 14–16 rays; base length of dorsal equals distance from dorsal origin to eye; base length of dorsal fin equal to or slightly shorter than base length of anal fin. Anal fin with 6–7 spines and 17–18 rays; pelvic fin thoracic, with 1 spine and 5 rays; pectoral fin elongate, and when laid forward across cheek reaching eye; caudal fin slightly forked. Scales ctenoid, in lateral line 34–44; lateral line complete. Chromosomes 2n = 48 (W. LeGrande, pers. comm.).

Back and upper head dark green with blue, green, and silvery reflections; sides lighter, with irregular pattern of distinct dark blotches, and no vertical bands (although in some individuals partial bands on upper back and caudal peduncle); ventral region of head and belly whitish. Eyes yellow-brown. Irregular, dark (often diffuse) opercle spot scarcely larger than diam of pupil of eye. Dorsal, caudal, and anal fins heavily vermiculated alternating with round to oblong yellow to pale green spots; paired fins unpigmented to lightly pigmented. Individuals from clear water show sharply contrasting patterns; fish from turbid waters look pale.

Breeding male head and breast dark, usually darker and more iridescent than in female.

Hybrids: Black crappie × white crappie (Hubbs 1955, Trautman 1957). Artificial black crappie × bluegill, black crappie × warmouth, black crappie × largemouth bass, black crappie × rock bass (Hester 1970).

DISTRIBUTION, STATUS, AND HABITAT

The black crappie occurs in all three drainage basins in Wisconsin. This glacial species is well distributed throughout the state, except in the streams of the driftless area of southwestern Wisconsin.

The black crappie originally did not range through the central and northcentral portions of Wisconsin, in the area bounded by Waushara, Forest, Bayfield, and Dunn counties (Greene 1935). Within this area, which represents over 25% of the surface area of Wisconsin, only a few collection sites were known up to the late 1920s. Greene did not encounter this species in the counties along Lake Michigan north of Ozaukee County, except for those draining into the western edge of Green Bay. Since the 1920s, however, the black crappie has been extensively introduced into many lakes and ponds throughout the state, including those areas from which it was not originally known. Between 1920 and 1925, the Wisconsin Department of Natural Resources made available large numbers of fish for stocking, mostly black crappies rescued from Mississippi River backwaters.

The black crappie is common in lakes and larger rivers throughout the state. It is abundant in the

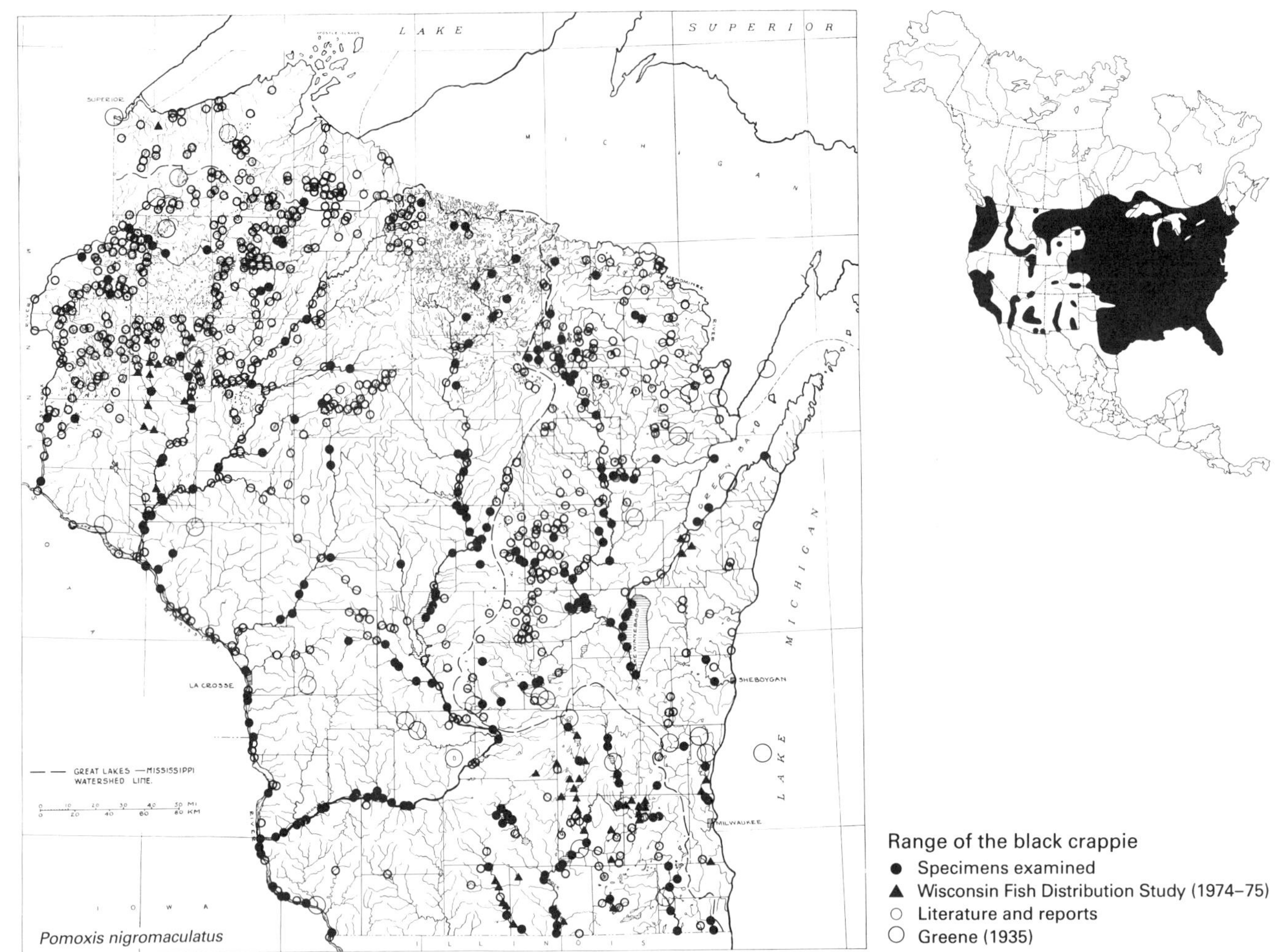

sloughs and backwaters of the Wisconsin and Mississippi rivers, and it is occasionally captured in the lower extremities of the larger tributaries of the Wisconsin River. It is abundant in Pewaukee Lake and Lake Poygan (Becker 1964a, 1964b), and in Lake Winnebago it is the most abundant species of the sunfish family (Priegel 1967a). In Waukesha County, the black crappie and the bluegill appeared in 32 of 40 lakes sampled (Poff and Threinen 1963)—the highest frequency of occurrence of all fishes in those lakes. In the upper Mississippi River, the black crappie is more common than the white crappie (Barnickol and Starrett 1951, Kittel 1955, P. W. Smith et al. 1971). At the barriers of tributary streams to Lake Superior, the black crappie occurs sporadically, and is "occasionally taken from 4 Wisconsin streams" (McLain et al. 1965). This species is the native crappie of Lake Wingra (Dane County), and was ranked as a dominant fish species in the lake during the first two decades of this century (Noland 1951). However, in the 1944 carp seining in Lake Wingra, the black crappie was outnumbered 3.5 to 1 by the white crappie, and in 1972–1974, by a ratio of 3 to 1 (Churchill 1976).

The black crappie is usually found in the clear, quiet, warm water of ponds, small lakes and bays, and in the shallow waters of large lakes, sloughs, backwaters, and landlocked pools. It is almost always associated with abundant growths of aquatic vegetation. In Wisconsin, it was encountered in clear to slightly turbid water, over substrates of sand (32% frequency), mud (20%), gravel (18%), silt (9%), rubble (9%), boulders (9%), clay (2%), hardpan (1%), and detritus (1%). It occurred in streams of the following widths: 1.0–3.0 m (2%), 3.1–6.0 m (9%), 6.1–12.0 m (10%), 12.1–24.0 m (38%), 24.1–50.0 m (31%), and more than 50 m (10%). It prefers clearer, deeper, and cooler waters than does the white crappie (Schneberger 1972a).

BIOLOGY

In Wisconsin, the black crappie usually spawns in May and June; however, during a colder season, spawning may be delayed until July. Favorable spawning temperatures range from 17.8 to 20°C (64 to 68°F), although activity may begin at 14.4°C (58°F) (Sigler and Miller 1963). The male sweeps out a nest of 20–23 cm diam, near *Chara* or other vegetation, in sand or fine gravel; nests also have been observed on muddy bottoms. Nests are built in shallows of 25 cm–0.6 m, as well as at depths up to 2 m or more. The nests are generally spaced 1.5–1.8 m apart.

Pearse (1919) observed about a dozen male black crappies on nests in a lagoon of Lake Wingra (Dane County) on 20 May. The nests were bare places on a clay bottom, adjacent to submerged aquatic plants along the edge of an undercut clay bank, in 0.6 m of water. In Illinois, a black crappie nest was hollowed out under the leaves of a water parsnip, and was surrounded by smartweed and *Juncus* (Richardson 1913). Some of the eggs had adhered to fine roots in the bottom of the nest, but most were on the leaves of the water parsnip, 5–10 cm above the bottom of the nest. This nest was guarded by a 15-cm-long male, who was so gentle that he moved away when a hand reached toward him. Normally, the male black crappie guarding a nest is quite belligerent and will attack intruders or objects within his territory. He guards the nest and protects the young until they start to feed.

The female black crappie may spawn with several males and may produce eggs several times during the spawning period. Water-hardened eggs average 0.93 mm diam (Merriner 1971a). The number of eggs produced by fish 3–8 years old was 3,000–188,000, or approximately 132,000/kg (60,000/lb) of fish (Vessel and Eddy 1941). In Indiana, 3- and 4-year-old black crappies averaged 33,700 and 41,900 eggs respectively (Ulrey et al. 1938). The fecundity of Lake Wingra females that were 163–180 mm TL on 25 May was 11,400 (7,900–19,100) eggs (Churchill 1976). The median hatching time in the laboratory was 57.5 hr at 18.3°C (65°F) (Merriner 1971b).

In Vilas County lakes, black crappie larvae first appeared during the first half of June and continued to appear in small numbers through most of July (Faber 1967).

Characteristics useful in separating larval black crappies from larval white crappies, are given in the white crappie species account (p. 860).

In southern Wisconsin, young-of-year black crappies were 25 mm long at the end of June, 45 mm long in July, 51 mm long in August, and 64 mm long at the end of September (R. Lorenz, pers. comm.). The growth of black crappies in the Fountain City backwater areas (Buffalo County) was generally faster than in any other Wisconsin waters reported.

More than 50% of male and female black crappies are mature at age II; 83% of the males and 79% of the females mature at age III (Nelson 1974).

In the Mississippi River (Pools 4–6) during 1955, Kittel (1955) noted the following frequency of occurrence in survey samples of each age class from I through VII: 106, 120, 67, 5, 10, 11, and 1. From this limited sample, it appears that after age III the mortality of black crappies is high and that few large crappies remain in the fishery. Kelley (1953) noted a decline in trap-net catches of 4- and 5-year-old fish from May to September, and concluded that the principal cause was natural mortality. In Murphy Flowage (Rusk County) from 1955 to 1969, the natural mortality of black crappies was 42%, and the estimated mortality through angling was 11% (Snow 1978). In Illinois, a natural death rate of more than 50% occurred in large broods of white and black crappies during their third year of life; anglers took about 7% of the harvest of catch-sized crappies, and the remainder was largely lost through natural mortality (Starrett and Fritz 1957).

In 1947, a 457-mm, 1.70-kg (18-in, 3-lb 12-oz) black crappie was caught from Mirror Lake (Sauk County). A 457-mm, 1.79-kg (18-in, 3-lb 15-oz) fish was taken from Blue Spring Lake (Jefferson County) in 1961 [Wis. Conserv. *Bull.* 1961 26(6):22]. A 502-mm, 2.04-kg (19.75-in, 4-lb 8-oz) crappie was hooked from the Gile Flowage (Iron County) on 12 August 1967 (Wis. Dep. Nat. Resour. 1977); although listed as a white crappie, it was more than likely a black crappie since white crappies are not known from the Lake Superior drainage. A 489-mm, 2.27-kg (19¼-in, 5-lb) black crappie was taken from the Santee-Cooper Reservoir in South Carolina in 1957 (*World Almanac* 1976).

The black crappie is carnivorous in its feeding habits. The food of very young black crappies is primarily *Cyclops* and Cladocera; small insect larvae are less important (Pearse 1919). The food of 140 black crappies 165–200 mm long, taken between February

Age and Growth (TL in mm) of the Black Crappie in Wisconsin

Location	1	2	3	4	5	6	7	Source
Drainage lakes, northwestern Wis.[a]	61	124	173	203	229	249	246	Snow (1969)
Seepage lakes, northwestern Wis.[a]			163	168	196	229	239	Snow (1969)
Mississippi R., Pools 4–6	84	137	187	234	269	282	302	Kittel (1955)
Mississippi R. (Buffalo Co.)	69	145	216	262	290			Christenson and Smith (1965)
L. Wingra (Dane Co.)	73	133	170	202	269	296	352	Churchill (1976)
Spauldings Pond[a] (Rock Co.)	114	152	165					Threinen and Helm (1952)

[a]Actual lengths at time of capture, not calculated to annulus.

and October in Lake Wingra (Dane County), was composed of Cladocera (33% volume), chironomid larvae and pupae (24%), amphipods (11%), fish (9%), ephemeropteran nymphs (6%), copepods (5%), adult (flying) chironomids (4%), and Odonata nymphs (2%); other food items, each forming less than 1% of the digestive tract materials included hemipteran nymphs and adults, caddisfly larvae, grasshoppers, beetles, ostracods, mites, snails, leeches, algae, miscellaneous plants, silt, and debris. In Lake Mendota (Pearse 1921a), the black crappie had consumed the following foods: fish (16.6% volume), insect larvae (13.3%), insect pupae (10.8%), insect adults (19.2%), cladocerans (16%), copepods (4.2%), ostracods (6.6%), and plants (13.3%).

In the diet of black crappies from northwestern Wisconsin lakes, Van Engel (1941) found that fish outranked invertebrates in importance when measured by the volume of food in stomachs, although the latter were found in a greater number of the stomachs; e.g., in Silver Lake, fly nymphs were present in 44% of the stomachs and fish in 38.7% of the stomachs, but the fish accounted for 88.2% of the total volume of food and the nymphs for only 2.7%. In January and February collections at Big Round Lake, *Leptodora* and fish were absent from the diet, and *Chaoborus* larvae were found in 94–97% of the stomachs and accounted for 30–50% of the volume of food. In July, fish appeared in the diet of only those crappies over 14 cm SL; the fish consumed were bluntnose minnows, perch, bluegills, and largemouth bass. In a Mississippi River study (Ranthum 1969), 21 of 36 black crappies contained fish, including gizzard shad and one small bullhead. Fish were an important summer food, particularly in July and August. In November and December, cladocerans made up most of the food volume.

A study of feeding periodicity in Illinois (Childers and Shoemaker 1953) indicated that the black crappie feeds most actively at dusk, from 1600 to 1800 hr, and that a second less active feeding period occurs at dawn, from 0600 to 0800 hr. Light feeding continues at night from 1800 to 0600 hr; there is practically no feeding during the day.

The black crappie is a midwater feeder. It feeds among aquatic vegetation in the open water, and to some extent at the surface. The black crappie's numerous gill rakers permit it to consume planktonic crustaceans at least until it reaches a large size, if not throughout life. The success of the black crappie in many waters may be attributed to its ability to consume foods of all types and sizes. The black crappie is one of the few members of the centrachid family that continues to feed during the winter and that does not go into semihibernation.

Although Reynolds and Casterlin (1977) determined that the black crappie had the lowest temperature preference [24°C (75.2°F)] of the fish tested, Neill and Magnuson (1974) noted that the preferred temperature of crappies from Lake Monona (Dane County) was 28.3°C (83°F) in both the field and the laboratory. Black crappies in the heated area of a South Carolina reservoir had higher length-weight relationships and higher mean coefficients of condition than those from unheated portions (Bennett 1972).

Moore (1942) determined an oxygen threshold for the black crappie at 1.4 ppm at near-freezing temperatures. In Lake Traverse, Minnesota, crappies were distressed but alive at 1.1 ppm oxygen (Moyle and Clothier 1959). The thresholds found by Cooper and Washburn (1949) in Michigan winterkill lakes were notably lower: In one lake, with an approximate minimum concentration of dissolved oxygen of 0.8–0.5 ppm in the upper 0.3–1.2 m of water there was good survival of black crappies; in a lake with a concentration of 0.3–0.1 ppm, there was still some survival of that species, although black crappies and other species also sustained heavy mortalities.

The black crappie, more than any other species, suffered sudden mortality in waters of Lake Waubesa and the Yahara River (Dane County) which were supersaturated with dissolved oxygen as a result of algal bloom (Woodbury 1941). All of the fish looked normal in death except for small gas bubbles under the skin and in the fin rays. The gills contained gas emboli large enough to obstruct the blood flow, and death was due to respiratory failure.

The black crappie is a gregarious fish that travels in schools. Moyle (1969) observed schools of 20–25 fish; during the day each school was located around a submerged tree, usually at a depth of 1–3 m, but during the evening the schools moved out over deep water, where they remained within 1–3 m of the surface. Keast (1965) has noted some nocturnal movement into the shallows by the black crappie and the rock bass. Young black crappies may often be found swarming in shallow, quiet, or protected waters. Adult fish may rest suspended and motionless, except for occasional flicks of the pectoral fins.

The movements of the black crappie include migrations. Black crappies living in large bodies of water may migrate several kilometers (Schneberger 1972a). Evidence of winter movement under the ice by black crappies in a backwater channel of the Mississippi River was determined by Greenbank (1956); the greatest movement occurred in early February when the ice had its greatest snow cover.

In Glass Lake (Grant County) of the Mississippi River, 509 black crappies were found with these species: longnose gar (1), gizzard shad (32), bigmouth buffalo (2), spotted sucker (4), white sucker (1), golden shiner (76), pugnose minnow (4), spotfin shiner (2), spottail shiner (32), weed shiner (1), tadpole madtom (4), grass pickerel (4), northern pike (5), white bass (3), yellow bass (3), yellow perch (36), walleye (8), logperch (6), johnny darter (1), mud darter (1), largemouth bass (112), bluegill (2), white crappie (6), and brook silverside (28).

IMPORTANCE AND MANAGEMENT

While black crappies are carnivorous in their feeding habits, they are also eaten by a number of other animals. Fish that prey on black crappie fry and fingerlings include perch, walleyes, bass, northern pike, and muskellunge. Yearling and adult crappies are suitable prey for the larger muskellunge and northern pike (Schneberger 1972a). Fish-eating birds that feed on black crappies include the great blue heron, American merganser, kingfisher, and bitterns. Otter and mink are probably the only predatory mammals that feed on the black crappie. Schneberger suggested that snapping turtles and water snakes may occasionally feed on this species.

The black crappie is host to the glochidia of the following mollusks: *Amblema plicata*, *Fusconaia ebena*, *Fusconaia flava*, *Megalonaias gigantea*, *Quadrula nodulata*, *Elliptio dilatata*, *Anodonta grandis*, *Actinonaias carinata*, *Lampsilis radiata luteola*, and *Lampsilis teres* (Hart and Fuller 1974).

Schneberger (1972a) has suggested that the activities of the carp may benefit the feeding and breeding activities of the black crappie by converting the habitat from a weedy to a more open-water environment. Crappies have been known to be relatively abundant in areas populated by carp.

In Iowa, Neal (1961) noted that there was a shift in the dominant population in Clear Lake from black crappies to white crappies. He suggested turbidity as a reason for this change. The spread northward into Wisconsin of the white crappie, its greater incidence in Wisconsin waters in recent years, and the increased turbidity of our waters imply that a similar population shift may be occurring in Wisconsin. The shift in crappie species incidence in Lake Wingra, noted above, supports this view.

The black crappie ranks high as a sport fish and a panfish. It is caught on small minnows, worms, and a wide variety of artificial lures, and occasionally it will rise to a dry fly. The black crappie has a tender mouth, from which hooks are easily torn. Because it is active and feeds throughout the winter, this species is a popular quarry for ice fishing enthusiasts in some parts of Wisconsin.

The rank of the combined crappie species in the Mississippi River sport catch was fourth in 1957 and second in 1962–1963 (Nord 1967). The estimated catch of all crappies for Pools 4, 5, 7, and 11 in 1967–1968 was 277,369 fish weighing 68,090 kg (150,100 lb), or a weight of 245 g (0.54 lb) for each fish caught (Wright 1970). Considering the relative abundance of the species, the figures undoubtedly represent more black crappies than white crappies for all pools, with almost a total dominance of black crappies in the upriver pools. In Pools 4–6 during 1955, the average number of black crappies taken per trap net lift was 17.5 out of a total of 32.4 fish of all species (Kittel 1955). By comparison, yellow and white bass averaged 3.6 fish per lift, carp 2.0, and white crappies 0.2.

In Escanaba Lake (Vilas County), the black crappie never exceeded 6% of the spring standing crop of sport fishes available to the angler from 1956 through 1969 (Kempinger et al. 1975). During the same period in which the other centrarchid populations declined, the black crappie population also decreased and remained low. From 1955 through 1969, 7,482 black crappies weighing 2,422 kg (5,339 lb) were caught by anglers from Escanaba Lake: this represents 2% of the total number of fish of all species caught, and 3.9% of the total weight harvested. In Murphy Flowage (Rusk County) from 1955 to 1970, the black crappies harvest represented 4.4% of all the fish caught and 5.8% of their weight (Snow 1978). The estimated total number of black crappies caught from June to August 1970 in Black Oak Lake (Vilas County) was 445 fish (190–290 mm); these constituted 5.3% of the total catch (Serns and McKnight 1974). The estimated catch from Laura Lake (Vilas County) was 121 black crappies (229–328 mm), or 1.7% of the total catch.

When large sport fish prove uncooperative, when human appetites have been whetted for a ready fish dinner, it is the crappie which often fills the bill.

The flesh of the black crappie is white, flaky, and tasty; however, fish from some waters may have a slightly muddy taste. An overnight soaking in cold saltwater, followed by a thorough rinsing before cooking, is said to improve the taste. Schneberger (1972a:13) has described methods for cooking black crappies:

> . . . They are usually fried in a heavy skillet after having been dipped in flour, in a flour and cornmeal mixture or in

a commercially prepared breading. Any number of cooking oils, shortenings or combinations with butter may be used depending on individual preferences. A well-known fishing guide prepares the cooking fat by first frying bacon in butter. Bacon sandwiches are then eaten along with the fried fish.

In 1976, crappies were bringing $1.89 per pound ($4.16/kg) in a Milwaukee food store.

In Wisconsin, commercial fishing for the black crappie is not allowed, but liberal sport fishing regulations are in force. The season in inland waters is year-round; there is no size limit, but there is a daily bag limit of 50 panfish, including the black crappie. In boundary waters there is no bag limit, except in Wisconsin-Minnesota waters, where the daily limit is 25 panfish. Up-to-date regulations should be consulted, since regulations are subject to change.

Many problems have been associated with the management of black crappies, some of them evolving from the widespread stocking of this species in waters formerly famed for their larger sport fish species. In the 1947–1948 Biennial Report of the Wisconsin Conservation Commission (1949) the black crappie was called the "carp of the north" because it became so abundant in many northern Wisconsin lakes, prevented the growth of other fishes, and often became stunted itself as a result of competition. By preying on the young of other species, especially predator fish species, black crappies may greatly alter other fish populations.

Undoubtedly the crappie has been blamed for imbalances among fish species which should be attributed to other factors. In the late 1800s, Long Lake had a reputation for being one of the best smallmouth bass lakes in Bayfield County (O'Donnell 1943). In 1891 carp were planted in the lake in order to "make fishing better." The bass fishing began to decline rapidly, and by 1920 had become so poor that angling had almost been abandoned. Around 1930, yellow perch were introduced, and in 1937 Long Lake received 700 adult black crappies, the first record of this species in that lake. Fishing remained poor. In 1941 the lake was netted and poisoned; the only species which seemed to have been holding its own was the dominant black crappie: all size groups from 51–305 mm were taken. O'Donnell viewed the black crappie as "ecologically dominant," although carp made up 55.1% of the total weight.

The removal of larger fishes through selective fishing causes crowded populations of stunted crappies. Even with liberal angling regulations, overpopulations are often a problem. Studies by the Wisconsin Department of Natural Resources at Murphy Flowage and at the Northern Highlands Forest Research Station show that angling is not able to control populations to prevent overcrowding. The stocking of large predator species to control overpopulation has not been successful because of the rapid removal of the predators by anglers (Schneberger 1972a).

The history of Spauldings Pond (Rock County) (Threinen and Helm 1952) also illustrates runaway black crappie populations. In 1945, bluegills made up 47% of the total fyke net catch from the pond; by 1946 this figure had declined to 8.3%; and by 1951 it had dropped to 4.6%. The incidence of crappies in the catch increased from 47% in 1945 to 87.5% in 1946, and to 91% in 1951. At the same time, stunting occurred among the crappies: the largest crappie in 1945 measured 284 mm (11.2 in), whereas the largest fish in 1951 measured a mere 178 mm (7 in).

Black crappies, carp, largemouth bass, and bluegills were stocked in a number of experimental ponds at the Delafield Hatchery (Waukesha County) (Mraz and Cooper 1957b). The adult fish were stocked during April and May, and the ponds were drained during December. For this 5-month period, the average survival rates for the four species were: carp 95.5%, largemouth bass 49.5%, bluegills 35.8%, and black crappies 44.0%. Reproduction of black crappies in these small ponds was uniformly low, never exceeding 1,258 per hectare, and failing entirely in two trials out of six.

Perch Family—Percidae

Eighteen species of percids in five genera are known from Wisconsin. This does not include the greenside darter *(Etheostoma blennioides)*, which has been incorrectly reported from southeastern Wisconsin. In the United States and Canada, 130 species in 5 genera are known (Robins et al. 1980).

The percidae appear to have originated in Europe from some basal percoid family during the Cenozoic, and to have spread to North America through at least two separate invasions. Percids have been known from the Upper Cretaceous and Oligocene of Europe, and from the Eocene of North America.

The darters, all of which are of North American origin, exhibit the greatest evolutionary development. The three genera, *Percina* (30 species), *Ammocrypta* (7 species), and *Etheostoma* (89 species), represent a cline from the primitive to the advanced.

By using 45 characters involving pigmentation, squamation, biochemistry, counts, and measurements, Page (1974) was able to develop a phylogeny for the genus *Percina*. *Percina* has a system of uninterrupted head canals and a complete lateral line (Page 1977). *Ammocrypta* is similar to *Percina*, but shows a reduction in some species in the number of pores in the head canal system. In the most advanced *Etheostoma*, the pores have been lost and the canals have become interrupted in the head canal and lateral line systems. Bailey and Gosline (1955) demonstrated the value of vertebral counts in the taxonomy of the Percidae and their utility in assessing relationships and deciphering phylogeny.

Members of the perch family are widely spread throughout Wisconsin. These are advanced fishes with ctenoid scales, and with the pelvic fins well forward and almost beneath the pectoral fins (thoracic position). All have one spine and five rays in the pelvic fins. The two dorsal fins are separate, the first dorsal with 6–15 spines and the second with only soft rays. The anal fin is small, with one or two spines, and the caudal fin is shallowly forked to rounded. The preopercle is smooth or serrate on its posterior edge, and the opercle usually ends in a single flat spine. The swim bladder is present in *Stizostedion* and *Perca*, but it is reduced or absent in *Percina, Ammocrypta*, and *Etheostoma*. If the swim bladder is present, it is without a duct to the pharynx (physoclistous condition).

Breeding tubercles are now known for 48 percid species. They function primarily in maintaining contact between the male and the female during the spawning act (Collette 1965). Walleyes, saugers, and perch lack these structures, and usually spawn in more slowly moving waters; they generally display little external sexual dimorphism. Males of most species of darters are much more brightly colored than females, especially during the spawning season.

The percids are limited in their range by high summer temperatures. They are adapted to temperature climates of the northern hemisphere, where water temperatures are less than 4°C (39°F) for more than 8 months of the year in the northernmost parts of their range, and may reach about 32°C (90°F) in the southernmost extremities of their native range (Collette et al. 1977).

The walleye, sauger, and perch are among the most valuable sport and commercial fishes in Wisconsin. As food fishes, these species rank among the favorites and command high prices.

The darters are considered important links in the food chains of fishes. Darters are also among the most beautiful of our native fishes; their colors are striking, and they make interesting aquarium pets, although some species are hard to keep alive.

The darters appear to be particularly sensitive to changes in their aquatic environments. Some react negatively to impoundments, since they need swift-running water over silt-free bottoms. In areas of heavy human settlement, most species of darters are quickly lost.

Walleye

Stizostedion vitreum vitreum (Mitchill). *Stizostedion*—pungent throat, according to Rafinesque; *vitreum*—glassy, from the large eye.

Other common names: yellow walleye, pickerel, yellow pickerel, yellow, yellow pike, perchpike, yellow pikeperch, walleye pike, walleyed pike, walleyed pikeperch, walleyed pickerel, dory, glasseye, white-eye, blue pike, gray pike, green pike, grass pike, jack, jack salmon, white salmon, okow, hornfish, blowfish, gum pike.

Subadult 205 mm, L. Winnebago, Aug. 1960

DESCRIPTION

Body elongate, almost cylindrical but slightly compressed laterally. Length 36–43 cm (14–17 in). TL = 1.21 SL. Depth into SL 4.9–5.4. Head length into SL 3.1–3.5. Preopercle serrated on posterior edge. Gill membranes extended forward, narrowly joined to one another, and narrowly joined to isthmus. Premaxillaries protractile, upper lip groove continuous over tip of snout. Mouth large, almost horizontal, upper jaw reaching about to back of eye, jaws equal anteriorly; strong caninelike teeth on premaxillaries, lower jaw and palatines; pharyngeal arches with short recurved teeth. Gill rakers on lower limb of first arch thin, long, about 8. Branchiostegal rays usually 7. Dorsal fins 2; first or spiny dorsal fin with 13 (12–14) spines; second dorsal fin with 1–2 spines, 18–21 rays. Anal fin with 2 spines and 13 (11–14) rays; pelvic fins thoracic, space between pelvic fins greater than one-half length of base of pelvic fin. Scales ctenoid; cheeks scaleless or nearly so; opercles mostly naked; breast and belly scaled. Lateral line complete, scales 77–87. Pyloric caeca usually 3, about same length as stomach. Vertebrae 46–47 (Bailey and Gosline 1955).

Dorsal region of head and back brown, olive, to brassy yellow; sides paler; ventral head and belly yellow to white. Sides and back variously speckled with dusky spots; in younger fish, vague dusky bands (about 9) across back and down sides. Eyes silvery in life; a reflecting layer (tapetum lucidum) causes glowing in dark. Membranes on the spiny dorsal fin diffusely pigmented, no definite horizontal rows of spots; last few membranes black. Second dorsal and caudal fins with dark spots in regular rows; ventral lobe of caudal fin often white-tipped. Pectoral fins pigmented with dark blotch at base; pelvics and anal largely clear.

Sexual dimorphism: In male, a single urogenital opening behind the anus; in female, 2 openings (genital and urinary) behind the anus (Moen 1959).

Breeding male without nuptial tubercles.

Hybrids: Walleye × sauger (Stroud 1948).

SYSTEMATIC NOTES

For many years the blue pike *(Stizostedion vitreum glaucum)* from Lakes Erie and Ontario, and possibly from other northern waters, has been recognized as a separate form. It is distinguished from the walleye by its blue color, slightly larger eyes set higher on the head, a different spawning time and place, a slower growth rate, smaller ultimate size, and different depth distribution (Scott and Crossman 1973). Today the blue pike is almost, if not entirely, extirpated (Committee on Rare and Endangered Wildlife Species 1966).

DISTRIBUTION, STATUS, AND HABITAT

It is believed that the walleye was originally confined to the larger lakes and waterways in Wisconsin. The extensive stocking of walleye fry and fingerlings that

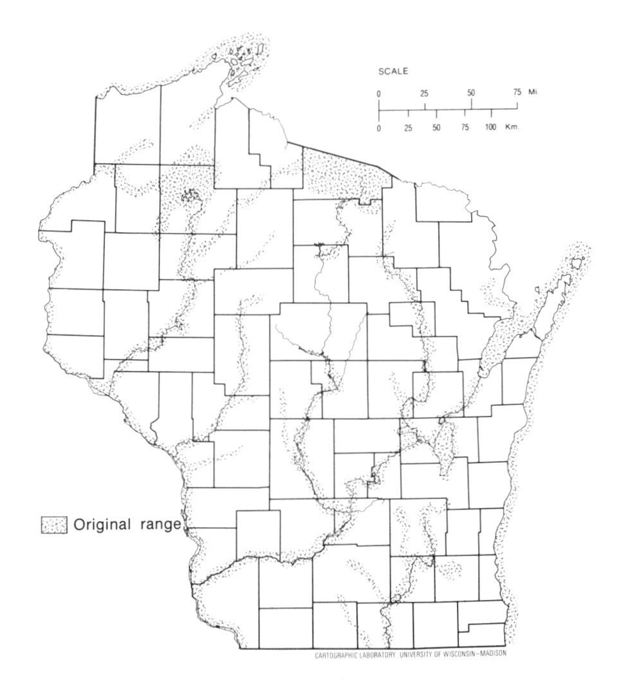

The original range of the walleye in Wisconsin (after Niemuth et al. 1959a:2)

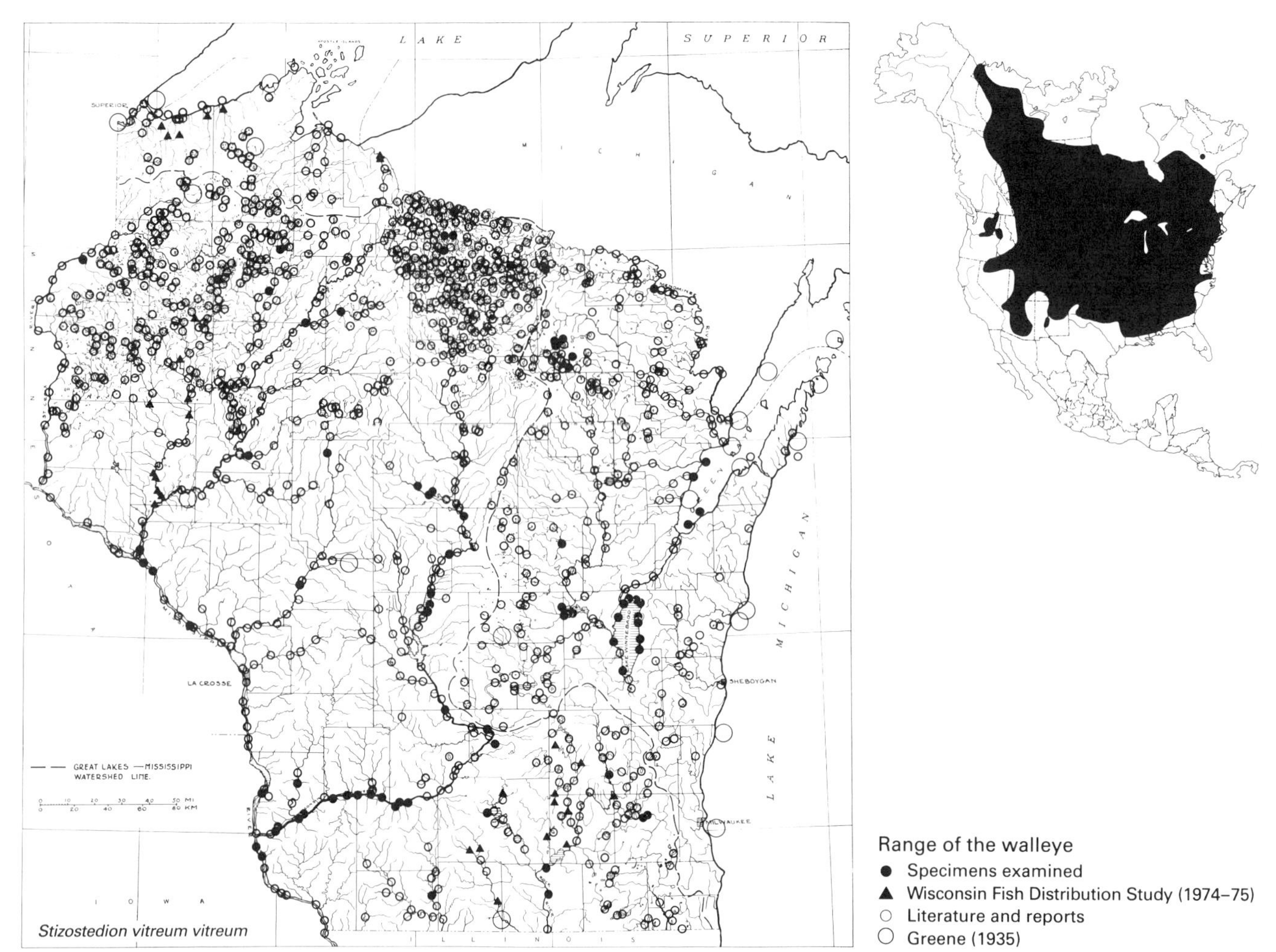

occurred early in many Wisconsin waters partly obscured the original distribution of the species. Today the walleye is present throughout Wisconsin.

The walleye is common locally in large rivers and in most large lakes in the state (Wis. Dep. Nat. Resour. 1971). It is uncommon at the barriers within tributaries to Lake Superior (McLain et al. 1965). The walleye fishery is particularly well known in the Fox and Wolf river basins and their connecting lakes, the boundary waters of the Lake Michigan drainage, the central and lower portions of the Wisconsin River, the northern resort waters, and the Mississippi River.

The walleye is generally associated with large rivers and drainage lakes, "although excellent populations are also sometimes found in smaller landlocked waters" (Klingbiel 1969). Many large impoundments also contain substantial walleye populations even in drainages where the species is not native.

The walleye was encountered most frequently in clear water, over substrates of sand, gravel, mud, rubble, boulders, clay, silt, and detritus (in decreasing order of occurrence). It is found mostly in the quiet water of lakes, backwaters, and sloughs, although during the spawning season it is frequently taken in moving water. Occasionally it occurs in the lower ends of small tributaries to large rivers. On the Mississippi River, walleyes frequent the main channel, the deeper side channels, Lake Pepin, and some other river lakes (Nord 1967). At certain times they occur below the dams and along riprap banks and wing dams.

According to Niemuth et al. (1959a), walleyes prefer moderately fertile waters, but they occur in all types of lakes, including the darkly stained dystrophic, or bog, lakes; the oligotrophic, or clear, softwater lakes; and the eutrophic, or fertile, hardwater lakes which combine the necessary spawning grounds and feeding areas. Most walleye lakes are more than 80 ha (200 acres) in size, and have substantial areas of open water. Reproduction is often sporadic in the more fertile waters.

BIOLOGY

The spawning migration of the walleye begins soon after the ice goes out, at water temperatures of 3.3–6.7°C (38–44°F). Walleyes have specific spawning habitat requirements, although no nests are built and the eggs are broadcast over a suitable substrate. In lakes with rocky shorelines, the rocky, wave-washed shallows are the primary spawning grounds. On lakes with inlet waterways, spawning occurs in inlet streams on gravel bottoms. In some places walleyes spawn on flooded wetland vegetation.

Spawning in Wisconsin generally occurs between mid-April and early May, although it may extend from the beginning of April to the middle of May. Walleye spawning ordinarily reaches a peak when water temperatures are 5.6–10°C (42–50°F); it has been observed, however, at temperatures as high as 17.2°C (63°F). Northern Wisconsin has a spawning season 1–2 weeks later than southern Wisconsin (Niemuth et al. 1959a).

Details of spawning by walleyes in the Wolf-Fox river system have been provided by Priegel (1970b). Walleyes from Lake Winnebago and connecting waters prefer to spawn in the flooded marsh areas adjacent to the Wolf and Fox rivers. These marshes are located in the flood plain, and in most cases they are old oxbows that are flooded only during the spring runoff; they all have inlets and outlets which provide a continuous flow of water over the marsh area during the period of high water levels in the rivers. This flowing water is considered to be the key to successful spawning by the walleye, and to the escape of walleye fry to the river.

Adjacent to the Wolf River there are 13 major spawning marshes, located 53–157 river kilometers (33–97 mi) from Lake Winnebago. In Spoehr's Marsh near Shiocton (Outagamie County), male walleyes in most years frequent the marsh over a 3- to 4-week period, while females occur there only during the actual spawning. Females are usually found near the outlet of the marsh, either in the adjacent river channel or in deeper areas of the marsh. There is a strong indication that females move into the marsh only when spawning is imminent and leave the marsh as soon as spawning has been completed—all within a 1-day period. Walleye eggs are usually found where the water is between 30 and 76 cm (12 and 30 in) deep, over vegetation mats of sedges and grasses. Walleye spawning also occurs in Lake Winnebago along the west shore, especially near the mouth of the Fox River, about a week after spawning on the river marshes (Priegel 1968c).

Walleyes migrating out of Lake Winnebago on the annual spawning run may move into the Fox River; when water levels are high, they may migrate beyond the Eureka Dam (Priegel 1966b). Once above the dam, it is possible for them to migrate into Lake Puckaway (Green Lake County), or as far as the Montello Dam (Marquette County), which is a distance of 123 river kilometers (76 mi) from Lake Winnebago. Active spawning occurs in the Montello River when water temperatures reach 5.6°C (42°F) in early April.

Spawning in the Eau Pleine Reservoir (Marathon County) occurred toward the end of April, and virtually ceased after 1 May (Joy 1975). In Pike and Round lakes (Price County), ice-out occurred on 7 May 1972 and spawning activity peaked on 10 May, probably because of unseasonably warm weather immediately following ice-out (Bever and Lealos 1974). Walleyes spawned in Escanaba Lake (Vilas County) in late April (Morsell 1970). In the Rock River below Hustisford (Dodge County), spawning occurred from 8 to 16 April, and was observed by H. Neuenschwander (pers. comm.) early in the morning and in the evening; he also observed spawning during the day and at times through the night.

In the Mississippi River, on 14 April 1969, a spawning concentration of walleyes and saugers was located over a rock-riprapped dike adjacent to Lock and Dam 6 (Trempealeau County) (Upper Miss. R. Conserv. Com. 1970, Gebken and Wright 1972b). Ripe males outnumbered ripe female walleyes by a factor of 7:1. Walleye eggs were recovered from the site. According to Gebken and Wright, earlier workers have suspected that flooding contributes to the varying year class strengths of walleyes and saugers. Gebken and Wright suggested that walleyes and saugers spawn in Pool 7 of the Mississippi River during periods of moderate or low flooding and that as flood waters rise suitable spawning areas become increasingly available, with suitability depending on the slope and size of the riprapped substrate.

The walleye is not a territorial fish at spawning time, but courtship behavior has been noted among fish grouped over shallow spawning grounds at night (Ellis and Giles 1965). Ellis and Giles have described courtship and spawning behavior (p. 360):

> . . . Overt courtship began by either males or females approaching another of either sex from behind or laterally and pushing sideways against it or drifting back and circling around pushing the approached fish backwards. The first dorsal fin was alternately erected and flattened during these approaches. The approached fish would either hold position or withdraw. Approaches and contact of this sort appeared to be the preliminary essentials of courtship and were promiscuous, i.e., there was no continued relationship between any particular pair of fish. Activity increased in frequency and intensity and individuals began to make preliminary darts forward and upward. Finally one or more females and one or more males came closely together and the compact group rushed upward. At the surface the

group swam vigorously around the compound until the moment of orgasm when swimming stopped and the females frequently turned or were pushed violently onto their sides. This sideways movement by the females was taken as an indicator of spawning even when no eggs or milt were seen. On one occasion during orgasm a male was clearly seen to have the first dorsal fin fully erected.

Similar observations have been made by Priegel (1970b) and O'Donnell (1938). O'Donnell estimated that 200–300 eggs were released with each spawning act, and that the act was repeated at 5-min intervals. Priegel observed that, once the upward rush began, only two males flanked each female, while the rest of the males followed in close pursuit. Females may spawn out completely in 1 night, whereas males have the potential for spawning over a longer period (Ellis and Giles 1965).

Walleyes usually broadcast their eggs; they exercise no parental care. After release, the adhesive eggs stick to one another and to objects they touch for the first hour or two. Water then hardens the external egg membrane, and the adhesive qualities are lost.

The diameter of mature eggs from ripe walleyes in Lake Winnebago varied from 1.8 to 2.1 mm (Priegel 1969c). The egg production of Lake Winnebago walleyes ranged from 43,255 eggs for a 442-mm, 680-g (17.4-in, 1.5-lb) fish to 227,181 eggs for a 615-mm, 2,359-g (24.2-in, 5.2-lb) fish.

The eggs hatch in 26 days at a water temperature of 4.4°C (40°F), in 21 days at a temperature of 10–12.8°C (50–55°F), and in 7 days at a mean temperature of 13.9°C (57°F) (Niemuth et al. 1959a). Allbaugh and Manz (1964) determined that walleye eggs and fry suffered no damage with rapid temperature fluctuations of 4.4°C (8°F).

On Spoehr's Marsh, newly hatched walleye fry averaged 7.6 (6.0–8.6) mm TL (Priegel 1970b). All indications are that, upon hatching, the fry must leave the marsh to reach a food source within 3–5 days, or they will perish. They are probably swept out of the marsh by water currents and carried by river currents into Lake Winnebago or into upriver lakes before the food supply in their yolk-sacs has been used up. The majority of the fry taken in the river channel as it enters Lake Winnebago have absorbed their yolk-sacs.

Newly hatched walleye fry have not yet developed paired fins, and their movement is restricted to vertical swimming. Fry sink in the water 15–20 cm, and then, with a vigorous motion of the tail muscle, move in a vertical direction to the surface again. When most walleye fry move down from the marshes, they travel in midriver near the surface of the water where the current is most rapid. Marking experiments have suggested that fry migrating out of marshes above Shiocton are able to reach Lake Winnebago within 3–5 days. In Lake Winnebago, the food supply is readily available and abundant.

Similar investigations by Priegel on the Fox River disclosed that the current was slow, especially in the wider sections of the river, and that it was probably not sufficient to carry the fry downstream. Evidence also showed that walleye fry passing over low-head dams, such as the Eureka Dam (Winnebago County), may either be killed or trapped in the eddies below the dam. The data indicated that, when water velocity was high, walleye fry were unable to survive passage over the dam; at lower velocities, they were able to pass safely over.

The early development of the walleye, from the 4-hour through the 6-day and hatching stages, has been illustrated and described by Deason (1934). Norden (1961) illustrated the 8- and 14.8-mm stages, and determined that the number of postanal myomeres in walleye larvae (26) can be used for separating them from yellow perch larvae (18). Fish (1932) illustrated and described the 7.8-, 12.5-, and 32-mm stages of the walleye. Scales first appeared on the caudal peduncle in 24-mm young from Lake Winnebago, and 45-mm fish were completely scaled (Priegel 1964c).

In lakes, walleye fry probably move into open water and lead a pelagic existence until a length of 2.5 cm or more is attained (Eschmeyer 1950). In northern Wisconsin lakes, Faber (1967) collected older larvae in both surface and bottom waters in June. In Escanaba Lake (Vilas County), fry move out to open water within a day or two after hatching, where they remain until they are about 30 mm long (Morsell 1970); in late June they return to inshore areas of the lake.

After the yolk-sac has been absorbed, walleye fry feed first on plankton crustaceans, then on insect larvae, principally chironomids. The greatest growth increase of the fry occurs from July to August, which probably indicates a change in the diet from zooplankters to insect larvae and forage fishes (Priegel 1969b). Lake Winnebago walleyes less than 75 mm long are plankton feeders, but turn to forage fishes if these are abundant. In Escanaba Lake, the yellow perch is clearly an important food of young-of-year walleyes, and appears to be selected over invertebrate food items (Morsell 1970).

In Lake Winnebago, young-of-year walleyes are generally over 75 mm TL at the end of July; by the end of October they are 130–137 mm TL (Priegel 1969b).

The age of walleyes is determined by reading scales. According to Priegel (1969a), the precise time of annulus formation has not been established, but it probably occurs in May or early June.

In Lake Winnebago, few walleyes live beyond 6 years (Priegel 1968c). Females reach a larger maximum size than males, and on the average are longer and heavier than males in a given year class, especially after the first 2 years of life. Weights for the Pike and Round lakes walleyes cited in the table below are as follows: age I—22 g; II—73 g; III—161 g; IV—268 g; V—347 g; VI—431 g; VII—530 g; VIII—637 g; IX—757 g; and X—836 g. Walleyes in the Mississippi River (Pool 7) weighed: I—86 g; II—241 g; III—431 g; IV—844 g; V—1,158 g; VI—1,249 g; VII—1,512 g; VIII—2,651 g; IX—2,701 g; X—2,978 g; XI—3,809 g; and XII—3,178 g.

The length-weight relation of the Lake Winnebago walleyes cited in table is expressed by the regression Log WT (lb) = −5.3596 + 3.2162 Log TL (in). Priegel has suggested that a lack of forage fishes, competition from other fish species (burbot, sauger, and yellow perch), and the long spawning migration (which must result in great energy loss) may be factors in the slow growth of Lake Winnebago walleyes.

Among Lake Winnebago walleyes, males mature at ages II–V, and females mature at ages V–VII (Priegel 1969a). Mississippi River males mature at an average age of 4.6 years, and females mature at 7.8 years (Gebken and Wright 1972b). In Pike Lake (Washington County), a high percentage of the males reach sexual maturity at age III, while most females mature at age IV (Mraz 1968).

In Wisconsin, the life span of walleyes appears to be about 7 years; few fish reach 10–12 years of age. An 18-year-old walleye, 838 mm long and weighing 4.65 kg (33 in, 10.25 lb), was caught in the Wisconsin River near Rhinelander in 1934 (Juday and Schloemer 1938). According to Louis Dornfeld (H. Neuenschwander, pers. comm.) a 9.3-kg (20.5-lb) walleye was speared in April 1896 below the Hustisford Dam (Dodge County). An 8.17-kg (18-lb) fish was caught from High Lake (Vilas County) in September 1933 (Wis. Dep. Nat. Resour. 1977). A 1.04-m, 11.34-kg (41-in, 25-lb) walleye was taken from Old Hickory Lake, Tennessee, in 1960 (*World Almanac* 1976).

Young walleyes (10–50 mm TL) in Lake Winnebago fed first on *Diaptomus, Leptodora*, and chironomid larvae, but the fry of white suckers, quillbacks, troutperch, and yellow perch were eaten to a limited extent (Priegel 1969b). In the diet of walleyes up to 100 mm long, planktonic crustaceans and chironomid larvae were still important, but in one collection fish remains occurred in 82.6% of the walleye stomachs; young freshwater drums were found in 42.9% of the stomachs. Even when substantial populations of young-of-year freshwater drums (8–18 cm TL) were available, only walleyes more than 38 cm long utilized them. The drum's rapid growth in length and body depth soon makes it unavailable to fish less than 28 cm long (Priegel 1963b).

In Vilas County lakes, Couey (1935) found that

Age and Growth (TL in mm) of the Walleye in Wisconsin

Location	1	2	3	4	5	6	7	8	9	10	11	12	Source
Northwestern Wis. drainage lakes	145	241	312	371	421	472							Snow (1969)
Trout L. (Vilas Co.)	135	221	348	421	483	526	551	566	587	592			Schloemer and Lorch (1942)
Pike L.–Round L. (Price Co.)	140	208	267	307	333	358	381	399	429	434			Bever and Lealos (1974)
Mississippi R., Pool 7[a]	196	290	356	427	472	480	526	605	607	630	663	673	Gebken and Wright (1972b)
Mississippi R., Pool 11	175	307	414	493	541	584	610	627	648	665	681		Vasey (1967)
Red R. (Dunn Co.)	162	264	328	373	419	452	474	490	514	537	562	618	Colvin (1975)
Big Eau Pleine Res. (Marathon Co.)	180	299	393	458	498								Joy (1975)
South Green Bay													
Males	226	333	399	470	493								Niemuth et al. (1959a)
Females	216	335	421	500	559	617	691	711					
L. Winnebago (Winnebago Co.)													
Males	142	259	323	361	384	396	411	427					Priegel (1969a)
Females	152	257	340	396	439	472	495	521					
L. Puckaway (Winnebago Co.)													
Males	190	323	394	432	460	480	498	516	541				Priegel (1966b)
Females	198	345	439	498	536	569	599	627	648				
Pike L. (Washington Co.)													
Males	173	287	358	401	432	457							Mraz (1968)
Females	178	292	376	439	480	533	574	630	653	701			

[a]Empirical lengths, not calculated to annulus.

fish, consisting of darters, minnows, and perch, amounted to 85% of the walleye's diet. The balance consisted of Diptera larvae, Ephemerida, entomostracans, caddisfly larvae, dragonfly nymphs, crayfish, and plant material (less than 1%). In one lake, insects were an important item of food, even in the largest walleyes caught. In the Eau Pleine Reservoir (Marathon County), fish ranked first in importance as food for walleyes of all sizes (Joy 1975). The stomach contents of walleyes less than 200 mm long consisted of fish (90.8% volume), insects (3.1%), and zooplankton (6.1%); walleyes more than 200 mm long had consumed fish (93.2% volume), insects (1.3%), crayfish (5.3%), and zooplankton (0.2%). The major prey species were bullheads and perch, but johnny darters, fathead minnows, carp, and black crappies were also identified. No cannibalism was noted in this study.

In summary, food habit studies have shown that walleyes consume almost all species of fish, as well as many of the larger invertebrates (Niemuth et al. 1959a). It is obvious that walleyes eat those food items which are most available. They are vigorous swimmers, capable of overtaking largemouth bass.

Walleye weight gain is greatest at the 20°C (68°F) temperature level, and the rate of food conversion is lower at variable temperatures than it is at constant temperatures. Maintenance requirements increase rapidly in the 12–20°C (54–68°F) interval (Kelso 1972). In Trout Lake (Vilas County), walleyes preferred water temperatures of 20.6°C (69°F) during the summer (Hile and Juday 1941). They are most active at temperatures of 12.8–23.3°C (55–74°F).

Characteristically, walleyes retire to the deeper, darker waters during the daytime. In the evening, they migrate to the bars and shoals to feed among the rocks or on the edge of weed beds. When waters are turbid or the weather is cloudy, they may be active during the daytime. In midsummer (July and early August) walleyes remain in deep water, where they continue to feed. They are active and feed throughout the winter, particularly when the ice first forms and again prior to the spring break-up (Niemuth et al. 1959a).

Walleyes often become the victims of winterkill in shallow lakes with low oxygen concentrations (Niemuth et al. 1959a). In Fox River marshes, embryo development was inhibited by low dissolved oxygen concentrations (Priegel 1970b). On the other hand, the walleye was one of several species of fish that suffered sudden mortality when the water of the Yahara River below Lake Waubesa (Dane County) became supersaturated with oxygen (Woodbury 1941). The fish looked normal in death except for small gas bubbles under the skin, in the fin rays, and in the gills, where most filaments contained gas emboli large enough to block the capillaries and to obstruct blood flow. It was theorized that oxygen was the gas causing the problem, and that death had resulted from respiratory failure.

In one study, DDT and its analogs in walleye egg samples ranged from 0.067 to 9.380 ppm. No relationship between the DDT content and the survival of walleye eggs and fry was established, however (Kleinert and Degurse 1968).

Schooling is common among walleyes, especially while they feed and during spawning periods. Walleyes seem to travel in loose aggregations in open water. They never become abundant in weedy waters.

In Lake Bemiji, Minnesota, walleyes traveled considerable distances, particularly during the spring and fall. Distances ranged from 0.8 km to 17.3 km (Holt et al. 1977). The mean daily distance moved was least during the summer season. The presence of overcast skies and precipitation appeared to be more important than changes in water temperature or dissolved oxygen concentrations in initiating long distance movements. Tagged walleyes were most active from late afternoon to early morning.

Tagging studies of walleyes in the Mississippi River below Lock and Dam 6, in the spring of 1959, demonstrated that movement out of the home pool is insignificant, but that locks and dams do not prohibit movement between pools (Hubley 1963b). Walleyes were recovered up to 63 km (39 mi) from the point of tagging.

An early study of walleyes tagged in the vicinity of the confluence of the Wolf and Waupaca rivers (Waupaca County) indicated that within 10 days a number of fish moved 81–97 river kilometers (50–60 mi) to the mouth of the Fox River and into Lake Winnebago (Herman 1947). Priegel (1968b) determined that the average distance walleyes traveled from Lake Poygan was 47 km (29 mi); from Lake Winneconne 45 km (28 mi); from Fox River marshes 36 km (22 mi); and from Wolf River marshes 53 km (33 mi). The maximum distance traveled was 157 km (97 mi), from Oshkosh on Lake Winnebago to Leeman (Outagamie County) on the Wolf River. During the course of the study, nine fish originally tagged in Lake Winnebago were recaptured in Lake Puckaway, a distance of 110 river kilometers (68 mi) from Lake Winnebago. These fish had to pass over four low-head dams in the Fox River at Eureka, Berlin, White River, and Princeton.

In many waters walleyes are associates of yellow

perch, and the predator-prey relationships of the two species are close. In Lake Pepin (Pool 4) of the Mississippi River, experimental gill nets caught saugers, which made up 19.2% of the catch; walleyes, which made up 2.7% (Upper Miss. R. Conserv. Com. 1967). Other species taken, in order of abundance, were: channel catfish 22.0%, yellow perch 10.3%, gizzard shad 8.2%, mooneyes 4.8%, and white bass 4.2%. In Pool 7, 68 walleyes were taken with 23 saugers, 20 common carp, 20 spotted suckers, 11 freshwater drum, 10 white crappies, 8 black crappies, 8 golden redhorse, 6 bluegills, 6 mooneyes, 4 quillbacks, 3 shorthead redhorse, 3 longnose gars, 2 largemouth bass, 1 white bass, 1 channel catfish, 1 black bullhead, 1 gizzard shad, and 1 shortnose gar (Gebken and Wright 1972b).

IMPORTANCE AND MANAGEMENT

The walleye is fair game for all fish-eating species. In Lake Poygan, a northern pike, 889 mm long and weighing 5.22 kg (35 in, 11.5 lb), had swallowed a 381-mm (15-in) walleye (Herman 1947). Young walleyes are often found in the stomachs of adult walleyes. Walleyes are subject to the usual fish-eating bird and mammal predators, but, because of their generally nocturnal habits, their preference for open water and deepwater areas, and their relatively large size as adults, this kind of predation is small. Incidents of adult walleyes being taken by eagles and herons have been observed in Wisconsin (Niemuth et al. 1959a).

Fishing surveys point out that the walleye is the most popular large sport fish in Wisconsin. In 1967, Wisconsin anglers alone took an estimated 4.5 million walleyes. In 1973, there were 1.2 million licensed anglers in Wisconsin, of whom one-half million pursued the sport of walleye fishing; they caught 5 million walleyes (Kempinger 1975). The walleye run on the Wolf River ranks with the top outdoor events of the year.

Walleyes are lured with a wide variety of live or artificial baits. They are taken with night crawlers, worms, minnows, frogs, and crayfish, and, on the Mississippi River, with the tadpole madtom. They respond to artificial spoons, plugs, spinners, streamer flies, poppers, and heavily weighted jigs. Twilight fishing is preferred, although walleyes will bite on cloudy days. They are one of the few sport fishes that will take minnows or jigging baits through the ice.

The walleye is an abundant sport fish in Lake Winnebago and connecting waters, and it attracts more fishermen to the Lake Winnebago area than any other sport fish. A recent tagging program showed that the harvest of walleyes in Lake Winnebago was consistently highest during the spawning migration (Priegel 1968c). Walleyes, however, are taken throughout the year from various sites; they are taken from reefs and rocky shores during the late spring, trolled from deep water over mud bottoms during the summer, caught along reefs and shorelines in the fall, and are taken in the tip-up or jigging fishery in winter.

In Escanaba Lake (Vilas County), which had an experimental year-round open season and no size limit on all species (except northern pike) from 1946 to 1969, walleyes ranked first in the catch in weight, with 23,253 kg (51,263 lb) harvested, and third in number of fish taken (following the yellow perch and pumpkinseed), with 63,029 caught. In Pike Lake (Washington County) the walleyes were harvested at the annual angler catch rate of 19–24%, while annual natural mortality did not exceed 5–10% (Mraz 1968).

On the Mississippi River, the walleye ranked sixth in the sport catch in 1957, and ninth in 1962–1963 (Nord 1967). The estimated sport fishery catch of walleyes in Pools 4, 5, 7, and 11 in 1967–1968 was 74,179 fish weighing 58,242 kg (128,399 lb) (Wright 1970).

In Wisconsin a number of rivers and inland lakes (including Lake Winnebago) have a continuous open season on walleyes; others have a closed period from 1 March to early May. The 1980 Wisconsin fishing regulations generally allow a daily combined total of five walleyes and saugers; for most waters there is no minimum size limit (Wis. Dep. Nat. Resour. 1979). Before fishing, the angler should consult current fishing regulations.

The flesh of the walleye is an epicurean delight—it is firm, white, fairly dry, and virtually free of bones. To many fish connoiseurs it is top table fare, delicately flavored and without a strong fishy taste. Since the flesh is not fatty and contains little oil, freezing and long storage are possible. Analysis indicates that the walleye is 79.7% water, 18.6% protein, 0.5% fat, and 1.4% ash (Niemuth et al. 1959a).

By law the commercial fishery for walleyes is restricted to the waters of Green Bay. Its status as a commercial fish in Lake Michigan has been summarized by Wells and McLain (1973). From 1899 to 1946, yearly production of walleyes averaged 58 thousand (14–157 thousand) kg. A pronounced production increase to 600 thousand kg in 1950 was followed by a decrease to 137 thousand kg in 1952, and another peak of 443 thousand kg in 1955. After 1955, production declined steadily to only 5,400 kg in 1970. The

Lake Michigan walleye fishery is centered in Green Bay, which produced an average of 97% of the total annual catch from 1947 to 1970. In 1974 the Green Bay production totaled 2,630 kg, and was valued at $3,921 (Wis. Dep. Nat. Resour. 1976c). To bolster this fishery, walleyes have been stocked from state hatcheries. In 1976, 5 million fry and 150,425 fingerlings were planted in Green Bay (Wis. Dep. Nat. Resour. 1976a).

As a commercial fish, the walleye has declined so greatly since 1956 that it is not now common in any part of Lake Michigan. Wells and McLain (1973:41–42) observed:

> . . . Reasons for the early decline in walleye abundance in southern Green Bay are not clear. The severe decrease of walleyes which occurred there . . . before 1882 . . . probably was the combined result of heavy fishing and deteriorating environment; the generally low abundance since 1930 might logically be blamed on the unsuitable habitat in that heavily polluted area. . . .
>
> Sea lamprey predation offers a possible explanation for the present poor state of the walleye stocks in Lake Michigan, but the relation is certainly not as conspicuous as in some cases of destruction of fish stocks by sea lampreys. . . .
>
> Alewives might have had an influence on walleye reproduction, but the relation is not obvious. If the walleye's decline has been a result of a long succession of year class failures, the earliest failures would have to have occurred before 1955, on the basis of production records. Interference by the alewife at that early date is extremely unlikely. It is not too far-fetched to suppose, however, that the earliest year class failures were due to natural causes (e.g., weather conditions) and that by the late 1950's alewives were abundant enough to prevent any further possibility of a good hatch.

Walleyes are important components in the predator-prey balances in lakes which have extensive open water and are essentially weed free. One successful plant of walleye fingerlings, beneficial to both walleyes and perch, was made in a lake in which perch was the dominant panfish (Threinen 1960), but poor control over bluegills occurred in lakes where the bluegill was the dominant species. Walleyes are a natural enemy of both largemouth and smallmouth bass, and, in lakes where walleyes are dominant, small bass eventually disappear from the populations and they become walleye lakes. This has been demonstrated in a number of lakes in Wisconsin that were originally bass lakes and were planted with walleyes (Doyle 1937, Niemuth et al. 1959a). In Minnesota, however, when smallmouth bass were introduced into four rocky, infertile lakes with established walleye populations, the walleyes declined in three lakes as the bass increased, and in the fourth lake there was a simultaneous rise in the number of walleyes and bass, followed by an increase in the abundance of walleyes and a decrease in the number of bass (F. H. Johnson and Hale 1977). Interspecific competition for spawning sites, for shoal habitat, or for food did not appear to be factors in the fluctuations in abundance. Predation of young walleyes by bass may have been a factor in failure of walleye year classes.

There is little evidence that there is significant predation on walleye eggs by other fish species, although it has often been suspect. Priegel (1970b) noted the presence of yellow perch, northern pike, suckers, and carp on the walleye spawning grounds of the Wolf River marshes and in Lake Winnebago, but he had no evidence of predation on walleye eggs. There was sufficient evidence, however, to show that the presence of spawning carp is detrimental to walleye eggs, since the carp roil up the bottom, dislodge the walleye eggs, and allow them to settle on the silt bottom where they quickly die from lack of oxygen.

The walleye is the most extensively propagated fish in Wisconsin. In 1976 the Wisconsin Department of Natural Resources (1976a) distributed 59,515,000 walleye fry and 3,261,329 fingerlings. The artificial rearing of this species has been described by Niemuth et al. (1959a:5):

> When eggs are taken for hatchery purposes, the eggs of a female are first extruded in a pan containing a little water by gentle pressure on the abdomen of a ripe female. Milt is then added by forcing a male in the same way. Eggs and milt are gently stirred by tilting the pan to accomplish fertilization. The fertilized eggs are then placed in a pail containing water and clay in suspension. Clay particles adhere to the eggs which are adhesive for the first hour. After hardening for an hour or so, the eggs can be transported and placed in battery jars where they will remain separated and roll freely. The hatch of artificially fertilized eggs is high, running 75 per cent or more.
>
> The walleye fry are reared to larger sizes in fertilized natural rearing ponds. Mean production of 48 pounds of fingerlings per acre has been achieved in Minnesota. Maximum production was 234 pounds per acre.

Fingerlings range from slightly over 25 mm to about 127 mm long, with a few somewhat larger. The most consistently successful walleye stockings are in new impoundments or rehabilitated lakes. Fry are usually used for this purpose. Wisconsin has a 9.3-ha (23-acre) drainable pond which has been used for walleye fingerling production for many years (Klingbiel 1969). Excluding 1 year in which production was very low, the harvest has averaged 130 kg/ha (116 lb/acre), and 83% survival has been obtained.

Stocking rates for walleyes vary according to a sliding scale for lakes of different sizes. The larger the lake, the smaller the per hectare stocking rate. A 40.5-ha lake receives 50 fingerlings per hectare, whereas a 405-ha lake receives 19.5 per hectare. Deviations are made, however, whenever conditions warrant.

In Wisconsin, walleye populations in many waters are quite stable, producing good natural year classes annually or every 2 or 3 years (Klingbiel 1969). Other waters, however, have tremendous population fluctuations. The causes of such fluctuations are not always known, but at times they are quite evident. High onshore winds, fluctuating water levels, and high predator populations are sometimes limiting factors.

The construction of artificial spawning beds holds promise for improved walleye reproduction. Although artificial reefs were not successful in establishing walleye year classes in Jennie Webber Lake (Oneida County), two of the three reefs were used for walleye spawning, and advanced egg development took place (McKnight 1975). Unexpected reproduction occurred when walleyes began to spawn on the rock riprapped bank and willow root entanglements just below a highway fronting on Lake Minocqua, Oneida County (Niemuth et al. 1959a). Among the few known walleye spawning sites in the Mississippi River are the riprapped wing dams below the locks (Gebken and Wright 1972b).

Bever and Lealos (1974) have suggested that an inverse relationship exists between walleye numbers and the abundance of panfish and related forage species. A decline in panfish numbers and an increase in walleye numbers has been observed in the Pike Lake Chain (Price County); however, this has not resulted in an associated increase in walleye biomass. They suggest increasing the forage base through intensive stocking of desirable food species (e.g., yellow perch).

F. H. Johnson (1977) determined that the removal of white suckers from lakes with a limited number of fish species appears to benefit walleye and yellow perch populations. In more productive waters where species composition is more diversified, the productivity released by removing white suckers might be assimilated by other species that feed on the same foods, with no measurable response by the percid populations.

Sufficient evidence has been presented above to indicate that successful walleye populations depend on spring flooding. Flooded marshes produce prime spawning sites. In 1964, when the marshes were dry along the Wolf River, walleyes were observed spawning on sand bars in the main river channel, as well as along the river's banks where grassy vegetation occurred, and in the deeper bayous. Although Priegel (1970b) followed egg development in numerous areas, no indication of a hatch was found. Though flooding may present problems to man in his many endeavors, it is beneficial to the walleye and to other fish species.

After a thorough study of the walleye spawning marshes along the Wolf and Fox rivers, Priegel (1970b) concluded that state ownership of existing spawning marshes was of primary importance for the maintenance of high quality spawning sites. All walleye spawning marshes along the Wolf and Fox rivers have been mapped and approved for acquisition by the state. Priegel recommended the following management practices for state-owned marshes: the prevention of level ditching or diking which would block the flow of water across the marshes; the use of controlled burning and brush cutting to curtail plant succession on marshes where desirable grasses and sedges were being replaced by undesirable woody vegetation; and the deepening of channels and removal of roads to improve current flow over the marshes.

According to Klingbiel (1969), the regulation of impoundment water levels to favor walleyes is becoming easier because of legislation and public opinion. The protection of natural spawning areas by land control and legislation is increasing.

Sauger

Stizostedion canadense (Smith). *Stizostedion*—pungent throat, according to Rafinesque; *canadense*—of Canada, the type locality.

Other common names: eastern sauger, sand pike, river pike, spotfin pike, ground pike, sand pike-perch, sand pickerel, blue pike, blue pikeperch, blue pickerel, gray pikeperch, gray pickerel, dory, walleye, pickering, jackfish, jack salmon.

Subadult 187 mm, Mississippi R., Dresbach Dam (La Crosse Co.), 13 June 1974

DESCRIPTION

Body elongate, almost cylindrical but slightly compressed laterally. Length 305–330 mm (12–13 in). TL = 1.20 SL. Depth into SL 5.0–5.9. Head length into SL 3.1–3.4. Preopercle serrated on posterior edge. Gill membranes extended forward, narrowly or not joined to one another, narrowly joined to isthmus. Premaxillaries protractile, upper lip groove continuous over snout. Mouth large, almost horizontal, upper jaw reaching to back of eye, jaws equal anteriorly; strong, caninelike teeth on premaxillaries, lower jaw, and palatines; pharyngeal arches with short, recurved teeth. Gill rakers on lower limb of first arch about 8. Branchiostegal rays usually 7. Dorsal fins 2: first or spiny dorsal fin with 12 (10–13) spines; second dorsal fin with 1–2 spines, 18 (17–19) rays. Anal fin with 2 spines and 11–13 rays; pelvic fins thoracic, space between pelvic fins greater than base of one pelvic fin. Scales ctenoid; cheeks well scaled; opercles, breast, and belly scaled. Lateral line complete, scales 79–87. Pyloric caeca usually 4–6, each usually shorter than stomach. Vertebrae 44–45 (Bailey and Gosline 1955).

Dorsal region of head and back brown to gray; sides paler, ventral region of head and belly white. Sides and back variously speckled with dusky spots; 4 dark saddles across back, some of which expand horizontally on sides. Eyes silvery in life; a well-developed reflecting layer (tapetum lucidum) causes glowing in dark. Membranes on the spiny dorsal fin with definite horizontal rows of spots, and last few membranes not solid black; second dorsal and caudal fins with dark spots in regular rows; ventral lobe of caudal fin sometimes white edged. Pectoral fins lightly speckled, and with a strong, black blotch at base; pelvic and anal fins clear to lightly speckled.

Breeding male without nuptial tubercles.

Hybrids: Sauger × walleye (Stroud 1948).

DISTRIBUTION, STATUS, AND HABITAT

In Wisconsin, the sauger occurs in both the Lake Michigan and Mississippi River drainage basins, but not in Wisconsin waters of the Lake Superior drainage.

In the Lake Michigan drainage, the sauger is abundant in Lake Winnebago, and is occasionally taken in Lakes Poygan, Winneconne, and Butte des Morts (Priegel 1969c). In the Upper Fox River, it has been taken as far upstream as the Eureka Dam. It occurs in Little Lake Butte des Morts, in the lower Fox River, and in Green Bay.

In the Mississippi River drainage, the sauger is common in the Mississippi River, and, according to Priegel, occurs in the following tributaries: the St. Croix River upstream to the dam at St. Croix Falls; the Kinnickinnic River from the River Falls Dam downstream to the St. Croix; the Chippewa River upstream to the dam at Eau Claire; the Eau Claire River to the dam at Lake Altoona; the Eau Galle River to the Eau Galle Dam; the Red Cedar River to the dam at Menomonie; the Black River upstream to the Jackson County line; the La Crosse River to the dam at Lake Neshonoc; and the lower reaches of the Bad Axe River. It is also found in the Wisconsin River upstream to lower Adams County, and in the lower reaches of two Wisconsin River tributaries, Otter Creek and the Kickapoo River. It is more common below the Prairie du Sac Dam than the walleye. Two saugers were reported from Jordan Lake (Adams County) in 1958.

Cahn (1927) reported the sauger from Lac La Belle and Forest Lake (Waukesha County); he suggested that it had been widely introduced in Waukesha County; however, no recent records are known, and it is doubtful that this species still exists there.

Greene (1935) doubted that the sauger was native to the Lake Michigan drainage of Wisconsin.

Greene had only a single report from Lake Winnebago, and failed to take any specimens himself while sampling from 1925 through 1928. He suggested that the sauger may have entered the Lake Michigan drainage by way of the Fox connectives—outlets of

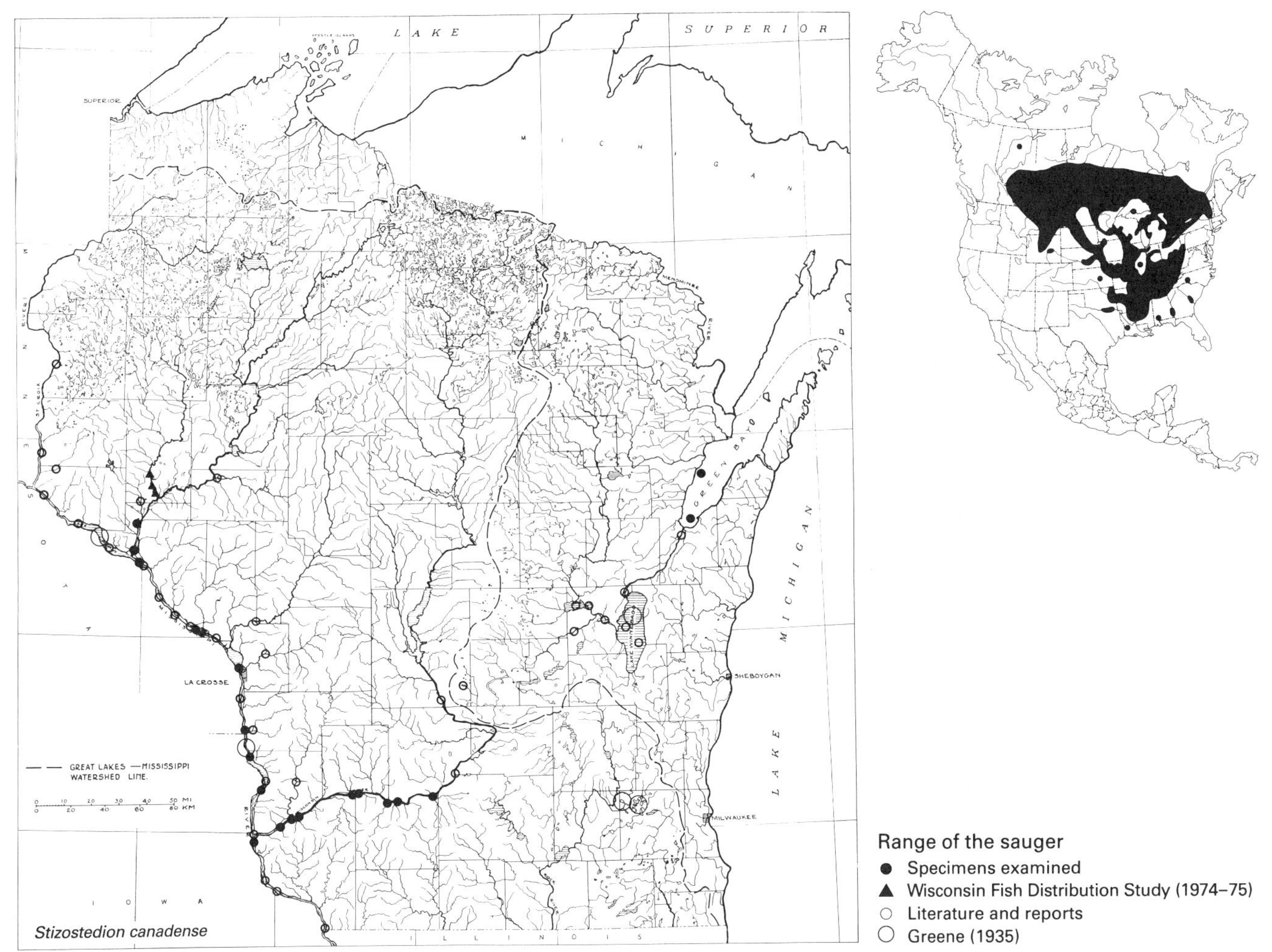

glacial Lake Oshkosh near the Portage Canal and Lake Winnebago. Priegel (1969c) learned from discussions with reliable, long-term residents, who knew the difference between the sauger and the walleye, that the Lake Winnebago sauger had "provided a fabulous fishery during the winter since the early 1920's."

In Wisconsin, the sauger appears to have extended its range since the 1920s. It is found in increasing abundance in both the Mississippi River and Lake Michigan drainages.

The sauger prefers large, turbid rivers and lakes. It occurs in large, deep waters of low gradients, except during spawning, when it may occur in the tailwaters of dams over rubble substrates. In the Mississippi River saugers prefer running water, except in areas such as Lake Pepin; they are generally found in the main channel, in the side channels, and in the tailwaters below the dams. It has been observed that young saugers sometimes frequent the shallow mud flats; they have been collected in such areas near the mouth of the Chippewa River in Lake Pepin and in other locations.

BIOLOGY

The life history of the sauger in Lake Winnebago has been thoroughly documented by Priegel (1969c). Unless otherwise indicated, the following account is from that source.

Saugers are known to spawn in both streams and lakes, but the choice of a stream or a lake apparently depends on local conditions in the waters concerned. Spawning generally occurs over hard bottoms in the reservoirs of streams, in the tailwaters of dams, and in the running water at the heads of major tributaries to reservoirs on large rivers. In Lake Erie, the sauger spawns on shallow bars of gravel or sand, and often runs up nearby rivers to spawn (Fish 1932); with the beginning of warm weather it is reported to work its way downstream again and to move into deep lake water.

The principal spawning sites of saugers in Lake

Winnebago extend almost without interruption for a distance of approximately 13 km (8 mi) along the north shore of the lake. Some spawning has been noted on the Calumetville reef along the east shore, and on the Long Point Island reef along the west shore. There is no indication of spawning migrations into either the Wolf or the Fox rivers.

Spawning occurs from late April through early May when water temperatures are between 6.1 and 11.7°C (43 and 53°F); peak activity occurs in May. The male saugers arrive on the spawning grounds before the females. No nest is built. Spawning occurs at night, and females leave the grounds soon after spawning (Scott and Crossman 1973). The eggs are shed in Lake Winnebago along the entire northern shore, in water depths up to 1.2 m on sand, rocks, and gravel, with a greater number on gravel. Spawning is essentially completed in less than 2 weeks.

In Pool 7 on the Mississippi River, spawning occurred 14 April 1969 (Upper Miss. R. Conserv. Com. 1970, Gebken and Wright 1972b). The water temperature was 8.3°C (47°F), and the river was 0.8 m above flood stage. The saugers, 50% of which were ripe, were found in 0.3–1.4 m of water over rock riprap. Very little is known about the spawning habits and the specific spawning sites of saugers and walleyes in the western Wisconsin boundary waters. It is suspected that flooding is responsible for strong year classes, since suitable spawning areas become increasingly available as flood waters rise over the rock-riprapped dikes adjoining dams.

The average number of eggs produced by saugers 257–371 mm TL, from Lake Winnebago, was 15,871. There was a range of 4,208 eggs for a 269-mm fish to 43,396 eggs for a 368-mm fish. In South Dakota, the estimated number of eggs ranged from 19,130 to 209,920; the average number of eggs per kilogram of body weight was 65,250 (W. R. Nelson 1969).

According to Priegel, the fertilized sauger eggs are not strongly adhesive; they are not found clinging to rocks or to any other substrates after water hardening. In Lewis and Clark Lake, South Dakota, the incubation period for sauger eggs was approximately 21 days at an average water temperature of 8.3°C (47°F) (W. R. Nelson 1968). The eggs of Wisconsin saugers averaged 1.3 (1.0–1.5) mm diam. In a fish hatchery they hatched into larvae 4.7–5.1 mm TL.

Priegel was able to separate very young saugers from walleyes by the absence of pigmentation on the dorsal surface of the sauger's midbrain area, which is visible through the top of the head. In walleye larvae this area is heavily pigmented, and appears dark to black.

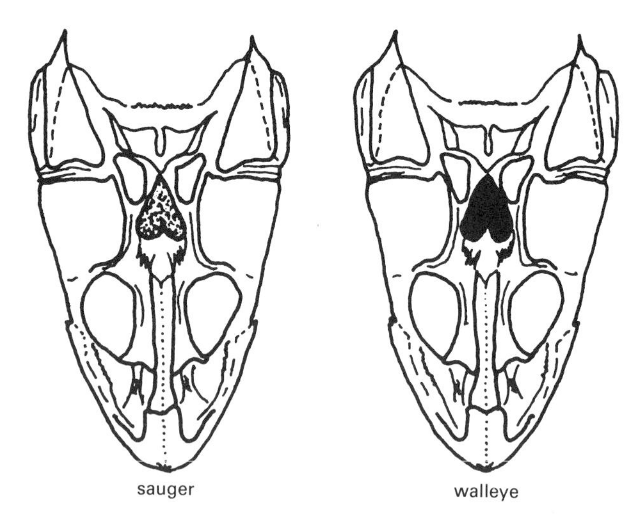

Identification of young saugers and walleyes by the "color spot" technique (Priegel 1969c:36)

M. Fish (1932) illustrated and described the 9-, 13-, 14.6-, and 27-mm stages. W. R. Nelson (1968) illustrated the 5.5-, 8.5-, 10.3-, 14.5-, and 17.5-mm stages, and described how very young saugers may be distinguished from young walleyes by the sauger's smaller size, fewer areas of pigmentation, and more oval yolk-sac shape.

In Lake Winnebago, the first young saugers were taken on 3 June; they averaged 17 (12–20) mm TL. Usually the first fry are captured after 20 June, and exceed 20 mm in length. By trawling in deeper, open-water areas of the lake, Priegel readily took saugers in the 12–50-mm size class. Young-of-year averaged 50 mm in mid-July, 75 mm in mid-August, 118 mm in mid-October, and up to 154 mm at the end of October.

The calculated lengths at the annuli of saugers from Wisconsin and elsewhere are given on the next page. The age of saugers is determined by scale analysis. The precise time of the annulus formation of Lake Winnebago saugers has not been established, but Priegel stated that it probably occurs in mid-May. No fish obtained during April had formed a new annulus. The calculated weights for Lake Winnebago saugers were: age I—9 g male (14 g female); II—91 g (104 g); III—195 g (204 g); IV—259 g (268 g); V—313 g (327 g); VI—372 g (390 g); VII—422 g (431 g); and VIII—468 g (468 g). A 5-year-old female was 460 mm (18.1 in) TL and weighed 953 g (2.1 lb) ; the heaviest male was 7 years old, 419 mm (16.5 in) long, and weighed 652 g (1 lb 7 oz).

Of 1,742 saugers sampled from Lake Winnebago, 54.9% were females; the sex ratio of males to females was 1:1.2. Few saugers live beyond 5 years in Lake Winnebago; only 10.8% of the males sampled were

Age and Growth (TL in mm) of the Sauger in Wisconsin and South Dakota

Location	1	2	3	4	5	6	7	8	Source
Mississippi R., L. Pepin, Pool 4	267	338	381	434	472	483			Upper Mississippi River Conservation Committee (1967)
Mississippi R., Pools 4–6	137	234	297	335	335	391			Kittel (1955)
Mississippi R., Pool 5A	124	229	302	345					Christenson and Smith (1965)
Mississippi R., Pool 7[a]	155	244	315	381	472	483	544		Gebken and Wright (1972b)
Mississippi R., Pools 7–10	249	300	351	391	411	427	478		Jergens and Childers (1959)
Mississippi R., Pool 11	145	269	356	414	450	480	513		Vasey (1967)
L. Winnebago (Winnebago Co.)									
Males	124	241	302	333	361	388	401	411	Priegel (1969c)
Females	135	241	297	325	358	394	417	434	
Lewis and Clark L., S. Dak.[b]									
Males	186	315	376	421	469				W. R. Nelson (1969)
Females	193	327	411	472	512	560	596	626	

[a]Empirical lengths, not calculated to annulus.
[b]Corrected, using an intercept of 29 mm.

over 5 years of age, compared to only 7% of the females.

Male saugers attain maturity at age II, while females attain maturity at age IV. The respective lengths at which more than 50% of the male and female saugers from Lake Winnebago attained maturity were 249 and 284 mm. On the Mississippi River, female saugers mature as early as age III (Gebken and Wright 1972b).

A 2.31-kg (5-lb 1.5-oz) sauger was caught from the Mississippi River (Buffalo County) on 26 May 1976 (Wis. Dep. Nat. Resour. 1977). Nord (1967) reported that an individual weighing more than 2.72 kg (6 lb) was taken by angling in 1964 below Lock and Dam 4 on the Mississippi River. A 711-mm, 3.97-kg (28-in, 8-lb 12-oz) sauger was taken from Lake Sakakawea, North Dakota, on 6 October 1971 (*World Almanac* 1976).

In Lake Winnebago, saugers in the 12–50-mm size class fed heavily on *Daphnia* sp., and to a lesser extent on *Cyclops* and chironomid larvae and pupae. The fry of trout-perch, white bass, and freshwater drum were found in 46.9% of sauger stomachs examined in 1966, and 64.7% of the stomachs examined in 1967. Saugers in the 51–75-mm class consumed young freshwater drum, trout-perch and white bass, but when these were not available in sufficient quantities they turned to *Cyclops*, *Daphnia*, chironomid larvae and pupae. Among saugers in the 76–150-mm class, chironomid larvae were the most important food item; in 1965, however, they positively sought and selected *Leptodora*, the least abundant (but large and attractive) zooplankton in Lake Winnebago. Fish remains, primarily trout-perch, were found in about half the stomachs.

In seven of eight samples during 1965, yearling saugers from Lake Winnebago fed primarily on fish. Fish were also the most important items consumed by adult saugers on all sampling dates from 1965 to 1968, occurring in 63.4–100% of the stomachs and accounting for 90.4–100% of the total food volume (Priegel 1969c). Trout-perch were the most frequently utilized forage fish; others eaten were young walleyes, saugers, burbots, black crappies, yellow perch, and white bass. When emerald shiners and trout-perch were present in abundance, the trout-perch were preferred by the saugers (Priegel 1962c). Saugers less than 279 mm long ate the most invertebrates, including chironomid larvae and leeches; saugers more than 279 mm long also ate midge larvae, leeches, and young-of-year freshwater drums. Priegel noted that walleyes showed a greater preference for emerald shiners, while saugers preferred trout-perch, thereby reducing competition between these closely related species.

Scott and Crossman (1973) noted that the northern distribution of the sauger is apparently related to the 15.6°C (60°F) July isotherm. In the Wabash River, Indiana, saugers avoided the three heated zones and consistently selected the coolest zones available; Gammon (1973) suggested a preferred water temperature of about 25.5°C (78°F). The preferred temperatures of saugers in the Norris Reservoir, Tennessee, were 18.6–19.2°C (65.5–66.6°F) (Ferguson 1958). The maximum temperature at which saugers were captured in the White River and Ipalco Discharge Canal, Indiana, was 33.6°C (92.5°F) (Proffitt and Benda 1971).

In the sauger the tapetum lucidum (reflecting layer behind the retina) is more uniformly developed within the eye, than it is in the walleye, in which it is well developed only in the ventral region (Collette et al. 1977). Apparently this sensitivity gives the sauger an advantage over the walleye in turbid water. In a bay of Lake Nipigon, Ontario, walleye dominance changed to sauger dominance a few years after turbid water had been diverted into the bay (Scott and Crossman 1973). Turbidity may prevent excessive egg adhesion and thereby reduce suffocation, it may protect the young from predators, and it may facilitate the feeding of the young by concentrating plankton near the surface. Saugers are more adapted to darkness and feed in deeper water than walleyes. In clearer water saugers are most active for short periods in the evening and early morning. In more turbid water, where light intensities are lower, the period of activity is longer. Collette et al. (1977) indicated that in shallow water the activity of saugers increases when the wind increases.

In large, deep lakes the sauger is generally found in bays in the region above the thermocline, although in Lake Huron Koelz (1929) reported gill netting specimens from depths of 146–183 m. In clear water at midday, saugers tend to stay in deep water, but they remain above the thermocline.

On rare occasions saugers are known to descend the St. Lawrence River to a point where the water is usually brackish (Scott and Crossman 1973).

Collette et al. (1977) stated that saugers are the most migratory of the percids. Tagged fish have been recovered at distances up to about 380 km (236 mi) from the point of release; their minimal mean swimming speeds have been estimated at 19.7 km/day upstream and 21.1 km/day downstream.

Studies of saugers tagged in the Mississippi River below Lock and Dam 6 in the spring of 1959 demonstrated that movement out of the home pool is insignificant, and that locks and dams do not prohibit movement between pools (Hubley 1963b). Saugers were recovered up to 57 km (35 mi) from the point of tagging.

In the Missouri River, the farthest distance traveled by saugers was 105 km (65 mi)—from the tailwaters of the Fort Randall Dam to the tailwaters of the Gavins Point Dam (W. R. Nelson 1969). Most saugers, especially mature fish, move out of Lewis and Clark Lake in the fall and winter to concentrate upstream in the Missouri River and in the tailwaters of the Fort Randall Dam. After the completion of spawning in the spring, the fish return to Lewis and Clark Lake.

IMPORTANCE AND MANAGEMENT

Saugers of various sizes are preyed on by saugers, walleyes, and northern pike, and probably by yellow perch, burbot, gars and bowfins. Although saugers consume most fishes, Scott and Crossman (1973) have suggested that they are not significant predators on any species of importance to man.

The sauger is host to the glochidial stages of a large number of mollusk species, including *Amblema plicata, Megalonaias gigantea, Quadrula metanevra, Plethobasus cyphyus, Actinonaias carinata, Lampsilis orbiculata, Lampsilis ovata, Lampsilis radiata luteola, Ligumia recta, Ellipsaria lineolata, Truncilla donaciformis,* and *Truncilla truncata* (Hart and Fuller 1974).

Where it is found in large numbers in Wisconsin, the sauger is an important sport fish. Its firm, white flesh is equal to the walleye's in taste, and some connoisseurs prefer it to walleye. Angling for saugers is largely confined to Lake Winnebago and to the Mississippi River and the extreme lower reaches of its major tributaries. The sauger is taken below dams, at the mouths of tributary streams, and below the rock wing dams in the Mississippi River. Anglers usually prefer to catch walleyes, since they are larger in size. Saugers respond readily to both artificial and live baits, including small bass plugs, spinner-minnow and spinner-fly combinations, streamer hair and feather wet flies, live minnows, small frogs, and nightcrawlers (Harlan and Speaker 1956).

The sauger is more abundant in the Mississippi River than the walleye. In the Burlington to Dubuque (Iowa) sector of the river, in an experimental netting, 68 saugers were taken with 17 walleyes (Barnickol and Starrett 1951). In a gill net sample taken in Lake Pepin during October 1965, 368 saugers were caught with 55 walleyes (Upper Miss. R. Conserv. Com. 1967); the saugers made up 19.2% of the total catch. In 1957, the sauger ranked third in the sport catch of the upper Mississippi River, and in 1962–1963 it ranked sixth (Nord 1967). The estimated sport fishery catch of saugers in Pools 4, 5, 7, and 11 of the

Sauger winter catch (Wisconsin DNR photo)

Mississippi River in 1967–1968 was 107,803 fish weighing 47,930 kg (105,666 lb) (Wright 1970).

In Lake Winnebago, the majority of saugers are caught through the ice, and this species usually constitutes more than half of the ice fisherman's catch (Priegel 1967a). On 28 January 1961, a creel census showed that 2,813 of the anglers checked had taken 3,998 saugers, which was 75% of all fish taken. Wind tipups baited with minnows are effective when fishing for saugers through the ice. When the water is open in the spring, saugers are effectively caught by trolling or drifting over sand bars and gravel along the north and northeast shores of the lake. The sauger harvest during the rest of the year is minimal at best, and at times there is no sauger fishing at all (Priegel 1968c).

In Wisconsin a number of rivers and inland lakes (including Lake Winnebago) have a continuous open season on saugers; others have a closed period from 1 March to early May. The 1980 Wisconsin fishing regulations generally allow a daily combined total of five saugers and walleyes; for most waters there is no minimum size limit (Wis. Dep. Nat. Resour. 1979). Before fishing, the angler should consult current fishing regulations.

Priegel (1969c) has suggested that the sauger in Lake Winnebago could stand a greater harvest and recommended that on Lake Winnebago a daily bag limit of five saugers should be tried to increase the sauger harvest. The daily bag limit of a combined total of five walleyes and saugers is not sufficient to harvest a sauger population that is shortlived, very stable, and attains high population levels. The argument that anglers cannot distinguish saugers from walleyes is not realistic in view of the fact that there are separate bag limits for northern pike and muskellunge, which resemble each other, and for largemouth bass and smallmouth bass, which are also similar.

Carlander (1955) determined that standing crops of saugers from Tennessee to Wisconsin averaged 2.0 kg/ha (0.5–6.3 kg/ha). Rapid growth rate of saugers is common in the expanding environments of new reservoirs (Carter 1968, W. R. Nelson 1969); Nelson noted that growth rate improved after impoundment of the reservoir (Lewis and Clark Lake) in 1955 but thereafter decreased and was quite stable between 1957 and 1963.

Yellow Perch

Perca flavescens (Mitchill). *Perca*—dusky, the ancient name of *Perca fluviatilis*, the Eurasian perch; *flavescens*—becoming gold colored.

Other common names: perch, lake perch, river perch, common perch, American perch, ringed perch, ringtail perch, raccoon perch, red perch, striped perch.

Adult 158 mm, Sugar Cr. (Door Co.), 19 Sept. 1965

DESCRIPTION

Body oval in cross section. Length 127–229 mm (5–9 in). TL = 1.20 SL. Depth into SL 3.3–3.8; deepest of all fishes in the perch family. Head length into SL 2.8–3.1. Preopercle serrated on posterior edge. Gill membranes extended forward, not joined to one another, and not joined to isthmus. Premaxillaries protractile, upper lip groove continuous over tip of snout. Mouth moderately large, slightly oblique, upper jaw reaching to pupil of eye, lower jaw equal to or slightly longer than upper jaw; minute, pointed teeth in brushlike pads on upper and lower jaws; no canines. Gill rakers on first arch heavy, close-set, about 18; branchiostegal rays usually 7. Dorsal fins 2: first or spiny dorsal fin with 13 (12–14) spines; second dorsal fin with 2 spines, 12–14 rays. Anal fin with 2 spines, 7–8 rays; pelvic fins thoracic, space between pelvic fins less than one-half base of 1 pelvic fin. Scales ctenoid; cheeks scaled, opercles mostly scaleless, breast, and belly scaled. Lateral line complete, scales 52–61. Pyloric caeca 3, short, thick. Vertebrae 40 (39–41) (Bailey and Gosline 1955). Chromosomes 2n = 48 (*Chromosome Atlas* 1973).

Dorsal region of head and back brown to green; sides yellow-green to yellow; ventral region of head and belly whitish; 6–7 dark, vertical bands extending over back and ending on lower sides. Eyes yellow to green. Spiny dorsal fin dusky, but black in the first 2 and the last 3–4 interradial membranes. Pectoral fins darkly pigmented anteriorly; pelvic fins generally clear; the paired fins yellowish to reddish in life.

Breeding male without nuptial tubercles, but more intensely colored than breeding female.

Sexual dimorphism: In male, urogenital opening behind the anus; in female, 2 openings (genital and urinary) behind the anus (Moen 1959).

DISTRIBUTION, STATUS, AND HABITAT

The yellow perch occurs in all three drainage basins in Wisconsin, in all of the state's boundary waters, and in Lakes Michigan and Superior. A glacial lake species, it is widely distributed except in the unglaciated region of southwestern Wisconsin.

The yellow perch is common locally in the Mississippi and lower Wisconsin rivers, and it is abundant in lakes, ponds, and impoundments on rivers. In Lake Pepin (Pepin County), its numbers have increased since the turn of the century. It is probably the most abundant panfish in Lake Poygan and in Pewaukee Lake (Becker 1964a,b). In Lake Winnebago, it is second only to the white bass in numbers (Priegel 1967a). The yellow perch is an important panfish in Lake Mendota (Dane County), Arbor Vitae Lake (Vilas County), Lake Geneva (Walworth County), and Little Lake Butte des Morts (Winnebago County). It is common in Chequamegon Bay (Johnson and Becker 1970), and at the barriers in tributaries to Lake Superior, especially in those streams with lakes in their systems (McLain et al. 1965). This species is also common in Green Bay and the inshore waters of Lake Michigan (Herman et al. 1959). Early in the century the yellow perch was the most abundant panfish in Lake Wingra (Dane County), but today it is far behind the bluegill, pumpkinseed, white crappie, and yellow bass (Noland 1951, Churchill 1976).

The yellow perch is adaptable to a wide variety of habitats; however, it prefers lakes, backwaters, and sloughs with modest amounts of vegetation and water of moderate fertility. In stream collection samples it has been encountered in slow, medium, and fast currents, although it occurred more commonly in pools of the following widths: 1.0–3.0 m (15%), 3.1–6.0 m (13%), 6.1–12.0 m (17%), 12.1–24.0 m (28%), 24.1–50.0 m (17%), and more than 50 m (10%). It occurred most frequently in shallows in clear to slightly turbid water, over substrates of sand (30% frequency), gravel (21%), mud (17%), silt (11%), rubble (9%), boulders (7%), detritus (3%), clay (1%), and marl (1%).

BIOLOGY

Spawning normally occurs shortly after ice-out in April or early May, at water temperatures of 7.2–11.1°C (45–52°F) (Herman et al. 1959, C. E. Johnson 1971). The spawning of the yellow perch closely follows that

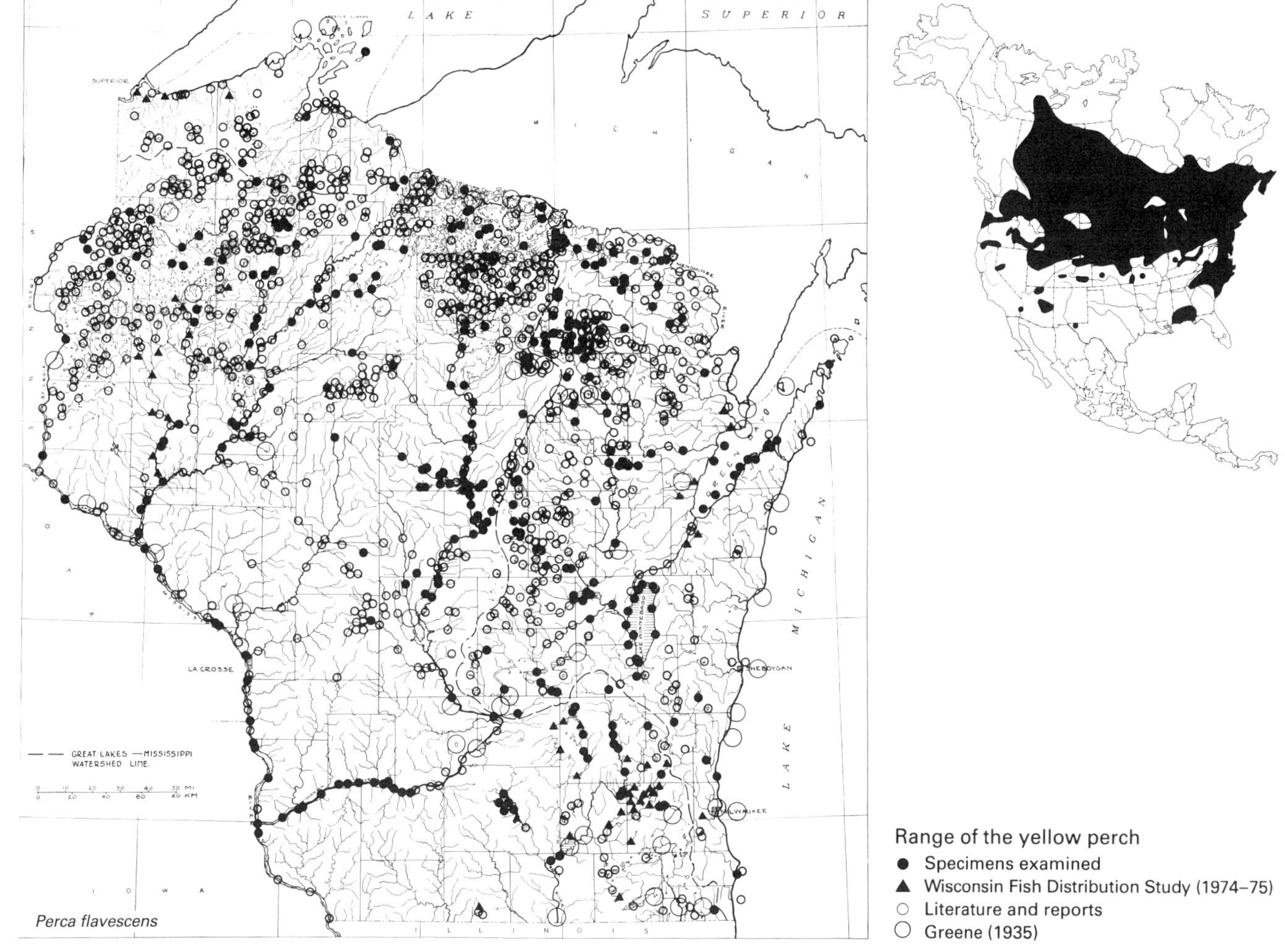

Perca flavescens

Range of the yellow perch
● Specimens examined
▲ Wisconsin Fish Distribution Study (1974–75)
○ Literature and reports
◯ Greene (1935)

of walleyes and often coincides with that of suckers. In Lake Winnebago, the spawning season usually starts between early April and early May, and once initiated may continue for 8–19 days (Weber 1975). Peak spawning occurs at water temperatures ranging from 6.7 to 19.0°C (44–66°F), and Weber noted that many yellow perch from Lake Winnebago migrate considerable distances to the upper Fox River to spawn—a round-trip journey of as much as 48–81 km (30–50 mi). In Lake Michigan, spawning occurs from 11 June to the end of June (R. Schumacher, pers. comm.).

Yellow perch are random spawners, and do not construct nests; nor do they guard their eggs and their young. The relatively unspecialized requirements of this species for spawning substrates allow yellow perch to use almost all slow-moving or static waters within their geographical range (Collette et al. 1977). The eggs are usually deposited in sheltered areas—most frequently they are draped over emergent and submergent vegetation or submerged brush in water depths of 0.6–3 m. Spawning generally occurs at night (Breder and Rosen 1966) although Harrington (1947) observed spawning after 0940 hr at a water temperature of 8.9°C (48°F) (p. 199):

> . . . A single, large, conspicuously gravid female was followed by a long queue of males. The first two males kept their snouts prodded against the belly of the female, and they were followed by a double row of males so close to one another that the retinue moved as one body led by the female. Several such retinues were formed, and maneuvered in the area at the same time. Each one was about a yard long, and numbered from 15 to 25 individuals. These queues followed a curved course, ranging from bottom in 2 to 4 feet of water, and often proceeding through spaces among the interlacing branches near the surface.

Activity continued at 1130 hr at 9.4°C (49°F), but fewer fish appeared to be present. The eggs were draped on branches of birch and pine which had toppled into the water. At the time of egg deposition, the males shed milt close to the female's vent.

Spawning by yellow perch in aquariums was observed by Hergenrader (1969:840):

> . . . At 1125 hr one of the females, who was in and facing the corner of the aquarium, attended by three males which were beside and beneath her near her vent, began a series

of rapid swimming movements. The female's tail beats increased in frequency until expulsion of the egg strand occurred. The strand was expelled over a period of 5 sec. Almost simultaneously the males released milt which appeared as a white cloud. Two strings of eggs were released although they probably represented a single mass that was torn in half. After release of the eggs the males left and did not approach the female again. The female did not attempt to protect the egg strand. . . .

Whenever a female made a quick turn or some other rapid movement, the males rushed to her and appeared to compete for the position just beneath and behind the vent. Quick movements invariably attracted the males who remained near the female for a few seconds, and then swam away if the movements did not persist. Hergenrader reported the release of seven fertilized egg strands, some about 60 cm long. Although the defense of eggs by the female yellow perch has been observed in a tank, it is not known if this occurs regularly in the wild (Collette et al. 1977).

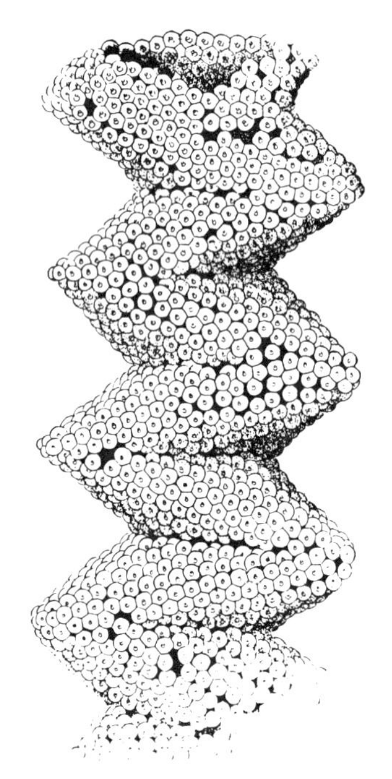

Yellow perch egg strand (Worth 1892:334)

Yellow perch egg strands are distinctive, and there is little possibility of confusing them with the eggs of any other species of fish. The eggs are held in a massive, gelatinous matrix known as a strand. These strands are accordion folded, about 38 mm thick, and slightly heavier than water; they float in the current until they become entangled in debris and fallen branches in the shallow water (Mansueti 1964). When water hardened, the strands attain lengths far exceeding that of the parent fish. Jordan and Evermann described an unusually large egg strand (1923:367):

. . . One yellow perch in a Fish Commission aquarium at Washington deposited a string of eggs 7 feet 4 inches long, 4 inches wide at one end and 2 at the other. After being fertilized this string weighed 2 pounds 9 ounces, while the weight of the fish before the eggs were discharged was only 1 pound 8 ounces.

The fecundity of yellow perch varies strikingly in different localities. Egg numbers range from 950 to 210,000; egg diameters vary from 1.0 to 2.1 mm (Thorpe 1977). In Minnesota, egg production varied from 10,000 to 48,000, with the largest fish producing the greatest number of eggs (Vessel and Eddy 1941). In Lake Winnebago, a 132-mm, age-II female held 4,200 eggs, and a 305-mm, age-VII female held 121,000 eggs (Weber 1975). The gonads of the yellow perch before spawning may make up more than 20% of the body weight of the female, and more than 8% of the body weight of the male; after spawning the ovaries or testes may shrink to about 1% or less of the body weight (Lagler et al. 1977).

The hatching time of yellow perch eggs is variable. Herman et al. (1959) reported incubation over 8–10 days at normal water temperatures in the spring; Mansueti (1964) reported a 27-day incubation period at temperatures of 8.5–12.0°C (47.3–53.6°F). Weber (1975) noted an incubation period of 17–20 days, and hatching over a period of 5–7 days. The prolarvae are 5.5–7.0 mm TL (Norden 1961).

The early development of Lake Winnebago yellow perch is discussed by Weber (1975) who provided photographs of embryos 1 day and 9 days after fertilization. The larvae are less than 5 mm long upon hatching. They swim up to the surface, where they remain in the upper 0.9–1.2 m of water for 3 or 4 weeks. The yolk-sac is absorbed in 3–5 days. Microscopic zooplankton become important to the survival of young yellow perch when they first begin to feed; if the zooplankton are too large for the young to eat, the fry will starve soon after their yolk-sacs and oil globules have been used up. Mansueti (1964) noted that in the laboratory there was an almost complete lack of feeding success among yellow perch in larval stages.

According to Mansueti (1964), fin formation starts at approximately 11 mm TL. All of the yellow perch's fins are formed at 13 mm TL. The formation of distinct body bands begins when the young are about 20 mm TL. M. Fish (1932) described and illustrated 5.6-, 7.3-, 9-, 12.5-, 14.4-, 20-, and 20.5-mm stages. Norden (1961) sketched the 5.8- and 12.0-mm stages, and provided means for separating perch and walleye larvae (see p. 874).

In Vilas County lakes, larval yellow perch were caught in varying numbers from the open water region between late May and early July (Faber 1967). In Lake Winnebago, the young live and feed near the surface until they are about 25 mm long (Weber 1975); at this size they gradually swim to the bottom of the lake. By mid-July, young yellow perch have attained 50% of their first year's growth; they are 102 mm (4 in) long by the end of the growing season in October.

The age of yellow perch is determined by markings on the scales. In this species, the time of annulus formation varies with the calendar year, with age (new growth starts earlier in younger fish), and possibly with locale. Growth is more rapid in southern Wisconsin waters than in northern waters.

The weights of yellow perch from the Lake Michigan study below (Schaefer 1977) were: I—13 g; II—58 g; III—84 g; IV—108 g; V—171 g; VI—233 g; and VII—307 g. Females grew faster and lived longer than males. Yellow perch of ages III to VIII from Lake Mendota (Dane County) showed the following total length and weight relationships: 188 mm—82 g; 213 mm—132 g; 236 mm—182 g; 251 mm—218 g; 264 mm—268 g; and 279 mm—281 g (Mackenthun and Herman 1949). The average yellow perch in the catch of Lake Mendota fishermen in 1947 measured 244 mm (9.6 in) and weighed about 179 g (6.3 oz) (Herman et al. 1959).

Yellow perch increase in length rapidly during the first 2 years of life. Thereafter they show only small annual length increments, but significant weight gains. Growth was significantly less at an average mean water temperature of 14.5°C in one year than at 16.0°C in another year (Coble 1966). The maximum observed longevity of yellow perch is 13 years (Brown 1957).

The male yellow perch in Lake Mendota attains sexual maturity in its second year of life, and the female attains it in the third year (Hasler 1945). In Lake Winnebago, females reach maturity in the third or fourth year of life at lengths of 190–229 mm, while males mature during their second year at a length of about 152 mm TL (Weber 1975). It is not unusual to find males from stunted populations that have matured at 102 mm (4.0 in) (Herman et al. 1959).

A 1.47-kg (3-lb 4-oz) yellow perch was caught from Lake Winnebago in 1954 (Wis. Dep. Nat. Resour. 1977). A large yellow perch was taken in New Jersey in 1865; it weighed 1.91 kg (4 lb 3.5 oz) (*World Almanac* 1976).

In a Minnesota lake, yellow perch young-of-year began to feed when they were 6 mm long, and yolk-sac absorption was completed at 7.1 mm (Siefert 1972). Copepod nauplii were the dominant food at the initiation of feeding, and remained a common food for all sizes of fish examined. Cladocera were nearly absent from digestive tracts until the fish reached 11 mm. Algae were negligible food items.

In northern Wisconsin lakes, yellow perch young eat entomostracans, but quickly change to an insect diet consisting, usually, of small dipterous larvae (Couey 1935). These, along with other aquatic insect larvae, constitute the principal foods until the perch is rather large. Although yellow perch begin to eat fish at an early age, fish does not become a major food item until the perch has reached a length of 180 mm or more. One 200-mm yellow perch had eaten a 65-mm perch.

Couey found considerable variety in the food habits of the yellow perch from year to year, even among fish in the same body of water. In Silver Lake (Vilas County), fish constituted 90% of the food volume consumed by yellow perch in 1932, but only 6.5% in 1931. In general, insects were the principal food in 1931; they consisted of Diptera larvae, mayflies, caddisfly larvae, dragonfly nymphs, *Sialis* larvae, and

Age and Growth (TL in mm) of the Yellow Perch in Wisconsin

Location	1	2	3	4	5	6	7	Source
Drainage lakes, northwestern Wis.	69	109	140	180	201	236		Snow (1969)
Seepage lakes, northwestern Wis.	66	99	127	150	168	183		Snow (1969)
Flora L. (Vilas Co.)	84	109	131	159	189	229	249	Parker (1958)
Mississippi R., Pools 4–6	97	135	185	229	259	285		Kittel (1955)
L. Mendota (Dane C.)								
Males	142	198	224	231				Herman et al. (1959)
Females	137	196	231	246				
L. Wingra (Dane Co.)	109	145	170	192				Churchill (1976)
Green Bay (Oconto Co.)[a]								
Males	79	127	160	173				Joeris (1957)
Females	84	130	165	193	183			
L. Michigan (Milwaukee Co.)	77	138	175	200	228	247	269	Schaefer (1977)

[a]Empirical lengths, not calculated to annulus.

miscellaneous insects, and constituted 48% of the volume of food consumed. Fish were the next most important food.

The stomachs of Mirror Lake (Waupaca County) yellow perch exceeding 20 cm TL, contained chironomid larvae and pupae (82% frequency) and *Daphnia* (36%); for fish less than 20 cm TL the figures were 28% and 83% respectively (O. Brynildson and Serns 1977). Pearse (1918), in studying the food of shore fish in lakes near Madison, found that yellow perch ate mostly insects, amphipods and entomostracans; even large adults had nothing in the alimentary canal except a large number of cladocerans. Later studies in Lake Mendota and Green Lake indicated a diet mostly of insect larvae and entomostracans, along with lesser amounts of crayfish, oligochaetes, mollusks, plant material, and traces of fish (Pearse 1921a).

In western Lake Superior, crustaceans were the predominant food of yellow perch during all months except February (Anderson and Smith 1971b). Amphipods were the principal crustaceans during April and May, *Mysis* during November, and isopods in February. Copepods and cladocerans also were eaten. Unidentified fish remains were the most important item in February. Fish eggs were eaten in February and November, and plant material in February. In Lake Michigan near Milwaukee, 98% volume of the summer diet of adult yellow perch consisted of slimy sculpins and alewives; the other 2% included insects, cladocerans, fish eggs, and other fish (Schaefer 1977).

The close-set gill rakers of the yellow perch effectively strain out small pelagic foods. Two feeding periods are known—morning and afternoon; the heaviest feeding occurs in the afternoon. An adult yellow perch eats about 7% of its weight in a day (Pearse and Achtenberg 1920). Pearse, Achtenberg and Hasler (1945) reported that, for the summer and winter seasons, yellow perch move into water devoid of oxygen, in close proximity to the lake bottom, to feed on chironomid larvae. When feeding yellow perch were observed on 16 July 1954, the oxygenless zone was very near the lake bottom, which forced the perch to tolerate brief periods without oxygen while feeding on the bottom (Hasler and Tibbles 1970).

In three Ontario lakes and four Wisconsin lakes, yellow perch were found at average temperatures of 19.7–21°C (67.5–70°F) (Ferguson 1958). At the Lake Monona (Dane County) power plant, Neill and Magnuson (1974) noted that perch avoided the thermal outfall and preferred nearby lake temperatures of 27.1°C (81°F); in the laboratory its preferred temperature was 23.4°C (74°F). Yellow perch made forays for food into water both warmer and cooler than the preferred temperatures. In southeastern Lake Michigan, yellow perch were usually found in water above 11°C (51.8°F) and were occasionally abundant in water as warm as 22°C (71.6°F); substantial numbers, however, were found at water temperatures as low as 8°C (46.4°F) (Wells 1968). The upper lethal temperature limit for yellow perch is reported at 32.2°C (90°F) (Clark 1969); a somewhat higher lethal temperature [about 33.5°C (92.3°F)] was reported by Collette et al. (1977).

The yellow perch is quite tolerant of low oxygen levels, and has been known to survive winterkill conditions under which bluegills, largemouth bass, and walleyes have suffocated (Herman et al. 1959). At oxygen tensions of 0.3–0.1 ppm in a southern Michigan lake, there was a heavy kill of yellow perch, but numbers of the species survived as well (Cooper and Washburn 1949). The toleration threshold of yellow perch for dissolved oxygen has been reported as approximately 0.4–0.3 ppm (Moore 1942). Pearse and Achtenberg (1920) noted that yellow perch may survive for more than 2 hr under field conditions in water containing only 0.07 ppm of oxygen at 15°C (59°F).

The relationship between the depth distribution of yellow perch in lakes and conditions with respect to temperature and dissolved gases (especially oxygen) is not clear-cut (Hile and Juday 1941:184–185): "In some lakes (Geneva, Mendota, and Muskellunge) perch appear to select the coldest water containing sufficient oxygen to support life, and may even penetrate strata in which the oxygen is deficient or even lacking (Mendota, Muskellunge?). . . . In other lakes (Silver, Trout, and Green) the perch exhibits a marked preference for shallow water in spite of an abundance of cold, well oxygenated water in the thermocline and hypolimnion."

Yellow perch can tolerate salinity of up to 10 ppt (Collette et al. 1977). On the other hand, they are among the fish most sensitive to antimycin (a fish toxicant), and in soft water situations they die in concentrations of 0.5 ppb (Radonski 1966).

Much evidence has been presented to show that the yellow perch is a strongly schooling fish. Schools of 50–200 fish are apparently stratified by size and by age. Schools of small yellow perch locate in the shallows among vegetation; schools of large fish locate in offshore, open waters. Many lone yellow perch have been captured in gill nets, however, which suggests schooling behavior is not strictly adhered to. Individuals often stray from a school (Hasler and Wisby 1958). Schooling is essentially a daytime behavior at a time when this species is actively feeding.

In Lake Mendota (Dane County), the daily and seasonal activity of the yellow perch has been extensively studied by Hasler (1945), Hasler and Wisby (1958), Hasler and Bardach (1949), and Hasler and Tibbles (1970). During summer daylight hours, yellow perch swim in large schools at depths between 8 and 11 m below the surface. Toward sundown they move in to shore until they touch bottom. Diving observations have shown that the fish move shoreward in the hour before sunset, and then cruise along the shore at the 6 m contour until the sun disappears. The school then disperses, and each fish quietly sinks to the sand and becomes motionless shortly after dark. Although yellow perch have a strong schooling instinct during daylight, they seem to lose it at night when they can no longer see one another. Predawn observations reveal yellow perch resting on the lake bottom. At daybreak, however, they rise, congregate into schools, and, shortly after sunrise, swim back into deeper water.

In Lake Mendota, yellow perch hug the bottom fairly closely during the fall, winter, and spring. During the winter they often inhabit the deepest parts of the lake. When gill nets were set where ice fishing had been most successful, yellow perch were caught in greater numbers over deep water, from 9 m down to the lake bottom. Large schools have been discovered 3–15 m below the ice. In the spring before spawning, yellow perch are evenly dispersed from the surface to the bottom of the lake. Most Lake Mendota yellow perch remain in the deepest water containing sufficient oxygen to maintain life. When yellow perch invade water which does not contain sufficient oxygen for breathing, they apparently draw on the supply in the swim bladder (Pearse and Achtenberg 1920).

In the Mississippi River (Ranthum 1969), yellow perch preferred shallow water and vegetated areas, and avoided flats, drop-off areas, and the channel. They were considerably more active during the day than at night; activity peaked between 1600 and 1800 hr. In Green Bay, most yellow perch were taken during the summer at the 9-m interval (Reigle 1969a); the several large catches made at 20 and 22 m in December and April indicated a seasonal movement into deeper water during the winter. In Lake Michigan off Milwaukee (Schaefer 1977), yellow perch entered shallow water (9 m) in June and remained there until September and October, when they gradually moved to water of intermediate depth (18–27 m); there they spent the winter.

In southeastern Lake Michigan, yellow perch in their first 2 years of life remain in water shallower than 5 m (Wells 1968); the movements of the older yellow perch are similar to those described by Schaefer. No yellow perch have been taken from southeastern Lake Michigan waters deeper than 46 m; however, this species has been reported at depths as great as 56 m (Thorpe 1977).

Manion (1977) noted that adult yellow perch entered a tributary stream of Lake Superior during flood stage, and that postspawning adults and their progeny moved downstream in the fall. In Green Bay, the majority of yellow perch that had been tagged were recaptured within the tagging area; 19.4% were recaptured in localities less than 32 km (20 mi) distant from the tagging site; 6.5% at distances of 32–65 km (20–40 mi); and 1.9% at distances of 65–81 km (40–50 mi) from the tagging areas (Mraz 1951). Movements of the yellow perch in this study appeared to be random. Migrations over some hundreds of kilometers have occurred in the Great Lakes (Collette et al. 1977).

In one study, the swimming speeds of yellow perch in Lake Mendota reached a peak during midsummer when water temperatures were 20–25°C (68–77°F). As the water cooled in autumn, the swimming speeds declined (Hergenrader and Hasler 1967). The highest rate of speed observed for a school of yellow perch was 54 cm/sec. The swimming speeds of individual yellow perch were commonly only one-half those of schools at a given temperature interval.

The yellow perch is afflicted with many parasites. Especially common and obvious are the eye grub, the yellow grub, and black spot. Black spot shows up as small, black cysts the size of sand grains, which pose no medical problem to man, but which detract from the appearance of the fish. Lake Mendota yellow perch have annual summertime mortalities which are presumably caused by the sporozoan *Myxobolus* (Herman et al. 1959). A die-off of an estimated 136 kilotons of yellow perch occurred in July and August 1884 in Lake Mendota. This event caused quite a stir, and as many as 38 men with wagons and teams of horses were employed in the clean-up at one time (Dunning 1884).

The yellow perch is widely associated with most species of fish found in Wisconsin, and, in Lakes Michigan and Superior, it occurs with the coldwater salmonids.

IMPORTANCE AND MANAGEMENT

Yellow perch are preyed on by walleyes, muskellunge, northern pike, burbot, smallmouth bass, lake trout, largemouth bass, bowfins, longnose gars, brown bullheads, and lampreys. At times yellow perch eat their own kind. Yellow perch eggs are eaten by aquatic birds and other animals, and the fish are eaten by gulls, terns, mergansers, herons, grebes, ospreys, and kingfishers (Adams and Hankinson 1926). In turn, yellow perch eat the spawn of other fishes, including walleyes, whitefish, and lake trout. Food studies indicate, however, that yellow perch do not create serious problems as predators of other fish species.

In Lake Michigan, recent trends in yellow perch populations undoubtedly have been related to alewife abundance. Yellow perch in Lake Michigan spawn in shallow areas in the spring when alewives are also concentrated inshore. The alewife seems to harm the yellow perch primarily by inhibiting reproduction; it also seems likely that alewives compete with or feed on yellow perch fry (Wells and McLain 1973). Evidence that the alewife may have been responsible for poor yellow perch hatches is provided by the exceptionally strong year class of yellow perch that developed in southeastern Lake Michigan in 1969, following the decline of alewives in 1967 and 1968.

Yellow perch are hosts to the glochidial stages of a number of mussels, including *Elliptio complanata, Elliptio dilatata, Anodonta grandis, Actinonaias carinata, Lampsilis ovata,* and *Lampsilis radiata luteola* (Hart and Fuller 1974).

Yellow perch can be caught on hook and line with worms, minnows, dragonfly naiads, mayfly nymphs, crayfish tails, and pieces of fish (including fish eyes). In the winter, anglers turn to small jigs, goldenrod grubs, salmon eggs, and small minnows for bait. Among Wisconsin's favorite yellow perch lakes are Mendota (Dane County), Arbor Vitae (Vilas County), Geneva (Walworth County), Winnebago and Little Butte des Morts (Winnebago County). Ice fishing on Lake Mendota has attracted as many as 5,000 men, women, and children on a nice winter day.

The recreational value of the yellow perch cannot be reduced to figures. Often the perch is the only species which does not disappoint the casual fisherman or vacationer, since it bites frequently when other fish do not, and it is more easily caught than any other Wisconsin species. It furnishes much amusement for persons unskilled in fishing, and for those who do not have expensive special equipment.

Lake Mendota yielded an estimated 1.5 million yellow perch to ice fishermen during the winter of 1956 (Hasler and Wisby 1958). In Escanaba Lake (Vilas County) during the 1946–1969 period, anglers caught 138,962 yellow perch weighing 16,744 kg (36,914 lb). Yellow perch ranked first in number of fish caught, (36.4% of the total catch), and ranked second in weight harvested (26.6%). During 1972 and 1973, yellow perch constituted 3.04% of the catch from the Point Beach Nuclear Plant (Manitowoc County) fishing pier: they were surpassed in numbers by rainbow trout, brown trout, brook trout, and carp (Spigarelli and Thommes 1976).

On the Mississippi River, yellow perch ranked tenth in the sport catch in 1957, and seventh in 1962–1963 (Nord 1967). In 1967–1968, the estimated sport fishery catch of yellow perch in Pools 4, 5, and 7 was 28,402 fish weighing 4,046 kg (8,919 lb) (Wright 1970).

The 1980 Wisconsin regulations (Wis. Dep. Nat. Resour. 1979) for inland waters allow year-round fishing for yellow perch, with no size limit; there is a daily bag limit of 50 panfish, including the yellow perch. In the Mississippi River, there are no restrictions on yellow perch fishing, except in the Wisconsin-Minnesota boundary waters, which have a daily bag limit of 25 fish. When caught as sport fish, yellow perch may not be sold, traded, or bartered. Current fishing regulations should be consulted.

The yellow perch has long had a reputation as the finest eating of Wisconsin's freshwater fishes. Jordan and Evermann wrote (1923:366):

> . . . As a pan-fish we do not know of any better among American freshwater fishes. We have experimented with the yellow perch and several other species, including both species of black bass, the bluegill, wall-eyed pike, and rock-bass, eating each for several days in succession, and found the yellow perch the sweetest and most delicious of them all. One does not tire of it so soon as of the other kinds.

The roe of yellow perch is often discarded, but it should be saved since it is delicious when fried with the perch.

Analysis of the edible portion of yellow perch shows that it is 79.3% water, 18.7% protein, 0.8% fat, and 1.2% ash. It has a low fat content and keeps well when frozen. The edible portion has a food value of 82 calories per 100 g of flesh (Herman et al. 1959).

The yellow perch has become increasingly important as a laboratory dissection animal (Chiasson 1966). Few of Wisconsin's native fishes are more attractive than yellow perch. They are often displayed in public aquariums, where they must be provided with cool, well-aerated water. Home aquariums of native fishes often include small yellow perch.

Commercial fishing for yellow perch is allowed in Green Bay, Lake Michigan, and Lake Superior. In Lake Michigan, commercial production has averaged 1.1 million kg (2.4 million lb) annually from 1889, when records began, through 1970 (Wells and McLain 1973). Three notable deviations from this average have occurred: in 1894–1896, when the average was 2.9 million kg (6.3 million lb); in 1961–1964, when the take averaged 2.2 million kg (4.9 million lb); and in 1965–1970, when production dropped abruptly to an average of only 404 thousand kg (890 thousand lb) (Wells and McLain 1973).

Green Bay of Lake Michigan usually has been a particularly heavy producer of yellow perch, although all shallow areas of the lake have yielded this species in commercial quantities. For Lake Michigan the 1974 commercial harvest of yellow perch was 378,722 kg (834,924 lb) a substantial increase over the 1973 production of 139,921 kg (308,468 lb). The value of the yellow perch fishery was reported at $327,261 in 1974; this represents the best year for yellow perch since 1964 (Wis. Dep. Nat. Resour. 1976c). More than 90% of the 1974 catch was produced from southern Green Bay. Fyke nets and 2½-in gill nets are the primary types of gear used to catch yellow perch. The production of yellow perch in the Wisconsin waters of Lake Superior is low; the 1973 catch of 227 kg was worth $280 (Pileggi and Thompson 1976).

The drop of yellow perch production since 1964 has been of concern to the Wisconsin Department of Natural Resources. Regulation of the commercial harvest may be necessary, especially in lower Green Bay. Suggestions for improving production call for the establishment of a refuge for yellow perch, increasing the size limit; phasing out the use of 2⅜-in (60-mm) nets; creating a half-mile closed strip along bay and lake shores; closing the season on yellow perch from 1 January to 11 June; and limiting the number of commercial fishermen or setting a harvest quota.

The yellow perch shows a consistent tendency to become overly abundant particularly in small, infertile lakes; the result of overabundance is poor growth. Even Lake Mendota had a history of under-sized, poorly growing yellow perch at the turn of the century (Bardach 1951). In some lakes, yellow perch are so dominant that the lakes have become "perch bound." Cannibalism, which would be a welcome antidote for such a condition, does not occur among yellow perch because of the similarity in size of the individuals making up the perch population.

Following the removal of 70 kg/ha (62.3 lb/acre) of yellow perch from Curtis Lake (Oneida County), the lengths (mm) of yellow perch in the lake showed the following increases (Churchill 1949b):

Age Class	1946	1949
I	81 mm	97 mm
II	117	155
III	175	173
IV	193	196
V	198	211

In 1946 about 1.5% of all yellow perch removed from Curtis Lake were 178 mm (7 in) or longer; in 1948, 16.3% were 178 mm or longer; and in 1949, 23.2%.

There is evidence that, under certain circumstances, walleye predation can be used to reduce a yellow perch population. Also since burbot are known to feed selectively on yellow perch, they have been introduced experimentally as a control measure into a northern Wisconsin lake with a stunted yellow perch population. Large lakes with abundant predator fish seem to have the best perch populations. Perch have been reduced or removed successfully through the use of selective fish toxicants (Radonski 1966, Lennon et al. 1970).

Since 1973, considerable attention has been given in Wisconsin to producing yellow perch on commercial farms. At the University of Wisconsin at Madison, yellow perch are raised entirely under controlled conditions, in which the best rate of growth is obtained at a water temperature of 20°C (68°F) and with a 16-hr photoperiod (Stuiber 1975). Growth has ranged from 79 to 343% during a 14-week period (Huh et al. 1976). Research at the University of Wisconsin-Madison is summarized in *Aquaculture: Raising Perch for the Midwest Market* (Univ. Wis. Sea Grant Coll. Prog. 1975).

Slenderhead Darter

Percina phoxocephala (Nelson). *Percina*—small perch; *phoxocephala*—tapering head.

Other common names: sharpnosed darter, long-headed darter.

Male 70 mm, Wisconsin R., near Orion (Richland Co.), 14 Aug. 1962

Female 72 mm, Wisconsin R., near Orion (Richland Co.), 14 Aug. 1962

DESCRIPTION

Body elongate, almost cylindrical, but slightly compressed laterally. Length 64 mm (2.5 in). TL = 1.18 SL. Depth into SL 4.5–6.0. Head length into SL 3.5–3.7. Preopercle smooth on posterior edge. Gill membranes moderately attached below to one another. Premaxillaries nonprotractile, upper lip groove not continuous over tip of snout. Snout pointed; mouth subterminal and horizontal. Upper jaw reaching to below front of eye; minute, sharp teeth in narrow bands on upper and lower jaws. Gill rakers on lower limb of first arch about 10; branchial apparatus discussed by Branson and Ulrikson (1967). Branchiostegal rays 6. Dorsal fins 2; first or spiny dorsal fin with 12 (13) spines, fin base into SL 3.3–3.5; second dorsal fin with 14 (12–14) rays, fin base into SL 5–5.5. Anal fin with 2 spines and 9–10 rays; pelvic fins thoracic. Scales ctenoid; cheeks naked, opercles scaled, nape with embedded scales; breast naked; 1 enlarged, modified scale at base of pelvic fins and 1 at apex of pelvic girdle; belly of female with naked median strip, of male with a row of enlarged, modified scales. Lateral line complete, scales 65–71; scales around caudal peduncle 23–25. Vertebrae 39 (38–40) (Bailey and Gosline 1955).

Back light brown or straw, with darker brown vermiculations and saddle-shaped blotches; sides a paler base color; belly and lower region of head white. Row of 10–16 rather obscure, more or less confluent, dark blotches on side. Small distinct black caudal spot, and a short, black vertical line extending from behind pectoral fin dorsally. A dark stripe from tip of snout extending backward to and occasionally through the eye to back of gill cover. Suborbital bar absent or faint. Submarginal band of bright orange in the spiny dorsal fin of the male (Page and Smith 1971). Breeding male without tubercles. Genital papilla in male a small triangular flap; in females, distinctly enlarged for a few weeks prior to spawning.

Sexual dimorphism: Males with a median row of enlarged, specialized scales extending from midpelvic area to the anus; absent in female. In late spring and early summer, male has closely spaced melanophores over breast, belly, and the ventral fins; female white below with only a few scattered melanophores on the anal fin. Spiny dorsal fin more heavily pigmented in male than in female, with the basal portion quite dark.

Hybrid: Slenderhead darter × blackside darter (Thomas 1970).

SYSTEMATIC NOTES

According to Page and Smith (1971), generalized characteristics of the subgenus *Swainia* (in which the slenderhead darter is the most widely distributed and best known species) include the modest specialization of the midventral row of scales in the male, lack of pronounced sexual dimorphism, highly pelagic habits, and high meristic counts. Winn (1958) suggested that the degree of reduction of swim bladder size could be used as an indicator of phylogenetic advancement of darters. Page and Smith found that 8 specimens had large bladders averaging 15% of standard length.

DISTRIBUTION, STATUS, AND HABITAT

In Wisconsin, the slenderhead darter occurs in the Mississippi River and Lake Michigan drainage basins. No records are known from the Lake Superior system. Only in Wisconsin has this species penetrated the Great Lakes drainage, and in the St. Croix River it reaches the northern limit of its restricted range.

This species is most commonly distributed in the lower Wisconsin, Pecatonica, Sugar, and Rock rivers; elsewhere it occurs in small, widely disjunct populations. Generally only 1 to 3 specimens are captured with each collection, but 40+ were taken by a state crew from the Pelican River (Oneida County) in 1975, and I took 23 from the Wisconsin River near Orion

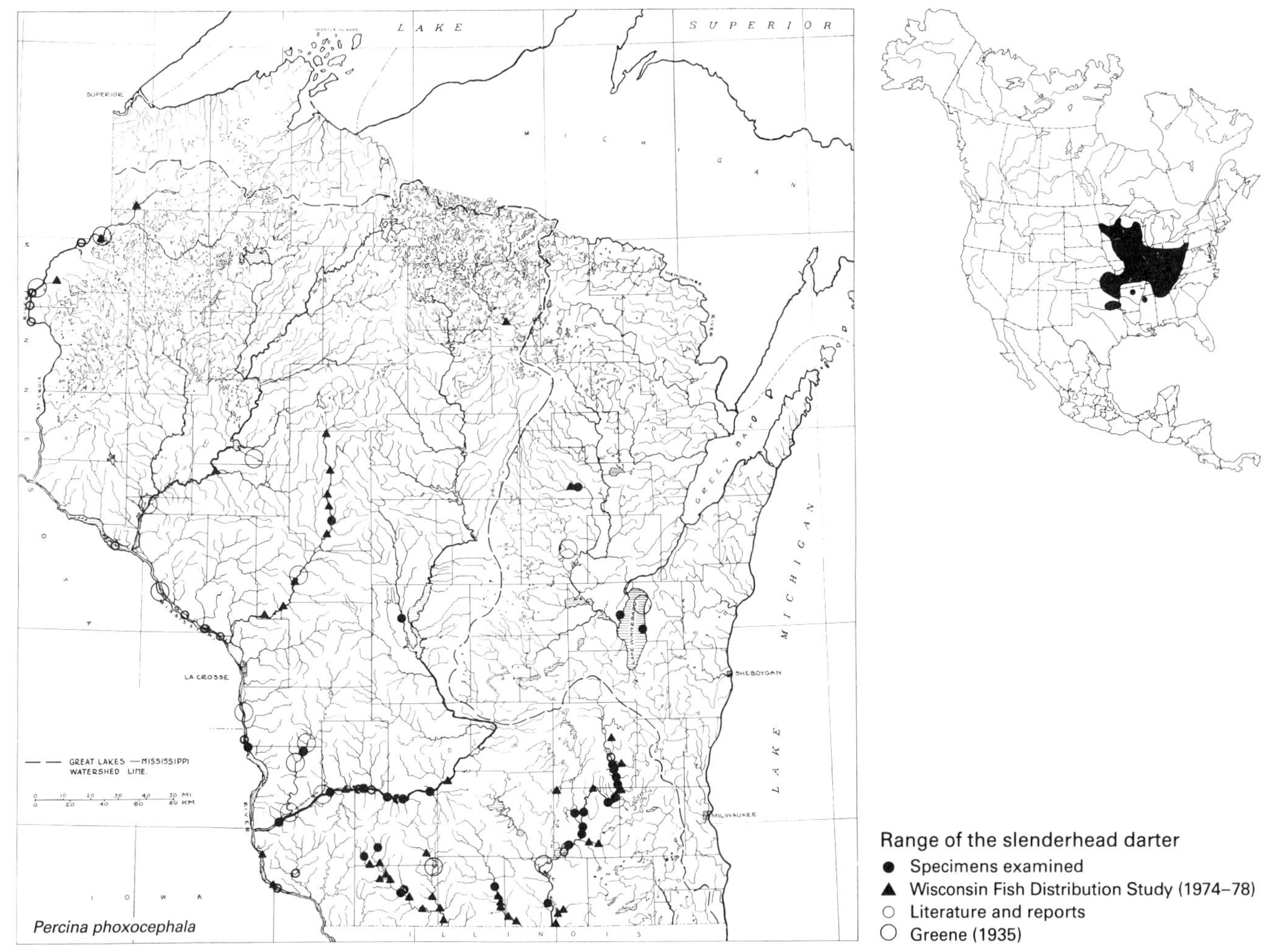

(Richland County) in 1962. The status of this species has remained the same in Wisconsin since the 1920s.

Much concern has been shown over the status of the slenderhead darter, especially along the periphery of its range. It is rare in Kentucky and South Dakota, and endangered in Pennsylvania (Miller 1972). In Kansas, it may require special attention to ensure its continued survival (Platt et al. 1973). In southern Ohio, the slenderhead darter's recent decline is related to increased siltation (Trautman 1957). The addition of this species to the federal rare and endangered fishes list has been proposed but additional information is needed to determine its status (Committee on Rare and Endangered Wildlife Species 1966).

The slenderhead darter inhabits moderate- to large-sized streams (more than 8 m wide to the largest rivers) with moderate to swift currents. Although sometimes taken in clear waters, it more frequently appears in slightly turbid to turbid waters. In Wisconsin, it was encountered most frequently in water at depths of more than 0.6 m, although in smaller streams it has been taken from shallow riffles 10–25 cm deep. It was found over the following substrates: gravel (26% frequency), sand (19%), rubble (16%), mud (16%), clay (13%), silt (7%), and bedrock (3%). Its appearance in lakes is unusual, and in Wisconsin it is known from Lake Winnebago, where it occurs over waveswept gravel shallows.

BIOLOGY

In Wisconsin, the slenderhead darter spawns in June. In central Illinois, spawning occurred from 5 to 14 June. However, it varies with climatic conditions and may be delayed for several weeks during periods of high water (Page and Smith 1971, Thomas 1970). Spawning occurs at 21.1°C (70°F) (Cross 1967).

According to Page and Smith, the mass movement of male slenderhead darters into the spawning habitat during May, well before the females, suggests that the species is territorial during the spawning season. Aquariums used to observe the slenderhead darter were probably too small to allow the establishment of territories, although males were consistently belligerent toward other males. In Illinois, spawning occurred in swift riffles over gravel and rubble, at water depths of 15–60 cm. The ratio of males to females prior to spawning was 11:2. After spawning, the adults returned to deeper water.

In Wisconsin, an age-II female slenderhead in June held 407 mature eggs (Lutterbie 1976). In June, the ovaries constituted 6–11% of the body weight; in July, 0.6%; in August, 0.9%; and in September, 1.4%—evidence that ovarian size increases shortly after spawning. In eastcentral Illinois, females held 500–2,000 eggs prior to spawning, of which 50–1,000 were mature and were laid during the spawning period (Page and Smith 1971). Egg production increases with the size of the female.

The eggs of the slenderhead darter have three stages of development: whitish at 0.5 mm diam, yellow at 0.6–1.1 mm, and yellow to orange at 1.1–1.3 mm diam. Mature eggs, which appear shortly before spawning, are transparent and adhesive, and contain one large oil droplet. Page and Smith noted that eggs which have not been spawned are resorbed.

Egg development and the growth of the young are rapid. A 22.4-mm slenderhead darter, collected in central Illinois on 23 June, was estimated to be 2 weeks old. It was almost fully scaled; the only areas lacking eventual scalation were the cheeks, opercles, and nape, and the anterior two-thirds of the belly. Scales are not present on the nape until specimens reach a standard length of 33 mm (Page and Smith 1971). It appears that young slenderheads attain half of their first year's growth in about 2 weeks. For 2–4 weeks after hatching, the young remain on gravel riffles in shallow water, 15–30 cm deep.

In southern Wisconsin, young-of-year slenderhead darters were 28 mm TL at the end of June, and 45 mm by mid-October (Lutterbie 1976). In northern Wisconsin, they averaged 45 mm by 18 August.

Slenderhead darters collected from southern Wisconsin streams showed the following growth (Lutterbie 1976:181):

Age Class	No. of Fish	TL (mm)		Calculated TL at Annulus (mm)			
		Avg	Range	1	2	3	4
I	25	49.48	42–58	40.24			
II	22	62.32	56–74	38.77	53.59		
III	21	72.29	65–77	37.67	54.90	66.62	
IV	6	77.67	69–83	38.83	54.33	67.17	73.67
Avg (weighted)				38.96	54.25	66.74	73.67

For 24 slenderheads from central and northern Wisconsin, the calculated lengths at annuli 1 through 4 were 44, 56, 68, and 80 mm TL respectively. In Illinois (Thomas 1970), lengths at annuli 1 through 3 were 45, 61, and 67 mm; in Iowa (Karr 1963), calculated lengths at annuli 1 through 4 were 34, 47, 49, and 56 mm.

The length-weight relationship for the slenderhead darter in northern and central Wisconsin was Log WT (g) = −12.3845 + 2.1667 Log TL (mm); and in southern Wisconsin it was Log WT (g) = −12.8709 + 3.2547 Log TL (mm) (Lutterbie 1976). In the Des Moines River, Iowa, the average K (TL) of slenderhead darters ranging from 35 to 78 mm long was 1.392 (Karr 1963).

There is little indication that sex influences the size of slenderhead darters. Although Page and Smith (1971) found that the largest specimens they collected were males, the differences between male and female lengths at various ages were not statistically significant. All age-I males are mature, as are age-I females larger than 42 mm.

In Wisconsin, an age-IV, 83-mm slenderhead from Black River (Clark County) weighed 4.5 g, and a fish of the same age and length from the Wisconsin River (Richland County) weighed 5.8 g. Trautman (1957) reported this species up to 102 mm (4 in) TL.

Young slenderhead darters feed mainly on midge larvae (Thomas 1970). Page and Smith noted that, as slenderhead darters increased in size, the composition of the diet, which had been dominated by dipteran larvae, changed to include substantially greater portions of the larger immature mayflies and caddisflies. Less frequently eaten items included amphipods, fish eggs, and terrestrial insects, as well as dragonfly naiads and water boatmen (Forbes 1880, Forbes and Richardson 1920, Cross 1967). Karr (1963) found stones and plant materials in the stomachs they examined, and concluded that these had been picked up incidentally in normal feeding.

The slenderhead darter probably feeds on whatever insect larvae are available and palatable, but Thomas (1970) indicated that there was some evidence of selective feeding since the fish appeared to avoid the abundant elmid beetle adults and plecopteran larvae in riffle areas. Feeding occurs throughout the daylight hours, and stops shortly after dark. Page and Smith (1971) found that the heaviest feeding occurred in May as the spawning period approached, and that the periods of least feeding were in the months following spawning (July and August) and in the colder months (November, February, and March).

Page and Smith observed an emigration of slenderheads from comparatively shallow raceways to deeper channels as winter approached.

Fish associated with 23 slenderhead darters taken from the Wisconsin River (Richland County) were: the bluntnose minnow (1), spottail shiner (9), yellow bullhead (1), stonecat (14), river darter (23), blackside darter (1), logperch (+), johnny darter (14), rainbow darter (1), fantail darter (9), and smallmouth bass (6).

IMPORTANCE AND MANAGEMENT

The slenderhead darter was not preyed upon by predator fish in Illinois streams studied, but in Kansas it was found in the stomach of a flathead catfish (Minckley and Deacon 1959).

In the Embarras River, Illinois, Page and Smith estimated a population of one slenderhead darter per 35.4 square meters of gravel habitat. In the Kaskaskia River, Thomas found one slenderhead for approximately 20 square meters at two sites; however, at many other sites the number of individuals per hectare was smaller than in the Embarras River study area.

Blackside Darter

Percina maculata (Girard). *Percina*—small perch; *maculata*—spotted.
Other common name: blacksided darter.

Male 81 mm, Eau Claire R. (Marathon Co.), 18 May 1968

Female 73 mm, Yellow R. (Taylor Co.), 27 Apr. 1974

DESCRIPTION

Body elongate to moderately robust, slightly compressed laterally. Average size 71 mm (2.8 in). TL = 1.18 SL. Depth into SL 4.7–5.5. Head length into SL 3.5–3.8. Preopercle smooth on posterior edge. Gill membranes narrowly attached below to one another. Premaxillaries nonprotractile, the upper lip groove not continuous over tip of snout. Snout pointed, mouth subterminal and horizontal, upper jaw reaching to below front of eye; minute, sharp teeth in narrow bands on upper and lower jaws. Gill rakers on lower limb of first arch long, narrow, wide-spaced, about 10. Branchial apparatus illustrated by Branson and Ulrikson (1967). Branchiostegal rays 6. Dorsal fins 2; first or spiny dorsal fin with 13 (12–15) spines, fin base into SL 3.3–3.5; second dorsal fin with 13 (13–15) rays, fin base into SL 5–6. Anal fin with 2 spines and 10 or 11 rays; pelvic fins thoracic. Scales ctenoid; cheeks naked or with embedded scales, opercles scaled, nape naked or with embedded scales; breast naked; 1 enlarged modified scale at base of pelvic fins, 1 or 2 at apex of pelvic girdle; belly of female with a naked median strip or a row of scarcely modified scales, of male with a row of enlarged modified scales (spikelike ctenii). Lateral line complete, scales 56–68; scales around caudal peduncle 20–23. Small air bladder present. Vertebrae 43 (42–44) (Bailey and Gosline 1955).

Back olive yellow with dusky vermiculations and 6–11 dark saddle-type markings or with a checkerboard design; sides yellow with an irregular, lateral black or brown stripe from snout through eyes across opercles and along body as 6–8 confluent longitudinal blotches; ventral region of head and belly whitish. Suborbital bar distinct, black. Black caudal spot present or absent. Spiny dorsal fin membranes with black pigment on about lower half, becoming less intense posteriorly; second dorsal and caudal fins lightly barred; remaining fins lightly pigmented, especially in female.

Breeding males without tubercles. Genital papilla in male a small triangular flap; in female distinctly enlarged and swollen. Male with more intense colors than female, especially during spawning act.

Sexual dichromatism: In male, fins and body slightly blacker than in female. Male capable of changing the intensity of black and white coloration at any time of year. In male, the membrane on the anterior edge of pelvic fins slightly thicker than in female.

Hybrids: Blackside darter × slenderhead darter, blackside darter × logperch (Thomas 1970, Trautman 1957, Wis. Fish Distrib. Study 1974–1979); blackside darter × Iowa darter (Wis. Fish Distrib. Study 1974–1979).

DISTRIBUTION, STATUS, AND HABITAT

In Wisconsin, the blackside darter is widely distributed in the Mississippi River and Lake Michigan drainage basins, but it is not known from the Lake Superior drainage. It is generally absent from the northern Wisconsin lakes regions. Its recent appearance in the upper St. Croix–Namekagon system suggests a recent introduction, and its widespread proliferation in the upper Red Cedar drainage since the single record noted by Greene (1935) may likewise be the result of an introduction.

The need of gravel for spawning probably explains the uncommon status of this species in the southern half of the driftless area, and may explain its relatively general distribution elsewhere, since moderate currents over sand and gravel are required only during spawning.

The status of this species is uncertain in a number of areas over its range. In Ohio, it is highly intolerant of mine wastes (Trautman 1957). In Illinois, human alterations such as dredging, channel straightening, and industrial and agricultural pollution affect at least the local distribution of the blackside darter (Thomas 1970). In eastern Iowa, the range is becoming constricted by the deterioration of the water quality (Harlan and Speaker 1956). In Kansas, the blackside darter is considered threatened (Platt et al. 1973).

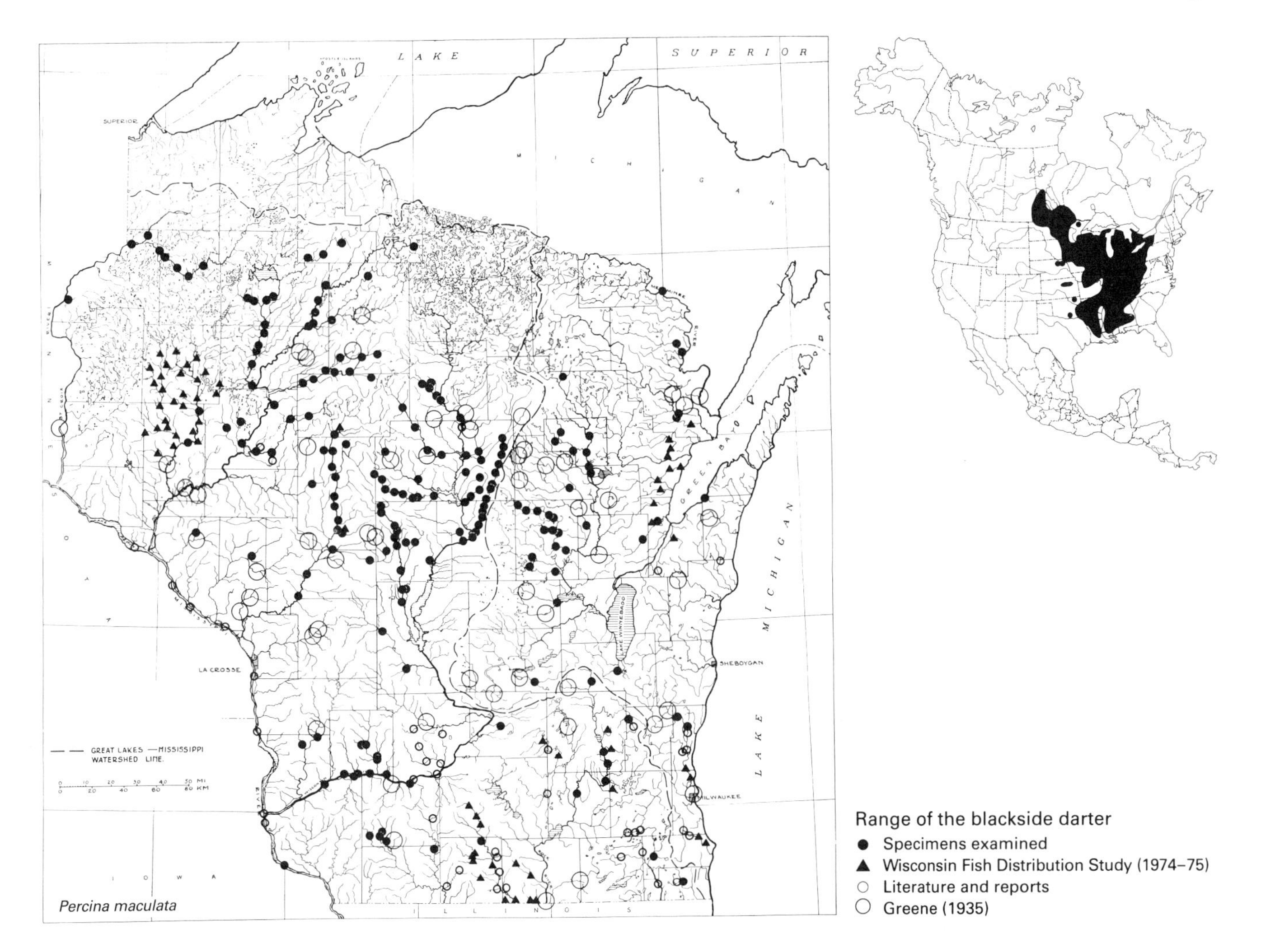

In Wisconsin, the blackside darter is common in medium- to large-sized streams. Although it is frequently observed, it is seldom abundant. In a central Wisconsin survey, it appeared in 58% of the collections, and, next to the johnny darter, it was the most common member of its family (Becker 1959). The blackside darter rarely appears in lakes. Greene (1935) noted that, out of 135 collections with blackside darters, 120 collections were from streams. Priegel (1967a) considered it rare in Lake Winnebago; I took a single specimen from Lake Poygan (Becker 1964b).

The blackside darter inhabits the quieter areas in marginal coldwater and in warmwater streams and rivers. It was found in clear to slightly turbid water at depths up to 1.5 m, often where considerable vegetation was present. It occurred over substrates of sand (27% frequency), gravel (19%), boulders (18%), mud (12%), silt (9%), rubble (9%), clay (4%), bedrock (1%), detritus (1%), and hardpan (1%). Sixty-five percent of the collections with blackside darters were taken from vegetated pools, which occurred in streams of the following widths: 1.0–3.0 m (8%), 3.1–6.0 m (17%), 6.1–12.0 m (15%), 12.1–24.0 m (29%), 24.1–50.0 m (17%), and more than 50 m (15%). The remainder of the collections came from shallow raceways or riffles.

BIOLOGY

In Wisconsin, the blackside darter spawns from April to June. Females collected from the Yellow River (Wood County) on 27 March were in spawning readiness one year, and in another year were spent or partially spent by 25 May (Lutterbie 1976). In southern Wisconsin, Cahn (1927) reported spawning in early June. In southern Michigan, spawning occurred at 16.5°C (61.7°F) and at pH 8.1 (Petravicz 1938). The eggs are laid in coarse sand or fine gravel, at depths of 30–60 cm (Winn 1958).

The blackside darter migrates from the deeper, often silt-covered, pools to raceways to spawn. The spawning migration may be postponed or even reversed by cold temperatures or by flooding. According to Thomas (1970), floods and increased turbidity may shorten the spawning period or increase the mortality rate of the young.

The following account of the spawning behavior of the blackside darter is derived mostly from Winn (1958) and Petravicz (1938). While the males are on the spawning grounds in waters with moderate current, the females remain in the deeper water until they are ready to spawn. No nest is built. The males move freely over the spawning grounds and do not establish territories. Instead, a male creates a completely "moving" territory around a female who swims onto the spawning ground. A male following such a female makes the area about 40 cm surrounding them into a territory, and makes brief dashes at any approaching male when the latter comes within it. Such moving territories are considered the most primitive and least complex type of territory.

The blackside darter male usually attacks only males of its own species. During the brief dash or during a fight between two males, the pelvic, anal, and caudal fins are held stiffly erect in a challenging position. When an intense fight ensues, the head is often lowered, and the erect caudal fin elevates the posterior region of the body. However, in this species the fight consists of only a short movement towards the intruder, which is sufficient to make him leave.

Little of the behavior of the blackside darter can truly be designated as courtship. Winn (1958) regards the recognition of the female by the male, and, as a consequence, his following her, as the simplest type of courtship. The subsequent movement by the female which stimulates the male to mount is also considered part of the courtship. Petravicz (1938:42) described the spawning behavior:

> . . . The female usually initiates the spawning by nervously and laboriously swimming to a desirable depression of sand or gravel, where she is pursued by males. Immediately after the female comes to rest, one male assumes the clasping position. . . .
>
> Simultaneously the pair vibrate their bodies for several seconds, meanwhile forcibly pressing genital apertures of their quivering bodies into the gravelly or sandy depressions where the eggs are deposited. When spawning on sand, the fish throw up a cloud of bottom material, and thus form a shallow depression. Their motions are not enough to disturb gravel.

When the pair has ceased vibrating, the male abandons the clasping position, and both fish lie exhausted on the bottom a few centimeters from the spawning location. Their fatigue is indicated by laborious gasping and the relaxed dorsal and caudal fins.

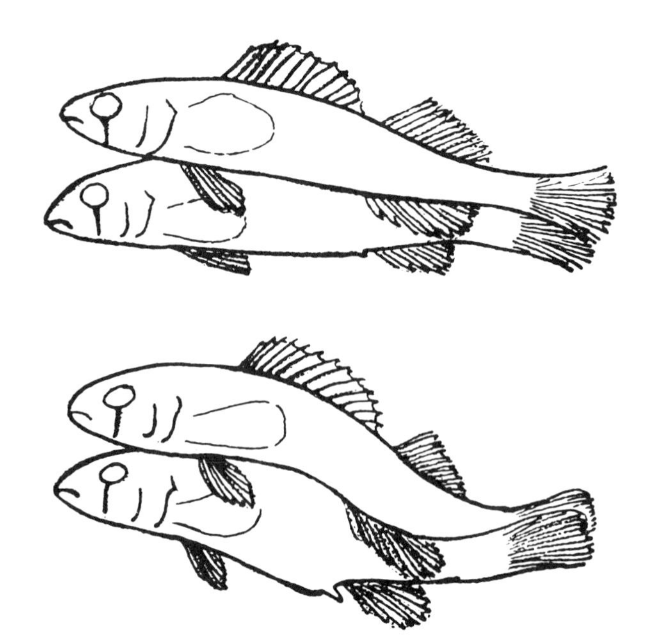

The spawning act of the blackside darter, showing the clasping position above, and the spawning act below. (Petravicz 1938:42).

Five minutes or even a half-hour may elapse before the spawning act is repeated. The female, who spawns periodically from early morning until late afternoon, is usually spent within about 2½ days. A female mates individually with several males, since she frequently shifts from one position on the spawning ground to another.

The eggs of the blackside darter are 1–2 mm diam, adhesive, and demersal. They are also colorless and transparent, and have a single, colorless oil droplet. More than 10 eggs are released with each mating, and a large female may lay up to 2,000 eggs during a spawning season.

In Wisconsin during May, four age-II females, 56–68 mm TL, held from 85 to 232 eggs; these fish probably were almost spent, since other age-II fish were spent (Lutterbie 1976). An age-II female, 70 mm TL, collected in April, held 502 mature eggs, and an age-II fish, 74 mm TL, taken in September, held 1,247 immature eggs. Egg numbers increase with the age and size of the individuals. Wisconsin specimens had ovaries which were 12.4% of the body weight during April, and 9.4% during May. In June, the ratio of ovary weight to body weight reached a low of 2%, this ratio increased in September and October to 2.6 and 3.4%. Testes constituted 1.2, 0.1, and 0.7% of the body weight in May, June, and July, respectively.

After the eggs are deposited, they receive no further attention from the parents. Blackside darter eggs hatch in about 6 days into larvae 5.75 mm long. Petravicz (1938) discussed embryonic development and illustrated the newly hatched larva and the postlarva 21 days after hatching. Fish (1932) illustrated and described the 41-mm stage. In Michigan, the estimated growth per day was 0.31 mm during a 30-day period early in the first summer of life (Hubbs 1921).

According to Petravicz, after hatching the young live in the surface strata; they may drop to the bottom strata within 3 weeks. Trautman (1957) found young blackside darters in stands of water willow and pondweed. Pflieger (1975) noted that the young commonly occur in backwaters, among accumulations of sticks, leaves, and other debris.

Young-of-year blackside darters in central Wisconsin were 29–47 mm TL in July and 34–60 mm in September. In northern Wisconsin, they were 45–60 mm in September.

Blackside darters collected from central Wisconsin streams showed the following growth (Lutterbie 1976:169):

Age Class	No. of Fish	TL (mm)		Calculated TL at Annulus (mm)			
		Avg	Range	1	2	3	4
I	32	58.53	50–68	48.62			
II	54	70.94	55–86	47.20	69.93		
III	11	78.54	70–87	47.36	69.18	78.54	
IV	3	94.00	89–104	49.67	76.67	85.33	92.67
Avg (weighted)				47.75	70.11	80.00	92.67

For 20 fish from northern Wisconsin, the calculated lengths at annuli 1 through 4 were 47, 74, 93, and 108 mm, respectively; for 8 fish from southern Wisconsin, 47, 70, 95, and 101 mm, respectively. In central and northern Wisconsin, the annulus had not been deposited by the latter part of May, but it appeared before June 11 in age-I and age-II fish, and by July 19 in age-III and age-IV fish.

The length-weight relationship of blackside darters in northern Wisconsin was Log W = −12.2535 + 3.1530 Log L; in central Wisconsin it was Log W = −11.8285 + 3.0335 Log L; and in southern Wisconsin, Log W = −13.0513 + 3.3825 Log L, where W is weight in grams and L is total length in millimeters (Lutterbie 1976).

The blackside darter generally reaches maturity when 2 years old; only rarely is a yearling fish mature (Winn 1958).

The largest Wisconsin blackside darter known (UWSP 551) is 111 mm (4.4 in) TL, 14.7 g—an age-IV fish from the East Branch of the Lily River (Langlade County), captured 18 July 1966.

Thomas (1970) found that young blackside darters selected microcrustaceans to eat, but that there was a rapid change to insect larvae. In central Wisconsin, blackside darters consumed mostly mayfly larvae, lesser quantities of diptera larvae, and small amounts of plant material which were probably ingested incidentally while feeding (R. Schwerdtfeger, pers. comm.). Cahn (1927) reported that blackside darters in southern Wisconsin ate largely entomostracans and copepods, as well as large numbers of insect larvae and nymphs.

Turner (1921) reported mayfly nymphs, chironomid larvae, corixid nymphs, copepods, fish remains, and silt in the digestive tracts of blackside darters. He thought that this darter was an opportunistic feeder, consuming whatever was available; however, Thomas (1970) reported that even where elmid beetles and Plecoptera nymphs were abundant they were avoided by blackside darters, while other forms were selected as food. Blackside darters have also been observed poking their heads in nests of *Nocomis*, suggesting that they were feeding on eggs (Hankinson 1932).

Unlike other darters, which remain relatively close to the bottom, the blackside darter is essentially a midwater form (Trautman 1957). At night both sexes are relatively inactive on the bottom, making only compensatory movements to maintain equilibrium (Winn 1958). Respiration rates are also reduced at night.

The migratory movements of blackside darters to spawning grounds have been documented by Winn (1958). He was able to follow "a large migrating population" upstream to the breeding area. After spawning, most blacksides leave the breeding grounds and migrate downstream, at least to the first permanent pool. In Bear Creek, Michigan, an intermittent stream which dries up in the summer and fall, the blackside darter has been known to migrate several miles upstream to permanent pools.

The blackside darter is essentially a moderate- to warmwater fish. It is seldom associated with such coldwater forms as brook trout and mottled sculpins, but it occurs commonly with rock bass and smallmouth bass at water temperatures of 20.7–21.4°C (69.3–70.6°F) (Hallam 1959). In Moccasin Creek (Wood County), 13 blackside darters were associated with the American brook lamprey (5), brook trout (2), northern hog sucker (13), white sucker (153), largescale stoneroller (3), blacknose dace (53), creek chub

(49), redside dace (9), bluntnose minnow (8), common shiner (27), bigmouth shiner (22), yellow bullhead (1), black bullhead (1), central mudminnow (2), johnny darter (29), and fantail darter (6). The species composition of that collection indicated that the water was in transition from cool to warm temperatures.

IMPORTANCE AND MANAGEMENT

The use of the blackside darter as food by other fishes and fish-eating birds is unknown, although it undoubtedly is used to a limited extent. This darter is not a bait fish, although Adams and Hankinson (1926) suggested that it may be "used as a bait, in the absence of anything better."

The blackside darter has been called "the fine gentleman of the family" (Petravicz 1938). It is attractive, quite hardy, and easily maintained in an aquarium. It can survive at least 40 days without being fed, although it becomes emaciated. It will take white worms, crushed crayfish, mayflies, and cubes of fresh beef and pork; it even attempts to swallow snails and caddisfly larvae.

Gilt Darter

Percina evides (Jordan and Copeland). *Percina*—small perch; *evides*—comely.
Other common name: gilded darter.

Adult 49 mm, Chippewa R. (Rusk Co.), 25 Sept. 1976

DESCRIPTION
Body elongate to moderately robust, slightly compressed laterally. Average length 66 mm (2.6 in). TL = 1.19 SL. Depth into SL 4.5–5.5. Head length into SL 3.5–4.0. Preopercle smooth on posterior edge. Gill membranes narrowly attached below to one another. Premaxillaries nonprotractile, the upper lip groove not continuous over tip of snout. Snout decurved, short; mouth subterminal and horizontal, upper jaw reaching to below or slightly beyond anterior edge of eye; minute, sharp teeth in narrow bands on upper and lower jaws. Gill rakers on lower limb of first arch long, narrow, about 11. Branchiostegal rays 6. Dorsal fins 2: first or spiny dorsal fin with 12 (11) spines, fin base into SL 3.3–3.5; second dorsal fin with 13 (12) rays, fin base into SL 4.5–5.0. Anal fin with 2 spines and 10 or 11 rays; pelvic fins thoracic. Scales ctenoid; cheeks naked or with a few embedded scales, opercles scaled or partially scaled; nape partially scaled near dorsal fin; breast naked; 1 enlarged modified scale at base of pelvic fins, 1 at apex of pelvic girdle; belly of female with a naked median strip or a few scarcely modified scales, of male with a row of modified scales with spikelike ctenii. Lateral line complete, scales 61–71; scales around caudal peduncle 24–29. Vertebrae 38–39 (Bailey and Gosline 1955).

Back dark olive, with 5–8 dark, squarish saddle bands across the dorsal ridge; sides with squarish green black blotches directly below saddle bands, and spaces between blotches yellow, orange, or copper red; belly yellowish or whitish. Suborbital bar distinct, black. Spiny dorsal fin mostly orange in life. In preserved specimens, spiny dorsal membranes more or less evenly pigmented except along the extreme outer margin, where they are clear (appearing white in individuals with darkly pigmented spiny dorsals); soft dorsal less pigmented than spiny dorsal; caudal fin pigmented along outer half of fin; remaining fins lightly pigmented except in breeding males.

Breeding male with 1–6 tubercles on rays of anal and pelvic fins and last few ventral rays of caudal fin. Single tubercles on midventral line scales, and on the first 3–4 rows of scales on either side of the anal fin. Tubercles have also been reported on the head, chin, and branchiostegal rays (Collette 1965), but these have not been seen on Wisconsin specimens. Each saddle band united with the blotch beneath to form 5–8 broad, green-black vertical bands with copper red areas between; 2 bright orange, roundish spots at base of caudal fin; ventral half of head and breast orange-red; dorsal fins mostly orange; anal and pelvic fins blue-black. In female, small tubercles may be present on anal and pelvic fins (Denoncourt 1969); pattern of markings similar to that of male, except all colors are subdued or lacking; vertical bands yellowish; anal and pelvic fins almost transparent. Young gilt darters resemble females.

DISTRIBUTION, STATUS, AND HABITAT
In Wisconsin, the gilt darter occurs in the Mississippi River drainage basin from the lower Black River to the upper Chippewa River and the St. Croix–Namekagon system, where it reaches the northern limit of its distribution. These populations appear to be isolated from one another.

Numerous 1956–1961 records of gilt darters from the Wisconsin-Minnesota boundary waters of the upper St. Croix River (Polk and Burnett counties) are kept in the Bell Museum of Natural History at the University of Minnesota and in the University of Kansas Museum.

Denoncourt (1969) examined the species upon which Greene (1935) had based his distribution: UMMZ 96070 (1) Bean Creek 2 mi S. Spring Brook (Washburn County), 1928; UMMZ 77969 (1) St. Croix River below the power dam at St. Croix Falls (Polk County), 1928; UMMZ 77844 (1) St. Croix River 11 mi N. of Danbury on Hwy. 35 (Burnett County), 1928; no specimen was reported to support Greene's record from Jackson County.

Recent specimens deposited in UWSP are: #2126 (13) St. Croix River above mouth of Rock Creek (Chisago County, Minnesota), 1968; #5288 (2) Black River T19N R5W Sec 10 (Jackson County), 1975; #5447 (12) Chippewa River T35N R7W Sec 21 (Rusk County), 1976; #5448 (4) Chippewa River T33N R8W Sec 1 (Rusk County), 1976; #5449 (1) Wood River T38N

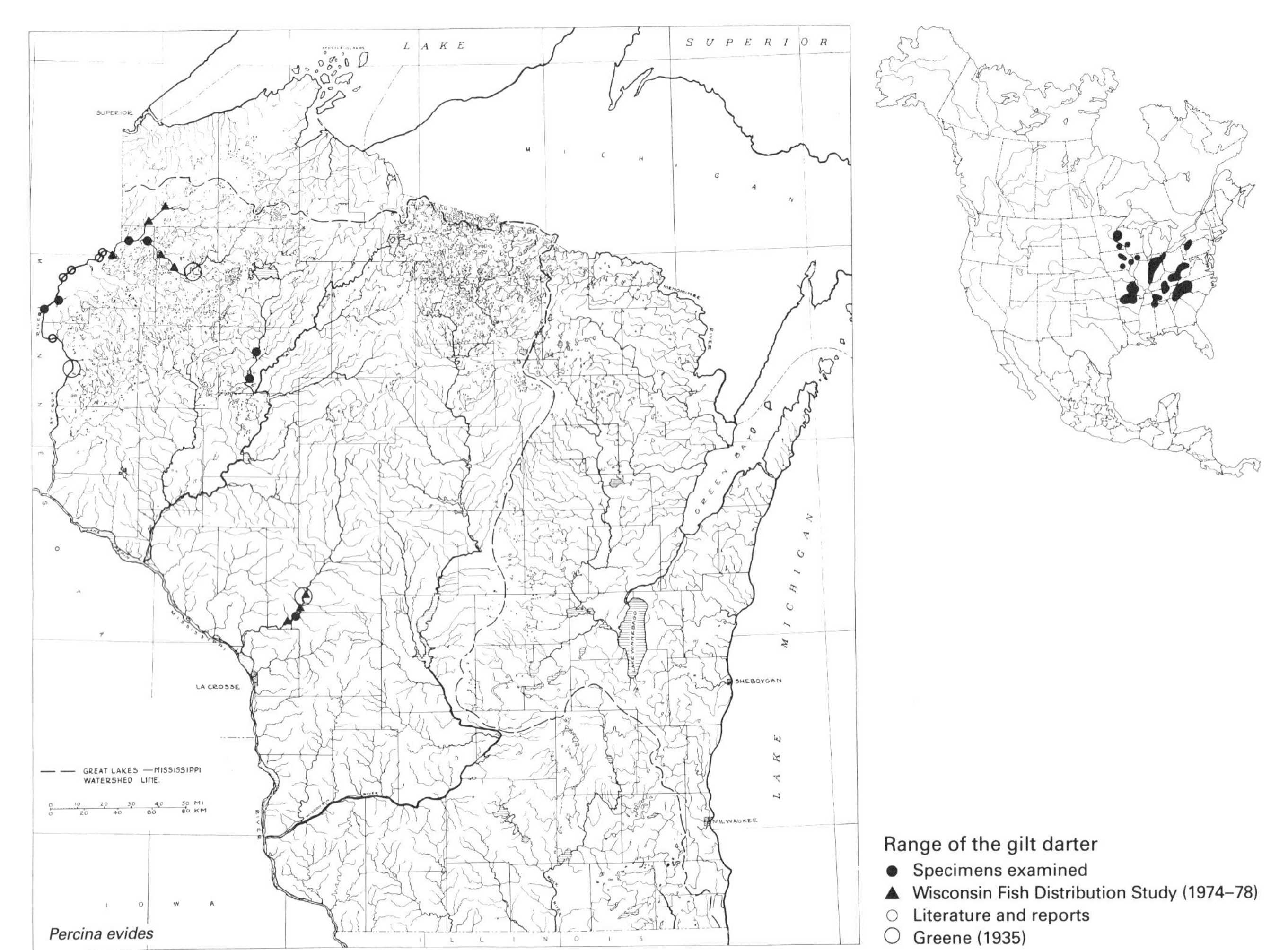

R19W Sec 19 (Burnett County), 1976; #5518 (2) Namekagon River T42N R14W Sec 33 (Burnett County), 1976; #5519 (1) St. Croix River T42N R15W Sec 33 (Burnett County), 1976; and #5708 (16) Black River T21N R4W Sec 33 (Jackson County), 1977.

The Wisconsin Fish Distribution Study (1974–1978) reported: three collections (2, 11, and 60 fish) from the Black River T19N R5W Sec 20 to T21N R4W Sec 33 (Jackson County), 1975 and 1977; two collections (3 and 11 fish) from the Yellow River T41N R16W Secs 27 and 28 (Burnett County), 1977; one collection (2) St. Croix River T43N R14W Sec 23 (Douglas County), 1977; (2) Moose River T44N R13W Sec 35 (Douglas County), 1977; and three collections (1, 2, and 1 fish) from the Namekagon River T42N R14W Sec 33 to T40N R12W Sec 18 (Washburn County), 1976 and 1977.

The known status of the gilt darter indicates a shrinking range, diminishing numbers in widely scattered populations, and extirpation in many states. The loss is especially evident in the northern portion of its range. The only Iowa records of the gilt darter go back to the last century, and it is undoubtedly extirpated there today (Harlan and Speaker 1956, Roosa 1977). In Illinois, the gilt darter occurred formerly in the Rock River, but it has not been collected in the state since 1932; it is believed to be extirpated (P. W. Smith 1965). In Indiana, it has decreased greatly in recent years (Gerking 1945), and it is listed as rare in Kentucky (Miller 1972). This species has been reported only twice from Ohio, and both reports were made before 1900 (Trautman 1957); it is probably extirpated in Ohio. Eddy and Underhill (1974) noted the disappearance of the gilt darter in some Minnesota waters, and suggested that the changes that have occurred in the Mississippi River drainage area during the past 50 years have eliminated the clearwater habitat preferred by the species. They regard the St. Croix population as (p. 379) "a modern relict population which has been isolated in recent times by habitat modification in its former range."

In Wisconsin, the status of the gilt darter at the sites where it is known to occur is difficult to assess.

Frequently only single specimens constitute a record for a given site. In most areas where its habitat is limited the gilt darter is rare. In parts of the St. Croix and the Black rivers it may be uncommon to common. Currently Wisconsin gives it endangered status (Les 1979). The required habitat of the gilt darter is threatened by man's economic interests, since the large, fastflowing sections of rivers lend themselves to a number of human enterprises which are attained with impoundment. When such areas are dammed, the gilt darter populations are immediately annihilated.

The gilt darter inhabits clear, medium-sized to large streams with clean, silt-free bottoms and permanently strong currents. It generally occurs in moderate to fast, deep riffles and pools, over gravel, rubble, and small boulders.

In the Black River (Jackson County), the gilt darter inhabits clear but brown-stained water 0.1–1.0 m deep and 18–30 m wide, over light-colored sand and fine gravel 6–12 mm diam, in a current of 0.6–1.2 m/sec (D. Becker, pers. comm.). Most specimens were collected within a meter of a shifting sand delta formed by the inflow of a tributary stream (Trout Creek). Fewer individuals were captured downstream in a current of 0.3–0.6 m/sec, which suggests that a faster current is preferred by this species.

BIOLOGY

In northwestern Wisconsin, the gilt darter probably spawns in mid-June. It was reported in breeding habit on 27 June in the Black River (Jackson County), where it was found over gravel riffles in 30 cm of water (D. Becker, pers. comm.). Sixty fish were collected, of which the majority appeared to be males. The females examined appeared to be spent. A 72-mm, 3.78-g female from that collection had ovaries 5% of body weight; of the eggs remaining 12 were mature, yellow, transparent eggs 1.3–1.6 mm diam; 115 were yellow, opaque eggs 0.8–1.1 mm diam; and the rest were numerous immature white eggs, 0.3–0.6 mm diam. In September the ovaries of a female gilt darter constituted 1.24% of the body weight (Lutterbie 1976).

In Virginia, gilt darters spawned in May when water temperatures were between 17.2 and 20°C (63 and 68°F) (Denoncourt 1969). The large males died shortly after spawning. In the Current River, Missouri, brilliantly colored males were taken the third week of June (Pflieger 1975).

Male gilt darters are significantly larger than the females. According to Winn (1958), this indicates that the males establish territories. The presence of large numbers of breeding tubercles and a midventral row of modified scales on males indicates that the male probably mounts the female in the spawning act. Collette (1965) reported breeding tubercles on gilt darter males from 10 March to 29 June; Denoncourt (1969), reported breeding tubercles from April to August, and noted that they appeared in the form of tubercular ridges as well as individual tubercles.

Young-of-year gilt darters from Wisconsin waters and from Wisconsin-Minnesota boundary waters were 35–37 mm TL in July, 33–52 mm in August, 33–44 mm in September, and 30–52 mm in October. Age-0 fish of both sexes in Virginia were 34–40 mm SL 3 months after hatching (Denoncourt 1969). Six months after hatching, males were significantly larger than females.

Gilt darters collected from Wisconsin boundary and inland waters showed the following growth (Lutterbie 1976:154):

Age Class	No. of Fish	TL (mm)		Calculated TL at Annulus (mm)			
		Avg	Range	1	2	3	4
I	39	52.9	38–65	38.4			
II	5	68.6	62–74	47.2	61.8		
III	2	73.0	71–75	44.5	61.5	73.0	
IV	2	75.5	75–76	46.0	60.0	69.0	75.5
Avg (weighted)				39.9	61.3	71.0	75.5

The length-weight relationship for 93 fish was Log WT (g) = −11.7037 + 2.9973 Log TL (mm).

The largest Wisconsin gilt darter observed (UWSP 5518) is an 81-mm (3.2-in), 5.9-g male collected from the Namekagon River (Burnett County) in 1976. According to Pflieger (1975), adult gilt darters reach a maximum size of about 89 mm (3.5 in).

A 59-mm male gilt darter taken from the Black River (Jackson County) in June had eaten mostly small diptera larvae (19), some caddisfly larvae (2), and small ephemeropteran nymphs (6). The digestive tract of a 72-mm female from the same collection held large caddisfly larvae (5), lesser quantities of small dipteran larvae (5), the remains of an ephemeropteran nymph, and unidentified insect remains. Both fish stomachs contained small stones, which had probably been ingested incidentally with the organic materials.

According to Denoncourt (1969), during the spring and summer the larger, more colorful male gilt darters occupy the deeper water with rubble and boulder bottoms; the females and smaller males are in the adjacent regions and tend to range more widely after the breeding season. Young-of-year are found in shallow water (15–31 cm) over gravel and small rubble. Schwartz (1965) found gilt darters in the deeper pools during the winter, and noted that in the spring they returned to the riffles with rapidly flowing water.

Twelve gilt darters were collected from the Chippewa River (Rusk County) along with the largescale stoneroller (3), hornyhead chub (10), mimic shiner (6), rosyface shiner (86), spotfin shiner (17), common shiner (91), silver redhorse (15), shorthead redhorse (3), white sucker (8), northern hog sucker (6), yellow bullhead (1), rock bass (1), smallmouth bass (1), walleye (1), yellow perch (1), and blackside darter (22).

IMPORTANCE AND MANAGEMENT

Because of its rarity, little is known about the gilt darter. Its use by fish-eating predators is undoubtedly small.

Breeding male gilt darters are among the most beautiful of Wisconsin fishes.

The gilt darter is difficult to collect since it is often found in fast water over bottoms of large gravel and rubble. It has been taken successfully (J. Underhill, pers. comm.) by fixing a seine in position directly downstream from a likely looking area, followed by stirring up the gravel and the rubble to dislodge the darters and to allow the current to sweep them into the net. Gilt darters are also collected with electrofishing gear, but manipulating heavy equipment in a rapid current while trying to capture a small fish is difficult.

Logperch

Percina caprodes (Rafinesque). *Percina*—small perch; *caprodes*—piglike, in reference to snout.
Other common names: zebra fish, Manitou darter, rockfish, hogmolly, hogfish.

Adult female 96 mm, Red Cedar R. (Dunn Co.), 19 Oct. 1974

DESCRIPTION
Body elongate, slightly compressed laterally. Length 94 mm (3.7 in). TL = 1.18 SL. Body depth into SL 5.0–6.0. Head length into SL 3.5–4.0. Preopercle smooth on posterior edge. Gill membranes narrowly attached below to one another. Premaxillaries nonprotractile, the upper lip groove not continuous over tip of snout. Snout pointed, elongate, often conical protuberance at tip and extending beyond lower lip; mouth inferior and horizontal, upper jaw not reaching to anterior edge of eye; minute, sharp to peglike teeth in narrow bands on upper and lower jaws. Gill rakers on lower limb of first arch short, wide-spaced, about 12. Branchial apparatus illustrated and described in detail by Branson and Ulrikson (1967). Branchiostegal rays 6. Dorsal fins 2: first or spiny dorsal fin with 13–15 spines, base in SL 3.3; second dorsal fin with 14 (14–16) rays, fin base into SL 4.8–5.5. Anal fin with 2 spines and 10 (9–11) rays; pelvic fins thoracic. Scales ctenoid; cheeks scaled, opercles scaled, nape naked to partially scaled; breast naked; belly in female usually with a naked median strip, in male usually with an interrupted row of enlarged modified scales. Lateral line complete, scales 71–79. Vertebrae 42 (41–44) (Bailey and Gosline 1955). Chromosomes 2n = 48 (W. LeGrande pers. comm.).

Back yellowish to dark olive; sides lighter, and belly whitish; 15–25 dark olive to black narrow, zebralike bands crossing over the back and vertically down the sides; bands alternating in length, with the shorter bands scarcely reaching lateral line in some instances. Dorsal and caudal fins lightly barred; remaining fins clear to lightly pigmented, especially along fin rays. Fin rays yellowish in life. Suborbital bar distinct to vague. Black caudal spot about size of pupil of eye.

Breeding male with tubercles on ventral scale rows, generally in the form of thickenings of the posterior portion of scale; these tubercles are usually not prominent, so that magnification and drying are necessary to trace their extent. Tubercles better developed and more persistent in southern populations of its range (Collette 1965).

Sexual dimorphism: Second dorsal and anal fins usually slightly larger in male than in female (Eddy and Underhill 1974). Males usually with an interrupted row of enlarged, modified scales on middle of breast; female usually with naked breast. Urogenital papilla in male coming to a sharp or blunt point; in female, it is broad and flat tipped. Anal and pelvic fins more pigmented in male than in female.

Hybrids: Logperch × blackside darter (Trautman 1957, Wis. Fish Distrib. Study 1974–1979). Numerous natural and artificial hybrids with *Ammocrypta*, *Etheostoma*, and *Percina* (Schwartz 1972).

SYSTEMATIC NOTES
The northern logperch, *Percina caprodes semifasciata* (De Kay), which occurs in Wisconsin, has a triangular, scaleless area on the nape, and lateral bars that are unevenly spaced and often expanded into blotches. The Ohio logperch, *Percina caprodes caprodes* (Rafinesque) has a closely scaled nape, and lateral bars more evenly spaced and scarcely expanded into blotches. Intergrades between these two forms were reported by Greene (1935) from the lower Milwaukee River (Milwaukee County). He suggested that this is evidence that *Percina caprodes caprodes* was once established in this locality, perhaps throughout the Milwaukee and Root river systems, but that it has been almost completely displaced by the encroachment of *P. c. semifasciata* from the west. I have observed considerable variation in the scalation of the nape in several other logperch populations, ranging from the naked to the fairly well scaled within the same collection. The squamational patterns appear to be determined by incompletely dominant genes at one or a few loci, and further investigation is warranted.

DISTRIBUTION, STATUS, AND HABITAT
In Wisconsin, the logperch occurs in all three drainage basins and in all boundary waters. It shows some avoidance of the driftless area, probably because of its need for gravel and washed sand for spawning sites. The logperch is largely absent from the northern sector of the Lake Michigan drainage.

The logperch is common in medium to large streams and rivers and in large lakes. With the excep-

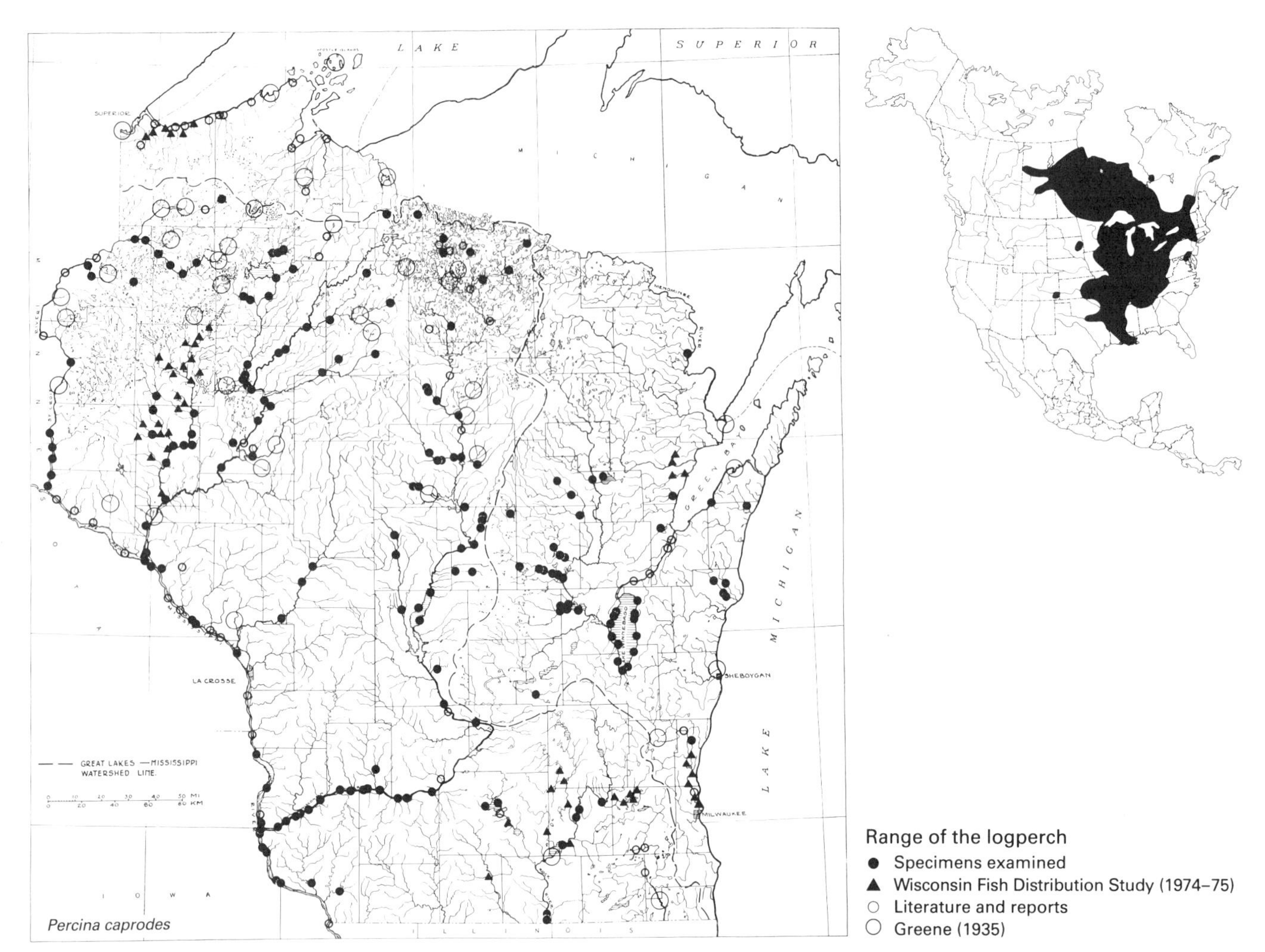

tion of the johnny darter and the Iowa darter, it is the most common darter in Wisconsin's inland lakes. In Lakes Winnebago and Poygan, it is distributed along wave-swept shores over bottoms of heavy gravel, rubble, or boulders, and seldom occurs in those areas protected from wind action. In Lake Superior, it is widespread and abundant in the barrier traps in the mouths of tributary streams (McLain et al. 1965). It is rare in Lake Michigan (Parsons et al. 1975).

The logperch is found in diverse habitats, including swift water, the quiet water of cutoff pools in rivers, and the open water of large lakes. In Wisconsin, it has been encountered most frequently in clear water at depths of 0.6–1.5 m, over substrates of sand (34% frequency), gravel (25%), boulders (14%), mud (10%), rubble (9%), silt (7%), and hardpan (1%). In streams it occurred in pools (50% frequency), riffles (33%), and sloughs (17%). River collections have been taken from streams of the following widths: 1.0–3.0 m (5%), 3.1–6.0 m (5%), 6.1–12.0 m (10%), 12.1–24.0 m (44%), 24.1–50.0 m (17%), and more than 50 m (20%). In southeastern Lake Michigan, the logperch has been trawled at depths of 9–22 m (Wells 1968). In eastern Lake Erie, it occurs to a depth of 40 m (Trautman 1957).

BIOLOGY

Winn (1958) has prepared a thorough history of the logperch, and, unless otherwise designated, the facts which follow are from that source. The logperch spawns from April to July in water 10–200 cm deep (Lutterbie 1976). No territory or nest is prepared.

In lake spawning, the male logperch form schools above an area of sand or gravel parallel to the shore line which may be up to 30 m in length—a much larger area than that covered by males spawning in streams. Such school formation is considered the most primitive reproductive behavior to be found among darters; Winn suggested that the males may need constant contact with other males in the school to maintain a sexually active state. Lake spawning logperch males are completely nonterritorial. They do not exhibit fighting behavior, and are the only darters not to do so. The females feed in deeper water beyond the male school, and after spawning they return to the deep water.

In streams, the male logperch school moves over sand and gravel, riffles, and raceways. A male protects a "moving territory" immediately surrounding a female which has come onto the breeding grounds. A male following a female makes brief dashes at an approaching male when the latter comes closer than approximately 40 cm. These attacks are directed against other logperch males and sometimes against blackside darter males. Such moving territories are considered to be the most primitive and the least complex type of territory. Territorial behavior is correlated with sexual dimorphism, and is less developed in those species, like the logperch, in which differences between the sexes are least evident.

Sexual recognition by the logperch is based more on behavior than on differences in color and form, which tend to confuse these fish. Winn noted that logperch males mount other logperch males much more frequently than do the males of other darter species. Logperch males follow females because they react to particular movements of the females, although it is not clear exactly what causes a "following" reaction. Male recognition of a ripe female and response to her behavior can be divided into the "following," "mounting," and "quivering" reactions which constitute the spawning process.

Spawning behavior has been described by Reighard (1913:238):

> The breeding males are found in groups of 15 or less. Among these are a few females, but most of the females are seen waiting in deeper water or about the borders of the group. When a female enters the group she is at once pursued by one or more males, usually by many. She continues to flee for some time in a tortuous course back and forth through the group in its neighborhood. The female finally settles to the bottom and a male takes position over her with his pelvic fins clasping her head and his tail at the side of hers. . . . A rapid vibration of the tail, pectoral and pelvic fins of both fish then follows and lasts about four seconds. This sends backward a whirl of sand and excavates a little pit in the sand beneath the fish. During this time, the eggs are emitted and fertilized and weighted by a coating of adhering sand grains. The spawning pair is usually enveloped by a group of supernumerary males, which are attempting to supplant the pairing male. When the spawning is completed, the spawning fish leave the pit or at least the female does so. She repeats the spawning in many other pits. When the spawning is finished at a pit the supernumerary males (and perhaps the pairing male) at once surround the pit and devour such eggs as they can get. The eggs were found in their stomachs. The eggs and young receive no care from their parents, but these, when the spawning period is ended, go into deeper water and are not again seen.

The logperch females release 10–20 eggs during each spawning act, and the spawning pair becomes almost completely buried by the swirling sand when vibrating. After spawning, the female darts out from under the male either to spawn again with a different male or with the same male or to return to deep water to rest.

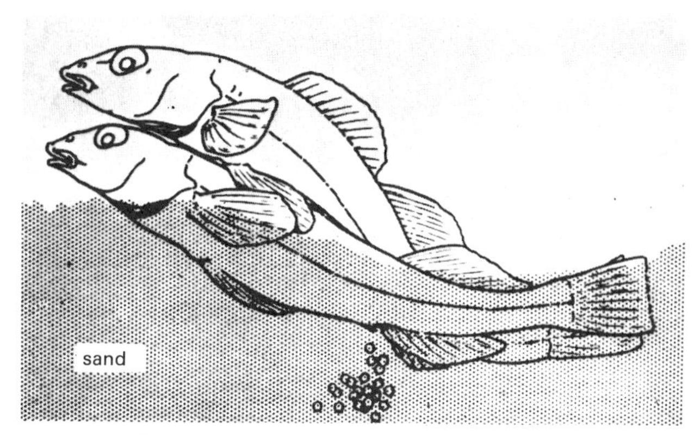

The spawning position of the logperch (Winn 1958:177. Copyright 1960, the Ecological Society of America)

Spawning occurs from early morning to early evening, but not at night, when this species remains relatively quiet on the bottom. A change in climatic conditions may cause logperch and other darters to leave the breeding area. After the spawning season, the adults migrate to the deeper waters of lakes or streams.

According to Winn (1958), the average number of eggs laid by a female logperch during a spawning season is about 2,000, although he listed a female, 84 mm SL, with 3,085 eggs. The number of eggs increases with the size and age of the individuals. The total complement of eggs is laid during the spawning season. Winn noted that there are large numbers of 3- and 4-year-old females in logperch populations compared with some other darter species.

In Wisconsin, the ovary weight of logperch in May was 10% of the body weight, but it was less than 1% from June to August (Lutterbie 1976). An age-III, 119-mm female, collected in May, held 846 eggs. An age-I, 71-mm female, taken in June, held 38 eggs.

The eggs of the logperch are demersal and adhesive, and average 1.3 mm diam. They are colorless and transparent, and usually have one colorless oil globule. The eggs and larvae may develop at a wide range of temperatures: in Texas (C. Hubbs 1961), logperch eggs and larvae developed between 22 and

26°C (71.6 and 78.8°F); in Ontario (Amundrud et al. 1974), the data suggest the development of eggs and larvae at approximately 8°C. (46.4°F).

Logperch eggs suffer many hazards which may reduce the hatch. Siltation may cover the eggs so deeply that the developing embryos suffocate. Heavy rains and flooding may wash the eggs out of the nesting area. The biggest threat is probably predation on the eggs by supernumerary male logperch and by other species of fish, such as the white sucker. In a Michigan lake, schools of suckers quietly entered the schools of logperch which were spawning in shallow water near shore and crowded the spawning fish aside to eat their recently laid eggs (Ellis and Roe 1917). This predation occurred throughout the day for nearly 2 weeks.

In Lake Opinicon, Ontario, the total length of free-swimming logperch at first appearance was 5.5 mm; at peak abundance from the end of May to the beginning of June it was 7.5–11.5 mm. In northern Wisconsin, logperch larvae appeared in June in the open water area of Little John Lake (Vilas County) (Faber 1967). Older young are often associated with dense beds of vegetation in shallow water.

M. Fish (1932) illustrated and described the 6.6-, 12.2-, 14.2-, and 20.5-mm stages. Taber (1969) illustrated the developmental stages from 5.3 to 25.3 mm.

In Michigan, the estimated growth of logperch was 0.4 mm per day during a 30-day period early in the first summer's existence (Hubbs 1921). In northern Wisconsin, young-of-year were 57–59 mm long in September; in southern Wisconsin, they were 59–72 mm long in July, and 63–79 mm long in August: and in central Wisconsin, they were 42–59 mm long in July, 41–83 mm long in August, and 50–81 mm long in September (Lutterbie 1976).

Logperch collected from central Wisconsin showed the following growth (Lutterbie 1976:144):

Age Class	No. of Fish	TL (mm)		Calculated TL at Annulus (mm)			
		Avg	Range	1	2	3	4
I	96	85.16	58–121	65.18			
II	47	106.23	77–134	62.09	95.49		
III	8	121.12	110–145	64.38	95.38	117.38	
IV	1	131.00		72.00	95.00	112.00	125.00
Avg (weighted)				64.23	95.46	116.78	125.00

For 33 logperch from southern Wisconsin, the calculated lengths at annuli 1 through 4 were 74, 105, 122, and 132 mm respectively. The length-weight relationship for central Wisconsin logperch was $\text{Log } W = -11.8965 + 3.0532 \text{ Log } L$; for southern Wisconsin fish it was $\text{Log } W = -11.9791 + 3.0742 \text{ Log } L$, where weight is in grams and total length in millimeters.

Maturity in the logperch occurs generally at age II, rarely by age I.

The largest specimen seen in the Museum of Natural History, Stevens Point, Wisconsin, is a 138-mm (5.4-in), 24.6-g female (UWSP 986), age IV, collected from the Little Platte River (Grant County). Wagner (1908), who found this species abundant in Lake Pepin, noted a few logperch 150–160 mm long. Trautman (1957) reported a specimen 180 mm long from Buckeye Lake, Ohio.

Young logperch feed on a variety of small organisms, but principally upon cladocerans and copepods. In its very early stages, the logperch is a surface feeder, but as it matures it becomes a bottom feeder (Turner 1921).

Logperch in the Madison, Wisconsin, area consumed fish eggs, insect larvae, pupae, and adults, amphipods, entomostracans, leeches, plant remains, algae, silt, and debris (Pearse 1918). In southeastern Wisconsin (Cahn 1927), they fed on bottom animal matter almost exclusively: *Chironomus*, *Simulium*, small crustacea, and small mollusks. Logperch from Dry Wood Creek (Chippewa County) had mostly eaten caddisfly and midgefly larvae, and lesser amounts of small mollusks, mayfly nymphs, small crustaceans, and riffle beetles (V. Buckley, pers. comm.).

Fish remains were found in one Ohio logperch (Turner 1921). Ten percent of the diet of logperch in Bull Shoals Reservoir, Arkansas, during the spring consisted of black bass eggs (Mullan et al. 1968). Logperch eat their own eggs; up to 20 logperch eggs have been found in logperch stomachs.

Turner considered the logperch to be a generalized feeder, and the period of maturity is marked by an omnivorous feeding habit. The logperch has a relatively long, narrow mouth, and feeds by darting forward, tilting its head down, and rapidly extending its highly protrusible jaw (Emery 1973). According to Emery, in Greenleaf Lake, Ontario, it is an active daytime feeder, and feeds in schools along the shore 1–3 m off the bottom. At night feeding ceases and the school breaks up, with the individual logperch taking refuge on the bottom in areas of cover such as the stalks of aquatic plants, the crevices in rocks, or the holes in sunken logs—anywhere it can rest with at least part of its body hidden. Emery observed that during the daytime, logperch did not often allow anyone to approach closer than 0.5 m. At night, however, it was possible for a diver to touch logperch while they were fully illuminated by a diving light.

On sunny days in clear water, the logperch retires

to the deeper waters, where it hides under rocks or buries itself in sand, leaving only its eyes exposed. It returns to shallower water in the evening (Trautman 1957). Clay (1962) noted that it avoided bright daylight by moving from the riffles into adjacent pools. In Douglas Lake, Michigan, the logperch during the nonbreeding season was found in the deeper waters off shore (Winn 1958).

In the Little Platte River (Grant County), 10 logperch were associated with the shorthead redhorse (1), white sucker (57), common carp (1), central stoneroller (73), blacknose dace (1), hornyhead chub (64), creek chub (1), bluntnose minnow (11), suckermouth minnow (39), common shiner (21), sand shiner (8), bigmouth shiner (2), johnny darter (4), fantail darter (1), and smallmouth bass (9).

IMPORTANCE AND MANAGEMENT

The logperch has been eaten by largemouth bass, northern pike, walleyes, lake trout, rock bass, and burbot, and by birds such as the tern and the red-breasted merganser. One of the serious predators on logperch are logperch themselves, specifically non-spawning males who feed on unburied or lightly buried eggs (Scott and Crossman 1973).

Jordan and Evermann (1896–1900) wrote (p. 1026): "The Log Perch is the giant of the family, the most of a fish, and therefore the least of a darter. . . . We often meet an urchin with two or three of them strung through the gills on a forked stick." Logperch are taken occasionally by hook-and-line fishermen when they are fishing for perch and sunfishes. The logperch is sometimes used as a bait minnow; however, it keeps poorly in a minnow pail. I have not seen this species in bait stations.

When fried, logperch are just as desirable a food fish as perch and sunfishes (Eddy and Surber 1947). However, individual logperch of sufficient size for human consumption are caught but rarely, and the larger fish are often highly encrusted with the parasitic trematode black spot, which renders them unpalatable to most people.

The logperch makes an interesting and hardy aquarium pet.

River Darter

Percina shumardi (Girard). *Percina*—small perch; *shumardi*—after its discoverer, Dr. G. C. Shumard, surgeon of the Pacific railroad survey.
Other common name: big-headed darter.

Male 67 mm, Wisconsin R., Port Andrews (Richland Co.), 16 Aug. 1962

Female 75 mm, Wisconsin R., Port Andrews (Richland Co.), 16 Aug. 1962

DESCRIPTION

Body elongate to moderately robust, slightly compressed laterally. Average length 64 mm (2.5 in). TL = 1.19 SL. Depth into SL 4.8–5.8. Head length into SL 3.5–3.8. Preopercle smooth on posterior edge. Gill membranes narrowly to moderately attached below to one another. Premaxillaries nonprotractile, the upper lip groove not continuous over tip of snout. Snout decurved, short; mouth horizontal to slightly oblique, lower jaw slightly included within upper jaw; upper jaw reaching to or extending slightly beyond anterior edge of eye; minute, sharp teeth in narrow bands on upper and lower jaws. Gill rakers on lower limb of first arch short, stout, bent, about 9. Branchial apparatus illustrated and described by Branson and Ulrikson (1967). Branchiostegal rays 6 (7). Dorsal fins 2: first or spiny dorsal fin with 10 (10–12) spines, fin base into SL 3.5–4.0; second dorsal fin with 14 (13–15) rays, fin base into SL 4.5–5.5. Anal fin with 2 spines and 11 (12) rays; pelvic fins thoracic. Scales ctenoid; cheeks scaled, opercles scaled, nape naked to scaled; breast naked; midline of belly naked or with a partial line of modified scales immediately before vent reaching about halfway to pelvic fin base. Lateral line complete, scales 48–60; scales around caudal peduncle 19–24. Vertebrae 39 (38–40) (Bailey and Gosline 1955).

Back brown to olive brown; sides lighter; and belly whitish; 6–7 faint saddle marks on back and 8–11 lateral blotches along sides that become short, vertical bars anteriorly. Distinct black suborbital bar. Caudal spot faint to prominent (especially in young). Spiny dorsal fin with black blotch on membrane behind first spine and a larger black blotch on membranes between last 3–4 spines. Second dorsal and caudal fins lightly speckled to barred. Anal, pelvic and pectoral fins clear to lightly pigmented.

Breeding male, with overall colors darker and colors more intensified than in females. In male tubercles present on anal fin, pelvic fins, ventral part of caudal fin, head, and midventral scales (Collette 1965).

Sexual dimorphism: Male usually with a line of modified scales extending from vent to about half the distance to pelvic fins; female generally with a naked midline strip or only a few midline scales. Males with thickened membrane on anterior edge of pelvic fins; female normal, without thickened membrane. Anal, pelvic, and pectoral fins more pigmented in male than in female; anal fin enlarged in males.

Hybrids: River darter × logperch (Schwartz 1972).

DISTRIBUTION, STATUS, AND HABITAT

In Wisconsin, the river darter occurs in the Mississippi River and Lake Michigan drainage basins. It is not known from the Lake Superior drainage. In the Mississippi drainage, it is present in the St. Croix River upstream to the St. Croix Falls Dam, the lower Red Cedar River, the Chippewa River upstream to Eau Claire, the Wisconsin River upstream to Wisconsin Dells, and the Mississippi River boundary water. In the Lake Michigan drainage, it occurs in Lakes Winnebago and Poygan, and in the lower parts of the upper Wolf River to at least its juncture with the Waupaca River. In the Waupaca River, it occurs upstream to within 3 km of Weyauwega (Waupaca County).

Greene (1935) had no record of the river darter from the Lake Michigan system. In all probability it is a recent immigrant from the Wisconsin River via the canal at Portage (Columbia County) and the upper Fox River system. It was first reported from the west shore of Lake Winnebago by Christenson (September 1963, Wis. Dep. Nat. Resour. Monthly Activity Report, Fishery, Nevin Hatchery), and from Lakes

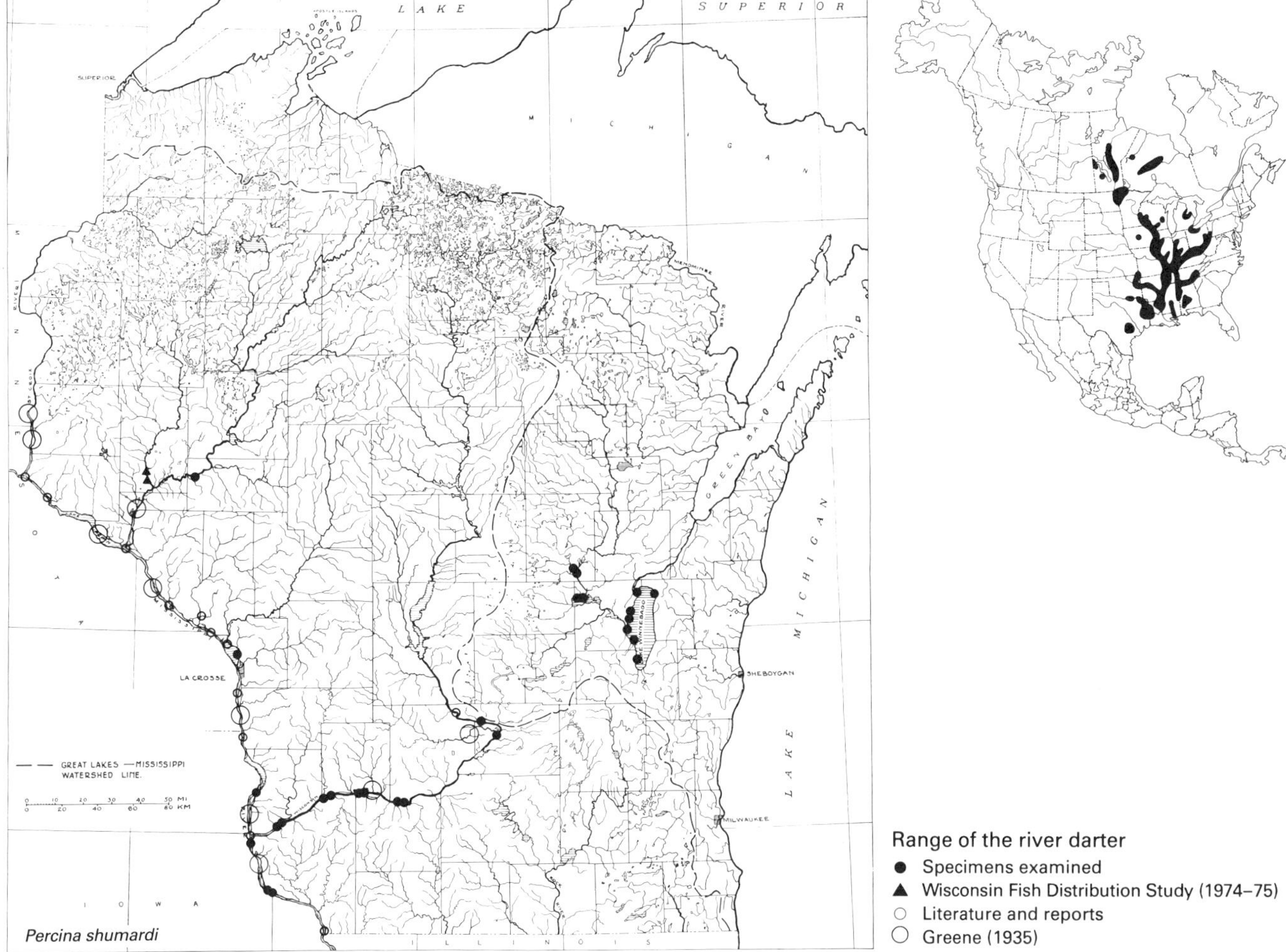

Range of the river darter
● Specimens examined
▲ Wisconsin Fish Distribution Study (1974–75)
○ Literature and reports
◯ Greene (1935)

Winnebago and Poygan and the Waupaca River by Becker (1964b). The spread of this species is similar to that indicated for the rainbow darter (Becker 1959). An early report of the river darter from southern Lake Michigan was noted by Hubbs (1926). Specimens were seen in the water system of Chicago; these had been taken up in the "cribs" offshore in Lake Michigan. The river darter's entry into southern Lake Michigan was probably through either glacial Lake Chicago, or more recently through the Chicago Sanitary and Ship Canal, which connects Lake Michigan with the Illinois River, a part of the Mississippi system (Greene 1935).

Although the river darter has appeared in a number of Wisconsin collections, at most sites only 1–3 individuals have been taken, and these have generally been young-of-year or yearling fish. It is probable that the river darter is more common in the state than my records indicate, and that part of the difficulty in assessing its distribution stems from a lack of adequate equipment with which to sample its habitat. Priegel (1967a) noted that the river darter is common in Lake Winnebago. Since Greene took his samples in the late 1920s, this species appears to have held its early range and to have expanded into the Lake Michigan system, where it has established a number of successful populations.

In lakes, the river darter occurs along wave-swept shores over sand, gravel, rubble, and bedrock. Young-of-year have been collected over sandy shallows in sluggish currents. Our collections were made with fine-mesh seines at depths up to 1 m, but we managed to take only a few age-II adults. That adult river darters are present in deeper chutes, riffles, and channels has been indicated by other investigators (Harlan and Speaker 1956, Pflieger 1975, Miller and Robison 1973, Thomas 1970). Trautman (1957) noted its presence in shallow waters only under turbid conditions; when the shallow water was clear, or collections were made at night, it was absent.

BIOLOGY

In Wisconsin, the river darter probably spawns from April to June. Cross (1967) reported river darters apparently spawning on 10 April in the Neosho River, Kansas, in water about 0.6 m deep over exposed bedrock, gravel, and larger stones. The river was unusually low and clear at the time, and the river darter was found only in strong, deep currents near shore. Scott and Crossman (1973) have suggested that the spawning behavior of the river darter is similar to that of the blackside darter.

On 8 June, the ovaries of an age-I female river darter from the Waupaca River (Waupaca County) contained a number of ripe eggs 1.2 mm diam. The ovaries constituted 2.2% of the body weight.

In central Wisconsin, young-of-year river darters were 36–54 mm TL in August; in southern Wisconsin, they were 42–56 mm long in August (Lutterbie 1976). In Illinois, young-of-year were 36–43 mm long in June (Thomas 1970).

For 17 river darters from southern Wisconsin, calculated growth at annuli 1 and 2 was 50 and 67 mm, respectively (Lutterbie 1976). In the Kaskaskia River, Illinois, the calculated lengths for 11 river darters at annuli 1 and 2 were 49 and 65 mm, respectively (Thomas 1970). Thomas estimated that this species attains 60 to 70% of its total growth by the first annulus; most growth occurred from June to mid-September. In these studies no river darter more than 2 years old was encountered. Maturity occurs in some river darters at age I.

In central Wisconsin, the length-weight relationship of river darters was $\text{Log } W = -13.364 + 3.4414 \text{ Log } L$; in southern Wisconsin, it was $\text{Log } W = -12.9628 + 3.3473 \text{ Log } L$, where W is weight in grams and L is length in millimeters (Lutterbie 1976).

The largest Wisconsin river darter known is a 2-year-old, 80-mm (3.2-in), 4.9-g female (UWSP 946), collected from the Wisconsin River (Richland County) on 4 August 1962. In Missouri (Pflieger 1975), adults of this species are commonly 58–84 mm long, but may grow to a maximum of about 89 mm (3.5 in).

Microcrustaceans are the main foods consumed by young river darters. The important food items of adults are Diptera (Chironomidae and Simuliidae), Trichoptera (Hydropsychidae), and crustaceans (copepods and cladocerans) (Thomas 1970). Feeding occurs during daylight hours.

In the Waupaca River below Weyauwega (Waupaca County), 3 river darters were associated with the shorthead redhorse (1), hornyhead chub (5), bluntnose minnow (76), fathead minnow (3), common shiner (56), rosyface shiner (48), spotfin shiner (33), spottail shiner (1), sand shiner (7), mimic shiner (9), northern pike (2), western sand darter (48), logperch (+), Iowa darter (1), and brook stickleback (29).

IMPORTANCE AND MANAGEMENT

The significance of the river darter as a forage species is probably minimal, and it is seldom if ever used as a bait fish.

Much is yet to be learned about the life history of the river darter, and it can become a prime research organism for the fish biologist seeking a challenge.

Crystal Darter

Ammocrypta asprella (Jordan). *Ammocrypta*—sand concealed, in reference to lying buried in the sand; *asprella*—little perch (from European genus *Aspro*).

Other common name: rough sand darter.

Female 125 mm, Wisconsin R., Orion (Richland Co.), 28 July 1962

DESCRIPTION

Body very slender, almost cylindrical. Length 140 mm (5.5 in). TL = 1.16 SL. Depth into SL 7.8–9.3. Head length into SL 4.0–4.5. Preopercle smooth on posterior edge. Gill membranes narrowly attached below to one another. Premaxillaries nonprotractile, the upper lip groove not continuous over tip of snout. Snout pointed; mouth horizontal, lower jaw included within upper jaw; upper jaw extending to below nostrils but not reaching eye; minute teeth in narrow bands on upper and lower jaws. Gill rakers on lower limb of first arch knoblike, about 11. Branchiostegal rays 6. Dorsal fins 2: first or spiny dorsal fin with 14 spines, fin base into SL 3.8–4.5; second dorsal fin with 15 (14–16) rays, fin base into SL 4.5–5.5. Anal fin with 1 spine and 15–16 rays; pelvic fins thoracic. Scales ctenoid; cheeks and opercles half to fully scaled; nape scaled; breast naked; belly generally naked but occasionally a few scattered scales before vent and at apex of pelvic girdle. Lateral line complete, scales 89–95; scales around caudal peduncle 25–28. Vertebrae 47–48 (Bailey and Gosline 1955).

Back and upper sides yellow-green; ventral region of head and belly whitish; 3–4 broad saddle marks over back extending forward to lateral line; 10–12 dark, confluent oblong blotches along sides. Dark stripe across snout through eyes and continuing posteriorly. Fins transparent to lightly pigmented; caudal fin often with wavy bands.

Breeding male with tubercles on anal and pelvic fins (Collette 1965).

SYSTEMATIC NOTES

The crystal darter is the sole member in the subgenus *Crystallaria*, formerly the generic name. The closely related western sand darter is in the subgenus *Ammocrypta*. *Crystallaria* and *Ammocrypta*, the 2 subgenera of the genus *Ammocrypta*, are recognized by some workers as distinct genera, since they are very different morphologically and represent different phyletic lines, although apparently these lines have a common origin (Williams 1975). Characteristics shared by the two subgenera are: a single anal spine; the arrangement of breeding tubercles; reduced frontal bones; narrow interorbital areas; narrowly conjoined branchiostegal membranes; and elongate median fin rays.

DISTRIBUTION, STATUS, AND HABITAT

In Wisconsin, the crystal darter occurs only in the Mississippi River drainage basin, where it reaches its northern limit of distribution.

Mississippi River records: UMMZ 76823 Cassville (Grant County); Minnesota Conservation Department, below railroad bridge at Winona (Winona County), Minnesota (Bailey and Gosline 1955); below Winona on the Wisconsin side (Buffalo County), 1945 (Eddy and Surber 1947). Recent specimens deposited in UWSP: #1156 (6) Wisconsin River at Orion (Richland County), 1962; #4788 (1) Trempealeau River T19N R10W Sec 11 (Trempealeau County), 1974; #5649 (5) Chippewa River T25N R13W Sec 9 (Pepin County), 1977; and #5650 (4) Chippewa River T26N R12W Sec 30 (Dunn County), 1977.

The Wisconsin Department of Natural Resources—La Crosse (E. Trimberger, pers. comm.) reported: Chippewa River T25N R13W Secs 1 and 2 (Pepin County), 1965, and T26N R12W Secs 11 and 30 (Dunn County), 1965. Specimen identified by me from Chippewa River R26N R12W Secs 29 and 30 (Dunn County), 1973 (J. Waybrant, Rice Div. of NUS Corp, Pittsburgh, Pa.). The Wisconsin Fish Distribution Study (1974–1978) reported: Chippewa River T25N R13W Secs 3, 4, and 9 (Pepin and Dunn counties), 1975; Red Cedar River T26N R12W Sec 30 and T26N R13W Secs 2, 11, 14, 24, and 35 (Dunn County), 1975.

The crystal darter is not abundant anywhere in its entire range. It is believed to be extirpated in Illinois, which is ironic, since the collection from which it was described came from a rocky creek in the Mississippi bluffs in Hancock County (Jordan and Evermann 1896–1900). In the Ohio River system, most records date from before 1900 (Trautman 1957, Gerking 1945, Clay 1975, P. W. Smith 1965), and it is probably extirpated from those waters. Trautman (1957) suggested that its probable extirpation in Ohio might have been caused by silt loads which covered its required

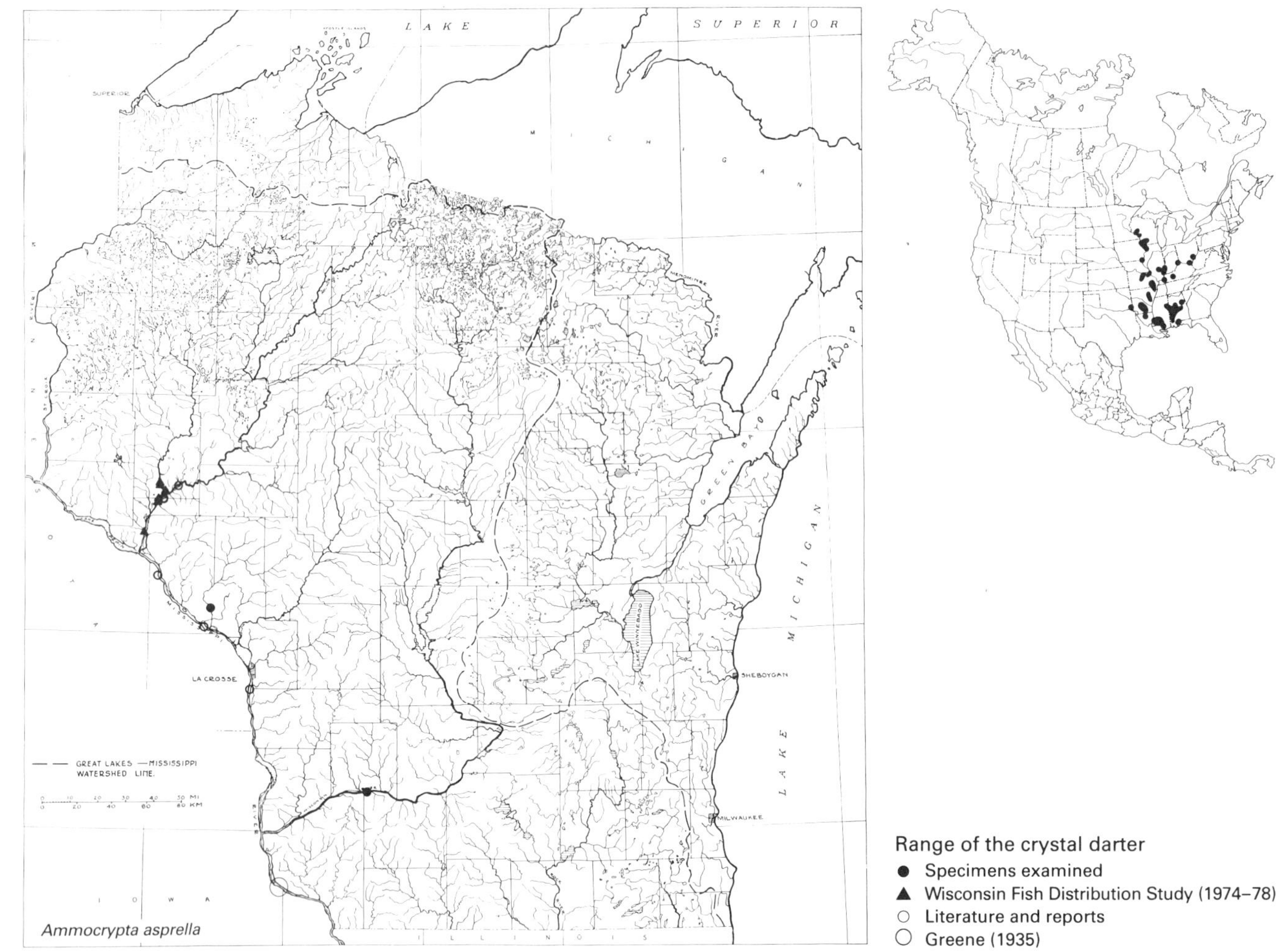

Range of the crystal darter
● Specimens examined
▲ Wisconsin Fish Distribution Study (1974–78)
○ Literature and reports
◯ Greene (1935)

spawning habitat. In Alabama and Mississippi, the crystal darter bears depleted status (Miller 1972).

In Wisconsin, the crystal darter is rare in the Mississippi, lower Wisconsin, and lower Trempealeau rivers, and uncommon to common in the lower Red Cedar River and in the Chippewa River between Durand (Pepin County) and Meridean (Dunn County). The northernmost population is probably the strongest remaining anywhere over its entire range. Wisconsin has accorded this species endangered status (Les 1979).

On the Mississippi River at Cassville, the crystal darter was collected from a gravelly bar with a moderate current. A young-of-year crystal darter from the Trempealeau River (Trempealeau County) was taken from brown-stained water, 0.6–1.1 m deep, over a sand substrate in a moderate to strong current. Collections in the Chippewa River (Pepin and Dunn counties) were taken over substrates of 10–25% sand and 90–75% gravel. In the Wisconsin River, it was found over an extensive rock shelf in about 0.3 m of moderately flowing water. It was taken in the Zumbro River, Minnesota, from driftwood and debris caught in a shifting sand bottom (J. Underhill, pers. comm.). Generally, the crystal darter is an inhabitant of extensive sandy riffles, bars, and pool bottoms. It usually occupies clear to slightly turbid waters of moderate to strong currents. The crystal darter prefers larger rivers and deeper waters than does the western sand darter.

BIOLOGY

The development of breeding tubercles in male crystal darters suggests spring spawning for this species. In specimens from Pearl River, Mississippi, Collette (1965) reported beginning tubercle development from late November to a maximum development in late January.

One male crystal darter (134 mm TL), taken from the Wisconsin River on 28 July, had testes that were 0.04% of the body weight; one female (123 mm TL) taken at the same time and place had ovaries that were 0.23% of the body weight (Lutterbie 1976). The testes were 27 mm long, while the right and left ovaries were 20 and 19 mm long, respectively. The ovaries contained 6,885 undeveloped eggs, averaging 0.2 mm diam.

A young-of-year crystal darter from the Trempealeau River was 81 mm long on 29 September.

Crystal darters collected in July from the Wisconsin River and Red Cedar–Chippewa river system showed the following growth (Lutterbie 1976:15):

Age Class	No. of Fish	TL (mm)		Calculated TL at Annulus (mm)		
		Avg	Range	1	2	3
I	11	118.36	97–142	86.73		
II	4	152.50	144–157	82.25	136.25	
III	1	166.00		99.00	145.00	160.00
Avg (weighted)				86.38	138.00	160.00

The length-weight relationship of crystal darters was Log W = −13.4213 + 3.2708 Log L, where weight is in grams and total length is in millimeters.

A 3-year-old crystal darter 166 mm (6.5 in) long and weighing 25.8 g (UWSP 1156) was captured from the lower Wisconsin River (Richland County) in July 1962.

The digestive tracts of two crystal darters taken from the Wisconsin River in July contained a total of 2 mayflies, 28 craneflies, 91 midgeflies, 1 blackfly, 38 caddisflies, 3 water scavenger beetles, and 3 nematodes. The midgeflies comprised 36% of the total weight of the organisms (Lutterbie 1976). Two crystal darters taken from the Red Cedar River in July contained 4 mayflies, 44 blackflies, and 2 caddisflies.

The data suggest that the crystal darter prefers deeper water (2–5 m) during the day, and moves into shallows at night or on heavily overcast days. Like the western sand darter, the crystal darter may burrow into the sand with only its eyes protruding, and dart out when a small prey organism comes into view (Miller and Robison 1973).

At Cassville (Grant County) on the Mississippi River, a number of crystal darters were seined along with the northern hog sucker, Mississippi silvery minnow, river shiner, and emerald shiner (Greene 1935). On one collection trip on the Wisconsin River (Richland County), 6 crystal darters were taken with shovelnose sturgeon (1), mooneye (4), quillback (1), river carpsucker (5), highfin carpsucker (2), shorthead redhorse (97), golden redhorse (47), northern hog sucker (65), common carp (12), silver chub (10), speckled chub (1), bluntnose minnow (1), emerald shiner (15), spotfin shiner (23), river shiner (1), sand shiner (36), sauger (6), walleye (1), river darter (3), slenderhead darter (11), logperch (31), smallmouth bass (21), black crappie (1), and freshwater drum (2).

IMPORTANCE AND MANAGEMENT

Considering its rarity, the crystal darter must play only a minor role in the ecological web. However, this does not detract from its being "a singularly interesting fish," as Jordan and Evermann (1896–1900) called it.

Study of the crystal darter is a unique challenge to the fish biologist, who must determine how to augment our scanty knowledge of this species' life history without endangering the remaining elements of its population. SCUBA observations of this darter in its native habitat may gain valuable information without any loss of seed stock.

Western Sand Darter

Ammocrypta clara Jordan and Meek. *Ammocrypta*—sand concealed, in reference to lying buried in the sand; *clara*—clear, referring to the clear or transparent flesh.

Other common name: sand darter.

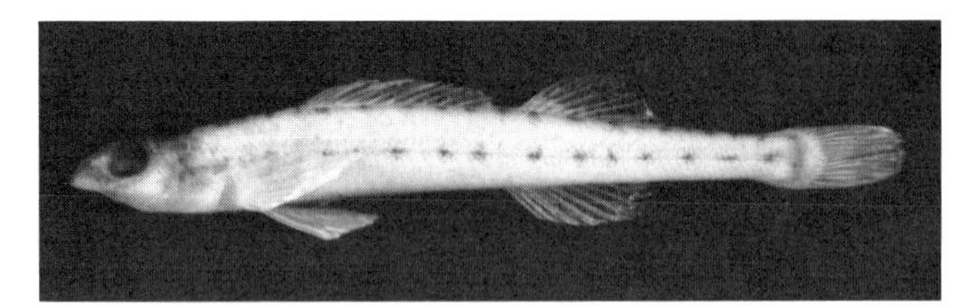

Female 65 mm, Black R. (Jackson Co.), 15 May 1976

DESCRIPTION

Body very slender, almost cylindrical. Average length 56 mm (2.2 in). TL = 1.17 SL. Depth into SL 6.5–8.0. Head length into SL 3.8–4.5. Preopercles smooth on posterior edge. Gill membranes narrowly to moderately attached below to one another. Premaxillaries nonprotractile, but the upper lip groove is continuous over tip of snout. Snout pointed; mouth horizontal, lower jaw included within upper jaw; upper jaw extending to below posterior nostril but not reaching eye; minute teeth in narrow bands on upper and lower jaws. Gill rakers on lower limb of first arch knoblike, about 8. Branchial apparatus illustrated and described by Branson and Ulrikson (1967). Branchiostegal rays 6. Dorsal fins 2: first or spiny dorsal fin with 10–12 spines, fin base into SL 3.8–4.5; second dorsal fin with 9–12 rays, fin base into SL 5.0–6.0. Anal fin with 1 spine and 7–10 rays; pelvic fins thoracic. Scales ctenoid; cheeks partially to fully scaled; opercles partially scaled; nape naked; breast naked; belly naked; body almost entirely naked with 3–4 rows of scales along the side (including the lateral line scale row) and broadening out on caudal peduncle to an almost completely scaled peduncle at base of caudal fin. Lateral line complete, scales 69–81. Vertebrae 39–40 (Bailey and Gosline 1955).

Pallid and transparent in life. Preserved head and body, light tan or straw-colored; small dark saddles, 12 or more on back; 10–12 small, oblong olive spots along midline of side (faint in life, darker when preserved); dark "moustache" on snout. Suborbital bar absent. Fins clear to weakly pigmented along spines and rays.

Breeding males with tubercles on pelvic, anal, and ventral rays of caudal fins.

SYSTEMATIC NOTES

Until recently the western sand darter was in synonymy with the eastern sand darter (*Ammocrypta pellucida*). Linder (1959) reviewed the specific status of *A. clara* and *A. pellucida*, and presented information to substantiate recognition of the two species, based on scale counts, opercle structures, and pigmentation. In contrast to the eastern form, the western sand darter has only 3–5 scale rows on the side of the body, a needlelike opercular spine, and less pigmentation in the mid-dorsal and lateral blotches. The description and range of the western form have been further clarified by Williams (1975).

DISTRIBUTION, STATUS, AND HABITAT

In Wisconsin, the western sand darter occurs in the Mississippi River and Lake Michigan drainage basins. In the Mississippi system it occurs in the St. Croix River upstream to St. Croix Falls, where it reaches the northern limit of its distribution; in the Chippewa River to the confluence of the Red Cedar River; in the Black River to Black River Falls; in the Wisconsin River upstream at least as far as Castle Rock Flowage (Juneau County), and in the flowage's tributary, the Yellow River. An old report from the Ashippun River places it in the upper Rock River system (Cahn 1927).

In the Lake Michigan drainage, the western sand darter was not known until 1960, when I reported it (UWSP 1155) from the Waupaca River (Becker 1965). In 1973, a specimen (UWSP 4404) was taken from the Wolf River (Outagamie County). These are the only known records from the Great Lakes drainage basin. The dispersal route into the Great Lakes system was probably via the Fox-Wisconsin canal at Portage (Columbia County), which links the Mississippi and Great Lakes drainages.

A number of sources report the declining abundance and extirpation of the western sand darter, especially in the central part of its range. It is listed as rare in Illinois (Lopinot and Smith 1973), depleted in Missouri (Miller 1972), threatened in Iowa (Roosa 1977), and extirpated in Kansas (Platt et al. 1973). Williams (1975) noted that it appears to be more abundant in the northern part of its range.

In Wisconsin, the western sand darter is common locally in the lower Wisconsin River, in the Mississippi River, and, according to Eddy and Underhill (1974), in the St. Croix River upstream to the St. Croix Falls Dam. It was common in the Waupaca River when 48 specimens were taken in 1960. In 1971, however, the upper Waupaca River was treated with fish toxicants during a carp control program,

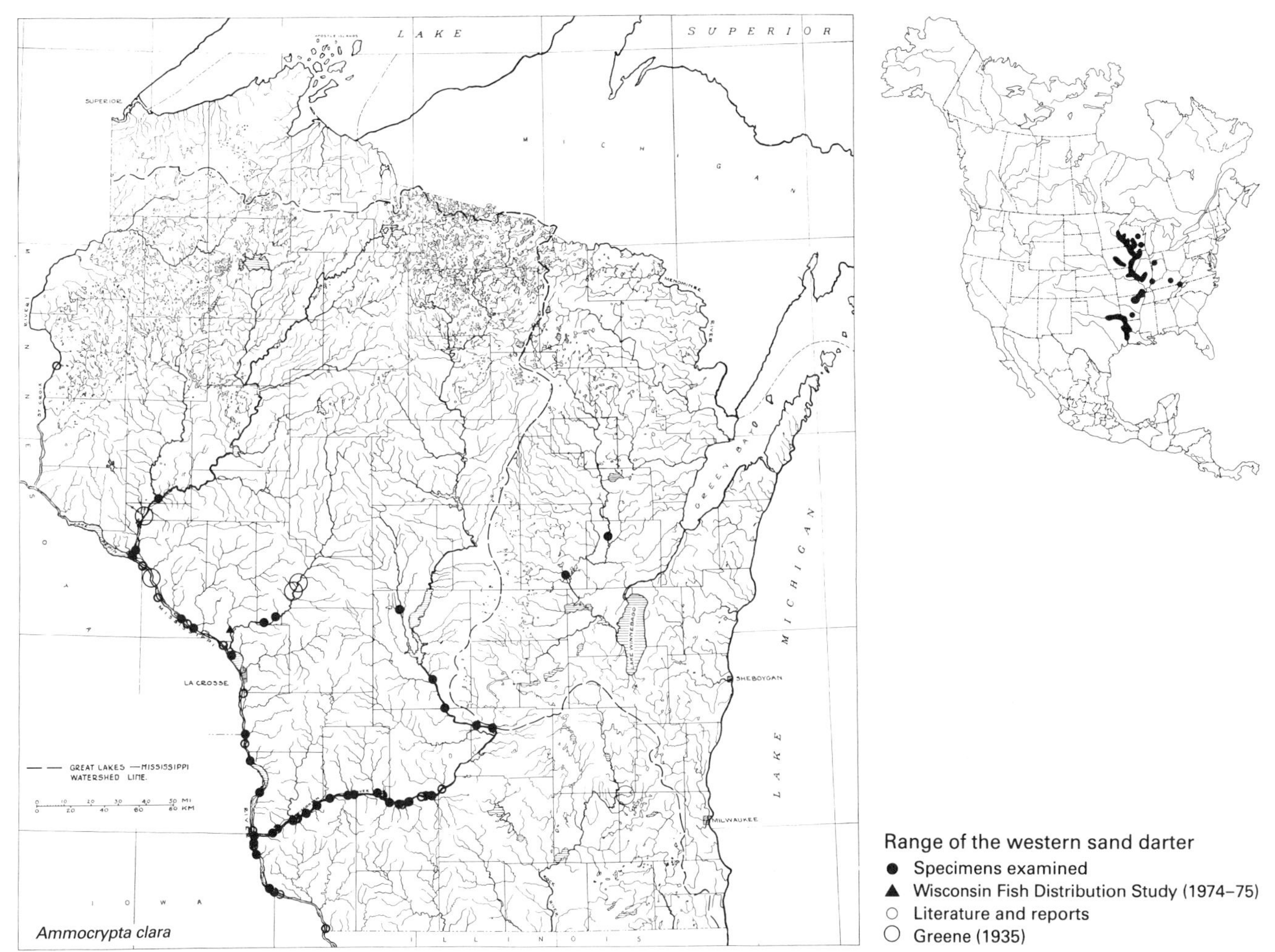

and, after the dam gates were closed at Weyauwega, the lower river containing the sand darter population was virtually without flow for several days. Repeated attempts to find surviving members of this population failed. According to Cross (1967), fluctuating water levels and increased siltation are especially detrimental to sand darters. Wisconsin has placed the western sand darter in the Lake Michigan system on watch status (Wis. Dep. Nat. Resour. Endangered Species Com. 1975).

The western sand darter occurs in medium-sized to large rivers in moderate to swift currents, over extensive sand flats, at depths of 0.2–0.9 m. It prefers clear to slightly turbid water.

Cahn (1927) took his single specimen in the Ashippun River from a 300 m stretch of clear sand "with not a sign of aquatic vegetation of any sort, or of a pebble larger than a sand grain." In the Waupaca River (Waupaca County), the site of capture was a hard-packed sand flat over the belly of a U-shaped bend in the river (Becker 1965); the depth of the water was 15 cm or less, the current was moderate, and width of the stream was about 18 m. No other fish were captured in this area.

BIOLOGY

In Wisconsin, the western sand darter spawns from late June through July (Lutterbie 1976). The ovaries of specimens taken in late June averaged 8.1% of the body weight (with a maximum of 11.6%); in early and mid-July, they averaged 7.9%; and in early August, 2.0%. Ovarian size increased to 3.1% in September; testicular development followed a similar pattern. By examining ovaries and the development of breeding tubercles, Williams (1975) placed the height of the spawning season in July and early August. He found females with mature eggs in late August.

In Wisconsin, maturing to mature eggs, 0.75–1.0 mm diam, averaged 203 (61–301) per adult female in June, 238 (152–324) in July, 54–88 in August, and 158 in September (Lutterbie 1976). The eggs appeared in three size classes: yellow eggs, 0.5 mm diam; orange eggs, 0.75 mm; and orange eggs, 1.00 mm.

Western sand darters from southern Wisconsin showed the following growth (Lutterbie 1976:24):

Age Class	No. of Fish	TL (mm)		Calculated TL at Annulus (mm)		
		Avg	Range	1	2	3
I	28	53.79	42–63	41.54		
II	76	58.64	53–66	44.62	55.86	
III	27	61.78	59–65	44.67	56.22	61.78
Avg (weighted)				43.97	55.95	61.78

For 47 western sand darters from central Wisconsin, the calculated lengths at the first three annuli were 43, 56, and 61 mm—almost identical to the calculated lengths for southern Wisconsin populations. The western sand darter reaches 71% of its total growth during its first year of life, and 91% during the second year. Females are usually larger and more numerous than the males.

The length-weight relationship for western sand darters was Log W = −12.5174 + 3.0949 Log L, where weight is in grams and total length is in millimeters (Lutterbie 1976). The largest western sand darter (UWSP 1149) collected from the Wisconsin River (Iowa County) is 66 mm (2.6 in) TL, 1.5 g, and 2 years old.

The western sand darter feeds on small or immature aquatic insects, such as mayflies and midge larvae, and on *Hyallela* (Eddy and Underhill 1974).

The western sand darter has the strange habit of burying itself in soft sand with nothing visible but its eyes and mouth (Cahn 1927). According to Linder (1953), the sand darter dives head-first into the sand, and, with rapid movements of the pectoral and caudal fins, completely buries itself. In aquarium observations, it has been found a couple of centimeters or more below the surface of the sand. Williams (1975) reported that the burying behavior of the related *Ammocrypta bifascia* consisted of a rapid dart along the bottom for a distance of 23–38 cm, after which a sudden headfirst plunge into the sand left the body buried. Only the eyes and snout were exposed. The midsection of the body was usually buried to a depth of 5–8 mm below the surface of the sand. The burying act usually required less than 3 seconds.

Williams summarized the functions of the burying habit (1975:30–31):

> The burying behavior of *Ammocrypta* has usually been explained in terms of protection from predators, however, this may not be the most important factor in the adaptive value of this behavior. The habitat of species of the subgenus *Ammocrypta* is shifting sand bottoms, generally considered to be the most unproductive lotic ecosystem. . . . The sterile nature of the habitat of sand darters generally precludes the presence of predatory species, with the exception of transient individuals. The absence of predators suggests that survival value of the burying behavior of *Ammocrypta* may not be due to the protection afforded. Actually this behavior may be more important in energy conservation than in protection. The energy required for an individual to maintain itself against a moderate current on a sand bottom would be considerably greater than the amount required for the same individual lying buried in the sand. Also, the lower temperature below the surface of the sand probably results in a reduction of the metabolic rate.

Over extensive sand flats where the water moves as a smooth sheet or a broad riffle, the western sand darter is generally the only species captured. In the Spring Green to Arena sector of the lower Wisconsin River, where the current was slow and the water was 0.3–0.6 m deep, the western sand darter was taken with the speckled chub and with an occasional bullhead minnow. In the lower Wisconsin River (Richland County), 60 western sand darters were collected alone from the typical habitat; from the immediately surrounding substrates (ranging from gravel to mud) I captured the longnose gar (1), shorthead redhorse (1), silver redhorse (1), golden redhorse (21), golden shiner (2), bullhead minnow (76), bluntnose minnow (13), emerald shiner (16), spotfin shiner (611), spottail shiner (1), river shiner (4), sand shiner (9), Mississippi silvery minnow (3), black bullhead (1), grass pickerel (2), yellow perch (23), walleye (16), blackside darter (1), johnny darter (72), rainbow darter (2), smallmouth bass (3), largemouth bass (481), pumpkinseed (1), bluegill (14), black crappie (25), white crappie (1), and brook silverside (3).

IMPORTANCE AND MANAGEMENT

The extent to which the sand darter is preyed upon by other animals is not known. Because of its small, thin body it is not a suitable bait fish.

The sand darter, with its restricted habitat and secretive habits, is little known. Many questions relating to its life history still need to be answered: What is its spawning behavior? Are the eggs and milt deposited on top of the substrate or within the sand bottom? Does the sand darter feed by swimming actively through the water after food organisms or does it, while buried in the sand, thrust after food particles moving overhead through the water column?

Johnny Darter

Etheostoma nigrum Rafinesque. *Etheostoma*—a straining mouth; *nigrum*—black, referring to the male, especially during spawning.
Other common name: central johnny darter.

Male 77 mm, Bear Cr. (Richland Co.), 28 July 1962

DESCRIPTION

Body slender, slightly compressed laterally. Average length 51 mm (2 in). TL = 1.20 SL. Depth into SL 4.5–5.8. Head length into SL 3.5–3.8. Preopercle smooth on posterior edge. Gill membranes narrowly to moderately attached below to one another. Premaxillaries protractile, the upper lip groove continuous over tip of snout. Snout decurved, short; mouth horizontal, lower jaw slightly included within upper jaw; upper jaw reaching below anterior edge of pupil; minute, sharp teeth in narrow bands on upper and lower jaws. Gill rakers on lower limb of first arch short, stout to knoblike, about 7. Branchial apparatus illustrated and described by Branson and Ulrikson (1967). Branchiostegal rays 6. Dorsal fins 2, scarcely to slightly separated: first or spiny dorsal fin with 8 (7–9) spines, fin base into SL 4.5; second dorsal fin with 13 (11–14) rays, fin base into SL 4.0–5.0. Anal fin with 1 spine and 7–9 rays; pelvic fins thoracic. Scales ctenoid; cheeks naked; opercles usually partially scaled; nape naked to scaled; breast naked, occasionally scaled; belly scaled, or, if naked, generally so behind pelvic fin base. Lateral line complete, scales 37–50. Vertebrae 38 (37–39) (Bailey and Gosline 1955). Chromosomes 2n = 48 (Ross 1973).

Back brown to straw yellow; sides paler; belly whitish yellow; 4–7 dark brown saddle marks on back; W-, J-, and S-shaped dark brown markings arranged along sides, suggesting a broken lateral stripe. Dark stripe extending from eye to snout, interrupted medially on snout. Suborbital bar short or absent. Caudal spot faint to absent. Spiny dorsal and soft dorsal fins usually with oblique rows of brown spots; caudal fin with wavy vertical brown bands; remaining fins lightly pigmented to transparent.

Breeding male becoming very dusky to black on the head and upper body and on the spiny dorsal, with increasing pigmentation on remaining fins. The pelvic spine and the first 2–3 pelvic rays and the ventral elements of the pectoral fins acquire whitened, knoblike tips.

Sexual dimorphism: All fins except the caudal fin larger in males. In male, urogenital papilla narrow, with 2 small lobes partially pigmented; in female, broad, swollen appearing, and unpigmented. In male, the first 3–5 spines of first dorsal fin with thickened, opaque white tips. Male larger than female.

SYSTEMATIC NOTES

Based on Wisconsin collections, Hubbs and Greene (1935) recognized two subspecies: the nominal central johnny darter, *Etheostoma nigrum nigrum*, and the scaly johnny darter, *Etheostoma nigrum eulepis*. The latter possesses scaled nape, breast, and cheeks. In the laboratory, Lagler and Bailey (1947) observed the phenotypic intermediacy of the F_1 intergrades. Analysis of large numbers of johnny darters in field collections from Minnesota (Underhill 1963) disclosed several collections containing intergrades, as well as both forms. Underhill concluded that scalation patterns were determined by incompletely dominant genes at one or a few loci, and that the morphological, ecological, and distributional evidence indicate that it is undesirable to recognize the scaly johnny darter as a subspecies.

DISTRIBUTION, STATUS, AND HABITAT

The johnny darter occurs in the Mississippi River, Lake Michigan, and Lake Superior drainage basins in Wisconsin. It is present in all boundary waters, and in the shallower waters of Green Bay and the Great Lakes. It is widely distributed in the streams and lakes of the state.

In Wisconsin, the johnny darter is the most successful member of the family Percidae, and is common to abundant in most waters. In northeastern Wisconsin, its frequency of occurrence in the Pine River basin was 39%, in the Popple River basin, 54% (Becker 1972). In a central Wisconsin fish distribution study (Becker 1959), the johnny darter appeared at 70% of the collection sites, and constituted more than 5% of all the fish handled. In a southwestern Wisconsin survey (Becker 1966), it was captured in 126 (78%) of 162 collections. It is common in Lakes Winnebago and Poygan (Priegel 1967a, Becker 1964b). Its abundance in Pewaukee Lake (Waukesha County) is a result of man's efforts to create suitable swimming areas by spreading gravel adjacent to piers. In the early 1940s, McCutchin (1946) reported the johnny darter as rare in Pewaukee Lake, but today it is com-

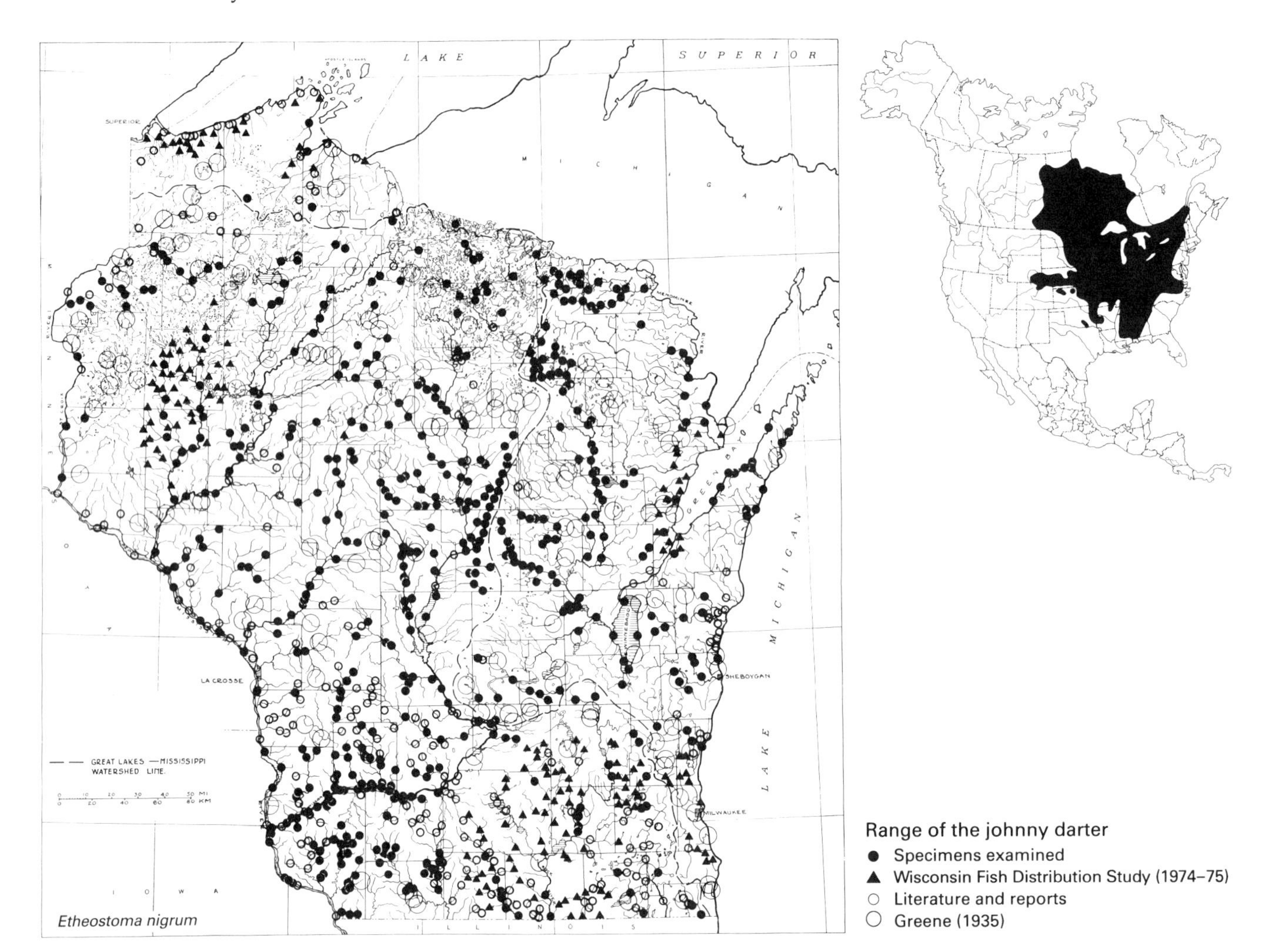

mon in such artificially created habitats. At the barriers in the mouths of streams tributary to Lake Superior, it is common to abundant (McLain et al. 1965).

The johnny darter inhabits most Wisconsin lakes and streams, but prefers small creeks with sand or mixed sand and gravel substrates. In Wisconsin, it was encountered in waters with varying silt loads, from the clear to the turbid. It occurred most frequently at depths of less than 0.5 m, over substrates of sand (25% frequency), gravel (21%), mud (13%), rubble (12%), silt (12%), boulders (9%), clay (6%), bedrock (2%), and detritus (1%). In two instances it was taken over marl. The johnny darter was taken in many lakes, but occurred more frequently in streams of the following widths: 1.0–3.0 m (23%), 3.1–6.0 m (25%), 6.1–12.0 m (15%), 12.1–24.0 m (18%), 24.1–50.0 m (13%), and more than 50 m (5%). In streams, 12% of the specimens collected were taken from sloughs, 51% from pools, and 37% from riffles.

In Lake Superior, nearly all johnny darters were captured from water less than 18 m deep, and none from water deeper than 25 m (Dryer 1966). In southeastern Lake Michigan, they were captured mostly between 22 and 31 m, but none from water deeper than 64 m (Wells 1968).

The johnny darter is a pioneer species which quickly becomes established in disturbed areas. In central Wisconsin, it moved into a newly dug stream channel and quickly became an important part of the fish community (Headrick 1976).

BIOLOGY

The johnny darter spawns from April to June at water temperatures ranging from 11.7 to 21.1°C (53 to 70°F). Changes in temperature, increased amounts of silt, or high water have been known to delay or interrupt the spawning of the johnny darter.

The spawning of the johnny darter has been treated in detail by Winn (1958) and by Atz (1940), and, unless otherwise designated, the following account has been drawn from those sources.

Males migrate to the spawning grounds in early or mid-April, slightly in advance of the females. The breeding area is usually in pools, slow raceways, and protected, shallow waters of lakes, which contain large rocks, logs, mussel shells, tin cans, or other objects on which eggs can be deposited. When the males arrive in these areas, they establish stationary territories 25 cm diam or larger, usually centered around one of the objects listed above. The males maintain only one territory, with the larger males dominating the smaller males. Two males of equal size desiring the same territory swim upstream alongside each other with their fins erect; once dominance is established, the superior male darts at the intruder with his fins erect, sending the intruder away. Males defend their territories against other species of fish that are up to 3 or 4 times their size. The johnny darter attacks by butting with its head and biting the fins of its opponent.

When establishing a territory, the male johnny darter assumes an inverted position, and with his anal, caudal, and pelvic fins cleans the undersurface of the rock or object chosen for a nesting site. Males increase the size of their nests by pushing coarse sand to either side with sweeping strokes of their bodies and tails, and/or by using their heads and pectoral fins. Males leave the nest only under great duress, although they do occasionally leave the territory for short periods of time. The territories are not maintained at night.

When a female johnny darter enters the territory, the male usually darts out at her as he would at any other intruder. He then returns quickly to his nest and swims actively upside down under the rock or object chosen as the nesting site; this activity appears to attract the female to the nest. The male recognizes a female by her complex behavior as she jerks back and forth, and at times takes an inverted position.

The female johnny darter enters the nest in the inverted position; if she is not in that position, the male quickly chases her out. Winn (1958) noted that both sexes maintain the inverted position most of the time while under the rock. An inverted female incites the male to move faster and to prod her sides while the two fish maintain a head-to-head relationship. Atz (1940) reported that this species may also assume a head-to-tail position. This activity stimulates the female to move continuously over the surface of the rock or object and to lay eggs. The male and female move jerkily over the area where the eggs are to be deposited. The female stops and presses her genital papilla against the rock and deposits an egg; seldom does she extrude more than one egg at a time. The male, maintaining the inverted position, then fertilizes the egg. It is not clear whether the eggs are fertilized immediately, or whether the male emits sperm intermittently during the course of spawning. The eggs are laid in an oblong patch up to 13 cm diam in a single layer, although in places the patch may contain two layers of eggs (Hankinson 1920).

Atz reported that one female spawned with the

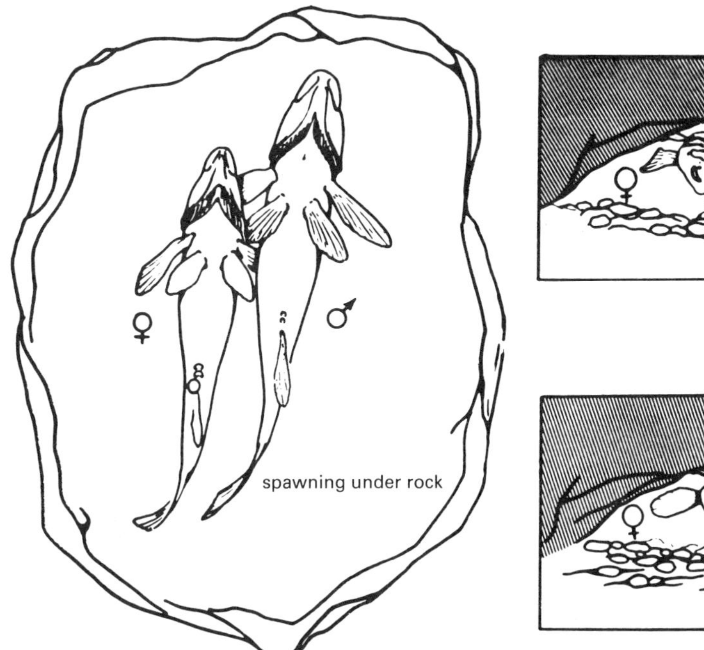

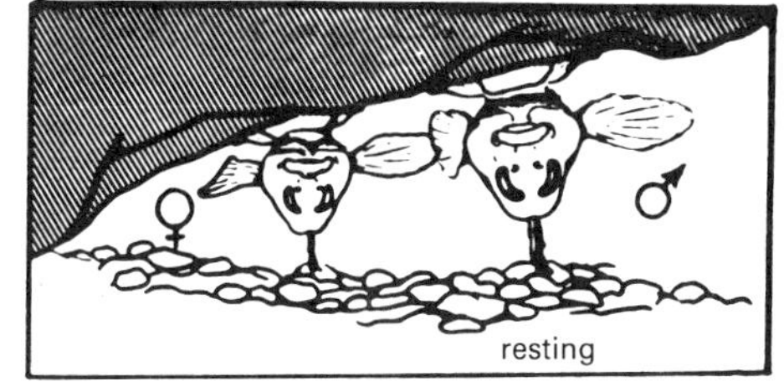

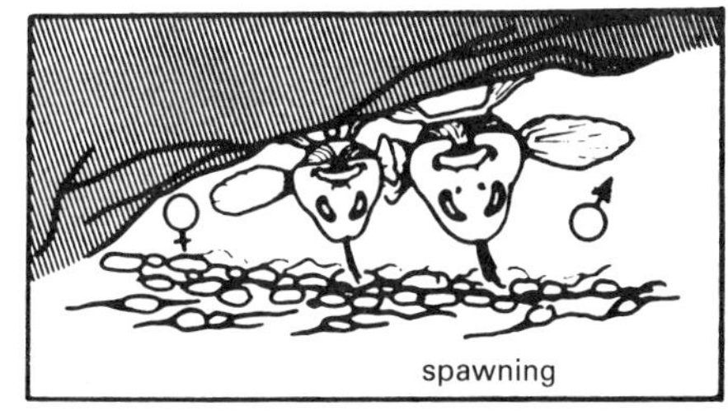

Side and top views of the positions of the johnny darter under rocks. The ventral view of the fish is obtained by looking down through the top of a hypothetically transparent rock, with the fish upside down on the underside of the rock (Winn 1958:178. Copyright 1960, the Ecological Society of America).

same male for 2 hr, during which 50 spawning acts took place. Winn counted 30, 47, 70, 870, 1080, 1100 plus, and 1150 eggs in individual nests; the small counts were made early in the spawning period. Both males and females are polygamous. A male spawns with more than one female, and a female may spawn with four to six different males and deposit between 30 and 200 eggs at each spawning.

Age-I female johnny darters from Wisconsin, 40–63 mm TL, held 169 (48–299) mature eggs; age-II females, 53–69 mm TL, held 323 (86–691) mature eggs (Lutterbie 1976). The mature egg is 1.5 mm diam and amber in color. The number of eggs produced is a function of age and size. Speare (1965) showed that three classes of eggs are produced by johnny darters, with diameters of 1.5, 1.0, and 0.5 mm; only the largest eggs are spawned. Lutterbie noted the greatest ovarian development in March and April, and a strong drop in ovarian size in June.

During spawning, and after its completion, the male johnny darter cares for the eggs. He moves over the eggs in an inverted position, rubbing them with his pelvic, anal, and caudal fins, about 13–16 times per half hour; each cleaning period lasts from 20 seconds to 5 minutes. The male also rubs the eggs with the swollen fleshy spines of his spiny dorsal fin, and fans them with his pectoral fins. He eats eggs that become covered with fungus. He also defends the eggs against predators, at least against the smaller fish.

Fertilized johnny darter eggs maintained at 22–24°C (71.6–75.2°F) hatch in 5.5–8 days. Speare (1965) noted that eggs laid in April hatch in 16 days at 12.8°C (55°F); in May, in 10 days at 20°C (68°F); and in June, in 6 days at 22.8°C (73°F). The larvae are 5 mm long upon hatching (Fish 1932). Fish illustrated and described the 5-, 5.6-, 7.1-, 9.6-, and 15-mm stages.

In southern Wisconsin, young-of-year johnny darters were 20–34 mm long in June, 24–38 mm in July, 25–48 mm in August, and 27–40 mm in September (Lutterbie 1976). In central Wisconsin, they were 25–48 mm long in July, 34–40 mm in August, and 29–54 mm in September.

Johnny darters from southern Wisconsin showed the following growth (Lutterbie 1976:115):

Age Class	No. of Fish	TL (mm)		Calculated TL at Annulus (mm)		
		Avg	Range	1	2	3
I	187	49.00	32–67	39.70		
II	68	56.59	37–77	35.25	50.64	
III	1	68.00		36.00	52.00	64.00
Avg (weighted)				38.50	50.66	64.00

For johnny darters from central Wisconsin the calculated growth at annuli 1 through 3 was 36, 51, and 66 mm; and for northern Wisconsin johnny darters, 39, 56, and 73 mm. Northern Wisconsin fish appear to have a slight growth advantage.

The length-weight relationship was Log W = −12.9211 + 3.2972 Log L, where weight is in grams and total length in millimeters. The largest johnny darter in the Musuem of Natural History, Stevens Point, (UWSP 1031), collected from the Tomorrow River (Portage County), is a 3-year-old male, 77 mm (3 in) TL.

The johnny darter at 15 mm feeds on entomostracans and minute midge larvae, and these items continue to appear in the diet throughout life (Turner 1921). In southeastern Wisconsin, the johnny darter's diet was composed of about 50% chironomid and blackfly larvae, with *Hyalella* and entomostracans (*Cyclops*, *Daphnia*, etc.) making up the other half (Cahn 1927). In fish from Lake Mendota (Dane County), 62.9% of the diet was insect larvae, 13.6% algae, 2.9% bottom ooze, and 20.7% sand (Pearse 1921a). In Green Lake (Green Lake County), it consumed insect larvae (82.1%), amphipods (2.5%), and sand (15.3%). In the Big Eau Pleine Reservoir (Marathon County), chironomids made up 66% and copepods 23% of the contents of 11 stomachs examined (D. Sanders, pers. comm.). Johnny darters from western Lake Superior had eaten chironomids (50%); the remaining contents of their stomachs were unidentifiable (Anderson and Smith 1971b).

Turner (1921) noted that there is no difference in the foods consumed by johnny darters in lake and stream habitats, and that organic and inorganic debris are ingested by fish of all ages. Emery (1973) observed that the johnny darter is a daytime feeder, and rarely feeds at night. The most important sense used by the johnny darter in the capture of food is sight (Roberts and Winn 1962); this species responds only slightly to olfactory cues.

The johnny darter is distinctly a shallow water darter, and is easily observed from shore. Forbes and Richardson noted (1920):

> . . . It often lies with its head up and its body bent to one side or supported partly by a stone. It can turn its head without moving its body; can roll the eye about in the socket; may rest suspended, as we have seen it do, on the under side of a floating board; and sometimes buries itself, with a whirl, in the soft sand, so that only its eyes are visible.

In some lakes, however, this species occurs at considerable depths. Moyle (1969) surmised that it inhabited deep water in Long Lake, Minnesota; many were captured in the fall in the shallow water into which they had migrated. A study of Lake Vermillion, Minnesota, disclosed few johnny darters in shallow waters, but trawl hauls revealed large populations at depths between 2 and 8 m; a few darters were captured in water as deep as 16 m.

The johnny darter is tolerant of many organic and inorganic pollutants, and it is able to inhabit siltier waters than are tolerated by many other fish species (Trautman 1957). Lotrich (1973) found that, although the total number of fish in a Kentucky stream was reduced by 50% following the influx of strip-mining wastes, the johnny darter's numbers were reduced by only a little more than 10%. Pflieger (1971) reported that the johnny darter avoids streams that are excessively turbid and silty.

In streams low in dissolved oxygen, the johnny darter moves out of the pools and sluggish areas into the faster riffles where oxygen levels are higher (Trautman 1957). In one population studied, a deficiency of dissolved oxygen (0.1–0.15 ppm) at night, caused by an overabundance of vegetation, resulted in increased mortality of the johnny darter and the Iowa darter (Roach and Wickliff 1934).

When johnny darters were pretreated with 2.3 ppb dieldrin for 30 days and then exposed to thermal stress, they had a significantly higher mortality rate than fish not pretreated with dieldrin and which had been exposed to the same thermal stress (Silbergeld 1973). Stress was applied by heating the water at a rate of 1°C/hr to a maximum of 9°C above ambient temperature.

Because of its ubiquitous distribution, the johnny darter comes into contact with most fish species in Wisconsin. In the Pine River (Richland County), 179 johnny darters were associated with the American brook lamprey (2), northern hog sucker (4), white sucker (72), central stoneroller (181), blacknose dace (176), creek chub (95), redside dace (50), bluntnose minnow (95), common shiner (190), bigmouth shiner (114), and fantail darter (82).

IMPORTANCE AND MANAGEMENT

The role of the johnny darter within the aquatic community, according to Scott and Crossman (1973), is probably to convert small food organisms to a larger form, and thus to serve as food for larger fishes. In the Big Eau Pleine Reservoir (Marathon County), the johnny darter is a major food item for the walleye (Joy 1975). The johnny darter has been eaten by lake trout, lake whitefish, burbot, smallmouth bass, and other fishes.

The johnny darter is a known host to the glochidial stages of the mussels *Alasmidonta calceola* and *Anodonta grandis*, and, as a result, aids in perpetuating those species (Hart and Fuller 1974).

The johnny darter is a useful species for behavioral studies in the laboratory. It makes an interesting and hardy aquarium species.

Bluntnose Darter

Etheostoma chlorosomum (Hay). *Etheostoma*—a straining mouth; *chlorosomum*—green bodied

Other common names: blunt-nosed darter, snubnose darter.

Young adult 36 mm, Miller Cr. (Alexander Co.) Illinois, 2 Sept. 1964

DESCRIPTION

Body slender, with a long slender caudal peduncle. Length 38–46 mm (1.5–1.8 in). TL = 1.20 SL. Depth into SL 6.0–7.2. Head length into SL 3.8–4.2. Preopercle smooth on posterior edge. Gill membranes moderately attached below to one another. Premaxillaries protractile, the upper lip groove continuous over tip of snout. Snout blunt and projecting slightly beyond the upper lip; mouth horizontal, lower jaw slightly included within upper jaw; upper jaw reaching below anterior edge of pupil; minute, sharp teeth in narrow bands on upper and lower jaws. Gill rakers on lower limb of first arch short, knoblike, about 6. Branchial apparatus illustrated and described by Branson and Ulrikson (1967). Branchiostegal rays about 6. Dorsal fins 2, slightly to widely separated: first or spiny dorsal fin with 8–9 spines, second dorsal fin with 9–11 rays. Anal fin with 1 spine and 7–8 rays; pelvic fins thoracic. Scales ctenoid; cheeks and opercles scaled; nape usually naked; breast and belly naked to scaled. Lateral line incomplete with fewer than 25 pored scales, lateral series scales 52–58. Vertebrae 39 (38–40) (Bailey and Gosline 1955).

Preserved: back yellow-brown (green-yellow in life) with 6–8 faint brown saddle marks; sides with 8–10 faint blotches similar to dorsal markings; belly whitish. Continuous dark stripe extending from eye to eye across snout. Suborbital bar faint to absent. Dorsal fins lightly speckled, caudal fin with wavy vertical bands; remaining fins clear.

Breeding male dark and with blackened dorsal fins. Thin elongate tubercles on first 2 pelvic rays and portions of remaining rays; poorly developed tubercles on middle portions of anal rays 2–5. In female, genital papilla a swollen rugose pad (Collette 1965).

DISTRIBUTION, STATUS, AND HABITAT

In Wisconsin, the bluntnose darter occurs upstream to Pool 8 in the Mississippi River and in closely adjacent waters. A southern species, it reaches its northern limit of distribution in Wisconsin, Minnesota, and Iowa.

In Minnesota, several specimens of the bluntnose darter were collected by survey crews from the Mississippi River in 1944, from Pine Creek in Houston County, and from an overflow pool of the Root River in 1945 (Eddy and Underhill 1974, R. E. Johnson and Moyle 1949). These specimens were examined by Eddy, but they were not deposited in the University of Minnesota collections, and their present location is unknown.

On 21 and 23 August 1944, four specimens were collected from small, isolated ponds of the Mississippi River between New Albin and Minnesota slough, Allamakee County, Iowa. These sites, virtually on the Iowa-Minnesota border, are just across the river from Victory (Vernon County), Wisconsin. Although these reports have been mentioned in the literature (Eddy and Surber 1947, Upper Miss. R. Conserv. Com. 1953, Harlan and Speaker 1956), the location of validating specimens was unknown until 1967, when M. Johnson found two vials labeled "*Boleosoma chlorosomum*" in the University of Wisconsin-Madison collections. Each contained a specimen from the two 1944 collection dates. The 21 August 1944 specimen, 26.5 mm SL, is now in the University of Michigan collections (UMMZ 186510), and the 23 August specimen is at the Museum of Zoology, University of Wisconsin–Madison.

A verified specimen of the bluntnose darter from the Wisconsin waters of the Mississippi River was seined on 11 August 1976 off Island 192, T3N R6W Sec 24 (Grant County) (Wis. Fish Distrib. Study 1974–1978). I have seen this specimen, which is presently housed in the Wisconsin Department of Natural Resources collections at the Nevin Headquarters in Madison.

In the northern portion of its range, the bluntnose darter is decreasing. At one time (before 1905), it was reported from the Lake Michigan drainage system at South Chicago, Illinois (Forbes and Richardson 1920), but it is probably extirpated in the Lake Michigan basin (Becker 1976). It has been placed on the threatened list in Iowa (Roosa 1977), it is rare in Kansas (Platt et al. 1973), and it has declined in Missouri since the 1940s (Pflieger 1971). Pflieger thought this was a result of increased siltation caused by the cultivation of prairies.

In Wisconsin, the bluntnose darter must be one of the rarest of fish species, although its specialized

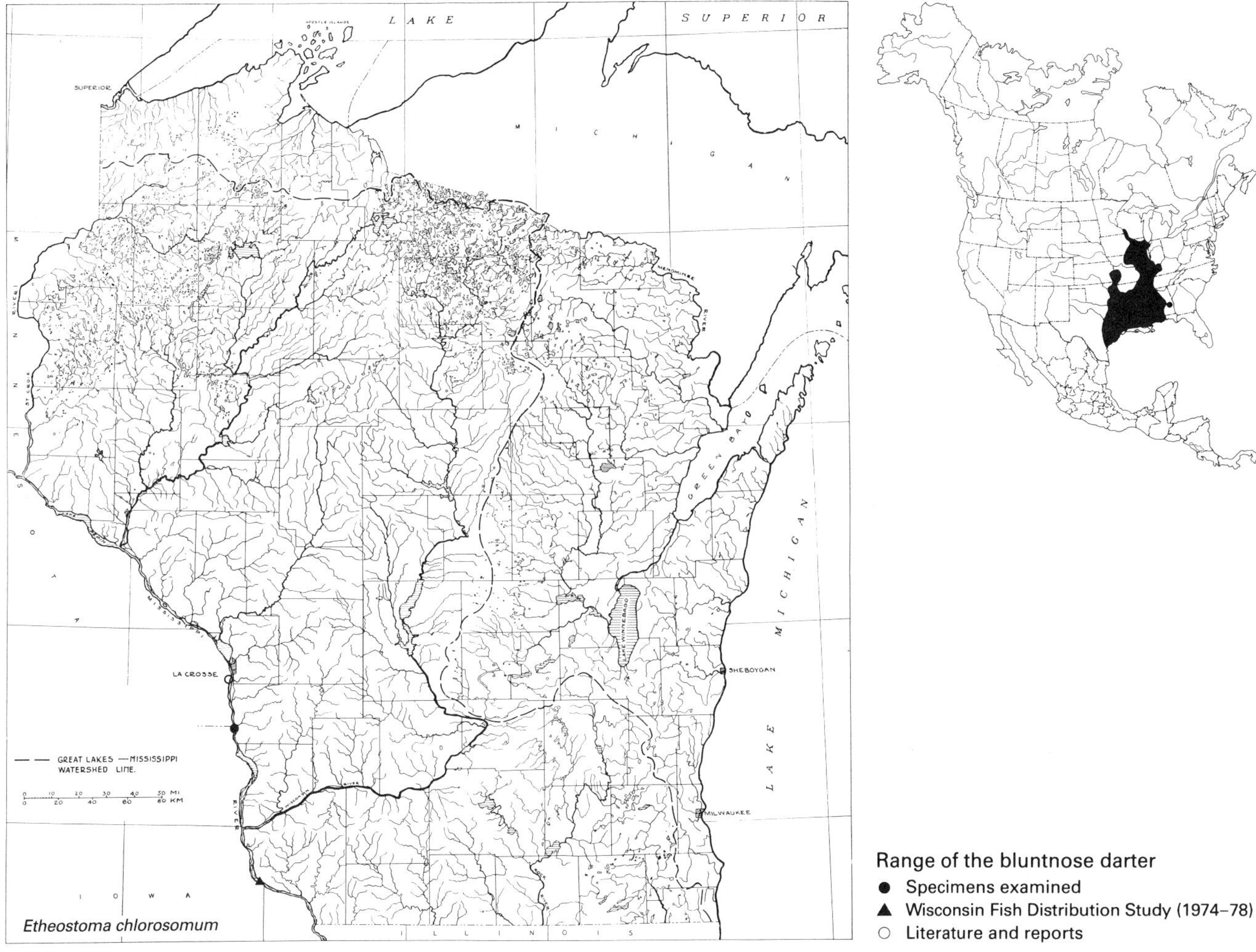

Etheostoma chlorosomum

Range of the bluntnose darter
- ● Specimens examined
- ▲ Wisconsin Fish Distribution Study (1974–78)
- ○ Literature and reports

habitat has not been adequately sampled. Wisconsin has accorded the bluntnose darter endangered status (Les 1979).

The bluntnose darter inhabits quiet waters of oxbows, ponds, sloughs, pools, and sluggish currents over mud, clay, and mixed sand and mud, often overlaid with vegetation debris. In Illinois, more than two-thirds of the collections have been taken from quiet waters, and about three-fifths have been taken over muddy bottoms (Forbes and Richardson 1920). The bluntnose darters captured from the Mississippi River at the Iowa-Minnesota border were seined from small, isolated ponds of unstained, stagnant water, over mud bottoms with scant or no vegetation. The ponds were as much as 2 m deep. In a Kentucky stream, this species occurred in a pool 6 m wide and 0.6 m deep, over a mud bottom "about half filled with leaves" (Clay 1975).

BIOLOGY

Nothing has been recorded about the breeding habits of the bluntnose darter in Wisconsin although it is likely that spawning occurs in the spring.

In Illinois, female bluntnose darters distended with eggs have been taken in late May. In Kansas (Cross 1967), this species came into breeding condition in April. In central Mississippi (Cook 1959), an individual fish collected on 15 April was in an advanced breeding condition.

Ten bluntnose darters from Miller Creek (Alexander County, Illinois), collected 2 September, were 34–39 mm TL and estimated to be age I. The calculated total length at the first annulus was 26 mm. In collections of the Mississippi Game and Fish Commission, 35 specimens ranged from 28 to 46 mm SL (estimated 34–55 mm TL) (Cook 1959). Clay (1975) noted that this species seldom exceeds 44 mm (1.7 in) TL in Kentucky. In Iowa it reaches a length of 64 mm (2.5 in) (Harlan and Speaker 1956).

In Kansas, specimens of bluntnose darters have been collected from streams that are somtimes intermittent during severe droughts and temporarily turbid (Cross 1967). The bluntnose darter is usually the only darter taken from a collection site, since it has adapted to an ecological niche differing from most darters. In Kentucky, the bluntnose darter was collected with the slough darter; other species present at the collection site were the spotted sucker, golden shiner, rosefin shiner, blackspotted topminnow, mosquitofish, pirate perch, four species of centrarchids, the common carp, and the black bullhead (Clay 1975). Pflieger suggested that the habits of the bluntnose darter are probably similar to those of the johnny darter.

IMPORTANCE AND MANAGEMENT

Although the bluntnose darter undoubtedly serves as a forage species for predatory fishes, it is of little consequence in Wisconsin because of its sparse numbers. So little is known about this species that a challenge remains for the research biologist: to document its life history, before it becomes extinct and a mere statistic.

Banded Darter

Etheostoma zonale (Cope). *Etheostoma*—a straining mouth; *zonale*—banded.
Other common names: eastern banded darter, zoned darter.

Male 60 mm, Tomorrow R. (Waupaca Co.), 29 Sept. 1971

DESCRIPTION
Body slender to moderately robust, slightly compressed laterally. Average length 51 mm (2 in). TL = 1.20 SL. Depth into SL 4.0–4.8. Head length into SL 3.5–4.0. Preopercle smooth on posterior edge. Gill membranes broadly attached to one another. Premaxillaries nonprotractile, the upper lip groove not continuous over tip of snout; snout strongly decurved, blunt; mouth horizontal, lower jaw slightly included within upper jaw; upper jaw reaching below anterior edge of eye; minute, sharp teeth in narrow bands on upper and lower jaws. Gill rakers on lower limb of first arch pointed, stubby or knoblike, about 7. Branchial apparatus illustrated and described by Branson and Ulrikson (1967). Branchiostegal rays 5. Dorsal fins 2: first or spiny dorsal fin with 11 (10–12) spines, fin base into SL 3.3–4.0; second dorsal fin with 12 (11) rays, fin base into SL 4.5–6.0. Anal fin with 2 spines and 8 (7–10) rays; pelvic fin thoracic; pectoral fin large, as long as or longer than head. Scales ctenoid; cheeks, opercles and nape scaled; breast partly to fully scaled. Lateral line complete, scales 41–53. Vertebrae 38–39 (Bailey and Gosline 1955).

Back mottled olive brown with 6–7 saddle marks; sides with indistinct dark blotches; belly yellow-white to white-green. Dark stripe extending from eye to eye around snout, interrupted medially on snout. Suborbital bar dark. Dorsal fins heavily pigmented to speckled; caudal fin with speckled wavy bands, pectoral fins with concentric bands.

Breeding male with 8–13 bright green vertical bands, which may or may not encircle body; sides of head olive, and ventral region of head and breast green; basal portion of spiny dorsal red, upper portion of spiny dorsal fin green with yellow-white margin; soft dorsal fin reddish at base anteriorly, remainder yellowish; caudal, pelvic, and anal fins greenish, with tips of spines and anterior rays whitish. Breeding female not as intensely colored, with olive replacing greens of male; fins more transparent, not containing greens or yellows.

Sexual dimorphism: Genital papilla twice as large in female and rectangular in shape. Spiny and soft dorsal fins larger in male (Lachner et al. 1950).

DISTRIBUTION, STATUS, AND HABITAT
The banded darter occurs in the lower two-thirds of Wisconsin in the Mississippi River and Lake Michigan drainage basins, where it reaches the northern limit of its distribution. It is not known from the Lake Superior system, nor is it known from the Lake Michigan drainage from Door County southward. Its distribution is spotty; it appears in stream systems which are widely separated from one another.

The banded darter is uncommon to common locally. In a survey of the larger streams in central Wisconsin, it appeared in 41% of the collections (Becker 1959). In the upper Rock River, it is uncommon (G. C. Becker 1972b). Usually it is not found in lakes, although Priegel (1967a) noted that it was rare in Lake Winnebago. It was eliminated from the Tomorrow and Waupaca rivers (Portage and Waupaca counties) when the stream was poisoned in 1971 (Becker 1975).

The banded darter prefers streams with a moderate to high gradient. In Wisconsin, it has been encountered most frequently in clear water at depths of 0.1–1.5 m, over substrates of sand (31% frequency), gravel (29%), rubble (10%), mud (10%), boulders (7%), silt (6%), hardpan (1%), clay (2%), bedrock (2%), and detritus (1%). It occurred in riffles (in 57% of the samples collected) and pools (43%), in streams of the following widths: 1.0–3.0 m (3%), 3.1–6.0 m (14%), 6.1–12.0 m (27%), 12.1–24.0 m (22%), 24.1–50.0 m (24%), and more than 50 m (11%). It occurs in small streams mostly in southern Wisconsin; northward it was found in medium-sized to large rivers. It is taken from habitats in which aquatic vegetation is absent to scarce.

BIOLOGY
In Wisconsin, the banded darter spawns from April to June, and possibly as late as July (Lutterbie 1976). Forbes and Richardson (1920) found females with distended abdomens from May to June in northern Illinois.

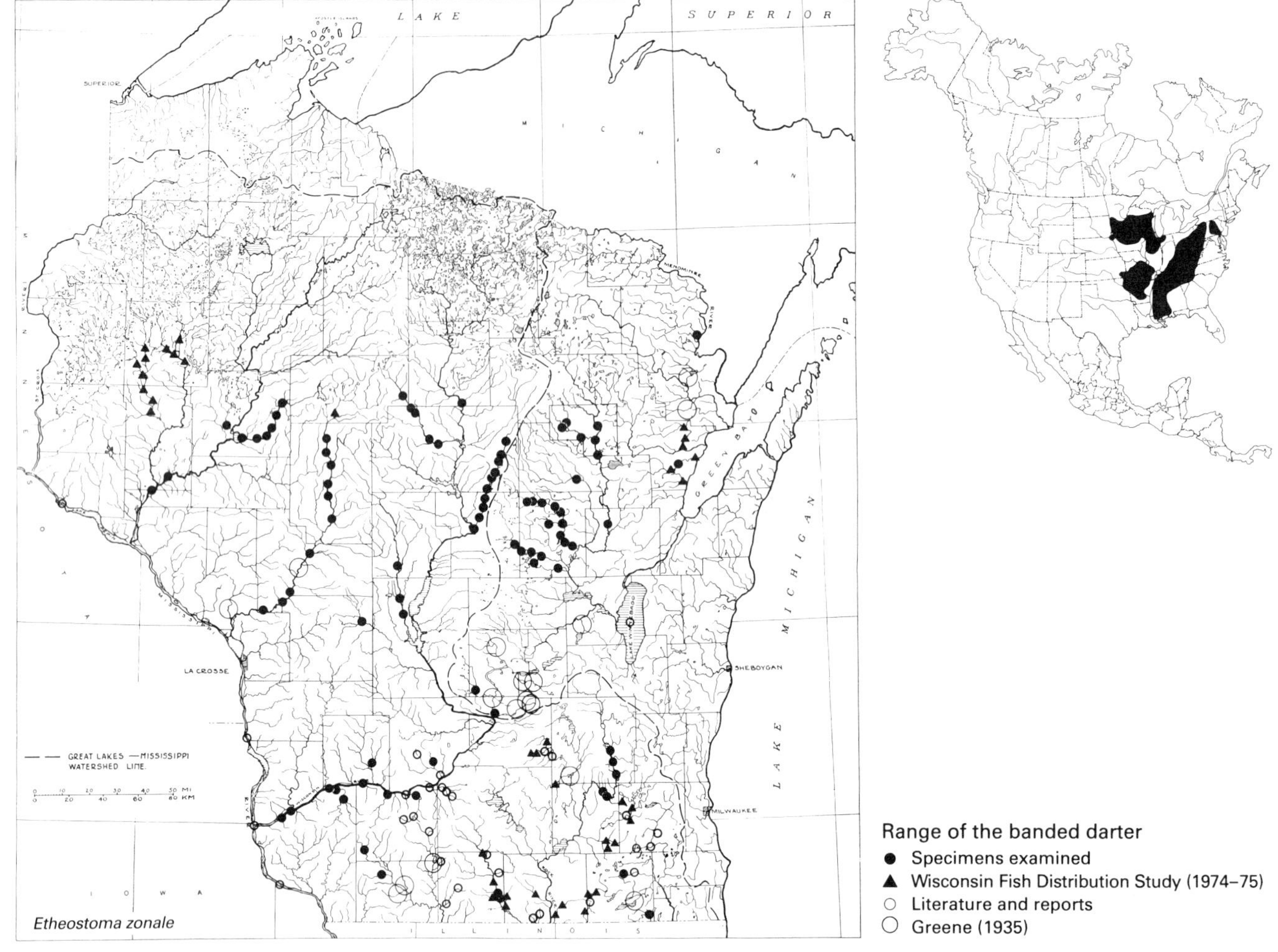

In Oklahoma, the banded darter spawns in algal clumps growing on large stones in the deeper riffles (Miller and Robison 1973). In Ohio, spawning areas are in the riffles of streams with moderate to high gradients which are less than 15 m wide and less than 0.6 m deep, and where there is an abundance of algae and aquatic moss on stones and boulders (Trautman 1957). Females deposit their eggs on these plant growths, and after the spawning season move downstream to overwinter in the deeper waters. In three Pennsylvania streams, a typical spawning area was 23 m long and 46–61 m wide, and had a depth of 0.6 m (Lachner et al. 1950).

In Wisconsin, the percentage of gonadal to body weight in banded darters was greatest from April to July; at that time, ovaries averaged 13.6% (9.4–18.6%) of body weight, and testes averaged 0.8% (0.6–1.1%) (Lutterbie 1976). The number of mature eggs in an age-II female, 54 mm long, was 225 in May; in age-II females, 59 and 57 mm long, 74 and 139 mature eggs in July. Age-III females, 49 and 54 mm long, held 49 and 141 mature eggs in June. These females were probably partly spawned at the time of capture.

Young-of-year banded darters in central Wisconsin were 27–40 mm TL in August. In Ohio, young-of-year were 20–43 mm long in October (Trautman 1957).

Banded darters from central Wisconsin showed the following growth (Lutterbie 1976:130):

Age Class	No. of Fish	TL (mm) Avg	TL (mm) Range	Calculated TL at Annulus (mm) 1	2	3	4
I	71	43.07	36–57	37.17			
II	117	52.10	44–60	36.36	50.95		
III	47	56.25	49–62	35.82	48.46	54.93	
IV	4	61.25	57–65	38.50	50.75	57.25	61.25
Avg (weighted)				36.53	50.24	55.11	61.25

For 23 banded darters from southern Wisconsin, the calculated lengths at annuli 1 through 3 were 36, 46, and 56 mm. Males are slightly longer than females of the same age, but females get older than males. In central Wisconsin, the annulus is deposited about 13 June. Lachner et al. (1950) observed that the breeding period of adult banded darters retards the formation of the annulus, and that little or no growth occurs until after spawning.

The banded darter attains 69% of its adult size in the first 2 months of life. No growth occurs from September to June in all year classes (J. Erickson, pers. comm.).

The length-weight relationship for banded darters in central Wisconsin was Log W = −12.5678 + 3.2697 Log L; for fish in southern Wisconsin, it was Log W = −12.020 + 3.1162 Log L, where W is weight in grams and L is TL in millimeters (Lutterbie 1976). The condition (K_{SL}) of 13 specimens collected from the Plover River (Portage County) in September was 1.07 (R. Duchrow, pers. comm.).

The banded darter reaches maturity at age II. No age-I fish examined by Lutterbie was mature.

A male banded darter 66 mm (2.6 in) long (UWSP 615) was collected from a branch of the Wolf River (Menominee County) in July 1966. A 4-year-old, 65-mm (2.5-in), 2.8-g male (UWSP 3817) was taken from the Crystal River (Waupaca County) on 25 September 1971.

In the Plover River (Portage County), 16 banded darters had eaten Diptera larvae, Ephemeroptera naiads, and some Coleoptera larvae; their digestive tracts also contained unidentifiable insect parts (R. Duchrow, pers. comm.). The intestine of the banded darter is short, which is indicative of a diet of animal food. Two individuals examined by Forbes (1880) had eaten nothing but small Diptera larvae, of which 65% were *Chironomus*.

In Missouri, adult banded darters occupied riffles over gravel and rubble, and the young were found in quieter waters around vegetation (Pflieger 1971). Reed (1968), studying the use of the riffle habitat by several species, found that the banded darter had a mean recapture rate of 23.6% from riffle areas; this was the lowest rate for the four darters studied—the rainbow, the barred fantail, the greenside, and the banded. In Minnesota, Eddy and Underhill (1974) found that the banded darter prefers the lower lips of pools at the point where the water begins to enter the rapids. In 43% of the collections in which this species was taken in Wisconsin, I found this species in pools adjacent to riffles.

A substrate seldom mentioned in connection with the banded darter is bedrock. This substrate in the lower Wisconsin River (Richland County) produced the largest collections of this darter (22 and 14 individuals) made in my southwestern fish survey (Becker 1966). The species collected with the 22 banded darters over bedrock, and over a wide variety of adjacent substrates, were: shovelnose sturgeon (1), mooneye (4), quillback (5), highfin carpsucker (2), shorthead redhorse (97), golden redhorse (47), northern hog sucker (65), common carp (12), silver chub (10), speckled chub (1), bluntnose minnow (1), emerald shiner (15), spotfin shiner (23), river shiner (1), sand shiner (36), sauger (6), walleye (1), crystal darter (3), slenderhead darter (36), logperch (31), smallmouth bass (21), black crappie (1), and freshwater drum (2).

From November to January, the banded darter was taken from ice-free riffles in the Waupaca River (Portage County) along with longnose dace, largescale stonerollers, hornyhead chubs, mottled sculpins, and northern hog suckers (Becker 1962).

IMPORTANCE AND MANAGEMENT

The banded darter is undoubtedly preyed upon by larger fish and by fish-eating birds because of its shallow water habits.

The banded darter is a beautiful fish, and, because of its brilliant colors, is often confused with the rainbow darter, which is frequently found in the same waters. The banded darter makes an attractive aquarium fish. This use is not encouraged, however, since even in a well-aerated aquarium it will generally die within a few weeks.

Rainbow Darter

Etheostoma caeruleum Storer. *Etheostoma*—a straining mouth; *caeruleum*—blue.

Other common names: rainbow fish, soldier darter, blue darter, banded darter.

Male 62 mm, Wisconsin R. at mouth of Plover R. (Portage Co.), 8 Oct. 1966

Female 46 mm, Wisconsin R. at mouth of Plover R. (Portage Co.), 8 Oct. 1966

DESCRIPTION

Body moderately robust, compressed laterally. Average length 64 mm (2.5 in). TL = 1.21 SL. Depth into SL 4.0–4.5. Head length into SL 3.3–3.5. Preopercle smooth on posterior edge. Gill membranes narrowly attached below to one another. Premaxillaries nonprotractile, the upper lip groove not continuous over tip of snout. Snout rather pointed; mouth almost horizontal, lower jaw slightly included within upper jaw; upper jaw reaching below anterior edge of eye to anterior edge of pupil; minute, sharp teeth in narrow bands on upper and lower jaws. Gill rakers long, stout, to knoblike, about 8. Branchiostegal rays 6. Dorsal fins 2: first or spiny dorsal fin with 10 (8–13) spines; fin base into SL 3.4; second dorsal fin with 12 (10–15) rays, fin base into SL 4.5. Anal fin with 2 spines and 7 (6–8) rays; pelvic fin thoracic; pectoral fin length generally slightly shorter than head length. Scales ctenoid; cheeks naked, except occasionally a row of scales along back border of eye; opercles scaled; nape partly naked to fully scaled; breast naked; belly scaled. Lateral line incomplete with 20–34 pored scales, lateral series scales 44 (37–49). Vertebrae 36 (34–37) (Dombeck 1974). Chromosomes 2n = 48 (Ross 1973).

In male: back mottled olive brown with 3–11 dark saddle marks; sides with 8–13 vertical blue-green bands, posterior to anus the bands more vivid and completely encircling body, while bands anterior to anus do not encroach on belly. Areas between bands reddish to orange, especially posteriorly; ventral region of head orange, breast blue-green, belly greenish. Spiny dorsal fin with 4 horizontal bands: first a red basal band, second a band of red dots, third a broad blue band, and fourth a green-blue margin; anal fin blue-green with reddish center. Suborbital bar faint to absent. In female: vertical bars less conspicuous, and much less colorful overall.

In breeding male the color very intense; breeding tubercles on belly scales and on midventral scales of caudal peduncle. Female color less intense, tubercles short (Collette 1965).

Sexual dimorphism. Male larger; anal, first dorsal, pectoral and pelvic fins larger in male than in female. In male, urogenital papilla small, conical; in female, swollen, broad, flat topped (Winn 1958).

Hybrids: Rainbow darter × orangethroat darter (Knapp 1964, Distler 1968, Martin and Richmond 1973). Artificial hybrids with *Etheostoma* and *Percina* (Schwartz 1972).

SYSTEMATIC NOTES

In a comparison of numbers of vertebrae, dorsal spines, dorsal rays, anal rays, pectoral rays, pored lateral line scales, lateral series scales, and body bars of rainbow darter populations from the Wisconsin River (Mississippi) drainage and the Fox River (Lake Michigan) drainage, Dombeck (1974) found significant differences in the number of dorsal rays (12.26 vs 13.13), pored lateral line scales (27.87 vs 26.21), lateral series scales (43.58 vs 44.85), and body bars (9.71 vs 10.65).

DISTRIBUTION, STATUS, AND HABITAT

In Wisconsin, the rainbow darter occurs in the Mississippi River and Lake Michigan drainage basins, where it reaches the northern limit of its range. Its range in central and northwestern Wisconsin coincides with the upper edge of the unglaciated portion of the state. Its other area of concentration is the glaciated lake region of southeastern Wisconsin, including the streams of the Rock River system.

In the Lake Michigan drainage basin, Greene (1935) captured the rainbow darter from the upper Fox River

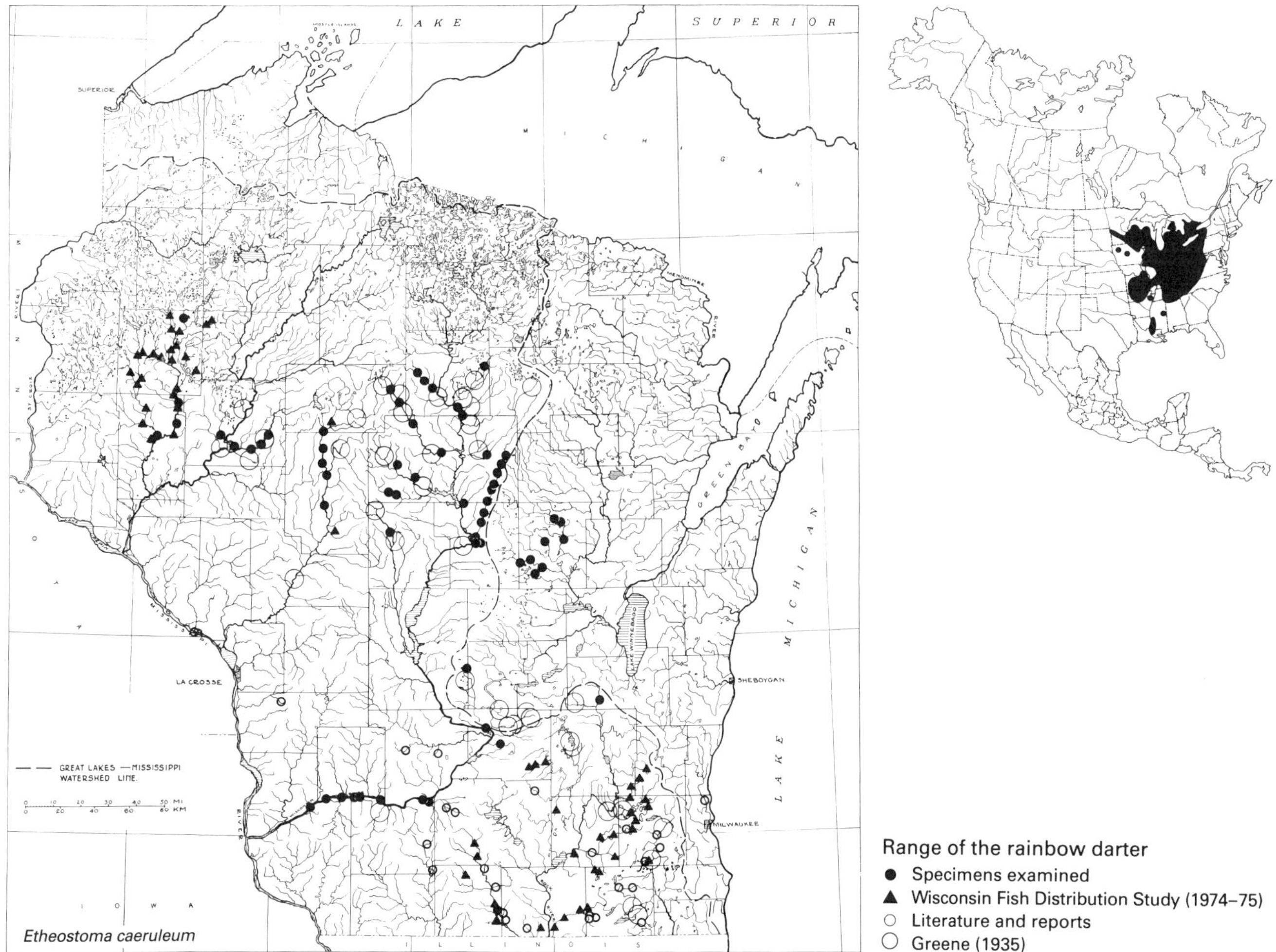

in a cluster of sites near Portage (Columbia County). Apparently the rainbow darter had at the time crossed over the divide from the Wisconsin River. Since 1958 it has been taken from several streams in Waupaca County. It seems probable that, if the rainbow darter had occurred in the Tomorrow-Waupaca and Little Wolf river systems during the 1920s in numbers comparable to those found in the 1960s, Greene would have recorded its presence.

The rainbow darter is common locally in central Wisconsin. In a survey of five large central Wisconsin streams (Becker 1959), the rainbow darter appeared in 27% of the collections. In the Plover River, it comprised 32% of all individuals collected at one site. It is common in southeastern Wisconsin, and uncommon in the southwestern quarter of the state. This species was probably eliminated from the Waupaca River downstream to Weyauwega (Waupaca County) when the stream was poisoned with antimycin in 1971 during a carp control program of the Wisconsin Department of Natural Resources (Becker 1975).

In Wisconsin, the rainbow darter was found most frequently in clear water at depths of 0.1–0.5 m, over substrates of sand (25% frequency), boulders (25%), gravel (20%), silt (13%), rubble (11%), clay (2%), bedrock (2%), and mud (2%). It has been collected from swift to moderate currents in streams—from riffles 40% of the time, and from pools 60% of the time. It was present in streams from 3 m to more than 100 m wide, but reached its greatest numbers in streams 12–24 m wide.

BIOLOGY

The rainbow darter spawns from April to June in Wisconsin. The following account of the spawning behavior of this species is derived largely from Winn (1958) and Reeves (1907), unless otherwise indicated.

Spawning does not take place until the water temperature is above 15°C (59°F). An abrupt drop in water temperature will interrupt spawning, as will increased turbidity, since vision is the most important sense used by rainbow darters in sexual activities. The spawning area consists of fine gravel, large gravel, rubble, or a mixture of gravel and rubble, in swift riffles about 0.3 m deep, with a flow of 23 m/min.

The large, brightly colored males defend territories which are generally restricted to specific areas, often where there is a large rock or a depression in the gravel. In the establishment of territories, the males participate in sham battles, in which rival males swim side by side in synchronized movements, with their dorsal fins erect and their heads held high so as to display their brightly colored breasts and ventral fins. This usually results in the larger, more colorful males establishing their territories in the center of the spawning grounds. A hierarchy is formed with such males in the most opportune spawning areas and the smaller males off to the sides. Territories may be from 12 to 30 cm diam. During the actual spawning, the diameter of the territory is reduced to the area immediately surrounding the female. The male rainbow darters defend their territories against members of their own species, and appear to ignore other species. A male chases an intruder if he approaches closer than about 30 cm. There is no territorial defense at night; the respiratory rates slow down, and the darters move only enough to maintain their positions.

Winn (1958) also calls attention to the moving territory created by a male rainbow when he follows a female for a distance of about 0.5–1.5 m as she moves onto the spawning ground to locate a suitable area for spawning. It is this area, restricted to a few centimeters immediately surrounding the female and the attending male, which the male defends against intruders of the same species.

When a female rainbow darter enters the riffle, she may swim through the spawning ground and circle back to the pool from which she came without stopping to spawn. As a female enters the spawning area, a male comes up from behind and follows, swimming parallel to the female and prodding her side with his snout by vibrating his head at a rate of 4–8 times/sec. When she is ready to spawn, the female buries her head in the gravel and raises her caudal region at an angle from 45° to nearly vertical to the substrate. Then, with a few vigorous strokes of the caudal fin, she pushes herself downward and forward, so that the ventral portion of her body and her pectoral fins are buried in the gravel. The pectoral fins are thought to serve as anchors to prevent the female from being displaced by the current. The burying process and the posture that the female assumes appear to stimulate the male to mount her. If the male tries to mount before the female has finished burying herself, she darts away. The male, when mounting, places his pelvic fins in front of the female's spiny dorsal fin and on her sides. The male uses his pectoral fins for stability, and his caudal fin is placed alongside the anal fin of the female.

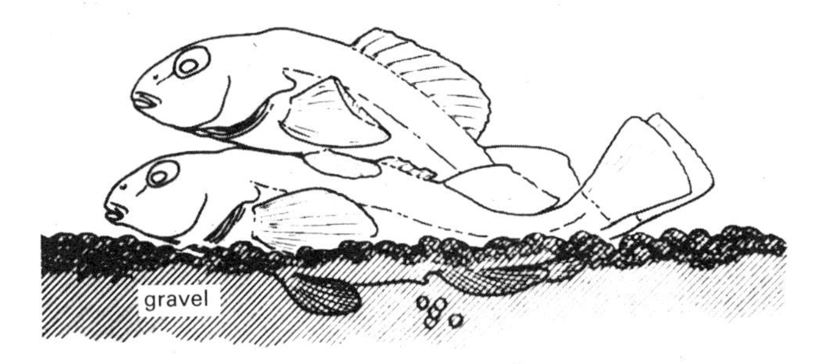

The spawning position of the rainbow darter (Winn 1958:177. Copyright 1960, the Ecological Society of America)

The simultaneous release of eggs and sperm is accomplished soon after the pair of rainbows starts to vibrate rapidly. The female then moves forward to be mounted again, either by the same male or by a different male. Three to seven eggs are released with each spawning act. After the female has completed a few spawnings, she returns to the pool at the bottom of the riffle to rest. The males may outnumber females 4 or 5 to 1 on the spawning grounds.

When two rainbow males follow the same female, they display to each other by lifting themselves up on their pectoral fins and exposing their brightly colored breasts and ventral fins; the dorsal fins are also erected. The defending male may attack the intruder, using his head and his caudal fin to strike the other fish in the opercular region, but no real injury appears to come to either of the contestants. Rival males of about the same size swim side by side in a sham battle similar to territorial battles, with the larger, more colorful male usually victorious. By this time the female has probably moved off, leaving the victor with nothing. Supernumerary males following females are usually chased away by the larger males. The completion of the spawning act takes precedence over fighting behavior when an intruder appears, but as soon as spawning has been completed the intruder is attacked and driven away. At times supernumerary males are seen next to a spawning pair, going through the same motions, and possibly even releasing some sperm. Supernumerary males occasionally slip in and spawn with a ready female when the pairing male is preoccupied with other males.

Winn (1958) noted that age-III male rainbow darters did not spawn with yearling females, probably because of the difference in sizes. He observed that yearling females and age-II males did spawn together.

In Wisconsin, the gonadal weights of rainbow darters peaked in May and June; they constituted 11% of the body weight for the females, and 0.85% for males. In July, they reached lows of 3.2% for females, and 0.4% for males. Lutterbie (1976) counted 167–450 mature eggs in females of ages I–III; Winn (1958), counted 508–1,462 eggs in females 34–50 mm TL. The largest egg production occurred in older and larger females. Not all of the eggs produced by rainbow darters are laid during the spawning season. Both Winn and Lutterbie found females after the spawning periods with eggs being resorbed.

Mature rainbow darter eggs are 1.0–1.8 mm diam, yellow to orange in color, with a single, large oil droplet. They are left buried in the gravel, and receive no further care from either parent. Neither the spawning pair nor supernumerary males have been observed eating the eggs in their natural setting, but they were seen eating the eggs in the laboratory. Hatching, according to Winn, occurs in 10–11.5 days at 17–18.5°C (63–65°F). Fish (1932) illustrated and described the 22.6-mm stage.

In southern Wisconsin, young-of-year rainbow darters were 20–26 mm in June and 27–37 mm in August; in central Wisconsin, they were 27–36 mm in July and 24–42 mm in September and October; and in northern Wisconsin they were 25–37 mm in September (Lutterbie 1976).

Rainbow darters from central Wisconsin showed the following growth (Lutterbie 1976:46):

Age Class	No. of Fish	TL (mm)		Calculated TL at Annulus (mm)			
		Avg	Range	1	2	3	4
I	59	42.00	34–52	33.75			
II	70	50.70	43–64	32.90	45.70		
III	48	58.56	48–74	34.14	48.35	55.43	
IV	5	61.40	57–63	31.30	46.60	54.60	59.20
Avg (weighted)				33.45	46.77	55.35	59.20

The calculated lengths at annuli 1 through 4 for rainbow darters from northern Wisconsin were 30, 45, 52, and 58 mm respectively. A 68-mm, 3.5-g fish (UWSP 1141) from the lower Wisconsin River had calculated lengths of 33, 48, 56, and 63 mm at annuli 1–4.

The length-weight relationship for rainbow darters in central Wisconsin was $\text{Log } W = -13.1003 + 3.4288 \text{ Log } L$, where W is in grams and TL in millimeters.

The rainbow darter reaches maturity at age I.

A large rainbow darter (UWSP 1145) was collected from the Lt. Eau Pleine River (Marathon County); it was 3 years old, weighed 4.9 g, and was 74 mm (2.9 in) long (Lutterbie 1976).

Rainbow darters up to the 15-mm stage eat large amounts of copepods, but soon their food habits resemble those of mature sport fishes, in that they capture and eat food animals that are very large in proportion to themselves (Turner 1921). The stomachs of rainbow darters 15–20 mm long contained 40% copepods; those of fish 35–40 mm long contained only 0.25% copepods. In southeastern Wisconsin, the food was mostly cladocerans and copepods, while crustacea (*Hyalella* and *Gammarus*) formed about 25% of the total bulk (Cahn 1927). In the Plover River (Portage County), 20 rainbow darter stomachs contained (in decreasing order of occurrence) Diptera larvae (Tendipedidae), Trichoptera larvae (Hydropsychidae), water mites, Ephemeroptera naiads (Baetidae), mollusks (*Sphaerium, Valvata*), and a Plecoptera naiad (G. David, pers. comm.).

Other food items consumed by rainbow darters include Coleoptera and Odonata larvae, young crayfish, and the eggs of stoneroller minnows, creek chubs, American brook lampreys, rosyface shiners, and white suckers (Lutterbie 1976). Reighard (1920) has described egg predation in a white sucker nest by rainbow darters (p. 13):

> . . . The black-nosed dace and the rainbow darter . . . gather at once in great numbers over the spot where the pairing suckers were. They come in a straight line from downstream attracted, no doubt, by the trail of milt, eggs or bottom materials swept down by the current. They gather in an area six or eight inches across and each burrows in the bottom with its snout as though seeking eggs. The whole little area is soon concealed by their wriggling tails, close-set like threads in the pile of velvet.

A reduction in the rainbow darter's numbers, or its absence from a habitat it normally would have occupied, is an indicator of chemical pollution and siltation. This species appears to have been eliminated from several sites in Wisconsin where it once occurred; its sensitivity to fish toxicants has been mentioned above. Katz and Gaufin (1953) found that the darters and black bass were highly sensitive to sewage pollution. However, the presence of the rainbow darter in the Rock River basin, where the waters are often heavily silted, is evidence that this species is able to tolerate normal agricultural pollution.

Apparently there is a differentiation in habitat selected by rainbow darters, depending on the sex and age of the individual (Winn 1958). Adult males remain in fast, large, rocky riffles during the winter and after the reproductive period; adult females are also found in such habitats during the winter. Before and after the reproductive period, however, females and young are more commonly found congregated in raceways and pools; the young are also found in these waters during the winter months. Cahn (1927) noted that the rainbow darter is very quick in its actions, and that it has the habit of seeking refuge under stones or sticks, although it does not remain under objects for any length of time.

In the Plover River (Marathon County), 101 rainbow darters were collected with the northern brook lamprey (13+), northern hog sucker (20), white sucker (68), blacknose dace (10), creek chub (13), northern redbelly dace (1), bluntnose minnow (6), common shiner (18), bigmouth shiner (3), blackside darter (6), johnny darter (31), banded darter (10), and fantail darter (11).

IMPORTANCE AND MANAGEMENT

Because it frequently inhabits shallow riffles, the rainbow darter is undoubtedly vulnerable to fish-eating birds as well as to predatory fishes. Apparently at one time it was used as a bait fish for white bass and perch, even though it is not very hardy (Cahn 1927).

The rainbow darter does not adapt well to the home aquarium, and soon expires. However, it can be kept successfully in a well-equipped laboratory or hatchery-type facility.

Scott and Crossman (1973) made the following remarks regarding the value of this species (p. 782):

> The rainbow darter is an exquisitely beautiful inhabitant of clean, gravelly Ontario streams and is of value for this reason alone, although we know of no direct economic importance. Perhaps it is of greatest value to man as an indicator of pollution for it is extremely sensitive to chemical pollution and silting.

Marked competition among species of darters occurs in many riffles, especially in the feeding and nursery areas (Trautman 1957). Whenever competition from one or more species of darters decreases or is absent, the rainbow darter shows a definite increase in number.

Mud Darter

Etheostoma asprigene (Forbes). *Etheostoma*—a straining mouth; *asprigene*—a kind of perch (from European genus *Aspro*).

Male 56 mm, channel between Trempealeau Lakes T18N R9W Sec. 36 (Trempealeau Co.), 7 Oct. 1967 (photo by M. Imhof)

DESCRIPTION
Body moderately robust, compressed laterally. Length 41–51 mm (1.6–2.0 in.). TL = 1.19 SL. Depth into SL 4.0–5.0. Head length into SL 3.0–3.5. Preopercle smooth on posterior edge. Gill membranes narrowly attached below to one another. Premaxillaries non-protractile, the upper lip groove not continuous over tip of snout. Snout decurved, blunt; mouth slightly oblique, upper jaw reaching below anterior edge of eye to anterior edge of pupil; minute, sharp teeth in narrow bands on upper and lower jaws. Gill rakers long, stout, about 8. Branchiostegal rays 6. Dorsal fins 2: first or spiny dorsal fin with 10 (10–12) spines, fin base into SL 3.8; second dorsal fin with 13 (10–14) rays, fin base into SL 3.8–4.5. Anal fin with 2 spines and 8 (8–9) rays; pelvic fin thoracic; pectoral fin length generally slightly shorter than head length. Scales ctenoid; cheeks and opercles scaled; nape partly to fully scaled; breast naked, belly scaled. Lateral line incomplete, pored scales ending under soft dorsal fin, 17–20 unpored scales; lateral series scales 47 (45–50). Vertebrae 37 (36–39) (Bailey and Gosline 1955).

Adult male back olive brown with 8–10 dark brown saddle marks; sides with 9–12 greenish brown blotches often fused into an irregular lateral stripe alternating with orange-yellow bars; belly orange. Often a narrow, horizontal unpigmented streak (whitish in preserved specimens) near lateral line along length of side. Suborbital bar dusky; dusky bar extending from eye onto snout. Spiny dorsal fin first with the basal half a broad blackish band, second a narrow orange band outward, and third a narrow black outer margin; soft dorsal and caudal fins mottled with brown wavy bars; remaining fins lightly pigmented. Three spots arranged vertically at base of caudal fin, occasionally interconnected. Female less brightly colored than male.

Breeding male with lower half of vertical bars on caudal peduncle blue-green; lower half of spiny dorsal fin blue-gray, with a prominent orange-red outer stripe twice as wide as the dusky edge; soft dorsal fin with dusky pigmentation and with a broad orange stripe through middle of fin; midportion of caudal fin orange-yellow. Interradial membranes of anal and pelvic fins with numerous dark chromatophores; pectoral fins with a few chromatopores edging soft rays. Breeding colors may be retained until August.

SYSTEMATIC NOTES
This species was formerly listed as *Etheostoma jessiae* by Forbes and Richardson (1920), and *Poecilichthys jessiae asprigenis* by Hubbs and Lagler (1947). The only Great Lakes record of the latter is now regarded as having probably been based on specimens of *Etheostoma exile*.

DISTRIBUTION, STATUS, AND HABITAT
In Wisconsin, the mud darter is known to occur only in the Mississippi River drainage basin. It reaches the northern limit of its distribution in Wisconsin and Minnesota. In Wisconsin, it has been collected in the Mississippi River proper, in the lower portions of larger tributaries, as well as in the lower portions of small tributaries to these waters. Although Cahn (1927) reported it as a "not uncommon species" in Waukesha County lakes, it was apparently confused there with the Iowa darter, and these records have not been plotted on the maps.

UWSP records: #1131 (1) Wisconsin River at Port Andrews T8N R2W Sec 2 (Richland County), 1962; #1132 (1) Sneed Creek T8N R3E Sec 21 (Iowa County), 1962; #1133, #1468, and #2774 (1 in each collection) Gran Grae Creek at Hwy 60 T7N R5W Sec 32 (Crawford County), 1962, 1966, and 1966; #1134 (1) Glass Lake on the Mississippi River at Bagley (Grant County), 1962; #1775 (1) channel between 2nd and 3rd Trempealeau lakes T18N R9W Sec 36 (Trempealeau County) 1967; and #5672 (4) Mississippi River at Jack Oak Island T3N R5W Sec 34 (Grant County) 1976.

The Wisconsin Fish Distribution Study (1974–1978) reported: 13 collections (1–16 specimens) Mississippi River T3N R5W Sec 34 to T8N R7W Sec 36 (Grant and Crawford counties), 1976; (14) Sandy Creek T5N R6W Sec 27 (Grant County), 1978; (12) unknown channel of Black River T17N R8W Sec 17 (La Crosse County), 1978; (1) Fleming Creek T18N R7W Sec 3 (La Crosse County) 1977; and (6) Sand Creek T19N

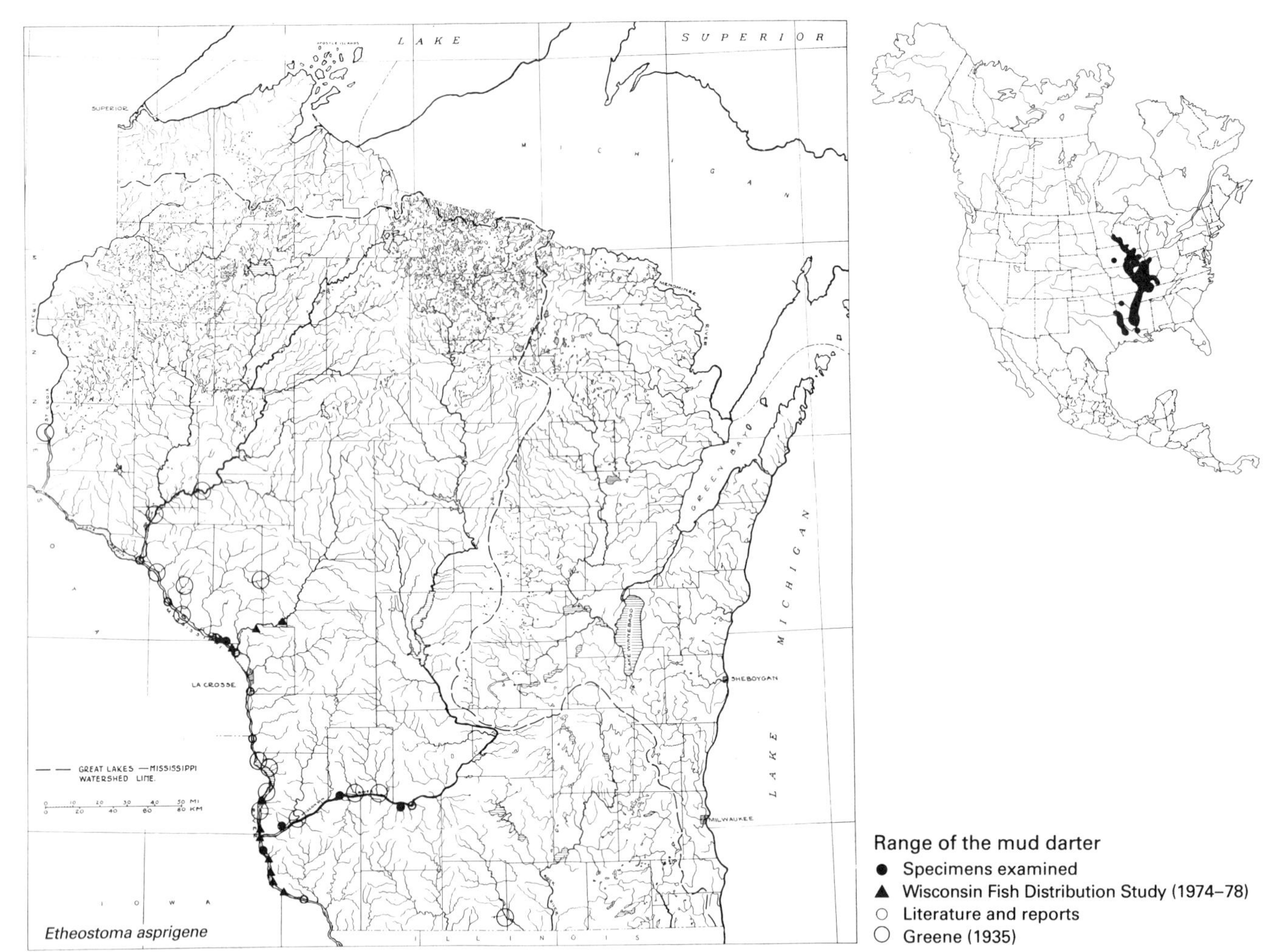

R5W Sec 29 (Jackson County) 1977. M. Johnson (pers. comm.) reported approximately six collections, usually of one or two specimens each, from the Mississippi River between Perrot State Park (Trempealeau County) and Wyalusing State Park (Grant County) from 1964 to 1966.

In Illinois, the mud darter was considered abundant early in the century (Forbes and Richardson 1920); in recent years it has been sporadic in large- and medium-sized streams throughout the state, except in northeastern Illinois, where it is absent (P. W. Smith 1965, 1971). P. W. Smith (1968) found that the mud darter has retreated from the Vermillion and Embarras rivers in Illinois because of a decrease in river size and a reduction in water flow. In Missouri, this species is common at some localities in the Lowlands (Pflieger 1975). Most Indiana records go back to the late 1800s; no mud darters have been taken in recent surveys (Gerking 1945 and 1955). The mud darter is rare and endangered in Kentucky (Miller 1972); threatened in Iowa (Roosa 1977); known only from McCurtain County in Oklahoma (Miller and Robison 1973); collected in only six localities in Mississippi (Cook 1959); on peripheral status in Texas (C. Hubbs 1976); and collected only from the Ouachita River drainage in Louisiana, where it is locally abundant (Douglas 1974).

The mud darter is one of the rarest of Wisconsin fishes. Seldom is more than a single specimen taken per collection. It is regarded as threatened in Wisconsin (Wis. Dep. Nat. Resour. Endangered Species Com. 1975, Les 1979), and Lutterbie (1976) has suggested giving it endangered status in the state.

The mud darter inhabits sloughs, overflow areas, sluggish riffles, and pools of large, low-gradient rivers, and the lower ends of tributaries. In Wisconsin it was encountered over substrates of mud, sand, clay, gravel, and bedrock, in waters as much as 1.5 m deep. At the Gran Grae Creek (Crawford County) collection site, the stream is 5–8 m wide and as much as 0.6 m deep; the current is moderate, over a bottom that is 95% sand and 5% gravel. At the Sneed Creek (Iowa County) site, the stream is 5 m wide and as much as 0.5 m deep, with a moderate current over a substrate of mud and clay; the banks are heavily shaded by trees. At the Port Andrews (Richland County) collection site on the Wisconsin River, a moderate current of water flows 8–20 cm deep over a rock shelf.

BIOLOGY

In Wisconsin, the mud darter apparently is a spring spawner, since testes from two males in July constituted only 0.7% of the body weight (Lutterbie 1976). At Havana, Illinois, spawning occurs in April and May; females in the middle of March carried large eggs, but others had not yet spawned on 12 May (Forbes and Richardson 1920).

In Wisconsin, young-of-year mud darters were 36–39 mm TL from August to September. Age-I fish averaged 47 (39–53) mm TL, and had a calculated total length at annulus of 41 mm (Lutterbie 1976). One age-II fish, 56 mm TL and 1.5 g, had calculated lengths of 43 and 52 mm at the first and second annuli.

The length-weight relationship, based on 11 fish, was $\text{Log } W = -9.7607 + 2.5199 \text{ Log } L$, where weight is in grams and total length in millimeters.

A large mud darter (UWSP 5671), a 3-year-old male, 65 mm (2.5 in) TL and 2.97 g, was taken from the Rock River at Milan, Illinois, from swift water (approximately 0.6 m/sec) at a depth of 1 m, over a sand and mud bottom (M. Miller, pers. comm.).

The diet of the mud darter consists of larvae of mayflies and *Chironomus* (Forbes and Richardson 1920).

On the Wisconsin River at Port Andrews (Richland County), a single mud darter was taken along with the creek chub (1), emerald shiner (4), spotfin shiner (43), spottail shiner (1), channel catfish (2), stonecat (9), river darter (11), slenderhead darter (9), logperch (5), johnny darter (21), banded darter (22), rainbow darter (2), fantail darter (41), smallmouth bass (4), largemouth bass (1), and bluegill (4).

IMPORTANCE AND MANAGEMENT

Nothing is known about the mud darter's natural predators and its use as a bait species.

Considering its rarity, the mud darter must play only a minor role in the ecological web. As is evident from the little information available on the mud darter, the opportunity exists for researchers to determine those phases of its life history which must be known in order to protect the species and ensure its continued existence. This information must be gained soon or the mud darter, over most of its range, will become a mere statistic.

Males in breeding habit are indescribably beautiful, and compete with such fish as the rainbow darter and the longear sunfish for possessing the most striking color combinations.

Iowa Darter

Etheostoma exile (Girard). *Etheostoma*—a straining mouth; *exilis*—slim.

Other common names: red-sided darter, yellowbelly, weed darter.

Male 63 mm, Squaw Cr. (Price Co.), 19 Sept. 1976

Female 60 mm, Squaw Cr. (Price Co.), 19 Sept. 1976

DESCRIPTION

Body elongate, slightly compressed laterally. Average length 51 mm (2 in). TL = 1.20 SL. Depth into SL 4.8–5.5. Head length into SL 3.5–3.8. Preopercle smooth on posterior edge. Gill membranes moderately attached below to one another. Premaxillaries nonprotractile, the upper lip groove not continuous over tip of snout. Snout rounded; mouth slightly oblique, upper jaw almost reaching below anterior edge of pupil; minute, sharp teeth in narrow bands on upper and lower jaws. Gill rakers short, stout to knoblike, about 7. Branchiostegal rays 5–6. Dorsal fins 2: first or spiny dorsal fin with 9 (8–12) spines, fin base into SL 4.0–4.6; second dorsal fin with 11 (10–12) rays, fin base into SL 6.0–7.0. Anal fin with 2 spines and 8 (7–9) rays; pelvic fin thoracic. Scales ctenoid; cheeks, opercles and nape scaled; breast partly scaled; belly scaled. Lateral line incomplete, pored scales ending near anterior edge of second dorsal fin, 27–42 unpored scales; lateral series scales 55–65. Vertebrae 37–38 (34–40) (Bailey and Gosline 1955).

Adult male back and sides dark brown to olive brown, becoming yellowish on belly. About 8 darker saddle marks on back; sides with 9–12 distinct vertical bars, and interspaces with small reddish blotches. Suborbital bar distinct, black. Spiny dorsal fin of 3 bands: the basal half of fin slate-colored, next a broad light-colored band (reddish in life), and on outer margin a narrow dusky stripe. Soft dorsal fin with brown speckles arranged in rows; caudal fin with speckles forming wavy vertical lines. Anal, pelvic and pectoral fins transparent to dark pigmented, especially along rays. Adult female with patterns much like those of the male but without the bright colors; lateral bars sometimes indistinct, more mottled with green-olive to yellow-brown.

Breeding male extremely colorful, but lacking breeding tubercles; sides with 9–12 dark blue bars, with the interspaces brick red; lower sides with an orange-yellow to red wash, becoming yellow to creamy white ventrally. Basal half of spiny dorsal fin with blue spots, then a broad orange to red outer band with transparent strips above and below, lastly a narrow blue margin on fin. Nonbreeding male colored the same, but less brilliantly, with reds subdued and blues replaced by dusky to olive brown.

Sexual dimorphism: Female larger. Anal and first dorsal fins larger in male (Winn 1958). Sides of male with short, vertical bars; female more mottled, with bars indistinct.

Hybrids: Iowa darter × blackside darter (Wis. Fish Distrib. Study 1974–1979).

DISTRIBUTION, STATUS, AND HABITAT

The Iowa darter occurs in the Mississippi River, Lake Michigan, and Lake Superior drainage basins in Wisconsin, where it is generally distributed, especially in the glaciated areas.

In the northern half of Ohio, this species has become greatly reduced in numbers, or has completely disappeared because of the destruction of its habitat (Trautman 1957). In Illinois its populations have been decimated because drainage of natural lakes, sloughs, and marshes has destroyed many of its habitats (P. W. Smith 1968).

In Wisconsin, the Iowa darter is uncommon to common locally. At a headwaters station of the Little Wolf River (Marathon County), 48 individuals constituted 26% of the total catch (Becker 1959). On the Little Eau Claire River (Marathon County), it ranked ninth in abundance in the total catch from five stations. In Waukesha County, it was reported as common in Oconomowoc, Pine, and La Belle lakes (Cahn 1927). Its appearance in large lakes, such as Poygan and Winnebago, is rare (Becker 1964b, Priegel 1967a). In the lower parts of the tributaries to Lake Superior, it is considered rare (McLain et al. 1965).

In Wisconsin, the Iowa darter is encountered most frequently in clear to slightly turbid, light brown water in small lakes, bog ponds, and the slow-moving brooks draining such waters, and in medium-sized

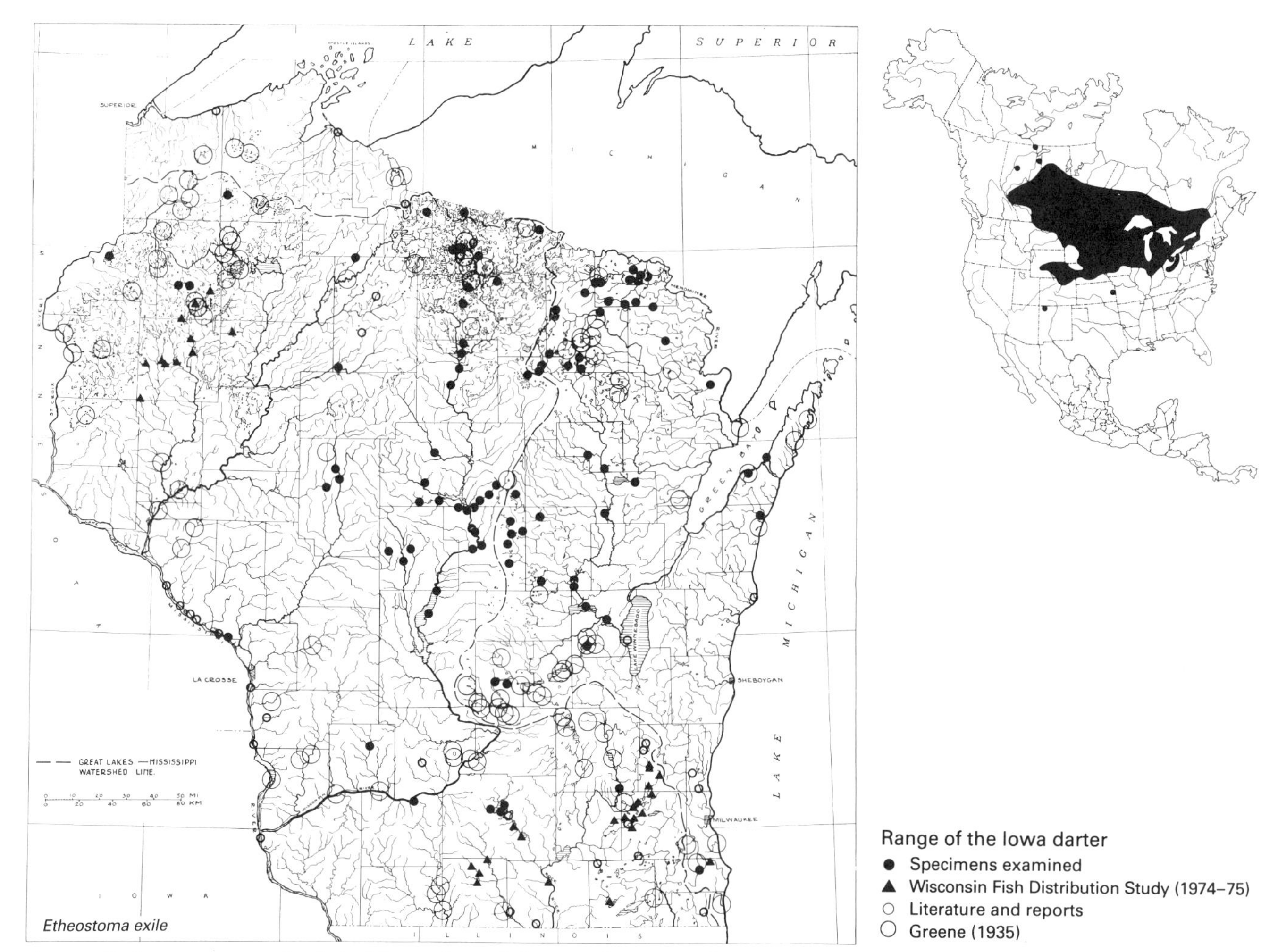

rivers. It less commonly inhabits oxbow lakes and overflow or impounded pools of large rivers. It occurred mostly at depths of less than 1.5 m, over substrates of sand (30% frequency), gravel (23%), mud (13%), silt (12%), detritus (6%), boulders (6%), rubble (5%), clay (3%), and bedrock (2%), and occasionally over marl. It was found in streams of the following widths: 0.1–3.0 m (35%), 3.1–6.0 m (20%), 6.1–12.0 m (15%), 12.1–24.0 m (20%), and 24.1–50.0 m (10%). It is commonly associated with submergent vegetation, particularly filamentous algae covering stones and plants; during seining, it frequently has to be disentangled from dense mats of algae.

BIOLOGY

In Wisconsin, the Iowa darter spawns from late April to mid-June (Lutterbie 1976). Unless otherwise designated, the spawning details which follow have been provided by Winn (1958).

In the spring, the Iowa darter migrates from the deeper portions of lakes and streams to shallow areas for spawning. Migration takes place from mid-March to late April in the Ann Arbor, Michigan, region. Males migrate slightly before females. Once the migration has started it can be stopped and even reversed with the onset of cold weather. In Sugarloaf Lake, Michigan, migration stopped when the water temperature dropped from about 13°C (55°F) to about 7°C (45°F), or when there was a drop of 10°C (18°F) accompanied by rain and running water. In Colorado, Jaffa (1917) found male Iowa darters with milt running and females with mature eggs, from 22 April to 1 June in pools 0.9–1.2 m deep at temperatures of 12–15°C (54–59°F).

Male Iowa darters establish stationary breeding territories in water 10–15 cm deep, along the shores of lakes, or where there is a current of 0.3–0.6 m/sec, along the banks of streams (Winn 1958, Copes 1970). These territories are located on submerged fibrous root banks with some vegetation. Winn also noted that some Iowa darters spawn successfully on gravel and sand, in the absence of fibrous roots. In aquariums, when given a choice, roots and filamentous algae are the preferred spawning sites; only occasionally are *Vallisneria* (with the leaves in a horizontal position) and gravel selected.

The larger and more brightly colored males maintain the prime spawning sites. The spawning territory has the shape of a semicircle, 30–60 cm diam, with the base against the bank or shore. The feeding range is thought to coincide with the breeding territory, with an escape range extending into the deeper water. The male is thought to mark his territory with visual cues on the shoreline or stream bank. Males exhibit pugnacious behavior only toward members of their own species, although Winn reported instances when Iowa darters chased least darters. When an intruder enters the territory, the defending male makes headlong dashes or sideways movements at the intruder with his fins erected. If the male is in the spawning position, he waits until the act has been completed before chasing the intruder away. Territories are thought to be maintained by males during the summer and winter.

The territorial society regulates the population size of Iowa darters in that the males can fertilize and care for only a limited number of eggs. The territory also serves as an area for undisturbed mating, and enables the sexes to find each other. Under crowded conditions, territories are not maintained and spawning is usually not successful. When Iowa darters were prevented by a dam from migrating up an inlet, hundreds gathered below the dam and attempted to spawn, but with little success.

The female Iowa darter migrates up from the deeper water and enters the male's territory when she is ready to spawn. The male follows the female, positioning himself between her and any intruders that are present. The male is stimulated to mount when the female comes to an abrupt stop, usually on fibrous roots, and maintains a horizontal to an acute position up to 45°, with the head at a higher level than the tail. The male mounts the female anterior to the spiny dorsal fin; his caudal region is then curved down, and presses against the caudal region of the female. The mounted position of the sexes is similar to that of the rainbow darter (see p. 934). The tactile stimulus of the male on the female triggers the spawning act, at which time both vibrate vigorously. From three to seven eggs are deposited and sperm is released. The eggs adhere to roots and other vegetation upon which they are deposited. The female then moves into several other territories and spawns with other males before returning to deeper water to rest. After the eggs have been deposited, they receive only indirect care by the male, who continues to guard the territory.

In most species that maintain well-developed territories, the male is larger than the female. However, in the Iowa darter, as well as in the least darter, the female is the larger fish; in such species, sex recognition and stationary territories are easily confused and disrupted. Consequently, under crowded conditions male Iowa darters at times mount other males.

In Wisconsin Iowa darters, the ovaries averaged 8.7% (4.5–12.6%) of body weight in April, and 10.1% (5.7–15.8%) in June (Lutterbie 1976). In July, the ovaries were 1.1% of the body weight. This ratio decreased slightly in August, and increased again in September and October. Testicular development followed a similar pattern. At peak development, the ovaries held immature, yellow eggs 0.5 mm diam, and mature, orange eggs 1.0 mm diam. The number of eggs per ovary appeared to be a function of the age and size of the fish. Age-I females, 42–46 mm TL, contained 429 (348–510) eggs; age-II fish, 51–58 mm long, 665 (312–970) eggs; and age-III fish, 64–66 mm long, 934 (905–962) eggs (Lutterbie 1976).

In the laboratory, the incubation period of Iowa darter eggs was 18–26 days at 13–16°C (55–61°F) (Jaffa 1917). The newly hatched darters are 3.4 mm long. The estimated growth is 0.30 mm per day during a 30-day period early in the first summer's existence (Hubbs 1921). Fish (1932) described and illustrated the 19.5-mm stage.

In central Wisconsin, young-of-year Iowa darters were 21–34 mm long in July, 21–52 mm in August, and 37–48 mm in September (Lutterbie 1976). In Wyoming, young-of-year ranged from 10 to 15 mm TL from July to 1 August. In September, the scales of Wyoming young had 4–12 circuli; the young were completely scaled at 25 mm TL (Copes 1975).

Iowa darters from northern Wisconsin showed the following growth (Lutterbie 1976:66):

Age Class	No. of Fish	TL (mm)		Calculated TL at Annulus (mm)			
		Avg	Range	1	2	3	4
I	45	46.82	34–55	37.11			
II	64	54.80	48–61	35.92	48.20		
III	41	63.44	58–68	36.46	50.34	59.12	
IV	2	68.50	68–69	38.00	49.00	55.50	66.50
Avg (weighted)				36.45	49.04	58.95	66.50

The calculated growths of 136 Iowa darters from central Wisconsin were 37, 51, and 63 mm at annuli 1 through 3. No age-IV fish were encountered in central Wisconsin collections.

In Wisconsin, the annulus of the Iowa darter forms

in June: on 6 June on fish in Little Sturgeon Bay (Door County); on 8 June, in the Waupaca River (Waupaca County); and on 28 June, in the North Branch of the Little Wolf River (Marathon County).

In central Wisconsin, the length-weight relationship for Iowa darters was Log W = −12.1951 + 3.0922 Log L; in northern Wisconsin, it was Log W = −12.5693 + 3.1799 Log L, where W is weight in grams and L is total length in millimeters (Lutterbie 1976).

An age-III Iowa darter 68 mm (2.7 in) long and weighing 2.3 g (UWSP 530) was collected from Mud Creek (Langlade County) in 1966.

In Wyoming, Copes (1970) noted that young-of-year Iowa darters consumed aquatic insects, copepods, amphipods, and rotifers. The food spectrum of adults (Copes 1975) was 33.5% (volume) Diptera adults and larvae, 18.1% Ephemeroptera, 15.2% crustaceans, 14.7% animal remains, and lesser amounts of Trichoptera, Odonata, mollusks, fish and fish eggs, and annelids. The eggs were probably those of the creek chub (*Semotilus atromaculatus*), since the Iowa darters were observed poking into creek chub nests.

In the Madison area (Dane County), the Iowa darter had consumed 58% (volume) amphipods, 21% *Chironomus* larvae, 16% beetle larvae, 3% gastropods, 1.6% oligochaetes, and 0.4% fine debris (Pearse 1918). In the stomachs of Iowa darters from Waukesha County lakes, Cahn (1927) reported finding mostly copepods, with some insect larvae and many small mayfly and stonefly nymphs.

In a Minnesota study, Moyle (1969) determined that only 39% of the estimated volume of food in the digestive tracts of Iowa darters consisted of bottom organisms. The remainder were classified as midwater organisms. Most of these were either *Hyallella azteca* (40%) or *Palpomyia larvae* (6%), which, during the day, were found on the bottom under rocks or among the aquatic plants, but which at night joined the plankton. There was no marked difference in the feeding of day- and night-captured fish. Apparently the Iowa darter fed both by capturing swimming organisms and by nipping them off the bottom.

The Iowa darter is able to survive low levels of oxygen. In a Michigan winterkill lake with less than 0.2 ppm dissolved oxygen, there was a complete kill of largemouth bass and bluegills, but some Iowa darters survived, along with bullheads, madtoms, bowfins, golden shiners, and other minnows. The Iowa darter did not survive oxygen levels of 0.1–0.15 ppm caused by an overabundance of vegetation (Roach and Wickliff 1934). According to Scott and Crossman (1973), the Iowa darter, like most darters, is intolerant of turbid, muddy waters of low visibility; such waters destroy its food supply.

The daily habits of the Iowa darter have been described by Emery (1973), who noted that most of his observations were made where there was a sandy bottom in shallow water (0.5–1.5 m), in areas of rugged, bouldery terrain, or near fallen and broken trees. The daytime coloration of the Iowa darter consisted of highly contrasting shades of dark brown and light brown, interspersed with bright flashes of red. At night, there was much less contrast in coloration than in the daytime, and the reds were barely discernible. At night, this species was extremely difficult to find. It was located in hidden rock crevices, far back in holes, in and under submerged trees, and occasionally resting in the obscurity of rocky overhangs. In the daytime, the Iowa darter was very active, and did not usually allow anyone to approach closer than 0.3–0.5 m. At night, however, the fish allowed divers to approach with hand lights to within approximately 10–15 cm; on a closer approach, the fish darted away, blundering into objects.

In the spring during breeding, the Iowa darter is found along stream banks, near shores in lakes, or in pools where vegetation or fibrous roots are plentiful. During the nonbreeding season it remains in the deeper waters of lakes and in pools of streams. Darters tentatively identified as Iowa darters were observed in rocky areas 5–6 m deep in Long Lake, Minnesota (Moyle 1969). The young are found in vegetated pools and lateral depressions (Copes 1970). In the winter, the Iowa darter is found under banks, near shelters in runs and small pools, or in thick organic debris and in plant zones 1.2 m deep (Copes 1970, Winn 1958).

When the Iowa darter is alarmed, it darts forward for 0.2–0.6 m, then comes to rest again on the bottom, or burrows into debris (Copes 1970). Copes observed 100 young-of-year fish in 1 m^2 which, when alarmed, scattered to cover 3–4 m^2.

In Moen Lake (Marathon County), 16 Iowa darters were associated with the creek chub (19), northern redbelly dace (40+), golden shiner (14+), bluntnose minnow (18+), common shiner (1), blackchin shiner (30+), black bullhead (4+), central mudminnow (2), yellow perch (1), and pumpkinseed (8+).

IMPORTANCE AND MANAGEMENT

The Iowa darter undoubtedly falls prey to predatory fishes and birds because of its shallow water habits and its showiness. Scott and Crossman (1973) cited a report which noted the absence of the Iowa darter in those areas where the northern pike is caught.

The Iowa darter is a host species to the glochidial stage of the mollusk *Anodonta grandis,* thus ensuring the success of that clam species (Hart and Fuller 1974).

Breeding Iowa darter males are among the most beautiful of our fishes, but unfortunately the bright colors tend to fade in captivity. Iowa darters also may be valuable as experimental fishes since they adapt readily to aquarium living, but crowding must be avoided. Lutterbie (pers. comm.) has brought adult Iowa darters into a large laboratory aquarium during early spring and has observed and filmed their spawning behavior.

Fantail Darter

Etheostoma flabellare Rafinesque. *Etheostoma*—a straining mouth; *flabellare*—fanlike, from the form of the tail.

Other common names: fan-tailed darter, striped fantail darter, barred fantail darter.

Male 53 mm, Mud Branch Cr. (Lafayette Co.), 29 June 1960

Female 52 mm, Mud Branch Cr. (Lafayette Co.), 29 June 1960

DESCRIPTION

Body elongate to moderately robust, compressed laterally, with deep caudal peduncle. Length 41–64 mm (1.6–2.5 in). TL = 1.20 SL. Depth into SL 4.5–5.0. Head length into SL 3.3–3.5. Preopercle smooth on posterior edge. Gill membranes broadly attached below to one another. Premaxillaries nonprotractile, the upper lip groove not continuous over tip of snout. Snout straight, not rounded; mouth slightly oblique, upper jaw reaching below anterior edge of pupil; small, sharp teeth (outermost teeth longest) in narrow bands on upper and lower jaws. Gill rakers short, pointed, often bent downward, about 7. Branchial apparatus illustrated and described by Branson and Ulrikson (1967). Branchiostegal rays 6. Dorsal fins 2: first or spiny dorsal fin with 8 (7) spines, fin base into SL 4.0–4.5; second dorsal fin with 13 (14) rays, fin base into SL 3.5–3.8. Anal fin with 2 spines and 7 (8) rays; pelvic fin thoracic. Scales ctenoid; cheeks, opercles and nape naked; breast naked, belly scaled. Lateral line incomplete, with 27–35 pored scales ending under second dorsal fin; lateral series scales 41–53. Vertebrae 34–35 (Bailey and Gosline 1955). Chromosomes 2n = 48 (Ross 1973).

Back brown to olive brown; sides lighter; belly yellow to whitish; 9–13 irregular vertical bars on sides, meshing on back into saddles of equal widths (these markings ill-defined in male). Lengthwise rows of dotted lines on sides and back. First dorsal fin with dark pigment along base. Second dorsal fin heavily speckled in female; in male, strongly dark-pigmented, especially lower half to base; caudal fin with 4–7 bars curving with contour of fin; remaining fins lightly pigmented to transparent.

Breeding male, lacking breeding tubercles, with head becoming intensely black during spawning act. Spiny dorsal with short spines topped by fleshy orange knobs; caudal fin with heavy dusky bands. Female lighter in color, lacking fleshy knobs on tips of dorsal spines; caudal fin with narrow brownish bands.

Sexual dimorphism: Male larger; anal, first, and second dorsal fins larger in male than in female. Male urogenital papilla extended; flattened and multicreased in female.

SYSTEMATIC NOTES

Two subspecies are recognized, the barred fantail *Etheostoma flabellare flabellare* Rafinesque, and the striped fantail *E. f. lineolatum* (Agassiz) (Hubbs and Lagler 1964). The first occurs in the eastern sector of the fantail darter's range west to lower Michigan and Indiana, and the latter southward from Minnesota, Wisconsin, and Upper Michigan. The Wisconsin form is distinquished by the lengthwise rows of spots or dashes in both sexes, which are absent in the eastern form, except in breeding males.

DISTRIBUTION, STATUS, AND HABITAT

In Wisconsin, the fantail darter occurs in the Mississippi River and Lake Michigan drainage basins, where it is at the northern limit of its range. It is not known from the Lake Superior drainage.

In a Plover River (central Wisconsin) survey (Becker 1959), the fantail darter constituted 15% of the darters taken, and 3.2% of all of the fish collected from 14 stations. Lake collections in Wisconsin are noted only from Lake Winnebago (Priegel 1967a), where the fantail darter is rare, and from the eastern shore of Green Bay (Door County). This species was probably eliminated from the Waupaca River (Waupaca County) downstream to Weyanwega by the Wisconsin Department of Natural Resources through poisoning with antimycin in a 1971 carp control project (Becker 1975).

The fantail darter is abundant over hard surfaces

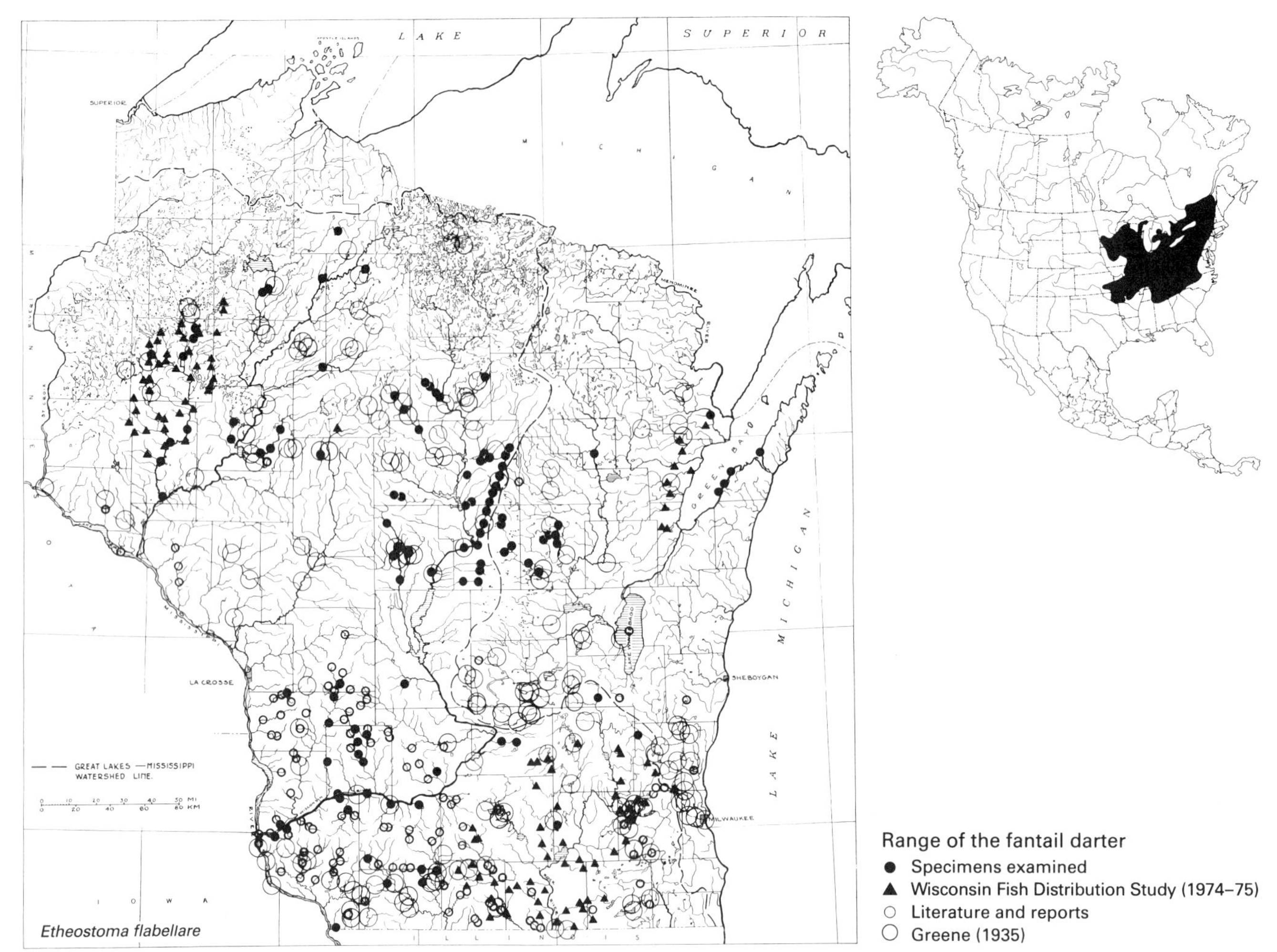

Range of the fantail darter
● Specimens examined
▲ Wisconsin Fish Distribution Study (1974–75)
○ Literature and reports
◯ Greene (1935)

in smaller streams, especially in southern Wisconsin, and it is occasionally found in medium-sized to large rivers. The fantail darter was encountered most frequently at warm water temperatures in clear to slightly turbid water, at depths of 1.5 m or less, over substrates of gravel (25% frequency), rubble (22%), sand (15%), silt (12%), boulders (11%), bedrock (6%), mud (4%), clay (3%), detritus (1%), and hardpan (1%). It occurred in moderate- to fast-flowing streams of the following widths: 1.0–3.0 m (38%), 3.1–6.0 m (32%), 6.1–12.0 m (14%), 12.1–24.0 m (11%), 24.1–50.0 m (2%), and more than 50 m (3%). According to Scott and Crossman (1973), it seems to be less sensitive to moderate turbidity and silting than the rainbow darter.

BIOLOGY

In Wisconsin, the fantail darter spawns from April to June (Lutterbie 1967). Spawning details have been provided by Lake (1936), Seifert (1963), and Winn (1958), from whom most of the following account is derived, unless otherwise indicated.

At water temperatures of 7–14°C (45–57°F), the male fantail darters migrate from the deeper, faster riffles up to shallow, more slowly flowing riffles, where stationary territories are established. Trautman (1957) found that, when silt deposits become so deep as to cover the spawning sites, the fantail darter spawns under rocks in the faster riffles. If a suitable habitat is not available, the males range over the entire spawning area, but do not establish territories. When territories are established, a hierarchy exists in the choice of territories, with the larger males, taking the preferred sites.

Territories are defended to establish the nest and to protect the eggs after spawning. When a fantail darter enters the territory of another, the two fish face each other. If the intruder moves, the defender attacks with fins erect, driving the intruder away. If contact is made, it is in the form of butts with the head and sometimes bites on the fins. The fantail darter also attacks other species of its own size. When a dead male was introduced into one territory, the defender attacked it until the dead fish was moved

38 cm away from the nest. However, dead females were accepted in both the upright and inverted positions. The male grows intensely dark when chasing an intruder.

The majority of fantail darter nests are found about halfway from the shore to the middle of the creek, where the bottom is hard. The nest cavities, located under rocks, are 13–25 mm deep. The depth of the cavity permits the resting female, while in the inverted position, to support herself with her dorsal fins on the bottom of the cavity while her belly and paired fins maintain contact with the bottom of the rock. The male's dorsal fin must also remain in contact with the undersurface of the rock when he is in the upright position during spawing. In preparing the nest, the male cleans off the debris and sediment on all sides of the rock by using the fleshy bulbs on his spiny dorsal fin, and the thickened flesh on top of his head. In most cases the nests are 1.2 m apart; some are only 0.3–0.5 m apart. One rock was found to have two nests under it. Nests with few entrances are considered prime sites.

The male fantail darter guards a territory of 0.3 m diam, with the nest at the center. Once he has established a territory, the male seldom leaves it, which indicates that a feeding territory is included within the breeding territory. A darter like the fantail, which has a complex breeding behavior, leaves the territory only under great duress; at such times it escapes to the deeper pools. At night there is no territorial defense.

About a week after the males migrate to the spawning area, the female fantail darters follow. The young and the females are found mainly in raceways and smaller pools. Defending males probably distinguish the males from the females on the basis of color and the complex behavior of the females.

Females entering the breeding area poke their heads under rocks and skip from rock to rock. During this time, the males dart out from under their rocks; whether this is to attract females or to forage for food is not known. When a female fantail enters a male's territory, the male may come out to meet her and lead the way back under the rock, or he may dash under the rock well in advance of the female and perform rapid movements where the eggs are to be laid. If two females enter the same nest to spawn, one is chased out by the male.

Breeding female fantail darters spawn with the most active males. The female may enter the nest in advance of the male, and the female or the pair may leave the nest several times before spawning. If the female is disturbed in the nest, she will leave and never return to that nest. The male, however, is quite bold and will usually not move unless he is touched.

Courting to spawning takes about 1 minute. When the female fantail darter is in the nest and ready to spawn, she rotates 180° to assume an inverted posi-

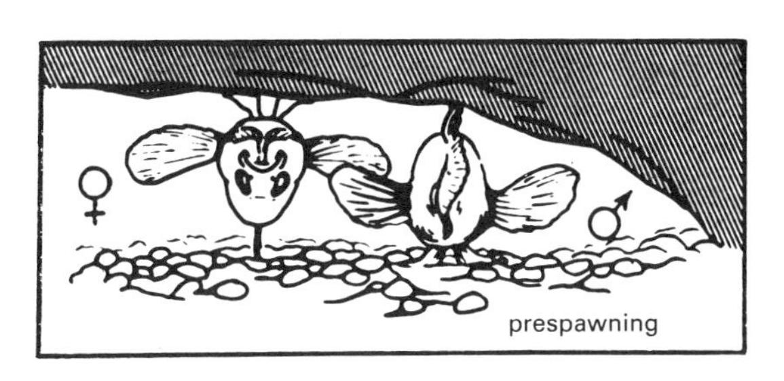

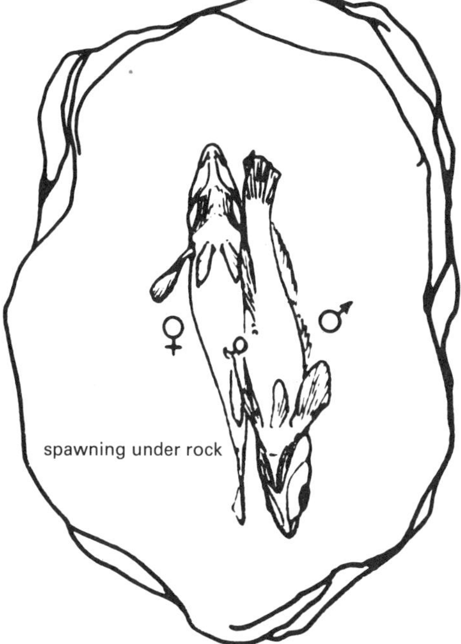

Side and top views of the fantail darters' positions under rocks. The ventral view of the fish is obtained by looking down through the top of a hypothetically transparent rock, with the fish upside down on the underside of the rock (Winn 1958:178. Copyright 1960, the Ecological Society of America).

tion, and the male assumes an upright, horizontal position in a head-to-tail relationship with the female. Together they move in circles and figure eights, as the the male butts and prods the caudal peduncle of the female to stimulate egg laying. As she gets ready to deposit an egg, she pushes against the rock and starts to vibrate. At this time, the male turns on his side so that his vent is alongside the female's vent. With tremendous vibration, egg and sperm are released simultaneously, and the egg is attached to the ceiling of the nest.

After the release of the sperm, the male immediately rights himself again, but the female may remain in the inverted position for as long as 2 hours. After a few minutes the spawning act is repeated; it will continue every 1–3 minutes until an average of 35 eggs has been deposited by the same female. Only 1 egg is laid at a time, and the average number for a large female fantail darter is 45 eggs laid with 1 male. After laying the eggs, the female is chased from the nest or darts out on her own. She returns to the pool to rest before spawning with another male. This species is polygamous; both males and females spawn with a number of partners. Females are known to spawn with as many as five different males in one season.

In Wisconsin, the gonads of fantail darters of both sexes reach their greatest development in May, and drop to their lowest weights in July (Lutterbie 1976). In May, the ovaries constituted 16% of the body weight, and the testes 0.7%. In May, three age-II females (49–52 mm TL) averaged 73 (39–91) mature eggs; in June, two age-II females (42 and 45 mm TL) averaged 46 (39 and 53) mature eggs; and four age-III females (48–50 mm TL) averaged 58 (40–80) mature eggs.

In northern New York, Lake (1936) reported that 23 female fantail darters contained an average of 226 eggs. Five different egg size groups were noticed, indicating that they had developed in stages during the spawning period. Lake suggested that each size group made up one clutch of eggs for each of the five separate spawnings engaged in during the breeding season. Females examined after the spawning season contained no eggs, indicating that all eggs, even the smaller ones, had matured. Winn (1958), however, noted that females remained ripe for 3 weeks, and found 10 females who contained from 5 to 100 eggs after the spawning season was over. Lake (1936) found an average of 169 eggs in 81 nests, with up to 562 eggs in some nests.

The eggs of the fantail darter are 2.2–2.3 mm diam. Incubation time is directly related to water temperature: 14–16 days at 23.5°C (74.3°F) and 30–35 days at 17–20°C (63–68°F) (Winn 1958). The male guards the nest and moves around under the eggs, brushing them with the bulbous tips of his dorsal spines and his soft dorsal fin. He also aerates the eggs by fanning them with his pectoral fins. Lake noted that the eggs quickly become infected if left untended, and Cross (1967) suggested that mucus from the male may have bactericidal and fungicidal effects, since males seem especially slimy during spawning. The greatest enemies to the eggs and the defending males are small crayfish and sculpins (Lake 1936, Koster 1937).

At hatching the fantail darter larvae are 6–7 mm long. According to Lake, the yolk-sac is absorbed within 7–10 days with little increase in larval length. The young are very active after hatching, and rest for only short periods of time. With this activity and the water current, they are soon dispersed throughout the stones and weeds. Descriptions of the developmental stages have been provided by Fish (1932) and Lake (1936).

In southern Wisconsin, young-of-year fantail darters collected in September are 24–36 mm TL; in northern Wisconsin, they are 23–29 mm (Lutterbie 1976).

The fantail darter from southern Wisconsin showed the following growth (Lutterbie 1976:85):

Age Class	No. of Fish	TL (mm)		Calculated TL at Annulus (mm)				
		Avg	Range	1	2	3	4	5
I	9	45.11	43–49	27.33				
II	76	47.15	34–61	32.21	45.59			
III	26	55.65	48–67	32.92	47.15	53.88		
IV	7	62.71	59–66	32.00	46.71	55.43	61.85	
V	4	71.75	69–74	31.50	46.25	59.50	66.25	72.50
Avg (weighted)				32.21	46.04	54.78	63.45	72.50

For 27 fantail darters from northern Wisconsin, the calculated lengths at annuli 1 through 3 were 23, 39, and 46 mm; for 108 darters from central Wisconsin, the lengths at annuli 1 through 4 were 28, 43, 56, and 60 mm.

The length-weight relationship for southern Wisconsin fantail darters was Log W = −11.3556 + 2.9747 Log L, where W is weight in grams and L is total length in millimeters (Lutterbie 1976).

Lake (1936) noted that age-I female fantail darters examined in November exhibited considerable egg development, suggesting that such females reach breeding readiness at age II.

A large Wisconsin fantail darter (UWSP 1110) was collected from Knapp Creek (Richland County) on 28

June 1962. It was 77 mm (3.0 in) TL, weighed 4.8 g, and was 5 years old. The fantail darter attained greater size in Wisconsin than in Iowa (Karr 1964), but it was smaller in Wisconsin than in Kentucky (Lotrich 1973).

The fantail darter's major food items belong to the orders Diptera, Ephemeroptera, Trichoptera, and Plecoptera (Lotrich 1973, Turner 1921, Karr 1964, Daiber 1956). Other foods consumed by this species are amphipods, Coleoptera larvae, Corixidae, ostracods, hyrachnids, and crayfish. The food of five fantail darters from the Madison (Dane County) area consisted of 42.7% (volume) Diptera larvae, 4.8% Trichoptera larvae, 48% amphipods, 0.2% cladocerans, 3% oligochaetes, and 1% plant items (Pearse 1918). In southeastern Wisconsin (Cahn 1927), fantail darters had eaten Diptera larvae (*Simulium* when available), mayflies, small dragonfly nymphs, *Planaria*, occasional young leeches, entomostracans, and small gastropods.

Turner (1921) found that 13-mm fantails contained Ephemeroptera and Diptera larvae as long as the fish themselves. The fantail darter is considered to be the most agile and active of all darters, and the large, active food organisms that appear in its diet are not taken by any other darter.

Although the fantail darter is apparently more tolerant than other darters of most pollutants, including silt, Lotrich found that its numbers dropped to 42% of the original population following an influx of strip mining wastes that caused heavy siltation. The absence of this species in portions of rivers in Oklahoma and Arkansas has been directly related to changes in the substrate (Moore and Paden 1950). When DDT was applied to a stream at a rate of less than 1.1 kilo/ha, specimens of the fantail darter were found dead after the fourth day of treatment (Hoffman and Surber 1945).

During the spawning season, the fantail darter inhabits the slower riffles. After spawning, the females move into the larger, deeper waters, where they overwinter; the males follow after the eggs have hatched (Trautman 1957).

In Kentucky, when the shallow gravel riffles dried up in later summer, fantail and rainbow darters moved to the deeper, quieter pools (Lotrich 1973). Cross (1967) suggested that the fantail darter in Kansas probably cannot tolerate an intermittent water flow, and that it must move or perish when flow ceases.

The base color of individual fantail darters changes according to the shade of the substrate where they occur. Light-colored individuals were found on sand, while the darker individuals were found on a darker substrate. Fantail darters also changed color with the time of day; in the laboratory they were all darker at night than when the lights were on during the day (Seifert 1963). The time that elapsed for this color change was 7 minutes. Only the dorsal portion of the body changed color.

The fantail darter reaches its highest level of abundance in warmwater streams. In Kuenster Creek (Grant County), 63 fantail darters were associated with the white sucker (49), central stoneroller (247), hornyhead chub (37), creek chub (2), southern redbelly dace (31), bluntnose minnow (187), suckermouth minnow (17), common shiner (62), bigmouth shiner (2), stonecat (2), and johnny darter (39).

IMPORTANCE AND MANAGEMENT

The fantail darter probably furnishes limited forage for predator fishes. It undoubtedly has the same bait value as other small darters—namely, it is useful in the absence of anything better.

Scott and Crossman (1973) have suggested that the fantail darter has no direct economic significance, but that the species offers unique opportunities for behavioral studies.

Few fishes have evoked more enthusiasm than the fantail darter. Jordan and Evermann (1896–1900) remarked that it was the "darter of darters—hardiest, wiriest, and wariest of them all and the one most expert in catching other creatures." It is reportedly very active and tenacious of life, and therefore is an excellent species for the aquarium.

Least Darter

Etheostoma microperca Jordan and Gilbert. *Etheostoma*—a straining mouth; *microperca*—small perch.

Other common name: northern least darter.

Male 32 mm, Plover R., Stevens Point (Portage Co.), 8 July 1965 (photo by M. Imhof)

DESCRIPTION

Body slender to moderately stout, compressed laterally. Average length 30 mm (1.2 in). TL = 1.25 SL. Depth into SL 4.3–4.8. Head length into SL 3.0–3.5. Preopercle smooth on posterior edge. Gill membranes moderately attached below to one another. Premaxillaries nonprotractile, the upper lip groove not continuous over tip of snout. Snout somewhat rounded, short; mouth strongly oblique (about 45°), upper jaw reaching below anterior edge of eye to anterior edge of pupil; small, sharp teeth in narrow bands on upper and lower jaws. Gill rakers short, irregularly shaped, about 4. Branchial apparatus illustrated and described by Branson and Ulrikson (1967). Branchiostegal rays 5 (6). Dorsal fins 2: first or spiny dorsal fin with 6 (5–7) spines, fin base into SL 4.5–5.5; second dorsal fin with 9–10 rays, fin base into SL 5.0–6.3. Anal fin with 2 (1) spines and 6 (5) rays; pelvic fin thoracic, extremely long reaching to vent or beyond. Scales ctenoid; cheeks, opercles and breast naked; nape naked (sometimes with embedded scales). Lateral line absent; lateral series scales 32–38 (0–7 pored scales). Vertebrae 32–34 (Bailey and Gosline 1955).

Back olive brown; sides lighter to straw-colored; belly creamy. Mottled with 6–9 small, irregular blotches along dorsal midline; 7–12 ill-defined rectangular blotches along midline of side; less mottling above, and least mottling below. First dorsal fin with diffuse brown pigment; second dorsal and anal fins with horizontal brown bars; remaining fins lightly pigmented. Suborbital bar prominent, black.

Breeding male with tubercles on all underside pelvic fin elements and occasionally on anal fin spines. An orange spot on membranes between each dorsal fin spine, base and outer edge of spiny dorsal black; anal and pelvic fins rusty orange. Breeding female lacking tubercles; pelvic, pectoral, and anal fins yellowish.

Sexual dimorphism: Female larger than male. Pectoral fin large in male. Pelvic fin reaching to base of anal fin in male; in female to vent. In male, pelvic fin cuplike, with an outer web of thickened skin. Urogenital papilla in male tubular and pointed; in female, conical and swollen.

DISTRIBUTION, STATUS, AND HABITAT

The least darter occurs in all three drainage basins in Wisconsin. It has been reported only once from the Lake Superior basin (Greene 1935). In the Mississippi River drainage, it is present in the St. Croix and Chippewa river systems of northwestern Wisconsin, in the Plover River of central Wisconsin, and in the Rock and Illinois-Fox systems of the southeastern corner of the state. It generally avoids the unglaciated region. In the Lake Michigan basin, it has two centers of distribution: the Wolf River system, and the streams of the heavily urbanized counties, including the Milwaukee, Menomonee, Root, and Pike rivers.

UWSP records: #1092 (11) creek draining Ebert Lake T23N R10E Sec 20 (Portage County), 1965; #1093 (29) Waterloo Creek T9N R11E Sec 24 (Dane County), 1965; #1094 (1), #1095 (2), #1096 (1), #1098 (12), #2053 (2), Plover River at Iverson Park, Stevens Point T24N R8E Sec 35 (Portage County), 1958–1968; #1097 (8) Allenton Flowage of Limestone Creek T11N R18E Sec 27 (Washington County), 1963; #3815 (8) and #3816 (162) Crystal River T21N R12E Sec 6 (Waupaca County), 1971; #3951 (13) White Clay Lake T27N R17E Secs 22 & 23 (Shawano County), 1971; #4592 (3) Yellow River T39N R15W Sec 23 (Burnett County), 1974; #5199 (1) Plover River T25N R9E Sec 19 (Portage County) 1975; #5329 (1) La Motte Lake T28N R16E Sec 19 (Menominee County), 1966; #5357 (1) No. Branch Lt. Wolf River T26N R10E Sec 7 (Marathon County), 1963; and #5450 (4) overflow pond adjacent to Chippewa River T38N R6W Sec 3 (Sawyer County), 1976.

The Wisconsin Fish Distribution Study (1974–1978) reported: (1) Tenmile Creek T32N R10W Sec 1 (Barron County), 1975; (1) Vermillion River T34N R13W Sec 3 (Barron County), 1975; (53) Lake Ripley T6N R13E Sec 7 (Jefferson County), 1974 and 1975; (18) Otter Creek T4N R14E Sec 18 (Rock County), 1975; (1) and (9) Allen Creek T5N R14E Secs 17 and 34 (Jefferson County), 1975; (1) Whitewater Creek T4N R15E Sec 10 (Walworth County), 1975; (3) Crooked Lake T7N

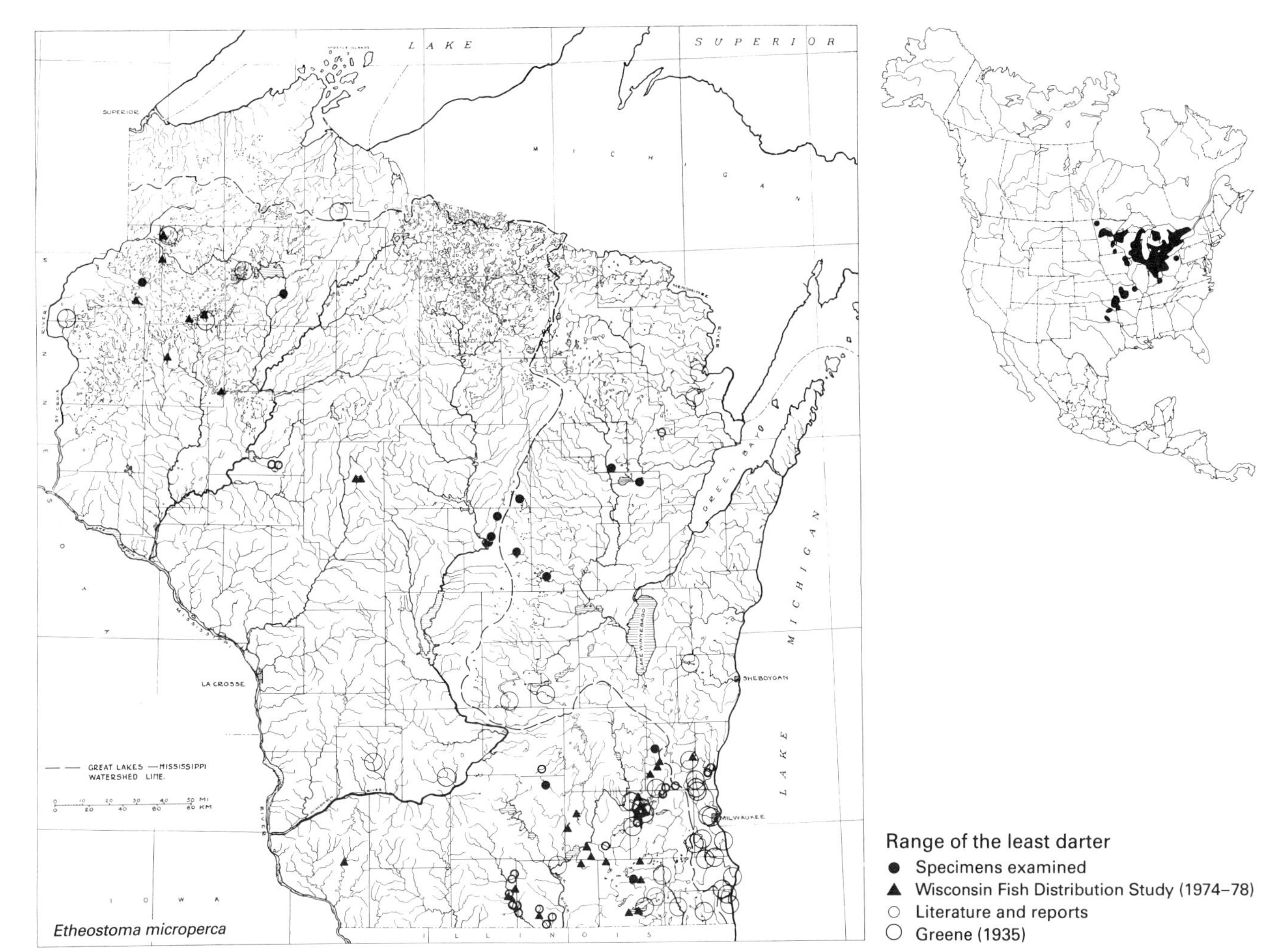

Range of the least darter
● Specimens examined
▲ Wisconsin Fish Distribution Study (1974–78)
○ Literature and reports
◯ Greene (1935)

R17E Sec 23 (Waukesha County), 1975; (193) Upper and Lower Nemahbin Lakes T7N R17E Sec 24 (Waukesha County), 1975; (2) Upper and Lower Nashota Lakes T7N R17E Secs 12 and 13 (Waukesha County), 1975; (2) Rock Lake T7N R13E Sec 15 (Jefferson County), 1974; (19) Oconomowoc Lake T7N R18E Secs 1, 3, and 35 (Waukesha County), 1975; (8) Ashippun Lake T8N R17E Sec 15 (Waukesha County), 1975; (1) Ashippun River T9N R18E Sec 4 (Washington County), 1975; (2) Rubicon River T10N R18E Sec 23 (Washington County), 1975; (10) Pike Lake T10N R18E Sec 27 (Washington County), 1974; (1) Upper Genesee Lake T7N R17E Sec 22 (Waukesha County), 1975; (46) East Fork Raccoon Creek T1N R11E Sec 12 (Rock County), 1974; (13) Raccoon Creek T1N R11E Secs 5 and 16 (Rock County), 1974; (2) Norwegian Creek T2N R9E Sec 14 (Green County), 1974; (8) Norwegian Creek T3N R10E Sec 31 (Rock County), 1974; (10) unnamed creek tributary to Norwegian Creek T3N R9E Sec 36 (Green County), 1974; (99) Platte River T4N R2W Sec 10 (Grant County), 1978; (99) unnamed Creek T27N R1W Sec 8 (Clark County), 1977; (1) Nelson Creek T27N R1W Sec 10 (Clark County), 1977; (2) Kekegama Lake T37N R12W Sec 26 (Washburn County), 1976; (1) Long Lake T37N R11W Sec 15 (Washburn County), 1976; (3) North Fork Clam River T38N R15W Sec 21 (Burnett County), 1976; (25) Fivemile Creek T42N R13W Sec 29 (Washburn County), 1977; and (11) McKenzie Creek T40N R13W Sec 6 (Washburn County), 1976.

M. Johnson (pers. comm.) reported: Green County—Allen Creek T3N R9E Sec 14 in 1964, Liberty Creek T4N R9E Sec 35 in 1964, Norwegian Creek T2N R9E Sec 11 in 1964, Sugar River T2N R9E Sec 26 in 1965; Rock County—Willow Creek T1N R10E Sec 7 in 1964, Taylor Creek T2N R10E Sec 31 in 1964, Coon Creek T1N R11E Sec 34 in 1966; Chippewa County—Clear Creek T28N R6W Sec 17 in 1966; Ozaukee County—Milwaukee River T10N R21E Sec 13 in 1967; Washington County—Bark River T9N R19E Sec 26 in 1968; Waukesha County—Bark River T8N R19E Sec 4 in 1968; Walworth County—Sugar Creek (Fox River drainage) T3N R16E Sec 12 in 1968; Columbia County—Crawfish River T10N R11E Sec 28 in 1968, collected by J. Mendelson; Sauk County—mouth of Honey Creek near Wisconsin River in 1968, collected by J. Mendelson; and Dane County—Waterloo Creek T9N R11E Sec 23 in 1966.

Over its range, the least darter has been declining. In Minnesota, it has been placed on watch status (Moyle 1975); in Kansas, it is vulnerable to extirpation (Platt et al. 1973); in Pennsylvania, it is endangered (Miller 1972); in Iowa, it is endangered and possibly extirpated (Roosa 1977). In Ohio, Trautman (1957) assumed that extensive ditching, dredging, draining, and polluting of prairie streams had decreased its abundance and constricted its distribution.

The numerous records of the least darter made by Greene (1935) in extreme southeastern Wisconsin in the late 1920s are not supported by recent reports, indicating that changed conditions (resulting from increased turbidity and habitat changes precipitated by agricultural, domestic, and industrial pollutants) have led to the elimination of this species in those waters. The widespread use of toxicants by the Wisconsin Department of Natural Resources in carp control programs has had a negative effect on its distribution. The least darter was noted as abundant in Waterloo Creek (Dane County) in 1966. Then the stream was poisoned, and repeated visits to the site of capture in 1967 produced no fish of any kind (M. Johnson, pers. comm.). The least darter has been recently placed on the watch list of Wisconsin fishes (Les 1979).

In Wisconsin, the least darter has been encountered most frequently in clear water at moderate to warm temperatures, at depths of 1.5 m or less, over substrates of gravel (39% frequency), sand (23%), silt (15%), boulders (8%), mud (8%), and clay (8%). It occurs within dense vegetation, including filamentous algal beds, in overflow ponds, pools, lakes and sluggish streams. It is typically found in quiet water, and is most frequently found in smaller waters associated with small streams, although it is occasionally taken along the edges of overflow waters adjacent to large rivers.

BIOLOGY

In Wisconsin, the spawning period of the least darter occurs from mid or late April to early July (Lutterbie 1976). In east central Illinois the spawning period extended from April to June (Burr and Page 1979). The spawning details and behavior which follow have been provided by Petravicz (1936) and Winn (1958), unless otherwise indicated.

Spawning occurred in Michigan in 0.2 m of water at a water temperature of 13.5°C (56.3°F) in the morning to 15.5°C (60°F) in the afternoon. The pH of the water was 7.9–8.0.

From March to May, the least darter migrates from the deeper portions of streams and lakes to the shallow areas to spawn. Males ripen 1–2 weeks earlier than females, and migrate slightly before them. Adverse weather conditions have been known to stop a spawning migration, and have even reversed its direction. Heavy rains causing high water, faster currents, and higher silt loads probably also delay spawning activities.

Least darter males establish and occupy stationary territories in heavily vegetated areas containing algae, *Potamogeton*, and other flowering aquatic plants. A male defends a territory of 30 cm diam, using a rock, or more often a plant, for the center of the territory. One territory, 25 cm in diameter, centered around a *Vallisneria* plant. The territory of the least darter has three dimensions, because it includes the vertical height of the plant or the center object in the territory, as well as its length and width. Other darters have only stationary territories of two dimensions. For the most part, the least darter attacks only individuals of its own species, which it does by making headlong assaults. Yearling males show less tendency than larger males to maintain territories, and larger males display dominance over the small males.

In most darter species that establish well-developed territories, the male is larger than the female. The least darter and Iowa darter are exceptions to this rule, the breeding females being somewhat larger than the breeding males. In darter species having stationary territories, there also appears to be an inherent protective mechanism wherein the males must keep in contact with other members of their own species in order to remain sexually active.

When ready to spawn, the female least darters move from the deeper parts of the stream or lake into the shallow areas occupied by the males. Frequently males are seen swimming after a female moving through the vegetated area. When the female slows down or comes to a stop the males contend for her, with the larger and more colorful male jostling away the other males and assuming the spawning position. Normally, if the female stops at a strongly acute to obtuse angle, the male is stimulated to assume the mounting position. The least darter spawns from an acute to a slightly obtuse angle, usually in a nearly vertical position. The female has an elongated, tubelike genital papilla, which is characteristic of darters that lay their eggs on gravel and plants, or in the vertical position.

The spawning position of the least darter (Winn 1958:177. Copyright 1960, the Ecological Society of America)

The modified pelvic fins of the male clasp the female just anterior to the spinous dorsal fin, extending down on both of her sides. His anal and caudal fins press against the caudal region of the female, and the female's soft dorsal fin presses against the side of the male. The male least darter induces the female to spawn by vibrating his head and the anterior region of his body. The breeding tubercles are thought to help maintain the position of the male on the female during the spawning act. When the female is ready to spawn, she reciprocates with the same type of vibration, curving her body so as to place the genital papilla on the twig, leaf, algae, or other spot selected for the one to three adhesive eggs. The egg or eggs are fertilized simultaneously upon release. The gaping mouths and the tense attitudes of the bodies indicate that the spawning act is unusually straining.

After spawning, the female darts off and goes through the entire process again with the same male or with a different male, engaging in several spawning acts before returning to the deeper water to rest. About 30 eggs are laid per day.

Since there is poor sex recognition among least darters and there are fewer color and behavioral differences in the sexes than in most darter species, mistakes of gender are frequently made. Least darter males mount other males much more frequently than the males of darter species in which sexual dimorphism and behavior is more pronounced.

The least darter lays its eggs only on plants, unless these are insufficient in number for the number of spawning pairs, in which case successful reproduction occurs on roots, rubble, or gravel. Occasionally the egg is laid in sand. After the female dives into the sand and is partly buried, the male assumes the spawning position, and the egg is laid and fertilized in the usual manner. This habit has been observed only in aquariums with bottoms of fine sand and few plants. According to Petravicz (1936), when a female begins to lay eggs on one material, such as the stems of plants, she rarely changes to another type, such as sand.

In Wisconsin least darters, the ovaries were best developed during May, when they were 19% of the body weight, and they remained highly developed through July, when they were 13% of the body weight (Lutterbie 1976). In September, ovaries made up only 1.9% of the body weight. The testes were largest in June and July, when they were 1.2 and 2.8% of the body weight respectively; in September they dropped to 0.4% of the body weight. In May, an age-I female held 146 eggs of 1 mm diam. In June, two age-I females held 150 and 194 mature eggs. Petravicz (1936) found that age-I fish held an average of 594 eggs, and age-II fish an average of 858 eggs. The eggs averaged 0.7 mm diam. The mature egg is usually transparent and yellowish, with one to several oil droplets. The male provides indirect care of eggs, and keeps at least other members of his own species away from them. In Illinois (Burr and Page 1979), neither sex gave any attention to the eggs after spawning.

At 18–20°C (64.4–68°F) incubation temperatures, hatching occurs in 6–6.2 days. According to Petravicz, the heart starts to beat after 50 hours of development, and has a rate of 150 beats per min just before hatching. Blood starts to flow at 80 hours. The total length of the least darter at hatching is 3 mm. Burr and Page (1979) illustrated and described the 3.5-mm hatchling, the 4.0-mm 3-day-old larva, and the 4.7-mm 7-day-old juvenile. At 12–13 mm all body scales were deposited.

Lutterbie determined that in central Wisconsin young-of-year least darters were 25–36 mm long in September; in southern Wisconsin, they were 24–26 mm long in August.

The growth of the least darter in central Wisconsin is shown on the following page (Lutterbie 1976:100). Least darters in southern Wisconsin were 30 and 35 mm at the first and second annuli.

The least darter is a short-lived fish; most individuals live through only two growing seasons (age I). Data suggest that most adults die shortly after their

Age Class	No. of Fish	TL (mm)		Calculated TL at Annulus (mm)	
		Avg	Range	1	2
I	38	35.00	28–41	31.21	
II	1	38.00		30.00	38.00
Avg (weighted)				31.18	38.00

first spawning. Of the museum specimens examined, only three had reached age II. They were 35–38 mm long, and the second annulus was at the margin of the scale. The length-weight relationship for least darters, based on 252 fish, was Log W = −11.7308 + 2.9805 Log L (Lutterbie 1976), where W is weight in grams and L is total length in millimeters.

The least darter reaches sexual maturity at a length of 27 mm at age I (Lagler et al. 1977). All age-I least darters are mature. It is the smallest of Wisconsin fishes in length, and among the earliest to mature. A large least darter (UWSP 3816) is an age-I specimen, 41 mm (1.6 in) TL, and 0.5 g. It was taken from the Crystal River (Waupaca County) in 1971. Trautman (1957) reported a specimen 46 mm (1.8 in) long.

The least darter feeds on all sorts of minute aquatic animal life. The stomachs of least darters taken from a pond adjacent to the Plover River (Portage County) contained large quantities of copepods and cladocerans (V. Starostka, pers. comm.). All food was of animal origin; no vegetation or sand appeared in any of the digestive tracts examined. In another sample from the same locale, the stomachs contained cladocerans, Diptera larvae, and unidentified plant seeds (A. Kossel, pers. comm.). Starostka noted that fall specimens had fat deposits on the viscera; the fat was absent in spring specimens, suggesting that fat was used for winter survival. In southeastern Wisconsin, the least darter's food consisted of about equal amounts of insect larvae, nymphs, and entomostracans (Cahn 1927).

The least darter is an inhabitant of cool to warm waters. In Canada, it was associated with the rock bass and smallmouth bass at an average summer water temperature of 21°C (70°F); it avoided the 16–17°C (60–62°F) temperature range inhabited by the brook trout and the mottled sculpin (Hallam 1959).

After the spawning period, the least darter moves back into deeper waters. In Whitmore Lake, Michigan, this species was found in the thick organic debris and plant zone in 1.2 m of water (Winn 1958). In the shallow periphery of a large pool below the Crystal tal River Dam (Waupaca County) I found numbers of least darters in cavities hollowed out under large stones, which provide a natural form of cover in the absence of vegetation.

In the Allenton Flowage (Washington County), 10 least darters were collected with the common carp (1), creek chub (13), northern redbelly dace (1), black bullhead (2), tadpole madtom (3), green sunfish (2), pumpkinseed (1), rock bass (1), and central mudminnow (+).

In an Illinois study (Burr and Page 1979) the greatest density was 33.09 least darters/m^2 collected in mid-October; the least density, 0.84 darters/m^2 in late March. During winter months the density decreased, and few individuals in the 1+ year class survived.

In an Ohio study of stream dessication, Tramer (1977) found that the least darter survived periods of drought by burrowing into the substrate. When rain refilled dry pools in the creek, the least darter reappeared.

IMPORTANCE AND MANAGEMENT

Little is known about the significance of the least darter in the food chain of other fishes. The black crappie and largemouth bass have fed on it to some extent (Cahn 1927). Petravicz (1936) indicated that supernumerary least darter males may devour eggs fertilized by rival males. Its close association with dense vegetation undoubtedly affords it considerable protection from predators, and perpetuates its secretive habits.

Drum Family—Sciaenidae

Only a single species of the drum family is known from Wisconsin. It is the only strictly freshwater member of a large number of saltwater forms, some of which occasionally move into nearby freshwater habitats. In the United States and Canada, 33 species in 18 genera are known (Robins et al. 1980). The drums are particularly well represented in Panama, and they should be thought of as primarily fishes of the sandy shores of tropical seas, although various members have traveled far in habit and form (Breder 1948). The family contains about 160 species, and has a fossil record beginning in the Paleocene.

The skull consists of heavy bones characterized by large cavities, which are adaptations for the mucous glands of the lateral line system. The jaws contain many small, sharp teeth in broad bands. The lower pharyngeal arches are large, sometimes fused, and contain buttonlike teeth for crushing. The spiny and soft dorsal fins are only slightly connected; the anal fin has two spines. Ctenoid scales cover the head and the body. The lateral line, which extends to the end of the caudal fin, is distinctive.

Another distinctive feature of the drum family is the large otolith located in the sacculus of the inner ear. In the freshwater drum, the otolith has white enameled surfaces, and is provided with peculiar grooves and markings. If an otolith is cut into thin sections and examined under a microscope, the layers formed in successive years are clearly visible as alternating light and dark zones. By a study of the otoliths, it is possible to obtain the age of any individual fish. Because of its toothlike nature and size, the otolith is often used as a "lucky bone" by youthful fishermen. When polished, otoliths may be converted into attractive jewelry.

Most species of the drum family have a complicated swim bladder with special muscles and tendons that are capable of producing audible sounds when vibrated against the bladder. The few species lacking the swim bladder sink to the bottom when they are not actually swimming, and are, of course, voiceless.

The drum family contains many species which reach a large size, and which are highly valued as food and sport fishes. The sea trout, the saltwater drums, the croakers, and the kingfishes are the saltwater counterparts of the freshwater centrarchids. They are easily caught, and are among the most edible of fishes.

Freshwater Drum

Aplodinotus grunniens Rafinesque. *Aplodinotus*—a simple or single back, in reference to the joined dorsal fin; *grunniens*—grunting.

Other common names: lake sheepshead, sheepshead, drum, sunfish, silver bass, gray bass, grunter, grinder, grunting perch, white perch, rock perch, perch, thunder-pumper, bubbler, gaspergou. Along the upper Mississippi River, commonly white perch or perch.

Subadult 246 mm, L. Winnebago (Fond du Lac Co.), 28 Aug. 1961

DESCRIPTION

Body deep, strongly compressed, especially dorsally; the back strongly arched forward. Length 254–356 mm (10–14 in). TL = 1.28–1.32 SL in fish more than 125 mm SL; 1.34–1.35 SL in fish less than 125 mm SL (Krumholz and Cavanah 1968). Depth into TL 3.3–3.8. Head length into TL 4.0–4.5. Snout rounded. Mouth ventral, horizontal. Upper jaw reaching below middle of eye; small teeth in broad bands on upper and lower jaws; pharyngeal arches heavy and with small, rounded, closely set teeth. Dorsal fins 2, connected by a narrow membrane: first or spiny dorsal fin with 8–9 spines; second dorsal fin with 1 spine and 24–32 rays. Anal fin with 2 spines (second greatly elongated and stouter than first) and 7 rays; pelvic fins thoracic, with 1 spine and 5 rays, the first ray elongated into a distinct filament. Scales ctenoid; scales on upper head, body, and extending onto bases of second dorsal and anal fins. Lateral line complete and extending through caudal fin (the only Wisconsin species in which this occurs). Lateral line scales 48–53 to hypural notch. Otolith of inner ear much enlarged (Priegel 1967c).

Back and upper region of head olive brown; sides silvery; belly and lower region of head white. Pectoral fins lightly pigmented; pelvic fins whitish; remaining fins dusky. General color of living fish from clear waters, bronzy; from turbid waters, grayish white.

Sexual dimorphism: In male, a single urogenital opening behind the anus; in female, 2 openings, genital and urinary, behind the anus (Moen 1959).

SYSTEMATIC NOTES

Marked similarities in the morphology of freshwater drum from Lake Winnebago, Wisconsin, and from the lower Ohio River, Kentucky, indicate that there is a remarkable stability within the species that has persisted essentially in its present form since early postglacial times (Krumholz and Cavanah 1968).

DISTRIBUTION, STATUS, AND HABITAT

In Wisconsin, the freshwater drum occurs in the Mississippi River and Lake Michigan drainage basins. It is not known from the Lake Superior basin. In the St. Croix River system above the St. Croix Falls (Polk County), it has been reported from Davis Brook, Minnesota, to the St. Croix reservoir (Kuehn et al. 1961); from the Danbury Flowage, Lt. Yellow Lake, Yellow Lake, and the Clam River in Burnett County (Blackman et al. 1966); and from the St. Croix River in Douglas County (Sather and Johannes 1973).

In the Wisconsin River system, the freshwater drum is known upstream to the Portage (Columbia County) area. In 1947, two drums were examined which had been caught in the Moen's Lake chain, part of the tributary system of the Wisconsin River in Oneida County (Priegel 1967c, L. O. Williamson memo to A. Oehmcke, DNR at Woodruff 17 July 1947). It is probable that these individuals were introduced as part of a fish rescue and transfer project. There are no other known records from the upper Wisconsin River drainage.

In the Lake Michigan drainage, the freshwater drum is abundant in Lake Winnebago and common in Lakes Poygan, Winneconne, and Lake Butte des Morts. It is fished commercially in Green Bay, but it is rare in Lake Michigan proper. A single specimen was reported from a 2-year creel census conducted at the Point Beach Nuclear Plant fishing pier (Manitowoc County) (Spigarelli and Thommes 1976).

In the Mississippi River system, the freshwater drum is common to abundant. It occurs in limited numbers in the Madison lakes (Dane County) and in Pewaukee Lake (Waukesha County). On the Wisconsin distribution map, open symbols on tributary streams indicate the upstream limits of this species.

In Wisconsin the freshwater drum appears secure, despite heavy commercial and state crew fishing. Fishing regulations for 1980 impose no bag limit and

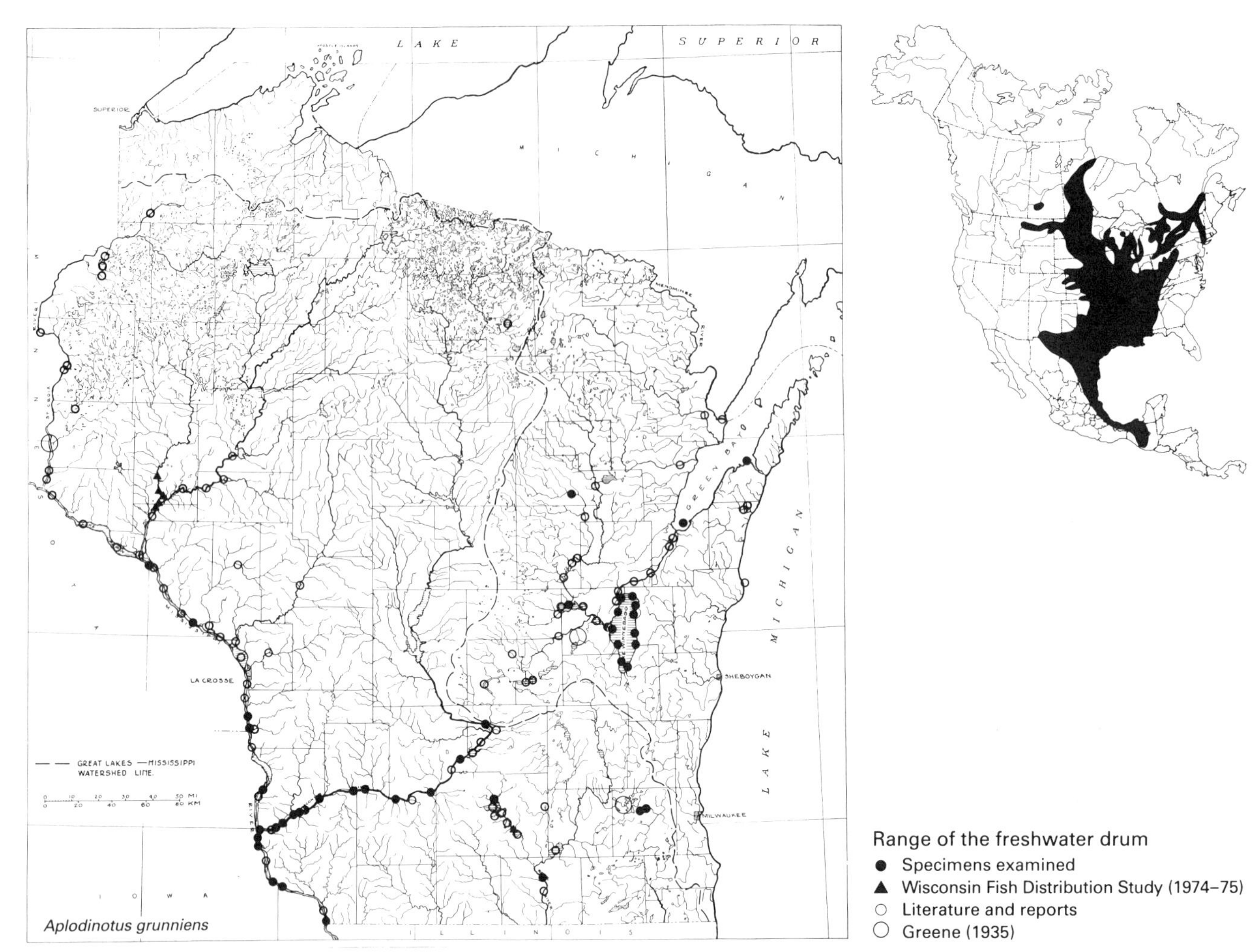

Range of the freshwater drum
● Specimens examined
▲ Wisconsin Fish Distribution Study (1974–75)
○ Literature and reports
◯ Greene (1935)

no size limit on this nongame species (Wis. Dep. Nat. Resour. 1979).

The freshwater drum inhabits large rivers, lakes, and impoundments. In streams it usually occurs in the larger pools. The open water areas of warm, sluggish lakes and streams with mud bottoms are the preferred habitats. The drum prefers turbid water, although it is occasionally found in clear water. It is seldom found in shallow, weedy areas. In the Great Lakes, it occurs mostly from shallows to waters 12–18 m deep.

BIOLOGY

On the Mississippi River, the freshwater drum spawns from the first of May to the end of June at water temperatures of 18.9–22.2°C (66–72°F) (Butler 1965, Nord 1967). In Lake Winnebago, spawning occurs at these temperatures during June and at times in July (Priegel 1967c). When water temperatures in Lake Winnebago remain below 18.9°C (66°F) until mid-July, some females may not spawn and their eggs are resorbed.

It is during late April and early May, as water temperatures rise in Lake Winnebago, that the male freshwater drum begins to produce his unusual sounds—first in short bursts between long intervals of silence (Schneider and Hasler 1960). Into late May the drumming sounds become longer and they are heard more often as the water temperature approaches the spawning level. According to Wirth (1958:30):

> It may well be that the males are serenading for the attention of the females. When this drumming or humming sound is heard, it is difficult to tell where the sound is coming from. It sounds like a motorcycle race in full swing several miles away, with increasing and falling volumes as if the wind varied in its strength to carry the sound.

Wirth also noted that, when freshwater drums are taken from the water, they often croak like bullfrogs. Whether this croaking sound is made in the same way as the drumming sound is not known. The intensity of drumming is greatest in Lake Winnebago during the spawning season in June. It diminishes gradually until it ceases in late August (Schneider and Hasler 1960).

The freshwater drum spawns pelagically in open water, usually far from shore. In Lake Winnebago the schools of spawning fish are easily observed on quiet days as they slowly mill at the surface with their backs out of water (Wirth 1958). At times, groups of fish come together and actually lift one or more individuals out of the water.

In Lake Erie (Daiber 1953), mature female freshwater drums had ovaries up to 12% of the body weight; they held from 43 to 508 thousand mature eggs about 1 mm diam. It is quite common for some female freshwater drums not to spawn even though their ovaries are full of eggs. Examination of such females in August or September has shown the eggs being resorbed.

In the Mississippi River, in Pool 3 and in Lake Pepin, strong year classes occurred when mean water temperatures exceeded the long-range mean water temperature for those waters (Butler 1965). This was particularly true for the month of May, but did not hold true for the entire month of June.

The eggs and larvae of the freshwater drum float on the surface of the water, a characteristic typical of saltwater fish and unique among freshwater fish in North America. The eggs require from 24 to 48 hours to hatch, and the larvae remain attached to the surface film for a similar length of time. Once the larvae are capable of swimming, they leave the surface. In Lewis and Clark Lake, South Dakota, the larvae, which are about 3 mm long at hatching, are scattered by water currents and wind and drift at the surface until they are about 10 mm long; they then move to deeper water (Walburg 1976). Priegel (1967c) noted that, after attaining a length of 25 mm, freshwater drums are found on or near the bottom, where they remain for most of their lives.

M. Fish (1932) illustrated and described the 13.3-mm stage, and described the 15.6-mm stage. Taber (1969) illustrated the developmental stages from 3.2 to 20.5 mm. Scales first appear on freshwater drums in the 15-mm class, and the young are fully scaled at 22 mm (Priegel 1966c).

In the Wisconsin River (Grant County), young-of-year freshwater drums were 29–43 mm long on 17 July; in Lake Winnebago (Calumet County), they were 32–68 mm long in mid-August; and in Lake Mendota, they were 78–82 mm long on 26 September.

According to Priegel, growth of Lake Winnebago freshwater drums is slower than that reported from most areas in the United States. However, growth of freshwater drums from the Mississippi River after the second year greatly exceeds the growth of this species in other locations.

In Lake Winnebago, freshwater drums showed the following length and weight relationships: 127–178 mm TL—average 45 g; 178–229 mm—113 g; 229–279 mm—204 g; 279–320 mm—363 g; 320–381 mm—567 g; and 381–432 mm—794 g (Priegel 1967c).

Slow growth appears to increase longevity. The fast-growing freshwater drums in the Mississippi River seldom reach 7 or 8 years of age. Priegel noted that few freshwater drums live to be more than 10 years of age, although there are records of individuals as old as 17 years. In Lake Winnebago, the age composition of the freshwater drum population has changed because of an intensive drum removal program initiated in 1954. In 1951, 73% of the freshwater drums caught were 7 years old or older, but by 1960, only 23% were 7 years or more in age. In 1963, only 12% were 7 years old or older.

In the Mississippi River, the first mature males were age II, and had a mean length of 310 mm. At age III, 63.4% of the freshwater drums were mature; they had a mean length of 351 mm (Butler and Smith 1950). Maturity was reached by 97% of the males by age IV, but not all were mature until age VI. Females first matured at age IV, at which time 46% were mature at an average length of 386 mm. All females beyond age V were mature. In Lake Winnebago, mature males are generally 3–4 years old and 254–305 mm long, while females are usually 4–5 years old and 279–305 mm long at maturity (Priegel 1967c). Freshwater drum females continue to reproduce year after year once sexual maturity is reached. In Lake Winnebago, there have been times when a small percentage of the older females did not reproduce each successive year. Males

Age and Growth (TL in mm) of the Freshwater Drum in Wisconsin and Lake Erie

Location	1	2	3	4	5	6	7	8	9	10	11	12	13	14	Source
L. Winnebago	130	218	277	312	338	356	368	381	391	427					Priegel (1969d)
Mississippi R., Pools 4A, 8, 10, 17	124	229	297	340	376	419	460	486							Butler and Smith (1950)
Mississippi R., Pool 5A	127	244	318	376	419	445	488								Christenson and Smith (1965)
L. Erie	132	201	254	292	335	358	396	419	432	460	472	483	460	480	Edsall (1967)

usually make up from 52 to 63% of the freshwater drum population.

Priegel (1963c) determined that the mean length of freshwater drums from Lake Winnebago is smaller today than the mean length of drums whose remains have been found at aboriginal campfire sites in the Lake Winnebago region. The calculated lengths of the latter, based on otolith size, are 460–472 mm (18.1–18.6 in). The sizes of the pharyngeal bones and molar teeth that are found in the campsites of American Indians indicate that in primordial times weights of about 90 kg (200 lb) were attained by freshwater drums (Hubbs and Lagler 1964). Witt (1960), however, after investigating drum otoliths found in Indian middens, suggested that the maximum size of this species is probably well under 45 kg (100 lb). Specimens weighing over 22.7 kg (50 lb) have been reported from Spirit Lake, Iowa (Harlan and Speaker 1956). A 24.7-kg (54-lb 8-oz) fish was captured from Nickajack Lake, Tennessee, in 1972.

In 1958, a freshwater drum weighing 14.1 kg (31 lb) and measuring 940 mm (37 in) was caught by an angler on Lake Winnebago (Priegel 1967c). In 1971, a fish weighing 11.8 kg (26 lb) was taken from the Fox River (Winnebago County) (Wis. Dep. Nat. Resour. 1977). A commercial fisherman (J. Diehl, pers. comm.) reported a 15.9-kg (35-lb) fish netted from the Mississippi River at La Crosse.

In Lake Winnebago, the food of young freshwater drums consists principally of minute crustaceans—the copepods and cladocerans. As the fish increase from 25 to 51 mm, insect larvae become an important part of their diet. The lake fly larva *Chironomus plumosus* becomes the most important item in the diet of all freshwater drums more than 38 mm long (Priegel 1967c,d). The leech *Helobdella* sp. was consumed by all freshwater drum groups of more than 60 mm. Freshwater drums also eat crayfish and small fish, but fish are a small part of their diet (Wirth 1958).

In the Mississippi River (Pool 19), 75% of the total stomach contents of freshwater drums consisted of *Hexagenia* naiads. Immature Coleoptera and Odonata, snails, and fish constituted the bulk of the remaining 25% (Hoopes 1960).

In Lake Winnebago, there is no evidence that adult freshwater drums feed on mollusks. Often the adult drum is characterized as feeding extensively on mollusks: the shells are crushed by the powerful pharyngeal jaws, the broken bits of shells are spewed out, and only the soft parts of the mollusks are swallowed. Krumholz and Cavanah (1968) noted that, although many general works indicate that the principal diet should consist of mollusks because of the strong molariform pharyngeal teeth, none of the more recent detailed studies bears this out.

The freshwater drum feeds chiefly by touch and taste, thus enabling it to endure more turbid water than sport fish species which feed principally by sight. Apparently it will feed at all hours, as full stomachs have been found at all hours of the day and night (Priegel 1967c). Trautman (1957) noted that, at twilight during the warmer months, freshwater drums come into waters less than 1.5 m deep, where they feed by moving rocks and stones with their snouts, capturing crayfishes, aquatic insects, darters, and other fishes that they have disturbed.

Although a hardy species, the freshwater drum has been observed in distress when water temperatures exceed 25.6°C (78°F), and when dissolved oxygen concentrations remain low over an extended period of time (Priegel 1967c). Gammon (1973) suggested that the optimum temperature for the freshwater drum in the Wabash River, Indiana, probably lies within the 29–31°C (84–88°F) range.

The tendency of freshwater drums to school begins early and continues throughout life. In the Mississippi River, movement and activity are largely governed by water temperature and water movement (Nord 1967). The drums usually move into the shallower waters in the spring and back into the deeper water of the main channel in the late fall. Activity and feeding are greatly reduced in winter. The freshwater drum has a wide range of habitats during warmer weather, and is found in practically all of the Mississippi River habitats except the shallow, slackwater areas. It is sometimes found in large concentrations in the tailwaters of the dams.

The drumming sound made by freshwater drums is produced by a special apparatus which is located in the body cavity, and is connected with the swim bladder. Two elongated muscles moving a tendon over the swim bladder are responsible for implementing the sound. Only sexually mature males possess this structure, which is fully developed by the third year of life (Priegel 1967c). The sounds were produced only during the daytime, from about 1000 per hr to sunset (Schneider and Hasler 1960).

IMPORTANCE AND MANAGEMENT

The freshwater drum has few natural enemies. Although apparently exposed and vulnerable, the eggs, larvae, and fry are seldom taken by other species. The young are eaten infrequently by walleyes, burbot, saugers, and white bass (Butler 1965, Priegel 1967c). The freshwater drum's covering of heavy ctenoid scales affords considerable protection for the Great

Lakes populations against attack by the sea lamprey (Scott and Crossman 1973). In most waters, commercial fishing is the major cause of adult mortality.

The freshwater drum has significance as an intermediary host for mussels, which pass through their metamorphosis on the drum's gills. Sometimes the freshwater drum carries an almost incredible number of glochidia (Surber 1913). Hart and Fuller (1974) list the following clams which use the freshwater drum as host: *Megalonaias gigantea, Anodonta grandis, Arcidens confragosa, Lampsilis orbiculata, Leptodea fragilis, Proptera alata, Proptera laevissima, Proptera purpurata, Truncilla donaciformis*, and *Truncilla truncata*.

In recent years, the number of Wisconsin anglers who catch the freshwater drum has been on the increase, although it is frequently taken incidentally to other sport fishes. On Lake Winnebago, the freshwater drum readily takes live bait such as worms, crayfish, and minnows. It also takes cut bait, and occasionally strikes spinner-minnows, wet flies, and small plugs. Unfortunately, this species bites well only during the summer months.

The estimated sport fishery catch of freshwater drums in Pools 4, 5, 7, and 11 of the Mississippi River in 1967–1968 was 90,412 fish weighing 27,414 kg (60,437 lb) (Wright 1970). This species ranked second in the sport catch in 1957, and fifth in 1962–1963 (Nord 1967).

Freshwater drums from Lake Winnebago are gamey fish on the hook, and when prepared for the table they are quite tasty. The edibility of the freshwater drum seems to vary from lake to lake, and small fish of 0.5–1 kg are usually more palatable than large fish. The flesh is white, with large flakes that are low in oil (Gebken and Wright 1972a). The values of the edible fillet are 16–18% protein, 1.5–6% oil, 1% ash, and 75–81% moisture. The protein content is higher than that of several other species of fish and about the same as that of beef and chicken; the fat content is lower than that of beef and chicken.

Wirth (1959) provided the following instructions for cooking freshwater drum (p. 10):

To prepare for cooking, season, roll the fillets or sticks in flour, cracker crumbs, or cornmeal and pan fry in oil. Or dip in a batter and drop them in deep fat. With either method, *drum fillets should not be fried too long* or they will dry out and become hard.

An excellent fish-frying batter is a beer batter. Merely mix beer with flour and salt to a thin enough consistency to stick to the fish and drop in a frying fat. This batter will impart a light crisp bubbly coating to the fillets or sticks with just a slight aroma of malt. If the use of beer is distasteful, use charged water or white soda for the same effect without the malt flavor.

Drum also are delicious smoked. They may be smoked in much the same manner as other fish suitable for smoking, but they *should not be heated too long* as they are not as oily as carp or catfish, and will tend to dry out. They are usually smoked whole with just the viscera removed. The head and scales may remain or be removed depending upon individual preference.

The otoliths (ear bones) of the freshwater drum were put to curious uses in ancient times. They were often worn on a string around the neck as a preventative and cure for colic (Priegel 1967c). Otoliths have been found in Indian middens throughout the range of the species. The Indians used the freshwater drum for food, and the otoliths for money and ornaments. Niehoff (1952) described five aboriginal otoliths found in Wisconsin that were perforated at two points, indicating that they had been strung, probably either for a necklace or a braclet. Aboriginal drum otoliths have been found in areas of Utah and California where the freshwater drum was not native; these otoliths must certainly have been carried there as some sort of trinket or wampum. Even today, otoliths have value as "lucky bones" for fishermen. Some people convert otoliths into attractive jewelry.

A considerable commercial freshwater drum fishery has developed in Wisconsin. In the Wisconsin portion of the Mississippi River, the freshwater drum ranks fourth in abundance and value in the catch. In 1977, the freshwater drum accounted for 12% of the total wholesale value of fish taken from the Wisconsin waters of the Mississippi, following the channel catfish (32%), buffalo (29%), and common carp (24%) (Fernholz and Crawley 1978). Between 1953 and 1977, the yearly catch of freshwater drums averaged 222,300 (112,800–435,400) kg. The 1977 catch was 250,167 kg (551,515 lb), and valued at $55,150 to the commercial fisherman. The seine accounts for the largest portion of the drum harvest; gill nets and set lines follow in importance. Freshwater drums are shipped to markets in large Midwest cities, where they sell quite readily, sometimes under the names of "white perch" or "perch." In 1975, the retail prices for freshwater drums were $1.08/kilo (49¢/lb) for fresh fish and $1.65/kilo (75¢/lb) for smoked fish in a Lansing, Iowa, fish market.

The 15.2 million kg of freshwater drums removed commercially from Lake Winnebago from 1955 to 1966 were valued at $1,012,840 (Priegel 1971b). In 1970, sales of 546,220 kg of freshwater drums in Wisconsin brought $40,444 (Miller 1971). Most of the freshwater drums that have been harvested in Lake Winnebago have been used for food in the mink industry.

According to Priegel (1967c), on Lake Winnebago

the Lake Erie–type trap nets were used to catch freshwater drums from 1955 through 1965, and were the most important gear in use until 1962, when trawling accounted for 61% of the catch. The effectiveness of the trawl continued to increase, so that by 1965 trawls accounted for 84% of the freshwater drum harvest. The drums are located by electronic sonar devices, which take the guesswork out of finding them. Priegel (1965) noted that in Lake Winnebago the catch per haul of adult freshwater drums increased during night trawling compared to the catch taken in day trawling.

In Lake Winnebago, the commercial harvest of freshwater drums was intensive enough to crop off the larger and older fish by 1962, so that the harvest after 1962 was composed of smaller and younger fish even though the rate of growth remained the same (Priegel 1971b). Priegel estimated that to keep the freshwater drum population at an optimum size in Lake Winnebago—i.e., less competitive with the sport species—1.1–1.4 million kg of drums should be removed annually.

In Lake Michigan, the freshwater drum population is concentrated in lower Green Bay, where it is harvested incidentally to the yellow perch fishery. The commercial harvest in 1974 was reported at 880 kg (1,941 lb), with a value of $155 (Wis. Dep. Nat. Resour. 1976c). Wells and McLain (1973) stated that in Lake Michigan the catch of freshwater drums since 1962 has been negligible because of poor market demand.

The standing crop of freshwater drums in Illinois and Wisconsin lakes averaged 7.7 (3.4–15.9) kg/ha (Carlander 1955). With the removal of freshwater drums from Lake Winnebago, increases have been noted in walleye, sauger, white bass, yellow perch, crappie, and channel catfish populations, especially since 1959 (Priegel 1971b); however, no positive correlation has been demonstrated between these increases and drum removal.

Sculpin Family—Cottidae

Four species of sculpins in two genera are known from Wisconsin. In the United States and Canada, 111 named species occur, three-fourths of which refer to the Pacific Ocean, including the western Arctic. In addition to the named species, some 30 little-known cottids have been recorded in the North American waters of Alaska alone (Robins et al. 1980). Although primarily marine fishes of arctic and temperate seas, one genus in particular, *Cottus*, is widely distributed in the fresh waters of the northern hemisphere. Twenty-one strictly freshwater species have evolved in North American waters, and, within that genus, several species are confined to only a spring or two. The family contains at least 300 species. The cottids are known from the Oligocene to Recent. They are among the most advanced of fishes.

Sculpins are characterized by enlarged, flattened heads and by expansive pectoral fins. The body tapers from the broad head to a relatively narrow caudal peduncle. The preopercle is variously armed with spines. The eyes are dorsal in position and occasionally are close set. The first dorsal fin is spiny, but the spines are soft. The pelvic fins possess a single spine which is bound by a membrane to the first pelvic ray, creating a single element. Scales are lacking, or are represented by dermal prickles.

Although freshwater sculpins are small fishes of 18 cm or less, some marine species may attain lengths of 61 cm or more. In Wisconsin, the sculpins are typical inhabitants of rocky, cool headwater streams; here they retreat under stones during daylight hours.

Sculpins are primarily carnivorous, feeding largely on microcrustaceans and aquatic insects. In trout streams they have long been accused of eating trout eggs and young. Probably most of the trout eggs consumed by sculpins are loose eggs that have not been buried in the nests. Little evidence is available to show that sculpins limit trout numbers. In fact, in large, deep lakes sculpins are an important forage fish for large trout and other predator species.

Sometimes a sculpin is used as bait by anglers.

From the accounts of sculpin species which follow, it is evident that life history information for some species is sketchy. W. Van Vliet, while working in deep water with scuba gear, lost his life in October 1968 as he attempted to unlock the mysteries of spoonhead and deepwater sculpin ecology and behavior in Heney Lake, Quebec (Delisle and Van Vliet 1968). The sculpins yield their secrets grudgingly—particularly those species in deep, coldwater habitats.

Deepwater Sculpin

Myoxocephalus thompsoni (Girard). *Myoxocephalus*—head like a dormouse; *thompsoni*—named for Rev. Zadock Thompson, the author of *History of Vermont*.

Other common names: Great Lakes fourhorn sculpin, sculpin, lake sculpin, deepwater blob.

Adult 173 mm, L. Michigan, near Sheboygan (Sheboygan Co.), 28 Oct. 1966. Lateral view above and dorsal view below.

DESCRIPTION

Head and anterior body flattened dorsoventrally; posterior body and caudal peduncle compressed laterally. Average length 137 mm (5.4 in). TL = 1.21 SL. Body depth into TL 4.4–6.0. Head length into TL 3.3–3.9. Snout blunt in lateral view. Mouth terminal, large. Upper jaw extending to below middle of eye or beyond; minute teeth in narrow bands on upper and lower jaws; palatine teeth present. Gill membranes meeting at an acute angle, free from isthmus. Four preopercular spines per side; uppermost spine directed upward, others downward. Dorsal fins 2, separated from each other about diam of eye; first or spiny dorsal fin with 7–8 soft spines; second dorsal fin with 12–14 rays. Anal fin rays 13–15; pelvic fins thoracic, small, of 1 spine and 3 rays but appearing as only 3 elements (the spine and first ray encased in a single fleshy membrane); pectoral fins large, fanlike, rays 16–17. Typical scales absent, and spines or prickles present only above lateral line, few in number and often arranged parallel to lateral line. Lateral line complete or nearly so.

Back and sides grayish brown to light brown; back occasionally with 4–7 saddle marks of varying size; belly and caudal peduncle lighter. Pelvic and anal fins generally unpigmented; first dorsal fin pigmented along edge; remaining fins variously speckled or barred.

Sexual dimorphism: In male, rays of second dorsal fin much elongated and reaching to base of caudal fin and beyond; in female, these rays not reaching to caudal fin. Pelvic fins notably longer in male than in female. Male with small tubercles on rays of second dorsal and pectoral fins; tubercles absent or weak in female (McPhail and Lindsey 1970). Vladykov (1933) noted that the upper caudal rays of the male tend to be more elongated than those of the female.

SYSTEMATIC NOTES

Until recently, the circumpolar form as well as the inland freshwater form were treated as a single species, the fourhorn sculpin *M. quadricornis* (see Bailey et al. 1970). Discriminate function analysis by McAllister et al. (1978) permits separation of the coastal brackish or saltwater form and the inland freshwater form into *M. quadricornis* and *M. thompsoni* respectively.

DISTRIBUTION, STATUS, AND HABITAT

In Wisconsin, the deepwater sculpin occurs in Lakes Michigan and Superior. In the Great Lakes system, the only inland water from which it has been reported is Torch Lake (Antrim County), Michigan (Hubbs and Lagler 1964). The first published record of the occurrence of this species in Lake Michigan was based on a specimen captured 26–32 km (16–20 mi) from Racine, Wisconsin, in 91–110 m of water (Hoy 1872a). In Lake Michigan, it has not been reported from southern Green Bay. Wisconsin records for Lake Superior cluster about the Apostle Islands. Eddy and Underhill (1974) reported it from Minnesota waters of Lake Superior off Grand Marais, Beaver Bay, and Isle Royale.

The deepwater sculpin is found in the Great Lakes and in deep, freshwater lakes of Canada. Scott and Crossman (1973) have discussed the effects of glaciation on its North American distribution (pp. 843–844):

> The deepwater sculpin is usually referred to as a glacial relict in both Europe and North America because, theoretically, it, together with the relict crustaceans *Mysis relicta* and *Pontoporeia affinis*, all originally occupying arctic, marine, or brackish waters, was pushed southward, along with the salt water, in front of the advancing ice sheets.

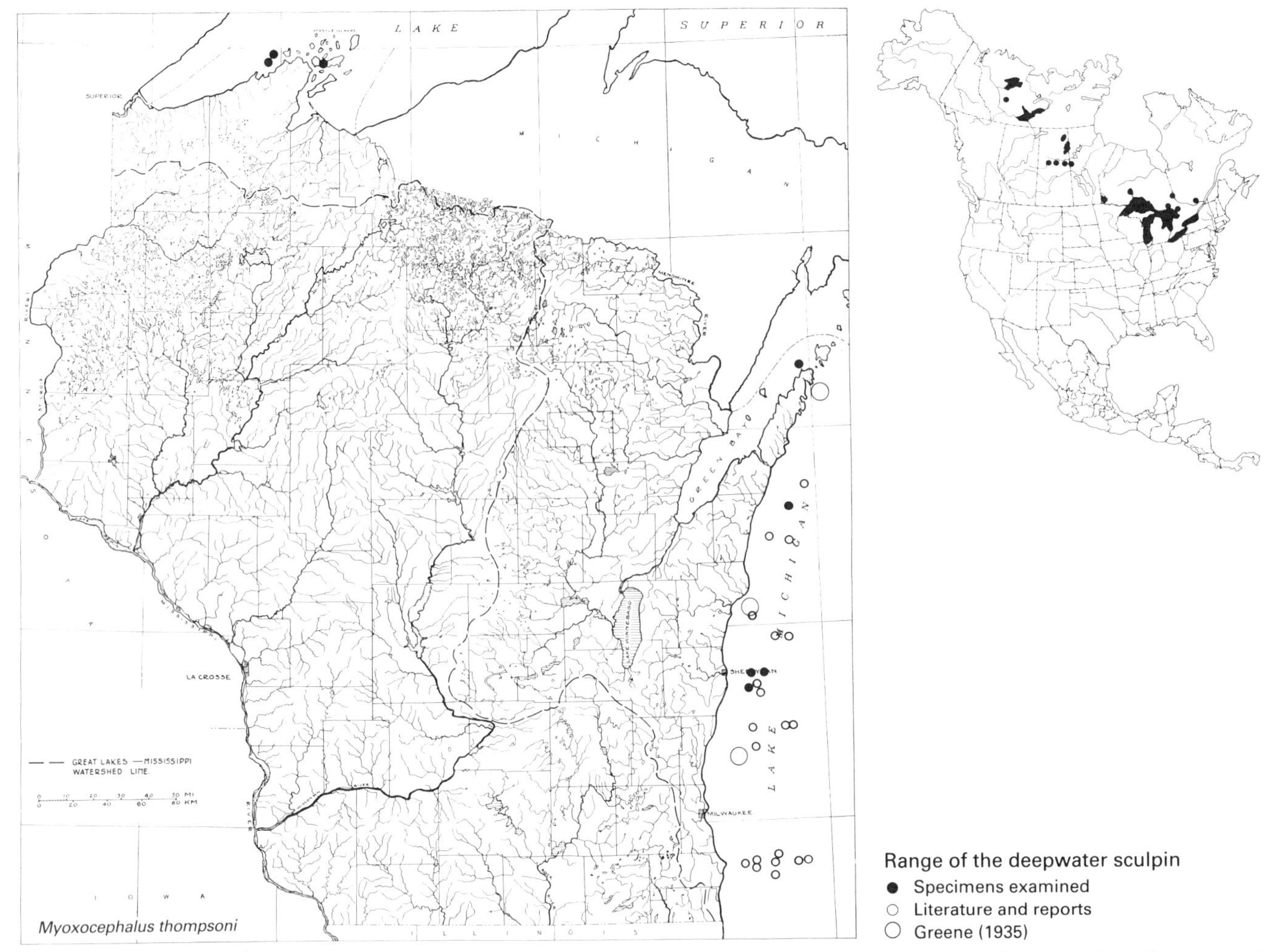

Range of the deepwater sculpin
● Specimens examined
○ Literature and reports
◯ Greene (1935)

Eventually the ice retreated, forming proglacial lakes as it did so, and leaving behind the deepwater sculpin and its ever-present invertebrate associates that form its food supply. Other theories proposed to explain this sculpin's freshwater distribution, which even now must be considered incompletely known, involve the voluntary migrations of marine sculpins into fresh water, and finally, dispersal by invasions of sea water up the St. Lawrence and inland from Hudson Bay.

Champagne et al. (1979) reported a 10,000-year-old fossil from Ottawa, Canada.

The future status of the deepwater sculpin is a matter of concern, especially in the light of what has occurred in Lake Ontario. At one time it was so abundant in Lake Ontario that it was considered to be a nuisance when caught in gill nets set for lake trout. It now appears to have been extirpated, for not a single specimen has been seen in 10 years, and even extensive experimental trawling has failed to capture a specimen (Scott and Crossman 1973). Scott and Crossman ascribed its extirpation to DDT pollution; S. H. Smith (1970) implied that the alewife was primarily responsible.

In Lake Huron, the deepwater sculpin continues to be abundant despite the large numbers of alewives present (Smith 1970). In Lake Michigan, its future is uncertain. Wells and McLain (1972 and 1973) noted that it had declined markedly in abundance in Lake Michigan after 1960, because of a deficiency in recruitment. The increase in reproduction of deepwater sculpins in Lake Michigan since the late 1960s, which has probably been related to the 1967–1968 decline in the number of alewives, may be reversed if the recovery begun by the alewife in 1969–1970 continues.

The common name, deepwater sculpin, is descriptive of its lake habitat. It does not occur in Green Bay at depths of 25–35 m (Deason 1939). In Lake Michigan, its preferred optimum depth range is between 73 and 128 m (Wells 1968). It is taken in the deepest part of the southern basin of Lake Michigan, at depths to 165 m, and at depths at least as great as 256 m in northern Lake Michigan. In Lake Superior, this species appears at depths from 73 m to at least 366 m (Dryer 1966).

BIOLOGY

In Lake Michigan, the deepwater sculpin spawns in deep water in the winter, and the eggs hatch in the spring (Wells and McLain 1973). In Canada, the available evidence indicates that this species spawns in the summer or early fall (Scott and Crossman 1973). Delisle and Van Vliet (1968) suggested that spawning in Heney Lake (Gatineau County), Quebec, occurred during June and July at water temperatures of 6.0–7.2°C (42.8–45°F), at depths of 15–27 m.

A 129-mm, 30.2-g deepwater sculpin, taken in mid-June 1968 from upper Green Bay had ovaries 5.9% of the body weight. These ovaries held fewer than 10 mature, clear orange eggs 1.8–2.1 mm diam, and several hundred immature, opaque eggs 1.0–1.3 mm diam. In Lake Superior, Eddy and Underhill (1974) found females with ripe eggs from late June through July. It is probable that year-round spawning occurs in the Great Lakes. In Great Bear Lake, Northwest Territories, ovaries contained well-developed eggs in late July.

Larval deepwater sculpins are found in the hypolimnion in deep areas of Lake Michigan (Wells 1968). In Lake Huron, young-of-year were taken in 5-minute tows from 20 April to 20 May along the inner basin of South Bay (Faber 1970). The presence of older larvae without yolk-sacs during the sampling period suggests that they either had hatched before the ice break-up within South Bay, or that they had moved into South Bay after hatching in Lake Huron. Other tow net data (unpublished) showed that deepwater sculpin larvae were numerous in certain years immediately outside the entrance into South Bay.

Deason (1939) reported 2 specimens, 102 and 109 mm SL (with calculated total lengths of 123 and 132 mm respectively), from near Two Rivers in Lake Michigan, which he believed were the largest individuals reported from the Great Lakes, but which, by comparison with more recent samples, are small fish. In 1966 and 1968, the average size of 18 individuals from upper Green Bay and off Sheboygan averaged 139 (125–173) mm TL. Wells and McLain (1973) have suggested that fluctuations in size reflect increasing and decreasing reproduction levels. For instance, in eastern Lake Michigan the average weight of deepwater sculpins in the catches climbed from 21 g in 1960 to 24–25 g in 1964 to 1968. The increase in average size from 1960 to 1968 was a result of a decreasing level of reproduction; few small individuals were taken in the catches of 1964–1968. In 1970 and 1971, the average weights of deepwater sculpins in the catch were 11 and 12 g respectively; these collections contained larger numbers of younger, smaller fish.

The largest deepwater sculpin in the UWSP collections is a male taken from Lake Michigan on 28 October 1966. It is 173 mm (6.8 in) TL, and weighs 60.29 g (preserved weight). A 199-mm (7.8-in) fish was taken from Lake Ontario (McPhail and Lindsey 1970).

The deepwater sculpin is strictly predacious, feeding on small crustaceans and the few species of aquatic insects found on the bottoms. The stomachs of 124 specimens from western Lake Superior disclosed that *Mysis* and *Pontoporeia* were eaten almost exclusively, with each equally important in the diet in most months (Anderson and Smith 1971b). Copepods and cladocerans were eaten occasionally. Unidentified insect remains and small numbers of coregonid eggs were taken in April, and plant material was consumed in September.

In southeastern Lake Michigan, the deepwater sculpin was always abundant at depths of 82 and 91 m, but was never abundant at other depths (Wells 1968). It extended its range slightly shoreward in the spring. No specimens were found in water shallower than 82 m on 13 February, but a few were found in water as shallow as 64 m on 11 March and 31 m on 15 April. The shallowest waters in which deepwater sculpins were caught off Saugatuck, Michigan, were 13 m on 26 May and 7 m in August.

Although deepwater sculpins are mostly restricted to water colder than 4.5°C (40°F), factors other than temperature probably exert a strong influence on the depth distribution of the species. In one study, it was found that they did not move into shallow water in numbers even where water temperatures were less than 4.5°C (Wells 1968).

McPhail and Lindsey (1970) have suggested that, at great depths, courtship and other social interactions among fishes must occur with little benefit of vision. Twice deepwater sculpins were kept captive in aquariums for 2 weeks before they died; during this time they were timid and passive, refusing even live food. How this little fish lives, how abundant it is, and what role it plays in the ecosystem of deep northern lakes are literally deep and dark secrets.

IMPORTANCE AND MANAGEMENT

The historical importance of the sculpin species has been their place in the diet of the lake trout. Deason (1939) recorded a total of 1,215 sculpins (species not designated) taken from 65 lake trout and burbot stomachs; as many as 139 specimens were secured from a single stomach. In southern and northern Lake Michigan, 15% of the lake trout stomachs examined which contained food held fourhorn sculpins; 26% of the burbot stomachs held deepwater sculpins (Van Oosten and Deason 1938). In Lake Superior, sculpins, including the deepwater sculpin, and their eggs are a significant part of the diet of lake trout and siscowets (Eddy and Underhill 1974).

A common associate of the deepwater sculpin in Lake Michigan is the alewife. Alewives are concentrated in deep water in winter when the sculpin spawns. Alewives are known to feed on fish eggs, and may well include the eggs of fourhorn sculpins in their diet (Wells and McLain 1973). Alewives may also compete with larval sculpins for plankton food, or prey upon the larvae. Alewives had so decimated the populations of large species of zooplankton in Lake Michigan by the mid-1960s that the actual presence of alewives among deepwater sculpin fry may not have been necessary to exert a negative effect on them.

The deepwater sculpin was taken commercially from Lake Michigan in trawls in the early 1960s for the animal food market, but only small quantities were harvested (Wells and McLain 1973).

To the biologist concerned with fish distribution, the deepwater sculpin presents a number of challenging problems. These include the postglacial dispersal of the species and its zoogeography.

Mottled Sculpin

Cottus bairdi Girard. *Cottus*—the bull's head, an old name of the European sculpin called miller's thumb; *bairdi*—for Spencer F. Baird, first U.S. Fish Commissioner.

Other common names: sculpin, common sculpin, Great Lakes mottled sculpin, northern muddler, muddler, blob, gudgeon, muffle-jaw, bullhead, springfish, lake sculpin, spoonhead, miller's thumb (called miller's thumb because its broad, flat head resembles the flattened thumb of the miller who had the misfortune to have his thumb crushed between millstones).

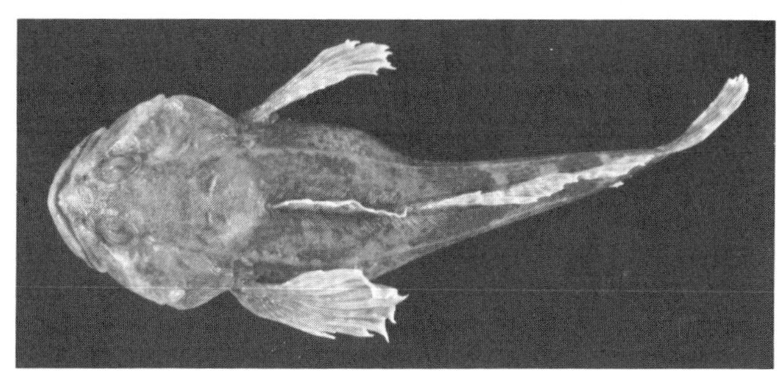

Adult 112 mm, Tomorrow R. (Portage Co.), 21 Mar. 1959. Lateral view above and dorsal view below.

DESCRIPTION

Head and anterior body flattened dorsoventrally; posterior body and caudal peduncle compressed laterally. Length 76–102 mm (3–4 in). TL = 1.23 SL. Depth into TL 4.4–5.6. Head length into TL 3.5–4.5. Snout rounded in lateral view. Mouth terminal, upper lip often protruding slightly beyond lower. Numerous short, blunt teeth in narrow bands on upper and lower jaws; palatine teeth usually present. Gill membranes broadly joined to isthmus. Upper preopercular spine large, directed upward, and curving slightly inward; lower 2 preopercular spines small, directed downward, and covered by skin. Dorsal fins 2, narrowly connected; first dorsal fin with 6–9 soft spines; second dorsal fin usually with 17–19 rays (last ray double; i.e., forked from base). Anal fin rays usually 13–15 (last ray double; i.e., forked from base). Pelvic fin thoracic, of 1 spine and 4 rays but appearing as only 4 elements (the spine and first ray encased in a single fleshy membrane); pectoral rays usually 14–15. Typical scales absent, but small prickles present on sides below lateral line at level of first dorsal fin. Lateral line incomplete, terminating under second dorsal fin. Chromosomes 2n = 48 (W. LeGrande, pers. comm.).

Upper region of head, back, and sides brown to tan, with dark brown to blackish mottling; lower region of head and belly whitish. First dorsal fin with small black spot anteriorly, and a larger black spot posteriorly; all fins speckled randomly, or banded; pelvic fin least pigmented.

Breeding male with a dark basal band on first dorsal fin, and a broad orange band on edge of fin; overall body color dark. Female lightly mottled.

Sexual dimorphism: In male a thin, elongated (like tip of leaf) genital papilla; in female genital papilla rudimentary or absent (Ludwig and Norden 1969). Male averages larger than females. Female with distended abdomen from approximately 2 months before spawning.

SYSTEMATIC NOTES

In the Great Lakes region, two subspecies have been recognized (Hubbs and Lagler 1964): the northern mottled sculpin, *Cottus bairdi bairdi* Girard, and the Great Lakes mottled sculpin *Cottus bairdi kumlieni* (Hoy). The northern mottled sculpin has distance between tip of snout and anus when measured backward from anus extending to a point nearer base than end of caudal fin; in the Greal Lakes mottled sculpin this distance extends to a point nearer end of the caudal fin. In the latter, the body is generally more slender and the dark bars are less distinctly developed. Greene (1935) recognized the Great Lakes mottled sculpin from the shores of Lake Michigan near Milwaukee and Port Washington, and near Bayfield on Lake Superior; however, he also reported records of the northern mottled sculpin in those vicinities. More work is needed to give such subspecific separation validity.

DISTRIBUTION, STATUS, AND HABITAT

In Wisconsin, the mottled sculpin occurs in the Mississippi River, Lake Michigan, and Lake Superior drainage basins. It is distributed in headwater streams and large lakes. Typically a stream species, it nevertheless avoids large sectors of the driftless area. This species inhabits the shoal waters of Lakes Michigan

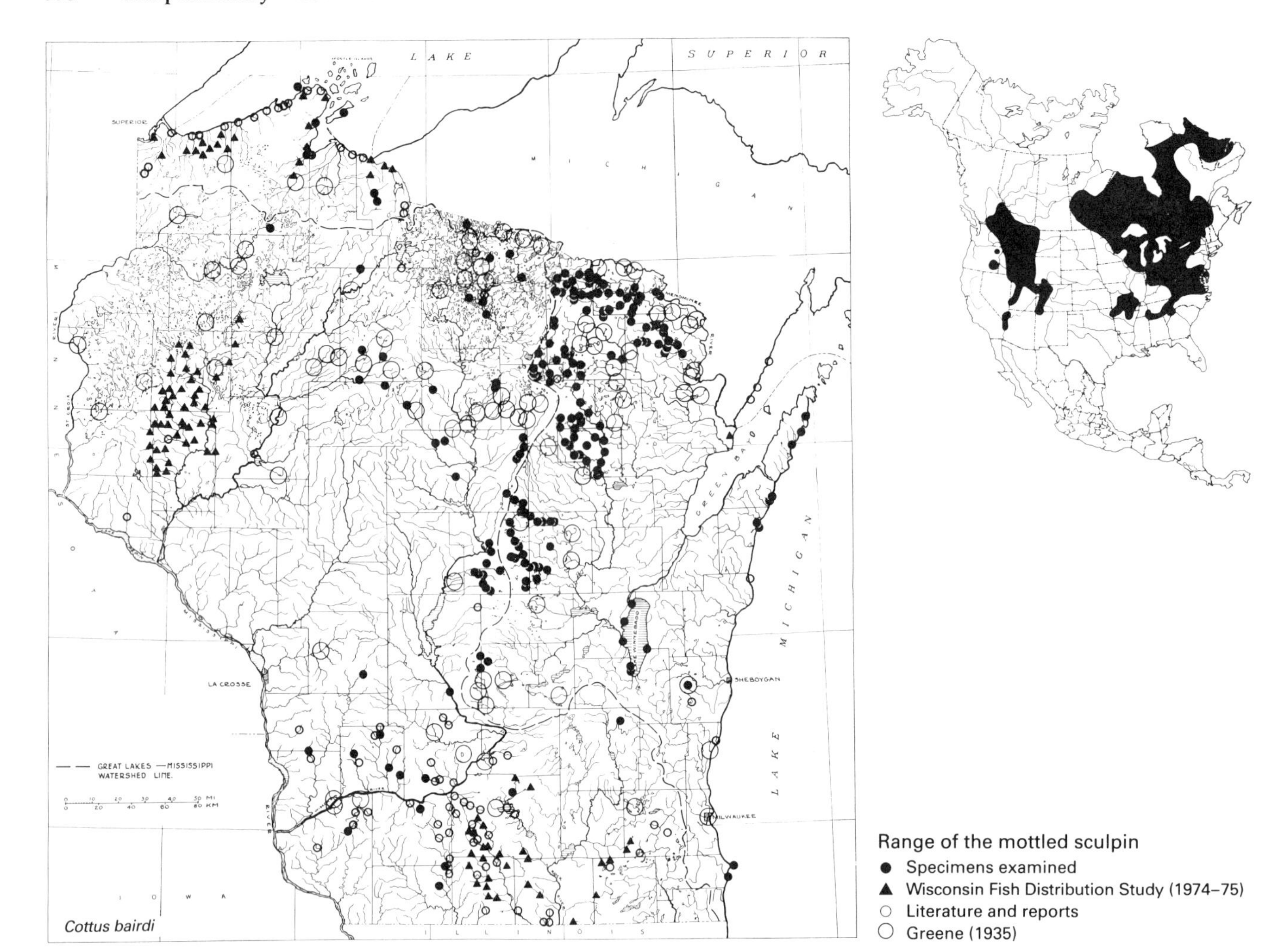

and Superior. Greene (1935) found it in 2.4% of the total river collections, 19.2% of the collections from smaller streams, and 4.9% of the lake collections.

The mottled sculpin is common in cold headwater streams throughout the state, where it is frequently the most common fish in the sample. It is common at barriers in the mouths of tributaries to Lake Superior (McLain et al. 1965). In Lake Winnebago, it is common along the shoreline (Priegel 1967b). It is rare along the shoals of southern Lake Michigan, but becomes more common northward.

In Wisconsin the mottled sculpin was encountered most frequently in clear or slightly turbid water at depths of 0.1–0.5 m, over substrates of sand (23% frequency), gravel (22%), silt (16%), rubble (12%), mud (12%), boulders (8%), detritus (4%), bedrock (1%), and clay (1%). It occurred in streams of the following widths: 1.0–3.0 m (41%), 3.1–6.0 m (20%), 6.1–12.0 m (16%), 12.1–24.0 m (17%), and 24.1–50.0 m (8%). It is found in pools and in medium to fast riffles in the vicinity of cover, which may be in the form of vegetation or of bottom materials such as gravel and rubble. The distribution of the mottled sculpin is more dependent on available shelter than on bottom type.

BIOLOGY

In Wisconsin, the mottled sculpin spawns in April and May. Ludwig and Norden (1969) observed spawning in Mt. Vernon Creek (Dane County), and unless otherwise designated the following account is derived from that source.

In Mt. Vernon Creek, spawning occurred from 1 April to 3 May at water temperatures of 8.9–13.9°C (48–57°F). The mottled sculpin nests consisted of cavities beneath flat rocks at depths of 22 cm, in areas of sufficient current to prevent silting. Other nests were observed in crevices among large gravel (5–8 cm diam), on Elodea, and in tunnels within loam material. The tunnels had openings of about 4 cm diam, and were more than 15 cm deep. One of the deepest tunnels contained the largest egg cluster (2,874 eggs), but it was not determined whether these holes were made by the sculpins. Entrances to the nests usually faced the middle of the stream or upstream. The bottoms of the nests were usually composed of small gravel, although rock, sand, silt, and mixtures of these were sometimes present.

Each nest was occupied by a single, mature male mottled sculpin in nuptial coloration. Ludwig and Norden occasionally observed gravid and spent females and immature sculpins in the nest with the adult male, but in no nest was more than one mature male found. The mature males were in their nests from the onset of spawning until the fry left at the end of May. Females remained in the nests only during spawning.

Each nest was guarded by the attending male. Koster (1936) reported a behavioral pattern resembling the movements of the barking dog, which he called "barking"—a characteristic warning to all other mottled sculpins from the nesting male. Koster observed an encounter in which a resident male bit an intruding male, who returned the bite.

Courtship commences when the male mottled sculpin first sights a female. Savage (1963) noted a ritualistic display of the head by the male, which consisted of one or more of the following elements: shaking, nodding, or gill-cover elevation. Undulations of the body also occurred, either alone or accompanying the head display. Shaking is a movement of the head in the horizontal plane, and nodding is a movement in the vertical plane. The rate of movement of the head was too rapid for accurate recording. Gill-cover elevation is a forward movement of the gill covers, which results in the visual enlargement of the head when viewed from the front. The movements which appeared most frequently were head shaking and gill-cover elevation.

In a laboratory study, the actual contact of the male with the female outside the nest was also observed by Savage (1963:320):

> Biting by the male was observed on 10 occasions and was of two types: (1) biting of the female's cheek, side, pectoral fin, or tail and (2) taking of the female's head into the mouth. A female was never observed to bite during encounters.

A ripe female always entered the nest when bitten on the head or pectoral fin. In each instance, the female turned upside down while inside the nesting cavity. Savage recorded the mottled sculpin's courtship and spawning behavior (p. 321):

> . . . Male A, positioned at the entrance [of the nest], shook and nodded vigorously and bit at the female, who turned away at first but soon turned back toward the shelter. Then the male took the female's head into his mouth, shook her, released and bit at the female's cheek twice. Each bite was followed by shaking. The male continued to shake and undulate as the female moved past him and into the shelter, turned upside down and remained there. The male turned partly upside down and his venter came into contact with the female's dorsum. His head and all his fins, except his pelvics, became jet black and his body became very pale. The male soon righted himself and placed himself across the entrance. The female remained in the nest for several days and was often seen in the upside-down position. Frequently the male also was seen to be upside down, pressed against the female.

Savage (1963) noted that, when the region of the urogenital pore became swollen, it was only a matter of a few hours before the female spawned. If she was isolated and unable to spawn with a male, the eggs were usually released; less often, the female became eggbound and died.

At spawning the gonadal products are released against the roof of the nesting cavity while both adults are in inverted positions. The majority of the eggs of the mottled sculpin were laid in an initial burst, followed by the apparent slow release of more eggs. Within several minutes after their release, the eggs had firmly adhered to the roof of the nest and had hardened; this was indicated by the fact that the activities of the two fish no longer moved the egg mass along the surface of the roof. The female had left the nest by the next morning.

The eggs were attached to the roof of the nest in clusters, which formed a fairly round, flattened mass that had 6–10 layers of eggs in the center. A mass contained an average of 1,205 eggs. Clusters were distinguishable from one another by color variations, which indicated that more than one female had spawned in each nest. There was an average of 3.3 color clusters per egg mass in 18 nests observed (Ludwig and Norden 1969).

According to Savage, the fanning of the eggs has been incorporated into the behavior of the male mottled sculpin during encounters with females, and does not appear to be necessary for the proper development of the eggs.

Eggs in preserved mottled sculpin females from Mt. Vernon Creek averaged 1.88 (1.50–2.06) mm diam. They were uniform in size and light orange-yellow in color. The average number of eggs in 39 females, 41–71 mm SL, was 328 (111–635).

In Mt. Vernon Creek, mottled sculpin prolarvae began to appear in the nests on 17 May. In the laboratory, eggs at 11.1–12.8°C (52–55°F) developed eye spots in 9 days, and hatched in 17 days. Larvae were 5.9 mm TL at hatching. At 14 days, when they had lost their yolk-sacs and were 6.7 mm long, they left the nest. In Erickson and Little John lakes (Vilas County), larval mottled sculpins were sporadically collected during May and June. Tow net data suggested that larval mottled sculpins located in open water areas for a short time (Faber 1967). Fish (1932) illustrated and described the 6.0-, 6.6-, 7.2-, 10-, and 11-mm stages.

In Mt. Vernon Creek 6.5 months after hatching, male mottled sculpins averaged 37.5 mm SL, and females, 33.8 mm SL (Ludwig and Norden 1969). In central Wisconsin, young-of-year from Lyndon Creek were 24–28 mm TL on 26 June; in northern Wisconsin, young from the Pine River (Florence County) were 18–25 mm on 22–23 July. In Lake Winnebago (Winnebago County), the young were 31–40 mm on 18 August, and in Lake Michigan shallows (Door County), they were 27–42 mm on 19 September.

By examining the otoliths of mottled sculpins, Ludwig and Norden (1969) determined that, in collections made from Mt. Vernon Creek in May, age-I males averaged 37.5 mm SL, and females, 32.7 mm SL; age-II males, 59.2 mm, and females, 53.1 mm; and age-III males, 74.5 mm, and females, 67.9 mm. In the Wisconsin collections, only one fish of age-IV was found—a female which contained 949 eggs (Ludwig and Lange 1975).

In the lower Jordan River, Michigan, the calculated total lengths of mottled sculpins at annuli 1 through 4 were 39.5 mm, 71.4 mm, 89.9 mm, and 87.8 mm; in the Ausable River, these lengths were 48.3 mm, 82.8 mm, 102.9 mm, and 102.3 mm (Quick 1971).

Sexual maturity is reached by some mottled sculpins at age II. Bailey (1952) noted that all females over 74 mm (2.9 in) TL were sexually mature. The largest male, collected from an irrigation canal which originated in the West Gallatin River, Montana, was 140 mm (5.4 in) TL. A large Wisconsin mottled sculpin (UWSP 586) is a female, 137 mm (5.4 in) TL, taken from Elton Creek (Langlade County) on 20 July 1966.

In the Madison area, mottled sculpins fed mainly on amphipods, mayfly nymphs, and chironomid larvae, and to a lesser extent on caddisfly larvae, ostracods, copepods, cladocerans, oligochaetes, leeches, plant remains, and algae (Pearse 1918). Mottled sculpins from the Lt. Plover River (Portage County) had eaten *Gammarus* sp., Diptera, and Trichoptera larvae; one stomach contained seeds (P. Brogan, pers. comm.). In the stomachs of mottled sculpins from southeastern Wisconsin, Cahn (1927) found stonefly larvae, small dragonfly and mayfly nymphs, chironomid and *Simulium* larvae, and rarely a small mollusk. A mottled sculpin from the Pine River (Florence County), 104 mm TL, contained a 51-mm central mudminnow.

Mottled sculpins from the West Gallatin River, Montana, had ingested mollusks (*Physa* and *Pisidium*), insects (Ephemeroptera nymphs, Plecoptera nymphs, Coleoptera larvae and adults, Hemiptera, Trichoptera larvae and pupae, Diptera larvae and pupae), Hydrachnidae, fish (longnose dace, mottled sculpins), and the eggs of mottled sculpins.

A few cases have been reported of mottled sculpins eating the eggs of trout, but evidence indicates that these eggs were improperly covered with gravel by the spawning trout. Most studies indicated that the mottled sculpin feeds on invertebrates that are found between and underneath rocks, where they are not available to most other fish (Moyle 1969). Mottled sculpins are more or less continuous feeders.

In southern Ontario, mottled sculpins were taken at average water temperatures of 16.6°C (62°F) when air temperatures averaged 22.9°C (73°F) (Hallam 1959). In Lake Monona (Dane County), Neill (1971) noted that this species tended to avoid the thermal plume of the Lake Monona steam generation plant. The unheated littoral zones, where this species occurred, rarely exceeded 29°C (84°F). In Lake Huron, the behavior of mottled sculpins was affected by a drop in water temperatures from 20 to 7°C (68 to 45°F) within a few seconds; the drop was caused by a sudden underwater seiche (Emery 1970). The mottled sculpins ceased feeding, and, in the cold water, often swam erratically. A number died as a result of thermal stress. In Iowa streams, M. Johnson (1971–1972) found the mottled sculpin in waters averaging 20°C (16–22°C).

The large pectoral fins of the mottled sculpin are used in darter fashion to support the body against the current, with the head upstream. The movements of the mottled sculpin are also darterlike in their rapidity; they often resemble hopping. The mottled sculpin hides under rocks during the major part of the day; large growths of vegetation provide secondary hiding places. Bailey (1952) noted that some small mottled sculpins hide in the quiet water near shore by stirring up clouds of silt which settle and cover them.

During the nonbreeding season, spatial isolation and aggressive behavior were not observed in mottled sculpins in a laboratory experiment. McCleave (1964) captured as many as six sculpins at one time in a 0.093-m^2 (1-ft^2) area, and fish often were seen touching one another. In Lake Huron, mottled sculpins occasionally reached densities of 2–5 per m^2 during the daytime, when feeding activity was rare (Emery 1973). Emery found that at night this species was more active than during the daytime, and was found more often in open, sandy areas. Feeding activity peaked at dusk, but continued after full darkness. Night coloration was similar to daytime coloration, but was somewhat paler.

In Trout Creek, Montana, where it was the most abundant species in the stream, the home range of the mottled sculpin was estimated at less than 50 m (McCleave 1964). The estimated population of sculpins was about 1.7–2.0/m^2. Homing was not exhibited in tagging experiments. About one-third of the displaced sculpins homed, one-third did not move, and one-third moved away from home. The longest upstream movement noted was 180 m, and the longest downstream movement was 153 m.

In a tributary of southern Lake Superior, mottled sculpins moved downstream chiefly in winter and during floods (Manion 1977). Headrick (1976) presented evidence that the mottled sculpin avoided newly ditched areas in central Wisconsin streams, although some fish did invade such areas eventually, probably when vegetative cover had become established.

In Mt. Vernon Creek (Dane County), associates of the mottled sculpin were the white sucker, brown trout, rainbow trout, brook trout, brook stickleback, redside dace, and the American brook lamprey; the last was common only during its short spring spawning run (Ludwig and Norden 1969). In a central Wisconsin tributary to the Waupaca River, I captured 122 mottled sculpins with the white sucker (95), largescale stoneroller (1), blacknose dace (10), creek chub (46), pearl dace (19), northern redbelly dace (1), golden shiner (3), bluntnose minnow (1), fathead minnow (4), common shiner (160), central mudminnow (17), johnny darter (4), pumpkinseed (3), and brook stickleback (134).

IMPORTANCE AND MANAGEMENT

The mottled sculpin has often been called a trout indicator, and it is a fact that, where good sculpin populations exist, the water generally holds trout populations as well. Small populations of mottled sculpins may inhabit the lower reaches of streams which no longer support trout, or, as in Lake Winnebago, lakes which support a warmwater fishery.

Mottled sculpins are known to form a part of the diet of large brook and brown trout. Adams and Hankinson (1926) reported that the mottled sculpin is eaten by American mergansers and northern pike. In a selection test in which equal numbers of mottled sculpins, creek chub, and brook trout of approximately the same size were presented to four mergansers, the ducks consumed about equal numbers of creek chubs and brook trout, but fewer mottled sculpins (Latta and Sharkey 1966). Deason (1939) reported finding six mottled sculpins in the stomachs of water snakes (*Natrix sipedon*).

From time to time, both the mottled sculpin and the slimy sculpin have been regarded as serious predators on trout eggs. Moyle (1977), in reviewing the problem of sculpin predation on salmonids, concluded that the limited evidence indicated that only under exceptional artificial conditions can sculpins severely limit salmonid populations through either predation or competition. In fact, sculpins are commonly an important prey of lake-dwelling salmonids, and occasionally of salmonids in streams. In one study, the sculpin was thought to serve as a buffer prey species for brook trout, by reducing brook trout predation on their own young. It is also possible that sculpin predation on predacious stoneflies may increase the supply of drifting herbivorous insects for trout, and perhaps reduce stonefly predation on trout eggs and young.

The mottled sculpin is host to the glochidial stages of the mollusks *Alasmidonta calceola* and *Anodontoides ferussicianus* (Hart and Fuller 1974), and so ensures the continued success of these clam species.

The mottled sculpin is caught incidentally by trout fishermen who use worms or nightcrawlers as bait. Some trout fishermen use the mottled sculpin as bait, particularly for large brown trout.

Slimy Sculpin

Cottus cognatus Richardson. *Cottus*—the bull's head, an old name of the European sculpin called miller's thumb; *cognatus*—related (to the European species *Cottus gobio*).

Other common names: slimy muddler, common slimy muddler, northern sculpin, sculpin, stargazer, Bear Lake bullhead, cockatouch, cottus, big fin, northern miller's thumb (called miller's thumb because its broad, flat head resembles the flattened thumb of the miller who had the misfortune to have his thumb crushed between millstones).

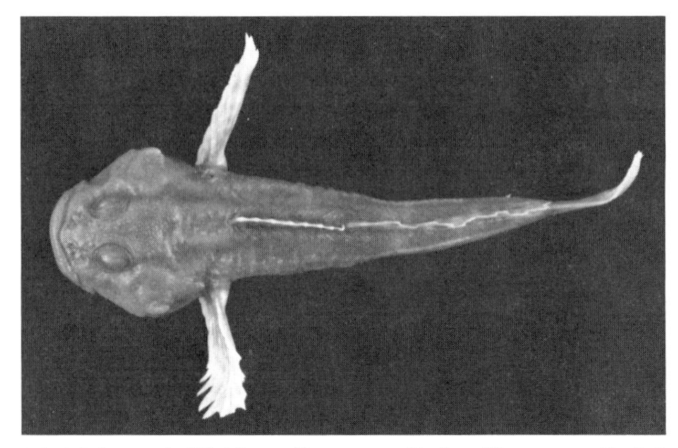

Adult 80 mm, L. Michigan, Kewaunee Harbor (Kewaunee Co.), 7 Apr. 1962. Lateral view above and dorsal view below.

DESCRIPTION

Head and anterior body flattened dorsoventrally; posterior body and caudal peduncle compressed laterally. Average length 76 mm (3 in). TL = 1.24 SL (in Citron Creek, Crawford County); TL = 1.19 SL (in Lake Michigan) (Foltz 1976). Depth into TL 5.0–5.9. Head length into TL 3.6–4.5. Snout rounded in lateral view. Mouth terminal, upper lip often protruding slightly beyond lower. Numerous teeth in narrow bands on upper and lower jaws; palatine teeth usually absent. Two midline mandibular pores. Gill membranes broadly joined to isthmus. Upper preopercular spine large, directed upward, and curving slightly inward; lower 2 preopercular spines small, directed downward, and covered by skin. Dorsal fins 2, narrowly connected; first dorsal fin with 7–9 soft spines; second dorsal fin usually with 16–18 rays (last ray usually single). Anal fin rays usually 11–13 (last ray usually single). Pelvic fins thoracic, with 1 spine and 3 pelvic rays but appearing as only 3 elements (the spine and first ray encased in a single fleshy membrane); pectoral rays usually 13–14. Typical scales absent, but small patch of prickles present on sides below lateral line at level of first dorsal fin. Lateral line incomplete, terminating under second dorsal fin. Chromosomes 2n = 48 (W. LeGrande, pers. comm.).

Upper region of head, back, and sides dark olive to dark brown, with dark mottling; often with 2 dark, oblique saddle marks under anterior and posterior parts of the second dorsal fin (especially evident in young); lower region of head and belly lighter to whitish. First dorsal fin darkly pigmented at base, with almost clear edge; remaining fins variously speckled, or banded as in the pectorals.

Breeding male dark overall, with a broad, reddish-orange edge on spinous dorsal fin; breeding female lighter overall, with distended abdomen.

Sexual dimorphism: Mature male with a subtriangular genital papilla, not present in female.

DISTRIBUTION, STATUS, AND HABITAT

In Wisconsin the slimy sculpin occurs in the Mississippi River, Lake Michigan, and Lake Superior drainage basins. In recent years this species has been discovered in isolated relict populations in the Mississippi drainage in and near the driftless area. These populations, except for a few in Iowa and Minnesota tributaries to the Mississippi, appear to be widely removed from the rest of the species' range in the Great Lakes drainage and throughout Canada.

In 1964, slimy sculpins were collected from Citron Creek (Crawford County) by M. Johnson and were sent to the University of Michigan Museum of Zoology for verification (Becker 1966). During July and August 1969, M. Johnson collected this species from 11 sites in southwestern Wisconsin—at 4 locales in the upper Coon Creek system (Vernon and Monroe counties); 1 locale on Rush Creek (Crawford County), a tributary to the Mississippi River; 4 tributaries to the Kickapoo River (Crawford, Vernon, and Richland counties); and 2 locales in the Green River system (Grant County). In 1975, this species was taken with the mottled sculpin in Rock Creek (Barron

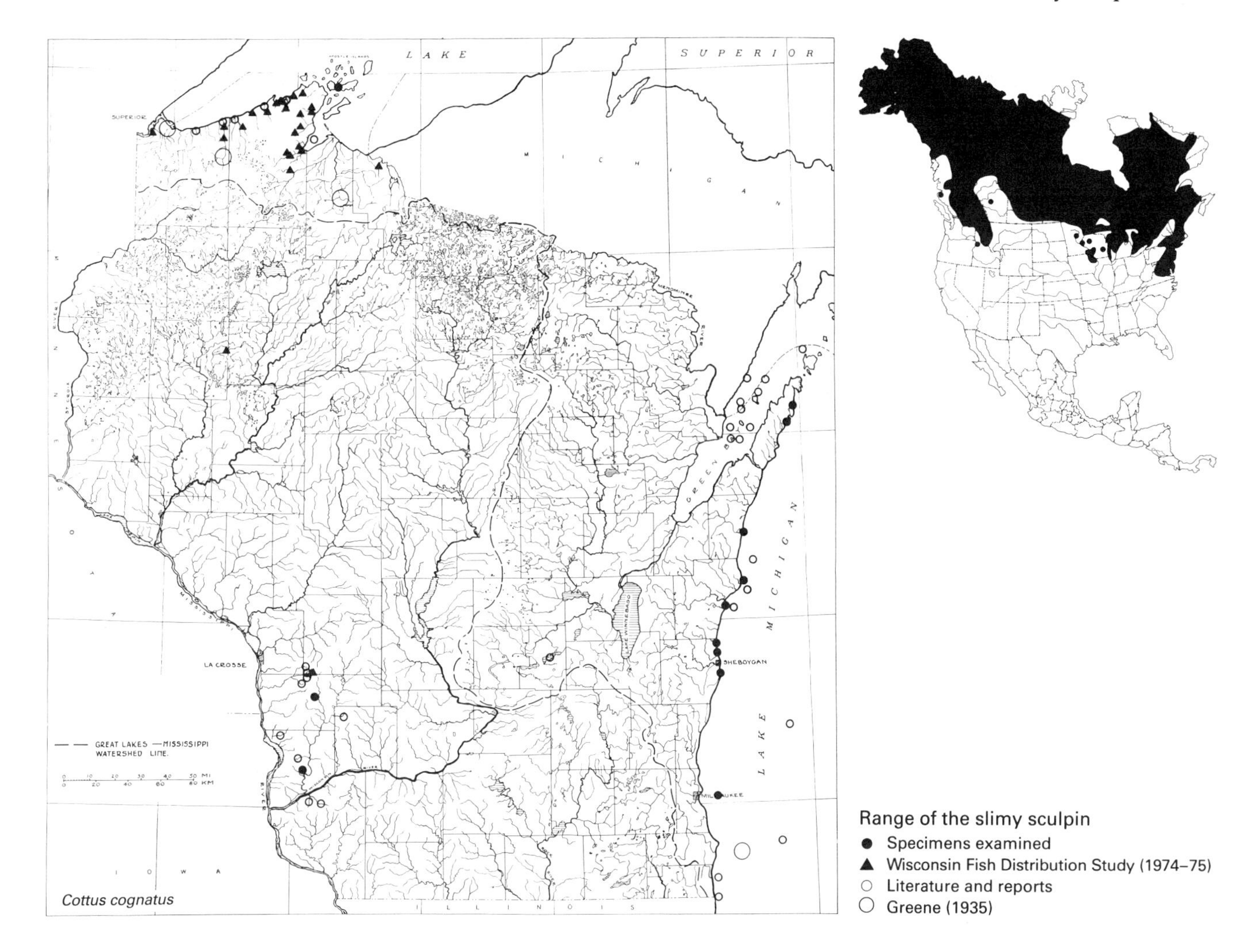

County) by the Wisconsin Fish Distribution Study (1974–1975). R. M. Bailey (1956) postulated that the slimy sculpin and the lake chub (*Couesius plumbeus*) are glacial relicts that survived in the driftless area during the Wisconsin glaciation.

In the Lake Michigan system, the slimy sculpin occurs in Lake Michigan and in Green Bay. In 1957, it was collected from Big Green Lake (Green Lake County) (V. Hacker, pers. comm.). Its presence in this deep lake suggests that other deep, inland lakes in Wisconsin may have populations of slimy sculpins. In addition to its occurrence in Lake Superior, it is found in numerous tributaries to the lake.

The slimy sculpin is uncommon to common in tributaries to Lake Superior. It is uncommon in streams of southwestern Wisconsin, where it is generally confined to springs and to short, spring-fed runs of only a few meters to several hundred meters in length. Such areas are vulnerable to any number of man-induced changes, including siltation. This species is not known in tributaries to Lake Michigan, but it does occur in the lake itself. In eastern Lake Michigan off Grand Haven, Michigan, slimy sculpins were almost four times as abundant in 1970 as in 1960. A large population of slimy sculpins was observed off Saugatuck, Michigan, in 1970 (Wells and McLain 1973).

Typical habitats of the slimy sculpin are deep, oligotrophic lakes, or swift, rocky-bottomed streams. Coldwater temperatures are obviously preferred, and the species is commonly found in association with trout or salmon. In streams it appears over substrates of rubble, boulders, silt, gravel, bedrock, and sand, where these are associated with dense growths of aquatic plants in moderate to fast currents.

In streams of southwestern Wisconsin, the slimy sculpin occurs in small springs and in headwater pools and riffles. It is found where the stream is 0.5–3.0 m wide and averages 13 cm deep, over substrates of sand, gravel, and rubble associated with abundant *Nasturtium* sp., *Ranunculus* sp., and filamentous algae (M. Johnson, pers. comm.).

BIOLOGY

Spawning by slimy sculpins in Wisconsin inland streams is probably similar to that of the same species in Valley Creek, a small Minnesota tributary to the St. Croix boundary water (Petrosky and Waters 1975). There spawning occurred in late April; the larger females appeared to have spawned first.

The spawning behavior of both slimy sculpins and mottled sculpins in streams is basically the same. Koster (Breder and Rosen 1966:548) made the following general observations:

> . . . The nest consists of a cavity usually beneath some flat object. It is constructed by the male who carries the larger objects out in the mouth and washes the lighter materials out by means of fanning and wriggling motions. The males sometimes fight over nests. The fight commences with a characteristic 'barking' action of the defending male and ends with the loss of the nuptial color by the conquered fish. The 'barking' actions are best likened to the barking of a dog. The courtship commences when the male first sights a female. The male flanks and drives the female into the nest after a few seconds or more of 'barking.' The eggs are deposited on the ceiling of the nest. Both sexes lie on their backs, the female often being pressed between the belly of the male and the nest cover. The female leaves after spawning. The males stay with the nest. Females mate but once a season. About a month after deposition the eggs hatch and the fry fall to the bottom of the nest. The yolk sac is absorbed in three to six days depending upon the water temperature, and the young begin to leave the nest. Males of *Cottus bairdii bairdii* and *Cottus cognatus* have been found guarding nests containing young that had already begun to feed.

The spawning behavior of lake populations of slimy sculpins is unknown, and may be different from that of stream populations. In southern Lake Michigan the slimy sculpin began to spawn some time before 5 May, at which time 66.4% of the sculpins were spent (Rottiers 1965). By 23 May, all but one eggbound female were spent. Fish in a deepwater sample (82 m), however, were totally unspent as late as 26 May. Collections of ripe females from Lake Michigan suggested that most spawning occurred at depths of 31–82 m. The bottom types where collections were made ranged from fine sand to mud. During the 1964 season, spawning peaked at 31 m early in the season, and at 46 m somewhat later in the season. The bulk of the specimens were captured in bottom water with a temperature of 6°C (42.8°F) or less.

According to Rottiers, in Lake Michigan the slimy sculpin is a bottom dweller and probably deposits its eggs in clumps on the bottom. In areas inhabited by the slimy sculpin, trawl tows indicate that the bottom is flat and quite free of debris, providing practically no material for nests and egg attachments.

The egg counts for 143 slimy sculpins from Lake Michigan (50–105 mm TL) averaged 291 (98–660). The eggs of 55 fish averaged 1.81 (1.41–2.07) mm diam (Rottiers 1965). Off Two Rivers (Kewaunee County), the number of eggs averaged 270 (84–653) per female (Foltz 1976). In Valley Creek, Minnesota, the egg counts for 34 females ranged from 59 eggs in an age-I fish which was 43 mm long to 645 eggs in an age-V fish which was 111-mm long (Petrosky and Waters 1975). The number of eggs produced increases with the size of the female.

Fish (1932) illustrated the 18-mm stage and described the 18- and 21.5-mm stages. Wells (1968) noted that, in Lake Michigan, larval slimy sculpins are found at midlevels, mostly in the hypolimnion. Little else is known about the young-of-year of this species, except that some apparently appear on the bottom in the fall. On 4 November, catches at 46 m and 55 m contained 72 and 5 individuals, respectively, which were between 25 and 38 mm long.

The calculated lengths at the annuli for slimy sculpins in the upper Jordan River, Michigan, were: 1—33.2 mm; 2—58.0 mm; 3—76.9 mm; and 4—91.9 mm; in the lower Jordan River, the calculated lengths were: 1—45.1 mm; 2—70.3 mm; 3—90.0 mm; and 4—105.0 mm (Quick 1971). The average lengths of slimy sculpins of ages I–VII from southern Lake Michigan were: I—39.4 mm; II—49.1 mm; III—71.8 mm; IV—83.4 mm; V—92.6 mm; VI—98.3 mm; and VII—108.0 mm (Rottiers 1965). The largest range in length within age groups was 45–89 mm in age-group III, and 65–109 mm in age-group IV.

The length-weight relationship (sexes combined) was determined from the postspawning specimens by the equation $\text{Log } W = -4.336 + 2.6354 \text{ Log } L$, where W is weight in grams and L is total length in millimeters. The annuluslike rings used in aging the otoliths are deposited between March and August in Lake Michigan slimy sculpins.

In southern Lake Michigan the average life expectancy of slimy sculpins is between 4 and 6 years. One specimen in a sample of 466 fish had reached 7 years.

In Lake Michigan, all slimy sculpins shorter than 55 mm (2.2 in) were immature, whereas all fish longer than 70 mm (2.8 in) were mature. No age-I sculpins were mature; 13.2% had reached maturity by age II, and 89% at age III; all slimy sculpins were mature by age IV (Rottiers 1965). In Valley Creek, Minnesota, one female was mature at age I, and most slimy sculpins of both sexes were mature at age II (Petrosky and Waters 1975).

In Valley Creek, an age-V female had reached a length of 111 mm (4.4 in). In Canada, the slimy sculpin has been reported to reach 120 mm (4.7 in) (McPhail and Lindsey 1970).

The food of slimy sculpins inhabiting Valley Creek was similar in most respects to that of the brook trout in the same stream. The most important food group was *Gammarus*, followed by Diptera larvae, Trichoptera larvae, and snails. Feeding on *Gammarus*, Trichoptera larvae, and snails increased with the age of the fish, whereas feeding on Diptera larvae decreased with age (Petrosky and Waters 1975). The slimy sculpin feeds by foraging on the bottom, while the brook trout feeds mostly on drift. The stomachs of slimy sculpins from the Duluth and Apostle Islands sectors of Lake Superior contained mostly crustaceans (mainly amphipods), followed in importance by chironomid larvae and other insects, coregonid and sculpin eggs, mollusks, plant material, oligochaetes, Hirudinea, and unidentifiable material (Anderson and Smith 1971b).

In the laboratory, slimy sculpins from southeastern Lake Michigan acclimated at water temperatures of 5° and 15°C (41° and 59°F) had preferred temperatures of 9° and 12°C (48° and 54°F), respectively, and an optimum temperature of about 10°C (50°F) (Otto and Rice 1977). Incipient upper lethal temperatures ranged from 18.5 to 23.5°C (65.3 to 74.3°F); the ultimate upper lethal temperature (at which 50% of the fish died) was about 26.5°C (79.7°F).

M. Johnson (1970) compared the slimy sculpin and the mottled sculpin from Wisconsin streams to determine how quickly heat narcosis (end point upon cessation of respiratory movements) would be reached at 30°C (86°F). Fish were taken directly from their natural habitats and tested immediately. Reaction times were significantly different for the two species: the slimy sculpin succumbed in 49.3 seconds, and the mottled sculpin in 60 seconds. Using a derived theoretical maximum temperature for instantaneous narcosis, the prediction was made that, with regard to temperature tolerance, the egg and larval stages were critical in the survival of both species. At these stages, the slimy sculpin would be restricted to waters of less than 10°C (50°F), while the mottled sculpin would tolerate temperatures up to 20°C (68°F.)

The summer field temperatures of slimy sculpin waters in Iowa average 14°C (57°F) [11–17°C (52–63°F)] (M. Johnson 1971–1972). Unpublished data collected from southwestern Wisconsin waters indicated an average summer water temperature of 13.8°C (56.8°F). Johnson postulated that, although winter water temperatures in the upper Midwest would allow movement of this species from one stream to another, the temperature requirements of the egg and larval stages would prohibit the establishment of the species in many streams. Johnson also suggested that the slimy sculpin may require a year-round water temperature which is fairly constant, since it is consistently found near springs; such water is of a nearly constant physical and chemical condition. Wells (1968) noted that, in southern Lake Michigan, the slimy sculpin seldom occurs in waters above 10°C (50°F), and most often is found in waters of 4–6°C (39–43°F), except during fall overturns when it is taken in waters up to 13°C (55.4°F).

In Lake Opeongo, Ontario, slimy sculpins at night were seen in water 3–5 m deep, resting on the sand with parts of their pectoral and pelvic fins covered with bottom materials (Emery 1973). During the daytime, they were observed at depths of 30–35 m; light levels at this depth approached full darkness. When disturbed, the sculpins moved in a quick circle and then dived straight down, burying themselves in the loose substrate.

In southern Lake Michigan, the depth distribution of slimy sculpins ranges from shore to 91 m, but it may occur at depths as great as 130 m (Rottiers 1965, Wells 1968, Foltz 1976). After thermal stratification, the range decreases somewhat, and the sculpins become more numerous between 46 and 64 m. Wells (1968) noted that in southern Lake Michigan they are distributed over a wide depth range in the winter, that they abandon shallow areas in the spring as soon as the waters warm significantly, and that they continue a gradual movement away from shore through the summer and fall. On 13 February, the greatest numbers of slimy sculpins were found at 18–64 m; after 15 March, and to the end of the year, they were found at all depths greater than 31 m.

In the Apostle Islands region of Lake Superior, slimy sculpins were concentrated in deeper water than in southeastern Lake Michigan (Dryer 1966). They were most common at depths greater than 73 m, and probably the greatest numbers were at 91–108 m. No evidence of seasonal changes in distribution could be detected.

In southwestern Wisconsin, M. Johnson (pers. comm.) captured 201 slimy sculpins at 11 collection sites. It was the only species collected at two of the sites, and it appeared with brown trout fingerlings at three sites, although Johnson noted that other sites also contained trout which were too elusive to catch in a seine. The number of individuals associated with the slimy sculpin at these sites were (number of collection sites given in parentheses): 38 longnose dace

(4), 29 blacknose dace (4), 15 creek chubs (4), 14 brook sticklebacks (3), 9 stonerollers (sp.?) (3), 17 fantail darters (2), 3 white suckers (2), and 1 johnny darter (1). Although the slimy sculpin and the mottled sculpin were not taken together in that collection series, equal numbers of the two species appeared in a Rock Creek (Barron County) collection (Wis. Fish Distrib. Study 1974–1975). In Valley Creek, Minnesota, the only species occurring in the study area besides the slimy sculpin were the brook trout, brown trout, rainbow trout, and the American brook lamprey (Petrosky and Waters 1975).

IMPORTANCE AND MANAGEMENT

Before the decline of the lake trout in Lake Michigan, the slimy sculpin was an important item in the diet of the large salmonids. Van Oosten and Deason (1938) noted that, in Lake Michigan and in Green Bay, 7.7% of the lake trout stomachs containing food held slimy sculpins, and that in southern and northern Lake Michigan, 1.6% of the burbot containing food held slimy sculpins.

The slimy sculpin has been accused of being a significant predator on salmonid eggs and larvae. Clary (1972) reported predation on hatching brown trout eggs and sac-fry by the slimy sculpin, but only at the time of hatching. Koster (1937) noted that there was virtually no evidence that slimy sculpins fed upon the eggs of lake trout and brook trout, and that only in rare instances did they prey upon young brook trout. Greeley (1932) suggested that sculpins probably feed only on loose trout eggs that have not been buried in the nests. In Valley Creek, Minnesota, where slimy sculpins 5 cm or longer were present in densities of about 7000/ha, no trout eggs were found in the stomachs examined (Petrosky and Waters 1975).

In Wisconsin, the slimy sculpin has little or no value as a bait minnow. According to Scott and Crossman (1973), in the Nipigon waters, Ontario, it is a favorite brook trout bait, and many of the trout that won the Nipigon Trophy were caught on "cockatouch."

In the upper Jordan River, Michigan, Quick (1971) estimated a density of slimy sculpins at 85,045 fish/ha; in the lower Jordan River, at 589 fish/ha. In Valley Creek, Minnesota, Petrosky and Waters (1975) calculated the density of slimy sculpins during the study period at about 20,000/ha. Comparisons with annual production estimates for brook and rainbow trout made previously suggested a normal total annual production for all fishes of about 200 kg/ha, with sculpins contributing about one-third and trout about two-thirds to the production.

Spoonhead Sculpin

Cottus ricei (Nelson). *Cottus*—the bull's head, an old name of the European miller's thumb; *ricei*—after its discoverer, M. L. Rice, then a student in zoology at Northwestern University in Evanston, Illinois.

Other common names: spoonhead muddler, Rice's sculpin, cow-faced sculpin.

Adult 77 mm, L. Superior (Bayfield Co.), June or July 1968. Lateral view above and dorsal view below.

DESCRIPTION

Head and anterior body flattened dorsoventrally; posterior body and narrow caudal peduncle compressed laterally. Average length 62 mm (2.4 in). TL = 1.20 SL. Depth into TL 5.1–6.2. Head spadelike in dorsal view; head length into TL 3.3–4.3. Snout flat in lateral view. Mouth terminal, small. Single midline mandibular pore. Numerous teeth in narrow bands on upper and lower jaws; palatine teeth absent. Gill membranes broadly joined to isthmus. Upper preopercular spine well developed, and hooked or curved upward and backward. Dorsal fins 2, always narrowly connected, but sometimes fins widely separated; first dorsal fin small with 7–9 soft spines; second dorsal fin usually with 16–18 rays. Anal fin rays usually 12–14. Pelvic fins thoracic, of 1 spine and 4 pelvic rays but appearing as only 4 elements (the spine and first ray encased in a single fleshy membrane); pectoral fins very large, 14–16 rays. Typical scales absent, but top of head and upper body more or less covered with small prickles. Lateral line complete.

Upper region of head and body light brown and tan, mottled with small dark speckles; ventral region of head and belly yellowish. Young occasionally with 4 dark saddle marks, the first 3 through base of second dorsal fin, the fourth on caudal peduncle. All fins lightly speckled, except pelvics which are clear. Distinct, narrow, vertical bar at caudal fin base.

Sexual dimorphism: Adult male with short, broad triangular genital papilla; much reduced in female.

SYSTEMATIC NOTES

The spoonhead sculpin was described from a specimen found on the shore of Lake Michigan near Evanston, Illinois (Nelson 1876). It is a distinctive sculpin with an unconfused taxonomy (McPhail and Lindsey 1970). Perhaps its closest relative is one of the Old World sculpins, *Cottus sibiricus*, *C. spinulosus*, or *C. gobio*.

DISTRIBUTION, STATUS, AND HABITAT

According to McPhail and Lindsey (1970), the spoonhead sculpin probably survived glaciation in the deeper waters of turbid rivers in the upper Mississippi basin. It moved northward in the wake of the retreating ice, and apparently died out in the southern portion of its original range. Although its tolerance of brackish waters is evidenced by its occurrence around Akimiski Island in James Bay, it has not extended its range up the east side of Hudson Bay. McPhail and Lindsey wrote: "In fact the distribution of this species is unique, and the factors governing its dispersal are unknown."

In Wisconsin, the spoonhead sculpin occurs in Lakes Michigan and Superior. In Lake Michigan it reaches the southern limit of its distribution.

The spoonhead sculpin is uncommon in Lake Superior, and rare to depleted in Lake Michigan. According to Wells and McLain (1973), the spoonhead sculpin, which once was common lakewide in Lake Michigan, has continually decreased in numbers and is now rare or absent in the southern portion of the lake. Several specimens were observed in trawl catches made by the Great Lakes Fishery Laboratory in that area in 1954, but none were seen in extensive trawling in 1960 and in 1964–1971. Although an occasional spoonhead sculpin might have been overlooked among slimy sculpins, it is doubtful that many would have gone undetected. The present status of

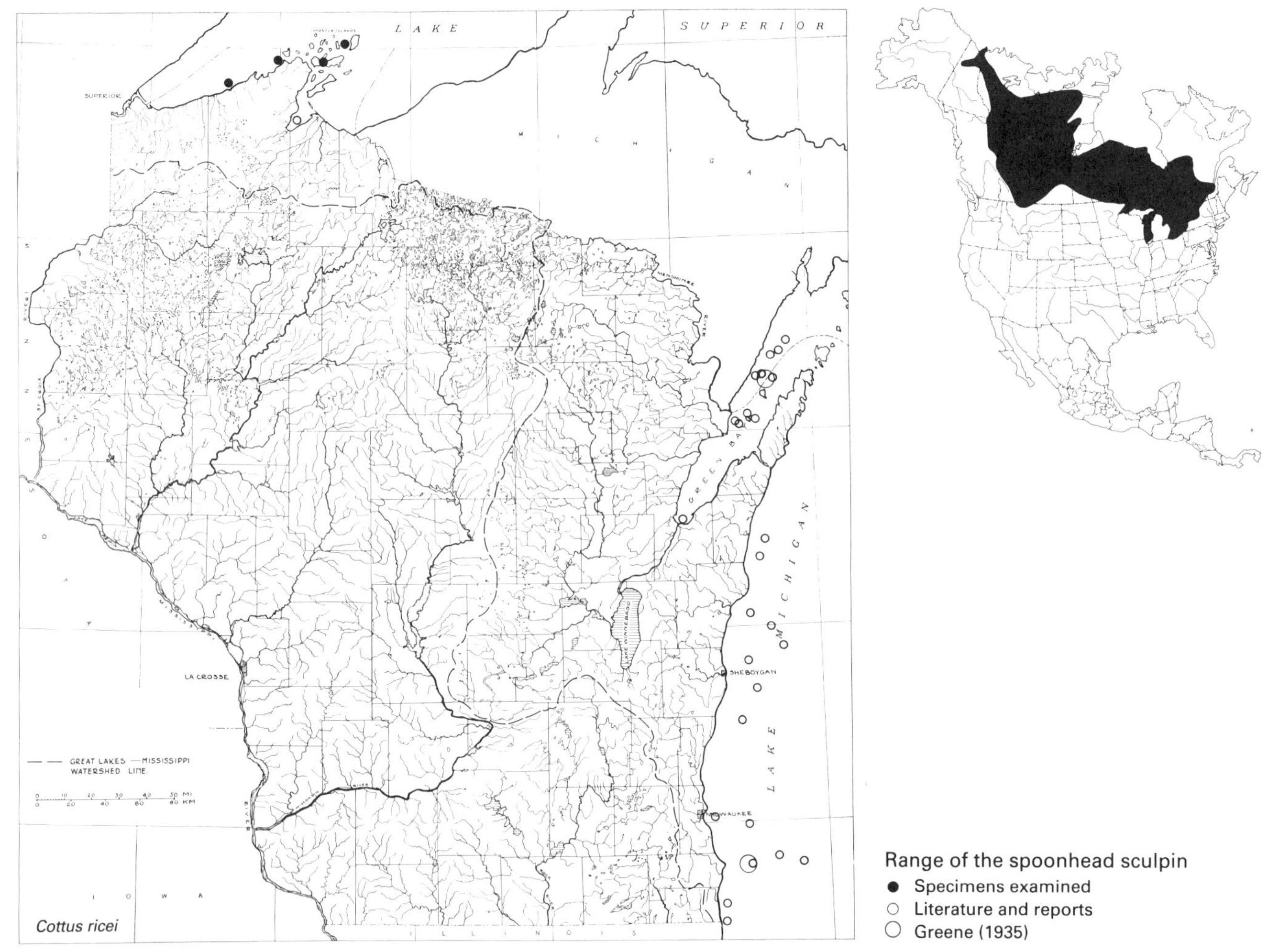

Range of the spoonhead sculpin
● Specimens examined
○ Literature and reports
◯ Greene (1935)

the spoonhead sculpin in northern Lake Michigan is not known; one was caught by trawl off Ludington, Michigan, in 1971. No causes have been suggested for the apparent disappearance of the spoonhead sculpin from southern Lake Michigan.

Over its range, the spoonhead sculpin is not known to be strikingly abundant or successful anywhere, despite the diversity of its habitats (McPhail and Lindsey 1970). In Michigan it is rare and depleted; in Montana it is rare; and in Ohio it is depleted (Miller 1972).

In Lake Michigan, the spoonhead sculpin occurs from shallows to depths of 134 m, and in Lake Superior it is found at depths of 37–110 m (Deason 1939, Dryer 1966). In the Great Lakes basin, it has been recorded from inland lakes only on Isle Royale and from Lake Charlevoix, Michigan. In the southern part of its range, this species is not known from any of the smaller lakes and streams, but in Canada, inland and northward, it has been caught in small, swift streams, turbid rivers, and the inshore shallows and deeper waters of lakes. Most northern collections are from the shallows of large, muddy rivers; a few are taken from lakes, and a few from tide pools in James Bay (McPhail and Lindsey 1970).

BIOLOGY

It is not known when the spoonhead sculpin spawns, but recent evidence suggests that it occurs in late summer or early fall. Delisle and Van Vliet (1968) reported that milt was exuded, under slight pressure, from males caught 1 August at a depth of 42.7 m in Pemichangan Lake, Quebec. At that depth the water temperature was 4.5°C (40°F). Scott and Crossman (1973) noted that Ontario specimens contained larger eggs in August than in June or July, and that they contained exceedingly small eggs in December.

In Lake Superior (Ashland County), an 84-mm, 7.54-g female spoonhead sculpin, collected 29 April, had ovaries 13.3% of the body weight; she held 638 orange eggs, which averaged 1.4 (1.0–1.7) mm diam. A 68-mm, 3.14-g female from the same collection had ovaries 8.2% of the body weight; she held 357 yellow to orange eggs, which averaged 1.12 (1.0–1.3) mm diam.

Fish (1932) illustrated and described the 27.5-mm stage from Lake Erie. The maximum size known for a spoonhead sculpin is a 134-mm (5.3-in) TL fish which was caught in gill nets in Pemichangan Lake, Quebec (Delisle and Van Vliet 1968). Eleven spoonhead sculpins, taken at 91 m from the Apostle Islands region of Lake Superior by trawl, ranged from 43 to 84 mm (1.7 to 3.3 in) TL.

The diet of 77 spoonhead sculpins from the Duluth-Superior sector of Lake Superior and of 64 spoonheads from the Apostle Islands was dominated by crustaceans; it also included insects, fish eggs, and other material (Anderson and Smith 1971b). Amphipods were the principal food of the spoonheads in both areas during all months. *Mysis* and copepods were consumed in lesser amounts in the two areas, and isopods were eaten only at Duluth-Superior. The consumption of insects (primarily chironomids), was not as important in the Apostle Islands region as it was in the Duluth-Superior area. Coregonid eggs were eaten during April and May in both areas. Plant material, oligochaetes, Hirudinea, and unidentified material constituted the balance of the stomach contents of spoonheads in both areas.

The spoonhead sculpin tolerates fresh and brackish waters.

In Lake Superior, the spoonhead sculpin is restricted to the deeper water, and no fish have been taken in water shallower than 37 m. The abundance of the species increases with depth to 73–90 m (Dryer 1966). In Lake Michigan, Hubbs reported (unpublished) that he collected several half-grown individuals from about 0.3 m of water near the head of the east arm of Grand Traverse Bay, and one individual from near the shore at Jackson Park, Chicago (Deason 1939).

IMPORTANCE AND MANAGEMENT

Historically, the spoonhead sculpin was preyed on by lake trout and burbot in Lake Michigan. Van Oosten and Deason (1938) noted that, in Lake Michigan and in Green Bay, 3.8% of the lake trout stomachs and 6.6% of the burbot stomachs containing food held spoonhead sculpins. According to Deason, as many as 33 spoonhead sculpins were found in a single stomach. Deason (1939) reported that the spoonhead sculpin was found in the stomachs of lake trout and burbot captured in gill nets at 24–134 m. Spoonheads have also been reported from the stomach of a whitefish caught in Charlevoix Lake, Michigan. As a result of its disappearance from southern Lake Michigan and its depletion in northern Lake Michigan, the spoonhead sculpin's use as a forage fish is limited.

Scott and Crossman (1973) noted that the spoonhead sculpin is of interest zoogeographically, since its presence in a body of water provides information on the geological or glacial history of the region.

References
Credits for Color Illustrations
Index

References

Adams, C. C., and T. L. Hankinson. 1926. Annotated list of Oneida Lake fish. pp. 283–542 *in* Bull. N.Y. State Coll. For., Roosevelt Wildl. Ann. 1(1–2).

Adams, L. A. 1942. Age determination and rate of growth in *Polydon spathula* by means of the growth rings of the otoliths and dentary bone. Am. Midl. Nat. 28:617–630.

Adelman, I. R., and L. L. Smith. 1970. Effect of oxygen on growth and food conversion efficiency of northern pike. Progr. Fish-Cult. 32(2):93–96.

Agassiz, J. L. R. 1850. Lake Superior. Its physical character, vegetation, and animals, compared with those of other and similar regions. Gould, Kendall, and Lincoln, Boston. 428 pp.

Agersborg, H. P. K. 1930. The influence of temperature on fish. Ecology 11(1):136–144.

Ahsan, S. N. 1966a. Cyclical changes in the testicular activity of the lake chub, *Couesius plumbeus* (Agassiz). Can. J. Zool. 44:149–159.

Ahsan, S. N. 1966b. Effects of temperature and light on the cyclical changes in the spermatogenetic activity of the lake chub *Couesius plumbeus* (Agassiz). Can. J. Zool. 44:161–171.

Allbaugh, C. A., and J. V. Manz. 1964. Preliminary study of the effects of temperature fluctuations on developing walleye eggs and fry. Progr. Fish-Cult. 26(4):175–180.

Allen, K. O., and K. Strawn. 1967. Heat tolerance of channel catfish, *Ictalurus punctatus*. Proc. Southeast. Assoc. Game Fish Commnrs. 21:399–410.

Allen, P. 1891. Icthyology [sic] of Dane County, Wisconsin. Part I. The Wis. Nat. 1(10):152–155.

Amundrud, J. R., D. J. Faber, and A. Keast. 1974. Seasonal succession of free-swimming perciform larvae in Lake Opinicon, Ontario, J. Fish. Res. Board Canada 31(10):1661–1665.

Anderson, E. D. 1969. Factors affecting abundance of lake herring (*Coregonus artedii* Lesueur) in western Lake Superior. Univ. Minn. Minneapolis. PhD Thesis. 316 pp.

Anderson, E. D., and L. L. Smith, Jr. 1971a. Factors affecting abundance of lake herring (*Coregonus artedii* Lesueur) in western Lake Superior. Trans. Am. Fish. Soc. 100(4):691–707.

Anderson, E. D., and L. L. Smith, Jr. 1971b. A synoptic study of food habits of 30 fish species from western Lake Superior. Univ. Minn. Agric. Exp. Stn. Tech. Bull. 279. 199 pp.

Anderson, W. C., and P. J. Manion. 1977. Morphological development of the integument of the sea lamprey, *Petromyzon marinus*. J. Fish. Res. Board Canada 34(1):159–163.

Andrews, A. K. 1970. Squamation chronology of the fathead minnow, *Pimephales promelas*. Trans. Am. Fish. Soc. 99(2):429–432.

Andrews, A. K., and S. A. Flickinger. 1974. Spawning requirements and characteristics of the fathead minnow. Proc. Southeast. Assoc. Game Fish Commnrs. 27(1973):759–766.

Andrews, L M., and C. W. Threinen. 1968. Surface water resources of Shawano County. Wis. Dep. Nat. Resour. Lake and Strm. Classif. Proj. 147 pp.

Angel, N. B., and W. R. Jones. 1974. Aquaculture of the American eel (*Anguilla rostrata*). N.C. State Univ., School Eng., Indus. Ext. Serv. 43 pp.

Anthony, J. 1963. Parasites of eastern Wisconsin fishes. Trans. Wis. Acad. Sci., Arts, Lett. 52:83–95.

Antonie, C. J., and W. H. Osness. 1963. Distribution and accumulation of copper following copper sulfate application on lakes. Trans. Wis. Acad. Sci., Arts, Lett. 52:69–175.

Applegate, V. C. 1943. Partial analysis of growth in a population of mudminnows, *Umbra limi* (Kirtland). Copeia 1943(2):92–96.

Applegate, V. C. 1950. Natural history of the sea lamprey, *Petromyzon marinus*, in Michigan. U.S. Fish Wildl. Serv. Spec. Sci. Rep.—Fish. No. 55. 237 pp.

Applegate, V. C., and J. W. Moffett. 1955. Sea lamprey and lake trout. pp. 9–16 *in* Twentieth-century bestiary. Simon and Schuster, N.Y.

Appleget, J., and L. L. Smith, Jr. 1951. The determination and rate of growth from vertebrae of the channel catfish, *Ictalurus lacustris punctatus*. Trans. Am. Fish. Soc. 80(1950):119–139.

Armstrong, J. W., C. R. Liston, P. I. Tack, and R. C. Anderson. 1977. Age, growth, maturity, and seasonal food habits of round whitefish, *Prosopium cylindraceum*, in Lake Michigan near Ludington, Michigan. Trans. Am. Fish. Soc. 106(2):151–155.

Armstrong, P. B. 1962. Stages in the development of *Ictalurus nebulosus*. Syracuse Univ. Press, Syracuse, N.Y. 8 pp. + 53 figs.

Atz, J. W. 1940. Reproductive behavior in the eastern johnny darter, *Boleosoma nigrum olmstedi* (Storer). Copeia 1940(2):100–106.

Avery, E. L. 1973. An experimental introduction of coho salmon into a landlocked lake in northern Wisconsin. Wis. Dep. Nat. Resour. Tech. Bull. 69. 8 pp.

Avery, E. L. 1974a. Experimental reclamation of trout streams through chemical treatment at Westfield Creek. Wis. Dep. Nat. Resour. Rep. 76. 12 pp. + tables.

Avery, E. L. 1974b. Reproduction and recruitment of anadromous salmonids in Wisconsin tributaries of Lake Michigan. Wis. Dep. Nat. Resour. Dingell-Johnson Proj. F–83–R, Stud. No. 108. 32 pp.

Avery, E. L. 1975. An evaluation of stocking fingerling trout in a "two-story" trout lake. Wis. Dep. Nat. Resour. Bur. Res. Rep. 83. 4 pp.

Bachay, G. S. 1944. Mississippi catfish. Wis. Conserv. Bull. 9(12):9–10.

Bailey, J. E. 1952. Life history and ecology of the sculpin *Cottus bairdi punctulatus* in southwestern Montana. Copeia 1952(4):243–255.

Bailey, M. M. 1963. Age, growth, and maturity of round whitefish of the Apostle Islands and Isle Royale regions, Lake Superior. U.S. Fish Wildl. Serv. Fish. Bull. 63(1):63–75.

Bailey, M. M. 1964. Age, growth, maturity, and sex composition of the American smelt, *Osmerus mordax* (Mitchill), of western Lake Superior. Trans. Am. Fish. Soc. 93(4):382–395.

Bailey, M. M. 1969. Age, growth, and maturity of the longnose sucker *Catostomus catostomus*, of western Lake Superior. J. Fish. Res. Board Canada 26(5):1289–1299.

Bailey, M. M. 1972. Age, growth, reproduction and food of the burbot, *Lota lota* (Linnaeus), in southwestern Lake Superior. Trans. Am. Fish. Soc. 101(4):667–674.

Bailey, R. M. 1938. The fishes of the Merrimack watershed. pp. 149–185 *in* N.H. Fish Game Dep. Surv. Rep. 3.

Bailey, R. M. 1951. A check-list of the fishes of Iowa, with keys for identification. pp. 187–238 *in* Iowa fish and fishing. Iowa Conserv. Comm., Des Moines.

Bailey, R. M. 1954. Distribution of the American cyprinid fish *Hybognathus hankinsoni* with comments on its original description. Copeia 1954(4):289–291.

Bailey, R. M. 1955. Differential mortality from high temperature in a mixed population of fishes in southern Michigan. Ecology 36(3):526–528.

Bailey, R. M. 1956. A revised list of the fishes of Iowa, with keys for identification. pp. 326–377 *in* Iowa fish and fishing. Iowa Conserv. Comm., Des Moines.

Bailey, R. M. 1959. Distribution of the American cyprinid fish *Notropis anogenus*. Copeia 1959(2):119–123.

Bailey, R. M., and M. O. Allum. 1962. Fishes of South Dakota. Univ. Mich. Mus. Zool. Misc. Publ. No. 119. 131 pp.

Bailey, R. M., and C. R. Gilbert. 1960. The American cyprinid fish *Notropis kanawha* identified as an interspecific hybrid. Copeia 1960(4):354–357.

Bailey, R. M., and W. A. Gosline. 1955. Variation and systematic significance of vertebral counts in the American fishes of the family Percidae. Univ. Mich. Mus. Zool. Misc. Publ. No. 93. 44 pp.

Bailey, R. M., and H. M. Harrison, Jr. 1948. Food habits of the southern channel catfish, *Ictalurus lacustris punctatus*, in the Des Moines River, Iowa. Trans. Am. Fish. Soc. 75:110–138.

Bailey, R. M., H. E. Winn, and C. L. Smith. 1954. Fishes from the Escambia River, Alabama and Florida, with ecologic and taxonomic notes. Proc. Acad. Nat. Sci. Phila. 106:109–164 + 1 fig.

Bailey, R. M., J. E. Fitch, E. S. Herald, E. A. Lachner, C. C. Lindsey, C. R. Robins, and W. B. Scott (Com. on names of fishes). 1970. A list of common and scientific names of fishes from the United States and Canada. 3d ed. Am. Fish. Soc., Wash., D.C., Spec. Publ. No. 6. 149 pp.

Baker, F. C. 1928. The fresh water mollusca of Wisconsin. Part II, Pelecypoda. Wis. Geol. Nat. Hist. Surv. 70(Part II). 495 pp.

Baldwin, N. S. 1968. Sea lamprey in the Great Lakes. Limnos 1(3):20–27.

Baldwin, R. E., D. H. Strong, and J. H. Torrie. 1961. Flavor and aroma of fish taken from four fresh water sources. Trans. Am. Fish. Soc. 90(2):175–180.

Ball, R. C., and E. H. Bacon. 1954. Use of pituitary material in the propagation of minnows. Progr. Fish-Cult. 16(3):108–113.

Ball, R. L., and R. V. Kilambi. 1973. The feeding ecology of the black and white crappies in Beaver Reservoir, Arkansas, and its effect on the relative abundance of the crappie species. Proc. Southeast. Assoc. Game Fish Commnrs. 26:577–590.

Balon, E. K. 1959. Die Entwicklung des akklimatisierten *Lepomis gibbosus* (Linné 1948) während der embryonalen Periode in den Donauseitenwässern. Z. Fischerei 8(1–3):1–27.

Bangham, R. V. 1944. Parasites of Northern Wisconsin fishes. Trans. Wis. Acad. Sci., Arts, Lett. 36:291–325.

Bardach, J. E. 1951. Changes in the yellow perch population of Lake Mendota, Wisconsin, between 1916 and 1948. Ecology 32(4):719–728.

Bardach, J. E. 1964. Downstream: a natural history of the river. Harper and Row, N.Y. 278 pp.

Bardach, J. E., M. Fujiya, and A. Holl. 1965. Detergents: effects on the chemical senses of the fish *Ictalurus natalis* (LeSueur). Science 148(3677):1605–1607.

Bardach, J. E., J. H. Ryther, and W. O. McLarney. 1972. Aquaculture. John Wiley and Sons, N.Y. 868 pp.

Bardach, J. E., J. H. Todd, and R. Crickmer. 1967. Orientation by taste in fish of the genus *Ictalurus*. Science 155(3767):1276–1278.

Bardach, J. E., J. J. Bernstein, J. S. Hart, and J. R. Brett. 1966. Tolerance to temperature extremes: animals. Part IV. Fishes. pp. 37–80 *in* Environmental biology, ed. P. L. Altman and D. Dittmer. Fed. Am. Soc. Exp. Biol., Bethesda, Md.

Bardack, D., and R. Zangerl. 1968. First fossil lamprey: a record from the Pennsylvanian of Illinois. Science 162(3859):1265–1267.

Barkalow, F. S. 1950. Largemouth bass following swimming animals. J. Wildl. Mgmt. 14:80.

Barney, R. L., and B. J. Anson. 1923. Life history and ecology of the orange-spotted sunfish, *Lepomis humilis*. Rep. U.S. Commnr. Fish. 1922, Append. XV, Bur. Fish. Doc. No. 938:1–16.

Barnickol, P. G., and W. C. Starrett. 1951. Commercial and sport fishes of the Mississippi River between Caruthersville, Missouri, and Dubuque, Iowa. Ill. Nat. Hist. Surv. Bull. 25(5):263–350.

Battle, H. I., and W. M. Sprules. 1960. Description of the semi-buoyant eggs and early development stages of the goldeye, *Hiodon alosoides* (Rafinesque). J. Fish. Res. Board Canada 17(2):245–266.

Baughman, J. L. 1947. The tench in America. J. Wildl. Mgmt. 11:197–204.

Baumann, P. C. 1975. An evaluation of the use of antimycin A for stream reclamation in the Rock River, Wisconsin. Univ. Wis., Madison. PhD Thesis. 119 pp.

Baumann, P. C., and J. F. Kitchell. 1974. Diel patterns of distribution and feeding of bluegill, *Lepomis macrochirus*, in Lake Wingra, Wisconsin. Trans. Am. Fish. Soc. 103(2):255–260.

Baxter, G. T., and J. R. Simon. 1970. Wyoming fishes. Wyo. Game Fish Dep. Bull. No. 4. 168 pp.

Beamish, R. J. 1972. Lethal pH for the white sucker *Catostomus commersoni* (Lacepède). Trans. Am. Fish. Soc. 101(1):355–358.

Beamish, R. J., and H. H. Harvey. 1969. Age determination in the white sucker. J. Fish. Res. Board Canada 26(3):633–638.

Beamish, R. J., and H. Tsuyuki. 1971. A biochemical and cytological study of the longnose sucker (*Catostomus catostomus*) and large and dwarf forms of the white sucker (*Catostomus commersoni*). J. Fish. Res. Board Canada 28(11):1745–1748.

Beamish, R. J., M. J. Merrilees, and E. J. Crossman. 1971. Karyotypes and DNA values for members of the suborder Esocoidei (Osteichthyes: Salmoniformes). Chromosoma 34:436–447.

Beard, D. B. 1943. Fading trails. Macmillan, N.Y. 279 pp.

Beard, T. D. 1971. Panfish literature review. Wis. Dep. Nat. Resour. Res. Rep. 71. 44 pp.

Beard, T. D. 1974. Impact of repeated antimycin treatments on the zooplankton and benthic organisms in Camp, Lamereau and Nancy lakes, Bayfield County, Wisconsin. Wis. Dep. Nat. Resour. Rep. 78. 7 pp. + tables.

Becker, C. D., R. G. Genoway, and M. J. Schneider. 1977. Comparative cold resistance of three Columbia River organisms. Trans. Am. Fish. Soc. 106(2):178–184.

Becker, G. C. 1959. Distribution of central Wisconsin fishes. Trans. Wis. Acad. Sci., Arts, Lett. 48:65–102.

Becker, G. C. 1961. Fading fins. Trans. Wis. Acad. Sci., Arts, Lett. 50:239–248.

Becker, G. C. 1962. Intra-specific variation in *Rhinichthys c. cataractae* (Valenciennes) and *Rhinichthys atratulus meleagris* (Agassiz) and anatomical and ecological studies of *Rhinichthys c. cataractae*. Univ. Wis., Madison. PhD thesis. 250 pp.

Becker, G. C. 1964a. The fishes of Pewaukee Lake. Trans. Wis. Acad. Sci., Arts, Lett. 53:19–27.

Becker, G. C. 1964b. The fishes of Lakes Poygan and Winnebago. Trans. Wis. Acad. Sci., Arts, Lett. 53:29–52.

Becker, G. C. 1965. The western sand darter, *Ammocrypta clara*, in the Great Lakes basin. Copeia 1965(2):241.

Becker, G. C. 1966. Fishes of southwestern Wisconsin. Trans. Wis. Acad. Sci., Arts, Lett. 55:87–117.

Becker, G. C. 1969. Preliminary list of fishes of Portage County, Wisconsin. Univ. Wis., Stevens Point, Mus. Nat. Hist. Fauna and Flora Wis. Rep. No. 1. 11 pp.

Becker, G. C. 1971. The pugnose shiner—a dodo? The Passenger Pigeon 33:199–201. [Corrections in 34(2):84.]

Becker, G. C. 1972a. Annotated list of the fishes of the Pine-Popple basin. Trans. Wis. Acad. Sci., Arts, Lett. 60:309–329.

Becker, G. C. 1972b. Preliminary survey of the fishes of the Rock River basin, Wisconsin, with suggestions for management. Univ. Wis., Stevens Point, Mus. Nat. Hist. Fauna and Flora Wis. Rep. No. 5. 16 pp.

Becker, G. C. 1975. Fish toxification: biological sanity or insanity? pp. 41–53 *in* Rehabilitation of fish populations with toxicants: a symposium, ed. P. H. Eschmeyer. North Cent. Div. Am. Fish. Soc. Spec. Publ. No. 4. 74 pp.

Becker, G. C. 1976. Inland fishes of the Lake Michigan drainage basin. Argonne Natl. Lab. ANL/ES-40. Vol. 17. 237 pp.

Becker, G. C., and J. R. Holland. 1972. A plan for the restoration of the Wisconsin River. Citizens Nat. Resour. Assoc. Rep., Loganville, Wis. 39 pp.

Becker, H. R. 1923. The habitat of *Aphredoderus sayanus*. Occas. Pap. Mus. Zool. Univ. Mich. No. 138. 4 pp.

Becker, S. H. 1972. Stream of a thousand isles. *In* Stream of a thousand isles; the Wisconsin River: its history and a plan for restoration. Citizens Nat. Resour. Assoc. Rep., Loganville, Wis. 33 pp.

Beckman, W. C. 1941. Increased growth rate of rock bass, *Ambloplites rupestris* (Rafinesque) following reduction in the density of the population. Trans. Am. Fish. Soc. 70:143–148.

Beeton, A. M. 1960. The vertical migration of *Mysis relicta* in Lakes Huron and Michigan. J. Fish. Res. Board Canada 17(4):517–539.

Behmer, D. J. 1965. Spawning periodicity of the river carpsucker *Carpiodes carpio*. Proc. Iowa Acad. Sci. 72:253–262.

Behmer, D. J. 1969a. A method of estimating fecundity; with data on river carpsucker, *Carpiodes carpio*. Trans. Am. Fish. Soc. 98(3):523–524.

Behmer, D. J. 1969b. Schooling of river carpsuckers and a population estimate. Trans. Am. Fish. Soc. 98(2):520–523.

Beitinger, T. L. 1974. Thermoregulatory behavior and diel activity patterns of bluegill, *Lepomis macrochirus*, following thermal shock. U.S. Fish Wildl. Serv. Fish. Bull. 72(3):1087–1093.

Beitinger, T. L., and J. J. Magnuson. 1975. Influence of social rank and size on thermoselection behavior of bluegill (*Lepomis macrochirus*). J. Fish. Res. Board Canada 32(11):2133–2136.

Beitinger, T. L., J. J. Magnuson, W. H. Neill, and W. R. Shaffer. 1975. Behavioral thermoregulation and activity patterns in the green sunfish, *Lepomis cyanellus*. Anim. Behav. 23:222–229.

Belonger, B. 1969. Lake trout sport fishing in the Wisconsin waters of Lake Superior. Wis. Conserv. Dep. Div. Fish Mgmt. Rep. No. 20. 18 pp. (mimeo).

Bennett, D. H. 1972. Length-weight relationships and condition factors of fishes from a South Carolina reservoir receiving thermal effluent. Progr. Fish-Cult. 34(2):85–87.

Bennett, G. W. 1937. The growth of the largemouthed black bass, *Huro salmoides* (Lacepède), in the waters of Wisconsin. Copeia 1937(2):104–118.

Bennett, G. W. 1938. Growth of the smallmouth black bass in Wisconsin waters. Copeia 1938:157–170.

Bennett, G. W. 1951. Experimental largemouth bass management in Illinois. Trans. Am. Fish. Soc. 80(1950):231–239.

Bennett, G. W., and W. F. Childers. 1957. The smallmouth bass, *Micropterus dolomieui*, in warm-water ponds. J. Wildl. Mgmt. 21(4):414–424.

Bennett, G. W., and W. F. Childers. 1966. The lake chubsucker as a forage species. Progr. Fish-Cult. 28(2):89–92.

Bennett, G. W., and L. Durham. 1951. Cost of bass fishing at Ridge Lake, Coles County, Illinois. Ill. Nat. Hist. Surv. Biol. Notes No. 23. 16 pp.

Benoit, D. E., and R. W. Carlson. 1977. Spawning success of fathead minnows on selected artificial substrates. Progr. Fish-Cult. 39(2):67–68.

Berg, D. R., W. R. Jones, and G. L. Crow. 1975. The case of the slippery eel, or: how to harvest, handle and market wild eels. N.C. State Univ. Sea Grant Prog. UNC–SG–75–20. 21 pp.

Berg, R. E. 1978. Growth and maturation of chinook salmon, *Oncorhynchus tshawytscha*, introduced into Lake Superior. Trans. Am. Fish. Soc. 107(2):281–283.

Berg, R. E., P. A. Doepke, and P. R. Hannuksela. 1975. First occurrence of the brook silverside, *Labidesthes sicculus*, in a tributary of Lake Superior. J. Fish. Res. Board Canada 32(12):2541–2542.

Berner, L. M. 1948. The intestinal convolutions: new generic characters for the separation of *Carpiodes* and *Ictiobus*. Copeia 1948(2):140–141.

Berra, T. M., and G. E. Gunning. 1972. Seasonal movement and home range of the longear sunfish, *Lepomis megalotis* (Rafinesque), in Louisiana. Am. Midl. Nat. 88(2):368–375.

Berry, F. H. 1955. Food of the mudfish (*Amia calva*) in Lake Newman, Florida, in relation to its management. Q. J. Fla. Acad. Sci. 18(1):69–75.

Bersamin, S. V. 1958. A preliminary study of the nutritional ecology and food habits of the chubs (*Leucichthys* spp.) and their relation to the ecology of Lake Michigan. Pap. Mich. Acad. Sci., Arts, Lett. 43:107–118.

Berst, A. H., and G. R. Spangler. 1973. Lake Huron, the ecology of the fish community and man's effects on it. Great Lakes Fish Comm. Tech. Rep. 21. 41 pp.

Bever, G. G., and J. M. Lealos. 1974. Walleye fishery in Pike and Round Lakes, Price County. Wis. Dep. Nat. Resour. Bur. Fish. Mgmt. Rep. No. 73. 16 pp.

Beyerle, G. B. 1971. A study of two northern pike-bluegill populations. Trans. Am. Fish. Soc. 100(1):69–73.

Bigelow, H. B., and W. W. Welsh. 1925. Fishes of the Gulf of Maine. Bull. U.S. Bur. Fish. 40(Part I). 567 pp.

Biggins, R. G. 1968. Centrachid feeding interactions in a small desert impoundment. Univ. Ariz., Tucson. MS Thesis. 44 pp.

Black, A., and W. M. Howell. 1978. A distinctive chromosomal race of the cyprinodontid fish, *Fundulus notatus*, from the upper Tombigbee River system of Alabama and Mississippi. Copeia 1978(2):280–288.

Black, E. C. 1953. Upper lethal temperatures of some British Columbia freshwater fishes. J. Fish. Res. Board Canada 10(4):196–210.

Black, J. D. 1944. "Carp problem" in 1901. Wis. Conserv. Bull. 9(7):6.

Black, J. D. 1945a. Natural history of the northern mimic shiner, *Notropis volucellus volucellus* Cope. Indiana Dep. Conserv. and Indiana Univ. Dep. Zool., Invest. Indiana Lakes and Strms. 2(18):449–469.

Black, J. D. 1945b. Winter habits of northern lake minnows. Copeia 1945(2):114.

Black, J. D. 1946. Nature's own weed killer—the German carp. Wis. Conserv. Bull. 11(4):3–7.

Black, J. D. 1948. The spawning of carp in holding ponds. Wis. Conserv. Bull. 13(3):6–7.

Black, J. D., and L. O. Williamson. 1946. Artificial hybrids between muskellunge and northern pike. Trans. Wis. Acad. Sci., Arts, Lett. 38:299–314.

Black, R. F. 1959. Friends of the Pleistocene. Science 130(3368):172–173.

Blackman, R. R., L. M. Sather, and C. W. Threinen. 1966. Surface water resources of Burnett County. Wis. Conserv. Dep. Lake and Strm. Classif. Proj. 165 pp.

Blaylock, B. G., and N. A. Griffith. 1971. A laboratory technique for spawning carp. Progr. Fish-Cult. 33(1):48–50.

Bodola, A. 1966. Life history of the gizzard shad, *Dorosoma cepedianum* (LeSueur), in western Lake Erie. U.S. Fish Wildl. Serv. Fish. Bull. 65(2):391–425.

Boesel, M. W. 1938. The food of nine species of fish from the western end of Lake Erie. Trans. Am. Fish. Soc. 67:215–223.

Booke, H. E. 1965. Increase of serum globulin levels with age in lake whitefish. Trans. Am. Fish. Soc. 94(4):397–398.

Booke, H. E. 1968. Cytotaxonomic studies of the coregonine fishes of the Great Lakes U.S.A.: DNA and karyotype analysis. J. Fish. Res. Board Canada 25(8):1667–1687.

Booke, H. E. 1970. Speciation parameters in coregonine fishes. Part I. Egg-size. Part II. Karyotype. pp. 61–66 *in* Biology of coregonid fishes, ed. C. C. Lindsey and C. S. Woods. Univ. Manitoba Press, Winnipeg.

Borell, A. E., and P. M. Scheffer. 1961. Trout in farm and ranch ponds. U.S.D.A. Farmer's Bull. No. 2154. 17 pp.

Borgeson, D. P., and W. H. Tody. 1967. Status report on Great Lakes fisheries. Mich. Dep. Conserv. Fish Mgmt. Rep. No. 2. 35 pp.

Born, S. M., T. L. Wirth, E. M. Brick, and J. O. Peterson. 1973b. Restoring the recreational potential of small impoundments. Wis. Dep. Nat. Resour. Tech. Bull. No. 71. 20 pp.

Born, S. M., T. L. Wirth, J. O. Peterson, J. P. Wall, and D. A. Stephenson. 1973a. Dilutional pumping at Snake Lake, Wisconsin. Wis. Dep. Nat. Resour. Tech. Bull. No. 66. 32 pp.

Bottrell, C. E., R. H. Ingersol, and R. W. Jones. 1964. Notes on the embryology, early development, and behavior of *Hybopsis aestivalis tetranemus* (Gilbert). Trans. Am. Microsc. Soc. 83(4):391–399.

Bouck, G. R. 1972. Effects of diurnal hypoxia on electrophoretic protein fractions and other health parameters of rock bass (*Ambloplites rupestris*). Trans. Am. Fish. Soc. 101(3):488–493.

Bouck, G. R., and R. C. Ball. 1965. Influence of a diurnal oxygen pulse on fish serum proteins. Trans. Am. Fish. Soc. 94(4):363–370.

Bowman, M. L. 1970. Life history of the black redhorse, *Moxostoma duquesnei* (LeSueur), in Missouri. Trans. Am. Fish. Soc. 99(3):546–559.

Boyer, R. L., and L. E. Vogele. 1971. Longear sunfish behavior in two Ozark reservoirs. pp. 13–25 *in* Reservoir fisheries and limnology, ed. G. E. Hall. Am. Fish. Soc. Spec. Publ. No. 8.

Braasch, M. E., and P. W. Smith. 1965. Relationships of the topminnows *Fundulus notatus* and *Fundulus olivaceus* in the upper Mississippi River valley. Copeia 1965(1):46–53.

Braatz, D. A. 1974. Invertebrate drift in a central Wisconsin brook trout stream. Univ. Wis., Stevens Point. MS Thesis. 63 pp.

Brandt, S. B. 1978. Thermal ecology and abundance of alewife (*Alosa pseudoharengus*) in Lake Michigan. Univ. Wis., Madison. PhD Thesis. 226 pp.

Branson, B. A. 1961. Observations on the distribution of nuptial tubercles in some catostomid fishes. Trans. Kans. Acad. Sci. 64(4):360–372.

Branson, B. A. 1962. Comparative cephalic and appendicular osteology of the fish family Catostomidae. Part I. *Cycleptus elongatus* (LeSueur). Southwest. Nat. 7(2):81–153.

Branson, B. A. 1966. The gar, a plea for a heritage of past. Ky. Happy Hunting Ground 22(July 1966):16–19.

Branson, B. A., and G. A. Moore. 1962. The lateralis components of the acoustico-lateralis system in the sunfish family Centrarchidae. Copeia 1962(1):1–108.

Branson, B. A., and G. U. Ulrikson. 1967. Morphology and histology of the branchial apparatus in percid fishes of the genera *Percina*, *Etheostoma*, and *Ammocrypta* (Percidae: Percinae, Etheostomatini). Trans. Am. Microsc. Soc. 86(4):371–389.

Brasch, J. 1950. The lampreys of Wisconsin. Wis. Conserv. Bull. 15(9):13–16.

Brasch, J., J. McFadden, and S. Kmiotek. 1973. Brook trout, life history, ecology, and management. Wis. Dep. Nat. Resour. Publ. 226. 15 pp.

Breder, C. M., Jr. 1935. The reproductive habits of the common catfish, *Ameiurus nebulosus* (LeSueur), with a discussion of their significance in ontogeny and phylogeny. Zoologica 19:143–185.

Breder, C. M., Jr. 1936. The reproductive habits of the North American sunfishes (family Centrarchidae). Zoologica 21(1):1–48.

Breder, C. M., Jr. 1948. Field book of marine fishes of the Atlantic coast from Labrador to Texas. G. P. Putnam's Sons, N.Y. 332 pp.

Breder, C. M., Jr., and D. R. Crawford. 1922. The food of certain minnows. Zoologica 2(14):287–327.

Breder, C. M., Jr., and D. E. Rosen. 1966. Modes of reproduction in fishes. Am. Mus. Nat. Hist. N.Y. 941 pp.

Brett, J. R. 1944. Some lethal temperature relations of Algonquin Park fishes. Univ. Toronto Stud. Biol. Ser. No. 52. 49 pp.

Brett, J. R. 1952. Temperature tolerance in young Pacific salmon, genus *Oncorhynchus*. J. Fish. Res. Board Canada 9(6):265–323.

Brice, J. J. 1898. A manual of fish culture based on the methods of the United States Commission of Fish and Fisheries (with notes on the cultivation of oysters and frogs). Rep. U.S. Commnr. Fish. 1897. 340 pp.

Britt, N. W. 1955. Stratification of western Lake Erie in summer of 1953: Effects on the *Hexagenia* (Ephemeroptera) population. Ecology 36(2):239–244.

Brooke, L. T. 1975. Effect of different constant incubation temperatures on egg survival and embryonic development in lake whitefish (*Coregonus clupeaformis*). Trans. Am. Fish. Soc. 104(3):555–559.

Brown, C. J. D. 1971. Fishes of Montana. Agric. Exp. Stn. Mont. State Univ., Bozeman. 207 pp.

Brown, E. H. 1968. Population characteristics and physical condition of alewives in a massive dieoff in Lake Michigan, 1967. Great Lakes Fish. Comm. Tech. Rep. No. 13. 20 pp.

Brown, E. H. 1970. Extreme female predominance in the bloater (*Coregonus hoyi*) of Lake Michigan in the 1960's. pp. 501–504 *in* Biology of coregonid fishes, ed. C. C. Lindsey and C. S. Woods. Univ. Manitoba Press, Winnipeg.

Brown, J. H., U. T. Hammer, and G. D. Koshinsky. 1970. Breeding biology of the lake chub, *Couesius plumbeus*, at Lac La Ronge, Saskatchewan. J. Fish. Res. Board Canada. 27(6):1005–1015.

Brown, M. E. 1957. Experimental studies on growth. pp. 361–400 *in* The physiology of fishes. Vol. 1, ed. M. E. Brown. Academic Press, N.Y.

Brues, C. T. 1928. Studies on the fauna of hot springs in the western United States and the biology of thermophilous animals. Proc. Am. Acad. Arts Sci. 63:139–228.

Brungs, W. A. 1971. Chronic effects of constant elevated temperature on the fathead minnow (*Pimephales promelas* Rafinesque). Trans. Am. Fish. Soc. 100(4):659–664.

Brynildson, C. L. 1955. The fish population of Stewart Lake at the time of its second fish removal. Wis. Conserv. Dep. Invest. Memo. No. 151. 10 pp.

Brynildson, C. L. 1957. The smallmouth in southern Wisconsin streams. Wis. Conserv. Bull. 22(8):20–22.

Brynildson, C. L. 1958. What's happening to northern pike spawning grounds? Wis. Conserv. Bull. 23(5):9–11.

Brynildson, C. L. 1959. Utilization of suckers and minnows. Wis. Conserv. Bull. 24(5):30–32.

Brynildson, C. L. 1960. Progress report of Wisconsin River catfish study May 1–October 5, 1960. Wis. Dep. Nat. Resour., Nevin Stn. 3 pp.

Brynildson, C. L. 1964. Progress report of the Wisconsin River catfish tagging study, 1959–1963. Wis. Dep. Nat. Resour., Nevin Stn. 5 pp.

Brynildson, C., and J. Truog. 1958. The structure of the forage fish populations in Milner Branch, Grant County, October 7–10, 1958. Wis. Conserv. Dep. Invest. Memo. No. 247. 8 pp.

Brynildson, C., and J. Truog. 1965. The structure of the smallmouth bass production in Livingston Branch, Iowa County, 1958–1964. Wis. Conserv. Dep. Invest. Memo. No. 258. 9 pp. (mimeo).

Brynildson, C., A. Ensign, and J. Truog. 1961. The fishery of the lower Wisconsin River. Wis. Conserv. Bull. 26(1):22–23.

Brynildson, C., D. B. Ives, and H. Druckenmiller. 1970. A two year creel census of Devil's Lake, Sauk County, Wisconsin. Wis. Dep. Nat. Resour. Bur. Fish Mgmt. Rep. No. 35. 11 pp.

Brynildson, O. M. 1958. Lime treatment of brown-stained lakes and their adaptability for trout and largemouth bass. Univ. Wis., Madison. PhD Thesis. 212 pp.

Brynildson, O. M. 1960. Growth of trout. Wis. Conserv. Dep. Annu. Progr. Rep. 9 pp. (mimeo).

Brynildson, O. M. 1961. Utilization of available food by trout. Wis. Conserv. Dep. Annu. Progr. Rep. 21 pp. (ditto).

Brynildson, O. M. 1966. Utilization of available food by splake. Wis. Conserv. Dep. Annu. Progr. Rep., Res. and Plan. Div., Cold Water Group. 12 pp. (mimeo).

Brynildson, O. M. 1969. The food of rainbow trout in Moose Lake, Waukesha County, Wisconsin. Wis. Dep. Nat. Resour., filed in Bur. Res. (unnumbered).

Brynildson, O. M., and C. L. Brynildson. 1978. Distribution and density of sculpins in a Wisconsin coulee stream. Wis. Dep. Nat. Resour. Res. Rep. 98. 5 pp.

Brynildson, O. M., and L. M. Christenson. 1961. Survival, yield, growth and coefficient of condition of hatchery-reared trout stocked in Wisconsin waters. Wis. Conserv. Dep. Misc. Res. Rep. 9. 23 pp.

Brynildson, O. M., and J. J. Kempinger. 1970. The food and growth of splake. Wis. Dep. Nat. Resour. Res. Rep. 59. 41 pp.

Brynildson, O. M., and J. J. Kempinger. 1973. Production, food and harvest of trout in Nebish Lake, Wisconsin. Wis. Dep. Nat. Resour. Tech. Bull. No. 65. 20 pp.

Brynildson, O. M., and J. W. Mason. 1975. Influence of organic pollution on the density and production of trout in a Wisconsin stream. Wis. Dep. Nat. Resour. Tech. Bull. 81. 14 pp.

Brynildson, O. M., and S. L. Serns. 1977. Effects of destratifcation and aeration of a lake on the distribution of planktonic crustacea, yellow perch, and trout. Wis. Dep. Nat. Resour. Tech. Bull. No. 99. 22 pp.

Brynildson, O. M., P. E. Degurse, and J. W. Mason. 1966. Survival growth and yield of stocked domesticated brown and rainbow trout fingerlings in Black Earth Creek. Wis. Dep. Nat. Resour. Res. Rep. 18. 10 pp.

Brynildson, O. M., V. A. Hacker, and T. A. Klick. 1963. Brown trout, its life history, ecology, and management. Wis. Conserv. Dep. Publ. 234. 15 pp.

Buchanan, A., M. Colvin, T. Joy, J. Kaster, G. Lutterbie, and T. Scullin. 1974. Evaluation of effects of thinning on panfish populations. Wis. Coop. Fish. Unit, Stevens Point, Rep. to Wis. Chap. Am. Fish. Soc. 41 pp.

Buchholz, M. 1957. Age and growth of river carpsucker in Des Moines River, Iowa. Proc. Iowa Acad. Sci. 64:589–600.

Buchholz, M. M., and K. D. Carlander. 1963. Failure of yellow bass, *Roccus mississippiensis*, to form annuli. Trans. Am. Fish. Soc. 92(4):384–390.

Budd, J. 1957. Introducton of the hybrid between the eastern brook trout and lake trout into the Great Lakes. Can. Fish Cult. 20:1–4.

Bulkley, R. V. 1970. Changes in yellow bass reproduction associated with environmental conditions. Iowa State J. Sci. 45(2):137–180.

Bunting, D. L., II, and W. H. Irwin. 1965. The relative resistances of seventeen species of fish to petroleum refinery effluents and a comparison of some possible methods of ranking resistances. Proc. Southeast. Assoc. Game Fish Commnrs. 17(1963):293–307.

Bur, M. T. 1976. Age, growth and food habits of Catostomidae in Pool 8 of the upper Mississippi River. Univ. Wis., LaCrosse. MS Thesis. 107 pp.

Burdick, G. E., M. Lipschuetz, H. F. Dean, and E. F. Harris. 1954. Lethal oxygen concentrations for trout and smallmouth bass. N.Y. Fish Game J. 1(1):84–97.

Burdick, M. E., and E. L. Cooper. 1956. Growth rate, survival, and harvest of fingerling rainbow trout planted in Weber Lake, Wisconsin. J. Wildl. Mgmt. 20(3):234–239.

Burnham, C. W. 1909. Notes on the yellow bass. Trans. Am. Fish. Soc. 39:103–108.

Burr, B. M. 1974. A new intergeneric hybrid combination in nature: *Pomoxis annularis* × *Centrarchus macropterus*. Copeia 1974(1):269–271.

Burr, B. M. 1976. Distribution and taxonomic status of the stoneroller, *Campostoma anomalum*, in Illinois. Chic. Acad. Sci. Nat. Hist. Misc. No. 194. 8 pp.

Burr, B. M., and M. A. Morris. 1977. Spawning behavior of the shorthead redhorse, *Moxostoma macrolepidotum*, in Big Rock Creek, Illinois. Trans. Am. Fish. Soc. 106(1):80–92.

Burr, B. M., and L. M. Page. 1979. The life history of the least darter, *Etheostoma microperca*, in the Iroquois River, Illinois. Ill. Nat. Hist. Surv. Biol. Notes No. 112. 15 pp.

Burr, B. M., and P. W. Smith. 1976. Status of the largescale stoneroller, *Campostoma oligolepis*. Copeia 1976(3):521–531.

Burrage, B. R. 1961. Notes on some captive minnows, *Pimephales promelas* Rafinesque. Trans. Kans. Acad. Sci. 64(4):357–359.

Butler, R. L. 1965. Freshwater drum in the navigational impoundments of the upper Mississippi River. Trans. Am. Fish. Soc. 94(4)339–349.

Butler, R. L. 1976. The underutilized and quality aquatic resource. Pa. Coop. Fish. Res. Unit. Presented at 13th Annu. Lake Superior Biol. Conf., Pigeon Lake, Wis. 15 pp.

Butler, R. L., and L. L. Smith, Jr. 1950. The age and rate of growth of the sheepshead, *Aplodinotus grunniens* Rafinesque, in the upper Mississippi River navigation pools. Trans. Am. Fish. Soc. 79(1949):43–54.

Buynak, G. L., and H. W. Mohr, Jr. 1978. Larval development of the northern hog sucker (*Hypentelium nigricans*) from the Susquehanna River. Trans. Am. Fish. Soc. 107(4):595–599.

Cahn, A. R. 1915. An ecological survey of the Wingra Springs region. Bull. Wis. Nat. Hist. Soc. 13(3):123–177.

Cahn, A. R. 1927. An ecological study of the southern Wisconsin fishes. The brook silverside (*Labidesthes sicculus*) and the cisco (*Leucichthys artedi*) in their relations to the region. Ill. Biol. Monogr. 11(1):1–151.

Cahn, A. R. 1936. Observations on the breeding of the lawyer, *Lota maculosa*. Copeia 1936(3):163–165.

Calabresa, T. A. 1977. Wisconsin groundwater 1977; an analysis. Wis. Nat. Resour. 1(3):8–13.

Calovich, F. E., and B. A. Branson. 1964. The supraethmoid-ethmoid complex in the American catfishes, *Ictalurus* and *Pylodictis*. Am. Midl. Nat. 71(2):335–343.

Campbell, J. S., and H. R. MacCrimmon. 1970. Biology of the emerald shiner, *Notropis atherinoides* Raf., in Lake Simcoe, Canada. J. Fish Biol. 2:259–273.

Campos, H. H., and C. Hubbs. 1973. Taxonomic implications of the karyotype of *Opsopoeodus emiliae*. Copeia 1973(1):161–163.

Carbine, W. F. 1939. Observations on the spawning habits of centrarchid fishes in Deep Lake, Oakland County, Michigan. Trans. 4th North Am. Wildl. Conf.:275–287.

Carbine, W. F. 1942. Observations on the life history of the northern pike, *Esox lucius* L., in Houghton Lake, Michigan. Trans. Am. Fish. Soc. 71(1941):149–64.

Carl, G. C., W. A. Clemens, and C. C. Lindsey. 1967. The freshwater fishes of British Columbia. B.C. Prov. Mus. Dep. Recreat. Conserv. Handb. No. 5. 192 pp.

Carlander, H. B. 1954. A history of fish and fishing in the upper Mississippi River. Upper Miss. R. Conserv. Com., Des Moines. 96 pp.

Carlander, K. D. 1955. Standing crops of named fishes in North American lakes and reservoirs. J. Fish. Res. Board Canada 12(4):543–570.

Carlander, K. D. 1969. Handbook of freshwater fishery biology. Vol. 1. Iowa State Univ. Press. Ames. 752 pp.

Carlander, K. D. 1977. Handbook of freshwater fishery biology. Vol. 2. Iowa State Univ. Press, Ames. 431 pp.

Carlander, K. D., and R. E. Cleary. 1949. The daily activity patterns of some freshwater fishes. Am. Midl. Nat. 41(2):447–452.

Carline, R. F. 1975. Influence of recruitment rates on production by three populations of wild brook trout (*Salvelinus fontinalis* Mitchill). Univ. Wis., Madison. PhD Thesis. 128 pp.

Carline, R. F., and O. M. Brynildson. 1977. Effects of hydraulic dredging on the ecology of native trout populations in Wisconsin spring ponds. Wis. Dep. Nat. Resour. Tech. Bull. No. 98. 40 pp.

Carline, R. F., O. M. Brynildson, and M. O. Johnson. 1976. Growth and survival of trout stocked in a northern Wisconsin spring pond. Wis. Dep. Nat. Resour. Res. Rep. 85. 21 pp.

Carlson, A. R., R. E. Seifert, and L. J. Herman. 1974. Effects of lowered dissolved oxygen concentrations on channel catfish (*Ictalurus punctatus*) embryos and larvae. Trans. Am. Fish. Soc. 103(3):623–626.

Carlson, D. A. 1966. Age and growth of stonecat *Noturus flavus* in the Vermillion River, South Dakota. Proc. S.D. Acad. Sci. 45:131–137.

Carlson, D. M., and P. S. Bonislawsky. (unpubl. manus.) Paddlefish resources of the Midwest (14 July 1978). Mo. Dep. Conserv. and Kans. Fish Game Comm.

Carlson, D. R. 1967. Fathead minnow, *Pimephales promelas* Rafinesque, in the Des Moines River, Boone County, Iowa, and the Skunk River drainage, Hamilton and Story counties, Iowa. Iowa State J. Sci. 41(3):363–374.

Carnes, W. C., Jr. 1958. Contributions to the biology of the eastern creek chubsucker, *Erimyzon oblongus* (Mitchill). N.C. State Coll., Raleigh. MS Thesis. 69 pp.

Carranza, J., and H. E. Winn. 1954. Reproductive behavior of the blackstripe topminnow, *Fundulus notatus*. Copeia 1954(4):273–278.

Carson, R. 1943. Fishes of the Middle West. U.S. Fish Wildl. Serv. Conserv. Bull. 34. 44 pp.

Carter, N. E. 1968. Age and growth of sauger in Pool 19 of the Mississippi River. Proc. Iowa Acad. Sci. 75:179–183.

Carver, D. C. 1967. Distribution and abundance of the centrarchids in the recent delta of the Mississippi River. Proc. Southeast. Assoc. Game Fish. Commnrs. 20:390–404.

Case, B. 1970. Spawning behavior of the chestnut lamprey (*Ichthyomyzon castaneus*). J. Fish. Res. Board Canada 27(10):1872–1874.

Casselman, J. M. 1974. External sex determination of northern pike, *Esox lucius* Linnaeus. Trans. Am. Fish. Soc. 103(2):343–347.

Cavender, T. M. 1970. A comparison of coregonines and other salmonids with the earliest known teleostean fishes. pp. 1–32 *in* Biology of coregonid fishes, ed. C. C. Lindsey and C. S. Woods. Univ. Manitoba Press, Winnipeg.

Chadwick, E. M. P. 1976. Ecological fish production in a small Precambrian shield lake. Environ. Biol. Fishes 1(1):13–60.

Chadwick, H. K., C. E. von Geldern, Jr., and M. L. Johnson. 1966. White bass. pp. 412–422 *in* Inland fisheries management, ed. A. Calhoun. Calif. Dep. Fish Game, Sacramento.

Champagne, D. E., C. R. Harington, and D. E. McAllister, 1979. Deepwater sculpin, *Myoxocephalus thompsoni* (Girard) from a Pleistocene nodule, Green Creek, Ontario, Canada. Can. J. Earth Sci. 16:1621–1628.

Chapoton, R. B. 1955. Growth characteristics of the northern redbelly dace, *Chrosomus eos* (Cope), in experimental ponds in northern Michigan. Mich. State Coll., East Lansing. MS Thesis. 49 pp.

Chen, T. R. 1971. A comparative chromosome study of twenty killifish species of genus *Fundulus* (Teleostei: Cyprinodontidae). Chromosoma 32:436–453.

Chen, T. R., and H. M. Reisman. 1970. A comparative chromosome study of the North American species of sticklebacks (Teleostei: Gasterosteidae). Cytogenetics 9:321–332.

Chen, T. R., and F. H. Ruddle. 1970. A chromosome study of four species and a hybrid of the killifish genus *Fundulus* (Cyprinodontidae). Chromosoma 29:255–267.

Chiasson, R. B. 1966. Laboratory anatomy of the perch. Wm. C. Brown Co., Dubuque. 53 pp.

Chidambaram, S., R. K. Meyer, and A. D. Hasler. 1972. Effects of hypophysectomy, pituitary autografts, prolactin, temperature and salinity of the medium on survival and natremia in the bullhead, *Ictalurus melas*. Comp. Biochem. Physiol. 43A:443–457.

Childers, W., and H. H. Shoemaker. 1953. Time of feeding of the black crappie and the white crappie. Trans. Ill. Acad. Sci. 46:227–230.

Childers, W. F. 1967. Hybridization of four species of sunfishes (Centrarchidae). Ill. Nat. Hist. Surv. Bull. 29(3):159–214.

Christenson, L. M. 1974. Notes on the blue sucker, *Cycleptus elongatus* (Lesueur), in the lower Chippewa and Red Cedar rivers, Wisconsin. Wis. Dep. Nat. Resour. Res. Rep. 75. 7 pp.

Christenson, L. M. 1975. The shovelnose sturgeon, *Scaphirhynchus platorynchus* (Rafinesque), in the Red Cedar-Chippewa river system, Wisconsin. Wis. Dep. Nat. Resour. Res. Rep. 82. 23 pp.

Christenson, L. M., and L. L. Smith. 1965. Characteristics of fish populations in upper Mississippi backwater areas. U.S. Fish Wildl. Serv. Circ. 212. 53 pp.

Christenson, L. M., A. E. Ehly, J. B. Hale, R. H. Hovind, J. M. Keener, C. Kabat, G. J. Knudsen, D. J. O'Donnell, and A. A. Oehmke. 1961. Beaver-trout-forest relationships. Wis. Conserv. Dep. 34 pp. + 2 append.

Chromosome Atlas: Fish, Amphibians, Reptiles, Birds. 1973. Vol. 2, ed. K. Benirschke and T. C. Hsu. Springer-Verlag, Berlin.

Churchill, M. A., and T. A. Wojtalik. 1969. Effects of heated discharges; the TVA experiences. Nuclear News 12(Sept):80–86.

Churchill, W. 1945. The brook lamprey in the Brule River. Trans. Wis. Acad. Sci., Arts, Lett. 37:337–346.

Churchill, W. 1949a. Do little bass always grow big? Wis. Conserv. Bull. 14(10):17–19.

Churchill, W. 1949b. The effect of perch removal on a small northeastern Wisconsin lake. Wis. Cons. Dep. Div. Fish Mgmt. Invest. Rep. No. 714. 7 pp.

Churchill, W. 1967. The cisco fishery in Wisconsin in 1966. Wis. Dep. Nat. Resour. Res. Plan. Surv. Rep. 3 pp. (mimeo).

Churchill, W. 1968. Muskellunge fishing in Wisconsin. Wis. Dep. Nat. Resour. Surv. Rep. (Nov 1968). 8 pp. (mimeo).

Churchill, W. 1971. Results of a mail survey of winter fishing in Wisconsin, 1970–71. Wis. Dep. Nat. Resour. Surv. Rep. 4 pp.

Churchill, W. 1972. A mail survey of open-water fishing in Wisconsin, 1971. Wis. Dep. Nat. Resour. Surv. Rep. 4 pp.

Churchill, W. 1976. Population and biomass estimates of fishes in Lake Wingra. Wis. Dep. Nat. Resour. Tech. Bull. No. 93. 8 pp.

Clady, M. D. 1967. Changes in an exploited population of the cisco, *Coregonus artedii* LeSueur. Pap. Mich. Acad. Sci., Arts, Lett. 52:85–99.

Claflin, T. O. 1963. Age and rate of growth of the goldeye, *Hiodon alosoides* (Rafinesque), in the Missouri River. Univ. S.D., Vermillion. MA Thesis. 28 pp.

Clark, C. F. 1950. Observations on the spawning habits of the northern pike, *Esox lucius*, in northwestern Ohio. Copeia 1950(4):285–288.

Clark, C. F. 1960. Lake St. Mary's and its management. Ohio Dep. Nat. Resour. Div. Wildl. Publ. W–324. 107 pp.

Clark, F. W., and M. H. A. Keenleyside. 1967. Reproductive isolation between the sunfish *Lepomis gibbosus* and *L. macrochirus*. J. Fish. Res. Board Canada 24(3):495–514.

Clark, J. R. 1969. Thermal pollution and aquatic life. Sci. Am. 220(3):19–27.

Clarke, R. M. 1973. The systematics of ciscoes (Coregonidae) in central Canada. Univ. Manitoba, Winnipeg. PhD Thesis. 260 pp.

Clary, J. R. 1972. Predation on the brown trout by the slimy sculpin. Progr. Fish-Cult. 34(2):91–95.

Clay, W. M. 1962. A field manual of Kentucky fishes. Ky. Dep. Fish Wildl. Resour., Frankfort. 147 pp.

Clay, W. M. 1975. The fishes of Kentucky. Ky. Dep. Fish Wildl. Resour., Frankfort. 416 pp.

Cleary, R. E. 1956. Observations on factors affecting smallmouth bass production in Iowa. J. Wildl. Mgmt. 20(4):353–359.

Clemens, H. P., and K. E. Sneed. 1957. The spawning behavior of the channel catfish *Ictalurus punctatus*. U.S. Fish Wildl. Serv. Spec. Sci. Rep.—Fish. No. 219. 11 pp.

Clifford, H. F. 1972. Downstream movements of white sucker, *Catostomus commersoni*, fry in a brown-water stream of Alberta. J. Fish. Res. Board Canada 29(7):1091–1093.

Clugston, J. P. 1973. The effects of heated effluents from a nuclear reactor on species diversity, abundance, reproduction, and movement of fish. Univ. Ga., Athens. PhD Thesis. Diss. Abstr. Int. 34(8)B:3580.

Coad, B. W. 1973. Modifications of the pelvic complex in ninespine sticklebacks, *Pungitius pungitius* (L.), of eastern Canada and the Northwest Territories. Le Nat. can. 100:315–316.

Coad, B. W., and G. Power. 1973. Observations on the ecology and meristic variation of the ninespine stickleback, *Pungitius pungitius* (L., 1758), of the Matamek River system, Quebec. Am. Midl. Nat. 90(2):498–503.

Coble, D. W. 1966. Dependence of total annual growth in yellow perch on temperature. J. Fish. Res. Board Canada 23(1):15–20.

Coble, D. W. 1967a. Relationship of temperature to total annual growth in adult smallmouth bass. J. Fish. Res. Board Canada 24(1):87–99.

Coble, D. W. 1967b. The white sucker population of South Bay, Lake Huron, and effects of sea lamprey on it. J. Fish. Res. Board Canada 24(10):2117–2136.

Coble, D. W. 1970. False annulus formation in bluegill scales. Trans. Am. Fish. Soc. 99(2):363–368.

Coble, D. W. 1973. Influence of appearance of prey and satiation of predator on food selection by northern pike (*Esox lucius*). J. Fish. Res. Board Canada 30(2):317–320.

Coble, D. W. 1975. Smallmouth bass. pp. 21–33 *in* Black bass biology and management, chrd. R. H. Stroud and ed. H. Clepper. Sport Fishing Inst., Wash., D.C.

Coker, R. E. 1930. Studies of common fishes of the Mississippi River at Keokuk. U.S. Dep. Commer. Bur. Fish. Doc. 1072:141–225.

Coker, R. E., A. F. Shira, H. W. Clark, and A. D. Howard. 1921. Natural history and propagation of fresh-water mussels. Bull. U.S. Bur. Fish. 37:75–182.

Colburn, R. 1946. Lawyer control. Wis. Conserv. Bull. 11(3):21.

Colby, P. J., and T. L. Brooke. 1970. Survival and development of lake herring (*Coregonus artedii*) eggs at various incubation temperatures. pp. 417–428 *in* Biology of coregonid fishes, ed. C. C. Lindsey and C. S. Woods. Univ. Manitoba Press, Winnipeg.

Colby, P. J., and G. N. Washburn. 1972. Feeding behavior of lake whitefish and lake herring in Torch Lake, Michigan. Progr. Fish-Cult. 34(3):151.

Collette, B. B. 1965. Systematic significance of breeding tubercles in fishes of the family Percidae. Proc. U.S. Natl. Mus. 117:567–614.

Collette, B. B., M. A. Ali, K. E. F. Hokanson, M. Nagiec, S. A. Smirnov, J. E. Thorpe, A. H. Weatherley, and J. Willemsen. 1977. Biology of the percids. J. Fish. Res. Board Canada 34(10):1891–1897.

Collier, J. E. 1959. Changes in fish populations and food habits of yellow bass in North Twin Lake, 1956–58. Proc. Iowa Acad. Sci. 66:518–522.

Colvin, M. A. 1975. The walleye population and fishery in the Red Cedar River, Wisconsin. Univ. Wis., Stevens Point. MS Thesis. 97 pp.

Commercial Fisheries Review. 1961. Lake Erie fish population survey for 1961 season begins. Commer. Fish. Rev. 23(6):23–24.

Commissioners of Fisheries of Wisconsin. 1876–1910. Annual and biennial reports of the commissioners of fisheries of Wisconsin. Madison.

Committee on Rare and Endangered Wildlife Species. 1966. Rare and endangered fishes and wildlife of the United States. U.S. Bur. Sport Fish. Wildl. Resour. Publ. 34 (7 sections, separately numbered).

Cook, F. A. 1959. Freshwater fishes in Mississippi. Miss. Fish Game Comm., Jackson. 239 pp.

Cook, R. S.(chmn), G. Becker, A. Beeton, P. N. Cook, P. H. Derse, A. D. Hasler, R. E. Lennon, P. Sager, and W. Selbig. 1972. Report of governor's study committee on the use of fish toxicants for fish management. State Wis. Off. of Gov., Madison. 5 pp. (mimeo).

Cooper, E. 1956. What's happened to the cisco? Wis. Conserv. Bull. 21(3):1–4.

Cooper, G. P. 1936. Some results of forage fish investigations in Michigan. Trans. Am. Fish. Soc. 65(1935):132–142.

Cooper, G. P., and G. N. Washburn. 1949. Relation of dissolved oxygen to winter mortality of fish in lakes. Trans. Am. Fish. Soc. 76(1946):23–33.

Cope, E. D. 1869. Synopsis of the Cyprinidae of Pennsylvania. Trans. Am. Phil. Soc. 13(2):351–399.

Copes, F. 1970. A study of the ecology of the native fishes of Sand Creek, Albany County, Wyoming. Univ. Wyo., Laramie. PhD Thesis. 281 pp.

Copes, F. 1975. Ecology of the brassy minnow, *Hybognathus hankinsoni* Hubbs. Univ. Wis., Stevens Point, Mus. Nat. Hist. Fauna and Flora Wis. Part III Rep. No. 10:46–72.

Copes, F. 1978. Ecology of the creek chub *Semotilus atromaculatus* (Mitchill) in northern waters. Univ. Wis., Stevens Point, Mus. Nat. Hist. Fauna and Flora Wis. Rep. No. 12:1–21.

Couey, F. M. 1935. Fish food studies of a number of northeastern Wisconsin lakes. Trans. Wis. Acad. Sci., Arts, Lett. 29:131–172.

Coutant, C. C. 1975. Temperature selection by fish—a factor in power-plant assessments. pp. 575–595 *in* Environmental effects of cooling systems at nuclear power plants. Oak Ridge Natl. Lab., Environ. Sci. Div. Publ. 701.

Cox, G. M. 1939. ". . . and little fishes." Wis. Conserv. Bull. 4(7):25–32.

Crabtree, K. T. 1972. Nitrate and nitrite variation in ground water. Wis. Dep. Nat. Resour. Tech. Bull. 58. 22 pp.

Crawford, R. H. 1966. Buoyancy regulation in lake trout. Univ. Toronto, Toronto. MA Thesis. 96 pp.

Creaser, C. W. 1925. The establishment of the Atlantic smelt in the upper waters of the Great Lakes. Pap. Mich. Acad. Sci., Arts, Lett. 5:405–423.

Creaser, C. W., and C. S. Hann. 1928. The food of larval lampreys. Pap. Mich. Acad. Sci., Arts, Lett. 10(1928):433–437.

Cross, A. S. 1938. A study of the fish parasite relationships in the Trout Lake region of Wisconsin. Trans. Wis. Acad. Sci., Arts, Lett. 31:439–456.

Cross, F. B. 1950. Effects of sewage and of a headwaters impoundment on the fishes of Stillwater Creek in Payne County, Oklahoma. Am. Midl. Nat. 43(1):128–145.

Cross, F. B. 1967. Handbook of fishes of Kansas. Univ. Kans. Mus. Nat. Hist. Misc. Publ. 45. 357 pp.

Cross, F. B., and W. L. Minckley. 1960. Five natural hybrid combinations in minnows (Cyprinidae). Univ. Kans. Mus. Nat. Hist., Publ. 13(1):1–18.

Crossman, E. J. 1962. Predator-prey relationships in pikes (Esocidae). J. Fish. Res. Board Canada 19(5):979–980.

Culp, R. L., and G. L. Culp. 1971. Advanced wastewater treatment. Van Nostrand Reinhold, N.Y. 310 pp.

Curtis, B. 1949. The life story of the fish. Dover Publications, N.Y. 284 pp.

Daiber, F. C. 1953. Notes on the spawning population of the freshwater drum (*Aplodinotus grunniens* Rafinesque) in western Lake Erie. Am. Midl. Nat. 50(1):159–171.

Daiber, F. C. 1956. A comparative analysis of the winter feeding habits of two benthic stream fishes. Copeia 1956(3):141–151.

Daly, R. I. 1968a. Preliminary notes on management of the rainbow trout in western Lake Michigan. Wis. Dep. Nat. Res. Bur. Fish Mgmt., Oshkosh, 4 pp. (mimeo).

Daly, R. I. 1968b. Progress report of fish management on Lake Michigan. Wis. Dep. Nat. Resour. Bur. Fish Mgmt., Oshkosh. 18 pp.

Daly, R. I. 1971. Chinook: the big one. Wis. Conserv. Bull. 36(5):22–23.

Daly, R. I., and L. W. Wiegert. 1958. "The smelt are running!" Wis. Conserv. Bull. 23(3):14–15.

Daly, R. I., V. A. Hacker, and L. Wiegert. 1962. The lake trout, its life history, ecology, and management. Wis. Conserv. Dep. Publ. No. 233. 15 pp.

Daly, R. I., J. Moore, and P. Schultz. 1974. Progress report of fish management on Lake Michigan, 1973. Wis. Dep. Nat. Resour. Bur. Fish Wildl. Mgmt. 39 pp. (mimeo).

Darnell, R. M., and R. R. Meierotto. 1962. Determination of feeding chronology in fishes. Trans. Am. Fish. Soc. 91(3):313–320.

Darnell, R. M., and R. R. Meierotto. 1965. Diurnal periodicity in the black bullhead. Trans. Am. Fish. Soc. 94(1):1–8.

Davidson, F. A., and S. J. Hutchinson. 1938. The geographic distribution and environmental limitations of the Pacific salmon (genus *Oncorhynchus*). U.S. Dep. Commer., Bur. Fish. Bull. 48(26):667–692.

Davis, B. J., and R. J. Miller. 1967. Brain patterns in minnows of the genus *Hybopsis* in relation to feeding habits and habitat. Copeia 1967(1):1–39.

Davis, H. S. 1956. Culture and diseases of game fishes. Univ. Calif. Press, Berkeley. 332 pp.

Davis, J. 1959. Management of channel catfish in Kansas. Univ. Kans. Mus. Nat. Hist. Misc. Publ. No. 21. 56 pp.

Deason, H. J. 1934. The development of fishes, tracing the natural developments from egg to fry. The Fisherman 3(11):1, 3.

Deason, H. J. 1939. The distribution of cottid fishes in Lake Michigan. Pap. Mich. Acad. Sci., Arts, Lett. 24(2)1938:105–115.

Deason, H. J., and R. Hile. 1947. Age and growth of the kiyi, *Leucichthys kiyi* Koelz, in Lake Michigan. Trans. Am. Fish. Soc. 74(1944):88–142.

Degraeve, G. M. 1970. Three types of burrowing behavior of the brook stickleback, *Culaea inconstans*. Trans. Am. Fish. Soc. 99(2):433.

Degurse, P. 1961. Common external parasites of fish. pp. 9–11 *in* Fish parasites. Wis. Conserv. Dep., Madison, Publ. 212–61.

Degurse, P. E., D. Crochett, and H. R. Nielsen. 1973. Observations on Lake Michigan coho salmon (*Oncorhynchus kisutch*) propagation mortality in Wisconsin with an evaluation of the pesticide relationship. Wis. Dep. Nat. Resour. Bur. Fish. Mgmt. Rep. No. 62. 11 pp. (mimeo).

Delco, E. A., Jr. 1960. Sound discrimination by males of two cyprinid fishes. Tex. J. Sci. 12(1, 2):48–54.

Delco, E. A., Jr., and R. J. Beyers. 1963. Reduced metabolic rates in males of two cyprinid fishes. Copeia 1963(1):176–178.

Delisle, C., and W. Van Vliet. 1968. First records of the sculpins *Myoxocephalus thompsonii* and *Cottus ricei* from the Ottawa Valley, southwestern Quebec. J. Fish. Res. Board Canada 25(12):2733–2737.

DeLoughery, F. 1975. New table delicacy. Environment 17(2):13, 15.

Denoncourt, R. F. 1969. A systematic study of the gilt darter *Percina evides* (Jordan and Copeland) (Pisces: Percidae). Cornell Univ., Ithaca. PhD Thesis. 209 pp.

De Sylva, D. P. 1964. Sea lamprey, *Petromyzon marinus*. pp. 778–779 *in* Standard fishing encyclopedia, ed. A. J. McClane. Holt, Rinehart & Winston, N.Y.

Dineen, C. F., and P. S. Stokely. 1954. Osteology of the central mudminnow, *Umbra limi*. Copeia 1954(3):169–179.

Dingerkus, G., and W. M. Howell. 1976. Karyotypic analysis and evidence of tetraploidy in the North American paddlefish, *Polyodon spathula*. Science 194(19 Nov 1976):842–844.

Dinsmore, J. J. 1962. Life history of the creek chub with emphasis on growth. Proc. Iowa Acad. Sci. 69:296–301.

Dintaman, R. C. 1975. A preliminary study of the occurrence of the American eel and finfish species in Maryland. Md. Dep. Nat. Resour., Wye Mills. 58 pp.

Distler, D. A. 1968. Distribution and variation of *Etheostoma spectabile* (Agassiz) (Percidae: Teleostei). Kans. Univ. Sci. Bull. 48:143–208.

Divine, G. 1968. A study of the smallmouth bass in ponds with special consideration of minnows and decapods as forage. Univ. Missouri, Columbia. MA Thesis. 115 pp.

Doan, K. H. 1938. Observations on dogfish (*Amia calva*) and their young. Copeia 1938(4):204.

Dobie, J. R., O. L. Meehean, and G. N. Washburn. 1948. Propagation of minnows and other bait species. U.S. Fish Wildl. Serv. Circ. 12. 113 pp.

Dobie, J. R., O. L. Meehean, S. F. Snieszko, and G. N. Washburn. 1956. Raising bait fishes. U.S. Fish Wildl. Serv. Circ. 35. 123 pp.

Dombeck, M. P. 1974. Meristic variation of the rainbow darter, *Etheostoma caeruleum* (Storer). Univ. Wis., Stevens Point. MS Thesis. 67 pp.

Dombeck, M. P. 1979. Movement and behavior of the muskellunge determined by radio-telemetry. Wis. Dep. Nat. Resour. Tech. Bull. No. 113. 19 pp.

Douglas, N. H. 1974. Freshwater fishes of Louisiana. La. Wildl. Fish. Comm., Claitor's Publishing, Baton Rouge. 443 pp.

Dow, R. L. 1972. The anadromous smelt fishery of Maine. Natl. Fisherman, June 1972. pp. 24–A, 29–A.

Dowell, V. E. 1962. Distribution of the blacknose shiner, *Notropis heterolepis* Eigenmann and Eigenmann, in Clay, Dickinson and Osceola counties, Iowa. Proc. Iowa Acad. Sci. 69:529–531.

Downs, W. 1974. Fish of Lake Michigan. Univ. Wis. Sea Grant Coll. Prog. WIS–SG–74–121. Sea Grant Commun. Off., Madison. 32 pp.

Downs, W. 1976. Fish of Lake Superior. Univ. Wis. Sea Grant Coll. Prog. WIS–SG–76–124. Sea Grant Commun. Off., Madison. 36 pp.

Doyle, B. 1937. Here's the answer. Wis. Conserv. Bull. 2(5):34.

Druschba, L. J. 1959. Are carp moving north? Wis. Conserv. Bull. 24(11):22–25.

Dryer, W. R. 1963. Age and growth of the whitefish in Lake Superior. U.S. Fish Wildl. Serv. Fish. Bull. 63(1):77–95.

Dryer, W. R. 1964. Movements, growth and rate of recapture of whitefish tagged in the Apostle Islands area of Lake Superior. U.S. Fish Wildl. Serv. Fish. Bull. 63(3):611–618.

Dryer, W. R. 1966. Bathymetric distribution of fish in the Apostle Islands region, Lake Superior. Trans. Am. Fish. Soc. 95(3):248–259.

Dryer, W. R., and J. Beil. 1964. Life history of the lake herring in Lake Superior. U.S. Fish Wildl. Serv. Fish. Bull. 63(3):493–530.

Dryer, W. R., and J. Beil. 1968. Growth changes of the bloater (*Coregonus hoyi*) of the Apostle Islands region of Lake Superior. Trans. Am. Fish. Soc. 97(2):146–158.

Dryer, W. R., and G. R. King. 1968. Rehabilitation of lake trout in the Apostle Islands region of Lake Superior. J. Fish Res. Board Canada 25(7):1377–1403.

Dryer, W. R., L. F. Erkkila, C. L. Tetzloff. 1965. Food of lake trout in Lake Superior. Trans. Am. Fish. Soc. 94(2):169–176.

Dudley, S., J. R. Graikoski, H. L. Seagran, and P. M. Earl. 1970. Sportsman's guide to handling, smoking, and preserving Great Lakes coho salmon. U.S. Fish Wildl. Serv. Circ. 346. 28 pp.

Dunning, P. 1884. Two hundred tons of dead fish, mostly perch, in Lake Mendota, Wisconsin. Bull. U.S. Fish. Comm. 4:439–443.

Dunst, R. C. 1969. Cox Hollow Lake, the first eight years of impoundment. Wis. Dep. Nat. Resour. Res. Rep. 47. 19 pp.

Dunst, R. C., and T. Wirth. 1972. Appendix O, the Chippewa Flowage fish population. pp. 0–43 *in* Chippewa flowage investigations. Part III A. Appendixes. Inland Lakes Demon. Stn. Proj., Upper Great Lakes Reg. Comm.

Dunst, R. C., S. M. Born, P. D. Uttormark, S. A. Smith, S. A. Nichols, J. O. Peterson, D. R. Knauer, S. L. Serns, D. R. Winter, and T. L. Wirth. 1974. Survey of lake rehabilitation techniques and experiences. Wis. Dep. Nat. Resour. Tech. Bull. No. 75. 179 pp.

Dupree, H. K., O. L. Green, and K. E. Sneed. 1966. Techniques for the hybridization of catfishes. Southeast. Fish Cult. Lab., Marion, Ala. 9 pp. (mimeo).

Durham, L. 1955a. Effects of predation by cormorants and gars on fish populations of ponds in Illinois. Univ. Ill., Urbana. PhD Thesis. 113 pp.

Durham, L. 1955b. Ecological factors affecting growth of smallmouth bass and longear sunfish in Jordan Creek. Trans. Ill. Acad. Sci. 47:25–34.

Dymond, J. R. 1926. The fishes of Lake Nipigon. Univ. Toronto Stud. Biol. Ser. 27, Ont. Fish. Res. Lab. Publ. 27:1–108.

Dymond, J. R. 1955. The introduction of foreign fishes in Canada. Int. Assoc. Theor. and Appl. Limnol. Proc. 12:543–553.

Dymond, J. R., J. L. Hart, and A. L. Pritchard. 1929. The fishes of the Canadian waters of Lake Ontario. Univ. Toronto Stud., Ont. Fish. Res. Lab. Publ. 37:3–35.

Eales, J. C. 1968. The eel fisheries of Eastern Canada. Fish. Res. Board Canada, Ottawa. Bull. 166:1–79.

Eastman, J. T. 1970. The pharyngeal bones and teeth of Minnesota cyprinid and catostomid fishes: functional morphology, variation and taxonomic significance. Univ. Minn., Minneapolis. PhD Thesis. 307 pp.

Eaton, T. H., Jr. 1935. Evolution of the upper jaw mechanism in teleost fishes. J. Morphol. 58(1):157–172.

Ebbers, M. A., and B. W. Hawkinson. 1978. Trapnetting survey of Pools 3–7 in the Mississippi River in 1957, 1963, 1970, 1977. Minn. Dep. Nat. Resour. Div. Fish Wildl., Sec. Fish. Rep. No. 12. 41 pp.

Echelle, A. A., and C. D. Riggs. 1972. Aspects of the early life history of gars (*Lepisosteus*) in Lake Texoma. Trans. Am. Fish. Soc. 101(1):106–112.

Eddy, S., and T. Surber. 1947. Northern fishes. Univ. Minn. Press, Minneapolis. 276 pp.

Eddy, S., and J. C. Underhill. 1974. Northern fishes. Univ. Minn. Press, Minneapolis. 414 pp.

Edsall, T. A. 1960. Age and growth of the whitefish, *Coregonus clupeaformis*, of Munising Bay, Lake Superior. Trans. Am. Fish. Soc. 89(4):323–332.

Edsall, T. A. 1964. Feeding by three species of fishes on eggs of spawning alewives. Copeia 1964(1): 226–227.

Edsall, T. A. 1967. Biology of the freshwater drum in western Lake Erie. Ohio J. Sci. 67(6):321–340.

Edsall, T. A. 1976. Electric power generation and its influence on Great Lakes fish. Proc. 2d Fed. Conf. on Great Lakes, 25–27 Mar. 1975. Interagency Comm. Mar. Sci. and Eng., Fed. Counc. Sci. & Tech., Great Lakes Basin Comm., Ann Arbor. pp. 453–462.

Eilers, J., M. Steimle, B. Martini, R. Becker, L. Anderson, F. Boettcher, M. Brilla, G. Glass, L. Heinis, J. Ilse, J. Rogalla, T. Poush, and C. Sandberg. 1979. Progress report—acid precipitation—investigation for northern Wisconsin. Wis. Dep. Nat. Resour., Rhinelander, and U.S. Environ. Prot. Agency, Environ. Res. Lab., Duluth. 15 pp. + append.

Ellis, D. V., and M. A. Giles. 1965. The spawning behavior of the walleye, *Stizostedion vitreum* (Mitchill). Trans. Am. Fish. Soc. 94(4):358–362.

Ellis, J. E. 1974. The jumping ability and behavior of green sunfish (*Lepomis cyanellus*) at the overflow of a 1.6 ha pond. Trans. Am. Fish. Soc. 103(3):620–623.

Ellis, M. 1973. Carp: a symptom, not a cause. "The Good Earth" feature in The Milwaukee J., 14 Jan:12.

Ellis, M. M., and G. C. Roe. 1917. Destruction of log perch eggs by suckers. Copeia 1917(47):69–71.

Ells, W. E. 1977. Incident at Winneconne. Wis. Nat. Resour. 1(2):22–23.

Elrod, J. H. 1974. Abundance, growth, survival, and maturation of channel catfish in Lake Sharpe, South Dakota. Trans. Am. Fish. Soc. 103(1):53–58.

Elrod, J. H., and T. J. Hassler. 1971. Vital statistics of seven fish species in Lake Sharpe, South Dakota 1964–1969. pp. 27–40 *in* Reservoir fishes and limnology, ed. G. E. Hall. Am. Fish. Soc. Spec. Publ. No. 8.

El-Shamy, F. 1976. A comparison of the growth rates of bluegill (*Lepomis macrochirus*) in Lake Wingra and Lake Mendota. Trans. Wis. Acad. Sci., Arts, Lett. 64:144–153.

Embody, G. C. 1922. Concerning high water temperature and trout. Trans. Am. Fish. Soc. 51:58–61.

Embody, G. C. 1934. Relation of temperature to the incubation periods of eggs of four species of trout. Trans. Am. Fish. Soc. 64:281–291.

Emery, A. R. 1970. Fish and crayfish mortalities due to an internal seiche in Georgian Bay, Lake Huron. J. Fish. Res. Board Canada 27(6):1165–1168.

Emery, A. R. 1973. Preliminary comparisons of day and night habits of freshwater fish in Ontario lakes. J. Fish. Res. Board Canada. 30(6):761–774.

Emery, A. R. 1975. Community structures. Sport Fishing Inst. Bull. 262(Mar 1975):2.

Emery, L., and E. H. Brown, Jr. 1978. Fecundity of the bloater (*Coregonus hoyi*) in Lake Michigan. Trans. Am. Fish. Soc. 107(6):785–789.

Emig, J. 1966a. Brown bullhead. pp. 463–475 *in* Inland fisheries management, ed. A. Calhoun. Calif. Dep. Fish Game.

Emig, J. 1966b. Smallmouth bass. pp. 354–366 *in* Inland fisheries management, ed. A. Calhoun. Calif. Dep. Fish Game.

Engel, S., and J. J. Magnuson. 1971. Ecological interactions between coho salmon and native fishes in a small lake. Proc. 14th Conf. Great Lakes Res. pp. 14–20.

English, T. S. 1952. A method of sectioning carp spines for growth studies. Progr. Fish-Cult. 14(1):36.

Eschmeyer, P. H. 1950. The life history of the walleye, *Stizostedion vitreum vitreum* (Mitchill), in Michigan. Mich. Dep. Conserv., Inst. Fish. Res. Bull. No. 3. 99 pp.

Eschmeyer, P. H. 1955. The reproduction of lake trout in southern Lake Superior. Trans. Am. Fish. Soc. 84(1954):47–74 + 3 figs.

Eschmeyer, P. H. 1956. The early life history of the lake trout in Lake Superior. Mich. Dep. Conserv. Misc. Publ. No. 10. 31 pp.

Eschmeyer, P. H. 1957. The lake trout (*Salvelinus namaycush*). U.S. Fish Wildl. Serv. Fish. Leaflet No. 441. 11 pp.

Eschmeyer, P. H., and R. M. Bailey. 1955. The pygmy whitefish, *Coregonus coulteri*, in Lake Superior. Trans. Am. Fish. Soc. 84:161–199.

Eschmeyer, P. H., and A. M. Phillips, Jr. 1965. Fat content of the flesh of siscowets and lake trout from Lake Superior. Trans. Am. Fish. Soc. 94(1):62–74.

Eschmeyer, P. H., R. Daly, and L. F. Erkkila. 1953. The movement of tagged lake trout in Lake Superior, 1950–1952. Trans. Am. Fish. Soc. 82(1952):68–77.

Evans, H. E. 1952. The correlation of brain pattern and feeding habits in four species of cyprinid fishes. J. Comp. Neur. 97(1):133–142.

Evans, H. E., and E. E. Deubler, Jr. 1955. Pharyngeal tooth replacement in *Semotilus atromaculatus* and *Clinostomus elongatus*, two species of cyprinid fishes. Copeia 1955(1):31–41.

Everhart, W. H. 1958. Fishes of Maine. 2d ed. Maine Dep. Inland Fish. Game, Augusta. 94 pp.

Everhart, W. H., and W. R. Seaman. 1971. Fishes of Colorado. Colo. Game, Fish Parks Div. 75 pp.

Evermann, B. W., and H. W. Clark. 1920. Lake Maxinkuckee: a physical and biological survey. Indiana Dep. Conserv. 1. 660 pp.

Ewers, L. A., and M. W. Boesel. 1935. The food of some Buckeye Lake fishes. Trans. Am. Fish. Soc. 65:57–70.

Eycleshymer, A. C. 1903. The early development of *Lepidosteus osseus*. Univ. Chic., Decennial Publications, 1st Ser., Vol. 10. Univ. Chic. Press, Chic. pp. 261–277.

Faber, D. J. 1967. Limnetic larval fish in northern Wisconsin lakes. J. Fish. Res. Board Canada 24(5)927–937.

Faber, D. J. 1970. Ecological observations on newly hatched lake whitefish in South Bay, Lake Huron. pp. 481–500 *in* Biology of coregonid fishes, ed. C. C. Lindsey and C. S. Woods. Univ. Manitoba Press, Winnipeg.

Fago, D. M. 1973. The northern's finicky spawning needs. Wis. Conserv. Bull. 38(2):18–19.

Fago, D. M. 1977. Northern pike production in managed spawning and rearing marshes. Wis. Dep. Nat. Resour. Tech. Bull. 96. 30 pp.

Fassbender, R. L., J. J. Weber, and L. M. Nelson. 1970. Surface water resources of Green Lake County. Wis. Dep. Nat. Resour. Lake and Strm. Classif. Proj. 72 pp.

Fee, E. 1965. Life history of the northern common shiner, *Notropis cornutus frontalis*, in Boone County, Iowa. Proc. Iowa Acad. Sci. 72:272–281.

Ferguson, D. E., and C. P. Goodyear. 1967. The pathway of endrin entry in black bullheads, *Ictalurus melas*. Copeia 1967(2):467–468.

Ferguson, R. G. 1958. The preferred temperature of fish and their midsummer distribution in temperate lakes and streams. J. Fish. Res. Board Canada 15(4):607–624.

Fernholz, W. B. 1966. Mississippi River commercial fishing statistics, 1965. Wis. Conser. Dep. Div. Fish Mgmt. Stat. Rep. 31 pp.

Fernholz, W. B. 1971. Mississippi River commercial fishing statistics, 1970. Wis. Dep. Nat. Resour. Bur. Fish Mgmt. Stat. Rep. 26 pp.

Fernholz, W. B. 1972. Mississippi River commercial fishing statistics, 1971. Wis. Dep. Nat. Resour. Bur. Fish Mgmt. Stat. Rep. 24 pp.

Fernholz, W. B., and V. E. Crawley. 1976. Mississippi River commercial fishing statistics, 1975. Wis. Dep. Nat. Resour. Bur. Fish Wildl. Mgmt. Stat. Rep. 25 pp.

Fernholz, W. B., and V. E. Crawley. 1977. Mississippi River commercial fishing statistics, 1976. Wis. Dep. Nat. Resour. Bur. Fish Wildl. Mgmt. Stat. Rep. 22 pp.

Fernholz, W. B., and V. E. Crawley, 1978. Mississippi River commercial fishing statistics, 1977. Wis. Dep. Nat. Resour. Bur. Fish Wildl. Mgmt. Stat. Rep. 22 pp.

Fetterolf, C. M., Jr. 1952. A population study of the fishes of Wintergreen Lake, Kalamazoo County, Michigan; with note on movement and effect of netting on condition. Mich. State Coll., East Lansing. MS Thesis. 127 pp.

Fine, I. V., and E. E. Werner. 1960. Economic significance of fishing in Wisconsin. Univ. Wis. School Commer., Madison, Wis. vacation-recreat. pap. Vol. 1. No. 10. 10 pp.

Finke, A. H. 1964. The channel catfish. Wis. Conserv. Bull. 29(2):18–19.

Finke, A. H. 1966a (June). Northern pike tagging study—Black River, La Crosse County, Wisconsin, 1964–1965. Wis. Dep. Nat. Resour. Bur. Fish Mgmt. Rep. No. 7. 10 pp. (mimeo).

Finke, A. H. 1966b. White bass tagging study—upper Mississippi River. Wis. Conserv. Dep. Div. Fish Mgmt. Rep. No. 6. 11 pp. (mimeo).

Finke, A. H. 1967. A five-year summary of commercial fishing for carp, buffalo, sheepshead, catfish and bullhead on the Wisconsin portion of the Mississippi River. Proc. 23d Annu. Meet. Upper Miss. R. Conserv. Com., 33-page addendum.

Fischthal, J. H. 1945. Parasites of Brule River fishes (Brule River survey: report no. 6). Trans. Wis. Acad. Sci., Arts, Lett. 37:275–278.

Fischthal, J. H. 1948. Stunted bluegills become prize fish. Wis. Conserv. Bull. 13(11):16–17.

Fischthal, J. H. 1950. Parasites of northwest Wisconsin fishes. Part II. The 1945 survey. Trans. Wis. Acad. Sci., Arts, Lett. 40(1):87–113.

Fischthal, J. H. 1952. Parasites of northwest Wisconsin fishes. Part III. The 1946 survey. Trans. Wis. Acad. Sci., Arts, Lett. 41:17–58.

Fischthal, J. H. 1961. Grubs in fishes. pp. 3–9 *in* Fish parasites. Wis. Conserv. Dep. Publ. 212–61.

Fish, M. P. 1932. Contributions to the early life histories of 62 species of fishes from Lake Erie and its tributary waters. Bull. U.S. Bur. Fish. 47(10):293–398.

Flemer, D. A., and W. S. Woolcott. 1966. Food habits and distribution of the fishes of Tuckahoe, Creek, Virginia, with special emphasis on the bluegill, *Lepomis m. macrochirus* Rafinesque. Chesapeake Sci. 7(2):75–89.

Flickinger, S. A. 1969. Determination of sexes in the fathead minnow. Trans. Am. Fish. Soc. 98(3):526–527.

Flittner, G. A. 1964. Morphology and life history of the emerald shiner *N. atherinoides*. Univ. Mich., Ann Arbor. PhD Thesis. 213 pp.

Foltz, J. W. 1976. Fecundity of the slimy sculpin, *Cottus cognatus*, in Lake Michigan. Copeia 1976(4):802–804.

Fontaine, P. A. 1944. Notes on the spawning of the shovelhead catfish, *Pilodictis olivaris* (Rafinesque). Copeia 1944(1):50–51.

Forbes, S. A. 1878. The food of Illinois fishes. Ill. Nat. Hist. Surv. Bull. 2:71–86.

Forbes, S. A. 1880. Various papers on the food of fishes. Bull. Ill. State Lab. Nat. Hist. 1(3):18–65.

Forbes, S. A. 1883. The food of the smaller fresh-water fishes. Bull. Ill. State Lab. Nat. Hist. 1(6):65–94.

Forbes, S. A. 1885. Description of new Illinois fishes. Bull. Ill. State Lab. Nat. Hist. 2(2):135–139.

Forbes, S. A., and R. E. Richardson. 1920. The fishes of Illinois. Ill. Nat. Hist. Surv. Bull. 3. 357 pp.

Forney, J. L. 1955. Life history of the black bullhead, *Ameiurus melas*, of Clear Lake, Iowa. Iowa State Coll. J. Sci. 30(1):145–162.

Forney, J. L. 1957. Raising bait fish and crayfish in New York ponds. Cornell Ext. Bull. 986:3–30.

Fowler, H. W. 1917. Some notes on the breeding habits of local catfishes. Copeia 1917(42):32–36.

Frankenberger, L. 1957. Whitefish and ciscoes—forgotten fish. Wis. Conserv. Bull. 22(12):21–23.

Frankenberger, L. 1968. Effects of habitat management on trout in a portion of the Kinnickinnic River, St. Croix County, Wisconsin. Wis. Dep. Nat. Resour. Bur. Fish Mgmt. Rep. No. 22. 14 pp. (mimeo).

Frankenberger, L. 1969. Evaluation of brown trout fingerling stocking programs in the lower Willow River and the economics thereof. Wis. Dep. Nat. Resour. Bur. Fish Mgmt. Rep. No. 24. 16 pp.

Frankenberger, L., and R. Fassbender. 1967. Evaluation of the effects of the habitat management program and the watershed planning program on the brown trout fishery in Bohemian Valley Creek, La Crosse County. Wis. Dep. Nat. Resour. Bur. Fish Mgmt. Rep. No. 16. 19 pp. (mimeo).

Franklin, D. R., and L. L. Smith. 1963. Early life history of the northern pike (*Esox lucius* L.) with special reference to the factors influencing strength of year classes. Trans. Am. Fish. Soc. 92(2):91–110.

Franklin, J. 1964. Aerobic bacteria in the intestine of the golden shiner. Progr. Fish-Cult. 26(4):160–166.
Fredrich, L. 1977. Ecological life history of juvenile whitefish in northern Lake Michigan. 20th Conf. Great Lakes Res., Int. Assoc. Great Lakes Res., Univ. Mich. Abstr.
Frey, D. G. 1940. Growth and ecology of the carp *Cyprinus carpio* Linnaeus in four lakes of the Madison region, Wisconsin. Univ. Wis., Madison. PhD Thesis. 248 pp.
Frey, D. G. 1942. Annulus formation in the scales of the carp. Copeia 1942:214–223.
Frey, D. G. 1963. Wisconsin: the Birge-Juday era. pp. 3–54 *in* Limnology in North America, ed. D. G. Frey. Univ. Wis. Press, Madison.
Frey, D. G., and H. Pedracine. 1938. Growth of the buffalo in Wisconsin lakes and streams. Trans. Wis. Acad. Sci., Arts, Lett. 31:513–525.
Frey, D. G., and L. Vike. 1941. A creek census on Lakes Waubesa and Kegonsa, Wisconsin, in 1939. Trans. Wis. Acad. Sci., Arts, Lett. 33:339–360.
Fuchs, E. H. 1967. Life history of the emerald shiner, *Notropis atherinoides*, in Lewis and Clark Lake, South Dakota. Trans. Am. Fish. Soc. 96(3):247–256.
Fukano, K. G., H. Gowing, M. J. Hensen, and L. N. Allison. 1964. Introduction of exotic fish into Michigan. Mich. Dep. Conserv. Inst. Fish. Res. Rep. No. 1689, 50 pp.
Funk, J. K. 1957. Movement of stream fishes in Missouri. Trans. Am. Fish. Soc. 85(1955):39–57.
Galat, D. L. 1973. Normal embryonic development of the muskellunge (*Esox masquinongy*). Trans. Am. Fish. Soc. 102(2):384–391.
Gale, W. F., and C. A. Gale. 1977. Spawning habits of spotfin shiner (*Notropis spilopterus*)—a fractional, crevice spawner. Trans. Am. Fish. Soc. 106(2):170–177.
Gammon, J. R. 1963. Conversion of food in young muskellunge. Trans. Am. Fish. Soc. 92(2):183–184.
Gammon, J. R. 1973. The effect of thermal input on the populations of fish and macroinvertebrates in the Wabash River. Purdue Univ. Water Res. Cent., Tech. Rep. No. 32. 106 pp.
Gammon, J. R., and A. D. Hasler. 1965. Predation by introduced muskellunge on perch and bass. Part I. Years 1–5. Trans. Wis. Acad. Sci., Arts, Lett. 54:249–272.
Gannon, J. E. 1976. The effects of differential digestion rates of zooplankton by alewife, *Alosa pseudoharengus*, on determinations of selective feeding. Trans. Am. Fish. Soc. 105(1):89–95.
Gapen, D. 1973. Why fish carp? Dan Gapen, Big Lake, Minn. 47 pp.
Garside, E. T., and C. M. Jordan. 1968. Upper lethal temperatures at various levels of salinity in the euryhaline cyprinodontids *Fundulus heteroclitus* and *F. diaphanus* after isosmotic acclimation. J. Fish. Res. Board Canada 25(12):2717–2720.
Gasaway, C. R. 1970. Changes in the fish population in Lake Francis Case in South Dakota in the first 16 years of impoundment. U.S. Bur. Sport Fish. Wildl. Tech. Pap. 56. 30 pp.
Gasith, A., and A. D. Hasler. 1976. Airborne litterfall as a source of organic matter in lakes. Limnol. Oceanogr. 21(2):253–258.
Gebken, D., and K. Wright. 1972a. Try the drum. Wis. Conserv. Bull. 37(2):23.
Gebken, D., and K. Wright. 1972b. Walleye and sauger spawning areas study, Pool 7, Mississippi River, 1960–1970. Wis. Dep. Nat. Resour. Bur. Fish Mgmt. Rep. No. 60. 27 pp.
Gee, J. H., and T. G. Northcote. 1963. Comparative ecology of 2 sympatric species of dace (*Rhinichthys*) in the Frazer River system, British Columbia. J. Fish. Res. Board Canada 20(1):105–118.
Geen, G. H., T. G. Northcote, G. F. Hartman, and C. C. Lindsey. 1966. Life histories of two species of catostomid fishes in Sixteenmile Lake, British Columbia, with particular reference to inlet stream spawning. J. Fish. Res. Board Canada 23(11):1761–1788.
Gerald, J. W. 1971. Sound production during courtship in six species of sunfish (Centrarchidae). Evolution 25(1):75–87.
Gerking, S. D. 1945. The distribution of the fishes of Indiana. Indiana Dep. Conserv. Indiana Univ. Dep. Zool., Invest. Indiana Lakes and Strms. 3(1):1–137 + Maps 1–113.
Gerking, S. D. 1952. The protein metabolism of sunfishes of different ages. Physiol. Zool. 25(4):358–372.
Gerking, S. D. 1953. Evidence for the concept of home range and territory in stream fishes. Ecology 34(2):347–365.
Gerking, S. D. 1955. Key to the fishes of Indiana. Indiana Dep. Conserv. and Indiana Univ. Dep. Zool. Contrib. 551, Invest. Indiana Lakes and Strms. 4(2):49–86.
Gibbons, J. W., and D. H. Bennett. 1971. Abundance and local movement of largemouth bass, *Micropterus salmoides*, in a reservoir receiving heated effluent from a reactor. Savannah R. Ecol. Lab. Annu. Rep. SRO–310–1 Aug 1971:90–99. Selected Water Res. Abstr. 6(2):72.
Gibbs, R. H., Jr. 1957a. Cyprinid fishes of the subgenus *Cyprinella* of *Notropis* I. Systematic status of the subgenus *Cyprinella*, with a key to the species exclusive of the *lutrensis-ornatus* complex. Copeia 1957(3):185–195.
Gibbs, R. H., Jr. 1957b. Cyprinid fishes of the subgenus *Cyprinella* of *Notropis* II. Distribution and variation of *Notropis spilopterus*, with the description of a new subspecies. Lloydia 20(3): 186–211.
Gilbert, C. R. 1953. Age and growth of the yellow stone catfish, *Noturus flavus* (Rafinesque). Ohio State Univ., Columbus. MS Thesis. 67 pp.
Gilbert, C. R. 1964. The American cyprinid fishes of the subgenus *Luxilus* (genus *Notropis*). Fla. State Mus. Bull. 8(2). 194 pp.
Gilbert, C. R., and R. M. Bailey. 1972. Systematics and zoogeography of the Amercan cyprinid fish *Notropis* (*Opsopoeodus*) *emiliae*. Occas. Pap. Mus. Zool. Univ. Mich. No. 664. 35 pp.
Giudice, J. J. 1965. Investigations on the propagation and survival of flathead catfish in troughs. Proc. Southeast. Assoc. Game Fish Commnrs. 17:178–180.
Gold, J. R., and J. C. Avise. 1977. Cytogenetic studies in North American minnows (Cyprinidae). I. Karyology of nine California genera. Copeia 1977(3):541–549.
Gold, J. R., C. W. Whitlock, W. J. Karel, and J. A. Barlow, Jr. 1980. Cytogenetic studies in North American minnows (Cyprinidae). VI. Karyotypes of thirteen species in the genus *Notropis*. Cytologia 44:457–466.
Goodyear, C. P. 1970. Terrestrial and aquatic orientation in the starhead topminnow, *Fundulus notti*. Science 168:603–605.
Gosline, W. A. 1966. The limits of the fish family Serranidae, with notes on other lower percoids. Proc. Calif. Acad. Sci. 33(6):91–112.
Gould, W. R., III, and W. H. Irwin. 1962. The suitabilities and relative resistances of twelve species of fish as bioassay animals for oil-refinery effluents. Proc. Southeast. Assoc. Game Fish Commnrs. 16:333–348.
Gowanloch, J. N., and C. Gresham. 1965. Fishes and fishing in Louisiana. State Conserv. Dep. Bull. No. 23. Claitor's Book Store, Baton Rouge. 701 pp.
Graham, J. J. 1954. The alewife in fresh water. Progr. Fish-Cult. 16(3):128–130.
Gravell, M., and R. G. Malsberger. 1965. A permanent cell line from the fathead minnow (*Pimephales promelas*). Ann. N.Y. Acad. Sci. 126:555–565.

Greeley, J. R. 1927. Fishes of the Genesee region with annotated list. pp. 47–66 *in* A biological survey of the Genesee River system. Suppl. 16th Annu. Rep. N.Y. State Conserv. Dep. 1926.

Greeley, J. R. 1929. Fishes of the Erie-Niagara watershed. pp. 150–179 *in* A biological survey of Erie-Niagara system. Suppl. 18th Annu. Rep. N.Y. State Conserv. Dep. 1928.

Greeley, J. R. 1932. The spawning habits of brook, brown, and rainbow trout, and the problem of egg predators. Trans. Am. Fish. Soc. 62:239–248.

Greeley, J. R. 1936. Fishes of the area with annotated list. pp. 45–88 *in* A biological survey of the Delaware and Susquehanna watershed. Suppl. 25th Annu. Rep. N.Y. State Conserv. Dep. 1935.

Greeley, J. R. 1938. Fishes of the area with annotated list. pp. 48–73 *in* A biological survey of the Allegheny and Chemung watersheds. Suppl. 27th Annu. Rep. N.Y. State Conserv. Dep. 1937.

Greeley, J. R., and S. C. Bishop. 1933. Fishes of the upper Hudson watershed. *In* Suppl. 22d Annu. Rep. N.Y. State Conserv. Dep. 1932.

Greeley, J. R., and C. W. Greene. 1931. Fishes of the area with annotated list. pp. 44–94 *in* A biological survey of the St. Lawrence watershed. Suppl. 20th Annu. Rep. N.Y. State Conserv. Dep. 1930.

Green, O. L. 1966. Observations on the culture of the bowfin. Progr. Fish-Cult. 28(3):179.

Greenbank, J. 1956. Movement of fish under the ice. Copeia 1956(3):158–162.

Greene, C. W. 1927. An ichthyological survey of Wisconsin. Pap. Mich. Acad. Sci., Arts, Lett. 7:299–310.

Greene, C. W. 1935. The distribution of Wisconsin fishes. Wis. Conserv. Comm. 235 pp.

Greene, G. N. 1962. White bass feeding: scent or sight. Trans. Am. Fish. Soc. 91(3):326.

Greenfield, D. W. 1973. An evaluation of the advisability of the release of grass carp, *Ctenopharyngodon idella*, into natural waters of the United States. Trans. Ill. Acad. Sci. 66(1–2):48–53.

Greenfield, D. W., and G. C. Deckert. 1973. Introgressive hybridization between *Gila orcutti* and *Hesperoleucas symmetricus* (Pisces: Cyprinidae) in the Cuyama River basis, California. Part II. Ecological aspects. Copeia 1973(3):417–427.

Greenfield, D. W., F. Abdel-Hameed, G. D. Deckert, and R. R. Flinn. 1973. Hybridization between *Chrosomus erythrogaster* and *Notropis cornutus*. Copeia 1973(1):54–60.

Grinstead, B. G. 1969. The vertical distribution of the white crappie in the Buncombe Creek arm of Lake Texoma. Okla. Fish. Res. Lab. Bull. 3. 37 pp.

Griswold, B. L. 1963. Food and growth of spottail shiners and other forage fishes of Clear Lake, Iowa. Proc. Iowa Acad. Sci. 70:215–223.

Griswold, B. L., and L. L. Smith, Jr. 1972. Early survival and growth of the ninespine stickleback, *Pungitius pungitius*. Trans. Am. Fish. Soc. 101(2):350–352.

Griswold, B. L., and L. L. Smith, Jr. 1973. The life history and trophic relationship of the ninespine stickleback, *Pungitius pungitius*, in the Apostle Islands area of Lake Superior. U.S. Fish Wildl. Serv. Fish. Bull. 71(4):1039–1060.

Grosslein, M. D., and L. L. Smith, Jr. 1959. The goldeye, *Amphiodon alosoides* (Rafinesque), in the commercial fishing of the Red Lakes, Minnesota. U.S. Fish Wildl. Serv. Fish. Bull. 60(157):33–41.

Gunderson, J. L. 1978. Vital statistics of the lake whitefish in three areas of Green Bay, Lake Michigan, with comparison to Lake Michigan east of Door County, Wisconsin. Univ. Wis., Stevens Point. MS Thesis. 84 pp.

Gunning, G. E. 1959. The sensory basis for homing in the longear sunfish, *Lepomis megalotis* (Rafinesque). Indiana Dep. Conserv. and Indiana Univ. Dep. Zool., Invest. Indiana Lakes and Strms. 5(3):103–130.

Gunning, G. E. 1965. A behavioral analysis of the movement of tagged longear sunfish. Progr. Fish-Cult. 27(4):211–215.

Gunning, G. E., and W. M. Lewis. 1956. Age and growth of two important bait species in a cold-water stream in southern Illinois. Am. Midl. Nat. 55(1):118–120.

Gunning, G. E., and C. R. Shoop. 1962. Restricted movement of the American eel, *Anguilla rostrata* (LeSueur), in freshwater streams with comments on growth rate. Tulane Stud. Zool. 9(5):265–272.

Haase, B. L. 1969. An ecological life history of the longnose gar, *Lepisosteus osseus* (Linnaeus), in Lake Mendota and in several other lakes of southern Wisconsin. Univ. Wis., Madison. PhD Thesis. 224 pp.

Hacker, V. A. 1957. Biology and management of lake trout in Green Lake, Wisconsin. Trans. Am. Fish. Soc. 86(1956):1–13.

Hacker, V. A. 1966. An analysis of the muskellunge fishery of Little Green Lake, Green Lake County, Wisconsin, 1957–65. Wis. Conserv. Dep. Div. Fish Mgmt. Rep. No. 4. 17 pp. (mimeo).

Hacker, V. A. 1973. The results of a ten-year voluntary muskellunge creel census at Little Green Lake, Green Lake County, Wisconsin, 1963–1972. Wis. Dep. Nat. Resour. Bur. Fish Mgmt. Rep. No. 58. 14 pp. (mimeo).

Hacker, V. A. 1975. Wisconsin waters with quillback, buffalo, sheepshead, carp, dogfish, garfish and eelpout removal 1947–1974. Wis. Dep. Nat. Resour., Oshkosh. 9 pp. (mimeo).

Hacker, V. A. 1976. Rough fish, under-utilized, delicious (some) and inexpensive. Wis. Dep. Nat. Resour. Publ. 7–8500 (76) n.p.

Hacker, V. A. 1977. A fine kettle of fish. Wis. Dep. Nat. Resour. Bur. Fish Mgmt. Publ. No. 17–3600 (77). 64 pp.

Hackney, P. A. 1966. Predator-prey relationships of the flathead catfish in ponds under selected forage fish conditions. Proc. Southeast. Assoc. Game Fish Commnrs. 19:217–222.

Hackney, P. A., W. M. Tatum, and S. L. Spencer. 1968. Life history study of the river redhorse, *Moxostoma carinatum* (Cope), in the Cahaba River, Alabama, with notes on the management of the species as a sport fish. Proc. Southeast. Assoc. Game Fish Commnrs. 21:324–332.

Hale, M. C. 1963. A comparative study of the food of the shiners *Notropis lutrensis* and *Notropis venustus*. J. Okla. Acad. Sci. 43:125–129.

Hall, G. E., and R. M. Jenkins. 1954. Notes on the age and growth of the pirateperch, *Aphredoderus sayanus*, in Oklahoma. Copeia 1954(1):69.

Hall, J. D. 1963. An ecological study of the chestnut lamprey, *Ichthyomyzon castaneus* Girard, in the Manistee River, Michigan. Univ. Mich., Ann Arbor. PhD Thesis. Diss. Abstr. 24(2):901–902.

Hallam, J. C. 1959. Habitat and associated fauna of four species of fish in Ontario streams. J. Fish. Res. Board Canada 16(2):147–173.

Hankinson, T. L. 1908. A biological survey of Walnut Lake, Michigan. Rep. State Biol. (Geol.) Surv. Mich. 1907:198–251.

Hankinson, T. L. 1920. Notes on life histories of Illinois fish. Trans. Ill. Acad. Sci. 12(1919):132–150.

Hankinson, T. L. 1932. Observations on the breeding behavior and habitats of fishes in southern Michigan. Pap. Mich. Acad. Sci., Arts, Lett. 15:411–425.

Hansen, D. F. 1951. Biology of the white crappie in Illinois. Ill. Nat. Hist. Surv. Bull. 25(4):211–265.

Hansen, D. F. 1965. Further observations on nesting of the white crappie, *Pomoxis annularis*. Trans. Am. Fish. Soc. 94(2):182–184.

Hanson, H. 1958. Operation fish rescue. Progr. Fish-Cult. 20(4):186–188.

Harkness, W. J. K., and J. R. Dymond. 1961. The lake sturgeon. The history of its fishery and problems of conservation. Ont. Dep. Lands For., Fish Wildl. Branch. 121 pp.

Harlan, J. R., and E. B. Speaker. 1956. Iowa fish and fishing. Iowa Conserv. Comm. 377 pp.

Harrington, R. W., Jr. 1947. Observations on the breeding habits of the yellow perch, *Perca flavescens* (Mitchill). Copeia 1947(3):199–200.

Harris, J. T., and R. T. Sauey. 1979. A guide to protecting Wisconsin wetlands. Citizens Nat. Resour. Assoc. Rep., Loganville, Wis., and Univ. Wis. Ext., Madison. 36 pp.

Harris, R. H. D. 1962. Growth and reproduction of the longnose sucker, *Catostomus catostomus* (Forster), in Great Slave Lake. J. Fish. Res. Board Canada 19(1):113–126.

Harrison, H. M. 1950. The foods used by some common fish of the Des Moines River drainage. pp. 31–44 *in* Biology seminar held at Des Moines, Iowa, 11 Jul 1950. Iowa Conserv. Comm. Div. Fish Game.

Hart, C. W., Jr., and S. L. H. Fuller. 1974. Pollution ecology of freshwater invertebrates. Academic Press, N.Y. 389 pp.

Hart, L. G. 1974. A telemetric study of homing and home range of flathead catfish *Pylodictis olivaris* (Rafinesque) in an 850 hectare Oklahoma reservoir. Okla. State Univ., Stillwater. MS Thesis. viii + 71 pp.

Hasler, A. D. 1945. Observations on the winter perch population of Lake Mendota. Ecology 26(1):90–94.

Hasler, A. D. 1947. Eutrophication of lakes by domestic drainage. Ecology 28(4):383–395.

Hasler, A. D. 1949. Antibiotic aspects of copper treatment of lakes. Trans. Wis. Acad. Sci., Arts, Lett. 39:97–103.

Hasler, A. D. 1963. Wisconsin 1940–1961. pp. 55–93 *in* Limnology in North America, ed. D. G. Frey. Univ. Wis. Press, Madison.

Hasler, A. D. 1973. Poisons, phosphates, preservation, people, and politics—a fish eye's view of ecology. Trans. Am. Fish. Soc. 102(1):213–224.

Hasler, A. D. 1975. Man-induced eutrophication of lakes. pp. 383–399 *in* The changing global environment, ed. S. F. Singer. D. Reidel Publishing, Dordrecht, Holland.

Hasler, A. D., and J. E. Bardach. 1949. Daily migrations of perch in Lake Mendota, Wisconsin. J. Wildl. Mgmt. 13(1):40–51.

Hasler, A. D., and J. J. Tibbles. 1970. A study of depth distribution of perch (*Perca flavescens*) using a rolling gill net. Berichte der Deut. Wissenschaft. Komm. für Meeresforsch. Sonderdruck 21(1–4):46–55.

Hasler, A. D., and W. J. Wisby. 1951. Discrimination of stream odors by fishes and its relation to parent stream behavior. Am. Nat. 85:223–238.

Hasler, A. D., and W. J. Wisby. 1958. The return of displaced largemouth bass and green sunfish to a "home" area. Ecology 39(2):289–293.

Hasler, A. D., R. K. Meyer, and H. M. Field. 1939. Spawning induced prematurely in trout with the aid of pituitary glands of the carp. Endocrinology 25:978–983.

Hasler, A. D., R. K. Meyer, and H. M. Field. 1940. The use of hormones for the conservation of muskellunge, *Esox masquinongy immaculatus* Garrard. Copeia 1940(1):43–46.

Hasler, A. D., H. P. Thomsen, and J. Neess. 1946. Facts and comments on raising two common bait minnows. Wis. Dep. Nat. Resour. Bull. 210-A-46. 14 pp.

Hasler, A. D., E. S. Gardella, H. F. Henderson, and R. M. Horrall. 1969. Open-water orientation of white bass, *Roccus chrysops*, as determined by ultrasonic tracking methods. J. Fish. Res. Board Canada 26(8):2173–2192.

Hasler, A. D., R. M. Horrall, W. J. Wisby, and W. Braemer. 1958. Sun orientation and homing in fishes. Limnol. Oceanogr. 3:353–361.

Hausle, D. A. 1973. Survival and emergence of young brook trout. Univ. Wis., Stevens Point. MS Thesis. 66 pp.

Havighurst, W. 1942. The long ships passing. Macmillan, N.Y. 219 pp.

Hayes, M. L. 1956. Life history studies of two species of suckers in Shadow Mountain Reservoir, Grand County, Colorado. Colo. Agric. Mech. Coll., Fort Collins. MS Thesis. 126 pp.

Hazzard, A. S. 1932. Some phases of the life history of the eastern brook trout *Salvelinus fontinalus* Mitchill. Trans. Am. Fish. Soc. 62:344–350.

Headrick, M. R. 1976. Effects of stream channelization on fish populations in the Buena Vista Marsh, Portage County, Wisconsin. Univ. Wis., Stevens Point. MS Thesis. 65 pp.

Hedges, S. B., and R. C. Ball. 1953. Production and harvest of bait fishes in Michigan. Mich. Dep. Conserv. Misc. Publ. 6. 30 pp.

Heding, R., and V. Hacker. 1960. A trout's thermostat: springs. Wis. Conserv. Bull. 25(5):19–22.

Heimstra, N. W., D. K. Damkot, and N. G. Benson. 1969. Some effects of silt turbidity on behavior of juvenile largemouth bass and green sunfish. U.S. Bur. Sport Fish. Wildl. Tech. Pap. 20. 9 pp.

Heinrich, J. W. 1977. Culture of larval alewives (*Alosa pseudoharengus*) in the laboratory. 20th Conf. Great Lakes Res., Int. Assoc. Great Lakes Res., Univ. Mich. Abstr.

Held, J. W. 1969. Some early summer foods of the shovelnose sturgeon in the Missouri River. Trans. Am. Fish. Soc. 98(3):514–517.

Held, J. W., and J. J. Peterka. 1974. Age, growth and food habits of the fathead minnow, *Pimephales promelas*, in North Dakota saline lakes. Trans. Am. Fish. Soc. 103(4):743–756.

Helle, J. H. 1970. Biological characteristics of intertidal and freshwater spawning pink salmon at Olsen Creek, Prince William Sound, Alaska, 1962–63. U.S. Fish Wildl. Serv. Spec. Sci. Rep.—Fish. No. 602. 19 pp.

Helm, J. M. 1960. Returns from muskellunge stocking. Wis. Conserv. Bull. 25(6):9–10.

Helm, W. T. 1958. A "new" fish in Wisconsin. Wis. Conserv. Bull. 23(7):10–12.

Helm, W. T. 1964. Yellow bass in Wisconsin. Trans. Wis. Acad. Sci., Arts, Lett. 53:109–125.

Helms, D. R. 1974a. Age and growth of shovelnose sturgeon, *Scaphirhynchus platorynchus* (Rafinesque), in the Mississippi River. Proc. Iowa Acad. Sci. 81(2):73–75.

Helms, D. R. 1974b. Shovelnose sturgeon in the Mississippi River, Iowa. Iowa Conserv. Comm. Fish. Res. Tech. Ser. 74-3. 68 pp.

Henderson, H. 1965. Observation on the propagation of flathead catfish in the San Marcos State fish hatchery, Texas. Proc. Southeast. Assoc. Game Fish Commnrs. 17:173–177.

Hergenrader, G. L. 1969. Spawning behavior of *Perca flavescens* in aquaria. Copeia 1969(4):839–841.

Hergenrader, G. L., and A. D. Hasler. 1967. Seasonal changes in swimming rates of yellow perch in Lake Mendota as measured by sonar. Trans. Am. Fish. Soc. 96(4):373–382.

Herman, E. F. 1947. Notes on tagging walleyes on the Wolf River. Wis. Conserv. Bull. 12(4):7–9.

Herman, E. F., W. Wisby, L. Wiegert, and M. Burdick. 1959. The yellow perch—its life history, ecology, and management. Wis. Conserv. Dep. Publ. 228. 14 pp.

Hester, F. E. 1970. Phylogenetic relationships of sunfishes as demonstrated by hybridization. Trans. Am. Fish. Soc. 99(1):100–104.

Hildebrand, S. F., and W. C. Schroeder. 1928. Fishes of Chesapeake Bay. Bull. U.S. Bur. Fish. 43(Part I). 388 pp.

Hile, R. 1936. Low production may not mean depletion. The Fisherman 5(2):1–2.

Hile, R. 1941. Age and growth of the rock bass, *Ambloplites rupestris* (Raf.), in Nebish Lake, Wisconsin. Trans. Wis. Acad. Sci., Arts, Lett. 33:189–337.

Hile, R. 1942. Growth of rock bass, *Ambloplites rupestris* (Rafinesque), in five lakes of northeastern Wisconsin. Trans. Am. Fish. Soc. 71:131–143.

Hile, R., and H. J. Buettner. 1955. Commercial fishery for chubs (ciscoes) in Lake Michigan through 1953. U.S. Fish Wildl. Serv. Spec. Sci. Rep.—Fish. No. 163. 49 pp.

Hile, R., and H. J. Deason. 1934. Growth of the whitefish, *Coregonus clupeaformis* (Mitchill), in Trout Lake, northeastern highlands, Wisconsin. Trans. Am. Fish. Soc. 64:231–237.

Hile, R., and H. J. Deason. 1947. Distribution, abundance and spawning season and grounds of the kiyi, *Leucichthys kiyi* Koelz, in Lake Michigan. Trans. Am. Fish. Soc. 74(1944):143–165.

Hile, R., and C. Juday. 1941. Bathymetric distribution of fish in lakes of northeastern highlands, Wisconsin. Trans. Wis. Acad. Sci., Arts, Lett. 33:147–187.

Hile, R., P. H. Eschmeyer, and G. F. Lunger. 1951a. Decline of the lake trout fishing in Lake Michigan. U.S. Fish Wildl. Serv. Fish. Bull. 52:77–95.

Hile, R., P. H. Eschmeyer, and G. F. Lunger. 1951b. Status of the lake trout fishery in Lake Superior. Trans. Am. Fish. Soc. 80:278–312.

Hine, R. L. 1970. Water on the land. Wis. Dep. Nat. Resour. 23 pp.

Hine, R. L., ed. 1971. A basic guide to water rights in Wisconsin. Wis. Dep. Nat. Resour. Publ. 1302–71. 39 pp.

Hinrichs, M. A. 1977. A description and key of the eggs and larvae of 5 species of fish in the subfamily Coregoninae. Univ. Wis., Stevens Point, Coop. Fish. Unit Abstr.

Hinrichs, M. A. 1979. A description and key of the eggs and larvae of five species of fish in the subfamily Coregoninae. Univ. Wis., Stevens Point. MS Thesis. 73 pp.

Hinrichs, M. A., and H. E. Booke. 1975. Egg development and larval feeding of the lake herring, *Coregonus artedii* LeSueur. Univ. Wis., Stevens Point, Mus. Nat. Hist. Fauna and Flora Wis. Rep. No. 10(4):73–90.

History of Sauk County, Wisconsin, The. 1880. Western Historical Society, Chicago. IV[19] + 825 pp.

Hoar, W. S. 1952. Thyroid function in some anadromous and landlocked teleosts. Trans. Royal Soc. Canada 46:39–53

Hocutt, C. H. 1973. Swimming performance of 3 warmwater fishes exposed to rapid temperature change. Chesapeake Sci. 14(1):11–16.

Hoffman, C. H., and E. W. Surber. 1945. Effects of an aerial application of wettable DDT on fish and fish-food organisms in Back Creek, West Virginia. Trans. Am. Fish. Soc. 75:48–58.

Hoffman, G. L. 1970. Parasites of North American freshwater fishes. Univ. Calif. Press, Berkeley. 486 pp.

Hogman, W. J. 1970. Early scale development on the Great Lakes coregonids, *Coregonus artedii* and *C. kiyi*. pp. 429–436 *in* Biology of coregonid fishes, ed. C. C. Lindsey and C. S. Woods. Univ. Manitoba Press, Winnipeg. 560 pp.

Hokanson, K. E. F., J. H. McCormick, and B. R. Jones. 1973. Temperature requirements for embryos and larvae of the northern pike, *Esox lucius* (Linn.). Trans. Am. Fish. Soc. 102(1):89–100.

Holder, D. R., and J. S. Ramsey. 1972. A case of albinism in the tadpole madtom, *Noturus gyrinus*. Trans. Am. Fish. Soc. 101(3):566–567.

Holey, M., B. Hollender, M. Imhof, R. Jesien, R. Konopacky, M. Toneys, and D. Coble. 1979. Never give a sucker an even break. Fisheries 4(1):2–6.

Hollander, E. E., and J. W. Avault, Jr. 1975. Effects of salinity on survival of buffalo fish eggs through yearlings. Progr. Fish-Cult. 37(1):47–51.

Holloway, A. D. 1954. Notes on the life history and management of the shortnose and longnose gars in Florida waters. J. Wildl. Mgmt. 18(4):438–449.

Holt, C. S., G. D. S. Grant, G. P. Oberstar, C. C. Oakes, and D. W. Bradt. 1977. Movement of walleye, *Stizostedion vitreum*, in Lake Bemidji, Minnesota, as determined by radio-biotelemetry. Trans. Am. Fish. Soc. 106(2):163–169.

Hooper, F. F. 1949. Age analysis of a population of the ameiurid fish *Schilbeodes mollis* (Hermann). Copeia 1949(1):34–38.

Hoopes, D. T. 1960. Utilization of mayflies and caddisflies by some Mississippi River fishes. Trans. Am. Fish. Soc. 89(1):32–34.

Hoover, E. E. 1936a. Contributions to the life history of the chinook and landlocked salmon in New Hampshire. Copeia 1936(4):193–198.

Hoover, E. E. 1936b. The spawning activities of fresh-water smelt, with special reference to sex ratio. Copeia 1936(2):85–91.

Horkel, J. D., and W. D. Pearson. 1976. Effects of turbidity on ventilation rates and oxygen consumption of green sunfish, *Lepomis cyanellus*. Trans. Am. Fish. Soc. 105(1):107–113.

Horn, M. H., and C. D. Riggs. 1973. Effects of temperature and light on rate of air breathing of the bowfin, *Amia calva*. Copeia 1973(4):653–657.

Horrall, R. M. 1962. A comparative study of two spawning populations of the white bass, *Roccus chrysops* (Rafinesque), in Lake Mendota, Wisconsin, with special reference to homing behavior. Univ. Wis., Madison. PhD Thesis. 181 pp.

Hough, J. L. 1958. Geology of the Great Lakes. Univ. Ill. Press, Urbana. 313 pp.

Houser, A. 1965. Growth of paddlefish in Fort Gibson reservoir, Oklahoma. Trans. Am. Fish. Soc. 94(1):91–93.

Houser, A., and B. Grinstead. 1961. The effect of black bullhead catfish and bluegill removals on the fish populations of a small lake. Proc. Southeast. Assoc. Game Fish Commnrs. 21:399–410.

Howell, W. M., and J. Villa. 1976. Chromosomal homogeneity in two sympatric cyprinid fishes of the genus *Rhinichthys*. Copeia 1976(1):112–116.

Hoy, P. R. 1872a. Deepwater fauna of Lake Michigan. Trans. Wis. Acad. Sci., Arts, Lett. 1870–1872:98–101.

Hoy, P. R. 1872b. Mortality of fish in the Racine River. Proc. Am. Assoc. Adv. Sci. 1872:198–199.

Hoy, P. R. 1883. Catalogue of the cold-blooded vertebrates of Wisconsin. Part III. Fishes. pp. 427–435 *in* Geology of Wisconsin, 1873–1879. Vol. 1, ed. T. C. Chamberlain. David Atwood Publishing, Madison, Wis.

Hubbs, C. 1961. Developmental temperature tolerances of four etheostomatine fishes occurring in Texas. Copeia 1961(2):195–198.

Hubbs, C. 1976. A checklist of Texas freshwater fishes. Tex. Parks Wildl. Dep. Tech. Ser. No. 11. 12 pp.

Hubbs, C. L. 1921. An ecological study of the life history of the fresh-water atherine fish *Labidesthes sicculus*. Ecology 2(4):262–276.

Hubbs, C. L. 1923. Seasonal variation in the number of vertebrae of fishes. Pap. Mich. Acad. Sci., Arts, Lett. 2(1922):207–214.

Hubbs, C. L. 1925. The life-cycle and growth of lampreys. Pap. Mich. Acad. Sci., Arts, Lett. 4:587–603.

Hubbs, C. L. 1926. A check-list of the fishes of the Great Lakes and tributary waters, with nomenclatorial notes and analytical keys. Univ. Mich. Mus. Zool. Misc. Publ. No. 15. 77 pp.

Hubbs, C. L. 1930a. Further additions and corrections to the list of the fishes of the Great Lakes and tributary waters. Pap. Mich. Acad. Sci., Arts, Lett. 11(1929):425–436.

Hubbs, C. L. 1930b. Materials for a revision of the catostomid fishes of eastern North America. Univ. Mich. Mus. Zool. Misc. Publ. No. 20. 47 pp.

Hubbs, C. L. 1934. Some experiences and suggestions on forage fish culture. Trans. Am. Fish. Soc. 63:53–63.

Hubbs, C. L. 1941. The relation of hydrological conditions to speciation in fishes. pp. 182–195 *in* A symposium on hydrobiology. Univ. Wis. Press, Madison.

Hubbs, C. L. 1942. Sexual dimorphism in the cyprinid fishes, *Margariscus* and *Couesius*, and alleged hybridization between these genera. Occas. Pap. Mus. Zool. Univ. Mich. No. 468. 6 pp.

Hubbs, C. L. 1951a. The American cyprinid fish *Notropis germanus* Hay interpreted as an intergeneric hybrid. Am. Midl. Nat. 45(2):446–454.

Hubbs, C. L. 1951b. *Notropis amnis*, a new cyprinid fish of the Mississippi fauna, with two subspecies. Occas. Pap. Mus. Zool. Univ. Mich. 530:1–30 + Pl. 1, Map 1.

Hubbs, C. L. 1955. Hybridization between fish species in nature. System. Zool. 4(1):1–20.

Hubbs, C. L., and R. M. Bailey. 1938. The smallmouth bass. Cranbrook Inst. Sci. Bull. No. 10. 92 pp.

Hubbs, C. L., and R. M. Bailey. 1952. Identification of *Oxygeneum pulverulentum* Forbes, from Illinois, as a hybrid cyprinid fish. Pap. Mich. Acad. Sci., Arts, Lett. 37(1951):143–152 + Pl.1.

Hubbs, C. L., and J. D. Black. 1947. Revision of *Ceratichthys*, a genus of American cyprinid fishes. Univ. Mich. Mus. Zool. Misc. Publ. No. 66. 56 pp.

Hubbs, C. L., and D. E. S. Brown. 1929. Materials for a distributional study of Ontario fishes. Trans. Royal Can. Inst. 17(1):1–56.

Hubbs, C. L., and G. P. Cooper. 1935. Age and growth of the long-eared and the green sunfishes in Michigan. Pap. Mich. Acad. Sci., Arts, Lett. 20(1934):669–696.

Hubbs, C. L., and G. P. Cooper. 1936. Minnows of Michigan. Cranbrook Inst. Sci. Bull. No. 8. 95 pp.

Hubbs, C. L., and W. R. Crowe. 1956. Preliminary analysis of the American cyprinid fishes, seven new, referred to the genus *Hybopsis*, subgenus *Erimystax*. Occas. Pap. Mus. Zool. Univ. Mich. No. 578. 8 pp.

Hubbs, C. L., and C. W. Greene. 1928. Further notes on the fishes of the Great Lakes and tributary waters. Pap. Mich. Acad. Sci., Arts, Lett. 8:371–392.

Hubbs, C. L., and C. W. Greene. 1935. Two new subspecies of fishes from Wisconsin. Trans. Wis. Acad. Sci., Arts, Lett. 29:89–101 + Pls. 2–3.

Hubbs, C. L., and K. F. Lagler. 1947. Fishes of the Great Lakes region. Cranbrook Inst. Sci. Bull. No. 26. 186 pp.

Hubbs, C. L., and K. F. Lagler. 1949. Fishes of Isle Royale, Lake Superior, Michigan. Pap. Mich. Acad. Sci., Arts, Lett. 33(1947):73–133.

Hubbs, C. L., and K. F. Lagler. 1958. Fishes of the Great Lakes region. rev. ed. Cranbrook Inst. Sci. Bull. No. 26. 213 pp.

Hubbs, C. L., and K. F. Lagler. 1964. Fishes of the Great Lakes region. Univ. Mich. Press, Ann Arbor. 213 pp.

Hubbs, C. L., and T. E. B. Pope. 1937. The spread of the sea lamprey through the Great Lakes. Trans. Am. Fish. Soc. 66(1936):172–176.

Hubbs, C. L., and M. B. Trautman. 1937. A revision of the lamprey genus *Ichthyomyzon*. Univ. Mich. Mus. Zool. Misc. Publ. 35. 109 pp.

Hubbs, C. L., and L. C. Hubbs, and R. E. Johnson. 1943. Hybridization in nature between species of catostomid fishes. Contr. Lab. Vertebr. Biol. Univ. Mich. 22:1–76.

Hubley, R. C., Jr. 1963a. Movement of tagged channel catfish in the upper Mississippi River. Trans. Am. Fish. Soc. 92(2):165–168.

Hubley, R. C., Jr. 1963b. Second year of walleye and sauger tagging on the upper Mississippi River. Wis. Conserv. Dep. Invest. Memo. No. 16. 4 pp.

Huck, L. L., and G. E. Gunning. 1967. Behavior of the longear sunfish, *Lepomis megalotis* (Rafinesque). Tulane Stud. Zool. 14(3):121–131.

Huggins, T. G. 1969. Production of channel catfish (*Ictalurus punctatus*) in tertiary treatment ponds. Iowa State Univ., Ames. MS Thesis. 120 pp.

Huh, H. T., H. E. Calbert, and D. A. Stuiber. 1976. Effects of temperature and light on growth of yellow perch and walleye using formulated feed. Trans. Am. Fish. Soc. 105(2):254–258.

Humphreys, J. D. 1978. Population dynamics of lake whitefish, *Coregonus clupeaformis*, in Lake Michigan east of Door County, Wisconsin. Univ. Wis., Stevens Point. MS Thesis. 69 pp.

Hunn, J. B., and L. M. Christenson. 1977. Chemical composition of blood and bile of the shovelnose sturgeon. Progr. Fish-Cult. 39(2):59–61.

Hunt, B. P., and W. F. Carbine. 1950. Food of young pike (*Esox lucius* L.) and associated fishes in Peterson's ditches, Houghton Lake, Michigan. Trans. Am. Fish. Soc. 80:67–83.

Hunt, R. L. 1962. Effects of angling regulations on a wild brook trout fishery. Wis. Conserv. Dep. Tech. Bull. No. 26. 58 pp.

Hunt, R. L. 1965a. Food of northern pike in a Wisconsin trout stream. Trans. Am. Fish. Soc. 94(1):95–97.

Hunt, R. L. 1965b. Dispersal of wild brook trout during their first summer of life. Trans. Am. Fish. Soc. 94(2):186–188.

Hunt, R. L. 1966. Production and angler harvest of wild brook trout in Lawrence Creek, Wisconsin. Wis. Conserv. Dep. Tech. Bull. No. 35. 52 pp.

Hunt, R. L. 1969. Effects of habitat alteration on production, standing crops and yield of brook trout in Lawrence Creek, Wisconsin. pp. 281–312 *in* Symposium on salmon and trout in streams, ed. T. G. Northcote. H. R. MacMillan lectures in fisheries, Univ. B.C., Vancouver.

Hunt, R. L. 1971. Responses of a brook trout population to habitat development in Lawrence Creek. Wis. Dep. Nat. Resour. Tech. Bull. No. 48. 35 pp.

Hunt, R. L. 1974. Annual production by brook trout in Lawrence Creek during eleven successive years. Wis. Dep. Nat. Resour. Tech. Bull. No. 82. 29 pp.

Hunt, R. L. 1975. Species-specific size limits for trout. Wis. Conserv. Bull. 40(4):12–13.

Hunt, R. L. 1976. Wild brook trout with two anal fins. Progr. Fish-Cult. 38(2):101.

Hunter, J. R. 1963. The reproductive behavior of the green sunfish, *Lepomis cyanellus*. Zoologica 48(1):13–24.

Hunter, J. R., and A. D. Hasler. 1965. Spawning association of the redfin shiner, *Notropis umbratilis*, and the green sunfish, *Lepomis cyanellus*. Copeia 1965(3):265–285.

Hunter, J. R., and W. J. Wisby. 1961. Utilization of the nests of green sunfish (*Lepomis cyanellus*) by the redfin shiner (*Notropis umbratilis cyanocephalus*). Copeia 1961(1):113–115.

Huntsman, G. R. 1967. Nuptial tubercles in carpsuckers (*Carpiodes*). Copeia 1967(2):457–458.

Hussakof, L. 1916. Discovery of the great lake trout, *Cristivomer namaycush*, in the Pleistocene of Wisconsin. J. Geol. 24:685–689.

Imhof, M. A., and H. E. Booke. 1976. Population genetics of Lake Michigan whitefish (*Coregonus clupeaformis*) using muscle isozymes as genetic markers. Univ. Wis., Stevens Point, Coop. Fish. Unit. 1 p. (mimeo).

Isaak, D. 1961. The ecological life history of the fathead minnow, *Pimephales promelas* (Rafinesque). Diss. Abstr. 22(6):2113–2114.

Jacobi, G. Z., and D. J. Degan. 1977. Aquatic macroinvertebrates in a small Wisconsin trout stream before, during, and two years after treatment with the fish toxicant antimycin. U.S. Fish Wildl. Serv. Invest. Fish Control No. 81. 24 pp.

Jacobs, D. L. 1948. Nesting of the brook stickleback. Proc. Minn. Acad. Sci. 16:33–34.

Jaffa, B. B. 1917. Notes on the breeding and incubation periods of the Iowa darter, *Etheostoma iowae* Jordan and Meek. Copeia 1917(47):71–72.

Jenkins, R., R. Elkin, and J. Finnell. 1955. Growth rates of six sunfishes in Oklahoma. Okla. Fish. Res. Lab. Rep. 49. 73 pp. (mimeo).

Jenkins, R. E. 1970. Systematic studies of the catostomid fish tribe Moxostomatini. Univ. Mich., Ann Arbor. PhD Thesis. 799 pp.

Jenkins, R. E. 1976. A list of undescribed freshwater fish species of continental United States and Canada, with additions to the 1970 checklist. Copeia 1976(3):642–644.

Jenkins, R. E., and E. A. Lachner. 1971. Criteria for analysis and interpretation of the American fish genera *Nocomis* Girard and *Hybopsis* Agassiz. Smithsonian Contr. to Zool. No. 90. 15 pp.

Jensen, A. L. 1976. Assessment of the United States lake whitefish (*Coregonus clupeaformis*) fisheries of Lake Superior, Lake Michigan, and Lake Huron. J. Fish. Res. Board Canada 33(4):747–759.

Jensen, A. L. 1978. Assessment of the lake trout fishery in Lake Superior: 1929–1950. Trans. Am. Fish. Soc. 107(4):543–549.

Jensen, A. L., and R. N. Duncan. 1971. Homing of transplanted coho-salmon. Progr. Fish-Cult. 33(4):216–218.

Jergens, G. D., and W. Childers. 1959. Ages at given lengths for some species taken in U.M.R.C.C. cooperative field survey, 1956, in the Wisconsin-Iowa-Illinois waters of the Mississippi River. Proc. 13th Annu. Meet. Upper Miss. R. Conserv. Com. Fish. Tech. Subcom. Suppl. Rep. pp. 113–121 (mimeo).

Jester, D. B. 1972. Life history, ecology, and management of the river carpsucker, *Carpiodes carpio* (Rafinesque), with reference to Elephant Butte Lake. N.M. State Univ. Agric. Exp. Stn. Res. Rep. No. 243. 120 pp.

Jester, D. B. 1973. Life history, ecology, and management of the smallmouth buffalo, *Ictiobus bubalus* (Rafinesque), with reference to Elephant Butte Lake. N. M. State Univ. Agric. Exp. Stn. Res. Rep. No. 261. 111 pp.

Jester, D. B. 1974. Life history, ecology, and management of the carp, *Cyprinus carpio* Linnaeus, in Elephant Butte Lake. N.M. State Univ. Agric. Exp. Stn. Res. Rep. No. 273. 80 pp.

Jobes, F. W. 1943. The age, growth, and bathymetric distribution of Reighard's chub, *Leucichthys reighardi* Koelz, in Lake Michigan. Trans. Am. Fish. Soc. 72(1942):108–135.

Jobes, F. W. 1949a. The age, growth, and distribution of the longjaw cisco, *Leucichthys alpenae* Koelz, in Lake Michigan. Trans. Am. Fish. Soc. 76(1946):215–247.

Jobes, F. W. 1949b. The age, growth, and bathymetric distribution of the bloater, *Leucichthys hoyi* (Gill), in Lake Michigan. Pap. Mich. Acad. Sci., Arts, Lett. 33(1947):135–172.

Joeris, L. S. 1957. Structure and growth of scales of yellow perch of Green Bay. Trans. Am. Fish. Soc. 86:169–194.

John, K. R. 1954. An ecological study of the cisco, *Leucichthys artedi* (LeSueur), in Lake Mendota, Wisconsin. Univ. Wis., Madison. PhD Thesis. 121 pp.

John, K. R. 1956. Onset in spawning activities of the shallow water cisco, *Leucichthys artedi* (LeSueur), in Lake Mendota, Wisconsin, relative to water temperatures. Copeia 1956(2):116–118.

Johnsen, P. B., and J. G. Heitz. 1975. Beep! Beep! Beep! Where are the carp? Wis. Conserv. Bull. 40(6):12–13.

Johnson, C. E. 1971. Factors affecting fish spawning. Wis. Conserv. Bull. 36(4):16–17.

Johnson, C. E., D. A. Stuiber, and R. C. Lindsay. 1974. Getting the most from your Great Lakes salmon. Univ. Wis. Sea Grant Coll. Prog. Publ. Inform. Rep. No. 120. 27 pp.

Johnson, F. H. 1977. Responses of walleye (*Stizostedion vitreum vitreum*) and yellow perch (*Perca flavescens*) populations to removal of white sucker (*Catostomus commersoni*) from a Minnesota lake, 1966. J. Fish. Res. Board Canada 34(10):1633–1642.

Johnson, F. H., and J. G. Hale. 1977. Interrelations between walleye (*Stizostedion vitreum vitreum*) and smallmouth bass (*Micropterus dolomieui*) in four northeastern Minnesota lakes, 1948–69. J. Fish. Res. Board Canada 34(10):1626–1632.

Johnson, L. D. 1954. And it didn't get away. Wis. Conserv. Bull. 19(8):16–17.

Johnson, L. D. 1958. Pond culture of muskellunge in Wisconsin. Wis. Dep. Nat. Resour. Tech. Bull. 17. 54 pp.

Johnson, L. D. 1960. Let's compare muskies. Wis. Conserv. Bull. 25(7):13–16.

Johnson, L. D. 1963. The travelling musky. Wis. Conserv. Bull. 28(4):10–11.

Johnson, L. D. 1965. The variable muskellunge. Wis. Conserv. Bull. 30(3):23–25.

Johnson, L. D. 1969. Food of angler-caught northern pike in Murphy Flowage. Wis. Dep. Nat. Resour. Tech. Bull. 42. 26 pp.

Johnson, L. D. 1971. Growth of known-age muskellunge in Wisconsin: and validation of age and growth determination methods. Wis. Dep. Nat. Resour. Tech. Bull. 49. 24 pp.

Johnson, L. D. 1974. Muskellunge survival in Wisconsin lakes, Minor Clark Fish Hatchery, Morehead, Kentucky. Proc. 6th Interstate Muskellunge Workshop. pp. 41–44.

Johnson, L. D. 1975. How many muskies aren't there anymore? Wis. Conserv. Bull. 40(5):20–21.

Johnson, L. D. 1978. Evaluation of esocid stocking program in Wisconsin. Am. Fish. Soc. Spec. Publ. No. 11:298–301.

Johnson, L. D. 1981. Comparison of muskellunge (*Esox masquinongy*) populations in a stocked lake and unstocked lake in Wisconsin, with notes on the occurrence of northern pike (*Esox lucius*). Wis. Dep. Nat. Resour. Res. Rep. 110. 17 pp.

Johnson, M. 1970. Reaction time of two species of sculpins to heat narcosis with comments on the role of temperature in their geographical distribution. Univ. Wis., Waukesha. 14 pp. (unpubl. manus.).

Johnson, M. 1971–1972. Distribution of sculpins (Pisces: Cottidae) in Iowa. Proc. Iowa Acad. Sci. 78:79–80.

Johnson, M., and G. Becker. 1970. Annotated list of the fishes of Wisconsin. Trans. Wis. Acad. Sci., Arts, Lett. 58:265–300.

Johnson, M. G. 1965. Estimates of fish populations in warmwater streams by the removal method. Trans. Am. Fish. Soc. 94(4):350–357.

Johnson, R. E., and J. B. Moyle. 1949. A biological survey and fishery management plan for the streams of the Root River basin. Minn. Dep. Conserv. Fish. Res. Invest. Rep. 87. 129 pp. (manus.).

Johnson, R. P. 1963. Studies on the life history and ecology of the bigmouth buffalo, *Ictiobus cyprinellus* (Valenciennes). J. Fish. Res. Board Canada 20(6):1397–1429.

Johnson, W. E., and A. D. Hasler. 1954. Rainbow trout production in dystrophic lakes. J. Wildl. Mgmt. 18(1):113–134.

Jones, R. A. 1964. Stonecat *Noturus flavus*. pp. 873–874 *in* McClane's standard fishing encyclopedia, ed. A. J. McClane. Holt, Rinehart, & Winston, N.Y.

Jones, T. C., and W. H. Irwin. 1962. Temperature preferences by two species of fish and the influence of temperature on fish distribution. Proc. Southeast. Assoc. Game Fish Commnrs. 16:323–333.

Jordan, D. S., and B. W. Evermann. 1896–1900. The fishes of north and middle America. Bull. U.S. Natl. Mus. 47(1–4). 3313 pp. + 392 pls.

Jordan, D. S., and B. W. Evermann. 1909. Descriptions of three new species of cisco, or lake herring (*Argyrosomus*), from the Great Lakes of America, with a note on the species of whitefish. Proc. U.S. Natl. Mus. 36(1662):165–172.

Jordan, D. S., and B. W. Evermann. 1923. American food and game fishes. Doubleday, Page and Co., Garden City, N.Y. 574 pp.

Jordan, D. S., and C. H. Gilbert. 1883. Synopsis of the fishes of North America. Bull. U.S. Natl. Mus. 16. 1vi + 1018 pp.

Joy, E. T., Jr. 1975. The walleye, *Stizostedion vitreum* (Mitchill), population and sport fishery of the Big Eau Pleine, a fluctuating central Wisconsin reservoir. Univ. Wis., Stevens Point. MS Thesis. 82 pp.

Juday, C., and A. D. Hasler. 1946. List of publications dealing with Wisconsin limnology, 1871–1945. Trans. Wis. Acad. Sci., Arts, Lett. 36:469–490.

Juday, C., and C. L. Schloemer. 1938. Fish facts. Wis. Conserv. Bull. 3(7):26–27.

Jude, D. J. 1973. Sublethal effects of ammonia and cadmium on growth of green sunfish. Mich. State Univ., East Lansing. PhD Thesis. 193 pp.

Karr, J. R. 1963. Age, growth, and food habits of johnny, slenderhead and blacksided darters of Boone County, Iowa. Proc. Iowa Acad. Sci. 70:228–236.

Karr, J. R. 1964. Age, growth, fecundity and food habits of fantail darters in Boone County, Iowa. Proc. Iowa Acad. Sci. 71:274–279.

Katz, M., and A. R. Gaufin. 1953. The effects of sewage pollution on the fish population of a midwestern stream. Trans. Am. Fish. Soc. 82(1952):156–165.

Kaya, C. M., and A. D. Hasler. 1972. Photoperiod and temperature effects on the gonads of green sunfish, *Lepomis cyanellus* (Rafinesque), during the quiescent, winter phase of its annual sexual cycle. Trans. Am. Fish. Soc. 101(2):270–275.

Keast, A. 1965. Resource subdivision amongst cohabiting fish species in a bay, Lake Opinicon, Ontario. Univ. Mich. Great Lakes Res. Div. Publ. No. 13:106–132.

Keast, A., and D. Webb. 1966. Mouth and body form relative to feeding ecology in the fish fauna of a small lake, Lake Opinicon, Ontario. J. Fish. Res. Board Canada 23(12):1845–1867.

Keast, A., and L. Welsh. 1968. Daily feeding periodicities, food uptake rates, and some dietary changes with hour of day in some lake fishes. J. Fish. Res. Board Canada 25(6):1133–1144.

Keenleyside, M. H. A. 1967. Behavior of male sunfish (genus *Lepomis*) towards females of three species. Evolution 21(4):688–695.

Keenleyside, M. H. A. 1972. Intraspecific intrusions into nests of spawning longear sunfish (Pisces: Centrarchidae). Copeia 1972(2):272–278.

Keeton, D. 1963. Growth of fishes in the Des Moines River, Iowa, with particular reference to water levels. Iowa State Univ., Ames. PhD Thesis. 208 pp.

Keleher, J. J. 1961. Comparison of largest Great Slave Lake fish with North American records. J. Fish. Res. Board Canada 18(3):417–421.

Kelley, D. W. 1953. Fluctuation in trap net catches in the upper Mississippi River. U.S. Fish Wildl. Serv. Spec. Sci. Rep.—Fish. No. 101. 38 pp.

Kelley, J. W. 1968. Effects of incubation temperature on survival of largemouth bass eggs. Progr. Fish-Cult. 30(3):159–163.

Kelly, H. A. 1924. *Amia calva* guarding its young. Copeia 1924(133):73–74.

Kelso, J. R. M. 1972. Conversion, maintenance, and assimilation for walleye, *Stizostedion vitreum vitreum*, as affected by size, diet, and temperature. J. Fish. Res. Board Canada 29(8):1181–1192.

Kempinger, J. 1975. Walleye fishing facts. Wis. Conserv. Bull. 40(4):19.

Kempinger, J. J., W. S. Churchill, G. R. Priegel, and L. M. Christenson. 1975. Estimate of abundance, harvest, and exploitation of the fish population of Escanaba Lake, Wisconsin, 1946–69. Wis. Dep. Nat. Resour. Tech. Bull. 84. 30 pp.

Kendall, W. C. 1921. Further observations on Coulter's whitefish (*Coregonus coulteri* Eigenmann). Copeia 90:1–4.

Kernen, L. T. 1974. Fishery investigations on the lower Fox River and south Green Bay in 1973–1974. Wis. Dep. Nat. Resour. 6 pp. + 2 tables (mimeo).

Keup, L. E., W. M. Ingram, and K. M. Mackenthun. 1967. Biology of water pollution. A collection of selected papers on stream pollution waste water and water treatment. U.S.D.I. Fed. Water Pollut. Control Adm. 290 pp.

Khan, N. Y., and S. U. Qadri. 1970. Morphological differences in Lake Superior lake char. J. Fish. Res. Board Canada 27(1):161–167.

Kilambi, R. V., J. Noble, and C. E. Hoffman. 1970. Influence of temperature and photoperiod on growth, food consumption and food conversion efficiency of channel catfish. Proc. Southeast. Assoc. Game Fish Commnrs. 24:519–531.

King, G. R., and B. L. Swanson. 1975. Progress report of fish management on Lake Superior, 1974. Wis. Dep. Nat. Resour. Div. For. Wildl. Recreat. 41 pp. (mimeo).

King, G. R., B. L. Swanson, and W. Weiher. 1976. Letter Oct 1976, Wis. Dep. Nat. Resour., Washburn.

Kinney, E. C., Jr. 1950. The life history of the trout perch, *Percopsis omiscomaycus* (Walbaum), in western Lake Erie. Ohio State Univ., Columbus. MS Thesis. 75 pp.

Kinney, E. C. 1954. A life history of the silver chub, *Hybopsis storeriana* (Kirtland), in western Lake Erie with notes on associated species. Diss. Abstr. 20(6):1978–1980. Vol. 35. Part. II. 30759.

Kitchell, J. F., and J. T. Windell. 1968. Rate of gastric digestion in pumpkinseed sunfish, *Lepomis gibbosus*. Trans. Am. Fish. Soc. 97(4):489–492.

Kitchell, J. F., and J. T. Windell. 1970. Nutritional value of algae to bluegill sunfish, *Lepomis macrochirus*. Copeia 1970(1):186–190.

Kitchell, J. F., J. F. Koone, R. V. O'Neill, H. H. Shugart, Jr., J. J. Magnuson, and R. S. Booth. 1974. Model of fish biomass dynamics. Trans. Am. Fish. Soc. 103(4):786–798.

Kittel, H. 1955. Report of test netting on Mississippi River 1955. Minn. Conserv. Dep., Lake City. 10 pp. (mimeo).

Klarberg, D. P., and A. Benson. 1975. Food habits of *Ictalurus nebulosus* in acid polluted water of northern West Virginia. Trans. Am. Fish. Soc. 104(3):541–547.

Kleinert, S. J. 1970. Production of northern pike in a managed marsh, Lake Ripley, Wisconsin. Wis. Dep. Nat. Resour. Res. Rep. No. 49. 19 pp.

Kleinert, S. J., and P. E. Degurse. 1968. Survival of walleye eggs and fry of known DDT residue levels from ten Wisconsin waters in 1967. Wis. Dep. Nat. Resour. Res. Rep. No. 37. 30 pp.

Kleinert, S. J., and P. E. Degurse. 1971. Mercury levels in fish from selected Wisconsin water. Wis. Dep. Nat. Resour. Res. Rep. No. 73. 16 pp.

Kleinert, S. J., and P. E. Degurse. 1972. Mercury levels in Wisconsin fish and wildlife. Wis. Dep. Nat. Resour. Tech. Bull. No. 52. 23 pp.

Kleinert, S. J., and D. Mraz. 1966. Life history of the grass pickerel (*Esox americanus vermiculatus*) in southeastern Wisconsin. Wis. Conserv. Dep. Tech. Bull. No. 37. 40 pp.

Kleinert, S. J., P. E. Degurse, and J. Ruhland. 1974. Concentration of metals in fish. Wis. Dep. Nat. Resour. Tech. Bull. No. 74:8–15.

Klingbiel, J. H. 1962. To catch a musky. . . . Wis. Conserv. Bull. 27(5):26.

Klingbiel, J. H. 1969. Management of walleye in the upper midwest. Wis. Conserv. Dep. Div. Fish Mgmt. Rep. No. 18. 14 pp. (mimeo).

Klingbiel, J. H., L. C. Stricker, and O. J. Rongstad. 1969. Wisconsin farm fish ponds. Univ. Wis. Coop. Ext. Prog. Man. 2. 44 pp.

Kmiotek, S. 1974. Wisconsin trout streams. Wis. Dep. Nat. Resour. Publ. 6–3600(74). 118 pp.

Knapp, F. T. 1953. Fishes found in the fresh waters of Texas. Ragland Studio and Litho Printing, Brunswick, Ga. 166 pp.

Knapp, L. W. 1964. Systematic studies of the rainbow darter, *Etheostoma caeruleum* (Storer), and the subgenus *Hadropterus* (Pisces: Percidae). Cornell Univ., Ithaca. PhD Thesis. 225 pp.

Knight, A. E. 1963. The embryonic and larval development of the rainbow trout. Trans. Am. Fish. Soc. 92(4):344–355.

Knudsen, G. J. 1962. Relationship of beaver to forests, trout and wildlife in Wisconsin. Wis. Conserv. Dep. Tech. Bull. No. 25. 50 pp.

Kobayasi, H., Y. Kawashima, and N. Takeuchi. 1970. Comparative chromosome studies in the genus *Carassius* especially with a finding of polyploidy in the ginbuna (*C. auratus langsdorfii*). Jap. J. Ichthyol. 17(4):153–160.

Koch, D. L. 1975. Non-game fish as a resource. pp. 41–46 *in* Symposium on trout/non-gamefish relationships in streams, ed. P. B. Moyle and D. L. Koch. Univ. Nev., Reno. Cent. Water Resour. Res. Misc. Rep. No. 17.

Koelz, W. 1921. Description of a new cisco from the Great Lakes. Occas. Pap. Mus. Zool. Univ. Mich. No. 104. 4 pp.

Koelz, W. 1924. Two new species of cisco from the Great Lakes. Occas. Pap. Mus. Zool. Univ. Mich. No. 146. 8 pp.

Koelz, W. 1929. Coregonid fishes of the Great Lakes. Bull. U.S. Bur. Fish. 43(1927)Part. II:297–643.

Koelz, W. 1931. The coregonid fishes of northeastern America. Pap. Mich. Acad. Sci., Arts, Lett. 13:303–432.

Konefes, J. L., and R. W. Bachmann. 1970. Growth of the fathead minnow (*Pimephales promelas*) in tertiary treatment ponds. Proc. Iowa Acad. Sci. 77:104–111.

Konrad, J. G. 1971. Mercury content of various bottom sediments, sewage treatment plant effluents and water supplies in Wisconsin. Wis. Dep. Nat. Resour. Res. Rep. No. 74. 16 pp.

Konrad, J. G., and S. J. Kleinert. 1974. Removal of metals from waste waters by municipal sewage treatment plants. Wis. Dep. Nat. Resour. Tech. Bull. No. 74. 7 pp.

Koster, W. J. 1936. The life history and ecology of the sculpins (Cottidae) of central New York. Cornell Univ., Ithaca. PhD Thesis (unnumbered).

Koster, W. J. 1937. The food of sculpin (Cottidae) in central New York. Trans. Am. Fish. Soc. 66:374–382.

Koster, W. J. 1939. Some phases of the life history and relationships of the cyprinid, *Clinostomus elongatus* (Kirtland). Copeia 1939(4):201–208.

Koster, W. J. 1957. Guide to the fishes of New Mexico. Univ. N.M. Press, Albuquerque. 116 pp.

Kraatz, W. C. 1923. A study of the food of the minnow *Campostoma anomalum*. Ohio J. Sci. 23(6):265–283.

Kramer, R. H., and L. L. Smith, Jr. 1960a. First-year of the largemouth bass, *Micropterus salmoides* (Lacepede) and some related ecological factors. Trans. Am. Fish. Soc. 89(2):222–233.

Kramer, R. H., and L. L. Smith, Jr. 1960b. Utilization of nests of largemouth bass, *Micropterus salmoides*, by golden shiners, *Notemigonus crysoleucas*. Copeia 1960(1):73–74.

Kraus, R. 1963. Food habits of the yellow bass, *Roccus mississippiensis*. Clear Lake, Iowa, summer 1962. Proc. Iowa Acad. Sci. 70:209–215.

Krohn, D. C. 1969. Summary of northern pike stocking investigations in Wisconsin. Wis. Dep. Nat. Resour. Res. Rep. No. 44. 35 pp.

Krumholz, L. A., and H. S. Cavanah. 1968. Comparative morphometry of freshwater drum from two midwestern localities. Trans. Am. Fish. Soc. 97(4):429–441.

Kudrna, J. J. 1965. Movement and homing of sunfishes in Clear Lake. Proc. Iowa Acad. Sci. 72:263–271.

Kudrynska, O. I. 1962. Cannibalism among the larvae and fry of the carp. Biol. Abstr. 41(6):21356.

Kuehn, J. H. 1949a. Statewide average total length in inches at each year. 2d rev. Minn. Fish. Res. Lab. Suppl. Invest. Rep. 51.

Kuehn, J. H. 1949b. A study of a population of longnose dace (*Rhinichthys c. cataractae*). Proc. Minn. Acad. Sci. 17:81–83.

Kuehn, J. H., W. Niemuth, and A. R. Peterson. 1961. A biological reconnaissance of the upper St. Croix River. Minn. and Wis. Conserv. Deps. 25 pp. + append. pp. A1–A21 (mimeo).

Kuehne, R. A. 1958. Studies on the schooling behavior of the minnows *Semotilus* and *Rhinichthys*. Diss. Abstr. 19(3):606.

Kutkuhn, J. H. 1955. Food and feeding habits of some fishes in a dredged Iowa lake. Proc. Iowa Acad. Sci. 62:576–588.

Laarman, P. W., W. A. Willford, and J. R. Olson. 1976. Retention of mercury in the muscles of yellow perch, *Perca flavescens*, and rock bass, *Ambloplites rupestris*. Trans. Am. Fish. Soc. 105(2):296–300.

Lachner, E. A. 1950. Food, growth and habits of fingerling smallmouth bass, *Micropterus dolomieui* Lacepede, in trout waters of western New York. J. Wildl. Mgmt. 14:50–55.

Lachner, E. A. 1952. Studies of the biology of the cyprinid fishes of the chub genus *Nocomis* of northeastern United States. Am. Midl. Nat. 48(2):433–466.

Lachner, E. A., E. F. Westlake, and P. S. Handwerk. 1950. Studies on the biology of some percid fishes from western Pennsylvania. Am. Midl. Nat. 43(1):92–111.

Lagler, K. F. 1956. The pike, *Esox lucius* Linnaeus, in relation to waterfowl on the Seney National Wildlife Refuge, Michigan. J. Wildl. Mgmt. 20(2):114–124.

Lagler, K. F., and R. M. Bailey. 1947. The genetic fixity of differential characters in subspecies of the percid fish, *Boleosoma nigrum*. Copeia 1947(1):50–59.

Lagler, K. F., and C. Hubbs. 1943. Fall spawning of the mud pickerel, *Esox vermiculatus* LeSueur. Copeia 1943(2):131.

Lagler, K. F., and B. T. Ostenson. 1942. Early spring food of the otter in Michigan. J. Wildl. Mgmt. 6:244–254.

Lagler, K. F., J. E. Bardach, and R. R. Miller. 1962. Ichthyology. John Wiley and Sons, N.Y. 545 pp.

Lagler, K. F., C. B. Obrecht, and G. V. Harry. 1942. The food and habits of gars (*Lepisosteus* spp.) considered in relation to fish management. Indiana Dep. Conserv. and Indiana Univ. Dep. Zool., Invest. Indiana Lakes and Strms. 2(8):117–135.

Lagler, K. F., J. E. Bardach, R. R. Miller, and D. R. M. Passino. 1977. Ichthyology. 2d ed. John Wiley and Sons, N.Y. 506 pp.

Lake, C. T. 1936. The life history of the fan-tailed darter *Catonotus flabellaris flabellaris* (Rafinesque). Am. Midl. Nat. 17(5):816–830.

Lam, C. N. H., and J. C. Roff. 1977. A method for separating alewife *Alosa pseudoharengus* from gizzard shad *Dorosoma cepedianum* larvae. J. Great Lakes Res. 3(3–4):313–316.

Lamsa, A. 1963. Downstream movements of brook sticklebacks, *Eucalia inconstans* (Kirtland), in a small southern Ontario stream. J. Fish. Res. Board Canada 20(2):587–589.

Langlois, T. H. 1929. Breeding habits of the northern dace. Ecology 10(1):161–163.

Langlois, T. H. 1936. A study of the small-mouth bass, *Micropterus dolomieu* (Lacepede), in rearing ponds in Ohio. Ohio State Univ. Stud., Ohio Biol. Surv. Bull. 33(6):189–225.

Langlois, T. H. 1941. Bait culturists guide. Ohio Div. Conserv. Nat. Resour. Bull. No. 137. 18 pp.

Langlois, T. H. 1954. The western end of Lake Erie and its ecology. J. W. Edwards, Ann Arbor. 479 pp.

Lapham, I. A. 1846. Wisconsin: its geography and topography. 2d ed. A. Hopkins, Milwaukee. 202 pp.

Larimore, R. W. 1950. Gametogenesis of *Polydon spathula* (Walbaum): a basis for regulation of the fishery. Copeia 1950(2):116–124.

Larimore, R. W. 1952. Home pools and homing behavior of smallmouth black bass in Jordan Creek. Ill. Nat. Hist. Surv. Biol. Notes No. 28:3–12.

Larimore, R. W. 1954. Dispersal, growth, and influence of smallmouth bass stocked in a warmwater stream. J. Wildl. Mgmt. 18(2):207–216.

Larimore, R. W. 1957. Ecological life history of the warmouth (Centrarchidae). Ill. Nat. Hist. Surv. Bull. 27(1). 84 pp.

Larimore, R. W., and M. J. Duever. 1968. Effects of temperature acclimation on the swimming ability of smallmouth bass fry. Trans. Am. Fish. Soc. 97(2):175–184.

Larimore, R. W., and D. W. Dufford. 1976. Hello, world! Bass number 2 calling. Ill. Nat. Hist. Surv. Rep. 161(Nov):1–2.

Larimore, R. W., and P. W. Smith. 1963. The fishes of Champaign County, Illinois, as affected by 60 years of stream changes. Ill. Nat. Hist. Surv. Bull. 28(2):299–382.

Laser, K. D., and K. D. Carlander. 1971. Life history of the red shiners, *Notropis lutrensis*, in the Skunk River, central Iowa. Iowa State J. Sci. 45(4):557–562.

Latta, W. C. 1963. Life history of the smallmouth bass, *Micropterus dolomieui*, at Waugashance Point, Lake Michigan. Mich. Conserv. Dep. Inst. Fish. Res. Bull. No. 5. 56 pp.

Latta, W. C., and R. F. Sharkey. 1966. Feeding behavior of the American merganser in captivity. J. Wildl. Mgmt. 30(1):17–23.

Lawler, G. H. 1954. Observations on the trout-perch, *Percopsis omiscomaycus* (Walbaum), at Heming Lake, Manitoba. J. Fish. Res. Board Canada 11(1):1–4.

Lawrie, A. H., and J. F. Rahrer. 1973. Lake Superior. A case history of the lake and its fisheries. Great Lakes Fish. Comm. Tech. Rep. No. 19. 69 pp.

Leach, W. J. 1940. Occurrence and life history of the northern brook lamprey, *Ichthyomyzon fossor*, in Indiana. Copeia 1940(1):21–34.

Leary, R. 1979. Population or stock structure of lake whitefish, *Coregonus clupeaformis*, in northern Lake Michigan assessed by isozyme electrophoresis. Univ. Wis., Stevens Point. MS Thesis. 40 pp.

LeCren, E. D. 1965. Some factors regulating the size of populations of freshwater fish. Mitt. Int. Verein. Limnol. 13:88–105.

Lee, D. C., C. R. Gilbert, C. H. Hocutt, R. E. Jenkins, D. E. McAllister, and J. R. Stauffer, Jr. 1980. Atlas of North American freshwater fishes. N.C. State Mus. Nat. Hist. 854 pp.

Lee, G. F. 1977. Effects of Madison metropolitan waste water effluent on water quality in Badfish Creek, Yahara and Rock rivers. Trans. Wis. Acad. Sci., Arts, Lett. 65:163–179.

Legendre, P. 1970. The bearing of *Phoxinus* hybridity on the classification of its North American species. Can. J. Zool. 48(6):1167–1179.

Legendre, P., and D. M. Steven. 1969. Denombrement des chromosomes chez quelques cyprins. Le Nat. can. 96:913–918.

LeGrande, W. H. 1978. Cytotaxonomy and chromosomal evolution in North American catfishes (Siluriformes, Ictaluridae) with emphasis on *Noturus*. Ohio State Univ., Columbus. PhD Thesis. 150 pp.

Lennon, R. E., and P. S. Parker. 1960. The stoneroller, *Campostoma anomalum* (Rafinesque), in Great Smoky Mountains National Park. Trans. Am. Fish. Soc. 89(3):263–270.

Lennon, R. E., J. B. Hunn, and R. A. Schnick. 1970. Reclamation of ponds, lakes, and streams with fish toxicants: a review. Food Agric. Organ. United Nations. Fish. Tech. Pap. 100. 99 pp.

Les, B. L. 1975. Common parasites of freshwater fish. Wis. Dep. Nat. Resour. Publ. 10–3600(75). 22 pp.

Les, B. L. 1979. The vanishing wild—Wisconsin's endangered wildlife and its habitat. Wis. Dep. Nat. Resour. 36 pp.

Les, B. L., and J. Polkowski. 1976. Wisconsin lakes directory. Wis. Dep. Nat. Resour. Bur. Fish Mgmt. Rep. No. 82. 49 pp.

Lewis, D. 1970. Trash fish makes good. The Milwaukee J. (1 Mar), Part IV.

Lewis, W. M. 1939. That "muddy taste" in fish. Wis. Conserv. Bull. 4(6):30–32.

Lewis, W. M. 1957. The fish population of a spring-fed stream system in southern Illinois. Trans. Ill. Acad. Sci. 50:23–29.

Lewis, W. M., and D. Elder. 1953. The fish population of the headwaters of a spotted bass stream in southern Illinois. Trans. Am. Fish. Soc. 82:193–202.

Lewis, W. M., and T. S. English. 1949. The warmouth, *Chaenobryttus coronarius*, in Red Haw Hill reservoir, Iowa. Iowa State Coll. J. Sci. 23(4):317–322.

Lewis, W. M., and S. Flickinger. 1967. Home range tendency of the largemouth bass (*Micropterus salmoides*). Ecology 48(6):1020–1023.

Lewis, W. M., M. Anthony, and D. R. Helms. 1965. Selection of animal forage to be used in the culture of channel catfish. Proc. Southeast. Assoc. Game Fish Commnrs. 17:364–367.

Lewis, W. M., R. Heidinger, and M. Konikoff. 1968. Loss of fishes over the drop box spillway of a lake. Trans. Am. Fish. Soc. 97(4):493–494.

Li, H. 1975. Competition and coexistence in stream fish. pp. 19–30 *in* Symposium on trout/non-gamefish relationships in streams, ed. P. B. Moyle and D. L. Koch. Univ. Nevada, Reno. Cent. Water Resour. Res. Misc. Rep. No. 17. 81 pp.

Liem, K. F., and L. P. Woods. 1973. A probable homologue of the clavicle in the holostean fish *Amia calva*. J. Zool. 170:521–531.

Linder, A. D. 1953. Observations on the care and behavior of darters, Etheostomatinae, in the laboratory. Proc. Okla. Acad. Sci. 43:28–30.

Linder, A. D. 1959. The American percid fishes *Ammocrypta clara* Jordan and Meek and *Ammocrypta pellucida* (Baird). Southwest. Nat. 4(4):176–184.

Lindsey, C. C. 1956. Distribution and taxonomy of fishes in the MacKenzie drainage of British Columbia. J. Fish. Res. Board Canada 13(6):759–886.

Loeb, H. A. 1964. Submergence of brown bullheads in bottom sediment. N.Y. Fish Game J. 11(2):119–124.

Loftus, K. H. 1958. Studies on river spawning populations of lake trout in eastern Lake Superior. Trans. Am. Fish. Soc. 87:259–277.

Long, W. L., and W. W. Ballard. 1976. Normal embryonic stages of the white sucker, *Catostomus commersoni*. Copeia 1976(2):342–351.

Lopinot, A. 1958. How fast do Illinois fish grow? Outdoors Ill. 5(4):8–10.

Lopinot, A. C., and P. W. Smith. 1973. Rare and endangered fish of Illinois. Ill. Dep. Conserv. Div. Fish. 53 pp.

Lord, R. F., Jr. 1927. Notes on the use of the blackhead minnow, *Pimephales promelas*, as a forage fish. Trans. Am. Fish. Soc. 57:92–99.

Lotrich, V. A. 1973. Growth, production, and community composition of fishes inhabiting a first-, second-, and third-order stream of Eastern Kentucky. Ecol. Monogr. 43(3):377–397.

Lovell, R. T. 1973. Put catfish offal to work for you. Fish Farm. Indus. Oct–Nov 1973:22–24.

Lovell, R. T., and L. A. Sackey. 1973. Absorption by channel catfish of earthy-musty flavor compounds synthesized by cultures of blue-green algae. Trans. Am. Fish. Soc. 102(4):774–777.

Lowry, G. R. 1971. Effect of habitat alteration on brown trout in McKenzie Creek, Wisconsin. Wis. Dep. Nat. Resour. Res. Rep. No. 70. 27 pp.

Luce, W. 1933. a survey of the fishery of the Kaskaskia River. Ill. Nat. Hist. Surv. Bull. 20(2):71–123.

Ludwig, G. M., and E. L. Lange. 1975. The relationship of length, age, and age-length interaction to the fecundity of the northern mottled sculpin, *Cottus b. bairdi*. Trans. Am. Fish. Soc. 104(1):64–67.

Ludwig, G. M., and C. R. Norden. 1969. Age, growth and reproduction of the northern mottled sculpin (*Cottus bairdi bairdi*) in Mt. Vernon Creek, Wisconsin. Occas. Pap. Nat. Hist. Milwaukee Public Mus. No. 2. 67 pp.

Lutterbie, G. W. 1975. Illustrated key to the Percidae of Wisconsin (walleye, sauger, perch, and darters). Univ. Wis., Stevens Point, Mus. Nat. Hist. Fauna Flora Wis. Rep. No. 10:17–43.

Lutterbie, G. W. 1976. The darters (Pisces: Percidae: Etheostomatinae) of Wisconsin. Univ. Wis., Stevens Point. MAT Thesis. 307 pp.

Lutterbie, G. W. 1979. Reproduction and age and growth in Wisconsin darters (Osteichthyes: Percidae). Univ. Wis., Stevens Point, Mus. Nat. Hist. Fauna Flora Wis. Rep. 15:1–44 + 19 figs., 21 tables.

Lux, F. E. 1960. Notes on first-year growth of several species of Minnesota fish. Progr. Fish-Cult. 22(1):81–82.

Lyles, C. H. 1968. Fishery statistics of the United States, 1966. U.S. Fish Wildl. Serv., Bur. Commer. Fish. Stat. Dig. No. 60. 679 pp.

McAfee, W. R. 1966a. Eastern brook trout. pp. 242–260 *in* Inland fisheries management, ed. A. Calhoun. Calif. Dep. Fish Game, Sacramento.

McAfee, W. R. 1966b. Rainbow trout. pp. 192–215 *in* Inland fisheries management, ed. A. Calhoun. Calif. Dep. Fish Game, Sacramento.

McAllister, D. E., R. Murphy, and J. Morrison. 1978. The complete minicomputer cataloging and research system for a museum. Curator 21(1):63–91.

McCann, J. A. 1959. Life history studies of the spottail shiner of Clear Lake, Iowa, with particular reference to some sampling problems. Trans. Am. Fish. Soc. 88(4):336–343.

McCarraher, D. B. 1960. Pike hybrids (*Esox lucius* × *E. vermiculatus*) in a Sandhill Lake, Nebraska. Trans. Am. Fish. Soc. 89(1):82–83.

McCarraher, D. B., and R. Thomas. 1968. Some ecological observations on the fathead minnow, *Pimephales promelas*, in the alkaline waters of Nebraska. Trans. Am. Fish. Soc. 97(1):52–55.

McCart, P. 1970. Evidence for the existence of sibling species of pygmy whitefish (*Prosopium coulteri*) in three Alaskan lakes. pp. 81–98 *in* Biology of coregonid fishes, ed. C. C. Lindsey and C. S. Woods. Univ. Manitoba Press, Winnipeg.

McCauley, R. W. 1963. Lethal temperatures of the developmental stages of the sea lamprey, *Petromyzon marinus* L. J. Fish. Res. Board Canada 20(2):483–490.

McCleave, J. D. 1964. Movement and population of the mottled sculpin (*Cottus bairdi* Girard) in a small Montana stream. Copeia 1964(3):506–513.

McComish, T. S. 1967. Food habits of bigmouth and smallmouth buffalo in Lewis and Clark Lake and the Missouri River. Trans. Am. Fish. Soc. 96(1):70–73.

McComish, T. S. 1968. Sexual differentiation of bluegills by the urogenital opening. Progr. Fish-Cult. 30(1):28.

McCoy, E. F. 1972. Role of bacteria in the nitrogen cycle in lakes. Environ. Prot. Agency Off., Res. and Monit. Prog. No. 16010 EHR. Supt. Doc., Wash., D.C. 3 pp.

McCutchin, T. N. 1946. A biological survey of Pewaukee Lake, Waukesha Co., Wisconsin. Wis. Conserv. Dep. Sec. Fish. Biol. Invest. Rep. No. 573. 28 pp. (mimeo).

McCutchin, T. N. 1949. Balancing an unbalanced lake. Wis. Conserv. Bull. 14(11):3–5.

McGregor, J. F. 1970. The chromosomes of the maskinonge (*Esox masquinongy*). Can. J. Genet. Cytol. 12:224–229.

MacKay, H. H. 1963. Fishes of Ontario. Ont. Dep. Lands For., Toronto. 300 pp.

MacKay, H. H., and E. MacGillivray. 1949. Recent investigations on the sea lamprey, *Petromyzon marinus*, in Ontario. Trans. Am. Fish. Soc. 76(1946):148–159.

McKechnie, R. J., and R. C. Tharratt. 1966. Green sunfish. pp. 399–401 *in* Inland fisheries management, ed. A. Calhoun. Calif. Dep. Fish Game, Sacramento.

Mackenthun, K. M. 1946. A preliminary report on the age, growth and condition factor of southern Wisconsin fishes. Wis. Conserv. Dep. Div. Fish Mgmt. Invest. Rep. No. 574. 21 pp.

Mackenthun, K. M. 1948. Age-length and length-weight relationship of southern area lake fishes. Wis. Conserv. Dep. Div. Fish Mgmt. Invest. Rep. No. 586. 6 pp.

Mackenthun, K. M., and E. F. Herman. 1949. A preliminary creel census of perch fishermen on Lake Mendota, Wisconsin. Trans. Wis. Acad. Sci., Arts, Lett. 39:141–150.

Mackenthun, K. M., and W. M. Ingram. 1967. Biological associated problems in freshwater environments, their identification, investigation and control. U.S.D.I. Fed. Water Pollut. Control Adm. Supt. Doc. 287 pp.

Mackenthun, K. M., E. F. Herman, and A. F. Bartsch. 1948. A heavy mortality of fishes resulting from the decomposition of algae in the Yahara River, Wisconsin. Trans. Am. Fish. Soc. 75(1945):175–180.

Mackenthun, K. M., W. M. Ingram, and R. Porges. 1964. Limnological aspects of recreational lakes. U.S. Dep. HEW Public Health Serv., Div. Water Supply & Pollut. Control. 176 pp.

McKenzie, J. A. 1974. The parental behavior of the male brook stickleback *Culaea inconstans* (Kirtland). Can. J. Zool. 52(5):649–652.

McKenzie, J. A., and M. H. A. Keenleyside. 1970. Reproductive behavior of ninespine sticklebacks (*Pungitius pungitius* L.) in South Bay, Manitoulin Island, Ontario. Can. J. Zool. 48(1):55–61.

McKnight, T. C. 1968. A comparison of growth between pellet-fed and minnow-fed largemouth bass fingerlings. Wis. Conserv. Dep. Div. Fish Mgmt. Rep. No. 14. 2 pp. (mimeo).

McKnight, T. C. 1975. Artificial walleye spawning reefs in Jennie Webber Lake, Oneida County. Wis. Dep. Nat. Resour. Bur. Fish Mgmt. Rep. No. 81. 16 pp.

McKnight, T. C., and S. L. Serns. 1974. Food habits of coho salmon (*Oncorhynchus kisutch*) in an inland Wisconsin lake. Trans. Am. Fish. Soc. 103(1):126–130.

McKnight, T. C., and S. L. Serns. 1977. Growth and harvest of coho salmon in Stormy Lake, Wisconsin. Progr. Fish-Cult. 39(2):79–85.

McKnight, T. C., R. W. Wendt, R. L. Theis, L. E. Morehouse, and M. E. Burdick. 1970. Cisco and whitefish sport fishing in northeastern Wisconsin. Wis. Dep. Nat. Resour. Bur. Fish Mgmt. Rep. No. 41. 15 pp. (mimeo).

McLain, A. L., B. R. Smith, and H. H. Moore. 1965. Experimental control of sea lamprey with electricity on the south shore of Lake Superior, 1953–60. Great Lakes Fish. Comm. Tech. Rep. No. 10. 48 pp.

MacLean, J. A., and J. H. Gee. 1971. Effects of temperature on movements of prespawning brook sticklebacks, *Culaea inconstans*, in the Roseau River, Manitoba. J. Fish. Res. Board Canada 28(6):919–923.

MacLean, N. G., and G. C. Teleki. 1977. Homing behavior of rock bass (*Ambloplites rupestris*) in Long Point Bay, Lake Erie. J. Great Lakes Res. 3(3–4):211–214.

McMillan, V. 1972. Mating of the fathead. Nat. Hist. 81(5):73–78.

McNaught, D. C. 1963. The fishes of Lake Mendota. Trans. Wis. Acad. Sci., Arts, Lett. 52:37–55.

McNaught, D. C., and A. D. Hasler. 1961. Surface schooling and feeding behavior in the white bass, *Roccus chrysops* (Rafinesque), in Lake Mendota. Limnol. Oceanogr. 6(1):53–60.

McPhail, J. D. 1963. Geographic variation in North American ninespine sticklebacks, *Pungitius pungitius*. J. Fish. Res. Board Canada 20(1):27–44.

McPhail, J. D., and C. C. Lindsey. 1970. Freshwater fishes of northwestern Canada and Alaska. Fish. Res. Board Canada, Ottawa. 381 pp.

McSwain, L., and R. M. Gennings. 1972. Spawning behavior of the spotted sucker *Minytrema melanops* (Rafinesque). Trans. Am. Fish. Soc. 101(4):738–740.

Magnuson, J. J. 1958. Some phases of the life history of troutperch, *Percopsis omiscomaycus* (Walbaum), in Lower Red Lake, Minnesota. Univ. Minn., Minneapolis. MS Thesis. 104 pp.

Magnuson, J. J., and R. M. Horrall. 1977. Univ. of Wis. 1977–1978 proposal to the National Sea Grant Program for continuing Sea Grant College support. *In* Vol. 2. Univ. Wis. Sea Grant Coll. Prog., Madison. 269 pp.

Magnuson, J. J., and L. L. Smith, Jr. 1963. Some phases of the life history of the troutperch, *Percopsis omiscomaycus*. Ecology 44(1):83–95.

Manion, P. J. 1967. Diatoms as food of larval sea lampreys in a small tributary of northern Lake Michigan. Trans. Am. Fish. Soc. 96(2):224–226.

Manion, P. J. 1968. Production of sea lamprey larvae from nests in two Lake Superior streams. Trans. Am. Fish. Soc. 97(4):484–486.

Manion, P. J. 1972. Variations in melanophores among lampreys in the upper Great Lakes. Trans. Am. Fish. Soc. 101(4):662–666.

Manion, P. J. 1973. Fecundity of the sea lamprey (*Petromyzon marinus*) in Lake Superior. Trans. Am. Fish. Soc. 101(4):718–720.

Manion, P. J. 1977. Downstream movement of fish in a tributary of southern Lake Superior. Progr. Fish-Cult. 39(1):14–16.

Manion, P. J., and A. L. McLain. 1971. Biology of larval sea lampreys (*Petromyzon marinus*) of the 1960 year class, isolated in the Big Garlic River, Michigan, 1960–1965. Great Lakes Fish. Comm. Tech. Rep. No. 16. 35 pp.

Manion, P. J., and H. A. Purvis. 1971. Giant American brook lampreys, *Lampetra lamottei*, in the upper Great Lakes. J. Fish. Res. Board Canada 28(4):616–620.

Manion, P. J., and T. M. Stauffer. 1970. Metamorphosis of the landlocked sea lamprey, *Petromyzon marinus*. J. Fish. Res. Board Canada 27(10):1735–1746.

Manner, H. W., M. VanCura, and C. Muehleman. 1977. The ultrastructure of the chorion of the fathead minnow, *Pimephales promelas*. Trans. Am. Fish. Soc. 106(1):110–114.

Mansueti, A. J. 1963. Some changes in morphology during ontogeny in the pirateperch, *Aphredoderus s. sayanus*. Copeia 1963(3):546–557.

Mansueti, A. J. 1964. Early development of the yellow perch, *Perca flavescens*. Chesapeake Sci. 5(1–2):46–66.

Mansueti, A. J., and J. D. Hardy. 1967. Development of fishes of the Chesapeake Bay region. Univ. Md., Baltimore, Nat. Resour. Inst., Part. I. 202 pp.

Manzer, J. I. 1968. Food of Pacific salmon and steelhead trout in the northeast Pacific Ocean. J. Fish. Res. Board Canada 25(5):1085–1089.

Manzer, J. I. 1969. Stomach contents of juvenile Pacific salmon in Chatham Sound and adjacent waters. J. Fish. Res. Board Canada 26(8):2219–2223.

Marcy, B. C., Jr., and R. C. Galvin. 1973. Winter-spring sport fishery in the heated discharge of a nuclear power plant. J. Fish. Biol. 5:541–547.

Marinac, P. 1976. The smallmouth bass population and fishery in a northern Wisconsin lake, Clear Lake, Oneida County. Univ. Wis., Stevens Point. MS Thesis. 60 pp.

Markus, H. C. 1932. The extent to which temperature changes influence food consumption in largemouth bass. Trans. Am. Fish. Soc. 62:202–210.

Markus, H. C. 1934. Life history of the blackhead minnow (*Pimephales promelas*). Copeia 1934(3):116–122.

Marshall, N. 1939. Annulus formation in scales of the common shiner, *Notropis cornutus chrysocephalus* (Rafinesque). Copeia 1939(3):148–154.

Marshall, N. 1947. Studies on the life history and ecology of *Notropis chalybaeus* (Cope). Q. J. Fla. Acad. Sci. 9(3–4):163–188.

Marshall, W., and N. C. Gilbert. 1905. Notes on the food and parasites of some freshwater fishes from the lakes at Madison, Wisconsin. Rep. U.S. Fish. Commnr. 24(1904):513–522.

Martin, F. D., and C. Hubbs. 1973. Observations on the development of pirate perch, *Aphredoderus sayanus* (Pisces: Aphredoderidae), with comments on yolk circulation patterns as a possible taxonomic tool. Copeia 1973(2):377–379.

Martin, F. D., R. C. Richmond. 1973. An analysis of five enzyme-gene loci in four etheostomid species (Percidae: Pisces) in an area of possible introgression. J. Fish Biol. 5(4):511–517.

Martin, L. 1932. The physical geography of Wisconsin. Wis. Geol. Nat. Hist. Surv. Bull. No. 36, Educ. Ser. No. 4. 608 pp.

Martin, R. G. 1977. PCBs—polychlorinated biphenyls. Sport Fishing Inst. Bull. 288(Sept 1977):1–3.

Marzolf, R. C. 1957. The reproduction of channel catfish in Missouri ponds. J. Wildl. Mgmt. 21(1):22–28.

Mason, J. W., O. M. Brynildson, and P. E. Degurse. 1966. Survival of trout fed dry and meal supplemented dry diets. Progr. Fish-Cult. 28(4):187–192.

Mason, J. W., O. M. Brynildson, and P. E. Degurse. 1967. Comparative survival of wild and domestic strains of brook trout in streams. Trans. Am. Fish. Soc. 96(3):313–319.

Mathiak, H. A. 1979. A river survey of the unionid mussels of Wisconsin, 1973–1977. Sand Shell Press, Horicon, Wis. 76 pp.

Mathur, D., and T. W. Robbins. 1971. Food habits and feeding chronology of young white crappie, *Pomoxis annularis* Rafinesque, in Conowingo Reservoir. Trans. Am. Fish. Soc. 100(2):307–311.

Mattingly, R. 1976. Great Lakes fish cookery. Mich. State Univ. Coop. Ext. Serv. Bull. E–932, Nat. Resour. Ser. 15 pp.

May, E. B., and C. R. Gasaway. 1967. A preliminary key to the identification of larval fishes of Oklahoma, with particular reference to Canton Reservoir, including a selected bibliography. Okla. Dep. Wildl. Conserv. Fish. Res. Lab. Bull. No. 5. Norman. 32 pp. + append., Figs. 1–58.

Mayers, L. J., and F. L. Roberts. 1969. Chromosomal homogeneity of five populations of alewives, *Alosa pseudoharengus*. Copeia 1969(2):313–317.

Meek, S. E., and S. F. Hildebrand. 1910. A synoptic list of the fishes known to occur within fifty miles of Chicago. Field Mus. Nat. Hist. No. 142 Zool. Ser. 7(9):223–338 + 62 figs.

Mendelson, J. 1972. Trophic relationships among species of *Notropis* (Pisces: Cyprinidae) in a small Wisconsin stream. Univ. Wis., Madison. PhD Thesis. 264 pp.

Menzel, B. W. 1976. Biochemical systematics and evolutionary genetics of the common shiner species group. Biochem. System. Ecol. 4:281–293.

Menzel, B. W., and E. C. Raney. 1973. Hybrid madtom catfish, *Noturus gyrinus* × *Noturus miurus*, from Cayuga Lake, New York. Am. Midl. Nat. 90(1):165–176.

Merriner, J. V. 1971a. Egg size as a factor in intergeneric hybrid success of centrarchids. Trans. Am. Fish. Soc. 100(1):29–32.

Merriner, J. V. 1971b. Development of intergeneric centrarchid hybrid embryos. Trans. Am. Fish. Soc. 100(4):611–618.

Metcalf, A. L. 1959. Fishes of Chautauqua, Cowley and Elk counties, Kansas. Univ. Kans., Lawrence, Publ. Mus. Nat. Hist. 11(6):345–400.

Meyer, F. A. 1970. Development of some larval centrarchids. Progr. Fish-Cult. 32(3):130–136.

Meyer, F. P. 1960. The life cycle of *Marsipometra hastata* (Linton, 1898) and the biology of its host, *Polyodon spathula*. Iowa State Univ., Ames. PhD Thesis. 148 pp.

Meyer, F. P., and J. H. Stevenson. 1962. Studies on the artificial propagation of the paddlefish. Progr. Fish-Cult. 24(2):65–67.

Meyer, W. H. 1962. Life history of three species of redhorse (*Moxostoma*) in the Des Moines River, Iowa. Trans. Am. Fish. Soc. 91(4):412–419.

Michigan Department of Natural Resources. 1975. List of the 5 largest specimens of certain species of fish from Michigan waters that have come to the attention of the Michigan Department of Natural Resources. Mich. Dep. Nat. Resour. Fish. Div. 28 pp. (mimeo).

Michigan Department of Natural Resources. 1976. Michigan's endangered and threatened species program. Mich. Dep. Nat. Resour. 30 pp.

Miller, B. 1974. The ling. Mont. Outdoors, Nov–Dec pp. 27–29.

Miller, H. C. 1963. The behavior of the pumpkinseed sunfish, *Lepomis gibbosus* (Linnaeus), with notes on the behavior of other species of *Lepomis* and pigmy sunfish, *Elassoma evergladei*. Behaviour 22 (1/2):88–151.

Miller, J. M. 1974. The food of brook trout fry from different subsections of Lawrence Creek, Wisconsin. Trans. Am. Fish. Soc. 103(1):130–134.

Miller, N. J. 1952. Carp: control and utilization. Wis. Conserv. Bull. 17(5):3–7.

Miller, N. J. 1971. Rough and detrimental fish removal—1970. Wis. Dep. Nat. Resour. 14 pp.

Miller, R. J. 1962. Sexual development and hermaphroditism in the hybrid cyprinid, *Notropis cornutus* × *N. rubellus*. Copeia 1962(2):450–452.

Miller, R. J. 1963. Comparative morphology of three cyprinid fishes: *Notropis cornutus*, *Notropis rubellus*, and the hybrid, *Notropis cornutus* × *Notropis rubellus*. Am. Midl. Nat. 69(1):1–33.

Miller, R. J. 1964. Behavior and ecology of some north American cyprinid fishes. Am. Midl. Nat. 72(2):313–357.

Miller, R. J. 1968. Speciation in the common shiner: an alternate view. Copeia 1968(3):640–647.

Miller, R. J. 1975. Comparative behavior of centrarchid basses. pp. 85–94 *in* Black bass biology and management, chrd. R. H. Stroud, and ed. H. Clepper. Sport Fishing Inst., Wash., D.C.

Miller, R. J., and H. W. Robison. 1973. The fishes of Oklahoma. Okla. State Univ. Press, Stillwater. 246 pp.

Miller, R. R. 1957. Origin and dispersal of the alewife *Alosa pseudoharengus* and *Dorosoma cepedianum* in the Great Lakes. Trans. Am. Fish. Soc. 86:97–111.

Miller, R. R. 1959. Origin and affinities of the freshwater fish fauna of western North America. pp. 187–222 *in* Zoogeography, ed. C. L. Hubbs. Am. Assoc. Adv. Sci. Publ. 51.

Miller, R. R. 1960. Systematics and biology of the gizzard shad (*Dorosoma cepedianum*) and related fishes. U.S. Fish Wildl. Serv. Fish. Bull. 173(60):371–392.

Miller, R. R. 1972. Threatened freshwater fishes of the United States. Trans. Am. Fish. Soc. 101(2):239–252.

Miller, R. R., and E. P. Pister. 1971. Management of the Owens pupfish, *Cyprinodon radiosus*, in Mono County, California. Trans. Am. Fish. Soc. 100(3):502–540.

Mills, H. B., W. C. Starrett, and F. C. Bellrose. 1966. Man's effect on the fish and wildlife of the Illinois River. Ill. Nat. Hist. Surv. Biol. Notes No. 57. 24 pp.

Milner, J. W. 1874a. Report on the fisheries of the Great Lakes; the results of inquiries prosecuted in 1871 and 1872. pp. 1–75 *in* Part II. Rep. U.S. Commnr. Fish. 1872 and 1873. Append. A.

Milner, J. W. 1874b. Report on the propagation of the shad (*Alosa sapidissima*) and its introduction into new waters by the U.S. Fish Commissioner in 1873. pp. 419–451 *in* Part II. Rep. U.S. Commnr. Fish. 1872 and 1873. Append. B.

Minckley, W. L. 1959. Fishes of the Big Blue River basin, Kansas. Univ. Kans., Lawrence, Publ. Mus. Nat. Hist. 11(7):401–442.

Minckley, W. L. 1969. Investigations of commercial fisheries potentials in reservoirs. Final Rep.—P.L. 88–309. Res. Ariz. Game Fish Dep., Ariz. State Univ., Tempe (mimeo).

Minckley, W. L., and J. E. Deacon. 1959. Biology of the flathead catfish in Kansas. Trans. Am. Fish. Soc. 88(4):344–353.

Minckley, W. L., J. E. Johnson, J. N. Rinne, and S. E. Willoughby. 1970. Foods of buffalofishes, genus *Ictiobus*, in Central Arizona reservoirs. Trans. Am. Fish. Soc. 99(2):333–342.

Modde, T., and J. C. Schmulbach. 1977. Food and feeding behavior of the shovelnose sturgeon, *Scaphirhynchus platorynchus*, in the unchannelized Missouri River, South Dakota. Trans. Am. Fish. Soc. 106(6):602–608.

Moen, T. 1953. Food habits of the carp in northwest Iowa lakes. Proc. Iowa Acad. Sci. 60:655–686.

Moen, T. 1959. Sexing of channel catfish. Trans. Am. Fish. Soc. 88(2):149.

Moen, T. E. 1974. Population trends, growth, and movement of bigmouth buffalo, *Ictiobus cyrpinellus*, in Lake Oahe, 1963–70. U.S. Fish Wildl. Serv. Tech. Pap. 78. 20 pp.

Moffett, J. W. 1957. Recent changes in the deep water fish population of Lake Michigan. Trans. Am. Fish. Soc. 86:393–408.

Monson, M., and J. Greenbank. 1947. Size and maturity of hackleback sturgeon. Proc. 3d Annu. Meet. Upper Miss. R. Conserv. Com. Progr. Rep. Tech. Com. Fish. pp. 41–44.

Moodie, G. E. E. 1977. Meristic variation, asymmetry, and aspects of habitat of *Culaea inconstans* (Kirtland), the brook stickleback, in Manitoba. Can. J. Zool. 55(2):398–404.

Moore, E. 1922. The primary sources of food of certain food and game, and bait fishes, of Lake George. pp. 52–63 *in* A biological survey of Lake George, New York. N.Y. State Conserv. Comm.

Moore, G. A. 1944. Notes on the early life history of *Notropis girardi*. Copeia 1944(4):209–214.

Moore, G. A. 1968. Fishes. pp. 31–210 *in* Vertebrates of the United States, ed. W. F. Blair, A. P. Blair, P. Brodkorb, F. R. Cagle, and G. A. Moore. 2d ed. McGraw-Hill, N.Y.

Moore, G. A., and W. E. Burris. 1956. Description of the lateral-line system of the pirateperch, *Aphredoderus sayanus*. Copeia 1956(1):18–20.

Moore, G. A., and J. M. Paden. 1950. The fishes of the Illinois River in Oklahoma and Arkansas. Am. Midl. Nat. 44(1):76–95.

Moore, H. H., and R. A. Braem. 1965. Distribution of fishes in U.S. streams tributary to Lake Superior. U.S. Fish Wildl. Serv. Spec. Sci. Rep.—Fish. No. 516. 61 pp.

Moore, H. H., F. H. Dahl, and A. K. Lemra. 1974. Movement and recapture of parasitic phase sea lampreys (*Petromyzon marinus*) tagged in the St. Mary's River and Lakes Huron and Michigan, 1963–67. Great Lakes Fish. Comm. Tech. Rep. No. 27. 19 pp.

Moore, R. H., R. A. Garrett, and P. J. Wingate. 1976. Occurrence of the red shiner, *Notropis lutrensis*, in North Carolina: a probable aquarium release. Trans. Am. Fish. Soc. 105(2):220–221.

Moore, W. G. 1942. Field studies on the oxygen requirements of certain freshwater fishes. Ecology 23(3):319–329.

Morgan, G. D. 1954. The life history of the white crappie, *Pomoxis annularis*, of Buckeye Lake, Ohio. Denison Univ. Sci. Lab. J. 43(618):113–114.

Morman, R. H. 1979. Distribution and ecology of lampreys in the lower peninsula of Michigan, 1957–75. Great Lakes Fish. Comm. Tech. Rep. No. 33. 59 pp.

Morris, D. 1958. The reproductive behaviour of the ten-spined stickleback (*Pygosteus pungitius* L.). Behaviour Suppl. 6. 154 pp.

Morris. L. A. 1965. Age and growth of the river carpsucker, *Carpiodes carpio*, in the Missouri River. Am. Midl. Nat. 73(2):423–429.

Morsell, J. W. 1970. Food habits and growth of young-of-the-year walleyes from Escanaba Lake. Prelim. Rep., Wis. Dep. Nat. Resour. Res. Rep. 56. 14 pp.

Morsell, J. W., and C. R. Norden. 1968. Morphology and food habits of the larval alewife, *Alosa pseudoharengus* (Wilson), in Lake Michigan. Proc. 11th Conf. Great Lakes Res. pp. 96–102.

Morton, M. C. 1970. The art of Viennese cooking. Bantam Books, N.Y. 139 pp.

Moss, D. D., and D. C. Scott. 1961. Dissolved oxygen requirements of three species of fish. Trans. Am. Fish. Soc. 90(4):377–393.

Mount, E. I., C. Fetterolf, S. J. Kleinert, J. C. MacLeod, L. L. Smith, and J. Whitely. 1970. Heavy metal contamination in North Central United States. Rep. of Ad Hoc Com. on Heavy Metal Contamination in Surface Waters to North Cent. Div., Fish. Soc. 7 pp.

Moy-Thomas, J. A., and R. S. Miles. 1971. Palaeozoic fishes. W. B. Saunders, Philadelphia. 259 pp.

Moyle, J. B. 1975. The uncommon ones. Minn. Dep. Nat. Resour. 32 pp.

Moyle, J. B., and W. D. Clothier. 1959. Effects of management and winter oxygen levels on the fish population of a prairie lake. Trans. Am. Fish. Soc. 88(3):178–185.

Moyle, J. B., and J. H. Kuehn. 1964. Carp, a sometimes villain. pp. 635–642 *in* Waterfowl tomorrow, ed. J. P. Linduska. U.S. Bur. Sport Fish. Wildl.

Moyle, P. B. 1969. Ecology of the fishes of a Minnesota lake with special reference to the cyprinidae. Univ. Minn., Minneapolis. PhD Thesis. 169 pp.

Moyle, P. B. 1973. Ecological segregation among three species of minnows (Cyprinidae) in a Minnesota lake. Trans. Am. Fish. Soc. 102(4):794–805.

Moyle, P. B. 1975. California trout streams: the way they were, probably. pp. 9–18 *in* Symposium on trout/non-gamefish relationships in streams, ed. P. B. Moyle and D. L. Koch. Univ. Nev., Reno, Cent. Water Resour. Res. Misc. Rep. No. 17. 81 pp.

Moyle, P. B. 1977. In defense of sculpins. Fisheries 2(1):20–23.

Mraz, D. 1951. Movements of yellow perch marked in southern Green Bay, Lake Michigan, in 1950. Trans. Am. Fish. Soc. 81:150–161.

Mraz, D. 1960. Preliminary report on the Lake Geneva smallmouth bass studies (1958–1959). Wis. Conserv. Dep. Div. Fish. Mgmt. Rep. No. 1. 22 pp. (mimeo).

Mraz, D. 1964a. Age and growth of the round whitefish in Lake Michigan. Trans. Am. Fish. Soc. 93(1):46–52.

Mraz, D. 1964b. Age, growth, sex ratio, and maturity of the whitefish in central Green Bay and adjacent waters of Lake Michigan. U.S. Fish Wildl. Serv. Fish. Bull. 63(3):619–634.

Mraz, D. 1964c. Evaluation of liberalized regulations on largemouth bass, Browns Lake, Wisconsin. Wis. Conserv. Dep. Tech. Bull. No. 31. 24 pp.

Mraz, D. 1964d. Observations on large and smallmouth bass nesting and early life history. Wis. Conserv. Dep. Fish. Res. Rep. No. 11. 13 pp.

Mraz, D. 1968. Recruitment, growth, exploitation and management of walleyes in a southeastern Wisconsin lake. Wis. Dep. Nat. Resour. Tech. Bull. No. 40. 38 pp.

Mraz, D., and E. L. Cooper. 1957a. Natural reproduction and survival of carp in small ponds. J. Wildl. Mgmt. 21(1):66–69.

Mraz, D., and E. L. Cooper. 1957b. Reproduction of carp, largemouth bass, bluegills, and black crappies in small rearing ponds. J. Wildl. Mgmt. 21(2):127–133.

Mraz, D., and C. W. Threinen. 1957. Angler's harvest, growth rate and population estimate of the largemouth bass of Browns Lake, Wisconsin. Trans. Am. Fish. Soc. 85:241–256.

Mraz, D., S. Kmiotek, and L. Frankenberger. 1961. The largemouth bass, its life history, ecology and management. Wis. Conserv. Dep. Publ. 232. 15 pp.

Mullan, J. W., and R. L. Applegate. 1968. Centrarchid food habits in a new and old reservoir during and following bass spawning. Proc. Southeast. Assoc. Game Fish. Commnrs. 21:332–342.

Mullan, J. W., R. L. Applegate, and W. C. Rainwater. 1968. Food of logperch (*Percina caprodes*) and brook silverside (*Labidesthes sicculus*) in a new and old Ozark reservoir. Trans. Am. Fish. Soc. 97(3):300–305.

Muncy, R. J. 1957. Distribution and movements of channel and flathead catfish in the Des Moines River, Boone County, Iowa. Iowa State Univ., Ames. PhD Thesis. 118 pp.

Murai, T., and J. W. Andrews. 1977. Effects of salinity on the eggs and fry of the golden shiner and goldfish. Progr. Fish-Cult. 39(3):121–122.

Muus, B. J., and P. Dahlstrom. 1971. Collins guide to the freshwater fishes of Britain and Europe. Collins, London. 222 pp.

Neal, R. A. 1961. White and black crappies in Clear Lake, summer, 1960. Proc. Iowa Acad. Sci. 68:247–253.

Needham, P. R. 1969. Trout streams. Holden-Day, San Francisco. 241 pp.

Needham, R. G. 1965. Spawning of paddlefish induced by pituitary material. Progr. Fish-Cult. 27(1):13–19.

Neess, J. 1947. Progress report to the Wisconsin Conservation Department on joint minnow project RF47:249. Univ. Wis. Dep. Zool. pp. 5–7.

Neess, J. C., W. T. Helm, and C. W. Threinen. 1957. Some vital statistics in a heavily exploited population of carp. J. Wildl. Mgmt. 21(3):279–292.

Neill, W. H., Jr. 1971. Distributional ecology and behavioral thermoregulation of fishes in relation to heated effluent from a steam-electric power plant (Lake Monona, Wisconsin). Univ. Wis., Madison. PhD Thesis. 203 pp.

Neill, W. H., Jr., and J. J. Magnuson. 1974. Distributional ecology and behavioral thermoregulation of fishes in relation to heated effluent from a power plant at Lake Monona, Wisconsin. Trans. Am. Fish. Soc. 103(4):663–710.

Neill, W. T. 1950. An estivating bowfin. Copeia 1950(3):240.

Nelson, E. W. 1876. A partial catalogue of the fishes of Illinois. Ill. Nat. Hist. Surv. Bull. 1(1):33–52.

Nelson, J. S. 1968a. Deep-water ninespine sticklebacks, *Pungitius pungitius*, in the Mississippi drainage. Copeia 1968(2):326–334.

Nelson, J. S. 1968b. Life history of the brook silverside, *Labidesthes sicculus*, in Crooked Lake, Indiana. Trans. Am. Fish. Soc. 97(3):293–296.

Nelson, J. S. 1968c. Ecology of the southernmost sympatric population of the brook stickleback, *Culaea inconstans*, and the ninespine stickleback, *Pungitius pungitius*, in Crooked Lake, Indiana. Proc. Indiana Acad. Sci. 77(1967):185–192.

Nelson, J. S. 1969. Geographic variation in the brook stickleback, *Culaea inconstans*, and notes on nomenclature and distribution. J. Fish. Res. Board Canada 26(9):2431–2447.

Nelson, J. S. 1971. Absence of the pelvic complex in ninespine sticklebacks, *Pungitius pungitius*, collected in Ireland and Wood Buffalo National Park region, Canada, with notes on meristic variation. Copeia 1971(4):707–717.

Nelson, J. S. 1973. Occurrence of hybrids between longnose sucker (*Catostomus catostomus*) and white sucker (*C. commersoni*) in Upper Kananaskis Reservoir, Alberta. J. Fish. Res. Board Canada 30(4):557–560.

Nelson, J. S. 1977. Evidence of a genetic basis for absence of the pelvic skeleton in brook stickleback, *Culaea inconstans*, and notes on the geographical distribution and origin of the loss. J. Fish. Res. Board Canada 34(9):1314–1320.

Nelson, M. N., and A. D. Hasler. 1942. The growth, food, distribution and relative abundance of the fishes of Lake Geneva, Wisconsin, in 1941. Trans. Wis. Acad. Sci., Arts, Lett. 34:137–148.

Nelson, W. R. 1968. Embryo and larval characteristics of sauger, walleye, and their reciprocal hybrids. Trans. Am. Fish. Soc. 97(2):167–174.

Nelson, W. R. 1969. Biological characteristics of the sauger population in Lewis and Clark Lake. U.S. Bur. Sport Fish. Wildl. Tech. Pap. 21. 11 pp.

Nelson, W. R. 1974. Age, growth, and maturity of thirteen species of fish from Lake Oahe during the early years of impoundment, 1963–1968. U.S. Bur. Sport Fish. Wildl. Tech. Pap. 77. 29 pp.

Netsch, N. F., and A. Witt, Jr. 1962. Contributions to the life history of the longnose gar (*Lepisosteus osseus*) in Missouri. Trans. Am. Fish. Soc. 91(3):251–262.

Neuenschwander, H. E. 1946. History and biology of the cisco in Lake Mendota. Univ. Wis. Lib. Lab. Limnol. (unpubl. manus.).

New, J. G. 1962. Hybridization between two cyprinids, *Chrosomus eos* and *Chrosomus neogaeus*. Copeia 1962(1):147–152.

Niazi, A. D. 1964. The development of the Weberian system and early embryology of *P. promelas*. Diss. Abstr. 25(4):2674.

Nichols, S. A. 1974. Mechanical and habitat manipulation for aquatic plant management, a review of techniques. Wis. Dep. Nat. Resour. Tech. Bull. No. 77. 34 pp.

Nickum, J. G. 1967. Some effects of sudden temperature changes upon selected species of freshwater fishes. South. Ill. Univ., Carbondale. PhD Thesis. 68 pp. Diss. Abstr. 27B, 3344 (1967).

Niehoff, A. 1952. Otoliths as ornaments. Wis. Archeol., n.s. 33(4):223–224.

Niemuth, W. 1959. For business or bait: the minnow. Wis. Conserv. Bull. 24(6):11–14.

Niemuth, W. 1967. A study of migratory lake-run trout in the Brule River, Wisconsin. Part I. Brown trout. Wis. Conserv. Dep. Div. Fish Mgmt. Rep. No. 12. 80 pp. (mimeo).

Niemuth, W. 1970. A study of migratory lake-run trout in the Brule River, Wisconsin. Part II. Rainbow trout. Wis. Dep. Nat. Resour. Bur. Fish Mgmt. Rep. No. 38. 70 pp.

Niemuth, W., W. Churchill, and T. Wirth. 1959a. The walleye, its life history, ecology and management. Wis. Conserv. Dep. Publ. No. 227. 14 pp.

Niemuth, W., W. Helm, and V. Hacker. 1959b. Life history, ecology and management of the longnose gar. Wis. Dep. Nat. Resour. Bur. Fish Mgmt. 16 pp. (unpubl. manus.).

Nigrelli, R. F. 1959. Longevity of fishes in captivity. *In* CIBA foundation colloquia on aging. Vol. 5, ed. G. E. W. Wolstenholme and M. O'Connor. Little, Brown, Boston.

Nikolsky, G. V. 1963. The ecology of fishes. Academic Press, N.Y. 352 pp.

Noble, R. L. 1965. Life history and ecology of western blacknose dace, Boone County, Iowa, 1963–1964. Proc. Iowa Acad. Sci. 72:282–293.

Noland, W. E. 1951. The hydrography, fish, and turtle populations of Lake Wingra. Trans. Wis. Acad. Sci., Arts, Lett. 40(2):5–58.

Nord, R. C. 1967. A compendium of fishery information on the upper Mississippi River. Upper Miss. R. Conserv. Com. 238 pp.

Norden, C. R. 1961. The identification of larval yellow perch, *Perca flavescens*, and walleye, *Stizostedion vitreum*. Copeia 1961(3):282–288.

Norden, C. R. 1967a. Age, growth and fecundity of the alewife, *Alosa pseudoharengus* (Wilson), in Lake Michigan. Trans. Am. Fish. Soc. 96(4):387–393.

Norden, C. R. 1967b. Development and identification of the larval alewife, *Alosa pseudoharengus* (Wilson), in Lake Michigan. Proc. 10th Conf. Great Lakes Res. pp. 70–78.

Norden, C. R. 1968. Morphology and food habits of the larval alewife, *Alosa pseudoharengus* (Wilson), in Lake Michigan. Proc. 11th Conf. Great Lakes Res. pp. 103–110.

Norden, C. R. 1970. Evolution and distribution of the genus *Prosopium*. pp. 67–80 *in* Biology of coregonid fishes, ed. C. C. Lindsey and C. S. Woods. Univ. Manitoba Press, Winnipeg.

Normandeau, D. A. 1969. Life history and ecology of the round whitefish, *Prosopium cylindraceum* (Pallas), of Newfound Lake, Bristol, New Hampshire. Trans. Am. Fish. Soc. 98(1):7–13.

Northcote, T. G. 1957. Common diseases and parasites of freshwater fishes in British Columbia. B.C. Fish Wildl. Serv.

Nuorteva, P., and E. Hasanen. 1975. Bioaccumulation of mercury in *Myoxocephalus quadricornis* in an unpolluted area of the Baltic. Ann. Zool. Fennici 12:247–254.

Nurnberger, P. K. 1928. A list of the plant and animal food of some fishes of Jay Cooke Park. Trans. Am. Fish. Soc. 58:175–177.

Nybakken, J. W. 1961. Analysis of the sympatric occurrence of two subspecies of the cyprinid fish, *Campostoma anomalum* (Rafinesque), in Wisconsin. Univ. Wis., Madison. MS Thesis. 35 pp.

Nyberg, D. W. 1971. Prey capture in the largemouth bass. Am. Midl. Nat. 86(1):128–144.

Nygren, A., P. Edlund, U. Hirsch, and L. Ashsgren. 1968. Cytological studies in perch (*Perca fluviatilis* L.), pike (*Esox lucius* L.), pike-perch (*Lucioperca lucioperca* L.), and ruff (*Ascerina cernua* L.). Hereditas 59:518–524.

Oberts, G. L. 1977. Water quality effects of potential urban best management practices: a literature review. Wis. Dep. Nat. Resour. Tech. Bull. No. 97. 25 pp.

Odell, T. T. 1934. The life history and ecological relationships of the alewife (*Pomolobus pseudoharengus* Wilson) in Seneca Lake, New York. Trans. Am. Fish. Soc. 64:118–126.

O'Donnell, D. J. 1938. Natural vs. artificial propagation. Wis. Conserv. Bull. 3(9):38–40.

O'Donnell, D. J. 1943. The fish population of three small lakes in northern Wisconsin. Trans. Am. Fish. Soc. 72:187–196.

Oehmcke, A. A. 1969. Muskellunge management in Wisconsin. Wis. Dep. Nat. Resour. Bur. Fish Mgmt. Rep. No. 19. 22 pp. (mimeo).

Oehmcke, A. A., and W. C. Truax. 1964. The Wolf River. Trans. Wis. Acad. Sci., Arts, Lett. 53(Part A):9–20.

Oehmcke, A. A., L. Johnson, J. Klingbiel, and C. Wistrom. 1965. The Wisconsin muskellunge, its life history, ecology and management. Wis. Conserv. Dep. Publ. 225. 12 pp.

Office of Federal Register. 1976. Code of federal regulations, 50 wildlife and fisheries. Natl. Archives and Rec. Serv. Supt. Doc., Govt. Print. Off. GS 4.108:50/976. 590 pp.

O'Gorman, R. 1974. Predation by rainbow smelt (*Osmerus mordax*) on young-of-the-year alewives (*Alosa pseudoharengus*) in the Great Lakes. Progr. Fish-Cult. 36(4):223–224.

O'Hara, J. J. 1968. Influence of weight and temperature on metabolic rate of sunfish. Ecology 49(1):159–161.

Ohno, S., W. Wolf, and N. B. Atkin. 1968. Evolution from fish to mammals by gene duplication. Hereditas 59:169–187.

Ohno, S., J. Muramoto, C. Stenius, L. Christian, W. A. Kittrell, and N. B. Atkin. 1969. Microchromosomes in holocephalian, chondrostean and holostean fishes. Chromosoma 26:35–40.

Okkelberg, P. 1922. Notes on the life-history of the brook lamprey *Ichthyomyzon unicolor*. Occas. Pap. Mus. Zool. Univ. Mich. No. 125. 14 pp.

Olson, D. E., and W. J. Scidmore. 1963. Homing tendency of spawning white suckers in Many Point Lake, Minnesota. Trans. Am. Fish. Soc. 92(1):13–16.

Otto, R. G., and J. O. Rice. 1977. Responses of a freshwater sculpin (*Cottus cognatus gracilis*) to temperature. Trans. Am. Fish. Soc. 106(1):89–94.

Otto, R. G., M. A. Kitchel, and J. O. Rice. 1976. Lethal and preferred temperatures of the alewife (*Alosa pseudoharengus*) in Lake Michigan. Trans. Am. Fish. Soc. 105(1):96–106.

Padfield, J. H., Jr., 1951. Age and growth differentiation between the sexes of the largemouth black bass, *Micropterus salmoides* (Lacepede). J. Tenn. Acad. Sci. 26(1):42–54.

Paetz, M. J., and J. S. Nelson. 1970. The fishes of Alberta. The Queen's Printer, Edmonton. 282 pp.

Page, L. M. 1974. The subgenera of *Percina* (Percidae: Etheostomatini). Copeia 1974(1):66–86.

Page, L. M. 1977. The lateralis system of darters (Etheostomatini). Copeia 1977(3):472–475.

Page, L. M., and P. W. Smith. 1971. The life history of the slenderhead darter, *Percina phoxocephala*, in the Embarras River, Illinois. Ill. Nat. Hist. Surv. Biol. Notes No. 74. 14 pp.

Page, L. M., and R. L. Smith. 1970. Recent range adjustments and hybridization of *Notropis lutrensis* and *Notropis spilopterus* in Illinois. Trans. Ill. Acad. Sci. 63(3):264–272.

Paloumpis, A. A. 1958. Response of some minnows to flood and drought conditions in an intermittent stream. Iowa State Coll. J. Sci. 32(4):547–561.

Paloumpis, A. A. 1963. A key to the Illinois species of *Ictalurus* (class Pisces) based on pectoral spines. Trans. Ill. Acad. Sci. 56(3):129–133.

Paloumpis, A. A. 1964. A key to the Illinois species of *Ictalurus* based on the supraethmoid bone. Trans. Ill. Acad. Sci. 57(4):253–256.

Paragamian, V. L. 1973. Population characteristics of smallmouth bass (*Micropterus dolomieui*) in the Plover and Red Cedar rivers, Wisconsin. Univ. Wis., Stevens Point. MS Thesis. 77 pp.

Paragamian, V. L. 1976a. Population characteristics of northern pike in the Plover River, Wisconsin. Progr. Fish-Cult. 38(3):160–163.

Paragamian, V. L. 1976b. Vulnerability of three species of forage fish to predation by smallmouth bass in a hatchery trough. Progr. Fish-Cult. 38(2):86–87.

Paragamian, V. L., and D. W. Coble. 1975. Vital statistics of smallmouth bass in two Wisconsin rivers, and other waters. J. Wildl. Mgmt. 39(1):201–210.

Parker, H. L. 1964. Natural history of *Pimephales vigilax* (Cyprinidae). Southwest Nat. 8(4):228–235.

Parker, N.C., and B. A. Simco. 1975. Activity patterns, feeding and behavior of the pirateperch, *Aphredoderus sayanus*. Copeia 1975(3):572–574.

Parker, P. S. 1960. Appalachian sport fishery investigations. U.S. Fish Wildl. Serv. Circ. 81:3–6.

Parker, P. S., and R. E. Lennon. 1956. Biology of the sea lamprey in its parasitic phase. U.S. Fish Wildl. Serv. Res. Rep. 44. iii + 32 pp.

Parker, R. A. 1956. A contribution to the population dynamics and homing behavior of northern Wisconsin lake fishes. Univ. Wis., Madison. PhD thesis. 81 pp.

Parker, R. A. 1958. Some effects of thinning on a population of fishes. Ecology 39(2):304–317.

Parker, R. A., and A. D. Hasler. 1959. Movements of some displaced centrarchids. Copeia 1959(1):11–18.

Parker, S. 1971. Wisconsin's troubled waters. Wis. Legis. Reference Bur. Res. Bull. 71–3. 47 pp.

Parker, W. D. 1971. Preliminary studies on sexing adult largemouth bass by means of an external characteristic. Progr. Fish-Cult. 33(1):54–55.

Parmalee, P. W. 1967. The freshwater mussels of Illinois. Ill. State Mus., Springfield, Popular Sci. Ser. Vol. 8. 108 pp.

Parsons, J. W. 1958. The study and management of the muskellunge in Tennessee. Tenn. Game Fish Comm. 23 pp. (mimeo).

Parsons, J. W. 1973. History of salmon in the Great Lakes, 1850–1970. U.S. Bur. Sport Fish. Wildl. Tech. Pap. No. 68. 80 pp.

Parsons, J. W., and T. N. Todd. 1974. Progress report on coregonine morphology, Sept 1974. U.S. Fish Wildl. Serv. Great Lakes Fish. Lab., Ann Arbor. 13 pp. (mimeo).

Parsons, J. W., T. Todd, and L. Emery. 1975. The status of some endemic fishes of the Great Lakes based upon changes in abundance. U.S. Fish Wildl. Serv. Great Lakes Fish. Lab., Ann Arbor. 6 pp. (mimeo).

Paruch, W. 1979. Age and growth of Ictaluridae in Wisconsin. Univ. Wis., Stevens Point. MST Thesis. 97 pp.

Patriarche, M. H., and E. M. Lowry. 1953. Age and rate of growth of five species of fish in Black River, Missouri. Univ. Mo. Stud. 26(2):85–109.

Patten, B. G. 1971. Predation by sculpins on fall chinook salmon, *Oncorhynchus tshawytscha*, fry of hatchery origin. U.S. Dep. Commer. Natl. Mar. Fish. Serv. Spec. Sci. Rep.—Fish. No. 621. 14 pp.

Pearse, A. S. 1918. The food of the shore fishes of certain Wisconsin lakes. Bull. U.S. Bur. Fish. 35:245–292.

Pearse, A. S. 1919. Habits of the black crappie in inland lakes of Wisconsin. Rep. U.S. Commnr. Fish. 1918. Append. 3:5–16.

Pearse, A. S. 1921a. Distribution and food of the fishes of Green Lake, Wisconsin, in summer. Bull. U.S. Bur. Fish. 37:253–272.

Pearse, A. S. 1921b. The distribution and food of the fishes of three Wisconsin lakes in summer. Univ. Wis. Stud. Sci. 3:1–61.

Pearse, A. S. 1924a. Observations on parasitic worms from Wisconsin fishes. Trans. Wis. Acad. Sci., Arts, Lett. 21:147–160.

Pearse, A. S. 1924b. The parasites of lake fishes. Trans. Wis. Acad. Sci., Arts, Lett. 21:161–194.

Pearse, A. S., and H. Achtenberg. 1920. Habits of yellow perch in Wisconsin lakes. Bull. U.S. Bur. Fish. 36:293–366.

Peck, G. W. 1943. Defense of the bullhead. Wis. Conserv. Bull. 8(9):17–18.

Peck, J. W. 1974. Migration, food habits, and predation on yearling coho salmon in a Lake Michigan tributary and bay. Trans. Am. Fish. Soc. 103(1):10–14.

Peckham, R. S., and C. F. Dineen. 1957. Ecology of the central mudminnow, *Umbra limi* (Kirtland). Am. Midl. Nat. 58:222–231.

Perlmutter, A. 1951. An aquarium experiment on the American eel as a predator on larval lampreys. Copeia 1951(2):173–174.

Perry, W. G. 1976. Black and bigmouth buffalo spawn in brackish water ponds. Progr. Fish-Cult. 38(2):81.

Peterman, L. G. 1969. Variations in pharyngeal arches of cyprinids. Univ. Wis., Stevens Point, Mus. Nat. Hist. 16 pp. (unpubl. manus.).

Peterson, J. E., J. P. Wall, T. L. Wirth, and S. M. Born. 1973. Eutrophication control: nutrient inactivation by chemical precipitation at Horseshoe Lake, Wisconsin. Wis. Dep. Nat. Resour. Tech. Bull. No. 62. 20 pp.

Peterson, L. I. 1956. Carp control on Lake Koskonong. Wis. Conserv. Bull. 21(5):25–28.

Petravicz, J. J. 1936. The breeding habits of the least darter, *Microperca punctulata* Putnam. Copeia 1936(2):77–82.

Petravicz, W. P. 1938. The breeding habits of the blackside darter, *Hadropterus maculatus* Girard. Copeia 1938(1):40–44.

Petrosky, C. E., and T. F. Waters. 1975. Annual production by slimy sculpin population in a small Minnesota trout stream. Trans. Am. Fish. Soc. 104(2):237–244.

Pfeiffer, R. A. 1955. Studies on the life history of the rosyface shiner, *Notropis rubellus* (Agassiz). Copeia 1955(2):95–104.

Pflieger, W. L. 1965. Reproductive behavior of the minnows *Notropis spilopterus* and *Notropis whipplii*. Copeia 1965(1):1–8.

Pflieger, W. L. 1966. Reproduction of the smallmouth bass (*Micropterus dolomieui*) in a small Ozark stream. Am. Midl. Nat. 76(2):410–418.

Pflieger, W. L. 1968. A checklist of the fishes of Missouri with keys for identification. Mo. Dep. Conserv. Div. Fish. D–J Ser. No. 3. 64 pp.

Pflieger, W. L. 1971. A distributional study of Missouri fishes. Univ. Kans., Lawrence, Publ. Mus. Nat. Hist. 20(3):225–570.

Pflieger, W. L. 1975. The fishes of Missouri. Mo. Dep. Conserv. 343 pp.

Phillips, G. L. 1967. Sexual dimorphism in the western blacknose dace, *Rhinichthys atratulus meleagris*. J. Minn. Acad. Sci. 34(1):11–13.

Phillips, G. L. 1969a. Morphology and variation of the American cyprinid fishes *Chrosomus erythrogaster* and *C. eos*. Copeia 1969(3):501–509.

Phillips, G. L. 1969b. Diet of the minnow *Chrosomus erythrogaster* (Cyprinidae) in a Minnesota stream. Am. Midl. Nat. 82(1):99–109.

Phillips, G. L. 1969c. Accuracy of fecundity estimates for the minnow *Chrosomus erythrogaster* (Cyprinidae). Trans. Am. Fish. Soc. 98(3):524–526.

Phillips, G. L., and J. C. Underhill. 1967. Revised distribution records of some Minnesota fishes, with addition of two species to the journal list. J. Minn. Acad. Sci. 34(2):177–180.

Phillips, G. L., and J. C. Underhill. 1971. Distribution and variation of the Catostomidae of Minnesota. Occas. Pap. Bell Mus. Nat. Hist. Univ. Minn. No. 10. 45 pp.

Piavis, G. W., J. H. Howell, and A. J. Smith. 1970. Experimental hybridization among five species of lampreys from the Great Lakes. Copeia 1970(1):29–37.

Pileggi, J., and B. G. Thompson. 1976. Fishery statistics of the United States 1973. U.S. Dep. Commer., Natl. Oceanic Atmos. Adm., Natl. Mar. Fish. Serv. Stat. Dig. No. 67. 458 pp.

Pister, E. P. 1974. Desert fishes and their habitats. Trans. Am. Fish. Soc. 103(3):531–540.

Pister, E. P. 1976. A rationale for the management of nongame fish and wildlife. Fisheries 1(1):11–14.

Pitt, T. K., E. T. Garside, and R. L. Hepburn. 1956. Temperature selection of the carp (*Cyprinus carpio* Linn.). Can. J. Zool. 34:555–557.

Platt, D. R., F. B. Cross, D. Distler, O. S. Fent, E. R. Hall, M. Terman, J. Zimmerman, and J. Walstrom. 1973. Rare, endangered and extirpated species in Kansas. Trans. Kans. Acad. Sci. 76(2):97–105.

Poff, R. J. 1973. Lake Michigan—state of the fishery. Wis. Dep. Nat. Resour. Bur. Fish Mgmt. Adm. Rep. No. 3. 6 pp.

Poff, R. J. 1974. Wisconsin's Lake Michigan commercial fisheries, 1940–1973. Wis. Dep. Nat. Resour. Bur. Fish Mgmt. Rep. No. 75. 45 pp. (mimeo).

Poff, R. J., and C. W. Threinen. 1963. Surface water resources of Waukesha County. Wis. Conserv. Dep. Lake and Strm. Classif. Proj. 69 pp.

Poff, R. J., and C. W. Threinen. 1964. Surface water resources of Milwaukee County. Wis. Conserv. Dep. Lake and Strm. Classif. Proj. 39 pp.

Potter, G. E. 1923(1924). Food of the shortnosed gar-pike (*Lepisosteus platostomus*). Proc. Iowa Acad. Sci. 30:167–170.

Potter, G. E. 1926. Ecological studies of the shortnosed gar-pike (*Lepisosteus platostomus*). Univ. Iowa Stud. Nat. Hist. 11(9):17–27.

Potter, I.C., and B. Rothwell. 1970. The mitotic chromosomes of the lamprey, *Petromyzon marinus* L. Experientia 26:429–430.

Power, M. E., and J. H. Todd. 1976. Effects of increasing temperature on social behaviour in territorial groups of pumpkinseed sunfish. Environ. Pollut. 10(3):217–223.

Prather, E. E. 1957a. Experiments on the commercial production of golden shiners. Proc. Southeast. Assoc. Game Fish Commnrs. 10(1956):150–155.

Prather, E. E. 1957b. Preliminary experiments on winter feeding small fathead minnows. Proc. Southeast. Assoc. Game Fish Commnrs. 11:249–253.

Prather, E. E. 1958. Further experiments on feeds for fathead minnows. Proc. Southeast. Assoc. Game Fish Commnrs. 12:176–178.

Prather, E. E., J. R. Fielding, M. C. Johnson, and H. S. Swingle. 1953. Production of bait minnows in the southeast. Ala. Polytech. Inst., Agric. Exp. Stn. Circ. No. 112. 71 pp.

Price, J. W. 1934. The embryology of the whitefish, *Coregonus clupeaformis* (Mitchill). Part I. Ohio J. Sci. 34(4):287–305. Part II. Ohio J. Sci. 34(6):339–414.

Price, J. W. 1935. The embryology of the whitefish, *Coregonus clupeaformis* (Mitchill). Part III. Ohio J. Sci. 35(1):40–53.

Priegel, G. R. 1960. Winnebago studies—annual progress report of the period Jan. 1 to Dec. 31, 1960. Wis. Conserv. Dep. Div. Fish Mgmt. Res. Sec., Oshkosh. 56 pp. (mimeo).

Priegel, G. R. 1962a. Plentiful but unknown. Wis. Conserv. Bull. 27(3):13.

Priegel, G. R. 1962b. Winnebago winter menu. Wis. Conserv. Bull. 27(1):20–21.

Priegel, G. R. 1962c. Food of walleye and sauger in Lake Winnebago. Wis. Conserv. Dep. Misc. Res. Rep. No. 6 (Fish.). 10 pp. (mimeo).

Priegel, G. R. 1963a. Dispersal of the shortnose gar, *Lepisosteus platostomus*, into the Great Lakes drainage. Trans. Am. Fish. Soc. 92(2):178.

Priegel, G. R. 1963b. Food of walleye and sauger in Lake Winnebago, Wisconsin. Trans. Am. Fish. Soc. 92(3):312–313.

Priegel, G. R. 1963c. Use of otoliths to determine length and weight of ancient freshwater drum in the Lake Winnebago area. Trans. Wis. Acad. Sci., Arts, Lett. 52:27–36.

Priegel, G. R. 1963d. What, no legs? Wis. Conserv. Bull. 28(4):23.

Priegel, G. R. 1964a. Lake Winnebago studies. pp. 14–16 *in* Wis. Conserv. Dep. 1965, Res. in Wis. 1964. 72 pp. (mimeo).

Priegel, G. R. 1964b. Review of Lake Poygan sturgeon management problems. Wis. Conserv. Dep., Oshkosh. 6 pp. (mimeo).

Priegel, G. R. 1964c. Early scale development in the walleye. Trans. Am. Fish. Soc. 93(2):199–200.

Priegel, G. R. 1965. Relative effectiveness of day and night trawling in Lake Winnebago. Wis. Conserv. Dep. Res. Plan. Div. Res. Rep. No. 14 (Fish.). 7 pp. (mimeo).

Priegel, G. R. 1966a. Age-length and length-weight relationships of bullheads from Little Lake Butte Des Morts, 1959. Wis. Conserv. Dep. Res. Plan. Div. Res. Rep. No. 17. (Fish.). 6 pp. (mimeo).

Priegel, G. R. 1966b. Lake Puckaway walleye. Wis. Conserv. Dep. Res. Rep. No. 19. (Fish.). 22 pp.

Priegel, G. R. 1966c. Early scale development in the freshwater drum, *Aplodinotus grunniens* Rafinesque. Trans. Am. Fish. Soc. 95(4):434–436.

Priegel, G. R. 1967a. A list of the fishes of Lake Winnebago. Wis. Conserv. Dep. Res. Rep. No. 27. 6 pp.

Priegel, G. R. 1967b. Identification of young walleyes and saugers in Lake Winnebago, Wisconsin. Progr. Fish-Cult. 29(2):108–109.

Priegel, G. R. 1967c. The freshwater drum—its life history, ecology and management. Wis. Dep. Nat. Resour. Publ. 236. 15 pp.

Priegel, G. R. 1967d. Food of the freshwater drum, *Aplodinotus grunniens*, in Lake Winnebago, Wisconsin. Trans. Am. Fish. Soc. 96(2):218–220.

Priegel, G. R. 1968a. Movement and harvest of tagged northern pike released in Lake Poygan and Big Lake Butte Des Morts. Wis. Dep. Nat. Resour. Fish. Res. Rep. No. 29. 7 pp.(mimeo).

Priegel, G. R. 1968b. The movement, rate of exploitation and homing behavior of walleyes in Lake Winnebago and connecting waters, Wisconsin, as determined by tagging. Trans. Wis. Acad. Sci., Arts, Lett. 56:207–223.

Priegel, G. R. 1968c. Lake Winnebago cousins. Wis. Conserv. Bull. 33(2):24–25.

Priegel, G. R. 1969a. Age and growth of the walleye in Lake Winnebago. Trans. Wis. Acad. Sci., Arts, Lett. 57:121–133.

Priegel, G. R. 1969b. Food and growth of young walleyes in Lake Winnebago, Wisconsin. Trans. Am. Fish. Soc. 98(1):121–124.

Priegel, G. R. 1969c. The Lake Winnebago sauger—age, growth, reproduction, food habits and early life history. Wis. Dep. Nat. Resour. Tech. Bull. No. 43. 63 pp.

Priegel, G. R. 1969d. Age and growth of the freshwater drum in Lake Winnebago, Wisconsin. Trans. Am. Fish. Soc. 98(1):116–118.

Priegel, G. R. 1970a. Food of the white bass, *Roccus chrysops*, in Lake Winnebago, Wisconsin. Trans. Am. Fish. Soc. 99(2):440–443.

Priegel, G. R. 1970b. Reproduction and early life history of the walleye in the Lake Winnebago region. Wis. Dep. Nat. Resour. Tech. Bull. 45. 105 pp.

Priegel, G. R. 1971a. Age and rate of growth of the white bass in Lake Winnebago, Wisconsin. Trans. Am. Fish. Soc. 100(3):567–569.

Priegel, G. R. 1971b. Evaluation of intensive freshwater drum removal in Lake Winnebago, Wisconsin, 1955–1966.Wis. Dep. Nat. Resour. Tech. Bull. No. 47. 28 pp.

Priegel, G. R. 1973. Lake sturgeon management on the Menominee River. Wis. Dep. Nat. Resour. Tech. Bull. No. 67. 20 pp.

Priegel, G. R. 1975. Age and growth of the yellow bass in Lake Poygan, Wisconsin. Trans. Am. Fish. Soc. 104(3):513–515.

Priegel, G. R. 1976. Age and growth of the white sucker in Lake Winnebago. Trans. Wis. Acad. Sci., Arts, Lett. 64:132–143.

Priegel, G. R., and D. C. Krohn. 1975. Characteristics of a northern pike spawning population. Wis. Dep. Nat. Resour. Tech. Bull. No. 86. 18 pp.

Priegel, G. R., and D. W. Morrissette. 1971. Carp migration in the Lake Winnebago area. Wis. Dep. Nat. Resour. Bur. Fish Mgmt. Rep. No. 42. 8 pp. (mimeo).

Priegel, G. R., and T. L. Wirth. 1971. The lake sturgeon, its life history, ecology and management. Wis. Dep. Nat. Resour. Publ. 240–270. 19 pp.

Priegel, G. R., and T. L. Wirth. 1975. Lake sturgeon harvest, growth, and recruitment in Lake Winnebago, Wisconsin. Wis. Dep. Nat. Resour. Tech. Bull. No. 83. 25 pp.

Pritchard, A. L. 1931. Taxonomic and life history statistics of the ciscoes of Lake Ontario. Univ. Toronto Stud. Biol. Ser. 35, Ont. Fish. Res. Lab. Publ. 41. 78 pp.

Privolnev, T. I. 1963. Threshold concentrations of oxygen in water for fish at different temperatures. Dokl. Akad. SSSR 151(2), Russian J. Water Pollut. Control Fed. 36(7):959–960.

Probst, R. T. 1954. Why study sturgeon? Wis. Conserv. Bull. 19(3):3–5.

Probst, R. T., and E. L. Cooper. 1955. Age, growth and production of the lake sturgeon (*Acipenser fulvescens*) in the Lake Winnebago region, Wisconsin. Trans. Am. Fish. Soc. 84:207–227.

Proffitt, M. A., and R. S. Benda. 1971. Growth and movement of fishes, and distribution of invertebrates, related to a heated discharge into the White River at Petersburg, Indiana. Indiana Univ. Water Resour. Invest. Rep. 5. 94 pp.

Purkett, C. A., Jr. 1958a. Growth of the fishes of the Salt River, Missouri. Trans. Am. Fish. Soc. 87(1957):116–131.

Purkett, C. A., Jr. 1958b. Growth rates of Missouri stream fishes. Mo. Fish Game Div. Dingell-Johnson Ser. No. 1. 46 pp.

Purkett, C. A., Jr. 1961. Reproduction and early development of the paddlefish. Trans. Am. Fish. Soc. 90(2):125–129.

Purkett, C. A., Jr. 1963. Artificial propagating of paddlefish. Progr. Fish-Cult. 25(1):31–33.

Purkett, C. A., Jr. 1965. Bowfin, *Amia calva*. pp. 142–143 *in* McClane's standard fishery encyclopedia, ed. A. J. McClane. Holt, Rinehart & Winston, N.Y.

Purvis, H. A. 1970. Growth, age at metamorphosis, and sex ratio of northern brook lamprey in a tributary of southern Lake Superior. Copeia 1970(2):326–332.

Pycha, R. L., and G. R. King. 1967. Returns of hatchery-reared lake trout in southern Lake Superior, 1955–1962. J. Fish. Res. Board Canada 24(2):281–298.

Pycha, R. L., and G. R. King. 1975. Changes in the lake trout populations of southern Lake Superior in relation to the fishery, the sea lamprey, and stocking, 1950–1970. Great Lakes Fish. Comm. Tech. Rep. No. 28. 35 pp.

Pycha, R. L., W. R. Dryer, and G. R. King. 1965. Movements of hatchery-reared lake trout in Lake Superior. J. Fish. Res. Board Canada 22(4):999.

Quick, R. F. 1971. The age and growth of brown trout (*Salmo trutta*) and sculpin (*Cottus* spp.) as it relates to eutrophication in the Jordan and Ausable rivers. Mich. State Univ., East Lansing. MS Thesis. 86 pp.

Quinn, J. R. 1976. The pirate perch, nature's anatomical wonder. Trop. Fish Hobbyist 24(11):86–89.

Radonski, G. C. 1966. The effects of low dosage applications of Fintrol (active ingredient—Antimycin A) on the yellow perch (*Perca flavescens*). Wis. Conserv. Dep. Div. Fish Mgmt. Rep. No. 10. 9 pp. (mimeo).

Ragotzkie, R. A. 1974. The Great Lakes rediscovered. Am. Scientist 62(4):454–464.

Rahrer, J. F. 1965. Age, growth, maturity, and fecundity of "humper" lake trout, Isle Royale, Lake Superior. Trans. Am. Fish. Soc. 94(1):75–83.

Rahrer, J. F. 1967. Growth of lake trout in Lake Superior before the maximum abundance of sea lamprey. Trans. Am. Fish. Soc. 96(3):268–277.

Raney, E. C. 1939. The breeding habits of the silvery minnow, *Hybognathus regius* Girard. Am. Midl. Nat. 21(3):674–680.

Raney, E. C. 1940a. Comparison of the breeding habits of two subspecies of black-nosed dace, *Rhinichthys atratulus* (Hermann). Am. Midl. Nat. 23(2):399–403.

Raney, E. C. 1940b. *Rhinichthys bowersi* from West Virginia, a hybrid *Rhinichthys cataractae* × *Nocomis micropogon*, Copeia 1940(4):270–271.

Raney, E. C. 1942. Propagation of the silvery minnow (*Hybognathus nuchalis regius* Girard) in ponds. Trans. Am. Fish. Soc. 71:215–218.

Raney, E. C. 1969. Minnows of New York. Parts I and II. The Conservationist 23(5):22–29 and 23(6):21–29.

Raney, E. C., and E. A. Lachner. 1946. Age, growth, and habits of the hog sucker, *Hypentelium nigricans* (LeSueur), in New York. Am. Midl. Nat. 36(1):76–86.

Ranthum, R. G. 1969. Distribution and food habits of several species of fish in Pool 19, Mississippi River. Iowa State Univ., Ames. MS Thesis. 207 pp.

Ranthum, R. G. 1971. A study of the movement and harvest of catfish tagged in the lower Trempealeau River and Trempealeau Bay. Wis. Dep. Nat. Resour. Bur. Fish Mgmt. Rep. No. 59. 21 pp. (mimeo).

Rasmussen, J. L., ed. 1979. A compendium of fishery information on the upper Mississippi River. 2d ed. Proc. 35th Annu. Meet. Upper Miss. R. Conserv. Com. Spec. Publ. 259 pp. + append.

Reckahn, J. A. 1970. Ecology of young lake whitefish (*Coregonus clupeaformis*) in South Bay, Manitoulin Island, Lake Huron. pp. 437–460 *in* Biology of coregonid fishes, ed. C. C. Lindsey and C. S. Woods. Univ. Manitoba Press. Winnipeg.

Reece, M. 1963. Fish and fishing. Meredith Press, N.Y. 224 pp.

Reed, H. D. 1907. The poison glands of *Noturus* and *Schilbeodes*. Am. Nat. 41(489):553–566.

Reed, R. J. 1954. Hermaphroditism in the rosyface shiner, *Notropis rubellus*. Copeia 1954(4):293–294.

Reed, R. J. 1957a. Phases of the life history of the rosyface shiner, *Notropis rubellus*, in northwestern Pennsylvania. Copeia 1957(4):286–290.

Reed, R. J. 1957b. The prolonged spawning of the rosyface shiner, *Notropis rubellus* (Agassiz), in northwestern Pennsylvania. Copeia 1957(3):250.

Reed, R. J. 1958. The early life history of two cyprinids, *Notropis rubellus* and *Campostoma anomalum pullum*. Copeia 1958(4):325–327.

Reed, R. J. 1959. Age, growth and food of the longnose dace, *Rhinichthys cataractae*, in northwestern Pennsylvania. Copeia 1959(2):160–162.

Reed, R. J. 1968. Mark and recapture studies of eight species of darters (Pisces: Percidae) in three streams of northwestern Pennsylvania. Copeia 1968(1):172–175.

Reed, R. J. 1971. Underwater observations of the population density and behavior of pumpkinseed, *Lepomis gibbosus* (Linnaeus), in Cranberry Pond, Massachusetts. Trans. Am. Fish. Soc. 100(2):350–353.

Reed, R. J., and J. C. Moulton. 1973. Age and growth of blacknose dace, *Rhinichthys atratulus*, and longnose dace, *R. cataractae*, in Massachusetts. Am. Midl. Nat. 90(1):206–210.

Reeves, C. D. 1907. The breeding habits of the rainbow darter (*Etheostoma coeruleum* Storer), a study in sexual selection. Biol. Bull. 14:35–59 + Figs. 1–3.

Regier, H. A. 1963. Ecology and management of largemouth bass and golden shiners in farm ponds in New York. N.Y. Fish Game J. 10(2):139–169.

Reighard, J. 1903. The function of the pearl organs of cyprinidae. Science 17:531.

Reighard, J. 1906. The breeding habits, development and propagation of the black bass (*Micropterus dolomieu* Lacepede and *Micropterus salmoides* Lacepede). Bull. Mich. Fish Comm. 7. 73 pp. + 29 figs.

Reighard, J. 1910. Methods of studying the habits of fishes, with an account of the breeding habits of the horned dace. Bull. U.S. Bur. Fish. 28(2):1111–1136 + Figs. 1–5, Pls. 114–120.

Reighard, J. 1913. The breeding habits of the logperch (*Percina caprodes*). Mich. Acad. Sci. Rep. 15:104–105.

Reighard, J. 1920. The breeding behavior of suckers and minnows. Biol. Bull. 38(1):1–32.

Reighard, J., and H. Cummins. 1916. Description of a new species of lamprey of the genus *Ichthyomyzon*. Occas. Pap. Mus. Zool. Univ. Mich. No. 31. 12 pp.

Reigle, N. J., Jr. 1969a. Bottom trawl explorations in Green Bay of Lake Michigan, 1963–1965. U.S. Fish Wildl. Serv. Bur. Commer. Fish. Circ. 297. 14 pp.
Reigle, N. J., Jr. 1969b. Bottom trawl explorations in northern Lake Michigan, 1963–1965. U.S. Fish Wildl. Serv. Bur. Commer. Fish. Circ. 318. 21 pp.
Reigle, N. J., Jr. 1969c. Bottom trawl explorations in southern lake Michigan, 1962–1965. U.S. Fish Wildl. Serv. Bur. Commer. Fish. Circ. 301. 35 pp.
Reinert, R. E., L. J. Stone, and H. L. Bergman. 1974. Dieldrin and DDT: accumulation from water and food by lake trout (*Salvelinus namaycush*) in the laboratory. Proc. 17th Conf. Great Lakes Res. pp. 52–58.
Reisman, H. M. 1961. The reproductive behavior of the five-spined stickleback, *Eucalia inconstans* (Kirtland). Am. Zool. 1(4):468.
Reisman, H. M., and T. J. Cade. 1967. Physiological and behavioral aspects of reproduction in the brook stickleback, *Culaea inconstans*. Am. Midl. Nat. 77(2):257–295.
Reynolds, W. W., and M. E. Casterlin. 1977. Temperature preferences of four fish species in an electronic thermoregulatory shuttlebox. Progr. Fish-Cult. 39(3):123–125.
Richards, F. P., and R. M. Ibara. 1978. The preferred temperatures of the brown bullhead, *Ictalurus nebulosus*, with reference to its orientation to the discharge canal of a nuclear plant. Trans. Am. Fish. Soc. 107(2):288–294.
Richardson, L. R. 1939. The spawning behavior of *Fundulus diaphanus* (LeSueur). Copeia 1939(3):165–167.
Richardson, R. E. 1913. Observations on the breeding habits of fishes at Havana, Illinois, 1910 and 1911. Bull. Ill. State lab. Nat. Hist. 9:405–416.
Richey, D. 1976. Salmon surprise. Mich. Dep. Nat. Resour. 45(5):36–38.
Riege, W. H., and A. Cherkin. 1971. One-trial learning in goldfish: temperature dependence. Behavorial Biol. 7(2):255–263.
Riggs, C. D. 1955. Reproduction of the white bass, *Morone chrysops*. Indiana Dep. Conserv. and Indiana Dep. Zool., Invest. Indiana Lakes and Strms. 4(3):87–110.
Rimsky-Korsakoff, V. N. 1930. The food of certain fishes of the Lake Champlain watershed. pp. 88–104 *in* A biological survey of the Champlain watershed. Suppl. 19th Annu. Rep. (1929) N.Y. State Conserv. Dep.
Roach, L. S., and E. L. Wickliff. 1934. Relationship of aquatic plants to oxygen supply, and their bearing on fish life. Trans. Am. Fish. Soc. 64:370–378.
Robbins, W. H., and H. R. MacCrimmon. 1974. The black bass in America and overseas. Biomgmt. Res. Enterpr., Sault Ste. Marie. 196 pp.
Roberts, F. L. 1967. Chromosome cytology of the Osteichthyes. Progr. Fish-Cult. 29(2):75–83.
Roberts, N. J., and H. E. Winn. 1962. Utilization of the senses in feeding behavior of the johnny darter, *Etheostoma nigrum*. Copeia 1962(3):567–570.
Robins, C. R., and E. E. Deubler, Jr. 1955. The life history and systematic status of the burbot, *Lota lota lacustris* (Walbaum), in the Susquehanna River system. N.Y. State Mus. Cir. 39. 49 pp.
Robins, C. R., R. M. Bailey, C. E. Bond, J. R. Brooker, E. A. Lachner, R. N. Lea, and W. B. Scott (Com. on names of fishes). 1980. A list of common and scientific names of fishes from the United States and Canada. 4th ed. Am. Fish. Soc., Bethesda, Md. Spec. Publ. No. 12. 174 pp.
Robinson, E. S., I. C. Potter, and C. J. Webb. 1974. Homogeneity of holarctic lamprey karyotypes. Caryologia 27(4):443–454.
Roelofs, E. W. 1957. Age and growth of whitefish, *Coregonus clupeaformis* (Mitchill), in Big Bay de Noc and northern Lake Michigan. Trans. Am. Fish. Soc. 87:190–199.
Roosa, D. M. 1977. Endangered and threatened fish of Iowa. Iowa State Preserves Advis. Board, Des Moines. Spec. Rep. No. 1. 25 pp. + append.
Rosen, D. E. 1964. The relationships and taxonomic position of the halfbeaks, killifishes, and silversides, and their relatives. Am. Mus. Nat. Hist. Bull. 127(5):217–268.
Ross, M. R. 1973. A chromosome study of 5 species of etheostomine fishes (Percidae). Copeia 1973(1):163–165.
Ross, M. R. 1976. Nest-entry behavior of female creek chubs (*Semotilus atromaculatus*) in different habitats. Copeia 1976(2):378–380.
Ross, M. R. 1977. Aggression as a social mechanism in the creek chub (*Semotilus atromaculatus*). Copeia 1977(2):393–397.
Ross, M. R., and T. M. Cavender. 1977. First report of the natural cyprinid hybrid, *Notropis cornutus* × *Rhinichthys cataractae*, from Ohio. Copeia 1977(4):777–780.
Rottiers, D. V. 1965. Some aspects of the life history of *Cottus cognatus* in Lake Michigan. Univ. Mich., Ann Arbor. MS Thesis. 49 pp.
Roy, J. M. 1973. Croissance, comportement, et alimentation de la lamproie du nord (*Ichthyomyzon unicuspis* Hubbs and Trautman) en captivité. Ministère de L'Industrie et du Commerce. Serv. de biologie, Dir. des Pêches. Travant sur les Pêcheries du Québec No. 41. 144 pp.
Rozin, P. N., and J. Mayer. 1961. Thermal reinforcement and thermoregularity behavior in the goldfish, *Carassius auratus*. Science 134(3843):942–943.
Ruedisili, L. C. 1972. Ground water in Wisconsin—quantity and quality protection: legal controls and management. Univ. Wis. Water Resour. Cent., Madison. 109 pp. + 6 maps.
Ruelle, R. 1977. Reproductive cycle and fecundity of white bass in Lewis and Clark Lake. Trans. Am. Fish. Soc. 106(1):67–76.
Rupp, R. S. 1965. Shore spawning and survival of eggs of the American smelt. Trans. Am. Fish. Soc. 94(2):160–168.
Rutledge, W. P. 1971. A contribution towards a bibliography of the white crappie, *Pomoxis annularis*, and the black crappie, *Pomoxis nigromaculatus*. Tex. Parks Wildl. Dep. Tech. Ser. No. 6:15–35.
Rutledge, W. P., and J. C. Barron. 1972. The effects of the removal of stunted white crappie on the remaining crappie population of Meridian State Park Lake, Bosque, Texas. Tex. Parks Wildl. Dep. Tech. Ser. No. 12. 41 pp.
Ryder, R. A. 1950. The great blue heron killed by carp. Condor 52(1):40–41.
Sadzikowski, M. R., and D. C. Wallace. 1976. Comparison of the food habits of size classes of three sunfishes (*Lepomis macrochirus* Rafinesque, *L. gibbosus* (Linnaeus) and *L. cyanellus* Rafinesque). Am. Midl. Nat. 95(1):220–225.
Saksena, V. P. 1963. Effects of temperature, light, feeding, and activity on the rate of aerial breathing of gar (*Lepisosteus*). Univ. Okla., Norman. PhD Thesis. Diss. Abstr. 24(6):2628.
Saksena, V. P., K. Yamamoto, and C. D. Riggs. 1961. Early development of channel catfish. Progr. Fish-Cult. 23(4):156–161.
Sather, L. M., and S. I. Johannes. 1973. Surface water resources of Douglas County. Wis. Dep. Nat. Resour. Lake and Strm. Classif. Proj. 166 pp.
Sather, L. M., and C. W. Threinen. 1963. Surface waters of Chippewa County. Wis. Conserv. Dep. Lake and Strm. Classif. Proj. 154 pp.
Sather, L. M., and C. W. Threinen. 1968. Surface water resources of Sawyer County. Wis. Dep. Nat. Resour. Lake and Strm. Classif. Proj. 213 pp.
Savage, T. 1963. Reproductive behavior of the mottled sculpin, *Cottus bairdi* Girard. Copeia 1963(2):317–325.

Scarola, J. F. 1973. Freshwater fishes of New Hampshire. N.H. Fish Game Dep. Div. Inland and Mar. Fish. 131 pp.

Schaefer, W. F. 1977. Growth patterns, food habits and seasonal distribution of yellow perch in southwestern Lake Michigan. Trans. Wis. Acad. Sci., Arts, Lett. 65:204–216.

Schloemer, C. L. 1936. The growth of the muskellunge *Esox masquinongy immaculatus* (Garrard) in various lakes and drainage areas of northern Wisconsin. Copeia 1936(4):185–193.

Schloemer, C. L. 1939. The age and rate of growth of the bluegill, *Helioperca macrochira* (Rafinesque). Univ. Wis., Madison. PhD Thesis. 113 pp.

Schloemer, C. L., and R. Lorch. 1942. The rate of growth of the wall-eyed pike, *Stizostedion vitreum* (Mitchill), in Wisconsin's inland waters, with special reference to the growth characteristics of the Trout Lake population. Copeia 1942(4):201–211.

Schlumpf, C. A. 1941. The spearing of sturgeon in Lake Winnebago. Wis. Conserv. Bull. 6(8):33–36.

Schmidt, J. 1922. The breeding places of the eel. Phil. Trans. Royal Soc. London, Ser. B. 211:179–208.

Schmitz, W. R., and R. E. Hetfeld. 1965. Predation by introduced muskellunge on perch and bass. II. Years 8–9. Trans. Wis. Acad. Sci., Arts, Lett. 54:273–282.

Schneberger, E. 1937a. The biological and economic importance of the smelt in Green Bay. Trans. Am. Fish. Soc. 66(1936):139–142.

Schneberger, E. 1937b. The food of small dogfish, *Amia calva*. Copeia 1937(1):61.

Schneberger, E. 1947. The sea lamprey—a menace to the Great Lakes fisheries. Wis. Conserv. Bull. 12(1):12–14.

Schneberger, E. 1972a. The black crappie—its life history, ecology and management. Wis. Dep. Nat. Resour. Publ. 243–72. 16 pp.

Schneberger, E. 1972b. White crappie—life history, ecology and management. Wis. Dep. Nat. Resour. Publ. 244. 14 pp.

Schneberger, E. 1972c. The white sucker, its life history, ecology and management. Wis. Dep. Nat. Resour. Publ. No. 245–72. 18 pp.

Schneberger, E. 1972d. Smallmouth bass—life history, ecology and management. Wis. Dep. Nat. Resour. Publ. No. 242. 16 pp.

Schneberger, E. 1973. Rock bass, life history, ecology and management. Wis. Dep. Nat. Resour. 16 pp.

Schneberger, E., and L. A. Woodbury. 1944. The lake sturgeon, *Acipenser fulvescens* Rafinesque, in Lake Winnebago, Wisconsin. Trans. Wis. Acad. Sci., Arts, Lett. 36:131–140.

Schneider, H., and A. D. Hasler. 1960. Laute and Lauterzeugung beim Süsswassertrommler *Aplodinotus grunniens* Rafinesque (Sciaenidae, Pisces). Z. vergleich. Physiol. 43(5):499–517.

Scholz, A. T., R. M. Horrall, J. C. Cooper, and A. D. Hasler. 1976. Imprinting to chemical cues: the basis for home stream selection in salmon. Science 192(18 Jun 1976):1247–1249.

Schontz, C. J. 1963. The effects of altitude and latitude on the morphology meristics, growth and fecundity of the eastern blacknose dace, *Rhinichthys atratulus atratulus* (Hermann). Diss. Abstr. 24(3):1303.

Schoumacher, R. 1968. Some observations on flathead catfish in the Mississippi River bordering Iowa. Trans. Am. Fish. Soc. 97(1):65–66.

Schultz, P. T. 1969. Prairie trout. Wis. Conserv. Bull. 34(1):16–17.

Schumacher, R. E., and S. Eddy. 1960. The appearance of pink salmon, *Oncorhynchus gorbuscha* (Walbaum), in Lake Superior. Trans. Am. Fish. Soc. 91(4):421–422.

Schumacher, R. E., and J. G. Hale. 1962. Third generation pink salmon, *Oncorhynchus gorbuscha* (Walbaum), in Lake Superior. Trans. Am. Fish. Soc. 91(4):421–422.

Schwartz, E., and A. D. Hasler. 1966a. Perception of surface waves by the blackstripe topminnow, *Fundulus notatus*. J. Fish. Res. Board Canada 23(9):1331–1352.

Schwartz, E., and A. D. Hasler. 1966b. Superficial lateral line sense organs of the mudminnow (*Umbra limi*). Z. vergleich. Physiol. 53:317–327.

Schwartz, F. J. 1962. Artificial pike hybrids, *Esox americanus vermiculatus* × *E. lucius*. Trans. Am. Fish. Soc. 91(2):229–230.

Schwartz, F. J. 1965. Densities and ecology of the darters of the upper Allegheny River watershed. Pittsburgh Univ. Pymatuming Lab. of Ecol. Spec. Publ. 3:95–101.

Schwartz, F. J. 1972. World literature to fish hybrids with an analysis by family, species, and hybrid. Gulf Coast Res. Lab., Ocean Springs, Miss. 328 pp.

Schwartz, F. J., and J. Norvell. 1958. Food, growth and sexual dimorphism of the redside dace *Clinostomus elongatus* (Kirtland) in Linesville Creek, Crawford County, Pennsylvania. Ohio J. Sci. 58(5):311–316.

Scidmore, W. J., and D. E. Woods. 1960. Some observations on competition between several species of fish for summer foods in four southern Minnesota lakes in 1955, 1956 and 1957. Minn. Fish Game Invest. Fish Ser. 2:13–24.

Scott, D. C. 1949. A study of a stream population of rock bass. Indiana Dep. Conserv. and Indiana Univ. Dep. Zool., Invest. Indiana Lakes and Strms. 3(3):169–234.

Scott, D. P. 1964. Thermal resistance of pike, muskellunge, and F_1 hybrid. J. Fish. Res. Board Canada 21(5):1045–1049.

Scott, W. B. 1967. Freshwater fishes of eastern Canada. Univ. Toronto Press, Toronto. 137 pp.

Scott, W. B., and E. J. Crossman. 1973. Freshwater fishes of Canada. Fish. Res. Board Canada, Ottawa. Bull. 184. 966 pp.

Scott, W. B., and S. H Smith. 1962. The occurrence of the longjaw cisco, *Leucichthys alpenae*, in Lake Erie. J. Fish. Res. Board Canada 19(6):1013–1023.

Scott, W. E. 1937. Conservation history. Wis. Conserv. Bull. 2(3):10–15.

Scott, W. E. 1965. Water policy evolution in Wisconsin; protection of the public trust. Trans. Wis. Acad. Sci., Arts, Lett. 54(Part A):143–197.

Seagran, H. L., J. T. Graikoski, and J. A. Emerson. 1970. Guidelines for the processing of hot-smoked chubs. U.S. Fish Wildl. Serv. Circ. 331. 23 pp.

Seeburger, G. 1975. Fishes of Walworth County. Univ. Wis., Stevens Point, Mus. Nat. Hist. Fauna Flora Wis. Rep. No. 10. 16 pp.

Seifert, M. F. 1963. Some aspects of territorial behavior of the fantail darter. Proc. Iowa Acad. Sci. 70:224–227.

Selgeby, J. H., W. R. MacCallum, and D. V. Swedberg. 1978. Predation by rainbow smelt (*Osmerus mordax*) on lake herring (*Coregonus artedii*) in Lake Superior. J. Fish. Res. Board Canada 35(11):1457–1463.

Serns, S. L., and T. C. McKnight. 1974. A summer creel census of Stormy, Black Oak and Laura lakes, Vilas County. Wis. Dep. Nat. Resour. Bur. Fish Mgmt. Rep. No. 71. 27 pp. (mimeo).

Serns, S. L., and T. C. McKnight. 1977. The occurrence of northern pike × grass pickerel hybrids and an exceptionally large grass pickerel in a northern Wisconsin stream. Copeia 1977(4):780–781.

Shaklee, J. B., M. J. Champion, and G. S. Whitt. 1974. Developmental genetics of teleosts: a biochemical analysis of lake chubsucker ontogeny. Dev. Biol. 38:356–382.

Sharp, R. W. 1950. Summary of farm-pond inspectors, 1949. Progr. Fish-Cult. 12(3):147–150.

Shepherd, M. E., and M. T. Huish. 1978. Age, growth, and diet of the pirate perch in a coastal plain stream of North Carolina. Trans. Am. Fish. Soc. 107(3):457–459.

Shetter, D. S. 1936. Migration, growth rate, and population density of brook trout in the north branch of the Au Sable River, Michigan. Trans. Am. Fish. Soc. 66:203–210.

Shetter, D. S. 1949. A brief history of the sea lamprey problem in Michigan waters. Trans. Am. Fish. Soc. 76:160–176.

Shields, J. T. 1957. Report of fisheries investigations during the second year of impoundment of Gavins Point Reservoir, South Dakota, 1956. S.D. Dep. Game Fish Parks Dingell-Johnson Proj. F–1–R–6. 34 pp. (mimeo).

Shields, J. T. 1965. Yellow bass *Roccus mississippiensis*. pp. 1023–1024 *in* McClane's standard fishing encyclopedia, ed. A. J. McClane. Holt, Rinehart & Winston, N.Y.

Shireman, J. V., R. L. Stetler, and E. E. Colle. 1978. Possible use of the lake chubsucker as a baitfish. Progr. Fish-Cult. 40(1):33–34.

Siefert, R. E. 1965. Early scale development in the white crappie. Trans. Am. Fish. Soc. 94(2):182.

Siefert, R. E. 1968. Reproductive behavior, incubation and mortality of eggs, and postlarval food selection in the white crappie. Trans. Am. Fish. Soc. 97(3):252–259.

Siefert, R. E. 1969a. Biology of the white crappie in Lewis and Clark Lake. U.S. Bur. Sport Fish. Wildl. Tech. Pap. No. 22 (Jan 1969). 16 pp.

Siefert, R. E. 1969b. Characteristics for separation of white and black crappie larvae. Trans. Am. Fish. Soc. 98(2):326–328.

Siefert, R. E. 1972. First food of larval yellow perch, white sucker, bluegill, emerald shiner, and rainbow smelt. Trans. Am. Fish. Soc. 101(2):219–225.

Siefert, R. E., A. R. Carlson, and L. J. Herman. 1974. Effects of reduced oxygen concentrations on the early life stages of mountain whitefish, smallmouth bass, and white bass. Progr. Fish-Cult. 36(4):186–191.

Siewert, H. F. 1973. Thermal effects on biological production in nutrient rich ponds. Univ. Wis. Water Resour. Cent. Tech. Completion Rep. A–020 and A–032. 23 pp.

Sigler, W. F. 1958. The ecology and use of carp in Utah. Utah Agric. Exp. Stn. Bull. 405. 63 pp.

Sigler, W. F., and R. R. Miller. 1963. Fishes of Utah. Utah Dep. Fish Game, Salt Lake City. 203 pp.

Silbergeld, E. D. 1973. Dieldrin. Effects of chronic sublethal exposure on adaptation to thermal stress in freshwater fish. Environ. Sci. Technol. 7(9):846–849.

Siler, R., Jr., and J. P. Clugston. 1975. Largemouth bass under conditions of extreme thermal stress. 333–341 pp. *in* Black bass biology and management, chrd. R. H. Stroud, and ed. H. Clepper. Sport Fishing Inst., Wash., D.C.

Skrypek, J. L. 1965. Three years of winter catfish angling of Lake Pepin, 1962–1965. Minn. Dep. Conserv. Invest. Rep. No. 286. 7 pp.

Slastenenko, E. P. 1957. A list of natural hybrids of the world. Hydrobiologi, Ser. B4(2–3):76–97.

Slastenenko, E. P. 1958. The freshwater fishes of Canada. Kiev Printers, Toronto. 383 pp.

Smith, A. J., J. H. Howell, and G. W. Piavis. 1968. Comparative embryology of five species of lampreys of the upper Great Lakes. Copeia 1968(3):461–469.

Smith, B. G. 1908. The spawning habits of *Chrosomus erythrogaster* Rafinesque. Biol. Bull. 15:9–18.

Smith, B. R., J. J. Tibbles, and B. G. Johnson. 1974. Control of the sea lamprey (*Petromyzon marinus*) in Lake Superior, 1953–70. Great Lakes Fish. Comm. Tech. Rep. 26. 60 pp.

Smith, G. R. 1963. A late Illinoian fish fauna from southwestern Kansas and its climatic significance. Copeia 1963(2):278–285.

Smith, H. M., and L. G. Harron. 1903. Breeding habits of the yellow catfish. Bull. U.S. Fish. Comm. 22(1902):149–154.

Smith, L. L., Jr., and R. H. Kramer. 1964. The spottail shiner in lower Red Lake, Minnesota. Trans. Am. Fish. Soc. 93(1):35–45.

Smith, M. W., and J. W. Saunders. 1955. The American eel in certain fresh waters of the maritime provinces of Canada. J. Fish. Res. Board Canada 12(2):238–269.

Smith, O. B., and J. Van Oosten. 1940. Tagging experiments with lake trout, whitefish, and other species of fish from Lake Michigan. Trans. Am. Fish. Soc. 69(1939):63–84.

Smith, O. R. 1935. The breeding habits of the stone roller minnow (*Campostoma anomalum* Rafinesque). Trans. Am. Fish. Soc. 65:148–151.

Smith, P. W. 1965. A preliminary annotated list of the lampreys and fishes of Illinois. Ill. Nat. Hist. Surv. Biol. Notes No. 54. 12 pp.

Smith, P. W. 1968. An assessment of changes in the fish fauna of two Illinois rivers and its bearing on their future. Trans. Ill. Acad. Sci. 61(1):31–45.

Smith, P. W. 1971. Illinois streams: a classification based on their fishes and an analysis of factors responsible for disappearance of native species. Ill. Nat. Hist. Surv. Biol. Notes No. 76. 14 pp.

Smith, P. W. 1973. A key to the fishes of Illinois. Ill. Dep. Conserv. Fish. Bull. No. 6. 43 pp.

Smith, P. W. 1975. Control mosquitoes with minnows. Ill. Nat. Hist. Surv. Rep. No. 151:1.

Smith, P. W. 1979. The fishes of Illinois. Univ. Ill. Press, Urbana. 314 pp.

Smith, P. W., A. C. Lopinot, and W. L. Pflieger. 1971. A distributional atlas of upper Mississippi River fishes. Ill. Nat. Hist. Surv. Biol. Notes No. 73. 20 pp.

Smith, R. J. F. 1970. Control of prespawning behavior of sunfish (*Lepomis gibbosus* and *L. megalotis*). Anim. Behav. 18:575–587.

Smith, R. J. F., and B. D. Murphy. 1974. Functional morphology of the dorsal pad in fathead minnows. Trans. Am. Fish. Soc. 103(1):65–72.

Smith, S. H. 1956. Life history of lake herring of Green Bay, Lake Michigan. U.S. Fish Wildl. Serv. Fish. Bull. 57(109):87–138.

Smith, S. H. 1957. Evolution and distribution of the coregonids. J. Fish. Res. Board Canada 14(4):599–604.

Smith, S. H. 1964. Status of the deepwater cisco populations of Lake Michigan. Trans. Am. Fish. Soc. 93(2):155–163.

Smith, S. H. 1968a. The alewife. Limnos 1(2):12–20.

Smith, S. H. 1968b. Species succession and fishery exploitation in the Great Lakes. J. Fish. Res. Board Canada 25(4):667–693.

Smith, S. H. 1970. Species interactions of the alewife in the Great Lakes. Trans. Am. Fish. Soc. 99(4):754–765.

Smith, S. H. 1972. Factors in ecologic succession in oligotrophic fish communities of the Laurentian Great Lakes. J. Fish. Res. Board Canada 29(6):717–730.

Smith, S. H. 1973. Application of theory and research in fishery management of the Laurentian Great Lakes. Trans. Am. Fish. Soc. 102(1):156–163.

Smith, W. E. 1975. Breeding and culture of two sunfish, *Lepomis cyanellus* and *L. megalotis*, in the laboratory. Progr. Fish-Cult. 37(4):227–229.

Smith-Vaniz, W. F. 1967. Freshwater fishes of Alabama. Auburn Univ. Agric. Exp. Stn. 209 pp.

Sneed, K. E. 1964. Southeastern fish cultural laboratory. U.S. Fish Wildl. Serv. Circ. 178:111–118.

Sneed, K. E., H. K. Dupree, and O. L. Green. 1961. Observations on the culture of flathead catfish (*Pylodictis olivaris*) fry and fingerlings in troughs. Proc. Southeast. Assoc. Game Fish Commnrs. 15:298–302.

Snelson, F. F., Jr. 1971. *Notropis mekistocholas*, a new herbivorous cyprinid fish endemic to the Cape Fear River basin, North Carolina. Copeia 1971(3):449–462.

Snelson, F. F., Jr. 1972. Systematics of the subgenus *Lythrurus*, genus *Notropis* (Pisces: Cyprinidae). Bull. Fla. State Mus. Biol. Sci. 17(1). 93 pp.

Snelson, F. F., Jr., and W. L. Pflieger. 1975. Redescription of the redfin shiner, *Notropis umbratilis*, and its subspecies in the central Mississippi River basin. Copeia 1975(2):231–249.

Snow, H. 1958. Northern pike at Murphy Flowage. Wis. Conserv. Bull. 23(2):15–18.

Snow, H. 1960. Bluegill at Murphy Flowage. Wis. Conserv. Bull. 25(3):11–14.

Snow, H. 1968. Stocking of muskellunge and walleye as a panfish control practice in Clear Lake, Sawyer County. Wis. Dep. Nat. Resour. Res. Rep. 38. 18 pp.

Snow, H. 1969. Comparative growth of eight species of fish in thirteen northern Wisconsin lakes. Wis. Dep. Nat. Resour. Res. Rep. 46. 23 pp.

Snow, H. 1971. Harvest and feeding habits of largemouth bass in Murphy Flowage, Wisconsin. Wis. Dep. Nat. Resour. Tech. Bull. No. 50. 25 pp.

Snow, H. 1974a. Effects of stocking northern pike in Murphy Flowage. Wis. Dep. Nat. Resour. Tech. Bull. No. 79. 20 pp.

Snow, H. 1974b. Notes on the zooplankton and benthos of Rush Lake, Douglas County, six years after application of antimycin. Wis. Dep. Nat. Resour. Res. Rep. 79. 4 pp.

Snow, H. 1978. A 15-year study of the harvest, exploitation, and mortality of fishes in Murphy Flowage, Wisconsin. Wis. Dep. Nat. Resour. Tech. Bull. No. 103. 22 pp.

Snow, H., A. Ensign, and J. Klingbiel. 1962. The bluegill—its life history, ecology and management. Wis. Conserv. Dep. Publ. 230. 14 pp.

Snow, H. E., and T. D. Beard. 1972. A ten-year study of native northern pike in Bucks Lake, Wisconsin. Wis. Dep. Nat. Resour. Tech. Bull. No. 56. 20 pp.

Snow, J. R. 1959. Notes on the propagation of the flathead catfish, *Pilodictis olivaris* (Rafinesque). Progr. Fish-Cult. 21(2):75–80.

Snyder, D. E., and S. C. Douglas. 1978. Description and identification of mooneye, *Hiodon tergisus*, protolarvae. Trans. Am. Fish. Soc. 107(4):590–594.

Solman, V. E. F. 1945. The ecological relations of pike, *Esox lucius* L., and waterfowl. Ecology 26(2):157–170.

Sorenson, L. 1971. Injections of carp with dried pituitary to control spawning time. Progr. Fish-Cult. 33(2):94.

Speare, E. P. 1965. Fecundity and egg survival of the central johnny darter (*Etheostoma nigrum nigrum*) in southern Michigan. Copeia 1965(3):308–314.

Spigarelli, S. A., and M. M. Thommes. 1976. Sport fishing at a thermal discharge into Lake Michigan. J. Great Lakes Res. 2(1):99–110.

Spoor, W. A. 1935. On the sexual dimorphism of *Catostomus commersonii* (Lacepède). Copeia 1935(4):167–171.

Spoor, W. A. 1938. Age and growth of the sucker, *Catostomus commersonii* (Lacepede), in Muskellunge Lake, Vilas County, Wisconsin. Trans. Wis. Acad. Sci., Arts, Lett. 31:457–505.

Spoor, W. A., and C. L. Schloemer. 1939. Diurnal activity of the common sucker, *Catostomus commersonii*, and rock bass, *Ambloplites rupestris*, in Muskellunge Lake. Trans. Am. Fish. Soc. 68:211–220.

Sroka, K. 1975. An effective hookless lure for members of the family Lepisosteidae. Univ. Wis., Stevens Point, Biol. Dep. 6 pp. (unpubl. manus.).

Staats, D. 1979. The problem is the (acid) solution. Great Lakes Communicator 10(3):3–4.

Starostka, V. J., and R. L. Applegate. 1970. Food selectivity of bigmouth buffalo, *Ictiobus cyprinellus*, in Lake Poinsett, South Dakota. Trans. Am. Fish. Soc. 99(3):571–576.

Starostka, V. J., and W. R. Nelson. 1974. Age, growth, sexual maturity and food of channel catfish in central Lake Oahe, 1968–1969. U.S. Fish Wildl. Serv. Tech. Pap. 81. 13 pp.

Starrett, W. 1950a. Distribution of the fishes of Boone County, Iowa, with special reference to the minnows and darters. Am. Midl. Nat. 43(1):112–127.

Starrett, W. 1950b. Food relationships of the minnows and darters of the Des Moines River, Iowa. Ecology 31(2):216–233.

Starrett, W. 1951. Some factors affecting the abundance of minnows in the Des Moines River, Iowa. Ecology 32(1):13–27.

Starrett, W. C., and P. G. Barnickol. 1955. Efficiency and selectivity of commercial fishing devices used on the Mississippi River. Ill. Nat. Hist. Surv. Bull. 26(4):325–366.

Starrett, W. C., and A. W. Fritz. 1957. The crappie story in Illinois. Outdoors in Ill. 4(2):11–14.

Starrett, W. C., W. J. Harth, and P. W. Smith. 1960. Parasitic lampreys of the genus *Ichthyomyzon* in the rivers of Illinois. Copeia 1960(4):337–346.

Stasiak, R. H. 1972. The morphology and life history of the finescale dace, *Pfrille neogaea*, in Itasca State Park, Minnesota. Univ. Minn., Minneapolis. PhD Thesis. 165 pp.

Stasiak, R. H. 1977. Morphology and variation in the finescale dace, *Chrosomus neogaeus*. Copeia 1977(4):771–774.

Stasiak, R. H. 1978. Reproduction, age, and growth of the finescale dace, *Chrosomus neogaeus*, in Minnesota. Trans. Am. Fish. Soc. 107(5):720–723.

Stauffer, J. B., Jr., J. H. Wilson, and K. L. Dickson. 1976. Comparison of stomach contents and condition of two catfish species living in ambient temperatures and in a heated discharge. Progr. Fish-Cult. 38(1):33–35.

Stauffer, T. M. 1972. Age, growth and downstream migration of juvenile rainbow trout in a Lake Michigan tributary. Trans. Am. Fish. Soc. 101(1):18–28.

Stauffer, T. M., and J. J. Hansen. 1958. Distribution of sea lamprey ammocoetes in Michigan tributaries of Lake Superior, 1955–1957. Mich. Dep. Conserv. Inst. Fish. Res. Misc. Publ. 11. 25 pp.

Steele, R. G., and M. H. A. Keenleyside. 1971. Mate selection in two species of sunfish (*Lepomis gibbosus* and *L. megalotis peltastes*). Can. J. Zool. 49(12):1541–1548.

Stegman, J. L. 1969. Fishes of Kinkaid Creek, Illinois. Trans. Ill. Acad. Sci. 52(1, 2):25–32.

Stein, R. A., J. F. Kitchell, and B. Knezevic. 1975. Selective predation by carp (*Cyprinus carpio* L.) on benthic molluscs in Skadar Lake, Yugoslavia. J. Fish. Biol. 7(3):391–399.

Stenton, J. E. 1951. Eastern brook trout eggs taken by longnose suckers in Banff National Park, Canada. Copeia 1951(2):171–173.

Stephenson, W. J. 1968. Coho, miracle fish of the midwest. Coho Unltd., Kalamazoo. 64 pp.

Sterba, G. 1973. Freshwater fishes of the world. T. F. H. Publications, Neptune City, N.J. 2 vols. 877 pp.

Stevens, L. A. 1971. Breakthrough in water pollution. Readers Dig. 98(590):167–168, 170–171, 175.

Stevenson, J. H. 1964. Fish farming experimental station. U.S. Fish Wildl. Serv. Circ. 178:79–100.

Stone, U. B. 1940. Studies on the biology of the satinfin minnows, *Notropis analostanus* and *Notropis spilopterus*. Cornell Univ., Ithaca. PhD Thesis. 98 pp. + vii + 14 pls.

Stone, U. B. 1947. A study of the deep-water cisco fishery of Lake Ontario with particular reference to the bloater, *Leucichthys hoyi* (Gill). Trans. Am. Fish. Soc. 74(1944):230–249.

Stroud, R. H., and H. Clepper. 1975. Black bass biology and management. Sport Fishing Inst., Wash., D.C. 534 pp.

Stroud, R. H. 1948. Notes on growth of hybrids between the sauger and the walleye (*Stizostedion canadense canadense* × *S. vitreum vitreum*) in Norris Reservoir, Tennessee. Copeia 1948(4):297–298.

Stroud, R. H. 1976. Status of grass carp. Sport Fishing Inst. Bull. 273(Apr 1976):4–6.

Stuiber, D. A. 1975. Aquaculture: facilities for the raising of yellow perch (*Perca flavescens*) in a controlled environment system. pp. 15–25 *in* Aquaculture: raising perch for midwest market. Univ. Wis., Madison, Sea Grant Coll. Prog., Advis. Rep. No. 13.

Stuntz, W. E. 1976. Habitat selection and growth of bluegills. Univ. Wis., Madison. PhD Thesis. 141 pp.

Summerfelt, R. C., and C. O. Minckley. 1969. Aspects of the life history of the sand shiner, *Notropis stramineus* (Cope), in the Smoky Hill River, Kansas. Trans. Am. Fish. Soc. 98(3):444–453.

Summerfelt, R. C., and P. R. Turner. 1971. Reproductive biology of the flathead catfish, *Pylodictus olivaris* (Rafinesque), in a turbid Oklahoma Reservoir. pp. 107–119 *in* Reservoir fishes and limnology, ed. G. E. Hall. Am. Fish. Soc. Spec. Publ. No. 8.

Suns, K., and G. Rees. 1977. The spottail shiner as an indicator of near-shore organochlorine contamination. 20th Conf. Great Lakes Res., Int. Assoc. Great Lakes Res., Univ. Mich. Abstr.

Surber, T. 1913. Notes on the natural hosts of freshwater mussels. Bull. U.S. Bur. Fish. 32:101–116.

Suttkus, R. D. 1958. Status of the nominal cyprinid species *Moniana deliciosa* Girard and *Cyprinella texana* Girard. Copeia 1958(4):307–318.

Svardson, G. 1945. Chromosome studies on Salmonidae. Rep. Swedish State Inst. Fresh-Water Fish. Res., Drottningholm. Vol. 23. 151 pp.

Swanson, B. L. 1973. Lake trout homing, migration and mortality studies, Lake Superior. Wis. Dep. Nat. Resour. Bur. Fish Mgmt. Rep. No. 65. 22 pp.

Swanson, B. L. 1976. Coho survey. Wis. Dep. Nat. Resour. Intra-Dep. Memo., Bayfield Stn. 3 pp. (mimeo).

Swee, U. B., and H. R. McCrimmon. 1966. Reproductive biology of the carp, *Cyprinus carpio* L., in Lake St. Lawrence, Ontario. Trans. Am. Fish. Soc. 95(4):372–380.

Swift, C. C. 1970. A review of the eastern North American cyprinid fishes of the *Notropis texanus* species group (subgenus *Alburnops*), with a definition of the subgenus *Hydrophlox*, and materials for a revision of the subgenus *Alburnops*. Fla. State Univ., Tallahassee. PhD Thesis. 515 pp.

Swingle, H. S. 1956. A repressive factor controlling reproduction in fishes. Oceanogr. Zool. Proc. 8th Pacific Sci. Congr. 3a(1953):856–871.

Swingle, H. S. 1957a. Commercial production of red cats (speckled bullheads) in ponds. Proc. Southeast. Assoc. Game Fish Commnrs. 10(1956):156–160.

Swingle, H. S. 1957b. Revised procedures for commercial production of bigmouth buffalo fish in ponds in the southeast. Proc. Southeast. Assoc. Game Fish Commnrs. 10(1956):162–165.

Swingle, H. S. 1964. Experiments with the flathead catfish (*Pylodictis olivaris*) in ponds. Proc. Southeast. Assoc. Game Fish Commnrs. 18:303–308.

Swingle, H. S. 1965. Growth rates of paddlefish receiving supplemental feeding in fertilized ponds. Progr. Fish-Cult. 27(4):220.

Swingle, H. S., and E. V. Smith. 1939. Increasing fish production in ponds. Trans. 4th North Am. Wildl. Conf.:332–338.

Swingle, H. S., and E. V. Smith. 1943. Factors affecting the reproduction of bluegill bream and largemouth black bass in ponds. Ala. Polytech. Inst., Agric. Exp. Stn. Circ. No. 87. 8 pp.

Taber, C. A. 1969. The distribution and identification of larval fishes in the Buncombe Creek arm of Lake Texoma with observations on spawning habits and relative abundance. Univ. Okla., Norman. PhD Thesis. 100 pp.

Tait, H. 1973. The impact of Great Lakes power generating plants on fish populations. Bur. Sport Fish. 5th Annu. Salmon Seminar, Michigan City, Indiana (27 Apr 1973). 12 pp. (mimeo).

Tarter, D. C. 1969. Some aspects of reproduction in the western blacknose dace, *Rhinichthys atratulus meleagris* Agassiz, in Doe Run, Meade County, Kentucky. Trans. Am. Fish. Soc. 98(3):454–459.

Tarzwell, C. M. 1941. The fish population of a small pond in northern Alabama. Trans. 5th North Am. Wildl. Conf.:245–251.

Tarzwell, C. M., ed. 1960. Biological problems in water pollution. Trans. 1959 Seminar, U.S. Dep. HEW Tech. Rep. W60–3. 285 pp.

Tarzwell, C. M., ed. 1965. Biological problems in water pollution. Trans. 3d Seminar, U.S. Dep. HEW Public Health Serv. Publ. No. 999–WP–25. 424 pp.

Taubert, B. D. 1977. Early morphological development of the green sunfish, *Lepomis cyanellus*, and its separation from other larval *Lepomis* species. Trans. Am. Fish. Soc. 106(5):445–448.

Taylor, W. R. 1954. Records of fishes in the John N. Lowe collection from the Upper Peninsula of Michigan. Univ. Mich. Mus. Zool. Publ. No. 87. 50 pp.

Taylor, W. R. 1969. A revision of the catfish genus *Noturus* Rafinesque with an analysis of higher groups in the Ictaluridae. Smithsonian Inst., U.S. Natl. Mus. Bull. 282. 315 pp.

Teichmann, H. 1957. Das Riechvermögen des Aales (*Anguilla anguilla* L.). Naturwissenschaften 44:242.

Tennant, L. T., and G. Billy. 1963. Articifical hybridization of the muskellunge and grass pickerel in Ohio. Progr. Fish-Cult. 25(2):68–70.

Thomas, D. L. 1970. An ecological study of four darters of the genus *Percina* (Percidae) in the Kaskaskia River, Illinois. Ill. Nat. Hist. Surv. Biol. Notes No. 70. 18 pp.

Thompson, D. H. 1933. The migration of Illinois fishes. Ill. Nat. Hist. Surv. Biol. Notes No. 1. 25 pp.

Thomsen, H. P., and A. D. Hasler. 1944. The minnow problem in Wisconsin. Wis. Conserv. Bull. 9(12):6–8.

Thorpe, J. E. 1977. Morphology, physiology, behavior, and ecology of *Perca fluviatilis* L. and *P. flavescens* Mitchill. J. Fish. Res. Board Canada 34(10):1504–1514.

Threinen, C. W. 1952. History, harvest and management of the Lake Koshkonong fishery. Wis. Conserv. Dep. Biol. Sec. Invest. Rep. No. 668. 32 pp.

Threinen, C. W. 1958. Life history, ecology, and management of the alewife. Wis. Conserv. Dep. Publ. 223. 8 pp.

Threinen, C. W. 1960. Results of walleye fingerling stocking in lakes with stunted panfish. Wis. Conserv. Dep. Summary Rep. 4 pp. (mimeo).

Threinen, C. W. 1964. An analysis of space demands of water and shore. Trans. 29th North Am. Wildl. Conf. pp. 353–372.

Threinen, C. W. 1969. An evaluation of the effect and extent of habitat loss on northern pike populations and means of prevention of losses. Wis. Dep. Nat. Resour. Bur. Fish Mgmt. Rep. No. 28. 25 pp. (mimeo).

Threinen, C. W., and W. T. Helm. 1952. Composition of the fish population and carrying capacity of Spauldings Pond, Rock County, as determined by rotenone treatment. Wis. Conserv. Dep. Invest. Rep. No. 656. 19 pp.

Threinen, C. W., and W. T. Helm. 1954. Experiments and observations designed to show carp destruction of aquatic vegetation. J. Wildl. Mgmt. 18(2):247–250.

Threinen, C. W., and E. Herman. 1958. Some notes on northern pike management (prepared for the Wis. Conserv. Congr.) Wis. Conserv. Dep. Fish and Trout Com. Meet. Burlington (10 Jan 1958) 2 pp. (mimeo).

Threinen, C. W., and A. Oehmcke. 1950. The northern invades the musky's domain. Wis. Conserv. Bull. 15(9):10–12.

Threinen, C. W., and R. Poff. 1963. The geography of Wisconsin's trout streams. Trans. Wis. Acad. Sci., Arts, Lett. 52:57–75.

Threinen, C. W., C. Wistrom, B. Apelgren, and H. Snow. 1966. The northern pike, life history, ecology, and management. Wis. Conserv. Dep. Publ. No. 235. 16 pp.

Thurston, C. E. 1962. Physical characteristics and chemical composition of two subspecies of lake trout. J. Fish. Res. Board Canada 19(1):39–44.

Tibbles, J. J. G. 1956. A study of the movements and depth distribution of the pelagic fishes in Lake Mendota. Univ. Wis., Madison. PhD Thesis. 193 pp.

Todd, D. K. 1970. The water encyclopedia. Water Info. Cent., Water Res. Bldg., Manhasset Isle, Port Washington, N.Y. 559 pp.

Todd, T. N. 1977. Revised status of Great Lakes coregonines, December 1976. U.S. Fish Wildl. Serv. Great Lakes Fish. Lab., Ann Arbor. 2 pp. (mimeo).

Todd, T. N. 1978. Revised status of Great lakes coregonines. U.S. Fish Wildl. Serv. Great Lakes Fish. Lab., Ann Arbor. 2 pp. (mimeo).

Todd, T. N., and G. R. Smith. 1980. Differentiation in *Coregonus zenithicus* in Lake Superior. Can. J. Fish. Aquatic Sci. 37(12):2228–2235.

Tomlinson, J. C., and D. J. Jude. 1977. Food of the trout-perch, *Percopsis omiscomaycus*, in southeastern Lake Michigan. 20th Conf. Great Lakes Res., Int. Assoc. Great Lakes Res., Univ. Mich. Abstr.

Trama, F. B. 1954. The pH tolerance of the common bluegill (*Lepomis macrochirus* Rafinesque). Phila. Acad. Sci. Notulae Naturae No. 256. 13 pp.

Tramer, E. J. 1977. Catastrophic mortality of stream fishes trapped in shrinking pools. Am. Midl. Nat. 97(2):469–478.

Trautman, M. B. 1957. The fishes of Ohio. Ohio State Univ. Press, Columbus. 683 pp. (rev. ed. 1981).

Traver, J. R. 1929. The habits of the black-nosed dace, *Rhinichthys atratulus* (Mitchill). J. Elisha Mitchell Sci. Soc. 45(1):101–120.

Trembley, F. J. 1960. Research project on effect of condenser discharge water on aquatic life. Inst. Res. Lehigh Univ. Progr. Rep. 1956–1959.

Triplett, J. R. 1976. Seasonal distribution and successional trends of fish in a new cooling reservoir. Univ. Kans., Lawrence. PhD Thesis. 153 pp.

Turner, C. L. 1921. Food of the common Ohio darters. Ohio J. Sci. 22(2):41–62.

Turner, P. R., and R. C. Summerfelt. 1971. Condition factors and length-weight relationships of the flathead catfish, *Pylodictis olivaris* (Rafinesque), in Lake Carl Blackwell. Proc. Okla. Acad. Sci. 51:36–40.

Tyus, H. M. 1973. Artificial intergeneric hybridization of *Ambloplites rupestris* (Centrarchidae). Copeia 1973(3):428–430.

Ulrey, L., C. Risk, and W. Scott. 1938. The number of eggs produced by some of our common fresh-water fishes. Indiana Dep. Conserv. and Indiana Univ. Dep. Zool., Invest. Indiana Lakes and Strms. 1(6):73–77.

Underhill, A. H. 1941. Estimation of a breeding population of chubsucker. Trans. 5th North Am. Wildl. Conf.:251–256.

Underhill, J. C. 1957. The distribution of Minnesota minnows and darters in relation to Pleistocene glaciation. Univ. Minn. Mus. Nat. Hist. Occas. Pap. No. 7. 45 pp.

Underhill, J. C. 1963. Distribution in Minnesota of the subspecies of the percid fish, *Etheostoma nigrum*, and of their intergrades. Am. Midl. Nat. 70(2):470–478.

Underhill, J. C., and D. J. Merrell. 1959. Intra-specific variation in the bigmouth shiner (*Notropis dorsalis*). Am. Midl. Nat. 61:133–147.

U.S. Fish and Wildlife Service. 1972. Grid map of Lake Michigan. U.S. Gov. Print. Off.:1979–666–501.

U.S. Geological Survey. 1974. Water resources data for Wisconsin—1972. Part I. Surface water records. Part II. Water quality records. U.S.D.I. Geol. Surv., Madison. 262 pp.

U.S. Geological Survey. 1976. Mineral and water resources of Wisconsin. Senate Com. on Inter. and Insular Aff., Wash., D.C. 185 pp.

U.S. Office of Water Planning and Standards. 1975. Fish kills caused by pollution in 1974. U.S. Environ. Prot. Agency Off. Water Plan. and Stand., Monitor. and Data Sup. Div. EPA–440/9–75–013. 28 pp.

U.S. Office of Water Planning and Standards. 1977. Fish kills caused by pollution in 1975. U.S. Environ. Prot. Agency Off. Water Plan. and Stand., Monitor. and Data Sup. Div. EPA–440/9–77–004. 84 pp.

University of Wisconsin Sea Grant College Program. 1975. Aquaculture: raising perch for the midwest market. Madison, Wis. Adv. Rep. No. 13. 87 pp.

Upper Mississippi River Conservation Committee. 1953. Proc. 9th Annu. Meet. Upper Miss. R. Conserv. Com., Fed. Bldg., Davenport, Iowa. 114 pp. (mimeo).

Upper Mississippi River Conservation Committee. 1967. Proc. 23rd Annu. Meet. Upper Miss. R. Conserv. Com., Fed. Bldg., Davenport, Iowa. 233 pp. + 22-page addendum.

Upper Mississippi River Conservation Committee. 1970. Proc. 26th Annu. Meet. Upper Miss. R. Conserv. Com., Fed. Bldg., Davenport, Iowa. 166 pp.

Uyeno, T. 1973. A comparative study of chromosomes in the teleostean fish order Osteoglossiformes. Jap. J. Ichthyol. 20(4):211–217.

Uyeno, T., and G. R. Smith. 1972. Tetraploid origin of the karyotype of catostomid fishes. Science 175:644–646.

Van Engel, W. A. 1940. The rate of growth of the northern pike, *Esox lucius* Linnaeus, in Wisconsin waters. Copeia 1940(3):177–187.

Van Engel, W. A. 1941. The food of the black crappie, *Pomoxis nigromaculatus*, in Wisconsin waters. Progr. Fish-Cult. No. 53:37.

Van Horn, W. M., J. B. Anderson, and M. Kotz. 1949. The effect of Kraft pulp mill wastes on some aquatic organisms. Trans. Am. Fish. Soc. 79:55–63.

Vanicek, D. 1961. Life history of the quillback and highfin carpsuckers in the Des Moines River. Proc. Iowa Acad. Sci. 68:238–246.

Van Oosten, J. 1932. The maximum age of fresh-water fishes. The Fisherman 1(11):3–4.

Van Oosten, J. 1936. Lake fisheries facing extermination. The Fisherman 5(11):1–3.

Van Oosten, J. 1937a. The age, growth, and sex ratio of the Lake Superior longjaw, *Leucichthys zenithicus* (Jordan and Evermann). Pap. Mich. Acad. Sci., Arts, Lett. 22(1936):691–711.

Van Oosten, J. 1937b. The dispersal of smelt, *Osmerus mordax* (Mitchill), in the Great Lakes region. Trans. Am. Fish. Soc. 66(1936):160–171.

Van Oosten, J. 1937c. The Great Lakes fisheries: their proper management for sustained yields. Trans. Am. Fish. Soc. 66(1936):131–138.

Van Oosten, J. 1940. The smelt, *Osmerus mordax* (Mitchill). Mich. Dep. Conserv. 13 pp.

Van Oosten, J. 1946. Maximum size and age of whitefish. The Fisherman 14(8):17–18.

Van Oosten, J. 1947. Mortality of smelt in Lakes Huron and Michigan during the fall and winter of 1942–43. Trans. Am. Fish. Soc. 74(1944):310–337.

Van Oosten, J. 1961. Records, ages and growth of the mooneye, *Hiodon tergisus*, of the Great Lakes. Trans. Am. Fish. Soc. 90(2):170–174.

Van Oosten, J., and H. Deason. 1938. The food of the lake trout (*Cristivomer namaycush namaycush*) and of the lawyer (*Lota maculosa*) of Lake Michigan. Trans. Am. Fish. Soc. 67(1937):155–177.

Van Oosten, J., and P. H. Eschmeyer. 1956. Biology of young lake trout, *Salvelinus namaycush*, in Lake Michigan. U.S. Fish Wildl. Serv. Res. Rep. No. 42. 88 pp.

Van Oosten, J., R. Hile, and F. W. Jobes. 1946. The whitefish fishery of Lakes Huron and Michigan with special reference to the deep-trap-net fishery. U.S. Fish Wildl. Serv. Fish. Bull. 50:297–394.

Vasey, F. W. 1967. Age and growth of walleye and sauger in Pool 11 of the Mississippi River. Iowa State J. Sci. 41(4):447–466.

Vessel, M. F., and S. Eddy. 1941. A preliminary study of the egg production of certain Minnesota fishes. Minn. Dep. Conserv. Fish. Res. Invest. Rep. No. 26. 26 pp.

Vilstrup, R. 1975. Potential—some economics of fish production. pp. 45–49 *in* Aquaculture: raising perch for midwest market. Univ. Wis. Sea Grant Coll. Progr. Advis. Rep. No. 13.

Vincent, R. E. 1960. Experimental introductions of fresh-water alewives. Progr. Fish-Cult. 22(1):38–43.

Vladykov, V. D. 1933. Biological and oceanographic conditions in Hudson Bay. Part IX. Fishes from the Hudson Bay region (except the Coregonidae). Contrib. Can. Biol. Fish., Toronto, n.s. 8(2)(Ser. A, Gen., No. 29):13–61.

Vladykov, V. D. 1949. Quebec lampreys, list of species and their economical importance. Quebec Dep. Fish. Contrib. No. 26. 67 pp.

Vladykov, V. D. 1950. Larvae of eastern American lampreys. Part I. Species with two dorsal fins. Le Nat. can. 77(3–4):73–95.

Vladykov, V. D. 1951. Fecundity of Quebec lampreys. Can. Fish Cult. 10:1–14.

Vladykov, V. D. 1964. Quest for the true breeding areas of the American eel. J. Fish. Res. Board Canada 21(6):1523–1530.

Vladykov, V. D. 1970. Pearl tubercles and certain cranial peculiarities useful in the taxonomy of coregonid genera. pp. 167–193 *in* Biology of coregonid fishes, ed. C. C. Lindsey and C. S. Woods. Univ. Manitoba Press, Winnipeg.

Vladykov, V. D., and J. M. Roy. 1948. Biologie de la lamproie d'eau douce (*Ichthyomyzon unicuspis*) après la métamorphose. Rev. can. de biol. 7(3):483–485.

Voigtlander, C. W., and T. E. Wissing. 1974. Food habits of young and yearling white bass, *Morone chrysops* (Rafinesque), in Lake Mendota, Wisconsin. Trans. Am. Fish. Soc. 103(1):25–31.

Vondracek, B. 1977. Life history characteristics of suckers from Green Bay and Lake Michigan with special reference to the white sucker. Univ. Wis., Madison. MS Thesis. 79 pp.

Wagner, C. C., and E. L. Cooper. 1963. Population density, growth, and fecundity of the creek chubsucker, *Erimyzon oblongus*. Copeia 1963(2):350–357.

Wagner, G. 1908. Notes on the fish fauna of Lake Pepin. Trans. Wis. Acad. Sci., Arts, Lett. 16(1):23–37.

Wagner, G. 1910a. *Argyrosomus johannae*, a new species of cisco from Lake Michigan. Science, n.s. 31(807):957–958.

Wagner, G. 1910b. On the stickleback of Lake Superior. Science, n.s. 32:28–30.

Wagner, G. 1911. The cisco of Green Lake, Wisconsin. Bull. Wis. Nat. Hist. Soc. 9:73–77.

Wagner, W. C. 1976. Pink salmon in Michigan tributaries of the Great Lakes, 1975. Mich. Dep. Nat. Resour., Marquette Fish. Res. Stn. 3 pp. (mimeo).

Wagner, W. C., and T. M. Stauffer. 1962. Sea lamprey larvae in lentic environments. Trans. Am. Fish. Soc. 91(4):384–387.

Wagner, W. C., and T. M. Stauffer. 1975. Occurrence of pink salmon in Michigan, 1963–1973. Mich. Dep. Nat. Resour. Fish. Div. Tech. Rep. No. 75–3. 8 pp. (mimeo).

Wahlquist, F. J. 1939. Brook trout albinos. Wis. Conserv. Bull. 4(1):24–25.

Walburg, C. H. 1964. Fish population studies, Lewis and Clark Lake, Missouri River, 1956–1962. U.S. Fish Wildl. Serv. Spec. Sci. Rep.—Fish. No. 482. 27 pp.

Walburg, C. H. 1976. Changes in the fish populations of Lewis and Clark Lake, 1956–74, and their relation to water management and the environment. U.S. Fish Wildl. Serv. Res. Rep. 79. 34 pp.

Walburg, C. H., and W. R. Nelson. 1966. Carp, river carpsucker, smallmouth buffalo, and bigmouth buffalo in Lewis and Clark Lake, Missouri. U.S. Fish Wildl. Serv. Res. Rep. No. 69. 30 pp.

Walden, H. T. 1964. Familiar freshwater fishes of America. Harper and Row, N.Y. 324 pp.

Wales, J. H. 1941. Development of steelhead trout eggs. Calif. Dep. Fish Game, Sacramento, 27(4):250–260.

Walker, T. J., and A. D. Hasler. 1949. Detection and discrimination of odors of aquatic plants by the bluntnose minnow (*Hyborhynchus notatus*). Physiol. Zool. 32(1):45–63.

Wallace, C. R. 1967. Observations on the reproductive behavior of the black bullhead (*Ictalurus melas*). Copeia 1967(4):852–853.

Walton, I. 1653. The complete angler. E. P. Dutton, N.Y. (Everyman's Library, 1906). 200 pp.

Ward, C. M., and W. H. Irwin. 1961. The relative resistance of thirteen species of fishes to petroleum refinery effluent. Proc. Southeast. Game Fish Comm. 15:255–276.

Washburn, G. N. 1948. Propagation of the creek chub in ponds with artificial raceways. Trans. Am. Fish. Soc. 75(1945):336–350.

Weber, J. J. 1971. Winnebago's bonus cod. Wis. Conserv. Bull. 36(6):23.

Weber, J. J. 1975. Golden strands. Wis. Conserv. Bull. 40(2):18–19.

Webster, D. A. 1942. The life histories of some Connecticut fishes. pp. 122–127 *in* A fishery survey of important Connecticut lakes. Bull. Conn. State Geol. Nat. Hist. Surv. 63.

Webster, D. A. 1945. Relation of temperature to survival and incubation of the eggs of smallmouth bass (*Micropterus dolomieu*). Trans. Am. Fish. Soc. 75:43–47.

Weeks, E. P., and H. G. Stangland. 1971. Effects of irrigation on streamflow in the central sand plain of Wisconsin. Wis. Dep. Nat. Resour. and Wis. Geol. Nat. Hist. Surv. 113 pp.

Weimer, L. 1980. Lake trout: the second time around. Wis. Nat. Resour. 4(4):13–16.

Weisel, G. F. 1957. Fish guide for inter-mountain Montana. Mont. State Univ. Press, Missoula. 88 pp.

Weisel, G. F., and J. B. Dillon. 1954. Observations on the pygmy whitefish, *Prosopium coulteri*, from Bull Lake, Montana. Copeia 1954(2):124–127.

Weisel, G. F., D. A. Hanzel, and R. L. Newell. 1973. The pygmy whitefish, *Prosopium coulteri*, in western Montana. U.S. Fish Wildl. Serv. Fish. Bull. 71(2):587–596.

Welker, B. D. 1962. Summer food habits of yellow bass and black bullheads in Clear Lake. Proc. Iowa Acad. Sci. 69:286–295.

Wells, L. 1966. Seasonal and depth distribution of larval bloaters (*Coregonus hoyi*) in southeastern Lake Michigan. Trans. Am. Fish. Soc. 95(4):388–396.

Wells, L. 1968. Seasonal depth distribution of fish in southeastern Lake Michigan. U.S. Fish Wildl. Serv. Fish. Bull. 67(1):1–15.

Wells, L., and A. M. Beeton. 1963. Food of the bloater, *Coregonus hoyi*, in Lake Michigan. Trans. Am. Fish. Soc. 92(3):245–255.

Wells, L., and R. House. 1974. Life history of the spottail shiner (*Notropis hudsonius*) in southeastern Lake Michigan, the Kalamazoo River and western Lake Erie. U.S. Bur. Sport Fish. Wildl. Res. Rep. 78. 10 pp.

Wells, L., and A. L. McLain. 1972. Lake Michigan: effects of exploitation, introductions, and eutrophication on the salmonid community. J. Fish. Res. Board Canada 29(6):889–898.

Wells, L., and A. L. McLain. 1973. Lake Michigan—man's effects on native fish stocks and other biota. Great Lakes Fish. Comm. Tech. Rep. No. 20. 55 pp.

Werner, E. E., and D. J. Hall. 1976. Niche shifts in sunfishes: experimental evidence and significance. Science 191(30 Jan 1976):404–406.

West, J. L., and F. E. Hester. 1966. Intergeneric hybridization of centrarchids. Trans. Am. Fish. Soc. 95(3):280–288.

Westman, J. R. 1938. Studies on the reproduction and growth of the bluntnosed minnow, Hyborhynchus notatus (Rafinesque). Copeia 1938:(2):57–61.

Westman, J. R. 1941. A consideration of population life-history studies in their relation to the problems of fish management research, with special reference to the small-mouth bass, *Micropterus dolomieui* Lacepede, the lake trout, *Cristivomer namaycush* (Walbaum), and the mud minnow, *Umbra limi* (Kirtland). Cornell Univ., Ithaca. PhD Thesis. 182 pp.

White, D. S. 1977. Early development and scale formation in the spotted sucker, *Minytrema melanops* (Catostomidae). Copeia 1977(2):400.

White, D. S., and K. H. Haag. 1977. Food and feeding habits of the spotted sucker, *Minytrema melanops* (Rafinesque). Am. Midl. Nat. 98(1):137–146.

White, G. E. 1971. The Texas golden green: a color mutation of the green sunfish. Progr. Fish-Cult. 33(3):155.

White, H. C. 1930. Some observations on the eastern brook trout (*S. fontinalis*) of Prince Edward Island. Trans. Am. Fish. Soc. 60:101–108.

White, R. J., and O. M. Brynildson. 1967. Guidelines for management of trout stream habitat in Wisconsin. Wis. Dep. Nat. Resour. Tech. Bull. No. 39. 65 pp.

White, R. J., and R. L. Hunt. 1969. Regularly occurring fluctuations in year-class strength of two brook trout populations. Trans. Wis. Acad. Sci., Arts, Lett. 57:135–153.

Whiteside, B. G., and N. E. Carter. 1973. Standing crop of fishes as an estimate of fish production in small bodies of water. Proc. Southeast. Assoc. Game Fish Commnrs. 26:414–417.

Whitfield, R. E. 1975. St. Lawrence River eel ladder. Ont. Minist. Nat. Resour. (East. Reg., Kemptville). 4 pp. (mimeo).

Whitley, G. P. 1950. New fish names. Proc. Royal Zool. Soc. New South Wales 1948–49:44.

Whitworth, W. R., P. L. Berrien, and W. T. Keller. 1968. Freshwater fishes of Connecticut. Bull. State Geol. Nat. Hist. Surv. Conn. 101. 134 pp.

Wiebe, A. H. 1931. Notes in the exposure of several species of fish to sudden changes in the hydrogen-ion concentration of the water and to atmosphere of pure oxygen. Trans. Am. Fish. Soc. 61:216–224.

Wiegert, L. W. 1958. Sport fishing on Green Bay. Wis. Conserv. Bull. 23(7):3–5.

Wiegert, L. W. 1966. A four-year study of the smallmouth bass in the outlying waters of Door County, Wisconsin. Wis. Conserv. Dep. Div. Fish Mgmt. Rep. No. 1. 11 pp. (mimeo).

Wiley, E. O. 1977. The phylogeny and systematics of the *Fundulus nottii* species group (Teleostei: Cyprinodontidae). Univ. Kans., Lawrence, Occas. Pap. Mus. Nat. Hist. No. 66. 31 pp.

Wiley, E. O., III, and D. D. Hall. 1975. *Fundulus blairae*, a new species of the *Fundulus nottii* complex (Teleostei, Cyprinodontidae). Am. Mus. Novitates No. 2577. 13 pp. + 5 figs., 9 tables.

Williams, J. D. 1975. Systematics of the percid fishes of the subgenus *Ammocrypta*, genus *Ammocrypta*, with descriptions of two new species. Bull. Ala. Mus. Nat. Hist. No. 1. 56 pp.

Williams, J. D. 1977. Endangered species: yesterday, today, and tomorrow? pp. 49–55 *in* Endangered and threatened plants and animals of North Carolina, ed. J. E. Cooper, S. S. Robinson, and J. B. Funderburg. N.C. State Mus. Nat. Hist. xvi + 444 pp.

Williams, W. E. 1959. Food conversion and growth rates for largemouth and smallmouth bass in laboratory aquaria. Trans. Am. Fish. Soc. 88(2):125–127.

Williamson, J., and R. O. Smitherman. 1975. Food habits of hybrid buffalofish, *Tilapia*, Israeli carp and channel catfish in polyculture. Proc. Southeast. Assoc. Game Fish Commnrs. 29:86–91.

Williamson, L. O. 1939. The fat-head minnow as a forage fish. Wis. Conserv. Bull. 4(6):50–51.

Winn, H. E. 1958. Comparative reproductive behavior and ecology of fourteen species of darters (Pisces—Percidae). Ecol. Mongr. 28(2):155–191.

Winn, H. E. 1960. Biology of the brook stickleback, *Eucalia inconstans*. Am. Midl. Nat. 63(2):424–440.

Winn, H. E., and J. F. Stout. 1960. Sound production by the satinfin shiner, *Notropis analostanus*, and related fishes. Science 132:222–223.

Wirth, T. L. 1958. Lake Winnebago freshwater drum. Wis. Conserv. Bull. 23(5):30–32.

Wirth, T. L. 1959. Drum for good eating. Wis. Conserv. Bull. 24(7):9–11.

Wirth, T. L., and P. T. Schultz. 1957. The 1957 lake sturgeon management report. Wis. Conserv. Dep., Oshkosh. 9 pp. (mimeo).

Wisconsin Conservation Commission. 1949. Twenty-first biennial report of the Wisconsin State Conservation Commission for the fiscal years ending June 30, 1947, and June 30, 1948. Wis. Conserv. Comm., Madison. 128 pp.

Wisconsin Conservation Commission. 1958. Wisconsin game fish. Wis. Conserv. Comm., Madison. Publ. 209–58. 24 pp.

Wisconsin Conservation Department. 1963. Wisconsin fish chronology. Wis. Conserv. Dep., Madison. 7 pp. (mimeo).

Wisconsin Department of Natural Resources. 1968a. Wisconsin muskellunge waters. Wis. Dep. Nat. Resour. Publ. 237–68. 25 pp.

Wisconsin Department of Natural Resources. 1968b. Smallmouth bass streams in Wisconsin. Wis. Dep. Nat. Resour. Publ. 224–68. 12 pp.

Wisconsin Department of Natural Resources. 1971. Wisconsin walleye waters. Wis. Dep. Nat. Resour. Publ. 241–71. 77 pp.

Wisconsin Department of Natural Resources. 1974. Wisconsin lakes. Wis. Dep. Nat. Resour. Publ. 7–3600(74). 79 pp.

Wisconsin Department of Natural Resources. 1976a. Fish distribution summary for 1976. Wis. Dep. Nat. Resour. 149 pp.

Wisconsin Department of Natural Resources. 1976b. Rough and detrimental fish removal—1976. State and contract. Wis. Dep. Nat. Resour. 9 pp. (mimeo).

Wisconsin Department of Natural Resources. 1976c. Wisconsin's Great Lakes commercial fisheries for 1974. Wis. Dep. Nat. Resour. Bur. Fish Mgmt. Sec. Rep. No. 86. 17 pp.

Wisconsin Department of Natural Resources. 1977. Freshwater angling records: world's record and Wisconsin's record fish. Wis. Dep. Nat. Resour. 2 pp. (mimeo).

Wisconsin Department of Natural Resouces. 1979. Wisconsin fishing regulations, 1980. Wis. Dep. Nat. Resour. Publ. 4-1020(79). 25 pp.

Wisconsin Department of Natural Resources. Endangered Species Committee. 1975. Endangered animals in Wisconsin. Wis. Dep. Nat. Resour. 10 pp. (mimeo).

Wisconsin Department of Resource Development. 1966. The outdoor recreation plan. Wis. Dep. Resour. Dev., Madison. 216 pp. + 17 maps.

Wisconsin Fish Distribution Study (D. Fago, proj. leader). 1974–1979. Computer printouts of the distribution of Wisconsin fishes. Wis. Dep. Nat. Resour.

Wisconsin Historical Collections. 1895. 13:345–347.

Wisconsin Legislative Reference Bureau. 1973. Blue book. State Wis. Dep. Adm., Madison. 900 pp.

Wisdom, J. L. A. 1972. Acceptability of flavor and aroma of smallmouth buffalo, river carpsucker, and carp from Elephant Butte Lake, New Mexico. N.M. State Univ., Las Cruces. MS Thesis. 26 pp.

Wissing, T. E. 1974. Energy transformation by young-of-the-year white bass in Lake Mendota, Wisconsin. Trans. Am. Fish. Soc. 103(1):32–37.

Wissing, T. E., and A. D. Hasler. 1971. Effects of swimming ability and food intake on the respiration of young-of-the-year white bass, *Morone chrysops*. Trans. Am. Fish. Soc. 100(3):537–543.

Witt, A., Jr. 1949. Experiments in learning of fishes with shocking and hooking as penalties. Univ. Ill., Urbana. MS Thesis. 60 pp.

Witt, A., Jr. 1960. Length and weight of ancient freshwater drum, *Aplodinotus grunniens*, calculated from otoliths found in Indian middens. Copeia 1960(3):181–185.

Witt, A., Jr., and R. C. Marzolf. 1954. Spawning and behavior of the longear sunfish, *Lepomis megalotis megalotis*. Copeia 1954(3):188–190.

Wohlfarth, G., and M. Lahman. 1963. Genetic improvement of carp. IV. Leather and line carp in fish ponds of Israel. Bamidgeh 15:3–8.

Wolff, R. C. 1974. A comparative age and growth study of the bluegill [*Lepomis macrochirus* (Rafinesque)] collected in May and June of 1974 in Lake Wazeecha, Wood County, Wisconsin, and Lake Sherwood, Adams County, Wisconsin. St. Mary's Coll., Winona. MS Thesis. 71 pp.

Woodbury, L. A. 1941. A sudden mortality of fishes accompanying a super saturation of oxygen in Lake Waubesa, Wisconsin. Trans. Am. Fish. Soc. 71:112–117.

Woods, L. P. 1970. The changing Great Lakes. Field Mus. Nat. Hist. Bull. 41(7):6–10.

Woodward, R. L., and T. E. Wissing. 1976. Age, growth and fecundity of the quillback (*Carpiodes cyprinus*) and highfin (*C. velifer*) carpsuckers in an Ohio stream. Trans. Am. Fish. Soc. 105(3):411–415.

Wootton, R. J. 1976. The biology of the sticklebacks. Academic Press, N.Y. 387 pp.

World Almanac. 1976. The world almanac and book of facts. Bicentennial ed. N.Y. Newspaper Enterprise Assoc., Inc., N.Y. 984 pp.

Worth, S. G. 1892. Observations on hatching of the yellow perch. Bull. U.S. Fish. Comm. 10(1890):331–334.

Worthington, V. 1976. Leave it to the fish. Natl. Wildl. Fed. Conserv. News 41(23):12–13.

Wright, K. J. 1970. The 1967–1968 sport fishery survey of the upper Mississippi River. Upper Miss. R. Conserv. Com. 116 pp. (mimeo).

Wright, K. J. 1973. An assessment of fish abundance, habitat, and fishing in a portion of Pool 8, Mississippi River, subject to highway intrusion. Wis. Dep. Nat. Resour. Bur. Fish. Mgmt. Rep. No. 63. 39 pp. (mimeo).

Wright, T. D. 1968. Changes in abundance of yellow bass (*Morone mississippiensis*) and white bass (*M. chrysops*) in Madison, Wisconsin, lakes. Copeia 1968(1):183–185.

Yellayi, R. R., and R. V. Kilambi. 1970. Observations on early development of white bass, *Roccus chrysops* (Rafinesque). Proc. Southeast. Assoc. Game Fish Commnrs. 23:261–265.

Yellayi, R. R., and R. V. Kilambi. 1975. Population dynamics of white bass in Beaver Reservoir, Arkansas. Proc. Southeast. Assoc. Game Fish Commnrs. 29:172–174.

Zahl, P. A., and D. D. Davis. 1932. Effects of gonadectomy on the secondary sexual characters in the ganoid fish, *Amia calva* Linnaeus. J. Exp. Zool. 63(2):291–304.

Zaporozec, A. 1974. Bibliography and index of Wisconsin ground water 1851–1972. Wis. Geol. Nat. Hist. Surv. and Wis. Dep. Nat. Resour. Spec. Rep. No. 2. 100 pp.

Zhiteneva, L. D. 1971. Composition of the blood of the ninespine stickleback [*Pungitius pungitius* (L.)] under conditions of adverse oxygen regime. J. Ichthyol. 11(3):409–417.

Zimmerman, C. J. 1970. Growth and food of the brook silverside, *Labidesthes sicculus*, in Indiana. Trans. Am. Fish. Soc. 99(2):435–438.

Zweiacker, P. 1967. Aspects of the life history of the shovelnose sturgeon, *Scaphirhynchus platorynchus* (Rafinesque), in the Missouri River. Univ. S.D., Vermillion. MA Thesis. 46 pp.

Credits for Color Illustrations

Sea lamprey (photos by S. L. Emery. U.S. Fish and Wildlife Service)
Lake sturgeon (portrait by Virgil Beck. Wisconsin DNR)
Paddlefish (portrait by Maynard Reece. Iowa State Conservation Commission)
Shortnose gar (photo by W. D. Schmid. University of Minnesota Press)
Longnose gar, adult (photo by W. D. Schmid. University of Minnesota Press)
American eel (Illinois Natural History Survey photo)
Skipjack herring (photo by W. L. Pflieger)
Brown trout (portrait by Virgil Beck. Wisconsin DNR)
Rainbow trout (portrait by Virgil Beck. Wisconsin DNR)
Pink salmon (photo by T. N. Todd. U.S. Fish and Wildlife Service)
Coho salmon (portrait by Virgil Beck. Wisconsin DNR)
Chinook salmon (portrait by Virgil Beck. Wisconsin DNR)
Brook trout (portrait by Virgil Beck. Wisconsin DNR)
Tiger trout (Wisconsin DNR photo)
Lake trout (portrait by Virgil Beck. Wisconsin DNR)
Lake whitefish (portrait by Virgil Beck. Wisconsin DNR)
Shortjaw cisco (photos by S. L. Emery. U.S. Fish and Wildlife Service)
Bloater, full view (photo by T. N. Todd. U.S. Fish and Wildlife Service)
Bloater, head view (photo by S. L. Emery. U.S. Fish and Wildlife Service)
Kiyi (photo by T. N. Todd. U.S. Fish and Wildlife Service)
Round whitefish (photo by J. Parsons. U.S. Fish and Wildlife Service)
Muskellunge (portrait by Virgil Beck. Wisconsin DNR)
Grass carp (Wisconsin DNR photo)
Hornyhead chub (photo by W. L. Pflieger)
Creek chubsucker (photo by L. M. Page)
Black redhorse (photo by W. L. Pflieger)
Shorthead redhorse (photo by W. D. Schmid. University of Minnesota Press)
River redhorse (photo by L. M. Page)

Flathead catfish (portrait by Virgil Beck. Wisconsin DNR)
Burbot (portrait by Virgil Beck. Wisconsin DNR)
Green sunfish (photo by W. L. Pflieger)
Bluegill (portrait by Virgil Beck. Wisconsin DNR)
Walleye (portrait by Virgil Beck. Wisconsin DNR)
Bluntnose darter (photo by L. M. Page)
Mud darter (photo by L. M. Page)

Index

Page numbers in italic type refer to color illustrations; page numbers in bold face type refer to species accounts.

TEXT DESIGNED BY GARDNER R. WILLS
JACKET DESIGNED BY QUENTIN FIORE
JACKET ILLUSTRATION BY VIRGIL BECK
COMPOSED BY GRAPHIC COMPOSITION, INC.
ATHENS, GEORGIA
MANUFACTURED BY MALLOY LITHOGRAPHING, INC.
ANN ARBOR, MICHIGAN
TEXT AND DISPLAY LINES ARE SET IN PALATINO

Library of Congress Cataloging in Publication Data
Becker, George C.
Fishes of Wisconsin.
Bibliography: pp. 985–1022
Includes index.
1. Fishes—Wisconsin.
I. Title.
QL628.W6B43 1983 639.9'77092'9775 81-69813
ISBN 0-299-08790-5